Smith and Hogan's
CRIMINAL LAW

David Ormerod is currently a Law Commissioner. He is seconded from Queen Mary, University of London, where he is Professor of Criminal Justice. David is the author of numerous journal articles and books and is: Editor-in-Chief of *Blackstone's Criminal Practice* (with Lord Justice Hooper); *Criminal Law Review* Cases Editor; and Consultant Editor of *Halsbury's Laws of England on Criminal Procedure* (2010). He also serves on the Editorial Boards of a number of legal journals. He lectures regularly to the profession and for the Judicial College on a range of topics.

He is a door tenant in the chambers of David Etherington QC, 18 Red Lion Court, and is a Bencher of Middle Temple.

He is a member of the Criminal Justice Council and of the Advocacy Training Council.

Other titles from David Ormerod:
Fraud: Criminal Law and Procedure (2008) with Clare Montgomery QC;
Smith's Law of Theft (9th edn 2007) with David Williams QC; and
Smith and Hogan Criminal Law: Cases and Materials (10th edn 2009).

Smith and Hogan's
CRIMINAL LAW

Thirteenth edition

David Ormerod

Barrister, Bencher of Middle Temple,
Law Commissioner for England and Wales,
Professor of Criminal Justice, Queen Mary University of London,
Door Tenant at 18 Red Lion Court

OXFORD
UNIVERSITY PRESS

OXFORD
UNIVERSITY PRESS

Great Clarendon Street, Oxford OX2 6DP

Oxford University Press is a department of the University of Oxford.
It furthers the University's objective of excellence in research, scholarship,
and education by publishing worldwide in

Oxford New York

Auckland Cape Town Dar es Salaam Hong Kong Karachi
Kuala Lumpur Madrid Melbourne Mexico City Nairobi
New Delhi Shanghai Taipei Toronto

With offices in

Argentina Austria Brazil Chile Czech Republic France Greece
Guatemala Hungary Italy Japan Poland Portugal Singapore
South Korea Switzerland Thailand Turkey Ukraine Vietnam

Oxford is a registered trade mark of Oxford University Press
in the UK and in certain other countries

Published in the United States
by Oxford University Press Inc., New York

Tenth edition 2002
Eleventh edition 2005
Twelfth edition 2008

British Library Cataloguing in Publication Data

Data available

Library of Congress Cataloging in Publication Data

Library of Congress Control Number: 2011931035

Typeset by Newgen Imaging Systems (P) Ltd, Chennai, India
Printed in Great Britain
on acid-free paper by
Ashford Colour Press Ltd., Gosport, Hampshire

ISBN 978–0–19–958649–3

3 5 7 9 10 8 6 4 2

For Elsie

 Online Resource Centre

This book is accompanied by an open access website which provides extremely comprehensive updates to the law, organized by chapter. These are intended to be printed and used with the book in order to help readers remain as up to date as possible with the latest changes to legislation and case law.

Also available on this website:

- An online chapter covering the offence of forgery
- A selection of useful web links
- A full bibliography and list of abbreviations.

Go to: www.oxfordtextbooks.co.uk/orc/smithhogan_textbook13e/

New to this edition

Key revisions in the 11th edition include –

Analysis of the latest case law developments (over 200 new appellate cases since the last edition):

- *R v Rahman* (2009) House of Lords on joint enterprise;
- *R v T* (2009 House of Lords on *doli incapax*;
- *R v Cooper* (2009) House of Lords on capacity in sexual cases;
- *R v G* (2008) House of Lords on strict liability and statutory rape;
- *Austin v MPC* (2008) House of Lords on public order and protest;
- *R v Sheppard and Whittle* (2010) on jurisdiction and extra-territoriality;
- *R v Yemoh* (2009), *R v Mendez and Thompson* (2010), *R v ABCD* (2010), *R v Badza*(2010), *R v Gnango* (2010), and *R v Lewis* (2010) – all decisions of the Court of Appeal Criminal Division on joint enterprise liability;
- *R v Inglis* (2011) on murder and mercy killing; and
- *R(Purdy) v DPP* (2009) on assisted suicides.

Discussion of new legislation:

- the Criminal Justice and Immigration Act 2008;
- the Coroners and Justice Act 2009;
- the Policing and Crime Act 2009; and
- the Bribery Act 2010.

Discussion of new Law Commission Consultation Papers and Reports:

- Law Commission Consultation Paper No 197 (2010) on unfitness to plead;
- Law Commission Consultation Paper No 195 (2010) on regulatory crime;
- Law Commission Consultation Paper No 193 (2009) on public nuisance and outraging public decency;
- Law Commission Report No 318 (2009) on conspiracy and attempts; and
- Law Commission Report No 314 (2009) on intoxication.

Preface

This edition has required significant revision to keep pace with statutory and common law developments. Chapter 15 has been substantially rewritten to deal with the new partial defences to murder (Loss of Self Control and Diminished Responsibility). Other statutory changes that are examined include the new offences of extreme pornography (Chapter 31), amendments to the Sexual Offences Act (Chapter 18), and more detailed analysis of some of the money laundering offences under the Proceeds of Crime Act 2002 is provided in Chapter 27. New cases examined in detail include the spate of cases on joint enterprise (*Rahman* (2009), *Yemoh* (2009), *Gnango* (2010), *ABCD* (2010), *Mendez and Thompson* (2010) and others) that has necessitated a rewriting of much of Chapter 8. There is consideration in Chapters 7 and 18 of *G* (2008) in the House of Lords on strict liability and sexual offences, and of *C* (2008) in the House of Lords on capacity to consent in sexual cases. Chapter 12 includes discussion of *T* (2009) in the House of Lords on *doli incapax* and of *Harvey* (2009) and *Keane* (2010) on self-defence. The House of Lords' final case – *Purdy* (2009) – and the DPP's guidance on suicide are discussed in Chapter 16. In addition to the dozens of new cases, I have as in previous editions incorporated greater discussion of academic material and I hope that this will be as enthusiastically received by readers as previously. The pressure of space has meant that in this edition the Forgery chapter, Chapter 28, which no longer features in many university courses, has been placed on the website where it is available to download free of charge: www.oxfordtextbooks.co.uk/orc/smithhogan_textbook13e/.

The Law Commission has maintained a prolific output since the last edition, and I have included discussion of the Consultation Papers and Reports on conspiracy and attempt, intoxication, criminal liability in regulatory contexts, and unfitness to plead. Since completing the 12th edition I have been privileged to be appointed as the Law Commissioner for England and Wales with responsibility for Criminal Law. I emphasize that the views expressed in this book do not represent those of the Law Commission. There should be no expectation that arguments advanced in this book will be those adopted by the Law Commission during my term as Commissioner.

My trepidation at following in the footsteps of Professors Sir John Smith and Brian Hogan persists. The more I work on the book the greater my admiration for what they achieved. To produce, as they did, such a scholarly, comprehensive, and accessible account of almost the entire criminal law continues to inspire me. I have sought to remain true to their ideal of producing a textbook which is valuable to a wide legal readership whilst providing a detailed exposition and doctrinal analysis of English criminal law. I hope, once again, that this is an edition of which they would have been proud.

The manuscript was delivered to the publishers in March 2011 and the law is stated as at 31 March, although it has been possible to accommodate a few more recent changes at proof stage.

Free online updates are produced every year and are available at: www.oxfordtextbooks.co.uk/orc/smithhogan_textbook13e/.

References to academic materials are provided in full in the footnotes. In addition, the online searchable bibliography which proved popular in the last edition has been updated and is available at: www.oxfordtextbooks.co.uk/orc/smithhogan_textbook13e/.

David Ormerod
London

Acknowledgements

I have been extremely fortunate to have many colleagues and friends in academia, at the Bar, and on the Bench who have been willing to discuss issues with me and in some cases comment on draft chapters. In particular, I would like to thank: Professors Peter Alldridge, William Wilson, and Valsamis Mitsilegas, Tracey Elliott, Damian Warburton, Rosa Freedman, Rudi Fortson QC, David Perry QC, Tony Shaw QC, David Williams QC, and HHJ Simon Tonking.

I am also grateful to the Law Commission for permitting me to take unpaid leave to finalize this edition, and for the forbearance of the Criminal Law team and my fellow Commissioners for my absences whilst doing so.

As with the last edition, I was determined to ensure that the level of discussion and analysis continued to meet the needs of undergraduate law students. I was fortunate in having assistance from current LLB students Kevin Nordin and Karl Laird and recent law graduates Tharini Sumanthiran and Diana Deju, who between them read a number of chapters. I thank them, and in particular Karl Laird, who also provided truly outstanding research assistance.

At OUP, John Carroll and Heather Smyth have been enormously helpful and patient in steering the book through the various stages of production. Jan Miles-Kingston and Gill Clack copy-edited and proofread the entire manuscript for which I am very grateful.

Contents

Part I General Principles

Part II Particular Crimes

Table of statutes

References in **bold** type indicate where the section of an Act is set out in part or in full.

Table of cases

EUROPEAN COURT OF HUMAN RIGHTS

Abbreviations

The following are the abbreviations used for the principal textbooks and legal journals cited in this book. References are to the latest editions, as shown below, unless it is specifically stated otherwise. The particulars of other works referred to in the text are set out in full in the relevant footnotes. A full bibliography of all references is available free online at **www. oxfordtextbooks.co.uk/orc/smithhogan_textbook13e/**.

Throughout the book the neutral citation system (UKSC, UKHL, UKPC, EWCA Crim, EWHC (Admin), etc) is commonly adopted in relation to cases in England and Wales since 2001.

Archbold	*Criminal Pleading, Evidence and Practice* by JF Archbold (2011) by PJ Richardson and others
Ashworth, POCL	*Principles of Criminal Law* (6th edn, 2009) by A Ashworth
Blackstone	*Blackstone's Criminal Practice* (2008) by Hooper LJ and D Ormerod (eds)
Blackstone, *Commentaries*, i	*Commentaries on the Laws of England* by Sir William Blackstone, vol i (4 vols) (17th edn, 1830) by E Christian
Butler	Report of the Committee on Mentally Abnormal Offenders (1975) Cmnd 6244
Cal Law Rev	California Law Review
Can Bar Rev	Canadian Bar Review
CLJ	Cambridge Law Journal
CLP	Current Legal Problems
Co I Inst	*Institutes of the Laws of England*, vol I (4 vols) (1797) by Sir Edward Coke
Col LR	Columbia Law Review
Cr App R	Criminal Appeal Reports
Crim LR	Criminal Law Review
Crime, Proof and Punishment	*Crime, Proof and Punishment: Essays in Honour of Sir Rupert Cross*, edited by CFH Tapper (1981)
Criminal Law Essays	*Criminal Law: Essays in Honour of JC Smith* edited by PF Smith (1987)
Draft Code	*A Criminal Code for England and Wales*, Law Com No 177 (1989)
Duff, *Answering for Crime*	*Answering for Crime: Responsibility and Liability in the Criminal Law* (2007) by RA Duff
Duff and Green, *Defining Crimes*	*Defining Crimes: Essays on the Special Part of the Criminal Law* (2005) by RA Duff and SP Green (eds)
East, I PC	*A Treatise of the Pleas of the Crown* by EH East, vol I (2 vols) (1803)
Edwards, *Mens Rea*	*Mens Rea in Statutory Offences* (1955) by J Ll J Edwards
Eighth Report	Criminal Law Revision Committee, Eighth Report, *Theft and Related Offences* (1966) Cmnd 2977
Emmerson, Ashworth and Macdonald, HR&CJ	*Human Rights and Criminal Justice* (2nd edn, 2007) by B Emmerson, A Ashworth and A Macdonald
Foster, *Crown Law*	*A Report on Crown Cases and Discourses on the Crown Law* by Sir Michael Foster (3rd edn, 1792) by M Dodson

Fourteenth Report	Criminal Law Revision Committee, Fourteenth Report, *Offences Against the Person* (1980) Cmnd 7844
Glazebrook, *Reshaping the Criminal Law*	*Reshaping the Criminal Law: Essays in Honour of Glanville Williams* edited by PR Glazebrook (1978)
Gordon	*Criminal Law of Scotland* (2nd edn, 1978) by GH Gordon
Green, *Lying Cheating and Stealing*	*Lying, Cheating and Stealing: A Moral Theory of White Collar Crime* (2006) by SP Green
Griew, *Theft*	*The Theft Acts 1968 and 1978* (7th edn, 1995) by EJ Griew
Hale, I PC	*The History of the Pleas of the Crown* by Sir Matthew Hale, vol i (2 vols) (1736)
Hall, *General Principles*	*General Principles of Criminal Law* (2nd edn, 1960) by J Hall
Halsbury	*The Laws of England* by the Earl of Halsbury and other lawyers (4th edn, 1973–) by Lord Hailsham of St Marylebone
Harv LR	Harvard Law Review
Hawkins, I PC	*A Treatise of the Pleas of the Crown* by W Hawkins, vol I (2 vols) (8th edn, 1795) by J Curwood
Horder, *Homicide Law*	*Homicide Law in Comparative Perspective* (2007) by J Horder (ed)
Howard, SR	*Strict Responsibility* (1963) by Colin Howard
J Cr L & Cr	Journal of Criminal Law and Criminology (USA)
J Crim L	Journal of Criminal Law (English)
JSPTL	Journal of the Society of Public Teachers of Law
Kenny, *Outlines*	*Outlines of Criminal Law* by CS Kenny (19th edn, 1965) by JWC Turner
LCCP	Law Commission Consultation Paper
LQR	Law Quarterly Review
LS	Legal Studies, the Journal of the Society of Public Teachers of Law
MACL	*The Modern Approach to Criminal Law* edited by L Radzinowicz and JWC Turner (1948)
Med Sci & L	Medicine, Science and the Law
MLR	Modern Law Review
NZ Essays	*Essays on Criminal Law in New Zealand* edited by RS Clark (1971)
OJLS	Oxford Journal of Legal Studies
Ormerod and Williams, *Smith's Law of Theft*	*The Law of Theft* (9th edn, 2007) by D Ormerod and DH Williams
Perkins, *Criminal Law*	*Criminal Law* (2nd edn, 1969) by R Perkins
Perkins and Boyce, *Criminal Law*	*Criminal Law* (3rd edn, 1982) by R Perkins and R Boyce
Pollock and Maitland, I HEL	*The History of English Law before the Time of Edward I* by Sir Frederick Pollock and FW Maitland, vol I (2 vols) (2nd edn)
RCCP	Report of the Royal Commission on Capital Punishment (1953) Cmd 8932
Russell	*Crime* by Sir WO Russell (12th edn, 1964) by JWC Turner (2 vols)
Simester, Spencer, Sullivan and Virgo, CLT&D	*Criminal Law Theory and Doctrine* (4th edn, 2010) by AP Simester, GR Sullivan, JR Spencer and G Virgo
Smith, *Justification and Excuse*	*Justification and Excuse in the Criminal Law* by JC Smith (The Hamlyn Lectures, 1989)
Smith, *Property Offences*	*Property Offences* (1994) by ATH Smith
Stephen, *Digest*	*A Digest of the Criminal Law* by Sir James Fitzjames Stephen (9th edn, 1950) by LF Sturge

Stephen, I HCL	*A History of the Criminal Law of England* by Sir James Fitzjames Stephen, vol I (3 vols) (1883)
Tadros, *Criminal Responsibility*	V Tadros, *Criminal Responsibility* (2005)
U Pa Law Rev	University of Pennsylvania Law Review
Williams, CLGP	*Criminal Law: The General Part* (2nd edn, 1961) by GL Williams
Williams, TBCL	*Textbook of Criminal Law* (2nd edn, 1983) by GL Williams
Wilson, *Central Issues*	*Central Issues in Criminal Theory* (2002) by W Wilson
YLJ	Yale Law Journal

Part I
General Principles

1
Defining crime

1.1 A universal definition of 'a crime'?

It is now rather unfashionable to begin law books with definitions.[1] One reason for this is the difficulty frequently encountered in defining the subject matter of a particular branch of the law; and nowhere has this been more greatly felt than in the criminal law. But this is a book about crimes, and if it did not at least attempt to tell the reader what a crime is, it would be deficient. It would allow the reader to proceed with preconceived notions about what constitutes a crime. In particular, there would be a danger that the reader might assume the popular meaning of crime which is different from, less precise, and narrower than, the legal meaning. A law book must be concerned with the legal meaning of crime; and the reader is entitled to know what it is, or at least why it is so difficult to describe.

Common definitions from non-legal dictionaries do not provide much help as a starting point, offering only bland definitions such as 'an act or omission prohibited and punished by law'. Although they may inform that the meaning of the word 'crime' can be traced to the Latin 'crimen' (accusation), that takes us no further forward to an understanding of the subject. A simple definition of a crime as a wrong, prosecuted and carrying a penalty might satisfy the layman without providing any sufficient answer for the lawyer. Arguably, an exercise in further definition is futile since every lawyer knows a crime when they see it, but a ready response to this claim is that not all crimes are readily identifiable even to the lawyer. This is inevitable when there are well in excess of 10,000 crimes in England and Wales[2] covering such diverse activities as murder, rape, being in possession of an unlicensed dangerous dog[3] and obstructing a clergyman in the discharge of his duties in a place of worship or on his way thither.[4] But given the importance of the criminal law in terms of what is at stake and how often it is used, surely a definition could and should be produced.

An attempt to define *a crime* at once encounters a difficulty. If the definition is a true one, it should enable us to recognize any conduct – *act* (or *omission*) – as a crime, or not a crime, by seeing whether it contains all the ingredients of the definition. But reflection will show that this is impossible. When Parliament enacts that a particular act shall become a crime or that an act which is now criminal shall cease to be so, the conduct does not change in nature in any respect other than that of legal classification. All its observable characteristics are precisely the same before as after the statute comes into force. Any attempt at definition of a crime will

---

[1] For classical accounts of the problem of definition see Kenny, *Outlines of Criminal Law* (15th edn, 1935) Ch 1; G Williams, 'The Definition of Crime' (1955) 8 CLP 107; G Hughes, 'The Concept of Crime: An American View' [1959] Crim LR 239 and 331. For more contemporary philosophical accounts, see in particular the collections of essays edited by RA Duff and SP Green, *Defining Crimes* (2005); Duff, *Answering for Crime*; A Halpin, *Definition in the Criminal Law* (2004); and essays in J Gardner, *Offences and Defences: Selected Essays in the Philosophy of Criminal Law* (2007).

[2] Not including the thousands of by-laws created at a local level.

[3] See the Dangerous Dogs Act 1991.

[4] Offences Against the Person Act 1861, s 36.

therefore either include the conduct at a time when it is not a crime, or exclude it when it is. Suicide was a crime until 3 August 1961, when, by the Suicide Act 1961,[5] it became perfectly lawful to kill oneself. The nature of the act in question, its morality or immorality and the consequence do not change overnight; but its legal nature does.

1.2 A universal purpose in criminal law?

Our quest for a definition of criminal law is not assisted greatly by looking for a declared purpose underlying the creation of criminal law in England and Wales. The criminal law of this country has developed over many centuries, and the purposes of those who have framed it, and of those who have enforced it, have undoubtedly been many and various. Consequently, it is not easy to state confidently today what the aims of the criminal law are. The authors of a completely new code of criminal law are, however, in a position to state their objectives at the outset. 'The general purposes of the provisions governing the definition of offenses' in the American Law Institute's Model Penal Code[6] might be taken as a statement of the proper objectives of the substantive law of crime in a modern legal system. The purposes are:

(1) to forbid and prevent conduct that unjustifiably and inexcusably inflicts or threatens substantial harm to individual or public interests;

(2) to subject to public control persons whose conduct indicates that they are disposed to commit crimes;

(3) to safeguard conduct that is without fault from condemnation as criminal;

(4) to give fair warning of the nature of the conduct declared to be an offense;

(5) to differentiate on reasonable grounds between serious and minor offenses.[7]

The reader will judge for himself how far these purposes are fulfilled by English criminal law while studying the general principles and particular offences discussed in the succeeding chapters. For example, whether our law is confined to forbidding conduct that is 'inexcusable', or whether it adequately safeguards conduct that is without fault from condemnation as criminal, are matters which are particularly considered in Ch 7 but which constantly arise elsewhere.

1.3 Universal characteristics of a crime?

Struggling to define crimes and even to identify a clear declared purpose in criminalizing forms of conduct, the student might turn instead to search for characteristics that are universal to every crime so that at least crimes can be identified even if not readily defined. Those hoping for a straightforward checklist of criteria guaranteed to identify a crime are destined for disappointment. It is nigh on impossible to agree any determinate criteria. There is considerable force in Professor Duff's recent concession that we should resist the:

desire to find some single concept or value that will capture the essence of crime or *the* essential characteristic in virtue of which crimes are properly punished ... in favour of a pluralism that recognises

---

[5] Below, Ch 16.

[6] Proposed Official Draft, Art 1, 1.02(1). cf N Walker, *The Aims of the Penal System* (1966).

[7] For criticism see PH Robinson, 'The Modern General Part – Three Illusions' in S Shute and A Simester (eds), *Criminal Law Theory* (2002) 79.

a diversity of reasons for criminalisation, matching the diversity of kinds of wrong which can legitimately be the criminal law's business.[8]

Despite the lack of a universally accepted definition of criminal law, it is possible to point to certain characteristics, which are *generally* found in conduct which is criminal, in particular, it usually involves a public wrong and a moral wrong.[9]

1.3.1 A 'public' wrong

Crimes are generally acts which have a particularly harmful effect on the public and do more than interfere with merely private rights. Sir Carleton Allen writes:

Crime is crime because it consists in wrongdoing which directly and in serious degree threatens the security or well-being of society, and because it is not safe to leave it redressable only by compensation of the party injured.[10]

This explains why acts have been made crimes either by judicial decision or by legislation, and it does not necessarily accurately represent the present state of affairs. A crime may remain a crime long after it has ceased to be a threat to the security or well-being of society.[11] Thus Allen's proposition tells us what – as he thinks – ought to be criminal rather than what is criminal.

There is a further dimension to the concept of public wrong.[12] This emphasizes not that the wrong is one done against the public, but rather that a 'public wrong' is significant for defining crimes because it reflects the important role that the public has in punishing crimes. As Duff explains:

we should be held criminally responsible for wrongdoings which are public in the sense that they properly concern all members of the polity, and merit a formal public response of censure and condemnation.[13]

As Duff acknowledges, that does not assist in determining what wrongdoing should count as 'public'.[14]

This 'public' nature of crimes is evidenced by the contrast between the rules of civil and criminal procedure. Any citizen can, as a general rule and in the absence of some provision to the contrary, bring a criminal prosecution, whether or not he has suffered any special harm over and above other members of the public. As a member of the public he has an interest in the enforcement of the criminal law. D steals V's watch. V may prosecute him – so may X, Y, Z or any other citizen.[15] As the Lord Chief Justice recently made clear in *Smith*[16] it was no defence to a charge of theft of drugs from V that V unlawfully possessed them. The law of theft protects the Queen's peace and is not a means of enforcing personal property rights.

---

[8] Duff, *Answering for Crime*, 139.

[9] Recent years have seen a huge outpouring of theoretical writing on the criminal law. For an interesting reflection on the last 25 years' worth see RA Duff, 'Theorising About Criminal Law' (2005) 25 OJLS 353.

[10] CK Allen, 'The Nature of a Crime' (1931) *Journal of Society of Comparative Legislation*, Feb, reprinted in *Legal Duties* 221 at 233–234.

[11] G Williams (1955) 8 CLP at 126–127.

[12] G Lamond, 'What is a Crime' (2007) 27 OJLS 609.

[13] Duff, *Answering for Crime*, 123. See generally Ch 6 of that work.

[14] Lamond argues it is because they represent blameworthy conduct, in terms of *mens rea*.

[15] The right of private prosecution is unaffected by the Prosecution of Offences Act 1985; but s 24 empowers the High Court, on the application of the AG, to restrain a vexatious prosecutor: *Ewing v Director of Public Prosecutions* [2010] EWCA Civ 70. The DPP may take over a private prosecution at any stage (s 6(2)) and may discontinue a prosecution during its 'preliminary stage': s 23. See R (*Gurja v CPS*) [2011] ENHC 472 (Admin).

[16] [2011] EWCA Crim 66.

In practice, of course, the vast majority of prosecutions are performed by the CPS or the Revenue and Customs Prosecutions Office or other public officers who have no personal interest in the outcome. The victim of an offence cannot prevent the prosecution of the offender.[17] The DPP's consent to a prosecution is not subject to judicial review in the absence of *mala fides*. Equally, proceedings may be stopped by the Crown through the entry of a *nolle prosequi* by the Attorney General who may stay the proceedings at any time[18] without the consent of the prosecutor.

If the prosecution succeeds and a sentence is imposed by the court, the instigator of the prosecution has no power to pardon the offender. This power belongs exclusively to the Crown, representing the public interest in the matter. It is important not to assimilate the position of the Crown with that of the victim. The recognition of the victim in the criminal process has been marked over the last decade or so, but in terms of substantive law, the formal position is that the prosecution is brought by the Crown, and the Crown is not seen as a surrogate victim.[19]

All this public control over the proceedings in criminal law stands in sharp contrast with the position regarding civil wrongs – torts and breaches of contract. There, only the person injured may sue. He (and only he) may freely discontinue the proceedings at any time and, if he succeeds and an award of damages is made in his favour, he may, at his entire discretion, forgive the defendant and terminate his liability.

Crimes, then, are wrongs which the judges have held, or Parliament has enacted, to be sufficiently injurious to the public to warrant the application of criminal procedure to deal with them. Of course this does not enable us to recognize an act as a crime when we see one. Some forms of conduct are so obviously public wrongs that *anyone* would say they should be criminal – murder or rape for example.[20] These are often referred to as the *mala in se* – intrinsically wrong. All such types of obviously harmful conduct almost certainly are criminal. But there are many other types of conduct – *mala prohibita* – about which opinions may differ widely: what of drug misuse, or prostitution?

It is important not to overstate the significance of public condemnation of a form of conduct. Parliament and the courts alone declare the range and scope of the criminal law. When a citizen is heard urging that, 'There ought to be a law against it . . .', he is expressing his personal conviction that some variety of act is so harmful to society that it ought to be discouraged by being made the subject of criminal proceedings. There will almost invariably be a body of opinion which disagrees. But even if *everyone* agreed with him, the act in question would not thereby become a crime. Public condemnation is ineffective without the endorsement of an Act of Parliament or a decision of a court.[21]

In recent years politicians have been too willing to accede to public condemnation of particular forms of conduct and the clamour to make new crimes. The Law Commission reports that:

Since 1997, more than 3000 criminal offences have come on to the statute book. That figure should be put in context, taking a longer perspective. Halsbury's Statutes of England and Wales has four volumes devoted to criminal laws that (however old they may be) are still currently in force. Volume 1 covers the offences created in the 637 years between 1351 and 1988. Volume 1 is 1382 pages long.

---

[17] See on victim waiver and settlement, G Dingwall and C Harding, *Diversion in the Criminal Law* (1998) Ch 3.

[18] The DPP may intervene and offer no evidence: *Turner v DPP* (1978) 68 Cr App R 70 (Mars Jones J), [1978] Crim LR 754; *Raymond v AG* [1982] QB 839, CA, [1982] Crim LR 826 and commentary.

[19] See *Weir* [2001] 1 WLR 421, HL.

[20] See the comments in the appeals against rape convictions on Pitcairn: *Christian* [2006] UKPC 47.

[21] Witness the Radio 4 poll to find the listeners' law, which prompted the Bill to redefine the defence of self-defence as applicable to householders injuring burglars, discussed in Ch 12 below.

Volumes 2 to 4 cover the offences created in the 19 years between 1989 and 2008. Volumes 2 to 4 are no less than 3746 pages long. So, more than 2 and a half times as many pages were needed in Halsbury's Statutes to cover offences created in the 19 years between 1989 and 2008 than were needed to cover the offences created in the 637 years prior to that. Moreover, it is unlikely that the Halsbury volumes devoted to 'criminal law' capture all offences created in recent times.[22]

There is, it is argued, just too much crime.[23] In particular, there has been a disproportionate use of the criminal law to deal with regulatory misconduct. The Law Commission has recently proposed that:

the criminal law should only be employed to deal with wrongdoers who deserve the stigma associated with criminal conviction because they have engaged in seriously reprehensible conduct. It should not be used as the primary means of promoting regulatory objectives.[24]

It is important at this point to emphasize one of the unique features of the criminal law of which it seems that Parliament may recently have lost sight. The criminal sanction is the most coercive method of regulating an individual's behaviour which the State can deploy. The whole criminal justice system involves State infringements of the personal autonomy from the possibility of investigation and surveillance, arrest, search, seizure, detention, questioning, public court hearings, a trial process which may include pre-trial detention, and lead to punishment, including the ultimate infringement – imprisonment. Even if no term of imprisonment is imposed, the range of other punishments available to the criminal courts all have one thing in common: a degree of stigma.[25] Even if individuals are not taken through the entire process of the criminal trial, but are diverted[26] before trial and dealt with by way of cautioning, conditional cautions, etc they suffer the stigma. There is a marked public condemnation which is publicly communicated.[27]

This degree of coercion is qualitatively different from the outcome in a dispute in civil law. For the liberal at least, criminalization should be a matter of last resort because of this stigmatization and the most intrusive forms of State intervention it entails. As Husak has stated, 'a criminal statute cannot be necessary to accomplish a purpose if other means could do so more easily'.[28] Readers will be able to judge for themselves whether English law really respects this principle of what Ashworth calls 'minimal criminalisation'.[29] The point is not so much to reduce criminal law to its absolute minimum, as to ensure that resort is only had to the criminalization in order to protect individual autonomy, or to protect those social arrangements necessary to ensure that individuals have the capacity and facilities to exercise their autonomy.[30]

---

[22] See LCCP 195 *Criminal Liability in Regulatory Contexts* (2010) para 1.17.

[23] See DN Husak, *Overcriminalisation* (2008) Ch 1.

[24] LC 195, para 1.29.

[25] See N Walker and C Marsh, 'Do Sentences Affect Public Disapproval?' (1984) British Journal of Criminology 27; N Walker, *Punishment, Danger and Stigma* (1980).

[26] See G Dingwall and C Harding, *Diversion in the Criminal Process* and more recently RA Duff, L Farmer, S Marshall and V Tadros, *The Trial on Trial*, vol 3 (2007) 180 et seq.

[27] See Tadros, *Criminal Responsibility*, 2.

[28] DN Husak, 'The Criminal Law as a Last Resort' (2004) 24 OJLS 207, 212.

[29] For an excellent and accessible account of the principles of criminalization see Ashworth, POCL, Chs 2 and 3. See the recent suggestion by Jeremy Horder that the focus is too narrow and fails to acknowledge the need for criminalization of conduct giving rise to remoter harms: J Horder, 'Bribery as a Form of Criminal Wrongdoing' (2011) 127 LQR 37.

[30] N Lacey, *Unspeakable Subjects* (1998); *State Punishment* (1988).

It is important also to note that in English law there is no category of 'violations' or 'administrative wrongs' that sit between criminal and civil wrongs as exist in some jurisdictions.[31]

1.3.2 A 'moral' wrong

The second characteristic of crimes which is usually emphasized is that they involve conduct which is morally wrong.[32] As with 'public wrong' the characteristic is hopelessly vague.

1.3.2.1 Morality

As seen above, the traditional attitude of the common law has been that crimes are essentially immoral acts deserving of punishment. Centuries ago, when the number of crimes was relatively few and only the most outrageous acts were prohibited – murder, robbery, rape, etc – this was, no doubt, true. But experience suggests that morality and the criminal law are not coextensive, and a review of the current vast range of criminal offences in England demonstrates that this proposition is undoubtedly true. Many acts are now prohibited on the grounds of social expediency and not because of their immoral nature. This is especially so in the field of summary offences – and summary offences are crimes.[33] Moreover, many acts which are generally regarded as immoral – for example, adultery – are not crimes in England.[34] The test of immorality is not a very helpful one in seeking to identify *universal* characteristics of a crime.[35]

There is a further difficulty which arises in classifying action as criminal on the basis of its purported immorality – whose morality should form the benchmark for criminalization? This problem is illustrated well by the problem of drawing appropriate legal limits on the level of physical harm to which a sane adult might consent being inflicted on him. Very different answers would be provided by, for example, the liberal,[36] the paternalist[37] and by the legal moralist.[38] The issue also arises in relation to the recently enacted Fraud Act 2006 in which the offences come close to criminalizing lying: it is sufficient that the defendant dishonestly makes a misleading statement with intent to gain.[39]

Whether an act ought to be a crime *simply* on the ground of its immoral nature has been the subject of vigorous debate on different issues through the decades. In the 1960s, the question was whether consensual homosexual conduct between men in private ought to be decriminalized. The Wolfenden Committee on Homosexual Offences and Prostitution reviewed the

---

[31] See LCCP 195, para 3.32 and the excellent discussion in R White, 'Civil Penalties: Oxymoron, Chimera and Stealth Sanction' (2010) 126 LQR 593 and K Reid, 'Strict Liability: Some Principles for Parliament' (2008) Stat LR 173.

[32] For an accessible account of this complex area see W Wilson, *Central Issues in Criminal Theory* (2000) Ch 1, and Duff, *Answering for Crime*, Chs 4 and 6.

[33] G Williams (1955) 8 CLP at 110. It is true that courts have frequently declined to attribute all the normal incidents of a crime to a regulatory offence on the grounds that it is 'not truly criminal' or is 'quasi-criminal': *Harrow London Borough Council v Shah* [1999] 3 All ER 302, [1999] Crim LR 992, DC, below, p 169. But this is a dubious argument. By any recognized test, the offence is criminal.

[34] Adultery is criminal in some countries. See Duff, *Answering for Crime*, 144.

[35] See LCCP 195, para 4.39 on the usefulness of the harm principle in general.

[36] With focus on whether harm is caused to another's interests.

[37] For whom it will be sufficient that harm is caused to another or the accused.

[38] For whom it is sufficient that the conduct is immoral. See the decision of the House of Lords in *Brown* [1994] AC 212, discussed in Ch 17 in full and LCCP 139, *Consent in the Criminal Law* (1995) Appendix C. cf P Roberts, 'Consent in the Criminal Law' (1997) 17 OJLS 389 and S Shute, 'The Law Commission's Second Consultation Paper on Consent' [1996] Crim LR 684.

[39] See D Ormerod, 'Criminalising Lying?' [2007] Crim LR 193 and Ch 23 below. Professor Horder categorizes this as a harm-centred, minimalist conception of the criminal law: Horder (2011) 127 LQR 37.

position. Its conclusion was that enforcement of morality is not a proper object of the criminal law. The function of the criminal law, as they saw it, is:

to preserve public order and decency, to protect the citizen from what is offensive or injurious, and to provide sufficient safeguards against exploitation and corruption of others, particularly those who are specially vulnerable . . . It is not . . . the function of the law to intervene in the private lives of citizens, or to seek to enforce any particular pattern of behaviour, further than is necessary to carry out the purposes we have outlined.[40]

This view was challenged by Lord Devlin,[41] who argued that there is a public morality which is an essential part of the bond which keeps society together; and that society may use the criminal law to preserve morality in the same way that it uses it to preserve anything else that is essential to its existence. The standard of morality is that of 'the man in the jury box', based on the 'mass of continuous experience half-consciously or unconsciously accumulated and embodied in the morality of common sense'. To this it was answered[42] that it is not proper for the State to enforce the general morality without asking whether it is based on ignorance, superstition or misunderstanding; that it is not a sufficient ground for prohibiting an act that 'the thought of it makes the man on the Clapham omnibus sick'. But if we are not to base criminal law on the general morality, does not this imply that 'our law making is or should be controlled by independent Gods of Pure Reason, installed somewhere in our political systems and endowed with power to determine such questions for society, free of the prejudices to which lesser men are subject'?[43] 'A free society is as much offended by the dictates of an intellectual oligarchy as by those of an autocrat.'[44]

In the midst of this controversy, the House of Lords made its controversial decision in *Shaw v DPP*,[45] in which Lord Simonds asserted that:

there remains in the courts of law a residual power to enforce the supreme and fundamental purpose of the law, to conserve not only the safety and order *but also the moral welfare of the state*;

and that the King's Bench was the custodian of the morality of the people and had the superintendency of offences *contra bonos mores*. 'Lord Devlin, regarded *Shaw's* case', as settling 'for the purpose of the law that morality in England means what twelve men and women think it means – in other words it is to be ascertained as a question of fact'.[46] Subsequently, however, the particular rule of law that caused the Wolfenden Committee to formulate its general principle[47] – that homosexual conduct between consenting male adults is an offence – was repealed by the Sexual Offences Act 1967. The House of Lords also repudiated the suggestion that it has power to extend the criminal law to enforce good morals.[48]

---

[40] (1957) Cmnd 247, para 13.

[41] *The Enforcement of Morals* (1965) 1.

[42] HLA Hart, *The Morality of the Criminal Law* (1964). Hart challenges the view that society is morally homogenous as Devlin's approach would require.

[43] EV Rostow, 'The Enforcement of Morals' [1960] CLJ 174 at 189.

[44] P Devlin, 'Law, Democracy and Morality' (1962) 110 U Pa Law Rev 635 at 642, reprinted in *The Enforcement of Morals* (1965) 86.

[45] [1962] AC 220, [1961] 2 All ER 446; below, p 478.

[46] 110 U Pa Law Rev at 648. See also HLA Hart, *Law, Liberty and Morality* (1963); G Hughes, 'Morals and the Criminal Law' (1962) 71 YLJ 662. For an excellent discussion of the whole controversy, see B Mitchell, *Law, Morality and Religion in a Secular Society* (1967).

[47] Above, n 40.

[48] *Knuller (Publishing, Printing and Promotions) Ltd v DPP* [1973] AC 435, below, p 457. Such judicial offence-creation would contravene Art 7 of the ECHR which protects against retrospective criminalization. See the recognition of the appropriate limits of judicial law-making in *Rimmington* [2005] UKHL 63.

The debate is echoed in more recent times with the question of what levels of harm or injury a sane adult might consent to in the course of consensual sexual sadomasochism. The issue divided the House of Lords in the case of *Brown*,[49] prompted two Law Commission Consultation Papers and provoked a torrent of legal academic writing.[50] Many other instances of the debate about morality and criminal law can be seen in recent years and will be replayed in the future.[51] For example, the Government recently introduced a new offence for an adult to possess extreme pornography depicting images of consenting adult conduct.[52]

1.3.2.2 Harms or wrongs to others[53]

Implicit in a requirement that a crime incorporates a moral wrong is the acceptance that a 'wrong' is done or harm to another or others is involved. Conduct can be treated as a 'wrong' if it violates some moral duty or rule, and harmful if it infringes the autonomy of another or causes serious offence to another. Conduct can be wrongful without being harmful (a white lie to V's benefit); and harmful without being wrong (D undercutting his competitors' prices and causing him to go out of business).

Again, this poses a problem since it is only if there is agreement as to the moral bases for criminalizing that there is likely to be agreement as to whether the conduct involves a harm.[54] What will be 'wrong' or 'harmful' for the paternalist will not necessarily be so for the liberal.

Academic writing has focused heavily on the issue of the harm principle in the last few decades. By far the most refined examination of this has been that of Professor Feinberg,[55] but he is not alone in recognizing the utility of the harm principle in defining what is characteristic about crimes.[56] In the late 1970s, Gross dealt with the issue as had Packer a decade earlier.[57]

The harm to others formula seems to me to have two uses that justify its inclusion in a list of limiting criteria for invocation of the criminal sanction. First, it is a way to make sure that a given form of conduct is not being subjected to the criminal sanction purely or even primarily because it is thought to be immoral. It forces an inquiry into precisely what bad effects are feared if the conduct in question is not suppressed by the criminal law. Second, it immediately brings into play a host of secular inquiries about the effects of subjecting the conduct in question to the criminal sanction. One cannot meaningfully deal with the question of harm to others without weighing benefits against detriments. In that sense, it is a kind of threshold question, important not so much in itself, as in focusing attention on the further considerations relevant to the ultimate decision. It is for these two instrumental reasons rather than for either its intrinsic rightness or ease of application that it deserves inclusion.[58]

It is easy to think of the harm principle in a narrow constrained way as meaning only direct harms to others. For some this fails to provide necessary protection against more remote

---

[49] [1994] AC 212.

[50] See the materials in Ch 17 below, p 618.

[51] See the special issue of the British Journal of Criminology 'Moral Panics – 36 Years On' (2009) 49(1).

[52] See below, p 1076.

[53] The philosophical literature on this topic is vast. See, *inter alia*, Wilson, *Central Issues*, Ch 1, and references therein.

[54] Harm can be defined to include endangerment to V's interests where D foresees that he might damage those interests although he is not acting intentionally to damage them. See further Duff, 'Criminalising Endangerment' in *Defining Crimes*; cf C Clarkson, 'Aggravated Endangerment' (2007) 60 CLP 279.

[55] See the review of the last 25 years by Duff (2005) 25 OJLS 353.

[56] For arguments that the harm principle is over and underinclusive see Duff, *Answering for Crime*, Ch 6.

[57] J Feinberg, *Harm to Others* (1984); H Packer, *The Limits of the Criminal Sanction* (1968) 266; H Gross, *A Theory of Criminal Justice* (1979) 119.

[58] Packer, ibid, 262.

harms.[59] A valuable refined statement of the harm principle is that by Professors Gardner and Shute:

It is no objection to the harm principle that a harmless action was criminalised nor even that an action with no tendency to cause harm was criminalised. It is enough to meet the demands of the harm principle that, if the actions were not criminalised that would be harmful.... Non-instrumental wrongs, even when they are perfectly harmless in themselves, can pass this test if their criminalisation diminishes the occurrence of them, and would detract from people's prospects – for example diminishing some public good.[60]

Classification of an activity as involving a 'setback to interests' or a 'diminution of a public good' will often be a controversial question.[61] As noted, Parliament has in recent years too readily accepted that a form of behaviour is sufficiently harmful or wrong to warrant criminalization (rather than some alternative less coercive form of regulation).[62] This has been particularly striking in the context of regulatory offences.[63] In identifying the interests to be protected by the criminal law, it is increasingly important to recognize the State's obligation to protect the rights of citizens as protected by the European Convention on Human Rights (ECHR). Thus, where Art 3 guarantees a right to be free from inhuman and degrading treatment, it is incumbent on the State through the process of the criminal law to provide adequate protection against the infliction of such harm as corporal punishment.[64] Similarly, where Art 2 of the ECHR guarantees a right to life, it is incumbent on the State to provide adequate protection of that right for each citizen.[65]

1.3.2.3 Agreed basis of criminalization?

Numerous scholarly analyses have devoted thousands of pages to an attempt to identify the basis on which conduct *ought* to be criminalized. These philosophical inquiries lie beyond the scope of this work which provides a doctrinal analysis of the criminal law.[66] A most recent and compelling examination of the criminalization problem is offered by Husak in his work *Overcriminalisation*.[67] He advances a number of factors which ought to guide whether conduct ought to be criminal. These are in brief: that the criminal law ought not to be used to prohibit 'non trivial harm or evil';[68] that a criminal offence must target some wrongful conduct by the defendant;[69] that punishment for an offence is justified only when and to the extent it is deserved';[70] the burden on justifying the creation of a criminal offence is on those who seek to introduce it;[71] that the crime to be created must identify a substantial and legitimate State

---

[59] Professor Horder advances a 'true' understanding of Mill's harm principle, based upon harm prevention and the risk of the harm that might result if the conduct were not criminalized. Horder (2011) 127 LQR 37. However, he does not propose any *de minimis* threshold nor does he establish how remote the risk of harm must be before it may be legitimately the subject of the criminal law.

[60] J Gardner and S Shute, 'The Wrongness of Rape' in J Horder (ed), *Oxford Essays in Jurisprudence* (2000), 216.

[61] Elaborate systems for differentiating levels of harm and relative offence seriousness have been devised, see A von Hirsch and N Jareborg, 'Gauging Criminal Harm: A Living Standard Analysis' (1991) 11 OJLS 1.

[62] See A Ashworth, 'Interpreting Criminal Statutes: A Crisis of Legality' (1991) 117 LQR 419.

[63] See LCCP 195.

[64] See below, p 643.

[65] See the discussion below, Ch 12.

[66] See n 57 and references therein.

[67] (2008).

[68] ibid, 66.

[69] ibid, 72.

[70] ibid, 82.

[71] ibid, 100.

interest to be protected,[72] and that the criminal law introduced will directly advance that interest;[73] and that criminalization will ensure that criminal law ought not to be more extensive in scope than is necessary to achieve its purpose.[74]

1.3.3 Definition by process?

It is impossible to define the intrinsic quality of conduct which renders it criminal, or of identifying any universal purpose and difficult to agree readily on any universal moral foundation for a crime. Because of this most writers – and the courts – have been driven to 'define' whether conduct is criminal by turning to the nature of the legal proceedings which may follow from its commission.[75] The criminal quality of an act cannot be discerned by intuition; nor can it be discovered by reference to any standard but one: is the act prohibited with penal consequences?[76]

The problem then becomes one of distinguishing criminal proceedings from civil proceedings. Any attempt to distinguish between crimes and torts comes up against the same kind of difficulty encountered in defining crimes generally: that most torts are crimes as well, though some torts are not crimes and some crimes are not torts. It is not in the nature of the act, but in the nature of the proceedings that the distinction consists; and both types of proceeding may follow where an act is both a crime and a tort.[77]

Kenny,[78] in a celebrated attempt to define a crime, directed his attention to ascertaining the essential distinction between civil and criminal procedure. He rejected any distinction based on: (i) the degree of activity manifested by the State in the two types of proceeding; for though the 'contrast is a genuine and vivid one', it was incapable of being applied with precision; (ii) the tribunals; for both civil and criminal cases may be heard in the magistrates' courts and the Supreme Court; (iii) the object of the proceedings; for, while 'the object of criminal procedure is always *Punishment*', the award of exemplary damages in civil actions is also punitive; (iv) the nature of the sanctions; for, while criminal sanctions never enrich any individual, it was not true to say that all civil actions do, since some civil actions for penalties could be brought only by the Crown. The action in civil law is subject to a limitation period which does not apply in criminal law – prosecutions for conduct 40 years ago have been successful.[79]

Kenny finally seized upon the degree of control exercised over the two types of proceedings by the Crown[80] as the criterion, and defined 'crimes' as:

wrongs whose sanction is punitive and is in no way remissible by any private person, but is remissible by the Crown alone, *if remissible at all*.[81]

---

[72] ibid, 120.

[73] ibid, 145.

[74] ibid, 153.

[75] See LCCP 195, para 3.39.

[76] *Proprietary Articles Trade Association v A-G for Canada* [1931] AC 310 at 324, per Lord Atkin.

[77] A civil action for assault or battery is barred by the Offences Against the Person Act 1861, ss 44 and 45 if criminal proceedings brought in the magistrates' court by or on behalf of the victim (i) have been dismissed and a certificate of dismissal has been issued; or (ii) have resulted in conviction and the defendant has paid anything he was ordered to pay or has served any imprisonment imposed. See *Stevens and Whitehouse* (1991) 155 JP 697.

[78] Kenny, *Outlines*, Ch 1.

[79] Note that there are some offences for which time limits apply: *Burwell v DPP* [2009] EWHC 1069 (Admin) dealing with the Computer Misuse Act 1990 provisions (subsequently repealed).

[80] Above, n 78

[81] ibid, 1.

He thought it necessary to bring in the elements of punishment only to exclude action for the recovery of the Crown's debts or other civil rights; and the italicized words were included so as not to exclude certain crimes which cannot be pardoned.[82] Kenny's definition has been much criticized. Winfield[83] thought it led to a vicious circle:

What is a crime? Something that the Crown alone can pardon. What is it that the Crown alone can pardon? A crime.[84]

Winfield thought it advisable not to accept this part of Kenny's definition; and he concentrated on the question, what is punishment? The answer he arrived at is that: 'The essence of punishment is its inevitability … no option is left to the offender as to whether he shall endure it or not'; whereas, in a civil case, 'he can always compromise or get rid of his liability with the assent of the injured party'.[85] Thus we seem to arrive back at the just rejected test of who can remit the sanction.

More substantial is the point made by Williams.[86] If we are going to define crime by reference to procedure, we ought to make use of the whole law of procedure, not just one item of it – the power to remit the sanction. If a court has to decide whether a particular act which has been prohibited by Parliament is a crime, it may be guided by a reference in the statute to any element which exists only in civil, or only in criminal, procedure as the case may be. A crime is:

an act that is capable of being followed by criminal proceedings, having one of the types of outcome (punishment, etc) known to follow these proceedings.[87]

This definition is by no means so unhelpful as at first sight it may appear; for there are many points of distinction between civil and criminal procedure, and the specification in a statute of any one procedural feature which is peculiar either to the civil or the criminal law will therefore point to the nature of the wrong. The question in issue may well be whether a rule of criminal, or a rule of civil, procedure should be followed.[88] While it may be that no statute or decision gives guidance on this precise point, the procedure test may yet supply the answer if a statute or decision indicates, as the appropriate procedure, some other rule which is peculiar either to civil or to criminal proceedings. Of course, the definition tells us nothing about what acts *ought* to be crimes, but that is not its purpose. Writers who set out to define a crime by reference to the nature of the act, on the other hand, inevitably end by telling us, not what a crime is, but what the writer thinks it ought to be; and that is not a definition of a crime.

There is a further problem with reliance on the procedural differences between crime and civil law to identify a crime. In recent years, Parliament has introduced a series of measures which although formally civil orders have a quasi-criminal nature: for example, Anti-Social Behaviour Orders, Football Banning Orders, Sexual Offences Prevention Orders, Serious Crime Prevention Orders.[89] Although civil procedures and civil rules of evidence may apply,

---

[82] A public nuisance while still unabated and offences under the Habeas Corpus Act 1679, s 11.

[83] *Province of the Law of Tort* (1931) Ch VIII.

[84] ibid, 197.

[85] ibid, 200.

[86] (1955) 8 CLP at 128.

[87] ibid, 123.

[88] cf PJ Fitzgerald, 'A Concept of Crime' [1960] Crim LR 257 at 259–260. See recently *Clipston* [2011] EWCA Crim 446.

[89] Serious Crime Act 2007, Part 1, on which see R Fortson, *Blackstone's Guide to the Serious Crime Act 2007* (2008).

the consequences of breaching such an order are criminal.[90] In addition, the stigma attached to such orders is greater than that which would usually be associated with a civil order.[91]

1.3.4 The practical test: is it a crime?

From time to time, the courts have found it necessary to determine whether a proceeding is criminal or not. Before the Criminal Evidence Act 1898, the defendant could not give evidence on oath on his own behalf in a criminal case whereas (since the Evidence Act 1851) he had been able to do so in a civil action. If he wished to give evidence the nature of the proceeding had to be ascertained.[92] The same problem could arise today if it were sought to *compel* the defendant to give evidence.[93] But a fruitful source of this problem was the Judicature Act 1873, s 47, and its successor, the Judicature Act 1925, s 31(1)(a), which, until 1968,[94] provided that no appeal should lie to the Court of Appeal 'in any criminal cause or matter'. The question whether a particular proceeding is a criminal cause or matter frequently came before the Court of Appeal and the House of Lords. In these cases the test which has regularly been applied is whether the proceedings may result in the punishment of the offender. If it may, then it is a criminal proceeding.[95] As a practical test, this seems to work well enough; but it must always be remembered that it is a rule with exceptions; for some actions for penalties are undoubtedly civil actions, and yet they have the punishment of the offender as their objective; for this reason the test of punishment is jurisprudentially unsatisfactory.[96]

The meaning of punishment itself is not easy to ascertain; for the defendant in a civil case, who is ordered to pay damages by way of compensation, may well feel that he has been punished. It has been suggested[97] that:

What distinguishes a criminal from a civil sanction and all that distinguishes it . . . is the judgment of community condemnation which accompanies and justifies its imposition.

According to this view it is the condemnation, plus the consequences of the sentence – fine or imprisonment, etc – which together constitute the punishment; but the condemnation is the essential feature. From this, it is argued that we can say readily enough what a 'crime' is:

---

[90] There is a danger that these orders can create personal criminal laws – while it is not an offence for a person to enter a particular shopping centre, if D is made subject to an order not to do so, his entering the shopping centre becomes a crime personal to him. Admittedly, he is criminally liable for the breach of the court order in the ASBO and not the entry *per se*, but the effect is the same and the dangers for misuse are obvious. See for recent discussion S Hoffman and S MacDonald, 'Should ASBOs be Civilized?' [2010] Crim LR 457; P Ramsay, 'Substantively Uncivilized ASBOs' [2010] Crim LR 761; S Hoffman and S Macdonald, 'Substantively Uncivilized ASBOs: A Response' [2010] Crim LR 764.

[91] See on these A Ashworth, 'Social Control and "Anti-Social Behaviour": The Subversion of Human Rights' (2004) 120 LQR 263. See also White (2010) 126 LQR 593.

[92] *Cattell v Ireson* (1858) EB & E 91; *Parker v Green* (1862) 2 B & S 299.

[93] He is compellable in a civil but not in a criminal case.

[94] Appeal now lies to the Court of Appeal (Criminal Division) as provided by the Criminal Appeal Act 1968. See LCCP 184, *The High Court's Jurisdiction in Relation to Criminal Proceedings* (2007), and Report of that name LC 324 (2010).

[95] eg *Mellor v Denham* (1880) 5 QBD 467; *Seaman v Burley* [1896] 2 QB 344; *Robson v Biggar* [1908] 1 KB 672; *Re Clifford and O'Sullivan* [1921] 2 AC 570; *Amand v Home Secretary and Minister of Defence of the Royal Netherlands Government* [1943] AC 147; *Re Osman (No 4)* [1991] Crim LR 533.

[96] It is thought not to be a substantial objection that exemplary damages may be awarded in some civil cases; for this is merely ancillary to the main object and the occasions for their award are now much restricted: *Rookes v Barnard* [1964] AC 1129 at 1221, [1964] 1 All ER 367 at 407, HL; *Cassell & Co Ltd v Broome* [1972] AC 1027, [1972] 1 All ER 801, HL. *AB v South West Water Services Ltd* [1993] QB 507.

[97] By HM Hart, 'The Aims of the Criminal Law' (1958) 23 Law and Contemporary Problems, 401, 404.

It is not simply anything which the legislature chooses to call a 'crime'. It is not simply anti-social conduct which public officers are given a responsibility to suppress. It is not simply any conduct to which a legislature chooses to attach a 'criminal' penalty. It is conduct which, if duly shown to have taken place, will incur a formal and solemn pronouncement of the moral condemnation of the community.[98]

But if 'the formal and solemn pronouncement' means the judgment of a criminal court (and what else can it mean?) we are driven back to ascertaining whether the proceeding is criminal or not. How is the judge to know whether to make 'solemn and formal pronouncement of condemnation' or to give judgment as in a civil action? Surely, only by ascertaining whether the legislature (or the courts in the case of a common law crime) have prescribed that the proceedings shall be criminal; and this must depend, primarily, upon whether it is intended to be punitive.

1.4 Conclusion

Readers will by now have realized that the task of defining 'crime' by reference to a universal purpose for criminalization or by identifying some universally accepted ingredients such as public wrongs and harms would be extremely difficult. There is no sufficient agreement as to what these purposes or ingredients are. The best that can be offered in practical terms is to consider the process and likely outcomes.

[98] ibid, 405.

2
Sources of criminal law

The task of identifying a clear definition of crime, or even identifying common characteristics as discussed in Ch 1, is not assisted by the diverse range of sources from which existing offences derive. An important consequence of this range of sources is that it is less easy to identify any unifying thread to the criminal law: in truth there no longer is one.[1] This inhibits certainty and consistency in application of the law. As Glazebrook observed,

> the materials of our criminal law [are] now so voluminous, chaotic and contradictory, [that] the Law Lords are left free to decide cases as the fancy takes them.[2]

This chapter offers a review of the principal sources from which the criminal law derives: common law, statute, EU law, international law and the ECHR.

2.1 Common law

A particular difficulty in English criminal law is that many important and serious offences, including for example, murder, manslaughter and conspiracy to defraud, derive from the common law rather than statute. It may seem surprising that the courts in the twenty-first century are still relying on definitions of offences from judicial pronouncements of centuries ago, or even from the common law writers and reporters of great antiquity – East,[3] Hale,[4] Coke,[5] Hawkins,[6] etc. This poses problems in terms of the principle of legality and of potentially retrospective application. Challenges to some of the best established common law offences – for example, the gross negligence manslaughter offence,[7] public nuisance[8] and conspiracy to defraud – have been mounted in recent years on the grounds of certainty and retrospectivity.

There has been a growing concern that these old common law offences are being used inappropriately. For example, in *Norris v USA*,[9] and *GG plc*[10] the House of Lords rejected attempts to use the ancient common law crime of conspiracy to defraud to deal with an alleged price fixing cartel. For centuries, the common law offence had been available but at no time

---

[1] A Ashworth, 'Is the Criminal Law a Lost Cause?' (2000) 116 LQR 225.
[2] P Glazebrook, 'How Old Did You Think She Was?' [2001] CLJ 26 at 30.
[3] EH East, *A Treatise of the Pleas of the Crown* (1803).
[4] M Hale, *The History of the Pleas of the Crown* (1736).
[5] Co I Inst, *Institutes of the Laws of England* (1797).
[6] J Curwood (ed), *A Treatise of the Pleas of the Crown* (8th edn, 1795).
[7] *Misra* [2004] EWCA Crim 2375, below Ch 15.
[8] *Rimmington* [2005] UKHL 63, below Ch 32. See also LCCP 193, *Simplification of Criminal Law: Public Nuisance and Outraging Public Decency* (2010).
[9] [2008] UKHL 16.
[10] [2008] UKHL 17.

had anyone, whether an individual or a company, been successfully prosecuted for being a party or giving effect to a price fixing agreement *per se*.[11] It was novel, inappropriate use.

It has been accepted repeatedly by the courts that they will not create new offences. This is to be welcomed since it is well recognized that judicial law-making is an undemocratic process with a tendency to create uncertainty. In *Jones et al*,[12] the House of Lords made clear that statute law was the sole source of new criminal offences and it was for those elected representatives of the country in Parliament, not the executive and not the judges, to decide what conduct should be treated as criminal. This echoed their lordships recent statements in *Goldstein and Rimmington*,[13] where it was observed that just as the courts had no power to create new offences so they had no power to abolish offences (public nuisance in that case).

A further problem with common law offences arises in relation to their overlap with statute. The House of Lords has now accepted that where Parliament has defined the ingredients of an offence, that statutory offence should ordinarily be charged rather than for a common law offence which might not include the same defences and for which the potential penalty is unlimited.[14] There have been repeated calls to abolish common law offences.[15] The problems posed by common law offences are examined further in the relevant chapters in which the offences are discussed.

It should not be forgotten that the common law also provides most of the defences in English law, including insanity, automatism, intoxication, mistake,[16] duress, duress of circumstances and necessity;[17] even self-defence which Parliament has claimed recently to clarify by statute rests firmly on common law principles.[18]

2.2 Statute

Notwithstanding the common law – with all its ambiguities and flexibility – most of the English criminal law is now contained in thousands of independent statutory offences. These are not collected together as a catalogue of 'criminal legislation', and many offences appear in an otherwise unrelated statute, as for example, with offences in the Companies Act 2006 or the Insolvency Act 1986. In addition there are thousands of statutory instruments to consider. Increasingly commonly, ministers and bodies such as local authorities are provided with powers to create criminal offences by subordinate legislation.

Even within the exclusively criminal statutes, it is often difficult to discern the present law since the statutes are too readily and heavily amended without being republished in consolidated form. As Toulson LJ noted recently in *Chambers*,[19] in a case dealing with tobacco importation:

To a worryingly large extent, statutory law is not practically accessible today, even to the courts whose constitutional duty it is to interpret and enforce it. There are four principal reasons.... First, the majority of legislation is secondary legislation.... Secondly, the volume of legislation has increased very

---

[11] Parliament criminalized price fixing cartels under the Enterprise Act 2002. See M O'Kane, *The Law of Criminal Cartels: Practice and Procedure* (2009); and C Montgomery and D Ormerod (eds), *Fraud: Criminal Law and Procedure* (2008) D6.

[12] [2006] UKHL 16.

[13] [2005] UKHL 63.

[14] ibid, [30].

[15] See recently G McBain 'Abolishing Some Obsolete Common Law Crimes' (2009) 20 KLJ 89.

[16] All dealt with in Ch 11.

[17] See Ch 12.

[18] See Ch 12 and the Criminal Justice and Immigration Act 2008, s 76.

[19] [2008] EWCA Crim 2467, [24]–[27]. On the unfairness this creates, see A Ashworth (2011) MLR 1, 21, and Ch 11 below.

greatly over the last 40 years.[20] Thirdly, on many subjects the legislation cannot be found in a single place, but in a patchwork of primary and secondary legislation. Fourthly, there is no comprehensive statute law database... This means that the courts are in many cases unable to discover what the law is, or was at the date with which the court is concerned, and are entirely dependent on the parties for being able to inform them what were the relevant statutory provisions which the court has to apply.

So extensive is the problem of criminalizing by secondary legislation that the Law Commission recently proposed that no new criminal offence making provision should be created otherwise than in primary legislation.[21]

Even once the relevant provision has been identified and it has been ascertained that it is in force, as any student of the English legal system will know, the fact that an offence is laid down in a statute does not mean that its meaning is guaranteed to be clear and undisputed. Many of the decisions discussed in this book involve the appellate criminal courts wrestling with matters of statutory construction. This has the potential to generate vast numbers of appellate decisions (all of which are now accessible via the internet and legal research databases) and there is a real danger that the principle under consideration in a given case is lost in the voluminous citation of authority.[22]

This is not the place to rehearse general principles of statutory construction. However, it is worth emphasizing one particular principle of statutory construction in criminal law: that if a provision is ambiguous it ought to be interpreted in the manner favourable to the accused.[23] The courts have recently acknowledged a new dimension to that principle where the ambiguity might be resolved by reference to Ministerial statements. It has been suggested that it is not permissible to use the doctrine in *Pepper v Hart*[24] and refer to the parliamentary debates to enlarge the scope of liability, according to *Thet v DPP*.[25] However, in *Tabnak,*[26] Lord Philips CJ, again giving the judgment of the court, qualified, *obiter,* what had been said in *Thet v DPP*:[27] the inappropriateness of reliance on *Pepper v Hart*, by the prosecution to admit parliamentary material in a criminal case as an aid to statutory construction may not have the same force where a defendant in a criminal case seeks to rely on parliamentary material. The criminal courts' use of *Pepper v Hart* continues to be rather unorthodox.[28]

2.3 EU[29]

The law of the European Union is an often overlooked source of English criminal law. There is little doubt that the domestic criminal lawyer in England is experiencing the influence of EU law in criminal process (with extradition and European Arrest Warrants etc). In terms of

---

[20] His lordship referred to the 'The Law Commission's Report on Post-Legislative Scrutiny' (2006) Law Com 302, which gave some figures in Appendix C. In 2005 there were 2,868 pages of new Public General Acts and approximately 13,000 pages of new Statutory Instruments, making a total well in excess of 15,000 pages (which is equivalent to over 300 pages a week) excluding European Directives and European Regulations, which were responsible for over 5,000 additional pages of legislation.' See also LCCP 195 *Criminal Liability in Regulatory Contexts*.

[21] See LCCP 195 (2010) 3.144.

[22] See *Erskine* [2009] EWCA Crim 1425, [2010] Crim LR 48 and commentary.

[23] *Tuck v Priester* (1887) 19 QBD 627.

[24] [1993] AC 593, HL.

[25] [2006] EWHC 2701 (Admin) at [15].

[26] [2007] EWCA Crim 380, [2007] 2 Cr App R 4.

[27] [2006] EWHC 2701, [2007] 2 All ER 425.

[28] See eg the decision in *JTB* [2009] UKHL 20 on *doli incapax*, discussed in Ch 11 in full and see F Bennion [2009] Crim LR 757.

[29] See for an accessible account, E Baker, 'The European Union's Area of Freedom, Security and (Criminal) Justice 10 years on' [2010] Crim LR 833. For more detailed analysis see V Mitsilegas, *EU Criminal Law* (2008). See also E Baker, 'Taking European Criminal Law Seriously' [1998] Crim LR 361; H Jung, 'Criminal Justice – a

substantive criminal law rather than process, although it might seem as if there is little English case law dealing explicitly with EU criminal law, in fact EU law does have an important influence on a number of areas of mainstream criminal law in this country. One way EU law may influence domestic criminal law is by introducing criminal law measures at EU level. Another way is to influence the interpretation of domestic law by EU principles. Obvious examples include: cartels in competition law that are now criminalized by the Enterprise Act 2002,[30] consumer protection offences, areas of VAT evasion and carousel frauds and environmental crimes.[31]

EU law is clearly an important source of statutory criminal law in England. The impact of the EU as a source of criminal law obviously increased with the Maastricht Treaty which introduced the three pillar structure with the European Union having some competence under the third pillar in criminal matters and those affecting security.[32] With the entry into force of the Lisbon Treaty in December 2009 EU criminal law will take on an even greater significance. The Lisbon Treaty abolished the third pillar and subsumed EU action in criminal matters under the full control of the EU institutions.[33] The Lisbon Treaty confirms that ECHR rights constitute general principles of EU law,[34] and EU criminal law measures and their implementation at the domestic level must be interpreted in accordance with fundamental rights.[35]

A recent decision of the ECJ also emphasizes the importance of EU law as a source of domestic criminal law, not just by imposing obligations on Parliament, but on the courts. In *Pupino* (Case C-105/03),[36] the ECJ concluded that the Italian courts were required to interpret Italian legislation, as far as is possible, to comply with the Framework Decision. The significance of the *Pupino* case lies in the fact that the Framework Decision in question was not one having a 'direct effect', that is, capable of being invoked by individuals in domestic courts. As a result of *Pupino,* domestic courts are under a duty to interpret domestic law as far as possible in conformity with third pillar law (pre-Lisbon). The impact of *Pupino* can be seen in the House of Lords in *Dabas,*[37] a case on the implementation of the European Arrest Warrant.

Under the Lisbon Treaty, the impact of EU provisions on the courts is even greater. The EU principle of direct effect allows an individual to invoke and rely upon EU law provisions

European Perspective' [1993] Crim LR 237; J Dine, 'European Community Criminal Law' [1993] Crim LR 246; N Bridge, 'The European Communities and the Criminal Law' [1976] Crim LR 88.

[30] C Graham, 'The Enterprise Act 2002 and Competition Law' (2004) 67 MLR 273; C Harding and J Joshua, 'Breaking up the Hardcore: the Prospects for the Proposed Cartel Offence' [2002] Crim LR 933. See generally, Arts 81–89, EC Treaty, but specifically Art 81, EC Treaty (above), Art 82, EC Treaty (abuse of a dominant position) and Art 87, EC Treaty (State aid) which are in force so as not to distort anti-competitiveness and allow punishment of those who do in and around the EU. See also *Norris v USA* [2008] UKHL 16.

[31] As an illustration of the way that EU law might impact on domestic criminal law see recently the realization that the Video Recordings Act 1984 was invalid since it was never referred to the EU Commission. The Video Recordings Act 2010 was enacted in identical terms. See *Buidimir* [2010] EWCA Crim 1486.

[32] Under the Lisbon Treaty criminal law will be adopted by qualified majority voting in the Council and co-decision with the European Parliament. The Union will have competence to legislate on a specific list of offences, subject to a process whereby the Member State can seek reconsideration of a proposal.

[33] The UK opt-out under Protocol 21 to the Lisbon Treaty extends to legislation amending existing measures which are binding upon the UK. The UK will decide on its participation on a case-by-case basis.

[34] The Charter of Fundamental Rights, in force since December 2009 with the final ratification of the Lisbon Treaty. See Chapter VI for the provisions relating to justice. They are similar to Arts 6 and 7 ECHR. See D Denman, 'The Charter of Fundamental Rights' [2010] EHRLR 349.

[35] See recently Case C-303/05 *Advocaten voor de Wereld* ECR [2007] I-3633.

[36] Judgment of the Court of Justice, *Pupino,* Case C-105/03 (16 June 2005).

[37] *Dabas v High Court of Justice, Madrid* [2007] UKHL 7 – the House of Lords interpreted the Extradition Act 2003 in such a way in order to facilitate the operation of the European Arrest Warrant in the light of the EU Framework Decision.

directly in *national* courts.[38] EU criminal law measures adopted after the Lisbon Treaty can have direct effect if the relevant conditions are met. Moreover, since the European Court of Justice regards EU law as having primacy over national law,[39] it may be that EU criminal law adopted following the Lisbon Treaty is held to take primacy over domestic criminal law.

In some instances, EU law provides the basis of a defence rather than an offence and the English courts are bound to have regard to it. In *Searby Ltd,*[40] the defendant company was charged with offences under the Control of Pesticides Regulations 1986 pursuant to the Food and Environment Protection Act 1985 alleging that it had stored and sold pesticides in the UK without Ministerial order. The company's claim that, by reference to the classification of the pesticides under EU law, it was not obliged to obtain such an order was not considered by the trial judge. The Court of Appeal quashed the conviction, since the trial judge had failed to give effect to 'directly applicable' EU law.[41]

Specific EC Treaty Articles may also be pleaded in defence. *Dearlove*[42] provides an example. V charged a substantially higher price for goods which the buyer intended to sell on the home market than for goods intended for export. It was accepted that this policy contravened Art 85(1) of the EEC Treaty (as it then was).[43] D conspired to obtain goods from V at the lower price by dishonestly representing that he intended to export them outside the EU to Australia. His conviction was upheld because the Theft Act 1968 could not be regarded as providing statutory support of the offending pricing policy and the prosecution was brought by the Crown to protect the public. The result would have been the same if V had brought a private prosecution – the nature of the criminal proceedings would have been the same. But the court accepted that, if the prosecution had undermined the effectiveness of Art 85(1) or favoured or reinforced the contravention, the appeal would have been allowed. And it might also have been different if the prosecution had been brought under a regulation made to enforce the offending policy. Other examples of EU law as a defence include unsuccessful attempts to rely on provisions of the Treaty which secure rights of free movement of goods as a defence to the importation of obscene articles.[44]

There are also instances where challenges have been launched in the ECJ against domestic criminal law on the basis that the domestic law provides a disproportionate penalty to the exercise of Community law rights. For example, a provision of national legislation requiring the exchange of a national driving licence issued by another Member State for a driving licence of that nation within a year of the holder's taking up residence may infringe free movement rights.[45]

There is a growing influence of EU law on the criminal process in the UK in more general terms following the gradual expansion of the EU's laws on Common Foreign and Security Policy. Under the changes implemented by the Treaty of Lisbon, there is now shared competence between the EU and the Member States with regard to common foreign and security

---

[38] See Case 26/62 *Van Gend en Loos* [1963] ECR 13. This applies even if EU law has not been (properly) implemented in Member States.

[39] Case 6/64 *Costa v Enel* [1964] ECR 585.

[40] [2003] EWCA Crim 1910.

[41] See European Communities Act 1972, s 2(1).

[42] *Dearlove, Druker* (1988) 88 Cr App R 279, CA.

[43] ie, restrictive agreements and concerted practices, now Art 81(1) following Amsterdam's EC Treaty 1999.

[44] Case 34/79, *Henn and Darby* [1979] ECR 3795; see also Case 121/85, *Conegate Ltd v Commissioners of Customs and Excise* [1986] ECR 1007. There is a vast amount of case law regarding free movement under the EC Treaty, with regard to 'market access', to which refer to P Craig and G de Búrca, *EU Law: Text, Cases and Materials* (4th edn, 2007) Chs 14–16.

[45] See, eg, *Skanavi and Chryssanthakopoulos* [1996] ECR I-929.

policy, as well as justice and home affairs. In particular, the impact will be felt in combating terrorism, corruption and fraud, immigration, trafficking of persons and drugs, and through the implementation of a uniform and EU-wide arrest warrant, through immigration and border control, and corruption and fraud.[46] In short, criminal law in England will continually require further examination in the light of EU developments.

2.4 International law

As supranational legal regimes have begun to exert more of an influence on English criminal law, the range of sources extends ever wider. There are several aspects to acknowledge. First, there are of course some crimes created by English law which can be committed abroad but these are not international at all, but simply extraterritorial.[47]

In addition there are numerous crimes of a transnational form in particular money laundering offences.

There is also the potential for international law to influence domestic law directly as was illustrated recently in *Jones*[48] where the appellants sought to argue that the definition of crime in s 3 of the Criminal Law Act 1967 should be interpreted to include the crime of aggression recognized in international law. This would have permitted them to argue that they were acting in prevention of a 'crime' (the international crime of aggression) when they damaged property at military establishments in England as a protest against the Iraq war. The House of Lords rejected that interpretation, recognizing that it was for Parliament to incorporate such international crimes into English law, and not for the courts.[49]

International law also influences domestic criminal law because the *origin* of domestic criminal law may be found in the UK's obligations to give effect to international law, specifically those obligations contained in treaties. For example, the offences contained in the International Criminal Court Act 2001 (genocide, war crimes and crimes against humanity as discussed in Ch 16) are defined by reference to the Rome Statute.

2.5 The ECHR and Human Rights Act 1998

The enactment of the Human Rights Act 1998 (HRA) was one of the most significant developments in English law in the last century. Its impact has been felt on the criminal law as elsewhere. Detailed consideration of the Act and the ECHR can be found in specialist texts, and the following pages offer simply an introductory overview of the most important aspects of the ECHR and its impact on substantive criminal law.[50] The Convention rights are dealt with at relevant points throughout the book.

As with other areas of law, the criminal court is, by virtue of s 2 of the Human Rights Act 1998, obliged to 'take account' of ECHR jurisprudence in construing English law. This is problematic since much of the Strasbourg jurisprudence is vague and general in nature and not in the familiar form of common law case precedents. In addition there is the problem

---

[46] See S Peers, *EU Justice and Home Affairs Law* (2nd edn, 2006); D Dinan, *Ever Closer Union* (2nd edn, 1999); T Tridimas, *The General Principles of EC Law* (1999); TC Hartley, *The Foundations of European Community Law* (5th edn, 2003) 261–267; Craig and de Búrca, *EU Law*, esp Ch 1 and pp 301–312.

[47] See P Alldridge, *Relocating Criminal Law* (2000) Ch 7.

[48] [2006] UKHL 16; see also the commentary at [2007] Crim LR 66.

[49] See Lord Bingham [2006] UKHL 16 at paras 12, 23, 28.

[50] See, generally, B Emmerson, A Ashworth and A Macdonald, *Human Rights and Criminal Justice* (2nd edn, 2007); J Cooper and M Colvin, *Human Rights in the Investigation and Prosecution of Crime* (2009).

that so often in criminal matters the ECtHR accepts that the actions of the relevant State are within the margin of appreciation. This accommodates the Member States' distinctive criminal law traditions and cultures, but renders the protection in substantive law relatively weak.[51] Under s 3 of the 1998 Act the courts must ensure that statutes 'so far as it is possible to do so, be read and given effect in a way which is compatible with the Convention rights'. Examples of the criminal courts' approach to that duty can be seen in numerous cases. Lord Bingham has recently summarized the position:

First, the interpretative obligation under s 3 is a very strong and far reaching one, and may require the court to depart from the legislative intention of Parliament. Secondly, a Convention-compliant interpretation under s 3 is the primary remedial measure and a declaration of incompatibility under s 4 an exceptional course. Thirdly, it is to be noted that during the passage of the Bill through Parliament the promoters of the Bill told both Houses that it was envisaged that the need for a declaration of incompatibility would rarely arise. Fourthly, there is a limit beyond which a Convention-compliant interpretation is not possible.... In explaining why a Convention-compliant interpretation may not be possible, members of the committee used differing expressions: such an interpretation would be incompatible with the underlying thrust of the legislation, or would not go with the grain of it, or would call for legislative deliberation, or would change the substance of a provision completely, or would remove its pith and substance, or would violate a cardinal principle of the legislation.... All of these expressions, as I respectfully think, yield valuable insights, but none of them should be allowed to supplant the simple test enacted in the Act: 'So far as it is possible to do so...'. While the House declined to try to formulate precise rules...it was thought that cases in which s 3 could not be used would in practice be fairly easy to identify.[52]

Where necessary the High Court, Court of Appeal or Supreme Court may declare a statute to be incompatible (HRA 1998, s 4) but cannot 'strike down' legislation. The courts have held some criminal statutes incompatible in controversial circumstances.[53] A court may 'read down' a statute to avoid a declaration of incompatibility. This has already proved necessary in some criminal cases.[54]

The ECHR imposes positive and negative obligations. Thus, the State cannot infringe a person's rights by, for example, denying his right to life (negative obligation). Equally, the State is obliged to provide protection for an individual's rights by ensuring the criminal law punishes and deters those who infringe rights (positive obligation).[55]

Some Articles of the Convention expressly impose such positive obligations,[56] as for example with Art 2 providing that the right to life 'shall be protected by law'. Many other guarantees under the Convention have been interpreted by the ECtHR to impose an obligation on the State to create laws which will protect the Convention rights of one individual from being infringed by another.[57]

---

[51] See K Cavanagh, 'Policing the Margins: Rights Protection and the European Court of Human Rights' [2006] EHRLR 422.

[52] A-G's Reference (No 4 of 2002) [2004] UKHL 43 at [28].

[53] See, eg, A v Secretary of State for the Home Department [2004] UKHL 56 on the Anti-terrorism, Crime and Security Act 2001.

[54] See, eg, Lambert [2002] 2 AC 545.

[55] See, further, J Rogers, 'Applying the Doctrine of Positive Obligations in the European Convention of Human Rights to Domestic Substantive Criminal Law in Domestic Proceedings' [2003] Crim LR 690. See also on the State's duty to protect life: Van Colle v CC of Hertfordshire [2008] UKHL 50.

[56] See generally S Fredman, Human Rights Transformed (2008).

[57] See Emmerson, Ashworth and Macdonald, HR&CJ, para 2.53.

2.5.1 'Criminal charge'

The meaning of a criminal offence in the context of the European Convention on Human Rights is a relatively new issue in domestic law. Enactment of the Human Rights Act 1998 increases the likelihood of the courts being compelled to decide whether proceedings are criminal, particularly when considering the protections of liberty in Art 5 and those of a fair trial in Art 6. However, the concept of a 'criminal charge' is an autonomous Convention concept, and the national courts can readily avoid any categorical determination for the purposes of English law.[58] The European Court has determined that if domestic law classifies the proceeding as criminal, this will be decisive, but where domestic law classifies the proceeding as non-criminal, the ECtHR will consider the true nature of the proceedings, taking into account the severity of the penalty which may be imposed looking especially at whether imprisonment is a possible penalty;[59] whether the rule applies only to a specific group or to the public generally;[60] whether there is a 'punitive or deterrent element' to the process;[61] whether the imposition of any penalty is dependent upon a finding of culpability;[62] and whether other Member States classify such conduct as criminal.[63] The impact of this context can be seen in domestic law: in H,[64] the House of Lords held that proceedings to determine whether D is unfit to plead under s 4 or s 4A of the Criminal Procedure (Insanity) Act 1964, do not involve the determination of a criminal charge since they do not result in a conviction or in any punishment.[65]

Ironically, this enhanced opportunity for clearer judicial definition of the concept of criminal proceedings occurs at a time when Parliament seems intent on blurring the boundaries of criminal law with the creation of quasi-criminal processes and orders such as those involving Anti-Social Behaviour.[66]

2.5.2 Convention rights and substantive criminal law

Although the ECHR impact is most significant in the context of evidence and procedure, the ECHR also has a direct impact on the operation of the substantive criminal law in many ways.[67]

---

[58] Engel v Netherlands [1976] 1 EHRR 647; Benham v United Kingdom [1996] 22 EHRR 293; see recently on 'criminal charge': R (R) v Durham Constabulary [2005] UKHL 21.

[59] Unless the 'nature, duration or manner of execution of the imprisonment' is such that it could not be 'appreciably detrimental': Engel, ibid.

[60] Weber v Switzerland (1990) 12 EHRR 508, para 33; Benham v United Kingdom (1996) 22 EHRR 293, para 56. See A Lester and D Pannick, Human Rights Law and Practice (2004) 4.6.13.

[61] Öztürk v Germany (1984) 6 EHRR 409, para 53; Bendenoun v France (1994) 18 EHRR 54, para 47.

[62] Benham v United Kingdom (1996) 22 EHRR 293, para 56.

[63] Öztürk v Germany (1984) 6 EHRR 409, para 53.

[64] [2003] 1 WLR 411, HL.

[65] See Ch 11 below.

[66] Crime and Disorder Act 1998, Part 1; Anti-social Behaviour Act 2003. See generally R (McCann) v Crown Court at Manchester [2003] 1 AC 787, HL. This trend in over-criminalization has caused Professor Ashworth to ask 'Is the Criminal Law a Lost Cause?' (2000) 116 LQR 225. 21.

[67] There was a substantial debate as to how significant an impact the Human Rights Act would have: for a minimalist view, see Buxton LJ, 'The HRA and Substantive Criminal Law' [1999] Crim LR 335; and for a more radical expectation see A Ashworth, 'HRA 1998 and Substantive Law' [2000] Crim LR 564.

2.5.2.1 Definition and interpretation

In terms of definition of crimes, the greatest impact might be under Art 7, which proscribes retrospective criminalization. Article 7 has been interpreted so as to prohibit vague criminal offences, as well as those that are truly retrospective. Article 7 provides:

(1) No one shall be held guilty of any criminal offence on account of any act or omission which did not constitute a criminal offence under national or international law at the time when it was committed. Nor shall a heavier penalty be imposed than the one that was applicable at the time the criminal offence was committed.

(2) This Article shall not prejudice the trial and punishment of any person for any act or omission which, at the time it was committed, was criminal according to the general principles of law recognized by civilized nations.

The European Court held in *Kokkinakis v Greece*,[68] and has reiterated many times since, that:

Article 7 is not confined to prohibiting the retrospective application of the criminal law to an accused's disadvantage: it also embodies, more generally, the principle that only the law can define a crime and prescribe a penalty (*nullum crimen, nulla poena sine lege*) and the principle that the criminal law must not be extensively construed to an accused's detriment, for instance by analogy ... it follows that an offence must be clearly defined in the law.

The Strasbourg Court looks to whether the individual can know from the wording of the relevant provision and, if need be, with the assistance of the courts' interpretation of it, which acts and omissions will make him criminally liable. This is not a prohibition on the development of the common law. As the Court noted in *SW*:[69]

However clearly drafted a legal provision may be, in any system of law, including criminal law, there is an inevitable element of judicial interpretation. There will always be a need for elucidation of doubtful points and for adaptation to changing circumstances. Indeed, in the United Kingdom, as in the other Convention States, the progressive development of the criminal law through judicial law-making is a well entrenched and necessary part of legal tradition. Article 7 of the Convention cannot be read as outlawing the gradual clarification of the rules of criminal liability through judicial interpretation from case to case, provided that the resultant development is consistent with the essence of the offence and could reasonably be foreseen.

In general, the English courts have taken a very narrow view of the protection afforded by Art 7[70] and have failed to accept that common law crimes such as manslaughter by gross negligence,[71] and public nuisance[72] are incompatible with Art 7 on the grounds of their vagueness. One striking example of the English courts' narrow approach is *Haw v Secretary of State*,[73] where the court held that there was no infringement when the Serious Organised Crime and Police Act 2005 imposing restrictions on demonstrations in Parliament Square was applied to someone whose protest there had started before the Act was even drafted.

The House of Lords[74] did rely on Art 7 in rejecting the Crown's use of conspiracy to defraud when that offence had never previously been used to prosecute the alleged wrongdoing – price fixing. The House acknowledged the 'consistent message ... through cases decided

---

[68] 25 May 1993 (Series A No 260-A, p 22), para 52.
[69] See *SW v United Kingdom* (1995) 21 EHRR 363, para 35.
[70] See C Murphy, 'The Principle of Legality in Criminal Law under the ECHR' [2010] EHRLR 194.
[71] *Misra* [2004] EWCA Crim 2375.
[72] *Rimmington* [2006] UKHL 63.
[73] [2005] EWCA Civ 532.
[74] *Norris v USA* [2008] UKHL 16; *GG* [2008] UKHL 17.

from 1875 through to 1984, was that price-fixing was not of itself capable of constituting a crime.... There was no reported case, indeed, it would appear, no unreported case, no text-book, no article which suggested otherwise.'[75] As such, it would infringe the principle of legality to impose the offence without warning. The House of Lords distinguished *SW* since in that case there was a gradual change in the law incrementally criminalizing marital rape and hence the availability of the charge had become reasonably foreseeable.

Many of the other Articles of the Convention will also affect the application of existing and future[76] crimes.

2.5.3 The Convention rights

Many of the ECHR rights as specified in the Human Rights Act 1998, Sch 1, are of importance in determining the appropriate scope and application of offences. There are numerous examples provided throughout the book, but a few simple examples show how widely the impact of the Convention can be felt in substantive criminal law:

- Article 2 will impact on the scope of the protection offered by the law of homicide and the qualifications on the scope of self-defence, on abortion and euthanasia.[77] In *Pretty v DPP*, as confirmed in *Pretty v UK*, Article 2 does not enshrine the right to self determination so as to require the State to permit the terminally ill to determine for themselves when they die;

- Article 3 will regulate the parental administration of corporal punishment;[78]

- Article 4 led to the introduction of a slavery offence in 2009.

- Article 5 will affect the manner in which defendants found unfit to plead or not guilty by reason of insanity will be treated,[79] and eg the definition of false imprisonment;[80]

- Article 6 may impact on the use of reverse burden of proof defences;[81]

- Article 8 will be relevant in protecting the rights of consenting adults to engage in sexual behaviour;[82]

- Article 9 could impact on the right of a religious group to conduct a service in public;

- Article 10 could offer a defence to those charged with offences in which they are expressing themselves in the form of protest – criminal damage or public order or obscenity;[83]

- Article 11 could affect the way the public order restrictions on a meeting are enforced;[84] and

- Article 14 could impact on the way that the criminal law discriminates against spouses or non-married couples.

---

[75] At [55].

[76] As the Minister must give an assurance to Parliament that any Bill is compatible with the ECHR: HRA 1998, s 19. Note, however, this was provided in the Bill in its original form when presented to Parliament. See, generally, ATH Smith, 'The Human Rights Act and the Criminal Lawyer: The Constitutional Context' [1999] CLR 251. The Law Commission's proposals are very keenly influenced by ECHR concerns; see, eg, LC 282, *Children: Their Non-Accidental Deaths or Serious Injury* (2003).

[77] See Chs 12–17.

[78] See Ch 17.

[79] See Ch 11.

[80] See Ch 17.

[81] See Ch 7.

[82] See Ch 18.

[83] Chs 29, 31, 32.

[84] Ch 32.

The relevant Articles are set out here for ease of reference.

Article 2

2. (1) Everyone's right to life shall be protected by law. No one shall be deprived of his life intentionally save in the execution of a sentence of a court following his conviction of a crime for which this penalty is provided by law.

(2) Deprivation of life shall not be regarded as inflicted in contravention of this Article when it results from the use of force which is no more than absolutely necessary:

(a) in defence of any person from unlawful violence;

(b) in order to effect a lawful arrest or to prevent the escape of a person lawfully detained;

(c) in action lawfully taken for the purpose of quelling a riot or insurrection.

Article 3

3. No one shall be subjected to torture or to inhuman or degrading treatment or punishment.

Article 4

(1) No one shall be held in slavery or servitude.

(2) No one shall be required to perform forced or compulsory labour.

(3) For the purpose of this article the term 'forced or compulsory labour' shall not include:

(a) any work required to be done in the ordinary course of detention imposed according to the provisions of Article 5 of this Convention or during conditional release from such detention;

(b) any service of a military character or, in case of conscientious objectors in countries where they are recognized, service exacted instead of compulsory military service;

(c) any service exacted in case of an emergency or calamity threatening the life or well-being of the community;

(d) any work or service which forms part of normal civic obligations.

Article 5

5. (1) Everyone has the right to liberty and security of the person. No one shall be deprived of his liberty save in the following cases and in accordance with a procedure prescribed by law:

(a) the lawful detention of a person after conviction by a competent court;

(b) the lawful arrest or detention of a person for non-compliance with the lawful order of a court or in order to secure the fulfilment of any obligation prescribed by law;

(c) the lawful arrest or detention of a person effected for the purpose of bringing him before the competent legal authority on reasonable suspicion of having committed an offence or when it is reasonably considered necessary to prevent his committing an offence or fleeing after having done so;

(d) the detention of a minor by lawful order for the purpose of educational supervision or his lawful detention for the purpose of bringing him before the competent legal authority;

(e) the lawful detention of persons for the prevention of the spreading of infectious diseases, of persons of unsound mind, alcoholics or drug addicts or vagrants;

(f) the lawful arrest or detention of a person to prevent his effecting an unauthorized entry into the country or of a person against whom action is being taken with a view to deportation or extradition.

(2) Everyone who is arrested shall be informed promptly, in a language which he understands, of the reasons for his arrest and of any charge against him.

(3) Everyone arrested or detained in accordance with the provisions of paragraph (1)(c) of this Article shall be brought promptly before a judge or other officer authorized by law to exercise judicial power and shall be entitled to trial within a reasonable time or to release pending trial. Release may be conditioned by guarantees to appear for trial.

(4) Everyone who is deprived of his liberty by arrest or detention shall be entitled to take proceedings by which the lawfulness of his detention shall be decided speedily by a court and his release ordered if the detention is not lawful.

(5) Everyone who has been the victim of arrest or detention in contravention of the provisions of this Article shall have an enforceable right to compensation.

Article 6

6. (1) In the determination of his civil rights and obligations or of any criminal charge against him, everyone is entitled to a fair and public hearing within a reasonable time by an independent and impartial tribunal established by law. Judgment shall be pronounced publicly but the press and public may be excluded from all or part of the trial in the interest of morals, public order or national security in a democratic society, where the interests of juveniles or the protection of the private lives of the parties so require, or to the extent strictly necessary in the opinion of the court in special circumstances where publicity would prejudice the interests of justice.

(2) Everyone charged with a criminal offence shall be presumed innocent until proved guilty according to law.

(3) Everyone charged with a criminal offence has the following minimum rights:

(a) to be informed promptly, in a language which he understands and in detail, of the nature and cause of the accusation against him;

(b) to have adequate time and facilities for the preparation of his defence;

(c) to defend himself in person or through legal assistance of his own choosing or, if he has not sufficient means to pay for legal assistance, to be given it free when the interests of justice so require;

(d) to examine or have examined witnesses against him and to obtain the attendance and examination of witnesses on his behalf under the same conditions as witnesses against him;

(e) to have the free assistance of an interpreter if he cannot understand or speak the language used in court.

Article 8

8. (1) Everyone has the right to respect for his private and family life, his home and his correspondence.

(2) There shall be no interference by a public authority with the exercise of this right except such as is in accordance with the law and is necessary in a democratic society in the interests of national security, public safety or the economic well-being of the country, for the prevention of disorder or crime, for the protection of health or morals, or for the protection of the rights and freedoms of others.

Article 9

9. (1) Everyone has the right to freedom of thought, conscience and religion; this right includes freedom to change his religion or belief and freedom, either alone or in community with others and in public or private, to manifest his religion or belief, in worship, teaching, practice and observance.

(2) Freedom to manifest one's religion or beliefs shall be subject only to such limitations as are prescribed by law and are necessary in a democratic society in the interests of public safety, for the protection of public order, health or morals, or for the protection of the rights and freedoms of others.

Article 10

10. (1) Everyone has the right to freedom of expression. This right shall include freedom to hold opinions and to receive and impart information and ideas without interference by public authority and regardless of frontiers. This Article shall not prevent States from requiring the licensing of broadcasting, television or cinema enterprises.

(2) The exercise of these freedoms, since it carries with it duties and responsibilities, may be subject to such formalities, conditions, restrictions or penalties as are prescribed by law and are necessary in a democratic society, in the interests of national security, territorial integrity or public safety, for the prevention of disorder or crime, for the protection of health or morals, for the protection of the reputation or rights of others, for preventing the disclosure of information received in confidence, or for maintaining the authority and impartiality of the judiciary.

Article 11

11. (1) Everyone has the right to freedom of peaceful assembly and to freedom of association with others, including the right to form and to join trade unions for the protection of his interests.

(2) No restrictions shall be placed on the exercise of these rights other than such as are prescribed by law and are necessary in a democratic society in the interests of national security or public safety, for the prevention of disorder or crime, for the protection of health or morals or for the protection of the rights and freedoms of others. This Article shall not prevent the imposition of lawful restrictions on the exercise of these rights by members of the armed forces, of the police or of the administration of the State.

Article 14

14. The enjoyment of the rights and freedoms set forth in this Convention shall be secured without discrimination on any ground such as sex, race, colour, language, religion, political or other opinion, national or social origin, association with a national minority, property, birth or other status.

Key issues of interpretation are worth emphasizing. In the case of Arts 2 and 3 the rights are absolute.[85] With Arts 8 to 10, the rights are qualified. Thus, although there may be a *prima facie* breach of the right, it is open to the Crown to show that the restriction on the exercise of that right is (i) prescribed by law (or in accordance with law); (ii) is necessary in a democratic society for one or more specified objectives (such as the protection of public order, health or morals, or the rights of others); and (iii) that it is a proportionate interference[86] with the right in order to promote those specified objectives. For example, where D is prosecuted for possession of cannabis and claims his conduct was in accordance with his religion, it will be for the Crown to establish that the law relating to misuse of drugs is sufficiently clearly prescribed by law, and that the offence and prosecution are necessary and proportionate to protect public order or prevent crime, etc.[87]

---

[85] What is meant by that is that the rights are absolute in their negative conception. However, when a claimant alleges a breach of the State's positive duty, these rights are subject to considerations of proportionality. See Lord Carswell in *Re Officer L* [2007] UKHL 36 [19] et seq.

[86] Even with absolute rights, there is some flexibility. For example in *Brown v Stott* [2000] UKPC D3 Lord Bingham stated that although Art 6 is absolute, its constituent elements are not. On the ECtHR approach see *O'Halloran and Francis v UK* (2007) Appn 15809/02.

[87] See Alldridge, *Relocating Criminal Law,* Ch 7.

2.5.4 Article 6(2) of the ECHR and the burden of proof[88]

The famous case of *Woolmington v DPP*[89] makes clear that the requirement for the prosecution to prove the guilt of the defendant beyond a reasonable doubt is a fundamental principle of English law. Article 6(2) of the ECHR reinforces this, providing that a person 'charged with a criminal offence shall be presumed innocent until proved guilty according to the law'. The effect of the presumption is that in any criminal trial the prosecution bear the burden of proving (beyond a reasonable doubt) that the defendant performed the relevant *actus reus* with the requisite *mens rea* in the crime alleged. The defendant will bear the burden of raising sufficient evidence to get any defences off the ground. For example, where it is alleged that D murdered V, the prosecution must establish all the elements of murder, and D will have an obligation to adduce sufficient evidence to raise his defence, for example, self-defence. The prosecution will then be obliged to rebut that defence to the criminal standard of proof, that is, making the jury satisfied so that they are sure that D was not acting in self-defence.

In exceptional circumstances, D bears a more onerous duty: to prove a fact on the balance of probabilities, rather than merely to adduce evidence of it. The first exception is where D pleads insanity. His obligation is to prove that it is more probable than not that he was 'insane' in law.[90] A second exception is where D pleads diminished responsibility under s 2 of the Homicide Act 1957. Again, it is for D to prove that it is more probable than not that he was in a diminished state at the time of the killing. Further exceptional categories are created by Parliament, but these must be treated with caution, since all must comply with Art 6(2).[91] Finally, there are implied statutory exceptions where the offence provides any 'exception, exemption, proviso, excuse or qualification whether or not it accompanies the description of the offence in the enactment creating the offence'.[92] It is rather unsatisfactory that such an important matter as the imposition of the burden of proof turns on the matter of form in the statutory drafting, and is not obvious in every offence creating provision.

Where an offence imposes a *legal burden* on the accused to *prove* a matter, rather than imposing merely an *evidential burden* to *raise* evidence of a matter, the question of compatibility with Art 6(2) arises. The leading ECHR authority on the application of Art 6(2) is *Salibiaku v France*.[93] The Court recognized that Art 6(2) does not regard presumptions of fact or of law provided for in the criminal law with indifference. It requires States to confine them within reasonable limits which take into account the importance of what is at stake and maintain the rights of the defence.[94]

The English courts have rapidly, though not consistently, developed a domestic jurisprudence on the imposition of a burden on the accused.[95] No fewer than four visits to the House of Lords have failed to produce definitive guidance on the matter.[96] In the most recent pronouncement, the House held that the court's responsibility in construing statutory provisions which appear to place a burden on a defendant is not to decide whether a reverse burden should be imposed on a defendant, but rather to evaluate whether Parliament's enactment unjustifiably

---

[88] See generally A Stumer, *The Presumption of Innocence, Evidential and Human Rights Perspectives* (2010).

[89] [1935] AC 462.

[90] See T Jones, 'Insanity, Automatism and the Burden of Proof on the Accused' (1995) 111 LQR 475.

[91] Arguably these are not so exceptional – see A Ashworth and M Blake, 'The Presumption of Innocence in English Criminal Law' [1996] Crim LR 306, who found around 40% of crimes imposing a burden on D.

[92] See the Magistrates' Courts Act 1980, s 101, in relation to summary offences. The House of Lords has applied the same essential criteria in finding implied burdens in indictable offences: *Hunt* [1987] AC 352.

[93] (1988) 13 EHRR 379.

[94] Para 28.

[95] See IH Dennis, 'Reverse Onuses and the Presumption of Innocence' [2005] Crim LR 901.

[96] See *R v DPP, ex p Kebilene* [2000] 2 AC 326; *Lambert* [2002] AC 545; *Johnstone* [2003] 1 WLR 736; *A-G's Reference (No 4 of 2002)* [2004] UKHL 43. See also *Chargot Ltd* [2009] UKHL 73.

infringes the presumption of innocence. Consider the case of a burden placed on the accused on a charge of membership of a proscribed organization under s 11 of the Terrorism Act 2000,[97] where Lord Bingham, identified five reasons[98] for his conclusion that the presumption was unjustifiably infringed:

(1) the reverse burden created a real risk that innocent individuals might be convicted, since the section is capable of applying to people who have no culpability;

(2) it could be difficult for any individual to prove that he has not participated in activities, since terrorist organizations do not often keep records;

(3) if the legal burden rested on defendants, courts would in some cases convict those who could not establish their innocence;

(4) the potential punishment is up to 10 years' imprisonment;

(5) the security considerations, although important, do not absolve Member States from their duty to ensure that basic standards of fairness are observed.

This can be contrasted with their lordships' conclusion in the conjoined appeal in *Sheldrake*, dealing with s 5(2) of the Road Traffic Act 1988 which provides a defence to the offence of drink driving.[99] The House of Lords held unanimously that Parliament had not acted unjustifiably in placing the burden on the accused in relation to that defence.[100]

The defendant has a full opportunity to show that there was no likelihood of his driving, a matter so closely conditioned by his own knowledge and state of mind at the material time as to make it much more appropriate for him to prove on the balance of probabilities that he would not be likely to drive than for the prosecutor to prove, beyond reasonable doubt, that he would...If a driver tries and fails to establish a defence under section 5(2), I would not regard the resulting conviction as unfair.

The guiding principles in determining the compatibility of a reverse onus provision appear to be the severity of sentence, the ease of proof for the defence and the risk of convicting the innocent.[101] These principles do not form a sufficiently solid or clear basis to guide the lower courts in future decision-making, and it is clear that the matter will require further appellate attention.[102]

2.6 A criminal code

It is an open question whether codified law necessarily equals better or even simpler law.[103]

England's lack of a code of criminal law – a single scheme of offences and elements of the general part of criminal law – adds to a lack of clarity, but also to a lack of accessibility. The Law Commission's[104] declared objective in its project to create a criminal code for England and Wales is to enhance the law's accessibility, comprehensibility, consistency and certainty.

---

[97] Section 11(2) provides: It is a defence for a person charged with an offence under subsection (1) to prove that the organisation was not proscribed on the last (or only) occasion on which he became a member or began to profess to be a member, and that he has not taken part in the activities of the organisation at any time while it was proscribed.

[98] [51]. See generally on the ECHR and terrorism, R Buxton [2010] Crim LR 533.

[99] Which provides that it is a defence for the defendant to prove that although he was in charge of the vehicle and was intoxicated beyond the legal limit 'the circumstances were such that there was no likelihood of his driving the vehicle whilst the proportion of alcohol' in his body exceeded the limit.

[100] [41]. See also *Chargot Ltd* [2009] UKHL 73.

[101] For cogent criticism, see A Ashworth, commenting in [2005] Crim LR 215.

[102] See especially Dennis [2005] Crim LR 901.

[103] J Horder, 'The Changing Face of the Law of Homicide', in J Horder (ed), *Homicide Law in Comparative Perspective* (2007) 31. Professor Horder was at that time the Criminal Law Commissioner.

[104] See www.lawcom.gov.uk. See also *Chargot Ltd* [2009] UKHL 73.

A criminal code has obvious attractions beyond these important objectives. A code would help to ensure that national law meets its international obligations. Symbolically also, the adoption of a criminal code provides an opportunity for the State to declare its position in relation to criminal behaviour in a transparent fashion.[105] A criminal law with a single accessible authoritative source, which is internally consistent and certain, would in most people's eyes be a welcome development, outweighing the risks that the code would be too inflexible and that judicial innovation would be stifled. Although historically England was a great exporter of criminal codes,[106] there is no sign of the adoption of the Draft Criminal Code produced in 1989 by a team of senior academic criminal lawyers.[107] There were calls for the implementation by successive Lord Chief Justices,[108] and by a former Chair of the Law Commission.[109]

One of the tremendous attributes of that Draft Code was the simplicity and succinct nature in which the offences were drafted. The value of concise and readily understood criminal law should not be underestimated. Some of the more recent Law Commission proposals have adopted more sophisticated and arguably more theoretically pure forms of offence. As so often happens, when transforming the proposals into legislation, the Government adds to the complexity of the drafting. The result is offences which are extremely complex. Whether these can be readily applied in all courts including the magistrates' court, in which 98 per cent of the criminal trials occur in England and Wales, is debatable. This is causing some to question whether the implementation of a code in this form is a beneficial exercise. As a simple illustration of the problem, readers will see in Chapter 13 that the offence of incitement which was settled common law and generated few problems in practice was redrafted in the 1989 code in the space of a page. The Law Commission's treatment of that offence in Report No 300 on *Inchoate Liability for Assisting and Encouraging* led to the enactment of Part 2 of the Serious Crime Act 2007 replacing the single offence of incitement with three new broader, more complex offences which require over 20 sections of the statute to define. This is not an isolated example.[110]

The Law Commission has been prolific in recent years in producing Consultation Papers and Reports affecting many areas of the substantive criminal law including in the last five years: murder, manslaughter, infanticide, provocation, diminished responsibility, incitement, conspiracy, attempt, secondary liability, bribery and corruption, intoxication and unfitness to plead. The papers produced are high quality with analysis of the present law and its defects, often providing empirical and comparative materials and stimulating discussion of the law. Reference to the Law Commission's valuable work is made throughout the book at the relevant points.[111]

---

[105] There is considerable literature as to the advantages of a code and what form a code might best take: see G de Búrca and S Gardner, 'Codification of the Criminal Law' (1990) 10 OJLS 559; RA Duff, 'Rule Violations and Wrong Doings', in S Shute and A Simester (eds), *Criminal Law Theory* (2002); P Alldridge, 'Making Criminal Law Known' (ibid). See, also, on recent developments in other jurisdictions PR Ferguson, 'Codifying Criminal Law: The Scots and English Draft Codes Compared' [2004] Crim LR 105; JP McCutcheon and K Quinn, 'Codifying Criminal Law in Ireland' (1998) 19 Statute Law Review 131; J Lavery (2010) 74 J Crim L 557.

[106] JF Stephen, *A Digest of the Criminal Law* and *A History of the Criminal Law of England* (1883).

[107] *A Criminal Code for England and Wales* (LC 177, 1989).

[108] See, eg, the statements by Lord Bingham of Cornhill, 'A Criminal Code: Must We Wait For Ever?' [1998] Crim LR 694.

[109] See M Arden, 'Criminal Law at the Crossroads: The Impact on Human Rights from the Law Commission's Perspective and the Need for a Code' [1999] Crim LR 439.

[110] See J Spencer, 'The Drafting of Criminal Legislation, Need it be so Impenetrable?' [2008] CLJ 585.

[111] It is worth reiterating that the views expressed in this book are the author's and not those of the Law Commission.

3

Procedure and sentencing

This book is about the substantive law of crime. That is, it attempts to state and to discuss the law which determines whether conduct amounts to a crime or not. The book is not about the procedure by which the law is enforced or the evidence by which criminal offences are proved, nevertheless it is necessary to provide an outline of:[1] the means by which offences are classified; the basic trial structure; the approach courts take to sentencing; and the structure of the appeals process.

3.1 Classification of offences

3.1.1 Indictable and summary offences

For procedural purposes crimes are classified as either indictable or summary offences. This describes the type of court hearing in which the trial will occur. Summary offences are offences which may be tried by courts having 'summary jurisdiction'. The trial is conducted by magistrates (whether a lay bench or a District Judge (magistrates' court)) without a jury. If the crime is one tried on indictment that means that the proceedings take place with a jury,[2] in the Crown Court.[3] For practical purposes it is the question of trial with or without a jury which is the important distinction between trial on indictment and summary trial. The importance of this distinction is that juries are the tribunal of fact and not law, unlike magistrates who are both. In most other respects the course and conduct of the trial are similar.[4]

The classification of offences as indictable and summary broadly reflects a distinction between serious and minor crimes. Some offences are so obviously serious that they are triable only on indictment (for example, robbery),[5] and some offences are so obviously minor

---

[1] For a more detailed treatment of the criminal process see P Hungerford-Welsh, *Criminal Procedure and Sentencing* (2009); A Ashworth and M Redmayne, *The Criminal Process: An Evaluative Study* (4th edn, 2010); A Sanders and R Young, *Criminal Justice* (3rd edn, 2006) and the practitioners' manuals D Ormerod and Hooper LJ, *Blackstone's Criminal Practice* (2011); PJ Richardson, *Archbold* (2011). See also the influential review – Auld LJ, *The Criminal Courts Review* (2001) Chs 3, 4, 5 and 7 at www.criminal-courts-review.org.uk/ccr-00.htm.

[2] Provision to allow for non-jury trial is provided in the Criminal Justice Act 2003, Part 7 in certain circumstances including, eg, cases where there has been jury tampering. There has been one such case to date : *Twomey* [2011] EWCA Crim 8. There was pressure for further extension of the exceptional categories, fuelled by collapses of lengthy trials which are claimed to be 'untriable' by a jury (see, eg, the 'Jubilee line fraud' which collapsed after almost two years at the Central Criminal Court, March 2005). On this see S Lloyd Bostock, 'The Jubilee Line Jurors' [2007] Crim LR 255; RF Julian, 'Judicial Perspectives on the Conduct of Serious Fraud Trials' [2007] Crim LR 751; see also the *Report on Interviews with Jurors in the Jubilee Line Case* (HMCPSI, 2006).

[3] Senior Courts Act 1981, s 46. When the Crown Court sits in the City of London it is known as the Central Criminal Court: Senior Courts Act s 8(3).

[4] An excellent overview of what has become an incredibly complex process is provided on the Home Office website: www.direct.gov.uk/en/CrimeJusticeAndTheLaw/index.htm .

[5] And some serious offences are more serious than others; consequently provision is made in the Senior Courts Act 1981, s 75(1) as amended by the Courts' Act 2003 for the allocation of cases as between suitably experienced

that they can be tried only summarily (for example, many road traffic offences). But for many crimes, their gravity turns upon the particular circumstances of the case. For example, the offence of theft catches the taking of £5 by an employee from a shop till and a multimillion pound bank heist. To reflect the need for the different treatment of cases charged under the same offence, many crimes can be tried in either the Crown Court or the magistrates' court: they are 'triable either way'.

Historically, the classification of offences was done on a piecemeal basis with each offence that was enacted, without any coherent overall plan. The Criminal Law Act 1977[6] restructured the system for allocating business between the magistrates' court and the Crown Court. It has been the subject of repeated amendment resulting in technical and complex provisions. The basic tripartite division remains: (a) offences triable only summarily; (b) offences triable only on indictment; and (c) offences triable either way.

3.1.1.1 Offences triable only summarily

A summary only offence is one which, if committed by an adult, is triable only in the magistrates' court.[7] Summary offences are all statutory. An offence which is classified as either way may be reclassified as summary only by Parliament where the need arises. Examples include drink-driving and assaulting constables in the execution of their duty which were made summary only by the Criminal Law Act 1977. Reclassification will usually be because of a desire to reduce the workload of the Crown Court, as with those examples. Other examples include the Criminal Justice Act 1988 reclassifying as summary only the offences of common assault and battery and taking vehicles without consent.

3.1.1.2 Offences triable only on indictment

An 'indictable' offence means an offence which, if committed by an adult, is triable on indictment. Confusingly, this label applies to offences triable *only* on indictment (in the Crown Court) as well as to those offences triable either way[8] (either in the magistrates' court or the Crown Court).

Offences triable *only* on indictment include any offence punishable by imprisonment for life on first conviction, causing death by dangerous driving and the more serious offences under the Theft Act 1968. Generally offences are made indictable only, because they are either of such exceptional gravity or because other reasons, such as anticipated complexity of issues, make them unsuitable for summary trial. All offences at common law were triable on indictment, therefore, in the absence of any specific statutory provision an offence will be triable on indictment. The trend has been to reserve indictable only offences for the most serious circumstances and most new offences are triable either way or summarily.

High Court Judges, Circuit Judges, Recorders and District Judges (Magistrates' Courts). See *Practice Direction (Criminal Proceedings: Criminal Proceedings)* [2002] 1 WLR 2870, para III.21, 'Classification of Crown Court business and allocation to Crown Court centres'. See also on levels of seriousness, LCCP 195 (2010) Ch 4.

[6] Based on the James Committee, *The Distribution of Criminal Business between the Crown Court and Magistrates' Courts* (1975) Cmnd 6323.

[7] Interpretation Act 1978, Sch 1. To conspire to commit a summary offence is an indictable offence (Criminal Law Act 1977, s 3); it is not an offence to attempt to commit an offence which is summary only, unless the statute so provides: Criminal Attempts Act 1981, ss 1 and 3, below, Ch 13. Under the Serious Crime Act 2007 Part 2, discussed in Ch 13 offences of assisting and encouraging crime are triable in the same fashion as the substantive crimes to which they relate. Thus, assisting or encouraging murder is indictable only; assisting or encouraging drink-driving is triable summarily only.

[8] Interpretation Act 1978, Sch 1.

3.1.1.3 Offences triable either way

An offence triable either way means an offence which, if committed by an adult, is triable either on indictment or summarily.[9] This class extends to (i) the offences listed in the Magistrates' Courts Act 1980, Sch I; and (ii) offences made triable either way by virtue of any other enactment.[10] The procedure for deciding whether a case should be tried in the magistrates' court or the Crown Court is outlined below.

3.1.1.4 Treasons, felonies and misdemeanours

At common law a crime might be classified either as treason, felony or misdemeanour. Originally the distinction between felony and misdemeanour was a distinction between serious and minor offences (the former involving penalties of a different order from the latter)[11] but over the years this distinction, though always broadly discernible, became blurred. But now, by s 1 of the Criminal Law Act 1967, all distinctions between felony and misdemeanour are abolished. From 1967, all offences are dealt with in the way that misdemeanours were before the Criminal Law Act. The terms appear regularly in pre-1968 cases and the reader must know to what they refer.

3.1.2 Arrestable offences

The law drew a distinction between arrestable and non-arrestable offences which had important implications for procedure and substantive criminal law. The Serious Organised Crime and Police Act 2005 abolished that distinction. The terminology will be seen in many of the cases decided prior to that date.

3.2 Procedure

It is impossible here to give anything other than a very bare outline of the stages of criminal procedure in England and Wales. Every element of the process rests on complex statutory provisions, with a mass of case law interpreting and applying them, all attracting a wealth of academic scholarship. Reference should be made to the specialist books on procedure.

In a serious case at least, following investigation and arrest, a suspect is detained and questioned. As a result of that investigation, if there is sufficient evidence the suspect will be charged with a criminal offence. In recent years there has been a proliferation of alternatives to formal prosecution – fixed penalty notices, civil orders such as ASBOs, cautions, conditional cautions etc[12] – these all seek to divert less serious offenders from the criminal court system, thereby saving court time and money.

If charged, the suspect is then likely to be released on bail, unless the offence is a serious one and there are risks associated with his being at liberty. If he is not bailed he can be held on remand in prison – even though he is still only a suspect. The CPS or other prosecution agency will review the evidence and decide whether to pursue the prosecution having regard to the CPS Code and other prosecutorial policies.[13] If the case is proceeded with,

---

[9] Interpretation Act 1978, Sch 1.

[10] Magistrates' Courts Act 1980, s 17.

[11] See generally, Pollock and Maitland, II HEL, Cap VIII, s 2.

[12] See G Dingwall and C Harding, *Diversion in the Criminal Process* (1998); see also the recent article by R White, ' "Civil Penalties": Oxymoron, Chimera and Stealth Sanction' (2010) 126 LQR 593.

[13] These can be very important in some cases – eg with assisted suicide allegations (see Ch 16 below, and the articles referred to therein) or with domestic violence (see M Madden Dempsey, *Prosecuting Domestic Violence:*

the question whether it is tried in the magistrates' court or the Crown Court depends on what class of offence has been charged – is it indictable only, triable either way or summary only?

3.2.1 Procedure for indictable only offences

The Crime and Disorder Act 1998 altered the procedure for offences triable *only* on indictment.[14] The 1998 Act removed the former requirement for 'committal proceedings'. These involved magistrates sitting as 'examining justices' to hear and review the evidence before committing (ie sending) a case to the Crown Court. Under the new regime, offenders charged with indictable only offences must be 'sent' to the Crown Court for trial without committal. Section 51 of the 1998 Act and Part 6 of and Sch 3 to the Criminal Justice Act 2003 result in a complex procedure whereby the court must send cases directly to the Crown Court without scrutiny of the evidence. The procedure allows for a challenge by the defence in the Crown Court for the charge to be dismissed if it appears to the judge that the evidence would not be sufficient for a jury to properly convict D.[15]

At trial in the Crown Court the trial judge deals with all aspects of the law and the jury with decisions of fact. The prosecution opens its case explaining what the charges on the indictment are and how it will prove them. The prosecution then calls its witnesses. They are examined in chief by the prosecution and then cross-examined by the defence. At the end of the prosecution case, the defence might claim that there is no case to answer – that the Crown has not produced enough evidence. The judge has an important power to be able to withdraw a case if there is no evidence that could justify a properly directed jury in convicting. In that case the jury will be formally directed to acquit.[16] If there is evidence on which a jury might convict the matter is left for them to return a verdict. As Moses LJ made clear recently in *Jabber*.[17]

The correct approach is to ask whether a reasonable jury, properly directed, would be entitled to draw an adverse inference. To draw an adverse inference from a combination of factual circumstances necessarily does involve the rejection of all realistic possibilities consistent with innocence. But that is not the same as saying that anyone considering those circumstances would be bound to reach the same conclusion. That is not an appropriate test for a judge to apply on the submission of no case. The correct test is the conventional test of what a reasonable jury would be en-titled to conclude.

If there is compelling evidence of guilt such that the *only* reasonable course would be for a properly directed jury to convict, the judge may comment in stronger terms than would otherwise be permissible when directing the jury at the end of the evidence, but *must not* direct the jury to convict.[18] If the case proceeds, the defence call their witnesses and these are cross-examined by the prosecution. Finally, the prosecution sums up its case in a closing speech and the defence makes a closing speech reiterating its position. The judge then directs the jury on the evidence and on the law in accordance with the Judicial Studies Board Bench book.[19] The jury retires to consider its verdict.

A *Philosophical Analysis* (2009)) or historic sexual abuse (see P Lewis, *Delayed Prosecutions for Childhood Sexual Abuse* (2005) Ch 2).

[14] Section 51 as substituted by the Criminal Justice Act 2003, Sch 3, para 18. There are complex provisions dealing with linked offences and offenders and linked offenders where one is a youth.

[15] Sch 3, para 2.

[16] *DPP v Stonehouse* [1978] AC 55 at 70, 79–80 and 94; P Devlin, *Trial by Jury* (Hamlyn Lectures, 1956) 78.

[17] [2006] EWCA Crim 2694 (at para 21): see also *Goring* [2011] EWCA Crim 2. The leading case is *Galbraith* [1981] WLR 1039.

[18] *Wang* [2005] UKHL 9.

[19] See the 2010 edition available at www.judiciary.gov.uk/Resources/JCO/Documents/benchbook_criminal_2010.pdf.

3.2.2 Procedure for either way offences

For offences falling under this head the procedure is regulated by the Magistrates' Courts Act 1980 as amended. Save for exceptional cases, D may opt for summary trial or trial on indictment. The magistrates' court may impose trial on indictment, but may (at present) not insist on summary trial if D[20] objects. The scheme obliges D to indicate a plea *before* the trial allocation decision is made.[21] If D indicates that he would plead guilty at trial, the court proceeds as if this were a guilty plea received at a summary trial. If D's indication is one of not guilty, the court listens to any representations from D and from the prosecutor, including revelations about D's antecedents, and decides on the trial allocation – should it stay in the magistrates' court or be sent to the Crown Court. The court (which can now comprise one magistrate for these purposes) takes into account the nature of the case and seriousness of the offence.[22] If the court considers summary trial more appropriate, that should be explained to D, as should the fact that he need not consent to summary trial but can opt for trial by jury. D may ask for an indication as to the likely sentence he will receive if tried summarily (that is, a custodial one or not), and this may then cause him to change his indication as to likely plea.[23] If D consents to summary trial, the case proceeds (at a later date fixed by the court if there is to be a trial). If D elects trial on indictment, the magistrates proceed to committal to transfer the case to the Crown Court.[24] If the court considers from the outset that trial on indictment is more appropriate it will proceed to send the case to the Crown Court and D effectively has no choice in the matter.[25]

There are some exceptional cases where this process is not applied. One such case worthy of note is where D is charged with a 'scheduled offence'. At the time the 1977 Act was drafted it was proposed,[26] with a view to relieving pressure on the Crown Court, that minor cases of theft and criminal damage should be triable only summarily. This proposal was accepted by Parliament[27] in relation to criminal damage but not in relation to theft on the ground that a conviction for the latter involved a stigma not involved in the former. The outcome is that where on a charge of criminal damage the value of the property does not exceed the relevant sum (currently £5,000) D must be tried summarily but, having regard to the loss of the former right to be tried by jury, the maximum punishment which the court can impose is three months' imprisonment and/or a fine at level 4. Though triable only summarily, 'low value criminal damage' remains an indictable offence for all other purposes.[28]

Trials occuring in the magistrates' court either before a bench of lay justices or a District Judge, have a procedure very similar to that for a trial on indictment. There is no jury, so the decisions as to the facts and as to the verdict are made by the justices or District Judge.

---

[20] In the case of adult joint defendants, if one consents to summary trial and the other elects for jury trial, the justices are not obliged to commit both for trial: *R v Brentwood JJ, ex p Nicholls* [1992] 1 AC 1 and see *R v Wigan JJ, ex p Layland* (1996) 160 JP 223.

[21] Magistrates' Courts Act 1980, ss 19–21 as substituted by the Criminal Justice Act 2003.

[22] Until s 19 is amended under the Ciminal Justice Act 2003.

[23] Clearly the provisions are designed to produce as many guilty pleas as early as possible in the system and to keep as many cases as possible from reaching the Crown Court.

[24] Criminal Justice Act 2003, Sch 3, para 7.

[25] Magistrates' Courts Act 1980, s 21.

[26] Cmnd 6323, paras 74–105.

[27] Magistrates' Courts Act 1980, s 22.

[28] *Fennell* (2000) 164 JP 386, [2000] Crim LR 677.

3.3 Crime and punishment

In Chapter 1, we considered how crimes might be defined, or at least identified. It is clear that while the definition of an offence can adequately *forbid* unjustifiable and inexcusable conduct, it can rarely prevent it. The mere fact that the Government pronounces that an activity is now criminal is, *in itself*, unlikely to stop its occurrence. Sometimes that happens. The Children and Young Persons (Harmful Publications) Act 1955 was said to have been 'completely successful' at a time when no prosecution had been brought under it.[29] But this is unusual. The fact that an act is known to be forbidden by the criminal law may, for many persons, be sufficient to ensure that they will not commit such an act, but for others this will not be enough. Hence our need for a law of criminal procedure – of evidence, and of sentencing.[30] The mere fact of conviction, being a public condemnation of the conduct in question, has some value in the prevention of crime, but it is far from being sufficient. Some, at least, of the purposes for which the criminal law exists can be fulfilled only through the imposition of sentences. It is therefore desirable at the outset to enquire to what ends sentences are directed – or professedly directed – by those who impose them.

As with procedure, sentencing is a complex process resting on layers of technical statutory provisions with thousands of appellate decisions and other guideline materials all aimed to produce a fair sentence for a particular offender given his offence and personal circumstances. A short descriptive account is offered to assist in putting the criminal law in context. For more detailed analysis see the many specialist works on sentencing theory and practice.

3.4 Wrongdoing and punishment

Crime has always been regarded by the courts as a moral wrong and conduct demanding retribution. The modern criminal law is based on an assumption that, in the absence of evidence to the contrary, people are able to choose whether to engage in criminal conduct or not, and that a person who chooses to commit a crime is responsible for the resulting wrong and deserves punishment.[31] The courts have generally seen their task as one of fitting the penalty to the particular degree of iniquity and dangerousness of the offender's conduct on that particular occasion. The sentence should adequately reflect the revulsion felt by citizens for the particular crime. Its purpose is seen not only as punishment but also as a public denunciation of the conduct in question. It may then satisfy the demand for retaliation by the public, or some members of the public, which serious crime sometimes arouses.

---

[29] HL, vol 299, col 451, 12 Feb 1969, quoted by G Zellick, 'Vidence as Pornography' [1970] Crim LR 192. But failure to prosecute does not mean that the harm has been eradicated. There were no prosecutions under the Prohibition of Female Circumcision Act 1985, but the practice continued and the Female Genital Mutilation Act 2003 was enacted to extend the scope of the offence. For ministerial confirmation of this and further attempts to eradicate the practice see www.theyworkforyou.com/wrans/?id=2010-11-03a.21378.h.

[30] On sentencing generally, see the accounts by A Ashworth, *Sentencing and Criminal Justice* (5th edn, 2010); DA Thomas, *Principles of Sentencing* (2nd edn, 1979) updated in looseleaf format; and M Wasik, *Emmins on Sentencing* (4th edn, 2001); R Banks, *Banks on Sentence* (5th edn, 2011).

[31] There are numerous philosophical accounts of the relationship between moral or mental responsibility and criminal responsibility. The topic lies beyond this work. See, *inter alia*, Duff, *Answering for Crime*; Tadros, *Criminal Responsibility*. For an account centred more on political theory, see A Brudner, *Punishment and Freedom: A Liberal Theory of Penal Justice* (2010).

The sentence must normally[32] be proportionate to the offence. The business of the court is to do justice and only by achieving some measure of proportion between one sentence and another can it do justice as between one offender and another. It is difficult to say, in absolute terms, that a particular sentence of imprisonment is proportionate to a particular rape or wounding – just as in the civil law it is difficult to put a cash value on the claimant's arm when it has been lost through the defendant's negligence. We are not weighing like against like. The courts have to do the best they can. In relative terms, the notion of proportionality is more practicable. It is possible to say that one wounding is worse than another; and that, if the first deserves, say, three years' imprisonment, the other deserves two.

To assist the courts in this process, the Sentencing Guidelines Council[33] and now its successor the Sentencing Council[34] publishes definitive guidelines for judges. These identify typical starting points for particular types of conduct falling within an offence. For example, someone convicted of robbery (Theft Act 1968, s 8) would be liable to a maximum sentence of life imprisonment. The Guidelines on Robbery assist the judge in sentencing such an offender by distinguishing five categories of robbery: street robbery or 'mugging'; robberies of small businesses; less sophisticated commercial robberies; violent personal robberies in the home; professionally planned commercial robberies. The Guidelines also provide lists of aggravating and mitigating features that the judge should have regard to (eg was D armed? was V vulnerable etc).

3.4.1 Sentencing purposes

When a sentence is to be imposed, the first decision to be made should be as to the object to be achieved by it.[35] Is the aim simply to mete out an appropriate punishment to a wrongdoer? Or is it to deter the wrongdoer and others from committing such offences in the future? Or to protect the public by shutting the offender away? Or is it the reform of the offender? Or a combination of these objects? Numerous theories of punishment have been advanced including those of deterrence, retribution, rehabilitation, restitution, incapacitation and denunciation. Parliament has regarded various of these theories as being more influential at one time or another, and its failure to adopt a single principled approach to sentencing for any sustained period has become a matter of concern in recent years.[36] The shift in attitude is illustrated by a comparison of the sentencing provisions of the Criminal Justice Act 1991 with those of the Criminal Justice Act 2003. In the 1991 Act the overriding principle was that criminals should 'get their just deserts'.[37] Retribution was

---

[32] There are now many circumstances in which a sentence will not appear proportionate to the individual wrongdoing if the conviction triggers an 'imprisonment for public protection', which is an indeterminate sentence under the Criminal Justice Act 2003 as amended by the Criminal Justice and Immigration Act 2008. If the judge considers that the offender poses a significant risk of serious harm as defined in the statutory criteria. Those so sentenced are required to serve the minimum term for their offence, with the Parole Board then assessing their case for release.

[33] The SGC, along with the Sentencing Advisory Panel (SAP), was abolished by s 135 of the Coroners and Justice Act 2009, which was brought into force on 6 April 2010 by SI 2010/816. Section 118 of the Act created the new Sentencing Council.

[34] On which see A Ashworth, 'Coroners and Justice Act 2009: Sentencing Guidelines and the Sentencing Council' [2010] Crim LR 389 and the Sentencing Council website: www.sentencingcouncil.org.uk.

[35] See DA Thomas, 'Sentencing: The Basic Principles' [1967] Crim LR 455 and 503.

[36] See the amendment to the Criminal Justice Act 1991 with the Criminal Justice Act 1993, the Criminal Justice and Public Order Act 1994, the Crime (Sentencing) Act 1997, the Youth Justice and Criminal Evidence Act 1999 and the consolidation in the Powers of Criminal Courts (Sentencing) Act 2000. All of the above were radically affected by the Criminal Justice Act 2003 and the Criminal Justice and Immigration Act 2008. See M Wasik, 'Going Around in Circles? Reflections on Fifty Years of Change in Sentencing' [2004] Crim LR 253. At the time of writing, the MOJ has published a Green Paper *Breaking the Cycle: Effective Punishment, Rehabilitation and Sentencing of Offenders* (2010) proposing radical changes to the system: www.justice.gov.uk/consultations/breaking-cycle-071210.htm.

[37] Crime, *Justice and Protecting the Public,* Cm 965, para 2.1.

central to the statutory framework for sentencing established by the Criminal Justice Act 1991.[38] The sentencing court was to have constant regard to the 'seriousness' of the offence. Custody was not to be imposed unless the seriousness of the offence required it or, in the case of a violent or sexual offence, custody was necessary to protect the public from the offender. If custody was imposed, it had to be commensurate with the seriousness of the offence unless a longer sentence was necessary to protect the public from a violent or sexual offender. If the offence was not serious enough to require custody, a non-custodial sentence involving some interference with liberty could be imposed – but only if the offence was serious enough to justify it.[39]

Under the 2003 Act, deterrence has assumed a more significant role. Section 142 of that Act provides the various aims of the sentencing court:

(1) Any court dealing with an offender in respect of his offence must have regard to the following:

    (a) the punishment of offenders,

    (b) the reduction of crime (including its reduction by deterrence),

    (c) the reform and rehabilitation of offenders,

    (d) the protection of the public, and

    (e) the making of reparation by offenders to persons affected by their offences.[40]

It is difficult to see how a court can have in mind all of these purposes in any one case and apply each appropriately and consistently.

The broader problem in identifying the dominant purposes of sentencing are exacerbated when more radical approaches to offender disposal are introduced into the system. Restorative justice, which seeks to include the victim in the process in an effort to make an offender appreciate the significance of his crime; apologize and gain forgiveness is one approach that has current popularity.[41]

3.4.2 Sentencing, moral fault and harm done

How is the gravity of the offence to be assessed? Section 143 of the Criminal Justice Act 2003[42] is intended to provide the courts with guidance on this.

(1) In considering the seriousness of any offence, the court must consider the offender's culpability in committing the offence and any harm which the offence caused, was intended to cause or might foreseeably have caused.

(2) In considering the seriousness of an offence ('the current offence') committed by an offender who has one or more previous convictions, the court must treat each previous conviction as an aggravating factor if (in the case of that conviction) the court considers that it can reasonably be so treated having regard, in particular, to –

    (a) the nature of the offence to which the conviction relates and its relevance to the current offence, and

    (b) the time that has elapsed since the conviction.

---

[38] As consolidated in the Powers of Criminal Courts (Sentencing) Act 2000 (hereafter 'PCC(S)A 2000').

[39] L Koffman, 'The Rise and Fall of Proportionality: The Failure of the Criminal Justice Act 1991' [2006] Crim LR 281.

[40] A von Hirsch and JV Roberts, 'Legislating Sentencing Principles: The Provisions of the Criminal Justice Act 2003 relating to Sentencing Purposes and the Role of Previous Convictions' [2004] Crim LR 639; I Edwards, 'Restorative Justice, Sentencing and the Court of Appeal' [2006] Crim LR 110.

[41] See G Johnstone and DW Vanness, *A Handbook of Restorative Justice* (2006); C Cuneen and C Hoyle, *Debating Restorative Justice* (2009); See also Edwards [2006] Crim LR 110 (last note).

[42] See for practical application DA Thomas, *Sentencing Referencer* (2010).

(3) In considering the seriousness of any offence committed while the offender was on bail, the court must treat the fact that it was committed in those circumstances as an aggravating factor.

In assessing gravity the courts must, therefore, have regard not only to the moral fault of the offender in terms of the harm that he intended or foresaw but also the amount of harm he has done. The assessment involves this explicit reference to the harm intended or *foreseen*, or, at least, foreseeable, rather than on the chance of what actually happens. However, the fact is that the law attaches greater significance to the harm done,[43] and that greater significance is ever more frequently reflected in the maximum sentences prescribed for crimes. For example, it is now an offence punishable with 14 years' imprisonment to cause death by careless driving when under the influence of drink or drugs.[44] 'Joyriding', as taking a vehicle without the owner's consent is popularly but inappropriately called, is punishable with six months' imprisonment but, if personal injury is caused, the maximum goes up to two years, and, if death is caused, 14 years.[45] In terms of the sentence actually handed down it has also long been accepted that the practice of the courts is to punish the attempt less severely than the complete offence. Less harm has been done.

3.4.3 Arriving at the right sentence in a given case

3.4.3.1 The statutory maximum

For many years Parliament's invariable practice was to fix a maximum but no minimum sentence and to leave it to the judge or magistrate to decide what sentence in the range from an absolute discharge to the specified maximum it is right to impose. Even where the maximum is imprisonment for life the court may grant an absolute discharge. The only significant exception to this rule was murder, where the court has no discretion and is required to impose a sentence of life imprisonment in all cases.

Recently, a marked unwillingness by politicians to trust the courts to impose a sufficiently severe sentence in certain types of case together with concern about persistent offenders has resulted in an increase in the number of offences and circumstances in which Parliament has decreed that mandatory penalties are to be imposed – for example for possession of a prohibited weapon[46] or burgling dwellings.[47] Except in these cases, the practice of Parliament is based on a recognition of the fact that the imperfections of offence definition are such that any definition, however carefully drafted, will embrace a wide range of culpability and that there will be some acts falling within it which are morally blameless and deserving of no punishment. Murder is no different from other crimes in this respect but it has always been treated differently for historical, emotional and, perhaps, political reasons.

3.4.3.2 The tariff

The statutory maximum gives very limited guidance to a court. It is useful only when it is not altogether out of proportion to contemporary attitudes to the crime in question. Many maxima have been revised recently but others have remained unchanged since the nineteenth century. Their origins can be traced to the terms of transportation which took the place of capital punishment in the 1820s and 1830s. Even in the case of modern revisions the

---

[43] cf the arguments advanced in particular by Professor Ashworth, see, eg, 'Defining Offences Without Harm', in PF Smith (ed), *Criminal Law Essays* (1987).
[44] Road Traffic Act 1988, s 3A, as amended; Criminal Justice Act 2003, s 285.
[45] Below, p 1141.
[46] Violent Crime Reduction Act 2006, s 30; Firearms Act 1968, s 51A.
[47] Section 111 of the PCC(S)A 2000.

practice of fixing a maximum high enough to cover the worst type of case results in maxima far above the normal range of sentences. In 1968 Parliament fixed the maximum sentence for theft at 10 years – an unrealistically long term which was almost never imposed.[48] The Criminal Justice Act 1991, s 26(1) reduces it to seven years but even this reduced maximum gives no guidance whatever to a magistrates' court and very little to a Crown Court, except in a very unusual case.

This is not to say that the maxima have no significance beyond the obligation not to exceed them. Where the judge imposed the maximum sentence of two years upon a man convicted of reckless driving (an offence now replaced by dangerous driving) in a case where the passengers in the other car narrowly escaped being burnt to death, the Court of Appeal reduced the sentence to 18 months. The court held that it was important to bear in mind that Parliament had drawn a distinction between reckless driving and causing death by reckless driving which was then punishable with five years' imprisonment.[49] That decision also demonstrates the principle that the maximum should be reserved for the worst type of case which comes before the court and a sentence which does not allow for this is wrong in principle.[50] The inconsistency in statutory maxima can produce strange anomalies.

3.4.3.3 The sentencing exercise

In principle, in the sentencing exercise the courts need to treat like cases alike and to deal consistently and transparently with relevant differences in criminal conduct between offenders. This is not an exercise in guesswork, nor can it be an exact science. As noted above, it is an attempt to maintain proportionality in the sentences imposed.[51] The courts rely on the guidelines issued from the Court of Appeal.[52] The Court of Appeal follows reports published by the Sentencing Guidelines Council[53] and now the Sentencing Council after widespread consultation. The Court of Appeal has a wide opportunity to issue guidelines in appeals from the defence, and on appeals by the Attorney General[54] (with leave of the Court of Appeal), on sentences that appear to the Attorney to be unduly lenient.

The court, having considered the relevant maximum sentence and the guideline cases, and having had regard to the Sentencing Guidelines, having heard counsel for the defence in mitigation, and having regard to any pre-sentence reports about the offender, may impose the appropriate sentence. The courts face a difficult task in securing equal treatment in sentencing while maintaining the flexibility necessary to do justice to the factual circumstances of the case.[55] In one sense, the task is made more complex, rather than assisted, by the range of disposal powers available to the court. Aside from discharges (conditional and absolute), there are custodial sentences which, under the 2003 Act, come in many forms.[56] In addition there

---

[48] I am grateful to Mr Simon Price for pointing out that occasionally, as in his case, 10-year sentences were imposed.

[49] *Staddon* [1992] Crim LR 70.

[50] Judges should not, however, use their imaginations to conjure up unlikely worst possible kinds of case: *Ambler* [1976] Crim LR 266; *Smith* [2006] EWCA Crim 2147; *Bright* [2008] 1 Cr App R(S) 102.

[51] See, generally, A von Hirsch and A Ashworth, *Proportionate Sentencing* (2005).

[52] See, eg, *Saw* [2009] EWCA Crim 01 on burglary, or *Milberry* [2003] 2 Cr App R 31 on rape. But note the Sentencing Guidelines on burglary and sex offences.

[53] www.sentencing-guidelines.gov.uk. These always influenced the Court of Appeal's decision-making: see the comments in *Oosthuizen* [2006] 1 Cr App R (S) 73.

[54] Criminal Justice Act 1988, s 36.

[55] To experience how difficult this is try the exercises – you be the judge: http//:ybtj.cjsonline.gov.uk.

[56] In recent years these included 'intermittent custody' (weekends in prison) although that scheme has now been abandoned and 'custody plus' (short terms of imprisonment with periods on licence) which seems likely to be abandoned having never been implemented.

is a range of community punishments available to the court.[57] Fines remain an enormously important disposal power for the less serious crimes. In the Crown Court fines are unlimited. The maximum fine for an either way offence tried in the magistrates' court is currently £5,000.[58] There is a standard scale of maximum fines for an adult on conviction of a summary offence,[59] with the maximum currently being £5,000. The Secretary of State is empowered by s 48 of the Criminal Justice Act 1982 to vary the maximum amount of fines, including the amounts specified in the standard scale, as appears to him to be justified by the charge.

References to the maximum sentence of imprisonment for an offence tried in the magistrates' court are, throughout the book, based on the law in February 2011. If, as seems increasingly unlikely, the Criminal Justice Act 2003, ss 280 and 281 are ever brought into force, many summary offences will carry a maximum term of imprisonment of 51 weeks where the offence is summary only, and 12 months where it is an offence triable either way.

3.5 Criminal appeals

Most of the decisions discussed in this work will be the reported decisions of the appellate courts – the Divisional Court, Court of Appeal Criminal Division, the House of Lords and now the Supreme Court.[60] It is important to have an understanding of the structure of the appeals process. It is unwieldy and unsatisfactory in many respects.[61] The material here offers only a short description.[62]

3.5.1 Appeals from the magistrates' court

3.5.1.1 Appeal to the Crown Court

A person convicted by a magistrates' court may appeal his conviction (if he pleaded not guilty) and/or his sentence to the Crown Court.[63] The appeal is in the form of a rehearing, heard before a Circuit Judge or Recorder, sitting with two lay magistrates unconcerned with the initial trial. The Crown Court may confirm, reverse or vary any part of the decision of the initial court.

3.5.1.2 Appeal to the High Court by 'way of case stated'

Both the prosecution and defence may appeal on the grounds that the magistrates' court was wrong *in law* or acted in *excess of jurisdiction*.[64] In hearing such an appeal, the High Court sits as a Divisional Court of the Queen's Bench Division. The lower court's finding of *facts* may not be disturbed by this type of appeal. The court may reverse, affirm or amend the

---

[57] These have recently included innovative forms of disposal such as electronic tagging, curfew orders, exclusion orders, supervision orders, and drug treatment and testing orders.

[58] Magistrates' Courts Act 1980, s 32.

[59] Criminal Justice Act 1982, s 37.

[60] From October 2009, the Supreme Court replaced the Appellate Committee of the House of Lords as the highest court in the United Kingdom. For more information on its constitution, procedures etc see www.supremecourt.gov.uk/index.html.

[61] See, for criticism, the Criminal Courts Review (2001); JR Spencer, 'Does our Present Criminal Appeal System Make Sense?' [2006] Crim LR 667. The Law Commission recently recommended reform of the appeal system impacting on criminal law, LC 324, *The High Court's Jurisdiction in Relation to Criminal Proceedings* (2010).

[62] For a more critical analysis see Ashworth and Redmayne, *The Criminal Process* (4th edn, 2010).

[63] Magistrates' Courts Act 1980, s 108(1).

[64] See the discussion in the Law Commission's CP No 184, *The High Court's Jurisdiction in Relation to Criminal Proceedings* (2007) and Report LC 324 at www.lawcom.gov.uk/docs/lc324_for_web.pdf.

magistrates' decision and may also remit the matter back to them with its opinion on the legal issues involved.

3.5.1.3 Application to the High Court for judicial review

The magistrates' courts are subject to the supervision of the High Court by means of judicial review. If it can be shown that the magistrates' court has acted *ultra vires* (ie beyond its power), the High Court has various powers to correct the error.

3.5.2 Appeals from the Crown Court

3.5.2.1 Defence appeal against conviction

Someone convicted of (or who pleaded guilty to) an offence on indictment may appeal to the Court of Appeal (Criminal Division).[65] The powers of the Court of Appeal have been the subject of continuing controversy.[66] Currently the court is empowered to quash a conviction if it is 'unsafe'. Section 2 of the Criminal Appeal Act 1995 provides that the Court of Appeal:

    (a) shall allow an appeal against conviction if they think that the conviction is unsafe; and

    (b) shall dismiss such an appeal in any other case.

The court will address the question of safety by looking at the case 'in the round'. If the court thinks that the appellant might be not guilty, it will quash the conviction. If there was an error of process, the court will consider the significance of that error and look at the question of safety. In some cases it will quash the conviction of a person who is accepted to be guilty of the offence charged. Where the Court of Appeal allows an appeal against conviction, it may order that the appellant be retried where it appears that this is required by the interests of justice.[67]

3.5.2.2 Defence appeal against sentence

A person who has been convicted of an offence on indictment may appeal to the Court of Appeal (Criminal Division) against his sentence. The court, if it considers that the appellant should be sentenced differently, may quash any sentence or order which is the subject of the appeal and substitute any other sentence or order that it thinks appropriate, provided that it would have been within the jurisdiction of the court below. The appellant may not, however, be dealt with more severely than by the court below, except that the court may bring a suspended sentence into effect. The court will interfere with the sentence if it is *manifestly excessive* or wrong in principle, or not justified by law, or where matters are improperly taken into account or improperly ignored, where fresh matters are to be taken into account.

3.5.2.3 Prosecution interlocutory appeal

Until the stage of the trial where the judge begins the summing up the prosecution has a right of appeal against points of law determined by the trial judge. The rights of appeal introduced under the Criminal Justice Act 2003, Part 9 apply only to trials on indictment and allow for an appeal to the Criminal Division of the Court of Appeal. The prosecution requires the leave

---

[65] The workload of the Court of Appeal Criminal Division is staggering. In 2009/2010 the CACD received 7,133 applications (5,653 sentence applications and 1,480 conviction applications). See the Court of Appeal Criminal Division Review of the Year 2009/10 (2011): http://www.hmcourtsservice.gov.uk/cms/files/Criminal_Div_Review_of_legal_year_2010.pdf.

[66] See Office for Criminal Justice Reform, *Quashing Convictions: Report of a Review by the Home Secretary, Lord Chancellor and Attorney General* (2006). See the provisions in the Criminal Justice and Immigration Act 2008 and for cogent criticism see JR Spencer, 'Quashing Convictions for Procedural Irregularities' [2007] Crim LR 835.

[67] Criminal Appeal Act 1968, s 7(l). See the recent Supreme Court decision in *R v Maxwell* [2010] UKSC 48.

of the judge or the Court of Appeal. Two rights of appeal are introduced. Section 58 allows for appeals to be made against 'adverse rulings', whilst s 62 allows for appeals against evidentiary rulings.[68] Appeals under s 58 may be brought on any ruling before the summing up. As a condition of its appeal, s 58(8) states that if the prosecution informs the court of their intention to appeal then they must also there and then inform the court of their agreement that if leave to appeal is refused or if the prosecution abandons the appeal D is acquitted. This is a heavy price for the prosecution to pay and thus will only be exercised by the prosecution where, in absence of the right of appeal, they would offer no evidence. The Court of Appeal can confirm, reverse or vary the ruling. Where the Court confirms the ruling then the defendant is acquitted. Where the ruling is varied or reversed the proceedings must be resumed or a fresh trial ordered unless the defendant could not receive a fair trial.

3.5.2.4 Prosecution appeals against sentence

Under the Criminal Justice Act 1988, ss 35 and 36 the Attorney General may refer certain sentences to the Court of Appeal (Criminal Division). The power may be exercised where 'it appears to the A-G that the sentencing of a person in a proceeding in the Crown Court has been *unduly lenient*'. The Court of Appeal may quash any sentence passed on the defendant, and in place of it pass such sentence (including a heavier sentence) as it thinks appropriate and as the court below had power to pass when dealing with him or her. This may seem like a harsh process, but there are strong arguments in favour of the reference procedure. Under-sentencing: (i) blunts the deterrent effect of the criminal law; (ii) causes outrage to the victim; (iii) is demoralizing to the police; (iv) causes injustice to those who were appropriately sentenced; (v) undermines public confidence in the administration of justice and the authority of the courts; (vi) may cause public danger; and (vii) hinders development of a rational sentencing policy by the Court of Appeal. The main contrary argument is that the procedure offends the principle against double jeopardy, by allowing the State two attempts to deal with an offender. As the offender has to face the prospect of being sentenced twice over, the Court of Appeal may make allowance and take this into account in the revised sentence in most cases.

3.5.2.5 Attorney-General's references

Section 36 of the Criminal Justice Act 1972 introduced a procedure whereby the Attorney General may refer a point of law to the Court of Appeal where the defendant in a trial on indictment has been acquitted. The point must actually have arisen in the case. The court gives its opinion and may thereafter refer the point to the Supreme Court. The reference has no effect on the trial or the acquittal. The aim of this procedure is to ensure that an erroneous direction by a trial judge on the law is corrected at the earliest opportunity and without the need for legislation. The procedure has been of value in providing authoritative guidance in a number of areas of criminal law, most notably that of conditional intention to steal, where the Court of Appeal's decision on a reference put an end to a line of argument that had led to a large number of undeserved acquittals.

---

[68] Section 62 is not yet in force. The evidentiary ruling must 'seriously weaken the prosecution case'. The Court of Appeal has now accepted that an evidentiary ruling can be appealed under s 58 if the Crown is prepared to accept that D will be acquitted if the leave to appeal is refused or the appeal is dismissed. See Y [2008] EWCA Crim 10. See generally, D Ormerod, A Waterman and R Fortson, 'Prosecution Appeals: Too Much of a Good Thing?' [2010] Crim LR 169.

3.5.2.6 Interlocutory appeals from preparatory hearings in serious cases

Preparatory hearings were initially available only in serious fraud cases, but now judges have the power to make binding rulings in all cases on any question as to the admissibility of evidence and any other question of law, at any point after a case is sent for trial in the Crown Court. These powers were introduced for all cases by the Criminal Procedure and Investigation Act 1996, ss 28 to 38. A preparatory hearing is an opportunity to resolve legal issues before a jury is sworn. An application may be made by either party, or the court may, of its own motion, initiate one. This type of hearing should be held where the judge believes that the indictment reveals 'a case of such complexity or a case whose trial is likely to be of such length that substantial benefits are likely to accrue'. The judge will make rulings on points of law and on the admissibility of evidence. The Act also introduced the opportunity to appeal from the judge's ruling at the preparatory hearing and this route to securing the opinion of the appellate courts has proved particularly useful in resolving difficult questions of law before the trial commences.

3.5.2.7 References by the Criminal Cases Review Commission

The Criminal Appeal Act 1995 established the Criminal Cases Review Commission[69] (CCRC) as a body to safeguard against miscarriages of justice. Where a person has been convicted of an offence on indictment, the Commission may *at any time* refer the conviction to the Court of Appeal and (whether or not they refer the conviction) any sentence (not fixed by law) imposed in relation to the conviction. There is no limit in time and a reference may be made from decades ago if there was a potentially unsafe conviction against the applicant on that date. The reference is treated as a defence appeal above. The case should also only be referred if an appeal has been unsuccessful or an application to appeal refused.

3.5.3 Appeals to the Supreme Court

Appeals lie from the Court of Appeal (Criminal Division) to the Supreme Court at the instance of either the defendant or the prosecutor. The Court of Appeal must certify that a point of law of general public importance is involved. In addition, leave must be obtained from either the Court of Appeal or the Supreme Court and this can only be granted where it appears that the point is one which ought to be considered by the Supreme Court. If leave is granted, the Supreme Court may in its discretion allow a point to be argued that is not connected with the point certified.[70]

---

[69] See www.ccrc.gov.uk/index.htm. Section 42 of the Criminal Justice and Immigration Act 2008 inserted s 16C into the Criminal Appeal Act 1968, giving the Court of Appeal power to dismiss appeals on reference by CCRC in post-conviction change of law cases where the sole ground of appeal is change of law and the Court of Appeal would not have extended leave.

[70] Judgments of the Supreme Court are available at www.supremecourt.gov.uk.

4

The elements of a crime: *actus reus*

4.1 Introduction

It is a fundamental principle of criminal law that a person may not be convicted of a crime unless the prosecution have proved beyond reasonable doubt both (a) that responsibility is to be attributed to D for certain behaviour or the existence of a certain state of affairs (in a conduct crime), in circumstances forbidden by criminal law and that D has caused any proscribed event (in a result crime) and (b) that D had a defined state of mind in relation to the behaviour, existence of the state of affairs or causing of the event. The event, behaviour or state of affairs, is called the *actus reus*, or the external element, and the state of mind the *mens rea*, or mental element, of the crime. The principle that a person is not criminally liable for his conduct unless the prescribed state of mind coincides with the prohibited *actus reus* also being present is frequently stated in the form of a Latin maxim: *actus non facit reum nisi mens sit rea.*[1]

4.1.1 Proof and the elements of the offence

As an example of these fundamental principles in operation, consider a charge of murder. If it is absolutely clear that D killed V – that is, he has caused an *actus reus* – he must be acquitted of murder if there is a reasonable possibility that the killing was accidental. If that is the case, it has not been proved beyond reasonable doubt that he had the requisite *mens rea*. It was so laid down by the House of Lords in *Woolmington v DPP*[2] where it was held, overruling earlier authorities, that it is a misdirection to tell a jury that D must *satisfy* them that the killing was an accident. The true rule is that the jury must acquit even though they are not satisfied that D's story is true, if they think it might reasonably be true. They should convict only if satisfied beyond reasonable doubt that it is *not* true. This rule is of general application[3] and there is only one exception to it at common law – the defence of insanity.[4] To raise other defences at common law – for example, loss of self-control, self-defence, automatism or duress – D need

---

[1] 'Properly translated, this means "An act does not make a man guilty of a crime, unless his mind be also guilty." It is thus not the *actus* which is "*reus*" but the man and his mind respectively' per Lord Hailsham in *Haughton v Smith* [1975] AC 476 at 491–492. It is, however, convenient to follow the established usage of '*actus reus*'. cf Lord Simon in *DPP for Northern Ireland v Lynch* [1975] AC 653 at 690, and Lord Diplock in *Miller* [1983] 2 AC 161 HL.

[2] [1935] AC 462. See Lord Cooke, 'One Golden Thread', in *Turning Points in the Common Law* (The Hamlyn Lectures, 1997) 28. See, generally, C Tapper, *Cross and Tapper on Evidence* (12th edn, 2010) Ch 10; IH Dennis, *The Law of Evidence* (4th edn, 2010) Ch 11.

[3] *Mancini v DPP* [1942] AC 1; *Chan Kau v R* [1955] AC 206; *Lobell* [1957] 1 QB 547 (self-defence); *Bratty v A-G for Northern Ireland* [1963] AC 386 (automatism); *Gill* [1963] 1 WLR 841 (duress). But the onus of proving procedural bars to trial such as *autrefois convict* or *acquit*, may be on D: *Coughlan* (1976) 63 Cr App R 33 at 36.

[4] Below, Ch 11.

do no more than introduce some evidence of all the constituents of the defence; whereupon it is for the Crown to satisfy the jury that at least one of those constituents did not exist. If there is evidence of a defence, though it has not been specifically raised by D, the judge must direct the jury to acquit unless they are satisfied that the defence has been disproved.[5] A statute may, however, expressly or impliedly[6] impose a burden of proof on D and frequently does so. Since the Human Rights Act 1998 such provisions may not always be fully effective,[7] and the court will be required to examine their compatibility with Art 6(2) of the ECHR. Where an onus of proof is put upon D, he satisfies it if he proves the issue on a balance of probabilities – the same standard as that on the claimant in a civil action – and he need not prove it beyond reasonable doubt.[8] The Law Commission's recent proposals in relation to a number of offences include defences for which D bears a legal burden of proof,[9] and this may become a more common feature in statutes.

4.1.2 Identifying elements of *actus reus* and *mens rea*

It is impossible to catalogue every type of conduct, circumstance or result that might constitute the *actus reus* of a crime. There are many thousands of offences, and in each case it is necessary to look to the specific terms of the offence, as defined by statute or common law, to determine what the elements of *actus reus* will be. As ever, care must be taken to be precise about the form of the *actus reus* of the particular offence. For example, the *actus reus* of murder is not simply the result – 'a killing' – but includes elements of conduct and circumstances: the causing of the death of a human being under the Queen's peace. Similarly, the *actus reus* of rape is not simply non-consensual sex, but more specifically, comprises elements of conduct (penile penetration of the vagina, anus or mouth of a person) and proscribed circumstances (without the person's consent). A key skill that the criminal lawyer must develop is the ability to identify which elements of an offence are those of *actus reus* and which relate to the *mens rea*. It is usually easier to identify the elements of a crime that comprise the *mens rea* since these are represented by common expressions – intentionally, knowingly, wilfully, recklessly, etc – all of which are examined fully in the next chapter.

It should be noted that the separation of elements into *actus reus* and *mens rea* in this manner is principally to allow for the most convenient exposition and discussion of any

---

[5] *Palmer v R* [1971] AC 814, [1971] 1 All ER 1077 at 1080; *Wheeler* (1967) 52 Cr App R 28 at 30–31; *Hamand* (1985) 82 Cr App R 65.

[6] *Hunt* [1987] AC 352, HL.

[7] See above, p 29. On the Human Rights Act and the burden of proof, see, *inter alia*, Emmerson, Ashworth and Macdonald, HR&CJ, Ch 29.

[8] *Carr-Briant* [1943] KB 607. The Criminal Law Revision Committee and the Law Commission have proposed that the law should be so amended that D would, in these cases, merely have to introduce sufficient evidence to raise the issue (an 'evidential burden') whereupon the onus of proof would be on the Crown: Eleventh Report, Cmnd 4991, paras 137–142; Draft Code, cl 13. Meanwhile, the House of Lords ruled in *Lambert* [2002] 2 AC 545 that the Human Rights Act 1998 may require a provision expressly imposing a reverse onus to be 'read down' to an evidential burden which is satisfied by raising a reasonable doubt. See also *Johnstone* [2003] UKHL 28. In a more recent pronouncement, the House of Lords held that the court's task is to ascertain whether the burden of proof imposed by Parliament *unjustifiably* infringes the presumption of innocence: *A-G's Reference (No 4 of 2002)* [2004] UKHL 43, para 31, [2005] Crim LR 215. See also IH Dennis, 'Reverse Onuses and the Presumption of Innocence: In Search of Principle' [2005] Crim LR 901; Duff, *Answering for Crime* (2007) 195–202 on the significance of proof for the interpretation of elements of offence or defence.

[9] See, eg, the defence of reasonableness in s 50 of the Serious Crime Act 2007 (LC 300, *Inchoate Liability for Assisting and Encouraging Crime* (2006), a similar defence proposed for conspiracy in LC 318, *Conspiracy and Attempts* (2009) (see Ch 13 below); and that proposed for duress to murder recommended in LC 304 (discussed in Ch 14 below)).

given crime.[10] In practical terms, there is no need for the prosecution to approach its case by breaking down the crime into constituent parts to prove each element in turn to the jury's satisfaction; it will commonly, and sensibly approach the task as one of proving the crime as a whole. Moreover, it is not always possible to separate precisely *actus reus* from *mens rea*.[11] Sometimes a word that describes the *actus reus*, or part of it, implies a mental element. Without that mental element the *actus reus* simply cannot exist. For example, there are many offences of possession of proscribed objects (drugs, knives, etc) and it has always been recognized that 'possession', which might appear to be an element of *actus reus*, consists also in a mental element.[12] The same is true of words like 'permits',[13] 'appropriates',[14] 'cultivates',[15] 'abandons'[16] and many more that appear across the range of offences. Having an offensive weapon in a public place is the *actus reus* of an offence; but whether an article is an offensive weapon depends, in some circumstances, on the intention with which it is carried. In the absence of that intention, the thing is not an offensive weapon and there is no *actus reus*.[17] Making a false representation is the *actus reus* of fraud, but the element of falsity requires knowledge that D knew the representation was untrue or misleading.[18] Similarly, transferring criminal property is an offence, but the definition of criminal property depends in part on whether D knows or suspects it is criminal.[19] The significance of this is that where the crime has an *actus reus* which incorporates a mental element, that necessarily becomes an element of the offence. It is the combination of the two which becomes the complete definition of the prohibited conduct.

4.1.3 No conviction without *actus reus*

It is possible for Parliament to dispense with *mens rea* in whole or in part by creating offences of strict or absolute liability, but, except in the anomalous case of an intoxicated offender,[20] the courts will not dispense with the *actus reus* element. There are no 'thought crimes'.[21] Thus, if an offence consists in 'possessing' or 'permitting', that offence cannot be proved if D cannot be shown to have 'possessed' or 'permitted'. The court may, of course, give effect to the word Parliament has chosen without requiring full *mens rea* as to every single element of the *actus reus*. For example, it was held that D was guilty of permitting the use of an uninsured vehicle where he intended to permit only the use of the vehicle (which was in fact uninsured) or cultivating a cannabis plant where he intended only to cultivate that plant (which was in fact a cannabis plant).

In some instances, the *actus reus* of a crime might be relatively minimal, and may even seem innocuous – as in conspiracy where the *actus reus* comprises 'an agreement'. This underlines

---

[10] See ATH Smith, 'On Actus Reus and Mens Rea', in Glazebrook, *Reshaping the Criminal Law*; see also the more recent analysis of the significance of the differentiation: Duff, *Answering for Crime*, 202–208.

[11] See ACE Lynch, 'The Mental Element in the Actus Reus' (1982) 98 LQR 109.

[12] See below, Ch 7. For an interesting analysis of possession offences, see MD Dubber, 'The Possession Paradigm' in Duff and Green, *Defining Crimes*.

[13] See Ch 7.

[14] See, below, Ch 19. In *Gomez* [1993] AC 442, 495, Lord Browne-Wilkinson regarded 'appropriation' as not involving any mental state; but this is hard to believe. See the discussion below, p 781.

[15] *Champ* (1981) 73 Cr App R 367, [1982] Crim LR 108 and commentary.

[16] *Hunt v Duckering* [1993] Crim LR 678, DC (abandoning a dog in circumstances likely to cause unnecessary suffering).

[17] Below, p 706.

[18] See Ch 23, s 2 of the Fraud Act 2006.

[19] See Ch 27.

[20] See *Lipman* [1970] 1 QB 152. See also the discussion of *Heard* [2007] EWCA Crim 725 below, p 318.

[21] For a theoretical analysis of why this is so, see Duff, *Answering for Crime*, 95 et seq. cf DN Husak, 'Does Criminal Liability Require an Act?', in RA Duff, *Philosophy and the Criminal Law* (1998).

the importance of keeping in mind the crime as a whole, and not allowing the fragmentation into elements of *actus reus* and *mens rea* to distort one's understanding of the offence.

It is important to note that every element of the *actus reus* must be proved. For example, taking the *actus reus* of assault – causing a person to apprehend immediate unlawful personal violence[22] – that might be broken down into elements of 'causing apprehension', of 'immediate', 'unlawful', 'personal violence'. If D's conduct failed to fulfil *all* of these requirements there would be no *actus reus*. Thus, if D caused V to apprehend personal violence, but not immediately, as where D telephoned V in Leeds and said 'I'm in London, but when I get back tomorrow I will hit you', there would be no assault. Similarly if D caused V to apprehend immediate personal violence, but D was acting with V's consent, there would be no unlawfulness and hence no assault.

4.1.4 Coincidence of *actus reus* and *mens rea*

Not only must the prosecution establish that every element of the *actus reus* of the crime in question and the relevant *mens rea* were present, they must, as a general rule, establish that they occurred at the same time – that there was a coincidence of *actus reus* and *mens rea*. This principle is examined in greater detail in the following chapter.

The *actus reus* amounts to a crime only when it is accompanied by the appropriate *mens rea*. To cause an *actus reus* without the requisite *mens rea* is not a crime and may be an ordinary, innocent act. For example, the offence of perjury[23] consists in the prescribed conduct of making a statement, whether true or not, in the prescribed circumstances of being on oath in a judicial proceeding, with the *mens rea* of knowing the statement to be false or not believing it to be true. Thus, every statement on oath in a judicial proceeding might be seen as the *actus reus* of perjury. When we say then, that a certain conduct comprises the *actus reus* of a crime, what we mean is that the conduct or result would be a crime if it were caused by a person with *mens rea*. The description of the conduct as an *actus reus* does not necessarily imply any judgment whatever as to its moral or legal quality. The analysis into *actus reus* and *mens rea* is for convenience of exposition only. The only concept known to the law is the crime; and the crime exists only when *actus reus* and *mens rea* coincide.

4.1.5 The nature of an *actus reus*

Since the *actus reus* includes all the elements in the definition of the crime except D's mental element,[24] it follows that the *actus reus* is not merely an 'act'. It may comprise conduct and its attendant circumstances or results. In some rare instances, the *actus reus* may consist in a set of circumstances or 'state of affairs', not including any conduct or action by D at all.[25] An example might be where D is charged with 'being found' drunk in a public place. Usually, however, the *actus reus* requires proof of an act or an omission by D (which might be better described as 'conduct'). In fraud, D's conduct (making a false representation) is the *actus reus*. For some crimes the *actus reus* comprises conduct and circumstances: perjury is committed as soon as D makes a statement (conduct) on oath (circumstance) that he does not believe to be true. It is irrelevant whether there is a result in terms of whether

---

[22] See, below, p 621.

[23] Perjury Act 1911, s 1(1), Stephen, *Digest*, 95–96.

[24] It should be said that this is not the only possible definition of an *actus reus*, and that a more limited view is taken of it by some writers. It is thought, however, that it is the most useful conception of the *actus reus* and is adopted throughout this book. cf Williams, CLGP, 16, who suggests that the elements of *actus reus* ought also to incorporate the absence of some defences. See also the discussion in Duff, *Answering for Crime*, 202.

[25] See, below, p 63.

his testimony is believed or not. But in many crimes it must also be proved that the pre-scribed conduct caused a particular result. In murder, for example, it must be shown that D's conduct caused the death. The *actus reus* of murder comprises elements of conduct, circumstance (that the victim was a human being under the Queen's peace) and result (that the victim died).

The different types of offence are usually designated[26] 'result crimes' and 'conduct crimes' respectively.[27]

4.1.5.1 Result crimes

There are many examples of result crimes, some of the most obvious being murder, man-slaughter, wounding, etc. It has been said[28] that in 'result crimes' the law is interested only in the result and not in the conduct bringing about the result. Similarly, a well-known definition of *actus reus* is 'such result of human conduct as the law seeks to prevent'.[29] But a dead person with a knife in his back is not the *actus reus* of a murder. It is putting the knife in the back thereby causing the death that is the *actus reus*. The law is no less interested in the conduct that brings about the result in a 'result crime' than in a 'conduct crime'.[30]

4.1.5.2 Conduct crimes

True conduct crimes, such as perjury, are rare. The term has been interpreted more widely by Glanville Williams to include rape and abduction – in these crimes, 'you do not have to wait to see if anything happens as a result of what the defendant does'.[31] This method of classifi-cation is controversial. If the test is whether you 'have to wait to see', wounding is a conduct crime if committed with a knife but a result crime if committed with a gun, crossbow or catapult. If the distinction is to be made at all (and, while interesting, it is not clear that it has, or should have, any practical consequences accept perhaps as to jurisdiction) these offences of wounding and abduction are better regarded as result crimes. A result has to flow from D's physical movements, whether you have to wait for it or not.

Since the Criminal Attempts Act 1981,[32] all indictable offences are now, in a sense, poten-tially conduct crimes because any act, done with intent thereby[33] to commit an indictable offence, may be an indictable attempt to commit it. D who aims a rifle at V and is about to shoot is, by that conduct, attempting to murder him. The *actus reus* of the offence attempted need never happen and may, indeed, be impossible. Its definition serves only to define the *mens rea* of the attempt.

A case can be made that the law should always have regard only to the conduct and not to the result. Whether the conduct results in harm is generally a matter of chance and does not alter the blameworthiness and dangerousness of the actor.[34] But the law has not gone so

---

[26] By Gordon, 61.

[27] Some crimes can be both – bribery can be committed by causing B to receive (result) or by offering to B (con-duct): SP Green, *Lying, Cheating and Stealing* (2005) 35. See the Bribery Act 2010, s 1 dealing with D who bribes and s 2 with R who receives.

[28] Gordon, 61.

[29] Kenny, *Outlines*, 17.

[30] See Lord Diplock in *Treacy v DPP* [1971] AC 537 at 560.

[31] 'The Problem of Reckless Attempts' [1983] Crim LR 365 at 366, 368.

[32] As interpreted in *Shivpuri*, below, p 482.

[33] ie, D intends to cause the result by that act; it is the last act D intends, and needs to do not a merely prepara-tory act. An earlier act is sufficient, if 'more than merely preparatory': below, Ch 13.

[34] A Ashworth, 'Belief Intent and Criminal Liability' in J Eekelaar and J Bell (eds), *Oxford Essays in Jurisprudence* (1989); 'Taking the Consequences' in S Shute, J Gardner and J Horder (eds), *Action and Value in Criminal Law* (1993) and 'Defining Offences Without Harm', in *Criminal Law Essays*.

far.[35] If D hurls a stone, being reckless whether he injures anyone, he is guilty of an offence if the stone strikes V but of no offence – not even an attempt – if no one is injured. From a retributive point of view, it might be argued that D should be equally liable in either event. This could be achieved by the creation of general offences of reckless endangerment.[36] On utilitarian grounds, however, it is probably undesirable to turn the whole criminal law into 'conduct crimes'. The needs of deterrence are probably adequately served in most cases by 'result crimes'; and the criminal law should be extended only where a clear need is established.

It has been argued that in some offences it may be that the *actus reus* can take different forms (result or conduct) depending on the circumstances.[37] Thus, theft can be committed where D assumes only one of the rights of the owner over his property (conduct crime)[38] or where he assumes them all (result crime). This ambiguity is all the less satisfactory because the different categorization of a crime as a conduct or result crime may have implications for procedure, in terms of the form of the indictment, and for jurisdictional issues.

The fact that an offence is a 'conduct offence' does not mean that it should automatically be classified as a 'continuing' offence. The term 'conduct' is being used to distinguish the type of crime from a 'result' crime. The conduct crime of perjury is completed once the testimony leaves the lips of the witness. It is not a continuing crime in any real sense. Identifying the starting and finishing points of the *actus reus* will be important in ensuring that the element of *mens rea* coincides in time, and may again be significant for procedural purposes of charging, in terms of the specific dates and actions alleged in the indictment and the territorial jurisdiction of the courts.

4.1.5.3 *Actus reus* includes circumstances

The *actus reus* is made up, generally but not invariably, of conduct and sometimes its consequences (result), and also of the circumstances in which the conduct takes place, or which constitute the state of affairs in so far as they are relevant. Circumstances, like consequences, are relevant if they are included in the definition of the crime. The definition of theft, for example, requires proof that D dishonestly appropriated property *belonging to another*. If the property belonged to no one (because it had been abandoned) D's appropriation in those circumstances could not constitute the *actus reus* of theft. However dishonest he might be, he could not be convicted of theft because an essential constituent of the crime is missing.[39] In child sex offences, the conduct of sexual touching, etc must be committed in the prescribed circumstance of the child being under a specified age (13 or 16 depending on the charge). In burglary, D's conduct of entering a building must be in prescribed circumstances: as a trespasser; and so on.

---

[35] As noted in the 12th edn, the Court of Appeal recently rejected this type of argument in a sentencing appeal where D who had stabbed V was guilty of her murder, even though unknown to anyone she had a very short life expectancy owing to a deep vein thrombosis. D claimed that his sentence ought to reflect this fact. He also sought to argue that his sentence should be reduced because V's pre-existing medical condition meant that she would die young and V's family had not been deprived of her 'long life': *Master* [2007] EWCA Crim 142.

[36] See, *inter alia*, the discussion in Duff, 'Criminalising Endangerment', in Duff and Green (eds), *Defining Crimes*; Duff, *Answering for Crime*, Ch 7; KJM Smith, 'Liability for Endangerment: English Ad Hoc Pragmatism and American Innovation' [1983] Crim LR 127; D Lanham, 'Danger Down Under' [1999] Crim LR 960; C Clarkson, 'Aggravated Endangerment Offences' (2007) 60 CLP 278.

[37] See M Hirst, *Jurisdiction and the Ambit of the Criminal Law* (2003) 128.

[38] See *Morris* [1984] AC 320 below, p 781.

[39] He might, however, be convicted of an attempt to steal. Below, p 413.

4.1.5.4 Victim's conduct/state as part of the *actus reus*

Sometimes a particular state of mind on the part of the *victim* is required by the definition of the crime. If so, that state of mind is part of the *actus reus* and, if the prosecution are unable to prove its existence, they must fail. If D is prosecuted for rape, it must be proved that V did not consent to the act. The absence of consent by V is an essential constituent of the *actus reus*. But in some crimes the consent of the victim is entirely irrelevant. If D is charged with the murder of V, it is no defence for him to show that V asked to be killed.

4.1.5.5 Summary

It is apparent from these examples that we can only see what elements comprise the *actus reus* by looking at the definition of the particular crime. We find this definition, in the case of common law crimes, in the decisions of the courts and, in the case of statutory crimes, in the words of the statute, as construed by the courts. Many factors may be relevant; for example, in bigamy, the fact that D is validly married; in treason committed abroad, that D is a British national (or under the protection of the Crown for some other reason);[40] in handling stolen goods, that the goods have, in fact, been stolen; and so on.

4.1.6 The effect of penalty provisions in determining the elements of the *actus reus*

Sometimes it happens that Parliament provides that an offence shall be more severely punishable when a particular fact, say 'X', is present. For example, causing a person to engage in sexual activity is an offence. If the sexual activity involves penile penetration, the maximum sentence is higher. When this happens, it is 'plain beyond argument that Parliament has created two offences', according to Lord Diplock (the whole House concurring) in *Courtie*.[41] The offence when X is present is a different and graver offence than when X is not present. X is an element in the *actus reus*, or the *mens rea*, or both, of the greater offence. The courts apply this principle where it can be presumed that Parliament intended to create two offences by giving one form of the offence a higher penalty; the courts will therefore disapply the principle if it would lead to such inconvenient and absurd results that, in the opinion of the courts, Parliament could not have intended it to apply: *DPP v Butterworth*.[42]

When *Courtie* applies, the effect is (i) that D can be convicted of the greater offence only if the charge alleges X, and (ii) it is for the jury to decide whether X is proved and to give their verdict accordingly, not a matter for the judge to decide after verdict. Thus, causing a person to engage in sexual activity (contrary to s 4 of the Sexual Offences Act 2003) carries a maximum sentence of 14 years' imprisonment , but the sentence for that offence is increased to a maximum of life where the activity involves penetrative acts (s 4(4)) and as such, there are two forms of the offence. If D is alleged to have caused an act of sexual penetration, that should be specified in the indictment.

Where Parliament provides an elaborate structure of maximum penalties, as in the case of drug offences, the substantive law is correspondingly complex.[43] But the principle is

---

[40] *Joyce v DPP* [1946] AC 347.

[41] [1984] AC 463 at 471, HL; *Grout* [2011] EWCA Crim 299.

[42] [1995] 1 AC 381, HL. Section 7(6) of the Road Traffic Act 1988 on its face creates only one offence of failing to provide a specimen of breath; but there is a higher penalty where the offender was driving or attempting to drive than when he was merely in charge. Nevertheless, there is only one offence. By contrast, s 5(1)(a) of the Act (driving/attempting to/being in charge of a motor vehicle on a road after consuming so much alcohol that the proportion of it in the breath/blood/urine exceeds the prescribed limit) creates nine offences, all punishable with the same penalty: *Bolton Justices, ex p Khan* [1999] Crim LR 912.

[43] *Shivpuri* [1987] AC 1, [1986] Crim LR 536 and commentary; *Ellis, Street and Smith* (1986) 84 Cr App R 235, [1987] Crim LR 44, CA, and commentary; *Bett* [1999] Crim LR 218. *Courtie* seems to have been completely overlooked in *Leeson* [2000] 1 Cr App R 233, [2000] Crim LR 195. See commentary at 196.

sound. Where proof of fact X entails liability to a higher penalty, the requirements of proof of X should be no less stringent than in the case of the other facts of the offence.

4.1.7 *Actus reus* and justification or excuse

There is a longstanding debate not only as to the value of the use of terms such as *actus reus* and *mens rea*,[44] but precisely how the terminology ought to be applied. In the terminology used by Glanville Williams:[45]

Actus reus includes…the absence of any ground of justification or excuse, whether such justification or excuse be stated in any statute creating the crime or implied by the courts in accordance with general principle…

An alternative view is that of David Lanham:[46]

As a matter of analysis we can think of a crime as being made up of three ingredients, *actus reus*, *mens rea* and (a negative element) absence of a valid defence.

Other variations on these two basic views can be advanced including, for example, the suggestion that the *actus reus* includes the absence of any elements of justification, but not those of excuse.[47]

A simple example illustrates these different approaches. Assuming the death penalty was still available in respect of certain crimes, if the public executioner carried out his duty to hang, say a convicted traitor, no offence would be committed – according to Williams because there is no *actus reus* (or, indeed, *mens rea*) and, according to Lanham, because, though there is both *actus reus* and *mens rea* (the intentional killing of a human being) there is a valid defence. Williams' opinion is attractive both because it seems strange to describe an act which is required or permitted by the law as an *actus reus*[48] and because there are practical difficulties in distinguishing (as Lanham's analysis requires) between the definitional elements of an offence and defence elements.[49] On the other hand, the enumeration of the elements of an offence becomes impossibly cumbersome if it has to include all conceivable defences – as the authors of the Draft Criminal Code put it, 'the inapplicability of every exception admitted by the definition of an offence must be treated as an element of it'.[50] Moreover, defences may also require mental as well as external elements. Duress is a defence but only, of course, if D is aware of the threatening facts.[51] If the object of the Latin terminology is convenience of exposition, there is much to be said for the Lanham usage and it is generally (but not invariably) followed in this book.[52]

---

[44] See PH Robinson, 'Should the Criminal Law Abandon the Actus Reus–Mens Rea Distinction?', in Shute, Gardner and Horder (eds), *Action and Value in Criminal Law*, arguing for the abandonment of the oversimplistic categorization which obscures the doctrines lying beneath the overarching labels. See also Duff, *Answering for Crime*, Ch 5.

[45] CLGP, 19. See also TBCL, Ch 2.

[46] [1976] Crim LR 276.

[47] See MS Moore, *Act and Crime: The Philosophy of Action and its Implications for Criminal Law* (1993) 177–183.

[48] But, as noted above, *actus reus* implies no moral judgement, the only point of the analysis being convenience in exposition.

[49] Although arguably the same is true of Williams' analysis since it requires us to exclude any ground of justification or excuse.

[50] Draft Code, vol 2, 7.2, 7.3.

[51] Below, p 347.

[52] The Latin terms are frequently used by the courts but no detailed analysis has been made of them and it cannot be said that there is a standard judicial usage. The recent judicial trend is to avoid Latin in the criminal trial. 'Throw Latin out of court' says Woolf: The Times, 20 July 2000.

4.1.8 An *actus reus* must be proved

Mens rea may exist without an *actus reus* but, if the *actus reus* of a particular crime does not exist or occur, that crime is not committed. Although D believes that he is appropriating V's property he cannot in any circumstances be guilty of theft if the property belongs to no one. D has the *mens rea* but the *actus reus*, the other fundamental element of the crime, is lacking. D may penetrate V with intent to have intercourse with her without her consent but, if in fact she consents, his act cannot amount to rape. D may intend to marry during the lifetime of his wife but if, unknown to him, she is dead, he cannot commit bigamy. If D makes a statement, which he believes to be false, with intent to gain, he cannot be convicted of fraud if the statement is, in fact, true. In each case, D may now be convicted of attempting to commit the crime in question.[53]

In *Deller*,[54] D induced V to purchase his car by representing (*inter alia*) that it was free from encumbrances, that is, that D had ownership and was entitled to sell it. In fact, D had previously executed a document that purported to mortgage the car to a finance company and, no doubt, D thought he was telling a lie. He was charged with obtaining by false pretences.[55] It then appeared that the document by which the transaction had been effected was probably void in law for the technical reason that it was as an unregistered bill of sale. If the document was void the car *was* free from encumbrances '... quite accidentally and, strange as it may sound, dishonestly, the appellant had told the truth'.[56] D's conviction was, therefore, quashed by the Court of Criminal Appeal, for, though he had *mens rea*, no *actus reus* had been established. Under the present law, D could be convicted of an attempted fraud.[57]

4.1.8.1 The problematic case of *Dadson*

A case which is sometimes said to be inconsistent with this fundamental principle, but which is worth discussing because it illustrates the difficulties that may arise in connection with its application, is *Dadson*.[58] A full discussion of the case occurs in the context of defences in Chapter 12.

D was a constable, employed to watch a copse from which wood had been stolen. He carried a loaded gun. V emerged from the copse carrying wood that he had stolen, and, ignoring D's calls to stop, ran away. D, having no other means of bringing him to justice, fired and wounded him in the leg. He was convicted of shooting at V with intent to cause him grievous bodily harm. V had been repeatedly convicted of stealing wood, but D did not know this. Under s 39 of the Larceny Act 1827, stealing wood was a felony if V had two previous convictions for the same offence. V was a felon. D did not know he was. It was lawful to wound an escaping felon[59] if this was the only way of arresting him.[60] Could D rely on what would be a compelling justifying circumstance when D was unaware of its existence? Erle J told the jury that the alleged felony, *being unknown to the prisoner*, constituted no justification. On a case reserved, the judges thought the conviction right: D was not justified in firing at V because the fact that V was committing a felony was not known to D at the time.

---

[53] Below, p 483.

[54] (1952) 36 Cr App R 184. cf *Brien* (1903) 3 SRNSW 410; *Dyson* [1908] 2 KB 454.

[55] Under the Larceny Act 1916, s 32, now replaced by the Fraud Act 2006, s 2, below, p 881.

[56] (1952) 36 Cr App R 184 at 191.

[57] Below, p 483.

[58] (1850) 2 Den 35. cf *Tooley* (1709) 11 Mod Rep 242 at 251, per Holt CJ; and see Williams, CLGP, 23 et seq.

[59] A term used before the Criminal Law Act 1967 to denote those committing serious offences.

[60] This was assumed in the case. On this point, see below, p 393

Many have argued that this case is wrong because, if we ignore D's state of mind and look at the actual facts, what he did was lawful; there was no *actus reus*.[61] It is submitted that this approach is incorrect. It is important to distinguish between two types of 'defence' that may be raised. In the first type, D merely denies the existence of an element (other than the *mens rea*) in the definition of the crime. If D successfully raises that plea he certainly cannot be convicted of that crime, whatever his state of mind. This is what happened in *Deller*.[62] In the second type, D admits that all the elements in the definition of the crime have been established and goes on to assert other facts that afford him a defence in law. As appears from the example of duress, above, the establishment of this type of defence may require D to assert the existence of a mental element as well as external facts.

In *Dadson*,[63] D did not deny that he shot at V or that he intended to cause him grievous bodily harm. He admitted the necessary constituents of the crime (other than 'unlawfulness') but went on to assert other facts that, he alleged, made his act lawful. He was pleading a defence. Whether his act was lawful depended on what were the constituents of the *defence* that he raised; and all that the case decided was that that defence, like duress and self-defence, required the assertion not merely of external facts but also of a state of mind.[64] *Dadson* then, is perfectly reconcilable with *Deller*. It does *not* decide that a person can be convicted where there is no *actus reus*. There was an *actus reus* for D did unlawfully wound V. All that the case decided was that the defence to wounding, 'I was arresting an escaping felon', was a defence which required a mental as well as a physical element and, because the mental element was lacking (D was not aware that V was a felon), the wounding was unlawful.[65]

4.2 Analysis of an *actus reus*

Some writers have suggested that 'an act' is nothing more than a willed muscular movement – for example, the deliberate crooking of a finger. But, if D crooked his finger around the trigger of a loaded pistol which was pointing at V, with the result that V was killed, to say 'D crooked his finger' would be a most misleading way of describing D's 'act'. 'Again, suppose a person orally demands money by threats of injury. Can the action of his vocal chords be separated from the resulting sound issuing from his mouth and its intended meaning to the hearer?'[66] We naturally say, 'D shot V' or 'D demanded money from V'. This way of describing the act takes account of the circumstances surrounding the actual movement of the body (in so far as they are relevant) and its consequences (again, in so far as they are relevant), and, for ordinary

---

[61] See Williams, CLGP, 22; Lady MacCauley, HM Trevalyen (ed), *The Works of Lord MacCauley: Volume 7* (1866) 552; PH Robinson, 'Competing Theories of Justification', in A Simester and ATH Smith (eds), *Harm and Culpability* (1996) 45. cf J Gardner, 'Justifications and Reasons', in A Simester and ATH Smith (eds), *Harm and Culpability*, 103.

[62] Above.

[63] Above, n 58.

[64] A doctrine of *actus reus* which says that such a course *must* be wrong, as contravening a fundamental principle, is much too constricting. Whether the defence should consist simply in the external facts, or in the facts plus the state of mind, is a matter of policy; and it was a not unreasonable decision of policy to say that a man who deliberately shot another should be guilty of an offence unless he knew of circumstances justifying or excusing his conduct.

[65] Below, p 393. For a defence of *Dadson*, see Hall, *General Principles*, 228 and Perkins, *Criminal Law*, 39. And cf the crime of perjury where D may be convicted if he makes a statement on oath which he believes to be false though it is in fact true.

[66] *Timbu Kolian v R* (1968) 119 CLR 47 at 69, per Windeyer J. D's act was demanding with menaces.

purposes, it is obviously the sensible way of describing it.[67] But for the purposes of the criminal law it is sometimes necessary to break down an 'act', so comprehensively described, into the constituents of (i) the conduct which is the central feature of the crime, (ii) the surrounding material circumstances, and (iii) the consequences. One reason for so doing is that the law may require different mental elements for the various constituents. For example, when a person is charged with an attempt to commit a crime it must be proved that he intended to do the act, and to cause the relevant consequence, but it may be that recklessness as to circumstances will suffice.

4.2.1 The conduct must be 'willed'[68]

If the *actus reus* of the crime includes an act, it must, of course, be proved that D did that act voluntarily. Although generally expressed as a requirement of 'voluntariness' there is a degree of confusion as to whether the law is truly concerned that D was 'conscious' of his actions, whether he 'willed' them, or whether they were 'voluntary'. These terms are not synonymous, and their precise definition involves complex questions of philosophy and neurology,[69] presenting distractions which for pragmatic reasons the criminal courts are keen to avoid. The requirement that the act was not involuntary is fundamental to the imposition of criminal liability since it reflects the underlying respect for the individual's autonomy and the principle that 'unless a man has the capacity and fair opportunity to adjust his behaviour to the law its penalties ought not to be applied to him'.[70]

The clearest cases of involuntariness might be thought to be those where D is unconscious. If D is unconscious or, for example, asleep, he *cannot* exercise his will, he cannot control his movement so any movements of his body that are made are involuntary. (This is subject to an important exception where the reason for the lack of consciousness is owing to voluntary intoxication.)

Even where D is conscious, there are many well-established circumstances in which the act will be found to be involuntary for the purposes of the criminal law. Suppose the act is 'wounding' and the evidence shows that, while D was holding a knife in his hand, E seized D's hand and, against D's will, plunged the knife still held by D's hand into V. Plainly D is not guilty of wounding because it was not his act. Similarly, D would not be guilty of a battery if he was afflicted by St Vitus' dance and his fist shot out in an uncontrolled spasm and struck V; or if D, startled by an unexpected explosion, dropped a weight, which he was carrying carefully, on to V's foot; or if D tripped onto V. If D, while driving, is attacked by a swarm of bees

---

[67] See, eg, the discussion of crimes involving hate speech in J Jaconelli, 'Context-Dependent Crime' [1995] Crim LR 771. For a more theoretical analysis of the significance of considering the *actus reus* as more than a bodily willed movement, see Duff, *Answering for Crime*, 98 et seq discussing how 'action' in this context cannot be seen as simply a natural or mechanical phenomenon.

[68] See, generally, RD Mackay, *Mental Condition Defences in the Criminal Law* (1995) Ch 1, and HLA Hart, *Punishment and Responsibility* (1968) Ch 4. There is considerable philosophical literature on the subject, including MS Moore, *Act and Crime: The Philosophy of Action and its Implications for Criminal Law* (1993). See also Wilson, *Central Issues*, Ch 4; A Norrie, *Crime, Reason and History* (2nd edn, 2000) 112–120.

[69] See, eg, DW Denno, 'How Psychological Research on Consciousness can Enlighten the Criminal Law' [2002] Amicus Curiae 28; R Schopp, *Automatism, Insanity and the Psychology of Criminal Responsibility: A Philosophical Inquiry* (1991); B McSherry, 'Voluntariness, Intention and the Defence of Mental Disorder: Towards a Rational Approach' (2003) 21(5) Behavioural Sciences and the Law 581; K Saunders, 'Voluntary Acts and the Criminal Law: Justifying Culpability Based on the Existence of Volition' (1988) 49 U Pitt LR 443. See also I Ebrahim et al, ' "Violence Sleepwalking and the Criminal Law" (1) The Medical Aspects' [2005] Crim LR 601; W Wilson et al, ' "Violence Sleepwalking and the Criminal Law" (2) The Legal Aspects' [2005] Crim LR 614, criticizing the current law and exposing the dissonance with medical knowledge.

[70] HLA Hart, *Punishment and Responsibility*, 181.

and disabled from controlling the vehicle, he may be held to be no longer 'driving'.[71] In each of these cases the movement of D's limbs was involuntary in that it did not flow from an exercise by D of his will.[72] The event happened either against, or at least without, his will. In these examples, note that D was conscious but exercised no control over his movements. Again, the involuntariness will not exclude liability if the reason for it was D's voluntary intoxication.

If D is conscious and the physical movement is voluntary, D may be liable for its consequences even though it is unintentionally misdirected, as where D put his foot on the accelerator of a bus instead of, as he intended, the brake.[73]

4.2.1.1 Self-induced involuntarism

As noted, there is an exception to the rule that there is no liability for an involuntary act: where the 'act' was done while in a state of self-induced intoxication.[74] The rule is a complex one to be examined in full in Chapter 11 below, but in short, it will, apparently, be no defence to crimes of 'basic intent' (that is, on an orthodox interpretation at least,[75] those which do not require proof of *mens rea* of intention) that D was unconscious or otherwise 'acting' involuntarily. Thus, where D, owing to his voluntary ingestion of LSD, kills his girlfriend V, mistakenly believing that he is slaying a serpent at the centre of the earth,[76] D's prior fault by voluntarily reducing himself to that drug induced state provides a sufficient basis of fault in law to regard his subsequent involuntary conduct as blameworthy. He is guilty of manslaughter. So, too, a person may be held liable for basic intent crimes (those which can be committed without proof of *mens rea* of intention) when he is aware of the risk of becoming unpredictable or aggressive when taking valium (a soporific or sedative drug) even though not on medical prescription.[77] A diabetic who fails to take sufficient food after a normal dose of insulin may rely on his consequent automatism as a defence to a charge of a crime of basic intent. His prior conduct lacks sufficient fault to be assigned to his subsequent act unless he was actually aware of the risk of becoming aggressive, unpredictable and uncontrolled.[78]

It has been argued[79] that this is part of a wider rule that any automatism induced by D's 'fault' whether involving drugs or not is no defence. 'Fault' means doing or omitting to do something that could reasonably be foreseen to be likely to bring about such a state. The decided cases, however, all appear to involve the use or misuse of drink or drugs (including prescribed medicines)[80] and it is thought that the anomalous rule whereby the courts hold a defendant liable despite his automaton state is properly confined to cases of voluntary intoxication. The basis for the courts adopting that exceptional course is the grave social danger presented by intoxicated individuals.[81] One can imagine (perhaps fanciful) scenarios in which D carelessly or knowingly sets up circumstances in which he will subsequently perform an

---

[71] *Hill v Baxter* [1958] 1 QB 277 at 286.

[72] Duff provides an interesting account of how, rather than focusing on action in terms of willed movement, this aspect of *actus reus* might be better described as turning on whether D had control: *Answering for Crime*, 99–106.

[73] *A-G's Reference (No 4 of 2000)* [2001] Crim LR 578 and commentary (causing death by dangerous driving).

[74] *Hardie* [1985] 1 WLR 64, CA. See the discussion in Ch 11 and LC 314, *Intoxication and Criminal Liability* (2009).

[75] cf *Heard* [2007] EWCA Crim 125 below, Ch 11, p 318.

[76] *Lipman* [1970] 1 QB 152; approved in *DPP v Majewski* [1977] AC 443. See below, p 312.

[77] *Hardie*, above.

[78] *Bailey* [1983] 1 WLR 760, below, p 314.

[79] RD Mackay, 'Intoxication as a Factor in Automatism' [1982] Crim LR 146, 147. See also RD Mackay, *Mental Condition Defences*, above.

[80] See *Poole* [2003] All ER (D) 448 (Mar) where D's failure to take his epilepsy medicine led to his loss of consciousness.

[81] These issues are discussed in full in Ch 11 below.

involuntary act, as where he visits a hypnotist to receive the suggestion that he should kill V and goes on to carry out that homicide when in the trance, but such circumstances have not been addressed by the courts.[82]

Of course, if the 'fault' exhibited by D's 'prior' conduct is in itself sufficient to found liability for the offence charged, then D is properly convicted of it under ordinary principles.[83] An elementary example is where a driver, feeling sleepy, continues to drive until he falls asleep and has an accident. His failure to stop may constitute the fault necessary to convict him of careless, or even dangerous, driving.[84] The subsequent conduct of falling asleep is not blame-less: D's culpability lies precisely in the failure to safeguard against its occurrence.

4.2.1.2 Voluntariness as *actus reus* or *mens rea*?

Writers dispute whether the voluntariness of D's conduct should be regarded as part of the *actus reus* or as part of the *mens rea*.[85] On the one hand, it is a mental element; on the other, it is said that it is an essential constituent of the act, which is part of the *actus reus*. It has been argued that the classification is important. The argument runs: some offences, known as offences of strict liability, do not require *mens rea*; so that, if voluntariness is part of the *mens rea*, a person charged with an offence of strict liability might be convicted for an involuntary act. But an *actus reus* must be proved, even for an offence of strict liability; therefore if vol-untariness is part of the *actus reus*, no one can be convicted of any crime if his act was invol-untary. As the latter result is thought to be not only desirable but also to represent the law, voluntariness can only properly be regarded as an element in the *actus reus*. The fallacy in this argument lies in the proposition that offences of strict liability require 'no *mens rea*' and the assumption that this means that the whole of the mental element involved in *mens rea* may be lacking.[86] This is not so. If the mental element is part of the *actus reus* (as in, for example, possession) there is certainly no way of dispensing with it;[87] but it does not follow that it must be dispensed with where an offence is held to be one of strict liability.

For 125 years, *Prince*[88] was regarded as the leading case on strict liability. Although now superseded by statute,[89] it remains a good illustration of the principle. *Prince* decided that D may be convicted of the offence (now repealed) of taking a girl under the age of 16 out of the possession and against the will of her father, even though D believed in good faith and on reasonable grounds that the girl he was taking was over 16. It is commonly said that no *mens rea* need be proved because the act which D *intended* – to take an 18-year-old girl (as she had told him she was) out of the possession of her parents – was not prohibited by law – it was not

---

[82] C Finkelstein, 'Involuntary Crimes, Voluntarily Committed', in S Shute and A Simester (eds), *Criminal Law Theory: Doctrines of the General Part* (2000) 143; PH Robinson, 'Causing the Condition of One's Own Defense: A Study in the Limits of the Criminal Law Doctrine' (1985) 71 Virg LR 1. See also *Finnegan v Heywood* (2000), 10 May, High Ct of Justiciary, where D's transitory state of sleepwalking (and driving) was induced by his volun-tary intoxication and he was aware of the likelihood of that outcome. The decision does not make it clear whether D would have had a defence of automatism if he was unaware of the likelihood. See also the valuable discussion by Wilson et al above, n 69, proposing a defence of 'not guilty by reason of sleep disorder'.

[83] The *dictum* of Martin JA in *Rabey* (1977) 79 DLR (3d) 414, 425 quoted by Mackay as a 'typical example of a dictum in support of "fault liability"' above, n 79, seems to be saying no more than this.

[84] *Kay v Butterworth* (1945) 173 LT 191, below, p 61 n 101.

[85] Turner (MACL, 195 and 199 and Kenny, *Outlines*, 23) thought 'voluntariness' an element of *mens rea*. Williams, CLGP, s 8 and I Patient, 'Some Remarks about the Element of Voluntariness in Offences of Absolute Liability' [1968] Crim LR 23 think it part of the *actus reus*.

[86] cf *Blackburn v Bowering*, below, p 661; Howard, SR 1; NZ Essays at 49; Packer, *The Limits of the Criminal Sanction* (1968) 126.

[87] Above, p 48.

[88] (1875) LR 2 CCR 154.

[89] At p 178.

an *actus reus*. But even if this was an offence 'requiring no *mens rea*', it is quite clear that it involved a substantial mental element, apart from the element of voluntariness. D would have to have been proved to have intended to take a girl out of the possession of her parents. If he thought the girl was in no one's possession, he was not guilty. If he thought the girl was a boy, he was probably not guilty. No one suggests, however, that we should say that his knowledge that the girl was in the possession of her parents is part of the *actus reus*. The fact is that, even in offences of strict liability, a limited degree of *mens rea* must be proved; and a jurist may, if he chooses, classify the voluntariness of D's act as part of the limited degree of *mens rea*. It is a matter of convenience only.

What is clear is that whether the act was involuntary is a more fundamental element of criminal liability than what we normally think of as *mens rea* – the intention to cause, or foresight of, results of the act and awareness of circumstances. If the conduct may have been involuntary the *actus reus* has not been proved by the Crown there can be no conviction.

What is missing in these cases appears to most people as a vital link between mind and body; and both the ordinary man and the lawyer might well insist on this by saying that in these cases there is not 'really' a human action at all and certainly nothing for which anyone should be made criminally responsible however 'strict' legal responsibility might be.[90]

4.2.1.3 Automatism

The plea of a lack of voluntariness is described as a plea of automatism, that is, that D was acting as an automaton. Automatism has narrow limits as a 'defence'. It is to be confined, according to Lord Denning,[91] to acts done while unconscious and to spasms, reflex actions and convulsions.[92] It commonly arises in driving cases, particularly where diabetic defendants claim that they were suffering from hyperglycaemic or hypoglycaemic states. In *Broome v Perkins*,[93] D, though in a hypoglycaemic state, was held guilty of driving without due care and attention because from time to time he apparently exercised conscious control over his car, veering away from other vehicles so as to avoid a collision, braking violently, and so on. Automatism is not a defence to a driving charge unless there is 'a total destruction of voluntary control'. A condition described by an expert witness as 'driving without awareness' was held to be no answer to a charge of causing death by reckless (or, now, dangerous) driving where it in fact amounted to merely reduced or imperfect awareness.[94]

Clearly policy plays a part in the courts' adoption of such a strict approach to the degree of involuntariness constituting automatism, particularly in road traffic offences. Some passages

---

[90] HLA Hart, 'Acts of Wills and Responsibility', Jubilee Lectures of the Faculty of Law, University of Sheffield (1960) 115 at 137. Note that Turner, while regarding voluntariness as *mens rea*, thought it a different and more fundamental element than foresight of consequences; MACL, 195–205.

[91] In *Bratty* [1963] AC 386, [1961] 3 All ER 523 at 532. It is confined to 'involuntary movement of the body or limbs of a person': *Watmore v Jenkins* [1962] 2 All ER 868 at 878, per Winn J. In a Canadian case, *Racimore* (1976) 25 CCC (2d) 143, a 'failure to remain' after an accident was held to be involuntary because D did not know there had been an accident. This seems to be an unsatisfactory device for introducing a requirement of *mens rea* into an offence of strict liability. cf *Davey v Towle* [1973] RTR 328.

[92] See the discussion in the Scottish case of *Ross v HM Advocate* (1991) SCCR 823 where the court identified four criteria: an external factor; which was not self-induced; which D was not bound to foresee; and which caused a total alienation of reason rendering him incapable of controlling or appreciating what he was doing. See on this P Ferguson, 'The Limits of the Automatism Defence' (1991) 36 JLSS 446.

[93] [1987] Crim LR 271, DC.

[94] *A-G's Reference (No 2 of 1992)* (1993) 99 Cr App R 429. It was argued that the cause of the condition was the 'external factor' of the motorway conditions. If those conditions produce total destruction of voluntary control, it is submitted that, assuming them to be no more than the ordinary stresses to which all drivers are subject, they would not constitute an external factor. The driver's exceptional susceptibility should result, however odd it may sound, in a special verdict of insanity. See also JC Smith, 'Individual Incapacities and Criminal Liability' [1999] Med L Rev 138 at 144–145 and *Rabey*, below p 300.

suggest that the requirement is one of a complete lack of consciousness rather than a lack of voluntariness. That seems unduly narrow and to risk losing sight of the focus on whether D had the capacity to control his actions. In relation to other crimes the courts have not consistently adopted such a strict approach. In the case of *Charlson*[95] for example, where the evidence was that D was 'acting as an automaton without any *real knowledge* of what he was doing' (emphasis added) as a result of a cerebral tumour, Barry J directed the jury to acquit if the defence might reasonably be true.

4.2.1.4 Physical involuntariness

Although the courts have confused the issue of consciousness and voluntariness in seeking to determine the scope of the defence of automatism, they have been clear and consistent in holding that the defence is of physical, not moral, involuntariness. Pleas of 'irresistible impulse' have been consistently rejected as a defence even where arising from insanity. The fact that, as a result of hysterical amnesia, or hysterical fugue, D was unaware of 'legal restrictions or moral concern', is no defence if he knew the facts which constitute the offence charged.[96] An irresistible craving for drink is not a defence to a charge of stealing alcohol.[97] Similarly if D has punched V it is no defence (though it may mitigate the sentence) to say that this was an immediate and irresistible reaction to provocation by V. But the borderline between this and a 'reflex action' must be a fine one. The legal nature and legal effect of a reflex action is, itself, uncertain. In *Ryan v R*,[98] D with one hand pointed a loaded shotgun at V whom he had robbed, while with the other hand he attempted to tie V up. V moved. D was startled and, he said, 'involuntarily' pressed the trigger because of a 'reflex action'. Barwick CJ thought that, if this story had been true, D would not have been responsible in law for the 'act' of pressing the trigger; but Windeyer J held that, while that act may have been 'involuntary' in a dictionary sense, it was one for which he was responsible in law and not properly analogous to an act done in convulsions or an epileptic seizure. With respect, however, it seems closer to these than to 'the sudden movement of a tennis player retrieving a difficult shot; not accompanied by conscious planning but certainly not involuntary'.[99]

It is, of course, very important to identify the precise conduct for which D is to be held responsible. In *Ryan v R*, the pointing of the loaded gun and the placing of the finger on the trigger were clearly voluntary acts and, provided that it could be said that these acts caused death, the accused would be liable for homicide, whether the pressing of the trigger was an act for which he was responsible or not. Similarly in the English civil case of *Gray v Barr*[100] D approached V with a loaded gun and fired a shot to frighten V. D and V grappled together and V fell on the gun and was shot and killed. The trial judge and Salmon LJ thought that the real cause of V's death was the accident of his falling on the gun; whereas Denning MR and Phillimore LJ thought that the cause was D's deliberate act in approaching V with the gun. All the judges agreed, however, that D could properly have been convicted of manslaughter on these facts. The act for which D would be held responsible was not the firing of the fatal shot – that was not his act – but deliberately approaching V in that threatening way. Again, a person may be immune from liability for an offence involving 'driving', though he is sitting at

---

[95] [1955] 1 All ER 859.

[96] *Isitt* [1978] Crim LR 159, CA.

[97] *Dodd* (1974) 7 SASR 151 at 157. See, generally, LS Tao, 'Legal Problems of Alcoholism' (1969) 37(3) Fordham LR 405; J Tolmie, 'Alcoholism and Criminal Liability' (2001) 64 MLR 688.

[98] (1967) 40 ALJR 488, discussed by ID Elliott, 'Responsibility for Involuntary Acts: *Ryan v The Queen*' (1968) 41 ALJ 497.

[99] Elliott, above.

[100] [1971] 2 QB 554; below, p 550. cf *Jarmain* [1946] KB 74; *Blayney v Knight* (1975) 60 Cr App R 269, DC. cf *A-G's Reference (No 3 of 2004)* [2005] EWCA Crim 1882, below p 219.

the controls of a moving vehicle, if he is unconscious through an epileptic fit; but, depending on the degree and frequency of epilepsy and the probability that he might have an attack, he might be liable through the conscious act of starting or continuing to drive.[101]

An interesting example arose recently in *Brady*[102] where, having voluntarily consumed alcohol and drugs, the defendant had fallen from a balcony in a nightclub onto the dance floor below and had landed on the victim, thereby causing her serious injuries. The Crown's evidence was to the effect that D had climbed onto the balcony railings and had jumped from them deliberately, D's account was that he perched his bottom against the railings and lost his balance and fell. The single issue in the trial was whether D had acted with the requisite *mens rea*. The Court of Appeal noted, *obiter*, that there was arguably evidence of 'deliberate non-accidental conduct on the part of the accused that inflicted grievous bodily harm', in that D had deliberately perched precariously on a low railing above a crowded dance floor and having consumed considerable quantities of alcohol and drugs. This deliberate act, on any view, led almost immediately and directly to the fall over the railing and to the inflicting of grievous bodily harm. It is submitted that there was an *actus reus*. A contrasting factual scenario would have been if a person was perched on the railings and fell because he lurched backwards involuntarily to avoid that unforeseen swarm of bees which academics often pray in aid.[103]

4.2.1.5 Distinguishing sane and insane automatism

A person who was in a state of automatism (other than one induced by voluntary intoxication) at the time he is alleged to have committed the offence, cannot be guilty of it and the only question is whether he is to be found simply 'not guilty' or 'not guilty by reason of insanity'. The outcome (which is of great importance) depends on how the automatism arose. If it was caused by 'a disease of the mind' the proper verdict is not guilty by reason of insanity. If it arose from any other cause the verdict is simply not guilty. But whether a cause is a 'disease of the mind' is a question of law and that phrase has a wide meaning. Any 'internal factor', mental or physical, is, in law, a disease of the mind. So automatism caused by a cerebral tumour or arteriosclerosis, epilepsy or diabetes arises from a disease of the mind. These are all 'internal' to the accused. External factors include concussion, the administration of an anaesthetic or other drug, or hypnosis. In a number of cases, acts done while sleeping have been treated as sane automatism[104] but it has now been held[105] that they are the product of a disease of the mind and thus insanity.

It will be recalled that the one exception at common law to the rule that the burden of proof is on the prosecution is the defence of insanity. So if D claims that he was in a state of automatism because of an internal factor, he is raising the insanity defence and it will be for him to satisfy the jury on the balance of probabilities that this was so; but if he relies on an external factor and lays a proper foundation for the automatism defence, the onus is on the prosecution to satisfy the jury beyond reasonable doubt that it was not so.[106] If he alleges that his condition was due to the administration of insulin (an external factor) inducing

---

[101] *Hill v Baxter* [1958] 1 QB 277 at 286, per Pearson LJ; *McBride* [1962] 2 QB 167. Similarly where D goes to sleep: *Kay v Butterworth* (1945) 173 LT 191.

[102] [2006] EWCA Crim 2413, [2007] Crim LR 564 and commentary.

[103] See further the commentary at [2007] Crim LR 564.

[104] *Boshears* (1961) The Times, 8 Feb; *Kemp* (1986) The Times, 3 May: D strangled his wife while experiencing a condition known as 'night terror'. Note that parasomnia caused by self-induced intoxication will not provide a defence of automatism. See further p 299.

[105] *Burgess* [1991] 2 QB 92, [1991] Crim LR 548, and see news reports for 21 March 2005 of a killing when sleepwalking which led to an acquittal.

[106] See *Roach* [2001] EWCA Crim 2698, below p 329.

hypoglycaemia (too little blood sugar), he will be acquitted unless the prosecution can disprove his claim;[107] but if he alleges that it was due to diabetes (an internal factor) causing hyperglycaemia (excessive blood sugar), the onus will be on him to prove the defence on the balance of probabilities; it must be supported by the evidence of two or more registered medical practitioners;[108] and, if he succeeds, he will be found not guilty by reason of insanity.[109]

A proper foundation for a defence of sane automatism may be laid by introducing evidence from which it may reasonably be inferred that the act was involuntary. Whether such a foundation has been laid is a question of law. Lord Denning has said that D's own word will rarely be sufficient,[110] unless it is supported by medical evidence. The difficult questions that arise where there is evidence that the automatism was caused partly by disease of the mind and partly by other factors are considered below.[111]

4.2.1.6 Involuntariness not arising from automatism

A person may have full control over his body but no control over events in which it is involved. A driver's brakes fail without his fault and, consequently, he inevitably fails to accord precedence to a pedestrian on a pedestrian crossing.[112] Although it is said that this offence is absolute,[113] requiring no evidence of negligence, it was held in *Burns v Bidder*[114] that such a driver has a defence. The court equated the driver's situation with that of one stunned by a swarm of bees, disabled by epilepsy,[115] or propelled by a vehicle hitting his car from behind. 'Voluntariness' is essential even in so-called crimes of 'absolute liability'.[116] On the other hand, it seems to have been held that it is no defence that the failure to accord precedence on the crossing arises inevitably from the unforeseeable behaviour of the pedestrian,[117] but the driver in such a case has no more power to avert the failure than where his brakes fail. It is submitted that D should never be held criminally liable for an 'act' or result of an 'act' over which he has no control.[118]

---

[107] Assuming he has not acted recklessly as to becoming automaton by failing to follow his prescription, etc.

[108] Criminal Procedure (Insanity and Unfitness to Plead) Act 1991, below, p 288.

[109] *Hennessy* [1989] 1 WLR 287, CA; *Bingham* [1991] Crim LR 433. cf *Pull* (1998) The Times, 20–21 Mar, discussed below. The distinction in terms of result highlights the unsatisfactorily incoherent nature of the law's categorization of automatism as sane or insane on the basis of its internal/external cause. See the cogent criticism of Wilson et al, n 69 [2005] Crim LR 614.

[110] In *Dervish* [1968] Crim LR 37, *Cook v Atchison* [1968] Crim LR 266 and *Stripp* (1978) 69 Cr App R 318, CA, it was held that D's evidence that he had a 'blackout' was insufficient to raise the defence (see also *C* [2007] EWCA Crim 1862).

[111] See p 327.

[112] Contrary to the Zebra, Pelican and Puffin Pedestrian Crossings Regulations and General Directions 1997, SI 2400, reg 25.

[113] *Hughes v Hall* [1960] 1 WLR 733.

[114] [1967] 2 QB 227.

[115] But see now *Sullivan* [1984] AC 156.

[116] An alternative explanation is the existence of a general defence of 'impossibility', below, Ch 11.

[117] *Neal v Reynolds* [1966] Crim LR 393. The case is only briefly reported and may be explained on another ground.

[118] See also KJM Smith and W Wilson, 'Impaired Voluntariness and Criminal Responsibility' (1993) 13 OJLS 69, considering the question of voluntariness in terms of a person's capacity to conform to the law's requirements. See also DN Husak, *Philosophy of Criminal Law* (1987) 102 and Duff, *Answering for Crime* on the significance of the issue of control. Duff suggests that use of the concept of control avoids many of the difficulties experienced in trying to distinguish acts and omissions.

4.3 A 'state of affairs' as an *actus reus*[119]

A crime may be so defined that it can be committed although there is no 'act' in the sense considered above. There may be no necessity for any 'willed muscular movement'. Instead, it may be enough if a specified 'state of affairs' is proved to exist. These offences are sometimes called 'status'[120] or 'situation'[121] offences. Under the Road Traffic Act 1988, s 4(2), for example, any person who, when in charge of a mechanically propelled vehicle on a road or other public place is unfit to drive through drink or drugs, commits an offence. One cannot take charge without consciously doing so, but it is not *taking* charge of the vehicle, or *becoming* unfit which is the offence, but simply *being* in charge and *being* unfit. So long as this state of affairs continues, the *actus reus* of the crime is committed. The *actus reus* may even be in the process of being committed while D is sleeping peacefully,[122] for he may still be 'in charge'. A further example is provided by the offence under s 25 of the Theft Act 1968 whereby a person commits an offence if, when not at his place of abode, he *has with him* any article for use in the course of, or in connection with, burglary, etc.[123] So long as he has the article with him, he is committing the offence. Of course, in all these examples D will, almost invariably, have done the acts of taking charge, getting drunk, or taking up the article, but these acts are not part of the crime. Although attempts have been made to defend these offences on the basis of D's prior fault, these are not wholly convincing.[124]

Offences of this type are treated with great caution. They are commonly associated with tyrannical regimes in which offences of 'status' are enacted, for example, offences of being a member of a particular political organization[125] or being of a particular race or religion (criminalization of which is yet worse because the person may have made no conscious choice to become such a member). It has recently been suggested that criminalizing such conduct may contravene the ECHR.[126]

Even in modern day England and Wales this type of offence has led to extraordinary results in offences of 'being found' in a particular situation. In *Larsonneur*,[127] D was convicted under the Aliens Order 1920 in that she, 'being an alien to whom leave to land in the United Kingdom has been refused' was found in the UK. She had been brought from Ireland into the UK against her will in the custody of the police. D, having been previously ordered to depart from the UK, went to the Irish Free State, which was not a 'departure' for the purposes of the Order; but the Free State was not part of the UK. She could not have been convicted of being found in the UK on 21 April if she had remained there. She was guilty of being found in the UK on that day; and she was in the UK on that day because she was brought here under arrest. Notwithstanding the wide condemnation of that decision,[128] similar results were reached in

---

[119] See P Glazebrook, 'Situational Liability', in *Reshaping the Criminal Law*, 108.

[120] Howard, SR, Ch 3.

[121] MD Cohen, 'The Actus Reus and Offences of Situation' (1972) 7 Israel Law Rev 186.

[122] *Duck v Peacock* [1949] 1 All ER 318; but see the defence provided by Road Traffic Act 1956, s 9(1) proviso, now re-enacted in Road Traffic Act 1988, s 4(3), on which see K Mc Cormac (ed), *Wilkinson's Road Traffic Offences* (24th edn, 2010) Ch 4.

[123] Theft Act 1968, s 25, below, p 970.

[124] See Norrie, *Crime, Reason and History*, 119.

[125] See *Scales v US* 327 US 203 (1961) re communist party membership.

[126] See GR Sullivan, 'Strict Liability and the ECHR', in A Simester (ed), *Appraising Strict Liability* (2005) 207.

[127] (1933) 24 Cr App R 74. cf *Walters* [1969] 1 QB 255 (being an incorrigible rogue). See the criticism of *Larsonneur* by Howard, sr, 47. For a spirited but unconvincing defence of the case, see DJ Lanham, '*Larsonneur* Revisited' [1976] Crim LR 276 and RC Doegar, 'Strict Liability in Criminal Law and Larsonneur Revisited' [1998] Crim LR 791 with response by JC Smith [1999] Crim LR 100, and DJ Lanham, Letter [1999] Crim LR 683.

[128] 'The acme of strict injustice', Hall, *General Principles*, 329 n 14; Williams, CLGP, 11; Howard, sr, 47; Gordon, 287; J Horder, *Excusing Crime* (2004), explains such cases as 'far from being exceptional', rather they were 'all too characteristic of the period', p 251.

respect of the offence under s 12 of the Licensing Act 1872 of being found drunk in a highway. In *Winzar v Chief Constable of Kent*,[129] D was taken to hospital on a stretcher but was found to be drunk and told to leave. When he was seen slumped on a seat in the corridor, the police were called and they took him to a police car stationed in the highway outside the hospital. He was convicted of being 'found drunk' in the highway. The words, 'found drunk', were held to mean 'perceived to be drunk'. But 'perceive' means 'to become aware of' and it seems that the police became aware of D's condition in the hospital and not in the highway.

Larsonneur and Winzar were convicted of offences the commission of which was in fact procured by the police;[130] and this seems peculiarly offensive. These offences of 'being found' are unusual[131] in that they require an act on the part of the finder but no act or *mens rea* on the part of the defendant. As a matter of principle, even 'state of affairs' offences ought to require proof that D either caused the state of affairs or failed to terminate it or act in order to do so when it was within his control and possible to do so.[132] Physical impossibility of compliance with the law should be a defence, at least where it is not proved that the impossibility arose through D's own fault.[133] Thus, situational offences are rightly condemned when they do not allow D to adjust his behaviour to remain within the law.[134]

It has been held by the Privy Council that the offence of 'remaining' in Singapore, having been prohibited from entering that Republic, could not be committed by one who was ignorant of the prohibition.[135] It is implicit in the case that to 'remain' because detained would not be an offence. It is true that 'remaining' may be said to be D's act while 'being found' is the act of another; but the substance of the two offences is the same.

It was held[136] at common law that 'being in possession' was an insufficient act to constitute the *actus reus* of a crime, but there are now many cases where, by statute, mere possession is enough. Thus, possession of dangerous drugs,[137] explosive substances, firearms and forged banknotes all constitute the *actus reus* of various crimes. 'Being in possession' does not involve an act in the sense of a muscular movement at all, for a person may possess goods merely by knowingly[138] keeping them in his house. Possession which is initially lawful may become

---

[129] (1983) The Times, 28 Mar, DC. cf *Palmer-Brown v Police* [1985] 1 NZLR 365, CA (D not 'found' behaving in a particular way when behaviour occurred some time after encounter with constable).

[130] It might be argued that the police action breaks the chain of causation between any prior wrongdoing of D and the ultimate forbidden status.

[131] But not unique. Being the parent of a child of compulsory school age was an offence under the Education Act 1944, s 39(1) if the child failed to attend school regularly. It was unnecessary to prove any knowledge or neglect on the part of the parent: *Crump v Gilmore* [1970] Crim LR 28. Glazebrook, 'Situational Liability', in *Reshaping the Criminal Law*, 108, contends that *Larsonneur*-type liability is by no means unusual, pointing, *inter alia*, to the similarity, from the defendant's point of view, of vicarious liability (on which see below, Ch 10).

[132] Patient [1968] Crim LR 23. cf *Burns v Nowell* (1880) 5 QBD 444 at 454 '...before a continuous act or proceeding, not originally unlawful, can be treated as unlawful by reason of the passing of an Act of Parliament, by which it is in terms made so, a reasonable time must be allowed for its discontinuance...' Other jurisdictions have avoided the result in *Larsonneur*: *Achterdam* 1911 EDL 336 (Burchell and Hunt, SACLP, 105); *O'Sullivan v Fisher* [1954] SASR 33. In the United States, similar offences have been held unconstitutional; *Robinson v California* 370 US 660, 8 L Ed 2d 758 (1962) (being addicted to the use of narcotics).

[133] See A Smart, 'Criminal Responsibility for Failing to do the Impossible' (1987) 103 LQR 532.

[134] Wilson, *Central Issues*, 83.

[135] *Lim Chin Aik v R* [1963] AC 160. See also *Finau v Department of Labour* [1984] 2 NZLR 396 (failure to leave New Zealand after revocation of permit not an offence where impossible to leave because of pregnancy). But cf *Grant v Borg* [1982] 1 WLR 638, HL, where an immigrant was held guilty of knowingly remaining beyond the time limit although, because of a mistake of law, he may have believed the time had been extended.

[136] *Heath* (1810) Russ & Ry 184; *Dugdale v R* (1853) 1 E & B 435.

[137] See, in particular, the comprehensive analysis in R Fortson, *Misuse of Drugs: Offences, Confiscation and Money Laundering* (5th edn, 2005) Ch 3.

[138] A person may possess a thing in the civil law although he does not know of its existence; but knowledge will usually be required in criminal law: cf *Warner v Metropolitan Police Comr*, below, p 162; *Cugullere* [1961] 1 WLR 858.

criminal because of a change of circumstances without any act by D,[139] but only after he has failed to divest himself of possession within a reasonable time.[140] 'Being in possession' is simply a state of affairs, which, in certain circumstances, involves criminal liability.

4.4 Omissions[141]

Considerable controversy rages over whether, and to what extent, the law ought to regard inactivity as a sufficient basis for criminal liability. There are powerful arguments of principle and practicality against the imposition of a general criminal liability for failing to act in circumstances which give rise to a prohibited harm.[142] The strongest argument against imposing any such general criminal liability is that to do so would infringe the autonomy of the citizen in a qualitatively different manner to circumstances where liability is imposed for positive action. So it is argued, it is legitimate for the law to criminalize holding someone under water so that they drown, but not to seek to compel a person to act by criminalizing, for example, his refusal to save a drowning stranger.[143] In some circumstances the law can, consistent with this principle of autonomy, impose liability for omission – as where the person is not a stranger but is D's child. These categories of exceptional liability for omission are examined below. Irrespective of the existence of these exceptions, the arguments of individual autonomy have been challenged for their failure generally to respect obligations of social responsibility, particularly where the potential harm that can be averted (for example, death) is disproportionate to the infringement of the person's liberty (for example, the simple act of plucking a child from a shallow pool of water).[144]

A further argument against the imposition of general liability for omissions is that to do so would infringe principles of legality. It is questioned whether the law can impose liability with sufficient clarity, specificity and certainty to respect adequately the principles of fair warning, fair labelling, maximum certainty, coherence with civil law, etc.[145] Again, there are counter arguments to these claims. In addition, there is the suggestion that failing to act cannot be regarded as a cause of harm, so that there should be no general liability for omission in result crimes. But these denials of causation often take an unduly simplistic approach. Further arguments against the imposition of general criminal liability for omissions include the practical difficulty in defining the standard of duty which the law would impose on the person required to act, and of the potential unfairness in singling out for punishment a particular individual from the population as a whole, or a group of individuals, none of whom acted. In the discussion that follows we can examine the extent to which the law has satisfactorily overcome these

---

[139] cf *Buswell* [1972] 1 WLR 64.

[140] *Burns v Nowell*, above, n 132. *Levine* [1927] 1 DLR 740 is contrary.

[141] There is a wealth of academic literature on the topic, see in particular: G Fletcher, *Rethinking Criminal Law* (1978) Ch 8; G Hughes, 'Criminal Omissions' (1958) 67 Yale LJ 590; Duff, *Answering for Crime*, Ch 5; P Glazebrook, 'Criminal Omissions: The Duty Requirements in Offences Against the Person' (1960) 76 LQR 386; A Ashworth, 'The Scope of Criminal Liability for Omissions' (1989) 105 LQR 424; JC Smith, 'Liability for Omissions in Criminal Law' (1984) 4 LS 88. See on Scots law: R Shiels, 'Scots Law and Liability for Omissions' (2006) 70 J Crim L 413.

[142] cf Tadros, *Criminal Responsibility*, 184.

[143] See G Williams, 'Criminal Omissions – the Conventional View' (1991) 107 LQR 86, for criticism see Tadros, *Criminal Responsibility*, 189 arguing that such cases are better dealt with by providing defences of justification.

[144] See especially A Ashworth (1989) 105 LQR 424. On qualitative moral differences between act and omission see A Simester 'Why Omissions are Special' (1995) 1 Legal Theory 311.

[145] For an accessible account of the academic concerns, see Wilson, *Central Issues*, 82–102. See A Ashworth, 'Ignorance of the Criminal Law and Duties to Avoid it' (2011) 74 MLR 1.

objections in those exceptional categories of case in which liability for failure to act has been recognized.

4.4.1 Offences of mere omission

Statutes frequently make it an offence to omit to do something. There are many legislative provisions requiring companies and others to submit returns of various kinds (tax, licences, etc) and making it an offence to fail to do so.[146] This type of offence is not restricted to corporate regulation: the driver of a vehicle which is involved in an accident must report the accident.[147] A motorist who fails to provide a police officer with a specimen of breath when properly required to do so commits an offence.[148] So does a person legally liable to maintain a child if he fails to provide him with adequate food, clothing, medical aid or lodging.[149] These offences, although they provide that D is liable for a criminal offence by omission, are uncontroversial provided that they respect the general principles of criminal law. Most of them are of a regulatory nature, but there are controversial examples relating to more serious crimes. Modern legislation has created a number of offences for failure to report criminal activities, such as ss 19 and 38B of the Terrorism Act 2000 (TA 2000),[150] which respectively criminalize failure to report suspicions of certain terrorist offences having been committed, when the information is acquired in a professional capacity, and failure to disclose information which would be of material assistance in the prevention of an act of terrorism.[151] There are also numerous examples of offences of failing to control others (even adult strangers) such as s 111A(1B) of the Social Security Administration Act 1992 (allowing false benefit claim).[152]

At common law, offences of pure omission are also to be found, though rarely. A police officer was held to be guilty of a common law misdemeanour when, without justification or excuse, he failed to perform his duty to preserve the Queen's peace by protecting a citizen who was being kicked to death.[153] A citizen is guilty of an offence if he fails to respond to a constable's call for assistance in keeping the peace.[154] The courts appear reluctant to extend common law offences to include liability for omission.[155]

---

[146] See, eg: Companies Act 1985, s 444 (as amended by the Companies Act 2006, Sch 3, para 1), (Secretary of State's power to require a company or individual to produce documents); Insolvency Act 1986, s 235 (duty on officers and employees of a company to cooperate with the 'office-holder' or official receiver of a company); Data Protection Act 1998, s 47 (failing or refusing to comply with an enforcement or an information notice).

[147] Road Traffic Act 1988, s 170(4).

[148] Road Traffic Act 1988, s 6.

[149] Children and Young Persons Act 1933, s 1(2)(a). Non-reporting of the harm caused by others to children could amount to 'neglect' under the Children and Young Persons Act 1933, s 1(1) (amended by the Children Act 1989, s 108(4), (5), Sch 12 para 2, Sch 3 para 2) (see *W* [2006] EWCA Crim 2723) or in the case of wilfully neglecting a mental patient contrary to the Mental Health Act 1983, s 127(1) (*Morrell* [2002] EWCA Crim 2547).

[150] See C Walker, *The Anti-terrorism Legislation* (2nd edn, 2010) para 3.89.

[151] Section 330 of the Proceeds of Crime Act 2002 (POCA 2002) also creates an offence for failing to disclose suspicions of money laundering.

[152] See *Tilley* [2009] EWCA Crim 1426 and [2009] Crim LR 162 and commentary.

[153] *Dytham* [1979] QB 722. For a definitive modern definition of misconduct in public office see *A-G's Reference (No 3 of 2003)* [2004] EWCA Crim 868, holding that D must be subjectively aware of the duty and subjectively reckless in its fulfilment, para 30. See also *Belton* [2010] EWCA Crim 2857 where it is not even clear D knew of her public office status.

[154] *Brown* (1841) Car & M 314, below, p 198. See D Nicholson, 'The Citizen's Duty to Assist the Police' [1992] Crim LR 611. PACE Code C para IK provides 'all citizens have a duty to help police officers to prevent crime and discover offenders'. This is a civic rather than a legal duty. cf J Wanik, 'Forcing the Bystander to Get Involved' (1985) 94 Yale LJ 1787.

[155] eg, rejection of perverting the course of justice by omission: *Clark* [2003] 2 Cr App R 23; cf the extension in relation to cheating the public revenue: *Mavji* (1987) 84 Cr App R 34, which may be explained on the basis of the Court of Appeal's exceptional preparedness to read dishonesty offences broadly, see below, p 779.

4.4.2 Offences of omission causing a result

Where, as in the above examples, the offence is defined in terms of the failure to act itself, there are no special difficulties. Problems with omissions arise when the offence requires proof of a result as, for example, in homicide and other offences against the person. Stephen stated the rule for these offences as follows: 'It is not a crime to cause death or bodily injury, even intentionally, by any omission...'[156]

He gave the following famous illustration:

A sees B drowning and is able to save him by holding out his hand. A abstains from doing so in order that B may be drowned, and B is drowned. A has committed no offence?

Stephen went on to state exceptional cases where the law imposes a duty to act. If A in the example were B's parent, A would have a duty to act and would be guilty of murder if he did not act and the child drowned. There are a number of problems which need to be considered.

(1) Is the offence in question one under which conviction can arise for omission?

(2) If so, is A under a duty to act?

(3) If so, can we truly say that A has 'caused' the prohibited result?

(4) Is the conduct in question properly regarded as an omission? In many cases the courts may strain the concept of an act so as to avoid difficulties, particularly in cases involving medical care terminating life.

4.4.2.1 Is the offence one capable of being committed by omission?

Assuming that D's conduct can properly be described as an omission, for example, standing by and watching a person drowning, or failing to feed a person, the question to determine is whether the offence with which he is charged can be fairly interpreted to apply to omissions.

Statutes generally

In statutory offences this question becomes one of construction. Is the verb, in its context, properly construed to include an omission? Glanville Williams has written:

In my opinion the courts should not create liability for omissions without statutory authority. Verbs used in defining offences and *prima facie* implying active conduct should not be stretched by interpretation to include omissions. In general the courts follow this principle. They do not say, for instance, that a person 'wounds' another by failing to save him from being wounded, or 'damages' a building by failing to stop a fire. At least, this has never been decided.[157]

But Professor Williams himself pointed out that the courts have often held offences to be capable of being committed by omission although the enactment did not expressly provide for it. As a matter of principle, it might be argued that the interpretation of a statute that is ambiguous in this regard ought to be resolved in D's favour. However, in many cases the words of the statute can be read to include omissions without straining their meaning.

There are numerous examples of the courts' construction of words to include liability for omission. In *Shama*,[158] a conviction for falsifying a document required for an accounting purpose contrary to the Theft Act 1968, s 17(1)(a) was upheld where D omitted entirely to fill

---

[156] JF Stephen, *Digest of the Criminal Law* (4th edn, 1887) art 212.
[157] Letter to the Editor [1982] Crim LR 773.
[158] [1990] 2 All ER 602, [1990] Crim LR 411.

in a form which it was his duty to complete. In *Firth*,[159] a doctor was held to have deceived a hospital contrary to the Theft Act 1978, s 2(1) (now repealed), by failing to inform the hospital that certain patients were private patients. 'Obstruct', 'falsify' and 'deceive' are all verbs which the courts have held to be capable of satisfaction by omission. So why not any other verb? The difficulty is to find any principle to limit such construction.

In *Ahmad*,[160] it was held that the words 'does acts' in a modern statute, the Protection from Eviction Act 1977, were to be strictly construed and were not satisfied by proof of an omission. A person commits an offence if he 'does acts' likely to interfere with the peace or comfort of a residential occupier with intent to cause him to give up occupation of the premises. D, having done such acts without any such intent, omitted, with the required intention, to rectify the situation he had created. He was not guilty. Yet even the word 'act' may sometimes be satisfied by an omission.[161] It was held that a man 'commits an act of gross indecency' with a child by totally passive submission to an act done by the child.[162] As noted, the courts often sidestep the issue by treating the whole of the circumstances as forming the basis for liability as in *B*[163] where the issue was regarded as whether D 'acted with or towards a child' by remaining motionless as the boy pressed his erect penis against D.

Homicide

The courts have long accepted without debate that murder and manslaughter are capable of commission by omission. Most cases of homicide by omission have resulted in convictions for manslaughter but there is at least one reported case of murder. In *Gibbins and Proctor*,[164] a man and the woman with whom he was living were convicted of murder of the man's child by withholding food. By living with the man and receiving money from him for food the woman had assumed a duty towards the child (see below). The judge was held to have rightly directed that they were guilty of murder if they withheld food with intent to cause the child grievous bodily harm, as a result of which she died. If the child had sustained grievous bodily harm but not died, it is difficult to suppose that the court would not have held the defendants guilty of an offence under s 18 of the Offences Against the Person Act 1861.[165] The commission of this offence seems to have been an essential constituent of the D's liability, as the case was left to the jury. It would be strange indeed if causing death should be capable of commission by omission and causing grievous bodily harm not. It would mean that D was not in breach of a duty to act until death occurred, at which point the duty was retrospectively imposed. That is surely unacceptable.

Non-fatal offences against the person

Although the courts have accepted that homicide can be perpetrated by omission, they have assumed that assault or battery require an act.[166] The words 'kill' and 'slay' in an indictment have been held to be satisfied by proof of an omission, so why not 'assault' or 'battery'? It is

---

[159] (1990) 91 Cr App R 217, [1990] Crim LR 326.

[160] (1986) 84 Cr App R 64, [1986] Crim LR 739. It will be noted that the court did not regard the act plus omission as an act. cf 'Creating a danger', below, p 72.

[161] This has particular significance because the entire law of attempts is based on the requirement of an 'act': Criminal Attempts Act 1981.

[162] *Speck* [1977] 2 All ER 859.

[163] [1999] Crim LR 594.

[164] (1918) 13 Cr App R 134, CCA.

[165] Below, p 652.

[166] Leaving aside for now the case where D creates a dangerous situation and fails to take steps within his power to avert that: *Santana Bermudez* [2004] Crim LR 471.

said that if D digs a pit for V to fall into, he commits an assault.[167] Why should it be different if he digs the pit without any such intention and then leaves it unfilled, intending V to fall in? Glanville Williams argues in respect of a similar case that 'in such circumstances of act-omission the total conduct should be regarded as an act...'[168] But 'should be regarded as' suggests a fiction and criminal liability should not turn on fictions. And his proposal would not meet the case where the hole has been dug by D's gardener and D, hearing that V is coming, decides to leave it unfilled.

Why should not the court legitimately interpret this as D causing V immediate unlawful violence? This view may derive some support from the decision in *Ireland*[169] that D's silent telephone call can constitute an assault. Again, however, it is likely that the courts would regard the assault as deriving from D's whole course of conduct by making the call coupled with his remaining silent. It is submitted that it would be realistic for the courts to recognize that one can 'assault', no less than 'kill', by omission.[170]

As for committing battery by omission, whereas assault only requires proof that D caused V to apprehend unlawful violence, battery requires the application of unlawful violence. Can it be said that D can apply force by omission? Such an interpretation of 'apply' might be a more difficult extension than with assault where the word 'cause' is the operative one.[171]

The discussion in the previous two paragraphs has dealt with the issue of whether there can be liability for assault and battery by omission, assuming that the elements of duty and causation can be established. As a separate matter, there can be liability for supervening fault in assault or battery – where D's course of conduct creates a dangerous situation towards any person and he omits to avert the risk. In *Fagan v Metropolitan Police Commissioner*,[172] where D accidentally drove his car onto a policeman's foot and then intentionally left it there, the majority of the court held that there was an assault (technically a battery) on the ground that, because D remained sitting in the car, there was a continuing act, not a mere omission. This again suggests, if not a fiction, a straining of words. Why should it be different if D had got out immediately, leaving the car on the officer's foot? The case would nowadays be decided under the exceptional category of duty recognized in *Miller*,[173] namely that D had created a dangerous situation by his act of driving onto V's foot and he then came under a duty to take reasonable steps to alleviate that danger. In *Santana Bermudez*,[174] this reasoning was applied to uphold D's conviction for assault occasioning actual bodily harm where D told a police officer who was about to search him that there were no needles on his person. The officer was pricked by a needle in D's pocket.

On the basis of *Gibbins* (above), it would seem that causing grievous bodily harm contrary to s 18 of the 1861 Act may be committed by omission. Although under s 20 of the 1861 Act the offence of wounding or inflicting grievous bodily harm would require proof of an 'infliction' of a 'wound' or grievous bodily harm, it is not clear that the words would be construed more narrowly than 'cause' in this context.[175] Since the offence under s 47 of the 1861 Act requires proof of an assault or battery and the 'occasioning', that is, 'causing' of actual bodily harm,

---

[167] The 'indirect violence' cases are doubted by M Hirst, 'Assault, Battery and Indirect Violence' [1999] Crim LR 577. cf Smith (1984) 4 LS 88.

[168] G Williams, 'What Should the Code do about Omissions?' (1987) 7 LS 92.

[169] [1998] AC 147.

[170] cf Wilson, *Central Issues*, 101.

[171] See Lord Hope in *Ireland* [1998] AC 147, 165.

[172] [1969] 1 QB 439 DC.

[173] [1983] 2 AC 161.

[174] [2004] Crim LR 471.

[175] *Mandair* [1995] AC 208.

subject to what was said above regarding assault, there is no reason to assume that this offence cannot also be committed by omission.

The CLRC recommended that liability for omissions in offences against the person should be confined to murder, manslaughter, and their proposed offences of causing serious injury with intent, unlawful detention, kidnapping, abduction and aggravated abduction.[176] The Home Office in its reform proposals[177] redrafted the offences against the person in terms of causing injury and serious injury. This approach would present few problems in relation to liability for commission by omission. The law would be simplified.

Offences against property

The Draft Criminal Code Team, being obliged to accept the CLRC recommendations, concluded that, if injury to the person was to be incapable of commission by omission, so, *a fortiori*, should be damage to property. This leads to the following illustration:[178]

D is employed as a night watchman at a factory. His duties are to take all reasonable steps to ensure the safety of the building. D sees that a small fire has broken out. There is an adjacent bucket of sand with which, as he knows, he could easily put out the fire. Having a grievance against his employer, he walks away and lets the fire burn. The factory is destroyed. He is not guilty of arson.

Such a conclusion may be unacceptable to the courts. If so, the remedy is in their hands. 'Destroy' and 'damage' in the Criminal Damage Act 1971[179] are capable of being construed to include omissions. It is submitted that in light of the shift in the proposals for reform of offences against the person this approach also needs to be reconsidered.

4.4.2.2 Who owes a duty?

Assuming that the offence itself is one capable of being committed by omission, the next question is, whether the individual defendant is one who may be under a duty to act.[180] Since most cases of omission have concerned homicide, the duties so far recognized[181] have been examined in the context of the duty to preserve life. This context is important because, when a fatality occurs there is an enhanced danger that the courts will find a duty in previously unrecognized circumstances where the enquiry involves an entirely *ex post facto* rationalization of the relationships involved.

Parents and other relations

Parents owe a duty to their children to act to save them from harm. Presumably children above the age of responsibility owe a corresponding duty to their parents.[182] Other close relationships, whether of a family,[183] domestic, business or other nature, possibly impose similar

---

[176] Fourteenth Report, *Offences Against the Person* (1980) Cmnd 7844, paras 252–255.

[177] *Violence: Reforming the Law of Offences Against the Person* (1998).

[178] LC 143, *Criminal Law: Codification of the Criminal Law – A Report to the Law Commission* (HC270) 212, 20(v).

[179] Below, p 1013.

[180] See, generally, L Alexander, 'Criminal Liability for Omissions: An Inventory of Issues', in A Shute and S Simester (eds), *Criminal Law Theory* (2002).

[181] Other than in cases of 'Supervening fault', below, p 72.

[182] eg, if a muscular 14-year-old leaves his fainting mother to drown in the notorious shallow pool. In *Evans* [2009] EWCA Crim 650 a teenager did not owe a duty on the basis of family relationships to her half-sister to whom she had supplied drugs.

[183] eg, marriage – in *Hood* [2004] 1 Cr App R (S) 431: D was convicted of gross negligence manslaughter for failing to call medical assistance for his wife for three weeks after she fell and broke bones. See also the discussion of the imposition of liability in such cases in J Horder and L McGowan, 'Manslaughter by Causing Another's Suicide' [2006] Crim LR 1035.

duties. The criminal law is increasingly willing to protect wide categories of individuals on the basis of their existence within an extended family,[184] but it is unclear whether it would be as willing to extend liability so broadly. The courts have managed to avoid identifying with precision those relationships which can be sufficient to ground liability. Indeed, they have failed to identify what is significant about those relationships in which a duty has been imposed. As a matter of principle, it can be argued that the important issue is not one of blood or formal legal relationship, but of interdependence.[185]

A further unresolved issue is what the relationship duty obliges D to do if it does arise. This would seem to be resolved on a case by case basis. One important issue will be whether the offence can be committed where D performed an act which he believed to be sufficient to fulfil his duty, or if he had a reasonable belief that what he was doing was sufficient. These issues will become intertwined with the *mens rea* of the offence.

It is equally unclear, when, if ever, the relationship duty ends. In the case of a parent and child, for example, a parent of a normal child may well be absolved on the attainment of the child turning 18, but this could hardly be so in the case of a disabled dependent child.

Voluntary undertakings

The need to define precisely the categories of relationship which trigger a duty has often been avoided by the courts because the particular case calling for adjudication has often involved a number of overlapping bases of liability including, significantly, the fact that D has voluntarily undertaken a position of responsibility towards V. For example, a person who has undertaken to care for a helpless and infirm relative[186] who has become dependent on him may be held to owe a duty, particularly where he is to receive some reward for caring for the other.[187] The holder of a public office requiring him to care for others may also incur criminal liability by failing to do so.

This category of duty would surely extend to unrelated persons who voluntarily undertake responsibility. It is arguable, therefore, that D who sees a stranger, V, drowning, but who voluntarily begins to go to V's assistance could be liable should he then abandon the rescue. Underlying bases for imposing a duty in such circumstances include the argument that in such cases D may be the best placed to act and that V may have relied to his detriment on D's actions – in the case of the drowning swimmer, V may be worse off by relying on D since he may, for example, have stopped calling for assistance from other potential rescuers.[188]

The extent to which the 'voluntary assumption of responsibility' is a free-standing basis for the imposition of a duty, and the scope of circumstances in which it might apply, remain unresolved. One of the most controversial cases may well turn on the existence of this duty. In *Stone and Dobinson*, although the defendants' liability for manslaughter arose in part from their family relationship, and their cohabitation with the victim, their voluntary undertaking of responsibility for the victim seems to have been significant in the court's conclusion that a duty was owed, although it seems that the voluntary undertaking was implied. As in other categories of duty, the courts have failed to define the content of the duty. The conviction of the defendants in *Stone and Dobinson*, both of whom had limited mental capacity, suggests that the courts might adopt a strict line when faced with claims that the accused had done what he believed to be sufficient to fulfil his duty. In terms of the termination of such a duty,

---

[184] See, eg, the extensive definition of family in the Sexual Offences Act 2003, s 27.

[185] Fletcher, *Rethinking Criminal Law*, 613.

[186] *Marriott* (1838) 8 C & P 425; *Nicholls* (1874) 13 Cox CC 75 (D was V's grandmother).

[187] *Instan* [1893] 1 QB 450 (D was V's niece, living in V's house, consuming food provided at V's expense but not supplying any to V); *Stone and Dobinson* [1977] QB 354.

[188] See for analysis of the problems, G Mead, 'Contracting into Crime: A Theory of Criminal Omissions' (1991) 11 OJLS 147.

one who has undertaken the duty can probably divest himself of it only by passing it on to some responsible authority or other person.

It is submitted that people who jointly engage in a hazardous activity whether lawful – like mountaineering – or unlawful – like drug abuse[189] – may also owe duties to one another. The courts have exhibited reluctance to impose obligations on this basis alone. In *Sinclair Johnson and Smith*,[190] manslaughter convictions were upheld against those who failed to seek medical care for a comatose fellow drug-taker, but the duty was based on the previous friendship and bond between the individuals, rather than the joint act of drug administration. In *Ruffell*,[191] a manslaughter conviction was upheld where D had been jointly involved in drug taking with the deceased. D, who had placed V outside in temperatures of six degrees, had also been a friend and host to V, and it is unclear on precisely which basis his duty arose. The matter is discussed further below in relation to the recent case of *Evans*.

Contractual duties

A contract may found a duty under criminal law to persons, including those not party to the contract but likely to be injured by failure to perform it. The most obvious examples in this category are those who are employed as carers or healthcare professionals. In *Pittwood*,[192] a railway crossing gate-keeper opened the gate to let a cart pass and went off to his lunch, forgetting to shut it again. Ten minutes later a haycart was struck by a train while crossing the line and V was killed. D was convicted of manslaughter. It was argued on his behalf that he owed a duty of care only to his employers, the railway company, with whom he contracted. Wright J held, however, that:

there was gross and criminal negligence, as the man was paid to keep the gate shut and protect the public… A man might incur criminal liability from a duty arising out of contract.[193]

Again, the courts have not addressed the issue of whether the duty owed under a contract exists strictly within the bounds of the terms of that contract. If D is a lifeguard whose terms of employment stipulate that he finishes at 5 pm daily, is he under a duty to save V who is drowning at 5.05 pm? It seems clear at least that the duty will terminate when the relationship ends, as when an employee leaves the service of his employer.

Creating a dangerous situation/supervening fault

Where D *does an act* which puts in peril V's person, his property, his liberty or any other interest protected by the criminal law, and D is aware that he has created the peril, he has a duty to take reasonable steps to prevent the harm in question resulting. The act may be done without any kind of fault but, if D fails to intervene, it is undoubtedly his act which is the cause of the harm. For this reason the principle may apply to a wider range of offences than can be committed by simple omission. This category of liability might therefore be treated as entirely separate from the four bases for imposing liability previously discussed.

---

[189] The point was not decided in *Dalby* [1982] 1 All ER 916. cf *People v Beardsley* (1967) 113 NW 1128.

[190] See, eg, *Sinclair Johnson and Smith* (1998) 21 Aug, CA.

[191] [2003] EWCA Crim 122.

[192] (1902) 19 TLR 37.

[193] Wright J said that this was not a mere case of nonfeasance, but of misfeasance. However, D's breach of duty was not in opening the gate, but in omitting to close it again. cf, however, *Smith* (1869) 11 Cox CC 210, where Lush J ruled that there was no duty because D's employer had no duty to provide a watchman. (If D makes a practice of seeing old ladies across the road, he is not responsible if one day he fails to be present and an old lady is killed.) H Beynon, 'Doctors as Murderers' [1982] Crim LR 17 at 22 suggests that opening and not shutting might be regarded as one 'act'; but would it really have been different if the gate had been opened by D's colleague who had just gone off duty? One hopes not.

The principle derives from *Miller*,[194] where D, a squatter in V's house, went to sleep holding a lighted cigarette. He awoke to find the mattress smouldering. He did nothing to put it out but moved into an adjoining room and went to sleep there. The house caught fire. D was convicted of arson contrary to s 1(1) and (3) of the Criminal Damage Act 1971. The House of Lords held that the judge had rightly directed the jury that, when D woke up, he was under a duty to take some action to put the fire out. Lord Diplock said:[195]

I see no rational ground for excluding from conduct capable of giving rise to criminal liability conduct which consists of failing to take measures that lie within one's power to counteract a danger that one has oneself created, if at the time of such conduct one's state of mind is such as constitutes a necessary ingredient of the offence.

The Court of Appeal had upheld the conviction on a different basis:

We would only say that an unintentional act followed by an intentional omission to rectify it or its consequences, or a reckless omission to do so when recklessness is a sufficient *mens rea* for the particular case, should only be regarded *in toto* as an intentional or reckless act when reality and common sense so require; this may well be a matter to be left to the jury. Further, in the relevant analysis we think that whether or not there is on the facts an element of adoption on the part of the alleged offender of what he has done earlier by what he deliberately or recklessly fails to do later is an important consideration.

The application of this 'continuous act' theory would apparently have produced a different result in *Ahmad*.[196] If the appellant could be deemed to have acted intentionally (that is, with intent to cause the residential occupier to give up occupation) when he rendered the flat uninhabitable, the difficulty of convicting him would have disappeared. This theory, again, involves an undesirable legal fiction. Fictions should have no place in the criminal law. Lord Diplock preferred the 'duty to avert danger' to the 'continuous act' theory but only on the ground that the former is easier to explain to a jury. It is submitted, however, that they are different in substance, as the example based on *Ahmad* shows.[197] Under *Miller*, D must have the *mens rea* required for the crime with which he is charged at the time of the omission to avert the danger he has created.

Again, one issue to be resolved is the extent of any such duty. Although expressed in terms of 'reasonable' steps, it is unclear how objective this test is to be in application, and in particular whether it is sufficient that D believes on the facts as he sees them that the remedial measures he took were sufficient. Moreover, it is unclear how the law would deal with an individual who claimed impossibility of performance of such a duty.[198]

The scope of the *Miller* doctrine remains unclear. The Court of Appeal has recently been prepared to adopt an extended interpretation of the *Miller* principle in the case of *Evans*. In that case D gave her sister, V, heroin to take, knowing that she was a recovering addict. V slipped into a coma. D became aware of that and chose not to call the emergency services but to sit with V. V died. The Court of Appeal upheld her conviction for gross negligence manslaughter. The court faced two difficulties in doing so – (1) identifying a duty (2) establishing that D's act caused V's death. For present purposes we are interested in the duty question. The court did not deal with the case on the basis of a sibling duty (they were both able teenagers)

---

[194] [1983] 2 AC 161. See [1982] Crim LR 527 and 773–774. The principle is replicated in the Home Office Draft Bill, cl 16 in *Violence: Reforming the Law of Offences Against the Person* (1998).

[195] [1983] 2 AC 176. See recently on Scots law application of the principle, J Chalmers, 'Fireraising by Omission', 2004 SLT 59.

[196] Above, p 68.

[197] See commentary [1982] Crim LR 527 and 773–774 and (1984) 4 LS 88 at 91.

[198] See Smart (1987) 103 LQR 532.

nor on the basis solely that D had supplied the drugs, nor on the basis that they were engaged in a dangerous activity together. The court focused on whether D owed a duty when her sister lapsed into a coma. In applying *Miller,* albeit in extended form, the court held that there was a duty.

The extension of *Miller* was significant. Although Miller was charged with criminal damage which at that time was satisfied by proof of objective recklessness, the House of Lords held that his duty only arose on his subjective realization of the danger. Gross negligence manslaughter is also a crime based on objective fault, but in *Evans* the court held that the duty arises when D realizes or *ought* to have realized the danger.[199] The Court did not provide further detailed examination of whether the duty arises from the creation or the realization of the danger.[200] It is certainly the case that the full scope of the *Miller* doctrine has not been satisfactorily explained. Nevertheless, it is submitted that the courts will be likely to continue applying a *Miller*-type analysis in these cases on various possible bases.

In these exceptional cases where D supplies drugs and remains present but fails to make reasonable efforts to seek medical attention when V experiences serious illness, Lord Diplock's statements in *Miller* are likely to be construed broadly to establish that a duty arises when D became aware (or ought to have become aware) of the events resulting from his act. A duty might also arise from V's death caused or contributed to by D's failure to act where a sufficient duty is imposed when D realized/ought to have realized V's post-injection predicament because (i) D is in a pre-existing relationship (parent, carer, etc) which persists irrespective of V's self-administration (eg the husband of a woman who has self-injected and who realizes or ought to have realized that she is having breathing difficulty); or (ii) because D and V were engaged in a dangerous joint enterprise; or (iii) where D has voluntarily assumed a duty to care for V who is in such a state. An example might be where V becomes dependent on D's assistance (eg where D starts to care for V, who has overdosed at a party, by moving him from one room to a more secluded space, but then abandons him, leaving V worse off as he is less likely to be seen and rescued by others).

One aspect of the scope of *Miller* is at least clear: it is necessary to invoke the *Miller* principle only in the case of a result crime requiring fault where the act causing the result is done without the relevant fault at that time. Where the offence requires no fault, there is no need to rely on it. In *Wings Ltd v Ellis*,[201] D Ltd, a tour operator, published a brochure which, unknown to D, contained misrepresentations. On discovering the truth, D did all they could to correct the errors but, subsequently, V read an uncorrected brochure and booked a holiday in reliance on it. D was convicted under the Trade Descriptions Act 1968, s 14(1)(a), of making a statement which they knew to be false and, s 14(1)(b), recklessly making a false statement. The statement was 'made' when it was read by V and, by then, D knew it was false. The Divisional Court, applying *Miller,* quashed both convictions. D had done all that could reasonably be expected to correct the false trade descriptions. The prosecutor appealed in respect of the offence under s 14(1)(a) only. The appeal was allowed. Subject to a statutory defence which was not pleaded, the House held that s 14(1)(a) created an 'absolute' offence.[202] D knew the statement was false and no other fault was required. There was no room for the application of *Miller.* Though any reader of s 14 would suppose that s 14(1)(a) is the more serious offence, s 14(1)(b) requires some element of fault, however 'reckless' is

---

[199] per Judge LCJ at [31].

[200] See also the detailed analysis by Glenys Williams, 'Gross negligence manslaughter and duty of care in "drugs" cases: *R v Evans*' [2009] Crim LR 631.

[201] [1984] 1 WLR 731; revsd [1985] AC 272, HL.

[202] See below, p 180.

interpreted, and Lord Hailsham thought that *Miller* might have been properly held applicable to that.[203]

Where the offence is one requiring fault, whether *mens rea* strictly so-called or negligence, it is submitted that the *Miller* principle is of general application.[204] If D, sitting alone in the passenger seat of a car, were accidentally to knock off the handbrake, so that the car rolled away, it is submitted that he could be convicted of murder if he wilfully omitted to put the brake on again, intending the car to run over and kill or cause grievous bodily harm to V. Similarly, D who locks the door of a room not knowing that V is inside and having learned that V is within, omits to unlock the door should be liable for false imprisonment.[205] Since the principle requires the appropriate element of fault at the time of the subsequent omission, it is submitted that liability should arise in such a case.[206]

Further clarification from the courts would be welcome on how it is to be determined when the duty under *Miller* comes to an end. In the case of *Lewin v CPS*,[207] a decision not to prosecute was upheld where D left his heavily intoxicated friend, V, asleep in a car in the summer heat in Spain where he died. The Divisional Court observed that D's responsibility for the welfare of his passenger 'persisted for so long as the vehicle was in motion, but... would normally have come to an end as soon as the vehicle was properly parked in a safe place at the end of its journey... [it] could only persist in a way which would be relevant to the offence of manslaughter if a reasonable person would have foreseen [the risk of death]'. The court went on 'the young man who was left in the unlocked car was an adult, not a small child or dog'.[208] Had not D created a dangerous situation by leaving V, heavily intoxicated, in the car? Was he not at fault for not summoning help when he realized the temperature had risen so high? Is the case distinguishable from *Evans*?

4.4.2.3 Causation and omissions[209]

Once it has been determined that there is an offence that can be committed by omission and a defendant who can be held liable owing to the existence of a relevant duty, there remains the question of whether his failure to act has caused the prohibited harm.

Considering again the example of the child, B, left to drown by his parent, A, Stephen saw no difficulty in saying that the death (or bodily injury) was caused by A's omission. Others have taken a different view.[210] Thus, it has been argued that B's death would have occurred in precisely the same way if his parent, A, had not come on the scene for any reason, so how can A be said to have caused it? He simply allowed it to happen. The cause of B's death could be said

---

[203] Lord Scarman thought the analogy with *Miller* 'ingenious, if far-fetched' and (it is submitted unfairly) an 'unhelpful and over-elaborate approach to the interpretation of an Act intended to protect the public...' [1984] 3 All ER 590–591.

[204] As, eg in *Green v Cross* (1910) 103 LT 279 – D innocently caught a dog in a trap. Instead of releasing it he left it until it was freed two hours later by the police. Held, Channell J dissenting, that there was evidence on which he could be convicted of 'cruelly ill-treating' the dog.

[205] Andenaes, GPCL of Norway, 135; and see *Fagan v Metropolitan Police Comr* [1969] 1 QB 439; above, p 69. See also the unusual case of *Bowell* [2003] EWCA Crim 3896 in which D falsely imprisoned V in his car, V jumped from the car and escaped, but D put V back in the car and falsely imprisoned her again before taking her to hospital several hours later: she was rendered paraplegic by these actions. The court suggested that D 'could have left her in the road without committing an offence' when she had jumped out.

[206] What of the case in which D hosts a party and X drinks alcohol to excess? If D allows X to drive home and X kills V, should D be liable? See the discussion of prosecutions under French law (2004) The Times, 26 Oct (news item).

[207] [2002] EWHC 1049 (Admin).

[208] Para 24.

[209] See Wilson, *Central Issues*, 186–192; H Beynon, 'Causation, Omissions and Complicity' [1987] Crim LR 539; Tadros, *Criminal Responsibility*, 171.

[210] See B Hogan, 'Omissions and the Duty Myth', in *Criminal Law Essays*.

to be simply his falling into the water. Nothing else had to happen. He just drowned. If A and strangers, C, D and E had walked by the pool together ignoring B's plight it is impossible to say that, as a matter of fact, A has caused the death but C, D and E have not.

There is a danger of oversimplifying things and seeking to resolve the entire issue of liability on the basis of causation without regard to the prior question of duty.[211] In the case of A, C, D and E, it is possible to describe their failure as *a* factual cause of B's death, and if A is under a duty towards B, it is therefore possible to say that A's failure to act may be *a* legal cause of B's death.[212] As the Draft Code puts it:

a person causes a result which is an element of an offence when…(b) he omits to do an act which might prevent its occurrence and which he is under a duty to do according to the law relating to the offence. (Cl 17(b))

It may be that this provision goes beyond the present law (and beyond what is desirable) in one respect: it extends liability to results which the act D omitted to do *might have* prevented. Arguably, it should be limited to results which that act *would have* prevented.[213] In the drowning child example, if A is B's parent and fails to act, under the present law it is submitted that the prosecution would have to establish that the failure on A's part *would* have, not might have, prevented B's death.

4.4.2.4 Act or omission?

It is not always easy to distinguish between an act and an omission. Some of the most difficult examples of the distinction arise in the context of a cessation of medical treatment. If a doctor is keeping a patient alive by cranking the handle of a machine and he stops, this looks like a clear case of omission. So too, if the machine is electrically operated but switches itself off every 24 hours and the doctor deliberately does not restart it. Switching off a functioning machine looks like an act; but is it any different in substance from the first two cases?[214] On the other hand, is it any different from cutting the high-wire on which a tight-rope walker is balancing?[215] – which is an act, if ever there was one. Is the ending of a programme of dialysis an omission, while switching off a ventilator is an act? Is the discontinuance of a drip feed, which is keeping a patient alive, by withdrawing the tube from his body an act[216] and failure to replace an emptied bag an omission? In theory, it might be possible to distinguish between these cases, but it seems offensive if liability for homicide is so heavily dependent on such very fine distinctions of this kind; but it appears to be so.[217]

A doctor is, no doubt, under a duty to make reasonable efforts, in the light of customary medical practice and all other relevant factors, to keep a patient alive.[218] Unfortunately, this does not solve the problem because the content of any duty there may be to 'keep alive' is different from that of the duty 'not to kill'. The issue has become further complicated with recognition that public authorities must respect not only the right to life under Art 2 of the

---

[211] See A Leavens, 'A Causation Approach to Criminal Omissions' (1988) 76 Cal LR 547.

[212] As considered below, p 84, it is sufficient that D's conduct is a substantial and operative cause of V's death for homicide; there is no need to prove that D's conduct is the sole cause of death.

[213] Williams, (1987) 7 LS 92 at 106–107, citing *Morby* (1882) 15 Cox CC 35.

[214] Examples put by I Kennedy, 'Switching off Life Support Machines: The Legal Implications' [1977] Crim LR 443.

[215] See Kennedy, ibid, at 452. See the discussion by Beynon [1982] Crim LR 17.

[216] Beynon, ibid.

[217] See also S Ost, *An Analytical Study of the Legal, Moral and Ethical Aspects of the Living Phenomenon of Euthanasia* (2003), discussing public perceptions of whether these types of act are equivalent.

[218] Williams, TBCL (1st edn, 1978) 236. See the discussion in *R (Burke) v GMC* [2004] EWHC 1879 (Admin), over-ruled and regarded as going too far in the discussion of some of these issues: *R (Burke) v GMC* [2006] QB 273, CA.

ECHR, but also the right to be free, in the course of treatment, from inhuman and degrading treatment under Art 3. The doctor must also respect the Art 8 privacy rights of the patient which might involve a declared wish to die, or for treatment to be withheld in specific circumstances. The Mental Capacity Act 2005 (ss 24–26) provides statutory recognition of the ability of a competent person to give a binding refusal of treatment (eg, 'do not resuscitate'). The individual can provide a binding advance refusal where he is presently competent but anticipates that he may lose that competence as his condition deteriorates.

The difficulties are brought into sharp focus where parents refuse their consent to operations on young children suffering from disabilities knowing that without the operation the baby will die. It has been held that such parents are not necessarily guilty of a criminal homicide if death ensues.[219] In *Re B (A Minor)*,[220] on these facts, the child was made a ward of court, and the court gave consent as being in the interests of the child. Dunn LJ said that the decision of the parents to allow the child to die was one which everyone accepted as 'entirely responsible'. It was a decision, it seems, that the parents could lawfully take, so that the death of the child, if it had followed, would not have been an *actus reus*. Templeman LJ thought there might possibly be cases 'where the future is so certain and where the life of the child is bound to be full of pain and suffering that the court might be driven to a different conclusion' – that is, to allow the child to die.[221] Yet there is no doubt that if the parents – or anyone – did any positive act to kill the child, they would be guilty of murder, subject to a relevant defence of necessity.[222] The undoubted duty of parents to preserve the life of their child is different from, and more restricted than, their duty not to kill it.

In *Arthur*,[223] a doctor, having noted that the parents of a Down's Syndrome child did not wish the child to survive, ordered 'nursing care only' and the administration of a drug, allegedly to stop the child seeking sustenance. At the trial of the doctor for attempted murder of the child, Farquharson J directed the jury that it was for them to decide whether 'there was an act properly so-called on the part of Dr Arthur, as distinct from simply allowing the child to die'. Simply allowing the child to die would apparently have been lawful,[224] and withholding food was, according to the medical evidence put by the judge to the jury, 'a negative act' – a mere omission. It is submitted that a better view is that an omission to provide such a child with food and the ordinary necessities of life ought to be equated with an act causing death rather than with an omission to perform an operation or to take some other extraordinary action. The position seems to be the same with a helpless, elderly person, incapable of taking decisions. It may be lawful for his family and the doctor to decide that an operation which would prolong a useless and painful life should not be performed; but it surely cannot be lawful to starve him to death, whether with the assistance of drugs or not?

Terminating life

The distinction between act and omission was the basis of the important decision in *Airedale National Health Service Trust v Bland*.[225] B, a victim of the Hillsborough stadium disaster,

---

[219] If it were an offence, it would (in the absence of diminished responsibility) be murder, because the parents intend the death of the child.

[220] [1981] 1 WLR 1421.

[221] cf the views in *R (Burke) v GMC* [2004] EWHC 1879 (Admin).

[222] See the discussion of *Re A* [2001] Fam 147, below, and *Inghs* [2010] EWCA Crim 2637.

[223] (1981) 12 BMLR 1, discussed by M Gunn and JC Smith, 'Arthur's Case and the Right to Life of a Down's Syndrome Child' [1985] Crim LR 705 and I Kennedy, *Treat Me Right* (1988) Ch 8.

[224] It is submitted that nothing turned on the fact that the charge had been reduced from murder to attempted murder – see [1986] Crim LR 760–762 and D Poole, 'Arthur's Case: A Comment' [1986] Crim LR 383; D Brahams, 'Putting Arthur's Case in Perspective' [1986] Crim LR 387.

[225] [1993] 1 All ER 821, [1993] Crim LR 877, HL. See J Keown, 'Restoring Moral and Intellectual Shape to the Law After *Bland*' (1997) 113 LQR 481. For a recent analysis of the *Bland* case and its implications for euthanasia

had been in a persistent vegetative state for three and a half years and medical opinion was that there was no hope of improvement or recovery. The Trust, with the support of B's parents, applied for a declaration that they might lawfully discontinue ventilation, nutrition and hydration by artificial means and end medical treatment except to allow B to die peacefully. The application was resisted by the Official Solicitor, who argued that the withdrawal of artificial feeding would constitute murder. The judge made the declaration and the House of Lords, affirming the Court of Appeal, upheld it. There was no doubt about the intention to kill. The object of the exercise was to terminate B's life. It was accepted that to kill by administering a lethal injection or any similar act would be murder; but what was proposed was held to be not an act, but an omission. Lord Goff said:

The question is not whether the doctor should take a course which will kill his patient, or even take a course which has the effect of accelerating his death. The question is whether the doctor should or should not continue to provide his patient with medical care which, if continued, will prolong his patient's life.

Lord Goff added that it might be difficult to say that it was in the patient's best interests that the treatment should be ended but that it could sensibly be said that it was not in his best interests that it should be continued. 'Ending' and 'not continuing' look uncommonly like the same thing; but the former expresses the conduct as an act, which could not be justified, and the latter as an omission, which could. In *Re A (Conjoined Twins: Surgical Separation)*, the Court of Appeal held, rightly, it is submitted, that surgery to separate twins was an act.[226] In *R (Burke) v GMC*,[227] Lord Phillips stated that *Bland* should not be read as requiring a persistent vegetative state (PSV) patient to be kept alive simply because he has made an advance directive to that effect. Section 26 of the Mental Capacity Act requires compliance with a valid advance directive to refuse treatment, but the crucial issue is what is in the best interests of a patient.[228]

ECHR concerns

In *Glass v United Kingdom*,[229] the ECtHR gave detailed consideration to the position under English law, acknowledging, at para 75: 'the regulatory framework . . . is firmly predicated on the duty to preserve the life of a patient, save in exceptional circumstances. Secondly, that same framework prioritises the requirement of parental consent [in the case of a child] and,

---

see D Price, 'What Shape to Euthanasia after *Bland*? Historical, Contemporary and Futuristic Paradigms' (2009) 125 LQR 142. The Scottish courts have reached the same result by a different route: *Law Hospital NHS Trust v Lord Advocate* [1996] 2 FLR 407. *Bland's* case was distinguished in *Re A (Children; Conjoined Twins: Surgical Separation)*, below, p 371. Note that the termination by non-feeding of a patient in a persistently vegetative state should normally only occur with the sanction of the High Court: *Practice Direction* [1994] 2 All ER 413. The approach has been held to be compatible with the obligations of the State to secure the right to life under Art 2 of the ECHR: *NHS Trusts, A v M* [2001] 1 All ER 801; *A Hospital v W* [2007] EWHC 425 (Fam). For a valuable review of the academic arguments in medical law, see A McGee, 'Finding a Way Through the Ethical and Legal Maze: Withdrawal of Medical Treatment and Euthanasia' (2005) 13 Med LR 357.

[226] For criticism of the approach in *Bland* and the consequences for the conjoined twin case see also J McEwan, 'Murder by Design: The Feel-Good Factor and the Criminal Law' (2001) 9 Med LR 246. See also M Wilks, 'Medical Treatment at the End of Life' in C Erin and S Ost, *Criminal Justice System and Health Care* (2007).

[227] [2006] QB 273. See, for discussion, C Dupre, 'Human Dignity and the Withdrawal of Medical Treatment: A Missed Opportunity' [2006] EHRLR 678, lamenting the CA's refusal to engage with the human dignity and ECHR arguments.

[228] [57].

[229] [2004] 1 FLR 1019 concerned the treatment of a child whom doctors thought was dying and to whom they administered diamorphine by way of palliative care despite the objections of the mother.

save in emergency situations, requires doctors to seek the intervention of the courts in the event of parental objection.'

In *R (Burke) v GMC*,[230] the High Court recognized that a withdrawal of artificial feeding and hydration which a competent patient wishes to continue or which an incompetent person has previously, when competent, directed to continue would infringe Art 8 of the ECHR.[231] It was also held that withdrawal of treatment would breach Art 3 if it exposed the patient to acute mental and physical suffering, irrespective of the awareness of the patient to that suffering. The court in *Burke* also suggested that it would be difficult to envisage circumstances in which the withdrawal of artificial feeding from a sentient patient would be compatible with the Convention. The Court of Appeal subsequently reversed the High Court's decision, upholding the legitimacy of the GMC Guidelines on the withdrawal of nutrition and hydration. The Lord Chief Justice emphasized the duty on doctors to take reasonable steps to keep the patient alive. The Court of Appeal concluded that the guarantees in Arts 2, 3 and 8 did not alter the common law position. The court endorsed the comments of Mumby J in the High Court,[232] that Art 2 does not entitle anyone to continue with life-prolonging treatment where to do so would expose the patient to 'inhuman or degrading treatment' breaching Art 3, but that at the same time, withdrawal of life-prolonging treatment within the common law parameters will not breach Art 2. Lord Phillips stated that this conclusion:

does not, however, lead to the further conclusion that if a National Health doctor were deliberately to bring about the death of a competent patient by withdrawing life-prolonging treatment contrary to that patient's wishes, Article 2 would not be infringed. It seems to us that such conduct would plainly violate Article 2. Furthermore, if English law permitted such conduct, this would also violate this country's positive obligation to enforce Article 2. As we have already indicated, we do not consider that English criminal law would countenance such conduct. However, the fact that Articles 2, 3 and 8 of the Convention may be engaged does not, in our judgment, advance the argument or alter the common law. [39]

In *NHS Trust A v M, NHS Trust B v H*,[233] it was held that the withdrawal of nutrition and hydration by artificial means from a patient in a persistent vegetative state would not infringe Art 2.

It will be appreciated from the discussion of these difficult medical cases that the courts struggle to distinguish between acts and omissions. The difficulty all too often leads to distinctions without any apparent difference, or in some cases to a sidestepping of the issue by a convenient treatment of the *actus reus* as the defendant's conduct viewed *in toto*.

4.4.2.5 'Easy rescue' statutes

As noted, there are hotly contested philosophical arguments about the desirability of creating liability for omissions in general, and much of the academic discussion has centred on the liability for failing to rescue.[234] Many jurisdictions have dealt with the 'shallow pool'

---

[230] [2004] EWHC 1879 (Admin). See also *Re OT* [2009] EWHC 633 (Fam): withdrawal of life-sustaining treatment which was no longer in the patient's best interests was not a breach of Art 2 or 8.

[231] On the GMC Guidelines, see J Keown, 'Beyond *Bland*: A Critique of the BMA Guidance on Withholding and Withdrawing Medical Treatment' (2000) 20 LS 66; cf D Price, 'Fairly Bland: An Alternative View of a Supposed New "Death Ethic" and the BMA Guidelines' (2001) 21 LS 618. See also the discussion of the Schiavo case in the USA – R A Destro, 'Lessons in Legal and Judicial Ethics from Schiavo' in C Erin and S Ost, *The Criminal Justice System and Health Care* (2007).

[232] [2005] QB 424, para 162.

[233] [2001] Fam 348.

[234] See, especially, J Feinberg, *Harm to Others* (1984) Ch 4. Compare H Gross, *A Theory of Criminal Justice* (1979) 61–65; M Menlowe, 'The Philosophical Foundations of a Duty to Rescue' and A McCall Smith, 'The Duty to Rescue and the Common Law', in M Menlowe and A McCall Smith (eds), *The Duty to Rescue: The Jurisprudence*

case by creating a specific offence for anyone failing to take steps which he could take without any personal risk, to save another from death or injury. It is important to note that these statutes do not equate omissions with acts. The offender is liable for the specific statutory offence of failing to rescue (with its own penalty) and not the harmful result which D may have prevented and has allowed to happen. Thus, he is not necessarily guilty of homicide if the victim dies.[235]

Some commentators have called for the enactment of an 'easy rescue' or 'Bad Samaritan' offence such as that adopted by our European neighbours,[236] certain American states,[237] and elsewhere. A clear example of the type of offence is provided in the Northern Territory in Australia Criminal Code Act, s 155. This makes it an offence for any person who, being able to provide rescue, resuscitation, medical treatment, first aid or succour of any kind to a person urgently in need of it and whose life may be endangered if it is not provided, to 'callously'[238] fail to do so. Powerful arguments have been made that such an offence would promote social cooperation, which is itself worthy of promotion by criminal regulation and that such laws are ultimately necessary for individual autonomy to be realized.[239]

The objections to Bad Samaritan laws are well rehearsed.[240] They have been criticized as being so vague that they are either unenforceable and/or contravene the principle of legality. Some of the examples from around the world, including those such as the Northern Territories offence, cast doubt on that. They are alleged to impose too great a burden on investigators and leave too much to prosecutorial discretion since there may be hundreds of potential defendants who failed to rescue (as opposed to the usual scenario with one criminal who acted). In addition, it is questionable how well they operate in practice since there seem to be very few prosecutions, at least in common law jurisdictions, which is not to say that they do not operate at a symbolic level in encouraging greater communitarianism.[241] More fundamentally they are claimed to represent a more significant infringement on autonomy (being told you must do X), impose ambiguous burdens (what to do if someone else has started to rescue) of uncertain duration (when does the duty end).

---

of Aid (1993). I am grateful to Tracey Elliott for discussion on this area in preparation for the article: 'Acts and Omissions: A Distinction Without a Defence' (2009) 39 Cambrian Law Review 40.

[235] Andanaes, GPCL, 132.

[236] eg France: C. Pén. Art 223–6 (which replaces Art 63 of the previous criminal code). See: A Ashworth and E Steiner, 'Criminal Omissions and Public Duties: The French Experience' (1990) 10 LS 152. For more recent analysis see M Vranken, 'Duty to Rescue in Civil Law and Common Law: Les Extrêmes se Touchent?' (1998) 47 ICLQ 934, at 937–938, and A Cadoppi, 'Failure to Rescue and the Continental Criminal Law' in MA Menlowe and A McCall Smith (eds.), *The Duty to Rescue: The Jurisprudence of Aid* (1993), p 93, which discusses the imposition of legal duties to rescue in European countries.

[237] 'Rescue' legislation has also been adopted in Rhode Island (Gen Laws R.I ss.11-37-3.1, 11-37-3.3, and 11-56-1), Massachusetts (Gen. Laws Ann. Ch.268, s.40), Minnesota (Stat. Ann. ss.604.01(a), 609.02), Hawaii (Haw. Rev. Stat. Ann. s.663-1.6) and Wisconsin (Wis. Stat. Ann. s.940.34 [1],[2]).

[238] 'Callous' here means with more than normal intent, which requires that 'it be proved that a person deliberately and consciously chose not to provide help or assistance': *Salmon v Chute* (1994) 115 FLR 176, Kearney J, at 199. For a brief discussion of this case see: JT Pardun, 'Good Samaritan Laws: A Global Perspective' (1998) 20 Loyola LA Int'l & Comp LJ 591, at 595–596. Murphy suggests that there is a greater need for imposing upon individuals a positive requirement to assist in the Northern Territory because its terrain and climate are particularly harsh and it is sparsely populated: L Murphy, 'Beneficence, Law and Liberty: The Case of Required Rescue' (2001) 89 Georgetown LJ 605, at 659, fn 234.

[239] A Ashworth, above n 141, at 432. cf A Norrie, *Crime, Reason and History* (2nd edn, 2001) 130–131. See also EJ Weinrib, 'The Case for a Duty to Rescue' (1980) 90 Yale LJ 247 and compare J Dressler, 'Some Brief Thoughts (Mostly Negative) about Bad Samaritan Laws' (2000) 40 Santa Clara LR 971.

[240] See JT Pardun, 'Good Samaritan Laws a Global Perspective' (1997–98) 20 Loy LA International and Comparative LJ 591.

[241] See Pardun above n 240, p 597.

Despite this, the Bad Samaritan laws are numerous[242] and have an ancient pedigree.[243] It is possible to draft legislation narrowly enough to meet or outweigh the objections. In particular, it is possible to include elements of *mens rea* such as that in the Northern Territories offence which requires callousness.[244]

4.4.2.6. Act omission or control?

The numerous complications which flow from the law's attempts to distinguish between acts and involuntary movement, states of affairs and omissions has prompted some academics[245] to argue that the problems can be avoided if the focus shifts to whether D had 'control' of the potential consequences of his behaviour at the relevant time[246] Duff suggests:

A control requirement does not distinguish action from omission: whether X is an outcome of my action or an event that I could do but do not prevent, I have the same degree of control over whether X ensues, and thus can be criminally responsible on just the same basis in both cases.[247]

Adopting a focus on whether the defendant had control will, Duff claims, make 'criminal responsibility for omissions unproblematic'.[248] There are many theoretical benefits to be gained from a control approach, but that the criminal law's practical response to omissions would nevertheless remain problematical in several ways.[249]

4.5 Causation[250]

In every result crime causation is, by definition, an issue. Although the issue often arises in the context of homicide, causation is important in all result crimes.[251] In many cases it is not a contentious issue because it is not disputed. When it is disputed, the prosecution must prove that D, by his own act or unlawful omission, caused the relevant result.[252] Theoretical disputes abound as to whether the element of causation can be properly seen as being exclusively an element of *actus reus* or whether it ought also to be seen as including consideration of D's fault. Tadros argues that the causal enquiry is sensitive to both moral factors and to the states of mind of the defendant.[253] There is no doubt that the cases are heavily policy laden, and it is clear that the courts are keen to avoid an unduly theoretical approach to the issue.

[242] See the appendix in Pardun's article above n 240.

[243] See Pardun above n 240, p 593 and references therein to similar laws in Ancient Egypt.

[244] See, eg, Duff, *Answering for Crime*. cf D Husak, *Philosophy of the Criminal Law* (2010) 38.

[245] *Answering for Crime*, 105.

[246] ibid, 107.

[247] ibid, 107.

[248] ibid, 107.

[249] See Elliott and Ormerod, above, n 234.

[250] See, generally, H Hart and T Honoré, *Causation in the Law* (2nd edn, 1985); A Norrie, *Crime Reason and History* (2nd edn, 2001) Ch 7; Wilson, *Central Issues*, Ch 6.

[251] Especially in cases of strict liability where, in the absence of *mens rea* elements, disputes over causation become the most critical, eg in environmental offences: N Padfield, 'Clean Water and Muddy Causation' [1995] Crim LR 683.

[252] On the issue of causing an event through the use of an innocent agent, see below, p 188.

[253] *Criminal Responsibility*, 159. Tadros poses an example (p 179) of D stabbing V in the leg. In the first scenario D is unaware that there is a bomb nearby. It explodes killing V. D would not be liable for murder even though he stabbed with intent to kill. In the second scenario, D stabs V and leaves him, being aware that a bomb is nearby. He concludes that in this second example the bomb would not break the chain of causation because D was aware of it.

4.5.1 Law or fact?

A common approach of the courts has been[254] to assert that causation is a question of fact to be answered by the application of common sense. The view that it is so simple is belied by the existence of a book on causation in law of over 500 pages with a 24-page table of cases.[255] What D did and what happened are certainly questions of fact. Whether D's act caused what happened is more complicated. If that is a question of fact it is one which is closely circumscribed by cases deciding what is incapable in law of being a cause, and what cannot reasonably be held not be a cause. Questions of fact *and law* are involved.

Whether D's act caused the result is a question that must be left to the jury, but in answering the question, they must apply legal principles, which it is the judge's duty to explain to them.[256] In one case[257] Lawton LJ said that where 'there is no conflict of evidence and all the jury has to do is to apply the law to the admitted facts, the judge is entitled to tell the jury what the result of that application will be'. Other cases,[258] however, show that the jury may have a substantial role in evaluating the primary facts, and that carries the attendant problems involved in their exercising moral judgement.

The judge may certainly direct the jury that they must acquit where there is no evidence that D caused the result, but it is not so clear whether he may tell them that they must find that D did cause death (or any other result) even where that is the only reasonable conclusion. If it is not for the judge to decide the issue, still less is it for expert witnesses. Where the question is whether the act caused a prohibited result such as certain injuries or death, the expert's function is to give the court his opinion on the medical issues. It is then for the jury to find the facts and apply the legal principles under the direction of the judge. Thus, cases such as *Jordan* (discussed below) have been criticized[259] because medical experts were permitted to say that the cause of V's death was certain medical treatment, and not wounds inflicted by D.[260] Whether the wound was capable of being 'a cause', for the purpose of the decision, was a question of law, not of medicine. Certainly it was relevant and proper for the court to know if the medical treatment was effective to cause death, either in conjunction with, or independently of, the wound; and perhaps all that the witnesses intended to say was that the treatment alone was the medical cause of death.[261] Of course, it is not necessary in every case for the trial judge to give detailed directions on every aspect of causation set out below.[262]

4.5.2 The 'but for' principle

The first legal principle to apply is that D's act cannot be regarded as the cause of an event if the event would have occurred in precisely the same way had D's act never been done. It must

---

[254] But see now the *Empress Car* case, below, p 90.

[255] Hart and Honoré, *Causation in the Law.*

[256] *Pagett* (1983) 76 Cr App R 279, CA.

[257] *Blaue* [1975] 3 All ER 446 at 450, CA, below, p 96. In *Malcherek*, below, p 94, it was held that the jury were bound to conclude that D caused V's death.

[258] eg, *Cheshire* [1991] 1 WLR 844, below, p 94.

[259] (1956) 40 Cr App R 152, below p 93. See G Williams, 'Causation in Homicide' [1957] Crim LR 431 and F Camps and J Havard, 'Causation in Homicide – A Medical View' [1957] Crim LR 576.

[260] cf *Cato* [1976] 1 All ER 260 at 264, below, p 85 where the medical experts said it was not for them to state the cause of death; they spoke to facts, and deductions therefrom were for the jury.

[261] The medical evidence may take on an additional significance in the case of an omission. See *Sinclair* (1998) above, p 72 and *Gowans* [2003] EWCA Crim 3935.

[262] See *Ogunbowale* [2007] EWCA Crim 2739. The new Crown Court Bench Book contains further guidance at Ch 5(9). See www.jsboard.co.uk/downloads/benchbook_criminal_2010.pdf.

be proved that, *but for* D's act or omission, the event would not have occurred.[263] Thus, if D poisons V's drink but V dies of natural causes before it has had any effect on V, D's conduct is not a 'but for' cause of V's death.[264] When deciding whether D's act was a 'but for' cause, a simple approach is to eliminate D's behaviour from the narrative and ask whether the result would have occurred anyway. If so, D is not liable.

In the traditional Latin terminology, D's act must be a *sine qua non* of the prohibited consequence (for example, death in murder). But this is only a starting point. There are many acts that are *sine qua non* of an event but are not, either in law or common sense, the cause of it. It is necessary to keep the test in perspective, otherwise blame could be attributed to D's ancestors! If D invites V to dinner and V is run over and killed on the way, V would not have died but for the invitation; but as a matter of common sense, no one would say 'D killed V', and in law D has not caused his death. In *Jordan*,[265] a wound inflicted by D stabbing V was certainly a *sine qua non* of the death of V because it led directly to the (badly performed) medical treatment that, according to the medical experts, caused death. It did not necessarily follow that the treatment was, in law, the only cause of the death. That depended on the application of the further principles considered below. The 'but for' principle is a starting point in the causation enquiry, but nothing more.

4.5.3 Contributory causes

It is clear that the act of D need not be the sole or the main cause of the result. It is wrong to direct a jury that D is not liable if he is, for example, less than one-fifth to blame.[266] Thus, where D struck V who was suffering from meningitis and died, it was enough that the death would not have been caused by the meningitis at the time when it occurred *but for* the blows (and it was immaterial that the blows would not have caused death but for the meningitis).[267]

Contributory causes may be the acts or omissions of others, including the conduct of the deceased himself. The contributory negligence of the claimant in civil actions of negligence was an absolute defence at common law, but no such principle applied in the criminal law. In *Swindall and Osborne*,[268] where one or other of the two accused ran over and killed an old man, Pollock CB directed the jury that it was immaterial that the victim was deaf or drunk or negligent and contributed to his own death. One or other of the two accused was a cause of death and, on the evidence, the other was an accessory.

An example of a case in which third parties contributed to V's death is *Benge*.[269] D, a foreman platelayer, employed to take up a certain section of railway line, misread the timetable so that the line was up at a time when a train arrived. He placed a flagman at a distance of only 540 yards, instead of 1,000 yards as required by the company's regulations, and entirely omitted to place fog signals, although the regulations specified that these should be put at 250-yard intervals for a distance of 1,000 yards. At D's trial for manslaughter it was urged that, in spite of his mistakes, the accident could not have happened if the other servants of the company had done their duty – if the flagman had gone the proper distance or if the engine driver had been keeping a proper look-out, which he was not. Pigott B ruled that this was no defence; if

---

[263] Even this basic rule may have exceptions, but only in very unlikely circumstances, eg, D and E, independently and simultaneously, shoot at V. D's bullet goes through V's heart and E's bullet blows his brains out. It seems safe to assume that both will be held to have caused V's death. cf Hall, *General Principles*, 267.

[264] See *White* [1910] 2 KB 124; D may be liable for the attempted murder of V.

[265] Discussed in detail below, p 93.

[266] *Henningan* [1971] 3 All ER 133. And see *Williams* [2010] ECWA Crim 2552.

[267] *Dyson* [1908] 2 KB 454.

[268] (1865) 4 F & F 504. *Ledger* (1862) 2 F & F 857 is contrary but was regarded by Stephen J as 'a very peculiar case': *Digest*, 161 n 4.

[269] (1846) 2 Car & Kir 230. See also *Walker* (1824) 1 C & P 320 (Garrow B).

D's negligence mainly or substantially caused the accident, it was irrelevant that it might have been avoided if other persons had not been negligent.

In *Warburton and Hubbersty*[270] the Court of Appeal rejected a submission that 'where a person has died from a number of injuries caused by different people and the defendant has caused (or been a party to causing) only injuries "A", then the defendant would not have caused the death unless the jury were sure that the deceased would have died from injuries "A" on their own'. Hooper LJ, delivering the judgment of the court, emphasized that 'the test for the jury is a simple one: did the acts for which the defendant is responsible *significantly contribute* to the victim's death'.

4.5.4 Connection between fault and result

The proscribed result is not attributable to D if the *culpable element* in his conduct in no way made a relevant contribution to the result. This is a difficult principle that is often misunderstood. A good illustration of its operation is in *Dalloway*.[271] D was driving a cart on a highway with reins not in his hands but loose on the horse's back. A three-year-old child ran into the road a few yards in front of the horse and was killed. Erle J directed the jury that, if D had reins and by using the reins could have saved the child, he was guilty of manslaughter; but that, if they thought D could not have saved the child by the use of the reins, then they should acquit him. If D had not been driving the cart at all the incident could not have occurred; and in that sense, he 'caused' it; but it was necessary to go further and show that the death was due to the culpable element in his conduct – his negligence in not using the reins.[272]

In the recent case of *Williams*[273] W was convicted of the draconian offence of causing death by driving without insurance and without a licence contrary to the Road Traffic Act 1988, s 3ZB. W drove his car without a driving licence or insurance. V crossed a dual-carriageway and stepped out in front of W's car. W argued that he could not avoid the accident. The Court of Appeal held W's driving was 'a cause' if it was 'more than negligible or de minimis'. The Court rejected the application of *Dalloway*. It is respectfully submitted that the case does assist. *Dalloway* serves to remind that the causation analysis must focus on the relevant act – which act is it alleged is the cause of the death? In *Dalloway* it was the negligent driving by misuse of the reins. In *Williams* it is submitted that the statute makes clear that it is the act of 'driving', not the existence of the car on the road. There has to be a causal link between the *driving* and not just the fact that the car was on the road at that time and the death. The Court of Appeal's interpretation focuses only on the link between the fact of the vehicle being on the road and the death. The statutory wording is not limited to that fact, but requires that the act of 'driving' causes the death. Consider a truly extreme case of a suicidal person jumping from a high motorway bridge and landing on D's uninsured car. Has D's *driving* caused V's death? V's death would have arisen if he had hit V's stationary car or the road. D's *driving* is not a cause of death.

4.5.5 Negligible causes

It is sometimes said[274] that D's conduct must be a 'substantial' cause, but the use of the word is misleading and seems to mean only that D's contribution must be more than negligible or not

---

[270] [2006] EWCA Crim 627, CA.

[271] (1847) 2 Cox CC 273, cf *Marsh* [1997] Crim LR 205.

[272] cf the discussion of *Clarke* (1990) 91 Cr App R 69.

[273] [2010] EWCA Crim 2552. See also *Carey* [2006] EWCA Crim 17 discussed below Ch 15.

[274] See, eg, *Benge*, above; *Smith* [1959] 2 QB 35 at 42–43, (below, p 94); Hall, *General Principles*, 283; Perkins (1946) 36 J Cr L & Cr at 393, and *Criminal Law*, 606–607.

be so minute that it will be ignored under the '*de minimis*' principle.[275] It may, therefore, be misleading to direct a jury that D is not liable unless his conduct was a 'substantial' cause.[276] For example, D and V are roped mountaineers. V has fallen over a 1,000-foot precipice and is dragging D slowly after him. D cuts the rope and V falls to his death five seconds before both V and D would have fallen. Any acceleration of death is killing but factors that produce a very trivial acceleration may be ignored. D's act is not a sufficiently substantial cause of V's death. Similarly, where two persons independently inflict wounds on V:

suppose one wound severed the jugular vein whereas the other barely broke the skin of the hand, and as the life blood gushed from the victim's neck, one drop oozed from the bruise on his finger ... metaphysicians will conclude that the extra drop of lost blood hastened the end by the infinitesimal fraction of a second. But the law will apply the *substantial factor* test and for juridical purposes the death will be imputed only to the severe injury in such an extreme case as this.[277]

These are, perhaps, rather unlikely examples but the principle would apply, for example, to a person visiting a dying man and contributing to his exhaustion by talking with him; and probably to the administration of pain-killing drugs which accelerate death.[278] In the context of homicide the problems raise controversial questions of science, law and morality as to the degree of acceleration that needs to be established to constitute a cause of death.[279]

The problem of an intervening cause, which is discussed below,[280] is sometimes put on the basis of substantial cause. Thus, Hall writes:

For example, a slight wound may have necessitated going to a doctor or drugstore, and *en route* the slightly injured person was struck by an automobile or shot by his mortal enemy. The slight wound, though a necessary condition of the death, did not contribute substantially to it.[281]

In *Williams*,[282] the court emphasized that the judge must explain to the jury what is meant by 'cause.' A simple reference to 'significant' or 'substantial' might be insufficient, as the terms could easily be misunderstood.

4.5.6 Intervening acts or events

Although D's culpable conduct is a factual (but for) and more than *de minimis* cause of the prohibited result, he is not necessarily legally responsible for it on that basis alone. If there is an intervening event (act or omission) either as a naturally occurring phenomenon or by

---

[275] *Cato* [1976] 1 All ER 260 at 265–266; '... it need hardly be added that [that cause] need not be substantial to render the accused guilty': *Malcherek* [1981] 2 All ER 422 at 428. But note that there is no defence of *de minimis per se* in English criminal law: *Scott* [2007] EWCA Crim 2757 (D 30 mins late in answering bail).

[276] *Hennigan*, above, n 266. Something more than a 'slight or trifling link' is required: *Kimsey* [1996] Crim LR 35. See also, eg, *Fitzgerald* [2006] EWCA Crim 1655.

[277] Perkins and Boyce, *Criminal Law*, 779. But cf *Garforth* [1954] Crim LR 936.

[278] Above, p 83.

[279] Numerous high profile cases involved doctors who have 'eased the passing' of a terminally ill patient. Examples include: *Cox* (1992) 12 BMLR 38 (see Editorial, 'Hard Cases Make Bad Law: Mercy Killing and Dr Cox' (1992) 142 NLJ 1293) and *Adams*, H Palmer, 'Dr Adams Trial for Murder' [1957] Crim LR 365. There was considerable comment following the case of David Moor: see A Arlidge, 'The Trial of Dr David Moor' [2000] Crim LR 31; JC Smith, 'A Comment on Moor's Case' [2000] Crim LR 41 and also J Goss, 'A Postscript to the Trial of Dr David Moor' [2000] Crim LR 568. The trial judge, Hooper J (as he then was) was prepared to leave the question of unlawfulness to the jury – if the act was proper treatment for the illness and pain management, it would be lawful even if the effect was fatal.

[280] Below.

[281] Hall, *General Principles* at 283, 393.

[282] Above n 266 see also *Barnes* [2008] EWCA Crim 2726.

some human conduct, it may operate to 'break the chain of causation', precluding D's liability for the ultimate result, (although D may remain liable for an attempt in many cases).

If, despite the intervening events, D's conduct remains a 'substantial and operative cause' of the result (for example, in murder, V's death), D will remain responsible; and if the intervention is by another person, that actor may also become liable in such circumstances. Subject to this, and some exceptional cases, the principles appear to be as follows:

(a) A subsequent act by D will not break the chain of causation so as to excuse him where the intervening act is part of the same transaction perpetrated by D. Eg D stabs V and then shoots him.

(b) D will not be liable if a natural event which is extraordinary or not *reasonably foreseeable*, supervenes and renders D's contribution merely part of the background.

(c) In relation to third party interventions D will not be liable if a third party's intervening act is either:

   (i) one of a *free deliberate and informed nature* (whether reasonably foreseeable or not);[283]

   (ii) if not a free deliberate informed act, one which was not reasonably foreseeable.

(d) D will not be liable if a medical professional intervenes to treat injuries inflicted by D and the treatment is so *independent* of D's conduct[284] and *so potent* as to render D's contribution part of the history and not a substantial and operating cause of death. The jury must remain focused on whether D remains liable, not whether the medical professional's conduct ought to render him criminally liable for his part. Even where incorrect treatment leads to death or more serious injury, it will only break the chain of causation if it is (i) unforeseeably bad, and (ii) the sole significant cause of the death (or more serious injury) with which D is charged.

(e) In relation to victims:

   (i) D *will* be liable if the victim has a pre-existing condition rendering him unusually vulnerable to physical injury as a result of an existing medical condition or old age, D must accept liability for any unusually serious consequences which result: *Hayward*;[285] *Blaue*.[286]

   (ii) D will not be liable if the victim's subsequent conduct in response to D's act is not within a range of responses that could be regarded as reasonable in the circumstances. Was V's act so daft as to be wholly disproportionate to D's act? If so it will break the chain.

Thus, in a homicide case D, who did what would have been a fatal act but for some independent intervention, is not responsible where the intervening independent act or unforeseen event is the immediate and sufficient cause of death. D administers poison to V but, before it

---

[283] This includes acts instinctively done for self-preservation and acts of an involuntary nature by the third party. cf *Empress* Cars [1999] AC 22, the case of a strict liability environmental offence only if the intervening act was extraordinary would it break causation.

[284] Although usually an act, it can be an omission to act. In *McKechnie* (1992) Cr App R 51 where doctors discovered that V had an ulcer but decided that it would be too dangerous to operate because V was still unconscious from D's beating. V died as a result of the ulcer bursting: 'The Recorder's statement of the question of the intervening events – the doctor's decision not to operate on the duodenal ulcer because [V's] head injuries made such an operation dangerous – properly directed the jury, not to the correctness of the medical decision, but to its reasonableness', per Auld J at 58.

[285] (1908) 21 Cox CC 692.

[286] [1975] 1 WLR 1411.

takes any effect on V's body, V is struck by lightning, shot dead by a burglar or dies of a heart attack not induced by the poison. In such cases, D may be guilty of attempted murder, but he cannot be convicted of murder.

The courts have struggled to produce a clear approach in this complex area. This problem is exacerbated by the diversity of factual circumstances in which such interventions arise, thereby encouraging the courts to distinguish cases too readily. Decisions have also been heavily influenced by policy considerations and this is illustrated by the willingness to conclude, for example, that interventions do not break the chain of causation where the intervention is by a health care professional. The courts have also adopted rather loose language in determining whether intervening events 'break the chain of causation', often resorting simply to the use of that metaphor. The best that can be offered by way of guidance is a series of principles, some of which are openly in conflict.

4.5.6.1 D's subsequent conduct

An intervening act by the original actor will not break the chain of causation so as to excuse him where the intervening act is part of the same transaction;[287] but it is otherwise if the act which causes the *actus reus* is part of a completely different transaction: for example D, having wounded V, visits him in hospital and accidentally infects him with smallpox of which he dies.[288]

4.5.6.2 Naturally occurring interventions

The accepted principle in relation to naturally occurring events is illustrated by the examples given by Perkins:[289]

if one man knocks down another and goes away leaving his victim not seriously hurt[290] but unconscious, on the floor of a building in which the assault occurred, and before the victim recovers consciousness he is killed in the fall of the building which is shaken down by a sudden earthquake, this is not homicide. The law attributes such a death to the 'Act of God' and not to the assault, even if it may be certain that the deceased would not have been in the building at the time of the earthquake, had he not been rendered unconscious. The blow was the occasion of the man's being there, but the blow was not the cause of the earthquake, nor was the deceased left in a position of obvious danger. On the other hand if the blow had been struck on the seashore, and the assailant had left his victim in imminent peril of an incoming tide which drowned him before consciousness returned, it would be homicide.[291]

In the second example, V's being drowned was a 'natural' consequence of D's action – that is, a consequence which might be expected to occur in the normal course of events. It was foreseeable as likely to occur in the normal course of events.[292] There is no break in the chain of causation by this naturally occurring intervening act and D remains liable for the result if the prosecution have established factual and legal causation as discussed in the principles above. In contrast, in the first example, V's being killed by the falling building was an abnormal and unforeseeable consequence. The act or event was not the natural consequence of D's act. This

---

[287] See below, p 89; Russell, 53–60, where the cases are set out; Williams, CLGP, 65; Hart and Honoré, *Causation in the Law*, 333.

[288] This paragraph was cited by the court in *Le Brun* (1991) 94 Cr App R 101, below, p 140.

[289] (1946) 36 J Cr L & Cr at 393.

[290] The result would appear to be the same if he were seriously hurt.

[291] cf *Hallett* [1969] SASR 141, where the court followed this passage in relation to similar facts.

[292] The courts use these terms interchangeably, but there is a difference. Not all naturally occurring events are foreseeable. In the most recent House of Lords case, *Empress Cars*, Lord Hoffmann used the term 'extraordinary' events rather than unforeseeable events in this context.

is sufficient to break the chain of causation. D may be liable for an attempted murder or some relevant offence against the person.

4.5.6.3 Third party interventions

Several categories of actor need to be considered.

Innocent agent

Where D knowingly employs an innocent agent[293] – for example, a person who is under the age of criminal responsibility, or insane, or merely someone without *mens rea* – to commit an offence, D, in law, causes the result, though the immediate causer is the innocent agent.

Involuntariness

A truly involuntary act clearly does not break the chain: D so startles E that E involuntarily drops a weight he is carrying which causes damage to V's property. There is no true intervening 'act' and D has caused the damage.

Justified and excused responses to D's act

The principles applicable to involuntary actors have been extended beyond innocent agency, and beyond what might naturally be regarded as 'involuntariness'. It is clear that human intervention, where it consists in a foreseeable act instinctively done for the purposes of self-preservation, or in the execution of a legal duty, does not break the chain of causation. In the case of *Pagett*,[294] D, to resist lawful arrest, held a girl in front of him as a shield and shot at armed policemen. The police 'instinctively'[295] fired back and killed the girl. D was held to have caused her death and to be guilty of manslaughter.[296] Though the court regarded the officers' instinctive act as 'involuntary', they also held that neither a reasonable act of self-defence nor an act done in the execution of a duty to prevent crime or arrest an offender, using such force as is reasonable in the circumstances, will break the chain of causation. It is not clear that such acts of self-defence or in the prevention of crime are necessarily in the same class as a truly 'involuntary' act. Moreover, it cannot be 'reasonable' for anyone intentionally to kill V, an innocent person, in order to save his own life[297] or to arrest X; and whether it is reasonable for him to take a risk of killing V must be doubtful. *Pagett* does not deal with the case where the officer's intervening act is unlawful. If it is, it does not necessarily follow that D's act is not a cause of death. There may be two unlawful causes.

The same principles should apply in determining whether the killing of an innocent bystander, or another policeman, by police bullets should be taken to be caused by D. It is obvious that the police marksman causes death.[298] His liability was not the issue in *Pagett*; but, if the shooting was a reasonable act of self-defence, the result, so far as he was concerned, was not an unlawful death.[299]

---

[293] Below, p 188.

[294] (1983) 76 Cr App R 279.

[295] Is not the purpose of firearms training to avoid acts of an instinctive nature such as this?

[296] Since the jury acquitted of murder, it must be taken that they were not satisfied D had the necessary *mens rea* as was then defined in *Hyam* [1975] AC 55 – that he knew it was highly probable that the girl would suffer death or grievous bodily harm.

[297] *Dudley and Stephens* (1884) 14 QBD 273, below, p 369; *Howe* [1987] AC 417, HL. cf commentary on *Pagett* [1983] Crim LR 394.

[298] cf *Malcherek*, below p 94.

[299] The court said that its comments were confined to homicide: but the same principles must surely apply to non-fatal offences.

Third party not free, deliberate, informed, but not reasonably foreseeable

If the third party human intervention is not a free, deliberate and informed one, but is not reasonably foreseeable, D will not have caused the result. In *Girdler*,[300] D had driven dangerously. D shunted the car driven by V into the path of oncoming traffic. V's car was avoided by most oncoming traffic but not by C. She drove into V killing him and herself. D was charged with causing both their deaths by dangerous driving. The Court of Appeal quashed the convictions after concluding that the trial judge's direction did not give sufficient assistance to the jury. The Court of Appeal concluded that if the immediate cause of the death of V was the 'free, deliberate, and informed' intervention of C then the chain of causation will be broken, but that there were problems in applying that test in this case. C's driving which led to the collision with V could not readily be described as falling within that category even if her driving was careless or dangerous. The court went on to recognize that a test based on reasonable foreseeability was applicable, but doubted whether directing a jury with those words would be apt. The court preferred a simpler expression of the concept:

a jury could be told, in circumstances like the present where the immediate cause of death is a second collision, that if they were sure that the defendant drove dangerously and were sure that his dangerous driving was more than a slight or trifling link to the death(s) then: *the defendant will have caused the death(s) only if you are sure that it could sensibly have been anticipated that a fatal collision might occur in the circumstances in which the second collision did occur.*

Third party voluntary actors

If the intervening event between D's act and V's death comprises the conduct of a third party acting in a 'fully voluntary' manner, the position should be straightforward. As Glanville Williams puts it:

What a person does (if he has reached adult years, is of sound mind and is not acting under mistake, intimidation or similar pressure) is his own responsibility and is not regarded as having been caused by other people. An intervening act of this kind, therefore, breaks the causal connection that would otherwise have been perceived between previous acts and the forbidden consequence.[301]

So, in a homicide case, the 'free, deliberate and informed' intervention by a third party has been held to have the effect of relieving the accused of criminal responsibility.[302] As a matter of principle, this seems right since the voluntary actor has chosen his course of action which leads to a prohibited result, and on orthodox principles of criminal liability he is liable for his voluntary actions which are now the immediate cause.

In *Latif*,[303] British customs officers in Pakistan intercepted heroin, which D intended to import into England. The officers brought it to England where D took delivery. It was held that D was not guilty of being concerned in the fraudulent evasion of the prohibition on importation because this had been effected by the 'free, deliberate and informed act' of the officers, exploiting the situation created by, but not acting in concert with, D. This broke the chain of causation. This can be contrasted with non-intentional intervening acts, for example, a failure by an employer to establish a safe system of work may remain a legal cause of death although the fatal accident would not have occurred but for the inadvertent, probably negligent, act of an employee operating the system.[304]

---

[300] [2009] EWCA Crim 2666.
[301] TBCL (2nd edn) 391. See, to the same effect, Hart and Honoré, *Causation in the Law*, 364–365.
[302] *Pagett* (1983) 76 Cr App R 279, 339.
[303] [1996] 2 Cr App R 92, [1996] Crim LR 414.
[304] *R v DPP, ex p Jones* [2000] Crim LR 858, DC.

This is a fundamental principle, but one that has given rise to difficulty in two categories of case that can be examined in more detail.

Empress Cars

In the *Empress Car* case,[305] D Ltd was held by the House of Lords to have caused the pollution of a river by bringing oil on to a site and failing to take precautions against the ever-present and foreseeable possibility that someone would release the oil into the river. The escape may have been caused by the fully voluntary national of a stranger, but it was also, in the opinion of the House, caused by the company. In reaching this conclusion Lord Hoffmann appears to confuse culpability with causation.[306] A householder may be blameworthy for forgetting to lock his door and set the burglar alarm at night but he could hardly be said to have 'caused' an ensuing burglary, though it would not have occurred if he had taken the proper precautions.[307] He may have been a factual cause, but as noted above with the example of the dinner invitation, that can never be enough to found liability in law. Lord Hoffmann put the case of a factory owner who carelessly leaves a drum containing highly inflammable vapour in a place where it could easily be accidentally ignited. He thought the owner would have caused an explosion if it occurred when a workman threw in a cigarette butt, believing the drum to be empty, but he would not have done so if a person knowing exactly what the drum contained, had thrown in a lighted match. In the former case the workman's act is not fully voluntary because he is making a fundamental mistake of fact; he is not acting with all the relevant information. In the latter case, the act is fully voluntary – and it appears to be indistinguishable from the actual facts of the *Empress Car* case. Lord Hoffmann concludes, it is submitted rightly, that, in the latter case, the carelessness of the owner had merely provided the person with an opportunity to do what he did – which appears to be equally true of the Empress Car Co Ltd. In suggesting that the chain of causation would be broken by the trespasser's act if it were an extraordinary one, but not merely by its being a free voluntary and informed act, his lordship seems to confuse the principles dealing with natural interventions and those with third party human interventions.

The principal authority relied on was that from the law of tort – Lord Hoffmann cited *Stansbie v Troman*.[308] In that case a decorator, left in charge of a house, went out to buy wallpaper, leaving the door open. He was held liable in negligence for an ensuing theft. Hart and Honoré[309] cite, along with *Stansbie v Troman*, an American case in which it was held a railway company would be liable if a girl they put down at nightfall in a dangerous area were raped. That may be true for the law of tort, but clearly, the railway or its officials could not be *criminally* liable for rape.

Empress ought to be regarded as an aberrant authority. On a charitable view, it might be explained on its own facts by the House of Lords being too heavily influenced by the policy of protecting the environment. In such cases the original actor has control of the potentially hazardous product and is under a duty to protect against environmental harm. Fortunately, the House of Lords has now confirmed in *Kennedy (No 2)*,[310] that the extreme interpretation of the principles as set down in *Empress* is applicable in relation to offences of pollution and is not of general application throughout the criminal law. The Court of Appeal decisions which had sought to apply *Empress* to, for example, manslaughter, were overruled.[311]

---

[305] *Environmental Agency (formerly National Rivers Authority) v Empress Car Co (Abertillery) Ltd* [1999] 2 AC 22, [1998] 1 All ER 481, HL.

[306] See his example of the irate wife at [1998] 1 All ER 487a–c.

[307] As we saw above, it may be accurate to describe the householder as *a* cause where he has a duty to lock up, p 83.

[308] [1948] 2 KB 48.

[309] See n 250.

[310] [2007] UKHL 38.

[311] *Finlay* [2003] EWCA Crim 3868 was the most striking example.

Lord Hoffmann further recognized in *Empress* that common sense is not a sufficient guide to resolving causation issues, and that legal principles are involved. This is valuable, but the guidance offered may be baffling to the courts, especially magistrates' courts, which are frequently required to decide cases like *Empress*. Causation, it appears, is a variable concept. According to Lord Hoffmann the answer to the question requires the court to ascertain the purpose and scope of the rule alleged to have been broken; and 'Not only may there be different answers to questions about causation when attributing responsibility to different people under different rules... but there may be different answers when attributing responsibility to different people under the same rule.' This suggests that the principles of causation have, in this narrow category of pollution and environmental offences, become merely a matter of fact to be determined on a case by case basis.[312]

Drug administration cases

The principle that a fully voluntary act breaks the chain of causation was overlooked, ignored and circumvented in a series of cases dealing with drug administration. The problem in these cases is simple to state. V self-injects what turns out to be a fatal overdose of drugs. D has either: supplied the drugs, made up the syringe, assisted by holding the tourniquet for V to find an injection site, or otherwise encouraged V's self-injection. In what circumstances is D liable for manslaughter? On a charge of unlawful act manslaughter, requiring proof of an unlawful, intentional and dangerous act causing death, the sticking point is in establishing causation. On orthodox principles of causation, V's free, voluntary deliberate informed act by self-injecting should break the chain of causation. As Glanville Williams explained:

The new intervening act (*novus actus interveniens*) of a responsible actor, who had full knowledge of what he is doing, and is not subject to mistake or pressure, will normally operate to relieve the defendant of liability for a further consequence, because it makes the consequence too remote... What a person does (if he has reached adult years, is of sound mind and is not acting under mistake, intimidation or other similar pressure) is his own responsibility, and is not regarded as having been caused by other people.[313]

The Court of Appeal adopted a confused approach to these cases in *Kennedy, Dias, Richards*,[314] *Rogers*[315] and *Finlay*.[316] In *Kennedy (No 2)*,[317] the conclusion was that 'if [D] either caused [V] to administer the drug or was acting jointly with the deceased in administering the drug, [D] would be acting in concert with [V] and there would be no breach in the chain of causation'. The jury is entitled to convict if it finds that the actions of the D and V are a 'combined operation'. The conclusion was heavily criticized.[318] The Court of Appeal certified the following question of general public importance:

When is it appropriate to find someone guilty of manslaughter where that person has been involved in the supply of a class A controlled drug, which is then freely and voluntarily self-administered by the person to whom it was supplied, and the administration of the drug then causes his death?

---

[312] This might reflect Lord Hoffmann's preference for issues to be left for jury determination in the criminal trial

[313] TBCL, 391.

[314] [2002] EWCA Crim 1.

[315] [2003] 1 WLR 137.

[316] [2003] EWCA Crim 3868.

[317] [2005] EWCA Crim 685.

[318] See D Ormerod and R Fortson, 'Drug Suppliers as Manslaughterers (Again)' [2005] Crim LR 819. For a defence of manslaughter charges in this scenario and proposals for a specific offence to achieve that see T Jones, 'Causation, Homicide and the Supply of Drugs' (2006) 26 Legal Studies 139, and see L Cherkassky (2008) 72 J Crim L 387.

The House of Lords, in a clear and concise unanimous judgment delivered by Lord Bingham, provided an unequivocal and welcome answer to the certified question. D who supplies drugs for V to self-inject can *never* be guilty of unlawful act manslaughter if V is a fully informed adult making a voluntary decision to self-inject. The House emphasized that the criminal law generally assumed the existence of free will; a defendant was not to be treated as causing an adult of sound mind to act in a certain way if the latter made a voluntary and informed decision to act in that way. The heroin was 'freely and voluntarily self-administered' by V who chose to inject himself knowing what he was doing. The House of Lords went further, and overruled *Rogers*,[319] where D had provided the drugs for V and had held the tourniquet for V as V freely and voluntarily injected himself with what turned out to be a lethal dose of heroin.[320] The House also overruled *Finlay*[321] where the Court of Appeal held that the question of whether V's act broke the chain of causation was one of fact for the jury and, following *Empress*, involved the assessment of whether V's act was extraordinary.

In *Burgess*[322] the Court of Appeal subsequently suggested that had the matter fallen for consideration (on the facts D had pleaded on a basis that could not stand in light of *Kennedy*) D raising the vein for V would suffice for a manslaughter conviction. It was held that 'if a defendant may be convicted on the basis that the fatal dose was jointly administered then it follows that he is not automatically entitled to be acquitted if the deceased rather than the defendant physically operated the plunger'.[323] There is obviously a difficult borderline between contributory acts which might properly be regarded as administering a noxious thing and acts which might not. The evidence is likely to be patchy – one participant is dead and the other, the defendant, likely to have been heavily intoxicated. *Burgess* might therefore serve as an example falling just the other side of the line from *Rogers*. Whether the necessary proximity existed between the actions of D and V is for the jury to determine. Liability for manslaughter will exist where D has provided the drugs to V whose act of self-administration was not free and voluntary.

The House of Lords in *Kennedy (No 2)* emphasized that nothing it had said cast doubt on liability for gross negligence manslaughter in such cases and the Court of Appeal in *Evans*[324] has confirmed that convictions for that offence can be secured although not for supply alone.[325]

4.5.6.4 Medical interventions

Largely for reasons of policy, the courts have adopted a particularly strict approach in cases where the alleged break in the chain of causation involves the conduct[326] of medical professionals. These are third parties who are intervening in a fully informed manner, (although not

---

[319] [2003] 2 Cr App R 10, [2003] Crim LR 555.

[320] It is submitted there will be few of the imaginable 'factual scenarios', aside from where D injects V, in which D can be said to be administering.

[321] [2003] EWCA Crim 3868. D was found to have 'caused to be administered'.

[322] [2008] EWCA Crim 516. See D Hughes (2008) 72 J Crim L 516. See also *Keen* [2008] EWCA Crim 1000.

[323] [12].

[324] [2009] EWCA Crim 650.

[325] See above p 74 for discussion and Ch 15.

[326] Although usually an act, it can be an omission to act, *McKechnie* (1992) Cr App R 51.

fully voluntarily since they are under a duty to act[327]), but whose conduct is generally insufficient to break the chain of causation in this context.

Before the advent of a rigorous science of forensic pathology, it was less easy to establish causes of death. The nineteenth-century cases[328] held that, where the immediate cause of death was the medical treatment received by V consequent upon his injury by D, D was guilty of homicide, whether the treatment was proper or improper, negligent or not. If the treatment was given *bona fide* by competent medical officers, evidence was not admissible to show that it was improper or unskilful. In the earlier cases, this rule was applied only where the wound was dangerous to life. Later, and logically, it was extended to less serious injuries. Those cases must now be regarded in the light of the modern decisions in *Jordan*,[329] *Smith*[330] and *Cheshire*.[331]

In *Jordan*, D stabbed V who was admitted to hospital and died eight days later. At the trial 'it did not occur to the prosecution, the defence, the judge or the jury that there could be any doubt but that the stab caused death'.[332] In the Court of Criminal Appeal, the fresh evidence of two doctors was allowed to the effect that, in their opinion, death had not been caused by the stab wound, which was mainly healed at the time of the death, but by the introduction (with a view to preventing infection) of terramycin after the deceased man had shown he was intolerant to it and by the intravenous introduction of large quantities of liquid. This treatment, according to the evidence, was 'palpably wrong'. The court held that if the jury had heard this evidence they would have felt precluded from saying that they were satisfied that the death was caused by the stab wound and they quashed the conviction.

The case has been interpreted by Williams[333] as one where the medical treatment was grossly negligent, but he argues[334] that any degree of negligence which would be recognized by the civil courts should be enough. The court did not say in express terms that there was evidence of negligence, gross or otherwise, though it may reasonably be inferred that 'palpably wrong' treatment is negligent. While anxiously disclaiming any intention of setting a precedent[335] they stated the basis of their decision in even broader terms. They were 'disposed to accept it as law that death resulting from any normal treatment employed to deal with a felonious injury may be regarded as caused by the felonious injury'; but it was 'sufficient to point out here that this was not normal treatment'. Surely, treatment that is 'not normal' is not necessarily negligent, even in the civil law?[336] The case gave rise to some concern in the medical profession and it was predicted[337] that the result of it would be that if, in future, the victim of a homicidal assault died as a result of the medical treatment instituted to save his life, it would not be considered homicide by the assailant if the treatment could be shown to be 'not normal'.

---

[327] As Wilson points out, 'doctors who have emergency surgery thrust upon them cannot be expected to get it right all the time', *Central Issues,* 181.

[328] Discussed in the sixth edition of this book, at 321.

[329] (1956) 40 Cr App R 152.

[330] [1959] 2 QB 35. Followed in *Gowans* [2003] EWCA Crim 3935.

[331] [1991] 3 All ER 670.

[332] See (1956) 40 Cr App R 152 at 155.

[333] [1957] Crim LR at 430.

[334] ibid, 513.

[335] But no court has the right to preclude future courts from considering the effects of its decisions.

[336] See *Bolam v Friern Hospital Management Committee* [1957] 1 WLR 582 and *Bolitho v City and Hackney HA* [1998] AC 232 and the discussion in WVH Rogers, *Winfield and Jolowicz on Tort* (18th edn, 2010) Ch 5.

[337] By Camps and Havard [1957] Crim LR 576 at 582–583.

Jordan was distinguished by the Court in *Smith*[338] and by the Court of Appeal in *Blaue*[339] as 'a very particular case depending upon its exact facts'.

In *Smith*,[340] in the course of a fight between soldiers of different regiments, D stabbed V twice with a bayonet. One of V's comrades, trying to carry V to the medical reception station, twice tripped and dropped him. At the reception station the medical officer, who was trying to cope with a number of other cases, did not realize that one of the wounds had pierced a lung and caused haemorrhage. He gave V treatment which, in the light of the information regarding V's condition available at the time of the trial, was 'thoroughly bad and might well have affected his chances of recovery'. D's conviction of murder was upheld and counsel's argument, that the court must be satisfied that the treatment was normal, and that this was abnormal, was brushed aside.

if at the time of death the original wound is still an operating cause and a substantial cause, then the death can properly be said to be the result of the wound, albeit that some other cause of death is also operating. Only if it can be said that the original wounding is merely the setting in which another cause operates can it be said that the death does not result from the wound. Putting it in another way, only if the second cause is so overwhelming as to make the original wound merely part of the history can it be said that death does not flow from the wound.[341]

In *Malcherek*,[342] the court thought that if a choice had to be made between *Jordan* and *Smith*, *Smith* was to be preferred; but they did not believe it was necessary to choose. In *Blaue*, *Jordan* was thought to be 'probably rightly decided on its facts'. It is submitted that this is so. *Smith* is distinguishable. *Jordan* was a case where a jury might have found, in the light of the new evidence, that the wound was, or may have been, merely the setting in which medical treatment caused death – as if a nurse had, with gross negligence, administered a deadly poison in mistake for a sleeping pill or, as in a Kentucky case, *Bush v Commonwealth*,[343] the medical officer attending V inadvertently infected him with scarlet fever and he died of that. None of these is an act which might be expected to occur in the ordinary course of events and they free D from liability. But, if the injured V is receiving proper and skilful medical attention and he dies from the treatment or the operation, D will be liable.

In *Cheshire*,[344] the bullet wounds which D inflicted upon V had ceased to be a threat to life and there was evidence that V's death was caused by the tracheotomy performed and negligently treated by the doctors so that it narrowed his windpipe and caused asphyxiation. The Court of Appeal held that the judge had misdirected the jury by telling them that only recklessness on the part of the doctors would break the chain of causation but upheld the conviction, asserting that 'the rare complication...was a direct consequence of the appellant's acts, which remained a significant cause of his death'. The test proposed by the court is not easy to apply:

Even though negligence in the treatment of the victim was the immediate cause of his death, the jury should not regard it as excluding the responsibility of the accused unless the negligent treatment was so independent of his acts, and in itself so potent in causing death, that they regard the contribution made by his acts as insignificant.

---

[338] [1959] 2 QB 35 at 43.
[339] [1975] 3 All ER 446. Likewise in *Evans and Gardiner (No 2)* [1976] VR 523 at 531.
[340] [1959] 2 QB 35 at 43.
[341] Per Lord Parker CJ [1959] 2 QB 35 at 42–43. The passage was applied in *Gowans* (above).
[342] [1981] 2 All ER 422.
[343] 78 Ky 268 (1880) (Kentucky Court of Appeals).
[344] [1991] 3 All ER 670, [1991] Crim LR 709.

It is difficult to know what 'so independent' and 'so potent' mean. In all these cases, D's act caused V to undergo the treatment and if that renders it 'dependent', D would be taken to have caused death, however outlandish the treatment; but it is clear that this is not intended. There is a similar problem with 'potent'. Suppose that the tracheotomy would have caused death even if the wound had been completely healed (this is not entirely clear).[345] No greater potency can then be imagined; but it is, at least, unlikely that the court intended that it should follow that D had not caused death. The wound would not have been an operating and substantial cause but the ultimate question is whether D's act was a cause and it is clear that it might be, even if the wound was not. The problem could well surface with a victim hospitalized by a wound from D who then, as the wound has healed, contracts MRSA in an unclean hospital.

It is submitted that the following propositions[346] at present represent the law:

(1) Medical evidence is admissible to show that the medical treatment of an injury was the cause of death and that the injury itself was not.[347] This is so whether or not the injury is life threatening. The conflict of medical evidence may present the jury with a difficult decision as to the potency of the medical intervention.[348] Juries will need careful guidance on such issues.[349]

(2) If an injury was an operating and substantial cause of death, D is guilty of homicide, however badly the injury was treated.[350]

(3) If an injury was not an operating and substantial cause of death (for example, it was effectively healed) but V was killed by, for example, the inadvertent administration of deadly poison by a nurse, the wrongful administration of terramycin, or the ill-treatment of a tracheotomy, D may or may not be guilty of homicide. The test we must now apply is the *Cheshire* independence/potency test. A better test, it is submitted, would be whether the treatment, or the manner of administering it, was so extraordinary as to be unforeseeable – which may be much the same thing as asking whether it was grossly negligent.

Jordan and *Cheshire* were cases where the medical treatment, not the wound, may have been the cause of death. The same principle applies where the injury prevents medical treatment for an independent condition which would have saved life: *McKechnie*,[351] where the injuries inflicted by D precluded medical treatment for the duodenal ulcer which killed V. Only an 'extraordinary and unusual' medical decision that the life-saving treatment was not possible would have broken the chain of causation.

It is important to keep in mind that where the question at D's trial is whether the medical professional has broken the chain of causation: the medical professional is *not* on trial. In *Malcherek*,[352] D inflicted upon V injuries which resulted in brain damage. She was put on a life-support machine. Some days later, after carrying out five of the six tests[353] for brainstem

---

[345] Indeed, according to the Court of Appeal (at 678) the judge directed the jury that the prosecution must prove that 'the bullets were one operative and substantial cause of death'; but the bullets (unless they were still in V's body) could not be an *operating* cause, if that is what is meant, in the sense that a wound might be.

[346] Approved in *Dear* [1996] Crim LR 595.

[347] *Jordan* must be authority for this at least. Moreover, at the trial in *Smith*, Dr Camps gave evidence that, with proper treatment, V's chances of recovery were as high as 75%.

[348] See, eg, *Gowans* [2003] EWCA Crim 3935 where V contracted fatal septicaemia in hospital.

[349] *Suratan* [2004] EWCA Crim 1246.

[350] But cf Hart and Honoré, *Causation in the Law*, 361, discussing *Blaue*, suppose that V had called for a blood transfusion and the doctor had refused because he wanted to play golf, whereupon V bled to death. They argue that death would have been 'caused by the doctor's callousness, not the original wound'. Surely, it would have been caused by both. The wound would certainly have been an operating and substantial cause.

[351] (1991) 94 Cr App R 51, [1992] Crim LR 194.

[352] [1981] 1 WLR 690. The appeal of *Steel*, heard at the same time, was materially the same.

[353] There were reasons for not applying the sixth test.

death prescribed by the Royal Colleges, doctors disconnected the machine and half an hour later she was pronounced dead. The judge withdrew the question of causation from the jury, ruling that there was no evidence on which they could decide that D did not cause V's death. On appeal, it was argued that there was evidence on which the jury could have found that the doctors caused death by switching off the machine. The appeal was dismissed. There was no doubt that the injury inflicted by D was an operating and substantial cause of death. Whether or not the doctors were also *a* cause of death was immaterial. They were not on trial;[354] D was. It was enough that a continuing and substantial cause of V's death was the injury inflicted by D.

4.5.6.5 Victim's conduct breaking the chain of causation

General principle – D takes his victim as found

It is a well-established principle in civil law that the defendant takes the victim of his wrong-doing as he finds him – with all V's subsisting weaknesses that might exacerbate the injury resulting from D's act, as where D pricks a haemophiliac with a pin, or slaps the head of a person with an egg-shell skull. According to *Blaue*,[355] in the criminal law, as in the civil, the defendant must 'take his victim as he finds him'.

If the principle is restricted to taking V as found in physical terms, little difficulty arises. It seems unnatural to describe V's body's 'response' to D's act as an intervening 'act' between D's infliction of injury and V's death. It is correct, therefore, that D takes V as he finds him with all V's subsisting physical conditions being taken into account.[356] However, controversially, the court in *Blaue* held that the principle applies so that D takes the victim as found in a more holistic sense – taking the victim's *mind* as well as his body as found.

In *Blaue*, D stabbed V, a young girl, and pierced her lung. She was told that she would die if she did not have a blood transfusion. Being a Jehovah's Witness, she refused on religious grounds. She died from the bleeding caused by the wound. D was convicted of manslaughter and argued that V's refusal to have a blood transfusion, being unreasonable, had broken the chain of causation. It was held that the judge had rightly instructed the jury that the wound was a cause of death. Lawton LJ said:[357]

It has long been the policy of the law that those who use violence on other people must take their victims as they find them. This in our judgment means the whole man, not just the physical man. It does not lie in the mouth of the assailant to say that his victim's religious beliefs which inhibited him from accepting certain kinds of treatment were unreasonable. The question for decision is what caused the death. The answer is a stab wound.

In this case, the wound was 'an operating cause and a substantial cause', so the *dictum* was unnecessary to the decision. It is unclear whether the court would take the same approach if V had not previously held the religious belief, but had adopted it to spite D (an unlikely scenario).[358]

---

[354] The court remarked, *obiter*, that they thought the suggestion that the doctors had caused the death 'bizarre' – they had done their skilful best to save life, but failed and so discontinued treatment. The policy dimension to causation in homicide where medical negligence is alleged is obvious.

[355] [1975] 3 All ER 446, [1976] Crim LR 648 and commentary. *Smithers* (1976) 34 CCC (2d) 427 (Sup Ct of Canada) is to the same effect. It was immaterial that death was caused in part by malfunctioning epiglottis, where a kick was a contributing cause, outside the *de minimis* range.

[356] See, eg, *Masters* [2007] EWCA Crim 142, D liable for murder where V had deep vein thrombosis which hastened death and would have killed her soon anyway.

[357] [1975] 3 All ER 446, 450.

[358] On advance decisions to refuse life-sustaining treatment see now Mental Capacity Act 2005, s 25.

The *Blaue* principle, if valid, would impose liability upon D for unforeseeable intervening events causing death and is probably confined to acts or omissions by the victim in person. If the parents of a rape victim were to kill their daughter on the ground that their religion required them to do so, it is thought that D would not be liable for the death. If, however, in *Blaue*, V had been too young to make a decision about a blood transfusion and her parents had succeeded on religious grounds in preventing a transfusion being given, it is thought that the wound would have remained an operating and substantial cause, so D would still have been liable. The parents might also have been guilty of some homicide offence.

Blaue followed *Holland*[359] in which D waylaid and assaulted V, cutting him severely across one of his fingers with an iron instrument. V refused to follow the surgeon's advice to have the finger amputated, although he was told that if he did not his life would be in great danger. The wound caused lockjaw, the finger was then amputated, but it was too late and V died of lockjaw. The surgeon's evidence was that if the finger had been amputated at first, V's life could probably have been saved. Maule J told the jury that it made no difference whether the wound was in its own nature instantly mortal, or whether it became the cause of death by reason of the deceased not having adopted the best mode of treatment. The question was whether, in the end, the wound inflicted by the prisoner was the real cause of death. The argument[360] that medical science has advanced greatly since 1841 and that a refusal to undergo medical treatment, reasonable then, would be unreasonable now, did not impress the court in *Blaue*. Whether V's conduct was reasonable or not was irrelevant.

The principle stated by the court in *Blaue*, if valid, is capable of wider application. Given that D would be liable for wounding or attempted murder, it is arguable that the principle can operate unduly harshly, but the same harshness would apply where the victim has an egg-shell skull, and that rule is not commonly criticized. The true force of the criticisms levelled against the decision are perhaps against the emphasis the law places on the result (death) rather than the blameworthiness of the life-threatening conduct (unlawful wounding).[361]

Self neglect by the victim

The common law rule is that neglect or maltreatment by the injured person of himself does not exempt D from liability for his ultimate death. In *Wall's* case,[362] where the former Governor of Goree was convicted[363] of the murder of a man by ordering the illegal infliction on him of a flogging of 800 lashes, there was evidence that V had aggravated his condition by drinking spirits. MacDonald LCB told the jury:[364]

there is no apology for a man if he puts another in so dangerous and hazardous a situation by his treatment of him, that some degree of unskilfullness and mistaken treatment of himself may possibly accelerate the fatal catastrophe. One man is not at liberty to put another into such perilous circumstances as these, and to make it depend upon his own prudence, knowledge, skill or experience what may hurry on or complete that catastrophe, or on the other hand may render him service.

In any event, the drink might have been regarded as a merely *de minimis* cause.

---

[359] (1841) 2 Mood & R 351. cf *Mubila* 1956 (1) SA 31.

[360] By Hart and Honoré, *Causation in the Law*, at 360.

[361] See the discussion above, p 50 and A Ashworth, 'Belief Intent and Criminal Liability', in Eekelaar and Bell (eds), *Oxford Essays in Jurisprudence*; 'Taking the Consequences', in Shute, Gardner and Horder (eds), *Action and Value in Criminal Law* and 'Defining Offences Without Harm', in *Criminal Law Essays*.

[362] (1802) 28 State Tr 51.

[363] 20 years after the event.

[364] At 145.

Subsequent *conduct* of the victim

A long line of cases has established that D will be held to have caused death or injury by so frightening V that V has jumped from a window or a car or behaved in some other manner dangerous to himself.[365] If D's unlawful conduct has prompted the response from V, D will remain liable if V's reaction was within the range of responses which might be expected from a victim in his situation.[366] If the reaction was 'so daft as to make it [V's] own voluntary act' the chain of causation is broken. So it seems D does not have to take a 'daft' victim as he finds him – unless, presumably he knows him to be daft – that is, likely to behave in an extraordinary fashion. The range of responses to be expected will, of course, vary according to the age and perhaps the sex of the victim.[367] This approach was followed recently in *Lewis*.[368] L chased V into the road following an argument, V was knocked down by an oncoming car. The Court of Appeal held, dismissing the appeal, that in cases of death during flight from an unlawful act it had to be shown that there was cause and effect, ie but for the unlawful act, flight and therefore death would not have taken place.

If the victim is a contributory cause of the incident, that does not preclude D's liability if D's act is a continuing and operative cause. In *People v Lewis*,[369] V, having received a mortal gunshot wound from which he would have died within the hour, cut his throat and died within five minutes. D was held liable for manslaughter on the ground that the original wound was an operating cause. 'Here, when the throat was cut, [V] was not merely languishing from a mortal wound; he was actually dying; and after the throat was cut he continued to languish from both wounds. Drop by drop the life current went out from both wounds, and at the very instant of death the gunshot wound was contributing to the event.'[370] The application of this principle would have provided a different answer if V had blown his brains out and died instantly, for then the bleeding from the original wound would not have been an operating cause. The conviction could then have been upheld only by applying a different principle – that the first act provided a reason for the second[371] – and the court would indeed have decided the case on that ground if they had been satisfied that the first act *was* the cause of the second; but they thought that V's suicide might have been out of remorse or a desire to shield D.

If the victim of a rape were to be so outraged as to commit suicide by shooting herself it might be argued that it was the bullet that caused the death and not the rape. Certainly the rape is not 'an operating and substantial cause' in the same sense as the wound in *Blaue*; but according to that case the rapist must take his victim as he finds her. His act caused the act that caused her death. This may be the effect of *Dear*[372] where D's conviction for murder was upheld, even though V may have intentionally caused his own death by aggravating the wounds inflicted on him by D. If V would not have killed himself but for those injuries, D caused his death. It would have been different if V had so acted only for some reason unconnected with D's attack on him – for example, shame at his own disgraceful conduct (paedophilia) which had led D to attack him. The decision is, perhaps, not quite conclusive of the rape victim/suicide case: the

---

[365] *Pitts* (1842) Car & M 284; *Halliday* (1889) 61 LT 701; *Curley* (1909) 2 Cr App R 96 at 109; *Lewis* [1970] Crim LR 647; *Mackie* [1973] Crim LR 54 (Cusack J); *Boswell* [1973] Crim LR 307 (Judge Gower); *Daley* (1979) 69 Cr App R 39.

[366] *Williams and Davies* (1991) 95 Cr App R 1, [1992] Crim LR 198; *Corbett* [1996] Crim LR 594. cf *Roberts* (1971) 56 Cr App R 95 at 102.

[367] Presumably, following *Blaue*, religions, no matter how esoteric cannot be regarded as 'daft'. What of an irrational but entrenched fear of hospitals?

[368] [2010] EWCA Crim 151.

[369] 124 Cal 551 (1899) Sup Ct of California.

[370] But was the contribution of the gunshot wound substantial or *de minimis* (slight or trifling)? cf the example given by Perkins, above, p 87 and Hart and Honoré, *Causation in the Law*, 243.

[371] Hart and Honoré, *Causation in the Law*, 244.

[372] [1996] Crim LR 595.

wounds as well as V's acts may have been the physical cause of death, whereas in the rape case the bullet is the sole physical cause of death. In *Dear* it was apparently regarded as immaterial that V's conduct was unforeseeable. In this respect the decision is not easily reconcilable with the line of authority establishing that V's 'daft' conduct will break the chain of causation.

In *D*,[373] the accused had struck his partner a minor blow on the forehead and she had then committed suicide. This was against a lengthy background of domestic abuse amounting to psychological, but not psychiatric, injury by D. The charge of manslaughter was dismissed since the Crown relied on the history of abuse as founding an unlawful and dangerous act.[374] In an *obiter dictum*, the Court of Appeal left open the possibility that a manslaughter conviction might be available: 'where a decision to commit suicide has been triggered by a physical assault which represents the culmination of a course of abusive conduct, it would be possible...to argue that the final assault played a significant part in causing the victim's death'. In terms of causation, even if D's conduct was treated as a sufficient unlawful and dangerous act, could it ever be a sufficient *cause* in law? There may be little doubt that in fact it operated as a cause of the suicide, but does V's action in choosing to commit suicide break the chain of causation? Can D ever be liable for manslaughter where V has committed suicide and D's act is not at that moment a continuing and operative cause of death? It has been argued that in such cases a jury might be willing to conclude that suicide was not outside the range of reasonable responses to be expected of someone in V's position, particularly where the jury were made aware of the history of abuse.[375] It should be noted that in none of the reported 'flight' cases does it appear that the victims have chosen to commit suicide; rather they have behaved in a dangerous fashion, being aware that their choice of escape may expose them to danger of injury or death.

4.5.6.6 Intended consequences

It is sometimes said that intended consequences cannot be too remote, that is, that D must always be liable for them. This, however, is an oversimplification,[376] and is not always accurate because the *sine qua non* rule remains applicable. Thus, in *White*,[377] the consequence intended by D – the death of his mother – occurred; but its occurrence – a fatal heart attack – had nothing to do with D's act in administering the poison and would have happened just the same if D had done nothing. Even where the *sine qua non* rule is satisfied, the consequence, though intended, may be too remote where it occurs as a result of the intervention of some new cause. So in the cases of *Bush*[378] and *Jordan*[379] it may be that D intended V's death, and V's death occurred; moreover, in neither case would death have occurred without D's act; but in the one case it was caused by scarlet fever and not by D's bullet; and in the other it was caused by medical treatment and not by D's knife.

Where the death occurs in the manner intended by D he will be guilty even if the course of events was not what he expected; for example, he shoots at V's head, but the bullet misses, ricochets and kills V by striking him in the back. The case of *Michael*[380] is perhaps a rather

---

[373] [2006] EWCA Crim 1139.

[374] The trial judge held that this was incapable of amounting to actual bodily harm absent psychiatric injury and the Court of Appeal agreed. See below, p 590.

[375] See further, Horder and McGowan [2006] Crim LR 1035.

[376] But note the rather stronger rejection by some – 'slogans like intended consequences are never too remote simply cannot be accepted': C Finkelstein, 'Involuntary Crimes, Voluntarily Committed', in Shute and Simester (eds), *Criminal Law Theory*, 150.

[377] [1910] 2 KB 124.

[378] 78 Ky 268 (1880); above, p 94.

[379] (1956) 40 Cr App R 152.

[380] (1840) 9 C & P 356.

extreme example of this. D's child, V, was in the care of a nurse, X. D, intending to murder the child, delivered to X a large quantity of laudanum, telling her it was a medicine to be administered to V. X did not think the child needed any medicine and left it untouched on the mantelpiece of her room. In X's absence, one of her children, Y, aged five, took the laudanum and administered a large dose to V who died. All the judges held that the jury were rightly directed that this administration by 'an unconscious agent' was murder. Hart and Honoré[381] criticize the case on the ground that the child was:

not in any sense an agent, conscious or unconscious, of the mother, who intended [X] alone to give the poison to the child; but the decision may be justified on the ground that, in our terminology, the act of the child of five did not negative causal connexion between the prisoner's act and the death.

According to this view, the result would have been different if Y had been, not five, but 15. It does not appear that Y knew, from the labelling of the bottle or otherwise, that this was 'medicine' for V. If she did know this, and acted on that knowledge, then there seems no difficulty in imputing the death to D, whatever Y's age. No such fact being reported, however, the case must be treated as one where Y's intervention was in no way prompted by D's instructions. Thus, if Y had taken the poison herself, her death would have been just as much caused by D's act as was V's in the actual case; but it would require an extension of the decision to hold D guilty in such a case, for Y's death was not an intended consequence.[382] If such an extension is not made, the result is quite arbitrary, for it was pure chance whether Y administered the poison to V, or to herself or another child.

4.5.7 Special instances of causation

There are a few instances of causation which require special mention, by reason of the state of the authorities.

4.5.7.1 Killing by mental suffering or shock

The view of earlier writers was that the law could take no cognizance of a killing caused merely by mental suffering or shock, because 'no external act of violence was offered, whereof the common law can take notice and secret things belong to God'.[383] Stephen thought that the fear of encouraging prosecutions for witchcraft was the reason for the rule and that it was 'a bad rule founded on ignorance now dispelled'.[384]

Suppose a man were intentionally killed by being kept awake till the nervous irritation of sleeplessness killed him, might not this be murder? Suppose a man kills a sick person intentionally by making a loud noise when sleep gives him a chance of life; or suppose knowing that a man has aneurysm of the heart, his heir rushes into his room and roars in his ear, 'Your wife is dead!' intending to kill and killing him, why are not these acts murder? They are no more 'secret things belonging to God' than the operation of arsenic.

This view now represents the law. Hale's proposition was first modified in *Towers*[385] where D violently assaulted a young girl who was holding a four-and-a-half-month-old child in her arms. The girl screamed loudly, so frightening the baby that it cried till it was black in the face. From that day it had convulsions and died a month later. Denman J held that there was

---

[381] *Causation in the Law*, 337.
[382] But the doctrine of transferred malice (below, p 136) would support such an extension.
[383] Hale, 1 PC, 429; and see East, 1 PC, 225.
[384] Stephen, *Digest*, 217 n 9.
[385] (1874) 12 Cox CC 530.

evidence to go to the jury of manslaughter. In the case of an adult person, he said that murder could not be committed by using language so strong or violent as to cause that person to die:

mere intimidation, causing a person to die from fright by working upon his fancy, was not murder,

but that rule did not apply to a child of such tender years as this:

if the man's act brought on the convulsions or brought them to a more dangerous extent, so that death would not have resulted otherwise, then it would be manslaughter.[386]

This was extended to the case of an adult person by Ridley J in *Hayward*.[387] D, who was in a condition of violent excitement and had expressed his determination to 'give his wife something', chased her from the house into the road using violent threats against her. She fell dead. She was suffering from an abnormal heart condition, such that any combination of physical exertion and fright or strong emotion might cause death. Ridley J directed the jury that no proof of actual physical violence was necessary, but that death from fright alone, caused by an illegal act, such as a threat of violence, was enough. D was unaware of V's condition, and following the general principle above, he must take his victim as found. It is irrelevant to the issue of causation whether the fright is one that would have an effect on a reasonable person or only one of exceptional timidity. D's awareness of the likely effect of his conduct will be a relevant issue in determining his *mens rea*.

4.5.7.2 Killing by perjury

With the abolition of the death penalty, discussion of D 'causing' V's death by giving false testimony leading to V's conviction for a capital crime seems now to be redundant. The principles are discussed in the 10th edition of this book, at 57.

4.5.8 Reform

The Criminal Law Team of the Law Commission produced a working paper on causation in 2002. The proposal was to codify the law as follows:

(1) Subject to subsections (2) to (5), a defendant causes a result which is an element of an offence when –

    (a) he does an act which makes a substantial and operative contribution to its occurrence; or

    (b) he omits to do an act, which he is under a duty to do according to the law relating to the offence, and the failure to do the act makes a substantial and operative contribution to its occurrence.

(2) (a) The finders of fact may conclude that a defendant's act or omission did not make a substantial and operative contribution to the occurrence of a result if compared with the voluntary intervention of another person, unless:

    (i) the defendant is subject to a legal duty to guard against the very harm that the intervention or event causes; and

    (ii) the intervention was not so extraordinary as to be unforeseeable to a reasonable person in the defendant's position; and

    (iii) it would have been practicable for the defendant to have taken steps to prevent the intervention.

    (b) The intervention of another person is not voluntary unless it is:

---

[386] ibid, 533.
[387] (1908) 21 Cox CC 692.

      (i) free, deliberate and informed; and

      (ii) performed or undertaken without any physical participation from the defendant.

(3) (a) The finders of fact may conclude that a defendant's act or omission did not make a substantial and operative contribution to the occurrence of a result if compared with an unforeseeable natural event;

    (b) A natural event is not unforeseeable unless:

      (i) the defendant did not foresee it; and

      (ii) it could not have been foreseen by any reasonable person in the defendant's position.

(4) A person who procures, assists, or encourages another to cause a result that is an element of an offence does not himself cause that result so as to be guilty of the offence as a principal except when –

    (a) section 26(1)(c) applies; or

    (b) the offence itself consists in the procuring, assisting or encouraging another to cause the result.[388]

---

[388] This was referred to in *Williams* [2010] EWCA Crim 2552.

5

The elements of a crime: *mens rea*

5.1 Introduction[1]

In the preceding chapter the *actus reus* or external elements of the offence were examined. This chapter deals with the *mens rea* or mental fault of the accused. An *actus reus* is, in the eyes of the law, a 'bad' thing. It is not necessarily a bad thing in everyone's eyes or even in the eyes of the majority of people. But the law requires us to accept its legal 'badness'. Many people think that, in certain circumstances, mercy killing is morally right. In law it is the *actus reus* of murder, legally very bad indeed.[2] It follows from the fact that an *actus reus* is treated in law as a bad thing that an intention to cause it is, in law, a bad intention, a guilty mind. Similarly, consciously taking an unjustified risk of causing an *actus reus* – that is being reckless whether the *actus reus* be caused – is also a bad state of mind, though less so than intentionally causing the *actus reus*. Inadvertently causing an *actus reus* by failing to take reasonable care – negligence – may also be regarded as legally blameworthy, though still less so. Intention, recklessness and negligence imply different degrees of 'fault' in the criminal law. This is set out concisely and clearly in the Draft Criminal Code Bill, cl 6, which provides:

fault element; means an element of an offence consisting –

  (a) of a state of mind with which a person acts; or

  (b) of a failure to comply with a standard of conduct; or

  (c) partly of such a state of mind and partly of such a failure …

All serious crimes and many minor offences require proof that D had the relevant blameworthy state of mind that is, fault element, but some – which we call 'offences of strict liability' – do not require proof of fault with respect to all the elements of the *actus reus*. For example, in the offence of assault, D must be shown to have caused V to apprehend immediate unlawful personal violence (the *actus reus*) and to have intended or been reckless as to whether his conduct would cause V to apprehend immediate unlawful violence. If D intended V to apprehend violence, but not *immediate* violence, he would be acquitted. The fault element for that part of the *actus reus* would not have been established. Contrast this with a case where D is charged with rape of a child under 13. The prosecution must establish that D penetrated V's vagina,

---

[1] For classic writings (which although largely historical are still pertinent) on the topic, see: J WC Turner, 'The Mental Element in Crimes at Common Law', MACL, 195; G Williams, *The Mental Element in Crime* (1965) and CLGP, in Ch 2; HLA Hart, 'Negligence, *Mens Rea* and Criminal Responsibility', in *Oxford Essays in Jurisprudence* (1961), 29; JC Smith, 'The Guilty Mind in the Criminal Law' (1960) 76 LQR 78; A Ashworth, 'Reason, Logic and Criminal Liability' (1975) 91 LQR 102; G Williams, 'Oblique Intention' [1987] CLJ 417. More recent theoretical analyses include RA Duff, *Intention, Agency and Criminal Liability* (1990); Tadros, *Criminal Responsibility,* esp Chs 8 and 9; A Brudner, *Punishment and Freedom: A Liberal Theory of Penal Justice* (2010) Ch 2.

[2] See *Inglis* [2010] EWCA Crim 2637 and Ch 16 below.

anus or mouth with his penis, and that at the time V was under 13. However, in terms of *mens rea* the prosecution is only required to prove that D intended to penetrate V with his penis. There is no requirement to prove that D knew or was reckless as to V being under 13 – liability as to that element of the *actus reus* relating to age is strict.[3]

The traditional term for the state of mind which must be proved, '*mens rea*', is unfortunately sometimes used by courts to include all degrees of fault, including failure to comply with a standard of conduct – negligence. Frequently the terminology is of no consequence, but it can lead to confusion.[4] In this book we use '*mens rea*' to mean the state of mind (intention, recklessness, knowledge, belief, suspicion, wilfulness, malice, etc), required by the particular crime and 'negligence' to describe failures by the defendant to comply with a prescribed standard of conduct irrespective of his personal state of mind.

5.1.1 Subjective and objective fault

There is an ongoing debate between: (i) 'subjectivists' who assert that, for serious crimes at least, the mental element should require proof that D has personal awareness of his actions and has himself perceived the relevant circumstances and consequences comprising the *actus reus* of the offence; and (ii) 'objectivists', for whom it is sufficient to prove that the reasonable person would have perceived the relevant circumstances/consequences comprising the *actus reus*, irrespective of whether the defendant himself was aware of them. This is, of course, a grossly oversimplistic summary of the competing positions. A more realistic view is that there are shades of subjectivism and objectivism along a spectrum. There are competing claims as to the merits of the approaches, both in terms of their principled foundations and their practical application.[5] Some subjectivists argue that the requirement of personal awareness on the part of D is crucial since it secures respect for the autonomy of the individual: D is punished where he has chosen to act in a way contrary to law. Objectivists point out that D might also be regarded as sufficiently culpable to deserve criminal punishment where his inadvertence related to a substantial and obvious risk of the proscribed harm, which D had the capacity to perceive.

Despite weighty academic opinion that 'the torch of orthodox subjectivism carried by Glanville Williams and Smith and Hogan and then by the Law Commission should be doused',[6] the subjective approach continues to be that favoured by the judiciary, at least in serious crimes, and this has been emphasized recently in the clearest terms from the highest tribunal. In the landmark case of *G*[7] Lord Bingham stated that:

it is a salutary principle that conviction of serious crime should depend on proof not simply that the defendant caused (by act or omission) an injurious result to another but that his state of mind when so acting was culpable. This, after all, is the meaning of the familiar rule *actus non facit reum nisi mens sit rea*. The most obviously culpable state of mind is no doubt an intention to cause the injurious result, but knowing disregard of an appreciated and unacceptable risk of causing an injurious

---

[3] *G* [2008] UKHL 37.

[4] Commentary on *Seaboard Offshore Ltd v Secretary of State for Transport* [1993] Crim LR 611; affd [1994] 2 All ER 99; *Peterssen v RSPCA* [1993] Crim LR 852.

[5] The major proponents of the subjectivist view have been Glanville Williams and Sir John Smith. The subjectivist view has been challenged by prominent academic writers including Andrew Ashworth, POCL; Anthony Duff, *Intention Agency and Criminal Liability* (1990); Alan Norrie, *Crime, Reason and History* (2nd edn, 2000) and Jeremy Horder, see the articles cited below in this chapter. For an excellent account of the positions in the context of manslaughter see LC 237, *Involuntary Manslaughter* (1996) Part IV.

[6] Ashworth (5th edn, 2006), POCL, 253. See also A Norrie, 'Between Orthodox Subjectivism and Moral Contextualism' [2006] Crim LR 486, 487.

[7] [2003] UKHL 50, [2004] 1 AC 1034.

result or a deliberate closing of the mind to such risk would be readily accepted as culpable also. It is clearly blameworthy to take an obvious and significant risk of causing injury to another. But it is not clearly blameworthy to do something involving a risk of injury to another if (for reasons other than self-induced intoxication: *R v Majewski* [1977] AC 443) one genuinely does not perceive the risk. Such a person may fairly be accused of stupidity or lack of imagination, but neither of those failings should expose him to conviction of serious crime or the risk of punishment.[8]

However, despite this strong endorsement of the subjectivist position from the House of Lords, Parliament has demonstrated a willingness to create serious offences in which the fault element is explicitly objective. Recent examples include many sexual offences in the Sexual Offences Act 2003, the Terrorism Acts and some of the money laundering offences in the Proceeds of Crime Act 2002.

5.1.2 *Mens rea* concerns legal not moral guilt

The literal meaning of '*mens rea*' – 'a guilty mind' – is misleading unless it is kept in mind that we are concerned with legal, not moral guilt. A person may – though only in exceptional circumstances – have *mens rea* though neither he, nor any reasonable person, would regard his state of mind as blameworthy.[9] *Mens rea* is the mental element required by the definition of the particular crime – typically, intention to fulfil the *actus reus* of that crime, or recklessness whether it be fulfilled. The word '*rea*' refers to the criminality of the act, not its moral quality. English courts focus on the accused's cognitive state – whether he foresaw risk, etc – rather than whether he was acting in a morally culpable manner.

In *Yip Chiu-cheung*,[10] D was charged with conspiring with E to export drugs from Hong Kong to Australia. E was an undercover drug enforcement officer who was called as a prosecution witness and testified that he made the agreement with D and intended, with the authority of his superiors, to carry it out. He was going to take the drugs to Australia to entrap other drug dealers. It takes two conspirators to make a conspiracy and D's unsuccessful defence was that E was not a conspirator because he lacked *mens rea*. It was held that E *did* have the *mens rea* of conspiracy – that is, an intention to commit the agreed crime. Neither E's good motives nor the superior orders under which he was acting would have been a defence if he had been charged. *Yip* was followed in *Kingston*.[11]

In *Kingston*,[12] D, a paedophile, was charged with indecent assault on a 15-year-old boy, V. D and V had both been drugged surreptitiously by P. P knew of D's tendencies, and he drugged D and V in the hope that D would indecently assault V and that he, P, would be able to video-record the events so as to blackmail D. D did indeed indecently assault V and P video-recorded the events. The House of Lords reinstated D's conviction; simply because blame or moral fault was absent did not mean that the necessary *mens rea* was also absent. Lord Mustill stated that:

Each offence consists of a prohibited act or omission coupled with whatever state of mind is called for by the statute or rule of the common law which creates the offence. In those offences which are not absolute the state of mind which the prosecution must prove to have underlain the act or omission – the 'mental element' – will in the majority of cases be such as to attract disapproval. The mental element will then be the mark of what may properly be called a 'guilty mind'. The professional burglar is guilty

---

[8] Per Lord Bingham at [32].

[9] *Dodman* [1998] 2 Cr App R 338, C-MAC, holding that 'Mens rea does not ... involve blameworthiness', citing the eighth edition of this book and disapproving the *Manual of Air Force Law* (6th edn, 1983) s 69, n 2.

[10] [1995] 1 AC 111.

[11] [1994] 3 WLR 519. See also *Hales* [2005] EWCA Crim 1118, on the difference between intention and motive.

[12] ibid.

in a moral as well as a legal sense; he intends to break into the house to steal, and most would confidently assert that this is wrong. But this will not always be so. In respect of some offences the mind of the defendant, and still less his moral judgment, may not be engaged at all. In others, although a mental activity must be the motive power for the prohibited act or omission the activity may be of such a kind or degree that society at large would not criticize the defendant's conduct severely or even criticize it at all. Such cases are not uncommon. Yet to assume that contemporary moral judgments affect the criminality of the act, as distinct from the punishment appropriate to the crime once proved, is to be misled by the expression 'mens rea', the ambiguity of which has been the subject of complaint for more than a century.[13]

The circumstances of these two cases are exceptional. An *actus reus* generally is, or includes, some very undesirable results – killing, wounding, theft or damage to property, etc – and an intention to cause it is nearly always a state of mind which ordinary people would regard as blameworthy; but moral blameworthiness is not the legal test.

5.2 Forms of *mens rea*

It is generally accepted that the different types of *mens rea* form a hierarchy, with intention and knowledge being the most culpable, followed by recklessness, belief and then by suspicion. There are other specific forms of *mens rea* arising in the context of individual offences, which it is difficult to fit within this hierarchy (eg dishonesty).

5.2.1 Intention[14]

Numerous offences are defined so as to require proof of 'intention' to cause specified results. These commonly include the more serious crimes. It might therefore be expected that the meaning of such a fundamental term would have been settled long ago, but this is not so. The cases are inconsistent, judicial opinion has recently changed and there is still some measure of uncertainty.[15] We may begin, however, with one well-settled proposition. Everyone agrees that a person intends to cause a result if he acts with the purpose of doing so. If D has resolved to kill V and he fires a loaded gun at him with the object of doing so, he intends to kill. It is immaterial that he is aware that he is a poor shot, that V is nearly out of range, and that his chances of success are small. It is sufficient that killing is his object or purpose, that he wants to kill, that he acts in order to kill.[16] Note that the focus is on D's purpose, not his desire[17] or wish as to the consequences. D can intend by having a result as his purpose without desiring

---

[13] At 526.

[14] The literature on this topic is voluminous. Many of the publications are very philosophical. See, *inter alia*, JC Smith, 'Intention in Criminal Law' (1974) 27 CLP 93; Lord Goff, 'The Mental Element in the Crime of Murder' (1988) 104 LQR 30; G Williams, 'The Mens Rea for Murder – Leave it Alone' (1989) 105 LQR 387; J Buzzard, 'Intent' [1978] Crim LR 5 and JC Smith, 'A Reply' [1978] Crim LR 14; AR White, *Misleading Cases* (1991) 47; J Finnis (1993) 109 LQR 329; N Lacey, 'A Clear Concept of Intention' (1993) 56 MLR 621; J Horder, 'Intention in the Criminal Law – A Rejoinder' (1995) 58 MLR 678; N Lacey, 'In(de)terminable Intentions' (1995) 58 MLR 692; MC Kaveny, 'Inferring Intention from Foresight' (2004) 120 LQR 81; I Kugler, *Direct and Oblique Intention in the Criminal Law* (2002); Tadros, *Criminal Responsibility*, Ch 8. See also the discussion in Law Com CP No 177, *A New Homicide Offence for England and Wales* (2006) Chs 3 and 4 (hereafter in this chapter LCCP 177); Law Com Report No 304, *Murder, Manslaughter and Infanticide* (2007) (hereafter in this chapter LC 304); G Coffey (2009) J Crim L 394.

[15] The fact that the main cases defining intention are all murder cases, with the difficult policy issues that offence entails, exacerbates inconsistency and uncertainty. See also the discussion in Tadros, *Criminal Responsibility*, 232.

[16] Duff suggests that this can be ascertained by asking: would D treat his action as a failure if he did not achieve the result? If so, D intended the result. Duff, *Intention, Agency and Criminal Liability*, 61.

[17] The danger of using this term was acknowledged in *Hales* [2005] EWCA Crim 1118 at [28].

it, as where D gives V a lethal injection to put him out of his pain, but wishes he did not have to. Note also that the definition of intention is wider than 'premeditation' where that term is used to denote planning or calculated acts. 'Intention' in English law extends beyond those cases to include spontaneous conduct.[18]

One view is that in law, 'intention' should be limited to the narrow definition of purposive or direct intention. On this view a result should never be regarded as intended unless it was the actor's purpose, that is, unless he acted in order to bring about that result. This is often considered to be the ordinary meaning given to the word.[19] However, the courts have frequently given the word a wider meaning, sometimes described as 'oblique' (as distinct from 'direct') intention.[20] Under this alternative approach, it may be sufficient that D has foreseen the prohibited result as one which is highly probably, or virtually certain to occur, even if achieving that result is not his purpose.[21]

5.2.1.1 Current legal position

The cases in which this issue arises almost always involve murder. The *mens rea* for murder is that D intends to kill or do gbh. The question that recurs is whether D has a sufficient *mens rea* where he does not have as his purpose that V will be killed or caused gbh by his conduct, but he foresees V's death or gbh as probable, or highly probable or virtually certain, to result.

Until relatively recently, the predominant judicial view was that an actor intended a result if he knew that it was a highly probable (or perhaps merely probable) result of his conduct, although it was not his purpose or object to cause that result. In 1979, Lord Diplock in *Hyam v DPP*[22] endorsed this view. A majority of the House in *Hyam* were certainly of the opinion that this was the law. The actual decision was that foresight of high probability of serious bodily harm was a *sufficient mens rea* for murder, not that such a state of mind *necessarily amounted* to an intention to cause serious bodily harm. In *Moloney*,[23] however, the House held that the *mens rea* of murder is intention to cause death or serious bodily harm so it was essential to determine the meaning of 'intention'. *Moloney* must be read in the light of the explanation of it by the House in *Hancock and Shankland*,[24] the Court of Appeal in *Nedrick*[25] and by the House in *Woollin*.[26] The effect of these numerous pronouncements from the appellate courts is that the current state of the law is:

(1) A result is intended when it is the actor's purpose to cause it.

(2) A court or jury *may also find* that a result is intended, though it is not the actor's purpose to cause it, when –

  (a) the result is a virtually certain consequence of that act, and

  (b) the actor knows that it is a virtually certain consequence.

It seems clear that (1) and (2) are distinct forms of intention. In *MD*,[27] the Court of Appeal described the second form of intention – oblique intention – as:

---

[18] See M Kremnitzer, 'On Premeditation' (1998) Buffalo Crim LR 627. LCCP 177 rejects it as an option owing to difficulties of proof.

[19] On the problems of using the ordinary language approach in this context see Lacey (1993) 56 MLR 621.

[20] cf J Bentham, *Principles of Morals and Legislation* (Harrison edn, 2007).

[21] Williams [1987] CLJ 417. See also A Norrie, 'Oblique Intention and Legal Politics' [1989] Crim LR 793; A Norrie, 'Intention – More Loose Talk' [1990] Crim LR 642; RA Duff, 'The Politics of Intention: A Response to Norrie' [1990] Crim LR 637; Tadros, *Criminal Responsibility*, 215–218 and 228–229; Kugler, *Direct and Oblique Intention*, Ch 1.

[22] [1975] AC 55.

[23] [1985] AC 905.

[24] [1986] AC 455.

[25] [1986] 1 WLR 1025.

[26] [1999] AC 82, [1998] Crim LR 890. See LCCP 177, para 4.38.

[27] [2004] EWCA Crim 1391.

designed to help the prosecution fill a gap in the rare circumstances in which a defendant does an act which caused death without the purpose of killing or causing serious injury, but in circumstances where death or serious bodily harm had been a virtual certainty (barring some unforeseen intervention) as a result of the defendant's action and the defendant had appreciated that such was the case. *Woollin* is not designed to make the prosecution's task more difficult, many murderers whose purpose was to kill or cause serious injury would escape conviction if the jury was only [directed under (2) (a) and (b)]. The man who kills another with a gun would be able to escape liability for murder if he could show[28] that he was such a bad shot that death or serious bodily harm was not a virtual certainty or that the defendant had thought that death or serious bodily harm was not a virtual certainty.[29]

5.2.1.2 Difficulties with the present law

The blurring of evidence and substantive law

The fact that the result was a virtually certain consequence of D's act is very good evidence that he knew that it was a virtually certain consequence; but it is difficult to see why it should be regarded as a necessary condition as a matter of substantive criminal law.[30] If D thinks that the result is virtually inevitable, but is making a mistake, surely he intends the result even though it was not, in fact, inevitable? If D fires a gun pointed at V's heart, his intention can hardly be affected by the fact, unknown to D, that V is wearing a bullet-proof vest. D's state of mind is as culpable whether V is wearing the vest or not. The difference is in the external circumstances. This point may not be of great practical importance because the best evidence that D knew that the consequence was virtually certain will be the fact that it *was* virtually certain; but this is not invariably so.

Equally, the fact that a result is virtually certain in fact is not proof of intention – the enquiry into intention is one involving an assessment of D's state of mind. Did he have the result as his purpose or foresee the result as virtually certain? It is easy to lose sight of this. In *Stringer*[31] M, aged 14, was alleged to have started a fire in his family home early one morning and walked off, knowing that five occupants were asleep upstairs. The Court of Appeal upheld the conviction:

if the jury were satisfied (as they must have been) that M started the fire after putting accelerant at the foot of the stairs, that he watched it take hold and then walked away, there *could be only one answer* to the question whether in fact it was a virtual certainty that somebody in the house would suffer really serious harm or death from M's actions. It would be wholly unrealistic to imagine all the occupants escaping from the house by jumping from the upstairs windows without any of them suffering any serious harm. This must have been obvious to any ordinary person at the time. Even taking account of M's age and the fact that his IQ was low/average, the inference that he must have appreciated it on that morning was also overwhelming. On the facts as the jury must have found them, the conclusion that M had the necessary intent was bound to follow.

---

[28] Surely this is a slip and the burden is on the Crown to rebut such a defence?

[29] The extended intention direction is only rarely needed. It is needed where D denies his purpose, not where, eg, D denies any part in the crime: *Phillips* [2004] EWCA Crim 112. The trial judge is best placed to make the decision on the appropriate direction. In *Allen* [2005] EWCA Crim 1344 the Court of Appeal emphasized that it 'is only in an exceptional case that the extended direction by reference to foresight becomes necessary. A case where reference to foresight of the consequences required, if the judge is convinced that, on the facts, and having regard to the way the case has been presented, some further explanation is necessary to avoid misunderstanding' [63]. See also *Hales* [2005] EWCA Crim 1118 at [27]; *Ogunbowale* [2007] EWCA Crim 2739.

[30] This criticism as stated in the 10th edition of this book was acknowledged by the Court of Appeal in *MD* [2004] EWCA Crim 1391.

[31] [2008] EWCA Crim 1222.

In practice that may be true, but strictly there is a difference between finding that the result was virtually certain and finding D foresaw it as such.

'Finding' intention

The second major criticism with the present description of the law offered in *Woollin* concerns the House's use of the phrase, italicized above, 'may also find'. There has been a long-standing debate about whether the descriptions of intention offered in the House of Lords' cases in recent decades define intention exhaustively, or whether they merely describe states of mind which a jury may choose to categorize as intention if they wish. Is D's foresight of a virtually certain result conclusive proof that he intended that result? Or is D's foresight of a virtually certain result merely evidence from which the jury may go on to find that he intended that result, if they wish so to categorize his state of mind?

In *Nedrick*, the Court of Appeal had stated that foresight of virtual certainty is merely evidence *from which intention may be inferred*. On that approach a jury may conclude that D foresaw V's death as virtually certain and yet choose not to treat that as intention. At one point in the judgment in *Woollin* Lord Steyn said that, 'The effect of the critical direction is that a result foreseen as virtually certain *is* an intended result' (emphasis added). That was welcomed by many commentators since it seemed to be an unequivocal statement from the House of Lords that there was no room for any 'finding' of intention by the jury. On a literal reading it ought to follow that once a court or jury was satisfied that D had such foresight, it *must* (not 'may') find that the result was intended by D. Such an approach, equating foresight of virtual certainty with intention would be advantageous, in terms of optimizing the certainty and consistency in application of this important *mens rea* element.

An alternative view was that *Woollin* did leave a degree of flexibility for the jury; the decision of the House of Lords was that the jury 'may' find intention. This suggests there is something further for the jury to decide once they have concluded that D foresaw[32] the result as virtually certain. It has been suggested by, amongst others, Professor Norrie, that a test in which foresight of virtual certainty *was* intention, rather than something from which intention *may* be found, would be over-inclusive and would not reflect the degree of 'moral malevolence' in D's act. The argument is that the jury, having decided that D did foresee some prohibited consequence as certain, should go on to consider whether, in all the circumstances, he was so wicked that an intention to cause the evil should be attributed to him.[33] Although this might enhance the prospects of achieving justice in the individual case, it does little to secure certainty and consistency in general application.

The Court of Appeal remains unwilling to interpret *Woollin* as laying down a clear rule that foresight of virtually certain consequences is intention. In *Matthews and Alleyne*,[34] M and A were convicted of robbery, kidnapping and murder. V was attacked on leaving a club in the early hours of the morning, and ultimately thrown off a bridge 25 feet high into a river 64 feet wide. V, being unable to swim, drowned. A co-accused gave evidence that V had said he could not swim. One ground of appeal against convictions for murder was that the judge had directed the jury that foresight of virtual certainty of consequences *was* intention. The Court of Appeal held that *Woollin* did not reach or lay down such a rule of substantive law; *Woollin* was concerned with the law of evidence. The judge had gone further than permitted.

---

[32] There is a further criticism that the word foresight adds to the confusion. It suggests that D must have a mental picture of the result in his mind, but that is not required. For this reason some prefer the use of the terms 'knowledge or belief', ie that the jury may find intention from D's knowledge or belief that the result will occur. See Tadros, *Criminal Responsibility*, 218–219.

[33] A Norrie, 'After *Woollin*' [1999] Crim LR 532; Norrie, *Crime, Reason and History*, 47–50. See, also, Kugler, *Direct and Oblique Intention*, 17.

[34] [2003] 2 Cr App R 30, [2003] Crim LR 553.

[T]he law has not yet reached a *definition* of intent in murder in terms of appreciation of a virtual certainty…On the contrary, it is clear from the discussion in *Woollin* as a whole that *Nedrick* was derived from the existing law, at that time ending in *Moloney* and *Hancock*, and that the critical direction in *Nedrick* was approved, subject to the change of one word.

The proper direction should have been in the terms from *Woollin* quoted above. However, the court acknowledged that once it was accepted that what was required was appreciation of virtual certainty, and not a lesser foresight of probable consequences, there was very little to choose between evidence and substantive law.

It seems then that following *Woollin*, the jury retain their 'moral elbow room'.[35] A defendant who is found to have (or admits to having) seen the result as virtually certain will not necessarily be found to have intended the result; the jury will have the discretion to find that he did. This is, it is submitted, an unsatisfactory position, leaving undefined a key term of fault applicable in the most serious crimes. The potential for inconsistent decisions on identical facts is stark. Professor Mitchell's empirical work for the Law Commission[36] confirms that the discretionary element in the definition has the potential to impact on the way crimes are investigated and prosecuted. It renders it more difficult to predict accurately the outcome of cases. This approach does not merely pose problems of a practical nature. If this 'moral threshold' test is to be applied to oblique intention so as to save hard cases from conviction, why should it not also apply to direct intention – that is, purpose? The typical mercy-killer acts with the purpose of killing – and his may be the hardest case of all.[37]

Lord Lane CJ recognized the force of the criticism of this aspect of his judgment in *Nedrick* in the debate on the Report of the House of Lords Select Committee on Murder when he stated:

in *Nedrick* the court was obliged to phrase matters as it did because of earlier decisions in your Lordships' House by which it was bound. We had to tread very gingerly indeed in order not to tread on your Lordships' toes. As a result, *Nedrick* was not as clear as it should have been. However, I agree with the conclusions of the committee that 'intention' should be defined in the terms set out in paragraph 195 of the report on page 50. That seems to express clearly what in *Nedrick* we failed properly to explain.[38]

The definition referred to is that stated in cl 18(b) of the Draft Code:

A person acts 'intentionally' with respect to…a result when he acts either in order to bring it about or being aware that it will occur in the ordinary course of events.

In *Woollin*, Lord Steyn, stressing '*will* occur', noted the similarity between the Code and the virtual certainty test. In *Moloney* Lord Bridge gave a notable example of a man who boards a plane which he knows to be bound for Manchester – the last place he wants to be – in order to escape pursuit: by boarding the Manchester plane, the man '*conclusively* demonstrates his intention to go there, because it is a moral certainty that that is where he will arrive'.[39] There is nothing here about this being merely evidence upon which the jury may find intention – intention is *conclusively* demonstrated.[40] Nevertheless, the Court of Appeal in *Matthews and*

---

[35] Horder (1995) 58 MLR 678, 688. V Tadros, 'The Homicide Ladder' (2006) 69 MLR 601, 604, argues that the moral elbow room allows for the jury to convict in cases where D believes that the result will occur where he does not desire it. See also the discussion in LCCP 177, paras 4.43–4.49 and 4.66, and LC 304, para 3.32.

[36] See LCCP 177, *Homicide* (2006) Appendix A; 'Distinguishing between Murder and Manslaughter in Practice' (2007) J Crim L 318.

[37] See *Inglis* [2010] EWCA Crim 2637.

[38] HL paper 78-I, 1989; HL vol 512, col 480, 6 Nov 1989.

[39] [1985] AC 905 at 926 (emphasis in original).

[40] This was the view taken by Ward and Brooke LJJ in *Re A (Conjoined Twins)* [2000] 4 All ER 961.

Alleyne, having been referred to the above passage in the 10th edition of this book, remained unconvinced that the law had yet reached that position.

In summary, aside from the complexity and lack of definition, the present law may be seen by some as too wide in treating as intention those cases in which D has foreseen as a very high probability that a particular consequence will arise, but asserts that that result was not his purpose. The Law Commission proposes a codification of the present law (see below), having provisionally considered and rejected various forms of exhaustive definition.[41]

5.2.1.3 Intention and results known to be a condition of achievement of purpose

It may be said that no one can ever know that a result is certain to follow from an act. This is why courts and writers are driven to speak of 'virtually' or 'morally' or 'almost' certain results. But a person may know that he cannot achieve his purpose, A, without bringing about some other result, B. If he is to bring about A, he knows he must also, at the same time or earlier, bring about B. It may be that, in any other circumstances, he would much rather B did not happen, indeed its occurrence may be abhorrent to him. But, the choice being between (i) going without A and (ii) having A and B, he decides to have A and B. It seems fair to say that he intends to cause B as well as A. Suppose that V has made a will, leaving the whole of his large estate to D. D loves V but he has an overwhelming desire to enjoy his inheritance immediately. If he gives V what he knows to be a fatal dose of poison, he intends to kill V, though he says truthfully that it causes him anguish. Similarly, consider D who wishes to injure his enemy, V, who is standing inside the window of the house of D's friend, Y. If, knowing the window to be closed, D throws the stone through it at V, can it be doubted that he intends to break his friend's window? Since result 'A' is the actor's purpose, it is immaterial that he is not certain that it will happen. He is not a good shot and he knows the stone may miss – but he intends to strike V. And, since he knows that, if he strikes V, it will be because he has broken Y's window, he intends to break the window. It seems from these examples that we might safely say that where D knows or believes a result to be a condition of the achievement of his purpose, D intends it.

Yet even this modest conclusion is not beyond doubt; there are a number of cases in which the generally accepted principles of intention seem to have been qualified in their application by the appellate courts. In *Moloney*,[42] Lord Bridge referred with approval to *Steane*[43] where D, who, during the Second World War in order to save himself and his family from the horrors of the concentration camp, gave broadcasts which would assist the enemy. He was held not to have had an 'intent to assist the enemy'. Steane may have been a loyal citizen who, in other circumstances, would have wished to do nothing to assist the enemy; but, being faced with the choice, 'Assist us – or back to the concentration camp', he chose to assist the enemy. Of course, his purpose was to stay out of the camp; but it seems plain that he knew that his purpose could only be achieved by assisting the enemy. Reading the script was assisting the enemy.[44] There

[41] See LCCP 177; Norrie [2006] Crim LR 486, 495. See below, p 115.

[42] [1985] AC 905 at 929.

[43] [1947] KB 997. See also Duff, *Intention, Agency and Criminal Liability*, 95. For an historical account see GR Rubin, 'New Light on Steane's Case' (2003) 24 Legal History 143.

[44] It might be argued that, even in these circumstances, B is not necessarily a condition of A. Someone might open the window while the stone is in flight towards it. The microphone into which Steane spoke might have been disconnected or the transmitter broken down. Lord Bridge's man who boards the plane for Manchester (the last place he wishes to go) to escape arrest intends (as Lord Bridge says [1985] AC at 986) to go to Manchester although it is possible that the plane will be diverted to Luton. Even in the case of D who gives V the fatal dose of poison to accelerate his inheritance, it is possible that V will die of natural causes before the poison takes effect: cf *White* [1910] 2 KB 124, CCA. See the discussion in Tadros, *Criminal Responsibility*, 219.

are numerous similar cases. In *Ahlers*,[45] a German consul who assisted German nationals to return home after the declaration of war in 1914 was held to have intended only to do his duty as consul. In *Sinnasamy Selvanayagam*,[46] the Privy Council said, *obiter*, that if D remained in occupation of his home in defiance of a lawful order to quit, knowing that the owner of the property would be annoyed, his 'dominant intention' was simply to retain his home and he was not guilty under the Ceylon Penal Code (as it then was) of remaining in occupation with intent to annoy the owner. In *Gillick*'s case,[47] some of the judges seem to have been of the opinion that a doctor, who knew or believed that his provision of contraceptive advice to a girl under 16 would encourage a man to have sexual intercourse with her, would not be guilty of abetting the offence, because his intention was to protect the girl, not to encourage sexual intercourse with her.

In some of these cases, it seems that the concept of intention is strained to do a job for which it is not fitted. The courts appear, in some of these admittedly hard cases, to examine the motives or justifications of the defendant while purporting to be determining his intention. Steane's acquittal would more properly have been based on duress and the case envisaged in *Gillick* seems to have been, in substance, one of necessity – a minor encouragement of sexual intercourse was a lesser evil than an unwanted pregnancy in the young girl.[48] In each of these cases, D had an 'honourable' purpose. Where D's purpose is disreputable, the court is most unlikely to interpret intention so narrowly. If Steane, being a chain smoker deprived of cigarettes, had read the script in order to get a packet, it is probable that Lord Goddard CJ would have had no hesitation in holding that, of course, he intended to assist the enemy. Yet, from the point of view of intention, there seems to be no difference between the cases.[49] If this is so, it produces an undesirable distortion of the concept of intention and it would be better if the true reason for the decision were articulated.[50] *Moloney*, and *Woollin* however, encourage such decisions – the jury appears to be left a measure of discretion to say whether they think the state of mind should be categorized as intention or not.

It is arguable that intention, in law, should extend to results known or believed by the actor to be conditions of the achievement of his purpose but should go no further. This would give effect to the constantly reiterated opinion of the courts that intention is different from desire. If D acts in order to cause 'A' and knows 'B' will follow, 'B' is not desired, at least it is not desired for its own sake; but it is intended. The court can avoid treating this as a case of recklessness as to B. D is not merely taking a risk of causing B; he *knows* or thinks he knows that, if he achieves his aim of causing 'A', 'B' will happen or will have already happened.

5.2.1.4 Results known or believed to be virtually certain to accompany achievement of purpose

Result B may also be intended, according to *Moloney*, where B is not a condition of A. It is possible for A (D's purpose) to occur without B also happening, but as D knows, causing A is

---

[45] [1915] 1 KB 616.

[46] [1951] AC 83.

[47] *Gillick v West Norfolk and Wisbech Area Health Authority* [1986] AC 112, [1986] Crim LR 113, HL and commentary. See also *Salford Health Authority, ex p Janaway* [1989] AC 537.

[48] See now the Sexual Offences Act 2003, s 73, below p 755.

[49] Williams, *The Mental Element in Crime*, 21.

[50] For consideration of the importance of the role of motive in defining intention, see Norrie, *Crime, Reason and History,* 36 et seq; D Husak, *The Philosophy of Criminal Law* (2010) Ch 2; Tadros, *Criminal Responsibility*, 202. After a lengthy philosophical account, Tadros concludes that D's intention must be motive-related. He suggests that where D does X believing that in doing X, D will also do Y, if Y is a reason that motivated D to do X, D intends Y. If D believes that Y was a reason against him doing X despite which he still did X, D intentionally did Y, although he did not intend to do Y (at p 225). The courts are best avoiding such sophistications.

virtually certain to cause B as well. D, wishing to collect the insurance on a cargo (result A), puts a time bomb in a plane to blow up in the mid-Atlantic. He has no wish to kill the crew. It is *possible* for the plane and cargo to be destroyed and the crew to escape – people do occasionally fall from aircraft at great heights and survive – but the possibility is so remote as to be negligible; and D knows that.[51] There is certainly a strong argument for saying that he intends to kill. This is so even if, as D knows, this type of bomb has a 50 per cent failure rate. There is an even chance that nothing will happen. But he wants the explosion (result A) to happen and, if it does, killing (result B) is, as he knows, a virtual certainty. So a jury may (not must) find that there is an intention to kill.[52]

The difficulty is that once we depart from absolute certainty, there is a question of degree and an uncertain boundary between intention and recklessness. In *Hyam*,[53] D, in order to frighten Mrs Booth, her rival for the affections of X, put blazing newspaper through the letter box of Booth's house and caused the death of two of her children. Ackner J directed the jury that D was guilty of murder if she knew that it was highly probable that her act would cause at least serious bodily harm. The jury convicted so they clearly found that she did know that. In the light of *Moloney*, that direction was wrong (foresight of virtual certainty is required before a jury can find intention) but Lord Bridge[54] thought that, on a proper direction, no reasonable jury could have failed to convict Hyam. Is that really so? Might not a jury have been satisfied that D knew that serious injury to occupants was a highly probable result without being satisfied that she knew it was virtually certain?

In *Moloney*,[55] Lord Hailsham and Lord Bridge put the case of a terrorist who plants a time bomb in a public building and gives a warning to enable the public to be evacuated. He knows that it is virtually certain that a bomb disposal squad will attempt to defuse the bomb. The squad does so, the bomb explodes and a member of the squad is killed. It is assumed that this is murder.[56] The bomber intends to endanger the squad's lives (because he knows that it is virtually certain they will attempt to defuse the bomb) but he does not, surely, know that it is virtually certain that one of them will be killed or even seriously injured. It is doubtful if this would be murder even under the 'highly probable' formula of *Hyam*. It looks like recklessness, which is not enough for murder. The example might be justified if it could be proved that the terrorist wants the bomb to go off *at a time* when he knows it is virtually certain that the squad will be attempting to defuse it. That would be indistinguishable from the 'bomb-in-the-plane' case, above, where the bomber wants the bomb to go off in the mid-Atlantic.

In *Moloney*, D shot his stepfather, whom he loved, when, in the course of a drunken game to establish who was quicker 'on the draw' with loaded shotguns, he pulled the trigger in response to a challenge, 'if you have [the guts] pull the trigger'. He may not have realized that the gun was aimed, at point-blank range, at V's head. His conviction was quashed because the judge misdirected the jury that D intended serious bodily harm if he foresaw that it would 'probably' happen. Lord Bridge insisted on the need for 'a moral certainty', a probability which is 'little short of overwhelming' and an act that 'will lead to a certain event

---

[51] This and the example in n 55, below, have prompted a voluminous literature, see A Pedain, 'Intention and the Terrorist Example' [2003] Crim LR 579 and references therein. Kaveny (2004) 120 LQR 81 argues that in the virtual certainty cases D's gross disregard for human life justifies D's conviction as a murderer.

[52] cf the view of I Kugler, 'Conditional Oblique Intention' [2004] Crim LR 284, seemingly suggesting that the question will depend on whether D has a guilty motive or Parliament's motive in creating an offence of that form or the degree of harm actually caused. It is difficult to see how these issues affect D's intention in substantive law.

[53] [1975] AC 55.

[54] [1985] AC at 926.

[55] [1985] AC at 913, 927.

[56] cf A Pedain [2003] Crim LR 579, suggesting that this is a form of intent because of D's 'motive'. Pedain argues that the terrorist in these cases is sufficiently morally culpable because of his willingness to risk another's death such that he can properly be regarded as having a direct intent for murder.

unless something unexpected supervenes to prevent it'.[57] Unfortunately, in summing up his opinion in the form of guidelines for trial judges, he used the term, 'natural consequence', to mean a consequence that is virtually certain to ensue.

In *Hancock and Shankland*,[58] two striking miners pushed from the parapet of a bridge heavy concrete blocks which struck a taxi taking a working miner to work and killed the taxi-driver. They said they intended to push the blocks on to the middle lane, not the inside lane in which the taxi was travelling, and that they intended to frighten the working miner and prevent him going to work, but not to hurt anyone. At their trial for murder, the judge closely followed the *Moloney* 'guidelines'. The Court of Appeal held that the conviction must be quashed. The guidelines were defective. The jury might well have understood 'natural consequence' to mean 'direct consequence' and not to convey the notion of moral certainty or overwhelming probability of which Lord Bridge spoke. The House of Lords agreed. Both courts stressed that even awareness that the consequence is virtually certain is not intention, but only evidence from which a jury may infer intention, if they are satisfied beyond reasonable doubt that this is the right inference. The difficulties with this approach are considered above.

5.2.1.5 Intention in crimes other than murder

Nearly all the leading cases relate to murder and Lord Steyn prefaced his decision in *Woollin* by remarking that 'intent' does not necessarily have precisely the same meaning in every context of the criminal law.

Earlier the House in *Moloney* said that they were laying down the law not only for murder but for offences requiring 'specific intent' generally (which, here, seems to mean merely offences requiring intent). The approval in *Moloney* of cases like *Steane* and the difficulty of reconciling the illustration of the bomber with intention as defined in that case suggests that the word may well be held to bear different shades of meaning in different contexts. Sometimes the context may indicate a narrower meaning – that nothing less than purpose will do. This may be the explanation of *Steane*, though that decision has been regularly cited in murder cases. A strong case can be made that the very nature of an attempt involves purpose, and that 'intent' in the Criminal Attempts Act[59] should be construed accordingly. The Draft Criminal Code recognizes that the context may require some modification of its proposed definition. But, while the context may require a narrower meaning, it is submitted that a court should be slow to give the term a narrower one. *Woollin* draws a clear line between intention and recklessness and it is desirable to preserve that clarity throughout the criminal law.

5.2.1.6 Intention as to conduct and circumstances

An act may be intentional with respect to circumstances as well as consequences. Intention here means either hope that the circumstance exists – which corresponds to purpose in relation to consequences – or knowledge (or belief that it is virtually certain) that the circumstance exists – which corresponds to foresight of certainty in relation to consequences.

> He who steals a letter containing a cheque, intentionally steals the cheque also if he hopes that the letter may contain one, even though he well knows that the odds against the existence of such a circumstance are very great.[60]

If D receives a car which he knows to be stolen, that is an intentional handling of stolen goods even though D would, perhaps, much prefer that the car was not stolen. If, however, D believed

---

[57] [1985] AC at 925, 926, 929. See recently *R(Tait) v CICAP* [2010] RTR 6.

[58] [1986] AC 455.

[59] Below, p 405. See LCCP, *Conspiracy and Attempts* (2007) para 14.27; LC 318.

[60] J Salmond, *Jurisprudence* (11th edn, 1957) 411 see below, p 128.

merely that it was probable, or highly probable, that the car was stolen, this would not be an intentional handling. He neither hoped it was stolen, nor knew it was.

5.2.1.7 Reform[61]

The definition in cl 18(b) of the Draft Code provides:

A person acts 'intentionally' with respect to . . . a result when he acts either in order to bring it about or being aware that it will occur in the ordinary course of events.

There were two possible defects in the definition proposed in the Draft Code: (i) It did not provide for the case where D knows that the relevant result will occur if, but only if, he succeeds in achieving some other purpose[62] and he is not certain that he will achieve that other purpose. This is exemplified by the case of the bomb with the 50 per cent failure rate.[63] (ii) In certain, admittedly rather unlikely, circumstances, the definition might mean that a person intended a result which it was his purpose to avoid – which does not seem to be very good sense. The starkest example is that of D who throws his child from the upper window of a burning house when he believes that death from the flames is inevitable.[64]

To avoid these difficulties, the Law Commission[65] proposed a definition of intention for the purposes of non-fatal offences against the person which, slightly modified, was included in the draft Bill, cl 14(1) in the Home Office Consultation Paper of February 1998:[66]

. . . a person acts intentionally with respect to a result if –

(a) it is his purpose to cause it; or

(b) although it is not his purpose to cause it, he knows that it would occur in the ordinary course of events if he were to succeed in his purpose of causing some other result.

Woollin, however, shows that this may be too narrow. D lost his temper and threw down his three-month-old son on to a hard surface, killing him. The Crown did not contend that his purpose was to kill or cause serious injury. He was convicted of murder on a direction that it was enough that he knew there was a 'substantial risk' that he would cause serious injury. His conviction was upheld by the Court of Appeal but quashed by the House of Lords. Even if Woollin knew that serious bodily injury was certain, he would not have an intention to cause it within cl 14 – it was not his purpose and he had no other purpose, except to vent his anger, which is not a purpose to cause a result. To meet this point it was suggested that the clause should be amended to read '. . . he knows that it *will occur in the ordinary course of events, or* that it would do so if he were to succeed in his purpose of causing some other result'. The Law Commission more recently rejected that suggestion on the ground that it presents problems where the result is the very thing that D is seeking to avoid (as in the case of the burning house and the father who throws his child to her virtually certain death).[67]

---

[61] See the discussion in LCCP 177, para 4.22.

[62] Above, p 113.

[63] Above, n 51.

[64] As to whether this is properly seen as a case of intention where a defence of necessity should apply, see the discussion at p 112. See also LCCP 177, para 4.26; Norrie [2006] Crim LR 486, 495.

[65] LC 218, paras 7.1–7.14 and cl 1 of draft Bill, following LCCP 122 (1992) paras 5.4–5.11 and JC Smith, 'A Note on Intention' [1990] Crim LR 85.

[66] JC Smith, 'Offences Against the Person: The Home Office Consultation Paper' [1998] Crim LR 317. See also A Khan, 'Intention in the Criminal Law: Time to Change' (2002) 23 Stat LR 235.

[67] LCCP 177, paras 4.26 and 4.42–4.44.

Parliament has accepted in one context at least that a person has intention in relation to a consequence where he means to cause the consequences or is aware that it will occur in the ordinary course of events.[68]

The Law Commission's homicide review led them to consider a number of proposals in relation to intention,[69] finally settling on one retaining the flexibility inherent in the present law (and the moral elbow room it provides):[70]

(1) A person should be taken to intend a result if he or she acts in order to bring it about.

(2) In cases where the judge believes that justice may not be done unless an expanded understanding of intention is given, the jury should be directed as follows: an intention to bring about a result may be found if it is shown that the defendant thought that the result was a virtually certain consequence of his or her action.

This definition removes the unnecessary requirement that the result was a virtual certainty.

5.2.1.8 The distinction between motive and intention

If D causes an *actus reus* with *mens rea*, he is guilty of the crime and on the orthodox view it is entirely irrelevant to his guilt that he had a good motive.[71] The mother who kills her disabled and suffering child out of motives of compassion is just as guilty of murder as is the person who kills for gain or hatred. On the other hand, if either the *actus reus* or the *mens rea* of any crime is lacking, no motive, however evil, will make a person guilty of a crime. The orthodox view that motive should not be confused with *mens rea* has come under challenge.[72] An American writer has argued:[73]

Suppose a grave felony is about to be committed under such circumstances that the killing of the offender to prevent the crime would be justified by law, and at that very moment he is shot and killed. If the slayer was prompted by the impulse to promote the social security by preventing the felony he is guilty of no offence; if he had no such impulse but merely acted upon the urge to satisfy an old grudge by killing a personal enemy, he is guilty of murder. The intent is the same in either case – to kill the person; the difference between innocence and guilt lies in the motive which prompted this intent.

It is submitted, however, that (assuming that D knew of the facts which justified the killing) this view is contrary to principle. If it were correct, it would seem to follow that D, the public executioner, would be guilty of murder in hanging X, who had been condemned to death by a competent court, if it were shown that D had postponed his retirement to carry

---

[68] See the International Criminal Courts Act 2001, s 66(3)(a).

[69] In LCCP 177 Ch 4, the Commission offered two models for consideration, one based on the clauses above, and one seeking to codify the common law position as set out in *Woollin*. The proposed revision of cl 18(b)(ii), to provide a definition of 'intentionally' for the offence of murder, was as follows: Subject to the proviso set out below: a person acts 'intentionally' with respect to a result when he or she acts either: (1) in order to bring it about, or (2) knowing that it will be virtually certain to occur; or (3) knowing that it would be virtually certain to occur if he or she were to succeed in his or her purpose of causing some other result. Proviso: a person is not to be deemed to have intended any result, which it was his or her specific purpose to avoid. Objections levelled at this provision by Norrie [2006] Crim LR 486 included that it concealed a defence of necessity.

[70] Academics tended to favour a full definition and practitioners and judges favoured the codification proposal adopting the present law (LC 304, para 3.17).

[71] See *A-G's Reference (No 1 of 2002)* [2002] EWCA Crim 2392, where D, a police officer, was prepared to fabricate evidence to convict a person who was factually guilty. Her 'good' motive was not an excuse for perverting the course of justice. It may affect sentence: *Inglis* [2010] EWCA Crim 2637.

[72] See Wilson, *Central Issues*, Ch 5; Norrie, *Crime, Reason and History*, 35–43; Norrie, *Punishment, Responsibility and Justice*, 170–181; J Horder, 'On the Irrelevance of Motive in Criminal Law', in Horder (ed), *Oxford Essays in Jurisprudence*; Tadros, *Criminal Responsibility*, Ch 8.

[73] RM Perkins and RN Boyce, *Criminal Law* (3rd edn, 1982) 930.

out this particular execution because he had a grudge against X and derived particular pleasure from hanging him. This can hardly be the law. If a surgical operation, though dangerous to life, is clearly justifiable on medical grounds, a surgeon who performs it with all proper skill cannot be said to be guilty of attempted murder, or, if the patient dies, murder, because he hopes the patient will die so that he can marry his wife, or inherit his property, or so that the patient will avoid the thoroughly miserable life he will face if he survives.[74]

One of the difficulties in determining the relevance of motive in criminal law lies in the ambiguity of language. Sometimes, when we speak of motive, we mean an emotion such as jealousy or greed, and sometimes we mean a species of intention. For example, D intends (i) to put poison in his uncle's tea, (ii) to cause his uncle's death, and (iii) to inherit his money. We would normally say that (iii) is his motive. Applying our test of intention, above, (iii) is certainly also intended but, the reason why it is considered merely a motive is that it is a consequence ulterior to the *mens rea* and the *actus reus*; it is no part of the crime. If this criterion as to the nature of motive be adopted then it follows that motive, by definition, is irrelevant to criminal responsibility – that is, a person may be lawfully convicted of a crime whatever his motive may be, or even if he has no motive. The courts are not always consistent in their terminology. If D dismisses E, an employee, who has given evidence against him, in accordance with the terms of E's contract, D will be guilty of contempt of court, it is said, if his 'motive' was to punish E for his evidence but not if it was for any other reason – for example, incompetence or redundancy.[75] A desire for consistency in terminology would suggest that in such a case we should speak of intent or purpose rather than motive. For example, if this variety of contempt were to be defined, the definition might say, 'with intent to punish the witness'.

In some exceptional cases motive does form an element of an offence. A conspicuous example is the series of 'racially aggravated offences' created by the Crime and Disorder Act 1998. Any of the existing offences specified in the Act[76] becomes a new racially aggravated offence with an enhanced penalty if, *inter alia*, 'the offence is motivated (wholly or partly) by hostility towards members of a racial group, based on their membership of that group'. In blackmail, contrary to the Theft Act 1968, s 21,[77] the accused's motive may be relevant in ascertaining whether his demand was unwarranted.[78] There are other circumstances in which motive may be relevant to the offence (for example, dishonesty) or defence (for example, revenge denies a defence of loss of self-control).[79]

As *evidence*, motive is always relevant.[80] This means simply that, if the prosecution can prove that D had a motive for committing the crime, they may do so since the existence of a motive makes it more likely that D in fact did commit it. People do not usually act without a motive.

In *sentencing*, motive is again important. When the law allows the judge a discretion in sentencing, he will obviously be more leniently disposed towards the convicted person who acted with a good motive.

---

[74] See ATH Smith in *Reshaping the Criminal Law*, 95.

[75] *A-G v Butterworth* [1963] 1 QB 696, [1962] 3 All ER 326, CA. cf *Rooney v Snaresbrook Crown Court* (1978) 68 Cr App R 78, [1979] Crim LR 109.

[76] See below, p 658.

[77] See below, Ch 26.

[78] cf *Adams*, below, p 495; *Chandler v DPP* [1964] AC 763.

[79] This restriction is made explicit in the new defences discussed in Ch 15.

[80] *Williams* (1986) 84 Cr App R 299, CA, not following *Berry* (1986) 83 Cr App R 7.

5.2.2 Recklessness

For many crimes, either intention to cause the proscribed result or recklessness as to whether that result is caused is sufficient to impose liability. A person who does not intend to cause a harmful result may take an unjustifiable risk of causing it. If he does so, he may be held to be reckless. Unjustifiably taking risks in conduct which might harm others is culpable behaviour. In some scenarios if we factor in the justifications for the conduct we might even say that some cases of intended action are less culpable than those involving recklessness.[81]

Not all risk-taking constitutes recklessness. Sometimes the accused will have identified a risk and rejected it as being so negligible as to be a reasonable one to take.[82] In other circumstances, the risk may have been rightly recognized to be much greater, but the social utility of the action justifies taking it.[83]

It can be justifiable to take a risk of causing harm to another's property or his person or even of causing his death. The operator of an aircraft, the surgeon performing an operation and the promoter of a tightrope act in a circus must all know that their conduct might cause death but none of them would properly be described as reckless unless the risk he took was an unreasonable one. The law allows the use of reasonable force in the lawful arrest of an offender or in private defence. If D forces V's car off the road, that cannot be reckless driving if it was reasonable to use that degree of force lawfully to arrest V.[84] If D, doing an act of reasonable self-defence, damages V's window, he is not guilty of reckless criminal damage.[85]

Whether it is justifiable to take a risk depends on the social value of the activity involved relative to the probability and the gravity of the harm which might be caused. The question is whether the risk was one which a reasonable and prudent person might have taken. It might be reasonable for D to shoot V's ferocious dog which is attacking his sheep, but it does not follow that it would be reasonable to take a risk of causing injury or death to V – still less a bystander, X. This element of the test is objective – that is to say, the court or jury lays down the required standard of care.

What degree of risk? It is impossible to say in general terms that recklessness requires any particular degree of probability of the occurrence of the harm in question.[86] If the conduct has no social utility – for example, a game of 'Russian roulette' or an armed robbery – the slightest possibility of any harm should be enough. If the act has a high degree of social utility – for example, the performance of a surgical operation – then only a very high degree of probability of grave harm that outweighs the social utility will suffice to condemn it as reckless.[87]

5.2.2.1 Subjective recklessness and malice

To establish recklessness it is necessary in all cases to show that D took an unjustifiable risk; but the prosecution must go further. The standard test of recklessness – traditionally called

---

[81] See, eg, the discussion in Kugler, *Direct and Obligue Intention*, 27. Considering D1 who intentionally terminates V's life to spare him pain, compared to D2 who shoots at an apple on V's head and misses, killing V.

[82] In LC 304 the definition of recklessness for the purposes of the Law Commission's proposed second degree murder requires awareness of a serious risk, where seriousness does not denote the degree of risk, but that the risk is one that should not be ignored. See LC 304, para 3.39.

[83] For discussion of the relative moral culpability of these two scenarios, see W Wilson, 'The Structure of Criminal Homicide' [2006] Crim LR 471; J Rogers, 'The Law Commission's Proposed Restructuring of the Law of Homicide' (2006) 70 J Crim L 223.

[84] *Renouf* [1986] 1 WLR 522.

[85] *Sears v Broome* [1986] Crim LR 461, DC.

[86] See *Vehicle Inspectorate v Nuttall* [1999] 1 WLR 629.

[87] See A Norrie, 'Subjectivism, Objectivism and the Limits of Criminal Recklessness' (1992) 12 OJLS 45; PH Robinson, 'The Modern General Part: Three Illusions' in S Shute and A Simester (eds), *Criminal Law Theory* (2002) 88–91.

'*Cunningham*' recklessness after the case of that name – requires not only proof of a taking of an unjustified risk, but proof that D was aware of the existence of the unreasonable risk. It is a subjective form of *mens rea*, focused on D's own cognition of the existence of a risk.

In *Cunningham*,[88] D tore a gas meter from the wall of the cellar of an unoccupied house to steal the money in it. He left the gas gushing out. It seeped into a neighbouring house and was inhaled by V whose life was endangered. D was convicted under s 23 of the Offences Against the Person Act 1861[89] of maliciously administering a noxious thing so as to endanger life. Because the judge directed the jury that 'malicious' meant simply 'wicked', D's conviction was quashed. The Court of Criminal Appeal quoted with approval the principle first propounded by Kenny in 1902.[90]

... in any statutory definition of a crime 'malice' must be taken not in the old vague sense of 'wickedness' in general, but as requiring either (i) an actual intention to do the particular *kind* of harm that in fact was done, or (ii) recklessness as to whether such harm should occur or not (ie the accused has foreseen that the particular kind of harm might be done, and yet has gone on to take the risk of it). It is neither limited to, nor does it indeed require, any ill-will towards the person injured.

The court reiterated: 'In our opinion, the word "maliciously" in a statutory crime postulates foresight of consequence.' Cunningham was not guilty unless *he* was aware, when he broke off the gas meter, or left the broken pipe with the gas gushing out,[91] that it might be inhaled by someone. In cases requiring 'malice' it is not sufficient that, if D had stopped to think, it would have been obvious to him that there was a risk. He must actually recognize the existence of the risk and deliberately take it. In a series of cases, of which the most important is *Parmenter*,[92] convictions of malicious wounding have been quashed because trial judges directed the jury that it was enough that D 'should have foreseen' the risk[93] thus leading the jury to think that it is enough that D ought to have foreseen. It is not. To be 'malicious', D must actually foresee some harm and the fact that he ought to have foreseen is, at best, some evidence that he did foresee.

In *Cunningham*, the court was considering the requirement of 'malice', a form of recklessness, but the definition in *Cunningham* applies generally to crimes of recklessness.[94]

It is well established that where D closes his mind to the risk he can be found reckless within the subjective definition, as where he claims that his extreme anger blocked out of his mind the risk involved in his action.[95] As Lord Lane put it, 'Knowledge or appreciation of a risk of the [proscribed harm] must have entered the defendant's mind even though he may have suppressed it or driven it out.'[96]

In the landmark case of *G* Lord Bingham based his definition of recklessness for the Criminal Damage Act 1971 on the Draft Criminal Code, cl 18(c):

---

[88] [1957] 2 QB 396.

[89] Below, p 673.

[90] *Outlines* (16th edn, 1952) 186.

[91] See on omissions, above, p 65.

[92] [1992] 1 AC 699, [1991] 4 All ER 698 at 706, HL.

[93] The trial judges fell into error by taking the words of Diplock LJ out of their context in *Mowatt* [1968] 1 QB 421 at 426.

[94] In one sense the definition in *Cunningham* is defective since it fails to make explicit that not only must D foresee the risk of the proscribed harm, but he must take it *unjustifiably* as discussed above, p 118.

[95] *Parker* [1977] 1 All ER 475 (D slammed phone down in anger and broke it).

[96] *Stephenson* [1979] QB 695, 704. See also the comments of Lord Bingham in *G* [2004] 1 AC 1034 at [39] and Lord Steyn at [58]. As a more striking example see *Booth* [2006] EWHC 192 (Admin), where D damaged V's car when he was knocked down by V. D was convicted of criminal damage since he was reckless as to the damage having seen the risk of being knocked down and closed his mind to that risk.

A person acts recklessly within the meaning of section 1 of the Criminal Damage Act 1971 with respect to –

(i) a circumstance when he is aware of a risk that it exists or will exist;

(ii) a result when he is aware of a risk that it will occur;

and it is, in the circumstances known to him, unreasonable to take the risk.

It is submitted that this subjective definition of recklessness ought to be applied in all statutory offences of recklessness unless Parliament has explicitly provided otherwise.[97] In *A-G's Reference (No 3 of 2003)*,[98] the Court of Appeal emphasized that although the House of Lords in *G* had stated that their decision was one specifically on recklessness under the Criminal Damage Act, 'general principles were laid down'. It was established that a defendant could not be culpable under the criminal law of doing something involving a risk of injury to another or damage to property if he genuinely did not perceive the risk.[99] The court refused to restrict the application of *G* to cases of positive action rather than those where liability arose by D's omission, and applied the subjective test to D's foresight of circumstances as well as consequences.[100]

Foresight of 'a' risk

It is only necessary for D to foresee *a* risk of the proscribed harm. In *Brady*,[101] D was drunk when he climbed on railings at a nightclub and fell onto the dance floor below causing serious injuries to V who was dancing there. The issue at trial was whether D inflicted the injury *maliciously*. D argued that the effect of the decision in *G*[102] was to require the jury to be directed that the Crown had to establish that D had foreseen 'an obvious and significant risk' of injury to another by his actions, or else that he would have done so had he been sober. The Court of Appeal rejected that argument. *G* does not require proof that D had foreseen 'an obvious and significant risk' in order to establish that he had acted recklessly; and it followed that there was no need for a trial judge directing a jury as to malice or recklessness to qualify the word 'risk' by the words obvious and significant. The court was surely right to reject this argument: to introduce a requirement that the risk was 'obvious and significant' would create uncertainty and complexity in an area of *mens rea* which desperately does not need it. The question would certainly arise whether the requirement was to prove that the degree of risk was 'obvious and significant', or whether that qualifying expression related to the consequences should the risk eventuate.[103]

---

[97] cf the offences relating to the Uranium Enrichment Technology (Prohibition on Disclosure) Regulations 2004, SI 1818, made under the Anti-terrorism Crime and Security Act 2001, s 80(2) where an objective form of recklessness is expressly adopted. For an argument that the *Caldwell* test applies in some consumer offence see Professor Cartwright in Appendix B to Law Commission Consultation Paper 195, *Criminal Liability in Regulatory Contexts* (2010) para B17.

[98] [2004] 2 Cr App R 367.

[99] [12].

[100] See also *Mbagwu* [2007] EWCA Crim 1068, where Hughes LJ noted at [20], 'the element of recklessness necessarily meant that the Defendant in question would have to be shown to be reckless in the sense understood in *Cunningham* (1957) 41 Cr App Rep 155. As is well known, recklessness in that sense requires (*and indeed these days in every sense requires*) that it be shown that the Defendant in question actually foresaw some harm to such a person' (emphasis added).

[101] [2006] EWCA Crim 2413. The trial judge's direction on the recklessness test was also flawed in not referring to the second limb – not only must the jury find that the accused personally saw a risk of the relevant harm, but that he went on *unreasonably* to take that risk.

[102] *G* [2004] 1 AC 1034.

[103] Difficulties with a similar qualification were experienced when the House of Lords in *Lawrence* [1982] AC 626 held that in reckless driving the risk must be an obvious and 'serious' one. On the difficulties of that aspect of

5.2.2.2 The rise and fall of objective recklessness

The *Cunningham*, subjective, approach to recklessness or 'advertent recklessness' as it is also called, was the accepted definition until a controversial, and, it is now accepted, erroneous turn by the House of Lords in the 1980s. Although the House of Lords has recently restored orthodoxy by affirming that the definition of recklessness is as stated in *Cunningham*, set out above, it is valuable to examine, briefly,[104] the temporary shift of English law towards objective recklessness in some offences.

Caldwell v MPC[105]

It was accepted that the *Cunningham* definition of recklessness applied, *inter alia*, to the offences of damaging property under the Malicious Damage Act 1861. The Law Commission in its Report on Criminal Damage[106] made many proposals for the reform of that law but considered that the mental element, as interpreted in *Cunningham*, was satisfactory. In relation to the *mens rea* it proposed only that it be 'expressed with greater simplicity and clarity' and that this should be achieved by using 'intentionally or recklessly' in place of the archaic and misleading term 'maliciously'. Parliament adopted the proposals in the Criminal Damage Act 1971. Unfortunately, the Commission proposed no definition of recklessness and the Act contains none. It was assumed that the definition under *Cunningham* would apply. The Court of Appeal held, though after some hesitation, that 'reckless' in the 1971 Act bore the *Cunningham* meaning. But in 1981, the House of Lords decided in *Caldwell*[107] (Lords Wilberforce and Edmund-Davies dissenting) and in *Lawrence*[108] that, where the statute uses the word 'reckless', a different test applied. In *Caldwell* Lord Diplock said that a person is reckless as to whether any property would be destroyed or damaged:

... if (1) he does an act which in fact creates an obvious risk that property would be destroyed or damaged and (2) when he does the act he (i) either has not given any thought to the possibility of there being any such risk or (ii) has recognized that there was some risk involved and has nonetheless gone on to do it.

Under both limbs (i) and (ii) of the direction, as formulated, it had to be proved that the risk taken was an 'obvious [and serious[109]] risk'. The further element of culpability was either –

(1) D's failure to give thought to whether there was 'such a risk' (which might be designated 'inadvertent recklessness'); or

(2) D's knowledge that there was 'some risk' ('advertent recklessness').

This represented a very different test to that in *Cunningham*.[110] It was sufficient to convict D for an offence to which the *Caldwell* recklessness test applied where the reasonable person

---

that test see: G Williams, 'Recklessness Redefined' [1981] CLJ 252, 276; J Brabyn, 'A Sequel to Seymour, Made in Hong Kong' [1987] Crim LR 84 at 90–91.

[104] For a full examination and compelling critique of the *Caldwell* definition and its implications, see the 10th edition of this book, and the references cited therein.

[105] [1982] AC 341. See, especially, EJ Griew, 'Reckless Damage and Reckless Driving – Living with *Caldwell* and *Lawrence*' [1981] Crim LR 743; J McEwan and J Robilliard, 'Recklessness: the House of Lords and the Criminal Law' (1981) 1 LS 267; G Syrota, 'A Radical Change in the Law of Recklessness?' [1982] Crim LR 97; G Williams [1981] CLJ 252; G Williams, 'The Unresolved Problem of Recklessness' (1988) 8 LS 74.

[106] LC 29 (1970), confirming proposals in Working Paper No 23 (1969).

[107] [1982] AC 341.

[108] [1982] AC 510. For discussion of these decisions see also the commentaries at [1981] Crim LR 393 and 410.

[109] According to the definition in *Lawrence*, decided in the House on the same day.

[110] The difference can be seen by considering post-*G* cases applying *Cunningham* to overturn convictions where the direction had, erroneously, been based on *Caldwell*: eg, *Castle* [2004] All ER (D) 289 (Oct); *Cooper* [2004] EWCA Crim 1382.

would have seen the risk even if D did not, nor even where D could not see the risk because of some limitation in his capacity.[111]

The 'model direction' contained inconsistencies and lacked precision,[112] in particular it left the knotty question whether there was a loophole or lacuna: D would not be reckless if he had considered the matter and decided that there was no risk. It was questionable whether such an individual was any less culpable than one who had given no thought (and who was therefore guilty).[113] There were also more principled objections to the test. First, it resulted in an indefensible distinction in law between the tests of recklessness applicable to various offences. To take an example based on *W (A Minor) v Dolbey*,[114] if D took an air rifle and, not even considering the possibility that it might be loaded (as was the fact), aimed and fired it at V, breaking V's spectacles and destroying his eye, D would, under *Caldwell*, have been be liable for recklessly causing criminal damage to the spectacles but would not have been criminally liable at all for the destruction of the eye because that offence imposes a test of subjective recklessness. The law appeared to give greater protection to spectacles than to eyes.

Secondly, it failed to respect the principle that for serious crimes at least, the defendant should be proved to have a culpable *state of mind*. *Caldwell* allowed for conviction on the basis of D having no state of mind as to the risk of the proscribed harm. This most significant principled failing of the *Caldwell* approach was its potential to create injustice, and this led, ultimately, to its downfall. The test worked harshly in cases of young people and those whose capacity to see risk was diminished for reasons which involved no fault on their part. It was sufficient that the reasonable person would have foreseen the risk even if D did not or could not because of his lack of experience or understanding or intelligence.[115] For example, in *Stephenson*,[116] a tramp sheltered in a hollow in a haystack. Feeling cold, he lit a fire in the hollow. The haystack was destroyed. Any reasonable person would have been aware of the risk but Stephenson was suffering from schizophrenia and may not have been aware of it. Because this was not clearly left to the jury, the court – pre-*Caldwell* – quashed his conviction. Even if he had stopped to think whether a risk existed, it is possible that, because of his condition, he might not have realized that there was a risk of damage. *Stephenson* would have been convicted under *Caldwell*. The objective test therefore had the potential to criminalize the blind person who damaged property being unaware of a risk which would have been obvious to a sighted person. And those with temporary disabilities – the person who strikes a match, being unaware because of his heavy cold that the premises reek with petrol fumes, could be convicted. Sir John Smith wrote of *Caldwell*: 'The decision sets back the law concerning the mental element in criminal damage in theory to before 1861.'[117]

---

[111] See S Field and M Lynn, 'The Capacity for Recklessness' (1992) 12 LS 74; S Field and M Lynn, 'Capacity Recklessness and the House of Lords' [1993] Crim LR 127.

[112] To whom must the risk be obvious? Was it always necessary for the risk to be obvious to a reasonable person? What if D was an expert who would have foreseen the risk but the reasonable person would not have done. (See further the commentary on the decision of the Court of Appeal in *Reid* (1989) 91 Cr App R 263 at [1991] Crim LR 269, 271.) Was the degree of risk that ought to have been foreseen restricted to serious risks?

[113] D Birch, 'The Foresight Saga: The Biggest Mistake of All' [1988] Crim LR 4. The relative culpability of one who gives no thought to the risk as compared to one who wrongly believes that there is no risk is difficult to assess. We need to know why the person had the state of mind. If it was because although he had the capacity to see the risk he was too careless or lazy to investigate the risks properly we would properly describe him as culpable: Tadros, *Criminal Responsibility*, 255.

[114] (1983) 88 Cr App R 1, [1983] Crim LR 681.

[115] 'The criminal law ought not to be used to criminalise the merely stupid or irrational' – Tadros, *Criminal Responsibility*, 239.

[116] [1979] QB 695.

[117] [1981] Crim LR 393. Note that inadvertent recklessness is established in other jurisdictions: see, eg, the discussion of German law in JR Spencer and A Pedain, 'Strict Liability in Continental Criminal Law', in A Simester (ed), *Appraising Strict Liability* (2005) 241.

R v G[118]

In *G*, Ds aged 11 and 12 went camping without their parents' permission. During the night they set fire to newspapers in the yard at the back of a shop and threw the lit newspapers under a bin. They left without putting out the fire. The fire spread to the wheelie bin and to the shop causing £1m worth of damage. Ds' case was that they expected the newspapers to burn themselves out on the concrete floor. Neither appreciated the risk of the fire spreading as it did. They were charged with arson contrary to s 1(1) and (3) of the 1971 Act. The judge directed the jury in accordance with *Caldwell*, expressing reservations about that being a harsh test in this context. The Court of Appeal upheld the convictions stating that *Caldwell* had been rightly applied and certified the issue of recklessness as one of general public importance. The House of Lords reviewed the history of the term 'recklessness' and unanimously overruled *Caldwell*. It was recognized that having regard to the Law Commission Report No 29 on which the Criminal Damage Act 1971 was based, and the parliamentary intent, the majority in *Caldwell* erred in concluding that 'reckless' in s 1 of the Act meant something different from 'malicious' under the previous law. That subjective test of recklessness required proof that the accused had foreseen the risk and yet had gone on unjustifiably to take it.[119] That was a much broader conclusion than was necessary to dispose of the certified question. The decision in *Caldwell* was acknowledged to be based on 'fragile foundations' because the House of Lords was not referred to the Law Commission Report. Moreover, Lord Bingham in *G* noted the fact that the majority decision in *Caldwell* had been in the face of a powerful dissent from Lord Edmund Davies, and had been subjected to sustained and cogent academic[120] and judicial criticism.[121]

Acknowledging the force of the principled criticisms outlined above, the House of Lords in *G* concluded that it should depart from *Caldwell* because it was 'just' to do so. *Caldwell* was castigated as being 'unfair', Lord Bingham referred to it as 'neither just nor moral', and Lord Steyn as a 'cynical strategy'. Lord Steyn also cited UK treaty obligations and the general shift in recent years towards greater subjectivity in *mens rea* as supporting the outright overruling of *Caldwell*. In short, as Lord Bingham observed, whilst it is clearly blameworthy to take a risk obvious to the individual, it is not 'clearly blameworthy' to do something involving a risk of harm when D has not perceived that risk.[122] Professor Keating's recent empirical work,[123] based on hypothetical scenarios similar to those in *G*, reveals that a large majority (69%) of members of the public *do* regard behaviour such as that of the boys as criminally blameworthy. Most of those believed that the boys of that age (11 and 12) were old enough to have realized the risks involved. Of those who would not support convicting such boys, the

---

[118] For criticism, see A Halpin, *Definition in the Criminal Law* (2004) Ch 3, especially pp 102–121; M Davies, 'Lawmakers, Law Lords and Legal Fault' (2004) 68 J Crim L 130, noting the 'delicious irony' that *G* was decided at a time when Parliament was introducing objective fault elements for serious sex offences in the Sexual Offences Act 2003. See also D Kimel (2004) 120 LQR 548 suggesting that the problem lay with the application of *Caldwell* in subsequent cases such as *Elliott*; and K Amirthalingham, 'Caldwell Recklessness is Dead: Long Live Mens Rea's Fecklessness' (2004) 63 MLR 491.

[119] *Cunningham* [1957] 2 QB 396.

[120] Seen n 105, above.

[121] Notably, Ackner LJ in *Stephen Malcolm R* (1984) 79 Cr App R 334, and Goff LJ in *Elliott v C (A Minor)* (1983) Cr App R 103.

[122] cf Lord Rodger of Earlsferry at [69], 'there is much to be said for treating as reckless D who does not trouble his mind to a risk that would have been obvious to him', and see the important article by J Horder, 'Two Histories and Four Hidden Principles of *Mens Rea*' (1997) 113 LQR 95. See also Kimel, above n 118, commenting that this conclusion of Lord Bingham is 'clearly unsatisfactory'. See recently the review of the two approaches by S Cunningham, 'Recklessness: Being Reckless and Acting Recklessly' (2010) 21 KLJ 445–467.

[123] 'Reckless Children' [2006] Crim LR 546.

majority were against doing so because of what they considered to be the inappropriateness of the application of the criminal process in such a case.

In *G*, their lordships rejected the narrower solution of a capacity-based exception to the *Caldwell* test. This approach had been suggested as a compromise between the subjectivism of *Cunningham* and the objectivism of *Caldwell*. It would have restricted *Caldwell* recklessness to cases in which D himself, having regard to his capacity to see risk, ought to have foreseen the risk of the proscribed harm. The House of Lords held that such an exception would be likely to create further difficulties in defining the relevant exceptional category, and would still impose liability generally on those who caused damage inadvertently. Lord Bingham noted that:

this refinement also has attractions, although it does not meet the objection of principle and does not represent a correct interpretation of the section. It is, in my opinion, open to the further objection of over-complicating the task of the jury (or bench of justices). It is one thing to decide whether a defendant can be believed when he says that the thought of a given risk never crossed his mind. It is another, and much more speculative, task to decide whether the risk would have been obvious to him if the thought had crossed his mind. The simpler the jury's task, the more likely is its verdict to be reliable.[124]

In practical terms, the House of Lords expressed concern at the complexity of *Caldwell* directions. Their lordships were confident that juries could be trusted to apply the *Cunningham* test without blindly accepting a defendant's assertion that he never thought of a certain risk when all the circumstances and probabilities and evidence of what he did and said at the time showed that he did or must have done. It was noted that there is nothing to suggest that this was seen as a problem before *Caldwell*.[125]

The decision in *G* is also welcome for its explicit adoption of the key provision from the Draft Criminal Code defining recklessness. Lord Bingham based his conclusion on the Draft Criminal Code, cl 18(c) as quoted above.

Does *Caldwell* still have a role to play?

At one stage in the mid-1980s it looked as if the *Caldwell* test was destined to be the principal form of recklessness in English criminal law. Lord Roskill, when holding the *Caldwell/ Lawrence* test to be applicable to manslaughter, said that 'reckless' should be given the *Caldwell* meaning in all offences, 'unless Parliament has otherwise ordained'.[126] Even before *G* it was clear that its application was much more limited. Lord Bingham explicitly limited his judgment in that case to overruling *Caldwell* in its application to criminal damage,[127] so the question remains: post-*G*, are there any offences to which the *Caldwell* formula applies? Other offences to which *Caldwell* had been applied included the Data Protection Act 1984, s 5[128] but that has now been repealed by the Data Protection Act 1998. *Halsbury's Laws* suggests *Caldwell* applies to the offence of recklessly providing false answers on being summoned for jury service,[129] and *Blackstone's Criminal Practice* (2003), immediately prior to *G* suggested *Caldwell* applied to recklessly making a declaration, etc which is false in a material particular;[130] recklessly giving false information in purported compliance with any

---

[124] [38].
[125] [39].
[126] *Seymour* [1983] 2 All ER 1058 at 1064, HL.
[127] [28].
[128] *Data Protection Registrar v Amnesty International* [1995] Crim LR 633.
[129] Juries Act 1974, s 2.
[130] Customs and Excise Management Act 1979, s 167(1).

obligation under the Misuse of Drugs Act,[131] and recklessly making a misleading or deceptive statement or forecast.[132] Although some authority supported these propositions, it is submitted that there is now no basis for applying anything other than the test set out in the Draft Criminal Code, cl 18 as applied in *G*, to each of these offences.

5.2.2.3 Subjective vs objective recklessness

The decision in *G* is important in reasserting the primacy of subjectivism, echoing other recent decisions in the House of Lords.[133] Lord Rodger acknowledged that there are academic arguments of substantial pedigree in favour of an objective approach to recklessness.[134] The choice is not simply between strict subjective and objective approaches. Many commentators have put forward versions of a compromise position in which the unacceptable harshness of a purely objective test is avoided. These approaches seek to reflect D's culpability in failing to advert to a risk that would have been obvious *to him*, that is, one that to was within his capacity to recognize.[135] Alternative suggestions have included tests of 'practical indifference'.[136]

5.2.2.4 Indifference

It is submitted that indifference to a particular risk, where it is proved to exist, is an aggravating factor, but not an element in the definition of the required fault.[137] A person who knowingly takes an unreasonable risk of causing a forbidden result may hope, sincerely and fervently, that it will never happen; but he is, surely, reckless. In *Reid* Lord Goff suggested that a person may be indifferent to a risk without being aware of its existence.[138] Surely, however, the most we can say is that D would have been indifferent to the risk if he had been aware of it. Such a conclusion could usually be drawn only from evidence as to his general character and habits which the law of evidence does not allow.[139]

The Law Commission did recently provisionally propose a form of reckless indifference in its offence of second degree murder. This concept was treated as a more culpable form of *mens rea* than 'simple' recklessness.[140] The Commission proposed that indifference to causing the proscribed result (in that case death) would be defined as follows:

D is indifferent, manifesting a 'couldn't care less' attitude to the result, when he or she realises that there is an unjustified risk of the result being caused by his or her conduct, but goes ahead with that conduct, causing the result. D's own assessment of the justifiability of taking the risk, in the circumstances, is to

---

[131] Misuse of Drugs Act 1971, s 18(3).

[132] Financial Services and Markets Act 2000, s 397(1)(c).

[133] *DPP v B* [2000] AC 428; *K* [2002] 1 AC 462 (strict liability); *(Morgan) Smith* [2001] 1 AC 146 (provocation).

[134] See Horder (1997) 113 LQR 95.

[135] See HLA Hart, 'Negligence, *Mens Rea* and Criminal Responsibility', in *Punishment and Responsibility* (1968). See also Tadros, *Criminal Responsibility*, Ch 9; Duff, *Answering for Crime*, 70.

[136] Duff, *Intention, Agency and Criminal Liability*, arguing that a test of practical indifference could be applied where D's conduct, 'including any conscious risk taking, any failure to notice an obvious risk created by her action and any unreasonable beliefs on which she acted, display a seriously culpable practical indifference to the interests which the agent's actions in fact threatened', p 172.

[137] cf *Gardiner* [1994] Crim LR 455 and commentary.

[138] (1992) 95 Cr App R 391, HL. L Leigh, 'Recklessness after *Reid*' (1993) 56 MLR 208.

[139] cf the proposals by V Tadros, 'Recklessness and the Duty to Take Care' in S Shute and A Simester (eds), *Criminal Law Theory* (2002) arguing that D should be liable if he did not fulfil his duty of investigating the risks which his 'background beliefs' led him to realize were present. See further Tadros, *Criminal Responsibility*, Ch 9.

[140] LCCP 177, para 3.21

be considered, along with all the other evidence, in deciding whether D was recklessly indifferent and 'couldn't care less' about causing the result.[141]

This would have created confusion by introducing a further test of recklessness into the law when it had only recently settled to a universally accepted test in G. The Law Commission resiled from this proposal in its final report, preferring a test based on one of subjective recklessness.[142]

5.2.2.5 Recklessness and indifference to circumstances

There is a particular difficulty in requiring proof of subjective recklessness as to an *actus reus* element which is of a morally indifferent nature. The definition of a crime sometimes draws an arbitrary line, as to a person's age, or as to time, weight, size and other matters of degree. Ignorance of the law is no defence but there is no reason why a person who is unaware of the law should direct his mind to the question whether the arbitrary line has been crossed in the particular case.[143] The possessor of a shotgun has no reason to consider whether the barrel is less than 24 inches in length unless he knows that, if it is, possession without a firearms certificate is an offence.[144] The case is different in a material respect from that of the person who has a positive but mistaken belief that the shotgun is under that length. Williams[145] sought to resolve the difficulty by distinguishing between cases of 'mistaken belief' (where there is a positive belief) which will negative recklessness and 'simple ignorance' (where there is no advertence to the question) which will not. This distinction gained some support from *Caldwell*.[146] D can truly be said to be indifferent as to the circumstance – he does not care whether the barrel of the gun is more or less than 24 inches, because he is unaware that it matters. This principle, however, could only be properly applicable in respect of age, time, weight, size and other circumstances which everyone knows to exist in some degree. D knows that the barrel has length and, *ex hypothesi*, he does not care what it is. Where the circumstance is not simply a matter of degree but of kind, it is no longer possible to say that D was indifferent.[147] D may buy and deliver to V a book with an attractive cover without looking at the contents and without considering whether it might contain obscene material, but to infer that he was indifferent would be quite unwarranted. It might be that, when he learned the facts, he might be quite horrified.[148] An objective form of *mens rea* may be appropriate in such a case.[149]

5.2.2.6 Wilfulness and recklessness

This *mens rea* term appears in hundreds of statutory offences including some which are commonly prosecuted (eg the offence under consideration and wilfully obstructing a police officer: Police Act 1996, s 89). It also features in important common law offences including

---

[141] LCCP 177, para 3.150. For criticism, see A Norrie, 'Between Orthodox Subjectivism and Moral Contextualism: Intention and the Consultation Paper' [2006] Crim LR 489, 491; Wilson, above, n 83 [2006] Crim LR 471; Rogers (2006) 70 JCL 223.

[142] LC 304, para 2.56.

[143] cf Horder [2001] Crim LR 15.

[144] Firearms Act 1968, s 1.

[145] Williams, CLGP (1st edn) 122, (2nd edn) 151. cf *A-G's Reference (No 1 of 1995)* [1996] 2 Cr App R 320, [1996] Crim LR 575.

[146] Above, p 121; cf *Pigg* (1982) 74 Cr App R at 358–359.

[147] There is an argument that in relation to sex offences the fact that V is under 16 renders D's acts towards her qualitatively different. See Horder [2001] Crim LR 15.

[148] The possessor of the shotgun might be equally horrified when they learned the *law*, but that is not the same thing. We are considering recklessness as to facts, not law. cf *Mousir* [1987] Crim LR 561 and commentary.

[149] Above, p 121.

misconduct in public office: *Attorney-General's Reference (No 3 of 2003)*.[150] It is surprising that the definition of the *mens rea* element 'wilful' or 'wilfully' is not as clear as it might be. Clarity of definition would certainly seem to be important. Historically, the term generated a great deal of inconsistent case law, particularly in the nineteenth century.[151]

The primary meaning of 'wilful' is 'deliberate' but it may also include recklessness, as accepted by the majority of the House of Lords in *Sheppard*.[152] In the context of the offence under the Children and Young Persons Act 1933, s 1, the parent must neglect the child 'intending, or at least foreseeing, that the probable consequence of neglect is that the child will suffer injury to his health'.[153] *Sheppard* left a number of ambiguities, but in light of subsequent case law, including the most recent pronouncement, *D*,[154] these appear to have been resolved. First, when it is alleged that the D's conduct was 'wilful' on the basis that his conduct was 'deliberate' or 'intentional', few if any problems arise in satisfying the wilfulness test in any offence. Second, when the allegation is that the alleged 'wilfulness' is demonstrated by D being reckless, it is now settled that the question is whether D was reckless in the subjective (*G*[155]) sense rather than the objective (*Caldwell*) sense of the word. In other words, if D has seen the risk of the proscribed circumstances or consequences and has nevertheless gone on unreasonably to take that risk, his conduct can be described as wilful. Third, the definition of wilful applies whether the allegation is that D performed acts or omissions within the definition of the relevant offence.[156] It would be illogical and create great practical difficulties if the definition of wilfulness for the offence differed depending on the form of harm alleged.

5.2.2.7 Reform

The Law Commission's draft Criminal Law Bill (cl 1) reproducing, with a slight modification, the definition in the Draft Code (cl 18(b)) provides that:

a person acts –

(b) 'recklessly' with respect to –

(i) a circumstance, when he is aware of a risk that it exists or will exist, and

(ii) a result when he is aware of a risk that it will occur,

and it is unreasonable, having regard to the circumstances known to him, to take that risk...

The draft Criminal Law Bill would apply this definition to non-fatal offences against the person, and the draft Code Bill would apply it to criminal offences generally. That would result in a great simplification of the law. It is submitted that it would also be a great improvement.

---

[150] [2005] QB 73.

[151] See J Edwards, *Mens Rea in Statutory Offences* (1955) Ch II; J Andrews, 'Wilfulness: A Lesson in Ambiguity' (1981) 1 LS 303. Andrews suggests (p 305) that one of the reasons that the meaning remained ambiguous in criminal law for so long was the 'relative sloppiness' in the 'construction and practice' of criminal law compared with the 'greater degree of intellectual discipline which is commonly observed by those who make and practice in' 'commercial, chancery and revenue' law!

[152] [1981] AC 394, at 408.

[153] At 408 per Lord Diplock.

[154] [2008] EWCA Crim 2360.

[155] [2003] UKHL 50.

[156] See also *Emma W* [2006] EWCA Crim 2723. Lord Diplock in *Sheppard* had equivocated on this. His lordship sought expressly to confine his definition to omissions, but rejected as not a 'natural meaning' a narrower meaning for positive acts which would limit wilful to mean only that the accused had *mens rea* as to the doing of the act and not its consequences: *Sheppard*, p 404.

5.2.3 Negligence[157]

After *G* and the eradication of *Caldwell* and *Lawrence,* it is possible once again confidently to draw a clear distinction between recklessness and negligence. Recklessness is the conscious taking of an unjustifiable risk, negligence is the inadvertent taking of an unjustifiable risk. If D is aware of the risk and decides to take it, he is reckless; if he is unaware of the risk, but ought to have been aware of it, he is negligent. Where D did consider whether or not there was a risk and concluded, wrongly and unreasonably, either that there was no risk, or the risk was so small that it would have been justifiable to take it, he is negligent.

5.2.4 Intention, recklessness and negligence as to circumstances

So far the discussion has focused on whether D intends or is reckless, etc as to the proscribed consequences – the death of V, the damage to property and so on. Intention, recklessness and negligence may also all be relevant with respect to the circumstance elements of the *actus reus*. In some crimes intention as to one or more elements of the *actus reus* is needed, but mere recklessness or negligence will suffice as to another or other elements. For example, in the offence of sexual touching of a child under 16, D must intend to touch, but he need not intend that the child is under 16; it is sufficient to found liability that he does not have a reasonable belief that she is 16 or older.

It would seem that, in determining whether D's fault amounted to intention, recklessness or negligence, the same criteria should be applied to circumstances as to consequences. So an act is intentional as to a circumstance[158] when D wants the circumstance to exist (where he hopes, perhaps faintly, that the letter he steals contains money, he intends to steal money)[159] or knows that it exists; or, if the broader view of intention[160] is accepted, he is virtually certain that it exists. He is reckless whether a circumstance exists or will exist when it is obvious that it may do so and D is aware of a risk that it exists or will exist. He is negligent with respect to a circumstance when, a reasonable person would know that it exists or will exist and D fails to appreciate that it exists, whether he has given thought to the question or not.

5.2.5 Knowledge

By comparison with *mens rea* elements such as intention and recklessness, knowledge has attracted comparatively little scholarship. Academic attention has focused on how knowledge plays a part in the general scheme of *mens rea* and to what extent it factors into negative fault elements (ie, mistaken beliefs) that displace *mens rea*. It is, however, a term deserving attention as it features in many statutes. It is usually considered to sit alongside intention in the *mens rea* hierarchy, but whereas intention is usually descriptive of state of minds as to consequences (for example, I intend to kill), knowledge is usually used in relation to circumstances (for example, importing a substance knowing it is prohibited).

Knowledge is not the only legislative term to describe prohibited states of mind as to circumstances. Parliament has deployed a range of terms: 'knowledge', 'belief', 'suspicion', 'having reasonable grounds to suspect' and even 'recklessness'. These different terms do not share the same meaning in law. The terms are used in many offences as alternative

---

[157] See Ch 6 below, and J Brady, 'Recklessness, Negligence, Indifference and Awareness' (1980) 43 MLR 381.

[158] This is not the same as saying that the circumstance is intended, because that implies a belief by D that he may be able to influence the existence of the circumstance.

[159] Salmond, *Jurisprudence*, 411.

[160] Above, p 114.

mens rea requirements.[161] The difficult issue lies in identifying the respective boundaries of each concept. More light has been shed on the matter by recent academic scholarship, with Professors Shute and Sullivan[162] in particular seeking to identify essential conditions which must exist before a state of mind might legitimately be described as 'knowledge'. The current definition of knowledge in English criminal law is that it is satisfied by proof of a true belief. D knows goods are stolen when he correctly believes they are.

The judicial view is clear: knowledge is true belief and one cannot know something or some circumstance that has yet to occur. As the Canadian Supreme Court explained in *USA v Dynar*:[163]

In the Western legal tradition, knowledge is defined as *true* belief: 'The word "know" refers exclusively to true knowledge; we are not said to "know" something that is not so'.

This view has been endorsed in the House of Lords in two recent cases. In *Montila*,[164] the House accepted that:

A person cannot know that something is A when in fact it is B. The proposition that a person knows that something is A is based on the premise that it is true that it is A. The fact that the property is A provides the starting point. Then there is the question whether the person knows that the property is A.[165]

Subsequently in *Saik* the House of Lords concluded:

the word 'know' should be interpreted strictly and not watered down. In this context knowledge means true belief.[166] In conspiracy for example, if D1 and D2 agree that they will, in the future, exchange money that comes into their bureau de change, they cannot be said to be agreeing to launder money which they *know* to be from a criminal source if they merely see the risk that it might be from a criminal source.[167]

5.2.5.1 Distinguishing knowledge from belief and suspicion

The orthodox view is that 'one cannot know a thing unless it is so',[168] and 'one cannot know a thing will be so unless it will be so'.[169] The critical feature distinguishing knowledge and belief is that the fact or circumstance 'is'.[170] As Shute acknowledges 'there are good reasons why the law should decline to extend its definition of knowledge generally to include knowledge that [the disputed proposition] is possible, likely, etc'.[171] Mere suspicion is therefore not knowledge.[172] The more difficult question lies in distinguishing knowledge from mere belief.[173]

---

[161] See the comprehensive catalogue provided by S Shute, 'Knowledge and Belief in the Criminal Law' in S Shute and A Simester (eds), *Criminal Law Theory* (2002) Ch 8, and see GR Sullivan, 'Knowledge, Belief and Culpability', ibid, Ch 9.

[162] Above n 161.

[163] Emphasis added [1997] 2 SCR 462.

[164] [2004] 1 WLR 3141.

[165] [27].

[166] [26]. See also Hooper LJ in *Liaquat Ali and others* [2005] EWCA Crim 87, [2005] 2 Cr App R 864 (at para 98).

[167] They might be said to intend that circumstance. See *Saik* [2006] UKHL 18.

[168] JC Smith, 'Conspiracy under the Criminal Law Act 1977 (1)' [1977] Crim LR 598, 603.

[169] ibid. See also G Williams, CLGP (1953) 133, and more generally writings on knowledge in philosophy – eg, AJ Ayer, *The Problem of Knowledge*, 'I conclude that the necessary and sufficient conditions for knowing that something is the case are first that what one is said to know be true, secondly that one be sure of it and thirdly that one should have the right to be sure' at 35, cited by R Buxton, 'Complicity in the Criminal Code' (1969) 85 LQR 252.

[170] As is made clear in *Hall* (1985) 81 Cr App R 260, knowing a fact might be is not the same as knowing it is.

[171] Shute, 'Knowledge and Belief in the Criminal Law', in Shute and Simester, *Criminal Law Theory*, 195.

[172] 'Suspicion in its ordinary meaning is a state of conjecture or surmise where proof is lacking: "I suspect but I cannot prove"': *Hussien v Chong Fook Kam* [1970] AC 942, 948. See also *Griffiths* (1974) 60 Cr App R 14, CA.

[173] *Hall* (1985) 81 Cr App R 260, 264, see below, p 994.

5.2.6 Belief

The relationship between knowledge and belief has been examined in close detail in the context of handling stolen goods. According to the Court of Appeal in *Hall*:[174]

Belief, of course, is something short of knowledge. It may be said to be the state of mind of a person who says to himself: 'I cannot say I know for certain that [the circumstance exists] but there can be no other reasonable conclusion in the light of all the circumstances, in the light of all that I have heard and seen'.

In *Forsyth*,[175] the court said that the judgment in *Hall* is 'potentially confusing'. In *Moys*,[176] the court suggested simply that the question whether D knew or believed that the proscribed circumstance existed is a subjective one and that suspicion, even coupled with the fact that D shut his eyes to the circumstances, is not enough.

5.2.7 Wilful blindness

The courts have for centuries[177] willingly interpreted knowledge as including 'shutting one's eyes to an obvious means of knowledge' or 'deliberately refraining from making inquiries the results of which the person does not care to have'.[178] Even the House of Lords controversially adopted this proposition:

It is always open to the tribunal of fact, when knowledge on the part of a defendant is required to be proved, to base a finding of knowledge on evidence that the defendant had deliberately shut his eyes to the obvious or refrained from inquiry because he suspected the truth but did not want to have his suspicion confirmed.[179]

A precise definition of wilful blindness or connivance[180] remains elusive.[181] Perhaps the best known exposition of the concept is that of Devlin J in *Roper v Taylor Garages (Exeter)*. His lordship distinguished (i) actual knowledge, (ii) wilful blindness (knowledge in the second degree) and (iii) constructive knowledge (knowledge in the third degree).[182] Actual knowledge has been considered: it means true belief. As for wilful blindness, Devlin J emphasized:

a vast distinction between a state of mind which consists of deliberately refraining from making inquiries, the result of which a person does not care to have [wilful blindness], and a state of mind

---

[174] (1985) 81 Cr App R 260 at 264, [1985] Crim LR 377.

[175] A *Hall* direction is not necessary in every case – *Toor* (1987) 85 Cr App R 116.

[176] (1984) 79 Cr App R 72, CA.

[177] See the discussion of the early case law in JL Edwards, *Mens Rea in Statutory Offences* (1953) Ch IX, 'The Criminal Degrees of Knowledge in Statutory Offences', 194.

[178] *Roper v Taylor's Garage* [1951] 2 TLR 284 (Devlin J). See also, eg, *Warner v Metropolitan Police Comr* [1969] 2 AC 256, 279 (Lord Reid); *Atwal v Massey* 56 Cr App R 6, DC.

[179] *Westminster City Council v Croyalgrange Ltd* (1986) 83 Cr App R 155, 164 (Lord Bridge).

[180] See *Winson* [1969] 1 QB 371, 383 (Parker LCJ). Old statutes often used the word 'connivance' but none currently seem to use wilful blindness.

[181] It seems this was owing to the confusion historically over its relationship with vicarious liability: Edwards, *Mens Rea in Statutory Offences*, 196–198.

[182] More sophisticated subdivisions have been attempted including Peter Gibson J's five categories in the *Baden* case [1993] 1 WLR 509, para 250. Although these were rejected as unhelpful by the House of Lords in the particular context of dishonesty in *Royal Brunei Airlines v Tan* [1995] 2 AC 378, they are worth noting: '(i) actual knowledge; (ii) wilfully shutting one's eyes to the obvious; (iii) wilfully and recklessly failing to make such inquiries as an honest and reasonable man would make; (iv) knowledge of circumstances which would indicate the facts to an honest and reasonable man; (v) knowledge of circumstances which would put an honest and reasonable man on inquiry.'

which is merely neglecting to make such inquiries as a reasonable and prudent person would make [constructive knowledge].[183]

Other judicial definitions[184] have variously incorporated elements of:

(1) a deliberate or intentional refusal to investigate the circumstances suspected;

(2) an opportunity to investigate them;

(3) an absence of doubt as to outcome or at least an awareness by D of the likely outcome of investigation and that the outcome would not be one D desired if he investigated his suspicions;

(4) a causal link between the refusal to investigate and the assumed likely outcome.[185]

The core elements appear to be a degree of awareness of the likely existence of the prohibited circumstances coupled with a blameworthy conscious refusal to enlighten oneself. Academic opinion seems united in requiring proof of more than mere suspicion.[186] Williams described it in terms of suspicion *'plus'* a deliberate omission to enquire.[187] More recently Sullivan described it in terms of 'suspicion coupled with *deliberate* failure to use *readily available* and effective means to resolve the suspicion'.[188] However described, the second limb of the test requires D must have possessed more than a state of awareness of the risk – he must demonstrate a blameworthiness[189] in his lack of enquiry that justifies treating his state of mind as akin to actual knowledge.[190]

The boundaries of 'wilful blindness' are imprecise. None of the core elements is defined with adequate precision. It is unclear what degree of awareness of risk D must hold. Is suspicion sufficient or must D hold a belief?[191] It is unclear how readily available the bases of enlightenment must be to D. Is he only wilfully blind if he can reasonably or immediately discover the truth, or is the matter one of proportionality depending on the degree of risk and the severity of the harm posed if the risk materializes? It is unclear how convinced of the outcome of investigation D must be – must it be proved, as Ashworth suggests, that D refrained from making inquiries because he was virtually certain that suspicion would be *confirmed*?[192] Further, to constitute wilful blindness it is unclear what motivation or purpose D must have in seeking to avoid the enlightenment for his refusal. In principle, there are strong arguments

---

[183] *Roper v Taylor's Garage* [1951] 2 TLR 284, 288.

[184] See those discussed by Edwards, *Mens Rea in Statutory Offences*, 199. The Draft Criminal Code also suggests that knowledge includes wilful blindness in cl 18(1)(a) a person acts knowingly 'with respect to a circumstance only when he is aware that it exists or will exist but also when he avoids taking steps that might confirm his belief that it exists or will exist'.

[185] See, eg, *Roper*; *Agip (Africa) v Jackson* [1990] Ch 265, 293 'deliberately shutting eyes to facts he would prefer not to know'; 'it is a commonplace that, if the accused had a suspicion but deliberately shut his eyes, the court or jury is well entitled to hold him guilty; *Warner v MPC* [1969] AC 256, 279 (Lord Reid). See also *Evan v Dell* [1937] 1 All ER 349, 353: 'deliberately refraining from making inquiries, the results of which [D] might not care to have'.

[186] Although that was not judicially accepted in the 19th century: see Edwards, *Mens Rea in Statutory Offences*, 207.

[187] CGLP (1953) 127, para 41. In his article on *mens rea* in secondary liability, 'Complicity, Purpose and the Draft Criminal Code' [1990] Crim LR 98, he described the element as 'an attempted fraud on the law', fn 4.

[188] See Sullivan, 'Knowledge, Belief and Culpability', in Shute and Simester, *Criminal Law Theory*, 214.

[189] See, generally, M Wasik and MP Thompson, 'Turning a Blind Eye as Constituting Mens Rea' (1981) 32 NILQ 324, 337–341.

[190] Described as 'purposeful avoidance' by W Wilson, *Criminal Law Doctrine and Theory* (2001) 167.

[191] G Williams agued that it should be 'realisation that the fact in question is probable, or at least possible above average', CGLP 127, para 41. The Law Commission proposed a formula based on D having 'no substantial doubt'. See Wasik and Thompson (1981) 32 NILQ 324, 333.

[192] Above, POCL, 185.

against the courts applying a *mens rea* element of wilful blindness unless its elements can be defined with much greater precision.

Some commentators[193] suggest that recklessness is akin to wilful blindness, but academic consensus seems to be that wilful blindness is a narrower category of *mens rea*.[194] It is narrower for several reasons including: (i) it assumes that D has the opportunity to avail himself of the facts or circumstances about which he has an awareness, (ii) that D's assessment of the likelihood of the fact is higher than foresight of *a* risk (as required for recklessness)[195] and (iii) he intentionally chooses not to enlighten himself. The distinction has been acknowledged in other jurisdictions, for example the Canadian Supreme Court recently observed:

Wilful blindness is distinct from recklessness because, while recklessness involves knowledge of a danger *or risk* and persistence in a course of conduct which creates *a risk* that the prohibited result will occur, wilful blindness arises where a person who has become aware of the need for some inquiry declines to make the inquiry because he does not wish to know the truth. He would prefer to remain ignorant.[196]

5.2.8 Suspicion and reasonable grounds to suspect

Parliament has demonstrated a greater willingness in recent years to create offences with low level *mens rea* requirements such as 'suspicion' and 'having reasonable grounds to suspect'. The money laundering offences in the Proceeds of Crime Act 2002 are some of the most obvious and draconian examples.[197] The Terrorism Acts also include offences based on suspicion. By s 18(1) of the Terrorism Act 2000, a person commits an offence if he enters into an arrangement which facilitates another person's retention or control of such property, but it is a defence for D to prove that he 'did not know and had no reasonable cause to suspect' that the arrangement related to terrorist property.[198] Requiring only that D 'suspects' relevant facts is a remarkably low threshold for a criminal offence; 'suspicion' and 'reasonable suspicion' have been criticized as too low even as a threshold for the exercise of certain police powers (in which area of law they are commonly found in statutes).

5.2.8.1 The meaning of 'suspicion'[199]

In *Da Silva*,[200] 'suspicion' was held to impose a subjective test: D's suspicion need not be based on 'reasonable grounds'. D must think that there is a possibility, which is more than fanciful, that the relevant facts exist. The court held that:

A vague feeling of unease would not suffice. But the statute does not require the suspicion to be 'clear' or 'firmly grounded and targeted on specific facts' or based on 'reasonable grounds'.[201]

---

[193] IH Dennis, 'The Mental Element for Accessories', in *Criminal Law Essays*. Edwards treated them as similar in his *Mens Rea in Criminal Statutes*, citing only very few instances where they were treated as synonymous, 203.

[194] See the characteristically forthright statements of EJ Griew, 'Consistency, Communication and Codification Reflection on Two Mens Rea Words', in *Reshaping the Criminal Law,* 73.

[195] Especially when recklessness is construed in its subjective sense following *G* [2004] 1 AC 1034.

[196] *R v Williams* [2004] 2 LRC 499 at [27], quoting from *Sansregret v R* [1985] 1 SCR 570 at 584 (McIntyre J).

[197] The offences are much broader in respect of *mens rea* than the international treaties demand as noted by their lordships in *Montila* [2004] UKHL 50 at [28].

[198] See the Terrorism Act 2000, s 18(2).

[199] For further discussion as to what is meant by 'knowledge', 'belief' and 'suspicion': see Glanville Williams, 'Handling, Theft and the Purchaser Who Takes a Chance' [1985] Crim LR 432 and see *Hall* [1985] Crim LR 377; *Toor* (1987) 85 Cr App R [116].

[200] [2006] EWCA Crim 1654.

[201] [16]. Applied in *Afolabi* [2009] EWCA Crim 2879.

The court stated that using words such as 'inkling' or 'fleeting thought' is liable to mislead.

More recently the Civil Division of the Court of Appeal has endorsed this subjective test of suspicion. In *Shah v HSBC*[202] the court held that a bank suspected property was criminal if it thought there was a possibility, which was more than fanciful. There was no requirement to show that that suspicion had been clear or firmly grounded and targeted on specific facts or based on reasonable grounds. The defence claims that the irrationality and negligently self-induced suspicion had no real prospect of success.

The courts have adopted the dictionary definitions, which are consistent with the previous judicial interpretations of the concept of suspicion in the related field of criminal procedure. One of the most famous statements is that of Lord Devlin in *Hussien v Chang Fook Kam*:[203]

Suspicion in its ordinary meaning is a state of conjecture or surmise where proof is lacking: 'I suspect but I cannot prove'. Suspicion arises at or near the starting point of an investigation of which the obtaining of prima facie proof is the end.

Further (albeit limited) guidance might be derived from the numerous decisions of the Court of Appeal on the *mens rea* of handling stolen goods, in which the distinction between belief and 'mere' suspicion has been problematic.[204] The court in *Da Silva* was right, it is submitted, not formally to impose a gloss on the definition by requiring that the suspicion be 'clear' or 'firmly grounded and targeted on specific facts', even though that approach has been adopted by the House of Lords in various civil law contexts.

The court in *Da Silva* expressed concern about the need for a more detailed direction in cases in which D has suspected but then 'honestly dismissed' his suspicion. This should not be made complicated. This is not a situation in which there is 'a lacuna' where D has failed to form the suspicion despite addressing his mind to it. The appropriate question is, it is submitted, whether D has formed the suspicion and whether he holds that state of mind at the time at which he performs the acts alleged to constitute the *actus reus*. If D had been suspicious, but by the time of the act those suspicions had been allayed by the receipt of other information, this will mean that he lacked the necessary *mens rea*.

5.2.8.2 'Reasonable grounds for knowing or suspecting'

In *Saik*,[205] the House of Lords held that the *mens rea* element 'reasonable grounds to suspect' in the context of s 93C(2) of the Criminal Justice Act 1988, and now found, for example, in many of the money laundering provisions[206] includes a requirement that the example, D had actual suspicion.[207] Lord Hope concluded that 'the first requirement contains both a subjective part – that the person suspects – and an objective part – that there are reasonable grounds for the suspicion'.[208]

It had previously been widely assumed that this fault element was a purely objective one,[209] requiring proof only that the reasonable person would have formed the suspicion

---

[202] [2010] EWCA Civ 31. The court's interpretation of suspicion was held to apply in the civil law relating to money laundering, *K Ltd v National Westminster Bank plc* [2006] EWCA Civ 1039.

[203] [1970] AC 942 at 948.

[204] See *Hall* (1985) 81 Cr App R 260, CA; *Forsyth* [1997] 2 Cr App R 299.

[205] [2006] 2 WLR 993, [2006] UKHL 18.

[206] The expression 'reasonable grounds for knowing or suspecting' appears in POCA, s 330 (failure to disclose: regulated sector), s 331 (failure to disclose: nominated officers in the regulated sector), and s 337 (protected disclosure). The shorter phrase 'reasonable grounds for suspecting' appears in many other sections of POCA.

[207] See principally Lord Hope's speech at paras 52–55. See further the commentary at [2006] Crim LR 998.

[208] Para 53.

[209] The assumption that the term 'reasonable grounds to suspect' was in this context a purely objective one is supported by the use of that term as a form of fault in some POCA offences (cf Lord Brown at [110]). For

on the facts available, irrespective of whether the individual defendant formed such suspicion himself. The test is now confirmed, in this context, as a mixed one comprising subjective (D suspects) and objective (there are reasonable grounds for D doing so) elements. This echoes the approach in police powers contexts, although arguably those are distinguishable because the dual requirement there serves as a check on abuse of authority. It is easy to envisage circumstances in which the Crown will fail to prove this element because D lacked suspicion (through naivety or stupidity) even though reasonable grounds existed for forming suspicion. But, in what circumstances is a prosecution ever likely to falter because D had suspicion, but his suspicion was one not based on reasonable grounds? There is a strong case for saying that, as a matter of policy, a person ought not to be criminally culpable for his failure to suspect even if, objectively viewed, there were grounds for suspecting.

5.2.9 Blameless inadvertence

A person may reasonably fail to foresee a consequence or reasonably fail to consider the possibility of the existence of a circumstance – as when goods, which are in fact stolen, are bought in the normal course of business from a trader of high repute. This state of mind would be classed as blameless inadvertence.

5.3 Further principles of *mens rea*

Mens rea is a term which has no single meaning. Every crime has its own *mens rea* which can be ascertained only by reference to its statutory definition or the case law. The most we can do is to state a general principle, or presumption, which governs its definition. Since *G*, we can say with confidence that, in crimes requiring *mens rea*, as distinct from negligence, the defendant should be liable only for that which he had *chosen* to bring about, or had chosen to take the risk of bringing about, that is, that he intended, or was reckless (in the subjective sense) or had knowledge, etc as to whether all the elements of the offence, both results and circumstances, should occur or exist. Because he had so chosen, he could fairly be held responsible for the occurrence of the *actus reus*. His intention, recklessness, knowledge, etc as to all the elements of the offence was *mens rea* or the basic constituent of it.

The general principle is expressed in the Draft Criminal Code as follows:

24 – (1) Unless a contrary intention appears, a person does not commit a Code offence unless he acts intentionally, knowingly or recklessly in respect of each of its elements...

5.3.1 The correspondence principle and constructive crime

The justification for requiring *mens rea* as to *every* element of the *actus reus* is that it must be presumed that every element contributes to the criminality of it. If it does not, it should not be there.[210] The requirement is therefore described as one of correspondence between the elements of *actus reus* and *mens rea*. This is an important aspect of the subjective approach to

example in s 330 of the 2002 Act it is a sufficient *mens rea* either that the defendant suspected, or that he had reasonable grounds to suspect the relevant facts.

[210] A view criticized by J Horder in writing on the requirement of *mens rea* as to age in sex crimes, 'How Culpability Can, and Cannot, be Denied in Under-Age Sex Crimes' [2001] Crim LR 15. See also the more general debate about the application of the correspondence principle and its merits: J Horder, 'A Critique of the Correspondence Principle' [1995] Crim LR 759; B Mitchell, 'In Defence of a Principle of Correspondence' [1999] Crim LR 195; Tadros, *Criminal Responsibility*, Ch 3 and 256–258; see also LCCP 177, Ch 2.

mens rea. In the present law many offences fall far short of precise correspondence; there are elements of the *actus reus* to which no corresponding *mens rea* attaches.[211]

A concept similar to that embodied in cl 24(1) of the Draft Code has been recognized by the courts[212] – a concept we might call basic *mens rea* – which describes those 'crimes whose definition expresses (or, more often implies) a *mens rea* which does not go beyond the *actus reus*'.[213] Basic *mens rea*, as so defined, is not required for all crimes, for even at common law there were many exceptions to it, and statutory crimes are frequently interpreted so as to exclude the necessity for either intention or recklessness with respect to some, one or more elements in the *actus reus*.

5.3.1.1 Constructive crime

Sometimes crimes may be satisfied by proof of the basic *mens rea* of a lesser offence than that charged – this is sometimes called 'constructive' crime. For example, an intention to cause serious bodily harm is the *mens rea* of murder. There is no need to prove that D intended to cause, or was reckless whether he caused, death – although death is the crucial element in the definition.[214] Lords Mustill and Steyn have criticized the application of this rule in murder as a 'conspicuous anomaly' and an example of 'constructive crime'.[215] Similarly, manslaughter may be committed by doing an unlawful and dangerous act which happens to cause death, although D has no *mens rea* as to the death.

Those are common law offences, but statutes are sometimes similarly interpreted. For example, constructive crime (that is, where the *mens rea* of a lesser offence suffices for a greater) is the general rule in offences against the person. D may be convicted of inflicting grievous bodily harm, if he foresaw some harm, not necessarily 'grievous', or of an assault occasioning actual bodily harm even though he foresaw no harm – the *mens rea* of common assault is enough.[216]

Some offences are so defined that it is sufficient to prove intention with respect to only one or more elements in the definition of the *actus reus*. Sometimes it is enough to prove only negligence; sometimes even this is not necessary and D may be convicted although he was blamelessly inadvertent as to a circumstance of the *actus reus*. In the latter case we shall say that the crime imposes 'strict liability' as to that circumstance.[217] Strict liability is discussed in Chapter 7.

---

[211] For the relationship between strict liability and constructive liability, see SP Green, 'Six Senses of Strict Liability', in A Simester (ed), *Appraising Strict Liability* (2005).

[212] Confusingly called 'basic intent' by Lord Simon in *DPP v Morgan* [1976] AC 182, [1975] 2 All ER 347 at 363; contrasting the term with 'ulterior intent' as used in the 3rd edition of this book and considered above

[213] Lord Simon's 'basic intent' does not go beyond but (it seems) does not necessarily go as far as the *actus reus* – it may not extend to every element of it. For this reason, and because it involves recklessness as well as intention, the term 'basic *mens rea*' is preferred.

[214] For criticism see LCCP 177, para 3.17 et seq, A Ashworth (2008) New Crim LR 232.

[215] In *A-G's Reference (No 3 of 1994)* [1998] 1 Cr App R 91, below, p 138 and *Powell and Daniels* [1999] AC 1, [1998] 1 Cr App R 261, below, p 215. Simester suggests that constructive crimes are not unfair if the element of *actus reus* to which lesser *mens rea* attaches is not unrelated to the *actus reus* for which D is required to have *mens rea*. So in an offence of causing death by dangerous driving, the fact that no *mens rea* as to death is required does not render the crime unfair since there is an element of *mens rea* as to the driving and the element of death is an 'intrinsic' risk to the element of driving. Seemingly, on this test, unlawful act manslaughter is not fair since although there is a requirement of *mens rea* as to some harm being caused to V, death (as to which no *mens rea* attaches) is not an intrinsic risk to that harm: see *Appraising Strict Liability* (2005) 46.

[216] cf the proposals of the Law Commission in its Report No 218, on offences against the person where the correspondence principle is respected in full. See Ch 17 below.

[217] See Ch 7.

5.3.1.2 Ulterior intent

The principle stated in cl 24(1), by itself, would amount to a definition of the *mens rea* of many crimes, but it does not meet all cases. A crime is frequently so defined that the *mens rea* includes an intention to produce some further consequence beyond the *actus reus* of the crime in question. Burglary is an example. It is not enough that D intended to enter a building as a trespasser, that is, to achieve the *actus reus* of burglary. It is necessary to go further and to show that D had the intention of committing one of a number of specified offences in the building. The actual commission of one of those offences is no part of the *actus reus* of burglary which is complete as soon as D enters. Instances of similar crimes include causing grievous bodily harm with intent to resist the lawful apprehension of any person,[218] and placing gunpowder near a building with intent to do bodily injury to any person.[219] Where such an ulterior intent must be proved, it is sometimes referred to as a 'specific intent'.[220] This term, however, is one which should be regarded with caution.[221] It is variously used to mean (i) whatever intention has to be proved to establish guilt of the particular crime before the court;[222] (ii) a 'direct' as distinct from an 'oblique' intention;[223] or (iii) an intention ulterior to the *actus reus*; or (iv) a crime where D may successfully plead lack of the prescribed *mens rea* notwithstanding the fact that he relies on evidence that he was intoxicated at the time.[224] The phrase 'ulterior intent' is therefore preferred to describe the third concept. The nature of the ulterior intent required varies widely from crime to crime – an intention to commit one of a number of specified offences in burglary, an intention to cause V to act to his prejudice in forgery, an intention permanently to deprive the owner in theft and so on.[225]

Where an ulterior *intent* is required, it is obvious that recklessness is not enough. On a charge of wounding with intent to cause grievous bodily harm, proof that D was reckless whether he caused grievous bodily harm will not suffice.[226]

It should again be emphasized that most crimes require only basic *mens rea* and no ulterior intent. In rape, for example, it is enough that D intentionally perpetrated the *actus reus* – penile penetration of a person without their consent – and no ulterior intention need be proved.

The result is that the best we can do by way of a general definition of *mens rea* is as follows: 'Intention, knowledge or recklessness with respect to all the elements of the offence *together with any ulterior intent which the definition of the crime requires.*'

5.3.2 Transferred malice[227]

If D, with the *mens rea* of a particular crime, causes the *actus reus* of the same crime,[228] he is guilty, even though the result, in some respects, is an unintended one. D intends to murder

---

[218] Offences Against the Person Act 1861, s 18.

[219] ibid, s 30.

[220] See R Perkins, 'A Rationale of *Mens Rea*' (1939) 52 Harv L Rev 905, 924.

[221] See R Cross, 'Specific Intent' [1961] Crim LR 510.

[222] *DPP v Beard* [1920] AC 479 at 501–502; below, p 312.

[223] Above, p 107. *Steane* [1947] KB 997 at 1004, [1947] 1 All ER 813 at 816.

[224] Below, p 311. See the discussion of *Heard* [2007] EWCA Crim 125, below, p 318.

[225] See J Horder, 'Crimes of Ulterior Intent', in A Simester and ATH Smith (eds), *Harm and Culpability* (1996) 153, arguing for more crimes of this nature to reflect more accurately the moral differences in wrongdoing.

[226] *Belfon* [1976] 3 All ER 46, where this passage was cited at p 49, [1976] 1 WLR 741, 744.

[227] See Ashworth in *Reshaping the Criminal Law*, 77–94 and in *Crime, Proof and Punishment*, 45–70; G Williams, 'Convictions and Fair Labelling' [1983] CLJ 85; J Chalmers and F Leverick 'Fair Labelling in Criminal Law' (2008) 71 MLR 217; J Horder, 'Transferred Malice and the Remoteness of Unexpected Outcomes from Intentions' [2006] Crim LR 383, and comparing the German system, M Bohlander, 'Problems of Transferred Malice in Multiple-Actor Scenarios' (2010) 74 J Crim Law 145.

[228] See *Hussain* [1969] 2 QB 567, [1969] Crim LR 433 and commentary; *Ellis, Street and Smith* [1987] Crim LR 44 and commentary; cf *Kundeus* (1976) 24 CCC (2d) 276 at 282–283.

X and, in the dusk, shoots at a person whom he believes to be X. He hits and kills the person at whom he aims, who is in fact V.[229] In one sense this is obviously an unintended result; but D did intend to cause the *actus reus* which he has caused and he is guilty of murder. Again, D intends to enter a house, No 6 King Street, and steal therein. In the dark he mistakenly enters No 7. He is guilty of burglary.[230]

The law, however, carries this principle still further. Suppose, now, that D, intending to murder X, shoots at a man who is in fact X, but *misses* and kills V[231] who, unknown to D, was standing close by. This is an unintended result in a different – and more fundamental – respect than the example considered above. Yet, once again, D, with the *mens rea* of a particular crime, has caused the *actus reus* of the same crime; and, once again, he is guilty of murder. So, where D struck X, who fell against V, who also fell and sustained a fatal injury, D was guilty of manslaughter: 'The criminality of the doer of the act is precisely the same whether it is [X] or [V] who dies.'[232] The application of the principle to cases of this second type is known as the doctrine of 'transferred malice'.

In *Latimer*,[233] D had a quarrel in a public house with X. He took off his belt and aimed a blow at X which struck him lightly, but the belt bounded off and struck V who was standing close by and wounded her severely. The jury found that the blow was unlawfully aimed at X, but that the striking of V 'was purely accidental and not such a consequence of the blow as the prisoner ought to have expected' – that is, he was not even negligent with respect to this result. It was held, on a case reserved, that D was properly convicted of unlawfully and maliciously wounding V.

It is important to notice the limitations of this doctrine. It operates only when the *actus reus* and the *mens rea* of the *same* crime coincide. If D, with the *mens rea* of one crime, does an act which causes the *actus reus* of a different crime, he cannot, be convicted of either offence. D shoots at V's dog with intent to kill it but misses and kills V who, unknown to D, was standing close by. Obviously he cannot be criminally liable for killing the dog, for he has not done so; nor can he be convicted of murder,[234] for he has not the *mens rea* for that crime. A similar result follows where D shoots at V with intent to kill him and, quite accidentally, kills V's dog: D is guilty of neither crime. As Horder puts it, such 'alchemy', translating fault elements and external elements between crimes is not permitted and would undermine the moral distinctiveness of each individual crime.[235] In such a case D would be liable for attempting to murder V and the availability of the attempt charge in most cases prompts Ashworth to question whether the transferred malice doctrine is needed.[236]

In *Pembliton*,[237] D was involved in a fight outside a public house, and, as a result, was charged with maliciously breaking a window. The jury found:

that the prisoner threw the stone which broke the window, but that he threw it at the people he had been fighting with, intending to strike one or more of them with it, but not intending to break the window.[238]

---

[229] Horder calls this an 'impersonality doctrine' [2006] Crim LR 383 at 384.

[230] See *Wrigley* [1957] Crim LR 57.

[231] What of the situation where D shoots at V intending to kill and does so, but the bullet continues and causes grievous bodily harm to X? Can D be convicted of grievous bodily harm to X? Or attempted murder of X?

[232] *Mitchell* [1983] QB 741, CA. cf *Haystead v Chief Constable of Derbyshire* [2000] Crim LR 758, DC. See for a more difficult case the decision in *Gnango* [2010] EWCA Crim 1691 discussed below p 218.

[233] (1886) 17 QBD 359.

[234] As to whether it could be manslaughter, see below, p 547.

[235] [2006] Crim LR 383, 393.

[236] ibid.

[237] (1874) LR 2 CCR 119.

[238] ibid, 120.

His conviction was quashed by the Court for Crown Cases Reserved, for there was no finding that he had the *mens rea* of the crime, the *actus reus* of which he had caused. Lord Coleridge pointed out that it would have been different if there had been a finding that he was reckless as to the consequence which had occurred – but there was no such finding.[239] The intent which is transferred must be a *mens rea*, whether intention or recklessness. If D shoots X with intent to kill, because X is making a murderous attack on him and this is the only way in which he can preserve his own life, he does not intend an *actus reus* (in the broader sense, above), for to kill in these circumstances is justified. If, however, D misses X and inadvertently kills V, an innocent bystander, he does cause an *actus reus* but he is not guilty of murder for there is no *mens rea* (in the broader sense) to transfer; the result which he intended was a perfectly lawful one.[240]

In *A-G's Reference (No 3 of 1994)*,[241] D stabbed a pregnant woman. Her child was born prematurely because of the stabbing and died in consequence of the premature birth. The fact that death resulted from premature birth, not directly from the stab wound, 'an unexpected difference of mode', was immaterial. Whether D was negligent in relation to the child was also irrelevant. In fact, D knew that the woman was pregnant but it seems that it would have made no difference if he had not known, and had had no reason to know that. His 'malice' against the mother was transferred to the child whose death he had in fact caused. The Court of Appeal gave full effect to the doctrine as described above, declining to impose two limitations advocated by Glanville Williams:[242] (i) that 'an unexpected difference of mode will be regarded as severing the chain of causation if it is sufficiently removed from the intended mode'; and (ii) that the doctrine 'should be limited to cases where the consequence was brought about by negligence in relation to the actual victim'.

The House of Lords, unenthusiastically, confirmed the existence of this ancient principle of transferred malice but declined to extend it to what they regarded as a double transfer of intent – from the mother to the foetus, and from the foetus to the child. D was not guilty of murder. Remarkably, however, they held he might be convicted of manslaughter by an unlawful and dangerous act – the assault on the mother. This looks like the application of the just rejected doctrine of transferred malice. But D did not intend a merely unlawful and dangerous act. He intended to cause grievous bodily harm; and the act, done with that intention, admittedly caused death – which looks like murder.[243] Horder argues that the correct question should have been whether murder was a representative label for D given that there was (i) an unintended victim and (ii) the death arose in a way that was not intended.[244] This is an attractive though complex theoretical model, but leaving the issue of the remoteness of the manner of infliction of the harm and the representativeness of the label of conviction to the jury is an impractical solution.

5.3.3 Coincidence in time of *actus reus* and *mens rea*[245]

The *mens rea* must coincide in point of time with the act which causes the *actus reus*.[246] 'If I happen to kill my neighbour accidentally, I do not become a murderer by thereafter

---

[239] Under *Caldwell*, recklessness was easy to establish in such a case and there was less need to rely on the doctrine of transferred malice.

[240] cf *Gross* (1913) 23 Cox CC 455.

[241] [1996] 1 Cr App R 351, [1996] Crim LR 268.

[242] CLGP, 48. He would abolish the doctrine for criminal damage. It results in 'unfair labelling' where the property damaged is more valuable than the property D intended to damage. He would retain it for offences against the person: [1983] CLJ 85. Injury to one person is (presumably) as bad as the same injury to any other person.

[243] For criticism see S Gough (1999) 62 MLR 128.

[244] [2006] Crim LR 383, 386–387.

[245] G Marston, 'Contemporaneity of Act and Intention' (1970) 86 LQR 208; A R White, 'The Identity and Time of the *Actus Reus*' [1977] Crim LR 148.

[246] *Jakeman* (1982) 76 Cr App R 223, [1983] Crim LR 104 and commentary thereon.

expressing joy over his death. My happiness over the result is not the same as a willingness to commit the illegal act.'[247] *Mens rea* implies an intention to do a present act, not a future act.[248] Suppose that D is driving to V's house, bent on killing V. A person steps under the wheels of D's car, giving D no chance to avoid him, and is killed. It is V. Clearly, D is not guilty of murder. One who walks out of prison while in a state of automatism does not commit the offence of escape[249] by deliberately remaining at large.[250] Suppose that D, having resolved to kill his wife, V, prepares and conceals a poisoned apple with the intention of giving it to her tomorrow. She finds the apple today, eats it and dies. D is not guilty of murder. He might be guilty of manslaughter on the ground that the act of leaving the apple where it might be found was reckless or grossly negligent.[251] However, if D does an act with intent thereby to cause the *actus reus*, and does so, it is immaterial that he has repented before the *actus reus* occurs. Where D dispatched suitcases which she knew to contain cannabis from Ghana to London, her repentance before the importation took place was no defence.[252]

Where, however, D has, with *mens rea*, gone beyond mere preparation and is in the course of committing an offence, it should be no answer that the final step was involuntary or accidental – as where D is on the point of pulling the trigger with intent to murder and, being startled by an explosion, does so involuntarily.[253]

Where the *actus reus* of the crime charged is a continuing act, it is sufficient that D has *mens rea* during its continuance.[254] Where the *actus reus* is part of a larger transaction, it may be sufficient that D has *mens rea* during the transaction, though not at the moment the *actus reus* is accomplished. D inflicts a wound upon V with intent to kill him. Then, believing that he has killed V, he disposes, as he thinks, of the 'corpse'. In fact V was not killed by the wound but dies as a result of the act of disposal. D has undoubtedly caused the *actus reus* of murder by the act of disposal but he did not, at that time have *mens rea*. In an Indian and a Rhodesian[255] case it was held, accordingly, that D must be acquitted of murder and convicted only of attempted murder. But in *Thabo Meli*,[256] the Privy Council held that it was:

> impossible to divide up what was really one series of acts in this way. There is no doubt that the accused set out to do all these acts in order to achieve their plan, and as parts of their plan: and it is much too refined a ground of judgment to say that, because they were at a misapprehension at one stage and thought that their guilty purpose was achieved before it was achieved, therefore they are to escape the penalties of the law.

This suggests that the answer might be different where there was no antecedent plan to dispose of the body. *Thabo Meli* was distinguished on this ground in New Zealand[257] and, at first, in South Africa.[258] But in England, in *Church*[259] the Court of Criminal Appeal applied *Thabo*

---

[247] Andanaes, GPCL of Norway, 194.

[248] 'There is no law against a man's intending to commit a murder the day after tomorrow. The law only deals with conduct': RM Holmes, *The Criminal Law* (John Harvard edn) 54.

[249] Sixth edition of this book, at 756.

[250] *Scott* [1967] VR 276; discussed by C Howard, 'Escaping from Gaol' [1967] Crim LR at 406.

[251] cf *Burke* [1987] Crim LR 480 and commentary at 484.

[252] *Jakeman*, above. cf *Wings Ltd v Ellis*, above, p 74.

[253] See commentary on *Burke* [1987] Crim LR 480. Note the possibility of applying the *Miller* principle (above, Ch 4) where D has created the dangerous situation and comes under a duty to avert risk.

[254] *Fagan v Metropolitan Police Comr* [1969] 1 QB 439, above, p 69. cf *Miller* [1983] 2 AC 161, HL; *Singh (Gurdev) v R* [1973] 1 WLR 1444, CA.

[255] *Khandu* (1890) ILR 15 Bom 194; *Shorty* [1950] SR 280.

[256] [1954] 1 All ER 373. Followed in *Moore and Dorn* [1975] Crim LR 229.

[257] *Ramsay* [1967] NZLR 1005.

[258] *Chiswibo* 1960 (2) SA 714.

[259] [1966] 1 QB 59.

Meli where D, in a sudden fight, knocked V unconscious and, wrongly believing her to be dead, threw her into the river where she drowned. He was charged with murder and his conviction for manslaughter was upheld. Here there was no antecedent plan. The point was not considered by the court, but it was apparently thought to be enough that the accused's conduct constituted 'a series of acts which culminated in [V's] death'. This is an extremely flexible approach to the principle of concurrence or contemporaneity as it is sometimes called, and it facilitates convictions in awkward fact scenarios.

In *Le Brun*,[260] the court followed *Church*, holding that it was immaterial that there was no preconceived plan and that the same principles apply to manslaughter as to murder.[261] D, in a quarrel, knocked his wife unconscious and while attempting to drag her body away dropped and killed her. The jury were rightly told that they could convict of murder or manslaughter, depending on the intention with which the blow was struck, if D accidentally dropped V while (i) attempting to move her to her home against her wishes and/or (ii) attempting to dispose of her body or otherwise cover up the assault. The court appears to uphold the manslaughter conviction on both of two alternative principles, as follows.

The transaction principle

This appears to operate so that D is guilty of homicide if he kills during the continuance of the transaction, the sequence of events initiated by the unlawful blow, and that transaction continues at least during the conduct described under (i) and (ii) above. This suggests that it certainly continues while D is engaged in some kind of wrongdoing arising out of, and immediately following, the unlawful blow. Though the case does not decide this, the result might have been different if D had dropped V in the same manner and at the same time and place while attempting to get her to hospital, or to her home if he had thought that was where she would wish to be taken; or, if he believed her to be dead, while he was attempting to deliver the corpse to the police. Under this principle it is immaterial that the second act is the sole cause of death.

The causation principle

This approach holds that the initial blow is a cause of death. As that blow was struck with *mens rea*, there is no further problem – Le Brun is guilty of murder or manslaughter as the case may be. The second event was also a cause of death but it is clear that there may be more than one cause (see above p 83). This may suggest that Le Brun would have been guilty if V had been similarly dropped by a passer-by who was trying to get her to hospital. But it may be that an intervening act by a third party is regarded as breaking the chain of causation, particularly where it is unforeseeable, whereas the same thing done by the original actor is not.[262] The causation principle represents the *ratio decidendi* of the South African case of *S v Masilela*.[263] D, intending to kill V, knocked him unconscious and, believing him to be dead, set fire to the house. V died from the fumes. If he had not been unconscious he would have been able to walk out, so knocking him unconscious was a cause of death. But it is probable that the chain of causation would be regarded as broken if the house had been set on fire by a tramp who happened to come along after D's departure.

In all these cases the second act was a cause of the death. Where it is impossible to say which act caused death, it has been held that D may be convicted only if it can be proved that he acted

---

[260] [1992] QB 61.

[261] In *A-G's Reference (No 4 of 1980)* [1981] 2 All ER 617 at 620, the court left open the question whether the principle applies to manslaughter and whether it was part of the *ratio decidendi* of *Church* that it does so.

[262] See the passage, above, cited by the court in *Le Brun*.

[263] 1968 (2) SA 558 (AD).

with *mens rea* (or other appropriate degree of fault) on both occasions. Where D knocked V downstairs and then, believing that he had killed her, cut her throat in order to dispose of the body, and it was impossible to say which act caused death, it was held that the jury should have been directed that they should convict of manslaughter if they were satisfied *both* (i) that knocking V downstairs was an intentional act which was unlawful and dangerous;[264] *and* (ii) that the act of cutting the throat was one of gross criminal negligence.[265] If manslaughter was committed, it was immaterial that it was impossible to prove on which of these two closely related occasions it occurred.[266] If the jury were not satisfied on both points, there was a 50 per cent chance that this was a case of accidental death, in which case acquittal must follow. But if *Thabo Meli* applies to manslaughter,[267] the direction is too favourable. Assuming it was all one 'transaction', it should have been enough to prove that D had the required *mens rea* on the first occasion.

5.3.4 Ignorance of the law is no defence[268]

In our discussion of the general principles of *mens rea* nothing has been said about whether D knows his act is against the law, for, in the great majority of cases, it is irrelevant whether he knows it or not: '...the principle that ignorance of the law is no defence in crime' said Lord Bridge, 'is so fundamental that to construe the word "knowingly" in a criminal statute as requiring not merely knowledge of facts material to the offender's guilt, but also knowledge of the relevant law, would be revolutionary and, to my mind, wholly unacceptable'.[269] This view has recently been powerfully criticized by Ashworth[270] who describes the proposition that ignorance of the criminal law is no defence as preposterous. He suggests that the doctrine is unfair and that it fails to recognize the State's duty to render the criminal law accessible to citizens to 'respect the right of individuals not to be convicted of offences for which it is not reasonable to expect them to have knowledge'.[271]

As the law presently stands, it must usually be proved that D intended to cause, or was reckless whether he caused, the event or state of affairs which, as a matter of fact, is forbidden by law; but it is quite immaterial to his conviction (though it may affect his punishment) whether he *knew* that the event or state of affairs was forbidden by law. This is so even though it also appears that D's ignorance of the law was quite reasonable and even, apparently, if it was quite impossible[272] for him to know of the prohibition in question. It was no defence for a native of Baghdad, charged with a sexual offence on board a ship lying in an English port, to show that the act was lawful in his own country and that he did not know English law.[273] It was held that a Frenchman might be guilty of murder in the course of duelling in England, even if he did not know that duelling was against English law.[274] In *Bailey*,[275] D was convicted of an offence

---

[264] This is manslaughter. Below, p 539.

[265] This may be considered to be manslaughter and indeed, was held to be so in this case. Below, p 552.

[266] *A-G's Reference (No 4 of 1980)* [1981] 1 WLR 705, CA, [1981] Crim LR 493 and commentary.

[267] This question was left open. *Church* suggests that it does; and that seems right in principle.

[268] See Ch 11, and A Ashworth, 'Excusable Mistake of Law' [1974] Crim LR 652; M Matthews, 'Ignorance of the Law is No Excuse' (1983) 3 LS 174.

[269] *Grant v Borg* [1982] 2 All ER 257 at 263, HL but cf *Curr* [1968] 2 QB 944. Acts done by D to V in the reasonable belief that V was committing a byelaw offence may be justified even if it turns out that the byelaw was void for uncertainty: *Percy v Hall* [1997] QB 924, (Civ Div).

[270] 'Ignorance of the Criminal Law, and Duties to Avoid it' (2011) 74 MLR 1.

[271] At p 25. This is particularly true of offence based on omissions, (ibid).

[272] *Bailey*, below.

[273] *Esop* (1836) 7 C & P 456.

[274] *Barronet and Allain* (1852) Dears CC 51.

[275] (1800) Russ & Ry 1.

created by a statute which was passed while he was on the high seas although he committed the act before the end of the voyage when he could not possibly have known of the statute.[276] In each of these cases it might be argued that D at least intended something immoral; but that makes no difference. A motorist's mistaken belief that a constable has no right in the particular circumstances to require a specimen of breath is not a reasonable excuse for not providing the specimen.[277] A mistaken belief that a firearms certificate was current was held to be incapable of being a reasonable excuse under the Firearms Act 1968, on the ground that it was a mistake of law.[278] Ignorance that certain banking transactions require the consent of the Bank of England is no defence to a charge of unauthorized deposit-taking.[279]

Since the courts are keen on saying that the meaning of an ordinary word in a statute is not a question of law[280] it is easy to see how many cases might involve an argument by D that he did not interpret the statutory words to apply to his conduct and therefore did not realize his act was criminal. If D studies the Public Order Act and concludes that the conduct in which he proposes to indulge is not 'insulting', but the court takes a different view, why cannot D rely on his mistake 'of fact'? It is thought that such a defence would be unsympathetically received by the courts and, indeed, regarded as subversive of the criminal law;[281] but, if it is accepted that *Brutus v Cozens* applies, it is difficult to see that it is bad in principle.[282]

In the case of the most serious crimes the problem does not arise; everyone knows it is against the law to murder, rob or rape.[283] In the case of many less serious crimes, however, a person may very easily, and without negligence, be ignorant that a particular act is a crime. In such cases there will usually be nothing immoral about the act; and the conviction of a morally innocent person requires justification. Various justifications for the rule have been advanced. Blackstone[284] thought that 'every person of discretion' may know the law – a proposition which is manifestly untrue today. Austin[285] based the rule upon the difficulty of disproving ignorance of the law, while Holmes,[286] who considered this no more difficult a question than many which are investigated in the courts, thought that to admit the plea of ignorance would be to encourage ignorance of the law. A more modern writer, Jerome Hall,[287] argued that to allow the defence would be to contradict one of the fundamental postulates of a legal order: that rules of law enforce objective meanings, to be ascertained by the courts:

If that plea [*sc,* ignorance of the law] were valid, the consequence would be: whenever a defendant in a criminal case thought that the law was thus and so, he is to be treated as though the law were thus and so, that is, *the law actually is thus and so.*[288]

---

[276] But the judges recommended a pardon. Where a continuing act was made unlawful it was held that a reasonable time must be allowed for its discontinuance and that ignorance of the law was relevant to determine this question: *Burns v Nowell* (1880) 5 QBD 444.

[277] *Reid* [1973] 1 WLR 1283, CA: '... if you choose at the street side to act out the part of Hampden, you have got to be right': per Scarman LJ.

[278] *Jones* [1995] 1 Cr App R 262. But was not this really a mistake of fact – though probably an unreasonable one?

[279] *A-G's Reference (No 1 of 1995) (B and F)* [1996] 2 Cr App R 320. The more difficult question was whether the ignorant directors 'consented' to the commission of the offence. Held, they did.

[280] *Brutus v Cozens* [1973] AC 854, HL.

[281] cf *Sancoff v Halford* [1973] Qd R 25. (Belief that books were not obscene is a mistake of law.)

[282] See Ashworth above, n 270.

[283] But see *Christian* [2006] UKPC 47 in which Pitcairn islanders charged with sexual offences claimed to have no access to English law, making that conduct criminal. See the fascinating article by H Power [2007] Crim LR 609.

[284] *Commentaries,* iv, 27.

[285] *Lectures on Jurisprudence* (1885) 497.

[286] *The Common Law* (1881) 48.

[287] 'Ignorance and Mistake in Criminal Law' (1957) 33 Ind LJ 1. cf *General Principles*, 382–383.

[288] (1957) 33 Ind LJ at 19. In *Cooper v Simmons* (1862) 7 H & N 707 at 717, Martin B thought that to allow the defence would be 'to substitute the opinion of a person charged with a breach of the law for the law itself'.

As Hall points out, the criminal law represents an objective code of ethics which must prevail over individual convictions and he therefore argues:[289]

Thus, while a person who acts in accordance with his honest convictions is certainly not as culpable as one who commits a harm knowing it is wrong, it is also true that conscience sometimes leads one astray. *Mens rea* underlines the essential difference. Penal liability based on it implies the objective wrongness of the harm proscribed – regardless of motive or conviction. This may fall short of perfect justice but the ethics of a legal order must be objective.

Much modern legislation is devoid of moral content, apart from the moral obligation to obey the law. One who, being ignorant of the law, sells goods at a price in excess of the maximum fixed by statute could hardly be said to have been led astray by his conscience while the 'harm proscribed' lacks 'objective wrongness'. Ashworth regards the rule as one based on shaky foundations.[290]

The common law rule is not universally followed and the arguments by which it is supported have been found 'not very convincing to those used to another system'.[291] In Scandinavian criminal law, ignorance of the law is, in varying degrees, a defence. Thus, in Norway, a person will not be excused for ignorance of 'the general rules of society which apply to everybody' or 'the special rules governing the business or activity in which the individual is engaged'. But 'a fisherman need not study the legislation on industry'; a servant may be excused for *bona fide* and reasonable obedience to illegal orders of his master; or a stranger for breaking a rule which he could not be expected to know about; or liability may be negatived because the legislation is very new, or its interpretation doubtful. Such rules seem to have much to commend them, compared with the rigid and uncompromising attitude of English law. They seek to relate guilt to moral responsibility in a way in which our rule does not.[292]

5.3.5 Mistake of law may negative *mens rea*[293]

If D, with *mens rea*, causes the *actus reus*, he is guilty and it will not avail him to say that he did not know the *actus reus* was forbidden by the criminal law. But the *actus reus* may be so defined that if D makes a mistake of law it may mean that he was not acting intentionally or recklessly with respect to some element in the *actus reus* and so he would lack *mens rea*. In such a case, his mistake, whether reasonable or not, is a defence. '…an honest belief in a certain state of things does afford a defence, including an honest though mistaken belief about legal rights'.[294] Unless the prosecution can prove that the mistake was not made, they have not established the requisite *mens rea*. For example, if D is charged with intentionally or recklessly damaging property belonging to another, even if he admits intentional damage to the property, his honest belief, arising from a mistake of law, that the property is his own, is

---

[289] 33 Ind LJ at 22.

[290] See above n 270.

[291] J Andenaes, '*Ignorantia Juris* in Scandinavian Law' in Mueller (ed), *Essays in Criminal Science* (1965) 217 at 222. For South African law see *S v De Blom* 1977 (3) SA 513 (AD) discussed by C Turpin [1978] CLJ 8.

[292] An exception to the general rule is created by the Statutory Instruments Act 1946, s 3. See D Lanham, 'Delegated Legislation and Publication' (1974) 37 MLR 510. On a charge brought under a statutory instrument it is a defence for D to prove that the instrument had not been issued at the time of the alleged offence; unless the Crown then proves that reasonable steps had been taken to bring it to the notice of the public, or persons likely to be affected by it, or D. See *Defiant Cycle Co Ltd v Newell* [1953] 2 All ER 38. The Privy Council has held that, in a jurisdiction where there is no similar provision, a person who is unaware that a ministerial order applying a prohibition to him has been made may set up his ignorance as a lack of *mens rea*: *Lim Chin Aik v R* [1963] AC 160, below, p 171.

[293] See Ch 11, p 330 below.

[294] *Barrett and Barrett* (1980) 72 Cr App R 212 at 216, CA, below, p 334.

a 'defence'. He will not have an intention or recklessness as to the element of *actus reus* – that the property belongs to another. The court so held, in *Smith*,[295] not because of any special provision in the Criminal Damage Act but by 'applying the ordinary principles of *mens rea*'. The plea of mistake is considered in full in Chapter 11.

5.3.6 Absence of a 'claim of right' as an element in *mens rea*

Sometimes the *mens rea* of an offence is so defined as to require the absence of a claim of right. In other words, if D believed he had a right to do the act in question, he had no *mens rea* and therefore was not guilty of the crime. This defence will prevail even if D's belief is mistaken and is based upon an entirely wrong view of the law. It is available in a number of important crimes, including theft,[296] criminal damage to property,[297] and a number of other offences requiring wilfulness or fraud. This is in accordance with the ordinary principle that a mistake of law may, indirectly, operate as a defence by preventing D from having *mens rea* in acting as he did. It is important to notice the limits within which this excuse operates. The mistake must be one which leads D to believe he has a right to act as he does; it is not enough that he simply believes his act is not a crime. Here too, the distinction between mistake as to the criminal and as to the civil law seems to be important. Thus, if D, having read in an out-of-date book on criminal law that it is not stealing to take another's title deeds to land,[298] were to take V's deeds, thinking that this was a way in which he could injure V without any risk of being punished, he could, no doubt, be convicted of theft under s 1 of the Theft Act 1968. He had no claim of right. It would be otherwise if D, owing to a misunderstanding of the law of property, thought that the title deeds were his, and that V was wrongfully withholding them from him. Here, clearly, he had a claim of right. Thus, while a mistake as to the criminal law only will not give rise to a claim of right, an error as to the civil law may do so.

It certainly cannot be asserted with confidence that the absence of a claim of right is a *general* requirement of *mens rea*, as it is in the case of theft and the other crimes referred to above. The question will therefore be considered in relation to specific crimes discussed throughout this book.

5.3.7 Proof of intention and foresight

There was formerly high authority[299] for the view that there is an irrebuttable presumption of law that a person foresees and intends the natural consequences of his acts. Proof that he did an act the natural consequence of which was death, was conclusive proof that he intended to kill, in the absence of evidence of insanity or incapacity to form an intent. To what extent, if at all, this actually represented the law was disputed: but it is now clear beyond all doubt that it is not the law. The question in every case is as to the actual intention of the person charged at the time when he did the act. Section 8 of the Criminal Justice Act 1967 provides:

A court or jury in determining whether a person has committed an offence,

(a) shall not be bound to infer that he intended or foresaw a result of his actions by reason only of its being a natural and probable consequence of those actions; but

---

[295] [1974] QB 354 , CA; below, p 330.

[296] Below, p 778.

[297] Below, p 1012.

[298] This was the rule at common law.

[299] *DPP v Smith* [1961] AC 290. The decision cannot be technically overruled by the Privy Council but five judges, all members of the House of Lords, declared that it was wrongly decided in *Frankland* [1987] AC 576, PC. cf the facts in *Hales* [2005] EWCA Crim 1118.

(b) shall decide whether he did intend or foresee that result by reference to all the evidence draw-ing such inferences from the evidence as appear proper in the circumstances.

To what extent intention or foresight need be proved in any particular case depends on the law relating to the crime which is in issue. Section 8 is concerned with *how* intention or foresight must be proved, not *when* it must be proved.[300] On a charge of unlawful act manslaughter, for example, it remains unnecessary to prove that D intended or foresaw that death was likely to result from his act.[301] Section 8 was once construed so as to affect the substantive law of murder[302] but this was exceptional and it is now clear that it applies only to proof and never affects the substantive law.

Although s 8 requires the court to have regard to *all* the evidence, that is, all the evidence relevant to the question whether D did intend or foresee, there is one exception. The courts have consistently held that evidence that D did not intend or foresee because he had taken drink or drugs is no defence, except in the case of crimes requiring 'specific intent'. This prac-tice has been reconciled with the words of s 8 by holding that where D relies on evidence that he had taken drink or drugs for the purpose of showing that he lacked any *mens rea*, there is a rule of substantive law that the prosecution need prove no *mens rea* unless the offence is one of 'specific intent'.[303] This is discussed further in Chapter 11.

It might be thought, at first sight, that proof of intention, foresight and knowledge presents almost insuperable difficulties. Direct evidence of a person's state of mind, except through his own confession, is not available. But the difficulties, in practice, are not so great. If D points a loaded gun at V's head, pulls the trigger and shoots him dead, it is reasonable to infer that D intended and foresaw V's death. A jury might well be convinced by such evidence that D intended to kill. If D offered an explanation of any kind – he thought the gun was unloaded, or he intended to fire above V's head – and the jury thought that it might reasonably be true, then they should acquit him of an intention to kill. If he offered no explanation, as s 8 makes clear, the jury would not be bound to convict him of having such an intention; they would have to ask themselves whether, in the light of all the evidence, they were satisfied beyond reasonable doubt. Sometimes D's acts may afford apparently overwhelming evidence of his intention to produce a particular result but evidence to the contrary is always admissible and the question must be left to the jury.[304] Similarly, the fact that any reasonable person would, in the circum-stances, have known of a fact is cogent evidence that D knew of it.

The difficulty of distinguishing between 'he foresaw' and 'he ought to have foreseen', 'he knew' and 'he ought to have known', is not a good reason for not drawing the line at this point. It is an inescapable difficulty when we have a law which requires us to look into individual's minds; and such a requirement is essential to a civilized system of criminal law.

[A] a lack of confidence in the ability of a tribunal correctly to estimate evidence of states of mind and the like can never be sufficient ground for excluding from enquiry the most fundamental element in a rational and humane criminal code.[305]

---

[300] *DPP v Majewski* [1997] AC 443, [1976] 2 All ER 142 at 151, 170.

[301] *DPP v Newbury* [1977] AC 500 HL.

[302] *Hyam v DPP* [1975] AC 55, above, p 107.

[303] *DPP v Majewski* [1977] AC 443, [1976] 2 All ER 142, HL.

[304] *Riley* [1967] Crim LR 656, is a striking instance of the rebuttal of apparently conclusive evidence of an in-tent. Expert evidence was admitted that D was suffering from psychoneurosis; but in the case of a normal person expert evidence as to the operation of the mind is not admissible. It is a question for the jury: *Chard* (1971) 56 Cr App R 268, CA. cf *Turner* [1975] QB 834, [1975] 1 All ER 70.

[305] *Thomas v R* (1937) 59 CLR 279 at 309, per Dixon J.

6
Crimes of negligence

6.1 Negligence as failure to comply with an objective standard[1]

Negligence describes conduct that departs from the standard to be expected of a reasonable person. Offences can be drafted with requirements to prove negligence as to consequences or circumstances. To establish negligence, the prosecution must prove that D's conduct failed to conform to what would be expected of the reasonable person in those circumstances. To establish that D was negligent it is not necessary for the prosecution to prove that D did not foresee a relevant risk. The question is whether his conduct falls below the reasonable standard. That might be because he has seen the risk of the proscribed consequence or circumstance but reacted unreasonably to it, or because he has not seen the risk when he ought to. If the reasonable person would have seen the risk of the proscribed harm or circumstance, D can be liable for crimes of negligence even if he personally failed to see the risk.

Negligence involves a failure by D to comply with an objective standard of behaviour set by the law. Intention, recklessness and negligence all involve a failure to comply with an objective standard of conduct; that is, they are all forms of fault.[2] It is important to appreciate the difference between negligence and intention or *Cunningham/G* recklessness.[3] Whereas intention and subjective recklessness require proof of D's state of mind – foresight of the risk of the proscribed harm – negligence may be conclusively proved by simply showing that D's conduct failed to measure up to an objective standard.

The now discredited form of *Caldwell* recklessness was also said by the House of Lords to involve proof of a state of mind; but this is misleading. *Caldwell* recklessness was only a state of mind in the sense that *not* giving thought is a state of mind.[4] An important distinction between *Caldwell* recklessness and negligence was the subject of much of the debate. Whereas under *Caldwell* recklessness, D would not have been liable if he had given thought to the matter of the risk of harm his conduct posed, and wrongly concluded that there was no risk,[5] in a crime of negligence D would be liable. In a crime based on negligence evidence of D's personal state of mind is no excuse. Negligence is proved by D's *conduct* failing to measure up to an objective standard. It is no answer for him to say, 'I considered whether there was a risk

---

[1] See generally, HLA Hart, in *Punishment and Responsibility* (1968) Ch VI, 'Negligence, *Mens Rea* and Criminal Responsibility'; liability for negligence in manslaughter and road traffic offences is considered in detail below, Ch 15 and Ch 33.

[2] cf the argument that since negligence involves no culpable choice by the accused it is not properly a fault element: RA Duff, 'Criminalising Endangerment', in Duff and Green, *Defining Crimes*, 48.

[3] Above, p 123.

[4] Above, p 121. See G Williams, 'Recklessness Redefined' [1981] CLJ 252 at 256–258. On the justification for culpability when D has not troubled to investigate risks that would be obvious to the reasonable person, see Tadros, *Criminal Responsibility*, Ch 3.

[5] Above, p 122.

and decided there was none'. Where the risk is one that he *ought to have* foreseen, that is an admission of negligence.[6]

It could also never be a 'defence' to a charge of negligence to show that the dangerous/ careless act was done recklessly or intentionally. If D were charged with manslaughter and the prosecution's case was that he killed V by gross negligence it is inconceivable that it could be a defence for him to say convincingly, 'I wasn't negligent; I *intended* to kill him'; or 'I took a quite deliberate risk of killing him'. The more blameworthy state of mind must include the less; so, if D failed to comply with the objective standard, he is liable whatever his state of mind.[7]

6.1.1 Negligence as *mens rea*

Writers differ as to whether negligence can properly be described as *mens rea*. If *mens rea* is used simply as a compendious expression for the varieties of fault that may give rise to crim-inal liability, then it does, of course, include negligence. If it is taken in its more literal sense of 'guilty mind', the usage is inappropriate. It is sometimes argued that the absence of fore-sight or knowledge is just as much a state of mind as its presence;[8] but, since negligence may be proved without establishing anything as to what was going on in D's mind, it seems more appropriate and convenient to restrict *mens rea* to intention, recklessness, knowledge, belief, dishonesty etc, and that is the sense in which it is used in this book. Crimes requiring *mens rea* are contrasted with crimes of negligence discussed in this chapter and strict liability crimes (discussed in the next).[9]

The courts have made abundantly clear that negligence is not a form of 'knowledge'. Devlin J emphasized that there is 'a vast distinction between a state of mind which consists of delib-erately refraining from making inquiries, the result of which a person does not care to have [wilful blindness], and a state of mind which is merely neglecting to make such inquiries as a reasonable and prudent person would make [constructive knowledge]'.[10] In *Flintshire County Council v Reynolds*,[11] it was recently reiterated that a person who has 'constructive notice' of a fact may be negligent, but this is not the same as 'knowing' that fact.[12]

6.1.2 Purely objective standards?

Although negligence is conduct that departs from the standard to be expected of a reasonable person, that is not to say that a person's state of mind is always completely irrelevant when negligence is in issue. Two issues need to be considered (i) is it permissible to take into account D's state of mind where that involves special knowledge that a reasonable person would not possess and (ii) is it possible to take into account D's state of mind where he has less knowledge or capacity to see a relevant risk?

---

[6] See generally J Brady, 'Recklessness, Negligence, Indifference and Awareness' (1980) 43 MLR 381. Note also the conclusion in *A-G's Reference (No 2 of 1999)* [2000] QB 796, that it is not necessary to produce evidence of the 'state of mind' of the accused on a charge of gross negligence manslaughter.

[7] A cold-blooded murderer does not behave reasonably, but we would not describe him as negligent.

[8] G Williams, *Salmond on Jurisprudence* (11th edn, 1957) 329. See also P Brett, *An Inquiry into Criminal Guilt* (1963) 99.

[9] cf Duff, *Answering for Crime* who summarizes Hart's position that if D was negligently responsible for bringing about the creation of the risk of the harm he is at 'fault', at 70–71.

[10] *Roper v Taylor's Garage* [1951] 2 TLR 284, 288.

[11] [2006] EWHC 195 (Admin) obtaining benefit contrary to Social Security Administration Act 1992, s 112.

[12] [17].

6.1.2.1 Where D possesses special knowledge

If D has special knowledge that an ordinary person would not possess, the appropriate question becomes whether a reasonable person, *with that knowledge*, would have acted as he did. For example, behaviour with a revolver that is possibly not negligent in the case of an ordinary person with no special knowledge might be grossly negligent if committed by a firearms expert.[13] D has *more* knowledge or capacity for foresight, and a higher standard will legitimately be expected of him.

The Road Traffic Act 1988, s 2A(3), defining dangerous driving[14] also recognizes that in deciding whether a driver drove dangerously, the standard is 'what would be expected of a competent and careful driver'; but, in determining that standard:

regard shall be had not only to the circumstances of which he could be expected to be aware, but also to any circumstances shown to be within the knowledge of the accused.

So, if D is aware of facts which would not be obvious to a reasonable driver, D may nevertheless be guilty since the Act provides that regard must be had to any circumstances shown to be within his knowledge. If D is reasonably unaware, for example, of the tendency of a car to swerve to the right when braked hard, D cannot be held to have driven dangerously or even carelessly, but once D becomes aware of this tendency he may properly be held to have driven dangerously if it would then be obvious to a competent and careful driver that to drive the car with this tendency would be dangerous.[15] Similarly, D's actual knowledge of an uneven road surface may count against him though other drivers would be unaware of the hazard.

Several cases have recently highlighted the difficulty in applying the objective test in situations where a driver has superior driving ability. The Court of Appeal has confirmed that the test is objective: *Bannister*.[16] The current state of the law is that the superior driving *ability* of the driver is irrelevant when a driver is charged with dangerous driving. To have regard to those *abilities* is inconsistent with the objective test of the competent and careful driver set out in the Act. These are not relevant to the dangerousness test because they go to the *standard* of the competent and careful driver and not the knowledge or circumstances. That distinction is a fine one.

6.1.2.2 Where D is unable to appreciate the relevant risk

More controversial is the question of whether the negligence test should take account of the individual defendant's personal *inability* to appreciate the risk of the proscribed harm. The orthodox answer is that if D has *less* knowledge or capacity for foresight than the reasonable person this will not generally help him. For example, on a charge of careless driving a learner driver, who was exercising all the skill and attention to be expected from a person with his short experience but who has failed to attain the required standard, would be held guilty.

A further example arises in the offence of harassment under the Protection from Harassment Act 1997, s 1(1)(b) read with s 1(2) imposes a requirement that the course of conduct (which is alleged to amount to harassment) must be one which D knew *or ought to have known* amounts to harassment. That is a statutory crime of negligence. The test of whether he knew or ought to have known is, under s 1, whether a reasonable person *in possession of the same information* as D would think the course of conduct did amount to harassment. In *C*,[17] the defendant, who suffered paranoid schizophrenia, had performed the conduct for the

---

[13] cf *Lamb* [1967] 2 QB 981; below, p 541.
[14] Below, p 1126.
[15] cf *Haynes v Swain* [1975] RTR 40, DC, above, p 1131.
[16] [2009] EWCA Crim 1571. Discussed in full in Ch 33. See also J Goudkamp [2010] CLJ 8.
[17] [2001] Crim LR 845 and commentary.

offence by sending offensive letters to his MP, on at least two occasions. He was convicted and appealed on the basis that the judge should have directed the jury to consider his mental disorder as a relevant condition of the hypothetical reasonable person in s 1(2). The Court of Appeal held that s 1(2) involved a purely objective test relating to the reasonable person and reasonable conduct. D's illness was not relevant to that question. Section 1(2) seeks to endow the reasonable person with knowledge of circumstances that would render otherwise seemingly innocuous conduct harassing (for example, when D knows that previous advances towards V have been rejected and continues to send gifts). In such cases D's inculpatory state of mind is taken into account. Why, then, should the reasonable person not also be possessed with knowledge about D's *exculpatory* states of mind in order to assess whether the conduct is harassment? This is not the same as asking whether a reasonable person with the characteristics of the accused would regard it as harassment, particularly where the characteristic inhibits cognition of the wrongdoing.[18]

However, the courts have accepted that strictness of the objective test ought, in some circumstances, to be modified where the defendant is a child. In *R (RSPA) v C*,[19] it was held that the question whether a juvenile (15) was negligent in not taking an injured cat to the vet should be judged by the standards of a reasonable girl of *her* age. It is submitted that this is a sensible qualification of the negligence standard, but it must be treated with caution. Should account of the defendant's age only be taken when that will affect his ability to appreciate the risk of the relevant harm? Some risks are obvious to very young children. Equally importantly the question arises whether taking into account the defendant's age (and capacity to appreciate risk) will undermine the policy of negligence based crimes. What of the 14-year-old tearaway who is driving a car illegally and causes injury? Should the evaluation of his carelessness in driving take account of his age? Surely not.

Some commentators have suggested that the objective standard ought to be qualified to the extent necessary to take account of the defendant's shortcomings that affect his ability to behave reasonably and which are not a result of his fault.[20] This would include characteristics such as age, hearing, sight, etc. It is doubtful that the courts would entertain such a radical qualification of the objective standard. The only English case following this approach seems to be *Hudson*.[21] In deciding whether a man who had sexual intercourse with a 'defective woman', contrary to s 7 of the Sexual Offences Act 1956 (repealed) had 'no reason to suspect her to be a defective', the court was bound:

to take into account the accused himself. There may be cases of which this is not one, where there is evidence before the jury that the accused himself is a person of limited intelligence, or possibly suffering from some handicap which would prevent him from appreciating the state of affairs which an ordinary man might realize.

The decisions in *Caldwell* and *Lawrence* in 1981 were open to the interpretation that an 'obvious' risk meant obvious to the particular defendant but the courts soon put paid to that notion. 'Obvious' under that test meant obvious to the reasonable person, even if the defendant was a 14-year-old schoolgirl with a learning disability.[22] Some academics rely on the cases decided under *Caldwell* to support the argument that the courts are (and ought to be) amenable to an

---

[18] Arguably the strong policy grounds of protection on which the Act is founded justify the court's rejection of any attempt to diminish the objective stance under this offence.

[19] [2006] EWHC 1069 (Admin).

[20] See Simester, Spencer, Sullivan and Virgo CLT&D, 155. See further T Hörnle 'Social Expectation in the Criminal Law: The Reasonable Person in a Comparative Perspective' (2008) 11 New Crim LR 1, at 19.

[21] [1966] 1 QB 448, But see now the many offences under the Sexual Offences Act 2003 where the issue turns on the reasonableness of D's belief.

[22] *Elliott v C (A Minor)* (1984) 79 Cr App R 334. *Stephen Malcolm R* (1984) 79 Cr App R 334.

interpretation of the concept of the reasonable person that is not entirely objective. Some further support for this might derive from the House of Lords decision in G. However, a response to this claim might be that these cases[23] are merely examples of the courts' desperate attempts to mitigate the harshness of the *Caldwell* formulation of recklessness which applied to serious offences, and that the cases do not provide support for any broader judicial willingness to subjectivize the test of negligence. In other contexts the court has rejected an opportunity to endow the reasonable person with the personal characteristics of the accused.[24] Attempts in other contexts to dilute the concept of the reasonable person have resulted in an unsatisfactory state of affairs.[25]

6.2 Negligence as the basis of liability

There are few serious crimes in English law in which negligence is the gist of the offence. Manslaughter, causing or allowing a child to die by an unlawful act contrary to s 5 of the Domestic Violence Crime and Victims Act 2004, and public nuisance[26] are the most conspicuous examples, although arguably manslaughter is a separate form of offence because it requires 'gross negligence'. Other examples where negligence *is* the central feature of the crime include the Road Traffic Act 1988, s 3, under which it is an offence to drive a mechanically propelled vehicle on a road without due care and attention or without reasonable consideration for other persons using the road. The offence may be committed by making an error of judgement of a kind that a reasonably prudent and skilful driver would not make. It will be noted that it is not necessary to prove that any harmful consequence ensued; it is enough to show that D drove in a manner in which a reasonable person would not have driven because he would have realized it involved an unjustifiable risk. The same considerations apply to the more serious offence of dangerous driving (see Chapter 33).

In a number of other serious crimes, negligence is not the gist of the offence, because intention or recklessness is required as to the central features of the offence, but negligence with respect to some subsidiary element in the *actus reus* is sometimes enough. So under s 9 of the Sexual Offences Act 2003, it is an offence intentionally to touch a person, B, aged under 16 where that touching is sexual and either B is under 16 and D *does not reasonably believe* that B is 16 or over, or B is under 13. The conduct element of the offence in the form of 'touching' has to be shown to be intentional, but as to the circumstance of B's age (where between 13 and 16), it is expressly provided that D is guilty if he does not reasonably believe B to be over 16. An honest but unreasonable belief that B is over 16 is no excuse. Negligence with respect to that circumstantial element of the *actus reus* will suffice. Such a provision, as well as catching the negligent person, disposes of another difficult case. It deals satisfactorily with the case of D who does not advert to B's age at all (simple ignorance),[27] for he cannot say that he reasonably believed B to be over 16.

It should be noted that the Sexual Offences Act, although moving from a purely subjective approach to recklessness as to consent, has not produced an offence of rape (nor other offences) in which the fault element is *exclusively* objective. The question for the jury in rape

---

[23] And those relating to driving such as *Reid* (1992) 95 Cr App R 391, HL.

[24] See, eg, *C* [2001] Crim LR 845 above. See more generally on negligence as an element of harassment, under the Protection from Harassment Act 1997, E Finch, 'Stalking the Perfect Stalking Law: An Evaluation of the Efficacy of the Protection from Harassment Act 1997' [2002] Crim LR 703, 714.

[25] See the discussion in relation to the old law of provocation, below, Ch 15.

[26] The Law Commission proposes making this a crime of recklessness. See Ch 32 below.

[27] For philosophical arguments about whether D who does not think about the risk in such circumstances can be described as reckless or culpable at all, see Tadros, *Criminal Responsibility*, Ch 3 and 255–258.

is whether the prosecution has made them sure that the particular defendant did not have a reasonable belief in consent in all the circumstances including whether any steps *he* took to ascertain consent were reasonable, and whether he intentionally penetrated the victim's vagina, anus or mouth.

6.2.1 Negligent mistakes

The rule, once supposed to exist, that a mistake was never a defence unless it was reasonable, was capable of turning almost any crime into a crime of negligence; but *Morgan*,[28] *B (A Minor)*[29] and *K*[30] have established that there is no such general rule. For example, before those cases, it was held that if D went through a ceremony of marriage, believing wrongly but without reasonable grounds that he was not married because his wife was dead, or his marriage has been dissolved or annulled, he was guilty of bigamy.[31] This, in effect, was to turn bigamy into a crime of negligence so far as this element of the offence is concerned. D was to be held liable because he did not take sufficient care to ascertain that his first marriage was at an end, before going through the second ceremony. It appears that these cases would be decided differently today. D would be guilty only if he knew that his wife was or might be alive, or that his first marriage was or might be subsisting, as the case may be.

6.3 Degrees of negligence

It has been said that there can be no 'degrees of inadvertence when that word is used to denote a state of mind, since it means that in the man's mind there has been a complete absence of a particular thought, a nullity; and of nullity there can be no degrees'.[32]

It is true that there can be no degrees of inadvertence but there can be degrees of fault in failing to advert. The more obvious the risk, and the greater D's capacity to advert to it, the greater his fault in failing to be aware of it. If negligence is regarded as non-attainment of a required standard of conduct then it is clear that there are degrees of it. One person may fall just short of the required standard, another may fall far short. The existence of degrees of negligence is recognized by s 2A of the Road Traffic Act 1988 (as substituted by the Road Traffic Act 1991)[33] when it provides that a person drives dangerously if:

(a) the way he drives falls far below what would be expected of a competent and careful driver, and

(b) it would be obvious to a competent and careful driver that driving in that way would be dangerous.

A driver whose driving falls below, but not *far* below, what would be expected of a competent and careful driver is negligent and probably guilty of careless driving contrary to s 3 of the 1988 Act; but he is not sufficiently negligent to be guilty of the more serious offence of dangerous driving.

---

[28] Below, p 330.

[29] Below, p 161.

[30] Below, p 162.

[31] *Tolson* (1889) 23 QBD 168, CCR; *Gould* [1968] 2 QB 65.

[32] Kenny, *Outlines*, 39, criticized by Hart, *Punishment and Responsibility*, above, who writes: 'Negligence is gross if the precautions to be taken against harm are very simple, such as persons who are but poorly endowed with physical and mental capacities can easily take.'

[33] Below, Ch 33.

The fault required for the present offence of causing death by dangerous driving probably falls short of that required by the law of manslaughter as restated in *Adomako*:[34] that is, '... whether, having regard to the risk of death involved, the conduct of the defendant was so bad as in all the circumstances as to amount in [the jury's] judgement to a criminal act or omission'. There are two possible distinctions. First, driving may fall far below what would be expected of a competent and careful driver without involving any apparent risk *to life*. The only apparent risk may be to property but, if the driving unforeseeably causes death, that will amount to a Road Traffic Act offence. Second, the Road Traffic Act offence is not subject to the jury's assessment of its 'badness'. True, the jury find, or, more accurately, have to accept the judge's direction, that even careless driving is a 'criminal act'; but the principle in *Adomako* has to be read against the background that the crime charged is manslaughter; and clearly the jury will be looking to see whether the conduct is bad enough to amount to that very serious crime, not careless driving. Conceivably, a jury of motorists might think that the particular driving, though falling far below the standard expected of a competent and careful driver, ought *not* to amount to a crime. It would be their duty to convict of causing death by dangerous driving, but not of manslaughter.[35] The more likely charge in such a case is now one of causing death by careless driving. Section 20(1) of the Road Safety Act 2006 creates an offence (inserting s 2B into the 1988 Act) of causing death by careless or inconsiderate driving.[36]

6.4 Should negligence be a ground of liability?

6.4.1 Negligence as a form of culpable fault

Distinguished academic writers have strongly contended that negligence should have no place in criminal liability.[37] Their arguments for the most part assume a clear-cut distinction between conscious and inadvertent risk-taking that clearly distinguishes *Cunningham/G* recklessness from negligence. *Caldwell* brought much inadvertent risk-taking within the criminal law, but it no longer has any application (although there are numerous serious offences with an objective element including, for example: manslaughter, dangerous driving, various terrorism offences,[38] money laundering offences[39] and many sexual offences under the Sexual Offences Act 2003).

Turner acknowledges that negligence connotes that D was 'in some measure blameworthy, and that we should expect an ordinary reasonable man to foresee the possibility of the consequences and to regulate his conduct so as to avoid them';[40] however, he also contends that the moral test, on which criminal liability should be (and, indeed, is) based, is the proof of subjective fault of foresight of the consequences of one's conduct. Hall goes further and finds it difficult to accept that negligently caused harm reflects a moral fault.[41] He rejects the view that punishment stimulates care, arguing that the deterrent theory postulates a person who weighs the possibility of punishment in the balance before acting; but the inadvertent harm-doer, by definition, does not do this. Hall appears to suggest that the courts themselves do not

---

[34] [1995] 1 AC 171, [1994] Crim LR 757, HL, below, p 552.

[35] There has to be a risk of death for gross negligence manslaughter: *Misra* [2004] EWCA Crim 2375, [2005] Crim LR 234. Below Ch 15, p 554.

[36] The maximum penalty on conviction on indictment is five years' imprisonment or a fine, or both.

[37] See, eg, J Hall, 'Negligent Behaviour Should be Excluded from Criminal Liability' (1963) 63 Col LR 632; L Alexander, K Ferzan and S Morse, *Crime and Culpability* (2009).

[38] Terrorism Act 2000, ss 15–18.

[39] Proceeds of Crime Act 2002, ss 330–333.

[40] MACL, 207.

[41] *General Principles*, 136.

really believe that punishment deters negligence, suggesting that sentences, even for negligent homicides, are relatively light. He rejects the thesis that negligent persons may be ethically blameworthy in so far as they are insensitive to the rights of others. In the case of negligently caused car accidents, for example, he argues that it seems much more probable that a dull mind, slow reactions, awkwardness and other ethically irrelevant factors were the underlying cause. Other commentators take a different view. Brett, for example, suggests that it is:

common knowledge that as soon as traffic police appear on the roads, drivers begin to pay greater attention to what they are doing and the standard of driving rises sharply.[42]

The negligent handling of certain articles – notably vehicles – can have such drastic consequences that society is almost bound to adopt any measures that seem to have a reasonable prospect of inducing greater care; and it seems reasonable to suppose that the threat of punishment does have an effect on the care used in their handling.

Glanville Williams acknowledges that 'it is possible for punishment to bring about greater foresight, by causing the subject to stop and think before committing himself to a course of conduct'; but thinks that this justification does not go very far and that the law is wise in penalizing negligence only exceptionally.

More recently, Lord Nicholls, rejecting the former rule that only a reasonable mistake will excuse, invoked a presumption against liability for mere negligence:

When [a person is held liable because his mistake, though negativing *mens rea*, was made without reasonable grounds] the defendant's 'fault' lies exclusively in falling short of an objective standard. His crime lies in his negligence. A statute may so provide expressly or by necessary implication. But this can have no place in a common law principle, of general application, which is concerned with the need for a mental element as an essential ingredient of a criminal offence.[43]

6.4.2 Negligence and capacity

Hart famously challenged the commonly accepted criterion of foresight. The reason why it is thought proper to punish (in most cases) the person who foresees the forbidden harm is that he can choose to cause it or not; but in some cases of negligence, at least, it may be said:

'he could have thought about what he was doing' with just as much rational confidence as one can say of an intentional wrong-doing, 'he could have done otherwise'.[44]

Hart's approach to negligence, however, differs from that so far generally adopted by the courts. He would not enforce an objective, external and impersonal standard which took no account of the individual's lack of capacity. He would recognize that punishment might be proper only if two questions are answered in the affirmative:[45]

(i) Did the accused fail to take those precautions which any reasonable man with normal capacities would in the circumstances have taken?

(ii) Could the accused, given his mental and physical capacities, have taken those precautions?

As noted above, the courts have not yet demonstrated a willingness to subjectivize the negligence standard in this way.

---

[42] Brett, *An Inquiry into Criminal Guilt*, 173.
[43] [2000] 2 AC 428, [2000] 1 All ER 833 at 837.
[44] *Oxford Essays in Jurisprudence*, 29.
[45] ibid, at 46. Hart was not advocating the punishment of negligence, only seeking to dispel the belief that negligence is a form of strict liability.

6.4.3 Due diligence defences

There have been many suggestions to include more negligence based liability in the criminal law by replacing strict liability offences – usually by accepting as a defence to strict liability offences that D acted with all due diligence. The 'no negligence' defence is examined further in the context of strict liability in the next chapter.

7
Crimes of strict liability

7.1 The nature of strict liability[1]

Crimes which do not require *mens rea* or even negligence as to one or more elements in the *actus reus* are known as offences of strict liability or, sometimes, 'of absolute prohibition'. An example is the Medicines Act 1968, s 58(2) which provides that no person shall sell by retail specified medicinal products except in accordance with a prescription given by an appropriate medical practitioner. In *Pharmaceutical Society of Great Britain v Storkwain Ltd*,[2] D, a pharmacist supplied specified drugs on prescriptions purporting to be signed by a Dr Irani. The prescriptions were forged. There was, therefore, no prescription given by an appropriate medical practitioner. There was no finding that D acted dishonestly, improperly or even negligently in acting on that prescription and providing X with the medicines. So far as appeared, the forgery was sufficient to deceive the pharmacists without any shortcoming on their part. Yet the House of Lords held that the Divisional Court was right to direct the magistrate to convict. The case highlights the difficulties with imposing strict liability, particularly in offences of a serious nature: there is a real sense of unfairness in convicting someone for conduct which on his part was 'faultless'.[3]

It should not be imagined that strict liability applies only in 'regulatory' offences, assuming indeed that that category can be defined.[4] For example, s 5 of the Sexual Offences Act 2003 creates an offence where D intentionally penetrates with his penis the vagina, anus or mouth of a child under 13. The conduct element of the offence – penetration – must be intentional; that much is clear. But what as to the circumstance element that V is under 13, the House

---

[1] For more detailed discussion of this topic, see especially J Horder, 'Strict Liability, Statutory Construction and the Spirit of Liberty' (2002) 118 LQR 458; the collection of essays edited by A Simester, *Appraising Strict Liability* (2005) and see K Reid, 'Strict Liability: Some Principles for Parliament' (2008) 29 St LR 173. For more historical accounts of the development of strict liability, see the seminal works by J Ll Edwards, *Mens Rea;* Howard, *Strict Responsibility;* F Sayre, 'Public Welfare Offences' (1933) 33 Col LR 55. See also M Smith and A Pearson, 'The Value of Strict Liability' [1969] Crim LR 516; WG Carson, 'Some Sociological Aspects of Strict Liability and the Enforcement of Factory Legislation' (1970) 33 MLR 396; B Hogan, *Criminal Liability without Fault* (1969); JC Smith, 'Responsibility in Criminal Law', in P Bean and DK Whynes (eds), *Barbara Wootton, Essays in Her Honour* (1986) – hereinafter 'Wootton' – 141; P Brett, 'Strict Responsibility: Possible Solutions' (1974) 37 MLR 417; L Leigh, *Strict and Vicarious Liability* (1982).

[2] [1986] 2 All ER 635, HL discussed by BS Jackson in 'Storkwain: A Case Study in Strict Liability and Self Regulation' [1991] Crim LR 892, who shows that the Society's policy was to prosecute only where the pharmacist had not acted with due diligence; but the Society does not have a monopoly of the right to prosecute; and if, in practice, fault is required, should not the decision whether it exists be made in court? See also R Cooke, *Turning Points* (Hamlyn Lectures, 1997) 40.

[3] Duff provides an interesting account of the relationship between strict liability and strict responsibility, classifying crimes into categories where liability is 'formally' strict (no intention, recklessness or negligence) and/or those where it is 'substantially' strict (ie no moral fault). See *Answering for Crime*, Ch 10.

[4] See below where the Law Commission Consultation Paper on *Criminal Liability in Regulatory Contexts* (2010) (LCCP 195) is examined.

of Lords[5] held that Parliament intended this element of the offence to be strict. The offence carries a maximum sentence of life imprisonment and, obviously, serious stigma. Numerous other serious criminal offences are strict as to at least one element of the *actus reus*, including possession of firearms,[6] terrorism offences, possession of indecent images of children[7] and many sexual offences.[8] The imposition of criminal liability and punishment (including imprisonment) for such conduct where D has not even considered that what he is doing might be wrong seems 'unjust'.[9]

The first case to impose strict liability is said[10] to be that of *Woodrow*.[11] D was found guilty of having in his possession adulterated tobacco, although he did not know it was adulterated. The prosecution emphasized the purpose of the statute – it was for the protection of the revenue – and the absence of 'knowingly' or any similar word in the form of the offence. The court, in interpreting the offence, relied on a section of the Act which gave the Commissioners of Excise a power not to prosecute where there was no 'intention of fraud or of offending against this Act' – the implication being that the crime was still committed even when there was no fraud or intention of offending against the Act. Practical problems were also weighed in the balance. Parke B thought that the prosecution would very rarely be able to prove knowledge in such cases; and that the public inconvenience which would follow if they were required to do so would be greater than the injustice to the individual if they were not. Even the exercise of reasonable care would not have saved D; according to Parke B, he was liable even if the adulteration was discoverable only by a 'nice chemical analysis'.[12] Liability was strict.

Notwithstanding the subsequent mass of case law, the considerations taken into account in this early case are very much the same as those which influence the decisions of the courts today when interpreting a statutory offence to determine whether it is one of strict liability: the public welfare purpose of the legislation, the precise statutory form of words in creating the offence, the relatively low penalty, and whether the offence would otherwise be impossible or almost impossible to prove. These issues will be considered later in this chapter.

It is important to appreciate that where an offence is interpreted to be one of strict liability, the fact that D could not have avoided the prescribed harm even if he had tried to will not absolve him of liability. For example, in *Hobbs v Winchester Corpn*,[13] the case turned on whether a butcher had sold unsound meat. The butcher was unaware, and *he could not have discovered* by any examination which he could reasonably be expected to make, that the meat was unsound. He was guilty of the crime of selling unsound meat. Kennedy LJ, having regard to the policy of the statute in protecting consumers said:[14]

---

[5] *G* [2008] UKHL 37; [2008] Crim LR 818.

[6] See *Deyemi* [2007] EWCA Crim 2060, [2008] Crim LR 327; *Zahid* [2010] EWCA Crim 2158.

[7] See, eg, *Price* [2006] EWCA Crim 3363 – Protection of Children Act 1978, s 1. For a comprehensive and accessible review of the issues, see A Gillespie, 'Child Pornography Balancing Substantive and Evidential Law to Safeguard Children' (2005) E & P 29.

[8] Some have argued that rape ought to be a strict liability offence: see, for discussion, K Huigens, 'Is Strict Liability Rape Defensible', in Duff and Green, *Defining Crimes* (2005) 196.

[9] See Duff, *Answering for Crime*, 231–232.

[10] By Sayre (1933) 33 Col LR 55. S Salako, 'Strict Criminal Liability: A Violation of the Convention' (2006) 70 J Crim L 531, erroneously attributes that conclusion, which he considers to be wrong, to the 6th edn of this book.

[11] (1846) 15 M & W 404.

[12] The judges suggested that D might have taken a warranty from the person from whom he bought the tobacco, indemnifying him against the consequences of a prosecution (fine and forfeiture). But there are difficulties with this. In *Askey v Golden Wine Co Ltd* [1948] 2 All ER 35 at 38, Denning J said: 'It is … a principle of our law that the punishment inflicted by a criminal court is personal to the offender and that the civil courts will not entertain an action by the offender to recover an indemnity against consequences of that punishment.'

[13] [1910] 2 KB 471, CA.

[14] ibid, at 483. Note the modern statutory defence, below, p 180.

I think that the policy of the Act is this: that if a man chooses for profit to engage in a business which involves the offering for sale of that which may be deadly or injurious to health he must take that risk, and that it is not a sufficient defence for anyone who chooses to embark on such a business to say 'I could not have discovered the disease unless I had an analyst on the premises'.

Similarly, in the famous case of *Cundy v Le Cocq*,[15] D was convicted of selling intoxicating liquor to a drunken person contrary to what was then s 13 of the Licensing Act 1872. It was proved that D did not know the person was drunk and nothing had occurred to show that he was drunk. While some sections of the Act contained the word 'knowingly', s 13 did not do so. The Divisional Court held that it was not necessary to consider whether D knew, or had means of knowing, *or could with ordinary care have detected*, that the person served was drunk. If he served a drink to a person who was in fact drunk, he was guilty.

In each of these cases D was not even negligent. He intended the conduct element of the offence – to sell medicine or meat or liquor or to possess tobacco – but he was blamelessly unaware of the crucial circumstance element in the *actus reus* – that the tobacco was adulterated, that the meat was unsound, that the person was drunk etc. In each case he was criminally liable despite not having been at fault in relation to this material element of the offence.

7.1.1 Irrelevance of *mens rea*

Where an offence is held to be one of strict liability, not only is it unnecessary for the prosecution to tender evidence of *mens rea* as to the matter of strict liability (that the prescription is duly signed by a practitioner, that the tobacco is adulterated etc), they *must* not adduce evidence of D's *mens rea* as to that aspect of the offence. Such evidence is irrelevant and, as it shows the defendant to be at fault, it is prejudicial. In *Sandhu*,[16] D was charged with the strict liability offence of causing a listed building to be altered without authority. Although D objected, the prosecution were allowed to prove that he knew the work went beyond what was permitted. This was an error and D's conviction was quashed.[17]

7.1.2 Distinction from 'absolute' liability

Until recently, relatively little academic attention had been paid to defining what we mean by strict liability. One particular problem is that there is no universally accepted definition of the terms strict liability and absolute liability and how they relate.

It is commonly said that 'no *mens rea*' need be proved in strict liability offences: 'D can be convicted on proof by the prosecution of *actus reus* only'.[18] In fact it is only in an extreme case[19] that this is true. The label 'absolute offence' is best reserved for those rare cases where the offence criminalizes D whose conduct has caused[20] an *actus reus* with no *mens rea* and who is precluded from relying on defences. Strict liability should be used to denote crimes in which one element or more (but not all) of the *actus reus* requires no proof of *mens rea*;

---

[15] (1884) 13 QBD 207.

[16] [1997] Crim LR 288 and commentary. See *Hill* [1997] Crim LR 459 for commentary on the sentencing implications.

[17] For proof of strict liability offence by D's previous similar misconduct, see eg *Vehicle and Operator Services Agency v Ace Crane and Transport Ltd* [2010] EWHC 288 (Admin).

[18] Howard, SR, 1.

[19] *Larsonneur*, above, p 552.

[20] In *Kilbride v Lake* [1962] NZLR 590, discussed by M Budd and A Lynch, 'Voluntariness, Causation and Strict Liability' [1978] Crim LR 74, D was acquitted of permitting a vehicle not displaying a current warrant of fitness to be on the highway, when the warrant was detached during his absence. The court took the view that there was an *actus reus* (*sed quaere?*) but that D had not caused it and he was not liable even if the offence was one of strict liability. cf *Strowger v John* [1974] RTR 124.

absolute liability denotes those crimes in which there is no *mens rea* attaching to any element of the *actus reus* or no due diligence defence available.[21] Even this definition of strict liability is problematical since it encompasses constructive crimes. Lord Edmund-Davies said that '…an offence is regarded – and properly regarded – as one of strict liability if no *mens rea* need be proved as to a single element in the *actus reus*'.[22] By this test, even murder is an offence of strict liability because no *mens rea* is required as to the crucial element of death.[23] Murder, however, does require an intention to cause grievous bodily harm, the *mens rea* of a lesser offence but nevertheless a substantial *mens rea*.[24]

Care should also be taken with loose definitions related to whether the offence can be committed without proof of moral fault: the focus is on whether there needs to be *mens rea*, and as the House of Lords has reminded us, *mens rea* is not necessarily synonymous with moral fault.[25] Unfortunately the courts and practitioners do not always adopt consistent and clear terminology.[26]

In our definition of strict liability, there must be one or more elements of *actus reus* as to which no *mens rea* is required. The element(s) as to which liability is strict will usually be one of great significance. In a great many cases, the courts have held that Parliament intended to impose strict liability and have convicted defendants who lacked *mens rea*, not merely as to some subsidiary matter, but as to the central feature of the *actus reus*. For example, in a case of sexual touching of a child under 13, liability to the age of the child is strict. D is guilty whether he thought the child was older, whether he had good reason to think so or not. If the child is under 13 that element of the offence is satisfied.

Even if the central element of the offence is strict, it by no means follows that *mens rea* will be required as to the remaining constituents of the offence. In one of the leading cases, *Gammon (Hong Kong) Ltd v A-G of Hong Kong*, construing the Hong Kong Building Ordinance, Lord Scarman said: 'Each provision clearly requires a degree of *mens rea*, but each is silent whether it is required in respect of all the facts which together constitute the offence created.' The Privy Council held that D was liable for deviating in a material way from the approved building plan, even though there was no evidence that he knew that his act constituted a material deviation from the plan – liability as to *that* element was strict.[27]

7.1.3 Common law and statute

Crimes of strict liability are almost invariably found in statutes. There are many thousands of these offences, mostly involving offences triable in the magistrates' court,[28] but with many

---

[21] See on this SP Green, 'Six Senses of Strict Liability: A Plea for Formalism', in A Simester (ed), *Appraising Strict Liability*. Green identifies six possible uses of 'strict liability' and concludes that the correct one is where the offence lacks *mens rea* as to at least one element. See also DN Husak, 'Varieties of Strict Liability' (1995) Canadian J of Law and Jurisprudence 189.

[22] *Whitehouse v Gay News Ltd* [1979] AC 617 at 656, quoting the 4th edition of this book, at 79. See on the constructive crime and strict liability relationship, S Green (above), p 2.

[23] It is for this reason that some eminent judges regard murder as an anomaly and an instance of 'constructive crime'. Above, p 135.

[24] Above, p 135. The misleading proposition that an offence of strict liability requires no *mens rea* seems to have been the cause of the trial judge's difficulties in *Blackburn v Bowering* [1994] 3 All ER 380, below, p 661.

[25] See Lord Mustill in *Kingston* [1995] 2 AC 355. For theoretical discussion of the moral issues see RA Duff, 'Strict Liability, Legal Presumption and the Presumption of Innocence', in A Simester (ed), *Appraising Strict Liability*.

[26] cf *Nicholson* [2006] EWCA Crim 1518 where the CA declined to adopt the term strict liability to describe an absence of a reasonable excuse. See also *Charles* [2009] EWCA Crim 1570 in the context of ASBOs.

[27] *Gammon (Hong Kong) Ltd v A-G of Hong Kong* [1985] AC 1, PC.

[28] See Justice, *Breaking the Rules* (1980).

triable on indictment.[29] There has been an increase of such offences being implemented by Parliament on matters of regulation.[30] This has been the subject of close scrutiny in the Macrory Report[31] which led to the Regulatory Enforcement and Sanctions Act 2008. That Act encourages the use of civil administrative sanctions rather than criminal offences. More recently, the Law Commission has addressed the problem in Consultation Paper No 195[32] in which more radical proposals are made to avoid the use of criminal offences in regulatory sectors.[33]

As for the common law, it used to be said that there were only two exceptions to the rule requiring *mens rea*. These were public nuisance and criminal libel. Public nuisance, however, is an anomalous crime and is treated in several respects rather as if it were a civil action than an indictable offence. Criminal libel has now been abolished, although Parliament has now expressly recognized the existence of strict liability in this context by the Contempt of Court Act 1981.[34] Other contempts of court at common law require *mens rea*.[35]

Apart from these instances, the common law generally required *mens rea*, though sometimes, the *mens rea* of a lesser offence – as in the case of murder where intention to cause grievous bodily harm is sufficient.

7.1.4 Strict liability and the presumption of innocence

The Human Rights Act 1998 prompted challenges to strict liability offences on the basis that they might infringe rights guaranteed under the European Convention. Since the Human Rights Act does not empower courts to 'strike down' statutes, the challenge is not in the same magnitude as that in, for example the USA, where it is possible for some strict liability offences to be held to be unconstitutional.[36] It has been argued that the imposition of strict liability might engage, for example, Art 3 (freedom from inhuman or degrading treatment),[37] Art 8 (respect for privacy),[38] Art 10 (freedom of expression),[39] and possibly Art 7 (guarantees against retrospectivity) owing to the ambiguity over whether the courts will hold liability to be strict.

---

[29] A Ashworth and M Blake, 'The Presumption of Innocence in English Criminal Law' [1996] Crim LR 306 found almost half of the offences in *Archbold* were strict in one sense.

[30] See R Baldwin, 'The New Punitive Regulation' (2004) 67 MLR 351.

[31] *Macrory Review of Regulatory Penalties* (2006). See J Norris and J Phillips, *The Law of Regulatory Enforcement and Sanctions* (2011).

[32] *Criminal Liability in Regulatory Contexts* (2010).

[33] The most radical suggestion in LCCP 195 is for all criminal offences with strict liability to be read subject to a defence for the accused to show that he had acted with all due diligence. See para 1.68.

[34] See *B* [2006] EWCA Crim 2692.

[35] *Akthar* [2006] EWCA Crim 469.

[36] See A Michaels, 'Imposing Constitutional Limits on Strict Liability: Lessons from the American Experience', in A Simester (ed), *Appraising Strict Liability*. See also the Irish Supreme Court decision in *CC v Ireland* (2006) IESC 33 noted by C Taylor, 'Irish Supreme Court: Sexual Offence: Constitutionality' (2006) 70 JCL 406. The English courts will of course read down statutes incompatible with the HRA – see, eg, the reverse burden case of *Keogh* [2007] EWCA Crim 528 (Official Secrets Act 1989), and *Webster* [2010] EWCA Crim 2819 (corruption).

[37] See GR Sullivan, 'Strict Liability for Criminal Offences in England and Wales following Incorporation into English Law of the ECHR', in A Simester (ed), *Appraising Strict Liability*, 206; A Michaels, above, 229–231. See also S Salako (2006) 70 J Crim L 531, arguing that 'it is degrading and inhuman to put a person who is not culpable through the process of a criminal trial'. The issue is most acute where D is sentenced to a lengthy term of imprisonment for a strict liability offence. The EU charter may well also influence developments here as Art 49(3) of the Charter of Fundamental Rights of the EU protects against disproportionate penalty.

[38] As in the *Barnfather* case below. See also on this A Michaels, above, 233.

[39] eg, in contempt of court cases: A Michaels, above. This might also be significant in offences involving communication: see *DPP v Collins* [2006] UKHL 40, p 1081 below, on the communication of racist views and the element of *mens rea*.

The greatest controversy has been over whether strict liability offences infringe the presumption of innocence guaranteed under Art 6(2) of the European Convention.[40] Some commentators argue that strict liability offences may offend against Art 6(2) because once the prohibited act is proved, D is 'presumed' to be liable.[41] It has been argued that the effect of the presumption and the imposition of strict liability is the same.[42] The functional equivalence is keenly disputed by others,[43] who regard the rules of procedure and substantive law as fundamentally distinct. Professor Ashworth has summarized the objection to strict liability as:

that it is wrong to convict people of serious offences without proof of culpability, and that is a separate argument from the presumption of innocence. It is not an argument about evidence and procedure at all but an argument about the proper preconditions of criminal liability.[44]

Although there is some faint support in the ECHR case law for the application of Art 6(2) to strict liability offences,[45] the European Court has held that strict liability offences are compatible with the Article: 'in principle the contracting States may, under certain conditions, penalize a simple or objective fact as such irrespective of whether it results from criminal intent or from negligence'.[46]

The English courts have taken account of that conclusion in holding that Art 6(2) is restricted to providing procedural protection and does not render the imposition of strict liability incompatible with Art 6(2).[47] As Lord Bingham stated in *Sheldrake*:[48]

The overriding concern is that a trial should be fair, and the presumption of innocence is a fundamental right directed to that end. The Convention does not outlaw presumptions of fact or law but requires that these should be kept within reasonable limits and should not be arbitrary. *It is open to states to define the constituent elements of a criminal offence, excluding the requirement of mens rea.* But the substance and effect of any presumption adverse to a defendant must be examined, and must be reasonable. Relevant to any judgment on reasonableness or proportionality will be the opportunity given to the defendant to rebut the presumption, maintenance of the rights of the defence, flexibility in application of the presumption, retention by the court of a power to assess the evidence, the importance of what is at stake and the difficulty which a prosecutor may face in the absence of a presumption.[49]

---

[40] A full examination of the issues of Art 6 belongs more properly in an evidence textbook. See C Tapper, *Cross and Tapper on Evidence* (12th edn, 2010) Ch III.

[41] See V Tadros and S Tierney, 'The Presumption of Innocence and the Human Rights Act' (2004) 67 MLR 402.

[42] See RA Duff, 'Strict Liability, Legal Presumptions and the Presumption of Innocence', in A Simester (ed), *Appraising Strict Liability*, 125.

[43] See P Roberts, 'Strict Liability and the Presumption of Innocence', in A Simester (ed), *Appraising Strict Liability*, 151.

[44] A Ashworth, 'Four Threats to the Presumption of Innocence' (2006) E & P 241, 252–253. cf the views of, eg, S Salako (2006) 70 J Crim L 53, who suggests such a distinction is 'artificial'.

[45] See *Hansen v Denmark* 28971/95.

[46] *Salibaku v France* (1998) 13 EHRR 379, Emmerson, Ashworth and Macdonald, HR&CJ, paras 9.74–9.77.

[47] *G* [2008] UKHL 37. See also *Barnfather v Islington LBC* [2003] EWHC 418 (Admin). On which see V Tadros and S Tierney (2004) 67 MLR 402, and J Horder, 'Whose Values Should Determine Whether Liability is Strict', in A Simester (ed), *Appraising Strict Liability*, 105 and see the valuable comment by B Fitzpatrick, 'Divisional Court – Strict Liability and Article 6(2) of the European Convention on Human Rights: School Non-Attendance Offence' (2004) 68 J Crim L 16

[48] [2005] 1 AC 246 at [21] (emphasis added).

[49] See also the comments of leading commentators such as Emmerson, Ashworth and Macdonald, HR&CJ, para 9.74, concluding that even the landmark decisions in *DPP v B* and *R v K* (below) have no bearing on the relationship between the presumption of innocence and the imposition of strict liability.

Recent examples of the domestic courts' approach include the rejection of the argument that strict liability offences restricting press publication of trial proceedings are incompatible with Arts 6 and 10,[50] that strict liability offences are incompatible with Art 7 on the basis of their ambiguity[51] and that the imposition of strict liability in sexual offences with children is incompatible with Art 6. In *G*,[52] G, who was aged 15, pleaded guilty to rape of a child under 13 (s 5 Sexual Offences Act 2003). G's basis of plea was that V consented and that he reasonably believed her to be older than 13, because she had so informed him. The House of Lords confirmed that s 5 creates an offence of strict liability to which belief in consent or the age of the victim has no application. The *actus reus* of the offence is vaginal, anal or oral sexual intercourse with a victim under 13, whether the victim consented or not and irrespective of how old the defendant thought she was. Section 5 created an offence even where the defendant reasonably believed that the child was over 16. The House of Lords reached that conclusion having regard to a number of factors including in particular the fact that in other sections of the 2003 Act[53] it is expressly stated that the offence is not committed if D believes that V is over 16; but in s 5 there is no reference to D having a reasonable belief as to age. In relation to the offences dealing with children under 13, liability as to age is strict. This may seem harsh, particularly where D is of similar age and had every reason to believe that V was over 13 (including because she told him so), but the court construed Parliament's intention to impose strict liability in order to protect such young children, but D would have been convicted of an offence on his admitted belief in any event.

7.2 The presumption of *mens rea*

Since strict liability offences are almost always found in statutes, the courts, in enforcing them, profess merely to be implementing the intention of Parliament, express or implied, as they find it in the statute. This has frequently been mere lip-service. In 1958, Devlin J wrote:

The fact is that Parliament has no intention whatever of troubling itself about *mens rea*. If it had, the thing would have been settled long ago. All that Parliament would have to do would be to use express words that left no room for implication. One is driven to the conclusion that the reason why Parliament has never done that is that it prefers to leave the point to the judges and does not want to legislate about it.[54]

The courts then have a fairly free hand in this matter, subject to any existing precedent. It is only rarely that the statute rules out *mens rea* expressly. A recent example is s 14 of the Policing and Crime Act 2009, criminalizing use of exploited prostitutes. It is made clear that it is 'irrelevant...whether [D] is, or ought to be, aware that [V] has engaged in exploitative conduct'.[55]

Aside from such rare cases, when strict liability has been imposed, it is then usually because the judges have regarded that interpretation as necessary or desirable in the public interest – effectively exercising a legislative function. In the past, judges were quick to state that there is a

---

[50] *O'Riordan v DPP* [2005] EWHC 1240 (Admin).

[51] *Muhammed* [2003] EWCA Crim 1852 and *Kearns* [2003] 1 Cr App R 7.

[52] [2008] UKHL 37, see Lord Hope at [28]–[29].

[53] cf the approach in *Ireland* in a very similar case: *CC v Ireland* (2006) IESC 33.

[54] *Samples of Lawmaking*, at 71. cf GC Thornton, *Legislative Drafting*, at 264. Lord Reid in *Sweet v Parsley* [1969] 1 All ER 347 at 351.

[55] The drafting of the offence is very poor in other respects.

presumption in favour of *mens rea*, commonly reciting the well-known statement by Wright J in *Sherras v De Rutzen*:[56]

> There is a presumption that *mens rea*, or evil intention, or knowledge of the wrongfulness of the act, is an essential ingredient in every offence; but that presumption is liable to be displaced either by the words of the statute creating the offence or by the subject-matter with which it deals, and both must be considered.

But the judges would then readily find the presumption rebutted. The position is said[57] to have reached its nadir when even bigamy was held to be a crime of strict liability in *Wheat*,[58] now happily overruled. The trend in the years before *Warner v Metropolitan Police Comr*,[59] (the first case on the point to reach the highest tribunal) seems to have been in favour of strict liability; but Lord Reid in that case (where he dissented) and in *Sweet v Parsley*[60] powerfully reaffirmed the presumption: '... whenever a section is silent as to *mens rea* there is a presumption that, in order to give effect to the will of Parliament, we must read in words appropriate to require *mens rea*'; and '... it is a universal principle that if a penal provision is reasonably capable of two interpretations, that interpretation which is most favourable to the accused must be adopted'.[61] In 1980, in *Sheppard*,[62] Lord Diplock noted that, 'The climate of both parliamentary and judicial opinion has been growing less favourable to the recognition of absolute offences over the last few decades...'[63]

The decisions of the House of Lords in *B (A Minor) v DPP*[64] and *K*,[65] signalled an emphatic reassertion of the presumption that all serious offences ought to be offences of *mens rea*.

7.2.1 A twenty-first century revitalized presumption of *mens rea*[66]

The House of Lords declared that there is a constitutional presumption of *mens rea* in offences. In interpreting a statute, the courts will ask whether that presumption is rebutted, with the consequence that the offence is one of strict liability: '... the test is not whether it is a reasonable implication that the statute rules out *mens rea* as a constituent part of the crime – the test is whether it is a *necessary* implication': *B*.[67] In *K*, the House followed this emphatically. Section 14 of the Sexual Offences Act 1956 (indecent assault – now repealed)[68] provided that neither a girl under 16 (s 14(2)) nor a 'defective' (s 14(4)) could give a consent which would prevent an act being an assault for the purposes of the section. It was, however, a defence for the person who had acted indecently towards a consenting 'defective' to prove that he did not

---

[56] [1895] 1 QB 918 at 921, below, p 170.

[57] Williams, CLGP, 178.

[58] [1921] 2 KB 119, overruled by *Gould* [1968] 2 QB 65, [1968] 1 All ER 849.

[59] [1969] 2 AC 256, [1968] 2 All ER 256, Lord Reid (whose speech still merits careful study) dissenting on this issue. The case is more fully considered below, p 172.

[60] [1970] AC 132, HL, below, p 174 but the House again imposed strict liability in *Alphacell Ltd v Woodward* [1972] AC 824, below, p 175.

[61] Per Lord Reid at 349–350.

[62] [1981] AC 394, [1980] 3 All ER 899 at 906.

[63] [1969] 2 AC 256.

[64] [2000] 2 AC 428.

[65] [2002] 1 AC 462.

[66] For strong criticism see J Horder, 'How Culpability Can, and Cannot, Be Denied in Under-Age Sex Crimes' [2001] Crim LR 15, commenting that the decision in *B v DPP* 'flies in the face of legislation and case law across much of the rest of the common law world'; PR Glazebrook, 'How Old Did You Think She Was?' [2001] CLJ 26. For criticism of the decision for failing to take a more radical look at the use of due diligence defences, see LCCP 195, para 6.15

[67] [2000] 2 AC 428, [2000] 1 All ER at 855d–e. Per Lord Hutton.

[68] Below, Ch 18, p 751.

know and had no reason to suspect her to be a defective. It necessarily followed that a person who failed to prove this was guilty, although he honestly believed the woman was not a defective; that is, subject to the statutory defence, the section imposed strict liability on that person. Section 14(3) provided that where D had gone through a ceremony of marriage with V which was invalid because she was under 16, it was a defence for him to prove that he believed, and had reasonable cause to believe, her to be his wife. Again, it necessarily followed that a person who was unable to prove that fact was guilty, although he honestly believed the girl to be his wife. Subject to the statutory defence, the section therefore imposed strict liability. But in contrast, there was no comparable statutory defence for the person who 'assaulted' the consenting girl under 16. Previous decisions over many years had held that, in this scenario, the section imposed unmitigated strict liability.

In *K*, the House overruled those cases and decided that it was for the prosecution to prove that D did not have the honest belief he asserted that V was 16 or over. As full *mens rea* with respect to age was not excluded expressly or by necessary implication in the section creating the offence, it was required. The decision was a controversial one. While Lord Bingham thought this result was not absurd, Lord Millett thought that, 'To afford a defendant who has not married the girl a more generous defence than one who believes he has is grotesque.'[69] Nevertheless, to do justice in the case before him, he concurred in the decision. He, at least, seemed ready to abandon all pretence that he was implementing the intention of Parliament. Parliament had signally failed to discharge its responsibility. Although the Sexual Offences Act 2003 has reversed the effect of the decision by creating offences in which liability as to age is strict,[70] the decisions in *B* and *K* afford a pre-eminence to the presumption of *mens rea* which, if applied generally, could result in a substantial diminution of strict liability in English law. It is important to note that the principle of these decisions is not confined to offences of this type. The judges thought that: 'In principle, an age-related ingredient of a statutory offence stands on no different footing from any other ingredient.'[71] The strength of the presumption of *mens rea* and of a requirement of *mens rea* in the subjective sense was endorsed in the strongest terms in the case of *G*[72] on recklessness.[73]

Arguably, all offences of strict liability are vulnerable to challenge by the revitalized presumption declared by the House.[74] For example, some of their lordships in *K*[75] refused, *obiter*, to apply the presumption to what was the offence of sexual intercourse with a girl under 13. That was an offence punishable with a maximum of life imprisonment and there was nothing in the words of that section itself which could possibly exclude *mens rea*. In *Kumar*,[76] the Court of Appeal applied *B* and *K* to hold that the offence of buggery (under the 1956 Act, now repealed by the Sexual Offences Act 2003) did *not* impose strict liability as to the age of the participants. A degree of caution must, however, be exercised as the impact of these cases begins to be felt in the lower courts. It would be misleading to think that since *B* and *K*, the courts have consistently rejected strict liability. Far from it. There are numerous instances of provisions

---

[69] [2001] 3 All ER 897, at [43].

[70] *G* [2008] UKHL 37.

[71] Lord Nicholls in *B* [2000] 2 AC 463, [2000] 1 All ER at 839. Lord Hobhouse in *K* [2001] 3 All ER at 911.

[72] [2003] UKHL 50, [2004] 1 AC 1034.

[73] [32]. Lord Steyn observed that the 'general tendency in modern times is towards adopting a subjective approach', at [55].

[74] A key contender must be the strictness as to age in offences of possession of indecent images of children, following *Land* [1999] QB 65, cf the commentary on *Smith and Jayson* [2002] Crim LR 659. Other likely challenges, eg, to the offences of possession of a weapon: see *Deyemi* [2007] EWCA Crim 2060 – liability for possession even where D was unaware it (stun gun) was a firearm, believing it to be a torch have been rejected.

[75] [2000] 1 All ER at 843g–h per Lord Steyn and 854h–j per Lord Hutton, [2001] 3 All ER [33] per Lord Bingham.

[76] [2005] Crim LR 470.

being interpreted as imposing strict liability as for example, in *Muhammed*[77] (materially contributing to insolvency by gambling carrying two years' imprisonment); *Matudi*,[78] (importing prohibited animal products); *Hart v Anglian Water Services Ltd*[79] (causing sewage effluent to be discharged); *Jackson*[80] (low flying aircraft); *K*[81] (possession of a ball-bearing gun constituting an imitation firearm); *Deyemi*[82] (possession of an electronic stun gun constitutes possession of firearm where D unaware it was a weapon); *Zahid* (possession of ammunition for a firearm).[83]

7.2.2 What *mens rea* is to be presumed?

Although stating, now with renewed zeal, that there is a presumption of *mens rea* in statutory offences, the courts do not usually tell us what they mean by *mens rea*. A much cited statement is that of Cave J in *Tolson*:[84]

At common law an honest...[85] belief in the existence of circumstances, which, if true, would make the act for which a prisoner is indicted an innocent act has always been held to be a good defence.

This is ambiguous. Does 'an innocent act' mean:

(1) not the crime charged or

(2) neither the crime charged nor some lesser offence or

(3) not a civil wrong or

(4) not a moral wrong?

The Draft Criminal Code, cl 20, 'General requirement of fault', would provide a clear rule based on (1):

(1) Every offence requires a fault element of recklessness with respect to each of its elements other than fault elements, unless otherwise provided.

If that were enacted, we would know exactly where we stood with respect to offences to which the Code applied. In the meantime there remains a degree of uncertainty.

7.3 Recognizing offences of strict liability

As noted, in some rare instances, Parliament makes it explicit that it is imposing an offence of strict liability. In all other cases the courts are obliged to divine the will of Parliament relating to the elements of *mens rea*.[86] The courts have not adopted a clear and consistent approach.

---

[77] [2003] EWCA Crim 1852.

[78] [2003] EWCA Crim 697.

[79] [2003] EWCA Crim 224.

[80] [2006] EWCA Crim 2380. The Court of Appeal's decision provides a very clear example of the discussion of the relevant factors to consider.

[81] [2006] EWCA Crim 2183.

[82] [2007] EWCA Crim 2060. See also *Rehman and Wood* [2006] 1 Cr App R (S) 404.

[83] [2010] EWCA Crim 2158.

[84] (1889) 23 QBD 168, CCCR, at 181.

[85] The words 'and reasonable' are omitted as being no longer applicable in the light of *B v DPP*.

[86] See generally LCCP 195 Part 6. Surely there is an argument for imposing an obligation on Parliament always to use one of a specified list of *mens rea* words when drafting offence-creating legislation and to make explicit if an offence is to be one of strict liability. The level of scrutiny of criminal legislation in Parliament is so poor that such matters do not always seem to be understood. An obligation of this nature on draftsmen would at least assist those in Parliament and clarify matters for the courts. See Reid (2008) 29 St LR 173.

Indeed, Glazebrook has suggested that there is an 'all too familiar litany of vague overlapping criteria which from time out of mind has signally failed to compel from judges predictable consensus'.[87] The court must start from the presumption of *mens rea*, and by reference to a number of interpretative techniques, decide whether Parliament displaced that presumption by necessary implication.

As Lord Scarman explained in *Gammon (Hong Kong) Ltd v A-G Hong Kong*:[88]

(1) There is a presumption of law that *mens rea* is required before a person can be held guilty of a criminal offence. (2) The presumption is particularly strong where the offence is 'truly criminal' in character. (3) The presumption applies to statutory offences, and can be displaced only if this is clearly or by necessary implication the effect of the statute. (4) The only situation in which the presumption can be displaced is where the statute is concerned with an issue of social concern ... (5) Even where a statute is concerned with such an issue, the presumption of *mens rea* stands unless it can also be shown that the creation of strict liability will be effective to promote the objects of the statute by encouraging greater vigilance to prevent the commission of the prohibited act.

7.3.1 The offence in its statutory context

One of the principal methods of determining if the presumption of *mens rea* is displaced is by reference to statutory terminology. The decisions in *B* and *K* in the House of Lords illustrate the supreme importance attached to the words of the statute. The presumption, we are told, 'can only be displaced by specific language, that is an express provision or a necessary implication'.[89] If that is taken literally many, if not most, cases of strict liability were wrongly decided; but subsequent case law has demonstrated that that is not the effect of *B* and *K*. In some instances the courts have taken *B* and *K* seriously. In *M*[90] in which the court upheld the judge's ruling that the offence of bringing a prohibited article into a prison[91] was not an offence of strict liability, Rix LJ said:

The default position is that, despite the absence of any express language, there is a presumption, founded in constitutional principle, that *mens rea* is an essential ingredient of the offence. Only a compelling case for implying the exclusion of such an ingredient as a matter of necessity will suffice. Therefore the absence of express language, even in the presence of express language elsewhere in the statute, is not enough to rebut the presumption unless the circumstances as a whole compel such a conclusion.

In other cases, the court has read *B* and *K* restrictively to mean that where there is an existing interpretation of an offence which holds it to be one of strict liability and that is a binding precedent, *B* and *K* are not sufficient in themselves to cause a reassessment.[92] In contrast, in *Cambridgeshire CC v Assoc Lead Mills Ltd*,[93] Walker J, having regard to the discussion in this book of the 'revitalised presumption' questioned whether even the offence based on 'use' on which there is plenty of binding authority is to be construed as one of strict liability.

[87] 'How Old Did You Think She Was?' [2001] CLJ 26.

[88] [1985] AC 1.

[89] Per Lord Steyn in *K*, at [32].

[90] [2009] EWCA Crim 2615.

[91] Contrary to the Prison Act 1952, s 40C(1), as inserted by the Offender Management Act 2007.

[92] See *Deyemi* [2007] EWCA Crim at [25]. See also the comments of Lord Phillips, President of the Supreme Court, in *R (Child Poverty Action Group) v Secretary of State for Work and Pensions* [2011] 2 WLR 1 describing the House in *B* as 'doing no more than applying a well-established common law presumption or requirement' [30].

[93] [2006] EHWC 1627 (Admin).

7.3.1.1 Verbs importing a mental element

We have already noticed that a particular verb may imply a mental element.[94] The obvious examples are to intend, be malicious or reckless, to know, to suspect, to have reasonable grounds to suspect, etc. With other verbs the courts take a less clear position. The use of one verb in the definition of an offence may import a requirement of fault when the use of a different verb with no such implication would result in an offence of strict liability.

A good recent example is M[95] in which the court upheld the judge's ruling that the offence of bringing, throwing or conveying a prohibited article into a prison[96] was not an offence of strict liability. Rix LJ had regard to the statutory language:

It is hard to think that the verb 'throws' does not involve an intentional act of some kind. It is difficult to conceive (but I do not say impossible) of a person throwing some [prescribed] article into or out of prison without knowing what he is doing. The verb 'brings' is perhaps more neutral, but it takes its colour from the verb 'throws'. The expression 'otherwise conveys', being of a catch-all nature, must plainly take its colour from what has gone before. These are therefore unpromising words with which to begin to find an offence of [strict] liability.

A further illustration is provided by the offence for a person to 'use or cause or permit to be used' a motor vehicle in contravention of certain regulations. 'Using', 'causing' and 'permitting' are three separate offences. In *James & Son Ltd v Smee*,[97] the court held that *using* a vehicle in contravention of a regulation (in that it had a defective braking system) was an offence of strict liability; but D was charged with *permitting* the use which, said the court, 'in our opinion, at once imports a state of mind', ie *mens rea*. A person might 'use' a vehicle with defective brakes although he had no idea that the brakes were defective; but he would not properly be said to 'permit' use with defective brakes unless he knew that the brakes were defective or, at least, was turning a blind eye to that fact. Knowledge is not necessarily the only mental element required. Does a person who knows that his premises are being used for producing or supplying drugs 'permit' if he does nothing about it? Is mere acquiescence enough?[98]

Unfortunately, the courts are inconsistent in their interpretation of this and similar words in other statutes. An example is the offence of 'permitting' a vehicle to be used without insurance. Take the common case where D lends his car to X on condition that it is only driven by an insured driver. If it is in fact driven by a person who is uninsured, the courts have held that D commits the offence. The court ignores the ordinary meaning of the word 'permit'. D who says: 'Here is my car, but you must not drive it until you have insurance' is taken in law 'to permit' what he actually forbids: driving without insurance.[99] In what appears to be the first case to reach the House of Lords on this, *Vehicle Inspectorate v Nuttall*,[100] it was said that the meaning depends on the context but it remains difficult to discern how and when the context operates. In *Nuttall*, two judges held that D had a duty to take reasonable steps to detect and prevent breaches and that, if he failed to do so, he 'permitted'. Two judges thought that

---

[94] Above, Ch 5.

[95] [2009] EWCA Crim 2615.

[96] Contrary to the Prison Act 1952, s 40C(1), as inserted by the Offender Management Act 2007.

[97] [1955] 1 QB 78, DC. cf *Lomas v Peek* [1947] 2 All ER 574.

[98] *Bradbury* [1996] Crim LR 808. Perhaps this is a case where the alternative verb, 'suffer', more appropriately describes the conduct. There are lots of other examples in drugs offences.

[99] *DPP v Fisher* [1991] Crim LR 787, distinguishing *Newbury v Davis* [1974] RTR 367.

[100] [1999] 1 WLR 629, HL (employer (D) permitting driver to contravene rules regarding rest periods). cf *Yorkshire Traction Co v Vehicle Inspectorate* [2001] RTR 518, DC.

a mental element of recklessness, in the sense of not caring whether a breach took place, was required. What is reasonable is an objective question and D's opinion is irrelevant.[101]

Similar inconsistency is to be found in the interpretation of the verbs, 'suffer', 'allow' and 'cause'.[102]

It seems that the courts will generally give verbs their natural meaning, including any mental element they imply, unless they consider that social policy requires them to decide otherwise. In relation to the offences of uninsured driving, the courts take a strict approach, presumably due to the danger to the public. In that context the courts refuse to give effect to what they recognize in other social contexts to be the natural meaning of the words used by Parliament. But is uninsured driving a greater social evil than driving with defective brakes?

7.3.1.2 The use of adverbs

'Knowingly'

The use of an adverb in a statute is a more explicit way in which Parliament can make clear that *mens rea* is required. The clearest word is 'knowingly'.[103] Devlin J has said that 'knowingly' only says expressly what is normally implied[104] – it does expressly what the presumption in favour of *mens rea* would do by implication. The use of the word suggests that Parliament wanted to make sure that the courts would not displace the presumption and hold the offence to be one of strict liability. Similarly, where Parliament provides that it is an offence to 'knowingly permit' something to be done, Parliament intends the presumption of *mens rea* to apply – perhaps the word 'permit' would have been sufficient to import *mens rea*, but the draftsman was taking no chances. When 'knowingly' is used, it should be difficult for any court to hold that *mens rea* is not required as to *all* the elements of the offence, though it might not extend to an exception clause in the definition of the crime.[105]

The requirement of 'knowingly' is satisfied by proof of what is sometimes called 'wilful blindness':[106] 'it is always open to the tribunal of fact, when knowledge on the part of a defendant is required to be proved, to base a finding of knowledge on evidence that the defendant had deliberately shut his eyes to the obvious or refrained from enquiry because he suspected the truth but did not want to have his suspicion confirmed'.[107] Sometimes, however, the courts take a stricter view, as in handling stolen goods, below, Chapter 27. In *Kwan Ping Bang*,[108] it was accepted that proof of knowledge by inference is possible provided the inference was compelling – 'one (and the only one) that no reasonable man could fail to draw from the direct facts proved'.

'Wilfully'

The word 'wilfully' looks like a '*mens rea* word' and it is sometimes treated as such. It was considered in Chapter 5. D does not 'wilfully' obstruct a police officer simply because he does a

---

[101] *Brock and Wyner* [2001] Crim LR 320 (permitting premises to be used for supplying drugs).

[102] A recent example is the approach in *Tilley* [2009] EWCA Crim 1426, interpreting the offence of dishonestly 'allowing' a person to fail to give prompt notification of a change in her social benefit circumstances under s 111A(1B) of the Social Security Administration Act 1992.

[103] See recently C Manchester, 'Knowledge Due Diligence and Strict Liability in Regulatory Offences' [2006] Crim LR 213.

[104] *Roper v Taylor's Central Garage (Exeter) Ltd* [1951] 2 TLR 284 at 288. See also S Shute, 'Knowledge and Belief in the Criminal Law', in S Shute and A Simester (eds), *Criminal Law Theory* (2002).

[105] cf *Brooks v Mason* [1902] 2 KB 743, DC and *Wings Ltd v Ellis*, above p 74.

[106] This is discussed in Ch 5 above.

[107] *Westminster City Council v Croyalgrange Ltd* [1986] 2 All ER 353 at 359, HL; *Manifest Shipping Co Ltd v Uni-Polaris Shipping Co Ltd* [2001] 1 All ER 743, HL.

[108] [1979] AC 609, 615.

deliberate act which in fact obstructs the officer; an intention to obstruct must be proved.[109] There are, however, cases in which the courts have imposed strict liability notwithstanding the use of this word. 'Wilful' in these cases is held to apply only to the conduct element of the offence but not to some circumstance or consequence which is an element of the crime. In these cases liability as to the consequences or circumstances elements of the offence have been held to be strict. So, for example, D was held guilty of wilfully fishing in private water, although he believed there was a public right to fish there;[110] of wilfully killing a house pigeon when he shot a bird, believing it was a wild pigeon;[111] and of wilfully destroying an oak tree in contravention of a tree preservation order when he was unaware of the order and believed that permission had been given for the tree to be felled.[112] In these cases, the fishing, the *conduct* of fishing, killing a bird, cutting down a tree were all 'wilful'; but in none of them was the commission of the crime 'wilful'.

Following the most important authority, *Sheppard*,[113] discussed in Chapter 5, it is arguable that 'wilfully' should be construed to mean wilfully committing *the crime*; but in practice it may be that the courts are still willing to interpret elements of an offence as imposing strict liability despite that word appearing in the statute.

7.3.1.3 Effect of usage of *mens rea* words in some sections but not others

Where a *mens rea* word is used in one section of a statute but not in another that may suggest that the second creates an offence of strict liability; but Lord Reid has said:

It is also firmly established that the fact that other sections of the Act expressly require *mens rea*, for example because they contain the word 'knowingly', is not itself sufficient to justify a decision that a section which is silent as to *mens rea* creates an absolute offence.[114]

In the celebrated example of *Sherras v De Rutzen*,[115] D was charged with supplying liquor to a constable on duty.[116] The policeman was not wearing his armband signalling that he was a police officer, and it was admitted that the failure to wear it was an indication that he was off duty. D, who was in the habit – quite lawfully – of serving constables in uniform but without their armlets, made no enquiry and took it for granted that this policeman was off duty. The Act provided an offence (in s 16(1)) for a licensee *knowingly* to harbour or suffer to remain on his premises any constable on duty. In contrast, the offence with which D was charged (s 16(2)) did not include the word 'knowingly', yet D's conviction was quashed. Day J said that the only inference to be drawn was that under s 16(1) the prosecution had to prove knowledge, while under s 16(2) the defendant had to prove he had no knowledge.[117]

---

[109] *Willmott v Atack* [1977] QB 498, DC.

[110] *Hudson v MacRae* (1863) 4 B & S 585, DC.

[111] *Cotterill v Penn* [1936] 1 KB 53.

[112] *Maidstone Borough Council v Mortimer* [1980] 3 All ER 552, DC.

[113] [1981] AC 394, HL. cf *Turner* [2008] EWCA Crim 272.

[114] *Sweet v Parsley* [1970] AC 132 at 149.

[115] [1895] 1 QB 918. cf *Harding v Price* [1948] 1 KB 695, DC (a defence to failure to report an accident was to show that D did not know an accident had occurred, even though the word 'knowingly' in the Motor Car Act 1903 was omitted when the section was repealed and replaced by the Road Traffic Act 1930). Reliance was unsuccessfully placed on the effect of additional new sections on the meaning of the original provisions of an Act in *Blake* [1997] Crim LR 207.

[116] Contrary to the Licensing Act 1872, s 16(2).

[117] This view was doubted by Devlin J in *Roper v Taylor's Central Garage* (above). If Day J intended to refer to the *evidential* burden only, the *dictum* is unobjectionable. See Edwards, *Mens Rea*, 90–97.

Wright J made no attempt to reconcile the two subsections, contenting himself with pointing out that:[118]

if guilty knowledge is not necessary, no care on the part of the publican could save him from conviction…since it would be as easy for the constable to deny that he was on duty when asked, or to produce a forged permission from his superior officer as to remove his armlet before entering the public house.[119]

This factor was influential in many recent cases including the cases of G in the House of Lords (dealing with sexual offences against under 13s where the statute is explicit about *mens rea* as to under 16s and silent as to under 13s); *Mohammad*[120] (Insolvency Act offences) and *Matudi*[121] (importation of endangered species).

7.3.2 The offence in its social context

In addition to the statutory form of the offence, the court must have regard to the context of the legislation and the purpose it was designed to serve, and this will be highly influential. Cases where strict liability was imposed primarily on social grounds may be even more vulnerable to attack after *B* and *K*. If *mens rea* is not ruled out expressly or by necessary implication from the text, it cannot, according to *dicta* in *K*, be excluded. As noted, this has not prevented the Court of Appeal subsequently imposing strict liability in cases such as *Muhammed*[122] and *Matudi*.[123]

7.3.2.1 'Real' or 'quasi' crime?[124]

An important matter is whether the court considers the offence to be a 'true' or 'real' crime or a 'quasi-crime'. Parliament makes no such distinction. Conduct either is, or it is not, declared by Parliament to be a crime.[125] Unlike many European jurisdictions, England does not create a separate category of administrative offences called 'violations' in which strict liability is imposed.[126] The Law Commission recently rejected the idea of adopting such a system.

Determining what is meant by 'real' crime is not easy. Mitchell J said that he did not regard the offence of selling a lottery ticket to a child under 16 as 'truly criminal in character' although it was punishable on indictment with two years' imprisonment.[127] This is a peculiar notion of 'truth'. The truth is that it is a crime. It is the courts that take it upon themselves to decide whether it is a 'real' or 'quasi' crime. They do so on the basis that an offence which, in the public eye, carries little or no stigma and does not involve 'the disgrace of criminality',[128] is only a quasi-crime. Then, strict liability may be imposed because 'it

---

[118] [1895] 1 QB 918 at 923.

[119] An example of this criterion as a determinant of strict liability is the case of *Matudi* [2003] EWCA Crim 697 dealing with the importation of endangered species.

[120] [2002] EWCA Crim 1856.

[121] [2003] EWCA Crim 697, (2004) J Crim L 186.

[122] [2003] EWCA Crim 1852.

[123] [2003] EWCA Crim 697.

[124] See J Horder (2002) 118 LQR 458, noting that regulatory offences are also stigmatizing for the accused. See also G Lamond, 'What is a Crime' (2007) 27 OJLS 609.

[125] See Ch 2, above.

[126] See the interesting discussion in Reid (2008) 29 St LR 173, and JR Spencer and A Pedain, 'Approaches to Strict and Constructive Liability in Continental Criminal Law', in A Simester (ed), *Appraising Strict Liability*.

[127] *London Borough of Harrow v Shah* [2000] Crim LR 692, DC. See further LCCP 195, Part 3.

[128] Per Lord Reid in *Warner v Metropolitan Police Comr* [1969] 2 AC 256 at 272.

does not offend the ordinary man's sense of justice that moral guilt is not of the essence of the offence'.[129]

The attempt to distinguish an offence on the basis of whether it is a regulatory or real crime is not particularly helpful.[130] In academic terms the question is often posed as whether the offence is *malum in se* (intrinsically morally wrong eg murder or rape) or merely *malum prohibitum* (wrong being prescribed by law) this too provokes as many disputes as it solves.[131]

Judicial utterances are no more helpful in giving the meaning of 'real' or quasi crime. In *Sherras v De Rutzen*, Wright J distinguished 'a class of acts... which are not criminal in any real sense, but are acts which in the public interest are prohibited under a penalty'.[132] Since we are assuming a defendant who is morally blameless, no stigma ought to attach to him anyway. In determining whether the offence involves a 'stigma', it is necessary to consider the case where the offence is committed intentionally. If Parliament prohibits the causing of results because it deems them in some measure harmful, the intentional causing of the harm in question probably deserves some measure of moral condemnation. Stigma attaches to, or should attach to, the person who deliberately sells lottery tickets to children or even the motorist who *deliberately* leaves his car in a parking space for longer than is permitted by law – it is an anti-social act, likely to cause inconvenience to others. But few people, even 'right-thinking' people, would consider such an act so iniquitous, even when done intentionally, that the actor ought to be locked up or even shunned and avoided. Since offences of strict liability do not distinguish between degrees of fault and no fault at all, a conviction fixes the offender with whatever stigma might attach to an intentional offender.[133]

Moreover, there is a danger in relying too heavily on judicial statements in relation to particular words used in different contexts and at different times. Society's attitude to what is blameworthy and 'truly' criminal changes. In *Hart v Anglian Water*, the Court of Appeal suggested that breaches of the Water Resources Act 1991, were not of a 'non-criminal' character.[134] In view of growing concerns over pollution and environmental matters in general, it is highly questionable whether the general public would share that view.

7.3.2.2 A crime of general or special prohibition?

A second factor which may be of great significance when considering social context is whether the provision is of general application or relates only to those following a particular trade, profession or special activity (especially where D has voluntarily engaged in that activity). In the latter type of case, the court may be much more ready to hold such a 'regulatory offence' to impose strict liability.[135] Lord Diplock put it as follows:[136]

Where penal provisions are of general application to the conduct of ordinary citizens in the course of their everyday life, the presumption is that the standard of care required of them in informing themselves of facts which would make their conduct unlawful is that of the familiar common law duty of care. But where the subject-matter of a statute is the regulation of a particular activity involving

---

[129] ibid. cf *Wings Ltd v Ellis*, above, p 74. See also *Matudi* [2003] EWCA Crim 697.

[130] cf A Simester, 'Is Strict Liability Always Wrong?', in A Simester (ed), *Appraising Strict Liability*, 37–41.

[131] See DN Husak, 'Malum Prohibitum and Retributivism', in Duff and Green (eds), *Defining Crimes* and SP Green, 'Why it is a Crime to Tear the Tag off a Mattress' (1997) 46 Emory LJ 1586.

[132] [1895] 1 QB 918 at 922.

[133] See JC Smith, in *Wootton*, 141 and in commentary on *B* at [2000] Crim LR 408. And see *Harrow v Shah*, above n 127.

[134] [2003] EWCA Crim 224. (that section has now been repealed by Sch 28, para 1 of the Environmental Permitting (England and Wales) Regulations 2010/675). See generally on this area C Abbott, *Enforcing Pollution Control Regulation* (2009).

[135] See further A Brudner, 'Imprisonment and Strict Liability' (1990) 40 U Toronto LJ 738.

[136] In *Sweet v Parsley* [1970] AC 132 at 163.

potential danger to public health, safety or morals, in which citizens have a choice whether they participate or not, the court may feel driven to infer an intention of Parliament to impose, by penal sanctions, a higher duty of care on those who choose to participate and to place on them an obligation to take whatever measures may be necessary to prevent the prohibited act, without regard to those considerations of cost or business practicability which play a part in the determination of what would be required of them in order to fulfil the ordinary common law duty of care.

So we find most instances of strict liability in statutes regulating the sale of food, and drugs, the management of industrial activities, the conduct of licensed premises and the like.[137] But the 'particular activity' may be one in which citizens generally engage, like driving a car. However, this is something which we choose to do and, as it involves potential danger to others, so it is not inconsistent with this statement of principle that some offences regulating the conduct of motorists should be strict.

Some commentators have argued that this factor, and in particular whether the activity involved is one for which a licence is required, is the most important in the courts' decision as to whether a statute should be interpreted as imposing strict liability.[138] Lord Clyde recognized this in *Lambert*:[139]

A strict responsibility may be acceptable in the case of statutory offences which are concerned to regulate the conduct of some particular activity in the public interest. The requirement to have a licence in order to carry on certain kinds of activity is an obvious example. The promotion of health and safety and the avoidance of pollution are among the purposes to be served by such controls. These kinds of cases may properly be seen as not truly criminal. Many may be relatively trivial and only involve a monetary penalty. Many may carry with them no real social disgrace or infamy.

7.3.2.3 Possibility of compliance

According to Devlin J, it is:

a safe general principle to follow...that where the punishment of an individual will not promote the observance of the law either by that individual or by others whose conduct he may reasonably be expected to influence, then, in the absence of clear and express words, such punishment is not intended.[140]

This principle has been restated many times, for example by the Privy Council in both *Lim Chin Aik*[141] and *Gammon (Hong Kong) Ltd v A-G of Hong Kong*[142] and by the Divisional Court in *Pharmaceutical Society of Great Britain v Storkwain Ltd*.[143] But, if implemented, it would seem to require negligence, though not perhaps of a high degree, rather than impose strict liability. D, it appears, must be shown to have fallen short in some respect of the standard to be expected of him. But was the principle applied in *Storkwain*? Are pharmacists expected to keep a handwriting expert on the premises to scrutinize the prescriptions? Or to telephone the doctor each time they receive a prescription for confirmation that he wrote it?[144] In *Harrow*

---

[137] See generally LCCP 195.

[138] See R Glover, 'Regulatory Offences and Reverse Burdens: The Licensing Approach' (2007) 71 J Crim L 259, arguing that the licence holders have accepted an obligation to prove defences to avoid liability, so that reverse burdens are not problematical in this context. See also Green (1997) 46 Emory LJ 1586; Husak, in Duff and Green, *Defining Crimes*, 82–84.

[139] [2002] AC 545 at [154].

[140] *Reynolds v G. H. Austin & Sons Ltd* [1951] 2 KB 135, [1951] 1 All ER 606, DC.

[141] [1963] AC 160 at 174, [1963] 1 All ER 223 at 228.

[142] [1985] AC 1 at 14–15, [1984] 2 All ER 503 at 508–509.

[143] [1985] 3 All ER 4, approved by the House of Lords [1986] 2 All ER 635 at 640.

[144] It appears that in *Storkwain* the pharmacist, not knowing Dr Irani, *did* telephone the number on the prescription but it was false and he was deceived by the forger or his accomplice who answered: Jackson [1991] Crim LR at 895.

v Shah, it was acknowledged that D had done all he could to ensure compliance with the law. What else could he do, except stop selling lottery tickets? Obviously, the courts do not expect such wholly unreasonable steps to be taken – but how then can the principle be satisfied in such cases?

The evidence from empirical studies is that use of strict liability crimes is not necessarily successful in securing compliance with regulations.[145]

7.3.2.4 Social danger

Fourthly, the courts are influenced by the degree of social danger which, in their opinion, will follow from breach of the particular prohibition. They take judicial notice of the problems with which the country is confronted. The greater the degree of social danger, the more likely is the offence to be interpreted as one of strict liability. Drugs, road accidents and pollution are constantly brought to our attention as pressing evils; and in each case the judges have at times invoked strict liability as a protection for society.

Dangerous drugs[146]

Legislation concerning dangerous drugs has had a chequered recent history. Lord Parker declared in 1966[147] that he took judicial notice of the fact that drugs are a great danger and the Divisional Court imposed strict liability of a most draconian character in a number of cases about that time. D was held to be guilty of being 'concerned in the management of premises used for the purpose of smoking cannabis' though he did not know and had no means of knowing that such smoking was taking place.[148] In other cases, it was held that D was guilty of being in unauthorized possession of a drug[149] if he knew he had control of a thing which was in fact a dangerous drug, even though he did not know, and had no reason to know, that it was either dangerous or a drug.[150] He might have reasonably believed that he had a bottle of sweets, but that would have been no defence.

Problems of possession[151]

The first case on strict liability ever considered by the House of Lords, *Warner v Metropolitan Police Comr*,[152] concerned possession of prohibited drugs. D, who as a sideline sold scent, collected two boxes which had been left for him at a cafe. One box contained scent, the other controlled drugs. D said he assumed both boxes contained scent. The jury were told that such a belief went only to mitigation. The Court of Appeal agreed. If D was in possession of the box and he knew the box contained something, he was in possession of the contents, whatever they were; and, as it was an 'absolute' offence, that was all the prosecution had to prove.

The House of Lords, Lord Reid dissenting, agreed with the courts below that the section created an 'absolute' offence, not requiring any *mens rea* as such. But it was, of course, necessary to prove the *actus reus*, that is, possession, and that involved proving a mental element. Lord Guest agreed with the Court of Appeal – D's knowledge that he had a box containing *something* under his control was enough – but the other judges held that more was required.

---

[145] G Richardson, 'Effective Means of Regulating Industry Strict Liability for Regulating Crime: The Empirical Evidence' [1987] Crim LR 295. See the Appendix A to LCCP 195 by Professor Black.

[146] See, generally, R Fortson, *The Misuse of Drugs and Drug Trafficking Offences* (5th edn, 2005).

[147] In *Yeandel v Fisher* [1966] 1 QB 440 at 446, [1965] 3 All ER 158 at 161.

[148] ibid.

[149] Contrary to s 1(1) of the Drugs (Prevention of Misuse) Act 1964.

[150] eg *Lockyer v Gibb* [1967] 2 QB 243, [1966] 2 All ER 653.

[151] See for a theoretical consideration of the issues raised by possession offences, MD Dubber, 'The Possession Paradigm', in Duff and Green (eds), *Defining Crimes*, 115.

[152] [1969] 2 AC 256, [1968] 2 All ER 356.

Though D's possession of the box gave rise to a strong inference that he was in possession of the contents, that inference might be rebutted. Their lordships' opinions are obscure and various but it seems that the inference certainly would be rebutted if (i) D believed the box contained scent, (ii) scent was something of 'a wholly different nature' from the drugs, (iii) D had no opportunity to ascertain its true nature, and (iv) he did not suspect there was 'anything wrong' with the contents. These issues (or at least some of them, for the majority of the House were far from being in complete accord) ought to have been left to the jury and, as they had not, three judges held that there had been a misdirection but upheld the conviction under the proviso.

Possession is a neutral concept, not implying any kind of blame or fault but experience has shown that, when it becomes the determinant of guilt, it tends to acquire a refined and artificial meaning of great complexity. It seems the most obvious common sense to say that a person firmly grasping a parcel is in possession of it and a distinction between the parcel and its contents is too absurd to contemplate; but, if it is a grave offence merely to possess the contents, courts will strive to find means to say that an innocent person is not in possession, by refining the meaning of that concept. Of course, this problem would not arise if it were held that the offence required some element of fault – possession, as observed, is neutral and in itself incapable of being 'fault' – but, sadly, of all the judges involved, only Lord Reid was willing to take this sensible course. The result was another calamitous decision by the House.

The five speeches delivered in *Warner* differ so greatly and it is so difficult to make sense of parts of them that courts in later cases have found it impossible to extract a *ratio decidendi*. The law has been modified by the Misuse of Drugs Act 1971 but the onus remains on the Crown to prove possession and the Act has nothing to say about that concept. It has, however, influenced the approach of the courts. In *McNamara*,[153] the Court of Appeal, while paying lip-service to the House of Lords, has gone back to the view of the Court of Appeal and the dissenting opinion (on this issue) of Lord Guest. D was in possession of a cardboard box containing cannabis resin. He said he thought it contained pornographic material. Because he knew he was in control of the box and that the box contained something, he was in possession of cannabis. The court was able to reach this conclusion without misgiving because it no longer followed that D was guilty of the offence. Under the Misuse of Drugs Act 1971, s 28, it was a defence to prove[154] that he neither believed nor suspected nor had reason to suspect that the thing of which he was in possession was a controlled drug.

McNamara provides a welcome simplification of the law where D knows he has the thing or a container with something in it but claims he thought it was something else. It does not solve the problem when he claims he was unaware of its existence. In *Warner*,[155] there was unanimous agreement about a hypothetical case posed earlier by Lord Parker CJ[156] – if something is slipped into a woman's shopping basket and she has no idea that it is there, she is not in possession of it. It is easy to find authority in the vast case law on possession to contradict that proposition but Parker LCJ, the Court of Appeal and the House were entirely confident about it: the woman is in possession of the basket and the known contents but not the thing secretly inserted. The judges shrank from saying that the hypothetical woman was in possession of the thing because they were thinking of a packet of controlled drugs and, if she was in possession, she would have been guilty of a grave offence. If the thing were a box of chocolates dropped in by a friend as a birthday present it is unlikely that they would have hesitated to

---

[153] (1988) 87 Cr App R 246, [1988] Crim LR 440 and commentary.
[154] Interpreted, *obiter*, by the House of Lords in *Lambert* [2002] AC 545 to mean not 'prove' but 'introduce evidence of' so as to comply with the Human Rights Act 1998.
[155] [1969] 2 AC at 282, 286, 300, 303 and 311.
[156] *Lockyer v Gibb* [1967] 2 QB 243 at 248.

hold that she was in possession of it. Suppose that, before she discovered it, the box had been removed by a pickpocket, would they have hesitated to hold that it was stolen from her (it was not stolen from anyone else) and that the pickpocket was a thief? Of course not. So far as possession is concerned, there is no rational distinction between the drugs and the chocolates.

In *Lewis*,[157] it was held that the judge had not misdirected the jury by telling them that the tenant of a house might be found to be in possession of drugs found on the premises although he did not know they were there, provided he had had an opportunity to find out that they were. But there is no material difference between planting drugs in a person's house and planting them in her basket.[158] The decision seems to contradict the one thing on which their lordships in *Warner* were unanimous. In introducing the idea of opportunity, the court relied on a statement of Lord Morris. But Lord Morris was dealing with a quite different question: possession, he said, was 'being *knowingly in control of a thing* in circumstances which have involved an opportunity (whether availed of or not) to learn or discover, at least in a general way, *what the thing is*'.[159] In *Lewis*, D was not knowingly in control of the thing.

Warner does not affect the law where the drug was not in a container. D must know he has the thing, but it is not necessary that he should know or comprehend its nature.[160] In *Marriott*,[161] D was convicted of being in possession of 0.03 grains of cannabis adhering to a penknife. It was held that the jury had been wrongly directed that he was guilty if he knew he was in possession of the penknife. It was necessary to prove at least that he knew that there was some foreign matter adhering to the knife. The court thought that no further *mens rea* was necessary – so that the accused would be guilty if he thought the matter was tobacco or toffee – but now, under the Misuse of Drugs Act, it would be a defence for him to prove[162] that he neither believed, nor suspected, nor had reason to suspect, that the matter was a controlled drug.

Being concerned in the management of premises

The second case concerning strict liability to reach the House of Lords was *Sweet v Parsley*.[163] On this occasion, the House overruled the cases which decided that being 'concerned in the management of premises used for the purpose of smoking cannabis' is an offence of strict liability. D, a schoolmistress, let the rooms of a country farmhouse, retaining one room for her own use and visiting the farm occasionally to collect rent and see that all was well. Cannabis was smoked in the farmhouse but it was found as a fact that she had no knowledge whatsoever of this. The Divisional Court nevertheless upheld her conviction.[164] She was 'concerned in the management' and that was enough. The House quashed her conviction. The 'purpose' referred to in the section must be that of the person concerned in the management; and D had no such purpose. Only Lord Wilberforce was content to stop with this 'prosaic interpretation of the paragraph'. The remainder relied, in varying degrees, on a presumption in favour of

---

[157] (1987) 87 Cr App R 270, [1988] Crim LR 517 and commentary.

[158] 'First of all man does not have possession of something which has been put into his pocket or into his house without his knowledge': *McNamara* (1988) 87 Cr App R 246 at 248.

[159] [1969] 2 AC at 289 (emphasis in original).

[160] *Boyesen* [1982] AC 768, [1982] 2 All ER 161. (It is immaterial how minute the quantity is provided only that it amounts to something and D knows he has it.)

[161] [1971] 1 WLR 187.

[162] Interpreted, *obiter*, by the House of Lords in *Lambert* [2001] 3 All ER 577 to mean not 'prove' but 'introduce evidence of' so as to comply with the Human Rights Act 1998.

[163] [1970] AC 132, [1969] 1 All ER 347.

[164] It has been suggested that strict liability in such a case might infringe Art 3 of the ECHR by subjecting D to degrading treatment. See Sullivan, 'Strict Liability for Criminal Offences', in A Simester (ed), *Appraising Strict Liability*, above, at 206.

mens rea. The actual decision in *Warner* was not affected,[165] but the attitude of the House, with the exception of Lord Reid, who saw no reason to alter what he had said in the earlier case, is very different. The judges are no less sensitive to the public's view of injustice than to their need for protection; and, for once, a case of strict liability had excited public interest. The public outcry and sense of injustice may not have been without influence.[166]

The corresponding provisions of the Misuse of Drugs Act require *mens rea* and leave the onus of proof, where it belongs, with the Crown. It is an offence if an occupier[167] or person concerned in the management of premises 'knowingly permits or suffers' the smoking of cannabis and other specified activities in connection with drugs. The word 'knowingly' was introduced for the first time in the Act; but it does not alter the decisions under the Dangerous Drugs Act 1965 that knowledge or wilful blindness is enough, but reasonable grounds for suspicion are not.[168]

Pollution

In view of the current concern about pollution it is scarcely surprising that modern examples of strict liability should arise in crimes to protect the environment. In *Alphacell Ltd v Woodward*,[169] the House of Lords held that D Ltd was guilty of causing polluted matter to enter a river, contrary to s 2(1)(a) of the Rivers (Prevention of Pollution) Act 1951.[170] They had built and operated settling tanks with an overflow channel into the river and provided pumps designed to prevent any overflow taking place. Because the pumps became obstructed with vegetation, an overflow of polluted water occurred. There was no evidence that D knew that pollution was taking place or that they had been in any way negligent. Lord Salmon stressed the public importance of preventing pollution and the risk of pollution from the vast and increasing number of riparian industries and said:[171]

If...it were held to be the law that no conviction could be obtained under the 1951 Act unless the prosecution could discharge the often impossible onus of proving that the pollution was caused intentionally or negligently, a great deal of pollution would go unpunished and undeterred to the relief of many riparian factory owners. As a result, many rivers which are now filthy would become filthier still and many rivers which are now clean would lose their cleanliness.

Another example is *Atkinson v Sir Alfred McAlpine & Son Ltd*,[172] where it was held that the company was guilty of failing to give written notice, as required by the Asbestos Regulations 1969, that they were going to undertake work involving crocidolite though they neither knew nor had reason to know that the work involved crocidolite. The court distinguished *Harding*

---

[165] *Fernandez* [1970] Crim LR 277 where it was held to be enough that D knew a package might contain some prohibited article and was prepared to take it, whatever the contents were.

[166] '...fortunately the press in this country are vigilant to expose injustice...', per Lord Reid, *Sweet v Parsley*, above, at 150.

[167] The occupier is a person whose degree of control is sufficient to enable him to exclude anyone likely to commit an offence under the Act. It is not limited to persons in legal possession and includes a student with rooms in college: *Tao* [1977] QB 141, [1976] 3 All ER 65.

[168] *Thomas* (1976) 63 Cr App R 65, [1976] Crim LR 517.

[169] [1972] AC 824,. cf *Empress Car Co (Abertillery) Ltd v National Rivers Authority* [1998] 1 All ER 481, HL, above, p 90; *Maidstone Borough Council v Mortimer* [1980] 3 All ER 552; *Kirkland v Robinson* [1987] Crim LR 643, DC (possession of live wild birds an offence of strict liability under the Wildlife and Countryside Act 1981, s 1(1)(a), taking into account the outstanding social importance of an Act designed to protect the environment).

[170] Now repealed.

[171] [1972] AC at 848.

[172] (1974) 16 KIR 220, [1974] Crim LR 668, DC.

v Price,[173] where Lord Goddard CJ, holding that D was not guilty of failing to report an accident, the happening of which he was unaware, said:

If a statute contains an absolute prohibition against the doing of some act, as a general rule *mens rea* is not a constituent of the offence, but there is all the difference between prohibiting an act and imposing a duty to do something on the happening of a certain event. Unless a man knows that the event has happened, how can he carry out the duty imposed? ... Any other view would lead to calling on a man to do the impossible.

In *McAlpine*, the court said that, unlike the accident, it was 'probably possible' to ascertain whether crocidolite was involved; but since they held that the mischief would not be met if 'knows or ought to know' were read into the regulation, it is clear that impossibility would not be regarded as a defence.

7.3.2.5 The severity of the punishment

It is often argued that the provision for a severe maximum punishment shows that strict liability could not have been intended by Parliament. To some extent, this is in conflict with the principle previously discussed, since the provision for only a slight punishment would suggest that Parliament thought the social danger involved to be slight. In the recent case of *Muhammed*,[174] accepting that materially contributing to the extent of insolvency by gambling was an offence of strict liability, the seriousness of the offence was described as the 'starting point' for the court in its determination. The court explained that the more serious the offence the greater the weight to be attached to the *mens rea* presumption and vice versa.

However, the courts do not seem to have been deterred in recent years from imposing strict liability in the case of offences carrying heavy maximum sentences – the offence under the Dangerous Drugs Act 1965 of which Ms Sweet was convicted was punishable on indictment with 10 years' imprisonment and causing death by dangerous driving was (originally) punishable with five. The fact that an offence under s 58(2) of the Firearms Act 1968 was punishable with three years' imprisonment did not deter the court from holding that an honest and reasonable belief that the firearm was an antique was no defence.[175] The House of Lords in *B and K* contemplated with equanimity strict liability for having sexual intercourse with a girl under 13 although the offence was punishable with life imprisonment.[176] The maximum life imprisonment in *G* did not prevent the House of Lords interpreting s 5 of the Sexual Offences Act 2003 as strict.[177] In *Gammon (Hong Kong) Ltd v A-G of Hong Kong*,[178] the Privy Council admitted that the fact the offence was punishable with a fine of HK$250,000 and imprisonment for three years was 'a formidable point'; but found 'there is nothing inconsistent with the purpose of the ordinance in imposing severe penalties for offences of strict liability'.

7.3.3 Other factors

It is impossible to catalogue all factors but in addition to those above, factors influencing the court's decision as to whether the presumption is necessarily rebutted, include the presence of

---

[173] [1948] 1 KB 695 DC.

[174] [2003] 2 WLR 105.

[175] *Howells* [1977] QB 614,. Section 19 of the Act (carrying a firearm in a public place) also imposes strict liability, although the penalty is seven years: *Vann and Davis* [1996] Crim LR 52.

[176] *B* and *K*, above, p 162.

[177] This is a striking example because G's argument was not that he should be acquitted because he was not at fault but that he should only be liable for the lesser offences (sex with under 16-year-old which on his version he had admitted) carrying a lesser sentence.

[178] [1985] AC 1 at 17.

due diligence defences, the stigma of the offence,[179] the need for such offences as a method of prosecuting corporate entities and the ease of proof for the prosecution unless strict liability is imposed. This final factor must be treated with caution since logically, it would allow for strict liability in, for example, murder because the prosecution face a difficult task in proving D's *mens rea* of intention.[180]

7.3.3.1 Liability is strict, not 'absolute'

It was observed at the beginning of this chapter that the fact that an offence is one of strict liability does not rule out the need for any mental element. It may be necessary to prove that D had *mens rea* as to the conduct or circumstances of the offence save the one element in respect of which strict liability was imposed. In addition, a strict liability offence does not preclude reliance on defences. When the court holds that it is an offence of strict liability to sell meat which is unfit for human consumption, it decides that a reasonable mistake as to that particular fact is not a defence. It does not decide that any other defence is unavailable to D; and indeed, we have seen that a mistake as to other circumstances of the *actus reus* may afford a defence.[181] There is no reason why all other defences should not be available as they are in the case of offences requiring full *mens rea*. Even when the former offence of dangerous driving was thought to impose strict liability,[182] it was held to be a defence if D was in a state of automatism when he 'drove' the vehicle.[183] Similarly, it is perfectly clear that a child under the age of 10 could in no circumstances be convicted of an offence of strict liability[184] and it is submitted that a child between 10 and 14 could be convicted only if it were proved that he knew his act was 'wrong'.[185] It is submitted, therefore, that other general defences – insanity,[186] necessity,[187] duress[188] and coercion – should be available equally on a charge of an offence of strict liability as in the case of any other offence.[189]

Larsonneur[190] and *Winzar v Chief Constable of Kent*[191] establish that *lawful* compulsion is not a defence to offences of 'being found'. It does not follow that unlawful duress would not be a defence. If D, being drunk, were forced at gunpoint into the highway he should not be guilty of being found drunk there. Nor does it follow that even lawful compulsion

---

[179] See *Barnfather v Islington Education Authority* [2003] EWHC 418 (Admin). In terms of the potential use of strict liability offences as evidence of D's bad character see *Goss* [2005] Crim LR 61.

[180] See the comparative study by J Spencer and A Pedain, 'Approaches to Strict and Constructive Liability in Continental Criminal Law', in A Simester (ed), *Appraising Strict Liability* noting that a reason for continental systems avoiding strict liability is that their procedures allow for proof more easily than the strict adversarial system in England.

[181] Above, p 158.

[182] cf *Gosney* [1971] 3 All ER 220.

[183] *Hill v Baxter* [1958] 1 QB 277; *Budd* [1962] Crim LR 49; *Watmore v Jenkins* [1962] 2 QB 572.

[184] Below, p 340.

[185] Below, p 341. cf Cave J in *Tolson* (1889) 23 QBD 168 at 182 and Lord Diplock in *Sweet v Parsley* [1969] 1 All ER 347 at 361.

[186] See *H v DPP* [1997] 1 WLR 1406 below in which insanity was wrongly regarded as a defence displacing *mens rea*.

[187] But see *Cichon v DPP* [1994] Crim LR 918 (defence of necessity not open under Dangerous Dogs Act 1991, s 1(2)(d), because an 'absolute' offence).

[188] See *Eden DC v Baird* [1998] CODS 209. *Hampshire CC v E* [2007] EWHC 2584 (Admin), below p 369 seems too narrow, and unfair. See J Donoghue (2011) 74 MLR 216, p 235 et seq.

[189] For discussion of this question see F Sayre, 'Public Welfare Offences' (1933) 33 Col LR 55 at 75–78; Howard, SR, Ch 9.

[190] (1933) 24 Cr App R 74; above, p 63.

[191] (1983) The Times, 28 Mar, above, p 64. cf *O'Sullivan v Fisher* [1954] SASR 33, discussed by Howard, SR at 193; *Achterdam* 1911 EDL 336 (Burchell and Hunt, SACLP, 114).

may not found a defence to other, less extreme, cases of strict liability than those of 'being found'.

7.3.3.2 ECHR

The arguments based on Art 6(2) have been considered above.

7.4 Arguments for and against strict liability

The proliferation of offences of strict liability, while generally deplored by legal writers, was welcomed by the distinguished social scientist, Lady Wootton, on the ground that 'nothing has dealt so devastating a blow at the punitive concept of the criminal process...'[192]

If, however, the primary function of the courts is conceived as the prevention of forbidden acts, there is little cause to be disturbed by the multiplication of offences of strict liability. If the law says that certain things are not to be done, it is illogical to confine this prohibition to occasions on which they are done from malice aforethought; for at least the material consequences of an action, and the reasons for prohibiting it are the same whether it is the result of sinister malicious plotting, of negligence or of sheer accident.[193]

Accepting that the primary function of the courts is the prevention of forbidden acts, there remains the question, which acts should be regarded as forbidden? Surely, only such acts as we can assert ought not to have been done. Suppose that a butcher, who has taken all reasonable precautions, has the misfortune to sell some meat which is unfit for human consumption. That it was so unfit is undiscoverable by any precaution which a butcher can be expected to take. Ought the butcher to have acted as he did? Unless we want butchers to stop selling meat, or to take precautions so extreme as to be unreasonable (like employing an analyst)[194] it would seem that the answer should be in the affirmative; we want butchers, who have taken all reasonable precautions, to sell meat – the act of this butcher was not one which the law should seek to prevent. The imposition of strict liability rather than negligence seems wholly inappropriate. Some commentators take a different view, arguing that strict liability offences perform a valuable role[195] in 'setting out schemes of conduct that have the effect of co-ordinating risk reduction or the promotion of certain goods'.

In the famous, but now overruled, case of *Prince* where D was convicted of taking a girl under 16 out of the possession of her parents, even though he had no *mens rea* as to her age, some of the judges reached their conclusion, on the ground that men should be deterred from taking girls out of the possession of their parents, whatever the girl's age. This reasoning can hardly be applied to many modern offences in which strict liability is adopted. We do not wish to deter people from driving cars, being concerned in the management of premises or canning peas.[196] These acts, if done with all proper care, are not such acts as the law should seek to prevent. The fallacy in the argument lies in looking at the harm done in isolation from the circumstances in which it was brought about. Many acts, which have in fact caused harm,

---

[192] *Crime and the Criminal Law* (2nd edn, 1963) 44. See also at 63, criticized by B Hogan, 'Criminal Liability without Fault' (1967); HLA Hart, *The Morality of the Criminal Law* (1965) 13 et seq.

[193] ibid, at 51.

[194] See Kennedy LJ cited above, p 157 and see below, p 180.

[195] Lamond (2007) 27 OJLS 609.

[196] See *Smedleys Ltd v Breed* [1974] AC 839. 'Obviously any consequence is avoidable by the simple expedient of not engaging in the process at all. But that clearly is not what is meant unless the process itself is open to serious criticism as unnecessary or inefficient', per Lord Hailsham [1974] 2 All ER 21 at 28.

ought to have been done. The surgeon performing a justified operation with all proper skill may cause death.

Another argument that is frequently advanced in favour of strict liability is that, without it, many guilty people would escape – 'that there is neither time nor personnel available to litigate the culpability of each particular infraction'.[197] This argument assumes that it is possible to deal with these cases without deciding whether D had *mens rea* or not, whether he was negligent or not. Certainly, D may be convicted without deciding these questions, but how can he be fairly sentenced? Clearly, the court ought to deal differently with (i) the butcher who knew that the meat was tainted; (ii) the butcher who did not know, but ought to have known; and (iii) the butcher who did not know and had no means of finding out. Sentence cannot properly be imposed without deciding into which category the convicted person falls. Treating the offence as one of strict liability, in the case of jury trial, merely removes the decision of these vital questions of fact from the jury and puts them in the hands of the judge; in the case of summary trial, it removes the questions from the sphere of strict proof according to law and leaves them to be decided in the much more informal way in which questions of fact relating purely to sentence are decided.[198]

There is a further problem with strict liability and sentencing. If the offence is one of strict liability, evidence is not admissible at the trial either to show that D was blameworthy – *Sandhu*[199] – or that he was not: *Gosney*.[200] On the assumption (held, on appeal, to be wrong) that the former offence of dangerous driving was one of strict liability, the judge, no doubt rightly, excluded evidence alleged to show that D was blameless. If the rules relating to proof at the trial have any value at all, it is extraordinary that they should not be applied to the most important facts in the case. That the sentence should be imposed by the judge on a basis of fact different from that on which the jury convicted is deplorable; but it is always possible in the case of strict liability unless the judge questions the jury as to the grounds of their decision – and there are difficulties about this.[201] A recent illustration of how *mens rea* may be relevant to sentence even where strict liability is imposed, is in cases of under-age sex. As a child under 13 cannot, in law, give consent to any sexual activity, an offender's belief in the age of the child, even if reasonably held, was irrelevant. However, when considering culpability, actual consent was recognized as being capable of being a mitigating factor.[202]

The argument which is probably most frequently advanced by the courts for imposing strict liability is that it is necessary to do so in the 'interests of the public'. Now it may be conceded that in many of the instances where strict liability has been imposed, the public does need protection against negligence and, assuming that the threat of punishment can make the potential harm-doer more careful, there may be a valid ground for imposing liability for negligence as

[197] H Wechsler, 'The Model Penal Code', in JL Edwards (ed), *Modern Advances in Criminology* (1965) 73. The argument was met by the authors of the code by 'the creation of a grade of offence which may be prosecuted in a criminal court but which is not denominated criminal and which entails upon conviction no severer sentence than a fine or civil penalty or forfeiture.'

[198] Disputed facts affecting sentence may be decided by the judge in a 'Newton hearing' after conviction – see *Newton* (1982) 77 Cr App R 13, [1983] Crim LR 198. In some cases judges have preferred the use of additional counts to obtain the jury's decision on important issues of culpability which would not appear from a verdict of guilty on a single count. See *Hoof* (intentional or reckless arson?), below, Ch 29. This course is not open where the offence is one of strict liability. In *Warner* (above, p 172) the recorder asked the jury after verdict whether D knew the box contained drugs but they said, reasonably, that they had not decided that question.

[199] [1997] Crim LR 288.

[200] [1971] 2 QB 674.

[201] cf comment on *Lockyer v Gibb* [1966] Crim LR 504 and on *Sheppard* [1981] Crim LR 171 at 172; *Dalas* [1966] Crim LR 692; *Warner* [1967] 3 All ER 93, [1967] Crim LR 528; *Lester* [1976] Crim LR 389; *Foo* [1976] Crim LR 456 and commentaries on these cases.

[202] *F* [2007] EWCA Crim 2550. See also the *obiter* comments in *Jackson* [2006] EWCA Crim 2380 above, p 164.

well as where there is *mens rea*. This is a plausible argument in favour of strict liability if there were no middle way between *mens rea* and strict liability – that is liability for negligence – and the judges have generally proceeded on the basis that there is no such middle way.

The case against strict liability then is, first, that it is unnecessary. It results in the conviction of persons who have behaved impeccably and who should not be required to alter their conduct in any way. Secondly, that it is unjust.[203] Even if an absolute discharge can be given (as in *Ball*)[204] D may feel rightly aggrieved at having been formally convicted of an offence for which he bore no responsibility. It is significant that Ball thought it worthwhile to appeal. Moreover, a conviction may have far-reaching consequences outside the courts,[205] so that it is no answer to say that only a nominal penalty is imposed.[206]

7.5 Negligence/lack of due diligence as a preferred approach

The imposition of liability for negligence would in fact meet the arguments of most of those who favour strict liability. Thus Roscoe Pound, in a passage which has been frequently and uncritically accepted as a justification for such offences, wrote:[207]

The good sense of the courts has introduced a doctrine of acting at one's peril with respect to statutory crimes which expresses the needs of society. Such statutes are not meant to punish the vicious but to put pressure upon the thoughtless and inefficient to do their whole duty in the interest of public health or safety or morals.

The 'thoughtless and inefficient' are, of course, the negligent. The objection to offences of strict liability is not that these negligent persons are penalized, but that others who are completely innocent are also liable to conviction.

7.5.1 Statutory due diligence defences

It is common for the drastic effect of a statute imposing strict liability to be mitigated by the provision of a statutory defence allowing the defendant to prove that he acted with all due diligence. The Law Commission has recently reviewed the use of due diligence defences and the various forms they take – the most general ones based on whether D has taken all reasonable precautions and exercised all due diligence to avoid the commission of the offence.[208]

As an example, the Trade Descriptions Act 1968 creates a number of offences, some of which replace earlier offences of strict liability, and s 24 provides that it is a defence to prove (i) that the commission of the offence was due (*inter alia*) to a mistake or accident and (ii) that D 'took all reasonable precautions and exercised all due diligence to avoid the commission of such an offence by himself or any person under his control'.[209] Thus, though the prosecution do not have to prove negligence, it is a defence for D to show that he was not negligent. Similar steps have been taken in the Misuse of Drugs Act 1971.

---

[203] See for a philosophical account, A Simester, 'Is Strict Liability Always Wrong?' and DN Husak, 'Strict Liability, Justice and Proportionality', in A Simester (ed), *Appraising Strict Liability*.

[204] (1966) 50 Cr App R 266 (blameless driver guilty of causing death by dangerous driving).

[205] As in the case of *Sweet v Parsley* [1970] AC 132, [1969] 1 All ER 347.

[206] This was accepted by the Privy Council in *Lim Chin Aik* [1963] AC 160 at 175 and by Lord Reid in *Warner* [1968] 2 All ER 356 at 366.

[207] *The Spirit of the Common Law* (1921) 52.

[208] LCCP 195, para 6.28.

[209] See generally, DL Parry, 'Judicial Approaches to Due Diligence' [1995] Crim LR 695. See P Cartwright, *Consumer Protection and the Criminal Law* (2001).

A further more recent example is in the Bribery Act 2010, s 7, which creates a new strict liability offence for a commercial organization where a person associated with it bribes another person intending to obtain or retain a business advantage. This is a very widely defined offence.[210] Section 7 provides:

(1) A relevant commercial organisation ('C') is guilty of an offence under this section if a person ('A') associated with C bribes another person intending –

    (a) to obtain or retain business for C, or

    (b) to obtain or retain an advantage in the conduct of business for C.

There is, crucially, a due diligence defence in s 7(2) for C to prove that C had in place adequate procedures designed to prevent persons associated with C from undertaking such conduct.

Sometimes due diligence defences are extremely complex with various specific elements that D must prove. Examples include those relating to the treatment and sale of food. The offences enacted by the first 20 sections of the Food Safety Act 1990 are mainly strict liability offences. Section 21(1), however, provides that it shall be a defence for the person charged with any of the offences to prove that he took all reasonable precautions and exercised all due diligence to avoid the commission of the offence by himself or by a person under his control;[211] but, where this defence involves an allegation that the offence was due to the act or default of another person, the defendant may not, without the leave of the court, rely on it unless within a prescribed period he has served on the prosecutor a notice in writing giving such information identifying or assisting in the identification of the other person as was then in his possession (s 21(5)).

The statutory due diligence defences usually impose on D a burden of proving both that he had no *mens rea* and that he took all reasonable precautions and exercised all due diligence to avoid the commission of an offence. The effect of such provisions is that the prosecution need do no more than prove that the accused did the prohibited act and it is then for him to establish, if he can, that he did it innocently. Such provisions are a distinct advance on unmitigated strict liability; but they are still a deviation from the fundamental principle that the prosecution must prove the whole of their case.

Arguments over what the due diligence defence requires D to prove can also arise. In the recent case of *Croydon LBC v Pinch a Pound (UK) Ltd*,[212] P Co sold knives. An employee at P Co sold a utility knife to two 15-year-olds. P was convicted in the magistrates' court under s 141A of the Criminal Justice Act 1988 ('selling' a knife to any one under 18). P argued successfully in the Crown Court that the company had exercised all due diligence and taken all reasonable precautions to prevent the commission of the offence, and therefore had the statutory defence in s 141A(4). The Divisional Court held that the Crown Court had misconstrued the due diligence test.[213] The defence in s 141A(4) comprised two elements: (i) taking reasonable precautions (eg a no sales policy, signage and staff training) and (ii) the exercise of due diligence in the management and operation of sales of the items (ensuring that the policy was adhered to, recording refused sales correctly etc). The Crown Court appeared to have focused

---

[210] Section 7 is triable only on indictment (s 11(3)). The maximum sentence is an unlimited fine. See the valuable analysis by S Gentle [2011] Crim LR 101. The offence will be in force from 1 July 2011.

[211] It has been held that there is no liability for D where he has taken all reasonable steps to delegate his duty to another who then fails to perform to the relevant standard. See, eg, *R (Keam) v DEFRA* [2005] EWHC 1582 (Admin).

[212] [2010] EWCA Crim 3238.

[213] Misapplying words from Lord Diplock's speech in *Tesco Supermarkets Ltd v Nattrass* [1972] AC 153 HL.

on whether D had shown an absence of negligence *and an absence of a reprehensible state of mind*. That was too generous to the defendant as it imported *mens rea* into the offence. The case was remitted with an order to convict.

7.5.2 Due diligence defences imposed at common law

In some common law jurisdictions it has become commonplace for the courts to adopt a 'halfway house' between strict liability and full *mens rea*. Once the *actus reus* has been proved an onus is imposed on D, sometimes to introduce evidence and sometimes to prove, that he had reasonable grounds for his failure to be aware of, or to foresee, relevant facts, as the case may be. The lead first came from Australia.[214] In Canada also, the Supreme Court, in a notable judgment delivered by Dickson J, held that public welfare offences *prima facie* fall into an intermediate class between offences requiring *mens rea* and offences 'of absolute liability'. The prosecution need prove only that D caused the *actus reus* but he may escape liability by proving that he took all reasonable care to avoid the commission of the offence.[215]

Where there is no such express due diligence provision in a statute, it is unlikely that the courts will hold it to be implied. It is true that the House of Lords in *Sweet v Parsley*[216] looked favourably on such a doctrine:[217]

When a statutory prohibition is cast in terms which at first sight appear to impose strict responsibility, they should be understood merely as imposing responsibility for negligence but emphasising that the burden of rebutting negligence by affirmative proof of reasonable mistake rests upon the defendant.[218]

However, the English courts have subsequently shown no inclination to put such a principle into practice. In *Gammon (Hong Kong) Ltd v A-G of Hong Kong*,[219] the Privy Council, while stressing the need for very high standards of care, regarded the choice as a straight one between *mens rea* and strict liability. Just as the judges invented the presumption in favour of *mens rea*, they could have invented a presumption of a negligence requirement in particular types of case. They chose not to do so. Lord Devlin has explained this:

It is not easy to find a way of construing a statute apparently expressed in terms of absolute liability so as to produce the requirement of negligence. Take, for example, an offence like driving a car while it has defective brakes. It is easy enough to read into a statute a word like 'wilfully' but you cannot just read in 'carelessly'. You cannot show that no one should carelessly drive a car with defective brakes; you are not trying to get at careless driving. What you want to say is that no one may drive a car without taking care to see that the brakes are not defective. That is not so easy to frame as a matter of construction and it has never been done.[220]

The judicial reluctance to read due diligence defences into strict liability is in part borne of a reluctance to impose a burden of proof on the defence. But as the former Law Lord, Lord Cooke of Thorndon observed:

---

[214] *Maher v Musson* (1934) 52 CLR 100; *Proudman v Dayman* (1941) 67 CLR 536.
[215] *City of Sault Ste Marie* (1978) 40 CCC (2d) 353.
[216] [1969] 1 All ER 347 at 351 per Lord Reid, at 357 per Lord Pearce and at 362 per Lord Diplock.
[217] As it had developed in Australia, see n 214 above.
[218] G Orchard, 'The Defence of Absence of Fault in Australia and Canada', in *Criminal Law Essays*.
[219] [1985] AC 1, [1984] 2 All ER 503 at 509.
[220] *Samples of Lawmaking*, 76.

It does seem odd that in the home of *Woolmington* absolute (or strict) liability is so extensively accepted by the courts, and with some equanimity. It is as if the great case has created a judicial mindset which recoils at a shifting of the onus, yet tolerates a harsher solution.[221]

There is nothing wrong, it is submitted, with the 'judicial mindset' which recoils at a shifting of the onus onto the defendant – that reflects a healthy commitment to the presumption of innocence – but when combined with a refusal to imply a requirement of either *mens rea* or negligence, it does indeed lead to an unduly harsh solution. The opportunity to adopt the halfway house was presented to the House of Lords in *B (A Minor) v DPP*[222] but was declined in favour of a requirement of full *mens rea*. It seems the halfway house has no future in England and Wales, except where it is embodied in a statute.

7.5.3 Reform

The Law Commission recently made the welcome recommendation that:

In an ideal world, criminal offences created by statute would always indicate when fault need not be proved, or if it needs to be proved what kind of fault (or defence) is involved. Since there are so many criminal offences under statute that fall short of the ideal, we believe that, subject to some possible exceptions, the courts should be given the power to apply a defence of due diligence in all the circumstances to statutory offences that would otherwise involve strict liability with no adequate defence. This approach has the advantage of leaving the strict basis of liability in the relevant provision intact. That means the courts will no longer need to search for what may be non-existent Parliamentary intention respecting fault requirements and will no longer need to decide whether a presumption that fault must be proved applies, and if so, whether the presumption has been displaced.[223]

---

[221] 'One Golden Thread', in *Turning Points of the Common Law* (Hamlyn Lectures, 1997) 28 at 47. See also *City of Sault Ste Marie* (1978) 85 DLR 3d 161 (Can). On defences of due diligence see G Orchard, 'The Defence of Absence of Fault in Australia and Canada', in *Criminal Law Essays*.

[222] [2000] 2 AC 428.

[223] Law Commission, CP 195, *Criminal Liability in Regulatory Contexts* (2010) para 6.92, recognising that in some contexts, eg road traffic, due diligence would not be an appropriate innovation.

8

Parties to crime[1]

8.1 Introduction

The person who directly and immediately performs the *actus reus* of an offence (the principal offender, in this chapter, P) is not necessarily the only one who is criminally liable for it. A person (in this chapter, D), might also be liable as an 'accessory', or as it is also called, a 'secondary party'. Specific common law and statutory rules govern whether a person is liable as an accessory; these rules apply to all offences, unless expressly[2] or impliedly excluded.[3] Where D is liable as an accessory, he is liable only because he aided, abetted, counselled or procured (for convenience we can say 'assisted or encouraged') P and the principal offence was committed. A person, D, other than the principal, P, might also be liable for an inchoate offence – assisting or encouraging P under the Serious Crime Act 2007 (SCA 2007) or for conspiring with P that the offence would be committed. There is a crucial difference from secondary liability: D's liability for inchoate offences does not depend on whether P has committed the offence.

In secondary liability we can describe D's liability as 'derivative' on the commission of the principal offence.[4] Logically therefore, the easiest way of ascertaining D's potential liability is to ascertain whether the principal offence has been committed, then to consider whether D has fulfilled the requirements of aiding and abetting that offence. This does not involve asking whether D fulfilled the elements of the principal offence, but whether he performed the relevant conduct sufficient to constitute assisting or encouraging and did so with the *mens rea* required for liability as an accessory. Occasionally, statutory offences are drafted in such a way that assisting or encouraging someone to commit an offence is criminal in its own right[5] and in those cases D can be liable for the statutory offence even if the offence D has assisted is not committed. There are also dozens of offences of 'being knowingly concerned in' a type of behaviour such as drug importation or supply of drugs, and the person 'knowingly concerned in' the conduct commits an offence of his own accord.[6]

The current law of secondary liability is unsatisfactorily complex, and displays many of the characteristic weaknesses of common law that has been allowed to develop in a pragmatic and unprincipled way. Reform would be welcome, although whether in the form the Law

---

[1] See, generally, KJM Smith, *A Modern Treatise on Complicity* (1991). For an excellent discussion of the current law see LC 305, *Participating in Crime* (2007) Part 2 and Appendix B.

[2] eg under the Corporate Manslaughter and Corporate Homicide Act 2007 there is no secondary liability for individuals.

[3] Arguably this occurs where a statute creates offences of 'using or causing or permitting to be used'. See *Carmichael & Sons (Worcester) Ltd v Cottle* [1971] RTR 11. cf *Farr* [1982] Crim LR 745, CA, and commentary.

[4] Russell, 128; *Surujpaul v R* [1958] 3 All ER 300 at 301, PC. This is now subject to the rule in *Millward* [1994] Crim LR 527, below, p 236.

[5] See, eg, Female Genital Mutilation Act 2003, below, p 640.

[6] See, eg, the Misuse of Drugs Act 1971, s 4(3)(b).

Commission proposes in its most recent recommendations (Report No 305 discussed below) is debated by some.[7]

8.2 Basis of liability

By the Accessories and Abettors Act 1861, s 8 as amended by the Criminal Law Act 1977:

Whosoever shall aid, abet, counsel or procure the commission of any indictable offence whether the same be an offence at common law or by virtue of any act passed or to be passed, shall be liable to be tried, indicted and punished as a principal offender.[8]

The section does not create an offence. It specifies the procedure and punishment for the aiders, abettors, counsellors and procurers, conveniently called 'accessories'.

8.2.1 Distinguishing accessories and principals

The law treats the accessory and principal in identical terms for the purposes of procedure and punishment. It has always been sufficient to prove that the defendant was either the principal[9] or accessory.[10] A person who is charged with an offence, say theft, may be convicted whether the evidence proves that he committed the theft (ie was a principal), or aided, abetted, counselled or procured it (ie was an accessory). But the charge should, wherever possible, specify whether the accused is alleged to have been the principal offender or an accessory.[11] The prosecution can nevertheless secure a conviction without specifying precisely what role they allege D played. Thus, in *Gianetto*, it was sufficient for the prosecution to allege that D killed his wife or that he was an accessory to her killing (by contracting a killer to do so).[12] The prosecution could not be sure whether D was the principal offender or an accessory, but could establish beyond doubt that he was involved in plotting her killing.

Difficulties of this type are commonplace where, for example, V is attacked by a group of individuals but the medical evidence points to death resulting from a single stab wound. Unless the evidence can establish that a particular member of the group must have been responsible for inflicting the fatal wound, the prosecution may have no alternative but to allege that each member was either the principal offender or an accessory. Considerable difficulty

---

[7] See R Buxton [2009] Crim LR 230; cf W Wilson, 'A Rational Scheme of Liability for Participation in Crime' [2008] Crim LR 3, suggesting the proposals generally 'succeed admirably'; cf GR Sullivan, 'Participating in Crime' [2008] Crim LR 19, suggesting the proposals on joint ventures show a 'disregard for the minimum standards of clarity and comprehensibility' and RD Taylor 'Procuring, Causation, Innocent Agency and the Law Commission' [2008] Crim LR 32, who is also critical of the complexity and incoherence of the proposals. For criticism of the 2007 Act see D Ormerod and R Fortson, 'The Serious Crime Act 2007 – The Part 2 Offences' [2009] Crim LR 359.

[8] Similar provisions relating to summary trial are to be found in the Magistrates' Courts Act 1980, s 44.

[9] The common law of felonies designated the actual perpetrator 'the principal in the first degree' and distinguished secondary parties into principals in the second degree – those who participated at the time when the felony was actually perpetrated – and accessories before the fact – those who participated at an earlier time. It was traditional to state that the distinction was that the principal in the second degree was *present* at the commission of the offence; but in fact he might be a considerable distance away – in an American case (*State v Hamilton and Lawrie* 13 Nev 386 (1878) – signals from mountain top, 30–40 miles away), so long as he was assisting or available to assist, at the time. Hawkins, II PC, c 29, ss 7 and 8; Foster, *Crown Law*, 350. The abolition of felonies in the Criminal Law Act 1967 renders the distinction redundant.

[10] *Mackalley's Case* (1611) 9 Co Rep 61b; *Fitzgerald* [1992] Crim LR 660.

[11] *DPP for Northern Ireland v Maxwell* [1978] 3 All ER 1140, HL; *Taylor* [1998] Crim LR 582.

[12] [1997] 1 Cr App R 1, CA and commentary [1996] Crim LR 722 for criticism. See also *Morton* [2004] Crim LR 73.

would arise in such cases if the prosecution had to choose. If there is only one fatal stab wound, the Crown cannot simply allege that each defendant was the principal. As a matter of fact that is most unlikely to be true; only one person will have plunged the knife in. Equally, the Crown would face difficulty if they alleged that each defendant was an accessory; unless the jury could be sure when considering the case against a particular defendant that he was not the principal he would have to be acquitted. In view of these forensic difficulties, the pragmatic solution of being able to charge D with being either an accessory or principal is understandable. The lack of precision in such an indictment has been held not to render it incompatible with Art 6 of the ECHR on the basis of the requirement that a defendant must know 'in detail' the nature of the case against him.[13]

Although the law treats the accessory and principal in identical terms for the purposes of procedure and punishment, it is important to distinguish them for several reasons. First, the accessory is only liable once the principal offence has been committed.[14] Secondary liability derives from the principal offence.[15] This derivative approach to secondary liability means that, with a murder for example, D may supply the weapon to P, who kills V, but it is not until that killing takes place (or is attempted) that D can be liable as an accessory. This contrasts with inchoate liability where D who supplies the weapon is liable (depending on his *mens rea*) as soon as he performs that act of supply, irrespective of whether P goes on to kill V. Second, in some cases, it is only an offence to do something *to another* and not to assist someone to do it to themselves (eg injecting drugs). Since in these cases there is no possibility of secondary liability, it is essential to establish if it is alleged that D helped P perform the conduct on himself, or performed it on P.[16] A third reason for distinguishing principals and accessories is that, even in offences of strict liability, accessories must always be proved to have *mens rea*.[17] Fourth, in some cases, offences are defined in such a way that they can be committed, as a principal offender, only by someone who is a member of a particular group or who has a particular qualification (eg, the 'driver' of a vehicle or the licensee of a pub).[18] Fifth, in some offences, vicarious liability may be imposed for the act of another who is a principal offender or does the act of a principal offender; but there is no vicarious liability for the act of an accessory.[19] Finally, in some exceptional cases the available sentencing differs significantly between principal and accessory.[20]

8.2.2 Secondary as distinct from inchoate liability

As noted, with inchoate offences D's liability arises as soon as he has assisted or encouraged P or agreed with him to commit an offence irrespective of whether the that leads to P

[13] *Mercer* [2001] All ER (D) 187.

[14] Committing the offence includes 'attempting' to commit the offence. If P, with D's encouragement, has attempted to murder V, D, as well as P, can be convicted of the offence of attempted murder.

[15] See GP Fletcher, *Rethinking Criminal Law* (1978) Ch 8; KJM Smith, *A Modern Treatise on Complicity* (1991) Ch 4; D Lanham, 'Primary and Derivative Criminal Liability: An Australian Perspective' [2000] Crim LR 707; LC 300, para 2.7 et seq. The law in application fails to remain true to this theory: Wilson describes English law as 'fudging' the theoretical basis: *Central Issues*, Ch 7. An alternative analysis sees the secondary as causally responsible for the principal's crime (see Smith, above, Ch 3; M Moore, *Causation and Responsibility An Essay in Law, Morals and Metaphysics* (2009); Gardner, *Offences and Defences*, Ch 4. See below p 193.

[16] *Kennedy (No 2)* [2008] 1 AC 269; cf *Empress Cars* [1999] 2 AC 22.

[17] Below, p 208.

[18] Below, p 282.

[19] Below, p 273. There is no vicarious liability at common law, as recently confirmed in *Craik v CC of Northumbria Police* [2010] EWHC 935 (Admin). See below.

[20] In road traffic offences, where disqualification of the principal is obligatory, disqualification of accessories is discretionary: Road Traffic Offenders Act 1988, s 34(5).

committing or attempting to commit the substantive offence.[21] Under ss 44 to 46 of the SCA 2007 there will be an overlap with secondary liability. Where D does an act which is capable of encouraging or assisting, eg supplying a gun to P for him to murder V, D will be liable under ss 44–46 (see Ch 13), subject to *mens rea*, irrespective of whether the anticipated offence is committed or attempted by P. The offences in ss 44–46 are extremely wide reaching. If P commits the murder, D can be charged as an accessory or under ss 44–46. There will often be little advantage in charging D as an accessory.[22] The procedure and sentence will be the same for the offence under the SCA 2007 as for the anticipated substantive offence.

There is an even more complex relationship between conspiracy and secondary liability. A conspiracy is complete as soon as A and B agree to commit an offence (say murder) with the intention,[23] that the offence should be committed. There is no secondary liability for anyone unless and until the murder is committed. If B commits murder, A is liable as an accessory to murder by having agreed with B and thereby provided B with encouragement.[24] It is also possible for A and B to be parties if, despite not having agreed to commit it, they share a common purpose to commit it.[25] If B commits the offence, A and B can also still be charged with conspiracy to do so (see Ch 13). Finally, there is the issue of being an accessory to a conspiracy – for example, A intentionally assists D1 and D2 (eg providing D1 and D2 with facilities to meet) when they are making an agreement to murder V; A does not assist in the murder itself, but merely in setting up the agreement. If D1 commits murder as part of his conspiracy with D2, D2 is liable as an accessory (as well as for the conspiracy) because D2 has encouraged D1. Arguably, A has assisted D1 and D2 to commit the conduct element of conspiracy, but it cannot reasonably be said that A has done any act that has assisted or encouraged[26] D1 to *perpetrate the conduct element* of murder. It is submitted that A's act is not enough to render him an accessory to murder.

8.3 The principal offender

It is important to identify the principal offender. Where there are several participants in a crime, the principal offender is the one whose act is the most immediate cause of the *actus reus*. In murder, for example, he is the person who, with *mens rea*, fires the gun or administers the poison which causes death; in theft, the person, who, with *mens rea*, appropriates the property which is stolen; in bigamy, the person who, knowing himself to be already married, goes through a second ceremony of marriage; and so on. With offences in which there is no result or consequence to be proved, the principal offender is perhaps more accurately the

---

[21] At common law D had no inchoate liability for assisting P to commit an offence which P did not subsequently commit or attempt to commit. The SCA 2007, ss 44–46, introduced such offences following the recommendation of the Law Commission in its Report, *Inchoate Liability for Assisting and Encouraging Crime* (2006) LC 300. See the discussion in Buxton, above.

[22] Section 45 requires that D should believe that P *will* commit the conduct element of the *actus reus* of the principal offence. In some respects this may actually be narrower than the present law. For example, D, sells P a knife believing that P will use it in the kitchen, if D also believes that P *might* use it to murder his wife, D is not liable under s 45, but may be liable under the present law as an accessory if P does commit murder. See Ch 13.

[23] cf *Anderson* [1986] AC 27 which is surely wrong on this.

[24] Even in the unusual case where it is not A's intention that the murder be committed. See below p 439.

[25] *Rook* [1993] 2 All ER 955, [1993] Crim LR 698 and commentary. cf Stephen, *Digest* (9th edn), art 28; Williams, CLGP, 363; *Pinkerton v United States* 328 US 640 (1946). See, however, D Lanham, 'Complicity, Concert and Conspiracy' (1980) 4 Crim LJ 276. Exceptionally, a conspirator, A, has no contact with, and is even unaware of the existence of conspirator B. If B commits the murder it is *arguable* that A has not in fact, assisted or encouraged (or in procuring caused) – B to commit it. A might in such a case be convicted of conspiracy to murder.

[26] Arguably there is no encouragement by A in this conduct. Some light may be shed on the meaning of that concept when the courts begin to grapple with the SCA 2007 provisions.

person who engages in the conduct element of the *actus reus*. In the case of statutory offences, whether a person is a principal offender will turn on whether he satisfies the precise form of words used to describe the conduct element of the offence.[27]

It is a fundamental principle that criminal liability arises from wrongdoing for which a person is himself responsible and not for the wrongdoing of others. If, by performing acts of assistance, an accessory were taken to have brought about the commission of the offence he would for all purposes become a principal offender. If D, having procured P to murder V, were taken to have caused V's death, that is, killed V, he would satisfy the definition of murder as a principal. Anyone whose assistance or encouragement in fact caused another to commit a crime would be a principal. The separate body of law of accessory liability is based on the assumption that the accessory does not cause the *actus reus*.[28]

The House of Lords in *Kennedy (No 2)*[29] has recently reaffirmed these fundamental principles.[30] As Lord Bingham made clear, referring to Glanville Williams's article 'Finis for Novus Actus' the doctrine of secondary liability was developed precisely because an informed voluntary choice was ordinarily regarded as a *novus actus interveniens* breaking the chain of causation:

Principals cause, accomplices encourage (or otherwise influence) or help. If the instigator were regarded as causing the result he would be a principal, and the conceptual division between principals (or, as I prefer to call them, perpetrators) and accessories would vanish. Indeed, it was because the instigator was not regarded as causing the crime that the notion of accessories had to be developed. This is the irrefragable argument for recognising the *novus actus* principle as one of the bases of our criminal law. The final act is done by the perpetrator, and his guilt pushes the accessories, conceptually speaking, into the background. Accessorial liability is, in the traditional theory, 'derivative' from that of the perpetrator.[31]

Despite these clear statements, the courts still occasionally refer to D as a 'cause' of P's act. In *Mendez and Thompson*[32] Toulson LJ, after a scholarly analysis of the historical position, concluded that 'at its most basic level secondary liability is founded on a principle of causation, that a defendant (D) is liable for an offence committed by a principal actor (P) if by his conduct he has caused or materially contributed to the commission of the offence (with the requisite mental element); and a person who knowingly assists or encourages another to commit an offence is taken to have contributed to its commission'.[33] If cause is read strictly, this approach seems to run contrary to the fundamental principle reiterated in *Kennedy (No 2)* and does not reflect the practical reality that D might be liable for providing assistance to someone who had already made up his mind to commit the offence. There would be no causal contribution to the offence in such a case.[34]

8.3.1 Innocent agency[35]

The *actus reus* of a crime may be directly brought about by the act of someone who is not a participant in the offence at all (that is, who has no *mens rea*, or who has some defence,[36]

---

[27] See, eg, *Corporation of London v Eurostar* [2004] EWHC 187 (Admin), where Eurostar were guilty as principals for 'landing' an Alsatian dog as prohibited under anti-rabies legislation.

[28] H Hart and T Honoré, *Causation in the Law* (2nd edn, 1985) 380; SH Kadish, *Essays* (1987) 143–144.

[29] [2007] UKHL 38, [2008] Crim LR 223.

[30] See above, p 91.

[31] [2007] UKHL 38, [17].

[32] [2010] EWCA Crim 516, criticized by G Virgo, [2010] Archbold Review; and D Ormerod [2011] Crim LR 151.

[33] [18], referring to *Foster's Crown Law* (3rd edn, 1809) p 369. Toulson LJ does add 'contributing to'.

[34] See, however, the argument advanced by Gardner *Offences and Defences* above.

[35] See P Alldridge, 'The Doctrine of Innocent Agency' (1990) 2 Criminal Law Forum 45; G Williams, 'Innocent Agency and Causation' (1992) 3 Criminal Law Forum 289; RD Taylor, 'Complicity and Excuses' [1983] Crim LR 656.

[36] Other than duress: *Bourne* (1952) 36 Cr App R 125.

such as infancy or insanity). Such a person is usually described as an 'innocent agent.' The principal offender in such a case is the participant whose act is the most immediate[37] cause of the innocent agent's act. Examples are plentiful. If D sends to V through the post a letter-bomb which injures V when it explodes, the postman who delivers the letter is an innocent agent. If D, intending to kill V, provides to V's daughter a poison which he says will cure V's cold, and the daughter innocently (that is, without knowing the true nature of the drug) administers the poison, causing V's death, then D is guilty as the principal offender and the daughter is an innocent agent.[38] If the daughter or the postman had *mens rea* then he or she would, of course, be a principal offender. Where D, an employee makes a false statement to his employer's accountant, knowing that the statement will be entered in the accounts, and the innocent accountant does enter it, D is guilty, as a principal offender, of falsifying his employer's accounts.[39] Where D induces a child, aged 9, to take money from a till and give it to D, D is a principal offender as the child is exempt from criminal liability. If the child is over 10 and liable to conviction, then he is the principal offender if he has *mens rea* and D is an accessory.[40]

There are some crimes to which the doctrine of innocent agency is inapplicable because it is impossible to say that D has personally performed the conduct required by the definition of the *actus reus*.[41] Bigamy – except in the case of a marriage by proxy – is a good example. Compare it with murder. If D causes an innocent person, say the postman E, to kill V by delivering a letter which he does not know contains a bomb, it is right for the law to take the view that *D has killed V* – the *actus reus* of murder. In contrast, if D knows that F is married, but induces E, an innocent person who has no knowledge of F's marital status, to marry F it is impossible to say that *D has married during the lifetime of his wife* – the *actus reus* of bigamy. He has not done so. The innocent agency doctrine seems equally inapplicable, it is submitted, in rape and other crimes involving sexual intercourse. There are *dicta* in *Cogan and Leak*[42] that rape may be committed through an innocent agent but these are contrary to principle. The Law Commission propose replacing the innocent agency doctrine with a specific offence; see below p 244.

8.3.2 Joint principal offenders

There may be more than one person engaged in perpetrating the conduct element of the *actus reus* of the principal offence. So there may be two or more principal offenders in the same crime. If D1 and D2 make an attack on V intending to kill or cause him serious injury and the combined effect of their blows is to kill him, both are guilty of murder[43] as joint principal offenders. A different type of joint responsibility is that where each of two or more parties does an act which is an element of, or part of, the *actus reus* of the principal offence.[44]

---

[37] This description of relative proximity can be problematical. D1 passes poison to D2, who passes it to D3 who, unaware that it is poison, passes it to V who dies. D3 is the innocent agent. Is D2 the principal offender and D1 a secondary party? Are both D1 and D2 principal offenders? See Smith, *A Modern Treatise on Complicity*, 98. I am grateful to David Hughes for pointing this out.

[38] *Anon* (1634) Kel 53; *Michael* (1840) 9 C & P 356.

[39] *Butt* (1884) 15 Cox CC 564.

[40] *Manley* (1844) 1 Cox CC 104 In *DPP v K & B* [1997] 1 Cr App R 36, DC, it was said, *obiter*, that if D procured a child under 10 to have sexual intercourse without consent, D could not be guilty of rape because there would be no *actus reus*. That seems wrong: see [1997] Crim LR 121, 122. See also *Mazeau* (1840) 9 C & P 676.

[41] cf *Woby v AJB and LCO* [1986] Crim LR 183, DC (boys under 18 not guilty of buying intoxicating liquor in licensed premises when they sent in an adult to buy it).

[42] [1976] QB 217 [1975] Crim LR 584 and commentary thereon; below, p 234.

[43] *Macklin and Murphy's Case* (1838) 2 Lew CC 225.

[44] *Bingley* (1821) Russ & Ry 446 (A and B each forged part of a banknote).

There is, however, no joint principalship if D induces another person, P (not an *innocent* agent), by persuasion or otherwise, to commit the offence: that does not amount to D causing the *actus reus*. P's voluntary intervening act 'breaks the chain of causation'[45] so that D is not a principal offender. P will be liable as the principal offender; D may be liable as an accessory.[46]

What if the principal offender himself is not present at the moment of the completion of the crime? If D1 and D2 conspire to employ an innocent agent, E, both D1 and D2 are liable as principal offenders for E's acts and it is immaterial that E was instructed by the one in the absence of the other.[47] The innocent agent's acts are considered the acts of both conspirators.[48] Where there is no innocent agent, the same considerations cannot apply. D encourages or assists P, who leaves poison to be taken by V, or sets a trap into which V falls. D is liable as a secondary party; P as the principal offender.

8.3.3 Joint principals or principal and accessory?

The distinction between a joint principal offender and a secondary party is sometimes a fine one. There is a view that all who act together with a common purpose – are principal offenders.[49] That would mean that if D provided assistance to P by providing a gun for him to murder V and P alone fired the shot, D might be liable as a principal for murder if he shared P's purpose to kill V, even though D did not perform the *actus reus* of murder.

This is not the law in England.[50] As noted, under s 8 of the 1861 Act, generally, it is immaterial whether D is alleged to have participated in the crime as principal or accessory. Either way, he is equally responsible and liable to conviction. When it is necessary to distinguish, the test would seem to be: did D by his own act (as distinct from anything done by P with D's advice or assistance) contribute to the *actus reus*? If he did, he is a principal offender. The distinction may be important where the jury acquit P and convict D. If D caused the *actus reus* by his own act, he is a principal offender and there is no problem. But, if he did not, there is a difficulty. If P is innocent, there is no crime which D can have aided or abetted. The difficulty can be overcome (i) if P can be regarded as an innocent agent, or (ii) under a somewhat uncertain principle[51] that it is an offence for D to procure the commission of P's *actus reus*;[52] but it is surely wrong to overcome it by a fiction, a pretence that D 'did it', if he did not.

Where the *actus* is a 'state of affairs'[53] – eg being in the UK illegally – the test for determining who is a principal offender is: ignoring D, does the statutory description of the state of affairs fit P?

---

[45] See *Kennedy (No 2)* [2007] UKHL 38.

[46] Or under ss 44 to 46 of the SCA 2007 depending on his *mens rea*.

[47] This qualifies the idea that generally the principal is the person who is the immediate cause of the conduct element of the *actus reus*.

[48] *Bull and Schmidt* (1845) 1 Cox CC 281. Arguably D1 is liable as an accessory to D2 who causes E to act.

[49] Some jurisdictions adopt such a rule. See in Australia *Osland v R* (1998) 73 ALJR 173, HC of A. See further JC Smith, 'Joint Enterprise and Secondary Liability' (1999) 50 NILQ 153, cf A Simester, 'The Mental Element in Complicity' (2006) 122 LQR 578.

[50] See, historically, Stephen's *Digest*, arts 37 and 38.

[51] Below, p 234.

[52] *Millward*, below, p 235.

[53] Above, p 63.

8.4 Secondary participation

To be liable, a person who is not the principal offender must be proved to have aided, abetted, counselled[54] or procured, though it is quite sufficient to show that he did one of these things.[55]

An accessory is liable when and where the principal offence he has aided, abetted, counselled or procured is committed. So an employer, D, who sends a lorry, which he knows to be in a dangerous condition, from Scotland to England may be held liable in England for a death caused here because of the lorry's condition.[56]

8.4.1 *Actus reus* of the accessory

The *actus reus* and *mens rea* of the principal offender will be prescribed by the relevant statute or common law, so with murder it would be killing a human being with malice aforethought, etc; with assault it will be intentionally or recklessly causing a person to apprehend immediate unlawful personal violence etc. If D is alleged to be an accessory to any crime, his liability as an accessory comprises the *actus reus* of aiding, abetting, counselling or procuring, with the relevant *mens rea* of an accessory (intention to assist, knowledge of the relevant circumstances rendering P's act criminal). The conduct sufficient to satisfy the elements of being an accessory will often contrast starkly with the requirements of the principal offence. In a case of murder, D can be convicted as an accessory as a result of conduct that consists of no more than knowingly acting as a lookout whereas P must be shown to have killed with intent to kill or do serious injury, but under s 8 of the 1861 Act both D and P will be convicted as murderers, labelled as such and punished as such.

It is important to remember that there is no secondary liability for a person whose participation in the relevant events does not involve him advising or encouraging P to commit the crime, and who does not assist P in the commission of it in any way. Accepting a lift on a motorbike known to have been taken without consent does not amount to aiding and abetting the use of the vehicle without insurance.[57] It would be different if D had participated in or assisted/encouraged the taking.[58] Liability as an accessory does not extend to cases where D has not assisted or encouraged in fact, but has merely attempted or conspired to do so.[59]

8.4.1.1 Aid, abet, counsel, procure

In *A-G's Reference (No 1 of 1975)* Lord Widgery CJ said:

We approach s 8 of the 1861 Act on the basis that the words should be given their ordinary meaning, if possible. We approach the section on the basis also that if four words are employed here 'aid, abet, counsel or procure', the probability is that there is a difference between each of those four words and

---

[54] 'Counselling' must not be taken literally. Mere incitement to commit an offence, not followed by its actual commission, is not 'counselling' – *Assistant Recorder of Kingston-upon-Hull, ex p Morgan* [1969] 2 QB 58, DC.

[55] *Ferguson v Weaving* [1951] KB 814.

[56] *Robert Millar (Contractors) Ltd* [1970] 2 QB 54. See Law Commission proposals on jurisdiction LC 305, Ch 6.

[57] *D (Infant) v Parsons* [1960] 1 WLR 797.

[58] *Ross v Rivenall* [1959] 1 WLR 713. cf the Theft Act 1968, s 12(1) and *Boldizsar v Knight* [1980] Crim LR 653, below, p 860.

[59] *Kenning* [2008] EWCA Crim 1534. Liability might arise under the SCA 2007, ss 44–46 or for conspiracy.

the other three, because, if there were no such difference, then Parliament would be wasting time in using four words where two or three would do.[60]

The four words had previously been regarded as technical terms and it is clear that they cannot be given their ordinary meaning in all respects.[61]

In the modern law, secondary participation almost invariably consists in 'assisting' or 'encouraging' the commission of the crime. The only possible exception may be the procurer who succeeds in causing the principal to commit the crime (as in the *A-G's Reference*) without doing anything which could be fairly described as encouragement or assistance. Assisting or encouraging can be by practically any means – supply of weapons, tools, information, support and encouragement, keeping watch, filming an attack on a mobile phone etc. It is generally irrelevant whether the accessory is present or absent or whether his assistance or encouragement was given before or at the time of the commission of the offence.

All four words – aid, abet, counsel, procure – may be used together to charge a person, D, who is alleged to have participated in an offence otherwise than as a principal offender.[62] So long as the evidence establishes that D's conduct satisfied one of the words, that is enough. However, where the indictment uses only one term – for example, 'procures' – it is necessary to prove that D's conduct fits that term.

Each element of the *actus reus* of the accessory deserves further brief examination to consider three particular issues: (i) what forms of conduct constitute aiding, abetting, counselling or procuring; (ii) whether there need be a causal link between the aiding, etc and the principal offence; and, (iii) whether there need be a meeting of minds or consensus between the aider, etc and the principal offender.

In short, the law is probably that:

(1) 'aiding' requires actual assistance but neither consensus nor causation;[63]

(2) 'abetting' and 'counselling' imply consensus but not causation;

(3) 'procuring' implies causation but not consensus.

Aiding

It has sometimes been said[64] that 'aid and abet' is a single concept, 'aid' denoting the *actus reus* and 'abet', the *mens rea*. The natural meaning of s 8 is however that stated in *A-G's Reference*. Moreover, the words aid and abet do connote different kinds of activity. The natural meaning of to 'aid' is to 'give help, support or assistance to'.[65] The courts have taken a broad view of what suffices for 'aid'. Although historically the term was commonly used to describe someone present assisting the principal at the time of the offence, there is now no such restriction.

---

[60] [1975] 2 All ER 684 at 686.

[61] Under the old law of felonies, 'aiding and abetting' was used to describe the activity of the principal 'in the second degree' and 'counselling and procuring' that of the accessory before the fact: *Ferguson v Weaving*, above, at 818–819; Stephen, *Digest* (4th edn), arts 37–39; *Bowker v Premier Drug Co Ltd* [1928] 1 KB 217 ('aid and abet' implies presence). Aid and abet was, however, sometimes used in relation to acts committed before the actual perpetration of the crime.

[62] *Re Smith* (1858) 3 H & N 227; *Ferguson v Weaving* [1951] KB 814.

[63] cf Stephen, *Digest* (4th edn) who argued that D who abets or counsels or commands (as well as procures) is liable and, by implication liable only, for an offence 'which is committed *in consequence* of such counselling, procuring, or commandment'.

[64] *Lynch v DPP for Northern Ireland* [1975] 1 All ER 913 at 941, per Lord Simon quoting the 3rd edition of this book and Devlin J in *National Coal Board v Gamble* [1959] 1 QB 11 at 20.

[65] *Oxford English Dictionary*.

Aiding can be satisfied by any act of assistance before or at the time of the offence.[66] Supplying a weapon or transporting P to the scene of the crime[67] are obvious examples.

Aiding does not imply any causal connection between D's act and P's. D may assist P and enable him to commit the offence more easily, earlier or with greater safety and, if so, D is surely guilty even if P would have committed the same offence if D had not intervened.[68] In *Bryce*,[69] however, the court seemed to imply a causal requirement. D was convicted of murder as an accessory. In the course of a drug dealers' dispute D assisted P, who was acting on the orders of the gang leader B. D transported P and a gun to a caravan near V's home. More than 12 hours later, P, acting alone, shot V. D's ground of appeal was that the delay meant that what D did (transporting P) was too remote in time and place to the killing to constitute assistance, particularly since at that stage P had not formed the intention to kill. The Court of Appeal, after a comprehensive survey of the case law, upheld D's conviction concluding that no intervening event occurred hindering the plan, this despite the fact that in the 12-hour delay P's gun barrel was shortened and B visited P to encourage him. The court concluded that there was no 'overwhelming supervening event' sufficient to break the chain of causation, nor had D effected a withdrawal in that time. This implies a causal requirement. More explicit statements to this effect were made in *Mendez*[70] discussed above. It is submitted that despite these *dicta*, it remains the case that there is no need for D's acts to have caused the commission of the *actus reus* of the principal offence. Although there must be some link between D and P in the sense that D must have provided assistance or encouragement in fact, that is a far cry from establishing causation.

Nor does aiding imply any consensus between D and P. If D sees P committing a crime and comes to his assistance by, for example, restraining the policeman who would have prevented P from committing the crime, D is surely guilty even though his assistance is unforeseen and unwanted by P and unknown to him. The same might apply to aid given beforehand. D, knowing that P is going to meet a blackmailer, V, slips a gun into P's pocket in the hope that he will kill V – which P does.[71]

Abetting

The natural meaning of 'abet' is 'to incite, instigate or encourage'.[72] Abetting is usually defined in term of encouragement. There is little to distinguish abetting from counselling;[73] perhaps there is no difference except that historically 'abet' was used to refer to encouragement at the time of the offence and 'counsel' encouragement at an earlier time.[74] It is clear that either type of activity is sufficient to found liability as an accessory.

The natural meaning of 'abet' does not imply any causal element because, the word, (like counselling[75]) does not even imply that the offence has been committed. As a matter of ordinary language one would say that D had instigated, incited, encouraged, counselled, P even

---

[66] *Coney* (1882) 8 QBD 534.

[67] See, eg, *Nedrick-Smith* [2006] EWHC 3015 (Admin) where D3 was a party to D2 and D1 attacking V in her home. D3 drove them and stood watching as they attacked. The magistrates were entitled to find her guilty as an accessory.

[68] See WR Le Fave and AW Scott, *Criminal Law* (1986) 504. See also *Luffman* [2008] EWCA Crim 1739 below. cf *Mendez* above n 32.

[69] [2004] EWCA Crim 1231. D would be liable for an offence under s 45 or 46 of the SCA 2007.

[70] [2010] EWCA Crim 516.

[71] D would on those facts be liable under s 44 of the SCA 2007. The passage in the text was quoted with approval by the Court of Appeal in *Fury* [2006] EWCA Crim 1258.

[72] *Oxford English Dictionary*.

[73] Lord Widgery's analysis of the four terms leaves considerable confusion. His lordship suggests that 'abet' and 'counsel' do imply different forms of activity.

[74] Per Lowry CJ in *DPP v Maxwell* [1978] 3 All ER 1140, 1158.

[75] See, eg, *Wilcox v Jeffery* [1951] 1 All ER 464; below, p 200; *Du Cros v Lambourne* [1907] KB 40.

though P did not then commit the principal offence. As a matter of law, however, the principal offence must have been committed before anyone can be convicted as an abettor or coun- sellor of it.[76] But, even when the principal offence has been committed, it is true to say that D 'abetted' or 'counselled' it, in the ordinary meaning of the words, even if his encouragement or counsel was ignored by P. Abetting and counselling may be treated alike on causation and although historically there was scholarly opinion to the contrary,[77] the courts have recently confirmed that there need not be any causal link between D's encouragement and P's com- mission of the offence in a case alleging counselling: *Luffman*.[78] Where the prosecution relies on counselling as the basis for secondary liability it must, however, establish that the com- mission of the offence was within the scope of the principal's authority.[79] Requiring proof of causation in abetting or counselling cases would present problems. To require that before D could be liable as an accessory his abetting/counselling must have caused P to commit the principal offence could, if causation is interpreted strictly, be to insist that, but for D's abet- ting/counselling, P's offence would not have been committed.[80] This would confine abetting and counselling much too narrowly. Moreover, D would then not be liable if when he encour- aged P, he knew that P had already made up his mind to commit the offence.[81] That is not to deny that D must have counselled in fact:[82] proffered advice or encouragement which has no effect on the mind of P is not counselling.[83]

As for consensus, there must be some connection between D's abetting (or counselling) and the commission of the principal offence. It is probably not necessary to prove that P was influenced in any way by D, but P must at least be aware that he has the authority, or the encouragement or the approval, of D to do the relevant acts.

For example, if the principal offender happened to be involved in a football riot in the course of which he laid about him with a weapon of some sort and killed someone who, unknown to him, was the person whom he had been counselled to kill, he would not, in our view, have been acting within the scope of his authority; he would have been acting outside it, albeit what he had done was what he had been counselled to do.[84]

It was suggested in *A-G's Reference (No 1 of 1975)* that in the case of abetting and counselling the concepts might require a meeting of minds of secondary party and principal. If coun- selling and abetting must be, in some degree, operative, as suggested above, this is clearly right.[85]

---

[76] Liability under the SCA 2007, Part 2 will arise if the anticipated offence does not occur. See p 187.

[77] Stephen argued that if D is charged with abetting or counselling, his acts must have caused P to commit the offence. Stephen, *Digest* (4th edn) art 39.On his view, D who abets or counsels or commands (as well as pro- cures) P is liable only for an offence by P 'which is committed *in consequence* of such counselling, procuring, or commandment'.

[78] [2008] EWCA Crim 1752.

[79] *Calhaem* [1985] QB 808 CA.

[80] '...it does not make any difference that the person [*sc*, the person counselled] would have tried to commit suicide anyway': *A-G v Able* [1984] 1 All ER 277 at 288, per Woolf J.

[81] *Giannetto* [1997] 1 Cr App R 1, [1996] Crim LR 722. Trial judge's example: 'I am going to kill your wife'; hus- band: 'Oh goody.'

[82] But, it is clearly the law that an attempt to counsel does not amount to counselling. Liability for D's acts capable of encouraging P arises under ss 44 to 46 of the SCA 2007, and this includes attempts by D to encourage P which fail to do so.

[83] *Clarkson* [1971] 1 WLR 1402, C-MAC.

[84] *Calhaem* [1985] QB 808, CA, per Parker LJ; *Schriek* [1997] 2 NZLR 139, 149. cf the view taken in W Wilson, *Criminal Law Doctrine* (2008) .

[85] Consider the case of D, a persistent troublemaker, who comes across P and V in the middle of an argument. D urges P to punch V. Just before doing so, P tells D to 'mind your own business'. See LC 305, Appendix B , para B.63.

Counselling

To 'counsel' means to advise or solicit or encourage. The relevance of causation and consensus has been examined in the discussion of abetting above.

Procuring

'To procure means to produce by endeavour.'[86] 'You cannot procure an offence unless there is a causal link between what you do and the commission of the offence.'[87] In *A-G's Reference*, D added alcohol to P's drink without P's knowledge or consent. P drove home and thereby committed a strict liability offence of driving with a blood/alcohol concentration above the prescribed limit.[88] D was held to have procured that offence by P if it was proved that D knew that P was going to drive and that the ordinary and natural result of the added alcohol would be to bring P's blood/alcohol concentration above the prescribed limit. D had caused the *actus reus* (circumstance element) of the offence by putting P over the limit. This is in accordance with the natural meaning of 'procure'.[89] It is different if the driver is aware of the 'lacing.' In that situation P has, by his free informed act of choosing to imbibe the laced drink, caused the *actus reus* (circumstance element) of the offence.[90] D might then be convicted as an accessory of P's offence of drink driving on the basis that, although D has not procured its commission, he has certainly assisted its commission.[91]

What must be proved by way of a causal link in procuring? Glanville Williams commented on the *A-G's Reference* that: 'in so far as [it] purports to decide that merely causing an offence can be said to be a procuring of it, it should be regarded as too incautious a generalisation'. Williams relied on the famous case of *Beatty v Gillbanks*.[92] In that case it was held that the Salvation Army was acting lawfully in holding its meeting in Weston-super-Mare although its officers knew from experience that this would cause a hostile organization, 'the Skeleton Army', to attack them. It would be absurd Williams argued to hold that the Salvationists were liable as accessories for the attack on themselves, but they might have known that the attack would result in damage to others, for example, broken shop windows. There are two possible answers to Williams's criticism: (i) Lord Widgery did not say that 'procure' means merely 'cause'. He said 'To procure means to produce by endeavour.' The Salvationists may have caused the Skeletons to make the attack (and to break the supposed windows) but these were certainly not results that they were 'endeavouring' to produce. Against this, it might be said that in *A-G's Reference*, D's awareness that he was causing the commission of the offence also fell short of proof of an endeavour to cause it; and, in *Blakely*,[93] the court thought *obiter* that D 'procured' a result if he contemplated it as a possible result of his act – which is far removed from endeavouring to produce it. (ii) The Skeletons knew exactly what they were doing and in *A-G's Reference* Lord Widgery made it clear the decision would not necessarily be the same where a driver knew that his drink was laced. The unaware driver 'in most instances . . . would have no means of preventing the offence from being committed', the aware driver would. Lord Widgery thus contemplated that the act of the aware driver might break the chain of causation even for the purposes

---

[86] *A-G's Reference (No 1 of 1975)* [1975] 2 All ER 684 at 686; *Reed* [1982] Crim LR 819. See KJM Smith, 'Complicity and Causation' [1986] Crim LR 663; H Beynon, 'Causation, Omissions and Complicity' [1987] Crim LR 539.

[87] ibid, 687.

[88] Road Traffic Act 1972, s 6(1), now replaced by Road Traffic Act 1988, s 5.

[89] cf P Glazebrook, 'Attempting to Procure' [1959] Crim LR 774.

[90] See *Kennedy (No 2)* [2007] UKHL 38.

[91] LC 300, para 5.25.

[92] (1882) 9 QBD 308; TBCL, 339.

[93] Below, p 207.

of secondary liability, but it is unclear whether his lordship meant that there would be no secondary liability.

If D procures X, an innocent agent, to commit an offence D is taken to have caused the *actus reus* for all purposes. If D procures P, a guilty agent, to commit the offence, to be liable as an accessory D must be proved to have in fact caused the act of P; but, in law, D is not regarded as having caused the *actus reus*. The driver whose drink, unknown to him is 'laced' is not an innocent agent because the offence he is guilty of is a strict liability offence.

In *A-G's Reference (No 1 of 1975)*, D's act of procuring was done without the knowledge or consent, and perhaps against the will, of P. The case decides that consensus is immaterial where 'procuring' is relied on.

How many modes of participation?

The terminological difficulties with four possible methods of participating in crime complicate the law. It has been suggested that in substance there are only two kinds of action involved – 'intentionally influencing the decision of the primary party to commit the crime and intentionally helping the primary actor to commit the crime'.[94] But does this cover a case like *A-G's Reference*[95] where the principal offender is strictly liable? D 'procured' P to drive with excess alcohol by secretly lacing P's drink. There was no 'decision of the primary party to commit the crime'; and 'helping the primary actor to commit the crime' also seems to imply that the purpose of the primary actor is to commit the crime, which was not so. If that kind of case is to be covered, the notion of procuring must also be included. The Law Commission proposes to abolish procuring as a form of offence. See below, p 243.

8.4.1.2 The timing of the accessory's assistance/encouragement

Assistance given by D before P even starts to commit the principal offence may be sufficient to found D's secondary liability if P then completes the offence. What is more important is to ascertain whether D has assisted or encouraged P before P has *concluded* the offence. Assistance given when P is no longer in the course of the commission of the offence – eg help to enable P to escape or to reap the benefits of the commission of the offence – does not make D an accessory. Where P broke into a warehouse, stole butter and deposited it in the street 30 yards from the warehouse door, D who then came to assist in carrying it off was held not guilty of abetting P's theft.[96] Assistance given by D to a murderer, after his victim is dead or to a rapist after the act of penetration has concluded does not render D an accessory.[97] D who, without any pre-arranged plan, joins P in an attack on V after V has received a fatal injury, is not guilty of homicide (though he may be guilty of an attempt) if his action in no way contributes to V's subsequent death.[98] If D1 and D2 carry out an armed robbery, and D3 drives past the bank as D1 and D2 flee from the scene of the crime with the proceeds, is D3 a party to the robbery if he allows D1 and D2 to get in the car to make good their escape?[99]

---

[94] Kadish, *Essays*, 151, supported by G Williams, 'Complicity, Purpose and the Draft Code – 1' [1990] Crim LR 4, 'Letters to the Editor – Criminal Complicity' [1991] Crim LR 930.

[95] Above, n 60.

[96] *King* (1817) Russ & Ry 332; see also *Kelly* (1820) Russ & Ry 421.

[97] The act is a continuing one: Sexual Offences Act 2003, s 79.

[98] *S v Thomo* 1969 (1) SA 385 (AD); Burchell and Hunt, SACLP 352. Some fine distinctions have begun to be drawn. In *Grundy* (1989) 89 Cr App R 333, it was held that if D struck a blow to V after P had caused grievous bodily harm, D might still be liable for assisting grievous bodily harm. In *Percival* [2003] EWCA Crim 1561, D who punched V after P had wounded V could not be liable as an aider and abettor to wounding.

[99] See also *Self* [1992] Crim LR 574 and commentary.

8.4.1.3 Omission as a sufficient *actus reus* of secondary liability?

As discussed in Chapter 4, the law does not generally impose criminal liability for a failure to act. In the context of secondary liability, the question arises whether D's omission to prevent P committing the crime is sufficient to make D an accessory. Two categories of case need to be distinguished.

First, there are the established categories in which the law imposes a *duty* on an individual to act. Thus, a husband who stands by and watches his wife drown their children is guilty as an accessory to the homicide.[100]

Secondly, the law extends liability even wider: where D has a *power or right to control* the actions of P and he deliberately refrains from exercising it, his inactivity *may* be a positive encouragement to P to perform an illegal act, and, therefore, an aiding and abetting by D. So, for example, if a licensee of a pub stands by and watches his customers drinking after hours, he is guilty of aiding and abetting them in doing so.[101] In *Du Cros v Lambourne*,[102] it was proved that D's car had been driven at a dangerous speed but it was not proved whether D or E was driving. It was held, nevertheless, that D could be convicted. If E was driving she was doing so in D's presence, with his consent and approval; for he was in control and could and ought to have prevented her from driving in a dangerous manner. D was equally liable whether he was a principal or an accessory.[103] The result would presumably have been different if it had been E's own car, for D would then have had no right of control, and could only have been convicted if proved to have actively encouraged E to drive at such speed.

In *Webster*,[104] the Court of Appeal approved *Du Cros v Lambourne*, holding that 'a defendant might be convicted of aiding and abetting dangerous driving if the driver drives dangerously in the owner's presence *and with the owner's consent and approval*'.[105] *Webster* emphasizes that it must be proved that D knew of those features of P's driving which rendered it dangerous and failed to take action within a reasonable time.[106] The court in *Webster* recognized the:

> need to establish not only knowledge of the dangerous driving but knowledge at a time when there was an opportunity to intervene. . . . We conclude that the prosecution had to prove that [D] knew that [P] was, by virtue of the speed the vehicle was travelling, driving dangerously at a time when there was an opportunity to intervene. It was [D's] failure to take that opportunity and, exercise his right as owner of the vehicle, which would lead to the inference that he was associating himself with the dangerous driving.

In *Baldessare*,[107] P and D unlawfully took X's car and P drove it recklessly and caused V's death. It was held that D was guilty of manslaughter as an accessory. In this case (as prosecuting counsel put it):

---

[100] *Russell* [1933] VLR 59.

[101] *Tuck v Robson*, [1970] 1 WLR 741, DC. The principal offence is committed by the drinkers, not the licensee.

[102] [1907] 1 KB 40; cf also *Rubie v Faulkner* [1940] 1 KB 571; *Harris* [1964] Crim LR 54. See D Lanham, 'Drivers, Control and Accomplices' [1982] Crim LR 419; M Wasik, 'A Learner's Careless Driving' [1982] Crim LR 411.

[103] cf *Swindall and Osborne* (1846) 2 Car & Kir 230: *Salmon* (1880) 6 QBD 79; *Iremonger v Wynne* [1957] Crim LR 624; G Williams, CLGP, 137 n 23.

[104] [2006] EWCA Crim 415.

[105] The court quashed the conviction in that case on the grounds that the trial judge had not directed the jury that they had to consider whether there was an opportunity for Webster to intervene.

[106] *Dennis v Pight* (1968) 11 FLR 458 at 463.

[107] (1930) 22 Cr App R 70.

The common purpose to drive recklessly was ... shown by the fact that both men were driving in a car which did not belong to them and the jury were entitled to infer that the driver was the agent of the passenger. It matters not whose hand was actually controlling the car at the time.

In the recent case of *Martin*,[108] D was convicted as an accessory to P's offence of causing death by dangerous driving. P was a learner driver and D was supervising him. P lost control of the vehicle on a bend, crashing, killing himself and a passenger.[109] Unlike *Baldessare*, there was no evidence that D had shared a common purpose with P to drive in this manner. The Court of Appeal, having considered *Webster*, tentatively proffered a direction that ought to have been given. D would be liable if (i) P committed the offence, (ii) D knew that P was driving in a manner which D knew fell far below the standard of a competent and careful driver, (iii) knowing that he had an opportunity to stop P from driving in that manner, D deliberately did not take that opportunity, (iv) *by not taking that opportunity D intended to assist or encourage P to drive in this manner and D did in fact by his presence and failure to intervene encouraged P to drive dangerously*.[110]

Whichever category of exception (duty or control) is relied on to prove the *actus reus* by omission, it is not necessary that the inactive accessory be present at the commission of the offence. A company and its directors may be convicted as accessories to the false making of tachograph records by the company's drivers if they knew that their inactivity was encouraging the practice on the roads miles away.[111]

8.4.1.4 Mere presence at the crime as a sufficient basis for secondary liability?

Can D's mere voluntary presence at P's commission of the principal offence, without anything more, satisfy the *actus reus* of secondary liability? If there is some conduct on the part of D which goes beyond 'mere' presence, then the principles already discussed will apply. The question will be whether D assisted or encouraged P by his actions or by his failure to act when under a duty/power to control. Where the case involves D's *mere* presence, several issues will commonly call for consideration including: whether D voluntarily attended the location where an offence is being or is about to be committed; the effect that D's presence has on P; and D's state of mind when present.

Mere presence at the scene of a crime is *capable* of constituting encouragement or assistance, but D is not necessarily guilty as an accessory merely because he is present and does nothing to prevent P's crime.[112] In some cases D's presence will constitute encouragement or assistance because he is present in pursuance of an agreement that the crime be committed. In other cases, D's presence may be sufficient even though there was no prior agreement,[113] and

---

[108] [2010] EWCA Crim 1450.

[109] The conviction for being an accessory to P causing his own death by dangerous driving was quashed as there is no such offence: it is an offence to cause the death of another by driving.

[110] [32] per Hooper LJ. A further possible element advanced by the court is not necessary (relating to D's foresight of death). See below at p 208 for discussion of the question whether liability might arise for D by reason of his participation in dangerous driving by P earlier in the journey, coupled with D's foresight that P might commit the offence of causing death by dangerous driving.

[111] *J F Alford Transport Ltd* [1997] 2 Cr App R 326, [1997] Crim LR 745, citing the 8th edition of this book, at 334. See also *Gaunt* [2003] EWCA Crim 3925, where D, the manager, failed to control P (employees) in racial harassment of V (employee).

[112] *Atkinson* (1869) 11 Cox CC 330; but it is an offence to refuse to assist a constable to suppress a breach of the peace when called upon to do so: *Brown* (1841) Car & M 314.

[113] *Rannath Mohan v R* [1967] 2 AC 187, [1967] 2 All ER 58.

no positive act,[114] provided his presence intentionally provides assistance or encouragement to the principal.[115]

There are numerous examples of these principles in operation. D who stands outside a building while his friends commit a burglary inside cannot be convicted of burglary without proof that he was assisting or encouraging by, for example, acting as lookout.[116] Similarly, for D to continue to sit beside the driver of a car, P, until the end of a journey after learning that P is uninsured does not amount to abetting P's uninsured driving.[117] If D continues to share a room with a person known to be in unlawful possession of drugs D is not an accessory unless encouragement or control is proved.[118] If prohibited drugs, found in a van belonging to a party of tourists, are the property of and under the exclusive control of one of them, the others are not guilty as accessories simply because they are present and know of the existence of the drugs.[119]

Both assistance or encouragement in fact *and* an intention to assist or encourage must be proved.[120] When these are proved, it is immaterial that D joined in the offence without any prior agreement.[121] The same principle applies in the case of omissions as in that of positive acts, and it has been held that where two drivers, without any previous arrangement between them, enter into competitive driving on the highway so as knowingly to encourage each other to drive at a dangerous speed or in a dangerous manner, the one is liable as a secondary party for a death or other criminal result caused by the other.[122]

Intention alone without encouragement or assistance in fact is insufficient. In *Allan*,[123] it was held that D who remains present at an affray, nursing a secret intention to help P if the need arises but doing nothing to evince that intention, does not thereby become an accessory. This was reiterated recently by the Privy Council in *Robinson*:[124]

The commission of most criminal offences, and certainly most offences of violence, could be assisted by the forbidding presence of another as back-up and support. If D's presence could properly be held to amount to communicating to P (whether expressly or by implication) that he was there to help in any way he could if the opportunity or need arose, that was perfectly capable of amounting to aiding. . . . It is important to make clear to juries that mere approval of (ie 'assent' to, or 'concurrence' in) the offence by a bystander who gives no assistance, does not without more amount to aiding.[125]

If some positive act of assistance or encouragement is voluntarily done, with knowledge of the circumstances constituting the offence, it is irrelevant that it is not done with the motive

---

[114] *Wilcox v Jeffery* [1951] 1 All ER 464.

[115] It is insufficient to prove that D arrived even only 30 seconds after P has finished attacking V if there is no evidence of D encouraging P: *Rose* [2004] EWCA Crim 764.

[116] *S v DPP* [2003] EWHC 2717 (Admin). See also *Rose* [2004] EWCA Crim 764 where D's only actions at the scene were to discourage P from his attack on V. cf *Ellis* [2008] EWCA Crim 886.

[117] *Smith v Baker* [1971] RTR 350.

[118] *Bland* [1988] Crim LR 41; see also *Kousar* [2009] EWCA Crim 139.

[119] *Searle* [1971] Crim LR 592 and commentary thereon.

[120] *Clarkson* [1971] 1 WLR 1402; *Jones and Mirrless* (1977) 65 Cr App R 250, CA.

[121] *Rannath Mohan v R* [1967] 2 AC 187.

[122] *Turner* [1991] Crim LR 57 and commentary. (Williams, TBCL, 360, thinks otherwise, citing *Mastin* (1834) 6 C & P 396.) If one of two racing drivers is killed, the other may be convicted of causing death by dangerous driving; and it is immaterial whether his act or that of the deceased was the immediate cause of death: *Kimsey* [1996] Crim LR 35; *Lee* [2006] EWCA Crim 240. See also *Martin* [2010] EWCA Crim 1450, above.

[123] [1965] 1 QB 130; see also *Tansley v Painter* (1968) 112 Sol Jo 1005; *Danquah* [2004] EWCA Crim 1248 (presence alone insufficient to show that Ds formed part of the gang that robbed V when no evidence of contribution to the intimidation or threats).

[124] [2011] UKPC 3.

[125] [14] per Sir Anthony Hughes.

or purpose of encouraging the crime.[126] Nevertheless, the onus on the Crown to prove D's intent can be a heavy one where liability is based solely on D's presence at the scene.[127]

In the case of *Coney*[128] it was held that proof of D's mere voluntary presence at a prizefight (illegal boxing match), without more, was, at the most, only *prima facie* and not conclusive evidence of abetting the offence of which the contestants were guilty. Presence at such an event is certainly capable of amounting to an actual encouragement. If there were no spectators there would be no fight and, therefore, each spectator, by his presence, contributes to the incentive to the contestants. Voluntary presence at such an event is some evidence on which a jury might find that D was there with the intention of encouraging P's fight. Coney's conviction was quashed because the majority of the court thought that the judge's direction was capable of being understood to mean that voluntary presence was *conclusive* evidence of an intention to encourage. If the direction had made it clear that presence was only *prima facie* evidence, no doubt the conviction would have been sustained. So, in *Wilcox v Jeffrey*,[129] D was found to be an accessory by his presence at a public jazz performance by P. P was the celebrated American saxophonist Coleman Hawkins, who had been given permission to enter the UK only on condition that he would take no employment. D's presence at P's performance was a sufficient aiding and abetting of P in his contravention of the relevant immigration provisions. D's behaviour before and after P's performance supplied further evidence of D's intention to encourage P; he had met P at the airport and D afterwards reported the performance in laudatory terms in his jazz periodical. There was no finding that D applauded the performance of P. Had there been such a finding then it would have been a case where the normal principles described above applied – it would not have been a case of 'mere' voluntary presence but one of active encouragement by D.

Public order offences often raise particular problems in this context since the principal offence will often turn on proof of acts by a specific number of individuals, and in cases of spontaneous violence between groups, it is difficult to identify who is a principal involved in the fight, who is present actively encouraging, and who is merely present without more.[130]

8.4.1.5 Problems of proving the accessory's *actus reus*

If all that can be proved is that the principal offence was committed either by P1 or by P2, both must be acquitted.[131] Only if it can be proved that the one who did not commit the crime as principal must have aided, abetted, counselled or procured the other to commit it can both be convicted.[132] Take the case of two nurses, P1 and P2, whose child V is injured while in their care. The injuries might have been inflicted by P1 alone, P2 alone, by P1 with P2's as accessory or vice versa. It is for the prosecution to prove to the criminal standard that the nurse who did not inflict the injuries must have aided or abetted the infliction either by positive acts or

---

[126] *National Coal Board v Gamble* [1959] 1 QB 11; below, p 202.

[127] eg *Miah* [2004] EWCA Crim 63.

[128] (1882) 8 QBD 534.

[129] [1951] 1 All ER 464. It is arguable that Art 11 of the ECHR may be engaged where the effect is to restrict D's right to assemble with others, see Ashworth, POCL, 416.

[130] See *Blackwood and others* [2002] EWCA Crim 3102 and *Ellis* [2008] EWCA Crim 886.

[131] *Richardson* (1785) 1 Leach 387; *Abbott* [1955] 2 QB 497.

[132] *Russell and Russell* [1987] Crim LR 494; *Lane and Lane* (1985) 82 Cr App R 5. For a valuable direction where one of two interrogating police officers has caused injury, see *Forman* [1988] Crim LR 677 (Judge Woods). See, generally, G Williams, 'Which of you Did it?' (1989) 52 MLR 179; EJ Griew, 'It Must Have Been One of Them' [1989] Crim LR 129. *Gibson and Gibson* (1984) 80 Cr App R 24 is misleading and should be used with care; see commentary at [1984] Crim LR 615.

by failure to fulfil the duty owed as a health care worker.[133] The problem often arises in this domestic situation. It differs from most other cases only because parents owe a duty to intervene to prevent the ill-treatment of their child when a stranger would have no such duty. The case of the parent or carer of the child or vulnerable adult who dies in their household is now governed by an exceptional procedure under the Domestic Violence, Crime and Victims Act 2004,[134] but the general principle remains.

8.4.2 *Mens rea* of the accessory

The *mens rea* requirements of the accessory are complex,[135] but can be summarized as follows:

(1) the accessory must intend to assist or encourage the principal's conduct, or in the case of procuring, to bring the offence about; and

(2) the accessory must have knowledge as to the essential elements of the principal's offence, (including any facts as to which the principal bears strict liability). This includes a requirement that D must be aware that the principal might act with *mens rea* when performing the conduct which constitutes the principal offence.[136]

8.4.2.1 Intention to aid, etc

It must be proved that D intended to do the acts which he knew to be capable of assisting or encouraging the commission of the crime. There are two elements – an intention to perform the act capable of encouraging or assisting, and an intention, or a belief, that that act will be of assistance. So, where D supplies a weapon to P, which P uses in a murder, proof of D's intention will turn on whether he meant to hand it over (as opposed to accidentally leaving it and P discovering it) and whether D intended that his supply would assist P; there is no further element that D must intend the consequences of P's conduct – that the murder be committed. As Devlin J said:[137]

If one man deliberately sells to another a gun to be used for murdering a third, he may be indifferent whether the third man lives or dies and interested only in the cash profit to be made out of the sale, but he can still be an aider and abettor.

Intention to perform the act of assistance

This element of the *mens rea* is unlikely to give rise to difficulty. D must intend to perform the act that does in fact provide assistance. There is only likely to be a problem in circumstances of potential involuntariness and other rare situations.

---

[133] See for an extreme case *Pinto* [2006] EWCA Crim 749 (D aided and abetted torture of V by P believing V to be possessed).

[134] Considered below at p 597. The Law Commission proposed a new offence of aggravated child cruelty under s 1 of the Children and Young Persons Act 1933, and an offence which dealt with both serious injury and death only in relation to children. For comment see P Glazebrook, 'Insufficient Child Protection' [2003] Crim LR 541.

[135] See LC 305, at para 1.16 which sets out the many permeations of *mens rea* which the case law would support.

[136] See LC 305, para 2.49.

[137] [1959] 1 QB 11 at 23, applied in *J F Alford Transport Ltd* [1997] 2 Cr App R 326, 334–335.

Intention thereby to assist

There is no judicial agreement on what the requirement of an intention to assist actually means. It is clearly a requirement of intention,[138] but must it be proved that D acted in order to assist P (direct intent); or is it sufficient to prove only that D knew his acts would be virtually certain to assist P (oblique intent)?[139] It seems to be generally accepted that D's knowledge that his act will assist is sufficient.[140] The weight of authority certainly supports the view that it is not necessary to prove that D had as his purpose or desire to assist and if D had the (oblique) intention, it is no excuse that D's motives in performing the act of assistance were unimpeachable.[141]

Oblique intention to assist sufficient

In *National Coal Board v Gamble*,[142] P, a lorry driver, had his employer's lorry filled with coal at a colliery belonging to the defendant Board [D1]. When the lorry was driven on to the weighbridge operated by the defendants' employee, D2, it appeared that its load greatly exceeded that permitted by the relevant regulation.[143] D2 informed P of this but P said he would take the risk, D2 gave him a weighbridge ticket and P committed the offence as principal by driving the overloaded lorry on the highway. The property in the coal did not pass until the ticket was handed over and, therefore, P could not properly have left the colliery without the ticket from D2. It was held that the Board, D1, through D2,[144] was guilty of the offence as an accessory. The decision was based on the assumption that D2 knew he had the right to prevent the lorry leaving the colliery with the coal. Had D2 not known this, he should have been acquitted. Presumably D2 was indifferent whether P drove his overloaded lorry on the road or not – he probably thought that it was none of his business – but D2's motive was irrelevant and it was enough that his positive act of assistance had been voluntarily done (that is, intentional performance of the act of assistance) with knowledge that by doing so he would be assisting P and knowledge of the circumstances constituting the offence.[145]

This principle – that D must have an oblique intention to assist P – has been adopted in numerous cases where D's assistance comprises an act of supply. In *Cook v Stockwell*,[146] D, a brewer, intentionally supplied large quantities of beer to some cottages, knowing very well that the occupants were reselling it, without being licensed to do so. In *Cafferata v Wilson*,[147] D, a wholesaler, voluntarily sold a firearm to P, who kept a general shop, but was not registered as a firearms dealer. Presumably D knew that P was going to resell the firearm, which in fact he did. In both these cases D was held liable as an accessory to the illegal sale. In both cases the suppliers were indifferent whether P's crime was committed or not. Both had voluntarily performed acts of assistance and had sufficient knowledge from which a jury could find that they intended by the act to assist P.

---

[138] The offence is therefore one of specific intent for the purposes of rules on voluntary intoxication: see Ch 11 below: *McNamara* [2009] EWCA Crim 2530.

[139] See RA Duff, 'Can I Help You? Accessorial Liability and the Intention to Assist' (1990) LS 165. See, generally, Smith, *A Modern Treatise on Complicity*, Ch 5.

[140] cf IH Dennis, 'The Mental Element for Accessories', in *Essays in Honour of J C Smith* (1987); contra GR Sullivan, 'Intent, Purpose and Complicity' [1988] Crim LR 641; and IH Dennis, 'Intention and Complicity: A Reply' [1988] Crim LR 649; Williams [1990] Crim LR 4, 12.

[141] Woolf J in *Gillick v West Norfolk and Wisbech Area Health Authority* [1984] QB 581 at 589. Woolf J's discussion of the criminal aspects of this case was adopted by Lords Scarman and Bridge in the House of Lords [1986] AC 112.

[142] [1959] 1 QB 11 DC, Slade J dissenting.

[143] Motor Vehicles (Construction and Use) Regulations 1955.

[144] See, however, below, p 205.

[145] D2 would commit an offence under s 45 of the SCA 2007.

[146] (1915) 84 LJKB 2187.

[147] [1936] 3 All ER 149.

The fact that D does not 'want' or 'aim' to assist does not prevent him being liable as an accessory if he has an oblique intent to assist. In *Lynch v DPP for Northern Ireland*, where D drove P to the place where he knew that P intended to murder a policeman, D's intentional driving of the car was aiding and abetting, 'even though he regretted the plan or indeed was horrified by it'.[148]

Confirmation of the sufficiency of oblique intent to assist comes from the recent case of *Bryce*,[149] where the Court of Appeal confirmed that D can be found to be intending to assist even if it is not D's purpose or desire that his acts will assist. The court approved an extract in *Blackstone's Criminal Practice* suggesting that the definition of intention in this context should reflect that in the law of murder. On this approach, the jury can 'find' an intention to assist from the evidence of D's voluntary performance of the act of assistance, even though his purpose or desire in performing that act is not to assist. In *Bryce*, D had transported P to the scene of the crime, he had clearly intended to perform that act of assistance, but D claimed that he lacked any intention to assist *by that act* since he did not know whether P would carry out the killing, indeed, D claimed that P himself did not finally decided to do so until 12 hours after D had left. The Court of Appeal held that the jury were entitled to find, from the evidence of D's performing the intentional act of transportation and the knowledge D had of P's potential crime that D had a sufficient intention to assist P to murder.

Authorities suggesting direct intent required

Although the overwhelming weight of authority supports a requirement of oblique intention to assist, some cases suggest that D must have a direct intent. It is submitted that these can each be distinguished or explained.

One case in which direct intent seems to have been required is *Fretwell*.[150] D reluctantly supplied an abortifacient to a woman, P, when she threatened to kill herself if he did not do so. He hoped she would not use it but she did so and died. At that time, at common law, this was self-murder by P. D was held not liable as an accessory because he was 'unwilling that the woman should take the poison'. A distinction between indifference and unwillingness of this nature is, however, too uncertain to form the basis of a legal rule. Applying the principles outlined above, D intentionally supplied the product and he intended to assist. *Fretwell* is perhaps best regarded as a case in which the court strained the principles governing the liability of accessories in order to mitigate the severity of the rule which treated suicide as murder.[151] Woolf J has subsequently suggested it is 'confined to its own facts'.[152]

Gillick's Case[153] (a civil action for a declaration) might also be thought to offer some support to the argument that intention to assist is restricted to purposive or direct intention. The House of Lords held that, in certain circumstances, a doctor may lawfully give contraceptive advice or treatment to a girl under the age of consent to sex (16) without her parents' consent. The conditions of lawful treatment could include cases where the doctor, D, knew that the provision of the advice or treatment would encourage or facilitate sexual intercourse by the girl with a man, P. The man would commit an offence.[154] The doctor's motives would no doubt be unimpeachable, but that is generally no answer. Why is not the doctor (and the parents if they concurred in the advice, for they have no more right than the doctor to aid and abet

[148] [1975] AC 653 at 678, per Lord Morris, approving the judgment of Lowry LCJ on this point. *Fretwell* (1862) Le & Ca 161, below, appears to be a merciful decision and unsound in principle.

[149] [2004] EWCA Crim 1231.

[150] Above, n 148; cf Williams, CLGP, s 124.

[151] As to which, see below, p 583.

[152] *A-G v Able* [1984] 1 All ER 277 at 287, citing the 4th edition of this book (1978) at 120–121. But cf *Gillick*, above, n 141 and *Janaway v Salford Health Authority*, below, p 378.

[153] Above, n 141.

[154] Sexual Offences Act 2003, below, p 762.

crime) guilty of aiding and abetting the man's offence?[155] The man's act may well be facilitated (through the girl's being more willing to have intercourse) and (if he knows of the contraception) encouraged by the doctor's acts.[156] The House of Lords decision that the doctor's advice is lawful clearly implies that he does not aid and abet a crime but the reason is nowhere clearly stated. It seems most likely that Woolf J at first instance and the majority of the House thought he lacked the necessary intention. This puts an undue strain on the concept of intention because it means that to be liable as an accessory D must not only intend to provide the assistance, but intend that the principal offence be committed. If a mother, knowing that her son is about to embark on an armed robbery and cannot be dissuaded, gives him a bullet-proof vest, with the sole and admirable motive of saving him from death or serious injury, is not her intention to enable him to perpetrate the robbery more safely an intention to aid and abet it? This should be a sufficient basis for her liability without proof that she intended that the robbery took place. It is submitted that *Gillick's Case* is better regarded as being based impliedly, if not expressly,[157] on necessity.

Recklessness insufficient

Mere recklessness, still less negligence, whether D's conduct assists P, is probably not enough. D's realization that he may have left his gun-cupboard unlocked and that his son has a disposition to commit armed robbery, is not sufficient to fix D with liability as an accessory to armed robbery and homicide which the son commits using one of D's guns. D has no intention to perform any act of advice or assistance nor that P would be assisted or encouraged by his conduct.

Intention in cases of assisting or encouraging by mere voluntary presence

The numerous difficult cases on this issue are discussed above (p 198). It is unclear, whether cases such as *Coney* (presence at prizefight) and *Clarkson* (presence watching a rape) should be seen as examples of the courts insisting on direct intention or whether oblique intention suffices. Consider *Clarkson*: it is certainly arguable that it was sufficient that D realized that his mere presence watching would encourage the rapist and there was no need to prove that his purpose was that his presence would do so.

'Intention' even if D is legally obliged to supply to P?

If P has loaned a weapon to D, and P demands it back, when D hands it over, it is arguable that D aids in the commission of P's subsequent crime committed with that weapon as much as if D had sold or lent the article to P in the first place, but this has never been held to be aiding in law.[158] *National Coal Board v Gamble* suggests a distinction between the cases:

(1) where the seller (D) is aware before ownership has passed to the buyer (P) of P's illegal purpose the delivery amounts to abetting,

but

(2) where the seller (D) learns of the illegal purpose for the first time after ownership has passed but before delivery to P the supply does not amount to abetting. The seller is merely complying with his legal duty to give P what is by then P's own property.

This seems to be an unsatisfactory distinction. If D delivers weedkiller to P, knowing that P intends to use it to murder his wife, it would be remarkable if D's guilt as an accessory to

---

[155] Although see now the exceptions in the Sexual Offences Act 2003, s 73, p 762.
[156] For a full discussion of this question, see [1986] Crim LR 114.
[157] See JR Spencer in *Criminal Law Essays*, 148, 164.
[158] [1959] 1 QB 11 at 20, per Devlin J.

murder turned on whether the ownership passed before or after D learned of P's intention.[159] The important thing is that D knows of P's intention when he makes delivery. It should not be an answer that P has a right to possession of the thing in the civil law because the civil law should not afford a right in such a case.[160] In *Garrett v Arthur Churchill (Glass) Ltd*,[161] D, who had bought a goblet as agent of P, was held guilty of being knowingly concerned in the exportation of goods without a licence, when, on P's instructions, he delivered P's own goblet to P's agent who was to take it to America.

... albeit there was a legal duty in ordinary circumstances to hand over the goblet to the owners once the agency was determined, I do not think that an action would lie for breach of that duty if the handing over would constitute the offence of being knowingly concerned in its exportation.[162]

Probably then the seller is liable whether or not the ownership has passed before delivery. Williams's view, however, is that the seller ought to be liable in neither case. He argues:[163]

The seller of an ordinary marketable commodity is not his buyer's keeper in criminal law unless he is specifically made so by statute. Any other rule would be too wide an extension of criminal responsibility.

A rule based on the nature of the thing as 'an ordinary marketable commodity' is not workable. Weedkiller is an ordinary marketable commodity but it may be acquired and used to commit murder. A more feasible distinction is one based on the seriousness of the offence contemplated:

The gravity of the social harm resulting from the unlawful conduct is used to determine whether mere knowledge of the intended use will be sufficient to carry the taint of illegality.[164]

This could operate on the basis of some balance of the respective harms,[165] but would have the disadvantage of being uncertain. No such distinction has been made in English law. Alternatively a distinction could be drawn between summary and indictable offences. This would create some arbitrary results.[166] A third approach would be to restrict the scope of the liability of the seller, D, to cases in which his purpose was to assist P. There would be difficulties in establishing that *mens rea* in some cases.

At present, English authorities suggest a general rule of liability for sellers subject to *mens rea*. This applies, *a fortiori*, in the case of lenders or those who rent out premises intended for unlawful purposes. In such cases the owner has a continuing interest in and right to control the property.[167]

---

[159] D would be liable under ss 44–46 of the SCA 2007.

[160] See G Williams, CLGP, s 124 and JC Smith, 'Civil Law Concepts in the Criminal Law' [1972B] CLJ 197 at 208. In *K v National Westminster Bank* [2006] EWCA Civ 1039, the court noted that if the criminal law (under Proceeds of Crime Act 2002) makes it an offence for a bank to honour a customer's instructions to transfer money which it is suspected is criminal property, there can be no breach of contract for the bank to refuse to do so.

[161] [1970] 1 QB 92. How far does this go? If X lends a picture to a museum, does the museum really commit an offence if, on demand, it returns the picture to X, knowing that he intends to export it without the licence required by law?

[162] [1969] 2 All ER at 1145, per Parker LCJ.

[163] CLGP, s 124 at 373. TBCL (1st edn), 293–294.

[164] Perkins and Boyce, *Criminal Law*, 746. See also G Williams, 'Obedience to Law as a Crime' (1990) 53 MLR 445.

[165] See Ashworth, POCL 413.

[166] GR Sullivan [1994] Crim LR 272.

[167] For example, the hotelier who lets a room to a man accompanied by a 15-year-old girl, knowing that he intends to seduce her.

Must D intend that his conduct 'will' or 'might' assist?
There is a potential difficulty where D believes his act is capable of assisting P but does not
believe that in fact it will assist P. An example is offered by the Law Commission[168] where
D, believing that P is going to murder V, sells P rat poison. If D believes that there is only a
50 per cent chance that P will use it to murder V but D foresees the risk that P *might* murder
V by some other means it cannot be said that D believes that his act *will* assist P. The Law
Commission suggest that the case law is inconclusive, as to whether D is liable.[169]

8.4.2.2 Knowledge of essential elements[170]
In addition to proof of intention to do the acts and to assist or encourage, there is a further, yet
more complex element of the accessory's *mens rea*: D must 'know' of, or at least turn a blind
eye to, the essential elements of P's offence. Before a person can be convicted of aiding and
abetting the commission of an offence he must at least know the essential matters which constitute that offence. He need not actually know that an offence has been committed, because
he may not know that the facts constitute an offence and because ignorance of the criminal
law is not a defence.[171]

Two questions arise:

(1) What does 'knowledge' mean in this context?

(2) As to what must D have knowledge – what are the 'essential matters that constitute the
principal offence'?

Knowledge/foresight/wilful blindness
A requirement to prove D's knowledge is especially difficult to apply in the context of secondary liability. D's knowledge must relate to P's conduct together with the prescribed circumstances and P's *men rea*. The conduct may or may not be happening contemporaneously
with D's act(s) of assistance or encouragement. Frequently D's acts of assistance or encouragement will have occurred before the commission of the offence by P, and D cannot have
'knowledge' of something that has yet to occur.[172] Where the circumstances have yet to arise
or materialize, D cannot know them because they are not yet in existence. The problem of
proving knowledge may even arise if the principal offence *has* materialized contemporaneously with D's assistance.

In the face of practical difficulties in applying a strict test of knowledge, the concept has
been diluted by the courts to such an extent that this element of *mens rea* required of D is
more accurately expressed as a realization of a possibility of the essential elements of P's
offence.[173] Knowledge in this context is equivalent to D foreseeing (or in some cases turning
a blind eye to) the likelihood of the essential matters. That seems a long way from a strict test

---

[168] Taken from LC 305, Appendix B, para B.75.

[169] See the speech of Lord Simon in *Lynch* [1975] AC 653, 698h.

[170] See, generally, KJM Smith, *A Modern Treatise on Complicity* above, Ch 6 and LC 305, Appendix B.

[171] *Johnson v Youden* [1950] 1 KB 544 at 546, per Lord Goddard CJ. See also *Ackroyds Air Travel Ltd v DPP*
[1950] 1 All ER 933 at 936; *Thomas v Lindop* [1950] 1 All ER 966 at 968; *Ferguson v Weaving* [1951] 1 KB 814;
Bateman v Evans [1964] Crim LR 601; *Smith v Jenner* [1968] Crim LR 99; *Dial Contracts Ltd v Vickers* [1971] RTR
386; *D Stanton & Sons Ltd v Webber* [1973] RTR 87, [1972] Crim LR 544 and commentary thereon.

[172] For discussion of the philosophical nature of knowledge and its relevance to the criminal law see S Shute,
'Knowledge and Belief in the Criminal Law' at 171 and GR Sullivan, 'Knowledge, Belief and Culpability' at 207
both in S Shute and A Simester (eds), *Criminal Law Theory: Doctrines of the General Part* (2002). See also the
essay by R Bagshaw, 'Legal Proof of Knowledge', in P Mirfield and R Smith (eds), *Essays in Honour of Colin Tapper*
(2003) on evidential influences of substantive law definitions of knowledge.

[173] See LC 305, para 2.65. For a defence of the dilution of *mens rea*, see A Simester (2006) LQR 578, at
588–592.

of knowledge. Various formulations can be found in the cases. In *Bryce*, the court held that it was sufficient that D did the act of assistance (transporting P to the scene), and at the time of doing that act D 'contemplated a real possibility' of the commission of an offence of the type that P committed.

The court adopted a similarly relaxed interpretation of 'knowledge' in *Carter v Richardson*[174] where D, the supervisor of a learner driver, P, was convicted of abetting P's driving with excess alcohol. The court said, *obiter*, that it was sufficient that D knew that it was 'probable' that P was 'over the limit' – that D was, in effect, 'reckless' in the *Cunningham* sense[175] to the essential element of the crime that P was over the limit. In *Carter v Richardson*, P's offence comprised two main elements: a conduct element – driving, and a circumstances element – with excess alcohol. D intentionally encouraged the act of driving and was reckless as to the circumstance of the excess alcohol, that was sufficient render him liable.

A different situation arose in *Blakely and Sutton v DPP*.[176] D, wanting P to stay the night with her, laced his drink without his knowledge. D proposed to tell P what she had done, knowing that P would not drive home when he was over the limit. But, P drove off before D could tell him. D's conviction for procuring P's driving with excess alcohol was quashed because the justices may have convicted D as a result of wrongly applying *Caldwell/Lawrence* recklessness. Though the court deplored the use of the word, 'reckless', the court said *obiter* that the conviction would have been upheld if it had been proved that D was aware of a risk that P would drive with excess alcohol. If so, this would go further than the decision or *dicta* (as the case may be) in *Carter v Richardson*. D's recklessness in this case relates to the conduct element (driving) whereas *Carter v Richardson* was concerned only with D's recklessness as to the circumstance element.

Not only is the requirement of knowledge read in an extremely broad fashion, to include belief, contemplation or foresight, but the courts have also held that it is sufficient that D foresees that the essential elements of P's offence *might* be committed, not that they *will* be committed as in *Carter v Richardson*. A more recent example of this can be seen in *Webster*.[177] The Court of Appeal allowed an appeal where D had been driving a vehicle and had then allowed P to drive, being aware that P was drunk. P drove dangerously and a passenger, V, was killed. P was charged with causing death by dangerous driving and D as an accessory to that crime. The court held that to establish secondary liability against D the prosecution had to prove that D foresaw that P was *likely* to drive dangerously.[178] Inadvertent recklessness or negligence would not suffice.[179]

The courts have then drawn the line at negligence. Although 'knowledge includes what ought to be known, so that wilful blindness cannot excuse. There is a vast distinction between deliberately refraining from making inquiries, the result of which the person does not care to have, and mere negligence. Negligence cannot amount to sufficient *mens rea*.'[180]

---

[174] [1974] RTR 314, discussed by G Williams [1975] CLJ 182 and TBCL, 309. But in *Giogianni* (1984) 156 CLR 473 the High Court of Australia held that recklessness is not sufficient on a charge of aiding and abetting.

[175] It is quite clear that inadvertent *Caldwell/Lawrence* recklessness was never enough: *Blakely and Sutton v DPP* [1991] Crim LR 763, DC.

[176] [1991] RTR 405, [1991] Crim LR 763, DC. D would presumably be liable under s 45 of the SCA 2007. On these drink driving cases see the discussion in LC 305, paras 4.31–4.36.

[177] [2006] EWCA Crim 415.

[178] [25]. Is foresight of the dangerous driving as 'likely' a different test?

[179] [25]–[26]. Elsewhere in the judgment at para [29] the court does refer to whether D 'knew', but it is clear that the focus is on foresight.

[180] Per Collins J in *R v Roberts and George* [1997] RTR 462, [1997] Crim LR 55.

D must 'know' of the 'essential matters' of P's offence[181]

'The essential matters which constitute the offence' are those existing at the time when the act of secondary participation is done by D. In summary, D must know (in practical terms that means foresee):

- the conduct element of P's offence, although not all of the details of when, where, etc the commission of the *actus reus* will occur;
- the possibility (not necessarily a probability)[182] of the proscribed consequences of P's conduct occurring[183] (D cannot 'know' of them before they arise), but he must foresee;
- the fact of P's *mens rea*. Thus, if D foresees that P might beat V up, but does not foresee that P will perform that action with the intention of killing or causing V grievous bodily harm, D will not have 'knowledge' of the 'essential matters' comprising the principal offence of murder.[184] D cannot be an accessory to P's murder of V unless he at least foresees that P might kill with intent to kill or do serious injury. It is important to note that D need not have the same *mens rea* as P. P must have the *mens rea* for the principal offence; D must have knowledge/foresight of P's *mens rea*. Difficulties involved in proving one person's contemplation of another's state of mind are obvious. The difficulty is even more apparent when it is realized that D may be found to have the relevant *mens rea* relating to P's *mens rea* even though at the time D performs the *actus reus* of assistance P has not yet formed that *mens rea*.[185]

Knowledge in abetting an offence of strict liability

Where P's offence is one of strict liability, D must have *mens rea*, namely 'knowledge' (however loosely interpreted) of the essential elements of P's wrongdoing. The principal may, but an accessory may not, be convicted without *mens rea*. The reason is that secondary participation is a common law notion.[186] Application of the normal common law principles of liability requiring *mens rea* highlights the peculiar nature of offences of strict liability. In a strict liability offence, an accessory who has no *mens rea* must be acquitted even if he was negligent,[187] whereas the principal who has caused the *actus reus* must be convicted even if he took all proper care and was not even negligent.

In *Callow v Tillstone*,[188] D, a veterinary surgeon, was charged with abetting the exposure for sale of unsound meat. At the request of a butcher, P, he examined the carcass and gave P a certificate that the meat was sound. The examination had been negligently conducted and the meat was tainted. P, relying on the certificate, exposed the meat for sale and was convicted. The magistrates, holding that D's negligence had caused the exposure, convicted him of abetting. It was held that his conviction must be quashed.[189] Arguably, D might have been liable if he had believed that the meat was 'probably' unsound.[190]

---

[181] See LC 305, para 2.51 et seq.

[182] *Powell* [1999] AC 1.

[183] See, generally, *Day* [2001] Crim LR 984, discussed below.

[184] There is, however, some authority for the view that the *mens rea* of the principal offender need not be known or foreseen by D. This is discussed below.

[185] *Bryce* [2004] Crim LR 963.

[186] It was never necessary for a statute creating an offence to specify that it should also be an offence to aid, etc, its commission. Above, p 185. cf *McCarthy* [1964] Crim LR 225.

[187] *Carter v Mace* [1949] 2 All ER 714, DC, is to the contrary, but in *Davies, Turner & Co Ltd v Brodie* [1954] 1 WLR 1364, DC, that case was said to lay down no principle of law and to be decided on its own particular facts. See J Montgomerie in 'Aiding and Abetting Statutory Offences' (1950) 66 LQR 222.

[188] (1900) 83 LT 411, DC.

[189] See also *Bowker v Premier Drug Co Ltd* [1928] 1 KB 217 at 227.

[190] cf *Carter v Richardson*, above p 207.

The principle would apply also in a case where, for example, P is charged with taking indecent images of a child under 18. If P had been assisted in his taking of the images by D, who had supplied the camera, it would have been a defence for D (even though not for P) to show that he believed the girl to be over 18 or even (at least if he was unaware of the relevance of the age of 18) that he did not know what age she was.

The same principle must apply, *a fortiori*, to offences where negligence as to circumstances will found liability for the principal. Take the offence of bigamy as an example. If D encourages P to marry, both believing honestly but mistakenly and on unreasonable grounds that P's husband is dead, P may be convicted of bigamy but D cannot be convicted as an accessory. This principle applies only to D's negligence as to circumstances forming part of P's crime. Whether a secondary party may be liable for unforeseen consequences of P's crime is considered below.[191]

Knowledge of what type of crime?

Liability for crimes of same type

If D aids, abets, counsels or procures, ie performs acts of assistance or encouragement to P and D intends or foresees that P will commit an offence of a certain 'type' (X), neither party specifying any particular victim, time or place, D may be convicted as a secondary party to any crime *of that type* which P commits. For example, D intentionally provides P with a knife, knowing that P intends to threaten someone. P does. D is liable.

The principle applies where, as is common, D and P have a shared common purpose to commit an offence, say burglary, but the act of P alone is be the immediate cause of the commission of that offence. D is liable as an accessory for that crime provided he intentionally performed acts of assistance or encouragement (driving P to the scene) intending thereby to assist/encourage.

The principle also applies where D does not have a common purpose with P, but assists/encourages being indifferent whether P commits the crime. A leading case is *Bainbridge*.[192] D purchased some oxygen-cutting equipment which was used six weeks later for breaking into a bank at Stoke Newington. D's story was that he had bought the equipment for P, that he suspected P wanted it for something illegal – perhaps melting down stolen goods – but that he did not know that it was going to be used for any such purpose as it was in fact used. It was held that it was essential to prove that D knew the *type of crime* that was going to be committed: it was not enough that he knew that some kind of illegality was contemplated; but that, if D knew breaking and entering and stealing were intended, it was not necessary to prove that D knew the precise details eg that the Midland Bank, Stoke Newington, was going to be broken into.[193] That would be too great a degree of specificity for the prosecution to establish and would narrow the scope of secondary liability unduly.

The principle applies equally whether D has assisted by supplying equipment or assisted or encouraged P in some other way. For example, D is liable as an accessory where he provides P with information on how to commit a crime of a particular type, although neither D or P has any particular crime in view when the advice is given.[194] Where D opened a bank account for

---

[191] Below, p 216.

[192] [1960] 1 QB 129, CCA. The result would be different under the LC 305 proposals because D can only be liable for those offences by P as to which D intended P commit the conduct element. If D has not intended P commit the conduct element of burglary (as opposed to handling) he is not liable. He would be liable under the SCA 2007, s 46.

[193] cf the narrower interpretation that the Law Commission placed on it in para B85 of Appendix B of LC 305.

[194] *Baker* (1909) 28 NZLR 536. G Williams thinks the case is wrongly decided: CLGP, s 125. But is it distinguishable in principle from *Bainbridge*? cf *McLeod and Georgia Straight Publishing Co Ltd* (1970) 75 WWR 161 (newspaper liable for incitement through article on how to cultivate marijuana).

P, giving P a false name, D was convicted of aiding and abetting P in the fraudulent use of the particular forged cheque which P subsequently drew upon the account. D had demonstrated an intention that the account be used as a vehicle for presenting forged cheques like the one in fact presented.[195] D knew the type of crime. D is liable even though he does not share P's intent that the offence be committed, as eg with the supplier of the gun in Devlin's example in *Gamble*. This principle might be regarded as unduly broad. Can it really be said that where D does not even know the precise crime that P will commit he 'knows the essential elements'?

In *DPP for Northern Ireland v Maxwell*[196] the House of Lords recognized the full effect of the principle in *Bainbridge*: that there was no strict requirement that D knows the precise offence P will commit. D assisted P by intentionally driving him to a pub, realizing that P intended to commit one or more of a number of offences, including: planting a bomb at the pub, shooting people at the pub or committing a robbery at the pub. In fact, P intended to plant, and did plant, a bomb there. D was liable as an accessory to that offence. The principle derived from *Maxwell* is that if D gives assistance to P, knowing that P intends to commit a crime, foreseeing that it is one or more of crime X, or crime Y, or crime Z, but being uncertain as to which, D will be liable as a secondary party to whichever of those crimes P in fact commits. He will not be liable for crime W, even if it is of the same (type) as XYZ, unless it was one D contemplated that P might commit with *mens rea*. On the facts of *Maxwell*, D would have been liable for murder if P had shot and killed: murder was an offence D had foreseen that P might commit in that manner with *mens rea* and P carried out that crime. D would not be liable if P had committed a 'type' of offence, not in D's contemplation when D performed his acts of assistance.[197] So, D would not have been liable if, on arrival at the pub, P had raped V. Nor would it be enough if D had a 'general criminal intention'. So an intention to abet another in the possession of a bag, whatever its contents may be, is insufficient to found an indictment for abetting the possession of cannabis.[198] If D had guessed that the bag contained either cannabis or some other article, proscribed or not, that should have been enough.

Where are the limits to such liability? If D has supplied P with the means of committing, or information on how to commit, a crime of a particular type, is D to be held liable for *all* the crimes of that type which P may thereafter commit? What if the Midland Bank at Stoke Newington was the second, third or fourth bank which P had burgled with Bainbridge's apparatus? Glanville Williams questioned whether D should be subject to such unforeseeable and perhaps far-reaching liability.[199] Yet, once it is conceded that D need not know the details of any specific crime, it is difficult to see why he should be liable for any one crime of *the type* contemplated and not for others of that type.[200]

There are further unresolved problems in relation to this principle. Whether a crime is of the 'same type' as another may not always be easy to discover. If D lends a jemmy to P, contemplating that P intends to enter a house in order to steal (burglary), is D guilty of any offence if P enters a house intending to commit grievous bodily harm (which is also burglary)? Clearly, D cannot be convicted of grievous bodily harm, because that is an offence of a different type; but he is probably guilty of burglary, because burglary was the crime he had in

---

[195] *Thambiah v R* [1966] AC 37 PC.

[196] [1978] 1 WLR 1350, HL.

[197] cf Lord Scarman who unlike Lord Hailsham who refers to the type of offence, relies on the judgment of Lowry LCJ in the Northern Ireland Court of Appeal, upholding the conviction on the basis that D 'knew' that P was going to commit one or more offences and although D did not 'know' which offence he knew that at least one would be committed and the offence P committed was one of those. I am grateful to David Hughes for discussions on this.

[198] *Patel* [1970] Crim LR 274 and commentary thereon. cf *Fernandez* [1970] Crim LR 277.

[199] CLGP, s 124.

[200] On the question of the withdrawal of an accessory before the fact, see below, p 236.

view – though this particular variety of burglary may be abhorrent to him. If D contemplates theft and P commits robbery, D is not guilty of robbery but might be convicted of the theft which is an essential element of robbery and included in it. Is theft an offence of the same type as removing an article from a place open to the public[201] or taking a motor vehicle without authority?[202] Is robbery an offence of the same type as blackmail? What of D who provides a stolen credit card to P assuming it will be used in fraud, but P uses it to slip the latch on V's door and commit theft. Is it sufficient that these are both dishonesty offences? This is an aspect of the law desperately in need of clarification, at least from a theoretical perspective; in practice the principle does not seem to have given rise to problems.

D not liable if P intentionally changes victim/target of crime X

If D aids, abets, counsels or procures ie assists or encourages P to commit a crime of a certain 'type' (X), against a particular person, or in respect of a particular thing, D is *not* liable if P *intentionally* commits an offence of the same type against some other person, or in respect of some other thing, unless D foresaw that P might do as he did.[203]

As an example of the principle in operation, consider D who intentionally provides P with a knife, knowing that P intends to threaten V. P deliberately threatens W instead. D had not foreseen that possibility. D is not liable. In *Reardon*,[204] (discussed below) it was accepted[205] that if D intentionally gives assistance to P to kill an identified person, V, D is not liable if P *deliberately* kills a different person, W.

This principle is described well by Hawkins:[206]

But if a man command another to commit a felony on a particular person or thing and he do it on another; as to kill A and he kill B or to burn the house of A and he burn the house of B or to steal an ox and he steal an horse; or to steal such an horse and he steal another; or to commit a felony of one kind and he commit another of a quite different nature; as to rob J S of his plate as he is going to market, and he break open his house in the night and there steal the plate; it is said that the commander is not an accessory because the act done varies in substance from that which was commanded.

As the second part of that quotation makes clear, the principle applies where there is an intentional substantial variation from the proposed course of conduct, even if the victim and property are the same. Hawkins also stated:[207]

[I]f the felony committed be the same in substance with that which was intended, and variant only in some circumstance, as in respect of the time or place, at which, or the means whereby it was effected, the abettor of the intent is altogether as much an accessory as if there had been no variance at all between it and the execution of it; as where a man advises another to kill such a one in the night, and he kills him in the day, or to kill him in the fields, and he kills him in the town, or to poison him, and he stabs or shoots him.[208]

The distinction depends on whether the variation is one 'of substance' and any such distinction must produce difficult borderline cases.

In *Dunning and Graham*, an unreported case at Preston Crown Court,[209] D had a grievance against V. P offered to set fire to V's house. D accepted the offer and gave P V's address.

[201] Theft Act 1968, s 11. Below, p 849.
[202] Theft Act 1968, s 12. Below, p 852.
[203] *Powell* [1999] AC 1 HL.
[204] [1999] Crim LR 392, CA.
[205] Referring to the 8th edition of this book, at 142.
[206] 2 PC c 29, s 21. See also Foster, *Crown Law*, 369. Stephen, *Digest* (4th edn), art 43.
[207] ibid, s 20.
[208] This is related to the principle in *Bainbridge* that D need not know all the detail of P's offence.
[209] December 1985, unreported.

P went to V's house, changed his mind, and set fire to V's Mercedes instead. D did not know that V owned such a car. Nevertheless, Macpherson J held that it was open to the jury to convict D on the ground that she must have authorized or envisaged the possibility of property such as a car in the driveway being damaged by fire. If the car had been so damaged as a consequence of P's setting fire to the house, D would have been liable for arson of the car on the basis of transferred malice discussed below. The actual case, however, seems to involve a deliberate variation from the plan. The result might be justified on this basis that D had authorized P to take revenge on V by damaging his property and that it did not really matter to her what the property was. Whether the variation is, or is not, one of substance, depends on the purpose of D as expressed to P.

The South African case of *S v Robinson*[210] provides a controversial illustration of the difficulties of applying this principle. It is an especially difficult case because there is no change of victim as such, but arguably a fundamental change of substance relating to the proposed offence. D1, D2 and P agreed with V that P should kill V to procure the money for which V's life was insured and to avoid V's prosecution for fraud. At the last moment, V withdrew his consent to die but P nevertheless killed him. It was not proved that D1 and D2 foresaw the possibility that P might kill V even if he withdrew his consent or that they had been reckless whether he did so kill him. It was held that the common purpose was murder with the consent of the victim and that P had acted outside that common purpose. D1 and D2, accordingly, were not guilty of murder – though they were guilty of attempted murder, since P had reached the stage of an attempt before V withdrew his consent. Holmes JA, dissenting, thought '...looking squarely at the whole train of events, the conspiracy was fulfilled in death, and there is no room for exquisite niceties of logic about the exact limits of the mandate in the conspiratorial common purpose'.

The division of judicial opinion in this case highlights the problem. What constitutes a change of 'substance' could be interpreted narrowly, being limited to changes which would alter the nature of the criminal charge that could be prosecuted. In *Robinson*, the offence planned was murder, that committed was murder, but we know from other high authority that a fundamental change might involve something that would not alter the nature of the charge – as where the manner of infliction is different.[211] A broader view of change of 'substance' seems more desirable, but the problem then arises of how to delimit 'changes of substance'. If P knows that a condition precedent of the agreement has not been performed (whether or not forming part of the definition of the crime), he might naturally be said to be no longer engaged on the joint enterprise. If D agrees with P that P shall murder V if he finds out that V is committing adultery with D's wife and P, having discovered that V is *not* committing adultery, nevertheless kills him, D should not be liable for murder, though, if this conditional intention is enough, he may be liable for conspiracy to murder.

D liable if P commits crime X by doctrine of transferred malice

If D intentionally aids, abets, counsels or procures P to commit a crime against a particular person V and P, endeavouring to commit that crime against V mistakenly, commits the crime against another, (W), P is liable under the doctrine of transferred malice;[212] and so, therefore, is D. To take an example, if D assists P by intentionally supplying a knife intending to assist P, and P kills W mistaking W for V, D is guilty as a secondary party, and P as a principal offender, of murder. It is important to note that in this scenario P has not *deliberately* departed from the course that D assisted him with; P was attempting to commit the crime which D has assisted

---

[210] 1968 (1) SA 666.

[211] *English* [1999] AC 1.

[212] Hawkins, 1 PC, Ch 29, s 22; Foster, 370; Stephen, *Digest* (4th edn) art 41, illustration (1). See also D Lanham, 'Accomplices and Transferred Malice' (1980) 96 LQR 110.

him with and D is as responsible for the unintended results of the acts he has assisted. The principle applies whether D and P share a common purpose that P's crime will be committed, or where D intentionally aids and abets, but is indifferent whether P commits the crime.

The old and famous case of *Saunders and Archer*,[213] in its result at least, is reconcilable with this principle. P, intended to murder his wife. Following the advice of D, P gave her a poisoned apple to eat. She ate a little of it and gave the rest to their child. P loved the child, yet he stood by and watched it eat the poison, of which it soon died. It was held that P was guilty of murder of the child, but the judges agreed that D, who, of course, was not present when the child ate the apple, was not an accessory to this murder. If P had been absent when the child ate the apple it is thought that this would have been a case of transferred malice and D would have been liable; but P's presence and failure to act made the killing of the child, in effect, a deliberate, and not an accidental, departure from the agreed plan. It was – as Kenny explained – 'as if Saunders had changed his mind and on a later occasion had used such poison as Archer had named in order to murder some quite different person of whom Archer had never heard'.[214]

8.5 Joint enterprise liability

The problem in identifying the scope of D's liability for P's offences arises most keenly in the context of joint enterprise liability. That term has given rise to a vast number of appeals and to much academic debate.[215]

8.5.1 Forms of joint enterprise

There are, it is submitted, five situations[216] in which the expression 'joint enterprise' appears to be used. Only some of them involve secondary liability.

(1) D and P participate together in the commission of crime(s). Each plays some part in the *actus reus* of the crime(s). Each is liable to be tried and convicted as a principal offender. This is often described as a joint enterprise, but is more accurately a case of D and P acting as joint principals. This is not a case of secondary liability.

(2) D and P participate together in the commission of crime X. Each plays a part in the commission of the *actus reus* of that crime. P (or another in the enterprise with P and D) also commits crime Y. D does not participate in the commission of the *actus reus* of that crime Y. D foresees that in the course of the commission of crime X P[217] (or another in the venture) might commit crime Y with *mens rea* in a manner not fundamentally different from that in which P does commit it. D and P are in a joint enterprise. D is liable as an accessory to crime Y (what might be called 'parasitic liablity').

---

[213] (1573) 2 Plowd 473.

[214] *Outlines* at 112. See the perceptive jury questions and clear directions in *Gordon-Butt* [2004] EWCA Crim 961 on changes of victim.

[215] See, JC Smith, 'Criminal Liability of Accessories: Law and Law Reform' (1997) 113 LQR 453; J Burchell, 'Joint Enterprise and Common Purpose' (1997) SACJ 125; cf A Simester, 'The Mental Element in Complicity' (2006) 122 LQR 578, for a review LC 305. See recently B Krebs, 'Joint Criminal Enterprise' (2010) 73 MLR 578.

[216] In *ABCD* [2010] EWCA Crim 1622 at [9], Hughes LJ refers to their being 'at least' 3, (his aligning with (1), (3) and (4) below). This is echoed in *Gnago* [2010] EWCA Crim 1691.

[217] If D is acting with a group as is commonly the case, it is not necessary for D to identify which of the group might commit crime Y provided he foresees that one might: *Yemoh* [2009] EWCA Crim 930.

(3) D and P share a common purpose[218] to commit crime(s). P alone commits the *actus reus* of the crime(s); D aids, abets, counsels or procures P to do so. P is liable as a principal and D as an accessory. Together they are rather misleadingly described by some as being in a joint enterprise.

(4) D and P share a common purpose to commit crime X (eg robbery). D foresees that in the course of doing so, P (or another member of the party to the venture) might commit other crime Y (eg murder). D does not have an intention that P commits crime Y, he does not share a common purpose with P that such a crime will be committed. If P commits crimes X and Y, he will be liable as principal for both. D will be liable as an accessory to crime X. D will also be liable as an accessory for crime Y committed by P provided D has foreseen as a possibility that P might with the relevant *mens rea* commit the offence Y in the manner in which P does commit it. This is a form of what might be called 'parasitic accessory liability'. D will be liable for the other offence (Y) perpetrated by P which D foresaw might be committed even if D did not intend that P would commit them. D and P will be said to be in a joint enterprise.

(5) D and P have no common purpose. D aids, abets, counsels or procures P to commit crime X (robbery). D does not share P's purpose to commit that crime. D foresees that in the course of committing crime X (robbery), P might commit another offence, Y (murder). If P commits robbery and murder he will be liable as a principal for both. D will be liable as an accessory to robbery. D will, in such circumstances also be liable as an accessory for any other offence committed by P provided D was an accessory to crime X, and has foreseen as a possibility that P might with the relevant *mens rea* commit the other offence (eg murder) in the manner in which P does commit it. It applies even though D and P do not share any common purpose.[219] This principle applies whether D is present with P or not.[220] This is a form of what might be called 'parasitic accessory liability'. D and P are said to be in a joint enterprise.

Consider some examples. D intentionally performs acts of assistance or encouragement to P: he gives P a gun to assist in his robbery. D is liable as an accessory for the robbery even though P is the one who completes the offence. That is orthodox accessorial liability at work. But, if in the course of the robbery P shoots and murders V, D is *also* liable as an accessory for murder which he did *not* intend or assist or encourage P to commit, provided (i) D intentionally encouraged or assisted P to commit robbery; (ii) D foresaw that in the course of[221] committing robbery, P might perform the conduct element of murder in the prescribed circumstances making that an offence; (iii) D foresaw that P might do so with the *mens rea* of murder,[222] and (iv) the manner of P committing the murder was not fundamentally different from what D foresaw might occur.[223]

---

[218] According to the Court of Appeal in *Gnango* [2010] EWCA Crim 1691, it is not enough that D and P have antagonistic purposes – eg to shoot each other, but to cause an affray in doing so.

[219] See *Reardon* [1999] Crim LR 392. See the JSB Bench book (2010) 61.

[220] *Rook* [1993] Crim LR 698.

[221] Irrespective of whether it is completed. Simester argues that it is a fiction to say that D aids and abets crime Y: above, p 190 n 49. But the *actus reus* of aiding is D's participated in crime X despite foreseeing that Y might occur.

[222] This is vital and all too often overlooked. It was reiterated in the clearest terms in *ABCD* [2010] EWCA Crim 1622. Several other recent Court of Appeal decisions seem to gloss over this requirement (*Badza* [2009] EWCA Crim 1363 [30]; *Willett* [2010] EWCA Crim 1620 [10]), but *ABCD* rightly and rigorously reasserts the requirement: it is necessary to prove that D foresaw not only what P might do but also that P might have the requisite *mens rea* for crime when he did it.

[223] This passage in the 11th edition was endorsed by the Court of Appeal in *Rahman* [2007] EWCA Crim 342 at [21].

Consider a second example. D, the accessory, intentionally assists or encourages P to commit burglary or robbery, contemplating that in the course of committing that offence P 'might well' do an act with intent to cause grievous bodily harm. If P does an act of the kind D foresaw/contemplated and causes grievous bodily harm, D is guilty as accessory to P's causing grievous bodily harm with intent, contrary to s 18 of the Offences Against the Person Act 1861. If V dies of the injury, P is guilty of murder and D is also guilty as accessory. If D assists or encourages P in the burglary/robbery, foreseeing/contemplating that P might act with intent to kill and P does so, both are guilty of attempted murder if V does not die.[224] The question is one of D's contemplation or foresight.

8.5.1.1 Joint enterprise distinct from joint principals

As noted, it is essential to identify whether D is a secondary party or a principal offender. It will be recalled that D1 and D2 are joint principal offenders where each does an act which is a cause of the *actus reus*. Where there are several participants in a crime the principal offender is the one whose act is the most immediate cause of the *actus reus*.[225] For example, each stabs V who dies from the combined effect of the wounds; or D1 and D2 together plant a bomb which goes off and kills V; but then each is liable for his own act, not because he has 'participated' in the act of another; and each is liable to the extent of his own *mens rea*. Suppose that, in the bomb case, D2 intends (and believes that D1 intends) that ample warning will be given to allow the area to be cleared, whereas D1 intends that no warning shall be given. The bomb goes off prematurely and kills V. D1 is *prima facie* guilty of murder, D2 of manslaughter.[226] Similarly where they jointly release a gas canister which D2 believes to contain tear gas and D1 knows to contain a deadly gas. There are two principal offenders and two offences.

8.5.2 Parasitic liability

The forms of joint enterprise liability that are most controversial are those involving parasitic liability as described above (ie those where D is liable for P's crime Y as well as crime X). This form of liability has been endorsed by the Privy Council in *Chan Wing-Siu v R*,[227] as interpreted in *Hyde* and *Hui Chi-ming* and approved by the House of Lords in *Powell and Daniels*[228] and *Rahman*.[229] It has been endorsed by numerous recent Court of Appeal decisions.[230]

---

[224] *O'Brien* [1995] 2 Cr App R 649, [1995] Crim LR 734.

[225] With offences in which there is no result or consequence to be proved, the principal offender is perhaps more accurately the person who engages in the conduct element, of the *actus reus*.

[226] Earlier editions of this book (see 6th edition, at 152–153) treated *Murtagh and Kennedy* [1955] Crim LR 315 as if it were a case of joint principals, a case where both parties were the cause of the *actus reus*. P, the driver, and D, the passenger in a car, were charged with murder by running down V. Glyn Jones J directed the jury that to drive a car at a person with intent to kill or cause grievous bodily harm was murder; but wilfully to drive on the pavement, not intending to hit anyone but intending to terrorize, would be manslaughter. The jury convicted P of murder and D of manslaughter. Both convictions were quashed on grounds which are immaterial for present purposes. The verdicts imply that P intended to run V down but D intended that he should not be run down but merely frightened. Are not driving at V to kill him, and driving close to V to frighten him, fundamentally different acts? And if D did not intend that, nor foresee a risk that P would drive at V, was not the act outside the scope of the joint enterprise and one for which D was not responsible? Only P did an act causing death and D could only be made liable if he foresaw that *that act* might be done: *Mahmood*, below, p 219.

[227] (1985) 80 Cr App R 117. See the 7th edition of this book, at 143–145, for an account of the cases ending in the final acceptance of the principle of *Chan Wing-Siu* in *Hyde* (1991) 92 Cr App R 131 and the decision in *Hui Chi-ming* (1992) 94 Cr App R 236, PC, that that result need not be authorized but merely foreseen. The case is discussed by the Law Com in LC 305, para 2.73.

[228] [1999] AC 1, [1997] 4 All ER 545, HL. See also the comment by G Virgo [1998] CLJ 3. See also *Neary* [2002] EWCA Crim 1736.

[229] [2008] UKHL 45.

[230] See, eg, *Smith* [2008] EWCA Crim 1342; *ABCD* [2010] EWCA Crim 1622; *Mendez* [2010] EWCA Crim 516; *Lewis* [2010] EWCA Crim 496; *Badza* [2010] EWCA Crim 1363.

The basis of D's parasitic liability turns on his contemplation or foresight – that is the 'touchstone' of D's liability.[231] He has foreseen crime Y as a possible incident of the common unlawful enterprise in the commission of crime X. The foresight must be of something more than a fleeting risk; it must be foresight of a real risk of crime Y.[232] It is a question of D's foresight in subjective terms – not what he ought to have foreseen. Proving it is not easy. In many cases it will be by inference. In *Gordon*,[233] it was held that a lack of surprise expressed by D as to the crime Y committed by P is not necessarily to be equated with foresight by D that the crime was one that P might commit. The criminal culpability lies in participating in the venture (crime X) with that foresight.[234] Liability is not based on whether D and P agree[235] tacitly[236] or otherwise, it is based on D's foresight of the offences P might commit. Foresight or contemplation by D is what matters.[237] As Hughes LJ explained in *ABCD*:[238]

as a matter of principle, the liability of D [...], rests...on his having continued in the common venture of crime [X] when he realises (even if he does not desire) that crime [Y] may be committed in the course of it. Where crime [Y] is murder, that means that he can properly be held guilty if he foresees that [P] will cause death by acting with murderous intent (viz either the intent to kill or the intent to do GBH). He has associated himself with a foreseen murder. If all he foresees is that death may be caused without either of those intentions, he has not associated himself with a foreseen murder; he has associated himself with foreseen manslaughter.[239]

The principle imposing parasitic liability in this way applies whether D is present with P or not.[240] It may be that D first contemplates that P might commit crime Y when D is already engaged in crime X as an accessory. Care must, however, be taken when the Crown's case is that D had no foresight of P committing the further crime (eg murder) until they were actively engaged in the basic crime to which D was an accessory (robbery/burglary). In such cases, particularly where events unfold quickly, there has to be evidence that D was continuing to participate with P having foreseen that P might go on to commit the other offence (murder). In *Willet*[241] for example, D and P set out to steal from V's van. D went to the van, P remained in the getaway vehicle. D was disturbed by the owner. D ran to the car and P drove off. As they turned the corner V blocked their path. P knocked him down killing him. D was at least an accessory to theft. D would only be liable for P's act of murder if D either (i) gave direct assistance or encouragement to that act of murder or (ii) having participated in the theft, D foresaw that P might commit at least gbh with intent when driving away and continued to participate in the criminal venture. The court concluded that D could not have foreseen that P might

---

[231] Per Lord Bingham in *Rahman* [2008] UKHL 45, [11], [21], per Lord Neuberger [103]. In *Mendez*, the Court seems to regard the 'fundamental difference' principle as based on causation: 'Conduct by P which involves a total and substantial variation from that encouraged by D could not properly be regarded as the "fruit" of D's encouragement, nor with propriety be said to have been committed under D's influence'[20]. Joint enterprise liability rests, it is submitted, not on whether D has made a causal contribution to the crime P eventually commits in the manner in which he does so, but on whether D has foresight or contemplation that P might do so with *mens rea* in the *manner* in which he did.

[232] See the comments of Lord Hutton in *English*.

[233] [2004] EWCA Crim 961.

[234] See for a clear statement of the law terms of contemplation: *Bryce* [2004] EWCA Crim 1321, [2004] Crim LR 963.

[235] See *Hyde* [1991] 1 QB 134

[236] See *Wakely* [1990] Crim LR 119 and commentary.

[237] See recently, *Willet* [2010] EWCA Crim 1620 where the Court suggested that the trial judge had also created difficulty by use of the expression 'tacit encouragement' or 'tacit agreement'.

[238] [2010] EWCA Crim 1622.

[239] [27].

[240] *Rook* [1993] Crim LR 698.

[241] [2010] EWCA Crim 1620.

drive at V with murderous intent until a few seconds before (when they turned the corner). It was necessary therefore for the Crown to prove that D actively assisted or encouraged. The court concluded that the fact that D continued to sit in the passenger seat could not of itself amount to assistance or encouragement.[242]

The most complex and difficult cases of parasitic liability to apply are those where D merely assists/encourages crime X being indifferent whether P commits that crime. The fact that D does not share P's purpose to commit crime X, does not prevent him from being liable for that crime X and, if he foresaw it might occur, crime Y.[243] This form of secondary liability was recognized in *Reardon*.[244] P shot two men, X and Y, in a bar and carried them, both dying, into the beer garden. He returned to the bar, said to D that one of them was still alive, and asked D for the loan of his knife. Medical evidence established that both men died from wounds inflicted by P with D's knife. D was charged with both murders. P did not specify which man was the victim he intended to stab. D intentionally assisted P in the crime of murder. The Court of Appeal held that he was rightly convicted as an accessory to both murders. There being no way of distinguishing between the victims, it was a case of liability for both murders or neither. The convictions were upheld on the ground that the jury must have found that D foresaw 'at least the strong possibility that if [P] found the other deceased alive, he might use the knife in the same way...' D intended to assist one murder and he knew there was a real risk that there might be two.

8.5.2.1 Parasitic liability for crimes *in furtherance of* commission of crime X

In a joint enterprise to commit crime X, D can be liable for P's crime Y if that conduct (and P's *mens rea*) was foreseen as a possibility by D *provided that crime Y arose in the course of or furtherance of the commission of crime X*.[245] This requirement provides further confirmation that joint enterprise cases are merely examples of the principles of secondary liability in operation. If D has intended to assist or encourage crime X and foreseen P's possible commission of crime Y in the course of that venture D has sufficient *mens rea* for accessorial liability. D has performed the *actus reus* of the offence of aiding and abetting by assisting or encouraging P in crime X. By doing so he has also assisted or encouraged crime Y *which is an incident to* or committed in furtherance of crime X. In practical terms, however, there can be problems in application of this scope of the venture principle to everyday examples in which joint enterprise arises. Consider D and P who commit a burglary (crime X), with D participating as joint principal or aider and abettor. P kills the householder as D foresaw he might. In most cases this will present no problem because the killing of the householder is in the furtherance of the burglary – to prevent detection/aid escape etc. What of the case where P kills a sleeping householder out of pure malice? D was downstairs at the time but has foreseen that P might intentionally cause gbh or kill. Is P's murder 'in the course of' the burglary?

---

[242] There was, however, evidence from a witness to whom D had confessed encouragement which was evidence from which a jury could reasonably conclude that he had participated in, and given encouragement to, the murder.

[243] As Lord Brown observed in *Rahman* [2008] UKHL 45, [63] a common purpose requirement would be superfluous as D must foresee P's crimes. That may be an oversimplification since although D's foresight subsumes all cases of D and P sharing a common purpose, it extends liability far wider. cf comments in *Badza* [2009] EWCA Crim 1363 at [41]. That decision must be treated with caution as several statements are contrary to established principle.

[244] [1999] Crim LR 392, CA. In *Gilmour*, D was roused from his bed and told to drive the car 'which he did not do willingly'. It seems his purpose was not to throw petrol bombs but to save his own skin; but he was treated as a party to a joint enterprise.

[245] *Hui Chi-ming* [1992] 1 A.C. 34; *Gnango* [2010] EWCA Crim 1691.

8.5.2.2 The significance of common purpose?

As we have seen not all forms of joint enterprise liability involve D and P sharing a common purpose. D can be liable if he intentionally assists P in the commission of crime X but does not share his purpose to commit that offence, and D foresees that P might intentionally commit crime Y in the course of his committing crime X.

In the recent case of *Gnango*[246] D had voluntarily engaged in an exchange of gunfire with an opponent (P) in a public place. One of P's shots, aimed at D, killed a passerby.[247] D was convicted of possessing a firearm with intent to endanger life, attempted murder and by way of joint enterprise, the murder of the passerby. The trial judge left the case to the jury on the basis that P had murdered V and that D was engaged with him in a joint enterprise to commit affray (crime X), D foreseeing that in the course of which P might commit intentional gbh or kill. D could be liable for murder perpetrated by P provided D had (i) jointly participated in the crime of affray or (ii) assisted/encouraged P in the commission of an affray and in either case had foreseen that P might intentionally kill etc. The Court of Appeal quashed the conviction. D and P shared no 'common purpose' in committing the affray: their purposes were antagonistic.[248] The court's conclusion is that in a case of joint enterprise *based on joint principalship*, in addition to proof that D foresees that P might intentionally commit crime Y, it is necessary for there to be an agreement to commit crime X and for a shared common purpose to commit crime X.[249] The judge and the Court of Appeal rejected[250] the argument that D might be convicted of murder on the alternative basis that D aided and abetted P in the crime of shooting at D. On that basis D would have aided and abetted crime X (shooting at D) and foreseen that P might kill in the course or furtherance of it.[251] The court rejected this strained approach. D shooting at P could not amount to encouragement of P to shoot at D with intent to kill himself. D could not be said to be intending to assist P: P's purpose (killing D) was directly contrary to the D's purpose.[252]

One alternative way of approaching this case is to argue that D and P were in a joint enterprise to shoot at each other and be shot. D was arguably engaged in a joint enterprise to shoot and be shot at. D and P have a common purpose to shoot and be shot at.[253] This is similar to the old prizefighting cases such as *Coney*[254] where D and P were guilty of prizefighting.

---

[246] [2010] EWCA Crim 1691. See [2011] Crim LR 151 for critical comment.

[247] P was not brought to justice, but would have been guilty of murder by the law of transferred malice.

[248] Are their purposes antagonistic *as far as the commission of the affray goes*?

[249] Cases like *Peters and Parfitt* [1995] Crim LR 501 make clear that there must be a shared common intent for joint principals.

[250] [46].

[251] For D to be liable on this basis the Crown would have to show: that by shooting at P with direct intent to kill him, D nevertheless also intended to encourage and did in fact encourage P to shoot back at D, and that D foresaw that in doing so P might intentionally kill a third person (or possibly him).

[252] Further, as the Court of Appeal put it, the judge had held that even if G had encouraged B to shoot at him, 'it would be odd for a victim of a murder to be a secondary party to that murder' [p 38]. Strictly of course we are speaking only about the *intended* victim.

[253] The Court of Appeal returns to the possibility of liability under this basis at the end of its judgment. Although expressing no concluded opinion, the clear inference from the discussion in paras 71–75 is that the court would have had less difficulty in supporting a conviction on this basis. The Court of Appeal have now certified a point of law for possible consideration by the Supreme Court, namely: If (1) D1 and D2 voluntarily engage in fighting each other, each intending to kill or cause grievous bodily harm to the other and each foreseeing that the other has the reciprocal intention, and if (2) D1 mistakenly kills V in the course of the fight, in what circumstances, if any, is D2 guilty of the offence of murdering V?

[254] Above p 204.

8.5.2.3 D not liable if P commits crime Y in a manner fundamentally different from what D contemplated as a real possibility

We have seen above that D will not be liable for a crime that P commits, even if it is of the same type that D foresaw might occur or that D shared P's purpose would occur, if P has *intentionally* changed the specified victim or target from that D intended or foresaw.

This principle has important implications in the context of joint enterprise liability. It commonly arises as a difficult issue, particularly in murder trials. Where D has intentionally assisted or encouraged P to commit crime X (whether sharing his intention or not) D will not liable for a crime (Z) committed by P in the course of committing crime (X) if the relevant act by P was *performed in a fundamentally different manner or was of a fundamentally different kind* from any act that D foresaw or contemplated that P might commit.

The leading cases are *English*[255] and *Rahman*.[256] In *English*, both D and P armed themselves with wooden stakes to attack a police officer (crime X). D knew that P might intentionally cause grievous bodily harm with a stake (crime Y), and if he had done and V had died D would have been guilty of murder. But P killed V with a knife (crime Z) which D did not know he had. The House of Lords quashed D's conviction for murder because it was not left to the jury to decide whether the killing with a knife was an act of a fundamentally different kind from any foreseen by D. An earlier illustration is *Mahmood*.[257] P and D took a car without the consent of the owner. There followed the usual police chase. P, the driver, abandoned the car in gear with the engine running so that the car ran on and killed a baby. The jury convicted D as well as P of manslaughter. Although the jury, being properly directed, must have found as a fact that D *did* foresee that P might do such an act, the Court of Appeal quashed D's conviction, holding there was no evidence on which they could find that D foresaw such an exceptional act of gross negligence by P. It would probably have been different if P had killed by excessive speed, going through a red light, etc, acts which commonly occur in cases of this kind and which a jury might properly have found that D did foresee.

This is a significant limit on the scope of D's liability. It is not so much an exception or qualification to the general principle of parasitic liability, rather it is the natural corollary of D's liability turning on whether he has foreseen or contemplated that P might commit the offence in the manner in which he did.[258] D is liable for the basic crime (X) committed by P, he is also liable for the crimes (Y) he foresees that P might commit with *mens rea*. The question is how much further is D's liability to be extended? If P acts in a way that is not precisely what D has foreseen can D be liable for these criminal acts (crime Z) of P as well?

D's plea that P's act was fundamentally different from what D foresaw can take on an enhanced significance in murder cases. Liability can turn on extremely fine factual distinctions. In *A-G's Reference (No 3 of 2004)*[259] the act which caused death was the deliberate discharge of a firearm deliberately aimed at V. The act contemplated by D was the deliberate discharge of a firearm in circumstances which excluded the deliberate causing, by the use of the firearm, of any physical injury, let alone the deliberate causing of death. The fact that D had not foreseen that possibility meant that he was not guilty of manslaughter even though he

---

[255] An appeal heard together with *Powell and Daniels*, above p 203.
[256] [2008] UKHL 45.
[257] [1995] RTR 48, [1994] Crim LR 368.
[258] See Lord Bingham in *Rahman* [2008] UKHL 45, [16] and Lord Rodger at [44].
[259] [2005] EWCA Crim 1882. Followed in *D* [2005] EWCA Crim 1985. cf *Briggs* [2007] Cr App R (S) 425, D drove P with gun into countryside with P's ex-girlfriend. P shot her dead and then killed himself. D convicted of manslaughter even though he foresaw only risk that P would threaten V. See also *Parsons* [2009] EWCA Crim 2693 shooting at someone to 'wing' them.

could have been guilty of manslaughter if the gun had been deliberately discharged and had accidentally killed V, or had accidentally been discharged with the same fatal result.[260]

This 'fundamental difference' principle requires more detailed analysis, and in particular it must be considered: (i) when D may rely on the claim that the act performed by P was fundamentally different from anything D foresaw, (ii) what 'fundamentally different' actually means, (iii) whether the law is too harsh.

In what circumstances can D raise a plea that P's act was fundamentally different?

Not all cases of P deviating from what D foresaw as likely will provide an opportunity for D to plead that P's acts were fundamentally different from what was foreseen so as to absolve D of liability for crime Y. The issue has arisen most keenly in the context of murder. There are a number of possible scenarios in which D might claim that P's act was fundamentally different.[261] The House of Lords in *English* dealt only with cases in which D foresaw that P might cause serious harm to V intending to cause serious harm.

The leading authority on this issue is now *Rahman* in the House of Lords.[262] The appellants were each convicted of murder. V had sustained two fatal stab wounds from a knife during an attack on him by a number of men, many of whom were armed with blunt instruments. The Crown alleged that each of the appellants had been a party to a joint enterprise to inflict unlawful violence on V. It could not be proved which person had inflicted the fatal blows. Each appellant denied possession of a knife and each asserted that he had not foreseen, believed, known or realized that anyone else in the group had a knife. Each claimed that the person who had inflicted the wound, whoever that was, had been acting outside the scope of any joint enterprise to attack. The trial judge allowed the jury to consider a plea that the principal's acts were fundamentally different even if they found that the appellant intended V to be killed. The Court of Appeal had suggested, *obiter*, that there was no reason why a party to a joint enterprise to inflict unlawful violence on a person would be entitled to the benefit of the 'fundamentally different' principle if he intended that V was to be killed or *if he foresaw that one of the attackers might kill V with an intention to kill*. The House of Lords took a different view. According to the House of Lords, D is now able to rely on the fundamental difference plea even where he foresaw that P might kill with intent. Arguably this is too generous to D. If D has committed himself to a venture seeing that P might kill with intent should it matter what *method* of killing D foresaw? D foresees that P might kill with a knife in the course of their burglary, P kills with a gun. Why should D be able to rely on that change?

Subsequently, in *Yemoh*[263] the Court of Appeal confirmed following *Rahman*, that the fundamental difference plea only has the potential to apply if D did not intend the victim to be killed and either:[264]

(i) D foresaw that one of the attackers might kill with intent to kill or cause really serious bodily harm;

---

[260] The prosecution must charge the secondary with alternative offences as well: *Greatrex* [1998] Crim LR 733.

[261] (i) D intends that V be killed and P kills with intent; (ii) D foresees that P may kill with intent to kill and P does so; (iii) D intends V to be caused gbh foreseeing that P may kill with intent and P kills; (iv) D foresees P's intentional infliction of gbh and that V might be killed; (v) D intends that V will be caused gbh with intent, but does not foresee V being killed; (vi) D foresees that P might intentionally cause gbh but D has no foresight of V being killed; (vii) where P has killed without intending to and D foresaw P might cause intentional gbh but did not foresee V's death.

[262] [2008] UKHL 45; cf the CA decision at [2007] EWCA Crim 342. For critical comment on the decision of the House of Lords see [2008] Crim LR 979.

[263] [2009] EWCA Crim 930.

[264] This was confirmed in *Mendez* [2010] EWCA Crim 516, [44].

(ii) D intended that really serious bodily harm would be caused;[265] or

(iii) D foresaw that one of the attackers might cause really serious bodily harm with intent to cause such harm.

The Ministry of Justice in its Consultation Paper *Murder, Manslaughter and Infanticide: Proposals for Reform of the Law* (2008)[266] recommended, *inter alia*, a more flexible statutory rule for fundamental difference based on whether P's act was 'within the scope of the joint criminal venture'. 'This would be the case where the act did not go far beyond that which was planned, agreed to or foreseen by the secondary party' (para 101). The fundamentally different qualification would only be available where D has not foreseen death of V as a possibility, and even when it is successfully applied it will result in a manslaughter conviction (cl 4).[267]

What does 'fundamentally different' mean?

The next problem that arises is, in those circumstances in which the plea is available, determining what will make P's act 'fundamentally different' from that which D foresaw. The case law has been unclear as to whether the enquiry is focused on the degree of difference in P's intentions, weapons, actions or the consequences of those? Despite the difficulty in practice, in *Rahman*,[268] Lord Bingham described the concept of 'fundamentally different' as having a 'plain meaning' and suggested that it is 'not a term of art'.[269] Similar suggestions about the ease with which this can be explained to the jury were made in *Mendez*[270] and *ABCD*.[271] It is accepted that this direction need not be given in cases where it is a theoretical or fanciful suggestion that there was a fundamental change by P.[272] Readers can judge for themselves how 'plain' the law is. In *Yemoh*,[273] the Court of Appeal emphasized that whether or not what P did was fundamentally different from anything foreseen by the D was a *question of fact*. In *Rahman* it was described as an objective question.[274]

In *Rahman*, Lord Brown restated the law on fundamental difference as follows:[275]

If D realises (without agreeing to such conduct being used) that P may kill or intentionally inflict serious injury, but nevertheless continues to participate with P in the venture, that will amount to a sufficient mental element for D to be guilty of murder if P, with the requisite intent, kills in the course of the venture *unless (i) P suddenly produces and uses a weapon of which D knows nothing and which is more lethal than any weapon which D contemplates that P or any other participant may be carrying and (ii) for that reason P's act is to be regarded as fundamentally different from*

---

[265] Arguably the method employed by P should not matter since D has sufficient *mens rea* for murder himself. The courts have not taken that strict line.

[266] The Consultation Document represented the next phase in the Homicide Law reform project begun by the Law Commission. It drew not only on the Law Commission Report on *Murder Manslaughter and Infanticide* (2006) No 304, but also the Law Commission's Report No 305 *Participating in Crime* (2007).

[267] This outcome is the one that Lord Parker thought would 'revolt the conscience of people today': *Morris* [1966] 2 QB 110, 120.

[268] [2008] UKHL 45.

[269] ibid [26].

[270] [2010] EWCA Crim 516.

[271] [2010] EWCA Crim 1622.

[272] See *Lewis* [2010] EWCA Crim 496; Lord Bingham emphasized this in *Rahman* at [26].

[273] [2009] EWCA Crim 930.

[274] At [57].

[275] At [68]. It is unclear whether his lordship thought himself merely to be describing the law as previously declared. His lordship uses the expression 'restatement'. The Ministry of Justice, *Murder Manslaughter and Infanticide* CP 19/08 (2008) regard this as a 'step in the right direction' at para 101. See also Buxton [2009] Crim LR 330 above.

anything foreseen by D. [The italicized words are in the original and designed to reflect the English qualification.][276]

Arguably the redefinition is too harsh on D: the fundamental difference plea is available only if there is a change of weapon (or the use of a weapon when none at all was contemplated).[277] With respect, it is doubtful whether that can be right. In *Attorney-General's Reference (No 3 of 2004)*,[278] the fundamental change was P firing the very weapon, of which D was well aware, *at* V rather than *near* V.

It is submitted that according to the House in *Rahman* the fundamentally different plea is likely to succeed only:

(i)   if there is a change of weapon (or the use of a weapon when none at all was contemplated).

(ii) in cases where D was unaware of the weapon which P uses to kill V. This is controversial. The courts have not previously gone as far as holding that as a matter of law D is precluded from relying on the qualification if he was aware that P had the weapon. Why should D who is aware that P has a weapon but does not foresee the possibility that P might use it be in a worse position than D who is unaware of the weapon? The only answer is one of policy: the message is clear – do not associate with those carrying weapons. In practical terms, the ramifications of this restriction are significant.

(iii) if the weapon used by P is different from that D foresaw might be used *and* more 'lethal'.[279]

(iv) if *because of* the change of weapon and its more lethal nature P's act may be regarded as fundamentally different. Thus, not every killing by P with an unforeseen weapon of a more lethal nature will necessarily amount to a fundamentally different act.[280]

Weapons

In practice, the question whether a weapon might render P's acts fundamentally different generates some of the most difficult issues in murder cases.[281] Great importance has always been attached to whether D knew when assisting in the commission of crime X that P was carrying the weapon with which crime Y was committed.[282]

If D knew,[283] that is cogent evidence that D contemplated an act of the kind done. But it is only evidence.[284] Applying the test laid down by Lord Brown in *Rahman*, it would seem that

---

[276] [2008] UKHL 45 Lord Neuberger agreed [72] as did Lord Scott [31] (although Lord Scott earlier in that paragraph stated that if the death of V is a foreseeably possible consequence D should be liable no matter what weapon was used).

[277] See Lord Rodger at [47]; Lord Brown at [68], Lord Neuberger [88] (although his lordship was more flexible [102]).

[278] [2005] EWCA Crim 1882.

[279] Per Lord Brown at [68] see also Lord Neuberger at [88]–[89] describing the weapon as 'different and more lethal.' cf Lord Scott who regarded it as beside the point whether D may not have known the killer had been carrying the weapon actually used: [31].

[280] See also the comments of Lord Hutton in *English*.

[281] See, eg, *Greatrex* [1999] 1 Cr App R 126, CA. For jury to decide if kicking with 'a shod foot', which was contemplated by D, was fundamentally different from striking with a bar or spanner, which was not contemplated.

[282] For a recent example where D's denial was of knowledge of the weapon see *Parsons* [2009] EWCA Crim 64.

[283] See the comments in *ABCD* [2010] EWCA Crim 1622. The prosecution is obliged to prove knowledge, which can not be inferred from, eg, the closeness of D and P and their having been together for the hours prior to the attack in which P used a knife: *Parchment* [2003] EWCA Crim 2428.

[284] *Roberts* [1993] 1 All ER 583 at 590.

the fundamental difference plea might *only* succeed when P uses a weapon that D was unaware of or a different one from the one that D was aware of. That seems to be a very narrow
view, as noted above. In more recent cases a welcome attempt has been made to refine this. In
Mendez and Thompson,[285] the Court of Appeal accepted as sound in principle the argument
of the appellant's counsel:

In cases where the common purpose is not to kill but to cause serious harm, D is not liable for the
murder of V if the direct cause of V's death was a deliberate act by P which was of a kind (a) unforeseen by D and (b) likely to be altogether more life-threatening than acts of the kind intended or
foreseen by D.... The reference to 'a deliberate act' is to the quality of the act – deliberate and not
by chance – rather than to any consideration of P's intention as to the consequences.[286]

The court emphasized 'what matters is not simply the difference in weapon but the way in
which it is likely to be used and the degree of injury which it is likely to cause'.[287] Although the
court states its desire to avoid putting a gloss on *Rahman*, it is respectfully submitted that that
is precisely what it has done. Prosecution advocates may well seek to argue that Lord Brown's
statement in *Rahman* is what binds trial judges.

   The difference in outcome of the approach in *Mendez* as compared to that in *Rahman* can
be seen by considering the decision of Carswell J in the Northern Irish case of *Gamble*.[288] D,
who agreed to participate in 'kneecapping' V with a gun, was not guilty of murder when P cut
V's throat with a knife – an act D had not foreseen. There was a change of weapon, action and
intention. In *Powell and Daniels* and *English*, Lord Hutton approved the decision, but added:
'whether a secondary party who foresees the use of a gun to kneecap, and death is then caused
by the deliberate firing of the gun into the head or body of the victim, is guilty of murder is
more debatable...'[289] If D foresaw that P might use the gun in this way, then he would certainly
be liable; but otherwise, surely not. Their lordships again returned to *Gamble* as a 'hard case'
in *Rahman*. Lord Brown considered the case to 'stretch to breaking point' the fundamental
difference principle. Lords Scott, Brown and Neuberger queried whether Carswell J's ruling in
Gamble was correct. Lord Roger took the view[290] that *Gamble* turned on its own special facts:

involving a situation where the two defendants could point to a definite limited purpose for which
they contemplated that violence would be used... In effect... it was as if the two defendants whom he
acquitted of murder had been about to kneecap the victim when two other men suddenly emerged
from the undergrowth and cut his throat...

Lords Bingham and Rodger regarded the throat cutting as 'of an entirely different character
in an entirely different context'.[291] If the act in *Gamble* is fundamentally different what makes
it so? Is it the increased likely lethality of the act?[292] 'Kneecapping', abominable though it is, is
unlikely to cause death, whereas blowing a man's brains out is certain to do so. D should not
be liable (for murder or manslaughter) simply because he foresaw the use of a gun with the
intention of causing non-lethal grievous bodily harm in the course of the venture and a gun
was used.[293] If the test in *Mendez* is applied, the question would be whether the *acts* of throat

---

[285] [2010] EWCA Crim 516.

[286] [2010] EWCA Crim 516 [44]–[47]. I am enormously grateful to counsel – Mr Adrian Waterman QC for
discussions on this and other aspects of joint enterprise liability.

[287] [42] per Toulson LJ.

[288] [1989] NI 268, NI Crown Court.

[289] [1997] 4 All ER 565h–j.

[290] At [40].

[291] [29]. Lord Rodger points out that it is unusual since D knew the limited purpose of P's intended violence.

[292] *Mendez* might support that approach.

[293] A conclusion approved in *Rahman* in the CA. In an unreported pre-*English* case, *Wei*, 96/5461/W3,
25 July 1997, five members of a Triad gang set out, four intending to murder V, the fifth, S, believing that the

slitting were fundamentally different from what D had foreseen. They surely are and D would be likely to be acquitted.

Particular problems arise if P arms himself in the course of the enterprise (for example, with a kitchen knife at the scene of the burglary). D may not have foreseen or be aware of P's possession of such a weapon.[294] Consider another difficult case. In *Webb*[295] D had master-minded a team of burglars, P1 and P2 etc, and sent them out to burgle the house of an elderly man. D knew that P1 was armed with screwdrivers and a knife and was a 'nutter' prone to violence. P killed V by stuffing a handkerchief in his mouth on which V suffocated. D's conviction was upheld on the basis that this was not an act of a fundamentally different kind from that D foresaw. He foresaw that P1 might commit gbh to silence V.

Actions

In terms of actions, cases such as *Mendez* and the *A-G's Reference (No 3 of 2004)*[296] demonstrate that the 'acts' of P have to be read to include the circumstances in which they were performed. It was not enough that D foresaw that P might pull the trigger of a gun. If P was firing it *at*[297] V that was fundamentally different from firing it into the air to frighten V. Even applying *Mendez*, it will be difficult for juries to ascertain how dangerous P's act was foreseen as likely to be. The dangerousness only makes sense if one asks how about the weapon to be used and the intent. It is unclear what factors will alter the nature of the act – what for example if P's attack is racially motivated and that was unforeseen by D.[298]

D's foresight of consequences of P's acts

In terms of foresight of consequences, whether D foresees the possible consequences of P's acts, might they occur, can be important. Consider the following case, P administers to V a particular drug, call it XYZ, which P knows is certain to kill, and is assisted and encouraged by D who knows the drug is XYZ but believes[299] XYZ's only effect will be to give V a headache. V is killed. P is guilty of murder. D is not guilty of murder. Whether D is guilty of manslaughter depends on whether the act done by P was 'fundamentally different' from any act contemplated by D. The administration of a deadly drug is fundamentally different from the administration of a drug which will cause mere discomfort. If the drug administered by P were a different drug – PQR – the answer, it is submitted, would be clear – D is not liable for the consequences of that unforeseen and fundamentally different act. Should it be different where D's mistake or ignorance relates not to the identity of the thing but to

common intention was only to frighten him, but by the firing of a loaded shotgun. When V was shot dead, the four were convicted of murder and S of manslaughter. The jury were not satisfied that S was aware of a real risk that the gun would be fired with intent to kill, S's conviction was upheld: he had 'authorized' the use of a loaded gun. But, surely, firing a gun at a person is fundamentally different from firing over his head in order to frighten him; and, if that is so, S was not responsible for that unforeseen act: *Bamborough* [1996] Crim LR 744 is similar.

[294] See C [2002] EWCA Crim 3154.
[295] [2006] EWCA Crim 962. cf *Daniel* [2007] UKPC 39, killing by 'bonfire rather than by gunfire' as D anticipated not outside the scope of the joint enterprise.
[296] [2005] EWCA Crim 1882, [2006] Crim LR 63.
[297] In *Rahman* [2007] 2 Cr App R 16, the Court of Appeal stated (at [43]) that in *A-G's Reference (No 3 of 2004)* what made the shooting of V a fundamentally different act was that the gun was deliberately fired at V and not that P must have intended to kill. It is the firing at V that makes it fundamentally different as Hooper LJ, who presided in the *Reference*, confirmed in *Rahman* (at [43]).
[298] See LCCP 177, para 5.37.
[299] Arguably, the differing levels of awareness of D and P might indicate whether there was a common purpose or not.

its attributes? If P and D had both believed that the only effect of XYZ was to cause a head-ache, then both would certainly be guilty of manslaughter. D has agreed to and assisted the mischievous act which caused death. He has not agreed to or foreseen a murderous act which causes death.[300]

Remember that where D and P have a shared purpose *to kill* V, the nature of the weapon used cannot matter.[301] If they have agreed that P should shoot V dead, and P cuts his throat or strangles him, D should be guilty of murder.[302]

D's foresight of P's mens rea

Following *Rahman*, it is now clear that for the crime of murder if D has foreseen that in the course of committing crime X, P might cause intentional gbh (crime Y), and P uses gbh with intent to kill, that change will not constitute a fundamental change. D remains liable for murder. Lord Bingham advanced two reasons against P's change of *mens rea* constituting a fundamental change. First, as practical matter it would avoid the law of joint enterprise becoming yet more complex and difficult for the jury, particularly in the typically fluid, fast-moving course of events. It is already hard enough for jurors to determine what D's subjective foresight of what P's future state of mind might be.[303] Secondly, drawing a distinction based on whether D foresaw P intending to kill or merely intending gbh is illogical since it is sufficient for P's *mens rea* for murder that P either intended to kill or to cause really serious injury.[304]

D's liability if D did not foresee that P might do an act of that kind

What should D's liability be if P has acted in a fundamentally different manner than that D foresaw? If P committed a crime (Y) that was fundamentally different from anything D had foreseen that he might, D is not guilty of that offence. What more commonly occurs is that P commits murder (crime Y) in the course of the joint enterprise to commit crime X. If D did not foresee that P might kill V with intent to kill or do gbh, can D be liable for actual bodily harm that he did foresee that P might intentionally commit? If P's conduct was not of a kind that D foresaw, D is entitled to an acquittal. If on the other hand D foresaw that P might engage in violent conduct but did not foresee that P might do so with *mens rea* for murder, D is liable for manslaughter. Stated as a matter of general principle, if the offence that P commits has the same *actus reus* as the one that D foresaw P might commit, but P's *mens rea* was greater than D foresaw, D can be liable as an accessory to the lesser offence that D foresaw P might commit.

In *Yemoh*[305] the Court of Appeal confirmed that P's greater *mens rea* from that which D foresaw will not prevent D being guilty of manslaughter. D, a member of the gang, knew

---

[300] Professor Taylor raises cogent objections, discussed by JC Smith in 'Commentary on *Day*' [2001] Crim LR 984: D's liability for manslaughter might depend on the prosecution proving that P did not have the *mens rea* for murder; and that, if the jury were not sure that P had the *mens rea* of murder and convicted him only of manslaughter, they could not be sure that D was guilty of manslaughter and would have to acquit him altogether.

[301] As confirmed in *Yemoh* [2009] EWCA Crim 930 and in *Mendez and Thompson* [2010] EWCA Crim 516 where the court drew on wide ranging sources from Foster's *Crown Law*, Criminal Law Commissioner's Reports of the 19th Century and the Indian Penal Code.

[302] cf Lord Hutton in *Powell* [1997] 4 All ER 566e–f.

[303] [24].

[304] [25]. In *O'Brien* [1995] 2 Cr App R 649. D's conviction for attempted murder was upheld only because he knew P might shoot *with intent* to kill.

[305] [2009] EWCA Crim 930. See also *Parsons* [2008] EWCA Crim 2693. The doctrine operates very harshly in manslaughter since D is liable for uncontemplated consequences (death) from an act he foresaw.

that another member of the gang, P, had a knife and intended that other to cause some injury to V or realized that he might cause some injury. The fact that P stabbed V *intending to kill* (ie with graver *mens rea*) did not absolve D.[306] If D intended or foresaw that one of the group might cause non-serious injury, D remains liable for manslaughter even if P kills with intent to kill or do gbh, unless P's manner of doing so is fundamentally different from that D foresaw.

The difficulty in such cases is well illustrated by the Northern Irish case of *Gilmour*,[307] D drove P to a place where he knew P intended to petrol-bomb a house. Petrol bombs, surprisingly, rarely cause injury to the person but this was an exceptionally large bomb which caused a great conflagration and three deaths. The lethal nature of the bomb satisfied the judge (in a 'Diplock' court – that is, one without a jury) that P intended, not merely to cause serious injury but to kill, that is, P must have known that it was virtually certain to do so. There was, however, no evidence that D was aware that this was not an 'ordinary' bomb. P was obviously guilty of murder and the judge convicted D as well on the ground that, knowing that the family was to be petrol-bombed, he remained near the scene in his car to enable P to escape. D's conviction for murder was quashed but a conviction for manslaughter substituted on the ground that a 'person acting as an accessory to a principal who carries out the very deed contemplated by both [is] guilty of the degree of offence appropriate to the intent with which he so acted.'[308] On the facts, it is submitted that it is difficult to see that the use of the big bomb was the 'very deed' contemplated by D. In an English (as opposed to a 'Diplock') court, it would have to be left to the jury to say whether they were satisfied that P's act was not fundamentally different from that contemplated by D. It seems unlikely that they would find that an act that was virtually certain to kill was not fundamentally different from one that was unlikely to cause injury, or that such a finding could be upheld.[309]

8.5.3 Spontaneous behaviour and joint enterprise

Do these same principles of joint enterprise apply in relation to spontaneous conduct by D and P? 'Joint enterprise' might be thought to suggest a planned offence, but it is clear from the authorities that the principles expounded above are readily applicable to the spontaneous conduct of two or more without pre-planning – usually an attack on person or property. The law is the same: *Greatrex*.[310] In *Mendez*[311] it was confirmed that the principles which apply to a pre-planned joint enterprise apply equally to a spontaneous joint enterprise.[312]

8.5.4 Liability for unforeseen consequences

It is by now obvious from the foregoing discussion that, where D is liable for an act done by P, D is liable for the unforeseen *consequences* of that act to the same extent as the law imposes

---

[306] This follows *Rahman* [2008] UKHL 45; cf the CA decision at [2007] EWCA Crim 342.

[307] [2000] NI 367, [2000] Crim LR 763, NI CA.

[308] Per Carswell LCJ, applying the principle stated (by Professor Richard Taylor) in *Blackstone* (2001) para A5.5.

[309] The criticism of the case in the 10th edition of this book was cited with approval in the case of *Van Hoogstraaten* (2 Dec 2003), CCC (Sir Stephen Mitchell). See also *Jairan* [2005] UKPC 19.

[310] *Greatrex*, above, at 138. Beldam LJ made a similar analysis in *Uddin* [1998] 2 All ER 744 at 751. See also *McCarthy* [2003] EWCA Crim 484, and *Reid* [2005] EWCA Crim 595.

[311] [2010] EWCA Crim 516

[312] See also *Greatrex* [1999] 1 Cr App R 126.

liability on P. In constructive crimes this extends liability significantly. For example, D foresees that P may do an act with intent to cause grievous bodily harm. P does so and kills: both are guilty of murder even if neither foresaw the possibility of death.[313] In manslaughter, the harshness is acute: D is liable for the uncontemplated consequences (death) of an act he didn't contemplate (eg stamping on V's head with intent to kill) albeit he would have been liable for the uncontemplated consequences (death) of an act he did contemplate (*mere injury* by beating) but which was never committed.[314]

If two persons participate in an event, but it is not proved that each intends to assist or encourage the other, neither is liable for acts done by the other which he did not assist or encourage the other to commit: *Petters and Parfitt*.[315] If one or other of them caused injury or death but it is not possible to prove which, neither can be convicted. If, however, D intentionally assists P, even without P's knowledge, D will be liable for the crime which he intended to assist P to commit and, it is submitted, any crime committed by P which D foresaw P might commit.

8.5.5 The significance of joint enterprise in murder

The consequences of the parasitic liability principle in joint enterprise are especially significant in a case of murder. Once it has been proved that a murder was committed, even if the principal cannot be identified, the fact that the jury cannot be sure which of the members of a group delivered the fatal blow does not prevent murder convictions for all or any members of the joint enterprise who foresaw that intentional gbh might occur: *Rahman*.[316]

There is a strongly held view that the present law is too strict[317] 'to hold D liable for murder on the foresight of a possibility is fundamentally unjust'.[318] The general public have also expressed unease with the position as demonstrated by the recent research conducted by Professors Mitchell and Roberts.[319]

D may be liable for an offence requiring proof of an intention on the part of the principal offender, P, although D is only reckless about P's likely intentional conduct. Recklessness whether death be caused is a sufficient *mens rea* for manslaughter but not for murder; yet D may be convicted if D is reckless as to whether P might intentionally perpetrate the conduct element of the *actus reus* of murder. This is certainly a controversial point; but D must foresee P's *intentional* act: recklessness *whether the conduct element of the offence of murder be committed* is a different and more culpable state of mind than recklessness *whether death be caused* – a point which was regarded as persuasive by Lord Steyn in *Powell and Daniels*.[320]

---

[313] However, there is, to the contrary, a single sentence in the speech of Lord Steyn in *Powell and Daniels, English* [1999] 1 AC 1, 14: 'it is just that a secondary party who foresees that the primary offender might *kill* with the intent sufficient for murder and assists and encourages the primary offender in the criminal enterprise on this basis, should be guilty of murder' (emphasis added). This implies that D, if he is to be convicted of murder, must foresee that the consequence element of murder might materialize. However, this contradicts *Chan Wing-siu* and is definitely not part of the *ratio* of *Powell and Daniels, English*. Thanks to Richard Taylor for this.

[314] See *Yemoh* above.

[315] [1995] Crim LR 501. cf *Mohan* [1967] 2 AC 187, PC.

[316] [2008] UKHL 45. See also *ABCD* [2010] EWCA Crim 1622 rightly rejecting a misreading of *Rahman* that D's foresight of P's mens rea was irrelevant in all cases. This was a misreading of *Rahman* predicted in the Commentary on that case in the Crim LR.

[317] An argument that it violated Art 6 of the ECHR was firmly rejected in *Concannon* [2002] Crim LR 211.

[318] Kirby J dissenting in *Clayton* (2006) HCA 58 at [108].

[319] *Public Survey of the Mandatory Life Sentence for Murder* (2010).

[320] [1997] 4 All ER at 550–551.

Some argue that D should not be held liable because he foresaw that P *might* do the act with intent in question, but only if he foresaw that P *would* do that act with that intent. This was the effect of some cases[321] decided after *Hancock* and *Nedrick*[322] but they seem to have been based on a misunderstanding of the effect of decisions on the *mens rea* of the principal in murder, which do not affect the principles of secondary liability. A further misunderstanding by some of the critics was that *Chan Wing-Siu* made the law stricter. On the contrary, it seems that the earlier common law rule was that an accessory to crime was liable, not only for that crime which he incited and encouraged, but also for any other crime committed by the principal that was a *probable* consequence of what he ordered or advised – an objective test.[323] In *Chan Wing-siu*, the Crown acknowledged that the test was subjective.[324] The issue was a narrow one: whether it was sufficient that D foresaw that P 'might well' do the fatal act, or that they must prove that he foresaw that it was more probable than not, as the appellant argued.[325] The Privy Council decided in favour of the Crown – it is sufficient that D foresaw that P 'might well' do the fatal act.

8.5.6 The underlying basis of joint enterprise liability?[326]

The courts have struggled in recent years in defining the scope of liability for an accessory where the principal offender has committed offences other than the most immediate one that D has assisted or encouraged. In part this is because of a failure to identify its underlying basis. It is submitted that although alternative approaches to 'joint enterprise', or 'joint venture liability'[327] have been postulated, the English courts have persistently adopted, albeit sometimes without discussion, the approach that joint enterprise is governed by the rules of secondary liability. This is expressly stated in a number of recent cases. As Hughes LJ explained in *ABCD*:[328]

It is necessary to remember that guilt based upon common enterprise is a form of *secondary* liability. The principle is that D is implicated in the guilt of P not only for the agreed crime X but for the further crime Y which he foresaw P might commit in the course of X. This form of liability therefore arises only where P has committed the further crime Y.[329]

In the House of Lords in *Powell and Daniels, English*, their lordships consistently treated parties to the joint enterprise as accessories. In *Rook*[330] it was held that the same ordinary principles of secondary liability apply to a party who is absent as to one who is present – and

---

[321] *Barr* (1986) 88 Cr App R 362; *Smith* [1988] Crim LR 616 and see David Poole QC, 'Letter to the Editor – Joint Enterprise and Intent: A Comment' [1989] Crim LR 236.

[322] Above, p 109.

[323] Foster, 370; Stephen, *Digest* (4th edn) art 20, Smith, *A Modern Treatise on Complicity*, 210–214.

[324] This has been reiterated in *ABCD* [2010] EWCA Crim 1620.

[325] On the problems with a 'probability' see *Darkan v The Queen* [2006] HCA 34 (High Ct of A).

[326] JC Smith, 'Criminal Liability of Accessories: Law and Law Reform' (1997) 113 LQR 453; J Burchell, 'Joint Enterprise and Common Purpose' (1997) 10 SACJ 125; cf A Simester, 'The Mental Element in Complicity' (2006) 122 LQR 578. B Krebb (2010) 73 MLR 578 offers discussion of a range of interpretations, suggesting it is *sui generis* and is an exculpatory doctrine seeking to limit the scope of D's liability.

[327] As LC 305 titles it.

[328] [2010] EWCA Crim 1622 (with lettering altered).

[329] [37].

[330] [1993] 2 All ER 955; *Wan and Chan* [1995] Crim LR 296.

rightly so, because the absent party may well be the 'mastermind' and the most culpable party.[331]

An alternative theory to the orthodoxy of treating joint enterprise cases as ones of secondary liability appeared in the Law Commission's Consultation Paper No 131, 'Assisting and Encouraging Crime',[332] and in *Stewart and Schofield*.[333] This novel theory is that a party to a joint enterprise is different from a 'mere aider or abettor, etc' or accessory. Distinguishing secondary participation, Hobhouse LJ said: 'In contrast, where the allegation is joint enterprise, the allegation is that one defendant participated in the criminal act of another'.[334] But this theory presents problems, if D and P set out together to rape (or to murder),[335] how does D 'participate' in P's act of penile penetration of V (or P's shooting V) except by assisting him or encouraging him – that is, aiding, abetting, counselling or procuring him – to do the act? It is submitted there is no other way. The only peculiarity of joint enterprise cases is that, once D has been shown to be aiding abetting counselling or procuring P in the commission of crime X, there is no need to look further for evidence of assisting and encouraging in relation to crime Y. It is simply necessary to apply the ordinary principles of secondary liability to the joint enterprise.[336]

Lord Hobhouse has written, extra-judicially, criticizing[337] the opinion that the law of joint enterprise is an application of the principles of accessory liability. He argues that the true basis is the civil law concept of agency which is also part of the criminal law: the party who does the deed (the principal in criminal law) is the agent of the others. Sometimes this is true, as where B and C hire P, a 'contract killer', to do the deed. But if P decides to commit murder and recruits B, C and D for reward to assist him by providing a weapon, driving him to and from the scene and keeping watch, it seems quite inaccurate to describe P as the agent of B, C and D. They are his agents. P is here the principal in the civil as well as in the criminal law. B, C and D are rightly held responsible for P's act; but their responsibility is surely not explicable on the ground that P is their agent. They are responsible because they aided and abetted him.

Professors Simester and Sullivan also advanced a theory that joint enterprise liability is to be distinguished from the ordinary principles of secondary liability. They argue that the joint enterprise liability arises from the collaboration or confederacy of the individuals in embarking on a criminal enterprise.[338] There is no English authority, apart from *Stewart and Schofield*, to support to this approach. Moreover, it is not clear that it assists in understanding or applying the law in all situations. First, it would require a distinction to be drawn between cases where D and P have a shared purpose to commit crime X and those cases where there

[331] Cf the view of the Law Commission that this case has been given a status it does not warrant: LC 305, para B.120.

[332] Criticized by JC Smith, 'Secondary Participation in Crime – Can We Do Without It?' (1994) 144 New LJ 679.

[333] [1995] 1 Cr App R 441, [1995] Crim LR 420 and commentary.

[334] Hobhouse LJ returned to this theme in a civil proceeding, *Crédit Lyonnais Bank Nederland NV v Export Credits Guarantee Department* [1998] 1 Lloyd's Rep 19 at 42–44. The effect seems to be the same as the opinion in *Osland*, above, n 19, that all the parties to a joint enterprise are principals in the first degree. The Australian approach is considered by the High Court in *McAuliffe v The Queen* (1995) 183 CLR 108 and *Gillard v The Queen* [2003] HCA 64, paras 108–113; *Clayton* (2006) HCA 58, although note Kirby J's powerful dissent. See also NSW Law Reform Commission Consultation Paper No 2, *Complicity* (2008).

[335] There is no justification for limiting the joint enterprise principles to murder, cf the statement in *Bryce* that it arises when 'two persons have already embarked upon and actually engaged in a course of criminal conduct in the course of which someone is killed', para 29, is too narrow.

[336] This passage in the last edition of this work was approved by the Court of Appeal in *Mendez* [2010] EWCA Crim 516.

[337] 'Agency and the Criminal Law', in *Lex Mercatoria (Essays in Honour of Francis Reynolds)* (2000).

[338] See A Simester and GR Sullivan CLT&D (2007), 228.

is no such shared purpose. As discussed above,[339] the cases – *Reardon, Mendez, ABCD*, etc – do not draw such a distinction. Second, it would only apply where two crimes are in issue, crime X – the one D assists P to commit – and crime Y, the one P goes on to commit separately. Presumably, until crime Y is commenced, the case is treated as one of normal aiding and abetting, but only after the second crime is committed does the joint enterprise label retrospectively apply. In terms of practicality, the approach would render an already very complex area yet more so.

The Law Commission reviewed the orthodox approach advanced here and that of Simester and Sullivan and concluded that the differences between the views did not in practice produce 'sufficiently significant differences' to matter[340] But preferred Simester and Sullivan's. The Court of Appeal has now firmly rejected that approach: *ABCD* (above).

8.6 Secondary participation and inchoate offences

It is an offence to do acts capable of assisting or encouraging,[341] or to conspire, or to attempt, to commit an offence.[342] It is *not* an offence to attempt[343] or, it is submitted, to conspire[344] to do an act which would involve no more than secondary liability for the offence if it were committed.

Secondary liability is triggered by the commission of the substantive principal offence. Knowing that P intends to drive his car, D2 urges D1 to 'lace' P's drink with so much alcohol that if P drives after consuming the drink he will inevitably commit an offence under s 5(1) of the Road Traffic Act 1988.[345] D1 agrees to do so and attempts to, or does, lace the drink. If P consumes the drink, drives his car and thus commits the offence under the Road Traffic Act 1988, D2 and D1 will be guilty as secondary parties;[346] but if P declines the drink, or does not drive the car, D2 is not guilty of conspiracy and D1 is guilty neither of conspiracy nor of attempt to commit the offence. The act encouraged, agreed upon, attempted and indeed done, lacing the drink, is not the offence.[347] D may be liable under the SCA 2007, s 44.

Assuming that P consumes the laced drink and drives, P could be guilty as the principal offender, notwithstanding his lack of *mens rea*, on the ground that the offence is one of strict liability. Where the offence is one requiring *mens rea*, which the actual perpetrator of the *actus reus* lacks, then those who procured him to act will be liable because they, or one of them, will be principal offenders.

In the case of conspiracy, one who abets or counsels the commission of the crime appears to be a principal offender in the conspiracy. It is also possible to abet or counsel an attempt.[348]

---

[339] At 217 et seq.

[340] See LC 305, para 3.56.

[341] The SCA 2007 replaced common law incitement with three statutory inchoate offences of assisting or encouraging in ss 44–46.

[342] Ch 13, below.

[343] Criminal Attempts Act 1981, s 1(4)(b); *Dunnington* [1984] QB 472 [1984] Crim LR 98, CA. cf *Chief Constable of Hampshire v Mace* (1986) 84 Cr App R 40, [1986] Crim LR 752. See the recent debate between M Bohlander and J Child in [2009] Crim LR, discussed below Ch 13, p 421.

[344] *Kenning* [2008] EWCA Crim 1534 ; *Hollinshead* [1985] 1 All ER 850 at 857–858, CA. The House of Lords left the question open: [1985] AC 975, [1985] 2 All ER 769. See JC Smith, 'Secondary Participation and Inchoate Offences', in *Crime, Proof and Punishment*, 21.

[345] Driving or being in charge of a motor vehicle with an alcohol concentration above a prescribed limit.

[346] *A-G's Reference (No 1 of 1975)*, above, p 191.

[347] The adulteration of the drink might possibly amount to the administration of a noxious thing, contrary to the Offences Against the Person Act 1861, s 24, below, Ch 17.

[348] *Hapgood and Wyatt* (1870) LR 1 CCR 221, CCR; *S v Robinson* 1968 (1) SA 666.

For the scope of D's liability for assisting or encouraging P to assist or encourage P2, see Chapter 13.

8.7 Conviction of secondary party and acquittal of principal offender/no principal

Even if the alleged principal offender has been acquitted, a conviction of another as an accessory may be logical. This is so even if it is assumed[349] that an accessory may be convicted only when the principal offender himself is guilty. The acquittal of the alleged principal offender, so far from being conclusive that no crime was committed, is not even admissible in evidence at a subsequent trial of the secondary parties.[350] A second jury may be satisfied beyond reasonable doubt that the crime was committed upon evidence which the first jury found unconvincing; evidence may be admissible against D which was not admissible against P, or fresh evidence may have come to light or P may have been acquitted because the prosecution offered no evidence against him.

The position would seem to be the same where D is tried first and convicted and P is subsequently acquitted[351] and when the parties are jointly indicted.[352] In *Hughes*,[353] after the prosecution had offered no evidence against P, he was acquitted and called as a witness for the Crown, with the result that D was convicted by the same jury as an accessory to P's alleged crime. Where principal and secondary parties are tried separately, this result is supported by the analogous rule laid down in *DPP v Shannon*[354] that the acquittal of one party to a conspiracy does not invalidate the conviction of the only other party on an earlier or later occasion. *Shannon* left open the question whether the one party may be convicted of conspiracy when the other is acquitted at the same trial;[355] and in *Anthony*[356] it was said, *obiter*, that a jury cannot acquit P and at the same time find D guilty of counselling him to commit the crime.

If P and D are tried together and the evidence tending to show that P committed the crime is the same against both, then it would be inconsistent to acquit P and convict D.[357] Where, however, there is evidence admissible against D but not against P that P committed the crime (as, for example, a confession by D that he counselled P to commit the crime and saw him commit it) it would be perfectly logical to acquit P and convict D of counselling him (and of conspiring with him). In *Humphreys and Turner*,[358] which was just such a case, Chapman J held that D might be convicted as an accessory, distinguishing the *dicta* in *Anthony* as applicable only to felonies. It is submitted that, ever since the Criminal Law Act 1967 came into force, the rule stated in *Humpheys and Turner* is applicable to all offences.

[349] Contrary to the view expressed below, p 834.

[350] *Hui Chi-ming v R* [1991] 3 All ER 897, PC. Under the Police and Criminal Evidence Act 1984, s 74, a conviction is now admissible to prove the commission of the offence by the principal: *Turner* [1991] Crim LR 57.

[351] In *Rowley* [1948] 1 All ER 570, D's conviction was quashed when, after he had pleaded guilty as an accessory, the alleged principals were acquitted by the jury. But the decision is criticized in *Shannon* [1974] 2 All ER 1009 at 1020 and 1049; below n 354. cf *Zaman* [2010] EWCA Crim, below, Ch 9, p 248.

[352] See also *Petch* [2005] 2 Cr App R 657.

[353] (1860) Bell CC 242.

[354] [1975] AC 717 HL; below, Ch 12.

[355] The point is now settled by the Criminal Law Act 1977, and *Longman and Cribben* (1980) 72 Cr App R 121, below, p 446; but *Shannon* is relevant to the common law governing secondary participation.

[356] [1965] 2 QB 189. cf *Surujpaul v R* [1958] 3 All ER 300 at 302–303.

[357] *Surujpaul v R* [1958] 3 All ER 300, [1958] 1 WLR 1050.

[358] [1965] 3 All ER 689 (Liverpool Crown Court). Followed in *Sweetman v Industries and Commerce Department* [1970] NZLR 139. cf *Davis* [1977] Crim LR 542, CA and commentary and *Fuller* [1998] Crim LR 61.

It is one thing for a court which is trying D alone to reject or ignore the holding of another court that P was not a principal offender and to hold that he was; and that, therefore, D might be convicted as an accessory to P's crime. It is quite another thing for a court to hold at one and the same time: (i) that P was, in law, not guilty[359] and (ii) that D was guilty, as a secondary party, of P's crime. These propositions seem, at first sight, to be inconsistent with the derivative nature of secondary liability.[360]

8.7.1 Secondary party guilty of a greater offence than the principal

Since secondary liability is said to derive from that of the principal offender, it is hard to see how the liability of the secondary party can properly be held to be greater than that of the principal offender. Historically,[361] distinctions were drawn based on the presence at the crime and it was thought that the liability of the accessory who was absent could never 'rise higher' than that of the principal offender. The distinctions depending on whether the accessory is present at, or absent from, the commission of the crime are no longer applicable.[362]

There are some cases where it seems obvious that a person who, at least, appears to be an accessory ought to be convicted of a greater offence than the immediate perpetrator of the *actus reus*. We have already noticed that offences may be committed through innocent agents and that if D, with intent to kill, sends a letter-bomb through the post to V who is killed by the explosion, D is guilty of murder as a principal offender and E, the postman, is an innocent agent. Suppose, however, that E notices some wires sticking out of the parcel and that he is aware that a number of letter-bombs have been sent by terrorists lately with fatal results. He thinks, 'This could be a letter-bomb – but it's not likely and I'm in a hurry, I'll risk it' and pushes the letter through V's letter box where it explodes and kills V. If these facts are proved, E behaved recklessly and is guilty of manslaughter. He is no longer an innocent agent. But it would be absurd if D who sent the letter with intent to kill should escape liability for murder.

Alternative approaches have been advanced by academics. Glanville Williams suggests that a person like our postman should be regarded as a semi-innocent agent.[363] Professor Kadish[364] prefers to say that D can properly be said to have caused V's death. Because P's actions are not 'fully voluntary' they do not break the chain of causation.[365] His approach explains the following difficult example:

[D] hands a gun to [P] informing him that it is loaded with blank ammunition only and telling him to go and scare [V] by discharging it. The ammunition is in fact live (as [D] knows) and [V] is killed. [P] is convicted only of manslaughter. . . . It would seem absurd that [D] should thereby escape conviction for murder.[366]

---

[359] Not merely that there was not enough evidence to convict him, but that there was evidence which established his innocence.

[360] Above, p 186.

[361] Hawkins 2 PC s 29, s 15.

[362] It depended on the distinction in the law of felonies between a principal in the second degree and an accessory which has been abolished.

[363] TBCL, 373.

[364] *Blame and Punishment* (1987) 183.

[365] eg P shoots at V, intending to kill but only wounds. D treats the wound recklessly and V dies of the maltreated wound. P and D have both caused V's death. P is guilty of murder and D of manslaughter. Both are principals.

[366] *Burke and Howe* [1986] QB 626 at 641–642, CA. Lord Mackay agreed with the CA who found this example convincing: [1987] AC 417, HL. See the similar examples in the 5th edition of this book, at 140.

P's act would be regarded by Kadish as not 'fully voluntary' because, through his ignorance of material facts, he was not fully aware of what he was doing or its consequences; so D has caused the death, intending to kill and is a principal murderer.[367]

For many years English law seemed to accept that D could not be liable for a more serious offence than P. This flowed from *Richards*,[368] which the Court of Appeal and Lord Mackay (in *Howe*) considered to be wrongly decided. D, a woman, hired P1 and P2 to beat up her husband 'bad enough to put him in hospital for a month'. She signalled to P1 and P2 when V left the house. They inflicted a wound upon V, not amounting to a serious injury. D was convicted of wounding with intent to cause grievous bodily harm but P1 and P2 were acquitted of that offence and convicted of the lesser offence of unlawful wounding. D's conviction was quashed and a conviction for unlawful wounding substituted.[369]

Richards was heavily criticized and, in view of the disapproval expressed in *Burke* (conjoined with *Howe* on appeal), though only *obiter*, may not be followed in future. It has some academic supporters.[370]

The anomaly of holding D liable for the greater offence is emphasized if it is supposed that V, by some unforeseeable mischance, had died of the slight injury inflicted by P1 and P2. This would have been manslaughter by P1 and P2. If D was guilty of the s 18 offence, it would follow logically that she was guilty of murder. It may be argued that this would be wrong (though she had the necessary *mens rea*), because no act was ever done with *intent thereby* to kill or cause serious bodily harm – there was no 'murderous act'. If, however, P1 and P2 had acted with intent to do serious bodily harm but succeeded in inflicting only a slight injury it would have been murder by all three if V had died of that. But then the act would have been done in pursuance of a joint enterprise to cause serious bodily harm. In fact there was no gbh committed and no charges of such. For that reason, though not for the reasons given, it may be that the decision in *Richards* was right after all.

The position is more straightforward where D and P both have the *mens rea* for the greater offence but P's liability is reduced for some reason to that of a lesser offence. If P causes the *actus reus* in carrying out the agreed plan but his liability is reduced 'for some reason special to himself',[371] such as loss of self control or diminished responsibility,[372] it seems clearly right that D should not be able to shelter behind P's personal exemption from liability for the greater offence.

In the case considered in *Burke* (conjoined with *Howe* on appeal), however, the reduction in P's liability did not depend on a personal consideration of this kind. P's defence was that he had agreed to shoot V out of fear of D, but that, when it came to the event, the gun went off accidentally. The killing was therefore unintentional and amounted to no more than manslaughter. The judge, following *Richards*, directed that, if the jury found P guilty only of manslaughter, then D could at most be guilty of manslaughter. The implication of the decision of the House is that this was wrong. It is submitted that it is correct; that the true position is that

---

[367] It is not so clear that the causation theory is a satisfactory explanation of the case where D intends the result and E is reckless whether he causes it – eg the postman case, above. It seems to be straining a bit to say that the postman's act is not 'fully voluntary'.

[368] [1974] QB 776 CA.

[369] This followed Hawkins view above n 36 It was assumed that, under the old law of felonies, D would have been an accessory and not a principal in the second degree. Above, p 232.

[370] Kadish ('Complicity and Causation' (1985) 73 Cal Law Rev 323 at 329) supports the *Richards* view arguing (i) that D did not cause the actions of P1 and P2 because they were not her unwitting instruments but chose to act freely as they did and (ii) she could not be held liable 'for an aggravated assault [ie an assault with intent to cause grievous bodily harm] that did not take place'.

[371] The phrase used by Lord Mackay in *Burke*, above, n 366.

[372] This case is covered by s 2(4) of the Homicide Act 1957. D's liability for murder is not affected by E's diminished responsibility. The Coroners and Justice Act 2009, s 54(8) applies the same rule to loss of self-control.

if P has gone beyond a merely preparatory act and is attempting to commit the crime when he 'accidentally' kills, both D and P are guilty of murder; but, if P is doing only a preparatory act when he happens to kill – he is driving to V's house with intent to blow it up when the bomb in his car goes off and kills V who has unexpectedly gone out for a walk – P is liable only for manslaughter and so is D. The killing which occurs is not the killing he intended, though the victim happens to be the same.[373]

8.7.2 Where the 'principal' is not guilty

Here we are concerned with cases where the immediate perpetrator of the *actus reus* is not guilty of the offence alleged and the offence is one which is incapable of being committed by a person as a principal offender acting through an innocent agent such as rape and other offences involving sexual intercourse, driving offences and bigamy (except where the bigamous marriage is by proxy). There are three possible situations:

(1) P has committed the *actus reus* of the offence with *mens rea* but has a defence;

(2) P has committed the *actus reus* but has no *mens rea*;

(3) P has not committed the *actus reus*.

Bourne[374]

D, by duress compelled his wife (P) to have sex with a dog. His conviction of abetting her to commit buggery was upheld although it was assumed that the wife, if she had been charged, would have been acquitted on the ground of coercion.[375] Sir Rupert Cross[376] argued that this was in accordance with principle because 'The wife committed the "*actus reus*" with the "*mens rea*" required by the definition of the crime in question and the husband participated in that "*mens rea*".' The wife had *mens rea* in the sense that she knew exactly what she was doing, though she was to be excused for doing it. According to some theorists, where the defence relied upon by the principal is excusatory, that does not preclude the accessory from being convicted.

Cogan and Leak[377]

D terrorized his wife, V, into submitting to sexual intercourse with P. P was convicted of rape and D of abetting him, but, on appeal, P's conviction had to be quashed because the jury had not been directed correctly, and it may have been that P lacked the *mens rea* as to V's consent. D's conviction was upheld but primarily on the ground that D was the principal offender acting through an innocent agent. The agency theory is misconceived. If it were right, a woman could be convicted of rape as the principal offender and it is plain that she cannot commit that offence; she does not have a penis. To suggest that D raped his wife V using P's penis is nonsense. The court's second reason was that D was rightly convicted as a procurer because V had been raped ('no one outside a court of law would say she had not been') and 'therefore the particulars of offence accurately stated what [D] had done, namely that he procured [P] to commit the offence'. But if P believed V was consenting, V had not, as a matter of law, been raped. If X's bike is taken from the place he left it by Y who owns an exactly similar model and thinks this is his, X, who has lost his bike for ever, reasonably believes it has been stolen, but he

---

[373] See commentary [1987] Crim LR 481 at 484.

[374] (1952) 36 Cr App R 125. See J Ll Edwards, 'Duress and Aiding and Abetting' (1953) 69 LQR 297; R Cross, 'Duress and Aiding and Abetting (A Reply)' (1953) 69 LQR 354.

[375] Below, p 375.

[376] (1953) 68 LQR 354.

[377] [1976] QB 217, [1975] Crim LR 584 and commentary.

is wrong. The court's distinguishing of *Walters v Lunt*[378] (trike not stolen goods because taken by a seven-year-old) was erroneous. If the hypothetical bike and trike were not stolen, and plainly they were not, V was not raped by P in *Cogan*. The court's opinion that D had procured not merely the *actus reus* but the offence of rape is wrong.

If a conviction is to be upheld in such a case – and policy and justice seem to require it[379] this could be on the ground that it is an offence to procure the commission of an *actus reus*; and this step was taken in *Millward*.[380] D instructed his employee, P, to drive on a road a vehicle which D knew, but P did not know, was in a dangerous condition. It was assumed that the *actus reus* of reckless driving was committed simply by the driving of the vehicle on the road. The condition of the vehicle resulted in a collision causing death. P was charged with causing death by reckless driving and D of abetting him. P was acquitted, D was convicted and his conviction upheld on the ground that he had procured the *actus reus*. This approach was advocated in the first seven editions of this book and it seems the best available to the courts; but there is force in the opinion of Kadish[381] that it 'at least technically... amounts to creating a new crime'. As there is no principal offender, there is no question of participation in the guilt of another or of 'secondary liability' and it becomes, in effect, a substantive offence to procure the commission of the *actus reus* of any crime.

Bourne, Cogan and Leak and *Millward* were all cases of alleged procuring and it is not certain whether the principle of *Millward* extends to other modes of secondary participation. Procuring is narrower than the other modes in that (i) it must be the cause of the conduct or circumstance element of the *actus reus* and, perhaps, (ii), it must be the procurer's purpose to cause the result – 'To procure means to produce by endeavour'[382] – but that may be too restrictive. Bourne and Leak were endeavouring to bring about the whole *actus reus*; but Millward, while he was 'endeavouring' to have the dangerous vehicle driven on the road, which was assumed to amount to reckless driving, was certainly not endeavouring to have anyone killed. If the driver had been guilty of reckless driving, then both he and Millward would certainly have been guilty of causing death by reckless driving; but it does not necessarily follow that Millward should be guilty of that offence when the driver is not guilty. If 'procure' does imply purpose and if the principle is limited to procuring, then he ought to have been convicted only of reckless driving and not of causing death. The cases may also be approached in terms of justification and excuse, although it is doubtful that this sheds any greater light on the issue – the principal offender in each case was acquitted on the basis of an excusing factor (duress or lack of *mens rea*), and according to the theory this does not preclude secondary liability.[383]

Morris v Tolman[384]

D was charged with abetting the owner of a vehicle in using that vehicle for a purpose for which the vehicle had not been licensed. The statute (the Roads Act 1920) was so phrased

---

[378] [1951] 2 All ER 645, below, p 979.

[379] The conduct may well be caught by the offences in the SCA 2007, ss 44–46.

[380] [1994] Crim LR 527. See RD Taylor, 'Complicity, Legal Scholarship and the Law of Unintended Consequences' (2009) 29 LS 1. In *DPP v K and B* [1997] 1 Cr App R 36, [1997] Crim LR 121, DC, the female procurers of 'rape' by an unidentified boy who may have been under 14, and may have been *doli incapax* (ie at that time incapable of committing the crime), were held guilty of rape. It was said that it would have been different if the unidentified boy had been, or may have been, under 10 because then there would have been no *actus reus* of rape. It is submitted that that is wrong. The *actus reus* was the voluntary penetration of the vagina by the penis, whatever the age of the boy.

[381] *Essays in Criminal Law*, 180.

[382] Above, p 195.

[383] See JC Smith, *Justifications and Excuses in Criminal Law* (1989); G Williams, 'Theory of Excuses' [1982] Crim LR 722, especially 735–738; Taylor [1983] Crim LR 656.

[384] [1923] 1 KB 166.

that the offence could be committed only by the licence-holder. It was held that, there being no evidence that the licence-holder, P, had used the vehicle for a purpose other than that for which it was licensed, D must be acquitted. Though he, in fact, had so used the vehicle, that was not an *actus reus*. Again, in *Thornton v Mitchell*,[385] D, a bus conductor, negligently signalled to the driver of his bus, P, to reverse. Two pedestrians, whom it was not possible for the driver to see, were knocked down and one of them killed. The driver having been acquitted of careless driving, it was held that the conductor must be acquitted of abetting. Again, there was no *actus reus*. The driver's acquittal shows that he committed no *actus reus*, for careless driving is a crime which requires no *mens rea* beyond an intention to drive and D could not be said to have driven the bus. There would have been no such obstacle in the way of convicting D for manslaughter. That would, at that time, simply have raised the question whether D's negligence was sufficiently great.[386]

Thornton and Mitchell was distinguished in *Millward* on the ground that there was no *actus reus* of careless driving in the former case. And in *Loukes*[387] where the facts were similar to those in *Millward*, D's conviction for procuring the offence of causing death by *dangerous* driving was quashed. The *actus reus* of dangerous driving[388] is more precisely defined and a condition of the liability of the driver, P, in this situation is that 'it would be obvious to a competent and careful driver that driving the vehicle in its current state would be dangerous'. The judge directed an acquittal of the driver on the ground that there was no evidence that the dangerous condition of the vehicle would have been obvious to a competent and careful driver. The conviction of Loukes, who was responsible for the maintenance of the vehicle, for procuring the commission of the offence, was quashed. There being no *actus reus*, he could not be held to have procured one.[389]

8.8 Withdrawal by a secondary party[390]

Where D has counselled P to commit a crime, or is present, aiding P in the commission of it, it may yet be possible for him to escape liability by withdrawal before P goes on to commit the crime. An effective withdrawal will not, however, affect any liability he may have already incurred for conspiracy, or, if the withdrawal took place after P had done a more than merely preparatory act,[391] attempt, to commit the crime.[392] It is important also to note that the Serious Crime Act offences in ss 44 to 46 allow for D to be prosecuted where he has done acts *capable of* assisting or encouraging P, irrespective of whether P commits any offence. Liability arises once D performs the acts capable of assisting or encouraging, irrespective of whether the acts do in fact assist or encourage. There is no withdrawal defence.

---

[385] [1940] 1 All ER 339. See Taylor [1983] Crim LR 656, and (2009) 29 LS 1.

[386] See above, Ch 5, and below, p 552.

[387] [1996] Crim LR 341. See commentary doubting whether there was an *actus reus* in *Millward*. And cf *Roberts and George* [1997] Crim LR 209.

[388] Below, p 1127. It seems that there is no room for procuring the *actus reus* as distinct from the offence because there is no *actus reus* unless the fault element is present – ie the full offence is committed: *Roberts and George* [1997] Crim LR 209 and commentary.

[389] In *Pickford* [1995] 1 Cr App R 420, 429–430 it was held that it was not an offence to aid and abet a boy under the age of 14 (at that time presumed to be incapable of sexual intercourse) to commit incest with his mother. The act would not be an *actus reus*.

[390] See D Lanham, 'Accomplices and Withdrawal' (1981) 97 LQR 575; Williams, TBCL, 310–311; KJM Smith, 'Withdrawal and Complicity' [2001] Crim LR 769.

[391] Below, p 411.

[392] Withdrawal does not affect liability for an attempt; below, p 423.

Although the principle that 'a person who unequivocally withdraws before the moment of the actual commission of the crime by the principal offender should not be liable for that crime',[393] is clear, it is less easy to identify not only what is meant by 'unequivocal withdrawal' but also on what basis the defence operates. It is unclear whether it is designed primarily to serve as an incentive to D to withdraw or to reflect his diminished degree of blameworthiness.[394] There are at least three bases on which such a defence might be constructed:

(1) The defence operates only where D brings to an end the *actus reus* of assisting or encouraging P. On this interpretation the defence would be relatively narrowly constructed.

(2) The defence may operate because D's withdrawal negates his *mens rea* of intention to assist or encourage. Such an approach would create an extremely broad defence, potentially D's unannounced unilateral decision to take no part would suffice. That would seem unworkable. It also seems to be unprincipled. If D does acts assisting or encouraging with the requisite *mens rea,* his subsequent withdrawal cannot negate his *mens rea* in relation to his completed *actus reus.*

(3) It is possible to construe the defence as a 'true' defence operating despite the presence of D's continuing *actus reus* and *mens rea* as a secondary party.

English law has yet to address these issues in detail. The Law Commission identifies the basis of the defence as 'negating the effect of the assistance, encouragement or agreement'[395] with the ultimate decision whether D has so managed being one for the jury.[396]

8.8.1 An effective withdrawal?

For any withdrawal to be effective, it must be voluntary, real and effective and communicated in some form in good time.[397] If D is arrested, he can hardly be said to have 'withdrawn'. His arrest does not necessarily demonstrate any repentance on his part, nor undo any aid, advice or encouragement he may have already given.[398] Of course, it usually precludes any future secondary participation by him;[399] but in this section we are concerned with absolution from the potential liability arising from D's past acts. Withdrawal has no part to play if D denies that he was involved in the offence in any way.[400]

In addition to a general voluntary awareness on D's part, a clear precondition for the defence to operate is an unequivocal communication of withdrawal.[401] This can be communication to the principal offender, and if more than one to all principal offenders, or by communication with the law enforcement agency.[402]

Mere repentance, without any action, is not a sufficient or necessary condition for the defence.[403] D's 'innocent' state of mind at the time of the commission of the crime is no

---

[393] *O'Flaherty* [2004] EWCA Crim 526, [2004] Crim LR 751; applied recently in *Mitchell* [2008] EWCA Crim 2552 and *Campbell* [2009] EWCA Crim 50.

[394] For a comprehensive discussion of these approaches see KJM Smith [2001] Crim LR 769.

[395] LC 305, para 3.60.

[396] LC 305, para 3.65.

[397] *Otway* [2011] EWCA Crim 3.

[398] *Johnson and Jones* (1841) Car & M 218. *Jackson* (1673) 1 Hale PC 464 at 465 appears contra but is an obscure and unsatisfactory case. See Lanham (1981) 97 LQR 575 at 577.

[399] For an infamous example where it did not, see *Craig and Bentley* (1952) The Times, 10–13 Dec.

[400] *Gallant* [2008] EWCA Crim 111.

[401] *O'Flahery* [2004] EWCA Crim 526.

[402] cf the Law Commission's view that D ought not to be automatically denied the defence if he has not informed all parties: LC 305, para 3.65.

[403] Hale, 1 PC, 618; Stephen, *Digest* (4th edn), art 42; Williams, CLGP, s 127; *Croft* [1944] 1 KB 295; *Becerra,* below, n 410.

answer if he had *mens rea* when he did the act of counselling or aiding. English courts are generally reluctant to enquire into questions of motive. D may have seen the error of his ways, or he may be acting out of malice against his accomplices or because of fear of detection or because he has decided that the risks outweigh the possible rewards. It is submitted that it should make no difference. It has been recognized, for example, that if D neutralizes the effect of any assistance or encouragement he has given, he is not liable, even if he did not intend to neutralize its effect.[404]

Preventing or attempting to prevent the crime

To be effective must D's withdrawal involve his taking all reasonable steps to prevent the crime? It is submitted that this is not a necessary, although clearly it should be a *sufficient* basis for the defence. Where D gives timely warning to the police, the effect ought in most cases to be that the crime will be prevented; but this may not always be so and, even where it is, there remains D's potential liability for abetting P's attempt, if P has gone beyond mere preparation. Surely, however, efforts to prevent the commission of the crime by informing the police ought to be an effective withdrawal, whether D has or has not attempted to persuade P to desist. Apart from being the best evidence of repentance, it is conduct which the law should and does encourage.[405]

Withdrawal by cancelling assistance provided

The question of withdrawal is usually approached by ascertaining whether D has 'neutralized' any input his assistance or encouragement might have had irrespective of whether that will in fact prevent the crime being committed. However, this is a difficult test to apply. For example, where D has supplied information it may be impossible in any meaningful sense to cancel the effect of that assistance by merely communicating withdrawal to P and suggesting that D will have no further part to play. In such cases D's communicated countermand must go further if it is to be effective in neutralizing *the effect* of the assistance. It may be that D in such cases would be obliged to inform the police or do some act to prevent the crime, but the courts have not insisted on this.

Although no clear test has evolved, what seems to be involved in these cases is an unarticulated proportionality test, assessing the exculpatory conduct (what was done or said, to whom, at what stage of the criminal conduct), and the mode of D's participation in the contemplated offence (supply of weapons or advice, mere encouragement, presence at the crime, having been the instigator[406]). In *O'Flaherty*, the court suggested that in evaluating the effectiveness of the withdrawal, account will be taken of 'the nature of the assistance and encouragement already given and how imminent the [principal offence], as well as the nature of the action said to constitute the withdrawal'.[407] The court emphasized that it is not necessary for D to have taken reasonable steps to prevent the crime in order to have successfully withdrawn.

If D's assistance consisted only in advising or encouraging P to commit the crime, it may be enough for him to tell P to desist.[408] If P then commits the crime he does so against D's advice and without his encouragement. It may be that P would never have committed the crime if D had not put it into his head in the first place; but then D may be properly and adequately dealt with by conviction under the SCA 2007, ss 44 to 46. If D has counselled more than one

---

[404] *Rook* [1993] 2 All ER at 963. See the discussion in LC 305, para 3.126.

[405] cf the large 'discounts' on sentence which may be earned for information given after D has become liable for and been convicted of the offence.

[406] *Mitchell* [2008] EWCA Crim 2552 (D started fight, paused for short period while some other fetched weapons including a mace, and violence recommenced with D present. V killed. D guilty of murder).

[407] Para 60.

[408] *Saunders and Archer* (1573) 2 Plowd 473.

person, then it seems that he must communicate his countermand to all of those who perpetrate the offence, for otherwise his counselling remains operative.[409] To be effective, the communication must be such as 'will serve unequivocal notice upon the other party to the common unlawful cause that if he proceeds upon it he does so without the further aid and assistance of those who withdraw'.[410] The position might be different where D has supplied P with the means of committing the crime. Aid may be no less easily neutralized than advice.

In *Grundy*,[411] D had supplied P, a burglar, with information which was presumably valuable to P in committing the crime; but, for two weeks before P did so, D had been trying to stop him breaking in. It was held that there was evidence of an effective withdrawal which should have been left to the jury. In *Whitefield*,[412] there was evidence that D had served unequivocal notice on E that, if he proceeded with the burglary they had planned together, he would do so without D's aid or assistance. The jury should have been told that, if they accepted the evidence, that was a defence. D would now be liable for an offence under ss 44 to 46 of the SCA 2007.

If a rejected countermand may be an effective withdrawal, as in *Grundy*, it is arguable that an attempt to countermand should be the same. D has done all in his power to communicate his countermand to P but failed. In all these cases, the countermand has, *ex hypothesi*, failed; and, if the question is whether D has done his best to neutralize his input, the answer does not depend on the reasons for the failure.[413] It could be argued that, where D has failed to communicate, he can escape only by going to the police; but this was not insisted on in *Grundy* when persuasion failed. This suggests that the basis for the defence lies not in neutralizing the *actus reus* of assisting so far performed by D, but on some broader principle operating to exculpate D despite his continuing *actus reus*.

An effective withdrawal may often be made more easily at the preparatory stage than where the crime is in the course of commission. Thus, in *Beccara* where D handed P a knife so that he could use it on anyone interfering in a burglary, D did not make a sufficient communication of withdrawal when, on the appearance of V, he said 'Come on, let's go', and got out through a window. Something 'vastly different and vastly more effective' was required and, possibly, nothing less than physical intervention to stop P committing the crime would be required.[414] In that case, the 'withdrawal' occurred at a very late stage. When the knife is about to descend, the only effective withdrawal may be physical intervention to prevent it reaching its target. This reasoning has been echoed in numerous recent cases.[415]

Spontaneous violence

In all the cases discussed above the offence was pre-planned. It was held in *Mitchell and King* that cases of spontaneous violence are different.[416] On this view, if A and B spontaneously attack V, they are aiding and abetting one another, so long as each is aware that he is being assisted and encouraged by the other; but, if B simply withdraws, his participation in the offence apparently ceases without the need for any express communication to A, so that he will not be liable for acts done by A thereafter.

---

[409] *State v Kinchen* (1910) 52 So 185, quoted by Lanham, above, at n 390.

[410] *Whitehouse* [1941] 1 WWR 112, per Sloan JA (Court of Appeal of British Columbia) approved in *Becerra* (1975) 62 Cr App R 212, CA. cf *Fletcher* [1962] Crim LR 551; *Grundy* [1977] Crim LR 543, CA.

[411] [1977] Crim LR 543.

[412] (1984) 79 Cr App R 36.

[413] Lanham, above, at n 390.

[414] *Becerra*, above, n 410. cf *Baker* [1994] Crim LR 444.

[415] See *Campbell* [2009] EWCA Crim 50; *Mitchell* [2008] EWCA Crim 2552.

[416] *Mitchell and King* (1998) 163 JP 75, [1999] Crim LR 496, DC.

The appropriateness of this test depends on which basis the defence rests. If it is regarded as a defence which operates by D neutralizing his *actus reus*, it can be seriously doubted: if A was encouraged by B's participation and was unaware that B had withdrawn, A continues to be encouraged. There is still an effective *actus reus*. As noted above, there are cases in which the defence has been successful where D has failed to neutralize the effect of his acts of assistance.

Fortunately, in the case of *Robinson*,[417] the Court of Appeal explained *Mitchell and King* as an exceptional case. Referring to the criticisms above, the court stated that:

> it can only be in exceptional circumstances that a person can withdraw from a crime he has initiated. Similarly in those rare circumstances communication of withdrawal must be given in order to give the principal offenders the opportunity to desist rather than complete the crime. This must be so even in situations of spontaneous violence unless it is not practicable or reasonable so to communicate as in the exceptional circumstances pertaining in *Mitchell* where the accused threw down his weapon and moved away before the final and fatal blows were inflicted.

More recently, however, in *O'Flaherty*, the court followed the distinction between 'planned' and 'spontaneous' violence drawn in *Mitchell and King*. The Court of Appeal concluded that 'in a case of spontaneous violence such as this where there has been no prior agreement, the jury will usually have to make inferences as to the scope of the joint enterprise from the knowledge and actions of individual participants'.[418] The courts seem to avoid a more precise definition, favouring to regard the matter as one of fact and degree to be left to the jury.

The confusion surrounding the availability of the defence and its elements renders it all too easy for the courts to apply it in a confusing fashion. A good illustration is the case of *Rafferty*.[419] D and his co-defendants, P1 and P2 attacked V. D punched V twice. He then left the scene with V's cash card headed for an ATM. Meanwhile, P1 and P2 continued the attack on V escalating the violence by kicking him in the head and finally, drowning him in the sea. D returned to find V dead. The trial judge left to the jury the question whether D had withdrawn from the enterprise (and if so whether he was then liable for causing the death as a principal). The Court of Appeal concluded, rightly it is submitted that D could not be guilty as a principal – he was not a cause of death. Nor, applying *Rahman* was D a secondary party: the acts of P1 and P2 in drowning V were of a fundamentally different nature from the enterprise with which D had been involved. It is submitted that there was no issue of withdrawal.

8.9 Victims as parties to crime[420]

It has been noted[421] that when a statute creates a crime it does not generally provide that it shall be an offence to aid, abet, counsel or procure it. Such a provision is unnecessary, for it follows by implication of law. There is, however, one exception to this rule. Where the statute is designed for the protection of a certain class of persons it may be construed as excluding by implication the liability of any member of that class who is the victim of the offence, even though that member does in fact aid, abet, counsel or procure the offence.

---

[417] [2000] 5 Archbold News 2, CA. See also *Mitchell* [2008] EWCA Crim 2552.

[418] Para 65.

[419] [2007] EWCA Crim 1846.

[420] See LC 305, para 5.24. See also: B Hogan, 'Victims as Parties to Crime' [1962] Crim LR 683; G Williams, 'Victims as Parties to Crimes – A Further Comment' [1964] Crim LR 686; G Williams, 'Victims and Other Exempt Parties in Crime' (1990) 10 LS 245; Criminal Law Revision Committee, Fifteenth Report (Cmnd 9213), Appendix B.

[421] Above, p 184.

In *Tyrrell*,[422] D, a girl between the ages of 13 and 16, abetted P to have unlawful sexual intercourse with her. This was an offence by P under the Criminal Law Amendment Act 1885, s 5.[423] It was held, however, that D could not be convicted of abetting because the Act 'was passed for the purpose of protecting women and girls against themselves'.[424] In *Pickford*,[425] the court held (though it was probably not necessary to the decision) that *Tyrrell* was applicable to the case of a woman committing incest with her 13-year-old son, but it is not obvious that s 11 of the Sexual Offences Act 1956 (which made it an offence for the woman to permit 'her grandfather, father, brother or son' to have intercourse with her) was intended for the protection of anyone. Under the Sexual Offences Act 2003, there is nothing to prevent the boy being treated as a principal offender.

It has been held that a woman who is not pregnant can be convicted of abetting the use upon herself by another of an instrument with intent to procure her miscarriage, although the clear implication of the statute[426] is that such a woman cannot be convicted of *using* an instrument on herself with that intent.[427] However, a pregnant woman can be convicted (under the same section) of using an instrument on herself so it cannot be argued that this section was passed for the protection of *women* and it would be curious that Parliament should have intended to protect non-pregnant women from themselves, but not pregnant women. How far the rule in *Tyrrell* extends has not been settled. The court referred to 'women' as well as girls and it may well be that it extends to the offences of procuration of women to be prostitutes and of brothel keeping which were in the 1885 Act and then in the Sexual Offences Act 1956.[428] It was held that it applied to the prostitute who abets a man who is living off her earnings.[429]

In all these cases, it seems clear that the protection of the law extended only to a person of the class who is a *victim*. Thus, a child under 16 could be convicted of abetting P in having intercourse with another child under 16; a boy under 14 could be convicted, even before the Sexual Offences Act 1993, of abetting P in intercourse with another boy under 14; a prostitute could abet P in keeping a brothel in which she was not a participant, or of living on the earnings of another prostitute. There are many instances other than sexual offences where laws are passed for the protection of a particular class of persons.

The Law Commission propose to preserve the *Tyrell* principle. There will be no liability where the principal offence is for the protection of a particular category of persons and both (i) D falls within that category and (ii) he is the victim.[430]

---

[422] [1894] 1 QB 710.

[423] See now Sexual Offences Act 2003, s 9; below, p 758.

[424] Per Lord Coleridge CJ at 712. Both the Chief Justice and Mathew J pointed out that there was nothing in the Act to say that the girl should be guilty of aiding and abetting; but, it is submitted, no importance could be attached to that, for statutes hardly ever do.

[425] [1995] 1 Cr App R 420, 428.

[426] Offences Against the Person Act 1861, s 58; below, Ch 16.

[427] *Sockett* (1908) 72 JP 428; below, p 607.

[428] Sections 22–24, 28 and 29. Repealed, see now Sexual Offences Act 2003, ss 52–55.

[429] *Congdon* [1990] NLJR 1221 (Judge Addison); Hogan [1962] Crim LR at 692–693; Williams (1990) 10 LS 245 at 248–249. The offence is repealed by the Sexual Offences Act 2003, under which children are a protected class, but liable to conviction for participating in the sexual activity. *Tyrell* seems to be largely ignored in the 2003 Act. See the article developing this point and cataloguing the instances in which the Act deviates from the principle: M Bohlander, 'The Sexual Offences Act 2003 – The Tyrrell Principle – Criminalising the Victims' [2005] Crim LR 701.

[430] LC 305, c16 of the Draft Bill.

8.10 Instigation for the purpose of entrapment[431]

Police or other law enforcement officers or their agents sometimes do acts for the purpose of entrapping, or getting evidence against offenders, which would certainly amount to counselling or abetting an offence if they were not done for that purpose. The difficult question is how far an officer may go without himself incurring liability for the offence. Law enforcement officers have no general licence to aid and abet crime.

Two separate questions are involved: (i) in what circumstances will the law enforcement agency official have committed a crime by his encouragement?; (ii) in what circumstances will the person encouraged by the officer be entitled to rely on such entrapment to excuse his conduct? We are concerned here only with the first of those questions, the second being a matter of 'defence' (and in English law only by way of procedural defence in terms of stay of proceedings).[432]

It should be noted that where charges are brought in these circumstances for offences under ss 44 to 46 of the SCA 2007, a defence is available under s 50 where D proves, (i) that he knew[433] certain circumstances existed; and (ii) that it was reasonable for him to act as he did in those circumstances.

8.10.1 Secondary liability for the agent provocateur

As long ago as 1929, the Royal Commission on Police Powers expressed:[434]

As a general rule, the police should observe only, without participating in an offence, except in cases where an offence is habitually committed in circumstances in which observation by a third party is *ex hypothesi* impossible. Where participation is essential it should only be resorted to on the express and written authority of the Chief Constable.

In *Sang*,[435] Lord Salmon said:

I would now refer to what is, I believe and hope, the unusual case, in which a dishonest policeman, anxious to improve his detection record, tries very hard with the help of an agent provocateur to induce a young man with no criminal record to commit a serious crime; and ultimately the young man reluctantly succumbs to the inducement . . . The policeman and the informer who had acted together in inciting him to commit the crime should . . . both be prosecuted and suitably punished.

It is not clear that the word 'dishonest' adds anything to the postulated facts and it should make no difference that the policeman's motive is hatred of crime. It can hardly be necessary that the person induced to act should be 'young'; and it might be even more serious to induce a person with a bad record who was 'going straight', for the consequences for him would be worse. These matters go to sentence, not liability.

The essence of the *dictum* seems to be that a person who would not otherwise have committed a particular crime is induced to do so,[436] and the House of Lords in *Looseley* confirmed that this is the essential basis of the concept of entrapment in English law:

---

[431] Williams, CLGP, s 256.

[432] See below, p 399. See, generally, the decision of the House of Lords in *Looseley* [2001] UKHL 53, [2002] 1 Cr App R 360; A Ashworth, 'Redrawing the Boundaries of Entrapment' [2002] Crim LR 161; D Ormerod and A Roberts, 'The Trouble with *Teixera*: Developing a Principled Approach to Entrapment' (2002) Int J E & P 38; A Ashworth, 'Testing Fidelity to Legal Values: Official Involvement in Criminal Justice' (2000) 63 MLR 633, 642–652.

[433] Note that it is not enough that D believed they existed.

[434] Cmd 3297 (1928) 116.

[435] (1979) 69 Cr App R 282 at 296.

[436] cf *Birtles* [1969] 2 All ER 1131n, [1969] 1 WLR 1047.

Whether the police conduct preceding the commission of the offence was no more than might be expected from others in the circumstances?[437]

An officer who agrees, and intends, to participate in such an offence is guilty of conspiracy.[438] Merely to provide the opportunity for, and temptation to commit an offence will be lawful,[439] as is participation in an offence which has already been 'laid on' and is going to be committed in any event, in order to trap the offenders.[440] In such a case it makes no difference that the police intervention may have affected the time or other circumstances of the commission of the offence.[441]

Where there is a continuing general conspiracy – for example, to supply drugs to anyone asking for them – it seems that a law enforcement officer commits no offence by inducing the general conspirators to enter into a particular conspiracy within the ambit of the general conspiracy, for example, to supply him with specified drugs.

It cannot be the law that the police may properly participate in a crime to the point at which irreparable damage is done. A policeman who assists P to commit murder in order to entrap him must be guilty of murder. It is submitted that the same must be true of any injury to the person, unless it is trivial and V consents to it; and probably to any damage to property, unless the owner consents.

The Law Commission propose a new defence where D shows (on the balance of probabilities) that he was acting in order to prevent the commission of an offence or occurrence of harm and it was reasonable to act as he did.[442]

8.11 Reform of secondary liability

The recommendations in Law Commission Report No 305 will, if implemented, transform the scope of accessorial liability. Taken together with Part 2 of the SCA 2007, there will, in effect, be eight types of liability for conduct that assists or encourages crime or is capable of doing so. Only a very short overview can be offered here.

(1) First, D may be liable for an inchoate offence where he intentionally does acts capable of assisting or encouraging the commission of a crime by P. D must believe or be reckless as to whether P will act with the *mens rea* of the offence and D must intend or believe that any relevant consequences or circumstances of P's offence will be satisfied (SCA 2007, s 44). This offence can be charged whether or not P commits the full offence.

(2) Second, D may be liable for an inchoate offence where he does acts capable of assisting or encouraging the commission of a crime by P, and believes that the conduct element of the *actus reus* of the crime will be committed by P, believing or being reckless as to whether P will have the *mens rea* for the offence, and believing or being reckless as to whether any relevant consequences or circumstances of P's offence will be satisfied (SCA 2007, s 45). The offence can be charged whether or not P commits the full offence.

---

[437] Lord Nicholls, para 23.

[438] *Yip Chiu-cheung v R*, above, p 105. See the Law Commission proposals on Conspiracy discussed below p 430.

[439] *Williams v DPP* (1993) 98 Cr App R 209, DC where the 'bait' was cartons of cigarettes left in a vulnerable position. The court said that the police had not aided, abetted, etc: but had they not procured the commission of the offence? They would have regarded the operation as a failure if no one had stolen the cartons.

[440] *McCann* (1971) 56 Cr App R 359.

[441] *McEvilly* (1973) 60 Cr App R 150.

[442] cf s 50 of the SCA 2007, discussed below, p 470 in which Parliament corrupted the Law Commission's similar proposals in relation to incitement.

(3) Third, D may be liable for an inchoate offence where he does acts capable of assisting or encouraging the commission of one of a number of specified crimes by P, and
believes that one of those crimes will be committed by P, believing or being reckless as
to whether P will possess any *mens rea* required for one of the offences, and believing
or being reckless as to whether any relevant consequences or circumstances of one of
those offences will be satisfied (SCA 2007, s 46). This offence can be charged whether or
not P commits the full offence.

In each of these offences under the SCA 2007, liability is inchoate. It is arguable that the scope
of criminal liability has extended too far by allowing for conviction and sentence for serious
offences where D's conduct is so remote from the harm of the full offence – P need not even
have attempted the principal crime.

(4) Fourth,[443] D may be liable as an accessory[444] if D's conduct assists or encourages P in
fact, whether directly or not, and whether the assistance or encouragement is substantial
or not. The assistance or encouragement may be by acts (words or conduct), or omission
if D is under a relevant duty (for example by contract or relationship), but not by failure
to control P where D has a specific entitlement to do so. D must have a direct or oblique
intent[445] that P commit the conduct element of the offence. This strict *mens rea* element
is central to the Commission's proposals reflecting the need for parity of culpability between D and P[446] if D is to be prosecuted, labelled and sentenced in the same manner as
P. It is not necessary that D intends P to commit the full offence. D must believe that the
circumstances and consequences of P's offence will be satisfied, *or* D must himself have
the *mens rea* for the full offence of which P commits the conduct element.[447]

(5) Fifth, D will be liable for a joint venture[448] where he agrees with P to commit an offence
or shares a common intention with P and D intended (directly or obliquely) that P
or another party to the venture should commit the conduct element of the principal
offence or believed that P or another would or might commit the conduct element of the
offence. D would not be liable if P's act is outside the scope[449] of the joint venture.[450]

It is significant that these fourth and fifth forms of liability above replace aiding and abetting,
counselling and procuring. They are considerably narrower than the present secondary liability presumably because there is no need to extend liability in view of the offences under ss
44 to 46 of the SCA 2007.

(6) Sixth, in the case of homicide,[451] a joint venture will be caught by the fifth category
above – D will be liable for murder[452] if D intended to assist or encourage P to commit
the relevant offence or D engaged in a joint criminal venture with P and realized that
P or another to the venture might commit the relevant offence. D would also be liable
for manslaughter if D and P were parties to a joint venture, P committed murder in

---

[443] LC 305, Part III, especially at para 3.15 et seq.

[444] Neither term is defined.

[445] LC 305, para 3.88. cf Wilson arguing that it should be purposive intent – [2008] Crim LR 16.

[446] LC 305, para 3.80.

[447] LC 305, para 3.109.

[448] Which is undefined.

[449] Not defined.

[450] For criticism, see Sullivan [2008] Crim LR 19, commenting on the absence of definition, heavy reliance on the
existing law and the undue complexity resulting, and Buxton [2009] Crim LR above who regards them as 'unreasonably and unnecessarily' extending the scope of criminal liability and being 'very burdensome' to apply, 243.

[451] Special proposals for joint venture were made in the Law Commission's *Murder, Manslaughter and
Infanticide* Report No 304 (2006) Part 4.

[452] As defined in the LC Report, see Ch 14 below.

relation to the fulfilment of that venture and D intended or foresaw that non-serious harm or the fear of harm might be caused by a party to the venture and a reasonable person in D's position and with D's knowledge of the relevant facts would have foreseen an obvious risk of death or serious injury being caused by a party to the venture.[453]

(7) Seventh, D may be liable under a new statutory form of innocent agency.[454] D will be liable if he intentionally caused P to commit the conduct element of the offence, but, although P does commit the conduct element, P is not guilty of the full offence because he is under 10, insane or lacks *mens rea*.[455] D must also be proved to have the *mens rea* element of the offence he intended to cause. In the case of strict liability offences, D must know or believe that P would commit the offence (which he would even if he lacked *mens rea*) in the circumstances and with the consequences it requires.[456] The new offence will extend to cases where the offence committed by P is only capable of being committed by a person of a particular description (for example a licensee), even if D is not such a person. There is no requirement that D needs to believe that the full offence will be committed nor that it will be committed by P himself.[457]

(8) Eighth, D may be liable where he intentionally causes a 'no fault' offence[458] to be committed by P and D knew or believed that his conduct would cause the offence to be committed.[459] It will be sufficient that D causes the circumstances of the no fault offence to be committed, for example with drink driving, it is enough that D laces P's drinks causing the circumstance element (that P is over the limit) without causing the conduct element (the driving of a motor vehicle).

The Law Commission also propose to preserve the *Tyrell* principle, and create a defence for those acting in order to prevent the commission of an offence or occurrence of harm where it was reasonable to act in that way.

The Law Commission's proposals for secondary liability as set out in its Report No 305[460] were designed to represent a coherent scheme complementing the inchoate offences recommended by the Commission in Report No 300. However, the coherence has been lost, or at least not yet achieved. First, Parliament enacted the inchoate liability provisions in the SCA 2007, but in doing so made fundamental changes to the scope of those provisions. Secondly, although the SCA 2007 is in force, the proposals in relation to secondary liability are not even before Parliament at the time of writing. Finally, and more worryingly, the Government's amendment of the scheme for incitement proposed in Report No 300 and enacted in the SCA 2007 led to wider offences and a change to the scope of the defences available. To maintain coherence, it seems that the Law Commission proposals on secondary parties will have to be similarly expanded. The logical conclusion is that in its future proposals in this area the Commission is now forced to offer wider offences to maintain consistency and coherence with the Serious Crime Act 2007 provisions.[461]

---

[453] The proposal was supported by the government in its paper *Murder, Manslaughter and Infanticide* (2008), 19/08 at paras 89–90. The proposals were not taken forward into the Coroners and Justice Act 2009.

[454] See LC 305, Part IV.

[455] It is not enough that P was under duress, etc.

[456] D aged 10 tells P aged 9 to have sex with V aged 9. D must know or believe that V will be under 13 (circumstances as to age being strict under s 5 of the Sexual Offences Act 2003).

[457] For critical comment, see RD Taylor [2008] Crim LR 19.

[458] ie a strict liability offence – where no proof of *mens rea* is required as to one or more elements of the *actus reus*.

[459] LC 305, para 4.31.

[460] (2007) on which see Wilson [2008] Crim LR 3; Taylor [2008] Crim LR 32; Sullivan [2008] Crim LR 19.

[461] See the proposals on conspiracy and attempts discussed in Ch 13.

9

Assistance after the offence

9.1 Impeding the apprehension or prosecution of offenders[1]

Someone who assists or encourages another to commit a crime may be liable as a secondary party under the common law and s 8 of the Accessories and Abettors Act 1861 as discussed in the previous chapter. In addition, there are specific offences for those who offer assistance to an offender after the commission of his offence. The general offence is found in Criminal Law Act 1967, s 42[2]:

> (1) Where a person has committed a relevant offence,[3] any other person who, knowing or believing him to be guilty of the offence or of some other relevant offence, does without lawful authority or reasonable excuse any act with intent to impede his apprehension or prosecution shall be guilty of an offence.
>
> (1A) In this section and section 5 below, 'relevant offence' means –
>
>> (a) an offence for which the sentence is fixed by law,
>>
>> (b) an offence for which a person of 18 years or over (not previously convicted) may be sentenced to imprisonment for a term of five years (or might be so sentenced but for the restrictions imposed by section 33 of the Magistrates' Courts Act 1980).
>
> (2) If on the trial of an indictment for a relevant offence the jury are satisfied that the offence charged (or some other offence of which the accused might on that charge be found guilty) was committed, but find the accused not guilty of it, they may find him guilty of any offence under subsection (1) above of which they are satisfied that he is guilty in relation to the offence charged (or that other offence).
>
> (3) A person committing an offence under subsection (1) above with intent to impede another person's apprehension or prosecution shall on conviction on indictment be liable to imprisonment according to the gravity of the other person's offence, as follows: –
>
>> (a) if that offence is one for which the sentence is fixed by law, he shall be liable to imprisonment for not more than ten years;

---

[1] G Williams, 'Evading Justice' [1975] Crim LR 430; KJM Smith, *A Modern Treatise on Complicity* (1991) Ch 1.

[2] Which replaced the common law position by which anyone who gave to any party to a felony any assistance whatever, tending to and having the object of, enabling him to evade arrest, trial or punishment, was guilty of the felony as accessory after the fact. Similar offences are provided for in specific contexts, including the wide offences of failing to disclose information related to terrorism: s 38B(1)(B) and s 38B(2) of the Terrorism Act 2000. See C Walker, 'Conscripting the Public in Terrorism Policing: Towards Safer Communities or a Police State?' [2010] Crim LR 441, and on the relationship with s 4 see *Girma* [2009] EWCA Crim 912; *Sherif* [2008] EWCA Crim 2653.

[3] The Serious Organised Crime and Police Act 2005 abolished the concept of 'arrestable offence'; and in this context replaced it with the term 'relevant offence'.

(b) if it is one for which a person (not previously convicted) may be sentenced to imprisonment for a term of fourteen years, he shall be liable to imprisonment for not more than
seven years;

(c) if it is not one included above but is one for which a person (not previously convicted)
may be sentenced to imprisonment for a term of ten years, he shall be liable to imprisonment for not more than five years;

(d) in any other case, he shall be liable to imprisonment for not more than three years.

(4) No proceedings shall be instituted for an offence under subsection (1) above except by or with
the consent of the Director of Public Prosecutions.[4]

The effect of *Courtie*[5] is that the section creates four offences, punishable with ten, seven, five
and three years' imprisonment respectively.

The CPS suggests that examples of the type of conduct appropriate for a charge of assisting
an offender include: hiding a principal offender; otherwise assisting a principal offender to
avoid arrest; assisting a principal offender to abscond from bail; lying to the police to protect principal offenders from investigation and prosecution; hiding the weapon used in an
assault/robbery; washing clothes worn by a principal offender to obstruct any potential forensic examination.[6] In some instances those who have assisted offenders are charged with
perverting the course of justice rather than s 4.[7]

9.1.1 *Actus reus*

There are two elements in the *actus reus* where D is charged with impeding the apprehension or prosecution of an offender, O: (i) a relevant offence must have been committed by the
offender, and (ii) D must have done 'any act' with the appropriate intent. No one may be convicted of an attempt to commit this offence.[8]

9.1.1.1 Proof of a relevant offence

The relevant offence alleged to have been committed by O must be specified in the indictment.[9] If, however, it turns out that O was not guilty of the specified offence, D may still be
convicted if O was guilty of another relevant offence for which O might have been convicted
on an indictment for the original specified offence.[10] So, for example, if it is alleged that O
committed murder and it transpires at D's trial that O was not guilty of murder but was guilty
of manslaughter or attempted murder, because O could, at his trial for murder, have been convicted of those offences, D may be convicted. It is not necessary to direct the jury to find what

---

[4] Consent may be granted after charge but must be before committal proceedings (indictable offences) or mode
of trial (either way offences). Consent must be obtained before proceedings are started by way of summons.

[5] Above, p 52. ie if the maximum sentence differs depending on how the crime is committed, each form of
offence with a different maximum is a separate offence.

[6] Charging Standard for Public Justice Offences: www.cps.gov.uk/legal/p_to_r/public_justice_offences_
incorporating_the_charging_standard/#Assisting_an_Offender.

[7] On which see SM Edwards, 'Perjury and Perverting the Course of Justice Considered' [2003] Crim LR 525.
The CPS suggests that perverting the course of justice should be considered when: the assisting is aimed at preventing or hindering the trial process (as opposed to the arrest or apprehension of an accused); the facts are so
serious that the court's sentencing powers for the statutory offence are considered inadequate; admissible evidence of the principal offence is lacking: Charging Standard for Public Justice Offences. Cf *R v T* [2011] EWCA
Crim 729.

[8] Criminal Attempts Act 1981, s 1(4)(c).

[9] Presumably this can include O's liability for secondary or inchoate offences.

[10] Criminal Law Act 1967, s 6(3); *Morgan* [1972] 1 QB 436, [1972] 1 All ER 348. *Quaere* whether the same principle is applicable to other provisions allowing conviction of offences other than that charged. NB: n 5 above.

offence D thought O had committed, though this may be a material factor in the imposition of sentence.[11]

It is only necessary to prove that the offence was committed, not that O was guilty. If O is tried first, it is immaterial that O is acquitted if it can be proved at D's later trial that O was guilty. Even where O and D are tried together, O's acquittal should not, in principle, be conclusive if it can be proved, as against D, that O committed the offence.[12] However, O's conviction is presumptive evidence that he did commit the offence: PACE 1984, s 74. If D is tried first, it is not necessary to prove O's guilt, merely that the offence was committed. In *Zaman*,[13] D pleaded guilty before O was even tried. O was subsequently acquitted. D appealed claiming that there could be no offence under s 4. The Court of Appeal rightly rejected that argument. The court rejected as immaterial whether D 'knew' or merely 'believed' of O's commission of the offence. With respect, it is submitted that a distinction may need to be drawn in practice between cases of belief and knowledge. In a case where D merely *believes* O has committed the offence, D's plea does not establish that O has committed the offence. Whereas, in a case where D *knows*[14] that O has committed the offence, the plea can fulfil the prosecution's obligation to establish that the offence was committed. Perhaps D ought not to have pleaded at all unless he knew (and not merely believed) that O had committed the offence.

9.1.1.2 An act of assistance

Once O's relevant offence has been proved, the remaining element in D's *actus reus* – 'any act' – is almost unlimited. There must be an *act* – an omission will not suffice[15] – but it need not be an act having a natural tendency to impede the apprehension or prosecution of an offender. Where the act does not have such a tendency, however, it will be difficult to prove the intent, in the absence of an admission. Common examples of sufficient 'acts' will be concealing the offender, providing him with a car, food or money to enable him to escape, or destroying evidence against him. The mere making of an oral offer of accommodation may be a sufficient act for these purposes.[16] It does not matter that D regrets his acts and persuades O to turn himself in. The offence is committed.[17]

According to the Criminal Law Revision Committee,[18] in drafting this offence, 'The requirement that there should be an attempt to "impede" a prosecution will exclude mere persuasion not to prosecute.' Yet words are no doubt a sufficient act; so that the offence would be committed by intentionally misdirecting police who were pursuing an offender, or by making a false statement to the police.[19]

An act done through an agent would be sufficient. Indeed, when done with intent to impede, the mere authorization of the agent would be a sufficient act to constitute the offence, though the agent never acted on it.

[11] ibid.

[12] cf *Shannon* [1975] AC 717, [1974] 2 All ER 1009, HL; *Donald* (1986) 83 Cr App R 49, [1986] Crim LR 535; *Williams* [1975] Crim LR at 432. On the use of an offender's incriminating statements at a joint trial, see *Hayter* [2005] UKHL 6 and *Y* [2008] EWCA Crim 10, cf *Girma* (above).

[13] [2010] EWCA Crim 209 citing with approval this paragraph in the 12th edition. See further commentary at [2010] Crim LR 574.

[14] ie had belief of a true fact: *Saik* [2006] UKHL 18; [2007] 1 AC 18.

[15] cf the offence under s 38B of the Terrorism Act 2000 whereby a person may commit the offence through total inactivity, eg by not answering police questions or by not volunteering information.

[16] *Sherif* [2008] EWCA Crim 2693.

[17] That is a matter of mitigation in sentence: *Roberts* [2008] EWCA Crim 59; *Robinson* [2008] 2 Cr App R (S) 201(35), CA.

[18] Cmnd 2659, para 28.

[19] This would amount to other offences as well. See Law Commission, *Offences Relating to Interference with the Course of Justice* (1979), Law Com No 96, HC Paper No 213 (Session 1979/80) Pt III.

9.1.1.3 Relationship to escape

It is clearly not an offence under s 4 to enable a convicted offender (as opposed to one awaiting trial) to escape from gaol; but this is not important as such acts will amount to other offences.[20] Whether it is an offence to assist such an offender who has escaped to remain at large depends on the interpretation of 'apprehension' in s 4. Does it extend beyond its obvious meaning of apprehension with a view to prosecution and include the re-arrest of the escaped convicted prisoner? There seems to be no reason why it should not be so interpreted.

9.1.2 *Mens rea*

There are two elements in the *mens rea*: (i) D must know or believe the offender to be guilty of the relevant offence which he had actually committed, or some other relevant offence; and (ii) D must intend to impede the apprehension or prosecution of the offender.

9.1.2.1 Know or believe

'Know' presumably means hold a true belief.[21] Belief is, presumably, to be construed as elsewhere eg as in handling stolen goods; if so it adds little to 'knowing'.[22] If the *mens rea* was limited to knowledge alone, it would be difficult to prove. Is wilful blindness sufficient? If D has a mere suspicion that O is an offender and, shutting his eyes to an obvious means of knowledge, assists O, he can hardly be said to 'believe' in O's guilt. Arguably, the subsection is unduly narrow in this respect.[23] In *Sherif*,[24] dealing with the offence under the Terrorism Act 2000, S was held to have known or believed that the London bombings of 21 July 2005 were to take place and failed to give information under s 38B. The judge was entitled in his direction to make it plain '...that it was not sufficient for the prosecution to establish that a defendant had closed his eyes, but that the jury was entitled to conclude, if satisfied that he had deliberately closed his eyes to the obvious because he did not wish to be told the truth, that that fact was capable of being evidence to support a conclusion that that defendant either knew or believed the fact in question'.

Where the allegation is that D knew *or* believed of '...*the* offence' – the relevant offence which has actually been committed – the *mens rea* is probably governed both by 'knowing' and 'believing'. Where the allegation is that the knowledge or belief relates to some 'other relevant offence' the issue must be governed only by 'believing' since, *ex hypothesi*, the offence has not been committed and, therefore, D cannot 'know' it has.

9.1.2.2 Knowledge or belief as to what?

In order to know or believe that a relevant offence has been committed, D need not know the law. It will be enough that he believes in the existence of facts which, whether D knows it or not, amount in law to a relevant offence.[25] His ignorance of the law cannot afford a defence.

It is immaterial that D is unaware of O's identity.[26] What if he makes a mistake of identity? If D thinks he sees R committing a relevant offence and acts, intending to impede his apprehension or prosecution, is D guilty under s 4 if he was in fact witnessing O commit the crime?

---

[20] Prison breaking, escape and rescue are offences at common law. See the 6th edition of this book, at Ch 19.3.

[21] *Saik* [2006] UKHL 18.

[22] *Ismail* [1977] Crim LR 557, CA; *Grainge* [1974] 1 All ER 928, CA; *Griffiths* (1974) 60 Cr App R 14, CA; below, p 994.

[23] Above, p 132.

[24] [2008] EWCA Crim 2653; [2009] 2 Cr App R (S) 33 (p 235) at [27].

[25] cf *Sykes v DPP* [1962] AC 528 at 563, [1961] 3 All ER 33 at 42.

[26] *Brindley* [1971] 2 QB 300, [1971] 2 All ER 698.

Perhaps the question should be answered by making a distinction. If D does an act which he intends to assist the person whom he in fact observed, his mistake of identity should be immaterial. For example, D sends a police officer, who is pursuing the offender, in the wrong direction. Here D knows that the *person he is assisting* has committed a relevant offence, and that person has in fact done so. Suppose, on the other hand, that D fabricates evidence the following day so as to provide an alibi for R and this evidence could not, and was of course not, intended to assist O, of whom D has never heard. Here he does not intend to assist the person whom he in fact observed. An indictment in these circumstances charging D with doing an act, knowing O to be guilty of a relevant offence and with intent to impede his prosecution is plainly bad. If R has never committed a relevant offence, it would seem that D is not guilty under the section;[27] if R once did commit a relevant offence, then D is guilty unless the limitation tentatively suggested in the previous paragraph be imposed.

9.1.2.3 Some other relevant offence

'Some other relevant offence' must refer to an offence which O has not committed, for otherwise the words are redundant.[28] If D thinks he has seen O commit a robbery and acts with intent to conceal this, he will be guilty, though O had in fact committed a murder and not a robbery. This is obviously as it should be, where, as in this example, D's belief relates to the transaction which constituted the actual offence. Suppose, however, that unknown to D, O committed murder last week. D believes, wrongly, that O committed bigamy two years ago. If D does an act with intent to impede O's prosecution for bigamy – such as burning O's letters – it would seem very odd indeed that D should be liable only because O committed murder last week – the murder has nothing to do with the case. This suggests that the supposed offence must arise from the same transaction as the actual offence (and, undoubtedly, this will normally be the case) but to so hold would require the imposition of some limitation on the express words of the section.[29]

9.1.2.4 With intent

D's act must be done with intent to impede the offender's apprehension or prosecution. It does not matter that D's act done with intent proves to be of no assistance to O whatsoever. It must be proved that D's *purpose* was to impede; it is not enough that D knew his act would certainly impede if that was not his object or one of his objects; ie a 'direct' and not merely an 'oblique' intention is required.[30] At least, this seems to be the Criminal Law Revision Committee's view of the clause which became s 4. Discussing the case of harbouring, they wrote:

If the harbouring is done with the object of impeding apprehension or prosecution . . . it will be within the offence; if it is done merely by way of providing or continuing to provide the criminal with accommodation in the ordinary way, it will not; and juries will be able to tell the difference.[31]

If this is the correct interpretation of the section, then a handler of stolen goods will not be guilty of an offence under s 4, even where he knows that his conduct has the effect of impeding the apprehension or prosecution of the thief, if that is not his object or purpose.[32] Nor is D guilty if, by acts done with the object of avoiding his own arrest or prosecution, he knowingly

---

[27] Nor could D be convicted of an attempt to commit the offence. See Criminal Attempts Act 1981, s 1(4)(c), below, p 421, for discussion of the offence as a specific form of preparatory offence see Duff, *Answering for Crime*, 160.

[28] NB: p 247 above.

[29] cf the discussion of s 5, below, p 251.

[30] Above, pp 107–114.

[31] Cmnd 2659, para 30.

[32] *Andrews and Craig* [1962] 3 All ER 961n.

impedes the arrest or prosecution of another.[33] Where there is *prima facie* evidence of the necessary intent, it is for D to lay a foundation for a defence by introducing evidence that his sole purpose was of a different character. In the absence of such evidence, there is no duty to direct a jury to consider whether D might have had a different intent.[34] If D has the dual object of saving himself and the other from arrest or prosecution then, no doubt, he is guilty.

9.1.2.5 Lawful authority

Even though the act is done with intent to impede, it is not an offence if there is 'lawful authority or reasonable excuse' for it. According to the Criminal Law Revision Committee:[35]

The exception for 'lawful authority' will cover an executive decision against a prosecution, and that for 'reasonable excuse' will avoid extending the offence to acts such as destroying the evidence of an offence (for example a worthless cheque) in pursuance of a legitimate agreement to refrain from prosecuting in consideration of the making good of loss caused by that offence.

It is possible that the exception may have some application outside this situation.[36] As with the Prevention of Crime Act,[37] it enables the courts to afford a defence in circumstances in which they think it reasonable to do so.

9.1.3 The sentence

Section 4(3)[38] provides for a sliding scale of sentences which is related to the relevant offence which has actually been committed. Where D believes that some other relevant offence has been committed, the punishment to which he is liable is fixed according to the *actus reus*, not according to the *mens rea*. If D acts with intent to impede the apprehension of O whom he believes to have committed malicious wounding[39] (maximum, five years), he is liable to three years' imprisonment if his belief is correct; but if O has in fact committed murder, he is liable to ten years.

It is clear that the relevant offence which fixes the maximum under s 4 must have been committed when the act of impeding takes place. D, rightly believing O to be guilty of malicious wounding, acts to impede his arrest. Subsequently, O's victim, V, dies, and O becomes guilty of murder. D is liable to only three and not ten years' imprisonment.

9.2 Compounding an offence[40]

Section 5(1) of the Criminal Law Act enacts an offence, triable either way, as follows:

Where a person has committed a relevant offence,[41] any other person who, knowing or believing that the offence or some other relevant offence has been committed, and that he has information

---

[33] *Jones* [1949] 1 KB 194, [1948] 2 All ER 964.

[34] *Brindley* [1971] 2 QB 300 at 304.

[35] Cmnd 2659, para 28.

[36] Would a wife have a reasonable excuse for assisting her husband? See P Pace, '"Impeding Arrest": A Wife's Right as a Spouse?' [1978] Crim LR 82. According to *Lee Shek Ching v R* Hong Kong, CA, 1985, No 53, being O's wife is not, as such, a reasonable excuse. See *T* [2011] EWCA Crim 729.

[37] Below, p 705.

[38] Above, p 246.

[39] Below, p 648.

[40] Williams [1975] Crim LR 430 at 609.

[41] The Serious Organised Crime and Police Act 2005, Sch 7, replaced 'arrestable offence' with 'relevant offence'.

which might be of material assistance in securing the prosecution or conviction of an offender for it, accepts or agrees to accept for not disclosing that information any consideration other than the making good of loss or injury caused by the offence, or the making of reasonable compensation for that loss or injury, shall be liable on conviction on indictment to imprisonment for not more than two years.

Proceedings may not be instituted without the consent of the Director of Public Prosecutions.[42] Section 5 replaced two much wider common law misdemeanours: 'compounding a felony' and 'misprision of felony'.[43] The former consisted in an agreement for consideration not to prosecute, or to impede a prosecution for, a felony. The latter consisted simply in an omission to report a felony to the police. Section 5 is narrower than misprision in that the offence is committed only if D accepts or agrees to accept a consideration for not disclosing the information relating to the relevant offence. It is narrower than compounding in that it is not now criminal to accept or agree to accept consideration for not disclosing information relating to the relevant offence, if the consideration is no more than the making good of loss or injury caused by the offence or the making of reasonable compensation for that loss or injury. No one may be convicted of attempting to commit an offence under s 5(1).[44]

9.2.1 *Actus reus*

There are two elements in the *actus reus*: (i) a relevant offence must actually have been committed; and (ii) D must accept or agree to accept consideration for not disclosing information which he knows or believes to be material.

The offence extends to all relevant offences. The limit on the scope of s 5 is provided by s 5(5): 'The compounding of an offence other than treason shall not be an offence otherwise than under this section.' D commits no offence by agreeing to accept any consideration for not prosecuting a non-relevant offence, though whether the resulting contract is enforceable is another matter.

The offence is committed only where D 'accepts or agrees to accept' the consideration. The section envisages an offer being made to D; if the offer comes *from* D, then he might also be guilty of the more serious offence of blackmail.[45] Consideration presumably bears much the same meaning as in the law of contract and extends to money, goods, services, or any act or forbearance.

9.2.2 *Mens rea*

There are two elements in the *mens rea*. It must be proved that (i) D knew or believed that a relevant offence had been committed and (ii) D intended to accept or to agree to accept consideration other than the making good of loss or the making of reasonable compensation.

9.2.2.1 Knowledge or belief

These terms should be construed in the same manner as in s 4 above.

9.2.2.2 Knowledge or belief as to what?

Where D's knowledge or belief relates to the relevant offence (A) which has actually been committed, the application of the section seems quite straightforward. But D's belief may

---

[42] Section 5(3).
[43] See the 1st edition of this book, at 539–544.
[44] Criminal Attempts Act 1981, s 1(4)(c), below, p 421.
[45] Below, Ch 26.

relate to some other relevant offence (B) which, *ex hypothesi*, has not been committed. Here D's acceptance, or agreement to accept consideration, must relate to the offence B which D believes to have been committed and thus not to the offence which has actually been committed since they are different. Under this section D's belief need not – as, under s 4, it probably must[46] – be that a relevant offence has been committed by the same person who has in fact committed such an offence. If D wrongly supposes that he has seen a relevant offence committed by R and accepts consideration for not disclosing what he saw, he will be guilty if, in fact, he saw O committing a relevant offence.

The argument advanced in connection with s 4, that D's belief must relate to the transaction which resulted in the actual offence, is much stronger in relation to s 5. If D wrongly supposes that R has committed a relevant offence and accepts consideration for not disclosing that fact, his guilt can hardly be established by proving that some time, somewhere, someone committed a relevant offence – for example, that Dr Crippen committed murder. The offence which D supposes to have been committed must have something to do with the offence which has actually been committed. The most obvious point of connection is that the real and the supposed offence must both arise out of the same transaction. An alternative view might be that it is sufficient if either (i) the two offences arise out of the same transaction or (ii) they both relate to the same person. Unknown to D, O committed murder last week. D believes, wrongly, that O committed bigamy two years ago. O offers money to D 'to keep his mouth shut'. D, believing that O is talking about the bigamy, accepts. According to the first view put above, D is not guilty; according to the alternative view, he is. It is submitted that the first view is better; according to the second, D's liability depends entirely on chance.

If D's acceptance of consideration relates to the transaction in question, then it seems that it will be immaterial that he is mistaken as to both (i) the nature of the relevant offence and (ii) the identity of the perpetrator. He supposes he saw R perpetrating a robbery. Actually, he saw O committing murder. If he accepts consideration for not disclosing what he saw he should be guilty.

The Criminal Law Revision Committee stated:[47]

the offence will not apply to a person who refrains from giving information because he does not think it right that the offender should be prosecuted or because of a promise of reparation by the offender. It would be difficult to justify making the offence apply to those cases.

It is difficult to see, however, how it can be a defence for D simply to say that he did not 'think it right that the offender should be prosecuted', if he has accepted consideration for not disclosing information. Even if he convinces the court of his views as to the impropriety of the contemplated prosecution, he still falls within the express words of the section. He could be acquitted only if the section were interpreted so as to require that D's object or motive be the acquisition of the consideration. As we have seen,[48] on a charge under s 4, it is probable that a *purpose* of impeding must be proved, but this may be justified by giving a narrow meaning to the ulterior intent specified in that section. No ulterior intent is specified in s 5 and, consequently, it is difficult to see how the section can be limited in the same way.

[46] See above, p 250.
[47] Cmnd 2659, para 41.
[48] Above, p 250.

9.2.2.3 Relationship with advertising for return of stolen goods

It may seem a little surprising that a specific offence of advertising rewards for the return of goods stolen or lost has been retained.[49] Section 23 of the Theft Act provides:

Where any public advertisement of a reward for the return of any goods which have been stolen or lost uses any words to the effect that no questions will be asked, or that the person producing the goods will be safe from apprehension or inquiry, or that any money paid for the purchase of the goods or advanced by way of loan on them will be repaid, the person advertising the reward and any person who prints or publishes the advertisement shall on summary conviction be liable to a fine not exceeding one hundred pounds.

In so far as an advertisement states that 'no questions will be asked' this is only proposing what is perfectly lawful under s 5(1) of the Criminal Law Act.[50] It is not clear why this should be an offence because it is done through a public advertisement. Nor is it clear why it should be an offence to offer a reward for the return of stolen goods, even their return by the thief. The promise to pay the reward might be unenforceable for lack of consideration but, if it were actually paid, there would be nothing unlawful about that. Possibly the theory is that, if such advertisements were common, theft might be encouraged in that thieves would have an easy and safe way of disposing of the stolen goods for reward. This cannot apply to an advertisement addressed to the bona fide purchaser offering to recompense him if he will return the stolen goods; this seems quite a reasonable thing to do, especially since the *bona fide* purchaser commits no offence by retaining the goods for himself.[51]

The section creates what the courts are pleased to call a quasi-criminal offence, not requiring *mens rea*, so the advertising manager of a company was liable for the publication of an advertisement which he had not read.[52] 'Stolen' bears the wide meaning given to that word by s 24(4) of the Theft Act so the *bona fide* purchaser may indeed have become the absolute owner of the goods where, for example, they have been obtained by fraud and the property in the goods passed.

9.3 Refusal to aid a constable[53]

It is a common law offence for D to refuse to go to the aid of a constable who, on seeing a breach of the peace, calls on D to assist him in restoring the peace. A ticket collector was held to be guilty of the offence when he failed to come to the assistance of a policewoman struggling with a thief. His defence that he had obeyed instructions not to leave his post was not accepted.[54] There must be a reasonable necessity for the constable to request assistance. It is no defence that D's aid would have been ineffective. So where a constable requested D to assist him in suppressing a breach of the peace among four or five hundred people at a prizefight, Alderson B directed that D's refusal was an offence.[55] It seems that it

---

[49] The section replaced the Larceny Act 1861, s 102 which provided for a penalty of £50 recoverable by a common informer. The fine increased to £100 by the Common Informers Act 1951. The CLRC hesitantly recommended retention 'as advertisements of this kind may encourage dishonesty': Eighth Report, *Theft and Related Offences* (1966) Cmnd 2977, para 144.

[50] Above, p 251.

[51] Below, p 1000.

[52] *Denham v Scott* (1983) 77 Cr App R 210, [1983] Crim LR 558, DC.

[53] See the valuable article by D Nicholson, 'The Citizen's Legal Duty to Assist the Police' [1992] Crim LR 611.

[54] *Waugh* (1976) The Times, 1 Oct (Knightsbridge Crown Court).

[55] *Brown* (1841) Car & M 314. cf *Sherlock* (1866) LR 1 CCR 20.

was no answer that he had his horses to take care of. Alderson B[56] recognized that physical impossibility or a lawful excuse would be an answer; but it is not clear what would constitute 'lawful excuse'. Is the citizen required to act where there would be a grave risk of death or serious injury? Surely the State cannot criminalize D for a failure to put his life on the line?

By s 65(3) of the Serious Crime Act 2007 a person does not perform an act capable of assisting or encouraging crime by the offender merely because he fails to respond to a constable's request for assistance in preventing a breach of the peace.

[56] In *Brown*, ibid.

10
Corporate and vicarious liability

10.1 Liability of corporations[1]

10.1.1 Introduction

This chapter deals with the potential criminal liability of organizations, focusing predominantly on corporations. It is common to speak of criminal liability of companies, but of course a company is only one type of incorporated business. Corporations include public limited companies (plc) and private limited companies (Ltd) as well as limited liability partnerships (LLP) and other organizations such as local authorities. The formality of incorporation and its extensive legal ramifications need not detain us.[2] What is important for present purposes is that corporations have a separate legal identity. They are treated in law as having a legal personality distinct from the natural persons – members, directors, employees, etc – who make up the corporation. That presents the opportunity, in theory, of imposing liability on the corporation separately from any criminal liability which might be imposed on the individual members for any wrongdoing.

The number of corporations and the involvement they have in diverse aspects of daily life has expanded dramatically over the last century. In more recent years it appears that the public perception of corporations has moved towards the true legal position: that the corporation is a free-standing entity, distinct from the people who manage and control it.[3] With this perception has come an expectation that a corporation might properly be regarded as culpable in criminal law separately from, although in addition to, its directors for deaths, breaches of health and safety, etc.[4]

---

[1] For detailed study see C Wells, *Corporations and Criminal Responsibility* (2nd edn, 2001); D Bergman, *The Case for Corporate Responsibility* (2000); J Gobert and M Punch, *Rethinking Corporate Crime* (2003); A Pinto QC and M Evans, *Corporate Criminal Liability* (2003); C Harding, *Criminal Enterprise: Individuals Organisation and Criminal Responsibility* (2007); J Gobert, 'Corporate Criminality: New Crimes for the Times' [1994] Crim LR 722; GR Sullivan, 'Expressing Corporate Guilt' (1995) 15 OJLS 281. The meaning of the corporation for the purposes of the criminal law was also recently reviewed in a valuable appendix to the Law Commission Consultation Paper 195 *Criminal Liability in Regulatory Contexts* (2010) (hereafter LCCP 195) by Professor Wells. See also Wells, 'Corporate Crime: Opening the Eyes of the Sentry' (2010) 30 LS 370, at 380–382.

[2] See the Companies Act 2006, s 1300(2) et seq.

[3] See Wells, above, n 1, and N Lacey, 'Philosophical Foundations of the Common Law', in Horder, *Oxford Essays in Jurisprudence,* 33. See also P Alldridge, *Relocating Criminal Law* (2000) considering how corporate liability challenges our perceptions of personhood, at 76–82.

[4] As this perception develops, there is a stronger argument that the appropriate basis for imposing criminal liability should be on culture within the corporation towards risk and harm. See below p 271. See also Wells, above, n 1. There is now growing pressure for corporations to be accountable for their contribution to offences in international law (eg by supplying dictators) See W Kalick 'Corporate Accountability for Human Rights Violations Amounting to International Crimes' (2010) 30 LS 370.

The pressure for the imposition of criminal liability has focused specifically on the issue of punishing companies for manslaughter. The various disasters, each with large loss of life – in particular the *Herald of Free Enterprise* ferry disaster and various rail crashes (Southall, Ladbroke Grove, Paddington, Hatfield) – all prompted calls for new legislation fixing the corporation with liability. The Corporate Manslaughter and Corporate Homicide Act 2007 (hereafter in this chapter 'the 2007 Act') seeks to meet these demands, and is examined in detail in Chapter 15. The 2007 Act imposes liability for manslaughter on 'organizations'. This concept is much wider than corporations.[5] The special policy considerations that flow from the unique harm of causing a death make it desirable for the corporate manslaughter provisions to apply to a wide range of organizations. This chapter deals with the potential criminal liability of associations – including corporations – beyond manslaughter.

As the expectation that corporations will be held criminally liable has grown, so too has the concern that English law's approach to corporate criminal liability is unsatisfactory at a fundamental level. This chapter considers the different methods by which corporations may be held liable in English law and examines the problems each poses.

Although a corporation is, in law, a separate legal entity, in relation to most serious offences, English law still relies on the culpability of the individual directors in fixing liability on the corporation. To take an example, if a company is alleged to have committed fraud by making false representations in order to secure lucrative contracts, the criminal culpability of the company will depend on the actions and fault of the directors and managers of the company. The traditional concepts of *actus reus* and *mens rea* can be applied to the company via its human controllers. A controller of the company must be proved to have had the relevant *mens rea* of the offence (acting dishonestly) and to have fulfilled the conduct element of the offence. At one level this seems logical, since although the company is in law a separate legal entity, it can only operate through the medium of its human actors. There are, however, difficulties. At a practical level, as we will see, there are problems in fixing blame on the company through relevant controllers. Moreover, at a principled level some argue that the criminal law ought to be capable of attributing blame to a corporation on account of wrongs done and harms caused by its corporate culture or policies. With larger corporations an ethos or culture can develop quite independently of the controlling officers. These arguments are keenly contested socio-legal and economic issues which lie beyond the scope of this work.[6] Some of the language of the courts in recent years has also emphasized the systemic failings – in the Hatfield rail prosecution, the failings of *Balfour Beatty* were described in such terms,[7] and the judge castigated the 'total vacuum of management' in the relevant area.[8] Such comments suggest a failure of the corporation rather than any individual.

Historically, it was thought that a corporation could not be indicted for a crime at all.[9] As a matter of procedure, personal appearance was necessary at court in the assizes and quarter-sessions. Since the corporation has no physical person, it could not appear. In the Court of King's Bench, however, appearance by attorney was allowed and the difficulty was

---

[5] By s 25, 'corporation' does not include a sole corporation but includes any body corporate wherever incorporated. This includes companies incorporated under companies legislation, as well as bodies incorporated under statute (as is the case with many non-Departmental Public Bodies and other bodies in the public sector) or by Royal Charter.

[6] See GR Sullivan, 'The Attribution of Culpability to a Limited Company' [1996] CLJ 515, and N Lacey, above, n 3.

[7] Note also the oft-quoted description of corporate 'sloppiness' in the P&O prosecution (1990) 93 Cr App R 72. See for comment on the Balfour decision and others C Wells (2010) 30 LS 370.

[8] [14].

[9] *Anon* (1701) 12 Mod Rep 560, per Holt CJ.

circumvented by removing the indictment into that court by writ of *certiorari*;[10] but now this is unnecessary and, by statute,[11] a corporation may appear and plead through a representative. Further objections which have been raised to imposing criminal liability are that, since a corporation is a creature of the law, it can only do such acts as it is legally empowered to do, so that any crime is necessarily *ultra vires*; and that the corporation, having neither body nor mind, cannot perform the acts or form the intents which are a prerequisite of criminal liability. The *ultra vires* doctrine, however, seems to have been ignored in both the law of tort and crime and to apply only in the law of contract and property.[12]

Recent reform proposals urge the use of innovative enforcement and civil law methods of dealing with corporate wrongdoing where the conduct involves breaches of regulations as opposed to commission of 'real' crimes such as those leading to injury or loss of property.[13] These civil law proposals lie beyond the scope of this work. The focus here is on the use of the criminal law.[14]

10.1.2 Bases of criminal liability

There are currently six ways in which a prosecution may be brought against a corporation or its directors.

10.1.2.1 Personal liability of corporate directors, etc

Firstly, individuals within a corporation can be prosecuted for their personal wrongdoing as any other human being. For example, a managing director of a company who bribes an agent of a company with whom he is making a contract will be at risk of personal prosecution. So too will a manager who commits offences of driving carelessly while on company business, or committing frauds, etc. No more need be said about such criminal liability since it is discussed throughout the book. If a corporation has been found to be criminally liable, the individual employee or director, etc can also be liable as a secondary party to the corporation's wrongdoing under s 8 of the Accessories and Abettors Act 1861 (see Chapter 8). A director can also in some cases be liable for conspiring with the company (see Chapter 13). Occasionally Parliament excludes personal liability when creating corporate offences as, for example, with the corporate manslaughter offence.[15]

10.1.2.2 Strict liability offences

Secondly, offences of strict liability can be committed by a corporation. Since there is no need for proof of *mens rea,* there is no difficulty in establishing any fault on the part of the corporation. Corporate liability for strict liability offences is, in theory, no different from strict liability imposed on human actors. It is, of course, important in the application of strict liability to corporations to consider the availability of due diligence defences, allowing the corporation an opportunity to prove that it took all reasonable steps to avoid the commission of

---

[10] *Birmingham and Gloucester Rly Co* (1842) 3 QB 223.

[11] Criminal Justice Act 1925, s 33.

[12] cf W V H Rogers, *Winfield and Jolowicz on Tort* (18th edn, 2010) Ch 1.

[13] In LCCP 195 the Commission seeks to apply the principles espoused in the Macrory Report – Regulatory Justice: Making Sanctions Effective (2006) in trying to reduce the volume of criminal offences that exist in relation to regulatory behaviour.

[14] See the valuable discussion in Appendix A to the LCCP 195 by Julia Black, examining the merits of these alternatives such as public civil sanctions, administrative sanctions, private civil law, warning notices, restorative justice initiatives, etc.

[15] 2007 Act, s 18(1).

the offence. No more need be said about this form of liability and the due diligence defence.[16]
They are considered in full in Chapter 7.

10.1.2.3 Statutory offences imposing duties on corporations

Thirdly, the corporation, as distinct from its employees or managers, can be criminally liable
for offences laid down by Parliament as applying specifically to corporations. A corporation
is a legal person but it has no physical existence. As a legal entity, a corporation may be placed
under a duty by Parliament to conduct itself in a particular way on pain of criminal sanction
for non-compliance. The type of case where it is most obviously proper that a corporation
should be held liable arises where a statute imposes a duty upon a corporation to act and the
corporation breaches that duty by failing to act. It was in such cases that the earliest developments in corporate liability took place. In 1842, in *Birmingham and Gloucester Rly Co*,[17]
a corporation was convicted for failing to fulfil a statutory duty. Four years later, in *Great
North of England Rly Co*,[18a] counsel sought to confine the effect of that decision to cases of
non-feasance where there was no agent who could be indicted, arguing that, in the case of
misfeasance, only the agents who had done the wrongful acts were liable. The court held that
the distinction was unfounded. Even if it were discoverable, it was incongruous that the corporation should be liable for the one type of wrong and not the other.

A recent example of an offence specifically created for corporations is that in s 7 of the
Bribery Act 2010, creating an offence for a commercial organization to fail to prevent bribery
by a person associated with it, intending to obtain or retain a business advantage. This is a
very widely defined offence. The due diligence defence in s 7(2) will be crucial as will be the
guidance published by the Justice Secretary under s 9.[18b]

10.1.2.4 Vicarious liability

It was not a great step forward from holding that a corporation could be liable for breach of
statutory duty, as in *Birmingham and Gloucester Railway*, to the courts imposing liability vicariously in these circumstances.[19] Fourthly, then, a corporation can be vicariously liable for
the acts of its employees and agents where a natural person would similarly be liable for such
acts; for example when a statute imposes vicarious responsibility.[20] Vicarious liability will be
considered in full below, p 273.

10.1.2.5 The identification doctrine

Aside from these four categories, prosecuting the corporation within the orthodox model of
criminal law creates difficulties. The criminal law's solution to the lack of a corporate body to
perform the *actus reus* and a corporate mind capable of forming *mens rea* has been to treat the
minds and bodies of the officers and servants of the corporation as supplying its mental and
physical faculties. The fifth way that the corporation can be liable for offences is therefore on
the basis that the controlling officers of the corporation performed the proscribed conduct
with the relevant fault element. This is the so-called 'identification' doctrine.[21]

---

[16] For a discussion of the difference types of due diligence defences and their merits, see LCCP 195, Part 6. See
also the valuable appendix by Professor Cartwright examining the use of due diligence defences in consumer
regulation in particular.

[17] (1842) 3 QB 223. cf *British Steel plc* [1995] Crim LR 654.

[18a] (1846) 9 QB 315.

[18b] See S Gentle [2011] Crim LR 101.

[19] *Mousell Bros Ltd v London and North-Western Rly Co* [1917] 2 KB 836; *Griffiths v Studebakers Ltd* [1924] 1 KB 102.

[20] *Griffiths v Studebakers Ltd* [1924] 1 KB 102; *Mousell Bros Ltd v London and North-Western Rly Co* [1917] 2
KB 836.

[21] See LCCP 195, Part 5 and Appendix C by Professor Wells.

Within every corporation there are certain persons (designated 'controlling officers' in the Draft Criminal Code)[22] who are the 'directing mind and will'[23] of the corporation and who, when acting in the company's business, are considered to be the 'embodiment of the company'.[24] Their acts and states of mind are the company's acts and states of mind and the company is held liable, not for the acts of others, but for what are deemed to be its own acts. The court looks to which person performed the proscribed conduct and then whether that person is sufficiently senior to be treated as a person who is a directing mind and will of the company.

The courts' willingness to attribute the blameworthy acts and *mens rea* of the controlling officers to the company developed rapidly in criminal law in the mid-1940s.[25] In *DPP v Kent and Sussex Contractors Ltd*,[26] the fraud alleged required an intention to deceive and it was held that the transport manager's intent was the intent of the company. *Kent* was approved in *ICR Haulage Ltd*[27] and applied to common law offences. The company was convicted of a conspiracy to defraud, with the act and intent of the managing director being the act and intent of the company. The doctrine was memorably described by Denning LJ:[28]

A company may in many ways be likened to a human body. It has a brain and a nerve centre which controls what it does. It also has hands which hold the tools and act in accordance with directions from the centre. Some of the people in the company are mere servants and agents who are nothing more than hands to do the work and cannot be said to represent the mind or will. Others are directors and managers who represent the directing mind and will of the company and control what it does. The state of mind of these managers is the state of mind of the company and is treated by the law as such.[29]

A person is not a 'controlling officer' simply because his work is 'brain' work (as opposed to physical work) and he exercises some managerial discretion, since not all such persons 'represent the directing mind and will of the company and control what it does'.[30] Nor is someone occupying a position entitled 'manager' necessarily a controlling mind. The manager of a supermarket belonging to a company owning hundreds of supermarkets is not the company's 'brains' and does not act as the company.[31] Companies have been held not to be criminally liable for the acts of a depot engineer[32] or a weighbridge operator,[33] or the European Sales Manager of the company.[34] Only the very senior managers will be likely to fit the description as the directing mind and will of the company. This illustrates one of the major shortcomings of the identification doctrine – that it fails to reflect the reality of the modern day large

---

[22] LC 143, para 11.6, and cl 34.

[23] *Lennard's Carrying Co Ltd v Asiatic Petroleum Co Ltd* [1915] AC 705, 713 per Viscount Haldane LC. Applied in *J F Alford Transport Ltd* [1997] 2 Cr App R 326 at 331.

[24] *Essendon Engineering Co Ltd v Maile* [1982] RTR 260, [1982] Crim LR 510.

[25] See for discussion of the development of the doctrine LCCP 195, paras 5.14–5.80.

[26] [1944] KB 146.

[27] [1944] KB 551, cf *McDonnell* [1966] 1 QB 233, below p 428.

[28] *HL Bolton (Engineering) Co Ltd v T. J. Graham & Sons Ltd* [1957] 1 QB 159 at 172. Though this *dictum* has been frequently followed, the Privy Council has said in the *Meridian* case, below, p 262, that the anthropomorphism distracts attention from what the Board regarded as the true principle determining whether acts should be attributed to the corporation – ie the interpretation of the particular statute.

[29] Thus, it is thought that a company could be guilty of abetting an offence through its managing director – though there is no *vicarious* liability in abetting, below, p 282. See *Robert Millar (Contractors) Ltd* [1970] 2 QB 54.

[30] *Tesco Supermarkets Ltd v Nattrass* [1972] AC 153 at 171, HL, per Lord Reid, at 187 per Lord Dilhorne and at 200 per Lord Diplock. See Gobert and Punch, *Rethinking Corporate Crime* (2003) 59–70.

[31] ibid.

[32] *Magna Plant Ltd v Mitchell* [1966] Crim LR 394.

[33] *John Henshall (Quarries) Ltd v Harvey* [1965] 2 QB 233.

[34] *Redfern and Dunlop Ltd (Aircraft Division)* [1993] Crim LR 43.

multinational corporation.[35] Although there are instances of a wide application, in general, it produces what many regard as an unsatisfactorily narrow scope for criminal liability. It also renders it disproportionately easy to prosecute smaller companies in which the controllers are more readily identifiable and allows larger corporations to avoid liability by disguising their true organizational structure.[36] There are also difficulties because the test remains so ambiguous – it is unclear which individuals will qualify, and whether the same approach is applicable in all contexts. It is difficult to apply the test to companies of all sizes and structures working in different sectors.

How are the courts to determine which individuals are controllers? In the leading case of *Tesco Supermarkets Ltd v Nattrass*,[37] it was said that the company may be criminally liable only for the acts of:

the board of directors, the managing director and perhaps other superior officers of a company [who] carry out the functions of management and speak and act as the company,[38]

or of a person:

who is in actual control of the operations of a company or of part of them and who is not responsible to another person in the company for the manner in which he discharges his duties in the sense of being under his orders.[39]

Lord Diplock[40] thought that the question is to be answered by:

identifying those natural persons who by the memorandum and articles of association or as a result of action taken by the directors or by the company in general meeting pursuant to the articles are entrusted with the exercise of the powers of the company.

Lord Pearson too thought that the constitution of the company concerned must be taken into account; and Lords Dilhorne, Pearson and Diplock thought that the reference in the 'common form' provision, discussed below,[41] to 'any director, manager, secretary or other similar officer of the body corporate' affords a useful indication. If the persons who are responsible for the general management of the company delegate their duties to another, then the acts of that other will be the acts of the company.[42]

Once the facts have been ascertained, it is a question of law whether a person, in doing particular things, is to be regarded as the company or merely as the company's employee or agent.[43] Accordingly the judge should direct the jury that if they find certain facts proved then they must find that the act and intention of the agent is the act and the intention of the company. It is not sufficient to direct that the company is liable for its 'responsible agents' or 'high executives', for such persons are not necessarily the company.[44] The test is the same whether the offence be serious or trivial.

The decision in *Tesco* failed to provide the clarity of definition that is needed in fixing the scope of criminal liability, and was heavily criticized.[45]

---

[35] For criticism see LCCP 195, Part 5 and appendices B and C; Wells, *Corporations and Criminal Responsibility*.

[36] 96 per cent of UK businesses have between 0–9 employees. See LCCP 185, para 7.6.

[37] Above, n 30.

[38] Per Lord Reid at 171.

[39] Per Viscount Dilhorne at 187.

[40] At 200, followed in *Seaboard Offshore Ltd v Secretary of State for Transport* [1994] 2 All ER 99, 104, HL.

[41] See below, p 265.

[42] [1972] AC 153 at 193.

[43] [1972] AC 153 at 170, 173, per Lord Reid.

[44] *Sporle* [1971] Crim LR 706.

[45] See LCCP 195 and references in Part 5; RJ Wickins, 'Confusion Worse Confounded: The End of the Directing Mind Theory' [1997] J Bus Law 524.

Meridian – all a matter of statutory construction?

In the more recent *Meridian* case,[46] the Privy Council, in a valuable review of the nature of corporate liability, held that where the criminal liability alleged is under a statutory offence, whether an act is to be attributed to a corporation is a question of the construction of the particular statute under which proceedings are brought. Thus, the statute may impose corporate liability in respect of an employee who could not be said to be the 'directing mind and will' of the corporation under the primary rules of attribution. This is a controversial extension of the potential scope of corporate liability. For many it represents a welcome relaxation of the identification doctrine, with the potential to impose corporate liability more flexibly in a broader range of circumstances, but in doing so it reduces the degree of certainty in the law. Indeed, Buxton LJ, in a powerful dissent in the Court of Appeal (Civil Division), has commented that *Meridian* represents an 'imperfect guide to the approach to the rule for attribution of a crime'.[47]

The Privy Council in *Meridian* contrasted the *Tesco* case with *Re Supply of Ready Mixed Concrete*.[48] In *Tesco* a narrow approach to liability was adopted. In the *Concrete* case the House of Lords held a company liable for contempt of court for the act of a regional employee, who made an arrangement in breach of an undertaking given by the company to the Restrictive Practices Court. The board of directors knew nothing of the arrangement and had given instructions that no such arrangements were to be made. But the arrangement made by the regional employee was an agreement binding on the company.[49] The company had given an undertaking that no such arrangement would be made and it had made such an arrangement. Should it not have been exactly the same if the undertaking had been given by an individual employer and the arrangement made by an employee with ostensible authority?[50] *Ready Mixed Concrete* was a case of civil contempt of court and the result would not necessarily have been the same if it had been a criminal offence requiring *mens rea*. In *Meridian* itself, it was held that the acts of the company's investment manager were properly attributed to the company for the purposes of the New Zealand Securities Act 1988. Perhaps all that these cases demonstrate is that a statute imposes liability if that appears to be the intention of the legislature. The Court of Appeal has subsequently emphasized that the *Meridian* approach is only applicable to offences of statutory origin.[51] It has been endorsed by the Law Commission in LCCP 195, where it is recommended that courts should look at the underlying purposes of the statutory scheme for guidance on the bases for holding a company liable.[52]

It is unclear how far the *Meridian* approach develops the identification doctrine in practice. The case of *Moore v I Bresler Ltd*,[53] which has been criticized for going too far down the scale in identifying a controlling officer,[54] was approved in *Meridian* by the Privy Council as an example of its 'construction' principle. The company was convicted of making false returns with intent to deceive, contrary to the Finance (No 2) Act 1940, when the returns were made by the company secretary and a *branch* sales manager.[55]

---

[46] *Meridian Global Funds Management Asia Ltd v Securities Commission* [1995] 2 AC 500. See E Ferran (2011) 127 LQR 239.

[47] *Re Odyssey (London) Ltd v OIC Run Off Ltd* (2000) The Times, 3 Mar, Court of Appeal (Civ Div).

[48] [1995] 1 AC 456. See C Wells, 'A Quite Revolution in Corporate Liability for Crime' (1995) 145 NLJ 1326.

[49] Lord Nolan [1995] 1 All ER at 150–151.

[50] 'In my opinion . . . the act [in breach of an injunction] need not be done by the person himself': Warrington J in *Stancomb v Trowbridge UDC* [1910] 2 Ch 190 at 193–194, a decision which Lord Nolan said should have been followed in *Ready-Mixed Concrete*.

[51] *A-G's Reference (No 2 of 1999)* [2000] QB 796.

[52] See in particular Part 5 and recommendation at para 5.110.

[53] [1944] 2 All ER 515, DC.

[54] By R Welsh, 'The Criminal Liability of Corporations' (1946) 62 LQR 345 at 358, Williams, TBCL, 973.

[55] But the company secretary might perhaps be regarded, when acting within the scope of his authority, as the company's 'directing mind and will' for this purpose. *Kent and Sussex Contractors* [1944] KB 146 seems more doubtful in this respect, as only the transport manager was involved.

Acting 'as' and yet 'against' the corporation

The *Moore v I Bresler Ltd*,[56] decision is also subject to criticism because the object was to conceal the fraudulent sale by these two officers of the company's property.[57] The Draft Code, cl 30(6), would reverse it by providing that a corporation is not liable for the act of a controlling officer when it is done with the intention of doing harm, or concealing harm done, to the corporation.

Acting within the scope of corporate duty

The controlling officer must be acting within the scope of his authority as a corporate officer at the time that he performs the necessary elements of the offence in terms of *actus reus* and *mens rea* before these can be treated as the criminal acts of the corporation itself under the identification doctrine.

A corporation's 'state of mind'

Having identified the relevant controlling individual with whom the corporation may be identified, it is necessary to prove that he performed the relevant *actus reus* with the accompanying *mens rea*. Where the offence is one of strict liability, the corporation may be held liable for the acts of any of its employees or agents where those acts are, in law, the company's acts, under the attribution principle discussed below (p 279).[58] Wherever the offence requires *mens rea*, it must be proved that a controlling officer had the *mens rea*.[59] Similarly, where a defence requires evidence of a belief or other state of mind, this must usually be the belief or state of mind of a controlling officer;[60] but the belief of one officer, A, will not suffice if another, B, especially if he is superior to A, knows that A's belief is ill-founded.[61] Probably, each controlling officer who is concerned in the offence must have the required state of mind. If, however, no controlling officer is involved and all the employees or agents who are involved do have the required state of mind, the defence ought clearly to be available. If a branch manager, not being a controlling officer, finds a controlled drug in supplies delivered to his branch and takes control of it, intending to hand it to the police, the company may surely rely on this intention to establish the defence provided by s 5(4) of the Misuse of Drugs Act 1971, if it is charged with unlawful possession of the drug.[62]

No aggregation of several controlling individuals' culpability[63]

A question that was raised by many critics of the identification doctrine was whether it must be proved that an individual controlling officer (whether identifiable or not) was guilty of the crime alleged against the company or whether it is permissible to 'aggregate' the conduct of a number of officers, none of whom would individually be guilty, so as to constitute in sum, the elements of the offence. It is submitted that it is not possible artificially to construct the *mens rea* in this way.[64] Two (semi) innocent states of mind cannot be added together to produce

---

[56] [1944] 2 All ER 515, DC.

[57] Williams, TBCL, 973, refers to *Belmont Finance Corpn Ltd v Williams Furniture Ltd* [1979] Ch 250 as 'a much more sensible decision of a civil court'.

[58] Agent's acts are the principal's act in law.

[59] *Tesco Supermarkets Ltd v Nattrass* [1972] AC 153. Draft Criminal Code, cl 34(2).

[60] *G J Coles & Co Ltd v Goldsworthy* [1985] WAR 183. See G Orchard in *Criminal Law Essays*, 114, 117, 118–119.

[61] *Brambles Holdings Ltd v Carey* (1976) 15 SASR 270 at 280.

[62] See Law Com No 177, Draft Criminal Code, Appendix B, Example 30 (vi).

[63] See especially C Wells, 'Culture, Risk and Criminal Liability' [1993] Crim LR 551, 563.

[64] cf *Armstrong v Strain* [1952] 1 KB 232, Devlin J: 'You cannot add an innocent state of mind to an innocent state of mind and get as a result a dishonest state of mind.'

a guilty state of mind.[65] Any such doctrine could certainly have no application in offences requiring knowledge, intention or recklessness. It is in relation to offences of negligence (particularly gross negligence) that the aggregation principle has been most forcefully advocated. The argument proceeds as follows: a company owes a duty of care and if its operation falls far below the standard required it is guilty of gross negligence. A series of minor failures by officers of the company might add up to a gross breach by the company of its duty of care. There is authority for such a doctrine in the law of tort[66] and the concept of negligence is the same in the criminal law, the difference being one of degree – criminal negligence must be 'gross'. It is immaterial that the doctrine of vicarious liability in tort does not apply in criminal law, because this is a case not of vicarious, but of personal, liability and that is a proper concern of the criminal law. Thus it was argued that a corporation ought to be open to prosecution for manslaughter by gross negligence on the aggregation principle.[67] This argument was rejected by the Court of Appeal in the *A-G's Reference (No 2 of 1999)*.[68] The prosecution arose from the Southall train crash in which seven passengers died. The trial judge ruled that the gross negligence manslaughter offence required negligence to be proved under the identification doctrine. The Court of Appeal approved that ruling, holding that unless an identified individual's conduct, characterized as gross criminal negligence, could be attributed to the company, the company was not, in the state of the common law, liable for manslaughter.[69] The specific statutory offence under the Corporate Manslaughter and Corporate Homicide Act 2007 will now apply, but the general principle in corporate liability that the identification doctrine cannot be satisfied by an aggregation of several officers' states of mind remains good law for all other offences.

Several interesting issues remain in relation to the aggregation argument, including to what extent the requirement that an individual controlling mind be identifiable is necessary for conviction. Can a company waive the need to establish that by pleading guilty on the basis that, although no controller was identifiable, the corporation is prepared to accept liability? There would seem no reason in principle why not. The bar on aggregation is to protect the company and if it chooses it may waive that protection. It would not be akin to a company pleading guilty to an offence that was not known to law. Consider the case where the company accepts that it must have been director A or B who performed the criminal acts, but it cannot be established beyond reasonable doubt which of them did. Surely the company should be capable of accepting guilt? Indeed, it is arguable that in such a case the law ought to allow the Crown to establish corporate liability in a contested trial.

Impact of the Corporate Manslaughter and Corporate Homicide Act 2007

The 2007 Act imposes liability for manslaughter on the basis of a breach of a relevant duty by the organization *as a result of the way the activities are managed or organized*. The italicized words are designed to ensure that the focus is on a 'management failure'; at least for

---

[65] Celia Wells argues to the contrary that 'aggregation needs to be seen as a recognition that individuals within a company contribute to the whole machine; it is the whole that is judged not the parts': *Corporations and Criminal Responsibility*, 155. See also LCCP 195, Appendix C.

[66] *W B Anderson & Sons Ltd v Rhodes (Liverpool) Ltd* [1967] 2 All ER 850, Cairns J, discussed by M Dean, 'Hedley Byrne and the Eager Business Man' (1968) 31 MLR 322; *Salmond on Torts* (21st edn, 1996) 406–409; *Fleming on Torts* (8th edn, 1992) 376–385.

[67] See below, p 564. In the *P&O* case, Turner J seems to have proceeded on the basis that recklessness must be proved.

[68] [2000] QB 796; considering *Great Western Trains Co* (1999) 3 June, CCC. It was also rejected in Scotland in *Transco v HM Advocate* 2004 SLT 41.

[69] The court's conclusion that there can *in general* be no corporate liability in the absence of an identified human offender ignores the principle discussed above of corporate liability where a duty is specifically imposed on the corporation as a legal person: *Birmingham & Gloucester Railway* (1842) 3 QB 223.

manslaughter the limitations of the identification doctrine are removed. Some commentators suggest that this would be a better approach to adopt in determining corporate liability for all offences.[70]

The Act does, however, place a restriction on the test. Under s 1(3), the offence is committed by an organization only if 'the way in which its activities are managed and organised *by its senior management* is a substantial element in the breach referred to in subsection 1'. Who are the senior managers? By s 1(4)(c):

'senior management', in relation to an organisation, means the persons who play significant roles in –

(i) the making of decisions about how the whole or a substantial part of its activities are to be managed or organised, or

(ii) the actual managing or organising of the whole or a substantial part of those activities.

This extends beyond the narrow category of senior individuals who would be caught at common law by being regarded as the directing mind and will under the identification doctrine. The merits of this test in the context of the offence are considered in Chapter 15 below. The test is linked to a senior level of management but also considers how an activity was managed within the organization as a whole. It will in manslaughter now be possible to aggregate the shortcomings of a wide variety of individuals within the organization to prove a failure of management *by the organization*. The language is designed to reflect the concentration of things done consistently within the organization's culture and policies more generally.[71]

It remains to be seen whether the courts will draw upon this definition of 'senior managers' from the 2007 Act in its consideration of the scope of the 'relevant controlling minds' in application of the identification doctrine more generally.[72]

10.1.2.6 Statutory liability of corporate officers

The sixth way in which liability may apply is by statute. The following provision commonly appears in statutes creating offences likely to be committed by corporations:[73]

Where an offence...committed by a body corporate is proved to have been committed with the consent or connivance of, or to be attributable to any neglect on the part of, any director, manager, secretary or other similar officer of the body corporate or any person who was purporting to act in any such capacity, he as well as the body corporate shall be guilty of that offence and shall be liable to be proceeded against and punished accordingly.

Whether a director or other officer is under a duty is a question which can be answered only by looking at the facts of each case; and the onus of proving that there was a duty which has been neglected is on the prosecution.[74]

---

[70] See the discussion in LCCP 195, Part 5 and Appendices B and C.

[71] For discussion of the advantages of basing liability on corporate organizational models see LCCP 195 and Appendix C in particular, considering the Australian experience.

[72] See the discussion by Cartwright in LCCP 195, App B.

[73] eg Outer Space Act 1986, s 11(3). The provision in the Fraud Act 2006, s 12 is even wider: '(1) Subsection (2) applies if an offence under this Act is committed by a body corporate. (2) If the offence is proved to have been committed with the consent or connivance of – (a) a director, manager, secretary or other similar officer of the body corporate, or (b) a person who was purporting to act in any such capacity, he (as well as the body corporate) is guilty of the offence and liable to be proceeded against and punished accordingly. (3) If the affairs of a body corporate are managed by its members, subsection (2) applies in relation to the acts and defaults of a member in connection with his functions of management as if he were a director of the body corporate.'

[74] *Huckerby v Elliott* [1970] 1 All ER 189. 'Manager' means someone managing the affairs of the company and not, eg, the manager of a store: *Tesco Supermarkets Ltd v Nattrass* [1972] AC 153 at 178.

So far as 'consent' and 'connivance' are concerned, these provisions probably effect only a slight extension of the law; because the officer who expressly consents or connives in the commission of the offence will be liable as a secondary party under the principles considered in Chapter 8. There may, however, be a case of consent which does not amount to counselling or abetting, however; and the words 'attributable to any neglect on the part of'[75] clearly impose a wider liability in making the officer liable for his negligence in failing to prevent the offence.

Note that this common form of provision[76] does not create an offence. It creates an extended form of secondary liability for an offence committed by a body corporate under some other provision of the relevant Act. It is submitted that, like the general law of secondary liability, it applies automatically and does not have to be, and indeed is incapable of being, charged as an offence.[77]

In the most recent House of Lords case dealing with such sections, *Chargot Ltd*,[78] a case under the Health and Safety Act 1974, s 37. Lord Hope (with whom the other Lords agreed) said:

No fixed rule can be laid down as to what the prosecution must identify and prove in order to establish that the officer's state of mind was such as to amount to consent, connivance or neglect. In some cases, as where the officer's place of activity was remote from the work place or what was done there was not under his immediate direction and control, this may require the leading of quite detailed evidence of which fair notice may have to be given. In others, where the officer was in day to day contact with what was done there, very little more may be needed...the question, in the end of the day, will always be whether the officer in question should have been put on inquiry so as to have taken steps to determine whether or not the appropriate safety procedures were in place.

The Law Commission has recently examined the use of this type of provision,[79] and concluded that in principle there cannot be true consent and connivance without at least a subjective awareness that wrongdoing is or will be taking place, and that a requirement for proof of at least that level of fault is desirable. On this recommendation it would not be possible to establish individual directors' liability for an offence committed by the company, unless there was true, subjective consent or connivance at the offence by the director in question. This would be:

in keeping with an understanding of the doctrine of consent and connivance as an extension of the complicity doctrine, to fit the reality of corporate decision-making. Moreover, where crimes requiring proof of fault or involving stigma are in issue, a requirement of at least subjective awareness on a director's part would appear to be essential, in point of justice, given that a finding of consent and connivance makes a director (or equivalent person) guilty of the offence itself.[80]

The Commission's proposal is that rather than for these connivance provisions being extended to include instances where the company's offence is attributable to mere neglect, instead, where appropriate, for new offences to be created based on liability for the conduct of an individual whom the company has negligently failed to prevent from committing the offence.[81]

---

[75] These words are omitted from the Theft Act 1968, s 18.

[76] Commonly used examples are discussed in LCCP 195, Part 7 including the Trade Descriptions Act 1968, s 20 and the Food Safety Act 1990, s 14.

[77] Contra, *Wilson* [1997] Crim LR 53 and commentary.

[78] [2008] UKHL 73.

[79] LCCP 195, Part 7.

[80] LCCP 195, para 7.34.

[81] ibid.

10.1.3 Limits of corporate liability

When any statute makes it an offence for 'a person' to do or omit to do something, that offence is capable of commission by a corporation, unless the contrary appears: the Interpretation Act 1889 (and now the Interpretation Act 1978) defined 'person' to include 'a body of persons corporate or unincorporate' unless the contrary appears and provided that the definition, so far as it includes bodies corporate, applies to any provision of an Act whenever passed, relating to an offence punishable on indictment or summary conviction.[82] The fact that the offence requires *mens rea* does not preclude corporate liability since, as discussed above, the state of mind of the corporation's controlling officers, as well as their acts, may be attributed to the corporation. However, the nature of the offence may be such that a corporation is physically incapable of committing it even through its controlling officers.

There are numerous other limitations on the liability of a corporation.

10.1.3.1 Categories of offence

There are offences which it is extremely unlikely that an official of a corporation could commit within the scope of his employment; for example, bigamy,[83] rape, some other sexual offences and, possibly, perjury.[84]

10.1.3.2 Penalty and punishment

A corporation cannot be sentenced to a physical punishment such as imprisonment. A corporation cannot therefore be guilty of murder. The lack of imagination in the law's response to sentencing corporations when they are found liable has been cogently criticized.[85] One of the most welcome aspects of the 2007 Act lies in the innovative sentencing and disposal powers available to the courts. The court may, if the prosecution apply, impose a remedial order. A remedial order under s 9 is one 'requiring the organisation to take specified steps' to remedy the breach or anything resulting from it which caused death, or any deficiency as to health and safety matters of which the breach appears to be an indication.[86] Under s 10 a publicity order may be made 'requiring the organisation to publicise in a specified manner' its conviction, specified particulars, the amount of any fine and the terms of any remedial order. This provision, added during the Bill's passage in the Lords, is clearly intended to deter by impact of adverse publicity.[87]

10.1.4 Unincorporated bodies

An unincorporated association, such as a partnership or trade union, is not a legal person at common law and therefore could not incur criminal liability, though its members could. This is still the position for common law offences. Statutory offences are different.

---

[82] See the Interpretation Act 1978, s 5 and Sch 1.

[83] Even in some of these cases it is not inconceivable that a corporation might be held liable as a secondary party. Eg the managing director of an incorporated marriage advisory bureau negotiates a marriage which he knows to be bigamous. Or a pornographic film company liable as an accessory to rape.

[84] In *Re Odyssey (London) Ltd v OIC Run Off Ltd* (2000) The Times, 3 Mar, CA (Civ Div), the majority considered, *obiter*, that a company could be liable for perjury through acts of director and managing director, if he had the 'status' of the company when testifying.

[85] See, generally, on the sentencing of corporations: Gobert and Punch, *Rethinking Corporate Crime,* Ch 7; and for a review of the punishments that might be available see M Jefferson, 'Corporate Criminal Liability: The Problems of Sanctions' (2001) 65 J Crim L 235.

[86] Failure to comply is an offence punishable with a fine.

[87] See the Sentencing Guidelines Council definitive guidance on these powers: www.sentencingcouncil.org.uk/docs/web__guideline_on_corporate_manslaughter_accessible.pdf.

10.1.4.1 Liability for what offences?

The effect of the Interpretation Act 1889 was that in all enactments relating to offences, whenever passed, the word 'person' includes bodies corporate (s 2) and, in enactments passed after 1889, both bodies corporate *and unincorporate* (s 19). The Interpretation Act 1978 preserves this position.[88] Since 1889 unincorporated bodies have been able to commit any offence under an enactment passed after 1889 which makes it an offence for a 'person' to do or omit to do anything which an unincorporated body is capable of doing. The potential liability of unincorporated bodies seems to have been little noticed. In *A-G v Able,* Woolf J, dealing with an alleged offence under the Suicide Act 1961 said, 'It must be remembered that the [Voluntary Euthanasia Society] is an unincorporated body and there can be no question of the society committing an offence';[89] but since that offence may be committed by 'a person' it seems that it may be committed by an unincorporated body. An unincorporated body, being the registered keeper of a vehicle, was held capable of liability as a 'person' to fixed penalties for illegal parking under the Transport Act 1982.[90]

Schedule 1 to the Interpretation Act 1978 provides that 'person' includes a body of persons corporate or unincorporate', and by s 5 of the Act 'in any Act, unless the contrary intention appears, words and expressions listed in Schedule 1 to this Act are to be construed according to that Schedule'. In determining whether 'a contrary intention appears' there is no form of words applied universally in the statutes. The Court of Appeal in *L*[91] has recently accepted that although several statutes do make specific provision for the criminal liability of unincorporated associations the provisions are so varied that no settled policy can be discerned from them. The court found it impossible to derive any general proposition that:

there is a form of enactment which is to be expected if an unincorporated association is to be criminally liable, and of which the absence signals a contrary intention for the purposes of section 5 of the Interpretation Act.[92]

The court accepted that the absence of procedural provisions to govern such prosecutions is not determinative of whether they were intended to apply to unincorporated associations. Different considerations may apply in *mens rea* offences and those at common law than from strict liability statutory offences. According to the Court of Appeal in *W Stevenson & Sons (a partnership)*,[93] in relation to partnerships one consideration may be whether there is some restriction upon the assets that will properly be available to meet any penalty imposed. It is submitted this is a doubtful interpretation. The court does not address in detail the impact of s 10 of the Partnership Act 1890.[94] It is arguable that once a partnership (or indeed a partner)

---

[88] Sch 2, para 4(5) maintains the existing application of 'person' to corporate bodies (and, implicitly, its non-application to unincorporated bodies) in pre-1889 statutes creating offences. The definition of 'person' in Sch 1 applies to all statutes passed after the commencement of the 1889 Act, so that they continue to be capable of commission by unincorporated bodies.

[89] [1984] QB 795.

[90] *Clerk to Croydon Justices, ex p Chief Constable of Kent* [1989] Crim LR 910, DC.

[91] [2009] EWCA Crim 1970.

[92] [22].

[93] [2008] EWCA Crim 273. W was convicted under an offence for failing 'to submit a sales note which accurately indicated the quantities and price at first sale of each fish species'. The question for the Court of Appeal was whether it was possible for legislation to render a partnership criminally liable as a separate entity from the individual partners.

[94] 'Where, by any wrongful act or omission of any partner acting in the ordinary course of the business of the firm, or with the authority of his co-partners, loss or injury is caused to any person not being a partner in the firm, or any penalty is incurred, the firm is liable therefore to the same extent as the partner so acting or omitting to act.'

has been convicted if s 10 applies, all the partners are liable to pay the fine as a matter of partnership law.[95]

It is disappointing that the law offers no clearer definition on these matters.

10.1.4.2 Which members of the unincorporated association can be liable?

It was thought that when an unincorporated association is prosecuted the courts would normally proceed by analogy to the law relating to corporations and that only officials corresponding to the controlling officers of corporations would bear some liability. The Court of Appeal has rejected that narrow approach, adopting an interpretation with the potential to impose liability on many thousands of individuals. In *L*,[96] the chairman and treasurer of a golf club with 900 members were prosecuted for the strict liability offence of polluting a watercourse by an escape of heating oil from the premises caused directly by an independent contractor. The question arose as to whether it was correct to prosecute the individuals rather than the association. The trial judge ruled that the individuals could not be prosecuted. The Court of Appeal disagreed. Irrespective of the lack of personal fault, liability arose as a result of membership. Criminal liability of unincorporated associations was said to involve quite separate principles from those relating to corporations:

A corporation has, for all legal purposes, independent legal personality. It is also regulated, often heavily. It must have a registered address and registered directors and secretary. An unincorporated association may indeed look very like a corporation in some cases, and it may have standing and de facto independence, but equally it may not. A prosecution which could only be brought against an informal grouping of building workers, or sportsmen, or campaigners would be likely to be wholly ineffective. It is a necessary consequence of the different nature of an unincorporated association that all its members remain jointly and severally liable for its actions done within their authority.[97]

The court's conclusion is that liability can be imposed on the individual members irrespective of the lack of personal fault of any individual member. It appears to be heavily influenced by the potential ineffectiveness of a prosecution against a body which might be as informal as some unincorporated ones no doubt are.[98] This has very serious potential ramifications for the presumably tens of thousands of members of unincorporated bodies that exist in England and Wales. Personal criminal liability might result simply by virtue of a person's voluntary membership of a lawful association. Liability is not dependent on any personal fault. Where individual members of an unincorporated association are prosecuted it is not on the basis of some form of vicarious liability. Nor, unlike corporations, does liability turn on the person holding a position of responsibility or office so that he might be regarded as a controlling officer. Given the enormous number of strict liability offences that such organizations might transgress in the course of performing their usual business the prospect of personal liability of all members seems astounding. Of course, there is the potential for prosecution agencies to select individuals within a club since it is for the CPS to determine the defendants in any given case and the courts will interfere only if there is an abuse of process. As Hughes LJ commented in *L*, relevant considerations will no doubt include 'the extent of the association's stability and

---

[95] Even if only the partnership is liable to pay, as the Court of Appeal thought, then if the partnership assets are insufficient to pay the fine, s 10 would require an additional contribution from the partners' own assets in any event since it is by definition a partnership liability. If that is right, the court's careful attempts to avoid unjust imposition of penalties on individuals are thwarted.

[96] [2008] EWCA Crim 1970.

[97] [33] per Hughes LJ.

[98] It should be noted that this has not prevented the imposition of injunctions against such bodies albeit with necessary elaboration eg *Huntingdon Life Sciences v Stop Huntingdon Animal Cruelty* [2003] EWHC 1967 (QB).

assets and the nature of the act or omission said to constitute an offence'. Exceptionally, the Crown might choose to prosecute both the association and members.

If the decision is correct, it is submitted that the potential criminal liability of members of unincorporated associations deserves parliamentary consideration. Provisions akin to those dealing with the criminal liability of company officers would produce fairer results.

10.1.5 Rationale and reform of corporate criminal liability

The English courts have created the identification principle through which corporate liability might be imposed without addressing the broader social purposes of imposing such liability,[99] nor (leaving aside the 2007 Act) of the effectiveness of the punishments administered. The fines imposed are ultimately borne by the shareholders who, in most cases, are not responsible in any sense for the offence. If they really had control over the directors and so over the management of the company, this might afford some justification; but it is generally recognized that they have little control over large, public companies.[100] Moreover, fines may be inflicted on the boards of nationalized industries, where there are no shareholders and the consumers of the product, who ultimately pay the fine, have no rights whatever to appoint or dismiss the officials concerned. Since the persons actually responsible for the offence may, in the great majority of cases, be convicted, it has been questioned whether there is any need to impose this additional penalty.

Arguments in favour of corporate liability include that there may be difficulty in fixing individuals with liability where someone among the 'brains' of the corporation has undoubtedly authorized the offence. Corporate liability, of course, also ensures that the offence will not go unpunished and that a fine proportionate to the gravity of the offence may be imposed, when it might be out of proportion to the means of the individuals concerned. Further, the imposition of liability on the organization gives all of those directing it an interest in the prevention of illegalities – and they are in a position to prevent them, though the shareholders are not. In the recent case of *Balfour Beatty Rail Infrastructure Ltd*,[101] the company appealed against a sentence of £10m imposed on the company for a conviction under s 3 of the Health and Safety at Work etc Act 1974 arising from the Hatfield train crash where several people died and many were injured. The Lord Chief Justice noted that the knowledge that a breach can result in a fine of sufficient size to impact on the shareholders 'will provide a powerful incentive for management to comply with the duty' while accepting that the fine need not always be so high as to affect dividends or share prices.[102] Since, moreover, the names of the officers will mean nothing to the public only the conviction of the corporation itself will serve to warn the public of the wrongful acts – operating buses with faulty brakes, trains on defective tracks, or selling mouldy pies – which are committed in its name.

As noted above, the courts have taken a relatively simplistic approach to imposing criminal liability on corporations by shoehorning them into the orthodox model of criminal liability via the identification doctrine.[103] This has pre-empted discussion of the more fundamental question, namely whether an entirely separate model of criminal responsibility ought to be created to reflect corporate structures and activities.[104] For some the company

---

[99] cf other jurisdictions, and, eg, J Gobert and E Mugnai, 'Coping with Corporate Criminality – Some Lessons from Italy' [2002] Crim LR 617; S Adam, N Cosette-Basecqz and M Nihoul (eds), *Corporate Criminal Liability in Europe* (2008).

[100] R Pennington, *Company Law* (8th edn, 2001) Part III.

[101] [2006] EWCA Crim 1586.

[102] [42].

[103] See A Norrie, *Crime Reason and History* (2nd edn, 2000) Ch 5.

[104] See further the discussion in LCCP 195, particularly the Appendices.

is no more than the collection of individuals which make it up, for others the company has a distinct personality which should be reflected in the law's treatment. Whether a company as a non-human entity can properly be found to be morally culpable in its own right raises issues extending well beyond the scope of this work, but four options for corporate criminal liability deserve mention.[105]

10.1.5.1 Aggregation

This approach has been noted above and involves aggregating the *mens rea* of various individuals within the corporation to combine as a sufficient blameworthy 'state of mind' of the company. This approach has been considered and rejected by the Court of Appeal.[106] This approach would, however, be practically attainable and would not require radical deviation from the orthodox model of criminal responsibility. But for this reason some commentators would regard it as an inadequate solution. It would serve only to maintain the fiction of attributing liability through the acts of the company controllers rather than looking deeper for a culpable corporate culture or ethos. As Fisse and Braithwaite argue 'organisations are systems...not just aggregations of individuals'.[107]

10.1.5.2 Culpable corporate culture

Professor Wells has also criticized the narrow understanding of the aggregation approach, arguing that it is not simply the sum of the parts – addition of director A's *mens rea* and director B's knowledge to comprise the relevant *mens rea* for the offence. Wells rejects the identification doctrine as too narrow and advocates an extension of the availability of direct corporate liability.[108] Having regard to the organizational structures of corporations and the corporate policies and practices, she argues that the law should recognize that 'responsibility can...be found in the corporation's structures themselves'.[109] Wells concludes that there should be a form of corporate *mens rea* approach. Under this proposal a corporation can be responsible for the corporation's acts. The difficulty with such a proposal lies in determining how errant the policy and/or practice of the company must be to be treated in law as being equally deserving of blame as the *mens rea* of an individual offender.

Some jurisdictions have introduced a corporate culture-based approach to liability. In the Australian Capital Territories, for example, the statutory equivalent to the corporate manslaughter offence[110] turns on proof of a culpable corporate culture, with corporate culture defined as an: 'attitude, policy, rule, course of conduct or practice existing within the corporation generally or in that part of the corporation where the relevant conduct happens'.

English law has not adopted anything quite so radical, even in the 2007 Act. Under the corporate manslaughter offence the jury's duty in relation to determining the breach of duty is provided in s 8 and includes an obligation to consider whether the evidence shows that the organization failed to comply with any health and safety legislation[111] that relates to the

---

[105] J Gobert, 'Corporate Criminality: Four Models of Fault' (1994) 14 LS 393; J Gobert, 'Corporate Criminality: New Crimes for the Times' [1994] Crim LR 722; R Grantham, 'Corporate Knowledge: Identification or Attribution?' (1996) 59 MLR 732.

[106] *A-G's Reference (No 2 of 1999)* [2000] QB 796. See also Bingham LJ in *R v HM Coroner for East Kent, ex p Spooner* (1989) 88 Cr App R 10.

[107] B Fisse and J Braithwaite, 'The Allocation of Responsibility for Corporate Crime: Individualism, Collectivism and Accountability' (1988) 11 Sydney LR 468, 479.

[108] See also the summary in LCCP 195, Appendix C.

[109] Wells, *Corporations and Criminal Responsibility*, 157.

[110] Crimes (Industrial Manslaughter) Amendment Act 2003, s 51, ACT Criminal Code, s 51. See generally LCCP 195, Appendix C.

[111] Defined in s 8(5): ' "health and safety guidance" means any code, guidance, manual or similar publication that is concerned with health and safety matters and is made or issued (under a statutory provision or otherwise)

alleged breach, and if so – how serious that failure was; how much of a risk of death it posed. The jury *may* also – consider:

the extent to which the evidence shows that there were attitudes, policies, systems or accepted practices within the organisation that were likely to have encouraged any such [health and safety] failure..., or to have produced tolerance of it; having regard to any health and safety guidance that relates to the alleged breach.

This section does not prevent the jury from having regard to any other matters they consider relevant. Section 8(3) emphasizes that the jury may have reference to general organizational and systems failures. One difficulty with this provision, as with establishing something as vague as a 'corporate culture',[112] is how the 'attitudes, etc' are proved. There is the potential for lengthy arguments and evidence comparing practices across the particular sector or industry. Imagine a prosecution of a rail company and the potential for the defence to adduce evidence of safety procedures and policies across the rail sector to demonstrate the quality of their own. No doubt the jury will have regard to the organization's overall objectives, published policy statements on safety, monitoring and compliance policies, attitudes to development of safety and to training and awareness, approaches to remedying previous health and safety infringements, etc.

There have been suggestions that English law could adopt a model of general corporate liability based on the 2007 Act approach.[113]

10.1.5.3 Reactive corporate fault

A yet more radical approach derives from the work of Australian academics, Fisse and Braithwaite.[114] In short, they propose a model under which the company can become liable to court orders to investigate and remedy its conduct where there is an alleged criminal wrongdoing. Criminal liability would follow where the company subsequently failed to take adequate remedial measures.

10.1.5.4 Specific statutory offences

Another alternative is to create specific corporate forms of offences. A recent example is the Bribery Act 2010, s 7. The s 7 offence provides:

(1) A relevant commercial organisation ('C') is guilty of an offence under this section if a person ('A') associated with C bribes another person intending –

(a) to obtain or retain business for C, or

(b) to obtain or retain an advantage in the conduct of business for C.

There is a due diligence defence in s 7(2) for C to prove that C had in place adequate procedures designed to prevent persons associated with C from undertaking such conduct.

The difficulties of the identification doctrine are avoided by providing specifically which individuals associated with a company will trigger liability for the company by their actions. In the case of s 7 it is a very wide range of individuals indeed. A person associated with a commercial organization is defined by s 8 as a person who performs services for or on behalf of the organization including employees, agents or subsidiaries. Employees are presumed to

by an authority responsible for the enforcement of any health and safety legislation'. See, generally, on Health and Safety legislation the helpful website of the Health and Safety Executive: www.hse.gov.uk/legislation.

[112] Arguably it is no more difficult than proving a subjective state of mind such as recklessness of a human defendant, See Wells, *Corporations and Criminal Responsibility*, 155.

[113] See LCCP 195, Part 5 and Appendices B and C.

[114] *Corporations, Crime and Accountability* (1993).

be performing services for their employer but otherwise the question is to be determined by reference to all the relevant circumstances. A person 'bribes' another for the purposes of this section if he commits an offence under s 1 and 6 of the Act or aids and abets such an offence. It is irrelevant whether there has been a prosecution for it (s 7(3)), provided the prosecution show that the person would be guilty of the offence were that person prosecuted under this Act. There is no need for A to have a close connection to the UK as defined in s 12, provided C is a 'relevant commercial organisation'. 'Relevant commercial organisation' is defined (at s 7(5)) as: a body incorporated under the law of any part of the UK and which carries on business whether there or elsewhere, a partnership that is formed under the law of any part of the UK and which carries on business there or elsewhere, or any other body corporate or partnership wherever incorporated or formed which carries on business in any part of the UK.

Other safeguards can be built into such offences. For example, s 7 is triable only on indictment (s 11(3)). No prosecution may be instituted in England and Wales except by or with the consent of the DPP, the Director of the Serious Fraud Office, or the Director of Revenue and Customs Prosecutions (s 10(1)). In the case of a partnership proceedings must be brought in the name of the partnership (not in that of any of the partners) (s 15).[115]

10.1.5.5 Extended vicarious liability

An alternative model would be to extend the approach to vicarious liability, as in some other jurisdictions such as some states in the USA, and introduce broader due diligence defences available to corporations.[116] The application of due diligence defences is considered in full in Chapter 7. Again, this may not involve a drastic change from the present position. We turn now to consider the scope of vicarious liability.

10.2 Vicarious liability[117]

10.2.1 Nature and scope of doctrine

The doctrine of 'vicarious liability' is a mechanism by which the law attributes blame for the acts of another. Common examples include retail companies being responsible for the sale of items by managers and shop assistants in their stores, and of licensees being responsible for the acts of their employees. Unfortunately, English law's approach has the potential to operate very harshly. As the Law Commission recently commented, the doctrine can operate wholly unfairly and disproportionately by imposing liability on D for an offence committed by someone even though D had no reason to think that the delegated person would do as he did.[118] The doctrine ought therefore to be kept within strict limits; disappointingly, it remains of uncertain scope.

---

[115] The maximum sentence is an unlimited fine. A fine imposed on a partnership is to be paid out of partnership assets (s 15(3)). See S Gentle [2011] Crim LR 101.

[116] See GR Sullivan [1996] CLJ 515.

[117] Williams, CLGP, Ch 7, and 'Mens Rea and Vicarious Responsibility' (1956) 9 CLP 57; P Glazebrook, 'Situational Liability', in Reshaping the Criminal Law, 108; PJ Pace, 'Delegation – A Doctrine in Search of a Definition' [1982] Crim LR 627; LH Leigh, Strict and Vicarious Liability (1982); FB Sayer, 'Criminal Responsibility for the Acts of Another' (1930) 43 Harv LR 689; T Baty, Vicarious Liability (1916) especially Ch X. For proposals for the reform of the law, see Law Com WP No 43; LCCP 195.

[118] See LCCP 195, para 1.89.

10.2.1.1 Vicarious liability distinguished from personal duty

It is important to distinguish vicarious liability from liability for breach of a personal duty. Many statutes, particularly dealing with regulatory offences, create specific offences that can be committed by the specified person (for example, the employer) in person. If the specified person is in breach of that duty, he commits the *actus reus* of the offence and, if it imposes strict liability, he is personally, not vicariously, guilty of the offence, though he may say with truth that he would not have been in breach but for the fault of his employees or agents. A good example is the Health and Safety at Work etc Act 1974. By s 3(1), the Act imposes on every employer a duty 'to conduct his undertaking in such a way as to ensure, so far as is reasonably practicable' that persons not in his employment are not exposed to risk. In *British Steel plc,*[119] D's subcontractor, negligently conducting D's undertaking, caused V's death. D had not ensured so far as was, in the opinion of the court, reasonably practicable, that persons were not exposed to risk and D was therefore guilty. D was liable, not vicariously for the acts of the subcontractor which caused death, but for his own failure to ensure that there was no risk of such a thing happening. This was a case of personal liability being imposed by the statute.[120]

10.2.1.2 Strict liability and vicarious liability distinguished

Vicarious liability is by no means the same thing as strict liability.[121] The point requires emphasis for there is an unhappy judicial tendency to confuse the two concepts. A statute may require *mens rea* and yet also impose vicarious responsibility under the delegation principle (below). It has already been noted that supplying liquor to a constable on duty was an offence requiring *mens rea,*[122] yet a licensee may be vicariously liable for his agent's act in so doing.[123] Conversely, it is clearly possible for a statute to create strict liability without imposing vicarious responsibility. Once a statute has been held to impose a duty with strict liability on a particular person, it is likely to be held that that person is liable for the acts of anyone through whom he performs that duty.[124] Where, however, the duty with strict liability is not imposed on particular persons but on the public generally, vicarious liability is inappropriate. For example, the former offence of causing death by dangerous driving was, at one time, held to be an offence of strict liability, but it is surely inconceivable that vicarious liability would have been imposed.

10.2.1.3 Relationship with tortious doctrine

True vicarious liability is the general rule in the law of tort. An employer is held liable for all acts of his employee performed in the course of his employee's employment, or, as the courts now prefer to say, performed in close connection with it.[125] In the criminal law, an employer is

---

[119] [1995] 1 WLR 1356, [1995] Crim LR 654. If work is part of D's undertaking – a question of fact – D is in breach of his duty if independent contractors whom he engages to perform it unreasonably expose others to risk: *Associated Octel Ltd* [1996] 4 All ER 846, HL. See also *Environment Agency v Biffa Waste Ltd* [2006] EWHC 1102 (Admin). *Alphacell Ltd* (above, p 175) was, it is submitted, a case of personal liability and wrongly treated as a precedent for vicarious liability in *National Rivers Authority v Alfred McAlpine Homes (East) Ltd* [1994] 4 All ER 286, DC, [1994] Crim LR 960 and commentary.

[120] See for a recent example: *Hatton v Traffic Management* [2006] EWCA Crim 1156.

[121] *Seaboard Offshore Ltd v Secretary of State for Transport* [1993] Crim LR 611; affd [1994] 2 All ER 99, HL.

[122] *Sherras v De Rutzen*, above, p 170.

[123] *Mullins v Collins* (1874) LR 9 QB 292.

[124] *Dicta* to the effect that an offence of strict liability necessarily imposes vicarious responsibility are not difficult to find: see, eg, *Barker v Levinson* [1951] 1 KB 342 at 345, [1950] 2 All ER 825 at 827; *James & Son Ltd v Smee* [1955] 1 QB 78 at 95, per Slade J; *Bradshaw v Ewart-James* [1983] 1 All ER 12 at 14.

[125] The doctrine has undergone a radical change in the law of tort, with a much wider scope of liability being imposed by the courts. Examples include *Dubai Aluminium v Salaam* [2003] AC 366, where their lordships held that it is not a condition of vicarious liability that all the wrongful acts for which an employee was responsible had

generally not so liable. In one of the leading civil cases, *Lloyd v Grace, Smith & Co*,[126] a solicitor's managing clerk, without the knowledge of his employer, induced a widow to give him instructions to sell certain property, to hand over the title deeds and to sign two documents which were neither read over nor explained to her, but which she believed were necessary for the sale. The documents were, in fact, a conveyance to the clerk of the property, of which he dishonestly disposed for his own benefit. It was held that, since the clerk was acting within the scope of his authority, his employer was liable. Today it is very likely that the clerk was guilty of certain criminal offences; but it is perfectly clear that his employer could never have been made criminally liable for those acts even though the employer bore civil liability.

An employer is similarly liable in tort where the employee acting in the course of his employment commits a fraud involving a forgery,[127] and for acts which amount to fraud, assault and battery, manslaughter and so on; but in none of these cases would the employer be *criminally* liable solely on the ground that his employee was acting in the course of his employment.

The doctrine of vicarious liability in tort developed in the early part of the eighteenth century, but there was to be no parallel development in the criminal law, as was made clear by the leading case of *Huggins*.[128] Huggins, the warden of the Fleet (equivalent to a prison governor), was charged with the murder of a prisoner whose death had been caused by the servant of Huggins' deputy. It was held that, though the servant was guilty, Huggins was not, since the acts were done without his knowledge. Raymond CJ said:[129]

It is a point not to be disputed, but that in criminal cases the principal is not answerable for the act of the deputy as he is in civil cases: they must each answer for their own acts, and stand or fall by their own behaviour. All the authors that treat of criminal proceedings proceed on the foundation of this distinction; that to affect the superior by the act of his deputy, there must be the command of the superior which is not found in this case.

This has been confirmed recently in *R (Chief Constable of Northumbria) v Newcastle Magistrates' Court*,[130] where the court, referring to the previous paragraph in this work concluded that there is no doctrine of criminal vicarious liability at common law (except in relation to public nuisance, criminal libel (as was) and some form of contempt of court).

10.2.2 Identifying criminal vicarious liability

An employer can be held liable for his employee's crimes, as a general rule, only where he is a participant in them within the rules governing secondary liability as discussed in Chapter 8. Three exceptions to the general rule have already been noted:[131] in public nuisance,[132]

---

to have been committed in the course of employment, rather vicarious liability would not be imposed unless all the acts or omissions which were necessary to make him personally liable had taken place in the course of employment. See also *Lister v Hesley Hall Ltd* [2002] 1 AC 215; and *Mattis v Pollock* (nightclub owner liable for bouncer stabbing V when club encouraged bouncer to be aggressive). See, generally, on tortious liability Rogers, *Winfield and Jolowicz on Tort* (18th edn, 2010), Ch 20; P Atiyah, *Vicarious Liability in the English Law of Torts* (1967) and on the recent developments C McIvor, 'The Use and Abuse of the Doctrine of Vicarious Liability' (2006) 35 CLWR 268.

[126] [1912] AC 716, HL. As approved by the House of Lords in *Lister v Hesley Hall* [2001] UKHL 22.
[127] *Uxbridge Permanent Building Society v Pickard* [1939] 2 KB 248.
[128] (1730) 2 Stra 883.
[129] ibid, 885.
[130] [2010] EWHC 935 (Admin). The court offered an interesting analysis of the history of the principle.
[131] Above, p 159.
[132] Although in *Rimmington* [2005] UKHL 63, Lord Bingham commented that this is hard to reconcile with the modern approach to that subject in cases potentially involving the severest penalties, and may well be explained, as Mellor J did in *R v Stephens* (1866) LR 1 QB 702 at 708–709, [1861–73] All ER Rep Ext 2059 at 2060–2061, by the civil colour of the proceedings, at [39].

criminal libel (prior to its abolition – see Chapter 31) and contempt of court an employer has been held liable for his employee's acts although he is, personally, perfectly innocent. These were the only exceptions at common law; but now, by statute, there are many such offences. Parliament is, of course, always at liberty to impose vicariously criminal liability.

As in the case of strict liability, in truth it appears that the imposition of vicarious liability is the work of the courts rather than of Parliament. Statutes do occasionally say, in terms, that one person is to be liable for another's crimes.[133] It is more common, however, for the courts to 'detect' such an intention in statutes. This judicial willingness to impose vicarious liability arises particularly in summary offences. The reason most commonly advanced by the judges for holding a person (usually an employer, but independent contractors may also be caught)[134] liable is that the statute would be 'rendered nugatory'[135] – and the will of Parliament thereby defeated – if he were not. It may seem rather odd for the courts to be willing to impose liability for the acts of another on grounds of expediency when the foundation of the criminal law is that a person should be liable only for his personal wrongdoing. This would be particularly unsatisfactory in the absence of clear evidence that the prosecution of an employer will render the legislation more effective by deterring that and other employers from similar breaches.

Atkin J in *Mousel Brothers Ltd v London and North-Western Railway Co*[136] provided guidance on the identification of statutory vicarious liability:

while *prima facie* a principal is not to be made criminally responsible for the acts of his servants, yet the legislature may prohibit an act or enforce a duty in such words as to make the prohibition or the duty absolute; in which case the principal is liable if the act is in fact done by his servants. To ascertain whether a particular Act of Parliament has that effect or not regard must be had to the object of the statute, the words used, the nature of the duty laid down, the person upon whom it is imposed, the person by whom it would in ordinary circumstances be performed, and the person upon whom the penalty is imposed.

The decision of the House of Lords in *Environment Agency v Empress Cars*[137] also has an impact in this area. As noted above, their lordships took an unorthodox, and it is submitted, erroneous approach to the issue of causation in the strict liability offences of 'causing' pollution under the Water Resources Act 1991. The House held that the conduct of a third party unknown to the defendants that released the pollutant from the defendant's storage tanks did not break the chain of causation. Hence the defendants remained liable.[138]

10.2.3 The application of vicarious liability

Two quite distinct principles, differing somewhat in their effect, underlie the various decisions on vicarious liability. In the first place, a person may be held liable for the acts of another where he has delegated to that other the performance of certain duties cast on him by Act of

---

[133] A striking example is the Road Traffic Offenders Act 1988, s 64(5), which provides that the owner of a vehicle (even if a corporation) shall be conclusively presumed to have been the driver at the time of the commission of certain offences and, 'accordingly, that acts or omissions of the driver of the vehicle at the time were his acts or omissions'.

[134] See, eg, *Quality Dairies (York) Ltd v Pedley* [1952] 1 KB 275.

[135] *Mullins v Collins* (1874) LR 9 QB 292 at 295, per Blackburn and Quain JJ; *Coppen v Moore (No 2)* [1898] 2 QB 306 at 314, per Lord Russell CJ; *Allen v Whitehead*, below.

[136] [1917] 2 KB 836 at 845.

[137] [1999] 2 AC 22.

[138] See *Milford Haven Port Authority* [2000] 2 Cr App R (S) 423. See also *Environment Agency v Biffa Waste Ltd* [2006] EWHC 1102 (Admin) which may appear to cast doubt on this, but is, it is submitted, a case turning on the facts of the subcontractual arrangement.

Parliament. In the second place, an employer may be held liable because acts which are done physically by his employee may, in law, be the employer's acts. These two types of case require separate consideration.

10.2.3.1 The delegation principle[139]

A good illustration of the application of this principle may be found in the case of *Allen v Whitehead*.[140] The Metropolitan Police Act 1839, s 44, provides an offence for a keeper of a refreshment house to 'knowingly permit or suffer prostitutes or persons of notoriously bad character to meet together and remain in a place where refreshments are sold and consumed'.

D, the occupier of a café, although receiving the profits of the business, did not himself manage it, but employed a manager. Having had a warning from the police, D instructed his manager that no prostitutes were to be allowed to congregate on the premises and had a notice to that effect displayed on the walls. He visited the premises once or twice a week and there was no evidence that any misconduct took place in his presence. Then, on eight consecutive days, a number of women, known to the manager to be prostitutes, met together and remained there between the hours of 8 pm and 4 am. It was held by the Divisional Court, reversing the Metropolitan Magistrate, that D's ignorance of those facts was no defence. The acts of the manager and his *mens rea* (knowing that the women present were prostitutes) were both to be imputed to his employer, not simply because he was an employee, but because the management of the house had been delegated to him.

So in *Linnett v Metropolitan Police Comr*[141] it was held, following *Allen v Whitehead*,[142] that one of two co-licensees was liable for the acts of the other in knowingly permitting disorderly conduct in the licensed premises, contrary to s 44 of the same Act, although the other was neither his servant nor his partner,[143] but simply his delegate in 'keeping' the premises.

The argument that vicarious responsibility is necessary if the statute is to be effective applies with special force to cases of this type. Where the statute is phrased in such a way that the offence can be committed only by the delegator, there would indeed be a real difficulty in making the statute effective without vicarious liability. For example, under the Metropolitan Police Act 1839, s 44 (above), the offence may be committed only by a person 'who shall *have or keep* any house...' Presumably the mere manager in *Allen v Whitehead* was not such a person and if, therefore, the absentee 'keeper' were not liable for his manager's acts, the statute could be ignored with impunity. The position is the same in many of the offences under the Licensing Acts;[144] only the licensee can commit the offences. The difficulty has been well put by Lord Russell CJ:[145]

We may take as an illustration the case of a sporting publican who attends race-meetings all over the country, and leaves a manager in charge of his public-house; is it to be said that there is no remedy under this section[146] if drink is sold by the manager in charge to any number of drunken persons?

---

[139] See Pace [1982] Crim LR 627.

[140] [1930] 1 KB 211.

[141] [1946] KB 290.

[142] Above, n 140.

[143] Both were, in fact, the employees of a limited company. The company was not charged, no doubt for the good reason that it was not the licensee.

[144] See, generally, S Mehigan, J Phillips and J Saunders (eds), *Paterson's Licensing Acts 2011* (119th edn, 2011) and by the same authors, *The Licensing Act 2003* (2004) paras 8.11–8.12.

[145] In *Police Comr v Cartman* [1896] 1 QB 655 at 658. Yet when Parliament adds 'or his servant', the court holds that the delegation still applies to the licensee: *Howker v Robinson*, below. In *Boucher v DPP* (1996) 160 JP 650, it was held that where D is the licensee and owns a shop with P who is not a licensee, D cannot be vicariously liable for P's sales to a minor since P is not a servant but a co-owner.

[146] Licensing Act 1872, s 13. cf *Cundy v Le Cocq*, above, p 157, which establishes that the offence is also one of strict liability.

It is clear that there is no machinery by which the person actually selling can be convicted; a penalty can only be inflicted on the licensee.

Sub-delegation

It has been recognized that vicarious liability might be extended to cover the case where A delegates his responsibilities to B who sub-delegates them to C. Thus, if the licensee's delegate sub-delegates his responsibilities, the licensee is liable for the sub-delegate's acts,[147] but he is not liable for the acts of an inferior servant to whom control of the premises has not been delegated.[148]

What constitutes effective delegation?

There is some doubt as to the degree of delegation which is necessary to bring the principle into operation. In a leading case, *Vane v Yiannopoullos*,[149] Parker LCJ said that: 'It must be shown that the licensee is not managing the business himself but has delegated the management to someone else...'[150]

Lord Evershed[151] agreed with that and Lord Hodson said that the principle '...has never so far been extended so as to cover the case where the whole of the authority of the licensee has not been transferred to another'.[152] Lord Reid appears to have confined the principle to cases where the licensee is absent from the premises but leaves another in charge.[153] It was held that the principle was inapplicable in that case where the licensee was on the premises, but not on the same floor as, a waitress whom he had instructed as to her rights to sell intoxicating liquor, at the time she made an illegal sale. However, in *Howker v Robinson*,[154] a licensee who was serving in one room of the pub (the public bar) was held liable for an illegal sale made by his barman in another room (the lounge). This does not seem to be a case where the whole authority of the licensee had been transferred or where he was not managing the business himself. The court regarded the question of whether there had been delegation as one of fact, which had been properly decided by the magistrates. *Winson*,[155] which the court followed, was entirely different, for there the licensee visited the premises only occasionally and had a manager who was in control.

In *Howker v Robinson,* the degree of delegation was no greater than is essential in any public house with more than one bar and it is submitted that not only does it go too far but it leaves the law in an uncertain state. It is apparently open to the magistrates to find as 'a fact' that there has or has not been delegation where the licensee is on the premises. The principle ought to be confined to the case where the licensee is not 'doing his job', but has handed it over to another. Where a licensee who is employed by a brewery is suspended, the brewery has the right, under an implied term in the contract of employment, to delegate the rights and duties of licensee to another employee. Thus, sales of liquor on the licensed premises continue to be lawful and, presumably, the suspended licensee is liable for offences committed by the delegate.[156]

---

[147] *Crabtree v Hole* (1879) 43 JP 799; *Sopp v Long* [1970] 1 QB 518, [1969] 1 All ER 855.
[148] *Allchorn v Hopkins* (1905) 69 JP 355.
[149] [1965] AC 486, HL.
[150] [1964] 2 QB 739 at 745.
[151] [1965] AC 486 at 505.
[152] ibid, 510.
[153] At 497; cf Pace [1982] Crim LR 627 at 629, 636.
[154] [1973] QB 178, DC. Contrast *McKenna v Harding* (1905) 69 JP 354.
[155] [1969] 1 QB 371.
[156] *DPP v Rogers* [1992] Crim LR 51, DC.

No delegation principle in strict liability offences?

According to Lord Parker, the delegation principle comes into play *only* in the case of offences requiring *mens rea*.[157] Where liability is strict, 'the person on whom liability is thrown is responsible whether he has delegated or whether he has acted through a servant'. According to this view, if D, the licensee, not having delegated his duties, is serving in the bar and E, the barmaid, without his knowledge, sells liquor (i) to a constable on duty and (ii) to a drunken person, D is liable for the latter but not the former offence, since (i) requires *mens rea* but (ii) does not. If this is right, strict liability offences must be dealt with under the 'attributed act' principle (below).

Legitimacy of the delegation principle

Some doubt was cast on the validity of the delegation principle by the House of Lords in *Vane v Yiannopoullos*.[158] Since there was no delegation in that case their lordships' remarks were *obiter*. Lords Morris and Donovan could find no statutory authority for the doctrine and, though they did not find it necessary to pronounce on its validity, Lord Donovan thought that 'If a decision that "knowingly" means "knowingly" will make the provision difficult to enforce, the remedy lies with the legislature.' Lord Reid found the delegation principle hard to justify; but while it may have been unwarranted in the first instance, it was now too late to upset such a long-standing practice. Lord Evershed thought that a licensee may 'fairly and sensibly' be held liable where he has delegated his powers and Lord Hodson expressed no opinion. Subsequent cases[159] show that the doctrine continues unimpaired. Such a long-standing principle is perhaps unlikely now to be overruled by the House of Lords. It should not, however, be readily extended.[160] In *Bradshaw v Ewart-James*,[161] the court declined to apply it to the case where the master of a ship delegated the performance of his statutory duty to his chief officer. That, however, was not a case of the full delegation which the doctrine seems to require, for the master remained on board and in command. As the master cannot personally direct the ship for 24 hours a day, some delegation is inevitable.

10.2.3.2 The 'attributed act' principle

This second principle occurs in cases of strict liability where the *actus reus* of the employee, etc is attributed to D. It arises in statutory offences involving acts of selling, possessing, using, etc.

Many of the reported cases are those in which 'selling' is the central feature of the *actus reus*, under statutes like the Trade Descriptions Act, the Food and Drugs Acts, etc. A 'sale' consists in the transfer of property in goods from A to B[162] and the seller, in law, is necessarily the person in whom the property is vested at the commencement of the transaction. It is not a great step and no surprise, therefore, for the court to say that the employer has committed the *actus reus* of 'selling' even though he was nowhere near when the incident took place. In *Coppen v Moore (No 2)*,[163] D owned six shops, in which he sold 'American hams'. He gave strict instructions that these hams were to be described as 'breakfast hams' and were not to be sold under any specific name of place of origin. In the absence of D, and without the

---

[157] *Winson* [1969] 1 QB 371 at 382.

[158] [1965] AC 486, HL.

[159] *Ross v Moss* [1965] 2 QB 396; *Winson* [1969] 1 QB 371.

[160] cf *Howker v Robinson*, above, n 154. Yet Bristow J, while considering himself bound by the authorities to apply the delegation principle, hoped that it might be overturned by the House of Lords: [1972] 2 All ER at 791.

[161] [1983] QB 671, DC.

[162] This is so in the criminal as well as the civil law: *Watson v Coupland* [1945] 1 All ER 217.

[163] [1898] 2 QB 306. One partner may similarly be liable for the acts of another: *Davies v Harvey* (1874) LR 9 QB 433. cf *Parsons v Barnes* [1973] Crim LR 537.

knowledge of the manager of the branch, one of the assistants sold a ham as a 'Scotch ham'. D was convicted[164] of selling goods 'to which any...false trade description is applied'. Lord Russell CJ said:[165]

It cannot be doubted that the appellant [the owner] sold the ham in question, although the transaction was carried out by his servants. In other words he was the seller, although not the actual salesman. It is clear also, as already stated, that the ham was sold with a 'false trade description' which was material. If so, there is evidence establishing a *prima facie* case of an offence against the Act having been *committed by the appellant*.

The court was clearly influenced by the fact that D (like many other employers) carried on his business in a number of branches and could not possibly be in direct control of each one so that, if actual knowledge of the particular transaction had to be proved, he could hardly ever be made liable. The court did not, however, apply the principle of delegation which is to be found in the licensing cases. By construing the Act in accordance with the principles of the civil law and so holding that D had himself committed an *actus reus*, the court introduced a more far-reaching principle. Comparison with *Allchorn v Hopkins*[166] will show that, under the delegation principle, D would not have been liable for the act of the assistant to whom control of the premises had not been delegated.[167] D is not liable unless the delegate is acting within the scope of the delegation. So, for example, D was not liable where an employee, who had no authority to sell anything, supplied his employer's whisky to a customer out of hours.[168]

A modern instance of the application of the attributed act principle is *Harrow London Borough Council v Shah and Shah*.[169] The Shahs, newsagents, were convicted of selling a national lottery ticket to a boy under 16, contrary to the National Lottery Act 1993, s 13(1) (c), although they had taken all reasonable steps[170] to ensure that the regulations were complied with and, though one of them was on the premises, neither was present in the shop when the ticket was sold by their employee, H, who reasonably believed the boy was at least 16 years old.

The limits of the attribution principle

There are many cases not involving a sale where a similar principle has been invoked. Just as it is the employer who, in law, 'sells' goods with which his employee is actually dealing, so too is he 'in possession' of goods which are actually in his employee's hands[171] and so can be made liable for offences of 'being in possession' (of which there are many)[172] through his employees. A producer of plays was held under s 15 of the Theatres Act 1843 (now repealed),[173] to have 'presented' a play even though he was miles away when it is performed, and words were

---

[164] Under the Merchandise Marks Act 1887, s 2(2).

[165] [1898] 2 QB 306 at 313.

[166] Above, p 278, n 148.

[167] It was within the scope of the employee's authority in *Coppen v Moore*, above, to sell hams.

[168] *Adams v Camfoni* [1929] 1 KB 95.

[169] [1999] 3 All ER 302, [2000] Crim LR 992, DC. It is submitted that the court attributed excessive authority to *Moussell Bros Ltd v London and North-Western Rly Co Ltd* [1917] 2 KB 836, DC in holding that the offence imposed vicarious liability. The ruling of strict liability is also questionable, in the light both of the terms of the section and the subsequent decisions in *B (A Minor) v DPP* and *K* above, p 162. See [2000] Crim LR 694–696.

[170] This is a common defence in such statutory offences. See, for a recent discussion in the context of vicarious liability: *R (Keam) v DEFRA* [2005] EWHC 1582 (Admin) (D's independent contractor allowing cow to go lame and not calling vet – whether D taken all reasonable steps), and see Ch 7 above.

[171] Below, n 188.

[172] For examples, see above, p 172.

[173] See Theatres Act 1968; below, p 1083.

introduced into the performance, without his knowledge, which had not been allowed by the Lord Chamberlain.[174]

More controversially, it has been held that the owners of a van which they have supplied to a bailiff of their farm, nevertheless commit the offence of 'keeping' a van which is not 'used solely for the conveyance of goods or burden in the course of trade' without a licence[175] if the bailiff uses it, without their knowledge or authority, to take his wife for a day out at Clacton.[176] An employer 'uses' his vehicle in contravention of the Motor Vehicles (Construction and Use) Regulations if his employee so uses it.[177] It is quite understandable that a court should hold that an employer 'presents' a play or 'keeps' a vehicle, for these verbs are apt to describe his function and inapt to describe that of his employees. It is less clear that this is so in the case of 'uses'.[178] This could very well refer to the employee's use.

Another case serves to illustrate the proper limits of the doctrine and the need for the statute to be considered in its context. In *A-G's Reference (No 2 of 2003)*,[179] D was held not to be vicariously liable for 'keeping' an embryo contrary to s 3(1)(b) and s 41(2)(a) of the Human Fertilisation and Embryology Act 1990 ('keeping or using' an embryo, except in pursuance of a licence) where he was the consultant responsible for the supervision of two clinics licensed under the 1990 Act. The embryologist working within one of the clinics was convicted of offences, but D, the supervisor, was unaware of those activities and had not participated in them. In approving the trial judge's decision to acquit D, Judge LJ commented that the offence is committed by the person who contravenes s 3(1), and regarded it as difficult to see how the language could extend to create criminal liability for 'keeping' to D, who 'notwithstanding his statutory responsibilities, does not in fact keep the embryo at all'.[180]

Sales by a licensee

A new principle seemed to have emerged in *Goodfellow v Johnson*:[181] a licensee is liable for the act of another which can lawfully be performed only by virtue of the licence, even though the other is not his employee. A brewery employed D, a licensee, and P, a barmaid. The barmaid sold watered down gin. The gin was at all times owned by the brewery. D, the licensee, who had no knowledge of the sale was prosecuted.[182] *Coppen v Moore* (the hams case) did not apply since D (licensee) was not the owner of the gin; the brewery was. The delegation principle did not apply because there was no delegation. It was thought that this case meant that there could be no prosecution of, for example, a brewery whose defective beer a licensee is selling.[183] It is submitted that that is wrong. The brewery was certainly the seller in law, but it was not charged. The offence in question was not a licensing offence. What if the barmaid had sold adulterated lemonade (a sale for which no licence is required)? It would be absurd to say that the brewery (and the barmaid) could be guilty of selling adulterated lemonade but not

---

[174] *Grade v DPP* [1942] 2 All ER 118. The defendant had in fact been called up for service in the RAF. The result would have been different if D had been charged with 'causing' the play to be presented: *Lovelace v DPP* [1954] 1 WLR 1468.

[175] Contrary to the Revenue Act 1869, s 27 (repealed).

[176] *Strutt v Clift* [1911] 1 KB 1.

[177] *Green v Burnett* [1955] 1 QB 78; but not where a partner, or person authorized *ad hoc*, uses the vehicle, if there is also an offence of permitting: *Crawford v Haughton* [1973] QB 1, DC; *Garrett v Hooper* [1973] Crim LR 61; *Cobb v Williams* [1973] Crim LR 243.

[178] See especially the disagreement in the Divisional Court in *Cambridgeshire CC v Associated Lead Mills Ltd* [2005] EWHC 1627 (Admin).

[179] [2004] EWCA Crim 785.

[180] [20].

[181] [1966] 1 QB 83, [1965] Crim LR 304 and commentary.

[182] Contrary to the Food and Drugs Act 1955.

[183] *Allied Domecq Leisure Ltd v Paul Graham Cooper* [1999] Crim LR 230 and commentary.

adulterated gin. In *Nottingham City Council v Wolverhampton and Dudley Breweries,*[184] it was acknowledged that the owner (brewery) could be convicted of an offence of selling intoxicating liquor below the tolerance allowed in the Food Labelling Regulations under the Food Safety Act 1990. Kennedy LJ, accepted that in *Goodfellow,* Lord Parker had misunderstood the provisions of the Food and Drugs Act 1955 by treating them as absolute offences, and had misunderstood *Hotchin v Hindmarsh.* Kennedy LJ observed that the owner (brewery) through the barmaid could make an effective sale regardless of the licensee (D) and that such a sale could involve the owner (brewery) and not just the licensee, D, in criminal liability.[185] Thus, the responsibility of the licensee, D, under licensing legislation does not relieve the owner of responsibility in relation to all other products.

10.2.4 Mode of participation of employer and employee

Where the statute creates an offence specifically for designated people to do the act in question (eg licensees), the designated person who is held vicariously liable for the acts of his employee is the principal offender. He alone possesses the personal characteristic which is an essential part of the *actus reus* and no one else is qualified to fill that role. The employee who actually performs the act is plainly incapable of being a principal, since he is not a licensee, etc, but he may be convicted as an accessory.[186] This seems strange since the employee is the only participant in the crime who is present and doing anything.

The position is different where the *actus reus* of the offence can be committed by someone who does not have to possess a personal characteristic, such as being a licensee. In such a case, if the employee is capable of being a principal, then it seems that he may be held to be a joint principal with his employer (the licensee). In crimes of 'selling' and being 'in possession' the court allows the prosecution the best of both worlds by having regard to the legal act when dealing with the employer and the physical act when dealing with the employee. So it is held that the employee, as well as the employer, 'sells'[187] or is 'in possession';[188] and the employee whose 'use' of a vehicle was held to be use by his employer was convicted in *Green v Burnett* (above) as a principal. It is submitted that when the employee is capable of being a principal it is logical to hold him liable as such (for he is the real offender) and not as an accessory.

Determining whether the employee is a principal or accessory, etc is of more than academic interest for two reasons. First, if the crime is one of strict liability, *mens rea* must nevertheless be proved if he is to be convicted as an accessory but not if he is a principal.[189] Secondly, where there is a statutory defence enabling someone held vicariously liable to escape if he can bring the 'actual offender' before the court, it is difficult to suppose that the production of an accessory (even though he is the real offender) will suffice. However, a joint principal certainly will in this scenario.[190]

10.2.5 No vicarious liability for abetting or attempting crimes

Abetting is a common law notion and therefore, as we have seen,[191] requires *mens rea* even where the principal offence is one of strict liability. For the same reasons there can be no

---

[184] [2004] 2 WLR 820.

[185] [18].

[186] *Griffiths v Studebakers Ltd* [1924] 1 KB 102; *Ross v Moss* [1965] 2 QB 396.

[187] *Hotchin v Hindmarsh* [1891] 2 QB 181. cf *Goodfellow v Johnson* [1966] 1 QB 83, but note the *Nottingham* case above.

[188] *Melias Ltd v Preston* [1957] 2 QB 380.

[189] Above, p 208.

[190] *Melias Ltd v Preston* [1957] 2QB 830.

[191] Above, p 208.

vicarious responsibility for abetting an offence, even though the offence itself may be one imposing vicarious liability. In *Ferguson v Weaving*,[192] D, a licensee, was charged with abetting several of her customers in consuming liquor on the licensed premises outside the permitted hours.[193] It appeared that she had taken all proper means to ensure that drinking ceased when 'Time' was called. But the waiters in the concert room, contrary to their instructions, made no attempt to collect the customers' drinks and, while D was visiting the several other rooms in the premises, the offence was committed. It was assumed that control of the concert room had been delegated. The principal offence was committed by the customers. While accepting that the waiters might have been guilty of abetting the customers who were the principal offenders, the court was emphatic that D could not be. Lord Goddard CJ said:[194]

She can aid and abet the customers if she knows that the customers are committing an offence, but we are not prepared to hold that their knowledge can be imputed to her so as to make her, not a principal offender, but an aider and abettor. So to hold would be to establish a new principle in criminal law and one for which there is no authority.

Had there been a substantive offence of *permitting* drinking on licensed premises after hours, it is fairly clear that the court could have held D guilty; for in that case the acts, and the *mens rea*, of the servant would have been attributed to her. Likewise it has been said that there can be no vicarious liability for attempting to commit a crime, even though the crime attempted imposes vicarious liability.[195]

10.2.6 Reform of vicarious liability

Clause 29 of the Law Commission Draft Criminal Code would impose a welcome restriction on the application of vicarious liability to those circumstances in which Parliament expressly imposed such. Far greater clarity and certainty would follow.

The Law Commission has recently provisionally recommended that a preferable method of imposing criminal liability in place of vicarious liability and delegation would be to create offences drafted in specific terms of 'failing to prevent someone to whom a duty of care has been delegated' from committing the offence.[196]

---

[192] [1951] 1 KB 814. See also *Thomas v Lindop* [1950] 1 All ER 966; *John Henshall (Quarries) Ltd v Harvey* [1965] 2 QB 233. *Provincial Motor Club Co Ltd v Dunning* [1909] 2 KB 599 overlooks this principle and is a doubtful decision.

[193] Contrary to the Licensing Act 1921, s 4.

[194] [1951] 1 KB 814 at 821.

[195] *Gardner v Akeroyd* [1952] 2 QB 743.

[196] See LCCP 195.

11
Mental conditions, intoxication and mistake

11.1 Introduction

In this and the next chapter the most commonly occurring 'defences' are considered. There is no accepted hierarchy of defences in English law and none is adopted in this book.[1] It should also be noted, that considerable disagreement persists over the precise theoretical lines between elements which ought properly to be regarded as part of the offence and those comprising defences.[2]

In this chapter, the pleas of insanity, intoxication and mistake are examined. It would be misleading to treat all of these as 'defences' in the true sense of the word since some involve a plea which simply puts the Crown to proof of the relevant issue. The 'defences' or 'pleas' of insanity and intoxication are based on denial of sufficient capacity to deserve the imposition of a criminal sanction. At the core of these topics – insanity, intoxication, mistake – is the basic principle of English criminal law that the defendant should be held liable only where he is of sufficient capacity.[3] As Professor Hart famously explained, a person is only to be blamed if he has the 'capacity and fair opportunity to change or adjust his behaviour to the law'.[4]

Chapter 12 deals with substantive defences in the true sense – where D has caused an *actus reus* with the appropriate *mens rea*, but despite both these elements of the offence being proved by the Crown, D is entitled to an acquittal owing to some justifying or excusing circumstance or condition. There are special defences which apply to particular crimes (for example, loss of self-control and diminished responsibility in murder), they are dealt with separately throughout the book although where appropriate their interrelationship with general defences is considered.

11.1.1 Defences and theories of justification and excuse

Historically, the common law distinguished between justification and excuse, at least in relation to homicide. Some homicides, like that done by the public hangman in carrying out the sentence of the court, were justifiable. Others, like killing by misadventure and without

---

[1] See, however, the theoretical approach in P Robinson, 'Criminal Law Defences: A Systematic Analysis' (1982) 82 Col LR 199; and for a ladder of defences see J Horder, *Excusing Crime* (2004) 103.

[2] See, generally, G Williams, 'Offences and Defences' (1982) 2 LS 233; K Campbell, 'Offence and Defence', in IH Dennis (ed), *Criminal Law and Criminal Justice* (1987). Tadros, *Criminal Responsibility* emphasizes the significance of the distinction. Defences, he argues, describe the conditions of criminal responsibility, but do 'not constitute essential features of D's conduct which express why he is deserving of conviction, where the defence is unavailable' (at 109). Thus, lack of consent is an element of offence in rape.

[3] Numerous theories abound as to whether criminal responsibility and defences are properly explained on the bases of D's capacity, choice or character. These philosophical arguments lie beyond the scope of this work. See, *inter alia*, Horder, *Excusing Crime* and Tadros, *Criminal Responsibility*, Ch 2.

[4] HLA Hart, *Punishment and Responsibility* (1968) 181.

culpable negligence, were merely excusable. In both cases the accused who successfully raised the defence was acquitted of felony but, if the homicide was merely excusable, his goods were forfeited. In 1828, forfeiture was abolished and, ever since, there has been no difference, so far as the defendant is concerned, between the various general defences. If successfully raised, they result in a verdict of not guilty. Insanity is distinct in this respect because it results in a verdict of not guilty by reason of insanity.

There has been a revival of academic interest in a distinction between justification and excuse.[5] On one simple version of the theory, an act is justified when society does not disapprove of it or where it is permitted.[6] An act is merely excused when society disapproves of it but thinks it is not right to punish D. The distinction is often described in simple terms: whereas the justification speaks to the rightness of the act, the excuse relates to the circumstances of the individual actor.[7] Clearly, some such distinction exists in fact. There are examples which obviously fall into one category or the other. The nine-year-old child who deliberately kills his playmate is excused but no one would say his act of killing is justified. In contrast, nearly everyone would approve of the conduct of a man who in self-defence wounds an aggressor when that is the only way he can save the lives of his family.

However, these systems of classification into justifications and excuses suffer from a number of drawbacks. First, there is no agreement on the precise hierarchy,[8] nature or definition of either classification. Duff suggests that they have 'bred needless confusion'.[9] A number of sophisticated models of justification and excuse have been developed by legal philosophers.[10] Recent suggestions propose a four-fold system of classification with justifications,[11] warranted acts,[12] excuses[13] and exemptions.[14] Secondly, there is no consensus as to which classification applies to which defence – for example, many see duress as excusatory but some treat it as justificatory. Thirdly, there seems to be little agreement as to what practical difference, if any, would result from classification of a particular defence into one category or another.

[5] G Fletcher, *Rethinking Criminal Law* (1978) Ch 10; S Yeo, *Compulsion in the Criminal Law* (1990); JC Smith, *Justification and Excuse* (1989); G Williams, 'The Theory of Excuses' [1982] Crim LR 732; Robinson (1982) 82 Col LR 199; J Gardner, 'The Gist of Excuses' (1998) Buffalo Crim LR 575; Horder, *Excusing Crime*; Tadros, *Criminal Responsibility*; Duff, *Answering for Crime* (2007) Ch 11.

[6] It is problematical to suggest that the question is whether society 'approves' of the conduct. A better basis for the classification is that it is 'permitted'. See, generally, the account in Duff, *Answering for Crime*, Ch 11. cf P Westen (2008) 28 OJLS 563.

[7] For criticism, see J Gardner, 'Wrongs and Faults', in A Simester (ed), *Appraising Strict Liability* (2005) 61–67.

[8] See D Husak 'On the Supposed Priority of Justification to Excuse' (2005) 24 Law and Phil 557.

[9] *Answering for Crime*, 263.

[10] Debate continues as to whether D who relies on a justification should be seen as having done no wrong, or as having done wrong but being justified in doing it (see G Fletcher, 'The Nature of Justifications', in S Shute, S Gardner and J Horder (eds), *Action and Value in Criminal Law* (1993) 175). As for excuses, there is debate over whether D is excused because he has acted 'out of character' or because he lacked capacity (ie he has not lived up to the standards we can reasonably expect of someone in his circumstances). See, generally, J Gardner (1998) Buffalo Crim LR 575; V Tadros, 'The Characters of Excuses' (2001) 21 OJLS 495; and Horder, *Excusing Crime*, Ch 3.

[11] There are many theories of justification ranging from those based on whether the outcome of D's act was a good one; whether he acted for good reasons; whether the outcome was good and was a result of D's acting for good reasons etc. See Tadros, *Criminal Responsibility*, Ch 10; J Dressler, 'New Thoughts About the Concept of Justification in the Criminal Law' (1984) 32 UCLA Rev 61; J Gardner (1998) Buffalo Crim LR 575.

[12] See Duff, *Answering for Crime* at 277 et seq. These arise where D had sufficient reason to believe he acted for a good reason.

[13] The theories of excuse are also numerous, with many accepting that there is no single definition. In short, it might be said that an excuse arises where D admits that his act was wrong, but claims not to deserve punishment because of the circumstances pertaining. See fully: Horder, *Excusing Crime*, especially Ch 6, Tadros, *Criminal Responsibility*, Ch 11; C Finkelstein 'Excuses and Dispositions in Criminal Law' (2002) 6 Buffalo Crim LR 317.

[14] Advocated by Horder, *Excusing Crime*, 103–106; Tadros, *Criminal Responsibility*, Chs 4, 10 and 11. D is exempted where his lack of capacity is a general continuing one whereas he will be excused if his lack of capacity relates to the particular incident alleged.

Few suggest that there is any difference so far as the acquittal of the person relying on the defence is concerned[15] but it has been argued more widely that the distinction affects third parties in that (i) it is lawful to resist an aggressor whose aggression is merely excused but not one whose aggression is justified; and (ii) there may be a conviction for aiding and abetting one who is merely excused[16] but not one who is justified. Some would also argue that particular judicial decisions on excuses are not to be regarded as being of any wider significance in precedent terms.[17] As Fletcher (whose work inspired the current interest) acknowledges,[18] Anglo-American criminal law has never expressly recognized these (as he thinks) fundamental distinctions.

Applying the version of the theory as expounded by Fletcher, a person arresting 'anyone who is in the act of committing an offence' would be justified but a person arresting 'anyone whom he has reasonable grounds for suspecting to be [but who is not in fact] committing an offence' is merely excused. But both acts are equally sanctioned by English law – the Police and Criminal Evidence Act 1984, s 24, declares that both are acts that a person *may* do. In doing so, he incurs no civil or criminal liability. It is true, however, that the first 'arrestee' would not be entitled to use force in self-defence (if the arrestor was using only reasonable force) whereas the second might be.[19] The law does recognize that a person's act may be excused in the criminal law, while incurring civil liability. A person who makes an unreasonable mistake of fact which, if it were true, would amount to reasonable grounds for suspecting another to be in the act of committing an offence, has a defence to a criminal prosecution for false imprisonment or assault (because he lacks *mens rea*) but remains liable for the corresponding torts: the act done is not the act which the 1984 Act says he *may* do. Here the terminology of justification and excuse seems appropriate. The act is 'unlawful', but the actor is excused from criminal liability.

Any attempt to rely on the theories of justifications or excuses as the guiding principle by which to structure an analysis of defences would, in the present state of the law, be premature, and no such attempt is made in either this or the subsequent chapter.

11.1.2 Relationship between mental condition defences

Some of the pleas in this chapter may overlap since they are concerned with D's denial that he was a responsible actor at the time of the commission of the offence. Their interrelationship may be usefully summarized at the outset. In short, there are three categories:

(1) Situations where D suffers some malfunctioning of his body or mind owing to some disease or *internal* cause. These factors are treated in law as 'diseases of the mind' which render D liable to a verdict of not guilty by reason of insanity. The category includes such everyday conditions as sleepwalking, epilepsy and diabetes. The label 'insanity' is profoundly misleading.

(2) Situations where, because of some *external* factor that has affected D's mind or body in such a way that he acts involuntarily, he is entitled to an acquittal. Examples include concussion, taking a *medically prescribed* drug or anaesthetic in accordance with instructions, and other 'external' factors. These may give rise to a defence of sane[20] automatism, but that defence is hedged with qualification and approached by the courts with considerable scepticism. A defence of sane automatism is available only where D suffers a complete loss of control. In addition, where the automatism is self-induced by

---

[15] cf Robinson (1982) 82 Col LR 199 considering special verdicts for those who are excused.
[16] As in *Bourne* (1952) 36 Cr App R 125 and *Cogan and Leak* [1976] QB 217, above, p 234.
[17] Robinson, above.
[18] *Rethinking Criminal Law*, above.
[19] Below, p 684.
[20] Sometimes called non-insane automatism.

taking alcohol or drugs, it will be a defence but to crimes of specific intent (as explained below) but only in relation to basic intent offences (explained below) where D's conduct in inducing the state of automatism is not reckless in inducing that state.

(3) Situations where the factors affecting D's capacity do not amount to a defence at all. Examples include the voluntary taking of drink or drugs (discussed below, p 314), which will provide no defence in crimes other than those of specific intent.

11.2 Insanity[21]

A defence of insanity is crucial to the criminal justice system.[22] It recognizes that the imposition of criminal punishment should be reserved for those who are rational and responsible beings. There are two ways in which an accused person's sanity may be relevant in a criminal trial. First, where the accused is claiming that he lacked mental capacity at the time of the commission of the acts alleged to constitute the criminal offence. Secondly, the accused may be claiming that at the time of trial he lacks mental capacity and is therefore not fit to be tried. It is convenient to deal with this second category here because of its very close relationship with the defence of insanity, although technically it is a matter not of substantive law but of procedure.

11.2.1 Insanity and unfitness to be tried

11.2.1.1 Mental condition rendering trial impracticable

In some cases, where D is held in custody awaiting trial, his mental state will be so bad that he is transferred to hospital. If the Home Secretary is satisfied by reports from at least two medical practitioners that D is suffering from mental disorder,[23] he may order that he be detained in a hospital, if that person is suffering from mental disorder of a nature or degree which makes it appropriate for him to be detained in a hospital for medical treatment; and he is in urgent need of such treatment; and appropriate medical treatment is available for him.[24] The defendant is normally brought to trial when he is well enough.[25] The basis for this practice is:

that the issue of insanity should be determined by the jury whenever possible and the power should be exercised only when there is likely to be a scandal if the prisoner is brought up for trial... [26]

Clearly to maintain compatibility with Art 5(1) (deprivation of liberty only in accordance with law) and Art 6 (fair trial) of the European Convention on Human Rights (ECHR) it is essential that the power to detain is exercised in accordance with law and sparingly.[27]

---

[21] See generally the excellent, though now quite dated discussion in RD Mackay, *Mental Condition Defences in Criminal Law* (1995). Proposals for the reform of the law are made in the Report of the Committee on Mentally Abnormal Offenders (The Butler Report – hereinafter in this chapter Butler) Cmnd 6244, 1975. See also the philosophical discussion in Tadros, *Criminal Responsibility*, Chs 11 and 12. The Law Commission is currently reviewing the law of insanity.

[22] Some have suggested that the defence could be abolished and the absence of *mens rea* would serve as a determinant of D's liability. See below, n 171 and C Slobogin 'An End to Insanity: Recasting the Role of Mental Illness in Criminal Cases' (2000) 86 Virginia LR 1199.

[23] For definitions, see Mental Health Act 2007. The 2007 Act amends the Mental Health Act 1983, redefining 'mental disorder' as 'any disorder or disability of the mind'.

[24] Mental Health Act 1983, s 48 (as amended).

[25] Butler, para 3.38.

[26] RCCP, Cmd 8932, above. See as a recent example *Ghanbary* [2006] EWCA Crim 2374.

[27] cf the statistics revealed by RD Mackay and D Machin, *Transfers from Prison to Hospital – The Operation of s 48 of the Mental Health Act 1983* (Home Office Research Directorate, 1998) No 84. See also P Bean, *Madness and Crime* (2008) Ch 3.

11.2.1.2 Unfitness to be tried[28]

Introduction

It is an important principle that D should, wherever possible, have an opportunity to contest his guilt in a normal criminal trial.[29] Finding someone to be 'unfit' and therefore subjecting him to some alternative process ought therefore to be the exception.

Someone who is certifiably insane may often nevertheless be fit to plead to the indictment and follow the proceedings at the trial and that, if he is, he should ordinarily be allowed to do so, because it is in principle desirable that a person charged with a criminal offence should, whenever possible, be tried, so that the question whether he committed the crime may be determined by a jury.[30]

At any trial in the Crown Court it might be alleged by the defence or the prosecution that D is 'unfit to plead'. If D is unfit, the normal trial process is not applied to him. Instead, a jury determines the narrow question whether he did the act complained of (without considering his *mens rea*). At that hearing D might be acquitted (having been found not to have done the act) or be found to have done the act, and thereby be subjected to a range of disposal powers.[31]

The issue of unfitness can be raised at any time. If raised at the start of the trial on arraignment, the Crown Court follows the procedure to determine D's fitness under ss 4 and 4A of the Criminal Procedure (Insanity) Act 1964.[32] The issue may also arise where D has been found unfit, he has been hospitalized and his condition has improved so that he is brought back to court to determine whether he remains unfit.[33] If, before the court has begun to decide on the next issue of whether D did the acts alleged, D is found to have recovered so as to be fit to stand trial, the court should revisit the question of fitness to plead.

What constitutes unfitness?

At the stage of enquiring whether D is unfit, the question is whether D has sufficient understanding to be tried. Astonishingly, the law is based on a test derived from a case decided in 1836 when any concern for mental illness and the impact that might have on the ability of an individual to participate in the trial was limited.[34] In its modern day incarnation, that test

---

[28] See Law Commission Consultation Paper No 197 *Unfitness to Plead* (2010); Mackay, *Mental Condition Defences*, Ch 5; for trends in the use of the plea see RD Mackay and G Kearns, 'An Upturn in Unfitness to Plead?' [2000] Crim LR 532; RD Mackay, B Mitchell and L Howe, 'A Continued Upturn in Unfitness to Plead – More Disability in Relation to the Trial under the 1991 Act' [2007] Crim LR 530. Research appended to the Law Commission CP 197 reveals that the number of unfitness cases increased and has levelled off at around 100 per year. Legal guidance for the conduct of such cases is provided by the CPS: www.cps.gov.uk/legal/l_to_o/ mentally_disordered_offenders/index.html#mens.

[29] *R (Hasani) v Blackfriars CC* [2005] EWHC 3016 (Admin).

[30] As expressed by witnesses before the *Royal Commission on Capital Punishment* Report, Cmd 8932, at 78. The judge must generally exercise this discretion to postpone where there is a reasonable chance that the prosecution case will be successfully challenged: *Webb* [1969] 2 QB 278. On the other hand, 'the case for the prosecution may appear so strong and the suggested condition of the prisoner so disabling that postponement of the trial of the issue would be wholly inexpedient': *Burles* [1970] 2 QB 191, per Parker LCJ.

[31] See LCCP 197, Part 6.

[32] As substituted by the Criminal Procedure (Insanity and Unfitness to Plead) Act 1991 and amended by the Domestic Violence, Crime and Victims Act 2004, discussed by S White, 'The Criminal Procedure (Insanity and Unfitness to Plead) Act 1991' [1992] Crim LR 4; P Fennell, 'The Criminal Procedure (Insanity and Unfitness to Plead) Act 1991' (1992) 55 MLR 547. The 1964 Act replaced the Criminal Lunatics Act 1800. See LCCP 197, Part 2 for a history of the developments.

[33] Section 4A is mandatory and must be complied with in full in such cases: *Ferris* [2004] EWHC 1221 (Admin).

[34] *Pritchard* (1836) 7 C and P 303. See LCCP 197, Part 2.

was explained in *M*.[35] The trial judge directed that the defendant had to have sufficient ability in relation to all of the following six things: (i) to understand the charges, (ii) to understand the plea, (iii) to challenge jurors, (iv) to instruct counsel and his solicitor, (v) to understand the course of the trial, and (vi) to give evidence if he chooses. If he is able to do these things, he has *a right* to be tried if he so wishes, even though he is not capable of acting in his best interests.[36] The same principle must, theoretically, be applicable where the prosecution contend that D is fit to plead and he denies it; but it might be more leniently applied in such a case.

It was held in *Podola*[37] that a person is fit to plead where an hysterical amnesia prevents him from remembering events during the whole of the period material to the question whether he committed the crime alleged, but whose mind is otherwise completely normal. The court was prepared to concede that a deaf mute[38] is 'unfit' but declined,

to extend the meaning of the word to include persons who are mentally normal at the time of the hearing of the proceedings against them and are perfectly capable of instructing their solicitors as to what submission their counsel is to put forward with regard to the commission of the crime.[39]

But is a person suffering from hysterical amnesia so capable? If the facts justify a defence of accident or alibi but D is unable to remember them, the defence cannot be raised unless there are witnesses who come forward. On the other hand it would be unsatisfactory if, for example, there could be no trial of a motorist who had suffered concussion in an accident, alleged to have been caused by his dangerous driving, and who could not remember what he did. It would be still less satisfactory in the case of one whose failure to recall the relevant events arose from drunkenness.[40]

The procedure for determining unfitness

The issue of unfitness may be raised by the judge on his own initiative or at the request of the prosecution or the defence. It is usually at the request of the defence at the start of the trial. Where neither party raises the issue, the judge should do so if he has doubts about the accused's fitness.[41]

If the question is raised by either party, or if the judge has doubts, the issue used to be tried by a jury.[42] Following the Domestic Violence, Crime and Victims Act 2004, s 22, the issue is now to be determined by a court without a jury. Such proceedings do not constitute 'criminal

---

[35] [2003] EWCA Crim 3452. See also *Walls* [2011] EWCA Crim 443 suggesting use of special measures.

[36] *Robertson* [1968] 3 All ER 557, [1968] 1 WLR 1767, CA. See also *R (Kenneally) v Snaresbrook Crown Court* [2002] QB 1169. For insights into how psychiatrists view these see T Rogers et al, 'Fitness to Plead and Competence to Stand Trial' (2008) 19 J Forensic Psychiatry and Psychology 576.

[37] [1960] 1 QB 325. The jury had found that Podola was not suffering from hysterical amnesia and the question before the Court of Criminal Appeal concerned the onus of proof of that issue; but the court held that this question could only arise if the alleged amnesia could in law bring Podola within the scope of s 2 of the Criminal Lunatics Act 1800. The court's decision on this point thus appears to be part of the *ratio decidendi* of the case.

[38] See also *Sharif* [2010] EWCA Crim 1709.

[39] [1960] 1 QB at 356. The word 'insane' was the one under consideration as that was the word used in the Criminal Lunatics Act 1800 not used in s 4 of the 1964 Act; but the law is unchanged. cf Cmd 2149, at 7.

[40] *Broadhurst v R* [1964] AC 441 at 451PC. Butler (by majority) recommended the retention of the *Podola* rule.

[41] *MacCarthy* [1967] 1 QB 68, discussed by AR Poole, 'Standing Mute and Fitness to Plead' [1966] Crim LR 6.

[42] Criminal Procedure (Insanity) Act 1964, s 4(5). See now *B* [2008] EWCA Crim 1997; [2009] Crim LR 608 on the position where D1 is unfit and D2 fit at the same trial. See also *MB* [2010] EWCA Crim 1684; on difficulties this creates see LCCP 197, para 7.27.

proceedings' since they cannot result in a conviction; the procedure is to ensure the protection of the defendant and the public. Accordingly, Art 6 of the ECHR does not apply.[43]

The general rule is that the question of fitness is to be determined as soon as it arises. If the accused is found by the judge to be fit and the trial proceeds the case will be tried by a jury in the normal way. Where, exceptionally, the question of fitness falls to be determined at a later time the issue is to be determined by the same jury by which the accused is being tried.[44] The defendant may not be found unfit to plead unless there is written or oral evidence to that effect by two or more registered medical practitioners at least one of whom is approved by the Home Secretary as having special experience in the field of mental disorder.[45] This goes some way to ensuring that the criminal process is in step with medical practice. The medical evidence is required to prove unfitness (not fitness).[46]

When trial of fitness to plead occurs

The case against a person who is undoubtedly unfit to plead may be weak and capable of demolition by cross-examination of the prosecution witnesses by his lawyers. It would be wrong if he were to be found unfit and subjected to the restraints (including detention) which may follow from that finding without having an opportunity to test the prosecution's case. The matter is now regulated by the Criminal Procedure (Insanity) Act 1964, as amended by the Criminal Procedure (Insanity and Unfitness to Plead) Act 1991 and the Domestic Violence, Crime and Victims Act 2004. As we have seen, the general rule is that the question of fitness is to be determined by the judge as soon as it arises; but if the judge, having regard to the nature of the supposed disability, thinks that it is expedient and in the interests of the accused to do so, he may postpone consideration of the question of fitness to be tried until any time up to the opening of the case for the defence. This gives the defence the opportunity to test the prosecution's case. If it is insufficient to justify a conviction, the jury will be directed to acquit and the question of fitness to plead will not arise. If there is a case to answer, that question will then be determined by the jury by whom D is being tried.

The trial of the facts

Where D is found to be unfit, either on arraignment or at the end of the prosecution case, the trial shall not proceed, or proceed further.[47] If the matter rested there, D might again be subject to restraint though he has done nothing wrong. Even if the prosecution's evidence has been heard and amounts to a case to answer, there may be an answer to it in the shape of evidence – for example, of alibi – available to the defence. Section 4A (introduced by the 1991 Act, and amended by the 2004 Act) therefore provides for a further hearing. The court (that is, the jury) shall then decide on the evidence (if any) already given and such evidence as is adduced by the prosecution or the defence whether D 'did the act or made the omission

---

[43] *H* [2003] UKHL 1, [2003] Crim LR 817, affirming *M Kerr and H* [2002] Crim LR 57. On ECHR concerns with the operation of the procedure see E Baker, 'Human Rights and McNaughten and the 1991 Act' [1994] Crim LR 84; Mackay, 'On Being Insane in Jersey Part Two' [2002] Crim LR 728, 'On Being Insane in Jersey Part Three – the Case of the *Attorney General v O'Driscoll*' [2004] Crim LR 219.

[44] Section 22 of the 2004 Act, amending the Criminal Procedure (Insanity) Act 1964, s 4(5) as substituted by the Criminal Procedure (Insanity and Unfitness to Plead) Act 1991, s 2.

[45] The 1964 Act as amended, s 4(6). See also *Borkan* [2004] EWCA Crim 1642.

[46] See *Ghulam* [2009] EWCA Crim 2285; [2010] Crim LR 796 and commentary.

[47] The judge in *O'Donnell* [1996] 1 Cr App R 286 went wrong at this point by allowing the trial to proceed, by failing to appoint someone to put the case for the defence and by not directing the trial jury that, now, the only question for them was whether D did the act. Conviction annulled and *venire de novo* ordered. See also *Norman* [2010] EWCA Crim 1810 – duty on court to appoint best person to represent D.

charged against him as the offence'.[48] The judge should not direct the jury as to what disposal powers might then be used against the defendant if the jury were to find that he did the act.[49] The objective of such a hearing is to test the evidence rather than to hold D to account.[50]

In relation to this s 4A hearing, it was held in *Antoine*[51] that the words 'act' and 'omission' mean the *actus reus* of the offence and that, accordingly, D could not rely on the defence of diminished responsibility.[52] The decision creates problems by its presumption that all offences divide neatly into elements only of *actus reus* and *mens rea* that can be readily identified. On the House of Lords approach, at a s 4A hearing, the defence can deny *actus reus* elements but not *mens rea* elements.[53] The confusion is exemplified in the judgment. For example, Lord Hutton, with whom all their lordships agreed, said that the jury should take into account any objective evidence of mistake, accident or self-defence and should not find that D did the act unless it is sure that the prosecution has negatived the defence. But the 'defences' of mistake and accident are simply denials of *mens rea*, not of the *actus reus*, and self-defence has a vital mental element. If this *dictum* is right, it is hard to see why any other evidence, other than of a defect of reason from disease of the mind, suggesting the absence of *mens rea*[54] should not be admissible, thus undermining the whole decision. Subsequently, it was held that D could not invoke the defence of provocation.[55] That defence also applied only where all the elements of murder are proved so 'the act' of murder and of manslaughter by reason of provocation seems to be identical. It appears that his lordship was anticipating that the s 4A enquiry is directed not merely to the *actus reus*, not to the full offence of *actus reus* and *mens rea*, but to an 'unlawful act'. It is possible to envisage some relatively straightforward cases where 'objective defences' ought to be capable of being pleaded. Difficult examples to test the precise limits of Lord Hutton's 'objective defences' might include a case in which the defence of sane automatism would have been advanced at trial. For example, where D has been hit on the head and in a state of concussion hit and killed V, D has by trial become so traumatized by the event that he is unfit. Is the plea a denial of *mens rea* and forbidden? Or is it a denial of a 'voluntary act' and expressly recognized by Lord Hutton? Or is it in some third category of 'not unlawful act'? The Court of Appeal acknowledged the problem in *M*[56] where it was accepted that the *actus reus*/*mens rea* distinction was not one that could be rigidly adhered to in every case given the diverse nature of crimes. It also poses special problems in cases of secondary liability.

---

[48] Problems arise where D has been found unfit to plead and his condition improves so that by the time of the trial of the facts he is potentially fit to stand trial. See *Omara* [2004] EWCA Crim 431.

[49] *Moore* [2009] EWCA Crim 1672.

[50] See LCCP 197, para 2.30.

[51] [2001] 1 AC 340, HL, [2000] Crim LR 621, overruling *Egan* [1998] 1 Cr App R 121 which had 'held' that the words meant all the ingredients of the offence – a surprising construction, but that intended by the Butler Committee (Cmnd 6244, 1975, para 10.24) on whose recommendations these provisions are based. RD Mackay and G Kearns, 'The Trial of the Facts and Unfitness to Plead' [1997] Crim LR 644, however, demonstrated that this was not the meaning intended by ministers who introduced the Bill in Parliament. The same words used in the Trial of Lunatics Act 1883, s 2, refer only to the *actus reus*: *Felstead* [1914] AC 534, HL. An application to Strasbourg was rejected as manifestly ill-founded: *Antoine v United Kingdom* 62960/00. See also Mackay, [2002] Crim LR 728. For discussion see LCCP 197, Part 6. The Law Commission proposes reversing *Antoine*.

[52] That defence applies only when the *actus reus* (and, indeed, the *mens rea*) of murder has been established.

[53] See *Norman* [2010] EWCA Crim 1880 as a good illustration of the problems – D was charged with child abduction and suffered from Huntingdon's disease.

[54] Clearly, the finding of an act or omission may include some elements of *mens rea* where they are a composite element of the *actus reus*. *R (Young) v Central Criminal Court* [2002] 2 Cr App R 12, [2002] Crim LR 588 and commentary by JC Smith.

[55] *Grant (Heather)* [2002] QB 1030.

[56] [2003] 2 Cr App R 21. On the difficulties involved see RD Mackay and W Brookbanks, 'Protecting the Unfit to Plead' [2005] Juridical Review 173.

The broader problem lies in defining with sufficient precision the level of enquiry that is appropriate at a trial of the facts under s 4A so as to (i) avoid assessment of the accused's mental state at the time of the offence, because although he is the person best able to know that, by definition, he is now unfit to provide such evidence, or rebut allegations, and (ii) prevent the detention of those who would have secured a complete acquittal at a normal trial for reasons other than those of mental illness. The irony is that by seeking to protect defendants from a full trial and enquiry into a mental state that they are unable to defend, the system might place them in a worse position by subjecting them to a s 4A hearing.

Where D has been found to be unfit and to have committed the *actus reus*, but his condition then improves and the question arises whether he is fit to be tried, the determination of his fitness and of whether he performed the *actus reus* must both be re-litigated. The prior determination of the *actus reus* being satisfied cannot be relied upon.[57]

Onus of proof

Podola's case decided, overruling earlier authorities, that, where D raises the issue of fitness to plead, the onus of proving that he is unfit is on him. By analogy to the rule prevailing when a defence of insanity is raised at the trial,[58] D is required to prove his case, not beyond reasonable doubt, but on a balance of probabilities. If the issue is raised by the prosecution and disputed by the defence then the burden is on the prosecution and the matter must be proved beyond reasonable doubt.[59] If the issue is raised by the judge and disputed by D, presumably the onus is again on the prosecution.[60]

The effect of *Podola*'s case is that a person may be convicted although a court was not satisfied that he was capable of making out a proper defence at his trial. Moreover, the reasoning of the court has been criticized[61] on the ground, *inter alia*, that the prosecution, in bringing the charge at all, is implicitly alleging that D is fit to stand his trial; and that he, in denying that he is so fit, is merely denying that the prosecution have established all the elements in their case.

Disposal powers in relation to a person unfit to plead who 'did the act'

Until the reforms made by the 1991 Act took effect, the court had to order that any person found unfit to plead had to be admitted to the hospital specified by the Home Secretary where he might be detained without limitation of time, the power to discharge him being exercisable only with the Home Secretary's consent. Since the 1991 Act a person who is found unfit to plead but following a s 4A hearing, not to have done the act or made the omission charged simply goes free. Where he is found to be unfit *and* to have done the act or made the omission a wider range of disposals is now generally available.[62] Under s 24 of the 2004 Act inserting a new s 5 into the 1964 Act, in any case other than one of a fixed sentence, the court may make:

(1) a hospital order (with or without a restriction order);[63]

(2) a supervision order; or

(3) an order for absolute discharge.

---

[57] *Ferris* [2004] EWHC 1221 (Admin); cf *Omara*, above n 48.

[58] Per Edmund Davies J at first instance, [1960] 1 QB 325 at 329; *Robertson* [1968] 1 WLR 1767, CA.

[59] *Antoine* [2001] AC 340. According to Podola's counsel, Mr Lawton, it had been the normal practice in recent years for the prosecution to call the evidence.

[60] By M Dean, 'Fitness to Plead' [1960] Crim LR 79 at 82.

[61] Section 5 of the 1964 Act as amended.

[62] See LCCP 197, paras 2.36–2.42.

[63] See *Narey v Customs and Excise* [2005] All ER (D) 199 (Apr).

Magistrates' and Youth Courts

In the magistrates' court and the Youth Court[64] the procedure is quite different, It is contained in s 37 of the Mental Health Act 1983.[65] In cases of alleged unfitness *if* there exists medical evidence to justify making a hospital or guardianship order under s 37 the court has the power to do so in all cases. Ordinarily the court should first address whether the act alleged was done or the omission made by D. If it is not proved that D did the act or omission he will be acquitted. If the court finds that he did the act or omission it can make an order under s 37. However, if appropriate, where the court finds that D performed the act it can, instead of making an order under s 37 conduct a trial of the insanity plea.[66] At the conclusion of that trial the court's powers of disposal under s 37 remain available.

Reform

The Law Commission in 2010 highlighted numerous problems presented with the present law. It is based on an historic test unrelated to psychiatric understanding. As Toulson LJ stated in 2008, there is a 'mismatch between the legal test and the psychiatric understanding'.[67] The procedure has been cogently criticized for its focus on D's communicative ability and its failure to address the true problem – whether D is capable of providing a rational account of the incident to instruct his lawyer.[68] The present test creates difficulties in practice. It fails to protect mentally ill defendants who, despite the unfitness procedure, are often tried in the normal way[69] although in some cases displaying bizarre behaviour.[70] It fails to protect enough defendants. Estimates are that 10 per cent of men on remand display signs of psychosis, but only a very small number of unfitness pleas are made each year.[71] The Law Commission has proposed a test based on decisional competence.[72]

The s 4A hearing is also defective since it fails to provide the maximum opportunity for the accused to be acquitted. The Law Commission provisionally proposes amendment to allow for a verdict of acquittal or 'that D did the act without grounds for acquittal', or that 'D did the act with a mental disorder'. This will assist in more effective disposal.[73]

11.2.2 A plea of insanity[74]

If at trial D is found fit to plead, or if that issue is not raised, he may raise the plea of insanity. The plea will be that D was insane at the time of the commission of the offence alleged.

---

[64] *P v Barking Youth Court* [2002] EWHC 734 (Admin), [2002] Crim LR 637.

[65] See A Samuels, 'Hospital Orders without Conviction' [1995] Crim LR 220. On the need to consider the suitability of such disposal see *A* [2006] Crim LR 79. Note that under the Mental Health Act 2007, Sch 1, s 37, powers will be available if D is suffering from any disorder or disability of mind (the limitation to cases of mental illness or severe mental impairment will be removed). See LCCP 197, Ch 8.

[66] *R (Singh) v Stratford MC* [2007] EWHC 1582 (Admin).

[67] *Murray* [2008] EWCA Crim 1792, [6].

[68] See also the psychiatrist's view – D Grubin, 'What Constitutes Unfitness to Plead' [1993] Crim LR 748, cf RA Duff, 'Fitness to Plead and Fair Trials' [1994] Crim LR 419.

[69] Recent examples include *Erskine* [2009] EWCA Crim 1425; *Moyle* [2008] EWCA Crim 3059.

[70] See *Shulman* [2010] EWCA Crim 1034; *Grant* [2008] EWCA Crim 1870.

[71] See LCCP 197, para 2.61.

[72] See LCCP 197, Part 3. See RD Mackay [2004] Crim LR 219. See also the Scottish Law Commission Report No 195 (2004) Ch 4 and cl 4. See LCCP 197, provisionally proposing a test of decisional competence, but awaiting a test being devised by psychiatrists. For critical comment see RD Mackay [2011] Crim LR, forthcoming.

[73] See LCCP 197, Part 6. For critical comment see Mackay [2011] Crim LR, forthcoming.

[74] See, generally, Mackay, *Mental Condition Defences in Criminal Law*, Ch 2, and for a more philosophical account see Tadros, *Criminal Responsibility*, Ch 12. The CPS provides guidance on prosecuting people with a mental disorder: www.cps.gov.uk/publications/research/offenders_with_mental_health_problems .html.

Although rarely raised in a magistrates' court, it applies in a summary trial as well as a trial on indictment.[75] The rules governing the plea of insanity derive from the common law, but in trials on indictment the procedure for dealing with the plea has been regulated by statute; the unamended common law operates in magistrates' courts.[76] A successful plea of insanity at a trial on indictment formerly resulted in a mandatory order that D be admitted to a special hospital where he might be detained indefinitely. That was a significant deterrent to raising the plea. Now, by the 1991 Act as amended by the Domestic Violence, Crime and Victims Act 2004, a verdict of not guilty by reason of insanity means that the judge has more discretion in the disposal and can order hospitalization, a supervision order or an absolute discharge. Statistics suggest that this may be leading to more frequent reliance on the defence.[77]

11.2.2.1 Operation of the defence

Whereas the plea of unfitness is concerned with the accused's mental state at the time of the trial, insanity is concerned with the accused's mental state at the time when he is alleged to have performed the criminal act.

As a preliminary point it is worth emphasizing that legal and psychiatric understanding of 'insanity' are completely different. Strangely, the fact that D suffers an extreme mental illness recognized by psychiatrists will not necessarily be sufficient to afford a defence in law. Conversely, the fact that D suffers an illness that no psychiatrist would normally regard as a form of 'insanity' (eg diabetes) does qualify him for the defence. It seems astonishing that in the twenty-first century the law remains based not on any medical understanding of mental illness but on a distinct legal criterion of responsibility defined by the common law and set out in authoritative form in the 'M'Naghten Rules', formulated by judges as long ago as 1843.[78] Daniel M'Naghten, intending to murder Sir Robert Peel, killed Peel's secretary by mistake. His acquittal of murder[79] on the ground of insanity provoked controversy and was debated in the legislative chamber of the House of Lords, which sought the advice of the judges and submitted to them a number of questions. The answers to those questions became the famous 'Rules'. Answers to hypothetical questions, even by all the judges, are not, strictly speaking, a source of law; but in *Sullivan*[80] it was accepted by the judicial committee of the House of Lords that the Rules have provided a comprehensive definition since 1843.[81] The M'Naghten Rules are binding law.

The importance of the Rules diminished greatly on the introduction of the defence of diminished responsibility and the abolition of the death penalty. Diminished responsibility is a (partial) defence only to murder. Insanity pleas remain rare, even on charges for murder. Defendants seemingly prefer to risk conviction rather than incur the stigma of a not guilty by reason of insanity verdict. This remains true even though, since 1991, the disposal powers are not limited to automatic indefinite detention. But the stigma of the label 'insanity' remains: it

---

[75] See *R (Singh) v Stratford MC* [2007] EWHC 1582 (Admin).

[76] *Horseferry Road Magistrates' Court, ex p K* [1996] 2 Cr App R 574, [1997] Crim LR 129. See T Ward, 'Magistrates, Insanity and the Common Law' [1997] Crim LR 796.

[77] See RD Mackay, 'Fact and Fiction About the Insanity Defence' [1990] Crim LR 247; RD Mackay and G Kearns, 'The Continued Under use of Unfitness to Plead and the Insanity Defence' [1994] Crim LR 546; RD Mackay and G Kearns, 'More Fact(s) about the Insanity Defence' [1999] Crim LR 714; Mackay, Mitchell and Howe [2006] Crim LR 399.

[78] (1843) 4 St Tr NS 847.

[79] (1843) 10 Cl & Fin 200.

[80] *Sullivan* [1983] 2 All ER 673 at 676.

[81] In *Johnson* [2007] EWCA Crim 1978 the Court of Appeal referred enigmatically to the fact that the Rules must, given their provenance, be treated with 'some caution'.

is strikingly inappropriate when so much progress has been made regarding public attitudes to mental illness.

In some cases defendants will even prefer to plead guilty rather than risk a special verdict on grounds of insanity. The propriety of accepting a plea of guilty by a person who, on the evidence, is not guilty seems doubtful but it has not been questioned in the Court of Appeal and the House of Lords has left the matter open. It is regrettable that the state of the law is such that people suffering from a mental condition feel compelled to plead guilty. One undesirable consequence is the disproportionately high number of inmates in prison with mental disorders.[82]

11.2.2.2 The test of insanity

Whatever the effect of the recent changes on procedure and disposal, the M'Naghten Rules remain of great importance symbolically both because they provide the legal test of responsibility of the mentally abnormal and because they set a limit to the defences of automatism and, in theory, of diminished responsibility. The basic propositions of the law are to be found in the answers to Questions 2 and 3 of the M'Naghten Rules:[83]

the jurors ought to be told in all cases that every man is presumed to be sane, and to possess a sufficient degree of reason to be responsible for his crimes, until the contrary be proved to their satisfaction; and that to establish a defence on the ground of insanity, it must be clearly proved that, at the time of the committing of the act, the party accused was labouring under such a defect of reason, from disease of the mind, as not to know the nature and quality of the act he was doing, or, if he did know it, that he did not know he was doing what was wrong.

It will be seen that there are two lines of defence open to an accused person (often called the 'two limbs'):

(1) he must be acquitted if, because of a disease of the mind, he did not know the nature and quality of his act (effectively a denial of *mens rea*); or

(2) even if he did know the nature and quality of his act, he must be acquitted if, because of a disease of the mind, he did not know it was 'wrong'.

The Rules have been heavily criticized for being over-inclusive; 'disease of the mind' has been widely construed as to include within the scope of insanity such everyday illnesses as diabetes. In addition, in some instances D qualifies for the defence even though he was responsible for his inability to appreciate the nature or wrongness of his actions. As Mackay has recently pointed out, some commentators have argued that the first limb is superfluous as anyone who did not know the nature and quality of the act must also not have known it was wrong. Others, including Glanville Williams, argued that the second limb was superfluous since anyone who did not know the nature and quality of his act must also have lacked awareness that it was wrong.[84] The Rules are also criticized for focus on the cognitive state of D (has he appreciated the nature or wrongness) rather than on whether D had the *capacity* to be held responsible or to conform with criminal regulation.[85]

---

[82] See in particular Lord Bradley's report, *People with Mental Health Problems or Learning Disabilities in the Criminal Justice System* (2009).

[83] 10 Cl & Fin at 210. R Moran, *Knowing Right From Wrong: The Insanity Defence of Daniel McNaghten* (1981).

[84] See RD Mackay 'Righting the Wrong? Some Observations on the Second Limb of the M'Naghten Rules' [2009] Crim LR 80.

[85] See, recently, Tadros, *Criminal Responsibility*, Ch 12; A Brudner, *Punishment and Freedom: A Liberal Theory of Penal Justice* (2009). See also the important distinction drawn by the LCCP 197 on unfitness to plead.

Disease of the mind

The two limbs of the Rule require separate consideration but the first question, under either limb, is whether D was suffering from 'a defect of reason from a disease of the mind'. If D was unaware of the nature and quality of his act for some reason *other than* a defect of reason from a disease of the mind (such as mistake) he will usually be entitled to a straightforward acquittal on the ground that he lacked the necessary *mens rea*. Moreover, in such a case the onus of proof remains on the Crown, whereas it shifts to D once he tenders evidence of a defect of reason arising from disease of the mind.[86] If D was unaware that his act was 'wrong' for some reason other than from a defect of reason from a disease of the mind, this will generally not amount to a defence at all. It is a cardinal principle that neither ignorance of the law,[87] nor good motive will normally afford a defence.

The question whether D has raised the defence of insanity is one of law for the judge.[88] Whether D, or indeed his medical witnesses, would call the condition on which he relies, 'insanity' is immaterial. The expert witnesses may testify as to the factual nature of the condition but it is for the judge to say whether that is evidence of 'a defect of reason, from disease of the mind', because, as will become apparent, these are legal, not medical, concepts. In the leading case of *Sullivan*,[89] the defence to a charge of assault occasioning actual bodily harm was that D attacked V while recovering from a minor epileptic seizure and did not know what he was doing. The House of Lords held that the judge had rightly ruled that this raised the defence of insanity. D had then pleaded guilty to the charge of which he was manifestly innocent, and his conviction was upheld.

It seems that any disease which produces a malfunctioning of the mind is a disease of the mind.[90] Commonly the insanity plea will involve mental illness (schizophrenia being the most common basis)[91] but it is not restricted to diseases of the brain. Arteriosclerosis, a tumour on the brain, epilepsy, diabetes, sleepwalking, pre-menstrual syndrome and all physical diseases, may amount in law to a disease of the mind if they produce the relevant malfunction. The lack of correlation with medical definitions of mental illness renders this aspect of the test potentially incompatible with the ECHR (see below) where it results in D's loss of liberty or loss of private life.

It is critical to reiterate the distinction between pleas of insanity and pleas of sane automatism. A transitory malfunctioning of the mind is not a disease of the mind when it is caused by some external factor – a blow on the head causing concussion, the consumption of alcohol or drugs, or the administration of an anaesthetic. In such cases sane automatism may be pleaded. That 'defence' imposes no burden of proof on D and, if successful, results in a complete acquittal. Insanity on the other hand must be proved by D (on the balance of probabilities) and results in a special verdict of not guilty by reason of insanity. In terms of process and outcome much turns on this distinction between internal and external causes of the malfunction of the mind, yet the basis for the distinction is unsatisfactory.

In determining whether D suffers a disease of the mind, it is clear that the law considers not only D's state of mind at the time, but how it came about.[92] Devlin J thought that the object of the inclusion of the words 'disease of the mind' was to exclude 'defects of reason caused simply by brutish stupidity without rational power'; but it seems the words exclude

---

[86] The application of the burden of proof in these cases is critically explored by T Jones, 'Insanity, Automatism and the Burden of Proof on the Accused' (1995) 111 LQR 475. It is surprising that there has not been a direct ECHR challenge on this basis other than *H v UK* (1990) Appn No 15023/89 in which Commission dismissed the application. That decision has been very heavily criticized: see T Jones, above.

[87] cf the challenge to that made by A Ashworth 'Ignorance of the Law, and Duties to Avoid it' (2011) 74 MLR 1.

[88] See *Roach* [2001] EWCA Crim 2698.

[89] [1984] AC 156, [1983] 2 All ER 673, HL.

[90] *Kemp* [1957] 1 QB 399 at 406, per Devlin J, approved by Lord Denning in *Bratty*, below, n 98.

[91] See Mackay, Mitchell and Howe [2006] Crim LR 399.

[92] Contrary to the *dictum* of Devlin J in *Kemp* [1957] 1 QB 399 at 407.

more than that. In *Quick*,[93] D who had inflicted actual bodily harm called medical evidence to show that he was a diabetic and that he was suffering from a hypoglycaemic attack at the time of the alleged offence and was unaware of what he was doing. Bridge J ruled that he had thereby raised a defence of insanity, whereupon D pleaded guilty. On appeal it was held that D's mental condition at the time of the offence was caused not by D's diabetes (an internal factor) but by his use of insulin prescribed by the doctor coupled with his failure to follow that prescription by eating after injecting insulin (an external factor). This use of the prescribed drug was an external factor and the plea of sane automatism should have been left to the jury. If D's mental condition had been caused by his diabetes the plea would have been insanity, being based on that internal factor of disease. The case illustrates the fine line between the two pleas although the consequence of pleading them successfully is markedly different.[94] The unsatisfactory nature of this distinction is further discussed in the next section.

Disease of the mind includes physical illnesses that manifest themselves by affecting reasoning. In *Kemp*,[95] D made an entirely motiveless and irrational attack on his wife with a hammer. He was charged with causing grievous bodily harm to her with intent. D suffered from arteriosclerosis which caused a congestion of blood in his brain, leading to a temporary lapse of consciousness during which he made the attack. It was conceded that D did not know the nature and quality of his act and that he suffered from a defect of reason but it was argued on his behalf that this arose, not from any mental disease, but from a purely physical one. It was argued that, if a physical disease caused the brain cells to degenerate (as in time, it might), then it would be a disease of the mind; but until it did so, it was said, this temporary interference with the working of the brain was like a concussion or something of that sort and not a disease of the mind. Devlin J rejected this argument and held that D was suffering from a disease of the mind. He said:

The law is not concerned with the brain but with the mind, in the sense that 'mind' is ordinarily used, the mental faculties of reason, memory and understanding. If one reads for 'disease of the mind' 'disease of the brain,' it would follow that in many cases pleas of insanity would not be established because it could not be proved that the brain had been affected in any way, either by degeneration of the cells or in any other way. In my judgment the condition of the brain is irrelevant and so is the question of whether the condition of the mind is curable or incurable, transitory or permanent.

In the earlier case of *Charlson*,[96] where the evidence was that D was 'acting as an automaton without any real knowledge of that he was doing' as a result of a cerebral tumour, Barry J directed the jury to acquit if the defence might reasonably be true. Devlin J distinguished *Charlson* on the ground that there the doctors were agreed that D was not suffering from a mental disease.[97] As this is a question of law the distinction seems unsound and in *Bratty*[98] Lord Denning approved *Kemp* and disagreed with *Charlson*. Lord Denning put forward his own view of a disease of the mind:

it seems to me that any mental disorder which has manifested itself in violence and is prone to recur is a disease of the mind. At any rate it is the sort of disease for which a person should be detained in hospital rather than be given an unqualified acquittal.

---

[93] [1973] QB 910, [1973] Crim LR 434 and commentary; cf *Hennessey*, below, p 298. See also LC 314, para 2.88.

[94] See *Bingham* [1991] Crim LR 433.

[95] [1957] 1 QB at 407.

[96] [1955] 1 WLR 317.

[97] A similar argument was rejected in *Sullivan* [1983] 2 All ER 673 at 677. The nomenclature adopted by the medical profession may change but the meaning of 'disease of the mind' in the M'Naghten Rules remains unchanged.

[98] *Bratty v A-G for Northern Ireland* [1963] AC 386 at 410–412, HL.

Quick casts some doubt on this *dictum*, and it is surely right to do so. The definition might fit a diabetic, but 'no mental hospital would admit a diabetic merely because he had a low blood sugar reaction', and it might be felt to be 'an affront to common sense' to regard such a person as insane; yet the court saw the weakness of the argument, agreeing with Devlin J that the disease might be 'curable or incurable ... transitory or permanent'; and the fact that the Home Secretary might have had a difficult problem of disposal did not affect the matter. Lord Denning's *dictum* has also been rightly criticized on the ground that it is tautologous and that a disease of the mind may manifest itself in wrongful acts other than violence, such as theft.[99]

'External' and 'internal' factors

The distinction between external causes, which may give rise to a defence of sane automatism, and internal factors which can only give rise to a defence of insanity has been subjected to sustained and cogent criticism.[100] The supposed justification is that the internal factor will usually be a continuing condition which may cause a recurrence of the prohibited conduct whereas the external factor – the blow on the head, the injection, the inhalation of toxic fumes,[101] etc will usually have a transitory effect which will not recur. However, it is surely wrong to assume such a precise correlation between the source of the defect in D's 'mind' and likelihood of recurrence. The blow on the head may inflict permanent damage, which would be viewed thereafter as an internal factor giving rise to a defence of insanity. In cases of diabetes, it can hardly be suggested that there is a greater risk of recurrence from the diabetes itself causing a hyperglyacaemic state (insanity) than from D forgetting to eat after taking insulin and going into a hypoglycaemic state (sane automatism). Distinguishing between external and internal causes is an unsatisfactory and deficient way of addressing the true mischief – the likelihood of danger posed by uncontrolled recurrence of the mental condition leading to a lack of capacity. The deficiency is exposed in Lord Lane's judgment in *Burgess*:

> if there is a danger of recurrence that may be an added reason for categorising the condition as a disease of the mind. On the other hand, the absence of the danger of recurrence is not a reason for saying that it cannot be a disease of the mind.[102]

The passage serves to emphasize that the underlying bases for the courts' approach are pragmatism and policy rather than principle.

Range of conditions treated in law as 'a disease of the mind'

The reach of the M'Naghten Rules in extending to epileptics,[103] diabetics,[104] pre-menstrual syndrome sufferers,[105] sleepwalkers,[106] etc is astonishingly wide. Its application to sleepwalking has prompted recent interest[107] following first instance decisions taking a generous

---

[99] N Walker, *Crime and Insanity in England* (1963) 117.

[100] See the dissent by Dickson J in *Rabey* (1981) 114 DLR (3d) 193; RD Mackay, 'Non-Organic Automatism' [1980] Crim LR 350; Williams, TBCL, 671.

[101] *Oakley* (1986) 24 CCC (3d) 351 at 362, per Martin JA.

[102] [1991] WLR 1206 at 1212.

[103] *Sullivan* [1984] AC 156. RD Mackay and M Reuber, 'Epilepsy and the Defence of Insanity – Time for a Change' [2007] Crim LR 782.

[104] *Hennessey* [1989] 2 All ER 9. See on diabetes and driving cases in particular J Rumbold, 'Diabetes and Criminal Responsibility' (2010) 174 CLJW 21.

[105] *Smith* [1982] Crim LR 531 and see V St John, 'Premenstrual Syndrome in the Criminal Law' [1997] Auckland Uni LR 331; SM Edwards, 'Mad, Bad or Pre-Menstrual' (1988) 138 NLJ 456.

[106] *Burgess* [1991] 2 All ER 769. Irene Mackay, 'The Sleepwalker is Not Insane' (1992) 55 MLR 714. cf the Canadian Supreme Court in *Parks* (1990) 95 DLR (4th) 27.

[107] See W Wilson et al, 'Violence, Sleepwalking and the Criminal Law' [2005] Crim LR 601 and 614; RD Mackay and B Mitchell, 'Sleepwalking, Automatism and Insanity' [2006] Crim LR 901 reviewing Canadian law which adopts a more holistic approach to the question rather than relying solely on the internal/external bifurcation.

approach and allowing a defence of sane automatism to be run.[108] Even if sleepwalking is classified as insanity, a more liberal approach is evident in some cases. For example, in one recent case D had killed V in the course of his sleepwalking/night terror, and pleaded insanity. The CPS discontinued the case as the result of an insanity verdict would have been hospitalization for D and that was not in the public interest.[109] Pressure has also been mounting for the reclassification of epilepsy to avoid the stigma of being labelled insane.[110]

Most if not all of the reported cases involve apparently purposive conduct. In *Bratty v A-G for Northern Ireland*,[111] D took off a girl's stocking and strangled her with it. There was medical evidence that he was suffering from psychomotor epilepsy which might have prevented him from knowing the nature and quality of his act. It was held to be evidence of insanity. This seems very far removed from a convulsive movement of the body of an epilepsy sufferer. It is a complex operation which has every appearance of being controlled by the brain. Whether or not D could have prevented himself from acting in this way, he appears to be a dangerous person and, in the absence of some other form of protection for the public, a simple verdict of acquittal seems inappropriate. Sullivan's conduct, like that of Kemp, Charlson, Quick and Rabey (below) also seems to have been apparently purposive and, though he was less obviously a danger to the public than Bratty, his case may be indistinguishable in principle. Even the examples of epilepsy referred to in recent research into insanity suggest that commonly the actions are complex purposive ones. Of course, a convulsive movement of a person in an epileptic fit may result in injury to person or property but it would seem absurd either to convict the epileptic or hold him to be insane. If insanity is available as a defence for seemingly purposive action, it is not fanciful to suggest, bearing in mind the increased flexibility of the courts' powers of disposal, that some unscrupulous pleas of insanity will be advanced, and the courts need to be alert to that fact.

It remains deeply unsatisfactory for this crucial 'disease of the mind' element to remain so ill-defined. Firstly a person with a mental condition of a non-severe nature and who poses no real future risk to society might end up labelled and treated as insane. Secondly, a challenge to the overbroad definition of disease of the mind may arise under the ECHR. Article 5(1)(e), in guaranteeing protection against arbitrary detention, allows for the detention of those suffering from mental illness where it is necessary for the protection of the public. The European Court of Human Rights has accepted that the State's power to detain in these circumstances is limited to cases where the mental illness is one recognized by objective medical expertise, and where the medical and legal definitions of mental illness have a close correlation.[112] If a defendant were to be detained as a result of a special verdict of insanity when the 'disease' he was suffering from was one which medical professionals would not normally classify as insanity, there might be an incompatibility. That may be unlikely as detention is regulated by the Mental Health Act. Although medical professionals are now required to be involved in the

---

[108] See *Lowe* unreported (2005), discussed in Wilson et al, and *Pooley* (2007) unreported, discussed in Mackay and Mitchell, note above. This has prompted CPS guidance: www.cps.gov.uk/legal/d_to_g/defences_-_sleepwalking_as_a_defence_in_sexual_offence_cases/index.html. See also I Ibrahim and P Fenwick, 'Sleep Related Automatism and the Law' (2008) 48 Med Sci Law 124.

[109] See www.cps.gov.uk/news/press_releases/156-09/index.html.

[110] See Mackay and Reuber [2007] Crim LR 782.

[111] [1963] AC 386.

[112] *Winterwerp v Netherlands* [1979] 2 EHRR 387, [1994] Crim LR 84; *Luberti v Italy* (1984) 6 EHRR 440; *Reid v UK* (2003) 37 EHRR 9. See P Sutherland and C Gearty, 'Insanity and the ECHR' [1992] Crim LR 418; Baker, above; Emmerson, Ashworth and Macdonald, HR&CJ, para 18.23 et seq. On the success of challenges in Jersey see Mackay [2002] Crim LR 728.

trial of insanity,[113] it is debatable whether this ensures compatibility.[114] Medical professionals might well, in the course of providing expert evidence, be obliged to state that the disease is one that satisfies the legal test of insanity, but that is quite different from a medical professional recognizing the disease as a matter of psychiatry as one of mental illness.

Borderline cases – disease of mind (insanity) or external factor (sane automatism)?

Some of the most controversial problems on classification arise in relation to 'psychological blows'. Cases in other jurisdictions have addressed directly the question of whether a 'dissociative state' resulting from a 'psychological blow' amounts to insane or sane automatism. In the Canadian case *Rabey*,[115] D, a student who had become infatuated by a girl, V, discovered that V did not regard him particularly highly and reacted to that news by hitting her on the head with a rock that he had taken from a geology laboratory. He was acquitted of causing bodily harm with intent on the ground of automatism. The trial judge accepted that D was in a dissociative state caused by the psychological blow of his rejection, which, it was held, was an external factor, analogous to a blow to the skull, where the skull is thin, causing concussion. The Ontario Court of Appeal allowed the prosecution's appeal and ordered a new trial. A further appeal to the Supreme Court of Canada was dismissed. That court approved the judgment of Martin J, who took the view that 'the ordinary stresses and disappointments of life which are the common lot of mankind do not constitute an external cause...'[116] The exceptional effect which this ordinary event had on D 'must be considered as having its source primarily in the [D's] psychological or emotional make-up'. Notwithstanding the powerful dissent by Dickson J, it is submitted that this is right and that in such a case if the evidence as to D's dissociative state is accepted at all,[117] it should be treated as evidence of insanity. Once the judge has so categorized the defence, D had the burden of proving on a balance of probabilities that he was in a dissociative state. If he and his medical witnesses are to be believed, he was not guilty, but he is a highly dangerous person.[118] Who is to say that the next ordinary stress of life will not lead him unconsciously to wield a deadly weapon? Policy clearly has a significant part to play here.

Martin J left open the question of the effect of an extraordinary event of such severity that it might reasonably be expected to cause a dissociative state in the average person. This would, it is submitted, be a case of sane automatism because D has done nothing to show that he is any more dangerous to others than anyone else; and he should be simply acquitted. It is of course difficult to identify what should constitute such a degree of extraordinariness. In *T*,[119] where the defendant had committed a robbery when suffering from Post Traumatic Stress Disorder as a result of being raped, the trial judge ruled that the rape was to be treated as an external factor. It would be uncontroversial to regard the rape as an extraordinary event, but it is unclear which if any other traumatic events will suffice. Further judicial clarification of the scope of this exceptional category of sane automatism would be welcome.

---

[113] By s 1 of the 1991 Act, a jury shall not return a special verdict of not guilty by reason of insanity (NGRI) except on the written or oral evidence of two or more registered medical practitioners of whom at least one is approved by the Home Secretary as having special experience in the field of mental disorder.

[114] In addition, Mackay, Mitchell and Howe [2006] Crim LR 399 identify cases in which NGRI verdicts have been returned without medical evidence.

[115] (1977) 37 CCC (2d) 461; affd [1980] SCR 513, 54 CCC (2d) 1. See also *Parnerkar* [1974] SCR 449, 10 CCC (2d) 253 and cases discussed by Mackay [1980] Crim LR 350.

[116] (1980) 54 CCC (2d) at 7.

[117] cf the scepticism of Williams about the acceptance of the evidence of 'over enthusiastic psychiatrists' in relation to the similar case of *Parnerkar* [1974] SCR 449, 10 CCC (2d) 253; Williams, TBCL (1st edn) at 612–613.

[118] In fact, D's expert witness said D had no predisposition to dissociate; but the court, while bound to take account of medical evidence, may also take account of the facts of the case and apply its common sense to all the evidence.

[119] [1990] Crim LR 256. And see *Huckerby* [2004] EWCA Crim 3251.

Defect of reason

The disease of the mind must have given rise to a 'defect of reason'. It seems that D's powers of reasoning must be impaired and that D's mere failure to use powers of reasoning which he possesses does not bring him within the M'Naghten Rules. When D claimed that she had taken articles from a supermarket without paying for them because of absentminded-ness resulting from depression, it was held that, even if she was suffering from a disease of the mind (which is arguable), she had not raised the defence of insanity but was simply denying that she had *mens rea*.[120] Tadros has recently suggested that this element of the defence warrants closer attention, since it could help to identify those who are morally re-sponsible for failing to recognize either the nature and quality or wrongness of their act. This element should cause the courts to focus on whether there was a diminution of D's reasoning powers.

The nature and quality of his act – the 'first limb'

The phrase 'nature and quality of his act' refers to the physical nature and quality of the act and not to its moral or legal quality.[121] In modern terms, it means simply that D 'did not know what he was doing'.[122] It is of narrow application; illustrations given by leading writers are:

A kills B under an insane delusion that he is breaking a jar[123]
   and
the madman who cut a woman's throat under the idea that he was cutting a loaf of bread.[124]

Of course, a person who was under a delusion such as these, apart altogether from insanity, could never be convicted of murder, simply because he had no *mens rea*. The important prac-tical difference, however, is that, if the delusion arose from a disease of the mind, he will be liable to be indefinitely detained in a special hospital[125] whereas, if it arose from some other cause, he will go entirely free. A person whose acts are involuntary because he is unconscious does not 'know the nature and quality of his act'.[126]

Those who advocate abolition[127] of the defence of insanity suggest that the ability to plead absence of *mens rea* can deal with those lacking mental responsibility. The approach has been adopted in some US states, but has been criticized. The Scottish Law Commission concluded that such an approach distorts the *mens rea* test to accommodate 'cases where the accused suffered from a mental disorder but could still form a mental element for specific offences'.[128] Abolishing insanity and relying on the question of *mens rea* also fails to accommodate the cases where D's mental illness led him to believe he had a defence, and those for whom *mens rea* is present because of the mental illness.

Knowledge that the act is 'wrong' – the 'second limb'

This second, alternative limb is not concerned with whether the accused is able to distinguish between right and wrong in general, but whether he was able to appreciate the wrongness

---

[120] *Clarke* [1972] 1 All ER 219. For discussion see Tadros, *Criminal Responsibility*, 333.
[121] *Codère* (1916) 12 Cr App R 21; see recently *Johnson* [2007] EWCA Crim 1978. For cogent criticism see Mackay [2009] Crim LR 80.
[122] *Sullivan* [1983] 2 All ER 673 at 678.
[123] Stephen, *Digest* (8th edn) 6.
[124] Kenny, *Outlines*, 76.
[125] The disposal powers for those found not guilty by reason of insanity in cases of murder are limited.
[126] *Sullivan* [1983] 2 All ER 673 at 678, HL.
[127] eg N Morris, 'The Criminal Responsibility of the Mentally Ill' (1982) 33 Syracuse LR 477.
[128] Report para 2.16.

of the particular act he was doing at the particular time alleged to constitute a crime. It has always been clear that if D knew his act was contrary to law, he knew it was 'wrong' for this purpose. Thus in their first answer the judges in *M'Naghten*'s case said:[129]

notwithstanding the party accused did the act complained of with a view, under the influence of in-sane delusion, of redressing or revenging some supposed grievance or injury, or of producing some public benefit, he is nevertheless punishable, according to the nature of the crime committed, if he knew at the time of committing such crime that he was acting contrary to law; by which expression we understand your lordships to mean the law of the land.

Even if D did not know his act was contrary to law, he was still liable if he knew that it was wrong 'according to the ordinary standard adopted by reasonable men'.[130] The fact that D thought his act was right was irrelevant if he knew that people generally considered it wrong. This again seems to be supported by the Rules:[131]

If the question were to be put as to the knowledge of the accused solely and exclusively with reference to the law of the land, it might tend to confound the jury, by inducing them to believe that an actual knowledge of the law of the land was essential to lead to a conviction: whereas the law is administered upon the principle that everyone must be taken conclusively to know it, without proof that he does know it. If the accused was conscious that the act was one which he ought not to do, and if that act was at the same time contrary to the law of the land, he is punishable.

Modern cases, however, suggest that the courts are concerned only with D's knowledge of legal, not moral, wrongness. In *Windle*,[132] D was unhappily married to a woman, V, who was always speaking of committing suicide and who, according to medical evidence at the trial, was certifiably insane. D killed V by the administration of 100 aspirins. He then gave himself up to the police, saying, 'I suppose they will hang me for this'. A medical witness for the de-fence said that D was suffering from a form of communicated insanity known as *folie à deux*. Rebutting medical evidence was called, but the doctors on both sides agreed that he knew he was doing an act which the law forbade. Devlin J thereupon withdrew the issue from the jury. So far the decision accords perfectly with the law as stated above but, in the Court of Criminal Appeal, Lord Goddard CJ, in upholding the conviction, said:[133]

Courts of law can only distinguish between that which is in accordance with the law and that which is contrary to law.... The law cannot embark on the question and it would be an unfortunate thing if it were left to juries to consider whether some particular act was morally right or wrong. The test must be whether it is contrary to law....

In the opinion of the court there is no doubt that in the M'Naghten Rules 'wrong' means contrary to law and not 'wrong' according to the opinion of one man or of a number of people on the question whether a particular act might or might not be justified.

Windle is in accordance with authority in rejecting the arguments of the defence that D should be acquitted if, knowing his act to be against the law, he also believed it to be morally right. In the Court of Appeal in *Johnson*,[134] it was recently confirmed that 'wrong' means only 'wrong' according to law. If D appreciates that his conduct is wrong according to law, he cannot rely on insanity. In practice it seems that juries commonly accept the defence in such cases.[135]

---

[129] (1843) 10 Cl & Fin at 209.
[130] *Codère* (1916) 12 Cr App R 21 at 27.
[131] (1843) 10 Cl & Fin at 210.
[132] [1952] 2 QB 826.
[133] [1952] 2 QB 826 at 833, 834.
[134] [2007] EWCA Crim 1978. See RD Mackay [2009] Crim LR 79, for a valuable review.
[135] See Mackay and Kearns [1999] Crim LR 714 at 722.

The High Court of Australia has refused to follow *Windle*. In *Stapleton v R*,[136] they made a detailed examination of the English law, before and after *M'Naghten* and came to the conclusion that *Windle* was wrongly decided. Their view was that if D believed his act to be right according to the ordinary standard of reasonable people he was entitled to be acquitted even if he knew it to be legally wrong. This would extend the scope of the defence, not only beyond what was laid down in *Windle*, but beyond what the law was believed to be before that case. While such an extension of the law may be desirable, it is difficult to reconcile with the M'Naghten Rules and to justify on the authorities.[137] In *Johnson*, the court discussed *Stapeleton* and rejected that approach.[138] It is not followed by the courts in England. This will be an important issue for the Law Commission in its pending reform. Should the defence be available where D kills a prostitute, knowing that to do so is murder, but believing that it is morally right to rid the streets of such women?[139]

Insane delusions and insanity

Whereas the defence of insanity is excessively broad in defining diseases of the mind, it is unsatisfactorily narrow in respect of what constitutes a sufficient awareness of wrongdoing. The judges were asked in *M'Naghten*'s case:

If a person under an insane delusion as to existing facts commits an offence in consequence thereof, is he thereby excused?

They replied:[140]

the answer must, of course, depend on the nature of the delusion: but making the same assumption as we did before, namely, that he labours under such partial delusion only, and is not in other respects insane, we think he must be considered in the same situation as to responsibility as if the facts with respect to which the delusion exists were real. For example, if under the influence of his delusion he supposes another man to be in the act of attempting to take away his life, and he kills that man, as he supposes, in self-defence, he would be exempt from punishment. If his delusion was that the deceased had inflicted a serious injury to his character and fortune, and he killed him in revenge for such supposed injury, he would be liable to punishment.

This seems to add nothing to the earlier answers. The insane delusions that the judges had in mind seem to have been factual errors of the kind which prevent a person from knowing the nature and quality of his act or knowing it is wrong. The example given seems to fall within those Rules.

The proposition that the insane person 'must be considered in the same situation as to responsibility as if the facts with respect to which the delusion exists were real' must be treated with caution. It should always be remembered that there must be an *actus reus*, accompanied by the appropriate *mens rea*, for a conviction. Suppose that D strangles his wife's poodle under the insane delusion that it is her illegitimate child. If the supposed facts were real he would be

---

[136] (1952) 86 CLR 358; see also *Weise* [1969] VR 953, especially at 960 et seq, per Barry J. See also *Chaulk* [1990] 3 SCR 1303; *Oomen* [2004] 2 SCR 507. See generally for a comparative review S Yeo, 'The Insanity Defence in the Criminal Law of the Commonwealth Nations' [2008] Sing JLS.

[137] *Stapleton v R* is discussed in a note by N Morris, '"Wrong" in the M'Naghten Rules' (1953) 16 MLR 435, which is criticized by J Montrose, 'The M'Naghten Rules' (1954) 17 MLR 383.

[138] Referring with approval to this para in the 11th edition.

[139] cf *Peter Sutcliffe* (1981) 30 Apr, CCC. See A Norrie, *Crime, Reason and History* (2nd edn, 2000) 192–193; cf Tadros, *Criminal Responsibility*, 326.

[140] (1843) 10 Cl & Fin at 211.

guilty of murder – but that is plainly impossible as there is no *actus reus*.[141] In respect of the dog there is no crime of *mens rea*. The Rule seems merely to emphasize that delusions which do not prevent D from having *mens rea* will afford no defence. As Lord Hewart CJ rather crudely put it, 'the mere fact that a man thinks he is John the Baptist does not entitle him to shoot his mother'. A case often discussed is that of a man who is under the insane delusion that he is obeying a divine command. Some American courts have held that such a belief affords a defence. Yet if the accused knows that his act is forbidden by law, it seems clear he is liable. Stephen certainly thought that this was so:

My own opinion is that if a special divine order were given to a man to commit murder, I should certainly hang him for it, unless I got a special divine order not to hang him.[142]

Irresistible impulse

It is recognized by psychiatrists that a person may know the nature and quality of an act, may even know that it is wrong, and yet perform it under an impulse that is almost or quite uncontrollable. Such a person has no defence under the M'Naghten Rules. The matter was considered in *Kopsch*:[143] D, according to his own admission, killed his uncle's wife. He said that he strangled her with his tie at her own request. (If this was an insane delusion, it would not, of course, afford a defence under the Rules stated above.) There was evidence that he had acted under the direction of his subconscious mind. Counsel argued that the judge should have directed the jury that a person under an impulse which he cannot control is not criminally responsible. This was described by Lord Hewart CJ as a 'fantastic theory . . . which if it were to become part of our criminal law, would be merely subversive'.[144]

The judges have steadily opposed acknowledging such a defence on the ground of the difficulty – or impossibility – of distinguishing between an impulse which proves irresistible because of insanity and one which is irresistible because of ordinary motives of greed, jealousy or revenge. The view has also been expressed that the harder an impulse is to resist, the greater is the need for a deterrent.[145]

English law does not recognize irresistible impulse even as a symptom from which a jury might deduce insanity within the meaning of the Rules.[146] If, however, medical evidence were tendered in a particular case that the uncontrollable impulse, to which the accused in that case had allegedly been subject, was a symptom that he did not know his act was wrong, it would be open to the jury to act on that evidence.[147] But it is not permissible for a judge to make use in one case of medical knowledge which he may have acquired from the evidence in another, in his direction to the jury.[148]

Although the M'Naghten Rules remain unaltered, a partial defence of irresistible impulse has now been admitted into the law of murder through the defence of diminished responsibility.[149]

---

[141] Nor, notwithstanding *Shivpuri*, below, p 336 should an insane delusion entail liability for an attempt.

[142] 2 HCL 160, n 1. In some jurisdictions statutory reformulations have expanded the defence to accommodate decisions. See, eg, *Phillip v The Queen* [2007] UKPC 31.

[143] (1925) 19 Cr App R 50, CCA. See also *True* (1922) 16 Cr App R 164; *Sodeman* [1936] 2 All ER 1138, PC.

[144] (1925) 19 Cr App R 50 at 51.

[145] As Canadian judge, Riddell J, put it: 'If you cannot resist an impulse in any other way, we will hang a rope in front of your eyes, and perhaps that will help': *Creighton* (1909) 14 CCC 349.

[146] *A-G for State of South Australia v Brown* [1960] AC 432, [1960] 1 All ER 734, PC.

[147] ibid. See also *Sodeman* (1936) 55 CLR 192 at 203.

[148] [1960] AC 432 at 449.

[149] See p 527.

11.2.2.3 Burden of proof

The M'Naghten Rules laid down that:

every man is presumed to be sane, and to possess a sufficient degree of reason to be responsible for his crimes, until the contrary be proved to [the jury's] satisfaction; and that to establish a defence on the ground of insanity, it must be clearly proved, etc.[150]

It seems from these words that the judges were intending to put the burden of proof squarely on the accused, and so it has always been subsequently assumed.[151] Insanity is stated to be the one exception at common law to the rule that it is the duty of the prosecution to prove the accused's guilt in all particulars.[152] He does not have to satisfy that heavy onus of proof beyond reasonable doubt which rests on the prosecution but is entitled to a verdict in his favour if he proves his case on a balance of probabilities, the standard which rests on the claimant in a civil action. If the jury think it is more likely than not that he is insane within the meaning of the Rules, then he is entitled to their verdict.

When, however, consideration is given to what has to be proved to establish insanity under the first limb of the Rules, there is an apparent conflict with the general rule requiring the prosecution to prove *mens rea*. This requires proof that the accused had the required *mens rea* with respect to all those consequences and circumstances of his act which constitute the *actus reus* of the crime with which he is charged. But, this is a requirement to prove that the accused *did* know the nature and quality of his act – at least in cases where the *mens rea* of the offence is intention or knowledge. The general rule, therefore, says that the prosecution must prove these facts; the special rule relating to insanity says that the defence must disprove them![153] Williams argued[154] that the only burden on the accused is the 'evidential' one of introducing sufficient evidence to raise a reasonable doubt in the jury's minds; and that the burden of *proof* is on the prosecution.[155] This solution appears to be the best way of resolving the inconsistency.[156]

This problem does not arise when D's defence takes the form that he did not know that his act was wrong. Here he is setting up the existence of facts which are quite outside the prosecution's case and there is no inconsistency in putting the onus on him. It is very strange that the onus of proof should be on the Crown if the defence is based on the first limb of the Rules and on D if it should be on the second. Yet the authorities[157] seem clearly to establish that the onus in the case of the second limb is on the accused. It is not possible to argue that the courts really meant the evidential burden for they have said very clearly that the burden is one of proof 'on balance of probabilities', the same standard that the claimant in a civil action must satisfy. Whatever may be the position regarding the first limb of the defence then, it seems clear that, under the second, the onus is on the accused.

The anomaly is emphasized by the decision of the House of Lords in *Bratty v A-G for Northern Ireland*[158] that, where the defence is sane automatism (that is, arising otherwise than through a disease of the mind), the burden of proof is on the prosecution. It is difficult to see why a person whose alleged disability arises from a disease of the mind should

---

[150] (1843) 10 Cl & Fin at 210.

[151] *Stokes* (1848) 3 Car & Kir 185; *Layton* (1849) 4 Cox CC 149; *Smith* (1910) 6 Cr App R 19; *Coelho* (1914) 30 TLR 535; *Bratty v A-G for Northern Ireland* [1963] AC 386, [1961] 3 All ER 523.

[152] *Woolmington v DPP* [1935] AC 462.

[153] See further, Jones (1995) 111 LQR 475 for a compelling critique.

[154] CLGP, at 165.

[155] In coroners proceedings insanity has to be disproved to the criminal standard to sustain a verdict of unlawful killing – *R (O'Connor) v HM Coroner for Avon* [2009] EWHC 854 (Admin).

[156] cf, however, *Cottle* [1958] NZLR 999 at 1019, per North J.

[157] *Sodeman v R* [1936] 2 All ER 1138; *Carr-Briant* [1943] KB 607.

[158] [1963] AC 386.

be convicted whereas one whose alleged disability arises from some other cause, would, in exactly the same circumstances, be acquitted.[159]

11.2.2.4 The scope of the defence

Hale[160] thought insanity was a defence only to capital charges but that opinion is no longer tenable. In *Horseferry Road Magistrates' Court, ex p K*,[161] the court accepted the misleading proposition in *Archbold*,[162] relied on by the applicant, that the defence of insanity 'is based on the absence of *mens rea*'. This may be true where D asserts that he did not know the nature and quality of his act, but it is not true where he asserts that he did not know the act was wrong.[163] Awareness of 'wrongness' is not an element in *mens rea*. It seems that *Ex p K* misled the court in *DPP v H*[164] into holding that the defence does not apply to an offence of strict liability – in that case driving with excess alcohol. It is submitted that the defence is of general application. Hawkins,[165] cited by the court in *Ex p K*, states: 'those who are under a natural disability of distinguishing between good and evil, as ... ideots and lunaticks ... are not punishable *by any criminal prosecution whatsoever*' [the court's italics].

11.2.2.5 The special verdict of insanity and the right of appeal

The Trial of Lunatics Act 1883 as amended provides that if it appears to the jury that the defendant 'did the act or made the omission charged but was insane as aforesaid at the time the jury shall return a special verdict that the accused is not guilty by reason of insanity'. In *A-G's Reference (No 3 of 1998)*,[166] it was held that the words 'act' and 'omission' mean the *actus reus* of the offence.[167] The prosecution do not have to prove *mens rea*. To require them to do so would be inconsistent with the rule that the onus is on D to prove that he did not know the nature and quality of his act.

A right of appeal to the Court of Appeal and the Supreme Court is provided by s 12 of the Criminal Appeal Act 1968, subject to the same conditions as apply in criminal appeals generally.

11.2.2.6 Function of the jury

It has been laid down for defences of both insanity and diminished responsibility that:[168]

it is for the jury and not for medical men [*sic*] of whatever eminence to determine the issue. Unless and until Parliament ordains that this question is to be determined by a panel of medical men, it is to a jury, after a proper direction by a judge, that by the law of this country the decision is to be entrusted.

The law regarding insanity, however, is now modified by s 1 of the 1991 Act which provides that a jury shall not return a special verdict of not guilty by reason of insanity except on the written or oral evidence of two or more registered medical practitioners of whom at least

---

[159] The Butler proposals on onus of proof appear below, p 308.

[160] I PC, c 4, and Walker, *Crime and Insanity in England*, I, 80; S White (1984) 148 JPN 412 at 419.

[161] Above, n 76.

[162] 1996 edn, at 17.109.

[163] See also *Moore v The State* [2001] UKPC 4.

[164] [1997] 1 WLR 1406. This is perhaps another manifestation of the fallacy that an offence of strict liability requires 'no *mens rea*'. The error of the trial judge in *Blackburn v Bowering*, below, p 661.

[165] Hawkins, 1 PC 1–2.

[166] [1999] 3 All ER 40, [1993] Crim LR 986.

[167] As defined in the 8th edition of this book, at 28. See above, p 3.

[168] *Matheson* [1958] 2 All ER 87, 42 Cr App R 145; *Bailey* (1961) 66 Cr App R 31n, [1961] Crim LR 828; *Sanders* [1991] Crim LR 781 – all cases concerning diminished responsibility – but the same principle surely applies to insanity.

one is approved by the Home Secretary as having special experience in the field of mental disorder.[169] The jury may still have to decide between conflicting medical evidence; but if the medical evidence is wholly in favour of a special verdict (or of diminished responsibility) and there is *nothing* in the facts or surrounding circumstances which could lead to a contrary conclusion, then a verdict of guilty (or guilty of murder as the case may be) will be upset.[170] If there are facts which, in the opinion of the court, justify the jury in coming to a conclusion different from that of the experts, their verdict will be upheld.

11.2.3 Proposals for reform of the insanity defence[171]

Almost from the moment of their formulation the Rules have been subjected to vigorous criticism, primarily by doctors, but also by lawyers. The Rules, being based on outdated psychiatric views, are too narrow, it is said, and exclude many persons who ought not to be held responsible. They are concerned only with defects of reason and take no account of emotional or volitional factors whereas modern medical science is unwilling to divide the mind into separate compartments and to consider the intellect apart from the emotions and the will.

In 1923, a committee under the chairmanship of Lord Atkin recommended that a person should not be held responsible 'when the act is committed under an impulse which [he] was by mental disease in substance deprived of any power to resist'.[172]

The recommendation was not implemented. In 1953, the Royal Commission on Capital Punishment[173] made much more far-reaching proposals. It thought that the question of responsibility is not primarily a matter of law or of medicine, but of morals and, therefore, most appropriately decided by a jury of ordinary people. The best course, it was recommended would be to abrogate the rules altogether and 'leave the jury to determine whether at the time of the act the accused was suffering from disease of the mind (or mental deficiency) to such a degree that he ought not to be held responsible'.[174]

This meant abandoning the assumption that it is necessary to have a rule of law defining the relation of insanity to criminal responsibility; but the Commission thought this assumption had broken down in practice anyway.[175] As an alternative, thought to be less satisfactory but better than leaving the Rules unchanged, the Commission recommended that a third limb be added to the Rules: that the accused 'was incapable of preventing himself from committing it...'[176]

It should be noted that there are some defenders of the present rules, and the case for them was most cogently put by Lord Devlin who emphasized that a test based on responsibility is:

---

[169] On the true input of the jury in practice see Mackay, Mitchell and Howe [2006] Crim LR 399.

[170] See recently *Khan* [2009] EWCA Crim 1569 where the evidence of diminished responsibility was not challenged or contradicted but D's conviction for murder was upheld. The murder verdict was rightly left to the jury.

[171] S Dell, 'Wanted; An Insanity Defence that Can be Used' [1983] Crim LR 431. For a recent reappraisal of the defence seeking to explain its operation by reference to lay conceptions of abnormality, see A Loughnan, 'Manifest Madness: Towards a New Understanding of the Insanity Defence' (2007) 70 MLR 379. See Mackay [2009] Crim LR 80, and calls for a more fundamental review made by M Hathaway 'The Moral Significance of the Insanity Defence' (2009) 73 J Crim L 310.

[172] Cmd 2005.

[173] Cmd 8932.

[174] ibid, para 333. cf Walker's criticism, *Crime and Insanity in England*, at 110–111: 'By what criterion could one tell whether this or that case "ought" to have been included? Could the criterion be expressed in words, or was it ineffable?'

[175] The Commission was impressed by Lord Cooper's view that 'However much you charge a jury as to the M'Naghten Rules or any other test, the question they would put to themselves when they retire is – "Is this man mad or is he not?"'; Report, para 3.22.

[176] Cmd 2005.

what distinguishes him from the animals, which emotional disorder does not; it is what makes him man; it is what makes him subject to the law. So it is fitting that nothing other than a defect of reason should give complete absolution.[177]

11.2.3.1 The Draft Criminal Code

The Butler Committee proposed a new approach which was substantially incorporated in to the Draft Code. There would be a new verdict of 'not guilty on evidence of mental disorder' – 'a mental disorder verdict'. As under the M'Naghten Rules, such a verdict would be returned in two types of case: (i) where the mental disorder precludes the required fault (corresponding to the 'nature and quality' limb), and (ii) where all the elements of the offence are proved but the mental disorder nevertheless should result in an acquittal (corresponding to the 'wrong' limb). The Code reverses the order.[178] Clause 35 provides:

> (1) A mental disorder verdict shall be returned if the defendant is proved to have committed an offence but it is proved on the balance of probabilities (whether by the prosecution or by the defendant) that he was at the time suffering from severe mental illness or severe mental handicap.

'Severe mental illness' is defined in the terms proposed by Butler as follows:

'Severe mental illness' means a mental illness which has one or more of the following characteristics –

> (a) lasting impairment of intellectual functions shown by failure of memory, orientation, comprehension and learning capacity;
>
> (b) lasting alteration of mood of such degree as to give rise to delusional appraisal of the defendant's situation, his past or his future, or that of others, or lack of any appraisal;
>
> (c) delusional beliefs, persecutory, jealous or grandiose;
>
> (d) abnormal perceptions associated with delusional misinterpretation of events;
>
> (e) thinking so disordered as to prevent reasonable appraisal of the defendant's situation of reasonable communication with others.

'Severe mental handicap' means: 'a state of arrested or incomplete development of mind which includes severe impairment or intelligence and social functioning', a definition adapted from that in the Mental Health Act 1959. These definitions would need to be updated to accord with the Mental Health Acts 1983 and 2007.

If the Code had stopped here, as Butler intended, this would have involved a major change of principle in that there need be no causal connection between the mental disorder and the commission of the act. Butler thought that the disorders specified are of such severity that a causal connection could safely be presumed. D's belief that he was John the Baptist, presumably 'a grandiose delusional belief', would be a defence to a charge of murdering his mother.[179] More realistically, D would have a defence to a charge of robbing a bank or of dangerous driving because he had a jealous delusional belief that his wife was committing adultery. The Law Commission thought such a result unacceptable and so cl 35(2) provides:

---

[177] 'Mental Abnormality and the Criminal Law', in R St J MacDonald (ed), *Changing Legal Objectives* (1963) 71 at 85. cf A F Goldstein, *The Insanity Defence* (1967).

[178] For an alternative approach to reform see the recent Scottish proposals – *Insanity and Diminished Responsibility*, Report No 195 (2004) in which the M'Naghten approach is rejected in favour of a model found in the USA where the defence is based on a lack of criminal responsibility due to mental disorder.

[179] Above, p 304. See also M Moore, 'Causation and Excuses' (1985) 73 Calif LR 1091.

Subsection (1) does not apply if the court or jury is satisfied beyond reasonable doubt that the offence was not attributable to the severe mental illness or severe mental handicap.

The effect is that there is a presumption that the commission of the offence was attributable to the disorder but it is rebuttable by proof beyond reasonable doubt.

Clause 36 provides the other limb of the defence:

A mental disorder verdict shall be returned if –

(a) the defendant is acquitted of an offence only because, by reason of evidence of mental disorder or a combination of mental disorder and intoxication, it is found that he acted or may have acted in a state of automatism, or without the fault required for the offence, or believing that an exempting circumstance existed; and

(b) it is proved on the balance of probabilities (whether by the prosecution or by the defendant) that he was suffering from mental disorder at the time of the act.

The clause applies only where the mental disorder (or mental disorder combined with intoxication) is the *sole* cause of D's condition, lack of fault, or mistake. Like the Rules, it applies to a person who, because of mental disorder, is under a delusion that he is the victim of a deadly attack and kills, as he supposes, in self-defence ('an exempting circumstance').

11.2.3.2 Onus of proof under the Code

The onus of proving *mens rea* or, when the issue has been raised, of disproving automatism or belief in an exempting circumstance, is on the prosecution. If they fail in this respect, D must be acquitted and the only question (where there is some evidence of mental disorder) is whether there should be an absolute acquittal or an acquittal on evidence of mental disorder. It seems right in principle that D should be entitled to an absolute acquittal, unless the jury are satisfied (either by the prosecution or the defence) that he was suffering from mental disorder; and cl 36(b), following Butler, so provides. Under cl 35 the choice for the jury is between conviction ('the defendant is proved to have committed an offence') and a mental disorder verdict so it might be thought the onus should be on the prosecution to prove one or the other. Butler, however, proposed that, to avoid confusing the jury, the onus of proving mental disorder should again be on the party alleging it, whether prosecution or defence; and cl 35 follows that proposal.

The Code would produce substantial improvements on the present position. It has been suggested however that it would still be incompatible with Art 5 of the ECHR.[180]

11.3 Sane automatism

A claim by D that his consciousness was so impaired that he was acting in a state of physical involuntariness is a claim of automatism. Someone is an automaton or in a state of automatism where his conscious mind is dissociated from that part of the mind which controls action.[181] This concept – a denial of a voluntary act – has been discussed in Chapter 4 above in the context of the *actus reus*.[182] A brief summary is presented here in juxtaposition to the analysis of

---

[180] See Ashworth, POCL, at 212.

[181] Wilson et al [2005] Crim LR 614, 615.

[182] See the discussion in Scots law as to whether the defence is one of a denial of *mens rea* or *actus reus* (PR Ferguson, 'The Limits of the Automatism Defence' (1991) 36 J Law Soc Scotland 446; I MacDougall 'Automatism – Negation of *Mens Rea*' (1992) 37 J Law Soc Scotland 57; – JM Ross, 'A Long Motor Run on a Dark Night: Reconstructing *HMA v Ritchie*' [2010] Edin LR 193).

insanity and intoxication to assist in understanding all three. It should be noted that where D makes this automatism claim the defence will only succeed if his loss of control was complete; an impaired consciousness is not automatism.[183] This is arguably an unduly strict approach. In an indication of how strictly the courts police this defence, particularly in relation to diabetic drivers, the Court of Appeal recently held, in an interlocutory prosecution appeal, that if D wants to advance a plea of sane automatism, he must provide evidence that: he was totally unable to control his actions (driving) due to an unforeseen hypoglycaemic attack; he could not reasonably have avoided the attack; and there were no advance warnings of its onset.[184]

The plea of automatism can be made in relation to all offences (subject to what is said below regarding self-induced automatism).

The defence of sane automatism can arise only where D's loss of consciousness is caused by the operation of some *external* factor on D. Automatism may arise where D suffers: a reflex spasm in response to being attacked by a swarm of bees,[185] a blow to the head causing concussion, an injection of insulin,[186] a rape or other serious violent attack causing post traumatic stress disorder, etc.[187] This external requirement is critical in distinguishing sane automatism from insanity and is discussed in the preceding section.

11.3.1 Self-induced automatism

Where D's state of automatism arises from his voluntary conduct (usually, ingesting substances), the following rules apply. The automatism plea is only available if D had a total loss of control.

(1) Where the automatism arises from D's taking a substance in *bona fide* compliance with his[188] medical prescription the defence is a complete one to all crimes. Eg D has an adverse reaction to an anaesthetic and hits V. D will be acquitted on charges (whether they be murder or assault) if he was totally automaton.

(2) Where the automatism arises otherwise than from D's taking a substance in accordance with a medical prescription, if the crime with which D is charged is one of specific intent (discussed below, p 314) the defence will result in acquittal. Eg D, a diabetic, takes insulin but ignores his prescription and takes too much, going into a coma. He punches V causing gbh. D will be acquitted.

(3) Where the automatism arises from D voluntarily taking a substance otherwise than in accordance with his medical prescription and the crime with which D is charged is one of basic intent (below, p 314) the automatism plea will fail if the substance ingested was one commonly known to create states of unpredictability or aggression (alcohol, heroin, cannabis, cocaine, etc). Thus, D charged with reckless criminal damage will have no success with a defence based on his claim that he was 'completely out of it' and unconscious when he swung his leg out and damaged V's property.

(4) Where the automatism arises from D's taking a substance otherwise than in accordance with his medical prescription and the crime with which D is charged is one of

---

[183] *A-G's Reference (No 2 of 1992)* [1992] QB 91. This is not always easy to establish see *Nelson* [2004] EWCA Crim 333 (reliance on hearsay). The Draft Code would permit the defence in circumstances of impaired consciousness (cl 33).

[184] *C* [2007] EWCA Crim 1862. See also *JG* [2006] EWCA Crim 1812.

[185] *Hill v Baxter* [1958] 1 QB 277.

[186] *Quick* [1973] QB 910.

[187] *R v T* [1990] Crim LR 256.

[188] See the odd acceptance of the defence where D took his friend's 'pills' and mixed them with alcohol: *Buck* (2002), discussed by K Roberts (2002) 99 Law Soc Gaz 40.

basic intent, and where the substance is not commonly known to create a state of un-predictability or aggression, the defence will result in an acquittal only if in taking the substance D was not subjectively reckless as to the effect it would have. Thus, D who is charged with reckless criminal damage after taking a soporific drug, will not succeed in his plea of automatism if he was aware when taking the drug that it posed the risk for him of a state of unpredictability of aggression.

Although the defence of automatism operates to deny the *actus reus* of the offence, in cases of self-induced automatism, the approach is founded on the same policy concerns that underpin the rules relating to the plea of intoxication which, if accepted at all, operates as a denial of *mens rea*.

11.4 Intoxication[189]

It will come as no surprise to hear that the law in this area is heavily policy based. There is often little by way of principle underpinning the operation of the law. The relationship be-tween intoxication and crime, particularly violent crime and public disorder, needs no elu-cidation here.[190] The following discussion analyses the three key distinctions drawn by the courts in their application of the plea of intoxication:

(1) Is the intoxication voluntary or involuntary?

(2) If voluntary, is the crime charged one of specific 'intent' or 'basic' intent?

(3) If basic intent, is the drug involved one of a dangerous nature (is it one known to create states of unpredictability or aggression)?

Before analysing these three issues, it is important to emphasize the general limits on the plea of intoxication. Intoxication is not, and never has been, a 'defence' in itself.[191] It is never a de-fence for D to say, however convincingly, that but for the drink he would not have behaved as he did.[192] Because alcohol and other drugs weaken the restraints and inhibitions which nor-mally govern our conduct, a person may do things when drunk that he would never dream of doing when sober. This is echoed recently in the controversial judgment of the Court of Appeal in *Heard*[193] discussed in full below.

11.4.1 Intoxication as a denial of criminal responsibility

Intoxication impairs a person's perception and judgement so he may fail to be aware of facts, or to foresee results of his conduct, of which he would certainly have been aware, or have fore-seen, if he had been sober. So, intoxication may be the reason why the defendant lacked the *mens rea* of the crime charged. When D relies on evidence of intoxication he does so for the purpose of disputing *mens rea*. This is its only relevance so far as liability to conviction (as opposed to sentence) is concerned.

---

[189] The focus in this chapter is exclusively on D's intoxication. V's intoxication may affect the substantive law, for example, in relation to sexual offences discussed below, p 723. See Law Commission Report No 314 *Intoxication and Criminal Liability* (2009). The report provides a useful summary of the current law in Part 2. See for critical comment on the propsoals J Child, 'Drink, Drugs and Law Reform: A Review of Law Commission Report No 314' [2009] Crim LR 488.

[190] See generally G Dingwall, *Alcohol and Crime* (2005); LC 314, para 1.1.

[191] See the recent review by A Simester, 'Intoxication is never a defence' [2009] Crim LR 3; LC 314, para 1.15.

[192] *DPP v Beard* [1920] AC 479 at 502–504.

[193] [2007] EWCA Crim 125.

It must always be borne in mind when considering intoxication that if D has the *mens rea* for the crime charged he is guilty. A drunken or drugged intent suffice for a crime of intention, a drunken or drugged awareness of a risk of the prohibited harm will suffice for a crime of recklessness. This is so even though drink or drugs impaired or negatived D's ability to judge between right and wrong or to resist temptation or provocation. It is so even though, in his drunken state, D found the impulse to act as he did irresistible. And if the state of intoxication was not self-induced by the accused – as where his drinks are laced. A drunken *mens rea* is still *mens rea*.

In many of the cases where intoxication is relevant, the plea, in substance, is one of mistake and the evidence of intoxication is circumstantial evidence that the mistake was made. Two examples quoted by Lord Denning[194] are: (i) where a nurse got so drunk at a christening that she put the baby on the fire in mistake for a log of wood;[195] and (ii) where a drunken man thought his friend, lying in bed, was a theatrical dummy and stabbed him to death.[196] Lord Denning said there would be a defence to murder in each of these cases. These mistakes were highly unreasonable and, in the case of a sober person, it would be extremely difficult to persuade a jury that they were made. The relevance of the evidence of intoxication is simply that it makes these mistakes much more credible. Similarly, where D denies that he foresaw some obvious consequence of his action. A denial which would be quite incredible in the case of a sober person may be readily accepted when there is evidence that D was intoxicated.

In *Beard,* it was said that intoxication was a 'defence' only if it rendered D *incapable* of forming the *mens rea*.[197] This goes too far. Proof of a lack of capacity to form *mens rea* is of course conclusive that *mens rea* was not present; but it is now established that it is not necessary to go so far. It is sufficient that D lacked *mens rea* on that occasion even though he was capable of forming the necessary intent. Equally, an intoxicated person may be capable, notwithstanding his intoxication, of forming the intent to kill and yet not do so. The nurse at the christening was capable of forming the intent to tend the fire, so she was probably capable of forming an intention to kill. The important thing is that she did not do so – and the intoxication was highly relevant to rebut the inference which might otherwise have arisen from her conduct. The correct question is, taking D's intoxicated state into account, did he in fact form the necessary *mens rea*?[198] The onus of proof – again contrary to certain *dicta* in *Beard*[199] – is clearly on the Crown to establish that, notwithstanding the alleged intoxication, D formed the *mens rea*.[200]

In a spate of recent cases, the courts have taken the unwelcome and it is submitted unduly restrictive approach to the question of when an intoxication plea gets off the ground. In *Soolkal and another v The State*,[201] *McKnight*[202] and *P*,[203] the courts have suggested that D is required to provide specific evidence to show that he was intoxicated and that he lacked *mens rea*. This burden is not satisfied by evidence that he had consumed so much drink/drugs

---

[194] In *A-G for Northern Ireland v Gallagher* [1963] AC 349 at 381m.

[195] (1748) 18 *Gentleman's Magazine* 570; quoted in Kenny, *Outlines*, 29.

[196] (1951) The Times, 13 Jan.

[197] [1920] AC 479 at 501–502, HL.

[198] *Pordage* [1975] Crim LR 575, CA, following *dicta* in *Sheehan* [1975] 2 All ER 960, [1975] Crim LR 339 and commentary, CA, *Cole* [1993] Crim LR 300. To the same effect are *Menniss* [1973] 2 NSWLR 113 and *Kamipeli* [1975] 2 NZLR 610. But cf *Groark* [1999] Crim LR 669.

[199] [1920] AC 479 at 502.

[200] *Sheehan*, above. *Bowden* [1993] Crim LR 379. When evidence emerges, whatever its source, of such intoxication as might have prevented D's forming a specific intent the judge must direct the jury on it: *Bennett* [1995] Crim LR 877. cf *McKinley* [1994] Crim LR 944, where the point was left open. The absence of a *Sheehan* direction seems to be a fertile ground of appeal: see *Golding* [2004] EWCA Crim 858. See LC 314, paras 2.27–2.33.

[201] [1999] 1 WLR 2011, PC.

[202] (2000) The Times, 5 May.

[203] [2004] EWCA Crim 1043.

that he was intoxicated or by a loss of memory owing to intoxication. The courts are surely imposing too onerous a duty on D who is not raising a defence in the true sense but rather denying the element of *mens rea* which it is always incumbent on the Crown to prove.

11.4.1.1 Intoxicated *mens rea*

If D had the *mens rea* for the crime charged, it makes no difference whether his intoxication was voluntarily or involuntary, nor whether the crime was one of specific or basic intent, nor whether the drug was of a dangerous or non-dangerous variety. In *Kingston,*[204] D may have given way to his paedophiliac inclinations only because E had surreptitiously laced his drink with intent that he should do so. D, however, knew what he was doing; he intended to commit a sexual assault on a 15-year-old boy. That was the *mens rea* of the offence. The judge had rightly directed the jury that a drugged intention is still an intention. The fact that, but for the secretly administered drug, he would not have formed the intent was a matter going only to mitigation of the penalty.[205]

11.4.2 Involuntary intoxication

Where, as a result of involuntary intoxication, D lacks the *mens rea* of the offence, it is submitted that he must be acquitted. This is so whether the crime charged is one of specific or basic intent. The offence has not been committed and there is absolutely no reason why the law should pretend that it has.[206] On a charge involving an offence of strict liability, the involuntary intoxication will not avail D since there is no *mens rea* for it to displace. In cases of alleged negligence, in principle, D ought only to be liable if the reasonable person would have acted in the same way had he suffered the effects of the involuntary intoxication.

In *Kingston,* Lord Mustill referred to a number of Scottish decisions to the effect that a defence is made out if it is 'based ... on an inability to form *mens rea* due to some external factor which was outwith the accused's control and which he was not bound to foresee'. The *dicta* quoted all required an inability to form the intent. Inability is certainly a conclusive answer; but, it is submitted that, whatever the position in Scotland, in England the ultimate question is whether D did form the *mens rea* and, if he did not — perhaps because he made a drunken mistake of fact – he must be acquitted, even though he was capable of forming the intent. This is the law in those cases where voluntary intoxication may be the basis of defence to an offence of specific intent, and it ought to apply, *a fortiori*, to involuntary intoxication.

Involuntary intoxication is narrowly defined. If D knew he was drinking alcohol, he cannot claim that the resulting intoxication was involuntary merely because he underestimated the amount he was consuming[207] or the effect it would have on him. Intoxication is 'involuntary' if D was unaware that he was taking an intoxicant. Where D's lemonade is laced with vodka and he is unaware that he has consumed any alcohol, he can rely on evidence of his drunken condition.[208]

---

[204] [1994] 3 All ER 353, HL. See J Horder, 'Pleading Involuntary Lack of Capacity' [1993] CLJ 298; R Smith and L Clements, 'Involuntary Intoxication, The Threshold of Inhibition and the Instigation of Crime' (1995) 46 NILQ 210. See LC 314, para 2.75.

[205] The case prompted interesting calls for a new defence applicable where D acted out of character. See GR Sullivan, 'Involuntary Intoxication and Beyond' [1994] Crim LR 272; 'Making Excuses', in S Shute and A Simester (eds), *Harm and Culpability* (1996) 131; Tadros (2001) 21 OJLS 495; Tadros, *Criminal Responsibility*, Ch 11; and for a recent review see C Crosby, 'Culpability, Kingston and the Law Commission' (2010) 74 J Crim L 434.

[206] See LC 314, para 1.22. See also the discussion in LC 314, Part 4.

[207] *Allen* [1988] Crim LR 698; cf the definition of voluntary intoxication proposed by the Butler Committee at para 18.56 and that in the Home Office Bill (below) cl 19(3). LC 314, Part 3 proposes a non-exhanstive list of situations amounting to involuntary intoxication.

[208] Above, n 204. In *Majewski*, below, the Lord Chancellor pointed out that the drugs taken were not medically prescribed.

Similarly, perhaps, where he has taken drink under duress.[209] It also covers the special case where a person becomes intoxicated through taking drugs (presumably including alcohol) voluntarily in *bona fide* pursuance of medical treatment or prescription. This will rarely, if ever, be applicable to drink but it might apply where, for example, brandy is administered to D after an accident.

As intoxication is nearly always voluntary, it is probably for D to raise the issue if he wishes to contend that it is involuntary. The onus of proof will then generally be on the Crown:[210] but the Public Order Act 1986, s 6(5), for the purposes of offences under that Act, requires D to 'show' that his intoxication was not self-induced or caused by medical treatment. This was presumably intended to put the onus of proof on D; but 'show', in contrast with 'prove' which is used in other sections of the Act, might be taken to impose no more than an evidential burden – more especially under the Human Rights Act 1998 giving force to Art 6(2) of the ECHR.[211]

11.4.3 Voluntary intoxication

11.4.3.1 Basic and specific intent crimes[212]

D is entitled to an acquittal where his voluntary intoxication is such that he did not form the *mens rea* for the offence of specific intent. It must be emphasized, once again, that this applies where there is a lack of *mens rea*, not merely a reduction of inhibition; a drunken intention is nevertheless an intention. The prosecution must prove *mens rea*.

In the case of a crime of basic intent, D may be convicted if he was voluntarily intoxicated at the time of committing the offence by a drug known to create unpredictability or aggression, though he did not have the *mens rea* required in all other circumstances for that offence and even though he was in a state of automatism at the time of doing the act; if he would have had *mens rea* if sober.

The problem lies in identifying a way of distinguishing between crimes of basic and specific intent. Until very recently, it appeared to be settled that the distinction was between whether the predominant *mens rea* element of the crime was one of intention knowledge or dishonesty which would lead to classification as a specific intent crime, or of something less (recklessness, negligence or strict liability) in which case the crime was one of basic intent. This was a largely pragmatic, but not unprincipled method of classification. The decision of the Court of Appeal in *Heard*[213] casts doubt on this simple and established method of classification. Although, technically the comments of the court on the basic/specific distinction are *obiter*.

The rule in *Majewski*

In *DPP v Majewski*,[214] the House of Lords confirmed the rule, obscurely stated in *Beard*,[215] that evidence of self-induced intoxication negativing *mens rea* is a defence to a charge of a crime requiring a specific intent but not to a charge of any other crime. In *Majewski*, D had assaulted a number of police officers when he was being restrained and arrested. He had taken a combination of drink and drugs and was very heavily intoxicated. He claimed that

---

[209] cf *Kingston*, above. But what of the much more common case where D has voluntarily taken some drink and his companions surreptitiously add more? Probably, the jury should be told to convict only if satisfied that the drink voluntarily taken *contributed* to his lack of awareness. cf LC 314, para 3.125.

[210] *Stripp* (1978) 69 Cr App R 318 at 323; *Bailey* [1983] 2 All ER 503 at 507.

[211] cf *Lambert* [2001] 3 All ER 577; *A-G's Reference (No 4 of 2002)* [2004] UKHL 40, [2005] Crim LR 200 above, p 30.

[212] See, recently, J Horder, 'The Classification of Crimes and the General Part', in Duff and Green (eds), *Defining Crimes*.

[213] [2007] EWCA Crim 125. See LC 314, paras 2.2–2.28.

[214] [1977] AC 443, [1976] 2 All ER 142, [1976] Crim LR 374 and commentary; G Williams, 'Intoxication of Specific Intent' (1976) 126 NLJ 658; AD Gold, 'An Untrimmed Beard' (1976) 19 Crim LQ 34; A Dashwood, 'Logic and the Lords in *Majewski*' [1977] Crim LR 532 and 591. Discussed in LC 314, paras 2.35–2.70.

[215] [1920] AC 479.

his self-induced intoxication prevented him forming the *mens rea*, and that the evidence of the intoxication ought to be admissible to support that plea, relying on s 8 of the Criminal Justice Act 1967. He was convicted and this was upheld by the House of Lords. He was charged with a crime of basic intent and it has long been recognized that voluntary intoxication was no defence to such a charge even if it did cause D to lack *mens rea*. Unfortunately, the House did not offer a unanimous basis for the distinction between crimes of specific intent and basic intent.

(a) Rule of substantive law

On one interpretation, the case imposes a rule of substantive law that, where D relies on voluntary intoxication to a charge of a crime not requiring 'specific intent', the prosecution need not prove any intention or foresight, whatever the definition of the crime may say, nor indeed any voluntary act. It follows that s 8 of the Criminal Justice Act 1967[216] has no application. There is, it appears, an implied qualification to every statute creating an offence and specifying a *mens rea* other than a specific intent. The *mens rea* must be proved – except, we must infer, where the accused was intoxicated through the voluntary taking of drink or drugs. It is assumed that D has the *mens rea* if he would have had it if sober. In *Richardson and Irwin*,[217] where DD dropped a fellow student from a balcony when drunk causing him grievous bodily harm, they were charged under s 20 of the 1861 Act. Their convictions were quashed by the Court of Appeal holding that the trial judge should have directed that the jury had to be sure that DD would have foreseen the risk of injury had they been sober.

On this interpretation it is fatal for a person charged with a crime not requiring specific intent who claims that he did not have *mens rea* to support his defence with evidence that he had taken drink and drugs. By so doing he dispenses the Crown from the duty, which until that moment lay upon them, of proving beyond reasonable doubt that he had *mens rea*. Could the Crown escape from this duty by leading evidence, or extracting an admission in cross-examination, that D had taken drink so as to diminish his capacity to foresee the consequences of his acts? According to Lord Salmon[218] in *Majewski* the question the House was deciding was whether the accused could rely *by way of defence* on the fact that he had voluntarily taken drink. But there are other *dicta* which suggest that D is held liable without the usual *mens rea* because he has taken the drink – the taking of the drink is the foundation of his liability[219] – a variety of *mens rea* – though not in the sense in which that term is used in this book. It is a form of 'prior fault', with D's liability for the crime based on his conduct at that time coupled with his fault in becoming intoxicated. If that is right, there is no reason why the Crown should not set out to prove it, instead of seeking to prove *mens rea* in the sense of intention or recklessness.

In principled terms this approach is problematical. It deems the defendant's negligence or recklessness in becoming voluntarily intoxicated – his 'prior fault' – to be sufficient *mens rea* for the crime. This is despite the fact that there is no contemporaneity between the fault in becoming intoxicated and the commission of the *actus reus* of the crime. And more importantly, despite the fact that the degree of fault in becoming intoxicated (foresight or awareness of becoming intoxicated) bears no correlation to the *mens rea* that would normally be

---

[216] Above, p 69. see Simester, above n 191, p 6.

[217] [1999] 1 Cr App R 192, see Simester, above n 191.

[218] [1977] AC 443.

[219] 'His course of conduct in reducing himself by drugs and drink to that condition in my view supplies the evidence of *mens rea*, of guilty mind, certainly sufficient for crimes of basic intent': per Lord Elwyn-Jones LC [1976] 2 All ER 142 at 150. 'There is no juristic reason why mental incapacity (short of M'Naghten insanity) brought about by self-induced intoxication to realize what one is doing or its probable consequences should not be such a state of mind stigmatized as wrongful by the criminal law; and there is every practical reason why it should be': per Lord Simon at 153. For critical comment see LC 314, Part 2.

required – foresight or awareness of a risk of a prohibited harm specified in the offence. It is, with respect, not enough to say as Hughes LJ suggests in *Heard* (below) that there is 'broadly equivalent culpability'.

It seems that this rule applies whatever the degree of intoxication, if D claimed that it prevented him from foreseeing or knowing what he would have foreseen or known had he been sober he is guilty of the basic intent offence. It is true that Lord Elwyn-Jones at one point[220] posed the question before the House much more narrowly. His lordship spoke of a person who 'consciously and deliberately takes alcohol and drugs not on medical prescription, but in order to escape from reality, to go "on a trip", to become hallucinated...' Such a person is readily distinguishable from the ordinary 'social drinker' who becomes intoxicated in the course of a convivial evening. The former, intending to reduce himself to a state in which he will have no control over his actions, might well be said to be in some sense reckless as to what he will do while in that state. The same cannot be said of the latter. But the general tenor of the speeches, as well as earlier and subsequent cases, is against any such distinction.[221]

Professor Duff has recently suggested that we can make moral sense of *Majewski* if we accept that:

recklessness can be constituted either by awareness of a relevant risk [as elsewhere in criminal law] or by unawareness that is due to voluntary intoxication: recklessness must be presumed given proof of such unawareness not because it can be inferred but because it is constituted by such.[222]

(b) A rule of evidence?

An alternative view is that *Majewski* does not create a rule of substantive law, but one of evidence. On this view, once D has been shown to be voluntarily intoxicated in a basic intent crime the evidence of intoxication is irrelevant to the question whether D held the *mens rea*, but the prosecution is still obliged to prove that D had the relevant *mens rea*. There is some authority that a jury must be directed to decide whether D was reckless, disregarding the evidence that he was intoxicated. In *Woods*,[223] D, charged with rape under the old sexual offences law, claimed that he was so drunk that he did not realize V was not consenting. He relied on s 1(2) of the Sexual Offences (Amendment) Act 1976[224] which required the jury to have regard to the presence or absence of reasonable grounds for a belief that the woman was consenting, 'in conjunction with any other relevant matters'. He said his intoxication was a relevant matter. The court said that self-induced intoxication is not 'a legally relevant matter' but 'the subsection directs the jury to look carefully at all the other relevant evidence before making up their minds on this issue'. The evidence of intoxication is undoubtedly logically relevant and may be the most cogent evidence. To ignore it in coming to a conclusion, is to answer a hypothetical question. It is no longer, 'did he believe she was consenting?' and must become, 'would he have known she was consenting if he had not been drunk?' This is most obviously so in the case where D's intoxication has rendered him unconscious.

This interpretation of *Majewski* as a rule of evidence also poses problems. Take *Lipman*, where D strangled V after taking LSD and believing that he was fighting off a serpent at the centre of the earth.[225] How can a judge seriously tell a jury to decide whether D *did* intend to do an unlawful and dangerous act to V – ignoring the undisputed evidence that he was

---

[220] [1977] AC 443 at 471.

[221] ACE Lynch, 'The Scope of Intoxication' [1982] Crim LR 139 makes a quite different distinction between 'complete intoxication' (to which *Majewski* would apply) and 'partial intoxication' (to which it would not); but there are many degrees of intoxication and the suggested distinction seems unworkable.

[222] *Answering for Crime*, 240–241.

[223] (1981) 74 Cr App R 312.

[224] Now repealed.

[225] [1970] 1 QB 152.

unconscious at the time? Without this 'legally irrelevant' evidence, the *only* question the jury can sensibly answer is, 'would he have known that such an act was dangerous if he had not been intoxicated'? On facts like those in *Lipman*, there is only one possible answer. It is most regrettable that juries should be faced with questions which are, with all respect, nonsensical, even if their common sense will lead them to consider the only matter really in issue.

Distinguishing specific and basic intent crimes[226]

In view of the rule in *Majewski*, the nature of 'specific intent' is a matter of great importance but a careful scrutiny of the authorities, particularly *Majewski* itself, fails to reveal any consistent principle by which specific and basic are to be distinguished.[227] A number of possible interpretations are possible. It is regrettable that the distinction is so obscure that the Law Commission recently felt unable confidently to state what the law was.[228]

Ulterior intent

One interpretation is that specific intent crimes are those in which there is an element of *mens rea* going beyond the immediate *actus reus*. There is, as it is often described, an 'ulterior intent'. For example in the crime of indecent exposure, it is necessary for D to have intentionally exposed his genitals with intent that someone will see them and be caused alarm or distress. There is a 'bolt on element of *mens rea*' beyond that relating to the immediate conduct of exposing his genitals. The crime would therefore on this analysis be treated as one of specific intent. This approach derives some support from *Majewski* and from the recent decision in *Heard*. Lord Justice Hughes suggested, *obiter*, that if an offence requires 'proof of a state of mind addressing something beyond the prohibited act itself, namely its consequences'. It is one of specific intent. The court 'regard[ed] this as the best explanation of the sometimes elusive distinction between specific and basic intent in the sense used in *Majewski*'.[229] It is submitted that it is a flawed basis for distinguishing between offences. The most compelling basis for rejecting this approach is that some crimes requiring no ulterior intent – conspicuously murder – have been consistently and unequivocally treated as crimes of 'specific intent' by all levels of court including the House of Lords. If the 'ulterior intent' approach is incapable of providing the correct classification for such an obvious example as murder, it cannot be worth serious consideration.[230] In addition, this approach produces some very odd results. For example, an offence can be one of specific intent even if it contains no element of intent at all – provided there is an ulterior *mens rea*: reckless criminal damage being reckless as to whether life is endangered thereby would be a crime of specific *intention*. What of intentionally causing grievous bodily harm under s 18? On the simple form of the charge, there is no bolt on *mens rea* to be added. It looks then like a crime of basic intent, but every precedent confirms that it is one of specific intent.

Purposive intent

An alternative method of distinguishing between specific and basic intent is to ask whether the *mens rea* of the crime requires a direct or purposive intention (specific) or some other form of *mens rea* or strict liability (basic). This also derives some support from the speech of Lord Simon in *Majewski* who suggested that the distinguishing factor is that 'the *mens rea*

---

[226] A Ward, 'Making Some Sense of Self-Induced Intoxication' [1986] CLJ 247. See LC 314, para 2.29 et seq.

[227] cf Gardner (1994) 14 OJLS 279 and J Horder, 'Intention in the Criminal Law – A Rejoinder' (1995) 58 MLR 678, who views the specific intent crimes as those in which the intent is integrally bound up with the nature and definition of the wrong involved. See the recommendation in LC 314.

[228] See Law Com Report No 229, para 3.27. In LC 314, Part 2, it was accepted again that the law was in a confused state.

[229] [31].

[230] Indeed this was one of the principal bases on which *Majewski* was criticized. See G Williams, TBCL, 429.

in a crime of specific intent requires proof of a purposive element'. Lord Simon put it in this way:[231]

The best description of 'specific intent' in this sense that I know is contained in the judgment of Fauteux J in *Reg v George* (1960) 128 Can CC 289, 301 – 'In considering the question of mens rea, a distinction is to be made between (i) intention as applied to acts considered in relation to their purposes and (ii) intention as applied to acts apart from their purposes. A general intent attending the commission of an act is, in some cases, the only intent required to constitute the crime while, in others, there must be, in addition to that general intent, a specific intent attending the purpose for the commission of the act.'

In *Heard*, Lord Justice Hughes also endorsed this distinction between basic and specific intent found in the speech of Lord Simon,[232] [above] '...that crimes of specific intent are those where the offence requires proof of purpose or consequence, which are not confined to, but amongst which are included, those where the purpose goes beyond the *actus reus* (sometimes referred to as cases of "ulterior intent")'. It is submitted that it is also a flawed basis on which to distinguish crimes of specific and basic intent. The crimes of murder and rape, for example, have been consistently and unequivocally accepted by the Court of Appeal and House of Lords as crimes of specific intent, yet there need be no purposive element in the *mens rea* of either.[233]

Predominant mens rea

A third approach to distinguishing between crimes of basic and specific intent is based on whether the crime in question is one for which the predominant *mens rea* is (a) intention knowledge or dishonesty (specific) or (b) (basic) some lesser *mens rea* recklessness, or negligence or strict liability. In *Majewski*, Lord Elwyn-Jones LC suggested that the test is that crimes not requiring specific intent are crimes that may be committed recklessly.[234] In *Heard*, in an *obiter dictum*, the Court of Appeal rejected this simple practical approach.

The decision in *Heard*

The decision in *Heard* is a controversial one and a number of points are worth emphasizing. First, on its facts, it should never have given rise to problems. The accused had, while drunk, exposed his penis and rubbed it against the thigh of a police officer. D's plea was that he had no recollection of the incident. That is never a basis for a plea of intoxication and that should have been the end of the matter. However, D relied on his voluntary intoxication as negating his *mens rea* of an intention to touch for the purposes of s 3(1)(a) of the Sexual Offences Act 2003. The trial judge ruled that the intentional touching element of the offence required proof of a basic intent, and that it followed that voluntary intoxication was not a defence. Applying the predominant *mens rea* interpretation of *Majewski*, on a charge such as that under s 3 with the requirement of an 'intentional' touching, it was arguable at least that the crime was one of specific intent.[235] The court rejected that.

Secondly, we can assume that sexual offences under the 2003 Act in which the conduct is 'intended'[236] will be treated as basic intent crimes unless there is a clear ulterior purpose, as in indecent exposure, and offences in which D is acting 'for the purpose of obtaining

---

[231] At 478H.

[232] At 478B–479B.

[233] See LC 314, para 2.8 et seq.

[234] Lord Edmund-Davies, a party to *Majewski*, was dismayed to think that, as a result of *Caldwell*, this opinion prevailed [1982] AC 341 at 361, [1981] 1 All ER 961 at 972.

[235] R Card, *Sexual Offences: The New Law* (2004) para 1.31; P Rook and R Ward, *Sexual Offences Law and Practice* (2004) para 2.72.

[236] See *Grout* [2011] EWCA Crim 299.

sexual gratification'.[237] On policy grounds the court was clearly entitled to assume that Parliament had not intended to change the law, although it should be noted that under the pre-2003 law, the offence of indecent assault was not always a basic intent crime. The court could have adopted the predominant *mens rea* and created an exception for sex offences.

Thirdly, the court's radical reinterpretation of *Majewski* aligning specific intent with an ulterior or purposive *mens rea* produces difficulties, even within the scope of the s 3 offence. Someone like Lipman[238] who becomes so intoxicated that he thinks he is stroking an animal at the centre of the earth when in fact he is stroking a woman's breast will, on the court's approach, be guilty under s 3. But, it is submitted that in such a case it would be difficult in any ordinary sense of the word to say that D 'intended' to touch V sexually as s 3 requires.

Fourthly, the court makes some very broad qualifications to the approach in s 3 (and other sexual offences and beyond one assumes) in respect of accidents. Lord Justice Hughes states that:

To flail about, stumble or barge around in an unco-ordinated manner which results in an unintended touching, objectively sexual, is not this offence. If to do so when sober is not this offence, then nor is it this offence to do so when intoxicated. It is also possible that such an action would not be judged by the jury to be objectively sexual, on the basis that it was clearly accidental, but whether that is so or not, we are satisfied that in such a case this offence is not committed. The intoxication, in such a situation, has not impacted on intention. Intention is simply not in question. What is in question is impairment of control of the limbs.... '[A] drunken intent is still an intent', the corollary [is] that 'a drunken accident is still an accident'.

In respect of someone who simply trips on the dance floor and grabs at the nearest thing to steady himself this makes perfect sense. But, consider someone who,[239] fooling around when heavily intoxicated pretends to strike the bottom of a woman who is bending and who misjudges the distance and strikes her bottom. He will be acquitted on the basis that his conduct is 'accidental'.[240] It is submitted that it would be a misuse of the word 'intention' to say that he had intended to touch her sexually. He intends to move his arm and intends to come close to touching her, but not to do so. It is also misleading to say it is accidental: D is reckless about that consequence, he has seen the risk and gone on to take it. There is a risk that the category of' drunken accident' endorsed by *Heard* will be misunderstood and applied in cases of what are plainly recklessness.

Finally, there are several reasons why it is submitted that the court's *obiter dicta* rejecting the predominant *mens rea* interpretation of *Majewski* in favour of a purposive approach should not be applied throughout the criminal law: it is more difficult to look for the 'bolt-on' element of additional *mens rea* in a crime in order to categorize it appropriately; the approach creates no fewer anomalies than the established interpretation of *Majewski*; and it creates confusion because specific intent might encompass crimes with no element of intent at all such as reckless criminal damage being reckless as to whether life is endangered thereby.

11.4.3.2 The current law on basic and specific

Despite its obscure exposition in the House of Lords, and its unsatisfactory theoretical underpinnings, the *Majewski* approach had subsequently been knocked into pragmatic shape: the predominant was an approach, familiar and universally applied. Those virtues ought not

---

[237] Section 12.
[238] *Lipman* (1969) 55 Cr App R 600, CA.
[239] cf *Shimmen* [1986] Crim LR 800, (1987) 84 Cr App Rep 7.
[240] [23].

to be undervalued. Despite *dicta* in *Hughes* it is submitted that any offence which may be committed recklessly ought to be held an offence of 'basic' and not 'specific' intent.

The safest approach seems to be that 'crime requiring specific intent' means a crime where evidence of voluntary intoxication negativing *mens rea* is a defence. It may be easier to accept that the designation of crimes as requiring, or not requiring, specific intent is based on no principle but on policy. In order to know how a crime should be classified for this purpose we can look only to the decisions of the courts. The following are crimes requiring specific intent: murder,[241] wounding or causing grievous bodily harm with intent,[242] theft,[243] robbery,[244] burglary with intent to steal,[245] handling stolen goods,[246] endeavouring to obtain money on a forged cheque,[247] causing criminal damage contrary to s 1(1) or (2) of the Criminal Damage Act 1971 where only intention to cause damage or, in the case of s 1(2), only intention to endanger life, is alleged,[248] an attempt to commit any offence requiring specific intent and possibly some forms of secondary participation in any offence.[249]

The following crimes do not require specific intent: manslaughter (apparently in all its forms);[250] rape,[251] sexual assault,[252] maliciously wounding or inflicting grievous bodily harm;[253] kidnapping and false imprisonment;[254] assault occasioning actual bodily harm;[255] assault on a constable in the execution of his duty;[256] common assault;[257] taking a conveyance without the consent of the owner;[258] criminal damage where intention or recklessness, or only recklessness, is alleged[259] and possibly an attempt to commit an offence where recklessness is a sufficient element in the *mens rea*,[260] as in attempted rape.[261]

It will be noted that for most specific intent offences there exists a basic intent offence that can be charged in the alternative (murder and manslaughter, ss 18 and 20 of the Offences Against the Person Act 1861 (OAPA 1861), etc). The prosecution are usually therefore able

---

[241] *Beard*, above; *Gallagher* [1963] AC 349; *Sheehan* [1975] 1 WLR 739, CA.

[242] *Bratty v A-G for Northern Ireland* [1963] AC 386, per Lord Denning; *Pordage* [1975] Crim LR 575; *Davies* [1991] Crim LR 469.

[243] *Ruse v Read* [1949] 1 KB 377, [1949] 1 All ER 398 and *Majewski* per Lord Simon at 152.

[244] As a corollary of theft.

[245] *Durante* [1972] 3 All ER 962, [1972] 1 WLR 1612.

[246] *Durante*, above.

[247] *Majewski*, per Lord Salmon at 158.

[248] *Caldwell* [1981] 1 All ER 961 at 964.

[249] *Clarkson* [1971] 3 All ER 344 at 347. But in *Lynch v DPP for Northern Ireland* [1975] 1 All ER 913 at 942, Lord Simon said, approving the decision of the Northern Irish Court of Criminal Appeal, that they held that the *mens rea* of aiding and abetting did not involve a 'specific intent'. But (i) he may have used the term in a different sense; and (ii) there may be a difference depending on the nature of the alleged secondary liability – an intent to procure is different from an intent to aid; above, p 191.

[250] *Beard, Gallagher* and *Bratty v A-G Northern Ireland* [1961] 3 All ER at 533, per Lord Denning; *Lipman* [1970] 1 QB 152, [1969] 3 All ER 410.

[251] *Grout* [2011] EWCA Crim 299. *Majewski*, above, per Lords Simon and Russell and *Leary v R* (1977) 74 DLR (3d) 103, SCC, discussed 55 Can Bar Rev 691. But if this is right, and it seems almost certain that it is, *Cogan and Leak* above, p 234 is wrongly decided; and *Morgan* above, p 330 might have been decided simply on this ground. cf *Fotheringham* (1988) 88 Cr App R 206, [1988] Crim LR 846 and commentary.

[252] *Heard* [2007] EWCA Crim 125.

[253] *Bratty* at 533, per Lord Denning; *Majewski*, above, per Lords Simon and Salmon.

[254] *Hutchins* [1988] Crim LR 379.

[255] *Bolton v Crawley* [1972] Crim LR 222; *Majewski*, above.

[256] *Majewski*, above.

[257] *A fortiori*.

[258] *MacPherson* [1973] RTR 157; *Gannon* (1987) 87 Cr App R 254. *Diggin* (1980) 72 Cr App R 204 is not, as it first appeared: [1980] Crim LR 656, an authority on intoxicated taking: [1981] Crim LR 563; but see S White, 'Taking the Joy Out of Joyriding' [1980] Crim LR 609.

[259] Below, Ch 29.

[260] Commentary on *Pullen* [1991] Crim LR 457 at 458.

[261] Below, p 321.

to avoid an acquittal in cases of self-induced intoxication. Two problems arise in this regard however. First, the jury will face confusing directions on charges such as ss 18 and 20 as to what use they may make of the evidence of intoxication. Secondly, there are some specific intent offences for which there is no basic intent equivalent: theft is an obvious example.

Specific and basic – a legitimate basis of distinction?

A classification of all crimes as offences of either specific or basic intent is over simplified. The Court of Appeal in *Heard* even hints at rejecting the twofold classification by suggesting that it is not to be assumed that every offence is one of basic or specific intent.[262] It is submitted that this aspect of the Court of Appeal's should be taken to be emphasizing is that an offence is likely to have more than one element of *mens rea*. The question is what is the predominant *mens rea*.

Consider the offence under s 18 of the OAPA 1861 of unlawfully and maliciously wounding with intent to resist lawful apprehension. There is abundant authority to the effect that the words 'unlawfully and maliciously' when used in s 20 import only a basic intent, that is, *Cunningham* recklessness. Presumably they have the same effect in s 18. So as far as wounding goes, s 18 is an offence of basic intent. But the intent to resist lawful apprehension seems a clear case of specific intent. So it seems that a drunken person who intends to resist lawful arrest but, because of his drunkenness, does not foresee the risk of wounding, might be convicted, notwithstanding his lack of *Cunningham* recklessness. If, on the other hand, because of drunkenness, he does not realize that he is resisting lawful arrest, he must be acquitted.[263] Rape is another example. A reasonable belief whether the person is consenting is a basic intent; but presumably there must be an actual intention to perform the penile penetration. But it is difficult to envisage a man, however drunk, having sexual intercourse without intending to do so. In *Fotheringham*, D had intercourse with the 14-year-old babysitter who was in his matrimonial bed. She did not resist, but did not in fact consent. D, who was drunk, said that he believed she was his wife. It was not, at that date, rape for a man to have intercourse with his wife without consent. His appeal was dismissed. His drunken belief that V was his wife was no more a defence than his belief that she was consenting.[264]

Intoxication and *Caldwell* recklessness

Where the offence is one of *Caldwell* recklessness, assuming that any such offences still exist, the impact of *Majewski* is reduced. Where, because he was intoxicated, D gave no thought to the existence of the risk, he was reckless and is liable to conviction without the invocation of the rule in *Majewski*.[265] This was the position in *Caldwell* itself. But *Majewski* may still have a significant sphere of operation.[266] D might say that he did consider whether there was a risk and decided there was none. He was then not *Caldwell*-reckless. But, if he would have appreciated the existence of the risk had he been sober, he will still be liable because of *Majewski*.

11.4.4 Dangerous or non-dangerous drugs in basic intent crime

In the case where D has become voluntarily intoxicated and the offence with which he is charged is one of basic intent, there remains one important issue to consider – whether the

---

[262] [14]. But what is this other category that now exists? And what offences might fall into it? See the Law Commission's rejection in LC 314, Part 2.

[263] *Davies* [1991] Crim LR 469.

[264] (1988) 88 Cr App R 206, [1988] Crim LR 846. But, according to *Richardson and Irwin* [1999] 1 Cr App R 392, [1999] Crim LR 494, D may rely on a drunken mistaken belief in consent, where consent would be a defence to a charge under OAPA 1861, s 20. Since this is a basic intent offence, the decision seems doubtful.

[265] This point was overlooked in *Cullen* [1993] Crim LR 936.

[266] This is overlooked by Lord Diplock at [1981] 1 All ER 968a.

substance ingested is 'dangerous', that is, commonly known to create states of unpredict-ability or aggression.

The law in this area has developed principally in cases where D was intoxicated by alcohol. In *Lipman*[267] it was held that the same principles apply to intoxication by other drugs but two later cases, *Bailey*[268] and *Hardie*,[269] suggest that drugs must be divided into two categories. Where it is common knowledge that a drug is liable to cause the taker to become aggressive or do dangerous or unpredictable things, that drug is to be classed alongside alcohol. Where there is no such common knowledge, as in the case of a merely soporific or sedative drug, dif-ferent rules apply. There are obvious difficulties about classifying drugs in this way and, it is surprising that it has not generated more case law.

In *Bailey*,[270] a diabetic failed to take sufficient food after insulin. He caused grievous bodily harm and his defence to charges under ss 18 and 20 of the Offences Against the Person Act was that, because of this failure, he was in a state of automatism. The recorder's direction to the jury that this was no defence was obviously wrong so far as s 18 was concerned for that is an offence of specific intent. The Court of Appeal held that it was also wrong for s 20 because 'self-induced automatism, other than that due to intoxication from alcohol or drugs, may pro-vide a defence to crimes of basic intent'.[271] The court went on:

The question in each case will be whether the prosecution has proved the necessary element of reck-lessness. In cases of assault, if the accused knows that his actions or inaction are likely to make him aggressive, unpredictable or uncontrolled with the result that he may cause some injury to others and he persists in the action or takes no remedial action when he knows it is required, it will be open to the jury to find that he was reckless.

The automatism seems to have been treated as arising from the failure to take food, rather than from the taking of the insulin, but the court hinted at a distinction between two types of drug:

It is common knowledge that those who take alcohol to excess or certain sorts of drugs may become aggressive or do dangerous or unpredictable things.... But the same cannot be said, without more, of a man who fails to take food after an insulin injection.

In *Hardie*,[272] the court developed this. D's defence to a charge of damaging property with intent to endanger the life of another or being reckless whether another's life be endangered, was that he had taken valium, a sedative drug, to calm his nerves and that this had resulted in intoxication precluding the *mens rea* for the offence. The judge, following *Majewski* and *Caldwell*, directed that this could be no defence. The Court of Appeal quashed the conviction. *Majewski* was not applicable because valium:

is wholly different in kind from drugs which are liable to cause unpredictability or aggressive-ness.... if the effect of a drug is merely soporific or sedative the taking of it, even in some excessive quantity, cannot in the ordinary way raise a conclusive presumption against the admission of proof of intoxication for the purpose of disproving *mens rea* in ordinary crimes, such as would be the case with alcoholic intoxication or incapacity or automatism resulting from the self-administration of dangerous drugs.[273]

---

[267] [1970] 1 QB 152, ; above, p 316.
[268] [1983] 1 WLR 760.
[269] [1985] 1 WLR 64.
[270] [1983] 1 WLR 760, CA.
[271] Above, p 310.
[272] [1985] 1 WLR 64.
[273] This overlooks the fact that the *Majewski* principle is stated by the House of Lords to be a rule of sub-stantive law and that the Criminal Justice Act 1967, s 8, precludes conclusive presumptions of intention or

This qualification to the normal rule for basic intent crimes applies where intoxication is self-induced otherwise than by alcohol or dangerous drugs. In these cases the test of liability is stated to be one of recklessness: 'If [D] does appreciate the risk that [failure to take food/taking the non-dangerous drug] may lead to aggressive, unpredictable and uncontrollable conduct and he nevertheless deliberately runs the risk or otherwise disregards it, this will amount to recklessness.'[274]

It is clear that the recklessness which must be proved is:

(1) subjective, an actual awareness of the risk of becoming aggressive, but

(2) 'general' – not requiring foresight of the *actus reus* of any particular crime, such as is required in the case of a sober person charged with an offence of *Cunningham* recklessness. D will be liable for any crime of recklessness the *actus reus* of which he happens to commit under the influence of the self-induced intoxication. This flows from the rule in *Majewski*.

Further:

(3) being aware that one may lose consciousness may be sufficient where a failure to exercise control may result in the *actus reus* of a crime, as in the case of careless or dangerous driving.

11.4.5 Intoxication and defences

11.4.5.1 Statutory defences prescribing a belief in circumstances

The *Majewski* rule has been held inapplicable where statute expressly provides that a particular belief shall be a defence to the charge. If D held that belief, he is not guilty, even though it arose from a drunken mistake that he would not have made when sober. In *Jaggard v Dickinson*,[275] D had a friend, H, who had invited her to treat his house as if it were her own. When drunk, D went to a house which she thought was H's but which in fact belonged to R, who barred her way. D gained entry by breaking windows and damaging the curtains. Charged with criminal damage, contrary to s 1(1) of the Criminal Damage Act 1971, she relied on s 5(2) of that Act[276] which provides that a person has a lawful excuse if D believed that the person entitled to consent to the damage would have done so had he known of the circumstances. D said that she believed that H would, in the circumstances, have consented to her damaging his property. Since s 1(1) creates an offence not requiring specific intent, D could not have relied on her drunkenness to negative her recklessness whether she damaged the property of another, but, it was held, she could rely on it to explain what would otherwise have been inexplicable and give colour to her evidence about the state of her belief. The court thought this was not the same thing as using drunkenness to rebut an inference of intention or recklessness. It seems, however, to be exactly the same thing.[277] Moreover, thought the court, s 5(2) provides that it is immaterial whether a belief is justified or not if it is honestly held, and it was not open to the court to add the words 'and the honesty of the belief is not attributable only to self-induced intoxication'. Yet the courts have not hesitated to add similar words to qualify Parliament's express requirement of 'malice', that is, *Cunningham* recklessness. The result is anomalous. Where the defendant did not intend any damage to property (but was reckless) he may be held

---

foresight. Above, p 143. The distinction is also unsatisfactory in pharmacological terms: M Weller and W Somers, 'Differences in the Medical and Legal Viewpoint Illustrated by *Hardie*' (1991) 31 Med Sci Law 152.

[274] *Bailey* [1983] 2 All ER 503 at 507.

[275] [1981] QB 527. cf the unsatisfactory case of *Gannon* (1987) 87 Cr App R 254, criticized by G Williams, 'Two Nocturnal Blunders' (1990) 140 NLJ 1564.

[276] Below, p 1024.

[277] See above, p 53.

liable because he was drunk; but where he did intend damage to property but thought the owner would consent he is not liable, however drunk he may have been. Suppose that D, because he is drunk, believes that certain property belonging to V is his own and damages it. His belief is not a matter of defence under s 5(2)[278] but negatives recklessness whether property *belonging to another* be damaged.[279] If D, being drunk, destroys X's property believing that it is the property of Y who would consent to his doing so, this is a defence; but if he destroys X's property believing that it is his own, it is not. The latest Law Commission proposals would reverse the approach in *Jaggard*,[280] which is a welcome reform proposal.

11.4.5.2 Common law defences

In relation to common law defences, the law has gone quite the other way. It is now settled that when D sets up self-defence, he is to be judged on the facts as he believed them to be, whether reasonably or not.[281] A mistake arising from voluntary intoxication cannot be relied on, according to *O'Grady*[282] and *Hatton* even on charge of murder or other crime requiring specific intent. In *O'Grady,* this was plainly *obiter* because the appellant had been acquitted of murder and was appealing only against his conviction for manslaughter; but in *O'Connor,*[283] the court, inexplicably, treated it as binding, while quashing the conviction of murder on another ground. This was followed in *Hatton.* H who had drunk more than 20 pints of beer killed V with at least seven blows from a sledgehammer. H stated that he could not recall V's death but that he had a vague recollection that a stick fashioned in the shape of a Samurai sword had been involved. H said that he believed that V had hit him with the stick and that he must have believed that V was attacking him. H wished to raise self-defence based on his own mistaken belief that he thought he was being attacked by an SAS officer (as V had earlier pretended to be) with a sword. The Court of Appeal, upholding his conviction, confirmed that the decision in *O'Grady*[284] applied equally to cases of manslaughter and murder: a defendant seeking to rely on self-defence could not rely on a mistake induced by voluntary intoxication. The case is controversial in extending the scope of *O'Grady* to murder, and in accepting unequivocally that the decision in *O'Connor* and *O'Grady* were binding (but not, implicitly, feeling bound by *Gladstone Williams*).

This approach is flawed in a number of ways. First, it contradicts the approach taken in relation to mistakes in self-defence. If D has made a genuine but unreasonable mistake as to the need for force, he will be judged on the facts as he unreasonably believed them to be. If this is so when D is sober, surely it ought to be so when he is intoxicated since his intoxication explains the basis for the unreasonableness of his mistake. (The Law Commission rejects this argument (at para 3.59).) Secondly, it is inconsistent with the application of the rules relating to specific and basic intent for offences. If D is charged with murder and pleads that he was too intoxicated to know what he was doing, he is, if believed, entitled to an acquittal on that specific intent charge. He will be convicted of manslaughter by gross negligence if the jury judge his unreasonable mistake as to the need for force as a grossly negligent mistake (which

---

[278] *Smith (DR)* [1974] QB 354, [1974] 1 All ER 632.

[279] ibid.

[280] LC314, para 2.94.

[281] *Gladstone Williams* [1987] 3 All ER 411, 78 Cr App R 276, below, p 381.

[282] [1987] QB 995, [1987] 3 All ER 420, criticized by the Law Commission, Law Com No 177, para 8.42, by H Milgate [1987] CLJ 381 and JC Smith [1987] Crim LR 706.

[283] [1991] Crim LR 135; cf *Hatton* [2005] EWCA Crim 2951.

[284] [1987] 3 WLR 321. Note also the Criminal Justice and Immigration Act 2008, s 76(5) which precludes D relying on a mistake in such circumstances which was attributable to him being voluntarily intoxicated. See also LC 314, para 2.54–2.61.

a drunken mistake almost certainly is).[285] If self-defence is a defence to murder it does not necessarily follow that it needs to be a defence to manslaughter. The Court of Appeal, in a purely policy driven series of decisions has created inconsistencies in an attempt to ensure that D cannot plead intoxicated self-defence: the basis for this seems to be a fear that jurors would acquit of all offences.[286] These decisions are difficult to defend. The court's attention does not appear to have been drawn to the recommendations of the Criminal Law Revision Committee, which complements those which the court followed in *Gladstone Williams*.[287] The more logical view, it is submitted, is that a mistake arising from voluntary intoxication by alcohol or dangerous drugs ought to found a defence to crime requiring specific intent but not to one of basic intent if the prosecution prove that but for the intoxication the defendant would not have made the mistake.

11.4.6 Intoxication induced with the intention of committing crime

Has D a defence if, intending to commit a crime, he takes drink or drugs in order to give himself 'Dutch courage' and then commits the crime, having, at the time of the act, induced insanity within the M'Naghten Rules or such a state of drunkenness as to negative a 'specific intent'? The problem was raised by *A-G for Northern Ireland v Gallagher*.[288] D, having decided to kill his wife, bought a knife and a bottle of whisky. He drank much of the whisky and then killed his wife with the knife. The defence was that he was either insane or so drunk as to be incapable of forming the necessary intent at the time he did the act. The Court of Criminal Appeal in Northern Ireland reversed his conviction for murder on the ground that the judge had misdirected the jury in telling them to apply the M'Naghten Rules to D's state of mind at the time before he took the alcohol and not at the time of committing the act. The majority of the House of Lords apparently did not dissent from the view of the Court of Criminal Appeal that such a direction would be 'at variance with the specific terms of the M'Naghten Rules which definitely fix the crucial time as the time of committing the act'.[289] They differed, however, in their interpretation of the summing up and held that it did direct the jury's attention to the time of committing the act. In that case, of course, it was not necessary to decide the problem because the jury, by their verdict, had found that D had *mens rea* and was not insane. Lord Denning, however, seems to have taken the view that the Court of Criminal Appeal's interpretation of the summing up was correct and that the direction, so interpreted, was right in law. He said:[290]

My Lords, I think the law on this point should take a clear stand. If a man, whilst sane and sober, forms an intention to kill and makes preparation for it knowing it is a wrong thing to do, and then gets himself drunk so as to give himself Dutch courage to do the killing, and whilst drunk carries out his intention, he cannot rely on this self-induced drunkenness as a defence to a charge of murder, nor even as reducing it to manslaughter. He cannot say he got himself into such a stupid state that he was incapable of an intent to kill. So also, when he is a psychopath, he cannot by drinking rely on his self-induced defect of reason as a defence of insanity. The wickedness of his mind before he got drunk is enough to condemn him, coupled with the act which he intended to do and did do.

---

[285] By Smith [1987] Crim LR 706. cf the rejection arguments in LC 314, paras 3.59–3.64.

[286] See the critical comments by A Ashworth [2006] Crim LR 353; JR Spencer [2006] CLJ 267; G Dingwall (2007) 70 MLR 127.

[287] See above, n 281.

[288] [1963] AC 349.

[289] See [1963] AC 349 at 376.

[290] [1963] AC 349 at 382.

The difficulty about this is that an intention to do an act some time in the future is not *mens rea*.[291] The *mens rea* must generally coincide with the conduct which causes the *actus reus*. If D, having resolved to murder his wife at midnight, drops off to sleep and, while still asleep, strangles her at midnight, it is thought that he is not guilty of murder (though he may be liable for manslaughter on the ground of his negligence). The case of deliberately induced drunkenness, however, is probably different. The true analogy, it is thought, is the case where a man uses an innocent agent as an instrument with which to commit crime. It has been seen[292] that if D induces an irresponsible person to kill, D is guilty of murder. Is not the position substantially the same where D induces in himself a state of irresponsibility with the intention that he shall kill while in that state?[293] Should not the responsible D be liable for the foreseen and intended acts of the irresponsible D? So regarded, a conviction would not be incompatible with the wording of the M'Naghten Rules. The result, certainly, seems to be one required by policy and it is thought the courts will achieve it if the problem should be squarely raised before them.

11.4.7 *Majewski* in other jurisdictions

Majewski was followed by the Supreme Court of Canada by a majority of four to three in *Leary*[294] but that court, by a majority of six to three, then held, in *Daviault*,[295] that *Leary*, that is, the *Majewski* rule, violates the Canadian Charter of Rights and Freedoms in that it eliminates the fundamental requirements of voluntariness and of *mens rea* in offences of basic intent. The High Court of Australia rejected *Majewski* in *O'Connor*,[296] holding that evidence of voluntary intoxication is admissible in all cases to show that an act was involuntary or that any required mental element was lacking, and approving the New Zealand Court of Appeal decision in *Kamipeli*[297] to similar effect. In South Africa the Appellate Division reached the same conclusion in *Chrétien*.[298]

11.4.8 Reform of intoxication

England is becoming isolated in clinging to the *Majewski* principle. Its abolition elsewhere does not seem to have led, as some anticipated, to increased crime or a collapse in respect for the law.[299] The Law Commission reached a provisional conclusion in 1993 that *Majewski* should be abolished in a Consultation Paper.[300] The radical proposal was to introduce a new offence of criminal intoxication which would better reflect, in terms of label, the responsibility of the individual who commits a crime in a state of voluntary intoxication.[301] The consultation however persuaded the Commission to change its mind. In LC 229 it was recommended[302] that the rule be codified with minor amendment and attempted clarification, but in a draft Bill so complex and clumsy that it is impossible to commend it.[303] That has not been taken

---

[291] Above, p 49.

[292] Above, p 88.

[293] See the discussion in Ch 4, p 61.

[294] [1978] 1 SCR 29, 33 CCC (2d) 473. See LC 314, Appendix C for a review of other jurisdictions.

[295] (1994) 118 DLR (4th) 469.

[296] (1980) 146 CLR 64.

[297] [1975] 2 NZLR 610.

[298] 1981 (1) SA 1097 (A). In Scotland the position is less clear. See S Gough, 'Surviving without *Majewski*' [2000] Crim LR 719; J Chalmers, 'Letter to the Editor' [2001] Crim LR 258. On the Irish position, see K Spencer, 'The Intoxication "Defence" in Ireland' (2005) ICLJ 2.

[299] G Orchard, 'Surviving without *Majewski*' [1993] Crim LR 426.

[300] LCCP No 127 (1993).

[301] For a defence, see G Virgo, 'Reconciling Principle and Policy' [1993] Crim LR 415; for criticism, see S Gardner, 'The Importance of *Majewski*' (1994) 14 OJLS 279.

[302] LC 229 (1995). See J Horder, 'Sobering Up' (1995) 58 MLR 534; E Paton, 'Reformulating the Intoxication Rule' [1995] Crim LR 382.

[303] See S Gough, 'Intoxication and Criminal Liability' (1996) 112 LQR 335.

forward. The Home Office then proposed a simplified model which it intended to enact in relation to offences against the person. That too has not been taken forward.[304]

The Law Commission's latest proposals in LC 314 would provide a statutory framework, replacing the specific/basic intent distinction. The replacement for the 'specific intent' rule is to create a statutory list of 'integral fault elements' (intention, knowledge, belief, fraud and dishonesty), and if D is charged with an offence with such an 'integral fault element' D will only be liable if the prosecution proves he had the relevant fault element despite being voluntarily intoxicated [para 3.42]. The general rule for all other offences (eg, those requiring recklessness) is that if D was voluntarily intoxicated he will be treated 'as having been aware at the material time of anything which D would then have been aware of but for the intoxication' [para 3.35]. This effectively replaces the basic intent rule. In relation to D's mistakes induced by voluntary intoxication D's mistaken belief should be taken into account only if D would have held the same belief if D had not been intoxicated [para 3.53]. If D's intoxication is involuntary (administered without consent or under duress or under proper medical instruction or without knowledge it was an intoxicant) or 'almost entirely involuntary', that can be considered in all cases where D is charged with a crime of subjective fault [para 3.105–3.126]. Separate complex rules are proposed in relation to secondary and inchoate liability [para 3.85–3.104].[305]

The Code Team's report[306] to the Commission offered a simpler scheme. Other proposals for a *via media* have been made[307] but have not attracted support and are not pursued here.

11.5 Combined, consecutive and concurrent causes of loss of capacity

The internal and external factors which cause an individual defendant to lack capacity may operate consecutively or concurrently. There is little authority on the complex questions which may arise and such as there is does not seem well thought out. It is sufficient to demonstrate, however, that this is a practical and not merely an academic problem. Some answers to the questions which may arise are suggested here.

11.5.1 Consecutive operation

11.5.1.1 Intoxication causes automatism

D, because he is drunk, sustains concussion and does the allegedly criminal act in a state of automatism resulting from the concussion. In *Stripp,*[308] the Court of Appeal thought, *obiter*, that D should be acquitted on the ground of automatism. That seems right – the intoxication is too remote from the act. The Law Commission concluded that the case suggests '*obiter*, the possibility that where there is a course of automatism clearly separable in time or effect from the intoxication and supported by a foundation of evidence, then a defence of automatism may be available, but when the causal factors are less easily separable it would seem that the presence of the intoxication will on policy grounds adopted in *Majewski* exclude reliance on automatism'.[309] Distinguishing the degree of separateness of the factors will not always be easy.

---

[304] See JC Smith, 'Offences Against the Person: The Home Office Consultation Paper' [1998] Crim LR 317.
[305] For critical comment see J Child, 'Drink, Drugs and Law Reform' [2009] Crim LR 488.
[306] LC 143 (1985) cl 26.
[307] See the 7th edition of this book, at 230.
[308] (1979) 69 Cr App R 318,323, CA. No foundation for automatism was laid.
[309] LCCP 127 (above) para 2.33, Report (above) para 6.44. LC 314, para 2.90.

11.5.1.2 Automatism causes intoxication

D having sustained concussion, drinks a bottle of vodka under the impression that it is water and does the allegedly criminal act, not knowing what he doing because he is intoxicated. Since the intoxication is involuntary, both causes lead to an acquittal and D must be acquitted.

11.5.1.3 Intoxication causes insanity

Beard settles that insanity caused by drink operates in the same manner as insanity arising from any other cause. If excessive drinking causes actual insanity, such as delirium tremens, then the M'Naghten Rules will be applied in exactly the same way as where insanity arises from any other causes: 'drunkenness is one thing and the diseases to which drunkenness leads are different things; and if a man by drunkenness brings on a state of disease which causes such a degree of madness, even for a time, which would have relieved him from responsibility if it had been caused in any other way, then he would not be criminally responsible'.[310]

It has already been seen[311] that there are serious difficulties in defining a 'disease of the mind' and the distinction between temporary insanity induced by drink and simple drunkenness is far from clear-cut. The distinction becomes important in the case of a person who does not know that his act is wrong because of excessive drinking. If he is suffering from temporary insanity he is entitled to a verdict of not guilty on the ground of insanity; but if he is merely drunk he should be convicted.[312]

11.5.1.4 Insanity causes intoxication or automatism

'Insanity' in the *M'Naghten* sense can strictly have no application here because it applies only in relation to a particular criminal act, whereas getting drunk or causing oneself concussion is probably not a criminal act at all and certainly not the criminal act with which we are concerned. However, D may not know the nature and quality of the act which causes the condition. The resulting intoxication is involuntary, so D should be acquitted. In so far as automatism is caused by insanity, it is the result of an internal cause which looks as if the net result should be, not guilty on the ground of insanity; but it would seem odd that, if D's insanity leads him to drink excessively, he should be acquitted absolutely whereas if it takes the form of banging his head against a wall until he does not know what he is doing he should be subject to restraint. Policy may be best served by a verdict of not guilty on the ground of insanity in both cases.

11.5.1.5 Automatism causes insanity

Such cases will surely be rare, but, if one should arise, probably the answer should be as in the case where automatism and insanity are concurrent causes and for the same reason.[313]

11.5.2 Concurrent operation

11.5.2.1 Intoxication and automatism

The circumstances of non-insane automatism being pleaded where D's level of intoxication renders him automaton are discussed above (p 310).

---

[310] *Davis* (1881) 14 Cox CC 563 at 564, per Stephen J approved by the House of Lords in *DPP v Beard* [1920] AC 479 at 501.

[311] Above, p 298.

[312] In a case of simple drunkenness the judge should not introduce the question whether the prisoner knew he was doing wrong – for 'it is a dangerous and confusing question' – per Lord Birkenhead in *DPP v Beard* [1920] AC 479 at 506. Note that in the Scottish case of *Finegan v Heywood* (2000) The Times, 10 May, a defence of sleepwalking triggered by intoxication was treated as not being one of 'automatism'.

[313] Below, p 329.

11.5.2.2 Intoxication and insanity

D does not know what he is doing, partly because of a disease of the mind and partly because he is drunk. The choice is (or should be) between a verdict of not guilty on the ground of insanity and, in a crime not requiring specific intent, one of guilty. Two difficult cases cast doubt on this and illustrate the difficulty in dealing with combined causes in practice.

In *Burns*,[314] D was charged with indecent assault, a crime not requiring specific intent. He may not have been aware of what he was doing, partly because of brain damage and partly because of drink and drugs. It is unclear whether the drugs were prescribed to B.[315] The court accepted that, if D did not know what he was doing, he was entitled to an absolute acquittal. If the only causes are alcohol and insanity it is difficult to see how this can be right, since neither of the concurrent causes entitled D to be absolutely acquitted. If the causes are alcohol, prescribed drugs and insanity the position is more complex. Since the crime is one of basic intent, it is arguable that the non-dangerous drugs that D was taking require the prosecution to establish that D was not reckless in becoming aggressive and unpredictable.[316] Williams took the view that in such a case insanity was the correct verdict,[317] and analogy with *Beard* might suggest that this is the right verdict, but the House of Lords in *A-G for Northern Ireland v Gallagher*[318] thought otherwise, unless the alcohol caused some quite different type of disease, such as delirium tremens.[319]

11.5.2.3 Automatism and insanity

In *Roach*,[320] the Court of Appeal adopted a more pragmatic approach, focusing on which of the multiple concurrent causes of the lack of control was dominant. D was convicted of wounding with intent to cause grievous bodily harm having attacked V with a knife after a minor dispute. D claimed to have no knowledge or memory of the incident. D claimed that his voluntary intoxication by alcohol, coupled with his prescribed drugs might have had some causative effect on his latent mental illness being triggered leading to his lack of awareness. The expert evidence described a 'disease of the mind' and not surprisingly that was treated by the prosecution as the basis of a plea of insanity. Defence counsel argued that the 'disease of the mind' should lead to a defence of automatism, but the judge did not leave that defence to the jury.[321] The Court of Appeal upheld the appeal. It was accepted that automatism was sufficiently widely defined that if external factors were operative on an 'underlying condition which would not otherwise produce a state of automatism', then a defence of non-insane automatism ought to be left to the jury.[322] The court considered this to be a borderline case as identified in *Quick*, where the 'transitory effect caused by the application to the body of some external factor such as violence, drugs etc cannot fairly be said to be due to disease'. With respect, it is not clear that this is a faithful application of that principle. In *Quick* the lack of control was due to hypoglycaemia, caused by taking insulin (an external event) on an underlying internal condition (diabetes). Is it true to say (as the Court of Appeal would) that the underlying condition in *Quick* would not otherwise have produced a state of automatism if the

---

[314] (1973) 58 Cr App R 364, [1975] Crim LR 155 and commentary.

[315] In earlier editions, it was suggested that the combination of the causes was intoxication and insanity alone. Mackay, *Mental Condition Defences*, at 158 criticizes that narrow view of the facts.

[316] See Mackay, ibid, at 159.

[317] TBCL, 681.

[318] [1963] AC 349, [1961] 3 All ER 299, above, p 325 (effect of drink on a psychopath).

[319] Combination of mental abnormality and drink resulting in a substantial impairment of mental responsibility did not amount to a defence of diminished responsibility: *Fenton*, below, p 535. NB the new diminished responsibility defence, below p 536.

[320] [2001] EWCA Crim 2698.

[321] [17].

[322] [28].

insulin had not been administered? Surely it would. D would have gone into a hyperglycaemic state if he had not taken the insulin. The state of automatism which would have resulted if the underlying condition had been left to its own devices would be hyperglycaemia, which is different from the state of automatism that resulted from the insulin – hypoglycaemia – but does that matter?

The court seems to accord precedence to the prescribed drugs rather than the internal cause and the voluntary intoxication. The lack of control seems to have been a combination of (i) the 'psychogenic' personality (which would alone result in a special verdict); (ii) prescribed drugs (which alone if taken as per the prescription would have resulted in acquittal); and (iii) the voluntary intoxication (which on a specific intent charge such as this could have resulted in acquittal). It is submitted that the decision in *Roach* should be approached with considerable caution. It may be regarded as correctly decided on its facts since the judge gave confusing directions as to the relevant burdens of proof.

11.6 Mistake

The rules relating to mistake are simply an application of the general principle that the prosecution must prove its case, including the *mens rea* or negligence which the definition of the crime requires and rebuttal of excuses raised. The so-called 'defence' is simply a denial that the prosecution has proved its case. Accordingly, only mistakes which relate to an issue which the prosecution have to prove will have any bearing on D's liability.

11.6.1 Mistakes as denials of *mens rea*

The 'landmark decision'[323] in *DPP v Morgan* endorsed by the House of Lords in *DPP v B*,[324] holds that D's mistake of fact will result in acquittal in all crimes of *mens rea* where it prevents D from possessing the relevant *mens rea* which the law requires for the crime with which he is charged. It is not a question of defence, but of denial of *mens rea*. As Lord Hailsham explains in *Morgan*:

Once one has accepted ... that the prohibited act is [x], and that the guilty state of mind is an intention to commit [x], it seems to me to follow as a matter of inexorable logic that there is no room either for a defence of honest belief or mistake, or of a defence of honest and reasonable belief or mistake. Either the prosecution proves that the accused had the requisite intention, or it does not. In the former case it succeeds, and in the latter it fails.[325]

Historically, mistake had been treated as a special defence and there were many *dicta* by eminent judges that *only* reasonable mistakes would excuse.[326] Lord Lane CJ[327] and the House of Lords,[328] in the light of *Morgan*, doubted these pronouncements and the House in *B v DPP*[329] has now made it very clear that they are wrong.

---

[323] [1976] AC 182.

[324] And subsequently by its ringing endorsement *K* [2002] 1 AC 462 and *G* [2003] UKHL 50.

[325] Per Lord Hailsham at 214. For a powerful critique, see J Horder, 'Cognition, Emotion and Criminal Culpability' (1990) 106 LQR 469.

[326] See, for historical accounts, E Keedy, 'Ignorance and Mistake in the Criminal Law' (1908) 22 Harv LR 75; Williams, CLGP, Ch 5; Hall, *General Principles*, Ch XI; G Williams, 'Homicide and the Supernatural' (1949) 65 LQR 491; C Howard, 'The Reasonableness of Mistake in the Criminal Law' (1961) 4 Univ QLJ 45.

[327] *Taaffe* [1983] 2 All ER 625, 628.

[328] *Westminster City Council v Croyalgrange Ltd* [1986] 2 All ER 353 at 399.

[329] See, particularly, Lord Nicholls at [2000] 1 All ER 836–839.

11.6.1.1 Evidence and proof

It should not be imagined that all D has to do is say 'I made a genuine mistake' to be acquitted. The reasonableness of his conduct will be important in evidential terms. Where the natural inference from D's conduct in the particular circumstances is that he intended or foresaw a particular result, the jury are very likely to convict him if he introduces no testimony that he did not in fact foresee; but the onus of proof remains throughout on the Crown and, technically, D does not bear even an evidential burden.[330] Although D's belief need not be reasonable to excuse him, as a matter of practice, the more unreasonable it is, the less likely the jury is to accept that it was genuinely held.

11.6.1.2 Mistakes in crimes of subjective *mens rea*

Where the law requires intention, knowledge, belief, or subjective recklessness with respect to some element in the *actus reus*, a mistake, whether reasonable or not, which precludes that state of mind will excuse D. The fact that a genuine though unreasonable mistake will negative D's *mens rea* or provide an excuse stems from the courts' endorsement of subjectivism in *mens rea*. Obviously, if a particular crime requires D's *mens rea* as to the proscribed conduct, circumstance or result to be based on his subjective intentions or beliefs, and because of a mistake of fact the intentions or beliefs D holds do not relate to the proscribed conduct, circumstance or result, D cannot be liable. Thus, where D genuinely though unreasonably believes that the thing he is shooting at is a scarecrow and not a human, he will lack the *mens rea* for murder – an intention to kill or do grievous bodily harm *to a person in being.*

Many commentators have suggested that the wholesale application of the subjectivist principles in the context of mistake is too simplistic an approach.[331] For example, in the context of sexual offences and consent, the ease with which D can ascertain the consent of his partner and the gravity of the harm done if the sexual act is non-consensual suggest that D's mistakes as to consent should be assessed objectively. This is in fact what Parliament has required in the Sexual Offences Act 2003. Beyond sexual cases, it can be argued that where D's mistake is unreasonable, in the sense of 'holding it or acting on it in a particular situation displays an unreasonable lack of the kind of respect and concern for others that the law demands' it should not lead to acquittal.[332] However, the present law generally adopts the subjectivist stance as stated in *Morgan* and *DPP v B.* As Lord Nicholls observed in *B v DPP*, 'considered as a matter of principle, the honest belief approach must be preferable. By definition the mental element in crime is concerned with a subjective state of mind such as intent or belief'.[333]

11.6.1.3 Mistakes and crimes of negligence

Where the law requires only negligence in respect of an element of the *actus reus*, then only a *reasonable* mistake can afford a defence; for an unreasonable mistake, by definition, is one

---

[330] G Williams, 'The Evidential Burden' (1977) 127 NLJ 156 at 158. But there is an evidential burden on D to get a particular mistake before the jury. 'Mistake is a defence in the sense that it is raised as an issue by the accused. The Crown is rarely possessed of knowledge of the subjective factors which may have caused an accused to entertain a belief in a fallacious set of facts': *Pappajohn v R* (1980) 52 CCC (2d) 481 at 494, per Dickson J. The judge does not have to direct the jury in every case of murder: 'You must be satisfied that D did not believe V was a turkey'; but he must give such a direction if D has testified that, when he fired, he thought V was a turkey.

[331] See Horder (1990) 106 LQR 469; Ashworth, POCL, 189; R Tur, 'Subjectivism and Objectivism: Towards Synthesis', in S Shute, J Gardner and J Horder (eds), *Action and Value in Criminal Law* (1993) 213; P Alldridge, *Relocating Criminal Law* (2000) 88.

[332] Duff, *Answering for Crime*, 294.

[333] For criticism see J Horder, 'How Culpability Can and Cannot be Denied in Under-age Sex Crimes' [2001] Crim LR 15, arguing that D's mistake should be relevant if it relates to his 'guiding moral reason'.

which a reasonable person would not make and is, therefore, a negligent one.[334] In cases of gross negligence manslaughter, D's unreasonable mistake may excuse provided it is not regarded by the jury as a grossly unreasonable mistake. Parliament may, of course, specify in relation to any crime that only reasonable beliefs will excuse. A recent example of this is the Sexual Offences Act 2003 (see below, Chapter 18).

11.6.1.4 Mistakes in crimes of strict liability

Where a crime is interpreted as imposing strict liability, then even a reasonable mistake as to that element of the *actus reus* for which liability is strict will not excuse. It is an oversimplification to say that mistakes are irrelevant in strict liability crimes since there are few such crimes in which every element of *actus reus* is regarded as strict.[335] Thus, in a sexual offence such as sexual assault on a child under 13 where liability as to the age of the victim is strict, D will still have to be proved to have *intentionally* touched V. Where he claims that because of a mistake he had not meant intentionally to touch a person, he will be denying *mens rea*, and an honest mistake will excuse. If he claims to have made a mistake about age, that is irrelevant because liability as to age is strict.

Bigamy – a special case?

On the explanation so far, the application of the principles of mistake would seem to be straightforward. However, there are skeletons lurking in the common law cupboard which suggest that in some cases D's mistake as to an element of *actus reus* must *always* be reasonable to provide an excuse. One particular problem relates to the cases on bigamy. In *Morgan*, the House showed no inclination to interfere with the line of authority[336] which asserted that D's mistaken belief in the death of his first spouse, or the dissolution or nullity of his first marriage, was a defence only where that mistake was reasonable. But in *B v DPP*, Lord Nicholls expressly disapproved of the requirement of reasonableness of belief in the leading bigamy case of *Tolson*.[337] It is submitted that a genuine though unreasonable belief ought now to be a sufficient excuse on a charge of bigamy. In general terms the *Tolson* approach may be tolerable where we are concerned with so-called 'quasi-criminal', 'regulatory' or 'welfare' offences; but it should have no place in serious crimes – and, after *B v DPP*, *K* and *G* it seems less likely to do so, as discussed above in Chapter 7.

11.6.1.5 Identifying the relevant mistake

What the discussion on bigamy exposes is the broader problem in many crimes of identifying which elements of *actus reus* require a corresponding *mens rea* requirement. In many serious offences there will usually be a strong if not complete correspondence, ie that elements of the *actus reus* will each have corresponding elements of *mens rea* to be proved. For example, in *Westminster City Council v Croyalgrange Ltd*,[338] Robert Goff LJ referred to 'the ordinary principle that, where it is required that an offence should have been knowingly committed, the requisite knowledge must embrace all the elements of the offence'. On orthodox subjective principles intention knowledge, belief or recklessness is required as to all the elements of the

---

[334] Above, Ch 6.

[335] See SP Green, 'Six Senses of Strict Liability', in A Simester (ed), *Appraising Strict Liability* (2005) Ch 1.

[336] *Tolson* (1889) 23 QBD 168, CCR; *King* [1964] 1 QB 285; *Gould* [1968] 2 QB 65. As the opinions in *Morgan* relating to defences have been reconsidered (below, p 333) so too may the opinions regarding bigamy, if the matter ever arises. The House also accepted the requirement of reasonable grounds for believing the use of force to be necessary in self-defence, but see *Beckford* and *Williams*, below, p 381.

[337] (1889) 23 QB 168 CCR.

[338] [1986] 83 Cr App R 155, [1986] Crim LR 693.

actus reus unless that is excluded expressly or by implication; and the more serious the crime, the more reluctant should the court be to find an implied exclusion.[339]

11.6.1.6 Summary

The most logical approach to mistakes is, it is submitted, (i) to identify the relevant mistake D claims to have made; (ii) identify to which element of the *actus reus* of the offence it relates; (iii) ascertain what *mens rea*, if any, attaches to that element of the *actus reus* in dispute; (iv) apply the relevant rule as stated in the previous paragraphs: if the *mens rea* element is subjective D is entitled to acquittal on a genuine mistake; if it is objective/negligence, D's mistake must be a reasonable one to lead to acquittal; if liability on that element of *actus reus* is strict, D's mistake is irrelevant.

11.6.2 Mistakes and defences

Morgan also left untouched the traditional requirement that mistakes as to the elements of defences had to be reasonable if they were to operate to excuse the accused. *Morgan*, although a case on the *mens rea* for rape, was a landmark case in relation to mistake generally. In *Beckford v R* the Privy Council recognized this:

Looking back, *Morgan* can now be seen as a landmark decision in the development of the common law, returning the law to the path upon which it might have developed but for the inability of an accused to give evidence on his own behalf.[340]

Beckford v R is itself of great importance in that it takes the principle of *Morgan* even further than the majority of the House were, at that time, prepared to go. In *Morgan* the plea was a simple denial of the prosecution's case. By charging rape, the prosecution alleged that D had intercourse with a woman who did not consent and that he either knew that she did not consent or was reckless (at that time subjective recklessness was the prescribed *mens rea* for rape) whether she did so. D denied that he knew or was reckless, as alleged.

Where on the other hand D pleads a true defence, D admits the allegations made by the prosecution but asserts further facts which, in law, justify or excuse his action. Self-defence is an example. D admits that he intentionally killed or wounded V but asserts that he did so because V was making a deadly attack on him and this was the only way he could save his own life. It may transpire that D was mistaken. V was not in fact making a deadly attack. The courts, until the 1980s, were consistent in asserting that the defence failed if there were no reasonable grounds for his belief. The majority of the House of Lords in *Morgan* did not intend to interfere with defences. They were concerned with a mistake as to an element of the offence. *Beckford* related to a mistake as to an element of a defence. The Privy Council rejected any distinction. They followed *Morgan* and approved the ruling of Lane LCJ in *Gladstone Williams*.[341] Discussing the offence of assault, he said:

The mental element necessary to constitute guilt is the intent to apply unlawful force to the victim. We do not believe that the mental element can be substantiated by simply showing an intent to apply force and no more.[342]

---

[339] There are, admittedly, many exceptions to this principle. The Law Commission Consultation Paper 195 *Criminal Liability in Regulatory Contexts* (2010) also contains discussion of the significance of this principle and of the hierarchy of *mens rea*, see the discussion in Ch 7.

[340] [1987] 3 All ER 425 at 431.

[341] [1987] 3 All ER 411, 78 Cr App R 276, CA.

[342] This important ruling may be threatened by the Human Rights Act, Art 2 (right to life), setting a more demanding standard than 'honest belief', see below, Ch 12.

If D believed, reasonably or not, in the existence of facts which would justify the force used in self-defence, he did not intend to use *unlawful* force. *Beckford* clearly applies to all instances of private defence.[343] However, in duress, for example, the courts continue to state that D's belief in the alleged compelling facts must be based on reasonable grounds.[344] If, however, D is to be judged on the facts as he believed them to be when he sets up self-defence it is difficult to see why it is different in principle when he sets up duress. In both cases D is saying that, on the facts as he believed them to be, his act was not an offence. It is submitted that the principle of *Beckford* should be applicable to defences generally.

Since *Beckford*, *Albert v Lavin*[345] must be taken to be wrong in making a distinction in relation to assault between the definitional elements of an offence and the definitional elements of a defence. The same subjective test applies to both. *Barrett and Barrett*[346] is more complex. D was convicted of assault occasioning actual bodily harm to bailiffs who were executing a warrant to take possession of his house. D intended to assault the bailiffs but claimed that he was justified because he believed the court order had been obtained by fraud, though his application to have it set aside had been unsuccessful. Not surprisingly, this refusal to accept the judgment of the courts was held to be no defence. If D was making a mistake, it was one of law, admittedly the civil law,[347] but of a rather special kind. It does not necessarily follow that the result would have been the same if D had believed the men were not bailiffs at all but imposters, or that the court had made no order. He was entitled to use force to repel a trespasser. An honest belief arising from a mistake of fact, reasonable or not, that the men were trespassers should certainly have been an answer;[348] *Morgan* was discussed, in relation not to this, but to a second point. It was argued that D was justified because he honestly believed that the force the bailiffs were using was excessive. But a mistake as to the amount of force which the law permits is certainly a mistake of law which is incapable of founding a defence. If it were otherwise, every person would, in effect, fix his own standards, whereas standards are fixed by law.

Morgan, properly understood, had nothing to do with either of these points and the court's remark that it was inapplicable because it related to rape was inappropriate. Indeed, the court spoke with approval of the *Tolson*[349] principle but, as they phrased it, it was the *Morgan*[350] principle – 'an honest belief in a certain state of things does afford a defence, including an honest though mistaken belief about legal rights' – not, be it noted, an honest *and reasonable* belief. The subjectivist could not ask for more; but the principle was inapplicable here because (i) refusal to accept the validity of a court order, if it is properly called a mistake at all, is not the sort of mistake that a court can, as a matter of policy, admit as a defence; and (ii) standards are conclusively settled by the law.

11.6.2.1 Summary

Whether the law recognizes the mistake made by D as to facts which if they existed would provide a valid defence, and whether to be recognized the mistake must be one of a reasonable or merely genuine nature, must be considered in the context of each defence (see the next chapter). Intoxicated mistake has been discussed above (p 323).

---

[343] Below, Ch 12.
[344] *Hasan* [2005] UKHL 22, below, Ch 12.
[345] [1982] AC 546, [1981] 1 All ER 628, DC.
[346] (1980) 72 Cr App R 212.
[347] See below, p 338.
[348] *Blackburn v Bowering*, below, p 661; *Faraj* [2007] EWCA Crim 1033.
[349] See above, pp 164, 332.
[350] Above, p 330.

The courts have adopted the subjective principle in some categories (for example, self-defence),[351] but not others (for example, duress).[352] Some commentators seek to distinguish the categories on the basis of whether the defence is one of a justificatory or excusatory kind, or whether the defence relates to a 'definitional element' of the offence. Since the law does not adopt such classifications, and they cannot be universally applied, it seems that these may confuse rather than illuminate matters.[353]

The correct approach is, it is submitted, (i) to identify the relevant mistake of fact the defendant claims to have made; (ii) identify to which element of the defence it relates; (iii) ascertain whether that element of the defence is one in which the courts have imposed an objective interpretation; (iv) if the defence is one assessed objectively – (for example, the requirement of a reasonable belief in a threat of death or serious injury in duress) D will only be able to rely on the mistake if it is reasonable; if the element of the defence is subjective (for example, the requirement that D believes in the need for force in private defence) he will be entitled to rely on the mistaken belief as to the facts even if unreasonable.

11.6.3 Irrelevant mistakes

A mistake which does not preclude *mens rea* (or negligence where that is in issue) is irrelevant and no defence. Suppose D believes he is smuggling a crate of Irish whiskey. In fact the crate contains Scotch whisky. Duty is, of course, chargeable on both. D believes he is importing a dutiable item and he is importing a dutiable item. The *actus reus* is the same whether the crate contains Irish or Scotch. He *knows*, because his belief and the facts coincide in this respect, that he is evading the duty chargeable on the goods in the crate. If D had believed the crate to contain only some non-dutiable item, for example, foreign currency (even if he had mistakenly believed it was dutiable) he would have lacked the *mens rea* for the offence.[354]

A much misunderstood case is that of *Taaffe*.[355] T imported 3.7 kilos of cannabis believing that he was importing large sums of money and that currency was subject to an import prohibition. The House of Lords upholding the decision of the Court of Appeal[356] concluded that an accused is to be judged upon the facts as he believed them to be. Taaffe held two mistaken states of mind. His mistake of fact was that he was importing currency when he was in fact importing cannabis. His mistake of law was that he thought currency was subject to a prohibition. T's belief as to the fact meant that he was not *knowingly* importing prohibited goods at all. If the jury accepted as genuine his mistaken belief as to the facts, there would be no knowing importation of prohibited goods. This is analogous to the example of D shooting the scarecrow above. On that basis his mistaken belief negatived the *mens rea*. He could not be convicted of the substantive offence under s 170.

T's mistaken belief as to the scope of criminal law is quite different. That belief could not, even if the jury accepted that he held it, have rendered him liable for importing the currency: there would be no criminal offence with which he could be charged either as a substantive offence under s 170 or an attempt under s 1 of the Criminal Attempt Act 1981. The criminal law, even when inchoate forms of offending are involved, cannot extend that far: if D visits

---

[351] *Williams* [1987] 3 All ER 441.

[352] *Graham* [1982] 1 All ER 801; *Hasan* [2005] UKHL 22.

[353] See TBCL, 138; Tur, 'Subjectivism and Objectivism: Towards Synthesis', in Shute, Gardner and Horder (eds), *Action and Value in Criminal Law*, 213.

[354] See commentary on *Taaffe* [1983] Crim LR 536 at 537, CA; affd [1984] AC 539. See *Forbes* [2001] UKHL 40 where D believed he was importing prohibited goods (adult pornography) and he was importing prohibited goods (child pornography). D evaded the prohibition on imports and intended to do so. See also *Matrix* [1997] 8 Archbold News.

[355] [1984] AC 539, HL.

[356] (1983) 77 Cr App R 82, CA.

England and believes that adultery is an offence, he cannot be liable for any crime by committing adultery while here, nor for attempting to do so (see Chapter 13 below).

The case of *Taaffe* provides for a defence only where D's belief is that he is importing goods of a particular description which if it were true, would mean that as a matter of law he was not in fact importing goods which were subject to any prohibition. This should be contrasted with a second category of case of mistake: that in which D believes that he is importing or attempting to import prohibited goods, but in fact he is importing something not subject to a prohibition or restriction. This is illustrated by the decision in *Shivpuri* discussed below, p 483. Shivpuri believed he was importing one type of prohibited goods when he was importing harmless material. The House of Lords concluded that there was no difficulty in convicting him of an attempt to import the prohibited goods. The case is, in one sense, the converse of *Taaffe*. Where D makes a mistake of fact that, if believed, would mean that he was not knowingly importing prohibited goods he is to be acquitted: *Taaffe*. Where D makes a mistake of fact that, if believed, would mean that he was importing goods subject to a prohibition, he can be convicted of an attempt to import those goods.

11.6.4 Mistakes of law[357]

If D makes a mistake by thinking that some form of conduct is criminal when it is not, he cannot be guilty of an offence – there is no offence with which he can be charged, as the example of the tourist who believes adultery is a crime in England. These are exceptional and unlikely ever to come to light. It does not apply where D refuses, however honestly, to accept the judgment of a court,[358] just as it would be hopeless for him to argue that he did not accept the validity of an Act of Parliament.

Suppose that X obtains goods from V by fraud and gives them to D, who knows all the facts. We have already seen that it will not avail D to say he does not know handling stolen goods is a crime. Equally, it is thought it will not avail him to say that he did not know that it is against the criminal law to obtain goods by fraud and that goods so obtained are 'stolen' for this purpose. 'Stolen' is a concept of the criminal, not the civil law, and ignorance of it is no defence.

On the other hand, the 'leave' granted to a visitor to remain in the United Kingdom looks like a civil law concept, but the House of Lords has held that a mistake of law is no answer to a charge of knowingly remaining without leave.[359]

11.6.4.1 Mistake of criminal law

If D mistakenly believes that conduct which is a crime in England is not criminal he will, generally, have no defence.[360] This is because *usually* knowledge that the act is forbidden by law is no part of *mens rea*.[361] Where, for example, D, a visitor to England believes that his conduct is

---

[357] See DN Husak and A von Hirsch, 'Culpability in Mistake of Law' in Shute, Gardner and Horder (eds), *Action and Value in Criminal Law*.

[358] ibid.

[359] *Grant v Borg* [1982] 1 WLR 638.

[360] Above, p 141.

[361] cf the comments of Lord Woolf in the appeal in the Privy Council in the Pitcairn Case discussed below: *Christian v The Queen* [2006] UKPC 47. His lordship stated that 'in this case the appellants suffered no prejudice in view of their state of knowledge an argument based on abuse of process would not be established. It may be the case that the argument under this head could be freestanding and not based on abuse of process. However if this be so the need for prejudice would still be a requirement. The great majority of criminal offences require *mens rea*. *If you do not know and are not put on notice that the conduct with which you are charged was criminal at the time you are alleged to have committed the offence, it can be the case that you do not have the necessary criminal intent.'* [Emphasis added.]

lawful because it does not constitute a crime in his homeland,[362] he will have no defence if that conduct is an offence in England. The harshness of the rule is tempered somewhat by the fact that most serious criminal offences are also well recognized as moral 'wrongs'. However, it is no defence even where the crime is not one commonly known to be criminal. Thus ignorance of any of the thousands of regulatory offences is no defence. This position is ameliorated only slightly by s 3(2) of the Statutory Instruments Act 1946 providing a defence for D charged with an offence created by Statutory Instrument to prove that, at the time of the offence, the instrument had not been published nor reasonable steps taken to bring its contents to the notice of the public or the accused.[363] By analogy, where an offence in English law involves an issue of foreign law, it is arguable that D should only be liable if it is reasonable for him to discover that law.[364] Andrew Ashworth has recently advanced a powerful argument against the present position. He suggests the rule is based on shaky foundation, examines many circumstances in which the rule gives rise to unfairness and identifies government obligations to provide clearer criminal law. (See above, p 141.)

The arguments that every citizen has access to a clear statement of the law is a constitutional principle supported by Art 7 of the ECHR. As Lord Bingham observed in *Rimmington*,[365] 'Article 7 sustains [the] contention that a criminal offence must be clearly defined in law, and represents the operation of "the principle of legal certainty".'[366] The principle enables each community to regulate itself:

with reference to the norms prevailing in the society in which they live. That generally entails *that the law must be adequately accessible – an individual must have an indication of the legal rules applicable in a given case – and he must be able to foresee the consequences of his actions, in particular to be able to avoid incurring the sanction of the criminal law.*[367]

The ease with which a defendant could discover the law and whether he might rely on a mistake as to the scope of the law where it was not readily discoverable were recently in issue in the prosecution of a number of men in the Pitcairn Islands for sexual abuse of young women on the islands. In *Christian & Others v The Queen (The Pitcairn Islands)*,[368] the defendants argued that the case should have been stayed as an abuse of process on the grounds, *inter alia*, that they did not know that English law applied and that they had no access on their remote Pacific Island to English legal texts. Lord Woolf[369] accepted that:

it is a requirement of almost every modern system of criminal law, that persons who are intended to be bound by a criminal statute must first be given either actual or at least constructive notice of what the law requires. This is a requirement of the rule of law, which in relation to the criminal law reflects the need for legal certainty.

He had no difficulty with the principle of such an argument but found it had no application on the facts: it was clear that DD, although probably unaware of the terms of the Sexual Offences Act or even that there was legislation of that name or the sentences that could be

---

[362] See *Esop* (1836) 7 C & P 456.

[363] cf A Ashworth, 'Excusable Mistake of Law' [1974] Crim LR 652 and p 141, n 270 above.

[364] See, eg, the argument in relation to sex tourism where D in England might mistakenly believe that to have sex with a 15-year-old in the host country is not criminal in that country. See Alldridge, *Relocating Criminal Law*, 149, discussing the Sexual Offences (Conspiracy and Incitement) Act 1996.

[365] [2005] UKHL 63.

[366] See, eg, *Brumarescu v Romania* (2001) 33 EHRR 35 at para 61 and *Kokkinakis v Greece* (1993) 17 EHRR 397 at para 52.

[367] *SW v United Kingdom; CR v United Kingdom* (1995) 21 EHRR 363 (emphasis added).

[368] [2006] UKPC 47. See H Power, 'Pitcairn Island' [2007] Crim LR 609.

[369] [40].

imposed for those offences, were aware that their conduct was contrary to the criminal law. The moral wrong of rape and sexual abuse were so obvious that the claim of a lack of awareness of specific offences was irrelevant. Similarly, the Privy Council rejected the argument that the defendants could not have discovered the law had they tried[370] because the precise terms of the Sexual Offences Act had not been published on the island because the fact that there were offences such as rape and possibly indecent assault was generally known because they had to be dealt with by the Supreme Court, requiring as they did greater punishment than was otherwise possible.

Interestingly, Lord Woolf acknowledged that:

The sheer volume of the law in England, much of which would be inapplicable..., creates real problems of access even to lawyers unless they are experts in the particular field of law in question. The criminal law can only operate...if the *onus is firmly placed on a person*, who is or ought to be on notice that conduct he is intending to embark on may contravene the criminal law, to take the action that is open to him to find out what are the provisions of that law.[371]

This places the emphasis on the duty of the citizen to ascertain the law rather than on the State to bring the law to every citizen's attention.

11.6.4.1 Erroneous advice given to D

Where D has relied on erroneous advice provided by the relevant State authority he may in some circumstances be successful in an application to stay proceedings as an abuse of process.[372]

11.6.5 Mistake of fact or law?

Identifying whether a mistake which D alleges he made is one of criminal law or fact is not always easy. For example, if D mistakenly believes that the person grabbing hold of him is a thug about to rob him and he resists, he has made a mistake of fact and cannot be guilty of assaulting with intent to resist arrest what was in fact a police officer. Where however, D is aware that the person who is grabbing him is a police officer, but mistakenly believes that the officer has no power of arrest on the facts as they exist, D has made a mistake of criminal law. But what of D who makes a mistake as to antecedent facts which, if they were as he believed them to be, would indeed preclude the officer's power of arrest?[373]

Where the *mens rea* involves some legal concept[374] or the absence of a claim of right then mistake may negative *mens rea* and be a defence.

An honest though unreasonable mistake as to the *civil* law may lead to acquittal where it prevents D from holding the *mens rea* of the criminal offence. For example, in *Smith (David)*,[375] D damaged property in his rented flat believing it was his own property – he made a mistake as to the ownership of the property. His conviction for criminal damage was quashed since D had no intent to damage property *belonging to another*. His mistake as to ownership prevented him having the relevant *mens rea*. As James LJ explained:

---

[370] cf Lord Hope at [83] who had he not concluded that they were aware of the wrongs which were criminal at common law, would have granted a stay.

[371] Para 44, emphasis added. See above, p 141.

[372] See A Ashworth, 'Testing Fidelity to Legal Values' (2000) 63 MLR 633, 635–642 identifying the importance of Art 7 of the ECHR. One of the strongest examples is *Postermobile v LBC* (1997) 8 Dec, unreported, DC and the Editorial at [1998] Crim LR 435 (D receiving erroneous information from planning agency). See also G Williams, 'The Draft Code and Relevance of Official Statements' (1989) 9 LS 177.

[373] See *Lee* [2001] Cr App R 293, below p 663.

[374] Above, p 141.

[375] [1974] QB 354.

Applying the ordinary principles of *mens rea*, the intention and recklessness and the absence of lawful excuse required to constitute the offence have reference to property belonging to another. It follows that in our judgment no offence is committed under this section if a person destroys or causes damage to property belonging to another if he does so in the honest though mistaken belief that the property is his own, and provided that the belief is honestly held it is irrelevant to consider whether or not it is a justifiable belief.[376]

[376] ibid, 360.

12
General defences

This chapter deals with defences in the broader sense, not just those focused on the mental condition of the accused. In the cases in this chapter, D will usually have performed the *actus reus* with the appropriate *mens rea*, but despite both these elements of the offence being proved by the Crown, the question is whether D is entitled to an acquittal owing to some justifying, excusing or exempting circumstance or condition. There are special defences which apply to particular crimes (for example, loss of self-control and diminished responsibility in murder) which are dealt with separately although where appropriate their interrelationship is considered. Some reference back to the general discussion of defences at the beginning of Chapter 11 may be necessary, particularly to the introductory comments on the theoretical underpinnings of defences and the theories of justifications and excuse.

12.1 Infancy[1]

Infants or, in more modern terminology, minors, are persons under 18 years of age. Although minors may be restricted from performing certain civil law activities (eg writing a will) the law imposes no such limitations on their ability to commit crimes, for, as Kenny put it, 'a child knows right from wrong long before he knows how to make a prudent speculation or a wise will'.[2] The common law, for the purposes of the criminal liability, divided infants into three categories, but under the present law only two categories remain.

12.1.1 Children under 10 years

A child was entirely exempt from criminal responsibility at common law until the day before his seventh birthday.[3] By statute, responsibility now begins on the child's tenth birthday.[4] The common law rule was stated as a conclusive presumption that the child is *doli incapax*, and the statute uses the same language: 'It shall be conclusively presumed that no child under the age of 10 years can be guilty of any offence.' Even though there may be the clearest evidence that the child caused an *actus reus* with *mens rea*, he cannot be convicted once it appears

---

[1] See, H Keating 'The Responsibility of Children in the Criminal Law' [2007] CFLQ 183, and 'Reckless Children' [2007] Crim LR 546 and for an historical account see G Williams, The Criminal Responsibility of Children' [1954] Crim LR 493. Broader issues of youth justice are discussed in C Ball, 'Youth Justice: Half A Century of Responses to Youth Offending' [2004] Crim LR 167; J Fionda, *Devils and Angels: Youth, Policy and Crime* (2005); L Hoyano and C Keenan, *Child Abuse: Law and Policy* (2007).

[2] Kenny, *Outlines*, 80.

[3] A person attains a particular age at the commencement of the relevant anniversary of the date of his birth: Family Law Reform Act 1969, s 9(1).

[4] Children and Young Persons Act 1933, s 50, as amended by the Children and Young Persons Act 1963, s 16, which raised the age from eight. The Ingleby Committee had recommended that the age be raised to 12. Cmnd 1911 (1960).

that he had not, at the time he did the act, attained the age of 10. Nor is this a mere procedural bar; no crime is committed by the child with the result that the one who instigated him to do the act is a principal and not a secondary party.[5] And where a husband and wife were charged with receiving from their son (aged seven) a child's tricycle, knowing it to have been stolen, it was held that they must be acquitted on the ground that, since the child could not steal, the tricycle was not stolen.[6] Ten is a comparatively low age for the beginning of criminal responsibility, it is certainly much lower than many other European states; but, as the Ingleby Committee pointed out:[7]

In many countries the 'age of criminal responsibility' is used to signify the age at which a person becomes liable to the 'ordinary' or 'full' penalties of the law. In this sense, the age of criminal responsibility in England is difficult to state: it is certainly much higher than [ten].[8]

Numerous organizations including the UN Committee on the Rights of the Child (2002) and the European Committee on Social Rights (2005), have urged reform of English law. There is, of course, no international agreement on what the age should be.[9]

As the Beijing Rules, adopted by the United Nations General Assembly in 1985 observe in their commentary on the United Nations Standard Minimum Rules for the Administration of Juvenile Justice (Beijing Rules), Art 4(1):[10]

The minimum age of criminal responsibility differs widely owing to history and culture. The modern approach would be to consider whether a child can live up to the moral and psychological components of criminal responsibility; that is, whether a child, by virtue of her or his individual discernment and understanding, can be held responsible for essentially antisocial behaviour. If the age of criminal responsibility is fixed too low or if there is no lower age limit at all, the notion of criminal responsibility would become meaningless. In general, there is a close relationship between the notion of responsibility for delinquent or criminal behaviour and other social rights and responsibilities (such as marital status, civil majority, etc).

12.1.2 Children aged 10 and above

At common law, there was a *rebuttable* presumption that a child aged not less than 10 but under 14 years ('a young person') was *doli incapax*: incapable of committing crime. The presumption was rebutted only if the prosecution proved beyond reasonable doubt, not only that the child caused an *actus reus* with *mens rea*, but also that he knew that the particular act was not merely naughty or mischievous, but 'seriously wrong'. If there was no evidence of such knowledge, other than that implicit in the act itself, the child had no case to answer. In *C v DPP*,[11] the Divisional Court held that this ancient rule of the common law was outdated and

---

[5] Above, p 188.

[6] *Walters v Lunt* [1951] 2 All ER 645; and cf *Marsh v Loader* (1863) 14 CBNS 535.

[7] Cmnd 1191, at 30. For the special rules governing the sentencing of children, see *Blackstone's Criminal Practice 2011*, Parts E9 and E11. For comparative materials on child prosecution, see A Nicol in *Child Offenders: UK and International Practice* (Howard League for Penal Reform, 1995).

[8] The age then was eight. Above, n 4.

[9] See generally D Cipriani, *Children's Rights and the Minimum Age of Criminal Responsibility: A Global Perspective* (2009). The age in Scotland has now increased to 12 – Justice and Licensing (Scotland) Act 2010, s 52.

[10] See further, the helpful discussion in Emmerson, Ashworth and Macdonald, HR&CJ, paras 11.01–11.05 concluding that it is 'difficult to see how the [current] age of criminal responsibility is in the child's best interests'. See also J Gillen, 'Age of Criminal Responsibility: The Frontier Between Crime and Justice' [2007] Int Fam LJ 7. There is mounting pressure for reform. See, eg, letter to the Times by distinguished experts in the area, 2 July 2010. See also A Ashworth, 'Child Defendants and the Doctrines of the Criminal Law' in J Chalmers, L Farmer and F Leverick (eds), *Essays in Criminal Law in Honour of Sir Gerald Gordon* (2010).

[11] [1996] AC 1, [1995] 2 All ER 43, HL. See the 8th edition of this book for detail, at 195.

no longer law; but the House of Lords reversed this, ruling that it was not open to the courts so to hold. That decision was followed by a series of acquittals which caused disquiet.

In the Crime and Disorder Act 1998, Parliament responded by abolishing the rebuttable presumption.[12] This was intended to put children aged 10 and above on an equal footing with adults, so far as liability (but not sentencing or mode of trial and procedure) is concerned. The Act is not well drafted. Section 34 of the Crime and Disorder Act 1998 provides:

The rebuttable presumption of criminal law that a child aged 10 or over is incapable of committing an offence is abolished.

It was cogently argued by Professor Walker that the section does not affect the substantive law,[13] leaving it open to a child under 14 to introduce evidence that he did not know that what he did was seriously wrong, whereupon it will be for the prosecution to prove, not only the usual *mens rea*, but also that the child did know that.[14] Some support for this view came from Smith LJ obiter in *CPS v P*.[15] The terms of the section seemed clear – it is the presumption that is being abolished. Whether that is what the Government thought it was abolishing is less certain. Contradictory statements appear in the Home Office White Paper.[16] Parliamentary debates were, inconclusive.[17] It was disappointing that almost 10 years after its purported abolition, no one was clear whether it had been abolished, or whether the defence rather than the mere presumption had ever existed.

In *T*[18] the House of Lords concluded that there was no authority for the existence of the defence separate from the presumption and that Parliament's intention was clearly to abolish the concept of *doli incapax* as having any effect in law. There is no separate defence of *doli incapax* after the Crime and Disorder Act 1998, s 34.[19] This is a disappointing though predictable outcome. The statute is clear that it is abolishing the presumption. The House of Lords' interpretation of the parliamentary debates is strained to achieve the pragmatic result desired.

In the last decade, the law relating to the procedure for trials of child defendants has developed[20] somewhat and this may assist some children. It has been recognized explicitly that a child defendant must be able to participate effectively in proceedings.[21] One of the criteria for determining whether a child has a sufficient understanding to be tried is whether he understands the seriousness of the consequences of his actions. In some cases,

---

[12] Crime and Disorder Act 1998, s 34. See in particular: N Walker, 'The End of an Old Song' (1999) 149 NLJ 64; L Gelsthorpe and A Morris, 'Much Ado about Nothing – A Critical Comment on Key Provisions Relating to Children in the Crime and Disorder Act 1998' [1999] CFLQ 209; J Fionda 'New Labour, Old Hat: Youth Justice and the Crime and Disorder Act 1998' [1999] Crim LR 36; C Webb, 'Irrational Presumptions of Rationality and Comprehension' [1998] 3 Web JCLI.

[13] See Walker (1999) 149 NLJ 64.

[14] This is supported by the Solicitor General's statements in Parliament, as cited by Walker, ibid.

[15] [2007] EWHC 946 (Admin). *CPS v P* remains a very important authority on the process which a judge ought to adopt before deciding whether to continue with a trial involving a child where there are doubts as to his capacity to understand the nature of the wrongdoing.

[16] *No More Excuses* (1997) para 4.4, para 4.5.

[17] cf Lord Ackner, *Hansard* 12, Feb 1998, col 1318.

[18] *T* [2009] UKHL 20; [2009] 1 AC 1310 (HL) For critical comment see F Bennion, 'Mens Rea and Defendants Below the Age of Discretion' [2009] Crim LR 757.

[19] T, aged 12 at the time of offending, pleaded guilty to 12 counts of causing or inciting a child under 13 to engage in sexual activity. This may be the sort of behavior where a child might know that what he is doing is wrong or naughty, without seeing it as being seriously wrong.

[20] See references above, n 1.

[21] *T & V v United Kingdom* (2000) 30 EHRR 121.

the child's lack of understanding of the wrongness of his conduct will be so great that it might preclude a trial.[22]

The *presumption* still poses problems in prosecutions for historic sexual abuse alleged against defendants who were between the ages of 10 to 14 at the time of their commission.[23]

12.2 Duress

12.2.1 Duress by threats and circumstances[24]

For centuries the law has recognized a defence of duress by threats. The typical case is where D is told, 'Do this [an act which would be a crime if there were no defence of duress] – or you will be killed', and, fearing for his life, D does the required act. Quite recently, the law has recognized another form of duress – duress of circumstances. Again, D does the act alleged to constitute the crime, feeling compelled to do so out of fear, but this time no human being is demanding that he do it.[25] D does it because he reasonably believes himself to be threatened with death or serious injury and that his only reasonable way of escaping the threat is to perform the conduct element of the offence. The defences are clearly closely related. For example, D is told he will be killed unless he acts as a getaway driver for a robbery. The compulsion on D to do the act is exactly the same whether the threat comes from someone demanding that he do it, or from an aggressor, or other circumstances. His moral culpability, or lack of it, seems exactly the same.[26] The discussion of the relationship of duress, duress of circumstances and necessity is postponed until each has been examined in detail (p 374 below).

The law relating to duress by threats is now well developed. Duress of circumstances is still relatively new (20 years old), but it has developed by analogy to duress by threats so that there is a ready-made set of principles to govern it. By a strange coincidence, all the early cases on duress of circumstances concerned road traffic offences but there is no reason why it should be limited to such offences. *Pommell*,[27] *Safi*,[28] *Shayler*[29] and a host of other cases decide that it has the same range and is governed by the same principles as duress by threats. There are only a few differences between the two defences in application. The result is that either form of

---

[22] Where there is evidence that D cannot understand, at the judge's discretion the process should switch to determining as a matter of fact whether the child performed the act alleged. There may be a sufficient delay between the act and the trial for D to have matured sufficiently to now understand the seriousness. See LCCP 197, *Unfitness to Plead* (2010). On special measures for children at trial see recently L Hoyano, 'Coroners and Justice Act 2009: Special Measures Directions Take Two: Entrenching Unequal Access to Justice?' [2010] Crim LR 345.

[23] *Andrew N* [2004] EWCA Crim 1236; *H* [2010] EWCA Crim 312.

[24] Although somewhat dated, there is a valuable discussion of the defences in LCCP 122, *Legislating the Criminal Code: Offences Against the Person and General Principles* (1992); LCCP 218, *Legislating the Criminal Code: Offences Against the Person and General Principles* (1993); LCCP 177, *A New Homicide Act for England?* (2005) Ch 7; LC 304, *Murder Manslaughter and Infanticide* (2007) Ch 6. On the Commission's proposals, see A Ashworth, 'Principles, Pragmatism and the Law Commission Recommendations on Homicide Reform' [2007] Crim LR 333, at 340. The Law Reform Commission of Ireland has also produced a valuable analysis in its Consultation Paper, *Duress and Necessity* (2006): www.lawreform.ie; see also the review in the Victorian Law Reform Commission Report, *Defences to Homicide* (2006) www.lawreform.vic.gov.au.

[25] *Cole* [1994] Crim LR 582; *Ali* [1995] Crim LR 303.

[26] See the judicial affirmation that the defences are this closely linked: *Safi* [2003] Crim LR 721; *Shayler* [2001] 1 WLR 2206, citing the 6th edition of this book, but note p 374 below.

[27] [1995] 2 Cr App R 607. The case was subsequently analysed as one of necessity rather than duress of circumstances because there is no immediate threat of death to D: see *Quayle* [2005] EWCA Crim 1415.

[28] [2003] Crim LR 721.

[29] [2001] 1 WLR 2206.

duress is a general defence, except that neither applies to some forms of treason, or to murder or attempted murder, whether as a principal or a secondary party.

12.2.1.1 Duress and voluntariness[30]

It has often been said that the duress must be such that D's act is not 'voluntary'. We are not, however, concerned here with the case where a person is compelled by physical force to go through the motions of an *actus reus* without any choice on his part. In such cases he will almost invariably[31] be guilty of no offence on the fundamental ground that he did no act.

If there be an actual forcing of a man, as if A by force takes the arm of B and the weapon in his hand and therewith stabs C whereof he dies, this is murder in A but B is not guilty.[32]

Nor are we concerned with the kind of involuntariness which arises from automatism where D is unable to control the movement of his body. When D pleads duress (or necessity) he admits that he was able to control his actions and chose to do the act with which he is charged, but denies responsibility for doing so. He may say, 'I had no choice' but that is not strictly true.[33] The alternative to committing the crime may have been so exceedingly unattractive that no reasonable person would have chosen it; but there was a choice. The courts recognize this. Where D is required to kill an innocent person, they insist that he must choose to defy the threat or threatening circumstance – and the courts 'threaten' him with conviction for murder and life imprisonment if he does not. In Canada, the Supreme Court (holding that necessity may be an excuse, but not a justification) described the act of a person under duress as 'morally involuntary', the 'involuntariness' being 'measured on the basis of society's expectation of appropriate and normal resistance to pressure'.[34] This seems to mean only that even a person of goodwill and reasonable fortitude might have chosen to do the 'criminal' act. Duress in English law cannot be said to be a form of involuntariness. A person, who kills when acting under duress, cannot rely on that plea. His act is voluntary. It would be illogical to say his act was involuntary if he only succeeded in wounding V. The conviction implies both that the act was voluntary and the result intended.[35] D intends to do the act which, but for the duress, would be a crime.

It has been recognized by the Court of Appeal and the House of Lords that the defence is not a denial of *mens rea*, but a true defence operating despite the existence of the *actus reus* and *mens rea* of the offence.[36]

In short, duress is a defence because '... threats of immediate death or serious personal violence so great as to overbear the ordinary powers of human resistance should be accepted as a justification for acts which would otherwise be criminal'.[37]

---

[30] See M Wasik, 'Duress and Criminal Responsibility' [1977] Crim LR 453; A Norrie, *Crime, Reason and History* (2nd edn, 2000) 165–170; ATH Smith, 'On *Actus Reus* and *Mens Rea*', in *Reshaping the Criminal Law* (1978) 104–106.

[31] cf *Larsonneur*, above, p 63.

[32] Hale, II PC, 534.

[33] *Hasan* [2005] UKHL 22, per Baroness Hale at [73]. See also Duff, *Answering for Crime*, 287.

[34] *Perka* (1984) 13 DLR (4th) 1.

[35] *Howe* [1987] AC 417, [1987] 1 All ER 771 at 777, HL, per Lord Hailsham, LC, citing Lords Kilbrandon and Edmund-Davies in *DPP for Northern Ireland v Lynch* [1975] AC 653 at 703 and 709–710.

[36] *Fisher* [2004] EWCA Crim 1190, [2004] Crim LR 938; see also *Hasan* [2005] UKHL 22 per Lord Bingham at [18].

[37] *A-G v Whelan* [1934] IR 518, per Murnaghan J (Irish CCA). The judge probably did not have in mind any distinction between justification and excuse. If there is a material distinction, duress seems to be an excuse. cf RA Duff, 'Rule Violations and Wrongdoing', in S Shute and A Simester (eds), *Criminal Law Theory* (2002) 63.

12.2.1.2 The onus of proof

The onus of disproving duress of either kind is on the Crown.[38] If no facts from which duress might reasonably be inferred appear in the prosecution's case, then D has the 'evidential burden' of laying a foundation for the defence by introducing evidence of such facts.[39] There is considerable judicial scepticism regarding defences of duress and the defendant's burden to get the defence on its feet will not always be straightforward.[40] There is a particular judicial anxiety when the defence is raised late in the trial process. The Law Commission's proposal in relation to the availability of the duress defence in murder is to reverse the burden, so that the accused would be obliged to prove on the balance of probabilities that the elements of the defence were made out.[41] This is a controversial approach.[42] It is a clear compromise, with the Commission being keen to see the defence of duress available to murder (which at present it is not), but prepared to reverse the burden to deter spurious and unmeritorious defences being run. The Commission acknowledges the difficulty the Crown may face in duress cases where D is often the sole source of evidence supporting the defence.[43]

12.2.1.3 The elements of the defence

Lord Bingham in the leading modern authority from the House of Lords, *Hasan*, summarized the elements of the defence:[44]

(1) there must be a threat of death or serious injury;

(2) that threat must have been made to D or his immediate family or someone close to him or, someone for whom D would reasonably regard himself as responsible;

(3) D's perception of the threat and his conduct in response are to be assessed objectively – his belief that he is under such a threat must be reasonable and his decision to commit the crime in response must be reasonable;

(4) the conduct it is sought to excuse must have been directly caused by the threats D relies on;

(5) there must have been no evasive action D could reasonably take;

(6) D cannot rely on threats to which he has voluntarily laid himself open;

(7) the defence is unavailable to murder, attempted murder or treason.

---

[38] *Hasan* [2005] UKHL 22, at [37]; *Gill* [1963] 2 All ER 688, [1963] 1 WLR 841, CCA; *Giaquento* [2001] EWCA Crim 2696; *Bianco* [2001] EWCA Crim 2156, endorsed in *Bloomfield* [2007] EWCA Crim 1873.

[39] Radically, recent Law Commission proposals would reverse the burden of proof on this defence. In relation to the application of duress to non-murder cases the Commission proposed, 'We repeat that in our view the reasons we have given for recommending that the defendant should bear the persuasive burden of proving duress are unique to the case of that defence. We also believe that they are sufficient to justify that step, and that it would not result in injustice to the defendant who genuinely acted under duress. The closing words of cl 25(2) and cl 25(4) of the Criminal Law Bill provide accordingly.' Report, para 33.16. It is doubtful whether this would be compatible with the ECHR (Art 6(2)). See the doubts expressed by Lord Bingham in *Hasan* at [20]. The Law Commission has subsequently recommended that the burden be reversed should the defence become available to a charge of murder: LC 304, Ch 6.

[40] See *Hasan* at [20].

[41] LC 304, para 6.115.

[42] For analysis of the potential ECHR implications, see LC 304, para 6.116 et seq.

[43] cf LCCP 177, para 7.66 where it is suggested that the days when it was easy to raise and difficult to rebut are 'long gone'!

[44] *Hasan* [2005] UKHL 22, at [21]. On the decision see, *inter alia*, D Ibbetson [2005] CLJ 530; R Ryan and D Ryan (2005) 56 NILQ 421.

(1) Threat of death or serious injury

The type of qualifying threat or danger

As a matter of policy the law places strict limits on the type of threat sufficient to trigger the defence. It is not simply a question of balancing in each case the gravity of the threat D faced against the gravity of the offence D committed in response. There is a minimum threshold below which the threats will never be sufficient to allow the defence of duress to operate. That threshold is set at a high level. The only threat or danger which will found a defence in either type of duress is one of death or serious[45] personal injury.[46] It has been held that serious psychiatric injury can be grievous bodily harm for the purposes of the Offences Against the Person Act and it is probable that a threat to cause such injury could amount to duress.[47] A threat to make a person a nervous wreck could be just as terrifying as a threat to cause serious physical injury.

This criterion of serious injury is narrowly construed by the courts. In *Brown*,[48] the court refused leave to appeal a conviction for possession of drugs when D, suffering from a degenerative disease was cultivating cannabis for personal use to alleviate his pain. The court regarded the threat of 'injury' he faced as being only that additional pain he would suffer by having to rely on prescribed medication rather than the lower level of pain suffered with his condition if he used cannabis. The difference between the two levels of pain was not sufficient to constitute 'serious' injury.[49] In *Quayle*,[50] the Court of Appeal went further and rejected the pain experienced by an multiple sclerosis sufferer as sufficient to qualify as 'harm' as the defence of duress of circumstances requires.

The House of Lords in *Hasan*, Lord Lane CJ in *Graham*,[51] and Woolf LJ in *Conway*,[52] all required a threat of death or serious personal injury. This is in keeping with most modern codes in other jurisdictions.[53] Lord Goddard, in *Steane*,[54] spoke of violence *or imprisonment* but in that case duress was held not to be in issue. While a threat of serious personal injury is the minimum which is acceptable to found the defence for offences to which it is available, a higher minimum may be required for crimes of great gravity. Thus, Hale required threats of death and so did the judges in *M'Growther*[55] and *Purdy*[56] but those were cases of treason. The Law Commission recently proposed that in a case of murder, duress will require proof that D was under a threat of death or 'life threatening injury'.[57]

The following *dictum* of Lords Wilberforce and Edmund-Davies no longer applies to killing but is good for other acts:

the realistic view is that, the more dreadful the circumstances of the killing, the heavier the evidential burden of an accused advancing such a plea, and the stronger and more irresistible the duress needed before it could be regarded as affording any defence.[58]

---

[45] In *Aikens* [2003] EWCA Crim 1573, it was doubted that a threat to punch V in the face would suffice.

[46] *Radford* [2004] EWCA Crim 2878. cf the Criminal Damage Act 1971, s 5(2)(b).

[47] *Baker v Wilkins* [1997] Crim LR 497.

[48] [2003] EWCA Crim 2637.

[49] A duress of circumstances case.

[50] [2005] EWCA Crim 1415, [2006] Crim LR 142 and commentary.

[51] [1982] 1 All ER 801, [1982] 1 WLR 294.

[52] [1989] QB 290, [1988] 3 All ER 1025.

[53] LC 218, para 29.1: 'the overwhelming tendency of the authorities as of modern codes, is to limit the defence to cases where death or serious injury is threatened....Consultation strongly supported that limitation on the defence of duress, which is imposed by clause 25(2)(a) of the Criminal Law Bill'.

[54] [1947] KB 997 at 1005.

[55] (1746) Fost 13.

[56] (1946) 10 JCL 182.

[57] LC 304, para 6.75.

[58] *Abbott v R* [1976] 3 All ER at 152.

Threats of blackmail, no matter how effective, are not sufficient.[59] There is no modern[60] case in which a threat of injury to property has been admitted.[61] In *M'Growther*,[62] it was held there was no defence where the Duke of Perth had threatened to burn the houses and drive off the cattle of any of his tenants who refused to follow him. But that was a case of treason and it does not necessarily follow that such a threat would not be enough on some lesser charge.

If the evil D caused by submitting to the threat (for example theft of a chocolate bar) was clearly less than that which would have been inflicted had he defied it (for example burning down his house), there are cogent reasons for allowing a defence; even if the threat was not of death or even grievous bodily harm. Williams argued strongly in favour of such a principle, which is, of course, closely analogous to that adopted in the American Model Penal Code in relation to necessity.[63] But this would in some cases still deny a defence to D even though the injury threatened was one which no ordinary person could be expected to endure; and there would be grave difficulty in balancing the two evils against one another when they are of a completely different character.[64] 'Proportionality' may be requisite for necessity[65] but it seems inappropriate for duress.

From whom/what threat must emanate

The threat must have some source extraneous to the defendant himself. In *Rodger and Rose*,[66] D who was serving a life sentence was informed that his tariff had been substantially increased. He broke out of prison and raised duress as a defence at his trial for prison-breaking. It was conceded for the purpose of the appeal that he broke out because he had become suicidal and would have committed suicide had he not done so. So there was a threat to his life, but since the threat did not come from an extraneous source, it was no defence. To allow it, said the court, 'could amount to a licence to commit crime dependent on the personal characteristics and vulnerability of the offender'. The Court of Appeal in *Quayle* relied upon this limitation to the defence to preclude the defence of duress of circumstances where D cultivated cannabis for personal use to alleviate pain for his multiple sclerosis.[67]

No threat need exist in fact

There is no requirement for there to be a threat in fact. It is sufficient that D believes that there is a threat of the relevant gravity. If the defence was only available where there was a threat in fact, D could not plead duress where threatened with an unloaded gun, nor where D escaped from prison erroneously believing it to be on fire. This would be unduly restrictive.

In *Safi and Others*,[68] Afghan hijackers who had landed at Stansted airport claimed that their fear of persecution at the hands of the Taliban constituted a defence of duress of

---

[59] *Singh* [1973] 1 WLR 1600.

[60] cf *Crutchley* (1831) 5 C & P 133.

[61] '...the threat may be to burn down [D's] house unless the householder merely keeps watch against interruption while a crime is committed. Or a fugitive from justice may say, "I have it in my power to make your son bankrupt. You can avoid that merely by driving me to the airport." Would not many ordinary people yield to such threats, and act contrary to their wish not to perform an action prohibited by law? Faced with such anomaly, is not the only answer, "Well, the law must draw a line somewhere; and, as a result of experience and human valuation, the law draws it between threats to property and threats to the person"', per Lord Simon [1975] AC 653, [1975] 1 All ER at 932.

[62] Above, n 55.

[63] Below, p 373.

[64] Law Com Working Paper No 55, paras 14–17.

[65] *S (DM)* [2001] Crim LR 986 below, p 374.

[66] [1998] 1 Cr App R 143.

[67] [2005] EWCA Crim 415. See M Watson, 'Cannabis and the Defence of Necessity' (1998) 148 NLJ 1260. See, for a philosophical consideration of such matters, SJ Morse, 'Diminished Capacity', in S Shute, S Gardner and J Horder (eds), *Action and Value in Criminal Law* (1993) 250–263.

[68] [2003] EWCA Crim 1809, [2003] Crim LR 721.

circumstances. The trial judge directed that the defence failed unless there was evidence that there was in fact, or might in fact have been, an imminent peril to the defendants or their families. S appealed on the basis that the defence should be available if he *reasonably* believed that if he had not acted in the way he had, he (and/or the family) would have been killed or seriously injured. The Court of Appeal allowed the appeal. Duress (or duress of circumstances) does not depend on there being an actual risk of death or serious injury to the accused; the defence can be made out if the accused was impelled to act as he did because, as a result of what he reasonably believed to be the situation, he had good cause to fear that otherwise death or serious injury would result.

The situation of the defendant who is not personally aware of the threat but which would cause a reasonable person to commit crime has not been addressed.[69]

(2) Threats against whom?

Most of the cases naturally involve a threat or danger to the life or safety of D himself, but the defences are not limited to that situation. In *Hurley and Murray*,[70] the Supreme Court of Victoria held that threats to kill or seriously injure D's *de facto* wife amounted to duress. In *Wright*,[71] threats against D's boyfriend sufficed. In *Conway*,[72] the threat was to the passenger in D's car; and in *Martin*,[73] D's wife's threat to commit suicide if he did not drive while disqualified was held capable of founding a defence of duress of circumstances – though in fact it seems to have been one of duress by threats – 'Drive or else...'[74] So threats against the life or safety of D's family certainly suffice. In *Shayler*,[75] the Lord Chief Justice, approving a statement of Rose LJ in *Hussain*, stated that:

the evil must be directed towards the defendant or a person or persons for whom he has responsibility or, we would add, persons for whom the situation makes him responsible; ... [this extends], by way of example, [to] the situation where the threat is made to set off a bomb unless the defendant performs the unlawful act. The defendant may have not have had any previous connection with those who would be injured by the bomb but the threat itself creates the defendant's responsibility for those who will be at risk if he does not give way to the threat.

Lord Bingham in *Hasan* also suggested that the threat must be 'directed against the defendant or his immediate family or someone close to him or for whom he is responsible'. So, threats to D, his family and others to whom he owes a 'duty' will qualify, but arguably this is too narrow. If a bank robber threatens to shoot a customer in the bank unless D, the clerk, hands him the keys, D surely has a defence to a charge of assisting the robbery. The concept of those for whom D is 'responsible' is ill-defined, and ought to be given a liberal construction. The defence is so heavily qualified by the requirement of a threat of death or serious injury and the other objective elements, that there is little need to impose restrictions on the categories of individual to whom the threat must be made.

---

[69] cf *O'Too* [2004] EWCA Crim 945 where D2 in cross-examination suggested that D1 was threatened with death if he did not comply with demands to deal drugs. D1's defence was a denial of involvement and therefore the defence was not raised and not left to the jury.

[70] [1967] VR 526.

[71] [2000] Crim LR 510.

[72] [1989] QB 290, [1988] 3 All ER 1025, CA.

[73] [1989] 1 All ER 652. See also *Wright* [2000] Crim LR 510.

[74] See also *M* [2007] EWCA Crim 3228, where M sought to smuggle drugs into prison being threatened with violence by X, and hearing threats from Y in prison that if he did not get the drugs he would commit suicide.

[75] [2001] 1 WLR 2206, para 49. This was accepted in *Hasan* [2005] UKHL 22, per Lord Bingham.

(3) Evaluating D's response to the threat

Several difficult issues arise in determining whether by committing the crime in response to the threats D's conduct should be excused. In particular, the courts have struggled with questions of whether it is sufficient that the particular defendant regarded it as a reasonable response to the threat he believed that he faced, or whether the defence is only available if the reasonable person would have responded in the same way if faced with the threat D genuinely believed he faced.

In *Howe* the House of Lords held that the defence fails if:

the prosecution prove that a person of reasonable firmness sharing the characteristics of the defendant would not have given way to the threats as did the defendant.

The House held that the correct direction was that stated by Lane LCJ in *Graham*:[76]

(1) Was [D], or may he have been, impelled to act as he did because, as a result of what he reasonably believed [E] had said or done, he had good cause to fear that if he did not so act [E] would kill him or … cause him serious physical injury? (2) If so, have the prosecution made the jury sure that a sober person of reasonable firmness, sharing the characteristics of [D], would not have responded to whatever he reasonably believed [E] said or did by taking part in the killing?

The direction contains three objective elements.

(1) D must have *reasonably* believed in the circumstances of the threat;[77]

(2) D's belief must have amounted to *good cause* for his fear;

(3) D's response must be one which might have been expected of a *sober person of reasonable firmness*.

A fourth element is usually considered although not deriving from the *Graham* judgment:

(4) D must have had no *reasonable* opportunity to escape the threat.

In imposing this objective regime on the defence Lord Lane in *Graham* equated duress with self-defence which, it was then generally accepted, imposed an objective test. But less than two years later in *Gladstone Williams*,[78] Lord Lane, influenced by the judgment of Lawton LJ in *Kimber*,[79] held that an unreasonable belief, if honestly held, might found self-defence. Lawton LJ appreciated and applied the general effect of *DPP v Morgan*[80] which was not cited in *Graham*. Logically, if *Morgan* applies to self-defence, it ought equally to apply to duress.[81] It is arguable, however, that the defences are distinguishable since duress is generally regarded as excusatory and self-defence as justificatory in nature.[82] The decision in *Graham* may thus have been an unfortunate accident – but, subsequently it has been approved by the House of

---

[76] [1982] 1 All ER 801 at 806, 74 Cr App R 235 at 241. cf *Lawrence* [1980] 1 NSWLR 122.

[77] The element of reasonableness was firmly endorsed in *Hasan* [2005] UKHL 22, at [23] per Lord Bingham. See also the Law Com, LC 304, para 6.77. In LCCP 177, para 7.46, n 26 the Commission suggested that in an unpublished codification project, the reasonableness test would be endorsed, reversing an earlier Law Commission Report recommendation.

[78] Above, p 324.

[79] [1983] 3 All ER 316 (an honest belief that V was consenting was a defence to indecent (now sexual) assault).

[80] Above, p 330. See JC Smith, 'The Triumph of Inexorable Logic', in *Leading Cases of the Twentieth Century* (2000).

[81] In *Martin (DP)* [2000] 2 Cr App R 42, CA (discussed in [2000] 7 Archbold News 6), Mantell LJ said at 49 – apparently in error – that the subjective test in self-defence had been applied to duress in *Cairns* [1999] 2 Cr App R 137 where Mantell LJ also gave the judgment. See, generally, on the merits of the subjective and objective approaches P Alldridge, 'Developing the Defence of Duress' [1986] Crim LR 433.

[82] See S Yeo, *Compulsion in the Criminal Law* (1990).

Lords in *Howe* and more recently still the House of Lords in *Hasan* certainly did not seem to be inclined to depart from it.[83]

It is submitted that, in the first two respects, the direction in *Graham* lays down too strict a rule. D should surely be judged on the basis of what he honestly believed and what he genuinely feared.[84] If his genuine fear was such that no person of reasonable firmness could have been expected to resist it, he should be excused. He may have been unduly credulous or stupid, but he is no more blameworthy than a person whose fear is based on reasonable grounds.[85] The Court of Appeal in *Martin (DP)*[86] held that D's characteristics – in that case a schizoid affective disorder, making him more likely to regard things said as threatening and to believe that threats would be carried out – must be taken into account. This seems to be a substantial mitigation of the objective test. It is doubtful whether that decision can stand in the light of the emphasis on the objective nature of the defence in *Hasan*.

As with mistake generally, lack of faith in the jury to detect the 'bogus defence' and the additional hardship for the prosecution probably lies at the root of the objective requirements. Also as with mistake generally, the more tenuous the grounds for his claim, the less likely is D to be believed.

The confusion and tension in this area is illustrated by the case of *Safi* (the Afghan hijack case above). At the first trial the judge directed the jury that D's genuine belief in the threat of death was sufficient, on a retrial the second judge adopted an objective formulation. The Court of Appeal failed to clarify the position but seemed implicitly to be adopting an objective test.[87] Similarly, in the case of *M*,[88] the Court of Appeal adopted an apparently subjective approach to the first question holding that the jury should be instructed that the defence fails if the prosecution satisfied them of any of the following:

(1) that the defendant did not genuinely believe that unless she committed the offence there was a real possibility of at least serious harm to herself or her family,

(2) that an ordinary person of reasonable firmness, sharing the accused's characteristics, would not in reaction to threats, real or perceived, have acted as she did, or that there was a rejected opportunity to escape or avoid the threat without injury to herself or her family which a reasonable person, in a like situation, would have taken.

In two subsequent cases, the Court of Appeal has again endorsed the objective approach in the first limb.[89] Further clarification from the House of Lords was not forthcoming in *Hasan*, but the tenor of the speech of Lord Bingham leaves little doubt that the *objective* formulation would be preferred. That would follow the decision in *Graham* which was approved in *Howe*.

---

[83] Lord Bingham rejected comparison with other defences in *Hasan*. cf LCCP 177, para 7.32. It is dangerous to place too much emphasis on comparisons with other defences when seeking to interpret the scope of duress. These common law defences evolved over centuries to meet the needs of individual cases and were not the product of a coherent structured scheme as one might expect from Parliament.

[84] See W Wilson, 'The Structure of Defences' [2005] Crim LR 108, 115–116. Courts occasionally lapse into such a formula, see *Mullally v DPP* [2006] EWHC 3448 (Admin).

[85] In *DPP v Rogers* [1998] Crim LR 202, DC, Brooke LJ seems wrongly to have assumed that this is now the law, apparently anticipating a reform proposed by the Law Commission. cf *Abdul-Hussain* [1999] Crim LR 570. If D reasonably believes there is a threat, it is immaterial that there is no threat in fact: *Cairns* [1999] 2 Cr App R 137, CA. For a criticism of the Commission's 'slavish adherence to subjectivism', see J Horder, 'Occupying the Moral High Ground' [1994] Crim LR 334 at 341 and comments by JC Smith, 'Individual Incapacities and Criminal Liability' (1998) 6 Med L Rev 138 at 155–157.

[86] [2002] 2 Cr App R 42, CA.

[87] Para 25.

[88] [2003] EWCA Crim 1170. See also *Sewell* [2004] EWCA Crim 2322.

[89] *Blake* [2004] EWCA Crim 1238 at [18]; *Bronson* [2004] EWCA Crim 903 at [23].

The person of reasonable steadfastness[90]

Since duress is (according to Lord Hailsham in *Howe* and Lord Bingham in *Hasan*) a concession to human frailty[91] and some people are frailer than others, it is arguable that the standard of fortitude required should also vary, and that a subjective test should apply.[92] That is not the approach adopted in English law. *Graham* is consistent with a common approach of the law in deciding that the standard is an objective one. It is for the law to lay down standards of conduct. When attacked, D may use only a reasonable degree of force in self-defence. Under the loss of self-control defence, D must display a reasonable degree of tolerance and self-restraint. Similarly, *Graham* decides that a person under duress is required to display 'the steadfastness reasonably to be expected of the ordinary citizen in his situation'.[93] The court relied particularly on the analogy with the law of provocation as was then in force and the decision in *Camplin*.[94] That case suggests that account should be taken of not only the gravity of the threat to D but also the sex and age of D and such of D's characteristics[95] as would affect the gravity of the threat to him. The leading case on this issue in duress is *Bowen*.[96]

In *Bowen*, it was held that for a duress plea D's age[97] and sex may be relevant, depending on the circumstances, as may pregnancy and serious physical disability. These might affect the gravity of the threat and D's ability to seek evasive action. In *Bowen*,[98] the court also accepted that a 'recognized mental illness or psychiatric condition, such as post traumatic stress disorder leading to learned helplessness'[99] would be relevant. But, D's low IQ, short of mental impairment or mental defectiveness, is not relevant: a person of low IQ may be expected to be as courageous and able to withstand threats as anyone else. That does not necessarily answer the argument – belatedly advanced on appeal – that D's ability to seek the protection of the police might have been impaired.

Cases of 'learned helplessness' are particularly difficult. In *Emery*,[100] a case of cruelty to a child, it was said, *obiter*, that it would be right to admit 'an expert account of the causes of the condition of dependent helplessness, the circumstances in which it might arise and what level of abuse would be required to produce it'. 'A woman of reasonable firmness suffering from a condition of dependent helplessness' may seem a contradiction in terms; but the point appears to be that the alleged history of violence by D's partner, said to have produced that condition, was part of the duress.[101] That explanation does not however seem to have appealed to the court in *Bowen*. This is a question for the jury and expert evidence has been held inadmissible to show that D was 'emotionally unstable' or in 'a grossly elevated neurotic state',[102] or that he

---

[90] See KJM Smith, 'Duress and Steadfastness: In Pursuit of the Unintelligible' [1999] Crim LR 363. See also Tadros, *Criminal Responsibility*, Ch 13, on the need for defences including duress to take account of D's characteristics.

[91] *Howe* [1987] 1 All ER 771 at 779–780; *Hasan* [2005] UKHL 22 at [18].

[92] 'It is arguable that the standard should be purely subjective and that it is contrary to principle to require the fear to be a reasonable one': per Lord Simon [1975] 1 All ER at 931. cf Law Com Working Paper No 55, paras 11–13 and LC 83 at paras 2.27–2.28; and *Hudson* [1965] 1 All ER 721 at 724.

[93] (1982) 74 Cr App R at 241.

[94] [1978] AC 705, [1978] 2 All ER 168, below, p 523.

[95] Such as the schizoid affective disorder afflicting *Martin (DP)* above, n 86.

[96] [1996] 2 Cr App R 157, [1996] Crim LR 577. In *Flatt* [1996] Crim LR 576, it was held that drug addiction was a self-induced condition, not a characteristic. For criticism of the approach in general for its failure to reflect psychiatric understanding, see A Buchanan and G Virgo, 'Duress and Mental Abnormality' [1999] Crim LR 517.

[97] cf *Ali* [1989] Crim LR 736.

[98] [1996] 2 Cr App R 157.

[99] This was held to be insufficient in *Moseley* [1999] 7 Archbold News 2.

[100] (1992) 14 Cr App R (S) 394. See recently J Loveless, 'Domestic Violence, Coercion and Duress' [2010] Crim LR 93 analysing how the defence is formulated in such a way as to exclude battered women.

[101] Arguably, in such a case D is still a person of reasonable firmness, just one with greater sensitivities.

[102] *Hegarty* [1994] Crim LR 353.

is unusually pliable or vulnerable to pressure;[103] nor is evidence admissible of sexual abuse as a child, resulting in lack of firmness, not amounting to psychiatric disorder: *Hurst*,[104] where Beldam LJ said, 'we find it hard to see how the person of reasonable firmness can be invested with the characteristics of a personality which lacks reasonable firmness...'

It is no less difficult when the condition is a 'recognized mental illness'. The acceptance of such an illness as a relevant characteristic suggests that this element of objective test has broken down and that we are moving closer to the test once proposed by the Law Commission: 'the threat is one which in all the circumstances (including any of [the defendant's] characteristics that affect its gravity) he cannot reasonably be expected to resist'.[105] The Commission's latest proposal in relation to murder is that the jury should be permitted to take account of all the circumstances except D's capacity to withstand the duress.

The court will be faced with drawing some fine distinctions between unusual vulnerability and recognized psychiatric conditions affecting the ability to withstand pressure.[106] The increasing shift towards subjectivity in this limb of the defence stands in contrast to the increased objectivity in the first limb. It highlights the incoherence of the defence as it has evolved at common law, underlining the need for a legislative response.

(4) The conduct it is sought to excuse must have been directly caused by the threats D relies on

Threats as a concurrent cause of the crime

It is said that D's will, must have been 'overborne' by the threat.[107] Presumably this means only that he would not have committed the offence 'but for' the threat and that the threat was one which might cause a person of reasonable fortitude to do as he did. If the prosecution can prove that he would have done the same act even if the threat had not been made, it seems that the defence will fail.[108] But the threat need not be the only motive for D's action. In *Valderrama-Vega*,[109] D was under financial pressure and had been threatened with disclosure of his homosexual behaviour – neither matter being capable of amounting to duress – but it was wrong to direct the jury that the threats of death or serious injury also alleged to have been made must have been the sole reason for his committing the offence. If D would not have committed the offence but for the latter threats the defence was available even if he acted because of the cumulative effect of all the pressure on him. It is probably going too far to say that it is enough that the threats of death were 'the last straw' because the law will look for something more substantial than 'a straw' for an excuse; but threats of death or serious bodily harm can never be trivial, so it is probably sufficient to tell the jury that D has the defence if he would not have acted but for the threats. A direction that the defence was available only if D acted *solely* because of the relevant threats was upheld where it was suggested that he might also have been influenced by greed but the court thought it inadvisable to use that word 'solely' in a summing up.[110]

---

[103] *Horne* [1994] Crim LR 584: 'not a hero nor a coward'.

[104] [1995] 1 Cr App R 82 at 90.

[105] Draft Criminal Law Bill, cl 25, Law Com No 218.

[106] See *Antar* [2004] EWCA Crim 2708.

[107] cf the discussion of *Steane* [1947] KB 997, [1947] 1 All ER 813. See also GR Rubin, 'New Light on Steane's Case' (2003) 24 Legal History 143. See, eg, the continued use of such statements which shed little light on the defence: *Rahman* [2010] EWCA Crim 235.

[108] In *DPP v Bell (Derek)* [1992] Crim LR 176, DC, D, in terror of an aggressor, began to drive with excess alcohol. Although he admitted that, before the threat, he intended to drive, it was found as a fact (a finding with which the DC could not interfere) that he drove because of terror and so had a defence of duress of circumstances. But for the threat he might have changed his mind or been persuaded by his passengers not to drive.

[109] [1985] Crim LR 220 and commentary.

[110] *Ortiz* (1986) 83 Cr App R 173.

A nominated crime demanded?

In the paradigmatic case of duress by threats, the defendant will have been told 'perform this crime or else'. The question has arisen how specific the nomination of the crime must be for D to be able to rely on the threats. In *Cole*,[111] D was convicted of robbing two building societies and pleaded duress on the basis that he had been threatened by money lenders to whom he was in debt. The Court of Appeal held that a plea of duress was not available as the money lenders had not stipulated that he commit robbery to meet their demands. This would place a very strict limitation on the defence. The Court of Appeal held, in addition, in *Cole* that there was not the degree of immediacy and directness required between the peril threatened and the offence charged. That is a better basis for the decision.

Subsequently, in *Ali*,[112] D, a heroin addict, was convicted of robbing a building society and D claimed that his supplier, X, who had a reputation for violence, had demanded repayment of the monies D owed him. Further, that X had provided D with a gun and told D to get the money by the following day from a bank or a building society. The Court of Appeal upheld his conviction but appeared to accept that a threat is capable of amounting to duress when D is charged with robbing a particular building society not specified by the person threatening him.

In a case of duress of circumstances there can be no nominated crime: D faced with an approaching tidal wave or tornado is not 'told' to 'steal that car to drive away', but he is entitled to the defence should he do so.

(5) There is no evasive action D can take

This element of the defence is more properly seen as part of a broader question which is whether the threat is still effective at the time D performs the conduct element of the offence. Historically it was recognized that:

> The only force that doth excuse, is a force upon the person, and present fear of death; and his force and fear must continue all the time the party remains with the rebels. It is incumbent on every man, who makes force his defence to show an actual force, and that he quitted the service as soon as he could.[113]

The Court of Appeal has recently reiterated the 'requirement that the accused must know or believe that the threat is one which will be carried out immediately or before the accused or the other person threatened, can obtain official protection'.[114] But in *Abdul-Hussain*,[115] where Iraqis hijacked an aircraft because they feared they would be killed if they were returned to Iraq, the court reinterpreted the requirement of immediacy, holding that the question was whether D's response to the 'imminent' threat was proportionate and reasonable.[116] This relaxation of the defence was controversial. In *Hasan*, Lord Bingham was at pains to reassert the primacy of the requirement of the 'immediacy of the threat' and D's inability to avoid it, which he described as the 'cardinal feature' of the defence.[117] His lordship opined that the

---

[111] [1994] Crim LR 582. In *Hasan*, Lord Bingham approved the decision regarding the threat as lacking immediacy.

[112] [1995] Crim LR 303.

[113] *M'Growther* (1746) Fost 13 at 14, per Lee CJ.

[114] *Hurst* [1995] 1 Cr App R 82 at 93; *Flatt* [1996] Crim LR 576.

[115] [1999] Crim LR 570.

[116] See *Abdul-Hussain* [1999] Crim LR 570, where the court added '... if Anne Frank had stolen a car to escape from Amsterdam and been charged with theft, the tenets of English law would not, in our judgment, have denied her a defence of duress of circumstances, on the ground that she should have waited for the Gestapo's knock on the door'. But the requirement of proportionality is questionable.

[117] [25]–[26].

defence would not be available if there was a delay of a day between D being threatened with being shot and his commission of the crime.

Duress where D has an opportunity to inform the police

If D is able reasonably to resort to the protection of the law, he must do so or the defence will be lost. In *Hasan*, Lord Bingham observed that it should be made clear to juries that unless D reasonably expects the threats to be carried out 'immediately or almost immediately' the defence may be lost because there may be little room for doubt that the could take evasive action. The question whether D had a reasonable opportunity to take evasive action ought *not* in his lordship's opinion to be subsumed within the question whether D had a reasonable belief in the existence of the threat and whether a reasonable person in D's circumstances would have responded as D did.[118]

When the threat is withdrawn or becomes ineffective, D must desist from committing the crime as soon as he reasonably can. If, for example, having consumed excess alcohol, D is threatened and drives off in fear of his life, he commits a drink drive offence only if the prosecution can prove that he continued to drive after the terror ceased.[119]

Where the threats operate, or D reasonably perceives them as operating on someone other than himself, the question whether the threat is still operative may be more difficult to determine. For example, in *Hurley*, D had ample opportunity to place himself under the protection of the police but the court held that the defence of duress might still be available because his *de facto* wife was held as a hostage by his oppressors. Though he himself was physically out of range, the threats against her were presently operative on his mind.

Hudson[120] went further. Two young women, called as witnesses for the prosecution, gave false evidence because they had been threatened by a gang with serious physical injury if they told the truth, and they saw one of the gang in the public gallery of the court. The young women were charged with perjury. Duress was accepted as a defence even though they could have put themselves under the protection of the law by informing the court; and there were no threats to third parties. The court thought it immaterial that the threatened injury could not follow at once since (in its opinion) there was no opportunity for delaying tactics and they had to make up their minds whether to commit the offence while the threat was operating. The threat was no less compelling because it could not be carried out there if it could be effected in the streets of Salford the same night. The case thus turns on the point that police protection could not be effective. It was recognized to extend the possible ambit of the defence widely for there would be few cases where the police can offer effective and permanent protection against such threats.[121] However, in *Hasan*, Lord Bingham regarded *Hudson and Taylor* as having had 'the unfortunate effect of weakening the requirement that execution of a threat must be *reasonably* believed to be imminent and immediate'.[122] Such a strict standard may be

---

[118] [24].

[119] *DPP v Bell (Derek)*, above, n 108. See this reiteration of this in *Malcolm v DPP* [2007] EWHC 363 (Admin); *Mullaley* [2006] EWHC 3448 (Admin) and in *Brown v CPS* [2007] EWHC 3274 (Admin).

[120] [1971] 2 All ER 244; followed by *Lewis* (1992) 96 Cr App R 412 at 415. Described by Ryan and Ryan (2005) NILQ 421, commenting on *Hasan* as a 'historical anomaly', at 427.

[121] See comment in [1971] Crim LR 359 and (by Goodhart) in 87 LQR 299 and 121 NLJ 909 and (by Zellick) in 121 NLJ 845. In *K* (1983) 78 Cr App R 82, CA, it was held that duress might be available as a defence to contempt of court committed in the witness box by a prisoner who had been threatened with reprisals against himself and his family, by the accused, a fellow prisoner. The Law Commission originally proposed: 'The threat must be, or the defendant must believe that it is, one that will be carried out immediately, or before he (or the person under threat) can obtain official protection: Criminal Law Bill, clause 25(2)(b). This provision, by allowing the defence if the defendant believes that official protection will be ineffective, differs from previous treatments of the point' – Report, para 29.2. In LC 304, the LC now prefers an objective test.

[122] [27]. Lord Bingham at one point suggests that the defence in *Hudson* should fail because there was no question that DD had 'no opportunity to avoid'. That is surely too strict a view. The question is whether they had a

supported by the need to prevent the defence being misused and pleaded in spurious cases, but is it right that a defendant who reasonably fears he will be shot tomorrow after perjuring himself today ought not to be allowed a defence of duress? His lordship seems to be focusing the question on whether D could avoid compliance with the threat, which is in one sense practically always possible. The real question is whether D could take action which would negative the *threat* itself. If D genuinely, and perhaps reasonably, believes that the police or others cannot protect him from the threat, should he be denied the defence?[123] What if those under threat are held overseas beyond the protection of the British police?

As with the question whether the reasonable person would have withstood the pressure, similar principles apply to the doctrine requiring D to escape from duress if possible. His defence will fail if an ordinary person of his sex, age and other relevant characteristics would have taken an opportunity to escape. Obviously, physical disabilities, for example that he had difficulties in walking, would be taken into account.[124] Following *Graham*, however, he must presumably be taken to have been aware of opportunities of which he ought reasonably to have been aware at the time the opportunity arose.[125] A better view, it is submitted, is that if he was not in fact aware of the opportunity to escape, he should not be penalized for his stupidity or slow-wittedness. In view of recent judicial pronouncements in this area such an approach would probably be seen as too generous to the accused.

If the defence of duress is left to the jury and D seeks to explain his decision not to seek assistance from the authorities rather than commit the crime, it is not necessarily incumbent on the judge to spell out each of the risks to D if he had taken such a route.[126]

(6) D cannot rely on threats to which he has voluntarily laid himself open

A further important limitation on the defence is that the threat cannot be one that arises from D having voluntarily exposed himself to threats of violence. This has become an increasingly problematic area and the courts have sought to prevent the defence being too readily available to those involved in drug related and terrorist crime in particular where their involvement demonstrates a degree of prior culpability. The restriction is hedged in with qualifications. In *Hasan*,[127] the House of Lords expressed concern at the way in which the defence was being relied on more readily by defendants in more cases and that there was a danger that the restrictive elements of the offence were not being applied rigorously enough.[128]

Voluntary exposure to threats

D will be denied the defence if he voluntarily exposed himself to a risk of threats. An example is *Sharp* where D, who was a party to a conspiracy to commit robberies, said that he wanted to withdraw when he saw his confederates equipped with guns, whereupon E threatened to blow his head off if he did not carry on with the plan. In the course of the robbery, E killed V. D's conviction for manslaughter was upheld after a jury had rejected his defence of duress. This had been the approach adopted in Northern Ireland in *Fitzpatrick* (duress no defence

---

reasonable chance to avoid the threats. For a recent example of the strictness of *Hasan* being applied, see *N* [2007] EWCA Crim 3479 and see *Hussain* [2008] EWCA Crim 1117.

[123] Consider the recent High Court of Australia case of *Taiapa* [2009] HCA 53 in which D was denied the opportunity to rely on the compulsion defence where, having been threatened at gun point that he, his pregnant girlfriend and his mother would be shot unless he couriered drugs, D drove to collect the drugs and did not report to the police. His asserted belief that the police would not protect him and his family was found not to give rise to the defence.

[124] But the fact that he was voluntarily drunk or drugged might be considered irrelevant.

[125] *Aikens*, above n 45.

[126] See *Arldridge* [2006] EWCA Crim 1970 where D had been threatened that his children would be beheaded with a samurai sword if he did not participate in a robbery.

[127] [2005] UKHL 22.

[128] See especially Lord Bingham's speech at [22].

to a charge of robbery committed as a result of threats by the IRA because D had voluntarily joined that organization)[129] and the *dicta* of Lords Morris, Wilberforce and Simon in *Lynch*.[130] It would be different of course if D was compelled to join the violent organization by threats of death or serious bodily harm then, in principle, he should not be deprived of the defence. Whether any lesser threat should suffice at this stage has not been decided. As Baroness Hale persuasively put the matter in *Hasan*, the question ought to be whether D by his joining exposed himself to the risk 'without reasonable excuse'.[131]

The types of organization

Most cases involve D joining a criminal gang. In *Sharp*, the gang were armed robbers; in *Fitzpatrick*, a paramilitary organization. In *Lewis*,[132] the court construed this limitation on the defence strictly to be limited to associations such as 'a para-military or gangster-tyrant style of organization'. In *Shepherd*,[133] where D voluntarily joined a gang of burglars but wanted to give up after his first outing and raised the defence of duress by the gang to a charge of a later burglary, it should have been left to the jury to decide whether he was taking a risk of being subjected to such a threat of violence when he joined the gang.

In *Ali*[134] the Court of Appeal held that if D has joined with others whom he ought to have realized might subject him to threats of violence, he is denied the defence of duress. The defence is lost irrespective of whether he has joined an existing criminal gang. D was convicted of the robbery at knife point of a vehicle owner. His plead of duress had been rejected at trial on the basis that D had voluntarily joined with the alleged duressor, BH, a co-accused in the robbery. D knew that BH carried a knife and had been warned not to associate with BH. The trial judge directed the jury that duress does not apply if:

the defendant chooses voluntarily to associate with others where he ought to foresee that he might be subjected to compulsion by threats of violence... If you choose to join very bad company, such bad company that you can foresee that you are going to be liable to threats of some kind to do things, then you cannot complain and say I was forced to do them when you had voluntarily associated with those people.

The judge elaborated on what was meant by 'bad company' explaining that joining bad company:

doesn't just mean people who are going about doing bad things, it means people who you should have realised could would be likely to, or may, subject you to compulsion by threats of violence.

The Court of Appeal upheld the conviction. In *Hasan*[135] Lord Bingham, answered the certified question by saying that:

the defence of duress is excluded when as a result of the accused's voluntary association *with others engaged in criminal activity* he foresaw or ought reasonably to have foreseen the risk of being subjected to any compulsion by threats of violence (emphasis added).

---

[129] [1977] NI 20, CA.

[130] [1975] AC 653.

[131] [78]. See also the problems arising for trafficked women who have evaded formal immigration, but are then forced into prostitution. In some cases the defence of duress will be available to their immigration offences. See *Ajayi* [2010] EWCA Crim 471. In other cases the prosecution policy should respect the protocol under the Council of Europe Convention on Action Against Trafficking in Human Beings. See *LM* [2010] EWCA Crim 2327 and the earlier cases of *O* [2008] EWCA Crim 2835 (and the related issues in *Asfaw* [2008] 1 AC 1061).

[132] (1992) 96 Cr App R 412; *Kleijn* [2001] All ER (D) 143 (May).

[133] (1987) 86 Cr App R 47.

[134] [2008] EWCA Crim 716.

[135] [2005] UKHL 22 [39].

The italicized words might suggest that the defence is only lost where D joins an existing criminal gang. *Ali* rejects any such limitation.

Active membership

It is too late if D attempts to withdraw from the organization, when the particular enterprise which resulted in the charge is in contemplation. No defence of duress is available. But a person who joined a paramilitary organization in his youth can hardly be held to have forfeited his right to plead duress by that organization for life. If he has done all he can to sever his connection with it before the particular incident was in contemplation, should he not be able to rely on the defence?

The risk to which D was exposing himself

In *Lewis*, D, who was serving a sentence for armed robbery, was savagely attacked in the prison yard by E, who was serving a sentence for the same robbery. D refused to testify against E because he was terrified of reprisals and was charged with contempt of court. It was held that duress ought to have been left to the jury as a defence to that charge. There was no evidence that D knew that he was exposing himself to the risk of this *sort of threat* when he participated in the armed robbery with E much earlier in time.

Initially the courts held that D would be denied the defence only where he voluntarily put himself in a position where he was aware of the risk of being subjected to pressure by way of violence *to commit offences of the type alleged* (*Baker and Ward*[136]). Subsequently a stricter view has been adopted. D will be denied the defence if he exposed himself to unlawful threats more generally: *Heath*,[137] *Harmer*.[138] Despite the cogent academic criticism of this approach,[139] the House of Lords in *Hasan* has now confirmed this strict view. Lord Bingham explained that:

The defendant is, *ex hypothesi*, a person who has voluntarily surrendered his will to the domination of another. Nothing should turn on foresight of the manner in which, in the event, the dominant party chooses to exploit the defendant's subservience. There need not be foresight of coercion to commit crimes, although it is not easy to envisage circumstances in which a party might be coerced to act lawfully.[140]

In *Ali*[141] the Court suggested a very narrow approach whereby D could not rely on the defence if he foresaw/ought to have foreseen that he was likely to be subjected to compulsion by threats. The court drew on the approval by Lord Bingham of the trial judge's direction in *Hasan*.[142] The approach in *Ali* and in *Hasan* is to deny the defence not on the basis of D's association with a criminal gang, but on associating with anyone he ought to have foreseen *might* put him under compulsion by threats.

---

136 [1999] 2 Cr App R 355.

137 *Heath* [2000] Crim LR 109 (indebted drug user, aware that he might be subjected to threats, required to transport £300k of cannabis), distinguishing *Baker and Ward* (above) (inadequate direction).

138 [2002] Crim LR 401.

139 As JC Smith noted in commenting on *Heath* [2000] Crim LR 109, 'it is one thing to be aware that you are likely to be beaten up if you do not pay your debts, it is another that you may be aware that you may be required under threat of violence to commit other, though unspecified crimes, if you do not'.

140 [37]. cf Baroness Hale's example of the battered woman compelled to perform lawful tasks of ironing [77].

141 [2008] EWCA Crim 716.

142 'Did the defendant voluntarily put himself in the position, in which he knew he was likely to be subjected to threats? You look to judge that in all the circumstances … if someone voluntarily associates with the sort of people who he knows are likely to put pressure on him, then he cannot really complain, if he finds himself under pressure. If you are sure that he did voluntarily put himself in such a position, the defence fails and he was guilty. If you are not sure and you have not been sure about all of the other questions, then you would find him not guilty.' [14]

D's awareness of the risk to which he is exposing himself

Hasan confirms that the duress defence is unavailable where the risk to which D exposes himself is pressure to commit any crime. A further question arises whether the defence can only be denied D where he is proved to have been aware of that risk (subjectively), or whether it is sufficient that he ought to have been aware of that risk (objectively). As a matter of policy the House of Lords in *Hasan* suggests that the test is whether D ought to have known. Again this restricts the availability of the defence.[143]

In *Ali* the Court of Appeal took the objective approach, holding that duress is not available if D *ought to have foreseen* that the others might threaten him. The interpretation will operate very harshly for those involved in, *inter alia*, drug misuse. Many users of drugs will associate themselves with drug dealers and in many, if not most cases, the users ought to realize that the dealer might be likely to threaten them with violence. If the dealer does threaten the user with violence unless the user commits crimes (usually to pay the dealer), the user will be denied the defence of duress.[144] Baroness Hale's minority speech in *Hasan* adopts a more subjective approach, suggesting that the defence is denied only where D has himself foreseen a risk that he will be compelled by threats of violence to commit crime. It is submitted this is preferable approach, but it is not the law.

The policy of the law is clearly to discourage association with known criminals, and to be slow to excuse the criminal conduct of those who do so. If a person voluntarily becomes or remains associated with others engaged in criminal activity in a situation where he knows or ought reasonably to know that he may be the subject of compulsion by them or their associates, he cannot rely on the defence to excuse any act which he is thereafter compelled to do by them. It is not necessary in this case to decide whether or to what extent that principle applies if an undercover agent penetrates a criminal gang for *bona fide* law enforcement purposes and is compelled by the gang to commit criminal acts.[145]

(7) Offences to which duress/duress of circumstances available

Duress by threats has been accepted as a defence to manslaughter,[146] criminal damage,[147] arson,[148] theft,[149] handling,[150] perjury and contempt of court,[151] perverting the course of justice,[152] offences under the Official Secrets Acts[153] and drug offences.[154] The courts have also assumed that it would apply to buggery[155] (presumably therefore to sex offences under the 2003 Act) and conspiracy[156] to defraud. It is available to strict liability crimes,[157] but, depending on the terms of the offence, not always to status crimes.[158]

---

[143] cf Baroness Hale commenting on the attractions of the subjectivist approach advanced by the Law Commission [75].

[144] cf *Heath* [2000] Crim LR 109. See also *Lal* [2010] EWCA Crim 2393.

[145] Lord Bingham at [38].

[146] *Evans and Gardiner* [1976] VR 517 and (*No 2*) 523.

[147] *Crutchley* (1831) 5 C & P 133.

[148] *Shiartos* (Lawton J, 19 Sept 1961, unreported but referred to in *Gill* (below).

[149] *Gill* [1963] 2 All ER 688, [1963] 1 WLR 841, CCA.

[150] *A-G v Whelan* [1934] IR 518.

[151] *K* (1983) 78 Cr App R 82, CA; *Lewis* (1992) 96 Cr App R 412.

[152] *Hudson v Taylor* [1971] 2 QB 202.

[153] *Shayler* [2001] Crim LR 986.

[154] *Valderrama-Vega* [1985] Crim LR 220; *Ortiz* (1986) 83 Cr App R 173.

[155] *Bourne* (1952) 36 Cr App R 125.

[156] *Verrier* [1965] Crim LR 732. In *Abdul-Hussain*, [1999] Crim LR 570, the court doubted whether duress can be a defence to conspiracy; but if it is a defence to doing the act, it must surely be a defence to agreeing to do it.

[157] *Eden DC v Braid* [1998] COD 259.

[158] See *New Forest Magistrates v E* [2007] EWHC 2584 (Admin), below, n 160.

Duress of circumstances has been held to be a defence to various road traffic offences to hijacking, contrary to s 1(1) of the Aviation Security Act 1982[159] and to unlawful possession of a firearm. It now seems safe to say that either kind of duress may be a defence to any crime,[160] except some forms of treason, murder and attempted murder.[161]

Duress and treason

Although it is not uncommon for treason to be mentioned as a crime where duress is not a defence, it is quite clear that it may be a defence to at least some forms of treason.[162] As long ago as 1419 in *Oldcastle*'s case,[163] the accused, who were charged with treason in supplying victuals to Sir John Oldcastle and his fellow rebels, were acquitted on the grounds that they acted through fear of death and desisted as soon as they could. The existence of the defence was admitted, *obiter*, by Lee CJ in *M'Growther*,[164] a trial for treason committed in the 1745 rebellion and by Lord Mansfield in *Stratton*:[165]

if a man is forced to commit acts of high treason, if it appears really force, and such as human nature could not be expected to resist and the jury are of that opinion, the man is not guilty of high treason.

Much more recently, in *Purdy*,[166] Oliver J directed a jury that fear of death would be a defence to a British prisoner of war who was charged with treason in having assisted with German propaganda in the Second World War. Against this, Lord Goddard CJ said in *Steane*[167] that the defence did not apply to treason, but this remark appears to have been made *per incuriam*. Treason is an offence which may take many forms varying widely in seriousness and it would be wrong to suppose that threats, even of death, will necessarily be a defence to every act of treason. In *Oldcastle*'s case,[168] Hale emphasizes that the accuseds' act was *only* furnishing of victuals and he appears to question whether, if they had taken a more active part in the rebellion, they would have been excused. Stephen thought the defence only applied where the offender took a subordinate part.

Duress and murder[169]

It was stated in the books from Hale onwards that duress could not be a defence to a charge of murder. As Blackstone put it, a man under duress 'ought rather to die himself than escape by the murder of an innocent'.[170] There was, however, no clear judicial authority in point and in 1969 in *Kray*,[171] an inroad was made into the supposed rule when Widgery LJ said that a person charged as an accessory before the fact to murder might rely on duress. In 1975, in *Lynch v DPP for Northern Ireland*,[172] the House of Lords, by a majority of three

---

[159] *Abdul-Hussain* [1999] Crim LR 570.

[160] Its use in relation to a charge under s 444 of the Education Act 1996, where a parent was charged with failing to secure the attendance of a child was doubted: *New Forest Local Education Authority v E* [2007] EWHC 2584 (Admin). Richards LJ stated that the section 'looks not to the conduct of the parent or even to the parent's failure to act, but simply to whether the child has failed to attend regularly at school and whether the defendant is the parent of that child. There is no obvious scope for a defence that the parent acted or failed to act by reason of some necessity or duress of circumstances', at [10].

[161] It is not available to civil tax penalties: *Mu v Customs and Excise* [2001] STI VADT.

[162] [1975] AC 653, [1975] 1 All ER at 920, per Lord Morris; 940, per Lord Simon; 944, per Lord Kilbrandon. In *Gotts* [1992] 2 AC 412, [1992] 2 WLR 284 at 300, Lord Lowry excepts 'most forms of treason'. This passage was cited by Lord Bingham in *Hasan*.

[163] (1419) Hale, I PC, 50, East, I PC, 70.

[164] (1746) Fost 13, 18 State Tr 391.

[165] (1779) 21 State Tr 1045.

[166] (1946) 10 JCL 182.

[167] [1947] KB 997 at 1005, [1947] 1 All ER 813 at 817.

[168] (1419) Hale, I PC, 50.

[169] See LCCP 177, Ch 7; LC 304, Ch 6

[170] Blackstone, *Commentaries*, iv, 30.

[171] [1970] 1 QB 125, [1969] 3 All ER 941.

[172] [1975] AC 653.

to two, held that a person charged with aiding and abetting murder – one who would have been a principal in the second degree under the law of felonies – could have a defence of duress. The position of the actual killer was left open and in *Abbott*[173] in 1976, again by three to two, the Privy Council distinguished *Lynch* and held that the defence was not available to the principal offender, the actual killer. This was an illogical and unsatisfactory position because it is by no means always the case that the actual killer is the most dominant or culpable member of a number of accomplices, but he alone was now excluded from the defence. The distinctions involved were technical and absurd.[174] Accordingly, when the matter came before the House in *Howe*,[175] there was a strong case for either going forward and allowing the defence to all alleged parties to murder, or backward, and allowing it to none. The House chose the latter course, overruling its own decision in *Lynch*. The speeches emphasize different aspects, but the following reasons for the decision appear among them.

(1) The ordinary person of reasonable fortitude, if asked to take an innocent life, might be expected to sacrifice his own.[176] Lord Hailsham would not 'regard a law as either "just"; or "humane" which withdraws the protection of the criminal law from the innocent victim and casts the cloak of its protection on the coward and the poltroon in the name[177] of a "concession to human frailty."'

(2) One who takes the life of an innocent person cannot claim that he is choosing the lesser of two evils.[178]

(3) The Law Commission had recommended[179] 10 years previously that duress should be a defence to the alleged principal offender, but Parliament had not acted on that recommendation.[180]

(4) Hard cases could be dealt with by not prosecuting – in some cases the person under duress might be expected to be the principal witness for the prosecution[181] – or by the action of the Parole Board in ordering the early release of a person who would have had a defence if duress had been an available defence.[182]

It is submitted that none of these reasons is at all convincing.[183]

(i) If the defence were available, it would apply only when a jury thought a person of reasonable fortitude *would* have yielded to the threat. The criminal law should not require

---

[173] [1977] AC 755, [1976] 3 All ER 140.

[174] *Graham* [1982] 1 All ER 801 at 804 per Lane LCJ. See also IH Dennis, 'Duress Murder and Criminal Responsibility' (1980) 106 LQR 208.

[175] [1987] AC 417, [1987] 1 All ER 771, [1987] Crim LR 480 (sub nom *Burke*) and commentary. See also H Milgate, 'Duress and the Criminal Law: Another About Turn by the House of Lords' [1988] CLJ 61; L Walters, 'Murder under Duress and Judicial Decision Making in the House of Lords' (1988) 18 LS 61; Horder, *Excusing Crime*, 133–137.

[176] *Howe* [1987] 1 All ER 771 at 779–780.

[177] Referring to the 5th edition of this book, at 215.

[178] Lord Hailsham, *Howe* (above) at 780. Art 2 of the ECHR will be engaged in cases of intentional killing.

[179] Lord Bridge, ibid, at 784 and Lord Griffiths at 788.

[180] Law Commission, *Defences of General Application* (Law Com No 83).

[181] Lord Griffiths, *Howe* (above) at 790.

[182] Lord Griffiths, ibid, at 791 and Lord Hailsham at 780–781. In non-murder cases the suggestion that the defence should be kept within strict limits and that no injustice will result because of the availability of sentencing discretion met with approval from Lord Bingham in *Hasan*, at [22], but cf Baroness Hale for convincing arguments against.

[183] This opinion was endorsed by Judge Stephen who, with Judge Cassese, was, however, dissenting in *Prosecutor v Drazen Erdemovic* (Case No IT-96–22-A) in the Appeals Chamber of the International Tribunal for the Prosecution of Persons for Serious Violations of International Humanitarian Law in the Former Yugoslavia. For an interesting discussion of whether the defence of duress ought to have been available to someone charged with war crimes for killing innocent civilians when he was threatened with death if he did not comply, see L Chiesa, 'Duress, Demanding Heroism, and Proportionality' (2008) 41 Vanderbilt Jnl of Transnational Crime 741.

heroism. Moreover, there are circumstances in which the good citizen of reasonable fortitude not only would, but probably should, yield to the threat because –

(ii) to do so might clearly be to choose the lesser of two evils, as where the threat is to kill D and all his family if he does not do, or assist in, an act which he knows will cause grievous harm but not death (though, *ex hypothesi*, it has resulted in death and so constitutes murder).

(iii) Parliament's failure to act on the Law Commission recommendation proves nothing. The Government has not given Parliament the opportunity to consider the matter. By parity of reason, Parliament might be taken to have approved of *Lynch*'s case, because there has been no move to overrule it.

(iv) Even if he were not prosecuted, the 'duressee' would be, in law, a murderer and, if he were called as a prosecution witness, the judge would, at that time, have been required to tell the jury that he was an accomplice in murder on whose evidence it would be dangerous to act in the absence of corroboration. A morally innocent person should not be left at the mercy of administrative discretion on a murder charge.

There is clearly a strong argument for reversing *Howe*.[184] Lord Bingham recently suggested that the logic of the argument is 'irresistible'.[185] *Wilson*[186] illustrates the difficulties when duress cannot be a defence to a charge of murder, even if the person seeking to rely on that defence is a child and even if his alleged role in the murder was that of a secondary party acting out of fear of an adult perpetrator. The 13-year-old defendant was not able to plead duress, but argued instead that he had 'not known what he was doing in that his mind did not go with his actions'.[187] The Court of Appeal observed in *Wilson* that there 'might be grounds for criticising' a rule that denied a child any defence to a charge of murder on the grounds of adult or parental duress, but had no choice but to apply the law as it stood.[188]

The Law Commission in its *Murder, Manslaughter and Infanticide* Report recommended allowing the defence to the charge of murder, but controversially, recommended reversing the burden of proof.[189] The Commission setting out the arguments for and against the defence applying in murder cases,[190] addresses a range of options and concludes, rightly it is submitted, that if the jury find that the accused acted under duress within all the stringent requirements of the defence, he ought to be totally exonerated.[191]

Attempted murder and other related offences

In *Howe*, only Lord Griffiths[192] expressed a clear view that duress is not a defence to attempted murder but it has since been so held by a majority of three to two in *Gotts*.[193] This is logical. If it were otherwise the effect would be that an act, excusable when done, would become

---

[184] On the need for reform see A Reed, 'The Need for a New Anglo American Approach to Duress' (1996) 61 J Crim L 209.

[185] *Hasan* at [21].

[186] [2007] EWCA Crim 1251.

[187] His police interview did not support this defence, but suggested that he acted under duress from his father – the very defence he was precluded from running.

[188] See commentary by A Ashworth [2008] Crim LR 138.

[189] LC 304, para 6.116. See also LCCP 177 in which the Commission took a different view. cf O Quick and C Wells, 'Getting Tough with Defences' [2006] Crim LR 514.

[190] LCCP 177, paras 7.18–7.19.

[191] LC 304, para 6.53.

[192] *Howe* (above) at 780 and 790.

[193] [1992] 2 AC 412, [1992] 1 All ER 832, HL. Lord Lowry, dissenting, thought it is 'the stark fact of death' which distinguishes murder from all other offences. See S Gardiner, 'Duress in Attempted Murder' (1991) 107 LQR 389. The issues are discussed in LCCP 177, para 7.60.

inexcusable if death resulted. But logic would also require the exclusion of the defence on a charge under s 18 of the Offences Against the Person Act 1861 of causing grievous bodily harm with intent because here also, the offence becomes murder if death results from it. A distinction might be made between murder committed with intent to kill, where duress would not be a defence, and murder committed with intent to cause serious bodily harm, where it would. This would be reconcilable with the traditional statement of the law – a person 'ought rather to die himself than escape by the murder of an innocent' – which seems to postulate a decision to kill; but *Howe* seems too emphatic and uncompromising a decision to allow of any such refinement. *Gotts* indicates that the line is to be drawn below attempted murder, leaving the defence applicable to conspiracy to murder and assisting or encouraging murder.

There is no point in raising the defence of duress to a murder charge; but suppose, as is frequently the case, that the evidence is such that the jury might properly acquit of murder and convict of manslaughter. If there is evidence that D may have been acting under duress[194] it is submitted that the judge should direct the jury that they must not convict of manslaughter either, unless they are sure that D was not acting under duress.

12.2.2 Duress of circumstances

12.2.2.1 The emergence of the defence[195]

The recognition of this defence occurred, more or less by accident, in *Willer*.[196] D was charged with reckless driving after he had driven very slowly on a pavement in order to escape from a gang of youths who were obviously intent on doing violence to him and his passengers. The trial judge declined to leave the defence of necessity to the jury. The Court of Appeal quashed D's conviction. They said that there was no need to decide on any defence of necessity that might have existed because 'the defence of duress[197] arose but was not pursued', as it ought to have been. It should have been left to the jury to say whether D drove 'under that form of compulsion, ie, under duress'. But this was not an instance of the previously recognized defence of duress by threats – the youths were not saying, 'Drive on the pavement – or else...' There is a closer analogy with self-defence.[198] But in substance the court was simply allowing the defence of necessity which it purported to dismiss as unnecessary to the decision. It should surely make no difference whether D drove on the pavement to escape from the youths, or a herd of charging bulls, a runaway lorry, or a flood, if he did so in order to escape death or serious bodily harm.

Subsequent cases have not dismissed *Willer* as a case decided *per incuriam*. They have treated it as rightly decided but have recognized that it is not the long-established defence of duress but an extension of it, 'duress of circumstances', the relationship of which to necessity has not been settled (see below). In *Conway*,[199] another case of reckless driving, D's passenger, Tonna, had been the target of an attack on another vehicle a few weeks earlier when another man was shot and Tonna had a narrow escape. According to D, when two young men in civilian clothes came running towards D's parked car, Tonna shouted hysterically, 'Drive off'. D drove off because he feared a deadly attack on Tonna. Being pursued by the two men in an unmarked vehicle, he drove in a manner which the jury adjudged to be reckless. The two men

---

[194] cf *Gilmour* [2000] 2 Cr App R 407 where D was roused from his bed and, unwillingly, drove the terrorist murderers to and from the scene of the crime.

[195] See S Gardner, 'Necessity's Newest Invention' (1991) 11 OJLS 125.

[196] (1986) 83 Cr App R 225.

[197] The 'very different' defence of duress according to the court in *Denton* (1987) 85 Cr App R 246 at 248.

[198] Below, p 379.

[199] [1989] QB 290, [1988] 3 All ER 1025.

were police officers who wished to interview Tonna. D's conviction was quashed because the defence of duress of circumstances had not been left to the jury.

Willer and *Conway* were followed in *Martin (Colin)*.[200] D, while disqualified, drove his stepson, who had overslept, to work. He said that he did so because his wife feared that the boy would lose his job if he were late and threatened to commit suicide if D did not drive him. The wife had suicidal tendencies and a doctor stated that it was likely that she would have carried out her threat. The defence ought to have been left to the jury. According to the Court of Appeal the defence:

can arise from other objective dangers threatening the accused or others.... the defence is available only if, from an objective standpoint, the accused can be said to be acting reasonably and proportionately in order to avoid a threat of death or serious injury.... [The] jury should be directed to determine these two questions: First, was the accused, or may he have been impelled to act as he did as a result of what he reasonably believed to be the situation he had good cause to fear that otherwise death or serious physical injury would result; Second, if so, would a sober person of reasonable firmness, sharing the characteristics of the accused, have responded to that situation by acting as the accused acted?[201]

On the facts, the case seems to be strictly a case of duress by threats, where D is told, 'Commit the crime or else...' The defence, as with duress by threats, is available only so long as the 'circumstances' continue to threaten. It may have been available (though the court did not decide the point) to a driver who drove off with excess alcohol in his blood to escape assailants; but it was not necessary for him to drive the two and a half miles to his home.[202] But where it was found that D, having consumed excess alcohol, drove off in fear of his life, he was guilty of an offence only if the prosecution could prove that he continued to drive after the terror ceased.[203] Similarly, in *Arnaot*,[204] where the court doubted there was any evidence that D was compelled by fear for her safety to drive dangerously following a road traffic incident.

In the recent case of *S and L*,[205] S was charged with an offence of using unlicensed guards and sought to plead 'necessity' in that he had to deploy unlicensed guards in an emergency. The Court of Appeal referred to the trial judge's 'immaculate judgment' containing a clear and correct statement of the law of 'necessity'. For such a defence there had to be material on which a reasonable jury might conclude that:

(i) it had not been possible for S to obtain a licence before the threat to the premises became so acute as to compel them to deploy unlicensed guards. Although no specific threat must be identified as a matter of law, in the absence of such, it may be very difficult to identify material fit to go to a jury;[206]

(ii) the deployment of the guards was directly caused by an immediate or imminent threat of death or serious injury;

(iii) no other means could reasonably have been taken to avoid the risk. The judge found that the material relied on by the defence did not support the ingredients of the defence.

With respect, this sounds very much like a defence of duress of circumstances rather than one of necessity.

---

[200] [1989] 1 All ER 652.

[201] Per Simon Brown J at 653.

[202] *DPP v Jones* [1990] RTR 34, DC. Nor to drive 72 miles when intoxicated to escape a threat, *DPP v Tomkinson*, above.

[203] *DPP v Bell (Derek)*, above, n 108. See also *Brown v CPS* [2007] EWHC 3274 (Admin).

[204] [2008] EWCA Crim 121.

[205] [2009] EWCA Crim 85.

[206] That is a rather ambiguous but potentially wide opportunity for a defence to be run.

The Court of Appeal is clearly anxious to keep a tight degree of control over the defence of duress of circumstances (as with duress by threats).[207] In *Quayle*,[208] the court heard a number of appeals and a related reference by the Attorney General. The issue in each case was whether the defence of necessity or 'necessity of circumstances' as it preferred to say, should be left to the jury in respect of offences of: possession, cultivation or production of cannabis where D genuinely and reasonably believed that such activities were necessary to avoid him suffering pain arising from a pre-existing medical condition or from conventional medicine to which he would otherwise resort to reduce the pain. Some of the appeals related to importation or possession with intent to supply cannabis for the purpose of alleviating pain suffered by others in similar circumstances. The defence argument was, in short, that the 'evil' of non-compliance with the Misuse of Drugs Act 1971 and the Customs and Excise Management Act 1979 was relatively minor compared with the risk of serious injury or pain to an individual defendant. It was argued that in any particular case it should be for the jury to weigh such potential ill-effects against the potential benefits to the particular defendant. This argument was supported by reference to the right to private life under Art 8 of the ECHR. The Crown argued, on policy grounds, that since Parliament had clearly and precisely regulated the medicinal use of drugs and had not provided for the use of cannabis there were strong public policy grounds against allowing the defence of necessity. Alternatively, if the policy argument was rejected, the defence of necessity was not made out: an accused who was seeking to avoid his own pain was unable to show that there was an extraneous circumstance allegedly causing the commission of the offence. Similarly, in the case of those who were seeking to avoid pain for others, they could not reasonably be said to have a responsibility towards those for whose benefit they claimed to be acting. The Attorney General submitted further that the defence of necessity did not include the avoidance of serious pain, and should not be extended (in the present context at least) to do so.

The Court of Appeal held there was no overarching principle applicable in all cases of necessity to be derived from individual authorities. 'Necessity' should be developed on a case by case basis. The court made more general comments about the defence of 'necessity', including that the defence required extraneous circumstances capable of objective scrutiny by judge and jury, capable of being checked and, where appropriate, met by other evidence. Otherwise abusive defences might arise.[209] It was emphasized also that there had to be an imminent danger of physical injury; otherwise, where pain was concerned (which required a large element of subjectivity in its assessment), there would be no clear objective basis by reference to which to test or determine the defence. Perhaps predictably, the court rejected the Art 8 argument, concluding that Parliament had sanctioned interference with the private life of the sufferer in its legislative policy.

In *Altham*,[210] the Court of Appeal dismissed an appeal in similar circumstances where the drug user who was convicted of possession sought to rely on Art 3 of the ECHR to support his claim of necessity. The Court of Appeal concluded that the condition of the appellant was made no worse by the State and that there was no Art 3 claim.

One further restriction which the Court of Appeal has recently sought to impose on the defence is, it is submitted, unwarranted. In *Jones*,[211] involving intentional criminal damage

---

[207] See, eg, statements in *Patel* [2010] EWCA Crim 976, [47]. Imminent danger that prevents a person from acting lawfully is a necessary ingredient of the defence.

[208] [2005] EWCA Crim 1415; see further the commentary at [2006] Crim LR 148.

[209] At para [73].

[210] [2006] EWCA Crim 07, discussed with commentary by Ashworth [2006] Crim LR 633.

[211] [2005] Crim LR 122. Discussed by S Gardner, 'Direct Action and the Defence of Necessity' [2005] Crim LR 371, although not on this point. For an analysis of the international law dimension to the case see R Cryer, 'Aggression at the Court of Appeal' (2005) 10 J of Conflict Law & Soc 209.

to an air force base in an attempt to prevent the USAF and UK services continuing their bombardment of Iraq, the defendants sought to rely, *inter alia*, on defences of duress of circumstances to the charges. In particular, the defendants argued that the war on Iraq was illegal in international law and that their actions were therefore necessary to avert that crime being committed on civilians in Iraq. On an interlocutory appeal, the Court of Appeal held that the defence was not available, declaring that it is limited to a case of D being faced with a crime in national law. With respect, that cannot be right. The defence was available to *Martin* when his wife was threatening suicide (not a crime), moreover one can envisage many circumstances in which D, or those for whom he is responsible, face a threat of death or serious injury by non-criminal means (for example, a rapidly engulfing forest fire leads D to steal a car to escape to safety). The House of Lords subsequently dealt with the appeal on the basis of the defence under s 3 of the Criminal Law Act 1967, and did not deal with the issues of duress of circumstances or necessity.[212]

12.3 Necessity

As with duress, we are again concerned with situations in which a person is faced with a choice between two unpleasant alternatives, one involving his committing a breach of the criminal law and the other some evil to himself or others. If the latter evil outweighs any evil involved in the breach of the letter of the law, it is arguable that the actor should have a defence of necessity. The courts have never recognized a defence in these broad terms and to what extent a defence of necessity prevails in English law is uncertain. As early as 1552, Sergeant Pollard in an argument which apparently found favour with the judges of the Exchequer Chamber said that breaking the letter of laws might be justified 'where the words of them are broken to avoid greater inconveniences, or through necessity, or by compulsion...'[213] More than 300 years later Stephen thought the law so vague that it was open to the judges to lay down any rule they thought expedient; and that the expediency of breaking the law in some cases might be so great that a defence should be allowed – but these cases could not be defined in advance.[214]

In spite of these doubts, Williams in 1953 submitted 'with some assurance' that the defence of necessity is recognized by English law[215] and, particularly, by the criminal law,[216] arguing that the 'peculiarity of necessity as a doctrine of law is the difficulty or impossibility of formulating it with any approach to precision'.

Williams' confidence was entirely justified. Lord Goff has, on several occasions recognized the existence of the defence and it was applied by the House of Lords in the *Bournewood Trust* case[217] to justify the detention of a person suffering from mental disorder where there was no statutory authority in point.[218] From an early period other particular instances of necessity were recognized. It was justifiable (in the conditions of those days) to pull down a house to

---

[212] [2006] UKHL 16, [2007] Crim LR 66.

[213] *Reniger v Forgossa* (1552) 1 Plowd 1 at 18.

[214] 2 HCL 108.

[215] 6 CLP, 216.

[216] CLGP, 724 et seq.

[217] [1998] 3 All ER 289, HL, at 297–298, 301–302.

[218] Note that the ECtHR in *HL v United Kingdom* (App No 45508/99) held that his being kept at Bournewood Hospital by doctors against the wishes of his carers under the common law of necessity amounted to a breach of Art 5(1) of the ECHR (deprivation of liberty) and of Art 5(4) (right to have lawfulness of detention reviewed by a court). Section 50 of the Mental Health Act 2007 amends the Mental Capacity Act 2005 so that it is unlawful to deprive a person of his liberty in a hospital or care home unless a standard or urgent authorization under Sch A1 to the 2005 Act is in force, or under an order of the Court of Protection.

prevent a fire from spreading,[219] for a prisoner to leave a burning gaol contrary to the express words of a statute, and for the crew of a ship or a passenger[220] to jettison the cargo in order to save the lives of the passengers. It was once held that prison officials may – indeed, must – forcibly feed prisoners if that is necessary to preserve their health and, *a fortiori*, their lives.[221] It was a defence to the statutory felony of procuring an abortion to show that the act was done in good faith for the purpose only of preserving the life of the mother,[222] although at that time there was no provision for such a defence in any statute.[223] More recently it has been recognized that a constable may direct other persons to disobey traffic regulations if that is reasonably necessary for the protection of life and property.[224]

An important case law development is the emergence of duress of circumstances above, which in many cases is treated simply as an instance of necessity. On some occasions the court has even merged the terms as in *Quayle* where the reference is to 'necessity of circumstance'. The relationship of the defences is discussed below. Despite the explicit recognition of the defence the courts adopt a persistently restrictive approach to its application. There is an underlying anxiety that the defence must be kept within strict limits to prevent defendants claiming generally that they thought their actions in breaking the law were reasonable and represented the lesser of two evils. This would be a Trojan horse for anarchy.[225] The speech of Lord Bingham in *Hasan* underlined these judicial anxieties with defences of circumstantial pressure.

12.3.1 Nature of threat

The traditional examples of necessity – escaping from the burning gaol, etc – do, like duress and duress of circumstances, involve danger to life. In relation to lesser threats, writers from Hale[226] onwards have denied that necessity can be defence to a charge of theft of food or clothing. In modern times, Lord Denning has justified that limit on the ground that '. . . if hunger were once allowed to be an excuse for stealing, it would open a door through which all kinds of lawlessness and disorder would pass'.[227]

In that case, a civil action, it was held that homelessness did not justify even an orderly entry into empty houses owned by the local authority: 'If homelessness were once admitted as a defence to trespass, no one's house could be safe. Necessity would open a door which no man could shut'.[228] Probably, it is now the law that if the taking or the entry was necessary to prevent death or serious injury through starvation or cold there would be a defence of duress of circumstances; but if it were merely to prevent hunger, or the discomforts of cold or homelessness, there would be no defence.

---

[219] See now the Criminal Damage Act 1971, below, Ch 29.

[220] *Mouse's Case* (1608) 12 Co Rep 63.

[221] *Leigh v Gladstone* (1909) 26 TLR 139 (Alverstone LCJ), not followed by Thorpe J in *Secretary of State for the Home Department v Robb* [1995] 1 All ER 677. The decision is heavily criticized – see G Zellick, 'The Forcible Feeding of Prisoners: An Examination of the Legality of England Therapy' [1976] PL 153 at 159 – and no longer applied in practice.

[222] *Bourne* [1939] 1 KB 687, [1938] 3 All ER 615. cf *Morgentaler* (1975) 20 CCC (2d) 449 (SCC), discussed by L Leigh, 'Necessity and the Case of Dr Morgentaler' [1978] Crim LR 151.

[223] See now Abortion Act 1967, below, Ch 16 and *T v T* [1988] 1 All ER 613, Fam Div.

[224] *Johnson v Phillips* [1975] 3 All ER 682, [1976] 1 WLR 65, DC. cf *Wood v Richards* [1977] RTR 201, [1977] Crim LR 295, DC.

[225] cf Norrie, *Crime Reason and History*, at 160.

[226] I PC, 54, and see Blackstone, *Commentaries*, iv, 31.

[227] *Southwark London Borough v Williams* [1971] 2 All ER 175 at 179.

[228] ibid.

There are some cases where what was in substance a defence of necessity was allowed without identifying a threat to life or serious injury. In *Gillick*'s case, one of the conditions stated of the lawfulness of the contraceptive advice or treatment given to a girl under 16, was that unless she receives it 'her physical or mental health or both are likely to suffer'.[229] In *F v West Berkshire Health Authority*,[230] it was held that it was lawful to carry out a sterilization operation on a woman who lacked the mental capacity to consent because otherwise there would be a grave risk of her becoming pregnant which would be disastrous from a psychiatric point of view.[231] Lord Goff founded his judgment on necessity. These cases would, however, involve at most a slight extension of duress of circumstances – comparable to MacNaghten J's interpretation of 'preserving the life of the mother' to include preserving her from becoming 'a physical or mental wreck' in *Bourne*,[232] a case which must now be regarded as one of duress of circumstances. Lord Goff has also said, 'That there exists a defence of necessity at common law, which may in 'some circumstances be invoked to justify what would otherwise be a trespass to land, is not in doubt. But the scope of the defence is by no means clear'. He found it unnecessary to decide the important question raised in that case, whether the defence could justify forcible entry (which would otherwise be a crime) into the private premises of another in the *bona fide*, but mistaken, belief that there exists an emergency on the premises by reason of the presence there of a person who has suffered injury and who may require urgent attention.[233]

12.3.1.1 Statutory implication or exclusion of necessity defence

In England it has been argued that there is a principle of statutory interpretation:

that it requires clear and unambiguous language before the courts will hold that a statutory provision was intended to apply to cases in which more harm will, in all probability, be caused by complying with it than by contravening it.[234]

This principle, if it exists, seems to be little noticed in modern times. In *Buckoke v Greater London Council*,[235] Lord Denning MR said, *obiter*:

A driver of a fire engine with ladders approaches the traffic lights. He sees 200 yards down the road a blazing house with a man at an upstairs window in extreme peril. The road is clear in all directions. At that moment the lights turn red. Is the driver to wait for 60 seconds or more, for the lights to turn green? If the driver waits for that time, the man's life will be lost.

Lord Denning accepted the opinion of both counsel that the driver would (at that time) commit an offence against the Road Traffic Regulations if he crossed the red light. But the threat to the fictional man at the upstairs window seems to be no less than the threat to Willer, to the passenger in Conway's car or to Martin. Lord Denning was stating the effect of the law as he then believed it to be; but he added that the hypothetical driver 'should not

---

229 Per Lord Fraser [1986] AC 112 at 174.

230 [1989] 2 All ER 545, HL.

231 See now the Mental Capacity Act 2005.

232 [1939] 1 KB 687, [1938] 3 All ER 615, below, p 614.

233 *Richards and Leeming* (on appeal from 81 Cr App R 125) (10 July 1986, unreported), HL. The House agreed with Lord Goff's speech (thanks to Sir Anthony Hooper for this material). By s 17(5) of the Police and Criminal Evidence Act 'all the rules of common law under which a constable has power to enter premises without a warrant are hereby abolished'. But does this abolish a justification which (if it exists at all) is available, not only to constables, but to persons generally?

234 P Glazebrook, 'The Necessity Plea in English Criminal Law' [1972A] CLJ 87 at 93.

235 [1971] 1 Ch 655, [1971] 2 All ER 254 at 258. Statutory regulations now exempt the driver of the fire engine; but a contractor with a ladder on his lorry might find himself in the same position.

be prosecuted. He should be congratulated' – so he might welcome this development. As Professor Packer says:

> it seems foolish to make rules (or to fail to make exceptions to rules) that discourage people from behaving as we would like them to behave. To the extent that the threat of punishment has deterrent efficacy, rules such as these would condition people confronted with dilemmas to make the wrong choice, either through action or inaction. And the actual imposition of punishment would serve no useful purpose since we assume these people are not in need of either restraint or reform.[236]

The terms of a statute may, in effect, 'build in' a defence of necessity or, on the other hand, positively exclude one; and in either of these situations there is no room for the application of a general, common law defence. *Quayle*[237] is a good example of the courts rejecting a possible defence on the basis of the conflict it would create with a statutory scheme in which no such defence for possession or supply of drugs was included. A defence of duress by threats or of 'necessity by circumstances' might be available where the general scheme and policy of the legislation was not in question, but the use of cannabis on an individual basis conflicted with the purposes and effect of the legislation.

12.3.1.2 Necessity and responses to non-criminal threats

As noted in the case of *Jones* above, the Court of Appeal sought to limit the defence to cases where D faced a criminal threat (in fact it was stipulated that the crime must be one under national law not international law). It is submitted that no such restriction applies. D may rely on the defence where he is faced with naturally occurring disasters, accidents caused by human actors or criminal threats.

12.3.1.3 Necessity and negligence?

In *DPP v Harris*,[238] McCowan LJ was inclined to think that necessity can never be a defence to what would otherwise be the offence of driving without due care because the term 'due' in the section allows for consideration of all the circumstances that would be taken into account if the general defence applied. In *Backshall*,[239] the court preferred the opinion of Curtis J who thought it contrary to common sense to allow the defence in relation to the graver offence of reckless (now dangerous) driving and not to the lesser offence of careless driving; but the court recognized that it may make no difference. A person driving as a necessity, as required, is not failing to exercise 'due' care. The reasoning of McCowan LJ might be applicable to any crime where the prosecution must prove that an act was done unreasonably: if it was necessary so to act, it could hardly be unreasonable to do so. In *Harris*, the court was concerned with a statutory regulation which prescribes the circumstances in which a fire, police or ambulance vehicle may cross a red light; and such a specific provision may well be taken to exclude a defence of necessity when such a vehicle crosses in other circumstances. In *Harris*, all was *obiter* because the court found that there was no necessity for D to drive as he did.

---

[236] H Packer, *The Limits of the Criminal Sanction* (1969) 114.

[237] [2005] EWCA Crim 1415.

[238] [1995] 1 Cr App R 170, [1995] Crim LR 73, DC. Curtis J thought that if necessity (in effect, duress of circumstances) applied to reckless driving, it must apply to the lesser offence of careless driving. cf *Symonds* [1998] Crim LR 280.

[239] [1999] 1 Cr App R 35 at 41.

12.3.1.4 Necessity in strict and situational liability offences

In *Cichon v DPP*,[240] the court held that prohibition against allowing a pit bull terrier to be unmuzzled in a public place was 'absolute' and said that it followed that Parliament had excluded any defence of necessity; but if a general defence such as self-defence, duress – or necessity – is available even in offences requiring *mens rea*, it should *a fortiori* be available to an offence of strict liability. If the owner had removed the dog's muzzle on the orders of an animal rights fanatic armed with a sawn-off shotgun, he would surely have had a defence of duress. So too with necessity – though the fact that the dog in *Cichon* was afflicted with kennel cough might well be held insufficient to ground any such defence.

In *New Forest Educational Authority v E*[241] the court held that the mother of a truanting child could not plead duress to a charge of 'being a parent of a child of compulsory school age' who was truanting.[242] The offence required no act by the mother, and thus the threats (from the child) could not affect her liability. Presumably no defence of necessity would be available to her either, which is a harsh result indeed, and seems wrong in principle.

12.3.1.5 Necessity and murder

One of the reasons given by the House of Lords in *Howe*[243] for refusing to allow a defence of duress to murder was that it had been decided in the famous case of *Dudley and Stephens*[244] that necessity was not a defence to murder. Whether that was the *ratio decidendi* of the case has been debated. One interpretation of the judgment is that the court found that no necessity existed[245] and the House of Lords has now held that the case does decide the point. The facts are well known, three men and a boy of the crew of a yacht were shipwrecked. After 18 days in an open boat, having been without food and water for several days, the two accused suggested to the third man that they should kill and eat the boy. He declined but, two days later, Dudley killed the boy who was now very weak. The three men then fed on the boy's body and, four days later, they were rescued. The accused were indicted for murder. The jury, by a special verdict, found that the men would probably have died within the four days had they not fed on the boy's body, that the boy would probably have died before them and that, at the time of the killing, there was no appreciable chance of saving life, except by killing one for the others to eat. The accused were convicted of murder, but the sentence was commuted to six months' imprisonment.

In *Dudley and Stephens*,[246] Lord Coleridge CJ examined the pronouncements of writers of authority and found nothing in them to justify the extension of a defence to such a case as this. Killing by the use of force necessary to preserve one's own life in self-defence was a well-recognized, but entirely different, case from the killing of an innocent person. Moreover, '[i]f...Lord Hale is clear – as he is – that extreme necessity of hunger does not justify larceny, what would he have said to the doctrine that it justified murder?'[247]

Apart from authority, the court clearly thought that the law ought not to afford a defence in such a case. They thought, first, that it would be too great a departure from morality;

---

[240] [1994] Crim LR 918, DC.

[241] [2007] EWHC 2584 (Admin)

[242] Education Act 1996, s 444.

[243] [1987] AC 417 at 429, 453, above, see J Donoghue (2011) 74 MLR 216, p 235 et seq.

[244] (1884) 14 QBD 273. On the instructions of Huddleston B the jury found the facts in a special verdict and the judge then adjourned the assizes to the Royal Courts of Justice where the case was argued before a court of five judges (Lord Coleridge CJ, Grove and Denman JJ, Pollock and Huddleston BB).

[245] Arguably this case is one of duress of circumstances as there is a threat of death or serious injury posed by the circumstances.

[246] On the case generally, see AWB Simpson, *Cannibalism and the Common Law* (1984).

[247] (1884) 14 QBD at 283.

and, secondly, that the principle would be dangerous because of the difficulty of measuring necessity and of selecting the victim. The second reason is more convincing:

Who is to be the judge of this sort of necessity? By what measure is the comparative value of lives to be measured? Is it to be strength or intellect, or what? It is plain that the principle leaves to him who is to profit by it to determine the necessity which will justify him in deliberately taking another's life to save his own.[248]

Williams finds as the 'one satisfying reason' in the judgment that it was no more necessary to kill the boy than one of the grown men and adds: 'To hinge guilt on this would indicate that lots should have been cast...'[249] If the boy had agreed to be bound by the casting of lots, he would have been consenting to die; and arguably, consent in such a situation may be a defence. Captain Oates took his life when he left Scott and his companions; yet he was regarded, not as a criminal, but as a hero.[250] If the boy had not consented, the drawing of lots would be hardly more rational than trial by ordeal – yet more civilized than a free-for-all. In fact, the court disapproved, *obiter*, of a ruling in an American case, *United States v Holmes*,[251] that the drawing of lots in similar circumstances would legalize a killing. Holmes, a member of the crew of a wrecked ship, was cast adrift in an overcrowded boat. In order to prevent the boat sinking, the mate gave orders to throw the male passengers overboard and Holmes assisted in throwing over 16 men. No doubt, if his act was criminal at all, it was murder; but a grand jury refused to indict him for murder and so he was charged with manslaughter. The judge directed that the law was that passengers must be preferred to seamen; only enough seamen to navigate the boat ought to have been saved; and the passengers whom necessity requires to be cast over must be chosen by lot. As this had not been done (none of the officers or crew went down with the ship) the jury found him guilty.

Stephen thought the method of selection 'over refined'[252] and Lord Coleridge thought this 'somewhat strange ground... can hardly... be an authority satisfactory to a court in this country'.[253]

The English judges offered no alternative solution and, presumably, their view was that, in the absence of a self-sacrificing volunteer, it was the duty of all to die. This was also the view of the distinguished American judge, Cardozo J:

Where two or more are overtaken by a common disaster, there is no right on the part of one to save the lives of some, by the killing of another. There is no rule of human jettison.[254]

The principle in *Dudley and Stephens* is distinguishable if there is no problem of selection. D, a mountaineer who cuts the rope seconds before he would be dragged over a precipice by E, his falling companion, surely commits no offence. There is no question of choosing between D and E. E is going to die in a matter of seconds anyway. The question is whether he alone should die a few seconds earlier, or whether they should both die seconds later. At the inquest following the Zeebrugge disaster a witness, an army corporal, gave evidence that he and numerous other passengers were trapped in the stricken ferry and in grave danger of drowning. A possible way of escape up a rope ladder was barred by a man, petrified by cold or fear, who could move neither up nor down. After fruitless attempts to persuade him to move, the corporal ordered those nearer to push him off the ladder. They did so, he fell into the water and

---

[248] 14 QBD at 287.
[249] CLGP, 744.
[250] Should it matter that Oates killed himself?
[251] 26 Fed Cas 360 (1841).
[252] 2 HCL 108.
[253] 14 QBD at 285.
[254] *Selected Writings*, 390.

was not seen again. The trapped passengers were then able to climb up the ladder to safety. The coroner expressed the opinion that a reasonable act of self-preservation, or the preservation of others, is 'not necessarily murder'. So far as is known, no legal proceedings against the corporal were ever contemplated. Unlike the cabin boy, but like the falling mountaineer, the man frozen on the ladder was chosen by fate as the potential victim by his immobility there. He was preventing the passengers from going where they had a right and a most urgent need to go. He was, unwittingly, imperilling their lives.[255]

Similarly, the commander of an Australian naval ship 'took the decision to save the rest of his crew by sealing four sailors in the blazing engine room, consigning them to certain death, after rescuers were beaten back by the flames'.[256] It seems likely that the decision taken by the officer is that which any prudent officer of sound judgement would have taken. If so, it is inconceivable that he would ever be charged with, or convicted of, murder. Surely the law should recognize this. In these examples the evil avoided outweighs that caused – one dies instead of two, or instead of many – not only is there extreme duress – the conduct is justified. Indeed the Australian officer would probably have been in breach of his duty if he had allowed his ship and most of her crew to be lost. So, notwithstanding the approval of *Dudley and Stephens* by *Howe*, it is submitted that it would be premature to conclude that *necessity* (as opposed to duress) can never be a defence to murder.[257]

Re A – the conjoined twins

In the case of the conjoined twins,[258] the court held that, in the special circumstances of that case, it was lawful to kill the weaker twin, B, in order to save the life of the stronger, A. But this was not a simple choice between A and B, which the court would have been unwilling to make. The situation presented to the court was that if the operation was performed B would be killed but A would probably live – as indeed occurred – but, if the operation was not performed, both would die. Brooke LJ based his decision on necessity. The three requirements for the defence were stated to be:

(1) the act is needed to avoid inevitable and irreparable evil;

(2) no more should be done than is reasonably necessary for the purpose to be achieved; and

(3) the evil inflicted must not be disproportionate to the evil avoided.[259]

His lordship distinguished *Dudley and Stephens*. There was no problem of who was to be selected to be killed in this case. Like the man on the rope in the Zeebrugge case and the falling mountaineer dragging his companion to his death, A was selected by the circumstances. Brooke LJ preferred necessity to private defence (discussed below) because here there was no 'unjust' aggression by B. But B was imperilling A's life and the private defence solution avoids

---

[255] See, further, JC Smith, *Justification and Excuse*, Ch 3. And cf, self-defence against a 9-year-old or insane person.

[256] (1998) The Times, 5 May.

[257] In *Selvaratnam* [2006] EWCA Crim 1321, counsel sought to argue that necessity was a defence to murder. It was raised only on appeal and rejected swiftly by the court, at [35]. It is submitted that what counsel was seeking to rely on was duress of circumstances which, by analogy with *Howe*, is not available as a defence to murder under the present law.

[258] *Re A (Children)* [2000] 4 All ER 961, [2001] Crim LR 400 and commentary. See also J Rogers, 'Necessity, Private-Defence and the Killing Mary' [2001] Crim LR 515. cf the approach of the Canadian Supreme Court in *Latimer* [2001] 1 SCR 3, denying D a defence where he killed his severely disabled daughter. The court pronounced a defence based on three criteria: (i) imminent peril; (ii) no reasonable legal alternative being available; (iii) D's reaction being proportionate. See S Ost, 'Euthanasia and the Defence of Necessity' in C Erin and S Ost, *The Criminal Justice System and Health Care* (2007).

[259] *Re A (Children)*, above, at 1051.

the argument, valid or not, that necessity can never justify killing. Whatever its basis, the principle appears to be that it is lawful for D to kill B where, as D knows, B is doomed to imminent death but even the short continuation of his life will kill A as well.

Shooting down hijacked aircraft

Following the destruction of the World Trade Center in New York by hijacked aircraft, it now appears to be recognized that it would be lawful to shoot down a plane, killing all the innocent passengers and crew if this were the only way to prevent a much greater impending disaster. This is doubted by Bohlander,[260] but without reference to the explicit statements in the Select Committee on Defence,[261] making it clear that the Government policy is to permit shooting down of civilian aircraft in such circumstances and that the basis for such action would be by application of a necessity principle:

In the last resort, it might be necessary to shoot down the civilian aircraft. MoD officials assured us...that they had properly examined the legal aspects of any such decision...we have satisfied ourselves with lawyers that there is a proper basis for doing this.

The MoD and Committee took the view that the test to be applied is that the act will be necessary and proportionate if:

(1) the act is needed to avoid inevitable and irreparable evil;

(2) no more should be done than is reasonably necessary for the purpose to be achieved; and

(3) the evil inflicted must not be disproportionate to the evil avoided.[262]

Even if duress cannot be a defence to murder, it seems quite clear that necessity can.

The issue of intentional killing in order to save lives also arose in the most striking and tragic circumstances with the shooting of Jean Charles de Menezes at the Stockwell Tube Station on 22 July 2005. The police shot him dead, mistakenly believing that he was a suicide bomber. They used immediate lethal force because the use of anything less is futile when a suicide bomber is able to detonate a bomb by a single movement. No prosecution for murder or manslaughter was brought against the officers.[263] If they had been so prosecuted, a defence of private/self-defence would have been the principal defence.

12.3.1.6 A doctor's defence of necessity[264]

Without expressly acknowledging it, the courts appear to have recognized a special defence to murder by doctors. Although a doctor knows that treatment will accelerate the death of his patient significantly – that is, kill him – he is not guilty of murder if his purpose is to give what, in the circumstances as he understands them, is proper treatment to relieve pain.[265] Even if this is right, there remains the possibility, where the doctor has made a grossly negligent assessment of the circumstances, of a conviction for manslaughter.

---

[260] 'In Extremis? Hijacked Airplanes, Collateral Damage and the Limits of Criminal Law' [2006] Crim LR 579. See for detailed analysis T Hornle, 'Hijacked Planes: May they be Shot Down?' (2007) 10 New Criminal Law Review 582.

[261] Sixth Report, *Defence and Security in the UK 2001–2002*, HC 518-I, para 8.

[262] ibid, para 9.

[263] See *R (da Silva) v DPP* [2006] EWHC 3204 (Admin). See also J Rogers, 'Shoot, Identify and Repent?' (2005) 155 NLJ 1273

[264] See S Ost, 'Euthanasia and the Defence of Necessity' [2005] Crim LR 255, arguing that necessity would provide a better basis for a defence of euthanasia for doctors.

[265] Dr Moor's case, discussed by A Arlidge QC, 'The Trial of Dr David Moor' [2000] Crim LR 31 and a comment by JC Smith, 'A Comment on Dr Moor's Case' [2000] Crim LR 41. See also A Ashworth, 'Criminal Liability in a Medical Context: The Treatment of Good Intentions', in A Simester and ATH Smith (eds), *Harm and Culpability* (1996).

12.3.1.7 Necessity and a duty to act

Where D owes a duty of care to E it seems that necessity may impose on him a duty to act to the detriment of – even to kill – others. The Australian naval officer referred to above probably had a duty to kill the four sailors. While the doctors in the conjoined twins remained in control, they apparently had a duty to kill the weaker twin. When the 'conflict of duties'[266] is resolved, D must fulfil the prevailing duty. If A, B and C are members of a mountaineering party and A sees that B is dragging C to the deaths of both, is he not bound to cut the rope, accelerating B's death but saving the life of C, if he can do so without risk? But what about a passer-by, D, who found himself in the same position as A? Presumably he would be justified in cutting the rope but probably not bound to do so.[267]

12.3.1.8 Necessity in other jurisdictions

In other parts of the common law world a general defence of necessity is now recognized.[268]

The courts of Victoria have recognized the existence of a general, if limited, defence in *Loughnan*[269] where D's defence to a charge of escaping from prison was that he feared he would otherwise be killed by other prisoners – but the defence was not made out on the facts. In *Perka*,[270] the Supreme Court of Canada held that necessity may be an 'excuse' but not a 'justification' (there seems to be no practical difference except that it perhaps made the court feel better) for an act which is 'inevitable, unavoidable and afford(s) no reasonable opportunity for an alternative course of action that does not involve a breach of the law'.

The American Model Penal Code, which has been adopted in many states of the USA, propounds a general defence of necessity:

Conduct which the actor believes to be necessary to avoid a harm or evil to him or to another is justifiable, provided that:

(a) the harm or evil sought to be avoided by such conduct is greater than that sought to be prevented by the law defining the offence charged...[271]

No such general principle exists or is likely to be developed by English courts. Edmund Davies LJ has clearly formulated the judicial attitude:

the law regards with the deepest suspicion any remedies of self-help, and permits these remedies to be resorted to only in very special circumstances. The reason for such circumspection is clear – necessity can very easily become simply a mask for anarchy.[272]

Until recently, it seemed that, except in cases where necessity had already been recognized as a defence, the courts were likely to be satisfied by their power to grant an absolute discharge in hard cases.[273] Recent developments suggest they may now be more adventurous.

---

[266] See the discussion of the judgment of Wilson J in *Perka v R* (1984) 13 DLR (4th) 1 at 36 by Ward LJ at [2000]4 All ER 1015–1016, by Brooke LJ at 1048–1050 and by Walker LJ at 1065–1066.

[267] On the 'duty' to assist in such cases see Ch 4 above.

[268] See recently for a review of the position in Oceanic countries M Forsyth, 'The Divorce or the Marriage of Morality and Law?: The Defence of Necessity in Pacific Island Countries' (2010) 21 Criminal Law Forum 121.

[269] [1981] VR 443.

[270] (1984) 13 DLR (4th) 1.

[271] Art 3, s 3.02. It is subject to qualifications not necessary to be noted here. See the fascinating discussions in L Alexander, 'Lesser Evils: A Closer Look at the Paradigmatic Justification' (2005) 24 Law and Phil 611; M Berman, 'Lesser Evils: A Less Close Look' (2005) 24 Law and Phil 681.

[272] *Southwark London Borough v Williams* [1971] Ch 734, [1971] 2 All ER 175 at 181.

[273] Glazebrook [1972A] CLJ 87 at 118–119.

12.3.1.9 Reform of necessity

The Law Commission, departing from the views of its Working Party, at one time recommended that there should be no general defence of necessity; and that, for the avoidance of doubt, it should be enacted that any such defence as does exist is abolished.[274] They thought that provision should be made by statute for a defence to particular offences where appropriate. The Commission is now persuaded that the defence of duress of circumstances should be provided and it is to be found in cl 43 of their Draft Code. More recently, the Law Commission[275] has also accepted that as part of the policy of retaining common law defences, a 'specific defence of necessity should be kept open as something potentially separate from duress. That is provided for by clause 36(2) of the Criminal Law Bill, which expressly saves "any distinct defence of necessity" when abrogating the common law defences of duress by threats and of circumstances.' This provides a welcome confirmation.

The Code would leave it open to the courts to develop such a defence at common law and Lord Mustill in *Kingston*[276] recognized the ability of the courts to establish new defences, though he found no justification for doing so in that case. The conjoined twins case illustrates a more open judicial approach.

12.3.2 The relationship between duress, duress of circumstances and necessity[277]

It seems now to be generally accepted that duress and duress of circumstances will be treated as identical by the courts as regards all elements other than the obvious one of the source of the threat. This seems unobjectionable. However, in *S (DM)*,[278] it was stated that *Abdul-Hussain* 'reflects other decisions which have treated the defences of duress and necessity as being part of the same defence and the extended form of the defence [that is, duress of circumstances] as being different labels for essentially the same thing'.[279] But there are strong objections to this view.

(1) It is established that duress cannot be a defence to murder or attempted murder but, following *Re A* (the case of the conjoined twins) it is now clear that necessity may be.

(2) Imminent threats of death or grievous bodily harm are the only occasions for a defence of duress but not for necessity. It is surely a defence to a charge of battery that D was pushing a child to save him from some quite minor injury or even damage to his clothing. Suppose that in *Martin (Colin)* D's wife's threat had been, not to kill herself but to

---

[274] Law Com No 83, *Defences of General Application* (1977); criticized by G Williams, 'Necessity' [1978] Crim LR 128 under the Crim LR heading Defences of General Application: The Law Commission's Report No 83; R Huxley, 'Proposals and Counter-Proposals on the Defence of Necessity' [1978] Crim LR 141.

[275] Law Com No 218, *Legislating the Criminal Code: Offences Against the Person and General Principles* (1992).

[276] Above, p 313.

[277] See Wilson, *Central Issues*, Ch 10, p 303 et seq; I Dennis, 'On Necessity as a Defence to Crime: Possibilities, Problems and the Limits of Justifications and Excuses' (2009) 3 Criminal Law and Philosophy 29 examining the theoretical bases for the defence. See also P Westen and J Mangiafico, 'The Criminal Defense of Duress as Justification not Excuse and Why it Matters' (2003) 6 Buffalo Crim LR 833.

[278] [2001] Crim LR 986.

[279] C Clarkson, 'Necessary Action: A New Defence' [2004] Crim LR 81, has recently made a more radical suggestion that the defences of duress, necessity, duress of circumstances and self-defence should be collapsed into one defence of 'necessary action'. This would succeed in achieving its aim of avoiding the inconsistencies of the present law, but only by adopting a lowest common denominator for the defences which seems to be simply that the jury scrutinizes D's conduct to ascertain whether he faced a crisis and responded proportionately. It would be most unlikely to be adopted by the courts since they would be concerned that it opens the floodgates for spurious claims and perverse verdicts.

leave D; and suppose further that the consequences of her doing so would have been disastrous for D and his family. Duress of circumstances is not open. Should it be a defence for D to demonstrate that the break-up of his marriage would be a social disaster beside which any effect of his driving a short distance while disqualified would pale into insignificance?

(3) Necessity is a defence only if the evil D seeks to avoid would be greater than that which he knows he is causing whereas if D yields to torture which no ordinary person could be expected to resist, he should be excused however grave the consequences.

(4) Recent cases allowing evidence of the vulnerability to duress of the particular defendant have nothing to do with the proportionality of evils which is said to be required for necessity but are highly relevant to whether he should be excused for giving way to threats.

(5) Necessity may create a duty to act but mere duress can hardly do so.

(6) Duress is (generally accepted to be) an excuse, and necessity a justification.[280] It is quite inappropriate to talk of a surgeon's will being 'overborne' when he decides that it is necessary to carry out a sterilization or other operation, as in the *West Berkshire case*,[281] on a person who is unable to consent. The surgeon is making a reasoned and reasonable decision. Lord Brandon thought that not only would it be lawful, but that it would be the doctor's duty to operate. There is no question of excusing 'human frailty'. All this is true, *a fortiori*, of the decision of the court when it authorizes such an operation as in *Re A* (the conjoined twins).

It is disappointing that the appellate courts, and recently a Lord Chief Justice, are prepared to state that 'the distinction between duress of circumstances and necessity has, correctly, been by and large ignored or blurred by the courts'.[282]

12.4 Marital coercion

Though the terminology used by judges and writers is by no means uniform, the term 'coercion' is generally reserved for a special defence that was available at common law only *to a wife* who committed certain crimes in the presence of her husband. It was then presumed that she acted under such coercion as to entitle her to be excused, unless the prosecution were able to prove that she took the initiative in committing the offence. The exact extent of the defence at common law is uncertain. It did not apply to treason or murder; Hale[283] excluded manslaughter as well and Hawkins ruled out robbery.[284] Earlier authorities allowed the defence only in the case of felonies but later it seems to have been extended to misdemeanours – but excluding brothel-keeping; 'for this is an offence touching the domestic economy or government of the home in which the wife has a principal share'.[285]

Various theoretical justifications were advanced for the rule – the identity of husband and wife, the wife's subjection to her husband and her duty to obey him – but the practical reason for its application to felonies was that it saved a woman from the death penalty when her husband was able, but she was not, to plead benefit of clergy.[286] This reason disappeared in

---

[280] See on this S Gardner, 'Direct Action and the Defence of Necessity' [2005] Crim LR 371.

[281] Above, p 313.

[282] *Shayler* (above) para 55; in *Hasan* [2005] UKHL 22, Lord Bingham seems to use the term necessity interchangeably with duress, eg at [22].

[283] 1 PC, 45.

[284] 1 PC, 4; but the editor of the 8th edition (J Curwood) doubted this.

[285] Blackstone, *Commentaries*, iv, 29.

[286] Hale, I PC, 45; 2 Lew CC 232n.

1692 when benefit of clergy was extended to women, yet the rule continued and its scope increased.

In 1925, however, the presumption was abolished by the Criminal Justice Act 1925, s 47:

> Any presumption of law that an offence committed by a wife in the presence of her husband is committed under the coercion of the husband is hereby abolished, but on a charge against a wife for any offence other than treason or murder, it shall be a good defence to prove that the offence was committed in the presence of, and under the coercion of, the husband.

At first sight, it would seem that all Parliament has done is to shift the burden of proof. But there are difficulties about this, for the question at once arises, proof of what? And it is not very easy to answer. 'Coercion' at common law was really a fiction applied when the wife committed a crime in the presence of the husband and there was no evidence of initiative by the wife. The common law gives little guidance as to what is required now coercion is a matter of affirmative proof. In *Shortland*,[287] a case of procuring a passport by deception, the court said that the wife must prove on the balance of probabilities that her will was overborne by the wishes of her husband so that she was forced unwillingly to participate in the offence. Neither physical force nor the threat of it is required.

12.4.1 Coercion

Coercion is a wider defence than duress and is available to wives in addition to that general defence.[288] 'The Act can be regarded as merely an incomplete statement of the common law, and the common law still exists to supplement its deficiency'.[289] In the debate on the Criminal Justice Bill, the Solicitor General told the House that the section gives the married woman:

> a rather wider and more extended line of defence than pure compulsion, because coercion imports coercion in the moral, possibly even in the spiritual realm, whereas compulsion imports something only in the physical realm.[290]

The recommendation of the Avory Committee[291] that wives should be put in the same position as persons generally was not adopted. Far from there being the 'endless litigation' which one member feared there are only four reported cases[292] in which the defence has been relied on.[293] It is by no means clear what a wife has to prove to succeed – moral and spiritual, as distinct from physical, coercion are somewhat intangible.

12.4.2 Restriction of marriage

The defence is available only to a woman who is validly married to her coercer. The woman must prove on the balance of probabilities that she is married to him. It is not enough that she believes on reasonable grounds that she is validly married: *Ditta*[294] where Lord Lane seems to have questioned whether the defence applies in the case of an Islamic polygamous marriage.

---

[287] [1996] 1 Cr App R 116, [1995] Crim LR 893.

[288] CLGP, 765. See *Richman* [1982] Crim LR 507 (Bristol Crown Court).

[289] CLGP, 765, approved by Lord Edmund-Davies [1975] 1 All ER 954. See also Lord Wilberforce at 930.

[290] HC, vol 188, col 875 (1925).

[291] Cmd 1677.

[292] *Pierce* (1941) 5 JCL 124, *Richman, Ditta* and *Shortland*, supra. cf *Bourne* (below, p 614) where duress rather than coercion seems to have been relied on.

[293] Perhaps the view of Mr Greaves-Lord, MP, has proved correct: 'how many women are there who have been coerced like that, who dare go into the witness box in order to convict the very persons under whose coercion the woman had committed the crime?', HC, vol 188, col 870 (1925).

[294] [1988] Crim LR 43.

There are obvious difficulties with such a discriminatory definition of the defence. It is questionable whether it would be regarded as compatible with Art 14 of the ECHR if D was convicted and imprisoned (therefore suffering deprivation of liberty) or suffering some other penalty infringing her right to respect for private life (Art 8) when facing coercion which would have entitled her to rely on the defence had she been married to the threatening party. The defence seems to be restricted to the 'wife' but, if it is to be retained at all, there is an argument that it ought to be available to a party in a civil partnership under the Civil Partnerships Act 2004. But which party?

12.4.3 Reform of coercion

If the defence has any rational basis in the modern law, it must (however unfounded in fact) be that wives are, or may be, under such domination by their husbands that they ought to be excused from criminal liability by threats of much less gravity than will avail persons generally. If so, it ought to be available to a woman who has an honest and reasonable (or even unreasonable) belief that she is married to her coercer. There is no reason to suppose that a wife by an Islamic polygamous marriage is any less under this supposed domination by her husband than a wife by a monogamous marriage; or a woman who lives as the 'partner' of a man and under his domination. The defence is a relic of the past which ought to have been abolished long ago.

The Law Commission has recommended its abolition.[295]

12.5 Superior orders[296]

It is not a defence for D merely to claim that the act was done by him in obedience to the orders of a superior, whether military or civil. Where a security officer caused an obstruction of the highway by checking all the vehicles entering his employer's premises, it was no defence that he was obeying his employer's instructions.[297] Both the House of Lords and the Privy Council have asserted, probably *obiter*, that there is no defence of superior orders in English law.[298] Both approved the statement of the High Court of Australia[299] that 'It is fundamental to our legal system that the executive has no power to authorize a breach of the law and that it is no excuse for an offender to say that he acted under the authority of a superior officer.'

The fact that D was acting under orders may, nevertheless, be very relevant. It may negative *mens rea* by, for example, showing that D was acting under a mistake of fact or that he had a claim of right[300] to do as he did, where that is a defence; or, where the charge is one of negligence,[301] it may show that he was acting reasonably.

---

[295] Law Com No 83 (1977) paras 3.1–3.9. The Irish Law Reform Commission also recently recommended abolition of the defence: see LRC CP 39, *Consultation Paper on Duress and Necessity* (2006).

[296] See S Wallerstein, 'Why English Law Should Not Incorporate the Defence of Superior Orders' [2010] Crim LR 109 considering the influence of international law. See also P Rowe, 'The Criminal Liability of a British Soldier Merely for Participating in the Iraq War 2003' [2010] Crim LR 752, at 757.

[297] *Lewis v Dickson* [1976] RTR 431, DC.

[298] *Clegg* [1995] 1 All ER 334 at 344, HL, below, p 389; *Yip Chiu-cheung* [1994] 2 All ER 924 at 928, PC, below, p 389. The implications of *Clegg* for firearms officers and servicemen are considered in S Skinner, 'Citizens in Uniform: Public Defence, Reasonableness and Human Rights' [2000] PL 266; J Rogers, 'Justifying the Use of Firearms by Policemen and Soldiers: A Response to the Home Office's Review of the Law on the Use of Lethal Force' (1998) 18 LS 486.

[299] *A v Hayden (No 2)* (1984) 156 CLR 532 at 540.

[300] *James* (1837) 8 C & P 131.

[301] *Trainer* (1864) 4 F & F 105.

12.5.1 Military law

Since 1944, the *Manual of Military Law*[302] has asserted that the fact that a war crime was committed in pursuance of superior orders does not deprive the act in question of its character as a crime. The rule is capable of operating particularly harshly in the case of military orders. At one time it was asserted that a soldier may be 'liable to be shot by a court-martial if he disobeys an order and to be hanged by a judge and jury if he obeys it'.[303] Servicemen are trained to obey orders instantly so that their response to commands is almost a reflex action. Although it would not be realistic to suggest that the action was involuntary, there is a cogent argument that the serviceman should have a defence if he did not know that the order was illegal and it was not so manifestly illegal that he ought to have known it.[304] The so-called soldiers' dilemma has long been a source of controversy.[305] The *Manual of Service Law*[306] now provides that:

A person who is bound to obey a superior is under a legal duty to refuse to carry out an order received from that superior, to do some act or make some omission, if the order is manifestly illegal. If the illegal order is carried out, an offence may be committed. Where the order is not manifestly illegal, an accused will not be excused if they carried out the order and in doing so commits an offence. However, the accused may have a defence on other grounds because, for example, the order may negate a particular intent on the accused's part (which may provide a complete defence) or it may reduce the offence to one of a less serious nature or it may excuse what otherwise appears to be negligence. Evidence of superior orders which fall short of providing the accused with a defence to the offence may still be a strong mitigating factor.'[307]

In a South African case,[308] which has been much cited, Solomon J said:

I think it is a safe rule to lay down that if a soldier honestly believes he is doing his duty in obeying the commands of his superior, and if the orders are not so manifestly illegal that he must or ought to have known they are unlawful, the private soldier would be protected by the orders of his superior officer....

One old English authority[309] directly on the point holds that it is not a defence to a charge of murder for D to show that he fired under the mistaken impression that it was his duty to do so. D was, no doubt, making a mistake of law, but there is no finding as to its reasonableness.

---

[302] *Manual of Military Law* (1972) Part 1, Ch VI, para 24; Part III, para 627. See Ministry of Defence, *The Manual of the Law of Armed Conflict* (2004). See, generally, AP Rogers, *Law on the Battlefield* (2nd edn, 2004); On the relevant judicial process for such a plea see HHJ Blackett, *Rant on The Court Martial and Service Law* (3rd edn, 2009).

[303] AV Dicey, *Introduction to the Study of the Law of the Constitution* (10th edn, 1959) 303. cf Stephen, I HCL, 204–206, Williams, CLGP, 105 and TBCL, 455–456, and Commander J Blackett, as he then was, (1944) RUSI Journal, Feb, p 12. See also DB Nichols, 'Untying the Soldier by Refurbishing the Common Law' [1976] Crim LR 181.

[304] See I Brownlee, 'Superior Orders – Time for a New Realism' [1989] Crim LR 396; see also for an interesting overview in the context of mistreatment of Iraqi prisoners, G Solis, 'Obedience to Orders' (2004) 2 J Int Crim Just 988; JN Maogoto, 'The Defence of Superior Orders', in O Olusanya (ed), *Rethinking International Criminal Law* (2007).

[305] See recently Wallerstein (above) and P Rowe, above n 296. See also *R(Smith) v Assistant Deputy Coroner for Oxfordshire* [2009] EWCA Civ 441 [105] per Clarke MR. Cf the argument by Wallerstein above rejecting as a sufficient basis for the defence that the subordinate faces the dilemma of disobeying an order or the criminal law.

[306] MOD, *Manual of Service Law*, (2011).

[307] Vol 1, s 2, para 1–12–7.

[308] *Smith* (1900) 17 SCR 561, 17 CGH 561. But the case has not always been followed in South Africa. See Burchell and Hunt, SACLP, 298–299.

[309] *Thomas* (1816) Ms of Bayley J, JWC Turner and AL Armitage, *Cases on Criminal Law* (1964) 67. For an instance of a concealed defence of superior orders, see *Salford Area Health Authority, ex p Janaway* [1989] AC 537, [1988] 2 WLR 442, CA; affd sub nom *Janaway v Salford Area Health Authority* on other grounds [1989] AC 537, [1988] 3 All ER 1079, HL, discussed, Smith, *Justification and Excuse*, 70–72.

12.5.2 Other provisions dealing with the defence

In an international context, the Statute of the International Criminal Court provides in Art 30 that 'the commission of a crime pursuant to an order of a government or of a superior does not relieve a person of criminal responsibility unless: (a) that person is under a legal obligation to obey orders of the government or the superior in question; (b) the person did not know that the order was unlawful; (c) the order was not manifestly unlawful'.[310]

The position of the superior officer is also worth noting. Under s 65 of the International Criminal Courts Act 2001 (ICC Act), criminal liability arises in English law for commanders and other superiors who fail to prevent crimes of their subordinates under the ICC Act: genocide, crimes against humanity, and war crimes or where the superior fails to submit the matter to the competent authorities for investigation and prosecution.

12.6 Public and private defence[311]

Force causing personal injury, damage to property, or even death may be justified or excused because the force was reasonably used in the defence of certain public or private interests. Public and private defence is therefore a general defence to any crime of which the use of force is an element or which is alleged to have been committed by the use of force.[312] The use of the word 'unlawfully' in a statutory definition is a reminder of the existence of the general defences but they apply whether or not the statute uses that word[313] unless expressly or impliedly excluded. It is clear that the burden of disproving claims of public or private defence rests on the prosecution.[314]

The law is to be found in a variety of sources. Defence of the person, whether one's own or that of another, is still regulated by the common law (a defence of private defence as it is called in this chapter); defence of property by the Criminal Damage Act 1971; and arrest and the prevention of crime by s 3 of the Criminal Law Act 1967. Because of its haphazard growth, the law contains some inconsistencies and anomalies. In many cases the common law plea of self-defence overlaps with the plea under s 3 of the Criminal Law Act 1967. It is important to bear in mind that s 3 is only available where D uses force in the prevention of a crime. If D is attacking someone who is not committing a crime, he must fall back on the common law as now largely restated in s 76 of the Criminal Justice and Immigration Act 2008 (CJIA). Although the principles are very similar, technically they are different defences. Section 76 provides:[315]

Reasonable force for purposes of self-defence etc.

(1) This section applies where in proceedings for an offence –

    (a) an issue arises as to whether a person charged with the offence ('D') is entitled to rely on a defence within subsection (2), and

---

[310] By Art 33(2) all orders to commit genocide or crimes against humanity are manifestly unlawful. See further H McCoubrey, 'From Nuremberg to Rome: Restoring the Defence of Superior Orders' (2001) 50 ICLQ 386, and Wallerstein above. Rowe, above, n 296 asserts that a soldier should disobey an order that will impose criminal liability on him under international law, n 296.

[311] See, *inter alia,* F Leverick, *Killing in Self-Defence* (2006); B Sangero, *Self Defence in Criminal Law* (2006).

[312] *Renouf* [1986] 2 All ER 449 (reckless driving). Force was not an element of the offence of reckless driving (now abolished) but the use of force was alleged to constitute the recklessness in that case.

[313] *Renouf,* above; *Rothwell* [1993] Crim LR 626.

[314] The judge must give clear direction on the issue: *O'Brien* [2004] EWCA Crim 2900.

[315] Section 76 fails to clarify the law (cf s 76(9)), seeking merely to put some common law on a statutory footing.

(b) the question arises whether the degree of force used by D against a person ('V') was reasonable in the circumstances.

(2) The defences are –

(a) the common law defence of self-defence; and

(b) the defences provided by section 3(1) of the Criminal Law Act 1967....

(9) This section is intended to clarify the operation of the existing defences mentioned in subsection (2).

(10) In this section –

(a) 'legitimate purpose' means –

(i) the purpose of self-defence under the common law, or

(ii) the prevention of crime or effecting or assisting in the lawful arrest of persons mentioned in the provisions referred to in subsection (2)(b);

(b) references to self-defence include acting in defence of another person; and

(c) references to the degree of force used are to the type and amount of force used.

12.6.1 General principle

The defences at common law and under s 3, as now both also regulated by s 76, can be conveniently described in terms of trigger and response – the trigger being D's belief that the circumstances render it reasonable or necessary for him to use force, and the response being his use of a proportionate amount of force to the threat he believes he faces.[316] The general principle is that the law allows such force to be used as is objectively reasonable in the circumstances as D genuinely believed them to be. The trigger is assessed subjectively; the response objectively. For example, if D believed that he was being attacked with a deadly weapon and he used only such force as was reasonable to repel such an attack, he has a defence to any charge of an offence arising out of his use of that force. It is immaterial that he was mistaken. Indeed, it is immaterial that he was unreasonably mistaken. Section 76 of the 2008 Act confirms this established common law principle.

In terms of the force D uses in 'response' to the threat as he genuinely perceives it to be, the question, 'Was the force used reasonable in the circumstances as D supposed them to be?'[317] is a question to be answered by the jury or magistrates having regard to s 76. If D's use of force was reasonable on the threat he believed he faced, he is not liable for any harm that arises, even if the reasonable force he uses results in some greater harm which he had not foreseen. For example, D wrestles with V who is trying to steal D's wallet. V dies of a heart attack. If it was reasonable to use the amount of force to wrestle with V, D commits no offence even though it would not have been reasonable to kill V. In the recent case of *Keane*[318] Hughes LJ summarized the law on these general principles set out in this paragraph.

12.6.1.1 D's belief in need for force – the trigger – is subjectively assessed[319]

Section 76(3) of the Criminal Justice and Immigration Act 2008 provides:

---

[316] See recently Wilson [2005] Crim LR 108.
[317] But not in relation to 5 of the Criminal Damage Act 1971, below, p 1024.
[318] [2010] EWCA Crim 2514. See also *Noye* [2011] EWCA Crim 650 at [9] and [55].
[319] See Leverick, *Killing in Self Defence*, Chs 5 and 9.

(3) The question whether the degree of force used by D was reasonable in the circumstances is to be decided *by reference to the circumstances as D believed them to be*, and subsections (4) to (8) also apply in connection with deciding that question. (emphasis added).

By s 76(4) of the 2008 Act:

If D claims to have held a particular belief as regards the existence of any circumstances –

- (a) the reasonableness or otherwise of that belief is relevant to the question whether D genuinely held it; but

- (b) if it is determined that D did genuinely hold it, D is entitled to rely on it for the purposes of subsection (3), whether or not –
  - (i) it was mistaken, or
  - (ii) (if it was mistaken) the mistake was a reasonable one to have made.

Section 76(4) makes clear that the reasonableness of the force D uses is to be assessed on the facts and circumstances as D genuinely believed them to be, even if his belief as to the circumstances was mistaken and unreasonable.

The common law authority for the proposition that D is to be judged on the facts as he believed them to be is *Gladstone Williams*,[320] repeatedly applied in the Court of Appeal[321] and by the Privy Council in *Beckford v R*. Williams was charged with an assault occasioning actual bodily harm to V. D's defence was that he was preventing V from committing an assault on X. But V may have been lawfully arresting X. The jury was directed that if V was acting lawfully, D had a defence only if he believed *on reasonable grounds* that V was acting unlawfully. It was held that this was a misdirection. D had a defence if he honestly held that belief, reasonably or not. The court referred to the recommendation of the Criminal Law Revision Committee that the common law of self-defence should be replaced by a statutory defence providing:

a person may use such force as is reasonable in the circumstances as he believes them to be in the defence of himself or any other person.[322]

The court declared that this proposition represented the common law, as stated in *Morgan*[323] and *Kimber*.[324]

If D is voluntarily intoxicated he cannot rely on any mistaken belief attributable to that intoxication: s 76(5).[325]

12.6.1.2 Reasonableness of force – the response – is to be assessed objectively

The reasonableness of D's response and the amount of force used are to be assessed objectively on the facts as D believes them to be. By s 76(6) of the 2008 Act.

---

[320] (1984) 78 Cr App R 276, CA. But, where D is drunk, see *O'Grady* [1987] QB 995 and *Hatton* [2005] EWCA Crim 2951 discussed above, p 324.

[321] *Jackson* [1985] RTR 257; *Asbury* [1986] Crim LR 258, CA; *Fisher* [1987] Crim LR 334, CA; *Beckford v R* [1988] AC 130, [1987] 3 All ER 425, PC. Failure to follow this closely will render the conviction unsafe see *Duffy v Cleveland* [2006] EWHC 3169 (Admin).

[322] Fourteenth Report, para 72(a). The phrase 'may use' is inappropriate. The CLRC was concerned only with establishing a defence in criminal proceedings. The act should not be regarded as justified in the civil law; and, if the mistake was grossly negligent and caused death, it might be manslaughter.

[323] [1976] AC 182.

[324] [1983] 3 All ER 316, CA (D guilty of indecent assault only if he did not believe V was consenting and 'couldn't care less').

[325] See Ch 11, p 324 above.

The degree of force used by D is not to be regarded as having been reasonable in the circumstances as D believed them to be if it was disproportionate in those circumstances.

At common law, in *Shaw (Norman) v R*,[326] the Privy Council accepted the proposition that in determining whether D's response by using force is proportionate, D is to be judged on the circumstances *and danger* as he believed them to be. This is, it is submitted a preferable approach. It was endorsed by the Court of Appeal in *Harvey*.[327]

D's belief that he is doing only what is reasonable may be evidence, but no more, that it was reasonable.[328] Lord Morris has said:[329]

If there has been an attack so that defence is reasonably necessary it will be recognized that a person defending himself cannot weigh to a nicety the exact measure of his necessary defensive action. If a jury thought that in a moment of unexpected anguish a person attacked had only done what he honestly and instinctively thought was necessary that would be most potent evidence that only reasonable defensive action had been taken. A jury will be told that the defence of self-defence, where the evidence makes its raising possible, will only fail if the prosecution show beyond doubt that what the accused did was not by way of self-defence.

This principle relates to self-defence but similar considerations apply to force used to prevent crime or to effect an arrest, etc.

12.6.1.3 Evidence of D's beliefs

There may be an issue as to what circumstances D genuinely believed to exist, especially where his claimed belief is, viewed objectively, an unreasonable one. In such a case evidence of D's personal characteristics must, in principle, be admissible in so far as they bear upon his ability to be aware of, or to perceive, the circumstances.[330] Sections 76(4)–(8) of the CJIA seek to explain, based on the common law, what may be relevant to the question of D's beliefs. In particular, under s 76(7) in deciding whether D had a genuine belief in the need to use force:

the following considerations are to be taken into account (so far as relevant in the circumstances of the case) –

(a) that a person acting for a legitimate purpose may not be able to weigh to a nicety the exact measure of any necessary action; and

(b) that evidence of a person's having only done what the person honestly and instinctively thought was necessary for a legitimate purpose constitutes strong evidence that only reasonable action was taken by that person for that purpose.

By s 76(8):

Subsection (7) is not to be read as preventing other matters from being taken into account where they are relevant to deciding the question mentioned in subsection (3).

---

[326] [2002] Crim LR 140, [2002] 1 Cr App R 10, PC.

[327] [2009] EWCA Crim 469.

[328] *Scarlett* [1993] 4 All ER 629 appeared to have significantly modified this rule but *Owino* [1996] 2 Cr App R 128, [1995] Crim LR 743, CA and *DPP v Armstrong-Braun* [1999] Crim LR 416, DC, decide that *Scarlett* in no way qualifies the law as stated in *Gladstone Williams* (1984) 78 Cr App R 276.

[329] *Palmer v R* [1971] 1 All ER 1077 at 1078, PC, applied in *Shannon* (1980) 71 Cr App R 192, [1980] Crim LR 438 and *Whyte* [1987] 3 All ER 416.

[330] Remorse is not necessarily evidence of reasonableness on D's part: *Dewar v DPP* [2010] EWHC 1050 (Admin).

At common law, *Martin (Anthony)*[331] decided, on policy grounds, that psychiatric evidence that D would have perceived the supposed circumstances as being a greater threat than would a normal person is not admissible. The court rejected an analogy with provocation[332] where such evidence would be admissible because provocation applied only to murder and was not a complete defence. But the court did not consider duress where such evidence is admissible for a defence which applies to virtually all crimes except murder and is a complete defence. In *Martin (DP)*,[333] psychiatric evidence was admitted that D was suffering from a schizoid affective disorder which made him more likely than a normal person to regard things said as threatening, and to believe that threats would be carried out. The court in *Martin (Anthony)* conceded that evidence of D's *physical* characteristics may be admissible. Circumstances which would not be seen as threatening by a robust young man may appear so to a frail elderly woman. The enactment of s 76(8) might lead to a renewed argument on the relevance of D's personal characteristics.

There is no clear coherence of approach between the extent to which the personal characteristics of the defendant are relevant to the defences of duress, loss of self-control[334] and self-defence. There may be good reason for this if each of the defences has a separate theoretical foundation, but the courts continue to make occasional comparisons between the defences without exploring the theoretical distinctions, explaining the bases for taking different approaches, nor even adopting a consistent approach within each defence. Since private defence is accepted as a justificatory and complete defence there may be stronger case for imposing an objective test in private defence.

Within self-defence, the balancing of the characteristics of the relevant individuals can give rise to difficult issues. What of the relatively slight woman who uses lethal force against a physically stronger male whom she believes is about to attack her?[335] The Law Commission in its 2004 consideration of the Partial Defence to Murder recognized the difficulty that this posed in many trials and recommended a new Judicial Studies Board Direction:

It is insufficient to weigh the weapons used on each side; sometimes there is an imbalance in size and strength. You must also consider the relationship between the defendant and [the other party]. A defendant who has experienced previous violence in a relationship may have an elevated view of the danger that they are in. They may honestly sense they are in greater danger than might appear to someone who has not lived through their experiences. All these matters should be taken into account when considering the reasonableness of the force used.[336]

12.6.1.4 The effect of the Human Rights Act 1998

There are arguments of some force[337] that the effect of Art 2 of the ECHR – the right to life – may be to invalidate the principle of *Gladstone Williams* and *Beckford* that a defendant is to

---

[331] [2002] Crim LR 136.

[332] See, below, p 506.

[333] [2002] 2 Cr App R 42.

[334] Under the defence of loss of control in the Coroners and Justice Act 2009 any circumstances which affected D are relevant otherwise than if they affected only his ability to exercise self-control and restraint, p 508, below.

[335] She might now rely on s 54 of the Coroners and Justice Act 2009 if she had lost self-control. If she had not lost self-control she must rely on the defence of self-defence.

[336] Law Com No 290, *Partial Defences to Murder* (2004) para 4.14 (adapted from suggested formulation by Justice For Women). cf s 76(7). See Crown Court Benchbook (2010) Ch 16.

[337] By A Ashworth, commenting on *Andronicou and Constantinou v Cyprus*, ECHR, 9/10/97, [1998] Crim LR 823. But see Buxton LJ, 'The Human Rights Act and the Substantive Criminal Law' [2000] Crim LR 331 at 336–337. See F Leverick, 'The Use of Force in Public or Private Defence and Article 2' [2002] Crim LR 347; JC Smith, 'The Use of Force in Public or Private Defence and Article 2' [2002] Crim LR 958; and F Leverick, 'The Use

be judged on the facts as he genuinely, though unreasonably believed them to be. Article 2 provides:

(1) Everyone's right to life shall be protected by law. No one shall be deprived of his life intentionally save in the execution of a sentence of a court following his conviction of a crime for which this penalty is provided by law.

(2) Deprivation of life shall not be regarded as inflicted in contravention of this article when it results from the use of force which is no more than absolutely necessary:

    (a) in defence of any person from unlawful violence;

    (b) in order to effect a lawful arrest or to prevent the escape of a person lawfully detained;

    (c) in action lawfully taken for the purpose of quelling a riot or insurrection.

It is argued by some eminent commentators including in particular Ashworth and Leverick that the present English law may be incompatible with this provision since a person's right to life is not sufficiently protected if he may be killed by force used without reasonable grounds.[338]

The arguments of incompatibility highlight a number of issues. First, the Article allows for life to be taken only where 'absolutely necessary'. A defendant in England could be acquitted even though his attack turns out to have been completely unnecessary. Furthermore, the European Court has underlined the restrictive nature of the exceptional circumstances in which killing is permitted.[339] In *McCann v UK* and in *Andronicou*, the Court has referred to the fact that the accused must have had 'good grounds' to use force. This looks like an objective test, which is not what English law requires: *Gladstone Williams* requires only a genuine belief in the need to use such force. Finally, it is noted that Art 2 restricts the circumstances in which a life may be taken to purposes of quelling riots, etc or in defence of unlawful *violence*. In English law, it is possible for a defendant to be acquitted where he uses lethal force even in response to an attack merely on property.[340]

Despite these arguments of incompatibility, it is not clear that Art 2 or the ECtHR's jurisprudence (which is typically vague) *demands* a change in the law to an objective test. The test of 'absolute necessity' applied in Strasbourg is not an inflexible one. Moreover, the ECtHR has not condemned English law which it has had the opportunity to do. The European Court's test was reiterated recently in *Bubbins v UK*[341] where the Court stated that D had an 'honest belief which was perceived for good reason to be valid at the time but which was mistaken'. There was no outright condemnation of the English test. As Emmerson and Ashworth[342] point out, the truth is that there is no case yet before the Strasbourg Court in which a use of lethal force in English law has been based on a wholly irrational mistake. If such a case arose, the court would have to face the conflict between the Strasbourg jurisprudence and English law. In recent pronouncement from the English courts, it has been accepted that the current rules of English law on the use of potentially lethal force by the police are not incompatible with the European Convention: *R (Bennett) v HM Coroner for Inner London*.[343] The proceedings involved judicial review of a coroner's decision. B's son had died as a result of

---

of Force in Public or Private Defence and Article 2: A Reply to Professor Sir John Smith' [2002] Crim LR 963. See also Leverick, above, n 311, Ch 10; Ashworth, POCL, 115.

[338] See Leverick, previous note.

[339] See *Andronicou*, para 171; *Gul v Turkey* (2002) 34 EHRR 28, para 77; *McCann v UK* (1996) 21 EHRR 95. More recently, see *Ramsahai v Netherlands* (2006) 43 EHRR 39; *Huohuanainen v Finland* [2007] EHRLR 472.

[340] See the Joint Committee on Human Rights 15th Legislative Report 2007–8, para 2.35.

[341] [2005] 41 EHRR 458. See N Martin (2006) 69 MLR 249 for comment.

[342] HR & CJ, para 18.33.

[343] [2006] EWHC 196 (Admin).

being shot by a police officer. A witness had told the police that the deceased was carrying a gun and two firearms officers attended the scene. In 30 seconds, one officer fired six shots, four of which struck the deceased in the back and side and one of which was fatal. At the inquest the coroner decided not to leave a verdict of unlawful killing to the jury and the jury returned a verdict of lawful killing. B sought judicial review on the grounds that the coroner's direction on self-defence had failed to pay heed to Art 2. In the High Court, Collins J held, having regard to the case law, that:

the European Court of Human Rights has considered what English law requires for self defence, and has not suggested that there is any incompatibility with Article 2. In truth, if any officer reasonably decides that he must use lethal force, it will inevitably be because it is absolutely necessary to do so. To kill when it is not absolutely necessary to do so is surely to act unreasonably. Thus, the reasonableness test does not in truth differ from the Article 2 test as applied in *McCann*.

The Court of Appeal upheld that decision.[344]

Looking at the subject more broadly, one can argue that notwithstanding some unguarded language by the Criminal Law Revision Committee and the courts, English law does not say that D may take the life of another where there are no reasonable grounds for doing so. It says only that he is not guilty of a criminal offence, if he believes honestly though unreasonably that such ground exists. Parliament has now endorsed that principle in s 76. Where D's belief is unreasonable that will of course be a powerful reason for disbelieving his account and convicting him. The killing is unlawful, but not criminal. D remains liable in tort. But that is not all. The criminal law itself provides protection. If D's mistake is so unreasonable as to amount to gross negligence, D will be guilty of manslaughter.[345] That is, D will be guilty of criminal homicide if the jury think his conduct bad enough to amount to a crime – or, as is submitted below, bad enough to deserve condemnation as manslaughter. The criminal law therefore does offer some protection. The fact that it is a conviction for manslaughter with a maximum life sentence cannot mean that the protection is inadequate. The right to life of the road user can hardly be said to be insufficiently protected against the dangerous motorist because he is guilty only of manslaughter and not murder.

Moreover, most force used in public or private defence is not intended to, and does not have, fatal results. Is the *Beckford* principle to be outlawed only where it has fatal results? There would not seem to be any logic in that. The alternative is that it is invalidated entirely. It is submitted that this would be an undesirable and unnecessary conclusion and the English courts should not arrive at it unless compelled to do so. The present law, at least as regards protection against violence to the person, balances the need to protect life – and limb – against the ordinary rights of persons accused of crime.

In addition to the right to life guaranteed in Art 2, the European Court has recognized that the rights in Arts 3 (freedom from torture and inhuman and degrading treatment) and 5 (right to liberty) are subject to an implied exception for injuries inflicted in self-defence.[346] D, who is protecting himself against an unlawful attack from V, will not infringe V's Art 5 rights by detaining him to prevent further attack.

---

[344] [2007] EWCA Civ 617. The basis of appeal was principally that it had been a misdirection not to direct the jury to consider whether the officer's claim to have acted in self-defence was reasonable in light of the requirement in the relevant ACPO manual to reassess at all times whether it was 'absolutely necessary' to shoot.

[345] cf Leverick [2002] Crim LR 347 at 361. See Leverick, *Killing in Self Defence*, Ch 10 See on the need for careful direction *Maddocks* [2006] EWCA Crim 3112. Use of lethal force is a last resort: *Noye* [2011] EWCA Crim 650.

[346] *Rivas v France* [2005] Crim LR 305; *RL v France* [2005] Crim LR 306.

12.6.2 Force used in the course of preventing crime or arresting offenders

The common law on this subject was both complex and uncertain;[347] but, by the Criminal Law Act 1967, s 3:

(1) A person may use such force as is reasonable in the circumstances in the prevention of crime, or in effecting or assisting in the lawful arrest of offenders or suspected offenders or of persons unlawfully at large.

(2) Subsection (1) above shall replace the rules of the common law on the question when force used for a purpose mentioned in the subsection is justified by that purpose.[348]

Section 3 states a rule both of civil and criminal law. When the force is 'reasonable in the circumstances' it is justified in every sense. No civil action or criminal proceeding will lie against the person using it. The section says nothing specifically about any criminal liability of the user of the force. When that is in issue the ordinary principles of *mens rea* should apply. The use of force may be unjustified in the civil law because it is not in fact 'reasonable in the circumstances'; but D, while liable in tort, may nevertheless be excused from criminal liability if it was 'reasonable in the circumstances *as he believed them to be*'. It has been held in a civil action in Northern Ireland[349] that, for the purpose of an identical provision, the objectives of the use of force are to be determined, not by the evidence of the user of the force, but by the court, applying an objective test. D, a soldier, said that his purpose in shooting was to arrest the occupants of a vehicle whom he believed on reasonable grounds to be determined terrorists who would probably continue to commit terrorist offences if they got away; but the court held that the use of force was not reasonable to make an arrest but was justified because it was reasonable to prevent crime.[350] If this is right (and it is a persuasive opinion) in a civil action, it is also right in criminal law. The only difference is that in the criminal case, D need not have reasonable grounds for his honest belief in the circumstances.

In *Ashley and Others v Chief Constable of Sussex Police,*[351] the House of Lords compared self-defence when used as a defence to a criminal charge and a defence in civil proceedings. In both criminal and civil proceedings, the conduct/degree of force in self-defence must objectively be reasonable but, in judging what was reasonable, the court must in either case have regard to all the circumstances, including the fact that the action may have been taken in the heat of the moment. However, there are differences: (i) In cases of mistaken self-defence an honest but unreasonable mistake may operate as a defence only in criminal proceedings. In civil proceedings, a mistaken view of the facts provides no defence in the absence of reasonable grounds for that mistake. (ii) The burden of proof is different: in criminal proceedings, the burden of negativing self-defence is on the prosecution; but in civil proceedings the burden is on the defendant to establish that he acted in reasonable self-defence.[352]

---

[347] See the 1st edition of this book, at 230–238.

[348] See s 76 of the Criminal Justice and Immigration Act 2008, above, p 379.

[349] *Kelly v Ministry of Defence* [1989] NI 341. On whether the defence applies to British soldiers abroad see P Rowe, above, n 296.

[350] The ECtHR (App No 17579/90) observed that the 'prevention of crime' does not appear in the justifications for taking life in Art 2 of the ECHR, but held that the shooting was justified to effect a lawful arrest. This decision is cogently criticized by JC Smith, 'The Right to Life and the Right to Kill in Law Enforcement' (1994) 144 NLJ 354.

[351] [2008] UKHL 25; see the CA's decision: [2006] EWCA Civ 1085.

[352] cf the decision at first instance [2005] EWHC 415 (QB).

12.6.2.1 What is a crime for the purposes of s 3?

Section 3 operates only where D responds to prevent a 'crime'. In *Jones*,[353] the House of Lords concluded that the concept of 'crime' in this context can only have been intended to mean a 'domestic' crime (that is, not something which constitutes a crime only in international law).[354] The Criminal Law Revision Committee[355] explained the proposed s 3 in very broad terms:

the court, in considering what was reasonable force, would take into account all the circumstances, including in particular the nature and degree of force used, the seriousness of the evil to be prevented and the possibility of preventing it by other means; but there is no need to specify in the clause the criteria for deciding the question. Since the clause is framed in general terms, it is not limited to arrestable[356] or any other class of offences, though in the case of very trivial offences it would very likely be held that it would not be reasonable to use even the slightest force to prevent them.

Despite the breadth of this statement the House of Lords' limitation in *Jones* seems warranted if the defence is to retain the degree of certainty desirable.

The definition of 'crime' may also cause problems at a more mundane level where the question arises whether the offence is occurring when D uses any force. In *Bowden*,[357] the issue was whether V had completed his appropriation of an article before D used violence to prevent what he understood to be a theft being perpetrated by V, but that is not a strong example. Similarly, in *Attwater*[358] D sought to rely on s 3, when he was charged with dangerous driving. He claimed that he drove in that manner (crashing with other vehicles) so that he could apprehend another driver X because X had been in an earlier incident and failed to stop. In short D claimed to be apprehending X for his crime of failing to stop after a road traffic accident. On the facts, X's offence was probably already over.[359]

12.6.2.2 When is the use of force reasonable in s 3?

The Criminal Law Revision Committee,[360] the authors of the section, described it as set out in the last paragraph: 'reasonable force, would take into account all the circumstances, including in particular the nature and degree of force used, the seriousness of the evil to be prevented and the possibility of preventing it by other means'.[361]

It cannot be reasonable to cause harm unless (i) it was *necessary* to do so in order to prevent the crime or effect the arrest and (ii) the evil which would follow from failure to prevent the crime or effect the arrest is so great that a reasonable person might think himself justified in causing that harm to avert that evil. It is likely, therefore, that even killing will be justifiable to prevent unlawful killing or grievous bodily harm, or to arrest a person where there is an imminent risk of his causing death or grievous bodily harm if left at liberty. The European Court has emphasized that the use of lethal force to stop a person suspected of a non-violent offence who does not pose an immediate risk of harm to anyone is contrary to Art 2.[362] The whole question is somewhat speculative. Is it reasonable to kill or cause serious bodily harm in order

---

[353] [2005] Crim LR 122.

[354] See Lord Bingham at [31]; Lord Hoffmann at [54] and Lord Mance at [105].

[355] Cmnd 2659, para 23.

[356] Since the Serious Organised Crime and Police Act 2005, all offences are potentially arrestable.

[357] [2002] EWCA Crim 1279.

[358] [2010] EWCA Crim 2399.

[359] *Jackson* [1985] RTR 257. The court left open whether this was strictly speaking a matter that should have been left to the jury. The court had no doubt that a jury would have rejected the defence.

[360] Cmnd 2659, para 23.

[361] Note s 76, above.

[362] See *Nachova v Bulgaria* (2004) 39 EHRR 37.

to prevent rape?[363] Or robbery, when the property involved is very valuable?[364] How much force may be used to prevent the destruction of a great work of art? The cases in which the police use lethal force because they believed D to be a terrorist suicide bomber and in which any lesser force would have been futile are the most extreme.

It seems that the question, 'What amount of force is reasonable in the circumstances?' is always for the jury and never a point of law for the judge.[365] If the prosecution case does not provide material to raise the issue, there is an evidential burden on the accused. If that burden is satisfied, that question for the jury is:

Are we satisfied that no reasonable person (a) with knowledge of such facts as were known to the accused[366] believed by him to exist (b) in the circumstances and time available to him for reflection (c) could be of the opinion that the prevention of the risk of harm to which others might be exposed if the suspect were allowed to escape, justified exposing the suspect to the risk of harm to him that might result from the kind of force that the accused contemplated using.[367]

At common law it was recognized that the standard of reasonableness should, as noted above, take account of the nature of the crisis in which the necessity to use force arises for, in circumstances of great stress, even the reasonable person cannot be expected to judge the minimum degree of force required to a nicety. This is now reflected in s 76(7) of the 2008 Act. In holding quite considerable force to be justified to prevent an obstruction of the highway by a violent and abusive driver, Geoffrey Lane J said: 'In the circumstances one did not use jewellers' scales to measure reasonable force . . .'[368]

12.6.2.3 Section 3 provides a defence only if force used

Section 3 excuses only the use of *force*. In *Blake v DPP*,[369] D, demonstrating against the Iraq war, wrote with a felt pen on a concrete pillar near the Houses of Parliament. He was charged with criminal damage and argued that his act was justified by, *inter alia*, s 3. The court held that his act was 'insufficient to amount to the use of force within the section'. This suggests that the defence might not have been ruled out on this ground (though it almost certainly would on other grounds) if D had used a hammer and chisel. It is odd that force should be excused when less serious acts might not be; but that is the effect of the section.[370]

In *Jones*, the House of Lords expressed doubt as to whether s 3 ought to be relied on in cases of alleged damage to property. Section 5 of the Criminal Damage Act provides the appropriate defence. The House also doubted whether s 3 was intended to apply to peaceable protest activities such as those used by the defendants in that case – cutting wire and chaining themselves to armed service vehicles.

---

[363] See Leverick above n 311 Ch 8.

[364] There are plenty of reported instances where the courts seem to have approved of the killing: eg the action of a butcher who used a knife to frustrate the robber of his takings, was approved by the coroner, though the robber died: (1967) The Times, 16 Sept. See the more recent cases discussed by E Tennant (2003) 167 JP 804.

[365] *Reference under s 48A of the Criminal Appeal (Northern Ireland) Act 1968 (No 1 of 1975)* [1976] 2 All ER 937 at 947, HL, per Lord Diplock.

[366] Lord Diplock used the word 'reasonably' here and, in the light of his often stated opinion, it is likely that he would wish to continue to use it, were he still alive; but his remarks, in the light of *Gladstone Williams* and the cases following it, should be read as if 'reasonably' were omitted.

[367] ibid.

[368] *Reed v Wastie* [1972] Crim LR 221.

[369] [1993] Crim LR 586, DC.

[370] The illogicality of this restriction as noted by Brooke LJ in *Bayer v DPP* [2003] EWHC 2567 (Admin), [2004] Crim LR 663, calling for reform of the defences.

12.6.3 Force used in private defence

The Criminal Law Act 1967 made no reference to the right of private defence – the right to use force in defence of oneself or another against an unjustifiable attack.[371] In so far as that differed in effect from s 3 of the 1967 Act, the common law was probably modified by s 3. Private defence and the prevention of crime are sometimes indistinguishable. If D goes to the defence of E whom V is trying to murder, he is exercising the right of private defence but he is also seeking to prevent the commission of a crime. It would be absurd to ask D whether he was acting in defence of E or to prevent murder being committed and preposterous that the law should differ according to his answer. He was doing both.[372] The law cannot have two sets of criteria governing the same situation: s 3 of the Criminal Law Act is applicable. This is supported by the application of the same tests in s 76 of the 2008 Act to both the common law and s 3 defences. The 1967 Act may be taken to have clarified the common law. Before the Criminal Law Act, the Court of Criminal Appeal equated the defence of others with the prevention of crime. In *Duffy*,[373] it was held that a woman would be justified in using reasonable force when it was necessary to do so in defence of her sister, not because they were sisters, but because 'there is a general liberty as between strangers to prevent a felony'. That general liberty now extends to all offences. The principles applicable are the same whether the defence is put on grounds of self-defence or on grounds of prevention of crime. The degree of force permissible should not differ, for example, in the case of an employer defending his employee from the case of a brother defending his sister – or, indeed, that of a complete stranger coming to the defence of another under unlawful attack. As s 76(10)(b) of the 2008 Act makes clear, references to self-defence include acting in defence of another. The position is the same where D acts in defence of property, whether his own or that of another, which V seeks to steal, destroy or damage.

Where D is acting in defence of his own person it may be less obvious that he is also acting in the prevention of crime but this will usually be in fact the case. D's purpose is not the enforcement of the law but his own self-preservation; yet the degree of force which is permissible is the same.[374] An enquiry into D's motives is not practicable.[375]

As with s 3, the private law defence is limited to cases in which D responds to an unjustified attack by using force. However, there is no requirement with the private law defence at common law that D is responding to a 'crime'. Thus where D believes that V's actions are unjustified because they are, for example, unlawful in international law, his use of force to prevent V's action may be justified.

12.6.4 Further elements of private and public defence

12.6.4.1 A duty to retreat?

There were formerly technical rules about the duty to retreat before using force, or at least fatal force. This is now simply a factor to be taken into account in deciding whether it was necessary to use force, and whether the force was reasonable.[376] If the only reasonable course is to re-

---

[371] Thus where D knows that the actual or imminent danger he faces is not from an unlawful or criminal act he cannot rely on the defence: *Bayer v DPP* [2003] EWHC 2567 (Admin). See also *Cresswell v DPP* [2006] EWHC 3379 (Admin) where the defendants could not be acting to prevent a crime when DEFRA officials were within the law to take the badgers in dispute.

[372] See *Clegg* [1995] 1 All ER 334 at 343.

[373] [1967] 1 QB 63, CCA.

[374] *Devlin v Armstrong* [1971] NI 13 at 33; *McInnes* [1971] 3 All ER 295 at 302.

[375] Above, p 116.

[376] *McInnes*, above. But cf *Whyte* [1987] 3 All ER 416 at 419, CA.

treat, then it would appear that to stand and fight must be to use unreasonable force. There is, however, no rule of law that a person attacked is bound to run away if he can. In *Duffy v DPP*[377] where the judge found that D could have retreated, the Divisional Court, following the 'classic pronouncement' in *Palmer v R*,[378] reiterated that:

the proposition that the old rule of law, that a man attacked must retreat as far as he can, has disappeared. Whether the accused did retreat is nevertheless an element for consideration in determining whether he was acting in self-defence, as is his ability or inclination to do so. The fact that a man engages in violence to defend himself does not justify the continued use or threat of violence beyond such time as is reasonable and necessary to defend himself.[379]

A demonstration by D at the time that he did not want to fight is, no doubt, the best evidence that he was acting reasonably and in good faith in self-defence; but it is no more than that. A person may in some circumstances so act without temporizing, disengaging or withdrawing; and he should have a good defence.[380]

Trial judges must be careful not to impliedly undermine the defence in directions on this matter.[381] In *Jones*, the House of Lords emphasized the view that it is not for the citizen who apprehends a breach of the law to take matters into his own hands if there is an opportunity to summon official help.[382]

12.6.4.2 Pre-emptive strikes

It has been accepted that a defendant need not wait for the attacker to strike the first blow before he defends himself. In *Devlin v Armstrong*,[383] following serious disturbances in Londonderry, D exhorted crowds of people who were stoning the police to build a barricade and keep the police out and fight them with petrol bombs. D claimed that she had acted in this manner because she honestly believed that the police were about to behave unlawfully in assaulting people and damaging property in the area. The Court of Appeal acknowledged that a 'plea of self-defence may afford a defence [where D used force] not merely to counter an actual attack, but to ward off or prevent an attack which he honestly anticipated. In that case, however, the anticipated attack must be imminent'.[384] In *Beckford*,[385] the Privy Council also acknowledged that circumstances may justify a pre-emptive strike in self-defence. The availability of the defence in circumstances of pre-emptive strike has been narrowly construed by the courts. Where there is no evidence to support a suggestion that D has acted in pre-emptive defence, no direction on the issue is needed.[386]

The requirement of imminence, strictly construed, prevents the widespread reliance on the defence where battered spouses kill their abusive partners. Commonly, the physical disparity between the parties means that the woman will seize her opportunity to kill the abuser when

---

[377] [2007] EWHC 3169 (Admin).
[378] [1971] AC 814, PC.
[379] Per Henriques J at [8].
[380] This passage was approved by the Court of Appeal in *Bird* [1985] 2 All ER 513 at 516. cf Ashworth, POCL, 115 arguing that this should be seen as an exception to the general principle of a duty to avoid conflict.
[381] See *M (ZM)* [2007] EWCA Crim 376.
[382] See Lord Mance at paras 78–81.
[383] [1971] NI 13.
[384] Per Lord MacDermott LCJ at 33.
[385] [1987] 3 All ER 425 PC.
[386] *Williams* [2005] EWCA Crim 669, cf *Carter* [2005] All ER (D) 372 (Apr); *Murphy* [2007] EWCA Crim 2810.

he is not poised about to strike her, but in a position of vulnerability. This caused such individuals to rely on the partial defences of provocation and diminished responsibility.[387]

Under s 54 of the Coroners and Justice Act 2009, a defendant who kills with malice aforethought may rely on a defence of loss of control (LOSC) if he has lost his self-control and, *inter alia*, he fears serious violence from V towards himself or an identified person. The relationship between the LOSC defence and self-defence or defence of others under s 76 of the Criminal Justice and Immigration Act 2008 needs to be approached with caution. Self-defence is available on any charge; LOSC defence is available only on a charge of murder.[388] Self-defence results in an acquittal; LOSC in a verdict of manslaughter. With LOSC, D can rely on fear of future non-imminent attack; with self-defence he can only rely on a threat of (or believed threat of) imminent attack. The defence of self-defence is available if D holds a genuine, though mistaken and unreasonable, belief of the threat to him of *any* violence). Violence is undefined in the LOSC defence but includes sexual violence.[389][390] The LOSC defence is available if D genuinely, though mistakenly and unreasonably, believes himself to be at risk of *serious* violence.[391] If the degree of force used by D in killing V is, viewed objectively, excessive, that will deprive D of the defence of self-defence,[392] but will not automatically deprive D of the LOSC defence.

12.6.4.3 Defence against a provoked attack

In *Browne*,[393] Lowry LCJ said, with regard to self-defence, 'The need to act must not have been created by conduct of the accused in the immediate context of the incident which was likely or intended to give rise to that need.'

Self-defence is clearly not available where D deliberately provoked the attack with the intention of killing purportedly in self-defence.[394] Where D's act was merely 'likely' to give rise to the need, the proposition, with respect, is more questionable. If D did not foresee that his actions would lead to an attack on him, it is submitted that he should not be deprived of his usual right of self-defence. Even if he did foresee the attack, he may still be entitled to act in self-defence if he did not intend it. D intervenes to stop V from ill-treating V's wife. He knows that V may react violently. V makes a deadly attack on D. Surely D's right of self-defence is unimpaired. This suggestion was cited *obiter* with approval in *Balogun*.[395]

In *Rashford*,[396] the Court of Appeal made it clear that self-defence is available to the person who started the fight, if the person whom he attacks not only defends himself but goes over to the offensive. As a matter of principle, the defence ought to be available where D has prompted V's attack, and even where D has foreseen that V was likely to respond with violence, subject

---

[387] See, generally, the discussion below, p 507 and C Wells, 'Battered Woman Syndrome and Defences to Homicide: Where Now?' (1994) 14 LS 266; A McColgan, 'In Defence of Battered Women Who Kill' (1993) 13 OJLS 508; J Dressler, 'Battered Women Who Kill Their Sleeping Tormentors', in S Shute and A Simester (eds), *Criminal Law Theory* (2002) arguing for a duress type defence and J Horder, 'Killing the Passive Abuser: A Theoretical Defence', in S Shute and A Simester (eds), *Criminal Law Theory*, 285.

[388] If there are multiple counts relating to different victims, care will be needed in directing the jury.

[389] MOJ CP 19/08 para 44.

[390] Fortson, below, p 508 n 21, argues that it includes psychological harm.

[391] See MOJ Circular 2010/13, para 25. cf Leigh below, p 508 n 21 who states that the test is objective.

[392] And therefore of a complete acquittal. See *Clegg* [1995] and Ch 12 above. See also Leverick, *Self Defence* (2007) pp 172 et seq.

[393] [1973] NI 96 at 107, CCA, discussed 24 NILQ 527. On 'prior fault' generally, see S Yeo, *Compulsion* (1990) Ch 5.

[394] cf *Mason* (1756) Fost 132. Under the Coroners and Justice Act 2009, the loss of self-control defence is not available in such circumstances. See below Ch 15, p 507.

[395] [1999] 98/6762/X2.

[396] [2005] EWCA Crim 3377, [2006] Crim LR 547.

to the restriction that it should not be available where D deliberately provoked the attack with the intention of killing purportedly in self-defence. Considerable care will be necessary in directing the jury in such cases. In *Rashford* Dyson LJ approved the Scottish decision in *Burns v HM Advocate*[397] as an important decision which should be more widely known. In that case[398] it was said that the question:

depends upon whether the violence offered by the victim was so out of proportion to the accused's own actings as to give rise to the reasonable apprehension that he was in an immediate danger from which he had no other means of escape, and whether the violence which he then used was no more than was necessary to preserve his own life or protect himself from serious injury.

As the commentary in the Criminal Law Review points out, that test is inaccurate for English law as it suggests that the apprehension which D must have as to the threat of danger must be a reasonable one.[399]

The principles were reiterated in *Harvey*.[400] In relation to self-defence relied on by an initial aggressor, the court followed *Rashford*. This is subject to a principle that D cannot rely on self-defence where he has set out to engineer an attack by V which will allow him, D, to respond with greater violence under the guise of self-defence. The difficulty of course lies in how to explain that to a jury. The court in *Harvey* emphasised that the direction on self-defence for initial aggressors is not always necessary simply because there is a dispute about 'who started it'.

The Court of Appeal has once again returned to this in *Keane*,[401] which provides a useful review, endorsing the guidance given in *Harvey* on the application of the defence where D provokes violence from another but on whom the tables are turned. Hughes LJ said:

It seems to us that that kind of homely expression, like 'the roles being reversed', can quite well encapsulate the question which may arise if an original aggressor claims the ability to rely on self-defence. We would commend it as suitable for a great many cases, subject only to this reminder.[402] ... We need to say as clearly as we may that it is not the law that if a defendant sets out to provoke another to punch him and succeeds, the defendant is then entitled to punch the other person. ... The reason why it is not the law is that underlying the law of self-defence is the common-sense morality that what is not unlawful is force which is reasonably necessary. ... Of course it might be different if the defendant set out to provoke a punch and the victim unexpectedly and disproportionately attacked him with a knife.

12.6.4.4 Defence against lawful force

Lowry LCJ stated in *Browne*:[403]

Where a police officer is acting lawfully and using only such force as is reasonable in the circumstances in the prevention of crime or in effecting the lawful arrest of offenders or suspected offenders, self-defence against him is not an available defence.

---

[397] 1995 SLT 1090.

[398] At 1093H.

[399] cf *Williams (Gladstone)* [1987] 3 All ER 411; *Beckford v R* [1988] AC 130; Criminal Justice and Immigration Act 2008, s 76.

[400] [2009] EWCA Crim 469.

[401] [2010] EWCA Crim 2514.

[402] His lordship added that: 'Lord Hope's formulation of the rule [in *Burns*] makes it clear that it is not enough to bring self-defence into issue that a defendant who started the fight is at some point during the fight for the time being getting the worst of it, merely because the victim is defending himself reasonably. In that event there has been no disproportionate act by the victim of the kind that Lord Hope is contemplating. The victim has not been turned into the aggressor. The tables have not been turned in that particular sense. The roles have not been reversed'[18].

[403] [1973] NI 96 at 107.

Again, it may be respectfully suggested that this proposition is too wide. If D, an innocent person, is attacked by the police who mistakenly believe him to be a gunman and the police attack is such that it would be reasonable if D were the gunman, does the law really deny D the right to resist?[404] Again, if D reasonably supposes that the police are terrorists, he surely commits no crime by resisting, even if the police are in fact acting lawfully and reasonably.

A person is not to be deprived of his right of self-defence because he has gone to a place where he might lawfully go, but where he knew he was likely to be attacked.

There is no question of any duty to retreat at least until the parties are in sight of one another and the threat is imminent.[405]

In a very few cases, the attacker may not be committing a crime because, for example, he is a child under 10, insane, in a state of automatism or under a material mistake of fact. If D is unaware of the circumstances which exempt the attacker, then s 3 of the Criminal Law Act will still, indirectly, afford him a defence to any criminal charge which may be brought, provided he is acting reasonably in the light of the circumstances as they appear, reasonably or not, to him; for he intends to use force in the prevention of crime, as that section allows, and therefore has no *mens rea*.

Where D does know of the circumstances in question, then s 3 is inapplicable, but it is submitted that the question should be decided on similar principles. A person should be allowed to use reasonable force in defending himself or another against an unjustifiable attack, even if the attacker is not criminally responsible.[406] Authority can now be found in the case of the conjoined twins, *Re A (Children)*.[407] The court granted a declaration that it would be lawful to carry out an operation to separate the twins to enable A to live even though the operation would inevitably kill B. B's heart and lungs were too deficient to keep her alive. She lived only because A was able to circulate sufficient oxygenated blood for both. The evidence was that, if the operation was not done, both would die. The *ratio decidendi* of the three judges differed but it is submitted that Ward LJ rightly held that this was a case of self-defence. B was, of course, completely innocent but she was killing A. He equated the case with that of a six-year-old boy shooting all and sundry in a playground. It would be lawful to kill him if that was the only way to prevent the deaths of others. There is a great difference between the boy's active conduct and the pathetic inactivity of B; but neither is committing a crime. Whatever the position regarding necessity and duress, it has always been held that private defence may be an answer to a charge of murder.

12.6.4.5 D's reliance on unknown justifying circumstances[408]

What of D who seeks to rely on facts that existed and would justify his use of force, but of which he was unaware at the time of acting? The test proposed in the CLRC's Fourteenth Report and adopted as the law in *Gladstone Williams* is stated exclusively in terms of D's be-

---

[404] *Mckoy* [2002] EWCA Crim 1628 suggests that D may resist unlawful restraint by a police officer. The judgment of Winn LJ in *Kenlin v Gardiner* [1967] 2 QB 510, is ambivalent. *Albert v Lavin* [1982] AC 546, DC (reversed by the House of Lords on another point) supports the view in the text. And see *Ansell v Swift* [1987] Crim LR 194 (Lewes Crown Court). The question is elaborately discussed in *Lawson and Forsythe* [1986] VR 515. Young CJ thought it may be reasonable to assume that, in some circumstances, D may defend himself against a lawful attack; McGarvie J said that he may do so, approving the 5th edition of this book, at 327–328, but Ormiston J thought self-defence was only lawful against an unlawful attack. cf *Fennell* [1971] 1 QB 428, [1970] 3 All ER 215, [1970] Crim LR 581 and commentary; below, p 397.

[405] *Field* [1972] Crim LR 435; cf *Beatty v Gillbanks* (1882) 9 QBD 308.

[406] *Bayer v DPP*, above n 371.

[407] [2000] 4 All ER 961, [2001] Crim LR 400, CA (Civ Div) and commentary.

[408] See TM Funk, 'Justifying Justifications' (1999) 19 OJLS 630, arguing that *Dadson* represents a 'very principled, precedented, coherent and logically compelling decision'. See also PH Robinson, 'Competing Theories of Justification: Deeds v Reasons', in S Shute and A Simester (eds), *Criminal Law Theory*, at 45; R Christopher,

lief. Its terms do not apply where D is unaware of existing circumstances which, if he knew of them, would justify his use of force. This line of reasoning accords with *Dadson*.[409] This is no accident. The Committee gave careful consideration to the matter and concluded that the *Dadson* principle was correct.[410]

On some interpretations where the circumstances justify the act, it is immaterial that D is not aware of them; where they can merely excuse the act, they do so only if he is aware of them.[411] Force used to make an arrest is said to be justified, not merely excused, so, it is argued, *Dadson* was a case of justification and is wrongly decided. Duress, which obviously requires awareness, is distinguishable because according to most commentators it merely excuses. But such an analysis based solely on justification and excuse is overly simplistic and does not provide a satisfactory explanation of *Dadson*. A boy who, knowing it is a wicked thing to do, deliberately kills his playmate has a defence if he was aged only nine at the time. Ten is the minimum age of criminal responsibility. He is excused, but no one would say he was 'justified' in killing his playmate because he was only nine. Is he to be liable for murder if he thought he was 10? Obviously not. He is excused by the fact, whether he knows of it or not. It is the policy of the law that a child under 10 shall not be convicted of crime and the child's mistake cannot be allowed to defeat that policy.

Self-defence is still governed by the common law. Suppose that D shoots at V with intent to murder him and kills him. It turns out that D did so in the nick of time because, unknown to D, V was about to shoot D dead.[412] If D had only known he would certainly have had the defence of self-defence. Is D guilty of murder? According to orthodox justification/excuse theory, it depends on whether self-defence provides a justification or an excuse for the use of force. Glanville Williams, who at one time thought self-defence merely an excuse, later concluded that it is a justification,[413] so he thought D would have a defence. But can it really be right that a person who has fired a gun at another with intent to murder should be beyond the reach of the law? One answer is that, though not guilty of murder, he is guilty of attempted murder under the Criminal Attempts Act 1981 (since, by that Act, he is to be treated for the purpose of an attempt charge as if the facts were as he believed them to be). But how can it be said that his act was both (i) justified and (ii) attempted murder? What would a jury make of a direction to that effect? The better view is that the *Dadson* principle applies and that it is generally applicable to defences unless policy (as in the case of the nine-year-old, above) otherwise requires.

12.6.4.6 Defence of property[414]

Where D is charged with criminal damage and his defence is that he was acting in defence of his own property – as where he kills V's dog which, he claims, was attacking his sheep, the matter is regulated by the Criminal Damage Act 1971, which is considered below, p 1029. Where D is charged with an offence against the person, or any other offence, and his defence is

---

'Unknowing Justification and the Logical Necessity of the *Dadson* Principle in Self-Defence' (1995) 15 OJLS 229; J Gardner, *Offences and Defences*, Ch 5.

[409] (1850) 2 Den 35.

[410] The discussion is not included in the Fourteenth Report, paras 281–287.

[411] See in general GP Fletcher, *Rethinking Criminal Law* (1978); Smith, *Justification and Excuse*; ML Corrado (ed), *Justification and Excuse in the Criminal Law: A Collection of Essays* (1994); A Eser, G Fletcher, K Cornils et al (eds), *Justification and Excuse: Comparative Perspectives* (1987). For monographs and essays providing sophisticated analyses of the theories, see especially R Schopp, *Justification Defences and Just Convictions* (1988) and Horder, *Excusing Crime*.

[412] This paradox of the unknowing justification is analysed by R Christopher (1995) 15 OJLS 229.

[413] Compare CLGP (1961) 25, (1982) 2 LS 233, 250.

[414] See D Lanham, 'Defence of Property in the Criminal Law' [1966] Crim LR 368.

that he was defending his property, he will generally be acting in the prevention of crime and, as in defence of the person, s 3 is likely to be held to provide the criterion.

In *Faraj*,[415] the Court of Appeal considered the defence of protection of property where D had made a mistake in thinking that a gas repair man was a burglar and had threatened him with a knife. The court could see no reason why a householder should not be entitled to detain someone in his house whom he *genuinely* believed to be a burglar. 'The householder must honestly believe that he needs to detain the suspect and must do so in a way which is reasonable': *Gladstone Williams* applies to mistakes in relation to defence of property.

It can rarely, if ever, be reasonable to use deadly force merely for the protection of property.[416] Would it have been reasonable to kill even one of the Great Train Robbers to prevent them from getting away with their millions of pounds of loot, or to kill a man about to destroy a priceless painting? – even assuming that no means short of killing could prevent the commission of the crime. It will be recalled that Art 2 of the ECHR does not permit the use of lethal force otherwise than in preventing riot, etc, or unlawful 'violence'.

In the case of *Hussey*,[417] it was stated that it would be lawful for a person to kill one who would unlawfully dispossess him of his home. Even if this were the law at the time, it would seem difficult now to contend that such conduct would be reasonable; for legal redress would be available if the householder were wrongly evicted. In so far as the householder was preventing crime, his conduct would be regulated by s 3 of the Criminal Law Act 1967 which replaces the rules of common law. It is thought that, in any event, the rule in *Hussey* would not extend to a trespasser who did not intend to dispossess the householder, even if the trespasser were guilty of an offence under Part II of the Criminal Law Act 1977.[418]

Following the conviction of the Norfolk farmer Anthony Martin for murder when he killed a burglar entering his isolated farmhouse,[419] there was considerable public concern, fuelled by misinformed newspaper reports, and a resulting clamour for a new law to protect the rights of householders.[420] The issue became a political one, and a number of excessively wide defences were drafted as Private Members' Bills.[421] The result was finally the enactment of s 76 of the 2008 Act, which is a very strange provision, merely partially restating the common law.

In the recent case of *Burns*[422] the Court emphasized the narrow scope of defences in such cases. B was convicted of causing actual bodily harm to V, a prostitute whom B had picked up and driven to a secluded spot. Having decided not to have sex with V, and having paid her, B requested V to leave the car and when she refused, used force. The Court of Appeal upheld his conviction. B had not acted in self-defence nor in defence of anyone else; he had not been defending his property against threat or risk of damage; he was not acting for any purpose within s 3 of the Criminal Law Act 1967. The defence was one of 'self help'. That defence was always a last resort. It was a defence which the common law would be reluctant to extend. Lord Judge CJ added:

Recognising that to be lawful the use of force must always be reasonable in the circumstances, we accept that it might be open to the owner of a vehicle, in the last resort and when all reasonably

---

[415] [2007] EWCA Crim 1033.

[416] See Leverick, *Killing in Self-Defence*, Ch 7.

[417] (1924) 18 Cr App R 160, CCA.

[418] cf *Taylor v Mucklow* [1973] Crim LR 750 and commentary. See also the civil law case of *Revill v Newbury* [1996] All ER 291.

[419] See S Yeo, 'Killing in Defence of Property' (2000) 150 NLJ 730.

[420] A poll on the Radio 4 programme, 'Today' in 2004 revealed that this was the listeners' most desired legislative change.

[421] See the Criminal Justice (Justifiable Conduct) Bill 2004, and the Criminal Law (Amendment) (Householder Protection) Bill 2004 criticized by S Skinner, 'Populist Politics and Shooting Burglars' [2005] Crim LR 275.

[422] [2010] EWCA Crim 1023.

practicable alternatives have failed, forcibly to remove an individual who has entered into his vehicle without permission and refuses to leave it. However, where that individual entered the car as a passenger, in effect at the invitation of the car owner, on the basis that they mutually understood that when their dealings were completed she would be driven back in the car from whence she had come, the use of force to remove her at the appellant's unilateral whim, was unlawful.

The court also doubted, as a matter of legal theory, whether the car owner's rights could be treated as analogous to those of a landowner to remove trespassers. However, caution is required since it does not seem the point was argued in full.

12.6.4.7 To what offences is public or private defence an answer?

These defences are most naturally relied on as answers to charges of homicide, assault, false imprisonment and other offences against the person. It is not clear to what extent public or private defence may be invoked as defences to other crimes.[423]

In *A-G's Reference (No 2 of 1983),*[424] D made and retained in his shop petrol-bombs at a time when extensive rioting was taking place in the area. He was acquitted of an offence under s 4(1) of the Explosive Substances Act 1883 of possessing an explosive substance in such circumstances as to give rise to a reasonable suspicion that he did not have it for a lawful object. It was a defence under the terms of the section for D to prove that he had it for a lawful object. The Court of Appeal held that there was evidence on which a jury might have decided that the use of the petrol-bombs would have been reasonable force in self-defence against an apprehended attack. If so, D had the bombs for 'a lawful object' and was not guilty of the offence charged. Yet it was assumed[425] that he was committing offences of manufacturing and storing explosives contrary to the Explosives Act 1875. The court agreed with the Court of Appeal in Northern Ireland in *Fegan*[426] that possession of a firearm for the purpose of protecting the possessor may be possession for a lawful object, even though the possession was unlawful being without a licence. The judgment is strangely ambivalent.

[D] is not confined for his remedy to calling in the police or boarding up his premises. He may still arm himself for his own protection, if the exigency arises, although in so doing he may commit other offences. That he may be guilty of other offences will avoid the risk of anarchy contemplated by the reference.

To say 'He may do it – but he will commit an offence if he does' seems inconsistent. There is, however, a clear statement that acts immediately preparatory to justifiable acts of self-defence are also justified. This must surely be right. If D becomes caught up in a shoot-out between police and dangerous criminals, picks up a revolver dropped by a wounded policeman and fires in order to defend his own and police lives, it would be astonishing if he had a defence to a charge of homicide but not to possessing a firearm without a licence.[427] Possibly, then, the passage above refers to preparatory, but not immediately preparatory acts. This does not resolve the ambivalence. The law must say whether a person may, or may not, do such acts; and if it says they are crimes, he may not.

---

[423] Clause 44 of the Draft Code ('Use of force in public or private defence') would not justify or excuse any criminal conduct not involving the use of force (except acts immediately preparatory to the use of such force); but the Code would leave it open to the courts to develop a wider defence at common law.

[424] [1984] QB 456, [1984] 1 All ER 988, [1984] Crim LR 289 and commentary.

[425] *A-G's Reference (No 2 of 1983)* [1984] 1 All ER 988 at 992–993.

[426] [1972] NI 80. cf *Emmanuel* [1998] Crim LR 347.

[427] cf *Georgiades* [1989] Crim LR 574; see recently *Salih* [2007] EWCA Crim 2750; *McAuley* [2009] EWCA Crim 2130.

The matter must now be considered in the light of the defence of duress of circumstances. A person may save himself from injury by an attacker by using force or by running away and *Willer* and *Conway*[428] are cases where this form of self-defence was an answer to a charge of reckless driving. In *Symonds*,[429] where a driver, charged under s 20 of the Offences Against the Person Act and with dangerous driving, raised self-defence it was held that the same considerations applied to the driving charge as to the s 20 offence. Calling the defence to driving charge 'duress of circumstances' may make no difference – but sometimes it may, because duress requires an objective test where the test for self-defence (*Gladstone Williams*) is certainly subjective. As a matter of policy there is a great deal to be said for encouraging a threatened person to escape, even where that involves committing a minor offence, rather than using force against the aggressor. It now seems that those defendants would have had a defence if they had driven through a red light, or while disqualified, or with excess alcohol, providing that it was necessary to do so in order to escape death or serious bodily harm. The hypothetical user of the revolver was also acting under duress of circumstances. A successful defendant will not care whether his defence is called 'duress of circumstances' or 'private defence'; but whether the defence succeeds may well depend on how it is categorized, for the former is limited to threats to the person whereas the latter extends to defence of property; and the former is governed by an objective test whereas a subjective test is applied to the latter. A disqualified driver who drove his Rolls Royce to avoid its destruction by an aggressor could not plead duress; nor would possession of the revolver without a licence be excused by duress if the possessor's honest belief that life was in danger was not based on reasonable grounds – though his defence to a charge of homicide would not be impaired. For the avoidance of such anomalies, acts immediately preparatory to public or private defence are better regarded as justified or excused by those defences.

The fears of the courts regarding a general defence of necessity[430] probably militate against a recognition that public and private defence may constitute a defence to crime generally; but, where contravention of *any* law is (i) necessary to enable the right of public or private defence to be exercised, and (ii) reasonable in the circumstances, it ought to be excused. It is open to the courts to move in this direction.

12.6.4.8 Use of force, excessive in the known circumstances

Generally, where D, being under no mistake of fact, uses force in public or private defence, he either has a complete defence or if he uses excessive force, no defence. In murder, if D used excessive force and lost his self-control he may (subject to the other elements of the defence being satisfied) be able to rely on the loss of self-control defence to reduce the offence to manslaughter. However, even in murder, if D has not lost his self-control, but has used excessive force, he will be guilty for the full offence of murder even if he genuinely (and reasonably) believed some force was necessary. This was affirmed by the House of Lords in *Clegg*.[431] D, a soldier on duty in Northern Ireland, fired four shots at a car (in fact stolen) which did not stop at a checkpoint. The judge, sitting in a 'Diplock' court without a jury, accepted that the first three shots had been fired in self-defence or defence of a colleague but that the fourth, which killed, was not, as the car had passed the soldiers and was already 50 feet down the road. D's conviction of murder was affirmed by the House of Lords, holding that it is established law that killing by excessive force in self-defence is murder and that if a change is to be made, it is

---

[428] Above, p 348. See DW Elliott, 'Necessity, Duress and Self-Defence' [1989] Crim LR 611.

[429] [1998] Crim LR 280.

[430] Above, p 365.

[431] [1995] 1 All ER 334, [1995] Crim LR 418 and commentary. See also M Kaye, 'Excessive Force in Self Defence After *Clegg*' (1996) 61 J Crim L 448.

for Parliament, not the courts, to make it. Where D has not lost control, but has used excessive force, there is no partial defence resulting in a manslaughter conviction, as with loss of control and diminished responsibility. The possibility was considered and rejected immediately after the *Clegg* decision.[432]

For 30 years, a line of cases in Australia held that killing by excessive force, even where there is no mistake of fact, should be manslaughter and not murder, if some force was justified:

if the occasion warrants action in self-defence or for the prevention of felony or the apprehension of the felon but the person taking action acts beyond the necessity of the occasion and kills the offender the crime is manslaughter – not murder.[433]

According to the High Court in *Howe*,[434] in relation to self-defence the defence applied where (i) D honestly and reasonably thought he was defending himself; and (ii) homicide would have been justified if excessive force had not been used; but (iii) D used more force than was reasonably necessary. This principle was mainly applied in self-defence cases,[435] but it originated in *McKay*,[436] which concerned the use of excessive force in the arrest of a criminal and the defence of property and it is logical that, if it applies at all, it should apply to any of the defences now being considered.[437]

In *Palmer*,[438] the Privy Council explained why they saw no need for this refinement of the law in England:

If there has been an attack so that defence is reasonably necessary it will be recognized that a person defending himself cannot weigh to a nicety the exact measure of his necessary defensive action. If a jury thought that in a moment of unexpected anguish a person attacked had only done what he honestly and instinctively thought was necessary that would be most potent evidence that only reasonable defensive action had been taken. A jury will be told that a defence of self-defence, where the evidence makes it[s] raising possible, will only fail if the prosecution show beyond doubt that what the accused did was not by way of self-defence.[439]

In *Zecevic*,[440] the Australian High Court overruled its previous decisions and followed *Palmer*, bringing Australian law into line with that of England. It did so, not because it thought the principle applied in those cases was a bad one, but because of the complexity which had arisen from the court's attempt to state the law in a form which took account of the onus of proof. The law was to be changed because it was too difficult for juries to understand and apply. The principle of *Gladstone Williams*[441] – which has not yet been followed in Australia – removes some

---

[432] See the *Inter-Departmental Review of the Law on Lethal Force in Self-defence or the Prevention of Crime* (1996) paras 83–84.

[433] *McKay* [1957] ALR 648 at 649, per Lowe J.

[434] (1958) 100 CLR 448; *Bufalo* [1958] VR 363; *Haley* (1959) 76 WNNSW 550; *Tikos* [1963] VR 285; *Tikos (No 2)* [1963] VR 306.

[435] ibid.

[436] [1957] VR 560.

[437] It has been argued the principle is of general application and should govern duress, coercion and necessity. Thus, even if duress, coercion and necessity do not afford a complete defence to murder, they might reduce the offence to manslaughter: Morris and Howard, *Studies in Criminal Law* (1964) 142. The idea is undeniably attractive but it is as yet unsupported by authority.

[438] [1971] AC 814, [1971] 1 All ER 1077.

[439] On the importance of this direction and the potential for it to be underestimated see the Law Com No 290, Part 4, paras 4.11–4.14.

[440] *Zecevic v DPP for Victoria* (1987) 61 ALJR 375. See Editorial [1988] Crim LR 1; D Lanham, 'Death of a Doubtful Defence' (1988) 104 LQR 239.

[441] Above, p 381.

of the complexity from the law and it ought to be capable of being stated in a form readily comprehensible by juries.

The CLRC was persuaded that *Howe* was right in principle and recommended its adoption in relation to private defence of person and property and the prevention of crime.[442] It is submitted that the soundness of this recommendation is not impaired by *Zekevic* or by *Clegg*.[443]

12.6.5 Reform of sef-defence/private defence

The Law Commission's general proposals on defences are contained in Report No 218 which provides:

27(1) The use of force by a person for any of the following purposes, if only such as is reasonable in the circumstances as he believes them to be, does not constitute an offence –

  (a) to protect himself or another from injury, assault or detention caused by a criminal act;

  (b) to protect himself or (with the authority of that other) another from trespass to the person;

  (c) to protect his property from appropriation, destruction or damage caused by a criminal act or from trespass or infringement;

  (d) to protect property belonging to another from appropriation, destruction or damage caused by a criminal act or (with the authority of the other) from trespass or infringement; or

  (e) to prevent crime or a breach of the peace.

  (6) Where an act is lawful by reason only of a belief or suspicion which is mistaken, the defence provided by this section applies as in the case of an unlawful act, unless –

  (a) D knows or believes that the force is used against a constable or a person assisting a constable, and

  (b) the constable is acting in the execution of his duty.

12.7 Entrapment[444]

Unlike some jurisdictions, such as the USA,[445] there is no defence of entrapment in English law in the sense of a substantive law plea advanced at trial.[446] Originally it was thought to be a necessary corollary that a judge has no discretion to exclude evidence of the commission of an offence which was induced by the trap for such exclusion would indirectly provide the defence which the law did not allow. While the substantive law is unchanged, it is now clear that the judges' duty to ensure that the accused receives the fair trial as emphasized by the

---

[442] Fourteenth Report, para 228. cf PF Smith, 'Excessive Defence – A Rejection of Australian Initiative' [1972] Crim LR 524.

[443] The Law Commission in cl 59 of the Draft Code have implemented the recommendation.

[444] JD McClean, 'Informers and Agents Provocateurs' [1969] Crim LR 527; J Heydon, 'The Problems of Entrapment' [1973] CLJ 268; Law Com Working Paper No 55 and Law Com No 83, *Report on Defences of General Application* (1977) where it is recommended that there should be no defence of entrapment but that consideration should be given to the creation of a new *offence* of entrapment. See A Ashworth, 'Entrapment' [1978] Crim LR 137.

[445] *Jacobsen v US* 112 S Ct 1535 (1992).

[446] *Sang* [1980] AC 402; *Latif* [1996] 1 WLR 104; *Looseley* [2001] UKHL 53. For consideration of the merits of a defence see A Choo, *Abuse of Process and Judicial Stays of Criminal Proceedings* (2nd edn, 2008).

Human Rights Act entitles or requires the judge in some circumstances to stay proceedings as an abuse of process or exclude the evidence in the discretion under s 78 of PACE.

12.7.1 Basis of stay for abuse of process

As the remedy is one properly regarded as a matter of criminal procedure, it is dealt with here in only brief outline.[447] In short, the question is whether the State officials[448] have done more than afford the accused an opportunity to break the law, of which he freely took advantage, or whether they have persuaded him by shameful or unworthy conduct to commit an offence which he would not otherwise have committed.[449] If the latter, the court should stay proceedings in order to avoid bringing the administration of justice into disrepute and respect the fact that it is not fair to try the defendant for a State-created crime. Determining whether the State has overstepped the mark or merely offered D an 'unexceptional' opportunity to commit crime will give rise to difficult decisions particularly since there will not always be an objective benchmark on what is an unexceptional opportunity. This may be easier to discover in the case of a drug deal (have the police offered a better deal than the average local price for that drug) than in cases of police offering to act as contract killers (price dependent on victim and means of killing). Numerous factors will be influential in determining whether the case should be stayed including: the type of crime involved, the degree of pressure or inducement offered, the circumstances in which it is offered, the particular vulnerability of the accused, the circumstances of the police operation – was it based on reasonable suspicion of a particular target and was it an authorized operation in accordance with the Regulation of Investigatory Powers Act 2000, Part II.[450] The House of Lords in *Looseley* rejected the emphasis placed on the accused's 'predisposition' to commit the crime in the European Court in *Teixeira de Castro v Portugal*.[451] It is submitted the House was right to do so and that *Teixeira*, although followed more recently by the ECtHR,[452] ought to be regarded with caution.[453]

12.7.1.1 Sentencing

Entrapment is also a matter which may be taken into account in fixing the sentence so, where there was a possibility that, say, a theft might not have been committed but for a police trap, D was sentenced as if he had been convicted of a conspiracy to steal rather than the actual

---

[447] Since the remedy is by way of a stay it will, under the Criminal Justice Act 2003, s 58, be appealable by the prosecution. See, generally, D Corker and D Young, *Abuse of Process* (3rd edn, 2009).

[448] Where the entrapment is from a private citizen – usually the 'fake Sheikh' of the *News of the World* newspaper – the abuse of process argument has not often proved successful (see *Shannon* [2001] 1 WLR 51; *Hardwicke and Thwaites* [2001] Crim LR 220). See also K Hofmeyr, 'The Problem of Private Entrapment' [2006] Crim LR 319. Arguably it should, since the court and prosecuting authorities as agencies of the State are endorsing the impropriety of the private individual and that in itself could be seen as an abuse of process. The possibility that a prosecution based on private entrapment could infringe Art 6 has been confirmed in *Shannon v United Kingdom* [2005] Crim LR 133.

[449] *A-G's Reference (No 3 of 2000)* [2002] Crim LR 301 and commentary; *Nottingham City Council v Amin* [2000] 2 All ER 946, DC; A Ashworth, 'Redrawing the Boundaries of Entrapment' [2002] Crim LR 161; S Mackay, 'Entrapment, Competing Views on the Effect of the HRA on the English Criminal Law' [2002] EHRLR 764. On post-*Looseley* developments see D Ormerod, 'Entrapment–Development Since *Looseley*' [2006] Covert Policing Review 82.

[450] See, eg, the decision to allow the appeal in *Moon* [2004] All ER (D) 167 (Nov) where D had dealt drugs to an undercover officer in an unsupervised operation when there was no prior suspicion against D; cf *Procter* [2004] EWCA Crim 1984; *M* [2011] EWCA Crim 648.

[451] (1998) 28 EHRR 101.

[452] *Eurofin* [2005] Crim LR 134.

[453] See D Ormerod and A Roberts, 'The Trouble with *Teixeira*: Developing a Principled Approach to Entrapment' (2002) Int J E & P 38.

theft.[454] But if the police have given D an unexceptional opportunity to deal drugs, which he has taken, there is no obligation to discount the sentence.[455]

12.8 Impossibility[456]

Where the law imposes a duty to act, it has sometimes been held that it is a defence that, through no fault of his own, it was impossible for D to fulfil that duty. A driver is not liable for failure to report an accident if he does not know the accident has happened.[457] The secretary of a limited company is not liable for failure to annex to an annual return a copy of a balance sheet laid before the company in a general meeting where there is no such balance sheet in existence: 'nobody ought to be prosecuted for that which it is impossible to do'.[458] A person is not liable for failure to leave a particular place if he is unaware of the order requiring him to do so.[459] In New Zealand, it has been held that a failure to leave the country after a revocation of a permit was not an offence if no airline would carry D because of the advanced state of her pregnancy.[460] Impossibility is a defence to a charge of failure to assist a constable to preserve the peace when called upon to do so.[461]

On the other hand, the failure of a driver to produce a test certificate is not excused by the fact that it is impossible for him to do so, the owner of the vehicle being unable or unwilling to produce it.[462] Failure by the owner of a vehicle to display the excise licence is not excused by the fact that, without any negligence or default on his part, it has become detached in his absence.[463]

We find here the inconsistency which is so common in relation to strict liability. It cannot be asserted, therefore, that any *general* defence of impossibility is recognized at the present time. It has to be regarded as a question of the interpretation of the particular provision, with all the uncertainty that this entails.

When impossibility might be available as a defence, it will presumably fail if the impossibility has been brought about by D's own default.[464] The defence would also seem to be confined to cases where the law imposes a duty to act and not to cases of commission where the corresponding defence, if any, is necessity.[465]

---

[454] *McCann*, above, p 384.

[455] See *Thornton and Hobbs* [2003] EWCA Crim 919.

[456] CLGP, at 746–748. See A Smart, 'Responsibility for Failing to do the Impossible' (1987) 103 LQR 532.

[457] *Harding v Price* [1948] 1 KB 695, [1948] 1 All ER 283, DC.

[458] *Stockdale v Coulson* [1974] 3 All ER 154 at 157, DC, per Melford Stevenson J.

[459] *Lim Chin Aik v R* [1963] AC 160, [1963] 1 All ER 223, PC.

[460] *Finau v Department of Labour* [1984] 2 NZLR 396.

[461] *Brown* (1841) Car & M 314, per Alderson B.

[462] *Davey v Towle* [1973] RTR 328, DC.

[463] *Strowger v John* [1974] RTR 124, DC; cf *Pilgram v Dean* [1974] 2 All ER 751, DC.

[464] But cf *Stockdale v Coulson*, above, and comment at [1974] Crim LR 375.

[465] See *Canestra* 1951 (2) SA 317 (AD) and Burchell and Hunt, SACLP, 293–296.

13
Inchoate Crime

13.1 Introduction

Attempts, conspiracies and assisting and encouraging under the Serious Crime Act 2007 are known collectively as 'inchoate offences'. 'Inchoate' means 'just begun, incipient; in an initial or early stage...' Criminalizing inchoate offences raises particular difficulties because the conduct involved will often be far removed from the type of harm that would be needed to give rise to a charge under the relevant substantive offence.[1] For example, where A and B agree to burgle V's house, a conspiracy to burgle is complete even though they have never been near the house and have taken no further steps to perpetrate that crime. It does not follow that inchoate offences will never involve a tangible harm – attempted murder can be charged as appropriately where D shoots V who survives as where D is arrested before he has taken aim to shoot.

The *actus reus* of inchoate offences can extend to cover a wide range of behaviour, sometimes seemingly innocuous, as for example with 'an agreement' in conspiracy, or mere words of encouragement in assisting and encouraging. However, there are sound reasons of policy and principle for punishing these types of wrongdoing, a central one being that the defendant has demonstrated by his actions his willingness that a substantive offence be committed. There is a clear risk of overcriminalization.[2] Since the *actus reus* is so broad, it is important that inchoates are kept within reasonable limits by requirements of serious *mens rea*. But, this emphasis on *mens rea* does not mean that inchoates can be regarded as thought-crimes; there remains a requirement that the defendant's blameworthy state of mind manifests itself by some words or other conduct.

Inchoate offences always relate to a substantive offence. Thus, there is no crime of attempt *per se*, only crimes of, for example, attempted theft, attempted murder, etc. It should also be noted that liability for inchoate offences exists independently of accessorial liability. In the latter, the secondary party's liability derives from the commission of the full offence by the principal offender. Inchoate offences are completed and can be prosecuted before the commission of any full offence. Significant consequences flow from this. For example, there are defences of withdrawal for secondary parties who demonstrate a change of heart before the commission of the principal offence; whereas inchoate liability is complete with the act of conspiracy or attempt or doing an act capable of assisting or encouraging; and any subsequent withdrawal goes only to mitigation in sentencing.[3] Arguably, inchoate offences better respect the principle of fair-labelling, since the description of D's conduct accurately reflects his personal behaviour; whereas in secondary liability the accessory's conduct may be fundamentally misdescribed as being derivative

---

[1] See, generally, the Law Commission's Consultation Paper No 183, *Conspiracy and Attempt* (2007) hereafter in this chapter 'LCCP 183'; and its Report No 318, *Conspiracy and Attempts* (2009) hereafter LC 318.

[2] See D Husak, *Overcriminalisation* (2008), 160 et seq. See on the importance of this, LCCP 195, para 4.61.

[3] There have been suggestions that by analogy with counselling, such a defence should be available to. For discussion see Ashworth, POCL, 463 and Wilson, *Central Issues*, 243–249.

on the conduct of another – the principal (as where the getaway driver in a fatal armed robbery is convicted as a 'murderer').[4]

It is likely that inchoate offences will be of increasing importance in the future, especially in prosecuting certain types of crime, the obvious example being the supply and importation of prohibited drugs. A number of other factors suggest that inchoates will become more commonplace, including, in particular, the recent shift from coercive to 'intelligence-led' policing where new powers and technological advances allow the police to gather evidence and intervene before substantive crimes are committed. Aside from their prevalence, the study of inchoate offences is also of increased importance because of Parliament's willingness to enact new forms of substantive offence that take the form of inchoate offences.[5] Recent examples include the offence of 'grooming' (seducing children to a meeting),[6] offences of 'inciting' another to engage in sexual activity,[7] assisting or encouraging suicide[8] expansive terrorist offences[9] and the wide-ranging offences under the Proceeds of Crime Act 2002.[10] Inchoates discussed in this chapter may also take on enhanced significance if the Law Commission's recent proposals in relation to regulatory crime are adopted. The proposals include preventing the creation of more separate statutory regulatory offences in inchoate form.[11]

The Government enacted a series of offences in Part 2 of the Serious Crime Act 2007 to replace the common law offence of incitement. The Law Commission recently reviewed the offences of conspiracy and attempt, and reference is made to the proposals throughout this chapter although the Government has stated that it has no plans to enact any of the proposals at this time.[12]

13.2 Attempt[13]

The common law of attempt[14] was repealed by the Criminal Attempts Act 1981 (in the rest of this part of the chapter referred to as 'the Act').[15] Section 1(1) creates a statutory offence:

---

[4] See above, Ch 8, and the discussion of the Law Commission's proposals in respect of secondary liability, LCCP 131 (1993), on which see JC Smith, 'Secondary Participation in Crime – Can We Do Without It?' (1994) 144 NLJ 679. See further the Report LC 305.

[5] LCCP 183, para 1.4.

[6] See s 15 of the Sexual Offences Act 2003, and Ch 18 below, p 763. On the prevalence of this, see A Gillespie, 'Child Protection on the Internet' (2002) 14 CFLQ 411; 'Children, Chatrooms and the Law' [2001] Crim LR 435, and B Gallagher et al, 'International and Internet Child Sexual Abuse and Exploitation – Issues Emerging from Research' (2003) 15 CFLQ 353–370.

[7] Sexual Offences Act 2003, s 8, see below, p 765.

[8] See Ch 16 below.

[9] See, eg, Terrorism Act 2000, s 59; Anti-terrorism, Crime and Security Act 2001, s 50, discussed by C Walker, *The Anti-terrorism Legislation* (2nd edn, 2009). In *Rowe* [2007] EWCA Crim 635, the LCJ noted at [53] that s 57 of the 2000 Act creates an inchoate offence in relation to terrorism. Comparing it to attempt, his lordship commented that: 'Section 57, for good and obvious reason, makes criminal conduct that is merely preparatory to the commission of terrorist acts. While such conduct is highly culpable, it is not as culpable as attempting to commit, or actually committing, the terrorist acts in question. But the seriousness of the offence consists not merely in the culpability of the offender but the potential of his conduct to cause harm.' The use of statutory inchoates is considered by the Law Commission: LCCP 183, Ch 15.

[10] See the discussion at p 1000, below and references therein.

[11] See LCCP 195, *Criminal Liability in Regulatory Contexts* (2010), para 1.38.

[12] As stated on the Law Commission website. cf the MOJ, *Report on the Implementation of Law Commission Proposals* (2011).

[13] See LCCP 183, Ch 14 for a review of the present law. For a valuable theoretical examination of the offence, see RA Duff, *Criminal Attempts* (1996) see also G Yaffe, *Attempts* (2010).

[14] See LCCP 183, Ch 13 for a review of the common law and see the fourth edition of this book, at 246–264.

[15] See, generally, IH Dennis, 'The Criminal Attempts Act 1981' [1982] Crim LR 5. See also P Glazebrook, 'Should We have a Law of Attempted Crime?' (1969) 85 LQR 28; Wilson, *Central Issues*, Ch 8.

If, with intent to commit an offence to which this section applies, a person does an act which is more than merely preparatory to the commission of the offence, he is guilty of attempting to commit the offence.

Liability turns on D doing more than merely preparatory acts with intent to commit an offence – in this chapter referred to as the 'substantive offence'. It is always essential to have in mind which substantive offence it is alleged D is intending to commit. Thereafter, it is a question of assessing D's conduct and *mens rea*.

13.2.1 *Mens rea* in attempts[16]

Exceptionally, *mens rea* is discussed before *actus reus* here because, as has often been remarked,[17] the mental element assumes paramount importance in attempts. The *actus reus* may be a seemingly innocent and harmless act, as where D puts sugar in V's tea. If D intends to murder V and believes that the substance is a deadly poison when it is in fact sugar, he has committed attempted murder. The *actus reus* may be *any* act, provided it is done with intent to commit the offence and goes beyond mere preparation (see below). Although the terms of s 1 suggest that the *mens rea* requirement is straightforward – 'with intent' – the position is more complex, and requires discussion of a number of elements of fault.

13.2.1.1 'Intentional' conduct

D must intend to perform the relevant *act* that goes beyond mere preparation towards the commission of the substantive offence. That is the conduct element of this offence. This can only sensibly be understood to mean a 'purposive' or direct intent rather than an oblique intent. If D carrying a knife trips and accidentally stabs V, D does not intend to wound V. He is not guilty of attempting to murder him.

13.2.1.2 Intention as to consequences

Where the substantive offence requires proof of a result or consequence, the offence of attempt will require proof of an intention as to that consequence. Wounding contrary to s 20 of the OAPA requires a result – a break in the continuity of V's skin. For a charge of attempted wounding, D must intend that consequence.

This is straightforward enough where the *mens rea* of the substantive offence requires an intention as to the consequence: the *mens rea* is the same on the attempt. However, many substantive offences require proof of some mental element short of intention (for example, recklessness or malice) as to consequences. On a charge of attempt, an intention and nothing less must be proved as to any result element of the *actus reus* of the substantive crime.[18] So, for example, recklessness whether the relevant harm is caused is a sufficient *mens rea* for most non-fatal offences against the person, for criminal damage and many other offences, but it is not a sufficient *mens rea* on a charge of attempting to commit any of them.[19] Equally, although an intention to cause grievous bodily harm is a sufficient *mens rea* for murder, that is plainly

---

[16] See Duff, *Criminal Attempts*, Ch 1; Yaffe, *Attempts,* Ch 4. LC 318, Part 8.

[17] See, eg, *Whybrow* (1951) 35 Cr App R 141.

[18] On one interpretation of *Attorney-General's Reference (No 3 of 1992)* [1994] 2 All ER 121, it may be sufficient that D has the *mens rea* (short of intention) sufficient for the full offence if he has completed that element in the course of his attempt. For discussion see LCCP, 183 para 16.68. The final proposal in LC 318 was that the 1981 Act be amended to provide that, for the purposes of s 1(1), an intent to commit an offence includes a conditional intent to commit it: para 8.106.

[19] *Millard and Vernon* [1987] Crim LR 393. cf D Stuart, '*Mens Rea*, Negligence and Attempts' [1968] Crim LR 647.

not an intention to commit murder and so is insufficient on a charge of attempted murder. Nothing less than an intention to kill will do on that charge.[20]

Purposive or oblique intention as to consequences?

As has been seen,[21] intention has a variable meaning in the criminal law so the question arises, what does 'intent to commit an offence' mean in s 1(1) of the Act? It was held in *Pearman*[22] that 'intent' in s 1 has the same meaning as in the common law of attempts, applying *Mohan*[23] where the court held that there must be proved:

a decision to bring about, in so far as it lies within the accused's power, the commission of the offence which it is alleged the accused attempted to commit, no matter whether the accused desired that consequence of his act or not.

The concluding words are difficult to reconcile with the main proposition, which certainly seems to embody the notion of 'trying' to cause, or striving for, a result.[24]

In *Pearman* the court thought that these words:

are probably designed to deal with a case where the accused has, as a primary purpose, some other object, for example, a man who plants a bomb in an aeroplane, which he knows is going to take off, it being his primary intention that he should claim the insurance on the aeroplane when the freight goes down into the sea. The jury would not be put off from saying that he intended to murder the crew simply by saying that he did not want or desire to kill the crew, but that was something that he inevitably intended to do.[25]

This is the meaning given to intention in criminal law generally after the series of cases culminating in *Woollin*.[26] Intention encompasses direct (purposive) intent and a jury may find intent from D's foresight of virtually certain consequences (oblique intent). This was applied to the offence of attempt by the Court of Appeal in *Walker*.[27] It seems, therefore, that the requirement of intention as to consequences is satisfied by proof of oblique intention.

On the facts of *Walker,* these refinements may not have been in point, since the jury had convicted on a direction that they must be satisfied that D was *trying* to kill. If he was trying to kill it was immaterial, as a matter of law, whether death was, or was known by D to be, virtually certain, highly probable, or merely possible: a person may intend to kill even though the possibility of doing so is, and he knows it is, remote. Probability is no more than relevant evidence of the sufficient state of mind – it is easier to infer that D was trying to kill if he threw V from the window of the twentieth floor than if he threw him from the window of the ground floor. It was only if he was *not* trying to kill that the degree of probability assumed the

---

[20] cf *Whybrow, O'Toole* [1987] Crim LR 759, CA. As the CA accepted in *Morrison* [2003] All ER (D) 281 (May), an indictment containing a count of attempted murder includes, implicitly, an intention to cause grievous bodily harm with intent which can therefore be left as an alternative count. For comment on the need for proof in attempts of an intention as to the completed offence, see J Horder, 'Varieties of Intention, Criminal Attempts and Endangerment' (1994) 14 LS 335.

[21] Above, Ch 5, p 107.

[22] (1984) 80 Cr App R 259, CA. For the common law position, see R Buxton, 'Inchoate Offences: Incitement and Attempt' [1973] Crim LR 656.

[23] [1976] QB 1, CA. See K Arenson, 'The Pitfalls in the Law of Attempt' (2005) 69 JCL 146; LC 318, para 8.87.

[24] See the discussion in Duff, *Criminal Attempts;* and Yaffe, *Attempts.*

[25] (1984) 80 Cr App R 259 at 263.

[26] [1999] AC 82, [1998] 4 All ER 103, above, p 107.

[27] (1989) 90 Cr App R 226, [1990] Crim LR 44. In that case the court condoned the use by the judge of the phrase, 'very high degree of probability', but it is now clear that foresight of 'virtual certainty' is the minimum from which a jury may find intention.

character of a rule of law, and then *Woollin* requires foresight of virtual certainty and nothing less will do.[28,] This issue of intention has been the subject of law reform proposals.[29]

13.2.1.3 Intention as to circumstances forming part of *actus reus*?

Where the substantive offence requires proof of intention or knowledge as to a circumstance, and recklessness will not suffice for the complete offence, it is clear that it will not suffice for the attempt. So if D attempts to receive goods, being reckless whether they are stolen, he is not guilty of an attempt to handle stolen goods because the full offence of handling requires knowledge or belief as to the circumstance that the goods are stolen goods.

Where the fault element relating to circumstances forming part of the *actus reus* of the substantive offence is specified to include states of mind less than intention or knowledge, is it necessary always to prove intention as to that circumstance on a charge of attempt? For example, the *mens rea* as to consent in the substantive crime of rape is satisfied by D not reasonably believing in V's consent. For the offence of attempted rape, it is necessary to prove that D intended that V was not consenting or is it sufficient that he did not reasonably believe in her consent? Note that s 1 of the 1981 Act describes fault only in terms of 'intention'.

It is submitted that although the case law is confusing, the position is that if the substantive offence requires proof of intention with respect to material circumstances then the attempt must also require intention. But, it is not necessary to prove intention as to circumstances where the charge is of an attempt to commit an offence for which the fault element relating to circumstances forming part of the *actus reus* of the substantive offence is specified to include states of mind less than intention or knowledge.

Stating the precise nature of the relevant *mens rea* for attempt is far from easy. Both 'direct' and 'oblique' intention can properly be used to describe *mens rea* in relation to circumstances as well as consequences. D could be said to have a direct intention as to circumstances where the existence of the circumstance is part of the package of results he desires. So for example in *Pigg*,[30] before the Act, it was assumed without argument that a man might be guilty of attempted rape if he tried to have sexual intercourse with a woman, with intention as to penetration, but being reckless[31] whether or not she consented to his doing so (that is, the circumstance of her consent). Though the point was not spelled out in any case, it is submitted that this was right in principle.

It is submitted that the *mens rea* of the complete crime should be modified only in so far as it is necessary in order to accommodate the concept of attempt. If subjective recklessness as to circumstances is a sufficient *mens rea* for the substantive crime, it should be so for an attempt. If D, seeking to remove hi-fi wiring from his rented accommodation sets out to damage the cable (intention as to a result), and at the time is reckless as to the ownership of the cable (a circumstance) because he is aware of the risk that it is the landlord's but is prepared to run that risk unjustifiably, he ought to be open to conviction for attempted criminal damage once

---

[28] For discussion of the philosophical dimensions of a distinction between trying to do something and trying to succeed, see J Hornby, 'On What's Intentionally Done', in S Shute, J Gardner and J Horder, *Action and Value in Criminal Law* (1993) 60; Horder (1994) 14 LS 335: those who try without an intention to succeed are equivalent to those who recklessly endanger. See also Yaffe, *Attempts*, Ch 2.

[29] The Law Commission provisionally proposed that *Woollin* should apply in attempts (LCCP 183), and that conditional intent would suffice: para 16.68. In LC 318 it was recommended that an intent to commit an offence includes a conditional intent to commit it: paras 8.96–8.106. cf the earlier proposals in Law Com No 143; R Buxton, 'The Working Party on Inchoate Offences: Incitement and Attempt' [1973] Crim LR 656, 662; Draft Code, cl 49(2) and G Williams, 'Intents in the Alternative' [1991] CLJ 120.

[30] (1982) 74 Cr App R 352, [1982] Crim LR 446 and commentary. See also S White, 'Three Points on *Pigg*' [1989] Crim LR 539, 541.

[31] That being the *mens rea* in 1981 when the Act was passed.

he has gone beyond an act of mere preparation. The counter argument to this is that, as with all inchoate crimes, liability might arise where D has caused little if any tangible harm, and to avoid overbreadth, attempts ought to require proof of a high level of culpability – in *mens rea* terms intention (perhaps even purposive intention) or knowledge.[32]

In *Khan*,[33] the court, after considering the conflicting opinions, held that, for the purposes of the Criminal Attempts Act, a man has an intention to commit rape if he intends to have sexual intercourse with a person, being reckless whether that person consents.[34] As Duff argues, D would be liable for the substantive offence if he succeeded in doing what he was trying to do with that level of *mens rea* as to circumstance, and it is logical therefore that he should be guilty of the attempt if he was unsuccessful in committing the substantive offence with the same *mens rea*.[35] In practical terms it would be virtually impossible to prove that D *intended* that the person with whom he had intercourse did not consent. The valuable protection offered by the offence of attempt would be severely curtailed.

Unfortunately, the courts have subsequently complicated the picture. *Khan* was followed (and arguably extended) in *A-G's Reference (No 3 of 1992)*[36] where the offence charged was attempted arson being reckless whether life be endangered, contrary to s 1(2) of the Criminal Damage Act 1971. DD had thrown petrol bombs at an occupied car and missed. The Court of Appeal stated a general principle:

a defendant, in order to be guilty of an attempt, must be in one of the states of mind required for the commission of the full offence, and did [*sic*] his best, so far as he could, to supply what was missing from the completion of the offence. It is the policy of the law that such people should be punished notwithstanding that in fact the intentions of such a defendant have not been fulfilled.[37]

Several comments must be made about this approach.[38] First, the decision goes beyond *Khan* by allowing a conviction for attempt where D's *mens rea* comprises only recklessness as to the existing *consequences* if there is an intention as to the missing *circumstances*. The full offence under s 1(2) of the Criminal Damage Act 1971 requires proof of a consequence: that property is damaged. There has never been a requirement in s 1(2) of an actual endangerment of any life. The required circumstance is that the property belonged to someone (not necessarily another). In addition, there was then a requirement that an ordinary prudent observer would have realized that life might be endangered by the damage.[39] Since the court in the

---

[32] See GR Sullivan, 'Intent, Subjective Recklessness and Culpability' (1992) 12 OJLS 381, 385 (relying on a concept of 'knowledge in the second degree'). cf RA Duff, 'The Circumstances of an Attempt' [1991] 50 CLJ 100 at 100–101.

[33] [1990] 2 All ER 783, (1990) 91 Cr App R 29. See further G Williams, 'The Problem of Reckless Attempts' [1983] Crim LR 365; R Buxton, 'Circumstances, Consequences and Attempted Rape' [1984] Crim LR 25; Duff [1991] CLJ 100 and the response by Williams [1991] CLJ 120. See LCCP 183, para 14.46; LC 318, para 8.129.

[34] This was of course before the Sexual Offences Act 2003 redefined rape. Note the error in the Sexual Offences Act 2003, s 77: definitions and application of rebuttable and conclusive presumptions in ss 75 and 76 are, by s 77, applicable only in respect of the substantive offences, not inchoate versions. What then of D charged with attempted rape and rape, where the prosecution are unsure with what V was penetrated if anything, and D pleads consent, whereas the complaint alleges that the penetration occurred while she was sleeping? See below Ch 18.

[35] Above, p 406.

[36] (1993) 98 Cr App R 383, [1994] Crim LR 348. For cogent criticism, see DW Elliott, 'Endangering Life by Destroying or Damaging Property' [1997] Crim LR 382, 393.

[37] See further on this approach J Stannard, 'Making Up for the Missing Element: A Sideways Look at Attempts' (1987) 7 LS 194.

[38] See RA Duff, 'Recklessness in Attempts (Again)' (1995) 15 OJLS 309 for an approach which seeks to explain the decision without distinctions between consequences and circumstances, focusing instead on the question whether D would have necessarily committed the full offence if he had carried out the actions.

[39] The latter requirement flowed from the application of the objective test in *Caldwell* as in *Sangha* (1988) 87 Cr App R 88. It is worth noting that since *Caldwell* has been overruled by *G*, it is arguable that the requirement

A-G's Reference concluded that it was sufficient if D was (*Caldwell*) reckless as to that element of life endangerment, it would seem that recklessness as to present consequences (where that is sufficient *mens rea* for the full offence) may also suffice for the *mens rea* of an attempt. This is, it is submitted, contrary to the clear wording of the Act which requires an intent as to consequences.

Secondly, the statement is overbroad.[40] Read literally, this approach would lead to the conviction for attempt of D who is merely reckless as to a consequence element of the offence provided he had an intention as to the relevant missing circumstance element(s). This is clearly not what the Act was intended to mean. Consider D who is reckless as to whether his slapdash DIY will damage the hi-fi cabling he is just about to try to remove (reckless as to consequence), but who intends/knows that it is property belonging to his landlord (intention as to circumstance). He ought not to be guilty of attempt.

Thirdly, even if the case does not extend the law as regards the *mens rea* for consequences in attempt, it produces problems for the *mens rea* as to circumstances. On a broad interpretation, the case would introduce strict liability into the law of attempts. For example, if D tries to touch sexually a girl, V, whom he believes on reasonable grounds to be aged 16 but who is in fact only 12, he would be guilty of an attempt to commit the offence under s 7 of the Sexual Offences Act 2003. He has the state of mind required for the commission of the full offence (an intention to touch a person, who is in fact, whether he knows it or not, under the age of 13); and he has done his best 'to supply [in the quaint language of the court] what was missing from the commission of the full offence' – sexual touching. There is a logical argument in favour of such an extension of inchoate liability;[41] but it goes beyond anything actually decided and beyond any recommendation of the Draft Code Team. It seems unlikely that the court in the *A-G's Reference* appreciated the point and the *dictum* should be regarded with reserve.

Finally, at the time of the decision, it was settled that *Caldwell* recklessness was sufficient for the full offence under the Criminal Damage Act and the court held that this was also the right test on the attempt charge. Subjective recklessness (*Cunningham/G* recklessness) has long been thought to be an acceptable *mens rea* as to circumstances in attempt because it is a true state of mind. However, a person may be *Caldwell* reckless even if the possibility of the relevant risk (a bystander's perception of a danger to life), never enters his head. To hold that such an objective fault element is sufficient for attempt is, arguably, an unacceptable extension of liability for an inchoate offence.[42] The point does not appear to have been considered explicitly by the court. Given the overruling of *Caldwell* in *G*,[43] the issue assumes less significance in relation to criminal damage, but if it is interpreted more broadly so that recklessness, negligence or even strict liability as to a circumstance will suffice, it remains of fundamental importance.

In addition to exposing the lack of clarity and certainty on the *mens rea* of attempts, the *A-G's* case highlights the absence of any general offence of reckless endangerment in English criminal law. If such an offence existed, it might serve as an alternative charge where D failed to bring about the proscribed harm of the substantive offence, but had exhibited a sufficient

---

relating to the perception of endangerment of life is not purely one of D's *mens rea* – that D intends or is subjectively reckless as to that danger – because recklessness requires also that the risk taking is unjustified, which implicitly requires that the risk is objectively present.

[40] See also for criticism: LCCP 183, para 14.42 et seq.

[41] See JC Smith, 'Two Problems in Criminal Attempts' (1957) 70 Harv LR 422 at 433 and 'Two Problems in Criminal Attempts Re-examined' [1962] Crim LR 135. See for further discussion Duff (1995) 15 OJLS 309, defending the more radical view.

[42] What of the person who does not give a thought to the relevant circumstance? Perhaps he should be held sufficiently reckless if he was indifferent? cf commentary on *Mousir* [1987] Crim LR 561 at 562.

[43] [2004] 1 AC 1034.

degree of culpability to deserve criminal sanction. A conviction could be achieved without straining the natural scope and meaning of the law of attempts. The argument for such an offence might be at its most compelling when the conduct creates a risk of injury, rather than risk merely to property.[44]

The Law Commission has recently recommended that for substantive offences which have a circumstance requirement but no corresponding fault requirement (ie strict liability as to circumstances), or which have a corresponding fault requirement which is objective (such as negligence), it should be possible to convict D of attempting to commit the substantive offence only if D was subjectively reckless as to the circumstance at the relevant time.[45] In addition, it is recommended that where a substantive offence has fault requirements not involving mere negligence (or its equivalent) – ie recklessness or knowledge – in relation to a fact or circumstance, it should be possible to convict D of attempting to commit the substantive offence if D possessed those fault requirements at the relevant time.[46]

13.2.1.4 Conditional intention

Great practical difficulty and much academic debate was caused by the decision of the Court of Appeal in *Husseyn*.[47] The defendants opened the door of a van in which there was a holdall containing valuable sub-aqua equipment. They were charged with attempted theft of the equipment. The judge directed the jury that they could convict if the defendants were about to look into the holdall and, if in the defendants' opinion its contents were valuable, to steal them. The Court of Appeal held that this was a misdirection: 'it cannot be said that one who has it in mind to steal only if what he finds is worth stealing has a present intention to steal'. This caused particular difficulties in the law of burglary because most persons charged with that crime intend to steal, not some specific thing, but anything they find which they think is worth stealing.[48] The Court of Appeal[49] got over this difficulty by holding that *Husseyn* applied only where, as in that case, the indictment named the specific thing which the defendant was alleged to have attempted to steal (the sub-aqua equipment). The Court of Appeal held that there would be no problem in convicting of an attempt if the indictment had charged an attempt to steal 'some or all of the contents' of the holdall – or car, handbag or house, as the case may be. This purely procedural device was rightly criticized. In *Husseyn*, for example, the only thing in the holdall was the sub-aqua equipment. If the defendant was guilty of attempting to steal 'some or all of the contents' he was obviously guilty of attempting to steal the sub-aqua equipment – there were no other contents; but if the indictment charged him with that he had to be acquitted!

---

[44] See the Scottish model in the Draft Code, cl 43, 'a person who intentionally or recklessly causes a risk of injury to another person is guilty of an offence of causing an unlawful risk of injury'. As the commentary makes clear, this deals with the person who, eg, drops a heavy object from a tall building onto a busy road, missing all road users. See generally KJM Smith, 'Liability for Endangerment: English Ad Hoc Pragmatism and American Innovation' [1983] Crim LR 127; RA Duff, 'Criminalising Endangerment', in RA Duff and SP Green, *Defining Crimes* (2005); Duff, *Answering for Crimes,* 148.

[45] LC 318, para 8.133.

[46] LC 318, para 8.137.

[47] (1977) 67 Cr App R 131n, [1978] Crim LR 219 and commentary; AR White, *Misleading Cases* (1991) 63. See also G Williams, 'The Three Rogues Charter' [1980] Crim LR 263. Described in LCCP 183 as 'wrong': para 16.74. See also LC 318 para 8.96 et seq.

[48] Similarly, a person may be guilty of attempted burglary with intent to commit gbh if he attempts to enter, hoping to find someone inside whom he would wish to beat up. It is immaterial that there is no one in the house: *Toothill* [1998] Crim LR 876; LC 318, para 8.129.

[49] *A-G's References (Nos 1 and 2 of 1979)* [1980] QB 180, [1979] Crim LR 585; see also *Walkington* [1979] 2 All ER 716, [1979] Crim LR 526 and commentary. For discussion, see LCCP 183, para 5.11.

Conditional intent under the 1981 Act

The Act does not expressly do anything about this absurd and unworthy distinction, and it remains part of the law.[50] The Act has however solved the problem because it is possible in such a case to charge D with attempting to steal something in the holdall even if it was empty. It is no bar to conviction under the Act if it is impossible for D to commit the substantive offence (because the holdall is empty). This reverses the common law position in *Haughton v Smith*.[51] In *Husseyn*, the jury must have found that D intended to steal anything in the holdall that he found to be of value. If he would have taken the sub-aqua equipment had he found it, he had certainly done an act that was more than merely preparatory to stealing it and he ought to be found guilty of attempting to do so. It might not, however, be possible for the jury to be satisfied that he would have taken that item. If he would not have taken it, it follows that he was looking for other things – we know not what and perhaps he did not know either – which were not there. He was attempting to steal all right, but his attempt was doomed to failure. This no longer matters since the Act reversed *Haughton v Smith*. He was no different in this respect from the person who attempts to steal from an empty pocket.

A practical difficulty remains in how to form the indictment. The formula approved by the Court of Appeal, 'some or all of the contents', is unsatisfactory because the jury may not be satisfied that D intended to steal *any* of the actual contents and may indeed be satisfied that he did not intend to steal any of them. The indictment would be accurate, however, if it simply stated, 'attempted to steal from a holdall'. This represents the truth, whether there is anything there that he would have stolen or not. The failure to specify any subject matter is not an objection because there is in fact no subject matter to be specified. D must be dealt with on the basis that he intended to take anything he thought worth taking, whatever it might be. The problem is exactly the same in the empty pocket case.

In *Husseyn*, the court followed *Easom*,[52] where D picked up a woman's handbag in a theatre, rummaged through the contents and put it back having taken nothing. The handbag was attached by a thread to a policewoman's wrist. D's conviction for stealing the handbag and the specified contents – tissues, cosmetics, etc – was quashed because there was no intention permanently to deprive the owner of these. Consequently, the court held, he was not guilty of attempting to steal the handbag or contents. Whether he was rightly acquitted of theft is debated[53] but, assuming he was, he was also innocent of attempting to steal the specific contents, but he was clearly guilty of an attempt to steal what was not there. Plainly, he was looking for money and therefore the handbag was, in effect, empty. The court posed a much-discussed example: 'If a dishonest postal sorter picks up a pile of letters intending to steal any which are registered, but, on finding that none of them are, replaces them, he has stolen nothing.' This is true; but he was then (before *Haughton v Smith*) and is now, guilty of attempting to steal registered letters.

Academic writing has produced a diverse range of classifications and terminology of conditional intentions but three broad categories are accepted: (i) 'non-comprehensive conditional intentions' – D intends to *do* 'x' if 'y';[54] (ii) 'comprehensive conditional intentions – D intends 'x' only if 'y' – D has a declared intentions as to his course of conduct in both eventualities: where *y* materializes and not; (iii) unconditional intentions – D intends 'x' even if 'y'.[55] These have not been explicitly examined by the courts.

---

[50] *Smith and Smith* [1986] Crim LR 166, CA.

[51] [1975] AC 476 below, p 483. Though there was an understandable inclination on the part of the Court of Appeal to carry on as if that case did not exist. See *Bayley and Easterbrook* [1980] Crim LR 503 and commentary.

[52] [1971] 2 QB 315.

[53] See Williams, TBCL, 651–653 and [1979] Crim LR 530; below, p 840

[54] K Campbell, 'Conditional Intention' (1982) 2 LS 77 at 84–85.

[55] cf the view in LCCP 183, Part 5, see below p 436.

The Law Commission has recently recommended that the 1981 Act be amended to provide that, for the purposes of s 1(1), an intent to commit an offence includes a conditional intent to commit it.[56]

13.2.2 *Actus reus* in attempt[57]

Although the *mens rea* of the offence is of primary importance, the *actus reus* of attempts remains significant. It ensures that the offence does not extend to criminalizing thoughts, but rather applies only when D has exhibited some physical willingness to bring his criminal intentions to fruition. This, of course, begs the question how much of a physical manifestation of that intention it is necessary for D to perform in order for his conduct to be regarded as an attempt to commit the crime.

The sufficiency of an act to prove attempt is an extremely controversial issue on many levels. Firstly, at a practical level, the more broadly the law extends the scope of attempt liability to include even the slightest conduct towards the commission of an offence, the greater the protection that can be afforded and the earlier the police can intervene. The cost of that approach is in potentially overbroad criminalization and oppressive policing.[58]

Secondly, on a theoretical level, there is a division between the 'subjectivist' and 'objectivist' schools of thought. In short, it has been said that 'subjectivists require the relevant acts to manifest an *intention* to commit the substantive offence whereas objectivists require the relevant acts to manifest the *actual* attempt'.[59]

Thirdly, there is an even broader related question which is why the criminal law places as much emphasis as it does on the *consequences* of the criminal actor's conduct. Why should the outcome of the defendant's intentional conduct make so much difference to his criminal liability? In the context of attempt, this raises specific questions whether and why D ought to be treated differently in terms of liability and punishment when he embarks on carrying out his criminal intentions, but the proscribed harm does not occur.[60]

13.2.2.1 Common law

Before the 1981 Act, there was a sufficient *actus reus* for an attempt if D's steps towards commission of the offence were properly described as 'an attempt', in ordinary meaning. This did not maximize legal certainty nor clarity. Many steps may be taken towards the commission of a crime that could not properly be described in this fashion. D, intending to commit murder, buys a gun and performs target practice, studies the habits of V, reconnoitres a suitable place to lie in ambush, puts on a disguise and sets out to take up his position. All are acts of preparation but could scarcely be described as attempted murder. D takes up his position, loads the gun, sees V approaching, raises the gun, takes aim, puts his finger on the trigger and squeezes it. D has now certainly committed attempted murder; but he might have desisted or been interrupted at any of the stages described. At what point had D gone far enough to be guilty

---

[56] LC 318, para 8.106.

[57] See Duff, *Criminal Attempts*, Ch 2; Yaffe, *Attempts*, Ch 10; D Stuart, 'The *Actus Reus* in Attempts' [1970] Crim LR 505.

[58] For a discussion of an even broader approach in which attempt liability is founded not on D's physical manifestation to commit crime but his disposition to do so, see PH Robinson, 'The Modern General Part: Three Illusions', in S Shute and A Simester, *Criminal Law Theory: Doctrines of the General Part* (2003) 92–93.

[59] Wilson, *Central Issues*, 237. See also Yaffe, above, Ch 1.

[60] See, generally, Duff, *Criminal Attempts*, Ch 12, Yaffe, *Attempts*, Ch 10; JC Smith, 'The Element of Chance in the Criminal Law' [1963] Crim LR 63; and in particular the writings of Professor Ashworth: 'Belief, Intent and Criminal Liability', in J Eekelaar and J Bell (eds), *Oxford Essays in Jurisprudence* (1987) and 'Criminal Attempts and the Role of Resulting Harm under the Code and under the Common Law' (1988) 19 Rutgers LR 725.

of an attempt? At common law it was a matter of fact: was D's act sufficiently proximate to murder to be properly described as an attempt to commit it?

More detailed formulations of the principle proved unsuccessful, being capricious in their operation or simply unhelpful.[61] This is not surprising when it is recalled that the principle has to apply to all crimes and that crimes are very diverse in their nature. The only well-settled rule was that if D had done the 'last act' that, as he knew, was necessary to achieve the *consequence* alleged to be attempted, he was guilty of the attempt.[62] The converse, however, did not apply. An act might be sufficiently proximate although it was not necessarily the last act to be done. For example, in *White,*[63] D was held guilty of attempted murder by the attempted administration of a dose of poison, though he may well have contemplated further doses, and further doses may have been necessary, to kill.

13.2.2.2 Common law and 1981 Act compared

The Law Commissioners when proposing the 1981 Act found that there is no 'magic formula' to define precisely what constitutes an attempt. The proximity test (that is, whether D's act is 'proximate' to the offence) was the only one broadly acceptable. Even its imprecision was not without advantages: 'its flexibility does enable difficult cases to be reconsidered and their authority questioned'; and 'where cases are so dependent on what are sometimes fine differences of degree, we think it is eminently appropriate for the question whether the conduct in a particular case amounts to an attempt to be left to the jury'. The purpose of the proximity test was to prevent too great an extension of criminal liability, by excluding mere acts of preparation. The test stated in s 1(1) of the Act is, in substance, that proposed by the Law Commission in formulating the provisions which led to the Act.[64] The Commission thought it 'undesirable to recommend anything more complex than a rationalization of the present law'. But, a definition expressly in terms of proximity was rejected. There was concern with any formula which suggested that only the 'last act' could be an attempt.[65]

The formula in the 1981 Act, it was decided, should direct attention not to when the commission of the offence begins, but to when mere preparation ends. The resulting 'preparatory act' test is more apt in one respect. 'Proximity' suggested that the attempter had to come 'pretty near'[66] to success; yet, where the attempt is to do the impossible (as where D attempts to murder using sugar that he believes to be poison), success is an infinity away. In contrast, there is no such conceptual difficulty about preparatory acts to do the impossible – by one who does not know it is impossible, of course!

It seems that no substantial change in the law was intended by the introduction of the test of 'going beyond mere preparation'. If any change has been made, it is to extend the scope of attempts because, if there is any 'middle ground' between mere preparation and a proximate act, an act in the middle ground now constitutes an attempt whereas formerly it did not do so.[67] It might be suggested, for example, that the assassin in the example above was

---

[61] The most interesting effort was called the 'equivocality theory' discussed in the fourth edition of this book, at 253–255. It is probably now of only historical interest, so far as English law is concerned.

[62] Even this, not very ambitious, rule was doubted by Lord Edmund-Davies in *Stonehouse* [1978] AC 55 at 86 but his lordship's doubts seem to relate to the last act of a secondary party which, admittedly, does not necessarily constitute an attempt. See [1977] Crim LR 547–549.

[63] [1910] 2 KB 124; see also *Linneker* [1906] 2 KB 99.

[64] See LC 102, paras 2.45–2.52. Criticized by G Williams, 'Wrong Turnings on the Law of Attempt' [1991] Crim LR 416.

[65] In particular, a test based on whether D had taken 'substantial steps'. cf the American Model Penal Code, s 5.01(1)(c).

[66] *Commonwealth v Kennedy* 170 Mass 18 (1897) O W Holmes J.

[67] See the section below on Reform, p 423.

not proximate when he merely left home to the site of the assassination, but that conduct might now be regarded as being beyond mere preparation. However, it seems more likely that preparation and commission overlap than that there is any gap between them.[68]

13.2.2.3 Interpreting 'beyond mere preparation'

Every step towards the commission of an offence, except the last one, could properly be described as 'preparatory' to the commission of the offence. The assassin crooks his finger around the trigger preparatory to pulling it. If the section were so interpreted, only the last act would amount to an attempt – a result which the Act designed to, and does, avoid: D may be guilty of attempted murder where he has not yet fired the gun and D can be guilty of attempted rape though he has not physically attempted penile penetration.[69]

The key word in interpreting the 1981 Act is 'merely'.[70] Not all preparatory acts are excluded. When does an act cease to be *merely* preparatory? The answer, it seems, must be when D is engaged in the commission of the offence which he is attempting – as Rowlatt J put it many years ago, when D is 'on the job'.[71] Whether he is engaged in the commission of the offence, seems to be, as it was before the Act, the ultimate question. The question whether D is in the 'executory stage' of committing the offence is another way of describing this.[72]

The first step for the court should be to determine precisely the nature of the substantive crime alleged to be attempted. In *Nash*,[73] D, who had left notes for paper boys inviting them to meet him and perform indecent acts with him, was held to be guilty of attempting to procure acts of gross indecency.[74] What the court overlooked was that an act is not 'procured' until it is committed; so the charge was, in substance, one of attempting to *commit* an act of gross indecency.[75] D's conduct fell far short of that. The nature of the crime is also important since it has been recognized that where the substantive offence turns on the commission of a single act (for example, killing or wounding) early acts are less likely to be regarded as beyond mere preparation than where the crime in question is one continuing over time (for example, fraud), where the 'moment of embarkation' may arise far earlier. This depends of course on

---

[68] The Law Commission suggested that the law must allow the flexibility judges need: LCCP 183, para 16.3.

[69] *A-G's Reference (No 1 of 1992)* (1992) 96 Cr App R 298, [1993] Crim LR 274. cf *Paitnaik* [2000] 3 Archbold News 2, CA, D straddled V but yet to remove his or her clothes or perform unequivocal sexual acts – sufficient evidence of attempt to be left to jury. See also *MH* [2004] WL 137 2419 where D struck the complainant, dragged her to a quiet lane, removed her trousers and boots and struggled with her asking her to make love: sufficient evidence of attempt to rape.

[70] E Griew, *Current Law Statutes* (1981) says that, 'If "merely" adds anything at all, it is only emphasis'; but elsewhere in his note he recognizes that all acts but the last are in one sense preparatory and that the phrase, 'merely preparatory', indicates that 'there may, in any criminal transaction, be a point before which it is appropriate to describe the actor as not yet engaged in the commission of the offence but as *only* preparing to commit it' (emphasis added). 'Only' equals 'merely'. Thus, Griew seems to agree that not all preparatory acts are excluded, but only those that are 'only' or 'merely' preparatory. In *Tosti* [1997] Crim LR 746, the court held that D's acts were 'preparatory, but not merely so'.

[71] *Osborn* (1919) 84 JP 63.

[72] LCCP 183, para 14.5.

[73] [1999] Crim LR 308 and commentary. cf *Toothill*, below, p 953 where the act which had to be attempted was the entry, not the intended rape. See now the offence of committing an offence with intent to commit a sex offence under the Sexual Offences Act 2003, s 62.

[74] Under the Sexual Offences Act 1956, s 13 now repealed (see the offences of inciting a child under 13 to engage in sexual activity, below, p 756).

[75] See PR Glazebrook, 'Attempting to Procure' [1959] Crim LR 774, commenting on *Miskell* (1954) 37 Cr App R 214. See LCCP 183 – proposed offence of criminal preparation not adopted in LC 318. See for critical comment and discussion of the merits of such an approach see J Rogers, 'The Codification of Attempts and the Case for Preparation' [2008] Crim LR 937.

the method by which the killing or the fraud is to be achieved.[76] Particular care is needed if the charge is one of an attempt to commit an offence which has, in its substantive form, an inchoate nature.[77]

Having identified the nature of the substantive crime and the nature of the conduct alleged to constitute acts beyond mere preparation, the court must determine whether the acts are indeed 'more than merely preparatory to the commission of the offence'. This is a question of fact. In a jury trial, it is of course for the judge to decide whether there is evidence sufficient in law to support such a finding and it is then for the jury to decide (i) what acts D did, and (ii) whether they were more than merely preparatory.[78] If the judge decides there is not sufficient evidence, he directs a verdict of not guilty. Where he decides there is sufficient evidence, he must leave both questions of fact to the jury, even where the only possible answer in law is that D is guilty.[79] Where, for example, the evidence is that D has done the 'last act', he may not tell the jury that, if they find that D did that act, that *is* an attempt even though, in law, this is so. The judge may express a strong opinion, but he must not appear to take the question of fact out of the hands of the jury.[80]

The decision of the judge is not always easy. As a recent example, in *K*[81] the defendant was convicted of attempting to cause a child to watch a sexual act. K spoke to some children playing near his office and asked a 6-year-old if he wanted to look at pornography on K's laptop computer. There was no direct evidence that the laptop was in fact in K's nearby office. The judge explained that the jury had to be sure that an invitation had been issued to the children and that the jury had to be sure that the laptop had been in the office and that it had been used to show pornography. If they were sure about that then the acts were more than merely preparatory. The Court of Appeal quashed the conviction. There was insufficient evidence in law to go before the jury and the directions given were inadequate. The mere invitation and the presence of a laptop computer did not amount to an attempt in law. There were acts that were merely preparatory and the judge should not have allowed the matter to go before the jury.[82] Contrast this with *R*[83] in which it was held that D's text message to a prostitute asking if she knew of any 12-year-olds available for sex was capable of constituting an attempt to arrange a sexual offence with a child (Sexual Offences Act, s 14).

It has been argued[84] that the judge and jury, in performing their respective functions, are not entitled to have regard to the word 'attempt'. The question to be determined is, in the words of s 4(3), simply whether D 'did an act falling within subsection (1) of [s 1]'; and that subsection does not use the word 'attempt'. While there is great force in this argument, it is

---

[76] *Qadir* [1997] 9 Archbold News 1, CA.

[77] See *Shergill* [2003] CLY 871 where the court rejected an indictment alleging an attempt to be knowingly concerned in the making of arrangements for facilitating entry of illegal entrants in to the UK (contrary to the Immigration Act 1971, s 25).

[78] See s 4(3) of the Act, which, in substance, codifies the common law as to the functions of judge and jury: *Stonehouse* [1978] AC 55. On the difficulty in application for jurors see JA Andrews, 'Uses and Misuses of the Jury', in *Reshaping the Criminal Law*, 55–56.

[79] *Wang* [2005] UKHL 9.

[80] *Griffin* [1993] Crim LR 515, CA. If the judge does and the jury convict, the Court of Appeal used to have an easy route to upholding the conviction under the proviso to the Criminal Appeal Act 1968, s 2. Since the Criminal Appeal Act 1995, there is no proviso, and the court would have to quash the conviction if it was regarded as unsafe. LCCP 183 provisionally proposed removing this problem by leaving the judge to decide the issue of whether there has been an attempt: para 16.89. The proposal was dropped in LC 318.

[81] [2009] EWCA Crim 1931. The full offence is only committed if the child does watch – cf *Nash*, above.

[82] The substantive offence involved is that contrary to s 12 of the Sexual Offences Act 2003, (for the purpose of obtaining sexual gratification, D intentionally causes a child to watch a third person engaging in an activity, or to look at an image of any person engaging in an activity), below, p 760.

[83] [2009] 1 WLR 713. The full offence requires that there is an 'arrangement' not that a sex act occurs.

[84] Griew, *Current Law Statutes*.

submitted that it should not prevail. As observed above, all acts but the last one are preparatory. How then are we to determine whether an act is more than *merely* preparatory? To be more than merely preparatory, it must also be something else. What? Some other concept not mentioned in the section must be invoked to give it a sensible meaning. The answer seems to be that the act must be part of the commission of the intended offence, an act that is done by D 'on the job', that it is, in a word, an 'attempt'.

The Act is, in this respect, a codifying Act so, applying *Bank of England v Vagliano Bros*,[85] 'the correct approach is to look first at the natural meaning of the statutory words, not to turn back to earlier case law and seek to fit some previous test to the words of the section'.[86]

Since the Act provides a statutory definition of attempt, the cases on attempt at common law are no longer binding. The citation of pre-Act cases has been discouraged.[87] They may, however, be regarded as persuasive because the Act is (in this respect) intended to be no more than a rationalization of the common law.

Judicial interpretations of the concept of attempt

A number of tests have been proposed at one time or another:

- whether D's act is the last act necessary; ie for there to be a completed attempt, not the completed crime. It would be enough for attempted murder that D was about to pull the trigger; there is no need for the victim to have died, which is the last act of murder;
- whether D's act is proximate to the commission of the full offence;
- whether D's act was one of a series which would lead to the crime if uninterrupted;
- whether D's act was immediately connected with the substantive offence.

The narrowest interpretation[88] was that of Lord Diplock in *Stonehouse*[89] where, having cited the opinion in *Eagleton*[90] that only acts 'immediately connected' with the offence can be attempts, he continued: 'In other words the offender must have crossed the Rubicon and burnt his boats.' The 'Rubicon test' was initially accepted as representing the law under the 1981 Act[91] but was rejected in *Gullefer*.[92] In *Gullefer*, D, seeing that the dog he had backed in a greyhound race was losing, jumped onto the track to stop the race. He hoped that the stewards would declare 'no race' whereupon punters would be entitled to have their money back and he would recover his £18 stake. His conviction for attempting to steal the £18 was quashed. His act was held to be merely preparatory. It remained for him to go to the bookmaker and demand his money.

In *Jones*,[93] applying *Gullefer*, the court upheld D's conviction of attempted murder where he got into V's car and pointed a loaded sawn-off shot gun at him, despite an argument by D that he had at least three acts to do: remove the safety catch, put his finger on the trigger and pull it. When he pointed the gun, there was evidence to leave to the jury. In the same vein is

---

[85] [1891] AC 107 at 144.

[86] *Jones* (1990) 91 Cr App R 351 at 353, discussed by KJM Smith, 'Proximity in Attempt: Lord Lane's Midway Course' [1991] Crim LR 576.

[87] The rule in *Vagliano* recognizes that where a provision is 'of doubtful import' resort to the previous law is perfectly legitimate.

[88] On which see Duff, *Criminal Attempts*, 390.

[89] [1978] AC 55 at 68. LCCP 183 suggests that Lord Diplock actually endorsed the proximity test despite his Rubicon comments.

[90] (1855) Dears CC 376, 515.

[91] *Widdowson* (1985) 82 Cr App R 314 at 318–319.

[92] [1990] 3 All ER 882, 91 Cr App R 356n. cf *Boyle* (1986) 84 Cr App R 270. cf *Stevens v R* [1985] LRC (Crim) discussed by L Blake (1986) J Crim Law 247.

[93] Above, n 86.

Litholetovs,[94] where D had done sufficient to be guilty of attempted arson by pouring petrol on V's door. It was unnecessary to prove that D had gone further by producing and operating the cigarette lighter he was carrying.

In *Gullefer,* Lord Lane also referred to an alternative 'test' formulated by Stephen:[95] 'An attempt to commit a crime is an act done with intent to commit that crime and forming part of a series of acts which would constitute its actual commission, if it were not interrupted.' Lord Lane recognized the unhelpful nature of this test. It does not define where the 'series of acts' begins. Moreover, many acts that are obviously merely preparatory could be said to be part of such a series.[96] Lord Lane said the 1981 Act requires a 'midway course' and that the attempt begins 'when the defendant embarks on the crime proper'. This seems the same as Rowlatt J's 'on the job' test.

The courts have failed to apply *Gullefer* consistently, adopting overly strict interpretations in some cases, with unsatisfactory results. This is demonstrated most vividly in *Campbell*[97] where D was arrested by police when, armed with an imitation gun, he approached within a yard of the door of a post office with intent to commit a robbery therein. His conviction for attempted robbery was quashed: the court held there was no evidence on which a jury could 'properly and safely' find that his acts were more than merely preparatory. From the viewpoint of public safety it is an unhappy decision. Though the police may lawfully arrest a person doing such preparatory acts because he is, or they have reasonable grounds for suspecting that he is, about to commit an offence,[98] they may feel obliged to wait until he has entered the post office and approached the counter before arresting him. The extra danger to post office staff, the public and the officers themselves is obvious.[99]

Geddes[100] is similarly unsatisfactory. D was found in the boys' toilet of a school, equipped in such a way as to suggest strongly that his purpose was kidnapping. His conviction for attempted false imprisonment was quashed. Even clear evidence of what D had in mind 'did not throw light on whether he had begun to carry out the commission of the offence'. Lord Bingham CJ distinguished between evidence that D was 'trying to commit the offence . . . [and that] he had only got himself ready to put himself in a position or equipped himself to do so'. *Campbell* and *Geddes* have served as a significant catalyst for the Law Commission's recent proposals for reform.[101] The narrow approach in *Geddes* was echoed in the decision in *K*[102] above relating to the pornography on the laptop. A similar approach was taken in *Mason v*

---

[94] [2002] EWCA Crim 86.

[95] *Digest of Criminal Law* (5th edn, 1894) art 50.

[96] LCCP 183 considers this in examining the appropriate definition for the new offence of criminal attempt which is narrower than that at present.

[97] [1991] Crim LR 268. But cf *Kelly* [1992] Crim LR 181.

[98] PACE, s 24(1) below, p 683.

[99] Campbell was convicted of the offence of carrying an imitation firearm and in similar cases it may be possible to convict of 'going equipped'; but the police may not know whether the suspect is armed or equipped and, whether they know or not, they will naturally wish to obtain a conviction for the more serious offence which they believe he intends to commit.

[100] [1996] Crim LR 894, per Bingham LCJ. The offence would now be one of trespass with intent to commit a sex offence contrary to the Sexual Offences Act 2003, s 63. This case is not easy to reconcile with *Tosti* [1997] Crim LR 746, where DD were examining a door to decide how best to break in, it was held to fall on the other side of the line and to be sufficient evidence of attempted burglary.

[101] Is it an overreaction to just a couple of bad cases in which the defendants could have been convicted of other offences in any event? See LCCP 183, Part 12. The Commission accepted it was unduly influenced by that case: LC 318, para 8.13. For suggestions of non-criminal responses to D who never gets beyond preparation, see D Ohana, 'Desert and Punishment for Acts Preparatory to the Commission of a Crime' (2007) 20 Canadian J of Law and Jurisprudence 113 and 'Responding to Acts Preparatory to the Commission of a Crime' (2006) 25 Criminal Justice Ethics 23.

[102] [2009] EWCA Crim 1931.

DPP[103] holding that the act of opening a car door could not be characterized as more than merely preparatory to the act of driving the vehicle and, accordingly, D could not properly be convicted of an attempted drink driving offence. The Divisional Court quashed the conviction. Nicol J said:[104]

In this case, the substantive offence, or the 'full offence', as it is referred to in the 1981 Act, is driving. In my view the appellant could not be said to have embarked on the 'crime proper' . . . until he did something which was part of the actual process of putting the car in motion. Turning on the engine would have been such a step, but starting to open the door of the car in my view was not capable of being so.[105]

It was thought that some pre-Act cases which were considered by judicial and academic critics to take too restrictive a view of attempts might be decided differently under the Act. Given the approach in *Geddes*, *K* and *Mason* this seems unlikely. One example is *Robinson*.[106] D, a jeweller, having insured his stock against theft, concealed some of it on his premises, tied himself up with string and called for help. He told a policeman who broke in that he had been knocked down and his safe robbed. The jewellery was insured for £1,200. The policeman was not satisfied with the story and discovered the property concealed on the premises. D confessed that he had hoped to get money from the insurers. His conviction for attempting to obtain by false pretences was quashed. If this case still represents the law, a judge, on these facts, should direct a jury to acquit of the attempt to commit that offence.[107] Notwithstanding the criticisms of the result, it is by no means clear that this conduct ought to be regarded as more than merely preparatory. The stage had been set; but the business of obtaining money from the insurance company was yet to begin. D was undoubtedly preparing to commit a crime but it is not obvious that he had yet begun to commit it. *Widdowson*, decided under the Act, was a rather similar case and the conviction was quashed.

In *Comer v Bloomfield*,[108] D went a step further than Robinson. Having crashed his van, he pushed it into a nearby wood, reported to the police that it had been stolen and wrote to his insurers stating that the van had been stolen and enquiring whether he could claim for it. He was acquitted of an attempt to obtain money by deception and the Divisional Court held that the magistrates were entitled to conclude that the making of a preliminary enquiry was insufficiently proximate to the actual obtaining. If the magistrates had convicted D, it may be that the conviction would have been upheld on the ground that there was evidence on which they might find that the act was sufficiently proximate (under the old law). Some such inconsistency in result must be anticipated when the question is treated as one of fact. Even if *Robinson* does represent the law under the 1981 Act, Bloomfield's enquiry might well be held to be evidence of a more than merely preparatory act; D had set about the business of getting money from the insurers. He was on the job. This might be compared with the

---

[103] [2009] EWHC 2198 (Admin).

[104] [19]–[20].

[105] As above, the distinction between fact and law is important in s 4(3). Turning on the engine *may* be considered to be something more than mere preparation to drive, but whether it *does* in fact amount to an attempt remains a pure question of fact in each case. M might have committed the offence of 'being in charge of a motor vehicle on a road or other public place', when over the limit, contrary to s 5(1)(b), provided he was on a road or public place. In *Moore v DPP* [2010] EWHC 1822 (Admin), a court was fully entitled to find that D had attempted to drive on a public road where D started his car on private property (the inside perimeter fence of an atomic weapons establishment) and was stopped by an officer a few metres from the public road to which he was heading.

[106] [1915] 2 KB 342, CCA. cf *Button* [1900] 2 QB 597, CCR.

[107] Interestingly it might be argued (as LCCP 183 assumes, para 13.15 n 31) that D has attempted to defraud under the Fraud Act 2006 by making a false representation through conduct. But is it by the false representation of being tied up that he intends to gain? See below p 888.

[108] (1970) 55 Cr App R 305.

case of *Bowles and Bowles*,[109] in which DD had befriended a vulnerable old lady and completed her last will and testament naming themselves as beneficiaries, but had not sought to execute the document and had it languishing for months in a drawer. The Court of Appeal held that there was insufficient evidence of an act more than merely preparatory to making a false instrument. Perhaps the most striking case of all the common law cases is *Komaroni and Rogerson*[110] where DD followed a lorry for 130 miles, waiting in vain for the driver to leave it unattended so that they could steal it. Streatfield J held that this was mere preparation. It seems likely that this would, rightly, be held to be evidence of an attempt under the 1981 Act.

The Law Commission recently suggested that the judicial interpretation of the test is so defective as to require at least rectification by specific guideline examples, and preferably full-blown statutory revision by the creation of new offences. Identifying the point at which D has moved from mere preparation into the territory of attempt is so difficult that the Law Commission initially proposed that the existing offence should be subdivided into an offence of criminal preparation, which is based on the conduct of D when performing acts which are more than merely preparatory to the commission of the substantive offence, and an offence of attempt which will be narrower than the present law, requiring D to be performing the last acts needed to commit the intended offence. That was an odd solution which did not meet with support on consultation. The present problem is in identifying the boundary between mere preparation and attempt. The Commission proposed creating two boundaries between three categories: no liability, more than mere preparation, and attempt. On consultation, the Commission rejected its initial proposals.

13.2.2.4 Attempt by omission

Section 1 of the 1981 Act is drafted in terms of an 'act' being more than merely preparatory. A crime of omission where the *actus reus* does not include any consequence resulting from the omission is, by its nature, incapable of being attempted.[111] This is not true of an offence including a consequence that may be committed by one having a duty to act. If the parents of a child deliberately withhold food from the child with the intent to kill it, they have set out to commit murder.[112] In fact, they are attempting to commit murder but, in the rare case where it cannot be proved that they did any act contributing to the death, it seems possible that, under the Criminal Attempts Act, they are no longer guilty of that offence.[113] They have done no 'act', as required by s 1(1). Though the Government seems to have supposed that an attempt could be charged in such a case,[114] it would require bold judicial interpretation to read 'act' to include 'omission', although reference to the Parliamentary debates would support liability for omissions in such a case.[115]

---

[109] [2004] EWCA Crim 1608.

[110] (1953) 103 L Jo 97.

[111] For discussion of inchoate crimes as result or conduct crimes, see M Hirst, *Jurisdiction and the Ambit of the Criminal Law* (2003) 134 et seq.

[112] *Gibbins and Proctor* (1918) 13 Cr App R 134, above, p 68. cf M Gunn and JC Smith, 'Arthur's Case and the Right to Life of a Down's Syndrome Child' [1985] Crim LR 705 at 706.

[113] They are, of course, guilty of the offence of wilful neglect of a young person under the Children and Young Persons Act 1933. See also the offence under the Domestic Violence, Crime and Victims Act 2004, s 5, discussed in Ch 16.

[114] See IH Dennis, 'The Criminal Attempts Act 1981' [1982] Crim LR 5, 7. LCCP 183, paras 12.24, 16.83; LC 318, para 8.142.

[115] See also the discussion of the nurse who, intending to kill a terminally ill patient, omits to replace a life sustaining drip: P Palmer, 'Attempt by Act or Omission: Causation and the Problem of the Hypothetical Nurse' (1999) 63 J Crim L 158.

Cases will be rare where an intention to commit an offence by omission can be proved. In *Nevard*,[116] D seriously injured his wife by striking her with an axe and a knife. He then forced her to abandon her attempt to dial 999 to call for assistance. Despite D's efforts to prevent the emergency services attending, V was found with non-fatal injuries. D was charged with wounding with intent and with attempted murder. The judge directed to regard D's conduct in preventing the emergency services being contacted as an element of the overall evidence of D's intention to kill. The Court of Appeal upheld the conviction, but suggested that the judge should have made explicit to the jury that attempting to divert the emergency services could not in itself constitute attempted murder. But was not D's conduct in taking the return call and lying a sufficient 'act'? He took positive steps to prevent the emergency services responding to his wife's call. If V dies because D prevents the emergency services from reaching her, or from helping her if they do arrive (for example, by keeping them away at gunpoint), that must make D a substantial cause of V's death, even if D was not the one who inflicted the original injuries. If D takes such positive measures to prevent the emergency services arriving, but despite his best efforts V lives, D must surely have attempted to cause V's death.

The Law Commission Report No 318 recommends that that 1981 Act be amended so that D may be convicted of attempted *murder* if (with the intent to kill V) D failed to discharge his or her legal duty to V (where that omission, unchecked, could have resulted in V's death).[117] The Commission's proposal to extend liability in relation to murder only appears somewhat arbitrary.

13.2.3 Successful attempts

It has sometimes been argued that failure is essential to the very nature of an attempt so that success precludes a conviction for attempting to commit a crime.[118] For a rather technical reason, this was true of attempts to commit felonies at common law. The Criminal Law Act 1967 abolished felonies so this problem disappeared. Section 6(4) of that Act provided:

where a person is charged on indictment with attempting to commit an offence or with an assault or other act preliminary to an offence, but not with the completed offence, then (subject to the discretion of the court to discharge the jury with a view to the preferment of an indictment for the completed offence) he may be convicted of the offence charged notwithstanding that he is shown to be guilty of the completed offence.

This provision does not extend to summary trial. However, in *Webley v Buxton*,[119] it was held that an attempt to commit a misdemeanour does not merge in the completed offence at common law. D was charged with attempting to take a conveyance for his own use without the consent of the owner, having sat astride a motorcycle and used his feet to push it eight feet across a pavement. The slightest movement of the conveyance is enough to constitute the full offence.[120] It was held that, though the justices were satisfied that he was guilty of the full offence, they had properly convicted him of the attempt.

---

[116] [2006] EWCA Crim 2896.

[117] Para 8.151.

[118] Hall, GPCL, 577: '…attempt implies failure…'; GP Fletcher, *Rethinking Criminal Law* (1978) 131. In *Commonwealth v Crow* 303 Pa 91 (1931) at 98, the court said 'A failure to consummate a crime is as much an essential element of an attempt as the intent and performance of an overt act towards its commission.'

[119] [1977] QB 481, [1977] Crim LR 160, overlooked in *Velasquez* [1995] 7 Archbold News 3, which is therefore wrong.

[120] Below, p 854.

The 1981 Act makes no provision for this problem[121] so the matter is governed by the common law as stated in *Webley v Buxton*. As a matter of principle, this seems right. At a certain point in the transaction, D is guilty of an attempt. The attempt may fail for many reasons, or it may succeed. There is no reason why, if it succeeds, it should cease to be the offence of attempt which, until that moment, it was. The greater includes the less. If D is convicted of attempted murder while his victim, V, is still alive and V then dies of injuries inflicted by D, D is now liable to be convicted of murder; but the conviction for attempt is not invalidated. It would, of course, be improper to convict D of both the attempt and the full offence at the same time. To that extent, the attempt merges in the completed offence.

13.2.4 Categories of offence which may be subject to an attempt

There are a number of limitations on the scope of the liability for attempt.

13.2.4.1 No liability for attempting summary only offences

At common law it was doubtful whether an attempt to commit an offence triable only summarily was a crime. Under the Act, it is clear that it is not, unless the provision creating the offence expressly provides that it shall be. The indictable offence of criminal damage is now triable only summarily if the damage is not more than £5,000,[122] but it has been held that such 'low-value' criminal damage remains an indictable offence.[123] It is therefore still an offence to attempt to commit it, however low the value of the damage attempted.

Since 1981, the policy aimed at disposing of more cases in magistrates' courts has resulted in an increase in the number of offences that are triable only summarily, including common assault and battery. The effect was to abolish the former offence of attempted assault, which leaves an undesirable gap in the law. There seems to be no good reason why it should not be an offence to attempt to commit a summary only offence and the policy should be reconsidered.[124]

13.2.4.2 Limits on liability for attempts of conspiracy and other secondary liability

Given that inchoate liability is, by definition, some distance removed from the full offence, there are obvious dangers in imposing double inchoate liability – prosecuting D for attempting to conspire with X to encourage Y to steal is preposterous. Limits on double inchoate liability need to be set.

By s 1(4),[125] there can be no liability for attempting to commit crimes of conspiracy, whether common law or statutory,[126] nor offences of assisting an arrestable offender or compounding an arrestable offence contrary to ss 4(1) and 5(1) respectively of the Criminal Law Act 1967.[127] Liability for attempting these offences would be a considerable extension of the law, with the conduct involved being doubly remote from the substantive offence. Nevertheless, somewhat

---

[121] LCCP 102, para 2.113.

[122] Magistrates' Courts Act 1980, s 22 and Sch 2. Only damage to the property itself is relevant, not any consequential damage: *R (on the Application of Abbott) v Colchester Magistrates' Court* [2001] Crim LR 564, DC.

[123] *Bristol Magistrates' Court, ex p E* [1999] Crim LR 161, DC; *Fennell* [2000] Crim LR 677.

[124] The Law Commission provisionally proposed to reverse the present rule: LCCP 183, para 6.67, cf LC 318, para 8.154.

[125] This result was achieved, rather curiously, by s 8 of the Computer Misuse Act 1990.

[126] Below. cf the statements in *Harmer* [2005] Crim LR 482 and comment.

[127] Above, Ch 9. Reasons for excluding the offences under the Criminal Law Act 1967 are given in LCCP 102 at paras 2.124–2.126.

surprisingly, it is an offence under the Act,[128] to attempt to commit an offence of assisting or encouraging under the Serious Crime Act 2007.[129]

The 1981 Act makes clear that it is not an offence to attempt to aid, abet, counsel, procure or suborn the commission of an offence: s 1(4)(b).[130] Where, however, a substantive offence is drafted in terms of aiding and abetting, an attempt to aid, etc is an offence. Section 1(4)(b) does not apply because these are not instances of aiding, etc *an offence*. An 'attempt under a special statutory provision' (s 3(1) of the Act) is now governed by the same principles as attempts under the Act.[131]

13.2.4.3 Other exceptional cases where no liability for attempt

Apart from the statutory exceptions there may be other crimes where an attempt charge cannot be pursued. Stephen thought there were a large number of such offences,[132] but his examples are not wholly convincing. In addition to those cases discussed above (summary only offences, conspiracy and aiding and abetting), offences where no attempt charge is possible include:

(1) Where any act done with the appropriate intent amounts to the complete crime.[133] Such crimes are rare but one may be the form of treason known as compassing the Queen's death. The offence requires proof of an overt act but it seems that any act done with intent to kill the Queen would be enough.

(2) A crime defined as an omission[134] where the *actus reus* does not include any consequence of the omission, as in the case of misprision of treason or some statutory offences of omission.

(3) It is difficult to conceive of an attempt where the *actus reus* is a state of affairs, such as 'being found' in particular circumstances.[135]

(4) It has been argued that there ought to be no liability for an offence that may be committed recklessly or negligently but not intentionally. The example most often used which comes readily to mind is involuntary manslaughter. The essence of this crime is that the killing is unintentional. An intentional killing (in the absence of diminished responsibility, the conditions for infanticide, loss of self-control[136] or a suicide pact) is necessarily murder. Section 1(1) of the Act requires an intention to commit the offence which D is charged with attempting and on this view an intent to commit involuntary

---

[128] As it was at common law, to attempt to commit the common law offence of incitement: *Dunnington* [1984] QB 472, [1984] 1 All ER 676, (1984) 78 Cr App R 171. For the common law, see JC Smith, 'Secondary Participation and Inchoate Offences', in *Crime, Proof and Punishment*, 21.

[129] It is possible for D to assist or encourage an attempt: s 44, SCA 2007.

[130] For arguments as to whether the section is superfluous now that the Serious Crime Act 2007 (SCA 2007), Part 2 is in force see M Bohlander, 'The Conflict Between the Serious Crime Act and s 1(4)(b) of the Criminal Attempts Act 1981' [2010] Crim LR 483 and J Childs who rejects the claim at [2010] Crim LR 924. It is submitted that the conflict may be avoided by reference to s 49 of the SCA 2007.

[131] The Law Commission's proposals in relation to double inchoate offences in LCCP 183, Ch 7 recommended that it should be an offence to attempt to conspire: para 7.57. This surely goes too far.

[132] II HCL, 227.

[133] In *Rogers v Arnott* [1960] 2 QB 244, [1960] 2 All ER 417, it was said that, for this reason, there could be no attempt to commit fraudulent conversion under s 20 of the Larceny Act 1916; but it is clear that there may be an attempt to appropriate property belonging to another, ie, to steal, contrary to s 1 of the Theft Act 1968, which has repealed fraudulent conversion.

[134] Attempt by omission generally is considered, above, p 418.

[135] Above, p 64.

[136] For attempted infanticide, see *KA Smith* [1983] Crim LR 739, below, p 593; and for attempt under provocation, *Bruzas* [1972] Crim LR 367, below, and *Campbell* [1997] Crim LR 495 (Sedley J) and commentary.

manslaughter is not a concept known to law. What, however, of D who intends to commit a strict liability offence but is foiled in the process – why should he not be liable for attempting to commit that offence? If liability can arise for strict liability, why not for offence of manslaughter?[137]

13.2.5 Jurisdictional issues[138]

13.2.5.1 Attempt in England to commit an offence abroad[139]

The Act now[140] allows for the prosecution for attempt of an offence intended by D to be committed outside England and Wales, provided that the more than merely preparatory act is done in England or Wales and the result attempted would be both an indictable offence as defined by English law and an offence by the law of that place. If D, a British citizen, posts a letter bomb from England to V in France, intending to kill V, he is liable to conviction for attempted murder as soon as the letter is posted;[141] but, if he intends only to injure V, he is not guilty of an attempt to cause him grievous or actual bodily harm. This is because murder abroad by a British citizen is triable in England but lesser offences against the person are not. If D were an alien, then he could not be tried in England for attempted murder. This seems anomalous, particularly since two foreigners acting in concert could, since 1977, be convicted of conspiracy in England to commit murder abroad.[142] The jurisdiction of the court has also been extended to certain cases where an act is done in England and Wales that would be an indictable attempt under the Act, but for the fact that the offence, if completed, would not be triable in England and Wales.[143]

13.2.5.2 Attempt abroad to commit an offence in England

It was settled before the Act by the decision of the House of Lords in *DPP v Stonehouse*[144] that an act done abroad with intent thereby to cause the commission of an offence in England was indictable here (even if done by an innocent agent[145]), at least if it had an effect in England. D, in Miami, falsely staged his death by drowning with the intent that his innocent wife in England should claim life assurance monies. He was guilty of attempting to enable his wife to obtain by deception. His acts abroad would have the 'effect' of communicating through the media to his wife and the insurance companies the false statement that he had died.[146] In *Somchai Liangsiriprasert v United States Government*,[147] the Privy Council, holding that a conspiracy abroad to commit an offence in England is indictable even though no overt act has been done within the jurisdiction, said, *obiter*, that the same rule applies to attempt. The Act has nothing to say on the question so it remains a matter of common law. This may be taken to have been settled by *Liangsiriprasert*.

---

[137] cf Simester Spencer, Sullivan and Virgo, CLT&D 334.

[138] See, generally, Hirst, *Jurisdiction and the Ambit of the Criminal Law*, Ch 4.

[139] cf conspiracy, below, p 446.

[140] Subsection (1A), inserted by Criminal Justice Act 1993, s 5(2).

[141] Below, p 578.

[142] Below, p 446.

[143] This applies to an offence under s 3 of the Computer Misuse Act 1990: s 1(1A) and (1B) of the Act; and to a 'Group A offence' as defined in Part 1 of the Criminal Justice Act 1993: s 1A of the Act. This includes all the major offences under the Theft Acts 1968 and 1978, the Forgery and Counterfeiting Act 1981 and the common law offence of cheating the public revenue.

[144] [1978] AC 55, [1977] Crim LR 544.

[145] cf *Latif* [1996] 2 Cr App R 92, HL, [1996] Crim LR 414 and commentary. But if D knows or believes E to have *mens rea*, he is guilty, not of an attempt, but under the offences in the SCA 2007, Part 2.

[146] Lord Keith insisted that an effect within the jurisdiction was essential but Lord Diplock thought otherwise. Why should the result have been different if D had been rescued from the sea and confessed before any report of his death appeared in England?

[147] (1991) 92 Cr App R 77 at 87–90.

13.2.5.3 Attempt abroad to commit an offence abroad

D, a British citizen, being in France, attempts to kill V in France or, knowing himself to be married, attempts to go through a ceremony of marriage there with X. If he succeeds he will be liable to conviction in England of murder and bigamy. Exceptionally, English law assumes jurisdiction over these crimes when committed abroad by a British citizen. Literally, then, the attempt is an offence under the Act. It has been argued that the presumption against the extra-territorial operation of the criminal law[148] requires the words 'does an act' to be construed as applicable only to acts done within the jurisdiction, or having, or being intended to have, some effect therein; but this argument has less weight after *Liangsiriprasert*. If the court has jurisdiction over the full offence when wholly committed abroad, why not over the attempt?

13.2.6 Withdrawal[149]

It is logical that, once the steps taken towards the commission of an offence are sufficiently far advanced to amount to an attempt, it can make no difference whether the failure to complete the crime is due to a voluntary withdrawal by D, the intervention of the police, or any other reason. In *Taylor*,[150] it was held that an attempt was committed where D approached a stack of corn with the intention of setting fire to it and lit a match for that purpose but abandoned his plan on finding that he was being watched. In some jurisdictions, logic has given way to policy and a defence of free and voluntary desistance is allowed.[151] Following the recommendation of the Law Commission,[152] the 1981 Act made no change to the common law in this respect. The principal argument in favour of a withdrawal defence is that it might induce the attempter to desist – but this seems unlikely. The existence of the defence would add to the problems of law enforcement authorities.

13.2.7 Reform of attempt

In its Consultation Paper 183 the Law Commission provisionally proposed radical new changes with the introduction of two offences of 'attempt' and 'criminal preparation'. After consultation, the Commission abandoned this scheme. It was accepted that the existing law works satisfactorily in practice. The Report No 318 proposed no change to the conduct element of attempt. Minor changes were recommended in relation to *mens rea* as noted above.

13.3 Conspiracy

13.3.1 Introduction

A criminal conspiracy is, in simple terms, an agreement between two or more persons to commit a crime. At common law conspiracy was defined as an agreement to do an unlawful

---

[148] See Griew, *Current Law Statutes*, General Note.

[149] See M Wasik, 'Abandoning Criminal Intent' [1980] Crim LR 785; Duff, *Criminal Attempts*, 65–75; Yaffe *Attempts*, Ch 11.

[150] (1859) 1 F & F 511; see also *Lankford* [1959] Crim LR 209. It is doubtful whether Taylor's desistance was 'free and voluntary' in the sense that he was motivated by a desire to avoid detection.

[151] See D Stuart, 'The *Actus Reus* in Attempts' [1970] Crim LR at 519–521. See the Draft Scots Code which provides a defence where D 'voluntarily abandons his attempt as a result of repentance before all acts necessary for the commission of the offence were done', cl 18(2).

[152] Law Com Report No 102, paras 2.131–2.133.

act or a lawful act by unlawful means.[153] The word 'unlawful' was used in a broad sense. The offence therefore included agreements to perform not only any crime triable in England, even a crime triable only summarily, but also at least (i) fraud, (ii) the corruption of public morals, (iii) the outraging of public decency, and (iv) some torts. In this respect it went far beyond the other inchoate offences of incitement and attempt, where the result incited or attempted must be a crime. For many years until *DPP v Withers*,[154] in 1974 the crime of conspiracy was believed to be even wider, including any agreement to effect a public mischief.

It has long been the generally approved aim of the Law Commission that:

[t]he crime of conspiracy should be limited to agreements to commit criminal offences: an agreement should not be criminal where that which it was agreed to be done would not amount to a criminal offence if committed by one person.[155]

The Criminal Law Act 1977 created a new offence of statutory conspiracy based on this policy. It is an offence to agree with another that a crime (whether statutory or common law) will be committed. However, the present law retains instances in which a crime is committed by agreeing to engage in conduct which would not be criminal if performed alone. This remains the case with conspiracy to defraud, conspiracy to corrupt public morals or to outrage public decency.[156] The retention of these common law conspiracies is controversial. The Law Commission has repeatedly proposed abolition,[157] but the Government remains unwilling to run the risk by removing flexible common law offences that might prove necessary to deal with some unforeseen scenario that would fall outside the scope of statutory conspiracy.[158]

Despite amendment by the Criminal Attempts Act 1981 and the Criminal Justice Act 1987, the Criminal Law Act 1977, which is the principal topic under examination in this part of the chapter remains an ill-drafted piece of legislation presenting numerous problems of interpretation. The arguments for reform to clarify the position seem compelling. The Law Commission recently produced proposals in which recommendations for a wider, and yet more complex form of conspiracy are advanced.[159]

13.3.2 Summary of present law

Whether a particular agreement between D1 and D2 is a statutory conspiracy under the Criminal Law Act or a conspiracy at common law, or both, the offence involves an agreement. That is not a mere mental operation, but must involve spoken or written words or other overt acts. If D1 repents and withdraws immediately after the agreement has been concluded, he is

---

[153] By Lord Denman in *Jones* (1832) 4 B & Ad 345 at 349. But a few years later in *Peck* (1839) 9 Ad & El 686 at 690 he declared, 'I do not think the antithesis very correct.' For an historical account, see LCCP 183, Ch 3.

[154] [1975] AC 842. Conspiracy to commit the common law offence of public nuisance continues to be a potential source of expansion of the criminal law. See commentary on *Soul* (1980) 70 Cr App R 295, [1980] Crim LR 233, CA. The House of Lords confirmed the ECHR compatibility of the offence of public nuisance: *Rimmington* [2005] UKHL 63.

[155] Law Com No 76, para 1.113; see also LC WP 50.

[156] Cases since the 1977 Act (*May* (1989) 91 Cr App R 157, CA; *Gibson* [1990] 2 QB 619, CA; *Rowley* [1991] 4 All ER 649, [1991] Crim LR 785, CA) confirming that it is an offence for a person acting alone to do acts tending to corrupt public morals create a doubt whether there is any scope for the operation of common law conspiracy to do these things.

[157] As with the recent call for abolition of conspiracy to defraud in its *Fraud* Report No 276 (2002). See further, D Ormerod and D Williams, *Smith's Law of Theft* (9th edn, 2007) Ch 5.

[158] There is the irony – if it is so unforeseeable, prosecuting it is likely to run into difficulty under Art 7. See also *Norris v USA* [2008] UKHL 16 holding that while price fixing in itself was not, prior to 2002, an offence under English law, when combined with other elements such as deliberate misrepresentation, it could lead to various offences such as fraud or conspiracy to defraud. See also *R v GG plc* [2008] UKHL 17.

[159] See LCCP 183; LC 318.

guilty[160] and his repentance is a matter of mitigation only. This reflects the crucial distinction between inchoate offending and liability as a secondary party.

13.3.2.1 Statutory conspiracy

It is an offence of conspiracy, triable only on indictment, to agree to commit any criminal offence even an offence triable only summarily.[161] This is a 'statutory' conspiracy under the Criminal Law Act 1977. It is not limited to agreements to commit a statutory crime – agreements to commit the common law offence of murder are charged under this offence – rather the term 'statutory conspiracy' is used to distinguish it from 'common law conspiracies'.

13.3.2.2 Common law conspiracies

It is an offence triable only on indictment to agree:

(1) to defraud, whether or not the fraud amounts to a crime or even a tort;[162]

(2) to do an act which tends to corrupt public morals or outrage public decency, whether or not that act amounts to a crime.

The 1977 Act has no part to play in the prosecution of such offences.

13.3.2.3 Relationship between common law and statutory conspiracies

Section 1(1) of the 1977 Act creates the offence of statutory conspiracy. It provides in effect that it is a conspiracy to agree to commit *any* offence. On a literal reading this would mean that it dealt with common law conspiracies to defraud, etc but s 1(1) is subject to s 5(1) and (2) which[163] now provide:

(1) Subject to the following provisions of this section, the offence of conspiracy at common law is hereby abolished.

(2) Subsection (1) above shall not affect the offence of conspiracy at common law so far as relates to conspiracy to defraud.

Section 5, was amended to this form to rectify an error in earlier drafting which rendered statutory and common law conspiracies mutually exclusive.[164] Statutory conspiracies and common law conspiracies to corrupt public morals or to outrage public decency remain mutually exclusive. But the Criminal Justice Act 1987, s 12, provides that statutory conspiracy and conspiracy to defraud are not mutually exclusive. An agreement to commit a crime involving fraud or dishonesty is both a statutory conspiracy and a conspiracy to defraud. The prosecutor will frequently have a choice.[165] The broad and flexible nature of the conspiracy to defraud offence ensures its continued popularity with prosecutors. It is a 'not yet rusty and still trusty' weapon.[166]

---

[160] As in the *Bridgewater Case*, unreported, referred to by Lord Coleridge CJ in the *Mogul Steamship Case* (1888) 21 QBD 544 at 549.

[161] LCCP 183, para 6.58 on summary conspiracies. In LC 318 it was recommended to remove the present requirement for the DPP to give consent if proceedings to prosecute a conspiracy to commit a summary offence are to be initiated: para 4.35.

[162] See the House of Lords decision on the scope of the common law offence in *GG* [2008] UKHL 17.

[163] As amended by the Criminal Justice Act 1987.

[164] See *Ayres* [1984] AC 447, [1984] 1 All ER 619. The House substantially modified the effect of *Ayres*, as generally understood, in the decision in *Cooke* [1986] AC 909.

[165] To be exercised in accordance with the Attorney General's guidance of 2007 issued to ensure appropriate use of conspiracy to defraud after the Fraud Act 2006 came into force and the guidance in the Code for Crown Prosecutors issued by the DPP under s 10(1) of the Prosecution of Offences Act 1985, See further www.cps.gov.uk.

[166] Auld LJ in *Norris* [2007] EWHC 71 (Admin), para 66.

13.3.3 Statutory conspiracy[167]

The offence of statutory conspiracy is defined by s 1(1) and s 1(2) of the Act. Section 1(1) (as amended by s 5 of the Criminal Attempts Act 1981) provides:

Subject to the following provisions of this part of the Act, if a person agrees with any other person or persons that a course of conduct shall be pursued which, if the agreement is carried out in accordance with their intentions, either –

(a) will necessarily amount to or involve the commission of any offence or offences by one or more of the parties to the agreement, or

(b) would do so but for the existence of facts which render the commission of the offence or any of the offences impossible,

he is guilty of conspiracy to commit the offence or offences in question.

Conspiracy is a crime where it is more difficult than usual to distinguish between *actus reus* and *mens rea*. The *actus reus* is said to be the agreement: but agreement is essentially a mental operation, though it must be manifested by or inferred from acts of some kind. 'In the case of conspiracy as opposed to the substantive offence, it is what was agreed to be done and not what was in fact done which is all important.'[168] The elements of the offence are best listed and examined separately rather than divided into sub-categories of *mens rea* and *actus reus*. They are:

(i)   an agreement;

(ii)   that a course of conduct will be pursued;

(iii) the course of conduct will necessarily amount to the commission of an offence if carried out in accordance with the defendants' intentions;

(iv)   the defendants had an intention to agree;

(v)   the defendants had an intention that the agreement will be carried out;

(vi)   the defendants had an intention or knowledge as to any circumstances forming part of the substantive offence.

13.3.3.1 The agreement

Surprisingly, the courts have failed to define with precision what conduct suffices to constitute the completed agreement. It may be that it is not necessary to prove an agreement in the strict sense required by the law of contract,[169] but the parties must at least have reached a decision[170] to perpetrate their unlawful object. Difficult questions may arise in cases where parties at the stage of negotiating subject to final details being agreed, eg D1 agrees to sell D2 certain goods, known to both to be stolen, at 'a price to be agreed between us'.[171] In *Walker*,[172]

---

[167] For the background to Part I of the Criminal Law Act, see LC WP 50 (*Inchoate Offences*, 1973), 56 (*Conspiracy to Defraud*, 1974), 57 (*Conspiracies Relating to Morals and Decency*, 1974) and 63 (*Conspiracies to Effect a Public Mischief and to Commit a Civil Wrong*, 1975); and Report LC 76, *Conspiracy and Criminal Law Reform* (1976). For the interpretation of the Act, see EJ Griew, 'Annotations on the Act', in *Current Law Statutes*; JC Smith, 'Conspiracy under the Criminal Law Act 1977' [1977] Crim LR 598 and 638; DW Elliott, '*Mens Rea* in Statutory Conspiracy' [1978] Crim LR 202; G Williams, 'The New Statutory Offence of Conspiracy' (1977) 127 NLJ 1164 and 1188; D Ormerod, 'Making Sense of Statutory Conspiracies' (2006) 59 CLP 185.

[168] *Bolton* (1991) 94 Cr App R 74 at 80, per Woolf LJ.

[169] See G Orchard, 'Agreement in Criminal Conspiracy' [1974] Crim LR 297 at 335.

[170] cf Williams, CLGP, 212.

[171] *May and Butcher Ltd v R* [1934] 2 KB 17n, HL.

[172] [1962] Crim LR 458; *Mulcahy v R* (1868) LR 3 HL 306 at 317. Careful jury direction is needed: *Webster* [2003] EWCA Crim 1946 (conspiracy to cheat the Revenue).

a conviction was quashed although it was 'perfectly clear' that D1 had discussed with D2 and D3 the proposition of stealing a payroll, because it was not proved that they had got beyond the stage of negotiation when D1 withdrew. Once the parties have agreed, the conspiracy is complete, even if they take no further action because, for example, they are arrested.

Conspiracy is a continuing offence.[173] The offence offers a significant attraction for prosecutors because of this opportunity to roll together a course of criminal conduct under one charge and on one indictment.[174]

The offence lies in agreeing with another that a crime will be committed. That is different from agreeing that D will commit the crime himself. D can be convicted of conspiracy even though he personally will not be participating in the commission of the substantive offence. The Law Commission has recently recommended that a conspiracy 'must involve an agreement by two or more persons *to engage in the conduct element of an offence* and (where relevant) to bring about any consequence element of the substantive offence'.[175] The recommendation would make a radical change to the law if it means that each D must agree that he will engage in the conduct of the commission of the substantive offence. That is surely not what is meant. What is required is that D agrees and intends that the conduct of the substantive offence be performed by at least one party to the agreement.

Wheel and chain conspiracies

It may not be necessary to show that the persons accused of conspiring together were in direct communication with one another. Thus, it may be that the conspiracy revolves around some third party, X, who is in touch with each of D1, D2, D3, though they are not in touch with one another (a 'wheel conspiracy'). Provided that the result is that they have a common design – for example, to rob a particular bank – D1, D2 and D3 may properly be indicted for conspiring together though they have never been in touch with one another until they meet in the dock. The same is true of a chain conspiracy where D1 communicates with D2, D2 with D3, etc. In either case it must be proved, of course, that each accused has agreed with another guilty person in relation to that single conspiracy.[176]

What has to be ascertained is always the same matter: is it true to say...that the acts of the accused were done in pursuance of a criminal purpose held in common between them?[177]

These propositions are well established,[178] but some of the leading cases demonstrate some questionable application of the principles. In *Meyrick*,[179] D1 and D2, nightclub proprietors, each separately offered bribes to a police sergeant, E, to induce him to ignore breaches of the licensing laws in respect of their own premises. They were convicted of conspiring, *inter alia*, to contravene the licensing laws. The jury were directed that there must be a 'common design'. D1 and D2 were convicted, but it is difficult to see how the evidence justified this finding. The intent of each nightclub proprietor was simply to evade the licensing laws in respect of his own premises. There was no common design merely parallel equivalent ones. *Meyrick* was distinguished in *Griffiths*[180] on the rather unconvincing ground that it related to a small geographical area (Soho), so the jury could come to the conclusion that 'the nightclub proprietors

---

[173] *DPP v Doot* [1973] AC 807, HL.

[174] See the comments of Lord Hope in *Saik* [2006] UKHL 18.

[175] LC 318, recommendation 1, p 159. This would enact the error in *Anderson* [1986] AC 27.

[176] *Ardalan* [1972] 2 All ER 257 at 261.

[177] *Meyrick* (1929) 21 Cr App R 94 at 102 and *Griffiths* [1966] 1 QB 589, applied in *Chrastny* [1991] 1 WLR 1381, CA; *Mintern* [2004] EWCA Crim 7.

[178] See, eg, *Cooper and Compton*, above; *Sweetland* (1957) 42 Cr App R 62.

[179] See above, n 177.

[180] (1965) 49 Cr App R 279.

in that district well knew what was happening generally in relation to the police'.[181] But this cannot be right. Even if D1 and D2 each knew that the other had made a similar agreement with E, it would seem that there were two separate and specific conspiracies, not one general one. Consider the following powerful example:

I employ an accountant to make out my tax return. He and his clerk are both present when I am about to sign the return. I notice an item in my expenses of £100 and say: 'I don't remember incurring this expense.' The clerk says: 'Well, actually I put it in. You didn't incur it, but I didn't think you would object to a few pounds being saved.' The accountant indicates his agreement to this attitude. After some hesitation I agree to let it stand. On those bare facts I cannot be charged with fifty others in a conspiracy to defraud [Inland Revenue] of £100,000 on the basis that this accountant and his clerk have persuaded 500 other clients to make false returns, some being false in one way, some in another, or even all in the same way. I have not knowingly attached myself to a general agreement to defraud.[182]

It is submitted that the position would be no different if the accountant had said: 'We do this for all our clients'; there would still have been a series of conspiracies, not one general conspiracy.[183]

Who can be a party to the agreement?
Corporations
A company may be convicted of an offence of conspiracy.[184] It must be proved that D conspired with another person but that other need not be identified.[185] If the managing director of a company resolves to perpetrate an illegality in the company's name, but communicates this to no other person, there is no conspiracy between him and the company.[186]

Statutory exceptions
In statutory conspiracies there are three cases in which the requirement of two parties is not satisfied. By s 2(2) of the Act, a person is not guilty of a statutory conspiracy:

if the only other person or persons with whom he agrees are (both initially and at all times during the currency of the agreement) persons of any one or more of the following descriptions, that is to say –

(a) his spouse [or civil partner];

(b) a person under the age of criminal responsibility; and

(c) an intended victim of that offence or of each of those offences.

Spouses (a) almost certainly states the rule of the common law, although no English case has ever been so decided.[187] The common law rule was based upon the fiction that husband and

---

[181] ibid, 291.

[182] Paull J ibid. cf the argument of Maddocks in *Meyrick* (1929) 45 TLR 421 at 422.

[183] The convictions in *Griffiths* were quashed as the evidence did not establish the single 'wheel conspiracy' alleged.

[184] *R v ICR Haulage Co Ltd* [1944] KB 551, CCA.

[185] *Phillips* (1987) 86 Cr App R 18, discussed [1988] Crim LR at 338.

[186] To allow such an indictment would be to 'offend against the basic concept of a conspiracy, namely an agreement of two or more to do an unlawful act . . . it would be artificial to take the view that the company, although it is clearly a separate legal entity can be regarded here as a separate entity or a separate mind . . .' *McDonnell* [1966] 1 QB 233 (Nield J). cf *ICR Haulage Co* [1944] KB 551. A conviction might ensue if D agrees with his company in his capacity as a person responsible for the acts of another corporation rather than as the person responsible for his company: see the Canadian cases cited in *McDonnell*.

[187] See, eg, Hawkins, I PC, c 27, s 8 and *Mawji v R* [1957] AC 126, [1957] 1 All ER 385, PC. There may be a conspiracy between husband and wife in the civil law: *Midland Bank Trust Co Ltd v Green (No 3)* [1979] Ch 496, [1979] 2 All ER 193 (Oliver J).

wife were one person with one will. The application of the rule to statutory conspiracies is based upon a social policy of preserving the stability of marriage.[188] The common law rule applies only where the parties are married at the time of the agreement. Marriage after the conspiracy or during its continuance is no defence.[189] Clearly, the same rule applies under the Act. A wife is guilty, though she agrees only with her husband, if she knows that there are other parties to the conspiracy.[190] There is no protection against prosecution should the married couple be charged with the substantive offence having perpetrated the offence as they agreed. The protection extends only to conspiracies exclusive to the married couple; if they agree with a third party the conspiracy can be prosecuted.[191] It is anomalous and anachronistic and the Law Commission has recommended abolition.[192]

Infants.[193] For the purposes of paragraph (b) a person is under the age of criminal responsibility 'so long as it is conclusively presumed by s 50 of the Children and Young Persons Act 1933,[194] that he cannot be guilty of any offence'[195] – that is, he is under the age of 10.

Victims. The Act does not define 'victim'. It is suggested that a person is a victim of an offence when the offence is held to exist for his protection with the effect that he is not a party to that offence when it is committed by another with his full knowledge and cooperation.[196] Thus there would be no conspiracy where D agreed with a person to kidnap him with his consent. There will be an offence of conspiracy where D and V agree on a course of conduct that would involve their both being guilty of an offence if the act takes place. It is unclear whether D and V who agree to engage in sadomasochistic activity would commit a conspiracy to commit gbh or abh at the time of the agreement.[197] Again there seems to be no common law authority in point and the question seems unlikely to arise on a charge of conspiracy at common law since an agreement to defraud with the victim of the fraud is difficult to imagine.

The Law Commission recommended that the present exemption for a non-victim co-conspirator should be abolished but that the present exemption for a victim (D) should be retained if the conspiracy is to commit an offence that exists wholly or in part for the protection of a particular category of persons; D falls within the protected category; and D is the person in respect of whom the offence agreed upon would have been committed.[198]

Solo conspirators

The 1977 Act does not deal with other cases where one of two parties to the agreement would not be liable to prosecution for the ulterior offence. It is clear that there may be a conspiracy although only one party is capable of committing the ulterior offence as a principal. If, for example, the offence can be committed only by the holder of a justices' licence and A, a licensee, agrees with B, a customer who is incapable of committing the offence as a principal, that he, A, will do so, there is a conspiracy to contravene the licensing legislation. The course of conduct

---

[188] LCCP 76, paras 1.46–1.49.

[189] *Robinson's Case* (1746) 1 Leach 37.

[190] *Chrastny* [1991] 1 WLR 1381, CA; *Lovick* [1993] Crim LR 890.

[191] *Chrastny* [1991] 1 WLR 1381, CA.

[192] See LC 318, para 5.16.

[193] The Law Commission recommended that the rule that an agreement involving a person of or over the age of criminal responsibility and a child under the age of criminal responsibility gives rise to no criminal liability for conspiracy should be retained. LC 318 para 5.45.

[194] Above, p 340.

[195] Section 2(3) of the Act.

[196] Above, p 241.

[197] See *Brown* [1994] AC 212, below, p 619.

[198] LC 318, para 5.35. D1, aged 15 conspires with D2 16 that P, 18 should have sex with D1. D1 has the defence, D2 does not.

will necessarily amount to the commission of the offence by one of the parties. B will be liable as a secondary party if the offence is committed. The controversial case of *Whitchurch*[199] is thus readily explicable. D, believing herself to be pregnant, agreed with two others that they would procure her miscarriage. It was not proved that D was in fact pregnant. A person who unlawfully uses instruments on a woman to procure an abortion commits an offence whether the woman is pregnant or not; but a woman who does the same acts to herself is guilty only if she is in fact pregnant. It was held that all three were guilty of conspiracy and it is submitted that the result would be the same if D had agreed with only one other person. D is guilty as a secondary party if the ulterior offence is committed by using the instruments on her,[200] so she is not a 'victim' under the principle of *Tyrrell*.[201]

In *Duguid*,[202] D agreed with E to remove a child of whom E was the mother from the possession of her lawful guardian. This would have been a crime by D under the Offences Against the Person Act 1861, s 56, but it was provided that a mother should not be liable to prosecution on account of taking her own child. It was held that E's 'immunity from prosecution for an act done by herself' was no bar to the conviction of D for conspiracy. The court did not find it necessary to decide whether E could have been convicted of the conspiracy.[203] This suggests that there may be a conspiracy with only one guilty party but the case is far from clear because the court may have accepted the argument of the prosecution that any bar to the prosecution of E was of a procedural nature. The better view is that there must be two conspirators.[204]

Mentally disordered conspirators

The Act does not deal with an agreement with a mentally disordered person so the common law, whatever it may be, applies to all conspiracies. In 1976 the Law Commission thought express provision unnecessary because 'a purported agreement with a person who is so mentally disordered as to be incapable of forming the intent necessary for the substantive offence will not be an agreement within clause 1(1) of the draft Bill [now, in substance, s 1(1) of the Act]'.[205] This seems to be right in the case of a mentally disordered person who does not know the nature and quality of the proposed act; but a person who, through mental disorder, does not know the proposed act is 'wrong' may be perfectly capable of forming the intent to commit it with full knowledge of the facts and circumstances.[206] In such a case it is arguable that a mentally normal party to the agreement is guilty of a statutory conspiracy though the mentally abnormal person is not because it is sufficient that the carrying out of the agreement will amount to an offence by *one of the parties*.[207]

An agreement creating multiple conspiracies?

A single agreement between D1 and D2 may involve them in two or more conspiracies. There is nothing to prevent their being charged as such. Where D1 and D2 agreed to buy cannabis in Thailand and import it into the UK, a conviction in Thailand for conspiracy to possess

---

[199] (1890) 24 QBD 420, criticized by Williams as 'gravely wrong for it sets at naught the limitation upon responsibility imposed by Parliament': CLGP, 673. But see B Hogan, 'Victims as Parties to Crime' [1962] Crim LR 683.

[200] *Sockett* (1908) 72 JP 428.

[201] Above, p 241.

[202] (1906) 21 Cox CC 200. cf *Sherry and El Yamani* [1993] Crim LR 537.

[203] The language used suggests that she might well have been guilty of conspiracy and of secondary participation in the ulterior offence if D had committed it, whether or not she could have been prosecuted. Section 56 has been repealed by the Child Abduction Act 1984, below, p 692 but the similar problems which could arise under that Act should be resolved in the same way.

[204] cf *Yip Chiu-cheung*, below, p 445.

[205] Law Com No 76, 22, n 67.

[206] cf *Matusevich v R* (1977) 51 ALJR 657 at 670, per Aickin J.

[207] Section 1(1), above, p 426.

cannabis for sale did not bar a prosecution in England for conspiracy to import the cannabis into England.[208] But where there is a general conspiracy to commit offences of a certain type, perhaps extending over a lengthy period, agreements to commit particular offences of that type may be treated simply as evidence of the general conspiracy.[209]

Agreements to commit more than one offence

It has been held to be legitimate to charge an offence alleging a single agreement embracing conduct involving several offences.[210] So, for example, D can be indicted for conspiracy to rob *and* murder as part of one agreement. Moreover, in some cases there is nothing to prevent charges being laid for conspiracy where D1 and D2 agree to commit offences 'X *or* Y' as one agreement.[211] The problem frequently arose in the context of money laundering conspiracies where until recently there were two categories of substantive offence. Dealing with money from drug related crime was one form of offence, and dealing with money from non-drug related crime was another. If D1 and D2 agreed to deal with monies from X in the future, being unaware whether the money from X would be from drug crime or other crime, but knowing it will be one or the other, that the agreement, if carried out, would 'necessarily lead to the commission of the offence contrary to the Drug Trafficking Act and/or to the offence contrary to the Criminal Justice Act. Such a count is not bad for duplicity; it alleges one agreement': *Suchedina*.[212] These cases on the procedure for indicting conspiracy effect significant extensions of an already broad offence.[213] It would be preferable for two counts to be included where that is possible.[214]

Timing of agreement

It is probably not essential that the agreement should have been made prior to the concerted action to effect the criminal purpose. If, when D1 is taking steps towards the commission of a crime, D2 comes to his assistance and the two work in concert, they might thereby be held to have conspired;[215] but if D1 is unaware of, or rejects D2's assistance, there is no conspiracy,[216] though D2 might be held to be an accessory of any offence or attempt consummated by D1.[217] Some of these principles derive from common law conspiracy cases, but, it is submitted that they apply equally to statutory conspiracy.

Proof of the agreement

The question of what conduct amounts to a sufficient agreement to found a charge of conspiracy is one of several questions in the criminal law aggravated by a confusion between the substantive law and the law of evidence. In most cases the agreement will probably be made in private. Direct evidence of it, even in an era of covert surveillance and telephone tapping,

---

[208] *Lavercombe* [1988] Crim LR 435.

[209] *Hammersley* (1958) 42 Cr App R 207, discussed in [1958] Crim LR 422–429 (acts alleged ranged over eight years and involved numerous illegal agreements with others, yet CCA contrived to hold that only one conspiracy to obstruct the course of justice, evidenced by a large number of overt acts, was disclosed by the indictment). *Barratt and Sheehan* [1996] Crim LR 495 is a similar case. cf *Edwards* [1991] Crim LR 45.

[210] *Roberts* [1998] 1 Cr App R 441; *Greenfield* [1973] 1 WLR 1151; *Taylor* [2002] Crim LR 205.

[211] *Hussain* [2002] Crim LR 407. Many of the cases on this involve the pre-POCA money laundering offences and are complicated by what are recognized in the wake of *Saik* [2006] UKHL 18 to be erroneous statements about the *mens rea* of conspiracy: *El-Kurd* [2001] Crim LR 234. The Law Commission discusses these in LC 318, Part 4.

[212] [2006] EWCA Crim 2543, and see LCCP 183, para 5.19 and Ch 6.

[213] Similarly where the parties agree to import 'prohibited drugs' which might be Class A or B or C – three separate offences: *Taylor (RJ)* [2002] Crim LR 203.

[214] See LC 318, Part 4, and para 4.25.

[215] *Leigh* (1775) 1 Car & Kir 28n; *Tibbits and Windust* [1902] 1 KB 77, CCR.

[216] *State v Tally* (1894) 102 Ala 25; *Michael and Wechsler's Cases* 699; *Hawkesley* [1959] Crim LR 211 (QS).

[217] *Rannath Mohan v R* [1967] 2 AC 187, PC.

will rarely be available. Agreements are frequently proved by showing that the parties concerted in the pursuit of a common object in such a manner as to show that their actions must
have been coordinated by arrangement beforehand.[218] The danger is that the importance
attached to the acts done may obscure the fact that these acts do not in themselves constitute
a conspiracy, but are only evidence of it. If the jury are left in reasonable doubt, when all the
evidence is in, whether the two or more accused persons were acting in pursuance of an agreement, they should acquit, even though the evidence shows that they were simultaneously
pursuing the same object.[219]

13.3.3.2 A 'course of conduct' which has been agreed

The words, 'the agreement', mean the agreement that a 'course of conduct' shall be pursued.
To consider an accused's liability for conspiracy, we therefore have to imagine that the course
of conduct he intended was pursued and to ask, would it, when completed, have necessarily
amounted to or involved the commission of any offence?[220] But the phrase, 'course of conduct', is ambiguous. It might mean (a) only that the defendants have to agreed on the actual
physical acts which they propose shall be done; or it might mean (b) that they must also have
agreed on the consequences which they intend to follow from their conduct and/or (c) on
the relevant circumstances which they know, or believe, or intend, to exist.[221] The broader
interpretation in (b) and (c) is, it is submitted, the correct interpretation. This deserves more
detailed discussion.

The narrow view

At common law, in *DPP v Nock*,[222] the House of Lords interpreted 'course of conduct' to
mean proof only of the physical acts. The defendants agreed to extract cocaine from a particular substance by subjecting it to a certain process. The substance contained no cocaine.
They were not guilty of conspiracy to produce a controlled drug. The 'course of conduct' was
the conduct involved in applying the process to that substance. If D1 and D2 agreed on that
course of conduct, it would not *necessarily* amount to or involve the commission of the offence
of producing a controlled drug.[223]

   Nock is a case where the 'existence of facts' – that is, that there was no cocaine in the substance – rendered the commission of the offence of producing a controlled drug impossible;
and, but for that fact, the course of conduct would necessarily have resulted in the production

---

[218] *Cooper and Compton* [1947] 2 All ER 701; *Hammersley* (1958) 42 Cr App R 207. Lord Diplock thought that
it is 'a legal fiction' (*DPP v Bhagwan* [1970] 3 All ER 97 at 104) and 'the height of sophistry' (*Knuller (Publishing,
Printing and Promotions) Ltd v DPP* [1972] 2 All ER 898 at 921) that the offence lies not in the concerted action but
in the inferred anterior agreement; but the law is clear that it is the agreement that is the offence. The concerted
action is evidence of the crime, but not the crime itself. cf JC Smith, 'Proving Conspiracy' [1996] Crim LR 386 and
'More on Proving Conspiracy' [1997] Crim LR 333.

[219] Where there are counts for both conspiracy and the ulterior crime, and the only evidence of conspiracy
is the collaboration of the parties in the completion of the ulterior crime, the only logical verdicts are guilty
of both conspiracy and the ulterior crime or not guilty of both. Thus in *Cooper and Compton* [1947] 2 All ER
701, the court quashed a verdict of guilty of conspiracy as inconsistent with a verdict of not guilty of larceny.
Conversely, in *Beach and Owens* [1957] Crim LR 687, a verdict of guilty of attempt to pervert the course of justice
was quashed as inconsistent with a failure to agree on a conspiracy count. See below on the use of substantive
and conspiracy counts.

[220] cf *Barnard* (1979) 70 Cr App R 28, [1980] Crim LR 235, CA and commentary.

[221] See LC 318, Part 2 for discussion of what this should mean.

[222] [1978] AC 979, [1978] Crim LR 483 and commentary. A case of common law conspiracy committed before,
but decided after, the Act came into force.

[223] They would now be guilty because of the addition of s 1(1)(b), above, which was added by the Criminal
Attempts Act 1981.

of a controlled drug. Section 1(1)(b), above, which was added by the Criminal Attempts Act 1981, is designed to ensure that in a case of statutory conspiracy the fact that the course of conduct relied on rendered the substantive offence impossible does not prevent a conviction for conspiracy. The section provides that if D1 and D2 agree that a course:

shall be pursued which, if the agreement is carried out in accordance with their intentions, either –

(a) will necessarily amount to or involve the commission of any offence or offences by one or more of the parties to the agreement, or

(b) would do so but for the existence of facts which render the commission of the offence or any of the offences impossible

On the facts in *Nock*, but for the existence of a fact (the non-existence of cocaine in the substance), the course of conduct agreed on (applying the process to the substance) would necessarily have resulted in the production of a controlled drug. There could now be liability for the conspiracy even though the intended result was impossible. Section 1(1)(b) removes any problem concerning the existence of facts at the time of the agreement and, as a corollary, consequences which depend on the existence of those facts – for example, the production of cocaine. The subsection has nothing to say, however, about (i) other consequences, not dependent on the existence of facts believed to exist by the defendants or (ii) the existence of facts precluding the commission of the crime at the time it is to be carried out.

Consequences as part of the course of conduct

Suppose the defendants D1 and D2 agree to kill V by putting poison in his tea. This, surely, must be conspiracy to murder; but the act of putting poison in the tea will not necessarily result in murder. V may decide not to drink it. So, if the course of conduct is putting poison in the tea, it is not conspiracy to murder – which is absurd.[224] Subsection (1)(b) has nothing to say in the matter because there is no question of impossibility. To avoid the absurdity, 'course of conduct' must be read to include the intended consequences – in this case, the death of V.[225]

Circumstances as part of the course of conduct

In determining whether conspiracy is committed, we have to look forward from the time of the agreement – will the agreed course of conduct necessarily amount to or involve the commission of an offence? Circumstances change. The commission of the offence may be perfectly possible at the time of the agreement and become impossible by the time it is to be performed. Where this may happen, how can we say that the pursuance of the course of conduct will *necessarily* amount to or involve the commission of an offence? Defendants agree to receive certain goods next Monday, which they know to be stolen; but, before next Monday, the goods may cease to be stolen goods by being restored to lawful custody. D1 and D2 may agree to marry next Tuesday, knowing that D1's wife is alive; but, before next Tuesday, she may die. These events may be unlikely, but they are possible, and therefore it cannot be said that the receipt of the goods or the going through with the marriage ceremony will *necessarily* amount to, or involve, the offences of handling stolen goods and bigamy respectively. If the contemplated receipt of the goods, or the marriage ceremony, is the 'course of conduct', the

---

[224] It would be conspiracy to attempt to commit murder, since putting poison in the tea necessarily amounts to an attempt. The Criminal Attempts Act 1981 does not rule out the possibility of such an offence, but it is an strange concept. An agreement to attempt to do something is, in practical terms, an agreement to do it. See LCCP 183, para 4.19. See LC 318, Part 3.

[225] This argument is discussed in full in Ormerod (2006) 59 CLP 185 and by JC Smith in [1977] Crim LR at 601–602. See also G Williams (1977) 127 NLJ 1164 at 1165 and see LCCP 183, para 4.19.

agreements do not amount to conspiracy to handle or commit bigamy.[226] Clearly, they ought to do so.

The obvious way out of this difficulty is to construe 'course of conduct' to include material circumstances *which the parties believe will (not may) exist.* There are two difficulties about this approach. First, under s 1(2) of the Act (discussed below) a person is not guilty of conspiracy unless he 'intends or knows' that circumstances necessary for the commission of the offence shall or will exist at the time when the conduct constituting the offence is to take place.[227] In the examples just given, D cannot 'know' that the circumstances will exist because, as we have seen, they may not do so. This was confirmed in *Saik*,[228] where the House of Lords held that it is not enough that D 'believes';[229] that the circumstances will exist; knowledge requires true belief. In the case of a conspiracy in relation to a future event this will not always be possible to prove. For example, if D1 and D2 are charged with conspiring to handle stolen goods, if they are to receive the goods at a future date, they cannot, at the time of the agreement, know that the goods will be stolen. That is a future circumstance. They may be guilty if they can be shown to have intended that the goods they will handle were to be stolen goods. It seems strange to say that D1 and D2 'intend' that they shall exist when the pair have, and know they have, no control over their existence.[230] The circumstance may, however, be held to be intended because it is part of an intended result.

The second difficulty, which applies to both consequences and circumstances, arises following the amendment made by the Criminal Attempts Act 1981, which added s 1(1)(b). If 'course of conduct' includes the circumstances believed by the parties to exist, this provision is entirely unnecessary. It is necessary only if the narrow *Nock*[231] interpretation of 'course of conduct' is right. Arguably, by enacting s 1(1)(b) Parliament has accepted that interpretation, but to have taken the sting out of it so far as impossibility at the time of the agreement is concerned. The trouble with this approach is that it leaves other stings elsewhere. However, the argument that 'course of conduct' must include intended consequences and foreseen circumstances is so compelling that s 1(1)(b) might reasonably be regarded as an 'avoidance of doubt' provision, strictly unnecessary, but there for the guidance of the unwary. *Nock* is a discredited, though not overruled,[232] decision on the common law and should not be applied in interpreting the 1977 Act.

The Law Commission has recently recommended that a conspirator must be shown to have intended that the conduct element of the offence, *and* (where relevant) the consequence element (or other consequences), should respectively be engaged in or brought about.[233]

Conditional agreements[234]

The question of conditional agreements requires separate consideration, particularly in the light of s 1 (1) of the Act. The parties may agree on alternative courses of action depending on the existence of some fact to be ascertained or some event which may or may not happen.

---

[226] They might be conspiracies to attempt. See LCCP 183, Part 7.

[227] Below, p 442.

[228] [2006] UKHL 18. The decision prompted the Government to refer the subject to the Law Commission: LCCP 183, para 1.20. Since the decision and the Court of Appeal's clarification of the approach in *Suchedina* above, it seems not to have given rise to problems in practice. See LC 318, Part 4.

[229] Lord Nicholls at [26]; Lord Hope at [78]; cf Lord Brown at [119]; nor of suspicion: Lord Nicholls at [30].

[230] For a further discussion of 'intend or know', see Ormerod (2006) 59 CLP 185 and the 4th edition of this book, at 220–222.

[231] Above, p 432.

[232] See below, p 481.

[233] LC 318, para 2.56.

[234] See Campbell (1982) 2 LS 77. See LCCP 183, Part 5, taking a different view of these categories.

It seems settled that there will be a conspiracy where the parties' objective is to commit a crime – but not if it proves too difficult or too dangerous – as where D1 and D2 agree that they will abandon their intention to commit burglary if they find the house surrounded by police. They agree to commit the burglary only if it is safe. If they go through with the agreed conduct *as intended* they must, of necessity, commit burglary. The fact that an agreement to commit a crime is subject to express or implied reservation does not necessarily preclude liability for conspiracy.[235]

There are far more difficult aspects to conditional intentions. If one of the courses of action agreed upon involves the commission of a crime and the other does not, is this a conspiracy to commit the crime? Can it be said that, if the agreement is carried out in accordance with their intentions, the course of conduct pursued will *necessarily* amount to or involve the commission of an offence? Is not the agreement carried out in accordance with their intentions if, in the event, they take the non-criminal course? For example, D1 and D2 may agree that they will transfer money brought into their bureau de change even if it is criminal property. Is this an agreement to launder criminal property? What if, when it is delivered, the money is not from criminal activity and so is not criminal property after all? Can it be said that, if the agreement is carried out in accordance with their intentions, the course of conduct pursued will *necessarily* amount to or involve the commission of an offence?[236] This is a complex area and only an outline can be offered here by reference to scenarios involving the putative money launderers who agree to transfer monies brought into their bureau de change.[237]

Agreements to do 'x' if 'y'

If D1 and D2 declare 'we will transfer the money if it is non-criminal property', there is no declared intention about what course of conduct they would adopt if the money is illicit. This is not, it is submitted, sufficient to constitute an agreement to launder money. D1 and D2 have, implicitly, seen the risk that the money will be illicit, but have not declared an intention to deal with criminal money. It cannot be said that D1 and D2 have agreed on a course of conduct that will *necessarily* involve them in the commission of an offence if carried out in accordance with their intentions. In fact, acting in accordance with their declared intentions, all we can assert is that they will *not* commit a money laundering offence.[238] The defendants' state of mind is declared only in relation to one possible eventuality.

Agreements to do 'x' only if 'y'[239]

The money laundering duo might say: 'we will transfer the money *only if* the money is non-criminal property, if it is criminal we will not transfer it'. There is no intention to pursue a course of conduct that will necessarily involve the commission of an offence: there can be no liability for conspiracy.[240] They differ significantly from the previous category because D1 and D2 have declared intentions as to their course of conduct in both eventualities: where *y* materializes and not.[241]

---

[235] *Mills* (1963) 47 Cr App R 49, [1963] Crim LR 181, CCA, and commentary. cf *Hussein* [1978] Crim LR 219, CA.

[236] See further, Ormerod (2006) 59 CLP 185; *Saik* [2006] UKHL 18; I am grateful to Tony Shaw QC for the very many valuable discussions on this topic and conspiracy in general.

[237] cf *Saik* [2006] UKHL 18. See LCCP 193 and LC 318, Part 2.

[238] Kenneth Campbell in his useful analysis of the concepts describes these as 'non-comprehensive conditional intentions' Campbell (1982) 2 LS 77 at 84–85.

[239] The courts got muddled with this in the theft and burglary cases in the 1970s, in particular *Easom* [1971] 2 QB 315. See also L Koffman, 'Conditional Intention to Steal' [1980] Crim LR 463 and J Parry, 'Conditional Intents: A Dissent' [1981] Crim LR 6. See also the cogent criticism by Campbell (1982) 2 LS 77 at 78–80.

[240] Campbell calls these 'comprehensive conditional intentions' ibid.

[241] As Lynch observes ('Further Comment' [1978] Crim LR 205), conditional intentions provide that 'if A then B, if not A then C', at 207.

Agreements to do 'x' even if 'y'

Our money launderers D1 and D2 might acknowledge that 'the monies involved in the business might be criminal, and agree to pursue such conduct *even though* some of the monies we transfer will be criminal property'. Their agreement could be reconstructed as one which includes a confirmed intention: 'we intend to pursue a course of conduct (transferring money) which is not criminal and if certain circumstances transpire (the money is criminal property), we intend nevertheless to pursue a course of conduct (transferring money)'. The agreement will, if completed in accordance with one of their intentions, necessarily involve the commission of a crime. Campbell calls these unconditional intentions. They are generally regarded as a form of direct intention.[242]

In *Saik*, members of the House took different approaches to conditional agreements,[243] but the majority recognized that it has no part to play on the facts as only suspicion and not intention was proved. Baroness Hale, dissenting provided what is, it is submitted, a powerful example to support her conclusion that a conditional intention suffices for liability in a conspiracy. Where D1 and D2 consider having sex with a woman and agree that they will do so *even if* she turns out not to be consenting they should be guilty of conspiracy since they have expressed an intent to rape.[244] The complex issue of conditional intentions may need to be addressed in further detail on a future occasion if it arises directly.[245]

Conditional agreements in the case law

The courts have been untroubled by these theoretical difficulties and have taken a broad brush approach to conditional intention in a series of cases. In *Reed*,[246] D1 and D2 were guilty of conspiring to aid and abet suicide (as the offence was then drafted) where they agreed that D1 would visit suicidal individuals and either discourage or actively help them, depending on his assessment of the appropriate course of action. D1 and D2 have agreed on a course of conduct which if carried out in accordance with their intentions will necessarily involve an offence. The court held that the following hypothetical case is distinguishable: D1 and D2 agree to drive from London to Edinburgh in a time which can be achieved without exceeding the speed limits, but only if the traffic which they encounter is exceptionally light. In this example, as in *Reed* itself, the parties have apparently agreed that, in a certain event, they will commit a crime. The difference appears to be that exceeding the speed limit is only incidental to the main object of the agreement – getting from London to Edinburgh in a certain time. In *Jackson*,[247] D1 and D2 agreed with D3 that D3, if convicted of the burglary for which he was on trial, should be shot in the leg so that the court would sentence him more leniently. They were guilty of conspiring to pervert the course of justice. This was an agreement that D1 and D2 intended to shoot D3 if he was convicted. D1 and D2 agreed on a course of conduct which if carried out in accordance with their intentions will necessarily involve an offence. In *O'Hadhmaill*,[248] it was held that an agreement by IRA members

---

[242] The Law Commission regards these as forms of recklessness not conditional intention. But that seems doubtful. In recklessness D has awareness of a risk. Here, D has beyond mere awareness of the risk, and demonstrated a commitment to perform the conduct even if the risk eventuates. See LC 318, Part 2.

[243] Lord Nicholls seems, strictly speaking, not to reject it outright [5]. Lord Brown finds it beguiling but reluctantly rejects it.

[244] [99]. See the rejection of this in LC 318, Part 2, para 2.115.

[245] The Law Commission considers the matter in detail in LCCP 183, Part 5 and LC 318, Part 2. See also Appendix B.

[246] [1982] Crim LR 819, CA. cf *O'Hadhmaill* [1996] Crim LR 509, below.

[247] [1985] Crim LR 442, CA.

[248] [1996] Crim LR 509. See LCCP 183, para 5.8.

during the period of the IRA ceasefire to make bombs with a view to causing explosions, if, but only if, the ceasefire came to an end was a conspiracy to cause an explosion.[249]

13.3.3.3 The object of the conspiracy

An agreement to commit any offence, is a conspiracy contrary to s 1 of the Act, triable on indictment.[250]

Summary offences

Proceedings for conspiracy to commit summary offences[251] may not be instituted without consent of the DPP.[252] The availability of trial on indictment for conspiracy to commit summary offences was introduced to meet the fear of[253] 'social danger involved in the deliberate planning of offences on a widespread scale'.

Conspiracies to commit inchoate offences

Although technically possible, conspiracies to commit other inchoate offences would be rare and in principle ought to be treated with caution since the remoteness from the substantive offence is substantial.[254] The matter is discussed in the recent Law Commission Report No 318.[255]

Conspiracies to aid and abet

The Criminal Attempts Act 1981[256] makes it clear that there can be no attempt to aid and abet an offence but it leaves open the question whether there can be a conspiracy to do so.[257] D1 and D2, knowing that E intends to commit a burglary, agree to leave a ladder in a place where it will assist him to do so. E is not a party to that agreement so is not a co-conspirator. If E uses the ladder and commits burglary, D1 and D2 will be guilty of aiding and abetting him to do so. Are they guilty of conspiracy to commit burglary? Conspiracy requires an agreement that will involve 'a course of conduct' amounting to or involving 'the commission of an offence'. If the course of conduct is placing the ladder, it seems clear that they are not guilty. Placing the ladder is not an attempt to aid and abet burglary, since the Criminal Attempts Act 1981[258] makes it clear that this is not an offence known to the law. However, it is argued above[259] that 'course of conduct' should be interpreted to include the consequences intended to follow from

---

[249] Sullivan suggests that the decision is useful in 'refut[ing]' any notion that, in legal discourse, one can never be found to have knowledge of facts relating to the future'. But, does this overlook the fact that the decision is more readily if not equally explicable on the basis of future intentions without detracting from the orthodox view that one cannot know the future? See also J Parry, 'Conditional Intents: A Dissent' [1981] Crim LR 6. cf LCCP 183, para 5.5. Arguably the agreement was subject to further necessary agreement of the parties as to whether the ceasefire had ended, and was not a concluded intention on the unusual facts of this case. cf LC 318, para 2.112.

[250] There is one exception: Trade Union and Labour Relations (Consolidation) Act 1992 s 242. Section 3 of the Conspiracy and Protection of Property Act 1875 is repealed by 1977 Act: s 5(11). See JC Smith [1977] Crim LR 638.

[251] But cf s 5(6) which limits this.

[252] Section 4(1) or, where prosecution for the summary offence itself so requires, that of the A-G: s 4(2). The Law Commission recommends abolishing that requirement: LC 318, para 4.35.

[253] LC 76, para 1.85. The Commission refer to *Blamires Transport Services Ltd* [1964] 1 QB 278, [1963] 3 All ER 170 as a typical example of the sort of case they had in mind. The conspiracy to contravene certain provisions of the Road Traffic Acts extended over two years and included a large number of offences, all triable only summarily.

[254] It is an offence to conspire to attempt and to conspire to commit an offence under SCA 2007, ss 44–46.

[255] Part 3.

[256] Section 1(4)(b).

[257] The question is discussed by JC Smith in *Crime, Proof and Punishment*, 21, 35–36 and 40–41. See also LC 318, Part 3.

[258] Above, p 420. See the possible offences under the SCA 2007, below p 472.

[259] Above, p 433.

the conduct agreed upon, including the action of a person not a party to the agreement – for example, V, who takes up poisoned tea left by D and E and drinks it. So it might be argued, consistently with that, that the course of conduct ought to include E's use of the ladder in committing burglary. If that should be accepted, the next question would be whether the burglary is 'the commission of any offence by one or more of the parties to the agreement'. E is not a party to the agreement, so the question becomes, do the words 'commission of any offence' include participation in the offence as a secondary party? Since all the parties to a conspiracy to commit an offence will be guilty of that offence if it is committed, but s 1(1) contemplates that it may be *committed* by only one of them, it is clear that 'commission' means commission by a principal. It is submitted, therefore, that an agreement to aid and abet an offence is not a conspiracy under the Act.

The previous paragraphs were approved by the Court of Appeal in *Hollinshead*.[260] DD agreed to sell to X 'black boxes', devices for altering electricity meters to show that less electricity had been used than was the fact. They expected X to resell the devices to consumers of electricity for use in defrauding the electricity supplier. The House of Lords[261] did not find it necessary to decide whether there could be a conspiracy to aid and abet and Lord Roskill said that it should be treated as open for consideration *de novo* if the question arises again. But there was clearly an agreement to aid and abet the consumers to commit offences under what was then s 2 of the Theft Act 1978[262] against the electricity supplier. By upholding the conviction for conspiracy to defraud, the House implicitly[263] decided that an agreement to aid and abet the consumers to commit an offence against the suppliers was not a statutory conspiracy.[264] This, it is submitted, is the position under the Act. In *Kenning*,[265] Lord Phillips CJ confirmed this interpretation:

an agreement to aid and abet an offence is not in law capable of constituting a criminal conspiracy under section 1(1) of the 1977 Act.

The Supreme Court of Hong Kong has held that there may be a *common law* conspiracy to aid and abet an offence in *Po Koon-tai*.[266]

Conspiracy and voluntary manslaughter

What is the position where there is an agreement by D1 and D2 to kill where D2 would have a defence of diminished responsibility on a charge of murder? If the killing is to be done by D1 it will be murder and so the agreement is a conspiracy to murder. If it is to be done by D2, D1 will still be guilty of murder by virtue of s 2(4) of the Homicide Act 1957.[267] However if, as submitted above,[268] 'commission of any offence' means commission as principal in the first degree, this appears to be a conspiracy to commit manslaughter.

13.3.3.4 An intention to agree

Clearly, if D1 is unaware that his conduct is being construed by D2 as an assent or agreement to a criminal proposal he will have no liability for conspiracy since he will not be intending

---

[260] [1985] 1 All ER 850 at 858.

[261] [1985] AC 975.

[262] The conduct in *Hollinshead* is now an offence under s 7 of the Fraud Act 2006.

[263] If that agreement were a statutory conspiracy, it could not under the then prevailing (though now repealed) rule in *Ayres* above, p 425 be a conspiracy to defraud.

[264] See commentary on *Hollinshead* [1985] Crim LR 653 at 656.

[265] [2008] EWCA Crim 1534.

[266] [1980] HKLR 492.

[267] Below, Ch 14.

[268] Above, n 265.

to form the necessary agreement. It might be argued that there are two elements to this part of the *mens rea*. First, it must be shown that D intended to perform the acts/speak the words that were capable of constituting an offer or acceptance of the agreement. This provides a very limited scope for denial of *mens rea*, but this might succeed where D is so intoxicated that he uses language or actions without being aware of their likely interpretation.[269] Secondly, the requirement of *actus reus* that there is an agreement suggests a corresponding *mens rea* requirement that D intentionally used conduct that he was aware might be understood to constitute an offer/acceptance in the non-contractual sense.[270]

13.3.3.5 Intention that the agreement will be carried out

Section 1 of the 1977 Act assumes the existence of an intention of the parties not merely to agree, but also to carry out their agreement. This is not surprising because the essence of conspiracy, like attempt, is the intent to cause the forbidden result. The Law Commission understood this well enough and their Report[271] was quite unequivocal in 1976. The draft Bill, and the Bill which was introduced into Parliament, also expressly required proof of intention. Unwisely, this provision was deleted from the Bill because it was thought too complex; but, in agreeing to the amendment, the Lord Chancellor stated that the speeches in Parliament had conceded that 'the law should require full intention and knowledge before conspiracy can be established'.[272]

However, in *Anderson*,[273] Lord Bridge, in a speech with which all of the House agreed, said that it was sufficient that an alleged conspirator had agreed that the criminal course of conduct be pursued and that he would play his role, but that it was not necessary to prove in addition that he intended the crime to be committed.[274] Lord Bridge was concerned with cases like that of the owner of a car, D, who agrees with a gang to hire it to them for use in a robbery. D may be quite indifferent whether the robbery is committed or not. In that situation the gang members are certainly guilty of conspiracy for they do intend to carry out the robbery; and D is guilty of abetting the conspiracy by giving encouragement to its continuance. There was no need to dilute the requirement that the conspirators must intend the commission of a crime.[275]

In *Anderson*, D was convicted of conspiring with a number of other persons to effect the escape of one of them from prison. D had agreed to supply diamond wire to cut bars. He had certainly intended to be a party to that agreement. But D said that he never intended the plan to be put into effect and believed that it could not possibly succeed. It was held that this was no defence. It was clear in that case that two or more of the alleged conspirators did intend

---

[269] The Law Commission has recommended that it should be possible for a defendant to deny that he or she possessed the fault element for conspiracy because of intoxication, whether voluntary or involuntary, even when the fault element in question is recklessness (or its equivalent): LC 318, para 2.164. In other words, the proposed offence will be treated as a specific intent offence even though it contains elements of recklessness.

[270] cf *Prior* [2004] Crim LR 849 and commentary discussing the *mens rea* for an 'offer' to supply drugs.

[271] *Report on Conspiracy and Criminal Law Reform* (LC 76) paras 1.25–1.41. For the common law, see *Mulcahy* (1868) LR 3 HL 306 at 317, per Willes J. *Yip Chiu-cheung*, above, p 105, assumes that a person is guilty of conspiracy at common law only if he intends to carry out the agreement. See per Lord Griffiths [1994] 2 All ER at 928c.

[272] HL, vol 379, col 55.

[273] [1986] AC 27, [1985] Crim LR 651, HL, and commentary. See also PW Ferguson, 'Intention Agreement and Statutory Conspiracy' (1986) 102 LQR 26.

[274] It might be argued that D1 and D2 agreeing to the course of conduct is sufficient because if they intend that they can be inferred to intend its consequences – the offence. This is a very strained interpretation. *Anderson* is criticized in LCCP 183, paras 4.26–4.41. In LC 318 the Law Commission recommends that a conspirator must be shown to have intended that the conduct element of the offence, and (where relevant) the consequence element (or other consequences), should respectively be engaged in or brought about (para 2.56) See also LC 318, para 4.30.

[275] Sections 44–46 of the SCA 2007 will now extend to deal with such cases.

to carry out the agreement, so D's conviction could have been upheld on the ground that he aided and abetted that conspiracy – which he undoubtedly did, encouraging the making or continuance of it by his offer to help.[276]

The decision that no intention need be proved on the part of one alleged principal offender in conspiracy would significantly alter the scope of the offence. If no intention needs to be proved on the part of conspirator A, then none needs to be proved on the part of another, B. But if A and B are the only parties, and neither has the intention that it should be carried out, how can there be a crime of conspiracy: a conspiracy which no one intends to carry out is an absurdity, if not an impossibility. Moreover, s 1(2)[277] of the Act requires the conspirators to have intention or knowledge as to facts or *circumstances* constituting an offence, and it would be very remarkable indeed if intention or knowledge were required for the circumstances of the principal offence and not for its *consequences*.

It is submitted that *Anderson* should not be followed in this respect. It has been overlooked or ignored more than once by the Court of Appeal.[278] In *Edwards* where D had agreed to supply amphetamine but there was a possibility that he intended to supply ephedrine, it was held that the judge had rightly directed the jury that they could convict of conspiracy to supply amphetamine only if D intended to supply amphetamine – that is, it was not sufficient that D agreed to supply amphetamine unless he intended to carry out the agreement.

Anderson was distinguished in *McPhillips*,[279] where the Court of Appeal of Northern Ireland, accepted the proposition in this book[280] that s 1(1) of the 1977 Act[281] assumes the existence of an intention of the parties to carry out the agreement. Lord Lowry CJ held that D, who had joined in a conspiracy to plant a bomb, timed to explode on the roof of a hall at 1 am when a disco would be at its height, was not a party to the conspiracy to murder of which his accomplices were guilty because, unknown to his accomplices, he intended to give a warning enabling the hall to be cleared. He did not intend that anyone should be killed. *Anderson* was distinguished relying on Lord Bridge's *dictum* that a 'perfectly respectable citizen' who joins in an agreement 'without the least intention of playing any part in the ostensibly agreed criminal objective but rather with the purpose of frustrating and exposing the objective of the other parties' is not guilty of conspiracy. The *dictum* may be correct[282] but hardly seems to fit *McPhillips*, whose convictions, arising out of the same facts, for conspiracy to cause explosions and offences under the Explosive Substances Act 1883, were upheld. He was rightly acquitted of conspiracy to murder as a principal offender simply because he lacked the required intention. More debatable is the decision that he was not guilty as an abettor of the conspiracy to murder. He intentionally gave assistance or encouragement to what he knew to be a conspiracy to murder and that is normally sufficient for liability. This suggests that an intention to frustrate the object of the conspiracy is a special defence. There are clear public policy grounds for allowing such a defence, although any such withdrawal-type defence will need

---

[276] See commentary on the decision of the Court of Appeal [1984] Crim LR 551, and, on conspiracy to aid and abet, above, p 438.

[277] Below, p 442.

[278] *Edwards* [1991] Crim LR 45; *Ashton* [1992] Crim LR 667; *Harvey* [1999] Crim LR 70.

[279] (1990) 6 BNIL.

[280] See the 6th edition of this book, at 259.

[281] Art 9(1) of the Criminal Attempts and Conspiracy (Northern Ireland) Order 1983 is identical with s 1(1).

[282] *Edwards* [1991] Crim LR 45, above, n 278. But cf *Yip Chiu-cheung v R*, above, p 105, and *Somchai Liangsiriprasert v United States Government* (1990) 92 Cr App R 77 at 82 where the Privy Council left open the question whether law enforcement officers who entered into an agreement to import drugs into the USA with the object of trapping the dealers should be regarded as conspirators. For valuable discussion on the liability of state officials see A Ashworth, 'Testing Fidelity to Legal Values: Official Involvement and Criminal Justice', in S Shute and A Simester (eds), *Criminal Law Theory: Doctrines of the General Part* (2002) 299, 324–5.

to be carefully prescribed in the context of inchoate liability.[283] Arguably it should be limited to conduct of the conspirator which serves unequivocal notice of withdrawal on his co-conspirators and seeks to nullify the effects of any overt acts D has performed as part of the conspiracy.[284] It has been held that where D1 intends that the offence should be carried out he is guilty of conspiracy although he had an ulterior motive to gather evidence of the criminal wrongdoing and expose it.[285] The Law Commission recommends that the defence of acting reasonably provided for by s 50 of the Serious Crime Act 2007 should be applied in its entirety to the offence of conspiracy.[286]

The 1977 Act does not deal specifically with the case where E purports to conspire with D but has no intention of going through with the plan. The question was formerly of no practical importance because D could be convicted of an attempt to conspire, but the Act rules that out. The point has not arisen in England but in some jurisdictions it has been decided that there is no conspiracy.[287] It might be argued that, looking at the facts objectively, there is such an agreement as (apart from the illegality) would be enforceable in the law of contract and that therefore there is an *actus reus*. D, who, with *mens rea*, has caused the *actus reus* should be guilty. An answer to this argument is that there is no *actus reus* unless E agrees in fact, that is, that an actual subjective agreement is required. If *Anderson*[288] is followed and E held to be guilty of conspiracy notwithstanding his lack of intention, the problem disappears.

13.3.3.6 Intention to play some part in carrying out the agreement

According to Lord Bridge in *Anderson*[289] the *mens rea* of conspiracy is established:

if, and only if, it is shown that the accused, when he entered into the agreement, intended to play some part in the agreed course of conduct in furtherance of the criminal purpose which the agreed course of conduct was intended to achieve.

No authority was cited for this novel *dictum* and the Court of Appeal has subsequently held that Lord Bridge is not to be taken as saying what he plainly did say (above); the court in *Siracusa* said that participation in conspiracy can be active or passive and D's intention to participate 'is established by his failure to stop the unlawful activity'.[290] D's liability is, however, complete when he joins the agreement, intending that it be carried out, and his failure to stop it is, at most, evidence of his agreement and intention. In truth, O'Connor LJ in *Siracusa* appears to have been using this as a mechanism to circumvent *Anderson*.

It is submitted that the correct statement of the law is that there is nothing in the section, nor in the common law, to require participation in the carrying out of the agreement by each conspirator. All that need be contemplated is the commission of the offence 'by one or more of the parties to the agreement'. So an agreement between A and B that A will supply a proscribed drug to B is a conspiracy between them to supply the drug.[291]

---

[283] The Law Commission rejects a withdrawal defence in LC 318, paras 2.35–2.45.

[284] cf the discussion above in relation to secondary withdrawal, p 236.

[285] *Jones and Warburton* [2002] EWCA Crim 735.

[286] LC 318, Part 6.

[287] *Harris* [1927] NPD 347 (South Africa); *O'Brien* [1954] SCR 666 (Canada); *Delaney v State* 164 Tenn 432 (1932) (Tennessee); *State v Otu* [1964] NNLR 113 (Nigeria). cf *Thomson* (1965) 50 Cr App R 1. See GHL Fridman in (1956) 19 MLR 276.

[288] Above, p 439.

[289] [1986] AC 27 at 39. Read literally, the Law Commission recommendatoins (para 2.45) endorse this.

[290] *Siracusa* (1989) 90 Cr App R 340, [1989] Crim LR 712; cf *Chambers* [2009] EWCA Crim 2742, following *Anderson*.

[291] *Drew* [2000] 1 Cr App R 91, [1999] Crim LR 581. But an indictment alleging a conspiracy to supply 'another' will be taken to mean a conspiracy to supply someone other than the conspirators: cases cited in commentary at [1999] Crim LR 582.

Unforeseen but inevitable consequences

As noticed above, Parliament deleted the provision in the Bill requiring an intention to cause any consequence which is an ingredient in the crime the parties are alleged to have conspired to commit. It is, however, submitted above that, notwithstanding *Anderson*, the parties must intend that at least one of them will pursue the course of conduct agreed upon. If so, they must be proved to have intended the foreseen consequences. Exceptionally, the agreed course of conduct may be such that it will necessarily cause a consequence not foreseen by the parties. For example, they agree to inflict a particular type of bodily harm, not appreciating that it will necessarily cause death. On a literal interpretation of the Act they are guilty of conspiracy to murder. In principle, that would be a wrong result, because killing is not intended and possibly not even foreseen as a possibility. It is thought that, as in interpreting other aspects of the offence, the answer lies in the construction of 'course of conduct'.[292] This should be read not only to include the consequences which are intended by the parties, but also to be limited to such consequences, whether they will in fact necessarily result or not. This is justifiable because it is the *agreed* course of conduct that we are concerned with; and the agreement does not include causing death.

If D1 and D2 agree to cause grievous bodily harm to V they are guilty of conspiring to commit an offence under s 18 of the Offences Against the Person Act 1861 but they are not guilty of conspiracy to murder although, if they carry out their intention and consequently V dies, they will be guilty of murder.[293] Similarly, an agreement to behave with gross negligence towards V is not a conspiracy to commit manslaughter, even though the parties will be guilty of manslaughter if they carry out the agreement and kill V.[294]

13.3.3.7 Intention or knowledge as to circumstances

Section 1(2) of the Act provides:

Where liability for any offence may be incurred without knowledge on the part of the person committing it of any particular fact or circumstance necessary for the commission of the offence, a person shall nevertheless not be guilty of conspiracy to commit that offence by virtue of subsection (1) above unless he and at least one other party to the agreement intend or know that the fact or circumstance shall or will exist at the time when the conduct constituting the offence is to take place.

The provision is intended to reflect the general principle that elements of *mens rea* in inchoate offences ought not to be diluted since that *mens rea* often forms the core of the wrongdoing in the absence of any tangible harm resulting from the *actus reus*. The aim of this section is to ensure that even if strict liability and recklessness as to circumstances are sufficient *mens rea* for the substantive crime, these are to have no place in conspiracy. Intention or knowledge as to *all* the circumstances of the *actus reus* is required *even* where the agreement is to commit a crime which in its substantive form may be committed recklessly, or is a crime of strict liability or one committed on the basis of D's suspicion or negligence.[295] Although the aim of

---

[292] Above, p 432.

[293] For an argument to the contrary, see 4th edition of this book, at 222–223 and [1977] Crim LR 638–639. cf Williams (1977) 127 NLJ at 1169 and Williams, TBCL (1st edn, 1978) 357–359.

[294] A conspiracy to commit manslaughter seems a theoretical possibility in the case of a suicide pact or where the party to do the killing is suffering from diminished responsibility. Above, p 430.

[295] The Law Commission proposes to reverse this position. Two provisions are proposed. Where the agreement relates to a substantive offence for which fault as to circumstances is strict liability or negligence an alleged conspirator must be shown at the time of the agreement to have been merely reckless whether a circumstance element of a substantive offence (or other relevant circumstance) would be present at the relevant time, (LC 318, para 2.137). Where the agreement relates to a substantive offence with fault requirements not involving mere negligence (or its equivalent), in relation to a fact or circumstance element, an alleged conspirator may be found

s 1(2) is clear enough, a number of problems arise in its interpretation. These have now been addressed by the House of Lords in *Saik*.[296]

Scope of application

First, there is no express provision in s 1(1) requiring intention or knowledge as to circumstances. Section 1(2) is expressed to apply *only* to those conspiracies which involve an offence which in its substantive form has an element of strict liability as to a circumstance or requires only recklessness as to a circumstance. A strict interpretation would lead to the conclusion that the section does not apply where the conspiracy alleged is one involving a substantive crime in which there is a requirement of intention or knowledge (and not mere recklessness) as to a circumstance.[297] In *Saik*,[298] the House of Lords accepted that Parliament could not have intended a scandalous paradox[299] whereby the requirement of *mens rea* should be greater on a charge of conspiring to commit an offence of strict liability or recklessness than on a charge of conspiring to commit an offence requiring knowledge.[300]

What constitutes knowledge?[301]

The knowledge required relates to the fact or circumstance which must be proved as part of the *actus reus*. The full reading of s 1(2) might be, though it is unclear, that the parties are not liable for conspiracy to commit any crime where the *actus reus* includes proof of a circumstance which they do not know exists or intend will exist. In *Saik*, the House of Lords confirmed that within s 1(2) the requirement of 'knowledge' or 'intention' as to the fact or circumstances necessary for the commission of the substantive offence is not to be diluted. Knowledge is not satisfied by proof of 'belief'[302] nor of suspicion.[303] These states of mind will not suffice for the conspiracy even if they would for the substantive offence. In this respect the offence of conspiracy is stricter than that of attempt where the courts have accepted that recklessness as to circumstances is a sufficient *mens rea* where that would suffice for the substantive crime attempted.[304]

What are the 'facts or circumstances' which must be known?

Suppose that D1 agrees to help D2 move out of his flat. D2 is unsure whether the cabling he has installed for his hi-fi belongs to him or to his landlord. D1 and D2 confer together and are uncertain, but agree, nevertheless, to remove it knowing their actions will result in damage in the process. They therefore have an intention to cause damage, and are reckless as to whether the property belongs to another. The substantive offence of criminal damage requires that D intends or is reckless as to the causing of damage (the result), *and* that D knows or is reckless as to whether the property belongs to another (circumstance).[305] If D1 and D2 went ahead, they would have sufficient *mens rea* to be convicted of the substantive

---

guilty if shown to have possessed those fault requirements at the time of his or her agreement to commit the offence. (para 2.146). The intention is to simplify the law.

[296] [2006] UKHL 18, [2007] AC 18.

[297] Elliott [1978] Crim LR 204; LCCP 183, para 4.65.

[298] Lord Nicholls at [18].

[299] Elliott, above.

[300] Smith [1977] Crim LR 606; Williams (1977) 127 NLJ 1166. See LCCP 183, para 4.45 et seq.

[301] See, generally, S Shute, 'Knowledge and Belief in the Criminal Law' (at 187) and GR Sullivan, 'Knowledge, Belief and Culpability' (at 215) in S Shute and A Simester (eds), *Criminal Law Theory: Doctrines of the General Part*, Chs 8 and 9 respectively.

[302] Lord Nicholls at [26], Lord Hope at [78]; cf Lord Brown at [119].

[303] Lord Nicholls at [30].

[304] *Khan* (1990) 91 Cr App R 29, above p 406. LCCP 183, para 4.145 et seq.

[305] *Smith (David Raymond)* [1974] QB 354. See below, p 1020.

offence. As for the conspiracy, in the *actual* circumstances that exist, the carrying out of the agreement 'will necessarily amount' to criminal damage; but on an orthodox reading of s 1(2), it is not a conspiracy to commit criminal damage. It would not be criminal damage in the circumstances which the parties *intend, or know, shall or will exist.* D1 and D2 are reckless as to the circumstance. Recklessness as to the circumstance of the *actus reus* (property belonging to another) is not a sufficient *mens rea* on a charge of conspiracy to commit a crime (criminal damage) even where it is a sufficient *mens rea* for the crime itself. If the Law Commission proposals are accepted, the law will extend considerably. It is submitted that the law would be overbroad.

For s 1(2) to apply there must be a fact or circumstance in the *actus reus* on which liability in the substantive offence is strict, based on negligence or for which D's recklessness suffices.[306] This has caused problems. For example, in a series of cases involving conspiracies to commit criminal damage being reckless as to whether life is endangered,[307] the Court of Appeal has held that it is sufficient to establish recklessness (rather than knowledge) on the part of the conspirators. These cases were based on the false assumption that the substantive offence requires proof of a fact that life is endangered. It does not: *Parker*.[308] Since life endangerment is not 'a circumstance' that needs to exist for the full offence, it is unnecessary in a conspiracy to prove that DD 'knew of' or intended it.[309]

Conspiring to import prohibited drugs

The offences of evading the prohibition on the importation of drugs come within s 1(2).[310] They are offences for which liability may be incurred without knowledge on the part of the defendant that the drug was of a particular class. For the substantive offence, it is sufficient that D knew the goods were subject to a prohibition on importation. If he is charged with importing pethidine (a Class A drug – penalty, life imprisonment) it is no defence that he believed the drug to be pemoline (a Class C drug – penalty, five years). But that the drug *was* pethidine is, of course, a fact necessary for the commission of the offence. On a charge of conspiracy, it must be proved that the defendant and at least one other party intended or knew that that fact should or would exist.[311] An indictment for conspiracy to import 'prohibited drugs' is different. It embraces agreements to import Class A, B and C drugs and, as these are different offences carrying different penalties, it appears at first sight to allege three distinct conspiracies. But s 1, defining statutory conspiracy, speaks of 'any offence or offences' and s 3

---

[306] This is discussed in full in Ormerod (2006) 59 CLP 185.

[307] *Mir* (1994) 22 Apr; *Browning* (1998) unreported; *Ryan* (1999) The Times, 13 Oct.

[308] [1993] Crim LR 856.

[309] See *Saik* [2006] UKHL 18. There are two arguments that these cases are not wrongly decided. First, they were all heard at a time when *Caldwell* recklessness was a sufficient *mens rea* for criminal damage. As such, although the offence did not require proof of a circumstance of a life being endangered, it did require proof of the reasonable person's awareness of a risk of life endangerment. That it is said could be a 'circumstance' in the substantive offence for which D must be held to have knowledge for the charge of conspiracy. Secondly, since *G* [2004] 1 AC 1034, the *mens rea* as to the endangerment of life is subjective. Arguably, however, there is still an 'objective circumstance' that must exist because even in a case of subjective recklessness, there must be proof that D 'unreasonably' took the risk he foresaw. Thanks are due to Rudi Fortson QC for discussions on this point.

[310] Above, p 442.

[311] *Siracusa* [1989] Crim LR 712 and commentary. In *Patel* (89/4351/S1, CA, 7 Aug 1991), Archbold, para 34–16, it was said that an agreement to deal with a drug believing it to be of a higher class than was in fact the case would be a conspiracy to deal in the drug of the lower class. That seems irreconcilable with s 1(2). But the parties appear to be guilty of a conspiracy to deal with the drugs of the higher class! The commission of the offence is impossible, but that is immaterial. See further *Taylor (RJ)* [2002] Crim LR 203 and commentary, and 301; *Hussain* [2002] 2 Cr App R 363, [2002] Crim LR 407 and commentary.

provides that, where the penalties for the substantive offences differ, the maximum for the conspiracy is the longer or longest of these.[312]

Where only one party has *mens rea*

Section 1(2) makes it clear that, so far as the relevant circumstances are concerned, both parties to the agreement (or, where there are more than two parties, at least two of them) must have *mens rea*. If D1 and D2 agree to touch V sexually and D1 knows that she is only 15, there is no conspiracy if D2 reasonably believes that she is 16.

The Law Commission's rejected subsection from 1976 would have made similar provision for foresight of consequences, but there is no such provision in the Act. If, however, 'course of conduct' is construed, as suggested above, to include intended consequences, and only intended consequences, the result is the same. As Lord Griffiths said in *Yip Chiu-cheung*,[313] 'The crime of conspiracy requires an agreement between two or more persons to commit an unlawful act with the intention of carrying it out. It is the intention to carry out the crime that constitutes the *mens rea* of the offence.' If D1 intends death and D2 intends grievous bodily harm, this is a conspiracy to cause grievous bodily harm but not a conspiracy to murder.

Ignorance of criminal law no defence

There is no requirement that DD have knowledge of the relevant criminal law which renders their proposed conduct illegal.[314]

13.3.4 Procedural issues relating to conspiracies

13.3.4.1 Conspiracy where the contemplated offence is committed

The courts discourage the charging of conspiracy where there is evidence of the complete crime.[315] However, one attraction of conspiracy charges is that evidence is admissible on a conspiracy charge which would not be admissible on a joint trial for the complete crime. The real objection to conspiracy being charged, as it has been commonly used in recent years, has been pointed out by Williams.[316] It is:

to the use of a conspiracy count to give a semblance of unity to a prosecution which, by combining a number of charges and several defendants, results in a complicated and protracted trial. The jury system is unworkable unless the prosecution is confined to a relatively simple issue which can be disposed of in a relatively short time.[317]

The length and complexity of trials for conspiracy raises doubts whether justice can be done.[318]

---

[312] Conspiracy thus appears to be a statutory exception to the rule in *Courtie* [1984] AC 463, that, when Parliament provides that an offence shall be more severely punishable when a particular fact is present, it necessarily creates two offences. See also the interesting decision of the Privy Council in *Karpavicius* [2002] UKPC 59 construing the New Zealand drugs legislation, although the ruling turns largely on the particular statutory words in s 6(2A)(c) of the Misuse of Drugs Act 1975 (NZ) which are not present in the English legislation. See also J Evans, 'Dilemma of Proof and the Extension of Criminal Statutes' [2003] Crim LR 181.

[313] [1994] 2 All ER 924, PC at 928.

[314] *Churchill v Walton* [1967] 2 AC 224; *Broad* [1997] Crim LR 666.

[315] Cockburn CJ, in *Boulton* (1871) 12 Cox CC 87 at 93. *West* [1948] 1 KB 709 at 720, [1948] 1 All ER 718 at 723 and see *Gray* [1995] 2 Cr App R 100, sub nom *Liggins* [1995] Crim LR 45.

[316] CLGP, 684; and see *The Proof of Guilt* (3rd edn, 1963) Ch 9 and 'The Added Conspiracy Count' (1978) 128 NLJ 24.

[317] See also the speech of Lord Hope in *Saik* [2006] UKHL 18.

[318] eg the Jubilee Line Fraud. See S Lloyd Bostock, 'The Jubilee Line Jurors: Does their Experience Strengthen the Argument for Judge-only Trial in Long and Complex Fraud Cases?' [2007] Crim LR 255.

Acquittal of the other alleged conspirators

Where D is alleged to have conspired with one other person, E, the acquittal of E, either before or after the trial of D, was no bar to, or ground for quashing, as the case may be, the conviction of D.[319] This was where the parties were tried separately. Where they were tried together there was some doubt whether it was ever right to convict D and acquit E – or vice versa.[320] These doubts are resolved by s 5(8) and (9) of the Act, which governs both common law and statutory conspiracies:

> 5 (8) The fact that the person or persons who, so far as appears from the indictment on which any person has been convicted of conspiracy, were the only other parties to the agreement on which his conviction was based have been acquitted of conspiracy by reference to that agreement (whether after being tried with the person convicted or separately) shall not be a ground for quashing his conviction unless under all the circumstances of the case his conviction is inconsistent with the acquittal of the other person or persons in question.

> (9) Any rule of law or practice inconsistent with the provisions of subsection (8) above is hereby abolished.

There may be evidence – usually a confession, but not necessarily so[321] – which is admissible against D but not against E, which shows that D conspired with E. In these circumstances it is perfectly logical for the jury to be satisfied, as against D, that he conspired with E, but not satisfied, as against E, that he conspired with D. It is only when the evidence against D and E is of equal weight, or nearly so, that the judge should direct the jury that they must either acquit both or convict both – being careful to add that, if they are unsure about the guilt of one, both must be acquitted.[322] The difficult question for the judge remains in deciding whether there is a sufficient inequality between the weight of the cases against each conspirator. The required degree of difference has been explained as 'marked'[323] or 'substantial'.[324] Ultimately the question would seem to be whether the difference is sufficient to displace a juror's reasonable doubt that they might otherwise have had. There is nothing to prevent the conviction of one conspirator at a retrial where his co-conspirator was acquitted at the original trial.[325]

13.3.4.2 Jurisdiction

The situation where there is an agreement in England to commit an offence abroad is now regulated by s 1A[326] of the Criminal Law Act 1977. The section applies where the pursuit of the agreed course of conduct would involve an act by one or more of the parties, or the happening of some event, in a place outside England and Wales which (a) would be an offence by the law of that place, and (b) would be an offence triable here but for the fact that it was committed abroad. Then, if, in England or Wales, (i) a person became a party to the agreement, or (ii) a party to the agreement did anything in relation to it before its formation, or did or omitted

---

[319] *DPP v Shannon* [1975] AC 717, HL. See recently *Zaman* [2010] EWCA Crim 209 (above, Ch 9). See also CW Coulter, 'The Unnecessary Rule of Consistency in Conspiracy Trials' (1986) 135 U Pa LR 223.

[320] ibid. D1 and D2 can be tried even if D3 has been acquitted earlier: *Austin* [2011] EWCA Crim 345.

[321] See *Testouri* [2004] Crim LR 372.

[322] *Longman and Cribben* (1980) 72 Cr App R 121, [1981] Crim LR 38 and commentary. cf the similar problem which arises with secondary parties, above, p 231. *Roberts* (1983) 78 Cr App R 41, [1985] Crim LR 218.

[323] *Longman*, at 125.

[324] *Roberts*, at 47.

[325] *James* [2002] EWCA Crim 1119; *Austin* [2011] EWCA Crim 345.

[326] Inserted by the Criminal Justice (Terrorism and Conspiracy) Act 1998 and amended by the Coroners and Justice Act 2009, s 72. See also C Campbell, 'Two Steps Backwards: The Criminal Justice (Terrorism and Conspiracy) Act 1998' [1999] Crim LR 941; J Holroyd, 'The Reform of Jurisdiction over International Conspiracy' (2000) 64 J Crim L 323. See further LCCP 183, Part 11; LC 318, Part 7.

anything in pursuance of it, the agreement is indictable as a conspiracy, contrary to s 1(1) of the 1977 Act.[327] In the Crown Court the question is to be treated as one of law to be decided by the judge. This is a significant extension of the scope of the already broad-reaching offence of conspiracy.[328] It is indicative of Parliament's approach to extending the scope of the criminal law beyond the physical limits of the jurisdiction in general.[329]

The 1977 Act makes no express provision for agreements abroad to commit an offence in England. It has been clear since 1973[330] that, at common law, an agreement abroad to commit a crime in England is indictable here if an overt act is done in England in pursuance of the agreement. The Privy Council held in *Somchai Liangsiriprasert v United States Government*[331] that it is unnecessary to prove that any overt act was done in England. The only purpose of requiring an overt act could be to establish the link between the conspiracy and England or to show that the conspiracy was continuing and any other evidence that establishes this is just as good.

Agreements abroad to commit offences abroad deserve a brief mention. D1 and D2, British citizens in France, agree to kill V in France or to go through a ceremony of marriage there, both knowing that D1 is married. The offences contemplated are triable in England so, literally, these are indictable conspiracies under the Act. It may be, however, that the presumption against the extraterritorial application of the criminal law will exclude agreements not made within the jurisdiction and not intended to have any effect therein, but this seems less likely after *Liangsiriprasert*.[332]

The Law Commission recently made proposals on jurisdiction which would if enacted bring the law for conspiracy broadly into line with that for assisting and encouraging under the Serious Crime Act 2007, as discussed below.[333]

13.3.5 Common law conspiracies

All common law conspiracies require proof of an agreement as considered in relation to statutory conspiracies above.

13.3.5.1 Conspiracy to defraud[334]

This offence is one of the most controversial in English criminal law, and there has been sustained pressure for its abolition.[335] It is excessively broad, vague and criminalizes conduct by

---

[327] There is, in effect, a presumption that the act or event is an offence by the foreign law unless the defence gives notice that, in their opinion, for which they must show grounds, it is not, and requires the prosecution to prove it: s 1A(8).

[328] Section 1A is not an offence in its own right: *Patel* [2009] EWCA Crim 67. cf M Hirst, *Jurisdiction and the Ambit of the Criminal Law* (2003).

[329] See, generally, Hirst, *Jurisdiction and the Ambit of the Criminal Law*, 142–148 for critical analysis of the provisions.

[330] *DPP v Doot* [1973] AC 807.

[331] (1990) 92 Cr App R 77, PC (a case of extradition from Hong Kong to the USA, but applying the common law of England), followed in *Sansom* [1991] Crim LR 126 where, however, one of the conspirators had acted in England in pursuance of the conspiracy. *Somchai* was applied in *Re Goatley* [2002] EWHC 1209 (Admin) to a case of cannabis importation. For discussion see LC 318, para 7.53.

[332] cf the corresponding problem in attempts, above p 422.

[333] See LC 318, Part 7.

[334] See Smith, *Property Offences*, Ch 19; C Montgomery and D Ormerod (eds), *Fraud: Criminal Law and Procedure* (2008) Ch D7; Ormerod and Williams, *Smith's Law of Theft*. For an historical account see T Hadden, 'Conspiracy to Defraud' [1966] CLJ 248. See also JC Smith, 'Fraud and the Criminal Law', in P Birks (ed), *Pressing Problems in the Law* (1995) vol 1, 49.

[335] See for discussion LC WP 56 (1974); 104 (1988) and ATH Smith, 'Conspiracy to Defraud' [1988] Crim LR 508; LC 228, *Conspiracy to Defraud* (1994) and JC Smith, 'Conspiracy to Defraud: Some Comments on the Law

two or more that would not be criminal or even tortious when performed by an individual. It offends against the principles of legality, certainty and fair warning, and results in an offence which is commonly defined by reference only to the concept of dishonesty – a concept that is ill-suited to shoulder that responsibility.[336] The Law Commission commented recently that the offence is 'so wide that it offers little guidance on the difference between fraudulent and lawful conduct'.[337] Even the Home Office has acknowledged that the offence was 'arguably unfairly uncertain and wide enough potentially to encompass sharp business practice'.[338] The Commission's conclusion was that the offence should be abolished with the implementation of the Fraud Act, but the government was insistent that conspiracy to defraud was retained – as a safeguard against lacunae being revealed in the new scheme.[339]

Following the enactment of the Fraud Act 2006, a prosecutor should only select a charge of conspiracy to defraud having had regard to the A-G's guidelines which provide that, in selecting charges in fraud cases, the prosecutor should first consider: whether the behaviour could be prosecuted under statute – whether under the Fraud Act 2006 or another Act or as a statutory conspiracy; and whether the available statutory charges adequately reflect the gravity of the offence. Statutory conspiracy to commit a substantive offence should be charged if the alleged agreement satisfies the definition in s 1 of the Criminal Law Act 1977, provided that there is no wider dishonest objective that would be important to the presentation of the prosecution case in reflecting the gravity of the case.[340]

Scope of the offence

It was stated by the House of Lords in *Scott v Metropolitan Police Comr*[341] that:

it is clearly the law that an agreement by two or more by dishonesty to deprive a person of something which is his or to which he is or would be or might be entitled[342] and an agreement by two or more by dishonesty to injure some proprietary right of his, suffices to constitute the offence of conspiracy to defraud.[343]

In *Scott*, D agreed with the employees of cinema owners that in return for payment, they would abstract films without the consent of their employers, or of the owners of the copyright, in order that D might make copies infringing the copyright, and distribute them for profit.

Commission's Report' [1995] Crim LR 209. The Law Commission offered a defence of its approach: S Silber, 'The Law Commission, Conspiracy to Defraud and the Dishonesty Project' [1995] Crim LR 461, and see JC Smith, Letter [1995] Crim LR 519.

[336] See the discussion below in Ch 23. As noted by the Law Commission in LCCP 155, *Legislating the Criminal Code: Fraud and Deception* (1999) in rejecting the idea of an offence based on an element of dishonesty because of anxiety that it would not be compatible with Art 7. See also D Ormerod, 'A Bit of a Con' [1999] Crim LR 789.

[337] LC 276, *Fraud* (2002) para 1.6.

[338] See Home Office, *Fraud Law Reform: Consultation on Proposals for Legislation* (2004) para 6. For comment, see P Binning, 'When Dishonesty is Not Enough' (2004) 154 NLJ 1042 and the references cited in Ch 23.

[339] See for detailed comment Ormerod and Williams, *Smith's Law of Theft*, para 5.65 et seq. The *Review of the Investigation and Criminal Proceedings relating to the Jubilee Line Case* (2006): para 11.88.

[340] Available from www.attorneygeneral.gov.uk/Publications/Documents/conspiracy%20to%20defraud%20 final.pdf.

[341] [1975] AC 819, [1974] 3 All ER 1032.

[342] In *Tarling v Government of the Republic of Singapore* (1978) 70 Cr App R 77, [1978] Crim LR 490 the House of Lords by a majority held that the intention of company directors to make and retain a secret profit for which they would have been accountable to the shareholders was not evidence of an intention to defraud. See, however, JC Smith, 'Theft, Conspiracy and Jurisdiction: Tarling's Case' [1979] Crim LR 220 at 225–226. In *Adams v R* [1995] 1 WLR 52, PC, the court seems to have been of the view that, even if the agreement to make and retain the secret profit is not an offence, the agreement to take positive steps to conceal it is. See commentary [1995] Crim LR 561, 562.

[343] Per Viscount Dilhorne at 1039.

It was held that D was guilty of a conspiracy to defraud. It was held to be immaterial that no one was deceived. The offence is one of defrauding. Although the well-known definition of 'defraud' by Buckley J in *Re London and Globe Finance Corpn Ltd*,[344] includes a reference to deceit ('to defraud is by deceit to induce a course of action'), there can be fraud without deceit. For example, larceny was an offence which had to be committed 'fraudulently', but deceit has never been a necessary ingredient of theft.

There are two versions of the offence of conspiracy to defraud. The most commonly encountered is that involving economic prejudice.[345]

Defrauding by imperilling economic interests

The breadth and flexibility of the offence are its vice and its virtue. The Law Commission in its Report No 276 catalogued those forms of conduct that are capable of being prosecuted only as conspiracy to defraud.[346]

The scope of the conspiracy offence clearly includes cases where the agreement is to do an act that would not be theft. In *Button*,[347] DD were convicted of conspiracy to use their employer's vats and dyes to dye articles which they were not permitted to dye in order to make profits for themselves and so to defraud their employer of the profit. The dyes were no doubt stolen; but the employer did not have a proprietary interest in the profit so that the appropriation of it did not constitute a substantive offence.[348] The great majority of agreements to defraud in this category will be agreements to commit offences under the Theft Act and/or the Fraud Act 2006 but clearly there are cases amounting to fraud within the definition in *Scott* that are not substantive offences. An example is the appropriation of the profit in *Button*. The offence as defined in *Scott* also applies to agreement to deprive someone temporarily of their property. Parliament chose not to create a general offence of temporarily depriving another of his property in the Theft Act;[349] but it remains the case that an agreement so to do is clearly capable of amounting to conspiracy to defraud under *Scott*.[350] Likewise it is a conspiracy to defraud where D1 and D2 agree to shift D1's boundary fence so as to appropriate V's land – an act which is not, by specific decision of Parliament, theft.

It is clear that V is defrauded if he is induced to take an economic risk which he would not have taken but for a deception.[351] It is no answer that D believed that the speculation was a good one and that V had a good chance of making a profit. If V is induced to part with

<hr/>

[344] [1903] 1 Ch 728 at 732, 733.

[345] There is no need for any deprivation.

[346] These included: deception which obtains a benefit which does not count as property, services or any of the other benefits defined in the Theft Acts; deception which causes a loss and obtains a directly corresponding gain, where the two are not the same property (other than a transfer of funds between bank accounts); deception which causes a loss and obtains a gain where the two are neither the same property nor directly correspondent; deception which does not obtain a gain, or cause a loss, but which prejudices another's financial interests; deception for a non-financial purpose; deception to gain a temporary benefit; deceptions which do not cause the obtaining of a benefit; conduct involving a view to gain or an intent to cause loss, but not deception; making a secret gain or causing a loss by abusing a position of trust or fiduciary duty; obtaining a service by giving false information to a machine; 'fixing' an event on which bets have been placed; dishonestly failing to fulfil a contractual obligation; and, dishonestly infringing another's legal right. Most are now caught by the general fraud offence in the Fraud Act 2006, s 1.

[347] (1848) 11 QB 929.

[348] JC Smith, 'Embezzlement and the Disobedient Servant' (1956) 19 MLR 39. But see *A-G for Hong Kong v Reid* [1994] 1 AC 324 and p 815.

[349] The CLRC rejected such an offence: Eighth Report, para 29.

[350] The defendants intended to deprive the owners temporarily of the films but permanently of the profits the owners would otherwise have made; and the defrauding was the loss of the profits: [1974] 3 All ER 1032 at 1038.

[351] *Allsop* (1976) 64 Cr App R 29, [1976] Crim LR 738, CA and commentary; cf *Hamilton* (1845) 1 Cox CC 244; *Carpenter* (1911) 22 Cox CC 618.

something of economic value, he is probably defrauded even if he does receive the promised return.[352]

Agreement to deceive V to act contrary to public duty

The proposition in *Scott* is not an exclusive definition of conspiracy to defraud. A person is also defrauded if he is deceived into acting contrary to his public duty.[353] So it would be a conspiracy to defraud if DD agree by deception to induce a public official to grant an export licence,[354] or to supply information[355] or to induce a professional body to accept an unqualified person as a member,[356] assuming, in each case, that it was the duty of the person so deceived not to do as asked in the actual circumstances of the case. If the public official is persuaded by means other than deception – for example, bribes or threats – to act contrary to his duty, he is obviously not defrauded and the agreement is not a conspiracy to defraud unless it can be said that those affected by the breach of duty have been defrauded – for example, those persons about whom the confidential information is disclosed or, more likely, perhaps, the official's superiors whose duty to keep the information secret has been vicariously violated. Most conspiracies to pervert the course of justice consist in agreements to deceive a public official so that he acts contrary to his duty and are conspiracies to defraud.

Some of their lordships in *Withers*[357] thought that this principle was strictly confined to public officials, and did not extend to the case, for example, of a bank manager deceived into breaking his contractual duty.[358] However, in *Wai Yu-tsang v R*,[359] the Privy Council said that the cases concerned with public duties are not to be regarded as a special category but as examples of the general principle that conspiracy to defraud does not require an intention to cause economic loss. The Board, disapproving Lord Diplock's more restrictive statement in *Scott*,[360] preferred the broad propositions of Lord Denning – 'If anyone may be prejudiced in any way by the fraud, that is enough' – and Lord Radcliffe, who agreed with Lord Denning and used similar language, in *Welham*.[361] This seems to open a very broad vista of potential criminal liability.

'Intention' to defraud

If a person is defrauded when he is 'prejudiced', conspirators clearly have a sufficient *mens rea* if it is their purpose to cause that prejudice by carrying out their agreement. There are *dicta* to the effect that such 'direct' intention in the form of a 'purpose' is required, but in *Wai Yu-tsang* the Privy Council thought this too restrictive and that it is enough that the parties have *agreed to cause* the prejudice. If they have agreed to cause it, that is, to defraud, they intend to defraud, and it is immaterial that defrauding is not their purpose.

---

[352] *Potger* (1970) 55 Cr App R 42.

[353] *Welham v DPP* [1961] AC 103. *Welham* was followed in *Terry* [1984] AC 374, HL (D, who uses an excise licence belonging to another vehicle intending to cause police officers to act on the assumption that it belongs to his vehicle, has an intention to defraud, even though he intends to pay the licence fee).

[354] *Board of Trade v Owen* [1957] AC 602.

[355] *DPP v Withers* [1975] AC 842.

[356] *Bassey* (1931) 22 Cr App R 160, CCA.

[357] [1975] AC 842.

[358] On the broad interpretation of public duty in the offence of misconduct in public office, see *A-G's Reference (No 3 of 2003)* [2004] EWCA Crim 868.

[359] [1991] 4 All ER 664 at 670, PC.

[360] [1975] AC 819 at 840–841. But the court in *Wai* made no reference to *Withers* [1975] AC 842, decided by the same judicial committee at the same time as *Scott*, where Lords Simon and Kilbrandon agreed with Lord Diplock.

[361] [1961] AC 103 at 133 and 124 respectively.

The purpose of fraudsters is almost always to make a profit for themselves and not to cause loss to another. They act out of greed, not spite. Since they know that they can make a gain only by causing loss or prejudice, they intend to cause the loss or prejudice, even though they have no 'wish' to cause it and perhaps regret the 'necessity' of doing so in order to achieve their object.

In the light of these principles *A-G's Reference (No 1 of 1982)* (the 'whisky-label case')[362] is a doubtful decision. The defendants were charged with conspiracy to defraud X Co by causing loss by unlawful labelling, sale and supply of whisky, falsely purporting to be 'X label' products. The agreement was made in England but the whisky was to be sold in Lebanon. The *ratio decidendi* was that the trial judge had rightly held that he had no jurisdiction to try the indictment because the contemplated crime in Lebanon (obtaining by deception from the purchasers of the whisky) would not have been indictable in England (see now below on jurisdiction). One reason for holding that there was no conspiracy to defraud X Co was that this was not the 'true object' of the agreement. Damage to X Co would have been 'a side effect or incidental consequence of the conspiracy and not its object'.[363] This must now be considered in the light of the decision of the House of Lords in *Cooke*.[364] British Rail stewards boarded a train, equipped with their own food which they dishonestly sold to passengers, instead of that provided by their employers, intending to keep the proceeds of sale for themselves.[365] The House had no difficulty in holding that they were guilty of conspiracy to defraud British Rail. It is true that the House was preoccupied with the problem of distinguishing *Ayres*, the 'whisky-label case' was not cited and it does not appear that it was argued that the loss to British Rail was 'a side effect or incidental consequence'. Nevertheless, it is clear that this was a case where the object of the conspirators was to make a profit out of the customers, not to defraud British Rail.

Of course, one must agree with Lord Lane CJ in the 'whisky-label case'[366] that, 'it would be contrary to principle, as well as being impracticable for the courts, to attribute to defendants constructive intentions to defraud third parties based on what the defendants should have foreseen as probable or possible consequences'. Constructive intentions are to be abhorred; but presumably the House in *Cooke* thought that a jury could properly find that the defendants must have known that their conduct would, inevitably, cause loss to British Rail. If so, it was right to hold that they *intended*[367] to defraud British Rail and it should be immaterial that this was not their *purpose*.

The intention must always be proved. Thus, the use abroad of a stolen cheque book and cheque card is capable of being fraud on a bank in England because the effect is to cause the bank in England to meet its legal or commercial obligation to honour the cheque; but, if D is charged with conspiracy to defraud the bank, the jury must be directed that he appreciated that his conduct would have this effect.[368] Subject to the jurisdictional problem, considered below, it is submitted that, on a proper direction, the whisky-label conspirators might properly have been convicted of conspiracy to defraud the X Co. They might have been more

---

[362] [1983] QB 751, [1983] Crim LR 534 and commentary.

[363] [1983] 2 All ER 724. But in *Governor of Pentonville Prison, ex p Osman* (1990) 90 Cr App R 281 at 298 it was held, distinguishing the whisky-label case, that a conspiracy to deprive V of dollars in the United States was only the means to effecting the 'true object' of the conspiracy which was the defrauding of V in Hong Kong. The distinction is not blindingly obvious.

[364] [1986] AC 909, [1987] Crim LR 114.

[365] They were probably guilty in law of going equipped to cheat the passengers and, when they sold food to them, of obtaining the price by deception. See below p 970.

[366] [1983] 2 All ER at 724.

[367] Above, p 107, Ch 5.

[368] *McPherson and Watts* [1985] Crim LR 508.

sophisticated in this respect than the stewards in *Cooke* and better able to appreciate the effect of their actions on third parties.

Prejudice includes putting at risk

If the conspirators know that the effect of carrying out the agreement will be to put V's property at risk, then they intend prejudice to V and, if they are dishonest, they are guilty of conspiracy to defraud him.[369] This is so notwithstanding that it turns out that V's property is unimpaired, or even that he makes a profit out of the transaction. A clear example would be where the conspirators agree to take V's money without his consent and then bet with it on a horse with odds at 20 to 1. They have agreed to defraud him and the conspiracy is not undone even if the horse wins and, as they intended throughout, they pay half the winnings into his bank account. This, it is submitted is the best explanation of *Allsop*.[370] The judgment is difficult because of its reliance on two *dicta* of Lord Diplock which were mutually inconsistent and have both since been disapproved; but the decision on the facts is readily explicable. D was a 'sub-broker' for a hire-purchase finance company, V. His function was to introduce prospective hire-purchasers who wished to acquire cars. In collusion with others, he filled in application forms with false statements about the value of the cars and the payment of deposits so as to cause V to accept applications for hire-purchase finance which, otherwise, they might have rejected. He expected and believed that the transactions he introduced would be duly completed, so that V would achieve their contemplated profit to the advantage of all concerned, including D who got his commission. His defence was that he did not intend V to suffer any pecuniary loss or be prejudiced in any way. The court found that V was defrauded when he was induced to do the very acts which D intended him to do. V paid an excessive price for cars and advanced money to persons who were not as creditworthy as they were alleged to be. This not merely put him at risk of being defrauded, but actually defrauded him: 'Interests which are imperilled are less valuable in terms of money than those same interests when they are secure and protected.'[371] The result intended by D was, in law, the defrauding of V; and V was in law defrauded. It is wholly immaterial whether D would have regarded that result as 'fraud'. If he did not, he was making a mistake of criminal law.

According to this explanation D intended to prejudice V. The facts admitted of no other interpretation. But the judge had directed the jury that they could convict if they were satisfied that D realized that his conduct was *likely to lead* to the detriment or prejudice of V. If this is taken literally, it is sufficient that D is reckless (in the *Cunningham/G* sense) whether prejudice – that is, defrauding – occurs. It is submitted that this would be going too far and take common law conspiracy out of line with statutory conspiracy. In *Wai Yu-tsang*, the Privy Council expressed a reluctance 'to allow this part of the law to become enmeshed in a distinction, sometimes artificially drawn between intention and recklessness'; but they then said, of *Allsop* and the instant case, that it is enough that:

the conspirators have dishonestly agreed to bring about a state of affairs which they realize will *or may* [emphasis in original] deceive the victim into so acting, or failing to act, that he will suffer economic loss or his economic interests will be put at risk.

The use of the words, 'or may', admit recklessness as a sufficient *mens rea* – it is enough that the parties have taken a conscious risk of causing prejudice. This was probably not necessary to the decision since the trial judge had directed the jury that D was guilty if he knew what he had done 'would cause detriment or prejudice to another'.

---

[369] See Ormerod and Williams, *Theft*, para 5.28.
[370] (1976) 64 Cr App R 29.
[371] (1976) 64 Cr App R at 32.

Dishonesty in putting property at risk

The intention to defraud is readily discernible in *Allsop* where there could be no question of V believing he had any right to do what he did. More difficult is the case where company directors take a risk with the company's property, perhaps hoping to make a large profit and so benefit the shareholders. If the risk taken was such that 'no director could have honestly believed... it was in the interest of that company that the risk should be taken',[372] then the company is defrauded. Whether a risk is unjustifiable is a question of judgement and a matter of degree. There is no clear dividing line between right and wrong, such as was crossed in *Allsop* when false statements were made, or in *Wai Yu-tseng* where the dishonouring of cheques was concealed in a bank account. Whether the risk is so grave that no director could believe it justified is equally a matter of judgement and degree. Conspiracy to defraud thus lacks the precision that we should normally look for in any offence, and certainly in one of this seriousness. The courts have made clear that care needs to be taken in drafting indictments to ensure that sufficient detail is provided,[373] *and* in particular making clear a distinction between the agreement alleged and the reasonable information given in respect of it.[374]

Dishonesty is an essential constituent of the *mens rea* but there has been controversy about what 'dishonesty' means in this context. In *Landy,*[375] the court appeared to think that the ultimate test was whether the *defendant* thought his conduct dishonest. In *McIvor,*[376] the court reiterated this view, holding that the test in theft is different; but, shortly afterwards in *Ghosh*[377] it was held that the same test should be applied in conspiracy to defraud as in theft. The standard of honesty is that of ordinary decent people and D is dishonest if he realizes he is acting contrary to that standard. In theft, D is not dishonest if he believes he has a right to do the act in question and this must also apply in conspiracy. If, however, he knows for example, that no 'ordinary decent company director' would take the risk in question, then he knows that the risk is an unjustifiable one and it is dishonest for him to take it.[378] The test proposed in *Sinclair*[379] accords with this. If *no* director could have believed the risk was justified, it follows that the defendant did not; but it would seem right that the jury should be directed that they must find this is so.

Fraud – by whom?

In statutory conspiracy it is expressly provided that the contemplated offence is to be committed 'by one or more of the parties to the agreement'.[380] In *Hollinshead,*[381] the Court of Appeal held that this was a restatement of the common law, so the same principle applied to conspiracy to defraud: the contemplated fraud must be one which is to be perpetrated by one of the parties to the agreement in the course of carrying it out. But complete execution of the agreement to sell the black boxes in that case would not defraud anyone. The parties contemplated that the fraud would be carried out by other persons, not yet ascertained, who

---

[372] *Sinclair* (1968) 52 Cr App R 618.

[373] See for example *Landy,* (1981) 72 Cr App R 237.

[374] *K* [2004] EWCA Crim 2685, [2005] Crim LR 298. It was noted, however, that it is only necessary to specify in detail in the indictment the agreement, and not how the participants intended individually to go about (or had gone about) defrauding V; and see *Giannakopolous* [2005] All ER 54 (Feb). See also *Fussell* [1997] Crim LR 812.

[375] [1981] 1 All ER 1172 at 1181.

[376] [1982] 1 WLR 409.

[377] [1982] QB 1053, See *Cox and Hodges* [1983] Crim LR 167 and commentary (fraudulent trading).

[378] For a remarkable difference of opinion in the House of Lords as to whether there was evidence of dishonesty, see *Tarling v Government of the Republic of Singapore* (1978) 70 Cr App R 77. See, on this case, Smith [1979] Crim LR 220.

[379] Above, n 372.

[380] Criminal Law Act 1977, s 1(1)(a), above, p 425.

[381] [1985] 1 All ER 850 at 857, above, p 438.

would buy the boxes and use them to defraud the electricity suppliers. The court therefore quashed the convictions for conspiracy to defraud – but they were restored by the House of Lords. The House held that the 'purpose' of the defendants was to cause economic loss to the electricity suppliers. This is difficult to understand. Their purpose was to make a profit by selling the devices to the (as they thought) middleman. Presumably they did not care what happened to the boxes after that. If they had been accidentally destroyed in a fire, they would not consider that their enterprise had failed. On the contrary, they might have been pleased at the prospect of selling some more. The House seems to have been much influenced by the fact that the boxes were 'dishonest devices' with only one 'purpose', which was to cause loss. But 'purpose' is here used in the sense of 'function'. An inanimate thing cannot have a 'purpose' (any more than it can be 'dishonest') in the sense in which that word is used in the law of conspiracy. However that may be, *Hollinshead* seems to broaden the law of conspiracy to defraud to include the case where the defendants contemplate that the execution of their agreement will enable some third party to perpetrate a fraud.

Jurisdiction over conspiracy to defraud[382]

An agreement in England or Wales to carry out a fraud abroad is not indictable at common law in England or Wales as a conspiracy to defraud. This is now regulated by s 5(3) of the Criminal Justice Act 1993 which provides that, where the conspiracy would be triable in England but for the fraud, which the parties had not envisaged intending to take place in England and Wales, a person may be guilty of conspiracy to defraud if:[383]

(1) a party to the agreement constituting the conspiracy, or a party's agent, did anything in England and Wales in relation to the agreement before its formation, or

(2) a party to it became a party in England and Wales (by joining it either in person or through an agent), or

(3) a party to it or a party's agent, did or omitted anything in England and Wales in pursuance of it.

ECHR

As has been noted, the offence is heavily dependent on the concept of dishonesty, and that test is one lacking in certainty.[384] Concerns were raised by Liberty and the Joint Parliamentary Committee on Human Rights as to whether the offence was compatible with Art 7 of the ECHR which prohibits criminal laws which lack sufficient certainty. The Law Commission acknowledged the force of the argument in its Report on *Fraud* by stating:

We continue to believe that a general dishonesty offence, by not requiring as an element some identifiable morally dubious conduct to which the test of dishonesty may be applied, would fail to provide any meaningful guidance on the scope of the criminal law and the conduct which may be lawfully pursued. We do not accept the argument that inherent uncertainty is satisfactorily cured by the promise of prosecutorial discretion.[385]

These views were echoed by the Joint Parliamentary Committee on Human Rights which, when scrutinizing the Fraud Bill, concluded:[386]

---

[382] See, generally, Hirst, *Jurisdiction and the Ambit of the Criminal Law*, 175–178.
[383] Hirst argues that s 5(3) should be charged separately from and in addition to conspiracy to defraud, above, p 426.
[384] Below, p 831.
[385] Para 5.28.
[386] Para 2.25.

we remain concerned that the common law offence of conspiracy to defraud is a general dishonesty offence and as such is not compatible with the common law and ECHR requirements of legal certainty for the reasons given above.

A challenge seems most likely if the conspiracy to defraud offence is used in a case where it amounts to an allegation of an agreement to act dishonestly, even though that action would not constitute an agreement to perform a criminal offence.[387]

There is plenty of authority supporting the argument against such a broad common law offence being expanded.[388] Recent examples include confirmation from the House of Lords in *Jones*[389] that criminal law can only be extended by Parliament and that the English common law does 'not permit the creation of new offences nor applying existing offences to activity previously regarded as outside the remit of the criminal law.'[390] Similarly in *Goldstein and Rimmington*,[391] the House of Lords stated that:

Where Parliament has defined the ingredients of an offence, perhaps stipulating what shall and shall not be a defence, and has prescribed a mode of trial and a maximum penalty, it must ordinarily be proper that conduct falling within that definition should be prosecuted for the statutory offence and not for a common law offence which may or may not provide the same defences and for which the potential penalty is unlimited.[392]

In the recent extradition case of *Norris v USA*,[393] the particular form of conduct that had not been previously charged as a conspiracy to defraud involved the dishonest agreement between suppliers, to fix prices or limit production. Such anti-competitive cartels are now proscribed by a series of specific offences introduced by the Enterprise Act 2002.[394] The allegation in *Norris v USA* and the related case of *GG* was that the conspirators routinely sold product to their customers pursuant to their agreement to avoid price competition. In effect, that the conspirators 'defrauded their customers by requiring that they pay higher prices than they might otherwise have paid had there been no conspiracy'. The argument that this charge infringed Art 7 was rejected by the Administrative Court and the Court of Appeal.[395]

---

[387] The challenge to the offence of cheating on this basis failed in *Pattni* [2001] Crim LR 570 (Southwark CC).

[388] See in the case of the conspiracy to defraud offence *Zemmel* (1985) 81 Cr App R 279, CA.

[389] [2006] UKHL 16.

[390] [29].

[391] [2005] UKHL 63.

[392] [30]. See also the ECHR decision in *Hashman and Harrup v UK* (2000) 30 EHRR 241.

[393] [2008] UKHL 16. The issue for the court was whether the English common law offence of conspiracy to defraud is capable of application to price fixing, so as to constitute an extradition offence within s 137 of the Extradition Act 2003. The prosecution chose to allege the conspiracy to defraud on the basis of a mere agreement secretly to fix prices. The defendants submitted that mere entry into a secret cartel was not criminal and was to be distinguished from positive action such as deceptive misrepresentation. There had been no previous prosecution for such conduct *per se*. The House of Lords accepted that the prosecution could well have charged the defendants with conspiracy to defraud based on allegations of lies and positive deception. They had not done so.

[394] Sections 188–202 create offences involving agreements to fix prices, limit production or supply, rig bids, etc where the agreement is a horizontal one between providers. The elements of the cartel offence were examined in *G* [2010] EWCA Crim 1148. S 188 is based on a 'dishonest' agreement between two or more undertakings to make or implement, or to cause to be made or implemented, a prohibited price-fixing arrangement concerning the supply of goods or services in the UK. The court held that the only dishonesty that must be proved is that of the defendant not the person he agreed with. See also *IB* [2009] EWCA Crim 2575. For detailed analysis see C Harding and J Joshua, 'Breaking up the Hardcore' [2002] Crim LR 933; M Furse and S Nash, 'Partners in Crime – the General Cartel Offence in UK Law' (2004) 15 Int Company and Commercial Law Review 138; K MacDonald and R Thompson, 'Dishonest Agreements' [2003] Competition LR 94.

[395] The court was influenced by Sir Jeremy Lever QC and J Pike, 'Cartel Agreements, Criminal Conspiracy and the Statutory "Cartel Offence" ' (2005) 26 ECLR vol 2, at 70–77.

In the House of Lords[396] the House rejected the lower courts' approach, acknowledging the 'consistent message... through cases decided from 1875 through to 1984, was that price-fixing was not of itself capable of constituting a crime.... There was no reported case, indeed, it would appear, no unreported case, no textbook, no article which suggested otherwise'.[397] Their lordships, having regard to *Jones* and *Rimmington*, concluded that it would infringe the principle of legality to allow a first prosecution for conspiracy to defraud on the terms alleged.

Conspiracy to defraud and the Fraud Act 2006

In view of the breadth of offences created under the Fraud Act 2006, very little fraudulent conduct will now be chargeable *only* as conspiracy to defraud. The Home Office suggested that possibly the only instances of conspiracy to defraud not covered by the 2006 Act would be dishonestly failing to fulfil a contractual obligation;[398] deception for a non-financial purpose; 'fixing' an event on which bets have been placed and, dishonestly infringing another's legal right.[399] In respect of those situations, it is questionable whether they ought to be criminal at all: hence the Law Commission's 2002 Report recommendation that conspiracy to defraud should be abolished.[400] Indeed, the Law Commission went so far as to describe the continued existence of the offence as 'indefensible'.[401] The Home Office had also stated:

if we achieve a proper and full definition of fraud there should be no need for a fall back offence of this kind.[402]

On public consultation by the Home Office the majority were opposed to abolition of the offence.[403] The main arguments for retention of the offence of conspiracy to defraud despite the incredible breadth of the Fraud Act offences were that: abolition might leave an unforeseen lacuna in the law;[404] retention would be necessary, even with the availability of the new fraud offences where, for example, a person allows his bank account to be used by a third party as a vehicle in the transfer of funds (typically from overseas) which form part of a conspiracy to defraud; retention was needed to deal with cases like *Hollinshead*;[405] most importantly, there are cases in which the use of the conspiracy to defraud charges, although not necessary, would render a prosecution far easier than if charges were brought under the 2006 Act.[406]

13.3.5.2 Conspiracy to corrupt public morals

In *Shaw v DPP*,[407] the House of Lords (Lord Reid dissenting) held that a conspiracy to corrupt public morals is an offence. D published the Ladies' Directory which advertised the names and addresses of prostitutes with, in some cases, photographs and, in others, particulars of sexual activities which they were willing to perform. He was convicted of *inter alia* conspiring to corrupt public morals and Obscene Publications Act offences. The House of Lords held that there was an offence of conspiring to commit a public mischief and that the corruption of public morals was a public mischief; but he did not reject the view of the Court of Criminal

---

[396] *Norris v USA* [2008] UKHL 16; *GG* [2008] UKHL 17.

[397] [55].

[398] Now possibly an offence under s 3 of the Fraud Act 2006.

[399] Home Office, *Fraud Law Reform* (2004) para 38.

[400] See also LC 228, *Conspiracy to Defraud* (1994).

[401] *Fraud*, Law Com No 276 (2002) para 1.4.

[402] Home Office, *Fraud Law Reform* (2004) para 37.

[403] See Home Office, *Fraud Law Reform Responses to Consultation* (2004).

[404] See *Fraud Law Reform Responses to Consultation* (2004) paras 39–45.

[405] This is misplaced. The conduct would be caught by s 7 of the Fraud Act 2006.

[406] Ormerod and Williams, *Smith's Law of Theft*, para 5.65.

[407] [1962] AC 220, [1961] 2 All ER 446.

Appeal that to corrupt public morals is a substantive offence. Lord Simon in *DPP v Withers*[408] concluded that there were three possible *rationes decidendi*.

(1) There is a substantive offence of corrupting public morals, so an agreement to do so is a conspiracy.

(2) The corruption of public morals is a separate head of conspiracy.

(3) There is an offence of conspiracy to affect a public mischief and the corruption of public morals is a public mischief.

Lord Simon held that it was open to the House to reject *ratio* (3) and, indeed, the decision does so. Since Lord Tucker did not decide that there is a substantive offence of corrupting public morals, it seems clear that the *ratio* must be taken to be (2).

It is therefore uncertain whether an agreement to corrupt public morals is a statutory conspiracy which should be charged under the 1977 Act; but judges of first instance may consider themselves bound by the decision of the Court of Criminal Appeal to hold that it is. *Shaw* was followed in *Knuller*[409] where, Lord Diplock dissenting, the House held that an agreement to publish advertisements to facilitate the commission of homosexual acts between adult males in private was a conspiracy to corrupt public morals, although such conduct was no longer a crime.[410] Lord Reid maintained his view that *Shaw* was wrongly decided but held that it should nevertheless be followed in the interests of certainty in the law. Given the existence of the offence, he thought there was sufficient evidence of its commission on these facts.[411] In *Shaw*, Lord Simonds used language which suggested that the House was asserting the right to expand the scope of the criminal law:[412]

In the sphere of criminal law I entertain no doubt that there remains in the courts of law a residual power to enforce the supreme and fundamental purpose of the law, to conserve not only the safety and order but also the moral welfare of the State, and that it is their duty to guard it against attacks which may be the more insidious because they are novel and unprepared for.

In *Knuller*, however, the House was emphatic that there is no residual power to create new offences. That is a task for Parliament. 'What the courts can and should do (as was truly laid down in *Shaw*'s case) is to recognize the applicability of established offences to new circumstances to which they are relevant.'[413] This is no longer tenable. Moreover, a finding that conduct is liable to corrupt public morals was said to be one not lightly to be reached. It is not enough that it is liable to 'lead morally astray'. Lord Simon of Glaisdale went so far as to say that, 'The words "corrupt public morals" suggest conduct which a jury might find to be destructive of the very fabric of society.'[414]

There are very strong objections of principle to an offence based on such vague notions of morality. It is doubtful whether such an offence would withstand challenge under Art 7 of the ECHR for its uncertainty. If the allegations involve the publication of material it may also be that a defence under Art 10 arises.[415] In view of the range of specific statutory offences dealing with obscenity and indecent images, it is doubtful whether there is

---

[408] [1974] 3 All ER 984 at 1003. Above, p 424.

[409] [1973] AC 435.

[410] Below, Ch 18.

[411] See [1972] 2 All ER at 904.

[412] [1962] AC 220 at 267. For a judicial view to the contrary, see Stephen, III HCL, 359. See S Davies, *Annual Survey of English Law* (1932) 276–277. For criticism of *Shaw*, see D Seaborne Davies (1962) 6 JSPTL (NS) 104; A Goodhart (1961) 77 LQR 560; Williams (1961) 24 MLR 626; and [1961] Crim LR 470.

[413] [1972] 2 All ER at 932, per Lord Simon of Glaisdale. This is impossible to square with *Rimmington*.

[414] cf Lord Devlin's views, above, p 9.

[415] This is discussed below in Ch 31 on 'Obscenity'.

any need to retain the offence of conspiracy to corrupt public morals.[416] Unfortunately, the offence did not form part of the comprehensive review of sexual offences recently conducted.[417]

It is important to recall the House of Lords' confirmation in *Rimmington* that where Parliament has defined the ingredients of an offence, the statutory offence and not the common law offence should be relied on.[418]

13.3.5.3 Conspiracy to outrage public decency

A majority of the House in *Knuller* (Lords Reid and Diplock dissenting) held that there is a common law offence of outraging public decency[419] and, consequently, it is an offence to conspire to outrage public decency. But:

'outrage', like 'corrupt' is a very strong word. 'Outraging public decency' goes considerably beyond offending the susceptibilities of, or even shocking, reasonable people... [T]he offence is concerned with recognized minimum standards of decency, which are likely to vary from time to time... [N]otwithstanding that 'public' in the offence is used in a locative sense, public decency must be viewed as a whole; and... the jury should be invited, where appropriate, to remember that they live in a plural society, with a tradition of tolerance towards minorities, and that this atmosphere of tolerance is itself part of public decency.[420]

This is a strict test. In *Choi*,[421] the defendant had secretly filmed women using a public lavatory in a supermarket. The court considered the meaning of the expression 'outraging public decency' and concluded that it involved activity which 'fills the onlooker with loathing or extreme distaste or causes them extreme annoyance'. Following the recent decisions of the Court of Appeal, including most recently *Hamilton*,[422] recognizing the existence of a substantive offence of outraging public decency, it may well be prudent to charge the offence under s 1 of the 1977 Act. Statutory conspiracies and common law conspiracies to corrupt public morals or to outrage public decency remain mutually exclusive, under s 5(3) of the 1977 Act. The prosecutor cannot therefore hedge his bets.

13.3.6 Onus of proof

Whether common law or statutory, the Crown must prove the conspiracy even where, on a charge of committing the ulterior offence, it would be on the defendant. So on a charge of conspiring to produce a controlled drug (an offence under s 4(2) of the Misuse of Drugs Act 1971) the prosecution must prove that D knew that the thing he was producing was the controlled drug alleged, although on a charge of committing the offence under the Misuse of Drugs Act the onus of proving lack of knowledge or suspicion would, by s 28 of that Act, have been on D.[423]

---

[416] A Hamilton, 'Live Streamed Sex Videos' (2003) 14(2) Computers and the Law 29, considers the possibility of prosecution for live video broadcasts on the internet.

[417] See especially *Setting the Boundaries* (2001) and the discussion in Ch 18, below.

[418] [30].

[419] See below, p 1083; following *Mayling* [1963] 2 QB 717 CCA.

[420] [1972] 2 All ER at 936, per Lord Simon.

[421] [1999] 8 Archbold News 3.

[422] [2007] EWCA Crim 2062, Ch 31 below. The Law Commission has recommended abolition of this common law conspiracy: LC 193, *Simplification of the Criminal Law: Public Nuisance and Outraging Public Decency (2010)*.

[423] *McGowan* [1990] Crim LR 399; *R v A-G, ex p Rockall* [1999] All ER (D) 726 (statutory presumption of corruption under the Prevention of Corruption Act 1916, s 2 not applicable on conspiracy charge) adopting the view in the 8th edition of this book, at 285.

13.3.7 Rationale of conspiracy

Why should the mere agreement to commit an offence be a crime?[424] A commonly accepted reason is that it enables the criminal law to intervene at an early stage to prevent the harm involved in the commission of the ulterior offence.[425] This argument is not completely convincing, however, for it does not explain why agreements differ from other acts manifesting an intention to commit a crime, which are not offences unless sufficiently proximate to amount to attempts. A declaration by one person of his unshakeable resolution to commit a crime and the taking of preparatory steps (not in themselves offences) do not amount to a crime. The law thus attaches importance to the act of agreement, 'over and above its value as an indicator of criminal intent'.[426] It is a step towards the commission of a crime to which the law has long attached a peculiar significance. The combination of minds, bent on the commission of the unlawful act, is taken to dispense with the need for proximity where only one person is involved.

It is argued that the effect of the combination of two individuals is to increase the risk that the crime will be committed and the danger to the proposed victim, or to the public. Yet the risk and the danger are not necessarily greater than those arising from the resolve and the preparatory acts of a determined sole individual. Perhaps the basis, never clearly articulated by our courts, is that there is something inherently wicked in a 'plot' to commit crime.[427]

None of this explains why an agreement to do an act, which is not a crime, may be a conspiracy. The traditional explanation is as follows.

The general principle on which the crime of conspiracy is founded is this, that the confederacy of several persons to effect any injurious object creates such a new and additional power to cause injury as requires criminal restraint; although none would be necessary were the same thing proposed, or even attempted to be done, by any person singly.[428]

This, however, does not explain why the confederacy, however powerful, should be criminal when even the actual achievement of the same injurious object by an individual – or, indeed, by the confederates – is not in itself an offence. The rationale of this aspect of conspiracy is now generally rejected and we are moving to a stage where it will be of historical interest only: '…the offence of conspiracy to do an unlawful, though not criminal, act ought to have no place in a modern system of law'.[429] The only significant exception to this principle is now the law of conspiracy to defraud.

In practical prosecution terms, the opportunity to charge counts of conspiracy, presenting the jury with a clear picture of the combined course of conduct of multiple defendants in one indictment is undeniable. There are in addition evidential advantages of cross admissibility of material against each of the conspirators. Conspiracy is a useful and powerful weapon.

13.3.8 Reform of conspiracy

Conspiracy is one of the most complex offences in English law. It is ill-defined and lacks even a clear rationale. Few would deny that reform is desirable. However, many of the complexities

---

[424] See IH Dennis, 'The Rationale of Criminal Conspiracy' (1977) 93 LQR 39; Williams, CLGP, para 226; F Sayre, 'Criminal Conspiracy' (1922) 35 Harv LR 393; PE Johnson, 'The Unnecessary Crime of Conspiracy' (1973) 61 Calif LR 1137, cf D Fitzpatrick, 'Variations on Conspiracy' (1993) 143 NLJ 1180, suggesting wider use of aiding and abetting conspiracy.

[425] LC WP 5. para 12: 'the most important rationale'. The Law Commission agreed: LC 76, para 1.5.

[426] Dennis, above, n 411.

[427] See Dennis, above, n 424, at 51–52.

[428] Criminal Law Commission, *Seventh Report* (1843) 90.

[429] LC 76, para 1.9.

have developed as a result of a willingness of prosecutors to stretch the offence to breaking point, using it as a convenient 'device' for presenting a continuing course of conduct involving numerous defendants. Arguably, reform should look to deter prosecutors from stretching the boundaries of the offence, not encourage it. The Law Commission's proposals in LC 318 will extend the scope of the offence dramatically. Take D1 and D2 who own a bureau de change. If they intend that people transfer money in their business and foresee a risk that criminal property might be transferred by a third party through their business (this is surely inevitable in any such exchange) and agree nevertheless to continue to transfer any monies that do come into their business, it would appear that they have committed the offence of conspiring to launder money. Their foresight of a risk that some money will be the proceeds of crime, coupled with their willingness to take that risk constitute a sufficient *mens rea*. That stands in stark contrast to the House of Lords' recent interpretation of the offence of conspiracy in *Saik* as requiring proof of intention or knowledge that criminal property will be transferred.

13.4 Encouragement and assistance under the Serious Crime Act 2007[430]

13.4.1 Introduction

At common law it was an offence for D to incite another person, P, to do or cause to be done an act or acts which, if done by P, would involve the commission of the offence or offences by P. It had to be shown that D intended or believed that P, if he acted as D encouraged him would do so with the fault required for the offence or offences. The second element of *mens rea* required proof that D knew (or had deliberately closed his eyes) to any material circumstances which were necessary elements alongside the conduct and consequences (if any) of the offence he was inciting. For example, if D was inciting P to sexually assault V (a child under 13), D must intend that P will sexually touch her (conduct) and know that V will be under 13 (circumstance). D did not need to do any more than incite with that state of mind. D could be liable irrespective of whether P committed the offence.[431]

This was a simple offence that generated very few appeals. Unfortunately it has been swept away with one of the most complex pieces of criminal legislation to have been drafted in recent times.[432]

The Serious Crime Act 2007, Part 2, has been in force since October 2008. It abolished the common law offence of incitement[433] replacing it with three new offences. They are based on the Law Commission's Report No 300[434] although the provisions as finally enacted differ

---

[430] See, for detailed analysis, R Fortson, *Blackstone's Guide to the Serious Crime Act 2007* (2008) Ch 6. I am extremely grateful to Rudi Fortson QC for his valuable comments on a draft of this part of this chapter. I have drawn on our collaborative piece: D Ormerod and R Fortson, 'Serious Crime Act 2007: The Part 2 Offences' [2009] Crim LR 389.

[431] For a discussion of the offence see earlier editions of this work.

[432] For critical comment see Ormerod and Fortson [2009] Crim LR 389; JR Spencer and G Virgo, 'Encouraging and Assisting Crime' (2008) 9 Archbold News 7.

[433] Section 59. The many statutory offences of incitement have been retained and are set out in Sch 3. They include soliciting murder. See Ch 16. Statutory conspiracy under s 1 of the Criminal Law Act 1977, and criminal attempts under s 1 of the Criminal Attempts Act 1981 are unaffected. Similarly, liability as an accessory under s 8 of the Accessories and Abettors Act 1861 is not altered by the provisions. There will be a considerable degree of overlap.

[434] *Inchoate Liability for Assisting and Encouraging Crime*, Cm 6878. See also the HL Research Paper, 07/52, and the Home Office Green Paper, *New Powers Against Organised and Financial Crime* (2006) Cm 6875, at 24 et seq.

considerably from the Commission's recommendations. In summary, the Serious Crime Act 2007, Part 2 creates offences where:

- D does an act that is *capable* of encouraging or assisting another, P, *intending* to encourage or to assist P, to commit an offence (s 44);
- D does an act that is *capable* of encouraging or assisting P, *believing* that the offence by P will be committed and, D *believes* that his act will encourage or assist its commission (s 45);
- D does an act that is *capable* of encouraging or assisting the commission of one or more of a number of offences by P, and he *believes* (i) that one or more of those offences will be committed (without having any belief as to which particular crime); and (ii) that his act will encourage or assist the commission of one or more of them (s 46).

13.4.2 Background to the Act

It is doubtful whether these tortuously complex offences were necessary. The law of incitement was well settled. It seemed to present little difficulty in practice, although the Law Commission and the Government were at pains to point to the ease with which organized criminals could escape liability, despite the extraordinary breadth of the offence of conspiracy above.[435] It is questionable whether there were persons beyond the reach of pre-existing laws against whom general but wider crimes are needed. Sullivan argues that the Law Commission's scheme was warranted given the career criminals and terrorist support networks.[436] But it is arguable that these are adequately tackled by the extremely broad and dedicated offences in the Terrorism Acts and by the Proceeds of Crime Act 2002. Even if the breadth of offences was necessary, the complex drafting style was not.

According to the Law Commission the common law on incitement suffered from the following defects:[437]

(1) There is uncertainty as to whether it must be D's purpose that P should commit the offence that D is inciting; (2) the fault element of the offence has been distorted by decisions of the Court of Appeal. These decisions have focused, wrongly, on the state of mind of P rather than on D's state of mind; (3) there is uncertainty as to whether and, if so, to what extent it is a defence to act in order to prevent the commission of an offence or to prevent or limit the occurrence of harm; (4) there is uncertainty as to the circumstances in which D is liable for inciting P to do an act which, if done by P, would not involve P committing an offence, for example because P is under the age of criminal responsibility or lacks a guilty mind; (5) the rules governing D's liability in cases where D incites P to commit an inchoate offence have resulted in absurd distinctions; (6) D may have a defence if the offence that he or she incites is impossible to commit whereas impossibility is not a defence to other inchoate offences, apart from common law conspiracies. The offence of incitement is therefore in need of clarification.

The principal point here is that there is *one* gap in the law:[438] an offence of facilitation was needed to deal with the apparently rare cases in which D assisted P without also encouraging him and P did not commit the substantive crime which D had assisted. In that case there was no incitement because there is no encouragement and no secondary liability because

---

[435] See the statements in *New Powers Against Organised and Financial Crime* (2006) 25.

[436] [2005] Crim LR 1047.

[437] See in particular Ch 3 of LC 300.

[438] LC 300, para 3.2. As pointed out by Glanville Williams, TBCL; see also JR Spencer, 'Trying to Help Another Person Commit an Offence', in *Criminal Law Essays*, 148. cf the view that there was no gap P Glazebrook, 'Structuring the Criminal Code: Functional Approaches to Complicity and Incomplete Offences and General Defences', in A Simester and ATH Smith, *Harm and Culpability* (1996) 195, 202.

the substantive offence is not committed. The consequence of this was, arguably, to lead the courts to adopt ever wider interpretations of conspiracy.[439] Examples of this cited by the Law Commission included the cases of *Anderson*[440] and *Hollinshead*,[441] discussed above. In these cases the House of Lords extended the scope of conspiracy to include, in *Anderson*, circumstances in which none of the conspirators intend to carry out the agreement. In *Hollinshead*, the House held that D1 and D2 were guilty of conspiracy where they foresaw that X, who was not a conspirator, would be able to commit a fraud.[442] Whether these were powerful bases for a new offence is debatable.[443]

A simple facilitation offence might have been introduced to supplement the existing settled, well-established and well-understood offence of incitement.[444] In Law Commission Report No 300, the Law Commission went far beyond that solution, recommending two broad new offences. The first was relatively uncontroversial at least in terms of its breadth, if not its complexity: encouraging or assisting the commission of a criminal act *intending*[445] that the criminal act should be committed. This has been enacted in s 44 of the Serious Crime Act. The second proposal was for an offence with a wider *mens rea* for the assister or encourager: it would be sufficient if D *believed* that his encouragement or assistance would (not might) encourage or assist P in the commission of the criminal act, believing that P would (not might) commit it. Parliament produced a scheme of broader and more complex offences with wider *mens rea*.

In Part 4 of Report No 300, the Commission addressed the possible pros and cons of offences of assisting and encouraging. In support of such are arguments that these inchoate offences: (i) allow enforcement agencies to combat serious crime at an earlier stage; are based on strong utilitarian principles; (ii) eliminate the element of risk inherent in making D's liability turn on whether P will act or not; (iii) reflect D's culpability for the actions he has taken; contribute to a coherent scheme of offences; and (iv) provide appropriate labels for the criminal conduct. Against the imposition of such inchoate liability are arguments that the offences: (i) are too broad and criminalize D's lawful conduct on the basis of his *mens rea* alone; (ii) are too premature and may saddle D with liability unfairly; (iii) create a disparity between the criminality of the assister who will be liable in every case and the principal who will only be liable if he performs the full offence; and (iv) the offences created are likely to be in vague form with too great a degree of dependence on D's *mens rea*. The Law Commission rebutted the arguments against, being driven by the moral principle that D is deserving of punishment once he has performed his acts of assistance or encouragement irrespective of whether P performs the conduct of the substantive offence.[446]

---

[439] See the comments of Professor Spencer quoted in LC 300, para 3.9.

[440] *Anderson* [1986] AC 27. LC 300, para 3.12.

[441] [1985] AC 975. LC 300, para 3.15.

[442] LC 300, para 3.17. *Hollinshead* no longer poses a problem: such conduct would now give rise to liability under s 7 of the Fraud Act 2006.

[443] *Anderson* was largely ignored by subsequent decisions and did not seem to have distorted the law as much as was feared. See *Yip-Chiu-Cheung* [1995] 1 AC 111; *Edwards* [1991] Crim LR 45; *Siracusa* (1990) 90 Cr App R 340. In the House of Lords' most recent pronouncement on conspiracy, Lord Nicholls expressly stated that the 'conspirators must intend to do the act prohibited by the substantive offence': *Saik* [2006] UKHL 18.

[444] cf the Law Commission's view that it was 'complex, unsatisfactory and arbitrary'. Readers who study the previous section of this chapter on incitement and this chapter on the new law can judge for themselves.

[445] See LC 300, para 5.89.

[446] LC 300, para 4.18. See also the valuable discussion in RD Taylor, 'Procuring, Causation, Innocent Agency and the Law Commission' [2008] Crim LR 32; W Wilson, 'A Rational Scheme of Liability for Participating in Crime' [2008] Crim LR 3.

13.4.3 The scope and forms of liability

Four situations need to be distinguished.[447] First, and most obviously, the offences create inchoate liability. D will be liable as soon as he has performed any act *capable*[448] of assisting or encouraging P irrespective of whether it has any effect on P or whether P goes on to commit the offence. As the Law Commission suggested:

If D sells P a weapon that D intends P will use to murder V, D has done everything that he or she intends to do. Nothing more turns on D's subsequent conduct whereas P has yet to take the step of attempting to commit the offence.[449]

Secondly, the offences apply also where D has done any act capable of assisting and encouraging P and it *has* assisted or encouraged. D will be liable in such circumstances even if P did not commit the anticipated offence. Again, D's liability is inchoate.[450]

Thirdly, the offences are also available against D even if P *has* committed the offence if D has done any acts capable of assisting or encouraging: s 49(1). This overlaps with D's secondary liability under the Accessories and Abettors Act 1861. This was a specific aim of the Law Commission. The result is to add to the breadth and confusion of the law. Under s 44 of the 2007 Act, for example, D will be liable in relation to the criminal act that he *intended* (say murder) rather than the actual offence committed by P (perhaps only wounding). In some cases the Crown would have the choice of charging D with aiding and abetting wounding or assisting and encouraging murder. There is a significant advantage in charging D with the offence under s 44 rather than as an accessory to P's act because it does not matter whether P has deliberately changed the manner of offence, or the identity of the victim.[451] Furthermore, D could be liable under these provisions of the 2007 Act where P is incapable of committing the offence which D has done acts to assist or encourage.[452]

Fourthly, the offences are also available not only against D, but also against P, the person D has assisted or encouraged. This may seem rather surprising, but is a logical application of the terms of the offences. Again, to take an example from the Law Commission's Report No 300, P will be liable if:

P asks D to supply him or her with an article so that P can commit an offence, P is doing an act capable of encouraging D to do an act capable of assisting P to commit an offence. In other words, if D supplies the article to P, not only is D committing the [s 45] offence but, by encouraging D to commit the [s 45] offence, P is committing the [s 44] offence.

The extent to which prosecutors will abandon reliance on other offences and rely on these offences to charge those whom we would currently regard as principals and secondary parties as well as inciters is open to debate. At the time of writing there are no reported cases.

13.4.3.1 Interpreting the 2007 Act

The offences are rendered complex because the sections (and the rest of that Part of the Act) include extended definitions of (i) what suffices as relevant conduct by D; and (ii) the subdivision of the elements of the offence to be committed by P, into conduct, circumstances and

---

[447] The discussion is based on s 44 because it is the simplest of the offences. The distinctions apply to the other sections.

[448] LC 300, para 5.22.

[449] LC 300, para 4.25.

[450] Where D does acts capable of encouraging P, his liability is in one sense wider than liability for conspiracy between D and P because P need not share his intention.

[451] See LC 300, para 5.5. This is markedly different from the position where D is a secondary party, see Ch 8.

[452] LC 300, paras 4.22–4.26.

consequences. Unfortunately, several of the fundamental terms in the offences are left undefined, including core elements of the *actus reus*: 'encouraging' and 'assisting'.[453] The Law Commission Report No 300 will serve as an important interpretative document, but given the degree of difference between what was proposed and what was enacted, considerable caution is warranted. In addition, caution must be exercised in reading the statute itself since the true scope of the offences in ss 44 to 46 cannot be appreciated without reference to the ensuing 20 sections.

Understanding and applying the provisions is rendered yet more difficult by the fact that they represent only half the overall package of offences governing secondary and inchoate liability which the Law Commission has devised.[454] The Law Commission's recommendations in LC 300 are only properly appreciated when read with LC 305 where the Law Commission provides a new range of offences to deal with all aspects of secondary liability. If enacted, there will be eight separate offences to deal with assisting and encouraging.[455] Unless the recommendations in LC 305 are enacted, which seems highly unlikely, the law will be left in a rather imbalanced state. The inchoate offences in the 2007 Act were designed by the Law Commission to be of wide application, in part because the Commission proposed that the offences to replace secondary liability will be much narrower. If those recommendations are not introduced, we are left with the wide offences of the new regime and the wide offences of secondary liability at common law.

13.4.4 Intentionally assisting or encouraging a crime: s 44

By s 44 of the Serious Crime Act 2007:

(1) A person commits an offence if –

    (a) he does an act capable of encouraging or assisting the commission of an offence; and

    (b) he intends to encourage or assist its commission.

(2) But he is not to be taken to have intended to encourage or assist the commission of an offence merely because such encouragement or assistance was a foreseeable consequence of his act.[456]

This is the most straightforward of the offences. A simple example illustrates how the section is intended to operate, D commits the offence by supplying P with a gun, intending that P will use it in the murder of V. D is liable under s 44 (subject to *mens rea*) as soon as he has done the act of supply that is capable of encouraging P. D's liability is not affected by whether P commits the crime, as made clear in s 49. D is liable if P does nothing further because P gets cold feet, or drops dead; or P attempts to commit the crime but fails because V is untraceable, or survives; or even where P does succeed and murders V. In all these cases D is liable for assisting or encouraging murder, and liable to be sentenced to life imprisonment.

The section goes beyond the common law incitement offence. It includes doing an act capable of assisting, even if not encouraging, where the full offence is not committed. The offence is wider than accessorial liability (discussed in Chapter 8) because, under s 44, D's liability is triggered as soon as D does acts capable of assisting; it is not dependent on whether P commits the crime or attempts to.

---

[453] This has been a feature of recent legislation in which the draftsman introduces undue technicality in some aspects of the statute whilst failing to define the essentials. See the Sexual Offences Act 2003 and the Fraud Act 2006 for other recent examples.

[454] See Wilson [2008] Crim LR 3 discussing the coherence that will be brought to bear when they are both enacted.

[455] See also the comments on LC 300 by GR Sullivan, 'Inchoate Liability for Assisting and Encouraging' [2005] Crim LR 1047.

[456] To be understood, this section must be read together with s 47(2), (5), (7), (8), and s 49(1) and (2).

Section 44 is triable in the same way as the 'anticipated offence' (ie the offence which D is intentionally assisting or encouraging P to commit but which P does not in fact need to commit[457] (in our example the murder)). Where the anticipated offence is murder, the sentence on conviction under s 44 is life.[458] Where the anticipated offence is any offence other than murder the maximum sentence is that available for the full anticipated offence if it had been committed.[459] A number of other procedural issues are dealt with below.

13.4.4.1 *Actus reus*

D's conduct must be 'capable' of 'assisting or encouraging' P. The focus is on D's conduct, not P's.[460] D's conduct can include a 'course of conduct'[461] as where D supplies a number of articles to P over time. This follows the Law Commission recommendation that D is liable if he performs 'a number of acts, none of which would be regarded as having the capacity to encourage or assist the doing of a criminal act, if the cumulative effect of D's course of conduct would be regarded as having the capacity to encourage or assist'.[462]

There is no requirement that D's act does in fact encourage or assist P, or anyone. P might ignore D's assistance or encouragement, or find it of no encouragement or assistance at all. It is arguable that there is not even any need for P to be aware of D's acts which were intended to assist or encourage him. The Law Commission suggested that it is immaterial if no one was aware of D's words of encouragement.[463] This extends the scope of liability from that at common law for incitement where it was necessary that the incitement should have at least been communicated.[464]

The scope of the *actus reus* is extended further in three ways by ss 65 and 66. First, s 65 provides that D's act is capable of encouraging or assisting the commission of an offence if D's conduct includes taking steps to reduce the possibility of criminal proceedings being brought in respect of that offence. D's assistance in providing a disguise for P who is about to commit a bank robbery is a simple example. An interesting question arises whether D's acts, which are capable of assisting or encouraging P, can include those relating to P's conduct after the entire *actus reus* of the substantive offence is committed by P. What of D who provides the getaway car which is available to P only *after* the robbery, or D providing false passports for P to flee the country after the robbery? Perhaps the Crown can get round such objections by arguing that the cases are the same: the provision of the disguise, getaway car, false passports, etc, 'encourage' P to commit the anticipated offence.

Secondly, by s 65(2)(b) D is liable if he fails to take reasonable steps to discharge a duty.[465] Whether there had been a failure to take reasonable steps to discharge a duty is a question of fact. To borrow the Law Commission's example, D would incur criminal liability in situations

---

[457] Section 55(1). Note that by 51A as introduced by the Coroners and Justice Act 2009, s 44 does not apply to an offence under s 2(1) of the Suicide Act 1961.

[458] Section 58(1).

[459] Section 58(2). See LC 300, para 5.43 and para 5.65.

[460] Note the trap for the unwary of confusing the use of the term 'act' in this part of the statute. 'Act' is used inconsistently and without clarification. Although from a reading of s 47, it might appear as if D's 'act' that is capable of giving assistance or encouragement might include 'a failure to act; the continuation of an act that has already begun; an attempt to do an act (except an act amounting to the commission of the offence of attempting to commit another offence)'. In fact the 'act' being discussed in that section is P's. cf s 65(2)(b) where 'the act' refers to D. See further Fortson, *Blackstone's Guide to the Serious Crime Act 2007*, Ch 6.

[461] Section 67.

[462] LC 300, para A.101, n 108.

[463] LC 300, para 5.29.

[464] *Banks* (1873) 12 Cox CC 393.

[465] By s 65(3) a person is not to be regarded as doing an act that is capable of encouraging or assisting the commission of an offence merely because he fails to respond to a constable's request for assistance in preventing a breach of the peace. See Ch 9 above. LC 300, para 5.46.

where he is a disgruntled security guard who fails to turn on a burglar alarm with the intention of assisting P to burgle the premises of D's employer.[466] Whether a duty existed is a matter of law, to be decided by the judge. Rudi Fortson makes the important point that s 65(2)(b) is restricted to cases in which D *deliberately* failed to take reasonable steps to discharge a duty 'but it does not apply where D failed to discharge a duty through inadvertence or forgetfulness'.[467] The third extension of the *actus reus* is by s 66. If D arranges for P to do an act capable of encouraging or assisting X and P does that act, D is liable, being deemed also to have done it. This is not necessarily the same as encouraging/assisting D2 to encourage or assist P to commit an offence. The Law Commission provided an illustration:[468]

if D arranges for another person P to do something which has the capacity to encourage or assist another person to commit a criminal act, then D is also to be regarded as having done P's act. Thus, a person such as a gang leader can be held liable for the encouragement or assistance provided by a member of his gang in carrying out his instructions.

Encouraging

The 2007 Act offers no definition of this core term.[469] The Law Commission intended that 'encouraging' would have the same meaning as it had developed under the common law offence of incitement. It would include 'instigating', 'persuading', 'threatening' and 'coercing'.[470] That seems uncontroversial. In LC 300, the Commission proposed that the definition should also extend to conduct which 'emboldens a person who has already decided to commit an offence'. What of the getaway car in the example above? Section 65 provides that an act that is capable of encouraging the commission of an offence includes words or conduct and includes both positive encouragement and hostile threats.[471] There need not be actual encouragement – that is, that which is effective – as is apparent from the fact that the 'act' need only be 'capable of' encouraging or assisting another person to commit an offence.

Some guidance on the likely interpretation of the concept of encouragement might be drawn from the case law on common law incitement. In *Marlow*,[472] for example, D was convicted on the basis of 'encouraging' others by his publication of a book on cannabis cultivation.[473] Encouragement can be by hostile threats or pressure as well as by friendly persuasion.[474] It may be implied as well as express. It was held to be an incitement to advertise an article for sale, representing its potential to be used to do an act which is an offence, is an act capable of encouraging P to commit that offence[475] – even when accompanied by a warning that the act

---

[466] LC 300, para 5.62; LC 305, para 3.34.

[467] *Blackstone's Guide to the Serious Crime Act 2007*, above n 430, para 6.55.

[468] LC 300, para A.95.

[469] See Wilson [2008] Crim LR 3 at 12.

[470] LC 300, para 5.37. See further Wilson [2008] Crim LR 3.

[471] It includes 'by threatening another person [P] or otherwise putting pressure on another person to commit the offence': s 65(1).

[472] [1997] Crim LR 897, [1998] 1 Cr App R (S) 273. (A statutory offence of incitement, contrary to the Misuse of Drugs Act 1971, s 19.)

[473] Note the danger in using synonyms – see *Smith* [2004] EWCA Crim 2187, referring to the 10th edition of this book and suggesting that use of the word 'stimulation' did not render the conviction for inciting rape unsafe where D and E had met to examine a pair of girl's knickers and to urge each other on to commit paedophile offences.

[474] *Race Relations Board v Applin* [1973] QB 815 at 827, CA, Civil Div, per Lord Denning MR, followed in *Invicta Plastics Ltd v Clare* [1976] RTR 251, [1976] Crim LR 131.

[475] *Invicta Plastics*, above. (Indication that 'Radatex' may be used to detect police radar traps was incitement to an offence under s 1(1) of the Wireless Telegraphy Act 1949. Note that the licensing requirement was removed by SI 1989 No 123, and that no offence of 'obtaining information' is committed by the user of the apparatus: *R v Knightsbridge Crown Court, ex p Foot* [1999] RTR 21.) cf the reports in The Times, 6 Aug 1998 that a student was

is an offence. But the courts held that the mere intention to manufacture and sell, wholesale, a device which has no function other than one involving the commission of an offence was not an intention to incite the commission of that offence.[476] Offering such devices for sale seems to be an encouragement. Under s 44 it seems more likely that the offence is committed (subject to *mens rea*).

The Court of Appeal adopted an expansive view of the concept at common law in holding that there was encouragement where P, invites D, to ask him, P, to commit an offence. Thus, in *Goldman*,[477] it was held that D was liable where P published an advertisement inviting readers to buy indecent photographs of children. D replied to the advertisement offering to buy the photographs of children under 16. D was guilty of attempting[478] to incite E to distribute indecent photographs of children under 16,[479] contrary to s 1 of the Protection of Children Act 1978.[480] Under s 44, D would, it seems, also be liable for encouraging.

Following *O'Shea*,[481] it also seems likely that encouragement will be interpreted to include conduct such as subscribing to a website with indecent images of children. In doing so D may be held to have encouraged P, the business offering for supply on the site, to continue doing so even though his communication had been with a wholly automated computer system. At common law there had to be contact with a person. Under s 44 it would seem that D is liable as soon as he sends his subscription details.[482]

Assisting

Again, unfortunately, there is no definition of this fundamental term. As noted, s 65 provides an extended definition to include D taking steps to reduce the prospect of criminal proceedings being brought[483] or by failing to take reasonable steps to discharge a duty.[484] Read literally, D should be liable if his or her act is capable of assisting (or encouraging) another person to *any* extent.[485] There is no requirement that D's conduct was, or could have been, a substantial contribution or assistance to P.[486]

Assisting or encouraging multiple offences

If D's act is capable of encouraging or assisting the commission of a number of offences, then by s 49(2), s 44 will apply separately in relation to each offence that he intends to encourage or assist to be committed. Presumably, therefore, each instance must be treated as a separate count and not rolled up into one count. If D provides P with a gun which he intends P to use

---

convicted of 'inciting speeding offences' by the sale of a 'speed trap jammer'. In *Parr-Moore* [2003] 1 Cr App R (S) 425, the court described the appellants' publication of disclaimer on such a device serving only to illustrate their realization that the trade was illegal, at [3].

[476] *James and Ashford* (1985) 82 Cr App R 226 at 232, distinguishing *Invicta Plastics*, above. See also *Maxwell-King* (2001) The Times, 2 Jan: incitement to commit offence contrary to the Computer Misuse Act 1990, s 3, by supply of device to allow unauthorized access to satellite TV channels.

[477] [2001] Crim LR 894, CA.

[478] There is no explanation as to why the acts were not charged as incitement *per se*. They should have been. cf *Jones* [2007] EWCA Crim 1118; see also [2007] Crim LR 979 and commentary.

[479] See now the Sexual Offences Act 2003, s 45.

[480] If P in this scenario is a State official, care must be taken to avoid a plea of 'entrapment', which, if successful, will lead to the proceedings being stayed as an abuse of process.

[481] [2004] Crim LR 948.

[482] The court in *O* did not discuss whether a corporation might be incited.

[483] Section 65(2)(a).

[484] Section 65(2)(b).

[485] LC 300, para 5.5.

[486] LC 300, para 5.51. cf the discussion by KJM Smith [1994] Crim LR 239, 246.

in threatening a number of debtors, D will be liable for each offence of robbery, blackmail, etc, which P commits provided that it was D's purpose to assist those offences.

13.4.4.2 *Mens rea*

There are four elements of *mens rea* to be proved under s 44.

Intention to do acts capable of assisting or encouraging

There must be an intention to do the *act* which is capable of encouraging or assisting. In the example above, D must intend to do the act of supplying the gun which he intends P to use in the murder. This excludes liability where D has only been reckless or negligent about performing conduct which might assist P, as where D leaves his gun cupboard open and P helps himself.

Intention to assist or encourage

D must intend to encourage or assist.[487] Section 44(2) makes clear that this is not satisfied by proof that the encouragement was a foreseeable consequence of D's intentional acts. This surely means (and should have said) D must have as his purpose to encourage or assist.[488] This element of the *mens rea* is in contrast with that in secondary liability where D's intention is satisfied by oblique intention.[489] It is unclear precisely why the *mens rea* requirement is stricter, but presumably this is because of the general concern discussed above that the *mens rea* requirements of inchoate crimes ought to be strictly construed to avoid over-criminalizing.[490]

D's *mens rea* as to P's mens rea

Where the anticipated crime is one of *mens rea*, D must believe or be reckless as to whether P *will* (not might) perform the conduct element for the anticipated offence and that P will, at that time, act with the prescribed *mens rea*. Section 47(5)(a) provides that it must be proved that:

(i)   D believed that, were the act[491] to be done, it would be done with that fault;

(ii)   D was reckless as to whether or not it would be done with that fault; or

(iii)   D's state of mind was such that, were he to do it, it would be done with that fault.

As an example of how this will operate, consider D who encourages P to touch V sexually. D is liable under s 44 for encouraging the offence if he does acts capable of encouraging P to do so and (i) intends purposively to encourage *and* (ii) intends or is (subjectively) reckless as to whether P would sexually touch V with intent (which is the *mens rea* required under s 3 of the Sexual Offences Act 2003).[492] Section 47(5)(a)(iii) deals with the cases where D would have *mens rea* if he committed the anticipated crime himself, even though he does not believe and is not reckless as to whether P would have such *mens rea*. For example, D encourages P to rape V. P has sex with V but lacks *mens rea* for rape. D is guilty of encouraging rape if D himself had the *mens rea* for rape even though he did not commit it and nor did P. Where this limb is

---

[487] LC 300, para 5.89.

[488] See Sullivan [2005] Crim LR 1047.

[489] See above, p 107. See LC 305, paras 2.63–269.

[490] The argument is a weak one in this context since the offence is close to one of assisting and encouraging as a secondary party.

[491] The act in question here is not D's, but P's. The Act uses the term 'act' inconsistently without clarifying whether the reference is to D or P. See Fortson, *Blackstone's Guide to the Serious Crime Act 2007*, para 6.47.

[492] Care will be needed here to distinguish between intending to encourage or assist – and the states of mind set out in s 47(5).

relied on, D is to be assumed to be able to do the act in question, ie there is no defence of impossibility for him (s 47(6)). So, in this example, D can be guilty for encouraging rape even if D is a woman.

D's *mens rea* as to consequences and circumstances of P's offence

D must also have *mens rea* as to the consequences and circumstances, if any, of the anticipated offence. By s 47(5)(b) if the offence is one requiring proof of particular circumstances or consequences (or both), it must be proved that:

(i) D believed [or (purposively[493]) intended[494]] that, were the act to be done, it would be done in those circumstances or with those consequences; or

(ii) D was reckless as to whether or not it would be done in those circumstances or with those consequences.

Thus, in the previous example of the sexual touching of a child, D must intend, or believe or be reckless as to whether the child whom he has encouraged P to touch sexually would be under 13 when the act (by P) was done.

Similarly this will apply where the anticipated crime is one of constructive liability. To take an example provided by the Home Office, D gives P a baseball bat and intends P to use it to inflict minor bodily harm on V. P, however, uses the bat to attack V and intentionally kills V. It would not be fair to hold D liable for encouraging and assisting murder, unless he also believes, or is reckless as to whether, V will be killed.[495]

Rudi Fortson demonstrates how technical this provision might be in practice, discussing the example of D who hopes that P will cause grievous bodily harm to V and supplies P with a baseball bat to do so, being unclear what P's exact intention might be. Assuming that P does not harm V, D cannot be liable for assisting or encouraging murder because although D would have acted with the fault for murder if he himself had committed the conduct element of that offence, s 47(5)(b) is not satisfied 'because *D does not believe that V will be killed* (and it was not D's purpose that V should be killed)'.[496]

13.4.4.3 Defences and exemptions to s 44

The standard defences that are discussed in Chapters 11 and 12 above will apply. If when he hands P a weapon D is an infant, or insane or acting in self-defence, he will be entitled to an acquittal.[497] Four other issues relating to specific defences or exemptions need also to be considered. Two preliminary ones are: first, it is no defence that D is unaware that the conduct by P that D is intentionally encouraging or assisting would be a criminal offence.[498] Secondly, as

---

[493] Section 47(7)(b) provides that D is not to be taken to have intended that an act would be done in particular circumstances or with particular consequences merely because its being done in those circumstances or with those consequences was a foreseeable consequence of his act of encouragement or assistance. Once again, it seems that this should have said purpose.

[494] In this offence, by s 47(7)(a), the word belief is to be read as if it were a reference to intended or believed.

[495] Explanatory Notes, para 135.

[496] Fortson, *Blackstone's Guide to the Serious Crime Act 2007*, para 6.133. D is, however, liable for intentionally encouraging or assisting the offence of causing grievous bodily harm with intent (Offences Against the Person Act 1861, s 18).

[497] But, what if D gives P a bat anticipating that P would use it to unlawfully assault V. In the event, P uses the bat but, ironically, P acts in self-defence against V who got in his attack first and used excessive force! D has no defence since his liability is not dependent on P's.

[498] This is spelled out in s 47(2) 'If it is alleged under section 44(1)(b) that a person (D) intended to encourage or assist the commission of an offence, it is sufficient to prove that he intended to encourage or assist the doing of an act which would amount to the commission of that offence.'

noted, it is no defence for D to claim that no offence is actually committed by P: s 49(1). Two other more significant defences need to be discussed in detail.

Reasonable conduct

It is a defence for D to prove on the balance of probabilities that he acted reasonably. Section 50 provides:

(1) A person is not guilty of an offence under this Part if he proves –

    (a) that he knew[499] certain circumstances existed; and

    (b) that it was reasonable for him to act as he did in those circumstances.

(2) A person is not guilty of an offence under this Part if he proves –

    (a) that he believed certain circumstances to exist;

    (b) that his belief was reasonable; and

    (c) that it was reasonable for him to act as he did in the circumstances as he believed them to be.

(3) Factors to be considered in determining whether it was reasonable for a person to act as he did include –

    (a) the seriousness of the anticipated offence (or, in the case of an offence under section 46, the offences specified in the indictment);

    (b) any purpose for which he claims to have been acting;

    (c) any authority by which he claims to have been acting.

The defence is broader than that proposed in LC 300, where no such defence was recommended for intentional assisting or encouraging under s 44. Note that it is not enough that D thinks that his conduct is reasonable; it must be found to be reasonable by the jury. It remains to be seen whether this invitation for every possible line of defence to be taken, whether good bad or indifferent, is exploited. Some individuals may think they have little to lose. What, for example, of the money launderer who claims that it was reasonable for him to run his business, knowing it would assist P, and in the knowledge that inevitably some of the money passing across his desk would be criminal. No doubt challenges will be mounted to the ECHR compatibility of the imposition of the burden on D. Perhaps that burden will itself serve to prevent spurious claims being made.[500]

Little guidance as to the precise scope and operation of the defence can be gleaned from the Law Commission Report because the Commission did not recommend such a defence in relation to s 44. In fact, if the Commission is right that it is unreasonable to perform acts of assistance with direct intent that the offence be committed, the defence will rarely if ever succeed under s 44.[501]

Three specific examples of the defence in operation were offered:[502]

D, a motorist, changes motorway lanes to allow a following motorist (P) to overtake, even though D knows that P is speeding; D, a reclusive householder, bars his front door to a man trying to get into his house to escape from a prospective assailant (P); D, a member of a DIY shop's check-out staff, believes the man (P) purchasing spray paint will use it to cause criminal damage.

---

[499] Note that it is not enough that D believed they existed.

[500] cf Fortson, *Blackstone's Guide to the Serious Crime Act 2007*, para 6.133.

[501] See the discussion by Sullivan [2005] Crim LR 1047 as to whether the defence is truly one of justification which its name suggests or an excuse.

[502] LC 300, para A.63.

Nor can much guidance be gained from scrutiny of the parliamentary debates. Baroness Scotland of Asthal explained that it would be available to a civil servant whistleblower, but that the success of the defence turns on whether the jury accepts that argument.[503] It was recognized in Parliament, and by the Home Office and Law Commission, that 'unmeritorious defendants' will seek to rely on the defence. The breadth of the defence is also indicated, implicitly, by the Government's decision that a separate defence of 'good purpose' is not necessary. The Law Commission had recommended such a defence for D whose acts capable of assistance or encouragement were reasonable and performed with the purpose of preventing or limiting harm.[504] It seems likely that the defence was felt to be necessary for undercover police officers and security service agents who may need to encourage criminal offences when undercover.

If the defence is appropriate and does amount to justification, perhaps this should be a defence generally available in all crimes.

Defences for victim assisters

The *Tyrrell* principle is put in statutory form.[505] D will have a defence if he is a 'victim' of the offence that D intends to encourage P to commit – for example where a 13-year-old, D, encourages her boyfriend, P, to have sex with her. Section 51 provides that a person does not commit an offence if:

(1) ... (a) he falls within the protected category; and (b) he is the person in respect of whom the protective offence was committed or would have been if it had been committed.

(2) 'Protective offence' means an offence that exists (wholly or in part) for the protection of a particular category of persons ('the protected category').

This works well enough where, for example, D (14) encourages P (35), to have sex with her. But what of D aged 12 encouraging P aged 12? What of adult D encouraging adult P to engage in sadomasochism? Again, far from the law being clear and certain, the lack of definition will lead to legal argument at trial and inevitably appeals will arise.

13.4.4.4 Relationship with other forms of culpability

Relationship with liability as a principal

In some circumstances, D's liability under s 44 will be greater than that of the principal offender who carried out an offence, as for example, where D encourages P to murder and P merely wounds V. The Act also provides for an extended form of principal liability for D in cases where D has assisted or encouraged, and where the anticipated offence has been committed in full. In such a case, if it is unclear whether D merely assisted or encouraged or himself committed the full offence, by s 56 he may be convicted of the s 44 offence. As with accessorial liability, D may be convicted of an offence if the prosecution cannot prove whether he was a perpetrator, or an accessory, but it can be proved that he must have been one or the other.[506] Once again the breadth of the scheme is obvious.

Relationship with secondary liability

If P commits the anticipated offence D may also be liable as an accessory in the usual way. The elements of D's conduct as an accessory are considered in Chapter 8 above. If D has performed acts *capable* of assisting or encouraging P, that will not necessarily mean that he will have

---

[503] *Hansard*, HL, 25 Apr 2007, col 744.
[504] See LC 300, para A.57.
[505] cf *Tyrrell* [1894] 1 QB 710.
[506] cf s 56(2). The purpose of s 56(2) is obscure.

done enough to render him liable as an accessory. P might never have heard D's words of encouragement, so D will not have aided in fact.[507] As for *mens rea*, if D has the *mens rea* for s 44, he will be likely to have the *mens rea* necessary to be an accessory. Again, this is not always going to be the case: where P has deliberately changed the victim or the manner of the commission of the offence D will be liable under s 44 but not as an accessory.

Relationship with conspiracy

D may be liable under s 44 in a wider range of circumstances than for conspiracy. Crucially, in a conspiracy, D1 must share a common purpose to commit the offence. Under s 44, D is liable irrespective of whether P has any intention to commit the anticipated offence.[508]

13.4.4.5 What must D's conduct have been capable of assisting or encouraging?

The Act describes D's conduct in terms of acts capable of encouraging or assisting the commission of '*an offence*'. Read literally, this is certainly wide enough to embrace substantive crimes as well as attempts and conspiracies and cases in which D does an act that is capable of encouraging/assisting. There is a significant difference from the Law Commission proposal which focused on whether D's acts were capable of assisting or encouraging P's 'criminal act', by which the Commission meant the conduct element of P's offence.[509] The Law Commission accepted that D ought not to be liable because he intends or believes that P should or will commit 'an "act" that is criminal. The "act" that is criminal in theft is the appropriation of property. It would be absurd if D could be criminally liable for doing nothing more than encouraging P to do that act.'[510] The difference is significant because in some cases, D's act of assistance or encouragement will be with intent towards a result which goes beyond the conduct element of P's offence.

13.4.4.6 Double inchoate liability
Attempting or conspiring to commit: ss 44–46

Since D's acts need only be capable of assisting or encouraging, there would seem to be little practical scope for liability for D to be guilty of an attempt to commit a ss 44–46 offence. The possibility arises where, for example, D is about to post the letter to P containing details of how to break into V's safe. In addition, D may be liable for an attempt to commit a ss 44–46 offence where he mistakenly believes that the acts he will perform are capable of assisting or encouraging P, but they are not, as a matter of fact, capable of doing so. The Act is ambiguous whether D can be liable for an attempt in either of these circumstances. As Fortson points out, it is not possible to impose liability on D for an attempt to assist or encourage by reference to s 47(8)(c) which deals with proving offences under s 44,[511] s 47(8)(c) 'must not be read as meaning that it is sufficient to found liability for an offence under ss 44–46 if D attempts to encourage or assist D2 to commit an offence'.[512] However, the fact that the *attempt* by D is not provided for in s 47(8) does not necessarily preclude the existence of that form of liability: D can attempt to commit a ss 44–46 offence.

There seems to be nothing to prevent liability for conspiring to commit offences under ss 44–46: D1 agreeing with D2 that D1 will perform acts capable of assisting or encouraging P to commit an offence against V. Perhaps D1 and D2, serious drug villains, agree that D1 should supply a local hoodlum, P, with a weapon so that he will kill V, a competitor in the local

[507] See Ch 8, p 186 above.
[508] See the discussion of *Anderson* above, p 439.
[509] See LC 300 Draft Bill, cl 17(2).
[510] LC 300, para 5.100. For telling criticism see Fortson, *Blackstone's Guide to the Serious Crime Act 2007*, 634.
[511] Section 47 focuses on P's acts, and includes expressly P attempting to do an act.
[512] Fortson, *Blackstone's Guide to the Serious Crime Act 2007*, para 6.87.

drug market.[513] D can conspire to commit an offence under ss 44–46. Again, this is stretching liability so far that one begins to ask where it will all end.

Assisting or encouraging attempts or conspiracies[514]

The Law Commission[515] proposed that D should be liable for the inchoate offence of doing an act which is capable of encouraging or assisting P to *attempt* to commit an offence, but *only if* it was his *direct intention* that P should do so. Under s 44,[516] D can be convicted of an offence if he performs acts capable of assisting or encouraging P to *attempt* to commit an offence.[517] The Law Commission noted that at common law, a charge of incitement to commit attempt is uncommon because D will nearly always be encouraging P to commit the full offence.[518]

As for assisting or encouraging conspiracy, under the Criminal Law Act 1977, s 5(7) it was no offence to incite a conspiracy,[519] but the Law Commission has been recommending repeal of that provision for 20 years.[520] In LC 300, the Commission recommended that D should be liable for acts capable of encouraging or assisting P to *conspire* to commit an offence, but only if it was D's *direct intention* that P should do so. D can be liable under s 44[521] where he does acts capable of assisting or encouraging P1 and P2 to *conspire* to commit an offence. Section 5(7) of the Criminal Law Act is repealed.[522]

Assisting or encouraging the act of assisting or encouraging

D can, it seems, be liable for performing acts capable of encouraging or assisting P to encourage or assist P2. If D supplies a weapon to P knowing that the weapon will be passed to P2 to perpetrate a murder, D is liable under s 44. As the Law Commission explained:

If it is D's intention that P should encourage or assist X, his or her conduct should not be considered too remote from the principal offence merely because, were P to encourage or assist X, P would not intend X to commit the principal offence.[523]

13.4.5 Assisting or encouraging believing offence will be committed: s 45

By s 45 of the Act a person commits an offence if:

(a) he does an act capable of encouraging or assisting the commission of an offence; and

(b) he believes –

    (i)   that the offence will be committed; and

    (ii) that his act will encourage or assist its commission.

---

[513] D1 and D2 might also separately (or jointly) be charged with a s 44 offence.

[514] cf the original proposals in LCCP 131: *Assisting and Encouraging Crime* (1993) para 4.184 and see for discussion Fortson, *Blackstone's Guide to the Serious Crime Act 2007*, para 6.78.

[515] LC 300, para 7.23.

[516] But not s 45 or 46 since Sch 3 to the Act removes attempt from the scope of their application.

[517] But not an act of assisting or encouraging an attempt to attempt: s 47(8)(c).

[518] LC.300, para 7.22.

[519] cf *Sirat* (1985) 83 Cr App R 41.

[520] See the *Criminal Law: A Criminal Code for England and Wales, Vol 2: Commentary on Draft Criminal Code Bill* (1989) LC 177, para 13.15; and see LC 300, para 7.19.

[521] But not under s 45 or 46 as Sch 3 removes statutory conspiracy from the scope of their application. See below as to common law conspiracies.

[522] Para 54 of Part 2 of Sch 6 to the SCA 2007.

[523] LC 300, para 7.15.

A simple example of this section in operation is where D supplies a gun to P, *believing* that P will use it to commit a murder. Under the previous law, D would not be liable for assisting or encouraging unless P committed the murder. D would not have been liable for conspiring with P unless there was a common agreement. Arguably, D could not have been charged with incitement unless there was encouragement rather than pure assistance. Under s 45, D can now be convicted of this new inchoate offence of assisting or encouraging the commission of a crime, even if P does not commit the crime. The s 45 offence is triable in the same way as the 'anticipated offence' (that is, the offence that P would commit if he did as D believed).[524] Where the anticipated offence is murder, the sentence on conviction under s 45 is life: s 58(1). Where the anticipated offence is any offence other than murder the maximum sentence is that available for the full anticipated offence if it had been committed: s 58(2).

13.4.5.1 *Actus reus*

D's conduct needs only to be *capable* of assisting or encouraging. This will be satisfied by, for example, the provision of weapons, tools, advice, etc. There is no requirement that the conduct does in fact encourage or assist P or anyone. As under s 44, D fulfils the *actus reus* by a 'course of conduct'.[525] Similarly, conduct capable of assisting or encouraging includes threats or putting pressure on another person.[526] The extended definitions from s 65[527] (taking steps to reduce the possibility of criminal proceedings being brought, and failing to fulfil a duty) apply to s 45. Failing to assist a police officer preventing a breach of the peace does not amount to encouraging or assisting in the commission of an offence under s 45.[528] As with s 44, if D arranges for P to do an act capable of encouraging or assisting X, and P does that act, D is treated as also having done it: s 66.

13.4.5.2 *Mens rea*

This differs significantly from that under s 44. There are three elements of the *mens rea*. They turn on the requirement that D has a 'belief'. Belief is a state of awareness short of knowledge, but greater than mere suspicion.[529] Unlike s 44, D need not *intend* that the criminal act by P should be done; D must *believe* that the offence *will* be done and that his or her own act *will* encourage or assist the doing of the criminal act.

Belief that acts will assist or encourage

D must be proved to have *believed* that his act (for example, supplying the gun to P) *will* (not might) encourage or assist the P in his performance of the conduct element of the offence (eg murder).[530] It is sufficient to prove that D believed that the act of supply would encourage or assist the doing of P's act in using the gun to kill V.[531]

Belief that offence will be committed

It is sufficient that D believes that the anticipated offence *will* be committed.[532] Although in secondary liability the courts purport to apply a test of knowledge of what P might do, in

---

[524] Section 55(1).
[525] Section 67.
[526] Section 65(1).
[527] (a) taking steps to reduce the possibility of criminal proceedings being brought in respect of that offence; (b) failing to take reasonable steps to discharge a duty.
[528] Section 65(3).
[529] See Ch 27 below on handling.
[530] Section 45(b)(ii).
[531] Section 47(3)(b).
[532] Section 49(7).

practice they apply a much lower *mens rea* requirement satisfied by contemplation of the risk of a real possibility that P will commit it.[533]

Under s 45, D must believe that an act will be done which 'would amount to the commission' of the anticipated offence.[534] In the example with the supply of the gun, D must believe that P will use the gun to cause death to be liable for assisting in the commission of a murder.

D's *mens rea* as to P's *mens rea*

Where the anticipated crime is one of *mens rea*, D must believe or be reckless as to whether P would perform the conduct element of the offence with the prescribed *mens rea* for that offence with which P would be charged.[535] As with s 44 above, s 47(5)(a)(iii) deals with the cases where D would have *mens rea* if he committed the offence, even though he does not believe and is not reckless as to whether P would have it. For example, if D encourages P to touch V sexually, D is liable for encouraging the offence if he does acts capable of encouraging P and believes that they will encourage/assist and believes that P will sexually touch V with intent (which is the *mens rea* required under s 3 of the Sexual Offences Act 2003).

D's *mens rea* as to circumstances and consequences

D must also have *mens rea* as to the consequences and circumstances of the anticipated offence.[536] For example, in the previous illustration D must believe or be reckless as to whether the child whom he has encouraged P to touch sexually would be under 13 if the act (by P) was done. As a second example, in a case of encouraging P to use violence on V, D would only be liable for murder if D believed or was reckless as to that consequence, ie that level of fatal violence.

13.4.5.3 Defences and exemptions to s 45

As under s 44, there is no need to prove that the anticipated offence did in fact occur. It is sufficient to prove that D believed that an offence would be committed and that his act would encourage or assist its commission, and that he *believed* that an act would be done which would amount to the commission of that offence; and that his act would encourage or assist the doing of that act: s 47(3). There is no requirement that any offence is actually committed by P: s 49(1). It is a defence for D to prove that he acted reasonably under s 50. D cannot be liable if he is a 'victim': s 51. These defences were considered above when discussing s 44.

13.4.5.4 To which offences does s 45 apply?

Unlike s 44, there are several offences specifically listed by Parliament as not being capable of being assisted or encouraged under s 45. None of the listed statutory incitement offences in Sch 3 can be committed under s 45. In addition, if D does an act capable of encouraging/assisting P to encourage or assist X, that is not an offence under s 45. D *cannot* be convicted under s 45 of encouraging or assisting a conspiracy to commit an offence, on mere belief that the offence (conspiracy) will be committed.[537] (He can be if he intends it: s 44.) Nor can D be liable under s 45 doing an act that is capable of encouraging or assisting P to attempt to commit an offence, on a mere belief that the attempt will be committed.[538] (If he intends the attempt to be committed he is liable under s 44.) Nor can D be liable under s 45 for encouraging or assisting P to do an act which is capable of assisting X to commit a crime.[539] Under s 45 there is no double inchoate liability.

---

[533] *Bryce* [2004] EWCA Crim 1231; cf *Webster* [2006] EWCA Crim 415.

[534] Section 47(3)(a).

[535] Section 47(5).

[536] Section 47(5)(b).

[537] Sch 3, Part 2, para 32.

[538] Sch 3, Part 2, para 33.

[539] Section 49(4). The Law Commission regarded this as an over-extension of criminal liability: LC 300, paras 7.12–7.13.

13.4.6 Encouraging or assisting one or more offences D believes will be committed s 46

By s 46 D is guilty of this offence if:

(a) he does an act capable of encouraging or assisting the commission of one or more of a number of offences; and

(b) he believes –

    (i)   that one or more of those offences will be committed (but has no belief as to which); and

    (ii)   that his act will encourage or assist the commission of one or more of them.

(2) It is immaterial for the purposes of subsection (1)(b)(ii) whether the person has any belief as to which offence will be encouraged or assisted.

It is not necessary for the prosecution to specify in the indictment every offence that D potentially might have encouraged or assisted. Note that an offence charged under s 46 of the Serious Crime Act 2007 is triable only on indictment: s 55(5).

This is the broadest, most complex and most controversial of the three offences. It is introduced to deal with the problem encountered under secondary liability where D gives assistance and D is aware that P is likely to commit one of a number of offences, but is unsure which. D drives P to a pub, being unsure whether D is going to commit robbery, murder, explosives offences or offences against the person.[540] In secondary liability, the adequacy of D's *mens rea* has proved difficult to define with any precision. Section 46 creates an offence for D who does acts capable of encouraging more than one criminal act where D believes: that at least one of those acts *will* be done but without having any belief as to which it will be; and that his conduct *will* encourage or assist the doing of at least one of those acts. Note that this is markedly different from the form of secondary liability that may arise under *DPP v Maxwell*. First, D need only do acts capable of assisting or encouraging; they need not assist or encourage in fact. Secondly, P need not perform any act or commit any offence; D's liability is inchoate, not dependent on P, and is complete as soon as D has performed his act. Thirdly, D's *mens rea* under s 46 must be a belief that one of the crimes will be committed. Fourthly, it is unnecessary for the prosecution to specify in the indictment every offence that D potentially might have encouraged or assisted but the indictment must specify all the offences which the crown allege D contemplated might be committed: s 46(3).[541]

As an example of its operation, D will be liable if:

(1) he supplies a weapon which is capable of encouraging or assisting the commission of one or more of a number of offences (for example, one or more robberies or murders); and

(2) D believes that his act of supplying the weapon to P *will* (not might) encourage or assist the commission of at least one of those offences; and

(3) although it cannot be proved that D had a belief or intent as to which *one* will be committed, it can be proved that D *believes* that one or more such offences *will* (not might) be committed;[542] and

---

[540] As in *DPP for N Ireland v Maxwell* [1978] 1 WLR 1350. As the Law Commission puts it: 'D, a taxi driver, is asked by a group of armed men to drive to a public house in the East End of London. D believes that they *will* commit an offence of violence and, from their comments to each other, he concludes that the offence *might* be robbery or it *might* be causing grievous bodily harm with intent', LC 300, para A.52.

[541] Fortson, above, n 430, para 6.71.

[542] Section 46(1)(b)(i).

(4) D believes or is reckless as to whether, when P is to perform the conduct element of the offence, P will do so with the *mens rea* required for that offence (or D's state of mind is such that were he to do it, it would be done with the fault required); and

(5) D believes or is reckless as to whether, were the conduct to be done by P, it would be done in those circumstances or with those consequences, if any, of which the offence requires proof.

It is as easy as that.

The maximum penalty for an offence under s 46 is life imprisonment if one of the anticipated offences is murder: s 58(5). If none of the anticipated offences is murder but one or more is an imprisonable offence, the maximum penalty is that for whichever offence has the highest or an unlimited fine.

13.4.6.1 *Actus reus*

D's conduct needs only to be *capable* of assisting or encouraging. There is no requirement that the conduct does in fact encourage or assist P or anyone. As under s 44, D's conduct can be a 'course of conduct.[543] Similarly, conduct capable of assisting or encouraging includes threats or putting pressure on another person.[544] The extended definitions from s 65 apply[545] (taking steps to reduce the possibility of criminal proceedings being brought, and failing to fulfil a duty) but failing to assist a police officer preventing a breach of the peace does not amount to an offence.[546] Under s 66 if D arranges for P to do an act capable of encouraging or assisting X, and P does that act, D is treated as also having done it.

13.4.6.2 *Mens rea*

There are no fewer than five elements of *mens rea* to be proved.

D's belief that he will assist or encourage

D must believe that his act *will* encourage or assist one or of more of the offences. It is not necessary that the Crown establish a belief as to which offence will be committed.

D's belief as to offences

D must believe that one or more of the offences *will* be committed. It is sufficient that D believes that the offence or one of the offences will be committed if certain conditions apply (s 49(7)). So, for example, if D encourages P to burgle the house and to use force to enter if necessary, D will be encouraging criminal damage and burglary.

D's belief as to one of a number of offences

If the allegation is that D believed one or more of a number of offences would be committed and that his act would encourage or assist the commission of one or more of them, by s 47(4), it is sufficient to prove that D believed:

(a) that one or more of a number of acts would be done which would amount to the commission of one or more of those offences; and

(b) that his act would encourage or assist the doing of one or more of those acts.

---

[543] Section 67.
[544] Section 65(1).
[545] (a) taking steps to reduce the possibility of criminal proceedings being brought in respect of that offence; (b) failing to take reasonable steps to discharge a duty.
[546] Section 65(3).

The aim of the provision is to allow for a conviction where, although it cannot be proved that D had a belief or intent as to which *crime* will be committed, it can be proved that D *believes* that one or more such offences *will* (not might) be committed. However, the section refers to the 'act' of P. This suggests that if D does an act which might assist in murder or arson, it is enough that he believes one of the acts (setting fire to a deserted building) would be done which *would* (not might) amount to the crime.[547]

D's *mens rea* as to P's *mens rea*

Where the anticipated crime is one requiring *mens rea*, D must believe or be reckless as to whether P would act with the *mens rea* for one[548] of the anticipated offences with which he would be charged: s 47(5). For example, where D encourages P to commit sexual touching or rape on V, D is liable for encouraging the s 46 offence if he does acts capable of encouraging P, and believes or is reckless (subjectively) as to whether P would commit either *one* of the offences with the *mens rea* for that offence. It is also sufficient under s 47(5)(a)(iii) that D's state of mind was such that, were he to do it, it would be done with that fault. This deals with the cases where D would have *mens rea* if he had committed the offence, even though he does not believe and is not reckless as to whether P would have the *mens rea*.

D's *mens rea* as to circumstances and consequences of P's act

If the offence is one requiring proof of particular circumstances or consequences (or both), D must also have *mens rea* as to the consequences and circumstances of one of the[549] anticipated offences: s 47(5). D must either believe that, were the act to be done, it would be done in those circumstances or with those consequences; or be reckless as to whether or not it would be done in those circumstances or with those consequences. Using the previous example, D must believe or be reckless as to whether the person, V, whom he has encouraged P to touch sexually/rape would lack consent if P performed the relevant act (penetration or sexual touching). It is sufficient that D believes/is reckless as to the existence of the circumstances for *either* one offence.

13.4.6.3 Defences

There is no need for any of the anticipated offences to occur: s 47(4). It is sufficient to prove that D believed that one or more of a number of acts would be done which would amount to the commission of one or more of those offences; and that his act would encourage or assist the doing of one or more of those acts. There is no requirement that any offence is actually committed: s 49(1). It is a defence for D to prove that he acted reasonably under s 50. D cannot be liable if he is a 'victim': s 51.

13.4.6.4 Which offences are capable of being assisted or encouraged

In deciding under s 46 whether an act is capable of encouraging or assisting the commission of one or more of a number of offences, listed offences in Sch 3 are to be disregarded.[550] D *cannot* be convicted under s 46 of encouraging or assisting a conspiracy to commit an offence.[551] Nor can D be liable under s 46 for doing an act that is capable of encouraging or assisting P to attempt

---

[547] See further Fortson, *Blackstone's Guide to the Serious Crime Act 2007*, para 6.71.
[548] See s 48(2).
[549] Section 48(2).
[550] Sch 3 offences are dozens of statutory forms of incitement including solicitation to murder.
[551] Sch 3, para 32.

to commit an offence.[552] Nor can D be liable under s 46 for encouraging or assisting P to do act which is capable of assisting X to commit a crime.[553] Nor is an offence of encouraging or assisting P to commit a statutory incitement of X.[554]

13.4.7 Procedure

Where a prosecuting authority has power to prosecute the substantive offence which D is alleged to have assisted or encouraged, it will also have power to initiate a prosecution for an offence of encouraging or assisting the commission of that substantive offence: s 54(2)(b).

Under s 55 if D is acquitted of an offence contrary to ss 44 to 46 of the Act, he may be found guilty of an 'alternative offence' as defined by s 57(4) and (9).

Where the substantive offence which D is alleged to have assisted or encouraged requires the consent of the Attorney General or the DPP before a prosecution can commence, that consent must be obtained before proceedings are initiated under Part 2 of the 2007 Act: s 54(2).

13.4.8 Jurisdiction

D may be liable in England and Wales no matter where he was at the time of the acts of encouragement or assistance provided he knows or believes that what he anticipates might take place wholly or partly in England and Wales: s 52(1). Where D does not know or believe that the acts of encouragement or assistance might take place in England and Wales he may only be guilty under s 45 if Sch 4 applies (as above in relation to s 44). Paragraph 1 of Sch 4 provides jurisdiction where D does an act in England and Wales, capable of encouraging or assisting an offence, and knows or believes that what he anticipates might take place *outside England and Wales* but the full offence is one for which P could be tried in England and Wales if it were committed outside England and Wales, or relevant conditions exist that would make it so triable. D in England who sends P in Madrid a gun to shoot V can be tried under s 44 because if P shot V the murder would be triable here.

Schedule 4, para 2, provides jurisdiction where D does an act *in England and Wales*, capable of encouraging or assisting an offence, and knows or believes that what he anticipates might take place in a country *outside England and Wales* but what he anticipates is also an offence under the law in force in that country. D in England who sends P in Paris a letter telling him to rape a child. D is guilty of the s 44 offence since rape of a child is an offence in French law.

Schedule 4, para 3, provides jurisdiction where D does an act *outside England and Wales,* capable of encouraging or assisting an offence, and knows or believes that what he anticipates might take place *outside England and Wales* but the offence is one for which it would be possible to prosecute the person who provides encouragement or assistance in England and Wales if he were to commit the offence as a principal in that place. D on holiday in Spain sends to his friend P in France, instructions on how to assassinate V in Paris. Since the murder could be tried in England, D would be liable for the s 44 offence.

Where the offence is one listed in Sch 4, the Attorney General's consent is required: s 53.

---

[552] Sch 33, para 33.

[553] Section 49(4). The Law Commission regarded this as an over-extension of criminal liability: LC 300, paras 7.12–7.13.

[554] As noted above, if D arranges for P to do an act capable of encouraging or assisting and P does that act D is treated as also having done it: s 66.

13.5 Inchoate crime and impossibility[555]

The problem of impossibility is peculiar to the 'inchoate' offences that are the subject of this chapter. If it is impossible to commit a crime, obviously no one can be convicted of committing it. It does not follow that no one can be convicted of attempting or conspiring or assisting/encouraging another to commit the crime. It is a fact that people sometimes do attempt, conspire and encourage others to do what is impossible. This happens only when D does not realize that what he has in view is impossible, that is, he is making a mistake of some kind, as when he tries to kill someone who (unknown to him) is already dead.

It is well established that in some circumstances, a conviction for attempt conspiracy or assisting/encouraging to commit an offence might be proper, although the commission of that offence was impossible. There has been great controversy about the circumstances in which impossibility will afford a defence and those in which it will not.

Several different categories of impossibility need to be considered in detail.

13.5.1 Impossibility and non-existent crimes

One category of case can be disposed of easily. That is where the crime is 'impossible' in the sense that the intended result is not a crime at all but D, because of his ignorance or mistake of criminal law, believes that it is. Here, the law is the same for all inchoate offences and it is clear that none of them is committed. Suppose that D comes from a country where adultery is a crime and he thinks that it is a crime in England. He may attempt the commission of adultery by chatting up his wife's friend. The 'offence' he has in mind is non-existent in England, its 'commission' is impossible and he is guilty of no offence.[556]

13.5.2 Impossibility in fact

In all the other cases to be considered below, we are discussing cases where there is a crime that exists and is capable of being committed and D has the *mens rea* of the ulterior offence – he intends that it shall be committed; but because of some *fact* as to which he is ignorant or mistaken, either:

(1) the result he intends cannot be achieved, or

(2) the result he intends, if achieved, will not be the crime that he believed would be committed.

Into category (1) fall cases where the means used are inadequate to achieve the intended result and where the subject matter or victim of the intended offence does not exist. Category (2) comprises cases where some circumstance, which is an element of the intended crime, does not exist. D believes that he is committing a crime, because he is making a mistake, not of criminal law, but of fact. For example, D intends that he (or the person with whom he conspires[557]) shall have sexual intercourse with V, whom he believes to be 15. V is 16 and consequently the 'result' (intercourse with V) will not be the crime that D intended. At one time,[558] it was thought that the distinction between categories (1) and (2) was material but, as the law now stands, it makes no difference. The law now is that:

---

[555] See generally Duff, above, Ch 3, and see recently S Christie 'The Relevance of Harm as the Criterion for the Punishment of Impossible Attempts' (2009) 73 J Crim L 153.

[556] See the discussion in Ch 11, p 330, of the case of *Taaffe* [1983] 2 All ER 625, CA; *Taaffe* [1984] AC 539, HL. See commentary on the decision of the CA: [1983] Crim LR 536.

[557] The 2007 Act makes no provision for impossibility under the new ss 44–46 offences. See below.

[558] See the first three editions of this book. See also, RA Duff, 'Attempts and the Problem of the Missing Circumstance' (1991) 42 NILQ 87; and White, *Misleading Cases*.

(1) common law conspiracies are governed by the common law;

(2) statutory conspiracy and attempt are governed by the Criminal Law Act 1977, s 1(1), as amended,[559] and the Criminal Attempts Act 1981, s 1(2) and (3), respectively. Assisting and encouraging are governed by the Serious Crime Act 2007.

13.5.2.1 Impossibility in common law conspiracies

DPP v Nock,[560] holds that impossibility *is* a general defence for common law conspiracies. It seems that the only exception is that D may be convicted where the impossibility results merely from the inadequacy of the means used, or to be used, to commit the offence.

So, for example, D will *not* be guilty of common law conspiracy where:

(1) The subject matter of the offence does not exist. D agrees with E to defraud V of her diamond ring. V has already sold it before D and E agreed.

On the other hand, D *may be* guilty of common law conspiracy to defraud where:

(1) He agrees with E to use a phishing scam on the internet to defraud investors, but the programme will not operate on his computer.[561]

13.5.2.2 Statutory conspiracies and attempts

For statutory conspiracies the law is to be found in the Criminal Law Act 1977, s 1(1)[562] as amended by the Criminal Attempts Act 1981 and, for attempts, it is in the Criminal Attempts Act 1981, s 1(2) and (3) which provides:

(2) A person may be guilty of attempting to commit an offence to which this section applies even though the facts are such that the commission of the offence is impossible.

(3) In any case where –

(a) apart from this subsection a person's intention would not be regarded as having amounted to an intent to commit an offence; but

(b) if the facts of the case had been as he believed them to be, his intention would be so regarded, then for the purposes of subsection (1) above he shall be regarded as having an intent to commit that offence.

Section 1(3) is strictly unnecessary but it was wise to include it as a matter of caution. It is unnecessary because under it no one will 'be regarded as having an intention to commit that offence' who does not in fact have that intent. It would be wholly wrong to impute a non-existent intent to a defendant and the Act does not do so. In other words, the subsection does nothing – except forestall the following fallacious argument:

(1) D (believing them to be stolen) intends to handle certain goods.

(2) Those goods are not stolen.

(3) Therefore D does not intend to handle stolen goods.

Section 1(3) says he shall be regarded as having an intention to handle stolen goods. Of course, he has such an intention anyway. The fact that the goods are not stolen, being unknown to him, is wholly irrelevant in determining his intention.

The gist of the two provisions is that for both statutory conspiracy and attempt there must be an intention to commit the offence[563] contemplated. Once that intention is proved, it is

---

[559] Above, p 426.

[560] [1978] AC 979, above, p 432.

[561] Where D agrees with E being unaware that E is a police officer D's plea of impossibility will fail *Gleeson* [2003] EWCA Crim 3557, [2004] 1 Cr App R 29.

[562] Above, p 426.

[563] For conspiracy, *pace* Lord Bridge in *Anderson*, above, p 439.

immaterial that it is *in fact* impossible to commit the substantive offence if, in the case of conspiracy, there has been an agreement to commit it and in the case of an attempt, a more than merely preparatory step towards its commission. The provisions have no application to the cases considered above where there is no crime to commit despite D's intention to do so, (eg adultery in England).

As an example of the section in operation, if D tries to break into V's safe to steal a diamond but there is no diamond present. D is guilty of attempting to steal the diamond. Similarly, if D and E agree that they will use D's jemmy to break into V's safe and steal a diamond, but there is no diamond, D and E are guilty of conspiracy to steal the diamond.

The proper construction of the Criminal Attempts Act was controversial but it is now settled by the decision of the House of Lords in *Shivpuri*.[564] It seems reasonable to assume that the same interpretation will be put on the amended s 1(1) of the Criminal Law Act 1977 (statutory conspiracy), for that section was amended by the Criminal Attempts Act 1981, s 5, to keep the law of attempt and conspiracy in line in this respect.

In the case of attempts, it must be proved that D had an intention to commit the crime in question. Once that is established, the only question is whether, with that intent, he has done an act which is 'more than merely preparatory' to the commission of the offence. Since, *ex hypothesi*, the offence is impossible, it is the offence envisaged by D to which the act in question must be more than merely preparatory. The effect is that the court must ask, 'would the act (eg breaking into the safe) have been more than merely preparatory to the commission of the offence (theft of the diamond) if the facts had been as D believed them to be (diamond within the safe)?'

In the case of conspiracy, it must be proved that D agreed with another or others that a course of conduct is to be pursued (breaking into the safe) which, in the circumstances believed by the parties to exist (diamond in the safe), will, in the event of their intention being achieved (theft of the diamond), amount to or involve the commission of the offence (theft).[565] It is then immaterial that the circumstances are in fact such that the offence is impossible, or that the results can never be achieved.

In the following example, D *will be guilty* both of statutory conspiracy and attempt:

(1) D and E agree that they will administer a poison, which D has acquired, to V in order to kill him. D administers the poison. As a matter of fact, the poison is too weak ever to kill anyone. D and E are guilty of conspiracy, and D of an attempt to murder V.

(2) D and E agree that they will steal from V's safe. D attempts to break open the safe. It is empty. D and E are guilty of conspiracy, and D of an attempt to steal from the safe.

(3) D and E agree that they will murder V. D shoots at V's heart but V is already dead. D and E are guilty of conspiracy to murder, and D of attempted murder.[566]

(4) D and E agree that they will receive from F certain goods which they believe to be stolen goods. D takes possession of the goods. The goods are not stolen goods. D and E are guilty of conspiracy, and D of an attempt to handle stolen goods.

(5) D and E agree that D will have consensual sexual intercourse with V, a girl whom they believe to be aged 15. D has sexual intercourse with her. In fact she is 16. D and E are guilty of conspiracy, and D of an attempt to engage in sexual activity with a child under the age of 16.

---

[564] [1987] AC 1, [1986] Crim LR 536.

[565] It has been argued above that this is the only sensible interpretation of the phrase 'course of conduct' and that the amendment by the 1981 Act was strictly unnecessary. The 1981 amendment may, however, be taken to reinforce this opinion.

[566] See also the example of *Brown* [2004] Crim LR 665 where D was rightly convicted of attempting to pervert the course of justice having put in train the machinery of public justice (by alleging he had been abused by V) which, if the matter were carried through in a way he wished or foresaw, would cause a risk to an innocent person (who was, unknown to D, already dead).

Examples (2) and (3) would not have been offences at common law under the principles established in *Haughton v Smith* and *Nock*, but those decisions are now generally recognized to have been unduly restrictive. It is the cases exemplified by illustrations (4) and (5) which have been the subject of much controversy.[567] The reason is that, in these cases, if D succeeds in doing the precise thing that he set out to do, he will not commit a crime. D takes possession of the very goods he intended to take possession of – no other – and that is no offence, for the goods are not stolen goods. D has sexual intercourse with the girl he intends to have intercourse with. She is 16 and consents so there is nothing unlawful. How then can his taking steps towards the accomplishment of something that is no crime be a conspiracy or an attempt to commit it? Bramwell B ridiculed the idea in *Collins*[568] in 1864. He put the case of D who takes an umbrella from the stand near the door of his club, intending to steal it, but it turns out to be his own umbrella. Bramwell B thought it absurd that D should be convicted of attempting to steal it. Arguments of this kind prevailed in the House of Lords in *Anderton v Ryan*[569] but were then rejected in *Shivpuri*[570] barely a year later.

In *Anderton v Ryan*, D bought a video recorder for £110. Later she said to police, 'I may as well be honest, it was a stolen one I bought...' She was charged with handling and attempted handling. The prosecution, presumably believing that they were unable to prove that the video had in fact been stolen, offered no evidence on the first charge. The magistrates were not satisfied that the video had been stolen, though D believed it had. They dismissed the charge. The Divisional Court allowed the prosecution's appeal[571] but the House of Lords, Lord Edmund-Davies dissenting, restored the decision of the magistrates. The Criminal Attempts Act 1981, s 1(3), said Lord Roskill, 'does not compel the conclusion that an erroneous belief in the existence of facts which, if true, would have made his completed act a crime makes him guilty of an attempt to commit that crime'. Because the House thought the conclusion absurd, they were not going to reach it unless compelled to do so.

In *Shivpuri*, D was arrested by customs officials while in possession of a suitcase. He admitted that he knew it contained prohibited drugs. Analysis showed that the material in the suitcase was not a prohibited drug but a vegetable material akin to snuff. He was convicted of attempting to be knowingly concerned in dealing with a prohibited drug, contrary to s 1(1) of the Criminal Attempts Act 1981 and s 170(1)(b) of the Customs and Excise Management Act 1979. His appeal was dismissed by the Court of Appeal[572] and, overruling *Anderton v Ryan*, by the House of Lords. No distinction is to be drawn between 'objectively innocent' acts (taking one's own umbrella, receiving non-stolen goods, handling snuff) and 'guilty' acts, for the purposes of the law of attempts. The law is as stated above.[573]

Since it must be proved that D intended to commit the crime in question, he is argued to be morally at least as bad as the person who actually commits the offence and, where the offence may be committed with some lesser degree of *mens rea*, perhaps worse; and he is as dangerous to whatever interest the particular law is designed to protect as the person who actually commits the offence. It is sometimes objected that he is punished solely for his thoughts but this is not true because it must be proved (in the case of an attempt) that he has taken such steps to put his intention into execution as would (if the facts were as he believed) be more than merely

---

[567] The powerful article which influenced the decision in *Shivpuri* is G Williams, 'The Lords and Impossible Attempts' [1986] CLJ 33. For earlier writing, see B Hogan, 'The Criminal Attempts Act and Attempting the Impossible' [1984] Crim LR 584, 'Attempting the Impossible and the Principle of Legality' (1985) 135 NLJ 454; G Williams, 'Attempting the Impossible – the Last Round?' (1985) 135 NLJ 337 and commentaries at [1985] Crim LR 44, 504, [1986] Crim LR 51.

[568] (1864) 9 Cox CC 497 at 498.

[569] [1985] AC 560.

[570] [1987] AC 1.

[571] [1985] 1 All ER 138, [1984] Crim LR 483.

[572] [1985] QB 1029, [1985] 1 All ER 143.

[573] At p 481.

preparatory to the commission of the offence. In the case of conspiracy (not expressly considered in *Shivpuri* but presumably governed by the same principles) he must have agreed with another that the offence be committed – the usual *actus reus* of conspiracy.

It is also argued that the conclusion offends against the principle of legality (no one shall be convicted of doing something which has not been declared by the law to be an offence).[574] But the issue in these cases was the proper construction of the statute. If Parliament has said (and the House ultimately decided that it has) that it is to be an offence (attempt) to do any act which is more than merely preparatory with intent to commit an offence, the law may be criticized for being too wide-ranging; but the conviction of one who does any such act with that intent can no longer be criticized for breaching the principle of legality.

The breadth of the law is such that there may be cases where prosecution would be ill-advised. Bramwell B's man who took his own umbrella would no doubt be surprised to find himself charged with attempting to steal his own umbrella. D who has *succeeded* in having consensual sexual intercourse with V, a 16-year-old, might be astonished to find himself charged in consequence with *attempting* to commit an offence against a person under 16. As such acts are objectively innocent, the offence is unlikely to come to light unless D advertises the fact that he acted with *mens rea*. There will be other cases, however, where a prosecution is in the public interest. The would-be drug smuggler, exemplified by *Shivpuri*, is an instance. It may well be that their Lordships' change of mind was influenced by the fact that *Anderton v Ryan* would have required them to turn such dangerous persons loose on the public. Perhaps the most important case in practice is that of the person who receives goods wrongly believing them to be stolen. Mrs Ryan's was an unusual and trivial case. Typical of the case where a prosecution is likely to be brought is *Haughton v Smith* itself. A van, heavily laden with stolen corned beef, was intercepted by the police. Having discovered that the intended recipient was D, the police allowed it to proceed on its way, but under the control of disguised policemen. D received the goods, believing them to be stolen. However, the beef ceased to be stolen goods when the police took control of it.[575] The House held that he was not guilty of attempted handling but now he could plainly be convicted. The public interest called for his conviction no less than if the police had never intercepted the goods.

Two doubtful cases

Mistakes of civil law

It has been noted that an intention to commit a non-existent crime (adultery) arising from a mistake as to the criminal law involves no liability.[576] A more difficult case is that where D has an intention to commit an existing offence because he is making a mistake of civil law. Believing that the law requires him to use money for a particular purpose, D dishonestly uses the money for another purpose. If his belief was true, he would be guilty of theft. Actually the law allows him to do what he likes with the money and he commits no substantive offence.[577] He intends to steal and has done his best to do so. In principle, the case is difficult to distinguish from those where the intent to commit an offence is attributable to a mistake of fact; but the use of the word 'facts' in s 1(3)(b) is likely to exclude liability.

Reckless impossible attempts

The recognition in *Khan*[578] of the reckless-as-to-circumstances attempt raises the spectre of the reckless/impossible attempt.[579] D burns V's rubbish on his bonfire, and V consents in

---

[574] B Hogan, 'The Principle of Legality' (1986) 136 NLJ 267.
[575] Below, p 980.
[576] Above, p 480.
[577] Commentary on *Huskinson* [1988] Crim LR 620 at 622.
[578] Above, p 407.
[579] G Williams [1983] Crim LR 365 at 375.

fact to that act, but D is not sure whether V consented or not. Is he guilty of attempted criminal damage? In the context of subjective reckless rape, Glanville Williams thought a person who was not sure if V was consenting must be guilty of attempted rape even if V was consenting, but he thought that no prosecution should ensue. A possible answer is that s 1(3) of the Criminal Attempts Act requires us to treat D as if the facts were 'as he *believed* them to be' which removes the impossibility defence. This affords some ground for holding that the reckless/impossible attempt is still no offence.

13.5.2.3 Assisting and encouraging

The SCA 2007 makes no reference to the position regarding impossibility. The Law Commission believed that impossibility would be no defence under its scheme,[580] and that that is what the Act achieves by its silence.[581] It is not clear that this aim has been achieved. If D encourages P or assists by providing him with the gun to kill V (who unknown to D is already dead) there are strong arguments for saying that D ought to be liable for assisting or encouraging murder. His conduct is no less blameworthy than those who attempt or conspire to murder in such circumstances. D has done an act capable of encouraging P to perform the conduct element of the offence or murder. The Act would seem to provide no defence of impossibility for D in such a case. The Commission provides the following example:

> if D...provides P with a weapon believing that P will use it to attack V1 (intending to kill V1), D is guilty of assisting murder irrespective of whether P uses the weapon to attack anyone. Were P to attack and murder V2, instead of V1, D would be equally guilty of encouraging or assisting murder. If P attacked V2 because V1 was already dead at the time that D provided the weapon, D would still be guilty of encouraging or assisting murder. It may have been impossible for V1 to be murdered but, nonetheless, D had done an act capable of encouraging or assisting the conduct element of murder, namely an attack on any human being. [582]

This case would appear to be dealt with by the Act. The position is less obvious in a case where D provides P with an article which he thinks is capable of assisting in the commission of a crime, but it is never going to be of assistance in committing any crime. Consider D who provides P with a plastic card which D believes is capable of assisting P to enter hotel bedrooms to steal therein. The card is not capable of opening any door. There is no magnetic strip and no data can be held on it. It would be arguable that because the card will not be 'capable of assisting or encouraging P' to commit the conduct element of the offence of burglary, that impossibility is a defence. Consider D who sends P in prison a Monopoly 'get out of jail free' card. That act is clearly not capable of assisting or encouraging escape. What then of D who provides the would-be assassin with what he thinks are live bullets but are blanks? One answer is to charge D with attempting to assist or encourage in such situations.

13.5.3 The future of impossiblity

In *Shivpuri* Lord Hailsham, with whom Lord Elwyn-Jones and Lord MacKay concurred, offered reasons why *Anderton v Ryan* was distinguishable (even though they concurred in overruling it). That might suggest that *Shivpuri* was open to challenge. It is now surely too late to resurrect arguments which were in substance rejected in *Shivpuri*[583] and which have been settled for 25 years.

---

[580] LC 300, para 6.61.
[581] LC 318, para 5.42. The Law Commission conclusion appears in a footnote only.
[582] LC 300, para 6.63.
[583] See the analysis of Lord Hailsham's speech at [1986] Crim LR 539–541. For attempts to reconcile the two decisions see RA Duff, 'Regarding Intention: The Criminal Attempts Act 1981 s 1(3)' (1990) XII(2) Liverpool Law Review 161, and Duff, *Criminal Attempts*, 378–384.

Part II
Particular Crimes

14
Murder

Murder remains relatively rare in England and Wales. In 2009/10, there were 615 recorded homicides.[1]

14.1 Definition

Although it is generally regarded as the most serious crime (apart perhaps from treason) the offence of murder has not been defined by statute. The Law Commission recently described it as a 'rickety structure set upon shaky foundations'.[2] Indeed, the classic definition derives from a book from the seventeenth century. That definition provided by Coke is:

Murder is when a man of sound memory, and of the age of discretion, unlawfully killeth within any county of the realm any reasonable creature *in rerum natura* under the king's peace, with malice aforethought, either expressed by the party or implied by law, [so as the party wounded, or hurt, etc die of the wound or hurt, etc within a year and a day after the same].[3]

The Law Commission recently conducted a comprehensive review of the existing scope of the offence and made far reaching proposals for reform.[4] These are discussed later in the chapter. The Government has, after initially indicating that it would consider legislative change,[5] now decided not to take forward the proposals.[6]

14.1.1 Who can commit murder

'A man of sound memory and of the age of discretion' means simply a person who is responsible according to the general principles which have been discussed above. Such a person is over the age of nine. If he was at the time of the killing under 14, there is no longer a need to prove that he knew it was seriously wrong.[7] The other limitations are that the offender is not insane within the M'Naghten Rules, and since 1957,[8] he does not suffer from diminished responsibility.[9]

---

[1] Homicide includes murder, manslaughter and infanticide. See J Flatley et al, *Crime in England and Wales 2009/10, Findings from the British Crime Survey and Police Recorded Crime* (2010) table 2.04.

[2] Law Commission Consultation Paper No 177, *A New Homicide Act for England and Wales?* (2005) (hereafter in this chapter LCCP 177) para 1.4. The history of the offence is summarized in LCCP 177 at paras 1.92–1.103.

[3] 3 Inst 47. As to the words in parentheses, see below, p 494.

[4] See LCCP 177 and Law Com Report No 304, *Murder Manslaughter and Infanticide* (2006) (hereafter in this chapter LC 304). Both these documents contain valuable analysis of the existing law meriting close attention.

[5] See the written Ministerial Statement of Maria Eagle, 12 Dec 2007.

[6] MOJ Report on the Implementation of Law Commission Proposals (2011), para 55.

[7] See the discussion of the *doli incapax* defence above, p 341.

[8] See s 2 of the Homicide Act 1957, as substituted by the Coroners and Justice Act 2009, see below Ch 15.

[9] The fact that D suffers ADHD does not necessarily preclude D having formed an intent: *Osborne* [2010] EWCA Crim 547 [36]

A corporation or other organization cannot be tried for murder because it cannot suffer the only penalty allowed by law, life imprisonment.[10]

14.1.2 Where murder can be committed[11]

If the killing is by a British citizen, it need no longer take place within 'any county of the realm'. Murder and manslaughter are among the exceptional cases where the English courts have jurisdiction over offences committed abroad. By s 9 of the Offences Against the Person Act 1861 and s 3 of the British Nationality Act 1948 a murder or manslaughter committed by a British citizen on land anywhere out of the United Kingdom may be tried in England or Northern Ireland as if it had been committed there.[12] Homicides on a British ship[13] or air-craft[14] are also triable here, whether committed by a British subject or not; those on a foreign ship (outside territorial waters[15]) may be triable if committed by a British citizen who 'does not belong' to that ship.[16] There are other statutory extensions under which murder may be tried in England and Wales irrespective of the killer's nationality.[17]

14.1.3 Who can be the victim[18]

Though it is only in relation to murder that a discussion arises as to who qualifies as a victim, it is clear that, in principle, the same rules must apply to assaults and offences against the person generally.[19] Coke's 'reasonable creature in *Rerum natura*' is simply the 'person' who is the victim of an offence in the modern law of offences against the person – that is, any human being.[20] The problems are at what stage in the process of birth a foetus becomes a person; and at what stage in the process of death a person becomes a corpse. Article 2 of the ECHR provides a right to life, and this imposes on the State certain obligations to protect life, and investigate the taking of life, but the European Court has not directly addressed the issue of when life begins and ends.[21]

---

[10] See below p 562 for possible liability for manslaughter.

[11] See, generally, on jurisdiction M Hirst, *Jurisdiction and the Ambit of the Criminal Law* (2003) 226–232.

[12] See CLRC, Offences Against the Person Working Paper 67; Offences Against the Person Report 125. There is no provision enabling a murder committed in Scotland to be tried in England. See for discussion M Hirst, 'Murder in England or Murder in Scotland' [1995] CLJ 488. Homicides committed abroad by non-British citizens may be tried here if the offences are under the War Crimes Act 1991, see *Sawoniuk* [2000] Cr App R 220.

[13] As defined in the Merchant Shipping Act 1995, s 1. The jurisdiction applies not only when sailing on the high seas, but also when in the rivers of a foreign territory at a place below bridges, where the tide ebbs and flows and where great ships go: *Anderson* (1868) LR 1 CCR 161. See further the Merchant Shipping Act 1995, ss 281–282.

[14] Civil Aviation Act 1982, s 92. The Civil Aviation (Amendment) Act 1996, s 1(2) extends the jurisdiction to offences on foreign aircraft in specified circumstances. See also the Aviation Security Act 1982, s 6.

[15] Jurisdiction over offences within territorial waters is given by the Territorial Waters Jurisdiction Act 1878, s 2.

[16] Merchant Shipping Act 1995, ss 281–282.

[17] See especially the Suppression of Terrorism Act 1978, s 4. In relation to British service personnel see the Armed Forces Act 2006, s 42 and below, n 45.

[18] See the discussion in IM Kennedy and A Grubb, *Medical Law Text with Materials* (2000). For historical accounts, see D Seaborne Davies, 'Child-killing in English Law' (1937) 1 MLR 203; G Williams, *Sanctity of Life and the Criminal Law* (1957) 19–23; and see recently J Keown and D Jones, 'Surveying the Foundations of Medical Law: A Reassessment of Glanville Williams' *The Sanctity of Life and the Criminal Law*' (2008) 16 Med LR 85; SB Atkinson, 'Life, Birth and Live Birth' (1904) 20 LQR 134.

[19] In *Tait* (1990) Cr App R 44, the court held that the offence of threatening to kill under s 16 of the OAPA 1861 was not made out by threats to kill a foetus.

[20] Draft Code, cl 53.

[21] See, generally, Emmerson, Ashworth and Macdonald, HR&CJ, para 18.44. See also E Wicks, 'Terminating Life and Human Right: The Fetus and the Neonate' in C Erin and S Ost, *The Criminal Justice System and Health Care* (2007).

14.1.3.1 Child or foetus?

It is not murder to kill a foetus/child in the womb or in the process of leaving the womb. If the child is not capable of being born alive, destruction may be an offence under s 58 of the Offences Against the Person Act 1861.[22] Where the child is capable of being born alive, it is an offence under the Infant Life (Preservation) Act 1929.[23] If the child has 'an existence independent of its mother' it is capable of being murdered. To have such an existence the child must have been wholly expelled from its mother's body and be alive.[24] The cord and afterbirth need not have been expelled from the mother nor severed from the child.[25] The tests of independent existence which the courts have accepted are that the child should have an independent circulation, and that it should have breathed after birth. But there are difficulties about both these tests.

In *Brain* Park J said:[26]

it is not essential that it should have breathed at the time it was killed; as many children are born alive and yet do not breathe for some time after their birth.

It appears that there is no readily available means of determining at what instant the foetal and parental circulations are so dissociated as to allow the child to live without the help of the parental circulation; and this dissociation may precede birth. There is thus some uncertainty about the precise moment at which the child comes under the protection of the law of murder, though the question does not seem to have troubled the English courts in recent years. The last reported case that the CLRC could trace was in 1874.[27] The Committee recommended that the test should be that the victim should have been born and have an existence independent of its mother. With the rapid developments in medical science and the increasing ability to keep alive children born prematurely, the law should be careful to avoid any more rigid form of definition. As Brooke LJ observed, in holding that a conjoined twin with useless heart and lungs, dependent on her twin, was protected by the law of murder: '[a]dvances in medical treatment of deformed neonates suggest that the criminal law's protection should be as wide as possible, and a conclusion that a creature in being was not reasonable would be confined only to the most extreme cases of which this is not an example'.[28] In *Iby*,[29] the New South Wales Court of Appeal held that the decision of viability be left largely to the jury. This is, with respect, not one that will engender certainty and consistency in the law. It is hoped that it will not be adopted by the English courts.

The European Court of Human Rights has declined to decide directly whether the foetus is protected by the right to life in Art 2. In *Vo v France*,[30] a doctor negligently caused fatal injury

[22] Below, p 602. A foetus of 24 weeks' gestation is presumed capable of being born alive: Human Fertilisation and Embryology Act 1990, s 37. The prescription, supply, administration or use of the contraceptive pill, minipill and morning-after pill does not contravene s 58 of the OAPA. *R (on the application of Smeaton) v Secretary of State for Health* [2002] All ER (D) 115 (Apr); [2002] Crim LR 664. Abortion in compliance with the 1967 Act does not contravene Art 2 of the ECHR: *Paton v United Kingdom* [1980] 3 EHRR 408. At common law, it was a 'great misprision' (misdemeanour) 3 Co Inst 50. According to Hale, I PC, 433, 'a great crime'. Willes J said in 1866 (BPP 21 at 274) that the crime was obsolete. (See MACL at 310.)

[23] Below, p 602. See, generally, DM Katkin and R Ogle, 'A Rationale for Infanticide Laws' [1993] Crim LR 903.

[24] See *Poulton* (1832) 5 C & P 329; *Enoch* (1850) 5 C& P 539.

[25] *Reeves* (1839) 9 C & P 25.

[26] (1834) 6 C & P 349 at 350. But see *C v S* and *Rance v Mid-Downs Health Authority*, below, p 603.

[27] *Handley* (1874) 13 Cox CC 79, followed by Wright J in *Pritchard* (1901) 17 TLR 310. Fourteenth Report, para 35.

[28] Per Brooke LJ in *Re A* [2001] Fam 147, [2001] 2 WLR 480.

[29] [2005] NSWCCA 178, discussed at [2005] Crim LR 742.

[30] [2004] 2 FCR 577, on which see K O'Donovan, 'Taking a Neutral Stance on the Legal Protection of the Fetus' (2006) 14 Med LR 115 and E Wicks, above n 21.

to a viable foetus after mistaking the mother's identity for that of a similarly named patient. The French Criminal Court acquitted him on the basis that the foetus was not a human being for the purposes of the offence. On application to the ECtHR, the Court ruled that the issue of life's commencement was within the margin of appreciation for Member States to determine. The Court acknowledged that in:

the circumstances examined to date by the Convention institutions – that is, in the various laws on abortion – the unborn child is not regarded as a 'person' directly protected by Article 2 of the Convention and that if the unborn do have a 'right' to 'life', it is implicitly limited by the mother's rights and interests. The Convention institutions have not, however, ruled out the possibility that in certain circumstances safeguards may be extended to the unborn child... It is also clear from an examination of these cases that the issue has always been determined by weighing up various, and sometimes conflicting, rights or freedoms claimed by a woman, a mother or a father in relation to one another or *vis-à-vis* an unborn child.[31]

The interpretation of Art 2 has involved the Court in balancing legal, medical, philosophical, ethical and religious issues. Since there is no consensus at national level, it is unsurprising that the Court has left States with considerable discretion in the matter – the issue of when the right to life begins comes within the margin of appreciation.[32]

14.1.3.2 Prenatal injury and post natal death

Where D intentionally causes injury to, or attempts to kill, the foetus, but the child is born alive and dies of the injury sustained, D has caused the death of a person in being – the *actus reus* of murder. Coke[33] stated that he was guilty of murder. In *West*, Maule J directed the jury that a woman was guilty of murder if, in attempting to procure an abortion, she caused the premature birth of her child who, consequently, died five hours later. The basis of that decision, however appears to be that D caused the death by a felonious act, a type of 'constructive murder', which was abolished by the Homicide Act 1957. In *A-G's Reference (No 3 of 1994)*,[34] D stabbed his girlfriend, V, who was 26 weeks' pregnant with his child, X. V recovered but, because of the wound, X was born prematurely and, as a result of the premature birth, died after 120 days. The House of Lords accepted, *obiter*, as an established rule, that 'Violence towards a foetus which results in harm suffered after the baby has been born alive can give rise to criminal responsibility even if the harm would not have been criminal (apart from statute) if it had been suffered in utero'.

However, difficulties arose in establishing *mens rea* in such a case. Since an intention to cause death or injury to the foetus is not the *mens rea* of murder,[35] it seems that it could not be that offence. If D intended the child to be born alive and then die or suffer serious injury, that would be murder. And it might be manslaughter by gross negligence, if there was an obvious and unjustifiable risk of, for example, premature birth and consequent early death.

The Court of Appeal had held that the foetus is an integral part of the mother before birth, no less than her arm or leg. If that were so, an intention to kill or cause serious harm

---

[31] Para 80.

[32] In *X v Norway* (App No 867/60); *X v Austria* (1976) 7 DR 87; *X v United Kingdom* (1980) 1 DR 244, the Convention institutions declined to determine the issue of the time at which life begins.

[33] 3 Co Inst 50; Hawkins, I PC, c 31, s 16; East, I PC, 228; contra Hale, I PC, 433; *West* (1848) 2 Cox CC 500. See also *Kwok Chak Ming* (Hong Kong, 1963) discussed in [1963] Crim LR 748 and J Temkin, 'Pre-Natal Injury, Homicide and the Draft Criminal Code' [1986] CLJ 414.

[34] [1997] 3 All ER 936 at 942, HL, reversing [1996] 1 Cr App R 351, [1996] Crim LR 268, CA.

[35] cf Temkin [1986] CLJ 414, and the Draft Code, cl 53.

to the foetus would be an intention to cause such harm to the mother – the *mens rea* of murder. But the House held that it was wrong. 'The mother and foetus were two distinct organisms living symbiotically, not a single organism with two aspects.' The House declined to extend the doctrine of transferred malice to what it regarded as a double transfer of intent – from the mother to the foetus and from the foetus to the child. It was not murder. Oddly, the House of Lords went on to hold that it was manslaughter of the child by the unlawful and dangerous act of stabbing the mother – which looks exactly like transferred malice.[36] Moreover, the act was not merely unlawful and dangerous – it was done with the *mens rea* of murder and, as it is acknowledged that it caused the death of the child, it is hard to see why it is not murder.

It was held in *Senior*[37] that where the pre-natal injury was caused by gross negligence or with a *mens rea* sufficient only for manslaughter, and that conduct caused death to the child after it had been born, a conviction for manslaughter was appropriate. It would be logical to go on to hold that gross pre-natal neglect of the child by the mother, resulting in death after birth, should also be manslaughter; but the courts have stopped short of this conclusion.[38] Neglect of the child by the mother after birth may give rise to liability, neglect before the birth does not. A woman is entitled to refuse medical treatment, even though she knows that the result may be the death of the foetus, or the child if it is born alive.[39]

14.1.3.3 Death

Similar problems could arise in determining the moment at which life ends, though these do not seem, in practice, to have troubled the courts. Is V dead, and therefore incapable of being murdered, if his heart has stopped beating but a surgeon confidently expects to start it again, by an injection or mechanical means?[40] Is V dead if he is in a 'hopeless' condition and 'kept alive' only by an apparatus of some kind?[41] There is, at present, no certain answer to these questions. The current medical view is that the test is one of brainstem death and that this can be diagnosed with certainty.[42] The law has not yet evolved a definition of its own and the CLRC declined to propose one[43] both because of the fluid state of medical science and the repercussions that such a definition might have on other branches of the law.[44]

---

[36] cf J Horder, 'Transferred Malice and the Remoteness of Unexpected Outcomes from Intentions' [2006] Crim LR 383.

[37] (1832) 1 Mood CC 346.

[38] *Knights* (1860) 2 F & F 46; *Izod* (1904) 20 Cox CC 690 (Channell J); and see the discussion by Davies, MACL at 308–309.

[39] *St George's Healthcare NHS Trust v S* [1998] 3 All ER 673, 685–692 (Civ Div).

[40] G Williams, *Sanctity of Life and the Criminal Law* (1957) 18.

[41] Kennedy and Grubb, *Medical Law*, Chs 16, 17, 18 and references therein; IM Kennedy, 'Alive or Dead?' (1969) 22 CLP 102; 'Switching Off Life Support Machines' [1977] Crim LR 443; B Hogan 'A Note on Death' [1972] Crim LR 80; P Skegg, 'Irreversibly Comatose Individuals: Alive or Dead?' [1964] CLJ 130; Report of the Broderick Committee (1969) Cmnd 4810, paras 808–812 and Law Com No 230 (1995).

[42] *Re A* [1992] 3 Med LR 303; *British Medical Journal* and *The Lancet*, 21 Feb 1979. cf *Malcherek* [1981] 2 All ER 422, [1981] 1 WLR 690, above, p 94. For detailed medical discussion on the test, see C Pallis and D Harley, *ABC of Brain Stem Death* (2nd edn, 1996) and MD Bell, E Moss and PG Murphy, 'Brainstem Death Testing in the UK: Time for Reappraisal?' (2004) 92 Br J Anaesthesia 633–640. See further, Kennedy and Grubb, *Medical Law*, 2141.

[43] Fourteenth Report, para 37.

[44] See also the discussion above relating to omissions and the termination of patients' life sustaining treatment, p 77 on omissions.

14.1.3.4 Under the Queen's peace[45]

All persons appear to be 'under the Queen's peace' for this purpose, even an alien enemy, 'unless…in the heat of war, and in the actual exercise thereof'.[46] In *Page*,[47] an argument that an Egyptian national who had been murdered in an Egyptian village by a British soldier serving there was not within the Queen's peace, was rejected.[48] Enemy soldiers who have been taken prisoner or have surrendered are protected by the law of murder.[49] In his recent analysis of the position of British service personnel in Iraq, Rowe concludes that the term is vague and in particular, insufficiently precise to establish whether it applies to 'non-international armed conflict abroad to which the UK is a party'.[50]

14.1.4 Death within a year and a day[51]

The rule stated by Coke that the death must occur within a year and a day has been abolished by the Law Reform (Year and a Day Rule) Act 1996. If an act can be shown to be the cause of death, it may now be murder, any other homicide offence, or suicide, however much time has elapsed between the act and the death. The Act, however, requires the consent of the Attorney General to the prosecution of any person for murder, manslaughter, infanticide or any other offence of which one of the elements is causing a person's death, or assisting or encouraging suicide, (i) where the injury alleged to have caused the death was sustained more than three years before the death occurred or (ii) where the accused has previously been convicted of an offence committed in circumstances alleged to be connected with the death. The Attorney General's consent is therefore required if D has been convicted of wounding V, who has subsequently died of the wound within three years of D's causing it and it is proposed to prosecute D for murder or manslaughter. It would seem that consent is also required if D has been convicted of a robbery, burglary or driving offence in the course of which V sustained an injury from which he subsequently died. This is not incompatible with the guarantee against double jeopardy in Art 4 of Protocol 7 of the ECHR.[52]

The year-and-a-day[53] rule continues to apply where any act or omission causing death was committed before 17 June 1996.

14.1.5 Unlawful

The requirement that the killing is unlawful is an important element of the offence. The most obvious example of its application is where the killing is in self-defence.[54] The element applies

---

[45] See M Hirst, 'Murder Under the Queen's Peace' [2008] Crim LR 541, arguing that the element ought now to focus on whether D is subject to the English law of homicide. On this see also ACE Lynch, 'British Subjects' Involvement in Foreign Military Clashes' [1978] Crim LR 257; P Rowe, 'The Criminal Liability of a British Soldier Merely for Participating in The Iraq War' [2010] Crim LR 752.

[46] Hale, I PC, 433.

[47] [1954] 1 QB 170, [1953] 2 All ER 1355 (C–MAC). See further P Rowe, 'Murder and the Law of War' (1991) 42 NILQ 216.

[48] The real issue in that case was whether the court-martial assembled in the Suez Canal Zone had jurisdiction to try the case. It was admitted that, if D had been brought to this country and tried here, no question could have arisen as to the nationality of the victim. The court-martial was held to have jurisdiction under the Army Act.

[49] Note also that a civilian of an enemy state in the custody of British forces is protected by Art 2 of the ECHR: *R (Mazin Jumaa Gatteh Al SKeina) v Secretary of State for Defence* [2007] UKHL 26.

[50] Above n 45.

[51] For historical material on the rule, see D Yale, 'A Year and A Day in Homicide' [1989] CLJ 202, and on the reform see LCCP 136, *The Year and a Day Rule in Homicide* (1994).

[52] *Young* [2005] EWCA Crim 2963.

[53] For further details, see 7th edition of this book, at 330.

[54] See generally F Leverick, *Killing in Self Defence* (2007).

more widely; for example, it was accepted by the Court of Appeal in the *A-G's Reference (No 3 of 1994)*[55] that the doctor who performed a lawful abortion would not be liable for murder should the foetus be born alive and die from injuries sustained in the termination procedure. The doctor in such a case would have performed a lawful act under the Abortion Act 1967. Consent, which in many offences will render conduct lawful, has no part to play in the context of murder. So, also, it is murder at common law if a person condemned to death be executed by someone other than the officer lawfully appointed, or if the officer lawfully appointed carries out the execution by an unauthorized method, as where he beheads a person condemned to be hanged.[56]

14.1.6 Causing death[57]

It must be proved that D, by his own act or unlawful omission, caused death. For this purpose, D, who, for example, procures E to murder D's wife, does not cause her death. D does not kill; E does. D is guilty of murder but as a secondary party. The principles of causation apply to 'result crimes' generally and are considered in detail in Chapter 4, above. In fact, most of the leading cases concern causing death in homicide offences.

14.1.6.1 Accelerating death

What must be caused is some acceleration of death. Since everyone must die sooner or later, it follows that every killing is merely an acceleration of death; and it makes no difference for this purpose that the victim is already suffering from a fatal disease or injury or is under sentence of death. Thus, in *Dyson*,[58] Lord Alverstone CJ said:[59]

The proper question to have been submitted to the jury was whether the prisoner accelerated the child's death by the injuries which he inflicted in . . . For if he did the fact that the child was already suffering from meningitis from which it would in any event have died before long, would afford no answer to the charge of causing its death.

The administration of pain-saving drugs presents difficult problems. In the case of *Adams*,[60] Devlin J directed the jury that there is no special defence justifying a doctor in giving drugs which would shorten life in the case of severe pain: 'If life were cut short by weeks or months it was just as much murder as if it were cut short by years.' He went on:

But that does not mean that a doctor aiding the sick or dying has to calculate in minutes or hours, or perhaps in days or weeks, the effect on a patient's life of the medicines which he administers. If the first purpose of medicine – the restoration of health – can no longer be achieved, there is still much for the doctor to do, and he is entitled to do all that is proper and necessary to relieve pain and suffering even if measures he takes may incidentally shorten life.

These passages are not easy to reconcile. If the doctor gives drugs with the sole object of relieving suffering of a dying man knowing that the drugs will certainly shorten his life, then he

---

[55] [1996] 2 All ER 10.

[56] ibid. The death penalty is abolished for all crimes in England and Wales: Crime and Disorder Act 1998, s 36.

[57] H Hart and T Honoré, *Causation in the Law* (2nd edn, 1985), especially Chs XII–XIV; G Williams, 'Causation in Homicide' [1957] Crim LR 429 and 510; F Camps and J Harvard, 'Causation in Homicide – A Medical View' [1957] Crim LR at 576. See also the discussion above, Ch 4 and references therein.

[58] [1908] 2 KB 454 at 457.

[59] [1908] 2 KB 454. And see Hale, I PC, 428; *Fletcher* (1841) Russell 417; *Martin* (1832) 5 C & P 128 at 130. See L Hoyano and C Keenan, *Child Abuse: Law and Policy* (2007) 135.

[60] [1957] Crim LR 365; S Bedford, *The Best We Can Do* (1958) 192; P Devlin, *Easing the Passing* (1985); Hart and Honoré, *Causation in the Law*, at 344.

intends to shorten life, that is, he intends to kill. If, as Devlin J held, the doctor has a defence it cannot be because his act has not caused death nor because he did not intend so to do. It seems that the courts now do recognize a special defence for a doctor in these circumstances.[61] In *Airedale NHS Trust v Bland*,[62] Lord Goff referred, *obiter*, to:

the established rule that a doctor may, when caring for a patient who is, for example, dying of cancer, lawfully administer painkilling drugs, despite the fact that he knows that an incidental effect of that application will be to abbreviate the patient's life.

Lord Goff added:

Moreover, where the doctor's treatment of his patient is lawful, the patient's death will be regarded in law as exclusively caused by the injury or disease to which his condition is attributable.

But this is surely a fiction and therefore undesirable. It is not the doctor's *purpose* to kill but the brutal truth is that the doctor has foreseen death as virtually certain and he kills his patient. The ambiguity of the definition of intention in *Woollin*[63] allows the jury flexibility to conclude that the doctor is not a murderer, see Chapter 5 above. If an unqualified and unauthorized person did the same act with the same knowledge he would presumably be guilty of murder. For the doctor the killing is likely to be treated as unintentional or justified.[64]

It is not however permissible, even for a doctor acting in good faith, purposely to kill in order to terminate pain. When painkilling drugs were no longer effective, Dr Cox,[65] in order to end the great suffering of his patient, administered a drug to stop her heart and end her suffering, not by the palliative effect of drugs but by death. He was held guilty of attempted murder (it was no longer possible to prove the actual cause of death). If he had administered a large dose of sedative causing her to lapse into a coma, he would probably have been on the right side of the law – even though that would have shortened life. In *R (Burke) v GMC*,[66] it was noted *obiter* that a doctor would have no defence to a charge of murder if he interrupted life-sustaining treatment in the face of the patient's express wish to be kept alive. The Mental Capacity Act 2005, s 4 deals with the circumstances in which treatment or its withdrawal is in the best interests of the patient. It is stipulated in s 4(5) that where the determination of what is in the best interests of the person relates to life-sustaining treatment, the person making the decision 'must not in considering whether the treatment is in the best interests of the person concerned, be motivated by a desire to bring about his death'.[67]

In *Inglis*[68] the Court of Appeal confirmed that there is no defence of mercy killing in English law. D appealed against her conviction for the attempted murder and murder of her son, V, who

---

[61] cf *R v David Moor*(1999) (Hooper J) discussed by A Arlidge, 'The Trial of Dr. David Moor' [2000] Crim LR 31 and JC Smith, 'A Comment on Moor's Case' [2000] Crim LR 41, above, p 372. See also J Goss, 'Postscript on the Trial of David Moor' [2000] Crim LR 568. The broader issues raised by assisted suicide and euthanasia lie beyond the scope of this work. See, in particular, R Dworkin, *Life's Dominion* (1993); Kennedy and Grubb, *Medical Law*, above, Ch 17; H Briggs, *Euthanasia, Death with Dignity and the Law* (2002); J Glover, *Causing Death and Saving Lives* (1977); S Ost, *An Analytical Study of the Legal, Moral and Ethical Aspects of the Living Phenomenon of Euthanasia* (2003); P Lewis, *Assisted Dying and Legal Change* (2007); M Wilks, 'Medical Treatment at the End of Life: A British Doctor's Perspective' in C Erin and S Ost, *The Criminal Justice System and Health Care* (2007).

[62] [1993] 1 All ER 821 at 868h–j. See also *R (Burke) v GMC* [2006] QB 273 and C Dupre, 'Human Dignity and the Withdrawal of Medical Treatment' (2006) 6 EHRLR 678.

[63] [1999] AC 82.

[64] On the significance of offences and defences in murder, see Duff, *Answering for Crime*, 211–216.

[65] (1992) 12 BLMR 38.

[66] [2006] QB 273.

[67] The Law Commission declined to engage in reform of mercy killings and euthanasia, preferring to see that as part of a free-standing review: LC 304, para 1.6.

[68] [2010] EWCA Crim 2637.

had been seriously injured in an accident and suffered catastrophic head injuries when aged 27. D tried to kill V by injecting him with heroin in his hospital bed. V was resuscitated but suffered substantial deterioration in his condition as a result. D was charged with attempted murder. While on bail she then injected V with a fatal dose of heroin. The court reviewed the current state of the law relating to 'mercy killing'. It was recognized that mercy killing is murder subject to any partial defences that apply.[69] The law does not distinguish between murder committed for malevolent reasons and murder motivated by familial love.[70]

14.1.7 The *mens rea* of murder[71]

14.1.7.1 Malice aforethought

The *mens rea* of murder is traditionally called 'malice aforethought'. This is a technical term and it has a technical meaning quite different from the ordinary popular meaning of the two words. The phrase, it has been truly said, 'is a mere arbitrary symbol... for the "malice" may have in it nothing really malicious; and need never be really "aforethought"'.[72] The House of Lords has confirmed that this means intention.[73] Thus a parent who kills a suffering child out of motives of compassion is 'malicious' for this purpose; and there is sufficient aforethought if an intention to kill is formed only a second before the fatal blow is struck. Neither ill-will nor premeditation[74] is necessary. The concept of premeditation is one which has been considered as an option for reform and wisely rejected. The fact that killing is premeditated is not necessarily an aggravating feature, as for example where an abused spouse plans a killing of her abuser.[75]

The meaning of the term malice aforethought is of the utmost importance, for it is the presence or absence of it which determines whether an unlawful killing is murder or manslaughter. Murder is unlawful homicide with malice aforethought. Manslaughter is an unlawful homicide without malice aforethought.[76]

Malice aforethought is a concept of the common law. It has a long history but, since *Moloney*,[77] it is no longer necessary to explore this in order to expound the modern law. We can now state that it consists in:

(1) an intention to kill any person or,

(2) an intention to cause grievous bodily harm to any person.

---

[69] The Law Commission summary of the law on mercy killing in Ch 7 of its Report No 304 *Murder Manslaughter and Infanticide* (2006) was endorsed as an accurate statement of the law.

[70] The latest statute to address the problem of mercy killing, (Criminal Justice Act 2003, s 269 and Sch 21), presented a problem as it treated precisely the same actions as both aggravating and mitigating factors. Although the statute expressly includes as mitigation for the offence the offender's subjective belief that he or she was acting out of mercy, that belief and motivation, however genuine, does not and cannot constitute any defence to the charge of murder.

[71] See Lord Goff, 'The Mental Element in the Crime of Murder' (1988) 104 LQR 30 and G Williams, 'The *Mens Rea* for Murder: Leave it Alone' (1989) 105 LQR 387. For discussion of the comparative approaches to the fault element in murder, see S Yeo, *Fault in Homicide* (1997), and the extensive discussion in LCCP 177 and LC 304.

[72] Kenny, *Outlines* (15th edn) 153.

[73] *Moloney* [1985] AC 905.

[74] For a suggestion for reform on this basis, see B Mitchell, 'Thinking About Murder' (1992) 56 J Crim L 78. See also the support for such a view derived from the research by Professor Mitchell appended to Law Com Report No 290, *Partial Defences to Murder* (2004). The Law Commission rejected redefinition in these terms in LC 304.

[75] See, generally, M Kremnitzer, 'On Premeditation' (1998) 1 Buffalo Crim LR 627. LCCP 177 rejected the approach on the basis of difficulties of proof. See also J Horder and D Hughes, 'Comparative Issues in the Law of Homicide', in J Horder (ed), *Homicide Law in Comparative Perspectives* (2007).

[76] Per Stephen J in *Doherty* (1887) 16 Cox CC 306 at 307.

[77] [1985] AC 905, [1985] 1 All ER 1025, above, p 107.

'Intention' has the meaning attributed to it in *Woollin*[78] as applied in *Matthews and Alleyne*.[79]

'Grievous bodily harm', at one time broadly interpreted to mean any harm sufficiently serious to interfere with health and comfort, must now be applied in its ordinary natural meaning. 'Grievous' means 'really serious'[80] and the word 'really' probably adds nothing but emphasis to the fact that the harm intended must be (actually or really) serious.[81] The Court of Appeal in *Bollom*[82] confirmed that the words are to be construed as ordinary English words and not assigned a specific legal definition.[83] The evaluation of whether the harm is sufficiently serious is based on the jury's assessment of the harm caused to the particular victim. The age and vulnerability of the victim will therefore be important. It is not a question of whether D thought that the harm he was causing was serious. This can present problems since it may, theoretically, give rise to murder by pinprick if D stabs with a needle V who is a haemophiliac, and the stabbing is judged to have been really serious bodily harm.[84] In its provisional proposals the Law Commission defined the term as 'harm of such a nature as to endanger life or as to cause or be likely to cause permanent or long-term damage to a significant aspect of physical integrity or mental functioning'.[85] The final proposal was to retain the common law position, replacing the word injury for harm.

Although the expression is ambiguous and forms a core element of the definition of such a serious offence carrying a unique sentence and stigma, it has been held, in Northern Ireland at least, to be compatible with the requirement in Art 7 of the ECHR of certainty.[86] There seems little doubt that this view would be followed by the courts in England.

In 1960, in the notorious case of *DPP v Smith*, the House of Lords laid down a largely objective test of liability in murder – the test was 'not what the defendant contemplated, but what the ordinary reasonable man or woman would in all the circumstances of the case have contemplated as the natural and probable result'. In *Hyam*,[87] the House declined to overrule *Smith*, holding that its effect had been modified by s 8 of the Criminal Justice Act 1967; but, in *Frankland and Moore v R*,[88] the Privy Council (comprising five judicial members of the House of Lords), acting on the *dicta* of Lord Diplock in *Hyam*,[89] Lord Bridge in *Moloney*[90] and Lord Scarman in *Hancock*,[91] held that in so far as it laid down an objective test, *Smith* did not represent the common law of England. Though the Privy Council cannot formally overrule a decision of the House of Lords, it can probably be taken, for all practical purposes, that *Smith* is overruled. Section 8 did not, after all, modify the law of murder; and the function of that section in relation to murder, as to all other crimes, is not to define what *mens rea* must

---

[78] [1999] AC 82, [1999] 1 Cr App R 8.

[79] [2003] 2 Cr App R 30, [2003] EWCA Crim 192, above, p 109.

[80] *DPP v Smith* [1961] AC 290 at 334, [1960] 3 All ER 161 at 171.

[81] *Saunders* [1985] Crim LR 230. It is for the judge to decide in each case whether it is necessary to direct the jury that the harm intended must be 'really serious'. Where the act was stabbing with a five-and-half-a-inch knife blade, it was not necessary: *Janjua* [1999] 1 Cr App Rep 91.

[82] [2003] EWCA Crim 2846.

[83] cf other jurisdictions in which definitions based on lethality are used. See LCCP 177, para 3.65 et seq.

[84] See LCCP 177, para 3.81. See also on the issues of this lack of definition: W Wilson, 'Murder and the Structure of Homicide', in B Mitchell and A Ashworth (eds), *Rethinking English Homicide Law* (2000).

[85] LCCP 177, para 3.159.

[86] *Anderson* [2003] NI 12, CA.

[87] [1975] AC 55 at 70–71.

[88] [1987] AC 576.

[89] [1975] AC 55 at 94.

[90] [1985] AC 905 at 921 and 928.

[91] [1986] AC 455 at 473.

be proved, but only *how* the *mens rea* required by the common law or other statutes, is to be proved.

14.1.7.2 Constructive malice

The common law of malice aforethought is now fully stated in the rule requiring an intention to cause death or grievous bodily harm. It is, however, still necessary to refer to s 1 of the Homicide Act 1957 which modified the common law.

(1) Where a person kills in the course or furtherance of some other offence, the killing shall not amount to murder unless done with the same malice aforethought (express or implied) as is required for a killing to amount to murder when not done in the course or furtherance of another offence.

(2) For the purposes of the foregoing subsection, a killing done in the course or for the purpose of resisting an officer of justice, or of resisting or avoiding or preventing a lawful arrest, or of effecting or assisting an escape or rescue from legal custody, shall be treated as a killing in the course of furtherance of another offence.

The purpose of this section was, as the side-note in the statute indicates, to limit malice aforethought by the 'abolition of "constructive malice"'. This took two forms: (i) it was murder to kill in the course or furtherance of a violent felony (or possibly any felony) so that an intention to commit the felony (for example, rape or robbery) was a sufficient *mens rea* where death resulted;[92] (ii) it was murder to kill while attempting to prevent lawful arrest or bring about escape from lawful arrest or custody, so that an intention to do these things was also malice aforethought where the act caused death. Section 1(1) abolishes the first, and s 1(2) the second form of constructive malice. While eliminating constructive malice, the section leaves in existence 'express' and 'implied' malice. Although these terms have been used for centuries, their meaning is obscure and they certainly do not have any ordinary natural meaning.[93] In the light of the common law, as we know it to be, 'express malice' must be taken to mean the intention to kill and 'implied malice' the intention to cause grievous bodily harm. Though the terms remain on the 'statute book', there is in practice no need to use them and the sooner they are buried the better.

It was at one time argued that s 1 also abolished intention to cause grievous bodily harm as a head of malice aforethought – an argument which required some other meaning to be given to 'implied malice' since that is expressly preserved.[94] In *Cunningham*,[95] the House confirmed that intention to cause grievous bodily harm survived the Homicide Act as a head of *mens rea*.[96]

Recently Lords Mustill and Steyn have criticized the rule that an intention to cause serious bodily harm is a sufficient *mens rea* for murder as a 'conspicuous anomaly' and an example of

---

[92] This form of murder exists in some US states and in former British colonies, see, eg, *Griffith* [2004] UKPC 58 (Barbados) and *Foster* [2007] UKPC 20. See generally C Finkelstein, 'Merger and Felony Murder', in Duff and Green (eds), *Defining Crimes.*

[93] See Lord Hailsham in *Cunningham* [1982] AC 566, [1981] 2 All ER 863 at 867.

[94] The argument was that the only reason why intention to cause grievous bodily harm was malice aforethought before 1957 was that in 1803 Lord Ellenborough's Act created a felony of causing grievous bodily harm with intent to do so. If death resulted, that was murder because, and only because, the killing was in the course or furtherance of that felony. The argument was rejected in *Vickers*[1957] 2 QB 664 (a court of five judges). As the LCCP 177 discusses at para 1.119, the LCJ in that case took a different approach to that which only a short time before he had assured Parliament he would take in such a case. Parliament had therefore enacted the 1957 Act on a misunderstanding as to the law. Lords Diplock and Kilbrandon accepted the argument in *Hyam* but the matter was left open because Lord Cross was not prepared to decide between the conflicting views.

[95] [1982] AC 566.

[96] It ante-dated Lord Ellenborough's Act as a form of malice aforethought, distinct from constructive malice.

a 'constructive crime'.[97] Lord Steyn spoke of the result of the present definition being defendants 'classified as murderers who are not in truth murderers'.[98] The grievous bodily harm rule has been defended by some academic commentators, either as reflecting a general principle that the law imposes an obligation on an attacker to take the unforeseen consequences of his actions,[99] or as an appropriate response in cases of death caused by an 'attack'.[100]

The House of Lords missed its opportunity in *Cunningham* to rid the law of the anomaly by requiring at least awareness of the risk of causing death. It seems unlikely that the Supreme Court will go to the lengths of overruling decisions in this area. The House of Lords endorsed the current gbh rule in *Rahman*.[101]

14.1.8 The relationship between murder and manslaughter at trial

Murder and manslaughter share a common *actus reus*. What distinguishes them is the *mens rea*. One important and complex practical issue that arises is whether in every murder trial it is desirable or necessary to include manslaughter as an alternative count in case the jury cannot agree on murder.[102] In *Coutts*,[103] C was charged with murder, and claimed that he had engaged in an act of consensual sex involving asphyxiation, and that V's death was an accident. The prosecution claimed it was a straightforward intentional killing. C claimed it was an accident. Both the prosecution and defence took the view that it would be undesirable to direct the jury on manslaughter: it would be likely to provide an opportunity for a compromise verdict which did not reflect the case as put or defended. The trial judge did not direct the jury on manslaughter, and C was convicted. His appeal was allowed by the House of Lords. The manslaughter count ought to be left to the jury.

In some cases where the defence case includes partial defences such as loss of control and/or diminished responsibility, coupled with denials of *mens rea,* even if the jury return a manslaughter verdict there will often be difficulty in deciphering on what basis this was reached.[104]

14.2 The sentence for murder

Until the Homicide Act 1957,[105] all persons convicted of murder were automatically sentenced to death. By s 5 of that Act certain types of murder were singled out and designated 'capital murder'. These continued to be punishable by death, while the remaining types of murder were punishable by imprisonment for life. In effect there were two degrees of murder.

---

[97] *A-G's Reference (No 3 of 1994)* [1998] AC 245, [1998] 1 Cr App R 91, 93, HL; *Powell and Daniels* and *English* [1999] AC 1, [1998] 1 Cr App R 261 at 267–268, and *Woollin* [1999] 1 AC 82, [1999] 1 Cr App R 8 at 13.

[98] ibid. cf Scots law and the requirement of wicked recklessness.

[99] J Horder, 'Two Histories and Four Hidden Principles of *Mens Rea*' (1997) 113 LQR 9.

[100] W Wilson, 'Murder and the Structure of Homicide', in Ashworth and Mitchell (eds), *Rethinking English Homicide Law.*

[101] *Rahman* [2008] UKHL 45 see above Ch 8.

[102] Murder is excluded from the general rule on alternative verdicts laid down in the Criminal Law Act 1967, s 6(3).

[103] [2006] 1 WLR 2154. cf *Foster* [2007] EWCA Crim 2869. Judges are encouraged to give written directions to juries.

[104] See also B Mitchell, 'Distinguishing Between Murder and Manslaughter in Practice' (2007) 71 J Crim L 318.

[105] See M Wasik, 'Sentencing in Homicide', in Ashworth and Mitchell (eds), *Rethinking English Homicide Law,* 167.

The distinction between the two degrees of murder proved to be most unsatisfactory, and the death penalty for murder was suspended by the Murder (Abolition of Death Penalty) Act 1965.[106] All persons convicted of murder must now be sentenced to imprisonment for life. The mandatory sentence was at that time unique in English law and the CLRC considered whether or not the judge should have discretion as in all other crimes. They were deeply and almost evenly divided on the issue. Their Report[107] set out the arguments on both sides in some detail but made no recommendation.

Subsequently the matter was considered by a Select Committee of the House of Lords (the Nathan Committee) which recommended, with one dissentient, that the mandatory sentence be abolished. Murder should be punishable with a maximum sentence of life but the judge should have the same discretion to impose lesser sentences as he has for other crimes.[108] The arguments in favour of this approach are overwhelming. Murders vary as greatly in their gravity and murderers in their dangerousness, as for any other crime. The recommendation has not, however, found favour with the Government, despite public opposition to the mandatory sentence,[109] and there seems to be no prospect of its implementation at the present time.

On sentencing a murderer, formerly the judge would make a recommendation to the Home Secretary of the minimum period which should elapse before the prisoner is released on licence.[110] That power was successfully challenged as incompatible with Arts 5 and 6 of the ECHR since the Minister was not an independent and impartial arbiter of the term of imprisonment.[111] (The mandatory sentence itself has been held not to be incompatible with Arts 3 and 5 of the ECHR.)[112]

The Criminal Justice Act 2003 imposed a new regime for the sentencing and procedure for release of those sentenced to life imprisonment.[113] Under Sch 21 to the Criminal Justice Act 2003 the judge must determine the length of the minimum term which will be served by the offender before he is eligible to be considered for release on licence. There are three starting points for adult offenders. First, a whole life term (that is, where the offender will serve the rest of his life in prison). This is reserved for those exceptionally serious cases, such as premeditated killings of two or more people, sexual or sadistic child murders or politically motivated murders. The second starting point is a 30-year minimum tariff for serious cases such as murders of police or prison officers, murders involving firearms, sexual or sadistic killings or killings aggravated by racial or sexual orientation. The final category is a 15-year minimum starting point for murders not falling within the two higher categories. In the latter two categories the judge will have the opportunity to take into account aggravating and mitigating features: the starting points of 30 and 15 years are just that.[114]

---

[106] This, by virtue of affirmative resolutions of both Houses of Parliament on 16 and 18 Dec 1969, was to be permanently in force. See L Blom-Cooper, 'Life Until Death' [1999] Crim LR 899.

[107] Fourteenth Report, para 19.27.

[108] HL Paper 78–I, (1989). See A Ashworth, 'Reform of the Law of Murder' [1990] Crim LR 75.

[109] See recently B Mitchell and J Roberts, *Public Opinion and Sentencing for Murder: An Empirical Investigation of Public Knowledge and Attitudes in England and Wales* (2010).

[110] See the review of the process over the last 50 years – S Shute, 'Punishing Murderers: Release Procedures and the "Tariff"' [2004] Crim LR 873.

[111] *R v Home Secretary, ex p Anderson* [2002] UKHL 46; *Stafford v United Kingdom* [2002] 35 EHRR 121.

[112] *Pyrah* [2003] 1 AC 903, [2003] 1 Cr App R 33.

[113] See *Practice Direction (Crime: Mandatory Life Sentence)* [2004] 1 WLR 1874; *Practice Direction (Crime: Mandatory Life Sentence) No 2* [2004] WLR 2551; and Criminal Justice Act 2003, s 269 et seq. For academic comment, see N Padfield, 'Tariffs in Murder' [2002] Crim LR 192.

[114] On public attitudes and expectations in sentencing of murder, see B Mitchell, in LCCP 177, Appendix A. Sch 21 has affected other sentencing policy: D Jeremy, 'Sentencing Policy of Short Term Expediency' [2010] Crim LR 593.

14.3 Proposals for reform

Given the seriousness involved in the offence,[115] the sanctity of life, the unique stigma and the mandatory sentence it is surprising that the offence remains so ill-defined in so many respects. Three main areas have been the subject of sustained criticism and focus for reform proposals. First, there is the ambiguity over the definition of the concept of intention (as examined in Chapter 5). This increases the opportunity for inconsistency in application and generates uncertainty in the law. Secondly, there is the grievous bodily harm rule which, in creating a constructive crime, carries with it all of the criticisms normally levelled at such offences for a failure to respect principles of fair labelling and correspondence between *actus reus* and *mens rea*.[116] Thirdly, there is the sustained and cogent criticism of the mandatory sentence.[117] It is often assumed that the mandatory sentence is retained to reflect the will of the populus, but research does not always bear out such a conclusion.[118]

Although the Government has been content to add, piecemeal, to the stock of homicide offences over the last century (see the infanticide offence, causing death by dangerous driving, the offence under s 5 of the Domestic Violence, Crime and Victims Act 2004, corporate manslaughter,[119] causing death by driving while uninsured, etc[120]), over the last 50 years it has avoided the reform of the most serious offence of them all – murder. Numerous reform proposals have been advanced, only a brief outline of which can be discussed here.

14.3.1 Abolishing murder and manslaughter?

One unlikely way forward, which was rejected by the Law Commission in its 2006 Report would be to replace murder and manslaughter with a single offence of unlawful killing in which the sentence is at the discretion of the trial judge (within guidelines). This view had some academic[121] and judicial support (from Lord Kilbrandon in *Hyam*) but was rejected by the CLRC.[122] Since this would remove the specific label and uniqueness that attaches to it, the option is unlikely ever to find much general support.[123] It is an unrealistic prospect in political terms,[124] but it has the merit of simplicity.

[115] See LCCP 177, Appendix G on the background information about murder.

[116] As regards labelling, Lord Steyn cited above, n 98 that people are labelled murderers who are in truth not such. As for correspondence, the *mens rea* of intent to do gbh does not correspond with the *actus reus* – death. See, in particular, B Mitchell, 'In Defence of the Correspondence Principle' [1999] Crim LR 195; J Horder, 'A Critique of the Correspondence Principle in Criminal Law' [1995] Crim LR 759. See also N Lacey, 'Partial Defences to Homicide', in Ashworth and Mitchell, *Rethinking English Criminal Law*, Ch 5. Some might argue that there is no difficulty in holding D liable in a gbh case because his act of intentional gbh is an attack on V which shows sufficient culpability by its practical indifference for V's life. See Duff, *Answering for Crime*, 253–255

[117] See, generally, B Mitchell, *Murder and Penal Policy* (1990).

[118] See the reports of Professor Mitchell's research as appended to Law Com Report No 290, revealing that 62.9% of the population surveyed thought that there ought *not* to be a mandatory sentence. cf the findings in the LCCP 177, Appendix A.

[119] Corporate Manslaughter and Corporate Homicide Act 2007.

[120] See the Road Safety Act 2006.

[121] See L Blom-Cooper and T Morris, *With Malice Aforethought: A Study of the Crime and Punishment for Homicide* (2004).

[122] In its Fourteenth Report on *Offences Against the Person* (1980). See R Buxton, 'The New Murder' [1980] Crim LR 521.

[123] For fascinating studies into the public perceptions of the scope of the offence, see B Mitchell, 'Public Perceptions of Homicide and Criminal Justice' (1998) 38 Brit J Crim 453 and 'Further Evidence of the Relationship Between Legal and Public Opinion on the Homicide Law' [2000] Crim LR 814.

[124] See J Horder and D Hughes, 'Comparative Issues in the Law of Homicide', in Horder (ed), *Homicide Law in Comparative Perspectives*, 7. See also B Mitchell (2007) 71 J Crim L 318 recognizing that it would devalue the enormity of the worst cases.

14.3.2 A victim-specific model?

A second model which has found little support would be to reform the law with a hierarchy of forms of homicide turning on categories of victim. The most serious form of homicide would, under such a model, be applicable to those who kill children or the elderly or police officers, etc. This would, it is submitted, be an unsatisfactory reform.

14.3.3 Law Commission Consultation Paper 177

The Law Commission's provisional proposals in LCCP 177[125] were to create a new ladder of homicide offences in a hierarchical structure respecting the correspondence principle. This follows the model adopted in many other jurisdictions where the seriousness of the wrong-doing is reflected in a graduated scheme of offences.[126] The proposals were for a crime of first degree murder which would carry the mandatory life penalty. This would be restricted to cases of intentional killing. Second degree murder would be a wholly new form of offence and would be much broader with a discretionary life maximum penalty. Second degree murder would include killing where D did not intend to kill but did intend to do serious harm, and 'recklessly indifferent' killing, where D realized that his or her conduct involved an unjustified risk of killing, but pressed on with that conduct without caring whether or not death would result. Second degree murder would also encompass the partial defences to what would otherwise be 'first degree murder'. Below second degree murder would lie an offence of manslaughter capable of commission in one of two ways: by gross negligence; or through an intentional act intended to cause injury or involving recklessness as to causing injury. Both would carry a discretionary life sentence.

The Commission carried out extensive reviews of public perceptions of the offence of murder and the approach taken in other jurisdictions.[127]

14.3.4 Law Commission Report No 304

In its final recommendations in Report No 304,[128] the Law Commission made some significant changes. Most significantly, the Law Commission extended the proposed offence of first degree murder (which would still carry a mandatory life penalty). This offence would, under the final proposal, include both: (a) killing intentionally, and (b) killing where there was an intention to do serious injury, coupled with an awareness of a serious risk of causing death.

Second degree murder (which would carry a discretionary life maximum penalty) would include: (a) killing where D intended to do serious injury; (b) killing where D intended to cause some injury or a fear or risk of injury, and was aware of a serious risk of causing death as well as (c) killing in which there is a partial defence (loss of self-control (gross provocation or fear of serious violence); diminished responsibility; participation in a suicide pact) to what would otherwise be first degree murder.

---

[125] On the Commission's proposals see: W Wilson, 'The Structure of Criminal Homicide' [2006] Crim LR 471; A Norrie, 'Between Orthodox Subjectivism and Moral Contextualism: Intention and the Consultation Paper' [2006] Crim LR 486; C Wells and O Quick, 'Getting Tough with Defences' [2006] Crim LR 514; V Tadros, 'The Homicide Ladder' (2006) 69 MLR 601–618; J Rogers, 'The Law Commission's Proposed Restructuring of Homicide' (2006) 70 J Crim Law 223.

[126] See J Horder, 'The Changing Face of the Law of Homicide', in Horder (ed), *Homicide Law in Comparative Perspectives*.

[127] See also Horder, above, n 126.

[128] See A Ashworth, 'Principles, Pragmatism and the Law Commission's Recommendations on Homicide Law Reform' [2007] Crim LR 333; R Taylor 'The Nature of "Partial Defences" and the Coherence of (Second Degree) Murder' [2007] Crim LR 345.

Manslaughter (also carrying a discretionary life maximum penalty) would include: (a) killing through gross negligence as to a risk of causing death; and (b) killing through a criminal act which is (i) intended to cause injury; or (ii) where there was an awareness that the act involved a serious risk of causing injury.[129] These provisions relating to manslaughter are considered in the following chapter.

Special provision was also made for an offence of participating in a joint criminal venture in the course of which another participant commits first or second degree murder. This would be an offence of manslaughter where the circumstances are such that it should have been obvious that first or second degree murder might be committed by another participant.

The Government has now decided it will not act upon these proposals from the Law Commission.

[129] See LC 304 (2006) para 1.67.

15
Manslaughter

At common law, all unlawful homicides which are not murder are manslaughter. The offence has a broad scope, being limited by murder at one extreme and accidental killing at the other. There is an increasing number of statutory offences of unlawful killing including, for example, causing death by dangerous driving and corporate manslaughter.[1] Some of these statutory offences preclude prosecution for manslaughter (notably corporate manslaughter) but in most cases manslaughter remains available as an alternative charge to the specific statutory offences.[2]

It is customary and useful to divide manslaughter into two main groups: 'voluntary' and 'involuntary' manslaughter. The distinction is based on D's intention at the time of the killing. Where there is no intention to kill or cause grievous bodily harm the offence falls within the category of involuntary manslaughter. In contrast, voluntary manslaughter comprises cases where D had the intention to kill or do grievous bodily harm but some defined mitigating circumstance – loss of self-control, diminished responsibility or killing in pursuance of a suicide pact – reduces his crime to the less serious grade of criminal homicide.[3] These partial defences to murder were originally introduced to avoid the death penalty. Today they subsist unsatisfactorily in order to avoid the mandatory life sentence for murder. The partial defences to murder were radically overhauled in the Coroners and Justice Act 2009. The account that follows focuses on the new law in force since October 2010.[4]

Three partial defences to murder exist:

(i) where D kills with the *mens rea* for murder but he has lost his self-control and one of the statutory qualifying triggers is satisfied (governed by ss 54–56 of the Coroners and Justice Act 2009);

(ii) where D kills with the *mens rea* for murder but he was suffering from diminished responsibility (under s 52 of the 2009 Act);

(iii) where D kills in pursuance of a suicide pact.[5] The problem of the suicide pact is looked at in the next chapter alongside the statutory crime of assisting or encouraging suicide.[6]

---

[1] These offences, their theoretical implications and the relationship with 'normal' manslaughter are considered in the valuable collection of essays edited by C Clarkson and S Cunningham (eds), *Criminal Liability for Non-Aggressive Death* (2008); see, in particular, A Ashworth, 'Manslaughter Generic or Nominate Offences' in that volume.

[2] See also V Tadros, 'The Limits of Manslaughter', in Clarkson and Cunningham, *Criminal Liability for Non-Aggressive Death* (2008), who argues that the special offences discriminate and fail to optimize coherence in the law; see also Tadros, *Criminal Responsibility,* 348 et seq.

[3] *A-G of Ceylon v Perera* [1953] AC 200, PC; *Lee Chun Chuen v R* [1963] AC 220; *Parker v R* [1964] AC 1369, *Smith (Clean) v R* [2002] 1 Cr App R 92; contra, per Viscount Simon in *Holmes v DPP* [1946] AC 588 at 598, HL.

[4] For analysis of the defences of provocation and diminished responsibility under the law before the Coroners and Justice Act 2009, see the previous edition Ch 15.

[5] Section 4, below.

[6] Below, p 583.

15.1 Loss of self-control

15.1.1 Provocation

The common law had recognized a defence of provocation for centuries.[7] The common law defence reduced murder to manslaughter where D killed with *mens rea* for murder, provided at the time of the killing he had been subjected to:

some act, or series of acts, done by the dead man to the accused, which would cause in any reasonable man, and actually causes in the accused, a sudden and temporary loss of self-control, rendering the accused so subject to passion as to make him or her for the moment not master of his mind.[8]

That common law rule was modified (but not codified) by the Homicide Act 1957, s 3. The elements of that defence were that if, when D killed, he had *mens rea* for murder he would be guilty of manslaughter if:

(i) things said or done provoked him, and

(ii) he suffered a sudden and temporary loss of self-control, and

(iii) the provocation was enough to make a reasonable man do as D did (with the reasonable man sharing those of D's characteristics that would affect the gravity of the provocation but not those which affected his ability to exercise self-control).

The defence was extremely controversial.[9] Courts faced increasing difficulty with its application, exacerbated by the House of Lords attempts to do justice in hard cases made harder still by the mandatory sentence for murder. There were disagreements as to the terms of the defence,[10] with numerous high profile appeals including several in recent decades to the House of Lords and Privy Council in which majority and plurality judgments added to the confusion. The core disagreement centred on whether, when addressing the question whether a reasonable person would have done as D did, the jury were to have regard to D's personal characteristics, and if so, which. The appellate courts failed to adopt a consistent approach, in some cases taking an objective view, but in others concluding that the jury ought to take a subjectivist view taking into account D's characteristics. For the appellate courts to fluctuate so often and so significantly on the interpretation of a defence in cases of such seriousness led to confusion and presented a disappointing spectacle.

Even the theoretical foundation for the defence remained unclear: was the defence properly regarded as one of partial justification (D has gone beyond what would be an acceptable response to the provoking conduct, or that the deceased deserved it) or of partial excuse (D's loss of self-control was uncharacteristic, the bad character exhibited exceeds that to be expected in the circumstances)?[11]

---

[7] For a comprehensive academic review of the theoretical issues and the historical context of the defence, see J Horder, *Provocation and Responsibility* (1992). See also JM Kaye, 'Early History of Murder and Manslaughter' (1967) 83 LQR 365.

[8] *Duffy* [1949] 1 All ER 932n. On this case see S Edwards 'Justice Devlin's Legacy' [2009] Crim LR 851.

[9] There is a wealth of literature on the topic. The Law Commission's Report No 290, *Partial Defences to Murder* (2004) (hereafter LC 290) is a valuable starting point. The Law Commission documents leading to the new Act also include valuable discussion –see Law Com, Consultation Paper No 177, *A New Homicide Act for England* (2005) (hereafter in this chapter LCCP 177) and Law Com Report No 304, *Murder, Manslaughter and Infanticide* (hereafter in this chapter LC 304). Valuable articles and essays include the seminal piece by A Ashworth, 'The Doctrine of Provocation' [1976] CLJ 292.

[10] See LCCP 177, para 2.78.

[11] Horder, *Provocation and Responsibility*, Chs 6–9, in particular at 130–135. See further, J Dressler, 'Provocation: Partial Justification or Partial Excuse' (1988) 51 MLR 467; F McAuley, 'Anticipating the Past: The

One of the most powerful influences for reform was the claim that the defence operated in a discriminatory fashion, which given its historical origins is hardly surprising.[12] Women who killed abusive partners were disadvantaged if they did not act in a state which could legally be described as one of 'sudden and temporary loss of control'.[13] In addition, until relatively recently, the cumulative effect of years of abuse was not considered. Further, the mental characteristics arising from an abusive relationship (including what some recognize as battered woman syndrome)[14] could only be taken into account if that was relevant to the gravity of the provocation (ie the sting of the words or conduct that provoked D), but not to D's ability to exercise her self-control.[15] The abused woman is unlikely as a matter of fact, to kill in self-defence (as that term is understood in law). Owing to relative limited physical strength, it is uncommon for women to respond lethally when facing an attack by an abusive male partner.[16] Women charged with murder were forced to rely on diminished responsibility, which aside from requiring expert evidence and imposing a burden of proof on the accused, stigmatized them as mentally abnormal.

A further general difficulty with the defence was its relationship with the partial defence of diminished responsibility. The elements were very different, with different burdens of proof, but they overlapped in many cases.[17]

These serious problems with the provocation defence prompted reform. Law Commission papers examined numerous options for reform including whether it was even necessary or desirable to retain the defence if the mandatory sentence were to be abolished.[18] Fundamental questions included whether the purpose of the defence was to unshackle the judge from imposing the mandatory sentence[19] or to label more distinctly those killers whose conduct might be regarded as morally different, despite their malice aforethought, owing to some mitigating feature of the killing. The unique stigmas and heightened emotions aroused by the stark fact of death in a murder case generate strong views on these issues. Many other jurisdictions have faced similar difficulties where defence and reform proposals have been widely canvassed.[20]

Defences of Provocation in Irish Law' (1987) 50 MLR 133; V Tadros, 'The Characters of Excuses' (2001) 21 OJLS 495. See also the discussion in LC 290, para 3.22 et seq and the Irish Law Reform Commission, LRC Consultation Paper No 27, *Homicide: The Plea of Provocation* (2003).

[12] See Horder, *Provocation and Responsibility, above.*

[13] S Edwards, *Sex and Gender in the Legal Process* (1996) Ch 6; O'Donovan (1991) 18 J Law & Soc 219; C Wells (1994) 14 LS 266; A McColgan, 'In Defence of Battered Women who Kill' (1993) 13 OJLS 508. For a valuable summary see LCCP 173, Ch 10.

[14] See L Walker, *Battered Women Syndrome* (1st edn, 1984); (3rd edn, 2008).

[15] See C Wells, 'Provocation: the Case for Abolition', in A Ashworth and B Mitchell (eds), *Rethinking English Homicide Law* (2000).

[16] On the availability of the defence, see A McColgan (1993) 13 OJLS 508; C Wells (1994) 14 LS 266; J Dressler, 'Battered Women Who Kill Their Sleeping Tormentors' and J Horder, 'Killing the Passive Abuser: A Theoretical Defence', both in S Shute and A Simester (eds), *Criminal Law Theory* (2002).

[17] There were calls to merge the defences in something similar to that in the US Model Penal Code, s 210(3)(1)(b). See also Law Com 304, para 5.22. On the merits of such overlap and a potential merging of the defences, see R Mackay and B Mitchell, 'Provoking Diminished Responsibility: Two Pleas Merging into One?' [2003] Crim LR 745; J Chalmers, 'Merging Provocation and Diminished Responsibility: Some Reasons for Scepticism' [2004] Crim LR 198; J Gardner and T Macklem, 'No Provocation Without Responsibility: A Reply to Mackay and Mitchell' [2004] Crim LR 213; R Mackay and B Mitchell, 'Replacing Provocation: More on a Combined Plea' [2004] Crim LR 219. See also R Holton and S Shute, 'Self Control in Modern Provocation Defence' (2007) 27 OJLS 49.

[18] See LC 290, Ch 2 and para 3.35 et seq and the responses discussed to the Consultation Paper No 173. Horder considers the arguments for abolition in *Provocation and Responsibility*, Ch 9.

[19] See C Wells, 'The Death Penalty for Provocation' [1978] Crim LR 662.

[20] See, eg, New South Wales Law Reform Commission, *Partial Defences to Murder: Provocation and Infanticide* (1997) No 83; Irish Law Reform Commission, LRC Consultation Paper No 27 (2003), above, n 11, and Law Com Paper

15.1.2 The new law[21]

By s 56 of the Coroners and Justice Act 2009 the common law defence of provocation is abolished and replaced by a new defence in ss 54 and 55. The provisions derive from the Law Commission Report No 304[22] and earlier Law Commission Reports[23] and papers. Since the enacted provisions differ in important respects from the proposal put forward by the Law Commission, care is needed in relying on these documents as a source for interpretation.[24]

Sections 54 and 55 replace the common law defence with a related but significantly different defence labelled 'loss of control' (in this chapter ('LOSC'). This is designed to be a much narrower defence than at common law and under s 3 of the 1957 Act. Section 54 provides:

> (1) Where a person ('D') kills or is a party to the killing of another ('V'), D is not to be convicted of murder if –
>
>   (a) D's acts and omissions in doing or being a party to the killing resulted from D's loss of self-control,
>
>   (b) the loss of self-control had a qualifying trigger, and
>
>   (c) a person of D's sex and age, with a normal degree of tolerance and self restraint and in the circumstances of D, might have reacted in the same or in a similar way to D ...
>
> (7) A person who, but for this section, would be liable to be convicted of murder is liable instead to be convicted of manslaughter.

The LOSC defence is further defined in s 55. It comprises three main elements. In short, there must be:

1. A loss of self-control (not necessarily sudden),

2. D's loss of control must have been attributable to one or both of two specified 'qualifying triggers':

   (i) D's fear of serious violence from V against D or another identified person

   and/or

   (ii) things done or said (or both) which

      (a) constitute circumstances of an extremely grave character, and

      (b) cause D to have a justifiable sense of being seriously wronged.

3. A person of D's sex and age, with a normal degree of tolerance and self-restraint and in the circumstances of D, might have reacted in the same or in a similar way to D.

No 173 for a valuable summary of the position in a number of jurisdictions. For comparative material generally, see S Yeo, *Unrestrained Killings and the Law: Provocation and Excessive Self Defence in India, England and Australia* (1998). See also eg the proposals in Victoria, Victoria Law Reform Commission, 'Law Reform Defences to Murder' [2005] Crim LR 256.

[21] See on the new law: A Norrie, 'Loss of Control – The Coroners and Justice Act 2009 – Partial Defences to Murder' [2010] Crim LR 275; R Fortson and A Keene, *Current Law Statutes Annotation* (2010); J Glasson and J Knowles, *Blackstone's Guide to the Coroners and Justice Act 2009* (2010), Ch 8. L Leigh, 'Two New Partial Defences to Murder' (2010) 53 Criminal Law and Justice Weekly 53; S Edwards, 'Anger and Fear as Justifiable Preludes for Loss of Self Control' (2010) 74 J Crim L 223; C Withey [2011] Crim LR 263.

[22] *Murder Manslaughter and Infanticide* (2006)

[23] No 290 – *Partial Defences to Murder* (2004) See also Law Commission Consultation Paper No 173 (2003) and Law Commission Consultation Paper No 177: *A New Homicide Act for England and Wales?* (2005).

[24] The Law Commission proposal had no loss of control requirement nor did it exclude reliance on sexual infidelity as a sufficient trigger, see below for discussion.

15.1.2.1 Commencement

Sections 54–56 were brought into force on 4 October 2010.[25] Since the provisions relate exclusively to a matter of substantive law, they will apply in relation to any murder which occurred after that date.[26] The new law will only apply if both D's act and V's death occurred after 4 October.[27]

15.1.2.2 The defence applies only to murder

The LOSC defence is available only to a charge of murder whether as a principal or secondary party.[28] Loss of self-control is not a defence to a charge of attempted murder or any charge other than murder. The defence should, it is submitted, have no relevance to the determination of whether D committed the acts or omissions[29] causing death when he has been found unfit to plead under s 4A of the Criminal Procedure (Insanity) Act 1964.[30]

15.1.2.3 Procedure

One of the problems with the provocation defence was that judges were obliged to leave the defence to the jury in every case in which there was some evidence of provocation even if the defence was not pleaded by D (and even if it ran counter to D's interests[31]). The LOSC defence need not be left in every case: s 54(6). Under that section the defence must be left only if 'sufficient evidence is adduced to raise an issue with respect to the defence' and this is when 'evidence is adduced on which, in the opinion of the trial judge, a jury, properly directed, could reasonably conclude that the defence might apply'. Trial judges will be likely to leave the new defence to the jury where the evidence given in the case is capable of satisfying the test in s 54(6) even if the defence have not, for tactical or other reasons, sought to rely on loss of control as a defence.

Sufficient evidence of LOSC may appear in the case presented by the Crown. If not, there is an evidential burden on D.[32] If no evidence is adduced by the Crown or D that D lost his

---

[25] The Coroners and Justice Act 2009 (Commencement No 4, Transitional and Saving Provisions) Order 2010, SI 2010 No 816.

[26] For some considerable time after 4 October 2010 many homicide trials will relate to offences alleged to have been committed 'wholly or partly' before that date: see Sch 22, para 7 of the Coroners and Justice Act 2009.

[27] Para 7 of Sch 22 to the 2009 Act provides, as follows: (1) No provision of Chapter 1 of Part 2 affects the operation of – (a) any rule of the common law, or (b) any provision of an Act or of subordinate legislation, in relation to offences committed wholly or partly before the commencement of the provision in question. (2) For the purposes of this paragraph an offence is partly committed before a particular time if – (a) a relevant event occurs before that time, and (b) another relevant event occurs at or after that time. (3) 'Relevant event' in relation to an offence means any act, omission or other event (including *any consequence of an act) proof of which is required for conviction of the offence.*

[28] Section 54(8), 'The fact that one party to a killing is by virtue of this section not liable to be convicted of murder does not affect the question whether the killing amounted to murder in the case of any other party to it.' This follows the position in relation to provocation: *Marks* [1998] Crim LR 676. It has been suggested that provocation (and diminished responsibility) should be available to all offences – J Horder, *Excusing Crime* (2003) 143–146.

[29] It is possible to have an omission causing death and plead LOSC as where D is so angry by his wife's perpetual taunts that he refuses to help her when she has fallen down the stairs and is critically injured. He leaves her to die despite having a duty to assist.

[30] That was the position with the defence of provocation: *Grant* [2001] EWCA Crim 2611, [2002] QB 1030.

[31] For example, if D was claiming that he killed V in self-defence and remained in control of his temper, if there was evidence of provocation and loss of self-control the provocation defence would be left to the jury even though that would undermine the defendant's plea of self-defence: *Bullard v R* [1957] AC 635; *Rolle v R* [1965] 3 All ER 582; *Lee Chun-Chuen v R* [1963] AC 220. In an interesting article based on empirical work B Mitchell, 'Distinguishing Between Murder and Manslaughter in Practice' (2006) 71 JCL 318, reveals that 75 per cent of provocation pleas are accompanied by one or more other defence. Difficulties are created for the judge where a jury returns a verdict in these cases.

[32] It is submitted that as under the s 3, defence mixed statements could be relied on: *Jama* [2004] EWCA Crim 960. Care will need to be taken with reliance on D's lies: *Davies* [2004] EWCA Crim 1914.

self-control, then the judge will withdraw the defence from the jury. Since the burden of proof is on the Crown, evidence which might leave a reasonable jury in reasonable doubt whether or not D lost his self-control is sufficient. There must be evidence of loss of self-control and of a qualifying trigger, mere speculation will not suffice.[33] On a murder charge, in deciding whether D intended death or grievous bodily harm, the jury must consider evidence of LOSC with all other relevant evidence.[34] If they are not satisfied that D had the necessary *mens rea*, they must acquit. But even if they decide he did have *mens rea*, LOSC may still be a defence, entitling D to be convicted of manslaughter.

15.1.2.4 No considered desire for revenge

The defence cannot apply where there is 'a considered desire for revenge' (s 54(4)) even if D lost control as a result of a qualifying trigger. This is a very important qualification and in many cases will be worth considering before any other element of the defence. The restriction must also be seen in combination with the requirement in s 55(6)(a): even if D has lost his self-control, if D's loss of control was caused by a thing which D incited to be done or said for the purpose of providing an excuse to use violence, the qualifying triggers are not available.

The law has long struggled to distinguish revenge killings, of a premeditated or calculated nature, from killings committed in the heat of the moment for which the partial defence is available. Under the old law the requirement of the sudden loss of self-control in the provocation defence was a mechanism for drawing this distinction. It provided rather an imperfect tool for doing so. In *Duffy* it was said that:[35]

circumstances which induce a desire for revenge are inconsistent with provocation, since the conscious formulation of a desire for revenge means that a person has had time to think, to reflect, and that would negative a sudden temporary loss of self-control, which is of the essence of provocation.

The Law Commission's reform proposal did not include any requirement for a loss of self-control, but did propose an explicit safeguard against the defence being used for revenge killings. The Commission recognized that in many cases a person would be acting with mixed motives (eg in a so-called 'honour' killing). The Law Commission proposals posed a complex test requiring a decision whether the killing was in fear and/or anger (defence) or motivated by a considered desire for revenge (no defence). The Commission was nevertheless confident that:

in many mixed motive cases the judge might take the view that, even if there is no 'considered desire for revenge', it is nonetheless a case where [for other reasons] no reasonable jury would find that the defence applies. We regard it as significant that of the provocation cases studied... in the two involving honour killing both the accused were convicted of murder. We are confident that the result would be no different under our recommendations.

With the section as enacted, including a requirement for D to have lost self-control, the position is even more complex. The judge is required to identify whether there was a 'considered desire for revenge' bearing in mind that D must have lost control and be acting in fear and/or anger. Aside from the theoretical incoherence which results from the insertion of a loss of self-control element (see below), the dual existence of a loss of self-control element and a restriction on considered revenge killings may generate problems in practice. It is easy to see how an abused spouse who kills after years of torment might be described as having both motives.

---

[33] See in relation to provocation: *Miao* [2003] EWCA Crim 3486; *Van Dongen* [2005] EWCA Crim 1728.

[34] Section 8 of the Criminal Justice Act 1967, above, p 144. Applied in relation to provocation in *Ives* [1970] 1 QB 208, [1969] 3 All ER 470.

[35] [1949] 1 All ER 932n.

The judge and jury will have a difficult task and the word 'considered' which suggests that there is some element of premeditation, is likely to be significant, but is unfortunately undefined.[36]

It is important to note also that under the new law there is no requirement for the loss of control to be 'sudden': s 54(2). The removal of that restriction means that in some cases it will be even harder for the court to determine whether the killing is one that is a motivated by a considered desire for revenge or from other emotions. For example, to take cases from the old law, there was held to be sufficient evidence to go to the jury in *Thornton*[37] where a wife had previously declared an intention to kill her brutally abusive husband, and after a fresh provocation she went to the kitchen, took and sharpened a carving knife and returned to another room where she fatally stabbed him. Is that a 'considered desire for revenge'? Similarly, under the old law, in *Pearson*,[38] although DD had armed themselves in advance with the fatal weapon and the killing was a joint enterprise provocation was left. Is arming oneself evidence of a 'considered desire for revenge'? In *Baillie*,[39] where D, being greatly enraged, fetched a gun from an attic and drove his car to V's house (stopping for petrol on the way) before shooting him, provocation was also left to the jury. Would this be regarded as a 'considered desire for revenge'?

The defence is not denied only where the desire for revenge exists before any potential qualifying trigger – fear of serious violence or things said or done. It is enough that having been taunted, D goes away for a couple of hours to brood and returns to stab V. It was suggested in Parliament that the courts should look to D's dominant motive at the time of the killing. That view was rejected by Ministers[40] who stated a belief that:

the expression 'considered desire for revenge' achieves the right balance in ensuring that thought-out revenge killings are excluded without automatically barring every case where revenge may be part of a complex range of motivations.

It is disappointing that what could be a very significant element of the defence has received so little attention.

15.1.2.5 Loss of control

The requirement of a 'loss of control' lies at the heart of the new defence but what that means is undefined. As observed in parliamentary debates it could refer to the failure to exercise self-control or the inability to do so.[41] It is a subjective test. If D is of an unusually phlegmatic temperament and it appears that he did not lose his self-control, the fact that a reasonable person in like circumstances would have done so will not assist D in the least. It is submitted that the test may be best understood as founded on whether D has lost his ability to maintain his actions in accordance with considered judgment or whether he had lost normal powers of reasoning.[42]

Removal of the requirement of suddenness may make the defence harder to get off the ground.[43] In practical terms, it may be difficult to establish whether there was a loss of control

---

[36] The provisional language the Law Commission used to describe this element was adopted in the statute despite the statement that the Commission was not engaged in statutory drafting: LC 304 para 5.27.

[37] [1992] 1 All ER 306. The jury rejected the defence, presumably being satisfied that there was no 'sudden and temporary' loss of self-control.

[38] [1992] Crim LR 193. See on this under the old law M Wasik, 'Cumulative Provocation and Domestic Killing' [1982] Crim LR 29.

[39] [1995] Crim LR 739.

[40] See the letter from Maria Eagle at www.justice.gov.uk/publications/docs/coroners-justice-letters-public-bill-comm.pdf.

[41] See *Hansard*, HL, 7 July 2009, col 572.

[42] See the discussion on the old law in R Holton and S Shute, 'Self Control in Modern Provocation Defence' (2007) 27 OJLS 49.

[43] cf *Duffy* [1949] 1 All ER 932.

if it was not 'sudden'.[44] The removal of the requirement for the loss of self-control to be sudden is a significant change from the position at common law and under the 1957 Act. Under the old law the requirement of a 'sudden and temporary loss' of control was regarded as problematic. The test had the potential to operate in a discriminatory way, rendering the defence too readily available to those who are quick to temper (more commonly men), and less accommodating of those who endure the provoking circumstances before responding with lethal force (often women who kill abusive partners).[45] The courts did not remove the requirement of a sudden and temporary loss of self-control under the old law, but the requirement was tempered by decisions such as *Thornton*[46] and *Ahluwalia*[47] to bring within the partial defence persons whose reaction to circumstances was delayed rather than instantaneous.[48]

Under the new law it remains the case that there must be a loss of control in fact. In deciding this question of fact the jury are, naturally, entitled to take into account all the relevant circumstances; the nature of the conduct which constitutes the qualifying trigger, and all the relevant conditions in which it took place, the sensitivity or otherwise of D,[49] and the time, if any, which elapsed between the qualifying trigger and the act which caused death. The length of time between the qualifying trigger and the killing will remain important, but it is no longer essential that the time gap is short.[50] D's failure to testify to his loss of self-control is not, it is submitted, necessarily, fatal to his case. In their evaluation of the defence as a whole, the jury should, it is submitted, be directed to consider the loss of control element before examining the qualifying triggers.[51]

The requirement that there must be a loss of control is not satisfied by evidence that D acted 'instinctively', for example where a boxer punches V who had taunted him.[52] In one tragic case[53] under the old law in which D yielded to the entreaties of his incurably ill and suffering wife to put an end to her life, it was held that D had not lost his self-control, indeed the evidence was that he was so in control as to stop immediately when he thought, wrongly, that she had changed her mind. The case highlights the arbitrariness of a defence partially absolving those who kill in a state of anger or outrage, but not those who exercise mercy.[54]

---

[44] The test at common law suggested that the longer the period to cool off and calm down the more likely the killing is a revenge killing. But this assumption was not borne out by psychological/physiological evidence see P Brett, 'The Physiology of Provocation' [1970] Crim LR 634. The requirement of suddenness was criticized for restricting the provocation defence and removing from its ambit the cases of outraged retaliation: Horder, *Excusing Crime*, 69–71If.

[45] For a broader ranging critique of the s 3 defence for its 'gendered and heterosexualist' nature and of measuring the reasonableness of killing across cultures, see H Power, 'Provocation and Culture' [2006] Crim LR 871. Other defences are also difficult to apply to these circumstances. See J Loveless, 'Domestic Violence, Coercion and Duress' [2010] Crim LR 93.

[46] [1992] 1 All ER 306, [1992] Crim LR 54. For a further appeal, see [1996] 2 Cr App R 108, [1996] Crim LR 597.

[47] [1992] 4 All ER 889, [1993] Crim LR 63. On which see D Nicolson and R Sanghvi, 'Battered Women and Provocation: The Implications of *R v Ahluwalia*' [1993] Crim LR 728.

[48] The issue has generated immense literature, see, generally, K O'Donovan, 'Defences for Battered Women Who Kill?' (1991) 18 J Law and Soc 219; C Wells, 'Battered Women Syndrome and Defences to Homicide: Where Now' (1994) 14 LS 266; and n 13, above.

[49] See, under s 3 the recent case of *Gregson* [2006] EWCA Crim 3364 (epileptic and mentally abnormal).

[50] See *Hansard*, HC Public Bills Committee, 3 March 2009, col 434.

[51] This was the case under s 3: *Brown* [1972] 2 All ER 1328 at 1333.

[52] *Serrano* [2006] EWCA Crim 3182 decided under s 3.

[53] *Cocker* [1989] Crim LR 740, discussed by PR Taylor, 'Provocation and Mercy Killing' [1991] Crim LR 111.

[54] The focus of the defence on the element of anger and spontaneous loss of control as an excusing feature is critically examined by J Horder, 'Reshaping the Subjective Element in the Provocation Defence' (2005) 25 OJLS 123 who considers a defence akin to what is now s 55 of the 2009 Act.

The 'loss of self control' element in s 54 raises several further issues. First, the loss of control must, presumably, still be temporary otherwise it would be a case of insanity.[55] Secondly, the burden is on the Crown to disprove the element once D has raised evidence of it. It is important to note that the judge has greater control of this LOSC defence than the defence of provocation. The judge will not have to leave the defence to the jury unless there is evidence on which a jury, properly directed, could conclude that the defence might apply.[56] Thirdly, a further element (considered below) of the LOSC defence is that D must be judged on the basis that he possesses a 'normal degree of tolerance and self restraint' (s 54(1)(c)). It would therefore seem relevant when considering whether at the moment that V was killed D had lost his self-control for the jury to consider the period available to D to reflect and to cool off. The cooling-off period was construed generously to D in a number of cases under the old law.[57]

By including a loss of control element, it has been argued that the Government has rendered the new defence incoherent.[58] The loss of control requirement was not part of the Law Commission's scheme for the proposed defence.[59] It was added by Government as a result of concerns that there was a risk of the partial defence being used inappropriately, for example, where D killed in cold blood, or the killing was gang-related, or the killing was a so-called 'honour killing',[60] and 'where a defendant has killed while basically in full possession of his or her senses, even if he or she is frightened, other than in a situation which is complete self-defence'.[61] The Law Commission's model was based on the qualifying triggers of fear and a sense of 'justified anger'.[62] To retain these qualifying limbs but to add a loss of control element renders the scheme unnecessarily complex and lacking logic; a person who has lost control cannot easily be described as acting in a state of 'justified' anger.[63]

Critics have also questioned the retention of the loss of control element given the Government's expressed intention to amend the law to rectify imbalances that exist in the treatment of men and women. The Law Commission recognized that women's typical reactions might make it harder for them to demonstrate a loss of self-control, and hence rejected that element in its final proposal. By retaining a requirement of loss of control the Government may actually have reduced the availability of the defence for abused women. It may be difficult to describe as a 'loss of control' circumstances where a person executes a plan to protect herself – as with abused women who kill their abusers while they sleep.

15.1.2.6 Qualifying triggers – s 55

Under the old law, there was no restriction on the words or conduct that were capable of founding the provocation defence, provided D lost his self-control. The provocation could arise from perfectly legal acts by V or others. Thus, to take an extreme example, in *Doughty*,[64] provocation should have been left to the jury as a defence where there was evidence that the persistent crying of D's two-week-old baby had caused D to lose his self-control and kill it.

---

[55] The 'temporary' nature of the loss of self-control seems irrelevant, provided only that it extended to the fatal act. D should not be deprived of defence because he continued to be berserk for days thereafter – but sudden losses of self-control are, in practice, temporary.

[56] Section 54(6). This follows a recommendation of the LC 304, para 5.11(5); and see paras 5.25–5.32.

[57] *Pearson* [1992] Crim. L.R. 193; *Baillie* [1991] Crim LR 383; *Ibrams* (1981) 74 Cr App R 154.

[58] See A Norrie, above, n 21. S Edwards, 'Anger and Fear as Justifiable Preludes for the Loss of Self Control' (2010) 74 J Crim L 223 discussing difficulties it will pose for abused spouses.

[59] The Law Commission recommended abolishing the positive requirement that D lost his self-control on the grounds that the requirement was unnecessary and undesirable and see LC 304, para 5.19.

[60] Ministry of Justice Consultation Paper 19/2008; CP 19/08.

[61] CP 19/08, para 36.

[62] What Norrie describes as 'imperfect justifications' [2009] Crim LR 278.

[63] See the powerful critique by A Norrie above n 21.

[64] (1986) 83 Cr App R 319. See J Horder, 'The Problem of Provocative Children' [1987] Crim LR 655.

Section 55 seeks to restrict the scope of the partial defence. Now, only qualifying triggers which cause the loss of self-control will be recognized. Section 55 provides:

(2) A loss of self-control had a qualifying trigger if subsection (3), (4) or (5) applies.

(3) This subsection applies if D's loss of self-control was attributable to D's fear of serious violence from V against D or another identified person.

(4) This subsection applies if D's loss of self-control was attributable to a thing or things done or said (or both) which –

    (a) constituted circumstances of an extremely grave character, and

    (b) caused D to have a justifiable sense of being seriously wronged.

(5) This subsection applies if D's loss of self-control was attributable to a combination of the matters mentioned in subsections (3) and (4).

Two preliminary points in relation to the qualifying triggers may be noted. First, the statute requires that the loss of self-control is 'attributable to' a qualifying trigger and this raises the question whether it might be construed as requiring something less than a formal causal link. Despite the ambiguity of the word, it is submitted that the courts will treat this as a requirement of causation. Secondly, what would otherwise be sufficient for a qualifying trigger is to be disregarded if D brought that state of affairs upon himself by, for example, looking for a fight by inciting something to be said or done (s 55(6)(a) or (b)), as the case may be. The restriction in s 56(6) is:

(a) D's fear of serious violence is to be disregarded to the extent that it was caused by a thing which D incited to be done or said for the purpose of providing an excuse to use violence;

(b) a sense of being seriously wronged by a thing done or said is not justifiable if D incited the thing to be done or said for the purpose of providing an excuse to use violence;

This is probably stricter than the previous law on which there was conflicting case law.[65] Under the old law, the jury were told to take into account everything both done and said according to the effect which, in their opinion, it would have on a reasonable person, even where that which was done and said was a predictable result of D's own conduct. That was the decision in *Johnson*,[66] not following *dicta* of the Privy Council in *Edwards v R*.[67] D's unpleasant behaviour in a nightclub resulted in an attack on him by V in response to which D killed V. D was not prevented from relying on provocation even if V's attack was a predictable result of D's behaviour.

Read literally, however, the new defence would only be removed from the jury in a case like *Johnson* if in engaging in the aggressive conduct D's *purpose* was subsequently to use violence. That suggests a narrow restriction and a person in Johnson's position would not necessarily be denied the defence. He may have been obnoxious in the nightclub not with the purpose of fighting, but of being obnoxious. Similarly, D will not be able to rely on LOSC where D *deliberately* induces a state of affairs that will generate a qualifying trigger – D taunts V whom he wants to kill, to do an act so that D may kill him and rely on the defence and be convicted of manslaughter only. Such a situation may seem far-fetched.[68]

---

[65] *Johnson* [1989] 1 WLR 740 is preferred to the *dicta* of the Privy Council in *Edwards* [1973] AC 648.

[66] [1989] Crim LR 738.

[67] [1973] AC 648 PC.

[68] Analogy should be drawn with law on self-defence where D is the initial aggressor see *Harvey* [2009] EWCA Crim 469; *Keane* [2010] EWCA Crim 2514, above Ch 12.

Fear of serious violence: s 55(3)

Section 55(3) provides:

This subsection applies if D's loss of self-control was attributable to D's fear of serious violence from V against D or another identified person.

And by s 55(6):

In determining whether a loss of self-control had a qualifying trigger –

(a) D's fear of serious violence is to be disregarded to the extent that it was caused by a thing which D incited to be done or said for the purpose of providing an excuse to use violence;

This qualifying trigger is the one which renders the new defence quite distinct from the defence of provocation. It flows from a Law Commission recommendation.[69] It is designed primarily to accommodate within the partial defence regime those women who kill their violent and abusive partners. The sudden and temporary requirement of the common law of provocation frequently proved a stumbling block for such women. This qualifying trigger will however, apply more widely. It clearly encompasses two quite distinct sets of circumstances: (i) where D kills in order to thwart an anticipated (albeit not imminent) attack, and (ii) where D over-reacts to what he perceived to be an imminent threat.[70] In the first category the defence will be particularly useful for abused spouses who kill. In that regard the reform is welcome. However, in relation to the second category, there is scope for the defence to be used in a very broad range of killings that are currently classed as murder and which attract no defence. For example, D who stabs V in a fight in pub might claim that he stabbed V having feared that V was going to stab him first. Even if D has used excessive force given the threat he thought he faced, and even if D has made an unreasonable mistake about the need for any force at all, he will, if the jury believe his story may be true, be convicted only of manslaughter. This is a significant change in the law.

The relationship between the LOSC defence and self-defence or defence of others under s 76 of the Criminal Justice and Immigration Act 2008 needs to be approached with care. Self-defence is available on any charge; LOSC defence is available only on a charge of murder.[71] Self-defence results in an acquittal; LOSC in a verdict of manslaughter. With LOSC, D can rely on fear of future non-imminent attack; with self-defence he can only rely on a threat of (or believed threat of) imminent attack. The defence of self-defence is available if D holds a genuine though mistaken and unreasonable belief of the threat to him of *any* violence (including sexual violence[72]). The LOSC defence is available if D genuinely, though mistakenly and unreasonably, believes himself to be at risk of *serious* violence.[73] Violence is undefined.[74] If the degree of force used by D in killing V is, viewed objectively, excessive, that will deprive D of the defence of self-defence,[75] but will not automatically deprive D of the LOSC defence. Section 54(1)(c) (below) requires a comparison of D's behaviour with that of a person of normal self-restraint. It has therefore been argued that if D uses excessive force in self-defence and kills, and a person of normal tolerance and self-restraint would, by

---

[69] LC 304, para 5.55. Historically the common law defence of provocation *did* encompass reactions prompted by fear: LC 304, para 5.49.

[70] See MOJ CP 19/08, para 28.

[71] If there are multiple counts relating to different victims, care will be needed in directing the jury.

[72] MOJ CP 19/08, para 44.

[73] See MOJ Circular 2010/13, para 25. cf Leigh above n 21 who states that the test is objective.

[74] Fortson, above, argues that it includes psychological harm. It includes sexual harm: MOJ CP19/08, para 27.

[75] And therefore of a complete acquittal. See *Clegg* [1995] and Ch 12 above. See also Leverick, *Self Defence* (2007) Ch 6.

definition, not use excessive force, the defence ought not to be available. This view appears to be too strict. The requirement in s 54(1) (c) is to consider whether the person of normal self-restraint '*might* have reacted' as D did. Even people of normal self-restraint sometimes use excessive force and kill. It is submitted that it is not appropriate to read the LOSC defence as restricted in such a way.[76]

Particular problems may arise where on the facts there is evidence that might support self-defence or LOSC. If D has lost self-control, self-defence is not available, but LOSC may be. If D has used excessive force, the complete defence of self-defence will fail, but D may still be able to rely on LOSC; the excessive amount of force being explicable by reference to the 'loss of self control.' Directions to the jury will need to be approached with great case. A further problem is posed by s 54(5):

On a charge of murder, if sufficient evidence is adduced to raise an issue with respect to the defence under subsection (1), the jury must assume that the defence is satisfied unless the prosecution proves beyond reasonable doubt that it is not.

At first sight this seems to suggest that in a case where D pleads self-defence, the Crown will automatically be entitled to a manslaughter conviction in any case where D lost his self-control. However, when applied properly, this provision does not create the conflict it appears.[77] Section 54(5) requires only that sufficient evidence is adduced to raise an issue under s 54(1). Thereafter, the prosecution shoulders the legal burden of proving, to the criminal standard of proof, that the defence is not satisfied. Unless the prosecution discharges that burden, s 54(5) requires the jury to assume that the defence is satisfied.

(6) For the purposes of subsection (5), sufficient evidence is adduced to raise an issue with respect to the defence if evidence is adduced on which, in the opinion of the trial judge, a jury, properly directed, could reasonably conclude that the defence might apply.

It is essential in cases where D pleads self-defence and LOSC that the jury deal with self-defence before LOSC. If jurors address these matters in the wrong order, a manslaughter conviction becomes compulsory. This seems to be a case in which written directions instructing jurors of the steps to verdict would be valuable.

Further problems may arise if D's fear of serious violence was based on an entirely mistaken interpretation of the facts by D. Under the old law the authorities suggested that, where D was provoked partly as the result of a mistake of fact he was entitled to be treated as if the facts were as he mistakenly supposed them to be. This line of reasoning accords with the approach to other defences. Given that the LOSC defence based on this first qualifying trigger is similar in many respects to self-defence, and a mistaken belief in the need for self-defence will not deprive a defendant of that defence, it is submitted that the defence is available if D has a genuine mistaken belief in facts that would amount to a qualifying trigger of a fear of serious violence.

It is unclear whether a mistake induced by voluntary intoxication precludes reliance on the defence. In self-defence, on policy grounds, mistakes due to intoxication are irrelevant, notwithstanding that murder is a crime of specific intent.[78] That would suggest that the defence of LOSC was not available. However, there are several arguments that could be

---

[76] cf the suggestion by J Miles: 'A Dog's Breakfast of Homicide Reform'; Archbold News, 2009, issue 6, 2009, p 8. See on this R Fortson, above, n 21.

[77] Maria Eagle stated that s 54(5) was to 'clarify where the burden of proof lies when a partial defence of loss of control arises in a case' and that 'the usual principles apply in relation to the burden of proof in the new partial defence'. *Hansard*, HC, 3 March 2009, col 437; See also the speech of Baroness Scotland of Asthal: *Hansard*, HL, 7 July 2009, col 585.

[78] *Hatton* [2006] 1 Cr App R 247, CA.

marshalled in favour of adopting a more generous approach in LOSC. First, the policy driven approach in relation to self-defence and intoxicated mistakes has been heavily and cogently criticized.[79] Secondly, this is a partial defence which leads to a manslaughter conviction – it is not the case that D will leave with a complete acquittal if he is permitted to found his plea on an intoxicated mistaken view of the facts.[80] It is established that a drunken mistake may negative the *mens rea* of murder[81] and it is therefore consistent that such a mistake should be relevant in determining whether the killing should be reduced to manslaughter on the ground of LOSC. Thirdly, under the provocation defence an intoxicated mistake as to the facts did not preclude reliance on the defence. In *Brown*,[82] D, a soldier, wrongly, but apparently reasonably, supposed that V was a member of a gang who were attacking him and his comrade. He struck V with a sword and killed him. The judges were clearly of the opinion that this was only manslaughter. In the other cases the mistake arose from drunkenness. In *Letenock*,[83] the Court of Criminal Appeal substituted a verdict of manslaughter in the case of a soldier who had stabbed a corporal, where the 'only element of doubt in the case is whether or not there was anything which might have caused the applicant, *in his drunken condition*, to believe that he was going to be struck'.[84] Against this is of course the requirement that D has by definition lost his self-control.[85]

The defence is limited under this qualifying trigger to cases where D fears violence from V to himself or an identified other. That acts as restriction, but it is unclear how narrowly it will be interpreted. What if D, who is in V's presence, hears V informing X to commit an act of violence on D's fellow gang member who is miles away. D loses his self-control and kills V. Is this sufficient?

Things said or done; circumstances of an extremely grave character, etc: s 55(4)

This form of the defence bears greatest similarity to the old law of provocation. This version of the LOSC defence is available in s 55(4) if D's loss of self-control was:

attributable to a thing or things done or said (or both) which –

(a) constituted circumstances of an extremely grave character, and

(b) caused D to have a justifiable sense of being seriously wronged.

Section 55(6) further provides that:

In determining whether a loss of self-control had a qualifying trigger –

...

(b) a sense of being seriously wronged by a thing done or said is not justifiable if D incited the thing to be done or said for the purpose of providing an excuse to use violence.

Under the old law a wide range of situations in which D claimed that he had been provoked by things said and/or done, could be left for the jury's consideration (for example the crying of a 17-day-old baby in *Doughty*[86]). This broad interpretation of the trigger for the defence

---

[79] See Ch 11 above, p 324.

[80] Although that is also true in relation to self-defence in murder because an unreasonable intoxicated mistake will lead to a conviction for manslaughter despite the courts' gloss on this in *O'Grady*. See above p 324.

[81] Above, p 312.

[82] (1776) 1 Leach 148.

[83] (1917) 12 Cr App R 221, CCA. cf p 324, above.

[84] ibid, 224.

[85] This is one example of how the insertion of the loss of control element to the Law Commission's original proposal creates difficulties and illogicalities.

[86] (1986) 83 Cr App R 319, CA.

meant that there was no requirement that the provoking acts or words were performed consciously, let alone with the deliberate intention to provoke.[87] The test under the new section is much stricter although the statutory language is disappointingly vague. Even if a person with a normal degree of tolerance and self-restraint might have reacted in the circumstances as D did (see s 54(1)(c) and s 54(3)), this will not be enough unless those circumstances meet the thresholds as specified in s 55(4) of the 2009 Act.

Things done or said

As under the old law, mere circumstances (rather than something said or done) no matter how provocative, cannot be a sufficient basis for this qualifying trigger.[88] Loss of control by a farmer on his crops being destroyed by a flood, or his flocks by foot-and-mouth, or an author on his manuscript being destroyed by lightning, cannot, it seems, constitute a qualifying trigger. An 'Act of God' could hardly be regarded as 'something done' within s 55(4). There is no requirement that the things said or done be said or done by the victim, (subject to the other elements of the defence). This follows the old law. For example, in *Davies*, D killed his wife, V having been provoked by X, her lover.[89] Bearing in mind that there is no restriction on the source of the words or conduct which case D to lose control, it seems odd to distinguish cases where the trigger is words by a third party (defence available) and mere circumstances (defence unavailable). If D may rely on the defence where the crops or the manuscript were destroyed by an unknown arsonist why should it be different where no human agency was involved?

There must be some evidence of the qualifying trigger. The new law follows the old on this. In *Acott*,[90] it was held by the House of Lords that for the old defence of provocation it was not enough that D's loss of control may possibly have been the result of some unidentified words or actions by another. There must be 'some evidence of *what* was done or *what* was said to provoke the homicidal reaction' (the court's emphasis). The trial judge is best placed to make this assessment.

There is no express provision in the 2009 Act to deal with the situation where D mistakenly believes that things were done or said. Several different situations need to be distinguished. First, there is the position where D mistakenly believes that things were said or done when nothing was in fact said or done at all. In that case it would be hard to see how the qualifying trigger is satisfied on a literal interpretation of the section. Secondly, there is the case in which words or acts occur, but D mistakes what was said or done. What of D who mishears V and thinks that V has issued a racist taunt when in fact V's words were completely innocuous? In that case, it would seem that the defence ought to be available (subject to the other elements), even if D's mistake is an unreasonable one. That raises the question of whether D can rely on this trigger for the LOSC defence if D acts on a mistaken belief induced by voluntary intoxication? Arguably, since the 'things done or said' must lead to a 'justifiable' sense of being seriously wronged, it will be appropriate to ignore intoxicated mistakes unless the mistake was one which D would have made had he been sober.

It is submitted that the defence will be available, as under the old law, if D sought to kill the person responsible for the acts or words but, by accident, missed him and killed an innocent person. The doctrine of transferred malice[91] should operate and D would be guilty of only

---

[87] This dilution of the concept of 'provocation' to mean merely words or conduct that *cause* the loss of control in the defendant has been heavily criticized by academics. See, in particular, T Macklem and J Gardner, 'Provocation and Pluralism' (2001) 64 MLR 815, and Tadros, *Criminal Responsibility*, 355–368. See LCCP 173, paras 4.8–4.11.

[88] *Acott* [1997] 2 Cr App R 94.

[89] [1975] QB 691, [1975] 1 All ER 890. cf the earlier decision to the same effect by Lawton J in *Twine* [1967] Crim LR 710, where D's girlfriend's conduct caused D to lose his self-control and strike and kill the man she was with.

[90] [1996] Crim LR 664; affd [1997] 1 All ER 706, HL; [1997] Crim LR 541. See also *Bharj* [2005] EWCA Crim 499 emphasizing that the jury would be looking at *all* the evidence.

[91] Above, p 136.

manslaughter. In *Gross*,[92] D, provoked by blows from her husband, shot at him, intending to kill him but missed and killed V. It was held that:

if the firing at the person intended to be hit would be manslaughter, then, if the bullet strikes a third person not intended to be hit, the killing of that person equally would be manslaughter and not murder.[93]

If D knew it was virtually certain that he would hit V, he would have an independent *mens rea* with respect to V, probably sufficient to fix him with liability for murder[94] at common law; but now the acts or words of the third party would be a defence even for D's acts towards V.

Historically, it used to be said that there was no defence if acts or words were not done to the defendant;[95] but the 2009 Act, as with the 1957 Act has no such explicit requirement. D can rely on the defence if V does acts to P, that might cause D to lose his self-control and in circumstances of extreme gravity, to kill V with intent and with a justifiable sense of being seriously wronged. For example, D might find V raping his daughter P.[96]

There is no limitation to prevent a third party account being sufficient to satisfy the trigger, as where D loses his temper following X's report of V's admission that V had attacked D's daughter. That is of course, subject to the other elements of the defence, and in particular it must be noted that the less plausible the account relayed to D the less likely it will cause a loss of self-control and the less likely it will give rise to a justifiable sense of being seriously wronged.

There is nothing to prevent a lawful act by V being sufficient to constitute the trigger, although the fact that the acts or words were lawful will cast doubt on whether D had a justifiable sense of being seriously wronged (below).[97] In particular, where the act is one which is not merely permitted, but which is positively praiseworthy, it is doubtful that a jury would find that it would cause D to lose his temper and to have a justifiable sense of being seriously wronged and that such action might have been performed by a person of normal tolerance and self-restraint in D's position.

Must constitute circumstances of an 'extremely grave character'

For the purposes of this second 'qualifying trigger' (s.55(4)), the threshold is that things said and done must constitute circumstances of an 'extremely grave character'. Presumably, grave to D, in his circumstances. The intention is to restrict the scope of the defence from what was the position under the defence of provocation. The Law Commission offered the following guidance:

The jury should be trusted to evaluate the relative grossness of provocation, in whatever form it comes, according to their own sense of justice in an individual case.[98]

It is disappointing that such a key term of the defence is left undefined.

'justifiable sense of being seriously wronged'

The defendant must have been caused by the things done or said to have a 'justifiable sense of being seriously wronged' (s 55(4)). This is much narrower than the previous law. It is intended to be an objective test.[99] It is, again, disappointing that the Act provides no further guidance on how the jury will approach this question. It was intended that it would provide an

---

[92] (1913) 23 Cox CC 455 (Darling J); and see *Porritt* [1961] 3 All ER 463, [1961] 1 WLR 1372.

[93] 23 Cox CC at 456.

[94] Above, p 107.

[95] But see *Fisher* (1837) 8 C & P 182 (Park J, *obiter*) (D coming upon V raping D's son) and *Harrington* (1866) 10 Cox CC 370 (Cockburn CJ contemplating the possibility of a defence where D found his daughter being violently assaulted by her husband).

[96] Examples under the 1957 Act included *Pearson* [1992] Crim LR 193.

[97] *Doughty* (1986) 83 Cr App R 319.

[98] LC 304, p 85 n 31.

[99] Some commentators (eg Liberty) suggested that the provision was insufficiently clear and that it might be construed subjectively.

opportunity to take into consideration cumulative abuse, which will be particularly important in domestic killings by abused women. At the same time it was intended to exclude from the scope of the defence the cases of racist or honour killings. For example, it is difficult to see how the defence could be left to the jury if D, a white supremacist, killed V, a black man, because V refused to give way to D on the staircase. No reasonable jury properly directed could conclude that D had a *justifiable* sense of being seriously wronged. The defence should be withdrawn from the jury. Similarly where D, a devout Muslim, kills his daughter because she has a sexual relationship before marriage, he cannot be said to have a justifiable sense of being seriously wronged.[100] In some cases, the judge will be obliged to leave the defence to the jury for their good sense. Note that the question for them is not whether D's act in *killing* was justifiable, but whether D had a justifiable sense of being seriously wronged. Again, it is presumably a question of whether the sense of serious wrong would be felt by someone in D's circumstances.

Sexual infidelity

Historically, one of the classic examples of extreme provocation recognized by the courts for centuries was where D killed having found his spouse in the act of adultery.[101] The Government's intention was to prevent the LOSC defence from being run in such a case and to prevent obsessively jealous men using suspected infidelity on the part of the spouse or partner as a defence for killing.[102]

Under the new law D's loss of control that is attributed to anything said or done, and which constitutes sexual infidelity, is to be disregarded (s 55(6)(c)). This limitation was introduced amid much controversy in the debates in Parliament. It did not form part of the Law Commission's original proposals. The restriction was met with anxiety by Lord Phillips who admitted he was 'uneasy about a law which so diminishes the significance of sexuality infidelity as expressly to exclude it from even the possibility of amounting to provocation'.[103]

It is important to be clear about what s 55(6) forbids:

In determining whether a loss of self-control had a qualifying trigger...

(c) the fact that a thing done or said constituted sexual infidelity is to be disregarded.

The restriction on the defence is likely to present difficulties; it may well fail to achieve the Government's aim. It is not even clear that the statute attacks the mischief. The concern is that men are able to rely on loss of self-control defences when their anger and loss of control results from sexual jealousy. The defence is denied defendants whose loss of self-control results from the fact of sexual infidelity.

Numerous problems arise. Firstly, there is no definition of what 'sexual infidelity' means. Clearly there can be infidelity outside of marriage, but how 'solid' a relationship must there be

---

[100] cf *Mohammed* [2005] EWCA Crim 1880 where in cross examination, D claimed that 'it is part of our religion' to do as he did in killing his sexually active unmarried daughter. His perception is not determinative of what is justifiable.

[101] Killing, in such a case, 'is of the lowest degree of [manslaughter]; and therefore...the court directed the burning in the hand to be gently inflicted, because there could not be a greater provocation': Blackstone, *Commentaries*, iv, 192. See also the case of *Manning* (1671) T Raym 212. For a recent case of exactly these facts, see *Christie* [2004] EWCA Crim 1338, D was convicted of murder. As an example of how significant this factor was see *Evans* [2009] EWCA Crim 2243 where the CA accepted that had E been aware of the infidelity of his wife he might have been able to plead provocation.

[102] See *Hansard*, HC Public Bills Committee, 3 March 2009, col 439.

[103] The Times, 7 Nov 2008.

before sexual acts with others outside of that relationship constitute infidelity?[104] It could be read narrowly to extend to only long-term relationships. Secondly, the term 'sexual' infidelity can, it might be argued, be read narrowly, so as to comprise only those incidents of and conduct directly related to sexual activity.

Thirdly, s 55(6)(c) read literally only forbids regard being had to the *fact* that the thing said or done constituted sexual infidelity when determining if there is a qualifying trigger sufficient for the defence to be left to the jury. The effect of the sexual infidelity is not to be disregarded, merely the words or acts that constituted it. This is a disappointing piece of legislative drafting.

Fourthly, the question arises when can words constitute sexual infidelity? It seems they can where, for example, D overhears his wife V saying 'I love you' to her lover, X. But what of words spoken by V telling D that she loves X? Do her words 'I love someone else' constitute infidelity or are they a report of her infidelity? On a narrow view of the section, it can be argued that the words do not constitute sexual infidelity and they are not to be disregarded under s 55(6)(c). In the debates in Parliament, in response to a question whether V bragging to D that he had been having an affair with D's wife would be covered, the Government spokeswoman said that the defence would turn on the facts, but that:

sexual infidelity in itself cannot and should not be an acceptable reason for a defence for murder. (emphasis added)[105]

Fifthly, s 55(6)(c), read literally, forbids only regard to the sexual infidelity. Provided there is some other thing said or done which amount to extreme circumstances which could have caused D to lose his self-control and to have a justifiable sense of being seriously wronged, the trigger will be satisfied. It may be difficult to discern whether D's loss of self-control is attributable to things done or said by his sexual partner *other than* her act of infidelity. What related aspects can be taken into account in determining if the trigger is present? The MOJ[106] makes clear that:

it is only the fact of sexual infidelity that must be disregarded. The thing said or done can still potentially amount to a 'qualifying trigger' if (ignoring the sexual infidelity) it amounts to circumstances of an extremely grave character which caused the defendant to have a justifiable sense of being seriously wronged.[107]

Examples of the sorts of activity that might trigger the defence and would not be excluded by s 55(6)(c) include, D who has found his wife in bed with her lover and killed the lover saying in defence of the killing that it was not the act of sex that triggered the loss of self-control but the fact that the lover was D's best friend. Some such defences will be plausible: D will claim the thing that caused him to lose self-control in extremely grave circumstances having a justifiable sense of being seriously wronged was not the sex but eg, 'the fact that V threatened to take the kids', or 'the fact that she taunted me about my erectile dysfunction' or 'the fact that she smashed up my prized possession as she was leaving' etc. In debates the Government spokeswoman stated:

it is important to set out the position precisely and uncompromisingly-namely that sexual infidelity is not the kind of thing done that is ever *sufficient on its own* to found a successful plea of loss of control so as to reduce the verdict from murder to manslaughter. (emphasis added)[108]

---

[104] The debates in Parliament do not reveal what types of relationship will qualify, but the references are usually to spouses, civil partners and in some instances to 'partners'.

[105] *Hansard*, HC, 9 Nov 2009, col 82 (Claire Ward).

[106] MOJ Circular 2010/13.

[107] Para 30. This echoes statements in Parliament where the spokeswoman stated: 'If other factors come into play, the court will of course have an opportunity to consider them, but it will not be able to make the decision exclusively on the ground of sexual infidelity.' *Hansard*, HC, 9 Nov, col 80 (Claire Ward).

[108] *Hansard*, HC, 9 Nov 2009, col 83 (Claire Ward).

More extreme examples are easier and were recognized in the debates: eg where D comes home to find her husband, V, having sex with his young stepdaughter. In such a case, if D killed V, it would be open to D to argue that it was the fact of sexual abuse and not the sexual infidelity per se that formed the qualifying trigger.

What is perhaps most astonishing is that the drafting means that s 55(6)(c) *only* forbids regard to the sexual infidelity when considering whether there is a trigger. Provided there is some other thing said or done which amount to extremely circumstances which could have caused D to lose his self-control and to have a justifiable sense of being seriously wronged, the trigger will be satisfied. If the trigger is satisfied, s 54(1)(c) then requires the jury to consider whether:

(c) a person of D's sex and age, with a normal degree of tolerance and self restraint and in the circum-stances of D, might have reacted in the same or in a similar way to D.

And by s 54(3):

(3) In subsection (1)(c) the reference to 'the circumstances of D' is a reference to all of D's circum-stances other than those whose only relevance to D's conduct is that they bear on D's general capacity for tolerance or self-restraint.

It is therefore arguable that the statute does not *at this final stage of the defence* preclude con-sideration of the fact of sexual infidelity. There are really two arguments. First, it can be said that what is being considered in s 54(1)(c) is not the sexual infidelity but the effects of the sexual infidelity on D. A defendant in such cases might be exceptionally vulnerable in the sense of being more easily 'wounded' by such actions.[109] In psychiatric terms the act causing the loss of control would be the *effects* of the unfaithfulness and the betrayal rather than the 'things said or done' which constitute sexual infidelity.[110] Section 54(1)(c) does not preclude reliance on such factors provided they are 'circumstances' and that they are relevant. They clearly are, and do not solely bear on D's general capacity for tolerance and self-restraint. Secondly, it can be argued that the terms of s 54(1)(c) do not preclude reliance on the 'circum-stance' of D discovering the sexual infidelity itself. This would allow the jury to have regard to the act/words in determining whether a person of D's age and sex etc in his 'circumstances' (ie just discovering sexual infidelity) might have reacted as he did.

On one view, these interpretations of s 54(1)(c) would seem to undermine the purpose of the provision in s 55. On another view, there is no conflict because there must be some trig-ger other than the mere fact of sexual infidelity for the defence to get to the jury, and what the Government was seeking to prohibit was sexual infidelity as a sole basis for the trigger. It was acknowledged that:

Judges are perfectly used to directing juries about what they can and cannot consider – they do it every day in court. It is not beyond the ability of judges to tell juries that sexual infidelity cannot be a qualifying trigger for a loss of self-control. If something else is relied on as the qualifying trigger, *any sexual infidelity that forms part of the background can be considered* but it cannot be the trigger. That is essentially what the legislation seeks to do – to stop the act of sexual infidelity being the trig-ger that enables people to say that these are extremely serious and grave circumstances. (emphasis added)[111]

---

[109] See, eg, the acceptance that someone who was sexually abused is more likely to take offence at sexual advances than someone who has not – *Hill* [2008] EWCA Crim 76.

[110] But the Government rejected an amendment that would have limited s 55(6)(c) to cases in which the motive for killing was punishment, sexual jealousy or sexual envy. *Hansard*, HC, 9 Nov, col 84 (Claire Ward).

[111] *Hansard*, HC 9 Nov 2009, col 94 (Claire Ward).

Combined qualifying triggers: s 55(5)

Section 55(5) provides:

This subsection applies if D's loss of self-control was attributable to a combination of the matters mentioned in subsections (3) and (4).

It is possible for D to rely on both qualifying triggers under s 55 in combination – that he killed having lost control because he was in fear of serious violence and that he also had a justifiable sense of being seriously wronged. A striking example would be D who kills V whom he found raping his daughter at knife point. The two limbs might also be relied on by the woman who kills her abusive partner after years of torment when she lost control fearing another violent attack by him.

One problem that may arise is whether a judge should withdraw the defence in a case if, where D who relies on both limbs, there is insufficient evidence of each limb in isolation, but in combination the evidence would satisfy s 54(5). It is submitted that the defence ought to be left.

15.1.2.7 Degree of tolerance and self-restraint: s 54(1)(c)

In addition to the loss of control and the qualifying trigger, the third element of the defence is an important limitation on its scope in the form of an objective requirement enacted in s 54(1)(c). The requirement is that 'a person of D's sex and age, with a normal degree of tolerance and self-restraint and in the *circumstances* of D, *might* have reacted in the same or in a similar way to D' (emphasis added). By s 54(3):

In subsection (1)(c) the reference to 'the circumstances of D' is a reference to all of D's circumstances other than those whose only relevance to D's conduct is that they bear on D's general capacity for tolerance or self-restraint.

In some respects the test is similar to the test under the 1957 Act which centred on whether a reasonable man might have done as D did. This element of the old test gave rise to confusion and numerous visits to the House of Lords.[112]

Background

Before the Homicide Act 1957 the judges took it upon themselves to instruct the jury as to the characteristics of the reasonable man. The test was rigidly objective, so, for example, D might have been mentally ill[113] or impotent but the jury still had to consider the effects of the provocation on a normal person.[114] The 1957 Act removed the power of the judge to dictate to the jury what amounted to the characteristics of the reasonable person. In *Camplin*,[115] D, a 15-year-old boy, killed V with a chapatti pan. D's story was that V had raped him and then laughed at him when he was overcome by shame, whereupon D lost his self-control and made the fatal attack. The trial judge directed that the test was the effect of the provocation, not on a reasonable boy, but on a reasonable man. The House of Lords held that this was wrong. Lord Diplock explained that the jury should be told that the reasonable man is a person having the power of self-control to be expected of an ordinary person of the sex and age of the accused, but in other respects sharing such of the accused's characteristics as they

---

[112] *Camplin* [1978] AC 705; *Morgan Smith* [2001] AC 146: not followed in *Attorney General from Jersey v Holley* [2005] 2 AC 580.
[113] *Alexander* (1913) 9 Cr App R 139.
[114] *Smith* (1915) 11 Cr App R 81; *Bedder v DPP* [1954] 1 WLR 1119.
[115] [1978] AC 705.

think would affect the gravity of the provocation to him; and that the question is not merely whether such a person would in like circumstances be provoked to lose his self-control but also would react to the provocation as the accused did. Age and sex – characteristics which everyone possesses – were to be taken into account in determining the degree of *self-restraint* required of D; but his other characteristics are said to be relevant only in so far as they affect the *gravity* of the provocation (ie the likely sting they carried for this particular defendant), not in their impact on the ability of D to exercise self-control.[116] The distinction was central to subsequent decisions of the House of Lords. In *Morhall*,[117] it was held that a discreditable characteristic of D (drug addiction) affecting the gravity of the provocation (D called 'a druggie') is material even though discreditable. Similarly in the Privy Council in *Luc Thiet Thuan v R*,[118] D's mental abnormality, was only relevant if it formed the subject of the taunts, otherwise it was not a relevant characteristic for the purposes of the objective test as it went only to D's self-control. Against this view, there developed a line of Court of Appeal cases which took a more generous approach, accepting that the reasonable man might be endowed with D's mental characteristics.[119] On this view, the jury could have regard to D's characteristics that affected his ability to exercise self-control not just where they were the subject of the taunts.

The division of judicial opinion came to a head in the controversial House of Lords decision in *Smith (Morgan)*.[120] The House held, Lords Hobhouse and Millett dissenting, that the jury may take into account, in addition to age and sex, other characteristics of the defendant which affect powers of self-control, whether or not they are also relevant to the gravity of the provocation. The decision met with strident criticism because it failed to respect the language of s 3. As the Court of Appeal subsequently put it, the 'reasonable man' became 'an archetype…left lurking in the statutory undergrowth'.[121] It also created considerable and confusing overlap with the defence of diminished responsibility under s 2. Moreover, it provided an opportunity for all of D's characteristics to be adduced,[122] including not only those which would have affected the gravity of the provocation, but those which affected the accused's ability to exercise self-control. In short, it left the jury with no benchmark against which to assess the defendant's conduct in killing when out of control. One impact was that by relaxing the objective criterion it more readily allowed for

---

[116] This line of reasoning accords with the argument made earlier by Ashworth in a seminal article. The proper distinction is that individual peculiarities which bear on the gravity of the provocation should be taken into account, whereas individual peculiarities bearing on the accused's level of self-control should not: [1976] CLJ 292. cf the distinction made between provocativeness and provocability made in the commentary on *Morhall* [1995] Crim LR 890. For consideration of whether the questions can be kept separate see A Norrie, 'From Criminal Law to Legal Theory: The Mysterious Case of the Reasonable Glue Sniffer' (2002) 65 MLR 538 at 547.

[117] [1996] AC 90, [1995] 3 All ER 659, HL, [1995] Crim LR 890. A unanimous decision of the House which was virtually ignored in *Smith* [2001] AC 146.

[118] [1996] 2 All ER 1033 (Lord Goff, Sir Brian Hutton and Sir Michael Hardie Boys, and Lord Steyn). Noted, [1996] Crim LR 433.

[119] *Ahluwalia* [1992] 4 All ER 889 and *Thornton (No 2)* [1996] 2 Cr App R 108, [1996] Crim LR 597; *Dryden* [1995] 4 All ER 987; *Humphreys* [1995] 4 All ER 1008.

[120] [2001] AC 146, [2000] 4 All ER 289, [2000] Crim LR 1004, HL. For critical comment see, *inter alia*, T Macklem and J Gardner, 'Compassion without Respect: Nine Fallacies in *R v Smith*' [2001] Crim LR 623; 'Provocation and Pluralism' (2001) 64 MLR 815. For a defence of the case see B Mitchell, R Mackay and W Brookbanks, 'Pleading for Provoked Killers: In Defence of Morgan Smith' (2008) 124 LQR 675 arguing that the approach allowed for those who lacked capacity to control themselves to rely on the defence.

[121] *Rowland* [2003] EWCA Crim 3636, para 41.

[122] Professor Ashworth's commentary on *Weller* [2003] Crim LR 724 at 725–727, and see *Rowland* [2003] EWCA Crim 3636.

the mental characteristics resulting from physical and emotional abuse to be considered by the jury. This was a positive consequence for victims of domestic abuse who kill. However, the relaxation applied equally to the mental characteristics often found in domestic abusers who kill – obsessiveness and jealousy.[123] In addition, it created widespread confusion in the trial courts, trial judges were faced with the prospect of directing juries with practically no guidance as to which characteristics, if any, ought not to be drawn to the attention of the jury.[124]

In *A-G for Jersey v Holley*,[125] a specially convened nine-member Board of the Privy Council concluded, by a majority of 6 to 3, that *Smith* was wrongly decided. The majority in the Privy Council accepted that within the 'objective limb', a distinction should be drawn between characteristics of the accused that were to be taken into account because they affected the gravity of the provocation and those relating to the ability to exercise self-control which were not to be taken into account.[126] In *James and Karimi*,[127] the Court of Appeal took the radical and controversial step of endorsing the Privy Council decision in *Holley* over that of the House of Lords in *Smith*.[128]

The new law

The requirement is that 'a person of D's sex and age, with a normal degree of tolerance and self-restraint and in the *circumstances* of D, *might* have reacted in the same or in a similar way to D'. It is submitted that it would therefore be wrong to assume that the combined effect of s 54(1)(c) and s 54(3) is to codify the decision of the majority of their lordships in *Holley*.[129] What constitutes a 'normal degree of tolerance and self restraint' is a matter for the jury to determine according to their judgement and their collective experience of life. The reference to 'D's sex and age' is consistent with statements made in *Camplin*, and *Holley* that the 'powers of self-control possessed by ordinary people vary according to their age and...their sex'.[130] Why sex was included at all and why these are always relevant circumstances is not clear. Difficulties may arise for defendants of mental abnormality for their age since if read restrictively it is the age that is to be taken into account.[131]

---

[123] See Part 2 of LCCP 173, especially paras 21–22; LC 304, para 5.41.

[124] *Weller* [2004] 1 Cr App R 1, it was held that the trial judge's failure to direct the jury to consider W's 'unduly possessive and jealous nature' did not render the conviction for murder unsafe provided the characteristics were not specifically removed from the jury's consideration; see also *R (Farnell) v CCRC* [2003] EWHC 835 (Admin).

[125] [2005] UKPC 23. For commentary see Ashworth [2005] Crim LR 966; Virgo [2005] CLJ 532. See also the discussion in LC 304, paras 5.34–5.39.

[126] The minority disagreed. Lords Bingham and Hoffmann suggest that it is not rationally possible to consider the two in isolation. The majority regarded any difficulties of 'mental gymnastics' required of jurors in having regard to a defendant's 'characteristics' for one purpose of the law of provocation but not another as having been exaggerated. [26]. Lord Carswell in dissent challenged that view, at [73].

[127] [2006] EWCA Crim 14, [2006] 1 Cr App R 29.

[128] On the precedent issue, see J Elvin, 'The Doctrine of Precedent and the Provocation Defence' (2006) 69 MLR 819. Numerous convictions from trials pre-*Smith* were, in light of the more generous approach that case applied, referred to the Court of Appeal by the CCRC. By the time they got to be heard, *Holley* had been decided and the law was as when the appellant's were convicted: *Moses* [2006] EWCA Crim 1721; *Hill* [2008] EWCA Crim 76.

[129] See on *Holley* the comments of Lord Lloyd,*Hansard*, HL, 7 July 2009, col 572, and Lord Thomas, col 579.

[130] *Holley* [2005] UKPC 23, para 13.

[131] cf Norrie, above, n 21, p 281.

However, in other respects the test is quite different. Firstly, the words that a person *'might* have reacted in the same or similar way to D' creates a test that is more generous to D than the requirement in s 3 of the 1957 Act which was that 'the provocation is enough *to make* reasonable man do as he did'. There is no express restriction that D's acts must be proportionate to the threat/trigger he faced.[132]

Secondly it is important to note that s 54(3) clarifies s 54(1)(c) so that the reference to 'the circumstances of D' includes *'all* of D's circumstances' except those which bear on D's 'general capacity for tolerance and self-restraint' (eg a propensity to violent outbursts). The words 'in the circumstances of D' may enable a jury to adopt a more generous approach when judging D's response than might have been possible under s 3 as interpreted in *Holley*. This opens up a broader range of subjective considerations than under the *Holley* test. Judges will have to be vigilant to ensure that the broad nature of the test for including D's circumstances in considering how a person of his age etc might have reacted does not lead to evidence of tenuous relevance being admitted and distracting the jury from the central enquiry.

A third distinguishing feature from the old law is that s 54(3) only appears to exclude a circumstance on which D seeks to rely if its *sole* relevance is to diminish D's self-restraint. This could open up the opportunity for D to adduce all sorts of evidence. In particular, D might claim that his intake of alcohol or other intoxicants was a relevant circumstance and that the intoxication did not simply diminish his self-restraint, but also had some other relevance – eg that it caused a relevant mistake. This may amount to no more than a plea of lack of intent on grounds of intoxication, but it will make directing the jury more complex. The majority in the Privy Council in *Holley* held that D's voluntarily intoxicated state was not a matter to be taken into account by the jury when considering whether D exercised ordinary self-control. Equally, evidence that D was suffering from chronic alcoholism was *not* (unless the taunts related to D's alcoholism) a matter to be taken into account by the jury when considering whether, having regard to the actual provocation and their view of its gravity, a person having ordinary powers of self-control would have done what the defendant did.[133]

Suppose under the new law that D, an alcoholic, is taunted by V with his addiction and instantly responds with a fatal blow. However drunk D may have been at the time, the jury must it seems be instructed to consider the effect of the taunts given that D is an alcoholic.

A final point to note on s 54(3) is that it excludes circumstances 'whose only relevance to D's conduct is that they bear on D's general capacity for tolerance or self restraint'. That restriction is similar to the old law in *excluding* certain features. However, there is now no positive requirement that D's individual circumstances have to affect the gravity of the triggering conduct in order for them to be *included* in the jury's assessment of what the person of D's age and sex might have done. So, where D has a learning disability is provoked, his disability will be relevant even if the taunts relate to something completely different. Again there is a need to be vigilant in avoiding evidence of marginal relevance from distracting the jury.

---

[132] cf *Van Dongen* [2005] EWCA Crim 1728 where the Court of Appeal seemed to imply such despite the decision against in *Phillips v R* [2005] Crim LR 971.

[133] See also the post-*Smith* case law supporting this position: *Keaveney* [2004] EWCA Crim 1091 and *Rowland*, above.

15.2 Diminished responsibility[134]

The Homicide Act 1957, s 2, introduced a new defence to murder: 'diminished responsibility'. The defence has been substituted with one of the same name contained in the Coroners and Justice Act 2009, s 52.

If successful, the defence allows D to be found guilty only of manslaughter.[135] By s 2(2) of the 1957 Act the burden of proof is on D. It has been held that, as in the case of insanity, the standard of proof required is not beyond reasonable doubt but on a balance of probabilities.[136] Diminished responsibility is not a general defence, but applies only to murder. It is not available as a defence to attempted murder,[137] nor can it be raised on a finding of unfitness to plead.[138]

15.2.1 The old law

Under s 2 of the 1957 Act as enacted, the defence was available on a charge of murder where D could prove that 'he was suffering from such abnormality of mind (whether arising from a condition of arrested or retarded development of mind or any inherent causes or induced by disease or injury) as substantially impaired his mental responsibility for his acts and omissions in doing or being a party to the killing'.

The elements of the defence were therefore (i) an abnormality of mind (ii) which arose from one of the specified conditions (iii) which substantially impaired (iv) D's mental responsibility. None of the elements was defined with any precision and arguably the courts in collusion with psychiatrists were content to avoid definition so that the defence maintained its flexibility, thereby allowing for its application in deserving cases in which the mandatory sentence for murder would otherwise apply.[139]

There had been numerous calls for reform. The Law Commission, in its Report No 290 on *Partial Defences to Murder,* concluded that[140] there was 'overwhelming support' for reform. The old law was regarded by many as 'chaotic' and it was suggested that a rational sentencing exercise would be a better response for meeting the needs of mentally ill defendants. It was

---

[134] For historical and general accounts see RD Mackay, 'Diminished Responsibility and Mentally Disordered Killers', in Ashworth and Mitchell (eds), *Rethinking English Homicide Law* (2000); E Tennant, *The Future of the Diminished Responsibility Defence to Murder'* (2001); S Dell, *Murder into Manslaughter: The Diminished Responsibility Defence in Practice* (1984); G Williams, 'Diminished Responsibility' (1960–1961) 1 Med Sci & L 41; B Wootton, 'Diminished Responsibility – A Layman's View' (1960) 76 LQR 224; R Sparks, 'Diminished Responsibility in Theory and Practice' (1964) 27 MLR 9; N Walker, *Crime and Insanity in England* (1968) 138–164; EJ Griew, 'The Future of Diminished Responsibility' [1988] Crim LR 75.

[135] The defence derives from the law of Scotland, where it was a judicial creation, originating in the decision of Lord Deas in *HM Advocate v Dingwall* (1867) 5 Irv 466. See TB Smith, 'Diminished Responsibility' [1957] Crim LR 354 and Lord Keith, 'Some Observations on Diminished Responsibility' [1959] Jur Rev 109. The Scottish version has recently been redefined in *Galbraith v HM Advocate (No 2)* 2002 JC 1. The Scottish Law Commission has proposed putting the definition from that case on a statutory footing. See Law Com Report No 195, *Insanity and Diminished Responsibility* (2004). Available from www.scotlawcom.gov.uk/download_file/view/231. cf the recommendation of the New South Wales Law Reform Commission, Report No 83, *Partial Defences to Murder: Provocation and Infanticide* (1997). See Victoria Law Reform Commission [2005] Crim LR 256.

[136] *Dunbar* [1958] 1 QB 1, [1957] 2 All ER 737. This rule is not affected by the Human Rights Act 1998: *Ali and Jordan* [2001] 1 All ER 1014, CA. Where the medical evidence of diminished responsibility is based on certain facts, it is for the defence to prove those facts by admissible evidence: *Ahmed Din* (1962) 46 Cr App R 269; *Bradshaw* (1985) 82 Cr App R 79, [1985] Crim LR 733 and commentary.

[137] *Campbell* [1997] Crim LR 495, Sedley J. See also Farrar [1992] 1 VR 207.

[138] *Antoine* [2001] AC 340.

[139] LC 304, para 5.107.

[140] LC 290, para 5.10 and see the Scottish Law Commission, *Insanity and Diminished Responsibility Report*, No 195 (2004).

noted that the defence was 'grossly abused' and whether a defendant 'finds a psychiatrist who will be prepared to testify that, for example, depression was responsible for his behaviour is "a lottery"'. There was some pressure for abolition, particularly if the mandatory sentence was removed, but the Law Commission identified several arguments[141] for retention, including the need for 'fair and just labelling'.[142]

The Commission refined its original proposal from the Partial Defences Project.[143] The proposals were taken forward by the MOJ and the new defence as enacted in 2009 is very similar to those proposals (but note the omission of a defence of developmental immaturity).

15.2.2 The new defence[144]

The Coroners and Justice Act 2009, s 52 provides:

(1) In section 2 of the Homicide Act 1957 (c. 11) (persons suffering from diminished responsibility), for subsection (1) substitute –

'(1) A person ("D") who kills or is a party to the killing of another is not to be convicted of murder if D was suffering from an abnormality of mental functioning which –

(a) arose from a recognised medical condition,

(b) substantially impaired D's ability to do one or more of the things mentioned in subsection (1A), and

(c) provides an explanation for D's acts and omissions in doing or being a party to the killing.

(1A) Those things are –

(a) to understand the nature of D's conduct;

(b) to form a rational judgment;

(c) to exercise self-control.

(1B) For the purposes of subsection (1)(c), an abnormality of mental functioning provides an explanation for D's conduct if it causes, or is a significant contributory factor in causing, D to carry out that conduct.

Section 52 was brought into force on 4 October 2010.[145] Since the provision relates exclusively to a matter of substantive law, it will apply in relation to any murder which occurred on or after that date.[146]

---

[141] Justifications included the need for some defence other than insanity given the 'out-dated nature of the insanity defence' and its unsatisfactory scope and operation; the stigmatization of the label 'insanity'; the need to prevent jurors being faced with only the option of murder or acquittal lest they perversely acquit; allowing the central issue of culpability to be determined by a jury and not by the judge as part of the sentencing process; the need to ensure public confidence in sentencing which is more likely on a diminished verdict than on murder; the need for a jury, to evaluate the expert evidence; the need to retain the defence for abused women 'driven to kill'; and the opportunity for the defence to provide a merciful but just disposition of mercy killing cases.

[142] ibid, para 5.18.

[143] See V Tadros, *Criminal Liability for Non-Aggressive Death* (2008).

[144] See in particular, R Fortson and A R Keene, *Current Law Statutes Annotation* (2010); J Glasson and J Knowles, *Blackstone's Guide to the Coroners and Justice Act 2009* (2010), Ch 8; L H Leigh, 'Two New Partial Defences to Murder' (2010) Criminal Law and Justice Weekly 53; R Mackay, 'The New Diminished Responsibility Plea' [2010] Crim LR 290.

[145] The Coroners and Justice Act 2009 (Commencement No 4, Transitional and Saving Provisions) Order 2010, SI 2010 No 816.

[146] Para 7 of Sch 22 to the Coroners and Justice Act 2009.

15.2.2.1 The elements of the defence

Section 52 makes significant changes to the defence of diminished responsibility. The main aim is to modernize and clarify the defence. In particular, the aim is to redraft the provision with the needs and practices of medical experts in mind, and to clarify what is involved in the 'substantial impairment of the defendant's mental responsibility'. Strikingly, the word 'responsibility' no longer features in the terms of the defence at all. The practical effects are, it would appear, to narrow the scope of the defence and to create the opportunity for experts to have even greater influence over the outcome. Because the experts have more opportunity to provide a more definitive opinion on more of the elements of the offence, it is unclear whether this will lead to a greater proportion of cases in which there will be accepted pleas. Professor Mackay conducted empirical research for the Law Commission[147] in which of the 157 cases studied, the prosecution accepted a diminished responsibility plea in 77.1 per cent of cases.[148] Statistics reveal that the total number of successful diminished responsibility pleas under the old law was around 20 per year.[149]

The elements of the new defence are:

(i)   An 'abnormality of mental functioning'. In itself this is not intended to be a change of substance, but rather one to adopt language preferred by psychiatrists.[150]

(ii) The abnormality must arise 'from a recognised medical condition.' This is designed to be wider than the old list of bracketed causes in the original definition in s 2 of the 1957 Act. Again, it is designed to allow expert evidence to be received on a more meaningful basis.

(iii) D's 'mental responsibility' must be substantially impaired. This means that his *ability* to do one or more of the things in s 2(1A), must be substantially impaired. The three things are:

    (a) to understand the nature of D's conduct;

    (b) to form a rational judgment;

    (c) to exercise self-control.

This is a dramatic change from the old law. It is more specific and leaves less moral elbow room for the jury and is arguably harder for D to prove.

(iv) The abnormality of mental functioning from a 'recognised medical condition' must be a cause or contributory cause of D's conduct in killing. There is some ambiguity as to whether the section requires a cause or merely an explanation.

Each element of the offence deserves more detailed consideration.

(i) 'an abnormality of mental functioning'

Under the old s 2 test (of 'abnormality of mind') the determination of 'abnormality' could be left to the jury. In *Byrne*[151] Lord Parker CJ stated[152] that 'abnormality' of mind:

means a state of mind so different from that of ordinary human beings that the reasonable man would term it abnormal. It appears to us to be wide enough to cover the mind's activities in all its aspects, not only the perception of physical acts and matters and the ability to form a rational judgment

---

[147] LC 290.

[148] Para 5.34.

[149] See LC 290; LC 304, para 5.84.

[150] See LC 304, para 5.114. It received support in Parliament from Baroness Murphy (Visiting Professor of Psychiatry at Queen Mary University of London) *Hansard*, HL, 30 June 2009, vol 712, col 177.

[151] [1960] 2 QB 396.

[152] At 403.

whether an act is right or wrong, but also the ability to exercise will-power to control physical acts in accordance with that rational judgement.

That formula was appropriate when a jury was considering a concept as loose and general as the 'mind' and asking itself whether D's 'mind' deviated from the norm. But the expression 'abnormality of mind' has been superseded by the test of abnormality of 'mental functioning'. That test is, even if not a formal psychiatric test, one with a psychiatric flavour. The jury cannot have a sound grasp of that concept without expert evidence. Nor, therefore, can the jury understand how far D's mental functioning deviates from the norm without expert evidence to assist them. As such, it is doubtful whether they can be left with as open a direction as in *Byrne*. Experts will express an opinion on whether there is an abnormal mental functioning. If there is uncontradicted expert evidence it is questionable whether the element of the defence must be left for the jury to determine, but it is submitted that it should.

There is no doubt that the new law is stricter than the original s 2. Nevertheless, there is little doubt that on facts such as those in *Byrne*, the defence would still be available. Byrne strangled a young woman in a YWCA hostel and mutilated her corpse. Evidence was tendered that from an early age he had been subject to perverted violent desires; that the impulse or urge of those desires was stronger than the normal impulse or urge of sex, that he found it very difficult or, perhaps, impossible in some cases to resist putting the desire into practice and that the act of killing the girl was done under such an impulse or urge.[153] That would be an abnormality of mental functioning.

(ii) 'a recognised medical condition'

The abnormality of mental functioning must arise 'from a recognised medical condition'. This is designed to be wider than the familiar list of sufficient causes in the original s 2 of the 1957 Act.[154] It is intended to produce clearer expert evidence from psychiatrists and psychologists and to allow sufficient flexibility for the new defence to develop in line with medical understanding and practice.[155] The immediate questions arising are: What kind(s) of medical condition? Recognized by whom?

'Medical condition'

This new element of the definition will provide a clearer foundation for the defence. As the Royal College of Psychiatrists explained, it will:

encourage reference within expert evidence to diagnosis in terms of one or two of the accepted internationally classificatory systems of mental conditions (i.e. the World Health Organisation: International Classification of Diseases (ICD-10); and the American Psychiatric Association: Diagnostic and Statistical Manual of Mental Disorders (DSM-1V)) without explicitly writing those systems into the legislation.[156]

---

[153] The defence of irresistible impulse, which is not within the defence of insanity, is therefore included into the law (but only of murder) by way of diminished responsibility.

[154] The Law Commission originally wanted a wider formulation: that source of the abnormality should be an 'underlying condition' (CP 177, para 10.21), to include a mental condition existing independent of the external circumstances that gave rise to the commission of an offence. It would therefore have 'include[d] cases in which the origins of the condition itself lie in adverse circumstances with which the offender has had to cope': CP 177, para 6.54.

[155] See the MOJ Consultation Paper 19/08 at www.justice.gov.uk/consultations/docs/murder-manslaughter-infanticide-consultation.pdf.

[156] LC 304, para 5.114. See MOJ CP 19/08, fn 13.

It, must be noted that *any* medical condition will suffice. It will include physical conditions as well as psychological or psychiatric ones.[157] Alcoholic dependency will qualify as a medical condition irrespective of whether it resulted in brain damage,[158] as will conditions such as diabetes or ADHD. Depressive illnesses resulting from prolonged abuse will qualify, and hence the defence remains available to battered women on those terms.[159] Although this element of the defence is much broader than the equivalent element under the 1957 Act, it should not create excessive breadth in the defence overall since the other elements are all, arguably, narrower. One consequence will be that if pleas based on spurious 'medical conditions' are made, it will lead to fewer pleas being accepted than under existing law. It will be interesting to see whether there are attempts to use this broad element of 'any medical condition' and the diminished responsibility defence as a method for getting some evidence before the jury of circumstances which will be precluded by the narrower defence of loss of control under s 54 (above).

In discussions on reform, groups expressed concern that this element may in some circumstances be narrower than the old law because it will not apply to those who kill terminally ill relatives when the killer has 'acted rationally in response to persistent requests from a seriously ill loved-one'.[160] However, the defence will only be categorically ruled out in such cases if there is no 'medical condition'. It may be that some depressive illness would be likely to be diagnosed.[161]

'Recognised'

The requirement that the medical condition is a 'recognised one' is also intended to prevent 'idiosyncratic diagnosis', being advanced as a basis for a plea of diminished responsibility.[162] However, during the debates in Committee in Parliament, the Government recognized that it is important that the legislation must be sufficiently flexible to cater for emerging medical conditions. It expressed the view that it is open to the defence to call a 'recognized specialist who has had their work peer-reviewed, although it has *not quite got on the list* (ie in DSM IV or ICD-10) and that it would be for the jury to decide whether the evidence met the partial defence requirements'.[163] Care will be needed to ensure that 'quack' opinions are not received. The comment in Parliament might have been better expressed in terms of the recognized specialist being not *yet on the list*. This would reflect the desire to ensure flexibility for development.

Developmental immaturity as a 'medical condition'? The new defence differs from the Law Commission's proposal principally because the new definition does not include, as a cause of impairment, 'developmental immaturity in a defendant under the age of 18', alongside abnormality of mental functioning arising from a mental condition. So, as it was put in debates:

An adult who acts like a 10-year-old gets that taken into account, but a 10-year-old who acts like a 10-year-old does not.[164]

---

[157] See the MOJ Consultation Paper 19/08, www.justice.gov.uk/consultations/docs/murder-manslaughter-infanticide-consultation.pdf, para 49.

[158] See *Tandy* [1989] 1 All ER 267; *Wood* [2008] EWCA Crim 1305; *Stewart* [2009] EWCA Crim 593; *Stewart (No 2)* [2010] EWCA Crim 2159. Arguably, acute intoxication will also constitute a recognized medical condition.

[159] Battered women's syndrome, having been included in 1992 in the standard British classification of mental diseases, is a relevant condition: *Hobson* [1998] 1 Cr App R 31.

[160] See the evidence of 'Dignity in Dying' to Joint Committee on Human Rights, 8th Report, 2008–2009, para 1.150; evidence 44–45. cf *Cocker* [1989] Crim LR who would not fit within this defence nor LOSC.

[161] See Public Bill Committee, 3 February 2009, written evidence (CJ/01); Joint Committee on Human Rights, 8th report, 2008–2009; para 1.151.

[162] LC 304, para 5.114.

[163] Public Bill Committee Debates, 3 March 2009, col 414.

[164] Public Bill Committee Debates, 3 March 2009, col 411.

The Government rejected this proposal on the grounds that this was unnecessary and be-cause the concept of a 'recognised medical condition' is designed to be wide enough to cover relevant conditions affecting those under 18 (eg learning disabilities and autistic spectrum disorders).[165]

There was widespread support for the Law Commission proposal.[166] Lord Phillips is on record as regretting the omission of any reference to developmental immaturity, saying:

The Government has not accepted this argument for two reasons. The first is that they do not be-lieve that the absence of such a provision is causing serious problems in practice. The second is, I quote:

> We think there is a risk that such a provision would open up the defence too widely and catch inappropriate cases. Even if it were to succeed only rarely (as the Law Commission suggest), we think it likely that far more defendants would at least try to run it, so diverting attention in too many trials from the key issue. I believe that there is something of a paradox in this reasoning. At present natural developmental immaturity in a child who has reached the age of 10 does not con-stitute a defence. That may be why developmental immaturity is not causing problems in practice. But it is surely offensive to justice that a child whose brain has not yet developed to the extent ne-cessary to provide the self-control that is found in an adult should be unable to pray this fact in aid, at least as a partial defence. Children develop at different speeds. If (and it may be a big if) some are sufficiently mature at the age of 10 to have full criminal responsibility, those who are not should, I feel, be entitled to pray this in aid.[167]

Since there is now no defence of *doli incapax*[168] the child killer has limited defence options. Arguably, there will be cases where a young defendant might be able to bring his devel-opmental immaturity within the rubric of a 'recognised medical condition' for the pur-poses of the new defence. However, whatever the cause of the developmental immaturity, whether it is nature or nurture, unless it results in an *abnormal* functioning, D will not be able to meet the requirement under new s 2(1)(a). The Law Commission was concerned that experts may find it impossible to distinguish between the impact of developmental im-maturity on D's functioning and the impact of a mental abnormality on that functioning process. It concluded that it was 'wholly unrealistic and unfair' to expect medical experts to assess the impact of mental abnormality whilst disregarding developmental immaturity.[169] The harshness of the inability to rely on developmental immaturity to found a diminished responsibility plea might be felt most keenly in some cases of joint enterprise for murder where a young vulnerable defendant has joined with an older gang, one of whose members kills V.

It must not be forgotten that the mere fact that D suffers from a particular medical condi-tion is only one part of the defence; all the elements need to be established by D.[170]

---

[165] See CP 19/08: www.justice.gov.uk/consultations/docs/murder-manslaughter-infanticide-consultation. pdf, para 55.

[166] Supported by the Crown Court Judges, the Criminal Bar Association, the Youth Justice Board, the Royal College of Psychiatrists, Dr Eileen Vizard, the NSPCC, and a number of lawyers in Parliament.

[167] Lord Phillips' Essex University/Clifford Chance lecture on *Reforming the Law of Homicide*, delivered on 6 November 2008. His lordship's position also creates an arbitrary distinction between those children who are at different stages of maturity. What should matter, it is submitted, is whether there is disfunction of ability to exercise control and judgement etc.

[168] *R v T* [2009] UKHL 20, above, Ch 12.

[169] LC 304, para 5.128.

[170] Under the old law it was held that D's ADHD was not of itself enough to satisfy the defence: *Osborne* [2010] EWCA Crim 547 where D killed V in an unprovoked attack in anger and his illness was not a cause of the conduct.

(iii) 'a substantial impairment of mental ability'

Under the old law, the matter that had to be substantially impaired was D's *mental responsibility* for acting as he did.[171] The test of *substantial* impairment of responsibility[172] was one of moral responsibility.[173] Under the new law, the matter that now has to be shown to be substantially impaired is D's *ability to do* any of the things mentioned in new s 2(1A).

Following *Lloyd*[174] 'substantially impaired' was interpreted in the 1957 Act to mean more than trivial and in the recent case of *R*[175] the Lord Chief Justice rejected the argument that the meaning of 'substantial' had been inconsistently applied under the 1957 Act:

Substantially is an ordinary English word...Its presence in the statute is deliberate. It is designed to ensure that the murderous activity of a defendant should not result in a conviction for manslaughter rather than murder on account of any impairment of mental responsibility, however trivial and insignificant; but equally that the defence should be available without the defendant having to show that his mental responsibility for his actions was so grossly impaired as to be extinguished. That is the purpose of this defence and this language. The Concise Oxford Dictionary offers 'of real importance' and 'having substance' as suggested meanings for 'substantially'. But, in reality, even the Concise Oxford Dictionary tells us very little more about the ordinary meaning and understanding to be attached to the word 'substantially'.

Under the new s 2, 'substantial' will, presumably, be interpreted in the same way. However, under the new s 2, the approach to the meaning of 'substantial' may well give rise to problems. What must be impaired is D's ability to (a) understand the nature of *his own* conduct; (b) to form a rational judgment; (c) to exercise self-control. Whether D has that ability is a matter of psychiatry. The question is whether there is a 'substantial impairment' of one or more of these. It is a psychiatric question how far D's ability deviates from the normal level of ability to do those things. Arguably therefore there will be greater input from experts and little for the jury to decide, although obviously, the ultimate decision on whether the defence is made out is for the jury.[176]

D has to show a substantial impairment of his ability to do one or more of these:

(a) to understand the nature of his own conduct;

(b) to form a rational judgment;

(c) to exercise self-control.[177]

If (a) and (b) are construed narrowly, they will be very similar to insanity and hence may be difficult for D to satisfy. If they are akin to insanity, in many cases D might well plead that complete defence rather than the partial defence of diminished responsibility.

(a) *'to understand the nature of D's conduct'*

As commentators have observed this is similar to the first limb of the insanity plea.[178] An example of how this element might be satisfied provided by the Law Commission[179] was of a 10-year-old boy with a recognized medical condition[180]:

---

[171] *Byrne*, above; *Simcox* [1964] Crim LR 402; *Lloyd* [1967] 1 QB 175. But cf Sparks, above, n 134, at 16–19.

[172] *Campbell* (1986) 84 Cr App R 255 at 259.

[173] A person whose impulse is irresistible bears *no* moral responsibility for his act, for he has no choice; a person whose impulse is much more difficult to resist than that of an ordinary person bears a diminished degree of moral responsibility for his act.

[174] [1967] 1 QB 175.

[175] [2010] EWCA Crim 194, para 15.

[176] See also the suggestion of the Law Com 304, para 5.198 that it will be a question for the jury.

[177] See *Byrne* [1960] 2 QB 396; and *Khan* [2009] EWCA Crim 1569.

[178] See Fortson, above n 144; Mackay, above, n 144.

[179] No 304, para 5.21.

[180] To reflect the provision as enacted we must amend the example so that he has an *abnormality* of mental functioning.

who has been left to play very violent video games for hours on end for much of his life, loses his temper and kills another child when the child attempts to take a game from him. When interviewed, he shows no real understanding that, when a person is killed they cannot simply be later revived, as happens in the games he has been continually playing.

One aspect of this form of the defence is that the focus is exclusively on whether D has the ability to understand the nature of his own conduct; it does not encompass his ability to understand anyone else's. Will this accommodate D who believes that his victim is, for example, possessed? Does this apply to the person with a very distorted thinking process? Baroness Murphy raised doubts about these in Parliament,[181] and such cases may be difficult to fit within limb (a).

b) 'Substantially impaired capacity to "form a rational judgement"'

Examples from the Law Commission included:

(i)   a woman who has been diagnosed as being in a state of learned helplessness conse-quent upon violent abuse suffered at her husband's hands comes to believe that only burning her husband to death will rid the world of his sins;

(ii) a mentally sub-normal boy believes that he must follow his older brother's instruc-tions, even when they involve taking take part in a killing. He says, 'I wouldn't dream of disobeying my brother and he would never tell me to do something if it was really wrong';

(iii) a depressed man who has been caring for many years for a terminally ill spouse, kills her, at her request. He says that he had found it progressively more difficult to stop her repeated requests dominating his thoughts to the exclusion of all else, so that 'I felt I would never think straight again until I had given her what she wanted.'

(c) The 'ability to exercise control'

This might be construed very much more widely and render the defence available in a broader range of circumstances than under (a) and (b).

(iv) An explanation (or cause) of the killing

The defence is narrowed further by the requirement that the abnormality of mental func-tioning, arising from a 'recognised medical condition' substantially impairing D's ability in a relevant manner must also 'explain' his acts in killing. By s 2(1B) 'an explanation' for D's conduct is provided 'if it causes, or is a significant contributory factor in causing, D to carry out that conduct'. Several problems arise. Section 2(1B) does not say that for the defence to succeed a sufficient explanation can *only* be provided if the abnormality of mental function-ing is a 'cause'.[182] On this basis a causal link is just one of the ways in which the killing might be 'explained. Although the wording of s. 2(1B) might lend itself to the argument that the sub-section provides merely one way in which the killing might be "explained", the language of the debates was clearly envisaging a causal link . . . ' There may be cases where the abnormality provides an explanation sufficient to mitigate the conduct to manslaughter even if there is no causal link. However, the language in debates was clearly envisaging a causal link. In debates, the Minister stated that:

We do not believe that the partial defence should succeed where random coincidence has brought together the activity of the person and the recognised medical condition. . . . *there must have been at least a significant contributory factor in causing the defendant to act as he did. We do not require the*

---

[181] *Hansard*, HL, 30 June 2009, vol 712, col 180.
[182] See further *Blackstone's Criminal Practice* (2011) B1.

corporations.[414] Section 1(2) also applies the offence to police forces, partnerships,[415] (Limited Liability Partnerships Act 2000 are caught by the definition of corporation in any event), trade unions[416] and employers' associations,[417] if the organization concerned is an employer. Schedule 1 lists the government departments to which the offence applies. There are some 40 such departments.[418] These include some in which it is not difficult to imagine how corporate manslaughter liability might arise because of the functions they perform, for example Department of Transport, Department of Health, Forestry Commission. With some it may seem a little less likely, for example Revenue and Customs, CPS, National Audit Office – but since liability can arise as a result of being an employer or occupier, it is not difficult so see how they might be liable for a death.[419]

In the course of debates in the House of Lords it was emphasized how important is the extension of the offence to public bodies:

[T]here is no reason why the death of an individual in one situation should be considered less of a death, or less deserving of justice, merely because that situation was presided over by government officials as opposed to privately employed foremen. Indeed, it is all the more of a tragedy and contravention of the natural principle of justice where the state itself acts with such gross negligence that the very lives of its own citizens are forfeit.[420]

Crown Immunity is removed by s 11. Section 11(2) provides that a Crown organization is to be treated as owing whatever duties of care it would owe if it were a corporation that was not a servant or agent of the Crown. However, as will be explained below there are a number of respects in which that liability is very heavily qualified in ss 3 to 7.

Partnerships are to be treated as owing whatever duties of care they would owe if they were a body corporate (s 14(2)).

15.4.3 Elements of the offence

In summary there must be:

- a relevant duty owed to the victim;
- the breach of the duty by the organization must be as a result of the way the activities are managed or organized;

---

[414] By s 25, 'corporation' does not include a corporation sole but includes any body corporate wherever incorporated. This includes companies incorporated under companies legislation, as well as bodies incorporated under statute (as is the case with many non-Departmental Public Bodies and other bodies in the public sector) or by Royal Charter.

[415] By s 25, 'partnership' means: (a) a partnership within the Partnership Act 1890, or (b) a limited partnership registered under the Limited Partnerships Act 1907, or a firm or entity of a similar character formed under the law of a country or territory outside the United Kingdom. See also *Stevenson & Sons*, above p 268.

[416] By s 25, 'trade union' has the meaning given by s 1 of the Trade Union and Labour Relations (Consolidation) Act 1992.

[417] By s 25, 'employers' association' has the meaning given by s 122 of the Trade Union and Labour Relations (Consolidation) Act 1992.

[418] Provision is made in s 16 for the circumstances in which relevant functions are transferred between one government department and another or between the other bodies listed in Sch 1, and for cases in which a relevant government agency is privatized.

[419] The list of organizations to which the offence applies can be further extended by secondary legislation, eg, to further types of unincorporated association, subject to the affirmative resolution procedure (s 21). The list of government departments in Sch 1 may be changed by the negative resolution procedure (eg the name of a particular department) unless the change is to alter the range of activities or functions in relation to which the s 1 offence applies, in which case the affirmative resolution procedure applies.

[420] *Hansard*, HL, text for 15 Jan 2007, col GC189 (Lord Hunt).

- a substantial element of the breach of the duty must be due to the way the senior management managed or organized activities;
- the breach of the duty must be a gross one;
- V's death was caused by the breach of the duty.

15.4.3.1 A relevant duty

The definition of a 'relevant duty of care' is provided in s 2 of the Act:

(1) A 'relevant duty of care', in relation to an organisation, means any of the following duties owed by it under the law of negligence –

(a) a duty owed to its employees or to other persons working for the organisation or performing services for it;

(b) a duty owed as occupier of premises;

(c) a duty owed in connection with –

(i) the supply by the organisation of goods or services (whether for consideration or not),

(ii) the carrying on by the organisation of any construction or maintenance operations,

(iii) the carrying on by the organisation of any other activity on a commercial basis, or

(iv) the use or keeping by the organisation of any plant, vehicle or other thing;

(d) a duty owed to a person who, by reason of being a person within subsection (2), is someone for whose safety the organisation is responsible [arising where V is in custody].

...

(3) Subsection (1) is subject to sections 3 to 7.

The duties reflect the duties of care arising at common law. The duty is that owed in the common law of negligence,[421] or, where applicable the statutory duty which has superseded the common law duty, for example, the Occupiers' Liability Act 1957. It is made clear by s 2(4) that a duty owed under the law of negligence will apply if the common law duty of negligence has been superseded by statutory provision imposing strict liability. The Explanatory Notes give the example of the Carriage of Air Act 1961. The most important thing to remember is that the criminal offence does not impose new duties, it is based on the existing duties which are present in civil law – either by statute or common law. The requirement of proving a duty will add to the complexity of the prosecution.

The most frequently arising duties are likely to be from relationships as employers and occupiers, and duties arising from these activities are also of special significance when it comes to identifying the scope of the exemptions for certain types of organization/activity.[422]

It is easy to see how the categories might give rise to duties of care which, if breached, could lead to fatalities. Duties as employer would, for example, include duties to provide safe places of work. Note that the duty as an employer extends beyond the scope of employees as strictly defined and includes subcontractors, and volunteer workers, etc. Duties as occupier of premises will render organizations liable if there are, eg faulty electrical wiring, dangerous staircases, etc. 'Premises' includes land, buildings and moveable structures (s 25); a duty owed

---

[421] Section 2(7) specifies, for the avoidance of doubt, that 'the law of negligence' includes: (a) in relation to England and Wales, the Occupiers' Liability Act 1957, the Defective Premises Act 1972 and the Occupiers' Liability Act 1984.

[422] See below, p 572.

in connection with the supply by the organization of goods might arise from provision of foodstuffs; duties arising from the provision of services (whether for consideration or not), would include most obviously rail travel and other transport; duties from the carrying on by the organization of any construction or maintenance operations[423] would include building operations.[424] Duties arising from the carrying on by the organization of any other activity on a commercial basis was a category included in case activities such as farming or mining were not regarded as involving the provision of services, etc. Duties arising from the use or keeping by the organization of any plant, vehicle or 'other thing' could be extremely wide ranging.

The most controversial category is that relating to duties arising from detention. Lord Ramsbotham, former Chief Inspector of Prisons, was successful in the House of Lords in amending the Bill to include what is now s 2(1)(d). There was considerable Government opposition and the Bill almost lapsed. The final compromise position reached was that the commencement of this element requires the further approval of Parliament. By s 27, an order by the Secretary of State to commence s 2(1)(d) is subject to the affirmative resolution procedure, and will require approval in both Houses of Parliament before it takes effect. The most difficult issue, and one which engaged the House of Lords, was the question whether suicides in detention would give rise to liability where the relevant agency, for example the Prison Service, could or should have prevented it.[425]

Section 2(2) lists the various forms of custody or detention[426] which will trigger a duty:

(2) A person is within this subsection if –

  (a) he is detained at a custodial institution or in a custody area at a court or police station;

  (b) he is detained at a removal centre or short-term holding facility;

  (c) he is being transported in a vehicle, or being held in any premises, in pursuance of prison escort arrangements or immigration escort arrangements;

  (d) he is living in secure accommodation in which he has been placed;

  (e) he is a detained patient.

Deaths in custody give rise to problems because of the particular status of the victim; that by definition the activities will be occurring within 'premises'; and the fact that the organization providing the detention 'service' is one which will have to make public policy decisions as to allocation of resources, etc (and therefore in some cases the duty would be excluded under s 3).[427]

Although the Government intention was not to introduce liability in this category for a further three years, there may be circumstances in which the broad terms of s 2(1) trigger liability for a death in custody. The answer to whether there is a relevant duty involves a

---

[423] Section 2(7) further defines 'construction or maintenance operations' to mean 'operations of any of the following descriptions – (a) construction, installation, alteration, extension, improvement, repair, maintenance, decoration, cleaning, demolition or dismantling of – (i) any building or structure, (ii) anything else that forms, or is to form, part of the land, or (iii) any plant, vehicle or other thing; (b) operations that form an integral part of, or are preparatory to, or are for rendering complete, any operations within paragraph (a).'

[424] This provision overlaps significantly with the previous category of supply of goods or services. It was included to avoid any lacunae where the construction operator was not acting 'commercially' – as might be argued with some public sector bodies

[425] Under the new division of power, prisons come under the responsibility of the Ministry of Justice. The list of Government Departments as enacted in Sch 1 will need to be amended.

[426] The various categories are further defined in s 2(7). Section 23 provides a power to the Secretary of State to add to those categories listed in s 2(2), to whom a 'relevant duty of care' is owed by reason of s 2(1)(d).

[427] See below, p 574.

most convoluted evaluation of whether there is a duty and whether the exemptions apply. If the death is attributable to a resourcing issue, the duty of care will be one relating to a decision on a matter of public policy and therefore be totally excluded by s 3(1). Preventable deaths due to poor management of the resources provided (rather than due to public policy decisions about resource allocation which will be excluded by s 3(1)) may fall within s 2, but s 3(2) must be borne in mind. That section excludes the duty of care in relation to 'the exercise of an exclusively public function', and this would include detaining offenders in prison. However, that exclusion does not include duties under s 2(1)(a) or (b). It is unlikely that s 2(1)(a) would found a duty in relation to a suicide, etc, as it imposes the organization's duty as employer to, eg prison officers. There is, however, possibility of liability under s 2(1)(b) if the organization's duty is as occupier. As parliamentary debates accepted, if a brick fell off a wall because of poor maintenance and killed a prisoner that would trigger liability under the provisions already in force since the duty of care was the ordinary one owed by an occupier of premises.[428]

The question arises to what extent does the prison authority's duty arising from its position as an occupier, (under the Occupiers Liability Act 1957) apply not merely to the cases where injury arises from the state of the premises, but from activity on the premises? The 1957 Act imposes duties which an occupier of premises owes to his visitors 'in respect of dangers due to the state of the premises or to things done or omitted to be done on them'. As Taylor observes, 'the very fact that it was thought necessary to add s 2(1)(d) suggests that there are some aspects that are not covered by the duty as occupier . . . Perhaps a distinction has to be drawn (but not a very satisfying or persuasive one) between these "normal" occupier duties and those arising from the special problems arising from the fact that the "visitors" are in custody, are often disturbed or vulnerable and are subject to special risks such as suicide (or harm from other inmates or mistreatment by their custodians) as a result.'[429]

Duty issues under s 2

Given the potential breadth of the categories of duty and examination of the common law which might be necessary to determine whether a duty does exist, it is reassuring to see that the question whether a duty of care is owed is a question of law. It is for the judge to decide: s 2(5). Moreover, 'the judge must make any findings of fact necessary to decide that question'. This latter provision about the judge finding facts is highly unusual and should be contrasted with the common law position on gross negligence manslaughter[430] where whether a duty of care exists is a matter for the jury once the judge has decided that there is evidence capable of establishing a duty.

Section 2(6) makes it clear that the duty of care will not be excluded by *ex turpi causa* and *volenti* doctrines.[431] This is potentially very important. The scope of liability at civil law is restricted in practice by the operation of these doctrines. However, the reason that they are excluded as defences or limits on criminal liability in this context is easy enough to deduce. The victim will in many cases not be properly described as taking a truly voluntary risk since he will be compelled to do so by the organization acting as his employer, etc.

---

[428] See Taylor, above, n 398. See also S Griffin, 'Accountability for Deaths Attributable to the Gross Negligent Act or Omission of a Police Force: The Impact of the Corporate Manslaughter and Corporate Homicide Act 2007' (2010) 74 J Crim L 648.

[429] ibid.

[430] *Evans* [2009] EWCA Crim 650.

[431] *Wacker* [2003] QB 1203.

15.4.3.2 The breach must be as a result of the way the activities are managed or organized

This second element of the offence is designed to ensure that the focus is on the so-called 'management failure'. This test is not linked to a particular level of management but considers how an activity was managed within the organization as a whole. It will now be possible to combine the shortcomings of a wide number of individuals within the organization to prove a failure of management *by the organization*. The language is designed to reflect the concentration on things done consistently with the organization's culture and policies more generally. It remains to be seen how easily this can be proved.

Senior management

The Act does, however, place a significant restriction on the organizational failure test. Under s 1(3), the offence is committed by an organization only if 'the way in which its activities are managed and organised by its senior management is a substantial element in the breach referred to in subsection (1)'. Who are the senior managers? By s 1(4)(c): 'senior management', in relation to an organization, means the persons who play 'significant roles' in making:

decisions about how the whole or a substantial part of its activities are to be managed or organised, or the actual managing or organising of the whole or a substantial part of those activities.

This extends beyond the narrow category of senior individuals who would be caught at common law by the identification doctrine being the 'directing mind and will'.[432]

The senior managers' management and organization must be a 'substantial element' in the breach of duty leading to death. Two important consequence flow from this aspect of the offence. First, since the senior managers' involvement need only be a substantial element in the organization, etc, the involvement and conduct of others – 'non-senior managers' who are involved in the management and organization of activities – is also relevant. Secondly, when assessing the management failure the contribution of those individuals who are not senior management can be taken into account even if their involvement is 'substantial' provided it is not so great as to render the senior managers' involvement something less than substantial. There can be more than one substantial element. No doubt the courts will say that a 'substantial' involvement is something that the jury can evaluate as an ordinary English word meaning more than trivial.

15.4.3.3 A 'gross' breach of duty?

The requirement of a gross breach of duty is clearly designed to echo the gross negligence manslaughter offence at common law. Section 2(4)(b) provides a more detailed explanation of the concept – a breach of a duty of care by an organization is a 'gross' breach if the conduct alleged to amount to a breach of that duty *falls far below* what can reasonably be expected of the organization in the circumstances. The language chosen is similar to that proposed by the Law Commission as a suitable form of words to replace gross negligence. The test retains a degree of circularity, although not to the extent of that in the common law offence of gross negligence manslaughter.

The jury's duty in relation to determining the breach of duty is provided in s 8:

(1) This section applies where –

    (a) it is established that an organisation owed a relevant duty of care to a person, and

    (b) it falls to the jury to decide whether there was a gross breach of that duty.

---

[432] Is the test too restrictive? Will companies seek to avoid this by nominating people in less senior positions to take responsibility for all health and safety policies?

(2) The jury must consider whether the evidence shows that the organisation failed to comply with any health and safety legislation[433] that relates to the alleged breach, and if so –

    (a) how serious that failure was;

    (b) how much of a risk of death it posed.

(3) The jury may also –

    (a) consider the extent to which the evidence shows that there were attitudes, policies, systems or accepted practices within the organisation that were likely to have encouraged any such failure as is mentioned in subsection (2), or to have produced tolerance of it;

    (b) have regard to any health and safety guidance that relates to the alleged breach.

(4) This section does not prevent the jury from having regard to any other matters they consider relevant.

This section deals with factors to be taken into account by the jury (the offence is only triable on indictment). Note that the jury '*must*' consider these issues. Note also that the jury is obliged to consider whether the 'organization' complied, not just whether its senior management complied. This further supports the argument that the activities of non-senior managers are relevant in determining whether there has been a management failure. Section 8(3) emphasizes that the jury may have reference to general organizational and systems failures.[434] The inability to do so under the old law was a source of common complaint. How the 'attitudes, etc' are proved is problematic. There is the potential for lengthy arguments and evidence comparing practices across the particular sector or industry. Imagine a prosecution of a rail company and the potential for them to adduce evidence of safety procedures and policies across the sector to demonstrate the quality of their own. No doubt the jury will have regard to the organization's overall objectives, published policy statements on safety, monitoring and compliance policies, attitudes to development of safety and to training and awareness, approaches to remedying previous health and safety infringements, etc.

15.4.3.4 Causing death

There must be a death of a person. Causation must be established in accordance with orthodox principles.[435] Difficulties may arise where the organization alleges that the individual employee has, with his free voluntary informed fatal act, broken the chain of causation.[436]

15.4.4 Excluded duties

The most important aspect of the legislation is not the scope of relevant duty and of potential liability under s 1 and s 2, but rather what the Government excluded from the scope of liability under ss 3 to 7. The excluded categories of duty are considerable. The different categories and sub-categories of duty also make the interpretation of whether a duty is owed rather more complex to unravel.

---

[433] Defined in s 8(5): ' "health and safety guidance" means any code, guidance, manual or similar publication that is concerned with health and safety matters and is made or issued (under a statutory provision or otherwise) by an authority responsible for the enforcement of any health and safety legislation'.

[434] This section has been influenced, as has much of this Act, by the Australian legislation and academic comment in Australia. See further B Fisse and J Braithwaite, *Corporations, Crime and Accountability* (1993).

[435] See Ch 4.

[436] See *Kennedy (No 2)* [2007] UKHL 38. However, it is arguable that the decision in *Latif* [1996] 1 WLR 104 would apply because the employee and organization are acting in concert.

15.4.4.1 Public policy

The broadest exclusion is provided in s 3(1) and deals with decisions of public policy taken by public authorities.

Any duty of care owed by a public authority in respect of a decision as to matters of public policy (including in particular the allocation of public resources or the weighing of competing public interests) is not a 'relevant duty of care'.

This excludes liability where a death is due to a public authority's decision not to allocate appropriate resources to a particular service. The section is seeking to reflect the distinction between 'operational' and 'public' policy matters in the law of tort.[437] The manner in which a public authority implements its duty in practice is justiciable in negligence, but the way it exercises its statutory discretion is not. In *X v Bedfordshire County Council*,[438] Lord Browne-Wilkinson said that, 'a common law duty of care in relation to the taking of decisions involving policy matters cannot exist'.[439] The courts have continually struggled with the dividing line and it has been recognized that the test is very difficult to apply.[440] It remains to be seen to what extent will the criminal courts be willing to engage in detailed evaluations of the common law on this issue.

As an example of the difficulty, if a relevant public authority decides not to deploy resources to buy a particular drug for patients suffering a particular illness, no duty arises. If, having made the decision to supply the drug, there is negligence in the way it is supplied/administered, etc, liability may arise. Interesting issues could arise in a trial in which the breach is of a duty owed by a private company and a public body where they have joint responsibility for managing an activity. The effect of the exemptions would be stark.

Section 3(2) provides a less extensive exclusion in relation to things done 'in the exercise of an exclusively public function':

(2) Any duty of care owed in respect of things done in the exercise of an exclusively public function is not a 'relevant duty of care' unless it falls within section 2(1)(a), (b) or (d).

(3) Any duty of care owed by a public authority in respect of inspections carried out in the exercise of a statutory function is not a 'relevant duty of care' unless it falls within section 2(1) (a) or (b).

(4) In this section –

'exclusively public function' means a function that falls within the prerogative of the Crown or is, by its nature, exercisable only with authority conferred –

(a) by the exercise of that prerogative, or

(b) by or under a statutory provision;

'statutory function' means a function conferred by or under a statutory provision.

The duty of care owed as employer or occupier or custodian under s 2(1)(a) or (b) or (d) still applies in these circumstances. This excludes only public functions involved in s (2)(1)(c), notably the supply of goods or services and construction work, etc. The exemption was not supported by consultees in the Government's consultation exercise.[441]

---

[437] See *Anns v Merton Borough Council* [1978] AC 728, HL. See Horder, above, n 389, at 115.

[438] [1995] 2 AC 633, HL.

[439] ibid, 738.

[440] *Phelps v Hillingdon LBC* [2001] 2 AC 619, HL. See further, Horder, above, n 437.

[441] Home Office, *Summary of Responses to Corporate Manslaughter: The Government's Draft Bill for Reform*, March 2005, at para 9.

15.4.4.2 Military activities: s 4

Many of the activities performed by the armed forces[442] will be excluded by virtue of s 3(2) (above), but s 3(2) does not prevent liability arising as an employer or occupier. Section 4 goes further by providing a total exclusion for some activities. There is no relevant duty for:

operations, including peacekeeping operations and operations for dealing with terrorism, civil unrest or serious public disorder, in the course of which members of the armed forces come under attack or face the threat of attack or violent resistance.

Liability is also excluded for preparation and support of military operations of that description, nor training of a hazardous nature, or training carried out in a hazardous way, which it is considered needs to be carried out, or carried out in that way, in order to improve or maintain the effectiveness of the armed forces with respect to such operations.[443]

The armed forces will owe a duty as an employer[444] or occupier other than in those circumstances.[445]

15.4.4.3 The Police: s 5[446]

The exemptions provided for police activities are also complex. Two categories exist. Sections 5(1) and 5(2) create a total exemption – that is, no relevant duty arises for some types of policing activity – where, in short, there are operations in relation to terrorism or civil unrest. More fully, there is no duty on the organization where officers or employees[447] of the public authority[448] in question are engaged in operations for dealing with terrorism, civil unrest or serious disorder, which involve them coming under attack, or facing the threat of attack or violent resistance, or those involving the carrying on of policing or law-enforcement activities (s 5(2)). Nor is there a duty when the police are preparing for those types of operations, or training to enable them to carry out such operations.

In other circumstances, by s 5(3) a 'relevant duty of care' is owed where the organization is acting as employer, occupier or custodian (that is, s 2(1)(a), (b) or (d)). This exemption will exclude circumstances where a member of the public has been killed in the pursuit of law-enforcement activities. The Explanatory Notes suggest that this includes:

decisions about and responses to emergency calls, the manner in which particular police operations are conducted, the way in which law enforcement and other coercive powers are exercised, measures taken to protect witnesses and the arrest and detention of suspects.

---

[442] By s 12(1) 'the "armed forces" means any of the naval, military or air forces of the Crown raised under the law of the United Kingdom'.

[443] Will there be a problem in ECHR terms if the army cannot be prosecuted for killing? Arguably there will be no breach of Art 2 because an intentional killing will be prosecutable as murder on the part of the officer involved.

[444] By s 12(2), a person who is a member of the armed forces is to be treated as employed by the Ministry of Defence.

[445] There is no liability for special forces: 'Any duty of care owed by the Ministry of Defence in respect of activities carried on by members of the special forces is not a "relevant duty of care"' (s 4(3)). This is presumably necessary to allow for more extreme forms of training. By s 4(4), 'the "special forces" means those units of the armed forces the maintenance of whose capabilities is the responsibility of the Director of Special Forces or which are for the time being subject to the operational command of that Director'.

[446] See S Griffin, 'Accountability for Deaths Attributable to the Gross Negligent Act or Omission of a Police Force: The Impact of the Corporate Manslaughter and Corporate Homicide Act 2007' (2010) 74 J Crim L 648.

[447] Section 13 provides that police officers are to be treated as the employees of the police force for which they work (and are therefore owed the employer's duty of care by the force). It also ensures that police forces are treated as occupiers of premises and that other conduct is attributable to them as if they were distinctly constituted bodies.

[448] This could include other authorities such as SOCA or immigration officials: s 5(4).

Professor Horder has suggested[449] that the extent of the exceptions in ss 4 and 5 is unwarranted and that the result may be to leave individuals at risk of liability when the agency is the one at fault. He suggests also that the exemption was unnecessary having regard to the need for the DPP's consent.[450] This is debatable. For Parliament to have fixed these activities as off-limits is one thing. To expect the DPP to have to make policy decisions such as the exemption of the police in a case of fatality is to subject him to media censure for whatever decision is made, and to diminish the level of certainty in the law.

15.4.4.4 Emergency services: s 6

In the law of tort, considerable difficulties have arisen in identifying the scope of the duty of care owed by the emergency and rescue services in the course of performing rescue activity. Section 6 puts beyond doubt that the corporate manslaughter offence does not apply generally to these agencies when responding to emergencies.[451] Approximate consistency with the civil law is secured by excluding liability arising from delay in response to an emergency, or the level of skill exercised in responding to the operation. The relevant emergency services protected by this exclusion are: the fire and rescue authorities and other emergency response organizations providing fire and rescue services; NHS bodies and ambulance services or blood/organ transport; the Coastguard and RNLI;[452] the armed forces (either responding to military emergency such as a fire on a base or when assisting the civilian rescue services). By s 6(7), emergency circumstances are defined in terms of those that are life-threatening or which are causing, or threaten to cause, serious injury or illness or serious harm to the environment or buildings or other property.

The emergency services may still be liable for a death arising from their status as employer or occupier even where the death arises in the course of an emergency (s 6(5)). The exemption also does not apply to duties that do not relate to *the way in which* a body responds to an emergency, for example, duties to maintain vehicles in a safe condition; these will be capable of prosecution under the offence. There is no exemption from liability for medical treatment itself, or decisions about this (other than decisions that establish the priority for treating patients). Matters relating to the organization and management of medical services will therefore be within the ambit of the offence (s 6(4)).

15.4.4.5 Child protection and probation: s 7

Section 7 limits the duty of care that a local authority or other public authority owes in respect of the exercise of its functions under Parts 4 and 5 of the Children Act 1989. In relation to the carrying on of those duties, a relevant duty arises for the purposes of s 1 only in relation to its activities as employer, occupier and duties relating to detention (s 2(1)(a), (b), (d)). There is no relevant duty, for example, if a child was not identified as being at risk and taken into care and was subsequently fatally injured. Similarly, any duty of care that a local probation board or other public authority owes in respect of the exercise by it of functions under Part 1 of the Criminal Justice and Court Services Act 2000 is excluded. In relation to carrying out those duties a relevant duty arises for the purposes of s 1 only in relation to its activities as employer, occupier and duties relating to detention (s 2(1) (a), (b), (d)).

---

[449] Above, n 389, at 119.

[450] See www.cps.gov.uk/legal/a_to_c/corporate_manslaughter.

[451] Emergency circumstances include circumstances that are believed to be emergency circumstances: s 6(8). This deals with the circumstances in which the response is to a hoax call.

[452] Those effecting sea rescue are also exempt in a very wide exclusionary provision.

15.4.5 Procedure

The offence of corporate manslaughter is triable only on indictment (s 1(6)), and a prosecution may not be instituted without the consent of the DPP (s 17(1)). Proceedings against partnerships[453] for the offence are to be brought in the name of the partnership (and not in that of any of its members) (s 14(2)). Any fine imposed on a partnership is to be paid out of the funds of the partnership (s 14(3)). Further provision is made in s 15 for evidential and procedural mechanisms to apply to organizations which are not corporations. The section ensures that the relevant evidential and procedural provisions apply, in the same way as they apply to corporations, to all those government departments or other bodies listed in Sch 1, as well as to police forces and those unincorporated associations covered by the offence.

15.4.5.1 Jurisdiction

Section 28 deals with extent and territorial application. The Act extends to the whole of the United Kingdom. Section 1 applies if the harm resulting in death is sustained: in the United Kingdom; or within the seaward limits of the territorial sea adjacent to the United Kingdom; on a British registered ship, British-controlled aircraft; a British-controlled hovercraft; in, on or above, or within 500 metres of, an offshore installation in United Kingdom territorial waters or a designated area of the United Kingdom's continental shelf (s 28(3)).[454]

Section 28(4) provides that:

For the purposes of subsection (3)(b) to (d) harm sustained on a ship, aircraft or hovercraft includes harm sustained by a person who –

(a) is then no longer on board the ship, aircraft or hovercraft in consequence of the wrecking of it or of some other mishap affecting it or occurring on it, and

(b) sustains the harm in consequence of that event.

Section 1 will therefore still apply if the harm resulting in death is sustained as a result of an incident involving a British vessel, but the victim is not physically on board when he suffers that harm. It will not apply if the incident involves a non-British vessel in international waters.

15.4.5.2 Penalties

An organization guilty of corporate manslaughter is liable to an unlimited fine (s 1(6)). Geotech were fined £385,000. In addition, the court has power on the application of the prosecution to impose a remedial order against an organization convicted of corporate manslaughter requiring it to take specified steps to remedy: the breach; any matter appearing to have resulted from it and to have been a cause of the death; or any health and safety deficiency in the 'organisation's policies, systems or practices' appearing to be indicated by the breach (s 9(1) and (2)). This provision is also heavily influenced by Australian experience. Any such order must be on 'such terms (whether those proposed or others) as the court considers appropriate having regard to any representations made, and any evidence adduced, in relation to that matter by the prosecution or on behalf of the organisation' (s 9(2)).

Section 9(4) provides for the form of a remedial order. It must specify a period within which the remedial steps are to be taken and may require the organization to supply evidence of

---

[453] Other than limited liability partnerships, which are corporate bodies and covered by the new offence as such.

[454] For difficulties in international waters see the investigation into the death of a yachtsman 15 miles off Cherbourg after collision with the *Alam Pintar* which resulted in no prosecution. See P Binning, 'Corporate Manslaughter on the High Seas' (2010) The Times, 28 Oct.

compliance. Periods specified may be extended or further extended by order of the court on an application made before the end of that period or extended period. An organization which fails to comply with a remedial order commits an offence triable only on indictment and punishable with an unlimited fine (s 9(5)). There appears to be nothing to prevent the conviction of a director as an accessory to this offence.

In addition, the court has power to impose a 'publicity order' under s 10 'requiring the organisation to publicise in a specified manner' its conviction, specified particulars, the amount of any fine and the terms of any remedial order. Before imposing such an order, the court must ascertain the views of any relevant enforcement authority as it considers appropriate, and have regard to any representations made by the prosecution or the organization. The form of a remedial order must specify a period within which the publicity order must be complied with, and may require the organization to supply evidence of compliance. An organization which fails to comply with an order commits an offence triable only on indictment and punishable with an unlimited fine (s 10(4)). Section 10 was added to the Bill during its passage in the House of Lords. It is clearly predicated on the assumption (probably correct) that large organizations are more concerned about adverse publicity than a fine.

The Sentencing Guidelines Council has issued a definitive guideline in relation to corporate manslaughter applicable to sentencing of organizations from 15 February 2010.[455] The court should require information about the financial circumstances of D, ideally examining relevant information for a three-year period including the year of the offence (para 14). There is no fixed correlation between turnover and fine (para. 15). Paragraph 19 lists factors which may or may not be relevant when the court is assessing the financial consequences of a fine. Any fine must be punitive and sufficient to have an impact on the defendant. The appropriate fine will rarely be less than £500,000 and may be measured in millions of pounds. Part G concerns publicity orders. The order should particularize the matters to be published, the place where the public announcement is to be made, the size of any notice and the number of insertions (if to be made in a newspaper).[456]

---

[455] Corporate Manslaughter and Corporate Homicide Act 2007 (Commencement No 2) Order 2010, SI 2010 No 276.

[456] See www.sentencing-guidelines.gov.uk/docs/guideline_on_corporate_manslaughter.pdf.

16
Further homicide and related offences

16.1 Offences ancillary to murder

Murder remains a common law offence, but Parliament was not content to leave to the common law the punishment of acts preliminary to murder. The Offences Against the Person Act 1861 created offences of conspiracy, solicitation, attempt and threats to murder. The offences of attempt were particularly complicated[1] and were repealed by the Criminal Law Act 1967. Attempts to commit murder are now governed by the Criminal Attempts Act 1981.[2] The conspiracy provision was repealed by the Criminal Law Act 1977 and conspiracy to murder is governed by that Act. Those who assist or encourage murder might be convicted of offences under Part 2 of the Serious Crime Act 2007, as discussed in Chapter 13, but there is also a specific offence of soliciting murder.

16.1.1 Solicitation

By s 4 of the Offences against the Person Act 1861 (as amended by the Criminal Law Act 1977) it is an offence punishable with life imprisonment to 'solicit, encourage, persuade or endeavour to persuade or … propose to any person, to murder any other person'.

The offence is relied on commonly to deal with those who hire 'contract killers' (who turn out to be undercover officers)[3] and has been used in more recent years to prosecute fundamentalist preachers who encourage their congregations to kill.[4] Sentences for the offence are high.[5]

16.1.1.1 A person

A child in the womb is not a 'person', so D encouraging X to kill the foetus while in the womb does not commit this offence.[6] But, in *Shephard*,[7] D's conviction was upheld when he wrote to a pregnant woman, 'When the kiddie is born you must lie on it … Don't let it live …' The decision seems reasonable on the facts – D *was* soliciting murder, ie to kill the child once born – but the court based it on the strange ground that the offence only arose if the child was in fact born alive. This seems untenable.

---

[1] See the 1st edition of this book, at 250–253.
[2] Above, p 403.
[3] See, as an example, *Singh Rai (Jagjit)* [2006] 2 Cr App R (S) 98.
[4] See *El-Faisal* [2004] EWCA Crim 343 and *Abu Hamza* [2006] EWCA Crim 2918.
[5] See *Saleem* [2007] EWCA Crim 2692.
[6] See *In re F (in utero)* [1988] Fam 122. Nor is it the offence of assisting or encouraging grievous bodily harm to the mother, since the foetus is not part of the mother; above, p 493.
[7] [1919] 2 KB 125, a case found 'very hard to follow' in *Tait*, below, n 22.

16.1.1.2 Jurisdiction

Section 4 is applicable where the person to be murdered is not a British subject or within this jurisdiction. The section also catches an alien who, within this jurisdiction, incites the commission of murder abroad, and who might otherwise be immune at common law under the rule in *Board of Trade v Owen*.[8] In *El-Faisal*,[9] the solicitation was sufficient where it was to murder all 'Hindus, Jews and non-believers [in Islam]' and it was contemplated that the killings incited might occur in any part of the world. In *Abu Hamza*,[10] the Court of Appeal, after an extensive survey of case law, held that s 4 makes the solicitation of murder an offence in England, even where the inciter is not British, the proposed killer is not British, the killing will be abroad, and the proposed victim is not British. The act of incitement under s 4 may be an offence under English law, even if the act of murder, if carried out, would not be. Lord Phillips CJ, observed that the motivation for the enactment of s 4 appeared to have been the activities of aliens in England in support of murders, or attempts to murder, committed by foreigners outside the jurisdiction. If so, it would have made no sense to have restricted the offence to situations where the murderers were to be British subjects. There was nothing in the wording that suggested that the conspirators, or the person incited, should be British subjects.

16.1.1.3 Audience

The offence may be committed by the publication of an article in a newspaper and it is immaterial that the readers of the newspapers are not identified.[11] Logically, it must be capable of commission by email and by posts on the internet.[12] It seems, however, that the offence is not committed unless the mind of the person solicited, etc is reached: *Krause*.[13] In that case Lord Alverstone CJ applied this restricted reading even though the offence extends to an 'endeavour to persuade' which might be thought to cover an unsuccessful attempt to communicate. He held, however, that there was a common law attempt to commit the statutory offence where it was not proved that the offending letters, though sent, had ever reached the addressee.[14] If it is proved that the letter or other publication did reach the addressee, it is not necessary to prove that his mind was in any way affected by it.[15]

16.1.1.4 'Solicitation'

A soliciting to kill, not merely to do serious harm, must be proved.[16] In deciding whether the words amount to a solicitation, etc, the jury will take account of (i) the language used; (ii) the occasion on which it was used; (iii) the persons to whom the words were used; and (iv) the circumstances surrounding their use. In *Diamond*,[17] Coleridge J left the jury to decide whether an article extolling the virtues of the assassins of tyrants was sufficient. The publication was just after an attempt on the life of the Viceroy of India, and the persons addressed were not

---

[8] [1957] AC 602, cf M Hirst, *Jurisdiction and the Ambit of the Criminal Law* (2003) 149, a view rejected by the CA in *Abu Hamza* above n 4.

[9] [2004] EWCA Crim 343. See the discussion above para 12.6 relating to the application of a defence of self-defence.

[10] [2006] EWCA Crim 2918.

[11] *Most* (1881) 7 QBD 244 endorsed in *Jones* [2007] EWCA Crim 1118.

[12] See *Sheppard and Whittle* [2010] EWCA Crim 65, discussed in Ch 31. D could be tried in England because a substantial measure of his activities took place there.

[13] (1902) 66 JP 121. Contrast *Horton v Mead* [1913] 1 KB 154.

[14] See also *Banks* (1873) 12 Cox CC 393 at 399, per Quain J.

[15] *Diamond* (1920) 84 JP 211; *Most*, above; *Krause*, above.

[16] *Bainbridge* (1991) No 504/24/90, [1991] Crim LR 535 (not reported on this point).

[17] Above, n 15.

'a debating society of philosophers or divines' but 'anybody whom the paper would reach in this country or in Ireland'.

16.1.1.5 Offence solicited

It has been held to be sufficient that D incites P to act as an accessory to murder, as where D recruits P to act as the getaway driver in a murder.[18]

16.1.1.6 Victim

The proposed victim need not be named. If the solicitation is to kill members of a group, it must be a sufficiently well-defined one. Where D was charged with the offence and the indictment alleged he had incited murder of 'sovereigns and rulers of Europe', Phillimore J thought 'rulers' a somewhat vague word, but there were some 18 or 20 sovereigns in Europe and that was a sufficiently well-defined class.[19] In *El-Faisal,* the incitement was to kill all Jews, Christians, Americans, Hindus and non-believers, but it does not appear from the report to have been challenged as an insufficiently defined class.[20]

There is no scope for an argument that the offence restricts the right to freedom of expression under Art 10 of the ECHR, since the limitation will, most obviously, be justified as necessary and proportionate for the protection of others.

16.1.2 Threats to kill

Section 16 of the Offences Against the Person Act 1861 created an offence of making written threats to murder.[21] The Criminal Law Act 1977, Sch 12, replaces that provision with a new and broader s 16:

A person who without lawful excuse makes to another a threat, intending that that other would fear that it would be carried out, to kill that other or a third person shall be guilty of an offence and liable on conviction on indictment to imprisonment for a term not exceeding ten years.

A foetus is not 'a third person' and so a threat to a mother to kill the foetus in her womb is not this offence.[22] In *Tait* the court thought that if the threat had been to kill the child after it was born it would still not be an offence – if that were an offence, they asked, why should it not be an offence to threaten a non-pregnant woman to kill any child she might have in the future? – this, the court thought, 'seems to stretch the meaning of "any third person" altogether too far'. Perhaps so, but this was a threat to kill a particular person, already existing in embryo at least, which is altogether a different threat in terms of its impact on the mother – or anyone else. The decision in *Shephard* above,[23] if we ignore the strange and unsupportable *dictum,* suggests that this would have been the offence – how could it be soliciting to kill a person and not threatening to kill a person? Moreover, it *is* a threat to kill a person, which the foetus will by then have become.

---

[18] *Winter* [2007] EWCA Crim 3493.

[19] *Antonelli and Barberi* (1905) 70 JP 4.

[20] In *Rahman* [2008] EWCA Crim 2290, the offending words were made by D with a microphone referring to western forces in Iraq and Afghanistan. He said, among other things, 'We want to see them coming home in body bags. We want to see their blood running in the streets of Baghdad. We want to see their blood running in Fallujah. We want to see the Mujahideen shoot down their planes the way we shoot down the birds.' He then prayed to Allah, 'Don't leave any of them alive in Iraq. Don't leave any of them alive in Afghanistan.' D carried two different placards with slogans reading 'annihilate those who insult Islam' and 'behead those who insult Islam'.

[21] See the 3rd edition of this book, at 266.

[22] *Tait* [1990] 1 QB 290, [1989] Crim LR 834.

[23] [1919] 2 KB 125, above, p 578.

The threat may take any form[24] and may be implied as well as express.[25] There is no need for the words 'I will kill' to be explicitly used.[26] There is no need for the threat to be made to the person against whom the violence will be carried out.[27] In principle, it is thought that a threat should be 'made to another' only when communicated; but, since it has been held that a 'demand' is 'made' within s 21(1) of the Theft Act 1968 when and where a letter containing it is posted,[28] it is at least possible that the same might be decided in the case of a threat. The inclusion of the words 'to another' in this section makes no difference, since the demand under s 21 must impliedly be made to another. Threats to kill in England and Wales made by emails from abroad have been sufficient to constitute the offence.[29] The offence is triable either way.[30] The statute makes a single threat to kill an offence and therefore where D has made repeated threats to kill over a period of time these ought not all to be charged in one count in the indictment (infringing the rule against duplicity).[31]

There were 55 recorded offences of conspiracy to murder and 9,566 threats to kill in 2009/10.[32]

16.1.2.1 Lawful excuses

There would be a lawful excuse for making the threat if, in the circumstances known to D, the killing would be excusable if the threat were carried out, as where D makes the threat in self-defence.[33] A threat to kill may, however, be excusable where actual killing would not. To cause fear of death might be reasonable to prevent crime or arrest an offender, whereas actually to kill would be quite unreasonable.[34] In many cases it will be desirable to tell the jury this.[35] Where there is some evidence of a lawful excuse, the onus is on the Crown to prove its absence and the question is always one for the jury.[36]

16.1.3 Concealment of birth

This offence when first created by statute in 1623[37] was limited to (i) an illegitimate child who (ii) was born alive and whose body was disposed of so as to conceal its death (iii) by its mother. The current statute, the Offences Against the Person Act 1861, s 60, is subject to none of these limitations; it applies to any child, legitimate or not and whether born alive or not, whose body is disposed of so as to conceal its birth, by anyone. The section provides:

If any woman shall be delivered of a child, every person who shall, by any secret disposition of the dead body of the said child, whether such child died before, at, or after its birth, endeavour to conceal

---

[24] Below, n 26. See *Kennedy* [1998] Crim LR 739.

[25] cf *Solanke* [1970] 1 WLR 1. See *Boucher* (1831) 4 C&P 561.

[26] As in *Robinson* [2009] EWCA Crim 375 where D had said to a police officer who asked if D was making a loose threat: 'I am making a semi automatic one and it is loaded.'

[27] See recently eg *Donovan* [2009] EWCA Crim 1258 (D informs prison officers he will kill V when he is released from present sentence).

[28] *Treacy v DPP* [1971] AC 537, HL; below, p 943.

[29] *M* [2003] EWCA Crim 3067.

[30] Magistrates' Courts Act 1980, s 17 and Sch 1.

[31] See *Marchese* [2008] EWCA Crim 389.

[32] J Flatley et al, *Crime in England and Wales 2009/10, Findings from the British Crime Survey and police recorded crime* (2010), table 2.04.

[33] See above, p 379.

[34] The two preceding sentences were approved by the Court of Appeal in *Cousins* [1982] 2 All ER 115 at 117.

[35] *Cousins*, above.

[36] ibid.

[37] 21 Jac 1 c 27.

the birth thereof, shall be guilty of [an offence triable either way] and being convicted thereof shall be liable, at the discretion of the court, to be imprisoned for any term not exceeding two years...

There were six reported offences of concealing an infant death close to birth in 2009/10.[38]

The expressed object of the original statute was to catch those women who would otherwise escape on a charge of murder because of the difficulty of proving that there had been a live birth.[39] Under a later Act,[40] which repealed the 1623 provision, a woman could only be convicted if she was acquitted on an indictment for murder. But the current offence is an independent substantive crime for which an indictment will lie irrespective of any other offences being alleged.[41]

The test of a 'secret disposition' seems to be whether there was a likelihood that the body would be found. Bovill CJ held therefore that there would be a secret disposition, 'if the body were placed in the middle of a moor in the winter, or on the top of a mountain, or in any other secluded place, where the body would not be likely to be found'.[42] If a body were thrown from a cliff top to the seashore, it might be a secret disposition if the place were secluded, but not if it were much frequented.[43] So, where the body was left in a closed but unlocked box in D's bedroom in such a way as to attract the attention of those who daily entered the room, it was held that there was no secret disposition.[44]

D must be proved to have done some act[45] of disposition *after* the child has died. If the living body of the child is concealed and thereafter dies in the place of concealment, this offence is not committed,[46] though that is probably murder, manslaughter or infanticide.

According to Erle J in *Berriman*,[47] the child must have 'arrived at that stage of maturity at the time of birth that it might have been a living child'; so that the concealment of a foetus but a few months old would be no offence.[48]

16.1.4 Other offences

It is a common law misdemeanour to dispose of or destroy a dead body with intent to prevent an inquest from being held.[49] There is a common law offence of preventing the decent and lawful burial of a body. It is an offence under the Perjury Act 1911 wilfully to make a false statement relating to births or deaths, or the live birth of a child.[50] And it is a summary offence under the Births and Deaths Registration Act 1953, s 36, to fail to give information concerning births and deaths when under a duty, as defined in the Act, to do so.

---

[38] Flatley et al, *Crime in England and Wales 2009/10*, table 2.04.

[39] The original sentence was that the woman should suffer death as in the case of murder.

[40] 43 Geo 3, c 58.

[41] It was formerly the law that a person acquitted of murder, infanticide or child destruction might be convicted, on the same indictment, of concealment of birth; but this rule was abolished by the Criminal Law Act 1967, Sch 2. On its historical application, see MB Emmerichs, 'Trials of Women for Homicide in Nineteenth Century England' (1993) 5 Women and Criminal Justice 99.

[42] *Brown* (1870) LR 1 CCR 244.

[43] ibid.

[44] *George* (1868) 11 Cox CC 41. cf *Sleep* (1864) 9 Cox CC 559; *Rosenberg* (1906) 70 JP 264.

[45] *Derham* (1843) 1 Cox CC 56 (leaving body in privy where born not act of concealment).

[46] *Coxhead* (1845) 1 Car & Kir 623 (decided under 9 Geo 4, c 31, but the principle is the same); *May* (1867) 10 Cox CC 448.

[47] (1854) 6 Cox CC 388 at 390.

[48] *Colmer* (1864) 9 Cox CC 506 is to the contrary but is doubted by Russell, 611, n 69.

[49] cf *Hunter* [1972] Crim LR 369. See M Hirst, 'Preventing the Lawful Burial of a Body' [1996] Crim LR 96. See also *R(Ghai) v Newcastle City Council* [2010] 3 WLR 737.

[50] Perjury Act 1911, s 4(1).

16.2 Complicity in suicide and suicide pacts[51]

16.2.1 Position at common law

It was felony at common law for a sane person of the age of responsibility to kill himself either intentionally or in the course of trying to kill another.[52] Such a suicide was regarded as self-murder. Though the offender was, in the nature of things, personally beyond the reach of the law, his guilt was not without important consequences at common law, since it resulted in the forfeiture of his property. The results were more important, however, where the attempt failed, for then:

(1) since D had attempted to commit a felony he was guilty, under ordinary common law principles, of the misdemeanour of attempted suicide;

(2) if D, in the course of trying to kill himself, killed another, he was guilty of murder under the doctrine of transferred malice.[53]

Though suicide was regarded as 'not a very serious crime',[54] an intention to commit it was the *mens rea* of murder. Moreover, one who was an accessory to the suicide of another was likewise guilty of murder as an accessory. It followed that the survivor of a suicide pact was also guilty of murder, for, even if he did not actually kill, he was an aider and abettor, or at least an accessory before the fact, to the other party's self-murder.

16.2.2 The Suicide Act 1961

Suicide ceased to be a crime by virtue of the Suicide Act 1961 which simply provides that: 'The rule of law whereby it is a crime for a person to commit suicide is hereby abrogated.'

There were very sound reasons for the abolition of the felony of suicide. The 'felon' was dead and thus beyond the reach of punishment. The legal sanction was not an effective deterrent – there were some 5,000 suicides a year; and the effect was merely to add to the distress and pain of the bereaved relatives.

The most important practical effect of the Act, however, was its repeal by implication of the crime of attempted suicide. If it was not a crime to commit suicide, it could not be a crime to attempt it. This also recognized the realities of the situation for it had been the practice for many years to institute proceedings only where it was necessary for the attempter's protection, for example, because no relatives and friends were willing to give help. Thus, in 1959, of a total of 4,980 suicide attempts known to the police (and an estimated actual total of 25,000 concealed from the police) only 518 prosecutions were brought. The protection of the attempter may now be secured under the Mental Health Act 1983.

---

[51] For general discussions on the implementation of the offences, see G Williams, *The Sanctity of Life and the Criminal Law* (1957) Ch 7; St John Stevas, *Life, Death and the Law* (1961) Ch 6; Second Report of the Criminal Law Revision Committee (1960) Cmnd 1187. For more recent developments, see K Wheat, 'The Law's Treatment of the Suicidal' (2000) 8 Med LR 182; J Keown and D Price, 'Surveying the Foundations of Medical Law' (2008) 16 Med L Rev 85. The more recent literature has focused on the litigation surrounding the right to die and the right to assist another to commit suicide here or abroad, and the development of the new CPS policy on assisted suicide following the decision in *R (Purdy) v DPP* [2009] UKHL 45. See references below.

[52] Hawkins, 1 PC, 77.

[53] *Hopwood* (1913) 8 Cr App R 143; *Spence* (1957) 41 Cr App R 80. Above, p 136.

[54] *French* (1955) 39 Cr App R 192, per Lord Goddard CJ.

16.2.2.1 Complicity in another's suicide

Section 2 of the Suicide Act created a new offence for D to aid, abet, counsel, or procure P in his suicide or attempt to commit suicide. The form of the offence was, in theoretical terms, an odd one. Since there was no principal offence committed by the suicidal person, so there was no crime for D to aid and abet. This had to be viewed as a specific statutory offence involving the use of the language of aiding and abetting even though there was no principal crime. Since the aiding, etc was the principal offence it was possible to charge an attempt to aid, etc so that unsuccessful advice or encouragement was punishable.[55] The offence has now been replaced by one on defined in terms of doing acts capable of assisting or encouraging suicide.

From 1 February 2010, s 59 of the Coroners and Justice Act 2009 replaced s 2(1) of the Suicide Act with the following:

(1) A person ('D') commits an offence if –

(a) D does an act capable of encouraging or assisting the suicide or attempted suicide of another person, and

(b) D's act was intended to encourage or assist suicide or an attempt at suicide.

(1A) The person referred to in subsection (1)(a) need not be a specific person (or class of persons) known to, or identified by, D.

(1B) D may commit an offence under this section whether or not a suicide, or an attempt at suicide, occurs.

(1C) An offence under this section is triable on indictment and a person convicted of such an offence is liable to imprisonment for a term not exceeding 14 years.

The changes are designed to clarify the law.[56] There is no intended extension of the law. The main change is to shift the basis of the offence from one of 'aiding and abetting' and 'attempting' to an inchoate form of the offence as defined in the modern terminology under Part 2 of the Serious Crime Act 2007 relating to the inchoate offence of intentionally[57] encouraging and assisting crime. Moving to an inchoate form of offence (subsection (1B)) means that there is no need to prosecute under the Criminal Attempts Act 1981 for *attempt* to assist suicide where no one, as a result of the encouragement, actually commits or attempts to commit suicide. The *full* inchoate offence under s 2(1) is now committed by doing an act capable of encouraging or assisting suicide whether or not any suicide is committed or attempted. The only scope for the operation of the law of attempt is where D attempts to do, but does not succeed in doing, 'the act' he intended to do – eg posting the letter of encouragement.

Subsection (1A) makes it clear that one can be liable for doing acts capable of encouraging or assisting persons unknown to commit suicide. Material on a website is caught.[58] The Joint Parliamentary Committee on Human Rights expressed concern that the new offence might have a chilling effect on free speech.[59]

---

[55] *McShane* [1977] Crim LR 737, CA, discussed by JC Smith in *Crime, Proof and Punishment*, 21 at 32–33. See recently *Workman* [2007] 1 Cr App R 637. See *S* [2005] EWCA Crim 819.

[56] The Ministry of Justice has published a circular explaining the revised law on encouraging or assisting suicide, which came into effect on 1 February 2010, www.justice.gov.uk/publications/docs/circular-03-2010-assisting-encouraging-suicide.pdf.

[57] It is unclear whether the restricted interpretation of that term that applies to s 44 of the Serious Crime Act 2007 applies here. See above, Ch 13.

[58] The reform was prompted in part by concerns about internet sites offering encouragement. See *Safer Children in a Digital World: the report of the Byron Review* (2008), www.dcsf.gov.uk/byronreview.

[59] It was suggested that the new offence might capture the publication of morbid poetry. The DPP in evidence to the Public Bill Committee gave assurance that this would not be caught because there would be no relevant intent.

Section 59 of the 2009 Act[60] also inserts a new subsection 2A into s 2 of the Suicide Act as follows:

2A Acts capable of encouraging or assisting

(1) If D arranges[61] for a person ('D2') to do an act that is capable of encouraging or assisting the suicide or attempted suicide of another person and D2 does that act, D is also to be treated for the purposes of this Act as having done it.

(2) Where the facts are such that an act is not capable of encouraging or assisting suicide or attempted suicide, for the purposes of this Act it is to be treated as so capable if the act would have been so capable had the facts been as D believed them to be at the time of the act or had subsequent events happened in the manner D believed they would happen (or both).

(3) A reference in this Act to a person ('P') doing an act that is capable of encouraging the suicide or attempted suicide of another person includes a reference to P doing so by threatening another person or otherwise putting pressure on another person to commit or attempt suicide.

This new subsection 2A makes it clear: that the offence can be committed through an intermediary,[62] that there is no defence of impossibility,[63] and that encouragement by threats or other forms of pressure is covered.[64] Subsection 2B clarifies that D's liability need not be based on an individual act but may be based on a course of conduct over a period of time. Again, none of this is intended significantly to change the substance as opposed to the form of the previous law. That is doubtful. The breadth of the assisting and encouraging offences in the Serious Crime Act is yet to be tested.

Prosecutorial policies

The operation of such an offence has given rise to considerable controversy because its scope means that those who help other consenting adults to die fall within its terms.[65] To date the cases have arisen under the old definition, but the issues are as pertinent under the new offence.

Challenges to the offence were raised on the basis that it might even criminalize the distribution of a booklet giving advice to any person who wishes to commit suicide on how to do so efficiently and painlessly. It was held that this was not necessarily an offence under the pre-2009 law. In *A-G v Able*,[66] Woolf J, as he then was, refused to grant a declaration that the distribution was unlawful, holding that an offence would be committed only if the distributor intended that the booklet would be used by someone contemplating suicide and that he would be (and in fact was) assisted or encouraged to do so. This challenge was brought to the old s 2

---

[60] Section 61 and Sch 12 of the 2009 Act, will, 'regulate, in relation to encouraging and assisting suicide, the liability of (electronic) information society service providers within the EEA area in a manner consistent with the UK's obligations under the E-Commerce Directive. It extends the liability of domestically based providers to acts done within the EEA and also controls the institution of proceedings in relation to EEA based (as opposed to domestically based) service providers'. It provides for some limited exceptions in relation to 'mere conduits', and in relation to 'caching' and 'hosting' services. See the explanatory notes to the Act.

[61] This is problematical. D1 who merely encourages D2 to provide encouragement to P to kill himself does not seem to have 'arranged', unlike D1 who provides D2 with material to pass to P.

[62] D gives lethal pills to X to administer to V.

[63] eg D gives V harmless pills that D thinks are lethal.

[64] This could be very important with the types of bullying email and internet campaigns that lead to suicide.

[65] See the references in n 78 below.

[66] [1984] QB 795, QBD. See KJM See Mental Capacity Act 2005, s62 and Code, para 9.5. Smith, 'Assisting Suicide – The Attorney-General and the Voluntary Euthanasia Society' [1983] Crim LR 579. See Mental Capacity 2005, s 62 and Code, para 9.5.

offence based on aiding and abetting and was in accordance with the ordinary principles of the law of secondary participation.[67] The new offence requires only that the publisher intends to do acts capable of assisting or encouraging and that his act was intended to encourage or assist suicide or an attempt at suicide.

The crime covers a variety of situations varying in moral culpability from D who encourages V to commit suicide for the purpose of inheriting his property,[68] to that of D who supplies a final fatal (over)dose to V of a prescribed drug to alleviate V's suffering when V is anxious to accelerate the end,[69] or refastens the plastic bag over the head of his terminally ill spouse as she desired.[70] The consent of the DPP is required in order to achieve consistency in prosecution practice.[71]

In the landmark case of *R (on the Application of Pretty) v DPP* it was held that the DPP had no power to give an undertaking that he will not prosecute the spouse, D, of a person, V, who suffers from an incurable disease which prevents her from committing suicide unaided, if D supplies V with the means of doing so when V requests it.[72] In *Pretty v United Kingdom*,[73] the European Court of Human Rights accepted that Art 2's protection provides a right to life, not a right to death. It was accepted that Arts 2, 3 and 9 were not engaged by the claim of a right to assisted death; Art 8 was engaged in such circumstances, but the UK's criminal prohibition was within Art 8(2).[74] The doctor who complies with the request of a competent adult who refuses life-sustaining/saving treatment does not assist his suicide.[75] As Lord Goff observed in *Bland* the doctor who keeps a patient comfortable whilst he dies, cannot be said to assist suicide: '…there is no question of the patient having committed suicide nor therefore of the doctor of having aided or abetted him in doing so. It is simply that the patient has, as he is entitled to, declined to consent to treatment which might or would have the effect of prolonging his life, and the doctor has, in accordance with his duty, complied with the patient's wishes.' The Mental Capacity Act 2005 is now in force and provides for advance refusals of life-sustaining treatment.[76]

---

[67] Above, Ch 8.

[68] eg *Cumming* [2007] 2 Cr App R (S) 20.

[69] The Court of Appeal in *Kennedy (No 2)* [2005] EWCA Crim 685, suggested that 'it would be an abuse to prosecute someone assisting another to commit suicide for murder', at [32].

[70] See the prosecution of David March, discussed in S Burns, 'The Quality of Mercy' (2007) 157 NLJ 86.

[71] *R (on the Application of Pretty) v DPP* [2002] 1 AC 800. See also on prosecution policy *Dunbar v Plant* [1997] 3 WLR 1261. According to the DPP's 'Policy for Prosecutors in Respect of Cases of Encouraging or Assisting Suicide' (Feb 2010), www.cps.gov.uk/publications/prosecution/assisted_suicide_policy.html, the DPP will only consent where the full code test is met (para 14), and these cases are dealt with by the Special Crime Division, the head of which reports directly to the DPP (paras 49, 50)

[72] *R (Pretty) v DPP* [2002] 1 AC 800. The case decides that the ECHR does not oblige a state to legalize assisted suicide. For comment, see R Tur, 'Legislative Techniques and Human Rights – The Sad Case of Assisted Suicide' [2003] Crim LR 3. cf D Calvert Smith and S O'Doherty, 'Legislative Technique and Human Rights – A Response' [2003] Crim LR 384.

[73] [2002] 35 EHRR 1.

[74] The HL held that Art 8 was not engaged, since that article was directed to the protection of personal autonomy whilst an individual was alive but did not confer a right to decide how or when to die: Lord Bingham [26], Lord Steyn [61]–[62], Lord Hope [100]–[102]. However, in *R (Purdy) v DPP* [2009] UKHL 45,(below) the HL departed from its decision in *Pretty* on this point and found Art 8(1) to be engaged: Lord Hope [35]–[38], Baroness Hale [67]–[68], Lord Brown [83]–[84] and Lord Neuberger at [95]. For analysis, see M Freeman, 'Death, Dying and the Human Rights Act 1998' (1999) 52 CLP 218; 'Denying Death its Dominion' (2002) 10 Med LR 245; B Hale, 'A Pretty Pass – When is there a Right to Die?' (2003) 32 Common Law World Review 1; D Morris, 'Assisted Suicide under the European Convention on Human Rights: A Critique' [2003] EHRLR 65.

[75] *Re B (Refusal of treatment)* [2002] 2 All ER 449 – also known as *Mrs B v NHS Trust* – in fact a hospital commits assault if they continue to treat her against her will and Butler-Sloss LJ awarded (albeit small) damages for assault.

[76] See s 25(5) and (6). These provisions only apply to adults who have capacity: s 24(1). Note also: s 24 does not include the word 'care'. Para 9.28 CoP states: 'An advance decision cannot refuse actions that are needed to keep ?

A further landmark challenge was made as to sufficiency of the DPP's policy on prosecuting the offence, in *R (on the Application of Purdy) v DPP*.[77] P suffered from primary progressive multiple sclerosis for which there was no known cure. She would have liked to end her life when her continuing existence became unbearable, but at that stage in her disease she would be unable to travel to a country where assisted suicide was lawful without help. Her husband was willing to help her to travel. If P's husband wished to help her to travel outside the country, there was a substantial risk that he would be prosecuted. P challenged the lawfulness of the failure of the DPP to issue a crime-specific policy identifying the facts and circumstances that would be taken into account when deciding whether to prosecute an individual for assisting another to commit suicide. P sought information in order to make an informed decision about whether to ask for her husband's assistance in committing suicide.

In the House of Lords P argued that the prohibition in s 2(1) constituted an interference with her right to respect for her private life under Art 8(1) of the ECHR; and that the interference was not 'in accordance with the law' as required by Art 8(2), in the absence of an offence-specific policy. The House of Lords allowed her appeal holding that the right to respect for life contained in Art 8(1) was engaged. The ECtHR had determined that the very essence of the Convention was respect for human dignity and human freedom and it was under Art 8 that notions of the quality of life took on significance and covered the situation of people who were concerned that they should not be forced to linger on in old age or in states of advanced physical or mental decrepitude which conflicted with strongly held ideas of self and person identity. For the purposes of Art 8(2), in order for s 2(4) of the 1961 Act to comply with the requirement that the law should be formulated with sufficient precision to enable the individual, if need be with advice, to regulate his conduct, the DPP had to create a code giving guidance on principles to be applied by Crown prosecutors in determining, in any case, whether proceedings for an offence under s 2(1) should be instituted. Such a code would be regarded for the purposes of Art 8(2) as forming part of the law in accordance with which an interference with the right of respect for private life might be held to be justified. In that way the requirements of accessibility and foreseeability would be satisfied.

It followed that the DPP was required to promulgate an offence-specific policy identifying the facts and circumstances which he would take into account in deciding, in a case such as that which the claimant's case exemplified, whether or not to exercise his discretion to consent to a prosecution under s 2(4). The House did not prescribe what the guidance might say. The decision was controversial in constitutional terms with the highest court of the land compelling the DPP to provide such guidance.[78] Interim guidance was published and, after consultation[79] a final version was produced.[80]

---

person comfortable (sometimes called basic or essential care). Examples include warmth, shelter, actions to keep a person clean and the offer of food and water by mouth.'

[77] *R (on the application of Purdy) v DPP* [2009] UKHL 45.

[78] See in particular on the decision R Nobles and D Schiff, 'Disobedience to the Law – Debbie Purdy's case' (2010) 73 MLR 295; and K Greasley, '*R(Purdy) v DPP* and the case for Wilful Blindness' (2010) 30 OJLS 301. J Rogers, 'Prosecutorial Policies, Prosecutorial Systems, and the Purdy Litigation' [2010] Crim LR 542; N Cartwright, '48 Years On: Is the Suicide Act Fit for Purpose? (2009) 17 Med LR 467; A Mullock, 'Overlooking the Criminally Compassionate: What are the Implications of Prosecutorial Policy on Encouraging or Assisting Suicide?' (2010) 18 Med L Rev 442, P Lewis, 'Informal Legal Change an Assisted Suicide: The Policy for Prosecutors' (2011) 31 LS 119.

[79] See R Daw and A Solomon 'Assisted Suicide and Identifying the Public Interest in the Decision to Prosecute' [2010] Crim LR – for an illuminating insight into how the policy was drawn up.

[80] See J Rogers, 'Prosecutorial Policies, Prosecutorial Systems, and the Purdy Litigation' [2010] Crim LR 542; A Mullock, 'Prosecutors Making (Bad) Law' (2009) 17 Med LR 290; R Heywood, 'Prosecutorial Guidelines on Assisted Suicide' (2010) 21 King's LJ 425. The DPP published his final policy on prosecuting cases of assisted suicide on 25 February 2010. The final policy can be found at www.cps.gov.uk/publications/prosecution/assisted_suicide_policy.pdf.

The new policy

The new prosecution policy does not 'decriminalize' the offence of encouraging or assisting suicide and does not give any express assurance that a person will be immune from prosecution if he does an act that encourages or assists another's suicide or attempted suicide. Seventeen factors that will be relevant and will suggest that a prosecution is more likely to be required are listed. These include: the victim being under 18 years of age; the victim not having the capacity (as defined by the Mental Capacity Act 2005) to reach an informed decision to commit suicide; the victim not having reached a voluntary, clear, settled and informed decision to commit suicide; the victim not having clearly and unequivocally communicated his or her decision to commit suicide to the suspect; the victim not having sought the encouragement or assistance of the suspect personally or on his or her own initiative; the suspect not being wholly motivated by compassion; for example, the suspect was motivated by the prospect that he or she or a person closely connected to him or her stood to gain in some way from the death of the victim; the suspect pressurizing the victim to commit suicide; the suspect not taking reasonable steps to ensure that any other person had not pressured the victim to commit suicide; the suspect having a history of violence or abuse against the victim; whether the victim could have herself performed the act that D did to assist V in her suicide; the suspect being unknown to the victim and encouraging or assisting the victim to commit or attempt to commit suicide by providing specific information via, for example, a website or publication; the suspect giving encouragement or assistance to more than one victim who were not known to each other; the suspect being paid by the victim or those close to the victim for his or her encouragement or assistance; the suspect acting in his or her capacity as a medical doctor, nurse, other healthcare professional, a professional carer (whether for payment or not), or as a person in authority, such as a prison officer, and the victim was in his or her care; the suspect being aware that the victim intended to commit suicide in a public place where it was reasonable to think that members of the public may be present; the suspect acting in his or her capacity as a person involved in the management or as an employee (whether for payment or not) of an organization or group, a purpose of which is to provide a physical environment (whether for payment or not) in which to allow another to commit suicide.

A prosecution is less likely to be required if: the victim had reached a voluntary, clear, settled and informed decision to commit suicide; the suspect was wholly motivated by compassion; the actions of the suspect, although sufficient to come within the definition of the offence, were of only minor encouragement or assistance; the suspect had sought to dissuade the victim from taking the course of action which resulted in his or her suicide; the actions of the suspect may be characterized as reluctant encouragement or assistance in the face of a determined wish on the part of the victim to commit suicide; the suspect reported the victim's suicide to the police and fully assisted them in their enquiries into the circumstances of the suicide or the attempt and his or her part in providing encouragement or assistance. The first instance of public interest factors of policy being applied was consideration of whether to prosecute Caractacus Downs, son of Sir Edward and Lady Downs who committed suicide at the Dignitas clinic.[81]

---

[81] See www.cps.gov.uk/news/press_releases/113_10. And Keir Starmer QC's statement at: www.cps.gov.uk/news/press_statements/the_death_of_sir_edward_and_lady_downes.

Jurisdictional issues[82]

There was a dispute under the old law as to whether a prosecution could ensue if D assisted V's suicide abroad.[83] The issue gained a high profile with tragic cases such as that of Daniel James who travelled to the Dignitas clinic in Switzerland to commit suicide having been paralysed.[84] Concern was raised that relatives would be prosecuted. The House of Lords left this issue unresolved in *Purdy*. Lord Phillips made the *obiter*, and, it is submitted, doubtful suggestion that assisting suicide abroad could be murder.[85] The orthodox interpretation of s 3(3) is that suicide is no longer an offence under English law, and nor therefore was complicity in suicide equivalent to complicity in murder.[86] Under s 2 as substituted in the 2009 Act, there seems no doubt that D will commit the offence if he performs acts that in England and Wales are capable of assisting V to commit or attempt suicide abroad.[87]

Transferred malice in suicides

Since suicide is not a crime, where D kills V in the course of trying to kill himself, there is now no room for the doctrine of transferred malice for there is no 'malice' to transfer. Where D kills V in the course of trying to kill himself, his liability depends on the general principles of murder and manslaughter. Thus, if the death of V was utterly unforeseeable, it would be accidental death; if there was gross negligence as to causing death or recklessness as to whether death or serious bodily harm was caused, it may be manslaughter; and if D foresaw death or serious bodily harm as virtually certain, it may be murder.[88]

Mercy killing[89]

English law admits of no defence of mercy killing or euthanasia. In *Inglis*[90] where a mother killed her severely injured son in what she considered to be an act of mercy, she was prosecuted for murder. As the Lord Chief Justice emphasized, upholding her conviction:

---

[82] *In Re Z* [2004] EWHC 2817 (Fam), the court held that a local authority which was aware of Mr Z's intention to assist his wife in travelling abroad to die was not permitted to pursue an injunction to prevent the pair from leaving the country. Its obligation was strictly to investigate and inform the police and the DPP of the relevant facts for a decision on prosecution.

[83] M Hirst, 'Suicide in Switzerland: Complicity in England?' [2009] Crim LR 335 argued that if A helps or encourages B to travel from England to a jurisdiction (such as Switzerland) where assisted suicide is lawful, in the knowledge that B will commit suicide there, A does not thereby commit any offence under the Suicide Act 1961 s 2(1). Lord Hope rejected this argument after careful consideration, referring to: *Smith (Wallace Duncan) (No 4)* [2004] QB 1418.

[84] See www.timesonline.co.uk/tol/news/uk/article4969423.ece.

[85] 'It is … plain that section 1 does not apply to suicide committed outside England and Wales. If that falls to be treated as murder, so that assisting it is also murder, it would seem to follow that if a British subject accompanies a relative, who is also a British subject, to Switzerland and assists in Switzerland the relative to commit suicide with help from Dignitas, that person will under English law commit the crime of murder and will be subject to the jurisdiction of the courts of England and Wales in relation to that offence, ibid [12]–[13].

[86] His lordships' comments are clearly *obiter* and not adopted by any other member of the House of Lords.

[87] See M. Hirst, 'Assisted Suicide after *Purdy*: The Unresolved Issue' [2009] Crim LR 870.

[88] See above, p 107.

[89] On which, see generally: S McLean, *Assisted Dying: Reflections on the Need for Law Reform* (2007); R Huxtable, *Euthanasia, Ethics and the Law* (2007); M Otlowski, *Voluntary Euthanasia and the Common Law* (2000); H Biggs, *Euthanasia, Death with Dignity and the Law* (2001); J Keown, *Euthanasia, Ethics and Public Policy: An Argument against Legislation* (2002). See also more specifically in the criminal law context, S Ost, 'Euthanasia and the Defence of Necessity' [2005] Crim LR 355; M Wilks, 'Medical Treatment at the End of Life: A British Doctor's Perspective' in C Erin and S Ost, *The Criminal Justice System and Health Care* (2007).

[90] *Inglis* [2010] EWCA Crim 2637.

the law does not recognise the concept implicit in the defence statement that [V] was 'already dead in all but a small physical degree'. The fact is that he was alive, a person in being. However brief the time left for him, that life could not lawfully be extinguished. Similarly, however disabled [V] might have been, a disabled life, even a life lived at the extremes of disability, is not one jot less precious than the life of an able-bodied person. [V]'s condition made him especially vulnerable, and for that among other reasons, whether or not he might have died within a few months anyway, his life was protected by the law, and no one, not even his mother, could lawfully step in and bring it to a premature conclusion. Until Parliament decides otherwise, the law recognises a distinction between the withdrawal of treatment supporting life, which, subject to stringent conditions, may be lawful, and the active termination of life, which is unlawful.

...How the problems of mercy killing, euthanasia, and assisting suicide should be addressed must be decided by Parliament, which, for this purpose at any rate, should be reflective of the conscience of the nation. In this appeal we are constrained to apply the law as we find it to be. We cannot amend it, or ignore it.[91]

There is no defence of mercy killing nor that the killing is in the best interests of the victim in some general sense, nor is there a defence of physician-assisted suicide.[92] Medical practitioners' obligations regarding the withdrawal of life-sustaining treatment are considered in Chapter 4 above.[93] A competent but paralysed adult is entitled to refuse to continue medical treatment. This is not suicide and the health care professionals are not assisting such.[94] There is no breach of Art 2 of the ECHR by the withdrawal of treatment in such cases.

The European Court in *Pretty v UK* declined to express a view on whether an assisted suicide provision would be compliant with Art 2. The Court concluded that the regulation of suicide was for the Member State's law, and that there was no state obligation to facilitate death. It should be noted also that the ECtHR has recently held that there is no breach of Art 8 if a Member State does not facilitate assisted suicide: *Haas v Switzerland*.[95]

A Private Members Bill for the Assisted Dying of the Terminally Ill, which would have enabled a competent adult who is suffering as a result of a terminal illness to receive medical assistance to die at his own request; and to make provision for a person suffering from a terminal illness to receive pain relief medication, was rejected in 2005.[96]

Several law reform agencies have reviewed the possibility of such a defence (or special offence) being available.[97] Most recently, the Law Commission declined to engage fully in the issue in its Consultation Paper on Homicide[98] and accepted in its subsequent Report No

---

[91] ibid, [38]–[39]. cf *Webb* [2011] EWCA Crim 152.

[92] E Jackson, 'Whose Death is it Anyway? Euthanasia and the Medical Profession' (2004) 57 CLP 415; cf the Netherlands on which see J Griffiths, 'Assisted Suicide in the Netherlands' (1995) 58 MLR 232; J Griffiths, H Weyers and M Adams, *Euthanasia and the Law of Europe* (2009), J Keown, 'Euthanasia in the Netherlands' in J Keown (ed), *Euthanasia Examined* (1995) 261; P Lewis, *Assisted Dying and Legal Change* (2007).

[93] See especially the decisions in *R (Burke) v GMC* [2004] EWHC 1879 (Admin); overruled, in the Court of Appeal [2006] QB 273; and see the ECHR application (App No 19807/06). For comment see J Coggan, 'Could the Right to Die with Dignity Represent a New Right to Die in English Law?' (2006) 14 Med LR 219, and generally on the ECHR position Emmerson, Ashworth and Macdonald, HR&CJ, para 18.48 et seq.

[94] *B (Consent to Treatment)* [2002] 2 All ER 449.

[95] Application No 31322/07.

[96] See S Evan and D Hewitt, 'A Question of Choice' (2006) 156 NLJ 44. See also the MOJ Consultation Paper 2009/06 which discusses these Bills.

[97] See the CLRC Working Paper on Offences Against the Person (1976) paras 79–87.

[98] See Ch 8 of that Paper and the criticism levelled by J Rogers in 'The Law Commission's Proposed Restructuring of the Law of Homicide' (2006) 70 J Crim L 223 suggesting a distinction might be drawn in terms of availability of a defence to relatives as opposed to professional carers. The Law Commission rejected that argument – see LC 304, para 7.28.

304 that the Government ought to commission such a reform study. Public attitudes to mercy killing, as confirmed in Professor Mitchell's illuminating empirical research,[99] reveal that where there is clear evidence of the victim's wish to die, such cases are amongst the least serious homicides cases.[100] The Law Commission concluded:

There are three reasons why it is arguable that it would be more satisfactory if, in cases of rational 'mercy' killing, Parliament were to make 'mercy' killing a partial defence rather than purely a matter going to mitigation of the minimum term. First, for a genuine 'mercy' killer, a life long licence seems neither necessary nor appropriate. Secondly, if there is a dispute of fact as to D's motive for killing V, it might be thought better that the jury, rather than the trial judge, should decide the issue. Thirdly, a partial defence would avoid the need for the practice, which concerns some of our consultees, of dressing up rational 'mercy' killing cases as ones of diminished responsibility by means of a sympathetic report from a pliant psychiatrist which the court and prosecution are content not to challenge.[101]

In *Inglis*,[102] the Lord Chief Justice referred to the Law Commission's 'careful analysis of this profoundly sensitive issue'.

Reform

The Law Commission provisionally recommended that a verdict of assisting suicide might be left as an alternative verdict on a charge of murder or manslaughter where D proves that he and V had intended to take part in a suicide pact.[103] That proposal was withdrawn in the final Report.[104]

16.2.3 Suicide pacts

A party to a suicide pact who assists or encourages the other party to commit suicide is, of course, guilty of the offence above.[105]

The survivor of such a pact may, however, have either himself killed the deceased or have procured a third party to do it. Such cases do not fall within the Suicide Act, but within the Homicide Act 1957, s 4(1), which, as amended by the Suicide Act, provides:

It shall be manslaughter and shall not be murder for a person acting in pursuance of a suicide pact between him and another to kill the other[106] or be party to the other being killed by a third person.

'Suicide pact' is defined by s 4(3) of the Homicide Act as:

a common agreement between two or more persons having for its object the death of all of them, whether or not each is to take his own life, but nothing done by a person who enters into a suicide pact shall be treated as done by him in pursuance of the pact unless it is done while he has the settled intention of dying in pursuance of the pact.

---

[99] Extracted in the LCCP 177 and LC 304.

[100] LC 304, para 7.17.

[101] Para 7.48.

[102] [2010] EWCA Crim 2637.

[103] LCCP 177, para 8.95.

[104] LC 304.

[105] Until the enactment of the Suicide Act, this was manslaughter under the Homicide Act 1957, s 4. The public interest does not normally call for the prosecution of the survivor of a suicide pact: *Dunbar v Plant* [1997] 3 WLR 1261, CA (Civ Div) per Phillips LJ at 1285.

[106] If, otherwise than in pursuance of a suicide pact, D kills V at V's request, D is of course guilty of murder. cf *Robinson*, above, p 212.

The onus on a charge of murder of establishing the defence of suicide pact is put by s 4(2) on the accused and the standard of proof required is the balance of probabilities. This is not incompatible with Art 6(2) of the ECHR.[107]

There are, on average, 10 to 15 successful suicide pacts per year.[108]

The distinction between assisting or encouraging in suicide and manslaughter by suicide pact is not entirely satisfactory.[109] The latter, being punishable with life imprisonment, is evidently the more serious crime; yet, since the person guilty of it always intends to die himself, it is difficult to see how it can compare in moral heinousness with the case of D who, for example, incites V to die in order that he may live and enjoy V's property.

The distinction between the two crimes may be very fine. If D and V agree to gas themselves with car exhaust fumes and D alone survives, it appears that he will be liable under the Homicide Act if he turned on the engine,[110] and possibly under the Suicide Act if V did. It may frequently be difficult to establish who did such an act and this is recognized by the provision in s 2(2) of the Suicide Act that, on the trial of an indictment for murder or manslaughter, the jury may find D guilty of assisting or encouraging in suicide if that is proved. If D is charged with murder and he establishes on a balance of probabilities that V committed suicide in pursuance of a suicide pact, he is entitled to be acquitted of murder and may presumably be convicted of assisting or encouraging in suicide since he has, in effect, admitted his guilt. If, however, D was charged with complicity and it appeared that he had killed V, he would have to be acquitted. The Law Commission recently commented on the over and under inclusiveness of the offence. It provides an undeserved defence to D who, as a leader of a cult, encourages followers to kill themselves but does not go through with the act himself. Yet it fails to deal with D's consensual killing of a terminally ill spouse, V, where D has secretly planned to kill himself once V is dead, but fails to achieve his own demise.[111]

There is considerable pressure for reform of the law. The Law Commission described the offence as having 'long outlived its usefulness' and having been flawed from the outset,[112] resting as it does on a promise from D to V that he will kill himself – a promise of no intrinsic moral value.[113] Although the Commission also acknowledged that it presented no significant problem in practice.[114] Individuals prosecuted for manslaughter of their nearest and dearest may well receive low sentences, and the pain and anguish of their bereavement is exacerbated by the criminal process.[115] Supporters of the law point to the significant protection it affords the vulnerable who face pressure to commit suicide when they perceive themselves to be a burden on carers. The defence is certainly more common among the elderly, and interestingly, empirical work reveals that the defence is more commonly relied on by men, suggesting that this allows a defence for dominant and controlling male partners.[116]

---

[107] A-G's Reference (No 1 of 2004) [2004] 1 WLR 2111 at [130]–[132].

[108] See LCCP 177, para 8.60.

[109] The Law Commission was not able to consider suicide in its review of *Partial Defences to Murder* (LC 290, 2004). In its Homicide Review in 2006 (*Murder, Manslaughter and Infanticide*, LC 304) the Law Commission's proposals for homicide provide only that the offence would be reclassified as second degree murder. The label seems unsuited to the actions of many of the cases to which it would apply.

[110] But if D pours out a glass of poison and V takes it, he may be liable under the Suicide Act 1961.

[111] See also the discussion of the differences in culpability between 'die together' cases and 'you then me' (homicide suicide) cases.

[112] LCCP 177, para 8.8.

[113] Para 8.19.

[114] ibid, para 8.20.

[115] See *Blackburn* (2005) 14 Jan, CCC, suspended sentence for killing terminally ill wife in suicide pact, and see the news reports for 15 Jan 2005.

[116] See LCCP 177, paras 8.67–8.83.

The Law Commission provisionally proposed to repeal s 4, intending that all such cases would fall within its extended definition of diminished responsibility as cases where D suffered severe depression.[117] In its Report No 304, the Commission recognized that diminished responsibility would not deal with all depressed carer cases, nor with mercy killings. It was recommended that s 4 should not be repealed.[118] Some of the cases will fall within the new diminished responsibility defence (explained in Chapter 15).

16.3 Infanticide[119]

The Infanticide Act 1938, s 1(1), was recently amended. From 4 October 2010 it now provides:

Where a woman by any wilful act or omission causes the death of her child being a child under the age of twelve months, but at the time of the act or omission the balance of her mind was disturbed by reason of her not having fully recovered from the effect of her giving birth to the child or by reason of the effect of lactation consequent upon the birth of the child, then [if][120] the circumstances were such that but for this Act the offence would have amounted to murder [or manslaughter], she shall be guilty of felony, to wit infanticide, and may for such offence be dealt with and punished as if she had been guilty of the offence of manslaughter of the child.

There were five recorded offences of infanticide during the period 2006/7.[121]

The 1938 Act provision replaced a statute of 1922 which had confined the defence to killings by mothers of 'newly-born' children. The Court of Criminal Appeal had held that to be inapplicable to a child of 35 days, so that the mother was convicted of murder.[122] The 1922 Act was itself the result of an agitation over very many years during which it was practically impossible to convict mothers of the murder of their young children because of the disapproval by public and professional opinion of a law which regarded such killings as ordinary murders. Where a conviction was obtained, the judge had to pronounce a sentence of death which everyone, except perhaps the offender, knew would not be carried out. A number of reasons were advanced why infanticide should be considered less reprehensible than other killings: (i) the injury done to the child was less, for it was incapable of the kind of suffering which might be undergone by the adult victim of a murder; (ii) the loss of its family was less great; (iii) the crime did not create the sense of insecurity in society which other murders caused; (iv) generally, the heinousness of the crime was less, the motive very frequently being the concealment of the shame of the birth of an illegitimate child; and (v) where the killing is done by the mother, her responsibility may be reduced by the disturbance of her mind caused by the stress of the birth. It is, of course, the last of these considerations which is the governing

---

[117] The research reveals that as many as 79% of s 4 cases involve depressed individuals, para 8.63.

[118] See LC 304, Ch 7.

[119] See LCCP 177, Ch 8; LC 304, Ch 9. See also D Seaborne Davies, 'Child-Killing in English Law' (1937) 1 MLR 203; MACL, 301; G Williams, *The Sanctity of Life* (1957) 25–45; K O'Donovan, 'The Medicalisation of Infanticide' [1984] Crim LR 259; RD Mackay, 'The Consequences of Killing Very Young Children' [1993] Crim LR 21; A Wilczynski and A Morris, 'Parents who Kill their Children' [1993] Crim LR 31; D Maeir-Katkin and R Ogle, 'A Rationale for Infanticide Laws' [1993] Crim LR 903; M Jackson, 'Infanticide: Historical Perspectives' (1996) 146 NLJ 416; K Brennan, 'Beyond the Medical Model: A Rationale for Infanticide Legislation' (2007) 58 NILQ 505. The Court of Appeal recently called for its urgent reform: *Kai-Whitewind* [2005] EWCA Crim 1092.

[120] This replaced the words 'notwithstanding that'. In *Gore* [2007] EWCA Crim 2789 the Court of Appeal had construed that as meaning 'even if'. It is now clear it means merely 'if'.

[121] Nicholas et al, *HO Statistical Bulletin: Crime 06/07*, table 2.04.

[122] *O'Donoghue* (1927) 20 Cr App R 132.

one in the present legislation.[123] The killing of an infant by persons other than the mother, or by the mother if the balance of her mind is not disturbed, remains murder.

This section is unusual in that it provides both a charge of infanticide, and also a partial defence to murder: by s 1(2) as amended by the Coroners and Justice Act 2009 that a woman indicted for the murder of her child under the age of 12 months may be acquitted of murder and convicted of infanticide if the conditions of s 1(1) are satisfied. The new subsection (2) reads:

Where upon the trial of a woman for the murder of her child, being a child under the age of twelve months, the jury are of opinion that she by any wilful act or omission caused its death, but that at the time of the act or omission the balance of her mind was disturbed by reason of her not having fully recovered from the effect of giving birth to the child or by reason of the effect of lactation consequent upon the birth of the child, then the jury may, [if] the circumstances were such that but for the provisions of this Act they might have returned a verdict of murder [or manslaughter], return in lieu thereof a verdict of infanticide.[124]

Where the charge is murder, an evidential burden on the issue of disturbance will fall on D; but the onus of *proof* remains with the Crown. Where the charge is infanticide, the onus of proving disturbance appears to be on the Crown; but this, of course, is unlikely to be contested.[125]

The 2009 Act amendment to the section came about following the case of *Gore*.[126] In that case the Court of Appeal had construed the old section 1 as applying even if the mother was not charged with a homicide offence and held that it was available even if the mother lacked the *mens rea* for murder. The new section makes clear that infanticide as a defence and offence applies only in cases where the mother could otherwise have been convicted of murder *or manslaughter*.[127]

The CLRC thought that, because of the way in which the offence is drafted, it is not possible to charge a person with attempting to commit infanticide,[128] but McCowan J has held that such an indictment will lie.[129]

16.3.1 Reform

It is arguable that the principles on which the Infanticide Act was based may be no longer accepted and that mental illness is not now considered to be a significant cause of infanticide. In many cases the relationship of incomplete recovery from the effects of childbirth or lactation to the child-killing is remote.[130] If the true trigger for the killing is a range of other social factors associated with caring for a young child the offence/defence ought to apply to carers of either sex. The Court of Appeal recently drew attention to the unsatisfactory nature of the defence in this respect.[131] Moreover, when the Infanticide Act was passed, there was no defence of diminished responsibility to murder.[132]

---

[123] The validity of this psychiatric basis for the offence has been doubted, see N Walker, *Crime and Insanity in England* (1968) vol 1, 87–104, cf Maier-Katkin and Ogle [1993] Crim LR 903, 905–909.

[124] Was it also necessary to insert 'or manslaughter' in the first line of s 1(2)? The effect of inserting it also into the opening words would be to make it clear that infanticide is an alternative verdict to a charge of manslaughter as well as to a charge of murder.

[125] See the numerous instances in LC No 304, Appendix.

[126] [2007] EWCA Crim 2789.

[127] HC Research Paper 09/06, p 22. The Government rejected the Law Commission proposal for a trial judge to have power to order medical reports where any mother killed a child under 1 and was convicted of murder.

[128] Fourteen Report, para 113.

[129] *K A Smith* [1983] Crim LR 739 and commentary.

[130] Butler Report, Cmnd 6244 at paras 19.23–19.24.

[131] See *Kai-Whitewind* [2005] EWCA Crim 1092.

[132] For comparison of the defence and offence, see Mackay [1993] Crim LR 21.

There are several differences between the defence of diminished responsibility and infanticide. Infanticide requires that the balance of a woman's mind is disturbed at the time she kills her child, either by failure to make a full recovery from the effects of the birth or as a result of the effects of lactation; diminished responsibility requires proof of abnormality of mental functioning arising from a recognized medical condition that substantially impairs the defendant's ability to (a) to understand the nature of D's conduct; (b) to form a rational judgement; (c) to exercise self-control and that explains his killing. Infanticide is both a partial defence to a charge of murder and an offence in its own right; diminished responsibility is only a partial defence. In infanticide, the burden of proof is on the prosecution; in diminished responsibility it is on the defendant on the balance of probabilities. In infanticide, unlike diminished responsibility, the defendant can rely on the plea if at the time of the killing the balance of her mind was disturbed either by birth or by the effects of lactation irrespective of whether that caused[133] her to kill the child. Infanticide is applicable only to biological mothers of the deceased and the deceased must have been under 12 months old at the time of death.[134]

The Butler Committee thought that diminished responsibility even under the old (pre 2009 Act) law would probably cover all cases and recommended the abolition of the separate offence of infanticide.[135] The CLRC disagreed, at first on the ground that, so long as the prosecution are unable to charge manslaughter by reason of diminished responsibility, infanticide has the advantage that it avoids the necessity of charging the mother with murder;[136] and later on the ground that diminished responsibility might not cover all the circumstances which in practice may be held to justify an infanticide verdict.[137]

According to the Royal College of Psychiatrists, these circumstances include:

(1) overwhelming stress from the social environment being highlighted by the birth of a baby, with the emphasis on the unsuitability of the accommodation etc; (2) overwhelming stress from an additional member to a household struggling with poverty; (3) psychological injury, and pressures and stress from a husband or other member of a family from the mother's incapacity to arrange the demands of the extra member of the family; (4) failure of bonding between mother and child through illness or disability which impairs the development of the mother's capacity to care for the infant.

In order to bring the law into line with its practical operation, and because of the difficulty of establishing a direct connection between giving birth and the imbalance of the woman's mind, the CLRC recommend that the test should be whether the balance of her mind was disturbed by reason of the effect of giving birth to the child *or circumstances consequent upon that birth*.[138] A dissentient view was that the effect would be to make adverse social conditions a defence to child killing.[139] Because of the decision to recommend the broadening of the offence in this way (in law, if not in practice)[140] the CLRC abandoned its earlier tentative recommendation that the killing of older children of the family should be infanticide and not

---

[133] See the debate above p 534 on whether the new diminished plea requires a causal link.

[134] See *Gore*, above n 126, at para 20.

[135] ibid. For criticism, see Maier-Katkin and Ogle [1993] Crim LR 903. It has the advantage of applying to carers of either sex.

[136] Criminal Law Revision Committee, Working Paper on *Offences Against the Person* (1976) 26. The Committee tentatively suggested that a person apparently suffering from diminished responsibility should be indictable for manslaughter but later withdrew this proposal: CLRC/OAP/R, para 95.

[137] Research reveals that half of women who plead or are convicted are not suffering any mental disorder. See Wilczynski and Morris [1993] Crim LR 31. See also the data in Appendix D of LC 304.

[138] Fourteenth Report, paras 103–106.

[139] See Annexes 7 and 8 to the Report.

[140] On the use of the offence in modern times see Mackay above and Wilczynski and Morris, above.

murder;[141] and recommended that the maximum penalty should be five years' imprisonment and not two, as they had previously been disposed to think.[142]

The Law Commission reviewed the scope of infanticide in its CP 177 and Report No 304. In CP 177,[143] its provisional proposals were to make minor amendment to the offence/defence so that it would apply where the deceased child was under two, and the reference to lactation in the defence would be removed since medical evidence did not support its retention. In its Final Report No 304, the Law Commission[144] considered extensive medical and psychiatric research,[145] along with the empirical survey by Professor Mackay[146] and recommended that no change be introduced to the offence/defence, save for a procedural amendment to allow an expedited appeal on medical evidence where a mother convicted of murdering her child under 12 months denied the killing. The 1938 Act was, somewhat disappointingly, described as a 'practicable legal solution'.[147]

16.4 The Domestic Violence, Crime and Victims Act 2004

Insurmountable problems arose in prosecutions for the non-accidental serious injury or death of a young child when the only individuals who had access to the child at the time of the incident (usually the two primary carers) denied responsibility. Although clear that at least one of the carers was guilty of a serious crime, it was often impossible to prove beyond reasonable doubt that the ill-treatment was at the hand of one (or both) rather than the other. The death or injury may have occurred while one carer was absent. Further, it was also often impossible to prove whether the carer not directly responsible was guilty as an accomplice. Prior to the 2004 Act, if all that could be proved was that the offence was committed either by D1 or by D2, both had to be acquitted. Only if it could be proved that the one who did not commit the crime *must* have aided and abetted it could both be convicted. This was as true where carers were charged with injury to their child as it was in the case of any other defendants. The only difference was that one carer may have a duty to intervene to prevent the ill-treatment of their child by the other when a stranger would have no such duty. It was for the prosecution to prove that the carer who did not inflict the injuries must have aided and abetted the infliction by failure to fulfil that duty or otherwise.

In a series of cases the Court of Appeal reluctantly accepted that trials in such circumstances would not normally proceed beyond a defence submission of no case to answer.[148] The result proved too much for some courts, and strained attempts to circumvent the problem were adopted. These were unsatisfactory.[149] The problem was a substantial one. Research revealed that in the UK no fewer than three children under the age of 10 died or suffered serious injury each week, and only 27 per cent of cases led to a conviction.[150] The

---

[141] Para 106.

[142] Para 108.

[143] Ch 9.

[144] Ch 8.

[145] Appendix E. Note also that the Royal College of Psychiatrists preferred a merger of the offence/defence with diminished responsibility: LC 304, para 8.35.

[146] Appendix D.

[147] Para 8.3.

[148] *Russell and Russell* [1987] Crim LR 494; *Lane and Lane* (1985) 82 Cr App R 5. For a valuable direction where one of two interrogating police officers has caused injury, see *Forman* [1988] Crim LR 677 (Judge Woods).

[149] *Gibson and Gibson* (1984) 80 Cr App R 24. See commentary [1984] Crim LR 615.

[150] See the Law Commission, *Children: Their Non-Accidental Death or Serious Injury (Criminal Trials)* (LC 282, 2003) Part II.

difficulties had exercised great academic minds, but no consensus was reached as to the optimal solution.[151] Was it better to create a new offence to catch A, who *ought to have* been aware of the wrongdoing of the other carer, B, who caused the injury? Alternatively (or additionally) was it appropriate to alter the procedure in such cases to upset the traditional burden of proof and presumption of innocence, or to admit pre-trial incriminating statements made by A against B, or to provide a statutory obligation to account for the death or injury?[152]

Following detailed consideration by the Law Commission, proposals for new offences and procedural changes were made, and provisions based on, though differing significantly from, those recommendations were implemented in the Domestic Violence, Crime and Victims Act 2004, s 5.[153] To appreciate the full significance of the s 5 offence, it must be seen alongside s 6 of that Act,[154] which introduces controversial procedural changes whereby inferences can be drawn from a defendant's silence when charged with murder/manslaughter, and the s 5 offence even where no case to answer would otherwise be established.

Section 5 introduces the new offence, which provides:[155]

(1) A person ('D') is guilty of an offence if –

    (a) a child or vulnerable adult ('V') dies as a result of the unlawful act of a person who –

        (i) was a member of the same household as V, and

        (ii) had frequent contact with him,

    (b) D was such a person at the time of that act,

    (c) at that time there was a significant risk of serious physical harm being caused to V by the unlawful act of such a person, and

    (d) either D was the person whose act caused V's death or –

        (i) D was, or ought to have been, aware of the risk mentioned in paragraph (c),

        (ii) D failed to take such steps as he could reasonably have been expected to take to protect V from the risk, and

        (iii) the act occurred in circumstances of the kind that D foresaw or ought to have foreseen.

(2) The prosecution does not have to prove whether it is the first alternative in subsection (1)(d) or the second (sub-paragraphs (i) to (iii)) that applies.

(3) If D was not the mother or father of V –

    (a) D may not be charged with an offence under this section if he was under the age of 16 at the time of the act that caused V's death;

---

[151] See, generally, G Williams, 'Which of You Did It?' (1989) 52 MLR 179; E Griew, 'It Must Have Been One of Them' [1989] Crim LR 129.

[152] See LC 282, 2003, Part V.

[153] In particular the Law Commission had proposed a new offence of aggravated child cruelty under s 1 of the Children and Young Person Act 1933, and had produced an offence which dealt with both serious injury and death in relation to children only. For comment on the Law Commission proposals, see P Glazebrook, 'Insufficient Child Protection' [2003] Crim LR 541, proposing an extremely wide offence which it is submitted would extend the ambit of the criminal law too far.

[154] See *Ikram* [2008] EWCA Crim 586 on difficulties that can arise as defendants shift their case in the course of the trial. cf. *Reid (Jason)* [2010] EWCA Crim 1478.

[155] See L Hoyano and C Keenan, *Child Abuse: Law and Policy* (2007) 157–178; M Hayes, 'Criminal Trials Where the Child is the Victim: Extra Protection for Children or a Missed Opportunity' [2005] CFLQ 307; C Colby, 'The Quest For Truth: Substantiating Allegations of Physical Abuse in Criminal Prosecutions and Care Proceedings' (2006) 20 I JLPF 317.

(b) for the purposes of subsection (1)(d)(ii) D could not have been expected to take any such step as is referred to there before attaining that age.

(4) For the purposes of this section –

(a) a person is to be regarded as a 'member' of a particular household, even if he does not live in that household, if he visits it so often and for such periods of time that it is reasonable to regard him as a member of it;

(b) where V lived in different households at different times, 'the same household as V' refers to the household in which V was living at the time of the act that caused V's death.

(5) For the purposes of this section an 'unlawful' act is one that –

(a) constitutes an offence, or

(b) would constitute an offence but for being the act of –

(i) a person under the age of ten, or

(ii) a person entitled to rely on a defence of insanity.

Paragraph (b) does not apply to an act of D.

The offence carries a maximum sentence of imprisonment for 14 years, and two offences of causing or allowing the death of a child or vulnerable person were recorded in 2009/10.[156] The first reported cases under the provision were rather uncontroversial. In *Liu and Tan*,[157] there was physical abuse tantamount to torture of T's wife. T was aware of the gross mistreatment and was a participant. It has been used in high profile cases such as the prosecutions relating to the death of 'Baby P'.[158]

Despite the attempts to define the key elements, many arbitrary distinctions persist and numerous issues will fall for judicial consideration.[159] In some respects the offence is unsatisfactorily wide; in particular, the Crown need not specify whether it is alleged that D killed *or* failed to take reasonable steps to prevent the death by the other member of the household.

16.4.1 Who is protected?

The offence is limited to cases in which the victim is a child or vulnerable adult who dies. A child is simply anyone under 16. The application of s 5 to vulnerable adults is less straightforward. The category under protection is less easily defined. 'Vulnerable adult' involves the more expansive definition in s 5(6):

a person aged 16 or over whose ability to protect himself from violence, abuse or neglect is significantly impaired through physical or mental disability or illness, through old age or otherwise.

This might have been intended primarily to protect the elderly cared for at home, but it may apply to domestic violence on much younger victims. In *Khan and others*[160] S was convicted of murdering V, his wife aged 19. V came to the UK from Kashmir to marry S, her cousin. They lived with S's mother, P, and others who were members of the extended family. V spoke no English. She was completely dependent on S and his family. S severely beat and inflicted fatal injuries on V in the garage outside the house whilst the appellants slept. Evidence was adduced that S had violently abused V for weeks prior to killing her. S and others were convicted of allowing the death of a vulnerable adult, contrary to s 5(1). The Court of Appeal held

---

[156] Flatley et al, *Crime in England and Wales 2009/10*, table 2.04.

[157] [2006] EWCA Crim 3321.

[158] *Owen* [2009] EWCA Crim 2259.

[159] See also Home Office Circular 9/2005, *The Domestic Violence, Crime and Victims Act 2004*.

[160] [2009] EWCA Crim 2.

that V was vulnerable at least from the time she suffered serious injuries in the weeks prior to the fatal attack. Adults, or near adults over the age of 16 were vulnerable if their ability to protect themselves from 'violence, abuse or neglect' was significantly impaired. The state of vulnerability did not need to be long-standing.

The court was not prepared to exclude 'the possibility that an adult who is utterly dependent on others, even if physically young and apparently fit, may fall within the protective ambit of the Act'.[161] Moreover, the anticipation of a full recovery might not reduce the individual's temporary vulnerability. Such a broad interpretation has the potential to create problems. It may make an already broad offence undesirably wide. The court's interpretation gives 'otherwise' within s 5(6) a meaning unconstrained by all of the words preceding it. Where the statute is introducing such a radical concept as a positive duty to act, with a criminal sanction for failure to do so, a narrower approach to interpretation might have been expected. The s 5 offence applies to D2, who fails to protect a vulnerable person from death, as well as to D1 who actually kills. Those who fail to protect are judged on a negligence-based standard – that they were or *ought to have been* aware of the significant risk of serious injury to V. On a natural interpretation, there is no need for D2 to realize that V is a vulnerable adult: liability on that element of the offence is strict. If that is correct, D2's liability turns exclusively on the awareness/negligence as to V being at significant risk of serious injury from D1 and D2's failure to take reasonable steps to avoid that harm. If liability as to V's status is strict, and the definition of vulnerability is as ambiguous as it seems to be, the offence is remarkably wide. Since D2 need not (and arguably cannot) know whether V qualifies as a vulnerable adult, D2 is under a duty as soon as D2 ought to have realized that any member of the household is at significant risk of grievous bodily harm (gbh) from any other member of the household, whether V is a child or even a fit adult. If D2 ought to have been so aware, D2 will only be acquitted if either he took reasonable steps to avoid the harm or, *at trial* it is determined that V was not a vulnerable adult after all. However, it is implicit in the decision that the extent to which D2 did or did not know of V's vulnerability is highly material to what it was reasonable for D2 to be expected to do.[162]

16.4.2 What type of act or omission?

The *actus reus* of the offence is committed by either D's act or omission[163] which caused the death of the victim; or D's failure to take such steps as he could reasonably have been expected to take to protect V from the *significant*[164] risk of *serious* physical harm by the unlawful act of a person living in the same household as V and having frequent contact with V. There is no requirement that the failure on D's part to protect V is a legal cause of death.[165] The conduct which caused death is not limited to that which would form specific crimes provided it was unlawful – offences of violence are the most obvious examples, and in relation to children under 16, but not vulnerable individuals, offences of child neglect.

D1's conduct which results in V's death must occur in circumstances of 'the kind' which were/ought to have been foreseen by D2; there is no need for the conduct to be identical to

---

[161] [26].

[162] Problems of proof might arise in the case of a person who is apparently fit: the physically fitter V is, the less likely that D2 will be aware that he is at significant risk of gbh from D1 (unless D1's treatment of V is extreme), particularly where D1's conduct takes the form of neglect rather than physical attack.

[163] Section 5(6) makes it clear that an act includes an omission.

[164] See *Mujuru* [2007] EWCA Crim 1249, [2008] Crim LR 54 and commentary.

[165] D2's act in killing V will break the chain of causation, D1 will remain liable under this offence, not for an omission based on a duty (identified under the categories in Ch 4).

that which D2 ought to have foreseen.[166] In determining what is of the same kind, it is not appropriate to place reliance on principles of fundamental changes of weapon in joint enterprise. It is odd that the offence is restricted by this requirement. It means that D2 who foresees that D1 might use violence by punching V cannot be prosecuted if D1 kills V by poisoning.

The unlawful act by D1 of which D2 must be aware/ought to be aware can include a course of violent conduct and an *omission* to act. If D1 neglects a vulnerable member of the household to whom he owes a duty of care and is liable for gross negligence manslaughter, D2, a fellow member of the household, might then be liable under s 5 if he at least ought to have been aware of the risk of serious injury to V by D1's conduct. The fact that D1's act must be an 'unlawful' one (including an omission) does not mean that there must an unlawful act as an element of the gross negligence manslaughter charge; rather, the gross negligence manslaughter qualifies because it is an unlawful act, ie a crime: s 5(5).

16.4.3 Household

The Act deliberately leaves undefined the concept of 'household'.[167] This is disappointing for an offence of this seriousness, even with the additional qualifying requirement that D has contact with the victim. Some categories of carer who have regular contact – for example, nannies – are seemingly not caught by the Act unless under s 5(4)(b). The focus of the offence is clearly on imposing burdens on household members to police the risk of harm.[168] In that respect it is illogical that the offence is not triggered where D is/ought to be aware of the risk posed by other carers in regular contact with the victim.

In *Khan*, it was held that membership of a household was a question of fact. There had to be 'frequent contact' between the household member and the eventual victim. That was a question of fact. The lack of certainty is unsatisfactory in an offence of this nature.

16.4.4 What type of harm?

Serious harm is defined in the 2004 Act as 'harm that amounts to grievous bodily harm for the purposes of the Offences Against the Person Act 1861'.[169]

16.4.5 What *mens rea*?

In terms of *mens rea*, it is effectively a crime of negligence since the fault on D's part if he is not the direct cause of the death is a question of whether he *ought to have been* aware of the risk. The death must have occurred *in the circumstances* that D ought to have foreseen. D who is aware that X has previously shaken their baby, V, violently might not be guilty if X caused V's death by, for example, dipping its dummy in methadone to stop its incessant crying.[170]

---

[166] See *Khan* at [39].

[167] In the House of Lords debates (21 Jan 2004, col GC362), Baroness Scotland stated that it was a deliberate decision to leave the definition to courts.

[168] 'It is drafted with the idea that members of the household will know enough about the activities of the other members that they can be expected to be aware of the risk to the victim and take action. They are 'complicit' in the offence, either directly or by proximity, through standing by during the preceding abuse or neglect and doing nothing. Therefore, in this context, if one were to ask, "Am I my brother's keeper?", the answer would be, "Yes".' Baroness Scotland, *Hansard*, 21 Jan 2004, col GC361.

[169] Section 5(6).

[170] For an example of a s 5 case involving poisoning, see *V* [2010] EWCA Crim 721 where D drugged her children to make them sleep.

In *Khan* the court referred to the ... ME AND VICTIMS ACT 2004
their eyes to a risk of which they ought ... offence to 'those who chose to close
foreseen'.[171] Technically, this confuses wilfu... ware, and which they ought to have
risk (at least suspicion) with negligence where D ... here D has some awareness of the
sonable person would. The test in s 5 is one of what ...

Another limitation on the scope of liability is that in ... any awareness provided a rea-
against the steps he could be reasonably expected to make ... ve been aware.
ability this will be relevant to determining what he could be ... D's failure is to be assessed
is petrified of D2? In addition, in assessing the reasonableness of ... ld or has a learning dis-
been taken by D, the question for the jury is, seemingly, whether the ... do. What of D1 who
this particular defendant to take. Thus, juries might hesitate before con... that ought to have
an abusive and violent relationship with X, and is aware that X batters them ... e reasonable for
D. In *Khan* the Court of Appeal sought to allay fears[172] that the offence will be ... who lives in
priately to victimize further those who, because they are themselves subjected to ... as he does
abuse, have failed to take steps to protect a child or vulnerable adult from the risks pos... appro-
the abuser within the household. As the court observes, under s 5(1)(d)(ii) the protective step... by
which could have been expected of D2 depend on what reasonably could have been expected
of *him or her* and the jury might therefore conclude that such a person's failure was reasonable
in the circumstances.

It should also be noted that the offence is qualified: the risk of which D ought to have
been aware is a 'significant' one of 'serious injury'. The Law Commission had concluded
that the level of risk to the child which must exist before a person is exposed to criminal
liability ought to be 'relatively high'.[173] The Commission drew support for its proposal
that the risk should be a 'real risk' more than 'a possibility', from the interpretation of the
expression 'likely harm' in s 31 of the Children Act 1989 as construed in the House of Lords
in *Re H and others*.[174] The Law Commission also accepted, however, that a test of 'serious
likelihood' or 'serious risk' would set the standard too high and inhibit successful prosecution.[175] Parliament substituted the words 'significant risk' for the Law Commission's
formula 'real risk'. Some commentators suggest that Parliament may, therefore, have
intended to impose a higher threshold.[176] Comments made in the course of parliamentary debates also support that view. Baroness Scotland of Asthal stated that 'We should
remember too that we are talking about "a significant risk of serious physical harm". *That
is quite a high threshold.* The signs of that risk would be very evident. In many cases, the
risk of harm is all too evident from previous harm that a member of the household has
inflicted on the child or on others.'[177]

---

[171] [32].

[172] Organizations such as *Justice* and *Refuge* cautioned during the Act's consultation process against the
danger that the offence may be used to further victimize abused women by their prosecution for allowing their
abusive partners to kill the child See, eg, *Refuge Response to the Domestic Violence Crimes and Victims Bill 07/04*.
A view echoed by J Herring, 'Familial Homicide, Failure to Protect and Domestic Violence: Who's the Victim'
[2007] Crim LR 923. *Mujuru*, above n 164, is one of the examples cited.

[173] Para 6.21.

[174] [1996] AC 563 at 592 per Lord Nicholls.

[175] Para 6.23.

[176] R Ward and R Bird, *The Domestic Violence, Crime and Victims Act 2004: A Practitioner's Guide* (2005)
para 3.24.

[177] *Hansard*, HL, 9 Mar 2004, col 1158, emphasis added.

In *Khan* the court referred to the extension of the offence to 'those who chose to close their eyes to a risk of which they ought to have been aware, and which they ought to have foreseen'.[171] Technically, this confuses wilful blindness where D has some awareness of the risk (at least suspicion) with negligence where D need not have any awareness provided a reasonable person would. The test in s 5 is one of what D ought to have been aware.

Another limitation on the scope of liability is that in s 5(1)(d)(ii): D's failure is to be assessed against the steps he could be reasonably expected to make. If D is a child or has a learning disability this will be relevant to determining what he could be expected to do. What of D1 who is petrified of D2? In addition, in assessing the reasonableness of the steps that ought to have been taken by D, the question for the jury is, seemingly, whether the steps are reasonable for this particular defendant to take. Thus, juries might hesitate before convicting D who lives in an abusive and violent relationship with X, and is aware that X batters their child as he does D. In *Khan* the Court of Appeal sought to allay fears[172] that the offence will be used inappropriately to victimize further those who, because they are themselves subjected to domestic abuse, have failed to take steps to protect a child or vulnerable adult from the risks posed by the abuser within the household. As the court observes, under s 5(1)(d)(ii) the protective steps which could have been expected of D2 depend on what reasonably could have been expected of *him or her* and the jury might therefore conclude that such a person's failure was reasonable in the circumstances.

It should also be noted that the offence is qualified: the risk of which D ought to have been aware is a 'significant' one of 'serious injury'. The Law Commission had concluded that the level of risk to the child which must exist before a person is exposed to criminal liability ought to be 'relatively high'.[173] The Commission drew support for its proposal that the risk should be a 'real risk' more than 'a possibility', from the interpretation of the expression 'likely harm' in s 31 of the Children Act 1989 as construed in the House of Lords in *Re H and others*.[174] The Law Commission also accepted, however, that a test of 'serious likelihood' or 'serious risk' would set the standard too high and inhibit successful prosecution.[175] Parliament substituted the words 'significant risk' for the Law Commission's formula 'real risk'. Some commentators suggest that Parliament may, therefore, have intended to impose a higher threshold.[176] Comments made in the course of parliamentary debates also support that view. Baroness Scotland of Asthal stated that 'We should remember too that we are talking about "a significant risk of serious physical harm". *That is quite a high threshold*. The signs of that risk would be very evident. In many cases, the risk of harm is all too evident from previous harm that a member of the household has inflicted on the child or on others.'[177]

---

[171] [32].

[172] Organizations such as *Justice* and *Refuge* cautioned during the Act's consultation process against the danger that the offence may be used to further victimize abused women by their prosecution for allowing their abusive partners to kill the child See, eg, *Refuge Response to the Domestic Violence Crimes and Victims Bill 07/04*. A view echoed by J Herring, 'Familial Homicide, Failure to Protect and Domestic Violence: Who's the Victim' [2007] Crim LR 923. *Mujuru*, above n 164, is one of the examples cited.

[173] Para 6.21.

[174] [1996] AC 563 at 592 per Lord Nicholls.

[175] Para 6.23.

[176] R Ward and R Bird, *The Domestic Violence, Crime and Victims Act 2004: A Practitioner's Guide* (2005) para 3.24.

[177] *Hansard*, HL, 9 Mar 2004, col 1158, emphasis added.

16.5 Child destruction and abortion[178]

It has already been observed that it is not murder to kill a child in the womb or while in the process of being born. Nor is it, in itself, an offence against the person of the mother, since the foetus is not part of the mother.[179] Though the killing of the child in the womb after 'quickening'[180] was a misdemeanour at common law, the present law on the subject is statutory. There are two offences to consider:

- section 1 of the Infant Life (Preservation) Act 1929 prohibits the killing of any child which is 'capable of being born alive'; and
- section 58 of the Offences Against the Person Act 1861 (subject to the Abortion Act 1967)[181] prohibits attempts to procure miscarriage from any time after the conception of the child until its birth.

The two offences thus overlap. Procuring a miscarriage so as to kill a child capable of being born alive may amount to both offences. Killing a child in the process of being born is not procuring a miscarriage and can amount only to child destruction, of which there were three recorded offences in 2009/10.[182]

16.5.1 Child destruction[183]

Section 1 of the Infant Life (Preservation) Act 1929 provides:

(1) Subject as hereinafter in this subsection provided, any person who, with intent to destroy the life of a child capable of being born alive, by any wilful act causes a child to die before it has an existence independent of its mother, shall be guilty of an offence, to wit, of child destruction, and shall be liable on conviction thereof on indictment to imprisonment for life: Provided that no person shall be found guilty of an offence under this section unless it is proved that the act which caused the death of the child was not done in good faith for the purpose only of preserving the life of the mother.

(2) For the purposes of this Act, evidence that a woman had at any material time been pregnant for a period of twenty-eight weeks or more shall be prima facie proof that she was at that time pregnant of a child capable of being born alive.

While the actual physical condition in which a foetus would exist following birth is a matter for expert medical evidence, whether a foetus at that particular stage of its development can properly be described as 'a child capable of being born alive' is a question of law for the court. Differing interpretations have been proffered, including that the expression is limited to the child in the process of being born, that it extended to any viable foetus, and widest of all, that it extended to any foetus capable of being born alive, however short-lived its existence.[184]

---

[178] See I Kennedy and A Grubb, *Medical Law: Texts and Materials* (2000) Part III; Williams, *Sanctity of Life*, 139–223; 'The Legalization of Medical Abortion' (1964) The Eugenics Review; BM Dickens, *Abortion and the Law* (1966); B Bennett, *Abortion* (2004). See also the Select Committee Report on *Scientific Developments in Relation to the Abortion Act 1967* (2007) HC 1045–1. I am grateful to Tracey Elliott for valuable discussions on this part.

[179] *A-G's Reference (No 3 of 1994)*, above, p 138.

[180] 'Quickening' was an ambiguous term but was generally accepted to mean the time at which the mother felt the motion of the child. It was commonly treated as being around the 15th/16th week.

[181] See below, p 604.

[182] Flatley et al, *Crime in England and Wales 2009/10*, table 2.04.

[183] See J Keown, 'The Scope of the Offence of Child Destruction' (1988) 104 LQR 120.

[184] See J Keown for discussion of the merits of each interpretation. See also D Price, 'How Viable is the Present Scope of the Offence of Child Destruction' (1987) 16 Anglo Am LR 220. cf *R v McDonald* (1999) NICC (4 March) (sufficient that foetus had a real chance of being born alive).

In *C v S*,[185] the medical experts disagreed as to whether a foetus at the stage it will normally have reached by the 18th to the 21st week of pregnancy would be described as capable of being born alive. The court held, in the light of the evidence that it would never be capable of breathing, that it could not.[186] In *Rance v Mid-Downs Health Authority*,[187] a civil action, Brooke J as he then was thought the meaning of the phrase was clear and that a child is 'born alive' if 'after birth, it exists as a live child, that is to say breathing and living by reason of its breathing through its own lungs alone, without deriving any of its living or power of living by or through any connection with its mother'. It is not necessary that the child be capable of survival into old age or even for a period of days. Applying this test, Brooke J was satisfied to 'a very high standard of proof' that the particular child was capable of being born alive after 26 weeks of pregnancy and therefore to kill him would have been the offence of child destruction. The Abortion Act 1967 uses the phrase 'protecting the life of the viable foetus' in respect of the provisions of the 1929 Act; but, rejecting the view that 'viable' has a different and more restrictive meaning, Brooke J held that it was merely used as convenient shorthand for 'capable of being born alive' and its use in 1967 had no effect on the meaning of the 1929 Act.[188]

The *Rance* test has the merit of being reasonably clear. However, it is not applicable to all situations. For example, in *Re A*, M never breathed on her own and yet, since she was clearly alive was regarded as such by all involved and the point as to whether she was born alive was not taken with any seriousness.[189] The pressure on the law's ability to deal with these difficult issues will increase as medical advances allow, for example for pre-birth treatment. It is now possible for a foetus to undergo surgery prior to birth, during the course of which it may be removed from the womb before being replaced in the mother. Is the child born? What if an individual was to burst in on the operating theatre and stab the foetus with murderous intent?

The Select Committee Report *Scientific Developments Relating to the Abortion Act 1967*[190] recognized the difficulty in defining the viability of a foetus or neonate. In relation to neonates, the Committee reported that 'it has been subject to a range of interpretations. At one extreme a baby could be defined as viable simply because it was born showing signs of life, for example, breathing or a heart beat… at the other extreme it could mean that a baby is capable of surviving through childhood with no or minimal disabilities.'[191] There is, as ever, a danger with loose language. In general, viability might mean the minimum age of gestation at which any neonate could survive, the minimum age at which this neonate could survive, or the age at which the majority of neonates would survive.[192] The Committee heard evidence that viability means, in medical terms, capability of surviving into adulthood.[193]

In a controversial series of decisions the European Court has declined to decide whether the protection of Art 2 extends to the unborn child. It was acknowledged in *Vo v France*[194] that the Convention institutions have not 'ruled out the possibility that in certain circumstances safeguards may be extended to the unborn child'.[195] The Court noted that 'the unborn

[185] [1988] QB 135, CA.

[186] ibid, at 1238–1239 (Heilbron J). cf G Wright, 'Capable of Being Born Alive?' (1981) 131 NLJ 188; 'The Legality of Abortion by Prostaglandin' [1984] Crim LR 347; Tunkel and Wright [1985] Crim LR 133.

[187] [1991] 1 QB 587 QBD.

[188] The 1990 amendments provide that no offence is committed under the 1929 Act provided that the pregnancy is terminated in accordance with provisions of the 1967 Act (below).

[189] See p 371 above. For a view that M was not 'born alive', see JK Mason, 'Conjoined Twins: A Diagnostic Conundrum' (2001) 5 ELR 226. On pre-natal surgery, see (2011) N Engl J Med, Editorial 9 Feb.

[190] (2007) HC 1045–1. See C Foster, 'Forty Years On' (2007) 157 NLJ 1517.

[191] Para 22.

[192] Para 23.

[193] Para 27.

[194] [2004] 2 FCR 577.

[195] Para 82.

child is not regarded as a person directly protected by Article 2 of the Convention and that if the unborn do have a right to life it is implicitly limited by the mother's rights and interests'.[196] The decision has been cogently criticized.[197]

The jury may convict of child destruction on an indictment for murder, manslaughter, infanticide or an offence under s 58 of the Offences Against the Person Act 1861; and on an indictment for child destruction, they may convict of an offence under s 58.[198]

16.5.1.1 Interrelationship with the Abortion Act 1967

The Abortion Act 1967 legalizes abortion in certain circumstances and subject to certain formalities. It originally provided that it should not affect the offence of child destruction but, as amended by the Human Fertilisation and Embryology Act 1990,[199] s 5(1) of the 1967 Act states that:

No offence under [the 1929 Act] shall be committed by a registered medical practitioner who terminates a pregnancy in accordance with the provisions of [the Abortion Act 1967].

The effect of this provision is that:

- If the doctor is complying with the terms of the 1967 Act, and causes the death of a child capable of being born alive, it is not an offence under the 1929 Act.[200]

- If the death of such a child is caused by a doctor who is *not* complying with the provisions of the 1967 Act, or if it is caused by any other person, then it is *prima facie* child destruction. There will, however, be a defence to a charge of child destruction if the act is done for the purpose only of preserving the life of the mother.

- But, even where the operation is to save the life of the mother, that will not amount to a defence to a charge under s 58 of the 1861 Act unless the *Bourne* defence of necessity has survived the 1967 Act – a matter of some doubt, considered below.[201]

A wide meaning was given to the words 'for the purpose only of preserving the life of the mother' by MacNaghten J in *Bourne*.[202] This was *obiter*, so far as the Infant Life (Preservation) Act 1929 was concerned, since the charge was brought under the Offences Against the Person Act 1861; but MacNaghten J took the view that those words represented the common law and were implicit in the 1861 Act by virtue of the word 'unlawfully'. He said:

As I have said, I think those words ['for the purpose of preserving the life of the mother'] ought to be construed in a reasonable sense, and if the doctor is of opinion, on reasonable grounds and with

---

[196] Para 80.

[197] See JK Mason, 'What's in a Name: The Vagaries of *Vo v France*' (2005) 17 CFLQ 97, calling for an offence of feticide which can be committed without an intent to kill – in cases of gross negligence. See also A Plomer, 'A Foetal Right to Life' [2005] EHRLR 311 criticizing the judgment and suggesting that in cases of violence against the mother life might be treated as beginning at the point of foetal viability. See also E Wicks, 'Terminating Life and Human Rights: The Fetus and the Neonate' in C Erin and S Ost, *The Criminal Justice System and Health Care* (2007), discussing whether the right of the foetus might be subordinate to that of the mother, a violation of the foetus right to life ought not to be justified on the basis of post-natal disability and suffering (201).

[198] For an example of a conviction where D used violence against the pregnant woman with the intention of causing the death of the child, see *Virgo* (1988) Cr App R (S) 427.

[199] On which, see A Grubb, 'The New Law on Abortion: Clarification or Ambiguity' [1991] Crim LR 659. See also the Government's *Review of the Human Fertilisation and Embryology Act: Proposals for Revised Legislation (Including Establishment of the Regulatory Authority for Tissue and Embryos)* in December 2006 (Cm 6989). See now the Human Fertilisation and Embryology Act 2008.

[200] M Bohlander, 'Of Shipwrecked Sailors, Unborn Children, Conjoined Twins and Hijacked Airplanes – Taking Human Life and the Defence of Necessity' (2006) 70 J Crim L 147 derives support from this for a defence of necessity applying to murder.

[201] Below, p 613.

[202] [1939] 1 KB 687.

adequate knowledge, that the probable consequence of the continuance of the pregnancy will be to make the woman a physical or mental wreck, the jury are quite entitled to take the view that the doctor who under these circumstances and in the honest belief, operates, is operating for the purpose of preserving the life of the mother.[203]

Both before and after this, however, the judge stressed that the test was whether the operation was performed in good faith for the purpose of preserving the *life* of the mother and the passage may be intended to refer only to such inquiries to health as will shorten life because the judge had said '... life depends upon health and health may be so gravely impaired that death results'.[204]

Informed medical opinion construed the judgment in the wider sense[205] and this appears to have been vindicated. In *Bergmann and Ferguson*,[206] Morris J is reported to have said that the court will not look too narrowly into the question of danger to life where danger to health is anticipated. Then, in *Newton and Stungo*,[207] Ashworth J stated in his direction to the jury, 'Such use of an instrument is unlawful unless the use is made in good faith for the purposes of preserving the life *or health* of the woman', adding that this included mental as well as physical health. Newton was acquitted of manslaughter by criminal negligence, but convicted of manslaughter by unlawfully using an instrument and of the offence under s 58. He did not appeal (obviously the direction was favourable to him); but it is thought likely that Ashworth J's view would be accepted by the appellate courts.[208]

The criterion of the defence as it has been applied by the courts is a subjective one; that is, the question is not whether the operation is in fact necessary to preserve the life of the mother but whether D *believes* it to be necessary.[209] In answering this question, the court will take account of the size of the fee, a large fee being evidence of bad faith;[210] and whether D followed accepted medical practice.[211] What is the position if the operation was in fact necessary, but was performed by D in bad faith, to oblige, as he thought, the mere convenience of the woman, and for a high fee? One view might be that there is no *actus reus* here,[212] but it is thought more likely that the defence will be limited to the case of a *bona fide* belief.[213] Thus, in *Newton*, it does not seem to have been decided that an operation was unnecessary; only that Newton did not *bona fide* believe it to be necessary.[214]

These cases all relate to s 58 of the 1861 Act, where they are probably no longer in point.[215] Since they purport to be an interpretation of the proviso in the 1929 Act, however, they cannot be ignored in considering the child destruction offence. On the other hand it is quite possible

---

[203] [1939] 1 KB at 693, 694.

[204] [1939] 1 KB at 692.

[205] J Havard, 'Therapeutic Abortion' [1958] Crim LR 600 at 605.

[206] (1948) unreported; Williams, *Sanctity of Life*, 154; 1 BMJ 1008.

[207] [1958] Crim LR 469, fully considered by Havard [1958] Crim LR 600.

[208] See also *Paton v BPAS* [1979] QB 276: 'not only would it be a bold and brave judge ... who would seek to interfere with the discretion of the doctors acting under the Abortion Act 1967, but I think he would really be a foolish judge who would try to do any such thing, unless, possibly, where there is clear bad faith and an obvious attempt to perpetrate a criminal offence', per Sir George Baker P.

[209] *Bergmann and Ferguson* cited in *The Sanctity of Life*, 165.

[210] A significant difference between the case of *Newton* and that of *Stungo* (who was acquitted) seems to have been that Stungo took a very small fee, Newton a high one.

[211] See Havard [1958] Crim LR at 607, 608.

[212] cf the discussion of *Dadson*, above, p 54.

[213] cf Williams, *The Sanctity of Life*, 166, who would agree with this conclusion on the ground that the crime is in the nature of an attempt. But it is just as much a substantive crime as burglary.

[214] But even if it was necessary to carry out the operation, it was probably not necessary to carry it out in the way it was done – in a consulting room, the patient being sent back to a hotel in a taxi afterwards.

[215] Below.

that the court, when actually confronted with the interpretation of the proviso, might take a stricter and narrower view of what constitutes the preservation of the life of the mother.

16.5.2 Attempting to procure miscarriage

The common law misdemeanour of abortion applied only after the child had 'quickened' in the womb. To procure an abortion before this occurred was no crime. A statute of 1803[216] enacted that it should be a felony punishable by death to administer a poison with intent to procure the miscarriage of a woman quick[217] with child and a felony punishable with imprisonment or transportation for 14 years to administer poison with a like intent to a woman who was not proved to be quick with child. The distinction between 'quick' and 'non-quick' women gave rise to complications and it disappeared in the re-enactment of the law by the Offences Against the Person Act 1837[218] which established the law substantially in its modern form. The current statute is the Offences Against the Person Act 1861, which provides by s 58:

Every woman being with child who, with intent to procure her own miscarriage, shall unlawfully administer to herself any poison or other noxious thing, or shall unlawfully use any instrument or other means whatsoever with the like intent, and whosoever, with intent to procure the miscarriage of any woman, whether she be or be not with child, shall unlawfully administer to her or cause to be taken by her any poison or other noxious thing, or shall unlawfully use any instrument or other means whatsoever with the like intent, shall be guilty of an offence, and being convicted thereof shall be liable...to imprisonment for life...

The extension of the law was of great practical importance, since most self-induced abortions occur before quickening. Prescription, supply, administration or use of the contraceptive pill, mini-pill and morning-after pill does not contravene s 58 because the pill is not an abortifacient.[219] It has also been held that the fitting of an IUD was not an offence under s 58.[220] In the recent case of *BPAS v Secretary of State for Health*:[221] BPAS's claim to establish that it would be lawful to pilot and adopt a process of providing early medical abortion (EMA) whereby part of the treatment was administered at home was rejected by the Admin Court. 'Parliament has decided by section 1(3A) to give the Secretary of State the responsibility for approval of the types of medicine that can be used, the manner in which they can be used and the places where they can be used.'[222]

The statute makes it clear beyond all doubt that the offence may be committed by the woman herself as well as by others, the only distinction being that if the woman herself is charged, it must be proved that she is in fact pregnant, whereas this is not necessary if the accused is someone other than the mother herself.[223] The Act is not confined to the use of a 'poison or other noxious thing' or 'any instrument'; the 'other means' include manual interference, even though no instrument is employed and the medical evidence is that the act could not, in the

[216] 43 Geo 3, c 58.

[217] See above, n 180. ie whether the mother felt the foetus.

[218] 7 Will & 1 Vic, c 85.

[219] *R (on the Application of Smeaton) v Secretary of State for Health* [2002] All ER (D) 115 (Apr), [2002] Crim LR 664. For critical comment on the decision, see J Keown, '"Morning After" Pills, "Miscarriage" and Muddle' (2005) LS 296, and B Hewson, 'SPUC and the Morning-After Pill Saga' (2002) 152 NLJ 1004.

[220] *Dhingra* (1991) unreported but cited in E Jackson, *Medical Law: Text, Cases and Materials* (2nd edn, 2010) 693.

[221] [2011] EWHC 235 (Admin).

[222] [37].

[223] Section 2(3) of the Human Fertilisation and Embryology Act 1990 provides that 'for the purposes of the Act, a woman is not to be treated as carrying a child until the embryo has become implanted'.

circumstances, cause a miscarriage.[224] The *actus reus* consists simply in the *administration* of the poison or other noxious thing or the *use* of the instrument or other means. The offence can be committed where the pregnant woman is not aware that the administration of the drug has been performed.[225]

The Act distinguishes between 'poison' and 'noxious thing' and it has been held that in the case of something other than a 'recognized poison', the thing must be administered in such quantity as to be in fact harmful though not necessarily abortifacient.[226] A sleeping pill has been held not to be noxious;[227] and the administration in harmless quantities of oil of juniper was no *actus reus*;[228] but Denman J said that it would be otherwise if a thing, innocuous when administered in small quantities, were to be administered in such quantities as to be noxious. Field and Stephen JJ thought that if the thing were a 'recognized poison' the offence might be committed even though the quantity given was so small as to be incapable of doing harm. The distinction is hardly a logical one for 'recognized poisons' may be beneficial when taken in small quantities and in such a case the thing taken is no more poisonous than the oil of juniper was noxious.

The section makes a distinction between the case where the woman administers, etc the thing to herself, in which case she must be proved to be with child, and the case where it is administered to her by another, in which case she need not be. The importance of this distinction has been diminished by the decision in *Whitchurch*[229] that a woman who is not pregnant may be convicted of conspiring with another to procure her own abortion, and by the decision in *Sockett* that such a woman[230] may be convicted of aiding and abetting in the offence of the other, if it is complete. Thus, in effect, the woman will be excused on the ground that she is not with child only in cases where she is not acting in concert with another. One view is that this interpretation has wholly undermined the intention of Parliament.[231] But it has been argued elsewhere[232] that it would have been perfectly reasonable for Parliament to discriminate between the non-pregnant woman who calls in the back-street or professional abortionist and the non-pregnant woman who administers to herself an abortifacient in the solitude of her own bedroom. The point is perhaps not of great practical importance as it appears that it is not the practice to prosecute the woman.[233]

It is debatable whether s 1 of the Abortion Act allows for a defence only when a pregnancy is *successfully* terminated. There are cases where the abortion is unsuccessful.[234] In *RCN v DHSS*,[235] the House of Lords suggested that it would be 'absurd' and 'cannot have been the intention of Parliament' that anyone taking part in an unsuccessful termination would be unable to rely on defences in the Abortion Act so as to be guilty of offence under the 1861 Act. Lord Edmund-Davies observed that 'Were it otherwise the unavoidable conclusion is that doctors and nurses could in such cases be convicted of what in essence would be the extraordinary crime of attempting to do a lawful act.'

---

[224] *Spicer* [1955] Crim LR 772.

[225] See the case of *Magira* [2008] EWCA Crim 1939 where D secretly put into his wife's food abortifacient drugs that he had bought on the internet. D did not want a child.

[226] *Marlow* (1964) 49 Cr App R 49 (Brabin J); *Douglas* [1966] NZLR 45. cf *Marcus* [1981] 2 All ER 833, below, p 675.

[227] *Weatherall* [1968] Crim LR 115 (Judge Brodrick).

[228] *Cramp* (1880) 5 QBD 307.

[229] (1890) 24 QBD 420; above, p 430.

[230] (1908) 72 JP 428; above, p 430.

[231] Williams, CLGP, 673.

[232] B Hogan, 'Victims as Parties to Crime' [1962] Crim LR 683 at 690.

[233] Nor has it been for some time. cf *The Sanctity of Life* at 146; *Peake* (1932) 97 JPN 353.

[234] Or dealing with an attempt, where abortion is attempted, but the woman turns out not to be pregnant.

[235] [1981] AC 800.

16.5.3 Knowingly supplying or procuring poison, etc

Section 59 of the Offences Against the Person Act makes a substantive crime of certain pre-paratory acts, some of which might amount to counselling or abetting the offence under s 58. It provides:

Whosoever shall unlawfully supply or procure any poison or other noxious thing, or any instrument or thing whatsoever, knowing that the same is intended to be unlawfully used or employed with intent to procure the miscarriage of any woman, whether she be or be not with child, shall be guilty of a misdemeanour, and being convicted thereof shall be liable... to imprisonment... for any term not exceeding five years...

The word 'procure', on the first occasion on which it is used in the section, means 'get pos-session of something of which you have not got possession already';[236] so D's conviction was quashed when there was no evidence as to how or when he had come into the possession of the instruments and the judge had misdirected the jury that the word was 'wide enough to include getting instruments or getting them together or preparing them for use'.[237]
   This leaves a gap in the legislation. As Crown counsel said:[238]

if a defendant went to a chemist and bought an instrument to abort A, he would have committed an offence, but if he then put the instrument away in a cupboard and later, for the purpose of aborting B went to the cupboard and took the instrument he would not have committed an offence.

The meaning was further considered in the extraordinary case of *Ahmed*.[239] D was married to a woman who spoke no English who fell pregnant. D took her to an abortion clinic, telling her she was going for a minor operation for ovarian cysts. Staff at the clinic became con-cerned and provided an interpreter. No abortion occurred. D was convicted of an offence under s 59, but the conviction was quashed on appeal. One argument considered was that the surgical instruments which must have been available to carry out the intended abortion were procured by D, but the indictment referred only to medical or surgical procedures and not to instruments. The Court of Appeal noted that there was no evidence that any particular instruments had been selected for use at or brought to the place at which the operation would take place. 'Even if they had, we do not consider that the appellant could be said to have "pro-cured" those instruments.' Referring to *Mills* the court confirmed that the word 'procure' is not apt to describe a case in which the defendant brings about a situation in which a third person, here a nurse or doctor, will take possession of or use an instrument of some kind.
   The meaning of 'thing' in s 59 was also considered in *Ahmed*.[240] The Court of Appeal held that D did not supply or procure any poison, any other noxious *thing* or any instrument. The Crown argued that a 'thing' was anticipated medical or surgical procedure. The Court of Appeal rejected that view – 'the juxtaposition of the word "thing" with the word "instrument" which almost immediately precedes it, indicates that the *"thing" must be some sort of article or object rather than something such as a medical procedure which has no physical existence*'.[241]
   The court drew support for this interpretation by comparing ss 59 and 58 of the 1861 Act. Section 58 extends to D who unlawfully uses 'any instrument or other means whatsoever'.
   The words, 'knowing that the same is intended to be unlawfully used' have been con-strued in an extraordinarily wide sense and one highly unfavourable to the accused. Their

---

[236] *Mills* [1963] 1 QB 522, following *Scully* (1903) 23 NZLR 380.
[237] [1963] 1 QB at 524.
[238] Ibid, 526.
[239] [2010] EWCA Crim 1949.
[240] [2010] EWCA Crim 1949.
[241] Per Hughes LJ at [13].

natural meaning is surely that some person other than the accused must intend to be the unlawful user and that the accused must know of that intention. But it has been held that it is enough if the accused *believes* that the poison, etc is to be so used, so that it is no defence for him to show that the person supplied did not intend to use it[242] or that the person supplied was a policeman who had obtained the thing by false representations about a purely fictitious woman.[243] This construction was defended by Erle CJ, the rest of the court concurring, on the extraordinary ground that, 'The defendant knew what his own intention was, and that was that the substance procured by him should be employed with intent to procure miscarriage.'[244] This attitude contrasts strikingly with the strict construction of the word 'procure'; and these two cases, have been dissented from in Victoria,[245] though followed elsewhere in the Commonwealth.[246] In *Ahmed* the court noted that a defendant such as Ahmed will not necessarily be liable since his lies might, the court thought, not have prevented the doctors concerned from forming the relevant medical opinions in the 1967 Act. D would not have been knowing that the thing was 'intended to be *unlawfully* used or employed with intent to procure the miscarriage of any woman'.

16.5.4 The Abortion Act 1967[247]

The law relating to abortion was modified in important respects by the Abortion Act 1967. In the Act:

the law relating to abortion' means ss 58 and 59 of the Offences Against the Person Act 1861, and any rule of law relating to the procurement of abortion.

Section 1 of the Act, as amended by the Human Fertilisation and Embryology Act 1990, s 37, provides:[248]

(1) Subject to the provisions of this section, a person shall not be guilty of an offence under the law relating to abortion when a pregnancy is terminated by a registered medical practitioner if two[249] registered medical practitioners are of the opinion, formed in good faith –

(a) that the pregnancy has not exceeded its twenty-fourth week and that the continuance of the pregnancy would involve risk, greater than if the pregnancy were terminated, of injury to the physical or mental health of the pregnant woman or any existing children of her family; or

---

[242] *Hillman* (1863) 9 Cox CC 386, CCR.

[243] *Titley* (1880) 14 Cox CC 502 (Stephen J).

[244] (1863) 9 Cox CC at 387.

[245] *Hyland* (1898) 24 VLR 101.

[246] *Scully* (1903) 23 NZLR 380; *Nosworthy* (1907) 26 NZLR 536; *Neil* [1909] St R Qd 225; *Freestone* [1913] TPD 758; *Irwin v R* (1968) 68 DLR (2d) 485.

[247] See J Hoggett, 'The Abortion Act 1967' [1968] Crim LR 247. On the changes introduced by the Act see HLA Hart, 'Abortion Law Reform: The English Experience' (1972) 8 MULR 389; M Simms, 'Abortion Law Reform: Has the Controversy Changed' [1970] Crim LR 567, 573 and 'The Abortion Act: A Reply' [1971] Crim LR 86; JM Finnis, 'The Abortion Act: What Has Changed?' [1971] Crim LR 3; and generally S Sheldon, *Beyond Control* (1977).

[248] See the valuable discussion of the amended Act by A Grubb, 'The New Law of Abortion: Clarification or Ambiguity?' [1991] Crim LR 659.

[249] The Select Committee Report, *Scientific Developments Relating to the Abortion Act 1967* (2007) HC 1045–1 above, heard evidence that the practical reality of two doctors considering a case was a 'sham', para 86. See generally Ch 4 of that report. The Committee reported that it had not been presented with 'any good evidence' that in the first trimester of pregnancy the two signature rule safeguards the woman or the doctors or 'serves any useful purpose', at para 99.

(b) that the termination is necessary to prevent grave permanent injury to the physical or mental health of the pregnant woman; or

(c) that the continuance of the pregnancy would involve risk to the life of the pregnant woman, greater than if the pregnancy were terminated; or

(d) that there is a substantial risk that if the child were born it would suffer from such physical or mental abnormalities as to be seriously handicapped.

(2) In determining whether the continuance of a pregnancy would involve such risk of injury to health as is mentioned in paragraph (a) [or (b)] of subsection (1) of this section, account may be taken of the pregnant woman's actual or reasonably foreseeable environment.

By s 1(3) and 1(3A) unless the abortion is carried out for the immediate saving of the life of the mother, the operation must be carried out in hospitals or other places as approved by the Secretary of State.

Section 1(4) provides that the requirement for the opinion of two registered medical practitioners:

shall not apply to the termination of a pregnancy by a registered medical practitioner in a case where he is of the opinion, formed in good faith, that the termination is immediately necessary to save the life or to prevent grave permanent injury to the physical or mental health of the pregnant woman.

There were 189,100 abortions in the UK in 2009: 91 per cent of those were carried out at or under 13 weeks gestation; 75 per cent were at or under 10 weeks.[250] Where the pregnancy has not exceeded its 24th week[251] the doctor must balance risks involved in an abortion against the risks to the woman or the existing child involved in the continuance of the pregnancy, and may perform the abortion only if it is his opinion that the latter are greater than the former. The Select Committee on Science and Technology recently reviewed the 24-week time limit to assess whether recent developments in medical science warranted a change in the law. The medical evidence suggested that around 89 per cent of foetuses born at 20 to 22 weeks are born dead.

Where the pregnancy has exceeded 24 weeks the risks to the existing child are no longer a ground for abortion.[252] The abortion can now be justified only on the grounds of risk of grave permanent injury to the woman or her death, or of the birth of a seriously handicapped child.[253] In *Jepson v Chief Constable of Mercia Police*,[254] D sought judicial review of the refusal

---

[250] See www.dh.gov.uk/en/Publicationsandstatistics/Publications/PublicationsStatistics/DH_116039.

[251] It is uncertain when time starts to run. See the discussion by Grubb [1991] Crim LR 659. The Select Committee Report, *Scientific Developments Relating to the Abortion Act 1967* considered whether medical advances should lead to a period short than 24 weeks. The conclusion was that no evidence had been presented that 'survival rates below 24 weeks gestation time have significantly improved', Ch 2. See also Jackson, *Medical Law,* 673.

[252] E Wicks, M Wyldes and M Kilby, 'Late Termination of Pregnancy for Foetal Abnormality: Medical and Legal Perspectives' (2004) 12 Med Law Rev 285.

[253] On this criterion, see the Select Committee Report, Ch 3, which is critical of the ambiguity of the wording and the difficulty in which this leaves doctors.

[254] [2003] EWHC 3318 (QB). A Grear, 'The Curate, a Cleft Palate and Ideological Closure in the Abortion Act 1967 – Time to Reconsider the Relationship Between Doctors and the Abortion Decision' [2004] Web JCLI; R Scott, 'Interpreting the Disability Ground of the Abortion Act' [2005] CLJ 388. See the interesting analysis by E Wicks, 'Terminating Life and Human Rights: The Fetus and the Neonate' in C Erin and S Ost, *The Criminal Justice System and Health Care* (2007), considering the difference in the degree of protection afforded to a foetus with severe disability and a newly born baby with such disability. See also S Smith 'Dignity: The Difference Between Abortion and Neonaticide for Severe Disability' in the same volume.

to prosecute doctors who performed an abortion where the foetus had a cleft palate. The court concluded that the doctor had acted in good faith.[255]

Where the life of the woman is at risk, the doctor must engage in another balancing exercise and may terminate the pregnancy if he is of the opinion that this gives her a better chance of survival: 51/49 is enough. But where the risk is not to her life but of 'grave permanent injury' the pregnancy may be terminated only if abortion is 'necessary' to prevent this. If the doctor is of the opinion that the woman will certainly suffer grave permanent injury if the pregnancy is not terminated, then termination is, undoubtedly, necessary. It must be assumed, however, that Parliament, in distinguishing between grave permanent injury and death, intended that a higher degree of risk of grave permanent injury than of death is required to justify abortion. If so, termination is not 'necessary' simply because the doctor is of the opinion that grave permanent injury is more likely than not, that is, 51/49 is not enough. Whether necessity can be established somewhere between the balance of probabilities and virtual certainty is not clear. These balancing exercises do not pose problems under Art 2 of the ECHR. The European Court has recognized that 'if the unborn do have a "right to life" it is implicitly limited by the mother's rights and interests'.[256]

There is a similar problem of determining what is a 'substantial' risk of abnormality resulting in 'serious' handicap to the child – but these uncertainties have been with us since 1967 without troubling the courts (but note *Jepson* above), however much they may have troubled the doctors. Clearly, something a good deal less than certainty may amount to a substantial risk and it is thought that most people would regard something well below a 50 per cent chance as substantial in this context.

Section 1(1)(a), on a literal reading, could justify the termination of most pregnancies in their early stages, since some risk is necessarily involved in childbearing whereas the risks involved in an abortion operation at this early stage are very slight.[257] The 1967 Act allowed the interests of the existing children of the woman's family to be taken into account for the first time. These expressions are not defined in the Act, but it has been argued[258] that 'family' means the sociological and not the legal unit, so as to include illegitimate children and perhaps children who have been accepted as members of the family. The view has been expressed[259] that a person over 21 could be a child of the family for this purpose if, for example, he were severely disabled.

An incapacitated adult could be provided with an abortion if it was in her best interests.[260] The assessment would be in accordance with the Mental Capacity Act 2005.

---

[255] Jackson J did give leave, on the basis that the case raised an issue of public importance. West Mercia then reopened the case and the CPS decided not to prosecute, determining that the doctor had acted in good faith. See CPS press release: 16/3/2005. E Wicks, M Wyldes and M Kilby, 'Late Termination of Pregnancy for Reason of Fetal Abnormality: Medical and Legal Perspectives' (2004) 12 Med L Rev 285; S Sheldon and S Wilkinson, 'Termination of Pregnancy for Reason of Foetal Disability: Are there Grounds for a Special Exception in Law?' (2001) 9 Med L Rev 85.

[256] *Vo v France* [2004] 2 FCR 577, para 80.

[257] '. . . it follows that a pregnancy may lawfully be terminated in order to secure a relatively small improvement in the woman's medical condition': *A Guide to the Abortion Act 1967*, at 11. The Act is not, however, interpreted in this way by the medical profession and administrators: *Hart* (1972) 8 MULR at 393–394. See also www.bma.org.uk/ethics/reproduction_genetics/LawEthicsAbortion2007.jsp.

[258] Hoggett [1968] Crim LR 247 at 249.

[259] ibid.

[260] See, eg, *Re SG (Adult Mental Patient: Abortion)* [1991] 2 FLR 329; *Re B (Wardship: Abortion)* [1991] 2 FLR 426; *Re SS (An Adult: Medical Treatment)* [2002] 1 FLR 445 – decided under common law pre-Mental Capacity Act 2005.

16.5.4.1 Abortion and multiple pregnancies

Multiple pregnancies may be reduced by killing one or more of the foetuses. The Human Fertilisation and Embryology Act 1990 amended s 5(2) of the Abortion Act 1967 to deal with the matter as follows:

(2) For the purposes of the law relating to abortion, anything done with intent to procure a woman's miscarriage (or, in the case of a woman carrying more than one foetus, her miscarriage of any foetus) is unlawfully done unless authorized by section 1 of this Act and, in the case of a woman carrying more than one foetus, anything done with intent to procure her miscarriage of any foetus is authorized by that section if –

(a) the ground for termination of the pregnancy specified in subsection (1)(d) of that section applies in relation to any foetus and the thing is done for the purpose of procuring the miscarriage of that foetus, or

(b) any other grounds for termination of the pregnancy specified in that section applies.

So, if one or more of several foetuses is identified as being substantially at risk of becoming a child suffering from such a mental or physical abnormality as would lead to its being seriously handicapped, that foetus, or those foetuses, may be aborted. Where no foetus is so identified, but the continuance of the multiple pregnancy would satisfy one of the other conditions in s 1, the doctor may reduce the number of foetuses in order to eliminate or reduce the risk. In this situation, the doctor must select which of a number of healthy foetuses is to die.[261]

16.5.4.2 Good faith of medical opinion

The Secretary of State for Health has exercised the powers given to him by s 2 to require the opinion of medical practitioners to be certified in a particular form and notice of the termination of pregnancy and other information to be given. The question of the good faith of the doctors is essentially one for the jury. A verdict of bad faith where there is no evidence as to professional practice and medical probabilities is often likely to be regarded by the Court of Appeal as unsafe; but this depends on the nature of the other evidence.

An opinion may be absurd professionally and yet formed in good faith; conversely an opinion may be one which a doctor could have entertained and yet in the particular circumstances of a case may be found either to have been formed in bad faith or not to have been formed at all.[262]

If one or both of the doctors has expressed an opinion in bad faith but the operation is performed by a third, D, who is unaware of the bad faith, the conditions of the Act are not satisfied but it is submitted that D has a defence. He lacks *mens rea* for, on the facts as he believes them to be, his act is a lawful one. The doctor in bad faith might, however, be convicted under Part 2 of the Serious Crime Act 2007 (see Ch 13) or the doctrine in *Cogan and Leak* or *Millward*.[263]

16.5.4.3 Termination 'by a registered medical practitioner'

The defences provided by the Act are available 'when a pregnancy is terminated by a registered medical practitioner'. When the conditions in the Act are satisfied and the pregnancy is terminated by the doctor, there is no *actus reus*. Those who assist him are therefore guilty of no offence. The Act obviously did not contemplate that every action in the steps leading to an abortion would be done personally by the doctor. If, however, the doctor were to delegate more and more of the process to others, there would come a point when it could no longer

---

[261] See Jackson above, n 251, at 628. See also the Human Fertilisation and Embryology Act 2008.
[262] *Smith* [1974] 1 All ER 376 at 381, and [1994] Crim LR 527.
[263] [1976] QB 217, above; [1994] Crim LR 527, p 234.

be said that the pregnancy had been terminated 'by a registered medical practitioner' – and at that point it would become unlawful. In *Royal College of Nursing of the United Kingdom v Department of Health and Social Security*,[264] the House of Lords by a majority of three to two, reversing a unanimous Court of Appeal judgment and restoring the judgment of Woolf J, held that a particular process for the extra-amniotic method of termination of pregnancies was lawful, notwithstanding the substantial part played by nurses in that process.[265] According to Lord Diplock, what the 1967 Act requires is that:

a registered medical practitioner . . . should accept responsibility for all stages of the treatment for the termination of the pregnancy. The particular method to be used should be decided by the doctor in charge of the treatment for the termination of the pregnancy; he should carry out any physical acts, forming part of the treatment, that in accordance with accepted medical practice are done only by qualified medical practitioners, and should give specific instructions as to the carrying out of such parts of the treatment cf as in accordance with accepted medical practice are carried out by nurses or other members of the hospital staff without medical qualifications. To each of them, the doctor, or his substitute, should be available to be consulted or called on for assistance from beginning to end of the treatment.

Thus, if the doctor were to direct the whole procedure by correspondence, over the telephone or by webcam the operation would presumably be unlawful.

Treatment to terminate a pregnancy, which, if the treatment were successful, would be lawfully terminated, is lawful treatment,[266] notwithstanding (as apparently happens in one or two per cent of cases) an ultimate failure to terminate the pregnancy. If the conditions of the 1967 Act are otherwise fulfilled and known to be fulfilled, the steps taken to procure abortion are taken without *mens rea* – there is no intent *unlawfully* to administer anything or *unlawfully* to use any instrument. There is, moreover, no *actus reus* for the legalization of an abortion must include the steps which are taken towards it.

16.5.4.4 Necessity at common law

The provision in s 5(2) of the 1967 Act that, 'For the purposes of the law relating to abortion, anything done with intent to procure a woman's miscarriage . . . is unlawfully done unless authorized by section 1 of this Act . . .' appears to be intended entirely to supersede the law as stated in *Bourne*.[267]

Abortions, and the steps to procure them which are proscribed, are unlawful unless they can be justified by the Act. It is submitted, however, that this provision cannot have been intended entirely to eliminate the operation of general defences to crime. To take extreme examples, a child under the age of 10, or a person within the M'Naghten Rules, could surely not be convicted of committing or (slightly more likely) abetting an abortion. If this is conceded, then duress by threats ought equally to operate, so why not duress of circumstances or necessity? And so we are back to admitting *Bourne's* case into the law. A possible interpretation of the Act would be to allow general defences, other than necessity. Construing s 5(2) in the light of the previous law, a court might conclude that its obvious purpose was to overrule *Bourne*; and that it would be unreasonable to extend its operation beyond that.

---

[264] [1981] AC 800, above n 235.

[265] See also the Select Committee Report, *Scientific Developments Relating to the Abortion Act 1967*, recognizing the ability of nursing staff to perform the modern abortion process, para 103 et seq.

[266] Per Lord Edmund-Davies, citing the 4th edition of this book, at 346 [1981] 1 All ER at 573.

[267] Above, p 604. cf the Canadian case of *Morgentaler* [1976] 1 SCR 616, 20 CCC (2d) 449 discussed by LH Leigh, 'Necessity and the Case of Dr Morgentaler' [1978] Crim LR 151 and *Davidson* [1969] VR 667 (Menhennit J).

A limited defence of necessity would seem desirable in principle. The defence would necessarily be limited in scope by the fact that, in the great majority of cases where it is necessary to procure an abortion, this is lawful by statute so that there is no room for the operation of any broader defence. Having regard to *Quayle*,[268] in which necessity defences were held to be ousted by the statutory scheme under the Misuse of Drugs Act, a similar argument could be advanced. The Abortion Act is clearly intended to provide a scheme for the legalization of abortion – abortions outside the Act are unlawful and an offence. But suppose that a qualified doctor who is not a registered medical practitioner and so does not come within the terms of s 1(4) above, forms the opinion in good faith that immediate termination of a pregnancy is necessary in order to save the life of the mother who is in a remote place and beyond the help of any registered medical practitioner. Is it the law that he must let the woman die when he could save her by terminating the pregnancy?

In *Bourne*, MacNaghten J took the view that there was not only a right but a duty to perform the operation where a woman's life could be saved only by the doctor procuring an abortion:

if a case arose where the life of a woman could be saved by performing the operation and the doctor refused to perform it because of his religious opinions and the woman died, he would be in grave peril of being brought before this court on a charge of manslaughter by negligence. He would have no better defence than a person who, again from some religious reason, refused to call in a doctor to attend his sick child, where a doctor could have been called in and the life of the child could have been saved.[269]

Section 4 of the Abortion Act now provides:

(1) Subject to subsection (2) of this section, no person shall be under any duty, whether by contract or by any statutory or other legal requirements, to participate in any treatment authorized by this Act to which he has a conscientious objection:

   Provided that in any legal proceedings the burden of proof of conscientious objection shall rest on the person claiming to rely on it.

(2) Nothing in subsection (1) of this section shall affect any duty to participate in treatment which is necessary to save the life or to prevent grave permanent injury to the physical or mental health of a pregnant woman.

The same people whose acts are rendered lawful by s 1 are given by s 4 the right in conscience to object to performing those same acts. A person can only claim that right in respect of an act which would have amounted to an offence before the Abortion Act came into force. So, a secretary was not entitled, by s 4, to refuse to type a letter arranging an abortion rendered lawful by s 1. It was held that she would not, under the old law, have been guilty of the abortion as a secondary party; her intention would have been merely to carry out her contract of employment, not to counsel or procure.[270]

Section 4(2) does not create any duty, but it does appear to recognize at least the possibility of a duty at common law. The only authority for this appears to be *Bourne*. It will be noted that MacNaghten J dealt only with the case where the woman died, whereas the Act refers to grave permanent injury to physical or mental health. MacNaghten J appeared to regard the doctor's liability as one arising from gross negligence; and this, if a ground of liability at all, is indeed confined to cases where death is caused.[271] There is no general criminal liability for causing grievous bodily harm by gross negligence as distinct from recklessness.

---

268 [2005] EWCA Crim 1415.
269 [1939] 1 KB at 693.
270 *Salford Area Health Authority, ex p Janaway* [1989] AC 537, [1988] 2 WLR 442, CA.
271 Above, p 604.

If, however, the doctor is under a duty to act, and he knows all the circumstances giving rise to that duty and foresees the consequences of not fulfilling it, it would seem that he has the *mens rea* necessary to found a conviction for causing grievous bodily harm contrary to s 18 of the Offences Against the Person Act 1861.[272] The only doubtful link in this argument appears to be the existence of the duty; but the Act strengthens the case for its existence. Clearly, a doctor with conscientious objections[273] could fulfil his duty by referring the patient to another doctor who does not have such objections; and it is submitted that the doctor has a duty to do this where an abortion is necessary to save the woman from death or grave permanent injury. The question of a duty to participate in the operation can arise only where there is no effective substitute for the doctor concerned. Where the patient has conscientious objections there can be no duty to perform the operation since, clearly, it can only be lawfully performed with consent.

Abortion in compliance with the 1967 Act does not contravene Art 2 of the ECHR: *Paton v United Kingdom*.[274]

16.6 Genocide, crimes against humanity and war crimes

The Genocide Act 1969 gave effect to the Genocide Convention, Art II, and rendered it a domestic offence to commit genocide. That offence, and indeed the Genocide Act, was repealed by the International Criminal Court Act 2001.[275] Under s 51 of the 2001 Act, from 1 September 2001:[276]

(1) It is an offence against the law of England and Wales for a person to commit genocide, a crime against humanity or a war crime.

(2) This section applies to acts committed –

   (a) in England or Wales, or

   (b) outside the United Kingdom by a United Kingdom national, a United Kingdom resident or a person subject to UK service jurisdiction.

The offences can be prosecuted only with the consent of the Attorney General.[277] They are triable only on indictment and carry a maximum 30-year sentence, except that offences involving murder must be dealt with as such.[278]

In interpreting definitions of genocide, crimes against humanity and war crimes the domestic court must take into account any relevant elements of crimes, and must have regard to any relevant judgment or decision of the International Criminal Court. The House of Lords recently noted the limited types of international crime that have been incorporated, and that

---

[272] Below, p 652.

[273] See, for arguments that the ECHR might impact on this claim, L Hammer, 'Abortion Objection in the UK within the Framework of the ECHR' [1999] EHRLR 564.

[274] [1980] 3 EHRR 408. cf *Kelly v Kelly* 1997 SLT 896 and *Vo v France*, above.

[275] On which, see generally, R Cryer and O Bekou, 'International Crimes and ICC Cooperation in England and Wales' (2007) 5 J Int Crim Just 441; R Cryer, 'Implementation of the International Criminal Court Statute in England and Wales' (2002) 51 ICLQ 733–743.

[276] On the jurisdiction of the International Criminal Court, see generally, R Dixon and K Khan, Archbold, *International Criminal Courts: Practice, Procedure and Evidence* (2009). See also D McGoldrick, 'The Permanent ICC – An End to the Culture of Impunity' [1999] Crim LR 627; N Stewart, 'The New ICC' (2001) 151 NLJ 1381; R Cryer, *Prosecuting International Crimes* (2005).

[277] Section 53(3).

[278] Section 53(5).

the crime of aggression had been deliberately excluded from the Act. The House concluded that it would be 'anomalous' if it were to be deemed as a domestic offence.[279]

Corporal Donald Payne pleaded guilty to acts of inhumane treatment of Iraqi civilian detainees in Iraq, becoming the first person to be convicted under the 2001 Act.[280]

16.6.1 Genocide

Genocide is defined in the Act to mean any of the following acts committed 'with intent to destroy, in whole or in part, a national, ethnical, racial or religious group', as such: (1) killing members of the group; (2) causing serious bodily or mental harm to members of the group; (3) deliberately inflicting on the group conditions of life calculated to bring about its physical destruction in whole or in part; (4) imposing measures intended to prevent births within the group; (5) forcibly transferring children of the group to another group.[281]

16.6.2 Crime against humanity

Crime against humanity under the 2001 Act means any of the following acts when committed as part of a widespread or systematic attack directed against any civilian population, with knowledge of the attack:

(i) murder; (ii) extermination; (iii) deportation or forcible transfer of population; (iv) imprisonment or other severe deprivation of physical liberty in violation of fundamental rules of international law; (v) torture; (vi) rape, sexual slavery, enforced prostitution, forced pregnancy; (vii) persecution against any identifiable group or collectivity on political, racial, national, ethnic, cultural, religious, gender as defined in paragraph 3, or other grounds that are universally recognized as impermissible under international law, in connection with any act referred to in this paragraph or any crime within the jurisdiction of the Court; (viii) enforced disappearance of persons; (viiii) the crime of apartheid; (x) other inhumane acts of a similar character intentionally causing great suffering, or serious injury to body or to mental or physical health.[282]

16.6.3 War crime

'War crime' is defined in Sch 8 to mean:

(1) grave breaches of the Geneva Conventions 1949, namely, any of the following acts against persons or property protected under the provisions of the relevant Geneva Convention (a) wilful killing; (b) torture or inhuman treatment, including biological experiments; (c) wilfully causing great suffering, or serious injury to body or health; (d) extensive destruction and appropriation of property, not justified by military necessity and carried out unlawfully and wantonly; (e) compelling a prisoner of war or other protected person to serve in the forces of a hostile power; (f) wilfully depriving a prisoner of war or other protected person of the rights of fair

---

[279] See *Jones* [2006] UKHL 16, in which D had sought to argue that acts of criminal damage and protests to prevent preparation for the Iraq war at military bases were acts preventing the crime of aggression. The House confirmed that the defence under s 3 of the Criminal Law Act 1967 was available only in respect of preventing a crime in domestic law. The appellants had also sought to argue that the military bases were involved in aiding and abetting war crimes in Iraq. Proving the relevant degree of knowledge of the parties in the UK who were at the bases would be very difficult indeed.

[280] The Guardian, 20 Sept 2006. See N Rasiah 'The Court-Martial of Corporal Payne and Others and the Future Landscape of International Criminal Justice' (2009) 7 J Int Crim Just 177; see also G Simpson, 'The Death of Baha Mousa' (2007) 8 Melb J Int L 340.

[281] Sch 8.

[282] International Criminal Court Act 2001, s 50(6), Sch 8.

and regular trial; (g) unlawful deportation or transfer or unlawful confinement; (h) taking of hostages;

(2) other serious violations [as specified] of the laws and customs applicable in international armed conflict, within the established framework of international law... [283]

(3) in the case of an armed conflict not of an international character, serious violations of any of the specified acts committed against persons taking no active part in the hostilities, including members of armed forces who have laid down their arms and those placed hors de combat by sickness, wounds, detention or any other cause.

16.7 The War Crimes Act 1991[284]

The War Crimes Act 1991 provides that proceedings for murder, manslaughter or culpable homicide may be brought against a person who committed that crime during the period of the Second World War in part of Germany or a place under German occupation and the act constituted a violation of the laws and customs of war. The proceedings may be brought irrespective of the nationality of the accused at the time of the alleged offence.[285]

[283] On the potential for liability of individual service personnel who are engaged in armed conflict which is unlawful see the discussion by R Rowe, 'The Criminal Liability of a British Soldier Merely for Participating in the Iraq War' [2010] Crim LR 752, and p 755 for discussion of the soldier's liability as an accessory.

[284] See T Richardson, 'Crimes without Frontiers? The War Crimes Act 1991', in I Loveland (ed), *Frontiers of Criminality* (1995); Emmerson, Ashworth and Macdonald, HR&CJ, para 10.45.

[285] For the only successful prosecution, see *Sawoniuk* [2000] 2 Cr App R 220.

17

Non-fatal offences against the person

The 'person' who may be the victim of any of the offences discussed in this chapter is a human being. In this context associations, whether corporate or unincorporated, cannot be victims of these offences though these bodies might be guilty of committing some of the offences either as principal or as an accessory. If a corporation may be guilty of manslaughter[1] there is no logical reason why it should not be guilty of lesser offences against the person. The meaning of 'person' as a victim has been discussed almost exclusively in relation to murder but it seems clear that the same principles must apply to non-fatal offences. The common law[2] position is usefully summarized in the Draft Criminal Code which provides[3] that victim 'means a person who has been born and has an existence independent of his mother and, unless the context otherwise requires, "death" and "personal harm" mean the death of, or personal harm to, such a person'.[4]

A foetus or a child in the process of being born could not, therefore, be the victim of an assault or any other offence against the person.[5] The attack might be an offence against the mother where it affected her person, as distinct from the foetus which is not part of her. Statutory offences are probably to be construed in accordance with the common law.

Offences against the person are prevalent. In 2009/10 there were 871, 712 recorded offences of violence against the person.[6]

17.1 Assault and battery

Assault and battery were two distinct crimes at common law and their separate existence (though now as statutory offences) is confirmed by s 39 of the Criminal Justice Act 1988:

Common assault and battery shall be summary offences and a person guilty of either of them shall be liable to a fine not exceeding level 5 on the standard scale, to imprisonment for a term not exceeding six months, or to both.

---

[1] Above, p 562. The 2007 Act deals only with corporate killings. In *R (on the Application of Gladstone plc) v Manchester City Magistrates' Court* [2004] All ER (D) 296 (Nov), it was held that a private prosecution for assault may be brought by a registered company (the victim being the Chief Executive who was kneed in the groin at the AGM). The company's memorandum of association included power to lay an information in respect of the assault.

[2] cf *Tait*, above, p 578.

[3] Cl 53(1).

[4] For further reform see below, p 656.

[5] In *A-G's Reference (No 3 of 1994)*, above, p 492, the Court of Appeal held that the foetus is part of the mother; but the House of Lords decided that it is not: [1997] 3 All ER 936, 943. 'The mother and the foetus were two distinct organisms living symbiotically, not a single organism with two aspects', per Lord Mustill.

[6] J Flatley et al, *Crime in England and Wales 2009/10, Findings from the British Crime Survey and police recorded crime* (2010), table 2.04.

Section 39 offers a valuable simplification of the law,[7] replacing the complex provisions in the Offences Against the Person Act (hereafter in this chapter 'OAPA') 1861.

17.1.1 Definitions[8]

An assault is any conduct by which D, intentionally or recklessly,[9] causes V to apprehend immediate and unlawful personal violence.[10] A battery is any conduct by which D, intentionally or recklessly, inflicts unlawful personal violence upon V.[11] But 'violence' here includes any unlawful touching[12] of another, however slight. As Blackstone explained:[13]

the law cannot draw the line between different degrees of violence, and therefore prohibits the first and lowest stage of it; every man's person being sacred, and no other having a right to meddle with it, in any the slightest manner.

This reflects the fact that the offences against the person protect the individual's personal autonomy by providing at least the opportunity for criminal punishment for the slightest unjustified infringement. This is supported by the protection offered by the ECHR, in Art 8 (respect for private life).[14] The other dimension to autonomy in this context – the purported freedom to do as you will with your body[15] – is less well respected in the current state of the law.[16]

In modern times, Lord Lane CJ described battery in expansive terms:

an intentional touching of another person without the consent of that person and without lawful excuse. It need not necessarily be hostile, or rude, or aggressive, as some of the cases seem to indicate.[17]

However, in *Brown*,[18] the majority of the House of Lords seem to have thought that hostility is an element in assault. But their lordships then interpreted 'hostile' in such a way as to deprive the word of all meaning. The case concerned sadomasochistic acts performed by a group of men on each other. All the acts were done for the mutual enjoyment of the participants, so they could not conceivably be assaults if hostility, in any ordinary meaning of the word, were required. The House of Lords suggested hostility was required but then upheld the convictions! Lord Jauncey said, '[i]f the appellants' activities in relation to the receivers [of the painful acts] were unlawful they were also hostile and a necessary ingredient of assault was

---

[7] Common assault and battery were indictable offences at common law and under s 47, that element of s 47 was repealed by the 1988 Act, together with ss 42 and 43.

[8] P Carter and R Harrison, *Offences of Violence* (1987).

[9] *Venna* [1976] QB 421,CA (a case of battery but the same principle surely applies to assault); *Savage* [1992] 1 AC 699, 740.

[10] In *Ireland* [1998] AC 147, [1997] 4 All ER 225, 236, 239 the House of Lords applied this definition, originating in the 1st edition of this book, at 262, adopted in *Fagan v Metropolitan Police Comr* [1969] 1 QB 439, [1968] 3 All ER 442 at 445, below, p 624 and approved in *Savage* [1992] AC 699, 740.

[11] *Rolfe* (1952) 36 Cr App R 4.

[12] Note that the concept of touching may achieve a greater significance since it now forms the core of a number of offences under the Sexual Offences Act 2003. In *H* [2005] Crim LR 734, it was confirmed that touching of clothes would constitute the offence under s 3 of that Act. See below, Ch 18.

[13] *Commentaries*, iii, 120, cited by Goff LJ in *Collins v Wilcock* [1984] 3 All ER 374 at 378.

[14] For more serious infringements the protection lies in Art 3 – freedom from torture, inhuman and degrading treatment and Art 5 – freedom from unlawful deprivation of liberty. Note also Art 4 protecting against slavery, and the new offence in s 71 of the Coroners and Justice Act 2009. Below, p 656.

[15] On which see J Gardner, *Offences and Defences* (2007) 12.

[16] See the discussion of *Brown* below.

[17] *Faulkner v Talbot* [1981] 3 All ER 468 at 471, applied in *Thomas* (1985) 81 Cr App R 331 at 334; and see *Collins v Wilcock* [1984] 3 All ER 374 at 379, DC; *Wilson v Pringle* [1987] QB 237, CA (Civ Div), criticized by Wood J in *T v T* [1988] 2 WLR 189 at 200, 203 (Fam Div); *Brown* [1992] 2 WLR 441 at 446, CA.

[18] [1994] AC 212, [1993] 2 All ER 75, [1993] Crim LR 583.

present'. But the acts were only unlawful if they amounted to assaults. The reasoning appears to be circular. Notwithstanding the opinions of their lordships, it is submitted that the actual decision confirms the view that hostility is not an essential ingredient in the criminal offences of assault or battery. Some commentators suggest that there is value in requiring proof of hostility because otherwise an intentional touching which is nothing more than a *faux pas* – D's exuberant hug of a stranger at midnight on New Year's Eve – is potentially criminal.[19] It is submitted that such cases are not criminal because D will have a genuine belief in consent to that level of touching on that occasion. The concept of 'hostility' is unnecessary and ambiguous; it could cause undesirable complications in an offence which, because of the volume and summary nature of prosecutions, needs to be kept simple.

Assault and battery form the basis of many aggravated offences – for example, assaulting a police officer, assault with intent to resist arrest, etc.[20] It should be noted that assault and battery are also torts; and many, though not all, of the principles appear to be equally applicable in both branches of the law. Consequently, some of the cases cited below are civil actions.

The CPS Charging Standards advise that the appropriate charge is assault or battery (rather than aggravated assaults) where the injuries sustained amount to no more than: grazes; scratches; abrasions; minor bruising; swellings; reddening of the skin; superficial cuts; or a 'black eye'[21] and there are no aggravating features. The breadth of the offences results in wide prosecutorial discretion.

17.1.2 The relationship between assault and battery

Assault and battery are separate crimes, although they were not always recognized to be such.[22] The reason for this stems from the terminological problem: there is no acceptable verb corresponding to the noun, battery. As a result, 'assaulted' is almost invariably used to mean 'committed a battery against'. Sometimes, even statutes use the term 'assault' to mean 'assault or battery' but on other occasions both words are used.[23]

Problems of substance as well as terminology flow from the separateness of assault and battery and these have long been ignored. In *DPP v Little*,[24] an information alleging that 'D... did unlawfully assault and batter J' was held to charge two offences and so to be 'bad for duplicity'.[25] This has repercussions for aggravated offences which depend on proof of an assault or battery. Consider the offence under OAPA 1861, s 47: 'Whosoever shall be convicted of an assault occasioning actual bodily harm shall be liable to [imprisonment for five years].' If D is charged under s 47 is it necessary for the Crown to spell out whether he assaulted or

---

[19] Simester and Sullivan, CLT&D 435

[20] The Home Office identified over 70 such offences: *Violence. Reforming the Offences Against the Person Act 1861* (1998) para 3.5.

[21] See www.cps.gov.uk/legal/l_to_o/offences_against_the_person/#P48_1458. See also C Clarkson, A Cretney, G Davis and J Shepherd, 'Assaults: The Relationship between Seriousness, Criminalisation and Punishment' [1994] Crim LR 4.

[22] The CLRC Fourteenth Report, para 148, treated them as a single offence which may be committed in two ways and the Draft Code, cl 75, follows the CLRC's recommendation.

[23] There is a deplorable inconsistency in the statutory terminology. Even the Criminal Justice Act 1988, having made it crystal clear in s 39 that there are two offences, goes on in s 40(3)(a) to use 'common assault' in a context in which it can only sensibly mean – and has now been held to mean – 'common assault or battery': *Lyndsey* [1995] 3 All ER 654.

[24] [1992] 1 All ER 299, [1991] Crim LR 900, DC.

[25] ie that it makes more than one allegation in the same charge against the defendant. That is not generally permitted. Many earlier cases decided that a charge of assault and/or battery in a single count or information is duplicitous: *Jones v Sherwood* [1942] 1 KB 127, DC and *Mansfield Justices, ex p Sharkey* [1985] QB 613, DC. But a blind eye appears to have been turned in *Notman* [1994] Crim LR 518.

battered and occasioned abh as a result or is it enough to use the term 'assault'? In *Savage*[26] Lord Ackner's language when discussing s 47 suggests that that offence can be satisfied by proof of an assault only but it would be incredible if D, who battered V without assaulting him (eg by hitting him on the back of the head so V did not apprehend the violence), was not guilty of an 'assault occasioning actual bodily harm'. If the word 'assault' in s 47 embraces both the offence of assault and the offence of battery it seems to follow that the usual form of indictment for that offence – 'AB... assaulted JN, thereby occasioning him actual bodily harm'– is defective because it actually alleges two offences.[27]

There were further procedural problems which flowed from the failure to recognize the separateness of the offences,[28] but the Domestic Violence, Crime and Victims Act 2004 remedied these.[29]

17.1.3 Common law or statutory offences?

Section 39 of the 1988 Act does not, read literally, create any offence. It assumes the existence of offences of common assault and battery and merely prescribes the mode of trial and penalty. Nevertheless, in *DPP v Little*,[30] it was held that common assault and battery have been statutory offences since the enactment of s 47 of the OAPA 1861. The better view is that s 47 merely prescribed the penalty for the common law offences of common assault – as statutes do for other common law offences, for example, murder, manslaughter and conspiracy to defraud.[31] Those offences all continue to exist at common law. Although Laws LJ has asserted unequivocally that 'in truth, common assault by beating remains a common law offence',[32] the prosecutor is probably well advised, pending review by a higher court, to follow *DPP v Little* and to charge common assault or battery as a statutory offence, contrary to s 39.

17.1.4 *Actus reus* of assault

The typical case of an assault as distinct from a battery is that where D, by some physical movement, causes V to apprehend that he is about to be struck. D runs towards or drives at V, or acts so as to appear to V to be on the point of striking, stabbing or shooting him. Assault was once regarded as attempted battery: D had embarked on an act which, if not stopped, would immediately result in an impact of some kind on V. Many attempted batteries are assaults, but this is not necessarily so. D's acts may be unobserved by V, as where D approaches V from behind, or V is asleep, or insensible, or too young to appreciate what D appears likely to do. And there may be an assault where D has no intention to commit a battery but only to cause V to apprehend one.[33] The requirement is for apprehension, not fear.

---

[26] [1991] 4 All ER 698 at 711.

[27] The same considerations apply to other aggravated assaults. The effect is that thousands of people were convicted on defective indictments ever since 1861 – but this in no way detracts from the inescapable logic of the argument.

[28] An indictment alleging assault occasioning actual bodily harm required a separate count for s 39 assault because it was not an included offence for an alternative verdict: *Mearns* [1990] 3 All ER 989; *Disalvo* [2004] All ER (D) 316 (Jul). Arguably these were wrongly decided.

[29] Section 11 makes common assault an alternative verdict to more serious offences of assault, even if the count has not been preferred in the indictment.

[30] Above, n 24.

[31] See [1991] Crim LR 900; *Blackstone* (2011) B2.1. The court in *Lyndsey*, above, n 23, noted the criticisms that have been made of *Little* but found it unnecessary to express any opinion.

[32] *Haystead v Chief Constable of Derbyshire* (2000) 164 JP 396, [2000] Crim LR 758, DC. The defendant was in fact charged under s 39.

[33] *Logdon v DPP* [1976] Crim LR 121, DC.

17.1.4.1 Immediacy

There is a tendency to enlarge the concept of assault by taking a generous, arguably too generous, view of 'immediacy' and to include threats to V where the impending impact is remote. In more recent years this approach was precipitated by the courts' desire to provide protection for those suffering harassment at a time before the Protection from Harassment Act 1997 was in force.[34]

In *Lewis*,[35] D was uttering threats to V from another room but was convicted of maliciously inflicting grievous bodily harm and therefore impliedly of an assault.[36] In *Logdon v DPP*,[37] D committed an assault by showing V a pistol in a drawer and declaring that he would hold her hostage. In *Ireland*,[38] the House of Lords held that words alone, or even silent telephone calls, are capable of amounting to an assault; but they found it unnecessary to decide whether they did so in that case. If the caller said, 'There is bomb under your house which I am about to detonate', that would seem a clear case of assault. Lord Steyn said that the caller *may* be guilty of assault if he said, 'I will be at your door in a minute or two.' It seems to be a question of fact. Did the call in fact cause V to apprehend immediate unlawful violence? In *Constanza*,[39] V, who had for some time been harassed by D, received two letters from him eight days apart which she interpreted as clear threats. It was held that they amounted to an assault occasioning actual bodily harm. Was this two assaults or one continuing assault? It is easy to see that the letters might have caused V *immediate apprehension* of violence at some time in the future, but less easy to suppose that, as V read them, she apprehended *immediate violence*.

In *Smith v Chief Superintendent of Woking Police Station*[40] D was convicted of assault by looking through the window of a bed-sitting room at V in her night clothes with intent to frighten her. Kerr LJ limited his decision to a case where D 'is immediately adjacent, albeit on the other side of a window'. His lordship distinguished, without dissenting from, the opinion in the fourth edition of this book that 'there can be no assault if it is obvious to V that D is unable to carry out his threat, as where D shakes his fist at V who is safely locked inside his car'. There may, of course, be an assault although D has no means of carrying out the threat.[41] The question is whether D intends to cause V to believe that he can and will carry it out immediately and whether V does so believe. The question arises most obviously where D points an unloaded or imitation gun at V. If V knows the gun is unloaded or an imitation, there is no assault, for then he could not apprehend being shot.[42] If V believes it is, or may be a real, loaded gun, there is an *actus reus* by D, for now V suffers the apprehension which is an essential element of assault.[43]

[34] See C Wells, 'Stalking: the Criminal Law's Response' [1997] Crim LR 463.

[35] [1970] Crim LR 647, CA.

[36] But see now *Wilson* [1984] AC 242, below, p 650.

[37] Above.

[38] Above. See G Virgo, 'Offences Against the Person – Do-It-Yourself Law Reform' [1997] CLJ 251. J Horder, 'Reconsidering Psychic Assault' [1998] Crim LR 392, regards this dilution of the immediacy requirement as a welcome shift to an offence based on causing fear. On the merits of general threat offences, see P Alldridge, 'Threat Offences the Case for Reform' [1994] Crim LR 176.

[39] [1997] Crim LR 576. The court used ambiguous language, referring to the fact that she apprehended violence 'at some time not excluding the immediate future'. The HL refused leave to appeal, but that does not imply approval of the decision.

[40] (1983) 76 Cr App R 234.

[41] *Pace* Tindal CJ in *Stephens v Myers* (1830) 4 C & P 349.

[42] *Lamb*, above, p 541.

[43] *Logdon v DPP*, above.

17.1.4.2 Assault by words alone

Ireland has now settled that an assault can be committed by words alone. This seems right –
as a matter of fact, words, no less than a gesture, are capable of causing an apprehension of
immediate violence.[44] It follows from *Constanza* that an assault by writing, fax, email, tweet
or text is also possible.

Where D's actions would be an assault, but his words negate the effect of his actions, there
is no offence.[45] If D's words are such that they amount to an implied threat or a conditional
threat (eg 'as soon as we are alone I will hit you'), there may be an assault.[46]

It has generally been assumed that an act of some kind – even if it is only making a telephone
call and remaining silent – is an essential ingredient of assault. One case[47] seems to support
assault by omission but the court's actual decision was that D's conduct was a 'continuing act'.
Where D inadvertently causes V to apprehend immediate violence (D is checking the sights
on his gun when V walks into the room) and subsequently wilfully declines to withdraw the
threat (by lowering the gun), his 'omission' might constitute an assault.

17.1.4.3 Attempt to assault

There can be no conviction for attempt to commit a common assault since common assault
is a summary only offence.[48] There is no reason why there should not be attempt to commit
a more serious offence of which assault forms an element; as where D points an unloaded
gun at V, intending to frighten him in order to resist lawful arrest, but V, knowing the gun is
unloaded, is unperturbed.[49]

17.1.5 *Actus reus* of battery

The *actus reus* consists in the infliction of unlawful personal violence by D upon V. V need
not be aware of the touching, as for example, where he is asleep.[50] It used to be said that every
battery involves an assault; but this is plainly not so, for in battery there need be no apprehension of the impending violence. A blow from behind is not any less a battery because V
was unaware that it was coming. It is generally said that D must have done some act and that
it is not enough that he stood still and obstructed V's passage[51] like an inanimate object. But
suppose D is sitting at the corner of a corridor with his legs stretched across it. He hears V running down the corridor and deliberately remains still with the intention that V, on turning the
corner, shall fall over his legs. Why should this not be a battery? It would be if D had put out
his legs with the intention of tripping up V. It would not be too difficult to conclude that D has
a duty to V from the creation of the dangerous situation, applying the general principle recognized in *Miller*.[52] Further support for this proposition derives from *Santana-Bermudez*,[53]

---

[44] Previously the law was unclear although many authoritative writers asserted that words could not amount
to an assault. See, generally, G Williams, 'Assault and Words' [1957] Crim LR 219.

[45] See *Tuberville v Savage* (1669) 1 Mood Rep 3 – words 'if it were not assize time I would not take such language'
negatived what would otherwise be assault of D putting hand on sword in V's presence.

[46] See J Horder, 'Psychic Assault' [1998] Crim LR 392.

[47] *Fagan v Metropolitan Police Comr* [1969] 1 QB 439.

[48] The point was not argued in *Lewis* [2010] EWCA Crim 151 (manslaughter where D chased V into the path
of oncoming traffic).

[49] AF Noyes, 'Is Criminal Assault a Separate Substantive Crime or is it an Attempted Battery?' (1945) 33 Ky LJ
189; *State v Wilson* (1955) 218 Ore 575, 346 P (2d) 115. See also D White, 'Attempts: Initiatives in the Common Law
Caribbean' [1980] Crim LR 780.

[50] See also *Thomas* (1985) 81 Cr App R 331.

[51] *Innes v Wylie* (1844) 1 Car & Kir 257.

[52] [1983] AC 161.

[53] [2004] Crim LR 471, [2003] EWHC 2908 (Admin).

where D, an intravenous drug user, assured a police officer who was about to search him that he was carrying no 'sharps' and the officer stabbed her finger on a syringe in D's pocket. The court upheld the conviction, applying *Miller*:[54]

> where someone (by act or word or a combination of the two) creates a danger and thereby exposes another to a reasonably foreseeable risk of injury which materializes, there is an evidential basis for the *actus reus* of an assault occasioning actual bodily harm. It remains necessary for the prosecution to prove an intention to assault or appropriate recklessness.[55]

By having the needles in his pocket and assuring the police officer about the contents of his pockets, D created a situation of danger. There may also be a battery where D inadvertently applies force to V and then wrongfully refuses to withdraw it. In *Fagan*,[56] where D accidentally drove his car on to a constable's foot and then intentionally left it there, the court held that there was a continuing act, not a mere omission.

There is certainly no battery where D has no control over the incident which causes the touching of V, as where D's horse unexpectedly runs away with him and into V;[57] but this might equally be explained because there is no *mens rea*. It might be otherwise if D foresaw, when he mounted the animal, that there was an unacceptable risk that this might happen.

17.1.5.1 Battery with or via an instrument

Most batteries are *directly* inflicted, for example by D striking V with his fist or an instrument, or by a missile thrown by him, or by spitting upon V. But this is not essential: there can be an indirect battery. Where D punched W causing her to drop her baby, V, he was guilty of battery on V. It was found as a fact that D was reckless whether he injured V.[58]

In *Martin*,[59] Stephen and Wills JJ thought there would be a battery where D digs a pit for V to fall into, or, where he causes V to rush into an obstruction. The Divisional Court has since recognized a battery by indirect means: in *DPP v K*,[60] D was convicted where he poured acid into a hand-drier in a toilet so that the next user sprayed himself with it.[61]

The courts have now interpreted 'bodily' harm to include psychiatric harm, and that may be inflicted without any impact on V's body by, for example, harassment over the phone. That certainly does not involve a battery.[62] Where, however, D has caused an impact on V, indirectly with no fully voluntary intervening act, it is submitted that D should, subject to *mens rea*, be guilty of battery.[63]

It is not a battery (nor an assault) for D to pull himself free from V who is detaining him, even though D uses force.[64]

---

[54] [1983] AC 161.

[55] [10].

[56] [1969] 1 QB 439.

[57] *Gibbons v Pepper* (1695) 2 Salk 637.

[58] *Haystead v Chief Constable of Derbyshire* (2000) 164 JP 396, [2000] Crim LR 758, DC, citing the 9th edition of this work. D could, alternatively, have been held guilty of an intentional assault by reason of transferred malice: above, p 136.

[59] (1881) 8 QBD 54, CCR.

[60] [1990] 1 All ER 331, [1990] Crim LR 321, DC, overruled on other grounds by *Spratt* [1991] 2 All ER 210, CA.

[61] It has been argued (M Hirst, 'Assault, Battery and Indirect Violence' [1999] Crim LR 557) that these authorities are inconsistent with the decision of the House of Lords in *MPC v Wilson* ([1984] AC 242, below, p 650) but all that case decided was that, though the word 'inflict' does not necessarily imply an assault, an allegation of inflicting harm may do so, and assault is therefore an 'included offence'.

[62] cf D Ormerod and M Gunn, 'In Defence of *Ireland*' [1996] 3 Web JCLI.

[63] The criminal law is not governed by the ancient forms of action at common law which would require directness.

[64] *Sheriff* [1969] Crim LR 260.

It is submitted that it would undoubtedly be a battery to set a dog on another.[65] If D beat O's horse causing it to run down V, this would be battery by D.[66] No doubt the famous civil case of *Scott v Shepherd*[67] is equally applicable for the criminal law. D threw a squib (a firework) into a crowded area. First E and then F flung the squib away in order to save themselves from injury. It exploded and injured V. The acts of E and F were not 'fully voluntary' intervening acts which broke the chain of causation. This was battery by D.

If there is no violence at all, there is no battery; as where D puts harmful matter into a drink which is consumed by V.[68]

17.1.6 *Mens rea* of assault and battery

It is convenient to consider the *mens rea* of the two offences together. They are inextricably confused in some of the leading cases but need to be kept distinct if the separateness of the two offences is to be taken seriously. It was established by *Venna*[69] in 1975 that assault and battery may be committed recklessly as well as intentionally. *Venna* was a case of battery occasioning actual bodily harm but *dicta* concerning assault were relied on and it is safe to assume that the same principles apply to both offences.

The *mens rea* of assault is an intention to cause V to apprehend immediate and unlawful violence, or recklessness whether such apprehension be caused.[70] Technically there is an argument that D should be shown to have intended or been reckless not only as to V's apprehension, but to have intended or been reckless that V's apprehension would be of *immediate* violence.

The *mens rea* of battery is an intention to apply force to the body of another or recklessness whether force be so applied.

17.1.6.1 Subjective recklessness

Venna approved the test of subjective, *Cunningham*-style recklessness. Despite some attempts to apply the *Caldwell* formulation of recklessness in *DPP v K*,[71] that decision was quickly overruled by the Court of Appeal in *Spratt*[72] which was followed by that court in *Parmenter*.[73] The House of Lords was not asked to decide the point but *dicta*[74] assume that *Cunningham* recklessness is required; and with the overruling of *Caldwell* in *G*, the point is surely unarguable. D must actually foresee the risk of causing apprehension of immediate violence, or the application of it, as the case may be, and go on unjustifiably to take that risk.

---

[65] *Murgatroyd v Chief Constable of West Yorkshire* [2000] All ER (D) 1742. But note the court's caution in *Dume* (1986) The Times, 16 Oct, CA.

[66] *Gibbon v Pepper* (1695) 2 Salk 637 (*obiter*).

[67] (1773) 2 Wm Bl 892.

[68] *Hanson* (1849) 2 Car & Kir 912; but see below, p 673.

[69] [1976] QB 421.

[70] cf *Savage* [1992] 1 AC 699, [1991] 4 All ER 698 at 711, HL.

[71] [1990] 1 All ER 331, [1990] Crim LR 321, DC.

[72] [1991] 2 All ER 210, [1990] Crim LR 797.

[73] [1992] 1 AC 699.

[74] 'Where the defendant neither intends nor adverts to the possibility that there will be any physical contact at all, then the offence under s 47 would not be made out. This is because there would have been no assault, let alone an assault occasioning actual bodily harm' ([1991] 4 All ER at 707): Lord Ackner of course means 'no battery'. Other *dicta* show that he recognized that an assault in the strict sense suffices for an offence under s 47 if it occasions actual bodily harm.

17.1.6.2 Is the *mens rea* of assault and battery interchangeable?

Is it an offence to cause the *actus reus* of battery with the *mens rea* only of assault or the *actus reus* of assault with the *mens rea* only of battery? In principle, the answer is no.[75] D waves his fist, intending to alarm (assault) V but not to strike him and not foreseeing any risk of doing so; but V who does not see D, moves, and is hit. D creeps up behind V, intending to hit him over the head without attracting his attention (battery), but V unexpectedly turns round and moves to avoid the blow. Taking the distinction between assault and battery seriously, in the former case D does not commit a battery but is attempting to commit an assault; and in the latter he does not commit an assault but is attempting to commit a battery; and these 'attempts' to commit summary offences are not offences. It remains to be seen how seriously the courts will take the separateness of the offences.

17.1.6.3 Assault and battery by an intoxicated person

Assault and battery are classified as offences of 'basic intent'[76] so it is no defence that D had no *mens rea* because of his voluntary intoxication. The reason appears to be that the offences may be committed by recklessness. If, the prosecution specifically alleges D has *intentionally* assaulted or battered, it may be that they will be required to prove a 'specific intent' and intoxication will be a defence.[77] Given the demonstrable link between alcohol and offences of violence, the courts might find this approach unpalatable.

17.2 Defences to assault and battery

17.2.1 Consent[78]

It is clear that consent is an answer to a charge of common assault or battery (though not necessarily to the offence of assault occasioning actual bodily harm). It remains unclear why consent is a defence to assault or battery. Is it because the *absence of consent* is an essential element in the offence, as in rape;[79] or is *consent* a defence to the charge? In *Brown*, Lord Jauncey, with whose reasoning Lord Lowry agreed, said that, if it had been necessary to answer this question, which it was not, he would have held consent to be a defence. Lord Templeman also treated consent as a defence. Lord Mustill, on the other hand, regarded it as one factor negativing an *actus reus*; while Lord Slynn emphatically agreed with Glanville Williams that '[i]t is ... inherent in the concept of assault and battery that the victim does not consent'.[80] The Law Commission regarded it as a defence.[81] However, Lord Woolf CJ recently stated that 'it is a requirement of *the offence* that the conduct itself should be unlawful'.[82]

---

[75] Above, p 620.

[76] Subject to any radical reappraisal of that concept following *Heard* [2007] EWCA Crim 125, above, p 318.

[77] cf *Caldwell* [1982] AC 341, [1981] 1 All ER 961 at 964.

[78] There is a vast literature on this subject. Accessible discussions include LCCP 134, *Consent and Offences against the Person* (1994), on which see D Ormerod, 'Consent and Offences Against the Person: LCCP No 134' (1994) 57 MLR 928; and LCCP 139, *Consent in Criminal Law* (1995), on which see D Ormerod and M Gunn, 'Consent – A Second Bash' [1996] Crim LR 694; S Shute, 'Something Old, Something New, Something Borrowed – Three Aspects of the Consent Project' [1996] Crim LR 684. For a review of the philosophical arguments, see P Roberts, 'The Philosophical Foundations of Consent in the Criminal Law' (1997) 17 OJLS 389. On consent more generally, see D Beyleveld and R Brownsword, *Consent in the Law* (2007).

[79] *Larter* [1995] Crim LR 75, below, Ch 18, p 729, n 107.

[80] G Williams, 'Consent and Public Policy' [1962] Crim LR 74, 75.

[81] For criticism see S Shute [1996] Crim LR 684.

[82] *Barnes* [2005] EWCA Crim 3246, para 16, [2005] Crim LR 381.

This view – that it is an element of the offence – is, it is submitted, the better one. The importance of the question is demonstrated by the dissent of Lords Mustill and Slynn in *Brown*. The majority held that the sadomasochistic defendants were guilty of assaults occasioning actual bodily harm on, and unlawful wounding of, one another, notwithstanding the defendants' enthusiastic submission to, and the pleasure which they all derived from, the sadomasochistic 'assaults'. The question the majority asked themselves was 'Does the public interest require the invention of a new defence?' This is quite different from the question the minority were answering: 'Does the public interest require the offence to be construed to include sadomasochistic conduct?' It is not surprising that they led to different conclusions.[83]

While the distinction between offence and defence is fundamental in theory and in judicial law-making, in the practical functioning of the law in this area it is probably not very important.[84] It affects the evidential burden – if the absence of consent is an element of the offence, the prosecution must set out to prove it; if it is a defence, it is for the defendant to introduce evidence of it; but, in either case, the ultimate burden of proof is on the prosecution. In the recent case of *Shabbir*[85] S and others were acquitted by the magistrates of charges including assault. The charges arose from a prolonged violent attack in a city centre. The defendants raised the plea of consent, arguing that the Crown had the burden of proving that V had not consented to being assaulted. The magistrates found that the Crown had failed to prove that matter and acquitted. The Divisional Court held that a lack of consent could be inferred from evidence (violent attack on strangers shown on CCTV) other than the direct evidence of the victim.

Whether or not consent is properly regarded as a defence or as an element of the offences of assault and battery (and therefore as an element of the aggravated assaults discussed below) it is valuable to consider its meaning here. In recent years the courts have been forced to deal with difficult issues including defining what constitutes effective 'consent' (that is, whether frauds or pressure vitiate consent) and, if such factual consent is present, whether it ought to be recognized in law. In other words in what circumstances it is appropriate for the State to apply the criminal sanction to punish conduct voluntarily engaged in by adults of full mental capacity. There are three distinct questions to address:

(1) Was there implied or express consent?

(2) Did the 'victim'[86] give effective consent to the act? and

(3) Was the act one to which he could, in law, validly consent?

17.2.1.1 Implied consent

Since the merest touching without consent is a battery, the exigencies of everyday life demand that there be an implied consent to that degree of contact which is necessary or customary in the ordinary course of daily life.

Generally speaking, consent is a defence to battery; and most of the physical contacts of ordinary life are not actionable because they are impliedly consented to by all who move in society and so expose themselves to the risk of bodily contact. So nobody can complain of

---

[83] cf *Wilson*, below, p 640, where the court asked, 'Does public policy or the public interest demand that the appellant's activities [branding of wife's buttocks at her request] be visited by the sanctions of the criminal law?' and, unsurprisingly, answered, 'No.'

[84] The Criminal Injuries Compensation Appeal Panel takes the view that the victim's consent is not determinative of whether an offence of violence has been committed: *R (E) v CICA* [2003] EWCA Civ 234.

[85] [2009] EWHC 2754 (Admin) Goldring LJ expressed astonishment and disappointment that such a 'wholly spurious' point would be taken on the facts of that case.

[86] The term 'victim' is adopted throughout this chapter, although it acknowledged that if V has truly consented, it is illogical to view him as such.

the jostling which is inevitable from his presence in, for example, a supermarket, an underground station or a busy street; nor can a person who attends a party complain if his hand is seized in friendship, or even if his back is (within reason) slapped. Although such cases are regarded as examples of implied consent, it is more common nowadays to treat them as falling within a general exception embracing the limited physical contact which is generally to be expected and accepted in the ordinary conduct of daily life.[87]

Touching a person for the purpose of engaging his attention has been held to be acceptable[88] but physical restraint is not. A police officer who catches hold of a boy, not for the purpose of arresting him but in order to detain him for questioning, is acting unlawfully.[89] So is a constable who takes hold of the arm of a woman found soliciting in order to caution her. The fact that the practice of cautioning prostitutes is recognized by statute does not imply any power to stop and detain.[90] But to 'detain' without any actual touching cannot be a battery. If the detention is effected by the threat of force, then it may be false imprisonment.[91] Art 5 of the ECHR has potential significance, but has been interpreted to protect against a 'deprivation of liberty not a minor restriction on freedom of movement'.[92]

For this purpose touching the 'person' of the victim includes the clothes he is wearing. It is a battery if D touches V's clothes.[93] It is not necessary that V should be able to feel the impact through the clothes. In *Thomas*,[94] where D touched the bottom of V's skirt and rubbed it, the court said, *obiter*, 'There could be no dispute that if you touch a person's clothes while he is wearing them that is equivalent to touching him.' Note that s 79 of the Sexual Offences Act 2003 defines touching for that Act, as including touching with any part of the body, with anything else or *through anything*, and in *H*[95] the Court of Appeal confirmed that touching V's clothes sufficed.

In *Dica*,[96] the Court of Appeal confirmed that where V, who was unaware of D's infected state, had consented to the act of unprotected sexual intercourse she could not be said to have

---

[87] *Collins v Wilcock* [1984] 3 All ER 374 at 378, per Robert Goff LJ. In *F v West Berkshire Health Authority* [1990] 2 AC 1, [1989] 2 All ER 545 at 563, HL, Lord Goff was more emphatic that the consent rationalization is 'artificial', pointing out that it is difficult to impute consent to those who through youth or mental disorder are unable to give it. See *Mepstead v DPP* [1996] Crim LR 111, DC. In *Wainwright v Home Office* [2003] UKHL 53, Goff LJ was described as having 'redefined' the concept: para 9.

[88] *Wiffin v Kincard* (1807) 2 Bos & PNR 471; *Coward v Baddeley* (1859) 4 H & N 478. *Donnelly v Jackman* [1970] 1 All ER 987, [1970] 1 WLR 562, where a police officer was held to be acting in the execution of his duty although he persisted in tapping V on the shoulder when V had made it clear that he had no intention of stopping to speak, is 'an extreme case': [1984] 3 All ER 374 at 379.

[89] *Kenlin v Gardiner* [1967] 2 QB 510. See *McKoy* [2002] EWCA Crim 1628. See for a recent example *Wood v DPP* [2008] EWHC 1056 (Admin).

[90] *Collins v Wilcock*, above, n 87; see, eg, *McMillan v CPS* [2008] EWHC 1457 (Admin), (touching when steadying a drunk person).

[91] See below, p 678.

[92] See discussion below Emmerson, Ashworth, and Macdonald, HR&CJ, para 5.02 et seq; *Guzzardi v Italy* (1981) 3 EHRR 333, para 92. See the discussion of *Austin v MPC* [2009] UKHL 12, below, p 685. See also *R(AP) v Secretary of State for the Home Department* [2010] UKSC 24, in which it was held that when deciding if there is a deprivation of liberty within the meaning of Art 5 of the Convention regard should be had to the subjective factors peculiar to the particular individual.

[93] *Day* (1845) 1 Cox CC 207. D slashed V's clothes with a knife.

[94] (1985) 81 Cr App R 331 at 334, CA.

[95] [2005] EWCA Crim 732, [2005] Crim LR 734.

[96] [2004] EWCA Crim 1103, [2004] Crim LR 944 and commentary. The House of Lords refused leave to appeal – see House of Lords Session 2005–2006, 15 Dec 2005. See, for criticism of the case: M Weait, 'Criminal Law and the Transmission of HIV: R v Dica' (2005) 68 MLR 121; M Weait, 'Dica: Knowledge, Consent and the Transmission of HIV' (2004) 154 NLJ 826; cf for a positive view of the case: JR Spencer, 'Retrial for Reckless Infection' (2004) 154 NLJ 762. See also M Davies, 'R v Dica: Lessons in Practising Unsafe Sex' (2004) 68 J Crim L 498. For detailed examination of the appropriate uses of the criminal law to tackle HIV transmission, see

impliedly consented to the risk of infection from that intercourse. In *H v CPS*[97] the court rejected the submission that teachers in special needs schools must by their post 'impliedly consent' to the use of violence against them by pupils. The court accepted that the teachers were accepting a heightened risk of violence but that was not implied consent to it.

17.2.1.2 Effective consent

The principal problems to address in this context are:

- what mental capacity V must possess to be capable of issuing effective consent,
- what degree of knowledge V must have to be capable of giving a valid consent,
- what effect on V's apparent consent a fraud by D will have, and
- whether duress or pressure from D or another will vitiate consent by V.

We are not at this point examining D's belief in V's consent, but it must be borne in mind that D's belief that V is consenting to an act for which V's factual consent would be recognized in law[98] is a defence whether D's belief is based on reasonable grounds or not, provided D's belief is honestly held.[99]

Capacity[100]

Those with a mental disorder or learning difficulty may lack sufficient capacity to give consent,[101] as may someone who is temporarily incapacitated by intoxication or otherwise. Youth is clearly also a potential impediment to the giving of effective consent.[102] In *Burrell v Harmer*,[103] where D tattooed boys aged 12 and 13, causing their arms to become inflamed and painful the boys' apparent consent was held to be no defence to a charge of assault occasioning actual bodily harm. The court took the view that the boys were unable to understand the nature of the act. But in what sense did they not understand it? The case highlights the relative superficiality of the English criminal courts' approach to such fundamental questions underlying the issue of consent.

S Bronnit, 'Spreading Disease and the Criminal Law' [1994] Crim LR 21; D Ormerod and M Gunn, 'Criminal Liability for the Transmission of HIV' [1996] Web JCLI; D Ormerod, 'Criminalizing HIV Transmission – Still No Effective Solutions' (2001) 30 Common Law World Review 135; M Weait and Y Azad, 'The Criminalisation of HIV Transmission in England and Wales: Questions of Law and Policy' (2005) 10 HIV/AIDS Policy & Law Review 1. See, more generally, M Weait, *Intimacy and Responsibility: The Criminalisaiton of HIV Transmission* (2007). cf S Matthiesson 'Should the Law Deal with Reckless HIV Infection as a Criminal Offence or as a Matter of Public Health?' (2010) 21 KLJ 123 responding to Weait; R Bennett, 'Should we Criminalise HIV Transmission' in C Erin and S Ost, (eds) *The Criminal Justice System and Health Care* (2007) 225; L Cherkassky, 'Being Informed: The Complexities of Knowledge, Deception and Consent when Transmitting HIV' (2010) 74 J Crim Law 242. The CPS has a dedicated policy for prosecuting cases involving the intentional or reckless sexual transmission of infection. See www.cps.gov.uk/publications/prosecution/sti.html. The policy was reviewed after one year. See the results at www.cps.gov.uk/publications/research/sti_one_year_on.html. The policy is found to be 'broadly effective' (para 5.1). Note that it is not just HIV transmission. A conviction for inflicting gbh by transmitting hepatitis B through sex was secured: see news reports for 19.11.08.

[97] [2010] All ER (D) 56 (Apr).

[98] *Konzani* [2005] EWCA Crim 706.

[99] *Morgan* [1976] AC 182 HL; above, p 330 *Albert v Lavin* [1981] 1 All ER 628, DC.

[100] LCCP 139, Part V; Law Commission, *Mental Capacity* (LC 231, 1995); see I Kennedy and A Grubb, *Medical Law* (3rd edn, 2000) Ch 5; E Jackson, *Medical Law: Text, Cases, and Materials* (2nd edn, 2009) Chs 4 and 5.

[101] See *Re MB (An Adult) (Medical Treatment)* [1997] 2 FCR 541. Medical treatment in defiance of the (mentally normal) adult patient's wishes or in the case of a child in defiance of those of a parent will infringe Art 8: *Glass v United Kingdom* (2000) App No 61827/00.

[102] See, generally, *Gillick v West Norfolk and Wisbech AHA* [1986] AC 112.

[103] [1967] Crim LR 169 and commentary thereon. It is now an offence to tattoo a person under the age of 18, except tattooing by a doctor for medical reasons: Tattooing of Minors Act 1969.

The Mental Capacity Act 2005 provides a definition, at least for the purposes of that Act, of 'people who lack capacity'. It remains to be seen to what extent the criminal courts will draw upon the definition: 'a person lacks capacity in relation to a matter if at the material time he is unable to make a decision for himself in relation to the matter because of a temporary or permanent impairment of, or a disturbance in the functioning of, the mind or brain'. The section further provides that a lack of capacity cannot be established merely by reference to '(a) a person's age or appearance, or (b) a condition of his, or an aspect of his behaviour, which might lead others to make unjustified assumptions about his capacity.' Even if the criminal courts do not adopt that definition directly in the context of offences against the person, they may be influenced in deciding whether a person lacks capacity by the 'principles' set out in s 1 of the Mental Capacity Act 2005 which include that a person: must be assumed to have capacity unless it is established to the contrary, and that a person is not to be treated as unable to make a decision merely because he makes an unwise decision.[104] The Act provides 'official recognition that capacity is not a blunt "all or nothing" condition, but is more complex, and is to be treated as being issue-specific. A person may not have sufficient capacity to be able to make complex, refined or major decisions but may still have the capacity to make simpler or less momentous ones, or to hold genuine views as to what he wants to be the outcome of more complex decisions or situations.'[105]

Informed consent

In principle, V cannot consent to some form of conduct without adequate knowledge of its nature, and the degree of knowledge required should depend on the degree of harm and risk of that harm to which V is exposing himself. In offences against the person this issue seems to have received little attention until very recently. In sexual offences, it is implicit in the statutory formulation of the more serious non-consensual offences that V must have capacity and have 'freely agreed', and that there must have been adequate information available to V to render his consent effective.[106] The issue overlaps with the next to be discussed – that of V's apparent consent in the face of deception by D. In sexual offences, the 2003 Act provides, *inter alia*, that there is no consent where D has deceived V as to the nature or purpose of D's act.[107] In non-sexual offences against the person, it remains unclear whether V can be said to have consented without having knowledge of the *purpose* of D's conduct even if V is aware of its *nature*.

In *Konzani*,[108] the Court of Appeal confirmed that if D engages in unprotected sexual intercourse with V, and D recklessly infects V with HIV, any defence of consent D seeks to advance will not be available unless V had made an informed consent to the risk of infection.[109] As the court explained:

If an individual who knows that he is suffering from the HIV virus conceals this stark fact from his sexual partner, the principle of her personal autonomy is not enhanced if he is exculpated when he

---

[104] The Act is supplemented by a Code of Practice published in 2007: www.dca.gov.uk/legal-policy/ mental-capacity/mca-cp.pdf. See also C [2009] UKHL 42, dealing with the offence in s 30 of the Sexual Offences Act 2003, discussed below p 723.

[105] See *In re S and another (Protected Persons)* [2010] 1 W.L.R. 1082, [53] concerning powers of attorney.

[106] See below, Ch 18.

[107] See s 76 below, p 730.

[108] [2005] EWCA Crim 706; M Weait, 'Knowledge, Autonomy and Consent: *R v Konzani*' [2006] Crim LR 763 arguing that the case extends the criminal law too far by criminalizing *reckless* non-disclosure of HIV positive status. See, more generally, M Weait, *Intimacy and Responsibility: The Criminalisaiton of HIV Transmission* (2007) arguing that the act of recklessly exposing a sexual partner to the risk of HIV infection without her consent should be decriminalized and treated as a public health issue.

[109] For sentencing considerations in such cases, see *P (SJ)* [2006] EWCA Crim 2599 – 32 months on a plea.

recklessly transmits the HIV virus to her through consensual sexual intercourse. On any view, the concealment of this fact from her almost inevitably means that she is deceived. Her consent is not properly informed, and she cannot give an informed consent to something of which she is ignorant. Equally, her personal autonomy is not normally protected by allowing a defendant who knows that he is suffering from the HIV virus which he deliberately conceals, to assert an honest belief in his partner's informed consent to the risk of the transmission of the HIV virus. Silence in these circumstances is incongruous with honesty, or with a genuine belief that there is an informed consent. Accordingly, in such circumstances the issue either of informed consent, or honest belief in it will only rarely arise: in reality, in most cases, the contention would be wholly artificial.[110]

Several aspects of the decision are of importance. First, to be effective, V's consent must be to the risk of HIV infection; V might well have consented to the act of sexual intercourse without consenting to the risk of HIV infection. Secondly, V cannot in law consent to intentional infection; V's consent is only effective if D is merely reckless as to transmission.[111] Thirdly, the decision appears to criminalize D who suspects that he is HIV positive, without knowing that fact, if he then goes on to have unprotected intercourse with V without her consent as to the risk of infection.[112] This aspect of the decision has been heavily criticized for overcriminalizing.[113] Fourthly, the decision treats D's failure to disclose his HIV positive status to V as sufficient to preclude informed consent by V. Several commentators have been critical of this aspect of the decision, arguing that V has some responsibility for taking precautions about her sexual safety, and that by assuming that by D's concealment V is not consenting, the law ignores that responsibility on V.[114] The question of whether D is liable where he has not informed V of his HIV status, but despite using a condom he has infected V remains unresolved. D will surely argue that he was not reckless as to the risk of infection.

It was accepted in *Konzani* that there may be circumstances in which V will have informed consent without express disclosure from D, as where the fact of D's HIV status becomes known in the course of medical treatment. That qualification to the general principle – that informed consent depends on D's honest disclosure – also poses problems. D will be able to plead that he did not know that V was not consenting to the risk, since he had a genuine belief that she knew of his HIV status although he had not disclosed the fact to her. In addition, D may be acquitted where V has in fact consented to the risk even if D did not know that she had consented because he was unaware of her having secured knowledge of his status from other sources. If absence of consent is an element of the *actus reus*, D cannot be guilty in such a case because the *actus reus* is not complete where V has, in fact, consented. If consent is a defence, D will have *actus reus* (infection) and *mens rea* (recklessness as to infection); but can he rely on the defence of consent based on the fact of V's awareness of his infected state of which D was ignorant at the time as it derived from other sources? Does the defence require proof that D was aware of the circumstances which would render his conduct justified? Cooper and Reed[115] suggest that this resurrects the problems posed by *Dadson* (above p 54). They point to the fact that D will be relying on a justifying circumstance (V's consent) of which D was unaware at the time of the act, and that this drives 'a coach and horses' through established doctrines of informed consent.

[110] [23].

[111] See below.

[112] Some argue that D has a 'right' not to know what his HIV status is and a right to act on that lack of knowledge: Tadros, *Criminal Responsibility*, 247.

[113] See S Ryan, 'Reckless Transmission of HIV: Knowledge and Culpability' [2006] Crim LR 981.

[114] See Weait (2005) 68 MLR at 128 and [2006] Crim LR 763. See also V Munro, 'On Responsible Relationships and Irresponsible Sex' (2007) 19 CFLQ 112.

[115] S Cooper and A Reed, 'Informed Consent and the Transmission of Sexual Disease: *Dadson* Revivified' (2007) 71 J Crim L 461.

Parliamentary clarification of the issues would be welcome, but is unlikely given the controversial nature of such legislation in terms of broader public health policies and the desire to encourage responsible sexual activity.[116]

The approach in *Konzani*, by which V's informed consent rests on D providing information as to the relevant risk, does not sit easily with the courts' approach in sexual offences, where not every fraud by D as to the purpose of his actions will vitiate consent.[117]

Consent procured by fraud[118]

In offences against the person, D's fraud as to the conduct does not necessarily negative V's consent: it does so only if it deceives V as to D's identity or the nature of the act.[119] The common law approach to frauds vitiating consent remains unsatisfactorily complex and confused.

If V agrees to X touching her in a manner amounting to a mere battery, her consent is *prima facie* vitiated if D impersonates X and touches her. V's autonomy includes a right (generally) to choose *who* touches her. In *Richardson*,[120] D, a registered dental practitioner who was suspended from practice, carried out dentistry on patients who said they would not have consented had they known that D was suspended. D was convicted of assault occasioning actual bodily harm, the trial judge ruling that the mistake vitiated consent, being equivalent to a mistake of identity, the Court of Appeal disagreed; so to hold would be to strain and distort the everyday meaning of 'identity'. The fraud was not as to who she was but whether she was licensed as a dentist. There is, to date, no recognition of a principle in offences against the person whereby a fraud as to an attribute (for example, being medically qualified) suffices to vitiate consent. It could be argued that there are some situations in which the status or attribute of the individual is inextricably bound up with his or her identity for the purposes of the specific activity he is performing. Indeed, it could be that the attribute is actually *more* important than the identity. For example, would a patient visiting a general practitioner and being told that a new doctor is taking the surgery be more concerned as to the 'status' of the person or his 'identity'? The same argument might apply to the attribute of being a police officer.[121]

The courts have had even greater difficulty dealing with the effect of frauds as to the nature of the act, and in particular in distinguishing frauds that relate to issues that affect the nature of the act and frauds that relate to a collateral issue. It would be undesirable for the law to treat all frauds as vitiating consent; otherwise the most trivial lies about the conduct could give rise to liability.[122] In *Bolduc and Bird*, where D1, a doctor, by falsely pretending that D2 was a medical student, obtained V's consent to D2's presence at a vaginal examination of V, it was held that there was no assault because the fraud was not as to the nature and quality of what

---

[116] See J Rogers [2005] CLJ 20, 22 pointing out that no Government is likely to want to legislate.

[117] See *Jheeta* [2007] EWCA Crim 1699; below p 733.

[118] See generally, LCCP 139, Part VI.

[119] But cf the rule in trespass to land and, therefore, in burglary, below, p 955.

[120] [1998] 2 Cr App R 200. *Richardson* now has to be read with *Tabassum* [2000] 2 Cr App R 328, below, p 633.

[121] With powers to arrest, search etc. See *Wellard* [1978] 1 WLR 921. It could be argued that there are circumstances in which the attribute or status of the actor is so crucial as to alter the *nature* of the act performed, as perhaps in a medical context. This would require the court to adopt a much wider reading of 'nature' than the orthodox interpretation which restricts the meaning to the mechanical acts see, eg, *Williams* [1923] 1 KB 340. There is some Canadian authority supporting a wider test. See *Maurantonio* (1967) 65 DLR (2d) 674; *Harms* [1944] 2 DLR 61. The GMC has established a Memorandum of Understanding (7 June 2005) on the investigation of fraudulent doctors. See generally www.gmc-uk.org.

[122] In appropriate cases the law lowers the threshold of what constitutes a sufficient fraud or threat, as where the victim is mentally disordered – see Sexual Offences Act 2003, ss 30–44 below, p 723.

was to be done.[123] Similarly, a woman was held to have consented to the nature of the act by agreeing to the introduction of an instrument into her vagina for diagnostic purposes when the operator was secretly acting only for sexual gratification.[124]

One of the leading cases in this area, and one which gave rise to considerable controversy, was *Clarence*.[125] D was charged with causing grievous bodily harm to his wife, V, when knowing that he was suffering from a sexually transmitted disease, he had unprotected sex with her and infected her. It was held that V had consented to intercourse with D and, although she would not have consented to the act of intercourse had she been aware of the disease from which D knew he was suffering, this was no assault. The court concluded that she had not been defrauded as to the *nature* of the act of intercourse (that is, the mechanics of that act)[126] but merely as to the associated risk of disease. The flaw in this approach was in focusing on V's awareness of the nature of the act of intercourse. This was not a rape case where her understanding of the nature of sex might have been important. The court should have focused on the more important question: was V aware or was she deceived about the harm which D was charged with causing – that of the infection. It was her awareness of the nature of *that* risk that ought to have been considered.

In the important case of *Dica*,[127] where D had infected two sexual partners with HIV, *Clarence* was regarded by the Court of Appeal as being no longer of useful application.[128] Where V, who was unaware of D's infected state, had consented to the act of unprotected sexual intercourse she could not be said to have impliedly consented to the risk of infection from that intercourse. In *Dica*, the court focused, appropriately it is submitted, on the question of whether the fraud related to the infection – which represents the harm alleged – rather than the intercourse. The conclusion was that the victims had been defrauded as to the risk of infection and hence had not consented to bodily harm, but had not been defrauded as to the nature of the act of sexual intercourse and hence had not been raped.[129] The nature of intercourse is the same whether with a HIV infected person or not. Where V has not consented to the risk of infection, D could be liable under s 20 of the OAPA 1861 if he was reckless as to whether he might infect V.[130]

Subsequently, in *Konzani*,[131] the court emphasized that 'there is a critical distinction between taking a risk of the various, potentially adverse and possibly problematic consequences of sexual intercourse and giving an informed consent to the risk of infection with a fatal disease'.[132]

Frauds as to the *nature* of the act (which, as *Dica* demonstrates, must be accurately categorized) are clearly sufficient to vitiate consent. Following *Tabassum*, it became unclear whether

---

[123] *Bolduc and Bird* (1967) 63 DLR (2d) 82 (Sup Ct of Canada, Spence J diss), reversing British Columbia CA 61 DLR (2d) 494; cf *Rosinski* (1824) 1 Mood CC 19.

[124] *Mobilio* [1991] 1 VR 339. See D Ormerod, 'A Victim's Mistaken Consent in Rape' (1992) 56 J Crim L 407.

[125] (1888) 22 QBD 23; below, p 650. For an interesting historical account of the case, see K Gleeson, 'The Problem of *Clarence*' (2005) 14 Nottingham LJ 1.

[126] cf *Williams* [1923] KB 340.

[127] [2004] EWCA Crim 1103, [2004] Crim LR 944 and commentary. See, references in n 108 above.

[128] The various aspects of that decision had been eroded by the courts over recent years, with *R* [1992] 1 AC 599 dispensing with the marital rape exemption, and *Ireland and Burstow* [1998] AC 147 accepting that 'infliction' need not involve an assault or direct contact.

[129] The CA allowed the appeal overturning the trial judge's ruling that the decision in *Brown* [1994] 1 AC 212 deprived V of the legal capacity to consent to such serious harm and that consent provided no defence. At his retrial Dica was convicted of inflicting grievous bodily harm contrary to s 20 and sentenced to four and a half years' imprisonment. The HL refused leave to appeal – see House of Lords Session 2005–2006, 15 Dec 2005.

[130] If D intended to infect V he would be liable under s 18 irrespective of consent.

[131] [2005] EWCA Crim 706.

[132] [22].

a fraud as to the 'quality' of the act (rather than its nature) would be sufficient to vitiate consent. In that case, D had persuaded three women to allow him to examine their breasts by falsely informing them that he was medically qualified and conducting research work for a cancer charity. D's conviction for indecent assault was upheld. The court accepted that the women had been aware of the nature of the act of touching their breasts, but defrauded as to the 'quality' of the act – they believed it to be for a medical purpose – and that vitiated their consent.[133] This was recognized to have profound repercussions. Where D has sexual intercourse with V knowing (or possibly even being reckless as to whether) he is HIV positive, D's fraud as to the infection could, on the *Tabassum* approach, be regarded as a fraud as to the 'quality' of the act. This could render V's consent to the intercourse invalid and D would be a rapist.[134]

In *B*,[135] the Court of Appeal rejected the argument that D who has intercourse with V and conceals his HIV status is defrauding V as to the 'purpose' of the act of intercourse. In effect, the result in *Clarence* is confirmed. Under the Sexual Offences Act 2003, it is conclusively presumed that V did not consent if D has defrauded V as to the nature *or purpose* of his act. In interpreting that provision, the court in *B* has concluded that concealment of HIV will not be a fraud as to purpose. It is submitted therefore that at common law, in relation to offences against the person where the requirement is of a fraud or mistake as to the *nature* of the act and not merely its purpose, the court is now extremely unlikely to adopt a contrary view.

Duress

Duress may negative apparently valid consent. A threat to imprison V unless he submitted to a beating would probably invalidate V's consent to the beating. Possibly a threat to dismiss from employment[136] or to bring a prosecution[137] would have a similar effect. It is submitted that non-criminal threats and even threats of lawful action may also be sufficient. It is unclear whether, to negative consent, the threats must be such that they would have caused a person of reasonable firmness to succumb to the violence. An alternative view would be that consent should be invalid if D knew of the particular vulnerabilities of V which caused him to succumb although they might not have caused a reasonable person to do so. If the test is whether the threat would be sufficient to overcome the will of a reasonably steadfast person, the outcome must depend to some extent on the relationship between the gravity of the threat and the act to which V is asked to submit.

Duress may be implied from the relationship between the parties – for example where D is a teacher, and V is a young pupil.[138] As in sexual offences,[139] submission is not consent. As noted, if D genuinely believes that V is consenting, even though she is in fact only submitting, D will lack *mens rea*.

17.2.1.3 Legal limits on the validity of consent

Having examined the circumstances in which V's apparent consent will be invalidated, we must turn to the yet more difficult question: if V has in fact given valid consent, is that consent recognized in law? Fundamental questions of morality are raised by the extent to which the

---

[133] There is no guidance in *Tabassum* on what might constitute the 'quality' of a particular act.

[134] Under the Sexual Offences Act 2003, s 76 a fraud as to the 'nature or purpose' (not quality) of the act is conclusively presumed to vitiate consent.

[135] [2006] EWCA Crim 2945. For criticism see L Leigh, 'Two Cases on Consent in Rape' (2007) 5 Archbold News 6.

[136] *McCoy* 1953 (2) SA 4 (AD) (threat to ground air hostess negativing her apparent consent to being caned).

[137] *State v Volschenk* 1968 (2) PH H283 (threat to prosecute held *not* to negative consent on rape charge).

[138] *Nichol* (1807) Russ & Ry 130.

[139] Below, p 721. See *Doyle* [2010] EWCA Crim 119.

State ought to use criminal sanctions to restrict an adult with full mental capacity in his consent to the infliction of harm on his person.[140] On a public policy basis, English law restricts the validity of consent by reference to the level of harm *and* the circumstances in which it is inflicted. Factual consent to mere assault or battery is valid in law. Factual consent to actual bodily harm or more serious levels of harm (wounding, serious harm, death) is not legally recognized unless the activity involved is one which the courts or Parliament has recognized to be in the public interest. Thus, as a matter of public policy, it is no defence to a charge of murder for D to say that V asked to be killed. On the other hand, V's consent to D's taking a high degree of risk of killing him is effective where it is justified by the purpose of the act, as it may be in the case of a surgical operation. Where the act has some social purpose, recognized by the law as valid, it is a question of balancing the degree of harm which will or may be caused against the value of that purpose.

Three issues require elucidation: what level of harm is caused, what level of harm is foreseen or intended, and whether the activity in which the harm arises is one of the exceptional categories in which consent is recognized. Unfortunately, since this is an area in which the decisions of the appellate courts are based so heavily on public policy, it is not always easy to identify clear principles.

The level of harm

Consent to an assault or battery will always be valid consent, no matter what the circumstances (for example even if it is in a sadomasochist encounter) provided the consent is effective, as discussed above.

If D has caused actual bodily harm – injury of more than a merely transient or trifling nature – with intent to do so,[141] the factual consent of the victim will *not* be legally valid unless the conduct falls within one of the recognized exceptional categories below. It is arguable that this sets far too low a threshold at which the law should cease to recognize consent as a general defence. The Law Commission proposed raising the level of harm to which a person is entitled to consent in general circumstances to harm falling below its proposed concept of 'serious disabling injury'.[142]

The role of intention and foresight of harms

Where D has intended or has been reckless as to the causing of actual bodily harm, liability arises even if V consents, subject to the exceptional cases below. The law has struggled with cases where D has not caused that level of harm intentionally – where he intends or is reckless as to causing only assault or battery with consent, but the conduct leads to actual bodily harm. Some *obiter dicta* suggest that D is guilty if the harm was foreseen by D (if not intended), or even if it was objectively likely to occur. The problem flowed from an overbroad statement in the *A-G's Reference (No 6 of 1980)*[143] where two youths of 18 and 17 settled an argument by a fist fight and when one sustained a bleeding nose and bruises to his face, it was held that the other was guilty of assault occasioning actual bodily harm:

[I]t is not in the public interest that people should try to cause or *should cause* each other actual bodily harm for no good reason. Minor struggles are another matter. So, in our judgment, it is immaterial

---

[140] See Williams [1962] Crim LR 74 and 154; LCCP 139, Part II, Appendix C; P Roberts (1997) 17 OJLS 389; J Feinberg, *The Moral Limits of the Criminal Law, Vol 1: Harm to Others* (1984).

[141] And probably also in cases where he does so recklessly. See the discussion of *Dica* above.

[142] See LCCP 139. For criticisms of the proposal and its incoherence with the offences against the person, see Ormerod and Gunn [1996] Crim LR 694. Many jurisdictions adopt a much higher threshold: see LCCP 139, Appendix B.

[143] [1981] QB 715.

whether the act occurs in private or in public; it is an assault if actual bodily harm *is intended and/or caused*. This means that most fights will be unlawful regardless of consent.[144] (emphasis added)

This passage was quoted with approval by all three of the majority in the leading case of *Brown* (below). It is submitted, however, that it goes too far. The difficulty is the words 'or should cause' and 'and/or'. These words imply that an offence is committed if D assaults or batters V with V's consent and D does not intend to cause bodily harm, but does so in fact. The passage suggests D will be liable even if the bodily harm was not foreseen or even foreseeable. That seems a wholly unreasonable result. Subsequent case law is difficult to reconcile with the position, and it is submitted that the *dictum* no longer represents the law.

It is submitted that the following reflects the current state of the law:

(1) D intends to cause actual bodily harm and causes that level of harm (or worse) to V with consent (or belief in V's consent). D is liable for actual bodily harm. V's consent is invalid unless the harm occurs in conduct within an exceptional category below (p 637 et seq). A good illustration is *Donovan*[145] where D's caning of V, with her consent, for their mutual sexual enjoyment would render him liable under s 47.

(2) D is reckless as to causing actual bodily harm and has V's consent (or belief in V's consent) to the risk of causing that level of injury which actually occurs. It is less clear whether V's consent is invalid in all cases irrespective of whether they fall within an exceptional category. *Dicta* in *Brown* and some decisions such as *Dica* suggest that the law treats V's factual consent as invalid only in respect of intentionally inflicted harms.

(3) D intends only to make physical contact with V at the level of battery with V's consent (or belief in V's consent), but in fact, D causes actual bodily harm not intending or being reckless as to that result. According to the *dictum* in *A-G's Reference* D is guilty, it being sufficient that actual bodily harm *is* caused.[146] This *dictum* has recently been rejected. The Court of Appeal in *Meachen*[147] concluded, correctly it is submitted, that where D intends[148] to cause the level of harm amounting to battery and has V's consent to that level of harm, if D then causes actual bodily harm or worse, without being reckless in doing so or intending to do so, he is not guilty. There is no unlawful battery as the foundational element of the actual bodily harm.[149] The facts of *Meachen* illustrate how this operates. On D's account he intentionally digitally penetrated V's anus with her consent for their mutual sexual gratification. D had no intention to cause any injury, nor did he see the risk of doing so. V suffered serious anal injury and required a colostomy. D's conviction for inflicting grievous bodily harm contrary to s 20 (and indecent assault under the Sexual Offences Act 1956) was quashed because the trial judge had erroneously ruled that V's consent could not avail D in these circumstances.

The *dictum* from the *A-G's Reference* was also rejected in *Slingsby*:[150] D and V engaged in 'vigorous' sexual activity, including D inserting his hand into V's vagina and rectum. This battery was activity to which V could lawfully, and did, consent. D was wearing a signet ring which caused internal injury to V resulting in infection which led to her death. D was charged with manslaughter by an unlawful and dangerous act. Judge J,

---

[144] *A-G's Reference (No 6 of 1980)* [1981] 2 All ER 1057 at 1059.
[145] [1934] 2 KB 498.
[146] D has committed the *actus reus* of actual bodily harm. He has the *mens rea* for actual bodily harm (it being the same as for assault/battery).
[147] [2006] EWCA Crim 2414.
[148] The court did not have to consider the case where D is reckless as to that harm; see para 43.
[149] This passage in the 11th edition was referred to in *Meachen*, at [36].
[150] [1995] Crim LR 570.

as he then was, ruled that it would be contrary to principle to treat as criminal, activity which would not otherwise amount to an assault merely because an injury was caused. It is submitted that this is right.

The decision in *Boyea*,[151] also needs to be re-evaluated in light of the decision in *Meachen*. In *Boyea* D's act of inserting his hand into V's vagina and twisting it caused actual bodily harm. It was held that there was an assault because the act was 'likely' to cause harm and D was guilty of an (indecent) assault even if he did not intend or foresee that harm was likely to be caused. This suggests that if, objectively, D's conduct is likely to lead to actual bodily harm there can be no defence of consent, even if D does not intend or foresee any harm over and above the battery to which he has consent. The Court of Appeal in *Meachen*, following *dicta* in *Dica*, concluded that *Boyea* is best treated as a decision in which V had not consented even to the assault/battery in the circumstances in which it was inflicted.

(4) D intends actual bodily harm with V's consent (or belief in V's consent) but in fact causes only a battery. D ought not to be convicted of that offence. Consent is a valid defence to assault/battery; D has not caused actual bodily harm.[152] In *Barnes*,[153] Lord Woolf asserted that 'When no bodily harm is caused, the consent of the victim to what happened is *always* a defence to a charge.'[154] It is submitted that this is the correct approach, even though D intended a level of harm to which consent would be no defence.[155]

(5) D is reckless as to causing actual bodily harm with V's consent (or belief in V's consent) as to that risk, but in fact causes only a battery. Arguably, since D has caused only a battery and has consent to that level of harm, he ought to be acquitted.

It need hardly be said if this analysis is correct, that the law is in a dreadfully confused and unsatisfactory state.

Type of activity involved

In *Brown*, a group of sadomasochistic men who had engaged in consensual beatings and genital torture which had not resulted in any participant receiving medical attention, were convicted of offences of assault occasioning actual bodily harm. The House of Lords, by a majority of 3 to 2 upheld the convictions. In doing so the House recognized certain categories of activity in which the law would recognize effective factual consent to injury as valid in law.[156]

In *Barnes*,[157] Lord Woolf candidly admitted that whether a particular activity is regarded as one to which consent may be valid is a matter of public policy. This 'renders it unnecessary to find a separate jurisprudential basis for the application of the defence in various different factual contexts in which an offence could be committed'. This will do little to satisfy those advocating the need for a clear moral foundation to the law's approach, but is not a great surprise. This policy-based approach allows the courts to maintain the incoherent list of exceptions and to add or subtract from that list based on its perception of the social utility of

---

[151] (1992) 156 JP 505, [1992] Crim LR 574.

[152] cf the view in *Donovan* [1934] 2 KB 498, CCA.

[153] [2005] Crim LR 381.

[154] Para 7, emphasis added.

[155] Arguably D may be liable for attempted actual bodily harm.

[156] On this, one of the most controversial decisions of the HL in the last few decades, see LCCP 139. D Kell, 'Social Disutility and Consent' (1994) 14 OJLS 121; M Giles, 'Consensual Harm and the Public Interest' (1994) 57 MLR 101; M Allen, 'Consent and Assault' (1994) 58 J Crim Law 183; N Bamforth, 'Sadomasochism and Consent' [1994] Crim LR 661; P Alldridge, *Relocating Criminal Law* (2000) 122 et seq. See also the definition in s 66 of the Criminal Justice and Immigration Act 2008 relating to extreme pornography below p 1077.

[157] [2005] Crim LR 381.

particular conduct and the circumstances in which it occurs. Thus, the courts may continue to allow consensual buttock branding as akin to tattooing (*Wilson*)[158] but not sadomasochistic caning on the buttocks (*Brown; Donovan*).

The differentiation of activities to which consent may be validly given on grounds of perceived public utility can be illustrated by comparing the case of a fist fight and a boxing match, both of which are intended or likely to cause actual bodily harm or worse. Boxing under the Queensberry rules is lawful. A boxer, trying to knock out his opponent, certainly has an intention to cause harm, possibly even serious harm, which is a sufficient *mens rea* for murder, but no prosecutions have been brought against fighters operating under the professional rules and in *Brown* all of their lordships accepted that boxing is lawful. According to Lord Mustill, boxing is best regarded as a special case which, 'for the time being stands outside the ordinary law of violence because society chooses to tolerate it'.[159] Where, however, two youths decide to settle an argument by a fight with fists[160] and one sustains a bleeding nose and bruises to his face the other is guilty of assault occasioning actual bodily harm.

The court in *A-G's Reference* sought to catalogue the types of activity to which V will be entitled to consent in law:

Nothing which we have said is intended to cast doubt on the accepted legality of properly conducted games and sports, lawful chastisement or correction, reasonable surgical interference, dangerous exhibitions, etc. These apparent exceptions can be justified as involving the exercise of a legal right, in the case of chastisement or correction, or as needed in the public interest, in the other cases.

Exceptional categories in which consent to (intentionally inflicted)[161] harm has been recognized by the courts or Parliament to be valid include the following.

Sports[162]

The law has long recognized the social utility of sport in enhancing the fitness of the population. A number of principles seem to have developed. First, although by playing the sport V consents to whatever the rules permit, if the rules permit an unacceptably dangerous act, the law need not recognize the validity of V's factual consent. That is a matter of public policy. However, boxing continues to be lawful despite the life-threatening injury and participants' intention to cause grievous bodily harm. Secondly, where unlike boxing and martial arts, playing within the rules of the particular sport does not *necessarily* involve D causing actual bodily harm, but D intentionally inflicts actual bodily harm or worse, V's consent is irrelevant and D commits the offence: *Bradshaw*.[163] Thirdly, and most difficult in practical terms to apply, if in playing such a sport D was reckless only as to the causing of the injury, the question will be whether V impliedly consented to the risk of that level of injury in the context in which it was inflicted.

[158] [1996] 2 Cr App R 241.

[159] For a full discussion, see M Gunn and D Ormerod, 'The Legality of Boxing' (1995) 15 LS 181, and LCCP 139, XII. See also S Greenfield and G Osborn (eds), *Law and Sport in Contemporary Society* (2000); J Anderson, *The Legality of Boxing: A Punch Drunk Love?* (2007).

[160] A 'prize-fight' in public is unlawful at common law as a breach of the peace tending to public disorder. *Brown* [1994] AC 212, [1993] 2 All ER 75 at 79, 86, 106, 119, HL. Because the whole enterprise is unlawful, consent is not a defence even to a charge of common assault against the contestants: *Coney* (1882) 8 QBD 534.

[161] See above. Arguably the consent defence is only invalid where D has *intentionally* caused harm. See further *Dica* above.

[162] See LCCP 139, Part XII and M Cutcheon, 'Sports, Violence and the Criminal Law' (1994) 45 NILQ 267. For a recent analysis questioning the objective approach to consent in sports, but denying the need for a uniform approach throughout the criminal law, see B Livings, 'A Different Ball Game' (2007) 71 J Crim L 534, disputing the arguments in C Elliott and C de Than, 'The Case for a Rational Reconstruction of Consent in Criminal Law' (2007) 70 MLR 225 who call for a unitary approach to consent throughout the criminal law.

[163] (1878) Cox CC 83.

The question of whether the conduct was within the rules of the game is not the sole determinant of liability.[164] It would be too simplistic to suggest that V's consent is only valid for that which the rules of the game permit. V may well, as a matter of fact, impliedly consented to the *risk* of injury occurring in conduct outside the rules as in a late tackle in football, or an illegitimate bouncer in cricket.[165] It is therefore necessary to look to a broader range of factors. In *Barnes*, the Court of Appeal confirmed that it is appropriate to make an objective evaluation of these circumstances. The court adopted the approach in Canadian law[166] and advocated by the Law Commission.[167] Relevant circumstances include the type of sport, the level at which it was being played, the nature of the act, the degree of force used, the extent of the risk of injury and D's state of mind. Prosecution is usually reserved for sufficiently grave conduct deserving to be regarded as criminal, having regard to the fact that most organized sports have their own disciplinary procedures and to the availability of civil remedies. What is accepted in one sport might not be covered by the implied consent in another. In highly competitive sports, conduct 'outside the rules' might be expected to occur in the heat of the moment, but even if such conduct justified not only being penalized but, for example, being sent off, it might not reach the threshold required for it to be criminal.

Horseplay[168]

This exception is not confined to organized games. Consent by children to rough and undisciplined play may be a defence to a charge of inflicting grievous bodily harm if there is no intention to cause injury. Equally, a genuine belief in consent, even an unreasonable belief, apparently negatives recklessness: *Jones*[169] where boys were injured by being tossed in the air by schoolmates. The decision recognizes that children have always indulged in rough and undisciplined play among themselves and probably always will; but the non-consenting child is rightly protected by the criminal law. The 'horseplay' exception seems to have been taken to extreme lengths in *Aitken*,[170] where the 'robust games' of Royal Air Force officers at a celebration in the mess included setting fire to one another's fire resistant clothing. Two such incidents apparently caused no harm but on a third occasion V sustained severe burns. It was held that a ruling that it was not open to the court martial to find that the 'activities' were lawful was wrong. If V consented to them, or if D believed, reasonably or not, that V consented to them, it was open to the trial court to find that there was no offence.

The courts have emphasized that horseplay can only be relied upon where V is consenting or D genuinely believes that to be the case. In the case of *A*,[171] D dropped V, a non-swimmer, off a bridge into a river where V drowned. V had been fighting for this not to happen and was clearly not consenting, nor was it credible that D believed he was. D's conviction for manslaughter was upheld.

---

[164] ibid.

[165] See *Moore* (1898) 14 TLR 229.

[166] See *Cicarelli* (1989) 54 CCC (3d) 121.

[167] LCCP 134. That approach was criticized by S Gardiner, 'The Law and the Sports Field' [1994] Crim LR 513, see also S Gardiner, 'Should More Matches End in Court' (2005) 155 NLJ 998 but received generally favourable responses: LCCP 139, paras 12.6–12.23. On *Barnes* see also J Anderson 'No Licence for Thuggery: Violence, Sport and the Criminal Law' [2008] Crim LR 751.

[168] See LCCP 139.

[169] [1987] Crim LR 123, CA.

[170] [1992] 1 WLR 1006, at 1011 (C-MAC).

[171] [2005] All ER 38 (D).

Surgery[172]

Consent to a surgical operation for a purpose recognized as valid by the law is effective.[173] This includes a 'sex-change' operation[174] and, presumably, cosmetic surgery and organ transplants. Where an adult of full mental capacity refuses consent to medical treatment a failure to respect that decision will render the doctor liable for criminal offences, even in circumstances in which the treatment will be life-preserving.[175]

Body modification[176]

Having one's hair cut is clearly lawful. Since cutting hair might amount to actual bodily harm, it is implicit that the law recognizes that consent to that activity will prevent liability: *DPP v Smith*.[177] Ritual[178] circumcision of males,[179] ear-piercing and tattooing of adults are generally assumed to be lawful. Presumably the same is true of more exotic body-piercing of adults.[180] In *Wilson*,[181] D's branding of his initials on his wife's buttocks, at her request, in lieu of tattooing, was held to be equally lawful. The only distinction from *Donovan*[182] appears to be that Donovan's motive was sexual gratification whereas Wilson's was to bestow on his wife an adornment which she desired. Where the purpose of the act is one which the law condemns, consent may be no answer to the charge.[183]

Coke tells us that in 1604, 'a young strong and lustie rogue, to make himself impotent, thereby to have the more colour to begge or to be relieved without putting himself to any labour, caused his companion to strike off his left hand' and that both of them were convicted of mayhem.[184] Maiming, even with consent, was unlawful because it deprived the king of a fighting man. In early Victorian times when soldiers, as part of their drill, had to bite cartridges, a soldier got a dentist to pull out his front teeth to avoid the drill. Stephen J thought that both were guilty of a crime.[185] Denning LJ followed these instances in discussing, *obiter*,

---

[172] See LCCP 139, Part VIII.

[173] Stephen, *Digest*, art 310. See P Skegg, 'Medical Procedures and the Crime of Battery' [1974] Crim LR 693 and (1973) 36 MLR 370.

[174] *Corbett v Corbett* [1971] P 83 at 99.

[175] *St George's Health Care v S* [1998] 3 All ER 673. See also the discussion above of the Mental Capacity Act 2005.

[176] On consent in relation to medical treatment and body modification see T Elliott 'Body Dismorphic Disorder, Radical Surgery and the Limits of Consent' (2009) 17 Med LR 149. See also See LCCP 139, Part IX.

[177] [2006] EWHC 94 (Admin).

[178] ie that performed otherwise than for medical reasons. See further, LCCP 139. See *Brown* [1994] 1 AC 212 and *Re J* [2000] 1 FCR 307, CA (Civ). Professor Feldman advised the Law Commission that non-therapeutic circumcision might be in breach of Art 3 of the ECHR, para 3.25, see further H Gilbert, 'Time to Reconsider the Lawfulness of Ritual Male Circumcision' [2007] EHRLR 279; PW Edge, 'Male Circumcision after the Human Rights Act' (1998) 5 J of Civil Liberties 320, see also L Vickers, 'Circumcision – The Unkindest Cut of All?' (2000) 150 NLJ 1694.

[179] See the Female Genital Mutilation Act 2003 replacing the Prohibition of Female Circumcision Act 1985 with extended offences to catch those in the UK who aid and abet circumcision performed abroad. In June 2005, a survey showed that up to 76,000 women living in the UK may have undergone illegal operations. An estimated 7,000 girls are still thought to be at risk. See www.bbc.co.uk/ethics/femalecircumcision/femalecirc_1.shtml#h6. See also *K v Secretary of State for the Home Department* [2007] 1 All ER 671, HL.

[180] See *Oversby* (1990) unreported, cited in LCCP 139, para 9.7.

[181] [1996] Crim LR 573, CA.

[182] [1934] 2 KB 498.

[183] The court was also influenced by the fact that W was married to his victim, but this must be an irrelevance. If the criminal law governing consensual injury is applied differently to homosexuals and heterosexuals (or to men and women) or on the basis of marriage this would almost certainly involve a violation of Arts 8 and 14 of the ECHR taken together.

[184] 1 Co Inst 127a and b.

[185] *Digest* (3rd edn) 142.

the legality of a sterilization operation.[186] His opinion (that the operation is unlawful if done only to enable the man to have the pleasure of intercourse without the responsibility) is no longer tenable,[187] but it illustrates the continuing and changing influence of public policy.

In circumstances where the body modification is for religious reasons, reliance on Art 9 of the ECHR guaranteeing respect for religious freedom would support the validity of consent. However, the courts have been unwilling to accommodate foreign cultural practices involving children, such as incision of cheeks.[188] In view of the recognition that ritual male circumcision practised by Jews and Muslims is lawful, the law's approach appears incoherent.

Sadomasochism[189]

Public policy is also at the root of the decision in *Brown*. In the opinion of the majority, policy requires the conviction of men participating in consensual sadomasochistic homosexual encounters, resulting in actual bodily harm and wounding, to protect society against a cult of violence with the danger of the corruption and proselytization of young men and the potential for the infliction of serious injury: this notwithstanding that there was in fact no permanent injury, no infection and no evidence of medical attention being required. The majority's reasoning that this was violence rather than sexual activity led to the conclusion that the activity should be unlawful.

Public policy was invoked to justify conviction for a relatively slight degree of harm in *Donovan*.[190] D, for his sexual gratification, beat a 17-year-old girl with a cane in circumstances of indecency. He was convicted of both indecent assault and common assault. The judge failed to direct the jury that the onus of negativing consent was on the Crown, but the Court of Criminal Appeal held that, if the blows were likely or intended to cause bodily harm, this omission was immaterial because D was guilty whether V consented or not. The conviction was quashed because the question whether the blows were likely or intended to cause bodily harm was not put to the jury.

In *Brown*, the whole House agreed that consent is a complete defence to the two offences – common and indecent assault – with which Donovan was charged. The Court of Criminal Appeal's opinion (that he could have been convicted of these offences because he was guilty of assault occasioning actual bodily harm, an offence with which he was not charged), was unacceptable in *Brown* to both Lord Lowry[191] of the majority and Lord Mustill[192] of the minority. Subsequent cases nevertheless seem to treat the *dicta* in *Donovan* as correct, but in light of the decision in *Meachen* above, it is submitted that if D intended to inflict a battery, the consent he had to that level of harm should preclude liability unless D intentionally or recklessly inflicted actual bodily harm.

The *dicta* in *Donovan* were distinguished in *Wilson*[193] (buttock branding) on the basis that Donovan was seeking sexual gratification, whereas Wilson was not – his conduct was like that of a professional tattooist who embellishes (intimate) parts at the request of their owner. In *Laskey*, the European Court distinguished *Wilson* because the injuries were not at all

---

[186] *Bravery v Bravery* [1954] 3 All ER 59 at 67, 68.

[187] The National Health Service (Family Planning) Amendment Act 1972 first authorized vasectomy services.

[188] *Adesanya* (1974) The Times, 16 July. See S Poulter, 'Foreign Customs and the English Criminal Law' (1975) 24 ICLQ 136.

[189] See LCCP 139, Part X.

[190] [1934] 2 KB 498. See L Leigh, 'Sado-Masochism, Consent and the Reform of the Criminal Law' (1976) 39 MLR 130.

[191] 'If the jury, properly directed, had found that consent was not disproved, they must have acquitted the appellant of the only charges brought against him' [1993] 2 All ER at 97.

[192] 'There is something amiss here' [1993] 2 All ER at 112.

[193] [1996] Crim LR 573.

'comparable in seriousness' with those in *Brown* even though they equally amounted to assault occasioning actual bodily harm. The decision in *Wilson* was distinguished, and *Brown* followed in a further case of sadomasochism: *Emmett*.[194] D's conviction for recklessly occasioning actual bodily harm to V by, *inter alia*, setting fire to lighter fuel on her breasts with her consent, was upheld by the Court of Appeal. The court described the conduct as going 'beyond that which was established in *Wilson*'. But the charge was the same – assault occasioning actual bodily harm. Are the courts to start evaluating the validity of consent on the basis of some undeclared judicial barometer of the severity of harm? In *Meachen* and in *Dica*, *Emmett* appears to have been treated as a case of intentional infliction of actual bodily harm.

Religious flagellation

In *Brown*, Lord Mustill accepted this as a recognized, though rarely practised, exception. The protection of religious freedoms under Art 9 of the ECHR would support such a conclusion.[195]

The risk of sexually transmitted infection

The decision of the Court of Appeal in *Dica*[196] is that an adult is entitled to give valid consent to the risk of being infected with a potentially lethal sexually transmitted disease such as HIV. The court distinguished between consensual acts of sexual intercourse where there might be a known risk to the health of one or other participants (consent valid) and those cases where participants were intent on spreading, or becoming infected with, disease (consent invalid). The court took the view that criminalization of consensual taking of risks would involve an 'impracticality of enforcement' and would undermine the general understanding of the community that sexual relationships were 'pre-eminently private'. Such arguments had not persuaded the House of Lords in *Brown*, albeit that case involved intentional harm. *Dica* might be seen as against the trend of post-*Brown* cases that treat consent even to a risk of harm as invalid.[197] Many will find unconvincing the distinction in *Dica* between 'sexual' and 'violent' acts, with cases such as *Emmett* and *Boyea* treated as having 'sexual overtones' but being really concerned with 'violent crime'. These cases must all be read carefully in light of *Meachen*. In *Konzani*,[198] the court confirmed that the consent will only be valid if V is informed of the risk of infection.

ECHR compatibility[199]

The case of *Brown* was considered by the European Court of Human Rights in *Laskey v United Kingdom*,[200] with the Court unanimously holding that the prosecution, conviction and sentence did not contravene Art 8 of the Convention. It should be noted that the Court doubted whether the activities even fell within the protection of Art 8. On the assumption that they did, the Court concluded that the prosecution was necessary and proportionate to the legitimate aim of the protection of health (and possibly also the protection of morals).

---

[194] (1999) The Times, 15 Oct.

[195] See LCCP 139, paras 10.2–10.7. However, note the conviction of Syed Mustafa Zaidi, a Shia Muslim for child cruelty after he forced two boys (13 and 15) to whip themselves during a religious ritual using a handled implement with curved blades. See news reports for 28 August 2008.

[196] [2004] EWCA 1103, [2004] Crim LR 944 and commentary.

[197] eg *Emett* (1999) The Times, 15 Oct.

[198] [2005] EWCA Crim 706.

[199] LCCP 139, Part III.

[200] (1997) 24 EHRR 39; L Moran, 'Learning the Limits of Privacy' (1998) 61 MLR 77. See also *KA & AD v Belgium* (2005) App No 42758/98.

The Court recognized that the margin of appreciation provided national courts the scope to prescribe the level of physical harm to which the law should permit an adult to consent.

17.2.2 Lawful chastisement[201]

It was always the common law rule that punishment was unlawful:

If it be administered for the gratification of passion or rage or if it be immoderate or excessive in its nature or degree, or if it be protracted beyond the child's powers of endurance or with an instrument unfitted for the purpose and calculated to produce danger to life and limb...[202]

In *A v United Kingdom*[203] the rule of the common law entitling parents to inflict moderate and reasonable physical chastisement on their children was held to offend Art 3 of the ECHR, prohibiting torture and inhuman or degrading treatment or punishment. In that case a jury had acquitted a stepfather who had caned a nine-year-old boy. It was accepted that the law then needed reform but there was considerable disagreement as what form reform should take. The English courts continued to acknowledge the parental right to chastise: *H.*[204] The judge had to give detailed directions to the jury to take account of the nature, context and duration of D's behaviour, the physical and mental effect on the child, the reasons for the punishment, and so on.

17.2.2.1 The Children Act 2004

Section 58 of the Children Act 2004 now provides:

(1) In relation to any offence specified in subsection (2), battery of a child cannot be justified on the ground that it constituted reasonable punishment.

(2) The offences referred to in subsection (1) are –

   (a) an offence under section 18 or 20 of the Offences against the Person Act 1861 (wounding and causing grievous bodily harm);

   (b) an offence under section 47 of that Act (assault occasioning actual bodily harm);

   (c) an offence under section 1 of the Children and Young Persons Act 1933 (cruelty to persons under 16).

(3) Battery of a child causing actual bodily harm to the child cannot be justified in any civil proceedings on the ground that it constituted reasonable punishment.

(4) For the purposes of subsection (3) 'actual bodily harm' has the same meaning as it has for the purposes of section 47 of the Offences against the Person Act 1861.

The effect is that reasonable and proportionate punishment amounting only to an assault or battery (that does not involve cruelty) is still protected by the defence of lawful chastisement. There is no longer a defence of lawful chastisement for punishment that involves a touching of the child and which constitutes the higher level of harm – actual bodily harm or cruelty. Given the ambiguity of the boundary between assault and actual bodily harm,

---

[201] For a valuable discussion, see H Keating, 'Protecting or Punishing Children: Physical Punishment, Human Rights and English Law Reform' (2006) 26 LS 394.

[202] *Hopley* (1860) 2 F & F 202 at 206, per Cockburn CJ. cf *Smith* [1985] Crim LR 42, CA.

[203] [1998] TLR 578, (1999) 27 EHRR 611. See also *Costello-Roberts v UK* (1993) 19 EHRR 112 (7-year-old slippered at public school); *Y v UK* (1992) 17 EHRR 238 (16-year-old caned at school). See, generally, B Phillips, 'The Case for Corporal Punishment in the UK – Beaten into Submission in Europe' (1994) 43 ICLQ 153.

[204] [2002] 1 Cr App R 59. J Rogers, 'A Criminal Lawyer's Response to Chastisement in the European Court' [2002] Crim LR 98; for trenchant criticism of the present law, see C Barton, 'Hitting Your Children: Common Assault or Common Sense' [2008] Fam Law 65.

neither parents nor children have gained a clear position of their rights. Immigrant parents must conform to English standards.[205] Reliance on Art 9 of the ECHR by parents claiming a right to inflict corporal punishment as an aspect of their religion will not preclude prosecution.[206]

The CPS reviewed a sample of cases where a child was assaulted by a parent or an adult acting *in loco parentis* after the coming into force of Children Act 2004, s 58. The report identified 12 cases where the reasonable chastisement defence was raised, which resulted in an acquittal or discontinuance. The report concluded that there is 'evidence to suggest that there have been cases where defendants charged with common assault have been acquitted or the case was discontinued, after running the reasonable chastisement defence. Of those cases, the file review suggests that it was possible that some defendants could have been charged differently.'[207]

17.2.2.2 Corporal punishment in schools

At common law, school teachers were in the same position as parents with regard to the conduct of the child at, or on his or her way to or from school.[208] Now, by s 549(4) of the Education Act 1996, a 'member of staff' of a school, has no right, by virtue of his position as such, to administer corporal punishment to a 'pupil' as defined in s 548(3) of that Act.[209] Staff may use reasonable force to restrain pupils who are violent or disruptive (s 550A) or to search a pupil for a weapon (s 550AA)[210] or to avert an immediate danger of personal injury or damage to property (s 548(5)).

17.2.3 Necessity

As noted above, necessity may negative what would otherwise be an assault, as where D pushes V out of the path of a vehicle which is about to run him down. The fireman, the paramedic, the surgeon and nurse may all do things to a person rendered unconscious in an accident, or by sudden illness, which would ordinarily be battery (or, in the case of the surgeon, wounding or grievous bodily harm) if done without consent; but they commit no offence if they are only doing what is necessary to save life or ensure improvement, or prevent deterioration, in health.[211]

Perhaps this is based on the presumption that V would consent if he knew of the circumstances, a principle which excuses conduct in other parts of the criminal law.[212] This is consistent with the view[213] that intervention cannot be justified if it is against V's known wishes.

---

[205] *Derriviere* (1969) 53 Cr App R 637, CA.

[206] *R (on the Application of Williamson) v Secretary of State for Education and Employment* [2002] EWCA Civ 1820. Confirmed in *R (Williamson) v Secretary of State for Education* [2005] UKHL 15, Baroness Hale's speech warrants close attention on these matters. See also App No 8811/79, *Seven Individuals v Sweden* 29 DR 104, EComHR. The ECHR issues are discussed in Emmerson, Ashworth and Macdonald, HR&CJ, paras 18–19. See also the conviction of Syed Mustafa Zaidi for child cruelty after he forced two boys (13 and 15) to whip themselves during a religious ritual. See news reports for 28 August 2008.

[207] *Reasonable Chastisement Research Report* (2007), www.cps.gov.uk/publications/research/chastisement. html.

[208] *Cleary v Booth* [1893] 1 QB 465; *Newport (Salop) Justices* [1929] 2 KB 416; *Mansell v Griffin* [1908] 1 KB 160.

[209] As substituted by the School Standards and Framework Act 1998.

[210] As inserted by the Violent Crime Reduction Act 2006, s 45.

[211] *F v West Berkshire Health Authority* [1990] 2 AC 1, [1989] 2 All ER 545 at 564, 566, HL, per Lord Goff.

[212] eg the Theft Act 1968, ss 2(1)(b), 12(6), Criminal Damage Act 1971, s 5(2)(b).

[213] *F v West Berks*, above, at 566, per Lord Goff.

So it seems that a passer-by who prevents V, a sane adult, from committing suicide by dragging him from the parapet of a bridge is guilty of battery.[214]

17.2.4 Self-help

The circumstances in which a person may use reasonable force to protect himself or his property are dealt with in Chapter 12. The Criminal Justice and Immigration Act 2008 regulates most such circumstances. The recent case of *Burns*[215] dealt with a situation falling outside the scope of that Act. B was not in danger or protecting himself, others or his property. B was convicted of causing actual bodily harm to a prostitute V. B had picked her up, agreed a price for sex and driven her to a secluded place. He then changed his mind about the sex act and asked her to get out of his car. She refused to get out until he drove her back to where they had met. He forcibly removed her, causing minor injury. The Court of Appeal, having referred to authority from the seventeenth century dismissed B's argument that he was entitled to use force as V became a trespasser on his property when he asked her to leave and she refused. B had not acted in self-defence nor in defence of anyone else; he had not been defending his property against threat or risk of damage; he was not acting for any purpose within s 3 of the Criminal Law Act 1967. The defence was one of 'self help'. That defence was always a last resort. It was a defence which the common law would be reluctant to extend. Lord Judge CJ added:

Recognising that to be lawful the use of force must always be reasonable in the circumstances, we accept that it might be open to the owner of a vehicle, in the last resort and when all reasonably practicable alternatives have failed, forcibly to remove an individual who has entered into his vehicle without permission and refuses to leave it. However, where that individual entered the car as a passenger, in effect at the invitation of the car owner, on the basis that they mutually understood that when their dealings were completed she would be driven back in the car from whence she had come, the use of force to remove her at the appellant's unilateral whim, was unlawful.

17.3 Assault occasioning actual bodily harm

By s 47 of the OAPA 1861, 'whosoever shall be convicted on indictment of any assault occasioning actual bodily harm shall be liable to imprisonment for not more than five years'.

17.3.1 *Actus reus*

17.3.1.1 Assault or battery

On its face, the section does not appear to create a separate offence but merely to provide a higher penalty for an assault at common law where actual bodily harm is occasioned ie caused. Consequently the offence was treated as a common law offence until the decision in *Courtie*,[216] and indeed for a period thereafter because it took some time for 'the penny to drop'. We now know that s 47 created a separate statutory offence[217] or, more accurately, two offences, assault occasioning actual bodily harm and battery occasioning actual bodily harm. Confusion on this still persists. For example, Lord Ackner in *Savage*[218] at one point describes

---

[214] cf Williams, TBCL, 616. Otherwise, perhaps, if V is in police custody: *Kirkham v Chief Constable of the Greater Manchester Police* [1990] 2 QB 283, CA.

[215] [2010] EWCA Crim 1023.

[216] [1984] AC 463, [1984] 1 All ER 740, HL, above, p 52.

[217] *Harrow Justices, ex p Osaseri* [1986] QB 589, [1985] 3 All ER 185, DC.

[218] [1992] 1 AC 699, [1991] 4 All ER 698 at 707 and 711.

the *mens rea* of the offence exclusively in terms of the battery and, at another, exclusively in terms of the assault. It is safe to assume that there are two offences and that their constituents, so far as the word 'assault' goes, are precisely the same as those of common assault and battery discussed above. Most cases will involve battery, but not all. An assault occasioning actual bodily harm might be committed by words or gestures alone, without the need for any physical contact between the assailant and the body of the victim. D may cause V to apprehend immediate unlawful violence and V might injure himself in making reasonable escape attempts.

17.3.1.2 Occasioning

Once an assault or battery with appropriate *mens rea* is proved, it remains only to prove that it occasioned actual bodily harm. That is a question of causation[219] not requiring proof of any further *mens rea* or fault. This was established in *Roberts*,[220] where D in a moving car 'assaulted' V by trying to take off her coat (a battery), whereupon she jumped out and sustained injury. It was held that the only question was whether the 'assault' caused V's action – only if it was something that no reasonable person could be expected to foresee would the chain of causation be broken.[221] It is now firmly established that this is the law, after a remarkable series of cases had thrown the matter into doubt.[222] In *Savage* and *Parmenter*, the House of Lords held that the law was correctly stated in *Roberts*.[223]

The offence may be committed in circumstances of omission where D has created a dangerous situation, as in the case of *Santana-Bermudez v DPP*.[224]

17.3.1.3 Bodily harm

'Bodily harm', according to the House of Lords in *DPP v Smith*[225] 'needs no explanation'. Since '[g]rievous means no more and no less than really serious' it seems to follow that, under s 47, the harm need not be really serious. In *Miller*,[226] it was described as any hurt or injury calculated to interfere with the health or comfort of the victim. This is a very low threshold for an offence carrying a five-year maximum sentence. It includes a temporary loss of consciousness.[227] It would seem sufficient that the harm was more than merely transient and trifling.[228] It can include the cutting of a substantial amount of hair.[229] In *DPP v Smith*, the court held that having regard to the dictionary definitions, in ordinary language 'harm' was not limited to 'injury' and extended to 'hurt' or 'damage'. 'Bodily', whether used as an adjective or adverb, was 'concerned with the body'. It is settled law that evidence of external bodily injury,

---

[219] cf the view of J Gardner, 'Rationality and the Rule of Law in Offences Against the Person' [1994] CLJ 502 at 509; J Gardner, *Offences and Defences, Selected Essays in the Philosophy of Criminal Law* (2007). See also J Stanton Ife, 'Horrific Crimes' in Duff et al *Boundaries of the Criminal Law* (2010).

[220] (1971) 56 Cr App R 95, [1972] Crim LR 27.

[221] cf *Williams and Davies* (1991) 95 Cr App R 1.

[222] In *Spratt* [1991] 2 All ER 220. the court, very properly overruling *DPP v K* [1990] 1 All ER 331, held that only *Cunningham*, not *Caldwell*, recklessness would suffice to establish the assault but then went on, not referring to *Roberts*, to hold there must be recklessness as to the occasioning of actual bodily harm. *Savage* [1991] 2 All ER 210, decided on the same day, applied the law as stated in *Roberts* but without reference to that case. In *Parmenter* [1992] 1 AC 699, [1991] 2 All ER 225, CA. the court, confronted with this conflict, preferred *Spratt*, again without reference to *Roberts*.

[223] [1991] 4 All ER 698, reversing *Parmenter* and overruling *Spratt* on this point.

[224] [2003] Crim LR 471, discussed above.

[225] [1961] AC 290 at 334, [1960] 3 All ER 161 at 171.

[226] [1954] 2 QB 282.

[227] *T v DPP* [2003] Crim LR 622.

[228] ibid.

[229] *DPP v Smith* [2006] EWHC 94 (Admin). Presumably the same is true if D damages V's hair substantially by applying a permanent colouring.

or a break in or bruise to the surface of the skin, is not required for there to be actual bodily harm. 'Bodily' encompasses all parts of the body including the victim's organs, his nervous system and his brain. Physical pain consequent on an assault is not a necessary ingredient of the offence, otherwise there could be no conviction where V was unconscious. Bodily harm can occur whether the tissue is alive beneath the surface of the skin or dead tissue above the surface of the skin; thus hair is an attribute and part of the human body. There is no need for the harm to be permanent: a bruise suffices. The fact that hair will regrow is irrelevant; cutting hair is bodily harm.

It has been held that actual bodily harm is not limited to physical injury. It includes psychiatric injury. This represents a significant judicial extension of the offence. Neurotic disorders are included because they affect the central nervous system of the body, but emotions such as fear and anxiety ('brain functions') are not. While physical injury is within the ordinary experience of a jury, psychiatric injury is not; so, if the prosecution wish to rely on it, they must call expert evidence to prove that the alleged condition amounts to psychiatric injury.[230] Even where the victim can give evidence of physical and mental symptoms of psychiatric injury, expert evidence is necessary to prove causation.[231] The Court of Appeal has declined to extend the scope of the offence: psychological injury, not amounting to an identified or recognized psychological condition, cannot amount to 'bodily harm'.[232]

The CPS Charging Standard recommends that s 47 be charged for injury such as: loss or breaking of tooth or teeth; temporary loss of sensory functions, which may include loss of consciousness; extensive or multiple bruising; displaced broken nose; minor fractures; minor, but not merely superficial, cuts of a sort probably requiring medical treatment (for example, stitches); psychiatric injury that is more than mere emotions such as fear, distress or panic.[233]

17.3.2 *Mens rea*

The only *mens rea* that needs to be proved is that necessary for the assault or battery.

The absence of any requirement that D intends or foresees the additional harm for which he is punished over and above an assault or battery demonstrates the lack of correspondence of *actus reus* and *mens rea* in the offence and the conflict with the general principles of subjectivism.[234] This is a very clear example of a constructive crime.

17.4 Wounding and grievous bodily harm: OAPA 1861, s 20

Section 20 of the Offences Against the Person Act 1861 creates two forms of offence: wounding and inflicting grievous bodily harm. By s 20:

Whosoever shall unlawfully and maliciously wound or inflict any grievous bodily harm upon any other person, either with or without any weapon or instrument shall be guilty of [an offence triable either way] and being convicted thereof shall be liable to imprisonment for five years.

---

[230] *Ireland* [1998] AC 147, [1997] 4 All ER 225 at 23–233, HL, approving *Chan-Fook* [1994] 2 All ER 552, [1994] Crim LR 432.

[231] *Morris* [1998] 1 Cr App R 386.

[232] *Dhaliwal* [2006] 2 Cr App R 348, [2006] EWCA Crim 1139.

[233] (2005). See www.cps.gov.uk/legal/l_to_o/offences_against_the_person/#P189_14382.

[234] Its constructive nature is defended on the basis that D has 'altered his normative position' towards V by choosing to assault V, and therefore must take the consequences of the further harm. See Gardner [1994] CLJ 502; J Horder, 'A Critique of the Correspondence Principle in Criminal Law' [1995] Crim LR 759. cf B Mitchell, 'In Defence of a Principle of Correspondence' [1999] Crim LR 195. See on this the important article by A Ashworth, 'A Change of Normative Position: Determining the Contours of Culpability in Criminal Law' [2008] 11 New Crim LR 232. See also I Hare, 'A Compelling Case for the Code' (1993) 56 MLR 74.

The two ways of committing the offence are: (i) malicious wounding, and (ii) maliciously inflicting grievous bodily harm.

The element of unlawfulness should not be overlooked and should always be drawn to the jury's attention.[235]

17.4.1 Malicious wounding

17.4.1.1 To wound

In order to constitute a wound, the continuity of the whole skin must be broken.[236] Where a pellet fired by an air pistol hit V in the eye but caused only an internal rupturing of blood vessels and not a break in the skin, there was no wound.[237] It is not enough that the cuticle or outer skin be broken if the inner skin remains intact.[238] Where V was treated with such violence that his collarbone was broken, it was held that there was no wound if his skin was intact.[239] It was held to be a wound, however, where the lining membrane of the urethra was ruptured and bled. Evidence was given that that membrane is precisely the same in character as the membrane lining the cheek and the external and internal skin of the lip.[240] It is wrong to direct a jury that 'the surface of the skin' must be broken. On that direction a scratch would suffice which is clearly inadequate.[241]

Under a predecessor offence to s 20[242] it was held that there was no wounding where V, in warding off D's attempt to cut his throat, struck his hands against a knife held by D and cut them;[243] nor where V was knocked down by D and wounded by falling on iron trams.[244] That old offence did not contain the words 'by any means whatsoever', and it is probable that these cases would now be decided differently. Even under the earlier law, D was guilty where he struck V on the hat with a gun and the hard rim of the hat caused a wound.[245] It is unclear whether there can be a wounding by omission. It was formerly held that wounding must be the result of a battery but it is probably now sufficient that the wound be directly inflicted whether by a battery or not.[246]

It is doubtful whether this specific form of injury (or indeed others in the OAPA such as choking and throwing acid) warrants a separate offence in a modern code of offences. Some suggest that the specificity of label and the distinctions between the harms and the manner in which they are inflicted reflect important moral differences.[247]

17.4.1.2 Malice

It is settled that this word means 'intentionally or recklessly' and 'reckless' is used in the *Cunningham* sense of course.[248] In *Brady*,[249] the Court of Appeal held that G does not require

---

[235] *Stokes* [2003] EWCA Crim 2977.

[236] *Moriarty v Brooks* (1834) 6 C & P 684.

[237] *C (A Minor) v Eisenhower* [1984] QB 331, 78 Cr App R 48, DC.

[238] *M'Loughlin* (1838) 8 C & P 635.

[239] *Wood* (1830) 1 Mood CC 278.

[240] *Waltham* (1849) 3 Cox CC 442. Contrast *Jones* (1849) 3 Cox CC 441.

[241] *Morris* [2005] EWCA Crim 609.

[242] 7 Will 4 & 1 Vic, c 85, s 4.

[243] *Beckett* (1836) 1 Mood & R 526 (Parke B); *Day* (1845) 1 Cox CC 207. cf *Coleman* (1920) 84 JP 112.

[244] *Spooner* (1853) 6 Cox CC 392.

[245] *Sheard* (1837) 2 Mood CC 13.

[246] *Wilson*, below, p 650 cf *Taylor* (1869) LR 1 CCR 194; *Austin* (1973) 58 Cr App R 163, CA.

[247] See the illuminating account by Gardner [1994] CLJ 502 and in J Gardner *Offences and Defences* (2007) Ch 2.

[248] Above, [1992] 1 AC 699. *Savage* and *Parmenter* [1991] 4 All ER at 721, HL, affirming *Mowatt* [1968] 1 QB 421, [1967] 3 All ER 47.

[249] [2006] EWCA Crim 2413.

proof that D had foreseen 'an obvious and significant risk' in order to establish that he had acted recklessly. D was drunk when he climbed on railings at a nightclub and fell onto the dance floor below causing serious injuries to V. The court allowed the appeal, because the judge had failed to direct the jury as to recklessness in sufficiently clear and careful terms.

D must intend or be reckless, but what is 'the particular kind of harm' that must be intended or foreseen? As a matter of general principle, the answer might be expected to be that it is necessary that D has *mens rea* as to all the elements of the *actus reus* – including the wounding or grievous bodily harm.[250] The law has developed differently. It is enough that D foresaw that *some* bodily harm, not necessarily amounting to grievous bodily harm or wounding, might occur.[251] Diplock LJ said in *Mowatt*:[252]

the word 'maliciously' does import upon the part of the person who unlawfully inflicts the wound or other grievous bodily harm an awareness that his act may have the consequence of causing some physical harm to some other person. That is what is meant by 'the particular kind of harm' in the citation from Professor Kenny.[253] It is quite unnecessary that the accused should have foreseen that his unlawful act might cause physical harm of the gravity described in [s 20], ie, a wound or serious physical injury. It is enough that he should have foreseen that some physical harm to some person, albeit of a minor character, might result.

It is sufficient to prove that D foresaw that *some* harm *might* result. To tell the jury that it must be proved that D foresaw that it *would* result is too generous to the defendant.[254] It is not enough, however, whether the charge is one of wounding or inflicting grievous bodily harm[255] that D intended to frighten (unless he foresaw that the fright might result in psychiatric injury).

17.4.2 Maliciously inflicting grievous bodily harm

'Grievous bodily harm' was formerly interpreted to include any harm which seriously interferes with health or comfort;[256] but, in *Smith*,[257] the House of Lords said that the words should bear their ordinary and natural meaning. It is not always necessary for the jury to be told to look for 'really' serious harm,[258] and it is not clear precisely what that word means when it is included. The jury may take into consideration the totality of the injuries,[259] provided they have been inflicted in one attack or the charge accurately reflects the relevant period.[260] Although the determination of whether the injury constitutes grievous bodily harm is to be assessed objectively, and not merely on the basis of the victim's perception,[261] the characteristics of the victim may be taken into account – what is grievous bodily harm to a child might

---

[250] cf above, p 134.

[251] Above, n 234.

[252] [1968] 1 QB 421 at 426, [1967] 3 All ER 47 at 50. Reiterated recently post-*G* in *C* [2007] EWCA Crim 1068. See also *Dakou* [2002] EWCA Crim 3156, oversimplifying the issue of malice in s 18. Courts continue to make errors with this – see recently *DPP v W* [2006] EWHC 92 (Admin), where magistrates had acquitted on the basis that D had not foreseen the level of harm V suffered.

[253] *Outlines*, 211. The citation is the passage approved by the Court of Criminal Appeal in *Cunningham* [1957] 2 QB 396, [1957] 2 All ER 412; above, p 119.

[254] *Rushworth* (1992) 95 Cr App R 252 at 255, cited in *Pearson* [1994] Crim LR 534 which nevertheless left this point in the air. Earlier *dicta* by Lords Diplock and Ackner are ambiguous.

[255] *Flack v Hunt* (1979) 70 Cr App R 51; *Sullivan* [1981] Crim LR 46, CA.

[256] *Ashman* (1858) 1 F & F 88.

[257] [1961] AC 290, [1960] 3 All ER 161; above, n 225; followed in *Metharam* [1961] 3 All ER 200.

[258] *Janua* [1999] 1 Cr App R 91.

[259] *Grundy* [1977] Crim LR 543; *Birmingham* [2002] EWCA Crim 2608.

[260] See *Brown* [2005] EWCA Crim 359 (abuse of V over several days).

[261] *Brown* [1998] Crim LR 484.

not be for an adult.[262] There is no need for the injury to be permanent or life threatening.[263] Unconsciousness is capable of constituting grievous bodily harm.[264]

Grievous bodily harm may cover cases where there is no wounding as, for instance, the broken collarbone in *Wood*.[265] Conversely, there might be a technical 'wounding' which could not be said to amount to grievous bodily harm – as with an injection by a needle.[266] The absence of any clear definition of the term and the associated risk of inconsistent applications and a lack of predictability in verdicts is lamentable.

It is settled that *serious* psychiatric injury amounts to grievous bodily harm.[267] This results in the possibility of convictions for inflicting grievous bodily harm by telephone – for example, a series of extreme obscene phone calls.[268] There is no legal difficulty with the *actus reus* – that is established simply by proving that D inflicted the serious psychiatric injury. Proof of *mens rea* in such a case may be more difficult.

Although the level of harm is ill-defined and rests on the jury's interpretation in each individual case, it has been held in Northern Ireland not to be contrary to Art 7 for want of certainty.[269]

17.4.2.1 Inflict

In a series of cases[270] from 1861 until 1983, it was held or assumed that the words 'inflict' and 'wound' both imply an 'assault'. D could be convicted of an offence under s 20 only if it was proved that he wounded or caused grievous bodily harm by committing an assault. *Clarence*[271] held that D caused V harm by infecting her with gonorrhoea, but did not *inflict* it unless there was an assault. But a second line of cases[272] simply ignored the requirement of an assault and upheld convictions where D so frightened V that V jumped through a window,[273] or accidentally injured himself by putting his hand through a glass door under a 'well-grounded apprehension of violence'.[274] In *Martin*[275] where, shortly before the end of a performance in a theatre, D put out the lights and placed an iron bar across the doorway, he was convicted of inflicting grievous bodily harm on those injured in the panic. In 1983 the House of Lords in *Wilson*[276] resolved the matter by deciding, following the Australian case of *Salisbury*,[277] that 'inflict' does not, after all, imply an assault.[278]

---

[262] *Bollom* [2004] 2 Cr App R 50.

[263] ibid.

[264] *Hicks* [2007] EWCA Crim 1500 – the issue being raised by the jury! See also *Foster* [2009] EWCA Crim 2214, para 28 discussing the levels of unconsciousness and whether the 'Glasgow coma score' might assist in determining the severity of the unconsciousness in law.

[265] Above, n 239.

[266] Although that is often charged under s 47. See, eg, *Gower* [2007] EWCA Crim 1655.

[267] *Ireland*, above, p 623.

[268] *Gelder* (1994) The Times, 25 May (news item).

[269] See *Anderson* [2003] NICA 12.

[270] *Yeadon and Birch* (1861) 9 Cox CC 91; *Taylor* (1869) LR 1 CCR 194; *Clarence* (1888) 22 QBD 23; *Snewing* [1972] Crim LR 267; *Carpenter* (1979) 76 Cr App R 320n, cited [1983] 1 All ER 1004.

[271] (1888) 22 QBD 23.

[272] *Halliday* (1889) 61 LT 701; *Lewis* [1970] Crim LR 647, CA; *Mackie* [1973] Crim LR 54; *Boswell* [1973] Crim LR 307 and *Cartledge v Allen* [1973] Crim LR 530, DC.

[273] *Halliday* (1889) 61 LT 701.

[274] *Cartledge v Allen* [1973] Crim LR 530.

[275] (1881) 8 QBD 54, CCR.

[276] [1984] AC 242 at 260, [1983] 3 All ER 448 at 455.

[277] [1976] VR 452 at 461.

[278] The House nevertheless contrived to hold that a person charged under s 20 could be convicted on that indictment of a common assault by virtue of s 6(3) of the Criminal Law Act 1967 – a much-criticized decision but

Arguably, the case decided no more than that; but Lord Roskill cited the opinion of the Australian court that 'inflict' has a narrower meaning than 'cause' (as used in s 18 below) and requires 'force being violently applied to the body of the victim'. In *Burstow*,[279] the House of Lords decided that 'inflict' does not bear this narrow meaning and that grievous bodily harm might be inflicted over the telephone or by other harassment, not involving the use of violence to the body or an assault. It remains necessary, as noticed above, to prove that D foresaw that he might cause some harm, not necessarily serious psychiatric injury.

The distinction between 'cause' and 'inflict' seems then to have been substantially eliminated. The House thought that, while the words are not synonymous, there is 'no radical divergence' of meaning. Perhaps this is to be read to mean no 'material' difference.[280] If the courts were interpreting a modern statute, the use of different words in adjacent sections might compel the conclusion that different meanings were intended; but no such inference can be drawn in the 1861 Act because it was never intended, and does not purport, to be a consistent whole.[281] *Clarence* can no longer be justified on the ground that there was no assault or violent application of force or that V consented.[282] It was not overruled but it appears to have been wrongly decided.[283] Following *Dica*, it now seems clear that as a matter of practice the terms can be treated as synonymous in almost every instance.

In *Brady*, above, the Court of Appeal questioned, *obiter*, whether it may be arguable that there was no *actus reus*, that is, no 'deliberate non-accidental conduct on the part of the accused that inflicted grievous bodily harm'. On D's account, he had deliberately perched precariously on a low railing above a crowded dance floor having consumed considerable quantities of alcohol and drugs. D argued that the act of falling was not deliberate and must, therefore, have been accidental; and that, since the *actus reus* of the offence contrary to s 20 required the inflicting of grievous bodily harm, the physical act of the falling that had caused the injury was not a direct assault. With respect, that argument is difficult to follow. There is no doubt that V suffered grievous bodily harm as she was rendered paraplegic. There is also no doubt that that injury was inflicted by D. The question is whether it was inflicted by D's blameworthy conduct. If the jury were satisfied that D realized that in perching as he did there was a risk of his falling and causing injury to a person below, and that he went on unreasonably to take that risk it is submitted that he would have committed the s 20 offence. Although the act of perching may look innocuous viewed in isolation, that is not the *actus reus* of the offence: the *actus reus* is D's whole conduct in perching *and* the resulting harm to the victim on the dance floor. The incident of D losing his balance and falling does not represent a break in the chain of causation; it is the very incident about which D was alleged to have

approved by the House in *Savage* [1991] 4 All ER 698 at 711. See G Williams, 'Alternative Elements and Included Offences' [1984] CLJ 290 and commentary at [1984] Crim LR 37.

[279] Heard and decided together with *Ireland* [1998] AC 147. Arguably the case is restricted to those cases involving the infliction of psychiatric injury. This would create an undesirable confusion in the law.

[280] Lord Hope, however, said that 'inflict' implies that the consequence of the act is something that the victim is likely find unpleasant or harmful whereas 'cause' may embrace pleasure as well as pain. But, if that is so, the sadomasochists in *Brown* [1994] 1 AC 212, above, could not have been held to have been guilty of *inflicting* grievous bodily harm, contrary to s 20, because everyone was having a jolly good time. This would be surprising, as they were guilty of wounding, contrary to the same subsection on the ground that consent was no defence.

[281] CS Greaves, *The Criminal Law Consolidation and Amendment Acts* (2nd edn, 1862) at 3–4, cited by Lord Steyn at 234.

[282] cf above, p 633.

[283] The draft Bill in the Home Office Consultation Paper of Feb 1998 expressly excludes from the proposed offences recklessly (but not intentionally) causing anything by disease. See now *Dica* [2004] EWCA Crim 1103 above p 633.

been reckless/malicious. His reckless conduct in perching as he did caused the loss of balance which caused the fall and the resulting injury.[284]

17.4.2.2 Co-existence of s 20 and s 47

The co-existence of s 47 with that of maliciously inflicting grievous bodily harm contrary to s 20 of the same Act, also punishable with a maximum of five years' imprisonment, makes little sense.[285] The prosecutor's task is slightly easier under s 47 since it is not necessary to prove even the foresight of some bodily harm which is necessary under s 20. Proof of an assault or battery is required under s 47, but is not necessary under s 20; and s 20 no longer requires proof of a direct application of force. Section 20 is regarded in practice as the more serious offence. In *Parmenter*,[286] the Court of Appeal said that:

although the sentences imposed in practice for the worst s 47 offences will overlap those imposed at the lower end of s 20, nobody could doubt that the two offences are seen in quite different terms, whether by defendants and their advisers contemplating pleas of guilty, or by judges passing sentence under s 47 on defendants whose pleas of guilty have been accepted by the prosecution, or by subsequent sentencers casting an eye down lists of previous convictions.

This is reflected in the CPS Charging Standard which recommends s 20 in cases such as: injury resulting in permanent disability or permanent loss of sensory function; injury which results in more than minor permanent, visible disfigurement; broken or displaced limbs or bones, including a fractured skull; compound fractures, broken cheek bone, jaw, ribs, etc; injuries which cause substantial loss of blood, usually necessitating a transfusion; injuries resulting in lengthy treatment or incapacity; psychiatric injury.[287]

17.5 Section 18 of the Offences Against the Person Act 1861

By s 18, as amended by the Criminal Law Act 1967:

Whosoever shall unlawfully and maliciously by any means whatsoever wound or cause any grievous bodily harm to any person with intent to do some grievous bodily harm to any person or with intent to resist or prevent the lawful apprehension or detainer of any person, shall be guilty of [an offence triable only on indictment], and being convicted thereof shall be liable to imprisonment of life.

The elements of the *actus reus* have been considered in relation to s 20 above.

17.5.1 *Mens rea*

The *mens rea* of the offence differs slightly depending on which form of the offence is charged.

17.5.1.1 Intention

In every case the Crown must establish an ulterior intent which may be either intent to do grievous bodily harm or intent to resist or prevent the lawful apprehension or detainer of

---

[284] Part of the problem in the court's analysis is that the events are all categorized as either deliberate or accidental. It is unclear what is meant by this, but it stems from the limited way in which the case was presented.

[285] cf the view of Gardner [1994] CLJ 500, and Ashworth, n 234.

[286] [1991] 2 All ER at 233.

[287] See CPS Charging Standard, www.cps.gov.uk/legal/l_to_o/offences_against_the_person/#P189_14382.

any person. Recklessness is not enough.[288] Where the allegation is of intentionally causing grievous bodily harm, it is sufficient that D intended to cause the harm he did, irrespective of whether *he* would regard that as really serious harm. As noted above in the context of s 20, proving an intention to cause psychiatric injury may be very difficult.

Intention has the same meaning as in the law of murder.[289] The prosecution must prove either: (i) that it was D's purpose to cause grievous bodily harm, or, if it was not his purpose, (ii) that he knew that grievous bodily harm was a virtually certain consequence of his act. In case (ii), the jury may then find that he had the requisite intent.[290] The jury need not be directed on this oblique intention definition except in rare cases.[291]

If D intends to cause grievous bodily harm to X and, striking at X, he accidentally wounds another person, V, he may be indicted for wounding V with intent to cause grievous bodily harm to X.[292] If D intends to cause grievous bodily harm to X, and strikes the person he aims at, who is in fact V, he may be convicted of wounding V with intent to cause grievous bodily harm to V.[293]

Where the indictment specifies a particular form of the offence, the intent prescribed in that form of the offence must be proved; it is not enough to prove another variety of intent described in the section.[294] So D had to be acquitted where the charge was intent to do some grievous bodily harm and the jury found that the acts were done to resist and prevent D's apprehension *and for no other purpose*.[295] But if D intends to prevent his apprehension and, in order to do so, intends to cause grievous bodily harm, he may be convicted under an indictment charging only the latter intent. It is immaterial which is the principal and which the subordinate intent.[296]

A count was held not to be bad for duplicity because it specified the ulterior intent in the alternative, the intents specified 'are variations of method rather than creations of separate offences in themselves'.[297]

The courts continue to create difficulties with the form of the *mens rea*. In *Taylor*[298] the judge had directed that the jury on a s 18 charge must be sure that the prosecution had proved that D had intended to cause grievous bodily harm or to wound. This was a misdirection to the jury.

An intent to wound is insufficient. There must be an intent to cause really serious bodily injury.[299]

---

[288] *Re Knight's Appeal* (1968) FLR 81.

[289] *Bryson* [1985] Crim LR 669; cf *Belfon* [1976] 3 All ER 46, CA.

[290] Above, p 107.

[291] See *Phillips* [2004] EWCA Crim 112.

[292] *Monger* [1973] Crim LR 301, per Mocatta J holding that D could not be convicted where the indictment alleged intent to harm V. This is in accord with *Ryan* (1839) 2 Mood & R 213 and *Hewlett* (1858) 1 F & F 91 but contrary to *Hunt* (1825) 1 Mood CC 93 and *Jarvis, Langdon and Stear* (1837) 2 Mood & R 40. cf the doctrine of transferred malice, above, p 136 and the comment on *Monger* in [1973] Crim LR 301.

[293] *Smith* (1855) Dears CC 559 at 560; *Stopford* (1870) 11 Cox CC 643.

[294] There are numerous forms of the s 18 offence other than that commonly relied upon – grievous bodily harm with intent to do grievous bodily harm – dealing with the causing of injury with ulterior intents to resist arrest, etc, wounding with intention to do some grievous bodily harm; wounding with intent to resist lawful apprehension; wounding with intent to prevent lawful apprehension; wounding with intent to resist lawful detainer; wounding with intent to prevent lawful detainer; causing grievous bodily harm with intent to resist lawful apprehension; causing grievous bodily harm with intent to prevent lawful apprehension; causing grievous bodily harm with intent to resist lawful detainer; causing grievous bodily harm with intent to prevent lawful detainer.

[295] *Duffin and Marshall* (1818) Russ & Ry 365; cf *Boyce* (1824) 1 Mood CC 29.

[296] *Gillow* (1825) 1 Mood CC 85.

[297] *Naismith* [1961] 2 All ER 735, [1961] 1 WLR 952, C-MAC – though it is difficult to see how an ulterior intent can be equated with a 'method'.

[298] [2009] EWCA Crim 544. See also *Gregory* [2009] EWCA Crim 1374.

[299] ibid, [3].

There was no evidence, upon which the jury could have relied, to show that D had intended really serious injury. The conviction was quashed and was replaced with a conviction for unlawful wounding. In *Purcell*,[300] the Court of Appeal suggested that at a trial of a person charged with causing grievous bodily harm the following direction should be given to the jury on the issue of intent:

You must feel sure that the defendant intended to cause serious bodily harm to the victim. You can only decide what his intention was by considering all the relevant circumstances and in particular what he did and what he said about it.

17.5.1.2 Malice

The meaning of malice has been considered above in relation to s 20.

Where, under s 18, the charge is of causing grievous bodily harm with intent to do grievous bodily harm, the word 'maliciously' obviously has no part to play. Any *mens rea* which it might import is comprehended within the ulterior intent. Even if 'wounding' is not foreseen, it is 'malicious'. The Court of Appeal has emphasized that generally judges ought not to give a direction on malice under s 18 in these cases.[301]

Where the charge is of malicious wounding or causing grievous bodily harm with intent to resist lawful apprehension, there is no difficulty in giving meaning to 'maliciously' and it is submitted that meaning should be given to that word.[302] A mere intent to resist lawful apprehension should not found liability for a charge of wounding or causing grievous bodily harm. It is submitted that the Court of Appeal went too far in *Mowatt*[303] in saying that '[i]n section 18 the word "maliciously" adds nothing'.

The indictment should spell out the alleged *mens rea*.[304] It is clear that there must be proof that D actually foresaw the specified result. Any doubt there may have been about this was dispelled by the Criminal Justice Act 1967, s 8.[305] *Mowatt* was decided before the Act came into force, and certain observations in the case are therefore suspect. It was said[306] that where the act:

was a direct assault which any ordinary person would be bound to realize was likely to cause some physical harm to the other person ... and the defence put forward on behalf of the accused is not that the assault was accidental or that he did not realize that it might cause some physical harm to the victim, but is some other defence such as that he did not do the alleged act or that he did it in self-defence, it is unnecessary to deal specifically in the summing up with what is meant by the word 'maliciously' in the section.

This suggests that the jury need not be directed on the issue because they are bound to infer that D foresaw the result, by reason of its being a natural and probable consequence of his actions. This is directly contrary to the words of s 8. Under s 10 of the Criminal Justice Act 1967, formal admissions may be made; but, if D has not admitted his malice, then it is submitted that it must be proved like every other element in the crime. The fact that the evidence appears to the judge to be overwhelming is not a good reason for not leaving it to the jury.

---

[300] (1986) 83 Cr App R 45, CA.

[301] See *Brown* [2005] EWCA Crim 359, at [17].

[302] *Morrison* (1989) Cr App R 17. D seized by a WPC as she was arresting him. D dived through a window pane and the WPC was dragged with him suffering serious facial injury. D clearly *intended* to resist arrest, CA held he must also be subjectively (*Cunningham*) reckless as to the grievous bodily harm.

[303] [1968] 1 QB 421, [1967] 3 All ER 47. See R Buxton, 'Negligence and Constructive Crime' [1969] Crim LR 112. See also *Ward* (1872) LR 1 CCR 356.

[304] *Hodgson* [2008] EWCA Crim 895.

[305] Above, p 649.

[306] *Mowatt* [1968] IQB 421, per Diplock LJ.

17.5.2 Alternative verdicts

A charge of 'causing' grievous bodily harm with intent contrary to s 18 has been held to include a charge of 'inflicting' grievous bodily harm contrary to s 20[307] which, in turn, includes a charge of assault occasioning actual bodily harm contrary to s 47.[308] The effect is that, on an indictment for the s 18 offence, the jury may find D guilty of an offence under s 20, or under s 47; and, on an indictment for the s 20 offence, of an offence under s 47. Whether to direct the jury that, if they acquit of the offence charged they may convict of a lesser included offence is a matter for the discretion of the judge. Following *Coutts*,[309] if the possibility that D is guilty only of a lesser offence (s 20 or s 47) has been raised in the course of the evidence, the judge should leave the alternative offence to the jury, even in cases in which neither prosecution nor defence wants the alternative offence to be left to the jury.[310] The Court of Appeal has reiterated the importance of this recently.[311]

In *Lahaye*,[312] the Court of Appeal's *per curiam* recommendation seems to be that a s 20 offence ought to be included in the indictment from the outset in *any* s 18 case, and this goes beyond what was suggested by the House of Lords (Lords Mackay, Goff and Mustill) in *Mandair*,[313] namely that it may be desirable to include as an alternative where appropriate. Automatic inclusion of a s 20 count reduces the prosecution's freedom to select its indictment of choice, and increases the risk of compromise verdicts, but, it seems that such verdicts are already the practical reality.

Research has suggested that the moral distinction between the s 18 and s 20 offences has been eroded by the availability of the alternative verdicts and the frequency with which they are returned. In one study only 23 per cent of those indicted for s 18 were convicted of that offence, whilst 53 per cent were convicted of s 20 and only one in ten of the contested s 18 trials led to an outright acquittal.[314] Is the inclusion of a s 20 count in all s 18 cases desirable? Will it prevent appeals of this nature?

17.6 Torture and slavery

17.6.1 Torture

By s 134 of the Criminal Justice Act 1988 a new offence of torture was introduced into English law.

A public official or person acting in an official capacity, whatever his nationality, commits the offence of torture if in the United Kingdom or elsewhere he intentionally inflicts severe pain or suffering on another in the performance or purported performance of his official duties.

---

[307] *Mandair* (1994) 99 Cr App R 250, [1994] Crim LR 666, HL.

[308] *Wilson* [1984] AC 242, [1984] Crim LR 36, HL, above, p 650.

[309] [2006] 1 WLR 2154.

[310] See *Ali* [2006] EWCA Crim 2906; cf *Foster* [2007] EWCA Crim 2869.

[311] *Foster* [2009] EWCA Crim 2214; *Green* [2009] EWCA Crim 2609; *Mathew* [2010] EWCA Crim 29; *Hodson* [2009] EWCA Crim 1590, [2010] Crim LR 249 and commentary. If s 20 is a realistically available verdict on the evidence, as an interpretation properly open to the jury, without trivializing the offending conduct, then the alternative should be left to the jury. The court emphasizes that it is particularly important that an alternative verdict was left to a jury where the offence charged required proof of a specific intent (s 18) and the alternative offence (s 20) did not.

[312] [2005] EWCA Crim 2847.

[313] [1995] AC 208.

[314] E Genders, 'Reform of the Offences Against the Person Act: Lessons from the Law in Action' [1999] Crim LR 689.

The offence carries a maximum sentence of life imprisonment.

17.6.2 Slavery

To accompany the offence of torture (contrary to art 3 of the ECHR) we now have an offence of slavery contrary to Art 4.[315] The Coroners and Justice Act 2009, s 71 creates new offences of holding another in slavery, servitude or compulsory labour where D knew or ought to have known that the person is so held. The offences are enacted to ensure compliance with Art 4 of the EHCR.[316] The maximum penalty on indictment is 14 years' imprisonment. Section 71 provides:

> (1) A person (D) commits an offence if –
>
> > (a) D holds another person in slavery or servitude and the circumstances are such that D knows or ought to know that the person is so held, or
> >
> > (b) D requires another person to perform forced or compulsory labour and the circumstances are such that D knows or ought to know that the person is being required to perform such labour.
>
> (2) In subsection (1) the references to holding a person in slavery or servitude or requiring a person to perform forced or compulsory labour are to be construed in accordance with Article 4 of the Human Rights Convention (which prohibits a person from being held in slavery or servitude or being required to perform forced or compulsory labour).

This is more than a symbolic gesture. There are reported cases in English law, where vulnerable individuals have been kept in dreadful conditions in servitude as 'slaves'. Until now prosecutions had been pursued for false imprisonment and assault.[317]

17.7 Reform

The case for reform of these offences against the person (assault, battery, s 47, s 20, s 18) is compelling.[318] The Law Commission commented that the law 'was defective on grounds both of effectiveness and of justice'.[319] The Home Office, *Consultation Paper on Violence*,[320] proposed a structured hierarchy of offences as follows:

> 1. – (1) A person is guilty of an offence if he intentionally causes serious injury to another.
>
> (2) A person is guilty of an offence if he omits to do an act which he has a duty to do at common law, the omission results in serious injury to another, and he intends the omission to have that result...
>
> (4) A person guilty of an offence under this section is liable on conviction on indictment to imprisonment for life.

---

[315] The Coroners and Justice Act 2009 (Commencement No 4, Transitional and Saving Provisions) Order 2010 (SI 2010, No 816) brought s 71 of the Act into force on 6 April 2010.

[316] See *Siliadin v France* (2006) 43 EHRR 16.

[317] eg *Pearson-Gaballonie* [2007] EWCA Crim 3504

[318] Genders [1999] Crim LR 689.

[319] LCCP 122, *Legislating the Criminal Code: Offences Against the Person and General Principles* (1992), on which see S Gardner, 'Reiterating the Criminal Code' (1992) 55 MLR 839; ATH Smith, 'Legislating the Criminal Code' [1992] Crim LR 396. See also LC 218, *Offences Against the Person and General Principles* (1993).

[320] (1998) on which see JC Smith, 'Offences Against The Person: The Home Office Consultation Paper' [1998] Crim LR 317.

2. – (1) A person is guilty of an offence if he recklessly causes serious injury to another....

(3) A person guilty of an offence under this section is liable –

    (a) on conviction on indictment, to imprisonment for a term not exceeding 7 years;

    (b) on summary conviction, to imprisonment for a term not exceeding 6 months or a fine not exceeding the statutory maximum or both.

3. – (1) A person is guilty of an offence if he intentionally or recklessly causes injury to another....

(3) A person guilty of an offence under this section is liable–

    (a) on conviction on indictment, to imprisonment for a term not exceeding 5 years;

    (b) on summary conviction, to imprisonment for a term not exceeding 6 months or a fine not exceeding the statutory maximum or both.

4. – (1) A person is guilty of an offence if –

    (a) he intentionally or recklessly applies force to or causes an impact on the body of another, or

    (b) he intentionally or recklessly causes the other to believe that any such force or impact is imminent.

(2) No such offence is committed if the force or impact, not being intended or likely to cause injury, is in the circumstances such as is generally acceptable in the ordinary conduct of daily life and the defendant does not know or believe that it is in fact unacceptable to the other person.

(3) A person guilty of an offence under this section is liable on summary conviction to imprisonment for a term not exceeding 6 months or a fine not exceeding level 5 on the standard scale or both.

15. – (1) In this Act 'injury' means –

    (a) physical injury, or

    (b) mental injury.

(2) Physical injury does not include anything caused by disease but (subject to that) it includes pain, unconsciousness and any other impairment of a person's physical condition.

(3) Mental injury does not include anything caused by disease but (subject to that) it includes any impairment of a person's mental health.

(4) In its application to section 1 this section applies without the exceptions relating to things caused by disease.

Recently, suggestions have been made for a further specific offence against the person to be included in the reform programme. It is argued for example, that domestic violence is a distinctive form of wrongdoing because of the contexts in which it arises, its systematic nature and the destruction of trust it creates.[321] A new dedicated offence might also serve to educate the public and police attitudes.[322] One of the difficulties would obviously be how to define such an offence.[323]

---

[321] See also on domestic violence M Madden Dempsey, *Prosecuting Domestic Violence: A philosophical Analysis* (2009).

[322] See V Tadros, 'The Distinctiveness of Domestic Abuse: a Freedom Based Account', in Duff and Green, *Defining Crimes*, 119.

[323] The Sentencing Guidelines Council provided specific guidelines for domestic violence cases – defined so as to include threatening behaviour, violence or abuse (psychological, physical, sexual, financial or emotional) between adults who are intimate partners or family members regardless of gender or sexuality.

17.8 Racially or religiously aggravated assaults[324]

The Crime and Disorder Act 1998 created a new category of racially aggravated crimes, and the Anti-terrorism Crime and Security Act 2001 extended these to include religiously aggravated offences.[325] Racist crime is increasing alarmingly.[326]

Many commentators questioned the value of these additional offences as the element of racial hostility, or religious hostility, could be taken into account as a matter of sentencing aggravation as it is with sexual orientation and disability hate crime under s 146 of the Criminal Justice Act 2003.[327] Professor Sir John Smith, QC went so far as to say, 'it is deplorable that the government is able to find time for ill-considered, "politically correct" legislation of this kind'.[328] Doubts as to the value of the offences were also raised because they apply so widely. The Lord Chief Justice in *Rogers*[329] acknowledged the concern that the broad interpretation of the section will result in prosecutions for racially aggravated offences in circumstances which the legislation had not intended:

[t]he very width of the meaning of racial group for the purposes of section 28(4) gives rise to a danger that charges of aggravated offences may be brought where vulgar abuse has included racial epithets that did not, when all the relevant circumstances are considered, indicate hostility to the race in question.

However, in a clear statement the House of Lords has now given unequivocal support for such offences. Baroness Hale opined that they properly reflect the 'qualitatively distinct order of gravity' involved when racial hostility is demonstrated.[330] In addition, establishing separate offences rather than leaving matters of racial aggravation purely for sentencing means that the jury must be satisfied of that distinctive stigmatizing aspect of the alleged wrongdoing.

17.8.1 The offences

Section 28(1) of the Crime and Disorder Act provides two forms which the racial and religious aggravation can take. The difference between the two is extremely important but unfortunately appears to be frequently overlooked.[331] Section 28(1)(a) applies where at the time of[332] committing the relevant offence (assault, s 47, s 20, public order offences, harassment, etc) or immediately[333] before or after doing so, the offender demonstrates towards the

---

[324] See generally, E Burney, 'Using the Law of Racially Aggravated Offences' [2003] Crim LR 28.

[325] See generally, M Malik, 'Racist Crime: Racially Aggravated Offences in the Crime and Disorder Act 1998' (1999) 62 MLR 409; M Idriss, 'Religion and the Anti-Terrorism Crime and Security Act 2001' [2002] Crim LR 890; A Tomkins, 'Legislating Against Terror: The Anti-terrorism Crime and Security Act 2001' [2002] PL 205; PW Edge, 'Extending Hate Crime to Religion' (2003) 10 J Civ Lib 5.

[326] See T Fowles and D Wilson, 'Racist and Religious Crime Data' (2004) 43 Howard J of Crim Justice 441. See CPS Annual Hate Crime Report, www.cps.gov.uk/publications/docs/CPS_hate_crime_report_2010.pdf.

[327] It has been held that where D pleads to a non-aggravated form of the offence and no evidence is offered on the racially aggravated form of the offence the judge cannot then sentence on the basis that the offence was racially aggravated: *McGillivray* [2005] Crim LR 484, CA.

[328] Commenting on *Pal* [2000] Crim LR 757.

[329] [2006] Crim LR 351.

[330] See note I Hare, 'Legislating Against Hate – The Legal Response to Bias Crimes' (1997) 17 OJLS 415, at 416–417.

[331] See recently *Jones v Bedford and Mid Bedfordshire Magistrates' Court* [2010] EWHC 523 (Admin).

[332] Where D uttered racist words and then attacked V several minutes later, the CA regarded the incident as properly viewed as one in which D's racial hostility was present throughout: *Babbs* [2007] EWCA Crim 2737.

[333] This qualifies both acts before and after – a 20-minute delay after the act before D made the racist remark demonstrating hostility was too long: *Parry v DPP* [2004] EWHC 3112 (Admin).

victim[334] of the offence racial or religious hostility based on the victim's membership of a racial or religious group. The question is whether, objectively, D's words or conduct demonstrate hostility based on race or religion. D's motivation is not relevant.

Section 28(1)(b) applies where the relevant offence is motivated wholly or partly by hostility towards members of a racial or religious group based on their membership of that group. This is a subjective question. D's motivation for the use of the words or conduct is crucial in determining whether it was racially or religiously hostile.

For the purposes of this chapter, the relevant offences are contained in s 29. A person commits an offence under s 29 if he commits:

(i)   an offence under s 20[335] of the OAPA 1861 (malicious wounding or grievous bodily harm) or

(ii) an offence under s 47 of that Act (above, p 645) or

(iii) a common assault,

which is 'racially aggravated' for the purposes of s 29.

Offences (i) and (ii), above, are punishable on indictment with seven years' imprisonment (compared with five years for the basic, non-aggravated offence) and offence (iii) with two years, the basic offence being triable only summarily.

17.8.2 Definitions

'Race' is widely defined to include colour, nationality (including citizenship) or ethnic or national origins.[336] The courts have taken an extremely wide and non-technical view of what constitutes a 'race' and racial group. It has been confirmed that the terms will be satisfied by non-inclusive expressions if, for example, D demonstrates hostility to V by calling him 'non-white' or 'foreign'.[337] 'Religious group' means a group of persons defined by reference to religious belief or lack of religious belief. The Act gives no further guidance. Given the broad interpretation in Art 9 of the ECHR, it would seem likely that the domestic courts will interpret the offence as affording protection to a religion as widely understood.[338] By analogy with the interpretation of race, non-inclusive terms will suffice, for example, 'unbeliever' or 'gentile'.[339]

Racial or religious hostility can be demonstrated by D towards someone of his own racial or religious group.[340] Note also that there is no need for D's presumption about V's race or religion to be accurate: as where D calls V a 'Paki' when V is from India. In *Rogers*,[341] the House of Lords confirmed that though D must have formed the view about V's racial group, the words used by D and which are alleged to demonstrate racial hostility need not refer expressly to that group to which V belongs. A racially aggravated assault might also be committed by one

---

[334] Who need not be present: *Parry v DPP* [2004] EWHC 3112 (Admin).

[335] There is no need for aggravation for s 18 which carries the maximum life sentence.

[336] 'African' does not denote an ethnic, but does denote a racial group: *White* [2001] Crim LR 576, but see commentary on difficulties this creates. Applying the House of Lords' approach in *Rogers*, both terms are capable of being construed as demonstrations of hostility based on the victim's membership of a racial group.

[337] *Rogers* [2007] UKHL 8. See also *DPP v M* [2004] EWHC 1453, [2005] Crim LR 392; *A-G's Reference (No 4 of 2004)* [2005] EWCA Crim 889; *H* [2010] EWCA Crim 1931 (question for jury whether D's repeated references to V as a 'monkey' or 'black monkey' constituted a *demonstration* of hostility based wholly or partly on race or whether it was mere vulgar abuse unconnected with hostility based on race).

[338] See *Pendragon v UK* (1999) 27 EHRR CD 179.

[339] *DPP v M* [2004] EWHC 1453, [2005] Crim LR 392.

[340] *White* [2001] Crim LR 576, CA.

[341] [2007] UKHL 8.

white person on another if the former were, for example, to call the latter 'nigger lover'.[342] It is submitted that this is a perfectly appropriate interpretation of the Act. There is no need for the aggravating words to be repeated, or for the intended target to hear them or be present.[343]

17.8.2.1 Assault and contemporaneous demonstration of hostility

The courts have made clear that the offence under s 28 (1)(a) is not limited to cases in which D is motivated solely or even mainly by racial malevolence. It is designed to extend to cases which may have a racially neutral gravamen but in the course of which there is, *objectively viewed*, hostility demonstrated towards the victim based on V's race (or presumed membership of that race).[344] So, for example. the offence applies where other bases for hostility exist – because V has eg taken D's car parking space, etc. In relation to s 28(1)(a), it has been held that no subjective intent needs to be proved. It is not a question of D intending to express hostility; the test is objective and the Crown merely has to show the hostile behaviour.[345] As a matter of statutory interpretation, the key term in the section is that the hostility is '*based on*' V's race. By contrast, under s 28(1)(b) the motivation behind the behaviour has to be proved – that is a requirement expressed in the section.[346]

The parliamentary debates show that this broad interpretation of s 28(1)(a) was intended, since it was felt that proving a sole racial motive for the offence would be too difficult a task for the prosecution.[347] In consequence, s 28(1)(a) is extremely broad. Lord Monson in the debates on the Bill described the section as Orwellian in that it seeks to police people's emotions.[348] At present only insults relating to religion and race are criminalized in this way. This highlights the arbitrariness of the legislation – as Maurice Kay J noted calling someone a 'fat bastard' is not criminal (yet). In terms of broader social objectives of the legislation, the section may be regarded as a success if it deters individuals from using racist language in any context. Whether this will be the effect or whether those convicted will bear such resentment at the stigma as to become hardened in their racist attitudes is debatable.[349]

[342] *DPP v Pal* [2000] Crim LR 756 per Simon Brown LJ. cf *Johnson v DPP* [2008] EWHC 509 (Admin).

[343] *Dykes v DPP*[2008] EWHC 2775 (Admin).

[344] Per Maurice Kay J in *Woods* [2002] EWHC 85 (Admin) para 11. See also *DPP v Green* [2004] All ER (D) 70 (May); *DPP v MacFarlane* [2002] All ER (D) 78 (Mar); *DPP v M* [2004] EWHC 1453 (Admin), [2005] Crim LR 392.

[345] See *Jones v Bedford and Mid Bedfordshire Magistrates' Court* [2010] EWHC 523 (Admin), the magistrates erred in applying the reasoning from s 28(1)(b) when dealing with a case that was charged under s 28(1)(a).

[346] See *Jones v Bedford and Mid Bedfordshire Magistrates' Court* [2010] EWHC 523 (Admin). Section 28(3) provides that it is irrelevant whether in a s 28(1)(a) case D's hostility is 'also' based to any extent by another factor besides his racism. Read literally, this suggests that the section does include an examination of whether D had some racialist intent in his hostility. On that interpretation, if D's hostility was exclusively based on non-racialist grounds, he would not be within the s 28(1)(a) offence. The decision in *Iones* precludes that argument.

[347] In *Pal* [2000] Crim LR 756, the DC accepted that the racial statement 'whiteman's arse licker' was not in itself sufficient to prove hostility based on racial grounds. Simon Brown LJ stated that he did 'not regard the fact that D would not have used such a term but for V's race as a *sine qua non* of the racial hostility'. His lordship did note that the use of racially abusive insults will 'ordinarily no doubt be found sufficient'. *Pal* has since been described as turning on its own facts. In *Rogers*, Baroness Hale suggests at [15] that the case might also have been disposed of by arguing that the racial hostility was based on the caretaker's association with whites. With respect, that argument was addressed by the DC at [12] and it is not clear that that alternative approach meets the problem – the argument could still be made that the basis for hostility was the ejection and V's conduct, not his race or affinity with members of other races.

[348] HL, 12 Feb 1998, col 1266.

[349] See, generally, E Burney and G Rose. *Racially Aggravated Offences: How is the Law Working?* (2002) HORS 244.

17.8.2.2 Racially/religiously motivated assaults

The s 28(1)(b) offence is much narrower and less controversial, being focused on the defendant's state of mind and one of his *motivations* for the crime being one of racial or religious hostility, although not necessarily against the victim in person. It provides an interesting example of an offence in which the motivations rather than intentions of the defendant become crucial in substantive criminal law, and not merely as a matter of evidence.

An example of the section in operation is *DPP v Howard*.[350] D chanted 'I'd rather be a Paki than a cop' at his neighbours who were white police officers. The charges were based on s 28(1)(b). The magistrates concluded that there was insufficient evidence on which they could be satisfied that the racially aggravated offence had been made out. They found that the evidence showed that D's hostility was motivated *only* by his intense dislike of the neighbours and not even as a result of his intense dislike of the police. There was, they concluded, insufficient evidence to establish (even in part) that the reason why those words were shouted was hostility towards members of the Pakistani race. The Divisional Court dismissed the prosecution appeal, concluding that the magistrates were entitled to come to the conclusion they did: there was an abundance of evidence that the *sole* motivation for D's chanting was his hostility toward the officers personally. Moses LJ suggested that:

prosecutors should be careful not to deploy [s28(1)(b)] where offensive words have been used, but in themselves have not in any way been the motivation for the particular offence with which a defendant is charged. It diminishes the gravity of this offence to use it in circumstances where it is unnecessary to do so and where plainly it cannot be proved.[351]

It is a question of fact whether the motivation is found to be exclusively for non-racist reasons. Thus, in contrast to *Howard*, in *Kendall v DPP*[352] the magistrates were entitled to find that displaying posters of black men convicted of manslaughter with the title 'Illegal Immigrant Murder Scum' was evidence of motive even though D claimed that his purpose was to drum up support for the BNP.

17.9 Aggravated assaults

Assault forms the basis for a number of more serious offences. Three introductory points should be noted about this. First, a person cannot be convicted of an aggravated assault unless he is guilty of assault. Subject to what was said above relating to consents and assault, if D has a defence to the charge of assault, he is not guilty of the aggravated assault. This apparently self-evident proposition is not always as obvious as it appears. For example, in *Blackburn v Bowering*,[353] D was convicted of assaulting an officer of the court in the execution of his duty.[354] His defence was that he did not believe V was a bailiff – he thought he was using reasonable force against a trespasser. D's mistake was as to the status of the victim. The trial judge ruled correctly that liability as to that element of the offence was strict,[355] but, he held that D's

---

[350] [2008] EWHC 608 (Admin).

[351] [12]. cf *Johnson v DPP* [2008] EWHC 509 (Admin).

[352] [2008] EWHC 1848 (Admin).

[353] [1994] 3 All ER 380, CA (Civ Div). The appeal came to the Civil Division because the offence was in the nature of a contempt of court. Referred to by Lord Nicholls in *B v DPP* [2000] 2 AC 428 at 463: 'The Crown advanced no suggestion to your Lordships that any of these recent cases was wrongly decided. This is not surprising, because the reasoning in these cases is compelling.'

[354] Contrary to the County Courts Act 1984, s 14(1)(b)

[355] Following *Forbes and Webb* (1865) 10 Cox CC 362 (assaulting constable). In this regard s 14 was rightly treated as akin to s 51 of the Police Act 1964 which has now replaced by s 89 of the Police Act 1996, below, p 663.

mistaken belief was no defence, remarking on the 'extraordinary situation' if that could have been a defence to common assault. D's conviction was quashed. If D was not guilty of assault because he lacked *mens rea* owing to a mistake, he could not be guilty of the aggravated form of the offence of assault on an officer of the court. Liability is strict as regards the status of the person assaulted, but there must still be an assault.[356] If the assault had been proved – for example, if D had used force which was excessive even against a trespasser, it would have been no defence that he believed (even on reasonable grounds) that V was not an officer but a thug.

Secondly, this range of aggravated offences do not form a coherent scheme, let alone a nicely structured ladder of offences, rather they form a motley collection which have evolved over time. Many of the offences are found within the Offences Against the Person Act 1861. Some of these were, no doubt, intended to deal with matters causing public concern at the time, and appear rather curious today. Thus, obstructing or assaulting a clergyman in the discharge of his duties in a place of worship or burial place, or who is on his way to or from such duties, is an offence triable either way, punishable on indictment with two years' imprisonment under s 36![357] Assaulting a magistrate or other person in the exercise of his duty concerning the preservation of a vessel in distress or a wreck is an offence punishable on indictment with seven years' imprisonment under s 37. Such provisions are rarely invoked in the modern day and need not be considered further, save to note that for some, the explicit labelling and differentiation between the offences by reference to the manner and circumstances in which they were caused reflects important moral distinctions that ought to be retained and replicated in a modern criminal Code.[358]

Thirdly, these aggravated offences, including those considered in this chapter, represent some of the starkest examples of crimes which do not respect the correspondence principle – that is D may be convicted of an offence requiring proof of *actus reus* elements A *and* B even though he has *mens rea* relating only to element A.[359]

17.9.1 Assault with intent to resist arrest

By s 38 of the OAPA 1861:

Whosoever shall assault any person with intent to resist or prevent the lawful apprehension or detainer of himself or of any other person for any offence is guilty of an offence triable either way and punishable with two years' imprisonment.

It may be assumed that the section creates two offences, assault with intent and battery with intent. For each version, D must be shown to have committed all the elements of the assault/battery *and* that he intended to resist, etc. Thus, threatening the arrester (V) with a weapon to make him let go of the arrestee would be the assault, poking him with it would be battery. Dragging the arrestee from V's grasp, being reckless whether this causes V to fall to the ground will be a reckless battery with intent to resist arrest if V does fall. D has an intention to prevent 'apprehension' when he tries to prevent the arrest taking place, and an intention to prevent the 'detainer' when he tries to bring the arrest to an end. The section applies only where the arrest is 'for any offence'; so it does not apply to an arrest in civil process or for a

---

[356] Above, p, 618. This offence is an example of 'constructive crime' because the *mens rea* of a lesser offence, common assault, must be proved.

[357] There was one reported instance of this offence in 2001, and one in 2002: HC Written Answer, 21 Nov 2005 (Hazel Blears).

[358] See J Horder, 'Rethinking Non-Fatal Offences Against the Person' (1994) 14 OJLS 335 arguing that the offences serve valuable labelling functions and Gardner [1994] CLJ 500 arguing that they are valuable in terms of clarity.

[359] Horder [1995] Crim LR 759; cf Mitchell [1999] Crim LR 195, and see references in n 234 above.

breach of the peace not amounting to crime. It is immaterial whether the arrest is by a police officer or a citizen; but D's claim that he did not know the arrester was a plain-clothes officer may be crucial where his defence is that he believed he was being attacked by thugs.[360]

The intent must be to resist 'lawful' arrest.[361] It is important to distinguish between D's mistakes of fact and law. If D knows of the factual circumstances which make the arrest lawful, he probably has a sufficient intent even though he believes, on the circumstances known to him, the arrest to be unlawful: for example, having read in an out-of-date law book that conspiracy is not an arrestable offence, he resists arrest for conspiracy. The law of arrest is treated as part of the criminal law for this purpose[362] and his mistake or ignorance of criminal law is no defence.[363] D's honest and, indeed, true belief that he is not, in fact, guilty of any offence is not *per se* a defence: the arrest may be lawful because the arrester has reasonable grounds for suspicion. But, if D makes a mistake of fact he should be judged on the circumstances as he believed them to be – in accordance with general principle. Thus, if D believes the arrester has, and D believes that the arrester knows he has, no reasonable grounds to suspect that D is guilty – matters of fact – D should be acquitted if he resists. Whatever the true facts, D does not *intend* to resist *lawful* arrest. It may be that the principle of *Fennell*[364] leaves D liable for common assault or battery but it would be wrong in principle to convict him of the aggravated offence when *mens rea* with respect to the aggravating factor is not proved.

17.9.2 Assault on, resistance to, or obstruction of constables

By s 89 of the Police Act 1996:

(1) Any person who assaults a constable in the execution of his duty, or a person assisting a constable in the execution of his duty, shall be guilty of an offence and liable on summary conviction to a fine not exceeding level 5 on the standard scale or to imprisonment for a term not exceeding six months or to both,

(2) Any person who resists or wilfully obstructs a constable in the execution of his duty, or a person assisting a constable in the execution of his duty, shall be guilty of an offence and liable on summary conviction to imprisonment for a term not exceeding one month or to a fine not exceeding level 3 on the standard scale, or to both.

Though the section is headed 'Assaults on Constables', it contains three crimes, only one of which necessarily amounts to an assault. Resistance to a constable may occur without an assault, as where D has been arrested by V and D tears himself from V's grasp and escapes.[365] Obstruction, as appears below, embraces many situations which do not amount to an assault. On the other hand, both resistance and obstruction clearly may include assaults. The nature of assault and resistance requires no further consideration but obstruction presents problems and is examined in some detail below.

---

[360] *Brightling* [1991] Crim LR 364, CA; *Blackburn v Bowering*, above, p 661.

[361] *Lee* [2001] 1 Cr App R 293, CA, and see commentary at [2001] Crim LR 991. 'Whether or not an offence has actually been committed or is believed by the defendant not to have been committed is irrelevant', per Rose LJ.

[362] cf cl 25(2)(b) of the Code Team's Draft Code (Law Com No 143), a provision not included in the Law Commission's draft (Law Com No 177).

[363] Talfourd J put his decision on this ground in *Bentley* (1850) 4 Cox CC 406. See more recently *Hewitt v DPP* [2002] EWHC 2801 (Admin).

[364] [1971] 1 QB 428, [1970] 3 All ER 215. cf *Ball* (1989) 90 Cr App R 378; [1978] Crim LR 580. See the quashing of the conviction in *McKoy* [2002] EWCA Crim 1628.

[365] *Sheriff* [1969] Crim LR 260.

Common to all three crimes is the requirement that the constable[366] is acting in the course of his duty. But the *mens rea* of assault and resistance, on the one hand, and obstruction on the other require separate consideration.

17.9.2.1 A constable acting in the execution of his duty[367]

Identifying whether a police officer is acting in the course of duty is a question which can give rise to difficult problems.[368] There are numerous examples of an officer's action falling on the wrong side of the line. A constable directing a motorist to leave the road to take part in a traffic census, before there was a statutory power to do so[369] was not acting in the execution of his duty since his right at common law to regulate traffic derives only from his duty to protect life and property.[370] A constable who restrained D under the mistaken belief that D had been lawfully arrested by another officer was held not to be acting in the execution of his duty.[371]

Caution is required when interpreting the word duty. There are many things which a constable on duty may do (eg rescuing a stranded cat or helping to deliver a baby)[372] which he is probably not under any 'duty' in the strict sense to do; that is, he would commit no crime or tort or even breach of police regulations by not doing it. In *Coffin v Smith*,[373] the Divisional Court held that a constable could be in the execution of his duty for the purposes of this section even if he was doing something that he was not obliged to do.[374] Officers, who had been summoned to a club to ensure that certain people left, were assaulted. It was held that the officers were there in fulfilment of their duty to keep the peace and were plainly acting in the execution of their duty. But duty surely cannot be equated with being 'on duty'.

A constable may be acting in the execution of his duty by being present, and by intervening when a breach of the peace occurs or is imminent, but acting outside his duty if he takes it

---

[366] ie a person holding the *office*, not the rank of constable. A prison officer acting as such is a constable for this purpose: Prison Act 1952, s 8 see also the extended power in s 8A (but immigration detention centre officials are not constables – *Yarl's Wood Immigration v Bedfordshire Police Authority* [2008] EWHC 2207 (Admin)). It is also an offence to assault: a member of a joint international investigation team, see SOCPA 2005, s 57; traffic officers under the Traffic Management Act 2004, s 10; revenue and customs officers, under the Commissioners for Revenue and Customs Act 2005, s 32; designated Serious Organised Crime Agency staff, under SOCPA 2005, s 51; foreign surveillance teams acting under RIPA 2000, under the Crime (International Co-operation) Act 2003, s 84; as to assaults on immigration officers, see the UK Borders Act 2007, ss 22 and 23; as to assaults on accredited financial investigators exercising powers under the Proceeds of Crime Act 2002, see s 453A of that Act. On the protection for Police Community Support Officers see s 46 of the Police Reform Act 2002, and *D v DPP* [2010] EWHC 3400 (Admin).

[367] On the duties of the police, see the discussion in S Bailey, D Harris and N Taylor, *Civil Liberties, Cases and Materials* (6th edn, 2009) at Ch 4(2). See also *Metropolitan Police Comr, ex p Blackburn* [1968] 2 QB 118, [1968] 1 All ER 763, CA, and *(No 3)* [1973] QB 241, [1973] 1 All ER 324, CA; K Lidstone, 'A Policeman's Duty Not to Take Liberties' [1976] Crim LR 617; U Ross, 'Two Cases on Obstructing a Constable' [1977] Crim LR 187.

[368] It is for the prosecution to prove: *R(Ahmad) v Bradford MC* [2008] EWHC 2934 (Admin).

[369] See now the Road Traffic Act 1988, s 35 as amended.

[370] *Hoffman v Thomas* [1974] 2 All ER 233, DC. In the pursuance of that duty, a constable may require a motorist to disobey a traffic regulation: *Johnson v Phillips* [1975] 3 All ER 682, DC; and remove a vehicle to the police station when the driver is arrested; *Liepins v Spearman* [1985] Crim LR 229. cf *Saunders* [1978] Crim LR 98 (Judge Heald) and commentary.

[371] *Kerr v DPP* [1995] Crim LR 394.

[372] Or assisting a landlord to expel drunk and disorderly people under the Licensing Act 2003, s 143(4) (see *Semple v DPP* [2009] EWHC 3241 (Admin)).

[373] (1980) 71 Cr App R 221. cf the approval of Sedley LJ in *Porter v MPC* (1999) unreported, 20 Nov, CA (Civ).

[374] The Court doubted older cases: *Prebble* (1858) 1 F & F 325 and *Roxburgh* (1871) 12 Cox CC 8. See also *Betts v Stevens* [1910] 1 KB 1 and 4th edition of this book, at 361–372. *Prebble* may be distinguishable as a case where the officer was doing no more than assist a citizen in the enforcement of private rights.

upon himself to expel a trespasser.[375] In a leading case, *Waterfield*,[376] the Court of Criminal Appeal provided welcome clarification:

it would be difficult, and in the present case it is unnecessary, to reduce within specific limits the general terms in which the duties of police constables have been expressed. In most cases it is probably more convenient to consider what the police constable was actually doing and in particular whether such conduct was *prima facie* an unlawful interference with a person's liberty or property. If so, it is then relevant to consider whether (a) such conduct falls within the general scope of any duty imposed by statute or recognized at common law and (b) whether such conduct, albeit within the general scope of such a duty, involved an unjustifiable use of powers associated with the duty.

If the police officer's conduct falls within the general scope of the 'duty' to prevent crime and to bring offenders to justice, then it would seem to be within the protection of the statute, if it was lawful. The officer may ask questions of individuals whom he suspects to be involved in offending.[377]

If, in the course of carrying out his duty to prevent crime and to bring offenders to justice, the officer exceeds his powers, then he is no longer acting in the execution of his duty for this purpose.[378]

Where the charge against D is that he assaulted or obstructed etc a police officer, V, in the execution of his duty and the assault etc occurred in the course of V performing an arrest for a criminal offence, the fact that that offence for which the officer was effecting an arrest is subsequently not prosecuted to conviction does not mean that V was not acting in the execution of his duty.[379] However, where the constable has not arrested D and uses violence on D, D's resistance will not be an offence even if the constable would have been empowered to arrest D in the first place.[380]

Where D is arrested or detained by an officer unlawfully, for example, where the officer has not used words of arrest or told D the grounds of arrest, the officer is not acting in the execution of his duty.[381] In such a case D cannot be liable for resisting other officers in the execution of their duty when they are merely assisting the unlawful arrest.[382] An officer is not acting in the execution of his duty where he searches D without giving reasons.[383] In *B v DPP*[384] the court held that where a police officer in plain clothes sought to exercise his power to stop and search he must ordinarily produce his warrant card before so doing, in accordance with PACE Code A. A failure to do so renders the search unlawful and hence the officer would not be acting in the execution of his duty. Similarly, where an officer enters premises, otherwise

---

[375] In *Chief Constable of Devon and Cornwall, ex p Central Electricity Generating Board* [1982] QB 458, [1981] 3 All ER 826, 835, the Chief Constable appeared to take the view that he had no right to intervene to expel trespassers, even where they were committing a criminal obstruction, unless a breach of the peace was imminent. Lawton LJ said the CEGB had no right to call on the police to supply 'muscle-power' to remove the obstructors; and if the obstructors allowed themselves to be removed without struggling or causing uproar, 'the police will have no reason for taking action, *nor should they*': at 836–837. (Emphasis in original.) On the police powers to prevent breach of the peace see also P Thornton et al *The Law of Public Order and Protest* (2009) para 6.125 et seq.

[376] [1964] 1 QB 164 at 170, [1963] 3 All ER 659 at 661.

[377] *Sekfali v DPP* [2006] EWHC 894 (Admin); cf *D v DPP* [2010] EWHC 3400 (Admin) dealing with powers of a PCSO.

[378] *Ludlow v Burgess* [1971] Crim LR 238, CA; *Pedro v Diss* [1981] 2 All ER 59, 72 Cr App R 193.

[379] *Burrell v DPP* [2005] EWHC 786 (Admin).

[380] *Wood v DPP* [2008] EWHC 1056 (Admin).

[381] cf *Saliu v DPP* [2005] EWHC 2689 (Admin), D assaulted PC who had yet to arrest.

[382] *Cumberbatch v CPS* [2009] EWHC 3353 (Admin).

[383] *McBean v Parker* [1983] Crim LR 399; *Brazil v Chief Constable of Surrey* (1983) 77 Cr App R 237, DC; *Osman v DPP* [1999] 163 JP 725; *Linehan v DPP* [2000] Crim LR 816; *Bonner v DPP* [2004] All ER (D) 74 (Oct).

[384] [2008] EWHC 1655 (Admin). See also *Garjho* [2011] All ER(D) 211 (Apr).

than in accordance with the statutory power,[385] or acts beyond the powers incidental to the search when on the premises. In *McArdle v Wallace*,[386] V, a constable, was held to be acting in the execution of his duty when he entered a café to make enquiries regarding stolen property. He was told to leave but did not do so and was then assaulted. At the time of the assault he was no longer acting in the execution of his duty since he became a trespasser when he refused to leave: for a constable can hardly have a duty to break the law.[387] In *R (Fullard) v Woking Magistrates' Court*,[388] the court emphasized that an officer cannot be acting in the execution of his duty when he was unlawfully present on private property. However, it was held that even where the officer has no legal right to remain when required to leave, offensive remarks directed at the officer and telling him to 'go away' will not necessarily suffice to withdraw any implied permission to enter or remain,[389] and the officer must in any event be given a reasonable opportunity to leave once such permission has effectively been withdrawn. Whether a licence to enter has been revoked is to be objectively determined.[390] A constable who is not acting in the execution of his duty because he is a trespasser begins to act in the execution of his duty as soon as circumstances justifying his presence arise – as where he reasonably apprehends a breach of the peace. He does not have to leave the premises and re-enter.[391] Even if an officer is not acting in the execution of his duty, for example where he is trespassing, the conduct of the defendant might nevertheless constitute a simple assault.[392]

17.9.2.2 Trivial touchings by officers

A police officer investigating crime is entitled to speak to any person from whom he thinks useful information can be obtained, even though that person declares that he is unwilling to reply,[393] but the officer has no power to detain for questioning so the use of reasonable force to escape from such detention is not an assault;[394] (it may be obstructing[395]) and the use of excessive force, while a common assault (or wounding, etc) would not be an offence under s 89.

Where, however, V tapped D on the shoulder, not intending to detain him but in order to speak to him, it was held that V was acting in the course of his duties, though it seems clear that D did not consent to this contact. The court thought that '... it is not every trivial interference with a citizen's liberty that amounts to a course of conduct sufficient to take the officer out of the course of his duties'.[396] The decision amounts to judicial acceptance that a police

---

[385] cf *McLorie v Oxford* [1982] 3 All ER 480, [1982] Crim LR 603; *O'Loughlin v Chief Constable of Essex* [1998] 1 WLR 374; cf *Hobson v CC Cheshire* [2003] EWHC 3011 (Admin); *Odewale v DPP* [2001] 2 Archbold News 2; cf *Baker v CPS* [2009] EWHC 299 (Admin).

[386] [1964] Crim LR 467; cf *Davis v Lisle* [1936] 2 KB 434, [1936] 2 All ER 213; *Robson v Hallett* [1967] 2 All ER 407; *McGowan v Chief Constable of Kingston-upon-Hull* [1967] Crim LR 34; *Kay v Hibbert* [1977] Crim LR 226, DC; *Jones and Jones v Lloyd* [1981] Crim LR 340, DC.

[387] See, however, the novel power to detain and segregate in the course of a search *DPP v Meaden* [2004] Crim LR 587 criticized in the commentary.

[388] [2005] EWHC 2922 (Admin).

[389] See also *Gilham v Breidenback* [1982] RTR 382.

[390] [21].

[391] *Lamb* [1990] Crim LR 58, DC.

[392] See, eg, *Syed v DPP* [2010] EWHC 81 (Admin).

[393] Code of Practice A, code issued under the Police and Criminal Evidence Act (1984); *Weight v Long* [1986] Crim LR 746. See also *Sekfali*, below.

[394] *Kenlin v Gardner* [1967] 2 QB 510, [1966] 3 All ER 931; *Ludlow v Burgess* [1971] Crim LR 238; *Lemsatef* [1977] 1 WLR 812. cf *Daniel v Morrison* (1980) 70 Cr App R 142, DC.

[395] See *Sekfali* below.

[396] *Donnelly v Jackman* [1970] 1 All ER 987, criticized in JC Smith, 'Assault: *Donnelly v Jackman*' [1970] Crim LR 219 at 220 and 'Police Power to Stop Without Arrest' [1970] 33 MLR 438; and followed in *Pounder v Police* [1971] NZLR 1080 (constable committing 'a trivial trespass'). cf *Squires v Botwright* [1972] RTR 462, DC; *Inwood*

officer can commit a crime (or tort) of assault and be within his duty. This seems like an unacceptable proposition; and the case is an 'extreme' one,[397] explicable only on the ground that the trespass committed by the constable was a momentary and trivial incident in an otherwise lawful course of conduct. In *Bentley v Brudzinski*,[398] on very similar facts, a different result was reached.

Where the question is whether something is trivial or *de minimis*, it is perhaps to be expected that assessments will differ. In *C v DPP*,[399] the officer's taking hold of a 14-year-old girl's arm to escort her home when she was reported missing by her parents was not in the exercise of his duty and hence her boyfriend was not guilty of assaulting the officer in the execution of his duty.

Waterfield[400] is a difficult case. V, a constable, had been informed that a car had been involved in a serious offence. Evidently acting on the instructions of a superior officer, he attempted to prevent D, the owner of the car, from removing it from the place on the road where it was parked. D drove the car at V, thus assaulting him, in order to remove it. The court held that V was not 'entitled' to prevent removal of the car[401] and therefore was not acting in the execution of his duty. The difficulty is that the judgment nowhere specifies in what respect V's act was unlawful. He simply stood in front of the car. Why, if it was not an unlawful act, was it not one that V might properly do in fulfilment of the general duty to bring offenders to justice?[402] It may be, however, that the answer is that V was guilty of obstructing the highway under the Highways Act 1959;[403] but there was no finding that the road was a highway.

Officer preventing breach of peace

Probably the most important application of s 89 is in the context of the constable's duty to prevent breaches of the peace which he reasonably apprehends.[404] The power is one which must be scrutinized with the utmost care since it allows an officer (and indeed a civilian) to restrain or arrest D where D has not committed, and is perhaps not even about to commit, a crime. The House of Lords has confirmed that a power to arrest or take less intrusive action arises

[1973] 2 All ER 645, CA; *Mepstead v DPP* (1995) 160 JP 475, [1996] Crim LR 111, DC. See D Lanham, 'Arrest, Detention and Compulsion' [1974] Crim LR 288.

[397] *Collins v Wilcock* [1984] 3 All ER 374 at 378, above. See also *McMillan v CPS* [2008] EWHC 1457 (Admin) – steadying a drunken person.

[398] [1982] Crim LR 825, DC and commentary.

[399] [2003] All ER (D) 37 (Nov).

[400] [1964] 1 QB 164, [1963] 3 All ER 659.

[401] The case has since been doubted on this point: *Ghani v Jones* [1970] 1 QB 693 at 707, CA. Where a constable in uniform or a traffic officer requires a vehicle to stop under s 163 of the Road Traffic Act 1988, the driver commits an offence if he fails to do so. He has a duty to remain at rest for a reasonable period; but it seems that the constable has no right under the section physically to stop or to detain the driver or vehicle: *Lodwick v Sanders* [1985] 1 All ER 577 at 582–584, [1985] Crim LR 210, per Webster J. But if the constable reasonably suspects the vehicle to be stolen by the driver he is entitled to seize and detain it and arrest the driver: ibid; *Sanders v DPP* [1988] Crim LR 605, DC. Similarly, if he has reasonable suspicion to search it: *Smith v DPP* [2002] EWHC 113 (Admin).

[402] See PJ Fitzgerald, 'The Arrest of a Motor-Car' [1965] Crim LR 23.

[403] Now s 137 of the Highways Act 1980. In *Herrick v Kidner* [2010] EWHC 269 (Admin) Cranston J reviewed the authorities, concluding that 'these authorities establish a number of principles with regard to an obstruction of the highway: first, members of the public are in general entitled to unrestricted access to the whole and each part of a highway; secondly, their right to such access is principally to pass and repass but it is also to enjoy other amenity rights; thirdly, those other amenity rights must be reasonable and usual and will depend on the particular circumstances; fourthly, any encroachment upon the highway which prevents members of the public from the enjoyment of these access and amenity rights is an unlawful obstruction; fifthly, the law ignores *de minimis* , or fractional obstructions; and sixthly, a highway authority cannot deprive itself of the power to act against an unlawful obstruction by refraining from exercising its statutory powers against it, or by purporting to give it consent.'[33]

[404] *Duncan v Jones* [1936] 1 KB 218.

where (i) a breach of the peace has been committed, or (ii) a breach has occurred and a further breach is threatened or (iii) the officer reasonably believes that a breach will be committed imminently. If an officer reasonably believes one of the above three circumstances pertains, he is under a duty to take such steps, whether by arrest or otherwise,[405] as he reasonably thinks are necessary.[406] Where a reasonable apprehension of an imminent breach of the peace exists, the preventive action taken must be reasonable and proportionate; and there is no power to take action short of an arrest when a breach of the peace is not so imminent as would be necessary to justify arrest.[407]

The most difficult cases are likely to be those in which the police seek to intervene to prevent conduct which is not objectively violent nor provocative to others but which may amount to a breach of the peace. In *Laporte* Lord Rodger observed that:

Sometimes lawful and proper conduct by A may be liable to result in a violent reaction from B, even though it is not directed against B. If B's resort to violence can be regarded as the natural consequence of A's conduct, and there is no other way of preserving the peace, a police officer may order A to desist from his conduct, even though it is lawful. If A refuses he may be arrested for obstructing a police officer in the execution of his duty.[408]

In *Hawkes v DPP*,[409] a conviction was quashed where the constable had exercised his powers unlawfully by arresting for an alleged breach of the peace when D had not demonstrated any violent conduct.[410] But, even where no breach of the peace is anticipated, a constable may be under some other duty to give instructions to members of the public – for example, to remove an obstruction from the highway[411]– and a deliberate refusal to obey such an instruction may amount to an obstruction of the police.

A constable who makes a lawful arrest is acting in the execution of his duty even though the arrest subsequently becomes unlawful when he fails to communicate the ground to the arrestee.[412]

17.9.2.3 *Mens rea* in cases of assault and resistance

The only *mens rea* required in the case of an allegation of assaulting a constable is the *mens rea* for assault or battery. In a case of resisting, the *mens rea* is an intention to resist. A reckless battery might be inflicted by hitting or flailing arms or legs around at arresting officers or even by biting, as where D uses his teeth to try to snatch something from the hand of the officer restraining him, being aware that he might make contact with the officer's hand in the process.[413]

There is no requirement to prove that D knew that the person he was assaulting was a police officer, still less that V was on duty. Liability in relation to the status of the arrester and whether the constable was in the execution of his duty is strict. Although the original authority for this was a ruling by a recorder in a direction to a jury in *Forbes and Webb*,[414] this has now been

---

[405] *King v Hodges* [1974] Crim LR 424; *Blench v DPP* [2004] All ER (D) 86 (Nov). The requirement for an 'imminent' breach of the peace was interpreted very widely in *Wragg v DPP* [2005] EWHC (Admin).

[406] *Piddington v Bates* [1960] 3 All ER 660.

[407] *R (Laporte) v Chief Constable of Gloucestershire* [2007] 2 WLR 46, HL.

[408] [78]. See recently *R(Moos) v MPC* [2011] EWHC 957 (Admin).

[409] [2005] EWHC, 2 Nov, unreported.

[410] She could probably have been arrested for an anticipated imminent breach.

[411] It is in the course of a constable's duty to require pickets to move where they would otherwise obstruct lawful passage on the highway by others; *Kavanagh v Hiscock* [1974] QB 600, CA, applying *Broome v DPP* [1974] AC 587 HL. See also *Austin v MPC* below, text accompanying n 570.

[412] *DPP v Hawkins* [1988] 3 All ER 673, [1988] Crim LR 741.

[413] *DPP v D* [2005] EWHC 967 (Admin).

[414] (1865) 10 Cox CC 362, applying s 38 of the OAPA 1861.

repeatedly accepted.[415] It is submitted that a better view[416] is that D should only be liable if he was at least reckless as to whether V was a police officer in the execution of his duty when he committed the assault.[417] Such a view avoids any difficulty arising from the fact that s 36[418] of the 1861 Act used the words 'to the knowledge of the offender', whereas no such words were used in s 38 or its successors. Nevertheless, the present English law is that laid down in *Forbes*. This is implicit in *McBride v Turnock*,[419] where D struck at O, who was not a constable, and hit V, who was. Although he had no intention of assaulting V, the Divisional Court held he was guilty of assaulting a constable in the execution of his duty. The *mens rea* for this crime being only that of a common assault/battery, D's 'malice' was transferable.[420] No better illustration could be given of the unsatisfactory nature of strict liability in this context. Following the landmark decisions of the House of Lords in *DPP v B*[421] and *R v K*[422] it is arguable that this approach deserves reconsideration.

If D is unaware (whether reasonably or not) that V is a constable and believes in the existence of circumstances of justification or excuse for his use of force, he should be acquitted:[423] he will not intend or be reckless as to an unlawful assault. If, however, D knows that V is a constable, it seems that a mistaken belief – even an honest and reasonable belief – that the constable is acting outside the course of his duty will not always be a defence. In *Fennell*,[424] the court assumed that a father might lawfully use reasonable force to free his son from unlawful arrest by the police; but he acted at his peril and, if the arrest proved to be lawful, he was guilty. The court thought it would be otherwise if D mistakenly believed that a relative or friend was in imminent danger of injury and used reasonable force to prevent that.

17.9.2.4 Wilful obstruction[425]

The meaning of obstruction

There must be obstruction in fact. If D does an act with intent to obstruct but which fails to do so he commits no offence – and it cannot be an attempt.[426] A wide interpretation of 'obstruction' has been accepted in England. It is not necessary that there should be any interference with the officer himself by physical force or threats.

Where the police tell an offender to desist from an offence, his deliberate refusal may amount to an obstruction, as where D is obstructing the highway and refuses to obey the instructions of a constable to move.[427] It is not necessary that the constable should anticipate

---

[415] In *Prince* (1875) LR 2 CCR 154 (six judges accepted it as correct); *Maxwell* (1909) 73 JP 176, (1909) 2 Cr App R 26; *Mark* [1961] Crim LR 173 (Judge Maxwell Turner). See also *Blackburn v Bowering*, above, p 660. See F Fairweather and S Levy, 'Assaults on the Police: A Case of Mistaken Identity' [1994] Crim LR 817.

[416] See the dissenting judges in *Reynhoudt* (1962) 36 ALJR 26.

[417] This was the view of the majority of the court in *Galvin (No 2)* [1961] VR 740, overruling *Galvin (No 1)* [1961] VR 733. Barry J thought actual knowledge necessary. Scholl J adhered to his view in *Galvin (No 1)* that the offence was one of strict liability. See also *McLeod* (1954) 111 CCC 106.

[418] Above, p 662.

[419] [1964] Crim LR 456, DC. This was also assumed to be the law in *Blackburn v Bowering*, above, p 660.

[420] Above, p 136.

[421] [2000] 2 AC 428, above Ch 7.

[422] *K* [2002] 1 AC 462, above Ch 7.

[423] *Gladstone Williams* (1984) 78 Cr App R 276, above, p 381. *Mark*, supra, requiring reasonable grounds for the belief, can no longer be regarded as good law.

[424] [1971] 1 QB 428, [1970] Crim LR 581 and commentary, CA; and cf *Ball* (1989) 90 Cr App R 378, [1989] Crim LR 579 and commentary.

[425] See for an historical account J Coutts, 'Obstructing the Police' (1956) 19 MLR 411.

[426] Because it is triable only summarily. cf *Bennett v Bale* [1986] Crim LR 404, DC and commentary.

[427] *Tynan v Balmer* [1967] 1 QB 91; *Donaldson v Police* [1968] NZLR 32.

a breach of the peace. But a constable has no power to arrest D for obstructing him, unless the obstruction was such that it actually caused, or was likely to cause, a breach of the peace.[428]

Equally, to give a warning to a person who *has* committed a crime so as to enable him to escape detection by police is enough. Thus, in *Betts v Stevens*,[429] D committed the offence by warning drivers who were exceeding the speed limit that there was a police trap ahead. *Hinchliffe v Sheldon*[430] might be thought to go further than *Betts v Stevens* in that it was only *suspected*, and not proved, that an offence was being committed; but there the warning was tantamount to a physical obstruction.[431] D, a publican's son, shouted a warning to his parents that the police were outside the public house. It was 11.17 pm and the lights were on in the bar, so presumably the police suspected that liquor was being consumed after hours. There was a delay of eight minutes before the police were admitted and no offence was detected. The police had a right to enter under statute[432] whether an offence was being committed or not, an entry under this statutory right was in execution of their duty; and their *entry* was obstructed. Lord Goddard CJ defined 'obstructing' as '[m]aking it more difficult for the police to carry out their duties'.[433] This is far wider than was necessary for the decision.

Where defendants warn individuals who *are about to commit* offences, the courts have had difficulties. In *Green v Moore*[434] the distinction was drawn between advising a person to *suspend* his criminal activity, so that he will not be found out by the police (warning motorists so they do not speed until past the speed trap), which is an offence; and advising him to give it up altogether (ie never speed again) – in which case he will not be found out by the police – which is not an offence.[435] In *Green v Moore*, D was a probationer constable who 'tipped off' a landlord of his local pub that a police 'support group' were waiting to catch him in the dastardly act of selling liquor out of hours! Thereafter, naturally, the landlord kept strictly within the letter of the law. D was aware that 'the landlord did not give a high priority to the strict observance of licensing hours', and the court construed his warning as one that the sale of liquor out of hours had better be *suspended* until the support group moved on to tackle some other nefarious activity. If D had said, 'Fred, the sale of liquor out of hours simply isn't on – give it up, once and for all' – the efforts of the support group would have been equally frustrated but that would have been no offence. The 'suspension theory' can only operate where the person 'tipped off' is known or believed to be engaged in a continuing criminal activity or system. If he is dissuaded from persisting in what is or appears to be a 'one-off' offence, which he is about to commit, there is no room for the suspension theory. In *Green v Moore*, D knew of the landlord's illegal practice.

Presumably it must be proved that some named officer was obstructed;[436] it would hardly be enough that D warned E in general terms that if he did not stop committing an offence he would be found out; or if he advised E to get a television licence because the detector van was

---

[428] *Wershof v Metropolitan Police Comr* [1978] 3 All ER 540 (May J); *Gelberg v Miller* [1961] 1 WLR 153; *Riley v DPP* [1990] Crim LR 422, DC.

[429] [1910] 1 KB 1.

[430] [1955] 3 All ER 406, [1955] 1 WLR 1207.

[431] See Coutts (1956) 19 MLR 411.

[432] See now Licensing Act 2003, s 180(1).

[433] [1955] 3 All ER at 408.

[434] [1982] QB 1044, [1982] 1 All ER 428. cf *Moore v Green* [1983] 1 All ER 663, DC. Explaining *Bastable v Little* [1907] 1 KB 59. See also *DPP v Glendinning* [2005] EWHC 2333 (Admin), holding that warning motorists of a speed trap was not necessarily sufficient to amount to the offence of obstructing a police officer in the execution of his duty unless the drivers being warned were speeding or were likely to be speeding. How fine a line is that? How will anyone know if they are likely to be?

[435] What then of the maps published of all speed camera sites, or the devices which warn motorists as they approach a speed trap?

[436] *Syce v Harrison* [1981] Crim LR 110n.

visiting his street next week – apart from the fact that the operators of the van would not be constables.

Obstructing by not assisting

Lord Goddard CJ's *dictum* defining 'obstructing' as '[m]aking it more difficult for the police to carry out their duties'[437] goes too far. Surely a solicitor who advises his client to say nothing cannot be guilty of an offence, though he undoubtedly makes things more difficult for the police; and why should a solicitor be in a different situation from anyone else? The fact that the refusal is expressed in abusive and obscene terms should, in principle, make no difference.[438] If D's language amounts to some other offence, such as that under the Public Order Act 1986, s 4,[439] he should be charged with that. *Ricketts v Cox*[440] seems a doubtful decision. The court accepted the finding of the justices that the 'totality of [the defendants'] behaviour and attitude at this stage amounted to an obstruction…', but all that could be added to the total was the abusive, obscene and hostile attitude of the defendants, reprehensible, no doubt, and galling to the officers, but still the assertion of an actual right.[441] While the report does refer to some unspecified threat by D, the court attached no particular significance to it and the decision seems to be based on the generally 'obstructive' nature of D's behaviour.

It has been held that refusal to answer a constable's question, though it undoubtedly makes it more difficult for the police to carry out their duties, does not amount to wilful obstruction: *Rice v Connolly*.[442] However, where there is more than a mere refusal the offence may be committed. In *Sekfali v DPP*,[443] police officers approached the defendants who had been acting suspiciously. The officers identified themselves as such whereupon the defendants all ran off. They were convicted of wilfully obstructing police officers in the execution of their duty. The Divisional Court held that the police officers were entitled in the execution of their duty to approach the men and ask questions. The court confirmed that a citizen has no legal duty to assist the police, whilst noting that most people would accept that they have a moral and social duty to do so. The court then went on:

section 89(2) makes it an offence to willfully obstruct a police officer in the execution of his duty. The appellants would have been entitled to remain silent and not answer any questions put to them. They could have refused, if they had not been arrested, to accompany the police to any particular place to which they might have been requested by the police to go. They could have said that they had no intention of answering questions and they could, no doubt, have said that as a result they were intent on going on their way and have done so without giving rise to a case which would entitle the court to conclude that in departing they were intending to impede the police officers and obstruct the police officers in the execution of their duty. Had they responded in that way, then it would have been for the police to have decided whether to arrest them; but they ran off, as the magistrates found to avoid apprehension. That being a wilful act, taken so as to obstruct the police, was an act capable of constituting an offence contrary to section 89(2).

Telling the police a false story is also quite different from merely remaining silent and clearly an obstruction.[444] Refusing to reveal the whereabouts of a prohibited drug is not an obstruction; but burying it to hide it from an officer searching for it might be, when the officer's task is

---

[437] [1955] 3 All ER at 408.
[438] See Marshall J in *Rice v Connolly* at 420.
[439] Below, p 1096.
[440] (1981) 74 Cr App R 298, DC.
[441] See commentary at [1982] Crim LR 184. The partial retraction at [1982] Crim LR 484 seems unnecessary.
[442] [1966] 2 QB 414, [1966] 2 All ER 649, DC.
[443] [2006] EWHC 894 (Admin).
[444] *Rice v Connolly* (above); *Mathews v Dwan* [1949] NZLR 1037.

made more difficult.[445] These difficulties would not arise if the Act had been held to be limited to physical interference; and it has been held[446] to be so limited in Scotland where 'obstruct' has been construed *ejusdem generis* with 'assault' and 'resist'.[447] D was held not guilty when he told lies to the police to conceal an offence of which he was guilty. There is much to be said in favour of the Scottish view.[448]

Lawful acts as obstruction?

It is not necessary that the act relied on as an obstruction should be unlawful independently of its operation as an obstruction of the police.[449] The conferment of powers and imposition of duties on the police, may, impliedly, impose duties on others not to impede the exercise by the police of these powers and duties. The right of a constable to enter licensed premises where he believes an offence might be committed imposes an obligation on the licensee and others to let him in.[450] The right of a constable to require a driver in certain circumstances to provide a specimen of breath[451] implies a duty on the motorist (though he has not been arrested) to remain 'there or nearby' until the constable has had a reasonable opportunity to carry out the test.[452] If, when D is found to have consumed an excess of alcohol, it is the duty of a constable to remove D's car from the highway, there is an implied duty on D to hand over the keys of the car.[453]

Whether a duty thus to cooperate with the police is to be implied depends on whether this is a compelling inference from the nature of the police duty or right. To some extent it is a question of policy – so, the courts have held there is no duty to answer police questions but there is a duty not to give misleading answers.[454] Whether D's conduct is an act rather than an omission is only one factor in determining whether there is an obstruction. Omissions may amount to obstruction even when the omission is not an offence independently of s 89.[455] There is a separate common law offence of refusing to aid a constable who is attempting to prevent or to quell a breach of the peace and who calls for assistance.[456]

Mens rea for obstruction

Unlike 'assault' and 'resist', if D is charged with 'obstruction', it must be proved that that was 'wilful'. D must intend to behave in such a way as to make it more difficult for the police to carry out their duties. His conduct need be neither hostile to, nor aimed at, the police, as some cases have suggested.[457] So, in *Lewis v Cox*[458] where D persisted in opening the door of a van in which X, who had been arrested, was about to be driven away. D's purpose was not to obstruct the police but to find out where X was being taken, but, since he must have known that he was preventing the police officer from driving off, the justices were bound to find that

---

[445] See note on *Syce v Harrison* [1981] Crim LR 110n.

[446] *Curlett v M'Kechnie* (1938) JC 176.

[447] The rearrangement of these offences by the Police Act precludes the application of the *ejusdem generis* rule; but it could have been applied when they were contained in the Offences Against the Person Act 1861.

[448] See Coutts (1956) 19 MLR 411.

[449] *Dibble v Ingleton* [1972] 1 QB 480, [1972] 1 All ER 275. See G Williams, 'Criminal Law – The Duty Not To Obstruct Your Own Conviction' [1972] CLJ 193.

[450] Licensing Act 2003, s 180.

[451] Road Traffic Act 1988, s 7.

[452] *DPP v Carey* [1970] AC 1072 at 1097, [1969] 3 All ER 1662 at 1680.

[453] *Stunt v Bolton* [1972] RTR 435, [1972] Crim LR 561.

[454] *Rice v Connolly*, above.

[455] For example, *Stunt v Bolton*, above. Cf *Dibble v Ingleton*, above, n 449.

[456] *Waugh* (1976) The Times, 1 Oct 1976.

[457] *Willmott v Atack* [1977] QB 498, [1976] 3 All ER 794; *Hills v Ellis* [1983] QB 680, [1983] 1 All ER 667.

[458] [1985] QB 509, [1984] 3 All ER 672.

he intended to make it more difficult for them to carry out their duty.[459] Similarly, in *Hills v Ellis*,[460] D was liable where D laid his hand on a constable's arm to draw his attention to the fact that, as D believed, he was arresting the wrong man. The courts appear to alternate between looking to D's primary purpose and any additional ones.

In *Rice v Connolly*,[461] it was said that 'wilfully' means not only 'intentionally' but also 'without lawful excuse'. This is difficult to follow. 'Wilfully' must surely refer to the state of mind of the defendant. But whether he has a lawful excuse for what he does generally depends on D's conduct and the circumstances in which he acts.[462] In that case, D would have been no more 'wilful' if he had told a false story. The difference seems to lie in the conduct which the court considers to be permissible. 'Wilfully' may of course import the absence of any *belief* on D's part of circumstances of lawful excuse. If the story told by D were in fact false, but D believed it to be true, the constable might be obstructed, but he would not be 'wilfully' obstructed.

As to mistakes about the status of the officer, in cases of obstruction, liability is not strict. In *Ostler v Elliott*,[463] it was held that D's reasonable belief that the police officers were robbers was a defence to wilful obstruction. Now, since the decision in *Gladstone Williams*,[464] it is sufficient that the mistaken belief was genuinely held even if it was unreasonable.

Note also the summary offence of obstructing without reasonable excuse an emergency worker – fire and rescue personnel, paramedics, lifeboat crew, etc – under the Emergency Workers (Obstruction) Act 2006. By s 1(3) a person is responding to emergency circumstances if the person: (a) is going anywhere for the purpose of dealing with emergency circumstances occurring there; or (b) is dealing with emergency circumstances or preparing to do so. Emergency is defined in s 1(4).[465]

17.10 Administering poison

Sections 23 and 24 of the Offences Against the Person Act 1861 create offences, punishable with ten and five years' imprisonment respectively, with a similar *actus reus*.

17.10.1 Section 23

The section (as amended) provides:

Whosoever shall unlawfully and maliciously administer to or cause to be administered to or taken by any other person any poison or other destructive or noxious thing, so as thereby to endanger the life of such person, or so as thereby to inflict upon such person any grievous bodily harm, shall be guilty of [an offence] and being convicted thereof shall be liable... to [imprisonment] for any term not exceeding ten years...

By s 25, a person charged under s 23 may be convicted of an offence under s 24.

[459] cf the discussion of intention, above, p 668.
[460] [1983] QB 680.
[461] Above, p 671.
[462] See comment at [1966] Crim LR 390.
[463] [1980] Crim LR 584. Note that, if he had assaulted the officers, his reasonable belief that they were not officers would not, in itself, have been a defence to a charge of assaulting them in the execution of their duty. See commentary at [1980] Crim LR 585.
[464] [1987] 3 All ER 411, 78 Cr App R 276, CA, above, p 381.
[465] The offence can include eg making hoax calls: *McMenemy* [2009] EWCA Crim 42.

17.10.1.1 *Actus reus*

Administer, cause to be administered, cause to be taken

Lord Bingham described s 23 as providing three distinct offences: (1) administering a noxious thing to any other person; (2) causing a noxious thing to be administered to any other person; and (3) causing a noxious thing to be taken by any other person. His lordship explained:

Offence (1) is committed where D administers the noxious thing directly to V, as by injecting V with the noxious thing, holding a glass containing the noxious thing to V's lips, or (as in *R v Gillard* [466] spraying the noxious thing in V's face. Offence (2) is typically committed where D does not directly administer the noxious thing to V but causes an innocent third party TP to administer it to V. If D, knowing a syringe to be filled with poison instructs TP to inject V, TP believing the syringe to contain a legitimate therapeutic substance, D would commit this offence. Offence (3) covers the situation where the noxious thing is not administered to V but taken by him, provided D causes the noxious thing to be taken by V and V does not make a voluntary and informed decision to take it. If D puts a noxious thing in food which V is about to eat and V, ignorant of the presence of the noxious thing, eats it, D commits offence (3).[467]

The words 'administer' and 'take' are to be construed by the court and not left as a question of fact to the jury.[468] The words are disjunctive. 'Takes' assumes some 'ingestion' by the victim. It seems that the thing is not 'administered' until it is taken into the body.[469] To leave the poison, intending it to be taken by an unwitting victim, may be an attempt to administer it.[470] There is no requirement that the 'administration' under s 23 involves surreptitious conduct.[471]

In *Kennedy*,[472] D handed to V a syringe containing heroin with which V injected himself and, in consequence, died. At his trial he was convicted of manslaughter. The Court of Appeal said, *obiter*, that it could see no reason why D should not have been convicted of an offence under s 23. There is a very good reason, simply that D did not administer the thing to V or cause V to take it. V, a person of full age and capacity, not labouring under any mistake, administered it to himself. Such an act breaks the chain of causation. After seemingly returning to orthodoxy in *Dias*, the Court of Appeal again returned to this revolutionary approach to causation in *Rogers*,[473] and *Finlay*.[474] In *Kennedy (No 2)*,[475] the House of Lords has finally laid this heresy to rest. Where D hands V a syringe with which V injects himself, there is no administering by D. Nor is it possible to say that D is jointly responsible or jointly engaged in administering the heroin.[476] In *Kennedy (No 2)*, the House of Lords also rejected the approach of the Court of Appeal in *Finlay* which had adopted the *Empress* approach to causation. Since V has voluntarily taken the decision to inject himself, his free informed act breaks the chain of causation. It is different if D secretly puts the noxious thing into V's drink and V consumes

---

[466] *Gillard* (1988) 87 Cr App R 189. See also *Cronin-Simpson* [2000] 1 Cr App R (S) 54, D surreptitiously pouring petrol into neighbour's house through loft pipe; *Potter* [2005] EWCA Crim 3050 – splashing petrol on V and threat to ignite (surely better charged as a threat to kill?).

[467] *Kennedy (No 2)* [2007] UKHL 38 at [9]–[10].

[468] *Gillard* (1988) 87 Cr App R 189 at 194.

[469] *Cadman* (1825) Carrington's Supplement 237. The report to the contrary in Ryan and Moody 114 is said to be inaccurate: *Harley* (above) per Parke J: and 6 Cox CC 16 n (c). But see *Walford* (1899) 34 L Jo 116, per Wills J.

[470] Prior to the Criminal Attempts Act, a judge could tell a jury it was an attempt, as Wightman J did in *Dale* (1852) 6 Cox CC 14.

[471] It has, been prosecuted where, eg, D doused people with petrol and threatened to ignite it: *Potter* [2005] EWCA Crim 3050.

[472] [1999] Crim LR 65, above, p 91. cf *Khan* [1998] Crim LR 830.

[473] [2003] Crim LR 555.

[474] [2003] EWCA Crim 3868.

[475] [2005] EWCA Crim 685.

[476] See Ch 4 above for detailed comment. But see *Burgess* [2008] EWCA Crim 516.

it. V's consumption is then not a fully voluntary act – he believes he is drinking nothing but, say, coffee and has no intention to take the noxious thing. D has then 'administered' it to him or caused him to take it.[477]

Noxious

Some substances are noxious *per se*, as, for example, with radioactive isotope polonium-210 used to murder Russian dissident, Alexander Litvinenko. In *Marcus*,[478] a case under s 24, 'noxious' was broadly interpreted. A substance which may be harmless if taken in small quantities is noxious if administered in sufficient quantity to injure, aggrieve or annoy.[479] The meaning is taken to be coloured by the purpose which D may have in view. It is not necessary that the substance should be injurious to bodily health: '"noxious" mean[s] something different in quality from and of less importance than poison or other destructive things'. The court quoted the *Shorter Oxford Dictionary* meaning, 'injurious, hurtful, harmful, unwholesome', and suggested that the insertion of the celebrated snail allegedly in the ginger beer bottle in *Donoghue v Stevenson*[480] would create a noxious substance. It was held that the insertion of sedative and sleeping tablets into a bottle of milk was an attempt to commit an offence under s 24. While the tablets would cause no more than sedation or possibly sleep, they might be a danger to a person doing such normal but potentially hazardous acts as driving or crossing the street.[481]

The court 'explained' *Cato*,[482] a case under s 23, where it was said that a thing could not be noxious merely because it was harmful if taken in large quantities. That observation was not 'explicable' but wrong. The actual decision, however, that heroin is a noxious thing even where it is administered to a person with a high tolerance to whom it is unlikely to do any particular harm, is right.[483] Heroin is noxious because 'it is liable to cause injury in common use'.[484] It was no answer that V was experienced in taking heroin and had a high tolerance. Ecstasy has been held to be a noxious substance for these purposes.[485] It has been argued that HIV could be regarded as a noxious substance capable of being administered in the course of sexual activity.[486] Charges under s 20 (above) are more likely.

Whether consenting to the administration of a noxious substance that might cause grievous bodily harm or endanger life is valid consent in law must be subject to the policy on consent adopted in *Brown*.[487] The courts have repeatedly asserted that factual consent will not necessarily provide a legal defence to a charge under s 23.[488] However, it must be the case that V can consent in some contexts to the administration of a noxious substance, even one that is potentially fatal, otherwise, V could not consent to anaesthetic for surgery. The validity of consent will, it seems, turn on public policy factors, so that while informed adult consent in a medical context or in horseplay may be legally recognized, in other contexts it will not be. In *Dica*, it was accepted that V could validly consent to the risk of infection by HIV. The court

---

[477] *Harley* (1830) 4 C & P 369; *Dale* (1852) 6 Cox CC 14. D would have been more appropriately charged with 'causing...to be taken'.

[478] [1981] 1 WLR 774, CA.

[479] Following *Hennah* (1877) 13 Cox CC 547 and *Cramp* (1880) 5 QBD 307. cf *Marlow* (1964) 49 Cr App R 49 (Brabin J).

[480] [1932] AC 562.

[481] See also *T* [2006] EWCA Crim 2557, where D (46) plied V (14) with alcohol and amphetamines.

[482] [1976] 1 WLR 110; cf *Dalby* [1982] 1 WLR 425, CA.

[483] 'It is not in doubt that heroin is a noxious thing, and the contrary was not contended', per Lord Bingham in *Kennedy (No 2)* [2007] UKHL 38 at [10].

[484] [1976] 1 All ER at 268. See also *MK* [2008] 2 Cr App R (S) 437 (administering methadone to child).

[485] See *Gantz* [2004] EWCA Crim 2862.

[486] See Ormerod and Gunn [1996] 1 Web JCLI; Bronnit [1994] Crim LR 21.

[487] [1994] AC 212.

[488] *Cato*; *McShane* (1977) 66 Cr App R 97. cf the CLRC Fourteenth Report, para 190.

acknowledged that in some instances a person would be willing to take that risk, for example to conceive or to respect a religious prohibition on contraception. The court held that V could not consent to an intentional infection.

'Thereby'

The use of the term 'thereby' in s 23 could represent a significant restriction on the offence if it is interpreted in as narrow a fashion, as that term has been understood in relation to the life endangering offences under the Criminal Damage Act 1971. If the life endangerment arises from consequences other than the noxious substance itself, it is arguable that the offence is not committed. For example, if D laces V's coffee and V then drives to work, if V's life is endangered by the manner of his driving which was affected by the noxious substance which induced drowsiness,[489] but not by the noxious substance administered, it is arguable that life is not endangered thereby.

17.10.1.2 *Mens rea*

Under s 23, the only *mens rea* required is intention or recklessness as to the administration of a noxious thing. The use in the section of the word 'maliciously' makes this clear as held in the leading case of *Cunningham*.[490] Whereas in s 24 the offence uses the expression 'with intent to', in s 23, the expression is simply 'so as thereby to'. This suggests that in s 23 no additional *mens rea* is required as to the element of endangering life or inflicting grievous bodily harm. That was the interpretation adopted in *Cato*. The requirement of 'malice' was satisfied by the deliberate injection of heroin into V's body. No *mens rea* was required as to the danger to life or the infliction of grievous bodily harm. In *Cunningham*, the Court of Criminal Appeal thought the jury should have been told that D must have foreseen that the gas he caused to be administered to V by breaking the gas pipe might cause injury to someone. The court did not say D must have foreseen that life would be endangered. This is an extraordinary result, in that a less culpable state of mind is required for the more serious offence (s 23) than the less serious (s 24).

17.10.2 Section 24

The section as amended provides:

Whosoever shall unlawfully and maliciously administer to or cause to be administered to or taken by any other person any poison or other destructive or noxious thing, with intent to injure, aggrieve, or annoy such person, shall be guilty of a misdemeanor, and being...convicted thereof shall be liable to be kept in penal servitude...

By s 25 a person charged under s 24 may not be convicted of an offence under s 23.[491]

17.10.2.1 *Actus reus*

The elements of administration, etc have been considered above in relation to s 23. Section 24 might be seen as an inchoate offence, with the focus on the conduct whereas s 23 is a result-oriented crime.[492]

---

[489] cf *Steer* [1988] AC 111.

[490] [1957] 2 QB 396 D tore the gas meter from the wall of an unoccupied house to steal money from it. The gas seeped into the neighbouring houses and was inhaled by V, whose life was endangered. D's conviction under s 23 was quashed because the judge directed the jury only that 'malicious' meant 'wicked'. See now Criminal Damage Act 1971, s 1(2), below, Ch 29.

[491] cf *Stokes* (1925) 19 Cr App R 71.

[492] See A Ashworth, 'Defining Criminal Offences without Harm', in *Criminal Law Essays*, at 13.

It is arguable that V ought to be able to provide valid consent to the administration of a substance under s 24. However, the level of harm likely is that of injury, which seems to be on a par with the threshold at which consent is generally treated as invalid in *Brown*.[493] The public policy exceptions as in *Brown* will apply.

17.10.2.2 *Mens rea*

This offence requires an ulterior intent: 'with intent to injure, aggrieve, or annoy such person'.

When a drug is given to V with intent to keep him awake it seems that whether this amounts to an intention to injure depends on whether D has a malevolent or a benevolent purpose. If D, a paedophile, gives the drug to V, a child, with the motive of ingratiating himself with V or rendering him susceptible to sexual offences, he has an intention to injure: *Hill*.[494] It would probably be otherwise if D's intention was to enable V to stay awake to enjoy the fireworks or greet his father on return from work. The administration of a drug to the pilot of an aircraft to keep him awake is probably not an offence. The administration of the same drug for the purpose of carrying out a prolonged interrogation may be.[495] This casts doubt on *Weatherall*.[496] D put a sleeping tablet in V's tea to enable him to search her handbag for letters proving that she was committing adultery. It was held that there was insufficient evidence of intent to injure, aggrieve or annoy: but there was surely evidence of a 'malevolent' purpose, as there would be if D gave V a sleeping tablet with intent to rape her. The test of malevolence is presumably objective. The paedophile's belief that the drugged child will enjoy and profit from the sexual experience is never likely to be regarded as capable of being a 'benevolent' purpose. The question of intention comes perilously close to being one of motive, and at least on orthodox approaches to *mens rea*, these are irrelevant.

17.10.3 Other poisoning offences

17.10.3.1 Administering substances in relation to sexual offences

The Sexual Offences Act 2003 introduced two important changes. First, s 61 introduced an offence of intentional administration of a substance/causing it to be taken by V without consent with intent to stupefy/overpower to enable any person to engage in sex with V. This is a further response to the problem of drug-assisted rape. Secondly, there is a presumption of an absence of consent where V has been caused to take a stupefying substance, s 75(2)(f) below. These are dealt with in Chapter 18.

17.10.3.2 Terrorist related poisonings

The Public Order Act 1986, s 38 creates what is in effect an offence of food terrorism applicable where, for example, D puts poisons or harmful objects in food products in supermarkets.[497] The Anti-terrorism, Crime and Security Act 2001, ss 113 and 114 create very broad offences of using or threatening to use a noxious substance or thing to cause harm and intimidate.[498] These offences have been extended by the Terrorism Act 2006 to include acts designed to influence the Government *or an international governmental organization* or to intimidate the

---

[493] cf the remarks in sentencing in *Sky* [2000] 2 Cr App R (S) 260, para 6.

[494] (1986) 83 Cr App Rep 386, HL. The offence under s 61 of the Sexual Offences Act 2003 will apply, see below, p 770.

[495] Examples taken from *Hill*, above.

[496] [1968] Crim LR 115 (Judge Broderick).

[497] See, eg, *Cruickshank* [2001] EWCA Crim 98.

[498] See C Walker, *Blackstone's Guide to the Anti-terrorism Legislation* (2nd edn, 2009) para 6.15.

public or a section of the public. In *Bourgass*,[499] the ricin production case, D's conviction was for conspiring to cause a public nuisance – it might be different now that s 113 is available. The Crime (International Co-operation) Act 2003 extends the jurisdictional scope of that offence in certain circumstances – subject to the consent of the Attorney General.[500]

17.11 False imprisonment

False imprisonment, like assault and battery, is both a crime at common law and a tort.[501] The civil remedy is commonly invoked and most of the reported cases on this subject are civil actions, but it features as a count in many indictments. As will appear, there are some important distinctions between the crime and the tort.

False imprisonment is committed where D unlawfully and intentionally or recklessly restrains V's freedom of movement from a particular place without lawful justification. 'Imprisonment' is probably a wider term than, and includes, 'arrest'.[502]

Article 5 of the ECHR provides a guarantee against arbitrary deprivation of liberty, but that has been interpreted more narrowly than the concept of 'restricting movement' which lies at the heart of false imprisonment. 'Article 5 is concerned with the *deprivation* of liberty and not with mere *restrictions* on freedom of movement.'[503] The distinction is not always easy to identify since the difference is 'merely one of degrees or intensity, and not one of nature or substance'.[504] In *Gillan v MPC*[505] the House of Lords held that a brief stop (20 mins) could not be regarded as a 'deprivation of liberty' within the meaning of Art 5; those subjected to a stop and search were merely 'detained in the sense of kept from proceeding or kept waiting.' The ECtHR disagreed, unanimously finding a violation of Art 8, that the use of coercive powers to require an individual to submit to a detailed search of his person, his clothing and his personal belongings amounted to a clear interference with the right to respect for private life: *Gillan and Quinton v UK*.[506] The Strasbourg Court expressly disagreed with the assessment of the House of Lords that the safeguards provided by the English legislation provided adequate protection against arbitrary interference.[507] The decision of the ECtHR in *Gillan* casts doubt on the already controversial decision in *Austin v MPC*[508] where the House of

---

[499] [2006] EWCA Crim 3397.

[500] See s 113A as amended by the Counter-terrorism Act 2008.

[501] See WVH Rogers, *Winfield and Jolowicz on Tort* (18th edn, 2010) Ch 4; R Clayton and H Tomlinson, *Civil Actions Against the Police* (3rd edn, 2003) 147 et seq.

[502] *Rahman* (1985) 81 Cr App R 349 at 353, CA. *Brown* [1977] Crim LR 291, CA, and commentary thereon and articles by D Telling, 'Arrest and Detention – The Conceptual Maze' [1978] Crim LR 320 and K Lidstone, 'A Maze in Law!' [1978] Crim LR 332. Care must be taken with the articles' references to powers of arrest as these have changed significantly.

[503] *Engel v Netherlands* (1976) 1 EHRR 647, para 58; *Guzzardi v Italy* (1980) 3 EHRR 333, para 92; *Raimondo v Italy* (1994) 18 EHRR 237, para 39; *HM v Switzerland*, 26 Feb 2002 (App No 39187/98). See generally Emmerson, Ashworth and Macdonald, HR&CJ, Ch 5.

[504] *Guzzardi v Italy* (1980) 3 EHRR 333, para 92; *Ashingdane v United Kingdom* (1985) 7 EHRR 528, para 41; *Engel v Netherlands* (1976) 1 EHRR 647, paras 58–59. See also *Blume v Spain* (2000) 30 EHRR 632.

[505] [2006] UKHL 12; see [2006] Crim LR 751 and commentary.

[506] (2010) 50 EHRR 45. See also *R(AP) v Secretary of State for the Home Department* [2010] UKSC 24, in which it was held that when deciding if there is a deprivation of liberty within the meaning of Art 5 of the Convention regard should be had to the subjective factors peculiar to the particular individual.

[507] The authorization power under the Terrorism Act 2000, s 44 required only that it be expedient to make the authorization, not that it be necessary or proportionate. See Ashworth commentary [2010] Crim LR 415.

[508] [2009] UKHL 5, [2009] 2 WLR 372

Lords concluded that the police detention of several thousand people on Oxford Street did not amount to a deprivation of liberty within the meaning of Art 5.[509]

17.11.1 *Actus reus*

17.11.1.1 'Imprisonment'

For the purposes of the offence of false imprisonment, The 'imprisonment' may consist in confining V in a prison,[510] a house,[511] even V's own house,[512] a mine[513] or a vehicle;[514] or simply in detaining V in a public street[515] or any other place.

A false imprisonment may arise for a short duration. The restraint need be only momentary, so that the offence would be complete if D tapped V on the shoulder and said, 'You are my prisoner.'[516] It is not necessary that the victim be physically detained; there may be an arrest by words alone, but only if V submits. If V is not physically detained and does not realize he is under constraint, he is not imprisoned.[517] If V agrees to go to a police station voluntarily, he has not been arrested though the constable would have arrested him if he had refused to go.[518] If it is then made clear to V that he will not be allowed to leave until he provides a laboratory specimen, it has been suggested that, though he has never been 'arrested', he is 'under arrest'.[519] If this distinction is valid it would seem to be enough for false imprisonment that V is 'under arrest'.

It is enough that D orders V to accompany him to another place, and V goes because he feels constrained to do so. V is not imprisoned if, on hearing D use words of arrest, he runs away or makes his escape by a trick.[520] An invitation by D to V to accompany him cannot be an imprisonment if it is made clear to V that he is entitled to refuse to go. Thus Lord Lyndhurst CB thought there was no imprisonment where D asked a policeman to take V into custody, and the policeman objected, but said that if D and V 'would be so good as to go with him', he would take the advice of his superior.[521] The distinction between a command, amounting to an imprisonment, and a request not doing so, is a difficult one.[522] Probably Alderson B went too far

---

[509] See Ashworth commentary [2010] Crim LR 415.

[510] *Cobbett v Grey* (1849) 4 Exch 729; *R v Govenor of Brockhill Prison, ex p Evans No 2* [2001] 2 AC 19. On the difference between positive acts of imprisonment and omissions see *Iqbal v Prison Officers Association* [2009] EWCA Civ 1312.

[511] *Warner v Riddiford* (1858) 4 CBNS 180.

[512] *Termes de la Ley*, approved by Warrington and Atkin LJJ (1920) 122 LT at 51 and 53. See also *Secretary of State for the Home Department v JJ* [2007] UKHL 45 considering the power to make control orders, involving 18-hour home detention and other restrictions on movement and association, under s 1(2) of the Prevention of Terrorism Act 2005. See also *Secretary of State for the Home Department v E* [2007] UKHL 47; *Secretary of State for the Home Department v MB; Secretary of State v AF* [2007] UKHL 46.

[513] *Herd v Weardale Steel, Coal and Coke Co Ltd* [1915] AC 67.

[514] By driving at such a speed that V dare not alight: *McDaniel v State* 15 Tex Crim 115 (1942); *Burton v Davies* [1953] QSR 26. See also *Bowell* [2003] EWCA Crim 3896, single count of false imprisonment split where D detained V in the car, and detained her again when she escaped and injured herself.

[515] Blackstone, *Commentaries*, iii, 127; *Ludlow v Burgess* [1971] Crim LR 238; *Austin v MPC*, above.

[516] *Simpson v Hill* (1795) 1 Esp 431, per Eyre CJ; *Sandon v Jervis* (1859) EB & E 942, '…a mere touch constitutes an arrest, though the party be not actually taken', per Crowder J.

[517] *Alderson v Booth* [1969] 2 QB 216, [1969] 2 All ER 271.

[518] *Campbell v Tormey* [1969] 1 All ER 961, [1969] 1 WLR 189. See Emmerson, Ashworth and Macdonald, HR&CJ, para 5.03.

[519] ibid, per Ashworth J.

[520] *Russen v Lucas* (1824) 1 C & P 153.

[521] *Cant v Parsons* (1834) 6 C & P 504.

[522] G Williams in CR Sowle, *Police Power and Individual Freedom: The Quest for Balance* (1996) at 43.

in *Peters v Stanway*[523] in holding that V was imprisoned if she went to the police station with a constable voluntarily but nevertheless in consequence of a charge against her.

Though some of the older authorities[524] speak of false imprisonment as a species of assault, it is quite clear that no assault need be proved.[525] In *Linsberg*,[526] the Common Sergeant held that V, a doctor, was falsely imprisoned where D locked the door to prevent him leaving a confinement. A battery is not necessarily an imprisonment. In *Bird v Jones*,[527] V was involved in 'a struggle during which no momentary detention of his person took place'.

There is little authority on the question of how large the area of confinement may be. It is not an imprisonment wrongfully to prevent V from going in a particular direction, if he is free to go in other directions. This was decided in *Bird v Jones*,[528] where Coleridge J said: 'A prison may have its boundary large or narrow, visible and tangible, or, though real, still in the conception only;[529] it may itself be moveable or fixed: but a boundary it must have…' It would be otherwise if V could move off in other directions only by taking an unreasonable risk.[530] It could hardly be said that a man locked in a second-floor room was not imprisoned because he could have climbed down the drainpipe. It has been suggested that it would be tortious to confine V to a large country estate or the Isle of Man;[531] but it could hardly be false imprisonment to prevent V from leaving Great Britain, still less to prevent him from entering. However, a person who has actually landed and is not allowed to leave an airport building is imprisoned.[532] Is V also imprisoned, then, if he is not allowed to leave the ship which has docked in a British port?

Merely deciding to restrain a person if he attempts to leave does not amount to imprisonment.[533] But if steps are in fact taken to prevent his leaving, as by placing a policeman at the door, he is imprisoned although he is not aware of it: *Meering v Grahame-White Aviation Co Ltd*[534] where Atkin LJ said:

It appears to me that a person could be imprisoned without his knowing it. I think a person can be imprisoned while he is asleep, while he is in a state of drunkenness, while he is unconscious, and while he is a lunatic… though the imprisonment began and ceased while he was in that state.

A contrary decision[535] was not cited and *Meering* has been heavily criticized,[536] although cited with approval by the House of Lords in *Murray v Minister of Defence*;[537] the arguments

---

[523] (1835) 6 C & P 737, followed in *Conn v David Spencer Ltd* [1930] 1 DLR 805.

[524] eg, Hawkins, I PC, c 60, s 7; *Pocock v Moore* (1825) Ry & M 321.

[525] *Grainger v Hill* (1838) 4 Bing NC 212; *Warner v Riddiford* (1858) 4 CBNS 180.

[526] (1905) 69 JP 107.

[527] Below.

[528] (1845) 7 QB 742 (Denman CJ dissenting).

[529] For example, V is forbidden to move more than ten yards from the village pump.

[530] *Street on Torts* (11th edn, 2007) at 32; (12th edn, 2007) 248.

[531] ibid. But 'Napoleon was certainly imprisoned on St Helena': *Winfield and Jolowicz on Torts* (15th edn, 1998) at 71. In *Re Mwenya* [1960] 1 QB 241, [1959] 3 All ER 525, a writ of *habeas corpus* was sought for V who was confined to an area of some 1,500 square miles but he was released before it became necessary to decide whether he was imprisoned for the purpose of *habeas corpus*.

[532] *Kuchenmeister v Home Office* [1958] 1 QB 496, [1958] 1 All ER 485.

[533] *Bournewood Community and Mental Health NHS Trust, ex p L* [1998] 3 All ER 289 at 298, HL; but Lord Steyn, dissenting, more realistically thought (at 306): 'The suggestion that L was free to go is a fairy tale.' Note the European Court's finding of a breach of Art 5 in *HL v United Kingdom* (App No 45508/99), and see the Mental Health Act 2007, ss 4 and 5.

[534] (1919) 122 LT 44, Duke LJ dissenting, where two policemen were stationed outside the door of a room to prevent V leaving. He was as effectively imprisoned as if the door had been locked. *Meering* was approved in *Murray v Ministry of Defence* [1988] 2 All ER 521 at 529, HL.

[535] *Herring v Boyle* (1834) 1 Cr M & R 377 (Court of Exchequer).

[536] G Williams in *Police Power and Individual Freedom* at 45–46; *Street on Torts* (12th edn, 2007) Ch 3.

[537] [1998] 1 WLR 692.

advanced against awarding damages in this situation are, however, not applicable to the crime. D's conduct may not be damaging to V if V knows nothing about it, but it is not necessarily any less blameworthy for, in most cases, the fact that V remains in ignorance must be a matter of mere chance.

Like other crimes, false imprisonment can be committed through an innocent agent.[538] So D is responsible for the *actus reus* if, at his direction or request, a policeman takes V into custody,[539] or he signs the charge-sheet when the police have said they will not take the responsibility of detaining V unless he does.[540] However, if D merely gives information to a constable, which causes him to make an arrest, that is not a false imprisonment in tort by D, if D is *bona fide*.[541] A fortiori, it should not be *criminal*, because D will also lack *mens rea*. But this raises the question why should D not be guilty if he deliberately supplies false information to a constable who, acting on his own authority but relying exclusively on D's information, arrests V?[542] D has surely caused the *actus reus* with *mens rea*. Note that where D is initially liable for false imprisonment his liability ceases on the intervention of some judicial act[543] authorizing the detention or on any other event, breaking the chain of causation.[544] So, in the case of the false information leading to arrest, D may be liable for the act of the constable but not the judicial act of the magistrate.[545]

Whatever the position in the law of tort,[546] it should be immaterial in the criminal law that the imprisonment was not 'directly' caused by D; and it ought to be sufficient that D caused it with *mens rea* – as by digging a pit into which V falls and is trapped.[547]

Another issue in the law of tort is whether, in view of the requirement of a trespass, it is possible to falsely imprison by mere omission. In *Herd v Weardale Steel Coal and Coke Co Ltd*,[548] V voluntarily descended into D's mine and, in breach of contract, stopped work and asked to be brought to the surface before the end of the shift. D's refusal to accede to this request was not a false imprisonment: he was under no duty to provide facilities for V to leave in breach of contract. Clearly, the result would be different if D were to take positive steps to prevent V from leaving in breach of contract,[549] as by locking him in a factory. Buckley and Hamilton LJJ[550] thought that mere omission could not have been false imprisonment, even if it occurred

---

[538] There is no vicarious liability for false imprisonment (nor generally in criminal law for common law offences: *R (Craik) v Newcastle Magistrates' Court* [2010] EWHC 935 (Admin).

[539] *Gosden v Elphick and Bennett* (1849) 4 Exch 445. Note also the tort of procuring an arrest see *Martin v Watson* [1996] 1 AC 74.

[540] *Austin v Dowling* (1870) LR 5 CP 534. It is otherwise if D signs the charge sheet as a matter of form, when the police are detaining V on their own responsibility: *Grinham v Willey* (1859) 4 H & N 496.

[541] *Gosden v Elphick and Bennett*, above; *Grinham v Willey*, above; 'We ought to take care that people are not put in peril for making complaint when a crime has been committed', per Pollock CB. cf *O'Hara v Chief Constable of RUC* [1997] AC 286.

[542] See *Hough v Chief Constable of Staffordshire* [2001] EWCA Civ 39.

[543] *Lock v Ashton* (1848) 12 QB 871. cf *Marrinan v Vibart* [1963] 1 QB 528, [1962] 3 All ER 380.

[544] *Harnett v Bond* [1925] AC 669. D's report caused V to be taken to an asylum; D was not liable for the imprisonment after the doctor at the asylum had examined V and decided to detain him. cf *Pike v Waldrum* [1952] 1 Lloyd's Rep 431.

[545] See *Austin v Dowling* (1870) LR 5 C & P 534 at 540.

[546] Clayton and Tomlinson, *Civil Actions against the Police*, para 4–046. See also *Ahmed v Shafique* [2009] EWHC 618 (QB).

[547] cf *Clarence* (1888) 22 QBD 23 at 36, per Wills J.

[548] [1915] AC 67, HL.

[549] Unless, perhaps, the contract was that V should be entitled to leave only on the fulfilment of some reasonable condition: *Robinson v Balmain New Ferry Co Ltd* [1910] AC 295, PC. *Sed quaere* whether one is entitled to restrain another from leaving even if it is a breach of contract for him to do so? The contract can hardly be specifically enforceable.

[550] [1913] 3 KB at 787 and 793.

when the shift was over. V's only civil remedy would have been in contract; but the House of Lords expressed no opinion on this point.

In *Mee v Cruickshank*,[551] Wills J held that a prison governor was under a duty to take steps to ensure that his officers did not detain a prisoner who had been acquitted. In that case there were acts of imprisonment by the prison officers but they were not the servants of D, the governor, and it seems to have been D's omission which rendered him liable in tort. As the House of Lords accepted in *Ex p Evans*, the failure to release a prisoner on the due date gives rise to an action in false imprisonment, even if the failure was in good faith. And it ought to make no difference that D's duty to release V arises out of a contract:

If a man gets into an express train and the doors are locked pending its arrival at its destination, he is not entitled, merely because the train has been stopped by signal, to call for the doors to be opened to let him out.[552]

But if he is kept locked in for a day at his destination this surely ought to be false imprisonment. And even if there is no remedy in tort this is no reason why the omission should not be held to be criminal. The CLRC were of the opinion that the crime of false imprisonment is, and ought to be, capable of commission by omission.[553]

17.11.1.2 Unlawful restraint

The imprisonment must be 'false', that is unlawful. A convicted person sentenced to imprisonment may be lawfully confined in any prison and, as against prison officers so confining him in good faith, he has no 'residual liberty'. If he is subjected to intolerable conditions he may have other remedies[554] but he cannot sue (or, it may be assumed, prosecute) the officers for false imprisonment.[555] It might, however, be false imprisonment for a fellow prisoner, or an officer acting in bad faith outside the scope of his duty, to lock him in a confined space, such as a hut, within the prison. In *Iqbal v Prison Officers Association*,[556] the failure to allow I, a serving prisoner, out of his cell on the day of unlawful strike action by prison officers, did not give rise to a claim for false imprisonment against the officers.

A parent may lawfully exercise restraint over a child, so long as he remains within the bounds of reasonable parental discipline and does not act in contravention of a court order,[557] or the Children Act 2004, s 58. Where a girl of 14 or 15 was fostered out by her father with the consent and assistance of the local authority and he abducted her against her will and with intent to take her to her country of origin, it was for the jury to say whether they were satisfied that this was outside the bounds of legitimate parental discipline and correction.[558] A defendant charged with false imprisonment may rely on other justifications, such as the prevention of crime.[559]

---

[551] (1902) 20 Cox CC 210.

[552] *Herd v Weardale Steel Coal and Coke Co Ltd* [1915] AC 67 at 71, per Lord Haldane. See M Amos, 'A Note on Contractual Restraint of Liberty' (1928) 44 LQR 464; KF Tan, 'A Misconceived Issue in the Tort of False Imprisonment' (1981) 44 MLR 166.

[553] Fourteenth Report, paras 253, 254.

[554] See *Krgozlu v MPC* [2006] EWCA Civ 1691.

[555] *Hague v Deputy Governor of Parkhurst Prison* [1991] 3 All ER 733, HL. What if the conditions are so intolerable as to found a defence of necessity to a charge of escape (above, Ch 12)? Is it false imprisonment to prevent such a prisoner from leaving the prison?

[556] [2009] EWCA Civ 1312.

[557] *Rahman* (1985) 81 Cr App R 349, CA. cf *D* [1984] AC 778, [1984] 1 All ER 574.

[558] *Rahman*, above. In fact, D pleaded guilty, and his appeal was dismissed. Note the Forced Marriage (Civil Protection) Act 2007.

[559] D acting to prevent theft relied on s 3 of the Criminal Law Act 1967: *Bowden* [2002] EWCA Civ 1279. See also *Faraj* [2007] EWCA Crim 1033 (above Ch 12) 395.

The question of false imprisonment most commonly arises in connection with the exercise of powers of arrest. If such powers are exceeded, there is a false imprisonment. The principal powers are as follows.

Arrest by a constable under a valid warrant

Where a warrant is issued but the justice lacks jurisdiction to issue the warrant, the constable who arrests under the warrant is statutorily protected[560] from any 'action' if he acts in obedience to it. As the term 'action' is inappropriate to a criminal proceeding, a constable could not rely on the Act as a defence to criminal prosecution; but he would probably have a good defence on the ground of lack of *mens rea*.[561] An arrest under warrant for a civil matter is unlawful if the arresting officer does not have the warrant in his possession.[562]

Arrest by a constable

The Police and Criminal Evidence Act (PACE) 1984, s 24 provides:[563]

(1) A constable may arrest without a warrant –

    (a) anyone who is about to commit an offence;

    (b) anyone who is in the act of committing an offence;

    (c) anyone whom he has reasonable grounds for suspecting to be about to commit an offence;

    (d) anyone whom he has reasonable grounds for suspecting to be committing an offence.

(2) If a constable has reasonable grounds for suspecting that an offence has been committed, he may arrest without a warrant anyone whom he has reasonable grounds to suspect of being guilty of it.

(3) If an offence has been committed, a constable may arrest without a warrant –

    (a) anyone who is guilty of the offence;

    (b) anyone whom he has reasonable grounds for suspecting to be guilty of it.

(4) But the power of summary arrest conferred by subsection (1), (2) or (3) is exercisable only if the constable has reasonable grounds for believing that for any of the reasons mentioned in subsection (5) it is necessary to arrest the person in question.

(5) The reasons are –

    (a) to enable the name of the person in question to be ascertained (in the case where the constable does not know, and cannot readily ascertain, the person's name, or has reasonable grounds for doubting whether a name given by the person as his name is his real name);

    (b) correspondingly as regards the person's address;

    (c) to prevent the person in question –

        (i) causing physical injury to himself or any other person;

        (ii) suffering physical injury;

        (iii) causing loss of or damage to property;

        (iv) committing an offence against public decency (subject to subsection (6)); or

        (v) causing an unlawful obstruction of the highway;

---

[560] The Constables Protection Act 1750. See *O'Connor v Isaacs* [1956] 2 QB 288.
[561] Below, p 686.
[562] *De Costa Small v Kirkpatrick* (1978) 68 Cr App R 186, [1979] Crim LR 41.
[563] As amended by s 110 of the Serious Crime Act 2005.

    (d) to protect a child or other vulnerable person from the person in question;

    (e) to allow the prompt and effective investigation of the offence or of the conduct of the person in question;

    (f) to prevent any prosecution for the offence from being hindered by the disappearance of the person in question.

(6) Subsection (5)(c)(iv) applies only where members of the public going about their normal business cannot reasonably be expected to avoid the person in question.

The powers are now available in relation to any offence, not as previously an 'arrestable offence'. The 'general arrest powers' in the PACE 1984, s 25, were repealed by the Serious Organised Crime and Police Act (SOCPA) 2005, s 110(2). Section 24(4) is crucial in imposing a condition on all arrests that they are necessary.[564]

Civilian powers of arrest

A new s 24A of PACE defines the more restrictive powers of arrest for civilians:

24A. – (1) A person other than a constable may arrest without a warrant –

    (a) anyone who is in the act of committing an indictable offence;

    (b) anyone whom he has reasonable grounds for suspecting to be committing an indictable offence.

(2) Where an indictable offence has been committed, a person other than a constable may arrest without a warrant –

    (a) anyone who is guilty of the offence;

    (b) anyone whom he has reasonable grounds for suspecting to be guilty of it.

(3) But the power of summary arrest conferred by subsection (1) or (2) is exercisable only if –

    (a) the person making the arrest has reasonable grounds for believing that for any of the reasons mentioned in subsection (4) it is necessary to arrest the person in question; and

    (b) it appears to the person making the arrest that it is not reasonably practicable for a constable to make it instead.

(4) The reasons are to prevent the person in question –

    (a) causing physical injury to himself or any other person;

    (b) suffering physical injury;

    (c) causing loss of or damage to property; or

    (d) making off before a constable can assume responsibility for him.

(5) This section does not apply in relation to an offence under part 3 or 3A of the Public Order Act 1986.

These civilian powers are more restricted in a number of ways. First, they apply only to indictable offences (s 24A(1) and (2)). Secondly, if a civilian, D, arrests V under s 24A(2) for an offence D believes has been committed, that arrest will be unlawful unless an indictable offence was in fact committed.[565] Thirdly, a civilian must have reasonable grounds for believing that it is necessary to arrest V for a statutory reason under s 24A(4) and it must appear to him that it is

---

[564] See *R (C) v Chief Constable of A* [2006] EWHC 2352 (Admin).

[565] *Self* [1992] 3 All ER 476, CA. The powers were described in *Ahmed v Shafique* [2009] EWHC 618 (QB) as reflecting the position as at common law declared in celebrated cases such as *Walters v WH Smith* [1914] 1 KB 595. Note that under s 24A(2), the arrestee must be guilty, not merely have committed the act.

not practicable for a constable to make the arrest instead (s 24A(3)). Finally, it should be noted that the conditions under s 24A(4) are more limited than those under s 24(5).

Arrest under the powers preserved by Schedule 2 to the Police and Criminal Evidence Act 1984

Numerous statutory powers of arrest without warrant were abolished by s 26 of the 1984 Act which, however, preserved the powers specified in Sch 2.[566]

Arrests for breach of the peace

An arrest can be made if a breach of the peace is committed in D's presence, or where he reasonably believes[567] that such a breach will be committed in the immediate future by a person, or where a breach has been committed and he reasonably believes that a renewal of it is threatened.[568] The House of Lords held in *R (Laporte) v Chief Constable of Gloucestershire*[569] that an arrest for an anticipated breach of the peace can only be legitimate where there is a reasonable apprehension of an *imminent* breach of the peace. Moreover, in the absence of such an apprehension, there is no power to take preventive action falling short of arrest.

In *Austin v MPC*[570] the House of Lords held that the there was no false imprisonment when, in order to maintain order and public safety and to prevent the commission of offences, the police held several thousand people in a cordon on Oxford Street in London. Some of those people were not demonstrators. The containment of the individuals amounted to imprisonment, but that it was not false imprisonment because the police were acting lawfully. The police action was found to be necessary in order to avoid an imminent breach of the peace (and the causing of serious injury) by some members of the crowd. The circumstances in which the police can detain V in order to avoid danger because of an imminent breach of the peace by X were said to be very strictly limited to extreme and exceptional circumstances.

There is a breach of the peace whenever harm is actually done or is likely to be done to a person, or in his presence to his property, or a person is in fear of being so harmed through an assault, an affray, a riot or other disturbance.[571] Public alarm, excitement or disturbance is not of itself a breach of the peace, unless it arises from actual or threatened violence.

Breach of the peace is not an offence.[572] A person arrested for breach of the peace may be held in custody at a police station, but the officer concerned must have an honest belief, based upon objective and reasonable grounds, that detention is necessary in order to prevent a breach of the peace: *Williamson v Chief Constable of West Midlands Police*.[573]

Arrest unlawful, unless information given

Where a person is arrested, otherwise than by being informed he is under arrest, he must be so informed as soon as practicable afterwards: s 28(3).[574] Article 5(2) of the ECHR provides the right of 'everyone arrested to be informed promptly in a language he understands of the

---

[566] *Blackstone's Criminal Practice* (2011), D1.

[567] This is an objective test having regard to the circumstances as perceived by the arrester at the time: *Redmond-Bate v DPP* (1999) 163 JP 789.

[568] *Howell* (1981) 73 Cr App R 31 at 36; *Kelbie* [1996] Crim LR 862 and commentary; *Jarrett v CC West Midlands Police* [2003] EWCA Civ 397. See generally P Thornton et al, *The Law of Public Order and Protest* (2009) Ch 6.

[569] [2007] 2 WLR 46.

[570] [2009] UKHL 5, [2009] 2 WLR 372. See now *R (Moos) v MPC* [2011] EWHC 957 (Admin).

[571] *Howell*, above, at 37. Lord Denning has said that even the lawful use of force is a breach of the peace: *Chief Constable of Devon and Cornwall, ex p Central Electricity Generating Board* [1981] 3 All ER 826 at 832; but this can hardly subject the person using such force to arrest.

[572] It is treated as criminal for the purposes of the ECHR: *Steel v UK* (1999) 28 EHRR 603.

[573] [2004] 1 WLR 14.

[574] See *Taylor v Chief Constable of Thames Valley* [2004] EWCA Civ 858.

reason for his arrest'.[575] The detained person must be told 'in simple, non-technical language that he can understand, the essential legal and factual grounds for his arrest so as to be able, if he sees fit, to apply to a court to challenge its lawfulness'.[576]

No arrest is lawful unless the person arrested is informed of the ground of the arrest at the time or as soon as is practicable thereafter; and, where the arrest is by a constable, this is so even where the ground for the arrest is obvious. If the arrested person escapes before it is reasonably practicable for him to be informed that he is under arrest, or the ground for the arrest, the arrest is not rendered unlawful.[577] The arrester must have a valid ground for the arrest in mind when he makes it.[578] The existence of a valid ground cannot justify an arrest when it was not actually exercised by the arrester.[579]

Other police powers of detention

Stop and search powers are provided under PACE and various other statutes including, notably, the Terrorism Act 2000. In *Gillan and Quinton v United Kingdom*[580] police officers used powers under ss 44–45 of the Terrorism Act 2000, to stop people for around 20 minutes. The House of Lords accepted the police practice, and held that such a brief stop could not be regarded as a 'deprivation of liberty' within the meaning of Art 5; those subjected to a stop and search were merely 'detained in the sense of kept from proceeding or kept waiting'. In Strasbourg, the ECtHR held that under Art 8, using coercive powers to require someone to submit to a detailed search of his person, his clothing and his personal belongings amounts to a clear interference with the right to respect for private life. The interference was not 'in accordance with the law'. The safeguards provided by the Act did not provide adequate protection against arbitrary interference. The Court decided not to reach a final determination on the application of Art 5.[581]

The courts have also recognized that a police officer may detain people present on premises when executing a search warrant.[582] The absence of an express statutory power to do so created difficulties.[583]

17.11.2 *Mens rea*

Since the great majority of the reported cases are civil actions,[584] there is little authority on the nature of the *mens rea* required for false imprisonment, but, in *Rahman*,[585] the court stated that 'false imprisonment consists in the unlawful and intentional or reckless restraint of a victim's freedom of movement from a particular place'. This was confirmed by *Hutchins*[586] which held that the offence is one of 'basic intent' so that a belief caused by self-induced intoxication that the victim is consenting is no defence. The courts did not specify

---

[575] See *X v Germany* (1978) 16 DR 111.

[576] *Fox, Campbell and Hartley v UK* (1991) 13 EHRR 157, para 40.

[577] These rules, in s 28 of the 1984 Act, replace the common law as stated in *Christie v Leachinsky* [1947] AC 573, [1947] 1 All ER 567. See *DPP v Hawkins* [1988] 3 All ER 673, [1988] Crim LR 741; *Brosch* [1988] Crim LR 743 and (especially) commentary.

[578] *Edwards v DPP* (1993) 97 Cr App R 301, 306–307, DC.

[579] *Redman* [1994] Crim LR 914.

[580] (2010) 50 EHRR 1105.

[581] See Sir Richard Buxton, 'Terrorism and the European Convention' [2010] Crim LR 533.

[582] *DPP v Meaden* [2004] 1 WLR 955, DC; see also *Connor v CC Merseyside* [2006] EWCA Civ 1549.

[583] See the commentary at [2003] Crim LR 587.

[584] Reckless indifference suffices for the tort: *Muuse v Secretary of State for the Home Department* [2010] EWCA Civ 453.

[585] (1985) 81 Cr App R 349 at 353, CA, above, n 557.

[586] [1988] Crim LR 379.

what kind of recklessness they had in mind; but a common law offence would naturally require *Cunningham* recklessness. This may be taken to be established now that it is settled that assault requires *Cunningham* recklessness.[587] Assault and false imprisonment are both common law offences and are so closely related that it is inconceivable that they should be governed by different principles of *mens rea*.

17.12 Kidnapping

Kidnapping has long been regarded as an aggravated form of false imprisonment[588] so the rules of lawful excuse are, no doubt, the same. Both are common law offences, punishable with imprisonment or fine at the discretion of the court. It is generally regarded as important to have a separate offence of kidnap to reflect the distinctive wrongdoing involved in the taking or carrying away which distinguishes kidnap from false imprisonment.

In *R v D*,[589] the House of Lords gave what purported to be an authoritative account of the law of kidnapping:

First, the nature of the offence is an attack on, and infringement of, the personal liberty of an individual. Second, the offence contains four ingredients as follows: (1) the taking or carrying away of one person by another, (2) by force or by fraud, (3) without the consent of the person so taken or carried away and (4) without lawful excuse. Third, until the comparatively recent abolition by statute of the division of criminal offences into the two categories of felonies and misdemeanours (see s 1 of the Criminal Law Act 1967), the offence of kidnapping was categorized by the common law as a misdemeanour only. Fourth, despite that, kidnapping was always regarded, by reason of its nature, as a grave and (to use the language of an earlier age) heinous offence. Fifth, in earlier days the offence contained a further ingredient, namely that the taking or carrying away should be from a place within the jurisdiction to another place outside it; this further ingredient has, however, long been obsolete and forms no necessary part of the offence today. Sixth, the offence was in former days described not merely as taking or carrying away a person but further or alternatively as secreting him; this element of secretion has, however, also become obsolete, so that, although it may be present in a particular case, it adds nothing to the basic ingredient of taking or carrying away.

In defining the offence in that way, Lord Brandon's attempts to consolidate earlier interpretations resulted in a considerable degree of overlap. Following recent decisions in which the Court of Appeal has struggled to identify whether the core of the offence lies in the wrong of taking and carrying away by fraud or force or the harm in terms of deprivation of liberty, the law is in a state of some confusion.

In *Cort*,[590] D had on a number of occasions stopped his car at bus stops, falsely stating to women in the queue that the bus they awaited had broken down and offered them a lift. On two occasions women got into the car. One changed her mind and asked to be let out of the car and D complied; the other was taken to her destination without being assaulted by D in any way. D was convicted of two counts of kidnapping. The Court of Appeal upheld the conviction, finding that D had defrauded VV as to the nature of the act. In this case it was held that

---

[587] Above, p 625.

[588] East, 1 PC, 429. On the history, see D Napier, 'Detention Offences at Common Law', in P Glazebrook (ed), *Reshaping the Criminal Law*, 198. I am grateful to Simon Tabbush for many valuable discussions on this offence.

[589] [1984] AC 778, [1984] 2 All ER 449, [1984] Crim LR 558. Kidnapping had not previously been satisfactorily defined: see D Napier, above, n 588. The Law Commission Draft Criminal Code, cl 81, proposed radical amendment to the offence by restricting it to cases of carrying away for ulterior purposes – to commit a serious offence.

[590] [2003] EWCA Crim 2149, [2004] Crim LR 64.

the complainants did not consent to the events, VV only consented to a ride in the car, but that the ride in the car was a 'different thing' from that with which D was charged. That decision is no longer to be followed in light of the decision in *Hendy-Freegard*.[591] H was convicted of two offences of kidnapping and a number of offences of dishonesty. H had 'an astonishing capacity to deceive', and managed to persuade three victims that he was an MI5 agent who had been investigating an IRA cell at their college. He persuaded them to leave the college and travel around the country, with periods of settlement, for a period of up to 10 years. During that period, he financially exploited them. H's conviction for kidnapping was quashed as the Court of Appeal, rightly it is submitted, concluded that because H did not accompany the victims this meant that there was no kidnap. In the course of the judgment, the Lord Chief Justice emphasized that the prosecution had to establish that the victim was deprived of his or her liberty.

Confusion remains as to the relationship between the elements of: (i) the deprivation of liberty, (ii) the absence of consent, (iii) being taken or carried away, (iv) the use of force or fraud and (v) the absence of a lawful excuse. In particular, it is difficult to determine whether the force or fraud must be the means of carrying away (as Lord Brandon's speech and *Cort* suggest) or the reason for the lack of consent. A further question is whether the consent must be (a) to the taking or carrying away, (b) the deprivation of liberty, (c) both, or (d) being taken by force or fraud.

It is submitted that there must be an act of force or fraud which results in V being taken or carried away and that by that act of taking or carrying away without consent, V must be deprived of liberty without lawful excuse.

17.12.1 Deprivation of liberty

The definition offered in *D* fails to clarify whether the offence requires proof of a deprivation of liberty. Prior to *D*, commentators had expressly defined the offence in terms of a deprivation of liberty and carrying away from the place where the victim wanted to be.[592] It is difficult to see how there could be a kidnap if V was not deprived of his liberty. It is submitted that following the recent decision in *Hendy-Freegard*, this is now reconfirmed as a core element of the offence. Whether someone is deprived of his liberty is to be determined in the same way as for the offence of false imprisonment. A deprivation of liberty is a necessary but not a sufficient basis of liability for kidnap.

It seems clear that if V has consented to the deprivation of liberty there can be no kidnapping. If V consents, for example, to being locked up (either as part of a prank or a role play in sadomasochism, etc) there is no offence of false imprisonment or of kidnap. There is consent to the deprivation of liberty.

Applying orthodox principles discussed above in this chapter, if D has deprived V of her liberty by deceiving her as to the nature of the act or as to his identity, there will be no valid consent. The usual difficulties will arise as to whether the fraud was as to the nature or identity. The case of *Wellard*,[593] might be best interpreted as involving a fraud as to identity. In *Wellard*, D was held to have 'taken' V when by impersonating a police officer he tricked V into his car in order to submit to a 'drugs search'. That case also suggests that there is a sufficient deprivation of liberty if V does not believe that he can move. This will usually arise because of D's deception.

591 [2007] EWCA Crim 1236, CA
592 See the 5th edition of this book, at 388; *Archbold* (40th edn, 1979) para 2796.
593 [1978] 3 All ER 161.

17.12.2 Taking and carrying away

There is no doubt that this is also an important element of the offence. The requirements of carrying away and the use of force or fraud seem to be the only factors distinguishing kidnapping from false imprisonment. It seems that every kidnapping is also a false imprisonment but a detention without any taking away or force or fraud (eg D merely turns the key intentionally locking V in the room) is only the latter offence. Where D has taken or carried V away by force or fraud, he may be convicted of both offences.[594] The crime is complete when V is deprived of his liberty and carried away from the place where he wished to be.[595]

The courts have failed to define what the term taking or carrying away means. Lord Brandon used the terms as alternatives, which suggests that there is some difference between them. Carried implies some movement, and as we know from *Hendy-Freegard*, D must accompany V. If 'takes' implies a different action, it could mean 'seizes', but if that means no more than a stationary capture of V by D, that would be difficult to reconcile with the requirement in *Hendy-Freegard*. It is submitted that the word 'takes' here should not construed so as to extend the offence of kidnap to include stationary detention that would amount to no more than false imprisonment.

The courts have failed to spell out the relationship between the element of taking or carrying away and the deprivation of liberty. It is submitted that the most logical interpretation of the offence may be that the act of taking or carrying away must be the *cause of* the deprivation of liberty. The decision in *Hendy-Freegard* supports this interpretation by concluding that there is no kidnap where V is taken or carried away by force or fraud (as in *Cort*) if not also deprived of her liberty. In *Cort*, for example, it would now seem to be accepted that the passengers accepting the lifts were defrauded as to being carried away, but not deprived of their liberty since they would be free to leave at any time they wished – as demonstrated by the fact that D did let one of the women out of the car immediately when she so requested. D could be interpreted more narrowly, to require deprivation of liberty in the course of taking or carrying away.

In *Hendy-Freegard*, Lord Phillips CJ stated that:

We cannot see that there was justification for extending the offence of kidnapping to cover the situation in which the driver of the car has no intention of detaining his passenger against her will nor of doing other than taking her to the destination to which she wishes to go, simply because in some such circumstances the driver may have an objectionable ulterior motive. The consequence of the decision in Cort would seem to be that the mini-cab driver, who obtains a fare by falsely pretending to be an authorised taxi, will be guilty of kidnapping.[596]

It is clear, following *Hendy-Freegard*, that D must accompany V at the time that V is alleged to be taken or carried away. The Crown's expansive interpretation argued for in *Hendy-Freegard* would have rendered guilty the practical joker who telephoned V and induced him to attend a hospital and remain there on the pretext that his wife had been in an accident. That would clearly go too far.[597]

Interpreting *D*, the taking and carrying away must be by force or fraud (below). It is not enough, then, that D asks V to accompany him and practises no fraud and offers no menace

---

[594] *Brown* [1985] Crim LR 398, CA (five years' imprisonment concurrent on both counts upheld).

[595] *Wellard* [1978] 3 All ER 161, [1978] 1 WLR 921.

[596] [55]. The Lord Chief Justice referred to the criticisms of *Cort* made in the 11th edition. *Cort* was also doubted by the Court of Appeal in *Nnamdi* [2005] EWCA Crim 74.

[597] The difficulty is to identify any serious offence in such cases. If D phones V and tells her falsely that D holds X hostage and that he will kill X unless V goes to a particular venue and remains there, what crime has been committed? There is no threat to X, nor to V.

or threat to V, even if V is then deprived of liberty at their destination. As noted above, it is submitted that to constitute kidnapping, the taking or carrying away must also be such as will deprive V of his or her liberty at that time. On a narrow interpretation of *D*, it is not sufficient that D persuades V by some fraud to accompany him to a place where he proposes to deprive her of her liberty if, during the period of her transmission to that place, D is prepared to release her at any time she requests. That would seem to follow from the decision in *Hendy-Freegard* interpreting *Cort*.

In *D*, Lord Brandon states, in terms, that the taking or carrying away must be by force or fraud *and without consent*. If a deprivation of liberty is also an essential element of the offence, and a lack of consent is an integral part of that element of the offence, the question arises: what part does consent have to play in taking and carrying away? If V is not consenting to the deprivation of his liberty, D ought to be guilty of kidnap irrespective of whether the force or fraud used to take or carry V away was sufficient to vitiate V's consent *to that act* of being carried or taken away.[598]

17.12.2.1 'Force or fraud'

The formulation in *D* creates problems. It is necessary to prove a taking or carrying away by force or fraud and absence of consent (whether that absence of consent was because of the force or fraud or not). If D's force or fraud taking V away also causes V's lack of consent, then no problem arises. If D's force or fraud that causes V to be taken or carried away is not of such gravity that it vitiates consent (eg a deception about a peripheral matter), it must be shown that V did not consent for some other reason. More problematic still is a case where D uses force or fraud and V is not consenting for a reason unconnected to force or fraud (eg a general lack of capacity). There would, on a literal reading of *D* be no offence unless the taking was shown to be 'by' force or fraud.

Force or fraud and consent

For the reasons discussed in the previous paragraph, it is submitted that if the force or fraud vitiates the consent to the taking or carrying away and that taking or carrying away causes V to be deprived of his liberty without consent, the offence will be committed.

Force

Clearly where D forces V by violence or threats of violence to be taken or carried away that should be sufficient to satisfy this element of the offence. It may be that lesser threats or trivial force ought to be sufficient for kidnapping. The Court of Appeal has suggested that the element of force sufficient to vitiate consent may be established by no more than submission.[599] Presumably the same is true of force sufficient to lead to taking away. The force used must be sufficient to cause V to be taken or carried away. In addition, if it is alleged that the taking or carrying away is by force, that taking or carrying away (and hence the force used to achieve it) must be sufficient to deprive V of his liberty without his consent. The relationship between deprivation of liberty and being taken away once again arises.

Fraud

What types of fraud will suffice? The answer is, it is submitted, contained within the analysis above. The fraud used must be sufficient to cause V to be taken or carried away. Any fraud (not just those as to identity and nature) may suffice to cause V to be carried away. There is also a question of whether V is consenting to being taken and carried away. The absence of

---

[598] That may be an assault.
[599] See *Greenhalgh* [2001] EWCA Crim 1367.

consent may arise from D's fraud or from some other basis (eg lack of capacity). It is possible to envisage a case in which D uses fraud on V to cause him to be carried away, but in which V is not actually deprived of his liberty by that act of taking away. This would seem to follow from *Hendy-Freegard's* interpretation of *Cort*.

Adopting general principles to frauds vitiating consent, any fraud as to the identity of the actor should suffice. In this context, it is submitted that there is a stronger claim than in most circumstances for a fraud as to certain attributes of the actor and not just his correct name or identity being sufficient. Thus, as in *Wellard*,[600] the impersonation of a police officer should suffice to negative the consent of the person. Other examples might include impersonation of State officials, paramedics, etc.

In addition to frauds as to identity, it is recognized that frauds as to the *nature* of the act will vitiate consent. This is where the most significant difficulties arise, as illustrated by the cases on sexual offences discussed below in Chapter 18. There is also the question of whether a fraud as to the 'purpose' of the taking will suffice to vitiate consent? Consider D who falsely tells V that her husband is injured and he drives her home (because he enjoys her company). Or consider D, who tells his 17-year-old daughter that they are to travel abroad to visit an ailing relative when his true motive is for her to take part in an arranged marriage. The destination, manner of transport, etc are identical so the nature of the carrying a way is not affected by the fraud. But note the decision in *Nnamdi*,[601] in which on the facts the court did not find it necessary to determine, on a charge of conspiracy to kidnap, whether telling V that she should meet D to join his modelling agency would be a sufficient fraud.

Force or fraud sufficient to vitiate consent to deprivation of liberty

On this literal approach to *D*, the elements of force or fraud represent routes through which the prosecution might establish the absence of consent to the fundamental question whether V was consenting to the deprivation of liberty arising from the taking or carrying away. It is an interpretation which resonates with Lord Brandon's emphasis in *D* that, 'the nature of the offence is an attack on, and infringement of, the personal liberty of an individual'.

17.12.2.2 Without lawful excuse

What amounts to a lawful excuse is left completely at large; and whether a taking by a parent amounts to kidnapping is likely to be resolved in the same way whether the court proceeds by the route of deciding (as the majority in *Reid*[602] would), whether there is a lawful excuse or by deciding (as Lord Bridge would) whether the offence extends to those further circumstances. If a 12-year-old child refuses to return home from a visit to his grandmother's and his father forcibly carries him off, he surely commits no offence. The majority would say, presumably, because the father has a lawful excuse and Lord Bridge, because kidnapping does not extend to those circumstances. The result is the same. The question must be whether the parent has gone beyond what is reasonable in the exercise of parental authority.

Where V is not D's child and D is not acting in pursuance of any statutory authority or power of arrest, 'lawful excuse' is likely to be narrowly confined. In *Henman*,[603] D was guilty of attempted kidnapping when he tried to take by force an acquaintance whom he believed to be in moral and spiritual danger from a religious sect to which she belonged. There was no lawful excuse because there was no 'necessity recognized by the law as such' for D's conduct.

---

[600] [1978] 3 All ER 161.
[601] [2005] EWCA Crim 74.
[602] [1973] QB 299, [1972] 2 All ER 1350.
[603] [1987] Crim LR 333, CA.

17.12.2.3 Who may be kidnapped?

It was held in *Reid*[604] that a husband may be convicted of kidnapping his wife and in *D* that a father may be guilty of kidnapping his child. It was recognized that, until modern times, it may be that an indictment of a father for kidnapping his child would have failed because of the paramount stature of his position in the family; but common law principles adapt and develop in the light of radically changed social conventions and conditions. Lord Bridge held that parental kidnapping includes the case (as in *D*) where the parent acts in contravention of the order of a competent court, leaving open the question whether a parent might be convicted in any other circumstances; but the majority preferred to hold simply that the parent is guilty where he acts 'without lawful excuse'.

In cases of fraud, the offence might be regarded as seriously deficient in protecting children. V must be deprived of his liberty without consent, and it will be possible to say that in the case of a young child[605] who lacks the understanding or intelligence to give consent, the absence of consent is a necessary inference. However, the present definition requires there to be a carrying or taking away *by* force or fraud. In the case of a young child, D may not need to use force or fraud (unless those words are very broadly construed) to succeed in taking V away, as where a toddler is persuaded by true statements ('I'll buy you sweets') to accompany D. Arguably, such cases need not be kidnapping since they constitute false imprisonment which is equally punishable so, though it looks a little odd if a baby cannot be kidnapped,[606] no great harm is done.

17.13 Other abduction offences

17.13.1 Abduction of children

The Child Abduction Act 1984, as amended by the Children Act 1989, creates two offences of abduction of a child under the age of 16.

17.13.1.1 Abduction by parents/guardians

The first offence, under s 1, arises where a child is taken or sent out of the United Kingdom 'without the appropriate consent'.

The offence may be committed as a principal[607] only by a person 'connected with' the child. A person 'connected with' a child is (i) the child's parent; (ii) in the case of a child whose parents were not married at the time of birth, a man in respect of whom there are reasonable grounds for believing him to be the father; (iii) a guardian; (iv) a special guardian;[608] (v) a person in whose favour 'a residence order'[609] is in force with respect to the child; or (vi) a person having custody.

---

[604] [1973] QB 299, [1972] 2 All ER 1350.

[605] In the case of an older child, it is a question of fact for the jury whether (i) the child has sufficient understanding and, if so, (ii) it in fact consented. Lord Brandon thought that a jury would usually find that a child under 14 lacked sufficient understanding to give consent; but this surely underestimates the capacity of the modern child. Reliance might be placed on the Mental Capacity Act 2005, discussed above, cf *Cooper* [2008] UKHL 42 on the capacity concept in consent in sex cases (below p 723).

[606] See G Williams, 'Can Babies be Kidnapped?' [1989] Crim LR 473. See the comments of Munby LJ in *Re HM* [2010] EWHC 870 (Fam) calling for law reform in this rea.

[607] A person who is not 'connected with' the child may be convicted as a secondary party or conspirator: *Sherry and El Yamani* [1993] Crim LR 537.

[608] As inserted by the Adoption Act 2002.

[609] As defined in s 8(1) of the Children Act 1989.

The 'appropriate consent' is the consent of *each* of the child's mother, the child's father if he has 'parental responsibility'[610] for him, any guardian, any special guardian, any person in whose favour a residence order is in force with respect to the child *and* any person having custody of him; *or* the leave of the court under the Children Act 1989,[611] or, in the case of any person having custody, the leave of the court which awarded custody.

The offence is not committed where a person in whose favour a residence order is in force takes or sends the child out of the United Kingdom for a period of less than one month or if he is a special guardian of the child and he takes or sends the child out of the United Kingdom for a period of less than three months unless, in either case, this is a breach of an order under Part II of the Children Act 1989.

The Act provides defences for which D bears an evidential burden and the prosecution the burden of proof where:

(1) D believes that he has the appropriate consent or that he would have it if the person or persons whose consent is required were aware of all the relevant circumstances; or

(2) he has taken all reasonable steps to communicate with those persons but has been unsuccessful; or

(3) the other person has unreasonably refused to consent.

17.13.1.2 Abduction otherwise than by parents/guardians

The second offence, which arises under s 2, requires an intentional or reckless taking or detention of a child under the age of 16. It is committed where a person who is:

(a) not the mother of 'the child in question'[612] or,

(b) where the parents were married at the time of the birth, his father or guardian, custodian or a person in whose favour a residence order is in force,

takes or detains the child without lawful authority or reasonable excuse,

(i) so as to remove him from the lawful control of any person having lawful control of him; or

(ii) so as to keep him out of the lawful control of any person entitled to lawful control of him.

There are therefore four ways in which the offences can be committed.

'Detaining' is defined in s 3 to include causing the child to be detained or inducing the child to remain with the accused or another person. 'Taking' is defined in s 3 so as to include causing or inducing the child to accompany the accused or any other person or causing the child to be taken. 'Remove' does not require any 'geographical' removal – it is not the removal of the child but removal of control of the child which is material. 'Lawful control' is not defined in the Act and the courts have declined to define it. The concept varies according to the person said to have control – for example, parent, schoolteacher or nanny. A relevant question is whether the child was deflected by D from doing that to which his lawful controller had consented into some other activity. Has D substituted his authority or will for that of the lawful controller? There was evidence on which a jury could find that D had taken control where he

---

[610] As defined in s 3 of the Children Act 1989.

[611] Note the amendments under the Adoption and Children Act 2002, s 139(1).

[612] This means the child actually taken: *Berry* [1996] 2 Cr App R 226, [1996] Crim LR 574 where D, the father of S1, took S2, believing she was S1. For criticism, see the commentary by JC Smith in [1996] Crim LR.

persuaded a 14-year-old boy on his way home from school to go to D's flat,[613] and where he persuaded children to go with him to look for a bicycle which he said had been stolen.[614]

It is immaterial that the child consented to the lawful removal from the lawful control.[615] In the recent case of X,[616] D was convicted of abducting a child, V, contrary to s 2(1)(b). D, a woman, was a drug addict and prostitute and had befriended V aged 13. V persistently ran away from home. V was found in the company of D in the red light district. V was dressed in a manner suggesting she was soliciting.[617] V said in her evidence that she had no intention of returning to her mother whether she was with D or not. On those facts, it was debatable whether the conduct of D was any cause at all of V's absence, but the Court of Appeal held that the issue was rightly left to the jury.[618]

The words 'so as to' are ambiguous. Two conflicting decisions added to the confusion. In *Mousir*, the Court of Appeal held that the words import an element of *actus reus* (that D's conduct had the objective consequence of removing the child from lawful control) but not *mens rea* (that D intended to remove lawful control) but in the extradition case of *Re Owens*[619] the Divisional Court, without being referred to *Mousir*, concluded that proof of *mens rea* was required. The Divisional Court in *Foster*[620] favoured the conclusion in *Mousir*.

In *Mousir*, the court held that D's conduct had to bring about a sufficient degree of interference with the lawful control of the child,[621] but that the concept of control did not require an assessment of the individual child's maturity. The conclusion that the words import such an element of *actus reus* seems, with respect, to be correct in principle. The natural meaning of the term 'so as to' is 'with the effect of' removing the child from lawful control. It introduces a causal element additional to the *actus reus* of 'taking' or 'detaining'.[622] *Owens* does not contradict this. Simon Brown LJ stated that 'the words "so as to" mean "with the intention of" rather than *merely* with the effect of'.[623] In *Re Owens*, the Divisional Court expressly held that D must 'intend' to interfere with another person's lawful control of the child.[624] The court in *Mousir* had accepted counsel's concession that the phrase did not import an element of *mens rea* – that D had knowledge as to the effect of his conduct being the removal of the child from lawful control. Since the offence charged in that case was one of attempt, the element of intention would be required separately under the Criminal Attempts Act 1981.

In *Foster*,[625] the court concluded that the emphasis on *mens rea* in *Owens* was unnecessary to reach the result in that case, suggesting that *Owens* should have been treated as a case in which D had a lawful excuse rather than one in which she lacked *mens rea*. The court stated that the *mens rea* for the s 2 offence is:

---

[613] *Mousir* [1987] Crim LR 561.

[614] *Leather* (1993) 98 Cr App R 179. On difficulties of proof see also *Norman* [2008] EWCA Crim 1810 (D unfit to plead on facts).

[615] *A* [2001] Cr App R 418.

[616] [2010] EWCA Crim 2367.

[617] The judge's direction on recklessness was appealed but, although unnecessary on the facts, was held not to be in error following, as it did, *Foster v DPP* [2005] 1 WLR 1400 below.

[618] See also *R v A* [2000] 2 All ER 177.

[619] [2000] 1 Cr App R 195.

[620] [2004] EWHC 2955 (Admin), [2005] Crim LR 639.

[621] Where, as in that case, the charge is one of attempt, the issue is whether the acts are more than merely preparatory to that effect.

[622] It is possible that D might remove or detain a child without lawful excuse but without causing him to be removed from lawful custody where D also removed or detained the lawful custodian.

[623] Emphasis added, at 201.

[624] [2000] 1 Cr App R 195.

[625] [2004] EWHC 2955 (Admin).

an intentional or reckless taking or detention of a child under the age of sixteen, the effect or objective consequence of which is to remove or to keep that child within the meaning of section 2(1)(a) or (b).

Article 8 of the European Convention – the right to respect for private life – may impose positive obligations on the State to respect family life. This may include an obligation on the State to provide safeguards against abduction.[626]

17.13.2 Taking of hostages

The Taking of Hostages Act 1982 creates an offence of exceptional breadth in that it extends to a person of any nationality acting anywhere in the world, or indeed, in outer space. It is committed by anyone who detains another and, in order to compel a State, international governmental organization or person to do or abstain from doing any act, threatens to kill, injure or continue to detain the hostage. It is punishable with imprisonment for life. Proceedings may not be instituted except by or with the consent of the Attorney General.

17.14 The Protection from Harassment Act 1997[627]

Prior to 1997 the criminal law struggled to provide protection for those who suffered at the hands of so-called 'stalkers'. It was difficult for the law to tackle an activity which was in part an infringement of privacy,[628] in part an offence against the person, with some forms of the conduct also having a public order dimension. The use of tortious remedies to tackle behaviour which amounted to stalking was severely curtailed by the decision of the House of Lords in *Hunter v Canary Wharf*.[629] The Lords held that only those who had a right to exclusive possession of the land could sue in nuisance. Recourse was had to the criminal law and prosecutors relied on offences of public nuisance, specific offences relating to malicious communications or telecommunications where possible, or public order offences and offences against the person. These efforts to combat what was perceived as a growing social menace were assisted by the courts' acceptance that psychiatric injury was a sufficient basis for a finding of actual or grievous bodily harm[630] and by the House of Lords' acceptance that assault could be committed by words alone or even by a silent telephone call.[631] These extended interpretations were not always well received[632] but led to convictions.

Parliament nevertheless felt that a specific offence was needed and, following consultation[633] and an unseemly rush through Parliament, the Protection from Harassment Act 1997 was enacted.[634] The draftsman faced a formidable difficulty in defining 'stalking' without over-criminalizing. The conduct complained of as harassing behaviour may include acts of

---

[626] *Iglesias Gil and AIU v Spain* (2003) (App No 56673/00); *Maire v Portugal* (2003) (App No 48206/99); *D A Child) (Abduction: Rights of Custody)* [2006] UKHL 51.

[627] See R Babcock, 'The Psychology of Stalking', in P Infield and G Platford, *The Law of Harassment and Stalking* (2000); N Addison and T Lawson-Cruttenden, *Harassment Law and Practice* (1998). See also the information collected at www.harassment-law.co.uk. The offence is further amended by the Serious Organised Crime and Police Act 2005, s 125.

[628] See Alldridge, *Relocating Criminal Law*, Ch 4.

[629] [1997] 2 All ER 426. See also *Wong v Parkside Health NHS Trust* [2003] 3 All ER 932, CA.

[630] *Chan Fook* [1994] 2 All ER 552, CA; *Burstow* [1998] AC 147.

[631] *Ireland* [1998] AC 147.

[632] C Wells, 'Stalking the Law's Response' [1997] Crim LR 1.

[633] See Home Office, *Stalking the Solutions* (1996).

[634] See the analysis by E Finch, *The Criminalisation of Stalking* (2001); M Allen, 'Look Who's Stalking' [1996] Web JCLI 1. For a comparative review of stalking laws see B Clarke and L Meintjes-van der Valt (1998) 115 South African Law 729.

apparent kindness, such as repeated sending of flowers or seemingly innocuous conduct, such as walking by the victim's house. As the Minister stated:

Stalkers do not stick to activities on a list. Stalkers and other weirdos [*sic*] who pursue women, [*sic*] cause racial harassment and annoy their neighbours have a wide range of activity which it is impossible to define.[635]

As Wells observes, the Act follows a pattern all too common in recent years of 'addressing a narrowly conceived social harm with a widely drawn provision, often supplementing and overlapping with existing offences'.[636] The flexibility allows for the offence to be used in respect of stalking, persistent protestors, bullying,[637] etc.

The CPS has recently issued guidance on prosecuting harassment.[638] The CPS introduces the guidance by stating:

This legal guidance addresses behaviour which is repeated and unwanted by the victim and which causes the victim to have a negative reaction in terms of alarm or distress. Cases involving stalking and harassment can be difficult to prosecute, and because of their nature are likely to require sensitive handling, especially with regard to victim care. The provision of accurate and up-to-date information to the victim throughout the life of the case, together with quality support, and careful consideration of any special measures requirements are essential factors for the CPS to consider.

17.14.1 Harassment defined

 1. – (1) A person must not pursue a course of conduct –

  (a) which amounts to harassment of another, and

  (b) which he knows or ought to know amounts to harassment of the other.

 (1A) person must not pursue a course of conduct –

  (a) which involves harassment of two or more persons, and

  (b) which he knows or ought to know involves harassment of those persons, and

  (c) by which he intends to persuade any person (whether or not one of those mentioned above) –

   (i) not to do something that he is entitled or required to do, or

   (ii) to do something that he is not under any obligation to do.

 2. – (1) A person who pursues a course of conduct in breach of section 1(1) or (1A) is guilty of an offence.[639]

17.14.1.1 Course of conduct

The offences under the Act are dependent on proof of a course of conduct, which is merely an element of each offence and not a crime in itself.

---

[635] D MacLean, Home Office Minister, HC, col 827 (17 Dec 1996).

[636] C Wells [1997] Crim LR 1 at 2.

[637] See A Gillespie, 'Cyber-Bullying and Harassment of Teenagers: The Legal Response' [2006] JSWFL 123; N Geach, 'Regulating Harassment: Is the Law Fit for the Social Networking Age?' (2009) 73 J Crim Law 241. The House of Lords in *Majrowski v Guy's and St Thomas' Hospital* [2006] UKHL 34, [2007] 1 AC 224, held that the Act applies in the workplace and that employers may be vicariously liable for failing to take appropriate preventative action to prevent employees being bullied. Note also the new powers inserted by the Domestic Violence, Crime and Victims Act 2004, in respect of restraining orders in domestic violence cases.

[638] See www.cps.gov.uk/legal/s_to_u/stalking_and_harassment.

[639] Section 1A was added by the SOCPA, s 125.

By s 7:

(3) A 'course of conduct' must involve –

(a) in the case of conduct in relation to a single person (see section 1(1)), conduct on at least two occasions in relation to that person, or

(b) in the case of conduct in relation to two or more persons (see section 1(1A)), conduct on at least one occasion in relation to each of those persons.

(3A) A person's conduct on any occasion shall be taken, if aided, abetted, counselled or procured by another –

(a) to be conduct on that occasion of the other (as well as conduct of the person whose conduct it is); and

(b) to be conduct in relation to which the other's knowledge and purpose, and what he ought to have known, are the same as they were in relation to what was contemplated or reasonably foreseeable at the time of the aiding, abetting, counselling or procuring.

The course of conduct is at the core of both crimes (and the tort). The provision is far from clear, with little further elaboration other than that words are sufficient (s 7(4)). One of the major problems under the Act has been in determining when two incidents are sufficiently closely associated to constitute a course of conduct. Although seeking to identify the idea of 'persistence' that lies at the heart of stalking, Parliament refrained from attempting further to define the proscribed behaviour. In debates on the Bill, Michael Howard, then Home Secretary, referred to the lack of definition, but regarded harassment as a concept 'interpreted regularly by the courts since 1986'.[640] It is extremely wide in scope and applies to protest and neighbourhood disputes[641] as well as what might more usually be regarded as stalking.

It has been accepted that D's conduct can amount to a course of conduct even where that involves some action by V. In *James v CPS*[642] D was receiving care from a social services team in his area. D repeatedly phoned the services team to complain about his care. The team manager, V, returned D's calls as she was duty bound to do and D was abusive to her. That pattern of behaviour was repeated. The Divisional Court held that the fact that V returned the calls was irrelevant. As Elias LJ observed:

If I am continually abusive to someone who comes within my vicinity, that may still be capable of constituting a course of conduct, even if the victim chooses to come within my vicinity. The fact that he or she chooses to do so might arguably be relevant to the question of whether there is harassment, but not to the question of whether there is a course of conduct.[643]

As the court recently observed in *Curtis*,[644] s 7 of the Act does not provide an exhaustive definition of harassment. There will be conduct which might alarm or distress someone without being harassing.[645]

One act or two?

Is there a 'course of conduct' when an individual engages in one continuous activity – for example, sitting outside V's house for a whole day? In *Hills*,[646] it was stressed that it is not just

[640] HC, vol 287, col 784 (17 Dec 1996).
[641] Inciting a dog to bark is sufficient to form part of a course of conduct: *Tafurelli v DPP* [2004] EWHC 2791 (Admin).
[642] [2009] EWHC 2925 (Admin).
[643] [12].
[644] [2010] EWCA Crim 123.
[645] In that case repeated incidents of domestic violence.
[646] [2001] Crim LR 318.

enough to count the incidents, nor to direct the jury in such terms.[647] In *Kelly v DPP*,[648] D, who had just been released on licence after conviction for harassing V, made three abusive and threatening telephone calls to a mobile telephone belonging to V between 2.57 am and 3.02 am. V did not answer any of the calls at the time and they were recorded on her voice-mail. V subsequently listened to the messages one after the other, without pause. It was held that the closeness of time within which the calls were made was only *a* factor to be taken into account when determining whether there had been repetitious behaviour for the purposes of proving the commission of an offence of harassment. The case raises questions about where the courts will draw the line. Consider D who telephones V, V answers the call and immediately she identifies D and terminates the call. D calls back immediately. V sees that D's number appears on the 'caller id' facility. Is this a course of conduct?

In *Hills*, Latham LJ stated that repetition was a significant factor in determining whether there is a course of conduct, but there is no requirement that acts be similar or repeated. Any combination of bouquets of flowers, menacing calls or letters, loitering outside the victim's home, etc will suffice. As was suggested in *Lau*,[649] the question of whether there is a course of conduct should be determined by whether there is a sufficient nexus between the two acts, taking account of all of the circumstances. The courts have acknowledged that the question is a difficult one.[650] In *DPP v Hardy*[651] the court accepted that 95 phone calls made over a 90-minute period were capable of constituting harassment, especially since they included threats to continue that behaviour all night.[652]

One actor or two?

Section 7(3A)[653] ensures that where A performs an harassing act towards V aided by B, and subsequently A alone commits a further act of harassment towards V, the two acts may be regarded as a course of conduct. This extension of the scope of a 'course of conduct' was enacted to deal with protestors. A campaign of collective harassment by two or more people can amount to a 'course of conduct'. The knowledge and purpose of the aider, abetter, counsellor or procurer is judged at the time that the conduct was planned and not when it is carried out. The provision seeks to pre-empt a defence by A that when he counselled B to commit a second act towards V, A was unaware that his first act towards V had caused distress. Since it is enough that A ought to have known that the act would cause distress at the time that the subsequent act was commissioned, he will be liable.

The offence can be committed by D communicating with X which causes harassment to V.[654]

One victim or two?

The course of conduct under s 1(1) must relate to 'another'. In *DPP v Williams*,[655] D had put his hand through a bathroom window startling the occupant V1 who was showering. She then informed V2, her flatmate, who was scared by the event as reported to her. Two days later

---

[647] *Patel* [2005] Crim LR 649, [2004] EWCA Crim 3284.

[648] [2003] Crim LR 43, DC.

[649] [2000] Crim LR 580 and commentary.

[650] See recently eg *Buckley* [2008] EWHC 136 (Admin) graveside altercation and spitting at V in cemetery car park.

[651] [2008] All ER (D) 315 (Oct).

[652] D had called an employment agency to request information about why he had been rejected for a job, so his calls had been legitimate to begin with, but they had clearly escalated into conduct that was capable of constituting harassment.

[653] As inserted by the Criminal Justice and Police Act 2001.

[654] *C v CPS* [2008] EWHC 148 (Admin).

[655] *DPP v Williams* (DC, 27 July 1998, Rose LJ and Bell J).

D peered through the bedroom window, this time frightening V2 directly. The magistrate convicted, holding that 'another' could be read as 'others'. The Divisional Court decided the case on the basis that V2 had been distressed on both occasions and therefore the offence was made out. The interpretation was rightly criticized for extending the offence considerably and for giving rise to practical problems.[656] In *Caurti v DPP*,[657] it was held that in relation to the more serious s 4 offence (causing fear of violence, below) the course of conduct must have its impact on *one* complainant, even where it is aimed at another.

Under s 1(1A), it is clear that the harassment can be to two or more persons, provided the additional element of intention in s 1(1A)(c) can be established. The provision will prove useful in criminalizing the conduct of protestors who target people connected with animal breeding and vivisection organizations.[658] Section 1(1A) will catch threats and intimidation intended to force an individual or individuals to stop trading.

The complainant must be an individual and not a corporate body:[659] s 7(5) of the Act provides that references to a 'person' are references to 'a person who is an individual'. But a company can commit the offence.[660]

No need for temporal proximity or similarity

Is there a course of conduct where different acts are separated by a considerable period of time? For example, are two acts separated by one year, say, two birthday cards, a 'course of conduct'? In *Lau v DPP*,[661] two incidents four months apart were held to be capable of amounting to a course of conduct. The court observed that 'one can conceive of circumstances where incidents, as far apart as a year, could constitute a course of conduct'. The example given was of racial harassment outside a synagogue on the Day of Atonement. In *Baron v CPS*,[662] it was accepted that the less proximate in time and the more limited in number the incidents, the less likely that there was a course of conduct. In *Pratt v DPP*,[663] D threw water over his estranged wife and three months later chased her through the matrimonial home swearing and questioning her constantly. The justices found these to be a course of conduct and the Divisional Court did not find this to be an irrational decision. However, it was noted that prosecuting authorities should be cautious in bringing charges for the offence of harassment in circumstances where only a small number of incidents had occurred. The prosecution should ensure not merely that two or more incidents had occurred, but that such repetitious behaviour had caused harassment to the other person.[664] Examples of prosecution agencies overusing harassment charges persist. In *Curtis*[665] D had in the course of a relationship with V, a fellow police officer engaged in conduct including: minor assaults on V; pulling the hand-brake of a car V was driving, causing it to skid. This was charged as harassment. The court quashed the conviction. The court defined harassment as 'tormenting a person by subjecting

[656] A charge under the 1997 Act, s 1(1), might be bad for duplicity where it names two complainants when they are members of a 'close knit identifiable group': *Mills v DPP* (1998) 17 Dec, DC.

[657] [2002] Crim LR 131 and commentary.

[658] See the Home Office document: *Animal Welfare: Human Rights – Protecting People from Animal Rights Extremists* (2004). See SOCPA 2005, s 145.

[659] *DPP v Dziurzynski* (2002) 166 JP 545; cf *Daiichi UK Ltd and others v Huntingdon Animal Cruelty and others* [2003] EWHC 2337 (QB): person does not include a limited company as a victim.

[660] See *Kosar v Bank of Scotland* [2011] EWHC 1050 (Admin).

[661] [2000] Crim LR, [2000] 1 FLR 799.

[662] 13 June 2000, unreported.

[663] [2001] EWHC 483 (Admin).

[664] Note that the CPS acknowledges that the Act is 'widely drafted, and could incorporate many minor forms of behaviour'. Reference should be had to Home Office Circular 34/1997, making it clear that the Act is not intended to supplant existing powers to deal with incidents that do not reach the threshold of harassment.

[665] [2010] EWCA Crim 123.

them to constant interference or intimidation'. The conduct had to be oppressive, unreasonable and unacceptable to a degree that would sustain criminal liability. Although D's conduct had been deplorable and the incidents had been far from trivial, it could not be concluded that, in the course of a volatile relationship where there had been aggression on both sides, the six incidents over a nine-month period amounted to a course of conduct amounting to harassment within the meaning of the Act. Reference was made to *Majrowski* (above)[666] where it was emphasized that:

Courts are well able to recognise the boundary between conduct which is unattractive, even unreasonable, and conduct which is oppressive and unacceptable. To cross the boundary from the regrettable to the unacceptable the gravity of the misconduct must be of an order which would sustain criminal liability under section 2.

Baroness Hale observed[667] that the definition had been deliberately left wide open and it had been left to the wisdom of the courts to distinguish between the ordinary banter and badinage of life and genuinely offensive and unacceptable behaviour. It cannot be a requirement that each of the acts alleged to constitute part of the course of conduct is itself criminal.[668]

It is submitted that the events making up the 'course of conduct' under the Act require a nexus, as is implicit within the expression, which suggests a 'series' of events with some connection. The main connecting factor will be that the acts are aimed at a particular victim, but that will not of itself be sufficient, in the same way that two visits to the hospital by the same patient would not necessarily be described as a course of treatment. There must be something more connecting them – in the case of the treatment, one would expect it to be for the same ailment. The mere fact that D made two harassing calls to the same victim a year apart will not necessarily constitute a course of conduct. If the calls were made on a particular anniversary, there would be a greater nexus and the course of conduct would be more likely to be established. The question must turn on all the circumstances of the case.

When does the course of conduct begin?

In many instances, D will be involved in what might be considered to be, initially at least, neutral conduct towards V. Does his course of conduct only begin when he is aware of the distress he is causing V, or when it causes V harassment or when the reasonable person would see it as harassing? In *King v DPP*,[669] the alleged harassment was by offering the victim a plant, writing letters to her, rummaging in her rubbish, stealing her discarded underwear from refuse bags and filming her secretly. The Divisional Court held that 'repeated offers of unwelcome gifts or the repeated sending of letters could well amount to harassment, nevertheless, the *single* offer of a gift of modest value *and* the sending of one innocuous letter in the circumstances of this case cannot amount to harassment within the meaning of the 1997 Act. Nor could the letter and the gift be treated as the first stage or the first two stages of a course of conduct amounting to harassment...' The magistrates were wrong to treat these incidents as forming a part of a course of conduct. The decision is difficult to square with the terms of the section. There is no limitation as to the types of conduct amounting to harassment in the statute.

A victim may be held to be aware of a course of conduct through indirect knowledge, as where V is told that D has been calling her, provided there is evidence on the basis of which the court can properly conclude that D was pursuing a course of conduct with the necessary *mens rea*.[670]

---

[666] [2007] 1 AC 224. Per Lord Nicholls at [30].
[667] ibid [66].
[668] See *R (Jones) v Bedfordshire MC* [2010] EWHC 523 (Admin), [27].
[669] 20 June 2000, DC.
[670] *Kellett v DPP* [2001] EWHC 107 (Admin).

Mens rea as to the course of conduct

There is no requirement that the harasser intended or directed his conduct to harass V, it is sufficient that 'a reasonable person in possession of the same information would think the course of conduct amounted to harassment of another'.[671] The leading case is that of *Colohan*[672] where it was held that the test is entirely objective. In that case D's schizophrenia could not be taken into consideration in evaluating whether the reasonable person would have realized that the conduct was harassing. On the facts, it was unclear whether D was denying that he knew what he was doing in writing the allegedly harassing letters, or denying that he knew that the letters constituted a course of harassing conduct, or was claiming simply that the harassment was reasonable. Given the clear policy behind the legislation it is not surprising that the court rejected the defence claims. The prosecution of mentally disordered individuals under this offence not only ensures the protection for victims of stalking, but also increases the chances of the offender receiving psychiatric assessment and treatment.

To be liable under s 1(1A), D must also intend to persuade the person(s) to refrain from something that they are entitled or to do something they are not; for example, for an animal breeding unit to stop trading with a vivisection lab.

In possession of the same information

Section 1(2) is unusual in requiring that the person whose course of conduct is in question *ought to know* that it amounts to harassment of another if a reasonable person 'in possession of the same information' would do so. The section is designed to endow the reasonable person with knowledge of circumstances that would render otherwise seemingly innocuous conduct harassing (for example, when D knows that previous advances towards V have been rejected and continues to send gifts). In such cases D's inculpatory state of mind is taken into account. Should the reasonable person also be possessed with knowledge about D's exculpatory states of mind in order to assess whether the conduct is harassment? This is not the same as asking whether a reasonable person with the characteristics of D would regard it as harassment, particularly where the characteristic inhibits cognition of the wrongdoing. In *Colohan*, the strong policy grounds of protection on which the Act is founded justified the court's rejection of any attempt to diminish the purely objective stance. In *Pelham*,[673] D was charged under the racially aggravated form of the offence and denied that she had the *mens rea* on the basis that she was of low IQ and lacked an understanding of the racial nature of her comments. The court refused to allow expert evidence as to this aspect of the *mens rea*, in line with the general rule against expert evidence being permitted on *mens rea* issues.

Defences justifying the course of conduct

Section 1 provides:

(3) Subsection (1) or (1A) does not apply to a course of conduct if the person who pursued it shows –

(a) that it was pursued for the purpose of preventing or detecting crime;

(b) that it was pursued under any enactment or rule of law or to comply with any condition or requirement imposed by any person under any enactment, or

(c) that in the particular circumstances the pursuit of the course of conduct was reasonable.

---

[671] Section 1(2).

[672] [2001] EWCA Crim 1251, [2001] Crim LR 845. See above, Ch 6.

[673] [2007] EWCA Crim 1321.

Paragraph (a) seems clear, although debate might arise over whether it is restricted to State officials engaged in criminal investigations or whether investigative journalists might also be able to rely on this defence.[674] It might apply to the busybody neighbourhood-watch co-ordinator, although the courts have suggested that s 1(3)(a) was framed with law enforcement agencies and not private individuals in mind. If a private individual relies on s 1(3)(a) he must show some rational basis for his conduct, judged on an objective basis.[675]

Paragraph (b) is uncontroversial. It protects the right of free speech and expression. In a civil case which was one of the first cases under the Act, Eady J, commented that the Act was not intended to be used to stifle discussion of public interest on public demonstrations.[676]

More difficult is the defence under para (c), particularly in cases where D claims that his action was part of a campaign of legitimate protest. In *Baron v DPP*,[677] the court emphasized that:

a line must be drawn between legitimate expression of disgust at the way a public agency has behaved and conduct amounting to harassment. The right to free speech requires a broad degree of tolerance in relation to communications. It is a legitimate exercise of that right to say things which are unpleasant or possibly hurtful to the recipient.

The defence under s 1(3)(c) does not involve the question whether the reasonable person regards the course of conduct as harassment, but whether it *is* reasonable harassment.[678]

It seems to arise only where it is accepted that the course of conduct is harassing. Furthermore, the question is whether the conduct was, as a whole 'reasonable', which suggests a purely objective assessment. In some cases involving protest campaigns the courts may face difficult issues of evaluating the reasonableness of a form of protest. These may involve arguments based on rights of freedom of expression under Art 10 of the ECHR.[679]

The burden is on the defendant to prove, on the balance of probabilities,[680] that the conduct is reasonable. It has been held that pursuit of conduct in breach of an injunction will preclude a defence under s 1(3)(c).[681]

17.14.1.2 The s 2 offence

2. – (1) A person who pursues a course of conduct in breach of section 1(1) or (1A) is guilty of an offence.

(2) A person guilty of an offence under this section is liable on summary conviction to imprisonment for a term not exceeding six months, or a fine not exceeding level 5 on the standard scale, or both.

The offence is based on the course of conduct and it has been held that prosecutions are not therefore time barred if at least one of the incidents forming part of the course of

---

[674] Note also s 12 providing that the Secretary of State may issue certificates that render conduct of specified individuals conclusively reasonable (eg, security service operatives).

[675] *Howlett v Holding* (2006) The Times, 8 Feb, QBD (D conducted a campaign against the V, a local councillor, by flying banners from his aircraft referring to her in derogatory and abusive terms).

[676] *Huntingdon Life Sciences v Curtin* (1997) The Times, 11 Dec [1998] Env LR D9. See recently *Bayer Crop Science Ltd* [2009] WL 4872821.

[677] 13 June 2000, unreported.

[678] Nothing that involves cultural or racial differences should be taken into account, unless it is relevant and supported by proper evidence: *C v CPS* [2008] EWHC 148 (Admin).

[679] See *Debnath* [2006] 2 Cr App R (S) 25, where a restraining order against D prohibiting any publication against V whether true or not was upheld.

[680] See p 29 above, on the appropriateness of the burden under the Human Rights Act 1998 and Art 6(2).

[681] *DPP v Mosely* (1999) The Times, 23 June.

conduct occurs within the six-month limitation period for the laying of informations in the magistrates' court.[682]

The s 2 offence requires two or more acts by D constituting a course of conduct. There need be only one result from their cumulative effect – the harassment of the victim. Section 7(2) provides that 'harassing a person' includes 'alarming the person or causing the person distress' and this has been treated as a non-exhaustive definition.[683] There is no requirement that any violence is threatened (or feared) for the offence under s 2. The section criminalizes conduct such as that in *Chambers and Edwards v DPP*[684] where protestors persistently but non-violently blocked the surveyor's theodolite beam, since the Divisional Court held that such conduct would amount to harassment for the purposes of the Public Order Act 1986. In many cases the section has been used successfully in respect of 'classic' stalking behaviour.[685]

17.14.1.3 Causing a fear of violence: s 4

Section 4 provides:

(1) A person whose course of conduct causes another to fear, on at least two occasions, that violence will be used against him is guilty of an offence if he knows or ought to know that his course of conduct will cause the other so to fear on each of those occasions.

(2) For the purposes of this section, the person whose course of conduct is in question ought to know that it will cause another to fear that violence will be used against him on any occasion if a reasonable person in possession of the same information would think the course of conduct would cause the other so to fear on that occasion.

(3) It is a defence for a person charged with an offence under this section to show that –

   (a) his course of conduct was pursued for the purpose of preventing or detecting crime,

   (b) his course of conduct was pursued under any enactment or rule of law or to comply with any condition or requirement imposed by any person under any enactment, or

   (c) the pursuit of his course of conduct was reasonable for the protection of himself or another or for the protection of his or another's property.

Section 4 is triable either way, carrying a maximum sentence on indictment of five years' imprisonment, or a fine or both. This is a high maximum sentence for a negligence-based offence. A judge who rules that there is no case to answer on a charge under s 4 may allow the jury to consider an alternative verdict under s 2.[686]

The essential difference between this offence and that in s 2 (and the tort in s 3) is that the victim must be caused to fear on at least two occasions, that violence will be used 'against him'. The other important difference is that the only defence available to this charge is that the harasser proves that his conduct was for the purpose of preventing or detecting crime, was lawfully authorized, or was reasonable for the protection of *himself or another or of property*.[687]

---

[682] *DPP v Baker* [2004] EWHC 2782 (Admin).

[683] *DPP v Ramsdale* (2001) The Independent, 19 Mar.

[684] [1995] Crim LR 896.

[685] For critical comment on the scope of the offence, see E Finch, 'Stalking the Perfect Stalking Law: An Evaluation of the Efficacy of the Protection from Harassment Act 1997' [2002] Crim LR 702. See also J Harris, Home Office Research Study No 203, *An Evaluation of the Use and Effectiveness of the Protection from Harassment Act 1997* (2000).

[686] *Livesey* [2006] EWCA Crim 3344.

[687] A failure to direct on these defences may well render a conviction unsafe – *Wilkes* [2004] EWCA Crim 3136.

Section 4 has been criticized as being too narrow because of this requirement.[688] Whereas s 2 explicitly requires, *inter alia*, (1) a course of conduct (2) which must amount to harassment of another, s 4 requires that the victim is caused, by the course of conduct, to fear violence on at least two occasions. In *Curtis* the court concluded that the s 4 offence requires proof also that the course of conduct has to amount to harassment. Section 4 does not expressly require that the course of conduct which causes the victim to fear violence constitutes harassment. Section 4 contains the stricter limitation that the course of conduct has to cause fear (it being insufficient even to frighten the victim as to what might happen (*Henley*)). Arguably s 4 represents a distinct offence focused not on harassment, but on the graver wrong of creating fear of violence. However, the court's preferred interpretation is one which construes s 4 in the broader context of the Act and sits more comfortably with the fact that s 2 is an included alternative offence.[689] Interpreting s 4 so as not to require the course of conduct to constitute 'harassment' would only be of practical significance if there are circumstances in which two or more incidents with a sufficient nexus caused a fear of violence without also being harassing. That would seem unlikely.

Section 4 has no requirement of immediacy as in assault. Unlike s 8 of the Public Order Act 1986, no definition of violence is provided in the 1997 Act. In *Henley*,[690] H's harassment of the complainant and her family included threats to kill. He was charged under s 4. The trial judge failed properly to direct the jury, wrongly suggesting that to 'seriously frighten her' would suffice and failed to clarify that the person must *himself* fear violence, not violence towards others. It was emphasized that a direction on the *mens rea* under s 4(2) should be routinely given. It is 'good practice' for the judge to direct the jury to consider whether the incidents about which they were sure were so connected in type and in context as to justify the conclusion that they could amount to a course of conduct.[691]

A fear of violence may be inferred from threats and behaviour other than explicit threats of violence issued to the victim in person (for example, threats to his dog), but the victim must fear that violence will be used against himself.[692] Threats to burn down the family house will suffice.[693]

17.14.1.4 Racially and religiously aggravated harassment

The Crime and Disorder Act 1998, as amended by the Anti-terrorism Crime and Security Act 2001, provides racially and religiously aggravated offences of harassment and putting people in fear of violence.

Section 32:

(1) A person is guilty of an offence under this section if he commits –

    (a) an offence under s 2 of the Protection from Harassment Act 1997 (offence of harassment); or

    (b) an offence under s 4 of that Act (putting people in fear of violence),

which is [racially or religiously aggravated] for the purposes of this section.

---

[688] See Finch [2002] Crim LR 702, above, suggesting a new offence of intentional harassment to bridge the gap between the narrow s 4 and the wide and overused s 2.

[689] Furthermore, it is consistent with the approach that seems to have been taken in previous authorities holding that the victim has been put in 'fear of violence *by harassment*', such as *Patel* [2004] EWCA Crim 3284 (emphasis added).

[690] [2000] Crim LR 582. See also *Curtis* [2010] EWCA Crim 123.

[691] *Sahin* [2009] EWCA Crim 2616.

[692] *R v DPP* [2001] Crim LR 396; *Henley* [2000] Crim LR 582; *Caurti v DPP* [2002] Crim LR 131 and commentaries.

[693] *R (A) v DPP* [2005] ACD 61.

An aggravated offence under s 32(1)(a) is triable either way and punishable on indictment with a maximum sentence of two years' imprisonment. An offence under s 32(1)(b) is triable either way and carries a maximum seven years' imprisonment on conviction on indictment. The nature of racial and religious aggravation is discussed above.

17.14.1.5 Harassment in the home

Section 126 of SOCPA introduced a new offence into s 42A of the Criminal Justice and Police Act 2001:

(1) A person commits an offence if –

    (a) that person is present outside or in the vicinity of any premises that are used by any individual ('the resident') as his dwelling;

    (b) that person is present there for the purpose (by his presence or otherwise) of representing to the resident or another individual (whether or not one who uses the premises as his dwelling), or of persuading the resident or such another individual –

        (i) that he should not do something that he is entitled or required to do; or

        (ii) that he should do something that he is not under any obligation to do;

    (c) that person –

        (i) intends his presence to amount to the harassment of, or to cause alarm or distress to, the resident; or

        (ii) knows or ought to know that his presence is likely to result in the harassment of, or to cause alarm or distress to, the resident; and

    (d) the presence of that person –

        (i) amounts to the harassment of, or causes alarm or distress to, any person falling within subsection (2); or

        (ii) is likely to result in the harassment of, or to cause alarm or distress to, any such person.

This offence is triable summarily only[694] and carries a maximum sentence of six months' imprisonment or a fine not exceeding level 4 on the standard scale, or both. 'Dwelling' has the same meaning as in the Public Order Act, s 8 (below).[695]

17.15 Offensive weapons

Legislation regulating the possession and use of firearms and offensive weapons is of major importance in the prevention of offences against the person. In earlier editions of this book[696] an account was given of the principal offences under the Firearms Act 1968 and other legislation. This is omitted from the present edition and the reader is referred to *Blackstone's Criminal Practice* (2011) Part B12 and *Archbold Crown Court* (2011) Ch 24.[697] Consideration is, however, given here to an important offence of general interest, created by the Prevention of Crime Act 1953.

---

[694] Section 42A(4).

[695] Section 42A(7).

[696] See the 6th edition at 416–422.

[697] See also R Shields, *Offensive Weapons* (2nd edn, 1996). The Violent Crime Reduction Act 2006 introduced further offences in relation to imitation firearms, minding a weapon for a person, etc.

17.15.1 The Prevention of Crime Act 1953

The Prevention of Crime Act 1953 is, according to its long title, 'An Act to prohibit the carrying of offensive weapons in public places, without lawful authority or reasonable excuse.'
The Act provides:

1. – (1) Any person who without lawful authority or reasonable excuse, the proof whereof shall lie on him, has with him in any public place any offensive weapon shall be guilty of an offence, and shall be liable –

    (a) on summary conviction, to imprisonment for a term not exceeding six months or a fine not exceeding [the statutory maximum], or both;

    (b) on conviction on indictment, to imprisonment for a term not exceeding four years or a fine, or both.

(2) Where any person is convicted of an offence under subsection (1) of this section the court may make an order for the forfeiture or disposal of any weapon in respect of which the offence was committed.

17.15.1.1 Offensive weapons

'Offensive weapon' is defined by s 1(4), as amended by the Public Order Act 1986, to mean 'any article made or adapted for use for causing injury to the person, or intended by the person having it with him for such use by him or by some other person'.

It will be noted that this definition is narrower than that of 'weapon of offence' in s 10(1)(b) of the Theft Act 1968. It does not include, as the Theft Act does, articles made, adapted or intended for *incapacitating* a person.[698]

According to the Court of Appeal in *Simpson*[699] there are three categories of offensive weapon:

(1) Articles *made* for causing injury would include a rifle or bayonet, a revolver, a cosh, a truncheon,[700] a knuckle-duster,[701] a pair of 'sand gloves',[702] a dagger, swordstick[703] or flick knife.[704] It has been held that the fact that rice flails are *used* as weapons is sufficient evidence that they are *made* for that purpose[705] but this seems doubtful. Whether an article is 'made for' causing injury requires the jury to consider whether it is of a kind which is, generally speaking, made for such use.[706] Categorization is a matter of fact, although judicial notice has been taken of the fact that flick-knives and butterfly knives

---

[698] Below, p 967. Ormerod and Williams, *Smith's Law of Theft*, Ch 9.

[699] [1983] 1 WLR 1494.

[700] *Houghton v Chief Constable of Greater Manchester* (1986) 84 Cr App R 319.

[701] '...bludgeons, properly so-called, clubs and anything that is not in common use for any other purpose but a weapon are clearly offensive weapons within the meaning of the legislature' (the Smuggling Acts): (1784) 1 Leach 342 n (a).

[702] ie gloves into which iron powder is inserted to give weight and protect the knuckles: *R v R* [2007] EWCA Crim, 15 Nov, unreported.

[703] *Butler* [1988] Crim LR 695.

[704] An offensive weapon *per se* because judicially noticed as such: *Simpson* [1983] 3 All ER 789, [1983] 1 WLR 1494; cf *Gibson v Wales* [1983] 1 All ER 869, [1983] Crim LR 113, DC and commentary; and *DPP v Hynde* [1998] Crim LR 72, DC (butterfly knife).

[705] *Copus v DPP* [1989] Crim LR 577 and commentary. It was conceded at the trial in *Malnik* [1989] Crim LR 451 that a rice flail was an offensive weapon.

[706] *Warne* (1997) 7 Archbold News 2.

are offensive *per se*.[707] The judge is entitled to direct the jury that this element of the offence is established, but never to direct a conviction *per se*.[708]

(2) Articles *adapted* for causing injury would include razor blades inserted in a potato or a bottle broken for the purpose, a chair-leg studded with nails and so on. 'Adapted' probably means altered so as to become suitable.[709] It has been held that unscrewing a pool cue so that the butt end could be used for violence might amount to adapting it, but this seems to be taking things too far.[710] It is not certain whether the intention of the adaptor is relevant.[711] Is an *accidentally* broken milk bottle 'adapted for use for causing injury to the person'? It is submitted that it is not and that if the article was not adapted with intent, it can only be an offensive weapon in the third category.

(3) It is very important to distinguish the third category of articles which are neither made nor adapted for causing injury, but are *carried for that purpose*. Whether D carried the article with the necessary purpose is a question of fact.[712] Articles which have been held to be carried with such intent include a sheath-knife,[713] a shotgun,[714] a razor,[715] a sandbag,[716] a pick-axe handle,[717] a stone,[718] and a drum of pepper.[719] *Any* article is capable of being an offensive weapon; but if it is of such a nature that it is unlikely to cause injury when brought into contact with the person, then the onus of proving the necessary intent will be very heavy.

Articles adapted or intended by the carrier to injure himself

It was held by the Crown Court in *Bryan v Mott*[720] that a bottle broken for the purpose of committing suicide is 'adapted' for causing injury to the person. In *Fleming*,[721] on the other hand, the judge ruled that a large domestic carving knife carried by D to injure himself was not 'intended' for causing injury to the person: though the Act does not say 'another person', that is what it means. The view of the judge in *Fleming* is to be preferred. The question is whether the thing is 'an offensive weapon' and since 'offensive' implies an attack on *another* the injury which the adaptor or carrier must contemplate must be injury to another. The cases may, however, be distinguishable if 'adapt' does not imply any intention on the part of the adaptor. Breaking the milk bottle in fact makes it more suitable for injuring others, even if the adaptor intends injury only to himself. But such a distinction does not seem justified in principle.

---

[707] See also the Criminal Justice Act 1988 (Offensive Weapons) Order 1988, SI 2019.

[708] *Wang* [2005] UKHL 9; *Dhindsa* [2005] EWCA Crim 1198.

[709] cf *Davison v Birmingham Industrial Co-operative Society* (1920) 90 LJKB 206; *Flower Freight Co Ltd v Hammond* [1963] 1 QB 275, [1962] 3 All ER 950; and *Herrmann v Metropolitan Leather Co Ltd* [1942] Ch 248, [1942] 1 All ER 294; *Maddox v Storer* [1963] 1 QB 451, [1962] 1 All ER 831; *Formosa* (1990) 92 Cr App R 11, [1990] Crim LR 868, CA.

[710] *Sills v DPP* [2006] EWHC 3383 (Admin) the case is better seen as one of purposive carrying.

[711] *Maddox v Storer* [1963] 1 QB 451, [1962] 1 All ER 831.

[712] *Williamson* (1977) 67 Cr App R 35, [1978] Crim LR 229. See also *Dhindsa* [2005] EWCA Crim 1198 (ring with name of appellant across several fingers wrongly treated by judge as a weapon when matter should have been left to jury).

[713] *Woodward v Koessler* [1958] 3 All ER 557.

[714] *Gipson* [1956] Crim LR 281; *Hodgson* [1954] Crim LR 379.

[715] *Petrie* [1961] 1 All ER 466; *Gibson v Wales* [1983] 1 All ER 869.

[716] ibid.

[717] *Cugullere* [1961] 2 All ER 343.

[718] *Harrison v Thornton* (1966) 68 Cr App R 28, [1966] Crim LR 388, DC.

[719] 120 JP 250. Also, no doubt, a stiletto heel, which can be a very dangerous weapon: (1964) The Times, 25 Sept.

[720] (1975) 62 Cr App R 71. The point was not decided by the DC.

[721] [1989] Crim LR 71 (Judge Fricker QC).

Burdens of proof

In the case of articles 'made or adapted', the prosecution have to prove no more than possession in a public place.[722] D will then be convicted unless he can prove, on a balance of probability, that he had lawful authority or reasonable excuse.[723] But if the article falls into the third category the onus is on the prosecution to show that it was carried with intent to injure.[724] The prosecution must satisfy the jury that the article is either offensive *per se* (made or adapted) or, if it is not, that D had it with him with intent. If some of the jury think it is the one, and some the other, the case, it is submitted, is not made out.[725]

The requisite intention

The question in *Woodward v Koessler*[726] was whether D intends to 'cause injury to the person' if he intends merely to frighten or intimidate by displaying a knife rather than by making physical contact. It is now established that he does not. If there is no intention to cause physical injury, the offence is only committed if there is an intention to cause injury by shock, a psychiatric injury – and only in very exceptional circumstances could evidence of such an intention be found.[727] Recklessness as to use will not be sufficient *mens rea* for the offence.[728] A conditional intention to use the article is sufficient but it must be an intention to use the article in the future. If D sets out from Berkshire intending, if the occasion arises, to use a domestic knife for causing injury in Cornwall, the knife is an offensive weapon so long as it is carried in a public place and the intention continues. Once D believes that there is no possibility of the knife being used for causing injury – because, for example, his purpose has been accomplished – it ceases to be an offensive weapon.[729] It may, therefore, be no offence to carry the knife – whether or not it had been used – from Cornwall back to Berkshire.

Offences of carrying, not using

After some hesitation, the courts have construed the Act in the light of its long title. It is aimed at the *carrying* of offensive weapons *in public places*. It is not aimed at the actual *use* of the weapon, which can invariably be adequately dealt with under some other offence. Possession of a weapon does not necessarily lead to an offence against the person, but that does not mean that possession offences are not justified.[730] It has been suggested that there are a growing number of possession-type offences which are acquiring a greater significance in the criminal law.[731] They are often easy to detect and prove and can carry substantial sentences.[732]

In *Jura*,[733] D was holding an air rifle at a shooting gallery when, on being suddenly provoked, he shot and wounded a woman. It was held that he had a reasonable excuse for *carrying* the rifle though not, of course, for using it in that way. But he had committed one offence, not

[722] *Davis v Alexander* (1970) 54 Cr App R 398.

[723] See *L v DPP* [2003] QB 137.

[724] *Petrie* [1961] 1 All ER 466; *Leer* [1982] Crim LR 310.

[725] *Flynn* (1985) 82 Cr App R 319, [1986] Crim LR 239 and commentary.

[726] [1958] 3 All ER 557.

[727] *Edmonds* [1963] 2 QB 142, [1963] 1 All ER 828; *Rapier* (1979) 70 Cr App R 17; *Snooks* [1997] Crim LR 230.

[728] See *Byrne* [2003] EWCA Crim 3253, [2004] Crim LR 582 and commentary.

[729] *Allamby* [1974] 3 All ER 126, CA. cf *Ellames* [1974] 3 All ER 130.

[730] See on this D Husak, 'The Nature and Justifiability of Non-Consummate Offences' (1995) 37 Ariz LR 151.

[731] See, eg, the offences under the Terrorism Acts and see C Walker, above n 498 Ch 6. For an interesting account of possession offences see MD Drubber, 'The Possession Paradigm', in Duff and Green (eds), *Defining Crimes*, 91.

[732] The CPS has published its policy on prosecuting those who carry weapons: www.cps.gov.uk/legal/l_to_o/offensive_weapons_knives_bladed_and_pointed_articles; see also www.cps.gov.uk/legal/l_to_o/offences_against_the_person.

[733] [1954] 1 QB 503, [1954] 1 All ER 696, CA.

two. It was as if a gamekeeper at a shooting party were suddenly to lose his temper and shoot at someone. The position is therefore that if D is lawfully in possession of the article, whether it be an offensive weapon *per se* or not, his decision unlawfully to use, and immediate use of it, does not amount to an offence under the Act. In *Dayle*,[734] D took a car jack from the boot of his car and threw it at V in the course of a fight. In *Ohlson v Hylton*,[735] D, a carpenter, took a hammer from his tool bag in the course of a fight and struck V. In neither case was D guilty of an offence under the Act. It seems that if D is not in possession of the article until an occasion for its use arises and he then takes it up for immediate use, he commits no offence under the Act.[736] The law was so stated in *Ohlson v Hylton*:[737]

To support a conviction under the Act the prosecution must show that the defendant was carrying or otherwise equipped with the weapon, and had the intent to use it offensively before any occasion for its actual use had arisen.[738]

This interpretation avoids the formidable difficulty which would otherwise arise where D picks up an article in the course of a fight, allegedly for self-defence. The onus of proving that this was an unreasonable step for the purposes of self-defence is on the Crown but, if it was capable of being an offence under the Act, it would be for D to prove he had a reasonable excuse.

Duration of offence

An 'occasion' has a beginning and it must also have an end.[739] If D picks up a glass to defend himself in the course of a pub brawl he does not commit an offence under the Act; but suppose, when the fight is over, he declines to put the glass down and insists on carrying it home through two miles of streets? Probably the 'occasion' has come to an end, and the question is whether D has a reasonable excuse to carry the article.

17.15.1.2 Lawful authority or reasonable excuse

It may be that the existence of lawful authority is a pure question of law, whereas whether there is a reasonable excuse is a question of fact, subject to the usual judicial control.[740]

The term 'lawful authority' presents difficulties. Before the Act, it was presumably generally lawful to be in possession of an offensive weapon in a public place – otherwise there would have been no necessity for the Act. Now it is generally unlawful. 'Lawful authority' postulates some legal exception to the general rule of the Act; yet none is provided for and the words themselves are certainly not self-explanatory. In *Bryan v Mott* Lord Widgery CJ said[741] that 'lawful authority' refers to those 'people who from time to time carry an offensive weapon as a matter of duty – the soldier with his rifle and the police officer with his truncheon'. It seems that the 'duty' must be a public one – an employer cannot authorize his employees to carry offensive weapons simply by getting them to contract to do so.

---

[734] [1973] 3 All ER 1151. See recently *Sundas* [2011] EWCA Crim 985.

[735] [1975] 2 All ER 490, DC. See also *Police v Smith* [1974] 2 NZLR 32 (guest in restaurant using table knife offensively); *Humphreys* [1977] Crim LR 225, CA (penknife).

[736] A point seemingly overlooked in *Byrne* [2004] Crim LR 582.

[737] [1975] 2 All ER 490 at 496. The requirement that the intention to use the weapon has to be formed before the occasion of its use has been reaffirmed in *Veasey* [1999] Crim LR 158 and *C v DPP* [2002] Crim LR 202 and commentaries.

[738] *Powell* [1963] Crim LR 511, CCA, and *Harrison v Thornton* [1966] Crim LR 388, DC, therefore appear to be wrongly decided.

[739] cf *Giles* [1976] Crim LR 253 (Judge Jones).

[740] *Peacock* [1973] Crim LR 639; *Leer* [1982] Crim LR 310, CA.

[741] (1975) 62 Cr App R 71 at 73, DC.

Whether there is a reasonable excuse is said to depend on whether a reasonable person would think it excusable to carry the weapon,[742] and, in *Butler*,[743] D's argument that he had a reasonable excuse because he never considered whether the swordstick he was carrying was an article made or adapted for causing injury was left to the jury; but that may have been too generous. What did he suppose a swordstick was for, if not injuring people? A possible answer is that he thought it was made as a curio or 'collector's item'. Generally the courts have construed the provision strictly and exercised close control over magistrates and juries. It is not enough that D's intentions for use of the article were entirely lawful.[744] All of the circumstances must be considered, so, for example, it was a reasonable excuse for a male stripper to possess a truncheon as part of his uniform.[745]

A belief, however reasonable and honest, that an extendable baton (an offensive weapon) is an aerial or some other innocent article is not a reasonable excuse.[746] It is not necessarily a reasonable excuse that the weapon is carried only for self-defence. D must show that there was 'an imminent[747] particular threat affecting the particular circumstances in which the weapon was carried'.[748] One who is under constant threat it is said, must resort to the police. He commits an offence if he regularly goes out armed for self-defence.[749] So, there was held to be no excuse for carrying around an iron bar, though D had reasonable cause to fear and did fear that he would be violently attacked and intended to use the bar for defence only.[750] It is not reasonable for an Edinburgh taxi driver to carry two feet of rubber hose with a piece of metal inserted at one end, though he does so for defence against violent passengers whom taxi drivers sometimes encounter at night.[751] It has been held that possession of a broken milkbottle (an article adapted for causing injury) is not excused by the fact that D intended to use it to commit suicide.[752] It is an offence for security guards at clubs to carry truncheons 'as a deterrent' and as 'part of the uniform'.[753]

Unlawful possession may become lawful if circumstances change so as to give rise to a reasonable excuse. When a person is attacked he may use anything that he can lay his hands on to defend himself, so long as he uses no more force than is reasonable in the circumstances. It may, then, be reasonable to use an offensive weapon that he is unlawfully carrying. When Butler[754] was viciously attacked, his use of the swordstick to defend himself was justified, so possession of it must have become lawful, but that could not undo the possession offence

---

[742] *Bryan v Mott*, note above.

[743] [1988] Crim LR 695.

[744] *Bryan v Mott*, above.

[745] See *Frame v Kennedy* 2008 HCJAC 25 (K performed as 'Sergeant Eros').

[746] *Densu* [1998] 1 Cr App R 400, [1998] Crim LR 345.

[747] But this word does not appear in the statute and should not be elevated to such: *McAuley* [2009] EWCA Crim 2130 decided under the 1988 Act, s 139.

[748] *Evans v Hughes* [1972] 3 All ER 412 at 415, DC; *Evans v Wright* [1964] Crim LR 466. The case was misapplied by the trial judge in *Archbold* [2007] EWCA Crim 2125, where D had phoned the police to report that V was attacking D's home and car and D had then gone in search of him with a knife. The trial judge's direction gave the jury no opportunity to apply a defence of reasonable excuse if D was facing imminent attack. See also *McAuley* [2009] EWCA Crim 2130 decided under the 1988 Act, s 139, emphasizing that the matter should be left to the jury.

[749] For a comparative view see D Lanham, 'Offensive Weapons and Self Defence' [2005] Crim LR 85.

[750] ibid. See also *Bradley v Moss* [1974] Crim LR 430, DC; *Pittard v Mahoney* [1977] Crim LR 169, DC.

[751] *Grieve v MacLeod* 1967 SLT 70.

[752] *Bryan v Mott*, above. See also *Bown* [2003] EWCA Crim 1989, [2004] 1 Cr App R 13, decided under the 1988 Act, s 139. See also *Miller* [2007] EWCA Crim 1891, possession of butterfly knife having confiscated from girlfriend with history of self-harm.

[753] *Spanner* [1973] Crim LR 704.

[754] Above, n 743.

already committed.[755] The narrow interpretation of reasonable excuse may qualify the important principle that a person cannot be driven off the streets and compelled not to go to a public place where he might lawfully be because he will be confronted by people intending to attack him.[756] If he decides that he cannot go to that place unless armed with an offensive weapon, it seems that he must stay away. He commits an offence if he goes armed.[757] The effectiveness of the legislation in preventing the carrying of arms would be seriously impaired if anyone who reasonably feared that he might be attacked was allowed to carry a weapon.[758]

Where D had an explanation for possession of the weapon, for example, by putting it in his work trousers and forgetting 'that he was wearing those trousers' and was found in possession in public, the defence of a reasonable excuse ought still to have been to be left to the jury.[759] Forgetfulness alone is not a sufficient good reason, but coupled with other factors may be and should be left to the jury.[760] In *Jolie* the court offered two examples of facts on which there might be a valid good reason based on forgetfulness: a parent who, having bought a kitchen knife, put it in the glove compartment of a car out of the reach of a child (reason 1), forgetting (reason 2) later to retrieve it. Similarly, in *Glidewell*,[761] a taxi driver discovered weapons left by a passenger (reason 1), and forgot to remove them because he was busy (reason 2).

The imposition of a burden of proof on D can cause great difficulty where he is charged in a second count with another offence which imposes no such burden. In *Snooks and Sergeant*,[762] DD were also charged with possessing an explosive, contrary to OAPA, s 64. They relied on self-defence. For s 64, the onus was on the prosecution, under the 1953 Act the onus is on DD. The jury have an impossible task.

17.15.1.3 A 'public place'

Section 1(4) of the Prevention of Crime Act 1953 provides:

'public place' includes any highway and any other premises or place to which at the material time the public have or are permitted to have access whether on payment or otherwise.

This is very similar to the interpretation which has been placed upon s 192 of the Road Traffic Act 1988 and to the definition of public place, etc in other Acts. It should always be borne in mind that the same term may bear different meanings according to the context in which it is used and that whether a place is public is a question of fact.[763]

A public place could not include land adjoining that to which the public had access even if D could have inflicted harm from such land.[764] A householder impliedly invites persons having legitimate business to walk up his garden path to the door, but this does not render the garden a 'public place'. The class of persons invited to enter is too restricted for them to constitute 'the public'.[765] On the other hand, the communal landing of a block of flats has been held to be a public place on the ground that the public had access in fact, whether or not they

---

[755] Smith, *Justification and Excuse*, at 117–123.

[756] *Field* [1972] Crim LR 435.

[757] *Malnik v DPP* [1989] Crim LR 451, DC.

[758] *Salih* [2007] EWCA Crim 2750. See *Deyemi* [2007] EWCA Crim 2060 and *Zahid* [2010] EWCA Crim 2158 on this approach with firearms.

[759] *Bird* [2004] EWCA Crim 964.

[760] *Jolie* [2004] EWCA Crim 1543; *Tsap* [2008] EWCA Crim 2679; *Chahal v DPP* [2010] EWHC 439 (Admin).

[761] (1999) 163 JP 557.

[762] [1997] Crim LR 230.

[763] *Theodolou* [1963] Crim LR 573.

[764] *Roberts* [2004] 1 Cr App R 16, [2003] EWCA Crim 2753 (garden 1m wide).

[765] *Edwards and Roberts* (1978) 67 Cr App R 228, [1978] Crim LR 564 (a case under s 5 of the Public Order Act 1936).

were permitted to have it.[766] In the absence of a notice restricting entry, there was evidence on which justices could find that the unrestricted access of the public to a local authority housing estate extended to the stairways and landings of the flats.[767] The jury are, of course, entitled to draw reasonable inferences; so that where D produced an air pistol in a private dwelling-house which he was visiting, it was open to them to infer that he brought it to or took it away from the house through the public street.[768] Possession of an article (truncheon) in a car on a public road is possession in a public place.[769]

17.15.1.4 Possession and *mens rea*

It must be proved that D 'has with him' the article. The prosecution must prove the minimum mental element which is necessary to constitute possession, and in addition, the 'closer contact' than mere possession which the phrase 'has with him' implies.[770] The question then is whether the offence is one of strict liability or whether any *mens rea* is required. The case law is in disarray. Some cases suggest that the prosecution must prove D knowingly 'has with him': *Cugullere*,[771] *Russell*.[772] Subsequent decisions (*Martindale*,[773] and *McCalla*,[774]) have erroneously treated *Russell* as simply a decision, and therefore a wrong decision, on the meaning of possession. The prevailing view, following *McCalla*, is that the offence is one of strict liability; but the better opinion is that *Russell*, though treated as overruled, should be regarded as the binding authority.[775]

In *Jolie*,[776] D was found in possession of a knife in a car he was driving and claimed that he had forgotten it was there, although he admitted putting it there as he had used it to start the broken ignition. Kennedy LJ suggested that in the cases of *McCalla, Martindale* and *Buswell* it had been clear that the article had remained under D's control. His lordship suggested that the jury should be directed that they may find possession if either D was aware of the presence of the weapon or he was responsible for putting it where it was mislaid.[777]

As regards the relevant *mens rea* as to the offensiveness of the weapon, in *Densu*,[778] counsel abandoned an argument before the Court of Appeal that the ruling of the trial judge was wrong in so far as it suggested that the proof that D has with him is satisfied on proof that D knew that he had the weapon (a baton) with him but did not know that it was a weapon. The prevailing view is that liability is strict.

17.15.1.5 Articles with blades or points

The Prevention of Crime Act is supplemented by an offence triable either way, punishable on summary conviction by six months', and, on indictment, by four years' imprisonment[779] under

---

[766] *Knox v Anderton* (1982) 76 Cr App R 156, [1983] Crim LR 114, DC, and commentary. But, a public place is not synonymous with a place from which the public are not excluded: *Harriott v DPP* [2005] EWHC 965 (Admin).

[767] See also *Hanrahan* [2004] All ER (D) 144 (Nov) (rehabilitation centre to which access gained through intercom).

[768] *Mehmed* [1963] Crim LR 780.

[769] *Ellis* [2010] EWAC Crim 163.

[770] *McCalla* (1988) 87 Cr App R 372 at 378.

[771] [1961] 2 All ER 343. Arguably the court was concerned only with the question of possession.

[772] (1984) 81 Cr App R 315.

[773] (1986) 84 Cr App R 31.

[774] Above, n 770.

[775] See commentary on *Wright* [1992] Crim LR 596.

[776] [2003] EWCA Crim 1543, [2003] Crim LR 730.

[777] See also *Hilton* [2009] EWHC 2867 (Admin) on the importance of distinguishing whether D knew he had something with him and whether he had a good reason for possessing it (decided under s 139).

[778] [1998] 1 Cr App R 400.

[779] Increased from two years by the Violent Crime Reduction Act 2006, s 42.

the Criminal Justice Act 1988, s 139, of having with one in a public place an article 'which has a blade[780] or is sharply pointed except a folding pocket knife[781] [with a cutting edge not exceeding three inches[782]'. The article need not be made or adapted for causing injury, nor intended by D for such use. The fact that a blade might be used for other functions than as a weapon (for example, a Swiss Army knife) does not mean that it is not *prima facie* a bladed article within s 139.[783] Otherwise, the constituents of the offence are similar to those required by the 1953 Act. It is a defence for D to prove that he had *good reason* or lawful authority for having the article with him. In *Jolie*, the court regarded the words 'good reason' in the 1988 Act as intended to be narrower than 'reasonable excuse' in the 1953 Act. The court concluded that the words 'good reason' do not generally require a judicial gloss in directing the jury.[784]

Self-defence against an anticipated imminent attack may be a good reason.[785] In *Davis*,[786] the court thought that the section imposed 'a very significant limitation on the citizen's freedom. It should not be assumed that it has been achieved except by the use of clear words.' It is specifically provided that it is a defence for D to prove that he had the article with him for use at work,[787] religious reasons[788] or as part of national costume. It is necessary to prove that he had it with him for a specific reason *in public* on this occasion.[789]

A new s 139A was inserted by the Offensive Weapons Act 1996, creating offences of having on school premises (i) an article to which s 139 applies (punishable on indictment with four years' imprisonment[790]) and (ii) an offensive weapon within the meaning of the Prevention of Crime Act 1953 (punishable on indictment with four years' imprisonment). It is a defence to both offences to prove 'good reason or lawful authority'.

17.16 Hoax offences

17.16.1 Bomb hoaxes: Criminal Law Act 1977[791]

The bomb hoax, always irritating and sometimes frightening, was dealt with in a variety of ways before 1977. If a demand were made by the hoaxer, it might be treated as blackmail.[792] If, as is usually the case, it involved a threat to damage property, s 2 of the Criminal Damage

---

[780] This probably means a blade which has a cutting edge. A screwdriver, even if it may be properly described as having a blade, is not within the section: *Davis* [1998] Crim LR 564. However, in *Brooker v DPP* (2005) 169 JP 368, a butter knife with no cutting edge and no point was held to be a bladed article.

[781] Which means a knife which is 'readily and indeed immediately foldable at all times, simply by the folding process': *Fehmi v DPP* (1993) 96 Cr App R 235, DC, so that a pocket knife which locks into position is not 'folding': *Deegan* [1998] 2 Cr App R 121, [1998] Crim LR 562.

[782] On the difficulties on proving length where the weapon is lost see *Banton* [2009] EWCA Crim 240.

[783] *Giles* [2003] All ER (D) 68 (Feb). A grapefruit knife qualifies: *R (on the application of Windsor and Maidenhead RIBC) v East Berkshire Justices* [2010] EWHC 3020 (Admin).

[784] See *Chahal v DPP* [2010] EWHC 439 (Admin); *Hilton* [2009] EWHC 2867 (Admin).

[785] *Emmanuel* [1998] Crim LR 347.

[786] [1998] Crim LR 564. Contrast the attitude of the court in *Deegan*, above, n 781.

[787] A question of fact for the jury: *Manning* [1998] Crim LR 198 (knife carried to do repairs to D's own car). This can include casual or part time work: *Chahal v DPP* [2010] EWHC 439 (Admin).

[788] Which must be the dominant reason: *Wang* [2003] EWCA Crim 3228. D must show that the religion was the reason for his possession on this occasion, ie that he was to use it in some religious connection. The court acknowledged, *per curiam*, that Art 9 of the ECHR might require the State authorities to allow persons to carry bladed instruments in public in pursuit of their religious beliefs.

[789] *Giles*, above.

[790] Increased from two years by the Violent Crime Reduction Act 2006, s 42.

[791] See C Walker, *The Prevention of Terrorism in British Law* (2nd edn, 1992) Ch 12.

[792] Below, Ch 25. *King* [1976] Crim LR 200.

Act 1971[793] might be invoked. In other cases, the hoax amounted to the offence of wasting the time of the police.[794] On one occasion at least, the clumsy weapon of common law public nuisance was used.[795] The Criminal Law Act 1977, s 51, now provides a special offence:

51. (1) A person who –

    (a) places any article in any place whatever; or

    (b) dispatches any article by post, rail or any other means whatever of sending things from one place to another,

       with the intention (in either case) of inducing in some other person a belief that it is likely to explode or ignite and thereby cause personal injury or damage to property is guilty of an offence.

    In this subsection 'article' includes substance.

(2) A person who communicated any information which he knows or believes to be false to another person with the intention of inducing in him or any other person a false belief that a bomb or other thing liable to explode or ignite is present in any place or location whatever is guilty of an offence.

(3) For a person to be guilty of an offence under subsection (1) or (2) above it is not necessary for him to have any particular person in mind as the person in whom he intends to induce the belief mentioned in that subsection.

(4) A person guilty of an offence under this section shall be liable –

    (a) on summary conviction, to imprisonment for a term not exceeding six months or to a fine not exceeding the prescribed sum, or both;

    (b) on conviction on indictment, to imprisonment for a term not exceeding seven years.

The gist of the offences is the *mens rea*. The *actus reus* of s 51(1)(a) is an act which everyone does every day. Under s 51(2), the information communicated may in fact be true; it is sufficient that D believes it to be false. If he believes that the information is, or may possibly be, true, then it obviously cannot be an offence to pass it on.

17.16.2 Hoaxes relating to biological weapons[796]

Section 51 does not deal with hoaxes involving things that do not 'ignite or explode', such as sending powders or liquids through the post and claiming that they are harmful.[797] Section 114 of the Anti-terrorism, Crime and Security Act 2001 fills that gap. It is an offence to place anywhere or send any substance or article intending to make others believe that it is likely to be or to contain a noxious substance or thing which could endanger human life or health. A further offence is provided by subs (2) for a person to falsely communicate any information to another that a noxious substance or thing is or will be in a place and so is likely to cause harm to or endanger human life or health. The offences are triable either way. On summary conviction the maximum sentence is six months, or a fine up to the statutory maximum or both. On conviction on indictment a person may be imprisoned for up to seven years, or fined or both.

Section 113 of the Anti-terrorism Crime and Security Act 2001, as amended by the Terrorism Act 2006, s 34, makes it an offence for a person to use or threaten to use a biological,

---

[793] Below, p 104. *Farrell* [1976] Crim LR 318.
[794] Criminal Law Act 1967, s 5(2). *Bikram* [1974] Crim LR 55.
[795] *Madden* [1975] 3 All ER 155, CA; below, p 1118.
[796] See C Walker, above n 498 Ch 6.
[797] See *Rimmington and Goldstein* [2005] UKHL 63.

chemical, radioactive or other noxious substance to cause various kinds of serious harm in a manner designed to influence the government or an international governmental organization or to intimidate the public. The maximum sentence is 14 years' imprisonment. The offence has been further extended to conduct with the purpose of advancing a political, religious or ideological cause, even if committed abroad in some circumstances.[798]

[798] See the Crime (International Co-operation) Act 2003, s 53.

18

Sexual offences

18.1 Introduction[1]

The Sexual Offences Act 2003 (SOA 2003) came into force on 1 May 2004.[2] The Act represents the most comprehensive and radical overhaul of the law relating to sexual offences ever undertaken in England and Wales. Previously, most of the relevant law was contained in the Sexual Offences Act 1956, but that was itself merely a consolidation of various statutes dating back to the late nineteenth century, and the 1956 Act had been amended incrementally to tackle numerous specific problems.[3] The 2003 Act redefines many of the offences found in the old legislation, but introduces scores of new ones. It is not, however, a complete codification of sexual offences; some regulation remains elsewhere – for example that relating to prostitution[4] and indecent photographs.[5] Parliament continues to add new sexual offences and to amend those in the 2003 Act.[6]

---

[1] See generally on the Act: P Rook and R Ward, *Sexual Offences: Law and Practice* (4th edn, 2010); K Stevenson, A Davies and M Gunn, *Blackstone's Guide to the Sexual Offences Act 2003* (2004); R Card, M Hirst and A Gillespie, *Sexual Offences* (2008). See also for an interesting comparison, Scottish Law Commission Discussion Paper No 131, *Rape and Other Offences* (2006). For a discussion of the Scots proposals see P Ferguson, 'Reforming Rape and Other Sexual Offences' (2008) Edinburgh L Rev 302.

[2] Where the prosecution has not demonstrated whether the events constituting the charge occurred before or after this date, it was held that the prosecution cannot continue: *Newbon* [2005] Crim LR 738, (HHJ Glenn); *C* [2005] EWCA Crim 3533. The Government responded by introducing s 55 of the Violent Crime Reduction Act 2006. In short, s 55 applies if the offence now charged is an offence under the SOA 2003 and the conduct alleged amounts to an offence under one of the repealed offences listed in subsection (2), and the *only thing* preventing D being found guilty is that it cannot be proved beyond reasonable doubt whether the conduct took place before or after the commencement of the SOA 2003. If so, where the maximum penalty of imprisonment available was lower under the old law that will be conclusively presumed to apply. If the penalties are the same, then it shall be conclusively presumed that the conduct took place after the commencement of the SOA 2003. The section presents difficulties: how can it be known that the 'only thing' preventing the accused being guilty is that the date has not been proved? Many other issues will determine guilt. It is also potentially unfair: Why should it not be that the version of the offence (not penalty) which is more favourable to the defendant is adopted? In *C* [2009] EWCA Crim 52 it was held that s 55 'to have been relied upon each offence should have been charged in the alternative under the new regime and the old'. This is still not always understood by prosecutors. See also *F* [2008] EWCA Crim 994.

[3] For the previous law see the 10th edition, Ch 16.

[4] The Home Office consultation process on prostitution: *Paying the Price* (2004) (see on this B Brooks Gordon, 'Clients and Commercial Sex' [2005] Crim LR 425; M Madden Dempsey, 'Rethinking Wolfenden' [2005] Crim LR 444) led to the new offences in the Policing and Crime Act 2009: s 14 creates a new offence of paying for sexual services of a prostitute who is subject to exploitation; s 16 amends the Street Offences Act 1959, s 1. A new offence of soliciting is created by s 19 of the 2009 Act, which inserts s 51A into the SOA 2003; this offence effectively replaces the offences under the Sexual Offences Act 1985. See TK Paz and N Levenkron (2009) 29 LS 438.

[5] See the Protection of Children Act 1978; and s 160 of the Criminal Justice Act 1988 as amended by the Coroners and Justice Act 2009 See generally, S Ost, *Child Pornography and Sexual Grooming: Legal and Societal Responses* (2009); M Taylor and E Quayle, *Child Pornography: An Internet Crime* (2003); A Gillespie, 'Child Protection on the Internet' (2002) 14 CFLQ 411.

[6] See, eg, the possession of extreme image offences discussed in Ch 31 and the amendments in the Violent Crime Reduction Act 2006, the Criminal Justice and Immigration Act 2008, the Coroners and Justice Act 2009 and the Policing and Crime Act 2009.

The prevalence of sexual offending remains high. In 2009/10 there were 54,509 sexual offences recorded in England and Wales.[7] See recently The Stern Review.[8]

18.1.1 The need for new law

There had been a growing level of concern over the effectiveness of the 1956 Act. It was described by one commentator as 'cumbersome and inadequate',[9] and by Lord Falconer when introducing the Sexual Offences Bill as 'archaic, incoherent and discriminatory'.[10] This was a widely, though not universally held view. Despite the sometimes dramatic incremental development, both at common law[11] and by legislation,[12] the protection offered against sexual offending remained unsatisfactory. One consequence of the continued incremental development of the law was its incoherence. In more general terms, it was recognized that the 1956 Act failed adequately to reflect the morality and prevalent sexual attitudes and practices of the twenty-first century. It provided inadequate protection for the vulnerable whilst also failing to respect the sexual autonomy of those capable of making informed choices about their sexual behaviour.[13] Moreover, the language used throughout the legislation was archaic and in some instances offensively inappropriate as, for example, with the references to 'defectives' rather than people with learning disabilities and mental disorders.[14] Many essential terms such as 'consent' and 'capacity' remained ill-defined. Some elements of the previous law were incompatible with ECHR obligations: for example, criminalizing consensual homosexual intercourse and gross indecency between males,[15] and, arguably, the law failed to provide effective protection against sexual offending as the State is obliged to do.[16]

Recognition of the unsatisfactory nature of the law extended beyond the legal community. Greater public awareness of the nature and effect of sexual assaults on victims coupled with

[7] J Flatley et al, *Crime in England and Wales 2009/10, Findings from the British Crime Survey and police recorded crime* (2010) table 2.04.

[8] A Report by Baroness Vivien Stern CBE of an independent review into how rape complaints are handled by public authorities in England and Wales (2010). The website, http://copfs.gov.uk/Resource/Doc/13547/0000632. pdf, includes the report and the Government's interim response.

[9] J Temkin, 'Getting it Right: Sexual Offences Law Reform' (2000) 150 NLJ 1169, and see J Temkin, *Rape and the Legal Process* (2nd edn, 2002); J Temkin and B Krahé, *Sexual Assault and the Justice Gap: A Question of Attitude* (2008).

[10] HL, vol 644, col 771.

[11] eg, the House of Lords in *R* [1992] 1 AC 599 declaring that the historical exception whereby a man could not be found guilty of raping his wife was finally abolished. For a detailed history, see Temkin, *Rape and Legal Process*, 72–89; M Giles, 'Judicial Law-Making in the Criminal Courts: The Case of Marital Rape' [1992] Crim LR 407.

[12] eg rape was extended to include non-consensual anal intercourse with a person of either sex by the Criminal Justice and Public Order Act 1994, s 142; the jurisdictional reaches of the English criminal law were extended by the Sexual Offences (Conspiracy and Incitement) Act 1996 to criminalize sex tourism (on which see P Alldridge, 'The Sexual Offences (Conspiracy and Incitement) Act 1996' [1997] Crim LR 30). Other significant statutory involvement included the Sexual Offences (Amendment) Act 2000, on which see J Burnside, 'The Sexual Offences (Amendment) Act 2000: The Head of a "Kiddy-libber" and the Torso of a "Child-saver"?' [2001] Crim LR 425.

[13] There is a voluminous philosophical literature on criminalizing sexual behaviour and the significance of consent in the offences. See, in particular, N Lacey, *Unspeakable Subjects* (1998); S Schulhofer, *Unwanted Sex: The Culture of Intimidation and the Failure of Law* (1998); J Gardner and S Shute, 'The Wrongness of Rape', in Horder (ed), *Oxford Essays in Jurisprudence*; M Childs, 'Sexual Autonomy and the Law' (2001) 64 MLR 309; V Tadros, 'Rape Without Consent' (2006) 26 OJLS 515 and references therein.

[14] See the comments of Baroness Hale in *Cooper* [2009] UKHL 42, [8]–[16] on the protection being offered on the basis of the status of the complainant's disorder.

[15] See *ADT v UK* (2000) 31 EHRR 803.

[16] *MC v Bulgaria* [2003] ECHR 39272/98.

the increase in reporting of sexual crimes rendered awareness of the Act's failings increasingly acute. Research into the process of prosecuting rapes and the decreasing conviction rates[17] had generated considerable public unease.[18] It was felt that this failing was in part a consequence of the inadequacies of the substantive law as well as of the shortcomings of the law of evidence and procedure.[19]

Previous reform proposals including the Fifteenth Report of the CLRC had been largely ignored.[20] The 2003 Act began with a more fundamental review: the Home Office Review of sex offences, *Setting the Boundaries;*[21] and the *Review of Part 1 of the Sex Offenders Act 1997.*[22] Following consultation, these led to a Government White Paper, *Protecting the Public: strengthening protection against sex offenders and reforming the law on sexual offences.*[23] The laudable aims of these reviews cannot be criticized. Unfortunately whilst trying to achieve some of those aims, such as a measure of gender neutrality[24] and modernization of the language, the Act creates numerous difficulties, many of a significant and substantial nature.

18.2 Recurring fundamental concepts in the 2003 Act

18.2.1 Consent

At the core of some of the most serious offences in the 2003 Act is the element of consent. It has long been recognized that determining the consent of the complainant is not restricted to ascertaining whether there has been the use or threat of force,[25] nor whether the sexual acts were against his or her will.[26] However, beyond these negative observations the law has

---

[17] *Setting the Boundaries; Reforming the Law on Sexual Offences* (July 2000) Home Office, paras 2.3 and 2.8.5. See Temkin, *Rape and the Legal Process,* 1–3 and 60–67. See also the material referred to in this chapter on reform below.

[18] The conviction rates fell from 1/3 to 1/13 between 1977 and 1999. See *Report of the Joint Investigation into the Investigation and Prosecution of Cases Involving Allegations of Rape* (2002) HMCPSI. See also A Myhill and J Allen, *Rape and Sexual Assault on Women: The Extent and Nature of the Problem – Findings from the British Crime Survey* (2002) HORS No 237; Temkin and Krahé, above, n 9. See also C Thomas *Are Juries Fair?* (2010) See also *Hansard,* HL Debates on Violence Against Women, 13 Jan 2011, col 1594, Baroness Stern, 'The Ministry of Justice researchers carried out a one-off analysis that found that, of all the 2007 rape cases where the trial was completed by the end of 2008, 42 per cent of defendants were found not guilty and 58 per cent were convicted of an offence, of which 34 per cent were convicted of rape, 17 per cent of another sexual offence, 3 per cent of another violent offence, 3 per cent of another indictable offence, and 1 per cent of a summary – that is, a minor offence. Thus, 54 per cent were convicted of rape or another sexual or violent offence. This is new information and it is important that we have been provided with it.'

[19] As addressed in the Youth Justice and Criminal Evidence Act 1999.

[20] CLRC, Fifteenth Report, *Sexual Offences* (1984) Cmnd 9213; B Hogan, 'On Modernising the Law of Sexual Offences', in *Reshaping the Criminal Law,* 174; J Temkin, 'Towards a Modern Law of Rape' (1982) 45 MLR 399.

[21] (2000). See N Lacey, 'Beset by Boundaries' [2001] Crim LR 3; Temkin, *Rape and the Legal Process,* at 60–67.

[22] (2001). Described by Lord Ackner in the Debates as a 'pamphlet': HL, col 846, 13 Feb 2003.

[23] Cm 5668 (2002).

[24] cf the Gender Recognition Act 2004 relating to gender-specific offences. On the importance of gender neutrality see P Rumney and M Morgan-Taylor, 'Recognising the Male Victim: Gender Neutrality and the Law of Rape' (1997) 26 Anglo American Law Review 198.

[25] Until relatively recently courts continued erroneously to direct juries that the use of force by the defendant and resistance by the complainant were essential ingredients of the offence of rape. See *Dimes* 7 Cr App R 43; *Harling* [1938] 1 All ER 307, and *Howard* [1965] 3 All ER 684.

[26] *Camplin* (1845) 1 Cox CC 220: Tindal CJ and Parke B were of the view that rape was ravishing a woman 'where she did not consent' and not ravishing her 'against her will'.

struggled to define, in positive terms, the scope of consent.[27] It is important to remember that the absence of consent is an element of the *actus reus,* not an element of defence. As Duff points out,[28] the description of the conduct must be descriptive of the prescribed wrong, and if consent was part of the defence, sexual intercourse would have to be the wrong.[29]

Defining consent was acknowledged to be one of the major difficulties under the 1956 Act,[30] where the leading authority of *Olugboja*[31] simply left the question to the jury to apply their common sense, giving consent its 'ordinary meaning'. This approach prompted stringent academic criticism: Glanville Williams regarded it as 'one more manifestation of the deplorable tendency of the criminal courts to leave important questions of legal policy to the jury'.[32]

Remedying this shortcoming was one of the most important objectives of the law reform. *Setting the Boundaries* emphasized the need for clarity in 'the most private and difficult area of sexual relationships... so that the boundaries of what is acceptable, and of criminally culpable behaviour, are all well understood'.[33] It was stressed that this is particularly important because in sexual activity, consent often involves 'verbal and non-verbal messages [which] can be mistaken and where assumptions about what is and is not appropriate can lead to significant misunderstanding'.[34] Given such determination to clarify the law of consent, echoed as forcefully as it was by Ministerial statements,[35] the provisions in the 2003 Act are rather disappointing. Although there is greater clarity than under *Olugboja*, the jury is still left with considerable discretion since the statutory definitions are not as clear or as comprehensive as they could be. In particular, it is doubtful whether the Act succeeds in providing any solution to some of the more frequently encountered difficulties such as the complainant who was, at the time of the sexual act, voluntarily and heavily intoxicated[36] or who succumbed to threats or pressure short of violence, or to deceptions.[37]

18.2.1.1 'Definition' of consent

Three sections in the Act seek to clarify what is meant by consent. Under s 76, where the defendant, A[38], deceives the complainant, B, as to the nature or purpose of the act or his identity, it is conclusively presumed that there is a lack of consent and that A has no reasonable belief in consent. Under s 75, six specified circumstances give rise to a rebuttable presumption that there was no consent and that A did not have a reasonable belief in B's consent. Finally, s 74

---

[27] See, generally, the discussion in the Law Commission Policy Paper appended to *Setting the Boundaries.* For more philosophical analysis see, eg, H Hurd, 'The Moral Magic of Consent' (1996) 2 Legal Theory 168; J McGregor, 'Why When She Says No She Doesn't Mean Maybe and Doesn't Mean Yes' (1996) 2 Legal Theory 175.

[28] See Duff, *Answering for Crime,* 208–211.

[29] For an argument that it is *prima facie* wrong to penetrate a vagina or anus see M Demsey and J Herring, 'Why Sexual Penetration Requires Justification' (2007) 27 OJLS 467.

[30] For a review of circumstances in which consent was held to be absent under the old law, see *Setting the Boundaries,* para 2.2.2.

[31] [1981] 3 All ER 443.

[32] Williams, TBCL, at 551. Although, see S Gardner, 'Appreciating *Olugboja*' (1996) 16 LS 275 for a defence of this approach emphasizing that it focused correctly on the issue of the victim's autonomy. See also G Dingwall, 'Addressing the Boundaries of Consent in Rape' (2002) 13 KCLJ 31.

[33] ibid, para 2.7.2, para 2.10.1.

[34] ibid. See on this D Husak, *The Philosophy of Criminal Law* (2009) Ch 9. See also P Rumney, 'The Review of Sex Offences and Rape Law Reform: Another False Dawn' (2001) 64 MLR 890 emphasizing that consent should involve a dialogue between the parties.

[35] See Lord Falconer speaking of the need for 'crystal clarity', HL Debates, col 772, 13 Feb 2003. See also *Protecting the Public,* para 30.

[36] See *Bree* [2007] EWCA Crim 804 and discussion below, p 724.

[37] See *Jheeta* [2007] EWCA Crim 1699 discussed below, p 733.

[38] Throughout this chapter 'A' will be used to denote the principal defendant and 'B' the complainant.

provides a general definition of consent which may be relevant in combination with ss 75 and 76 in appropriate cases, and independently governs all other situations. It is unclear whether the three-tiered approach to consent reflects a hierarchy of circumstances in which consent is absent.[39]

These 'deeply ambiguous'[40] definitions apply throughout Part I of the Act (in particular for the non-consensual offences of rape, assault by penetration, sexual assault, and causing a person to engage in sexual activity without consent). One very significant failure of the drafts-man was not to extend ss 75 and 76 beyond the substantive offences, to inchoate forms of those offences.[41]

It is surprising that there have been very few cases in which consent has been examined by the Court of Appeal. Presumably, juries are applying their common sense. In *H*,[42] the Court of Appeal rightly emphasized that it is not necessary in every case for the judge to direct on all aspects of the law of consent when they do not arise on the facts.

Section 74

Section 74 provides that 'a person consents if he agrees by choice, and has the freedom and capacity to make that choice'. This definition, based on 'free agreement', is intended to em-phasize that the absence of the complainant's protest, resistance or injury does not necessarily signify his consent. Although the Act is silent as to the precise moment at which B's consent or agreement must be present, it is clear that the relevant time is that of the alleged sexual wrong-doing. This may present problems where, for example, B has indicated to A his willingness to engage in sexual activity later that evening, but then becomes so heavily intoxicated that at the time of the sexual act B is incapable of making any coherent decision.[43] *A fortiori* where B initially indicates his disinclination to engage in sexual activity but later does so when vol-untarily intoxicated.

'Freedom', it is submitted, is too loose a word to use in defining this crucial element of such serious offences. Freedom is a term which is heavily context dependent and always implies 'freedom from' something.[44] The jury will have to address the existence and weight of this 'other' pressure from which B might have been acting freely. It may therefore be desirable for the jury to address the question of freedom by reference to proportionality. The greater the 'pressure' facing B the less 'freedom' she has to make her choice to engage in sexual activity. This may involve the jury in a difficult assessment of a wide range of factors when the degree of freedom is inhibited by, for example, A's threat to terminate B's employment unless she has sex. This may lead into further difficulties such as the source of the pressures, particularly where the defendant is not directly responsible for bringing them to bear. Beyond freedom from physical pressure, it is unclear what degree of freedom is envisaged to validate consent. In particular, issues may arise as to B's economic freedom, as where B, an underprivileged employee of a wealthy businessman agrees to his sexual advances to retain her position. Other

---

[39] See the influential article by J Temkin and A Ashworth, 'Rape, Sexual Assaults and the Problems of Consent' [2004] Crim LR 328. See also J Miles (2008) 10 Archbold News 5, suggesting that s 74 should be construed subject to s 76. This seems to be a strained reading of the sections. For a summary of some of the key cases since the Act see J Elvin, 'The Concept of Consent under the Sexual Offences Act 2003' (2008) 72 J Crim L 519.

[40] See Tadros (2006) 26 OJLS 521.

[41] See HHJ Rodwell, 'Problems with the Sexual Offences Act 2003' [2005] Crim LR 290.

[42] [2006] EWCA Crim 853. See also *Taran* [2006] EWCA Crim 1498, where B was raped at gun point and there was no need to explain to the jury the intricacies of ss 75 and 76, below.

[43] See also the Law Commission's Policy Paper, para 4.54. See, generally, Temkin, *Rape and the Legal Process*, 90–116.

[44] As Temkin and Ashworth point out, above, n 39, freedom is only used to rule out the suggestion of some or all of its antitheses. See p 336, citing JL Austin, 'A Plea for Excuses', in H Morris (ed), *Freedom and Responsibility* (1961) 8.

examples might involve B's religious freedom as where a dependent young member of a strict religion agrees to sexual activity with an elder whom in all other respects she has been taught never to question.[45] In the case of *Kirk*[46] it was accepted by the Court of Appeal that the teenage homeless complainant, B, who had been sexually abused for years by A, had not consented to sex with A where she had done so to gain £3.25 from him in order to buy food.

This question of defining freedom also raises the difficult relationship between 'consent' and 'submission'. Under the 1956 Act, in *Olugboja*[47] the court placed considerable emphasis on the difference between consent and submission, but never fully identified what the distinction was. Thus, B may reluctantly submit to sexual intercourse only because her fiancé threatens that he will break off their engagement if she does not. Such a case is very far removed from rape but it seems to be one of submission. At the other extreme, B may submit because A is holding a knife at her throat. This is plainly rape; there is no consent.[48] In both cases B yields because a threat is made; it is not easy to see how the term 'submission' helps distinguish them. The confusion in addressing these terms was in part a result of the *dictum* of Coleridge J in *Day*:[49] 'every consent involves a submission; but it by no means follows that a mere submission involves consent'. It is submitted that this is wrong. B who joyously embraces her reluctant lover, A, undoubtedly consents to the acts that follow but it would seem inappropriate, to put it mildly, to say that B 'submits' to that which she ardently desires and provokes. On the other hand, B who 'gives in' to threats from her fiancé does in fact agree, although not freely. Whether any useful distinction can be drawn in this context between threats ('do this or I will sack you') and promises ('do this and I will give you a pay rise') is debatable.

The language of submission and consent was used in *Kirk* (above), and the Court of Appeal recently addressed this issue directly in *Doyle*[50] where A had used violence against his ex-partner (holding her head under water and tying her up) before demanding sex. B refused, protesting until he had penetrated her; she then ceased to resist explaining at trial that she 'just let him get on with it'. A's conviction for rape was upheld.[51] There was no consent. The court acknowledged that there would be circumstances where a jury would require assistance with the distinction between (i) reluctant but free exercise of choice, especially in a long-term loving relationship, and (ii) unwilling submission due to fear of worse consequences, but the instant case did not call for such assistance.[52]

Section 74 also uses the term 'choice' as a factor in determining consent. Choice presupposes that B has options from which to choose and that in turn surely presupposes B is possessed of adequate information about each to make an 'informed' choice between them.[53]

---

[45] Difficulties also arise because A will claim that he had a reasonable belief in B's consent.

[46] [2008] EWCA Crim 434 (under the old law).

[47] (1981) 73 Cr App R 344.

[48] This may now give rise to a presumption of non-consent under s 75(2)(a).

[49] (1841) 9 C & P 722 at 724.

[50] [2010] EWCA Crim 119.

[51] The judge directed that 'submission to do something which she did not want to happen does not amount to consent. In deciding if [B] consented or whether she merely submitted to something which she did not want, you should apply your combined good sense, your experience, and your knowledge of human behaviour and modern behaviour to all the relevant facts, including, obviously, their relationship and what you have heard about that. The law does not require a complainant to have resisted physically, and nor is it necessary to show that a woman's submission was induced by force or fear, although obviously, in this case, as you know, the prosecution evidence is that Miss C did say no, and physically resisted until the defendant penetrated her.'

[52] In cases where a direction on submission is needed, the current JSB direction 53 offers an illustration taken from Pill J's ruling in *Zafar*: 'V may not particularly want sexual intercourse on a particular occasion, but because it is her husband or her partner who is asking for it, she will consent to sexual intercourse. The fact that such consent is given reluctantly or out of a sense of duty to her partner i[t i]s still consent.'

[53] Tadros argues that there is a paradox in the present law in that it is possible for B to agree by choice while lacking freedom or capacity: if one lacks capacity and freedom one cannot agree by choice at all (2006) 26 OJLS 521.

Again, s 74 fails to offer any guidance as to the degree of information about the activity (such as penetration) that B is to engage in. One of the most controversial areas in which this issue arises is in cases where A is HIV positive and has not informed B of that fact. The Court of Appeal has confirmed that a complainant's consent to the risk of contracting HIV has to be an informed consent.[54] However, it is important to reiterate,[55] that the current position in English law is that if A who is HIV positive fails to inform B of that fact before having unprotected intercourse, A will not commit rape. A is regarded not as having deceived B as to the nature of the act (sex), but as to the risk of infection. The appropriate charge is therefore under the Offences Against the Person Act 1861. Indeed, it has been held that A's failure to disclose his HIV status did not affect the issue of consent in rape where there were no allegations that A had deceived B, rather that he had forcibly attacked B. The evidence of A's HIV status should have been excluded: the fact that a defendant may not have disclosed his HIV status is not relevant to the issue of consent under s 74.[56] Arguably, if A impliedly represented to B his HIV negative status, that may well be relevant in considering if B consented. Other difficult cases are equally easy to imagine: if A deceives B as to whether he is using a condom, has B chosen to have intercourse? Is the consent to 'unprotected' intercourse?

The element of 'capacity' is similarly not further defined. It is clearly 'integral to the concept of choice'.[57] In this context it is clearly intended to mean mental capacity. It is submitted that the crucial issue should be whether B has the capacity to choose to perform the specified act with A on the occasion in question.[58] The test is not one focusing on B's status – ie whether B has a particular mental disability or not. The question is focused on B's capacity to make the decision about engaging in this sexual act with this person.

The leading authority on the concept of capacity to consent under the 2003 Act is *Cooper* in which the House of Lords considered that term in the context of the offence under s30: sexual activity with a person with a mental disorder impeding choice.[59] Some aspects of the decision inform a general understanding of consent. B was a 28-year-old woman with a history of serious mental disorders manifesting themselves in episodes of impulsive and aggressive behaviour, delusions, hallucinations, depression or manic episodes. She developed irrational concerns for her safety. A befriended her, gave her crack cocaine, and made her perform oral sex on him and a co-defendant. B said that she had performed the acts out of fear of violence. A argued that B's capacity was only impaired and that she did not lack capacity to choose in the sense of lacking sufficient understanding of the nature of the act or its consequences. In short, A argued that B knew what oral sex was and that was sufficient for her to have capacity to consent. The judge directed the jury that if B had an irrational fear or confusion of mind arising from her mental disorder she may lack capacity to choose whether to agree to sexual touching. The Court of Appeal[60] took a much narrower view of capacity and held that an

---

[54] *Konzani* [2005] EWCA Crim 706.

[55] See the full discussion in Ch 17.

[56] *B* [2006] EWCA Crim 2945.

[57] Per Sir Igor Judge P in *Bree* [2007] EWCA Crim 256 at [23].

[58] C Elliott and C De Than, 'The Case for a Rational Reconstruction of Consent in Criminal Law' (2007) 70 MLR 225 argue that the test of capacity should focus on whether B was capable of understanding at the material time the nature and reasonable foreseeable consequences of the act and able to communicate her consent effectively, at 242.

[59] Technically these comments might be seen as *obiter* on the scope of capacity in s 74 since the appeal dealt with the meaning of the words 'unable to communicate' a choice in s 30(2). By s. 30(2) a person is unable to refuse if – (a) he lacks the capacity to choose whether to agree to the touching (whether because he lacks sufficient understanding of the nature or reasonably foreseeable consequences of what is being done, or for any other reason), or (b) he is unable to communicate such a choice to the alleged offender.

[60] [2008] EWCA Crim 1155. For critical comment see T Elliott (2008) 6 Arch News 5. The Court of Appeal relied heavily on Munby J in *X City Council v MB* [2006] EWHC Fam 168.

irrational fear that prevents the exercise of choice cannot be equated with a lack of capacity to choose. The House of Lords unanimously held that this approach was wrong. In a welcome judgment delivered by Baroness Hale,[61] it was stressed that the law on capacity recognizes that to be able to make a decision:

(a) a person must be able to understand the information relevant to making it, and

(b must be able to weigh that information in the balance to arrive at a choice.[62]

A mentally disordered person might appreciate the sexual nature of the act but not be able to weigh the information in the balance so as to be able to arrive at a choice. *The capacity to choose under the 2003 Act is situation and person specific.* 'One does not consent to sex in general but consents to this act of sex with this person at this time and place.'[63] These general sentiments in relation to capacity are important in construing s 74.

In short, there appear to be the following categories:

- B lacks mental capacity to make the choice – no consent;
- B lacks ability to refuse because of mental disorder – unable to refuse; if the inability also amounts to inability to choose B also gives no consent;
- B lacks ability to refuse for reasons unrelated to mental disorder – if inability amounts to inability to choose (for example being heavily intoxicated) also gives no consent;
- B has mental capacity to choose, but *mentally* (not physically)[64] incapable of communicating choice to this defendant – unable to refuse; arguably[65] also lacking consent.

Intoxicated consent

A engages in sexual activity with B who is intoxicated.[66] How intoxicated must B be to lack capacity for the purposes of the 2003 Act? This has provoked controversy and a number of high profile appeals. In the 2002 White Paper, *Protecting the Public*, the Home Secretary, when stating the Government's intention to create a set of evidential presumptions, indicated that these would not cover voluntary intoxication leading to incapacity falling short of sleep or a lack of consciousness:

I have rejected the suggestion that someone who is inebriated could claim they were unable to give consent – as opposed to someone who is unconscious for whatever reason, including because of alcohol – on the ground that we do not want mischievous accusations.

In *Dougal*,[67] the trial judge directed the jury to enter a 'not guilty' verdict when the prosecutor informed the judge that he did not propose to proceed further because the prosecution were unable to prove that the complainant had not given consent because of her level of intoxication.[68] The decision to drop the case was controversial since all that B had said was that she 'could not remember'. Following the furore over that case the Government raised the issue in

---

[61] The central issue was the scope of s 30. The issue of capacity under that section is made clear by the Act. As House concluded under s 30(2)(a), a person is unable to refuse if she lacks the capacity to choose to agree to the touching whether because she lacks sufficient understanding of the nature or reasonably foreseeable consequences of what is being done '*or for any other reason*'.

[62] [2009] UKHL 42 [24].

[63] Para 27 per Baroness Hale. Such an approach is in keeping with the concept of autonomy in matters of private life guaranteed by Art 8 of the ECHR.

[64] B lacks physical ability to communicate consent to this defendant – presumptively no consent (s 75).

[65] Stevenson et al, above n 1, regard these as all non-consensual cases.

[66] If B is involuntarily intoxicated by A's conduct, s 75(2)(f) might be applicable: presumption of no consent. Note also the offence under s 61, below, p 770.

[67] [2005] Swansea Crown Court.

[68] This CPS decision was criticized in *Bree* [2007] EWCA Crim 256.

a Consultation Paper, *Convicting Rapists and Protecting Victims,*[69] asking 'Does the law on capacity need to be changed. Should there be a statutory definition of capacity?' Subsequently, the Court of Appeal has sought to pre-empt the need for further legislative intervention by encouraging trial judges to leave the issue to the common sense of the jury where there is evidence that B might not have been consenting owing to intoxication.[70] That is likely to lead to inconsistency of decisions, but is a pragmatic response to a seemingly intractable problem.

In *Bree,*[71] A aged 25, and B, aged 19, had both voluntarily consumed a large amount of alcohol and it was accepted by both parties that sexual intercourse had taken place. A was charged with rape on the basis that B had effectively been unconscious throughout most of the sexual activity. B gave evidence that she was not unconscious. It was a fundamental part of A's case that B had been conscious throughout and had in fact consented. A claimed that B's intoxication did not mean that she had lacked the capacity to consent, indeed, she had removed her own pyjamas and responded to questions such as whether she had a condom. A was convicted, but the Court of Appeal allowed the appeal. In cases of rape arising after voluntary[72] consumption of alcohol, the question was whether the evidence had proved that A had had sexual intercourse with B without her consent. On the proper construction of s 74, where B had voluntarily consumed alcohol but remained *capable* of *choosing* whether or not to have intercourse, and in her drunken state agreed to do so, that would not be rape. However, if, through drink or some other reason, B had temporarily lost her capacity to choose whether to have intercourse on the relevant occasion, she was not consenting and, subject to questions about A's *mens rea,* if intercourse took place, that would be rape.[73] The question is not whether the alcohol had made either or both less inhibited than they would have been if sober, nor whether either or both might afterwards have regretted what had happened and indeed wished that it had not.[74] The court remarked pithily that the 'capacity to consent can evaporate well before unconsciousness occurs'.[75] The court also emphasized that the jury should in such cases be given assistance with the meaning of 'capacity'.

In *Hysa,*[76] a young girl on a New Year's Eve celebration in London became detached from her friends and after drinking half a bottle of vodka, and taking cannabis, ended up in a car with three strangers. One allegedly raped her and digitally penetrated her. She confirmed in her evidence that she did not want to have sex with the man, that she did not think that she did so willingly and she did not think that she would have consented. She said she could not remember what she had said to the man because she was drunk. The defence argued that, firstly, the complainant clearly had capacity to consent because she had rejected the advances of the first and third man, and at its highest, the Crown's case was that she could not remember

---

[69] (2006).

[70] On jury attitudes to intoxicated rape complainants see also E Finch and V Munro, 'Breaking Boundaries; Sexual Consent in the Jury Room' (2006) 26 LS 303.

[71] [2007] EWCA Crim 256. See for critical comment on the case P Rumney and R Fenton, 'Intoxicated Consent in Rape: *Bree* and Juror Decision-Making' (2008) 71 MLR 279 calling for better guidance and S Wallerstein 'A Drunken Consent is Still a Consent – Or Is It?' (2009) 73 J Crim Law 318 arguing that the law does not go far enough and that a drunken consent is not consent. Wallerstein proposes a two-step test: (1) was B drunk so as to make her incapable of giving a valid consent; and, if so, (2) was there pre-intoxication consent? If the answer to 2 is yes, there is consent. If not, there is no consent.

[72] See D Warburton (2007) 71 J Crim L 394 on whether the decision is restricted to cases of voluntary intoxication.

[73] Per Sir Igor Judge at [34]. See also the valuable commentary by Andrew Ashworth [2007] Crim LR 903.

[74] Moreover, it was not a question of whether either or both might have a very poor recollection of precisely what had happened. That might be relevant to the reliability of their evidence.

[75] [32]. The language echoes that of the law on intoxicated defendants, but the analogy is flawed: see Wallerstein (above n 71).

[76] [2007] EWCA Crim 2056. *Bree* was distinguished in *Wright* [2007] All ER (D) 267 (Nov) where B had been so heavily intoxicated as to be unconscious.

whether or not she had consented: the Crown simply could not exclude the possibility that the complainant had said 'yes'. The Court of Appeal, in an interlocutory appeal by the Crown, concluded that the judge erred in withdrawing the case from the jury. The pre-2003 Act case of *Malone*[77] was referred as authority for the proposition that:

there is no requirement that the absence of consent has to be demonstrated or that it has to be communicated to the defendant for the *actus reus* of rape to exist.... It is not the law that the prosecution in order to obtain a conviction for rape have to show that the complainant was either incapable of saying no or putting up some physical resistance, or did say no or put up some physical resistance.

The court was critical of the defence submissions 'based to a large extent on the premise that because the complainant cannot remember if she consented or not, that is fatal to the prosecution'. That was, in the court's words 'expressly disavowed' in *Bree*.[78]

The courts have yet to tackle the problem case of B who agrees when sober to have sex with A and whether her consent given when sober is lost when she is heavily intoxicated?[79]

Section 75 – evidential presumptions

If A is proved to have performed the relevant act[80] (for example, penile penetration), and it is proved that any of the circumstances listed in s 75(2) exists and A knows[81] it exists, B is taken not to have consented and A not to have a reasonable belief in B's consent unless sufficient evidence is adduced to raise the issue.

The circumstances in s 75(2) are:

(a) any person was, at the time of the relevant act or immediately before it began, using violence against the complainant or causing the complainant to fear that immediate violence would be used against him;

(b) any person was, at the time of the relevant act or immediately before it began, causing the complainant to fear that violence was being used, or that immediate violence would be used, against another person;

(c) the complainant was, and the defendant was not, unlawfully detained at the time of the relevant act;

(d) the complainant was asleep or otherwise unconscious at the time of the relevant act;

(e) because of the complainant's physical disability, the complainant would not have been able at the time of the relevant act to communicate to the defendant whether the complainant consented;

(f) any person had administered to or caused to be taken by the complainant, without the complainant's consent, a substance which, having regard to when it was administered or taken, was capable of causing or enabling the complainant to be stupefied or overpowered at the time of the relevant act.

Although A has to know that '*those* circumstances existed',[82] the requirement is in fact only that his knowledge of any *one* circumstance is proved.[83] The Act is silent on whether this must

---

[77] [1998] 2 Cr App R 447.

[78] Hallet LJ emphasized that it would be a rare case indeed where it would be appropriate for a judge to stop a case in which, on one view, a 16-year-old girl, alone at night and vulnerable through drink, is picked up by a stranger who has sex with her within minutes of meeting her and she says repeatedly she would not have consented to sex in these circumstances. At the recommenced trial the jury took just 40 minutes to convict.

[79] See *Ashlee* 212 CCC (3d) 477 where the Alberta CA held that consent becomes vitiated on unconsciousness.

[80] See s 77.

[81] Knowledge means 'true belief' as we have been reminded recently by the House of Lords in a different context: *Saik* [2006] UKHL 18.

[82] Section 75(1)(c).

[83] Section 75(1)(b).

be proof by the prosecution.[84] There is no requirement that the existence of the circumstances listed in (a) to (f) *caused* B's lack of consent.[85] The absence of consent is simply presumed. Controversially, s 75 relates to both the issue of consent and the issue of A's belief in consent. Section 75 creates a rather odd set of presumptions since A can raise evidence sufficient to rebut the presumption without challenging the actual circumstance on which the presumption arises. Thus, where the prosecution allege that B was asleep, A might raise evidence which will rebut the effect of the Crown's evidence without denying the fact that B was asleep. A can claim that he believed, reasonably, that B was consenting despite being asleep (based on their previous sexual practices).[86] A is obliged not to rebut the *fact* giving rise to the presumption, but the *legal consequences* of that presumption.

If the prosecution proves the three elements – the relevant act, A's knowledge and the circumstance giving rise to the presumption – A is obliged to raise sufficient evidence to rebut the issue. This can be done by calling evidence, testifying, or by cross-examination of a Crown witness.[87] The obligation on A to satisfy the judge, from the evidence, that there is a real issue about consent that is worth putting to the jury means the section is more likely to withstand ECHR challenge[88] than the original version in the Bill which incorporated reverse burdens for A's belief in consent.[89] Creating such presumptions has an important symbolic value,[90] and was widely welcomed in principle.[91] The Canadian courts have interpreted similar provisions as requiring that any claims by the defence have an 'air of reality'.[92] It is submitted that even if such an interpretation were adopted in the English courts, that should not render it necessary for the defence to produce corroborative independent evidence, in the formal sense, to rebut the presumption.[93]

A jury should not ordinarily be directed as to s 75 at all. If there is evidence that is capable of establishing consent (including A's testimony to that effect), s 75 ceases to have any application and the jury have no need to hear of it. In *White*,[94] A sent B a photo of him digitally penetrating her vagina. They had been in a sexual relationship. A claimed he took the image with her consent. B claimed he must have taken it while she slept. The Court of Appeal quashed the conviction where the judge had directed on s 75 in a confusing manner.[95] Under s 75, A is to be

---

[84] What if D2 seeks to prove the existence of the circumstance in the course of showing that he lacked knowledge of it but D1 did not?

[85] cf the proposals in *Setting the Boundaries*, para 2.10.9.

[86] Note however, that in *P* [2009] EWCA Crim 1110, Hughes LJ stated that 'We have no doubt that ⋯ there is no real prospect of a jury considering that a belief in consent might be reasonably based on the proposition that because a defendant has had sexual intercourse on a number of previous occasions with a comatose or unconscious or asleep complainant, who after discovery of those occasions has not overtly objected, that this gives rise to an advance consent which the defendant could reasonably rely upon in the future to indulge in like sexual activity whenever she was in a similar condition.' [29]

[87] Note that earlier version of the Bill specifically stated cross-examination of the victim would not be sufficient to raise issue as to V's consent unless the equivalent of an admission of consent.

[88] cf the views expressed in Stevenson et al, *Blackstone's Guide to the SOA 2003*, para 2.4.3.

[89] HL, cols 1062–1063, 2 June 2003 (Lord Thomas of Gresford).

[90] See Beverley Hughes, HC Standing Committee B, 15 Oct, col 26.

[91] See Home Affairs Committee Fifth Report 2002–3, HC 639.

[92] A striking example cited by Rook and Ward, *Sexual Offences: Law and Practice*, is of *Filice* (1999) Carswell Ont 1262 where evidence that B had (as was her custom) taken out her false teeth before sex was sufficient to give the claim an air of reality. See further *Pappajohn* [1980] 2 SCR 120 discussed by Lord Steyn in *R v A (No 2)* [2002] 1 AC 67. For discussion on this, see: Temkin, *Rape and the Legal Process*, 132.

[93] *Osolin* [1993] 4 SCR 595; *Park* [1995] 2 SCR 836.

[94] [2010] EWCA Crim 1929.

[95] The court approved the recommendation in *Blackstone Criminal Practice*. See now Hooper and Ormerod (eds), *Blackstone Criminal Practice* (2011) B3.

taken not to have reasonably believed that B consented *unless* sufficient evidence is adduced to raise an issue as to whether A reasonably believed it. The Court of Appeal stated:

There must be some foundation in the evidence and it must not be merely speculative or fanciful for there to be sufficient evidence. However, *it is vital to understand that if the trial judge decides (presumably at the close of the evidence) that there is sufficient evidence to raise an issue as to whether the complainant consented and/or the accused reasonably believed that the complainant was consenting, then the judge will put the issues to the jury in accordance with the key sections (ie 74 and 1(2)), and the section 75 route is barred.* In the relatively rare cases where the judge decides that there is not sufficient evidence on one or both of the issues, a section 75 direction must be given on that issue. (Emphasis added.)

The jury should then be directed to deal with the issue of consent under the general guidance in s 74. If sufficient evidence of consent has *not* been raised and there is no other defence available to A, the jury will be bound to find A guilty.

In view of the complexity of the s 75 provision, it is perhaps no surprise that there are few reported instances in which it has been relied on. They are very rarely relied on in practice. Section 75 will clearly have an impact on the process of the trial. In practical terms it will render it more likely that A will testify.[96] In addition, it will have a significant impact on the way that sexual offences are investigated and on the manner of police interviews. If the complainant alleges that one of the s 75(2) circumstances was present, the suspect will be under considerable pressure to offer an explanation in interview and advance his defence at an earlier stage.

Aside from these general concerns about creating presumptions, the individual circumstances listed in s 75(2) also pose problems.

Threats of violence

The use/threats of immediate violence need not emanate from A before they are treated, presumptively, as vitiating B's consent. This is a welcome extension of the law. Section 75(2)(a) will operate in circumstances such as those in *Dagnall*,[97] where A had grabbed B and dragged her off the road telling her he would rape her. Under threat, B told A that he could 'do what he liked as long as he did not harm her'. A was apprehended before penetrating B and convicted under the 1956 Act of attempted rape.[98] The fact that B had explicitly assented to sexual acts did not in these circumstances mean that she was consenting. However, there are difficulties with s 75(2)(a). It is unclear why the requirement is one of 'immediate' violence. Arguably, it should be sufficient that A threatens B that he will 'make her suffer one day' unless she has sex with him at once. It may be that the concept of 'immediacy' is interpreted expansively by the courts.[99] Of course, even without the presumption, in a case of threats of a non-immediate nature, B's consent might still be absent when applying the general test of free agreement under s 74.

Although it might appear sensible for a threat of violence to give rise to a conclusive presumption of non-consent, it is clear that in some circumstances even the most explicit

---

[96] See Explanatory Notes Sexual Offences Act 2003, Ch 42, which makes it clear that evidence given by the defendant himself may constitute 'sufficient evidence'.

[97] [2003] EWCA Crim 2441.

[98] See also *Low* [1997] Crim LR 692 where B performed oral sex on A after persuading him not to rape her vaginally as she was pregnant. Note that there is a potential problem with applying the s 75 presumption to attempts. See HHJ Rodwell QC [2005] Crim LR 290.

[99] See the interpretation of 'immediate' in assault, p 622. The court did not tackle the issue in the case of *C* [2007] EWCA Crim 378 where the threats were to mother and child. Counsel had wrongly advised as to whether s 75 could apply to allow the Crown to rely on earlier threats which lacked immediacy.

threats of violence to B might not vitiate consent as, for example, where A and B are sado-masochists.[100] The rebuttability of the presumption provides for this scenario.

'Violence' is not defined. It is clear from the parliamentary debates that it was intended to be limited only to violence to the person, but that does not appear on the face of the statute. Where A threatens to damage B's property unless she engages in sexual activity, s 75 does not apply and the jury are left to determine the question of B's consent by reference to the criteria in s 74.

It is lamentable that the 2003 Act provided no replacement for the offence under s 2 of the 1956 Act, despite contrary recommendations in *Setting The Boundaries*. Section 2 provided an offence of procuring sexual intercourse by threats. A broader gender-neutral version of causing sexual activity by threats would have provided a useful backstop offence for cases in which the threats fall short of violence so that the jury were not sure there was a lack of consent, but considered the conduct blameworthy. For example, in *Olugboja*,[101] reference was made to an unreported case in which Winn J held that a constable had no case to answer where he induced B to consent to sexual intercourse by threatening to report her for an offence; whereas in *Wellard*,[102] A was said to have a previous conviction for rape (for which he was sentenced to six years' imprisonment) by masquerading as a security officer and inducing a girl to consent by threatening to report to her parents and the police that she had been seen having intercourse in a public place. Other examples are easy to envisage: A threatens that, if B does not consent, he will (i) tell the police of a theft she has committed; (ii) tell her father of her previous immorality; (iii) dismiss her from her present employment; (iv) not give her a rise in salary; (v) never take her to the cinema again.[103] Clearly, a line must be drawn somewhere, but the boundary of consent in such cases is difficult to draw and the Act ought to have provided more guidance.

Section 75(2)(b) also relates to threats of violence, applying where B is caused to fear that violence was being used, or that immediate violence would be used against another person. This is an extremely broad presumption, but it has been welcomed as 'clarifying the common law regarding the fear of violence to third parties'.[104] There is no requirement that A is in any way involved in the causing of the complainant's fear. Thus, A who is aware that B, an immigrant, has heard on the TV of ongoing violent atrocities against the population of her homeland, who then performs a relevant sexual act with B is presumed to have done so without consent. Although this may seem like a fanciful example which is unlikely to present problems in practice, because of the ease with which the presumption could be rebutted, it demonstrates the unsatisfactory nature of the overbroad drafting.

Unlawful detention

Section 75(2)(c) seems to be an uncontroversial provision. Where, for example, B has been kidnapped, and A is aware of B's detained status, it is legitimate to presume that B is not consenting to sexual activity. This arises where, for example A kidnaps his former lover and sexually assaults her.[105] Although there are instances of hostages forming a sexual bond with their kidnappers, it is unlikely that A will be able easily to rebut this presumption.

---

[100] See N Bamforth, 'Sado-Masochism and Consent' [1994] Crim LR 661.

[101] [1982] QB 320 at 347–348.

[102] (1978) 67 Cr App R 364 at 368. See, above, p 688. The court made no comment on the propriety or otherwise of the conviction.

[103] Note that in the case of mentally disordered complainants ss 34–37 provides offences based on 'inducement, threat or deception' where the degree of threat is not limited – it could include a threat to break friends with the complainant.

[104] Temkin and Ashworth [2004] Crim LR 328.

[105] eg *David T* [2005] EWCA Crim 2668.

Unconsciousness

The presumption in s 75(2)(d) requires proof that A knows that B is unconscious.[106] At common law, it was held that unconsciousness (including lack of consciousness through sleep) was sufficient to vitiate consent.[107] There are numerous cases of sexual activity when the complainant was asleep resulting in a conviction.[108] Indeed, this seems to be more commonplace than one might imagine.[109] Arguably, the *presumption* in s 75(2)(d) provides less protection than had been afforded at common law where consent was conclusively rebutted. It is arguable therefore that this circumstance of 'unconsciousness' ought to give rise to a *conclusive* presumption of non-consent by B.[110] However, if B is unconscious and A is aware of that fact, there may be circumstances in which A will be readily capable of rebutting a presumption of non-consent. For example, A, who performs a relevant sexual act (note that the presumption applies to offences of touching and not just penetrative acts) on his sleeping partner as a gesture of intimacy to wake her, ought not to be conclusively presumed guilty.

There is no stipulation as to the cause of the lack of consciousness; it could arise from self-induced intoxication. At common law, if a complainant, through alcohol or drugs, was not capable of exercising a judgement on consent, she was not consenting.[111] Such circumstances now only give rise to *a presumption* of a lack of consent. It is clear that the Sexual Offences Review envisaged that consent would be lacking in such a case.[112]

Inability to communicate owing to physical disability

At common law, and under the 1956 Act, there was no requirement that the absence of consent has to be demonstrated or communicated to A.[113] As a matter of logic it is unclear why the physical inability to *communicate* should be seen as presumptive of a lack of consent. The statutory formula seems to presuppose that B has the capacity to make the choice of free agreement, but merely lacks the physical ability to communicate to this defendant. The Act makes specific provision for those with mental disorders who are unable to communicate (ss 30–44).[114]

It is notable that the presumption only applies if B's physical disability inhibits his communication with *this* defendant. This may be significant if B has a particular speech or sign pattern that can be understood by some individuals.

Causing to be taken by the complainant, without consent, a substance capable of causing or enabling the complainant to be stupefied or overpowered at the time of the relevant act

This provision was introduced late in the Bill's progress as a response to the growing concern over 'drug assisted rape'.[115] The Act seeks to combat this problem by the presumption in this section and the introduction of the new offence in s 61.[116] The presumption of non-consent applies to both sexes and to sexual acts other than intercourse.

[106] cf the view expressed in Stevenson et al, *Blackstone's Guide to the SOA 2003*, para 2.4.1.3.

[107] See *Larter and Castleton* [1995] Crim LR 75; *Howard* [1966] 1 WLR 13.

[108] See recently *Johnston* [2003] All ER (D) 266 (Jun).

[109] See, eg, *Garvey;* [2004] EWCA Crim 2672; *Blacklock* [2006] EWCA Crim 1740; *Ekatette* [2008] EWCA Crim 3137 where X filmed A having sex with unconscious B.

[110] See, eg, Temkin and Ashworth [2004] Crim LR 328.

[111] *Malone* [1998] 2 Cr App R 454. See *Bree* [2007] EWCA Crim 256 and discussion above. See also *Zhang* [2007] EWCA Crim 2018.

[112] See *Setting The Boundaries*, 18, para 2.10.7 et seq.

[113] *Malone* [1998] 2 Cr App R 447, [1998] Crim LR 834.

[114] See *Cooper* [2009] UKHL 42. In particular note Lord Rodger at [30] distinguishing physical inability to communicate and other bases.

[115] For comprehensive analysis, see E Finch and V Munro, 'Intoxicated Consent and the Boundaries of Drug Assisted Rape' [2003] Crim LR 773; 'The Sexual Offences Act 2003: Intoxicated Consent and Drug Assisted Rape Revisited' [2004] Crim LR 789.

[116] See, below, p 770.

Although targeted at drugs which induce states of incapacity such as Rohypnol and GHB (gamma hydroxyl butyrate acid), there is no statutory limitation on the type of substance which will trigger the presumption. Alcohol is certainly capable of satisfying the definition,[117] so A who surreptitiously laces B's soft drink with spirits will be caught. Similarly, there is no limitation on the manner of the administration. Unless it is established that A knew or believed that the substance was capable of rendering B stupefied or overpowered the presumption will not apply. This will depend on the type of drug involved. The section does not apply to the 'seductive blandishments to have "just one more drink" '.[118]

The presumption will also apply where A 'caused [the substance] to be taken by the complainant'; this includes A deceiving B into self-administration of the substance as where the substance is mixed with an innocuous one (laced drinks). If B's consumption is purely voluntary and fully informed the presumption does not apply.[119]

The section makes clear that it is irrelevant who administers or causes B to take the substance, provided that one is administered and that B is therefore presumed not to consent. The presumption would apply where X administers in the company of A, then B gets in a taxi home with A, who performs a sexual act on B.

In those cases in which the presumption applies, A can argue that although he administered the drug being aware of its effects, B nevertheless consented to the sexual acts that finally ensued. If, for example, B indicated at the beginning of the date that she would not have sex with A, and A surreptitiously laces B's drink with potent alcohol, it may be that B later willingly engages in sexual activity with him (not being unconscious nor stupefied); her inhibitions having been lowered.

Section 75(2)(f) will increase the pressure on A to testify and strengthen the hand of the police in interview since they can enquire why A thought that B was consenting given the circumstance of his administering the substance. It will also render prosecution far easier in some circumstances.

Section 76 – conclusive presumptions

If it is proved that A performed the relevant act[120] and any one of the circumstances specified in s 76(2) existed, it is to be *conclusively presumed* that the complainant did not consent to the relevant act, and that A did not believe that the complainant consented. There is an important labelling issue here: if A engages in these forms of conduct (deceiving the complainant) and commits the relevant act, he is conclusively proved to be a sexual offender, this is not merely a matter of evidence.[121] It is questionable whether since these are conclusive presumptions they are intended by Parliament to represent the worst forms of non-consent. It seems doubtful that they outrank the sexual offence in the course of a violent attack, but some would argue that the element of deception renders the position more serious because of the potential guilt felt by the complainant in being tricked.[122]

---

[117] See Beverely Hughes, HC Standing Committee B, 14 Oct, col 54.

[118] Per Igor Judge P in *Bree*, at [24]

[119] See recently *Abbess* [2004] EWCA Crim 1813 where there was no trace of GHB found.

[120] Section 77.

[121] See Tadros (2006) 26 OJLS 515.

[122] Similar arguments led the Sexual Offences Review to conclude that stranger rape was not worse *per se* than acquaintance rape where the complainant may feel an element of self blame in misjudging her attacker. Temkin and Ashworth [2004] Crim LR 328, 337, cf the debate on theft below regarding the relative seriousness of being deceived into acting as opposed to actions being performed against the will. See also C Gallavin, 'Fraud Vitiating Consent to Sexual Activity: Further Confusion in the Making' (2008) 23 NZLR 87.

The circumstances giving rise to a conclusive presumption are:

(1) the defendant intentionally deceived the complainant as to the *nature or purpose* of the relevant act;

(2) the defendant intentionally induced the complainant to consent to the relevant act by *impersonating a person known personally* to the complainant.

It is sufficient that any *one* of the deceptions is proved. In both instances, the section goes further than the common law. The provisions are immediately open to challenge on the basis that it is unclear why these are conclusive of anything beyond D's absence of a belief in consent.[123] These are also arguably objectionably wide as *conclusive* presumptions especially since they apply in relation to offences other than one of penetration, for example, touching. It is arguable that the breadth of such a conclusive presumption might be incompatible with Art 6 of the ECHR, if it presumes A's guilt despite evidence to the contrary.

There are many well-established difficulties in drawing a line between the kinds of fraud which ought to be treated as a matter of conclusive presumption that B is consenting. Should they be based on frauds which would render a contract invalid, should they relate only to the nature or purpose or identity, etc? Several suggestions have been made to move towards a more coherent approach to the issue in offences against the person and in sexual offences.[124]

Nature or purpose

At common law, a fraud as to the nature of the act vitiated consent.[125] Thus, there was no consent where B was unaware that she was submitting to sexual intercourse because, for example, she had been persuaded by A that he was performing a surgical operation as in *Flattery*.[126] She was deceived as to the very nature of the act, believing it was surgery rather than sexual intercourse. Similarly, in *Williams*,[127] A persuaded his voice pupil that he was opening an air passage to improve her singing voice when he was having sex with her.[128] In that case, B was unaware of sexual matters and was held not to have consented. When analysing what 'nature' means in this context it is important to note that in each of these cases, B was deceived as to the physical mechanics of what A was about to do to her. She had no idea of what sexual intercourse involved. Neither was a case in which B understood the mechanics of sex, ie penile penetration of the vagina but did not understand its significance, believing it was also a cure for fits/for a singing exercise. If that had been the case one might argue that B was deceived as to the purpose of the act (understanding it was sex but deceived also into thinking the act will also cure fits/improve vocal range).

Under the 2003 Act, where B has been defrauded as to the nature *or* purpose of the acts A performs, s 76 creates a conclusive presumption that B is not consenting.[129]

It is important to note that s 76 applies only in cases of *intentional* deceptions by A. Where A has not intentionally deceived B, s 76 has no application – as where B has unilaterally formed a

---

[123] cf Stevenson et al, *Blackstone's Guide to the SOA 2003* who regard this as unarguable, para 242.

[124] See, eg, R Williams, 'Deception Mistake and the Vitiation of the Victim's Consent' (2008) 124 LQR 132.

[125] See *Flattery* (1877) 2 QBD 410; *Williams* [1923] 1 KB 340.

[126] (1877) 2 QBD 410, CCCR.

[127] [1923] 1 KB 340, CCA. Williams, *Textbook of Criminal Law*, 561–562 thinks *Williams* 'clearly wrong' because it was not proved that B did not know the facts of life and may merely have been persuaded that sexual intercourse improves breathing. If that were all, it was not rape; but Hewart LCJ said that the girl never consented to sexual intercourse but only a necessary operation.

[128] Did she understand the mechanics of the act but misunderstand whether the act would improve her voice or simply misunderstand what he was about to do to her, having no idea about what sexual intercourse entailed?

[129] Read literally there is no need to establish that there was no consent. It is sufficient that A has deceived B about the nature/purpose of the act. This is another example of the extremely poor drafting in this Act.

false understanding as to the nature, purpose or identity.[130] In such cases, B's mistake, even if A is aware of it but has not intentionally caused it, will be relevant to the consideration under s 74 of whether B is consenting. It will be likely that B is not consenting within s 74 if the mistake is as to any of these matters listed in s 76.

Nature. Three further problems have arisen under s 76. First, there is the question of what the nature of sexual intercourse means. Can the 'nature of the act' be read widely so as to render A guilty of rape under s 76 for deceiving B as to whether he will use a condom in penetrative sex? Of course, under s 74, such a deception may be likely to remove any purported free agreement by the complainant. However, there is an argument that unprotected intercourse is different in *nature* from protected intercourse so that s 76 is engaged and A is conclusively presumed guilty of rape in such a case. Such a wide reading would not have been likely under the old law, but some argued that it should be under the new. The Court of Appeal's approach to the cases of HIV transmission seems to forestall that argument. In *Dica*,[131] knowing that he was HIV positive, A had engaged in consensual unprotected sexual intercourse with the two complainants, thereby infecting each of them with the disease. He was convicted of inflicting grievous bodily harm, contrary to s 20 of the Offences Against the Person Act 1861. It was the Crown's case that A had been reckless as to whether the complainants might become infected with the disease; and that, had the complainants known of his condition, they would not have consented to sexual intercourse. The Court of Appeal allowed A's appeal and ordered a retrial: the alleged concealment by A was not as to the nature of the sexual act itself, but as to the risk of infection, therefore he was not guilty of rape.[132] B knew the nature (sexual intercourse) of the acts and was not deceived as to that fact. She was deceived as to the risk of infection. That is a narrow reading of 'nature', but not indefensible. Even if s 76 is not engaged, there would seem to be no good reason why the fact that A deceived B should not be a factor which is considered by the jury when examining consent under s 74. In *B*,[133] the Court of Appeal held that evidence of the defendant's sexual diseases was inadmissible when considering s 74, but this, it is submitted, goes too far.

Quality. Secondly, there is a question as to how s 76 deals with frauds as to 'quality' rather than the nature of the act. Under the old law, it was unclear whether a deception as to 'quality' as opposed to the 'nature' of the act would be sufficient to vitiate consent. In *Tabassum*,[134] A, who was not medically qualified, persuaded women to allow him to measure their breasts by representing (perhaps truthfully) that he was doing so for the purpose of a breast cancer database he was preparing for doctors. His convictions for indecent assault were upheld, although the women were fully aware of the nature of the acts to be done because (i) they would not have consented to these acts if they had not believed that he had medical qualifications and (ii) the defendant knew that this was so. Following *Tabassum*, it seemed that although the complainant was aware of the nature of the act, her consent may be negatived if she was mistaken as to its *quality*. This appeared to be a new distinction for which there was no authority.[135] The concept of a deception as to 'quality' has not been explicitly included in the Act, but the inclusion of '*purpose*' in s 76(2)(a) confirms that the legislation is designed to extend the protection

---

[130] This seems to be underplayed in the radical proposals offered by J Herring, 'Mistaken Consent' [2005] Crim LR 511. cf M Bohlander, 'Mistaken Consent to Sex, Political Correctness and Correct Policy' (2008) 71 J Crim L 412. Bohlander suggests that Herring's approach demeans rape.

[131] [2004] EWCA Crim 1103, [2004] Crim LR 944 and commentary. See also *Konzani* [2005] EWCA Crim 706. The Canadian courts have approached things differently in *Cuerrier* (1998) SCR 371.

[132] See also *Tabassum* [2002] 2 Cr App R 328 and *Cort* [2003] 3 WLR 1300.

[133] [2006] EWCA Crim 2945.

[134] [2000] 2 Cr App R 328, [2000] Crim LR 686, CA.

[135] *Setting the Boundaries* gave the example of a false representation of a medical examination, para 2.10.9 at 19.

of the law. In any event, evidence of A's deception as to the quality of the act should be available to the jury in determining whether consent was present under s 74.

Purpose. Thirdly, there is the question of how widely the concept of 'purpose' should be construed under the Act. Deceptions as to the 'purpose' of the act are most likely to arise in relation to sexual touching and non-penile penetration, although it is possible that a deception as to the purpose of the act of intercourse will arise.[136] The presumptions apply in respect of male and female victims. They would operate for example in cases such as *Green*,[137] where a doctor had conducted bogus medical examinations of young men, including wiring them to monitors while they masturbated, allegedly so that he could assess their potential to become impotent.[138] The men understood the nature of the acts they were performing but were deceived as to the purpose for doing so. The issue is not one of A's motive, nor what the complainants thought, but whether the act (masturbation) was being performed for a different purpose than that which A alleged. The purpose of the act of masturbation was different in *Green* since it was not for a medical reason it was for sexual gratification. *Green* is a relatively easy case.

A slightly more difficult example is *Piper*,[139] where A's touching of B when measuring her for a bikini was a sexual assault given that he had invited B on the basis that he was running a modelling agency. A pleaded guilty. Here the act is one of sexual touching in the bikini area. The purpose which A alleged was that this was for the purpose of assessing her modelling statistics, etc. The true purpose was for his sexual gratification.

The question then arises whether s 76 permits a wider approach so as conclusively to presume guilt in cases such as *Linekar*.[140] In that case, A procured a prostitute to have intercourse with him by promising to pay her £25. He never intended to pay. It was held under the 1956 Act that this was not rape. The deception did not go to the 'nature' of the act, since the prostitute knew the nature of the conduct of intercourse. Under the 2003 Act, it might be argued that the deception as to payment alters the '*purpose*' of the act for the prostitute. On this interpretation, A would as a result of a conclusive presumption, be classified as a rapist. This would, it is submitted, have been an unwelcome extension of such serious offences. The complainant in *Linekar* has not been deceived as to the mechanics of the act of sexual intercourse. Nor has she been deceived as to its purpose – sexual gratification of the accused. She has been deceived as to a peripheral matter – payment. It is submitted that A's deception as to the payment may be taken into consideration with the other evidence when the jury assesses under s 74 whether she was freely agreeing to the act. This is not a conclusive presumption case.

The Court of Appeal in *Jheeta*[141] has taken a clear line in not overextending the scope of s 76. In this bizarre case, A deceived B in relation to the nature or purpose of the intercourse. A's deception to B, that she must have intercourse with him to avoid being fined by the police and to avoid his committing suicide, did not engage s 76. B knew what the act of intercourse entailed and agreed. It will no doubt be suggested by some that the Court of Appeal is taking too narrow a view of 'purpose', restricting it to almost the same meaning as 'nature'. In *Jheeta*, the complainant was not deceived as to the nature of the mechanics of intercourse (that is, vaginal penetration with a penis). Nor, it is submitted, was she deceived as to the purpose. She understood it to be for sexual gratification which is what it was for. It is submitted that this is

---

[136] eg where A claims it is to procreate but really it is for his gratification.

[137] [2002] EWCA Crim 1501.

[138] This passage was cited with approval by the Court of Appeal in *Jheeta* [2007] 2 Cr App R 34.

[139] [2007] EWCA Crim 2151.

[140] [1995] 2 Cr App R 49, [1995] Crim LR 320. See A Reed, 'Analysis of Fraud Vitiating Consent in Rape Cases' (1995) 59 Crim LR 310.

[141] [2007] EWCA Crim 1699. The pressure to treat such conduct as rape is increased because the Act fails to include any provision analogous to s 3 of the 1956 Act, criminalizing procuring sexual intercourse by false pretences (short of those which would vitiate consent).

the correct approach to limiting the draconian conclusive presumption provision in s 76. The question of A's deceptions can be left to the jury in their consideration of consent under s 74.

A more difficult case is *Devonauld*.[142] B, was a 16-year-old boy who had been in a relationship with A's daughter. The relationship had broken down and, believing B to have treated his daughter badly, A sought to teach B a lesson by deliberately embarrassing him. A set up a fake email account pretending to be a young woman. A then corresponded with B over the internet and persuaded B to masturbate in front of a webcam. A was convicted, having changed his plea to guilty following a ruling by the judge, of an offence of causing a person to engage in sexual activity without consent. The trial judge ruled that s 76(2)(a) applied. The Court of Appeal dismissed an application for leave to appeal, holding it was open to the jury to conclude that B had been deceived as to the purpose of the act. Was B deceived as to A's purpose? It was 'difficult to see how the jury could have concluded otherwise than that B had been deceived into believing that he was indulging in sexual acts with, and for the sexual gratification of, a young woman with whom he was having an online relationship'. B's act was undoubtedly sexual, A's purpose in causing B to engage in it was not to secure sexual gratification. A's purpose was to cause B to engage in a sexual act. It is submitted that the decision is out of step with that in *Jheeta*.[143]

There are dangers in taking a wider reading of purpose. If 'purpose' is read widely, many bigamists and adulterers would become rapists *on the basis of a conclusive presumption*.

Some commentators have argued for an even broader reading of s 76. Herring goes so far as to suggest that where B has *made a mistake* about a matter relating to the sexual conduct with A, including a mistake about A's state of mind, which, had she known the truth, she would not have agreed to, there is no consent and if he knows or *ought to have known*[144] that B was mistaken and would not have consented had she known the truth, he is guilty. This is frightening in its ramifications: where B discovers that she made a mistake about A's marital status, wealth, sexual prowess, or love for her, A becomes a rapist. The results are unrealistic in practical application.[145] The breadth of the proposal is striking since it includes a unilateral mistake by B as to a state of mind held by A. Of course, such a radical approach could not be brought within s 76 since it is based on B's mistakes when the 2003 Act is founded on A's frauds.[146]

It is submitted that deceptions by A as to peripheral circumstances which did not relate to the nature or purpose of the relevent act did not vitiate consent at common law, and the 2003 Act does not alter that position. They do not fall within s 76, and it is doubtful that they remove freedom of choice or capacity under s 74. A simple solution to these problems would be for a re-enactment of s 3 of the 1956 Act to criminalize procuring sexual activity by false pretences. The false promises as to matters other than the nature or purpose of the act – eg to

---

[142] [2008] EWCA Crim 527; see also the comment by J Rogers (2008) 72 J Crim L 268.

[143] Was there a deception as to the identity of a person known to B if that person (Cassie on the internet) did not really exist? See B Fitzpatrick (2008) 72 J Crim L 11 discussing this in the context of *Jheeta*.

[144] As Hyman Gross makes clear in his powerful response ('Rape, Moralism and Human Rights' [2007] Crim LR 220) why should A be liable on that basis for a mistake he has not induced?

[145] Herring himself appears to take a contrary view – that sex is unlike the activities to which contractual rules can apply in criminal law (above, n 130). cf Peter Alldridge's proposal that consent should be vitiated if without mistake, consent would not have been given and the person to whom it was given knew: 'Sex Lies and the Criminal Law' (1993) 44 NILQ 250.

[146] With mistakes unilaterally formed by B it is doubtful whether in such circumstances there is any legal obligation on A to disabuse B of his misconception, although if A admits to being aware of B's confusion, this may assist the prosecution in proving his *mens rea* – that he did not reasonably believe in B's consent to that sexual act. cf Miles (2008) 10 Archbold News 5, arguing that if B makes a mistake of a type governed by s 76 there is no consent and that if B makes a mistake other than one of the type within s 76 there is consent even if A induced the mistake. This seems to reduce the operation of s 74 too much. See Rook and Ward, para 1.99.

give the complainant a part in a film,[147] or to marry her – would bring A's conduct within the scope of the criminal law.

Section 76 might have little scope for application with penile penetration. It is difficult to conceive of many cases in twenty-first century England where a person is deceived as to the *nature* of penile penetration, or indeed its primary purpose.[148] With other sexual conduct, there is a much stronger argument for relying on s 76 – A may tell B he is digitally penetrating her for a medical purpose. She is not defrauded as to the 'nature' of the action (that is, a finger entering her vagina), but is as to purpose. She thinks it is for a medical purpose and it is actually for a sexual one. Arguably, this should trigger a conclusive presumption of lack of consent.

Difficulties may arise in all cases of deceptions where A acts with more than one purpose. It is possible for A to have multiple purposes, only some of which are legitimate and about which the accused has been honest with B. What for example, of A, a doctor performing a *necessary* intimate medical examination of B, with the additional aim of allowing his friend, X, to watch for his sexual gratification?[149] It is submitted that on these facts there is a deception as to the 'purpose'.

Section 76(2)(b) – identity fraud?

By s 142(3) of the Criminal Justice and Public Order Act 1994, it was rape for a man to induce a woman to have intercourse with him by impersonating her husband. At common law, this was extended to include impersonation of long-term heterosexual partnerships.[150] Section 76(2)(b) extends the law beyond any particular category or duration of relationship, it also extends beyond the offence of rape to other acts of penetration and sexual activity. This is a welcome extension.

The conclusive presumption in s 76(2)(b) is more limited than that in para (a) since it is not sufficient for A to have lied about his identity, or even to have lied successfully and deceived B, it must be *by that* impersonation that B is induced to consent. The prosecution must prove this causal link.

The section poses other difficulties in interpretation, particularly regarding the limitation expressed in the formula 'known personally to' the accused. This is clearly intended to prevent the presumption arising when A claims to be a celebrity with whom B has no personal acquaintance, but for whom B may be expected to hold an attraction. Are all people B has ever met 'known personally to' him? Is it only those with whom B has had some greater degree of intimacy? Can a person be known personally to B by email correspondence? Consider the couple who arrange to meet after internet dating. X gets cold feet and decides he cannot face meeting B. A, his friend, steps in. Is there a conclusive presumption that B was not consenting to any sexual acts which follow?

Disappointingly, despite Law Commission recommendations to the contrary,[151] the Act does not deal expressly with the problem of deception as to the defendant's attributes (for example A claiming to have a medical qualification, be a police officer, etc) or other personal

---

[147] As occurred in *Melliti* [2001] EWCA Crim 1563.

[148] Unless a much broader view of purpose is adopted so that eg sex for procreation is treated as purposively different from that for recreation.

[149] cf *Bolduc and Bird* (1967) 63 DLR (2d) 82.

[150] *Elbekkay* [1995] Crim LR 163.

[151] The Law Commission Report *Consent in Sex Offences* submitted to the Home Office, *Sex Offences Review* (2000) para 5.25. The Commission concluded 'that it should be open to a jury to decide that, for the purposes of a particular act, the "identity" of the actor included the possession of a professional qualification or other authority to do the act in question, and that if the defendant had no such authority then he or she did it without consent'.

authority to perform the act.[152] Thus, the position in cases such as *Richardson*[153] remains unchanged. In that case the defendant had continued to practice as a dentist although suspended. Patients claimed that they would not have allowed her to treat them if they had known of her suspension. She pleaded guilty to assault after the trial judge ruled that her deception had vitiated consent. The defence submission that the patients had consented to treatment despite their ignorance as to the circumstances was rejected. The Court of Appeal quashed her conviction, refusing to accept the prosecutor's argument that the concept of the identity of a person extended to cover the qualifications or attributes of the practitioner on the basis that the patients only consented to treatment by a qualified and not a suspended one. The court felt that this would be straining and distorting the definition of identity.

18.2.2 Sexual: s 78

Most offences in the Act involve proof of 'sexual' activity of one kind or another. The concept of 'sexual' is therefore of great significance, and the Act seeks to define it in a fashion similar to that propounded in the House of Lords in *Court*:[154]

[P]enetration, touching or any other activity is sexual if a *reasonable person* would consider that –

(a) whatever its circumstances or any person's purpose in relation to it, it is because of its nature sexual, or

(b) because of its nature it may be sexual and because of its circumstances or the purpose of any person in relation to it (or both) it is sexual.

The first limb requires consideration only of the nature of the act divorced from its circumstances. Where the nature of the activity is unambiguously sexual[155] (for example, penile penetration, oral sex, etc) the activity *is* sexual irrespective of the defendant's purpose. Even this limb may be difficult to apply.[156]

The second limb deals with cases where the nature of an activity is ambiguous. Such actions are only 'sexual' if the circumstances or the defendant's purpose render them such. The leading case is that of *H*[157] in the Court of Appeal. B was walking across some fields, when A said to her 'Do you fancy a shag?' She ignored that remark and continued walking. A then grabbed her tracksuit bottoms by the fabric, attempted to pull her towards him and, without succeeding, attempted to place his hand over her mouth. She broke free and escaped. A was convicted of sexual assault, contrary to s 3. It had been submitted that nothing had occurred which a reasonable person might regard as being 'sexual' within the meaning of s 78. According to the Court of Appeal in *H*, the approach should be as follows:

1. If the conduct is unambiguously sexual in the eyes of reasonable people, s 78(a) applies and the conduct is sexual irrespective of what A claims.

2. If the conduct is not unambiguously sexual in the eyes of reasonable people, the jury must ask themselves

---

[152] See *Richardson* [1999] Crim LR 62.

[153] [1998] 2 Cr App R 200.

[154] [1989] AC 28. See on this G Williams, 'The Meaning of Indecency' (1990) 12 LS 20; GR Sullivan, 'The Need for A Crime of Sexual Assault' [1989] Crim LR 331.

[155] The unambiguous nature of the indecency is relevant to whether a proved assault is indecent. It is not relevant to the question whether there is an assault in the first place. *Tabassum* [2000] 2 Cr App R 328, above, p 732. n 134, is surely wrong in this respect.

[156] What of A who pulls B's head towards his naked penis. It looks unambiguously sexual, but what if A claims he is confirming to B, his partner, that he has not had sex. I am grateful to Sally O'Neill QC for the example.

[157] [2005] EWCA Crim 732. See also A Gillespie, 'Indecent Images, Grooming and the Law' [2006] Crim LR 412.

(i) whether they as 12 reasonable people considered that the conduct in the particular circumstances before them because of its nature *might* be sexual and[158]

(ii) whether they, as reasonable people considered that in view of the circumstances or the purpose of the person in relation to the conduct or both it was in fact sexual.

The court's approach to s 78 has the effect of extending the potential scope of the offences dependent on proof of 'sexual' conduct well beyond the former offences in which the requirement was of indecency. In more general terms, the fact that jurors remain sole arbiters of what is 'sexual' is not conducive to the development of a consistent jurisprudence on a fundamental statutory term. Can a jury really be expected to keep the two questions under s 78(b) separate? Taking a shoe fetishist touching B's foot as an example, is there not a danger that the jury will, in answering (i), conclude that the conduct is capable of being sexual by referring, illegitimately, to A's secret motive, particularly when viewed against the backdrop of B having complained.

Few problems arise in relation to s 78(a) – if A's conduct is inherently sexual (for example, oral sex). The difficulty with s 78(a) is that it might be regarded as overly strict. For example, on facts such as those in *Court*,[159] A, an assistant in a shop, pulled a girl aged 12 who was in the shop across his knee and spanked her on her clothed bottom. When asked why he did it, he said 'Buttock fetish'. The House held (Lord Goff dissenting) that because the act was ambiguous, it was necessary to prove an indecent intention. Under the 2003 Act, on facts such as those in *Court*, if A had pulled down B's shorts, the case may well fall immediately into s 78(a), with the nature of the act rendering it unambiguously sexual. What, however, if in pulling down B's shorts, A had a merely (admittedly bizarre) disciplinary motive? Arguably there should be an opportunity for A's explanation, but that only arises if the case is decided under s 78(b).[160] Conversely there may be some acts of an unambiguously sexual nature where A's purpose is to perpetrate an act of violence not sex, but A's purpose is irrelevant.

The more significant aspect of the section is s 78(b). Examples of the operation of s 78(b) might include where A induces B to remove clothing, or an intimate examination involving digital penetration of the vagina or anus. If performed by a doctor for a medical purpose, and in appropriate medical circumstances, these would be non-sexual, A's purpose may make them sexual. As interpreted in *H* s 78(b) catches a wide range of conduct as sexual. It is submitted that practically any seemingly innocuous conduct *may* be capable of being regarded by a reasonable person as being sexual. Fetishism knows no bounds.[161] The s 78(b) test could give rise to difficulties in practice. Take the case of *Pratt*[162] as an example: A made two young boys strip and point a torch at each others genitals while he watched. A claimed that he was looking for cannabis. Under s 78, if the jury believed A's explanation for his actions it will be treated as a non-sexual purpose, and provided they do not conclude that the act is sexual *per se* (category (a)) A will be acquitted.

Section 78 also creates difficulties with odd sexual fetishes. In *George*,[163] A attempted to remove a girl's shoe from her foot because this gave him sexual gratification. Streathfield J,

---

[158] In relation to this first question, evidence as to the circumstances before or after the conduct was irrelevant.

[159] [1989] AC 28.

[160] A similar argument is developed by I Bantekas, 'Can Touching Always be Sexual When There is No Sexual Intent?' (2008) 72 J Crim L 251.

[161] For criticism of this interpretation see C Gallavin above, n 122.

[162] [1984] Crim LR 51. Note that he is not guilty of sexual assault since he does not touch the boys; the charge would be under s 4.

[163] [1956] Crim LR 52. Such cases are not uncommon: see *Price* [2004] 1 Cr App R 12, [2003] EWCA Crim 2405, where D stroked V's leg and boot and admitted it was because he had a shoe fetish. See news reports for 10 May 2006 discussing conviction of a man in New York who licked the boots of 70 women on the subway.

rejecting an argument that A's indecent motive made this an indecent assault, held that there were no circumstances of indecency. This decision was not followed under the 2003 Act in *H*. Stroking a woman's shod foot is not unambiguously sexual (leaving aside the extreme cases): s 78(a) does not apply. However, assuming a reasonable person would consider that stroking a woman's foot '*may be*' sexual, A's purpose would render it such: s 78(b). The less overtly sexual the fetish, the less likely the reasonable jury might regard it as being sexual and the less likely it will be caught by the section.

The significant shift from the 1956 Act offences based on 'indecent' conduct to the 2003 Act focus on 'sexual' conduct fails to address other difficulties. For example, in the case of *CW* [164] it was questioned whether A's touching of a 13-year-old's 'belly bar piercing' was 'indecent' under the 1956 Act. It is no clearer whether this is sexual under the 2003 Act than whether it was indecent under the old law. More commonly occurring questions might be whether a kiss is inherently sexual in which case its categorization depends on the circumstances and purpose of the kisser (thus, not where a hairy old aunt issues a slobbering greeting to a reluctant nephew). Distinguishing on the basis of whether the kissing involved is 'deep'[165] or otherwise is not an accurate basis of distinction. In *Davies*,[166] a 22-year-old woman kissing an 11-year-old girl on the mouth with an open mouth was sufficient for a s 7 offence – sexual touching of a child under 13.

Does an act which is seemingly sexual lose that quality if it is performed exclusively in A's mind for reasons of violence? In *AJ*,[167] A was convicted of s 3 sexual touching of B (his 19-year-old step-daughter) whom he had tied up (wrists and feet) and pinned down while he told her she needed to 'do more' around the house, that being part of an ongoing argument between them. B claimed that she thought that he was going to rape her. Her tracksuit bottoms 'fell down' in the course of the struggle with him, he did not touch her genitals.[168] In *Deal*,[169] A was convicted of two counts of sexual touching, one being for the act of standing behind a WPC and rubbing her arms with his hands, whilst making comments to her which she was unable to hear. It might even be argued in an extreme case that an act of penetration is not sexual: in *Hill*,[170] A had, in the course of a violent argument with his partner, 'forcefully inserted his finger in her vagina' as the Court of Appeal described it: 'without her consent and…as some form of aggressive humiliation rather than a sexual act'.[171] A nevertheless pleaded guilty to a 'sexual' penetration.

18.2.3 Touching: s 79(8)

Under the 1956 Act the offences other than those of intercourse centred predominantly on acts involving 'assault' as explained in the Court of Appeal in *Court*:[172]

The offence…included both a battery, or touching, and psychic assault without touching. If there was touching, it was not necessary to prove that the victim was aware of the assault or of the circumstances of indecency. If there was no touching, then to constitute an indecent assault the victim must be shown to have been aware of the assault and of the circumstances of indecency.

---

[164] *R v CW* [2004] EWCA Crim 340, CA.

[165] See Williams (1990) 10 LS 29 (presumably his definition turns on whether tongues are involved).

[166] [2005] EWCA Crim 3690.

[167] [2006] EWCA Crim 2956.

[168] Evidence was admitted to show that D had in the previous hour been viewing pornography on the internet.

[169] [2006] EWCA Crim 684.

[170] [2006] EWCA Crim 2575.

[171] ibid, [4].

[172] [1987] 1 All ER 120 at 122.

The 2003 Act creates offences based on 'touching' which includes touching –

(a) with any part of the body,[173]

(b) with anything else,

(c) through anything,[174]

and in particular includes touching amounting to penetration.

As elsewhere in the Act, there is no further definition of any of the terms, and this may lead to a regrettable inconsistency in the application of the law.

The leading case is *H* where the question was whether A's touching of B's tracksuit bottoms alone constituted a 'touching' of another person within the meaning of s 79(8). Although s 79(8) offers an extended and non-exhaustive interpretation of that term, including 'touching through anything' some commentators had suggested that the Act required physical contact with B's *body*.[175] The Court of Appeal held that where a person was wearing clothing, touching of that clothing constituted touching for the purposes of the Act. It was unnecessary for there to be some form of pressure brought against the body of the individual who was alleged to have been assaulted for touching to occur for the purposes of s 3.[176] This is consistent with the decisions in relation to battery generally. For example, in *Thomas*,[177] A had touched the bottom of B's skirt and the court said *obiter* that '[t]here could be no dispute that if you touch a person's clothes while he is wearing them that is equivalent to touching him'. There are numerous instances of convictions for sexual assault through clothing under the Act. For example, in *Swinscoe*,[178] A approached an eight-year-old and asked to see her knickers before touching her through her underwear (s 7).

The shift from 'assault' under the 1956 Act to 'touching' under the 2003 Act is significant. Although assault did not require any element of hostility,[179] 'touching' might appear to be broader than even a non-hostile assault. It is submitted that as with the old law, there is no room for any '*de minimis*' exception.[180] In other circumstances it seems that the law has been narrowed. Thus, sexual words do not constitute a touching but might well have been assaults. Similarly, where D walks towards someone with his penis exposed,[181] this could have been an assault: the old law did not require any apprehension of indecent touching.[182] Note that it is enough that A makes contact and the act is sexual; B need not be aware that there is a touching or, presumably, that the act is sexual.[183] So, in *Farrar*,[184] A committed the offence

---

[173] Note that under s 79(3) surgically reconstructed body parts are included as parts of the 'body' with which touching can occur.

[174] This covers D who engages in frottaging (rubbing his genitals against a fellow passenger on public transport): see, eg, *Tanylidiz* [1998] Crim LR 228.

[175] Professor Card suggested that 'lightly touching an outer garment so thick that no physical contact is made with B's body would not suffice'. Card, *Sexual Offences*, para 2.32

[176] Interestingly, A's counsel's argument had been that A had pulled the shorts away from B not touching her at all.

[177] (1985) 81 Cr App R 331, at 334.

[178] [2006] EWCA Crim 2412.

[179] Although cf the House of Lords in *Brown* [1994] 1 AC 212 and above p 637.

[180] *Ananthanarayanan* (1994) 98 Cr App R 1 at 5, per Laws J. See *Mills* [2003] EWCA Crim 3723, two-second touching of barmaid's breasts by customer.

[181] *Rolfe* (1952) 36 Cr App R 4.

[182] *Sargeant* (1996) 161 JP 127, [1997] Crim LR 50, where the assault was a threat with a knife and the circumstance of indecency was A's demand that B masturbate into a condom in a public place.

[183] *Bounekhla* [2006] EWCA Crim 1217 (A secretly ejaculating over B while dancing closely with her in a nightclub).

[184] [2006] EWCA Crim 3261.

by blindfolding a child, B, and masturbating on him. There is still the question whether it is sufficient that A ejaculates on B without touching B in the process.[185]

It is unclear whether there can be a touching by omission. What, for example, of cases such as *Speck*,[186] where A's failure to remove B's hand, which she had voluntarily placed on his penis, caused it to become erect? Does this constitute a touching? There is a touching between A and B, but it is more difficult to describe A as touching B. Is it a sexual touching if the sexual element derives from B and not A? It is submitted that it capable of being a sexual.[187]

18.3 Non-consensual offences

18.3.1 Rape

Rape was an offence at common law. Although placed on a statutory basis in the Sexual Offences Act 1956, s 1, there was no statutory definition of the offence, and this position continued until the Sexual Offences (Amendment) Act 1976[188] introduced a partial definition of the *mens rea* requirement and the Criminal Justice and Public Order Act 1994 extended the offence to include anal rape. There had been sustained calls for reform of the offence, particularly the mental element and the opportunity for an acquittal on the basis of a mere honest belief in the complainant's consent since the controversial decision in *Morgan*.[189] The need for this issue to be addressed and for clearer definition of this the most serious sexual offence were significant catalysts for reform, as was the low conviction rate for rape: by 1999, only one in 13 alleged rapes led to conviction.[190]

The 2003 reform prompted several radical suggestions for rape to be subdivided into different categories of offence. One suggestion was to distinguish between cases on the basis of whether there was a previous relationship between the accused and complainant (acquaintance rape) and the more stereotypical but less common stranger rape. This was rejected. There is no doubt that rape by an acquaintance, including as it does an abuse of trust, can be as traumatic as stranger rape.[191] The Court of Appeal has accepted that, in sentencing terms, there is in general no difference between a stranger rape and an acquaintance rape.[192] The 2003 Act

---

[185] The Scottish legislation specifically provides that such conduct is an offence: s 3(2)(d) of the Sexual Offences (Scotland) Act 2009, in force from 1.12.10.

[186] [1977] Crim LR 689. See also *B* [2004] EWCA Crim 319 where A had allowed B to touch his genitals and where B had placed A's hand on her genitals.

[187] cf the s 4 case of *Aveya* [2009] EWCA Crim 2640 where A forced B's hand onto A's penis and moved it.

[188] The Sexual Offences Act 1956, s 1(1), simply provided 'It is a felony for a man to rape a woman', whilst s 1(2) provided 'A man who induces a married woman to have sexual intercourse with him by impersonating her husband commits rape.'

[189] [1976] AC 182; see, below, p 744.

[190] *Rape and Sexual Assault of Women, Findings from the BCS* (2002) Home Office. See, also, the discussion of reform below, p 777.

[191] Statistics reveal that 45 per cent of rapes are by partners, 16 per cent are by acquaintances: Home Office Research Study No 237, *Rape and Sexual Assault of Women: The Extent and Nature of the Problem* (Mar 2002). See http://webarchive.nationalarchives.gov.uk/20110220105210/rds.homeoffice.gov.uk/rds/pdfs2/hors237.pdf. See also the report by Kelly, Lovett and Regan. See http://webarchive.nationalarchives.gov.uk/20110220105210/rds.homeoffice.gov.uk/rds/pdfs2/hors237.pdf – report in 2005 at 39 for analysis of the relationship between victim and offender for the full data-set (1987–2002) which reveals that the largest category of assailants are acquaintances (33 per cent), followed by strangers (28 per cent), current and ex-partners (19 per cent), known less than 24 hours (11 per cent) and family members (10 per cent).

[192] See also the Sentencing Advisory Panel's advice to the Court of Appeal, Foreword by the Chairman, 1 May 2002, paras 32–35. On the court's controversial qualification of this see P Rumney, 'Progress at a Price: The Construction of Non-Stranger Rape in the *Millbery* Sentencing Guidelines' (2003) 66 MLR 870.

also rejected the possibility of structuring different offences of rape based on the extent of mental fault.[193]

Despite the rejection of these more radical proposals, the new rape offence represents a significant change from the 1956 Act. It provides:

(1) A person (A) commits an offence if –

    (a) he intentionally penetrates the vagina, anus or mouth of another person (B) with his penis,

    (b) B does not consent to the penetration, and

    (c) A does not reasonably believe B consents.

(2) Whether a belief is reasonable is to be determined having regard to all the circumstances, including any steps A has taken to ascertain whether B consents.

Rape is triable only on indictment (except for certain cases where there is provision for trial in the Youth Court).[194] The maximum penalty is life imprisonment.[195]

18.3.1.1 *Actus reus*

Penile

The Sexual Offences Review team were eager for the offence of rape to resonate with the general public's understanding of the term, and concluded that, although it would perpetuate gender inequality, penile penetration should nevertheless remain an essential element of the offence. The Review considered that penile penetration was a distinctive act, carrying as it can risks of pregnancy and disease transmission, and that it should, therefore, be treated separately from other penetrative assaults. This strong commitment to the principle of fair labelling is especially important in sexual offences where the stigma of conviction is most acute. If jurors are to apply the offences appropriately it is also important that the offences reflect society's general understanding of the wrongdoing involved. By restricting rape to penile penetration,[196] s 1 reflects this principle.

Because the offence requires penetration by a penis, rape remains one of the few offences capable of being committed only by a male (as a principal offender).[197] However, in a welcome extension of the offence, a post-operative transsexual can commit rape with her reconstructed penis[198] (hence, presumably, the drafting in terms of 'a person' rather than 'a man').[199] A female can aid and abet the offence[200] as where she encourages or assists a man, A, to penetrate B without B's consent. It may be possible for the female aider and abettor to be convicted even

---

[193] See Temkin, *Rape and the Legal Process*, Ch 3, H Power, 'Towards a Redefinition of the *Mens Rea* of Rape' (2003) 23 OJLS 379, a view also considered by the Heilbron Committee, paras 79–80. For a proposal to subdivide the offence into categories based on the reason for the absence of consent (eg intoxicated, under threat of violence etc) see Tadros (2006) 26 OJLS 515.

[194] Magistrates' Courts Act 1980, s 24, as amended by the Powers of Criminal Courts (Sentencing) Act 2000, s 165(1) and Sch 9, para 64.

[195] SOA 2003, s 1(4). Attempted rape formerly carried a maximum of seven years' imprisonment: Sexual Offences Act 1956, s 37 and Sch 2. The maximum was increased to life by the Sexual Offences Act 1985, s 3(2).

[196] *Setting the Boundaries*, Ch 2, para 2.8.4.

[197] The Sexual Offences Act 1993 removed the common law presumption that boys under the age of 14 are incapable of intercourse. In a prosecution for historic offences pre-20 Mar 1993 a defendant cannot be guilty of charges involving acts of sexual intercourse perpetrated when he was aged under 14. See *R v W* (2003) 10 Archbold News 2 and D Ormerod, 'A Presumption of Intercourse' (2003) 1 Archbold News 2.

[198] Under s 79(3).

[199] Section 79(3). See *Setting the Boundaries* recommendation at para 2.8.4.

[200] *Ram* (1893) 17 Cox CC 609; *Lord Baltimore's case* (1768) 1 Black, W. 648.

though A is acquitted of rape on the basis of his lack of *mens rea*.[201] In such circumstances, a female can also now be charged with an offence under s 4 – causing a person to engage in sexual activity – and it is submitted that this is the more appropriate charge (see below).

The conclusive presumption that boys under 14 were incapable of sexual intercourse was abolished by the Sexual Offences Act 1993, s 1, for acts done after 20 September 1993. It has been held that a boy under 10 years old cannot commit an offence and so cannot be procured to commit rape,[202] but this reasoning seems flawed.[203]

Penetration

Penetration is not defined in the Act, although s 79(2) provides that it is a continuing act, thus putting on a statutory footing the decisions of the Privy Council in *Kaitamaki*[204] and the Court of Appeal in *Cooper and Schaub*.[205] Penetration continues until withdrawal,[206] and A can be convicted of rape where having initially penetrated B with consent, B subsequently withdraws that consent and A, being aware of that retraction of consent, does not remove his penis.[207] Presumably, A will not commit the offence until he either knows or could reasonably be expected to know that consent had been withdrawn.

The Act does not provide any clarification of the degree of penetration necessary. Presumably the common law rule applies so that the slightest degree of penetration will suffice. In relation to vaginal rape, this will include any penetration of the vulva,[208] and thus, the common law rule that it is not necessary to show that the hymen was ruptured remains.[209] In *F*,[210] 'vagina' was held to be used in the general sense of the female genitals, not in its strict anatomical sense.[211] There is no express provision making clear that rape is complete upon penetration without ejaculation,[212] but this must surely still represent the law. The fact that the Act creates numerous other offences of non-penile penetration supports this view.

If the prosecution fails to establish that there was penetration by a penis, a verdict of attempted rape may be returned if A's conduct amounted to more than mere preparation to penile penetration.

Of the vagina, anus or mouth

'Vagina' is to be interpreted as including the vulva.[213] Section 79 of the Act provides further relevant definition, including welcome confirmation that penetration of surgically reconstructed vaginas suffices.[214] At common law rape protected only against penetration of the

---

[201] *Cogan and Leak* [1975] 2 All ER 1059.

[202] *DPP v K and C* [1997] 1 Cr App R 36 at 42.

[203] See commentary in [1997] Crim LR 121, and above, p 189, n 40. See also *C* [2005] EWCA Crim 2817.

[204] [1985] AC 147.

[205] [1994] Crim LR 531.

[206] For criticism of *Kaitamaki* see 10th edition, where it was emphasized that the offence requires penetration without consent as an essential part of the *actus reus* of rape and this act of penetration must be accompanied by the *mens rea*.

[207] See *Leaver* [2006] EWCA Crim 2988 and under the previous law also *Tarmohammed* [1997] Crim LR 458; *Greaves* [1999] 1 Cr App R (S) 319.

[208] Section 79(3).

[209] *Hughes* (1841) 9 C & P 752; *Lines* (1844) 1 C & K 393; *Allen (Henry)* (1839) 9 C & P 31; *M'Rue* (1838) 8 C & P 641.

[210] [2002] EWCA Crim 2936.

[211] cf *Holland* (1993) 117 ALR 193, High Ct of Aus.

[212] cf s 44 of the Sexual Offences Act 1956.

[213] Section 79(9).

[214] Section 79(3). This puts on a statutory footing the ruling in *Matthews*, unreported, Oct 1996. See also M Hicks and G Branston, 'Transexual Rape – A Loophole Closed?' [1997] Crim LR 526.

vagina, indeed historically it was an offence protecting virginity.[215] The Criminal Justice and Public Order Act 1994, s 142, introduced the offence of anal rape. The 2003 Act extends the offence of rape yet further by including non-consensual penile penetration of the mouth. The Sexual Offences Review acknowledged that non-consensual oral sex is as 'abhorrent, demeaning and traumatising' as vaginal and anal penetration by the penis.[216] There is no doubt that this form of conduct deserves appropriate condemnation by the law in terms of labelling and sentence, but some argued that it would have been more appropriately dealt with as non-consensual penetration under s 2 (which also carries a life sentence). Jurors appear willing to convict of 'rape' for this conduct. There may of course be greater forensic difficulties in establishing oral sex as opposed to vaginal or anal penetration, although that in itself should not militate against it being classified as rape.[217] The Court of Appeal has confirmed that sentencing should not distinguish between the orifices penetrated.[218]

Without consent

The critical element of rape remains the absence of consent. Without that, penile penetration is not merely not criminal, it is an explicit expression of intimacy. The Act's approach to consent is discussed above.

18.3.1.2 *Mens rea*

Intentional penetration

The requirement that the defendant *intentionally* penetrate the relevant orifice should not give rise to difficulty in practice. One circumstance in which A might realistically claim that penile penetration was 'accidental' might include those where A intended to penetrate B's vagina with her consent, but accidentally penetrated her anus, for which act he knew he did not have consent, or to which he could not reasonably believe that he had consent (whether from previous knowledge or from B's expression of non-consent once A penetrated her anally).[219] It has been held that to charge A with rape where the allegation is that he penetrated either B's vagina or her anus is not to allege two offences.[220] Nevertheless, if A has a reasonable belief in consent to vaginal sex and unintentionally penetrates B's anus, it is submitted that he has not raped B.

Despite this element of the offence being expressed in terms of intention, it would seem, following *Heard*,[221] that a mistake of this nature induced by voluntary intoxication cannot be relied upon.[222] The offence is one of basic intent.

Mens rea as to consent

One of the most dramatic changes under the 2003 Act was to redefine the *mens rea* for rape. Under s 1(1) of the Act the prosecution has to prove A intentionally penetrated the vagina, anus or mouth of B, and A did not have a *reasonable* belief that B was consenting.

It will be recalled that it was held in *Morgan* that rape was not proved if the man may have honestly believed that the woman was consenting, even if that belief was unreasonable. Lord

---

[215] Temkin, *Rape and the Legal Process*, 57.

[216] *Setting the Boundaries*, para 2.8.5. See the Government response to the *Home Affairs Committee Fifth Report*.

[217] The Sentencing Advisory Panel proposed that which orifice is penetrated should not affect the starting point for sentencing, at 15.

[218] *Ismail* [2005] EWCA Crim 397.

[219] See, eg, *Pigg* (above) and discussion by S White, 'Three Points on *Pigg*' [1989] Crim LR 539.

[220] *K* [2008] EWCA Crim 1923.

[221] [2007] EWCA Crim 125.

[222] cf *Woods* (1981) 74 Cr App R 132. See now *Grewal* [2010] EWCA Crim 2448.

Hailsham in *Morgan* held that the *mens rea* required an 'intention of having intercourse, willy-nilly, not caring whether the victim consents or not'.[223] Another way of putting this was to ask, 'Was A's attitude one of "I could not care less whether B is consenting or not, I am going to have intercourse with her regardless"?'[224] Thus, the *mens rea* under the old law required proof that A intentionally had sexual intercourse with B, (i) knowing that B did not consent, or (ii) being aware that there was a possibility that B did not consent.

Following widespread public concern with this approach, the Heilbron Committee[225] reviewed the position and, while endorsing *Morgan*, recommended some statutory clarification. The Sexual Offences (Amendment) Act 1976 provides in s 1(2): 'It is hereby declared that if at a trial for a rape offence the jury has to consider whether a man believed that a woman or man was consenting to sexual intercourse, the presence or absence of reasonable grounds for such a belief is a matter to which the jury is to have regard, in conjunction with any other relevant matters, in considering whether he so believed.' This was largely a public relations provision explaining the jury's role in evaluating a defendant's mistaken beliefs of facts; it did not enact any rule peculiar to rape.

There was little empirical evidence that *Morgan* defences were successfully run, so jurors were presumably not readily believing defendants' spurious claims. Even if generally unsuccessful, the plea was easy to run and difficult to disprove, and sent an undesirable message to society – that it is acceptable to take unreasonable risks as to your partner's consent to sexual conduct.[226] Unsurprisingly, many submissions to the Sexual Offences Review were highly critical of the approach. *Setting the Boundaries* regarded this 'defence' as in direct conflict with the ordinary perceptions of contemporary society. A more objective approach to the issue of *mens rea* as to consent was desirable, or even necessary, but further difficulty lay in determining the appropriate degree of objectivity.

One key issue of the reform agenda became whether the *mens rea* (for rape in particular) ought to be rendered wholly objective (would a reasonable person have realized that B was not consenting?). Although the general trend of English criminal law has been increasingly favouring subjective approaches to *mens rea* – even in serious sexual offences[227] – there are powerful arguments against adopting a purely subjective approach in this context. When the conduct in question is of a sexual nature, the ease with which the defendant can ascertain the consent of his partner, coupled with the catastrophic consequences for the victim if the defendant acts without consent, militate strongly against the purely subjective approach. The generosity the law extends to accepting a defendant's genuine but unreasonable mistakes in, for example, matters of self-defence need not be replicated in sexual cases because the conduct in question calls for a qualitatively different degree of vigilance on his part.[228]

The Government took a strong stance on this aspect of the reform.[229] In early versions of the Sexual Offences Bill, it was proposed that the defendant would bear a *legal* burden (on the balance of probabilities) to show that he did believe that the complainant consented. This may

---

[223] [1976] AC 182 at 215. See also the Heilbron *Report of the Advisory Group on the Law of Rape* (1975) Cmnd 6352, para 77.

[224] *Taylor* (1984) 80 Cr App R 327; *Haughian* (1985) 80 Cr App R 334.

[225] Cmnd 6352 (1975). See [1976] Crim LR 97.

[226] See the Law Commission's Policy Paper in *Setting the Boundaries* (2000) vol 2.

[227] See *K* [2001] UKHL 41; *DPP v B* [2000] 2 WLR 452.

[228] See, generally, J Horder, 'Cognition, Emotion and Criminal Culpability' (1990) 106 LQR 469, 477; T Pickard, 'Culpable Mistakes' (1980) 30 U Toronto J 75; C Wells, 'Swatting the Subjectivist Bug' [1982] Crim LR 209. There have been suggestions for strict liability rape offences. For discussion see K Huigens, 'Is Strict Liability Rape Defensible', in Duff and Green, *Defining Crime,* 196 discussing a hypothetical case where B was under the self-imposed mistaken belief that A was a serial rapist, so she acquiesced in all A did. A was unaware and thought B was consenting.

[229] See HL, col 1089, 31 Mar 2003, Lord Falconer.

well have been in breach of Art 6(2) of the ECHR. The final version as enacted is less objective, and although to be welcomed for extending the *mens rea*, the Act is far from clear, and may still leave the opportunity for *Morgan*-type pleas to be run (although they will be even less likely to succeed).

The *mens rea* in rape and the other non-consensual offences (ss 1–4) comprises two elements:

(1) A does not reasonably believe B consents.

(2) Whether a belief is reasonable is to be determined having regard to all the circumstances, including any steps A has taken to ascertain whether B consents.

The new provisions do not render the test *wholly* objective.[230] The defendant's personal characteristics and beliefs remain important, but both the concluded belief as to consent and the manner by which A reached it are to be assessed by reference to some objective criteria.

A does 'not reasonably believe'

This encompasses cases in which (i) A's purpose is to act without B's consent; (ii) A is aware that B might not be consenting; (iii) A has no belief whether B is consenting or not; (iv) A holds a belief that B is consenting but that is an unreasonable belief. What remains unclear is whether in (iv) the question is as to (a) A's purely subjective belief about consent measured against a standard of reasonableness applied by the jury or magistrate, or (b) A's assessment that his own belief as to consent was reasonable. It is submitted that the correct interpretation is that in (a).[231] The dilution of the purely objective test originally proposed to accommodate those with limited capacity has not been that substantial. A, with a learning disability,[232] who believes B is consenting will have the *mens rea* if the reasonable juror concludes that belief was an unreasonable one, irrespective of the fact that the basis for belief is understandable, given A's limited capacity.

Reasonable having regard to all the circumstances including the steps taken

The reasonableness test does not oblige the defendant to have taken any specific steps to ascertain consent; the Government was keen to emphasize that there would be no need to have 'blank consent forms by the bedside'. However, where steps have been taken they must be taken into account by the jury in deciding whether the defendant's claimed belief in consent was reasonable.[233] Also, importantly, the issue of the reasonableness of belief will now be worth pursuing in interview with the suspect. The objective test has an impact on the evidential provisions regarding cross-examination of sexual complainants.[234]

Ministerial statements[235] suggest that the expression 'all the circumstances' in s 1(2) will allow juries when determining the reasonableness of the belief, to take account of any *relevant* characteristics of the defendant. Ministers rejected the idea that the very narrow interpretation of similar provisions in New Zealand might be followed, creating a purely objective test.[236] It is clear then that the defendant's age; general sexual experience; sexual experience with this complainant;[237] learning disability; and any other factor that could have affected his ability to understand the nature and consequences of his actions, and particularly the ability

---

[230] See above, Ch 6, for discussion of negligence.

[231] HC, col 639 refers ambiguously to the 'focus on the defendant's belief', at para 23.

[232] Under the old law A's Asperger's was relevant: see *Tipu Sultan* [2008] EWCA Crim 6.

[233] HC, 3rd reading, col 669, 17 June 2003.

[234] See *Bahadour* [2005] EWCA Crim 396 and J McEwan, 'I Thought She Consented' [2006] Crim LR 961.

[235] HC, col 1073, Lord Falconer of Thoroton, 2 June 2003; HC, col 674, Baroness Scotland of Asthal, 17 June 2003.

[236] HC, col 674, Baroness Scotland of Asthal, 17 June 2003.

[237] *McAllister* [1997] Crim LR 233.

to appreciate the risk of non-consent, may be relevant depending on the circumstance of the particular case. What weight will attach to these characteristics will be a matter for judicial direction.

Several difficulties flow from the breadth of this provision. First, there is the question as to which characteristics of the defendant might be *excluded* from the jury's deliberation. Should the jury be able to take into account the defendant's self-induced intoxication by drink or drugs? On the basis of the long-established position that rape is a crime of basic intent, it would seem not.[238] What of other characteristics, such as those which are inherently unreasonable in the context of sexual conduct? For example, what of A who claims that women who invite him for coffee are automatically agreeing to sex? Or that dressing in a short skirt is an invitation to be touched in a sexual manner?[239] Ministers reassured Parliament that the jury would not be asked to take into account such characteristics.[240] The crucial question for the courts will lie in defining the limits on which less strikingly unreasonable characteristics are legally relevant. This created difficulty elsewhere in the law, particularly with provocation.[241] Careful judicial direction will be critical. Once again it is disappointing that such an important issue is not resolved in the Act.

Secondly, and related to this point, the statute does not expressly preclude the most objectionable of the *Morgan*-type pleas from being advanced. A could claim that he had taken reasonable steps to ascertain the consent of the complainant by asking her friends, or by seeking the confirmation of her husband (as in *Morgan*). A could also claim that it was reasonable for him to ignore B's explicit 'no' since he believes that all women sometimes say 'no' and mean 'yes'.[242] Such pleas are never likely to be considered to be 'reasonable' by any right-thinking jury. Nevertheless, the 2003 Act provisions allows for the plea to be run adding to the distress of the complainant. It should be noted that *Setting The Boundaries* recommended a significantly wider list of circumstances presumptively vitiating consent including where a person has agreement given for them by a third party.[243] This was rejected because of concerns that a person with a learning disability, A, might be easily deceived by X and have sex with B believing her to be consenting on the basis of X's false statement.[244]

As the Court of Appeal noted in *Taran (Farid)*:[245]

A direction upon absence of reasonable belief clearly falls to be given when, but only when, there is material on which a jury might come to the conclusion that (a) the complainant did not in fact consent, but (b) the defendant thought that she was consenting. Such a direction does not fall to be given unless there is such material. It is, of course, the fact, as all trial judges know well, that a direction of

---

[238] *Heard* [2007] EWCA Crim 125; *Fotheringham* (1988) 88 Cr App R 206; *Grewal* [2010] EWCA Crim 2448.

[239] The disturbing report of Amnesty International revealed that one-third of the UK population believe that women who had flirted were wholly or partially responsible for a sexual assault on them. See the Home Office Report, *Convicting Rapists and Protecting Victims* (2006) below p 777.

[240] Lord Falconer of Thoroton stated 'Introducing a requirement that all of the personal characteristics of the defendant should be taken into account would mean that the jury would be asked to take into account characteristics that should not absolve him from his guilt: for example, the fact that he has a quick temper or that the sight of a girl in a mini-skirt will always turn him on and make him unable to resist her. That cannot be the intention.' HL, 17 June 2003.

[241] Especially in relation to provocation. Guidance may be derived from the Court of Appeal's approach in self-defence cases where D has a belief formed owing to a psychiatric condition: *Canns* [2010] EWCA Crim 2264.

[242] See also D Husak, above n 34, Ch 9. Note, however, that in *P* [2009] EWCA Crim 1100 the Court observed that 'Any counsel accordingly advising a defendant facing a charge of rape, whose instructions are that he had a genuine belief in consent, will have to advise him as to the likelihood of a jury nonetheless concluding that in the circumstances the belief was unreasonable.'

[243] Ibid, 20, para 2.10.9.

[244] See Temkin and Ashworth [2004] Crim LR 328, 339.

[245] [2006] EWCA Crim 1498.

this kind, as of many other kinds, may have to be given even when it is not the case of either the Crown or the defendant that it arises... Reasonable belief in consent on an indictment for rape can certainly be [an] example, but only where there is material on which a jury may think that there might have been a misunderstanding, that is to say that the complainant did not in fact consent but that the defendant may have thought that she did.[246]

Sober mistaken consent by A

What is the liability of A who claims that he thought on reasonable grounds that X would be consenting to the sexual act which he then mistakenly performed on B? Can A claim he has a reasonable belief in consent? In *Whitta*,[247] where A had agreed with X that they would have sex later after the party they were both attending. Both A and X were adults but drunk. A, having removed his glasses, later entered a bedroom and digitally penetrated B, the sleeping 51-year-old mother of the party host. B was also very drunk. A desisted as soon as he realized his mistake. The trial judge ruled that mistake as to the identity in this context was irrelevant – liability was strict. The judge's approach draws support from the peculiar drafting of the sections with their reference to A and B. The Court of Appeal disagreed with this analysis of the ruling. The effect of the judge's ruling was that it is not a defence to a charge if the defendant has made a mistake, however reasonable, as to the identity of the person to whom the sexual activity is directed. That is not the law. It would mean that A who kissed his wife's twin sister would be liable for sexual assault irrespective of the reasonableness of his mistaken belief that he was kissing his wife. It is submitted that the correct question is whether A's belief was a reasonable one.

18.3.1.3 Prosecutions for marital rape occurring before 1992

The rule of the common law from the time of Hale was that, with few exceptions, a husband could not be convicted of raping his wife. The rule was based on a fiction that a wife could not retract the consent to intercourse which she gave upon marriage – a proposition which family law had long since rejected. In 1991, in *R*,[248] the House of Lords decided that there was no rule that a husband cannot be guilty of rape of his wife and that the word, 'unlawful' in s 1 of the 1976 Act was 'surplusage'. It is arguable that this decision flouted the will of Parliament but the result was highly desirable.

A husband can be guilty of raping his wife even if the non-consensual sexual intercourse took place before the House of Lords' abolition of the exemption in *R v R* in 1991. The ECtHR expressly held that this will not violate Art 7 of the Convention,[249] rejecting this claim in *SW v United Kingdom, CR v United Kingdom*.[250] The Court held that Art 7 did not prohibit the gradual evolution and clarification of the common law rules of criminal liability through judicial interpretation, provided that the developments were consistent with the essence of the offence and could reasonably be anticipated. Since the House of Lords in *R* had continued a discernible trend of developing case law, incrementally removing the husband's immunity and this was a foreseeable development, there was no violation.

In *C*,[251] the Court of Appeal upheld the defendant's 2002 conviction for raping his wife in 1970. The court was confident that a solicitor would have told his client in 1970 that the courts had developed and continued to develop exceptions to the marital exemption, and that if the

---

[246] [12]. See also *Saad* [2009] EWCA Crim 2781.
[247] [2006] EWCA Crim 2626.
[248] *R* [1992] 1 AC 599.
[249] 'No one shall be guilty of any criminal offence on account of any act or omission which did not constitute a criminal offence under national or international law at the time when it was committed.'
[250] [1996] 1 FLR 434.
[251] [2005] Crim LR 238 and commentary by Ashworth.

appellate courts reconsidered the issue they might abolish it. With respect, this is very doubtful. At the time, the only exceptions to the application of the marital rape exemption appeared to be for an agreement to separate and a *decree nisi*.[252] This also ignores the fact that the House of Commons had expressly rejected a motion to change the law 15 years before *R*; the Law Commission had in its exhaustive treatment of the issue in 1990 listed the exceptions,[253] and noted that they extended only to specified judicial orders of separation, and not even to cases where judicial proceedings had been initiated.[254]

18.3.2 Assault by penetration: s 2

A person, A, commits an offence if he intentionally penetrates the vagina or anus of another person (B), sexually, with a part of his body or anything else, where B does not consent to the penetration, and A does not reasonably believe that B consents. This offence introduced in the 2003 Act carries a maximum life sentence. It is designed to reflect the seriousness of non-consensual penetration with objects other than the penis. Acts of penetration with bottles, knives, fingers, etc are caught by s 2. Such acts would have been charged as indecent assault under the old law, and thus lacked a sufficiently accurate or stigmatizing label and sentencing power.[255] The Court of Appeal has made clear that long sentences may be appropriate for some acts of digital penetration.[256] The offence has proved useful where B cannot recall, could not tell, or lacks the capacity to tell whether the penetration was by a penis or other object.[257]

18.3.2.1 *Actus reus*

Penetration is discussed above. Unlike rape the penetration need not be by a penis; where it is, the charge ought to be under s 1. Where there is doubt as to with what the complainant was penetrated the charge should be under s 2. The offence can be committed by a person of either sex on a person of either sex. The act of penetration is regarded as continuing until withdrawal. Since the degree of penetration need only be slight, and 'vagina' includes 'vulva',[258] oral sex performed on a woman is caught by s 2. The requirement that the penetration is 'sexual' (as discussed above) excludes medical examinations, intimate body searches, etc. If the prosecution cannot establish the 'sexual' element, there is no *actus reus*, and the offence is not committed even if the complainant is not-consenting to the penetration. Such acts should be charged as offences against the person. An allegation that A penetrated B's vagina or anus is not an allegation of two offences.[259]

The absence of consent is an element of the *actus reus* and if B has consented to the acts of penetration with any form of object, provided A's intention is only to perform acts amounting to a battery, his penetration of B will not render him liable for an offence of violence if injury is in fact caused. Where the act of penetration is intended or likely to cause actual bodily harm

---

[252] See *Miller* [1954] 2 QB 282. See also the explanation in the 1st edition of this book, at 291; *O'Brien* [1974] 3 All ER 663; *Steele* [1977] Crim LR 290.

[253] See Law Com Working Paper No 116 (1990) paras 2.12–2.16. See further LC Report No 205, *Rape within Marriage* (1992).

[254] cf the decision in *Laskey* [2003] All ER (D) 69 (May), where L was convicted of the rape in marriage between 1988–1995. At this point in time it would have been clear to any lawyer that the exemption was on the brink of being abolished.

[255] A maximum 10 years.

[256] *Corran* [2005] EWCA Crim 192.

[257] See, eg, *Minshull* [2004] EWCA 2673 (B severely disabled); and *Lyddaman* [2006] EWCA Crim 383.

[258] Section 79.

[259] *P* [2010] EWCA Crim 164, following *K* [2008] EWCA Crim 1923 in relation to rape.

or worse and is performed for a sexual purpose, A may be liable for an offence against the person, even if B consents.[260]

18.3.2.2 *Mens rea*

The penetration must be intentional; there is no crime of reckless sexual penetration.[261] However, following *Heard*,[262] the voluntarily intoxicated defendant cannot rely on his intoxicated state to support his claim that his penetration of V with an object/part of his body was not intentional. Such circumstances are however unlikely to be commonplace. The *mens rea* regarding consent is determined in accordance with the principles discussed above p 718. Sections 75 and 76 relating to presumptions on consent apply.

It remains unclear whether there is an element of *mens rea* as to the 'sexual' nature of the penetration. As a matter of principle, each element of the *actus reus* ought to have a corresponding element of *mens rea*. The fact that this element of *actus reus* (sexual) is to be determined by the jury does not of itself preclude a corresponding requirement of *mens rea*.[263] If this additional *mens rea* element is required, A might claim, for example, that his penetration of B's vagina with an object such as a bottle was motivated solely by a desire to cause injury, being performed with a violent and not a sexual intent. It is doubtful that such a plea would be successful, and A would, in any event, have thereby admitted an offence against the person.[264] There are bizarre instances of penetrative conduct that would appear to be motivated by such non-sexual motives.[265] It may be that penetrative acts would be dealt with, additionally, as offences against the person where performed as acts of torture.[266]

18.3.3 Sexual assault: s 3

Under the law prior to the 2003 Act there were separate offences of 'indecent assault', protecting men and women.[267] For the want of anything more specific, these offences dealt with all non-consensual conduct: non-penile penetrations of the vagina and anus, oral sex; the merest touching in an indecent manner; and even psychic assaults in circumstances of indecency. The label on conviction did not differentiate between the vastly different forms of conduct and their disparate gravity.[268] Many of the activities dealt with previously as indecent assaults would now be rape (oral sex) or s 2 (most commonly digital penetration of the vagina).

The 2003 Act introduces a much wider offence with greater ambiguity stemming from the broad definition of the central elements of 'sexual' and 'touching'.

A commits an offence if he intentionally touches another person (B), sexually, and B does not consent to the touching, and A does not reasonably believe that B consents. The maximum sentence of imprisonment is 10 years on indictment; and six months summarily.

---

[260] See *Meachen* [2006] EWCA Crim 2414, discussed above p 237.

[261] See *Phillips* [2008] EWCA Crim 2830 where A claimed to have digitally penetrated B while he, A, was asleep.

[262] [2007] EWCA Crim 125.

[263] The definition of grievous bodily harm is left to the jury but D must still be proved to have intended it for a s 18 charge under the OAPA 1861.

[264] See *Hill* [2006] EWCA Crim 2575– penetration with fingers in forceful manner. Section 18 of the OAPA 1861.

[265] In *C* [2001] 1 Cr App R (S) 533 D paid a prostitute to fellate him and surreptitiously inserted live maggots into her vagina.

[266] In *Aydin v Turkey* (1997) 25 EHRR 251 it was recognized that rape by a State official could constitute torture.

[267] Sections 14 and 15 of the Act.

[268] Temkin (2000) 150 NLJ 1169, 1170 described them as 'mindless' (by which presumably it is meant that they did not describe the essence of the wrongdoing, particularly in serious cases).

18.3.3.1 *Actus reus*

The elements of 'sexual' and 'touching' have been discussed above. In combination the terms render the offence very broad indeed. There is no element of hostility required; a kiss could be sufficient provided it is regarded as sexual, as could A stroking B's clothing without her awareness. Although described as 'sexual assault' there is no need for a technical assault or battery; a touching is what is needed. As such, conduct that constitutes a psychic assault will not satisfy the *actus reus*.[269] If the touching is in non-sexual circumstances there is no offence – for example, where a police officer pats down a suspect, or a rugby player grabs the testicles of an opponent in the scrum. If the complainant is not consenting to such touching the conduct should be charged, if at all, as an offence against the person.

The sexual touching must be proved to be without consent. The presumptions in ss 75 and 76 (discussed above) apply. Given the breadth of the activity covered, there is a potential for problems with the conclusive presumptions. What, for example, of the Dr A who tells B, accurately, that a breast examination is necessary, but who also nurses a secret sexual purpose in performing it? Is there a deception as to 'purpose'?[270]

18.3.3.2 *Mens rea*

The touching must be intentional. Applying the established interpretation of *Majewski*, on a charge such as that under s 3 with the requirement of an 'intentional' touching, it was at least arguable that the crime is one of specific intent.[271] However, following the decision in *Heard*, the offence should be treated as one of basic intent: it is no excuse for A to rely on his voluntary intoxication as an excuse that he did not intend to touch the complainant in a sexual manner. As noted,[272] on its facts, *Heard* should never have given rise to problems. A had, while drunk, exposed his penis and rubbed it against the thigh of a police officer, B. A's plea was that he had no recollection of the incident. That is never a basis for a plea of intoxication and that should have been the end of the matter. However, A relied on his voluntary intoxication as negating his *mens rea* of an intention to touch for the purposes of s 3(1)(a) of the SOA 2003. The trial judge ruled that the intentional touching element of the offence required proof of a basic intent, and that it followed that voluntary intoxication was not a defence. The Court of Appeal concluded that A could not rely on that voluntary intoxication to negative *mens rea*. The full implications are considered in Chapter 11 above. On policy grounds the court was clearly entitled to assume that Parliament had not intended to change the law (although it should be noted that under the pre-2003 law, the offence of indecent assault was not always a basic intent crime).

A claim that a touching was not intended to be 'sexual', but rather was one of pure violence could in some circumstances form the basis of a plausible plea, certainly more so than in circumstances of penetration under s 2 discussed above. It remains unclear whether the courts will entertain such a plea in any circumstances.

18.3.4 Intentionally causing someone to engage in sexual activity: s 4

A commits an offence if he intentionally causes another person (B) to engage in an activity, the activity is sexual, B does not consent to engaging in the activity, and A does not reasonably believe that B consents.

---

[269] cf *Rolfe* (1952) Cr App R 4 (above).

[270] See above p 732.

[271] Card, *Sexual Offences: The New Law*, para 1.31; Rook and Ward, *Sexual Offences Law and Practice*, para 2.72.

[272] [2007] EWCA Crim 125.

This is an entirely new and potentially very useful offence, which has as one of its purposes criminalizing the actions of women who compel or procure men to penetrate them. Under the old law this conduct would have been prosecuted as indecent assault only. Examples of other types of conduct caught by this offence would include requiring a person to masturbate him/herself[273] or to masturbate another person.[274] It is an extremely broad offence and could also include A, who for example, causes B to act as a prostitute.

Aggravated versions of the offence (which attract a maximum of life imprisonment rather than the standard maximum 10 years on indictment/six months summarily) are created by subs (4). These involve penetration of B's anus or vagina; penetration of B's mouth with a person's penis; penetration of a person's anus or vagina by B with his body or otherwise; or penetration of a person's mouth with B's penis. Applying *Courtie*,[275] there are separate offences created and this must be reflected in the indictment.

18.3.4.1 *Actus reus*

The offence can be committed by words alone, and there is no explicit requirement that A is present when B engages in the activity nor that A participate in the activity. It is commonly prosecuted for indecent text messaging where A incites B to have sex with him.[276] The offence could also involve a third party, who might also be a victim if neither the third party nor B consent.[277] However, this is not a preliminary offence: the sexual activity must take place for A to be guilty. Although A must 'cause' the action, following orthodox principles of causation[278] it appears to be sufficient for A to be 'a' cause of the sexual activity without being the 'sole' cause. It is doubtful that an omission to prevent sexual activity occurring is a sufficient *actus reus*.[279]

The presumptions regarding consent in ss 75 and 76 (discussed above) apply.

18.3.4.2 *Mens rea*

As with rape, discussed above, the reasonableness of belief is determined by reference to 'all the circumstances' including 'any steps A has taken to ascertain B's consent'.

There is a requirement of 'intention', which in this context would apparently include oblique intention – foresight by A that B's engaging in the sexual activity is a virtually certain consequence of A's action, even though it might not be his 'direct intention'.[280]

Despite the requirement of intention to cause B to engage in the activity, following *Heard*, s 4 creates a basic intent offence. A who in a voluntarily intoxicated state jokingly encourages B to strip might claim that there was no such intent, but drunken intent is still intent.

18.4 Offences against children under 13 (ss 5–8)[281]

The offences in ss 5 to 8 are very similar to those in ss 1 to 4, except that they relate only to offences against children under 13, and there is no requirement to prove the absence of consent.

---

[273] As in *Sargeant* [1997] Crim LR 50; see *Devonauld* [2008] EWCA Crim 527, above p 734.

[274] See *Basherdost* [2009] EWCA Crim 2883 where A forced B and C to engage in sex together while he filmed them.

[275] [1984] AC 463.

[276] eg *A* [2006] EWCA Crim 2103; *Hinton-Smith* [2005] EWCA Crim 2575.

[277] As in *Basherdost* [2008] EWCA Crim 2883.

[278] Discussed in Ch 4.

[279] See *Clarkson and Carroll* [1971] 3 All ER 344. Card, *Sexual Offences*, above.

[280] See above Ch 5, p 107.

[281] See generally F Bennion, 'Criminalizing Children under the Sexual Offences Bill' (2003) 167 JP 784; JR Spencer, 'Child and Family Offences' [2004] Crim LR 347; L Hoyano and C Keenan *Child Abuse: Law and*

- Section 5 criminalizes penile penetration of the vagina, anus or mouth of a child under 13
- Section 6 criminalizes penetration of the vagina or anus of a child under 13
- Section 7 criminalizes sexual touching of a child under 13
- Section 8 criminalizes causing or inciting a child under 13 to engage in sexual conduct.

Under the old law a child under 16 could not consent to indecent assault, but could consent to sexual intercourse.[282] Determining whether a child consented to sexual intercourse involved an assessment of her understanding of the activity.[283] Consent is no longer an issue. This shift proved to be very controversial as the legislation progressed through Parliament. The commendable underlying policy of the offences is to protect the child from the 'predatory' older offender, and to guard against exploitation of young people, but the breadth of the offences raises a number of problems.

First, the legislation makes no attempt to distinguish between exploitative sexual activity against a child under 13 (whether by older individual or not) and that of fully informed consensual sexual experimentation between children under that age.

Secondly, denying the relevance of the factual consent of the under-13-year-old clashes with the law's willingness to accept their capacity to consent to, for example, invasive medical procedures. The Home Secretary stated in a press release on the Act receiving Royal Assent that there would be no prosecution for sexual activity between children under the age of 16 where the activity is genuinely consensual. This rather begs the question why the Act is not drafted so as to include a requirement of an absence of consent. In the first eight months of the Act being in force there were 38 prosecutions with 21 convictions.[284]

Thirdly, this gave rise to challenges under the ECHR. In the controversial case of G,[285] the defendant who was aged 15, pleaded guilty to rape of a child under 13 (s 5). G's basis of plea was that V consented and that he reasonably believed her to be older than 13, because she had so informed him. One ground of appeal was that the offence was incompatible with Art 8 since G claimed he should have been charged under s 9 and 13 (sexual activity with a child under 16), if at all. The charge and conviction under s 5 (sex with child under 13) breached his right to respect for private life by labelling him publicly as a rapist, subjecting him to a maximum penalty of life imprisonment and attracting sexual offender notification requirements.[286] Compliance with the proportionality requirement in Art 8 would, he argued, mean that no prosecution should ensue;[287] or prosecution should be under ss 9 and 13, with its lower maximum penalty of five years and limited notification requirements. The House of Lords, (Lords Hope and Carswell dissenting) held that s 5 was compatible with Art 8. Convicting G of rape contrary to s 5 even in circumstances where the agreed basis of plea established that his

---

Policy (2007) pp 192-215 dealing with comparative materials. For sentencing guidance, see *Corran* [2005] EWCA Crim 192. See, also, L James, 'Children who Commit Sex Offences' (2007) Howard Jnl 493. The Criminal Justice and Immigration Act 2008 extends the territorial reach of a number of offences under the Act in relation to children: s 72 of the SOA 2003 as substituted by s 72 of the 2008 Act.

[282] It was arguable that since all acts of intercourse must include an indecent assault, the law was irremediably incoherent.

[283] *Howard* [1966] 1 WLR 13.

[284] See the Home Office, *The Sexual Offences Act 2003: A Stocktake of the Effectiveness of the Act since its Implementation* (2006) 9.

[285] [2008] UKHL 37; [2008] Crim LR 000 with a valuable commentary by Andrew Ashworth.

[286] See now the decision of the Supreme Court in *R(F) v Secretary of State for the Home Department* [2010] UKSC 17.

[287] The Government had given an assurance that consensual sexual activity between minors would not inevitably be prosecuted, but relied on prosecutorial discretion to achieve the correct balance, and this was not a satisfactory protection for rights. cf the position in Ireland: *CC v Ireland* [2006] $ IR 1 (Irish Supreme Court) and C O'Sullivan, 'Protecting Young People from Themselves' (2009) Dublin Uni LJ 386.

offence fell properly within the ambit of s 13 did not infringe Art 8. The issue drew some striking comments from the Law Lords.[288] Baroness Hale doubted whether Art 8 was engaged at all but, if it was, held there was no breach.[289] Similarly, Lord Mance accepted that Art 8 might be engaged, but that prosecution was justified to protect children. In the minority, Lord Hope concluded that the prosecution ought not to have pursued a s 5 conviction once G's basis of plea was accepted. His lordship did not go as far as to say that it was disproportionate to use s 5 even in cases where children had mutually agreed to have sex. Lord Carswell agreed, deprecating the use of the 'crude generalisation' using the term 'statutory rape'.[290]

There is no additional restraint on prosecution such as a requirement for the DPP's prior consent. In *R v R*,[291] the Administrative Court doubted whether criminal prosecution was always appropriate where the conduct is less serious conduct between children; in that case it was two children with learning disabilities with A touching B's breast over her clothes. In *R(S) v DPP*[292] the prosecutor did abandon the s 5 charge against a boy of 15 in favour of proceeding under s 13 when it appeared that the conduct had been consensual. Challenges to such decisions to prosecute will be rare: *R (Tolhurst) v CPS*.[293]

The final general point to note is that the breadth of the new offences means that in cases of consensual sexual activity between 12-year-olds they will both commit an offence – for example, as penetrator (s 5) and penetrated (s 9). In this context, the drafting undermines the principle in *Tyrrell*[294] whereby a child 'victim' could not be convicted as a participant in the offence.

The degree of overlap of ss 9 to 10 and s 13 with ss 5 to 8 is notable. For example, a person guilty of s 5 could be guilty of s 9 or s 13 also ('touching' including penetration). The sections have considerable sentencing discrepancy – s 5 is a maximum of life, s 9 (over 18s) maximum 14 years, s 13 (under 18s) maximum five years on indictment/six months if summary.

In relation to an adult defendant committing offences under ss 5 to 8, the CPS guidance[295] is that 'a prosecution will usually take place unless there are public interest factors tending against prosecution which clearly outweigh those tending in favour'. The CPS emphasizes that the 'overriding public concern is to protect children. It was not Parliament's intention to punish children unnecessarily or for the criminal law to intervene where it is wholly inappropriate'. The CPS view is that the 2003 Act does 'not change the principles or the decision-making process in deciding whether or not to prosecute youths for sexual offences'.[296] Prosecutors are to have regard to various factors including the age and understanding of the offender, her willingness, her emotional and physical development, the nature of the acts. This may include whether the offender has been subjected to any exploitation, coercion,

---

[288] Lord Hoffman opined that 'This case is another example of the regrettable tendency to try to convert the whole system of criminal justice into questions of human rights'[10]. Lord Hoffman went as far as to suggest that Convention rights have nothing to do with prosecutorial policy. This was denied by Lord Hope [34]. See the discussion by R Buxton 'Private Life and the English Judges' (2009) 29 OJLS 413.

[289] [54].

[290] [60].

[291] [2007] EWHC 1842 (Admin).

[292] [2006] EWHC 2231 (Admin).

[293] [2008] EWHC 2976 (Admin).

[294] [1894] 1 QB 710. For a catalogue of the circumstances in which the Act ignores the *Tyrrell* principle, see M Bohlander, 'The Sexual Offences Act 2003 and the *Tyrrell* Principle Criminalising Victims' [2005] Crim LR 703.

[295] See www.cps.gov.uk/legal/s_to_u/sexual_offences_act/index.html#Sexual_key_points.

[296] The Guidance emphasizes the need to gather as much information as possible from sources, such as the police, and any professionals assisting those agencies about the defendant's home circumstances and the circumstances surrounding the alleged offence, as well as any information known about the victim. See www.cps.gov.uk/legal/s_to_u/sexual_offences_act.

threat, deception, grooming or manipulation by another which has led him or her to commit the offence. The relative ages of the parties are also important.[297]

It is recognized that 'it is *not* in the public interest to prosecute children who are of the same or similar age and understanding that engage in sexual activity, where the activity is truly consensual for both parties and there are no aggravating features, such as coercion or corruption'. The abolition of the *doli incapax* defence renders the position more strict for young children.[298]

18.4.1 Rape of a child under 13: s 5

There had been much discussion of the merits of a 'statutory rape' offence, commonly found in the USA, and s 5 introduces one: a person commits an offence if he intentionally penetrates the vagina, anus or mouth of another person with his penis, and the other person is under 13.

As noted above, the Sexual Offences Review was anxious for the offence of rape to continue to reflect everyday conceptions of that term, hence the requirement of penile penetration. In this instance, the unique stigma of 'rape' has been applied to conduct which seems to be lacking the most important aspect of the everyday conception of the offence – an absence of consent. The maximum sentence is one of life imprisonment.[299] Given that it is rape, it will be more difficult for the CPS to declare that it is not in the public interest to prosecute, particularly in the face of pressure from the complainant's parents.[300]

18.4.1.1 *Actus reus*

Each element of the *actus reus* – penetration, with a penis, of the vagina, anus or mouth – has already been discussed in the section on rape. The additional element of the *actus reus* is that B is aged under 13. Given the significance of B's age, it is crucial that this element is proved strictly via the usual mechanisms. The defendant may be of any age, although criminal liability as a principal offender arises at the age of 10.[301] It has already been noted that this is a very broad offence: B, aged 12, who willingly performs oral sex on her 12-year-old boyfriend thereby renders him a rapist (and she commits offences under ss 7 and 9). The absence of any requirement of consent means that it is less likely that the complainant will face the ordeal of giving evidence.

18.4.1.2 *Mens rea*

Penetration must be intentional, as discussed above. There is no opportunity for a plea of consent, and thus no plea of mistaken belief as to consent, however reasonable.[302] Similarly there is no scope for a plea of mistake, however reasonable, as to the age of the complainant.

---

[297] In *G* [2008] UKHL 37 Lord Hope concludes that 'The context suggests however that a child under 18 ought not to be prosecuted under section 5 for performing a sexual act with a child under 13 of the kind to which that section applies unless the circumstances are such as to indicate that it plainly was an offence of such gravity that prosecution under section 13 would not be appropriate. It suggests that a child under 18 (and more especially a child as young as 15) should not be prosecuted under section 5 (rape of a child under 13) if the complainer says that he or she consented to sexual intercourse.'[23] (See also Baroness Hale at [48].)

[298] See *JTB* [2009] UKHL 20, and see Ch 12 above.

[299] On the relevance of mistake as to age on sentence, see *A-G's Reference (No 74 of 2007)* [2007] EWCA Crim 2550.

[300] See Mr Malins, HC Standing Committee B, col 107, 11 Sept 2003. In *G* [2008] UKHL 37 Lord Hope noted that 'The creation of an offence of this kind, carrying the stigma and maximum sentence of life as it does, applicable as it is to child defendants places a "heavy responsibility" on the prosecuting authorities, where both parties are of a similar young age, to distinguish the consensual experimentation from the exploitative' [14].

[301] See above, Ch 12 on defences.

[302] See the discussion in Ch 7 above.

In G,[303] G, who was aged 15, pleaded guilty to rape of a child under 13, where B consented and that he reasonably believed her to be older than 13, because she had so informed him. The House of Lords confirmed that s 5 creates an offence of strict liability; belief in consent or the age of the victim is irrelevant. The presumption of *mens rea* is negatived by necessary implication, arising from the contrast of the express references to reasonable belief that a child was over 16, in other sections – s 9 of the 2003 Act – and the absence of any such reference in relation to children under 13. This was Parliament's 'deliberate choice'.[304] The consequence is, as Lord Hoffman put it:

The policy of the legislation is to protect children. If you have sex with someone who is on any view a child or young person, you take your chance on exactly how old they are.[305]

The House of Lords also confirmed that s 5 as a strict liability offence is compatible with Art 6.[306]

18.4.1.3 Defences for secondary liability

Concern was expressed in Parliament as to the potential for such broad offences to criminalize the actions of teachers and health care workers who advise young people about sex education and safe sexual practices in general. For example, there was concern that the doctor who provided contraceptives to the 12-year-old girl to protect her in her consensual sexual acts with her partner would be aiding and abetting her 'rape'. To meet this difficulty, s 14 of the Act provides that there is no liability for aiding and abetting or counselling if the purpose of the actor is to protect the child from sexually transmitted diseases or pregnancy or to protect physical safety or promote emotional well-being, unless the actor's purpose is to gain sexual gratification or to cause or encourage the relevant sexual act.[307]

18.4.2 Assault of a child under 13 by penetration: s 6

It is an offence for a person intentionally to penetrate the vagina or anus of a person under 13 with a part of the body or anything else where that penetration is sexual.

This is an entirely new offence, identical to that in s 2, except that there is no requirement that the complainant is not consenting. Again there is no scope for a plea of mistaken belief in consent or mistaken reasonable beliefs as to the age of the victim. This is a very broad offence which criminalizes consensual sexual (for example, digital) penetration between 12-year-olds. As with the offence under s 5, there is no liability for aiding and abetting or counselling if the purpose of the assistance is to protect the child unless the actor's purpose is to gain sexual gratification or to cause or encourage the relevant sexual act.[308] Section 6 is triable on indictment only and carries a maximum sentence of life imprisonment.

18.4.3 Sexual assault of a child: s 7

It is an offence intentionally to touch a person under 13, where that touching is sexual. This new offence is identical to that in s 3 (above), except that there is no requirement that the complainant is not consenting. There is no scope for a plea of mistaken belief in consent or mistaken reasonable belief as to the age of the victim. This is an excessively broad offence which

---

[303] [2006] EWCA Crim 821, [2006] Crim LR 930,
[304] Lord Hope at [21]
[305] [3]. (See also Baroness Hale at [45-48]
[306] Art 6 is concerned with procedural protection not the substantive law. (See Lord Hoffman at and Lord Hope at [27]). See above Ch 7.
[307] Section 73.
[308] Section 73.

criminalizes consensual kissing between 12-year-olds.[309] It also applies, of course, where the adult offender preys on children.[310] The defence applicable to abetting or counselling applies as under ss 5 and 6.[311]

18.4.4 Causing or inciting a child under 13 to engage in sexual activity: s 8

It is an offence intentionally to cause a person under 13 to engage in an activity, which is sexual. It is also an offence intentionally to incite a person under 13 to engage in a sexual activity. These are entirely new offences, broader than the offence under s 4 above. Separate offences carrying a maximum of life imprisonment (rather than the standard 14 years on indictment/ six months summarily) are created under s 4(4) if the activity involves causing or inciting:

(a) penetration of B's anus or vagina,

(b) penetration of B's mouth with a person's penis,

(c) penetration of a person's anus or vagina by B, or

(d) penetration of a person's mouth with B's penis.

18.4.4.1 *Actus reus*

The offence can be committed by *causing* B to engage in sexual activity, in which case it is identical to that under s 4 above except that there is no requirement that B is not consenting. A, who persuades his 12-year-old girlfriend to touch herself sexually, commits the *actus reus* of this offence.

In addition, there is an offence of 'incitement' of B. It is submitted that the word incitement should carry its technical legal meaning.[312] The inclusion of a specific offence of incitement enables a prosecution where the child incited would not herself commit an offence (and would not be liable under a common law charge of incitement). This offence is much broader and does not require that any sexual activity occurs. It covers the case where A, the friend of B, aged 12, encourages B to have oral sex with B's boyfriend C. The Court of Appeal has taken a very wide interpretation of s 8 and of the concept of incitement in this context. In *Walker*,[313] the Court of Appeal rightly held that s 8 created two offences: (i) intentionally causing and (ii) intentionally inciting a child under 13 to engage in sexual activity. The allegation was centred on the concept of incitement and the court held that it was not a necessary ingredient for incitement of sexual activity that A had intended that sexual activity would take place. So, when A said over the phone to a child he was watching in a nearby public telephone booth, 'show us your fanny' there was no need for proof that he ever intended her to do anything sexual. But, how can there ever be an incitement without intention from A that the act by B will occur?

The Court of Appeal took an equally broad interpretation of the offence in *Jones*. The defendant wrote graffiti on train and station toilets seeking girls aged eight to 13 for sex in return for payment. He gave a mobile telephone number for them to contact. Following a complaint by a journalist, the police began an undercover operation using an officer pretending to be aged 12. The defendant was charged, with attempting to incite her to sexual activity.

---

[309] Section 7 is triable either way. The maximum sentence is 14 years on indictment; six months summarily.

[310] See, for an unusual example, *PE* [2007] EWCA Crim 231 where A, a scout leader, tied up young boys – clothed – and video recorded the incidents. A derived sexual gratification from the acts.

[311] Section 73.

[312] See Ch 13 above.

[313] [2006] EWCA Crim 1907. See now *Grout* [2011] EWCA Crim 299.

At trial the defendant alleged that the charge disclosed no offence known to law, because the defendant did not intend to incite any actual person under the age of 13 (the officer being older) and therefore could not have had the requisite intent. He was convicted. The Court of Appeal held that s 8 of the 2003 Act did not require incitement of an identified or identifiable child.[314] The criminality at which the offence was directed was the incitement. It mattered not that this was directed at a particular child, a very large group of children or whether they could be identified or not. There was no significance in the use of the term 'another' in s 8 as opposed to 'any other'; they meant the same. Therefore, the offence could have been charged without identifying a particular person, and it could not be said that the police created the offence. A who leaves messages on a children's website or scribbled on the walls of a children's play area inciting sex commits the s 8 offence. Whilst this may seem like a desirable result in terms of protection of under-13s, it presents problems. If it is unnecessary for A to be targeting the message at a particular individual, whenever A sends a message *capable* of being read by under-13s, the charges can now be brought under s 8. In other words, unless A targets a child over 13, he will always be at risk of prosecution for the more serious s 8 offence. What of A who leaves a message on a blog: 'sex is great: I recommend trying it with your first girlfriend/boyfriend'? This might have been intended only for consumption by older children, but, assuming it amounts to a sufficient encouragement to constitute incitement, it is now caught by s 8. Following *G,* liability is strict. The charge under s 10 below allows A an excuse if he has a reasonable belief that the person is over-16 (unless V is under-13). In cases of untargeted messages such as the blog example above, D will be denied the opportunity to rely on that excuse because he cannot know by whom his message will be read.

The offence is used where A incites B to have sex with him.[315] Unlike ss 5 to 7, there is no defence for 'abetting or counselling' to protect the child.[316] Thus, teacher, A, approached by B, 12, who asks whether she should engage in full sex with her boyfriend X as he would like, commits the offence if he, A, incites her by suggesting that since she and X are only 12 they should stick to other intimate activities short of sex (even perhaps just kissing). The offence applies where A causes or incites sexual activity abroad (see below p 777).[317]

18.5 Sexual offences against children aged 13 to 16

The legal age of consent remains at 16.[318] Under the old law the protection afforded to children under 16 years included specific offences[319] which had been incrementally amended and lacked coherence.

The 2003 Act creates a series of specific offences targeting a wider range of sexual activity with children under 16. These reflect the Act's policy of protecting children from sexual exploitation.

[314] The defendant's acts were more than merely preparatory and done with the intention of committing the offence. The fact that commission of the actual offence was on the true facts impossible because the police substituted an adult for a child did not mean that there was a defence in law to the charge. That is uncontroversial.

[315] eg *A* [2006] EWCA Crim 2103; *Hinton-Smith* [2005] EWCA Crim 2575, or even to cause V to show her bra strap: *Grout* [2011] EWCA Crim 299.

[316] Section 73.

[317] See, eg, *Charnley* [2010] All ER (D) 127 (Jun) A had used the internet to procure and watch the rape of children in the Philippines.

[318] *Setting the Boundaries,* recommended that age of consent remain at 16 – para 3.5.7 (recommendation no 17); the age of consent is lower in most other European countries – para 3.9.9.

[319] Unlawful sexual intercourse with a girl under 16 (s 6); buggery of a person under 16 (s 12); indecent assault against boys and girls under 16 irrespective of their consent (ss 14 and 15) and offences under the Indecency with Children Act 1960.

There is no time limit on prosecution as there was under some of the 1956 Act offences, which reflects the growing awareness of frequent delays in disclosing childhood sexual abuse.[320]

Widespread public concern that the Act criminalized consensual sexual activity between children produced only Ministerial assurances that the use of these offences in prosecuting children will be limited:

The creation of such broad ranging offences raises a number of difficulties. There are no convictions at present [for kissing]. The guidelines [for the CPS] will be strong and I do not think that there will be prosecutions in the future for less serious consensual activity between children.[321]

Parliament expressly rejected the approach in other jurisdictions whereby liability for consensual sexual activity with those under 16 would be criminal only where one of the parties was older than the other by a specified amount – for example, two years as in Canada.[322] One of the principal reasons for rejection was the recognition that many offences against children are committed by children.[323] As noted challenges under Art 8 of the ECHR were mounted by consenting 15-year-olds.[324]

18.5.1 Sexual activity with a child: s 9

It is an offence intentionally to touch a person, B, where that touching is sexual and either:

(1) B is under 16 and A does not reasonably believe that B is 16 or over, or

(2) B is under 13.

The offence under s 9 can be committed by a person aged 18 or over. The maximum sentence is 14 years' imprisonment. Sexual touching in these circumstances committed by offenders below 18 is criminalized in identical terms by s 13.[325]

A separate offence[326] is created by subs (2) where the touching involves penetration (a) penetration of B's anus or vagina, (b) penetration of B's mouth with a person's penis, (c) penetration of a person's anus or vagina by B, or (d) penetration of a person's mouth with B's penis. This offence carries a maximum penalty of 14 years' imprisonment and is triable on indictment only.

18.5.1.1 *Actus reus*

The elements of 'touching' and 'sexual' are discussed above. There is no requirement that B is not consenting. A, 18, kissing/touching his consenting 15-year-old girlfriend is guilty if his conduct is 'sexual touching' which is to be decided by the jury. Passionate embracing and kissing suffices.[327] The offence can of course be by women on young boys.[328]

18.5.1.2 *Mens rea*

The touching must be intentional as discussed above in relation to s 3. If B is under 13 there is no other element of *mens rea*. A's pleas of honest (and reasonable) beliefs in consent or age are

---

[320] See the problems created by *J* [2004] UKHL 42; *Cottrell* [2007] EWCA Crim 2016 and *K* [2009] EWCA Crim 2117.

[321] See Paul Goggins, HC, col 622, 3 Nov 2003.

[322] Criminal Code 1985, s 150.1.

[323] E Lovell, *Children and Young People who Display Sexually Harmful Behaviour* (2002) NSPCC.

[324] See *G* [2008] UKHL 37 above. cf the view in *E v DPP* [2005] EWHC 147 (Admin), in which it was held that Art 8 was not infringed by s 6 of the 2003 Act.

[325] The sentence is one of six months' imprisonment summarily, five years on indictment: s 13.

[326] See above.

[327] *Lister* [2005] EWCA Crim 1903.

[328] See *Angela C* [2006] EWCA Crim 1781 (43-year-old having sex with 14-year-old boyfriend of her daughter) in which numerous cases of this nature are reviewed.

irrelevant. Liability is strict.[329] If B is aged between 13 and 16, A must also be proved not to have had a reasonable belief that B was aged over 16. This is a more generous defence than the 'young man's defence' under the 1956 Act which was limited to cases where D faced his first charge of this nature and was under 24.[330] Beliefs in consent remain irrelevant in such a case.

18.5.1.3 Defences

As with ss 5 to 8 above, the defence under s 73 applies to aiding and abetting or counselling for the child's protection. A marriage defence was deleted in the final stages of the Bill.

18.5.2 Causing or inciting a child to engage in sexual activity: s 10

It is an offence intentionally and an offence to cause or to incite a person under 16, B, to engage in a sexual activity, if either – B is under 16 and A does not reasonably believe that B is 16 or over, or B is under 13.[331]

A separate offence is created by s 10(2) for penetrative touching (as in s 9 above). That offence carries a maximum penalty of 14 years and is triable on indictment only. These offences can be committed by a person under the age of 18, in which case the sentence is one of six months summarily, five years on indictment: s 13. These are extremely broad offences, technically capable of criminalizing much schoolyard banter. Section 10 is commonly used to prosecute the sender of explicit text messages by mobile phone.[332] It has also proved useful as an offence supporting that of 'grooming' under s 15.[333]

18.5.2.1 *Actus reus*

There are two offences: an act 'causing' B to engage, and any conduct 'inciting' B to engage in the activity. The relevant elements are discussed above in relation to s 8. The offences are very broad. A, 18, who begs his 15-year-old girlfriend to strip for him commits an offence whether she declines or willingly assents. Examples of inciting sexual activity might include the conduct in *DPP v B* where the defendant invited the girl to give him 'a shiner' (perform oral sex on him). It includes A causing/inciting B to engage in sexual activity with a third party. Following the decision in *Walker* (above), incitement is construed so broadly as to include circumstances in which A has no intention that the act will be carried out. Following *Jones*, where A has not targeted a specific child or age range, it will always be possible to prosecute him for the more serious offence under s 8.

The breadth of the *actus reus* in terms of causing or inciting leaves no room for the application of the defence under s 73.

18.5.2.2 *Mens rea*

A must 'intend' to cause or incite. It is submitted that in this context intention extends to oblique intention. There is no scope for a plea of consent. If B is under 13 there is no other element of *mens rea*. A's pleas of honest (and reasonable) beliefs in consent or age are irrelevant. Liability is strict. If B is aged between 13 and 16, A must also be proved not to have had a reasonable belief that B was aged over 16. Beliefs in consent remain irrelevant in such a case.

---

[329] This represents a direct reversal of the House of Lords' decisions in *DPP v B* [2000] AC 428 and *K* [2002] 1 AC 462.

[330] See *Kirk and Russell* [2002] EWCA Crim 1580.

[331] See the unusual case of *B (Piara)* [2010] EWCA Crim 315 where a Bangladeshi-born mother who spoke no English arranged a 'marriage' by custom (but not recognized in law) between her 15-year-old and a man in his late thirties who abused her sexually. The mother claimed not to know about the age of consent in England.

[332] See, eg, *Howell* [2007] EWCA Crim 1863.

[333] See A Gillespie, 'Indecent Images, Grooming and the Law' [2006] Crim LR 412.

18.5.3 Engaging in sexual activity in the presence of a child: s 11

It is an offence intentionally to engage in sexual activity, when a person under 16, B, is present or is in a place from which A can be observed, where for the purpose of obtaining sexual gratification A engages in it knowing or believing that B is aware, or intending that B should be aware that he is engaging in it, and either B is under 16 and A does not reasonably believe that B is 16 or over, or B is under 13.[334]

This is another entirely novel offence. It will cover much of the activity that might previously have been charged as gross indecency. It is triable either way. The maximum sentence is 10 years' imprisonment on indictment/six months summarily. The offence can also be committed by a person under 18, for which the sentence is one of six months summarily, five years on indictment: s 13.

18.5.3.1 *Actus reus*

A must engage in a sexual[335] activity. B's position is far from clear. There is no requirement that B is actually witnessing the act, merely that B is present or in a position from which A can be observed. Since observation includes viewing directly or viewing an image,[336] the offence can be committed via a web-cam. To that extent it is unclear what degree of physical proximity B must have to A. There is also no guidance as to whether the observation has to be in real time. There is no requirement that B is aware of the sexual activity, but B must actually be under 16; an undercover officer witnessing the event will not suffice. B's consent to being present or witnessing the events is irrelevant.

The offence is directed primarily at the defendant who masturbates in front of a child but it has the potential to criminalize a much wider range of conduct. Sexual thrill seekers ('doggers' as they are called) who have sex in public places might commit the offence by having sex in a park visible from the nearby children's play area.[337]

18.5.3.2 *Mens rea*

There are four elements of *mens rea*: (i) A must intentionally engage in the sexual activity; (ii) A must have as his 'purpose' (which is presumably narrower than his intention and is restricted to 'direct' intention[338]) to derive sexual[339] gratification from B's presence. It remains unclear whether A's *sole* purpose must be to derive sexual pleasure from B's watching? A and C will not commit the offence if their child, B, walks in on their sexual activity in the parental bedroom; (iii) A must 'know or believe' that B is aware or 'intend' that B should be aware of the activity; (iv) In the case of B being between 13 and 16, A must be shown not to have had a reasonable belief that B is 16 or over.

18.5.4 Causing a child to watch a sexual act: s 12

It is an offence intentionally to cause another person under 16, B, to watch a third person engaging in an activity, or to look at an image of any person engaging in a sexual activity, where

---

[334] See, eg, *Chevron* [2005] All ER (D) 91 (Feb), masturbating in sight of 12-year-old on beach.

[335] As defined in s 78 and discussed above, p 736.

[336] Section 79(4) and (5).

[337] See also the case of *WT* [2005] EWCA Crim 2448. Husband and wife convicted of taking photos of 14-year-old daughter naked and of having their 9-year-old daughter photograph them in acts of intercourse and in posed lewd positions.

[338] And renders the offence one of specific intent: *Heard* [2007] EWCA Crim 125

[339] Section 78 (above).

A acts for the purpose of obtaining sexual gratification, and is aware that B is under 16 and does not reasonably believe that B is 16 or over, or B is under 13.

This offence was included to supplement that in relation to grooming below. Research suggests that paedophiles often diminish the sexual inhibitions of children by exposing them to explicit pornography to facilitate subsequent sexual acts. The offence under s 12 is wider than that under s 11 because the activity/image B is watching is not restricted to one involving A. It is a very wide offence: A aged 18 who shows his willing 15-year-old girlfriend a pornographic film for their mutual sexual enjoyment commits the offence. The obvious cases of application will be where an adult gets a child to watch sexual DVDs, etc. It will apply to causing a child to read explicit text messages.[340]

The offence is triable either way and carries a maximum 10-year sentence on indictment. By s 13 it can be committed by a child under the age of 18, in which case the maximum sentence is five years' imprisonment.

18.5.4.1 *Actus reus*

A must cause B to watch the activity/image. Ordinary principles of causation apply here as elsewhere. Omitting to prevent B from watching the activity/image will not ground liability, as where a parent A turns a blind eye to B watching a pornographic film. In such a case A would also lack the *mens rea* of acting for the purpose of sexual gratification. 'Image' is widely defined to include moving or still images however produced and 3D images.[341] The broadest definition possible was created to include, for example, cartoons and 'etchings' as well as video and computer generated pseudo-images. The image must be sexual as defined in s 78. B must watch the activity or image. This involves using the visual sense. It must be proved that B was under 16, again, an undercover officer being caused to watch an act will not suffice.

In *Abdullahi*,[342] the Court of Appeal held that the act must be done 'for the purpose of obtaining sexual gratification' – but the gratification need not be contemporaneous; so A is guilty if his act is done in order to 'groom' a child with a view to sexual activity later. A caused the 13-year-old complainant, whom he plied with drink and drugs, to watch a pornographic film depicting heterosexual and homosexual sexual activity. Subsequently, in his room, A touched B's penis. A was charged with offences under the SOA 2003, ss 12 and 14. It was sufficient that A showed the images for the purpose of obtaining sexual gratification, either by enjoying seeing the complainant looking at the images or with a view to engaging in sexual activity with B later.

18.5.4.2 *Mens rea*

The elements of *mens rea* are that A must (i) intend to cause B to watch, (ii) act for the 'purpose' of sexual gratification. As in s 11 'purpose' is to be narrowly construed. If A has a dual purpose, for example, to explain sexual matters to B, but also to derive some sexual gratification from the activity, it is submitted that A commits the offence.

Although there is no explicit element of *mens rea* in relation to the 'sexual' nature of the activity in s 12(1)(b), the courts might imply a requirement of knowledge. This could create problems. Since what is 'sexual' is to be defined retrospectively by the jury, A might claim that he did not realize it was sexual when he caused B to watch the image. In particular this argument might be advanced when the images are regarded as 'art'.

---

[340] *L* [2006] EWCA Crim 2225 where images of the offender masturbating were sent by phone to B.
[341] Section 79(4).
[342] [2006] EWCA Crim 2060.

18.5.5 Arranging or facilitating commission of a child sex offence: s 14

It is an offence for A intentionally to arrange or facilitate something that A intends to do, intends another person to do, or believes that another person will do, in any part of the world, and doing it will involve the commission of an offence under any of ss 9 to 13 (above).

This is a controversial 'sweeper' provision. It is a form of inchoate offence and can be committed in a number of ways. Its breadth in the original Bill caused consternation among youth and health care workers (and teenage magazine advice columnists) anxious that by giving legitimate advice to teenagers about safe sexual practices they would expose themselves to prosecution. As a result, the offence is markedly narrower than its original draft.

18.5.5.1 *Actus reus*

The element of 'arranging' is not defined. The Home Office provides as an example the case where A approaches an agency and requests a 15-year-old girl for sex.[343] In *R*[344] A asked an adult prostitute whether she knew of any young girls, aged 12 or 13, who were working as prostitutes. She said that she did not. D then sent text messages to her asking whether she had, 'got the 12-year-old sorted yet?' The prostitute reported the matter to the police and D was prosecuted under s 14. The trial judge ruled that there was no conduct amounting to that offence or an attempt to commit it. The Crown appealed. The Court of Appeal reversed the trial judge's decision. The court held that s 14 does not require any 'agreement'.[345] D asked the prostitute to arrange things for him, but she did not so and therefore D could not be said to have done more than attempt to commit the s 14 offence. On the facts there was a possible attempt. Whether D's acts went beyond mere preparation for the purposes of an attempt would be a question of fact for the jury. Moses LJ suggested that:

The section does not require an agreement or arrangement. It does not require the consent or acquiescence of anyone else. An arrangement may be made without the agreement or acquiescence of anyone else. A defendant may take steps by way of a plan with the criminal objective identified in the section without involving anyone else and the mere fact that no-one else is involved would not necessarily mean that no arrangement was made. In those circumstances, we reject the submission...that, absent any agreement, formal or informal, there can be no arrangement.

Section 14 was acknowledged to be wider than attempt because it does not require proof of any act that is 'more than merely preparatory' to one of the relevant child sex offences. The section 'does not limit the stage at which criminal liability is imposed to what would hitherto be regarded as an attempt; in other words, to a proximate stage before the commission of the full offence. The section widens liability to steps taken with the requisite criminal intent by way of preparation.'

The case went back for trial and R was convicted. He appealed successfully on the basis that the judge had this time directed in such a way that the jury were bound to convict.[346] On a retrial he was convicted and appealed again seeking to distinguish the two earlier appeal decisions, in his own case. In this third appeal the Court of Appeal held that the agreement was not necessary for the offence of arrangement to be concluded.[347]

---

[343] See, eg, *Jordan* [2006] EWCA Crim 3311 where A asked a prostitute to get him an under-age girl. See also *R* (2008) EWCA Crim, 16 Jan, unreported.

[344] [2008] EWCA Crim 619.

[345] Since R's request had not been acted on by the prostitute it seems difficult to regard his conduct as amounting to 'arranging or facilitating' any ulterior offence.

[346] [2008] EWCA Crim 2912.

[347] [2009] EWCA Crim 1472. See A Gillespie (2009) 73 J Crim L 378.

The offence is extremely broad. A, 18, who agrees with his willing 15-year-old girlfriend to meet later for sex commits the offence. It is particularly wide since it governs arranging or facilitating acts anywhere in the world; it seems that A who arranges to marry B, 14, in her native country in which the age of consent is 14 commits the offence.

'Facilitating' is not defined. It is intended to cover the case where A lets his room to C so that C can have sex with B aged 15. This is also an overbroad offence. It applies also to suppliers of pornography which might be used in ss 11 and 12 offences. A, the father of a 15-year-old girl who would rather she had sex with boyfriend at home than elsewhere, appears to facilitate that action (although he may have a defence under s 14(3)(b) below).

18.5.5.2 *Mens rea*

A must intend the activity. In this context it would seem that oblique intention would be sufficient. However, the offence is limited in the sense that A must intend that an offence under ss 9 to 13 *will* be committed.

18.5.5.3 The exceptions

In view of the overbroad terms of the offence, the statutory exceptions provided in s 14 are extremely important. These provide:

> (2) A person does not commit an offence under this section if –
>
> > (a) he arranges or facilitates something that he believes another person will do, but that he does not intend to do or intend another person to do, and
> >
> > (b) any offence within subs (1)(b) would be an offence against a child for whose protection he acts.
>
> (3) For the purposes of subs (2), a person acts for the protection of a child if he acts for the purpose of –
>
> > (a) protecting the child from sexually transmitted infection,
> >
> > (b) protecting the physical safety of the child,
> >
> > (c) preventing the child from becoming pregnant, or
> >
> > (d) promoting the child's emotional well-being by the giving of advice, and not for the purpose of obtaining sexual gratification or for the purpose of causing or encouraging the activity constituting the offence within subs (1)(b) or the child's participation in it.

These are designed to safeguard the health care worker who provides condoms and sex education and the teacher who advises children under 16 on sexual matters. Although well-intentioned, major ambiguities remain, in particular in defining 'emotional well-being' in s 14(3)(d). The courts will be left to flesh out these issues.

18.5.6 Meeting a child following sexual grooming, etc: s 15

Paedophiles' use of the internet, in particular 'chatrooms' to contact and 'groom' children before meeting them with a view to committing sexual acts has become a widespread problem.[348] Under the old law the principal offences available were those of attempt which required the investigating authorities to wait until confident that the offender had gone beyond acts

---

[348] On the scale of this type of activity see A Gillespie, 'Child Protection on the Internet – Challenges for Criminal Law' (2002) 14 CFLQ 411. The offence was amended by the Criminal Justice and Immigration Act 2008, s 73.

of mere preparation to the substantive sexual offence.[349] This was unsatisfactory since it exposed the child to a risk of harm. In response, the Government created the much publicized grooming offence. The seriousness with which this risk is considered by the Government is evidenced by the maximum sentence of 10 years' imprisonment on indictment/six months summarily. The definition as amended[350] is:

> 15 (1) A person aged 18 or over (A) commits an offence if –
>
>> (a) A has met or communicated with another person (B) on at least two occasions and subsequently –
>>
>>> (i)   A intentionally meets B,
>>>
>>> (ii) A travels with the intention of meeting B in any part of the world or arranges to meet B in any part of the world, or
>>>
>>> (iii) B travels with the intention of meeting A in any part of the world,
>>
>> (b) A intends to do anything to or in respect of B, during or after the meeting mentioned in paragraph (a)(i) to (iii) and in any part of the world, which if done will involve the commission by A of a relevant offence,
>>
>> (c) B is under 16, and
>>
>> (d) A does not reasonably believe that B is 16 or over.
>
> (2) In subsection (1) –
>
>> (a) the reference to A having met or communicated with B is a reference to A having met B in any part of the world or having communicated with B by any means from, to or in any part of the world.

The offence can be committed by an adult where a child under 16 travels to meet the adult or the adult agrees to meet the child, following the two earlier communications and the adult intends to commit a relevant sexual offence during or after the meeting.

In one of the first reported cases under the provision, *Mansfield*,[351] Sir Douglas Brown explained the paternalist nature of the provision: 'The law is there to protect young girls against their own immature sexual experimentation and to punish much older men who take advantage of them.'[352] The offence also protects boys of course.[353] In 2009/10, there were 405 cases prosecuted under the section.[354]

18.5.6.1 *Actus reus*

There must be two communications. There is no restriction on the manner of communication, nor on the period of time between them. It is unclear whether two messages in the course of one dialogue in an internet chatroom will suffice. There is no requirement that the messages are sexual in nature.[355] The offence is headed 'meeting a child *following* sexual grooming etc' but that is rather misleading. The phrase 'sexual grooming', does not appear in the

---

[349] For a comprehensive analysis of the old law and its failings, see A Gillespie, 'Children, Chatrooms and the Law' [2001] Crim LR 435.

[350] By the Criminal Justice and Immigration Act 2008, s 73 and Sch 15.

[351] [2005] EWCA Crim 927.

[352] Endorsed in *Mohammed* [2006] EWCA Crim 1107.

[353] See, eg, *A-G's Reference (No 91 of 2007)* unreported.

[354] See Flatley et al, Crime in England and Wales 2009/10, Findings from the British Crime Survey and police recorded crime (2010), table 2.04.

[355] *Gaviria* [2010] EWCA Crim 1693, citing this para in the last edition with approval.

section.[356] The aim of the section is to penalize those who use relationships to break down children's inhibitions before arranging a meeting with a view to sexual offending. The initial communications need therefore not be sexual. They may well be seemingly innocuous. An offence is committed whether or not a meeting actually takes place. It is enough that having communicated with B twice before, A travels with the intention of meeting B or arranges to meet B or B travels with the intention of meeting A. What is crucial is proving A's intention to engage in a child sex offence on B during or after the meeting.

It is not enough that, during the course of a meeting, started without any such intention, A then decides to take advantage of the situation and commit an offence: the crime then will be the commission of or the attempt to commit that offence. The offence contained within s. 15 is not engaged.[357]

Moreover, there is no clear limit on the period of time between the previous meeting/communication and the planned meeting. This raises the problem at what point must A believe B to be over 16 – in the course of communication or at the time of the proposed meeting? What if B turns 16 in the interim?

Despite its laudable aims, anxieties must be raised by the breadth of the offence. A, 18, writes two love letters to B, 15, arranging to meet at the local disco. A might commit the offence depending on his *mens rea*.[358]

Arguably, however, the offence is too narrow. An elderly man A, who is a paedophile, posts internet messages to B, believing her to be 15. She is X, an undercover woman police officer aged over 16. No substantive offence is committed. A might be liable for an attempt.

18.5.6.2 *Mens rea*

There is a requirement of intention. It is submitted that given the lack of any requirement for manifest wrongdoing in communicating and setting out to meet B, this element should be very strictly construed by the courts. In lobbying Parliament during the passage of the Bill, the offence was likened to a 'thought-crime' because of the absence of any tangible harm.[359]

18.6 Offences of abuse of trust

The Sexual Offences (Amendment) Act 2000[360] created new offences of abuse of a position of trust.[361] The 2003 Act replaced them with four offences where A (aged over 18) in a position of trust to B (under 18): sexually touches B (s 16);[362] causes or incites B to engage in sexual activity (s 17); engages in sexual activity in B's presence for the purpose of sexual gratification (s 18); or causes B to watch a sexual image or activity for the purpose of obtaining sexual gratification.

The most notable feature of the offences is that they criminalize consensual conduct with those under 18. Although 16- to 18-year-olds may consent to sexual activity in other

---

[356] See Rook and Ward, *Sexual Offences Law and Practice*, para 4.137, noting that the government resisted amendments to the Bill to restrict the offence in that way.

[357] *Gaviria* [2010] EWCA Crim 1683 per Leveson LJ at [17].

[358] ie if he hopes that the evening may involve sexual conduct with B, he commits the offence when he travels to the disco.

[359] See Liberty and Criminal Bar Association responses to the Government's White Paper, *Protecting the Public*.

[360] See Burnside [2001] Crim LR 425.

[361] See the 10th edition, at 478.

[362] eg a teacher's kiss to a 6th former at the leavers' ball: *Lamb* [2007] EWCA Crim 1766; *Wootton* [2005] EWCA Crim 2137, teacher engaged in sex with 15- and 16-year-olds; *Wilson* [2007] EWCA Crim 2762.

circumstances, they cannot do so with those who regularly 'look after' them.[363] This reflects the Act's theme of preventing exploitation. The category of those in positions of trust is widely defined and includes, for example, pupils and students, but is not all embracing; there is no specific inclusion of categories such as clergy and non-professional carers such as scout leaders. Individuals in these positions may fall within the terms of the offence depending on the circumstances of their responsibility for B.

The offences place a burden on A where his position of trust arises in an institutional setting, to present evidence that he did not know nor could he reasonably be expected to know that he was in a position of trust towards B. This may well be a difficult plea to raise unless A and B are in a large institution.

No offence is committed where A has a reasonable belief that B is aged over 18 (unless B is under 13). There is a defence for A to prove that he was lawfully married to B (aged 16+) or that immediately before the position of trust arose there existed a lawful sexual relationship between them. This covers cases where, for example, A and B had a sexual relationship before A became a trainee teacher at B's school.

18.7 Family offences

The 2003 Act creates two sets of offences to deal with offences within the family. In relation to children, ss 25 and 26 criminalize the same forms of activity as ss 9 and 12 (above): sexual touching and causing a child to engage in sexual activity. These are welcome extensions, protecting vulnerable individuals against acts other than sexual intercourse. Sections 25 and 26 differ from ss 9 and 12 in two important respects: B must be under 18 and A must be a family member. Family membership is defined in very broad terms in the Act (and has been further extended by the Criminal Justice and Immigration Act 2008, Sch 15), extending well beyond blood relationships to reflect the diverse structures of modern families. It protects, for example, the step-child,[364] foster child,[365] and adopted child.[366] Family members, include adoptive relationships,[367] wider family members who live, or have lived, in the same household as the child or who are, or have been, regularly involved in caring for, training or supervising or being in sole charge of the child[368] and others who are living in the same household as the child and who hold a position of trust or authority in relation to the child at the time of the alleged offence.[369] The breadth of the extended family[370] caught by the Act reflects the shift in emphasis in the legislation from a blood relationship based offence of heterosexual intercourse

---

[363] As defined in ss 21 and 22. The requirement of regularity may be unduly restrictive. Does it catch the supply teacher? Guidance for Care Workers on the SOA 2003 can be found at www.teachernet.gov.uk/_doc/6674/care-workers.pdf.

[364] See, eg, *R (Danny)* [2005] EWCA Crim 1296 where D asked his 12-year-old daughter to allow him to perform oral sex on her.

[365] *Thomas (Robert)* [2005] EWCA Crim 2343.

[366] Criminal Justice and Immigration Act 2008, Sch 15, para 3.

[367] Parents, current or former foster parents, grandparents, brothers, sisters, half-brothers, half-sisters, aunts and uncles.

[368] Step-parents, cousins, stepbrothers and stepsisters, current or former foster siblings.

[369] This offence will not be committed if A has a lawful sexual relationship with the child after the familial relationship has ceased, even where the child is under 18.

[370] This is so wide that it has been argued that sports coaches will be caught: C Brackenridge and Y Williams, 'Incest in the "Family" of Sport' (2004) 154 NLJ 179. See the Safeguarding Vulnerable Groups Act 2006.

(incest)[371] to one based on gender-neutral exploitation of sexual vulnerability in the home environment.

There are defences in s 28 where A is lawfully married to B[372] at the time of engaging in the sexual activity, and under s 29 where A proves that a lawful sexual relationship existed between A and B immediately before the familial relationship arose.[373]

The 2003 Act also creates controversial sexual offences involving consenting adult relatives. Section 64 makes it an offence for A aged 16 or over to intentionally penetrate sexually (anally, vaginally or orally) a relative B who is aged 18 or over if he knows or could reasonably have been expected to know that B is his relative. The converse offence is provided for in s 65: A aged 16 or over commits an offence by consenting to being penetrated sexually by a relative B aged 18 or over if he knows or could reasonably have been expected to know that B is his relative. The concept of a 'relative' is broadly defined.[374] Where the prosecution establishes that A is related to B, A will be taken to have known or to have reasonably been expected to know that they were related in that way unless A raises sufficient evidence as to whether he knew or could reasonably have been expected to know. These are broad, gender-neutral offences. They have been heavily criticized.[375] Both offences are triable summarily or on indictment and have a maximum penalty of two years' imprisonment. Together ss 64 and 65 make both parties to sexual activity guilty, so who is the law trying to protect? Will this be found to be compatible with Art 8 of the ECHR for consenting adults?

18.8 Offences involving mental disorder

The Act provides three specific groups of offences to protect those with a mental disorder. In each category the types of behaviour criminalized are roughly the same as those in relation to children. In short the activities prohibited are:

- sexual touching of B;
- causing or inciting sexual activity by B;
- engaging in sexual activity in B's presence;
- causing B to watch sexual activity.

In the offences dealing with children, the Act has decreed that it is sufficient to prove that one of these activities is intentionally performed; liability as to the factor of vulnerability, ie age,

---

[371] Founded historically in part at least on eugenics arguments: V Bailey and S Blackburn, 'The Punishment of Incest Act 1908: A Case Study in Law Creation' [1979] Crim LR 708; S Wolfram, 'Eugenics and the Punishment of Incest Act 1908' [1983] Crim LR 308; J Temkin, 'Do We Need a Crime of Incest?' (1988) 44 CLP 185.

[372] Note the amended definition in the Civil Partnerships Act 2004.

[373] eg two 16-year-olds are in a sexual relationship and the girl's father and boy's mother subsequently marry. As amended by the Criminal Justice and Immigration Act 2008, Sch 15, para 4.

[374] Parent, grandparent, child, grandchild, brother, sister, half-brother, half-sister; and blood relationships of uncle, aunt, nephew or niece. Criminal Justice and Immigration Act 2008, Sch 15, adopted child/parent relationships are caught where A is over 18. The Human Fertilisation and Embryology (Parental Orders) Regulations 2010 (SI 2010 No 985), amended the Sexual Offences Act ss 64 and 65 so that references to an adoptive relationship include references to the comparable relationship under a parental order.

[375] See Spencer [2004] Crim LR 347 who doubts that they could ever be properly used. But what of the situation where, eg, X aged 17 penetrates his 19-year-old sister, Y, having secured her agreement with a threat which is not sufficient to vitiate consent under s 74. This constitutes an offence under s 64, but not any other serious offence, and it may well be proper to prosecute it. X commits the s 64 offence (X being over 16 and Y being over 18), but not the child offences (Y is over 16), nor the family offences (Y being over 18).

is strict. Applying strict liability would be too harsh in the present context[376] since there may not necessarily be physical signs that the adult complainant is a vulnerable person. Thus, only when these activities arise in an exploitative context are they criminalized. The three prohibited contexts for such activity are:

- sections 30 to 33 where B is mentally disordered and *'unable to refuse'*;[377]
- sections 34 to 37 where B is mentally disordered and the activity is caused by *'threats or deception or inducement'* which need not vitiate consent under s 74;
- sections 38 to 41 where B is mentally disordered and A is *'in a relationship as a carer'*.[378]

There are numerous welcome improvements in the 2003 Act scheme. Creating specific offences produces much fairer labelling – defendants are convicted of offences that better describe their actions. The language has been modernized, and gender specificity has been removed. This is not mere window dressing: for example, one result is that mentally disordered men are protected against heterosexual abuse. The offensive terminology of the 1956 Act was replaced by the appropriate (but technical) language of the Mental Health Acts. The Mental Health Act 2007 adopts broader definitions and produces yet wider offences. Mental disorder under the 2007 Act means any disability or disorder of the mind and will include conditions such as autism and bipolar.

As elsewhere in the Act, there is tremendous prolixity. Many of the definitions are complex and their interrelationship with other provisions in the Act exacerbates this problem. For example, the relationship between the s 30 offence of sexual touching with a person with mental disorder impeding the ability to refuse and the general offence of non-consensual sexual touching in s 3 is confusing. Thus, s 30(2) provides:

B is unable to refuse if:

(a) he lacks the capacity to choose whether to agree to the [activity] (whether because he lacks sufficient understanding of the nature or reasonably foreseeable consequences of what is being done, or for any other reason), or

(b) he is unable to communicate such a choice to A.

The definition of 'inability to refuse' includes cases where B lacks capacity: in such cases there is clearly no consent.[379] Inability to refuse includes, in the alternative, an inability to communicate a choice to this defendant. The House of Lords confirmed that s 30(2)(b) did not require that a complainant was physically unable to communicate by reason of her mental disorder. There is considerable overlap with the offences under ss 1–4.

It is arguable that too much discretion lies in the hands of the CPS who will face an especially difficult task in deciding whether to prosecute in cases where, for example, A and B are both mentally disordered, or where a carer claims that the actions were performed for the appropriate sex education of an individual with learning disability. In many instances it will

---

[376] *Setting the Boundaries*, para 4.6.4.

[377] In *Hulme v DPP* [2006] EWHC 1347 (Admin), the DC considered the offence under s 30, concluding that on the facts a magistrates' court was entitled to reach the decision that a woman suffering from a mental disorder was unable to refuse to be touched sexually. The defendant, a 73-year-old had touched the complainant, a cerebral palsy sufferer with a low mental age (aged 27). B was unable to refuse because she did not know what to say or how to say it. She was physically capable of speaking, but was too confused and scared to do so. This was held to be an inability to refuse. The conviction was upheld despite the magistrates having been incorrectly advised as to the interpretation of s 30.

[378] This is broadly construed as where B was suffering from post-natal depression and was in a vulnerable state when her social worker had sexual intercourse with her: *Bradford* [2006] EWCA 2495.

[379] See *C* [2009] UKHL 42.

still be necessary to determine the capacity of the complainant and this will involve her giving evidence – albeit under the Youth Justice and Criminal Evidence Act 1999 regime.

Symbolically it was very important for the Act to criminalize exploitative behaviour, but the message is confused when it overcriminalizes and potentially inhibits the appropriate sexual behaviour of those with a learning disability.[380]

Note that the offences involving mental incapacity do not have to be charged where the complainant has such a disability. It is possible to rely on the straightforward non-consensual offences of rape, penetration, etc.[381]

18.9 Other sexual offences

18.9.1 Prostitution and pornography

The Act provides specific protection against the sexual exploitation of children in pornography and prostitution. Section 47 provides an offence of paying (as widely defined) for the sexual services of a child and s 48 provides wider supporting offences of causing or inciting child prostitution or pornography, being designed to catch those who recruit vulnerable children into such activities.

Further broadly defined offences provide protection against controlling a child prostitute or a child involved in pornography[382] and arranging or facilitating child prostitution or pornography.[383]

Provisions to deal with adult sexual exploitation are strengthened with a range of offences introduced to deal with causing or inciting[384] or controlling prostitution for gain.[385] The rise in trafficking for prostitution is combated by offences of trafficking into, within and outwith the UK.[386]

18.9.2 Indecent photographs of children[387]

There are offences of taking, making, permitting to take, distributing, showing, possessing with intent to distribute, and advertising indecent photographs or pseudo-photographs of children under 18. There is a defence if the child is aged over 16 and A proves that he and the child were married or living together as partners in an enduring family relationship, that the child consented to the image being taken and that the image shows no one other than B (and A).[388] This is an area of considerable controversy.

---

[380] The *Twelfth Report of the Parliamentary Joint Committee on Human Rights* (2003) (HL 199; HC 765) concluded that the provisions were probably compatible with ECHR obligations under Art 8.

[381] See, eg, *Wragg* [2006] EWCA Crim 2022 (D touched V, who was a cerebral palsy sufferer, in a community home).

[382] Section 49.

[383] Section 50.

[384] Section 52.

[385] Section 53.

[386] Sections 57, 58, 59. See the recent Joint Parliamentary Committee on Human Rights Report on Human Trafficking HL 179 (2007). See also *Shaban Maka* [2005] EWCA Crim 3365 (a guideline sentencing case).

[387] See references above, n 333. On the prevalence of this activity, see B Gallagher, K Christmann, C Fraser and B Hodgson, 'International and Internet Child Sexual Abuse and Exploitation – Issues Emerging from Research' (2003) 15 CFLQ 353.

[388] On the complexity and unsatisfactory nature of the offences, see A Gillespie, 'The Sexual Offences Act 2003: (3) Tinkering With "Child Pornography"' [2004] Crim LR 361.

The strictness of the offences has given rise to concern in some cases, particularly as regards the definition of creation, which can occur by the act of downloading an image to view it on the screen of a computer and then immediately deleting it without consciously saving it. Because of the strictness of liability in relation to age other difficulties arise where D downloads images of teenagers claiming that he was led by the website to believe the models to be older. There are also broader concerns about freedom of expression.[389] Further offences have been enacted in the Criminal Justice and Immigration Act 2008, s 69 these are considered in Chapter 31.

18.9.3 Preliminary offences

18.9.3.1 Administering drugs

The Act introduces three important new preliminary sex offences. Section 61 introduces an offence of intentional administration of a substance/causing it to be taken by B without consent with intent to stupefy/overpower to enable any person to engage in sex with B.[390] This is a further response to the problem of drug assisted rape (see also s 75(2)(f) above).[391] The offence is much wider than that in s 4 of the 1956 Act, being gender-neutral and relating to all sexual activity rather than just sexual intercourse. The offence covers A spiking B's drinks as well as administering drugs such as GHB and Rohypnol. It does not extend to A encouraging B to get drunk so that A could more readily persuade B to have sex.

Section 61 applies where A himself administers the substance to B, and where A causes the substance to be taken by B, by for example persuading C to administer it to B. There is no requirement that the intended sexual activity involve A. It is a preliminary offence in the sense that there is no requirement that B actually is involved in any sexual activity. It is unclear whether those who manufacture or supply the drugs will be liable as aiders and abettors or for offences under s 61.

18.9.3.2 Committing an offence with intent to commit a sexual offence

Section 62 introduces an offence of 'committing an offence with intent to commit a sexual offence'. The offence was designed primarily to tackle cases where A kidnaps B so that he can rape her or assaults B to subdue her.[392] The offence as drafted is much wider: there is no requirement that the preliminary offence is directed at B, the person against whom the substantive sexual offence is committed. A, 18, speeding in his car to B, 15, to have consensual sex with her commits the offence. Stalking under the Protection from Harassment Act 1997 will suffice as the preliminary crime.[393] It will also apply in the more commonplace cases such as those of a physical assault by A in preparation for a sexual assault or rape.[394]

---

[389] See I Cram, 'Criminalising Child Pornography – A Canadian Study in Freedom of Expression and Charter-Led Judicial Review of Legislative Policy Making' (2002) 66 J Crim L 359 on the decision of the Canadian Supreme Court in *R v Sharpe* [2001] 1 SCR 45.

[390] See *Wright* [2006] EWCA Crim 2672; *Spall* [2008] 1 Cr App R (S) 250.

[391] cf the offences of poisoning under ss 23 and 24 of the OAPA 1861. See also *Coomber* [2005] EWCA Crim 1113 (scout leader drugging boys to abuse them when asleep). On the prevalence of intoxicated complainants see M Horvath and J Brown, 'The Role of Drugs and Alcohol in Rape' (2006) 46 Med Sci Law 219 concluding that the complainant's state of intoxication is more significant than the defendant's.

[392] See the first sentencing case on the offence: *Wisniewshi* [2004] EWCA Crim 3361. See recently *Vageesan S* [2008] EWCA Crim 346 (assault prior to rape).

[393] Where the preparatory offence is kidnapping or false imprisonment, the offence is triable on indictment only, and has a maximum penalty of life imprisonment. In all other cases, the offence is triable summarily or on indictment and has a maximum penalty of 10 years on indictment.

[394] See *Seevaratnarajah* [2008] EWCA Crim 346.

At common law it was uncertain whether the offence of assault with intent to rape exists.[395] There is no doubt that an indictment for assault with intent to rape would lie at common law but it is not certain whether it was a specific offence or an example of a wider common law offence of assault with intent to commit a felony. If the latter, it ceased to exist with the abolition of felonies by the Criminal Law Act 1967 and the repeal of the words in s 38 of the OAPA 1861 which provided that assault with intent to commit a felony was punishable with two years' imprisonment. The better view is that there was no general offence of assault with intent to commit a felony at common law, and that assault with intent to rape was, and is, a specific offence which was not abolished by the 1861 Act or by the repeal of the general statutory offence. Most significantly, it was treated by the draftsman of the 1861 legislation, CS Greaves, as continuing to exist after the 1861 Act.[396] Most cases of assault with intent to rape will amount to attempted rape under the Criminal Attempts Act 1981 but there will be instances where the assault is a 'merely preparatory' act.[397] In such cases the most obvious charge is that under s 62.

18.9.3.3 Trespass with intent to commit a sexual offence

The third preliminary offence is that under s 63: 'trespass with intent to commit a sexual offence'. This is committed where A commits a sexual offence whilst he is on any premises as a trespasser, either knowing or being reckless[398] as to whether he is trespassing. A person is a trespasser if he is on any premises without the owner's or occupier's consent, or other lawful excuse. This replaces the offence under the Theft Act 1968, s 9, in relation to burglary with intent to rape. It is clearly wider since it involves any trespass and includes sexual offences beyond rape.[399]

18.9.4 Miscellaneous sexual offences

18.9.4.1 Exposure

Section 66 creates an offence if A intentionally exposes his or her genitals with the intention that another person will see them and be caused alarm or distress. This extends the previous law to include female exposure, although that is a particularly rare phenomenon. It is not necessary that anyone should have seen the genitals or have been caused alarm or distress. In addition to the commonplace incidents of flashing, the offence has been used to tackle the more unusual exposers: see the case of *Bullen*,[400] where D went to a women's dress shop and exposed himself when trying on clothes.[401] There was much controversy over the offence when originally introduced since it was feared that it would criminalize naturism.[402] As finally enacted, the offence would not apply to a naturist unless his exposure is with intention to cause alarm or distress. Similarly, it is unlikely that 'streakers' at sports events will

---

[395] In *J* (Crown Court at Stafford, 9 June 1986), Turner J held that it does exist and in *P* [1990] Crim LR 323, Pill J held that it does not. In *Lionel* (1982) 4 Cr App R (S) 291, an appeal against sentence was dismissed, the assumption that the offence exists not being challenged. See S Spencer, 'Assault with Intent to Rape – Dead or Alive' [1986] Crim LR 110.

[396] CS Greaves (ed), *Russell on Crime* (4th edn, 1865) 927.

[397] Above Ch 11.

[398] This is one of the few offences in the 2003 Act that includes a reckless *mens rea* element.

[399] See, eg, *H* [2007] EWCA Crim 2622. The offence is triable summarily or on indictment and has a maximum penalty of 10 years. See Ch 26 below.

[400] [2006] EWCA Crim 1801.

[401] See also *Whitton* [2006] EWCA Crim 3229 (D masturbating and exposing himself to child pedestrians as he drove).

[402] See eg *Lindsky* [2009] All ER (D) 263 (Nov) where D was convicted having been naked in his own garden.

be prosecuted. For many people, the distress caused is by the disruption to play not by the exposure of genitals.[403]

18.9.4.2 Voyeurism

Section 67 creates an offence, where A, for the purposes of sexual gratification, observes another person doing a 'private act' in the knowledge that the other person does not consent to being observed for that purpose. The offence extends beyond simple peeping toms looking through keyholes.[404] Subsection (2) creates an offence of A 'operating equipment' with the intention of enabling another person, C, for their sexual gratification, to observe B doing a 'private act' in the knowledge that B has not consented to this being done for another person's sexual gratification. This provision was enacted in response to the numerous instances reported in the news of people setting up illicit cameras. In *Vigon v DPP*,[405] surreptitious viewing of customers changing into swimwear in a market stall cubicle was held capable of being 'insulting behaviour' for the purposes of the Public Order Act 1986, s 5.[406] The common law offence of outraging public decency was also prayed in aid when a defendant secretly filmed women urinating in a supermarket toilet. 'Disgusting conduct' was held to be that which fills an onlooker with loathing or extreme distaste or causes the onlooker extreme annoyance: *Choi*.[407] That offence is considered in Chapter 31 below, and it has been put to recent use in relation to conduct including 'up skirting' (filming illicitly up women's skirts).[408]

Similarly, s 67(3) makes it an offence for a person A to record B doing a 'private act' with the intention that A or a third person will, for the purposes of sexual gratification look at the recorded image, when it is known that B does not consent to being recorded for that purpose.[409] Finally, s 67(4) creates an offence for a person to install equipment, or to construct or adapt a structure,[410] with the intention of enabling himself, or another person, to commit an offence under s 67(1).[411]

For each of these offences a 'private act' is defined in s 68 as 'an act done in a place and in circumstances where the person would reasonably expect privacy and either the person's genitals, buttocks or female[412] breasts are exposed or covered only by underwear,[413] or the person is using a lavatory or the person is doing a sexual act that is not of a kind ordinarily done in public'. There is much scope for judicial interpretation.[414]

The leading case is *Bassett*.[415] A was convicted of voyeurism. He used a video camera hidden in a bag in men's changing rooms at a public swimming pool, to film B, a man, who was

---

[403] The offence is triable summarily or on indictment with a maximum penalty of two years' imprisonment.

[404] Or placing mirrors under changing room cubicles: *Sayed* [2009] EWCA Crim 1922.

[405] [1998] Crim LR 289, DC.

[406] It is sufficient that the defendant is aware that his conduct may be insulting, so there is no need to prove that he intended to insult the customer – it is no defence that he concealed the camera.

[407] (1999) 8 Archbold News 3.

[408] See A Gillepsie 'Upskirting and Down-Blouses: Voyeurism and the Law' [2008] Crim LR 370 on whether a voyeurism-based offence such as that in New Zealand should be adopted here.

[409] See the case of *Sippings* [2008] EWCA Crim 46 where D had video-recorded from his kitchen window B, his neighbour's teenage daughter, undressing in her bedroom when she left the curtains open.

[410] 'Structure' includes 'a tent, vehicle or vessel or other temporary or movable structure'.

[411] The offence is triable summarily or on indictment with a maximum penalty of two years' imprisonment.

[412] See *Bassett* [2008] EWCA Crim 1174.

[413] See the NI case of *PSNI v MacRitchie* [2008] NICA 26 holding that a bikini was not underwear when worn by B in a changing cubicle at the local swimming pool. A had sought to video her changing from his cubicle.

[414] See the sentencing cases of *Henderson* [2006] EWCA Crim 198 (filming in public toilets); *Turner* [2006] EWCA Crim 63 (sports centre manager filming changing rooms); *IP* [2004] EWCA Crim 2646 (filming 24-year-old stepdaughter in shower); *McCann* [2006] EWCA Crim 1078 (surveillance camera hidden in neighbour's bathroom).

[415] [2008] EWCA Crim 1174.

in the shower in his trunks. The showers were open to the general view of the changing room. A had 'observed' B for the purpose of obtaining sexual gratification, and B did not consent to that. The judge ruled that B was in a place in circumstances which would reasonably be expected to provide privacy. The Court of Appeal disagreed and allowed the appeal. The case is important in emphasizing the centrality of the privacy expectation element of the offence. A will escape liability even if he observes B in a state of nakedness, derives sexual gratification from doing so and lacks B's consent to being observed for the purpose of sexual gratification *unless* it is also proved that there is a reasonable expectation of privacy. The reason that no offence was committed in *Bassett* is that although it is possible to have a reasonable expectation of privacy without being wholly enclosed, there was no reasonable expectation of privacy in the circumstances. Hughes LJ remarked that it was 'normally inevitable' that users must expect to be observed unclothed by other users of public swimming pools and changing facilities in sports and leisure complexes. It is to be left to the jury to determine if there is reasonable expectation of privacy. In determining whether there is a reasonable expectation of privacy in the circumstances the court suggests that there A's purpose may be relevant, but it is 'the nature of the observation rather than the purpose of the observer which may be relevant to the expectation of privacy'.[416] Presumably then a casual glance at B naked in the communal shower from which A derives a sexual thrill is not enough, but determined ogling might be, *a fortiori* if A starts filming.

It is worth noting the position in relation to consent in such cases. It will not excuse A that B impliedly consented to being viewed in a state of nakedness in a place in which privacy would be expected if B has not consented to being observed *for the purposes of sexual gratification*.[417]

18.9.4.3 Bestiality

Section 69 creates an offence for A intentionally to penetrate the vagina[418] or anus of a living animal with his penis where he knows or is reckless as to whether that is what he is penetrating. It also creates an offence for A intentionally to cause or allow her vagina or his or her anus to be penetrated by the penis of a living animal where he or she knows or is reckless as to whether it is the penis of a live animal that is penetrating him/her. Note also the offences of extreme pornography discussed in Chapter 31.

18.9.4.4 Necrophilia[419]

Section 70 makes it an offence for A intentionally to penetrate sexually[420] any part of the body of a dead person B with A's penis, any other body part or any other object, knowing or being reckless as to whether A is penetrating any part of a dead body. A commits no offence if B dies during intercourse unless A realizes and continues to penetrate B.[421] The penetration must be

---

[416] [11].

[417] *See Sippings* [2008] EWCA Crim 46 in which D pleaded guilty to observing from his kitchen window V (aged 14–19) over a five-year period when she was undressing in her bedroom in a neighbouring house with the lights on and the curtains open. Is there a reasonable expectation of privacy in a room with the lights on and curtains open?

[418] The reference to vagina or anus in this context is further explained at s 79(9) and (10). References to 'vagina' include vulva and in relation to an animal, references to the vagina or anus include references to any similar part.

[419] The offence is triable summarily or on indictment and has a maximum penalty of two years. It could be charged in some extreme cases: eg Mark Dixie who claimed to have performed sex with the corpse of, but not to have killed, his victim: http://news.bbc.co.uk/1/hi/england/london/7254628.stm. He was convicted of murder.

[420] Hence pathology staff will not commit the offence by penetrating the corpse with his finger or instrument for medical purposes.

[421] The offence is triable summarily or on indictment and has a maximum penalty of two years' imprisonment.

sexual but it remains unclear whether D must have any *mens rea* in relation to that element of the *actus reus*. As a matter of principle that would be desirable.

18.9.4.5 Sexual activity in a public lavatory

Section 71 creates an offence for A to engage in sexual activity[422] in a public lavatory.[423] There is no requirement that any person is alarmed or distressed by the activity. This is the only offence in the Act which is triable summarily only.[424] Section 320 of the Criminal Justice Act 2003 has made the common law offence of 'outraging public decency' triable summarily as well as on indictment. The offence under s 71 is wider since there is no need for the act to have shocked, disgusted or revolted a member of the public.

18.10 Overarching problems with the 2003 Act

18.10.1 Undue complexity[425]

In terms of technicality and complexity there are several problems with the Act. First, it takes 80 sections to set out the many new offences, and these often contain numerous subcategories of offence. For example, many involve aggravated versions for penetrative acts, and since these are indictable only and carry a different sentence, following *Courtie*[426] each represents a separate offence. Although it might be argued that it is better to have too many offences than too few in an area dealing with serious matters such as these, it is questionable whether tighter drafting and structure could have achieved adequate protection. This is not just a criticism levelled at the length of the Act; practical problems arise when there are too many charging options.[427] It produces confusion and inhibits optimal development of case law, with no guarantee that similar conduct will be treated consistently by the CPS and by courts. Recognizing the extent of the options available to prosecutors, the CPS guidelines[428] state that:

Prosecutors should choose the most appropriate charge to fit the circumstances of the case, taking account of the courts' sentencing powers. As a general rule, where the circumstances of a case match a particular offence specified in the Act, this offence should be charged, for example s 25 (familial child sex offence) where the victim is 14 should be charged rather than s 9 (sexual activity with a child), so long as all the elements can be proved.

Parliament's decision to create so many offences is especially ironic given that the Sexual Offences Review was described as seeking to 'focus the law more sharply' and 'to abolish the unnecessary and useless offences which have accumulated over the years'.[429]

Secondly, the complexity is also exacerbated by the obsession with detail and with describing the manner in which the offence is committed rather than with the harm caused: whilst this shows commendable respect for the principles of fair labelling and maximum

---

[422] An activity is sexual if a reasonable person would, in all the circumstances but regardless of any person's purpose, consider it to be sexual.

[423] 'Public lavatory' is defined as a lavatory to which the public or a section of the public has or is permitted to have access, whether on payment or otherwise. See C Ashford, 'Sexuality, Public Space and the Criminal Law: The Cottaging Phenomenon' (2007) 71 J Crim L 506.

[424] It carries a maximum penalty of six months' imprisonment or a fine.

[425] See JR Spencer 'The Drafting of Criminal Legislation: Need It Be So Impenetrable?' [2008] CLJ 585.

[426] [1984] AC 463.

[427] See *Grout* [2011] EWCA Crim 299. In some instances, it would appear that the objective in including a new crime is to trigger the availability of possible sexual offender orders under Part 2 of the Act.

[428] See CPS guidance 2010 at www.cps.gov.uk/legal/s_to_u/sexual_offences_act/index.html.

[429] Temkin (2000) 150 NLJ 1169.

certainty, it creates confusion and density[430] in the legislation which renders it less accessible than it ought to be.[431] An example of this detail can be seen in s 67 (voyeurism) – A, for the purpose of obtaining sexual gratification, observes or records or enables another to observe (with equipment or otherwise) B doing a 'private act' knowing B does not consent to observation for that purpose. By s 68 'private acts' are those 'in a private structure in which one would expect privacy and B's genitals, buttocks or breasts are exposed or covered only with underwear, or B is using the lavatory, or B is doing a sexual act not of a kind ordinarily done in public.' This obsession with exhaustive definition is sadly lacking in some of the key definitions of fundamental issues such as 'consent'.

Finally, the number of offences and the minute definition of many elements produce some glaring examples of incoherence. One of the most striking is that although a person can engage in sexual activity at 16, it is still illegal to have a sexual relationship with her/his carer until over 18, or to engage in sexual conduct with certain members of the extended family even though s/he could marry them. Similarly, whilst it is legal for A to have intercourse with B aged 16, consensually taking or possessing her nude photo will not be legal unless A is married to her, or living with her in an enduring family relationship.

18.10.2 Overcriminalization?

In addition to the volume and complexity of the offences, there are many examples of the Act providing what are arguably overbroad offences. One obvious example is s 62 'committing an offence with intent to commit a sexual offence'. This contains no limitation to the types of offence and no requirement that the preliminary offence is directed at the person who will be the victim of the sex offence.[432] The offence has been used diversely to prosecute acts such as committing criminal damage with intent to commit a sexual offence where A wrote graffiti on trains inciting underage girls to text him for sex.[433] Ironically, despite the detail and number of other offences in the Act, this section has proved important in making up for the shortfalls in drafting elsewhere.[434]

A further argument that the Act overcriminalizes can be based on the jurisdictional reach of the offences. As amended by the Criminal Justice and Immigration Act 2008, many of the offences (including ss 1–4, 5–8, 10–19, 25, 26, 30–41) can be prosecuted in England and Wales even if performed abroad if the victim was under 18 and the offender is a UK national or UK resident.[435] In the case of a UK national it is no defence that the conduct was not criminal in the country in which it took place.

A further controversial aspect of the Act is the heavy reliance on strict liability in many contexts – most notably the offences committed against children under 13. There is of course a clear and legitimate objective in providing protection against sexual exploitation for young people. However, the criminal law should be reserved for the clearest cases of wrongdoing. The offences in relation to children, impose strict liability as to age and can be committed irrespective of the age of the offender, his reasonable belief in the age of the victim, or whether the acts were in a consensual or exploitative environment. Lord Millett's observations in the

---

[430] See the definition of foster siblings at s 27 for an example, p 766 above.

[431] Other memorable examples include the degree of detail in defining offences such as intercourse with an animal, where the Act goes so far as to extend the definition to the 'vagina or anus' to include references 'to any similar part' in animals – eg those functionally equivalent body parts in amphibians and crustaceans.

[432] A, 18, criminally damaging the condom machine to gain condoms to have consensual sex with B, 15, commits the offence.

[433] *Jones* [2007] EWCA Crim 1118, above, p 756.

[434] See the importance of this as noted by Woolf LCJ in *H*, above, p 736 and its use for kidnap cases, eg *Royle* [2005] EWCA Crim 279 (D kidnapped V at road side and forced her to undress before she escaped).

[435] Section 72 as amended by the Criminal Justice and Immigration Act 2008.

House of Lords only two years previously in *K* went unheeded: 'the age of consent has long ceased to reflect ordinary life, and in this respect Parliament has signally failed to discharge its responsibility for keeping the criminal law in touch with the needs of society'.[436]

Some of the offences introduced demonstrate the clashes of principle which arise when criminal law seeks to regulate activities such as sexual behaviour. Examples include the difficulty in providing adequate protection for children and those with learning or mental disability without denying them an opportunity to express their sexual behaviour in non-exploitative relationships. The Government claimed that it was not seeking to prosecute consensual conduct between youths that was not previously prosecuted. Given that the 2003 Act criminalizes a broader range of consensual sexual activities (such as watching sexual activity) this is doubtful. Moreover, even if the new offences were no broader and not prosecuted more frequently, this is not an adequate justification for creation of offences criminalizing consensual sexual activity (short of penetration) between minors and carrying a maximum of 14 years. The Act is supposed to modernize the law and to reflect the sexual mores of the twenty-first century. Implementing broad offences in the context of sexual conduct also poses a danger in sending conflicting messages to young members of society. In general, the new Act seeks to encourage and re-educate people about the significance of respecting the autonomy of individuals by obtaining their consent.[437] But with children under 16 that message may be undermined by a starker one – even if you do act responsibly and seek and gain consent in your sexual experimentation you will still commit a serious offence.

Parliament received repeated Ministerial assurances that the volume, strictness and breadth of the offences would not lead to overcriminalization in practice because the CPS would exercise their discretion not to prosecute.[438] Aside from the fact that the Act leaves some very hard decisions to be made, in terms of principle, it is undesirable that such significant issues are a matter of discretion not law. As the Joint Parliamentary Committee on Human Rights observed in the Twelfth Report.

Creating catch all offences and then relying on the prosecutor's discretion to sort things out satisfactorily undermines [the rule of law]. It leaves prosecutors to do the job that Parliament should be doing, and gives them discretion to prosecute (or not to prosecute) people who ought never to have been within the scope of criminal liability in the first place.[439]

Another unfortunate feature of the Act is that it perpetuates the growing trend of creating 'quasi-crimes' – civil orders that are backed by a criminal sanction for breach. These have become a common feature – ASBO, Football Banning Order, exclusion order, etc – and they pose many problems.[440] The 2003 Act introduced new orders including FTO (Foreign Travel Orders), SOPO (Sexual Offence Prevention Orders) and RSHO (Risk of Sexual Harm Orders).[441]

18.10.3 ECHR issues

In ECHR terms, the Act is only a partial success. Although succeeding in removing several incompatible offences (gross indecency, buggery, etc), it creates new problems of ECHR

---

[436] [2001] UKHL 41 at [44]. On the House of Lords' approach to strict liability and age in sexual offences see J Horder, 'How Culpability Can and Can't be Denied in Under Age Sex Crimes' [2001] Crim LR 15.

[437] On the criminal law's role in facilitating conditions in which autonomy can be promoted, see Lacey, *Unspeakable Subjects*, 151.

[438] The CPS policy is available from www.cps.gov.uk/legal/p_to_r/rape_manual/rape_manual.

[439] Para 2.11.

[440] See, generally, A Ashworth, 'Social Control and Anti-Social Behaviour: the Subversion of Human Rights?' (2004) 120 LQR 263.

[441] See S Shute, 'New Civil Preventative Orders: Sexual Offences Prevention Orders; Foreign Travel Orders; Risk of Sexual Harm Orders' [2004] Crim LR 417.

incompatibility. One of the most obvious and heavily criticized examples, is the criminalization of sexual conduct between consenting children, particularly those aged 13 to 16.[442] The
Parliamentary Joint Committee on Human Rights[443] suggested that some sections of the Act
were overbroad in criminalizing all sexual touching between children. The decision of the
House of Lords in *G* is disappointing.

18.11 Reform

There is a danger that the Act will be seen as a panacea for the problems of investigating
and prosecuting sexual offences, and for the high attrition rates. There are deeper underlying
causes for: the prevalence of sex offences, the reluctance to report and the problems of proof
at trial.[444] Redefining rape to include non-consensual oral sex and all penile penetration of
under-13s irrespective of consent will in one way increase the number of rape convictions.
Similarly, in relation to child pornography, by raising to 18 the age of those who must not be
photographed in circumstances of indecency, the defence will be much less likely to succeed
in claiming that they believed the pubescent child was above that age.

The Government soon published a document[445] analysing the success of the Act. The
summary of the main findings was that: the Act has succeeded in providing a clear legal
framework to tackle sexual offending in twenty-first century Britain; the extension of what
constitutes the offence of rape and the introduction of other new offences has been welcomed; in particular, it has provided a coherent regime of offences to tackle sexual offending
against children, especially against those aged under 13 years old; it has introduced a range
of civil orders that are a useful tool for public protection agencies and have made a positive
contribution to protecting the public from sex offenders; there is little evidence to show that,
to date, the Act has helped to secure a greater number of convictions against sex offenders,
particularly rapists; awareness about the Act and its provisions remains patchy and there is
a clear need for training for those investigating and prosecuting sexual offences and those
working with the victims and survivors of sexual violence; there is a need to consider how
best to raise the profile within government and across all relevant agencies of tackling sexual
offending.

---

[442] See G above. *Laskey v UK* (1997) 24 EHRR 39; *Sutherland v UK* (1997) 24 EHRR CD22; Note also the
Northern Irish case of *S* [2006] NICA 34 in which the CA concluded that A lacked status as a victim and inclined
to the view that the offence was justifiable to protect young girls from themselves.

[443] Twelfth Report 2002–3, *Scrutiny of Bills: Further Progress Report,* 2003 (HL 119; HC 765).

[444] See J Harris and S Grace, 'A Question of Evidence? Investigating and Prosecuting Rapes in the 1990s' (1999)
HORS No 196; J Gregory and S Lees, *Policing Sexual Assault* (1999) 60–66; Temkin, *Rape and the Legal Process,*
11–30.

[445] *SOA 2003: Stocktake* (2006).

19
Theft

19.1 Interpreting the Theft Acts

The law governing dishonesty related offences is to be found in the Theft Acts 1968, 1978, the Theft (Amendment) Act 1996 and the Fraud Act 2006.[1] These Acts are not a re-statement of the common law and its numerous statutory additions. They provide a code of the most important offences of dishonest dealing with the protection of property, (with the notable exception of forgery, and the common law offence of conspiracy to defraud), based on a fundamental reconsideration of the principles by the Criminal Law Revision Committee (CLRC)[2] and the Law Commission.[3]

The law of theft is concerned with invasions of the proprietary interests of others but the law of property is not to be found explained in any detailed fashion in the Theft Acts. It is a matter of civil law. The Theft Acts assume its existence. The criminal courts, including the appellate courts, have sometimes shown impatience with arguments based on 'the finer distinctions in civil law',[4] but many of the fundamental issues of criminal liability turn on these civil law concepts. For example, whether property 'belongs to another' for the purposes of theft 'is a question to which the criminal law offers no answer and which can only be answered by reference to civil law principles'.[5] Equally, the Acts provide no definition of what constitutes 'a proprietary right or interest' for the purposes of s 5 of the 1968 Act. Theft offences sometimes necessarily involve consideration of 'the finer distinctions in civil law'.[6] It follows, of course, that changes in the civil law may affect the scope of the criminal law.[7] The Acts, by protecting property rights *per se*, also serve to protect the vitally important mechanisms for creating and exchanging property rights.[8]

Unfortunately, the interpretation of the Theft Acts has produced a great deal of complex case law. In interpreting the Acts, the courts have usually aimed to give words and expressions their ordinary meaning so as to avoid undue technicality and subtlety. This is a sensible approach, but it has led to the practice of leaving the interpretation of 'ordinary'

---

[1] See D Ormerod and D Williams, *Smith's Law of Theft* (9th edn, 2007) (hereinafter Ormerod and Williams, *Theft*); EJ Griew, *The Theft Acts 1968 and 1978* (7th edn, 1995) (hereinafter Griew, *Theft*); ATH Smith, *Property Offences* (1994) (hereinafter Smith, *Property Offences*).

[2] Eighth Report, para 7. And see Thirteenth Report (1977) Cmnd 6733.

[3] See especially LC 276, *Fraud* (2002).

[4] *Baxter* [1971] 2 All ER 359 at 363, CA: *Morris* [1984] AC 320, [1983] 3 All ER 288 at 294, HL.

[5] *Dobson v General Accident Fire and Life Assurance Corpn plc* [1989] 3 All ER 927 at 937, CA, per Bingham LJ.

[6] See *Shadrokh-Cigari* [1988] Crim LR 465, CA, below, p 818; *Wheeler* (1990) 92 Cr App R 279, CA, below, p 796. See also JC Smith, 'Civil Law Concepts in the Criminal Law' [1972B] CLJ 197; GR Williams, 'Theft, Consent and Illegality' [1977] Crim LR 127 and 205; G Treitel, 'Contract and Crime', in *Crime, Proof and Punishment*, 81.

[7] See discussion of *Floyd v DPP*, below, p 813.

[8] See A Simester and GR Sullivan, 'On the Nature and Rationale of Property Offences', in Duff and Green (eds), *Defining Crimes*, 173–183.

words and expressions to the jury.[9] The interpretation, even of ordinary words, must sometimes be a matter for the court to maintain respect for the rule of law and to ensure certainty, consistency and clarity in the definition and interpretation of the law. To leave interpretation in the hands of the juries (or more frequently the magistrates) is to risk their taking different views on indistinguishable facts. Even such ordinary words in the Theft Act as 'dishonesty', 'force', 'building', etc may involve definitional problems on which a jury may require guidance if like is to be treated as like. This poses potential problems of compatibility with Art 7 of the ECHR which protects against retrospective criminalization, and includes a requirement that crimes are defined with sufficient certainty and predictability.

One final aspect of the interpretation of the Theft Acts should also be emphasized from the outset. The appellate courts have demonstrated a distinct willingness to uphold the convictions of those found to have been dishonest even though there are fundamental errors with the conviction in other respects.[10] This has not generated the level of clarity and certainty of principle in the law that is desirable. In addition, such an approach places a degree of emphasis on the concept of dishonesty, which as we shall see, it is ill-suited to bear.[11]

The offence of theft is an extremely broad one as will soon be appreciated. In a recent empirical study Green and Kugler have questioned the merits of having such a broad single offence which fails to distinguish the different harms and wrongs involved in various activities which all result in the same outcome – D acquiring V's property.[12]

19.2 The offence of theft

By s 1(1) of the Theft Act 1968:

A person is guilty of theft if he dishonestly appropriates property belonging to another with the intention of permanently depriving the other of it; and 'thief' and 'steal' shall be construed accordingly.

The maximum sentence is now seven years (s 7).[13] In 2009/10 there were 913,874 recorded thefts.[14]

There is much about this definition that is self-explanatory and the vast majority of thefts can be dealt with without further elaboration. This is worth emphasizing before turning to detailed consideration of the elements of the offence.

---

[9] See G Williams, 'Law and Fact' [1976] Crim LR 472; DW Elliott, 'Law and Fact in Theft Act Cases' [1976] Crim LR 707. See also *Brutus v Cozens* [1973] AC 854, cf *Chandler v DPP* [1964] AC 763, HL and DW Elliott, '*Brutus v Cozens*, Decline and Fall' [1989] Crim LR 323.

[10] See, eg, Lord Steyn in *Hinks*, at 844, discussed below, p 784.

[11] See further: Ormerod and Williams, *Theft*, Ch 1.

[12] The study involved students ranking relative blameworthiness of D acquiring V's bike by theft, robbery, embezzlement, fraud, burglary, blackmail etc. See S Green and M Kugler, 'Community Perceptions of Theft Seriousness: A Challenge to Model Penal Code and English Theft Act Consolidation' (2010) 7 *Journal of Empirical Legal Studies* 511.

[13] Criminal Justice Act 1991, s 26. Originally it was 10 years. Under the Penalties for Disorderly Behaviour (Amount of Penalty)(Amendment No 2) Order 2004, SI 2468, made under the Criminal Justice and Police Act 2001, s 3(1), a fixed penalty may be awarded. Few people ever received sentences over 7 years, but there were even some theft sentences as high as the maximum. I am grateful to Simon Price for pointing this out.

[14] J Flatley et al, *Crime in England and Wales 2009/10, Findings from the British Crime Survey and police recorded crime* (2010) table 2.04.

19.3 *Actus reus*

The *actus reus* of theft consists (i) in the appropriation of (ii) property (iii) belonging to another.

19.3.1 Appropriation[15]

By s 3 of the Theft Act 1968:

(1) Any assumption by a person of the rights of an owner amounts to an appropriation, and this includes, where he has come by the property (innocently or not) without stealing it, any later assumption of a right to it by keeping or dealing with it as owner.

(2) Where property, or a right or interest in property is or purports to be transferred for value to a person acting in good faith, no later assumption by him of rights which he believed himself to be acquiring shall, by reason of any defect in the transferor's title, amount to theft of the property.

The CLRC did not provide a full definition of 'appropriation' because they assumed that people would realize that it was simply a different label for what they saw as the 'familiar concept of conversion...'[16] Appropriation was preferred because it more aptly describes the kind of acts it is intended to cover. The CLRC were rather optimistic in assuming that laymen (jurors and magistrates) have a familiarity with 'conversion' in its legal sense of usurping rights of property belonging to another. 'Conversion' is a complex tort[17] and not even all criminal lawyers have a full understanding of the concept. Appropriation was intended to be broad enough to describe various types of conduct that had been separate offences under the previous law: 'taking and carrying away' – which was required for simple larceny; 'conversion' by a bailee; embezzlement[18] and fraudulent conversion.[19]

Three basic problems in interpreting 'appropriation' have arisen, each of which has had a significant impact on the overall scope of the offence of theft:

(1) Is there an appropriation if D assumes only *a right* of the owner, not *all* the rights of that owner?

(2) Can D 'assume' rights when the alleged assumption is an act done with the consent of the owner?

(3) Can there be an appropriation when the effect is that the entire proprietary interest in the thing then belongs indefeasibly to the alleged thief?

Controversially, all three questions have been answered in the affirmative by the House of Lords: the first two in *Gomez*,[20] and the third in *Hinks*.[21]

---

[15] For early comment on this element of the offence, see L Koffman, 'The Nature of Appropriation' [1982] Crim LR 331; D Stuart, 'Reform of the Law of Theft' (1967) 30 MLR 609.

[16] Cmnd 2977, para 34.

[17] See A Dugdale and M Jones (eds) *Clerk and Lindsell on Torts* (20th edn, 2010), ch 17.

[18] A statutory offence involving the misappropriation by an employee of any property delivered to him on account of his employer.

[19] A statutory offence of conversion by a trustee or fiduciary of property entrusted to him.

[20] [1993] AC 442, HL, [1993] Crim LR 304 and commentary. On which see also M Davies, 'Consent after the House of Lords: Taking and Leading Astray the House of Lords' (1993) 13 LS 308; S Cooper and M Allen, 'Appropriation After *Gomez*' (1993) 57 J Crim Law 186.

[21] [2000] 4 All ER 833. On which see especially: JC Smith [2001] Crim LR 162; ATH Smith, 'Theft or Sharp Practice: Who Cares Now?' [2001] CLJ 21; J Beatson and A Simester, 'Stealing One's Own Property' (1999) 115 LQR 372; S Shute, 'Appropriation and the Law of Theft' [2002] Crim LR 445.

19.3.1.1 Assumption of 'a' right – *Morris*

The section requires an assumption of 'the rights of an owner' which seems *prima facie* to mean all the rights, not one, or some, of the rights of the owner in question. But in *Morris* Lord Roskill, having conceded that there was force in that view, nevertheless held that it is an appropriation if D assumes a single right. His lordship said, 'the later words, "any assumption of a right" in subs (1) and the words in subs (2) "no later assumption by him of rights" seem to me to militate strongly against [the view that all rights must be assumed].' Remarkably, his lordship omitted the subsequent and important words, 'to it'. Surely, if D assumes *a right to* the thing, he treats it as *his*, something in which he owns *all* the rights. As for the reference to subs (2), it is hard to see how a reference to 'rights' can point to a conclusion that the assumption of 'a right' is sufficient.

Many think Lord Roskill's conclusion was obviously wrong,[22] but it formed an element in the *ratio decidendi* of *Morris*. It has been endorsed by the House of Lords in *Gomez* where Lord Keith said, without giving reasons, that it was obviously right. So, for better or worse, we must take it that the law is settled: any assumption of *any of* the rights of an owner amounts to an appropriation. This extends the scope of the offence so that acts which might naturally be regarded as mere preparation or attempts would, because they involve the assumption of a single right, constitute the *actus reus* of the full offence.

Morris was concerned with a formerly common scenario where D switches the labels on two articles displayed on the shelves of a supermarket with the intention of buying the more expensive article for the price of the less expensive one. The right to label the goods is a right of the owner, so the label switching amounted to an appropriation and theft. D, of course, intended to deceive the cashier and to obtain the goods by deception (at that time probably an offence under s 15 of the 1968 Act, and now an offence of making a false representation under ss 1 and 2 of the Fraud Act 2006). On the interpretation in *Morris*, D has appropriated the goods as soon as he switches the label even if D gets cold feet, abandons the venture and leaves the goods with the switched labels safely on the shelf. Even if D re-switched the labels and left the articles exactly as he found them, that could not undo the appropriation he had committed. It is important to remember that on these facts, to be guilty of theft D must be shown to have *mens rea* – the intention permanently to deprive and dishonestly; there would not necessarily be a completed theft where D moves articles in a supermarket as a prank.

19.3.1.2 Appropriation with consent – *Gomez*

Section 3 is not drafted in terms of requiring a 'misappropriation'. In *Morris*, Lord Roskill, for a unanimous House, said, 'In the context of s 3(1), the concept of appropriation involves not an act expressly or impliedly authorized by the owner but an act by way of adverse interference with or usurpation of those rights.'[23] This, however, was *obiter*, because the label switching was plainly unauthorized by the shop and there was no need to say anything about authorized acts. In *Gomez*, the House held that the Lord Roskill's *dictum* was wrong: there can be an appropriation even if D acts with V's consent in relation to the property.

Gomez, followed an earlier House of Lords decision in *Lawrence*,[24] in which D, a taxi driver, was convicted of stealing from V, an Italian who spoke little English. V showed D a note bearing an address and tendered £1 to be taken there. The authorized fare was about 50p but D

---

[22] E Melissaris, 'The Concept of Appropriation and the Offence of Theft' (2007) 70 MLR 581 supports the decision.

[23] [1983] 3 All ER at 292. See LH Leigh, 'Some Remarks on Appropriation in the Law of Theft after *Morris*' (1985) 48 MLR 167.

[24] [1972] AC 626, HL. For defence of *Lawrence* on pragmatic grounds, see P Glazebrook, 'Thief or Swindler: Who Cares?' [1991] CLJ 389.

indicated that £1 was not enough and took from V's still open wallet a £1 and a £5 note. V permitted him to do so. D was convicted of theft. On appeal D argued that he took the money with V's consent. This was rejected. One of the questions certified for the House was whether the offence of theft was to be construed as if it contained the words 'without the consent of the owner'. The answer was, rightly, an emphatic 'no'. The definition of theft was based on certain offences in the Larceny Act 1916.[25] Those offences did not include the phrase, 'without the consent of the owner' and it had never been suggested that someone acting with consent could be guilty of those offences.[26] The CLRC intended that 'appropriates' in the 1968 Act would mean the same as 'converts' in the 1916 Act, so it is no surprise that they did not include the words 'without consent'.

Gomez, the assistant manager of a shop, persuaded the manager to sell goods to the value of £17,000 to his accomplice, X, and to accept payment by two cheques. The cheques, as Gomez and X knew, were stolen and worthless. If they had been charged with obtaining the goods by deception, contrary to s 15 of the 1968 Act, the case would never have been heard of;[27] but, for some reason, they were charged with theft. The Court of Appeal, following *Morris*, quashed their convictions.[28] The court declined to follow *Dobson v General Accident Fire and Life Assurance Corpn plc*,[29] a decision of the Civil Division of the Court of Appeal, which applied *Lawrence*. In *Dobson*, the plaintiff had been deceived by a rogue, R, into accepting a worthless cheque when selling his expensive watch and ring. Dobson sought to recover from his insurers the value of the watch and ring. The policy covered only loss by theft. It was not enough for Dobson to prove (this being a civil case) that his property had been obtained by deception (as it undoubtedly had). The insurers argued that there was no theft.[30] Parker LJ held that the making of the contract over the phone days before the delivery constituted the act of appropriation – it was an assumption of ownership by R.[31] There was an appropriation even if Dobson had consented to R's conduct.

The House in *Gomez*, relying heavily on the judgment of Parker LJ in *Dobson*, restored the convictions holding that, on the issue of the effect of consent, *Lawrence* and *Morris* were irreconcilable. The proposition in *Lawrence* was *ratio decidendi*, that in *Morris* an *obiter dictum*. That was good enough for the majority: *Lawrence* prevailed.

19.3.1.3 The misinterpretation of the Theft Act scheme

Gomez involves an issue that has troubled the courts for centuries. This involves the distinction between obtaining *possession* of property and obtaining outright *ownership*. The old law had separate offences, one to deal with cases where D by deception caused V to transfer possession (larceny by trick) and one where D, by deception caused V to transfer ownership

---

[25] The offences of fraudulent conversion and larceny by a bailee. On the value of these distinct offences see, A Steele, 'Taking Possession: The Defining Element of Theft?' (2008) 32 Melbourne University Law Review 1030.

[26] A bailee who acted with consent would not 'fraudulently convert to his own use' the property in question. It would have been inept for the draftsman of the Larceny Act to write 'converts to his own use without the consent of the owner'.

[27] It would now be a straightforward case under s 2 of the Fraud Act 2006.

[28] The contract of sale was voidable for fraud but not void, ownership of the electrical goods passed to X, and the contract not having been avoided, he was entitled to take possession and he did so with the consent and express authority of the owner For consideration of when ownership passed see R Heaton, 'Deceiving without Thieving' [2001] Crim LR 712.

[29] [1990] 1 QB 274.

[30] Ownership passed when a contract of sale was made over the telephone two days before delivery so that R, when he collected the goods, was taking delivery of his own property.

[31] On the insurance implications of the definition of theft generally see M Wasik, 'Definitions of Crimes in Insurance Contracts' [1986] J Bus Law 45.

(obtaining by false pretences).[32] The two offences were complex in application but generally thought to be mutually exclusive.[33]

The CLRC when drafting the Theft Act, decided to create an offence of obtaining property by deception (s 15) to cover all cases of conduct that would have been larceny by a trick or obtaining by false pretences. So, under the Theft Act as enacted, the prosecutor could not go wrong if he charged s 15 whenever D had obtained any interest in property – whether possession or ownership – by any kind of trick or false pretence. Some cases in which D obtained possession of the property with consent but had not obtained ownership would be theft, as well as obtaining by deception, but the intention was that if a deception was involved, s 15 should be charged.[34]

Unfortunately, some prosecutors and judges failed to recognize the distinction in the new Act. Lawrence, the dishonest taxi driver should have been charged with obtaining by deception[35] but the argument was not properly presented to the House of Lords in that case.[36] Gomez should also have been charged with obtaining by deception. In *Gomez,* the appellant invited the House to look at the Report of the CLRC to discover the way the 1968 Act was intended to operate. The majority declined as it would 'serve no useful purpose' to do so. Lord Lowry, dissenting, demonstrated convincingly that reference to the Report would have shown that there was no intention for theft to include cases where D obtained ownership with V's consent. The law should have been as stated in the *dictum* in *Morris,* not the decision in *Lawrence*; and that Gomez was wrongly convicted of theft. Some may think that would have been 'a useful purpose' in looking at the CLRC Report.

19.3.1.4 Theft where consent is given without deception by D

The point of law of general importance certified for the decision of the House in *Gomez* was whether there is an appropriation where 'consent has been obtained by a false representation', as occurred in that case. It was not necessary for the House to go beyond that and consider cases in which no deception was involved.[37] Nevertheless, the House chose to confirm explicitly that there could be an appropriation even where D has practised no deception on V. This was illustrated by their example of the label switcher in the supermarket. Their lordships were in no doubt that D in that scenario appropriates property when he touches the article on the shelf, although he has, as yet, practised no deception.[38]

The conclusion in *Gomez* that an appropriation can occur with the owner's consent, irrespective of that consent being induced by deception, is further illustrated by the overruling

---

[32] See G Ferris, 'The Origins of Larceny by Trick and Constructive Possession' [1998] Crim LR 17.

[33] On the moral differences between the types of dishonest conduct and public perceptions of such see Green and Kugler (2010) 7 *Journal of Empirical Legal Studies* 511.

[34] cf Smith, *Property Offences,* para 5.17. See the confusion where both theft and deception were available: *Clarke v CPS* [2007] EWHC 2228 (Admin). The repeal of the deception offences means that the overlap will now be with the Fraud Act 2006.

[35] He obtained ownership of the excessive fare by deception, since V permitted him to take the money only because D had told him, falsely, that £1 was not enough.

[36] For an opinion as to the questions which the House ought to have been asked, see [1971] Crim LR 53, 54.

[37] There was powerful, though, it is submitted, mistaken, academic support suggesting that there can be an appropriation where the consent was by a false representation. See G Williams, 'Theft and Voidable Title' [1981] Crim LR 666, and see the reply by JC Smith at [1981] Crim LR 677. See also a letter by GV Hart [1982] Crim LR 391.

[38] Arguably he commits the general fraud offence contrary to s 1(2)(a) and s 2 of the Fraud Act 2006 in relation to *both* items as soon as he switches the labels. There is a false representation as to the more expensive item and by that representation D intends to cause loss to the shopkeeper. The cheaper item is now falsely represented to have a higher price. If D's intent is that X will pay that amount for it he intends to cause loss to X; if it is his intent that no one will, but if remains at its inflated price, he commits fraud against the shopkeeper because he intends the keeper to be exposed to the risk of loss on the sale of that item.

of *Fritschy*.[39] In that case the owner of some kruggerands instructed Fritschy to collect them from bullion dealers in England and take them to Switzerland. Fritschy did exactly what he was told to do until he arrived in Switzerland and then, as he had intended from the beginning, he disposed of the property for his own benefit. The court in *Fritschy*, held that, as everything he did in England was done with the consent and authority of the owner, he committed no appropriation and therefore no theft within the jurisdiction of the court. However, the House of Lords in *Gomez* held that Fritschy committed theft the moment he first got his hands on the property with intent to steal it, although there was no finding of any deception.

Gomez also overruled *Skipp*.[40] There D, 'posing as a genuine haulage contractor' (presumably that was itself an operative deception), collected three loads from different places in London with instructions to deliver them in Leicester. D deviated from the route to Leicester and transferred the goods to an accomplice, as he had planned all along. It was unsuccessfully argued that the charge he faced – a single count for theft of the entire load – was procedurally defective[41] because it actually alleged three separate appropriations and therefore should have been charged as three thefts. The court held that though D may have had a dishonest intention permanently to deprive at the time he received each of the three loads, he had done nothing inconsistent with the rights of the owners until he diverted the goods from their proper destination. According to the court in *Skipp* that was the point at which D stole. Since *Gomez* it is now clear that he committed three thefts when he collected the loads– each theft being also an offence of obtaining property by deception.

19.3.1.5 Appropriation of indefeasible title to property – *Hinks*

It was argued that despite the incredible breadth of the concept of appropriation as interpreted in *Gomez*, there remained one necessary limitation to that concept. In all the decided cases, any proprietary right acquired by D's appropriation was voidable:[42] the owner was entitled to rescind the transaction and get his property back. Following *Gomez* these appropriations could nevertheless constitute theft. In contrast, where D gets an absolute, indefeasible right to the property, he has the right to retain the property. It was thought by some to be unacceptable – impossible even – for a criminal court to hold that a transaction which resulted in D obtaining such a right amounted to a theft of the property by him. If D has a right to retain the property, or even to recover it from the alleged victim, it could hardly be held to be theft for him to take and keep it. If it were theft by D, the civil law would be assisting D to enjoy, or to recover, the fruits of his crime by providing protection through the law relating to conversion! This argument underestimated the determination of some judges including, as it happened, a majority of a particular committee of the House, to convict those deemed by a jury to be dishonest.

In each of a series of three cases, D received a substantial gift from V, a person of a vulnerable mental state, over whom D had acquired some influence. In each case V was of sufficient mental capacity in law to make a gift of property.[43] On those facts in civil law, in each case there was a valid gift to D. In the first case, *Mazo*,[44] it was 'common ground that the receiver

---

[39] [1985] Crim LR 745. A charge of obtaining property by deception was withdrawn from the jury.

[40] [1975] Crim LR 114.

[41] Technically called being 'bad for duplicity'.

[42] Where one party to a transaction is acting under a fundamental mistake the transaction is void and no property passes. Where, in contrast, the party is acting under a non-fundamental mistake the transaction is voidable and property does pass.

[43] The gift might, in civil law, have been voidable because of the exercise of undue influence by D, but the juries were not asked to consider that question, so we must take it that it was not.

[44] [1996] Crim LR 435.

of a valid gift *inter vivos* could not be the subject of a conviction for theft' – D's conviction was quashed. But, in *Hopkins and Kendrick*,[45] the Court of Appeal upheld the conviction of the recipients of the gifts. The court distinguished *Mazo*, but expressly doubted the validity of the parties' agreed premise on which *Mazo* was decided. In the third case, *Hinks*,[46] the Court of Appeal confronted the problem directly and held that it was immaterial whether there was a valid gift: *Mazo* was based on a mistaken premise. The only question was whether D, the recipient of the gift, was dishonest – and jury had found that she was. The House, Lords Hutton and Hobhouse dissenting, upheld the conviction.

The conduct of the accused in all three cases was despicable.[47] They were, as the jury must have found in each case, dishonestly taking an unfair advantage of a person with failing powers. If the donors were mentally incapable of making a valid gift owing to their diminished mental capacity, the cases were unanswerable. But the prosecutions were not made on the basis that the victims lacked mental capacity to make decisions to give their property away. We must assume they were capable and had done so. It should be reiterated at this point that the offence of theft was drafted with the purpose of protecting property rights, not protecting against exploitation *per se*.[48] With the advent of the new fraud offence of abusing a position of financial trust,[49] which is explicitly designed to criminalize exploitative dishonest conduct, there is a yet stronger argument that the courts should reconsider the *actus reus* of theft to return it to acceptable limits based on the protection of property rights.

The result of the decision of the House of Lords in *Hinks* is that the recipient of a valid gift may now be guilty of stealing it – provided only that a jury is satisfied that his mind was dishonest in the sense to be considered below. As Professor Smith commented, '[a]t its outer reaches theft becomes something akin to "thought crime"'.[50] Aside from creating an astonishingly broad offence of theft, this creates numerous problems.

First, although there is a theft there are sometimes no stolen goods because the donor, *ex hypothesi*, never has any right to restitution:[51] the property belongs absolutely to D for ever.

Secondly, there is the problem of the relationship between civil and criminal law.[52] There are very strong principled arguments for the criminal law not extending beyond the civil law, in particular in the area of theft where the criminal law is necessarily developed on the foundations of civil law concepts of property, ownership, etc. It is submitted that the Act was intended to be construed such that there could be no theft where D acted within the civil law. The majority of the House in *Hinks* acknowledged, with surprising equanimity, that their

[45] [1997] 2 Cr App R 524, [1997] Crim LR 359.

[46] [1998] Crim LR 904. The court derived 'some comfort' from Simon Gardner's article, 'Property and Theft' [1998] Crim LR 35.

[47] All would now be guilty of the offence of fraud under s 4 of the Fraud Act 2006.

[48] cf AL Bogg and J Stanton-Ife, 'Protecting the Vulnerable: Legality, Harm and Theft' (2003) 23 LS 402. See also S Shute, 'Appropriation and the Law of Theft' [2002] Crim LR 445.

[49] See below, p 980.

[50] 'Theft or Sharp Practice Who Cares Now?' [2001] CLJ 21, 22. For a view that even after *Hinks* the argument is still open that a valid gift cannot be dishonest see *Arlidge and Parry on Fraud*, paras 2.040 and 2.059.

[51] See s 24(3) of the Theft Act 1968, below, p 980. Assuming a valid gift, the goods were never out of lawful custody or possession and the donor never had a right to restitution. Hinks was ordered to pay £19,000 compensation to Dolphin. Compensation for what? For keeping a gift which she was in civil law entitled to keep? The jury's verdict did not decide that she did not have an *indefeasible* title to the property. Was the judge entitled to decide that her title was defeasible? – for misrepresentation, undue influence, or what? Could Hinks have an argument that the order was contrary to her right to peaceful enjoyment of her possessions under Art 1, protocol 1 of the ECHR?

[52] See on this more generally: Smith [1972B] CLJ 197; Williams [1977] Crim LR 127 and 205; ATH Smith, 'Gifts and the Law of Theft' [1999] CLJ 10.

decision creates a conflict between the civil and the criminal law. D who has V's consent to appropriate the property will commit no civil law wrong and, indeed, will be able to rely on the civil law to enforce the transfer of property, but will be exposed to prosecution for theft. In *Hinks*, Lord Steyn states, however, that '...it would be wrong to assume on *a priori* grounds that the criminal law rather than the civil law is defective' in creating this conflict. If we were constructing a new code of civil and criminal law, it would certainly be open to the legislator to prefer a principle of the criminal law to one of the civil law, but that is not the position. The Theft Acts assume the existence of the civil law of property rights and the criminal courts are, or should be, bound to take it as they find it.

The implications of the decision are significant. Suppose that D is selling a painting of Salisbury Cathedral. V becomes very excited on seeing the painting and, thinking he is about to get a bargain, offers D £100,000 for it. D realizes that V thinks the painting is by Constable, but D knows that it was painted by his sister and is worth no more than £100. He accepts V's offer. D has made an enforceable contract and he is entitled to recover and to retain the money.[53] Similarly, if a buyer, D2, knew that a picture was in fact by Constable and bought it for a very small sum from a seller, V2, who, as D2 was aware, did not know this, a jury might well regard the conduct in these examples as dishonest – and, of course, V would not have consented in either case, had he known the true facts. The effect of *Hinks* is that, if the jury is satisfied that these defendants were dishonest they are guilty of stealing the property – property to which they are absolutely entitled in civil law.

The third problem with the decision in *Hinks* is with the requirement that at the time of appropriation there must be property belonging to another. In the trilogy of cases *Mazo*, *Hopkins and Kendrick* and *Hinks*, the property belonged to the donor, V, until the instant when the dishonest act of receiving the gift (appropriation) was done. D's acquisition of the entire proprietary interest and the appropriation were simultaneous. If, however, D acquires the entire interest first and then, after an interval, does the act alleged to be an appropriation, it seems he cannot, even after *Hinks*, be guilty: he has not then appropriated property belonging to another – it is already his.[54] For example, consider a case where V, a poor person infatuated by a wealthy man, D, sends a valuable gift to D's house where it arrives while D is absent abroad. When D comes home, he treats it as his own – which it is. However dishonest a jury might think his conduct at that point in time, this cannot be theft. The property is already his. Consider also the effect of these cases on the actions of a motorist at a self-service station who fills his tank, intending to drive off without paying.[55] The ownership in the petrol probably passes to the motorist when he puts it into his tank; but after *Hinks* it is no answer to a charge of theft that he had acquired an absolute, indefeasible right to the property. Even now, however, it should be an answer to a charge of theft that he did not form the dishonest intent until after he had acquired the entire proprietary interest. The prosecutor is advised to charge making off without payment, contrary to s 3 of the Theft Act 1978.[56]

---

[53] cf *Smith v Hughes* (1871) LR 6 QB 597 (sale of oats enforceable by seller although he knew that the buyer thought they were old oats, new oats being useless to him, and that the oats were in fact new). The question was not 'what a man of scrupulous morality or nice honour would do in such circumstances'. Another example may be the case where a finder has in law a better right to the thing found than the landowner: below, p 800. However dishonest the finder may be, he should not be guilty of theft by appropriating that which the law says he may appropriate. Whether this is an offence under the Fraud Act is considered below, p 880.

[54] See Lord Hobhouse at [2000] 4 All ER 855f–g.

[55] In *McHugh* (1976) 64 Cr App R 92 it was assumed, without argument, that this was theft. If it was theft before *Gomez*, it is so still. cf *Edwards v Ddin* [1976] 3 All ER 705, DC.

[56] Below, p 882. See Ch 23 for the potential liability for fraud in such cases.

19.3.1.6 The consequences of the House of Lords' interpretation of appropriation

In the trilogy of cases – *Morris, Gomez* and *Hinks* – the House has adopted an interpretation of appropriation at odds with that intended and with very significant ramifications.[57]

(i) Overextending the scope of the offence

The effect of the overbroad reading of the element of appropriation is to render the offence of theft an extraordinarily wide one, embracing many acts which would more naturally be regarded as merely preparatory acts, not even amounting to an attempt to steal. Where V is the absolute owner of property the general principle in civil law is that only he has any right to do anything to or with it. Anyone else who does anything to or with it is therefore exercising a right of the owner. If V has consented to or authorized the exercise of that right by D we would not, it is submitted, ordinarily describe that exercise as an 'assumption' or 'appropriation'; but, since it has been decided that consent and authority are immaterial, it is both. And, since the assumption of any one of the owner's rights in the property is an appropriation of the property itself, this amounts to theft if done dishonestly and with an intention permanently to deprive. The effect is to overrule *Eddy v Niman*,[58] which had decided that a person who takes goods from the shelves of a supermarket and, with intent to steal, puts them into the wire basket provided does not commit theft because everything he has done was with the store's implied consent. There is an obvious difficulty in proving intent in such a case but, if that can be done, this is now theft.[59]

Theft might now be defined as follows:

Anyone doing anything whatever to property belonging to another, with or without his consent, appropriates it; and, if he does so dishonestly and with intent by that, or any subsequent act, permanently to deprive, he commits theft.

Prosecutors may, as a result of the broad interpretation find it easier to secure convictions for theft in most cases, but problems may arise in identifying the precise time and place of the act which constitutes the appropriation. Astonishing though it may sound, despite the incredible breadth of the offence as currently interpreted, prosecutors may well be advised to prefer the offence of fraud in many cases since that is even wider and requires no proof of loss, gain, appropriation or intention permanently to deprive.[60] It is obvious that the combination of the

---

[57] E Meliassaris, 'The Concept of Appropriation and the Offence of Theft' (2007) 70 MLR 581 has suggested that appropriation should be understood as occurring only when D develops a 'proprietary subjectivity' for the property, ie thinks of the property as his own. This might produce results which are as unpalatable as under the present law. For example, in *Fritschy*, as with other bailments, appropriation may be at the time of taking physical control of the goods even if within the terms of the bailment. The donee of a gift could, on this test, be held to have appropriated it, as in *Hinks*, See also on the interpretation of appropriation: N Weinrich, 'German Cures For English Ailments? Appropriation Versus Taking Away – Significance and Consequences of Conceptual Differences Between the English and the German Law of Theft' (2005) 69 J Crim Law 427.

[58] (1981) 73 Cr App R 237, [1981] Crim LR 502, DC. Parker LJ, in his judgment in *Dobson*, which was approved in *Gomez*, discussed the question and held that *Eddy v Niman* was inconsistent with the decision of the Court of Appeal in *McPherson* [1973] Crim LR 191. The latter case did not depend on the fact that the goods were concealed in a shopping bag – the offence was committed as soon as they were taken from the shelves.

[59] This is another case where the goods are stolen but are not 'stolen goods' for the purposes of the Act as they remain in the possession and ownership of the shop. But, unlike the situation in *Hinks*, the shopper has set out to do something – take the goods out of the possession of the owner – which would render them stolen. It is submitted that here the law of theft intervenes too early, whereas in *Hinks*, it should never interfere at all.

[60] See p 833 below.

interpretation of theft and the new offences of fraud provide English criminal law with some of the most wide-reaching dishonesty offences imaginable.

(ii) Overemphasis on *mens rea*

By reducing the *actus reus* almost to vanishing point theft becomes (too) dependent on *mens rea*, placing additional emphasis on dishonesty. It loses what Fletcher would describe as its 'manifest criminality'.[61] It should be noted that a minority of academics welcomed this shift. For example, Gardner regarded the decision in *Gomez* as 'unimpeachable' in following the decision in *Lawrence*, and 'desirable from first principles...[since] the quality of the dishonest conduct is not necessarily altered by the victim's consent'.[62]

(iii) The overlap with obtaining property by deception under s 15

The effect of *Gomez* was that virtually[63] all offences of obtaining property by deception contrary to s 15 were also theft (except obtaining land, which, the Act provides, cannot be stolen). The creation of this degree of overlap made life much easier for prosecutors, but was not what the Act intended,[64] which was to maintain a difference between offences of obtaining ownership by deception and theft.[65] In terms of labelling, 'theft' and 'deception' reflect separate moral wrongs, and in principle there ought not to be extensive overlap between the two.[66] The judicial blurring of such distinctions undermined the coherence of the Act's scheme of offences.

(iv) Creating confusion in the Court of Appeal

The initial reaction of the Court of Appeal to *Gomez* seems to have been one of incredulity. In *Gallasso*,[67] an appeal heard on the very day that judgment was given in *Gomez*, the court said that although a taking with consent may be an appropriation, 'there must still be a taking'. That would have imposed drastic limitations on theft, but it is an untenable opinion. It is certain that 'appropriation' includes what we formerly knew as conversion, as well as taking. In *Gallasso*, D, a nurse, received cheques on behalf of a patient with learning disabilities, V, and, instead of paying them into one of two existing accounts in V's name, opened a new account,

---

[61] G Fletcher, *Rethinking Criminal Law* (1978) 82. See M Giles and S Uglow, 'Appropriation and Manifest Criminality in Theft' (1992) 56 J Crim L 179, and see, Steele (2008) 32 Melbourne University Law Review 1030.

[62] S Gardner, 'Appropriation in Theft: The Last Word' (1993) 109 LQR 194. See also P Glazebrook, 'Revising the Theft Acts' [1993] CLJ 191 pointing out that D's moral blameworthiness is as great in these cases where V consents.

[63] R Heaton, 'Deceiving without Thieving' [2001] Crim LR 712, describes cases where the obtaining of goods may still not amount to theft, including, eg, goods delivered under a mail order contract.

[64] Strikingly, in *Briggs* [2004] Cr App R, the Court of Appeal resisted a wide reading of appropriation, by relying on an argument that to do otherwise would mean that there was too great an overlap between theft and deception. This is precisely the reasoning that had on three occasions failed to persuade the House of Lords against creating an almost total overlap between the offences. For an illustration of how the overlap caused courts to be too lax in their scrutiny of the allegations see *Clarke v CPS* [2007] EWHC 2228 (Admin).

[65] This is quite distinct from the expressly intended overlap between, eg theft and robbery, where all robberies must contain a theft. This point undermines the argument in S Gardner, 'Appropriation in Theft: The Last Word' (1993) 109 LQR 194.

[66] See in particular, S Shute and J Horder, 'Thieving and Deceiving: What is the Difference' (1993) 56 MLR 548, 'the thief makes war on a social practice from the outside, the deceiver is the traitor within'; C Clarkson, 'Theft and Fair Labelling' (1993) 56 MLR 554. See for a more pragmatic view: Glazebrook [1991] CLJ 389 and [1993] CLJ 191. Shute and Horder suggest that the true distinction lies in the voluntariness of the transfer. This test, it is submitted, carries its own substantial difficulties, some of which are addressed by Clarkson.

[67] [1993] Crim LR 459. See also [1993] Crim LR at 307. Griew, *Theft*, para 2.89 thinks the 'strange judgment' may 'defy rationalisation'; and Smith, *Property Offences*, para 5.56, concludes that it is 'simply wrong'.

also in V's name, and paid the cheques into that account. It was alleged that D's purpose was to make unauthorized withdrawals. The court held that, even if D was acting dishonestly and with intent permanently to deprive V, this was not theft because there was no taking and therefore no appropriation. But D was certainly exercising a right of the owner and, according to *Gomez*, it was immaterial that she was doing so with consent, provided that she was acting dishonestly and with intent to deprive. The case appears indistinguishable from *Fritschy*. *Gallasso* must be taken as wrongly decided.

The Court of Appeal's apparent disbelief at the breadth of the offence of theft in the wake of *Gomez* and *Hinks* continues to manifest itself. In *Ashcroft*,[68] D, a haulier, was alleged to have conspired to steal items from sealed containers in transit. The court regarded as 'some way removed from reality' D's argument that the theft occurred when D originally took possession of the goods in his lorries (in Scotland). Having referred to *Atakpu* (below), the court commented that in this case 'there never was in any ordinary sense of the word an "appropriation" of the stolen goods until the conspirators removed them from the containers . . .'[69] True enough, but since *Gomez*, the word appropriation does not bear the 'ordinary' meaning that its drafters had intended.[70] It is difficult to distinguish the case from *Skipp* or *Fritschy*, neither of which was cited by the court.

(v) The greater importance of timing

In some cases there will be a greater significance on the precise time at which the appropriation occurs. Consider the old case of *Hircock*:[71] D, by deception, obtained possession of a car under a hire-purchase agreement. Fourteen days later he dishonestly sold the car. It was held that he was guilty of obtaining property by deception (he would now be guilty of fraud) when he obtained the car, and of theft when he sold it. Applying *Gomez*, he would now be guilty of theft (and obtaining) when he got possession of the car and that theft would be finished before he sold the car (he was no longer 'on the job' of stealing). Once stolen by him, he could not steal it again. Similarly, in *Dip Kaur v Chief Constable for Hampshire*,[72] the theft would be complete much earlier in time. D found in a shop, in a rack of shoes which she knew to be properly priced £6.99 a pair, one of which was labelled £6.99 and the other £4.99. She took the pair to the cashier, and, as she hoped, the cashier saw the lower and not the higher price. She paid £4.99 and left the shop with the shoes. Her conviction for theft was quashed on the ground that the cashier had authority to accept D's offer to buy at the lower price and the ownership passed to D. It now seems clear in the light of *Gomez*, that D was guilty of theft as soon as she did anything with the shoes with a dishonest intent – probably when she picked them up and noticed the price discrepancy, certainly not later than when she tendered them to the cashier.

(vi) Jurisdictional matters

The significance of the timing of the appropriation can be important if there is a cross-jurisdictional aspect to the crime. The House of Lords decision in *Gomez* was therefore

---

[68] [2003] EWCA Crim 2365.

[69] Para 45.

[70] For an early discussion of the two senses of the word 'appropriation', see A Halpin, 'The Appropriate Appropriation' [1991] Crim LR 426 and A Halpin, *Definitions in the Criminal Law* (2004) 166–181.

[71] (1978) 67 Cr App R 278, [1979] Crim LR 184.

[72] [1981] 2 All ER 430, DC. D was probably guilty of obtaining by deception by representing that the authorized price was £4.99 when she knew it was £6.99. The transaction at the cash desk seems to be the same whether D has swapped labels herself, seen them swapped by a mischievous child or the article has been mislabelled by a careless assistant. If D knows she is presenting a 'false' price label to the cashier, she is committing a Fraud Act offence.

applied, with great reluctance, by the Court of Appeal in *Atakpu*.[73] D and E hired cars in Germany and Belgium and drove them to England, intending to sell them to *bona fide* purchasers. They were detained in Dover and charged with conspiracy to steal. The trial judge, applying the Court of Appeal's decision in *Gomez*, held that there was no theft outside the jurisdiction of the court (that is, England and Wales) because everything that was done there (Germany and Belgium) was done with the consent of the owner. The judge went on to hold that theft would have been committed in England when D and E retained the cars after the expiration of the hire period with the dishonest intention of permanently depriving the owners. It was *Fritschy* in reverse. D and E were guilty of conspiracy to steal in England. However, by the time *Atakpu* reached the Court of Appeal, the House of Lords had allowed the appeal in *Gomez*. The Court of Appeal felt bound to conclude that theft was committed outside the jurisdiction when the cars were obtained irrespective of the consent of the owner which D and E had induced by their deception. The court concluded that while theft may continue as long as the thief is 'on the job', and that this is a question for a jury, no jury could reasonably decide that these thefts were continuing days after D and E had first obtained the cars. Theft is a finite act and this theft ended outside the jurisdiction of the English courts. There was a conspiracy in England to steal in Germany and Belgium, but not to steal *in England*.[74] That conspiracy would now be indictable under and s 1 and s 1A of the Criminal Law Act 1977.[75]

(vii) Conflict with the civil law

Glanville Williams argued that no act should amount to theft unless it is contrary to the civil law. Nearly all thefts do amount to the civil wrongs of trespass, conversion or breach of trust but it does not follow that civil unlawfulness is a necessary constituent of the offence.[76] The definition of theft does not use the word 'unlawfully' nor does it say '*mis*appropriate'.[77] It has been argued[78] that a requirement of unlawfulness can be read into the concept of dishonesty. Thus, it has been suggested that the word 'dishonestly' has an objective, as well as a subjective, meaning and that actions that are lawful at civil law are not the dishonest conduct which the section requires.

The courts are extremely reluctant to admit consideration of civil law into criminal cases, even where it is inevitable, and these arguments have not been judicially accepted.[79] After *Gomez*, and *Hinks*,[80] the arguments appear untenable. The removal of goods from the shelves of a supermarket is not a civil wrong merely because the act is done with a secret dishonest

---

[73] [1994] QB 69.

[74] See Sullivan and Warbrick (G Sullivan and C Warbrick, 'Territoriality, Theft and *Atakpu*' [1994] Crim LR 650 at 659) for an argument that the court was misled by the phrase 'theft abroad is not triable in England' and that so-called 'theft abroad' is not theft under English law; D and E had come by the cars without stealing them so their later assumption of a right to the cars in England would have amounted to an appropriation; the cars were to be stolen in English law for the first time when appropriated in England. For a counter argument see the 12th edition of this work.

[75] Above, p 446. See further, M Hirst, *Jurisdiction and the Ambit of the Criminal Law* (2003) para 2.26.

[76] '…the aims and purposes of the civil law are not co-extensive with the criminal', Smith, *Property Offences*, para 5.06; but see also paras 5.11–5.52.

[77] Although this is regarded as 'the very essence of the offence' by Simester and Sullivan in Duff and Green, *Defining Crimes*, at 173.

[78] *Arlidge and Parry on Fraud*, para 1.10.

[79] A partner has been held guilty of theft of the partnership property, even though his act did not amount to the tort of conversion. The court did not think it necessary to look for any other civil wrong – in fact the act must have been a breach of contract: *Bonner* [1970] 2 All ER 97n.

[80] See Lord Hobhouse at [2000] 4 All ER 865b.

intent, but it is now theft. Fritschy committed no civil wrong by carrying out his employer's instructions to take the krugerrands to Switzerland, but we are now told he was a thief.

In *Hinks*, the House of Lords recognized that the decision led to a conflict, but took comfort from Gardner's argument that the criminal law can 'float free' of the civil law in this context. It is submitted that this ignores the underlying purpose of the offence of theft and others in the Theft Acts being designed to protect property – a civil law concept.[81] Shute suggests an alternative argument; dishonest conduct such as that in *Hinks*, might not constitute a civil law wrong, it 'may nonetheless have a *tendency* to undermine property rights either directly by attacking the interests that they protect, or indirectly by weakening an established system of property rights and so threatening the public good that the system represents'.[82] It is submitted that such vague concepts of harm do not form a sufficiently clear or solid foundation for an offence that is serious, commonplace, and for which a clear rationale – protecting property rights – has existed since its inception. The consequence of accepting the arguments supporting the *Hinks* proposition is, of course, that the offence becomes almost entirely dependent on the concept of dishonesty. It becomes an offence protecting against exploitation not property rights.[83]

19.3.1.7 Theft without loss

In *Chan Man-sin v A-G of Hong Kong*,[84] a company accountant drew a forged cheque on the company's bank account. It was held that he stole from the company the thing in action consisting in its credit balance, or its contractual right to overdraw, even though it was settled law that the honouring of the forged cheque and debiting of the company's account was a nullity and the company, on discovering the unauthorized debit, was entitled to have it reversed. In law, D's actions were wholly ineffective, the company was never a penny the worse off; but it was held that there was an appropriation – because D assumed the rights of an owner over the credit balance – and an intent permanently to deprive – because he intended to treat the thing as his own to dispose of regardless of the company's rights.[85]

The Privy Council has subsequently endorsed the broad effect of *Hinks*, rejecting an argument that it cannot apply where there is no loss to V.[86] In *Wheatley v The Commissioner of Police of the British Virgin Islands*,[87] D was a government official who had bestowed a lucrative contract on V and received payment from V for doing so: straightforward corruption. The charges alleged theft contrary to laws[88] which reflect ss 1 to 6 of the Theft Act 1968 in all relevant respects. The magistrate acquitted D on the theft charges but the Court of Appeal of the British Virgin Islands entered convictions on the theft counts. The Privy Council held that the convictions for theft were safe. As Lord Bingham opined:

it is certainly true that in most cases of theft there will be an original owner of money or goods who will be poorer because of the defendant's conduct. But in one of the two cases in *Morris* the defendant was arrested before paying the reduced price for the goods, so that the supermarket suffered no loss,

---

[81] See also J Beatson and A Simester, 'Stealing One's Own Property' (1999) 115 LQR 372. It is a decision described by Simester and Sullivan in Duff and Green, *Defining Crimes* as 'subversive', at 179.

[82] Shute [2002] Crim LR 445, 455.

[83] Simester and Sullivan in Duff and Green, *Defining Crimes*, at 180. See also SP Green, *Lying, Cheating and Stealing: A Moral Theory of White Collar Crime* (2006) Ch 6: recognizing that to steal is to violate 'in some fundamental way, another's rights of ownership [or possession]', at 89–90.

[84] [1988] 1 All ER 1.

[85] Presumably the same principle applies to tangible property.

[86] [2006] UKPC 24, [2006] 1 WLR 1683, [2006] 2 Cr App R 21.

[87] [2006] UKPC 24.

[88] Section 209(a) of the Criminal Code (Act No 1 of 1997) of the Laws of the British Virgin Islands.

and, in *R (A) v Snaresbrook Crown Court*,[89] it was accepted that the alleged theft was carried out for a purpose which could financially benefit the company.[90]

19.3.1.8 Appropriation by 'keeping' and 'dealing'

Section 3 provides that there can be an appropriation not only by assuming the right of an owner as discussed thus far, but also by keeping or dealing with property as owner. It is difficult to conceive of D being held to be 'dealing' with the property where he has done nothing at all in relation to the goods, even though he has made up his mind to steal them.[91] Arguably, however, 'keeping' goes somewhat further.

Suppose that D, having borrowed V's bike for a week, resolves at the end of the week to keep it. It would clearly be an appropriation, at the end of the week, to refuse to return it on demand,[92] or to deny V access to it, or for D to claim it as his own. Such conduct shows that he is keeping it as owner. It would also constitute appropriation if D were to use the bike after the end of the week because that use would be an assumption of one of the owner's rights. But what if D, on the expiry of the loan, merely leaves the bike where it is in his garage, hoping that V will forget about it, and intending to keep it? Literally the case falls within the s 3 since D is 'keeping...it as owner' and there is no justification for giving the words other than their plain meaning. Of course it would be very difficult to prove D's *mens rea* in the form of the intention permanently to deprive, but he satisfies the appropriation requirement of keeping as owner. Proof would be even more difficult in the case of some forms of property. As the court has recently underlined in *Gresham*[93] '"keeping" as owner in relation to a bank account may be difficult to prove in a case where [D] does no more than refrain from bringing the mistake to the attention of the bank'.[94] Some positive act such as drawing a cheque on the account may be necessary.

19.3.1.9 Appropriation – requirement of a positive act?

Theft requires proof of an 'act' by D towards the property that belongs to another, subject to what was said above about 'keeping' and 'dealing'. As appropriation is defined in terms of an 'assumption' of the right(s) of another, that seems to require conduct on D's part demonstrating such an assumption. What of cases in which D induces V to hand over property to him? Can there be an appropriation before the point in time at which D has physical contact with, possession or control of the property?

In *Hilton*,[95] where D, who had direct control of a bank account belonging to a charity, gave instructions for the transfer of the charity's funds to settle his personal debts, it was held that he stole the property[96] belonging to the charity. *Hilton* might be regarded as a straightforward case since D always had control of the bank account and instructed his agent (the bank) to act in relation to the property. D acted in relation to the property. Arguably it is different where D, by deception, induces, V, the owner and controller of the bank account, to transfer funds from it. Although in such a case V's property[97] has gone, D did not 'appropriate' it.[98] The Court of

---

[89] [2001] All ER (D) 123, para 25.

[90] [11].

[91] But see *A-G's Reference (No 1 of 1983)* [1985] QB 182, CA, below, p 816.

[92] cf *Wakeman* (1912) 8 Cr App R 18.

[93] [2003] EWCA Crim 2070.

[94] Approving the statements in *Ngan* [1998] 1 Cr App R 331 at 336, *Gresham*, para 22.

[95] [1997] 2 Cr App R 445, [1997] Crim LR 761 and commentary.

[96] A thing in action representing the charity's right to payment of that sum from its bank.

[97] The thing in action in the form of his credit balance, or part of it.

[98] *Caresana* [1996] Crim LR 667; *Naviede* [1997] Crim LR 662. See also JC Smith (1996) 9 Archbold News, 14 Nov.

Appeal recently affirmed this view in *Briggs*[99] where D had, by deception, induced her elderly relatives to transfer to her proceeds of their house sale. The Court of Appeal quashed a conviction for theft.[100] The court held that the word 'appropriation' connoted a physical act rather than a more remote action triggering the payment that gave rise to the charge.[101] The court relied heavily on Sir John Smith QC's commentary on *Caresena*:

It is true that D procures the whole course of events resulting in V's account being debited; but the telegraphic transfer is initiated by V and his voluntary intervening acts break the chain of causation. It is the same as if V is induced by deception to take money out of his safe to pay to D. D does not at that moment 'appropriate' it – V is not acting as his agent. D commits theft only if and when the money is put into his hands.

It is submitted that while this approach remains correct after *Gomez* and *Hinks,* those cases do make it very much harder to draw any clear distinction between (i) D's direct acts towards V's property, with V's fraudulently obtained consent (appropriation), and (ii) D's acts causing V to transfer his property with V's fraudulently obtained consent (no appropriation until D acquires it). The distinction seems to be that V's act of transfer in (ii) breaks the chain of causation.[102] D can of course be liable for theft if he induces another party to conduct a transfer on his behalf. If D uses an innocent agent, E, to effect the transfer of V's property, or to extinguish it, there would be no difficulty in establishing a theft charge at the moment that E assumes any right in relation to V's property. Similarly, where D deceives V as to the nature and quality of the act of transfer (as where V is naïve or vulnerable) that would suffice. The fact that V has the authority to act in this way by transferring the property and to consent is, according to *Gomez* and *Hinks,* irrelevant. By setting in motion the transaction D could, in that circumstance, be regarded as having started the continuing act of appropriation.[103]

19.3.1.10 Offers to sell as an act of appropriation?

Under the old law D could be liable for larceny by offering to sell property belonging to another. Under the 1968 Act, on a charge of theft, the question would now be whether he appropriated the property offered for sale. It has been argued that a purported sale of V's property by D might not be an assumption of a right of another.[104] The better view is that although D may lawfully *contract* to sell V's property to X at some future date (D hoping that he will be able to buy it from V in order to sell it to X the meantime);[105] but a purported present sale to a *bona fide* purchaser seems to be an appropriation. Theft, is an 'offence against ownership'; it does not matter that D never gets possession. The property D offered for sale nearly always continues to belong to the original owner, so theft generally has no effect on the owners' rights, as such.

Even in the light of *Gomez*, the earlier case of *Pitham* remains difficult to justify. D, knowing that V was in prison, took Pitham to V's house and offered to sell V's property to Pitham.

---

[99] [2004] EWCA Crim 3662, [2004] Crim LR 455.

[100] There was some confusion as to what D was alleged to have stolen. It appears to be the credit balance representing the proceeds of the sale.

[101] Despite the court's approving reference to the *Oxford English Dictionary* definition of appropriation involving a 'taking', it is submitted that a physical 'taking' or 'touching' is only a sufficient but not a necessary element of the offence, otherwise there would be no protection for intangible property.

[102] cf R Heaton, 'Cheques and Balances' [2005] Crim LR 747.

[103] I am grateful to Tony Shaw QC for clarifying my thinking on this issue. cf *Arlidge and Parry on Fraud*, para 9.113.

[104] Smith, *Property Offences*, 'whereas the owner has a right against others that they shall not deliver his property to third persons (because that involves a tortious interference) he has no general right that they shall not contract to sell it, or purport to pass ownership in it'. para 5.49.

[105] cf Sale of Goods Act 1979, s 5.

It was held that the offer amounted to a completed theft of V's property.[106] Pitham, the buyer, knew that D had no authority to sell V's property and D knew that Pitham knew that. D did not purport to be the owner or have the owner's authority to sell the property. It was not really an offer to sell at all, but a proposal for a joint theft of the property.[107]

19.3.1.11 Continuing appropriation[108]

An offence that is complete at a particular moment may nevertheless continue being committed for some time thereafter. It is often important to know how long a particular theft continued. A person may be guilty of a theft by aiding and abetting it while it is being committed by another, but he cannot aid and abet once the theft is over. A person may be guilty of robbery if he uses force while theft is being committed but not by using force when the theft is at an end. A person may be guilty of the offence of handling stolen goods only if he does a proscribed act 'otherwise than in the course of the stealing'. A person may use reasonable force in preventing a crime, in this case theft, while it is being committed.[109]

Theft may certainly be committed in an instant, so that D could be convicted of the offence even if he was immediately arrested. It does not follow that the offence is over in an instant, though that seems to have been the opinion of the court in *Pitham*.[110] In *Atakpu*,[111] after a careful review of the pre-*Gomez* authorities, Ward J summarized the law as follows:[112]

(1) theft can occur in an instant by a single appropriation but it can also involve a course of dealing with property lasting longer and involving several appropriations before the transaction is complete; (2) theft is a finite act – it has a beginning and it has an end; (3) at what point the transaction is complete is a matter for the jury to decide upon the facts of each case; (4) though there may be several appropriations in the course of a single theft or several appropriations of different goods each constituting a separate theft as in *R v Skipp*, no case suggests that there can be successive thefts of the same property...

The court thought that, on a strict construction, *Gomez* left 'little room for a continuous course of action'. The court did not welcome that consequence of the *Gomez* decision and preferred the view that appropriation continues so long as the thief can sensibly be regarded as in the act of stealing, or in more understandable words, so long as he is 'on the job'.[113] In *Atakpu*, it was not necessary for the court to decide the matter, because no jury could have reasonably concluded that the theft of the cars in Frankfurt or Brussels in that case, was continuing when the cars were brought, days later, into England. It is thought that this is the better view and that to treat appropriation simply as an instantaneous act would be inconsistent with the provisions of the Act relating to robbery and handling, which presuppose that there can be a course of stealing.

---

[106] This was significant because it meant that when the goods were delivered to Pitham he received them 'otherwise than in the course of the stealing' and was therefore guilty of handling stolen goods: see Ch 27 below.

[107] The jury acquitted Pitham of theft although 'The evidence that they had bought property knowing that it was stolen, arose from the fact that they said they had bought considerably under price', 65 Cr App R at 47. How can a buyer knowing that the seller, by selling the property, is stealing it, not be guilty of theft? See also Williams, TBCL (2nd edn, 1983) 764; Ormerod and Williams, *Theft*, para 2.103.

[108] G Williams, 'Appropriation: A Single or Continuous Act' [1978] Crim LR 69.

[109] See *Bowden* [2002] EWCA Crim 1279, where D claimed a defence under s 3 of the Criminal Law Act 1967 when detaining youths whom he believed to have stolen car keys. The Court of Appeal held that the judge was right to leave to the jury the issue of whether the youths' crime of theft of the keys was still continuing at the time of D's actions.

[110] Above, p 793.

[111] Above, p 790.

[112] [1993] 4 All ER 215 at 223.

[113] As it was put in the 7th edition of this book, at 513.

19.3.1.12 Appropriation – when and where?

Where the thief and the property are in different places does the theft take place where and when D acts, or where and when his act affects the property? The problem usually arises in relation to the theft of things in action – intangible property – but it is equally possible with tangible property. D, in England, may dishonestly assume V's rights of ownership over goods in a warehouse in Scotland by selling, or purporting to sell, them to E.[114] The cases have not all taken a consistent approach to the problem. In *Tomsett*,[115] the court of Appeal accepted without argument that the theft occurred at the location of the property in question. Similarly, in *Kohn*,[116] Lane LJ said, *obiter*, that where D had drawn cheques to himself on V's bank account, the theft did not take place until the account was debited. In extradition cases, the courts took different views. In *Ex p Osman*,[117] Osman, in Hong Kong, sent a telex assuming the rights of the owner of a bank account in New York. It was held that this could be theft in Hong Kong. In *Ex p Levin*,[118] the court held that a computer operator in Russia committed theft in the USA by operating on magnetic discs on a computer server in the USA.

In *Ngan*,[119] a large sum intended for V had been mistakenly paid into D's bank account in England. By virtue of s 5(4) of the 1968 Act (discussed below) this property was to be regarded as belonging to V. D dishonestly drew blank cheques on the account and sent them to her sister in Scotland who presented them there for payment. The court, equating the presentation of the cheque with the sending of the telex in *Osman*, held that the theft took place in Scotland. The act of presenting the cheque was the point of appropriation. The signing and issuing of the cheques were preparatory acts to the theft, but the appropriation occurred before the account was debited.

These problems are less likely to arise since the bringing into force of Part 1 of the Criminal Justice Act 1993 and s 1A of the Criminal Law Act 1977, but they are still significant and require resolution. In the light of the broad notion of appropriation followed since *Gomez*, it may be that the theft is committed where and when D does some act which only the owner could properly do; but that it continues to the time when and place where it affects the property.

19.3.1.13 The exception in favour of *bona fide* purchasers: s 3(2)

The definition of appropriation in s 3 includes an important exception:

Where property or a right or interest in property is or purports to be transferred for value to a person acting in good faith, no later assumption by him of rights which he believed himself to be acquiring shall, by reason of any defect in the transferor's title, amount to theft.

The CLRC explained this exception as follows:[120]

A person may buy something in good faith, but may find out afterwards that the seller had no title to it, perhaps because the seller or somebody else stole it. If the buyer nevertheless keeps the thing or otherwise deals with it as owner, he could … be guilty of theft. It is arguable that this would be right;

---

[114] See Ormerod and Williams, *Theft*, para 2.108.

[115] [1985] Crim LR 369. D, a telex operator had transferred funds from V bank to an account in Geneva. The theft occurred in Geneva. His conviction for conspiracy was quashed. This would not be so today. See Criminal Law Act 1977, s 1A, above, p 446.

[116] (1979) 69 Cr App R 395, below, p 797.

[117] *Governor of Pentonville Prison, ex p Osman* [1989] 3 All ER 701, DC. This issue was not discussed in the House of Lords: [1997] AC 741. The Divisional Court comprised of Lloyd LJ and French J, both members of the court in *Tomsett*.

[118] *Governor of Brixton Prison, ex p Levin* [1997] QB 65, DC.

[119] [1998] 1 Cr App R 331. The availability of theft charges was accepted in *Ali* [2009] EWCA Crim 1131.

[120] Eighth Report, para 37. But this exception may now be neutralized by the money laundering legislation, below, p 1000.

but on the whole it seems to us that, whatever view is taken of the buyer's moral duty, the law would be too strict if it made him guilty of theft.

The exception operates in favour only of a person acquiring his interest (eg by buying the property from D or by acquiring other rights over it) in good faith and for value – a 'BFP'. The 'BFP' who discovers that the property is stolen is not guilty of handling if he disposes of it to an innocent person.[121] But the property in the hands of the 'BFP' continues to belong to the owner from whom it was stolen. If the 'BFP', sells it and represents himself as having title to the property he may be guilty of fraud.[122]

19.3.2 Property

Those types of property which may be stolen are defined in s 4 of the Theft Act 1968. The broad effect of the section is that all property may be stolen subject to certain exceptions in relation to land, things growing wild and wild creatures. It is important to note that the offence is founded on orthodox civil law concepts of property.

Legal conceptions of property are constantly evolving to reflect developments in society, and in recent years the particular concern has been for the law to reflect the rapid developments in information technology and the way in which data is stored and accessed. There have been calls to expand the definition of property to provide protection in this area.[123] More radically, there is pressure for the law to recognize a diverse range of rights and interests as species of property (for example, environmental rights and welfare rights).[124] Irrespective of the validity of this re-conceptualization of property, it is submitted that the law of theft is certainly not the most appropriate mechanism for securing protection of these rights under the criminal law. Recent empirical research has also called into question whether thefts of different forms of property, even when equal in value, ought to be treated alike. Green and Kugler distinguish between 'thefts' of items of equal monetary value but different physical and legal form.[125] Subjects consistently ranked the theft of tangible goods as more blameworthy than the theft of intangibles, and the theft of intangible goods as more blameworthy than the theft of services.

Under the 1968 Act, the definition of property is extremely broad, and coupled with the breadth of the definition of appropriation this renders the *actus reus* minimal. The structure of the Act avoids defining offences by distinctions based on the type of property involved, and focuses instead on the manner of the harm being caused. Section 4(1) provides the general definition:

'Property' includes money and all other property, real or personal, including things in action and other intangible property.

The definition is wide enough to include property which is unlawful or illegal or prohibited. D can therefore be guilty of stealing from V the drugs V unlawfully possesses.[126] There are specified exceptions relating to land, animals and plants to be discussed below.

19.3.2.1 Things in action

The one limitation on the generality of the definition of property, apart from the specified exceptions, is that the property must be capable of appropriation. Intangible property may

---

[121] Below, p 872.

[122] See *Wheeler* (1990) 92 Cr App R 279, CA. D did not obtain by deception in selling stolen goods to V but only because the sale, though not the delivery, took place before D became aware that they were stolen.

[123] See, eg, J Lipton, 'A Revised Property Concept for the New Millenium' (1999) 7 Int J of Law and IT 171.

[124] See N Lacey, C Wells and O Quick, *Reconstructing Criminal Law* (4th edn, 2010) 399.

[125] These were: tangible good (a book in their example); an intangible good (a computer file downloaded from a website); a supply of a service which was not limited (attendance at a full lecture) and a service the supply of which was limited (attendance at a lecture in which the hall was half empty). See Green and Kugler (2010) 7 *Journal of Empirical Legal Studies* 511.

[126] See *Smith* [2011] EWCA Crim 66, citing Ormerod and Williams, p 80, with approval.

be appropriated by any assumption of any of the rights of an owner over it.[127] This is best illustrated by reference to one of the most commonplace forms of intangible property – bank accounts. Where a bank account is in credit, the relationship between banker and customer is that of a debtor and creditor. In law, the customer, V, does not have 'money in the bank';[128] there is no specific pile of money that is designated as his. The property that he has is a 'thing in action', a right to payment by the bank of the sum of money it owes him. Thus, if D dishonestly causes a bank to debit V's account, D does not appropriate V's money, he appropriates a thing in action belonging to V (V's right to payment of that sum from the bank) and may be guilty of theft of that property.[129] D has reduced or extinguished V's right to that payment from the bank. Where V has an overdraft with the bank, V has a right to payment from the bank of the sum up to the limit of that agreed overdraft, and that is property – a thing in action – that D may steal by dishonestly causing the bank to debit V's account. The operation of this aspect of the law of theft is illustrated by *Kohn*.[130] D, an accountant employed by a company to write cheques to pay the company's debts, made out cheques on the company's account to meet his personal liabilities and was held guilty of theft of the thing in action.

Care must always be taken to ascertain the state of V's account at the time of the alleged theft by D. If V is overdrawn and has no overdraft facility, D's drawing of a cheque on V's account cannot amount to theft because there is no property to steal – V has no contractual right to any payment from the bank. D's action might amount to attempted theft, like an attempt to steal from an empty pocket.

In terms of conduct by D in relation to bank accounts over which he has control, care must also be taken. In *Hilton*,[131] where D, who had direct control of a bank account belonging to a charity, gave instructions for the transfer of the charity's funds to settle his personal debts, it was held that he stole the thing in action belonging to the charity. On the other hand, D does not steal from his *own* bank where he uses his banker's card to make a purchase, knowing that his own account is overdrawn and that his authority to use the card has terminated.[132] The bank is obliged to meet the cheque and its own funds will be thereby diminished. D has caused the bank to become indebted but he has not assumed a right over any specific property of the bank. If D withdraws money from an ATM at his bank at his bank in excess of his overdraft and without authorization, he may commit theft of the cash.[133]

Stealing or obtaining cheques[134]

Where a cheque is alleged to have been stolen, a different problem arises. A cheque is a piece of paper which, if given for consideration, creates a thing in action – it gives the person in whose favour it is made out a right to sue the person who made out the cheque for the sum stated. So, where V writes a cheque payable to D, as well as obtaining the piece of paper into his physical

[127] See *Storrow and Poole* [1983] Crim LR 332.
[128] 'Although we talk about people having money in the bank, the only person who has money in the bank is the banker', *Davenport* [1954] 1 All ER 602, 603, per Goddard LCJ.
[129] *Chan Man-sin v A-G for Hong Kong* [1988] 1 All ER 1, PC, p 747 above; *Ex p Osman* [1989] 3 All ER 701, DC, above, p 795; *Williams* [2001] 1 Cr App R 362.
[130] [1997] 2 Cr App R 445, [1997] Crim LR 761 and commentary. As discussed above, p 792 it may be different where D, by deception, induces V, the owner and controller of the bank account, to transfer funds from it. V's credit balance, or part of it, has gone, but arguably D did not 'appropriate' it until he took control/possession of the property: *Caresana* [1996] Crim LR 667; *Naviede* [1997] Crim LR 662; *Briggs* [2004] Crim LR 455.
[131] *Navvabi* [1986] 1 WLR 1311, CA.
[132] (1979) 69 Cr App R 395, CA. See further EJ Griew, 'Stealing and Obtaining Bank Credits' [1986] Crim LR 356.
[133] See *Poland v Ulatowski* [2010] EWCA Crim 2673 (Admin).
[134] See JC Smith, 'Obtaining Cheques by Deception or Theft' [1997] Crim LR 396, 'Stealing Tickets' [1998] Crim LR 723 and commentaries on *Horsman* [1998] Crim LR 128 and *Aston* [1998] Crim LR 498; see also *Arlidge and Parry on Fraud*, para 9.151.

possession, D also obtains a thing in action – a right to sue V's bank for the sum specified on the cheque. However, it is crucial to note that the particular thing in action obtained by D is *not* an item of property that previously belonged to V; the thing in action D obtains is *his* right to sue V's bank. This is a new item of property, distinct from that which V owned before he wrote the cheque to D; the previous item of property was *V's* right to sue his bank. In *Preddy*[135] the House accepted this to be the correct state of the law. *Preddy* confirms that the thing in action D obtains belonged from the instant of its creation to him. It never belonged, or could belong, to V. A chose in action is, remember, a right to sue someone, and D could not sue himself!

Where D dishonestly induces V to draw a cheque in his favour, and D attempts to cash the cheque he would now commit fraud contrary to s 1 of the Fraud Act 2006. If D presents the cheque for the credit of his own account, he is at that point guilty of theft of a different thing in action which does belong to V, namely V's credit balance (or right to overdraw if such a facility exists) at his bank.[136] On presenting the cheque,[137] D has assumed V's right to destroy that part of V's property.[138]

D also acquires the cheque itself, the physical thing in the form of the piece of paper. *Preddy* did not decide whether D might be guilty of obtaining this item of property. Lord Goff noted that it does belong to V but said that D would not be guilty because he had no intention permanently to deprive – he knew that the cheque form would, after presentation, be returned to V via his bank (or at least be available for V's collection).[139] It is submitted that this was *obiter* (as well as wrong) but the Court of Appeal in *Graham*[140] treated it as *ratio* and in *Clark*[141] held that it was bound by that decision. So at present a cheque form – piece of paper – cannot be stolen, if D intends to present it for payment. A cheque is still a piece of paper and can be stolen if D intends merely to retain the piece of paper. For example, D might steal from V a cheque which V has never cashed because it was signed by someone famous and V retains it as a souvenir.[142]

So far the discussion has concluded that D does not obtain a thing in action from V (the one he acquires has never belonged to V), and does not steal the cheque form (that is, the paper). There is an argument that D could also be convicted of theft of the cheque not as a piece of paper, but as a 'valuable security'. A cheque is recognized as a 'valuable security' by s 20 of the 1968 Act. This is a highly technical area of law,[143] but it is easy enough to understand that a cheque is special – not just any piece of paper which will cause, say, a bank clerk to hand over £1,000; but a cheque will do that. Of course the cheque *is* (i) a piece of paper which (ii) *creates* a thing in action but it is also (iii) a valuable security. A valuable security is an item of property that may be stolen; and that means, not the theft of the thing in action, nor a mere piece of paper, but the instrument, the physical thing with certain writing on it.[144] The Supreme

---

[135] [1996] AC 815.

[136] *Burke*, above, and *Williams (Roy)* [2001] 1 Cr App R 362, [2001] Crim LR 253.

[137] *Ngan* [1998] 1 Cr App R 331.

[138] Prior to the Fraud Act coming into force (15.01.07) D committed no offence of obtaining property by deception because D's increased credit balance (a thing in action belonging to D – his right to sue his bank) was never 'property belonging to another', *Burke* [2000] Crim LR 413, applying *Preddy*.

[139] This assumes they will all be retained for V; modern banking practice is not to do so. D may intend to return the piece of paper, but not the valuable security: see below. That may make an allegation of theft of the valuable security an attractive one.

[140] [1997] 1 Cr App R 302.

[141] [2001] Crim LR 572, [2001] EWCA Crim 884.

[142] See *Roach* [2011] EWCA Crim 918 (blank cheque D never going to present).

[143] 'A cheque is not a piece of paper and no more.... It is a piece of paper with certain special characteristics', *Kohn* (1979) 69 Cr App R 395 at 409, per Lord Lane CJ.

[144] *Arnold* [1997] 4 All ER 1, [1997] Crim LR 833. D was convicted of stealing a valuable security, a bill of exchange, signed by V, creating a thing in action which V could never own, but was nevertheless, property belonging to him. But cf *Horsman*, above, n 134.

Court of Victoria in *Parsons*,[145] accepted this argument. The English Court of Appeal found it 'highly persuasive' but, unlike the Victorian court, was unable to follow it. The question of D's liability for theft may still be open to argument.[146] D will, of course, be liable under the Fraud Act if he makes any false representation relating to the account, the cheque form or his right to use them, provided he also has the relevant *mens rea*.

A final point to note is that a cheque creates a thing in action *only if it is given for valuable consideration*.[147] If D induces V to make him a gift of a cheque for £50, that cheque does not create a thing in action – but it is still a cheque and, it is submitted, a valuable security. Unless V stops it, the cheque will enable D to deprive V of £50. When D gets his hands on it, he has a valuable, tangible, thing in his possession. It is submitted that such a cheque is a valuable security capable of being stolen.

19.3.2.2 Other intangible property

The reach of the law of theft is extended yet further by s 4(1) beyond things in action to include 'other intangible property'. An illustration is provided by *A-G of Hong Kong v Chan Nai-Keung*,[148] The export of textiles from Hong Kong was prohibited except under licence, and exports were regulated by a quota system. An exporter who, in a given year, could not meet his quotas could sell his surplus export quotas to an exporter who could meet them, and there was a flourishing market in these quotas. D, a director of the A exporting company, without the authorization of the A company, sold surplus quotas at a gross undervalue to the B exporting company in which D had an interest as a director. It was held that the quotas, though they were not things in action, were nevertheless 'other intangible property' – the quotas were things of value which could be bought and sold and by knowingly selling them at an undervalue D had appropriated them.[149]

The definition of property is so broad that it is easier to focus on the things that do not constitute property for the purposes of the Act. Some of these limitations on what constitutes property are contained in the Act (land, wild animals, electricity) and some are the result of case law – eg confidential information. Each merits consideration.

19.3.2.3 Limitations on the theft of land

It would have been technically possible to make land generally stealable (eg where D moves his boundary fence a few inches into V's garden), since rights over land are just as capable of appropriation as rights in goods. But limitations have been imposed for reasons of policy. In drafting the Theft Act the CLRC considered that there were numerous reasons[150] for not treating this as theft, including: that appropriating land by encroachment was rare and could

---

[145] [1998] 2 VR 478; affd 73 ALJR 27, High Ct of Aust.

[146] A point of law of general importance was certified; the House refused leave on the ground that the offence of obtaining a money transfer by deception and other offences are adequate. That is not correct. In *Marshall*, considered below, p 808, it was argued that, if a cheque cannot be stolen from the drawer, a ticket cannot be stolen from the company issuing it. The court dismissed this argument as impossible, but it is submitted that it is right. The cheque and the ticket are both papers which create and embody a thing in action against the issuer. In neither case can the thing in action be stolen or obtained from the issuer – it cannot belong to him – but that is no reason why the paper, which does belong to him and which is a valuable thing, cannot be stolen from him. For an argument against this approach relying on the valuable security see *Arlidge and Parry on Fraud*, para 9.155.

[147] That is, any consideration sufficient to support a simple contract or an antecedent debt or liability: Bills of Exchange Act 1882, s 27(1).

[148] [1987] 1 WLR 1339, [1988] Crim LR 125, PC. The law of theft in Hong Kong was identical in this respect to the law of England.

[149] *Pilgram v Rice-Smith* [1977] 2 All ER 658, DC; *Bhachu* (1976) 65 Cr App R 261, CA.

[150] Eighth Report, paras 40–44. cf Smith, *Property Offences*, paras 3.32–3.33, 3.38.

be dealt with adequately by civil remedies;[151] and it might create conflict with the civil law (D could get good title by occupation for twelve years and it would be odd if he remained even theoretically guilty of theft for ever afterwards). Section 4(2) therefore limits the scope of theft of land, and provides:

A person cannot steal land, or things forming part of land and severed from it by him or by his directions, except in the following cases, that is to say –

(a) when he is a trustee or personal representative, or is authorized by power of attorney, or as liquidator of a company, or otherwise, to sell or dispose of land belonging to another, and he appropriates the land or anything forming part of it by dealing with it in breach of the confidence reposed in him; or

(b) when he is not in possession of the land and appropriates anything forming part of the land by severing it or causing it to be severed, or after it has been severed; or

(c) when, being in possession of the land under a tenancy, he appropriates the whole or part of any fixture or structure let to be used with the land.[152]

(1) *Appropriation by trustees etc.*[153] Exceptionally, land, or things forming part of the land, are capable of being stolen by trustees etc. Thus, a trustee may appropriate land held in trust by an unauthorized disposition. Of course an unauthorized dealing is not, of itself, theft since the other elements of the offence must be present. If, for example, a trustee is authorized to sell the land only to A and he sells it to B because B is offering a much better price, the unauthorized sale by the trustee might not be dishonest.

(2) *Appropriation by persons not in possession.* It is not theft for D to appropriate land without severing it, as where he moves his boundary fence so as to incorporate a strip of V's land into his own.[154] However, a person not in possession can steal anything forming part of the land by severing it or by appropriating it after it has been severed. Thus, it may be theft where D helps himself to the topsoil in V's garden, or to a gate, or to rose bushes, or even to growing grass.[155] In each case the appropriation is complete upon severance,[156] but where the thing is already severed, as where the gate is lying in V's yard for repair, the appropriation would be complete, at the latest, when D takes control of it.

(3) *Appropriation by tenants of fixtures.* A tenant cannot steal the land which he possesses by virtue of the tenancy, nor of things forming part of the land. If D, a tenant, removes topsoil from the premises, say to sell it to a neighbour, he is appropriating property of

[151] But the Committee observed (ibid, para 42) that moving boundaries was a 'real problem, especially in crowded housing estates'. Rarity did not prevent the CLRC creating the offence under s 11 (below, p 849) which seems to owe its origin to *three* known instances of its occurrence.

[152] For purposes of this subsection 'land' does not include incorporeal hereditaments; (eg easements) 'tenancy' means a tenancy for years or any less period and includes an agreement for such a tenancy, but a person who after the end of a tenancy remains in possession as statutory tenant or otherwise is to be treated as having possession under the tenancy, and 'let' shall be construed accordingly.

[153] See R Brazier, 'Criminal Trustees?' (1975) 39 Conv (NS) 29. Such individuals would be liable for fraud under s 4 of the Fraud Act 2006.

[154] The arguments for and against making land the subject of theft are summarized in the Eighth Report, at 21–22.

[155] By human hand or by grazing cattle: *McGill v Shepherd* (unreported), M Williams and C Weinberg, *The Australian Law of Theft* (3rd edn,1986) 116. In 1972, a man was prosecuted at Leeds Crown Court for stealing Cleckheaton railway station by dismantling and removing it. He was acquitted on the merits, the jury accepting that on this bold enterprise he was acting under a claim of right. But railway stations are stealable by severance.

[156] Note that if D is caught in the act of severing he is guilty only of an attempt. By attempting to sever D is, of course, assuming the rights of an owner and in other circumstances (above, p 792), this alone constitutes a complete appropriation. But in this case the effect of the subsection is to insist upon severance to complete the theft.

another (the landlord) but he is not guilty of theft. A tenant may be guilty of theft, however, where he appropriates (and here severance is not required) any fixture or structure let to be used with the land. A fixture here means something annexed to land for use or ornament, such as a washbasin, cupboards or a fireplace, and a structure seems to mean some structure of a moveable or temporary character, such as a garden shed or a greenhouse. A house would not be a structure in this sense.

(4) *Appropriation by persons not in possession.* In contrast, if D's son, who is living with D, the tenant, removes the topsoil to sell it the son would be guilty of theft because he is not 'in possession' of the land although he happens to live there.

To determine potential liability for theft, it may, therefore, be important to determine whether a particular article forms part of the land. Generally, appropriation will involve severance, so non-possessors will be caught by s 4(2)(b) while tenants are caught by s 4(2)(c). But if a licensee in possession appropriates a structure, it is vital to know whether it forms part of the land. This is a question of land law and the answer depends on the degree of annexation and the object of annexation.[157]

19.3.2.4 Limitations on the theft of things growing wild

There is a long-standing cultural tradition in Britain of picking fruits from the land for consumption.[158] Section 4(3) of the Act provides some limited protection from theft charges in such circumstances:

A person who picks mushrooms growing wild on any land, or who picks flowers, fruit or foliage from a plant growing wild on any land, does not (although not in possession of the land) steal what he picks, unless he does it for reward or for sale or other commercial purpose.

For purposes of this subsection 'mushroom' includes any fungus, and 'plant' includes any shrub or tree.[159]

In some ways it might be thought that s 4(3) is rather unnecessary. It exempts from liability for theft someone who picks wild mushrooms, or one who picks flowers, fruit or foliage '*from a plant*' (thus a person who takes the whole plant may be convicted of theft)[160] growing wild on land unless done for sale or other commercial purpose. Picking holly branches around about Christmas time for the purpose of sale may amount to theft, as may picking elderberries for making wine if the purpose is to sell the wine. The whole matter might have been left to the common sense of the prosecutor who would hardly institute proceedings where the appropriation was trivial. Of course this would leave the aggrieved landowner free to take proceedings in such trivial cases, but generally under the criminal law the person aggrieved is free to take proceedings in the most trivial case and this does not apparently lead to any serious abuse. However, the CLRC thought that, 'a provision could reasonably be criticized which made it even technically theft in all cases to pick wild flowers against the will of the landowner'.[161]

In some instances liability might also arise under the Criminal Damage Act 1971.

---

[157] See *Elitestone Ltd v Morris* [1997] 1 WLR 687, HL. The chattel must be actually fixed to the land, not for its more convenient use as a chattel, but for the more convenient use of the land Compare *Elitestone v Morris* [1997] 2 All ER 513 – timber bungalow on concrete stand on land only removable by destroying part of land, held to be part of land; cf *Chelsea Yacht and Boat Club v Pope* [2001] 2 All ER 409 – houseboat secured to riverbed pontoon and river walls by mooring ropes is not part of land.

[158] See M Welstead, 'Season of Mists and Mellow Fruitfulness' (1995) 150 NLJ 1499.

[159] For discussion of the legal protection of trees see the recent case of *Palm Developments Ltd v SoS for Communities and Local Govt* [2009] EWHC 220 (Admin).

[160] This raises interesting possibilities in the case of GM protestors who remove seedlings.

[161] Eighth Report, para 47. The Wildlife and Countryside Act 1981 makes it an offence to kill, possess or sell certain creatures; and to pick, uproot or destroy certain wild plants.

19.3.2.5 Limitations on the theft of wild creatures

Section 4(4) of the Act provides:

Wild creatures, tamed or untamed, shall be regarded as property; but a person cannot steal a wild creature not tamed nor ordinarily kept in captivity, or the carcase of any such creature, unless either it has been reduced into possession by or on behalf of another person and possession of it has not since been lost or abandoned, or another person is in course of reducing it into possession.

It is possible, therefore, to steal wild creatures where these have been tamed or are ordinarily kept in captivity. A tiger may be stolen from a zoo, and if it has escaped it may be stolen while at large because it is 'ordinarily' kept in captivity.

Wild animals while at large are not owned by anyone, nor does a landowner have a proprietary interest in such animals even where they constitute game. The landowner has, however, the right to take wild animals, and once a wild animal is caught or killed it immediately becomes the property of the landowner where this takes place. The taker (that is, the killer, trapper, etc) would be guilty of theft but for the protection afforded by s 4(4). He is guilty instead of a minor offence of poaching.[162] Poaching may amount to an offence under a variety of enactments[163] – the Night Poaching Act 1828, the Game Act 1831[164] as amended by the Game Laws (Amendment) Act 1960 and the Poaching Prevention Act 1862.[165] Deer are protected by the Deer Act 1991.

The CLRC recommended[166] that poaching should be theft when done 'for reward or for sale or other commercial purpose'. Parliament rejected that proposal. Poaching is unlawful but it was felt that it would be going too far, even in such cases, to turn this traditional country pastime into theft.

Wild animals may be stolen when they are in the process of being reduced into possession by or on behalf of another. A lazy poacher who picks up the pheasants shot from the skies by V is a thief, as is a gamekeeper who keeps for himself a pheasant which he shot for his employer. And if V, having shot a pheasant, cannot find it in the brush and gives up the search, a subsequent appropriation by D makes him a thief from the landowner.[167]

In *Cresswell v DPP*,[168] the Divisional Court considered whether badgers which had been enticed into traps set by officials from DEFRA had become 'property' for the purposes of the Criminal Damage Act 1971 (identically worded in this respect to the Theft Act). The defendants who had destroyed the traps sought to argue that the badgers were property and they had a defence to destruction of the traps on the basis that they were protecting property – the badgers. Keene LJ, rejecting the argument, stated that 'merely to entice a wild animal, whether it be a badger or a game bird or a deer, to a particular spot from time to time by providing food there, even with the objective ultimately of killing it in due course, does not form part of the course normally of reducing it into possession. If the creature were thereby to become the property, say, of the landowner providing the food, it would mean that it could not then be lawfully shot by the adjoining landowner on or over whose

---

[162] See *Halsbury's Laws of England*, vol 11, para 570. See K Cook, *Wildlife Law: Conservation and Biodiversity* (2004).

[163] See generally the Wildlife and Countryside Act 1981, ss 1, 9, and Sch 5.

[164] Section 24 protects against the destruction or taking of game eggs. Section 23 of the Game Act 1831 made it an offence to kill game without a game certificate. This section was repealed by art 2(h) of Regulatory Reform (Game) Order 2007, SI 2007, removing various licensing requirements to kill or take game.

[165] Which protects, *inter alia*, game eggs.

[166] Eighth Report, para 52.

[167] As to abandonment, see below, p 822.

[168] [2006] EWHC 3379 (Admin).

land it passed'.[169] Walker J was more hesitant, declining to express a concluded view on what constitutes property.[170]

19.3.2.6 Electricity

On the face of it all property is capable of appropriation, but there were formerly doubts whether electricity was capable of appropriation. The dishonest use, wasting or diverting of electricity was a separate offence under the Larceny Acts and the position was preserved by s 13 of the Theft Act. The CLRC observed that, 'This has to be a separate offence because owing to its nature electricity is excluded from the definition of stealing in ... [s] 1(1) of the [Act].'[171] The Committee's view was endorsed in *Low v Blease*[172] where it was held that, electricity not being property capable of appropriation, D could not be convicted of burglary in entering premises and making a telephone call from them.[173] Heat is a thing of value, as anyone paying the bills well knows, but it seems that it would not be theft to assume the right to heat belonging to V, by diverting V's hot water so as to warm D's premises.[174] The heat is energy (as is electricity) but is not property.

Section 13 of the Theft Act 1968 provides:

A person who dishonestly uses without due authority, or dishonestly causes to be wasted or diverted, any electricity shall on conviction on indictment be liable to imprisonment for a term not exceeding five years.

This provision will ordinarily be applied to the case where D dishonestly[175] uses some device to bypass his electricity meter, but beyond that it is capable of some curious applications.[176] There were 1,738 offences of dishonest use of electricity recorded in 2009/10.[177] Applied strictly there might be an offence under this section where D borrows an electrically driven vehicle such as an environmentally friendly car, golf buggy or disabled-person's scooter,

---

[169] [11].

[170] His lordship suggested that: '[i]n broad terms, (a) it is a question of law whether an animal is wild or domestic.... (b) Once a wild animal is killed or dies, absolute property in the dead animal vests in the owner of the land or, in a case where relevant shooting or sporting rights have been granted, in the owner of those rights. (c) While a wild animal is alive there is no absolute property in that animal. There may, however, be what is known as a qualified property in them in three circumstances. The first is described as a qualified property *per industriam*. Wild animals become the property of a person who takes or tames or reclaims them until they regain their natural liberty and have not the intention to return. Examples of that kind of property include animals such as deer, swans and doves. A second qualified property is described as *ratione impotentiae et loci*. The owner of land has a qualified property in the young of animals born on the land until they can fly or run away. A third type of qualified property is described as *ratione soli* and *ratione privilegii*. An owner of land who has retained the exclusive right to hunt, take and kill wild animals on his land has a qualified property in them for the time being while they are there but if he grants to another the right to hunt, take or kill them then the grantee has a qualified property.'[38].

[171] Eighth Report, para 85. See further Griew, *Theft*, paras 2.162–2.165; Williams, TBCL, 736–737; Ormerod and Williams, *Theft*, Ch 11.

[172] [1975] Crim LR 513, DC. cf *Flack v Baldry* [1988] 1 WLR 214, treating electricity as a 'noxious thing' for the purposes of Firearms Act 1968, s 5(1)(b).

[173] See *P* (2000) 11 Aug, CA, No 0003586 Y5, where D entered his neighbour's property as a trespasser and made phone calls to premium rate sex chat lines.

[174] *Clinton v Cahill* [1998] NI 200. Nor is it theft of the hot water, unless all, or substantially all, of the heat is exhausted, so as to deprive the water of its 'virtue'.

[175] See *Boggeln v Williams* [1978] 2 All ER 1061, [1978] Crim LR 242, DC, below, p 828. Care must be taken when the offence alleged is against a number of occupants of a property in which the meter has been bypassed – *Hoar and Hoar* [1992] Crim LR 606; *Collins and Fox v Chief Constable of Merseyside* [1988] Crim LR 247.

[176] cf Ormerod and Williams, *Theft*, para 2.176. It has been prosecuted where, eg, D has wired his house up to the nearby street lamp to run appliances free.

[177] See Flatley et al, *Crime in England and Wales 2009/10*, table 2.04.

though there would be no theft of the vehicle, nor an offence of taking a conveyance under s 12.[178] But proceedings under s 13 in such a case are perhaps very unlikely. There might be some reluctance to prosecute when the substance of what D does is not criminal, even though there is technically some incidental offence.[179]

In terms of *actus reus,* it is enough under s 13 that D causes electricity to be wasted or diverted; he need not be shown to have made any use of the electricity for himself. An employee who, out of spite for his employer, puts on all the lighting and heating appliances in the office would commit the offence; but a fellow employee, or even a stranger, who, knowing what D has done, chooses to stay in the office to enjoy the warmth, would not: 'use' implies some consumption of electricity which would not occur but for the accused's acts.[180] The offence extends only to the abstraction of electricity, whether from the mains or a battery source. Gas and water, if dishonestly appropriated, can form the subject of a theft charge. Despite the upsurge in using more environmentally friendly energy sources (solar and wind, etc) the s 13 offence only protects against the dishonest abstraction of these forms of power once converted.[181]

The *mens rea* of s 13 is dishonesty. The partial definition of dishonesty in s 2 (below) does not apply; the test of dishonesty in *Ghosh* does.[182] Although it has been held in cases of electricity meter tampering that the defendant must be shown to have an intention not to pay, this is too generous to the defence; it is one factor to be considered in the overall question of dishonesty.[183] There is a potential problem with *mens rea*: D may plausibly claim that he did not consider the fact that he was causing the electricity to be used, and thus lacks the necessary *mens rea,* as, for example, where D makes unauthorized use of a telephone. It was perhaps for these reasons that the law was amended by the Theft Act 1968[184] to create the specific offence of dishonestly using a communication system with intent to avoid payment.[185] This provides an appropriately labelled charge and avoids the prosecution appearing strained.

Parliament has created specific offences to deal with dishonesty in relation to particular conduct involving electronic equipment including, for example, receiving programmes broadcast via satellite and cable,[186] reprogramming,[187] or offering or agreeing to change or

---

[178] See below, Ch 21.

[179] Prosecutions have been brought for stealing the petrol consumed where D has borrowed a motor vehicle, but this was never regarded as satisfactory, and the offence of taking motor vehicles was introduced. cf *Low v Blease,* above, where it was apparently assumed that a dishonest user of a telephone may commit the offence under s 13. See also *R v Sui-Tak-Chee* (1984) unreported, in which abstracting electricity valued at one-eighth of a Hong Kong cent by using a computer without authorization led to a conviction; referred to in S Fafinski, 'Access Denied' (2006) 70 J Crim Law 424.

[180] This sentence was approved in *McReadie and Tume* (1992) 96 Cr App R 143, [1992] Crim LR 872 CA.

[181] There are strong policy arguments for saying that if D prevents V's solar panels from working by blocking the sun over his property or deprives V's turbines of wind, V's remedy should be through the civil law, and not the criminal law.

[182] *Melwani* [1989] Crim LR 565, CA.

[183] See *Collins and Fox v Chief Constable of Merseyside* [1988] Crim LR 247; Griew, *Theft,* para 2.164.

[184] Sch 2, Part 1, para 8, see now Communications Act 2003, s 125: dishonestly obtaining an electronic communications service with intent to avoid payment of a charge applicable to that service. But this does not cover 999 calls since no payment is involved; it is, however, an offence under s 5(2) of the Criminal Law Act 1967 to cause any wasteful employment of the police.

[185] Punishable, on summary conviction, by six months' imprisonment and/or a fine not exceeding the statutory maximum; and, on indictment, by two years' imprisonment. As to the intent, cf *Corbyn v Saunders* [1978] Crim LR 169, DC.

[186] Copyright Designs and Patents Act 1988, s 297(1) and s 297A inserted by the Conditional Access (Unauthorised Decoders) Regs 2000, SI 1175. See *Mainwaring* [2002] FSR 20. On the spate of prosecutions relating to unauthorized viewing of premiership football matches see S Clover, 'Confused Signals – Satellite Broadcasting and Premiership Football' [2007] Ent LR 234.

[187] Mobile Telephones (Re-programming) Act 2002.

interfere with, or offering or agreeing to arrange for another person to change or interfere with mobile phone SIM cards.[188]

19.3.2.7 Confidential information

It has been held[189] that confidential information, though it has a value and can be sold, is not property within s 4(1). Accordingly, an undergraduate was not guilty of theft where he unlawfully acquired an examination paper and returned that original piece of paper after he had read its contents.[190] The 'theft' of information is a serious problem, particularly in the form of industrial espionage, for which the civil law arguably provides inadequate remedies. However, as Griew observes,[191] the Theft Act is not the appropriate instrument to deal with this specialized kind of mischief. The Law Commission has reviewed the possibility of introducing a specific offence of the misuse of trade secrets,[192] and in view of the significance and prevalence of the problem, legislation would seem desirable. The Law Commission's proposal was to criminalize non-consensual use or disclosure of another's trade secrets.

19.3.2.8 Services

Services do not constitute property, so it is not theft for D dishonestly to walk off without paying for his haircut. Specific offences were originally included in the Theft Act 1978 to deal with this problem, and now the Fraud Act 2006 provides an offence of dishonestly obtaining services which was described by the Law Commission when drafting it as 'akin to theft'.[193]

19.3.3 Belonging to another

The third element of the *actus reus* of theft is that the property which D appropriates must belong to another.

19.3.3.1 The general rule

Section 5(1) of the Theft Act 1968 provides:

Property shall be regarded as belonging to any person having possession or control of it, or having in it any proprietary right or interest (not being an equitable interest arising only from an agreement to transfer or grant an interest).

The onus is on the prosecution to prove that the property in question belonged to someone.[194] Frequently this is self-evident and not disputed at trial, but not always.

---

[188] Violent Crime Reduction Act 2006, s 62 amending the 2002 Act.

[189] *Oxford v Moss* (1978) 68 Cr App R 183, [1979] Crim LR 119.

[190] But see commentary at [1979] Crim LR 119.

[191] Griew, *Theft*, para 2.25. See further R Hammond, 'Theft of Information' (1984) 100 LQR 252; JT Cross, 'Protecting Confidential Information under the Criminal Law of Theft and Fraud' (1991) 11 OJLS 264; AL Christie, 'Should the Law of Theft Extend to Information?' (2005) 69 J Crim Law 349; A Coleman, *Intellectual Property Law* (1994). See also L Weinreib, 'Information and Property' (1988) 38 UTLJ 117, and the Canadian Supreme Court in *Stewart* (1988) 50 DLR 1.

[192] See LCCP 150, *Legislating the Criminal Code: Misuses of Trade Secrets* (1997), and the reviews by J Hull, 'Stealing Secrets: A Review of the Law Commission Consultation Paper' [1998] Crim LR 246; A Trenton, and C Steele, 'Trade Secrets: The Need for Criminal Liability' (1998) 20 EIPR 188. For a recent review of the criminal law's general protection for intellectual property, see C Davies, 'Protection of Intellectual Property – A Myth?' (2004) 68 J Crim Law 398.

[193] See below, p 910.

[194] The person to whom the property belongs will usually be known and identified in the indictment, but if the owner is unknown D may be charged with stealing the property of a person unknown provided that this does not result in D being unable to ascertain the nature of the case he has to meet. cf *Gregory* [1972] 2 All ER 861 at

In the ordinary case, property is stolen from someone who both owns and possesses it, by someone who has no interest in the property whatever, as where V's wallet is stolen by a stranger, D. Section 5(1) covers this case, of course, but it goes much further. Two partners both own the whole of the partnership property; but, if one of them dishonestly makes off with it to the exclusion of the other, he steals it from the other.[195] As a further example of the breadth of s 5(1), suppose that V lends a book to X and that X is showing the book to Z when D snatches the book from Z's hands and makes off with it. Here D has stolen the book from Z (who has control of it), and X (who has possession of it), and V (who also has a proprietary interest – ownership – in it).

Moreover, under s 5(1), D can still be guilty of stealing an item of property if he has an interest (that is, possession or control) in that property, provided someone else, V, also has a proprietary interest in it at the same time and it is D's intention dishonestly to deprive V permanently of his interest. So, in the above illustration, if Z were dishonestly to appropriate the book he would steal it from both V and X,[196] and if X were dishonestly to appropriate the book he would steal it from V. An owner may even steal his own property. So, if A owns a book, and lends it to B, while the book is in B's possession it belongs to B for the purposes of s 5(1). When A appropriates it, there is 'another' who has a proprietary interest: B. It is important to note that s 5 does not place any limitations on the class of persons who may steal. Thus, there is nothing to say that a person cannot steal where he has a better proprietary claim than the victim. So, in our example D can be liable for theft of his book on loan to V even though D is the owner and V has mere possession of it.

Of course, it will be rare for D's appropriation of his own property to amount not just to an appropriation but to a complete theft because D will be unlikely to possess *mens rea*: he may easily be able to plead a claim of right,[197] or be unlikely to be found dishonest generally. But consider *Turner (No 2)*.[198] D had left his car with V for repair, promising to pay for the repairs when he returned to collect the car the following day. D, however, returned a few hours later and surreptitiously took back his car using the spare keys. Although D claimed that he was entitled to do as he did, it was clear from the circumstances that he was acting dishonestly, and his conviction for stealing the car from V was affirmed. At first sight this seems obviously right because D was out to cheat V of his right to retain the property until the debt for the service work was satisfied (technically his 'lien'). V had a proprietary right or interest in the property and, even as against the owner, D, the car could be properly regarded as belonging to V so long as he had his lien. Unfortunately the trial judge told the jury to disregard the question of the lien. Thus, the case is authority for a much broader proposition: that D may steal his own property from V who is D's 'bailee at will', (that is, where D is entitled to terminate the bailment *at any time*). It is obvious that so long as V remains in possession of D's property he has a 'proprietary right or interest' as against third parties. Should X have come along and taken Turner's car while it was in V's possession, there would be no difficulty in saying X stole it from V. But it seems odd to regard V as having a 'proprietary interest' as against D, when D could determine the bailment and take back his property as he is entitled to do.

866, CA (handling property of person unknown); and see *Anglim and Cooke v Thomas* [1974] VR 363 at 374 (SC of Victoria).

[195] *Bonner* [1970] 1 WLR 838.

[196] cf *Thompson* (1862) Le & Ca 225. D made off with a sovereign which V handed him to buy a ticket for her because she was unable to make her way through the crowd before a ticket office. This would be theft by D. cf *Rose v Matt* [1951] 1 KB 810, [1951] 1 All ER 361, DC.

[197] Below, p 825.

[198] [1971] 2 All ER 441, CA.

Turner is difficult to justify.[199] A better decision is that of Judge Da Cunha in *Meredith*.[200] D surreptitiously removed his car from a police pound where it had been lawfully placed by the police for causing an obstruction. It was held that D could not be convicted of stealing the car. The police were lawfully in possession of it so that a third party could have stolen it from them. But, they had no right to retain it from D: they had a right to enforce the statutory charge for its removal from the compound, but not to retain it from him. It is useful to compare the position of the police and the repairer in *Turner (No 2)*. There are differences,[201] but, if the police were not liable in *Meredith*, Turner should not have been be liable (ignoring the repairer's lien as the courts in that case did).

19.3.3.2 Possession or control

Possession and control may overlap, and it is not important to pursue any possible distinction between them because property is treated as belonging to V if he has *either* possession or control. It is the limits of these concepts which are important, not the difference between them.

Possession requires both an intention to possess and some degree of control in fact. If V and D both see a wallet on the pavement, both may have the same intent to possess it, but until one of them seizes it neither has possession. Once V seizes it he has both possession and control. If he hands it to D just to show D what he has got, it would normally be said that V retains possession while D has control.

Possession and control are not, however, always as clear cut as in this illustration where V's intent existed in respect of a specific article (wallet) and he reduced it into his actual control – he had it in his hands. But it is not necessary to have, or ever to have had, control of a thing in this sense in order to have possession. A drinks vending-machine supplier may have possession of the coins inserted in the machine without knowing at any given moment how many coins, if any, are in the machine.[202] Similarly, a householder normally has possession of the whole contents of his house even though he cannot itemize all his goods. He may consign unwanted articles to his attic or cellar and forget about them, but he still retains possession.

It is not, then, essential that V's intent to possess should exist in respect of a specific thing: it may be enough for V's intent to exist in respect of all the goods situated about his premises. In *Woodman*,[203] V owned some disused business premises. V sold all the scrap metal on the premises to X; X removed most of it but left some as being too inaccessible to be worth the expense of removal. D then entered the premises to take some of this scrap and was held to have been rightly convicted of theft from V. V continued to control the site and by erecting fences and posting notices V showed that he intended to exclude others; that was enough to give V control of the scrap which he did not wish to remove.

This principle was exemplified in the recent cases involving the theft of golf balls from lakes and water features on courses with a view to the balls being resold (reportedly producing a £15,000 to £30,000 annual turnover). In *Rostron*,[204] the Court of Appeal confirmed that the

---

[199] In so far as *Turner* decided that V's possession need not be lawful, it is obviously right and was approved on this point in *Kelly* [1998] 3 All ER 741 at 750. It may be theft to take the stolen property from a thief; the law protects his possession. But the point in *Turner* is that D (in the absence of a lien) had every right to take his own property back. If the owner takes his property from a thief who is unlawfully detaining it, does he steal it if he mistakenly thinks it is someone else's property?

[200] [1973] Crim LR 253.

[201] The police were not bailees of the car (they came into possession by a statutory power to take the car).

[202] cf *Martin v Marsh* [1955] Crim LR 781 (electricity meters). But see [1956] Crim LR 74.

[203] [1974] QB 754,CA. See also *Hibbert v McKiernan* [1948] 2 KB 142, DC (theft of golf balls 'lost' on club premises) criticized by R Hickey (2006) 26 LS 584 for its 'cavalier' reasoning, at 600; *Williams v Phillips* (1957) 41 Cr App R 5, DC (theft of refuse from dustbins). See below, p 822.

[204] [2003] All ER (D) 269 (Jul), [2003] EWCA Crim 2206.

issue was whether there was evidence that golf balls hit into a lake were property belonging to another – the club owning the course.[205] It remains necessary for the prosecution to prove that the golf ball retrievers were acting dishonestly in order to sustain a theft conviction, and that may be no easy task. Possibly a finder who was not trespassing – a visitor playing a round of golf or a person crossing the course under a public right of way – would have a better right than the club to the ball. If so (and it is a question of civil law turning on whether they had exercised control over the course to assert title to the property on it), it is submitted that he could not be guilty of theft.

Dependence on civil law

In some instances the question of who has a proprietary interest will turn on technical issues of civil law. In *Marshall*,[206] D obtained part-used underground tickets and travelcards from members of the public passing through railway barriers and resold them to other potential customers, so depriving London Underground Ltd (LUL) of the revenue it would have gained from the potential customers. D was convicted of theft of the part-used tickets from LUL. The court assumed that those tickets, though in the possession of the passengers, continued to belong to LUL because there was a contract term to that effect on the reverse of each ticket.[207] If reasonable efforts had been made by LUL to bring that term to the passengers notice the passenger was a mere bailee of the ticket[208] – he was in possession of a ticket belonging to LUL. It could be stolen from him and from LUL. If sufficient notice of the term was not given to the passenger, the ticket belonged only to the passenger who had originally purchased it, LUL had no proprietary interest in it, and D could not properly be convicted of stealing from LUL. The availability of the theft charge turns on the application of the law of contract. (See also below in relation to equitable interests).

19.3.3.3 Proprietary interests and treasure trove

At common law, the rules of treasure trove governed whether the Crown owned articles of gold or silver whose original owner or successors in title could not be found.[209] The Treasure Act 1996 abolished the law relating to 'treasure trove', replacing it by a wide concept of 'treasure' including, as well as any object which would previously have been treasure trove, other specified objects at least 300, or in some cases 200, years old.[210] When 'treasure' is found it vests in the Crown. The finder of treasure, D, who takes it for himself commits the *actus reus* of theft: he has appropriated property belonging to the Crown. To prove theft from the

---

[205] See L Toczek, 'Never Plead Guilty!' (2002) 146 SJ 455. See also the detailed analysis by Hickey (above) considering whether it would matter if the balls were in the ground (in a water feature or embedded, etc) or on the ground, and suggesting that the criminal courts ought to follow the civil law where the property is found on the land – asking whether the landowner had evidenced an intention to control the land and anything on it. Where the item is found in the land, title should be with the landowner.

[206] [1998] 2 Cr App R 282, discussed by JC Smith, 'Stealing Tickets' [1998] Crim LR 723. For consideration of the case and offences that may have been committed see also K Reid and J MacLeod, 'Ticket Touts or Theft of Tickets and Related Offences' (1999) 63 J Crim Law 593.

[207] Even if such a term existed, it is for the jury to determine whether LUL had taken reasonable steps to bring that condition to the notice of the 'buyer' – as the passenger probably thought himself to be: see the contract case of *Parker v South Eastern Rly Co* (1877) 2 CPD 416, CA.

[208] He was a buyer of the right to travel on the railway, a thing in action.

[209] See *Hancock* (1989) 90 Cr App R 422, [1990] Crim LR 125 and the discussion in earlier editions of this work.

[210] See, generally, EM Paintin, 'The Criminal Offence under the Treasure Act' (2001) Art Antiquities and Law 101 and J Marston and L Ross, 'Treasure and Portable Antiquities in the 1990s still Chained to the Ghosts of the Past: The Treasure Act 1996' [1997] Conv 273, criticizing the Act for offering only piecemeal protection.

Crown, it has to be shown that D knew the Crown was, or at least might be,[211] the owner – that is, that the property had the factual characteristics of treasure – for example, that a bracelet is at least 300 years old and is made of at least 10 per cent by weight of precious metal. But a defendant might know that the property had the factual characteristics of treasure and still be unaware of the Crown's proprietary interest because of his understandable ignorance of the law of treasure.[212] So, proving theft may be very difficult. It is possible instead to charge D with theft from the landowner on whose land the treasure was found. The proprietary interest of the owner of the land is much easier to prove than that of the Crown.[213] In *Waverley Borough Council v Fletcher*,[214] F, using a metal detector in a public park belonging to the council, found a mediaeval gold brooch. A coroner's inquest decided that it was not treasure trove and returned it to F. It was held that the council was entitled to a declaration that the brooch was its property. Auld LJ stated two principles:

(1) Where an article is found in or attached to land, the owner or possessor of the land has a better title than the finder.[215]

(2) Where an article is found unattached on land, the owner or possessor of the land has a better title than the finder only if he exercised such manifest control over the land as to indicate an intention to control the land and anything that might be found on it.[216]

19.3.3.4 Any proprietary right or interest

Property is also to be regarded as belonging to any person having in it 'any proprietary right or interest'. Obviously, then, property may be stolen from the owner although at the time of the appropriation the owner is not in possession or control, as where V lends his library book to X and D steals the book from X. Furthermore, property may be stolen from the owner even though he may never have been in possession or control. If X sells goods to V (ownership passing to V) but X remains in possession of them until V has collected, if D dishonestly appropriates them, he steals from both X and V.[217] Moreover on those facts, if X, after he has sold the goods to V, dishonestly appropriates them (eg by selling them to Y) X steals the property from V even though X was still in possession of the property; X has usurped V's proprietary right in the property. Similarly if V, dishonestly removed *his* property from X's premises (with V

---

[211] 'Might be' because the finder may be aware that 'reasonable steps' might reveal that the find was of silver and that it had been concealed, not lost: Theft Act 1968, s 2(1)(c), below, p 826.

[212] Ignorance of the civil law may negative *mens rea*: above, p 825.

[213] Under the doctrine of 'transferred malice', D's intention dishonestly to deprive the landowner of the property may be treated as an intention dishonestly to deprive the Crown. If the property turns out to be treasure, D may be guilty of stealing it both from the landowner and from the Crown. On the legal position of those who take property washed ashore, see the Merchant Shipping Act 1995, and the Protection of Wrecks Act 1973. See M Salter and C Bryden, 'Finders, Keepers and Illegal Sweepers' (2007) 151 SJ 1018.

[214] [1995] 4 All ER 756.

[215] In *Rowe* (1859) 8 Cox CC 139, R was convicted of larceny from a canal company of iron found in the bed of a canal when it was drained. The true owner of the iron was unknown but the canal company had a sufficient proprietary interest in it. *Rowe* was followed by Chitty J in *Elwes v Brigg Gas Co* (1886) 33 Ch D 562, and in *South Staffordshire Water Co v Sharman* [1896] 2 QB 44. And cf *Woodman* (1974) 59 Cr App R 200, CA above, p 807.

[216] In *Parker v British Airways Board* [1982] QB 1004, a passenger who found a gold bracelet in a British Airways executive lounge was held to have a better right to it than British Airways. On the other hand in *Hibbert v McKiernan* [1948] 2 KB 142, a trespasser on a golf course was held guilty of larceny of balls lost by golfers from the secretary and members of the golf club. He was aware of the intent of the club to exclude him as a 'pilferer' of lost balls, so the case is distinguishable, cf *Rostron* [2003] EWCA Crim 2206. See further the discussion by Hickey (2006) 26 LS 584, above.

[217] Frequently the thief will have no idea of the identity of the owner, or owners, of the property; it suffices that he knows the property belongs to *another*.

intent to avoid paying for the property) then V steals from X because he usurp's X's remaining interest in the property.[218]

D may appropriate property which belongs to V in any of the senses described in s 5(1). It does not matter that V's interest is precarious or that it may be short-lived; wild birds reared by V may belong to V although they may 'betake themselves to the woods and fields' as soon as they are old enough to fly,[219] and flowers left on a grave remain the property of the leaver.[220] Nor does it matter that someone exists who has a better right to the property than V: a thief may steal from a thief.[221] This is a well-established principle. It does not matter that it is impossible for the victim (the original thief) to assert his title in a civil court: public policy which prevents the wrongdoer from enforcing a property right should have no application to criminal proceedings brought in the name of the Crown. The criminal law is concerned with keeping the Queen's peace, not vindicating individual property rights.[222]

19.3.3.5 Equitable interests

The term 'any proprietary right or interest' in s 5 extends to both legal and equitable proprietary interests. Where property is subject to a trust it belongs to both the trustee (legal interest) and beneficiary (equitable interest) and it may be stolen from either. The question whether V has an equitable interest in property alleged to have been stolen from him may involve difficult issues of civil law as for example in *Clowes (No 2)*,[223] where the criminal court had to consider various Chancery decisions and to rely on the principles of equity relating to tracing into mixed finds to determine whether there was property belonging to another. The criminal law becomes dependent on the civil law here, and if the scope of the civil law's definition of who has a 'proprietary interest' changes, that affects the scope of the criminal law. See the discussion of s 5(4) below.[224]

Under s 5(1) property is not to be regarded as belonging to a person who has an equitable interest arising *only* from an agreement to transfer or grant an interest. A specifically enforceable contract to sell property may give the intending buyer an equitable interest in the property[225] and the provision makes it clear that the seller cannot commit theft by reselling the property to another, however dishonest this may be thought to be.

19.3.3.6 Trust property[226]

Section 5(2) of the Theft Act 1968 provides:

Where property is subject to a trust, the persons to whom it belongs shall be regarded as including any person having a right to enforce the trust, and an intention to defeat the trust shall be regarded accordingly as an intention to deprive of the property any person having that right.

---

[218] cf *Rose v Matt* [1951] 1 KB 810, DC (pledgor of clock dishonestly retook it from pledgee).

[219] cf *Shickle* (1868) LR 1 CCR 158.

[220] According to *Bustler v State* 184 SE 2d 24 (1944) (SC of Tennessee). cf *Edwards and Stacey* (1877) 13 Cox CC 384.

[221] cf *Clarke*, referred to at [1956] Crim LR 369–370; *Meech* [1974] QB 549, [1973] 3 All ER 939, CA and see *Rose* [2008] EWCA Crim 239.

[222] *Smith* [2011] EWCA Crim 66, citing this work and Ormerod and Williams on the point.

[223] [1994] 2 All ER 316. See also MC Davies, 'After *R v Clowes No 2*: An Act of Theft Empowered – A Jury Impoverished' (1997) 61 J Crim Law 99 commenting that with a trial based on complex legal issues the effect is to reduce the issues that fall to be determined by the jury, potentially displacing the importance of, eg, s 2(1)(a) of Theft Act 1968. See also the *Fraud Trials Protocol* (2005).

[224] Below, p 815.

[225] See Ormerod and Williams, *Theft*, para 2.196.

[226] Brazier (1975) 39 Conv (NS) 29.

In the ordinary case, appropriation of trust property by a trustee is covered not only by this subsection but also by s 5(1) because the beneficiary ordinarily has a proprietary interest and accordingly the trust property belongs to another – the beneficiary – within s 5(1). In *Sanders*,[227] D, the executor of a will appropriated £100,000 of the legacy. He admitted doing so and admitted that he did so dishonestly. He argued that this was not theft since subsequently it had come to light that there was a second will naming him as the beneficiary. The Court of Appeal upheld his conviction. Once probate had been granted a trust was established, and if D had discovered that he was the beneficiary under a second will he ought to have sought an amendment of probate. As the court noted, in some cases there would be a ground for arguing that D was not dishonest in such action.

In some exceptional circumstances there will be no ascertained beneficiary. This occurs in the case of 'purpose' trusts, whether charitable[228] or private,[229] where the object is to affect some purpose rather than to benefit ascertainable individuals. To meet such cases s 5(2) goes further than s 5(1) by providing that the property is to be treated as belonging to anyone who has a right to enforce the trust.[230] As far as charitable trusts are concerned, the trustees are the legal owners of the charity's funds but, if they misappropriate the money, they steal not from the donors to that charity, but from the Attorney General who has the right to enforce the trust.[231]

19.3.3.7 Property received for a particular purpose

Section 5(3) of the 1968 Act provides that:

When a person receives property from or on account of another, and is under an obligation to the other to retain and deal with that property or its proceeds in a particular way, the property or proceeds shall be regarded (as against him) as belonging to the other.

If there is no legal obligation on D to retain and deal with the property in a particular way, it is his to do as he likes with, and it cannot be theft for him to do what he is entitled to do. But where there is such an obligation, it seems right that the property should be capable of being stolen by D. A straightforward example would be where D agrees to do certain work for V and V makes an advance payment of £100, D's failure to do the work or return the £100 will be a breach of contract but no criminal offence.[232] But, if V had given D the money *for a specified purpose*, such as to buy materials for the job, that would create the obligation on D to retain and deal, so that D's dishonest disposal of the money for some other purpose would be theft under s 5(3).

Breadth of application

Section 5(3) covers a very wide range of cases. Every bailment seems to be included. So does every trust. Section 5(1) is so wide that in many cases it is unnecessary to rely on s 5(3). So where D has received property from or on account of V in the circumstances described in the subsection, V will usually have a legal or equitable interest in the property or proceeds.[233]

---

[227] [2003] EWCA Crim 3079.

[228] eg, where money is given to D in trust for the improvement of schools in a particular locality.

[229] eg, where money is given to D in trust for the maintenance of a tomb, or for the upkeep of animals.

[230] In the foregoing examples this would be, respectively, the A-G and the person entitled to the residue of the estate.

[231] *Dyke and Munro* [2002] Crim LR 153, [2002] 1 Cr App R 404.

[232] Of course, if D never intended to do the work, he would be guilty of fraud under s 2 of the 2006 Act and, since *Gomez*, of theft of it. But if he was acting honestly at the time he received the money, once he had received it he was the absolute owner of it and there was nothing belonging to another for him to steal.

[233] In *Klineberg and Marsden* [1999] Crim LR 419, the court said that this sentence did not anticipate the unreported case of *Smith (Paul Adrian)*, 14 May 1997, 'in which, when cheques from investors were paid into Intercity's [Smith's] bank account, the person on whose account the money was received (GRE) did not have

Should D dishonestly appropriate the property, he will be stealing it from V who has retained a proprietary right or interest. The case then is covered by s 5(1) and s 5(3) is unnecessary. Even where that is so, s 5(3) is useful because it allows the prosecution to make out its case more easily, without the need to resort to the technical question whether V retains an equitable interest.

'From or on account of another'

The section applies only where the property is 'received from or on account of another'. This creates a difficulty where the property is credited to D's account by a bank transfer.[234] *Preddy* decides that, since the credit is new property, a thing in action which belongs to D and has never belonged to anyone else, D could not be guilty of obtaining property *belonging to another* by deception. The property has only ever been D's. On one interpretation, D has not 'received' the property from another or on account of another. The property of the other, V, was the thing in action – V's right to sue his bank – and that was extinguished when D's new item of property was created. On that interpretation s 5(3) does not apply and D can be guilty of theft only if the person whose bank account has been debited retains an equitable interest in the new property owned by D. Although, in *Klineberg*,[235] the court did not distinguish between funds provided by cash, cheque or bank transfer, it is clear that the first two are property 'received' from another, the third is not. An alternative interpretation is to suggest that D has received the chose in action that never previously existed and never belonged to anyone other than him. On that interpretation s 5(3) would apply. The issue may be academic since D may be guilty of a Fraud Act offence in such cases.

'Obligation'

It is settled that an 'obligation' to retain and deal with property in a certain way in s 5(3) (and (4) to be discussed below) means a legal, not a merely moral or social, obligation. That much is straightforward, determining whether there is such an obligation is far less so. Where the relevant transaction which allegedly creates the obligation is wholly in writing, it is for the judge to decide as a matter of law whether it does create the legal obligation and to direct the jury accordingly.[236] Where the obligation is alleged to have been created wholly or partly by word of mouth, or by conduct, the judge should direct the jury that, if they find the necessary facts (which he must refer them to specifically) proved, there *is* an obligation – not that it is 'open to them' to find that there is an obligation.[237] Aside from the correct procedure for determining whether a legal obligation existed, the substance of that question will often involve complex issues of civil law.[238]

a legal or equitable interest in the credit balance but it was nevertheless to be regarded under s 5(3) as belonging to GRE'. Since Smith was under a contractual obligation to GRE to forward all the monies received, it was unnecessary to decide, and the court does not appear to have decided, whether GRE had an equitable interest. The case is an excellent illustration of the utility of the subsection as described above. *Klineberg* seems, in this respect, straightforward, since the money was paid to D on the understanding that it would be 'safeguarded by trusteeship'.

[234] Though it is commonly called a bank transfer, in law it is not a 'transfer' at all.

[235] [1999] Crim LR 417.

[236] *Clowes (No 2)* [1994] 2 All ER 316, holding that a brochure inviting the payment of money for investment in gilts was a contractual document creating a trust.

[237] *Dubar* [1995] 1 All ER 781, following *Mainwaring* (1981) 74 Cr App R 99 and disapproving *dicta* in *Hall* [1972] 2 All ER 1009 at 1012 and *Hayes* (1976) 64 Cr App R 82 at 85 and 87.

[238] See, eg, *Breaks and Huggan* [1998] Crim LR 349 (contractual obligations of insurance brokers placing insurance with Lloyds).

Obligation owed to V

It is plain that the obligation must be owed by D to V. It is not enough that D is under an obligation to a third party to deal with the property for the benefit of V. The case of *Floyd v DPP*[239] is difficult to square with this principle. D collected money in weekly premiums from colleagues who had ordered goods from a Christmas hamper company – V Ltd. She failed to pay the money to V Ltd and her conviction for stealing it from V Ltd was upheld in reliance on s 5(3). The court said it was unnecessary to show that V Ltd had any legal or equitable interest in the money. The only remaining source of an obligation seems to be a contract; but D had made no contract with V Ltd that she would collect and hand over the money. There was probably a contract between D and her colleagues that she would 'retain and deal' with the money they gave her for the benefit of V Ltd but V Ltd was not privy to that contract and acquired no rights at common law. The position is different now under the Contracts (Rights of Third Parties) Act 1999:[240] as the term in the contract between D and her colleagues requiring her to retain and deal with the money by paying it to V apparently 'purports to confer a benefit' on V, V will under s 1(1)(b) of the 1999 Act be able to enforce that term, 'in their own right'. The money will then be regarded as belonging to them under s 5(3).

Examples of s 5(3) in operation

If D is under no legal obligation to retain and deal with property which has been delivered to him, he can lawfully do what he likes with it and it is incapable of being stolen, as are its proceeds. This is ordinarily the position where money is lent. Assuming that when V lent money to D, he received the money honestly, D's subsequent decision to dispose of the money and never to repay it, however dishonest, cannot be theft. It is not always easy to determine whether D was under an obligation to retain and deal or at liberty to dispose of the property entirely as he wished. It is, to underline the point, a question of civil law.

Advance payments

As noted above, this includes if V has given D money *for a specified purpose*, as an advance such as to buy materials for the job. That would create the obligation on D to retain and deal, so that D's dishonest disposal of the money for some other purpose would be theft.

Deposits

If V were to pay a deposit to D, a trader, for goods to be supplied under a contract of sale, such a transaction would normally imply that D is under no obligation to deal with that deposit in a particular way. D might well pay the deposit into his trading account but he could draw on that account as he wished and would not be obliged to keep in existence a discrete fund representing V's deposit. If, on the other hand, V were to give D, his secretary, £100 with instructions to go to a travel agency and purchase a ticket for a flight, the normal inference would be that D is under an obligation to deal with the £100 in a particular way. The difficulties in application are well illustrated by *Hall*.[241] D, a partner in a firm of travel agents, had received money from V and others as deposits for air trips to America. The flights never materialized and the deposits, which had been paid into the firm's general trading account, were never returned to V and other customers. The Court of Appeal had no difficulty in accepting the jury's verdict that D had acted dishonestly in spending this money, but quashed D's conviction for theft on the ground that D had not received the money under an obligation to deal with it *in a particular way*. The court reached this conclusion with obvious reluctance (as ever when there has been a finding of dishonesty).[242]

---

[239] [2000] Crim LR 411, DC.

[240] Applying to contracts made on or after 11 May 2000.

[241] [1972] 2 All ER 1009, CA, and see *Hayes* (1976) 64 Cr App R 82.

[242] [1972] 2 All ER 1009 at 1011. See *Re Kumar* [2000] Crim LR 504, DC, where there was such an obligation.

The case shows that if D owes money to V and he dishonestly disposes of his assets so that when the time comes for payment to V he has no funds from which to meet his debts, he will not be under an obligation for the purposes of s 5(3). Moreover, it makes no difference, so far as the law of theft is concerned, that D has acted in this way in order to defeat his creditors. A liability to pay V is accordingly not enough under s 5(3) unless D is obliged to keep in existence a fund representing that property.

Breaches of contract

The subsection may apply to cases of mere breach of contract not covered by s 5(1). For example, D who buys a non-transferable ticket may become the owner of the ticket, but be under a contractual obligation to 'retain and deal with it in a particular manner' in the sense of 'not dealing' with it.[243] In the case of a rail ticket, such as that in *Marshall*, his ownership of the ticket involved his contractual obligation not to assign it to another. But note that the property must be 'received'. Where D enters into a contract to deal with his own property in his own possession the subsection does not apply.[244]

Charity sponsorship

A common situation in which s 5(3) is used is where D receives property from C for onward transmission to, or for the benefit of, E. The required obligation may be imposed on D either by D's relationship with C, or his relationship with E, or both. In *Lewis v Lethbridge*,[245] D obtained sponsorships in favour of a charity (E) and received £54 from sponsors (C). He failed to deliver the money. His conviction of theft was quashed because the magistrates had made no finding of any rule of the charity requiring D to hand over the actual cash received or to maintain a separate fund; there was no evidence that he was anything other than a debtor to the charity. No consideration was given to the question whether any obligation was imposed by the sponsors. They might have been surprised to learn that they were giving the money to D to do as he liked with. In *Wain*,[246] the Court of Appeal disapproved *Lethbridge*, holding that the approach was unduly narrow and that, on similar facts, the defendant was under such an obligation and, accordingly, guilty of theft.

Obligations imposed by statute

It is possible for the obligation to be imposed on D by statute. No doubt when the State pays housing benefit to D to enable D to pay his rent, the expectation is that D will use that money to pay his landlord, but it was held in *Huskinson*[247] that D was not guilty of theft where he spent some of the money received as housing benefit on himself. There was nothing in the relevant legislation suggesting that D was bound to pay *that* money or its proceeds to the landlord. D could have met his legal obligation to pay the rent from any source, such as an unexpected win on the lottery and spent the benefit as he chose.

---

[243] cf Smith [1998] Crim LR 723 at 726. It is pointed out that this is not theft of the thing in action, but whether it is theft of the thing in possession (the ticket) is not considered.

[244] It may, however, create an equitable interest. cf commentary on *Arnold* [1997] Crim LR at 834. The case involved an odd application of s 5(3).

[245] [1987] Crim LR 59, DC.

[246] [1995] 2 Cr App R 660, following *Davidge v Bunnett* [1984] Crim LR 297, DC, where, in pursuance of an agreement by flatmates to share the costs of gas, etc, D received money from the others for the gas bill and spent it on Christmas presents. Domestic arrangements are commonly not intended to give rise to legal relationships but here the parties were not members of the same family and presumably intended their agreement to be legally binding. More doubtful is the case where a woman was held guilty of stealing money entrusted to her by her cohabitee to buy food, etc for their household: *Cullen* (No 968/C74 of 1974, unreported).

[247] [1988] Crim LR 620, DC.

Obligations and agency

An obligation to deal with property in a specified way may be imposed on D in civil law through the acts of his agents. However, if D is unaware of the facts giving rise to that obligation, the prosecution cannot rely on s 5(3).[248] Moreover, if D knew the facts but owing to his mistake of civil law believed that there was no obligation and that the money was his to do as he liked with, he would not be dishonest and should be acquitted on that ground.

If D receives a bribe in contravention of his duty to his principal, V, the principal may recover the amount of the bribe in a civil action; but whether D can steal the amount of the bribe depends on whether he is a mere debtor to V or holds the bribe on trust for V. This is a complex question of civil law. In *Lister & Co v Stubbs*,[249] the Court of Appeal held V has no proprietary interest in the money; but in *A-G for Hong Kong v Reid*,[250] the Privy Council disagreed and held that a bribe should be treated as being held on constructive trust for V from the moment it is received.[251] The *Reid* approach would substantially enlarge the criminal law,[252] and it has now been followed by the High Court in *Tesco Stores v Pook*[253] and in *Daraydan Holdings Ltd v Solland International Ltd*.[254] However, this is only a Privy Council decision and technically as a matter of *stare decisis* the Court of Appeal ought to be followed.[255] However, it is now unlikely that the Court of Appeal Criminal Division will regard itself as bound by *Lister & Co v Stubbs*.[256]

For s 5(3) to apply, it is not necessary that the fiduciary duty arises out of the transaction between D and the person delivering the property to him; it is enough that D's fiduciary duty arises out of a relationship with a person other than the deliveror.

Where D, a broker, is engaged to collect premiums on behalf of V, if the terms of the agreement provide that the premiums vest in V,[257] D may steal them; if the agreement merely makes D a debtor to V for the amount of the premiums paid,[258] D will not be a thief if he keeps them. In both cases the broker has been dishonest and in both V is the loser, but in the first case the broker is a thief and in the second he is not; a distinction which may be effected by a few strokes of the pen in the agreement between V and D.[259]

19.3.3.8 Property got by mistake

Section 5(4) of the Theft Act provides:

Where a person gets property by another's mistake, and is under an obligation to make restoration (in whole or in part) of the property or its proceeds or of the value thereof, then to the extent of that

[248] *Wills* (1990) 92 Cr App R 297.
[249] (1890) 45 Ch D 1. See also *Cullum* (1873) LR 2 CCR 28; CLRC, Eighth Report, para 38; Williams, TBCL, 756; ATH Smith, 'Constructive Trusts in the Law of Theft' [1977] Crim LR 395; JC Smith (1956) 19 MLR 39, 46. It has been said that in none of the cases in which a fiduciary has been held liable to account for profits did the question arise whether the defendant was a trustee as opposed to being merely accountable: J Martin, *Hanbury and Martin, Modern Equity* (17th edn, 2005).
[250] [1994] 1 AC 324, [1994] 1 All ER 1, PC.
[251] See A Hudson, *Equity & Trusts*, (6th edn, 2010) 519–520.
[252] See JC Smith, 'Contracts – Mistake, Frustration and Implied Terms' (1994) 110 LQR 180.
[253] [2003] EWHC 823 (Ch).
[254] [2005] Ch 119. See Hudson, *Equity & Trusts*, 519–520. *Reid* has been followed, or discussed with approval, in numerous cases; *Clark v Cutland* [2003] EWCA Civ 810, *Smalley v Bracken Partners* [2003] EWCA Civ 1875. See also Companies Act 2006, s 176.
[255] See the recent decision in *Sinclair Investments v Versailles Trade Finance Ltd* [2010] EWHC 1614 (Ch) paras 37–54 per Lewison J.
[256] This is the attitude taken by the court in the law of provocation where a similar situation has arisen: *Karimi* [2006] EWCA Crim 14, albeit the Privy Council decision involved was one comprising nine members.
[257] *Brewster* (1979) 69 Cr App R 375, CA.
[258] *Robertson* [1977] Crim LR 629 (Judge Rubin QC).
[259] See also *Breaks and Huggan* [1998] Crim LR 349.

obligation the property or proceeds shall be regarded (as against him) as belonging to the person entitled to restoration, and an intention not to make restoration shall be regarded accordingly as an intention to deprive that person of the property or proceeds.

This provision was enacted to deal with the problem encountered in the case of *Moynes v Coopper*.[260] D, a labourer employed by V, was given an advance on his pay. Later that week, unaware that an advance had been made, V's wages' clerk paid D the full weekly wage. D dishonestly kept all of the money. The difficulty in treating this as theft by D is that in law the whole of the full weekly wage belonged to D. Under the old law D was acquitted. The wages clerk made a mistake of course, but his mistake was not such as would prevent ownership of all the money passing to D. Had the clerk known that D had been given an advance he would have paid D less, nevertheless, the clerk did intend to pay the full amount, and he was authorized as V's wages clerk to pay wages. This type of case is now covered by s 5(4): D steals the excess payment if he dishonestly appropriates it. Although D becomes the owner of the full weekly wage he is under a legal obligation, at the very least, to repay the value of the excess payment.

Section 5(4) was applied in these circumstances in *A-G's Reference (No 1 of 1983)*.[261] D's salary was paid into her bank account by direct debit and on one occasion her employers mistakenly overpaid her by £74.74. The question for the court was: assuming that she dishonestly decided not to repay that sum would she have been guilty of theft? In law she became the owner of the money and, as Lord Lane CJ pointed out, had no special provision been made for the case that would have been an end to the matter. But s 5(4) provided for the case. The 'money in the bank' was entirely hers to do as she liked with, but she was under an obligation to repay an equivalent sum (the value) to her employers. On these facts, subject to proof of dishonesty, her failure to do so meant she was guilty of theft.

The law is clear as to V's position in circumstances of making a mistaken payment: if, owing to a mistake of fact, V believes that he is legally obliged to make a payment and he does so, he is entitled in civil law to recover the equivalent of the sum he mistakenly paid.[262] It is less clear what D's civil law position is where he has received a payment made in error The issue whether D was under a legal obligation to repay the value was resolved in the *A-G's Reference (No 1)* without difficulty, but it will be appreciated that it will not always be so straightforward. The law of unjust enrichment[263] is one of complexity and subtlety which has developed considerably in recent years. In *Kleinwort Benson Ltd v Lincoln City Council*,[264] a bare majority of the House of Lords held that money paid under a mistake of law, as well as a mistake of fact, was recoverable on the ground that its receipt by D would, *prima facie*, lead to his unjust enrichment. The majority also held that money paid under a void contract may be recovered even though the void contract is fully performed. D's liability for theft may turn upon a consideration of fine points of civil law remote from the central question of D's dishonesty. Significantly, it was held by the House of Lords in *Westdeutsche Landesbank v Islington*[265] that if money was paid under a mistake, but in circumstances in which the recipient (D) was not aware of that mistake, then the payer (V) retains no proprietary right in that money if the recipient (D) has disposed of it in good faith. V's remedy is a purely personal

---

[260] [1956] 1 QB 439. See also the discussion in W Swadling, 'Rescission, Property and the Common Law' (2005) 121 LQR 123 at 135.

[261] [1985] QB 182,CA.

[262] *Norwich Union Fire Insurance Society Ltd v William H Price Ltd* [1934] AC 455.

[263] See R Goff and G Jones, *The Law of Restitution* (7th edn, 2010).

[264] [1999] 2 AC 349, followed in a number of other decisions, including *Deutsche Morgan Grenfell v IRC* [2006] UKHL 49, [2007] AC 558.

[265] [1996] AC 669.

remedy at common law, as opposed to being a right in property, for money had and received. It is only if D had knowledge of some factor in relation to the receipt of that money that D would be treated as holding that money on constructive trust for V, such that V would thereby have an equitable proprietary right in that money.[266]

There was no evidence in the *A-G's Reference* that D had spent the money that was overpaid or that she had done any act in relation to it. To meet a possible argument that in doing nothing D cannot intend permanently to deprive the owner, s 5(4) further provides that an intention not to make restoration shall be regarded as an intention permanently to deprive.[267]

A further difficulty with cases such as this follows from the decision in *Preddy* and the need to identify which item of property is in issue. In *Gresham* (below), D's mother had been in receipt of pension payments from her former employer which were made by automatic transfers to her bank account. D failed to inform her employer (the Department of Education) and the bank of his mother's death. The payments continued to be credited for 10 years after her death and D having had the power of attorney to act for her when she was alive, continued to use this power to cash cheques drawn on her account. The cheques drawn by D reduced the credit balance in his mother's account. D was convicted of theft and obtaining a money transfer by deception (contrary to the offence then in force under s 15A of the 1968 Act). The credit balance that D diminished by drawing cheques was not an item of property that belonged to the Dept of Education within the terms of s 5(1). The prosecution relied instead on the fact that the payments had been by mistake and that s 5(4) applied. The court upheld convictions for theft on this basis, rejecting an argument that s 5(4) has no application where D has induced V's mistake by deception as 'eccentric'.

Is s 5(4) superfluous?

The foregoing discussion of s 5(4) assumes, as seemingly did the CLRC, that the entire proprietary interest in the money mistakenly paid passes to D, who is no more than a debtor. That is the position *at law*. Section 5(4) was felt to be necessary to vest a fictitious interest in V who had paid money by mistake. However, some cases have now held that as a matter of equity, where V pays money by mistake to D, V retains an equitable interest. If that is right, V has a proprietary right or interest under s 5(1) in such cases and there would be no need for s 5(4).

In *Chase Manhattan Bank NA v Israel–British Bank (London) Ltd*,[268] the X bank by mistake paid $2 million.[269] Goulding J held that V who pays money (or, presumably, delivers any property) to D under a mistake of fact retains an equitable interest[270] in the money and the conscience of D is subject to a fiduciary duty to respect V's proprietary right.[271] The reasoning underpinning this decision was disapproved by Lord Browne-Wilkinson in *Westdeutsche Landesbank v Islington*[272] but commented *obiter*, that stolen monies should be treated as being held on constructive trust by the thief, and therefore would be traceable by the original

---

[266] See Hudson, *Equity & Trusts,* above, p 505.

[267] 'Keeping' is a sufficient appropriation. See above, p 792.

[268] [1981] Ch 105 – doubted, but not so as to affect its application in criminal cases, by Lord Browne-Wilkinson in *Westdeutsche Landesbank Girozentrale v Islington LBC* [1996] AC 669 at 715. *Westdeutsche* has been followed in *Bank of America v Arnell* [1999] Lloyd's Rep 399; *Clark v Cutland* [2003] EWCA Civ 810. For a helpful discussion see G Virgo, *Principles of the Law of Restitution* (2nd edn, 2006) 608–612.

[269] The payment was from X bank to the Y bank for the account of the Z bank which subsequently went into liquidation. The X bank was, of course, entitled to a dividend in the liquidation but it sought to recover the whole of its loss.

[270] Section 5(1) extends to equitable interests, see above, p 810.

[271] Accordingly, the X bank was entitled to the restoration of the whole of the money mistakenly paid and was not relegated to claiming a dividend in the liquidation.

[272] [1996] AC 669.

owner of those monies. Having regard to the decision in *Kleinwort*,[273] it is now the case that a mistake of fact or law may ground a claim in unjust enrichment, and so an obligation to make restitution may arise where the mistake caused the payment to be made (or other benefit to be transferred). In *Moynes v Coopper*, V retained an equitable interest in the money overpaid and D, on these facts, could now be convicted of theft even if s 5(4) had not been enacted.

The *Chase Manhattan* principle was relied on by the Court of Appeal (Criminal Division) in *Shadrokh-Cigari*.[274] The O bank had, in error, credited a child's account at the V bank with £286,000 instead of £286! D, the child's guardian, got the child to sign authority for the V bank to issue banker's drafts, and when D was arrested only £21,000 of the £286,000 remained in the account. Upholding D's conviction for theft from the V bank, the court said that the drafts belonged to the bank and although legal ownership passed to D by delivery, the bank retained an equitable interest by virtue of the *Chase Manhattan* principle and D had appropriated property belonging to another (V) within the broad terms of s 5(1). It was accordingly not necessary to rely on s 5(4) though that subsection provided an alternative route to conviction.[275] Subsequent decisions have applied *Shadrokh-Cigari* without hesitation. In *Webster*,[276] the Court Martial Appeal Court upheld D's conviction for theft of a medal which he had sold on ebay. The medal was sent in error to Captain X, (it was an unsolicited duplicate), X gave it to D, his admin officer to deal with. There was some confusion as to what the procedure was for the issue and return of medals, but the court had no doubt that medals are akin to gifts from the sovereign, and that in this case there had been a fundamental error by the Ministry of Defence in supplying a duplicate. The Crown retained an interest in that medal, it was property belonging to another as against D.[277]

Identifying the property got by mistake

Section 5(4), or the *Chase Manhattan* principle, applies though only part of the property is got by mistake. In *Moynes v Coopper*,[278] D appropriated only the amount by which he was overpaid. In such a case it would be impossible to identify the coins which represented the overpayment but the prosecution is not required to do so because the relevant property is sufficiently identified if it is proved to be part of an identifiable whole. This principle was applied in *Davis*.[279] By a computer error, D was sent two cheques a month in respect of housing benefit when he was entitled to only one. It was held that where D had cashed these cheques he could be convicted of stealing the proceeds (the cash) of one of the cheques and it was not necessary for the prosecution to establish which proceeds he had stolen and which he had not.[280]

Requirement of legal obligation

It will be evident from the foregoing discussion that 'obligation' in s 5(4) can only refer to a legal obligation imposed by the civil law. This is confirmed by *Gilks*,[281] though the case has

---

[273] Above, p 816.

[274] [1988] Crim LR 465, CA. See further G MacCormack, 'Mistaken Payments and Proprietary Claims' [1996] Conv 86.

[275] See also the statements in *Gresham* [2003] EWCA Crim 2070.

[276] [2006] EWCA Crim 2894.

[277] Was this not obvious? Was there not also X's proprietary interest? He had not authorized the sale, and after *Gomez* that would not matter in any event. See also the comments of the Administrative Court in *Re Holmes* [2004] EWHC 2020 (Admin) expressing the provisional view that the property which D had fraudulently transferred by automated process from a German to a Dutch bank was subject to a constructive trust. cf *Ngan* [1998] 1 Cr App R 331 in which s 5(4) was not discussed.

[278] Above, p 816.

[279] (1988) 88 Cr App R 347, CA.

[280] On the civil law position for tracing into mixed finds see *Westdeutsche Landesbank v Islington* [1996] AC 669.

[281] [1972] 1 WLR 1341, CA.

its complications. V, a bookmaker, mistakenly believing that D had backed a winning horse, overpaid D on the bets he had placed and D, aware of the error, dishonestly decided not to return the overpayment. Since V had made no mistake either as to the amount or the recipient, ownership of the money passed to D. The court was clear that s 5(4) was inapplicable. As this was a betting transaction, as a matter of civil law, V had no right of restitution in respect of the overpayment, so D could be under no legal obligation to make restoration. But the court went on, relying upon an antique and questionable authority under the law of larceny,[282] to uphold D's conviction on the grounds that since V would not have made the overpayment but for his mistake, ownership in the money did not pass to D. This is at odds with the civil law and the decision needs to be reconsidered. It is a further example of the courts striving to uphold the convictions of those found to be dishonest, at the expense of clarity and principle in the definition of the Theft Act offences. After *Westdeutsche Landesbank v Islington (above)*, it is clear under civil law that if D was aware that a part of the money had been mistakenly overpaid to him, then D would be required to hold that overpayment on constructive trust for the payer, V.

19.3.3.9 Property of corporations

A corporation such as a limited company or the University of London is, in law, a person distinct from its members. It can own property and be the victim of theft and other offences under the Theft Acts. A member of the corporation can be guilty of stealing the property of the corporation – it is property belonging to another: the company. If a director, D, of a limited company misappropriates the company's property the injury is suffered by the company's shareholders or, if it is insolvent, its creditors; but the property D has appropriated does not belong to the directors and D is guilty of theft, not from them, but from the company.[283] This is straightforward where D is misappropriating the property because he is acting without authority. The matter is more difficult if the alleged theft from the company is, say, an act authorized by the board of directors at a properly constituted meeting. Although it exists as a separate legal person, a company can act only through its human controlling officers and, in some contexts at least, they are identified with the company – their acts are the company's acts.[284] If company directors resolve to use the company's assets for their personal advantage instead of for the company's proper purposes, and if this act is the company's act (that is, the company authorizes it (albeit by the directors' decision)), it is hard to see how it can be theft; no one can steal from himself. It is different if the act is *ultra vires* the company because then it is not the company's act at all; but the courts seem to have regarded the question of *ultra vires* as irrelevant.

The problem is most acute where the directors, say, D and E, are also the sole shareholders. If D and E, as the controlling mind of the company, C, agree that C shall pay them money for their personal use, have they stolen the money from C? Judicial opinion, before *Gomez*, was divided about this situation. One view was that this was theft from the company.[285] The other was that an act done with the authority of the company cannot in general amount to an appropriation:[286] Since *Gomez* it is clear that this is wrong. A dishonest appropriation is now theft, even if the owner consents. In *Gomez*, Lord Browne-Wilkinson (with whom

---

[282] *Middleton* (1873) LR 2 CCR 38.

[283] *R (on the Application of A) v Snaresbrook Crown Court* (2001) 165 JPN 495.

[284] Above, Ch 10.

[285] *A-G's Reference (No 2 of 1982)* [1984] QB 624; *Phillipou* (1989) 89 Cr App R 290.

[286] *McHugh and Tringhamm* (1988) 88 Cr App R 385, CA at 393. See also *Roffel* [1985] VR 511, discussed by JC Smith (1985) 9 Crim LJ 320.

three judges, including Lord Lowry who dissented on the main issue, agreed) said that their lordships' decision rendered 'the whole question of consent by the company irrelevant'.

D and E in the example above might object, saying they were not merely acting with the consent of the company: they *were* the company. If I give away all my property with the intention of defrauding my creditors, it is impossible to hold that I have committed theft because I have not appropriated something belonging to another. However, Lord Browne-Wilkinson also said that even if consent was relevant to appropriation, there would still be a theft:[287]

Where a company is accused of a crime the acts and intentions of those who are the directing minds and will of the company are to be attributed to the company. That is not the law where the charge is that those who are the directing minds and will have themselves committed a crime against the company.

It must now be conceded, following *Gomez*, that in these cases D appropriates property belonging to another, but there is still difficulty in seeing how it can be a *dishonest* appropriation.[288] The act is not dishonest *vis-à-vis* the shareholders because they are the appropriators and therefore it is unreal to say that it is dishonest with respect to the company, which exists for the benefit of the shareholders. It may well be dishonest with respect to the company's creditors – but the property does not belong to them.[289] The illogicality of the position is demonstrated further when comparison is made with the position of partnership property. If D and E were not the directors of a company but the sole members of a partnership, they could not be guilty of theft of the partnership's assets, even if they disposed of them in riotous living with intent to defeat their creditors.[290] There does not seem to be any difference in substance.

19.3.3.10 Ownerless property

A person cannot be guilty of stealing property that is not owned by another at the time of the appropriation. If there is no person to whom the property belongs in any of the senses set out in s 5, that property cannot be stolen. Property that is capable of belonging to another may be ownerless because it has never been made the subject of ownership. D can commit no offence where, for example, he takes a swarm of bees not presently owned by another.

19.3.3.11 Property it is unlawful to possess

There is nothing to stop a theft charge where the property in question was held by V someone who had no lawful right to it. A thief can steal from a thief. Equally it does not matter whether the property is of a type that V was not lawfully permitted to possess. In *Smith*,[291] D was convicted of robbery having appropriated V's heroin by force. Initially D and others were charged with robbery of cash (£50) but the indictment was amended to charge robbery of drugs to the value of £50. D argued that the prohibited drugs did not amount to property within the meaning of the Theft Act 1968. In particular that they could not be guilty of theft (and hence of robbery) if the article that had been taken was unlawfully in the possession of V. Moreover, it was argued that there could be no appropriation of the rights of the owner where the owner had no rights of possession because possession was prohibited by law. The Court of Appeal rejected these arguments. On settled law, the sole question was whether the owner had possession or

---

[287] [1993] 1 All ER at 40.

[288] DW Elliott, 'Directors' Thefts and Dishonesty' [1991] Crim LR 732; Griew, *Theft*, paras 2.86–2.87.

[289] GR Sullivan, Letters to the Editor [1991] Crim LR 929 argues that the interests of the creditors of an insolvent or doubtfully solvent company are the interests of the company, and as such D and E are rightly guilty of theft in such circumstances. But it is not clear that this is an established principle or that it is the foundation of the cases holding the sole director may steal the company's property.

[290] Note the new offence of fraudulent trading by a sole trader under s 9 of the Fraud Act 2006.

[291] [2011] EWCA Crim 66.

control of the property. There was no ground whatever for qualifying the words 'possession or control', in any way. It was sufficient that the person from whom the property was taken, or to use the words of the Act, appropriated, was at the time in fact in possession or control of the property. The criminal law is concerned with keeping the Queen's peace, not with protecting private property rights.[292]

19.3.3.12 Corpses and living body tissue[293]

The common law rule was that there is no property in a corpse or part of a corpse. Executors or administrators or others with a legal duty to inter a body have a right to custody and possession of it until it is buried; but it seems the corpse is incapable of being stolen from them. In *Doodeward v Spence*,[294] a decision of the High Court of New South Wales where the English authorities are examined, it was held that a proprietary interest could be acquired by one who expended work and skill on the corpse with a view to its preservation on scientific or other grounds. This decision was applied in *Kelly*,[295] where parts of bodies preserved as anatomical specimens and taken from the Royal College of Surgeons were held to have been stolen.

In *Yearworth v North Bristol NHS Trust*,[296] the Court of Appeal (Civil Division) has moved away from this principle that recognised property rights in body tissue only on the basis of expended skill. The claimants who were undergoing cancer treatment had stored their sperm with the defendant hospital for future use; they sought damages when the hospital failed to store the sperm properly. One issue at trial was whether each man's sperm was 'property' belonging to him. It was removed from his body but unlike most other removed tissue was capable of performing the same function it had when in the body. The Court of Appeal, accepting that the men had ownership for the purposes of the claim, acknowledged that developments in medical science require a re-analysis of the common law's treatment of ownership of body products.[297] The Lord Chief Justice accepted that the storage of sperm in liquid nitrogen represented 'an application to the sperm of work and skill', but regarded *Doodeward* as illogical:

[W]e are not content to see the common law in this area founded upon the principle in *Doodeward*, which was devised as an exception to a principle, itself of exceptional character, relating to the ownership of a human corpse. [45]

The Human Tissue Act 2004[298] provides a framework for issues of donation, storage and use of body parts, organs and tissue. The Act is a response to the concerns raised by events at Alder

---

[292] If the argument of S in this case was accepted, it would, nevertheless, be an offence to steal drugs from the exhibit room in court or from a police officer.

[293] See ATH Smith, 'Stealing the Body and its Parts' [1976] Crim LR 622 and *Property Offences*, paras 3.03–3.06; P Skegg, 'Criminal Liability for the Unauthorized Use of Corpses for Medical Education and Research' (1992) 32 Med Sci Law 51; M Pawlowski, 'Dead Bodies as Property' (1996) 146 NLJ 1828; A Maclean, 'Resurrection of the Body Snatchers' (2000) 150 NLJ 174.

[294] (1908) 95 R (NSW) 107.

[295] [1998] 3 All ER 741. cf *Dobson v North Tyneside Health Authority* [1996] 4 All ER 474, CA (Civ Div).

[296] [2009] EWCA Civ 37. See M Quigley (2009) 17 Med LR 457; C Hawes 'Property Interests in Body Parts: *Yearworth v North Bristol NHS Trust*' (2010) 73 MLR 130.

[297] See the discussion at [31]–[45].

[298] The Human Tissue Act 2004 provides safeguards and penalties in relation to improper retention of tissue and organs without consent. The Act sets up an overarching authority which rationalizes regulation and introduces regulation of post mortems and the retention of tissue for purposes like education and research, and provides for the Human Tissue Authority to issue codes of practice giving practical guidance on the conduct of activities within its remit: Department of Health Guidelines: http://webarchive.nationalarchives.gov.uk/+/www.dh.gov.uk/en/Publichealth/Scientificdevelopmentgeneticsandbioethics/Tissue/index.htm. See also I Kennedy and A Grubb, *Medical Law: Text and Materials* (3rd edn, 2000) Ch 18.

Hay and Bristol Royal Infirmary.[299] Many difficult issues relating to proprietary interests in body parts arise in other areas of the law and these may have an impact on future interpretations of s 5. For example, in the recent case of *L v Human Fertilisation and Embryology Authority*[300] it was doubted whether there was anyone who had authority to remove or authorise removal from a deceased person's gametes without effective advance consent.

19.3.3.13 Property of the deceased

In *Sullivan and Ballion*,[301] the defendants had appropriated the £50,000 they found on their friend who had died of natural causes in their company the night before. The deceased was a drug dealer and the money represented his takings. They were charged with theft of the money. Dismissing the charges, the trial judge ruled that the property did not 'belong to another' when it was taken.[302] As pointed out in the commentary to the case, the property must have belonged to someone other than the thieves (who had no rights to it). Since there may be a conviction of theft of property of a person unknown, it follows that it is enough to show that the property must have belonged to someone and that the defendants knew it belonged to someone other than themselves. The money did not belong to those who had purchased drugs from the deceased (in this case a group known as 'The Firm') because, as the judge held, they had parted with their entire proprietary interest in the money; but the proprietary interest can hardly have vanished into thin air – it passed to the deceased or, if he was acting as an agent, his principal. At the time of the alleged theft, the money must have belonged either to the deceased's principal, if any; or to those entitled under his (or their) will or intestacy; or, if they did not exist, to the Crown as *bona vacantia*.[303] There remains the difficulty in establishing the defendants' *mens rea*. If the defendants supposed, or may have supposed, that the property belonged to no one and could be taken by the first person to come across it, then they are not guilty. But if they knew it must belong to someone other than themselves, it is immaterial that they did not know who that person was.

19.3.3.14 Abandonment[304]

Property which has at one time been owned may become ownerless by abandonment. But abandonment is not something to be lightly inferred: property is abandoned only when the owner is indifferent to any future appropriation of the property by others. It is not enough

---

[299] See Department of Health guidelines: *The Removal, Retention and Use of Human Organs and Tissue from Post-mortem Examination* (2001).

[300] [2008] EWHC 2149 (Fam).

[301] [2002] Crim LR 758.

[302] Hale, PC, 514: 'If A dies intestate, and the goods of the intestate are stolen before administration committed, it is felony, and the goods shall be supposed to be *bona episcopi* de D. ordinary of the diocese, and if he made B his executor the goods shall be supposed bona B tho he hath not proved the will, and they need not show specifically their title as ordinary or executor because it is of their own possession, in which case a general indictment as well as a general action of trespass lies without naming themselves as executor or ordinary, and so for an administrator.' East, PC, 652 and *Russell on Crime* (2nd edn, 1843) ii, 99 state the law in similar terms.

[303] A suggested direction for such cases is 'Before you can convict the defendants of theft, you must be sure (i) that the deceased died in possession of the money; (ii) that D took it for their own use; (iii) knowing that the money was not theirs to take; and that it must have belonged to someone other than themselves; (iv) intending to deprive whoever was entitled to the money permanently of it; and (v) that they did so dishonestly'. See commentary, n 301 above.

[304] On abandonment, see AH Hudson, 'Is Divesting Abandonment Possible at Common Law' (1984) 100 LQR 110; 'Abandonment' in N Palmer and E McKendrick (eds), *Interests in Property* (1993). See also the interesting article discussing the civil and criminal law approaches to abandonment: R Hickey, 'Stealing Abandoned Goods: Possessory Title in Proceedings for Theft' (2006) 26 LS 584. On the potential for theft charges against 'freegans' – those who take food from supermarket refuse areas when it has been discarded because it has passed its sell by date – see the detailed analysis by S Thomas, 'Do Freegans Commit Theft' (2010) 30 LS 98. The argument

that V had no further use for the goods. A farmer who buries diseased animals has no further use for them but he would clearly intend that others should not make use of them and retains ownership of the carcasses.[305] It is legitimate for magistrates to conclude that a person who leaves bags of goods outside a charity shop has not abandoned the items.[306] When D takes the bags he can be convicted of theft – subject to his *mens rea*. The person leaving the bags does so with the intention of making a legitimate donation and has attempted to effect delivery.[307] Whether the charity shop had either kept and resold those items or disposed of them, they still would have come within its possession and control but the shop did not have possession or control when D appropriated. Importantly then, a householder who puts rubbish in his dustbin has no further use for the rubbish, but he puts it there to be collected by the authorized refuse collectors and not as an invitation to all comers to help themselves.[308] A shipowner who runs aground and whose cargo is cast onto the land has not lost his proprietary interest in the cargo.[309] Nor is property abandoned because the owner has lost it and has given up the search.[310] A husband may have lost his wedding ring and long since given up the search but will not have abandoned it.

19.4 *Mens rea*

Theft requires an intention to appropriate property belonging to another,[311] and that the act be done dishonestly. As the Law Commission stated in its Consultation Paper No 155, 'in theft…dishonesty is now the principal determinant of criminality'.[312]

19.4.1 View to gain immaterial

Section 1(2) of the 1968 Act provides, 'It is immaterial whether the appropriation is made with a view to gain, or is made for the thief's own benefit.'

This section is designed to defeat arguments such as that which might be made by D, a shop worker who charged his friend, E, for only some of the goods in E's trolley. The fact that the gain was for E does not prevent D stealing from the shop owner. Similarly, the section renders prosecution easier in cases of D causing only loss to V, without a corresponding gain

advanced in that article that the goods are not abandoned may not be unlikely to persuade the courts, but the argument based on *mens rea* is, it is submitted, a stronger one.

[305] cf *Edwards and Stacey* (1877) 36 LT 30.

[306] *R (Ricketts) v Basildon Magistrates Court* [2010] EWHC 2358 (Admin).

[307] That gift would be complete when the shop took possession of the items. Until then, the donor had not even relinquished possession. D faced a second count of theft of bags left by the charity shop in its dustbin. The property was deemed to belong to the shop at the time of appropriation by D. See also *Rostron* [2003] EWCA Crim 2206. At trial, it would of course be important to deal fully with D's belief that he was not acting dishonestly, under s 2 of the Act and under *Ghosh* [1982] QB 1083, and that he lacked an intent to deprive.

[308] cf *Williams v Phillips* (1957) 121 JP 163. The availability of theft charges in such circumstances is important in dealing with those who rummage through the refuse of celebrities for information to sell to tabloid newspapers, and those who appropriate confidential industrial or financial information from refuse. There is a specific offence under s 60 of the Environmental Protection Act 1990 of interfering with waste receptacles.

[309] R Glover, 'Can Dishonesty be Salvaged? Theft and the Grounding of the MSC Napoli' (2010) 74 J Crim Law 53; J. Lowther, R. Glover and M. Williams, 'Salvage, Pollution or Looting? The Stranding of the *Napoli*'s Cargo' (2009) 15 Journal of International Maritime Law 65.

[310] *Hibbert v McKiernan* [1948] 1 All ER 860, DC, discussed in [1972B] CLJ at 213–215 (lost golf balls not abandoned), and see the references in n 304 above.

[311] *Ingram* [1975] Crim LR 457, CA (absent-minded taking a defence to charge of shop-lifting). *Small* [1987] Crim LR 777, CA (D, who believes, reasonably or not, that property has been abandoned, does not intend to appropriate property belonging to another (or, *ex hypothesi*, permanently to deprive)).

[312] Para 3.2.

to himself. Thus, if D takes V's letters and puts them down a lavatory or throws V's iPod off a cliff, he is guilty of theft notwithstanding the fact that he intends only to cause loss to V and not gain for himself or anyone else. It might be thought that these instances could safely and more appropriately have been left to other branches of the criminal law – criminal damage to property for instance. But there are cases where there is no such damage or destruction of the property which would be sufficient to found a charge under another Act. For example, D takes V's diamond and flings it into a deep pond. The diamond lies unharmed in the pond and a prosecution for criminal damage would fail. It seems clearly right that D should be guilty of theft.[313] As Lord Bingham observed, 'In providing that an appropriation may be dishonest even where there is a willingness to pay, [the section] shows that the prospect of loss is not determinative of dishonesty.'[314]

19.4.2 Dishonesty[315]

The CLRC thought that 'dishonesty' could probably be left undefined and they did not define it but merely sought to clarify its meaning in certain respects. By s 2 of the Act:

(1) A person's appropriation of property belonging to another is not to be regarded as dishonest –

    (a) if he appropriates the property in the belief that he has in law the right to deprive the other of it, on behalf of himself or of a third person; or

    (b) if he appropriates the property in the belief that he would have the other's consent if the other knew of the appropriation and the circumstances of it; or

    (c) (except where the property came to him as trustee or personal representative) if he appropriates the property in the belief that the person to whom the property belongs cannot be discovered by taking reasonable steps.

(2) A person's appropriation of property belonging to another may be dishonest notwithstanding that he is willing to pay for the property.[316]

It will be noticed that this section specifies three situations in which an appropriation of property belonging to another is *not* to be regarded as dishonest, and one in which it may be. By this negative approach, the section assists somewhat in defining the meaning of dishonesty, but the section does not specify any state of mind that *must* be regarded as dishonest. The approach to defining dishonesty raises interesting questions about the role that the element has to play in the offence of theft generally. Dishonesty operates both as a peg on which to hang claims of an exculpatory nature – that is, as equivalent to an element of unlawfulness or lack of blameworthiness – and also as a positive element of *mens rea*, requiring proof of D's state of mind. Professor Horder describes dishonesty as a concealed excuse, 'taking the form of a morally open textured mental element'.[317] This overlap between 'dishonesty' as a state of mind (requiring a factual enquiry from the jury) and as a concept describing the wrong done (requiring a moral evaluation by the jury) is perpetuated by the case law. A further complexity

---

[313] An alternative solution would be to consider creating an offence of unlawfully depriving the owner of the use of his property: see below, p 833.

[314] *Wheatley and Penn v Commissioner of Police of the British Virgin Islands* [2006] UKPC 24.

[315] See also Smith, *Property Offences*, Ch 7; *Arlidge and Parry on Fraud*, Ch 2; Law Com Report No 276, *Fraud* (2002) Part V.

[316] Care must be taken when considering the concept of dishonesty since s 2 is not applicable to all of the offences under the Theft Acts.

[317] *Excusing Crime* (2003) 49. See A Steel 'The Harms and Wrongs of Stealing: The Harm Principle and Dishonesty in Theft' (2008) 31 UNSWLJ 712.

with the element of dishonesty (beyond the law of theft *per se*) has been described by the Law Commission:

In some crimes, such as conspiracy to defraud, the other elements of the offence are not prima facie unlawful, so dishonesty renders criminal otherwise lawful conduct. However, in deception offences the other elements of the offence, if proved, would normally be unlawful in themselves. If someone has practised a deception in order to gain a benefit their conduct is prima facie wrongful. Therefore dishonesty can be raised to rebut the inference that conduct was in fact wrongful... The former type of crime [can be described] as having a *positive* requirement of dishonesty, and the latter as having a *negative* requirement.[318]

It is regrettable that there is no statutory definition of dishonesty, particularly since the common law definition which supplements s 2 is so vague, and as noted above, dishonesty has assumed an elevated importance following the excessively broad interpretations of the *actus reus* elements of the offence.[319]

19.4.2.1 Belief in the right to deprive

D is not dishonest if he believes, whether reasonably or not,[320] that he has the legal right[321] to do the act which is alleged to constitute an appropriation of the property of another. The prosecution must disprove any belief in such a right that D claims to have held.[322] The Act refers specifically to a belief in a right *in law* as inconsistent with dishonesty. This does not necessarily mean that a belief in a merely moral right will be insufficient to negative dishonesty.[323] The common law position was that taking another's property was not justifiable, even where it necessary to avoid starvation, and that suggests that even the strongest moral claim to deprive another is not enough to rebut dishonesty. However, under the 1968 Act it is now a jury question. There is nothing in the Act to say that a belief in a moral right does not rebut dishonesty, and a jury would be likely to find that a truly starving person was not dishonest.

D's belief in the legal right of another, X, will also negative D's dishonesty. Thus, in *Close*,[324] an employee, paying his employer's debt in kind by taking his employer's property without consent, was apparently held not to be dishonest by a jury. Where D specifically pleads a belief in a claim of right, the jury ought, it is submitted, to be directed in relation to s 2 and not left to deal with the issue under the general test in *Ghosh* (below).[325]

Since a belief in a claim of right should negate *mens rea* in all cases, it is arguable that this element of s 2 should have been made generally applicable throughout the Act rather than being restricted to cases of theft.

---

[318] Law Com No 276, above, para 5.12. For criticism of this as unhelpful, see P Kiernan and G Scanlon, 'Fraud and the Law Commission: The Future of Dishonesty' (2003) 24 Comp Law 4.

[319] cf the Law Commission's current view which is that no definition is possible: Law Com No 276, *Fraud*, above, Part V.

[320] See *Terry* [2001] EWCA Crim 2979.

[321] It is irrelevant that no such right exists in law. A *dictum* to the contrary in *Gott v Measures* [1948] 1 KB 234, [1947] 2 All ER 609, is irreconcilable with the decision in *Bernhard* [1938] 2 KB 264. The belief need not relate to a 'property' right: *Wood* [1999] Crim LR 564 and commentary.

[322] There must be some evidence of the belief in a claim of right to be left to the jury before the judge is obliged to leave it: *Hall* [2008] EWCA Crim 2086.

[323] A belief in a moral right was not a defence to larceny: *Harris v Harrison* [1963] Crim LR 497, DC. cf Williams, CLGP, 322.

[324] [1977] Crim LR 107.

[325] See *Rostron* [2003] EWCA Crim 2206, where D believed that he had a legal right to collect 'lost' golf balls. cf *Smith (Paul Adrian)* (1997) 7 Archbold News 4, CA. On charges to which s 2 does not apply *Ghosh* must perform the function: *Woods* (1999) 5 Archbold News 2, CA.

19.4.2.2 Belief that the owner would consent

It is sufficient that D holds a mistaken though genuine belief that the person to whom the property belonged would have consented had he known of the circumstances. Thus, D will not be dishonest where he helps himself to his flatmates' milk from the fridge if he holds a belief that this would be consented to. Numerous appropriations of this nature occur every day and a specific provision dealing with the matter precludes capricious prosecutions. Following *Hinks*, the issue of mistaken beliefs will be of particular importance in cases in which D claims that he was acting with the owner's consent.[326]

19.4.2.3 Belief that the person to whom the property belongs cannot be discovered by taking reasonable steps

Though the Act makes no reference to 'finding', this provision is obviously intended to preserve the substance of the common law rule relating to finding. The finder who appropriates property commits the *actus reus* of theft (assuming that the property does belong to another and has not been abandoned) but is not dishonest unless he believes the owner *can* be discovered by taking reasonable steps. There is no requirement that D's belief about the traceability of the owner is reasonable; merely that his belief about the steps necessary to trace the owner is reasonable. This will depend on the nature of the property in question.[327]

If D's initial appropriation of lost property is innocent (either because he does not believe that the owner can be discovered by taking reasonable steps or because he intends to return the thing to the owner when he takes it), a dishonest later assumption of a right to it by keeping or dealing with it as owner will be theft by virtue of s 3(1).[328] While this provision was intended primarily for the case of finding, it is not confined to that case and there are other instances where it would apply. Suppose that V arranges with D that D shall gratuitously store V's furniture in D's house. V leaves the town and D loses touch with him. Some years later D, needing the space in his house and being unable to locate V, sells the furniture.[329] This is undoubtedly an appropriation of the property of another and D is civilly liable to V in conversion; but he appears to be saved from any possibility of conviction of theft by s 2(1)(c). Though the purchase money probably belongs to V, D's immunity under the Act for lack of dishonesty must extend to the proceeds of sale.

Where property has come to D as a trustee or personal representative and he appropriates it, he may be dishonest even though he believes that the person to whom the property belongs cannot be discovered by taking reasonable steps. This seems to provide a particularly strict approach, with the intention being that the trustee or personal representative can never be personally entitled to the property (unless it is specifically so provided by the trust instrument or the will) for, if the beneficiaries are extinct or undiscoverable, the Crown will be entitled to the beneficial interest as *bona vacantia*. However, if the trustee or personal representative appropriates the property for his own use, honestly believing that he is entitled to do so, then it is submitted that he must be acquitted. But if he knows that he has no right to do this and that the property in the last resort belongs to the Crown, he commits theft from the beneficiaries, if they are in existence and, if not, from the Crown.

---

[326] See above, p 784. See especially Lord Hutton's dissent focusing on dishonesty and the question of whether D can be convicted if he has a claim of right – consent, but not if he has a mere belief in a claim of right – under s 2(1)(a). See the discussion in relation to freegans taking from supermarket rubbish bins: S Thomas, above n 304.

[327] See, eg, the implausible defence in *Sylvester* (1985) CO/559/84 where D alleged that the car he was stripping of parts in a car park was abandoned and therefore s 2(1)(c) applied.

[328] Above, p 792.

[329] cf *Sachs v Miklos* [1948] 2 KB 23; *Munro v Wilmott* [1949] 1 KB 295.

19.4.2.4 Dishonest appropriation, notwithstanding payment

Section 2(2) is intended to deal with the kind of situation where D takes bottles of milk from V's doorstep but leaves in its place the full price. Certainly D has no claim of right and he intends to deprive V permanently of his property. Doubts had, however, arisen as to whether this was dishonest. This subsection resolves them. The mere fact of payment does not negative dishonesty but the jury are entitled to take into account all the circumstances and these may be such that even an intention to pay for property, let alone actual payment, may negative dishonesty. The fact of payment, or intention to pay, may be cogent evidence where D's defence is that he believed V would have consented, as where D takes milk bottles from V's unattended delivery van and leaves the price, claiming that he assumed that V would have been very happy to sell him the milk had he been there, but that he had not time to wait for V to return. If D is believed – and the fact of repayment would be persuasive evidence – it would seem that he has no dishonest intent. The section is important in emphasizing that D's willingness to pay the market value for appropriated property will not necessarily negate dishonesty, otherwise there would be no theft where D takes V's original work of art that he has long coveted, leaving its listed valuation price.

19.4.2.5 Dishonesty as an element of the offence

In drafting the 1968 Act, the CLRC seem to have overlooked the limited role played by the equivalent word 'fraudulently' in the Larceny Act,[330] and in their Eighth Report[331] the word was assumed to have some large though unspecified role to play in the definition of the offence. In drafting the 1968 Act the CLRC used 'dishonestly' rather than 'fraudulently', not because the meaning was any different but because they thought it to be more easily understood:

'Dishonestly' seems to us a better word than 'fraudulently'. The question 'Was this "dishonest"?' is easier for a jury to answer than the question 'Was this "fraudulent"?' 'Dishonesty' is something which laymen can easily recognize when they see it, whereas 'fraud' may seem to involve technicalities which have to be explained by a lawyer.

This passage suggests that it is for jurors to decide whether 'this' (D's conduct) is dishonest. Of course, it is for jurors to decide all questions of fact, including the state of mind of the defendant – what was his intention and belief, including his belief as to his legal rights. But, under the Larceny Act, it was probably for the judge to say whether that state of mind was to be characterized in law as 'fraudulent' subject to the jury finding given facts.[332] The substitution of 'dishonestly' for 'fraudulently' has therefore led to an important change in the law. Possibly influenced by this misleading passage in the CLRC Report, the Court of Appeal in *Feely*[333] held that it is for the jury in each case to decide, not only what the defendant's state of mind was, but also, subject to s 2, whether that state of mind is to be categorized as dishonest.

---

[330] Commentators on the Larceny Act 1916 disagreed as to the function, if any, of the word 'fraudulently' (which was the precursor to 'dishonesty'). JWC Turner (writing as editor of *Russell on Crime* (12th edn,1964) 996), concluded that the word added nothing to 'without a claim of right' (now found in s 2(1)(a)). Others thought it had the limited function of exculpating the taker who believed the owner would have consented if it had been possible to ask him – a case now expressly covered by s 2(1)(b) of the 1968 Act: see Wing-Commander Lowe, 'The Fraudulent Intent in Larceny' [1956] Crim LR 78. Others that it exculpated the taker of money or other 'fungibles' (substitutable property) who intended to, and had no doubt that he could, return, not the identical thing, but an equivalent (a case which is not expressly provided for in the 1968 Act): JC Smith, 'The Fraudulent Intent to Larceny: Another View' [1956] Crim LR 238. See also the recent analysis by see A Steel, 'The Meanings of Dishonesty in Theft' (2009) 38 Common Law World Review 103.

[331] Para 39. On the CLRC intentions see also DW Elliott, 'Dishonesty in Theft: A Dispensable Concept' [1982] Crim LR 395 at 405.

[332] *Williams* [1953] 1 QB 660, CCA; *Cockburn* [1968] 1 All ER 466, CA.

[333] [1973] QB 530 [1973] Crim LR 193 and commentary.

Jurors, when deciding whether an appropriation was dishonest can be reasonably expected to, and should, apply the current standards of ordinary decent people. In their own lives they have to decide what is and what is not dishonest. We can see no reason why, when in a jury box, they should require the help of a judge to tell them what amounts to dishonesty.

Only a moment's comparison with the approach to other *mens rea* requirements is needed to illustrate how much of a departure from the old law and from orthodoxy this is. For example, in a case involving recklessness, the judge defines that concept and directs the jury to determine whether, on the facts as they find them to be, D's state of mind is within that legal definition. The jury are not invited to define recklessness themselves.[334]

The court in *Feely* was certainly much influenced by the opinion of the House of Lords in *Brutus v Cozens*[335] that the meaning of an ordinary word of the English language is not a question of law for the judge but one of fact for the jury. 'Dishonestly' is such a word and so it was for the jury to attribute to it such meaning as they thought proper. A major difficulty about this view is that juries – and magistrates – are likely to give different answers on facts which are indistinguishable. This creates very obvious injustices that bring the criminal law into disrepute. It also raises the potential for challenges to the law under Art 7 of the ECHR on the basis of lack of certainty. In relation to the offence of theft, the elements of *actus reus* – that there must be an appropriation of property belonging to another – are likely to be held to be sufficient, even after the extensive interpretation in *Gomez* and *Hinks*, to ensure that the offence of theft is not incompatible with Art 7. It is not yet an offence based solely on the concept of dishonesty (despite the best efforts of the House of Lords in *Morris*, *Gomez* and *Hinks*). It has been held at first instance that dishonesty under *Ghosh* is not itself incompatible with Art 7.[336]

Feely did at least provide a standard – that of 'ordinary decent people', as understood by the jury – against which the defendant's intentions and beliefs were to be tested. Other cases, however, went further. In *Gilks*,[337] D agreed that it would be dishonest if his grocer gave him too much change and he kept it, but he said bookmakers are 'a race apart' and there was nothing dishonest about keeping an overpayment from them. The judge invited the jury to 'try and place yourselves in [D's] position at that time and answer the question whether in your view he thought he was acting dishonestly'. The Court of Appeal thought this was a proper and sufficient direction, agreeing apparently that, if D may have held the belief he claimed, the prosecution had not established dishonesty. This applied, not the standards of ordinary decent people, but the defendant's own standards, however deplorable they might be. In *Boggeln v Williams*,[338] the court expressly rejected an argument that D's belief as to his own honesty was irrelevant and held that, on the contrary, it was crucial. D, whose electricity had been cut off, reconnected the supply through the meter. He knew that the electricity company did not consent to his doing so, but he notified them and believed, not unreasonably, that he would be

---

[334] It is interesting to contrast the position in Ireland. In Ireland, theft offences are contained in the Criminal Justice (Theft and Fraud Offences) Act 2001, which repealed the Larceny Act 1916 and 1990. Section 4(1) states, '…a person is guilty of theft if he or she dishonestly appropriates property without the consent of its owner and with the intention of depriving the owner of it'. Section 2 defines dishonestly as 'without a claim of right made in good faith'. The rationale for defining dishonestly was contained in para 15.52 of the Law Reform Commission's Report on the Law Relating to Dishonesty, which stated, 'To by-pass the judge and leave the definition of fundamental legal concepts to the jury would be an unwarranted exercise in misguided populism.' I am grateful to Karl Laird for researching this point.

[335] [1973] AC 854.

[336] *Pattni* [2001] Crim LR 570.

[337] Above, p 818; [1972] 3 All ER 280 at 283. On the very early cases see DW Elliott, 'Dishonesty Under the Theft Act' [1972] Crim LR 625.

[338] [1978] 2 All ER 1061, [1978] Crim LR 242 and commentary.

able to pay at the due time. It was held that the question was whether he believed that what he did was honest. A further complexity was introduced in *McIvor*,[339] where the Court of Appeal said that the test of dishonesty in conspiracy to defraud was different from that to be applied in theft.

The leading case is now *Ghosh*.[340] In that case, the Court of Appeal significantly improved the position by rejecting any distinction between the test of dishonesty in different offences. *Ghosh* itself was a case of obtaining by deception contrary to s 15 of the 1968 Act; and it is now reasonably clear that the same principle applies throughout the Theft Acts, the Fraud Act 2006 and the common law of conspiracy to defraud as well as other statutory offences[341] such as fraudulent trading under the Companies Act 2006. There is one test of dishonesty in English criminal law.[342]

The court in *Ghosh* also provided a new and more elaborate explanation of the approach to be taken in determining D's dishonesty. The test to be applied by the trier of fact is twofold:

(1) Was what was done dishonest according to the ordinary standards of reasonable and honest people? If no, D is not guilty. If yes:

(2) Did the defendant realize that reasonable and honest people regard what he did as dishonest? If yes, he is guilty; if no, he is not.

The Court of Appeal has frequently stressed that it is not necessary to give this *Ghosh* direction to the jury in every case.[343] Thus, it is unnecessary where D's claim is a lack of dishonesty owing to forgetfulness,[344] or where the question relates solely to the genuineness of D's belief rather than D's claim that the ordinary person would not regard it as dishonest.[345] Nor is it necessary where, for example D, a shop-worker, simply denies taking the property and does not claim for example that he borrowed it from the till.[346] If there is any evidence to suggest that D's attitude was, 'Whatever others may think, *I* did not consider this dishonest', the direction must be given. Where there is no such evidence it is probably unnecessary. Where this direction is necessary, the exact form of words ought to be used.[347]

---

[339] [1982] 1 All ER 491.

[340] [1982] QB 1053.

[341] eg Social Security Administration (Fraud) Act 1997 offences of deception: *Department for Work and Pensions v Costello* [2006] EWHC 1156 (Admin).

[342] In some circumstances the *Ghosh* test is applicable in civil cases: *Aktieselskabet Dansk Skibsfinansiering v Brothers* [2001] BCLC 324; *Royal Brunei Airlines Sdn Bhd v Tan* [1995] 2 AC 378 and see the discussion in *Twinsectra Ltd v Yardley* [2002] 2 WLR 802, [2002] UKHL 12, particularly at paras 27–33 and 115–134, on which see MP Thompson, 'Criminal Law and Property Law: An Unhappy Combination' (2002) 66 Conv 387; R Thornton, 'Dishonest Assistance: Guilty Conduct or a Guilty Mind' [2002] CLJ 524. In *Barlow Clowes Intl v Eurotrust* [2005] UKPC 37, *Twinsectra* was explained.

[343] See in particular *Roberts* (1985) 84 Cr App R 177; *Price* [1990] Crim LR 200. cf A Halpin, 'The Test for Dishonesty' [1996] Crim LR 289, at 291.

[344] *Atkinson* [2004] Crim LR 226.

[345] *Wood* [2002] EWCA Crim 832, CA where D claimed that his trespassing into empty premises to remove the entire stock of curtain fabric, was not dishonest since he believed it to be abandoned. cf *Rostron* [2003] EWCA Crim 2266, where the Court of Appeal seem to restrict *Ghosh* to cases where D would have a claim of right under s 2(1)(a). That must be wrong. Moreover, if the defendants had been aware that the golf club on whose land they were trespassing had a legal right to the balls that was still not enough to lead to a finding of dishonesty. They could have claimed that their behaviour was not to be regarded as dishonest by ordinary right thinking people: then they would have been entitled to a full *Ghosh* direction. See the discussion in Hickey above n 304 and in relation to freegans, S Thomas, above n 304.

[346] *Cobb* [2005] EWCA Crim 1549.

[347] *Hyam* [1997] Crim LR 439. Embellishments are to be avoided cf *Robertson* [2006] EWCA Crim 1289: the judge should not have added 'reasonable and honest people engaged in business'.

The first limb of *Ghosh* rarely gives rise to difficulties, although it can do. It was recently held that no reasonable magistrates' court could have concluded that the reasonable and honest person would not regard as dishonest the conduct of the accused manager of a tool hire shop who allowed customers to borrow items for a very short period of time for no payment (sometimes receiving a personal tip) as he would alter the company records to show that the item had been returned as faulty or incorrectly chosen.[348]

Several effects of the *Ghosh* test need to be noted. First, it gets away from the extreme and unacceptable subjectivism of *Gilks* and *Boggeln v Williams*. D is no longer to be judged by his own standards of honesty. Secondly, *Ghosh* attempts a compromise between a purely objective *Feely*-type test which might be regarded as too harsh, and a purely subjective test such as that in *Gilks* which would create a thief's charter. However, in seeking to achieve this compromise it introduces an unnecessary confusion in the form of the second limb. Campbell[349] cogently argues that this additional limb is superfluous if under the first limb the jury is properly directed to take account of all the circumstances. Taking the oft-quoted example of D who fails to pay a travel fare because he is new to the country and is accustomed to free public transport, it should not be necessary to rely on the second limb to conclude that D is not dishonest. A properly directed jury would so conclude under the first limb. Thirdly, the attempted compromise may fail in its intended purpose – to prevent the 'Robin Hood defence', that is, where D claims that the activity was not dishonest – but it is not clear that it does so. The defendant would have to be acquitted 'if the jury think *either* (a) that what Robin Hood did (rob the rich to feed the poor) was not dishonest *or* (b) that Robin Hood thought the reasonable and honest man would not consider what he did as dishonest'.[350] Taking a more modern example of a peace protestor who takes from an army depot armaments destined for a war zone because he knows they are being used against civilians. He would certainly not regard his own conduct as dishonest and so would escape under the rule as stated in *Gilks*. He might still do so under *Ghosh*.[351] A jury of pacifists would be likely to agree with him; and it might be difficult to satisfy any jury that the defendant did not believe that all right-thinking people would agree with him. Peace protestors probably do so believe. But this surely *should* be theft. One who deliberately deprives another of his property should not be able to escape liability because of his disapproval, however profound and morally justified, of the lawful use to which that property was being put by its owner. In deciding whether a certain state of mind should be regarded as dishonest it is not irrelevant to consider how the matter will be regarded by the ordinary decent citizen who is the victim of the offence. The owners of the armaments will certainly consider that their property has been stolen, even though they are fully aware of the state of mind of the takers. The law fails in one of its purposes if it does not afford protection to a person against what he quite reasonably regards as a straightforward case of theft.

---

[348] *Gohill v DPP* [2007] EWHC 23 (Admin).

[349] K Campbell, 'The Test of Dishonesty in *Ghosh*' [1994] 43 CLJ 349, Campbell suggests that if the aim is to provide this hybrid test it should be: whether a reasonable jury, applying ordinary standards of honesty, is prepared to excuse D's failure to recognize that his own behaviour would be regarded as dishonest by the standards of ordinary people.

[350] Such examples contradict the view of some commentators that apart from 'morons and lunatics' the only people likely to rely on a claim that they did not realize that ordinary honest people would regard their conduct as dishonest are business people who assert that their activities are the norm in that context, *Arlidge and Parry on Fraud* (2nd edn, 1996) para 1.027.

[351] This is an instance in which it appears motive, which is generally regarded as irrelevant to *mens rea* in practice, assumes an importance. The defendant's character may also take on an elevated significance: *Bailey* [2004] EWCA Crim 2530.

19.4.2.6 Critique and reform of dishonesty

Ghosh has generated much criticism and some valuable proposals for reform.[352]

Criticism

Perhaps the most trenchant critic of the *Ghosh* test was Professor Griew,[353] who catalogued its numerous deficiencies. Griew suggested that the test confuses the state of mind with the concept of dishonesty;[354] leaves a question of law to the jury[355] which may lead to inconsistent decisions with the potential for different juries to reach different verdicts on identical facts, thus presenting acute problems in respect of Art 7 of the ECHR;[356] leads to more trials as defendants have little to lose by pleading not guilty and hoping that the dishonesty element is not made out; leads to longer trials as the dishonesty issue is a 'live' one in all cases; assumes a community norm within the jury in that they must agree on the ordinary standards of honesty; assumes that jurors are honest, or at least that they can apply ordinary standards of honesty even if they do not adhere to them in their personal lives; and, is unsuitable in specialized cases such as complex commercial frauds where the 'ordinary' person is unlikely to understand the honesty or otherwise of the activities.[357] The CLRC view of dishonesty relied on the common sense of members of society and a consensus about the appropriate benchmarks for protecting private property. As Norrie[358] points out, this view of private property might not be an accurate reflection of current values, particularly in relation to specific types of misappropriation – for example, petty pilfering from the workplace and omissions from tax returns. A national survey in 2007 found that more than 33 per cent of people admitted that they had paid in cash to a cleaner, plumber or other tradesman to avoid paying tax, 20 per cent had taken something from work; just under a third, if handed too much change in a shop or business transaction, would just keep it, and one in ten avoids paying their television licence. About 6 per cent of people have 'padded out' an insurance claim.[359] Of course, it might well be that people do not generally assume their own moral standards when sitting as jurors.

---

[352] EJ Griew, 'Dishonesty – The Objections to *Feely* and *Ghosh*' [1985] Crim LR 341; M Wasik, 'Mens Rea, Motive and the Problem of Dishonesty in the Law of Theft' [1977] Crim LR 543; Elliott [1982] Crim LR 395 at 398. Elliott's solution is to dispense with the word 'dishonestly' altogether but to add a new s 3(2): 'No appropriation of property belonging to another which is not detrimental to the interests of the other in a significant practical way shall amount to theft of the property.'

[353] Author of *The Theft Acts 1968 and 1978* (7th edn, 1995) and 'Objections to *Feely* and *Ghosh*' [1985] Crim LR 341.

[354] See also K Campbell, 'The Test of Dishonesty in *Ghosh*' [1994] CLJ 349 at 354 criticizing *Ghosh* for confusing the state of mind and the defendant's standards of honesty.

[355] For an argument in support of leaving such issues to the jury, see R Tur, 'Dishonesty and the Jury Question', in A Phillips Griffiths (ed), *Philosophy and Practice* (1985). The Law Commission provisionally concluded that 'the circumstances in which such conduct may be found to be non-dishonest cannot be circumscribed by legal definition. Where dishonesty is a positive element, it *must* be open to the fact-finders to find that particular conduct is not dishonest, even if the legislation does not say so.' LCCP 155 (1999) para 5.6.

[356] Art 7 guarantees not only against retrospective criminalization in strict terms, but also that 'legal provisions which interfere with individual rights must be adequately accessible, and formulated with sufficient precision to enable the citizen to regulate his conduct', *G v Federal Republic of Germany* 60 DR 252 at 262 (1989). So vague are the elements of dishonesty under *Ghosh* that the LCCP 155 provisionally took the view that a Home Secretary could not safely be advised to make a statement of compatibility in relation to a Bill creating a general dishonesty offence. Subsequently, the Law Commission reversed its opinion in LC 276, *Fraud* (2002).

[357] On the suitability of dishonesty in these cases, see also Elliott [1991] Crim LR 732 arguing that insufficient attention has been paid to the issue of dishonesty in cases of sole traders committing theft from the company. In *Lockwood* [1986] Crim LR 244, the CA held that the *Ghosh* test is to be applied without embellishments such as 'current notions of fair trading among commercial men', cf *Robertson* [2006] EWCA Crim 1289.

[358] At 42. See also N Lacey, C Wells and O Quick, *Reconstructing Criminal Law* (4th edn, 2010) 399.

[359] See The Times, 24 June 2007; S Farrall and S Karstedt, *Law Abiding Majority?* (2007). The report found that 61% of 1,807 people in England and Wales aged between 25 and 65 had committed at least one of a number of offences against business, Government or their employers.

In terms of principle, the criticisms levelled at the *Ghosh* test are rendered all the more cogent for several reasons. First, the test applies in a great volume of cases in English courts – all those involving an element of dishonesty, which includes all Theft Act, Fraud Act and common law conspiracy to defraud cases, and many other offences under specific legislation (although it seems that dishonesty does not create enormous problems in practice).[360] Secondly, broad interpretations of the elements of *actus reus* have left dishonesty as the principal determinant of criminality in theft. As the Law Commission commented recently, 'where the conduct elements of an offence are morally neutral [as, eg, appropriation may be], the element of dishonesty has to do more than simply exclude specific types of conduct which, though *prima facie* wrongful, do not deserve to be criminal'.[361]

Ghosh has not been universally accepted in other jurisdictions. Before *Ghosh*, the Supreme Court of Victoria had refused to follow *Feely*, when construing the identical provision in Victorian legislation. In *Salvo*,[362] Fullagar J, with whom Murphy J seems to have agreed in substance, held that it was the duty of the judge to explain to the jury what 'dishonestly' meant; and he should tell them that it means 'with disposition to defraud, that is with disposition to withhold from a person what is his right'. There are, however, two difficulties about this interpretation. The first is that it seems to add nothing to what is expressly stated in s 2(1)(a) – that is, a person who has a claim of legal right is not dishonest – and leaves no function for the word 'dishonestly'.[363] Secondly, it seems too narrow as a matter of policy.[364] Such an approach leads to the conviction of D who, knowing that he has no right to do so, takes V's money with intent to spend it but with the certainty (in his own mind) that he will be able to replace it before it is missed, so that V will never know anything about it and suffer no detriment whatever.[365]

Reform

The Law Commission recently commented that it found the criticisms of the present law 'compelling'.[366] In the light of the volume and strength of such criticisms, it is not surprising, therefore, that numerous reform proposals have been advanced. Professor Elliott went so far as to suggest the removal of the element of dishonesty from the definition of theft. His proposal was to leave s 2 to deal with the bulk of cases and to add a further exculpatory element to the definition of the offence for conduct 'not detrimental to the interests of the owner in a significant practical way'.[367] It is unclear that such a proposal would offer any greater degree

---

[360] See, eg, Magistrates' Association response to the LCCP 155, reported in Law Com No 276, para 5.14. And see the Commission's conclusion at para 5.18.

[361] LCCP 155, para 5.6.

[362] [1980] VR 401.

[363] Williams, TBCL, 730.

[364] See Elliott [1982] Crim LR at 406.

[365] In Australia, the *Salvo* approach has been followed in *R v Bonollo* [1981] VR 633 (the full court of the Supreme Court of Victoria); *Love* (1989) 17 NSWLR 608, and *Condon* (1995) 83 A Crim R 335. In *Peters v The Queen* (1998) 192 CLR 493, the majority of the High Court distinguished *Salvo*, but declined to adopt the *Ghosh* test, preferring that the jury be directed by the standards of ordinary decent people – a test seemingly akin to *Feely*. The High Court's conclusion was that there is no obligation for the Crown to show that D realized that his acts were dishonest by the current standards of honesty: *McLeod* [2003] HCA 24 at [100]. New Zealand does not follow the *Ghosh* test. See *Williams* [1985] 1 NZLR 294. For an illuminating review of the law in common law countries see A Steel, 'The Meanings of Dishonesty in Theft' (2009) 38 Common Law World Review 103.

[366] LCCP 155, para 5.32.

[367] See Elliott [1982] Crim LR 395. See also Elliott [1991] Crim LR 732. cf G Williams, 'Innocuously Dipping into Trust Funds' (1983) 5 LS 183. This solution would require legislation and that seems very unlikely. Why should the taking of £20 from Bill Gates' wallet not amount to theft?

of certainty and promote any greater degree of consistency than the present law. There have been many other proposals, each with their strengths and defects.[368]

One attractive solution would be a provision that a person appropriating property belonging to another *is* to be regarded as dishonest unless one of the three existing exemptions (in s 2) apply or, fourthly:

he intends to replace the property with an equivalent and believes that no detriment whatever will be caused to the owner by the appropriation.

This would excuse the employee who 'borrows' £5 from the till when closing the shop on Saturday afternoon, having no doubt that he will be able to replace it when he opens up on Monday morning, only to be robbed and rendered penniless on his way home from the pub on Saturday night.[369] His actions would be unlawful (in civil law) although not dishonest. It probably would not save the postmaster who 'borrows' from the post office till to keep his ailing grocery business going, in the hope that business will improve.

This test might, however, be thought too severe, leaving no escape route for hard cases such as the parents taking food for their starving children. But perhaps the concept of dishonesty is not the right vehicle for such cases. Suppose that the person breaks a window to get at the food and is charged with criminal damage. The definition of criminal damage does not require dishonesty. It would not make much sense to acquit the parent of theft and convict instead of criminal damage. They should stand or fall together. The parent might claim he had a 'lawful excuse' for the doing the damage – that is the general defences of necessity or duress of circumstances – and this is the right approach for theft. If dishonesty were defined appropriately as a state of mind, exculpatory claims would be dealt with under the general defences which are applicable equally to theft and criminal damage. It is important, of course, to distinguish elements of unlawfulness and dishonesty. D may be acting unlawfully (and aware that he is), and yet not aware that he is acting dishonestly.

19.4.3 Intention permanently to deprive

The Theft Act preserves the rule of the common law and of the Larceny Act 1916 that appropriating the property of another with the intention of depriving him only temporarily of it is not stealing. There is no general offence in English law of stealing the use or enjoyment of a chattel or other property. The taking of motor vehicles and of articles from public places are exceptions, considered below. Apart from those cases, the 1968 Act left the law substantially unchanged; so that, if D takes V's horse without authority and rides it for an afternoon, a week or a month, he commits no offence under the 1968 Act if he has an intention to return the horse at the end of this period.[370]

---

[368] See, *inter alia*, Glazebrook [1993] CLJ 191 who provides a list of excepted circumstances that are not dishonest. This approach is developed by A Halpin, 'The Test for Dishonesty' [1996] Crim LR 283 at 294 – '1. The treatment by a person of the property of another is to be regarded as dishonest where it is done without a belief that the other would consent to that treatment if he knew of all the circumstances, unless the person believes that the law permits that treatment of the property. 2. The treatment by a person of the property of another is not to be regarded as dishonest if done (otherwise than by a trustee or personal representative) in the belief that the person to whom the property belongs is unlikely to be discovered by taking reasonable steps.' See further, Haplin, *Definition in the Criminal Law*, 162–166.

[369] This proposal goes back substantially to the explanation offered many years ago for the meaning of 'fraudulently' in the Larceny Act 1916 and to that made by JC Smith in the first two editions of *Law of Theft*.

[370] *Neal v Gribble* [1978] RTR 409, below, p 858.

19.4.3.1 Deprivation of persons with limited interests

As we have seen, theft may be committed against a person having possession or control of property or having any proprietary right or interest in it. The element of permanence relates to the deprivation of V, not to the proposed benefit to D. Where V has an interest less than full ownership, it appears that an intention by D to deprive him of the whole of that interest, whatever it might be, is sufficient.[371] Thus, if as D knows, V has hired a car from X for a month, and D takes it, intending to return it to X after the month has expired, this appears to be theft from V, who is permanently deprived of his whole interest in the property, but it is not theft from X. The question is one of intention; so, if in the above example, D, when he took the car, believed V to be the owner, he would apparently not commit theft from V (because he intended to return it) even though V was, in fact, deprived of his whole interest.

19.4.3.2 Section 6 and the common law

Under the law before the 1968 Act the phrase 'intention permanently to deprive' was held to include the cases where:

(1) D took V's property with intention that V should have it back only by paying for it – for example, he took V's property so that, pretending that it was his own, he could sell it to V[372] ('ransom' cases).

(2) D took V's property intending to return it to V only when he had completely changed its substance – for example, D, being employed by V to melt iron, took an axle belonging to V and melted it down in order to increase his output and consequently his earnings;[373] or D wrongfully fed V's oats to V's own horses;[374] or took V's horse intending to kill it and to return the carcass.[375]

(3) D took V's property and pawned it, intending to redeem and restore it to V one day but with no reasonable prospects of being able to do so.[376]

The draft Bill proposed by the CLRC contained no definition or elaboration of the phrase 'intention of permanently depriving'. The Committee assumed that the old law would be applied without any difficulty under that expression. The Government had other ideas and introduced a clause which, after much amendment, became s 6.[377]

Section 6(1) provides:

A person appropriating property belonging to another without meaning the other permanently to lose the thing itself is nevertheless to be regarded as having the intention of permanently depriving the other of it if his intention is to treat the thing as his own to dispose of regardless of the other's rights, and a borrowing or lending of it may amount to so treating it if, but only if, the borrowing or lending is for a period and in circumstances making it equivalent to an outright taking or disposal.

As Spencer has written,[378] and the Court of Appeal was inclined to agree,[379] s 6 'sprouts obscurities at every phrase'.

---

[371] cf Smith, *Property Offences*, para 6.05.

[372] *Hall* (1849) 1 Den 381. See recently *Raphael* [2008] EWCA Crim 1014 (below).

[373] *Richards* (1844) 1 Car & Kir 532.

[374] *Morfit* (1816) Russ & Ry 307.

[375] cf *Cabbage* (1815) Russ & Ry 292.

[376] *Phetheon* (1840) 9 C & P 552; *Medland* (1851) 5 Cox CC 292. cf *Trebilcock* (1858) Dears & B 453 and *Wynn* (1887) 16 Cox CC 231, which are inconclusive on the point.

[377] See JR Spencer, 'The Metamorphosis of Section 6 of the Theft Act' [1977] Crim LR 653. See more recently A Steele 'Permanent Borrowing and Lending: A New View of s6 Theft Act 1968' (2008) 17 Nottingham LJ 3.

[378] Spencer [1977] Crim LR 653.

[379] *Lloyd* [1985] QB 829 at 834.

On one view s 6 was intended to cover the cases that had been included under the old law and no more. In *Lloyd*,[380] the Court of Appeal approved academic opinions that s 6 only need be referred to in exceptional cases and then the question for the jury should not be 'worded in terms of the generalities' of the section but be related to the particular facts. The court cited the opinion of Edmund Davies LJ,[381] that 'Section 6...gives illustrations, as it were, of what can amount to the dishonest intention demanded by s 1(1). But it is a misconception to interpret it as watering down s 1', and concluded, 'we would try to interpret the section in such a way as to ensure that nothing is construed as an intention permanently to deprive which would not prior to the 1968 Act have been so construed'.

However, before and since *Lloyd*, courts have given the words of the section their wider ordinary meaning. In *Downes*,[382] the Court of Appeal held that D committed theft when, being in possession of vouchers belonging to the Inland Revenue and made out in his name, he sold them to others who, as he knew, would submit them to the Revenue so as to obtain tax advantages. The primary reason for the decision was that the document when returned to the Revenue would be in substance a different thing; but the court also held that s 6 was to be given its ordinary meaning – D intended to treat the vouchers as his own to dispose of regardless of the Revenue's rights. Subsequently, in *Chan Man-sin*,[383] the Privy Council held that, where a company accountant drew a forged cheque on the company's account, there was 'ample evidence' of intention permanently to deprive the company of its credit balance, even on the assumption that D contemplated that the fraud would be discovered and the company would lose nothing. He intended to treat the balance as his own to dispose of regardless of the company's rights. *Re Osman*,[384] another case of 'theft without loss', is similar. In *Bagshaw*,[385] the Court of Appeal said that the restrictive view taken in *Lloyd* was *obiter* and that 'there may be other occasions on which s 6 applies'.

The current judicial opinion seems to be that s 6 is to be given its wider ordinary meaning (whatever that may be) and is not necessarily restricted to the scope of the common law meaning of the concept. The court in *Raphael*[386] expressly doubted whether the statutory framework created by the Act should always be restrictively interpreted by reference to the previous law. Section 6 certainly has to be applied to situations which did not arise at common law, like the theft or obtaining of a thing in action.[387] Subject to that, it is submitted that, in view of the acknowledged obscurity of s 6, the better opinion is that it should, in general, be treated as a narrow restatement of the common law.[388]

19.4.3.3 Disposal of the property as one's own

Adopting the broader meaning of s 6 presents some difficulties. It is submitted that an intention merely to use the thing as one's own is not enough, and that 'dispose of' is not used in the sense in which a commander might 'dispose of' his infantry but rather in the meaning given by the *Shorter Oxford Dictionary*: 'To deal with definitely; to get rid of; to get done with, finish.

---

[380] [1985] QB 829.

[381] *Warner* (1970) 55 Cr App R 93 at 97.

[382] (1983) 77 Cr App R 260, [1983] Crim LR 819 and commentary.

[383] [1988] 1 All ER 1, [1988] Crim LR 319, PC.

[384] [1988] Crim LR 611.

[385] [1988] Crim LR 321.

[386] [2008] EWCA Crim 1014.

[387] Since the thing in action is often extinguished and replaced by another (eg V's bank credit being extinguished and D's being created), there can only be permanent deprivation of that item of property belonging to V. The question is of D's *mens rea* as to that deprivation.

[388] cf Griew, *Theft*, para 2.103.

To make over by way of sale or bargain, sell.'[389] In *DPP v Lavender*,[390] however, the Divisional Court seems to have held D's intention to treat the thing as his own, regardless of the owner's rights, as crucial and to have minimized the importance of 'to dispose of'. D, a council tenant, without authority, removed two doors from another property belonging to the council to replace doors in the council property he occupied. Did he not, in fact, treat the doors as the property of the council, like the rest of the premises he occupied? If a secretary surreptitiously swaps his keyboard for the similar model operated by a colleague (because he believes it works better), does he steal the keyboard from his employer? He may well steal it from his colleague whom he does intend to deprive permanently of his limited interest.

It is submitted that, on a similar basis, there is no reason why there should not be a conviction for theft (rather than having to rely on s 11) in a case like that of the taker of the Goya from the National Gallery: 'I will return the picture when £X is paid to charity.' Substantially, the taker is offering to sell the thing back and his case is, in principle, the same as those contemplated by s 6(1). Nor should it make any difference that the price demanded is something other than money. 'I will return the picture when E (who is imprisoned) is given a free pardon' – this should be sufficient evidence of an intention permanently to deprive. The general principle might be that it is sufficient that there is an intention that V shall not have the property back unless some consideration is supplied by him or another; or, more generally still, unless some condition is satisfied.

The Court of Appeal recently commented that it was hard to find a better example of an intention on the part of the thief to 'treat the thing as his own to dispose of regardless of the other's rights'[391] than on the facts of *Raphael*.[392] D had stolen V's car using violence and then contacted V offering to sell the car back to him.

19.4.3.4 Borrowing or lending

Where money or anything which is consumed by use – like petrol – is 'borrowed', the dishonest 'borrower' has an intention permanently to deprive even though he intends to replace the money or the article with another which is just as good. He intends to deprive the owner of the specific thing he has appropriated.[393] In the case of a true borrowing it appears that there can be no theft, however dishonest the borrower may be, because, by definition, he does intend to return the specific thing taken. Yet by s 6(1), if the borrowing 'is for a period and in circumstances making it equivalent to an outright taking...' the borrower may be regarded as having the intention of depriving the owner permanently. This is a rather puzzling provision, because it would seem, *prima facie*, that borrowing cannot be an 'outright taking'. Clearly, however, this part of the subsection is intended to do something and, therefore, certain borrowings are to be treated as the equivalent of outright takings. Once this is accepted, it is not difficult to divine the kind of borrowings which are intended to be covered: they are those where the taker intends not to return the thing until the virtue is gone out of it: D takes V's non-rechargeable battery, intending to return it to V when it is exhausted; or V's season ticket, intending to return it to V when the season is over. Similar in principle are those cases where D intends to return the thing only when it is completely changed in substance.[394]

Where property belonging to another has been entirely deprived of an essential characteristic, which has been described as its 'virtue', the matter seems reasonably clear as for example

---

[389] This passage was cited in *Cahill* [1993] Crim LR 141.
[390] [1994] Crim LR 297.
[391] [47].
[392] [2008] EWCA Crim 1014.
[393] *Velumyl* [1989] Crim LR 299.
[394] See cases cited above. *Dicta* in *Bagshaw* [1988] Crim LR 321 concerning the 'virtue' test seem inappropriate to the facts of that case.

with a person stealing a ticket which will be returned only after it has been used. What if the virtue has not been entirely eliminated – but very nearly? D takes V's season ticket for Arsenal's matches intending to return it to him in time for the last match of the season. Is this an 'outright taking' so as to amount to theft of the ticket? If it is, is it theft if D intends to return the ticket in time for two matches? – or three, four, five or six – where should the line be drawn? The difficulty of drawing a line suggests that it should not be theft of the ticket unless D intends to keep it until it has lost *all* (or, at least, substantially all) of its virtue.[395] (The difficulty might satisfactorily be overcome in this particular case by holding that the right to see each match is a separate thing in action, of which V is permanently deprived once that match is over.) This means, of course, that if D takes V's car and keeps it for 10 years, he will not be guilty of theft if, when, as he intended all along, he returns it to V, it is still a roadworthy vehicle, though the proportion of its original value which it retains is very small. If it can no longer be described as a car, but is scrap metal, then, if D intended to return it in this state, he has stolen it.[396]

The provision regarding lending appears to contemplate the situation where D is in possession or control of the property and he lends it to another, X. If D knows that the effect is that V will never get the property back again, he clearly has an intention permanently to deprive V. Similarly, if D knows that, when V gets the property back again, the virtue will have gone out of it, this is equivalent to an outright disposal. The examples of the non-rechargeable battery, season ticket, etc are applicable here, though they seem less likely to arise in the context of lending than of borrowing.

19.4.3.5 Parting with property under a condition as to its return

Section 6(2) provides:

Without prejudice to the generality of subsection (1) above, where a person, having possession or control (lawfully or not) of property belonging to another, parts with the property under a condition as to its return which he *may not* be able to perform, this (if done for purposes of his own and without the other's authority) amounts to treating the property as his own to dispose of regardless of the other's rights.

This is clearly intended to deal with the kind of case which gave difficulty under the old law, where D, being in possession or control of V's goods, pawns them. If D had no intention of ever redeeming the goods, there was no problem – he was guilty of larceny and he would now clearly be guilty of theft, apart from s 6(2). But what if D does intend to redeem? The answer now is that if he knows that he may not be able to do so, he is guilty of theft. The subsection does not seem to allow any distinction to be drawn between the case where D knows that the chances of his being able to redeem are slight and the case where he believes the chances are high; in either case, the condition is one which he knows he may not be able to perform.

The common law cases suggested that it was theft, notwithstanding an intention to redeem the goods, if the person pawning them had no reasonable prospects of being able to redeem them.[397] It is submitted, however, that the question under the Theft Act is a purely subjective one: D must *intend* to dispose of the property regardless of the other's rights, and s 6(2) merely describes what he must intend. If then D is in fact *convinced*, however unreasonably, that he

---

[395] cf *Chan Wai Lam v R* [1981] Crim LR 497.

[396] cf *DPP v J* [2002] EWHC 291 (Admin), holding that the magistrates were wrong to accept a submission of no case where D had taken V's headphones, snapped them and returned them.

[397] *Phetheon* (1840) 9 C & P 552; *Medland* (1851) 5 Cox CC 292. *Trebilcock* (1858) Dears & B 453 and *Wynn* (1887) 16 Cox CC 231 are inconclusive.

will be able to redeem the property, he does not come within the terms of s 6(2) because he intends *to dispose of it under a condition which he will be able to perform*.[398]

This is not necessarily conclusive, however, for s 6(2) is without prejudice to the generality of s 6(1); and it might reasonably be argued that even the person who is convinced, when pawning the goods, of his power to redeem them intends to treat the goods as his own to dispose of, regardless of the other's rights. This would be equally true if the person pawning the goods in fact had power to redeem; and, since pawning is not 'lending', there is no need to prove that it was equivalent to an outright disposal.[399]

On the whole it would seem that the better approach is to hold that D who is certain of his ability to redeem does not have an intention permanently to deprive. Such a person, in some circumstances, may well be found by the jury not to be dishonest. For example, D, a tenant for a year of a furnished house, being temporarily short of money, pawns the landlord's clock, knowing that he will certainly be able to redeem it and intends to do so before the year expires. A prosecution for theft of the clock should fail on the grounds both that he is not dishonest and that he has no intent permanently to deprive.

19.4.3.6 Abandonment of property

Early nineteenth-century cases on the taking of horses decided that there was no intention permanently to deprive, even though D turned the horse loose some considerable distance from the place where he took it. In the conditions of those times it might be supposed that D must have known that there was a substantial risk that V would not get his horse back. This lenient attitude may be contrasted with that adopted in the pawning cases, and the right course would seem to be to attach no importance to these old decisions in the interpretation of the Theft Act.

The case where the property is abandoned is not within s 6(2) for D does not part with the property under a condition. He might, however, be regarded as having an intention to treat the thing as his own to dispose of regardless of the other's rights. If D borrows the thing and then leaves it where he knows the owner or someone on his behalf will certainly find it, he clearly does not have an intention permanently to deprive. But if he abandons the thing in circumstances such that he knows that it is quite uncertain whether the owner will ever get it back or not, then it would not be unreasonable to hold that he has an intention to treat the thing as his own to dispose of regardless of the other's rights.

Care must be taken with arguments that property has been abandoned and that D has therefore demonstrated an intent to deprive permanently. In the recent case of *Mitchell*[400] D was charged with robbery having been one of four men who had seized V's vehicle having crashed their own vehicle in a police chase. They abandoned V's car and took another one which they subsequently abandoned and burnt out.[401] The trial judge ruled there was sufficient evidence from the taking of the first car and abandoning capable of amounting to an intention to dispose of property regardless of owner's rights pursuant to s 6(1) of the Act. The Court of Appeal

---

[398] See A Steele (2008) 17 Nottingham LJ 3 in a comprehensive review of the case law suggests that an intention permanently to deprive is established: 1. Automatically if D pawns V's property subject to a condition that D cannot control. There is no need to prove any intent in such cases; 2. If D's borrowing V's property is objectively equivalent to an outright taking but where D intends that it will be returned; 3. Where D lends V's property to X and D does not intend that V's property will be returned to him; 4. In all other cases the subjective intention of D must be proved.

[399] The difficulty about this interpretation is that it makes it very difficult to see why s 6(2) is there at all; if D's disposition of property under a condition which he is able to perform is theft under subs (1), why refer specifically to the case of a condition which he may not be able to perform?

[400] [2008] EWCA Crim 850.

[401] It was conceded by the prosecution that the second vehicle had not been stolen.

allowed the appeal confirming that s 6(1) was not intended to dilute the definition of theft in s 1(1). None of the earlier authorities extended the scope of s 6 to a case, even of violent taking of a car for its brief use before abandoning it where it could easily be discovered.

By analogy to the pawning case discussed above, it would seem that it should be immaterial whether D believes that the chances of V's getting the property back are large or small; it is sufficient that he intends to risk the loss of V's property. In *Fernandes*,[402] Auld LJ concluded that 'section 6 may apply to a person in possession or control of another's property who dishonestly and for his own purpose deals with that property in such a manner that he knows he is risking its loss'.[403] Suppose, for example, that D, being caught in the rain when leaving a restaurant in London, takes an umbrella to shelter him on his way to the station and abandons it in the train on his arrival at Leeds. He should be guilty of theft.[404]

19.4.3.7 Other things to be returned – but for a price

A problem arises with the theft of a railway ticket or any other ticket which entitles the holder to services or goods when he returns it.[405] If D takes the ticket from another passenger, V, there is no difficulty. D intends to deprive V permanently not only of the piece of paper but also of the thing in action (the contractual right to travel) which it represents; but if he takes the ticket from the rail company intending to use it, he may well intend to give it up at the end of the journey.[406] The rail company own the piece of paper but they cannot own the contractual right to travel. As with a cheque,[407] it may be said that D intends to return a different thing, a cancelled ticket with a hole punched in it; it has lost its virtue.

An alternative explanation is that D intends that the rail company shall have the ticket only by paying for it – through the provision of a ride on their train. That should be enough. This explanation has the advantage that it extends to things which are intended to be returned (but only for value) in an unchanged form. For example, D takes tokens from a coffee shop intending to return them in exchange for his espresso; or gaming chips from the proprietor of a gaming club, intending to return them in exchange for the right to play.[408] In all these cases there is probably a conditional intention permanently to deprive in the literal sense. The ticket, tokens and chips will probably not be returned at all if the taker realizes that he is not going to receive the value they represent.

19.4.3.8 Conditional intention to deprive

Consider a case where D takes V's bag, intending to take anything of value which he finds in it. Is such a 'conditional' intention sufficient? In *Easom*,[409] the Court of Appeal held, controversially, that 'a conditional appropriation will not do'. A difficulty with this proposition is

---

[402] [1996] 1 Cr App R 175. cf *Mitchell* [2008] EWCA Crim 850 in which D was not guilty of robbery where he had taken a car by force and abandoned it.

[403] At 188.

[404] cf the position in Scotland where temporary deprivation may suffice, and note the Scottish Draft Code proposing that recklessness as to permanent deprivation should be an alternative *mens rea*. See further the discussion by P Ferguson, 'Codifying Criminal Law (1): A Critique of Scots Common Law' [2004] Crim LR 49 and also P Ferguson, 'Codifying Criminal Law (2): The Scots and the English Draft Codes Compared' [2004] Crim LR 105.

[405] cf *Marshall* [1998] 2 Cr App R 282, above, p 808.

[406] At one time, everyone knew that all tickets had to be given to the collector at the end of the journey, but, in these days of 'open stations', this is not necessarily so. If I am travelling to King's Cross (an open station) I expect (and intend) to retain my ticket; but if I am travelling to Leeds (a closed station), I expect (and intend) to give it up.

[407] Above, p 797.

[408] cf correspondence in [1976] Crim LR 329 and commentary on *Pick* [1982] Crim LR 238 which should be read in the light of the Gaming Act 1968, s 16 which was overlooked.

[409] [1971] 2 QB 315 at 319, [1971] 2 All ER 945 at 947.

that all intention is conditional, even though the condition is unexpressed and not present to the mind of the person at that time. In that case, D picked up a woman's handbag in a cinema, rummaged through the contents and put it back having taken nothing. The handbag was attached by a thread to a policewoman's wrist. D's conviction for stealing the handbag and the specified contents – tissues, cosmetics, etc – was quashed because D never had any intention of permanently depriving V of any of those things. It followed that he was not guilty of attempting to steal any of them. No doubt he intended to steal things which were not there – presumably money – and might have been convicted of attempting to steal on a suitably worded indictment.[410] D had no intention permanently to deprive, and consequently, he was not guilty of attempting to steal the handbag, or the specified contents either.

In *Husseyn*,[411] DD opened the door of a van in which there was a holdall containing valuable sub-aqua equipment. They were charged with attempted theft of the equipment. The judge directed the jury that they could convict if DD were about to look into the holdall and, if its contents were valuable, to steal it. The Court of Appeal, following *Easom*, held that this was a misdirection: 'it cannot be said that one who has it in mind to steal only if what he finds is worth stealing has a present intention to steal'. In *Re A-G's References (Nos 1 and 2 of 1979)*,[412] the Court of Appeal held that these words were applicable only to an indictment which alleged an intention to steal a specific object, such as sub-aqua equipment. If the indictment had charged an attempt to steal 'some or all of the contents of the holdall' or, in *Easom*, of the handbag, there would be no problem. Yet, in *Husseyn*, the sub-aqua equipment *was* the contents of the holdall – there were no other contents; so, according to the court, D was not guilty of attempting to steal the equipment if it was described as such, but he was guilty if it was described as the 'contents of the holdall'. At that time it was clear law that there could be no conviction for attempting to steal a thing that was not there – it was the sub-aqua equipment or nothing. Since the Criminal Attempts Act 1981,[413] this is no longer so. A person looking for money in an empty handbag might now be convicted of attempting to steal money.

The real problem in cases of this kind is the form of the charges. The formula approved in the *A-G's References* is not satisfactory because, in these cases, the defendant did not intend (or it was not proved that he intended) to steal any of the contents. But he undoubtedly intended to steal something – something which was *not* 'all or any of the contents'.[414] The charge would be accurate if it alleged simply that D attempted to steal from the handbag, or holdall.[415] This is so whether or not there is anything there that D would have stolen. D's intention to steal anything he finds which he thinks worth stealing is a present intention to steal, at least so far as the law of attempts is concerned. The failure to specify any subject matter cannot be an objection since the Criminal Attempts Act 1981.[416]

It is submitted that the better view is that an assumption of ownership, which is conditional because there is an intention to deprive only in a certain event, is theft. For example, D takes V's ring intending to keep it if the stone is a diamond, but otherwise to return it. He takes it to a jeweller who says the stone is paste. D returns the ring to V. It is submitted that he committed

---

[410] Below.

[411] (1977) 67 Cr App R 131n, [1978] Crim LR 219 and commentary; discussed at [1978] Crim LR 444 and 644.

[412] [1980] QB 180, [1979] 3 All ER 143, [1979] Crim LR 585 and commentary.

[413] Above, p 409.

[414] cf *Bayley and Easterbrook* [1980] Crim LR 503 and commentary.

[415] cf *Smith and Smith* [1986] Crim LR 166 and commentary.

[416] As with the law of burglary, this is an instance in which it appears motive, which is generally regarded as irrelevant in *mens rea* in practice, assumes an importance below, p 962. It may be different where the charge is theft. A lorry driver was held (in a civil action) not guilty of theft of the goods loaded on his lorry when he drove off intending to steal the load 'if and when the circumstances were favourable': *Grundy (Teddington) Ltd v Fulton* [1983] 1 Lloyd's Rep 16, CA; but he had assumed a right of the owner (cf *Gomez*) and the only question is whether the conditional intention was enough: *Archbold*, para 21.80.

theft when he took the ring. The fact that he returned it is relevant only to mitigation in sentence. A similar problem may arise where D takes the property of V, say a ring, intending to claim a reward from V for finding it. If he intends to return the ring in any event and hopes to receive the reward, he is not guilty of stealing the ring though he is of fraud and of an attempt to steal the reward. But if he intends to retain the ring unless he receives the reward, he seems to be in substantially the same situation as the taker who sells the property back to the owner. It might be said, however, that in this example, the taker is not treating the property as his own. There are two possible answers to this: the assertion of a better right to possession might be regarded as treating the property as one's own; or, s 6 not providing an exclusive definition, this might be regarded as an analogous case falling within the general principle.

19.5 Reform

Over the last century the central focus of acquisitive crimes has shifted from protecting the possession of tangible goods against transportation to the protection of ownership of property (as broadly construed) against misuse. Those interests being protected, and which form essential elements of the *actus reus* – property and ownership – have expanded. The constant concept has been that of *mens rea* – fraud or dishonesty. So it seems that it will be in the future. It may be that the *actus reus* of the offences will disappear almost to vanishing point as the interests the law seeks to protect become more diffuse, diverse and indefinable.

There is also a growing pressure to use the criminal law to protect other 'interests' from misuse – trade secrets being a strong example. The law may need to be more forward-thinking by protecting 'rights' and 'interests' such as the 'use' and 'value' derived from 'having access' to facilities. As these interests are harder to define the mental element of dishonesty offences will become ever more important.

Although the Theft Acts have generated some complex and controversial case law, one view is that there is not very much wrong with them if properly handled.[417] An alternative view is that the Acts are now in need of some radical reappraisal since they represent a pragmatic but unprincipled patchwork of overlapping and technical offences.

19.6 Liability of spouses and civil partners for Theft Act offences[418]

For many purposes husband and wife and, since the Civil Partnership Act 2004 those in a 'civil partnership', occupy a special position under the law and have special rules relating to themselves. Section 30 of the Theft Act 1968 makes spouses and civil partners liable in respect of offences against each other's property as though they were not married. It is clear that a spouse may steal property belonging exclusively to the other, it is equally clear that a

---

[417] See JC Smith, 'The Sad Fate of the Theft Act 1968', in W Swadling and G Jones, *The Search for Principle, Essays in Honour of Lord Goff of Chieveley* (1999) 97. See also JC Smith, 'Conspiracy to Defraud: Some Comments on the Law Commission's Report' [1995] Crim LR 210 (a view shared by the Model Criminal Code Committee of the Attorney-General's Department, Australia, Final Report (1995) Chs 3, 6) and JC Smith, 'Reforming the Theft Acts' (1996) 28 Bracton LJ 27. See also DW Elliott, 'Dialogues on the Theft Act', in *Reshaping the Criminal Law*, 287.

[418] See Ormerod and Williams, *Theft*, Ch 14.4; Griew, *Theft*, Ch 1.

spouse/partner may steal property jointly owned with the other spouse/partner, since one co-owner may steal from another.[419]

By s 30(2), one spouse may prosecute the other for *any* criminal offence whether that offence is committed by a spouse on the person or property of the other, or whether by a spouse against a third party. That is subject to s 30(4), which provides that where the offence consists of 'stealing or doing unlawful damage to property which at the time of the offence belongs to that person's wife or husband or civil partner' proceedings may not be instituted except by or with the consent of the DPP.[420] Neither a wife nor a police officer, then, would need the Director's leave to institute proceedings for an assault on the wife by the husband, nor to prosecute the husband in respect of *any* offence committed by him on a third party. A wife might, for example, prosecute her husband for stealing property belonging to a child of the marriage or for assaulting his mother-in-law. There are further exceptional situations provided for in s 30(4) where either the spouses are jointly charged or where the spouses are, by order, no longer bound to cohabit.

19.7 Corporations and their officers

So far as offences under the Theft Acts generally are concerned, the liability of corporations for them falls to be determined in accordance with the general principles applicable to the liability of corporations for crime.[421] Where a corporation commits a crime it must be the case that the crime has been committed by a person, or persons, in control of the corporation's affairs.[422] Such persons are, of course, liable in accordance with the ordinary principles governing liability for crime. Section 18 contains a special provision relating to false accounting. This is considered in Chapter 24 below.

---

[419] See above, p 806.
[420] By the Prosecution of Offences Act 1985, s 1(7). The consent may be given by a Crown Prosecutor.
[421] See above, Ch 10.
[422] A corporation may, of course, be vicariously liable for crimes even though the crime is not committed by a person in control of its affairs: see above, p 273. But vicarious liability would not apply in connection with offences under the Theft Act 1968.

20
Robbery

20.1 Robbery under the Theft Act 1968

Robbery was a common law offence, put on a statutory footing in the 1968 Act, s 8:

(1) A person is guilty of robbery if he steals, and immediately before or at the time of doing so, and in order to do so, he uses force on any person or puts or seeks to put any person in fear of being then and there subjected to force.

(2) A person guilty of robbery, or of an assault with intent to rob, shall on conviction on indictment be liable to imprisonment for life.

Robbery[1] is an extremely serious offence, carrying a maximum life sentence, and attracting substantial sentences in practice.[2] It is triable only on indictment. In recent years there has been a steady increase in its incidence, and enhanced media attention focused on street 'muggings' (especially for mobile phones),[3] car jacking, and robberies of those using ATM (cash point) machines.[4] In 2009/10, there were 75,101 recorded robberies.[5]

The offence is very broad, applying to theft in many circumstances, ranging from the work of sophisticated gangs[6] and armed bank robbers,[7] to extreme forms of playground bullying.[8] There have been cogent calls for reform to subdivide the offence into categories based on the gravity of the threat or use of violence involved.[9] This would provide offences which would have more appropriate labelling and sentencing.

Since the offence necessarily includes theft,[10] and will usually also involve an offence against the person,[11] it might be thought that a separate offence of robbery is otiose and that

---

[1] See, generally, Ormerod and Williams, *Smith's Law of Theft*, Ch 7; J Andrews, 'Robbery' [1966] Crim LR 524; Griew, *Theft*, Ch 3; Smith, *Property Offences*, Ch 14.

[2] TheSentencingGuidelinesareavailableathttp://webarchive.nationalarchives.gov.uk/+/http://www.sentencingcouncil.org.uk/professional/guidelines/theft-acts.htm. See also www.cps.gov.uk/legal/s_to_u/sentencing_manual/robbery.

[3] See *A-G's Reference Nos 4 and 7* 'Q' [2002] 2 Cr App R (S) 345. A phone is stolen in around 52% of robberies and is the only item stolen in around 28%: Home Office Press Release, 25 June 2007. By criminalizing offers to re-program mobile phones it is hoped to reduce such offending: Violent Crime Reduction Act 2006, s 62, modifying s 1(1) of the Mobile Telephone (Re-programming) Act 2002.

[4] For a review of police data, see J Smith, *The Nature of Personal Robbery* (2003).

[5] J Flatley, et al, Crime in England and Wales 2009/10, *Findings from the British Crime Survey and Police Recorded Crime* (2010) 32.

[6] See M Gill, *Commercial Robbery* (2000).

[7] Armed robbery attracts very high sentences. See, generally, on armed robbery: I O'Donnell and S Morrison, 'Armed and Dangerous: The Use of Firearms in Robbery' [1997] 36(3) Howard Jnl 305. A relevant firearms offence ought to be added to the indictment: *Murphy* [2002] Crim LR 674. See, generally, Ormerod and Williams, *Smith's Law of Theft*, para 7.26, R Matthews *Armed Robbery* (2003).

[8] See *F A and others* [2003] 2 Cr App R (S) 503.

[9] See A Ashworth, 'Robbery Reassessed' [2002] Crim LR 851.

[10] *Guy* (1990) 93 Cr App R 108, CA.

[11] Robbery is not an offence of violence *per se*: *Baker* [2000] Crim LR 700, CA.

the combination of the two charges would cater adequately in terms of labelling and sentencing powers. Despite the overlap, it is submitted that a specifically labelled offence of robbery is desirable, not least because in cases of a theft with a threat of violence, unless the threat is to kill, the only offence against the person likely to have been committed will only be that of assault.[12] In short, with robbery the whole is greater than the sum of the parts.

20.1.1 Requirement of theft

As defined, robbery is essentially an aggravated form of theft; and if there is no theft, or attempted theft, there can be no robbery or attempted robbery. All of the elements of theft must be proved. So it would not be robbery where D by force takes a bag from V in the belief that he has the legal right to it (no dishonesty);[13] or where D is merely begging for money[14]; or where D by force takes a car from V not intending to deprive V permanently of it.[15] In the first case D may be guilty of an assault,[16] and in the latter of both an assault and an offence under s 12 of the Theft Act, but in neither case is he guilty of robbery. Robbery does not require that D keeps the property, rather only that he has the intention permanently to deprive V, as where D takes V's headphones by force, snaps and returns them in 'useless' form.[17]

The offence of robbery is complete when the theft is complete, that is when the appropriation is complete. Following recent interpretations of that concept,[18] a robbery can be completed much earlier than at common law, and than the drafters of the Theft Act intended. So, in *Corcoran v Anderton*,[19] where D and E sought to take V's handbag by force, it was held that the theft was complete when D snatched the handbag from V's grasp, though it then fell from D's hands and the defendants made off without it. It is now arguable that the theft in such a case is complete when D first touches the handbag, for by that conduct he is assuming a right of an owner.

For robbery, the appropriation element of theft will normally be by D 'taking' V's property since it is difficult to imagine realistic situations in which robbery might be effected by other modes of appropriation.[20] One possibility is where a bailee refuses to return property to the owner, and backs this refusal with a threat of force. It is unclear whether D can be said to have completed the robbery where he issues a threat to V and demands that V hand over his property and V is in the process of doing so, but D has not yet touched it.[21] A safer course is to charge an attempted robbery in such circumstances.

---

[12] Ashworth [2002] Crim LR 851 at 863.

[13] cf *Skivington* [1968] 1 QB 166, [1967] 1 All ER 483; *Robinson* [1977] Crim LR 173, CA; *Forrester* [1992] Crim LR 793, CA; *Hall* [2008] EWCA Crim 2086 – some evidence of the belief in right to the property is needed before the judge must leave it to the jury.

[14] cf *Codsi* [2009] EWCA Crim 1618.

[15] See *Raphael* [2008] EWCA Crim 1014; [2008] Crim LR 995 and commentary. R had been convicted of conspiracy to rob V by forcibly taking his car and then offering V the opportunity to buy it back. The Court of Appeal referred to s 6 (above) and concluded that this was clearly capable of amounting to robbery. Contrast that with *Mitchell* [2008] EWCA Crim 850 where DD took V's car as a getaway car and abandoned it later with no attempt to conceal it: no intention permanently to deprive, no theft and therefore no robbery.

[16] D's claim that he believes himself to be entitled to the property appropriated does not of itself legitimate his use of force. The fact that V unlawfully possesses the property does not preclude a robbery conviction if D takes it by force: *Smith* [2011] EWCA Crim 66.

[17] Magistrates wrong to accept submission of no case: *DPP v J* [2002] EWHC 291 (Admin).

[18] Discussed above, Ch 19. The significance of when robbery ends can be important in sentence in a murder case where D is alleged to have killed for gain: see Sch 21, para 5 of the Criminal Justice Act 2003 and *Cullen* [2007] 2 Cr App R (S) 394.

[19] (1980) 71 Cr App R 104, [1980] Crim LR 385.

[20] See Andrews [1966] Crim LR 524, for possible instances.

[21] cf *Briggs* [2004] Crim LR 495. cf *Farrell* (1787) 1 Leach 332n. D apprehended before V handed over the property.

20.1.2 Use or threat of force

Any use or threat of 'force' against the person suffices. 'Force' is wider than the concept of 'violence' used at common law, and might be regarded as a more neutral word. The courts have not defined it, and treat it as an ordinary English word, which should be left to the jury to determine.[22] It is submitted that no jury could reasonably find that the slight physical contact that might be involved where D picks V's pocket would amount to a use of force.[23] However, very little may be required to turn a case of theft into one of robbery and to push or nudge the victim so as to cause him to lose his balance is capable of being a use of force.[24] If D causes a substance to come into contact with V, in an effort to incapacitate V in order to facilitate theft, then it is submitted that D would be guilty of robbery.

The offence can be committed in one of three ways:

- Where D uses force. This poses few problems. It is no defence that V was unaware that D was using force, as where D strikes V from behind.

- Where D 'puts' any person in 'fear' of being then and there subjected to force. Here, the language of the section does leave some ambiguity. Is it a requirement of robbery that (a) V is put in 'fear' or (b) is it sufficient that he apprehends[25] that force may be used if he resists. The Divisional Court has recently confirmed in *R v DPP*[26] that robbery does not require proof that V was actually put in fear. It is submitted that this must be correct, otherwise the commission of the offence would turn on the courage of the victim. That case does not, however, answer the question whether it is necessary for the victim to apprehend that force will be used. In this form of the offence, it would seem to be a neces-sary element. Support for that proposition is derived from *Grant v CPS*,[27] although the court in *R v DPP* cast doubt on that case.

- Where the allegation is that D *seeks* to put V in fear of force. Here, there is no need for V to be in fear, nor it seems to apprehend force; the offence turns solely on D's intention. It is important to emphasize that it is sufficient that D's intent is to produce a state of mind where V *apprehends* force, it is not necessary for D to intend that V will be afraid. Hence, D cannot plead that he thought V was macho enough not to be afraid of the threats. *Tennant* makes clear that D may threaten a use of force and satisfy the requirement of the offence of robbery although V is not made to apprehend the immediate infliction of force on him which is necessary to constitute an assault.[28]

A threat of force may be implied as well as express. Where D threatens V with force unless V complies with D's demands and at a later stage D takes property from an unprotesting V, D may be convicted of robbery if he intends, and V understands, the threat to continue even though D's original threats were not made for the purpose of taking V's property.[29] This

---

[22] *Dawson and James* (1976) 64 Cr App R 170, CA.

[23] See, eg, *Monaghan and Monaghan* [2000] 1 Cr App R (S) 6 where 'jostling' to pick V's pockets was charged as theft.

[24] *Dawson*, n 22. See Williams, TBCL, 825, suggesting a distinction based on 'gentle force' used to take by stealth as opposed to force used to overcome resistance. See also Griew, *Theft*, para 3.05; Smith, *Property Offences*, para 14.10.

[25] Clearly a different state of mind from fear as is obvious from the law in relation to assault, see above p 622.

[26] [2007] EWHC 739 (Admin).

[27] *Grant v CPS* [2000] QBD unreported, 10 Mar.

[28] *Tennant* [1976] Crim LR 133, CC.

[29] *Donaghy and Marshall* [1981] Crim LR 644 (Judge Chavasse).

might be a common occurrence where D threatens V who subsequently escorts D to V's bank ATM and withdraws cash to hand over to D.

20.1.2.1 Force to the person

Prior to the Theft Act, robbery was thought of as stealing accomplished by force against the person, the force being used to overpower V's resistance and not merely to seize the property.[30] The CLRC, in drafting the 1968 Act had the same distinction in mind stating they would 'not regard mere snatching of property, such as a handbag, from an unresisting owner as using force for the purpose of the definition'.[31] That requirement that the force be administered directly to a person and not the property being stolen was meant to be retained by the words in s 8: '...if he steals...and in order to do so, he uses force *on any person* or seeks to put *any person* in fear of being then and there subjected to force'. But, in *Clouden*,[32] the distinction was rejected and D's conviction for robbery was upheld where he wrenched a shopping basket from V's hand and ran off with it. In the view of the court the old distinction could not stand with the words of s 8, and it was open to a jury to find on such facts that force had been used on V with intent to steal. *A fortiori,* it will be robbery where, for example, a struggle, even a fleeting one, takes place for possession of a handbag,[33] or where an earring is snatched tearing the lobe of the ear.[34] The decision in *Clouden* is an interesting illustration of the ambiguity over the true foundation of robbery: it is a hybrid offence protecting property and personal safety, and the courts refuse to narrow it down by defining its concepts in an unduly technical fashion.

20.1.2.2 In order to steal

If D assaults V and, having incapacitated him without any intention of stealing from him, opportunistically takes V's wallet, there is no robbery. D commits offences against the person and theft.[35]

20.1.3 On *any* person

In most cases of robbery, D will use or threaten force against the person in possession of the property. But the offence is not so limited. Provided the force is used or threatened *in order* to steal, it will be robbery.

If, for example, the only force used at the time of the [Great Train Robbery] in 1963 had been on a signalman, this would under the [Act] have been sufficient.[36]

It does not matter that the person against whom the force is used or threatened has no interest whatever in the property; it would be robbery to overpower a security guard in his office at X Co, because his office overlooks a factory Y Co across the road from which the thieves wish to steal, and they fear that he will notice them and raise the alarm.

It does not amount to robbery where D threatens to use force on X (who has no knowledge of the threat) in order to overcome V's reluctance to part with his money. Take the case of D a bank robber. If D hands V, a bank teller, a note which reads 'I have a gun pointed at

---

[30] *Gnosil* (1824) 1 C & P 304; *Harman's Case* (1620) 2 Roll Rep 154.

[31] Eighth Report, para 65.

[32] [1987] Crim LR 56, CA. Griew believes the case to be wrongly decided: para 3.05. See also, eg, *Symons* [2009] EWCA Crim 83 where D pulled at V's bag.

[33] *Corcoran v Anderton* (1980) 71 Cr App R 104, [1980] Crim LR 385, DC.

[34] cf *Lapier* (1784) 1 Leach 320.

[35] *Harris* (1998) The Times, 4 Mar; *James* [1997] Crim LR 598.

[36] Eighth Report, para 65. cf *Smith v Desmond and Hall* [1965] AC 960, [1965] 1 All ER 976.

a customer',[37] V who is safely behind the armour plated glass is not apprehending force to himself (not robbery). The customer is unaware of what D has in mind and has written on the note. He is not apprehending violence. However, if D reads the note aloud, that is sufficient for robbery if the customer, X, then apprehends violence. There is no glaring failing in the law in these situations since all cases of this type could be treated as blackmail under s 21 of the Act.

20.1.4 Immediately before or at the time of stealing

Strictly interpreted, this expression might suggest that force used only a second after the theft is technically complete would not suffice for robbery, a view which may be said to receive further support from the requirement that the force be used 'in order to steal'. The argument was advanced in *Hale*.[38] D and E entered V's house and while D was upstairs stealing a jewellery box, E was downstairs tying up V. Their convictions for robbery were upheld though the appropriation of the jewellery box might have been completed before the force was used. The court regarded appropriation, as a 'continuing act' and it was open to the jury on these facts to conclude that it continued while V was tied up. The matter needs to be looked at in a common sense way; while the force must be used at the time of the theft and *in order to steal*,[39] the theft needs to be looked at in its entirety.

There is, arguably, an ever greater need for the courts to adopt a pragmatic approach to this issue following the extension of the concept of appropriation. Technically, where D first touches V's property he has appropriated it, but it would render the offence of robbery useless if the theft was deemed complete at that time and D applied force a second later. Thus, where D has already gained access to V's car, and locked himself in, and V is only threatened by D's driving at him to escape, the theft might be said to be continuing and a robbery committed.[40] But, a line has to be drawn somewhere. If, having taken the car from V without using or threatening force, D is subsequently stopped by a police officer in the street and knocks him down in order to avoid arrest this would not amount to robbery. Force used to retain possession of property not obtained by force would not ordinarily be thought of as robbery.[41] Even on a broad view, the use of force is neither at the time of, nor in order to commit, the theft.[42] There may be merit in extending the offence by legislation to include force or the threat of force 'immediately after' a theft.[43] This would resonate with the existing underlying approach which is that robbery protects against the use of force in the acquisition of property.

'Immediately before' must add something to 'at the time of' the theft. The interpretation taken in some Australian decisions – that it means 'no intervening space or lapse of time or event of any significance'[44] – may be too restrictive. Clearly, if a gang overpower V, the security guard at the main gate of a depot, this would be a use of force immediately before the theft, although some minutes must elapse before the gang reaches the part of the depot where the safe is housed.[45] And it can make no difference that V is not present at the depot at

---

[37] *Taylor* [1996] 10 Archbold News 2, CA. cf *Reane* (1794) 2 Leach 616.

[38] (1978) 68 Cr App R 415, [1979] Crim LR 596, CA. Confirmed post-*Gomez* in *Lockley* [1995] Crim LR 656. cf *Gregory* (1981) 74 Cr App R 154, [1982] Crim LR 229, CA. cf *Atakpu*, above, p 790.

[39] Failure to direct the jury on this point renders the conviction unsafe: *West* (1999) 14 Sept, CA, unreported.

[40] *Hayward v Norwich Union Insurance Ltd* [2000] Lloyd's Rep IR 382. Whether the offence is one of theft or robbery may be of special significance for V's insurance claim: see, generally, M Wasik, 'Definitions of Crime in Insurance Contracts' [1986] JBL 45.

[41] *Harman's Case* (1620) 2 Roll Rep 154.

[42] cf Eighth Report, para 65.

[43] Griew, *Theft*, para 3.08.

[44] *Stanischewski* [2001] NTSC 86.

[45] It would surely be open to the jury so to find. cf *Hale* (1978) 68 Cr App R 415, [1979] Crim LR 596, above n 38.

all; it would be robbery where some members of the gang detain V by force at his home while their confederates open the safe in the depot miles away. It does not seem to be possible to put any specific temporal limit on 'immediately'. All the circumstances have to be considered including the time when, and the place where, the force was used or threatened in relation to the theft. Force converts theft into robbery only when its use or threat is in a real sense directly part of the theft, and is used in order to accomplish the theft.

It is not enough that D gets V to part with property by threatening to use force on a separate and/or future occasion. This may well amount to blackmail but the fact that V is intimidated or frightened is not in itself enough for robbery unless he is put in fear of being 'then and there' subject to force. But suppose a gang, by threats of force, persuade V, the depot security guard, to stay away from work the following evening, and on that evening they steal from the depot uninterrupted. At the time of the theft the threat of force still operates on V's mind; he stays at home because he is afraid of what will happen if he goes to work. But this does not seem to amount to robbery. At the time of the theft V is not put in fear of being 'then and there' subjected to force. In *Khan*,[46] V, at D's request, withdrew cash from his bank to hand over to D. V stated that he was in fear that D would be attacked by X, a violent man to whom D claimed to be in debt, and that he feared that if X beat up D, D would then come and beat up him, V. The Court of Appeal quashed D's robbery conviction: there was no evidence that V feared that he would be subjected *then and there* to force.

20.1.5 *Mens rea*

Obviously robbery requires at least an intention to steal, which in this context will usually be a purposive, direct intent.[47] But it seems to require more than this. What of the *mens rea* requirement in relation to the use or threat of force? It could be argued that liability in respect of the force is strict, and that if D intends to steal it will be robbery if in fact there is some use of force, or if in fact he puts someone in fear, whether he intends to do so or not. But in principle this would not be a desirable interpretation. It seems clear that D must use or threaten force *in order* to steal, and a merely accidental use of force would not be done in order to steal.[48] Moreover, it should be proved that D intended to use the force in relation to a person, and not merely to property.[49]

It is enough that D seeks to put another in fear of being subjected to force. Fear here means to apprehend, and it would be no less a robbery because V was not afraid. Even if V does not apprehend that he will be subjected to force (because, perhaps, plain-clothes policemen are present and D has walked into a trap), it will be robbery if D intended to make him fear. But it would not be enough that V is in fact put in fear unless D intended to put V in fear. A timorous witness to a smash and grab raid might well fear that the thieves will turn on him, but if the thieves do not intend to put him in fear of being there and then subjected to force, the offence cannot amount to robbery.

---

[46] [2001] EWCA Crim 923.
[47] See above, p 107.
[48] cf *Edwards* (1843) 1 Cox CC 32.
[49] Intention here might include oblique intention, above, p 107.

21

Offences of temporary deprivation

In general it is not an offence dishonestly to use the property of another unless there is an intention to deprive the other permanently of the property.[1] There may be a case for creating a general offence (which need not necessarily be termed theft) of dishonest use or unauthorized use of another's property.[2] Arguably, the case for such an offence is growing stronger as so much property derives its particular value to an individual or company from its availability for *immediate* use.

At the time of drafting the 1968 Act, the Criminal Law Revision Committee decided against any such offence and their view, though subject to vigorous assault in Parliament, was accepted. The Committee were of the opinion that such a considerable extension of the criminal law was not called for at that time by any existing serious evil.[3] But Parliament accepted particular cases in which temporary deprivation of property is considered to be a serious evil. The taking of vehicles (which was first made an offence by s 28 of the Road Traffic Act 1930) is one obvious instance; and the taking of vessels (which was first made an offence by s 1 of the Vessels Protection Act 1967)[4] is another. These offences are now dealt with in s 12 of the Theft Act 1968 that extends the offence to a much wider range of conveyances.

In addition, the Theft Act 1968 added a further and entirely new offence of temporary deprivation; that of removing articles from places open to the public. Before the Act there had been a number of notorious 'borrowings' such as the removal from the National Gallery of Goya's portrait of the Duke of Wellington, and the Committee thought the problem 'serious enough to justify the creation of a special offence'.[5]

21.1 Removal of articles from places open to the public

Section 11 of the Theft Act 1968 provides:

(1) Subject to subsections (2) and (3) below, where the public have access to a building in order to view the building or part of it, or a collection or part of a collection housed in it, any person who

---

[1] See, generally, Ormerod and Williams, *Smith's Law of Theft*, Ch 10; Griew, *Theft*, Ch 5; Smith, *Property Offences*, Ch 8.

[2] See, especially, G Williams, 'Temporary Appropriation Should Be Theft' [1981] Crim LR 129.

[3] Eighth Report, para 56.

[4] As repealed by the Theft Act 1968.

[5] CLRC, para 57 (ii). See recently the allegations against D Cartrain who visited Damian Hirst's installation *Pharmacy* at Tate Britain and removed a few of the rare 'Faber Castell dated 1990 Mongol 482 Series' pencils. Cartrain then produced a 'wanted' poster: 'For the safe return of Damien Hirst's pencils I would like my artworks back that DACS and Hirst took off me in November. It's not a large demand…Hirst has until the end of this month to resolve this or on 31 of July the pencils will be sharpened. He has been warned.' The pencils were worth £500,000. See news reports for 4 September 2009.

without lawful authority removes from the building or its grounds the whole or part of any article displayed or kept for display to the public in the building or that part of it or in its grounds shall be guilty of an offence. For this purpose 'collection' includes a collection got together for a temporary purpose, but references in this section to a collection do not apply to a collection made or exhibited for the purpose of effecting sales or other commercial dealings.

(2) It is immaterial for purposes of subsection (1) above, that the public's access to a building is limited to a particular period or particular occasion; but where anything removed from a building or its grounds is there otherwise than as forming part of, or being on loan for exhibition with, a collection intended for permanent exhibition to the public, the person removing it does not thereby commit an offence under this section unless he removes it on a day when the public have access to the building as mentioned in subsection (1) above.

(3) A person does not commit an offence under this section if he believes that he has lawful authority for the removal of the thing in question or that he would have it if the person entitled to give it knew of the removal and the circumstances of it.

(4) A person guilty of an offence under this section shall, on conviction on indictment, be liable to imprisonment for a term not exceeding five years.

It is questionable why special protection should be provided for the temporary deprivation of this category of items in such specific circumstances when the temporary removal of non-exhibited property of individuals or companies will commonly be a cause of much greater concern, and pose the risk of much greater financial hardship to the victim.

21.1.1 *Actus reus*

On the face of it the offence under s 11 is one of considerable complexity; the draftsman's intention was to deal with the specific mischief discussed, and care has been taken to confine the operation of the section to that mischief. Numerous points arise for consideration.

21.1.1.1 Public access to a building

The public must have access to the building, not merely the grounds. Access must be *public* access; access limited for a particular section of the public will not suffice.[6] It does not matter that members of the public are required to pay for the privilege of access, nor whether the purpose of imposing the charge is merely to cover expenses or to make a profit.[7] But the access must be to a building or part thereof. So if D removes a statuette displayed in the open in a municipal park this would not be within the section.[8] If, however, the park consists of a building and its grounds, and the public have access to the building in order to view, D's removal of the statuette would be within this section.

Normally, no doubt, D will have entered the building in consequence of the owner's invitation[9] to the public to view. But, so long as the public have access to view, D may commit the offence although he entered as a trespasser or although he is the owner's guest and is temporarily residing in the building.

21.1.1.2 In order to view

The access to the building must be *in order* to view the building (or part of the building) or a collection (or part of a collection) housed in it. It has been held that the question whether

---

[6] But the exclusion of a particular class, eg, the exclusion of children from an exhibition considered unsuitable for them, would not prevent access being public access.

[7] But see below, p 852.

[8] cf the discussion in relation to burglary, below Ch 26.

[9] *Barr* [1978] Crim LR 244 (Deputy Judge Lowry) and commentary.

access is 'in order to view' is to be determined by reference to the occupiers' intention in allowing access.[10] The public might have access to a building (a shopping precinct or arcade for example) where collections are from time to time exhibited in the lanes connecting the shops; but in such circumstances access exists in order to shop and access to view the collection is only incidental to that shopping purpose. If, however, the collection is housed in a cordoned off part of the precinct and access is given to that part specifically so that the collection may be viewed, it would be within the protection of s 11.

21.1.1.3 Articles displayed or kept for display

The offence proscribes the removal of *any* articles displayed or kept for display, and is not confined to works of art. The coronation stone in Westminster Abbey (something which the CLRC expressly considered)[11] is clearly for this purpose an article displayed to the public though it is not a work of art. The criterion is only whether the article, which may be priceless in either sense of the term, is displayed or kept for display to the public.

'Display' here is presumably used in the sense of 'exhibit' and not merely in the sense of able to be seen; the article must be displayed or exhibited *to the public*.[12] Consequently, the removal of a fire extinguisher from a building housing exhibits would not be within the section even though it can be seen by members of the public, but it would be within the section if the fire extinguisher was itself exhibited, perhaps as an example of an early type of extinguisher, or as an example of unique design, or even nowadays if it was acclaimed as a work of modern 'art'.

It is enough that the article, though not displayed, is 'kept' for display, as where a painting is kept in the gallery's store-room.[13]

21.1.1.4 Removal

To complete the *actus reus* of the offence the article must be removed from the building *or* from its grounds. Thus, removal from the building to the grounds or vice versa will suffice. The removal, as s 11(2) makes clear, need not be during the times at which the public have access. If the collection is permanently[14] exhibited (which would be the case, for example, with municipal galleries and museums) removal at any time, even on a holiday when the building is closed to the public, may amount to an offence. But if the exhibition is temporary only, the removal must take place on a day when the public have access to the building in order to view. This serves to illustrate how unduly complex the provision is as a result of its being tailored to meet such a particular mischief. It underlines the fact that the offence is driven in part by a desire to criminalize the abuse of trust of those given access to public exhibitions.[15]

21.1.1.5 Commercial exhibitions

This limitation on the scope of the offence creates considerable ambiguity. As has been seen,[16] s 11 applies notwithstanding that the owner charges the public for admission. It applies even though he admits the public only to make profit. But the section does not apply where the

---

[10] ibid.
[11] Eighth Report. cf *Barr* [1978] Crim LR 244, CA.
[12] So linked in *Barr*.
[13] cf *Durkin* [1973] QB 786, [1973] 2 All ER 872, CA.
[14] In this context 'permanently' means for an indefinite period: *Durkin* [1973] QB 786, [1973] 2 All ER 872, CA.
[15] See Griew, *Theft*, para 5.08.
[16] Above, p 850.

owner admits the public only to view a collection,[17] if the collection is 'made or exhibited for the purpose of effecting sales or other commercial dealings'.

If it is such an exhibition, s 11 has no application whether entry is free or not. It seems odd that the law draws this distinction. The reason for this restriction upon the offence was to avoid creating an unduly wide offence, involving a very substantial exception to the general principle that temporary deprivation should not be criminal.[18] It would have meant, for example, that a removal from the premises of an ordinary commercial bookseller would have been an offence even where D has no intent permanently to deprive. In addition, since the section protects things at risk because they are on display to the public, it is thought to be reasonable for that risk to be borne by the commercial exhibitor.

As it stands the limitation applies only where the collection is made or exhibited for *the purpose*[19] of sale or other commercial dealings. If then a commercial bookseller, for the purpose of encouraging local art, arranges exhibitions in a room of his bookshop to which the public are admitted, the removal by D of the paintings, or of any other article displayed or kept for display in his premises, would fall within the section whether or not it was available for sale.

21.1.2 *Mens rea*

D must intend to remove the article from the building *or* its grounds. Dishonesty is not required but D would not be guilty of an offence if he removed an article in the belief (and clearly the test of D's belief is here subjective) that he had lawful authority or that the person entitled to give consent would have done so. Strictly, it would be an offence for D to remove a statuette from the house to the garden because he thinks the setting better, provided D believes the person entitled to give consent would not have done so.

21.2 Taking conveyances[20]

Because of the ease of tracing intact vehicles via their identification numbers, it is often difficult to establish that D intended permanently to deprive V of his vehicle when taking it.[21] A recent example is *Mitchell*[22] in which D took V's car from her with violence in the course of his attempt to evade capture by the police who were pursuing him. He abandoned the car, intact with hazard lights flashing. There was no theft and no robbery.[23] Thus, a specific offence

---

[17] Note that if the owner admits the public to view the building as well as the collection D may commit the offence by removing anything displayed (including articles forming part of the collection) although the collection is exhibited for commercial purposes. cf Ormerod and Williams, *Smith's Law of Theft,* Ch 10.

[18] The clause as originally drafted would have excluded not only the case where the public was invited to view the contents for a commercial object, but also where the public was invited to view the building for a commercial object. The latter limitation was removed; cf n 17.

[19] Presumably it is the dominant one that matters.

[20] For a practical analysis, see K McCormac (ed), *Wilkinson's Road Traffic Offences* (24th edn, 2010) Ch 15; and for a more broad-ranging socio-legal review of car crime, see C Corbett, *Car Crime* (2003).

[21] See S White, 'Taking the Joy Out of Joy-Riding' [1980] Crim LR 609; Ormerod and Williams, *Smith's Law of Theft,* Ch 10; Griew, *Theft,* Ch 6; Smith, *Property Offences,* Ch 9.

[22] [2008] EWCA Crim 850.

[23] cf *Raphael* [2008] EWCA Crim 1014, discussed above p 834, where D took V's car and attempted to sell it back to him. This was theft as D had an intention permanently to deprive V within the extended meaning of s 6 of the Act.

criminalizing temporary deprivation of conveyances is necessary.[24] Section 12 of the Theft Act 1968 (as amended) now provides:

(1) Subject to subsections (5) and (6) below, a person shall be guilty of an offence if, without having the consent of the owner or other lawful authority, he takes any conveyance for his own or another's use or, knowing that any conveyance has been taken without such authority, drives it or allows himself to be carried in or on it.

(2) A person guilty of an offence under subsection (1) above shall… [be liable on summary conviction to a fine not exceeding level 5 on the standard scale, to imprisonment for a term not exceeding six months, or to both].

(3) [Repealed]

(4) If on the trial of an indictment for theft the jury are not satisfied that the accused committed theft, but it is proved that the accused committed an offence under subsection (1) above, the jury may find him guilty of the offence under subsection (1) [and if he is found guilty of it, he shall be liable as he would have been liable under subsection (2) above on summary conviction].

[Subs 4A–C deal with procedural issues for commencement of prosecution]

(5) Subsection (1) above shall not apply in relation to pedal cycles; but, subject to subsection (6) below, a person who, without having the consent of the owner or other lawful authority, takes a pedal cycle for his own or another's use, or rides a pedal cycle knowing it to have been taken without such authority, shall on summary conviction be liable to a fine not exceeding [level 3 on the standard scale].

(6) A person does not commit an offence under this section by anything done in the belief that he has lawful authority to do it or that he would have the owner's consent if the owner knew of his doing it and the circumstances of it.

(7) For purposes of this section –

(a) 'conveyance' means any conveyance constructed or adapted for the carriage of a person or persons whether by land, water or air, except that it does not include a conveyance constructed or adapted for use only under the control of a person not carried in or on it, and 'drive' shall be construed accordingly; and

(b) 'owner', in relation to a conveyance which is the subject of a hiring agreement or hire-purchase agreement, means the person in possession of the conveyance under that agreement.

By s 37(1) of the Criminal Justice Act 1988, the offence is now triable only summarily.[25] When a jury acquits of theft of a conveyance it may convict of an offence under s 12, whereupon the offender is punishable as he would have been on summary conviction.[26] Proceedings under s 12 can not be commenced after the end of a period of three years from the date on which the offence was committed, and six months after the date on which sufficient evidence to justify the proceedings comes to the knowledge of the prosecutor.[27] In 2009/10, there were 109,817 recorded instances of theft of, or unauthorized taking of, a motor vehicle.[28]

---

[24] Technically, charges of theft of the fuel might be brought.

[25] Punishable by a fine not exceeding level 5 on the standard scale, or by six months' imprisonment, or by both. Although triable summarily only, a count under s 12 may be included in an indictment under s 40 of the Criminal Justice Act 1988.

[26] For the position in the magistrates' court, see *R (H) v Liverpool City Youth Court* [2001] Crim LR 487. On the substitution of charges under s 12 when the original allegation is attempted theft, see *DPP v Hammerton* [2009] EWHC 921 (Admin).

[27] Vehicles (Crime) Act 2001, s 37(1).

[28] J Flatley et al, *Crime in England and Wales 2009/10, Findings from the British Crime Survey and Police Recorded Crime* (2010) 32.

21.2.1 Taking for own or another's use

21.2.1.1 Taking

The offence is committed where D 'takes any conveyance for his own or another's use.' D 'takes' when he (i) assumes possession or control *and* (ii) moves the conveyance, or causes it to be moved. Where possession is assumed, abandoned and resumed there is a second taking.[29] It is not enough that D uses the conveyance for some purpose (say to sleep or shelter in it) since he must also take it. The offence can be completed only by some movement, however slight, of the conveyance.[30] The taking must be intentional.[31] In the case of a motor vehicle the taking will be most frequently accomplished by driving but the taking may be accomplished in some other way, as by pushing or towing or even by removing the conveyance on a transporter. In *Pearce*,[32] D's conviction was upheld when he took an inflatable dinghy and drove off with it on his trailer; the court rejecting an argument that the offence could be committed only where D took the conveyance by moving it in its own medium. Nor was there a need for D to have been conveyed on the boat.

Although, the offence is commonly regarded as one relating to temporary deprivation of use, the requirement of a physical taking demonstrates that the offence does not protect against deprivation generally. Thus, where D intentionally hides V's car keys, depriving V of the use of the vehicle, he does not commit the offence under s 12.[33]

21.2.1.2 For his own or another's use

The essence of the offence was thought by the Criminal Law Revision Committee to be 'stealing a ride'.[34] Strictly, however, D may steal a ride without committing this offence. A hitch-hiker who jumps on to the back of a passing lorry literally steals a ride but does not commit the offence since in no sense has he *taken* the vehicle for his own or another's use. So too if D, releases the handbrake of a car so that it runs down an incline (without his being on board), or releases a boat from its moorings so that it is carried away by the tide, this would not fall within the section.[35] In neither case is the conveyance taken by D for his own or another's use.

Considering these last two examples the Court of Appeal in *Bow*[36] expressed the firm view that the reason why D was not guilty of an offence was that although the conveyance had been moved, it would not have been 'used' as a conveyance. In other words 'use' means, and means only, use as a conveyance. No doubt in the vast majority of cases D's purpose in taking the conveyance is to transport himself from one place to another, but it is not entirely clear that the offence is, or ought to be, confined to takings with that purpose. In *Pearce*, it does not clearly appear why D took the dinghy but in *Marchant and McCallister*,[37] the Court of Appeal

---

[29] *DPP v Spriggs* [1994] RTR 1, [1993] Crim LR 622.

[30] *Bogacki* [1973] QB 832, [1973] 2 All ER 864, CA. cf *Miller* [1976] Crim LR 147, CA (boarding boat anticipating journey but no movement in fact), and *Diggin* (1980) 72 Cr App R 204, [1980] Crim LR 565, CA. Because the offence is now summary only no attempt charge is available, but the Criminal Attempt Act 1981, s 9, creates a specific offence of interference with a motor vehicle with the intention that an offence under s 12(1) shall be committed.

[31] The offence was not committed where D accidentally put his foot on the accelerator in an automatic car: *Blayney v Knight* [1975] Crim LR 237.

[32] [1973] Crim LR 321, CA.

[33] The *actus reus* of theft does not of course require a physical moving of the vehicle. See also the discussion in relation to criminal damage below, p 1014.

[34] Eighth Report, para 84.

[35] Even though the owner temporarily loses the use of his car or boat and is equally inconvenienced.

[36] (1977) 64 Cr App R 54, [1977] Crim LR 176 and commentary.

[37] (1985) 80 Cr App R 361.

assumed that the conviction was based on D's intended use of the dinghy as a conveyance and confirmed that taking a conveyance with intent to use it on some future occasion as a conveyance sufficed.[38] *Bow* suggests, and *Marchant* appears clearly to confirm, that if D in *Pearce* had some use other than as a conveyance in mind (for example, to use the dinghy as a paddling pool for his children) he could not be convicted under s 12. *Stokes*[39] is to the same effect. There it was held that D did not commit the offence where he pushed V's car around the corner to make V think it had been stolen.[40]

The courts have interpreted s 12(1) as though the words 'as a conveyance' had been inserted after 'use'. But on the face of the provision 'use' is capable of extending to uses other than use as a conveyance.[41] It should be recalled that this provision was inserted to deal with the problem of temporary deprivations. The mischief aimed at is surely that the use of the conveyance is denied to V and it should not be significant to what use D puts it when he takes it.

Even if use is restricted to use as a conveyance any such use suffices. It is enough that D releases a boat from its moorings so that he can be carried downstream in it. So, in *Bow*,[42] where D released the handbrake of V's car and coasted some 200 yards down a narrow road in order to enable him to remove his own obstructed car, it was conceded that no distinction could be drawn between driving the motor and allowing it to freewheel. But it was argued that D had not used the car as a conveyance, merely to move it as an obstruction. The court accepted that to push an obstructing vehicle a yard or two to get it out of the way would not involve the use of the vehicle as a conveyance,[43] but where the vehicle was necessarily used as a conveyance, the taker cannot be heard to say that it was not for that use. Yet D did not use V's car in order to convey himself from one end of the lane to the other. It so happened, that to remove it as an obstruction required its removal not for two yards but for 200. It is not easy to see why the distance involved should make all that difference if all D is doing is to remove a conveyance as an obstruction.[44]

21.2.1.3 Taking by unauthorized use

The discussion so far has assumed that D is not in possession or control of the conveyance but it may happen that D already has lawful possession or control and the question arises whether D can be said to 'take' the conveyance by using it in an unauthorized way. Suppose, for example, that D, authorized to use V's van in the course of V's business, uses the van to take his family to the seaside. It seems clear that under this section he may commit the offence for he now 'takes [the van] for his own . . . use'. D does not have the consent of V for the taking for his, D's, own use. This was the view taken by the Court of Appeal in *McGill*,[45] a case decided under s 217 of the Road Traffic Act 1960. D, given permission to use V's car to drive E to the station and on condition that he returned it immediately, subsequently drove it elsewhere and did not return it for some days. D's conviction for taking the car without the consent of the owner, in relation to his use after the trip to the station, was upheld. The same result must follow under s 12 of the Theft Act even though there is no requirement for driving away and where the emphasis is squarely placed on taking 'for his own or another's use'. So,

---

[38] Equally a conditional intent (eg an intent to use should it prove suitable) will suffice.

[39] [1983] RTR 59, CA.

[40] The outcome of the case may have been different had D got into the car and steered it round the corner.

[41] See White [1980] Crim LR 609 at 611.

[42] (1977) 64 Cr App R 54.

[43] In such circumstances D might in any case have lawful authority for the removal, see below, p 856.

[44] In *Bow*, D was probably engaged in a poaching expedition and V's car had been deliberately placed to block D's egress. But if D finds a vehicle blocking the highway he is presumably entitled to remove it whether he is on his way to or from a crime.

[45] [1970] RTR 209, CA.

in *McKnight v Davies*,[46] the conviction of a lorry driver was upheld when instead of returning the lorry to the depot at the end of the working day he used it for his own purposes and did not return it till the early hours of the following morning. It would seem that an unauthorized use in terms of either the destination involved or time of taking,[47] or duration will constitute the offence. Equally, it has been held that the offence is committed where D allows some third party to drive the vehicle, being aware that the owner would not have consented to that person driving.[48]

McGill, McKnight v Davies and *McMinn* were cases where the use by D was plainly outside the scope of the terms of the bailment or the terms of the employment so there was no difficulty in finding that D took it for his own use. It is thought, however, that not every deviation by a bailee from the terms of the bailment, or of an employee from the terms of his employment, would constitute a taking for his own use. For the offence there must be a use that is sufficiently at variance with the terms of the contract to demonstrate that D has replaced use on behalf of another by use on his own behalf.[49] But there is an exception in the case of a hirer under a hire-purchase agreement. His unauthorized use cannot amount to an offence because by s 12(7) he is treated as owner for the purposes of the section.

21.2.1.4 Without owner's consent or lawful authority

The ordinary run of cases where D takes V's vehicle without reference to V presents no problem. It follows from the discussion in the previous paragraph that where D has obtained V's permission to use the vehicle for a particular purpose and for a given time, D may be convicted of the offence if he uses it beyond that time for a different purpose: *McGill*.[50] There is no difficulty in such a case in saying that D has taken the vehicle for his own use, and that particular use is clearly one to which V has not consented.

21.2.1.5 Consent by fraud

McGill is a clear case. Suppose, however, that D made some false representation to induce V to allow him to take the car. The falsity might relate to (i) some attribute of D (for example, his being licensed to drive); (ii) some fundamental issue such as D's identity; or, (iii) D's purpose in taking the vehicle.

Taking the first of these issues, what if D had falsely represented that he was licensed to drive in order to borrow V's car for the trip to the station? There is perhaps no compelling reason why D should not be guilty of the offence since he knows perfectly well that V has 'consented' only because he has been misled. But on a strict interpretation of the section all that is required is that V should have consented to D taking the car for the trip to the station (the taking for D's own use) and to this V may be said to have consented even though he would never have consented had he known that D was unlicensed. The point arose in *Whittaker v Campbell*.[51] D and E required a vehicle to transport goods but D was not licensed to drive and E had only a provisional licence. Somehow they came into possession of T's licence and D, representing himself as T, hired a vehicle from V. Their convictions for taking a vehicle

---

[46] [1974] RTR 4, DC.

[47] *Wibberley* [1966] 2 QB 214, [1965] 3 All ER 718, CCA.

[48] *McMinn v McMinn* [2006] 3 All ER 87 at 93, applying *McKnight*.

[49] 'Not every brief, unauthorized diversion from his proper route by an employee in the course of his working day will necessarily involve a "taking" of the vehicle for his own use', *McKnight v Davies* [1974] RTR 4 at 8, per Lord Widgery CJ. See also *Wibberley* [1966] 2 QB 214, [1965] 3 All ER 718, CCA; *Phipps* [1970] RTR 209, CA. In determining whether an employee has taken his employers' vehicle, it would seem proper to consider whether for civil purposes D is acting in the course of his employment.

[50] [1970] RTR 209, CA; above.

[51] [1984] QB 318, [1983] 3 All ER 582, DC.

without consent were quashed. The court thought that while there might be a taking without consent where the owner is by force compelled to part with possession,[52] where he is induced to do so by fraud it could not be said 'in commonsense terms' that he had not consented to the taking. Distinguishing between agreements induced by force and fraud in this manner is at odds with the general approach of the criminal law and undermines the principle that consent necessarily involves an agreement made freely, and which is based on adequate accurate information. On the other hand, the broad commonsense approach to consent is less problematic in this context given the mischief at which the section is aimed.

The court in *Whitaker v Campbell* also considered the second issue – whether the offence would be committed where the fraud is such as to induce a 'fundamental mistake'. The court thought that it would not make sense, having regard to the mischief at which the offence was aimed, to have D's liability turn upon whether the transaction was voidable for fraud or void for mistake. That distinction is one that presents complexity in civil law. Moreover, it does not sit easily with the criminal law's approach to the concept of consent. Suppose that D telephones V and impersonates V's brother, thereby inducing V to agree the loan of his car to his brother and to leave the keys in an accessible spot while V is out of town. If D then avails himself of this trick to take possession of the car while V is away, it would be an astonishing conclusion to say that V had consented to D taking his car. It is submitted that the issue of consent by fraud under s 12 deserves reconsideration.[53]

As for the third problem of falsity, in *Whittaker v Campbell* there was no suggestion of any misrepresentation as to the use to which D and E proposed to put the vehicle and their actual use was within the terms of the hire.[54] Suppose, however, that D obtains possession by describing to V a use that he knows V will consent to while proposing to use the vehicle for a use to which he knows V would not consent. D might, for example, secure V's consent to the use of his vehicle for the transportation of goods from Leeds to London knowing that V would not consent had he known that the goods were stolen. The case is essentially indistinguishable from *Whittaker v Campbell*. V has consented to the use of his vehicle for that journey though he would not have agreed to incur criminal liability as a handler of stolen goods.

Suppose, though, that D's *purpose* is not to drive to London and back but to take the vehicle on a fortnight's holiday to the south of France. The point arose in *Peart*.[55] D persuaded V to lend him a van by pretending that he needed it for an urgent appointment in Alnwick and that he would return it by 7.30 pm. In fact D wanted the van for a journey to Burnley where he was found with the van by the police at 9.00 pm, and he knew all along that V would not have consented to this use. It was held, quashing D's conviction, that V's consent was not vitiated by the deception since V had merely been deceived as to *the purpose* for which the car was to be used and reliance was placed on this decision by the court in *Whittaker v Campbell*.

But there are difficulties with *Peart*. By reason of the direction given to the jury by the trial judge, the Court of Appeal had to consider the position at the time when the van was borrowed in the afternoon:

There was no issue left to [the jury] whether, in this particular case, there could have been a fresh taking... at some time after it was originally taken away at 2.30 pm. The consent which has to be

[52] See *Hogdan* [1962] Crim LR 563.

[53] cf Smith, *Property Offences*, paras 9–23.

[54] In *Singh v Rathour (Northern Star Insurance Co Ltd, third party)* [1988] 2 All ER 16, CA, a civil case where the issue was whether D was insured under his policy which covered him when driving any vehicle 'provided he had the consent of the owner', it was held that D did not have the consent of the owner where he was aware that the consent given did not extend to the use to which he put the vehicle. See J Birds, 'Consent of the Owner under a Motor Policy' [1998] JBL 421.

[55] [1970] 2 QB 672, [1970] 2 All ER 823, CA.

considered is thus a consent at the time of taking possession of the van with licence to drive and use it.[56]

It seems then that even if he did not commit an offence at the time of the taking he would, like the defendants in *McGill* and *McKnight v Davies*,[57] have done so as soon as he departed from the Alnwick road and set course for Burnley.

There is, however, a difference. In *McGill* and *McKnight v Davies,* there was no evidence that the defendants had the unauthorized use in mind when they obtained possession but that proof was not lacking in *Peart* – D frankly admitted it – and it is submitted this case also ought to be reconsidered. Given the use for a journey to which V had consented, D *took* it for a journey for which no consent was given. As a practical matter of evidence, it will often be necessary to prove a departure from the stated use in order to prove that D intended to use the vehicle in other than the authorized way but this cannot affect the substantive criminal law.

21.2.1.6 Lawful authority

D commits no offence where he takes a vehicle, even without the consent of the owner, when acting under 'other lawful authority'. This is appropriate to cover the growing number of cases where local authorities or the police are authorized under various statutory powers to remove vehicles. No doubt D would be acting lawfully in moving V's vehicle a few yards so that he can obtain access to the highway for his own vehicle, even though he may know that V does not consent to the removal.[58]

It may fairly be assumed that general defences such as self-defence and duress are available on charges for this offence.

21.2.1.7 Conveyance

Section 12(7) provides:

For purposes of this section – (a) 'conveyance' means any conveyance constructed or adapted for the carriage of a person or persons whether by land, water or air, except that it does not include a conveyance constructed or adapted for use only under the control of a person not carried in or on it, and 'drive' shall be construed accordingly

'Conveyance' has been interpreted to mean a mechanical contrivance of some kind. While it includes conveyances such as cars and motor-cycles, it does not include horses;[59] horses are clearly not constructed, though they may be suitable, for the carriage of persons, and the argument that they might be 'adapted' by the use of halter and bridle was rejected. Because the essence of the offence was thought to be stealing a ride,[60] conveyance is defined, in effect, to exclude conveyances that are not meant for riding.[61] Thus, though it would be an offence to take an aircraft, hovercraft or railway engine, it is not an offence within this section to take a handcart or certain kinds of lawnmower which, though power driven, are operated by a person who is not carried in or on it.[62]

---

[56] [1970] 2 All ER 823 at 824. It seems surprising that the proviso which was then available to the Court of Appeal was not applied.

[57] Above, p 855.

[58] But see *Bow* (1977) 64 Cr App R 54, CA, above, n 36.

[59] *Neal v Gribble* (1978) 68 Cr App R 9, [1978] RTR 409.

[60] cf Eighth Report, para 84. Earlier (para 82) the Committee seemed to have viewed the mischief of the offence as the danger, loss and inconvenience which often result from it. See HL, vol 290, col 141.

[61] But on this see above, p 855.

[62] Recently, concern has arisen over electric cars and whether these can be 'stolen' or taken without the owner's consent. Insurance companies have been more concerned about the theft of the very expensive batteries on which

21.2.2 *Mens rea*

The taking must be intentional. It is not enough that the vehicle accidentally moves.[63]

Section 12(6) provides that a person does not commit an offence by anything done in the belief that he has lawful authority to do it or that the owner would have consented. The test of belief appears to be subjective. If D honestly believes that V has consented to his use of V's car, it is not relevant to enquire whether V did in fact consent or whether V would have consented had he known of the circumstances – for example, that D was uninsured,[64] or even that D was unlicensed to drive. If D takes a vehicle 'without having the consent of the owner' and does not believe that the owner would have consented had he known of the taking, he may be convicted though the owner subsequently says that he would have consented;[65] the offence is constituted not by taking a conveyance without the owner's consent, but in taking it without *having* the consent of the owner.

If D takes a conveyance not caring whether the owner would or would not have consented, it would seem that he may be convicted. For in such a case he does not *believe* that the owner would have consented.[66]

Taking a conveyance has been held to be a crime of basic intent so that evidence of intoxication is not relevant as tending to show that D lacked *mens rea*.[67] Arguably, where D's belief as to the consent of the owner is based on a mistake induced by voluntary intoxication he can rely on that mistake.[68]

21.2.3 Driving or being carried

Section 12 creates a second version of the offence to deal with the person who allows himself to be carried or who himself drives a vehicle which has already been taken, but who might not be caught by ordinary principles of accessorial liability since he might not have been a party to the taking.

If, when D allows himself to be carried, he is aiding and abetting the taking of the conveyance by E, he may be convicted of the primary offence as a secondary party. But if the 'taking' has come to an end, the primary offence has ceased and it is no longer possible to aid and abet it. In such a case the second version of the offence is applicable being based on D 'allowing' himself to be carried. 'Allow' is probably a word of wider ambit than 'aid, abet, counsel or procure'. If D allows himself to be driven by a person who, as he knows, would drive the car whether D was there or not, he may neither assist or encourage, nor intend to assist or encourage, the driver.[69]

Where E takes a conveyance without consent or other lawful authority, it is an offence for D, knowing the conveyance has been so taken, to drive it or allow himself to be carried in or on it. A hitch-hiker would therefore not be guilty of an offence where, unknown to him, the driver is using his employer's van, contrary to his instructions, to go to Blackpool for the day.

---

they run. See www.independent.co.uk/money/insurance/five-questions-about-insuring-electric-cars-2185008.html.

[63] *Blayney v Knight* (1974) 60 Cr App R 269.

[64] *Clotworthy* [1981] RTR 477, CA.

[65] *Ambler* [1979] RTR 217, CA.

[66] cf the discussion of recklessness above, Ch 5.

[67] *MacPherson* [1973] RTR 157, CA; *Gannon* (1988) 87 Cr App R 254, CA. G Williams is heavily critical of *Gannon*, 'Two Nocturnal Blunders' (1990) 140 NLJ 1564. For a contrary view, see White [1980] Crim LR 609.

[68] By analogy with the decision in *Jaggard v Dickinson* [1981] QB 527, DC, decided under s 5(2) of the Criminal Damage Act 1971 which uses similar terms. See Griew, *Theft*, para 6.20.

[69] cf above, Ch 8.

If the driver tells the hitch-hiker that he is so using the van then the hitch-hiker will be liable if he allows himself to be carried further.[70]

21.2.3.1 Carried

D's mere presence in or on the conveyance, knowing that it has been taken without consent or authority, does not suffice unless he allows himself to be 'carried' in or on it and this requires some movement of the conveyance.[71]

21.2.3.2 Driving

In *DPP v Alderton*,[72] merely sitting in the car with the engine on, gear engaged and the wheels spinning was held to be 'driving'. In *Planton v DPP*,[73] D stopped his vehicle on a causeway, awaiting an opportunity to cross at the low tide. D claimed he was not 'driving' for the purposes of a drink driving offence since his vehicle was not moving. The Divisional Court held that he was driving: a driver who had stopped at traffic lights was in a similar position but was still driving. It seems to be a question of fact and degree whether a cessation of movement has been so long that it could not reasonably be said that a person was still driving.

21.2.3.3 *Mens rea*

It must be proved that D *knew* that the conveyance had been taken without authority when he drove it or allowed himself to be carried in or on it as the case may be. The vehicle must actually have been taken; one cannot know a thing to be so, unless it is so.[74] 'Wilful blindness' may be enough as in the case of other statutes.[75] Such a state of mind is, dangerously close to that of belief that the conveyance had been so taken.[76] D would be wilfully blind where he thinks it quite possible that E might have taken the vehicle without authority but makes no enquiries to ascertain whether this is so or not. It could happen that E believes he has authority to take the conveyance but D knows that E has not. In such a case D would be guilty of an offence since he knows it was taken without authority. And no doubt D knows the conveyance has been taken without authority, and may be convicted under this provision, though he knows that E has in fact stolen the conveyance.[77]

Where E's conviction is proved by certificate under s 74 of PACE, and D was in the vehicle at the time of the taking to which E's conviction relates, that is *prima facie* evidence of E's guilt, but it must also be shown that D *knew* it was taken.[78]

21.2.4 Pedal cycles

Section 12(5) creates an offence of taking pedal cycles,[79] which has broadly similar elements to the offence under s 12(1). A small difference is that the offence under s 12(5) is not committed by one who allows himself to be carried on the cycle knowing that it has been

---

[70] *Boldizsar v Knight* [1980] Crim LR 653, DC. For more detailed analysis, see Ormerod and Williams, *Smith's Law of Theft*, paras 8–13. There are problems of proof where the prosecution seek to rely on D informing E that the vehicle has been taken: *Francis* [1982] Crim LR 694.

[71] *Miller* [1976] Crim LR 147, CA; *Diggin* (1980) 72 Cr App R 204, [1981] RTR 83, CA.

[72] [2004] RTR 367.

[73] [2001] EWHC 450 (Admin).

[74] See the discussion of the House of Lords of the concept of knowledge in *Saik* [2006] UKHL 18.

[75] Edwards, *Mens Rea in Statutory Offences*, 202–205; Williams, CLGP, 159.

[76] See s 22(1), below, p 975.

[77] cf *Tolley v Giddings* [1964] 2 QB 354, [1964] 1 All ER 201, DC.

[78] *DPP v Parker* [2006] EWHC 1270.

[79] It is a moot point whether this extends to electronically powered cycles or stand-on scooters.

taken without authority. The offence is summary only.[80] In 2009/10, there were 109,851 such offences recorded.[81]

21.3 Aggravated vehicle-taking[82]

The so-called 'joyrider' (or 'twocker') under s 12 is liable to relatively limited punishments. He is additionally liable for any offence involved in taking the vehicle (most obviously criminal damage caused in gaining access to the conveyance and in interfering with the locks and the electrics in order to get it started) and the driver, whether or not he is the original taker, is liable for any offence committed whilst driving the vehicle (for example, driving whilst uninsured, careless driving, dangerous driving). And, of course, a person who allows himself to be carried in or on a conveyance may be liable as a secondary party to these further offences under the principles which govern aiding and abetting or under the version of the s 12 offence discussed above.[83]

It might be thought therefore that s 12 was entirely adequate to deal with the taker, those who subsequently drive the taken conveyance and those who allow themselves to be carried in or on it. In the normal case the fine of £5,000 and/or six months' imprisonment would seem adequate. In the abnormal case where the driver drives dangerously, or kills whilst driving dangerously, a count can be added for that and again the punishment (imprisonment in this case) would seem to be adequate. But the abnormal case became not so abnormal in the early 1990s. The taking of motor vehicles increased to an extent that it was described as epidemic. As the activity increased, so did the risks. Youngsters (usually male) use the vehicles they have taken to demonstrate their driving 'skills' or become involved in high-speed chases when pursued by the police.[84] The hazards of either are obvious. Even in the face of this epidemic, it might be argued that s 12 and the range of driving offences and ordinary criminal charges for damage and injury inflicted were adequate in the sense that the activity would always be capable of being punished and the penalties provided seemed appropriate.[85]

There was an additional problem, in many cases the taking is performed by a group, and the vehicle is damaged or injury inflicted, but it is difficult to prove whether it was D or E or F who damaged the vehicle or caused the injury. One or more of them is able to claim that the damage was done before he joined the enterprise. And where, as not infrequently happens, the vehicle is found burned out, all three would say that this must have been done by someone else after they had abandoned the vehicle.

It was to deal with all of these problems, and what was seen as a rapidly growing social menace, that s 12A of the Theft Act 1968, was inserted by the Aggravated Vehicle-Taking Act 1992. It provides:

12A. – (1) Subject to subsection (3) below, a person is guilty of aggravated taking of a vehicle if –

    (a) he commits an offence under section 12 (1) above (in this section referred to as a 'basic offence') in relation to a mechanically propelled vehicle; and

---

[80] Thus there can be no attempt charge.

[81] Flatley et al, *Crime in England and Wales 2009/10*, 32.

[82] See JN Spencer, 'The Aggravated Vehicle Taking Act 1992' [1992] Crim LR 69.

[83] Above, Ch 8.

[84] See B Rix, D Walker and R Brown, *A Study of Deaths and Serious Injuries Resulting from Police Vehicle Accidents* (1997) HORS, noting that 27% of those in police vehicle accidents were in stolen cars at the time.

[85] It is not suggested that the answer or solution lies in the penalty, merely that the penalty is adequate in relation to the crime. The answer lies in foolproof (or is it expert-proof?) immobilizing devices.

(b) it is proved that, at any time after the vehicle was unlawfully taken (whether by him or another) and before it was recovered, the vehicle was driven, or injury or damage was caused, in one or more of the circumstances set out in paragraphs (a) to (d) of subsection (2) below.

(2) The circumstances referred to in subsection (1)(b) above are –

   (a) that the vehicle was driven dangerously on a road or other public place;

   (b) that, owing to the driving of the vehicle, an accident occurred by which injury was caused to any person;

   (c) that, owing to the driving of the vehicle, an accident occurred by which damage was caused to any property, other than the vehicle;

   (d) that damage was caused to the vehicle.

(3) A person is not guilty of an offence under this section if he proves that, as regards any such proven driving, injury or damage as is referred to in subsection (1)(b) above, either –

   (a) the driving, accident or damage referred to in subsection (2) above occurred before he committed the basic offence; or

   (b) he was neither in nor on nor in the immediate vicinity of the vehicle when that driving, accident or damage occurred.

(4) A person guilty of an offence under this section shall be liable on conviction on indictment to imprisonment for a term not exceeding two years or, if it is proved that, in circumstances falling within subsection (2)(b) above, the accident caused the death of the person concerned, fourteen years.[86]

(5) If a person who is charged with an offence under this section is found not guilty of that offence but it is proved that he committed a basic offence, he may be convicted of the basic offence.

Since there is a different maximum sentence for those cases in which death results there are technically two offences created by the section.[87] The offences are draconian, and have features that depart markedly from the principles that ordinarily govern liability, at least for serious crimes.

The prosecution must first prove that D has committed the basic offence under s 12(1) of the 1968 Act as described above in relation to a mechanically propelled vehicle – the offence does not apply to conveyances generally.

Secondly, the prosecution must prove that at any time after the vehicle was unlawfully taken (proof of the identity of the taker is not required) and before it was recovered (that is, restored to the owner or other lawful custody: s 12A(8)) the vehicle was driven or injury or damage was caused in one or more of the circumstances specified in s 12A(2). These circumstances, apart from dangerous driving which requires a measure of fault,[88] require no proof of fault on the part of D, or D and others involved in the enterprise, merely that either injury to the person or damage to property was owing to the driving,[89] or that damage was caused to the vehicle taken, whether by driving or not.[90] There is therefore strict liability in respect of all these consequences. D's driving might be impeccable, but he will not escape liability if the

---

[86] Criminal Justice Act 2003, s 285(1).

[87] Such should therefore be charged separately: *Courtie* [1984] AC 463; *Sherwood* [1995] RTR 60.

[88] See below, Ch 33.

[89] The Court of Appeal in *Marsh* [1997] 1 Cr App R 67 held that the words 'owing to the driving of the vehicle' were plain and simple and no gloss ought to be provided by referring the jury to the manner of the driving. See [1997] Crim LR 205 and comment. If D has used the car as a weapon, he will still be caught by the section: accident includes deliberate causing of injury *B* [2005] 1 Cr App R 140, [2005] Crim LR 388.

[90] *Dawes v DPP* [1995] 1 Cr App R 65 at 72, 73.

injury, damage or death arises.[91] Moreover, each of the participants in the enterprise commits the offence though he was not driving the vehicle. The section creates an offence of guilt by association.

So if D and E commit the basic offence (s 12) each of them is liable if either one of them causes injury or damage when driving the vehicle. More remarkably, if during the enterprise D chooses to damage the vehicle by slashing the seats, E commits the offence under s 12A though he does not abet D in slashing the seats or even if E tries to dissuade D from so doing.[92] This highlights the draconian nature of the provision. Even if E is no longer in the vehicle, he may be walking away from it when D decides to set fire to it.[93] E is liable provided he is still 'in the immediate vicinity' of the vehicle. Not only does the offence create guilt by association but guilt by approximation.

Section 12A(3) deals with the problem of proof identified above. The prosecution may prove, or D may admit, that D committed the basic offence but D may claim that he had left the enterprise before the injury or damage was done or that he joined the enterprise after the injury or damage had been done. In such circumstances it is for D to prove on the balance of probability that the dangerous driving or the accident or the damage took place before he committed the basic offence; or that, having committed the basic offence, he was no longer in, nor on, nor in the immediate vicinity of the vehicle when one of those events took place.

The activity known as 'car jacking' – where D causes V to stop his car and D then forcibly ejects V from the car and drives V's vehicle away – is more appropriately prosecuted by offences of theft, robbery, offences against the person, etc. In particular, in cases where V is caused to stop by D's minor collision with V's vehicle, aggravated vehicle-taking will not be a suitable charge because the damage will have occurred prior to the taking.

It is unclear whether an attempt to commit aggravated vehicle-taking is an offence. The s 12A offence requires proof of the basic offence under s 12 which is triable summarily only (and therefore can not be the subject of an attempt charge), but the s 12A offence itself is triable either way. It is submitted that in an appropriate case a charge of attempt would be available, as where D is apprehended trying to break into a high-powered vehicle and admits that his intention was to take it for an evening's 'racing' against his friends' car.

---

[91] See, eg, *Clifford* [2007] EWCA Crim 2442.

[92] 'A passenger may be liable even though the passenger has protested at the driving which has caused damage to the vehicle': *Dawes v DPP* [1995] 1 Cr App R 65 at 72, per Kennedy LJ. See also *Wiggins* [2001] RTR 37 on the sentencing implications in such cases.

[93] Or allow it to roll down hill causing damage to property. See *DPP v Hughes* [2010] EWHC 515 (Admin).

22
Making off without payment

22.1 Making off under the Theft Act 1978

By s 3[1] of the Theft Act 1978:

(1) Subject to subsection (3) below, a person who, knowing that payment on the spot for any goods supplied or service done is required or expected from him, dishonestly makes off without having paid as required or expected and with intent to avoid payment of the amount due shall be guilty of an offence.

(2) For purposes of this section 'payment on the spot' includes payment at the time of collecting goods on which work has been done or in respect of which service has been provided.

(3) Subsection (1) above shall not apply where the supply of the goods or the doing of the service is contrary to law, or where the service done is such that payment is not legally enforceable.[2]

By s 4 the offence, which is triable either way, is punishable on summary conviction by imprisonment and/or a fine not exceeding the prescribed maximum (presently £5,000), and on indictment by imprisonment for a term not exceeding two years and/or a fine.

This offence aims to deal in a simple and straightforward way with conduct that was commonly called 'bilking'. It deals with the person who, for example, having consumed a meal in a restaurant, or filled the tank of the car with petrol, or reached their destination in a taxi, decamps without paying. For all their factual simplicity, as we will see,[3] these cases create considerable difficulties if prosecuted as theft (or fraud). There are no such difficulties under s 3.

Under this section, there is no requirement whatever that D's conduct amounts to theft or fraud or that he has practised any deception at all. There is no requirement to prove that D was dishonest when he ordered the meal or began to fill his car; it is sufficient if the dishonesty occurs at the point of making off. The offence may have been rendered otiose in many situations by the Fraud Act 2006. Under the old deception offences D could only be liable if his deception occurred *before*, the relevant property passed to him (or the service was provided etc depending on which type of deception offence was charged). In contrast, under s 2 of the Fraud Act 2006, D may be liable even if he makes a false representation *after* the entire proprietary interest has passed to him. It follows that if, after D, a motorist, has filled his fuel tank and the entire proprietary interest in the petrol has passed to him, he falsely represents to V, the cashier, that it will be paid for by D's firm, D commits the offence under s 2.[4] Section 3 of

---

[1] See generally J Spencer, 'The Theft Act 1978' [1979] Crim LR 24, 35; G Syrota, 'Annotations to Theft Act 1978' in *Current Law Statutes* 1978; [1978] 42 MLR 301, 304; Ormerod and Williams, *Smith's Law of Theft*, Ch 6; Griew, *Theft*, Ch 13; Smith, *Property Offences*, Ch 20.

[2] Section 3(4) was repealed by the Serious Organised Crime and Police Act 2005, Sch 17(2), para 1.

[3] See, eg, *DPP v Ray* [1974] AC 370, [1973] 3 All ER 131, HL, below, p 890; *Edwards v Ddin* [1976] 3 All ER 705, [1976] 1 WLR 942.

[4] cf under the old law *Collis-Smith* [1971] Crim LR 716, CA.

the 1978 Act may nevertheless be preferable because it describes precisely what D did, and it does not involve proof of a false representation. Moreover, in some cases s 3 of the 1978 Act will be necessary because the fraud offence is limited to cases of intending to gain or cause loss in terms of property.[5]

The s 3 offence creates an exception to the general principle that it is not an offence dishonestly to avoid the payment of a debt.[6] This might be thought to pose a potential problem of over criminalizing. The exception is, however, limited and understandable. In the ordinary case a dishonest debtor (who can be traced) can be coerced into payment via civil remedies without resort to criminal sanctions; where bilking is involved enforcement can usually only occur on the spot, since the person becomes difficult, if not impossible, to trace.[7]

22.1.1 *Actus reus*

22.1.1.1 Makes off

The term 'makes off' might be thought of as having a pejorative connotation implying some requirement of stealth in the manner of the person making off. Certainly, the offence extends to such cases (the diner who waits until the manager leaves the room or decamps via the cloakroom window) but it cannot be confined to such cases. A diner who brazenly walks out of the restaurant after finishing his pudding is properly said to make off though his act is done openly and without stealth; so too, a heavyweight boxer whose departure cannot be prevented by a timorous restaurant owner.[8]

'Makes off' appears to mean simply that D leaves one place (the place where the payment is required) for another place. The offence does not necessarily require that D should have 'made off' from V's premises; the spot from which D makes off is simply the place where payment is required[9] and this may be a newsvendor's stand or an ice-cream van on the highway. In the case of a taxi ride it will be the agreed destination. If D has not left the first place he has not made off, but if he is in the process of leaving there may be an attempt.[10] Presumably, this element of the *actus reus* continues for such time as D can be said to be in the process of 'making off'.[11]

If D leaves with V's consent it may be more difficult to say that D has made off. Suppose that D, having determined never to pay, gives his correct name and address to V and is allowed to go. It would be a strained reading of the section to say that D had made off; D has left without paying but the offence requires something more than that. A more difficult case is that where E, who also intends never to pay, gives a false name and address to V and is allowed to go. The two cases differ in that D can be traced and coerced into payment under the civil law while E cannot be traced at all. Spencer[12] argues that the difference between these cases is material. The mischief aimed at by this section, he argues, is the bilking customer who cannot be traced.[13]

---

[5] See below, p 878.

[6] See further GH Treitel, 'Contract and Crime', in *Crime, Proof and Punishment*, 89.

[7] Hence originally by s 3(4) a power of arrest was conferred which was necessary since the offence carries only a maximum two-year sentence and was not, before SOCPA 2005, automatically arrestable.

[8] See F Bennion, 'Letter to the Editor' [1980] Crim LR 670.

[9] Payment may be legitimately required at more than one spot: *Moberly v Allsop* [1992] COD 190, 156 JP 514, DC. See also *Aziz* [1993] Crim LR 708.

[10] *Brooks and Brooks* (1982) 76 Cr App R 66, [1983] Crim LR 188, CA; making off, said the court, 'may be an exercise accompanied by the sound of trumpets or a silent stealing away after the folding of tents'.

[11] This was important for determining the lawfulness of arrests: *Drameh* [1983] Crim LR 322.

[12] [1983] Crim LR 573.

[13] He supported this argument by the fact that as originally enacted, V had a power of arrest; it would be highly undesirable if V could arrest a customer of whose identity he is aware, that power being required for the unidentifiable bilker.

Spencer's argument that the applicability of the offence turns on the traceability of the bilker has force, but is not easy to square with the language of s 3. It can lead to some illogical results. For example, assume that F is V's best customer of many years' standing. One day F determines not to pay and decamps from the premises via the toilet window. All the elements of the offence appear to be present unless it is to be said that F did not make off. It may puzzle us all to wonder why F should have thought that he could get away with his conduct but he seems clearly to have made off. A customer in a wheelchair would surely make off if he decamps without paying though he does not at all fancy his chances of outpacing the restaurateur.[14] If the untraceability of D was the touchstone of the offence, it is arguable that the offence would then fail to protect the proprietor (for example, the restaurant owner) who knows who D is, but is unlikely to pursue D's small debt via the civil courts.[15] The CLRC[16] regarded the purpose of the offence as to protect legitimate business.

Section 3 does not, on a natural interpretation, mean that D does not make off if he gives a correct identification but E does make off if he gives a false one. Suppose in the latter case that V orders a taxi for E and bids him a cheery farewell from the hotel lobby. Can it really be said that E has made off?[17]

If, however, V permits D to leave the spot where payment is required for a purely temporary purpose (for example to answer a telephone call or to collect his wallet from his overcoat which he has deposited in the cloakroom) expecting him to return to settle up, it is submitted that D commits the offence if he then decamps. In such cases V has not consented to D leaving without paying, quite the contrary, in the latter example he has consented to D facilitating payment. So where V, a taxi driver, permits D to leave so that D, as he claims, may go into his house to get the fare it would appear that D, if he then decamps, has made off within the meaning of this section.

22.1.1.2 Goods supplied or service done

The offence requires that the goods[18] be *supplied* or that a service be *done*. Most obviously goods are supplied where V delivers them to D but the offence cannot be limited only to cases of delivery by V. Petrol is clearly supplied to D at a self-service filling station though D supplies himself and, by similarly, goods taken by D from the shelves in a supermarket are supplied.[19] Supplied in this context connotes goods proffered by V and accordingly taken by D. Hence it would not be an offence under this section (though it may be theft) for D to take goods in a shop which is not self-service; such goods are not proffered until tendered by V or his assistant. It is submitted that goods may be supplied for the purpose of s 3 even though D has a dishonest intent from the outset and therefore steals the goods. It can hardly have been intended that theft and making off should be mutually exclusive since the effect of that would create difficulties for prosecutors.

Where 'service' is concerned the service must be 'done'. An obvious example of a service done is the provision of hotel accommodation, or a meal in a restaurant, but it will also apply to the collection of goods, such as clothes, shoes or cars, on which work (repair, etc) has been done. A service may be done (as goods may be supplied) though nothing is physically done

---

[14] For further views on this difficult aspect of the offence, see Williams, TBCL, 878; F Bennion, Letter, 'The Drafting of Section 3 of the Theft Act 1978' [1980] Crim LR 670; Letters [1983] Crim LR 205, 574; Griew, *Theft*, paras 13–16.

[15] See Griew, paras 13–16.

[16] Thirteenth Report, para 19 (1977) Cmnd 6733.

[17] cf *Hammond* [1982] Crim LR 611, below, n 27.

[18] As defined in s 34 of the 1968 Act, applicable to the 1978 Act by s 5(2).

[19] *Contra* ATH Smith, 'Shoplifting and the Theft Acts' [1981] Crim LR 586. cf Griew, para 13.07; Ormerod and Williams, *Smith's Law of Theft*, para 6.12.

by V other than proffering the service of which D takes advantage, as where D is permitted to park his car on V's parking lot.

There is no definition of 'service' in s 3. 'Service' is not the same as the extended meaning of 'services' which was contained in s 1 of the 1978 Act.[20]

22.1.1.3 Unenforceable debts

The offence under s 3, unlike the repealed offence under s 1 of the 1978 Act, cannot be committed where the supply of the goods or the doing of the service is contrary to law; or where the service done is such that payment is not legally enforceable.[21] Thus, it is no offence for D to make off from a brothel without paying.

Whether a supply of goods or services is contrary to law or whether payment for a service is not legally enforceable involves a consideration of the general law and cannot be detailed here.[22] But the distinction that s 3 makes may be illustrated by reference to transactions entered into by a minor.[23] As a matter of civil law, the supply of unnecessary services to a minor will not create a legally enforceable contract. If a landlord supplies 'intoxicating liquor' to a minor the transaction is contrary to law and the minor commits no offence in making off without payment. If the minor has a service provided which is not a 'necessary' one (say flying lessons) he commits no offence in making off since payment for that service is not legally enforceable. If the minor is supplied with non-necessary *goods* (say 11 fancy waistcoats) and makes off he commits the offence; while payment for the waistcoats is not legally enforceable, the supply of these *goods* is not contrary to law.

The courts do not seem to have been troubled by defence claims that although performance of the contract was not contrary to law, some collateral aspect of V's conduct in the supply of the goods or services was contrary to law and therefore unprotected by s 3. It was anticipated by some that this would give rise to problems in cases such as D bilking on the unlicensed taxi driver.[24]

22.1.1.4 Without having paid as required or expected

It is implicit in the section that V requires or expects payment on the spot and that the payment is due in fact and law. If a taxi driver, in the course of a journey, commits a breach of contract entitling his passenger to rescind the contract, the passenger does not commit an offence by making off.[25] Where the money is due, does a person who gives a worthless cheque in 'payment' of the debt commit the offence? The question was previously of little importance because D would have been guilty of the more serious offence under s 2(1)(b) of the 1978 Act. The offence would now be one under s 2 of the Fraud Act 2006 as D makes a false representation that the cheque will be honoured.[26] In the one reported case (although only at first instance)[27] in which the matter has arisen the judge ruled that the s 3 offence was not committed because a worthless cheque was not the same as counterfeit money, and that D was not

---

[20] See on that *Sofroinou* [2003] EWCA Crim 3681, and p 773 in the 11th edition of this work. Section 1 was repealed by the Fraud Act 2006.

[21] The reason for the distinction is that while the aim of s 1 was to punish fraud, the aim of s 3, as noted is to protect legitimate business.

[22] For a general review of the relationship and consideration of s 3, see Treitel, 'Contract and Crime', in *Crime, Proof and Punishment*, 81.

[23] cf P Rowlands, 'Minors: Can They Make Off Without Payment' (1981) 145 JP 410: cf Smith, *Property Offences*, para 20.69.

[24] See Griew, *Theft*, para 13.10.

[25] *Troughton v Metropolitan Police* [1987] Crim LR 138, DC.

[26] See G Syrota, 'Are Cheque Frauds Covered by Section 3 of the Theft Act 1978' [1980] Crim LR 413.

[27] *Hammond* [1982] Crim LR 611 (Judge Morrison).

making off because he departed with V's consent. The true answer may well be that D is guilty because he has not paid 'as required or expected'. V requires and expects payment in legal tender or by a good cheque. Payment by a worthless cheque no more satisfies his requirement or expectation than payment in counterfeit money. If, however, as is now almost inevitable, the cheque is backed by a cheque guarantee card, then, depending on the conditions of its issue, D may have paid as required or expected although his authority to use the card has been withdrawn or even if it has been stolen.[28] Similarly, with payment by credit card.[29] V has been paid if the bank or card issuer is bound to honour the cheque or card, and that is a question of civil law. The offence is not committed if the supplier consents to D's leaving without payment, even if the consent was obtained by fraud, as where D deceives V into accepting postponement of payment.[30] Payment in such a case is not required or expected at *that* time. This may be an offence under s 2 of the Fraud Act 2006.

22.1.2 *Mens rea*

The offence requires that D should make off (i) dishonestly; (ii) knowing that payment on the spot is required or expected from him; and (iii) with intent to avoid payment.

22.1.2.1 Dishonesty

Reference may be made to the general discussion of dishonesty.[31] It does not matter at what stage D decides to act dishonestly so long as he is dishonest when he makes off. While dishonesty is a question for the jury, D would not be dishonest in refusing to pay for goods or a service genuinely believed by him to be deficient.

22.1.2.2 Knowing that payment on the spot is required or expected of him

The offence is concerned only with cases where payment on the spot is required. Such transactions are difficult to define in abstract terms but are usually easy enough to identify[32] by reference to normal trading practices, although these may in particular instances be modified by the course of dealing between the parties.[33] If D honestly believes that the transaction is on credit terms, he cannot be convicted of this offence for he is not acting dishonestly and he does not *know* the transaction to be a spot transaction. Where D believes that payment is to be made by another (for example, where he believes that E will pay for the meal) he does not commit the offence because he neither acts dishonestly nor does he know that payment is to be required of him.[34] Presumably D would not be liable if, having drunk too much alcohol with his meal, he staggers out of the restaurant without paying when D is so intoxicated that he does not know what he is doing.

---

[28] cf *First Sport Ltd v Barclays Bank plc* [1993] 3 All ER 789, CA (Civ Div).

[29] cf *Re Charge Card Services Ltd* [1988] 3 All ER 702, [1988] 3 WLR 764, CA (Civ Div).

[30] *Vincent* [2001] Crim LR 488, [2001] 2 Cr App R 150, [2001] EWCA Crim 295, CA. See also *Evans v Lane* (1984) CO/137/84, CA.

[31] Above, p 824.

[32] Section 3(2) provides that it includes 'payment at the time of collecting goods on which work has been done or in respect of which service has been provided'. But this seems to have been added *ex abundanti cautela* and adds nothing.

[33] It cannot be enough that V requires a payment to be made on the spot, eg seeing D who owes him £10 lent a month ago, V demands payment on the spot. The reference is to those transactions where payment customarily follows immediately upon the provision of the goods or service.

[34] *Brooks and Brooks* (1982) 76 Cr App R 66, [1983] Crim LR 188, CA.

22.1.2.3 Intention to avoid payment

Section 3 does not in terms require an intention to make permanent default, and commentators tended to favour the view that a dishonest intention temporarily to avoid payment would suffice. However, *Allen*[35] holds that the offence requires an intention to make permanent default. D had left an hotel without settling his bill and the trial judge directed the jury that all that was required was an intention to make default at the time payment was required. The Court of Appeal held, however, that an intention to make permanent default was required because s 3 required both (i) a making off without paying on the spot; and (ii) an intention to avoid payment. In view of the requirement in (i), (ii) made sense only if permanent default was intended. The House of Lords endorsed this view and drew further support for it by reference to the fact that the CLRC had intended permanent default to be necessary.[36]

The Home Office recently rejected a reform proposal suggested by garage owners[37] which would have extended the offence to include cases where D acts with intent to defer payment.

[35] [1985] AC 1029, [1985] 2 All ER 641, [1985] Crim LR 739.

[36] Thirteenth Report, para 18 (1977) Cmnd 6733.

[37] Complaining of individuals who, having filled their cars with fuel, claimed to have left their wallets at home and promised to pay at a later date. That may be an offence under s 2 of the Fraud Act 2006.

23
The Fraud Act 2006

23.1 Background

23.1.1 Common law approaches to fraud

It may seem surprising that there has been no statutory general offence of fraud in modern times in England and Wales. Conspiracy to defraud and fraudulent trading come closest, but neither is truly a general fraud offence.[1] One consequence of this is that there has been no attempt to provide a clear definition of what constitutes fraud.[2]

23.1.2 Deception under the Theft Acts 1968, 1978 and 1996

The Theft Act 1968 included deception offences,[3] each requiring that D's conduct constituted a representation (whether by act or omission), that the representation caused V to form a false belief, that belief (caused by the representation) led V to behave in a prescribed way (transfer property, a valuable security, etc) and that as a result of the behaviour D (or another) gained. These offences which caused problems. The requirement for an operative deception meant that the offences were restricted in application. If V knew that D's statement was false,[4] or if V would have acted in the same way even if he had known it,[5] or if V did not rely on the false statement but arrived at the same erroneous conclusion from his own observation or some other source,[6] or, of course, if V did not read or hear the false statement made by D, no deception offence was committed. Numerous technical issues arose.[7] including such fundamental matters as: whether a representation could be made impliedly;[8] whether indifference as to the truth of a representation precluded a finding of an operative deception[9] and whether there

---

[1] Conspiracy because it requires conduct by two or more and fraudulent trading because it could only be committed by a corporate business.

[2] Astonishingly, the 2006 Act manages to introduce a general fraud offence, use the term fraud in labelling offences, but fails to provide any definition. cf N Yeo, 'Bull's Eye' (2007) 157 NLJ 212 at 213, suggesting that in practical terms the Government has succeeded in defining fraud.

[3] The offences were: obtaining property: 1968, s 15; obtaining a money transfer: 1968, s 15A; obtaining a pecuniary advantage: 1968, s 16; procuring the execution of a valuable security: 1968, s 20(2); obtaining services: 1978, s 1; securing the remission of a liability: 1978, s 2(1) (a); inducing a creditor to wait for or to forgo payment: 1978, s 2(1)(b); obtaining an exemption from or abatement of liability: 1978, s 2(1)(c).

[4] *Ady* (1835) 7 C & P 140; *Mills* (1857) Dears & B 205; *Hensler* (1870) 11 Cox CC 570; *Light* (1915) 11 Cr App R 111.

[5] *Edwards* [1978] Crim LR 49, CA, and commentary at 50.

[6] *Roebuck* (1856) Dears & B 24.

[7] For a detailed account see JC Smith, *The Law of Theft* (8th edn, 1997) Ch 4; and Ch 19 of the 11th edition of this book.

[8] *Ray* [1974] AC 370.

[9] *Charles* [1977] AC 177; *Lambie* [1982] AC 449.

could be a deception of a machine.[10] The courts were forced to adopt broad interpretations and the concept of deception was, arguably, being misconstrued.

Any amendment by Parliament would be unlikely to have the flexibility to deal with every fraudster's future initiatives. It was thought that to offer adequate protection from the growing problem of fraud, a more structured and coherent package of offences was necessary to keep pace with technology and modern methods of property transfer.[11] The Law Commission, Home Office (and the Attorney General in parliamentary debates on the Fraud Act[12]) catalogued the problems with the old law: too many offences; with too much overlap; too much technicality;[13] over-particularized offences;[14] difficulty in selecting charges where it was unclear how D proposed to receive the property (money order/cash/cheque each involving different offences); and obtaining by deception required an intention permanently to deprive.

The chosen solution to these problems was to repeal the deception offences and replace them with a general fraud offence in the Fraud Act 2006.[15]

23.1.3 Evolution of the Fraud Act 2006

The immediate history of the Fraud Act 2006 can be traced to the Law Commission Consultation Paper – No 155, *Legislating the Criminal Code: Fraud and Deception* (1999)[16] – followed by Law Commission Report No 276, *Fraud* (2002).[17] In turn, the Government responded with the Home Office Consultation Paper, *Fraud Law Reform* (2004)[18] which developed the Law Commission's proposals.

23.1.3.1 The merits of a general fraud offence

The merits of general fraud offences have been debated for decades.[19] Such an offence was considered by the CLRC when preparing the Theft Act 1968.[20] The Committee recommended an unusual form of fraud offence,[21] markedly different from that in the 2006 Act because it required that D deceived V. Once that proposal was rejected by Parliament, it seems that the general attitude, at least in the academic community, was against introducing such an offence. Several eminent commentators doubted whether a general fraud offence could ever be drafted which does not extend potential criminal liability too far.[22] There were, however,

---

[10] Belatedly the courts have taken a more robust stand on this and have been prepared to assume that there cannot be deception of machines for the purposes of dishonesty offences: see recently *Poland v Ulatowski* [2010] EWHC 2673 (Admin) at [32] and cf *Re Holmes* [2004] EWHC 2020 (Admin).

[11] Law Com Report No 276, *Fraud* (2002).

[12] See especially *Hansard*, HL, 22 June 2005, col 1652.

[13] See the comments in *Hansard*, HC, 12 June 2006, col 535 (Solicitor General).

[14] Law Com Report No 276, paras 3.11–3.24.

[15] In force from 15 Jan 2007: Fraud Act 2006 (Commencement) Order 2006, SI 3200; Fraud Act 2006, Sch 2, paras 2 and 3. See *Goldsmith* [2009] EWCA Crim 1840 below.

[16] (1999). See www.lawcom.gov.uk/docs/cp155.pdf.

[17] (2002). See www.lawcom.gov.uk/docs/lc276.pdf. Described by Dominic Grieve MP as a 'model of its kind' *Hansard*, HC, 12 June 2006, col 546.

[18] See www.homeoffice.gov.uk/documents/cons-fraud-law-reform.

[19] The merits were discussed in Law Com WP No 104, *Conspiracy to Defraud* (1987), and in LCCP 155, Parts 4 and 5. The model offered was an offence for 'Any person who dishonestly causes another to suffer [financial] prejudice, or who dishonestly makes a gain for himself or another', para 5.2.

[20] Eighth Report, paras 97–100.

[21] Cl 12(3) of the CLRC Draft Bill of 1966: 'A person who dishonestly, with a view to gain for himself or another, by any deception induces a person to do or refrain from doing any act shall on conviction on indictment be liable to imprisonment for a term not exceeding two years.'

[22] JC Smith, 'Fraud and The Criminal Law', in P Birks (ed), *Criminal Justice and Human Rights – Pressing Problems in the Law* (1995) vol 1, 49. Similar sentiments were expressed by another great theft scholar EJ Griew,

numerous strong supporters of such reform.[23] Most of the proponents of a general fraud offence argued for a model requiring not only that the prosecution prove that the defendant behaved dishonestly and with intent to gain/cause loss but also that there were economic interests actually imperilled by that conduct. This would certainly pose fewer problems than the model on which the Fraud Act is based, where there is no requirement to prove that the conduct has the potential to imperil economic interests or caused the victim to believe the representations.

23.1.3.2 Law Commission proposals

The Law Commission, in its Consultation Paper No 155, made recommendations to amend the deception offences, but declined to recommend any general fraud offence. This hesitant and unambitious approach was heavily criticized.[24] However, there was a discernable shift away from focusing on the wrong of 'deception'. The new focus was towards criminalizing instances of imperilling economic interests, with greater emphasis on the *mens rea* of D than on any objectively discernible harm.

The final Report No 276, *Fraud*, represented a complete *volte-face* from CP 155. The Report recommended a general fraud offence and the attached Draft Bill described three forms the offence should take. The proposals were endorsed by the Home Office in a further Consultation in 2004, in which additional proposals were suggested. The Government drew support for introducing broader, less technical offences from the deficiencies in the old law and from the need to combat the rising volume of fraud with estimates of £16bn lost in 2004.[25]

The Bill was, in general, very warmly received in Parliament where Law Lords approved of practically all of its terms (except the retention of the offence of conspiracy to defraud).[26] The Bill was passed almost unchallenged. The Act received Royal Assent on 8 November 2006.

23.2 The general fraud offence

The principal offence is the general fraud offence created by s 1 in the following terms:

(1) A person is guilty of fraud if he is in breach of any of the sections listed in subsection (2) (which provide for different ways of committing the offence).

(2) The sections are –

    (a) section 2 (fraud by false representation),

    (b) section 3 (fraud by failing to disclose information), and

    (c) section 4 (fraud by abuse of position).

The offence of fraud can be committed in one of three ways as proscribed by ss 2 to 4. Each is based on dishonest conduct against property interests, and carries a maximum 10-year

---

Theft, 141. See also the conclusions in Law Com WP No 56, *Criminal Law: Conspiracy to Defraud* (1974) paras 65, 81–82.

[23] See GR Sullivan, 'Fraud and Efficacy in the Criminal Law: A Proposal for a Wide Residual Offence' [1985] Crim LR 616; and 'Framing an Acceptable General Offence of Fraud' (1989) 53 J Crim L 92.

[24] See D Ormerod, 'A Bit of a Con' [1999] Crim LR 789.

[25] See HC Research Paper 06/31, at 3. See also press reports of 7 Mar 2007.

[26] See, eg, *Hansard,* HL, 22 June 2005, col 1661.

sentence on indictment.[27] They are incredibly wide offences deliberately drafted to avoid technicality.

23.2.1 General matters of interpretation

The 2006 Act is a short statute designed to be unburdened by the technicality which bedevilled the old law. The Act is not a codifying Act. It is modelled largely on the Law Commission Bill attached to the *Fraud* Report No 276 and that document will serve as a useful interpretative tool,[28] especially so given the Government's refusal to define many core elements of the offence in an attempt to ensure the broadest interpretation.[29]

The language of the statute is rather odd in places and in some respects more suited to the creation of statutory torts rather than crimes. Thus, for example, s 1 describes a person as being guilty if he is 'in breach of', and the principal offence ss 2 to 4 echo this by providing that 'a person is in breach of this section if...'

The offence of fraud can be charged in one of three forms: s 1(2)(a) (fraud by false representation under s 2); s 1(2)(b) (fraud by failure to disclose under s 3); s 1(2)(c) (fraud by abuse of position under s 4). The particularity and complexity of this scheme was unnecessary. Sections 2 to 4 could have been free-standing offences in their own right. If nothing else that would have rendered it easier for the courts to discern sentencing principles for the very different types of offending involved in each of these sections and may have generated greater clarity in prosecution policies.

Anecdotal evidence from prosecution policy makers is that the Act will be used in a restricted manner and that many of the most extreme possible uses of the legislation, identified throughout this chapter, will never see the light of a court room. It is to be hoped that this is the case. However, that does not excuse Parliament's creation of such wide and ill-defined offences, leaving to prosecutorial discretion the fair and efficient administration and application of the offences. Moreover, there is no guarantee that all prosecution agencies will adopt equally rigorous prosecution policies, nor that each agency will apply such policies with internal consistency.[30] Even if the prosecution agencies do all manage to achieve a sensible, measured, consistent approach to the Act, that does not prevent inappropriate use by private prosecution and malcontents. Such prosecutions may be taken over and stopped by the CPS, but the damage has by then been done – arrests have been made and accusations levelled from which individuals and companies suffer.

There was a great deal of overlap between the offences of theft and obtaining by deception under the old law. Under the new Act there will be considerable overlap with fraud and particularly with s 2. Prosecutors may well feel more comfortable charging theft where there is an overlap as theft is so wide, well established and uncontroversial (in practice at least) that few issues now arise on appeal: it is a safe and known option. Nevertheless, it should be noted that fraud requires no element of appropriation, no loss, no gain, no intention permanently to

---

[27] The Sentencing Guidelines Council produced a guideline on sentencing for the offences: www.sentencingcouncil.org.uk/docs/web_sentencing_for_fraud_statutory_offences.pdf.

[28] In addition to the Law Commission Consultation Paper and Report, valuable insights may be gleaned from the Home Office Consultation Paper, Home Office Paper of Responses to Consultation, and the House of Commons Research Paper 06/31.

[29] See, eg, the lack of definition of the term 'abuse' in s 4. In general, the Government were reluctant to provide a rigorous analysis of any terms.

[30] The larger scale frauds which come under scrutiny from the most senior lawyers are those to which more detailed attention is likely to be paid, and ironically it may be those to which the Act's provisions are applied most cautiously.

deprive and carries a higher sentence. The CPS reminds prosecutors of the particular benefit in banking cases.[31]

The courts' approach to the Act will depend on the way that the offences are prosecuted by the agencies. It is hoped that in the early cases to be dealt with on appeal some of the fundamental principles are established. Chief among those it is to be hoped is that the criminal law should not extend to those cases in which the defendant has a civil law *right* to be acting in the way that he has. The frontier of the criminal law ought, it is submitted, to be commensurate with that boundary. The likelihood is that the courts will adopt an approach treating the elements of the offences as 'ordinary English words' wherever possible. The legislation was designed to be non-technical and this will support what appears to be the Court of Appeal's current preferred approach to statutory interpretation in criminal law.

23.2.2 Jurisdiction

The courts continue to have jurisdiction when property is fraudulently gained/lost in England or Wales, even though the conduct causing this result has taken place in another country (or countries as where D in the USA makes false representations to V in Canada causing V's London bank account to be debited). The Criminal Justice Act 1993 provides that if any act or omission, proof of which is required for conviction of a relevant crime (a 'relevant event'), takes place here it will be capable of prosecution in England and Wales. Schedule 1 to the 2006 Act amends the 1993 Act to extend the meaning of 'relevant event' to include:

(a) if the fraud involved an intention to make a gain and the gain occurred, *that occurrence*; and

(b) if the fraud involved an intention to cause a loss or to expose another to a risk of loss and the loss occurred, *that occurrence* [emphasis added].

Where, however, D performs one of the elements of the fraud offence abroad (for example, making the false representation under s 2, or abusing the financial position under s 4), but intends to make a gain which will occur in England and Wales or cause a loss in this jurisdiction, the 1993 Act (as amended by the 2006 Act) will not apply unless *there is an actual gain or loss within England and Wales*. The Act could have extended the meaning of 'relevant event' to include the making of the false representation etc with intent rather than the result (given that these are now conduct crimes), but 'curiously'[32] did not do so.

23.2.3 Commencement

Transitional provisions are provided in the Act.[33] The old deception offences under the Theft Acts offences will continue to apply for any offences partly[34] committed before 15 January 2007, that is where a relevant event' occurs before that date.[35] In *Goldsmith*[36] the Court of

---

[31] The credit/debit status of any bank accounts debited is irrelevant to the Fraud Act offences. All that is in issue is D's right to use the account; it is not necessary to prove or demonstrate any consequences of fraud (though they will clearly be material to sentence, compensation and confiscation). 'Preddy' type difficulties will not arise (where the property obtained had not belonged to another); Fraud Act offences do not require an intent permanently to deprive; a charge should describe what actually happened and reflect the true criminality; and the indictment should be as simple as reasonably possible. See www.cps.gov.uk/legal/d_to_g/fraud_act.

[32] See *Blackstone*, B5.99.

[33] Set out in Sch 2. Under para 3(1) of Sch 2.

[34] Para 3(2) of Sch 2 defines an offence as being 'partly committed' when: a relevant event occurred before 15 Jan 2007, and another 'relevant event' occurred on or after 15 Jan 2007.

[35] Relevant event is, for these purposes, defined in para 3(3) of Sch 2 as: '...any act, omission or other event (including any result of one or more acts or omissions) proof of which is required for conviction of the offence'.

[36] [2009] EWCA Crim 1840.

Appeal noted that the date in an indictment is not normally to be regarded as a material aver-ment. Although not contentious in the case itself, it is submitted that the prosecution ought to be especially careful with dates in relation to transitional periods such as this.[37]

Where it is unclear whether a 'relevant event' occurred before or after commencement it will be necessary for the Crown to put alternative counts on the indictment under the 2006 Act and the previous legislation. This practice was endorsed in *Bellman*[38] where the House of Lords held that where there is *prima facie* evidence that a defendant has committed either crime A or crime B then both crimes may be charged and left to the jury, even though proof of crime A will establish that D cannot have committed crime B and *vice versa*. Where it is clear that D has committed crime A or crime B but there is no evidence to say when the crime has been committed then neither crime can be left to the jury.[39]

23.2.4 Common elements of the fraud offence

The forms of the offence are discussed fully below. In outline: s 2 involves making a false representation with dishonest intent to gain or cause loss; s 3 involves dishonestly failing to disclose information when under a legal duty to do so and with intent to gain or cause loss; and s 4 involves dishonestly abusing a position in which one is expected to safeguard the financial interests of another.

23.2.4.1 Dishonesty

The principal element of *mens rea* for the offence of fraud in each of its three forms is that of dishonesty. The Law Commission and the Home Office intended that the *Ghosh* definition should apply, and this was confirmed repeatedly[40] in the parliamentary debates. That test is examined in detail in Chapter 19 above.

Reliance on the *Ghosh* test, with its inherent unpredictability, increases the chances that more cases will go to trial as defendants have little to lose by 'trying their luck' with a jury. In terms of principle, the lack of certainty in the substantive law and inefficiency in the criminal justice system render this undesirable. There is also a sting in the tail: at some point in the future, it may well be that fraud cases are conducted without a jury on which D can chance his luck.[41]

Article 7

Particular difficulties are anticipated with Art 7 of the ECHR and challenges to the Act on that basis are anticipated.[42] The Joint Parliamentary Committee on Human Rights, in its Fourteenth Report[43] scrutinizing the Fraud Bill concluded that the new offence is compatible with the ECHR, Art 7 and common law requirements of certainty:

the new general offence of fraud *is not* a general dishonesty offence. Rather, it embeds as an element in the definition of the offence some identifiable morally dubious conduct to which the test of dis-honesty may be applied, as the Law Commission correctly observed is required by the principle of legal certainty. We are therefore satisfied that, as defined in the Bill, the new general offence of fraud

---

[37] This has caused problems in confiscation proceedings and in conspiracy charges where the tendency is to look to evidence of the first overt act performed by D and/or the date when D joined a conspiracy.

[38] [1989] AC 836.

[39] See on this *C* [2005] EWCA Crim 3533, Ch 18 above, p 716.

[40] See *Hansard*, HL Debates, 19 July 2005, col 1424 (A-G); House of Commons Research Paper 31/06, at 14; Standing Committee B, 20 June 2006, col 8 (Solicitor General).

[41] See the attempts to amend the Criminal Justice Act 2003, s 43, which has not yet been brought into force.

[42] See Ch 19.

[43] See www.publications.parliament.uk/pa/jt200506/jtselect/jtrights/134/13402.htm.

satisfies the common law and ECHR requirement that criminal offences be defined with sufficient clarity and precision to enable the public to predict with sufficient certainty whether or not they will be liable.[44]

The Committee did, however, confirm that:

a general dishonesty offence would be incompatible with the common law principle of legality. In our view it would also be in breach of the requirement of legal certainty in Articles 5 and 7 ECHR for the same reasons.[45]

The validity of this argument is questionable.[46] It is not strikingly obvious that in all cases there will have been 'morally dubious' conduct over and above dishonesty. In the s 2 offence, the additional morally dubious conduct seems to be little more than making a false representation – that is, lying, which might also be fairly described in many contexts at least as 'being dishonest'. That is, the 'additional' element which the Committee regards as preventing the offence being one solely of dishonesty! Similarly, in s 4, the morally dubious conduct additional to dishonesty seems hard to identify, it could be something as innocuous as failing to work for an employer as hard as one might. It is true that there is also the element of an intent to gain or cause loss, but that is extremely wide and can be morally neutral in some cases, particularly perhaps where D intends only to get that which is his (which is nevertheless an intent to gain[47]).

At its widest, D could be liable under s 2 for making a statement which he knew might be misleading with intent to gain his own property temporarily – provided that he is also dishonest.

Claim of right

It should also be noted that there is no equivalent to s 2 of the Theft Act 1968 and therefore, D's claims to be acting under a claim of right are no guarantee of acquittal. Dishonesty under the Act is based solely on *Ghosh*.[48] It is submitted that this is a fundamental flaw and that a claim of right is as inconsistent with dishonesty under ss 2 to 4 as it is for theft. If D has a claim of right to the property he should not ordinarily be at risk of criminal liability.[49] It is unlikely that in practice any defendant would be found to be dishonest under *Ghosh* in such circumstances. Equally, it is submitted that there should be no criminal liability for the defendant who genuinely believes he has a claim of right to the property which he seeks to gain, or indeed where D genuinely believes he has a claim of right to cause V to lose that property. It is unlikely, though not impossible, that someone in such circumstances would be found to be dishonest within the meaning in *Ghosh*. A jury might well think a person dishonest who had made a deliberately false representation even where he did so to get something to which he thought he was entitled.[50] It is doubtful that it is in the public interest to prosecute where the claim is a genuine one and substantiated by evidence.

---

[44] Para 2.14, emphasis added. See also the A-G's statements in debate: *Hansard*, 19 July 2005, col 1424.

[45] ibid, para 2.12.

[46] See above.

[47] See below, p 932.

[48] Above, p 829. See *Melwani* [1989] Crim LR 565, CA.

[49] cf the Law Commission recommending that a claim of right ought not be a defence in all cases, No 276, para 7.66, which was a reversal of its position in CP 155.

[50] In *Falconer-Atlee* (1973) 58 Cr App R 348 at 358, a case of theft, the judge's direction on dishonesty was held to be defective because he omitted to tell the jury that s 2(1)(a) expressly provided that a person with a claim of right was not dishonest. Yet, since D's mistake, if any, was a mistake of fact, the direction does not seem to have been necessary or, indeed, appropriate. The court in *Woolven* distinguished that case, not because it was a case of

It is submitted that a mistake of civil law giving rise to a belief in a claim of right ought to be a defence.[51] One argument in support of such an interpretation is the desire to maintain coherence between the offence of theft and that of fraud.[52] If D believes the property to be his own, whether through a mistake of fact or a mistake of law, he has a defence if the charge is brought as theft. There are good reasons to suggest that it would be wrong that he should have no defence if the charge is brought under s 1 of the 2006 Act. If the judge has to direct the jury expressly on the theft charge that claim of right is a defence (and it is submitted that he should), then it is desirable that he should also have to do so on the fraud charge, instead of leaving the jury to deduce this from the general *Ghosh* direction.[53]

If this interpretation is correct, D should have a defence in the following case: X bought D's car with a worthless cheque, X sold the car to a *bona fide* purchaser, V. V refuses to give up the car to D. D, believing that he is entitled to have the car back, recovers possession by pretending to be a mechanic from V's garage collecting the car for servicing. He would be able to rely on the defence in s 2 of the 1968 Act if charged with theft, and ought therefore to be acquitted if charged with fraud contrary to s 1(2)(a) and s 2 of the Fraud Act 2006. D has certainly made a false representation; but if he genuinely believes he is entitled to possession of the car, it is submitted that the jury should be told that he is not 'dishonest' for the purposes of the section.

Probably the same result should follow where D's belief relates not to any specific property but to the repayment of debt. For example, D has been V's mistress. On the termination of the relationship, V promises to pay D £100. Later he declines to do so. D is advised by a foreign lawyer that she is entitled to the money. By a false representation she seeks to persuade V to pay her £100.[54] In such a case there was, and no doubt is, a sufficient claim of right to negative an 'intent to steal'; and, if so, there should equally be a defence to an offence of fraud under s 1(2)(a) and s 2 for false representation. A more difficult case is that where D intends to gain something other than the thing to which he has a claim of right. Would people suppose, for example, that they have a right to behave fraudulently to a debtor to compel him to pay?

One important consequence of the absence of an automatic and complete defence of a claim of right is that under s 2, for example, D's attempts to qualify his false representations with a disclaimer will not automatically lead to acquittal unless the qualification is judged sufficient to displace any degree of falsity. If D makes a false statement in a company prospectus, it may not be sufficient that he includes a disclaimer that, for example, 'no investment should be made on the basis of the information in this document alone'. A jury may well find such conduct dishonest when viewed in the round.

theft but, apparently, on the ground that the direction in the instant case did, in effect, if not in so many words, tell the jury to acquit if they thought D might have a claim of right.

[51] The CPS has issued guidance to prosecutors stating that: 'The criminal law is not a suitable vehicle to regulate such disputes. Before a criminal charge can proceed the ownership of any property must be absolutely clear. If that ownership is in real dispute, the criminal law should not be invoked until ownership has been established in the civil courts. However, circumstances will arise where the issues are clear and the offences are serious. If so, prosecution may be required in the public interest. Prosecutors should ensure that the state of affairs between the parties has not changed prior to any trial. This may affect both the public interest and the evidential test.' See www.cps.gov.uk/legal/d_to_g/fraud_act.

[52] Arguably, the moral wrong in the two offences is quite distinct, with theft being designed to protect property rights and the associated rights of transfer of property, etc and fraud being to protect against dishonest exploitation of others. The House of Lords' broad interpretation of theft in *Hinks* and *Gomez* (above, p 787) undermines such a distinction.

[53] In *Parker* (1910) 74 JP 208, Ridley J held that a claim of right was no answer to a charge of demanding money upon a forged document with intent to defraud. In *Woolven*, the court thought that case was not a decisive authority against a claim of right defence under s 15; and *Parker* has been overruled by the Forgery and Counterfeiting Act 1981, s 10(2).

[54] cf *Bernhard* [1938] 2 KB 264.

In the event of a prosecution for an alleged fraud where D has a claim of right or a belief in a claim of right, it is important that the jury is directed that dishonesty is a separate element of the offence. D may deliberately make a false representation, yet not act dishonestly in doing so.[55] The jury should always be directed that they must be satisfied that the conduct alleged under ss 2 to 4 as appropriate was done dishonestly.[56]

23.2.4.2 With intent to gain or cause loss or to expose to a risk of loss

Section 5 defines the meaning of 'gain' and 'loss' for the purposes of ss 2 to 4.

(1) The references to gain and loss in sections 2 to 4 are to be read in accordance with this section.

(2) 'Gain' and 'loss' –

    (a) extend only to gain or loss in money or other property;

    (b) include any such gain or loss whether temporary or permanent;

and 'property' means any property whether real or personal (including things in action and other intangible property).

(3) 'Gain' includes a gain by keeping what one has, as well as a gain by getting what one does not have.

(4) 'Loss' includes a loss by not getting what one might get, as well as a loss by parting with what one has.

The definitions are essentially the same as those in s 34(2)(a) of the Theft Act 1968.[57] Under these definitions, 'gain' and 'loss' are limited to gain and loss in money or other property. 'Property', in this context is defined as in s 4(1) of the Theft Act 1968.[58] The definition of 'property' covers all forms of property; the Government was keen to ensure coherence with the Theft Act.[59] None of the special exceptions in s 4 of the 1968 apply: there can be fraud with intent to gain/cause loss of land, wild animals and flora, but they cannot be stolen.

Loss or gain

In most cases 'an intention to gain' and an 'intention to cause loss' will go hand in hand; V's loss will be D's gain. The phrase, 'intent to cause loss' is not, however, superfluous. There may be circumstances in which D intends to cause a loss to V without any corresponding gain to D, for example, where D lies to V to pay X. Problems arose in some cases under the old law because the deception might cause a gain which did not correspond to a loss.[60]

The consequence of making the intentions alternative[61] sufficient bases for liability is that the general fraud offence becomes even broader. For example, D who starts a false rumour that V is going out of business, commits the s 2 form of the offence if he does so with intent to lead customers away from V, intending V to lose or be exposed to a risk of loss and is regarded

---

[55] See *Wright* [1960] Crim LR 366, *Griffiths* [1966] 1 QB 589, [1965] 2 All ER 448 and *Talbott* [1995] Crim LR 396.

[56] Under the old law see *Potger* (1970) 55 Cr App R 42; cf *McVey* [1988] Crim LR 127 and commentary.

[57] cf in particular their use in relation to false accounting, Theft Act 1968 s 17, below, p 926. They are also used in the Trade Marks Act 1994.

[58] Above, Ch 19, p 796.

[59] See Standing Committee B, 20 June 2006, col 32 (Solicitor General).

[60] The *Guinness* case was one famous example of this. See *Saunders* [1996] Cr App R 463, and more generally, N Kochan and H Pym, *The Guinness Affair* (1987).

[61] C Withey, 'The Fraud Act 2006' (2007) 71 J Crim L 220 suggests that both an intent to gain and an intent to cause loss must be proved, but this is difficult to square with the words of the section.

as dishonest in doing so.[62] There is no requirement that D seeks to gain by these actions. It is debatable whether such conduct ought properly to be described as fraud.

Intention

Intention should bear its ordinary meaning, and should extend as elsewhere in the criminal law to include the foresight of a virtually certain consequence.[63] This may be significant in extending the scope of the offences. For example, it is sufficient that D makes a false representation foreseeing that it is virtually certain to cause loss to V although that is not his purpose, and although he hopes that V will not lose.[64]

23.2.4.3 Remoteness

It should be noted that although the fraud offences are not result-based crimes, the element of intent to gain/cause loss does involve a causal link that must be established. Under s 2, for example, it is '*by the*' false representation that D must intend to make the gain or cause the loss. This prompts the question: how remote can D's intentions be? Suppose that D makes false representations to induce V, a wealthy banker, to marry him. Is he guilty of the s 2 offence if one intention is to enrich himself? Presumably such matters will be left to the jury to determine.[65]

What of the more thoughtful defence: that it is not by the false representation (under s 2) or the failure to disclose (under s 3) or the abuse of position (under s 4) that D intends to gain/cause loss, but by some other aspect of his conduct?[66] One obvious example is where D makes a number of representations in relation to a sale: eg that a car is a genuine VW, that it has a specific mileage and that it has had one careful 'lady owner'. Can D argue that the final representation, though false, is not one by which he intended to make a gain? This may well become subsumed within his plea of a lack of dishonesty, but it is a distinct element of the offence and deserves to be drawn to the jury's attention. The jury will properly have regard to all the circumstances. The fact that the representation relates to a peripheral matter will not *entitle* the defendant to an acquittal.[67] What is in issue is solely a matter of D's intent. It seems then to be a question of fact and degree in every case whether what was said was intended to be a misrepresentation by which the gain or loss would be made.

The jury would have to be sure under, for example, s 2 that (i) D made a representation that was untrue or misleading, and in relation to *that* representation,[68] (ii) D knew it was or might have been false, and (iii) that D made the representation dishonestly, and (iv) that D, by making *that* representation, intended to make a gain/cause loss etc.

The problem may be dealt with more easily where D has made two or more false representations. In such a case the Crown may incorporate all the representations in one count indicting the conduct as, for example, 'falsely representing the details of the car for sale' and rely on the

---

[62] See No 276, para 4.13.

[63] See *Hansard*, HL, 19 July 2005, col 1414 (A-G). cf the definition advanced by the House of Lords in the context of murder in *Woollin* [1998] AC 82.

[64] See the explanation of the concept in Ch 5 above.

[65] The Court of Appeal seems reluctant to impose clear rules of remoteness in criminal law contexts. See, eg, *Kennedy (No 2)* [2005] EWCA Crim 785, cf the decision of the House of Lords [2008] UKHL 37. In *Idress* [2011] EWHC 624 (Admin) a conviction under s 2 was upheld where D had persuaded X to sit his driving test for him representing himself to be D. Presumably the property D was to gain was the driving licence.

[66] See the correspondence between Ormerod and Gardner [2007] Crim LR 661.

[67] A proposal that the misrepresentation must be a 'material' one was expressly rejected by the A-G during the debates: *Hansard*, HL, 19 July 2005, cols 1419–1420. See also *Lancaster* [2010] EWCA Crim 370 on the element of materiality not need to be causal in false accounting – below p 930.

[68] Each representation if there are many charged.

two statements (original form of vehicle and previous ownership) as evidence of the dishonest intent to gain. This raises a further problem which the Act does not address – must each false representation be alleged in a separate count in the indictment? There is every likelihood that prosecutors will wrap up a number of representations in one count. In a long-running investment fraud this matter might be critical and inhibit the defendant's case, especially if he wants to deny causal intent. It may also give rise to a 'Brown problem':[69] six jurors might think that D is guilty because of representation A and six because of representation B.

Less problematical is the case where D uses a false representation in order to secure a contract, and intends to fulfil the terms of the contract and give value for money. To be liable in such a case the Crown must surely have to show that D foresaw that it was virtually certain that his conduct in making the false representation would lead him to gain. There are numerous instances of convictions under the Act for D making a false representation as to his eligibility to work in the UK, securing employment and working to be paid,[70] or even making false representations as to having a clean driving licence which was a prerequisite for the job.[71]

Claims of entitlement to the gain

It is not necessarily a good defence that D believes he has a right to the gain or loss he seeks. If he has such a belief, then he might not be dishonest under *Ghosh*, but he still has the intention to gain (and/or to cause loss). Should it be an offence for A to lie to B to get back money owed to him? In view of the clear authority on the construction of the same expression in false accounting,[72] it seems hopeless to argue under the Fraud Act that there is in fact no gain where a person merely secures the payment of that which he is owed. The Court of Appeal has held that the element of intent to gain is also satisfied by proof of an intention to 'acquire' even that property to which D is entitled. *A fortiori*, there will be a relevant intention where D genuinely though mistakenly believes that he is entitled to the gain (or to cause the loss). Such cases will be rare. Greater emphasis will therefore be placed on the dishonesty element.

It can be argued that the definition in s 5 is too wide since it criminalizes the situation where D intends V not to get something which V might have gained, even though V was not entitled to it. For example, under s 2, if V asks D for a loan and D denies it him by saying falsely that he has no money to spare, D has made a false representation with intent to cause V not to gain that which he might[73] have obtained.[74] V has at most suffered a loss of a chance. D might avoid liability by arguing that a simple refusal, however malicious or dishonest is not a 'representation' but an explanation for the refusal. Even if it is a representation, D might claim the words were not intended to cause loss or damage but designed solely to ease the loss and damage caused by the refusal. D's additional, or alternative, saving grace is that he is probably not going to be regarded as dishonest in those circumstances.[75]

The extent of possible criminal liability may seem excessively broad since it includes making a misleading statement with intent to cause someone to be exposed to the risk of temporarily not being able to get that which he might otherwise have got. How will the prosecution prove the intention to cause loss by not getting what one might get? Is it enough in practice that D believes that there was a chance that V would make a gain?

---

[69] See *Brown* (1984) 79 Cr App R 115.

[70] See *Dziruni* [2008] EWCA Crim 667; *Haboub* [2007] EWCA Crim 3327.

[71] *Asif* [2008] EWCA Crim 3348.

[72] *A-G's Reference (No 1 of 2001)* [2002] Crim LR 844.

[73] The offence would have been much tighter with a requirement that D intended that loss/gain would occur.

[74] See GR Sullivan, 'Fraud and Efficiency in the Criminal Law' [1985] Crim LR 616.

[75] See Standing Committee B, 20 June 2006, cols 33–35.

Exposure to temporary loss

Unlike theft, there is no requirement that D acts with intent to deprive V *permanently* of any property. It would seem to be sufficient under s 2, for example, that D makes a false representation to V with intent to cause V to lend D property[76] which D intends to return in an unaltered form. The offence comes close to criminalizing dishonest deprivation of the value of an item's usefulness. This strains the property-based foundation of the offence. It supports the argument that the offence is one centred on the wrong of lying.[77]

Intention to expose another to a risk of loss

It is sufficient that D intends that V will be exposed to the risk of loss; there is no need for the Crown to prove that D had a more specific intention that V will actually lose. D who makes a false representation on his health insurance form will be liable (under s 2). He intends the insurance company to be exposed to a risk of loss, even though he desperately hopes that he will remain healthy and they will not incur actual loss.

D, who makes a false statement in a job reference for V, will be liable if he intends that V will thereby not be promoted and attain the higher salary appropriate to that post.

23.3 Section 2: fraud by false representation

The offence created by s 1(2)(a) of the Act is incredibly broad. It is heavily used. In 2009/10 there were 27,139 fraud offences recorded (false representation: cheque, plastic card and on-line bank accounts).[78]

This offence is described in s 2, which provides:

(1) A person is in breach of this section if he –

    (a) dishonestly makes a false representation, and

    (b) intends, by making the representation –

        (i) to make a gain for himself or another, or

        (ii) to cause loss to another or to expose another to a risk of loss.

(2) A representation is false if –

    (a) it is untrue or misleading, and

    (b) the person making it knows that it is, or might be, untrue or misleading.

(3) 'Representation' means any representation as to fact or law, including a representation as to the state of mind of –

    (a) the person making the representation, or

    (b) any other person.

(4) A representation may be express or implied.

(5) For the purposes of this section a representation may be regarded as made if it (or anything implying it) is submitted in any form to any system or device designed to receive, convey or respond to communications (with or without human intervention).

---

[76] Even that to which D is already entitled. cf *Zemmel* [1985] Crim LR 213, and the Law Commission Working Paper on *Conspiracy to Defraud* (1988) para 4.4 rejecting this as a sufficient basis for criminal liability.

[77] See D Ormerod, 'Criminalising Lying' [2007] Crim LR 193; cf J Horder (2011) 127 LQR 37.

[78] J Flatley et al, *Crime in England and Wales 2009/10, Findings from the British Crime Survey and police recorded crime* (2010) 32.

Section 1 provides that the maximum sentence on indictment is 10 years' imprisonment.

The *actus reus* requires proof that D: made a representation, which is untrue or mislead-ing, and the *mens rea* requires proof that: D knew the representation was, or knew that it might be, false, and he acted dishonestly, and with intent to gain or cause loss or expose to a risk of loss.

23.3.1 Conduct-based offence

Crucial to an understanding of the operation and scope of the offence is an appreciation of the conduct-based nature of liability. Under the old law,[79] it had to be proved that D's conduct ac-tually deceived V and caused him to do whatever act was appropriate to the offence charged. Under s 2, there is no need to prove: a result of any kind; that the alleged victim or indeed any person believed any representation; that any person acted on a representation; or that D suc-ceeded in making a gain or causing a loss by the representation.

This shift from a result-based to conduct-based offence has numerous other practical implications. The principal aim is to make the offence easier to prove, and there is little doubt that in most cases this objective will be achieved. The effect is that D may be liable for the false representations even where they had no bearing on V.

Classic problems which recurred under the old law are greatly diminished, if not eradi-cated. For example, in *Laverty*,[80] a case under s 15 of the 1968 Act, D changed the number plates and chassis identification plate of a car and sold it to V. It was held that this consti-tuted a representation by conduct that the car was the original car to which these numbers had been assigned; but D's conviction for obtaining the price of the car by deception from V was quashed on the ground that it was not proved that the deception operated on V's mind. There was no direct evidence to that effect – V said he bought the car because he thought D was the owner – and it was not a necessary inference.[81] Under s 2 of the 2006 Act, the offence is committed as soon as D dishonestly changes the number plate or at the latest offered it for sale with intent to gain.

23.3.1.1 Time of commission of the offence

One of the most important consequences of the shift to a conduct-based offence is that the s 2 crime is complete before the point in time at which any person acts in response to the false representation (as would have been required for a deception offence). A s 2 offence may also be completed later in time. For example, whereas under the old law D could only be liable if his deception occurred before the relevant property passed to him, under the s 2 offence, D can be liable if he makes a false representation after the entire proprietary interest has passed to him. If, after D, a motorist, fills his tank so that the entire proprietary interest in the petrol has passed to him, he falsely represents to V the garage cashier that it will be paid for by D's employer, he does not obtain the petrol *by* that deception. On the same facts, under s 2 once D falsely represents to V that it will be paid for by his firm, he commits the offence irrespective

---

[79] Even under the pre-1968 law, it was necessary to show that the false pretences *caused* the loss. cf S Farrell, N Yeo and G Ladenbury who suggest that the 2006 Act is a return to the pre-1968 position – *Blackstone's Guide to the Fraud Act 2006* (2007) para 1.09.

[80] [1970] 3 All ER 432. cf *Talbot* [1995] Crim LR 396.

[81] If the only flaw in the prosecution's case was that the representation did not influence V, the court had power to substitute a conviction for an attempt. They did not do so, possibly because there was also insufficient evidence that D intended to deceive V into buying the car by this representation. The purpose of changing the plates may well have been not to deceive the buyer, but to deceive the police, the true owner and anyone else who might iden-tify the vehicle. It would seem that the prosecution would have been on stronger ground had they alleged that D had made a representation by conduct that he had a right to sell the car.

of the fact that the property in the petrol has passed.[82] He intends by the false representation about payment to cause loss to the garage dishonestly.

23.3.1.2 A victimless crime?[83]

It seems that no specific victim(s) need to be identified, because no loss needs to have been incurred and no person needs to have believed or acted on D's representation. The fact that D must have acted with the intention to gain or cause loss[84] means, however, that the offence will remain focused on the potential effect a false representation might have had on the economic interests of others.

Under the old law, the normal way of proving that a deception was relied on was to call V to say that he had relied on it.[85] Under s 2, there is clearly no need to call a victim since there need be no result. In most instances, prosecutors may still prefer to call a victim or intended victim who can give unequivocal evidence of the representation being made and the surrounding circumstances which will support the allegations that it was made dishonestly, with knowledge as to its falsity and with intent to gain or cause loss. In some rare cases it might be possible to invite the jury to infer that the false representation was made without calling evidence of that fact.[86]

23.3.2 *Actus reus*

23.3.2.1 'Makes a representation'

Whether a representation is made is a question of fact for the jury.

By whom representation may be made

The offence can be committed by any 'person' who makes a false representation. Clearly this can include a corporation as where a false representation is contained in a corporation's prospectus for potential investors.[87]

D will be liable for his personal representations. He might also be liable for representations of third parties which he can be said unambiguously to have adopted, as for example where a manager adopts statements made by his predecessor. D will be liable as for the false

---

[82] cf under the old law *Collis-Smith* [1971] Crim LR 716, CA. He may also be guilty of making off without payment which is not abolished. See Ch 22.

[83] On this concept see H Packer *The Limits of the Criminal Sanction*, 151–152. Packer suggests that victimless crimes pose a peculiar problem for criminal justice because the State is more likely to resort to the use of covert surveillance. Unlike the paradigm examples offered by Packer, fraud is not a 'victimless crime'. Rather, by bringing forward in time the completion of the *actus reus* of the offence (ie completion being as soon as the relevant representation is made, the offence is committed without the requirement that anyone actually believes it, let alone acts on it), Parliament has therefore *created* a victimless crime that is quite unlike the traditional understanding of 'fraud'.

[84] Above, p 878.

[85] *Laverty* [1970] 3 All ER 432, CA; *Tirado* (1974) 59 Cr App R 80 at 87, CA. but it was possible to secure a conviction without a victim giving evidence or even making a statement, where the false representation could be proved from the documents or admissions made by D. It was, of course, always possible to prove the more onerous concept of deception by inference from other facts without direct evidence: *Tirado* (1974) 59 Cr App R 80 at 87, CA and see *PS* [2007] EWCA Crim, 12 July (unreported).

[86] See, eg, *Greig* [2010] EWCA Crim 1183 in which the reason for the payments by the vulnerable V to the cowboy builders were plain enough for the conviction to be safe.

[87] Such representations are already criminalized by the Financial Services and Markets Act 2000, s 397. Within that section a distinction is made between recklessly and knowingly making a false statement. See *Bailey* [2005] EWCA Crim 3487.

representations of his agents, either as the principal provided he has the relevant *mens rea*[88] or as an aider or abettor, counsellor or procurer of his agent's false representations. D may also be liable for making a false representation through an innocent agent.

It is important also to recall the significance of the fact that it is sufficient under s 2 that D intends *either* to gain *or* to cause loss. If D offers a credit card for payment for goods in a shop, he makes a representation to the shopkeeper that payment will be made and that he has the authority to use the card.[89] If the latter representation is false but D knows that the shop will be paid by the credit card company, D still commits the offence. He is making a false representation to the shopkeeper with intent to cause loss/expose to a risk of loss the credit card company (if they pay) or the shopkeeper (if the credit card company will not pay because, for example, D's card is outside the expiry date and the shop ought to have refused it).[90] However, only one offence is created despite the different elements of intent to gain, intent to cause loss and intent to expose to a risk of loss.

When is a representation made?

Although this seems like an unnecessary question, on closer analysis, there are a number of potential difficulties with this element of timing. It is arguable that the representation is made either (i) as soon as D articulates it? (ii) only if it is also addressed to something? (iii) only when it is actually perceived as such by a person, that is, when it is communicated? If D stands alone in the middle of an empty market and shouts 'Guaranteed solid gold watch for sale', if the watch is not solid gold and D knows that it is not, he is making a false statement, but is it a representation? Under the old law, where D had to cause V to believe the representation, the issue did not arise, because there had to be a completed communication.

It is significant that the Act uses the term 'representation' rather than 'communication'.[91] The latter term would ordinarily imply that there was a recipient, of the statement which D made, even if that recipient ignored the statement completely. However, even that restrictive interpretation of the concept of communication cannot be asserted beyond doubt. In *DPP v Collins*,[92] the House of Lords held that the offence making a grossly offensive communication[93] – could be committed even if no person was in receipt of the communication. It is submitted that under s 2 of the Fraud Act 2006 there need not be a completed communication in the sense that a person must read or hear or see D's statement in order for it to constitute a representation. A representation would seem to be 'made' as soon as articulated, but in accordance with the ordinary use of the word, a representation must be made 'to' someone or something.[94] A representation could include a statement being made to the whole world.[95] If this interpretation is correct, this could have significant repercussions for the scope of the offence. In most cases it will render the full offence complete far earlier in time than would

---

[88] cf the position in tort where an innocent principal is liable for the fraud of his agent, *Kingsnorth Trust Ltd v Bell* [1986] 1 WLR 119, CA. The agent is not liable under the Misrepresentation Act 1967, s 2(1), since no contract exists between the agent and the representee: *Resolute Maritime Inc v Nippon Kaiji Kyokai, The Skopas* [1983] 1 WLR 857.

[89] See below, p 892.

[90] See further below, p 892.

[91] cf C Withey, 'The Fraud Act 2006' (2007) 71 J Crim L 220, suggesting that the offence is not committed unless a communication is completed. This is difficult to square with the statutory wording and intent.

[92] [2006] UKHL 40, [2006] 1 WLR 2223.

[93] Communications Act 2003, s 127.

[94] In civil law, in misrepresentation the representee must be the person to whom the representation is made or those contemplated by D that the representation might reach or those whom it did reach and who acted on it: *Swift v Winterbotham* (1873) LR 8 QB 244 at 253.

[95] See *Silverlock* [1894] 2 QB 766, CCCR (fraudulent advert in newspaper).

have been possible with deception offences. In resolving this difficulty in interpretation, it is helpful to have regard to the Act's aim to criminalize the making of representations to a machine, and the specific provision in subs 5 included to ensure that such conduct constitutes a representation.

Representations to machines

The prevailing opinion under the old law was that it is not possible in law to deceive a machine.[96] 'To deceive is . . . to induce a man to believe that a thing is true which is false, and which the person practising the deceit knows or believes to be false.'[97] Deceit can be practised only on a human mind.[98] Where D obtained property, etc, or even a service, as the result of some dishonest practice on a machine, without the intervention of a human mind, he could not be guilty of an obtaining offence.[99] Whereas the only recourse used to be for D to be open to conviction for an offence of, for example, making off without payment contrary to the 1978 Act, s 3(1), he might now commit the s 11 offence considered below.

The problem of how to criminalize the 'deception' of a machine became an acute one as businesses relied increasingly on automated facilities to pay by credit card via automated telephone systems and the internet.[100] Such activity is not restricted to the consumer context. In Holmes,[101] for example, D faced extradition for his conduct when, as an official in a German bank he had dishonestly used a co-worker's password to credit an account under his control in a Dutch bank. The entirely automated banking practice, of which the court took judicial notice, was such that the transfer was not complete until the Dutch bank received confirmation from the German bank. In that case, the court observed that the old authorities, including, in particular, Davies v Flackett,[102] were not strictly binding authority for the proposition that deception of a machine or computer is not a deception, but accepted that the general view is that it is not possible to deceive a machine. The court regarded this as regrettable, and urged a new offence of theft or some cognate offence to deal with the problem. Sections 2 and 11 of the Act do so.

The Government was clearly not confident that, under s 2, a 'representation' would be interpreted to include any statements made to machines and computers as where D types in his PIN on a chip and PIN device.[103] To ensure that such conduct is within the scope of s 2, the Government introduced an amendment to cl 2. Section 2(5) now provides:

---

[96] Griew, Theft, paras 8–12; see also Williams, TBCL, 794 and Smith, Property Offences, para 11.02. Arlidge and Parry on Fraud, para 4.054, however, are more doubtful. Some devices used to operate machines are now 'instruments' for the purposes of the law of forgery. See also I Walden, Computer Crimes and Digital Investigations (2007) paras 3.50–3.53. See, however, the first instance civil decision of HHJ Seymour QC concluding that an action for deceit can be founded on lies told to a machine: Renault UK v Fleetpro Technical Service [2007] EWHC 2541 (QB).

[97] Re London and Globe Finance Corpn Ltd [1903] 1 Ch 728 at 732.

[98] See (1972) Law Soc Gaz 576 and Law Com WP 56, at 51.

[99] cf the recent decision of the Administrative Court in Poland v Ulatowski [2010] EWHC 2673 (Admin) in which Roderick Evans J was prepared to assume that an ATM machine could not be deceived by D using his own card beyond its overdraft limit [32].

[100] In 2009/10 there were 7,759 recorded crimes of theft from an automatic machine or meter, although some of these will have involved someone prising open the cash box and stealing its contents. Flatley et al, Crime in England and Wales 2009/10, 32. Following implementation of the Fraud Act 2006, offences involving theft from an automatic machine using a plastic card are now regarded, and recorded, as false representation (cheque, plastic card and online banks). The total for all offences for 2009/10 was 27,139.

[101] [2004] EWHC 2020 (Admin); [2005] Crim LR 229 and commentary.

[102] [1974] RTR 8.

[103] Hansard, HL, 14 Mar 2006, col 1108 (A-G).

For the purposes of this section a representation may be regarded as made if it (or anything implying it) is submitted in any form to any system or device designed to receive, convey or respond to communications (with or without human intervention).

The Home Office Explanatory Notes elaborate on the intention behind this subsection:

fraud can be committed where a person makes a representation to a machine and a response can be produced without any need for human involvement. (An example is where a person enters a number into a 'CHIP and PIN' machine.) The Law Commission had concluded that, although it was not clear whether a representation could be made to a machine, such a provision was unnecessary (see paragraph 8.4 of their report). But subsection (5) is expressed in fairly general terms because it would be artificial to distinguish situations involving modern technology, where it is doubtful whether there has been a 'representation', because the only recipient of the false statement is a machine or a piece of software, from other situations not involving modern technology where a false statement is submitted to a system for dealing with communications but is not in fact communicated to a human being (eg postal or messenger systems).[104]

Section 2(5) is not without its difficulties. Aside from the complexity of the drafting, difficulties also stem from the breadth of the subsection. The terms used in s 2(5) were obviously intended to provide the broadest scope of liability, but they are not unambiguous. For example, is a document 'submitted' when the defendant saves the typing to his hard drive on the computer, or is it only 'submitted' when he sends it via email? There is a clear argument for suggesting that the document is submitted as soon as D saves it. However, if that is the case, how is it any different from D who writes his false representation on a piece of paper and locks it in his safe? That would not, it is submitted, look like he has made a representation, but it is difficult to distinguish it from the case of saving data to a hard drive. Arguably, the individual who has submitted it to his computer is in a position in which he may more readily communicate it, but that mere possibility does not adequately justify any difference in criminality. The legislature might have intended to criminalize the conduct only when the representation was submitted to the ISP or system designed to act on it, but the section is not so narrowly drafted.

The criminal courts may follow the much narrower approach adopted in e-commerce. In business to business contracts it seems to be accepted that all contractually relevant communications only have operative effect when they are received.[105] In other contexts, it has been argued that the normal 'postal rule' of contract applies in relation to email contact so that the time of acceptance is the time when the electronic message was received by the ISP's network, and the place of acceptance is therefore where that 'node' of the network which received the message. The courts have permitted contracting parties to stipulate in advance where and when the relevant communications will have legal effect.[106] The implications are important. Consider D who types his false statements into a document on his computer and proposes to send that document to V later via email. If by saving it he has 'submitted' it in a form to a device designed to receive, etc he commits the offence at that point, even though it has not yet been released from D's control. For example, suppose D intends to circulate his false sales brochure by email at 8 am the following day, and he puts his false prospectus in his 'mail waiting to be sent' box. (In such a case, could D also argue that he was not intending by *that representation* to make a gain or cause loss. This is unlikely to succeed as a plea: D does intend to gain by *that* representation eventually – when it is sent.)

---

[104] Para 17, www.opsi.gov.uk/ACTS/acts2006/en/ukpgaen_20060035_en_1.htm.
[105] C Reed and J Angel, *Computer Law* (2003) 203.
[106] ibid.

Section 2(5) clearly extends the meaning of representation in cases involving 'submission to any system or device designed to receive, convey or respond to communications (with or without human intervention)', but what of those in which there is no 'submission' to such a system or device?[107] Is the concept of representation to be given an equally broad interpretation? What of the case in which D simply writes his representation on a piece of paper. Has he at that time made a representation? It is submitted that s 2(5) must be regarded as informing the general interpretation of the word representation. There is no need for completed communication to V. It suggests, implicitly that there is no requirement that a representation should be addressed to anyone specifically, or to a human being, provided of course that it is addressed to someone or something.

There will be few instances where this element of s 2 will give rise to problems in practice. The CPS goes so far as to assert that the problem will not arise: 'In practice, prosecutors are unlikely to receive a file unless the last stage was reached. If faced with a file where the final stage was earlier in the process prosecutors may wish to consider charging an attempt.'[108] There is no doubt that if D makes a statement otherwise than to a system or device as defined in s 2(5), and it cannot be proved that it was represented to someone or something, D may nevertheless be liable for an attempted offence under s 1(2)(a) and s 2.

Attempted representation?

Since the offence can be committed as soon as D has made a false representation, there is only limited scope for a charge of attempt. Possible examples include where D, having prepared documents containing false statements, is apprehended en route to post those to V. It may be that liability for the full offence arises even earlier if D decides to make his representations via a 'system' as defined in s 2(5) discussed above.

The most important circumstances in which an attempt will be charged may well be those in which D has unwittingly made a true statement. In *Deller*,[109] D induced V to purchase his car by representing, *inter alia*, that it was free from encumbrances, that is, that D had ownership and was free to sell it. In fact, D had previously executed a document that purported to mortgage the car to a finance company and, no doubt, he thought he was telling a lie. He was charged with obtaining by false pretences.[110] However, the document by which the transaction had been effected was probably void in law for the technical reason that it was as an unregistered bill of sale. If the document was void the car *was* free from encumbrances: '...quite accidentally and, strange as it may sound, dishonestly, the appellant had told the truth'.[111] D's conviction was, therefore, quashed by the Court of Criminal Appeal, for, though he had *mens rea*, no *actus reus* had been established. Under the 2006 Act, D could be convicted of an attempted fraud as soon as he made the true representation with intent.

Where the representation occurs

The *actus reus* requires that a representation is made, and hence the offence should be regarded as occurring in the place in which D acts in making that representation. The discussion above is pertinent. A representation may be articulated and communicated at different venues.

[107] Neither term is further defined. Presumably the Government was anxious not to use terminology which might become outdated or too difficult to define as, eg, with 'computer'.

[108] See www.cps.gov.uk/legal/d_to_g/fraud_act.

[109] (1952) 36 Cr App R 184. cf *Brien* (1903) 3 SRNSW 410; *Dyson* [1908] 2 KB 454.

[110] Under the Larceny Act 1916, s 32. The same principles are applicable.

[111] (1952) 36 Cr App R 184 at 191.

Representations by words, conduct or other means

The most obvious forms of the offence will involve D's physical action in the form of oral or written representations. D satisfies the 'making' element of the offence as much by saying to a customer: 'this is a genuine Chippendale chair I have for sale' as by describing the chair in like terms in his catalogue. Forms of physical conduct other than speech or writing will suffice as where D nods assent in response to the question 'Is this a genuine Chippendale chair?'

Conduct was capable of providing a relevant representation for the deception offences, and some of the old authorities remain valuable. In *Barnard*,[112] D went into an Oxford shop wearing a fellow-commoner's cap and gown. He induced the shopkeeper to sell him goods on credit by an express representation that he was a fellow-commoner; but Bolland B said, *obiter*, that he would have been guilty even if he had said nothing: he was making an implied representation that he was a fellow-commoner. In an Australian case,[113] the wearing of a badge was held to be a 'false pretence' when it indicated that the wearer was entitled to take bets on a racecourse. This would seem to constitute a 'representation'. Similarly, wearing a false press badge to gain entry to a sporting event or a members' tie in order to gain entry to the enclosure at Lords may constitute representations. There will remain some forms of conduct which give rise to doubt – is it enough that D represents that he is authorized to be 'present' in a virtual place, by having logged on illicitly to a website or secure terminal? The representation is not of course the entire offence – there must be a dishonest intention to gain or cause loss in terms of property for a completed offence.

Most instances in which s 2 is charged will involve representations made by words spoken or contained in documents. Classic examples will be false representations on mortgage application forms, or loan application forms,[114] or as to the need for building work to be performed on an elderly person's home;[115] or by use of false identity documents to secure work.[116] The s 2 form of the offence is also specifically designed to criminalize 'phishing' on the internet. D who posts on the internet a website purporting to be that of a bank or financial institution, encouraging account holders to reveal their passwords and confidential information will commit the offence. It does not matter that the website is ignored by everyone; a false representation has been made.

Representation by omission?

In early versions of the Bill the definition of 'representation' expressly referred to the fact that it could be by 'words or conduct' but that term is omitted from the section as enacted. Almost all representations will be by words or conduct, but Parliament's deletion of that expression raises the question whether the offence might also be committed by silent inaction. A simple example of a representation by omission is provided by the CPS: where D 'omits to mention previous convictions or County Court Judgments on an application form'. It seems clear that D would be falsely representing himself as being of 'good character or financial probity'. This could of course be seen as a case of positive action – completing a form with false information.

The interrelationship between ss 2 and 3 is important in this context. Section 3 of the Act criminalizes failing to disclose information. A broad reading of s 2 would overlap significantly with that section. However, s 3 is limited to cases in which D is under a 'legal duty' to

---

[112] (1837) 7 C & P 784.

[113] *Robinson* (1884) 10 VLR 131.

[114] See cases under the Act including: *Viera* [2009] EWCA Crim 528; *Cleps* [2009] EWCA Crim 894.

[115] See, eg, *Cowan* [2007] EWCA Crim 3402; *Hamilton* [2008] EWCA Crim 2518.

[116] See, eg, *Kapitene* [2010] EWCA Crim 2061; *Haboub* [2007] EWCA Crim 3320.

disclose information; a broad reading of s 2 would not be so limited. Several scenarios deserve to be considered in more detail.

(i) If D has not actively misled V in any of the representations he has made, but realizes that V is acting under a misconception as to the facts D has expressed, D may be liable under s 3 *if* he is under a legal duty to correct V's error. The criminal law must reflect the civil law's *caveat emptor* principle.

(ii) If D has not actively misled V, and is *not* under a duty to correct V's error, there can be no liability under s 3. Can D be liable under s 2? D cannot be liable under s 2 unless there is a *false* representation. Is D making a false representation by omitting to do something to disabuse V of his own error in interpretation? In a case almost 200 years ago it was held to be fraud in the civil law for the seller of a ship to remove her from a position out of the water where it might be seen that the keel was damaged, and instead to launch her afloat so that these defects were concealed by the water.[117] This amounts to a representation that the vessel was seaworthy and is relatively uncontroversial as conduct by D is readily construed as a representation. Suppose, however, that the ship was already in the water before any sale was in prospect. Would it be a representation for the seller to leave her there when viewed by the buyer and say nothing about the defects? Under the old law, there was a requirement that D deceived V by 'words *or conduct*', but no such restriction applies in s 2 of the 2006 Act.

Under the deception offences, in *Firth*,[118] a consultant was held to have deceived a hospital, contrary to the 1978 Act, s 2 (1), by failing to inform the hospital that certain patients were private patients, knowing that the effect would be that they would be exempted from liability to make a payment. The court apparently regarded an omission in breach of D's duty as 'conduct' for the purposes of determining whether there was a deception.[119] In similar circumstances, the courts might conclude that D was making an implied false representation, rendering him liable under s 3. It is important to emphasize that in the scenario under consideration D is *not* under a legal duty to correct any misunderstanding by V.[120] The question is whether it is necessary or desirable for the courts to extend the scope of criminal liability by interpreting s 2 to catch those circumstances where D is under no legal duty to correct V's misunderstanding of D's true representation. For the sake of clarity and to keep the criminal law on a more certain footing, it is submitted that such cases ought not to be within the scope of s 2. Liability for the failure to remedy V's misunderstanding of non-false statements ought to be restricted to that which may arise under s 3 where D has a legal duty to disclose.[121] Support for this approach derives from the Attorney General in early parliamentary debates on the Bill. when the A-G accepted that there are occasions when:

something that most of us naturally might think of as a non-disclosure is transformed by a fiction of the law into an implicit misrepresentation. But it is a fiction; it is not how people think about it. People will frequently say, 'I was not misled because I understand that he was implicitly making this representation to me. He just did not disclose something; he was dishonest in not disclosing it; and the purpose of that was to make a gain or to do something else'. One can think of many other examples where that would be the true basis on which a charge would be laid.[122]

---

[117] *Schneider v Heath* (1813) 3 Camp 506, approved by the Court of Appeal in *Ward v Hobbs* (1877) 3 QBD 150 at 162, CA. cf the Consumer Protection from Unfair Trading Regulations 2008, reg 9.

[118] (1989) 91 Cr App R 217, CA, [1990] Crim LR 326, and commentary. cf *Shama* [1990] 2 All ER 602, [1990] 1 WLR 661, CA, below, p 930.

[119] Such behaviour would now constitute an offence under ss 3 (if there was a legal duty to disclose) and 4 (if there was an expectation that D would not act contrary to the financial interests of the hospital).

[120] *Smith v Hughes* (1871) LR 6 QB 597.

[121] See, eg, *Chitty on Contracts* (30th edn, 2009) Ch 6.

[122] *Hansard*, HL, 19 July 2005, cols 1411–1412.

In the previous scenario, it was envisaged that there was a unilateral misunderstanding by V, with no change in circumstances after D's initial representation. A different scenario is that where D makes a representation to V which is not false within the meaning in s 2, but subsequently, to D's knowledge but not V's, circumstances change in a way that materially affects the accuracy of D's original representation. If D continues to act without correcting V's (mis)understanding of the position D might be said to be impliedly making a fresh, and now false, representation. Where D is under a legal duty to disclose the change in circumstances to V (for example, in a contract of insurance) he will be liable under s 3, but the question remains whether in those cases in which D is not under a legal duty, he ought to be liable under s 2.

Under the old law, in *DPP v Ray*,[123] it was established that one who enters a restaurant and orders a meal impliedly represents that he intends to pay for the meal before leaving,[124] and probably also represents, in the absence of an agreement for credit, that he has the money to pay.[125] In that case, D's implied representation was true when made and continued true until the end of the meal, but when D changed his mind and decided to leave without paying, it became false. Under the 1968 Act, it was essential to prove that V acted on the false representation and that the result of V's so acting was that D obtained the property or the service as the case may be.[126] It was held that the waiter acted on the false statement by leaving the room thereby allowing D an opportunity to leave, when he would not have done so had he known the truth, that D intended to leave without paying. Importantly for present purposes, Lord Pearson referred to there being a continuing representation: 'By "continuing representation" I mean in this case not a continuing effect of an initial representation, but a representation which is being made by conduct at every moment throughout that course of conduct...' If there is a representation in such a case where D made a true statement but later to his knowledge circumstances change materially, s 2 will apply.

Might a distinction be drawn between those cases in which the material change in circumstances is one over which D has control – as where he changes his mind about a willingness to pay and those in which he has no control? Suppose that D sends an order to V for a book, promising to pay the price within 10 days of delivery and that D does intend to pay when he posts the order, and makes that statement, but changes his mind before V reads the order. It is likely that the courts will regard the representation in such circumstances to be a continuing one.

(iii) A further scenario to be considered is that where D makes a false representation, but at the time he makes it, he believes it to be true. It is submitted that if D discovers that the statement is false and thereafter does not seek to rectify any misunderstanding, he may be liable.[127] This conclusion is not beyond doubt because of the manner in which s 2 is drafted. At the time of making the representation, D makes a statement which is inaccurate (untrue or misleading), but it is not false under s 2 unless at that time D also knows that it is or might be

---

[123] [1974] AC 370, [1973] 3 All ER 131, HL; *Nordeng* (1975) 62 Cr App R 123 at 129, CA.

[124] *DPP v Ray* [1974] AC 370 at 379, 382, 385, 388, 391, [1973] 3 All ER 131, HL.

[125] ibid, 379, 382.

[126] It was accepted that, if D had decided only while the waiter was out of the room that he would not pay and then made off while the waiter was out of the room, he would not have committed the offence. On the particular facts, D's continued presence was essential to the prosecution's case.

[127] cf *Rai* [2000] 1 Cr App R 242 under the old law where D failed to inform the council that his mother had died and allowed them to continue their installation of disability aids to which he was not entitled. See a similar scenario in *Ali* [2006] All ER (D) 270 (May), where D was not in receipt of student support when applying for local authority benefit, but when he received student support he failed to disclose this change in circumstances to the local authority. The prosecution was under s 111A of the Social Security Administration Act 1992. See also *R (Pearson) v Greenwich MC* [2008] EWHC 300 (Admin). For an example of the nuances in its interpretation see *Croydon LBC v Shanahan* [2010] EWCA Crim 98. See further *Arlidge and Parry on Fraud*, para 2.045.

false. The falsity of the statement is dependent on proof of an element of *mens rea*. If D believes he is making a true statement, then for the purposes of s 2, there is no false statement actually made. To avoid this problem, the courts will have to interpret the concept of representation as being a continuing one. Where D makes a statement which is in fact untrue or misleading and later comes to know that it is such, he can be said to be making a false statement at that later point in time. It will be at that point that he must also be found to be dishonest.

As a matter of general principle it is submitted that considerable caution should be exercised in interpreting s 2 to prevent undesirable extension of the criminal law where D is neither responsible or at fault in causing V to interpret the representation in an erroneous manner nor under a legal duty to disclose the fact of V's error. The criminal law ought to take its lead from the civil law. The maxim *caveat emptor* ought to operate to restrict the scope of liability. In commercial transactions, D, though under a duty to do nothing to confirm any misunderstanding by V, has no duty to correct it even though he is fully aware of it. '[T]he passive acquiescence of the seller in the self-deception of the buyer does not entitle the buyer to avoid the contract.'[128] This ought not to amount to a s 2 offence. The CPS has issued important guidance on the public interest test in prosecuting frauds which states that:

The borderline between criminal and civil liability is likely to be an issue in alleged Fraud Act offences particularly those under Section 1. Prosecutors should bear in mind that the principle of *caveat emptor* applies and should consider whether civil proceedings or the regulatory regime that applies to advertising and other commercial activities might be more appropriate. Not every advertising puff should lead to a criminal conviction but it is also the case that fraudsters prey on the vulnerable. Prosecutors should guard against the criminal law being used as a debt collection agency or to protect the commercial interests of companies and organisations. However, prosecutors should also remain alert to the fact that such organisations can become the focus of serious and organised criminal offending.[129]

A representation may be express or implied: s 2(4)

Section 2(4) was included late in the passage of the Bill through the House of Lords.[130] To have suggested in the absence of such a provision that a 'representation' could be express but not implied would have been most unlikely to have persuaded any court. Nevertheless, s 2(4) is included for the avoidance of doubt. Express representations will rarely give rise to difficulty, at least where they relate to facts (as opposed to states of mind). Greater difficulty is likely to arise in interpreting 'implied' representations, judging by experiences with the old law. A person who registers as a guest in a hotel represents that he intends to pay the bill at the end of his stay.[131] A wine waiter employed at a hotel impliedly represents that the wine he offers is his employer's, not his own.[132] A motor trader who states that the mileage shown on the odometer of a second-hand car 'may not be correct' represents that he does not know it to be incorrect.[133] A bookmaker, it is submitted, represents, when he takes a bet, that he intends to pay if the horse backed wins.[134] One who takes a taxi represents that he intends to pay, and has the means of paying, at the end of the ride.[135]

---

[128] *Smith v Hughes* (1871) LR 6 QB 597.

[129] See www.cps.gov.uk/legal/d_to_g/fraud_act.

[130] *Hansard*, HL, 14 Mar 2006, col 1107.

[131] *Harris* (1975) 62 Cr App R 28, CA.

[132] *Doukas* [1978] 1 All ER 1061, [1978] Crim LR 177, CA. The decision is to be preferred to *Rashid* [1977] 2 All ER 237, CA.

[133] *King* [1979] Crim LR 122.

[134] cf *Buckmaster* (1887) 20 QBD 182.

[135] cf *Waterfall* [1970] 1 QB 148, [1969] 3 All ER 1048, CA.

Representations and cheques

It is submitted that a person tendering a cheque impliedly makes three representations: (i) that he has an account on which the cheque is drawn; (ii) that he has authority to draw on the bank for that amount; and (iii) that the cheque as drawn is a valid order for that amount. This was the accepted orthodoxy from cases as early as *Hazelton*.[136] The doubt cast on that orthodoxy in *Metropolitan Police Comr v Charles*[137] can now surely be ignored since their lordships' approach was driven by their desire to find a deception in the face of the evidence in that case. Lord Edmund-Davies in *Metropolitan Police Comr v Charles*[138] quoted with approval the words of Pollock B in *Hazelton*[139] that the representation is that 'the existing state of facts is such that in the ordinary course the cheque will be met'. In *Gilmartin*, the Court of Appeal thought that 'this terse but neat epitome of the representation . . . should properly be regarded as an authoritative statement of the law'.[140] It is submitted that this approach should be followed in interpreting and applying s 2.

Where D post-dates a cheque, it may be his intention to pay in sufficient funds to meet it before presentation. Alternatively, he may believe that a third party is going to pay in such funds – as where he knows that his account is overdrawn but confidently expecting that he will have an ample credit balance tomorrow when his salary is paid into his account by his employer. There being no express representation, D must be taken to be saying that either, (a) there are sufficient funds in the account to meet the cheque; or, (b) he intends to pay in sufficient funds; or, (c) he believes that a third party will do so. Each is an implied representation of fact and is sufficient to constitute this element of the offence.

Credit cards and debit cards

When a person presents his credit or debit card he makes a representation (i) that he has the authority to use that card, and (ii) that payment will be made. Under the old law problems arose because the representation had to cause the obtaining. That difficulty is removed because under the 2006 Act the requirement is only that the representation that is made is false and D intends to gain/cause loss *by* that false representation. There are, however, three problems which do need to be considered.

The first relates to the falsity of the statements. The fact that payment will be made by the card-issuing company means that D's representation as to payment will in most cases *not* be false. The debit card contains an undertaking by the bank that, if the conditions on the card are satisfied, the payment will be honoured. The position with credit cards is similar.[141] The bank issuing the card enters into contracts with the trader, agreeing to pay the trader the sum shown on a voucher signed by the customer/confirmed by chip and PIN when making a purchase, provided that the conditions on the credit or debit card are satisfied. Conditions on both types of card may be satisfied although the holder is exceeding his authority. The trader accepting either type of card will usually do so simply because the conditions on the card are

---

[136] (1874) LR 2 CCR 134, the source of the proposition in Kenny, *Outlines*, 359, adopted in *Page* [1971] 2 QB 330 at 333.

[137] [1977] AC 177, [1976] 3 All ER 112, HL.

[138] ibid.

[139] (1874) LR 2 CCR 134 at 140.

[140] (1983) 76 Cr App R 238 at 244.

[141] In the case of credit cards, the contract between the bank and the trader precedes the purchase by the customer, whereas in the case of the debit card the contract is made when the trader accepts the customer's cheque, relying on the card which is produced. See *Paget's Law of Banking* (13th edn, 2006) paras 2.62–2.69; *First Sport Ltd v Barclays Bank plc* [1993] 3 All ER 789, [1993] 1 WLR 1229, CA (Civ Div), holding, Kennedy LJ dissenting, that the bank was bound even though the cheque was a forgery. Lord Roskill's opinion in *Lambie* (all their lordships concurring) that the customer was making a contract as agent for the credit card company is powerfully criticized by F Bennion, 'Credit or Theft: The *Lambie* Cases' (1981) 131 NLJ 431.

satisfied. He will not know whether the customer is exceeding his authority and using the card in breach of contract with the bank. He will get his money in any event. This is neither immoral nor unreasonable. The whole object of these cards is to avoid the trader concerning himself with the relationship between the cardholder and his bank. The trader is perfectly entitled to take advantage of the facility which the banks offer him.

If D is unaware of the banking practice whereby the trader is guaranteed to receive payment, he will unwittingly be making a true statement that payment will be made. Since he intends to make a false representation, he would theoretically also be liable for an attempt. However, resort to such technicalities is unnecessary. The fact that D makes a true representation that payment will be made is not the end of the matter because in many of these cases, D will be making a separate, false representation. When D presents the card knowing he is lacking authority to do so – because it is not his or because he is overdrawn, etc – he makes a false representation. If that representation is made (even impliedly), the element of the offence is satisfied. D will be aware that he is making that representation and that it is false.[142]

The second problem is the requirement that it must be *by the* false representation that D intends to gain/cause loss or expose another to a risk of loss. If D has made a representation as to his authority to use the card, it seems clear that he has *by* that false representation intended to expose another (the credit card company and or the trader) to a risk of loss. Arguably, by that false representation D also intends to gain by keeping that which he has (s 5(3)). Subject to dishonesty, all the other elements also appear to be satisfied:[143] it is no excuse that D also intends the trader to receive payment (that is, not to make a loss).

Finally, there is the question of representations as to authority to use the card. The trader apparently does not care that D has no authority or that D has exceeded his limit; he will receive his payment as explained above. Can D claim therefore that it was not *by* his false representation to the trader that he intended to make a gain/cause a loss? Although this is a plea that D can raise, alongside one of a lack of dishonesty in such circumstances, it is submitted that it will be unlikely to succeed. The trader's apparent disinterest in D's representations is in fact more apparent than real.[144] If D uses X's card because D knows X's PIN, D dishonestly makes a false representation. X might be recompensed by his bank for any loss and the trader might (probably will) be paid by the bank, but the bank will lose out. In that sense, it does appear that neither X nor the shopkeeper particularly 'care' if the card is misused – neither will lose out, but, there is an argument which suggests that beneath that superficiality they do 'care'. If X or the trader became aware that D was misusing the card, and chose to endorse that misuse, then he would become party to the fraud against the bank. X and the trader 'care' – not because they may suffer financial loss, but because they might otherwise become accessories to a criminal offence, and on becoming accessories, they would lose their right to recompense.

Some commentators argue that there is not a false representation in such circumstances.[145] It is submitted this interpretation places too much emphasis on the likely significance of the representation to V. That issue is no longer of relevance under the 2006 Act because the question is not whether V might be deceived or believe a matter, it is whether it is a representation to the trader that is false. If D has no authority to use the card, the trader would

---

[142] cf the recent decision of the Administrative Court in *Poland v Ulatowski* [2010] EWHC 2673 (Admin).

[143] Arguably the trader will also be exposed to the risk of loss.

[144] For consideration of the bank's obligation where it is suspected that there was no genuine transaction with an unauthorized card, see *Do-buy 295 Ltd v Nat West Bank* [2010] EWHC 2862 (QB).

[145] The argument is that there can only be a representation as to authority by D if he thinks that it will matter to V, and since the trader, V, will not care whether D is authorized, there is no false representation. *Arlidge and Parry on Fraud*, para 4.068.

not accept his card because otherwise the trader would be an accomplice to D's fraud on the bank.

Representations as to 'fact'

Representations as to present facts will present little difficulty for the courts. If D asserts that he is selling a solid gold watch and it is, to his knowledge, made of brass, he commits the offence. Greater difficulty arises if his statements included making a representation as to future facts. Section 2(3) defines a representation as meaning '*any* representation as to fact...', but the term 'any' relates to the type of representation, not the type of fact; it is designed to encourage the most expansive reading of 'representation'. Representations as to the occurrence of future events or the existence of future facts are best seen as cases of representations as to present states of mind – as where D says he promises that payment will be made tomorrow. That is a representation as to D's present state of mind about a future event.

Representations as to 'law'

Section 2(3) expressly provides that 'any representation' as to law will suffice. Representations of law ought to be caught, for example: D and V are reading a legal document and D deliberately misrepresents its legal effect. This would seem to be false representation of law since the construction of documents is a question of law. If D does so with the intent to gain or cause loss, for example, by inducing V to pay money for the release of his rights, this would seem to amount to fraud contrary to s 2. Greater difficulty will arise where the state of the law contained in the representation is uncertain. For a representation to be 'false' within s 2, not only must it be untrue or misleading, but D must know it is or might be untrue or misleading. Where there is some ambiguity as to the state of the law, D will only be making a false representation where it is untrue or misleading *and* he does not believe it to be true. The following proposition formulated by Street[146] for the law of the tort of deceit is probably equally true of the concept of representation in this context:

If the representations refer to legal principles as distinct from the facts on which those principles operate and the parties are on an equal footing, those representations are only expressions of belief and of the same effect as expressions of opinion between parties on an equal footing. In other cases where the defendant professes legal information beyond that of the [claimant] the ordinary rules of liability for deceit apply.[147]

Representations as to 'states of mind'

Section 2(3) provides that a representation as to a state of mind of any person will suffice. A representation as to a present intention of either D or some other person will therefore be sufficient. Representations as to present intentions may be expressed or implied.

If D states that his intention is that he will pay V tomorrow, he is making a representation as to his present state of mind. The Crown must of course go further and prove that the representation as to D's state of mind was false, that is, it must be proved that at the time of making the representation as to the present state of mind, D knew that it was false. It has long been recognized that a misrepresentation as to a present state of mind will found a civil action for deceit and this is no more difficult to prove in the criminal than in the civil case – though the standard of proof is, of course, higher. Evidence as to the circumstances in which the promise was made, or as to a systematic course of conduct by D or, of course, as to a confession are examples of ways in which a jury might be convinced beyond reasonable doubt that D was deceiving V as to his present intentions. If D, at the time of making the representation

---

[146] J Murphy, *Street on Torts* (12th edn, 2007) 334.
[147] ibid, 123.

intended to carry out his promise but later changed his mind he is guilty of a breach of contract. He is also guilty under s 3 of the 2006 Act if he is under a legal duty to disclose that information (that is, the change of intention).

Representations as to the present intentions of a person other than D seem to be rare. Examples would include where an agent obtains property for his principal by representing that the principal intends to render services or supply goods, well knowing that the principal has no such intention, or where an estate agent says that a particular building society is willing to advance half the purchase price of a house, knowing that this is not so. Where the representation is as to the state of mind of another, it may be more common for the Crown to allege, in proving falsity, that D knew not that it was untrue but that it *might* be untrue or misleading.

Statements of opinion

Difficulties have arisen in determining whether a statement of opinion is sufficient to constitute a representation. D who says 'this is a Swiss made watch' is making a representation of fact. But what of D who says 'the quality of the mechanism in this watch is as good as a Swiss made one'? is this a representation of fact? Is it a representation as to D's state of mind – also capable of being treated as a representation of fact under s 2?

In the old case of *Bryan*,[148] D obtained money from V by representing that certain spoons were of the best quality, equal to a famous brand – 'Elkington's A', and having as much silver in them as 'Elkington's A'. These statements were false to D's knowledge.[149] Nevertheless, 10 out of 12 judges[150] held that his conviction must be quashed on the ground that this was mere exaggerated praise by a seller of his goods to which that statute was not intended to apply. Erle J said, 'Whether these spoons … were equal to "Elkington's A" or not, cannot be, as far as I know, decidedly affirmed or denied in the same way as a past fact can be affirmed or denied, but it is in the nature of a matter of opinion.' It is submitted that the case went too far.[151] The statement that the spoons had as much silver in them as 'Elkington's A' is a statement of fact.[152] It is submitted that the second representation in *Bryan* ought now to be treated as a false representation as to fact sufficient for a conviction under s 2.

Difficulties will no doubt arise in distinguishing representations of fact from opinion, particularly when it comes to exaggeration as to value or excessive quotation. It has been held[153] that it is a misrepresentation of fact for D to state 'that they [had] effected necessary repairs to a roof [which repairs were specified] that they had done the work in a proper and workmanlike manner and that [a specified sum] was a fair and reasonable sum to charge for the work involved'. The evidence showed that nothing needed to be done to the roof, what had been done served no useful purpose and it could have been done for £5, whereas £35 was charged. It might be argued that representations as to quotations could be interpreted as including an implied representation of fact that the price quoted is one reflecting only a fair profit margin. But even this strained reading will not assist in all cases. What of the vendor's description of

---

[148] (1857) Dears & B 265.

[149] D's counsel said: 'I cannot contend that the prisoner did not tell a wilful lie …'

[150] Willes J *dissentiente* and Bramwell B *dubitante*.

[151] It may be a significant fact that at the time *Bryan* was decided, it was not possible for the prisoner to give evidence in his own defence. In *Ragg* (1860) Bell CC 208 at 219, Erle CJ, referring to *Bryan*, said, '… if such statements are indictable a purchaser who wishes to get out of a bad bargain made by his own negligence, might have recourse to an indictment, on the trial of which the vendor's statement on oath would be excluded, instead of being obliged to bring an action where each party would be heard on equal terms'.

[152] *Ardley* (1871) LR 1 CCR 301.

[153] *Jeff and Bassett* (1966) 51 Cr App R 28, CA. cf *Hawkins v Smith* [1978] Crim LR 578 ('Showroom condition throughout' a false trade description of a car which has interior and mechanical defects).

his tenant as 'a most desirable tenant' when the rent was in arrears and, in the past, had only been paid under pressure? This was held by the Court of Appeal to be a sufficient misrepresentation to found an action in deceit.[154]

In a case where the facts are equally well known to both parties, what one of them says to the other is frequently nothing but an expression of opinion. But if the facts are not equally well known to both sides, then a statement of opinion by one who knows the facts best involves very often a statement of a material fact, for he impliedly states that he knows facts which justify his opinion.[155] Deliberate misstatements of opinion will be likely to be generally condemned as dishonest, no less dishonest, indeed, than misstatements of other facts – for whether an opinion is held or not is a fact. The question now ought to be not 'Is it a matter of opinion?' but, 'If it is a matter of opinion, was it D's real opinion?' If the opinion is not honestly held there is a misrepresentation of fact, for D's state of mind is a question of fact.

23.3.2.2 'False' representation

Whether a representation is false usually depends on the meaning intended or understood by the parties and that too is a question for the jury, even where the statement is made in a document. Where the issue is as to the legal effect of a document, it is for the judge to decide.[156]

Section 2(2)(a) provides that a representation may be false by either being 'untrue', or 'misleading'. It is necessary for the Crown to establish as a matter of *actus reus* that the representation is false or misleading aside from any issue about D's knowledge as to its truth or otherwise. However, the states of mind of the parties are likely to be important. Indeed, rather oddly the Act provides that a statement is only false if D knows it is or knows it might be false. The definition of falsity turns not solely on the objectively discernible fact of its lack of accuracy, but on D's subjective awareness of that fact or its possibility.

Untrue

The word is an ordinary English word and no doubt the courts will suggest that juries should be directed to approach it as such. The only potential difficulties in application relate to those representations made by D which are not *wholly* untrue. It should be noted that there is no requirement that the falsity relates to a material particular. Where D's representation contains one falsity, even if it relates to a peripheral matter in his dealings with V, he may be convicted subject to the jury concluding that the use of that falsity was dishonest, and that it is *by that falsity*[157] that he intended to gain or cause loss. This may give rise to difficulties in a range of circumstances from the street trader who exaggerates his wares to the investment fraudster who falsely embellishes certain aspects of the deal.

Where the requirement to prove that D's statement was untrue requires the prosecution to prove a negative and the affirmative fact which, if it exists, will establish the truth of the statement is within D's knowledge, there may be an onus on him not to prove anything, but at least to introduce some evidence of the affirmative fact. In *Mandry and Wooster*,[158] street traders selling scent for 25p, said, 'You can go down the road and buy it for 2 guineas in the big stores.' The police checked on certain stores but it was admitted in cross-examination that they had not been to Selfridges. It was held that it was not improper for the judge to point out that it was impossible for the police to go to every shop in London and that 'if the defence knew of their own knowledge of anywhere it could be bought at that price . . . they were perfectly entitled to

---

[154] *Smith v Land and House Property Corpn* (1884) 28 Ch D 7.
[155] ibid, 15, per Bowen LJ.
[156] *Adams* [1994] RTR 220, [1993] Crim LR 525 and commentary. cf *Deller*, above, p 54.
[157] See above, p 879.
[158] [1973] 3 All ER 996; cf *Silverman* (1987) 86 Cr App R 213.

call evidence'. Even though no evidence was called to show that the perfume was on sale at Selfridges or anywhere else, the convictions were upheld.

D will always be able to argue that it was not *by* the particular falsity alleged that he intended to make the gain/cause the loss. This issue is discussed above.[159] Simply because D's representation relates to a peripheral matter will not *entitle* the defendant to an acquittal. It will be a question of fact and degree in every case whether what was said was intended to be a misrepresentation by which the gain or loss would be made. Ironically, the jury may be more likely to acquit a person whose lie is a whopper of such proportions that the jury accept that, although knowingly false, no one could have intended that it would be believed. In general the defence are going to be faced with the difficult obstacle which is the juror's natural inclination to ask – 'if D did not intend that his representation would lead to the gain or loss why did he make it?'

Or misleading

The inclusion of this alternative suggests that the draftsman intended that it constitute a distinct route to establishing falsity. The Home Office has suggested a very wide interpretation of the term 'misleading' proposing that it means 'less than wholly true and capable of an interpretation to the detriment of the victim'.[160] Being 'untrue' and being 'misleading' are, it is submitted, distinct behaviours.[161] An untrue statement is one which is literally false. A statement can be misleading even though it is literally true. Common examples are where D fails to provide a comprehensive answer to a question. For example, V asks D a car salesman 'Have you had many faults reported with this model?' and D replies, 'Only one this year'. That may be a literally true statement, but is highly misleading if there were 200 faults reported the previous year.[162] To display a cheap fake with a collection of original Lowry paintings may amount to a misleading representation that the fake is by Lowry.[163]

The potential for liability arises also with 'ambiguous' statements. It has been held in civil law, that 'if with intent to lead the plaintiff to act up on it [D] put forth a statement which [D] knew may bear two meanings, one of which is false to [his] knowledge and thereby the plaintiff putting that meaning on it is misled, I do not think [D] could escape by saying [the plaintiff] ought to have put the other'.[164]

There are, arguably, important moral distinctions between the conduct of someone who lies outright and someone who is merely economical with the truth, allowing the hearer to infer facts for which he must take some responsibility – *caveat auditor!*[165] These distinctions find no place in the 2006 Act.

Whether a representation is misleading can be a matter of degree. Is a 'trade puff' misleading? The main repost by a street trader to an allegation that he made a false representation may be that there was no dishonesty. The second argument that he may rely on is that he did not intend by his exaggerated banter to cause anyone to believe him and that he did not therefore intend by that admittedly false representation to gain or cause loss. Such arguments may

---

[159] At p 879.

[160] Para 19.

[161] Although Arlidge and Parry dispute this. See *Arlidge and Parry on Fraud*, para 4.085.

[162] There is little problem in practice in saying that the misrepresentation is by something not literally true but meant to be misunderstood: *Moens v Heyworth* (1842) 10 M and W 147. There are academic debates as to which conduct is more blameworthy and whether the victim of one or the other suffers greater harm. One view is that the victim who is misled feels more aggrieved since he has played a part in his own loss by inferring facts which D did not expressly represent. See, generally, Green, *Lying, Cheating and Stealing*.

[163] cf *Hill v Gray* (1816) 1 Stark 434, a doubtful decision, since it is not clear that the seller induced the buyer's mistake.

[164] *Smith v Chadwick* (1884) 9 App Cas 187 at 201 HL.

[165] See Green, *Lying, Cheating, and Stealing*, 78.

sometimes be difficult to sustain in a court remote in time and atmosphere from the theatre of a street market.[166]

Proof of falsity

Proving whether a representation is untrue will be far easier when it relates to a fact (or law) that exists at the time of the making of the representation[167] than when it relates to the state of mind of an individual. Since the requirement is both that the representation is untrue, as a matter of *actus reus*, and that D knew that it might be untrue, particular difficulties may arise as regards any representation as to future facts. This is likely when representations relate to states of mind.

If the representation is untrue, there is no explicit defence that the representation was made for good reason or with lawful excuse, as where D said he made the false representation in order to recover property (which he believed) belonging to him, in such a case the defendant must rely on the claim of a lack of dishonesty,[168] and, as noted, the Act does not provide a special defence of belief in claim of right.

In many cases of complexity, the question will be whether an individual representation can fairly be examined as false when taken out of the context of the others with which it was made.

23.3.3 *Mens rea*

23.3.3.1 'Knowing that the representation is' or 'knowing that it might be' false

Knowledge is a strict form of *mens rea*; much stricter than 'belief', 'suspicion', 'having reasonable grounds to suspect' and even 'recklessness'.[169] In this offence, knowledge is in a diluted form – the Crown need only prove knowledge that the representation either: (i) is untrue; or (ii) is misleading; or (iii) might be untrue; or (iv) might be misleading.

In the context of representations as to existing facts, the proof of knowledge will be least difficult to establish. It will require proof, often by inference, that D possessed knowledge of the existence of the falsity of the representation. More difficult will be cases where the falsity relates to the present state of mind as to the likely existence of future facts occurring, for example: 'we believe that the payment for the goods will be made to us by a creditor tomorrow and we will immediately pay you'. In many cases, it will be very difficult for the Crown to establish that D knew that his present statement was false. Even with the opportunity for the Crown to succeed on proof of knowledge that D knew that the representation might be misleading, difficulties may arise.

It is sufficient that D is shown to have known that his representation might be false. Is the offence rendered too wide by this alternative *mens rea*? D tells a customer that he has a Renoir for sale. D knows that there is a risk, as with all art, that the painting might be a fake. Does D know that the statement *might be* misleading? He will only be guilty if he made a false statement and he was dishonest. The element of dishonesty once again serves as the

---

[166] See above and the correspondence between Ormerod and Gardner [2007] Crim LR 661.

[167] The A-G accepted that it is implicit in the drafting of cl 2 that 'the only time at which one can make a judgment about whether the defendant thinks his representation is, or might be, untrue, is when he makes the representation. So if he believes it to be true at the time he makes it, he cannot have been dishonest', *Hansard*, HL, 19 July 2005, col 1420.

[168] See above, p 876.

[169] See the House of Lords discussion of the definition of knowledge in the context of conspiracy: *Saik* [2006] UKHL 18.

principal determinant of guilt.[170] Interestingly, the Attorney General had no difficulty with this example,[171] saying that it would be for a jury to decide if the art dealer was dishonest and thus guilty of fraud.

If an art dealer said, 'This is a painting by Renoir', knowing that that statement can have a huge impact on the value of the painting – but not knowing whether it is true and thinking that it might be untrue – it would be for a jury to decide whether he was dishonest. If he was dishonest, I see no difficulty in saying that he is guilty of fraud in those circumstances.[172]

Is this an oversimplification? Is the Attorney General treating as sufficient D's *thinking* that a statement might be untrue or misleading?[173] Many competent art dealers will acknowledge that there is always a risk that a painting might be a forgery. If the painting in question turns out to be a forgery, a representation has been made. But did the art dealer know it might be misleading? He might argue that acceptance or knowledge that a thing might be untrue is different from thinking that it in fact is or might in fact be untrue. In the former case, the dealer, while accepting that nothing can be certain in the art market, believes that his attribution is true, and therefore acts honestly. The dealer who actually thinks it might be untrue, acts dishonestly. The issue is properly regarded as one of dishonesty and not knowledge. In short, a dealer who believes that his attribution in respect of this painting is true, acts honestly. He has an honest belief based upon provenance, history, his own expertise, reliance on the expertise of others, or a combination of any of these factors. The dealer who actually thinks it might be untrue, acts, it is submitted, dishonestly. It is easy to see that a person who has bought an item which has been wrongly attributed by an auction house might use the criminal law in s 2 to support his civil claim for misrepresentation.

It seems inevitable then that in practice this *mens rea* element will blur unsatisfactorily into the element of dishonesty. The courts need to be alert to guard against reckless representations being treated as sufficient dishonest acts when the section actually requires *both* dishonesty and knowledge as to falsity.

Wilful blindness

The breadth of this fault element may extend even further if the courts interpret knowledge as including 'shutting one's eyes to an obvious means of knowledge' or 'deliberately refraining from making inquiries the results of which the person does not care to have'.[174] The concept is discussed in Chapter 5.[175]

Not negligence

What must certainly be guarded against is any slippage into regarding as a sufficient *mens rea* test negligence or constructive knowledge. The courts have rejected the idea that constructive knowledge is sufficient in the context of deception offences[176] and this state of negligence should have no part under the Fraud Act. It is worth noting that the Government rejected as too wide *mens rea* alternatives which were proposed on consultation, including a test based on whether D had 'no reasonable grounds for believing' the representation to be true, and that he 'ought to have known' it to be false.

---

[170] *Hansard*, HL, 19 July 2005, col 1416 (Lord Kingsland).

[171] Nor did the Home Office in its Response to Consultees, observing that if it caused sellers to be more careful that was a desirable result: para 18.

[172] *Hansard*, HL, 19 July 2005, col 1417. The Home Office thought likewise in its Responses to Consultation, para 17.

[173] cf the old law in which reckless deceptions sufficed: Theft Act 1968, s 15(4).

[174] *Roper v Taylor's Garage* [1951] 2 TLR 284, per Devlin J.

[175] See also *Manifest Shipping Co Ltd v Uni-Polaris Shipping Co Ltd and others* [2003] 1 AC 469.

[176] *Flintshire CC v Reynolds* [2006] EWHC 195 (Admin).

Knowledge and mistake of law

Where the alleged false representation is one relating to law, and D denies that he has knowledge as to the relevant law, if that is a denial of criminal law, there is no excuse, but if D is denying a knowledge of civil law that may be a sufficient excuse.

23.3.3.2 Dishonesty

The *Ghosh* test applies, as noted above. This is potentially problematical in the s 2 form of the offence since the criminality turns almost exclusively on dishonesty, and the definition of that term is left to the jury to determine on a case-by-case basis. In addition, as noted, there is no guarantee of acquittal where D has a claim of right or belief in a claim of right to the property he intends to gain by his false representation.

23.3.3.3 With intent to gain or cause loss

This element is discussed above, at p 878.

23.4 Section 3: fraud by failing to disclose information

Section 3 provides the second form of the general fraud offence introduced by s 1. It is far less heavily used. In 2009/10 there were 362 recorded offences.[177]

Section 3 provides:

A person is in breach of this section if he –

(a) dishonestly fails to disclose information to another person, which he is under a legal duty to disclose, and

(a) (b) intends, by failing to disclose the information –

(i) to make a gain for himself or another, or

(ii) to cause loss to another or to expose another to a risk of loss.

23.4.1 General

The elements of this version of the fraud offence are, as with s 2, easy enough to describe. None of the elements is, however, defined in detail in the section. The *actus reus* comprises: failing to disclose information to a person; being under a *legal* duty to disclose. The *mens rea* comprises acting dishonestly, with an intention to make a gain/cause loss/expose to loss.

The important overriding principle of interpretation is that criminal liability under s 3 should not be imposed where the civil law imposes no duty to speak. As has been emphasized throughout, it is desirable for the criminal law to respect the civil law foundations on which the offences are created.[178] This interpretation derives explicit support from the comments of the Attorney General in the course of parliamentary debates where he stated that 'the Government believe that it would be undesirable to create [a] disparity between the criminal and the civil law; it should not be criminal to withhold information which you are entitled to withhold under civil law'.[179]

This overriding interpretative principle is also underlined by the fact that the offence is much narrower than original formulations proposed by the Law Commission. These included

---

[177] Flatley et al, *Crime in England and Wales 2009/10*, 32.
[178] See Sullivan [1985] Crim LR 617.
[179] *Hansard*, HL, 19 July 2005, col 1426.

breaches of 'moral duties' or duties arising from an expectation in the mind of the person with whom D is dealing.[180] The Home Office expressly rejected these proposals as creating offences which would be too ambiguous and which would trespass on the *caveat emptor* principle.[181]

23.4.2 Relationship with s 2

This form of offence is much narrower than that under s 2, but their relationship warrants close attention.[182] Arguably, many if not all cases in which there is a legal duty to disclose information might be regarded as involving an implied false representation within s 2.[183] As a matter of principle, it is preferable for the charges to be brought under s 3. This ensures an accuracy of labelling in the offence and conviction, and in practical terms it will be easier for juries to understand the wrongdoing in terms of failing to disclose.

A good example of the potential application of s 3 is the case of *Rai*[184] decided under the 1978 Act. D obtained a grant from the city council to install a bathroom for his disabled mother. Before it was installed, she died. D did not disclose this fact and allowed the work to proceed. He was convicted of obtaining services by deception. The courts regarded D as engaged in a continuing implied representation. It could be regarded in the same way under the 2006 Act and the s 2 form of fraud could apply. However, this could equally be seen as a case where D was under a legal duty to inform the council when his mother died. That would allow for a charge under s 3.

23.4.3 *Actus reus*

23.4.3.1 A person

There is nothing to prevent a corporation being liable for a failure to disclose information under s 3 when the obligation is imposed by law on the corporate entity.[185]

23.4.3.2 Legal duty to disclose

For the purposes of determining when and where the offence occurs, it appears to be committed at the point at which the failure to disclose under the duty arises. D's duty must, it is submitted, be one arising under English law. It may arguably extend to some international law obligations to the extent that these are incorporated within domestic civil law.

Types of duty

The core element of the s 3 form of the fraud offence is the concept of 'legal duty'.[186] Unfortunately, this critical concept is not defined in the Act, nor even in the Home Office Explanatory Notes. It is necessary to turn to the Law Commission's Report for further guidance on which forms of legal duty were envisaged as being caught by the section. The Law Commission's Report on *Fraud*,[187] stated that:

---

[180] Home Office *Fraud Law Reform* (2004) paras 18–22.

[181] See HO, *Fraud Reform Responses to Consultation* (2004) paras 21–25.

[182] See above, p 888. See also *Hansard*, HL, 19 July 2005, col 1411.

[183] Provided the failure to disclose when under such a duty can be seen as synonymous with a false representation by omission.

[184] [2000] 1 Cr App R 242, [2000] Crim LR 192. The case rejects the idea that *Firth* is a general authority for a proposition that mere silence constitutes deception.

[185] For the liability of corporate officers see s 12 of the 2006 Act.

[186] The requirement of a legal duty was endorsed by the 'Rose Committee' of senior judges: *Hansard*, HL, 12 June 2006, col 536.

[187] Paras 7.28 and 7.29.

Such a duty may derive from statute (such as the provisions governing company prospectuses), from the fact that the transaction in question is one of the utmost good faith (such as a contract of insurance), from the express or implied terms of a contract, from the custom of a particular trade or market, or from the existence of a fiduciary relationship between the parties (such as that of agent and principal).

For this purpose there is a legal duty to disclose information not only if D's failure to disclose it gives V a cause of action for damages, but also if the law gives V a right to set aside any change in his or her legal position to which he or she may consent as a result of the non-disclosure. For example, a person in a fiduciary position has a duty to disclose material information when entering into a contract with his or her beneficiary, in the sense that a failure to make such disclosure will entitle the beneficiary to rescind the contract and to reclaim any property transferred under it.[188]

That opens an extremely broad vista of criminal liability. Some of the examples offered are already criminalized (for example, the failure to disclose information in a company prospectus is criminalized by the Financial Services and Markets Act 2000).[189] Other categories will also be straightforward, as, for example, with insurance contracts where a person fails to disclose that he has a medical condition when taking out life insurance; or with job applications where there is a failure to reveal criminal convictions.[190] There may be duties that arise in equity, contract, and even in tort. Some categories will, however, be less straightforward, particularly when this involves the criminal court in an assessment of complex matters of civil law. Difficult matters of proof will arise where the question is whether a duty arises in the trade or custom or was agreed to orally, etc.

Since liability only arises on proof of a 'legal' duty, the question must, it is submitted, be one of law for the judge, with the jury being directed to conclude that if they find certain facts, as identified by the judge, proved, they can conclude that in law there is a duty to disclose information.[191] Several Lords expressed doubts in Parliament as to whether judges would struggle in explaining this issue to the jury.[192] The element was, however, endorsed by the 'Rose Committee' – a committee of the Senior Judiciary.[193] The Home Office rather optimistically regarded this as a 'relatively uncomplicated' requirement.[194]

The criminal courts have demonstrated a marked reluctance to become embroiled in civil law issues in their interpretation of the Theft Acts.[195] This despite the fact that the offences in question, being specifically designed to protect property and property rights *must*, by definition, rely upon the civil law's explanation and understanding of those concepts. Under s 3, the criminal courts are statutorily obliged to have regard to the civil law. It remains to be seen whether this is a duty they accept and can fulfil without wasting vast amounts of court time bogged down in arcane points of civil law, and/or leading to confusion of jurors.[196]

---

[188] eg, where a person in a fiduciary position has a duty to disclose material information when contracting with a beneficiary: a failure to make such disclosure will entitle the beneficiary to rescind the contract and to reclaim any property transferred under it. This section might be applicable in acrimonious divorce settlements where D withholds disclosure of his true assets. See D Salter, 'It's Criminal Not to Disclose' (2007) 37 Fam L 432.

[189] One recent example is that in the case of *Butt* [2005] EWCA Crim 805, where D's duty arose from his directorship in the company making the representations about high-yield investment.

[190] See *Daley* [2010] EWCA Crim 2193. See also *Mashta* [2010] EWCA Crim 2595.

[191] cf the A-G's view that this was a question of fact: *Hansard*, HL, 19 July 2005, col 1428.

[192] *Hansard*, HL, 19 July 2005, col 1427 (Lord Lyell of Markyate).

[193] *Hansard*, HL, 12 June 2006, col 536.

[194] Home Office Responses 2004, para 21.

[195] See, especially, *Morris* [1984] AC 320 at 324.

[196] Cynics might suggest that the difficulty jurors express in understanding the civil law questions will in time be prayed in aid by the Government in its campaign to remove the jury from fraud trials.

Scope of duty

The difficulties in applying the civil law are exacerbated because the civil law will be essential not only in identifying the relevant circumstances in which a duty arises, but also in assessing whether, if D has revealed any information, it was a sufficient disclosure to satisfy the duty imposed upon him. This will be a further matter on which the jury will require careful direction. Clearly, where the Crown can show that D has failed completely to comply with his civil duty, he will be liable. Beyond that, where D claims that he has fulfilled the duty of disclosure it will be a matter of degree. Such issues go not only to the question of the duty and its scope, but also relate to D's dishonesty.

Awareness of a duty?

Liability appears to be strict as to the existence of a duty. It is no defence for D to claim that he lacked the knowledge or awareness of the duty to disclose. Any such claims will be subsumed within the general plea of a lack of dishonesty – once again that is the element of the offence which is the principal determinant of liability. It is interesting to note that the Law Commission in its original proposals suggested that liability as to the existence of the duty ought not to be strict. However, that recommendation was made in the context of a range of much broader proposals. Once the Government restricted its scope to cases of breach of a legal duty, it is arguable that imposing strict liability as to the existence of such duties is less problematical. Arguably, D ought to be aware of his duties in civil law. The counter argument is that his mistake as to the civil law ought not to give rise to criminal liability.

It will be interesting to see the courts' response to this problem. Despite the landmark decisions of the House of Lords in *DPP v B*[197] and *K*,[198] holding that there is a constitutional principle of a presumption of *mens rea* in English criminal law, the courts are willing to find that the presumption is rebutted by necessary implication. If the courts find that liability is strict as to the existence of the duty, D will be able to advance a plea of a lack of awareness of the duty, and/or the scope of the obligations it imposed, within a plea of a lack of dishonesty.

Information

The duty must be one which is to disclose 'information'. That concept is not defined. It is submitted that the word is an ordinary English word and that few difficulties in interpretation should arise. It will take its meaning in part from the circumstances and terms of the duty in question.

To whom duty must be owed?

The section does not limit liability to those cases in which D is under a duty to disclose to V and fails to disclose to V. For example, D might be a company director and in breaching his duties to the company he might intend to expose to a risk of loss V, an investor. Again, the scope of criminal liability is determined by the particular civil law obligation imposed.

23.4.3.3 Failing to disclose

As noted, the question of whether there has been a sufficient degree of failure in disclosure may give rise to problems. The opportunity for the defence to claim that there has been adequate disclosure may well be exploited.[199] If D has fulfilled his civil law duty in terms of the type/quantity of disclosure there should be no criminal liability. This may involve the courts in

---

[197] [2000] 2 AC 428.
[198] [2002] 1 AC 462.
[199] See the argument in *Ali* [2006] All ER (D) 207 (May) where D had failed to disclose a change in benefit entitlement.

some complex issues of civil law. Particularly difficult examples might include those in which the allegation of a failure to comply with a duty which arises from the trade or custom. Such duties are less likely to be clearly prescribed and must take their form, to some extent, from the circumstances in which they arise and from the parties' expectations. Expert evidence may need to be called.

23.4.4 *Mens rea*

23.4.4.1 Dishonesty

As discussed above, the *Ghosh* test will apply. The element of dishonesty will be especially important in cases where D claims that he was not aware of his duty and or that he believed that he had satisfied that duty. Arguably, the vague nature of the dishonesty test renders the offence too wide.[200]

23.4.4.2 With intent to gain or cause loss or expose to risk of loss

This element of the *mens rea* is discussed above. There is no requirement that the intention is to cause a loss by which D gains. Nor need there be any intention for the loss to be caused to the person to whom the duty is owed.

23.5 Section 4: fraud by abuse of position

The third form of the general fraud offence is perhaps the most controversial and is provided for in s 4. It is rarely prosecuted, in 2009/10 there were 1,159 recorded offences.[201] Section 4 provides:

(1) A person is in breach of this section if he –

   (a) occupies a position in which he is expected to safeguard, or not to act against, the financial interests of another person,

   (b) dishonestly abuses that position, and

   (c) intends, by means of the abuse of that position –

      (i) to make a gain for himself or another, or

      (ii) to cause loss to another or to expose another to a risk of loss.

(2) A person may be regarded as having abused his position even though his conduct consisted of an omission rather than an act.

23.5.1 Interpretation

As with ss 2 and 3 the terms of the offence are easy to describe. The *actus reus* comprises abusing a position of financial trust and the *mens rea* comprises acting dishonestly and intending by the abuse to make a gain/cause loss. Once again, it is lamentable that none of the terms of this form of the offence are defined in the Act. The provision met with some opposition in Parliament, being described as 'woolly',[202] and as a 'catch all provision that will be a nightmare of judicial interpretation . . . and help bring the law into disrepute'.[203]

---

[200] See comments of Brian Jenkins MP in *Hansard*, HC, 12 June 2006, col 554.

[201] Flatley et al, *Crime in England and Wales 2009/10*, 32.

[202] *Hansard*, HC, 12 June 2006, col 549.

[203] Standing Committee B, 20 June 2006, col 25.

23.5.2 *Actus reus*

23.5.2.1 A 'position'

Critical to understanding this offence is the concept of 'position'. Unfortunately, despite repeated requests for clarification in the course of parliamentary debates, the Government refused to define with any particularity what this element of the fraud means. The most obvious interpretation of this element would be to treat it as synonymous with a requirement that D owed a 'fiduciary duty' to the other. That would have involved the criminal courts in yet more close analysis of complex civil law questions, but it would have secured certainty and ensured coherence between the civil and criminal law. Unfortunately, the Government rejected this logical interpretation, being persuaded by arguments that the definition of 'fiduciary duty' would be unduly technical and would restrict the scope of the offence.[204] It preferred to allow s 4 to extend the criminal law into ambiguous territory, although, interestingly, few if any of the examples provided by government spokesmen or in government documents go beyond circumstances in which D does in fact owe a fiduciary duty.

The Home Office Explanatory Notes[205] provide little assistance, simply referring the reader back to the Law Commission explanation in its Report No 276. The Law Commission explained the meaning of 'position' at para 7.38:

The necessary relationship will be present between trustee and beneficiary, director and company, professional person and client, agent and principal, employee and employer, or between partners. It may arise otherwise, for example within a family, or in the context of voluntary work, or in any context where the parties are not at arm's length. In nearly all cases where it arises, it will be recognised by the civil law as importing fiduciary duties, and any relationship that is so recognised will suffice. We see no reason, however, why the existence of such duties should be essential. This does not of course mean that it would be entirely a matter for the fact-finders whether the necessary relationship exists. The question whether the particular facts alleged can properly be described as giving rise to that relationship will be an issue capable of being ruled upon by the judge and, if the case goes to the jury, of being the subject of directions.[206]

This offers a very broad and ill-defined scope of liability. The Home Office gave examples of relevant 'positions' as including those where D is given access to V's premises, equipment, records or customers.[207] It also provided other obvious examples, including that of a software company employee who abused his employment position to clone software products with the intention of selling them, and employees in care homes who were entrusted to look after the financial affairs of the elderly or disabled person and drew money for their own purposes.[208] These give no meaningful guidance on any limits of this serious offence.[209] The only other advice was that the offence applies wherever V has 'voluntarily' put D in such a position.[210] It would apply to cases of insider dealing, and to cases where auditors have acted dishonestly in not safeguarding investors etc.[211]

---

[204] See Standing Committee B, 20 June 2006, cols 24–27 (Solicitor General).

[205] Para 20.

[206] Referred to in debates by the A-G (*Hansard*, HL, 19 July 2005, col 1431) and the Solicitor General (*Hansard*, HC, 12 June 2006, col 558).

[207] Para 23.

[208] This would also be theft: *Hopkins and Kendrick* [1997] 2 Cr App R 524; *Hinks* [2001] 1 Cr App R 18.

[209] Section 4 will overlap with theft in some cases, eg, *Chan Man Sin v A-G for Hong Kong* [1988] 1 All ER 1; cf *A-G for HK v Reid* [1994] AC 314.

[210] No 276, para 7.37, repeated in the Home Office Consultation Paper (2004) para 23.

[211] See as an example of civil law duty, *Manutzfarg v Freightliner* [2007] EWCA Civ 910.

As noted, the Government was unwilling to accept that the scope of liability for s 4 should be restricted to circumstances of fiduciary duties arguing that the definition of fiduciary duty was too narrow and too complex. The Solicitor General referred to the definition of that concept provided by Millet LJ in *Bristol & West Building Society v Mothew*,[212] but interpreted his lordship's definition in a particularly narrow fashion to conclude that a fiduciary duty would restrict the offence unnecessarily because it would require proof that the person under the fiduciary duty has a single loyalty.[213]

It was pointed out to the Solicitor General that he had misunderstood the concept of fiduciary duty,[214] with regard to the use of 'single-mindedness', but an amendment which would have restricted liability to cases of fiduciary duty was defeated.

Cases of fiduciary duty

In the more obvious situations in which s 4 might be relied on, the existence of the duty will present no problem: D's civil law duties will saddle him with liability. Even in these cases, there may be practical problems with the criminal courts identifying with precision the duty, and its terms. This may pose further questions as to the respective functions of judge and jury. If the scope of liability under s 4 had been restricted to cases of fiduciary duty, there would have been a strong argument for saying that the judge must determine whether D's 'position' is within s 4 and to direct the jury as to what evidence of that they must find in order to convict. However, since a fiduciary duty will be a *sufficient* but not a *necessary* basis for liability, it is more questionable who has responsibility for determining D's status. The Law Commission clearly thought that whether the particular facts alleged can properly be described as giving rise to that relationship will be 'an issue capable of being ruled upon by the judge and, if the case goes to the jury, of being the subject of directions'.[215]

One area of fiduciary duty in which the s 4 offence will be useful is that relating to secret profits. The common law had become extremely confused on this issue. In *Tarling*,[216] the House of Lords held that the company directors' failure to disclose a secret profit made in breach of a fiduciary duty even if it was dishonest, did not constitute a conspiracy to defraud. In *Adams*,[217] the Privy Council held that the company director had been correctly convicted when making a secret profit. Adams seems to have gone further than Tarling by actively concealing the profits. The position was inconsistent and incoherent. Section 4 is wide enough to tackle both situations: it catches secret profiteers from the waiter who sells his bottle of wine, passing it off as one from the restaurant,[218] to the director who makes personal millions by trading company stock in breach of his fiduciary duty.

In cases involving a breach of a fiduciary duty, there may well be an overlap with s 3 where the fiduciary fails to disclose information, and/or under s 2 when there is a false representation. Note, however, that liability is potentially wider under s 4 because there is no need for the Crown to prove any positive act on D's part; an omission will do.

---

[212] [1998] Ch 1. J Martin, *Hanbury and Martin on Modern Equity* (18th edn, 2009) Ch 23.

[213] He referred to 'what Lord Justice Millett described as the "single-minded loyalty" of the fiduciary . . . It is on that basis that we put the wording in the clause, "he is expected to safeguard". Such a person is in a position where they are trusted, but it might not go as far as having a legal relationship which involves an entitlement on the part of the other person to their single-minded loyalty. The person may have loyalty to many others.' HC Standing Committee B, 20 June 2006, col 27.

[214] See cols 27–28.

[215] No 276, para 7.38.

[216] (1978) 70 Cr App R 77, HL. The application of the offence in this context is discussed in the Home Office, *Response to Consultation Document*, Annex B, para 14.

[217] [1995] 1 WLR 52, PC.

[218] *Doukas* [1978] 1 All ER 1071.

Liability in the absence of a fiduciary duty

The s 4 offence has the potential to criminalize acts or omissions by someone who is not under a formal legal duty of a fiduciary nature. Justice criticized the offence on these grounds when it was proposed, suggesting that it 'compromised legal certainty'.[219] The Law Commission's examples, above, which list the family and other voluntary arrangements as being caught, highlight the potential reach of s 4. Will the breadth of the offence open up the possibility of civil actions becoming the subject of prosecution?[220] Concerns were expressed in Parliament that the offence would for example, catch D who breaches a confidentiality agreement with his employer.[221]

Employee A of X Ltd will be caught by passing up an opportunity to seal a lucrative contract so that his friend B, working for Y Ltd can take advantage.[222] D who is employed to secure three tenders for a lucrative contract and chooses instead to obtain one which turns out to be a disastrous selection may be caught. Section 4 seems to apply whether A is motivated by malice or laziness. Beyond that the scope of the offence is astonishingly wide. Its ambit lies in the hands of those defining the qualifying 'position'. To take an extreme example, what of an employee who persistently arrives late for work? He occupies a position in which he is expected not to act against the financial interests of the employer. Arguably, he abuses that position intending thereby to make a gain. Subject to a finding of dishonesty, he may be guilty. Is it sufficient that D causes V to lose merely a chance of profit?

The offence is so wide that it also has the potential to apply to financial misgovernance by public officials. Many public officials are in a position in which they are expected to safeguard or not to act against the financial interests of another person (that is, the public or the Crown). There may be overlap with offences of corruption[223] and misfeasance in public office.[224]

Unless kept within sensible limits, the offence has the potential to elevate all sorts of trivial contractual and familial disputes into criminal matters. The Government suggested that 'something more than a breakdown of relationships' would be needed to trigger s 4, but did not elaborate on this.[225] Careful prosecuting will also be needed to ensure that the offence is not allowed to criminalize conduct which involves no civil law wrong. In those cases of non-fiduciary duty which are prosecuted, the element of dishonesty will carry a disproportionate burden in determining criminal liability. For the reasons expressed above, it is doubtful whether that ill-defined element can shoulder such a burden in an offence carrying a maximum of 10 years' imprisonment.

The CPS has listed examples of circumstances in which s 4 should be charged to guide prosecutors.[226] These demonstrate the reach of the offence. There have been few reported cases

---

[219] Briefing Document for HL, above (2006) para 8.

[220] This will be a significant stick with which employers can beat employees: Mr Geoffrey Cox QC, MP, Standing Committee B, 20 June 2006, col 15.

[221] Standing Committee B, 20 June 2006, col 15.

[222] The CPS has issued guidance on public policy interests of prosecuting fraud and has stated that 'The criminal law should not be used to protect private confidences.'

[223] See, eg, *Ross River v Cambridge FC* [2007] EWHC 2115 (Ch), where the fraudulent representations involved bribery of a member of the defendant's board. From July 2011 the offences will be replaced by the Bribery Act 2010.

[224] See C Nichols et al, *Corruption and the Misuse of Public Office* (2006) Ch 3.

[225] See Home Office, *Fraud Law Reform, Responses to Consultation* (2004) para 27.

[226] These include 'an employee of a software company who uses his position to clone software products with the intention of selling the products on his own behalf'; 'a person employed to care for an elderly or disabled person with access to that person's bank account who abuses that position by removing funds for his own personal use'; 'an employee who abuses his position in order to grant contracts or discounts to friends, relatives and associates'; 'a trader who helps an elderly person with odd jobs, gains influence over that person and removes money from their account'; 'the person entrusted to purchase lottery tickets on behalf of others'.

under s 4. In *Marshall* the offence was used to prosecute a care home worker who was mis-using residents' bank accounts.[227] In *Gale*[228] G had abused his position as a shipping handler when he certified cargo as 'approved' for shipment to the USA when he was in fact unaware of its contents (a prohibited substance).

23.5.2.2 'Occupies'

The section applies only in relation to the positions D 'occupies'. It is clear that the 'abuse' with intent to gain or cause loss must arise while D is in occupation of that position in order for s 4 to apply. Where D has, whilst in a position of trust, obtained financial information, and then after leaving his position uses that information with intent to gain or cause loss, has the s 4 offence been committed? Arguably, the answer will turn on whether D intends *at the time of the obtaining* to use the information to gain or cause loss. If he obtains the information with that intention he is abusing the position he then occupies. More difficult will be the case where D obtains such information while occupying a relevant 'position', and at the time of obtaining he has no intention by that obtaining to gain or cause loss then or in the future. Perhaps he has an intention to keep the information as a safeguard against any future allegation that he was involved in a dubious aspect of a particular deal that was being undertaken in the organ-ization within which he occupied the position.[229] Subsequently, having left that position, D realizes that there is the potential to use the information to make a gain or cause a loss and he decides to do so. He is not at that time abusing a position which he 'occupies'. Such a person commits the offence under s 6 of the Act possession of an article for use in fraud (below) if he intends it to be used in fraud–which is of course much narrower than intending to use it for gain or to cause loss or expose to a risk of loss.

According to the Solicitor General in the course of debates in the Standing Committee:

A person can occupy a position where they owe a duty that goes beyond the performance of a job. A contract that is entered into that obliges a person to have duties of confidentiality, perhaps, can go well beyond the time when that employment ceases. The duty may, however, still arise. The person entered into the duty at the beginning of the employment and it exists indefinitely. Therefore a person may still occupy a position in which there is a legitimate expectation. That may well, by virtue of a contract and the agreement that the employee entered into voluntarily, go beyond redundancy or the point when he leaves the post.[230]

23.5.2.3 Expectation

The scope of the concept of 'position' which D must occupy is to some extent dependent on the definition of the term 'position in which he is expected to safeguard'.[231] The critical question, and one which Parliament spectacularly left unanswered, is: whose expectation counts?[232] If it is the potential victim's this could be a very wide scope of liability subject to D denying liability by way of a lack of dishonesty. If it is a test based on what D thinks his financial duties are, it might be very limited and difficult to prove. The courts may choose to construe the requirement of expectation be objectively.

---

[227] [2009] EWCA Crim 2076.

[228] [2008] EWCA Crim 1344.

[229] Is that an abuse? It is doubtful that a jury would regard it as such where the defendant is protecting himself against allegations that he was involved in criminal conduct by the organization; that does not sound like abuse, even though it is contrary to the interests of that organization.

[230] Standing Committee B, 20 June 2006, col 23.

[231] If the conduct is perpetrated by a public official, there may be an offence of misconduct in public office.

[232] See the discussion in the Commons Standing Committee where it was proposed that the word 'expected' be replaced by a requirement that D had a 'fiduciary duty': HC, Standing Committee B, 20 June 2006, col 11; rejected by the Solicitor General at col 20.

23.5.2.4 Financial interests

The term is not defined. There is little doubt that the courts will be encouraged to adopt a very wide reading. There is no restriction that the financial interests be regarded as long-term ones.

23.5.2.5 Abuse

The term 'abuse' is not defined. The Home Office makes clear in the Explanatory Notes that it is deliberately left undefined as the term is intended to cover a wide range of conduct. Coupled with the breadth of the concept of 'positions' of responsibility this makes the offence extremely wide. If positions of financial responsibility were restricted to legal/fiduciary duty cases the issue of abuse would be resolved by asking simply whether the defendant had breached the legal/fiduciary duty he owed.

The word 'abuse' may well fall to be interpreted as an ordinary English word, which although straightforward, will do nothing to promote certainty and consistency in an offence of such seriousness. If guidance is needed, the dictionary definitions suggest that it involves acting 'wrongly' or 'improperly' or treating in a harmful or injurious way. Although not an element of the offence, jurors might be unwilling to conclude there has been abuse unless some loss is in fact caused (or some gain accrued) or at least that someone is exposed to the risk of loss.

The abuse is of the 'position', but it may be that D holds a position of financial responsibility towards B (for example, the company), but acts with intent to cause loss to C (an investor) by the abuse of his position *vis-à-vis* B.

It is notable that the original proposal contained a requirement of secrecy in D's actions of abuse,[233] but the Home Office removed this element, despite its widespread approval on the grounds that it was difficult to define and created unnecessary complication.[234]

23.5.2.6 Act or omission

Section 4(2) makes clear that the offence can be committed by omission as well as by positive action. An obvious example is where D, an employee, fails to perform his duty under the contract of employment so that a rival company wins the tender at the expense of D's employer.

23.5.3 *Mens rea*

It would appear that liability is strict as to whether D occupies a position in which he is expected to safeguard the financial interests of another. D's lack of awareness that he is in such a position must be subsumed in a plea of lack of dishonesty. There is no explicit *mens rea* requirement as to any awareness of the defendant as to the existence of the expectation that he must safeguard the financial interests of another.

23.5.3.1 Dishonesty

The elements have been discussed above. As noted there is a very heavy burden placed on dishonesty. It is interesting to consider the ECHR compatibility of this form of the fraud offence. In cases in which there is no legal or fiduciary duty on D, it is difficult to see what additional

---

[233] Indeed, the CPS said: 'In the absence of an element of secrecy, it is accepted that the new offence would probably be too wide.' However, the deletion of this requirement was supported by Lord Lloyd, *Hansard*, HL, 22 June 2005, col 1665.

[234] See Home Office, *Fraud Law Reform, Responses to Consultation* (2004) para 28. See also *Hansard*, HL, 19 July 2005, cols 1432–1433; *Hansard*, HC, 12 June 2006, col 538; Standing Committee B, 20 June 2006, cols 28–29.

element of conduct which is morally dubious prevents the offence being one based solely on dishonesty. As the Joint Parliamentary Committee on Human Rights recognized, such an offence would be likely to infringe Art 7.[235]

23.5.3.2 Intent to gain/cause loss

One particular aspect of this element to note in the context of s 4 is that the definition of gain and loss includes intangible property which may well have a significant role to play in the context of abuse of a financial position.

23.6 Section 11: obtaining services dishonestly

Section 11 replaces the offence of obtaining services by deception in s 1 of the Theft Act 1978.[236] As noted above, it was increasingly apparent that the Theft Acts failed to protect against the obtaining of services via wholly automated processes. The Law Commission's proposal as endorsed by the Home Office was to remove the troublesome element of deception from the offence and to place the emphasis on dishonesty.

The section provides:

(1) A person is guilty of an offence under this section if he obtains services for himself or another –

    (a) by a dishonest act, and

    (b) in breach of subsection (2).

(2) A person obtains services in breach of this subsection if –

    (a) they are made available on the basis that payment has been, is being or will be made for or in respect of them,

    (b) he obtains them without any payment having been made for or in respect of them or without payment having been made in full, and

    (c) when he obtains them, he knows –

        (i) that they are being made available on the basis described in paragraph (a), or

        (ii) that they might be, but intends that payment will not be made, or will not be made in full.

(3) A person guilty of an offence under this section is liable –

    (a) on summary conviction, to imprisonment for a term not exceeding 12 months or to a fine not exceeding the statutory maximum (or to both);

    (b) on conviction on indictment, to imprisonment for a term not exceeding 5[237] years or to a fine (or to both).

---

[235] See above, p 875.

[236] See, generally, the Home Office, *Fraud Law Reform* (2004) paras 32–35; the Home Office, *Fraud Law Reform, Responses to Consultation* (2004) para 35; the Home Office Explanatory Notes, paras 34–36; the House of Commons *Research Paper* 31/06, at 17.

[237] The Government rejected calls for the sentence to be a maximum of 10 years consistent with ss 2–4 of the Act: Standing Committee B, 20 June 2006, col 59.

23.6.1 Interpretation

This is a result crime, and is quite distinct from the three forms of fraud offence provided for in ss 1 to 4.[238] There must be an actual obtaining of a service. The *actus reus* comprises (i) an act resulting in the obtaining; (ii) of services (iii) for which payment is or will become due and (iv) a failure to pay in whole or in part. The *mens rea* comprises (i) dishonesty; (ii) knowing that the services are to be paid for or knowing that they might have to be paid for; (iii) with intent to avoid payment in whole or in part.

According to the Law Commission in its Report No 276, 'This offence would be more analogous to theft than to deception, because it could be committed by "helping oneself" to the service rather than dishonestly inducing another person to provide it.'[239]

23.6.2 *Actus reus*

23.6.2.1 An act

Unusually, the offence is restricted to conduct in the form of a positive act. It is made explicit that it is not possible to commit the offence by omission. If an unsolicited service is offered, perhaps in the mistaken belief that a customer has paid for it, no dishonest 'act' has taken place. A rather unconvincing example provided in Parliament was of D, who sits on a boat and does not alight when he hears an announcement that anyone who has not paid for the next trip should alight. It was suggested that he commits no offence under this section.[240] This restriction may be rather illusory in its practical impact. In this example there is no doubt that D commits a fraud offence under s 2 by making an implied representation by conduct that he will pay for the trip. He does so with intent to cause financial loss to the travel company and/ or to gain by keeping that which he has (s 5(3)). In addition, it is difficult to see why D is not obtaining a service in the form of the return trip by his positive act of sitting on the boat to take the return trip.

23.6.2.2 Obtaining

As noted, this is a result crime. D's dishonest act must be a cause of the obtaining of a service. The obtaining may be for D or another.

23.6.2.3 Service

Service is not further defined. But the offence is restricted in that it only applies to services for which payment is required. This follows the old s 1 of the 1978 Act offence which did not apply to gratuitous services. Some of the situations in which D obtains a service for free by making a false representation will be caught by s 2 (above). Note that ss 1 to 4 apply only in relation to *property* whereas s 11 applies in relation to dishonest obtaining of *services*. As under the old law, an application for a bank account or credit card will only be caught by this offence if the service is to be paid for: *Sofroniou*.[241] What is not made clear is whether the offence extends to services which are not legally enforceable? Can the offence occur, for example, in respect of prostitution or corrupt services?[242]

---

[238] cf *Arlidge and Parry on Fraud* who suggest that 'one who lies to obtain services is guilty of the same offences as one who lies to get property', para 9.003.

[239] Report No 276, para 8.8.

[240] The Government also emphasized the need to avoid criminalizing those who received unsolicited services from unscrupulous companies: Standing Committee B, 20 June 2006, col 54.

[241] [2003] EWCA Crim 3681.

[242] *Linekar* [1995] QB 250.

The offence obviously extends well beyond the electronic 'deception' type case. It covers, for example, the case where D climbs over a wall and watches a football match without paying the entrance fee (such a person is not deceiving the provider of the service directly, but is obtaining a service which is provided on the basis that people will pay for it). But, not to cases where D watches the game from the window of a property adjoining the ground.[243]

As the Home Office explains, it also covers the situation where a person attaches a decoder to his television to enable viewing access to cable/satellite television channels for which he has no intention of paying.[244] It was suggested that it would also catch illegally downloading music where the provision of the music constituted a service.[245]

23.6.2.4 Without payment

One problem with the s 11 offence which does not seem to have been foreseen was that it may be inapplicable in the commonplace situation where D obtains the relevant service by using a credit card or debit card. Even though the use of the card is unauthorized, the payment will be made by the bank/issuing company provided that the PIN is correct and the security number accurate, etc. The offence will not apply in such circumstances because the requirement is not that D himself does not pay, but that payment has not been made at all, or in part. The fact that D is unaware of the banking practice, and believes that no payment will be made cannot make him liable under s 11 if payment has in fact been made. He may, of course, be liable for an attempt.

In many cases where D obtains a service by use of a credit card in such circumstances he will also obtain some element of property (for example, the ticket for the travel, or for entry to the theatre, etc) and will therefore commit an offence under s 2 of the Act because his false representation (that he is authorized to use the card), coupled with a dishonest intention to cause either loss to the credit card company and/or expose to a risk of loss the service provider, suffice for that offence. He might also be regarded as making a false representation with intention to gain by keeping what he has – ie the money he would otherwise have had to spend. Alternatively, s 6 of the 2006 Act might be used with charges of possession of the article with intent to commit fraud.

23.6.3 *Mens rea*

23.6.3.1 Dishonesty

Dishonesty has been discussed above. *Ghosh*[246] applies. This is the principal *mens rea* element of the new offence.

23.6.3.2 Knowing that payment required/might be

The additional requirement that D knows that the services are to be paid for or knows that they might have to be paid for imposes a relatively strict test. Arguably, the offence is too wide in including cases where D knows only that payment *might* have to be made. This form of the *mens rea* was included to deal with electronic purchasing over the internet and cases where D might have alleged that he was unsure what the obligations to pay were.[247] Arguably, the statute is right to extend the offence this far: if D knows that it might be the onus is on him to make enquiries before he engages the services, and not to act dishonestly.

---

[243] Standing Committee B, 20 June 2006, col 52.
[244] See Home Office Explanatory Notes, para 36.
[245] ibid.
[246] [1982] QB 1053, CA.
[247] Home Office, *Fraud Law Reform* (2004) para 35.

Other difficulties might arise where there is uncertainty over whether the knowledge is that payment will be due immediately or at some later date.

23.6.3.3 Intention that payment avoided

This requirement that D acts with intent to avoid payment in whole or in part marks a departure from the old offence under s 1 of the 1978 Act and narrows the scope of the crime.

Intends that 'payment will not be made'

As noted, there is no liability for D who obtains a service by use of a credit card, where payment is made by the card issuing company, although D was unaware of that fact and intended that no payment would be made.

If D intends that payment will be made, whether by himself or by the card company, he will also be acquitted. The Law Commission was keen to emphasize the limits of the s 11 offence in this regard and provided an example that DD, parents of D, who lie about their religion in order to get D into a private school where they will be charged and pay the full fees, commit no offence under s 11.[248]

23.7 Section 6: possession of articles for fraud

The scope of the criminal law's proscription of acts merely preparatory to the commission of acquisitive crime is extended dramatically by s 6 which provides:

(1) A person is guilty of an offence if he has in his possession or under his control any article for use in the course of or in connection with any fraud.

(2) A person guilty of an offence under this section is liable –

(a) on summary conviction, to imprisonment for a term not exceeding 12 months or to a fine not exceeding the statutory maximum (or to both);

(b) on conviction on indictment, to imprisonment for a term not exceeding 5 years or to a fine (or to both).

This is a disturbingly wide new offence. In 2009/10 there were 1,541 recorded offences.[249] The Law Commission in its 2002 Report, *Fraud*, had proposed simply to replace that form of s 25 of the Theft Act offence of 'going equipped'[250] which covered going equipped with implements for 'deception'[251] with one covering going equipped for 'fraud'.[252] The going equipped offence is limited in two significant ways: (a) the offence cannot be committed by possession of the materials at the defendant's abode, thereby respecting the unique privacy rights

---

[248] There has been considerable controversy as to whether the Fraud Act applies in relation to parents making false representations in order to enhance their chances of securing places in state schools which the parents would like their children to attend. See C Monaghan, 'Fraudsters? Putting Parents in the Dock' (2010) 174 CJLW 581. It is difficult to identify what property D intends to gain. See also the Report to the Secretary of State for Children Schools and Families on Fraudulent or Misleading Applications for Admission to Schools (2009) see also http://news.bbc.co.uk/1/hi/8334503.stm and www.telegraph.co.uk/education/6486725/Warning-over-school-admissions-theft.html.

[249] Flatley et al, *Crime in England and Wales 2009/10*, 32.

[250] See below, Ch 26.

[251] Confusingly termed 'cheat' in s 25 of the 1968 Act.

[252] See Law Commission, *Fraud* (2002), Draft Bill, 'In section 25 (going equipped for burglary, theft or cheat) –(a) in subsections (1) and (3) for "cheat" substitute "fraud", and (b) in subsection (5) for "and 'cheat' means an offence under section 15(1) of this Act" substitute "and 'fraud' means fraud contrary to section 1 of the Fraud Act 2002".'

attaching to that space, (b) the s 25 offence is designed to deal with the defendant who has set out to commit the specified wrong – albeit this might be mere preparation and hence not an attempt, nevertheless, it does require evidence that D has a degree of proximity to the offence although the defendant need not be on his way to commit a crime at that moment and need not have identified a target.

The Home Office in its consultation exercise in 2004 proposed much wider reform, noting in particular the need to deal with the use of home computers for fraud.[253] The Home Office went on to explain its desire for an offence of mere possession of, for example, computer software for use in 'the course of or in connection with' a fraud.[254] One particular concern was the widespread use of software to read credit cards, and the impact this has on the volume of fraud and more generally the public's fear of fraud and of 'identity theft'.[255]

The Government's argument is not as compelling as it might at first seem. There is now the extremely wide offence (ss 2–4) in the 2006 Act with which to prosecute frauds. The fraudster who works from home is caught by those provisions just as easily as anyone else. There is also the scope for charging inchoate offences such as conspiracy to commit a s 6 offence.[256] Similarly, the fraudster who has *attempted* to commit frauds from his home will be caught. Section 6 extends to those who have not yet even attempted to commit fraud. Section 6 may turn out to be a powerful weapon in prosecuting the peripheral players in major frauds. If the key players are prosecuted under ss 2 to 4 or for conspiracy to defraud, there will be many who have assisted in some way who could be more easily prosecuted under s 6 than for assisting or encouraging or conspiring.

23.7.1 *Actus reus*

23.7.1.1 An article

The concept of article has been given a wide reading under the s 25 offence,[257] but the 2006 Act provides a yet broader definition of the term in s 8.

(1) For the purposes of –

(a) sections 6 and 7, and

(b) the provisions listed in subsection (2),[258] so far as they relate to articles for use in the course of or in connection with fraud,

'article' *includes* any program or data held in electronic form.[259]

The Home Office Explanatory Notes state that:

Examples of cases where electronic programs or data could be used in fraud are: a computer program can generate credit card numbers; computer templates can be used for producing blank utility bills; computer files can contain lists of other peoples' credit card details or draft letters in connection with 'advance fee' frauds.[260]

---

[253] Para 39.

[254] Para 41.

[255] The Home Office explained the target included articles which are specifically 'made or adapted' for committing frauds at para 42.

[256] See, eg, *Pakiyanthur* [2010] EWCA Crim 2312.

[257] See, ibid, para 50.

[258] Offences of having in possession and powers under PACE etc.

[259] Emphasis added. See on the wide interpretation of the concept of article in the Terrorism Act 2000, s 57, to include electronic data, the case of *M* [2007] EWCA Crim 218; cf *Rowe* [2007] EWCA Crim 635; *Zafar* [2008] EWCA Crim 184 as approved in this respect in *G* [2010] 1 AC 43.

[260] Para 26.

There is no requirement that the program or data is designed exclusively for fraud. Any word processing or spreadsheet program is capable of being used to produce false invoices or false utility bills. Any email software is capable of sending false representations and thus for committing frauds under s 2, and so on. It is difficult to see any restriction on the concept of article which might limit the offence. A printer and computer, an iPhone,[261] a memory stick,[262] paper[263] or even a humble pen are articles and capable of being used in the course of or in connection with fraud and are capable of being possessed.

23.7.1.2 A person

The offence is designed primarily to tackle the *individual* but would seem also on the application of general principles of interpretation to apply to corporate defendants. The company director who is aware of the DVD copying machine or the software for producing false bills, etc, which is loaded onto the company's computers may render the company liable.

23.7.1.3 Has in his possession

The concept of possession has given rise to problems for the courts, particularly in relation to drugs offences.[264] Possession is a neutral concept, not implying any kind of blame or fault but experience, especially in the old law of larceny, has shown that, when it becomes the determinant of guilt, it tends to acquire a refined and artificial meaning of great complexity.

There is no requirement that the articles are held in possession in any particular venue. Any article in the possession of the person whether at home, in public or at work is capable of satisfying this element of the offence. Whereas the concept of possession has created few problems with the going equipped offence, it might be suggested that this is in part at least because the offence only applies where D is not at his abode. That restriction makes it more likely that the articles will be on D's person or in very close proximity to him for the offence to be triggered. With the offence under s 6, there is no such restriction. A person might be said to have in his possession many thousands of articles around his home and workplace.

Personal possession?

One issue which the courts may be called on to resolve under s 6 is whether it is possible for D to be in possession through an agent or intermediary? Does D have in his possession the software held on his teenage son's computer? Does the employer possess all the software loaded onto each of his employees' computers? Such cases might be thought to be cases of 'control' by D, if within the offence at all. There is, however, nothing in the section to require the possession to be exclusive to D. There appears to be no obvious basis for the courts to take a restrictive interpretation.[265] The question therefore arises: what limits on liability are there? Does D possess an article in the form of data if it is stored only on a server outside the jurisdiction and accessible via the internet? If so, does D possess all that software or data on the internet to which he has instant access? Surely not. What about the case where D takes an annual

---

[261] See, eg, *Nimley* [2010] EWCA Crim 2752 – recording films in cinema to upload to website.

[262] Used for downloading data from ATM machines in *Ciorba* [2009] EWCA Crim 1800.

[263] As in *Kazi* [2010] EWCA Crim 2026 where D was going to pass the paper off as bundles of used banknotes that had been blacked out by the Bank of England. The victim would be told that these could be washed clean with a special chemical sold to them for a high price. This is commonly known as a 'wash wash' or 'black money' fraud. The victim is persuaded to buy the paper by the fraudster demonstrating the process on a real note on which an easily removable dye has been added.

[264] See, generally, R Fortson, *Misuse of Drugs, Offences, Confiscation and Money Laundering* (5th edn, 2005).

[265] cf other statutes in which specific provision is made, eg, Misuse of Drugs Act 1971, s 37(3): 'For the purposes of this Act the things which a person has in his possession shall be taken to include anything subject to his control which is in the custody of another.'

subscription to an electronic product, which can be used in fraud, stored on a server outside the jurisdiction, which by virtue of his subscription he can access from the UK? Might he have possession of an article, through the internet, for use in connection with fraud?

Knowing possession?

One way of restricting the scope of the concept of possession in this context would be for the courts to read in an element of *mens rea*. If it must be shown that D intended that the article be used in the course of fraud, as it is to be hoped and anticipated the courts will confirm, this will obviously impose a natural limitation on the scope of the offence as a whole, although it will do nothing to restrict the scope of the concept of possession.

One view is that there is no need to read in an additional element of mens rea as to possession, since the requirement of *mens rea* as to the intended use of the article will be a sufficient safeguard against the conviction of an innocent person for possessing articles which are *capable* of being used for fraud. An alternative view is that even though an additional *mens rea* element that D must *know* he is in possession of articles which he intends will be used for fraud is not necessary, it is nevertheless desirable since s 6 is so wide in its reach.[266] D who intends that the article will be used for fraud is almost inevitably likely to 'know' that it is his possession, but not always. What of D who is party to a gang of would-be fraudsters and is aware of a device that the gang possesses which could be used for fraud, and he intends that it should be used for their proposed fraud, but is unaware that it has been left in his garage by the gang. From such examples, it is certainly arguable that an element of knowing possession is desirable in the construction of the section.

In construing the concept of possession and its *mens rea*, it is unclear to what extent the courts might usefully and legitimately draw upon the jurisprudence regarding the concept of possession and its interpretation in other contexts. In the unlikely event that the courts refuse to read in the element of intention as to use, then there would be a greater similarity with the offences of drug possession where there is also no obligation on the Crown to establish any intent to use, etc. The CPS suggests in its guidance that it is 'probable' the courts are likely to draw on the case law on possession of drugs. In that context, the courts have held that D must 'know' that he is in possession of something which is, in fact, a controlled drug.[267]

If it must be proved that D 'knew' that he possessed the article that is alleged to be for use in fraud, particular difficulties may arise in the case of electronic data. Even in cases of tangible articles problems may arise: what of D who claims that he was unaware of the credit card cloning machine being stored in his son's bedroom or his office storeroom? In the drugs context, in *Lewis*,[268] it was held that the judge had not misdirected the jury by telling them that the tenant of a house might be found to be in possession of articles (drugs) found on the premises although he did not know they were there, provided he had had an opportunity to find out that they were. But this seems to go too far.[269] It is submitted that D does not possess 'articles' for use in fraud if the Crown can only establish that he had an opportunity to discover that they were on his property.

---

[266] The House of Lords has made very clear its position against strict liability offences unless Parliament has expressly or by necessary implication displaced the presumption of *mens rea: DPP v B* [2000] 2 AC 482.

[267] *Warner v Metropolitan Police Comr* [1969] 2 AC 256, *Boyesen* [1982] AC 768 and *McNamara* (1988) 87 Cr App R 246; *Lambert* [2002] 2 AC 545. cf in relation to firearms: *Zahid* [2010] EWCA Crim 2158.

[268] (1987) 87 Cr App R 270, [1988] Crim LR 517 and commentary.

[269] 'First of all man does not have possession of something which has been put into his pocket or into his house without his knowledge': *McNamara* (1988) 87 Cr App R 246 at 248.

Knowledge of the fraudulent 'nature' of the article

If the courts do incorporate an element of *mens rea* requiring proof that D must know he has the thing which he is alleged to possess, the question arises whether there is a further element which must be established – that D must know or comprehend the *nature* of the article?[270] What if D knows of the existence of the software that he possesses, but not its function? On one view, he is still in possession, a position akin to the container cases in drugs law. It is submitted that this should not pose any great problems for the courts. If there is a requirement that D intends that the article be used for fraud, it will be very rare for D to be able to raise a plausible plea of this type. Where the Crown have established D's intention as to fraudulent use, it will be possible but unlikely that he did not also know of the nature of the article. In contrast, if D lacks *any* understanding as to the nature of the article and its use, he must also lack an intention that it be used for fraud. Nor is any serious practical problem posed if the Crown establish D's intention that the article be used for fraud but D claims that he wrongly believed that the article can be used for fraud in one particular manner when it can in fact only be used for fraud in a different manner: D remains liable because the Crown must only establish a general intention as to its use.

The prosecution merely need to prove that D had possession and the relevant intent at some stage. If D asserts that he had forgotten that he had the article, by implication he is admitting knowing possession at some earlier time. If the prosecution can establish that at that stage he had the relevant intention he will be guilty.

Possession of electronic data

Where the article is electronic data on a computer, being perhaps one of many thousands on D's office machine, proving possession may be more difficult. The Crown's task will be even harder if the courts interpret the provision as requiring proof that D 'knew' he had possession of the article. What of a case where D claims to have deleted the relevant data or software and therefore not to have it in his possession even though an IT expert could recover the material from D's computer? This argument as a basis for denial of possession was accepted in the case of *Porter*[271] in the context of possession of indecent images of children. The Court of Appeal held that 'if a person cannot retrieve or gain access to an image, in our view he no longer has custody or control of it. He has put it beyond his reach just as does a person who destroys or otherwise gets rid of a hard copy photograph.'[272] It is questionable whether that is a faithful analogy. It is not as if D has burnt the hard copy photograph, rather he has put the hard copy in a safe and thrown away the key. Someone with the relevant skills can allow him to access it. Similarly, someone who has deleted the data from his computer could still be said to be in control of it in the sense that he possesses the machine on which it is stored and controls access to it, even if that access must be by another (more skilled) person. It is arguable that a charge of controlling such an article would be better suited in these circumstances. Again, the fact of deletion proves that D possessed the article pre-deletion and if it can be shown he had the relevant intent at that stage he is guilty.

23.7.1.4 'Control'

Use of the words possession *or* control must suggest that Parliament intended them to be capable of applying differently. Possession is intended to mean merely having custody of the article and the word 'or' does not extend the meaning of possession, but signifies that 'under

---

[270] *Boyesen* [1982] AC 768, [1982] 2 All ER 161. (It is immaterial how minute the quantity is provided only that it amounts to something and D knows he has it.)

[271] cf *Porter* [2006] EWCA Crim 560, [2006] Crim LR 748.

[272] [21].

his control' is a discrete, alternative version of the offence. The CPS guidance suggests that the phrase is intended to suggest something 'looser' than the concept of absolute possession.[273]

How far does the concept of control extend in this context? Does D control all material that is present on any of D's premises, or in his car etc? To what extent can D be said to be in control of an article which he cannot access instantly? In some offences in which the concept of having control of an article is used, the scope of the control is defined by the nature of the article or the illegal uses to which it is to be put. Given the breadth of the definition of article, there is no such implicit restriction in this offence. The courts might follow the interpretation in relation to electronic articles at least, in the offences under RIPA 2000,[274] in which the Court of Appeal recently held that a person has a right to control where he has the ability to authorize and forbid access.[275]

There is no obvious way in which 'control' will be limited by the courts to incorporate some requirement of D's physical proximity to or ease of access to the article. In the absence of any such limitation, the question arises whether any geographical limit can be placed on the concept in this context. Does D control the articles in his safety deposit box, or locked in his safe many miles away? If so, does it matter that the articles are in D's safe in Liechtenstein rather than in London? It does not seem to be an abuse of language to say that someone sitting at a computer terminal in London can be in control of data on his own server in the USA which he intends to be used to send false representations to the UK with intent to cause loss to the recipients here. In *Ex p Levin*,[276] an extradition case, the court thought that the fact that a computer operator was physically in Russia was of far less significance than the fact that he was looking at, and operating, on magnetic discs in the USA: he had committed theft in the USA and could be extradited to that country. That again prompts the question – can D be in control of data which is instantly accessible to him because it is posted on the internet? It is submitted that this would be going too far. The courts may be able to avoid such a broad reading by concluding that material/data etc stored on a site to which D does not have the ability to regulate access is not within his control. If D controls the website, he can regulate access to the data and can be said to be in control of it.

Knowing control?

As with the element of possession, there is a question mark over whether the Crown must show that D knows he is in control of the article. As above, if the courts read in the element of intention that the article be used for fraud, there is arguably no need to include a further element of *mens rea* that D knew he was in control of the article. D who intends that the article will be used for fraud is almost inevitably likely to know that it is under his control. But, as noted above, it is possible for D to be aware of the existence of an article for use in fraud, intend that it be used for such, but believe that it is under the control of an associate. The courts have construed the concept of control in s 5 of the Theft Act 1968 in a wide fashion such that a person may be in 'control' of property, even though unaware of its presence.[277]

---

[273] See www.cps.gov.uk/legal/d_to_g/fraud_act.

[274] Section 1(6) of that Act provides: 'The circumstances in which a person makes an interception of a communication in the course of its transmission by means of a private telecommunication system are such that his conduct is excluded from criminal liability under subsection (2) if – (a) he is a person with a *right to control* the operation or the use of the system; or (b) he has the express or implied consent of such a person to make the interception.'

[275] *Stanford* [2006] EWCA Crim 258.

[276] *Governor of Brixton Prison, ex p Levin* [1997] QB 65, [1997] 3 All ER 289, DC.

[277] *Woodman* [1974] QB 754 at 758.

23.7.1.5 'For use in the course of or in connection with'

This form of words is identical to that in going equipped. The offences of fraud are so wide that the items which might be used 'in connection with' such activities are endless. It is not necessarily a defence that D did not intend to use the article while in the physical commission of the contemplated crime. If, for example, he intended to use it only in the course of covering his tracks after the commission of the offence, this would be enough, being use 'in connection with' the offence. Similarly, if he intended to use the article while doing preparatory acts, the offence would be committed.

23.7.1.6 'Any fraud'

This clearly extends to offences under ss 2 to 4 of the 2006 Act. Presumably it also extends to ss 9 and 11. Is it limited to frauds under the Act? Is conspiracy to defraud caught as well? If the offence of fraudulent trading by a non-corporate business is caught (Fraud Act 2006, s 9), is the Companies Act 2006, s 993, offence of fraudulent trading by a corporation also caught? Is it restricted to the commission of the offence as principal or as an accessory or conspirator? The Act provides no guidance on whether 'fraud' is to be construed as meaning general fraud offence under s 1 or some wider collection of offences.[278] It is submitted that the offence does not extend to articles for use in connection with all dishonest offences. Some support for this is derived from the refusal of the Home Office in its responses to consultation to extend the proposal to include possession of articles for use in theft.[279]

23.7.2 *Mens rea*

The section makes no reference to *mens rea*.[280] The Home Office Explanatory Notes suggest that 'A general intention to commit fraud will suffice.'[281] It is submitted that this interpretation *must* be adopted by the courts to prevent the entire population being at risk of prosecution for the possession of pens, paper, etc.[282] Although the possession must be 'for' fraud, if there is no *mens rea* as to intention. D will be liable where, for example, he opens a cupboard in his new office and finds a credit card cloning machine. He has possession and it is for use in fraud – exclusively so. He has no defence of reasonable excuse for the possession since none is available under the Act. A *mens rea* requirement of intention is essential if s 6 is to work.

It is anticipated that the courts will apply *Ellames*[283] where in construing the s 25 offence the court said that:

In our view, to establish an offence under s 25(1) *the prosecution must prove that the defendant was in possession of the article, and intended the article to be used* in the course of or in connection with some future burglary, theft or cheat. But it is not necessary to prove that he intended it to be used in the course of or in connection with any specific burglary, theft or cheat; it is enough to prove a general

---

[278] For example, what of the offences involving copyright infringement under the Copyright Designs and Patents Act 1988 where D records films at the cinema on his iPhone and uploads them to a website for general viewing: see, eg, *Nimley* [2010] EWCA Crim 2752.

[279] Para 49.

[280] For criticism, see Justice, *Briefing for the Fraud Bill House of Lords Committee*, paras 18–21; and debates in Parliament: *Hansard*, HL Committee, 19 July 2005, col 1451; *Hansard*, HC, Standing Committee B, 20 June, cols 38–42; D Ormerod, 'The Fraud Act 2006 – Criminalising Lying' [2007] Crim LR 193.

[281] [25].

[282] In its original proposal, the Home Office had implicitly envisaged a strict liability offence of pure possession. This follows from the discussion in para 43 of the consultation document where it is explained that maximum sentencing powers will have to distinguish between 'simple possession where no intention can be proved... and possession with intent to commit a fraud'.

[283] [1974] 3 All ER 130.

intention to use it for some burglary, theft or cheat; we think that this view is supported by the use of the word 'any' in s 25(1).... Nor, in our view, is it necessary to prove that the defendant intended to use it himself; it will be enough to prove that he had it with him with the intention that it should be used by someone else.

A number of arguments can be marshalled in support of this interpretation. First, the Home Office had made clear in its response to consultation that the prosecution 'should have to prove a general intention that the article be used by the possessor (or someone else) for a fraudulent purpose, though they should not have to prove intended use in a particular fraud'.[284] The Home Office intention is clearly for this offence to follow the *mens rea* of the s 25 offence.[285] Secondly, the Attorney General[286] and Solicitor General[287] confirmed that the offence was not one of strict liability. Although they declined to amend the provision by the simple insertion of a requirement that D is in possession 'with intent that the article will be used for fraud', the Law Officers both confirmed that it was the Government's intention that the *mens rea* as laid down in *Ellames* would be 'attracted' by the use in s 6 of the same language as that in s 25 of the 1968 Act.[288] It is unfortunate that the amendment was rejected. The courts are naturally cautious in interpreting statutes by using analogous language from a different Act, particularly where the surrounding words are not identical.

23.7.3 Defences

Note that there is no defence of lawful excuse or lawful authority. The Home Office in its responses to consultation regarded this as unnecessary given the *mens rea* requirement – which is unfortunately not spelt out on the face of the statute. The investigative agency, which possesses such materials as a part of an undercover operation etc, will be protected by the lack of *mens rea* and/or by the absence of any public interest in prosecution.[289] The Home Office explanation for the absence of such a defence was that the 'dishonesty test' would protect those in undercover operations.[290] This seems to demonstrate a fundamental misunderstanding of s 6, which contains no dishonesty element!

23.7.4 Inchoate liability

The offences are capable of extending even further when inchoate versions are considered – eg D who seeks to purchase a device for use in fraud from a state agent in a sting operation attempts to possess.[291] However, it is submitted that it is not necessary to fall back on the use of an attempt charge where there is a potential impossibility problem.[292] The full offence may well be committed. For example, D is proved to be in possession of an article which he thinks will be able to clone credit cards, but which is in fact a useless piece of software which will be incapable of doing so. He is in possession of an article and he intends that the article will be used for fraud. He commits the full offence, even though it would be impossible for the article to be used to commit fraud.

---

[284] Paras 46–52.

[285] See *Ellames* [1974] 3 All ER 130.

[286] *Hansard*, HL, 19 July 2005, col 1452; *Hansard*, HL, 22 June 2005, col 1674.

[287] *Hansard*, HC, 12 June 2006, cols 541–542.

[288] See the Solicitor General's acceptance that he was making a '*Pepper v Hart*' statement to this effect: Standing Committee B, 20 June 2006, col 45. See also the Home Office Explanatory Notes, para 25. The CPS guidance clearly assumes that *Ellames* will apply: www.cps.gov.uk.

[289] Paras 47–48.

[290] Home Office, *Fraud Law Reform, Responses to Consultation* (2004) para 48.

[291] See also the liability for conspiracy in *Pakiyanthur* [2010] EWCA Crim 2312.

[292] See above, p 480.

23.8 Section 7: making or supplying articles for use in frauds

23.8.1 Section 7 of the Fraud Act 2006

Section 7 provides for a further broad offence:

(1) A person is guilty of an offence if he makes, adapts, supplies, or offers to supply any article –

    (a) knowing that it is designed or adapted for use in the course of or in connection with fraud, or

    (b) intending it to be used to commit, or assist in the commission of, fraud.

(2) A person guilty of an offence under this section is liable –

    (a) on summary conviction, to imprisonment for a term not exceeding 12 months or to a fine not exceeding the statutory maximum (or to both);

    (b) on conviction on indictment, to imprisonment for a term not exceeding 10 years or to a fine (or to both).

In 2009/10 there were 860 recorded offences.[293]

23.8.1.1 The forms of the offence

It is submitted that there are several distinct versions of the offence contained in s 7. There are obviously differences between making, adapting, supplying and offering to supply. There are also important differences between s 7(1)(a) which requires that the article *is*[294] for use in connection with fraud and s 7(1)(b) where there is no requirement that the article is so designed etc provided D intends it to be used. Section 7(1)(b) is in that respect much wider, and that difference may be important particularly where the charges allege supply/offer to supply.[295] In a different respect, s 7(1)(b) seems narrower than s 7(1)(a), being restricted to articles for use in the commission of fraud, whereas s 7(1)(a) is wider – encompassing use in connection with fraud. Whether the courts will be willing to draw such a distinction remains to be seen.

23.8.1.2 Scope of offence

This is far from being the straightforward offence that the Government proposed. The Home Office had suggested that the offence would extend only to cases where the article was 'specifically designed to commit fraud or where the manufacturer knows the article is to be used to commit frauds'.[296] Clearly, the offence extends much wider than this.[297] The only example of its operation provided in the Explanatory Notes to the Act is that where 'a person makes devices which when attached to electricity meters cause the meter to malfunction. The actual amount of electricity used is concealed from the provider, who thus makes a

---

[293] See Flatley et al, *Crime in England and Wales 2009/10*, 32.

[294] Otherwise, there could be no knowledge that it is for such use: *Montila* [2004] UKHL 50 and *Saik* [2006] UKHL 18.

[295] If the allegation is that D made or adapted the article, it is likely to be caught by s 7(1)(a) in any event.

[296] *Responses to Consultation* (2005) para 52.

[297] The variations include that D (i) makes an article knowing it is designed or adapted for use in the course of or in connection with fraud; (ii) D adapts an article knowing it is designed or adapted for use in the course of or in connection with fraud; (iii) D supplies an article knowing it is designed or adapted for use in the course of or in connection with fraud; (iv) D offers to supply knowing it is designed or adapted for use in the course of or in connection with fraud; (v) D makes an article intending it to be used to commit, or assist in the commission of, fraud; (vi) D adapts an article intending it to be used to commit, or assist in the commission of, fraud; (vii) D supplies an article intending it to be used to commit, or assist in the commission of, fraud; (viii) D offers to supply an article intending it to be used to commit, or assist in the commission of, fraud.

loss.'[298] Such conduct was capable of being prosecuted as conspiracy to defraud where there was more than one actor involved in the agreement, as in *Hollinshead*,[299] discussed above in Chapter 13.

Section 7 has the potential to apply to a much wider range of circumstances. It will catch the software manufacture who produces programs such as 'creditmaster IV' and others which are designed solely for criminal purposes. In that respect it is a welcome addition to the prosecution's armoury.

There seems to be no doubt that the section could apply to the corporate defendant. The companies producing blank cards for use in credit card cloning, or designing software for the production of phishing sites etc are all caught.

23.8.1.3 *Actus reus*
Any article

The definition of article has been considered above. By virtue of s 8, it includes electronic data. The scope of the *actus reus* is extremely broad. An allegation based on articles 'designed or adapted for' use in fraud will be relatively narrow but will still encompass, for example, computer software for credit card cloning etc. In comparison, if the allegation is that the article is 'intended for use in' fraud and it was made or supplied or offered for supply, the offence extends much wider and could include innocuous articles such as mobile phones. It seems clear that the offence is committed irrespective of whether the article is capable of being used by itself or in combination with other articles.[300]

As noted above, where the charge is laid under s 7(1)(a), it is necessary that the Crown establishes that the article *is* designed or adapted for use in fraud. The article must be such in order for D to know that it is such.

'Makes'

This is an ordinary English word, and in this context is used in the sense of 'manufactures'. It should not give rise to many difficulties in application. Where D has made the article, it will be most likely that he also knows that it is designed for or adapted for use in fraud and the charge will be under s 7(1)(a). It is possible, however, that D has made some article which is not designed or adapted for fraud, but which he nevertheless intends to use for that purpose. This would fall under s 7(1)(b) and could extend as widely as, for example, the making of paper which D intends to use to print false cheque forms.

Where the allegation involves electronic data, the courts might draw upon the interpretation of the word 'makes' from the offences dealing with indecent images of children. In that context, it has been held that D makes an image when he downloads it to his computer cache from the internet.[301] If such an interpretation is adopted under s 7, it will broaden the offence considerably. The individual who downloads software, even if he does not then adapt it or alter it or use it, may be liable if the Crown can establish either: (i) that it was designed or adapted for use in fraud (s 7(1), for example, credit card cloning software; or (ii) even if it is entirely innocuous software such as a spread sheet program, that D intended to use it for the commission of fraud (s 7(1)(b)).

---

[298] Para 27.
[299] [1985] 1 All ER 850 at 858, and commentary at [1985] Crim LR 653 at 656.
[300] cf Misuse of Drugs Act 1971, s 9A, inserted by Drugs Trafficking Offences Act 1986, s 34(1).
[301] *Atkins v DPP* [2000] 1 WLR 1427.

'Adapts'

Adapts is a term which may have been chosen with the application of this offence to electronic data in mind. To describe the action of creating software or other electronic data as 'making' an article would be an unnatural use of that word (unless the courts adopt the interpretation in the previous paragraph in which case downloading constitutes making). Moreover, it will often be the case that D has not created the software from scratch but has changed a form of software which has pre-existing legitimate uses and has 'adapted' it for fraudulent use. There is no requirement that the article which D adapts must have been in his possession, ownership or control.

As with the individual who 'makes' the article, it is most likely that the individual who has adapted the article will have done so knowing that it is designed or adapted for fraud. In that case the appropriate charge will be under s 7(1)(a).

'Supplies'

This is a term which, like possession, has created difficulties for the courts in a number of contexts. However, given that in this context we are dealing with the supply of articles for illegal purposes, it is unlikely that the courts will take a restrictive or unduly technical approach to the term. In the leading case on the interpretation of this term in the Misuse of Drugs Act, *Maginnis*,[302] the House of Lords held that the word 'supply' is to be interpreted by reference to the 'ordinary natural meaning of the word together with any assistance which may be afforded by the context'.

The word 'supply', in its ordinary natural meaning, conveys the idea of furnishing or providing to another something which is wanted or required in order to meet the wants or requirements of that other. It connotes more than the mere transfer of physical control of some chattel or object from one person to another. No one would ordinarily say that to hand over something to a mere custodian was to supply him with it. The additional concept is that of enabling the recipient to apply the thing handed over to purposes for which he desires or has a duty to apply it.[303] It is unlikely that the courts will need to become embroiled in the difficulties arising from the interpretation of the term 'supply' in the drugs offences where there is a transfer from A to B for a short period. In such cases, the Court of Appeal has concluded that a supply only occurs where there is a transfer for the benefit of the transferee rather than the transferor.[304]

There is no restriction that the supply has to be for money or money's worth or that it is restricted to commercial supply.[305] D handing over a blank credit card to his friend for free is as guilty as the commercial provider of software programs for, for example, decoding satellite television boxes.

Where D is alleged to have supplied an article, the prosecutor will have to exercise considerable care over the selection of the charges. If D has supplied the article and knows that it is designed or adapted for use in fraud, the correct charge is under s 7(1)(a). That charge will only be available where the article supplied is actually designed or adapted for use in fraud. Where the articles are not designed or adapted for fraud, the charges will have to be brought under s 7(1)(b),[306] and that form of offence will be available only where D has the intention that the articles are used for fraud.

---

[302] [1987] AC 303.

[303] Lord Keith at 309.

[304] *Dempsey* (1985) 82 Cr App R 291, CA.

[305] cf s 1(4) of the Video Recordings Act 1984 now re-enacted as the Video Recordings Act 2010 where an extended definition makes this clear.

[306] Or as attempts.

'Offers to supply'

This expression is also one with which the courts will be familiar from the Misuse of Drugs Act 1971, s 4(1)(b) and s 4(3)(a). It seems likely that the courts will follow the interpretation developed under that Act, and an offer will therefore be capable of being made by words or conduct. Whether the words or conduct amount to an 'offer', will be a question of fact. Further, it will not be necessary for D making the offer to have in his possession or control the article he is offering to supply. The manufacturer, or someone acting as his agent, who has yet to make the articles in question may be liable for offering to supply them.[307] Whether D intends to perform the act of supplying he is offering will be irrelevant; the offence is complete as soon as an offer to supply is made.[308] Perhaps most importantly, as an overriding principle, the courts have held that this is not an area in which it will be helpful to refer to principles of contract law in determining whether there is an offer.

Where the article is one designed or adapted for use in fraud and D knows that, his offer to supply it will be caught under s 7(1)(a). D's knowledge as to that fact is what matters; there is no need to show that D is aware/intends that the recipient intends to use it for fraud.[309] Where D merely has an intention that the articles he offers to supply will be used in the commission of fraud, he commits the s 7(1)(b) form of the offence, irrespective of whether the articles are in fact designed or adapted for fraud. Again, there is no need for the Crown to prove that D has any intent or knowledge of the offeree's *mens rea*. In this respect the offence is stricter than assisting and encouraging where D's liability turns in part on his *mens rea* as to the incitee's likely criminality.

In the course of or connection with any fraud

This expression suggests a very broad scope of application. It would seem to include articles not only for use in performance of the actual elements of the fraud offence, but also articles for use in preparation and/or concealment of the offence.

To commit or assist in the commission of

In contrast to the expression 'in the course of or connection with' this expression seems to be more restricted. A reasonable argument can be advanced that the expression denotes the elements of the fraud offence, and does not extend to the acts preparatory or ancillary to that offence whether before or after its commission.

For use in 'any fraud'

As with the s 6 offence, it is unclear whether the offence can be committed where the 'fraud' offence is one which is proscribed by common law (conspiracy to defraud) or by legislation other than the Fraud Act 2006. Are articles for use in a conspiracy to defraud caught? The Home Office's use of the example based on *Hollinshead* suggests that the s 7 offence does apply to conspiracy to defraud. Whether the s 7 offence extends further and applies, for example, to supply of articles for use in the commission of other dishonesty offences generally and in specific fraud-based offences such as those under the Taxes Management Act and the Value Added Taxes Act remains to be seen.

---

[307] *Mitchell* [1992] Crim LR 723; *Haggard v Mason* [1976] 1 WLR 187.

[308] *Gill* (1993) 97 Cr App R 215.

[309] cf, eg, the offence under s 125 of the Communication Act 2003 in which it is an offence to possess or supply apparatus knowing or believing that the intentions of the person to whom it is supplied are dishonestly to obtain etc communication services. See, similarly, the requirement of *mens rea* in s 2(3)(b) of the Mobile Telephone (Re-programming) Act 2002.

23.8.1.4 *Mens rea*

Section 7(1)(a)

'Knowing' that it is designed or adapted for such use

This is a relatively strict *mens rea* requirement. Knowledge involves a state of mind of true belief. As the House of Lords has recently acknowledged in *Montila*:

A person may have reasonable grounds to suspect that property is one thing (A) when in fact it is something different (B). But that is not so when the question is what a person knows. A person cannot know that something is A when in fact it is B. The proposition that a person knows that something is A is based on the premise that it is true that it is A.[310]

It is difficult to see how the doctrine of wilful blindness has any application in the context of design, although it is possible in the context of adaptation.

The Crown must establish that the article which D has made, adapted, supplied or offered to supply is designed or adapted for use in the course of or in connection with fraud. In addition, the Crown must prove that D knew that the article was designed or adapted for such use. There is no requirement that D intends or believes or knows that the person to whom the article is supplied or offered will commit any fraud offence. The CPS suggests, with some optimism, that the 'use to which the article can be put is likely to provide sufficient evidence of the defendant's state of mind'.[311]

Section 7(1)(b)

Intending it to be used to commit or assist in committing

The s 7(1)(b) form of offence is available where D makes, adapts, supplies or offers to supply any article, whether it is designed or adapted for use in fraud or not, with the intention that the article will be used in the commission of fraud or to assist in the commission of fraud. Intention here will presumably include not only direct intention in the sense of purpose, but also an oblique intention where D sees the use of the article for fraud as virtually certain.

It is submitted that it is not necessary that D intends that the person to whom he supplies or offers to supply the article will act with *mens rea*.

23.8.2 Reform

Although the 2006 Act has been in force for a short time, there is some likelihood of further legislative development in this area in the near future. The Government continues to keep under review the law of fraud and some proposals may involve changes to the substantive law.[312]

---

[310] [2004] UKHL 50.
[311] See www.cps.gov.uk.
[312] See R Sarker, 'Fighting Fraud – A Missed Opportunity' (2007) 28 Comp Law 243.

24

Other offences involving fraud

24.1 False accounting

Section 17 of the Theft Act 1968 provides:

> (1) Where a person dishonestly, with a view to gain for himself or another or with intent to cause loss to another, –
>
> > (a) destroys, defaces, conceals or falsifies any account or any record or document made or required for any accounting purpose; or
> >
> > (b) in furnishing information for any purpose produces or makes use of any account, or any such record or document as aforesaid, which to his knowledge is or may be misleading, false or deceptive in a material particular;
>
> he shall, on conviction on indictment, be liable to imprisonment for a term not exceeding seven years.

It has been suggested that the section creates six forms of the offence, although the courts acknowledge that 'false accounting' is the appropriate way to refer to the offence however committed.[1] False accounting is a useful charge to reflect accurately the scale of dishonest wrongdoing without the need to deal with the complex issues of when and where property transfers (whether as bank credits or otherwise) occurred. False accounting is often the most suitable charge where the conduct did not involve a scheme which was fraudulent from the outset but became so when, for example, a business got into financial difficulties. The offence overlaps with others, especially forgery and fraud. The offence under s 17 is wider than forgery; not every false statement renders the document a forgery.[2] False accounting is narrower than the general Fraud Act offence because it is restricted to falsity, etc in relation to accounts. The implementation of the Fraud Act may explain the reduction in the number of false accounting prosecutions.[3] The fraud offence under s 1 of the 2006 Act has the advantage of a higher sentence (10 years).[4]

The Fraud Act applies under s 2 to any false representation and under ss 3 and 4 where D is under a legal duty to reveal information or where he is in a position in which he is expected to safeguard V's financial interests as, for example, where he is the auditor or accountant.

---

[1] *Bow Street Magistrates, ex p Hill* (1999) 29 Nov, unreported, DC.

[2] See below Ch 28 and *Dodge* [1972] 1 QB 416, CA.

[3] There were 158 recorded offences of false accounting in 2008/9; J Flatley et al, *Crime in England and Wales 2009/10, Findings from the British Crime Survey and police recorded crime* (2010) table 2.04.

[4] The Sentencing Guidelines Council final guideline on sentencing statutory fraud offences which came into effect on 26 October 2009 includes guidance on sentencing in cases of false accounting. A new update to the Magistrates' Courts Sentencing Guidelines has been issued which, *inter alia*, reflects the guidelines on fraud. See www.sentencing-guidelines.gov.uk.

24.1.2 Section 17(1)(a)

24.1.2.1 *Actus reus*

The offence may be committed by any person who falsifies, etc any document 'made or required' for an accounting purpose. It is not necessary to prove that anyone accepted or acted on the falsified document; this is a conduct offence, not an offence of deception requiring a result caused by D's conduct. The falsification, etc is a sufficient manifestation of criminal intent to warrant criminalization irrespective of whether it causes loss or results in gain.

The account or record

'Account' is an ordinary English word. 'Any account or any record' encompasses a set of written financial accounts but is interpreted widely to include a mechanical or electronic or digital accounting device such as a computer or a taximeter. It has even been held to include[5] a turnstile which records the number of paying customers[6] as the admission of two people through one movement of the turnstile amounts to falsification by the omission of a material particular. A completely false set of accounts is also 'an account' for the purposes of the section.[7]

'Made or required for'

It is enough that the document was either made or required for an accounting purpose.[8] This restriction means that s 17 does not apply to all documents or records.

Unfortunately, the courts have failed to adopt a consistent approach to identifying whether particular documents were made or required for accounting purposes. Two issues arise: (i) whether a document is made or required for an accounting purpose (ii) on what evidence the jury is to be satisfied of that fact.

In relation to the first issue, neither 'made for' or 'required for' is to be read restrictively. Each should be given their ordinary meaning having regard to the context[9] and potential purpose for which the document was required. They should not be treated as technical terms of 'forensic accounting'.[10] It has been persuasively suggested that 'made for' refers to the purposes of the maker of the document and 'required for' to the purposes of the recipient.[11] A set of financial accounts is *prima facie* made for an accounting purpose. Any other record or document is 'made for' an accounting purpose where that is its primary purpose. It has also been held that it is enough that *one of the purposes* of the document or record is for an accounting purpose.[12] This is a controversial extension of the offence.[13]

In relation to the second issue, the question of what evidence is needed for the jury to be satisfied of the accounting purpose, the courts have distinguished between (i) those types of documents which a jury, with such experience and knowledge of the world as jurors may be expected to have, could by examining the document, be satisfied that it was required for an accounting purpose; and, (ii) those from which no such inference could safely be drawn. In the second category, the prosecution must adduce evidence of the purpose of

---

[5] cf *Solomons* [1909] 2 KB 980.

[6] *Edwards v Toombs* [1983] Crim LR 43, DC.

[7] *Scot-Simonds* [1994] Crim LR 933.

[8] *Baxter v Gov of HM Prison Brixton* [2002] EWHC 300 (Admin).

[9] See *Neil* [2008] EWCA Crim 476.

[10] ibid, Auld LJ, para 22.

[11] Some support for this view is implicit in Auld LJ's judgment in *Baxter*.

[12] *A-G's Reference (No 1 of 1980)* [1981] 1 All ER 366, [1981] 1 WLR 34, CA (personal loan proposal forms addressed to finance company).

[13] See *Arlidge and Parry on Fraud*, Ch 12.

the document. The court or jury may infer from the circumstances that the document is so required[14] but only if sufficient evidence exists for this conclusion to be drawn. One of the difficulties with the offence is that jurors cannot be assumed to know about accounting practices,[15] and the types of document that might be required for accounting purposes are extremely wide ranging.

A recent decision has sought to clarify the position of the evidence that may be required, at least in relation to the commonly occurring problem of false information on a commercial mortgage or loan application form. In *O and H*[16] (a prosecution appeal against an adverse ruling) the Court of Appeal held that an application made by a person for a mortgage was a document required for an accounting purpose because, if successful, it would lead to the lender providing funds and thus the opening of a mortgage account in favour of D in the books of the lender. That account would inevitably included the name and address of D as set out on the form and any bank details supplied by D. It would be inevitable (so the jury could find) that the account formed part of the accounting records of the lender. No direct evidence was required to prove that. A jury was entitled to conclude that an application for a mortgage or a loan made to a commercial institution was a document required for an accounting purpose.

The court conducted a comprehensive review of all the earlier authorities. It was accepted that not all of the decisions were reconcilable. In some earlier authorities the court had taken a wide view of the likely uses the recipient would make of such documents. For example, a 'Report on Title' was required by a building society for an accounting purpose'[17] namely to decide whether to grant a mortgage advance. Similarly, in *Osinuga v DPP*[18] a form claiming entitlement to housing benefit was held to be a 'document made or required for' an accounting purpose. In *Manning*,[19] it was held that it would be open to a jury to conclude that an insurer's cover note was 'required' in the terms of this section simply by looking at the document because it set out what the client owed – but it was a borderline case. On other occasions the court had taken a narrower view. For example in *Okanta*,[20] the court was not satisfied that a falsified letter which induced a mortgage advance was required for an accounting purpose. Similarly in *Sundhers*, the court had held that claim forms for an insurance company had not been demonstrated to be required for an accounting purpose.[21] The cases adopting this narrower view would be decided differently applying *O* because the focus would be on whether the forms would have led to the opening of account or the making of an account transfer. This is, with respect, one of the difficulties with the decision in *O*. Although it makes the prosecution's obligation on proof clear, caution must be exercised in applying the decision. The court is not saying, it is submitted, that an accounting purpose in s 17 can *only* arise where an account will be created or transfers into or from an account will be caused. That would render the offence far too narrow and would be irreconcilable with many earlier decisions. What the court is saying, it is submitted, is that because in cases of commercial mortgage or loan applications an account will be created, the application document is necessarily one that is required for an accounting purpose. *Mallett* is clear that it is the *document* that must

---

[14] *Osinuga v DPP* [1998] Crim LR 216, DC; *Baxter* (above).

[15] *Sundhers* [1998] Crim LR 497.

[16] [2010] EWCA Crim 2233; [2011] Crim LR 401 and commentary.

[17] *Cummings-John* [1997] Crim LR 660.

[18] [1998] Crim LR 216. cf at first instance HH Judge Jackson in *S* (1997) 4 Archbold News 1, which must be regarded as wrongly decided. NB the specific offence under the Social Security Administration Act 1992, s 111A, inserted by the Social Security Administration (Fraud) Act 1997, s 13.

[19] [1998] 2 Cr App R 461, [1999] Crim LR 151.

[20] [1997] Crim LR 451. Distinguished in *Doncaster* [2008] EWCA Crim 5.

[21] *Sundhers* [1998] Crim LR 497.

be made or required for an accounting purpose. A further reason for caution when applying this reasoning is that the focus on the fact that the application document leads to an account being created must not be allowed to cloud the very clear law holding that there is no requirement under s 17 to prove that D's false statement etc caused any result. False accounting is a conduct offence.

Given the inconsistent authorities on this element of the offence, prosecutors may well prefer, where possible, to rely on the general fraud offence under s 1 of the 2006 Act in which no such restriction as to the document applies.[22]

Particular difficulty arises where the document is one that is not a set of formal accounts and is being sent to a private individual rather than a lending company or equivalent. For example in alleged high-yield investment frauds and pyramid frauds, application forms sent to a potential investor which include false statements as to the rate of return on investments may constitute documents made or required for any accounting purpose since they would be retained by the investor: 'it was the sort of document he would put in a wall safe not a waste paper basket'.[23]

'Any accounting purpose'

The section further extends its reach to any document, so long as it is made or required for *any* accounting purpose, though the document itself is not in the nature of an account and though the falsification does not relate to figures. So if, in a hire-purchase proposal, form D enters false particulars relating to a company director, the case falls within the plain words of s 17(1)(a).[24]

Destruction, defacement etc

Some account or record must be destroyed, defaced, concealed or falsified by D or as a result of information provided by D. It is not enough that D is cheating V, for example by selling his own property as V's, if that transaction is not recorded in any account.[25]

The courts do not seem to have provided any detailed consideration of the terms destruction, defacement or concealment. Destruction and defacement should present few, if any, problems. Some cases of defacement might also constitute forgery under the Forgery and Counterfeiting Act 1981.[26] 'Concealment' raises the interesting question of whether it is necessary for D to be hiding some record etc, being aware that he is under a duty to disclose it, or whether it is sufficient simply that D conceals it. Arguably concealment requires some 'act' and cannot be committed by a mere omission. The issue will commonly be rolled up with that of dishonesty since knowing concealment commonly implies a lack of honesty. Secrecy and dishonesty are, however, not coextensive, nor are transparency and honesty.

Falsification

The more important issues arise in relation to falsification. Under s 17(1)(a) the offence is committed by falsification of the account, etc whereas under s 17(1)(b) it is committed by *use* of a falsified account, etc. Section 17(2) provides an extended though non-exhaustive definition of falsity:

For the purposes of this section a person who makes or concurs in making in an account or other document an entry which is or may be misleading, false or deceptive in a material particular, or

---

[22] The likelihood that the Fraud Act would be relied on was noted by the Court of Appeal in *O*.

[23] *Baxter v Gov of HM Prison Brixton* [2002] EWHC 300 (Admin).

[24] *A-G's Reference (No 1 of 2001)* [2002] Crim LR 844. The charge is available in relation to alleged fraud of parliamentary expenses and is not ousted by art 9 of the Bill of Rights 1688: *Chaytor* [2010] UKSC 52.

[25] *Cooke* [1986] AC 909, [1986] 2 All ER 985, HL.

[26] cf *Arlidge and Parry on Fraud*, para 11.058.

who omits or concurs in omitting a material particular from an account or other document, is to be treated as falsifying the account or document.

The extended meaning attaches only to documents and accounts, not records.[27] Falsification may be by omission, as where D omits to include information relating to his true income on an application form for housing benefit.[28] The case law has extended the scope of the *actus reus* far beyond that simple proposition. In *Shama*,[29] D, an international telephone operator, was required for each call to fill in a 'charge ticket' which was then used for an accounting purpose. He connected certain favoured subscribers without filling in a charge ticket, so they were not charged. The prosecution was unable to produce any falsified document. Upholding D's conviction, the court said that 'failure to complete a charge ticket by omitting material particulars from a document required for an accounting purpose' constituted the offence. But how can the omission to make a document at all be the omission of material particulars from it? The omission of material particulars seems necessarily to imply the existence of a document from which those particulars are omitted.[30]

The offence applies irrespective of whether D is under a formal duty to account, but if D is acting under such a duty that will prescribe the scope of his obligation to include material in the documents.[31]

Material particular

Where the allegation is of falsification, that must relate to a material particular.[32] This aspect of the offence has also been interpreted broadly. Information is 'material' if it is something that matters to V in making up his mind about action to be taken on the document.[33] It need not be material to the accounting purpose directly. In *Mallett*, the Court of Appeal approved the trial judge's description of a material particular as 'an important matter; a thing that mattered'. It was not specified to whom it must be shown to have been important. The particulars may be material precisely for the purpose of auditing and detecting fraud. Thus, omitting the name of an account holder to whom bank payments were to be made is a material particular since the name would have revealed instantly that the payment was unauthorized.[34] The particular can be material for the purposes of the section even if it would not have been the direct cause of the gain being made or the loss caused. That applies whether the allegation is one of positive falsification or omission. For example, if D, when completing an application form for a mortgage, omits to mention that he is married, although that information had it been revealed, might not have caused the mortgage to be refused, it can be regarded as a material particular for the purposes of s 17.[35]

---

[27] cf *Arlidge and Parry on Fraud*, para 11.058.

[28] See *Lancaster* [2010] EWCA Crim 370; [2010] Crim LR 776 and commentary.

[29] [1990] 2 All ER 602, [1990] Crim LR 411, CA.

[30] Presumably, D, at the end of his shift returned a bundle of charge tickets to his employers. Effectively it was his work record for the shift and was required for an accounting purpose. The 'record' might be regarded as a single document though it records each transaction on a separate page; on this view the document would be false by omitting to record some of the transactions. The best course now might be to charge under s 2 of the Fraud Act 2006: when the operator handed in the forms there was presumably an implied, if not an express, representation that there was a form for each call, it must still be shown that D intended to gain/cause loss.

[31] *Keatley* [1980] Crim LR 505 (Judge Mendl).

[32] If it is of destruction, etc, it is the whole document or record or, presumably, a relevant part.

[33] *Mallett* [1978] 3 All ER 10, [1978] 1 WLR 820, CA.

[34] *Taylor* [2003] EWCA Crim, 30 April, D dishonestly authorizing £73,000 payments from his employer to his parents.

[35] See *Lancaster* [2010] EWCA Crim 370. Toulson LJ did express doubt whether all incomplete or incorrect answers would be material (for example, ethnic monitoring in government forms, or profiling questions in commercial forms).

In cases of omission, it will only be possible to evaluate the materiality of the omitted particular in the context of the account as a whole. Whether the omission was significant would depend on the nature of the document and the context. The test is objective, although it is doubtful whether it would be helpful to the jury to use that term. Evidence may be admissible to explain significance. There is no hard and fast rule that any omission to supply information required by an application form must *necessarily* amount to the omission of a material particular.

There does not appear to be a clear *mens rea* requirement as to materiality: it is not clear that D must know or believe that the 'particular' he has omitted (or falsified) is or may be material.

24.1.2.2 *Mens rea*

The *mens rea* of the s 17(1)(a) offence requires that D:

(1) intentionally destroys, defaces, conceals or falsifies the document, and

(2) does so dishonestly, and

(3) acts with a view to gain for himself or another, or with intent to cause loss to another.

Given the breadth of the *actus reus* (above) it is desirable in principle for specificity and clarity in each element of *mens rea*. However, the courts have relied heavily on the dishonesty as the gravamen, avoiding unduly technical separation of the issues of knowledge and falsity.[36]

Intentionally making the statement in the account or record

Proving *mens rea* may be difficult if D is completing large numbers of similar records containing routine information. In *Atkinson,* a pharmacist completed forms to secure repayment of prescription costs. She admitted to filling in the forms while watching TV and playing with her children. Some forms were false in a material particular. The trial judge directed the jury to concentrate on her dishonesty, commenting that it was sufficient if the jury were sure that she knew it was *likely* that some of the forms were false in a material particular. The Court of Appeal regarded this as a dilution of the element of intention, coming close to mere recklessness. There must be a view to gain or intent to cause loss (below), which would not be satisfied by proof that D saw the falsity of a statement as 'likely'.[37] There is a distinct requirement that D 'deliberately and intentionally' makes the statement in the account or document. It is important to keep this element separate from the question of intention to gain since there are cases in which D will act with knowledge of falsity but with no ulterior intent to gain or cause loss.[38] This is an important element of the offence because the exercise of completing standard records and accounts is such that there is often great potential for recklessness or negligence in the recording of data. Such failings should not give rise to liability under this offence.

Knowledge as to falsity

Since s 17(2) extends the offence to cover cases in which the statement 'is or may be' misleading, false or deceptive, it is arguable that D is guilty if he intentionally makes statements in the account or record, knowing that they *may be false* and acts with a view to gain or intent to

---

[36] In *Atkinson* [2004] Crim LR 226, the court's suggestion that 'only lawyers would think of breaking [the *mens rea*] into component parts' is, with respect, an odd one. Is this not one element of the art of statutory construction?

[37] It is acceptable to say that D intends result A (causing loss/making gain) if he does an act B (making false statement) which is likely to bring about the result A, *provided* D also has an *intention* to perform act B.

[38] See further Ormerod and Williams, *Smith's Law of Theft*, Ch 4 and cases cited therein.

cause loss. The learned authors of Arlidge and Parry[39] suggest that it can hardly be intended that the subsection should apply where it is uncertain whether the proposition in question is true or false. The conclusion is that the expression 'or may be' must relate *only* to the s 17(1)(b) offence which includes the terms 'deception' and 'misleading'.[40]

'Dishonesty'

The term should be interpreted, as far as possible, consistently with its application in other sections of the 1968 Act. The concept of a claim of right includes a claim to the payment of a debt, and it is unclear whether the concept has any relevance here, as it does in s 1.[41] What of D who falsifies accounts to get property to which he believes he has a claim of right? One argument is that this should not excuse false accounting: the legitimacy of the end, or the belief in the legitimacy of the end, should not justify an illegality in the means of securing that end. D should not falsify documents. A further argument is that the essence of this offence is to recognize the separate obligation of honesty in the creation of documents that will serve as a *means* by which D can acquire property. If D has a genuine belief in the claim of right to the money to which he acts with a view to gain, there is no reason why he should use false means (evidencing his dishonesty) to acquire that money.

In the *A-G's Reference (No 1 of 2001)*,[42] X had been charged with an offence in the USA, which attracted high-profile media coverage. A fund was established with payments from well-wishers. An appeal committee placed donations received in the fund account, irrespective of whether the donors expressly stated whether the payment was for X and her parents (G and S) or for the fund. G and S submitted false invoices in respect of expenses incurred in attending their daughter's trial. That was alleged to amount to false accounting. The judge accepted the submission that because some of the money transferred to the fund was money originally donated to G and S to use as they chose, the prosecution could not prove that the amount of money obtained on the false invoice was not the money of G and S. No claim of a belief in a claim of legal entitlement was made. It is easy to see how even though G and S had a 'view to gain' in the sense of acquiring the property, a jury might have found that they were not dishonest in submitting the false invoices if they believed they had a legal right to acquire the property.

In *Gohill v DPP*,[43] D1 and D2 were charged with offences of theft and false accounting arising from their management of a plant hire shop. They had accepted 'tips' for allowing others to use the plant for a short time without payment. On these occasions D1 and D2 recorded each such short use as if the plant had not been hired at all. They claimed that these actions were not dishonest but were promoting customer relations. The justices acquitted, not being satisfied beyond a reasonable doubt that the defendants' actions had been dishonest by the ordinary standards of reasonable and honest people. The prosecution's appeal was allowed, Leveson LJ concluding that it was impossible to find that it was not dishonest by the ordinary standards of reasonable and honest people to falsify a record in this way, particularly since company policy, of which the defendants had been aware, did not permit an alteration of those records.

---

[39] *Arlidge and Parry on Fraud*, para 12.013.
[40] See *Arlidge and Parry on Fraud*, para 12.013. Would this have been a better charge for *Atkinson* (above)?
[41] *Wood* [1999] Crim LR 564. Williams, TBCL, 890.
[42] [2002] Crim LR 844.
[43] [2007] EWHC 239 (Admin).

Gain and loss

'Gain' and 'loss' are defined in s 34(2)(a) which is discussed elsewhere.[44] There might be a view to gain or an intention to cause loss in falsifying the account although the gain or loss has already taken place.

'Gain' includes a gain by keeping what one has. This has created some difficulties in interpretation. D commits an offence under s 17 where, having already appropriated property of V's, he destroys, defaces, conceals or falsifies an account so that he will not be found out, or to put off the evil day when he will be called to account: *Eden*.[45] *Golechha*[46] appears to decide that D acts with a view to gain or an intention to cause loss where D is in debt to V and D falsifies, etc an account with intent to cause V not to enforce the debt. It is submitted that in such circumstances D's act involves both an intent to gain and cause loss. It is not easy to reconcile this decision with *Eden*. Putting off the evil day when D will have to repay his debt would seem clearly to constitute a 'gain' to D. *Golechha* has been described as a case turning very much on its own facts.[47] A 'deed of postponement', postponing the priority of a registered charge in favour of another obligation does 'cause loss'.[48]

Where D falsifies accounts to exaggerate the profit which his department is making in order to induce his employer to continue his employment, it seems he has both a view to gain (he does this to keep his job and his salary) and an intent to cause loss (in so far as it causes him to continue to operate an uneconomic department).[49] It may be that there is no appropriation, or intended appropriation, of any money or goods belonging to the employer and therefore no theft; but, clearly, D is acting dishonestly. In *Masterson*,[50] D's falsification of invoices in an attempt to 'improve relations with his co-directors' who were unhappy with the acquisitions he had recently made was not sufficient to constitute the necessary view to 'gain'. D knew that there was no question of losing his position and could not therefore be said even to be falsifying them with a view to retaining that 'which he had'.

'With a view to gain' was construed, in a different context, in *Dooley*[51] as requiring more than foresight or awareness of a likelihood of the prohibited consequence. It is sufficient that D has the consequence (in this case 'gain') as 'one of' the reasons for acting in that fashion.

There can be a view to gain even if D has a (belief in a) claim of right to that which he is acquiring. In the *A-G's Reference (No 1 of 2001)*,[52] discussed above, G and S accepted that there was evidence that their expenses invoice was false, but argued that some of the money the committee had transferred to the trust was in fact money originally donated to G and S to use as they chose. On this basis they argued that the prosecution could not prove that the amount G and S sought to obtain via the false invoice was not theirs. They argued they had not 'gained' anything within the meaning of s 34(2)(a) because the trustees had incorporated into the trust some money which in fact belonged to G and S. The judge accepted that submission and ruled that G and S should be acquitted. The Court of Appeal held this was wrong. Where D has provided false information with a view to obtaining money or other property it is not necessary for the prosecution to prove that D had no legal entitlement to the money or other property in question.

---

[44] See above, p 878. cf *Lee Cheung Wing v R*, below, n 53.
[45] [1971] Crim LR 416, CA.
[46] [1989] 3 All ER 908, [1990] Crim LR 865 (sub nom *Choraria and Golechha*), CA.
[47] *Masterson* (1996), 30 Apr, unreported, CA.
[48] *Cummings (John)* [1997] Crim LR 660.
[49] cf *Wines* [1953] 2 All ER 1497, CCA.
[50] (1996) CA 94/2221/X5.
[51] [2005] EWCA Crim 3093.
[52] [2002] Crim LR 844.

In *Lee Cheung Wing*,[53] D was an employee of a company offering facilities for dealing in futures. Employees were not allowed to use these facilities. D, in breach of his employment contract, opened an account in the name of a friend, X. The transactions were profitable and D signed withdrawal slips in X's name. The question was whether the slips were made 'with a view to gain'. D said he was withdrawing money to which he was entitled. Since a person has a view to gain even if he is entitled to the property demanded,[54] Lee's conviction might perhaps have been upheld on that ground. The Privy Council, however, held that D was not entitled to the money because he would have been bound to account to his employer for a profit made by improper use of his position as an employee.[55] The Board added that, in any event, action by D to recover the profits would probably have been met by a plea of *ex turpi causa non oritur actio*. *Lee Cheung Wing*,[56] is not a sufficiently clear and weighty authority to cast doubt on the reasoning in the *A-G's Reference* because in *Lee Cheung Wing* it was not actually necessary to decide whether D would have been guilty had he been entitled to keep the money.

As for the intention to cause loss, it is unclear whether the intent must be direct or whether an oblique intention (where D sees a loss as virtually certain barring some unforeseen intervention) will suffice. The motives for intending to cause the loss are irrelevant. Thus, in *Leedham*,[57] D, a policeman, so disliked the Government ban on handguns (imposed after the Dunblane shootings) that he completed compensation forms falsely and dishonestly to cause loss to the Home Office by allowing claims for ineligible items owned by others.

Strict liability as to accounting purpose

The *actus reus* requires proof that the document is made or required for an accounting purpose. As a matter of principle, this ought to involve proof of *mens rea*. It has been held[58] however, that there is no requirement to prove D's intent or awareness of the purpose for which the document is required. A person may be guilty of false accounting although he has no idea, perhaps reasonably so, that this is what he is doing – as, for example, where the document is one which subsequently requires expert evidence to show that it is required for an accounting purpose. This imposition of strict liability as to an essential element of a serious offence seems objectionable.

Awareness of materiality?

Where the allegation is one of falsifying the document, etc a further element of *actus reus* is involved – the falsity must relate to a material particular. There has been no detailed judicial scrutiny of whether D must know or be aware of the materiality of the particular. In *Bowie and McVicar*,[59] HH Judge Atherton ruled that it was necessary for the prosecution to establish that additional element of *mens rea*.[60]

In most cases, this issue will be subsumed within the question of dishonesty. If, for example, D makes an application for insurance and in doing so he makes a false statement – perhaps out

---

[53] (1991) 94 Cr App R 355, [1992] Crim LR 440, PC.
[54] *A-G's Reference (No 1 of 2001)* [2002] Crim LR 844.
[55] *Reading v A-G* [1951] AC 507 at 516, 517.
[56] (1991) 94 Cr App R 355, PC.
[57] No 200200135/Y3.
[58] *Graham* [1997] 1 Cr App R 302 at 314.
[59] Manchester Crown Court, 19 Feb 2003.
[60] The charges arose from the sale of the defendants' portfolio of properties, which had been let to various tenants. The details of the properties were, in some cases, inaccurate in recording that the rents were paid from housing benefit rather than privately by the tenants. These were false statements, and arguably material since they would affect the security of future payments. The defendants denied that they had acted 'intentionally' or 'recklessly' either as to the falsehood or the materiality of that falsehood, but were convicted.

of embarrassment – as to his marital status, he knows that it is false, but is arguably unaware of the materiality of that status in enhancing the insurance rate he will be offered. Arguably, the lack of awareness or recklessness as to the materiality can be adequately addressed within the broader questions of whether D is dishonest and is acting with a view to gain. The overlap is so substantial that it is difficult to envisage circumstances in which D will be able to plead simultaneously that he accepts that he was dishonest, but that he lacked *mens rea* as to the materiality and should therefore be acquitted.[61] All such cases can, it is submitted, be prosecuted under s 1(2)(a) and s 2 of the Fraud Act 2006, where it is sufficient that D has made a false representation with intent to gain/cause loss irrespective of the materiality of the falsity.

24.1.3 Section 17(1)(b)

24.1.3.1 *Actus reus*

The offence under s 17(1)(b) involves 'using' rather than destroying, falsifying, etc the account. This is an extremely broad offence since it applies where D uses the document, etc for *any* purpose. A document may be misleading or false within the subsection by its failure to include material particulars, even though it is accurate in the sense that each statement which is contained is true.[62] It is notable that the prosecution need to show only that information in the account may be (not is) misleading or deceptive. Difficulties may arise in establishing the misleading, false or deceptive particular, and expert accounting evidence may be necessary. The elements relating to accounts and records or documents made or required for any accounting purpose are interpreted as in relation to s 17(1)(a), as are the requirements relating to falsity.

24.1.3.2 *Mens rea*

The *mens rea* for the s 17(1)(b) offence comprises: (i) intentionally using a document; (ii) knowing it is or may be false; (iii) dishonestly; and (iv) with a view to gain for himself or another, or with intent to cause loss to another. It is important to note that the *mens rea* differs here in one important respect from the elements as discussed in relation to s 17(1)(a). D may commit the offence in furnishing information not only where he knows that the material particular is false, but also where he knows that the document *may* be false or misleading in a material particular; evidently wilful blindness suffices.

24.2 Corporations and their officers

So far as offences under the Theft Acts generally are concerned, the liability of corporations for them falls to be determined in accordance with the general principles applicable to the liability of corporations for crime.[63] Where a corporation commits a crime it must be the case that the crime has been committed by a person, or persons, in control of the corporation's affairs.[64] Such persons are, of course, liable in accordance with the ordinary principles governing liability for crime. Section 18 contains a special provision relating to false accounting. The section provides:

---

[61] cf Smith, *Property Offences*, para 24.07a.

[62] See *Kylsant* [1932] 1 KB 442.

[63] See above, Ch 10.

[64] A corporation may, of course, be vicariously liable for crimes even though the crime is not committed by a person in control of its affairs: see above, p 259. But vicarious liability would not apply in connection with offences under the Theft Act 1968.

(1) Where an offence committed by a body corporate under section 17 of this Act is proved to have been committed with the consent or connivance of any director, manager, secretary or other similar officer[65] of the body corporate, or any person who was purporting to act in any such capacity, he as well as the body corporate shall be guilty of that offence, and shall be liable to be proceeded against and punished accordingly.

(2) Where the affairs of a body corporate are managed by its members, this section shall apply in relation to the acts and defaults of a member in connection with his functions of management as if he were a director of the body corporate.

This provision was explained by the Criminal Law Revision Committee as follows:[66]

The [section] follows a form of provision commonly included in statutes,[67] where an offence is of a kind to be committed by bodies corporate and where it is desired to put the management[68] under a positive obligation to prevent irregularities, if aware of them. Passive acquiescence does not, under the general law, make a person liable as a party to the offence, but there are clearly cases (of which we think this is one) where the director's responsibilities for his company require him to intervene to prevent fraud and where consent or connivance amount to guilt.

The Committee was suggesting that, without such a provision, in some circumstances the director might not be liable under the general principles governing liability for crime. The circumstances in which the director does not incur liability as a joint perpetrator or accessory will be relatively few. Suppose, for example, that D, a director, learns that E, a fellow director, proposes to falsify accounts but D does nothing about it. The effect of s 18 appears to be that D incurs criminal liability in respect of the false accounting because the offence has been committed with his consent. There would be no need to show that D communicated to E his approval of the falsification. Possibly, however, D would be liable under general principles for he has a clear duty to control the actions of E in this situation and his deliberate failure to perform his duty, coupled with his guilty knowledge, may make him an accessory.[69]

24.3 False statements by company directors

Section 19 of the Act provides:

(1) Where an officer of a body corporate or unincorporated association (or person purporting to act as such), with intent to deceive members or creditors of the body corporate or association about its affairs, publishes or concurs in publishing a written statement or account which to his knowledge is or may be misleading, false or deceptive in a material particular, he shall on conviction on indictment be liable to imprisonment for a term not exceeding seven years.

(2) For purposes of this section a person who has entered into a security for the benefit of a body corporate or association is to be treated as a creditor of it.

---

[65] See *Boal* [1992] 3 All ER 177, limiting this to those in positions of real power.
[66] Eighth Report, para 104.
[67] See further, above, p 265.
[68] Note that s 18 imposes criminal liability only on the management; this may include (s 18(2)) any member who is in fact in control even though he may not formally hold a managerial post.
[69] See above, p 197; *Tamm* [1973] Crim LR 115, CA.

(3) Where the affairs of a body corporate or association are managed by its members, this section shall apply to any statement which a member publishes or concurs in publishing in connection with his functions of management as if he were an officer of the body corporate or association.

The offence is designed to deal with cases where directors publish false prospectuses to members. It is one of a range of legislative provisions seeking to protect investors.[70]

In two senses the offence is a narrow one. First, it may be committed only by an officer[71] of a body corporate or unincorporated association. 'Officer' in relation to a body corporate includes a director, manager or secretary.[72] Secondly, it may be committed only where the intention is to deceive[73] members or creditors of the corporation or association, and not the public at large, about its affairs. This is much narrower than the scope of liability under s 2 of the Fraud Act 2006 which is not restricted to company officers nor does it require an intent to deceive.

In another sense, the offence is a wide one for it extends to the publication of any *written* statement of account that *may be* misleading in a material particular. Recklessness suffices. It is not necessary to show that there is any view to gain or intention to cause loss in publishing the statement or account, though no doubt either or both will often be present. There is no requirement that D acted dishonestly, although it has been suggested that there is no practical difference between defining the *mens rea* as an intent to deceive or dishonesty.[74] The prosecution will depend in many cases on the expert accountancy evidence as to whether the accounts were misleading. The offence might be committed where an officer, in order to inspire confidence in the company, falsely publishes that a well-known person has been appointed to the board. It might also include a false statement, 'made in order to appeal to persons interested in a particular area, that a company had arranged to build a factory in that area.'[75]

In view of the breadth of specific offences to protect investors, particularly the Financial Services and Markets Act 2000, s 397,[76] and the breadth of the general fraud offence under the Fraud Act 2006, it is surprising that s 19 was not considered for repeal in the Fraud Act 2006.

24.4 Suppression of documents

By s 20 of the Theft Act 1968:

(1) A person who dishonestly, with a view to gain for himself or another or with intent to cause loss to another, destroys, defaces or conceals any valuable security, any will or other testamentary document or any original document of or belonging to, or filed or deposited in, any court of

---

[70] See, generally, J Fisher, J Bewsey, M Waters and E Ovey, *The Law of Investor Protection* (2nd edn, 2003); *Arlidge and Parry on Fraud*, para 12.030; M Gale, 'Fraud and the Sale of Shares' (2001) 22 Company Lawyer 98. Investor protection has taken on a greater significance as increasing numbers of the general public have personal investment portfolios.

[71] The officers of a body corporate are frequently defined in the articles or by-laws of a corporation. See Companies Act 2006, Part 1, Ch 2. An auditor may be an officer: *Shacter* [1960] 2 QB 252.

[72] Companies Act 2006, s 1173(1).

[73] As to intent to deceive, see *Welham v DPP* [1961] AC 103, [1960] 1 All ER 805, HL.

[74] See *Shuck* [1992] Crim LR 209.

[75] Eighth Report, para 105.

[76] Creating offences for any person who makes a statement, promise or forecast which he knows to be misleading, false or deceptive in a material particular, or dishonestly conceals any material facts, whether in connection with a statement, promise or forecast made by him, or otherwise, or recklessly makes (dishonestly or otherwise) a statement, promise or forecast which is misleading, false or deceptive in a material particulars.

justice or any government department shall on conviction on indictment be liable to imprisonment for a term not exceeding seven years.[77]

This provision is not likely to be of great practical importance; it was included because:

It seemed to us that it might provide the only way of dealing with a person who, for example, suppressed a public document as a first step towards committing a fraud but did not get so far as attempting to commit the fraud. In accordance with the scheme of the [Act] the offence is limited to something done dishonestly and with a view to gain or with intent to cause loss to another.[78]

Section 20 (3) provides that:

For purposes of this section ... [79] 'valuable security' means any document creating, transferring, surrendering or releasing any right to in or over property, or authorising the payment of money or delivery of any property, or evidencing the creation, transfer, surrender or release of any such right, or the payment of money or delivery of any property or the satisfaction of any obligation.

The wide definition of valuable security renders this offence available in a diverse range of circumstances and it is rather surprising that it is not often prosecuted. Presumably, the evidential difficulties in establishing the destruction, etc of the document lie behind this. Note also that the Proceeds of Crime Act 2002 creates offences including that under s 327: concealing, disguising, converting or transferring criminal property or removing it from the jurisdiction.[80] In addition there are offences of making false statements in statutory documents.[81]

24.5 Cheating the public revenue[82]

Cheating was a misdemeanour at common law and was developed most vigorously during the eighteenth century. The authorities suggest an incredibly broad definition. Hawkins[83] defined cheating as '... deceitful practices, in defrauding or endeavouring to defraud another of his own right by means of some artful device, contrary to the plain rules of common honesty'.

The common law offence of cheating still retains significant importance because, though s 32(1) of the Theft Act abolished cheating (along with common law offences against property), it did so only 'except as regards offences relating to the public revenue'. The punishment is imprisonment and/or a fine without limit.

As a practical matter, the offence of cheating has been used, on any scale at all, only in connection with frauds against the other public revenue. Given the available sentence and the breadth of the offence it is not surprising that it is popular with the Revenue and Customs Prosecutions Office and is frequently prosecuted in preference to specific offences under the Theft Acts, Taxes Management Act and VAT Act.[84] It remains to be seen whether the broad general fraud offence will be used in preference to cheat. It is doubtful that prosecutors will see any advantage in doing so.

---

[77] Section 20(2) of the Theft Act 1968 created a very important offence of 'procuring the execution of a valuable security'. This was repealed by the Fraud Act 2006.

[78] Eighth Report, para 106.

[79] Words repealed by the Fraud Act 2006.

[80] See below, p 1003.

[81] Perjury Act 1911, s 5.

[82] D Ormerod, 'Cheating the Public Revenue' [1998] Crim LR 627; D Ormerod, 'Summary Evasion of Income Tax' [2002] Crim LR 3.

[83] 1 PC 318.

[84] Where large-scale cheats result in large (£1m+) losses to the public revenue, sentences will be substantially in excess of the maximum available under the statutes (7 years): *Meehan* [2007] 2 Cr App R (S) 155.

In *Hudson*,[85] the Court of Criminal Appeal upheld D's conviction on a charge of making false statements to the prejudice of the Crown and the public revenue with intent to defraud where it appeared that D had falsely stated to the Inland Revenue the profits of his business. It was argued that the indictment disclosed no offence known to the law, but the court, relying on *dicta* of Lord Mansfield CJ in *Bembridge*,[86] and statements by Hawkins[87] and East,[88] held that it was an offence for a private individual, as well as a public officer, to defraud the Crown and public. The argument that there was no such offence was raised again in *Mulligan*[89] and was just as forthrightly rejected by the Court of Appeal.

The CLRC was minded to abolish the offence, and its retention was the result of special pleading by the revenue authorities who wished to retain it for serious revenue frauds where penalties under other provisions were seen by them as inadequate. Perhaps, too, the Revenue was attracted by the expansive terminology of Hawkins' definition. At all events, the Revenue's fondest hopes for cheating must have been realized by *Mavji*.[90] D had dishonestly evaded value added tax to the tune of over £1,000,000. Charged, as he might have been, under what was then s 38(1) of the Finance Act 1972 with the fraudulent evasion of tax he would have been liable to a maximum of two years' imprisonment and/or a fine of £1,000 or three times the tax, whichever was the greater. Convicted, as he was, of cheating he was sentenced to six years' imprisonment and made criminally bankrupt in the sum of £690,000. The Court of Appeal, affirming D's conviction and sentence, rejected counsel's submission that cheating required a positive act such as a deception, and not merely an omission to make a VAT return. The court held that D was under a duty to make such a return and his failure to do so with intent to cheat the revenue of money to which it was entitled constituted the offence.[91] This conclusion was, with respect, a novel extension of the offence. *Hudson*,[92] which was treated in *Mavji* as the leading case, appears to assume that cheating requires the use of a false representation or false device. Even the expansive language of *Hawkins* is conditioned by the requirement 'by means of some artful device'. What artful device was employed by D in *Mavji*?

The *actus reus* of the offence has become so wide that the definition is almost best stated in negative terms. There need not be a dishonest act; an omission will suffice. The act or omission must be intended to prejudice the HMRC[93] or Department of Work and Pensions. The offence cannot be committed in respect of a local authority,[94] nor, it is submitted, against the EU.[95] There is no requirement of an operative deception,[96] nor of a need to prove actual loss to the revenue,[97] or to any other. It is not necessary to prove that the accused's conduct

---

[85] [1956] 2 QB 252, [1956] 1 All ER 814, discussed by 'Watchful' [1956] BTR 119.

[86] (1783) 22 State Tr 1 at 156.

[87] 1 PC 322.

[88] 2 PC 821.

[89] [1990] Crim LR 427, CA.

[90] [1987] 2 All ER 758, [1987] 1 WLR 1388, CA. *Mavji* was followed in *Redford* (1988) 89 Cr App R 1, CA. The proposition in *Mavji* that the statutory offences coexist with the common law offence of cheating the public revenue was confirmed by the House of Lords in *Revenue & Customs Commissioners v Total Network SL* [2008] UKHL 19 [136].

[91] Cheating is a 'conduct offence' and it is not necessary to prove that D caused any loss: *Hunt* [1994] Crim LR 747.

[92] Above.

[93] *Blake* (1844) 6 QB 126; *R v Tonner* [1985] 1 WLR 344.

[94] *Lush v Coles* [1967] 1 WLR 685.

[95] On fraud in the European Union, see L Kuhl, 'The Criminal Law Protection of the Communities' Financial Interests Against Fraud' [1998] Crim LR 259 and 323, especially at 264–266, and 330.

[96] *Mavji* [1987] 1 WLR 1388.

[97] *Hunt* [1994] STC 819 at 827, per Stuart-Smith LJ. Hence its use in VAT carousel frauds. See also *Matthews* [2008] EWCA Crim 423.

resulted in any gain to himself,[98] nor for the defendant to be a government official.[99] The types of behaviour caught include: failing to account for VAT,[100] withholding PAYE and National Insurance,[101] failing to register for VAT[102] or simply failing to disclose income.[103] It is unclear precisely when the offence commences. Is D cheating the Revenue when he has determined not to declare his profits but has yet to make a false declaration in his tax return?[104] Does it matter whether he has done some act – such as keeping a false set of books?[105] It is a particularly useful offence in cases of carousel frauds where there is no duty to pay VAT arising.

It is difficult to see how the offence could be stated in more expansive terms. The offence is of course even broader when charged as a conspiracy to cheat, as it often is. The breadth of the offence means that often the only live issue at trial will be dishonesty.

The jury's difficulty in applying the dishonesty test in commercial settings has been considered above in Chapter 19. In relation to carefully planned tax schemes the problems appear obvious: it seems ludicrous to ask jurors to apply the test of whether a reasonable and honest person would see it as dishonest when they (probably) have little or no understanding of the very complex civil law tax position or commercial background.[106] To ask them further whether they believe that the accused realized that the activity would be regarded as dishonest by the standards of reasonable people is expecting rather a lot. The activity engaged in might have been what D genuinely, and on expert advice, regarded as mere tax avoidance (acceptable in civil and criminal law), but which the jury considers to be dishonest and therefore to constitute a cheat. This is tantamount to retrospective criminalization and may well offend the protection in Art 7 of the ECHR.[107]

Notwithstanding the criticism of the cheating offence, the Government introduced a new statutory version of the offence which was triable either way. Section 144 of the Finance Act 2000 criminalized 'being knowingly concerned in the evasion of income tax'. This was an ill-defined and extremely broad offence, but for numerous reasons proved less successful than the Revenue anticipated.[108]

---

[98] *Hunt* [1994] STC 819, [1994] Crim LR 747.

[99] *Mulligan* [1990] Crim LR 427.

[100] *Ryan* [1994] STC 446, [1994] Crim LR 858.

[101] *Less* (1993), The Times, 30 Mar.

[102] *Redford* [1988] STC 845, [1989] Crim LR 152.

[103] *Anderson* (1992) 13 Cr App R (S) 564.

[104] This may be important in determining whether the property in the form of the tax not yet paid is already criminal property for the purposes of the Proceeds of Crime Act 2002, s 340.

[105] cf *Doncaster* [2008] EWCA Crim 5; *IK* [2007] EWCA Crim 491.

[106] eg the difficulty in cases where D is alleged to have created sham transactions and avoided tax: *Kumar* [2005] EWCA Crim 1979.

[107] cf *Pattni* [2000] Crim LR 570 at first instance. See LCCP 155, *Legislating the Criminal Code: Fraud and Deception* (1999) para 3.23.

[108] See D Ormerod, 'Summary Evasion of Income Tax' [2002] Crim LR 3. Section 144 was repealed on 1 April 2010 by Sch 10(2), para 1 of the Taxation (International and Other Provisions) Act 2010. The offence is now found in s 106A of the Taxes Management Act 1970.

25

Blackmail and related offences

25.1 Blackmail[1]

Originally the word blackmail was used to describe the tribute paid to Scottish chieftains by landowners in the border counties in order to secure immunity from raids on their lands. In the early stages of its development the crime of blackmail seems to have been coextensive with robbery and attempted robbery,[2] but over the years the definition has been extended to embrace more subtle methods of extortion. The law is now set out in s 21 of the Theft Act 1968:[3]

(1) A person is guilty of blackmail if, with a view to gain for himself or another or with intent to cause loss to another, he makes any unwarranted demand with menaces; and for this purpose a demand with menaces is unwarranted unless the person making it does so in the belief –

    (a) that he has reasonable grounds for making the demand; and

    (b) that the use of the menaces is a proper means of reinforcing the demand.

(2) The nature of the act or omission demanded is immaterial, and it is also immaterial whether the menaces do or do not relate to action to be taken by the person making the demand.

(3) A person guilty of blackmail shall on conviction on indictment be liable to imprisonment for a term not exceeding fourteen years.

When unravelled, this rather complicated provision comprises an *actus reus* of an unwarranted demand with menaces, and *mens rea* requirements of an intention to make the unwarranted demand with menaces, with a view to gain or intention to cause loss, in the absence of a belief that there are reasonable grounds for making the demand and that the menacing is a proper means of enforcing the demand. The offence is complete upon the demand being made, irrespective of whether any property is transferred.

Blackmail is triable only on indictment. In 2009/10, there were 1,458 recorded instances of blackmail.[4]

---

[1] Ormerod and Williams, *Smith's Law of Theft*, Ch 12; Griew, *Theft*, Ch 14; CLRC Eighth Report, paras 108–125.

[2] W Winder, 'The Development of Blackmail' (1941) 5 MLR 21; G Williams, 'Blackmail' [1954] Crim LR 7; J Lindgren, 'The Theory, History, and Practice of the Bribery-Extortion Distinction' (1993) 141(5) U Pa L Rev 1695; M Hepworth, 'The British Conception of Blackmail' (1975) 3 Int J of Criminology and Penology 1.

[3] B MacKenna, 'Blackmail' [1966] Crim LR 467; B Hogan, 'Blackmail' [1966] Crim LR 474; CR Williams, 'Demanding with Menaces: A Survey of the Australian Law of Blackmail' (1975) 10 Melb LR 118, especially at 136–144.

[4] See J Flatley et al, *Crime in England and Wales 2009/10, Findings from the British Crime Survey and police recorded crime* (2010) table 2.04.

There are relatively few reported appellate court decisions on the substance of the offence; those that are reported relate to sentencing, and it should be noted in that regard that the offence is one of the most serious in the criminal calendar attracting long-term imprisonment.[5] Mobile telecommunications, advances in information technology and the internet have created new opportunities for blackmail.[6]

Although the offence appears in the Theft Act 1968, and its requirement of an act with a view to loss or gain demonstrates that it serves to protect property, in many cases blackmail is more appropriately viewed as an offence against privacy.[7] Correctly identifying the harm or interest being protected by the offence has generated a wealth of academic literature.[8] It has been suggested that the wrong of blackmail is done even if the demand is nothing to do with payment[9] but that seems to be overinclusive: the offence as defined in English law is restricted to cases in which the demand is for property.

25.1.1 The demand

A demand may take any form, and may be implicit as well as explicit. It extends well beyond the obvious '£1,000 or I will publish the photographs exposing your adultery'. The demand could be oral, in writing, by gestures or by D's demeanour provided that, objectively viewed, it is a demand. The essence of this offence is that D's communication conveys the message to V that a menace will materialize unless V complies with the demand. D may be guilty of blackmail where, for example, he apprehends V in the act of stealing and, without any formal demand, makes it clear to V that if he pays D money he will hear no more of the matter.[10] D's humblest form of request may be a demand.[11] But, whether express or implied, there must actually be a demand. If, having caught V in the act of stealing, D receives and accepts an

---

[5] See, eg, *Hadjou* [1989] Crim LR 390; *Ablewhite* [2007] EWCA Crim 832 (12 years for conspiracy to blackmail animal breeders); and the strange case of *Wedell* [2007] EWCA Crim 2878 where D blackmailed V, who had sexually abused him as a child, leading V to kill himself. See recently *Aziz* [2009] EWCA Crim 2337, describing blackmail as 'ugly and cruel' [17].

[6] See recently the case of *Breakwell* [2009] EWCA Crim 2298, where D sent digitally altered images of Vs' faces on nude bodies with demands that they send him real photos of them nude on threat of him publishing the fakes on line. See also the increasingly common practice of hackers threatening to corrupt or to disable a company's website unless payment is made. See M Griffiths, 'Internet Corporate Blackmail: A Growing Problem' (2004) 168 JP 632. See also S Morris, *The Future of Netcrime* (2004) HORS 62/04, at 15. Greater difficulties of proof might arise: *Robinson* [2006] Crim LR 427. Blackmailers also plant viruses on women's computers and identify embarrassing material which they use to make demands: the CPS discuss such a case – *Ringland* (2006) 9 Nov, CC.

[7] See P Alldridge, 'Attempted Murder of the Soul: Blackmail, Privacy and Secrets' (1993) 13 OJLS 368 and *Relocating Criminal Law* (2000) Ch 4. See also the suggestion that blackmail is a 'serious offence against the person, even where the threat is one of exposure rather than violence': A Simester and GR Sullivan, 'The Nature and Rationale of Property Offences' in Duff and Green (eds), *Defining Crimes*, 188. For a sociological view of the activity, see M Hepworth, *Blackmail, Publicity and Secrecy in Everyday Life* (1975); for an historical account of its expansion in the last century, see A McLaren, *Sexual Blackmail* (2002).

[8] See, *inter alia*, 'Blackmail – A Symposium' (1993) 141(5) U Pa L Rev and L Katz, *Ill-gotten Gains: Evasion, Blackmail, Fraud, and Kindred Puzzles of the Law* (1996). For recent English material, see W Block, 'The Logic of the Argument of Legalising Blackmail' [2001] Bracton LJ 61; W Block and R McGee, 'Blackmail as a Victimless Crime' [1999] Bracton LJ 24.

[9] See Simester and Sullivan in Duff and Green (eds), *Defining Crimes*, 188.

[10] cf *Collister and Warhurst* (1955) 39 Cr App R 100, CCA: 'the demeanour of the accused' was sufficient. See also *Lambert* [2009] EWCA Crim 2860.

[11] cf *Robinson* (1796) East, 2 PC 1110, where the words 'Remember, Sir, I am now only making an appeal to your benevolence' were held in the circumstances capable of importing a demand. In *Miah* [2003] 1 Cr App R (S) 379, D sent videos of child pornography to Vs with a return address and when they returned them D contacted Vs informing them that their fingerprints were on the videos and 'urging' them or 'inviting' them to call a telephone number. D pleaded guilty and no issue arose as to whether these 'invitations' to call the number were a 'demand'.

unsolicited offer to buy his silence, D would not be guilty of blackmail (but might commit the offence of withholding for gain information relating to an offence).

A demand may be made through an intermediary.[12] It may be complete though it has not been communicated to V because, say, V is deaf. A demand by letter is made where and when it is posted.[13] Presumably the same is true of email communications, with the demand being complete as soon as the email has been sent. In these cases D has done the final act necessary to communicate the demand. The offence is complete irrespective of V's compliance with the demand. It has been argued that the wide interpretation of demand means that there is little or no room for a crime of attempted blackmail,[14] although there are hypothetical scenarios of D being intercepted on his way to the post, etc. Treating the full offence as committed before the demand has been communicated, emphasizes that the gravamen of the offence is the making of unwarranted demands *per se*.

Normally, D will demand money or other property but s 21(2) provides that 'the nature of the act or omission demanded is immaterial'. At first sight, this seems to undermine the foundation of the offence being one of protecting *property*. However, it does not go that far because the offence can be committed only if D also has a view to gain or an intention to cause loss in money or other property.[15] The purpose of s 21(2) seems to have been to forestall a possible argument that D cannot be guilty unless his demand is for some specific item of property.[16] If D demands with menaces that he be given paid employment or demands that V sign a promissory note provided by D,[17] he may be guilty of blackmail if he acts with a view to gain. Demands for sexual intercourse or other acts of a sexual nature are not within the scope of the offence and are dealt with under the Sexual Offences Act 2003.[18]

25.1.2 Menaces

The word 'menace' is an ordinary English word which in most cases will be understood by a jury without the need for elaboration.[19] On one view it might suggest only threats of violence to persons or property, but under the former law[20] 'menace' was given a much wider meaning. The CLRC intended to retain this extended meaning. The Committee was well aware of the meaning 'menace' had acquired and deliberately chose to use this word when they might have chosen another.[21] It extends to threats to damage property and to make damaging allegations whether truthful or not. In *Thorne v Motor Trade Association*,[22] Lord Wright said[23] that a menace was a threat of 'any action detrimental to or unpleasant to the person addressed'. This

---

[12] *Thumber* (1999) No 199900691, 29 Nov, CA.

[13] *Treacy v DPP* [1971] AC 537, [1971] 1 All ER 110, HL. See PJ Pace, 'Demanding with Menaces' (1971) 121 NLJ 242.

[14] See *Moran* (1952) 36 Cr App R 10 at 12; cf JL Edwards, 'Criminal Attempts' (1952) 15 MLR 345.

[15] Theft Act 1968, s 34; below, p 948.

[16] cf Eighth Report, Annex 2.

[17] cf *Phipoe* (1795) 2 Leach 673, where Mrs Phipoe, armed with a carving knife, 'in the French language threatened, amidst the most opprobrious expressions, to take away [V's] life' unless he signed a promissory note on paper and with materials provided by her.

[18] See above, Ch 18. Note that the offence of procuring a woman to have sexual intercourse by threats contrary to s 2 of the Sexual Offences Act 1956 has not been replicated in the 2003 Act. There are reported convictions for blackmail in these circumstances (eg *Downer* (2000) 17 Oct, CA), but these must be erroneous.

[19] *Lawrence and Pomroy* (1971) 57 Cr App R 64, CA.

[20] Although not called blackmail, see ss 29–31 of the Larceny Act 1916.

[21] Eighth Report, para 123.

[22] [1937] AC 797, [1937] 3 All ER 157, HL.

[23] [1937] AC at 817, [1937] 3 All ER at 167.

is a very wide definition.[24] The CLRC chose 'menaces' in preference to 'threats' because, 'notwithstanding the wide meaning given to "menaces" in *Thorne's* case... we regard that word as stronger than "threats", and the consequent slight restriction on the scope of the offence seems to us right'. In view of Lord Wright's definition of menaces, it might be thought that any theoretical distinction between menaces and threats is wholly illusory in practice,[25] but it does perhaps serve to emphasize that there is a limit below which conduct will not be regarded as a menace.

Three situations need to be distinguished.

(1) Where D has in fact made a demand with a 'menace' that would cause a person of ordinary firmness to succumb, V's *subsequent* refusal to accede to the demand cannot relieve D of liability. There can be a menace even if V is not intimidated. Thus, D may be guilty of blackmail where he threatens to assault V unless V pays him money, even though V is in no way frightened and squares up to D with the result that D runs away.[26]

(2) The law will not treat as a menace words or conduct which would not intimidate or influence *anyone* to respond to the demand. So, in *Harry*,[27] where the organizers of a student charity 'Rag' event had written to shopkeepers offering them immunity from any 'inconvenience' resulting from Rag activities, the trial judge ruled that there was not sufficient evidence of a menace. Some shopkeepers had complained of the veiled threat in the letter but this menace was not, to use the words of Sellers LJ in *Clear*,[28] 'of such a nature and extent that the mind of an ordinary person of normal stability and courage might be influenced or made apprehensive so as to accede unwillingly to the demand'.

(3) However, D's conduct may amount to a menace even though a person of ordinary firmness would not accede to the demand where, *to D's knowledge*, the particular victim, owing to such factors as infirmity, youth, timidity or even plain cowardice, will accede to the demand.[29] Indeed, the blackmailer will often select his victim precisely because he is aware of the victim's vulnerability.[30] If D intends that his menace should operate on the mind of V and knows of circumstances that will make V unwillingly accede to the demand, D may properly be convicted of blackmail. Since the offence is completed irrespective of the demand being successfully communicated to V, there is some tension with this aspect of the offence being interpreted by reference to the victim's susceptibilities.[31]

The recent case of *Lambert*[32] emphasized that it was still blackmail if D threatened that something would happen to V even if D could not carry out that threat. D in that case claimed to have X held hostage when he did not. D demanded money from V on threat of injuring X. It was not within D's power to carry out the threat to injure X there and then. At trial D argued that s 21 is limited to situations where the person making the demand is proposing

---

[24] For an argument that the offence be limited to threats to do unlawful acts, see Green, *Lying, Cheating, and Stealing*, Ch 17. For an argument that the definition is so wide that drug dealers might be guilty of blackmailing addicted customers by 'selling protection from withdrawal symptoms', see P Alldridge, *Relocating Criminal Law*, 205–206.

[25] See above, n 23 and L Katz, *Ill-gotten Gains: Evasion, Blackmail, Fraud and Kindred Puzzles of the Law* (1996) 157.

[26] cf *Moran* [1952] 1 All ER 803n, CCA. See also *Garwood* [1987] 1 All ER 1032 at 1034.

[27] [1974] Crim LR 32 (Judge Petre).

[28] [1968] 1 All ER 74 at 80, CA.

[29] *Clear* [1968] 1 All ER 74 at 80, CA; *Garwood* [1987] 1 All ER 1032, [1987] 1 WLR 319, CA.

[30] cf *Tomlinson* [1895] 1 QB 706, CCR.

[31] See Smith, *Property Offences*, 15–18.

[32] [2009] EWCA Crim 2860.

to carry out the menace or had it in his power to do so. That would certainly be the typical circumstances of many blackmail charges. The trial judge and Court of Appeal rejected the argument, referring to s 21(2) which states that it is 'immaterial whether the menaces relate to action to be taken by the person making the demand'. That provision was expressly inserted to confirm that there is no need for the demander to be the one who will carry out the menace.[33] However, it seems that s 21 does not quite meet *Lambert's* argument head on. His argument was that the person issuing the menaces must be capable of controlling the carrying out of the threat, even if it is be performed by another. Read literally there is nothing in the statute to justify such a restriction as a matter of law. Of course, the fact that the demander might not be in a position to carry out the action he threatens is something which might affect whether his conduct constitutes a menace in the particular case. A chain letter in which D asserts that some unpleasantness will befall X unless V pays Y may therefore satisfy the offence subject to the sufficiency of the menace. Nor is there any restriction that the menace will involve actions directly against the person to whom the menace/demand is issued. Such a limitation would render the offence very narrow indeed: it would be an offence to demand property backed by a threat to harm V, but not a threat to harm V's child. That cannot be right.

25.1.3 Unwarranted demand

Not every demand accompanied by a menace will amount to blackmail. It will be appreciated at once that it ought not to be blackmail to demand payment of a debt from V and threaten civil proceedings in the event of his failure to comply. There is a menace (a threat of action detrimental to or unpleasant to the person addressed) but it is in the circumstances a perfectly lawful demand accompanied by a justifiable threat. At the other extreme, a demand by D for property to which he is not legally entitled accompanied by a threat to kill V would be an obvious instance of blackmail.

25.1.3.1 The paradox of blackmail

Between these two extremes in the previous paragraph, less clear-cut cases emerge: D may threaten to publicize V as a defaulter unless he pays a gaming debt;[34] D may threaten to publish memoirs which expose V's discreditable conduct unless V 'buys' them from D;[35] or D may threaten to expose V's immoral relationship with D unless V pays money which he had promised D.[36] It is arguable whether the conduct in these cases *ought* to be blackmail. Indeed, there is an apparent paradox in that while it is lawful for D to make a demand for payment of a debt owed by V, and, it is lawful for D to expose or threaten to expose V's immorality, it is blackmail to perform the two in combination. This paradox has given rise to an extensive academic literature, and a diverse range of theories has been employed in an attempt to justify criminalizing that paradox and indeed the inclusion of the offence of blackmail in a coherent and principled code of criminal law.[37] These theories include: analyses of the offence in terms of its economic efficiency;[38] claims that blackmail is outlawed as a means of prohibiting private law enforcement,[39] and the growth of an industry trading on confidential material which

---

[33] *Eighth Report*, Annex 2, 131.

[34] cf *Norreys v Zeffert* [1939] 2 All ER 187, KBD.

[35] cf the case discussed in Lord Denning's *Report*, Cmnd 2152, paras 31–36.

[36] cf *Bernhard* [1938] 2 KB 264, [1938] 2 All ER 140, CCA.

[37] For an interesting review of many of the theories, see J Isenbergh, 'Blackmail from A to C' (1993) U Pa L Rev 1905.

[38] See further: DH Ginsburg and P Shechtman, 'Blackmail: An Economic Analysis of the Law' (1993) 141 U Pa L Rev 1849; R Posner, 'Blackmail, Privacy and Freedom of Contract' (1993) 141 U Pa L Rev 1817.

[39] JG Brown, 'Blackmail as Private Justice' (1993) 141 U Pa L Rev 1935.

generate fear and inhibit normal lifestyles;[40] and assertions that the offence prevents D being unjustly enriched through the use of another's interests (V's confidential information and/ or the public's 'right to know' about that information).[41] Some of the most cogent theoretical explanations for the offence are focused on the coercion and exploitation it involves, even in the paradox cases.[42] Far from seeing the paradox as creating an anomaly, some eminent American academics have treated blackmail as a paradigmatic crime with its core being D placing V in a subordinate position.[43]

25.1.3.2 Subjective approach

The Theft Act's pragmatic solution to defining the type of menace that will be lawful is provided in s 21(1). D's demand will be unwarranted unless made in the belief (a) that there are reasonable grounds for making it, *and* (b) that the use of the menaces is a proper means of enforcing the demand. The test is subjective: did D believe in the reasonableness of the grounds for making the demand and the propriety of using a menace to enforce the demand. D's belief in the reasonableness of the demand may derive from the fact that V owes him money, or from D's presumption that he has a legal claim against V, or from some other source.[44] D's belief that the use of menaces is a proper way of enforcing that demand may stem from such factors as his upbringing, and his relationship and past dealings with V.[45]

Suppose that V promises that he will pay D £100 for the sexual favours which he has received from her; V fails to keep his promise whereupon D threatens to expose the relationship to V's regular sexual partner unless he pays.[46] D's liability would turn upon whether she believed that she had reasonable grounds for demanding the £100, *and* that her threat to expose V was a proper way of enforcing the demand. All the circumstances have to be taken into account in so far as they are relevant as tending to show or negative the authenticity of D's beliefs. D might have believed (wrongly) that she was legally entitled to the £100 (reasonable grounds) and that it was lawful for her to threaten to expose V to get it (proper means of enforcement). Alternatively, D might have believed that she was morally entitled to enforce payment in this way; this would be enough provided she believed in fact that this was reasonable and proper. One person (a lawyer, for example) might feel that she was morally entitled to something and yet recognize that her moral claim would not afford her reasonable grounds for making the demand. Another person might genuinely think that her moral right affords her reasonable grounds. In practice, D may not think precisely in terms of the legality or morality of her conduct, but more in terms of whether or not it is, in a broad way, reasonable.

---

[40] R Epstein, 'Blackmail Inc.' (1983) 50 U Chi L R 553.

[41] See further on this, J Lindgren, 'Unravelling the Paradox of Blackmail' (1984) 84 Col L Rev 670.

[42] See further, S Altmann, 'A Patchwork Theory of Blackmail' (1993) 141 U Pa L Rev 1639; G Lamond, 'Coercion, Threats and the Puzzle of Blackmail', in A Simester and ATH Smith (eds), *Harm and Culpability* (1996).

[43] See G Fletcher, 'Blackmail: The Paradigmatic Crime' (1993) 141 U Pa L Rev 1617 and L Katz, 'Blackmail and Other Forms of Arm-Twisting' (1993) 141 U Pa L Rev 1567. The offence continues to excite public and academic interest. See, for example, SE Sachs, 'Saving Toby: Extortion, Blackmail and the Right to Destroy' (2006) 24 Yale Law & Policy Rev 251 discussing the case of a website where the owner of a rabbit (pictured) demanded money from readers to spare him from being killed and eaten.

[44] cf *Kewell* [2000] 2 Cr App R (S) 38, where V owed a debt to D but there was little difficulty in establishing that D knew it was improper to threaten to reveal embarrassing but consensually taken photos of V from their period of cohabitation. Similarly, in *St Q* [2002] 1 Cr App R (2) 440, where D's threat was to distribute videos of consensual sex to encourage his wife to agree a divorce settlement. See also *Walker* [2010] EWCA Crim 2184 where D threatened that unless paid he would kill V's dog which he had found.

[45] Car clampers do not commit the offence provided they believe that clamping is a proper means of enforcing the demand for payment: *Arthur v Anker* [1997] QB 564 at 577. cf cases such as *Havell and Miller* [2006] 2 Cr App R (S) 633 which are clearly within the scope of the offence.

[46] cf *Bernhard* [1938] 2 KB 264.

In *Harvey, Ulyett and Plummer*,[47] D and his associates paid V £20,000 for what V claimed was a consignment of cannabis but which turned out to be 'a load of rubbish'. Incensed by this swindle, the defendants kidnapped V's wife and child and made threats of serious bodily harm to them and to V unless the money was returned. No doubt a lawyer (or even a reasonably well-informed layman) would have appreciated that in these circumstances the money was not recoverable since it was paid in pursuance of an illegal contract. Such a person might have difficulty in forming a belief that there were reasonable grounds for the demand. But in *Harvey* the particular defendants felt that they had been swindled ('ripped off to the tune of £20,000' as the trial judge put it) and it was for the jury to determine whether as a matter of fact they believed that their demand was reasonable.[48]

It has been argued[49] that this goes too far: that it is not right that D's own moral standards should determine the rightness or wrongness of his conduct.[50] The criticism is that the *mens rea* turns not merely on D's subjective beliefs about the circumstances in which he is acting (as in recklessness, etc), but also on D's beliefs about appropriate moral standards. There are a number of responses to this. First, as a practical matter most people do act according to generally accepted legal and moral standards, and the cases must be rare where D can *genuinely* rely on his own moral standards where these are seriously at odds with accepted norms. Second, it is important to note that it is not enough that D feels that his conduct is justified or that it is in some way right for him; 'proper' in this context involves a consideration of what D believes would be generally thought of as proper. While the test of D's belief is subjective, that belief refers to an external standard – that of propriety; D cannot, therefore, take refuge in his own standards when he knows that these are not thought proper by members of society in general.[51] In this respect the test reflects that found in the *Ghosh*[52] formula of dishonesty. Third, there is a further limitation on the opportunity for D to claim that his own standards apply in evaluating what is a proper means of enforcing a demand. It has been held that if D knows that he is threatening to commit a crime, he cannot maintain that he believes such a threat to be proper.[53] This is a questionable limitation. The focus must surely remain on the question of D's belief as to the propriety of his use of menaces. The fact that D is aware that his menace would be a crime may be strong evidence that he did not believe it to be a proper means of enforcing the demand, but it is not conclusive.

One consequence of this subjective approach is that D may be guilty of blackmail where he believes that he has no reasonable grounds for his demand or that the use of the menaces is improper, even though, viewed objectively, his demand is perfectly reasonable and his threat perfectly proper. Concentrating to this extent on D's state of mind as the criterion of criminality represents something of an innovation in English criminal law, but cases where the matter arises must inevitably be rare.

---

[47] (1981) 72 Cr App R 139, CA.

[48] See also *Lambert* [2009] EWCA Crim 2860 where D's argument that the threat to injure to recover a debt was also rejected.

[49] By Sir Brian MacKenna, 'Blackmail' [1966] Crim LR 467 at 469.

[50] See *Lambert* [1972] Crim LR 422 (Newcastle Crown Court), where Judge John Arnold appears to have accepted that the effect of the section is that the law should give 'efficacy to the defendant's moral judgments whatever they may be'.

[51] cf Griew, *Theft*, para 14.30. In *Harrison* [2001] EWCA Crim 1314, where D had been demanding money to which he believed himself to be entitled as compensation for his being sacked by V, the judge directed the jury that '"proper" was a word of wide meaning – wider than lawful, but no act which was not believed to be lawful could be believed to be proper within the subsection. The test is not what the defendant regarded as justified but what he believed to be proper...' The Court of Appeal commented that the directions contain a rogue sentence 'proper in that sense... meant a suitable and apt way, not threats of unlawful or criminal actions'.

[52] [1982] QB 1053.

[53] *Harvey, Ulyett and Plummer* (1980) 72 Cr App R 139, CA.

It should be noted that s 21(2) provides that it is immaterial whether or not the menaces relate to action to be taken by the person making the demand. Consequently, it may amount to blackmail if D makes a demand of V and threatens that E will assault V if he does not comply. The express provision was included to prevent any possible argument on this matter.[54]

25.1.4 View to gain or intent to cause loss

It has been noted above[55] that the requirement of a view to gain or intent to cause loss operates as a limiting factor on the offence of blackmail. It anchors it, albeit rather precariously, in the scheme of offences protecting property interests.[56] A threat by D to prosecute V for a theft she has committed unless she has sexual intercourse with him, though it might constitute some other offence,[57] would not amount to blackmail under s 21(1) of the Act. The Theft Act 1968 is concerned with invasions of economic interests, and gain and loss are defined accordingly in s 34(2)(a):

'gain' and 'loss' are to be construed as extending only to gain or loss in money or other property, but as extending to any such gain or loss whether temporary or permanent; and –

(i) 'gain' includes a gain by keeping what one has, as well as a gain by getting what one has not; and

(ii) 'loss' includes a loss by not getting what one might get, as well as a loss by parting with what one has.

In the ordinary case of blackmail, D will have both a view to gain (for himself) and an intention to cause loss (to V), but either suffices. D may commit the offence where he intends to cause loss to V without making a gain for himself, as where, he demands by threats that Z destroy property belonging to V. In such a case, D clearly intends to cause loss to 'another' even though the person threatened is not the person to whom the loss is caused. Conversely, D may act with a view to gain although there is no intention to cause loss. D might demand that V appoint him as a paid director in V's company: here D has a view to gain for himself but it may well be that, far from intending to cause V loss, he intends to bring him increased profits.

Most often D's view to gain will be obvious: a blackmailer's prime objective is normally to get money or other property from V, intending to deprive V permanently of property. Section 34(2)(a) makes it clear, however, that there is no need for the intended gain or loss to be permanent. D might be guilty of blackmail, for example, where by menaces he demands that V make a loan of property. This again reflects the fact that the gravamen of the offence is that an unwarranted demand has been made. But will any view to gain – no matter how remote – suffice?[58] Clearly, there may be a view to gain although the gain is not to materialize for a period of time, or even though the gain may never materialize. D might, by threats, cause his sister to destroy their grandmother's will on the assumption that this shall be to D's financial advantage; it can make no difference that granny is on her death bed or is in the best of health, or that she has made another will revoking the

---

[54] Eighth Report, Annex 2. See also *Lambert* (above).

[55] At p 942.

[56] There is a view to gain where D at gun point demands that a doctor give him an injection of morphine (morphine is property) to relieve pain: *Bevans* (1987) 87 Cr App R 64, [1988] Crim LR 236, CA. It is not uncommon for blackmail charges to be laid where one drug gang has demanded drugs from another, backed by threats of violence, eg *Hart and Bullen* [1999] 2 Cr App R (S) 233.

[57] See above, Ch 18.

[58] See Ormerod and Williams, *Theft*, paras 12.20–12.21.

one destroyed.[59] The essence of blackmail is the demand with menaces and the offence is complete whether D succeeds in making a gain thereafter or not.[60] The interpretation of the concept of 'view to gain' has not been fully explored in the case law under s 21, although the courts have acknowledged that the expression does not connote motive.[61] The academic approach has been to interpret the expression as simply a form of intention.[62] What seems to be important is that D should have the view to gain in his mind at the time of making the demand; the fact that it has crossed his mind at some stage that there may be a gain involved might not be enough. While it is probably not necessary to show that D's primary purpose in making the demand was to make a gain for himself or another, it must be one of his objectives.[63] Equally, where it has to be shown that D *intended* to cause loss to another, the mere foresight that another might suffer some likelihood of loss would be insufficient. Arguably, it should be sufficient that D demands something and in doing so realizes that it is virtually certain to result in his causing loss to V. In *Dooley*,[64] the Court of Appeal expressly left open that question.[65]

Subparagraphs (i) and (ii) of s 34(2)(a) were introduced to meet a possible argument that D would not be acting with a view to gain, or with intent to cause loss, where the gain or loss had already taken place. An example might be where D owes V £10 and demands by threats that V forgo his claim to the debt; it is now quite clear[66] that D would be acting with a view to gain.

A further difficulty under this section is whether D can be said to have a view to gain or intent to cause loss where he acts under a supposed legal claim of right to the property demanded (the paradox position above). Suppose that D, who is owed £100 by V, threatens to expose to V's employers the fact that V is a paedophile unless V pays the debt. D can satisfy the requirement that he believes he has reasonable grounds for making the demand, but it may be supposed (as must almost invariably be the case) that D does not believe that the use of the menace is a proper means of reinforcing the demand. It was clearly intended by the CLRC that D might be guilty of blackmail if he failed to meet *either* of the criteria in paragraphs (a) and (b) of s 21(1), irrespective of whether or not D acted under a legal claim of right to the property demanded:

The essential feature of the offence will be that the accused demands something with menaces when he knows either that he has no right to make the demand or that the use of the menaces is improper. This, we believe, will limit the offence to what would ordinarily be thought should be included in blackmail. The true blackmailer will know that he has no reasonable grounds for demanding money as the price of keeping his victim's secret: *the person with a genuine claim will be guilty unless he believes that it is proper to use the menaces to enforce his claim.*[67]

---

[59] See *Custance* [2007] EWCA Crim 520.

[60] cf *Moran* [1952] 1 All ER 803n, CCA.

[61] Per Chitty LJ in *J Lyons and Sons v Wilkins* [1899] 1 Ch 255 at 269–270, considering the offence under s 7 of the Conspiracy and Protection of Property Act 1875. See also *Bevans* (1988) 87 Cr App R 64: D's unwarranted demand with menaces for painkiller was sufficient for blackmail as he did so with a view to gain even though his motive was to alleviate pain.

[62] See, eg, Williams, TBCL, 830.

[63] This sentence in the 11th edition was approved by the Court of Appeal in *Dooley* [2005] EWCA Crim 3093 at [14].

[64] [2005] EWCA Crim 3093.

[65] See further the commentary at [2006] Crim LR 544. In that case, it was held that D possesses child pornography 'with a view to' its being shown to others if he intends to do so; and it is not enough that he knew that others could access it from his computer if he did not actually 'want' this.

[66] Or is it? See *Golechha* [1989] 3 All ER 908, [1990] Crim LR 865, CA, above, p 933.

[67] Eighth Report, para 121, emphasis added.

The offence of blackmail is, however, governed in all cases by the requirement of view to gain or intent to cause loss. It might be argued[68] that where D demands property to which he is *legally* entitled (or believes himself to be legally entitled), he has no view to make a gain for himself or to cause loss to another: D makes no gain in getting what he is legally entitled to, and V sustains no loss in paying his lawful debts. In other statutory contexts, gain is sometimes treated as economic gain or profit. However, it has also been held to mean 'acquisition' and this is not necessarily to be equated with the narrower concept of 'profit'.[69] To construe it as meaning acquisition would certainly be consistent with the CLRC's intentions.[70] In *Lawrence and Pomroy*,[71] where D and E were convicted of blackmail in making threats to recover a debt, it appears to have been assumed by the Court of Appeal, though the point was not directly argued,[72] that D and E had a view to gain. This accords with s 21(2) which emphasizes that the 'nature of the act or omission demanded is immaterial'. A literal interpretation should mean that a demand for a debt legally owed will suffice for the offence.[73]

By the same token, D intends V to lose a particular item even if D is prepared to replace it with one of identical value.[74]

25.2 Unlawful harassment of debtors

Section 40 of the Administration of Justice Act 1970 creates an offence of unlawful harassment of debtors which may be noted at this point. The offence is summary only and punishable by fine,[75] is committed by one who, with the object of coercing another person to pay money claimed as a debt under a contract:

(a) harasses the debtor by demands which by reason of their frequency or manner of making are calculated to subject the debtor or members of his household to alarm, distress or humiliation; or

(b) falsely represents that criminal proceedings lie for non-payment; or

(c) falsely represents that he is authorized in some official capacity to enforce payment; or

(d) utters a document falsely represented to have an official character.

Whatever may be the position in relation to the offence of blackmail, it is clearly no defence to a charge under this provision that the debt was owed. The offence was created to curb the growing practice of enforcing the payment of debts in a fashion that is unreasonable, unfair or improper; such as where a creditor calls at the debtor's house to make a demand and is

---

[68] B Hogan, 'Blackmail' [1966] Crim LR 474, 476. cf Ormerod and Williams, *Smith's Law of Theft*, para 12.28. cf Griew, *Theft*, paras 14.25–14.28.

[69] cf Ormerod and Williams, *Smith's Law of Theft*, para 12.28; and authorities there cited. cf *Blazina* [1925] NZLR 407 on the meaning of 'extort or gain' in the New Zealand Crimes Act 1908.

[70] As expressed in the passage cited at n 67, above. But the Committee also characterized blackmail as an offence of dishonesty (cf paras 118 and 122) and one who demands that to which he believes he is legally entitled is not acting dishonestly: cf *Skivington* [1968] 1 QB 166, [1967] 1 All ER 483, CA, and *Robinson* [1977] Crim LR 173, above, p 844.

[71] (1971) 57 Cr App R 64, CA.

[72] The point was argued in *Parkes* [1973] Crim LR 358 (Judge Dean), where it was ruled that a person demanding money undoubtedly owed to him did have a view to gain and approved in *A-G's Reference (No 1 of 2001)* [2002] EWCA Crim 1768, [2003] 1 Cr App R 131.

[73] Considered in *A-G's Reference (No 1 of 2001)* [2002] EWCA Crim 1768, [2003] 1 Cr App R 131 in the context of false accounting.

[74] See Ormerod and Williams, *Smith's Law of Theft*, para 12.31.

[75] Level 5 on the standard scale.

accompanied by large, fierce and hungry-looking rottweilers. The offence is wider than black-mail in that it may cover conduct that the creditor believes to be proper as a means of enforcing the debt. Under paragraph (a) it is enough that the demands are 'calculated to' cause distress, and this is likely to be interpreted as importing an objective standard (calculated in the eyes of reasonable people) so that it will be no defence that D himself did not calculate to cause distress.

25.3 Other offences based on threats

There are numerous other offences based on threats including: threats to kill,[76] assaults,[77] robbery,[78] threats to damage property,[79] threats of food terrorism,[80] threats of violence for the purpose of securing entry to premises,[81] sending malicious communications[82] and demanding payment for unsolicited goods with threats.[83] There is disappointingly little coherence in English law's approach to threat offences.[84]

[76] OAPA 1861, s 16.
[77] Criminal Justice Act 1988, s 39.
[78] Theft Act 1968, s 8.
[79] Criminal Damage Act 1971, s 2.
[80] Public Order Act 1986, s 38.
[81] Criminal Law Act 1977, s 6(1).
[82] Malicious Communications Act 1988, s 1, as extended by the Criminal Justice and Police Act 2001, s 43.
[83] Unsolicited Goods and Services Act 1971, s 2(2).
[84] See P Alldridge, 'Threats Offences: A Case for Reform' [1994] Crim LR 176.

26

Burglary and related offences

Burglary is an offence under the Theft Act 1968. The offence is prevalent. There were a total of 540,655 recorded offences of burglary in 2009/10, including burglaries in a dwelling and aggravated burglaries.[1] The offence is much broader than the common (mis)understanding of a 'breaking and entering' in order to steal.

26.1 Burglary[2]

Section 9 of the Theft Act 1968 provides:

(1) A person[3] is guilty of burglary if –

    (a) he enters any building or part of a building as a trespasser and with intent to commit any such offence as is mentioned in subsection (2) below; or

    (b) having entered any building or part of a building as a trespasser he steals or attempts to steal anything in the building or that part of it or inflicts or attempts to inflict on any person therein any grievous bodily harm.

(2) The offences referred to in subsection (1)(a) above are offences of stealing anything in the building or part of a building in question, of inflicting on any person therein any grievous bodily harm [...][4] therein, and of doing unlawful damage to the building or anything therein.

(3) A person guilty of burglary shall on conviction on indictment be liable to imprisonment for a term not exceeding –

    (a) where the offence was committed in respect of a building or part of a building which is a dwelling, fourteen years;

    (b) in any other case, ten years.[5]

---

[1] J Flatley et al, *Crime in England and Wales 2009/10, Findings from the British Crime Survey and police recorded crime* (2010) table 2.04.

[2] For further analysis of the offence see Ormerod and Williams, *Smith's Law of Theft*, Ch 8; EJ Griew, *The Theft Acts* (7th edn, 1995) Ch 4, hereafter in this chapter Griew, *Theft*; ATH Smith, *Property Offences*, Ch 28.

[3] In *Deutsche Genossenschaftsbank v Burnhope* [1996] 1 Lloyd's Rep 113, 123, the majority of the HL found on the facts of that case that the company in question had not committed a burglary, however, Lord Steyn, dissenting, had no doubt that a company could commit burglary where, eg, a company chairman dishonestly instructs an innocent employee to enter V's warehouse and remove valuables.

[4] The offence of entering a building with intent to commit rape was repealed by the Sexual Offences Act 2003, Sch 7, para 1. Section 63 of that Act creates a much broader offence see below, p 969.

[5] For current sentencing practice see *Saw* [2009] EWCA Crim 1. Sentencing for burglary is controversial, arousing strong public emotion and common misunderstanding; see M Davies, 'Filling in the Gaps' [2003] Crim LR 243.

(4) References in subsections (1) and (2) above to a building, and the reference in subsection (3) above to a building which is a dwelling, shall apply also to an inhabited vehicle or vessel, and shall apply to any such vehicle or vessel at times when the person having a habitation in it is not there as well as at times when he is.[6]

Section 9(1)(a) describes three separate ways the offence can be committed (entering with intent to steal, commit grievous bodily harm or unlawful damage), each of which can be committed by entry into either a dwelling (a 'domestic burglary')[7] or other building. Because there are separate sentencing provisions depending on whether the building in question is a dwelling, s 9(1)(a) effectively creates six separate offences. All these offences are committed once D has entered as a trespasser with the necessary intent,[8] irrespective of whether or not he succeeds in the intended theft, grievous bodily harm, etc.[9]

Section 9(1)(b) creates four separate forms of burglary (attempting to steal, stealing, attempting to inflict grievous bodily harm and inflicting grievous bodily harm). Again, each of these forms can be committed as either a domestic burglary or otherwise, with separate sentencing regimes applying for domestic burglaries.

A person charged with an offence under s 9(1)(b) may be convicted of an offence under s 9(1)(a) because (however contrary to the facts it may seem) the allegation of an offence under s 9(1)(b) is held to include an allegation of an offence under s 9(1)(a).[10]

The law seems to be unduly technical, and is very different from the layman's conception of burglary. More importantly, the offence definition does not reveal the principal harm against which it offers protection – possibilities are the invasion of private space, the risk of violent confrontation or aggravated forms of theft.[11] There are powerful arguments that the offence encompasses so many qualitatively different types of wrongdoing under one label that it deserves reformulation.[12] It is qualitatively different from a mere attempt to commit a theft or damage or injury.[13]

26.1.1 *Actus reus*

26.1.1.1 Enters

At common law, the insertion of any part, however small, of the body into the building or structure was a sufficient entry. Where D pushed in a window-pane and the forepart of his finger was observed inside the building that was enough.[14] The 1968 Act gives no express guidance on this issue and Parliament seems to have assumed that the common law rules

---

[6] Section 9(3) and (4) as substituted by the Criminal Justice Act 1991, amended by the PCC(S)A 2000.

[7] Under s 111 of the PCC(S)A 2000. Burglary comprising the commission of, or an intention to commit, an offence triable only on indictment and burglary in a dwelling where any person in the dwelling was subjected to violence or the threat of violence are triable on indictment only: Magistrates' Courts Act 1980, Sch 1, para 28; *McGrath* [2003] EWCA Crim 2062, [2004] Crim LR 142; *Practice Direction (Criminal Proceedings: Consolidation)* [2002] 1 WLR 2870, para 51.

[8] *Watson* [1989] Crim LR 733; *Toothill* [1998] Crim LR 876.

[9] If successful, D can still be charged under s 9(1)(a): *Taylor* [1979] Crim LR 649.

[10] *Whiting* (1987) 85 Cr App R 78, applying *Wilson and Jenkins* [1984] AC 242, [1983] 3 All ER 448, HL. *Whiting* is criticized at [1987] Crim LR 473. See also the CLRC Eighth Report, para 76. See *Chevannes* [2009] EWCA Crim 2725 below n 104.

[11] See Ashworth, POCL, 386.

[12] B Mitchell, 'Multiple Wrongdoing and Offence Structure' (2001) 64 MLR 393.

[13] GR Sullivan and AP Simester 'On the Nature and Rationale of Property Offences', in Duff and Green (eds), *Defining Crimes*, 168 at 192 ; Duff, *Answering for Crime*, 127–128. See also G Yaffe *Attempts* (2010) Ch 12; J Gardner, *Offences and Defences* (2010).

[14] *Davis* (1823) Russ & Ry 499.

would apply.[15] In the celebrated case of *Collins*,[16] D, naked but for his socks, had climbed up a ladder onto a bedroom window-sill as a trespasser and with intent to rape the woman inside the bedroom. The woman, believing him to be her boyfriend and seeing him silhouetted with an erect penis invited him in. It was not clear whether he was on the sill outside the window or on the inner sill at the moment when he ceased to be a trespasser and became an invitee. Generations of law students have pondered whether any part of D might have been inside the building at that point in time. Edmund Davies LJ in *Collins* held that to constitute burglary there must be 'an effective and substantial entry' as a trespasser. Later cases, however, do not support this opinion. In *Brown*,[17] there was a sufficient entry where D's feet were on the ground outside a shop and the top half of his body was inside the broken shop window, as if he was rummaging for goods displayed there. The court said that the word 'substantial' did not materially assist but the entry must be 'effective' and here it was: D was presumably in a position to steal. In *Ryan*,[18] D became trapped by the neck with only his head and right arm inside the window, but the court rejected the argument that because D could not have stolen anything this was not capable of constituting an entry. But strictly, *Ryan* decided only that there was evidence on which a jury could find that D had entered.

It is submitted that it cannot be required that D must have got so far into the building as to be able to accomplish his unlawful purpose. D who intends to inflict grievous bodily harm is guilty of burglary when he enters through the ground floor window though V is on the fourth floor. The act of entry need not, therefore, be either an 'effective' or a 'substantial' entry. It is unsatisfactory that such a crucial *actus reus* element of a serious offence should be left for a jury to determine; the best course would be to accept the continued existence of the common law rule: any entry no matter how slight should suffice.

At common law, if D inserted an instrument into the building for the purpose of committing the ulterior offence (theft etc), there was an entry even though no part of the body was introduced into the building. It was enough that hooks were inserted into the premises to drag out the carpets (theft), or that the barrel of a gun was introduced with a view to shooting someone inside (gbh). However, the insertion of an instrument merely for the purpose of gaining entry and not for the purpose of committing the ulterior offence was *not* an entry if no part of the body entered.[19] If D bored a hole in a door with a drill for the purpose of gaining entry, the emergence of the point of the drill bit on the inside of the door was not an entry. Under the 1968 Act, even if the courts are willing to follow the common law in holding that the intrusion of any part of the body is an entry, they may be more reluctant to preserve these technical rules regarding instruments. The rules do seem to produce outlandish results – there would be an entry if a stick of dynamite is thrown into the building, or if a bullet is fired from outside the building into it, or if a bomb is sent by post (assuming that such acts are not done merely to gain access to the building). The 1968 Act was said to be written in 'simple language as used and understood by ordinary literate men and women', but these examples are not what an ordinary person would describe as an 'entry'. Perhaps D must at least be present at the scene, or 'on the job'. Arguably, a distinction should be drawn between cases where D causes an instrument to enter V's building (for example, by throwing it), and those where the instrument entering V's building represents an extension of D's body (as where he uses a telescopic pole).[20] These issues

---

[15] HL Deb, vol 290, cols 85–86.

[16] [1973] QB 100 at 106, [1972] 2 All ER 1105 at 1111. This was at a time when burglary included trespassing with intent to rape.

[17] [1985] Crim LR 212, CA.

[18] [1996] Crim LR 320, (1996) 160 JP 610, CA.

[19] eg recently *Horncastle* [2006] EWCA Crim 1736 (pole through letterbox to hook door keys from shelf).

[20] cf Griew, *Theft*, para 4.21. The offence has been used successfully where, eg, D has used a mechanical digger to steal a cash dispenser by ripping it from the wall of a bank: *Richardson and Brown* [1998] 2 Cr App R (S) 87;

do not seem to have given rise to difficulty under the Act, perhaps due to the sensible use of more suitable charges.[21]

If it is conceded that inserting an inanimate instrument is not an entry, are we to distinguish between inanimate and animate instruments? Suppose that, instead of an instrument, D sends in a monkey? Is that an entry? At common law, burglary could be committed by an innocent agent, as for example, if D sent a child under the age of 10 into the building to steal.[22] This is probably not burglary under the 1968 Act[23] because it seems it must be D's body that enters and as discussed, it is not enough that D uses some instrument to do so.

26.1.1.2 As a trespasser

Trespass is a legal concept and resort must be made to the law of tort in order to ascertain its meaning.[24] It would appear that as a matter of civil law any intentional, reckless or (possibly) negligent entry into a building is a trespass if the building is in fact in the possession of another who does not consent to the entry. In burglary the prosecution must show that D knew, or was reckless as to whether or not he was a trespasser.

In all cases of burglary, it must be shown that D entered the building as a trespasser. Trespass can be proved without evidence from the occupier in person.[25] Problems can arise when D has been invited to enter for a particular purpose or by a person in the household who is not the owner. In *Collins*,[26] the woman who invited D in to have sex with her was the daughter of the householder. It was held that, whatever the position in the law of tort, the woman's invitation, without the knowledge or consent of the occupier (parent), meant that D was not a trespasser for the purpose of burglary. Suppose, however, that she had invited her lover, D, into her father's house to steal her father's property. This surely ought to be burglary if D realized that she had no right to invite him in for this purpose. Where the invitation to enter is issued by a member of the household, it is submitted that the crucial question will often be that of D's *mens rea*: did D know, or was he reckless as to whether or not, the invitation from that person was issued without the relevant authority? This again highlights the problem that burglary protects against a number of harms – the trespass, and the ulterior harms – and the interests being protected may be those of different individuals.[27]

In *Jones and Smith*,[28] the occupier's son, D, had a general permission to enter his father's house. He entered the house with E for the purpose of stealing. This constituted burglary. D had knowingly exceeded the permission granted to him by his father. It is perhaps noteworthy that it was a case 'where [D and E] took elaborate precautions, going there at dead of night'; and that, even if D's entry was covered by his father's general permission, this would scarcely extend to the entry of his accomplice. If E's entry was unlawful, D abetted it. Glanville

---

cf *Sang* [2003] EWCA Crim 2411 (going equipped for burglary with fishing rod bound with sellotape to extract car keys through letterboxes).

[21] The CPS advises: 'When there are any factual difficulties with the degree of entry, consideration should be given to charging another offence, for example theft.'

[22] Hale, I PC, 555.

[23] cf *Wheelhouse* [1994] Crim LR 756.

[24] See especially WVH Rogers, *Winfield and Jolowicz on Tort* (18th edn, 2010) Ch 13.

[25] *Maccuish* (1999) 6 Archbold News 2, CA.

[26] [1973] QB 100 at 107, [1972] 2 All ER 1105 at 1111. cf *Robson v Hallett* [1967] 2 QB 939, [1967] 2 All ER 407 (invitation by occupier's son effective until withdrawn by occupier).

[27] Burglary does not require that the ulterior offence should concern the occupier. If D and E enter V's house without V's consent, it would strictly amount to burglary were D to steal E's wallet or inflict on E grievous bodily harm.

[28] [1976] 3 All ER 54, CA.

Williams[29] argued that *Jones and Smith* is wrongly decided, being inconsistent with *Collins*,[30] because Collins exceeded permission since he entered intending to rape *if necessary* ie if the woman in the bedroom had not consented. But as the girl saw him to be 'a naked male with an erect penis' it seems that she invited him in expressly for the purpose of sexual intercourse, that he knew he was so invited and that any intention to rape must have lapsed by the time of the trespass when he entered the building.

Mistake as to identity, where identity is material, generally vitiates consent. So, where V's invitation to enter is based on a mistake as to the identity of D who is being invited in, there will be a trespass if D knew the mistake was being made. If Collins had known of the woman's mistake as to his identity he would have intentionally entered as a trespasser.

In tort law, a mistake by the person entering a building is no defence: if D on a very dark night entered his neighbour's house by mistake he would be regarded as having intentionally entered and trespassed. It would be a tortious trespass even if D's mistake was a reasonable one, and even more so if it were negligent as, for example, if D made the mistake because he was drunk. In criminal law, for D to be guilty of burglary it is necessary to show he was a trespasser (as defined in the civil law) but that is not sufficient: the criminal law also requires *mens rea*. If D is charged under s 9(1)(a), it need not be proved that D knew that as a matter of *law* that he was a trespasser. It must, however, be proved that, when he entered, he knew *the facts* which caused him to be a trespasser, or at least that he was reckless as to whether or not those facts existed.[31] A merely negligent entry, as where D enters another's house honestly but unreasonably believing it to be his own, is not enough to constitute burglary. D would also lack the *mens rea* for burglary if he believed he had a right to enter. Imagine that D, being separated from his wife, wrongly supposes that he has a right to enter the matrimonial home of which she is the owner-occupier and D enters with intent to inflict grievous bodily harm upon her. Even if he is a trespasser in law, D is not a burglar.[32]

If D's entry is involuntary, he does not enter as a trespasser. So if, having been dragged against his will into V's house and left there by drunken companions, he steals V's vase and leaves, this is not burglary. If, however, D had intentionally entered the building, believing it to be his own house and committed theft on discovering it was someone else's, he would have committed theft after entering as a trespasser and thus committed the *actus reus* of burglary with the *mens rea* required by s 9(1)(b). That offence is committed, not at the time of entry, but when the ulterior crime is committed; at that time D knew that he had entered as a trespasser.[33]

Trespass by exceeding a permission

Where D gains entry by deception he enters as a trespasser.[34] For example, D is a trespasser if he gains admission to V's house by falsely pretending that he has been sent by the BBC to examine the radio in order to improve the reception. The cases have taken a broader reading of trespass and this has serious consequences for the offence of burglary.

---

[29] TBCL, 846–850.

[30] cf Mason J in *Barker v R* (1983) 7 ALJR 426 at 429: 'The foundation for this conclusion [*sc*, that of Williams] is too frail.'

[31] *Collins* [1973] QB 100 at 104–105, [1972] 2 All ER 1105 at 1109–1110. 'Reckless' is used in the subjective sense: *Cunningham* [1957] 2 QB 396 and *G* [2003] UKHL 50. See above, p 123. D need not know the civil law of trespass.

[32] There are of course other offences with which he could be charged.

[33] The common law doctrine of trespass *ab initio* was held not to apply to burglary under the Theft Act: *Collins* [1973] QB 100 at 107, [1972] 2 All ER 1105 at 1111. See JC Smith, *The Law of Theft* (2nd edn, 1972) at paras 377–378 and (4th edn, 1979) at paras 338–339.

[34] There is no need to distinguish between entry under a licence that is void and one that is merely voidable; entry under either is a trespass.

A person with limited authority to enter for a particular purpose enters as a trespasser, though he practices no deception, if he has an unlawful purpose outside the scope of that limited authority. Thus, in *Taylor v Jackson*,[35] D, who had express permission to go on V's land and hunt for rabbits, went there instead to hunt for hares. The Divisional Court held that this was evidence of trespass in pursuit of game, contrary to the Game Act 1831, s 30. In *Hillen and Pettigrew v ICI (Alkali) Ltd*,[36] members of a stevedore's gang who had permission to enter a barge for the limited purpose of unloading it were held to be trespassers when they placed kegs on the hatch covers, knowing that this was a wrong and dangerous thing to do.[37] Lord Atkin stated:

As Scrutton LJ has pointedly said: 'When you invite a person into your house to use the staircase you do not invite him to slide down the banisters.'[38] So far as he sets foot on so much of the premises as lie outside the invitation or uses them for purposes which are alien to the invitation he is not an invitee but a trespasser, and his rights must be determined accordingly.

In *Farrington v Thomson and Bridgland*,[39] an Australian court held that a police officer was a trespasser when he entered a hotel for the purpose of committing a tort. The implied invitation to the public to enter the hotel did not extend to persons entering for the purpose of committing torts or crimes. In *Barker v R*,[40] V asked his neighbour, D, to keep an eye on his house while he was away on holiday. Having been told the whereabouts of a concealed key in case he needed to enter, D entered in order to steal. The High Court of Australia held that D had committed burglary: 'If a person enters for a purpose outside the scope of his authority then he stands in no better position than a person who enters with no authority at all.'[41] One decision goes against this view. In *Byrne v Kinematograph Renters Society Ltd*,[42] Harman J held that it was not trespass to gain entry to a cinema by buying tickets with the purpose, not of seeing the film, but of counting the patrons. This decision is against the weight of authority and, it is submitted, should not be followed.

It seems, therefore, that a person who enters a shop for the *sole* purpose of shoplifting is a burglar, though two of the majority in *Barker* thought otherwise. In their view, where the permission to enter is not limited by reference to purpose, a person with permission to enter is not a trespasser merely because he enters with a secret unlawful intent. It was argued that the shopkeeper's invitation to the public is not limited by reference to a specific purpose: '...the mere presence of the prospective customer upon the premises is itself likely to be an object of the invitation and a person will be within the invitation if he enters for no particular purpose at all'.[43] It is doubtful, however, if the shopkeeper's invitation can be said to extend to those who enter for the *sole* purpose of shoplifting. It is only in the exceptional case that it will be

[35] (1898) 78 LT 555.

[36] [1936] AC 65.

[37] Therefore, they were not entitled to damages for injury when the covers collapsed.

[38] *The Carlgarth* [1927] P 93 at 110.

[39] [1959] VR 286 (Smith J). See also *Gross v Wright* [1923] 2 DLR 171.

[40] (1983) 7 ALJR 426 (Murphy J dissenting).

[41] Per Mason J at 429.

[42] [1958] 2 All ER 579 at 593; distinguished in *Jones*, above, p 955, and by Mason J in *Barker v R* (1983) 7 ALJR 426 at 429 on the ground that 'the invitation by the lessee of the cinema to the public to enter the cinema was in very general terms and could on no view be said to be limited in the way in which was contended'. See more recently *Taylor* [2004] VSCA 189 and *Lambourn* [2007] VSCA 187.

[43] Brennan and Deane JJ (1983) 7 ALJR at 436. See also Williams, TBCL, 'a person who has a licence in fact to enter does not become a trespasser by reason of his criminal intent', at 846, see further 846–849; PJ Pace, 'Burglarious Trespass' [1985] Crim LR 716; ATH Smith, 'Shoplifting and the Theft Acts' [1981] Crim LR 586. A burglarious shoplifter should be sentenced in accordance with shoplifting guidelines rather than burglary guidelines: *Creed* [2005] EWCA Crim 215.

possible to prove this particular intent at the time of entry – as where there is evidence of a previous conspiracy, or system, or preparatory acts such as the wearing of a jacket with special pockets. Such an entry may be no more than a merely preparatory act to stealing (and so not attempted theft); but it ought to be possible, where there is clear evidence, to secure a conviction for burglary. Few would object to the conviction of burglary of bank robbers who enter the bank flourishing pistols, for they are clearly outside the invitation extended by the bank to the public. A person who enters a shop for the sole purpose of murdering the manager is surely a trespasser; the case of the intending thief is no different in principle.

This extension of the law beyond what was intended by the CLRC[44] is significant in terms of the number of people potentially at risk of prosecution for burglary. The interpretation in *Jones and Smith* echoes the view expressed by Fletcher that the emphasis in burglary has shifted from an act of manifest illegality – 'breaking' and entering – to an illicit entry where the principal element of blameworthiness lies in the criminal intent.[45] The cumulative effect of the extension in *Jones and Smith* with that of recent decisions in theft cases must also be considered.[46] Consider D, an antiques dealer who calls on a gullible old lady with the intention of tricking her into selling him her priceless heirloom for a gross undervalue (fraud, but seemingly also now theft); D could be guilty of burglary.

The decision in *Jones and Smith* does, however, have the advantage of emphasizing the importance of *mens rea* and reducing the reliance within the criminal law on the intricacies of the civil law of trespass.[47] It has been suggested that to keep the *Jones and Smith* extension within desirable limits a distinction might be drawn between buildings that are open to the public and others that are not,[48] but such a distinction might create an unnecessary layer of technicality. Buildings are increasingly commonly quasi-public[49] (in large shopping centres, for instance) and this distinction might cast further doubts on the ability of the tort of trespass to provide a sufficiently clear foundation for the offence in this context.

26.1.1.3 The victim of the burglary

Trespass is an interference with possession. Burglary is therefore committed against the person in possession of the building entered. Thus, where the premises are rented, burglary is committed against the tenant and not against the landlord. The landlord could commit burglary of the premises, the tenant could not.[50] A century and a half ago, it was held that, where an employee occupies premises belonging to his employer for the more convenient performance of his duties (eg a caretaker living on site), the employer is not a trespasser if he enters the premises.[51] In such a case it is, of course, necessary to look at the precise terms of the arrangement between the parties. If the employee has been given exclusive possession; he would be the victim of a trespass. It does not necessarily follow that, because the employee is not the victim of a trespass by his employer, the employee is not a victim of trespass by a third party.[52] The position of a lodger depends on the precise terms of his contract. If he has

---

[44] See Eighth Report, para 35.

[45] See G Fletcher, *Rethinking Criminal Law* (1977) 128.

[46] See above p 780.

[47] Ashworth, POCL, 386.

[48] ATH Smith, *Property Offences*, paras 28–14, referring to the American Model Penal Code, s 221.1.

[49] See K Gray and S Gray, 'Civil Rights, Civil Wrongs and Quasi-public Space' [1999] 1 EHRLR 46, discussed in the breach of the peace case, *Porter v MPC* (1999) 20 Oct, CA Civ Div, unreported.

[50] In contrast, a guest in a hotel will not ordinarily have sufficient possession of his room in law to enable him to sue in trespass. A burglary of a hotel room will be against the hotelier. Sentencing in such cases is as if the burglary was a domestic one: *Cook* [2007] EWCA Crim 7.

[51] *Mayhew v Suttle* (1854) 4 E & B 347; *White v Bayley* (1861) 10 CBNS 227.

[52] Though in *White v Bayley* (above, n 51) Byles J thought, *obiter*, that an action could not have been maintained by the servant against a stranger (10 CBNS at 235).

exclusive possession so that he can refuse entry to the landlord then he may maintain trespass. Many lodgers, however, do not have such possession and in such cases an unauthorized entry by a third party is a trespass against the landlord.

It seems to follow that burglary is not committed where an hotelier enters the room of a guest, even though the entry is with intent to steal and is without the guest's consent. Depending on the terms of the contract, the same may be true in the case of an employer entering premises occupied by his employee for the purposes of his employment or a landlord entering the rooms of his lodger. There is no glaring deficiency in the law since charges of attempted or actual theft will lie in either case.

It is possible to charge burglary even though the indictment does not allege that the building was the property of anyone.[53] There must be a trespass, so evidence must be offered that someone other than the accused was in possession. If that is all that is necessary, evidence that A or B was in possession should suffice – it is equally a trespass in either event. But if a statement of ownership is required in the indictment, 'A or B' will hardly do. It is submitted that if the indictment alleges that D trespassed in a building, without alleging who is the owner of the building, that will suffice.

26.1.1.4 Any building or part of a building

The meaning of 'building' has frequently been considered by the courts in interpreting numerous statutes.[54] The meaning of the term varies according to context,[55] and many things that have been held to be buildings for other purposes (a garden wall, a railway embankment or a tunnel under the road, for example) will not be buildings for the purpose of the Theft Act: According to Lord Esher MR, its 'ordinary and usual meaning is, a block of brick or stone work, covered in by a roof'.[56] It seems clear, however, that for the purposes of the offence of burglary it is not necessary that the structure be of brick or stone to be a building. All dwellings are protected, regardless of their material of construction, and the Act expressly includes 'an inhabited vehicle or vessel'.

To constitute a building, the structure must have some degree of permanence.[57] Moveable structures which are intended for use as offices, workshops and stores ('portakabins') may fairly be regarded as buildings though their intended use on a given site is only temporary. It has been generally assumed that a tent cannot be a building,[58] notwithstanding that it is occupied on a particular site indefinitely. A structure may be a building even though its construction is flimsy.

The structure does not need to be one occupied by people. Farm outbuildings (such as stables, barns or silos) used to house animals or products are buildings for the purposes of burglary, as are factory buildings and stores. The detached garage, shed or greenhouse in the grounds of a dwelling are similarly protected.

---

[53] cf the Larceny Act 1916 which required that the breaking and entering be of the dwelling-house *of another*. See JN Adams, 'Trespass under the Theft and Firearms Act' (1969) 119 NLJ 655.

[54] An early example is *Manning and Rogers* (1871) LR 1 CCR 338.

[55] See the explicit statement to this effect from Lord Neuberger MR in *R(Ghai) v Newcastle City Council* [2010] EWCA Civ 59 at [22].

[56] *Moir v Williams* [1892] 1 QB 264. cf Byles J in *Stevens v Gourley* (1859) 7 CBNS 99 at 112 – 'a structure of considerable size and intended to be permanent or at least to endure for a considerable time'. This statement was put into context in the *Ghai* case where it was suggested that 'building in normal parlance is naturally used to describe a significantly wider range of structures than would be included in Lord Esher's inclusion of brick or stonework covered by a roof' [24].

[57] There is authority that a structure is capable of being a 'building' notwithstanding that it is 'implanted within another building': *Royal Exchange Theatre Trust v The Commissioners* [1978] VATTR 139.

[58] See CLRC Eighth Report, para 78. This is certainly questionable in the case of, for example, a substantial marquee housing many facilities. cf *Storn* (1865) 5 SCR (NSW) 26.

Potential problems also arise regarding at which point in the process of erection a structure becomes a building. In *Manning and Rogers*,[59] Lush J said: '...it is sufficient that it should be a connected and entire structure. I do not think four walls erected a foot high would be a building.' In that case all the walls were built and the roof was on, so it was obvious that the structure was a building. It is possible that a structure with a roof and no walls, such as a band-stand, is a building. So too, a structure which is intended to have a roof – a house where the walls are complete but not yet roofed or a house which has lost its roof in a hurricane. It has been held in a different context that 'a mere structure or superstructure composed of a steel and concrete frame [as yet] having no roof' could constitute a building.[60]

Lines must be drawn and it will not always be easy to do so.[61] The courts would probably hold, following *Brutus v Cozens*,[62] that 'building' is an ordinary word the meaning of which is 'a matter of fact and degree' to be determined by the trier of fact. The judge must at least rule whether or not there is evidence on which a reasonable jury could find the structure to be a building. As with the concept of entry, it is unfortunate that one of the essential elements of the offence is left to be determined by the trier of fact.

The extent of a 'building'

Under the very complex pre-1968 law, the entry had to be into a particular dwelling house, office, shop, garage, etc. A single structure might contain many dwelling houses (a block of flats, for example) many offices, shops or garages. If D entered through the window of Flat 1 with intent to pass through it, go upstairs and steal in Flat 45, the breaking and entering of Flat 1 was neither burglary nor housebreaking because D did not intend to commit a crime therein.[63]

Under the Theft Act, everything depends on the extent of a 'building'.[64] In its ordinary natural meaning, this term could certainly include a block of flats. Adopting that meaning, D's entry through the window of Flat 1 as a trespasser with intent to pass through, go upstairs and steal in Flat 45 is an entry of a building as a trespasser with intent to steal therein – it is burglary. The effect is to criminalize as burglary what was previously, at most, an attempt, and probably only an act of preparation. There seems no good reason, however, why the law should not be extended in this way. On the contrary, there is everything to be said for enabling the police to intervene at the earliest possible moment to prevent such offences, and for fore-stalling the unmeritorious plea by D: 'I had no intention to steal in the flat – I was only using

---

[59] (1871) LR 1 CCR 338.

[60] *R v Ealing London Borough Council, ex p Zainuddain* [1994] 2 PLR 1 at 4, per Tucker LJ.

[61] Contrast *B and S v Leathley* [1979] Crim LR 314 (Carlisle CC) and *Norfolk Constabulary v Seekings and Gould* [1986] Crim LR 167 (Norfolk CC). In the former it was held that a freezer container detached from its chassis, resting on railway sleepers and used to store frozen food, was a building; in the latter it was held that two similar containers, still on their wheeled chassis, remained vehicles though they were, as in the first case, being used by a supermarket to provide temporary storage space. cf *King* [1978] 19 SASR 118 (walk-in freezer could be a building).

[62] [1973] AC 854, [1972] 2 All ER 1297, HL.

[63] cf *Wrigley* [1957] Crim LR 57. It was probably not even an attempt, not being sufficiently proximate to the intended crime.

[64] In *Hedley v Webb* [1901] 2 Ch 126, Cozens-Hardy J held that two semi-detached houses were a single build-ing for the purpose of determining whether there was a sewer within the meaning of the Public Health Act 1875, s 4. In *Birch v Wigan Corpn* [1953] 1 QB 136, [1952] 2 All ER 893, the Court of Appeal (Denning LJ dissenting) held that one house in a terrace of six was a 'house' within the meaning of s 11(1) and (4) of the Housing Act 1936 and not 'part of a building' within s 12 of that Act. Since the sections were mutually exclusive, the house could not be both a 'house' and 'part of a building' for the purpose of the Act; otherwise, Denning LJ would have been disposed to say that the house was both. Romer LJ also thought that 'for some purposes and in other contexts two "houses" may constitute one building'. cf Ormerod and Williams, *Smith's Law of Theft*, paras 8.31–8.36.

it as a passage to another flat which I never reached'. It is submitted, therefore, that the word 'building' should be given its natural meaning.

Part of a building

It is sufficient if the trespass takes place in part of a building. So, for example, one lodger may commit burglary by entering the room of another lodger within the same house, or by entering the part of the house occupied by the landlord. Similarly, a guest in a hotel may commit burglary by entering the room of another guest. A customer in a shop who goes behind the counter and takes money from the till during a short absence of the shopkeeper would be guilty of burglary. He enters that part of the building as a trespasser, even though he entered the shop (the building) with the shopkeeper's permission. The permission did not extend to his going behind the counter.[65]

What is 'a part' of the building may be a difficult and important question. Take a case put by the CLRC:[66] D enters a shop lawfully[67] but conceals himself on the premises until closing time and then emerges with intent to steal. When concealing himself D may or may not have entered a part of the building to which customers are not permitted to go. Even if he did commit a trespass at this stage because the area was off limits to customers, D may not have done so with intent to commit an offence in that part of the building. For example, D hides in the broom cupboard of a supermarket, intending to emerge and steal goods. The broom cupboard is not an area that customers are permitted to enter. D's entry of the broom cupboard, even during opening hours, is a trespass. It is a trespass committed with intent to steal, but is not burglary, for D has no intent to steal in the part of the building (broom cupboard) that he has entered as a trespasser. When he emerges from the broom cupboard after the shop has closed, he is a trespasser. He is just as much a trespasser as if he had been told in express terms to leave the shop, for he knows perfectly well that his permission to remain on the premises terminated when the shop closed.[68] He has, then, entered a part of the building – the main floor of the shop – with intent to steal. Suppose, however, having entered lawfully, D merely remained concealed until after closing time behind a stack of tins of soup in the main hall of the supermarket. This was not a trespass because he had a right to be there. When he emerged and proceeded to steal, still in the main hall of the supermarket, was he entering another part of the building? It is submitted that every step he took was 'as a trespasser', but it is difficult to see that he entered any part of the building as a trespasser; the whole transaction took place in a single part of the building which he had lawfully entered.[69] It is illogical to treat these two cases differently.

The word 'part' has no precise meaning in relation to buildings. Its significance for the purpose of the section is that a person may lawfully enter one part of a building, yet be a trespasser on setting foot in another. This was the view taken in *Walkington*.[70] D, having entered a department store, went into an area bounded by a moveable three-sided counter where he opened a cash till. It was held that there was evidence on which the jury could find that the counter area was a 'part' of the building from which the public were excluded and that if D knew that, he entered it as a trespasser. For the purposes of burglary, buildings, it seems fall into two parts: those parts where D is entitled to be, and those where he is not.

---

[65] *Walkington* [1979] 2 All ER 716, [1979] 1 WLR 1169, CA.

[66] Eighth Report, para 75.

[67] ie, without intent to steal; above, p 957.

[68] The CLRC thought: 'The case is not important, because the offender is likely to go into a part of the building where he has no right to be, and this will be a trespassory entry into that part.' But he has no right to be in any part of the building after closing time and the only question, it is submitted, is whether he went into *another* part.

[69] cf *Laing* [1995] Crim LR 395.

[70] [1979] 2 All ER 716, [1979] 1 WLR 1169, CA.

If D is lawfully in Flat 1 and, without leaving the building, he enters Flat 2 as a trespasser with intent to pass through it into Flat 3 and steal therein, his entry into Flat 2 does not constitute burglary if each flat is regarded as a separate part. He has not entered *Flat 2* with intent to steal *therein*. Yet, as we have seen, if he had entered Flat 2 from outside the building as a trespasser, there would have been no problem; he would have entered the *building* as a trespasser with intent to steal *therein*.[71] Perhaps it may fairly be said, however, that the building is in two parts: one part comprising the flat, where D is lawfully present, and the other part comprising *all* the remaining flats, where D may not lawfully go. On this view D would commit burglary by entering that part (that is, the remainder of the building) as a trespasser with the appropriate intent.

Inhabited vehicle or vessel[72]

Whilst all 'buildings' are protected by the law of burglary, vehicles and vessels are protected only where they are 'inhabited'. The obvious cases which are brought within the protection of burglary by this provision are a caravan or houseboat which is someone's home. There seems to be no reason whatever why a home should lack the ordinary protection of the law because it is mobile.[73] The limits of the extended definition should be noted. 'Inhabited' implies not that there is someone present inside the vehicle at the moment of the entry as a trespasser, but that someone lives there. My sports car is not an inhabited vehicle because I happen to be sitting in it when D enters against my will. The caravan or houseboat that is a person's home is, expressly protected, whether or not the occupier is there at the time of the burglary.

Owners of camper vans might use them for the ordinary purposes of a car during most of the year but they live in them while on holiday. While the vehicle is being lived in, it is undoubtedly an inhabited vehicle.[74] When being used for the ordinary purposes of a car it is submitted that it is not. The exact moment at which the camper van becomes an inhabited vehicle may be difficult to ascertain.[75]

Applying ordinary principles of construction of criminal offences, to be guilty of burglary D must know of the facts which would make him, in law, a trespasser in a building. Just as *Collins*[76] shows that D must know (or be reckless as to) the facts which render him a trespasser, so too D should not be convicted of burglary unless he knew of the facts which make the thing entered 'a building' in law. Suppose D enters a camper van parked by the side of the road. If he knew that V was living in the vehicle, there is no problem. But what if he did not know? It would now seem that he must be acquitted of burglary unless it can be shown that he was at least reckless as to whether anyone was living there or not; this involves showing that the possibility was present to his mind.

'Dwelling'

Since the Criminal Justice Act 1991, it has become crucial to identify whether the building entered is a dwelling, rendering the offence a 'domestic burglary' for sentencing purposes. This issue is discussed below.

---

[71] cf S White, 'Lurkers, Draggers and Kidnappers' (1986) 150 JP 37 at 56.

[72] Section 9(3).

[73] Arguably, on this rationale, the offence should also extend to protect tent dwellers.

[74] Quaere whether the unoccupied boat or caravan, which is visited and lived in only during holidays is protected. See ATH Smith, *Property Offences*, paras 28–39 (no); Williams, TBCL, 841, (yes); Griew, *Theft*, paras 4–27 (no).

[75] Ormerod and Williams, *Smith's Law of Theft*, paras 8.43–8.46. cf *Bundy* [1977] 2 All ER 382, [1977] 1 WLR 914, CA, below, p 972.

[76] [1973] QB 100, [1972] 2 All ER 1105; above, p 954.

26.1.2 *Mens rea*

26.1.2.1 Intention to enter as a trespasser

Burglary requires proof that D knew (or was reckless as to) the facts that, in law, make his entry trespassory: *Collins*.[77] It would follow that if D sets up an honest belief in a right to enter, it would be for the Crown to prove that D's belief was not held.

26.1.2.2 The ulterior offence

It must be proved that D, *either*:

(i) entered with intent[78] to commit one of the following offences:

   (a) stealing,

   (b) inflicting grievous bodily harm,

   (c) unlawful damage to the building or anything therein;[79]
   or

(ii) entered and committed *or* attempted to commit one of the following offences:

   (a) stealing,

   (b) inflicting grievous bodily harm.

Where the charge is one of entering with intent, it must be proved that at the time of entry D held an intention to cause the harm in question. In many such cases D's intent may be conditional at the time of entry, in the sense that he intends to steal if there is anything worth stealing, or intends to cause grievous bodily harm if V, his enemy, happens to be in the building. It is no bar to D's conviction that there is nothing in the building worth stealing or that V is out of town.[80] If D intends to steal a specific item only (should it be present), it seems that the 9(1)(a) offence is not committed.[81]

Intention must be proved; it is not sufficient that D is shown to have been reckless at the time of entry as to whether or not the ulterior offence would be committed.[82] Although intention in this context will usually be direct or purposive, it is possible that D will have an oblique intention: as where he intends to remove from V's premises an item of property that is his, but foresees that in doing so he is virtually certain to cause criminal damage to V's property.

The offences in s 9(1)(a) may be accurately described as inchoate versions of the three ulterior offences. Since the trespassory intrusion represents a freestanding harm to V's interests, it is generally accepted that it is appropriate in principle to criminalize these actions by a specific offence – burglary.

Stealing

This clearly means theft, contrary to s 1 of the Theft Act 1968.[83] Following *Gomez* this has an especially broad meaning.[84]

---

[77] [1973] QB 100, [1972] 2 All ER 1105.

[78] The crime is one of specific intent: *Durante* [1972] 1 WLR 1612, above, p 969.

[79] The further alternative of intending rape was repealed by the Sexual Offences Act 2003. See below.

[80] *A-G's References (Nos 1 and 2 of 1979)* [1979] 3 All ER 143, CA. See the discussion above, p 840. This interpretation of intention illustrates the flexibility of that concept: A Ashworth, 'The Elasticity of *Mens Rea*', in *Crime, Proof and Punishment*, 45, 49.

[81] Ormerod and Williams, *Smith's Law of Theft*, para 8.51.

[82] *A v DPP* [2003] All ER (D) 393 (Jun).

[83] Electricity is not property for the purposes of theft and cannot therefore found a burglary charge, as where D enters property and makes a telephone call: *Low v Blease* [1975] Crim LR 513.

[84] *Dobson v General Accident Fire and Life Assurance Corpn plc* [1990] 1 QB 274, [1989] 3 All ER 927, CA, above, p 782.

Grievous bodily harm

The intention to inflict grievous bodily harm in s 9(1)(a) must be an intention to commit an offence, that is, to inflict that harm unlawfully. The offence in question would be causing grievous bodily harm with intent to do so, contrary to s 18 of the Offences Against the Person Act 1861. It is arguable that s 23 of that Act may also be a qualifying offence since it involves administering or causing to be administered poisons or noxious substances so as thereby to endanger life *or inflict grievous bodily harm.*

If there is no evidence of the intent at the time of entry, the charge under s 9(1)(a) should not be left to the jury, even if the occupiers have been assaulted.[85]

Section 9(1)(b) does not use the word 'offence', but simply requires that D inflicts or attempts to inflict on any person in the building any grievous bodily harm. The omission of the word 'offence' is in fact a legislative accident,[86] but in *Jenkins*[87] the Court of Appeal held that the infliction need not amount to an offence of any kind. The court gave this example:

An intruder gains access to the house without breaking in (where there is an open window for instance).[88] He is on the premises as a trespasser and his intrusion is observed by someone in the house of whom he may not even be aware, and as a result that person suffers a severe shock, with a resulting stroke ... Should such an event fall outside the provisions of s 9 when causing some damage to property falls fairly within it?

This is a question plainly expecting the answer, 'no'. It is submitted that the right answer is an emphatic 'yes'. Otherwise, a person may become guilty of burglary in consequence of a wholly unforeseen and unforeseeable event. The analogy with damage to property is misplaced: causing damage to property does not fall within the provisions of s 9(1)(b). There must be an actual intention to cause damage at the time of the trespassory entry to constitute the offence under s 9(1)(a). This requires a *mens rea* which is wholly absent in the example put by the court. The House of Lords allowed the appeal in *Jenkins*[89] but on a different point and no allusion was made to the interpretation by the Court of Appeal of s 9(1)(b). The case, therefore, stands as an authority – but, it is submitted, a bad one. When para (b) is read in the context of s 9(1) and (2), it is reasonably clear that the infliction of bodily harm required must be an offence – in effect, under s 18 or 20 (possibly s 23) of the Offences Against the Person Act 1861.

What if D enters with intent to murder? It would be very strange if an entry with intent to inflict grievous bodily harm amounted to burglary, and an entry with intent to murder did not. It is submitted that the greater includes the lesser and that an intention to kill is enough.

Unlawful damage to the building or anything therein

The damage intended must be such that to cause it would amount to an offence. It might be any of the offences of causing damage created by the Criminal Damage Act 1971. In the case of every one of the offences which is likely to be invoked under this provision, the *actus reus* must be committed intentionally or recklessly.

Is it necessary that the object of the ulterior crime be in the building before the trespassory entry? In other words, is it burglary if D drags V into a barn with intent to rob, or inflict grievous bodily harm on him?[90] Similarly, it might be asked what of D who enters with the aim of

---

[85] *O'Neill, McMullen and Kelly* (1986) The Times, 17 Oct.

[86] See JC Smith, 'Burglary under the Theft Bill' [1968] Crim LR 367 and commentary on *Jenkins* [1983] 1 All ER 1000, [1983] Crim LR 386, CA.

[87] [1983] 1 All ER 1000 at 1002. cf *Watson* (1989) 89 Cr App R 211 (death caused after entry is caused in the course of committing an offence under s 9(1)(a)).

[88] The relevance of the absence of breaking is obscure.

[89] [1983] 3 All ER 448, [1984] Crim LR 36 and commentary.

[90] See S White, 'Lurkers, Draggers and Kidnappers' (1986) 150 JP 37 at 56.

removing a piece of property to damage it outside. Must it be proved only that the property was in the building or part thereof, or that the damage would occur in the building or part thereof? The words of the section do not supply a clear answer, but the purpose of the offence – the protection of persons and things in a building – suggests that the crime does not extend to these cases.

It might be questioned why the offence of burglary is limited to the ulterior intent to commit such a limited number of specified offences, and to the commission of an even smaller number. There have been suggestions to criminalize trespass with intent to commit any indictable offence; that would create considerable overlap with offences of inchoate liability, and would not appear to be necessary.[91]

26.2 Burglary in respect of a dwelling

Since the Criminal Justice Act 1991, burglary in respect of a dwelling is a separate offence[92] – a new aggravated form of burglary. In *Miller*[93] the Court of Appeal has recognized that where it is alleged that a burglary has been committed in relation to a dwelling, it is necessary to specify as much in the particulars of the offence. Arguably, this represents a return to the origins of the offence being a crime against 'habitation',[94] and has significance in labelling the conduct appropriately. The only constituent of the offence that requires consideration is 'dwelling', but it must be looked at in respect of both *actus reus* and *mens rea*.

26.2.1 *Actus reus*

'Dwelling' is not defined but it presumably means substantially the same as 'dwelling house' in the former offence of burglary at common law and under the Larceny Acts.[95] 'House' would be too narrow a definition and the word 'dwelling' better describes many forms of accommodation that should be protected. A person dwells in that place where he sleeps, not that where he spends his waking hours where those places are different. A building, such as a block of flats, may contain many dwellings. Entering the 'public' parts of the block may be burglary but perhaps not burglary in 'a dwelling'. In *Le Vine v Director of Public Prosecutions*[96] the District Judge was held to be right to find that the laundry room within the sheltered housing was not a dwelling for the purposes of the Public Order Act. Premises that qualify as a dwelling will not cease to be such because of the temporary absence of the inhabitants, provided that at least one of them intends to return. A person may have more than one dwelling, as where he has a flat in London and a house in the country, sleeping sometimes in one and sometimes in the other.[97] The camper van considered above will probably be a dwelling while the owners are living in it, but will cease to be a dwelling when they stop doing so.

---

[91] See LCCP 183, *Conspiracy and Attempts* (2007) para 16.61.

[92] Above, p 953. See *Courtie*, above, Ch 4.

[93] [2010] EWCA Crim 809.

[94] Blackstone, *Commentaries*, iv, 220.

[95] See the 1st edition of this book (1965) 399; *Russell on Crime* (12th edn, 1964) 826. cf Public Order Act 1986, s 8: ' "dwelling" means any structure or part of a structure occupied as a person's home or as other living accommodation (whether the occupation is separate or shared with others) but does not include any part not so occupied, and for this purpose "structure" includes a tent, caravan, vehicle, vessel or other temporary or movable structure'. cf Terrorism Act 2000, s 121: ' "dwelling" means a building or part of a building used as a dwelling, and a vehicle which is habitually stationary and which is used as a dwelling...'

[96] [2010] EWHC 1128 (Admin).

[97] On whether a new house is a dwelling before it has been occupied see *Lees* [2007] EWCA Crim 1640. Arguably it must have been occupied as a dwelling for some time, however short.

26.2.2 *Mens rea*

As 'dwelling' is an aggravating element in the offence warranting a higher maximum sentence of imprisonment, it should, in principle, import a requirement of *mens rea*. A person who commits burglary in a dwelling should be convicted only of simple burglary if he believed that no one lived there ie unless he had awareness that it was a dwelling. In principle and by analogy to the construction of 'as a trespasser' in *Collins*,[98] recklessness should be enough. If D entered being aware that someone might be living there, and someone was, he should be guilty of burglary in respect of a dwelling.

26.3 Aggravated burglary

By s 10 of the Theft Act:

(1) A person is guilty of aggravated burglary if he commits any burglary and at the time has with him any firearm or imitation firearm, any weapon of offence, or any explosive; and for this purpose –

    (a) 'firearm' includes an airgun or air pistol, and 'imitation firearm' means anything which has the appearance of being a firearm, whether capable of being discharged or not; and

    (b) 'weapon of offence' means any article made or adapted for use for causing injury to or incapacitating a person, or intended by the person having it with him for such use; and

    (c) 'explosive' means any article manufactured for the purpose of producing a practical effect by explosion, or intended by the person having it with him for that purpose.

(2) A person guilty of aggravated burglary shall on conviction on indictment be liable to imprisonment for life.

The reason given by the CLRC for the creation of this additional offence is that 'burglary when in possession of the articles mentioned ... is so serious that it should in our opinion be punishable with imprisonment for life. The offence is comparable with robbery (which will be so punishable). It must be extremely frightening to those in the building, and it might well lead to loss of life.'[99] The offence can be committed in dwellings or other buildings.

26.3.1 The articles of aggravation

'Firearm' is not defined in the Act, except to the extent that it includes an airgun or air pistol. The term is given a very wide meaning by the Firearms Act 1968,[100] but since that statutory definition has not been incorporated in the Theft Act it is submitted that the word should not be given a meaning any wider than that which it naturally bears; and that the term 'imitation firearm' be similarly limited.[101]

The definition of 'weapon of offence' is marginally wider than that of 'offensive weapon' in s 1(4) of the Prevention of Crime Act 1953.[102] It includes (i) articles made for causing

---

[98] At p 954, above.

[99] Eighth Report, para 80.

[100] See s 57 and *Grace v DPP* (1989) 153 JP 491. Note that the possession of a firearm with intent to commit an indictable offence (including burglary) is an offence carrying a maximum life imprisonment: Firearms Act 1968, s 18.

[101] The term has been widely construed under the Firearms Act 1968. A jury cannot conclude that D pointing a finger inside his coat at V is sufficient: *Bentham* [2005] UKHL 18.

[102] Above, p 706. Note that defences of lawful authority or reasonable excuse available under the 1953 Act do not apply here.

injury to a person, (ii) articles adapted for causing injury to a person, (iii) articles which D has with him for that purpose, (iv) any article made for *incapacitating* a person, (v) any article adapted for *incapacitating* a person, and (vi) any article which D has with him for that purpose. Articles *made* for incapacitating a person might include a pair of handcuffs; articles *adapted* for incapacitating might include a pair of socks made into a gag; articles *intended* for incapacitating a person might include sleeping pills to put in the night-watchman's tea, a rope to tie him up, a sack to put over his head, pepper to throw in his face, and so on.

The definition of 'explosive' closely follows that in s 3(1) of the Explosives Act 1875 which, after enumerating various explosives, adds: '...and every other substance, whether similar to those above mentioned or not, used or manufactured with a view to produce a practical effect by explosion or by a pyrotechnic effect...'

It will be observed that the definition in the Theft Act is narrower. The Explosives Act, if read literally, is wide enough to include a box of matches – these produce a 'pyrotechnic effect' – but it seems clear that a box of matches would not be an 'explosive' under the Theft Act. The main difficulty about the definition (this is unlikely to be important in practice) lies in determining the meaning of 'practical effect'. Perhaps it serves to exclude fireworks which, so it has been said in connection with another Act, are 'things that are made for amusement'.[103]

26.3.2 'At the time' of commission of burglary

It must be proved that D had the article of aggravation with him *at the time* of committing the burglary. Where the charge is one of entry with intent (s 9(1)(a)) this is clearly at the time of entry. Where the charge is one of committing a specified offence, having entered (s 9(1)(b)), it is at the time of commission of the specified offence. Care must be taken to identity precisely whether the charge is under s 9(1)(a) or (b) and what articles were present at the time of entry and afterwards[104] and under whose control.[105]

Burglary is not aggravated merely because a weapon is used against the occupier outside the building or is held by an accomplice in a getaway car.[106] Nor is it enough to prove an armed entry by D as a trespasser unless that entry is accompanied by one of the specified intents. If D, having no such intent at the time of entry, discards his weapon and thereafter commits one of the specified offences he is not guilty of aggravated burglary[107] though he would be so guilty if he rearmed himself for this purpose.[108] It is debatable whether or not D who arms himself only to escape, having already completed the burglary (for example, by stealing), is guilty of the aggravated offence.[109] By analogy with the court's approach in *Watson*,[110] and the courts' willingness to treat Theft Act offences as continuing,[111] it is likely that the offence would be held to have been committed.

---

[103] *Bliss v Lilley* (1862) 32 LJMC 3, per Cockburn CJ and Blackburn J, but Wightman J thought that a fog-signal was a 'firework'. cf *Bouch* [1982] 3 All ER 918, CA; *Howard* [1993] Crim LR 213, CA. See also the definition in Sch 1 to the Fireworks Act 2003 [not yet in force].

[104] *Chevannes* [2009] EWCA Crim 2725.

[105] See *Downer* [2009] EWCA Crim 1361.

[106] *Klass* [1998] 1 Cr App R 453, CA.

[107] *Francis* [1982] Crim LR 363, CA.

[108] *O'Leary* (1986) 82 Cr App R 34, CA.

[109] See Smith, *Property Offences*, para 28.61.

[110] *Watson* (1989) 89 Cr App R 211, CA.

[111] *Atakpu* (1994) 98 Cr App R 254, CA above, p 790.

26.3.3 'Has with him'

The expression 'has with him' appears in the Prevention of Crime Act 1953 and reference should be made to the discussion of that Act,[112] particularly as regards the controversial issue of D claiming to have forgotten that he has with him the forbidden article.[113] The Court of Appeal has recently reiterated that what matters for the purpose of s 10 is whether the weapon was within D's control so that it could be taken up and used if necessary (not whether he was holding it).[114]

When the prosecution has proved that the article was made or adapted for causing injury or incapacitating, it need not prove that D intended to use the weapon in the course of the burglary. Where the article was not so made or adapted, but the prosecution proves D had it with him for such use, it is not necessary to show that he intended so to use it *in the course of the burglary.* D's conviction was accordingly upheld in *Stones*[115] where at the time of the burglary he had with him an ordinary kitchen knife that, he claimed, he was carrying to use in self-defence in case he was attacked by a gang. The court held that the mischief at which the section is aimed is that if a burglar has a weapon which he intends to use to injure some person unconnected with the premises burgled, he might nevertheless be tempted so to use it if challenged during the course of the burglary. Clearly, a conditional intent to use a weapon suffices for the offence.

Under the Prevention of Crime Act, it has been decided that a person carrying an inoffensive article for an innocent purpose does not become guilty of having an offensive weapon with him merely because he uses that article for an offensive purpose. The 1953 Act is directed against the *carrying* of articles intended to be used as weapons, not against the *use* of an article as a weapon. It was to be expected that the same construction would be put upon the similar words of s 10 of the Theft Act, but, in *Kelly*,[116] it was held that D, who had used a screwdriver to effect an entry to premises, became guilty of aggravated burglary when he used it to prod V in the stomach. The court purported to apply the ordinary meaning of the words of the subsection, but they seem indistinguishable in this respect from the words of the Prevention of Crime Act (and the same considerations of policy seem applicable to the two provisions). *Kelly* seems a dubious decision.

It has also been held under the 1953 Act that no offence is committed where a person arms himself with a weapon for instant attack on his victim;[117] if *Kelly* is right, it seems that such a decision can hardly apply to s 10. So if D is interrupted in the course of stealing after a trespassory entry, picks up a paperweight (or any object) and throws it with intent to cause injury, he will thereby become guilty of aggravated burglary. He could be adequately dealt with by a charge of simple burglary and a second count charging whatever offence against the person he has committed; it is submitted that this is the proper course. On the other hand, if D picks up a stone outside the building to use as a weapon should he be disturbed after entry, the subsequent burglary would properly be held to be aggravated: D has armed himself before an occasion to

---

[112] Above, p 706. See also *Pawlicki and Swindell* (1992) 95 Cr App R 246, [1992] Crim LR 584 ('have with him' under Firearms Act 1968, s 18(1)), and *North* [2001] EWCA Crim 544. In respect of the Firearms Act offence, it has been held that the question of propinquity is to be approached in a commonsense way. A person could not, therefore, be said to 'have with him' a firearm stored two or three miles away: *Bradish* (2004) 148 SJ 474, CA.

[113] See especially *Jolie* above, p 708.

[114] See *Chevannes* above, n 104.

[115] [1989] 1 WLR 156, 89 Cr App R 26, CA. See NJ Reville, 'Mischief of Aggravated Burglary' (1989) 139 NLJ 835.

[116] (1992) 97 Cr App R 245, [1993] Crim LR 763 and commentary.

[117] *Ohlson v Hylton* [1975] 2 All ER 490; *Giles* [1976] Crim LR 253; *Bates v Bulman* (1979) 68 Cr App R 21; *Byrne* [2004] Crim LR 582.

use violence has arisen; and the stone is a weapon of offence. In *O'Leary*,[118] D, having entered V's house as a trespasser, took up a kitchen knife and proceeded upstairs where by use of the knife he forced V to hand over property. It was held that he was rightly convicted of aggravated burglary. Burglary is committed under s 9(1)(b) at the time when the ulterior offence is committed; before its commission, D had armed himself for use in connection with it.

26.4 Trespass with intent to commit a sexual offence

Section 63 of the Sexual Offences Act 2003 introduced a new offence to replace burglary with intent to rape.[119]

(1) A person commits an offence if –

    (a) he is a trespasser on any premises,

    (b) he intends to commit a relevant sexual offence on the premises, and

    (c) he knows that, or is reckless as to whether, he is a trespasser.

(2) In this section –

    'premises' includes a structure or part of a structure;

    'relevant sexual offence' [is all those in that Part of the Act];

    'structure' includes a tent, vehicle or vessel or other temporary or movable structure.

The offence is significantly wider in a number of respects than the old law under where it was burglary to enter a building as a trespasser with intent to rape. Under s 63 any trespass is sufficient and there is no need to prove a trespassory *entry*. The trespass may arise as a result of D exceeding permission for the purposes which entry was granted; or exceeding permission in terms of the areas or parts of promises entered. Secondly, the trespass relates to 'premises', which is wider than the concept of a building or part of a building. It is a term used in many statutes, including criminal ones, and is usually widely construed.[120] Technically, it could extend to all areas of land which could be the subject of a lease and will include open spaces (fields and parks). Thirdly, the concept of 'structure' is widely defined, and will unlike in burglary, include a car or van.[121] Fourthly, as with s 9(1)(a) there is no need for the ulterior (sexual) offence to occur. Indeed, there is no need for any intended victim to be on the premises. Finally, the list of ulterior offences to which this section applies is much wider than under old law which applied only to rape; it extends to all those in Part 1 of the 2003 Act.[122] By s 72

---

[118] (1986) 82 Cr App R 341, CA.

[119] See generally P Rook and R Ward, *Sexual Offences Law and Practice* (4th edn, 2010) para 13.36 et seq.

[120] eg in the Criminal Law Act 1977, 'premises' means any building, any part of a building under separate occupation, any land ancillary to a building, the site comprising any building or buildings together with any land ancillary thereto: s 12(1)(a).

[121] 'Structure' is a term used in numerous statutes, but its interpretation is heavily dependent on context. A recent example is the Criminal Justice and Police Act 2001, where s 66 provides (as amended by the Marine and Coastal Access Act 2009, Part 8, s 253 (6)(b), in force from 12 January 2010) ' "premises" includes any vehicle, stall or moveable structure (including an offshore installation [or other marine installation]) and any other place whatever, whether or not occupied as land'. Section 48 of the RIPA 2000 similarly provides that 'premises' includes any vehicle or moveable structure and any other place whatever, whether or not occupied as land. This suggests that 'structure' is wider than 'building'. For proposals to extend the law see LCCP 183, above, para 16.61.

[122] See, eg, *Fulton* [2006] EWCA Crim 960 (D had forced his way into the house of a 60-year-old woman and forced her to watch him masturbate). See also *C* [2006] EWCA Crim 1024 and *Ralston* [2005] EWCA Crim 3279 (sexual touching); and *H* [2007] EWCA Crim 2622.

of the 2003 Act the offence is committed if D, who is a British national, does an act abroad against an under 18-year-old which would, if committed in the UK constitute an offence under s 63.

The *mens rea* of the offence requires proof that D intended to perform the relevant sexual offence, and knowledge or subjective recklessness as to the facts that render him a trespasser.

26.5 Going equipped

Many of the offences in the Theft Acts (and Fraud Act) have been criticized for their considerable breadth, particularly in view of the generally wide interpretations adopted by the courts. It is possible for D to be convicted of theft from the moment that he touches an item or acts in a way that assumes any single right of an owner, provided he has the proscribed state of mind.[123] Similarly, it is possible for D to be convicted of burglary where he has only entered as a trespasser with a proscribed intent.[124] With charges also available for attempted theft where D has gone beyond any act of mere preparation, the reach of the criminal law in this area is vast. The offence under s 25 (like those under ss 6 and 7 of the Fraud Act) goes further still, criminalizing conduct of a more preliminary nature than even attempt.

By s 25(1) and (2) of the Theft Act 1968:

(1) A person shall be guilty of an offence if, when not at his place of abode, he has with him any article for use in the course of or in connection with any burglary, theft.[125]

(2) A person guilty of an offence under this section shall on conviction on indictment be liable to imprisonment for a term not exceeding three years.[126]

This useful inchoate offence[127] is expressed to be directed against acts preparatory to:

(i)   burglary contrary to s 9;

(ii)   theft contrary to s 1;

     ... [128];

(iv)   taking and driving away a conveyance, contrary to s 12.[129]

26.5.1 *Actus reus*

The cross heading in the statute, 'Possession of house-breaking implements, etc', and the side note, 'Going equipped for stealing, etc', indicate that the offence[130] is aimed primarily at someone setting out on an expedition equipped with a jemmy, skeleton keys and such like. However, in *Re McAngus*,[131] an extradition case, it was held that there was evidence of the offence when undercover agents said that D had agreed to sell them counterfeit clothing and had shown them shirts, wrongly bearing an American brand name, in a bonded warehouse.

---

[123] See the discussion of *Gomez* [1993] AC 442 and *Hinks* [2001] 2 AC 241, above p 781.

[124] See s 9(1)(a), above p 781.

[125] The form of the offence in terms of going equipped to cheat was abolished by the Fraud Act 2006.

[126] See, generally, JK Bentil (1979) 143 JP 47; Williams, TBCL, 853–857; Griew, *Theft*, Ch 16; Smith, *Property Offences*, para 31.1.

[127] There were 3,676 recorded offences of going equipped in 2009/10: Flatley et al, *Crime in England and Wales 2009/10*, table 2.04.

[128] References to deception under s 15 of the Act were repealed by the Fraud Act 2006.

[129] By s 25(5), 'theft' in this section includes an offence under s 12(1).

[130] Like its predecessor, s 28 of the Larceny Act 1916.

[131] [1994] Crim LR 602, DC, and commentary.

D was certainly 'equipped' for criminal deception and, when visiting the warehouse, was not at his place of abode. If he had been hawking the shirts from door to door it would have been a straightforward case, but D did not 'go' anywhere with the articles. The side-note is not part of the section but might now be considered as a legitimate aid to statutory construction;[132] it might be taken to show that 'going' is the essence of the offence.[133] Presumably, it would have made no difference if the shirts had been kept in D's own warehouse (which does not seem substantially different from keeping them at home).

D must have with him 'any article'; the article need not be made or adapted for use in committing one of the specified offences. It is sufficient that D intended to use it in the course of, or in connection with, one of the specified offences. So, the article may be as innocuous as a tin of treacle (intended for use in removing a pane of glass), a diving suit (to allow D to steal balls from a lake on a golf course),[134] a pair of gloves (to be worn to avoid leaving fingerprints), or a charity collecting tin (which D is not authorized to use).[135] It was implicit in numerous decisions that the offence of going equipped to cheat caught such conduct as possession of a sliced loaf and a bag of tomatoes[136] or bottles of wine[137] which D intended to pass off as the property of his employer.[138]

D can hardly be committing an offence by wearing his shoes or any other item of everyday clothing, yet it was argued above that gloves for the avoidance of fingerprints would entail liability.[139] This suggests that one way of restricting the scope of the offence is to limit it to articles D would not be carrying with him 'but for' the contemplated offence. On this view, if it is something that he would carry with him on an innocent outing, it should not fall within this section. So there might be a difference between a pair of latex gloves and a pair of woollen gloves that D was wearing to keep his hands warm on a freezing night, even though he did intend to keep them on so as to avoid leaving fingerprints. The latter pair of gloves is hardly distinguishable, for this purpose, from D's overcoat, which seems to fall into the same category as his shoes. If D is carrying a pair of plimsolls in his car to facilitate his cat-burgling, this seems a plain enough case, but what if he has simply selected his ordinary shoes for wear because they are less noisy than his hobnail boots? Arguably, this 'but for' analysis is too simplistic. What of D who picks up his gloves with a view to avoiding leaving fingerprints at a burglary that he is about to commit, but on opening his front door sees that it is snowing and would ordinarily have picked up his gloves on seeing snow outside? There is no difference between wearing the woolly gloves, for a dual purpose, and wearing latex gloves for a sole purpose. In both cases, D wears the gloves in order to avoid detection.

The offence is extremely broad, and in some instances the *actus reus* might be regarded as negligible. The emphasis is on the proof of *mens rea*; for that reason, care must be taken to avoid overly broad application.

---

[132] *M* [2004] UKHL 50, [2005] Crim LR 479; cf R Munday, 'Bad Character Rules and Riddles: "Explanatory Notes" and True Meanings of s 103(1) of the Criminal Justice Act 2003' [2005] Crim LR 337.

[133] As the long title showed that 'carrying' was the essence of the offence under the Prevention of Crime Act 1953, above, p 706.

[134] *Rostron* [2003] EWCA Crim 2206.

[135] *Armson* [2005] EWCA Crim 2528.

[136] *Rashid* [1977] 2 All ER 237, 64 Cr App R 201, CA; cf *Cooke* [1986] AC 909, applied in relation to s 25 in *Whiteside* [1989] Crim LR 436.

[137] *Doukas* [1978] 1 All ER 1061, [1978] 1 WLR 372, CA.

[138] This series of cases place unwarranted emphasis on the question of whether the intended victim would be deceived, when the true issue is, it is submitted, whether D intends to obtain property by deception. See Ormerod and Williams, *Smith's Law of Theft*, para 3.96; Griew, *Theft*, paras 16.11–16.13.

[139] cf *Ellames* [1974] 3 All ER 130, CA; above para p 919, where gloves were included in the charge.

The expression 'has with him'[140] is the same as in s 10(1)(b) of the Act. Questions as to D's knowledge of the nature of the thing can hardly arise here, since it must be proved that he intended to use it in the course of, or (more broadly) in connection with, one of the specified offences. If a number of defendants are charged jointly with going equipped it must be proved that all the members of the enterprise knew of the existence of the articles and had the common purpose to use those articles in the specified offence.[141]

No doubt D has an article with him if it is in his immediate possession or control; he will be guilty if the article is only a short distance away and he can take it up as he needs it, as where a ladder has been left in a garden by an accomplice and D enters the garden intending to use the ladder to make an entry to the house. If the article is found in D's car some distance from the scene of the crime this will be evidence that D was in possession of the article when driving the car. The tenor of decisions on the interpretation of 'has with him' indicates that mere momentary possession will not suffice,[142] as where D is apprehended on picking up a stone which he intends to use to break a window in order to commit burglary. But, in *Minor v DPP*,[143] it seems to have been decided that D may be convicted of going equipped (in this case, to steal petrol from cars) though he did not take the equipment (petrol cans and a hose) with him but somehow came across it while he was removing the cap from the petrol tank of a car. It appears to have been regarded as enough that the theft 'was to be posterior to the acquisition of the articles'. On this view, the burglar who picks up a nearby stone to break a window to gain entry would commit the offence of going equipped; it is respectfully submitted that 'has with him' requires more than that the acquisition of the article should precede the theft.

'Place of abode' is a term that suggests a place, that is a site, where D lives.[144] Clearly, this offence is not committed when D has articles for housebreaking, etc, in his own home,[145] but place of abode is apt to cover the whole of the premises where D lives so that D does not commit the offence by having the articles in his garage or even in his car while that is on his premises. Once D steps into the street with the articles, or drives off with them in his car, the offence may be committed. The ambit of the exemption is presumably based on a respect for D's privacy. Though a car or a caravan may constitute a place of abode while stationary at some site, they can never constitute a *place* of abode while D is in transit; if he then has the articles with him, he may commit the offence.[146]

26.5.2 *Mens rea*

The *mens rea* for the offence would appear to consist in D's:

(1) knowledge that he possesses the article; and

(2) intention to use the article in the course of or in connection with any of the specified crimes.

It was held in *Ellames*[147] that the 'intent to use' must necessarily relate to use in the future so that D was not guilty of this offence where the evidence showed only that he was in possession of certain articles (masks, guns, gloves, etc) after a robbery and was trying to get rid of them. Given an intent to use the article in the future, the expression 'in the course

---

[140] See above, p 970.

[141] *Reader, Connor and Hart* [1998] 7 Apr 1998, CA.

[142] Above, p 968.

[143] (1987) 152 JP 30, DC.

[144] *Bundy* [1977] 2 All ER 382, CA; *Kelt* [1977] 3 All ER 1099, [1977] Crim LR 556 and commentary.

[145] It may be an offence under the Fraud Act 2006, s 6.

[146] *Bundy* [1977] 2 All ER 382, CA.

[147] [1974] 3 All ER 130, CA.

of or in connection with' any burglary, theft is wide enough to cover not only articles intended for use in the perpetration of the crime, but also articles intended for use before or after its commission. A car intended for use to make an escape after the commission of a robbery falls within the offence. But the article must be intended for some direct use in connection with the crime; it has been held that D's possession of a stolen driving licence so that he could obtain a job which would give him an opportunity to steal is not within the offence.[148]

In *Ellames*,[149] it was said that D could commit the offence where he possessed the articles for future use by another, so that D would have been guilty in that case had he been hiding away the guns, etc, for their future use by others. The court also thought that it was not necessary to show that D intended the article to be used in connection with a particular theft; the section requires only intended use in connection with *any* burglary or theft. No doubt a conditional intent (for example, possessing a jemmy to use if necessary) suffices, but D must have made up his mind, even if only contingently, to use the article. If D had not so determined he does not commit the offence.[150] Section 25(3)[151] provides:

Where a person is charged with an offence under this section, proof that he had with him any article made or adapted for use in committing a burglary or theft… shall be evidence that he had it with him for such use.

This is probably no more than enactment of the general rules regarding proof of intent.[152] It puts upon D an evidential burden. If he offers no explanation then the jury may be told that there is evidence upon which they may find that he had the necessary intent, but it is submitted that they should be told so to find only if satisfied so they are sure that he in fact had that intent.[153] If D does offer an explanation then the jury should be told to acquit if they think it may reasonably be true, and to convict only if satisfied beyond reasonable doubt that the explanation is untrue. The provision does not reverse the burden of proof and poses no difficulty under Art 6(2) of the ECHR.[154]

Where the article in question is not made or adapted for use in any specified offence, mere proof of possession without more will not amount to *prima facie* evidence – that is, the case will have to be withdrawn from the jury.[155] It is a question of law for the judge, at what point proof of other incriminating circumstances amounts to a case fit for submission to the jury.

The Fraud Act 2006 introduced offences of possession of articles for use in fraud (s 6) and making, adapting, supplying or offering to supply articles for fraud (s 7).[156] The Law Commission made provisional proposals for a wider general offence of possession of an article away from one's home with intent to use it in a specified offence.[157]

---

[148] *Mansfield* [1975] Crim LR 101, CA.

[149] [1974] 3 All ER 130, [1974] 1 WLR 1391, CA.

[150] So in *Hargreaves* [1985] Crim LR 243, CA, the jury were misdirected when told they could convict if satisfied that D might have used the article.

[151] As amended by the Fraud Act 2006, Sch 1, para 8.

[152] cf Criminal Justice Act 1967, s 8; above, p 144.

[153] cf the case where the alleged receiver is proved to have been in possession of recently stolen property and offers no explanation: *Abramovitch* (1914) 11 Cr App R 45, CCA.

[154] *Whiteside* [1989] Crim LR 436. See also A Ashworth and M Blake, 'The Presumption of Innocence in English Criminal Law' [1996] Crim LR 306.

[155] cf *Harrison* [1970] Crim LR 415, CA.

[156] See p 921.

[157] See LCCP 183, para 16.6.1. These were not taken forward.

26.6 Other trespass offences

English law criminalizes numerous other types of trespass.[158] These include trespassing on various types of property (railways,[159] aerodromes[160] etc) and areas protected for their significance in national security.[161] In addition there are offences of trespass with weapons.[162] Further, there are old offences of being found in specified places for unlawful purposes, eg: 'being found in or upon any dwelling house warehouse, coach house, stable or outhouse or in any enclosed yard garden or area for any unlawful purpose'.[163]

[158] See generally P Thornton et al, *The Law of Public Order and Protest* (2010) Ch 5.
[159] British Transport Commission Act 1949, s 55.
[160] Civil Aviation Act 1982.
[161] Official Secrets Act 1911.
[162] Criminal Law Act 1977, s 8.
[163] Vagrancy Act 1824, s 4 and see *L v CPS* [2008] 1 Cr App R 8.

27

Handling and related offences

27.1 Handling stolen goods

By s 22 of the Theft Act 1968:[1]

(1) A person handles stolen goods if (otherwise than in the course of the stealing) knowing or believing them to be stolen goods he dishonestly receives the goods, or dishonestly undertakes or assists in their retention, removal, disposal or realisation by or for the benefit of another person, or if he arranges to do so.

(2) A person guilty of handling stolen goods shall on conviction on indictment be liable to imprisonment for a term not exceeding fourteen years.

The maximum sentence is twice that available for theft,[2] reflecting Parliament's desire to deter the professional 'fence' so that the market for stolen goods will diminish and the incidence of theft will decrease.[3] The particular moral wrong involved lies in dealing in stolen goods – with the idea being that stolen goods 'are a form of contraband, like drugs or counterfeit currency, which law-abiding persons should not, knowingly, acquire'.[4] In practical terms the substantial differences between the sentencing of large-scale professional handlers and, for example, receiving low value stolen goods for personal use[5] prompts suggestions that the offence ought to be subdivided to reflect more accurately the criminality involved.[6]

The incidence of handling seems to be dropping significantly. In 1997, there were 33,574 recorded offences, and in 2009/10 only 9,425.[7] The increased use of money laundering offences may explain this. Other explanations may include: the reduction in the price of goods that

---

[1] See generally, Ormerod and Williams, *Smith's Law of Theft*, Ch 13; Griew, *Theft*, Ch 15; Smith, *Property Offences*, Ch 30; CLRC Eighth Report (1966) paras 127–132. The law is cogently criticized by DW Elliott, 'Theft and Related Problems – England, Australia and the USA Compared' (1977) 26 ICLQ 110, 135–144.

[2] Sentencing guidelines were provided in *Webbe* [2001] EWCA Crim 1217.

[3] *Shelton* (1986) 83 Cr App R 379; *Tokeley-Parry* [1999] Crim LR 578 (deterring removal of antiquities from Egypt). See also M Sutton, K Johnston and H Lockwood, *Handling Stolen Goods and Theft: A Market Reduction Approach* (1998); M Sutton, 'Supply by Theft: Does the Market for Second-Hand Goods Play a Role in Keeping Crime Figures High?' (1995) 35 Brit J Criminology 400; JL Schneider, 'Stolen Goods Markets' (2005) 45 Brit J Criminology 129.

[4] A Simester and GR Sullivan, 'The Nature and Rationale of Property Offences', in Duff and Green, *Defining Crimes,* 190. It is this same philosophy that lies behind the far-reaching and draconian offences in the Proceeds of Crime Act 2002, criminalizing dealing not just with stolen goods but the proceeds of criminal activity.

[5] Low monetary value goods received for a handler's own use will attract a modest fine or conditional discharge. For analysis of the activities of the professional handler, see CB Klockars, *The Professional Fence* (1975). See www.sentencingcouncil.org.uk/guidelines/guidelines-to-download.htm.

[6] See DA Thomas, 'Form and Function in Criminal Law', in *Reshaping the Criminal Law,* 23–24.

[7] J Flatley et al, *Crime in England and Wales 2009/10, Findings from the British Crime Survey and police recorded crime* (2010) table 2.04.

tended to be stolen for resale for example, TVs, videos DVDs etc; fewer armed robberies of jewellery stores etc (because of tougher sentences), and greater access to second hand goods at reasonable prices through 'ebay' and similar lawful trading schemes.

English law has since the nineteenth century provided a specific offence of handling, treating this conduct as an independent crime rather than one of being an 'accessory after the fact' to theft.[8] The diversity of the activities seeks to criminalize results in a broad and complex offence – Glanville Williams memorably described s 22 as a 'draftsman's omelette'.[9]

27.1.1 *Actus reus*

The *actus reus* is drafted in extremely broad terms, creating an offence that can be committed in many different ways.[10] It is obvious from the section that there is no requirement that the handler ever comes into physical possession of the stolen goods, and that the concept of stolen goods itself carries an extended meaning.

The questions that require detailed consideration are: what are 'goods'? when are they 'stolen'? and what is 'handling' (that is, undertaking or assisting in retention, removal, disposal or realization)?

27.1.1.1 Stolen goods

By s 34(2)(b), '... "goods", except in so far as the context otherwise requires, includes money and every other description of property except land, and includes things severed from the land by stealing'. This definition differs from that of 'property' for the purposes of theft. Since, however, land generally is excluded from theft by s 4(2), the effect is that, subject to the small exceptions discussed below, property which can be stolen can be the subject of a handling charge.

Land

A 'thing', attached to or forming part of the land, can be stolen (s 4(2)(b)[11]) and can therefore always be the subject of handling since the stealing necessarily involves severance of the thing in question. Under s 4(2)(c), on the other hand, a fixture or structure can be stolen whether severed from the land or not. Only if it is severed can it be the subject of handling. So, if E, an outgoing tenant, dishonestly sells to D, the incoming tenant, a fixture which actually belongs to V, the landlord, D cannot be guilty of handling if the fixture is not severed.[12] If after D's tenancy the incoming tenant is F who knows all of the facts about how D came to have the fixture, F is not guilty of handling even though F has knowingly taken possession of a stolen fixture.

Land which is stolen contrary to s 4(2)(a) (by trustees or personal representatives) will rarely be capable of being handled since the kind of conduct contemplated by s 4(2)(a) will not normally involve severance.

---

[8] J Hall, *Theft, Law and Society* (2nd edn, 1952) 55–58; cf Hale, I PC, 618. G Fletcher, *Rethinking Criminal Law* (1978) 645–646, regards this as an illustration of the gradual replacement of the offence of being an accessory after the fact.

[9] Williams, TBCL, 858.

[10] *Nicklin* [1977] 1 WLR 403.

[11] Above, p 800.

[12] This is true whether or not his act is in the course of stealing.

Land may be the subject of both fraud and blackmail, both of which create 'stolen' goods for the purposes of handling.[13] Again, severance of the land may or may not take place and handling is possible only if it does so.

Things in action

Things in action (an item of property comprising D's right to sue X) are expressly mentioned in s 4(1) of the 1968 Act as capable of being the subject of theft but are not mentioned in s 34(2)(b). They must, however, be included in the all-encompassing words 'every other description of property except land' within that section. Things in action may then constitute stolen goods, but a further question is whether they can be handled. Some forms of the *actus reus* in s 22 – for example, 'realisation' and 'disposal' – would, on a natural interpretation, extend to D's dealings with things in action. This is uncontroversial. Whether things in action can be the subject of a charge of 'receiving' is less clear. If 'receiving' in s 22 is interpreted in the same way it was under pre-Theft Act law (where it referred to taking control of a physical thing), it would not be apt to apply to things in action. But there would seem to be no good reason for fettering the interpretation of s 22 in this way. If 'receiving' is given its ordinary meaning there is no reason why D cannot receive a thing in action. So, if D opens a bank account into which he pays stolen money and subsequently assigns the balance in that bank account to E, on a natural use of the language E 'receives' that balance.[14] The Court of Appeal took this broad view in *A-G's Reference (No 4 of 1979)*[15] concluding:

[I]t is clear that a balance in a bank account, being a debt, is itself a thing in action which falls within the definition of goods and may therefore be goods which directly or indirectly represent stolen goods for the purposes of s 24(2)(a).

In *Forsyth*,[16] the court had no doubt that there could be an offence of handling of a thing in action. It is submitted that this view is in accord with the interpretation of the Act and makes good sense.

Meaning of 'stolen'

By s 24(4):

For purposes of the provisions of this Act relating to goods which have been stolen (including subsections (1) to (3) above) goods obtained in England or Wales or elsewhere either by blackmail or [, subject to subsection (5) below by fraud (within the meaning of the Fraud Act 2006)][17] shall be regarded as stolen; and 'steal', 'theft' and 'thief' shall be construed accordingly.[18]

---

[13] Below, p 978.

[14] This forestalls any argument that because only some forms of the conduct (realization, disposal, etc) specified in s 22 (but not receiving) are applicable to things in action, they can never be handled.

[15] [1981] 1 All ER 1193 at 1198, [1981] Crim LR 51 and commentary. But see now *Preddy* [1996] AC 815 and discussion above, p 812. If part of the balance in the thief's account is transferred to the credit of the receiver's it cannot 'represent the goods originally stolen with s 24(2)(a)' because following *Preddy* a new thing in action is created which belongs to the receiver and has never been in the hands of a thief or handler and so is not stolen. Section 24A must be relied on in such cases.

[16] [1997] 2 Cr App R 299, [1997] Crim LR 581, below, p 983. The conviction was quashed on other grounds.

[17] Words substituted by the Fraud Act 2006, Sch 1, para 6, in force from 15 Jan 2007.

[18] By s 24(5): 'Subsection (1) above applies in relation to goods obtained by fraud as if – (a) the reference to the commencement of this Act were a reference to the commencement of the Fraud Act 2006, and (b) the reference to an offence under this Act were a reference to an offence under section 1 of that Act.'

By s 24A(8):

References to stolen goods include money which is withdrawn from an account to which a wrongful credit[19] has been made, but only to the extent that the money derives from the credit.

And by s 24(1):

The provisions of this Act relating to goods which have been stolen shall apply whether the stealing occurred in England or Wales or elsewhere, and whether it occurred before or after the commencement of this Act, provided that the stealing (if not an offence under this Act) amounted to an offence where and at the time when the goods were stolen; and references to stolen goods shall be construed accordingly.

The effect of these provisions is that goods are 'stolen' for the purposes of the Act if they:

    (i)   have been stolen contrary to s 1;[20]

    (ii) have been obtained by blackmail contrary to s 21;

    (iii) have been obtained by fraud contrary to s 1 of the Fraud Act 2006;

    (iv) consist of money dishonestly withdrawn from a wrongful bank credit; or

    (v) have been the subject of an act done in a foreign country which was:

        (a) a crime by the law of that country and which

        (b) had it been done in England, would have been theft, blackmail or fraud contrary to s 1 or s 21 of the Theft Act 1968 or s 1 of the Fraud Act 2006.[21] The jurisdictional scope of the offence is such that if T steals property in, for example, Greece by performing an act that is theft under Greek law[22] and theft if performed in England, and D, in England, handles that property with *mens rea*, D can be convicted of handling under s 22.[23]

If the information or indictment specifies that the goods were stolen from a specific entity (person or corporation), the prosecution is obliged to prove that issue, if the ownership by the entity is integral to the case.[24]

The 'thief' must be guilty

Though s 22 does not say so expressly, the goods must have been stolen in fact.[25] To take a simple recent example, magistrates had erred when they concluded that a credit card was stolen when it was found in D's house three weeks after its owner had realized it was missing. D could, as he had claimed, have found it in the street but forgotten to hand it in to the

---

[19] See s 24A (dishonestly retaining a wrongful credit), below, p 998.

[20] This will include goods obtained by offences of robbery and burglary which involve theft. See, eg, *Pitham and Hehl* (1976) 65 Cr App R 45.

[21] Handling is a Group A offence for the purposes of the Criminal Justice Act 1993. See, generally, M Hirst, *Jurisdiction and the Ambit of the Criminal Law* (2003) 180 et seq.

[22] This will have to be proved and cannot be presumed: *Ofori and Tackie (No 2)* (1994) 99 Cr App R 223; *Okolie* [2000] All ER (D) 661, The Times, 15 May. Note also the Administration of Justice Act 1920, s 15.

[23] The question whether D commits theft in England if he performs acts in, eg, Greece amounting to theft under Greek law and transports the goods to England, is considered above, p 794; *Atakpu* [1994] QB 69; and GR Sullivan and C Warbrick, 'Territoriality, Theft and *Atakpu*' [1994] Crim LR 650. D who commits theft abroad and returns to England with the criminal property may commit a money laundering offence contrary to s 329 of the Proceeds of Crime Act 2002.

[24] *Iqbal v DPP* (2004) All ER (D) 314 (Oct).

[25] *Haughton v Smith* [1975] AC 476, [1973] 3 All ER 1109 at 1112, 1119 and 1124.

police. There was insufficient evidence that the card had been stolen at the time it came into D's possession.[26]

It is not sufficient for the prosecution to prove that D believed the goods to be 'stolen' if they were not. If, because of a mistake of fact (or of civil law) D wrongly believed the goods to be stolen, he might be guilty of theft or, since the Criminal Attempts Act 1981, of an attempt to handle. If D says he knew the goods were stolen because T told him so, this is evidence of D's *mens rea* but it is not evidence that the goods were stolen in fact.[27] T's admission based on D's hearsay[28] is of no more value than the hearsay itself. It is a misdirection to tell the jury that they are entitled to take such an admission into account, except as evidence of *mens rea*.[29] In contrast, D's admission of facts that he himself perceived (by, for example, seeing T steal the goods) is evidence of those facts from which a jury could infer that the goods were stolen. Thus, in a more likely scenario, D's admission that he bought goods in a pub at a ridiculously low price is *prima facie* evidence that those goods were stolen; similarly, where a television set is bought in a betting shop or where a publican buys cases of whisky from a lorry driver.[30] The conduct of a person, T, who offers a bag of jewellery to a stranger, D, for £2,000 and then accepts £100 for it, suggests strongly, as a matter of common sense, that the jewellery is stolen.[31]

If the alleged thief, T, is not guilty, the handler, D, cannot be convicted for there are no stolen goods for him to handle. So, for example, if the alleged thief turns out to have been under the age of 10 at the time of the alleged theft, then the goods appropriated cannot be stolen goods and there can be no conviction for handling them.[32] If D believed the 'thief' was 10 or above, he might be convicted of an attempt to handle.[33] Whatever his belief as to the 'thief's' age, the more appropriate charge would be theft of the goods. In considering the liability of the handler and the question of whether there has been a theft, the courts have not drawn any distinctions between cases in which the alleged thief is acquitted on the basis of a justification – for example, necessity – or an excuse – for example, insanity.

If the appropriator of the goods is guilty of theft (or the fraudster, or blackmailer guilty of those offences), it is submitted that the goods acquired may be the subject of handling although the appropriator is immune from prosecution by reason, for example, of diplomatic immunity.[34] The thief could be prosecuted for the theft if diplomatic immunity were waived. The handler may be convicted whether that immunity is waived or not – unless, of course, he too is entitled to diplomatic immunity.

It must be proved, as against an alleged handler, that another person was guilty of stealing the goods. If the thief, T, and handler, D, are tried together, the verdict acquitting T is not necessarily inconsistent with one convicting D; evidence admissible against D may have been inadmissible against T. In separate trials, the fact that T has been acquitted of stealing the goods is no bar to the prosecution of the handler and is, indeed, inadmissible in evidence. But the fact that T has been convicted of stealing the goods is now admissible at D's trial for handling and, when it is admitted, T must be taken to have committed the theft unless the contrary

---

[26] *Defazio v DPP* [2007] All ER (D) 262 (Jul).

[27] *Porter* [1976] Crim LR 58; *Marshall* [1977] Crim LR 106; *Lang v Evans (Inspector of Police)* [1977] Crim LR 286; *Hack* [1978] Crim LR 359; *Overington* [1978] Crim LR 692, CA.

[28] An out of court assertion relied on for the truth of its content; see now the impenetrable Criminal Justice Act 2003, s 115. See *Singh* [2006] 2 Cr App R 12. Under the new hearsay regime, such conduct will only be inadmissible hearsay if (one of) E's purpose(s) was to cause D to believe that fact or to act upon the basis that the goods were stolen.

[29] *Hulbert* (1979) 69 Cr App R 243, CA.

[30] An example put by Lawton LJ in *McDonald* (1980) 70 Cr App R 288, CA. See also *Barnes* [1991] Crim LR 132.

[31] *Korniak* (1983) 76 Cr App R 145, CA.

[32] *Walters v Lunt* [1951] 2 All ER 645, thus remains good law.

[33] See *Toye* [1984] Crim LR 555.

[34] cf *Dickinson v Del Solar* [1930] 1 KB 376; *AB* [1941] 1 KB 454; *Madan* (1961) 45 Cr App R 80.

is proved.[35] Under this controversial evidential provision, if D claims that T did not steal the goods – that T was wrongly convicted – it is for D to prove it on a balance of probabilities.

27.1.1.2 When goods cease to be stolen

It is obvious that goods that have once been stolen cannot continue to be regarded as 'stolen' so long as they continue to exist thereafter. A line must be drawn somewhere, and the Act draws it in the same place as the common law did. By s 24(3) of the Act:

But no goods shall be regarded as having continued to be stolen goods after they have been restored to the person from whom they were stolen or to other lawful possession or custody, or after that person and any other person claiming through him have otherwise ceased as regards those goods to have any right to restitution in respect of the theft.

So if T steals goods, but the stolen goods are taken back by the owner or someone acting on his behalf, or by the police,[36] but then in a police sting operation returned to the thief so that he may hand them over to a receiver, D that person will not be guilty of handling because the goods he receives are no longer stolen goods.[37] A charge of attempted handling is available, and it may also be theft. D might also be convicted of handling if his acts of 'arranging' occurred after the theft but before the goods had been 'restored'.

Difficult questions arise over whether goods have in fact been 'restored to the person from whom they were stolen or to other lawful possession or custody'. It cannot be enough that V (the owner or his agent) knows that T has stolen the goods and follows T to his destination so that the handler can be caught red-handed;[38] nor that V marks the goods after the theft so that they can be identified in the hands of the handler.[39] A more difficult case in this context is *King*.[40] A parcel containing a stolen fur coat was handed by T, the thief, to a policeman who was in the act of examining the parcel when the telephone rang. The caller was D, the proposed receiver. The policeman stopped his examination, and D was told to come along as arranged, he did so and received the coat. It was held that D was guilty of receiving stolen goods because the coat had not been reduced into the possession of the police – though it was admitted that in a few minutes it would have been, had the telephone not rung. The case has, however, been criticized. It is easy to accept that if the police are examining a parcel to see whether it contains stolen goods, they do not take possession of the contents until they decide that this is what they are looking for.[41] In *King*, however, T had admitted to the policeman the theft of the coat and produced the parcel. One might have expected, therefore, that the policeman had made up his mind to take charge of it before the telephone rang. The court presumably made the decision on the assumption that the police officer had not done so. On that assumption the decision would now be the same under the Theft Act.[42]

This view is supported by the decision in *A-G's Reference (No 1 of 1974)*[43] that whether the police officer has taken possession depends primarily on his intentions. In that case an

---

[35] See s 74 of PACE 1984, *O'Connor* (1986) 85 Cr App R 298 at 302, and *Cross and Tapper on Evidence* (12th edn, 2010).

[36] *A-G's Reference (No 1 of 1974)* [1974] QB 744, [1974] 2 All ER 899, CA.

[37] cf *Dolan* (1855) Dears CC 436; *Schmidt* (1866) LR 1 CCR 15; *Villensky* [1892] 2 QB 597.

[38] In *Haughton v Smith* [1975] AC 476, [1973] 3 All ER 1109, the police accompanied the driver of a van containing stolen goods to its destination to trap the handler. Lords Hailsham and Dilhorne questioned whether the prosecution was right to concede that the goods had been 'restored' to lawful custody.

[39] *Greater London Metropolitan Police Comr v Streeter* (1980) 71 Cr App R 113, DC.

[40] [1938] 2 All ER 662, CCA.

[41] cf *Warner v Metropolitan Police Comr* [1969] 2 AC 256, [1968] 2 All ER 356, HL.

[42] In *A-G's Reference (No 1 of 1974)* [1974] 2 All ER 899 at 904, Lord Widgery CJ said that *King* 'might be thought to be a rather bold decision'.

[43] ibid.

officer, correctly suspecting that goods in the back of a car were stolen, immobilized the car by removing the rotor arm from the engine and kept watch until T returned to the car. He questioned T and in view of T's unsatisfactory response arrested him. It was held that the jury ought to have been directed to consider whether the officer had decided, before T's appearance, to take possession of the goods or whether he was of an entirely open mind, intending to decide after he had questioned T. Possession[44] requires both an intention to possess and some act of possession. To immobilize a car does not necessarily involve an intention to possess the car or its contents but, along with other circumstances, it may be evidence of such an intention. This approach is hardly conducive to certainty and consistency in the law in deciding whether goods cease to be stolen.

It is clear that the goods cease to be stolen in the case where the police take control acting without the authority of the owner, for they are clearly in 'other lawful possession or custody of the goods'. Indeed, it would seem to be enough that the goods fall into the possession of *any* person provided that person intends to restore them to the person from whom they were stolen.

Section 24(3) also provides that the goods lose their character of being 'stolen goods' if the person from whom they were stolen has ceased to have any *right to restitution* in respect of them. Whether a 'right to restitution' exists is a complex question of civil law. A person whose goods have been wrongfully converted (under the Torts (Interference with Goods) Act 1977) does not have a *right* to have those goods restored to him. He has a right to damages to compensate him for the conversion, but it is in the discretion of the court whether to order the goods to be delivered to him.[45] Section 24(3) is not intended to be limited to only those cases in which a court would exercise its discretion to order the goods to be returned to V. In the criminal proceedings, it would be impossible to identify such cases and it is submitted that the subsection is applicable to all cases in which V *could* succeed in a civil action based on his proprietary interest in the thing, whether in conversion or for the protection of an equitable interest.[46]

As drafted, the provision seems to have been intended to bear a still wider meaning. The CLRC explained it as follows:[47]

if the person who owned the goods when they were stolen no longer has any title to them, there will be no reason why the goods should continue to have the taint of being stolen goods. For example, the offence of handling stolen goods will…apply also to goods obtained by criminal deception under [s 15[48]]. If the owner of the goods who has been deceived chooses on discovering the deception to ratify his disposal of the goods he will cease to have any title to them.

It is clear that 'title' is here used in a broad sense to include a right to rescind. The Committee clearly had in mind a case where property passes from V to D at the moment when the goods are obtained by fraud.[49] In such a case, V, strictly, has no 'title' and his right to recover the goods (or much more likely, their value) will only arise on his rescinding the contract.[50] Such a potential right is, it is submitted, clearly a 'right to restitution' within the Act.

---

[44] For the purposes of s 24(3) possession *or control* suffices. Arguably in both the above cases the police officer had at least control of the goods but control, like possession, must involve an intention to take charge.

[45] Torts (Interference with Goods) Act 1977, s 3. See, generally, WVH Rogers, *Winfield and Jolowicz on Tort* (18th edn, 2010) para 17.28.

[46] In view of the recent expansion of the opportunities to claim for restitution or unjust enrichment, this might be enlarged, particularly in cases where there has been a transfer of property under a mistake. See Ch 19, above p 816.

[47] Eighth Report, para 139.

[48] Now repealed.

[49] As discussed above, Ch 23.

[50] cf above, Ch 19, above p 784.

27.1.1.3 Goods representing those originally stolen may be stolen goods

By s 24(2) of the Act:

For the purposes of those provisions references to stolen goods shall include, in addition to the goods originally stolen and parts of them (whether in their original state or not), –

(a) any other goods which directly or indirectly represent or have at any time represented the stolen goods in the hands of the thief as being the proceeds of any disposal or realisation of the whole or part of the goods stolen or of goods so representing the stolen goods; and

(b) any other goods which directly or indirectly represent or have at any time represented the stolen goods in the hands of a handler of the stolen goods or any part of them as being the proceeds of any disposal or realisation of the whole or part of the stolen goods handled by him or of goods so representing them.

The CLRC[51] accepted that this provision:

[M]ay seem technical; but the effect will be that the goods which the accused is charged with handling must, at the time of the handling or at some previous time, (i) have been in the hands of the thief or of a handler, and (ii) have represented the original stolen goods in the sense of being the proceeds, direct or indirect, of a sale or other realisation of the original goods.

The effect is best explained by example. Suppose D steals an Audi car from V and subsequently that car passes, by way of sale, exchange or otherwise, through the hands of E, F and G. The Audi remains stolen until such time as it ceases to be stolen by virtue of s 24(3) (that is, until the Audi is restored to the owner or other lawful custody or until the owner ceases to have a right to restitution in respect of it). It follows that until such time any person acquiring the Audi may be convicted of handling it, if he acquires it knowing or believing it to be stolen. It is not necessary for every person in the chain to have been a handler for the Audi to remain stolen. So, where the person acquiring the Audi, say G, acquires it from F, knowing or believing it to be stolen, G handles it even though F's acquisition of the car did not constitute handling by F because F acquired it innocently.

The position with regard to the *proceeds* of stolen goods rather than the goods themselves is different. Assume that D steals the Audi from V, D exchanges the stolen Audi with E for a BMW. The BMW is now notionally stolen for the purposes of the offence because it directly represents the proceeds of the stolen Audi *in the hands of the thief*, D. Assume that E was aware that the Audi was stolen and he exchanges it with F for a Citroën. The Citroën is now notionally stolen because it represents the proceeds of the stolen Audi *in the hands of the handler*, E. Assume, then, that D sells the BMW to H who buys in good faith for £5,000. The BMW now ceases to be stolen goods as V has no right to restitution and (unlike with actual stolen goods in the example of the Audi with G and F above) once *notionally* stolen goods cease to be stolen goods they cannot revert to being notionally stolen because they are subsequently acquired by someone who is aware of their provenance.

The £5,000 now in D's hands, however, *is* notionally stolen because it indirectly represents the proceeds of the stolen Audi *in the hands of the thief* and a recipient of all or part of that £5,000 would, if aware of its provenance, be guilty of handling. The position may be a little more complex where D banks the £5,000. If the £5,000 represents all that D has in the account, money which D draws from the account is stolen goods and a receiver of it, having the requisite knowledge, would be guilty of handling. Where, however, D has other innocently acquired money in his account, say a further £5,000, it may be difficult to prove that a cheque drawn for £2,000 that is cashed by E represents the proceeds of the stolen £5,000. It is not enough to

[51] Eighth Report, 66.

establish that the recipient believed that the cheque for £2,000 represented proceeds of the stolen £5,000 – that it represented his share of the ill-gotten £5,000.[52] This will establish the recipient's *mens rea*, which would be enough to convict him of an attempt, but, to establish the full offence it must additionally be proved that D intended the £2,000 to represent the proceeds of the stolen money.

In the difficult case of *Forsyth*,[53] T stole funds in a company's bank account and transferred them to a series of other banks in which he had accounts. It was held that 'in the hands of' means 'in the possession or control of' and therefore that the new credit balances remained under T's control. This renders the handling offence even wider. The balances were new property, distinct from that stolen,[54] but they 'represented' that stolen money and, 'being in the hands of' the thief, were accordingly stolen goods. More difficult to follow is the court's assumption that the actual banknotes withdrawn, on T's instructions, by D from one of the accounts were also stolen, so that D was guilty of handling them when she took physical possession of them. The notes belonged exclusively to the bank and had never been in the hands of a thief or handler until D received them and therefore could not have been stolen goods under s 24(2). If A pays stolen money into a bank account and, in payment of a debt he owes to B, gives B a cheque drawn on that account, B, if he cashes the cheque, does not receive stolen money. The actual cash in the form of pound coins in the hands of the bank is not stolen goods. B is not the thief, nor is he receiving stolen goods. He is not guilty of handling. Nor is it permissible to argue that B is a handler and therefore that the goods are stolen because they are in his hands. That is a circular argument.

In that example, however, B is acting on his own behalf. In *Forsyth* D was acting as an agent for T, the original thief. For the reason given above, D (it is submitted) was not *receiving* stolen goods. But, because D, unlike B in the example, was acting as agent for the thief, the cash, though physically in D's hands, was, in law, 'in the hands of' T – that is, it 'indirectly represented the stolen goods in the hands of the thief' (s 24(2)(a)) – and was therefore stolen goods. D was not a receiver of stolen goods – the cash became stolen only when she received it. She then had stolen goods in her hands. That is not an offence; but she then went on to assist in the retention, etc, of the stolen goods for the benefit of T; and that is the offence of handling.

27.1.1.4 Forms of handling

Section 22 of the 1968 Act creates a broad offence[55] capable of being committed in any one of several (as many as 18) ways. These are:

(1) *Receiving* the goods.

(2) *Undertaking* the retention, removal, disposal or realization of the goods by or for the benefit of another person.

(3) *Assisting* in the retention, removal, disposal or realization of the goods by or for the benefit of another person.

(4) *Arranging* to do (1), (2), (3).

Although in the leading case of *Bloxham*,[56] Lord Bridge said, 'It is, I think, well settled that this subsection creates two distinct offences but no more than two', this must be wrong. It is

---

[52] *A-G's Reference (No 4 of 1979)* [1981] 1 All ER 1193, [1981] 1 WLR 667, CA.

[53] [1997] 2 Cr App R 299, [1997] Crim LR 589 and additional commentary, at 755.

[54] *Preddy* [1996] AC 815.

[55] Under the old law in s 33(1) of the Larceny Act 1916, the only way of committing the offence was by 'receiving' the stolen goods.

[56] [1983] 1 AC 109, [1982] 1 All ER 582 on which see L Blake, 'The Erstwhile Innocent Purchaser of Stolen Goods' (1982) 46 J Crim L 220.

generally accepted that s 22 creates only one offence[57] which may be committed in a variety of ways. What was well settled before *Bloxham* (and remains so) was that, where the evidence justified it, the proper practice was to have one count for receiving (or perhaps arranging to receive) and a second count for all the other forms of handling.[58] In law, however, the subsection creates only one offence.[59]

If D is charged specifically with receiving only, he may not be convicted on that indictment of some other form of handling;[60] and vice versa. Since receiving is 'a single finite act' each receipt of stolen goods is a separate offence. Therefore, a single count for receiving a whole quantity of goods found in D's possession will be defective because it alleges more than one offence in the single charge (it is 'bad for duplicity') if the receipt of various portions of that whole took place on more than one occasion.[61] The forms of handling other than receiving include 'an activity which may be continuing'; so that it is legitimate to charge D in a single count with handling a quantity of goods, parts of which have been received on different occasions. The word 'retention', in particular, would be apt to apply where a large quantity of goods is found in D's possession and has been received by him in portions over a long period of time. In order to obtain a conviction under the single count it would, of course, be necessary to prove, not merely that D received the goods, but that he was retaining them for the benefit of another person, or that he was assisting another person in retaining them.

Receiving

All forms of handling other than receiving or arranging to receive are subject to the qualification that it must be proved that D was acting 'for the benefit of another person'. If, as will frequently be the case, there is no evidence of this then it must be proved that D received or arranged to receive the goods and evidence of no other form of handling will suffice.[62]

So, to establish receiving, it must be proved that either:

(1) D took possession or joined with others to share possession (whether actual or constructive), intending to possess the goods, or

(2) D took control of the stolen property or joined with others to share control of it with intent to do so.

'Receiving' the thief by welcoming him as a person who has the goods in his possession does not necessarily amount to receiving the goods. If the thief, T, retains exclusive control, there is no receiving by D.[63] There may, however, be a joint possession by the thief and receiver, so it is unnecessary to prove that the thief ever parted with possession – it is sufficient that he shared it with the alleged receiver.

The question is what joint possession means in these circumstances. In *Smith*,[64] it was held that a jury had been correctly directed that they could convict D of handling if they believed that the stolen watch was in the custody of the thief, that D was aware of that and that D had

---

[57] *Griffiths v Freeman* [1970] 1 All ER 1117.

[58] *Willis and Syme* [1972] 3 All ER 797, CA; *Deakin* [1972] 3 All ER 803, CA.

[59] Thus in *Nicklin* [1977] 2 All ER 444, CA, [1977] Crim LR 221 it was held that an indictment alleging unparticularized handling was not bad for duplicity as it charges only one offence. Particulars should be given so as to enable the accused to understand the ingredients of the charge he has to meet: *Sloggett* [1972] 1 QB 430, [1971] 3 All ER 264. The maximum number of counts for a single instance of handling in the ordinary case is two: *Ikpong* [1972] Crim LR 432, CA.

[60] *Nicklin*, above.

[61] *Smythe* (1980) 72 Cr App Rep 8, CA. cf *Skipp*, above, p 784 (overruled, but still relevant on this issue).

[62] The Theft Act does not further define receiving and it must be assumed that old authorities all remain valid.

[63] *Wiley* (1850) 2 Den 37.

[64] (1855) Dears CC 494. See also *Gleed* (1916) 12 Cr App R 32, CCA.

absolute control over the thief to the extent that if D demanded it, the thief would hand it to him. Lord Campbell CJ said that if the thief had been employed by D to commit theft, so that the watch was in D's control, D was guilty of receiving. This situation is slightly odd because usually handling occurs because a previous theft has been committed. In this situation how-ever there has been no *previous* theft, so D may become a handler by some act done only *after* the theft. It is of course important to identify the point at which D receives the stolen goods, since it is at that point that he must have the relevant *mens rea*.[65] D would be guilty of theft and receiving, but since virtually all handling is now theft, it is the general rule that the two offences are committed simultaneously.[66]

As is clear from *Smith*, it is not necessary to prove personal physical possession or control by D. It is enough if the goods are received by his agent with D's authority.[67] There are few other limits on what constitutes receiving: D's receipt may be for a merely temporary purpose such as concealment from the police;[68] and, it is unnecessary that the receiver should receive any profit or advantage from the possession of the goods.[69] However, it is not enough that D took possession by 'finding' goods that were stolen; there must be a receipt *from* another.[70] If D took possession of goods from the thief without his consent, this appears to be capable of being both theft and handling, since it is clear that the two offences can be committed by one and the same act.[71]

In all cases of receiving, it continues to be essential for the judge to give a careful direc-tion as to possession or control.[72] If the only evidence against D is that he ran away on being found by the police in a house where stolen property had been left, there would appear to be no case to leave to a jury. Likewise, where the evidence is consistent with the view that D went to premises where stolen goods were stored with the intention of assuming possession but had not actually done so,[73] or where the only evidence of receiving for example, a stolen car, is that D's fingerprint was found on the rear-view mirror.[74] The mere fact that the stolen goods were found on D's premises is not sufficient evidence to establish receiving. It must be shown that the goods had come either by invitation or arrangement with him or that he had exercised some control over them.[75] It has even been held that D is not necessarily in possession of a stolen safe simply because he assists others in trying to open it.[76]

Arranging to receive

Where it is impossible to prove an actual receipt by D, the evidence may nevertheless show that D has arranged to receive the goods. Where D has merely made preparations to receive and has not yet reached the stage of attempting to do so, the preparations may constitute a sufficient arrangement. The difficulties in a case like *King*[77] (the fur coat case discussed above) will be overcome if it appears that the arrangement to receive was concluded before there was a possibility of the goods ceasing to be stolen. Presumably it is enough if the proposed receipt

[65] *Brook* [1993] Crim LR 455.

[66] *Sainthouse* [1980] Crim LR 506.

[67] *Miller* (1854) 6 Cox CC 353.

[68] *Richardson* (1834) 6 C & P 335.

[69] *Davis* (1833) 6 C & P 177.

[70] *Haider* (1985) unreported, discussed in Griew, *Theft*, para 13.

[71] This was formerly only larceny (from the thief) and not receiving: *Wade* (1844) 1 Car & Kir 739.

[72] *Frost and Hale* (1964) 48 Cr App R 284, CCA.

[73] *Freedman* (1930) 22 Cr App R 133, CCA. But this might be sufficient evidence of an arrangement to receive.

[74] *Court* (1960) 44 Cr App R 242, CCA.

[75] *Cavendish* [1961] 2 All ER 856, CCA; *Lloyd* [1992] Crim LR 361.

[76] *Tomblin* [1964] Crim LR 780, CCA.

[77] Above, p 980. And similarly the difficulties of *Haughton v Smith* [1975] AC 476, [1973] 3 All ER 1109, HL, above, n 25.

is by an agent of D. The arrangement must be made after the theft, since D must know or believe the goods to be stolen when he makes the arrangement.[78]

It is difficult to envisage an arrangement that does not involve an agreement with another, although there is no such express requirement in the Act. Such an agreement will therefore almost always amount to a conspiracy to receive so the breadth of the crime created by this provision is less far-reaching than might appear. Clearly, an arrangement made by D with an innocent person is enough (provided D has the relevant *mens rea*), as is an arrangement that does not involve another party at all, if that can be envisaged.

The offence of handling is complete as soon as the proposed receipt is arranged. It is immaterial (except as to sentence) that D repents or does nothing in pursuance of the arrangement. In this respect it is clear that the substantive offence of arranging to receive has developed as a form of inchoate offence, rather than a form of secondary participation.

Undertaking and assisting

Handling under the Act extends to acts of 'undertaking and assisting' in the retention, removal, disposal or realization. These acts were formerly not criminal at all, not even by way of an attempt. Section 22 creates far-reaching and overlapping forms of the offence. 'Undertaking' presumably covers the case where D sets out to retain, etc the stolen goods, on his own initiative. It appears more apt to describe the activity of the seller of stolen goods rather than that of the buyer. 'Assisting' seems more apt to cover the case where D joins the thief or another handler in doing so.[79]

Retention

In *Pitchley*,[80] the court suggested that retention means 'keep possession of, not lose, continue to have'. It is a continuing activity. The obvious cases of retaining will be where D stores stolen goods for the thief. An example of assisting in retention would be where D's 15-year-old son, T, brings home a bicycle which he has stolen: D assists in its retention if (i) he agrees that T may keep the bicycle in the house, or (ii) he tells the police there is no bicycle in the house, or (iii) he gives T a tin of paint so that he may disguise it.

Merely to *use* goods knowing them to be stolen does not in itself amount to assisting in their retention. D did not commit the offence by using a stolen heater and battery charger in his father's garage,[81] nor by erecting stolen scaffolding in the course of a building operation.[82] Nothing was done with the purpose, or with the effect, of assisting in retention. It must be proved that D assisted in retention by concealing the goods or making them more difficult to identify or some other such conduct. It has been held that it is sufficient that D's passive conduct may constitute such assistance.[83] But, according to *Kanwar*,[84] 'something must be done by the offender, and done intentionally and dishonestly, for the purpose of enabling the goods to be retained'. However, it was held to be sufficient in that case that D told lies to protect her husband who had dishonestly brought the stolen goods into the house. She knew that, if the deception succeeded, the effect would be that her husband would be enabled to retain the goods.

---

[78] *Park* (1987) 87 Cr App R 164, CA.
[79] But cf *Deakin* [1972] 3 All ER 803, CA.
[80] (1972) 57 Cr App R 30, CA.
[81] *Sanders* (1982) 75 Cr App R 84.
[82] *Thornhill* (unreported; discussed in *Sanders* (1982) 75 Cr App R 84).
[83] *Burroughes* (2000) 29 Nov, unreported, CA.
[84] [1982] 2 All ER 528, 75 Cr App R 87.

Disposal

This would most obviously cover cases of D destroying the stolen goods, or by using stolen money to pay for goods or services.[85] It extends beyond that to cases where D negotiates with E to sell him goods which D knows to have been stolen by T, although D is never in possession or control of the goods,[86] he would appear to have undertaken or assisted in the disposal of stolen goods.

A person does not 'assist' in the disposal of stolen property merely by accepting any benefit deriving from that disposition. There must be proof that D gave help or encouragement; an omission to act will not generally ground liability. In *Coleman*,[87] D knew that his wife was using stolen money to pay solicitors' fees relating to the purchase of a flat in the couple's joint names. That did not in itself amount to assisting though it was evidence from which a jury might infer that he had assisted by telling his wife to use the stolen money or agreeing that she should do so.

Removal

This would occur where, for example, D assists T to lift from a van a barrel of gin which he knows to have been stolen by T or another. Even if D never has possession or control[88] he has assisted or undertaken the removal of the stolen goods. D who lights the way for T to carry stolen goods from a house to a barn, so that he may negotiate for the purchase of them[89] has assisted in the removal of the goods and even if that were the full extent of his intended dealing with the goods he would still be liable to conviction (though his sentence might be lighter).

Realization

According to the House of Lords in *Bloxham*, this means 'exchanging goods for money or other property'. This form of the offence overlaps with disposal.

Assistance

The undertaking or assisting must relate to the retention, etc of the goods. The assistance can be by words or conduct. It was said in *Kanwar* that, '[t]he requisite assistance need not be successful in its object'. But is it true to say that one who attempts to assist and fails nevertheless 'assists'? This seems to involve reading the section as if it read, 'does an act with the purpose of assisting'. The would-be assister who fails to assist in any way would surely be more properly convicted of an attempt.

In all cases of undertaking it is necessary for the prosecution to prove that D was acting by or for the benefit of another, and in cases of 'assisting in' D must be assisting another.

Arranging to undertake or assist

The extension of the law to undertaking and assisting is far-reaching, but the Act goes further still. The mere arrangement to do any of the acts amounting to undertaking or assisting amounts to the complete offence of handling. The goods must, of course, be stolen by the time of such an arrangement. It is, presumably, enough that D agreed to negotiate the sale of the stolen goods, for example, to lift down the barrel of stolen gin or to do any act for the purpose of enabling T to retain, remove or dispose of the stolen goods.

---

[85] cf Williams, TBCL, 867, interpreting disposal as being limited to alienation.
[86] cf *Watson* [1916] 2 KB 385.
[87] [1986] Crim LR 56, CA.
[88] *Gleed* (1916) 12 Cr App R 32, CCA; *Hobson v Impett* (1957) 41 Cr App R 138, CCA.
[89] *Wiley* (1850) 2 Den 37.

27.1.1.5 Handling by omission

'Receiving', 'undertaking' and 'arranging' all suggest that some positive conduct is required, though as little as a nod or a wink might suffice in particular circumstances. 'Assisting', however, may be constituted by inactivity provided it is in circumstances where that inactivity does in fact provide assistance.[90] Take a simple case. D, a wife, could hardly be constituted a handler because T, her husband, each dawn returns to *his* house with the fruits of the night's burglaries. As has been shown above, D would not become a handler even if she used the goods, provided such use did not involve assistance in their retention, etc.

Knowledge of the whereabouts of stolen goods cannot suffice to make D a handler; nor does D become a handler simply by refusing to answer police questions as to the whereabouts of the goods[91] since there is no obligation to help the police with their enquiries.[92] So, in *Brown*,[93] where T secreted stolen goods in D's flat and told D he had done so, it was a misdirection to tell the jury that assisting in the retention of the goods could be inferred from D's refusal to reveal the presence of the stolen goods when questioned about them by the police. The conviction in *Brown* was, however, upheld by applying the proviso then available to the Court of Appeal. D had tacitly, if not expressly, permitted T to hide the goods on his premises and had thereby assisted in their retention. This is not to say that knowledge of the presence of stolen goods on his premises always renders the occupier a handler. Obviously, D does not assist in the retention of stolen goods where D knows that T is wearing a stolen coat and invites T into his premises, even if D puts it in the cloakroom for the duration of T's stay. But if D's premises are used, as they were used in *Brown*, to house the goods and D allows them to remain there he can properly be said to be assisting in their retention just as plainly as if he had initially given permission. What is important here is that D has control of premises and has chosen to allow their use for the storage of stolen goods.[94]

Pitchley[95] is similar. T, D's son, gave D stolen money telling him that he had won it on the horses and D paid it into his bank account. Two days later D became aware that the money was stolen but he did nothing about it until questioned by the police four days later. D's conviction for handling by assisting in the retention of the stolen money[96] was upheld because he had continued to retain possession after he became aware that the money was stolen. D had assumed control of the money and had, with guilty knowledge, retained control for the benefit of T. But the stolen money had in fact ceased to exist and it appears that the thing in action which replaced it was not 'stolen' because D was neither a thief nor a handler at the time

---

[90] See above, n 83.

[91] Though D may become a handler (assist in the retention of the goods) if lies are told to put the police off the scent: *Kanwar* [1982] 2 All ER 528, [1982] 1 WLR 845, above, n 84.

[92] See above, p 665. Although cf *Sekfali v DPP* [2006] EWHC 894 (Admin).

[93] [1970] 1 QB 105, [1969] 3 All ER 198, CA.

[94] cf the case of *Kousar* [2009] EWCA Crim 139 decided under the Trade Marks Act 1994 in which K's conviction for unauthorized use of a trademark was quashed. K's home was searched after her husband's market stall was found to be selling counterfeit goods. Counterfeit goods were in the loft and in a van parked outside. The van was not the family transport and K did not use it. K was prosecuted on the basis that she was in *possession, control or custody* of the goods as a principal offender, not as an aider and abettor of her husband. The Court of Appeal held that in terms of possession, proof of K's knowledge or acquiescence of the presence of the goods was not enough. There was no evidence that K was in possession of the goods in the loft, and *a fortiori*, she did not have possession of the goods in the van outside. As far as control was concerned, *actual* control of the goods was needed. It was not enough that she had the ability to control the storage of the goods.

[95] (1972) 57 Cr App R 30, CA. cf *Tamm* [1973] Crim LR 115.

[96] The decision overlooks the fact that when D acquired his knowledge there was no longer any 'stolen' money to handle (see Ormerod and Williams, *Smith's Law of Theft*, para 13.70, n 3) but this does not affect the point at issue.

of the 'realisation'.[97] It is thus very doubtful whether Pitchley was rightly convicted. A better charge would have been theft. The thing in action, being the proceeds of the stolen money, probably continued to belong to V; and D, by keeping it as owner, appropriated it: s 3(2).

27.1.1.6 Otherwise than in the course of the stealing[98]

The offence is committed only if the conduct that amounts to handling occurs otherwise than in the course of the original stealing, that is, causing the goods to be stolen goods in the first place before the alleged handling arose. (Almost every handling is also a second theft – the handler dishonestly appropriates property belonging to another with the intention permanently to deprive the other of it – but that is not significant for this issue.)

If D was a party to the original theft, his participation in that theft cannot also render him liable for the offence of handling stolen goods. This limitation is necessary to keep handling within proper bounds. Without it, virtually every instance of theft by two or more persons would also be handling by one or the other or, more likely, both of them. This restriction assists in separating these two distinct forms of conduct that carry vastly different sentences and particular labels to which different stigmas attach.

The courts have emphasized that charging and jury directions should be kept simple where these issues arise.[99] It is often a sensible course for alternative counts of theft and handling to be left to the jury.

The duration of stealing

Identifying when the stealing stops and the handling begins is important. The duration of 'the course of the stealing' depends on the extent to which appropriation is a continuing act.[100] The issue has become even more complex following *Gomez*, and the extension of the concept of appropriation, rendering what were previously mere preparatory acts to completed thefts. As noted, one case involving handling, *Pitham and Hehl*,[101] suggested that appropriation is an instantaneous act, concluded at the moment the goods are stolen. If this were right, the words 'in the course of the stealing' would be rendered nugatory. It is submitted that, in the light of *Hale*[102] and *Atakpu*,[103] cases concerned with robbery and theft respectively, *Pitham* must be wrongly decided in this respect.

Atakpu adopts the transaction test – was D still 'on the job'? Although providing a pragmatic guideline, this does not, of course, solve all the problems. A thief is likely to be held to be on the job while he is in a building that he has entered for the purpose of stealing and from which he intends to remove the stolen goods. But is he still in the course of theft as he walks down the garden path with the goods? as he drives home? and as he shows them to his wife at home? Griew[104] suggests that the scope of theft is determined by looking at the 'the total process of the effective appropriation, including the getaway,' but it is doubtful that this is any improvement on the test of the thief being 'on the job'.

It does not necessarily follow that the theft is still in the course of being committed because the stolen property has not yet been removed from the premises on which it was

---

[97] See Griew, *Theft*, paras 15–23, n 62; Williams, TBCL, 873: above.

[98] See, generally, ATH Smith, 'Theft and/or Handling' [1977] Crim LR 517, and *Property Offences*, paras 30.71–30.82.

[99] See *Bosson* [1999] Crim LR 596.

[100] Above, p 794. See also G Williams, 'Appropriation: A Single or Continuous Act?' [1978] Crim LR 69.

[101] (1976) 65 Cr App R 45, above, p 793.

[102] (1978) 68 Cr App R 415, above, p 847. The offence of robbery under s 8 requires theft 'at the time of' whereas s 22 focuses on 'the course of'.

[103] [1994] QB 69, above, p 794.

[104] Paras 15–46.

stolen. If D and T agree to steal from their employer V and in pursuance of the plan D steals goods which he places in T's locker so that T may remove them from the premises, T is a thief and not a handler even though some time elapses between D's appropriation of the goods and T's removal of them. It is one enterprise for the theft of V's goods. If, however, D steals V's goods and secretes them on the premises, a *subsequent* arrangement with T for T to remove them from the premises constitutes T being a handler.[105] T is not a party to the original theft.

Proof of handling or theft

It has been held that in an ordinary case, the words, 'otherwise than in the course of the stealing', have little importance and the jury should not even be told about them. But where the evidence is such that a reasonable jury might think it reasonably possible that the alleged handler was a participant in the theft, they should surely be told that, if this was so, the law says that he is not guilty of handling.

There have been some odd applications of this principle in various cases. In *Cash*,[106] it was held that the words 'otherwise than in the course of stealing' do not constitute an element in the offence that has to be proved in order to establish a *prima facie* case of handling. In *Cash*, stolen goods were found in D's possession on 25 February. The property was stolen (by a burglar) not later than 16 February. It was held that it was not open to the jury to infer that D was the burglar rather than a receiver. Perhaps the evidence was insufficient to satisfy the jury beyond reasonable doubt that D was the burglar but might they not, given the opportunity, have thought that it was reasonably possible, if not probable, that he *was* the burglar? Is it unheard of for burglars to retain possession of the stolen property for nine days? In *Greaves*,[107] it was held that the judge had properly left it open to the jury to convict of burglary where the time lapse was 17 days. More recently in *Wells*,[108] *Cash* was described as a decision which makes 'entirely good sense'[109] and held to apply in any case in which there is no evidence to be left to the jury suggesting that D was a burglar/thief.

There are at least four possible incriminating explanations for D's recent possession in these types of case: (i) that he is the thief, (ii) that he took part in the theft and received the goods in the course of it, (iii) that he was implicated in the theft and only received his proceeds later, (iv) that he was not involved in the theft and received the stolen goods at a later date.[110] If all that can be proved by the prosecution beyond a reasonable doubt, is that D was in possession with a dishonest state of mind, how can handling be satisfactorily established?

---

[105] cf *Atwell and O'Donnell* (1801) East, 2 PC, 768. D1 and D2 bent on stealing some of their employer's property moved it nearer the warehouse door during the course of the morning. Later that day E1 and E2 arranged to buy the goods from them and all returned later that evening to take away the goods from the warehouse. It was held that E1 and E2 were thieves and not receivers; the theft was a continuing transaction as to those (E1 and E2) who joined the plot before the goods were finally removed from the warehouse. Assuming this case was correctly decided under the former law of larceny, it is arguable that if these facts were to recur that E1 and E2 are handlers and not thieves. The theft (the appropriation) may have been complete before E1 and E2 became aware of it.

[106] [1985] QB 801, [1985] Crim LR 311 and commentary.

[107] (1987) The Times, 11 July. *Cash* was also distinguished in *Bruce* [1988] VR 579. Failure to add alternative theft counts can be fatal to the indictment *Suter* [1997] CLY 1339 (Judge Bull Guildford CC).

[108] [2004] EWCA Crim 79.

[109] Para 1. On inferences from possession, see recently *M v DPP* [2009] EWHC 525 (Admin) (inference) from M's claim to have bought a mobile phone from X very cheaply without packaging or charger, but with a SIM card). On the difficulty of proving continuity of the evidence – ie that the goods allegedly stolen are those allegedly handled etc see *Lamb v DPP* [2009] EWHC 238 (Admin).

[110] See M Hirst, 'Guilty but of What' (2000) 4 E & P 31.

27.1.1.7 For the benefit of another person

Each of the nouns, 'retention', 'removal', 'disposal' and 'realization' is governed by the words 'by or for the benefit of another person'.[111] It must therefore be proved that:

(1) D undertook or arranged the retention, removal, disposal or realization *for the benefit of another person*; or

(2) D assisted or arranged the retention, removal, disposal or realization *by another person*.[112]

There can hardly ever have been a thief who did not retain, remove, dispose of or realize the stolen goods, so this requirement of conduct being 'for the benefit of another' prevents all thieves from also being handlers. The italicized words are an essential part of the offence and the indictment must allege that the handling was 'by or for the benefit of another person'.[113] The thief may himself be guilty of handling (by undertaking) if he himself retains, removes, etc the goods for the benefit of another person. It would seem to be immaterial that the other person is guilty of no offence and even unaware of what is going on.

However, an important limitation was imposed in *Bloxham*[114] where it was held that a purchaser, as such, of stolen goods is not 'another person' within the meaning of the section. Thus, where D sells stolen goods to E, D's act is not for the benefit of the buyer, E, it is for D's own benefit. Sellers usually sell for their own benefit, not the benefit of the purchaser; that much is uncontroversial. However, in the opinion of Lord Bridge even if the sale could be described as for the purchaser's benefit, it would not be within the ambit of the section. This gives a special, though obscure meaning to the term 'another person'. Griew lucidly summarizes the interpretation – something will be for the benefit of another when it is 'an act done on behalf of another person; it is an act that the other might do himself'.[115]

In *Bloxham*, D, acting in good faith, purchased a stolen car for £1,300. Eleven months later, suspecting the truth, he sold it for £200 to a person unknown who was prepared to buy it without documentation. D was charged with handling by undertaking or assisting in the realization of the car for the benefit of the buyer. A submission of no case to answer was rejected, whereupon he pleaded guilty. His conviction was upheld by the Court of Appeal who thought that the buyer's use of the car, for which he had paid less than its true value, was a benefit to him. Maybe it was; but it seems a travesty to say that the sale was for his benefit. The House of Lords quashed the conviction. The buyer was not 'another person'. In fact, of course, he was 'another person'; but the sale was certainly not effected 'on his behalf'.

Bloxham was distinguished in *Tokeley-Parry*[116] where D was charged with undertaking or assisting in removal by E, whom he had procured to smuggle stolen antiquities from Egypt. An argument that D and E were one person was firmly rejected. E was 'another person' in fact and in law. Further, *Roberts*[117] decides that, if A and B are jointly charged in one count with an act of handling 'by or for the benefit of another,' the other must be some person other than A or B.

---

[111] *Sloggett* [1971] 3 All ER 264 at 267.

[112] cf L Blake, 'The Innocent Purchaser and Section 22 of the Theft Act' [1972] Crim LR 494, arguing that there is no need that the third party benefits if he retains, removes, realizes or disposes.

[113] *Sloggett* [1972] 1 QB 430, [1971] 3 All ER 264.

[114] Above, n 56.

[115] Paras 15–22. See also Spencer's suggestion '... the requirement that the act be "for the benefit of another" serves no intelligible purpose unless it limits the offence to those who act on another's behalf': 'The Mishandling of Handling' [1981] Crim LR 682 at 685, commenting on the Court of Appeal decision in *Bloxham*.

[116] [1999] Crim LR 578. It is questionable how this was for the benefit of anyone other than D.

[117] No 93/0075/Z2 (9 July 1993, unreported), see [1996] Crim LR 495 and see *Gingell* [2000] 1 Cr App R 88.

This seems logical if, indeed, only one act, jointly done by A and B, is alleged.[118] A might, however, arrange the disposition of the goods *by* B; and B might undertake the disposition *for the benefit of* A. In that case both have committed an offence under s 22 and there is no need to show that any third person was involved.

Conspiracy to handle

As s 22 creates only one offence (according to Lord Bridge in *Bloxham*) an indictment for conspiracy to handle contrary to s 22, without particularizing the form of handling, is acceptable: it is not an allegation of conspiracy to commit crime X *or* crime Y.

Notwithstanding *Roberts*, an agreement by A and B that B would, for example, dispose of the goods for the benefit of A is a conspiracy to handle. A and B have agreed that B will commit the offence of handling, and that is enough. If B does dispose of the goods as agreed, he commits the offence under s 22; and, obviously A has counselled or procured him to do so. They are both guilty of the same offence. There seems to be every reason, *pace* the court in *Roberts*, why A and B should be jointly charged with committing it.[119]

27.1.1.8 Innocent receipt and subsequent retention with *mens rea*

If D receives the stolen goods innocently, (ie either believing them not to be stolen or knowing them to be stolen but intending to return them to the true owner) he commits no offence.[120] Suppose he subsequently discovers the goods to be stolen or decides not to return them to the true owner or disposes of them. He has dishonestly undertaken the retention of, or has disposed of stolen goods knowing them to be stolen. Whether he is guilty of an offence depends on a number of factors.

(1) Where D does not get ownership of the goods (the normal situation where goods are the product of theft):

    (i) D gives value for the goods.

        (a) D retains or disposes of the goods for his own benefit. This is not theft because of s 3(2);[121] nor is it handling by undertaking, assisting or arranging since it is not for the benefit of another.[122] D might be guilty of handling by aiding and abetting the receiving by the person to whom he disposes of the goods, if that person has *mens rea*.

        (b) D retains or disposes of the goods for the benefit of another. This is not theft (s 3(2)) but is handling.

    (ii) D does not give value.

        (a) D retains or disposes of the goods for his own benefit. This is theft but not handling unless it amounts to aiding and abetting receipt by another.

        (b) D retains or disposes of the goods for the benefit of another. This is theft and handling.

(2) Where D gets ownership of the goods:

    (i) D gives value for the goods.

---

[118] Why this should only apply if they are jointly charged is less logical, see R Harrison, 'Handling Stolen Goods for the Benefit of Another' (2000) 64 J Crim L 156.

[119] See *Slater and Suddens* [1996] Crim LR 300.

[120] *Alt* [1972] Crim LR 552, CA.

[121] Above, p 795.

[122] *Bloxham* [1983] 1 AC 109, [1982] 1 All ER 582, HL.

Retention or disposal of the goods cannot be theft since V has no property in the goods. It is not handling since V has lost his right to restitution,[123] his right to rescind being destroyed on the goods coming into the hands of D who was a *bona fide* purchaser for value.

(ii) D does not give value.

Again this cannot be theft, since V has no property in the goods, but it may be handling since V's right to rescind and secure restitution of his property is not extinguished by the goods coming into the hands of one who does not give value. It will be handling if this is so *and* D either aids and abets a guilty receipt by another or disposes of the goods for the benefit of another.

27.1.1.9 Handling by the thief[124]

Any thief may be convicted of handling goods stolen by him by receiving them – if the evidence warrants this conclusion.[125] In the majority of cases the thief can only be guilty of handling by receiving where he is assisting or encouraging the receipt by another because he is already in possession or control and therefore cannot receive as the principal offender. In some circumstances, however, a thief might be convicted of handling the stolen goods by receiving them as the principal offender. For example, D steals goods and, in the course of the theft, delivers them to E. Two days later E returns the goods to D.

27.1.2 *Mens rea*

D's *mens rea* as described below must coincide in time with the conduct constituting the *actus reus*. In the case of receiving, this is when D first receives the goods or makes the arrangement to receive.[126] In the case of other forms of handling, which may be continuing in nature, it is sufficient that the *mens rea* exists at some point in that continuum, for example, where D has taken possession innocently, but has subsequently become aware of the provenance of the goods and then acts for the benefit of another.[127]

27.1.2.1 Knowledge or belief[128]

It must be proved that the goods were stolen and that D handled them 'knowing or believing them to be stolen goods'. It is vital that the belief or knowledge is D's, not merely that of the reasonable person, since this is a subjective *mens rea* requirement.[129]

The Criminal Law Revision Committee apparently intended to include the concept of 'wilful blindness', which is often held by the courts to be included in the word 'knowing':[130]

It is a serious defect of the [pre-1968] law that actual knowledge that the property was stolen must be proved. Often the prosecution cannot prove this. In many cases indeed guilty knowledge does not exist, although the circumstances of the transaction are such that the receiver ought to be guilty of an offence. The man who buys goods at a ridiculously low price from an unknown seller whom he meets

---

[123] Above, p 980.

[124] ATH Smith [1977] Crim LR 517.

[125] *Dolan* (1975) 62 Cr App R 36, CA; *Stapylton v O'Callaghan* [1973] 2 All ER 782, DC.

[126] *Alt* (1972) 56 Cr App R 45.

[127] See V Tunkel (1983) 133 NLJ 844.

[128] See in particular E Griew, 'Consistency, Communication and Codification – Reflections on Two *Mens Rea* Words', in *Reshaping the Criminal Law*, 57; S Shute, 'Knowledge and Belief in the Criminal Law', in S Shute and A Simester (eds), *Criminal Law Theory: Doctrines of the General Part* (2002) 171; GR Sullivan, 'Knowledge, Belief and Culpability', ibid, 207; AR White, *Misleading Cases* (1991) 133; Tadros, *Criminal Responsibility*, Ch 9.

[129] *Bellenie* [1980] Crim LR 43; *Brook* [1993] Crim LR 455.

[130] Above, p 130.

in a public house may not *know* that the goods were stolen, and he may take the precaution of asking no questions. Yet it may be clear on the evidence that he believes that the goods were stolen. In such cases the prosecution may fail (rightly, as the law now stands) for want of proof of guilty knowledge.[131]

If this was the Committee's intention, it has not been achieved. Wilful blindness postulates that D has a strong suspicion that something is so (in this case goods are stolen) and consciously decides not to take steps that he could take to confirm or deny that fact. But the courts have repeatedly said that, for the purposes of s 22, suspicion, however strong, is not to be equated with belief that the goods are stolen.[132] It is a misdirection to tell the jury that it is enough that D, 'suspecting that the goods were stolen deliberately shut his eyes to the consequences'.[133]

Proof of either knowledge or belief will suffice. What, if anything, does 'believing' add to 'knowing'? According to *Hall*:[134]

A man may be said to know that goods are stolen when he is told by someone with first-hand knowledge (someone such as the thief or the burglar) that such is the case. Belief, of course, is something short of knowledge. It may be said to be the state of mind of a person who says to himself: 'I cannot say I know for certain that these goods are stolen but there can be no other reasonable conclusion in the light of all the circumstances, in the light of all that I have heard and seen.'

This seems to be merely a distinction between two *sources* of D's state of mind. But s 22 suggests a distinction between two states of mind that might be held, not two modes of arriving at the same state of mind. The case suggests that if D had direct evidence, he knows; if he has mere circumstantial evidence, he believes; but, it would surely be more accurate to describe knowledge in terms of the accuracy of the belief, not the directness of the evidence leading to the belief? As Shute has recently suggested, the distinctions between the concepts are twofold: knowledge constitutes a true belief, and belief includes acceptance of the proposition in question whereas knowledge does not.[135] In *Forsyth*,[136] the court said that the judgment in *Hall* is 'potentially confusing'.[137] In *Moys*,[138] the court suggested simply that the question whether D knew or believed that the goods were stolen is a subjective one and that suspicion, even coupled with the fact that D shut his eyes to the circumstances, is not enough.

In practical terms, D may be left in varying degrees of certainty as to the provenance of the goods whether or not he has been told by the thief, or deduced the fact from his own observation. What matters is that D is caused to be certain that the goods are stolen, there is no significance for these purposes in the source of information. Although what seems to be implied in *Hall* is that the person with direct information is certain and the person with circumstantial evidence is nearly certain, it would be dangerous in such terms to direct a jury because 'near certainty' is strong suspicion and that is not enough. It is unclear whether it is sufficient that D

---

[131] Eighth Report, 64. cf *Woods* [1969] 1 QB 447, [1968] 3 All ER 709, CA. See also G Williams, 'Handling, Theft and the Purchaser Who Takes a Chance' [1985] Crim LR 432.

[132] *Forsyth* [1997] Crim LR 581, CA; *Grainge* [1974] 1 All ER 928, CA; *Saik* [2006] UKHL 18. cf *Woods* [1969] 1 QB 447, [1968] 3 All ER 709, CCA; *Ismail* [1977] Crim LR 557 and commentary. cf Griew, *Theft*, paras 15.30–15.33; Spencer [1985] Crim LR 101. See S Shute, 'Knowledge and Belief in the Criminal Law', in S Shute and A Simester (eds), *Criminal Law Theory: Doctrines of the General Part* (2002).

[133] *Griffiths* (1974) 60 Cr App R 14, CA. *Atwal v Massey* [1971] 3 All ER 881, DC, is definitely misleading on this point and seems to have misled the judge in *Pethick* [1980] Crim LR 242, where it was said that suspicion, 'however strong', does not amount to knowledge.

[134] (1985) 81 Cr App R 260 at 264, [1985] Crim LR 377.

[135] At n 132.

[136] Above, n 132. A *Hall* direction is not necessary in every case – *Toor* (1987) 85 Cr App R 116.

[137] It is the second part of *Hall* that present a problem: *Adinga* [2003] EWCA Crim 3201.

[138] (1984) 79 Cr App R 72, CA.

considers the likelihood that the goods are stolen to be 'virtually certain'; presumably not. It is clearly not enough for D to believe that the goods are 'probably' stolen.[139]

In general, it seems that a judge cannot go wrong by simply directing the jury in accordance with the words of the section and offering no elaboration or explanation of 'believing'.[140] Of course, it may be that the jury will then apply the word as if it included wilful blindness, but no one will ever know. This is another example of the judicial interpretation of definitional elements of crimes, which is unsatisfactory, but which remains uncorrected because the cloak of jury secrecy avoids the true shortcomings of the interpretation being exposed.

Some have called for a further extension of the offence to include reckless handling.[141] There are of course competing policy arguments: on the one hand there is the need to avoid stifling trade of honest dealers and on the other the recognition that in most cases dishonest defendants could escape liability by not confirming mere suspicions. If there were a high incidence of low value handling by individuals (dealing through ebay and car boot sales, etc) such arguments might have greater force. The argument would become greater still if different offences distinguished professional fences from individuals trading in low value items.

Knowledge or belief of what?

It is sufficient that D knows or believes that the goods, whatever they are, are stolen. His knowledge or belief need not extend to the identity of the thief, or the owner,[142] or the nature of the stolen goods.[143] If D knows he is in possession of a box containing stolen goods, it is no defence that he does not know what the contents are and is shocked to discover that the box contains guns; nor would it be a defence that he believed the box contained stolen watches. Equally, it is enough for D to know or believe that the goods are stolen in the extended meaning that term has under s 24. So, it does not matter that D believed the goods to be the product of blackmail when they were in fact the product of a theft. In line with general principle, it is not necessary for D to know the criminal law: it is sufficient that D has knowledge or belief as to the facts and circumstances that render it criminal.

27.1.2.2 Dishonesty

'Dishonestly'[144] shares the same meaning as elsewhere in the Theft Acts. D may receive goods knowing or believing them to be stolen and yet not be guilty if, for example, he intends to return them to the true owner or turn them in to the police.[145] A claim of right will negate dishonesty, but it will be difficult to establish such a claim where D knows or believes the goods to be stolen, except where he intends to return the goods to the owner.

27.1.2.3 Proof of mens rea

The general principles of evidence in criminal cases apply to the proof of offences of theft and handling as they apply to other crimes. This is not the place to examine those rules in full, but their application to these offences has created special problems and some brief examination is necessary.

---

[139] *Reader* (1977) 66 Cr App R 33 at 36, CA. For consideration of whether this ought to be a sufficient *mens rea*, see J Spencer, 'Handling, Theft and the Mala Fide Purchaser' [1985] Crim LR 92 at 95–96; Williams [1985] Crim LR 432 at 435; J Spencer, 'Handling and Taking Risks: A Reply to Professor Williams' [1985] Crim LR 440.

[140] *Reader* (1977) 66 Cr App R 33; *Harris* (1986) 84 Cr App R 75; *Toor* (1986) 85 Cr App R 116, [1987] Crim LR 122, CA.

[141] See J Spencer [1985] Crim LR 92.

[142] *Fuschillo* [1940] 2 All ER 489; but it may be necessary to name the owner where the property is of a common and indistinctive type: *Gregory* [1972] 2 All ER 861. See recently *Webster* [2002] EWCA Crim 1346.

[143] *McCullum* (1973) 57 Cr App R 645.

[144] cf *Ghosh* [1982] QB 1053, [1982] 2 All ER 689, CA; above, p 829.

[145] cf *Matthews* [1950] 1 All ER 137, CCA.

The 'doctrine' of recent possession

Where D is found in possession of, or dealing with, property which has recently been stolen, a jury may properly infer that he is guilty of an offence if he offers no explanation or if they are satisfied beyond reasonable doubt that any explanation he has offered is untrue. They are not bound so to infer and must not do so unless they are sure that D was in fact guilty of the particular offence. The onus of proof remains on the Crown throughout. Whether D offers an explanation or not, the jury must not convict unless they are sure that he committed the offence in question.[146]

These principles are frequently misleadingly referred to as 'the doctrine of recent possession'. The 'doctrine' is nothing more than the application of the ordinary principles of circumstantial evidence to this commonly recurring situation. Sometimes, the correct inference will be that D was the thief (or robber or burglar if the goods were stolen in the course of a robbery or burglary), sometimes, that he was a handler. If the lead is stolen off the church roof at midnight and D is found dragging it across a field at 1 am, this is very cogent evidence that he stole the lead from the roof. If it is found in his backyard the next day and he offers no explanation,[147] or an explanation which is shown to be untrue, as to how he came by it, this is slightly less cogent evidence that he was the thief but very persuasive that he either stole it or received it, knowing it to be stolen. As the time lengthens between the theft and discovery of D's connection with the stolen property, the weight of the evidence diminishes but it will vary according to the nature of the property stolen and other circumstances.[148] One relevant circumstance will be the nature of D's conduct in relation to the goods, but the same principles apply whether D is charged with receiving or with one of the other forms of handling. So, in *Ball*,[149] it was held that there was evidence of handling otherwise than by receiving where D assisted the thief in physically handling stolen goods and accompanying him on an expedition to sell the stolen property.

The difficulty which arises is that a jury may be quite certain that D was either the thief or a receiver but not satisfied beyond reasonable doubt that he was one rather than the other. Indeed, it may be that there is no evidence on which they could possibly be satisfied that he was the one rather than the other. In that case, it appears that neither offence is proved, and the only proper course is a complete acquittal – a conclusion satisfactory only to the accused. A solution which has been adopted in some jurisdictions, following *Langmead*,[150] is to direct the jury that, if they are satisfied beyond reasonable doubt that D was *either* the thief *or* a receiver, they may convict of the offence which they think more probable – that is, it is enough that they are satisfied on a balance of probabilities that D was the thief, or that he was the receiver. As the jury is unlikely to find that the evidence is exactly evenly balanced, this is a practical solution, and one that should be Art 6(2) compliant.[151] It was, however, rejected by the Privy Council in *A-G of Hong Kong v Yip Kai-foon*.[152] D was charged with robbery and with handling the goods stolen. The Privy Council held that the jury had been rightly directed

---

[146] *Abramovitch* (1914) 11 Cr App R 45; *Aves* (1950) 34 Cr App R 159; *Hepworth* [1955] 2 QB 600.

[147] Inferences at trial might be drawn under ss 34–38 of the Criminal Justice and Public Order Act 1994 for the failure. See, generally, C Tapper, *Cross and Tapper on Evidence* (12th edn, 2010) Ch XIV, Part 2. The court must be careful not to apply the inference in such a way as to reverse the burden of proof: *Camara v DPP* (2003) All ER (D) 264 (Oct).

[148] See, eg, *Mason* [1981] QB 881 (antique wine coasters in D's possession five months after theft).

[149] (1983) 77 Cr App R 131, [1983] Crim LR 546.

[150] (1864) Le & Ca 427.

[151] If the approach was applied more widely it would pose problems particularly where more than two alternatives are left, leading to possible conviction of an offence of which the jury are not even sure D is probably guilty. See further M Hirst, *Jurisdiction and the Ambit of Criminal Law* (2003).

[152] [1988] AC 642, [1988] 1 All ER 153, followed in *Foreman* [1991] Crim LR 702; but see commentary at 704.

to consider the robbery charge first. Once they had decided that they were not sure that D was guilty of robbery, he was to be presumed to be innocent of the theft of the goods and it followed that any handling that occurred took place 'otherwise than in the course of the stealing' so there was no need for more than a passing reference to those words. This is a novel use of the presumption of innocence against a defendant. Because the jury are not satisfied beyond reasonable doubt that D was guilty of theft it is apparently to be conclusively presumed that he was not guilty of that offence. If the jury are satisfied that he was guilty of one offence or the other, it follows inevitably that he was guilty of handling. But this is arbitrary. The outcome depends on which offence the jury consider first, and it becomes critical for the jury to be directed carefully as to the order in which they approach the verdicts.[153] A more fundamental objection is that the approach treats the acquittal as proof of innocence and may offend Art 6(2) of the ECHR.[154]

Because of the difficulty of proving guilty knowledge, the Theft Act has provides for the admission of certain evidence on a receiving charge that would not (at least at the time of enactment) be admissible in criminal cases generally. By s 27(3):

Where a person is being proceeded against for handling stolen goods (but not for any offence other than handling stolen goods),[155] then at any stage of the proceedings, if evidence has been given of his having or arranging to have in his possession the goods the subject of the charge, or of his undertaking or assisting in, or arranging to undertake or assist in, their retention, removal, disposal or realisation, the following evidence shall be admissible for the purpose of proving that he knew or believed the goods to be stolen goods:

(a) evidence that he has had in his possession, or has undertaken or assisted in the retention, removal, disposal or realisation of, stolen goods from any theft taking place not more than twelve months before the offence charged;[156] and

(b) (provided that seven days' notice in writing has been given to him of the intention to prove the conviction) evidence that he has within the five years preceding the date of the offence charged been convicted of theft or of handling stolen goods.[157]

The provisions have the potential to operate unjustly by allowing the police repeatedly to round up the 'usual suspects' and for the jury to reason from prejudice to guilt. The careful exercise of the trial judge's discretion in the use of the section is critical, as is the judicial obligation to warn the jury of the uses to which the evidence might legitimately be put. The Law Commission called for the abolition of the provisions.[158] The provisions supplement the statutory rules governing the admissibility of previous misconduct.[159] Thus, D's handling of goods stolen earlier than 12 months before the handling now charged might be admissible

---

[153] *Fernandez* [1997] 1 Cr App R 123.

[154] See Hirst (2000) 4 E & P 31.

[155] cf *Anderson* [1978] Crim LR 223 (Judge Stroyan).

[156] There is no requirement for D to have been convicted on this earlier occasion. As to what detail may be admitted see *Bradley* (1979) 70 Cr App R 200, [1980] Crim LR 173, CA, and commentary.

[157] These provisions have attracted both judicial and academic criticism: see *Hacker* [1995] 1 Cr App R 332, HL, overruling *Fowler* (1987) 86 Cr App R 219, [1987] Crim LR 769, CA; R Munday, 'Handling the Evidential Exception' [1988] Crim LR 345.

[158] See Law Commission, *Evidence of Bad Character in Criminal Proceedings* (2001) Cm 5257, paras 4.13–4.23, 11.53–11.55. On such prejudice generally, see S Lloyd-Bostock, 'The Effects on Juries of Hearing About the Defendant's Previous Criminal Record: A Simulation Study' [2000] Crim LR 734.

[159] See ss 98–112 of the Criminal Justice Act 2003. See Ormerod and Williams, *Smith's Law of Theft*, paras 13.102–13.120 for more detailed treatment.

under s 101 of the Criminal Justice Act 2003.[160] So too might a conviction of theft or handling after the date of the offence charged or more than five years before it.[161]

27.2 Dishonestly retaining a wrongful credit

Section 24A of the Theft Act 1968 (inserted by s 2 of the Theft (Amendment) Act 1996) provides:

(1) A person is guilty of an offence if –

    (a) a wrongful credit has been made to an account kept by him or in respect of which he has any right or interest,

    (b) he knows or believes that the credit is wrongful; and

    (c) he dishonestly fails to take such steps as are reasonable in the circumstances to secure that the credit is cancelled.

(2) References to a credit are to a credit of an amount of money.[162]

The offence is punishable on indictment with imprisonment for 10 years.

The effect is that D1, a thief or fraudster, who has credited to his account[163] a wrongful credit commits an offence if he does not take steps within a reasonable time to divest himself of his ill-gotten gains. The provision is not, of course, aimed at him but at D2, where D1 has procured the crediting, not of his own, but of D2's account. If this was done with D2's conniv-ance, D2 would be guilty as a secondary party to D1's original offence which generated the proceeds which were credited to D1's account. There would be no need to invoke s 24A.

Suppose, however, that the credit was made without D2's connivance. One day D2 finds that an unexpected credit has been made to his account by D1. As soon as he knows or believes that the credit has been made in such circumstances as to amount to an offence he comes under a duty to divest himself of this unforeseen windfall. If he fails to do so within a reason-able time he commits the offence. It is an offence of omission,[164] rather like theft where s 5(4) applies. Whereas, however, s 5(4) requires D to intend to 'make restoration' of the property, s 24A(1)(c) merely requires him to cancel the credit. Does he do this merely by withdrawing the money to spend on riotous living? It seems not. In *Lee*,[165] L relied on a passage in previous editions to the effect that if D withdraws the money to spend for his own benefit, he cancels the credit and might escape liability under s 24A – 'if the draftsmen meant "make restoration" he should have said so – but, by section 24A(8), the money withdrawn is stolen goods so he will be guilty of receiving stolen goods'. The Court of Appeal rejected this submission noting that if it were correct it would lead to a 'surprising conclusion, since it is clear from the terms of the section itself that the offence consists in retaining the credit rather than taking reasonable steps to cancel it'. The conclusion was that 'the word "cancelled" as used in section 24A(1)(c) means cancelling the original credit so as to achieve the same effect as if it had not been made

---

[160] Or in some odd cases at common law if s 98(a) applies. C Tapper, *Cross and Tapper on Evidence* (12th edn, 2010) Ch VIII; *Blackstone's*, F12.39.

[161] See *Adenusi* [2006] EWCA Crim 1059.

[162] As amended by the Fraud Act 2006, Sch 1.

[163] By Sch 1 to the Fraud Act 2006: (9) 'Account' means an account kept with – (a) a bank; (b) a person carry-ing on a business which falls within subsection (10) below; or (c) an issuer of electronic money (as defined for the purposes of Part 2 of the Financial Services and Markets Act 2000).

[164] The argument of the Law Commission that this is necessary is found in Law Com No 243 at 39.

[165] [2006] EWCA Crim 156.

in the first place. In many cases that will be achieved by a corresponding debit reversing the original entry in the account'.[166]

The section extends to other conduct which was not an offence even before the decision of the House of Lords in *Preddy*. Section 24A(2A)[167] provides:

(2A) A credit to an account is wrongful to the extent that it derives from

    (a) theft;

    (b) blackmail;

    (c) fraud (contrary to section 1 of the Fraud Act 2006); or

    (d) stolen goods.

So D2 may be guilty of the offence if:

(1) D1 steals money and pays it into D2's account;

(2) D1 obtains money by blackmail and pays that money into D2's account;

(3) D1 obtains money by fraud and pays that into D2's account;

(4) D1 receives stolen money and pays it into D2's account.

In each of these cases the credit in D2's account is a new item of property – a thing in action belonging to D2 – which has never been 'in the hands' of a thief or handler and so is not 'stolen goods' within s 24(2). D2 is not guilty of handling by retaining it. Now, however, he commits an offence under s 24A(1) if he dishonestly fails to cancel 'the wrongful credit' within a reasonable time. Cancelling, according to *Lee*, means cancelling it as if it had never been made and not simply withdrawing that amount. In any event, s 24A(8) provides that any money which is withdrawn from a wrongful credit will be stolen goods and subject to the general law of handling so D2 may commit an offence under s 22. An incidental effect is that the thief, blackmailer or handler who pays the proceeds of his offence into his own account commits another offence when he fails to take reasonable steps to cancel the credit. This is so because the Law Commission thought: 'It would be difficult, if not impossible, to devise a simple way of excluding the case where A dishonestly secures a credit to his own account, while including the case where A dishonestly secures a credit to B's.'[168]

Section 24A(5) provides that it is immaterial whether an account is overdrawn before or after a credit is made. So if D2's account is overdrawn to the tune of £100 when a wrongful credit of £50 arrives, he is under a duty, somehow, to get his overdraft restored to its former level. There is no provision corresponding to s 24(3).[169] Nor is there any exemption for the *bona fide* purchaser such as is to be found in s 3(2).[170] Suppose that D sells his car in good faith to A who pays him with stolen money. After learning that the money was stolen D spends it. He did not commit any offence before the enactment of s 24A. He still commits no offence if A paid him in cash and he spends the cash. But if D paid the cash into his own bank account, or if he was paid by a cheque which he has paid into that account, he has received a wrongful credit and it appears that he will (subject to proof of dishonesty) commit an offence under s 24A when he spends the money, because he has failed to take reasonable steps to disgorge.

---

[166] [22].

[167] As inserted by the Fraud Act 2006.

[168] Law Com No 243, paras 6.16–6.17. The Commission comforted itself with the consideration that there was already an enormous degree of overlap in the existing offences under the Theft Acts.

[169] Stolen goods cease to be 'stolen' when they are restored to lawful custody or when the owner and any others claiming through him have ceased to have any right to restitution of the goods, above, p 980.

[170] Above, p 795.

That would create not only an unsatisfactory anomaly but also a conflict with the civil law.[171] The money, whether in cash or in the bank, is surely his to dispose of as he chooses. How then can he be guilty of a crime by doing so? It may be that a court will think it necessary to read into s 24A(1)(c) some such qualification as 'except where no person has any right to restitution of the credit', on the ground that Parliament could not have intended to change, or create a conflict with, such a fundamental rule of the civil law. This would introduce a limitation to the same effect as that relating to stolen goods generally in s 24(4).

27.3 Advertising for the return of stolen goods[172]

The existence of this offence might come as a surprise given the number of such advertisements that are commonly seen.[173] By s 23 of the Theft Act 1968 it is an offence publicly to advertise for the return of stolen goods indicating that no questions will be asked about how the person returning the goods came by them. An offence of this type has existed since 1828[174] and it was retained, after some hesitation in the Theft Act because it was thought that advertisements of this kind might encourage dishonesty.[175] Though such advertisements may encourage dishonesty in other people, dishonesty is not required of the perpetrator. It operates harshly in preventing the advertiser offering to pay the (innocent) *bona fide* purchaser of the advertiser's stolen goods.

Indeed, the offence has been held to be one of strict liability so that the advertising manager of a newspaper in which such an advertisement appeared committed the offence, though he was unaware that it had appeared in the paper.[176] In the light of the House of Lords' reiteration of the presumption of *mens rea* a court may be persuaded that strict liability is inappropriate.[177] However, when analysing the offence, Goff LJ in *Denham* regarded the section as creating a 'quasi criminal' offence, and that is a factor pointing towards strict liability.

27.4 Money laundering[178]

In a series of complex and draconian statutes over the last two decades successive Governments have sought to combat serious crime by targeting not just the offenders (who may commit a money laundering offence in relation to their own criminal conduct), but those who assist in the disposal of criminal proceeds. Accordingly, Parliament has enacted a raft of measures providing for confiscation, asset recovery, civil recovery, restraint proceedings, and prevention

---

[171] A transferee of stolen currency for value and without notice gets a good title: *Miller v Race* (1758) 1 Burr 452.

[172] See JC Smith, 'Rewards for the Return of Lost or Stolen Property', in N Palmer (ed), *The Recovery of Stolen Art* (1998).

[173] eg 'Laptop stolen from library before exams no questions asked but please place the data on a disc and return to…'

[174] See *Hall* (1985) 81 Cr App R 260, [1985] Crim LR 377, p 945 on its history. See also Smith, *Property Offences*, Ch 31B.

[175] Eighth Report, para 144.

[176] *Withers* [1975] Crim LR 647; *Denham v Scott* (1983) 77 Cr App R 210, DC.

[177] See *DPP v B* [2000] 2 AC 428; *R v K* [2002] 1 AC 462. See above, p 162.

[178] See, generally, A Mitchell, S Taylor and K Talbot, *On Confiscation and the Proceeds of Crime* (3rd edn, 2010, looseleaf) Ch 9; *Blackstone*, B.22; for an accessible account see also R Fortson, 'Money Laundering Offences Under POCA 2002' in W Blair and W Brent, *Banks and Financial Crime: The International Law of Tainted Money* (2008) and for a more theoretical account see P Alldridge, *Money Laundering Law* (2003) Ch 9.

orders. In some respects the offences of money laundering share a similar rationale to hand-ling: to target the individuals who render criminal activity profitable rather than the person committing the substantive crime himself.[179]

However, the money laundering offences are concerned not just with stolen goods but with criminal proceeds more generally. The legislation has been driven by inter-national treaty obligations, and these are frequently relied upon by the courts as an aid to interpretation.[180]

The offences under the Criminal Justice Act 1988 (CJA 1988) and the Drug Trafficking Act 1994 (DTA 1944) provided a series of offences which criminalized entering into or being concerned in an arrangement involving the retention, acquisition, use, possession, etc of criminal proceeds (CJA 1988) or the proceeds of drug crime (DTA 1994).[181] This strict division between laundering 'drug' money and 'other criminal proceeds' (eg those from theft or any crimes other than drugs) created significant practical problems, as pre-dictably when D claimed that he thought that he was involved in something suspicious but was not sure what. Unless the Crown could establish that he knew or suspected it was drug money (DTA) *or* that he suspected it was proceeds of non-drug crime (CJA) he would be acquitted. This led to difficulties at trial with practitioners and juries having to grapple with complex indictments alleging that D laundered either drug, and/or other criminal property. Even greater complexity arose in prosecutions for conspiracies of these offences.[182]

The Proceeds of Crime Act 2002 (POCA) remedies some of these problems but creates offences of a no less draconian nature. These often contain *mens rea* of mere suspicion or even objective tests of fault. The legislation is extremely technical and cannot be dealt with in detail in this work. The Act creates important offences for those in the 'regulated sector'[183] to fail to disclose suspected money laundering and an offence of 'tipping off' another person that sus-pected money laundering has been reported. These offences are not dealt with in this work. This chapter offers only an overview of the three principal money laundering offences to serve as a contrast to the offence of handling.[184]

27.4.1 The Proceeds of Crime Act 2002[185]

Part 7 of the Act introduces three sections – ss 327, 328, 329 – replacing the separate categories of offence relating to drug and non-drug crime.[186] These are the 'money laundering' offences. Technically, by s 340(11), 'money laundering' is much wider and includes not only (i) the substantive offences under ss 327, 328 and 329, but also (ii) inchoate forms of those offences, (iii) secondary participation in those offences and (iv) any act which would constitute (i), (ii) or (iii) if it were done in the UK.

---

[179] On whether these should be seen as true crimes see D Husak, *Overcriminalization* (2008) 104–107.

[180] See *Montila* [2004] UKHL 50 [2005] Crim LR 479.

[181] For an excellent review of some of the problems under the old law, see J Fisher and J Bewsey, 'Laundering the Proceeds of Fiscal Crime' [2000] JIBL 11.

[182] See *El Kurd* [2001] Crim LR 234; *Hussain* [2002] Crim LR 407.

[183] Catalogued in Sch 9 to the Act (as amended).

[184] The offences are supplemented by the important provisions in the Money Laundering Regulations 2007, SI No 2157.

[185] See E Rees and A Hall, *Blackstone's Guide to the Proceeds of Crime Act 2002* (3rd edn, 2008); R Fortson, *Misuse of Drugs: Offences Confiscation and Money Laundering* (5th edn, 2005); *Mitchell, Taylor and Talbot on Confiscation and Proceeds of Crime* (2005) Ch VIII; C Montgomery and D Ormerod (eds), *Fraud: Criminal Law and Practice* (2008) Ch D9.

[186] See on the history *Bowman v Fels* [2005] 1 WLR 3083.

27.4.1.1 Criminal property

Sections 327–329 of POCA criminalize D's dealings (concealing, disguising, converting, transferring, acquiring, using, possessing etc) with 'criminal property'. Section 340 defines what constitutes criminal property and is therefore central to their operation. It is a complex provision.

Take a case where D runs a bureau de change and takes receipt of bags full of used £20 notes which he converts into Swiss francs. Leaving aside for the moment the requirements of the money laundering activity (probably 'converting' under s 327 in this case) and what that entails, it is worth beginning by looking at what the Crown must prove in order to show that the property (the bags of cash) was criminal property under s 340.

It is first essential for the prosecution to establish that the property that D is alleged to have laundered (by converting etc) is the product of 'criminal conduct'. This criminal conduct is often called the 'predicate offence' to distinguish it from the money laundering offence (in our example converting criminal property) which is being alleged. Criminal conduct includes the launderer's own criminal conduct.[187] It also includes conduct abroad that is not an offence under the laws of the state where the conduct occurred, but which would be such an offence if committed somewhere in the UK. Perhaps the used £20 notes are the product of drug trafficking, prostitution, tax fraud,[188] burglary etc. Secondly, the property must be 'criminal property.' That concept comprises not just money which is the product of criminality, but a much wider range of property,[189] and by s 340(3) property is 'criminal' if:

(a) it constitutes a person's benefit[190] from criminal conduct or it represents such a benefit (in whole or part and whether directly or indirectly), and

(b) the alleged offender knows or suspects that it constitutes or represents such a benefit.

Notice that the property only becomes criminal property if D knows or suspects it to be criminally tainted. It is not enough to show merely that the property constitutes someone's benefit from crime, eg that the £20 notes were from drug trafficking. There is an element of *mens rea* to be proved. In our example, D running the bureau de change must know or suspect that the £20 notes derive from criminal conduct. Equally, it seems now to be accepted that it is *not* enough that D suspects that the property he is dealing with is the proceeds (benefit) from criminal conduct[191] if it is not in fact (perhaps D suspects that a bag of used £20 notes is criminal, but in fact the person wanting to exchange them is just an eccentric who does not trust banks). Although the case law might not all seem to be consistent, on closer inspection it is. Some of the pronouncements are on the s 330 offence which criminalizes D's failure to report a suspicion that property is 'criminal property', and under s 330 it is immaterial whether the property is actually criminal property or not. Accordingly, in the High Court of Justiciary in *Ahmad v HM Advocate*,[192] it was held that the s 330 offence (based on reasonable grounds to

---

[187] *Greaves* [2010] EWCA Crim 709.

[188] cf P Alldridge and A Mumford, 'Tax Evasion and the Proceeds of Crime Act 2002' (2005) 25 LS 353.

[189] By s 340(9) 'property is all property wherever situated and includes – (a) money; (b) all forms of property, real or personal, heritable or moveable; (c) things in action and other intangible or incorporeal property'.

[190] A person 'benefits' from conduct if he obtains property as a result of or in connection with the conduct. By s 340(8) 'if a person benefits from conduct his benefit is the property obtained as a result of or in connection with the conduct'. By s 340(6) ' If a person obtains a pecuniary advantage as a result of or in connection with conduct, he is to be taken to obtain as a result of or in connection with the conduct a sum of money equal to the value of the pecuniary advantage.' And s 340(7): 'References to property or a pecuniary advantage obtained in connection with conduct include references to property or a pecuniary advantage obtained in both that connection and some other.'

[191] See *Montila* [2005] 1 WLR 3141 at [41].

[192] [2009] HCJAC 60.

suspect) may be committed even where D's suspicion that the property in question is 'criminal property' proves to be wrong.[193] However, in relation to ss 327–329 which are our concern, there must be criminal property in fact.[194] In *Shah v HSBC*[195] the High Court held that:

> If the property in question is not in fact 'criminal property' then no offence is committed. For the purpose of the present applications it should be assumed that it was not criminal property.... On that basis it would not therefore have been illegal for HSBC to execute the payment instructions and the rights under the contract cannot have been suspended by illegality.

The reach of the money laundering offences is greater still because criminal property is extended by s 340(4): it does not matter who carried out the 'criminal conduct', who benefited or even whether the conduct occurred before or after the passing of the Act. Clearly, there is considerable overlap with the offences of handling stolen goods and dishonestly retaining a wrongful credit.

The predicate offence[196]

As noted, the prosecution must prove that there is criminal property under s 340. Controversy has arisen over how much detail it is necessary for the Crown to establish about the criminal conduct which generated this criminal property. What must the prosecution prove about this 'predicate offence' (as it is known) which has generated the criminal property that it is now alleged D has concealed, disguised, transferred etc to render him liable for the money laundering offence under ss 327–329? In our example with the bureau de change, is it necessary for the Crown to prove precisely what offence generated the money?

The criminal courts have struggled with the question of the degree of specificity with which the Crown must identify the predicate offence. In *Craig*,[197] Gage LJ approved a passage from *Kelly* (unreported) in which Butterfield said: 'Whilst the prosecution must prove that the property is "criminal property" within the meaning of the statutory definition, there is nothing in the wording of the section which imports any further requirement that the property emanated from a particular crime or any specific type of criminal conduct.'[198] Gage LJ did however suggest, *obiter*, that the Crown would be 'well advised' to give full particulars of the relevant offending.[199] In *NW*[200] Laws LJ took a different view, imposing an obligation on the Crown to identify the predicate offending in 'type' at least. The predominant view is now accepted to be that there is no strict obligation to prove the predicate offence:

> ... there are two ways in which the Crown can prove the property derives from crime, a) by showing that it derives from conduct of a specific kind or kinds and that conduct of that kind or those kinds is

---

[193] This was based in part on the decision in *Squirrell v National Westminster Bank Plc* [2006] 1 WLR 637.

[194] See *Montila* [2005] 1 WLR 3141.

[195] [2009] EWHC 79 (QB) at [39]; per Hamblen J; a decision reversed on its merits in the Court of Appeal (Civil Division) [2010] EWCA Civ 31.

[196] See commentary on *NW* [2008] Crim LR 900 and V Walters 'Prosecuting Money Launderers: Does the Prosecution Have to Prove the Predicate Offence?' [2009] Crim LR 571 and *Ahmad (Mohammad) v HM Advocate* [2009] HCJAC 60 (HCJ); D McCluskey, 'Money Laundering: The Disappearing Predicate' [2009] Crim LR 719.

[197] [2007] EWCA Crim 2913.

[198] *Craig* [2007] EWCA Crim 2913 at [29].

[199] [41].

[200] Laws LJ in *NW* tried to avoid an 'anomalous' or 'bizarre' position where the Crown had a less onerous obligation in proving the source of criminal property in a prosecution than they would have under civil recovery. In civil proceedings for recovery under Part 5 of POCA a specified 'kind' of unlawful conduct must be proved to have occurred: *R (Director of the Assets Recovery Agency) v Green* [2005] EWHC 3168 (Admin); *Director of the Assets Recovery Agency v Olupitan* [2008] EWCA Civ 104.

unlawful, or b) by evidence of the circumstances in which the property is handled which are such as to give rise to the irresistible inference that it can only be derived from crime.[201]

In *F*,[202] it was made clear that the Crown can succeed in a prosecution without identifying even the type of offence from which the criminal proceeds were generated. In that case the inference that the property was criminal may not have been too difficult to draw as the two defendants had £1,184,670 in cash in their luggage on a plane to Iran. They were charged with being concerned in a money laundering arrangement contrary to s 329(1) and of transferring criminal property contrary to s 327(1)(d). The key question to be determined by the jury was whether or not the property was criminal property. The circumstances were such as to give rise to the irresistible inference that the cash could only have been derived from crime. Similarly, in *IK*[203] the Court of Appeal held that it was open to a jury to infer that very large sums which were being concealed in D's money transfer business represented criminal property even though 'the prosecution could not identify the provenance of the money'. Difficulties can arise, particularly where the property in question is something as innocuous as a plasma TV or a car. If the Crown alleges that these are criminal property that D is converting (perhaps D has them advertised on ebay), how easy will it be to infer that they are criminal property from the circumstances (D's low income, the circumstances in which he came to possess them etc)? In *Gabriel*,[204] the Court of Appeal provided further clarification of the Crown's responsibilities in proving that the property was property derived from criminal conduct:

In our judgment it is a sensible practice for the prosecution, either by giving particulars, or at least in opening, to set out the facts upon which it relies and the inferences which it will invite the jury to draw as proof that the property was criminal property.[205]

The courts have also emphasized the need for judges to prevent unfairness from arising from the Crown proceeding on such broad offences without identifying with sufficient specificity what the allegation against the accused really entails. D, the launderer need not be shown to know precisely what crime is involved. It is enough to show that he knew or suspected it was criminally tainted property. Further clarification, preferably from the Supreme Court is desirable bearing in mind how many appeals[206] have arisen on this point.[207]

The predicate offence must precede the money laundering

A money laundering offence can, it seems, be proved in the absence of a conviction for the predicate offence.[208] However, the prosecution must prove that the criminal conduct in s 340, which generates the proceeds of crime, coupled with D's knowledge or suspicion of that fact (and which thus constitutes 'criminal property') occurred before the alleged money laundering conduct took place, and not as part of it.[209]

---

[201] *Anwoir* [2008] EWCA Crim 1354 at [21].

[202] [2008] EWCA Crim 1868, following *Anwoir* [2008] EWCA Crim 1354.

[203] [2007] 1 WLR 2262.

[204] [2006] EWCA Crim 229.

[205] [29].

[206] Including *Craig* [2007] EWCA Crim 2913; *Anwoir* [2009] 1 WLR 980 and *F* [2008] EWCA Crim 1868.

[207] Some clarification from the Supreme Court is desirable given the seriousness of the POCA offences, the sentences they carry, the ease with which the prosecution can establish the other very widely defined elements of the offence (with *mens rea* of mere suspicion), and the Crown's willingness to charge POCA offences in such a wide range of circumstances (see *Rose; Whitwan,* below). A point of general importance was certified in *Anwoir*: 'whether in a prosecution under section 327 or 328 of the Proceeds of Crime Act 2002, section 340 requires the Crown to prove at least the class or type of criminal conduct that is alleged generated the proceeds of crime'.

[208] This was confirmed by the Court of Appeal in *Sabaharwal* [2001] 2 Cr App R (S) 81.

[209] *Geary* [2010] EWCA Crim 1925.

In *Loizou*,[210] L successfully appealed a ruling of the trial judge that the Crown would be entitled to put its case under s 327, on the basis that property transferred for a criminal purpose would thereby become 'criminal property' within the meaning of s 340. This is clearly not what the statute intended. The offence (under s 327) involves, *inter alia*, transferring criminal property. It is not an offence of criminally transferring property. The prosecution must prove that the property is criminal property within s 340 at the time of, or immediately before, the acts alleged to constitute the transfer etc. In the case of *IK*,[211] it was accepted that the Crown can rely on allegations of non-declaration of income as the predicate offence for s 327 provided D has, at the time of the conduct alleged to constitute money laundering, already made a false tax declaration to the Revenue or has committed some other cheat upon the Revenue.[212]

27.4.1.2 The s 327 offence

Section 327 creates an offence where D conceals, disguises, converts, transfers or removes criminal property from the UK. On one construction, the section appears to create five different offences and therefore the indictment should specify the relevant act to avoid the count being bad for duplicity. However, it is submitted that s 327 creates a single offence that can be committed in a number of ways.[213]

Actus reus

Section 327(3) defines concealing or disguising criminal property as including 'concealing or disguising its nature, source, location, disposition, movement or ownership or any rights with respect to it'. The offence is broadly drawn, and has the scope to apply in cases that would usually be thought of as classic instances of handling stolen goods. In *Thompson*,[214] for example, D was convicted under s 327 when he sold a train set to a specialist shop for £180 when its true value was £3500. The train set had been stolen five days earlier. D claimed to have bought it at a car boot sale. The jury found that the property was criminal property because it was the proceeds of crime (theft) and D suspected as much.

As indicated above, the property must be criminal property at the moment that it is concealed/disguised/converted/transferred etc. In *Loizou*,[215] Clarke LJ said:

In our view, the natural meaning of s. 327(1) of the 2002 Act is that the property concealed, disguised, converted or transferred, as the case may be, must be criminal property at the time it is concealed, disguised, converted or transferred (as the case may be). Put the other way round, in a case of transfer, if the property is not criminal property at the time of the transfer, the offence is not committed.[216]

The scope of the s 327 offence is demonstrated by the recent case of *Fazal*.[217] F was convicted on seven counts of *converting* criminal property contrary to s 327. F gave his bank details, debit card and PIN to a friend, P, who had said he needed an account to pay in his wages. F claimed that he did not use the account in question. Deposits were made into the account by people duped by P into paying for non-existent goods. The Crown alleged that F had facilitated the 'conversion' not that he had deposited or withdrawn monies himself. The question

---

[210] [2005] EWCA 1579, [2005] 2 Cr App R 37.
[211] [2007] 1 WLR 2262.
[212] cf Alldridge and Mumford (2005) 25 LS 353.
[213] cf *Griffiths v Freeman* [1970] 1 All ER 1117.
[214] [2010] EWCA Crim 1216.
[215] [2005] 2 Cr App R 37 [30].
[216] See also *Kensington International Ltd v Republic of Congo (formerly People's Republic of Congo) (Vitol Services Ltd and others, third parties)* [2008] 1 WLR 1144.
[217] [2009] EWCA Crim 1697.

was whether, even assuming *mens rea*, F's conduct could amount to converting criminal property within the meaning of s 327. F was charged as a principal offender, not as an accessory to P. The Court of Appeal upheld his conviction: if someone lodged, received, retained or withdrew money from his account each act would amount to a conversion for the purposes of s 327. A person with a bank account could be said to be converting the money through that account merely by allowing some third party to use the account.

In relation to the definition of 'conversion', the Court of Appeal stated that:

A person may lodge, receive, retain and withdraw monies from his account, each of which would amount to a converting of the monies concerned, and [counsel] does not suggest otherwise, by asking or allowing some other agent to do so. That other agent may have mens rea himself or may be an entirely innocent agent, but that does not prevent the owner of the account, who uses and operates his account, albeit with the help of an agent, innocent or otherwise, to be himself converting money which goes through that account by means of its operation in that way. There are probably several instances of converting down the line as the money is paid in, received, retained and withdrawn, and at various stages transfers or changes its features from a chose of action owned by one person into a chose of action owned by another person. When money goes through an account it changes its nature from money likely to be owned by one bank but representing a debt owed to one creditor into money owned by another bank and representing a debt owed to another creditor. Finally, when that money is withdrawn in cash, if it is withdrawn in cash, it becomes transferred into cash into the hands of the withdrawer.

Once there was a credit in F's account representing the fraudulently obtained sums, it is easy to see how that can be treated as property constituting or representing a person's benefit from criminal conduct (fraud/deception) under s 340. It is also easy to see how F has obtained an interest in it and how withdrawals from F's account constitute conversions. However, the court is equally clear that even mere 'receipt' of a deposit to F's account can amount to 'conversion'. (In automated bank transfers there is strictly no 'receipt' or 'transfer' of property; there is a transfer *of value*.) If the deposit to F's account was made by a fraudster who had obtained the victim's property, that would be uncontroversial. There would be a 'benefit' in the hands of the fraudster before the 'conversion' took place on receipt of the monies into F's account. However, in *Fazal*, the deposits into F's account were *automated* bank transfers made by the victims directly. There are difficulties with such a broad interpretation.[218] F's conduct in this case might more naturally be thought of as an offence under s 328 (see below).

Mens rea

There is no requirement to prove dishonesty. Nor is there any requirement that D is aware of the precise criminality which created the property. It is sufficient that he does one of the acts – concealing, disguising etc – and knows or suspects the property is the proceeds of criminal conduct.

The *mens rea* requirement is very wide. Suspicion is an ordinary English word. In *Da Silva*,[219] the judge directed the jury that 'to suspect something, you have a state of mind that is well short of knowing that the matter that you suspect is true. It is an ordinary English word…the dictionary definition of "suspicion" [is] an act of suspecting, the imagining of

---

[218] In the language of s 340, before the credit appearing in F's account, what was the property which constituted or represented P or F's conduct and in which either of them had obtained an 'interest'? When did they acquire that interest?

[219] [2006] EWCA Crim 1654. On suspicion see Rudi Fortson, above n 178 paras 7.46–7,49.

something without evidence or on slender evidence, inkling, mistrust'.[220] The Court of Appeal held that the word 'suspect' and its affiliates was that the defendant had to think that there was a possibility, which was more than fanciful, that the relevant facts existed. A vague feeling of unease would not suffice; however, the statute did not require that the suspicion had to be 'clear' or 'firmly grounded and targeted on specific facts', or based upon 'reasonable grounds' [16]. Where a judge feels it appropriate to assist the jury with the word 'suspecting', a direction along those lines would be adequate and accurate. Expressions such as 'inkling', 'fleeting thought' are liable to mislead and their use is best avoided. The only possible qualification was whether, in an appropriate case, a jury should also be directed that the suspicion had to be of a settled nature; a case might, for example, arise in which a defendant had entertained a suspicion in the above sense but, on further thought, had honestly dismissed it from his or her mind as being unworthy or as contrary to such evidence as existed or as being outweighed by other considerations. In such a case a careful direction to the jury might be required; however, before such a direction was necessary there would have to be some reason to suppose that the defendant had gone through some such thought process. This interpretation is consistent with earlier pronouncements including, notably, that of Lord Devlin in *Hussien v Chang Fook Kam*:[221]

Suspicion in its ordinary meaning is a state of conjecture or surmise where proof is lacking: 'I suspect but I cannot prove'. Suspicion arises at or near the starting point of an investigation of which the obtaining of prima facie proof is the end.[222]

The court's interpretation of suspicion has been held to apply in the civil law relating to this offence: *K Ltd v National Westminster Bank plc*.[223]

27.4.1.3 The s 328 offence

Section 328 creates only one offence of entering into or becoming concerned in an arrangement which, D 'knows or suspects facilitates (by whatever means) the acquisition, retention, use or control of criminal property by or on behalf of another person'. It has been held that this extraordinarily broad offence does not cover the normal conduct of litigation by professions.[224]

Actus reus

The concept of 'arrangement' is a vague one. Note that the property has to be criminal property *at the time of* the arrangement (ie the predicate offence must precede alleged arrangement).[225] The principle enunciated in *Loizou* applies to all the money laundering offences charged under ss 327–329. In *Geary*[226] G pleaded guilty to an offence under s 328 when he allowed a friend D to deposit money in G's bank account. D told G that he wanted to hide money from his wife who he was divorcing. The money was in fact the proceeds of a theft from a bank. G allowed his account to be used. G believed that he was merely helping D to conceal some of his assets so

---

[220] [2006] EWCA Crim 1654. See paras [16]–[19] for the correct approach.

[221] [1970] AC 942 at 948.

[222] See also the definition suggested in the JMLSG 2006 Guidance at para 7.9, 'A degree of satisfaction and not necessarily amounting to belief but at least extending beyond speculation as to whether an event has occurred or not'; and 'Although the creation of suspicion requires a lesser factual basis than the creation of a belief, it must nonetheless be built upon some foundation.'

[223] [2006] EWCA Civ 1039.

[224] *Bowman v Fels* [2005] EWCA Civ 328. See also *Squirrell Ltd v National Westminster Bank plc* [2006] 1 WLR 637 at [16].

[225] See also *Akhtar* [2011] EWCA Crim 146.

[226] [2010] EWCA Crim 1925; [2011] Crim LR 321 and commentary.

as to minimize the amount D would have to pay to his wife in a divorce settlement. Crucially, G did not believe the monies to be the result of criminal activities. The trial judge ruled that on those facts G would have committed a s 328 offence because on G's version of events, there had been a conspiracy between G and D to pervert the course of justice. The Court of Appeal held that on those facts there would have been no criminal property. Moore-Bick LJ said:

In our view the natural and ordinary meaning of section 328(1) is that the arrangement to which it refers must be one which relates to property which is criminal property at the time when the arrangement begins to operate on it. To say that it extends to property which was originally legitimate but became criminal only as a result of carrying out the arrangement is to stretch the language of the section beyond its proper limits. An arrangement relating to property which has an independent criminal object may, when carried out, render the subject matter criminal property, but it cannot properly be said that the arrangement applied to property that was already criminal property at the time it began to operate on it. Moreover, we do not accept that an arrangement of the kind under consideration in the present case can be separated into its component parts, each of which is then to be viewed as a separate arrangement. In this case there was but one arrangement, namely, that the appellant would receive money, hold it for a period and return it. To treat the holding and return as separate arrangements relating to property that had previously been received is artificial.

This did not mean that G had committed no offence under that part of the Act. On the assumption that the purpose for which the money was transferred to G involved perverting the course of justice, it became criminal property in his hands. Moore-Bick LJ considered that G could, therefore, have been charged with an offence of converting or transferring criminal property contrary to s 327(1)(c) or (d) rather than giving 'a strained and unduly broad interpretation to section 328(1) in order to bring within it conduct that falls within other sections of this Part of the Act'.[227] But even on this basis, proof of G's *mens rea* would have been crucial to establishing that the property was 'criminal property' within the meaning of s 340.

Mens rea

There is no requirement of dishonesty etc. D must know or suspect that the property is criminal property. The concept of 'suspicion' was considered above.

27.4.1.4 The s 329 offence

Section 329 creates three offences of acquisition, use and possession of criminal property. Subsection 3 provides that for the purposes of this section:

(a) a person acquires property for inadequate consideration if the value of the consideration is significantly less than the value of the property;

(b) a person uses or has possession of property for inadequate consideration if the value of the consideration is significantly less than the value of the use or possession;

(c) the provision by a person of goods or services which he knows or suspects may help another to carry out criminal conduct is not consideration.

---

[227] The Court of Appeal certified that the following points of law of general public importance are involved: (i) whether, as regards ss 327, 328 and 329 of the Proceeds of Crime Act 2002, the property in question had to have become criminal property as a result of some conduct which occurred prior to the act which was alleged to constitute the offence; (ii) whether, as regards s 328(1) of the Act, the arrangement to which it referred had to be one which related to property which was criminal property at the time the arrangement began to operate; and (iii) whether, as regards s 328(1) of the Act, the arrangement could be separated into its component parts, each of which could be seen as a separate arrangement.

Actus reus

The offence has a wide reach. The thief who retains possession of property that he has stolen commits an offence under s 329(1)(b) or (c). In this respect it is easier to prove than handling since there is no issue as to whether the money laundering occurred otherwise than in the course of theft. It has, however, been argued that the thief never obtains an interest (in the sense of a legal interest) in the stolen goods and that there is no criminal property to be laundered under s 329. The counter, and, it is submitted, stronger argument is that the thief would acquire possession of the property, and that is treated, in the law of theft at least, as a proprietary interest. The ease with which these offences can be proved by comparison with the offences under the Theft Act 1968 has led to some controversial convictions.[228]

In *Whitwam*[229] the Court of Appeal accepted the force of the argument in the previous paragraph. D was charged with acquiring criminal property, contrary to s 329(1) of the 2002 Act, when he was found in possession of a child's motorcycle that had been stolen in the course of a burglary. The issue arose as to whether this was criminal property as required under s 340 and, particularly, whether it could be criminal property if D had no 'interest', in the motorcycle. On appeal against conviction, D conceded that a thief obtained an 'interest' within the meaning of s 340(10) of the Act, in the property he stole because he obtained a right to possession of that property. Given the fact that the motorcycle had been obtained as a result of criminal conduct and constituted his benefit from that conduct, it was criminal property.

Mens rea

Dishonesty is not required under s 329. D must know or suspect that the property in question is criminal property. Suspicion is considered above.

A Specific defence to s 329

Section 329 provides a defence if D has acquired the property for adequate consideration. By s 329(3):

  (a) a person acquires property for inadequate consideration if the value of the consideration is significantly less than the value of the property;

  (b) a person uses or has possession of property for inadequate consideration if the value of the consideration is significantly less than the value of the use or possession;

  (c) the provision by a person of goods or services which he knows or suspects may help another to carry out criminal conduct is not consideration.

The defendant bears the evidential burden of raising the defence: *Hogan v DPP.*[230]

27.4.1.5 Defences to ss 327–329 offences

There are two defences common to ss 327–329. First, where a person makes an authorized disclosure to the authorities under s 338 or was intending to do so and had a reasonable excuse for failing to do. It was accepted in *Bowman v Fels*[231] that 'the issue or pursuit of ordinary legal proceedings with a view to obtaining the court's adjudication upon the parties' rights and duties is not to be regarded as an arrangement or a prohibited act within ss. 327–9'. It follows that lawyers conducting litigation are not required to make disclosure to SOCA and obtain SOCA consent merely because of a suspicion that the proceedings might in some way

---

[228] See, eg, *Hogan v DPP* [2007] 1 WLR 2944 and *Wilkinson v DPP* [2006] EWHC 3012 (Admin).
[229] [2008] EWCA Crim 239.
[230] [2007] 1 WLR 2944.
[231] [2005] 1 WLR 3083.

facilitate the acquisition, retention, use or control of criminal property by one or more of the parties.[232]

Secondly, by the amendments made in Serious Organised Crime and Police Act 2005[233] D will have a defence if he knows, or believes on reasonable grounds, that the relevant 'criminal' conduct occurred (or is occurring) in a country outside the UK, and is not (or was not at that time) criminal in that country.

27.4.2 Charging money laundering or handling?

The overlap between the offences in POCA and the offence of handling seems obvious. They are both regimes designed to deter the predicate criminal conduct, or at least to ensure that those who perform such conduct will have a more difficult time in disposing of their ill-gotten gains, and to deter those who engage in disposing of such gains. Questions have been raised about the extent to which the money laundering offences have rendered the handling offence obsolete.[234] There are certainly advantages for the prosecutor in charging money laundering. There is no need to prove that D was dishonest, nor that he 'knew or believed' that the property in question was stolen goods. Mere suspicion is sufficient *mens rea* for money laundering. Money laundering also has the advantage of capturing the conduct of the thief himself, who under s 22 and following *Bloxham*, cannot be convicted of handling unless he does so 'for the benefit of another'. Moreover, there are no difficulties in money laundering charges if the goods were allegedly stolen abroad.[235] However, some take the view that it is wrong to view the offences as overlapping, arguing that the purposes of the legislative regimes are different, with money laundering being 'intended to deal with those who operate with a veneer of respectability, under cover of which they clean up (launder) the proceeds of the activities of the front line criminals'.

In *R (on the application of Wilkinson v DPP)*,[236] the court recommended that POCA charges, (in that case s 329), charges should be resorted to only in serious cases, in accordance with CPS guidance, but the court accepted that if POCA was charged inappropriately where the facts suggest a simple handling offence the court could do no more than encourage the prosecution to charge handling stolen goods.

In *Whitwam* above, the court also addressed the appropriateness of charging a money laundering offence under Part 7 of the Act in respect of conduct which had the hallmarks of ordinary burglary, theft or handling. The Court of Appeal considered the CPS Code and prosecution guidance acknowledging that money laundering charges should normally be considered where a defendant had actively tried to conceal or transfer criminal proceeds. The Court of Appeal expressed concern at the use of POCA in such circumstances (although accepting that charging decisions were for the CPS rather than the courts).

---

[232] The defence applies if D: (a) he makes an authorized disclosure under s 338 and (if the disclosure is made before he does the act mentioned in subsection (1)) he has the appropriate consent;

(b) he intended to make such a disclosure but had a reasonable excuse for not doing so;

(c) the act he does is done in carrying out a function he has relating to the enforcement of any provision of this Act or of any other enactment relating to criminal conduct or benefit from criminal conduct.

[233] SOCPA 2005, s 102.

[234] cf the CPS guidance, and Criminal Law Week (2007) 19 Feb and see P Rule, 'An Alternative Handler' (2006) 170 JP 884.

[235] If handling is charged it is necessary to prove the foreign law, see *Ofori* (1994) 99 Cr App R 223 above.

[236] [2006] EWHC 3012 (Admin).

28
Forgery

Forgery and counterfeiting are now regulated by the Forgery and Counterfeiting Act 1981.[1] This Act is largely based upon the recommendations of the Law Commission.[2]

Forgery overlaps with many other offences. It is usually done as a preparatory step to the commission of some other crime, most often a crime involving fraud. Despite the many available dishonesty offences, forgery is retained as a separate offence because it has long been regarded as a serious offence, and the conduct is regarded as qualitatively distinctive enough to warrant a particular label within the criminal code.

The offences of forgery may be paraphrased as follows:

(1) making a false instrument (s 1);

(2) copying a false instrument (s 2);

(3) using a false instrument (s 3);

(4) using a copy of a false instrument (s 4);

(5) having custody or control of specified kinds of false instrument (s 5(1)); and

(6) making or having custody or control of machines, paper, etc for making false instruments of that kind (s 5(3)).

All of the forgery offences require proof that D intended to induce somebody to accept a false instrument as genuine, which as a result causes them to do or not to do some act to his own or any other person's prejudice. Forgery does not require proof of dishonesty.[3]

Forgery is triable either way.[4] The maximum sentence is 10 years' imprisonment on indictment; six months' imprisonment or a fine not exceeding the statutory maximum or both summarily.

A FULL DISCUSSION OF THE OFFENCE IS CONTAINED IN THE CHAPTER, AVAILABLE FREE ON THE WEBSITE:
www.oxfordtextbooks.co.uk/orc/smithhogan_textbook13e/

---

[1] Smith, *Property Offences*, Ch 23, *Arlidge and Parry on Fraud* (3rd edn, 2007) Ch 11.

[2] Law Com No 55, *Report on Forgery and Counterfeit Currency* (1973). See also Law Com Working Paper No 26, *Forgery* (1970). The history is considered by JWC Turner, 'Documents in the Law of Forgery' (1946) 32 Virginia Law Rev 939.

[3] *Campbell* (1984) 80 Cr App R 47; *Winston* [1999] 1 Cr App R 337.

[4] Forgery and Counterfeiting Act 1981, s 6.

29
Offences of damage to property

The principal offences of damage to property are governed by the Criminal Damage Act 1971 which replaced the complicated provisions of the Malicious Damage Act 1861. Like the Theft Act the Criminal Damage Act is a code, and it must be approached and interpreted in the same fashion.[1] The Criminal Damage Act is largely the product of a Law Commission Report, and reference to that helps in understanding the underlying policies and in elucidating the provisions of the Act.[2]

The Law Commission sought to align the law governing damage to property with that governing appropriating property as found in the Theft Act 1968. Complete parity for theft and criminal damage is neither practicable nor desirable, but it is important that there should be no conflict of principle if the criminal code as a whole is to be consistent and harmonious. Differences are obvious: while land cannot in general be stolen, there is no need for any similar limitation in relation to offences of criminal damage. On the other hand, it is clearly desirable that if it is not generally an offence to pick another's wild mushrooms, it should not be an offence to destroy or damage them and the Criminal Damage Act makes that clear.

The offence is commonplace: in 2009/10 there were 806,720 recorded offences of criminal damage.[3]

29.1 Destroying or damaging property of another

By s 1(1) of the Criminal Damage Act 1971:

A person who without lawful excuse destroys or damages any property belonging to another intending to destroy or damage any such property or being reckless as to whether any such property would be destroyed or damaged shall be guilty of an offence.

And by s 4 the offence is punishable by imprisonment for 10 years on indictment.[4]

---

[1] See above, p 778.

[2] See Law Com No 29, *Offences of Damage to Property* (1970). See also Law Com Working Paper No 23, *Malicious Damage* and generally DW Elliott, 'Criminal Damage' [1988] Crim LR 403.

[3] J Flatley et al, *Crime in England and Wales 2009/10, Findings from the British Crime Survey and police recorded crime* (2010) table 2.04.

[4] Although originally the same as theft, this is now more severe than theft (maximum 7 years). Penalty notices are often imposed: criminal damage contrary to s 1(1) attracts a fixed penalty: the Penalties for Disorderly Behaviour (Amount of Penalty) (Amendment) Order 2009.

29.1.1 Destroy or damage

The expression 'destroy or damage' was commonly used in the Malicious Damage Act 1861 and previous decisions on the meaning of these words, though no longer binding, retain a persuasive value.

'What constitutes criminal damage is a matter of fact and degree and it is for the [jury or magistrates], applying their common sense, to decide whether what occurred was damage or not'.[5] In *Samuels v Stubbs*,[6] Walters J said:

It seems to me that it is difficult to lay down any very general and, at the same time, precise and absolute rule as to what constitutes 'damage'. One must be guided in a great degree by the circumstances of each case, the nature of the article and the mode in which it is affected or treated ... It is my view, however, that the word ... is sufficiently wide in its meaning to embrace injury, mischief or harm done to property, and that in order to constitute 'damage' it is unnecessary to establish such definite or actual damage as renders the property useless, or prevents it from serving its normal function ...

Under the usual principles, a court or jury must not be allowed to find that the result constitutes damage when no reasonable tribunal could so find. A magistrates' court may be corrected, as a magistrate was in *Samuels v Stubbs*,[7] if it finds that the result was not damage when, in law, it was. This lack of firm definition does nothing to promote consistency in the law.

What is contemplated by 'destroy or damage' is actual destruction or damage; that is, some *physical* alteration, harm, impairment or deterioration. This will usually be capable of being perceived by human senses,[8] but it is the property that must be tangible for the purposes of this offence, not the damage.[9] The damage can be caused by act or omission.[10] It is not enough to show that what has been done amounts to a civil wrong, as for example a trespass to land or goods for neither requires proof of actual damage. So, in *Eley v Lytle*[11] D was not guilty when, during a game of football, he ran over V's land and committed trespass without actual damage. The same result would follow under the 1971 Act. Actual damage, however, need only be slight. Grass can be damaged by trampling it down,[12] and is easily and rapidly damaged by football, cricket or even bowls.[13] And even sterner stuff is susceptible of damage, as where a stalagmite is broken away.[14]

Should rendering property unfit for use constitute 'damage'? This poses difficulty in numerous situations. A thing may be damaged in the sense of being physically harmed though nothing is actually broken or deformed. A car is damaged just as much by uncoupling the brake cable as by cutting it with a pair of pliers. So a machine may be damaged by removing some integral

---

[5] *Roe v Kingerlee* [1986] Crim LR 735.

[6] [1972] 4 SASR 200 at 203. Following this, in *Previsic* [2008] VSCA 112 Ashley JA stated that absence of cost of repair is a circumstance that a jury might take into account in deciding whether it was satisfied to the criminal standard that the accused had damaged property.

[7] [1972] 4 SASR 200 at 201.

[8] But no doubt a non-rechargeable battery is damaged by exhausting the charge. The damage cannot be perceived by the eye but it has been rendered useless. Similarly with the erasure of recordings from audio, video and storage media: it was held that a card containing a computer program is damaged by erasure of the program: *Cox v Riley* (1986) 83 Cr App R 54, DC. But as to the modification of computers and computer material see now the Computer Misuse Act 1990 below, Ch 30 and s 10(5) of the Act (as inserted) discussed below. On these cases see also I Walden, *Computer Crimes and Digital Investigations* (2007) 172–173.

[9] See below, p 1016.

[10] *Miller* [1983] 2 AC 161, above, p 69.

[11] (1885) 50 JP 308, DC.

[12] *Gayford v Chouler* [1898] 1 QB 316, DC.

[13] cf *Laws v Eltringham* (1881) 8 QBD 283, DC, below, n 41.

[14] See (1964) The Times, 12 Sept.

part,[15] or by running it in an improper fashion so that physical impairment will result,[16] or tampering with some part so that it will not work although no part is removed or broken.[17] In *Lloyd v DPP*,[18] it was argued that clamping a car was, by itself, damage to the car, but the court rejected that and the decision was followed in *Drake v DPP*[19] where it was held that clamping involved no intrusion into the physical integrity of the vehicle. The clamp renders the vehicle useless for its purpose for the time being, just as the removal of an essential working part does. The distinction appears to be that the clamp renders the vehicle unworkable by being attached rather than by physically harming any integral part. In *Lloyd*, a large yellow sticker was also affixed firmly to the windscreen, rendering it impossible to drive the car until considerable effort had been put into removing it. Brian Hogan contended strenuously, and reasonably, that this must be criminal damage. But applying the court's test, did it intrude into 'integrity' of the vehicle any more than the clamp? Affixing with glue can hardly be more intrusive than affixing with steel bolts.

The courts' inconsistency of approach is demonstrated by other examples. The courts have accepted that damage was caused to a blanket and police cell where D stuffed the blanket in the toilet in his cell and repeatedly flushed the toilet causing flooding. The water was clean and the floor was waterproof, but the suggestion that this was not damage was 'incomprehensible'. The floor and blanket were rendered temporarily unusable.[20] The property was rendered inoperative and imperfect.

The question of damaging by impairing 'usefulness' might arise where the owner is deprived of access to a house or car by the theft or borrowing of keys to the front door or ignition keys. It would not be a natural use of language to describe these actions as damaging the house or car (even though the owner may be put to expense before he can put the house or car to their intended uses).[21] The physical integrity of the house or car is unaltered. The Scottish Law Commission proposed a new offence to combat this problem: interference with property or a person's lawful use of property which causes harm or inconvenience. This would catch the wheel-clamper and the borrower of car or house keys.[22]

Should rendering property less valuable constitute 'damage'? It has been held that property may be damaged though there is no interference with its performance if it is rendered less valuable.[23] A car is damaged if the paintwork is scratched and food is damaged by spoiling, as is milk where watered.[24] In each of those cases there is a physical interference. Smith[25]

---

[15] cf *Tacey* (1821) Russ & Ry 452. Charges of criminal damage were brought against the person who sabotaged floodlights at a premiership football game intending to fix bets: The Times, 13 Feb 1999.

[16] cf *Norris* (1840) 9 C & P 241.

[17] cf *Fisher* (1865) LR 1 CCR 7, DC, and see *Getty v Antrim County Council* [1950] NI 114 (dismantling). Though a machine or a structure may be damaged by the removal of a part or by dismantling, it does not necessarily follow that *the parts* are damaged by the removal or dismantling; if the parts are undamaged D can be charged only with damaging the whole machine: *Woolcock* [1977] Crim LR 104 and 161; *Morphitis v Salmon* [1990] Crim LR 48, DC. Care must be taken in drafting the charge accurately.

[18] [1992] 1 All ER 982, DC.

[19] [1994] RTR 411, DC, [1994] Crim LR 855. cf the position in Scotland discussed by A Phillips, 'Criminal and Civil Aspects of Wheel Clamping on Private Property' (1993) 38 J of the Law Soc of Scotland 187. Wheelclampers are regulated by the Private Security Industry Act 2001.

[20] *Fiak* [2005] EWCA Crim 2381.

[21] *Henderson and Battley* (1984), CA unreported but extensively cited in *Cox v Riley* (1986) 83 Cr App R 54, [1986] Crim LR 460, DC. See the rejection of the removal of keys as damage in *DPP v Fraser* [2008] NSWSC 244.

[22] See Draft Criminal Code for Scotland (2003) cl 83. This is less of a problem in Scotland as there is a common law offence of 'malicious mischief': *HM Advocate v Wilson* (1983) SCCR 420.

[23] cf *Foster* (1852) 6 Cox CC 25. cf *King v Lees* (1948) 65 TLR 21, DC (passenger urinating in taxi held to have caused injury for purposes of the London Hackney Carriage Act 1831, s 41).

[24] cf *Roper v Knott* [1898] 1 QB 868, DC.

[25] Smith, *Property Offences*, para 27.16.

argues that focusing on the impact of D's conduct on the value of V's property is an erroneous approach under the 1971 Act since it could lead to the prosecution for criminal damage in wholly unsuitable circumstances.[26] This serves to remind us that the offence requires that property must be physically altered.

In an attempt to avoid difficult decisions of whether damage is *de minimis*, the courts have occasionally been guided by the potential for expense to be incurred by the owner in rectifying the apparent harm.[27] In *Samuels v Stubbs*,[28] D had jumped on a policeman's hat resulting in 'temporary functional derangement'. This was held to constitute damage though there was no evidence that the cap might not have been restored to its original state without any real cost or trouble to the owner. By contrast, in *Hardman v Chief Constable of Avon and Somerset Constabulary*,[29] it was held that pavement drawings in water soluble paint constituted damage to the pavement where the local authority incurred expense in removing them with high-pressure water jets. This seems entirely right. No one would maintain that property which has been daubed by slogans or drawings was not damaged simply because the rain would eventually remove all trace of them[30] or because the householder could remove them more quickly with soap and water. *Samuels v Stubbs* is, perhaps, a less clear case. If an article is accidentally trodden upon (and for the purpose of determining whether there has been damage it can make no difference that it is intentionally trodden upon) and the owner finds that it takes a matter of moments to press it back into shape, surely he would say that no damage had been done? In *A (A Juvenile) v R*,[31] it was held that spitting on a policeman's raincoat did not damage the raincoat where the spittle could be removed by a wipe with a damp cloth. No doubt it would have been otherwise had the raincoat material been capable of being stained by the spittle.[32]

The defendant's opinion that what he did was not damage is irrelevant if damage is caused in law and fact. V's wall is damaged by D's graffiti irrespective of whether D regards it as an improvement.[33]

The principles used in interpreting 'destroy' or 'damage' apply equally when the question is whether D has damaged land or interests in land. To dump rubbish on another's land, even though there is no tangible hurt to the land beneath the rubbish, may amount to damage of

---

[26] The example given is that of the taking of the examination paper in *Oxford v Moss* (1978) 68 Cr App R 183, but the offence would surely not be made out in that case because the harm done (whether damage or not) is to the interest in confidentiality which does not constitute property for criminal damage (nor for theft).

/ [27] The problem arises disproportionately frequently with criminal damage because the activities of protestors commonly involve a symbolic act of minor damage – daubing slogans, decapitating statues of former Prime Ministers, snipping perimeter fencing of air force bases, etc.

[28] [1972] 4 SASR 200 at 203.

[29] [1986] Crim LR 330 (Judge Llewellyn Jones and Justices).

[30] For a call for criminal damage prosecutions of dog owners who allow their dogs to foul pavements see P Alldridge, 'Incontinent Dogs and the Law' (1990) 140 NLJ 1067.

[31] [1978] Crim LR 689 (Judge Streeter and Justices).

[32] But would the policeman have been unduly fastidious to insist that even a rain-proofed material should be dry-cleaned after it had been spat upon?

[33] Nor is D's motive (eg painting fig leaves over parts he considers indecent) relevant. cf *Fancy* [1980] Crim LR 171, CC (whiting out National Front slogans). See also M Watson, 'Graffiti – Popular Art, Anti Social Behaviour or Criminal Damage' (2004) 168 JP 668 and see the valuable discussion in I Edwards, 'Bansky's Graffiti: A Not So Simple Case' (2009) 73 J Crim Law 345, considering whether there is damage, whether D needs to be aware it is damage and whether there is a lawful excuse. Defacement Removal Notice powers were introduced by ss 48–52 of the Anti-social Behaviour Act 2003 as modified by Sch 4, para 18 of the Clean Neighbourhoods and Environment Act 2005. In force from 18 January 2008 by virtue of SI 2007/3371. These are notices for local authorities to impose on the owners of street furniture, etc whose property is defaced with graffiti obliging them to remove the specified graffiti within 28 days or the local authority can remove it and recover the costs.

the land if the owner is put to expense in removing the rubbish before the land can be put to his uses.[34]

The Police and Justice Act 2006 inserted a new s 10(5) which provides that for the purposes of the Criminal Damage Act 'a modification of the contents of a computer shall not be regarded as damaging any computer or computer storage medium unless its effect on that computer or computer storage medium impairs its physical condition'.[35]

'Destroy' clearly goes beyond damage and does not contemplate half measures. The word is a useful addition. It more accurately describes certain forms of conduct; for example: to 'destroy' structures by pulling them down or demolishing them, or to destroy crops or other growing things by laying them to waste, or to break machines, or to kill animals.[36]

29.1.2 Property

Section 10(1) of the Criminal Damage Act provides:

In this Act 'property' means property of a tangible nature, whether real or personal, including money and –

(a) including wild creatures which have been tamed or are ordinarily kept in captivity, and any other wild creatures or their carcasses if, but only if, they have been reduced into possession which has not been lost or abandoned or are in the course of being reduced into possession; but

(b) not including mushrooms growing wild on any land or flowers, fruit or foliage of a plant growing wild on any land.

For the purposes of this subsection 'mushroom' includes any fungus and 'plant' includes any shrub or tree.

The exceptions in paras (a) and (b) are of course to keep the law of damage to property in line with the law of theft.[37] But while there is a substantial measure of correspondence in the definitions of property for theft and damage, there are three significant differences.

In the first place land, which in general cannot be stolen, may be the subject of criminal damage. The policies which favour exempting land from the offence of stealing[38] have never applied to the offences of damaging property. While D cannot steal his neighbour's beautifully tended lawn by annexing it,[39] he may commit criminal damage by turning it over to grow vegetables.

Secondly, while it is now possible to steal intangible property, it is not possible to commit criminal damage to it. 'Offences of criminal damage to property', said the Law Commission, 'in the context of the present law connote physical damage in their commission, and for that reason we have not included intangible things in the class of property, damage to which should

---

[34] One might question the consistency of this with the decision in *Lloyd* [1991] Crim LR 904, DC, where as noted, the court took the view that a car was not damaged by placing a wheel clamp on it. Criminal damage charges had also proved ineffective in combating the menace of prostitutes' cards being stuck on public telephone boxes hence the offence under the Criminal Justice and Police Act 2001, s 46 (see Home Office, *New Measures to Control Prostitutes' Cards in Phone Boxes* (1999)).

[35] Police and Justice Act 2006, Sch 14, para 2.

[36] cf *Barnet London Borough Council v Eastern Electricity Board* [1973] 2 All ER 319, DC.

[37] But note that the destruction of, or damage to, wild animals and plants may be an offence under other legislation; see for example the Wildlife and Countryside Act 1981 and the Protection of Badgers Act 1992.

[38] See above, p 799.

[39] He might steal by removing the turf. The warden of a university hall of residence was once surprised to discover that, in his absence, his lawn had been carried away (though not 'dishonestly') by the Vice-Chancellor to make a bowling green.

constitute an offence'.[40] Consequently such intangible property as easements and profits, patents and copyrights, are excluded for the purposes of criminal damage.[41]

Thirdly, whereas it is theft to pick wild mushrooms, fruit and foliage, etc for commercial purposes, this would not result in a criminal damage charge irrespective of whether the picker had commercial motives.[42] It is important to note that the limitation extends only to fruit or foliage of plants growing on the land. The land itself may be damaged by, for example, environmental protest against GM crops.[43]

Turning to animals, in *Cresswell v DPP*,[44] the Divisional Court considered whether badgers which had been enticed into traps set by officials from DEFRA had become 'property' for the purposes of s 10. The defendants sought to argue that the badgers were no longer wild, but property under s 10 and that a defence to destroying the traps was available on the basis that the destruction of the traps was to protect property – the badgers. Keene LJ, rejecting the argument, stated that 'merely to entice a wild animal, whether it be a badger or a game bird or a deer, to a particular spot from time to time by providing food there, even with the objective ultimately of killing it in due course, does not form part of the normal course of reducing it into possession. If the creature were thereby to become the property, say, of the landowner providing the food, it would mean that it could not then be lawfully shot by the adjoining landowner on or over whose land it passed.'[45] Walker J was more hesitant, declining to express a concluded view on what constitutes property.[46]

A person does not constitute property for the purposes of this offence.[47]

29.1.3 Belonging to another

The offence under s 1(1) may be committed only where D destroys or damages property 'belonging to another'. Here, again, the policy of the law of criminal damage, which must be to protect interests in addition to ownership, is very much the same as that for the law of theft. Section 10 of the Criminal Damage Act therefore provides:[48]

(2) Property shall be treated for the purposes of this Act as belonging to any person –

[40] Law Com No 29, para 34.

[41] cf *Laws v Eltringham* (1881) 8 QBD 283, DC. D and others had been charged with damaging Newcastle Town Moor by playing bowls upon it. It was held that the property could not be laid in the freeman who had merely the (incorporeal) right of herbage; the property ought to have been laid in Newcastle Corporation as the freeholder.

[42] On the relationship of the provisions with the Wildlife and Countryside Act 1981, see M Welstead, 'Seasons of Mists and Mellow Fruitfulness' (1995) 145 NLJ 1499.

[43] See M Stallworthy, 'Damage to Crops' (2000) 150 NLJ 728 at 801.

[44] [2006] EWHC 3379 (Admin).

[45] [11].

[46] His lordship did express some more general views on the concept of wild animals: 'In broad terms, (a) it is a question of law whether an animal is wild or domestic.... (b) Once a wild animal is killed or dies, absolute property in the dead animal vests in the owner of the land or, in a case where relevant shooting or sporting rights have been granted, in the owner of those rights. (c) While a wild animal is alive there is no absolute property in that animal. There may, however, be what is known as a qualified property in them in three circumstances. The first is described as a qualified property *per industriam*. Wild animals become the property of a person who takes or tames or reclaims them until they regain their natural liberty and have not the intention to return. Examples of that kind of property include animals such as deer, swans and doves. A second qualified property is described as *ratione impotentiae et loci*. The owner of land has a qualified property in the young of animals born on the land until they can fly or run away. A third type of qualified property is described as *ratione soli* and *ratione privilegii*. An owner of land who has retained the exclusive right to hunt, take and kill wild animals on his land has a qualified property in them for the time being while they are there but if he grants to another the right to hunt, take or kill them then the grantee has a qualified property.' [38]

[47] *Baker* [1997] Crim LR 497.

[48] See for comparison s 5 of the Theft Act 1968 above, p 805.

    (a) having the custody or control of it;

    (b) having in it any proprietary right or interest (not being an equitable interest arising only from an agreement to transfer or grant an interest); or

    (c) having a charge on it.

(3) Where property is subject to a trust, the person to whom it belongs shall be so treated as including any person having a right to enforce the trust.

(4) Property of a corporation sole shall be so treated as belonging to the corporation notwithstanding a vacancy in the corporation.

It is, then, enough that V has some proprietary interest in the property which D damages, and it does not have to be shown that V is the owner of the property. D may, for example, damage property which V has borrowed or rented. Further, D may commit an offence where the property belongs to him provided that V *also* has a proprietary interest in the property. So, where D owns a car and loans it to V, but then D damages the car during the loan period, he damages property 'belonging to another'. In such cases, it may be difficult to prove that D acted with *mens rea* or without lawful excuse,[49] but, given that, D may commit criminal damage though he both owns, has custody and control of the property. Just as a co-owner of property may steal it by appropriating the other's share,[50] a co-owner may commit criminal damage by destroying or damaging the property.

V must have some *proprietary* right or interest in the property.[51] Where property is insured the insurer acquires an interest in the property, but the interest is not a proprietary one.[52] If D destroys his own property which he has insured with V, he does not destroy property belonging to another even though he may have destroyed it with a view to making a dishonest claim against V.[53] In *Appleyard*,[54] where D, the managing director of a company, set fire to the company's premises, it was argued that he could not be convicted of arson since he was 'in effect' the owner of the premises. D's conviction for arson was nevertheless upheld apparently on the basis that he was not the owner of the premises and knew he was not.

Property is also treated as belonging to a person who has a 'charge' on it because the Law Commission thought that this was an interest worthy of protection.[55] This expression does not, in terms, appear in s 5 of the Theft Act 1968 and is probably unnecessary in either Act, since a charge is almost certainly a 'proprietary interest'.

It will be noted that the definition of property belonging to another in the Criminal Damage Act, s 10, contains no provision equivalent to s 5(4) of the Theft Act – property got by another's mistake. This distinction can be of no practical importance: the getting of property by another's mistake may well excite acquisitive instincts but it is unlikely to excite an outburst of vandalism. There do not seem to have been difficulties over allegations of damaging abandoned property.[56] In *Cresswell*, it was accepted that there may well be some items of property which do not belong to another (for example, because abandoned) and some which

---

[49] See below, p 1022.

[50] *Bonner* [1970] 2 All ER 97n, [1970] 1 WLR 838, CA, above, p 1022.

[51] See above, p 806.

[52] An insurer has an interest in the safety of the insured property but, without more, this does not constitute a proprietary interest. cf *Lucena v Craufurd* (1806) 2 Bos & PNR 269, HL, per Lawrence J at 302.

[53] cf *Denton* [1982] 1 All ER 65, [1981] 1 WLR 1446, CA, below, p 1023. Such offences were included in the Malicious Damage Act 1861, ss 3 and 59.

[54] (1985) 81 Cr App R 319, [1985] Crim LR 723, CA.

[55] Law Com No 29, para 39.

[56] cf theft of 'abandoned' property: above, p 807.

are not capable of doing – for example, with wild animals in a state of being reduced into possession.[57]

Where D is the owner of property in which no other person has *any* proprietary right or interest, his destroying or damaging it cannot amount to an offence under s 1(1).[58] Nor generally is it an offence to damage one's own property apart from the special case dealt with in s 1(2).[59] It is not an offence for D to destroy a work of art which he owns or to lay waste to his plentiful stocks of food at a time of acute shortage. Such acts may be properly described as wanton but they are not criminal because there is no compelling policy reason for making them criminal. But where such a reason does exist, and cruelty to animals provides an illustration, particular offences can be created which extend to harm by an owner to his own property.[60]

29.1.4 *Mens rea*

Section 1(1) requires that the destruction or damaging of the property should be intentional or reckless, and without lawful excuse.

29.1.4.1 Intention and recklessness[61]

The *mens rea* requirement in the Malicious Damage Act offences was intention or malice. The Law Commission expressly stated its intention that the offences under the Criminal Damage Act 1971 should require the same *mens rea*. The only difference was to be a change of language from malice to 'recklessness', reflecting the Commission's aim for greater simplicity and clarity. The term 'maliciously',[62] was avoided because:

it gives the impression that the mental element differs from that which is imposed in other offences requiring traditional *mens rea*. It is evident from such cases as *Cunningham*[63] and *Mowatt*[64] that the word can give rise to difficulties of interpretation. Furthermore, the word 'maliciously' conveys the impression that some ill-will is required against the person whose property is damaged.[65]

The Law Commission's proposal was therefore to require proof that D's conduct was intended by D to cause the damage in question or was foreseen by D as creating a risk of causing that damage which risk he then went on unjustifiably to take. In other words, recklessness was to be interpreted in its subjective sense.

There must be *mens rea* proved as to the damage (consequences) and that the property damaged belongs to another (circumstances). It is not enough that D intends to do the act which causes the damage unless he intends to cause the damage itself; proof that D intended to throw a stone is not proof that he intended to break a window.[66] Nor is it enough that D intends to damage property if he does not intend to damage property *of another*. Since D commits no offence under s 1(1) of the Act in damaging or destroying his own property, it follows in principle that he ought to be guilty of no offence where he destroys V's property under the

---

[57] Walker J at [41].

[58] If, in a case like *Hinks*, above, p 784, the donee is given a chattel, he may steal it, but he can then damage or destroy it with impunity. Where the donee's title is voidable, it may be arguable that it is different.

[59] Below, p 1033.

[60] Examples would include protection of listed buildings.

[61] cf the general discussion of intention and recklessness, above, Ch 5.

[62] 'Maliciously' was the expression most commonly used in the Malicious Damage Act 1861 to describe *mens rea*.

[63] [1957] 2 QB 396, [1957] 2 All ER 412, CA, above, p 119.

[64] [1968] 1 QB 421, [1967] 3 All ER 47, HL, above, p 649.

[65] Law Com No 29, para 44.

[66] cf *Pembliton* (1874) LR 2 CCR 119.

mistaken impression that it is his own. Whether D's mistake is one of fact or law, he commits no crime for he lacks *mens rea*, and this view was firmly endorsed by the Court of Appeal in *Smith*.[67] Upon the termination of his tenancy of a flat D had caused £130 worth of damage in removing wiring which he had himself installed and boarded over. As a matter of property law, the landlord became the owner of the wiring and boarding as fixtures, and the trial judge directed the jury that D could have no lawful excuse since he had in law no right to do as he did. D's appeal against conviction was allowed. James LJ said on behalf of the court:[68]

Applying the ordinary principles of *mens rea*, the intention and recklessness and the absence of lawful excuse required to constitute the offence have reference to property belonging to another. It follows that in our judgment no offence is committed under this section if a person destroys or causes damage to property belonging to another if he does so in the honest though mistaken belief that the property is his own, and provided that the belief is honestly held it is irrelevant to consider whether or not it is a justifiable belief.

The mistake in *Smith* was a mistake as to the civil law; D knew all the facts and drew the wrong conclusion of law from them. The result is the same so far as criminal liability is concerned whether the mistake is one of fact or law so long as the mistake negatives *mens rea*.[69] As such, D commits no offence in pulling down a house if he honestly believes the house is his whether his mistake is one of fact or civil law and however egregious his error may have been.[70] It makes no difference that D's conduct might be described as wanton (as where he destroys a work of art) or that his purpose is a crime of fraud (for example, to defraud insurers). If D does not intend to destroy or damage property of *another*, nothing can render him liable to a charge under s 1(1). In *Appleyard*,[71] above, if D had believed that he owned the company's premises then he could not have been convicted whatever his motive (to defraud insurers or creditors, to inflict loss on the shareholders) may have been.

29.1.4.2 *Mens rea* as to damage – foresight of consequences?

The Act extends liability not merely to damage which is caused intentionally but also damage which is caused recklessly. That recklessness in this context was meant to connote foresight of consequences is apparent from the Law Commission's Report. This is reinforced by the Law Commission's proposed definition of recklessness[72] which, as Lord Edmund Davies pointed out,[73] was surely in the draftsman's mind when he drafted the Criminal Damage Act. This was not the view taken in *Caldwell*,[74] where the criminal law was plunged into unnecessary confusion and complexity,[75] and the breadth of the offence posed risks of serious unfairness.[76] Fortunately, the House of Lords has since acknowledged that the decision of the majority in *Caldwell* constituted a misinterpretation of the 1971 Act, and for that reason and for sound

---

[67] [1974] QB 354, [1974] 1 All ER 632, CA.

[68] [1974] 1 All ER 632 at 636.

[69] See generally above, p 330.

[70] cf *Langford* (1842) Car & M 602.

[71] (1985) 81 Cr App R 319, [1985] Crim LR 723, CA.

[72] 'A person is reckless if, (a) knowing that there is a risk that an event may result from his conduct or that circumstances may exist, he takes that risk, and (b) it is unreasonable for him to take it, having regard to the degree and nature of the risk he knows to be present': Working Paper No 31, *The Mental Element in Crime*. See also Law Com No 89, *Report on the Mental Element in Crime*.

[73] *Caldwell* [1981] 1 All ER 961 at 968, HL, [1982] AC 341.

[74] [1981] 1 All ER 961, [1982] AC 341.

[75] See Lord Steyn in G [2004] AC 1034, [2003] 4 All ER 765 at para 57.

[76] See per Lord Bingham in G, above, at para 33: 'It is neither moral nor just to convict a defendant (least of all a child) on the strength of what someone else would have apprehended if the defendant himself had no such apprehension. Nor, the defendant having been convicted is the problem cured by imposition of a nominal penalty.'

reasons of policy and principle as discussed above in Chapter 5, the orthodox subjective interpretation of recklessness which the Law Commission intended has been re-established. *Caldwell* is overruled.

In *G*,[77] the two defendants aged 11 and 12, when on a camping expedition without their parents' permission, entered the yard of a shop and set fire to bundles of newspapers leaving some lit newspaper under a large plastic wheelie-bin. The newspapers set fire to the wheelie-bin and the fire spread causing £1m worth of damage. The boys had expected the fires to extinguish themselves on the concrete floor; neither had appreciated that there was any risk of the fire spreading in the way that it did.[78] They were convicted of arson contrary to ss 1(1) and 1(3) of the Criminal Damage Act applying the *Caldwell* formula of recklessness, although the jury acknowledged some difficulty in applying fairly an objective standard to children whose capacity to see risk was limited by their immaturity.[79] In overruling *Caldwell*, Lord Bingham observed that:

section 1 as enacted followed, subject to an immaterial addition, the draft proposed by the Law Commission. It cannot be supposed that by 'reckless' Parliament meant anything different from the Law Commission. The Law Commission's meaning was made plain both in its Report (Law Com No 29) and in Working Paper No 23 which preceded it. These materials (not, it would seem, placed before the House in *R v Caldwell*) reveal a very plain intention to replace the old-fashioned and misleading expression 'maliciously' by the more familiar expression 'reckless' but to give the latter expression the meaning which *R v Cunningham*... and Professor Kenny had given to the former. In treating this authority as irrelevant to the construction of 'reckless' the majority fell into understandable but clearly demonstrable error. No relevant change in the mens rea necessary for proof of the offence was intended, and in holding otherwise the majority misconstrued section 1 of the Act.[80]

As Lord Bingham made clear, the definition of recklessness to be applied in criminal damage is now that found in cl 18(c) of the Draft Criminal Code:

A person acts recklessly within the meaning of section 1 of the Criminal Damage Act 1971 with respect to –

(i) a circumstance when he is aware of a risk that it exists or will exist;

(ii) a result when he is aware of a risk that it will occur;

and it is, in the circumstances known to him, unreasonable to take the risk.

The courts have applied the new test unhesitatingly. For example, in *Booth v CPS*,[81] the Divisional Court upheld a conviction for criminal damage against D, a pedestrian who had stepped out into the path of a car, causing £517 worth of damage. D was drunk but aware of the risk of a collision and implicitly aware of the risk of damaging the car.

The doctrine of transferred malice[82] applies to the offence, so that if D intends, or is reckless as to, damage to property of A, he may be liable where he in fact causes damage, neither intentionally nor recklessly, to property of B.

---

[77] [2004] AC 1034, [2003] 4 All ER 765.

[78] Lord Bingham noted that they would have had little defence to a charge in relation to the wheelie-bin, at [33].

[79] See the interesting article by H Keating, 'Reckless Children' [2007] Crim LR 546 on whether the children were likely to have foreseen damage and public attitudes to punishing such acts by children.

[80] ibid, para 29. See also Lord Steyn at para 45; and Lord Rodger at para 64.

[81] (2006) 170 JP 305.

[82] See above, p 136.

The intention or the recklessness need not be related to the particular property damaged, provided that it is related to another's property. If, for example, a person throws a stone at a passing motor car intending to damage it, but misses and breaks a shop window, he will have the necessary intention in respect of the damage to the window as he intended to damage the property of another. But if in a fit of anger he throws a stone at his own car he will not have the requisite intention if it misses and damages V's. In this case the question of whether he has committed an offence will depend upon whether in throwing the stone at his own car he was reckless as to whether any property belonging to another would be destroyed or damaged.[83]

D would not commit an offence of criminal damage where he throws a stone at V but misses him and breaks a window, unless of course D was subjectively reckless as to the risk of breaking the window.[84]

Arson, as we will see below, is a separate offence carrying a higher punishment than damage caused by other means and its *mens rea* requires not merely the intentional or reckless damaging of property but the intentional or reckless damaging of property *by fire*. Williams suggests[85] that transferred malice would not apply where D, intent on damaging property other than by fire, accidentally starts a fire in circumstances where there is no obvious and serious risk of fire. This, with respect, seems an acceptable conclusion.

Obviously, *mens rea* cannot be supplied by an afterthought. If D inadvertently breaks V's window he cannot become liable when, having learned that V is a tax inspector, he rejoices in the harm caused. On the other hand, if D inadvertently sets fire to V's property and subsequently becomes aware[86] that he has done so, he may be criminally liable if, intending or being reckless that *further* damage ensue to V's property, he lets the fire take its course when it lies within his power to prevent or minimize that further damage.[87]

It will be incumbent on the judge to provide careful direction on the issues of intention and recklessness if charged on the same indictment.[88]

29.1.5 Lawful excuse

The Law Commission took the view that in most cases:

there is a clear distinction between the mental element and the element of unlawfulness, and in the absence of one or other element no offence will be committed, notwithstanding that damage may have been done to another's property. For example, a police officer who, in order to execute a warrant of arrest, has to force open a door of a house is acting with lawful excuse although he intends to damage the door or the lock. On the other hand a person playing tennis on a properly fenced court who inadvertently hits a ball on to a greenhouse roof, breaking a pane of glass, acts without lawful excuse, but will escape liability because he has not the requisite intention.[89]

---

[83] Law Com No 29, para 45.

[84] cf *Pembliton* (1874) LR 2 CCR 119.

[85] (1983) 42 CLJ 85 at 86. cf A Ashworth, 'Transferred Malice and Punishment for Unforeseen Consequences', in *Reshaping the Criminal Law*, 77, 92. The issue is discussed in detail in J Horder, 'A Critique of the Correspondence Principle in Criminal Law' [1995] Crim LR 759 at 769–770. Horder argues that what really matters is 'the representative label: is it right to label D as an arsonist if he did not intend to start a fire . . .' cf B Mitchell, 'In Defence of a Principle of Correspondence' [1999] Crim LR 195.

[86] It is not enough that D ought to have been aware, or was not aware because he gave no thought to it: *Miller*, note below.

[87] *Miller* [1983] 2 AC 161, [1983] 1 All ER 978, HL. See above p 69.

[88] *Mason* [2005] All ER (D) 04 (Feb).

[89] Law Com No 29, para 49.

This distinction drawn by the Law Commission between the 'mental element' and the element of 'unlawfulness' may be a distinction of convenience but it is also a distinction generally adopted in this work. It is thought convenient to consider separately, so far as the situation permits, the issue of intention or recklessness as to the damaging of the property and the various grounds of exculpation or justification that may exist for damage deliberately done.

Under the pre-1971 law, it was not always clear in what circumstances it was justifiable to damage or destroy the property of another. Section 5 of the Act provides a partial definition of 'lawful excuse', and makes a clean break with the earlier law. The section in part provides:

(2) A person charged with an offence to which this section applies[90] shall, whether or not he would be treated for the purposes of this Act as having a lawful excuse apart from this subsection, be treated for those purposes as having a lawful excuse –

(a) if at the time of the act or acts alleged to constitute the offence he believed that the person or persons whom he believed to be entitled to consent to the destruction of or damage to the property in question had so consented, or would have consented to it if he or they had known of the destruction or damage and its circumstances; or

(b) if he destroyed or damaged or threatened to destroy or damage the property in question ... in order to protect property belonging to himself or another or a right or interest in property which was or which he believed to be vested in himself or another, and at the time of the act or acts alleged to constitute the offence he believed –

(i) that the property, right or interest was in immediate need of protection; and

(ii) that the means of protection adopted or proposed to be adopted were or would be reasonable having regard to all the circumstances.

(3) For the purpose of this section it is immaterial whether a belief is justified or not if it is honestly held.

(4) For the purposes of subsection (2) above a right or interest in property includes any right or privilege in or over land, whether created by grant, licence or otherwise.

29.1.5.1 Belief in consent

D's belief is judged by the single criterion that it be honestly held; a point which, if it is not clear enough from the wording of s 5(2)(a), is put beyond doubt by s 5(3). Section 5(2)(a) closely follows the pattern of s 2(1)(b) of the Theft Act 1968,[91] and it is right that it should since the parallel between theft and criminal damage is at this point exact.

The provision covers a number of mistaken beliefs. First, and most obviously this provision covers the case where D believes that the owner *has consented* to the destruction or damage. So, in *Denton*,[92] it was held that D was not guilty of arson in setting fire to his employer's mill when D believed that his employer had encouraged him to do so (even though this was in order to make a fraudulent claim against the insurers). Secondly, the provision covers the case where D comes across an injured animal and, believing that the owner *would have consented* had he been able to contact him, D kills the animal to put it out of its misery.[93] Thirdly, the provision covers the case where D rightly believes that X is a person *entitled to consent* to the destruction or damage and wrongly believes that he *has consented*. Thus, for example, an

---

[90] The section applies to an offence under s 1(1); as to other offences, see below.

[91] See above, p 824.

[92] [1982] 1 All ER 65, [1981] 1 WLR 1446, CA.

[93] There is also a specific defence under the Wild Mammals (Protection) Act 1996, s 2, for the attempted killing of a wild mammal as an act of mercy if D shows that the mammal had been so seriously disabled otherwise than by his unlawful act that there was no reasonable chance of its recovering. Note also the Animal Welfare Act 2006, ss 4–8 (as amended), which create offences of harm to protected animals.

employee destroying or damaging property belonging to the firm would commit no offence where he believed that some person in authority (say, a foreman) was entitled to consent, and had consented.[94] Fourthly, the provision applies where D honestly but wrongly believes that X is the person *entitled to consent* and also wrongly believes that he *would have consented* to the damage if asked. Mistakes as to the identity of the person entitled to consent, the status of the person, the presence of consent and the likelihood of conditional consent are therefore all accommodated in this extremely wide defence.

One controversial example of the breadth of the defence is that in *Jaggard v Dickinson*[95] where D had permission to treat the house of a friend, X, as her own. One night when D was heavily intoxicated she took a taxi to the street where X lived. D then attempted to enter what she mistakenly believed to be X's house, smashing a window in the process. The magistrates had rejected the s 5(2)(a) defence since D's belief in consent was brought about by self-induced intoxication. The Divisional Court quashed the conviction because of the explicitly subjective focus of s 5(3): 'a belief can be just as much honestly held if it is induced by intoxication, as if it stems from stupidity, forgetfulness or inattention'.[96] Williams exposes the breadth of the decision by posing the case of D, intoxicated by LSD who believes that the owner of a Rolls Royce has instructed him to roll it over a cliff.

Based on subjective beliefs though the defence is, it seems that a belief that God is entitled to, and does, consent to the damage is no answer.[97]

29.1.5.2 Defence of property

D has a lawful excuse within s 5(2)(b) if:

(i)   he destroyed or damaged the property in question in order to protect property which he *believed* to be vested in himself or another.[98] Some decisions have interpreted this as importing an objective element into the defence. It is submitted that this element ought, on a natural interpretation of the language, to be construed entirely subjectively.

(ii) he *believed* the property to be in immediate need of protection. The courts have construed this as importing an objective element ie is there a reasonable belief. That interpretation is more justifiable.

(iii) he *believed* that the means of protection adopted were reasonable having regard to all the circumstances. This is interpreted as an entirely subjective question.[99]

---

[94] cf *James* (1837) 8 C & P 131.

[95] [1981] 3 All ER 716.

[96] Per Mustill J at 532. See G Williams, 'Two Nocturnal Blunders' (1990) 140 NLJ 1564.

[97] *Blake v DPP* [1993] Crim LR 586, DC, above, p 388 and commentary suggesting difficulties also because God is not a 'person'.

[98] In *Cresswell*, the argument that these words were superfluous was rejected. They may be necessary to deal with abandoned property.

[99] cf the Northern Irish case of *McCann* the Court of Appeal summarized the position as follows: 'there are three elements to the defence...firstly, that the defendant acted in order to protect property; secondly that he honestly believed that that property was in immediate need of protection; and, thirdly, that he honestly believed that his actions were reasonable having regard to all the circumstances. It is clear that the second and third elements of the defence involve the application of a subjective test, ie did the defendant honestly believe that the conditions therein arose in the particular case. Different considerations arise in relation to the first element of the defence, however.' That interpretation was also the one of the Divisional Court in *DPP v Unsworth* [2010] EWHC 3037 (Admin).

Origin and type of threat

A person is entitled to take measures to protect his own property, real or personal, from harm caused by, or by the use of, property belonging to another. The origin of the threat to D's property might be animate (such as trespassing cattle) or inanimate (such as a caravan). If, for example, a dog is attacking sheep it may be shot if this is a necessary measure to protect the sheep.[100] A right of way over land belonging to another, being a 'right or privilege in or over land,' is 'property' and may be defended, in appropriate circumstances, by the demolition of a wall obstructing it.[101] The owner clearly has this right where the risk to his property exists in fact, but the Act goes further in providing defences.

In *Jones*,[102] the Court of Appeal concluded that there is no requirement that the threat to the item of property D believed to be in need of protection is a threat of *unlawful* damage. Certainly that restriction does not appear in the terms of the section. In *Cresswell* (the badgers case), however, the Divisional Court, in rejecting D's argument that he had believed the badgers to be in immediate need of protection, suggested that the s 5(2) defence was not available. It is not the purpose of the section to prevent an owner destroying or damaging his property.[103] There would be no unlawful act perpetrated against the badgers by the people D believed to be the owners (DEFRA) if those people killed badgers. Keene LJ suggested that if there was an unlawful act another defence would arise.[104]

Threat to 'property'

The property which D believes he is acting in order to protect must exist.[105] It is of course for the prosecution to disprove D's claim so long as D meets the evidential burden by laying a foundation for his claim to lawful excuse. The obligation is interpreted strictly: it is not for the judge to raise the defence and it has even been suggested that D must raise the defence by testifying.[106]

'In order to'

This aspect of the s 5(2)(b) provision has caused most difficulty. In a series of cases the courts have said that the words, 'in order to protect property' have an objective meaning. The insistence that the test is objective is difficult to reconcile with the wording of the statute which suggests a purely subjective test.

In *Hunt*,[107] D, who assisted his wife in her job as warden of a block of old people's flats, set fire to some bedding. He said he did so in order to demonstrate that the fire alarm was not working and so to protect the flats from immediate danger by getting it put right. The court asserted that, while this act was done in order to draw attention to the defective state of the fire alarm, it was not done in order to protect property. Roskill LJ was clear that the question whether or not a particular act of destruction or damage or threat of destruction or damage was done or made 'in order to' protect property belonging to another must be an objective test.

---

[100] Where there is no such justification, injuring the animal may constitute an offence under the Animal Welfare Act 2006, s 1 (as amended). cf *Isted v Crown Prosecution Service* (1997) 162 JP 513, DC, decided under the old law.

[101] *Chamberlain v Lindon* [1998] 2 All ER 538, DC.

[102] [2005] QB 259.

[103] Per Keene LJ at [16].

[104] If D peers through my window and sees me about to destroy my original Picasso in my living room, can he rely on s 5(2)(b) as a defence to breaking down my door? I would be committing no crime, but should D have a defence?

[105] Per Keene LJ in *Cresswell* above, at [10].

[106] And not through defence statements or counsel: *Jones* [2003] EWCA Crim 894, Buxton LJ at para 14.

[107] (1977) 66 Cr App R 105, CA. cf *Phillips v Pringle* [1973] 1 NSWLR 275 (CCA of New South Wales, action pursuant to a UN resolution against racialism not a lawful excuse for damaging goalposts).

In *Ashford and Smith*[108] and *Hill and Hall*,[109] the defendants were convicted of possessing articles with intent to damage property, namely the perimeter fences surrounding military bases. They claimed to have a lawful excuse because the bases, being an obvious target for enemy attack, constituted an immediate danger to property in the neighbourhood, and they acted in order to have the bases, and with them, the danger, removed. In both cases, the court said that the defence had rightly been withdrawn from the jury: *objectively*, the defendants did not act in order to protect property.[110]

In *Johnson v DPP*,[111] D, a squatter, damaged the door frame of a house in order to replace the locks with one of his own. He said that he did so in order to protect his property which he believed to be in immediate need of protection. The court purporting to apply an objective test (but in fact, it seems, simply disbelieving D) said that his purpose was not to protect property but to enable him to use the door; and, in applying a subjective test, that he did not believe his property was in immediate need of protection and that the means of protection were reasonable. It should be noted that a person may act with more than one purpose, and it is sufficient that one of those purposes was to protect property.[112]

As the court in *Hill and Hall* accepts, there are two distinct matters to be addressed. The first matter to be decided is D's actual state of mind. If D is asked, 'Why did you do this act?' and answers 'In order to protect the flats from fire', or 'To save the houses from damage by enemy attack' or 'To protect my property from thieves', he may be disbelieved but, if his answer is or may be true, if this was, or may have been, his reason for acting, it is impossible to say, rationally, that he did not act 'in order to' protect property. A purpose can exist only in the mind; it need not have an objective existence. If A sticks pins into a wax model of Buckingham Palace in order to destroy it, all reasonable people will agree that the act does not imperil the Palace. 'Objectively' the act is quite harmless; but no amount of objectivity can alter the fact that A acts 'in order to' destroy property if that is why he is acting. Similarly if he acts in order to *protect* property. This issue should be assessed on D's subjective belief.

It may be that all three decisions above can be justified without resort to the unacceptable view that 'in order to' bears an objective meaning. The more acceptable basis for the decisions is that in each case the need, even as asserted by the defendants, was not an *immediate* need.[113]

'In immediate need of protection'

The courts' importation of an objective element into this question of D's alleged belief that the property was 'in immediate need of protection' is also difficult to reconcile with the statutory language but is, in policy terms, easier to justify.

Under s 5(2)(b)(i) and (ii) it is irrelevant that the belief was wholly unreasonable if it was, or may have been, actually held. Unreasonableness is only evidence which assists the trier of fact in determining the ultimate question: whether the belief was honestly held or not. But, once D's belief is ascertained, however unreasonable the existence of the belief, the question

---

[108] [1988] Crim LR 682, CA.

[109] (1988) 89 Cr App R 74, CA.

[110] In *Hill and Hall*, it was added that there was no evidence on which it could be found that D believed the property was in immediate need of protection.

[111] [1994] Crim LR 673, DC.

[112] In *Chamberlain v Lindon* [1998] 1 WLR 1252, [1998] 2 All ER 538, above, n 101, it was held that it was immaterial that D may have had a second purpose of avoiding civil litigation. This attitude has not been reflected in other cases, including *Mitchell* [2004] Crim LR 139 where the court rejected the common law defence of recaption where D had removed wheel clamps. Self-help is a last resort.

[113] In *Chamberlain v Lindon*, above, it was held that D, within the meaning of the Act, believed the right of way was in immediate need of protection because the wall across it was an existing obstruction and delay would be evidence of acquiescence in it.

whether it is a belief of the kind specified in the section is an objective question – a question of law or, perhaps, mixed fact and law. Whether the need for protection, as seen by D, is an 'immediate' need is a question for the court or jury. For example, if Johnson had said that he believed his goods would be in need of protection when he moved them into the premises in a week's time, the court may believe him but not accept that this belief is a belief in an 'immediate' need for protection.

The courts have followed the approach in *Hill and Hall*, to deny the defence where protestors have caused criminal damage as a symbolic gesture of protest where there is no 'direct and proximate' threat to their property.[114] In *Jones*, D was convicted of causing £65,000 worth of damage to council premises in a protest over planning permission. Buxton LJ,[115] accepted that the objective evaluation of beliefs in the defence was no different from the court deciding whether a defendant's claim that his intent was to break the victim's nose amounted in law to grievous bodily harm.[116] The absence of any 'immediate' need for protection has also been used by the courts to prevent defendants relying on s 5(2)(b) when they have damaged wheel clamps attached to their vehicles.[117]

Belief in the reasonableness of the action

Once again the subjective terms of s 5(2)(b) need to be emphasized. There is no requirement that D's belief be reasonable, still less that D's conduct must meet some objective standard of reasonableness. The section does require that D must believe that it was reasonable for him to do as he did. In theory D might justify destroying an oil refinery because he believes its effluent is damaging his geraniums. However, a jury is unlikely to believe he did think, or could possibly have thought, that this was reasonable.[118] This example was discussed in *DPP v Unsworth*[119] where the court quashed D's conviction for criminal damage to her neighbour's trees which D claimed to have cut down to protect the right to light that she, D, believed she had. The defence had been misapplied at trial. Munby LJ pointed out that:

The protection, the safeguard, against such extravagant attempts to rely upon the defence is of course, ... that a jury is unlikely in the circumstances postulated to believe that the defendant did think or could possibly have thought that what he was doing was reasonable.[120]

The problem is that in practice, because of the theoretical availability of such a defence, protestors are able to advance the plea at trial, and maintain maximum publicity for their cause throughout the trial.

Relationship with other defences

Section 5(2)(b) is in line with general principles of defences in so far as it relates to beliefs in facts or circumstances. However, it goes well beyond the norm by providing that D's *belief* that the means employed *were reasonable* will excuse him. This must be contrasted with the position in self-defence/prevention of crime where D may use such force as *is found by a jury to be reasonable* in the circumstances which D believed to exist.[121] In self-defence, D's belief

---

[114] *Jones* [2003] EWCA Crim 894.

[115] Citing the 10th edition of this book with approval.

[116] *Jones* [2003] ECWA Crim 894 [19].

[117] See *Lloyd v DPP* [1992] 1 All ER 982; *Mitchell* [2004] Crim LR 139.

[118] *Hunt* might be different. There was some evidence that efforts had been made to get the Council to repair the fire alarm but these had proved unavailing. D may thus have reached the end of his tether and his claim that he believed the action reasonable might carry some credibility.

[119] [2010] EWHC 3037 (Admin).

[120] [42].

[121] Above, p 381. Note that an apparent attempt in *Scarlett* [1993] 4 All ER 629 to introduce a similar subjective standard into the law of self-defence and prevention of crime has been resoundingly rejected.

in the trigger for the defence is assessed on a subjective basis but the response to it is assessed objectively. The disparity between the 1971 Act and the common law was acknowledged in *DPP v Bayer*,[122] where Brooke LJ noted that the degree of incoherence provided a further illustration of the urgent need for codification.

The breadth of the defence in s 5(2) may be thought to carry subjectivity to excessive lengths. It departs from the general principle of criminal law that standards are set by the law, in practice by the jury or magistrates, not by every person for himself. The effect may be that D's right to use force to defend his dog, which is property, may be more fully protected by the law than his right to use force to defend his child, who is not property.[123]

Prophylactic measures in defence of property

D may not destroy or damage property of another merely because he honestly believes that harm may occur to D's property at some time in the future. On the other hand, it is not unlawful for D to take defensive measures in relation to his own property. It is an offence under s 31 of the Offences Against the Person Act 1861 to set traps so as to endanger life,[124] and it is an offence under s 1(2) of the Criminal Damage Act 1971 to destroy or damage property in order to endanger life,[125] but it is not otherwise an offence merely to take defensive measures (to set broken glass on walls, erect spiked fences, etc) for the purpose of discouraging or preventing incursions by persons on their property.[126] In such cases the question of criminal liability can arise only where some harm is caused to the person or property of another.

So far as harm to another's property is concerned, D will ordinarily have taken his defensive or protective measures at some stage before his property was in 'immediate need of protection', and when the harm occurs D may be absent and unaware of it. It is submitted that where what D has done is a normal method of protecting property, say a barbed wire fence erected by D, a farmer, he would not be liable though a trespasser tears his best suit in climbing through the fence, notwithstanding that D himself could not have justified ripping open the trespasser's suit as a use of reasonable force to eject him.[127] But where D adopts unusual defensive measures, say traps calculated to maim animals it would normally not be difficult to show that he did not honestly believe this was a reasonable way to protect his property.

What of D who leaves an unchained dog loose on his premises overnight? That would be an offence under the Guard Dogs Act,[128] but would he be liable, if property is damaged, under the Criminal Damage Act. The question would be whether the owner believed that the keeping of an uncontrolled guard dog was reasonable having regard to all the circumstances.[129]

---

[122] [2004] 1 Cr App R 38, [2004] Crim LR 663. Some of the broader statements in *Bayer* regarding defences were doubted in *Cresswell* (above).

[123] Section 5(2)(b) does not apply to damage to property in order to protect a person *Baker and Wilkins* [1997] Crim LR 497.

[124] See *Cockburn* [2008] EWCA Crim 316.

[125] Below, p 1033.

[126] cf potential civil liability under the Occupiers' Liability Act 1984, on which see W V H Rogers, *Winfield and Jolowicz on Tort* (18th edn, 2010) Ch 9.

[127] Note the specific powers to remove trespassers under the Criminal Justice and Public Order Act 1994, s 69.

[128] The Guard Dogs Act 1975, makes it a summary offence, punishable by a fine at level 3, to use or permit the use of a guard dog (that is, a dog kept for the purpose of protecting persons or property or a person guarding the same) unless a person capable of controlling the dog, the handler, is present and controlling it, except where the dog is secured and not at liberty to go about the premises: see ss 1, 7 and *Hobson v Gledhill* [1978] 1 All ER 945, [1978] 1 WLR 215, DC. The Act shall not be construed as conferring any civil right of action, or as derogating from any remedy (whether civil or criminal) in proceedings instituted otherwise than by virtue of the Act: s 5(2).

[129] In *Cummings v Granger*, the Court of Appeal held that keeping an uncontrolled guard dog was not, in the circumstances of that case, unreasonable; and conduct is not necessarily unreasonable even though it involves a breach of the criminal law. cf *Buckoke v Greater London Council* [1971] 1 Ch 655, [1971] 2 All ER 254, CA, above, p 367.

In determining whether D thought the measure was reasonable, regard would be had to D's knowledge of the risk of accidental as opposed to deliberate trespass, of the risk to children not capable of looking properly to their own protection, of the propensities of the particular dog and other similar factors.

Another common case calling for the protection of property is where a dog is worrying livestock. In such a case s 5(2)(b) will ordinarily provide a lawful excuse for the killing of the dog. The civil law provides further protection.[130] The law in such circumstances is further complicated by the availability of charges under the Animal Welfare Act 2006, but no offence is committed if an animal is destroyed in an appropriate and humane manner.[131]

Protecting interests that D believes he has

In most cases no doubt D will be the owner of the property which he seeks to protect, but even if D is not the owner he will not incur criminal liability if he honestly believes himself to be the owner and the other circumstances set out in the section exist.

The scope of the defence under s 5(2)(b) is again rather astonishing. By s 5(4), property is expressly defined to include any right or privilege in or over land. Consequently, D may commit no crime where, honestly but mistakenly believing he has a right of way across V's land, he tears down a hut erected by V which, as D thinks, obstructs his imagined right of way. Moreover, D is in the same position where he believes that he has a right or interest in property which he protects, but that imagined right is not a right or interest which is recognized by law. D has a defence in such a case because by s 5(3), it is immaterial whether a belief is justified or not so long as it is honestly held. Suppose, for example, that D has a right to kill and take game on O's land, and D kills V's dog which he sees chasing and destroying game. In such a case, there is in law no right or interest in property to protect; until D himself reduces the game into his possession he has no proprietary interest in it whatever.[132] But if D believes he has a right or interest in the game, he would incur no criminal liability in killing V's dog provided the other circumstances required for the defence exist.[133] In such a case as this, D's belief that he has a right in property to protect is understandable, but even if D's belief is absurd it suffices to provide him with the defence if honestly held.

Protecting interests of others

The position is essentially the same where D claims to act to protect the property of another. An employee who caused damage to V's property in defending property belonging to his employer would commit no offence given his belief that the measures were reasonable and were immediately needed. But there need be no nexus whatever between the person intervening to protect the property and the owner of it. An officious bystander who chooses to intervene to protect the property of another will be free from criminal liability if he acts honestly on the same terms.

D must have at least a belief that there is some *property interest* that he is protecting. Thus, the defence was correctly held to be unavailable where D decapitated a statue of Baroness Thatcher. He explained his motive as being that he held her responsible for developments in

---

[130] Under the Animals Act 1971, s 9(3)(a), D incurs no civil liability in this situation provided that D is a person entitled to act for the protection of the livestock and that he gives notice within 48 hours to the officer in charge of a police station of the killing or injury. That is true even if the dog *has been* worrying livestock – so there is no current threat to D's sheep: s 9(3)(b). It is submitted that in these circumstances D would commit no criminal offence. See the discussion of *Workman v Cowper* [1961] 1 All ER 683.

[131] Section 4(4).

[132] A point echoed in *Cresswell* at [41].

[133] On the facts of *Gott v Measures* [1948] 1 KB 234, [1947] 2 All ER 609, DC, D would now be acquitted.

world politics with which he disagreed and that he genuinely feared for the future of his son growing up in this world.[134] D had no belief that he was protecting property.

29.1.5.3 Cases not falling within the Act

By its terms, s 5(2) recognizes that there may be other circumstances which would constitute lawful excuse on a charge of criminal damage, and s 5(5) further provides:

This section shall not be construed as casting any doubt on any defence recognized by law as a defence to criminal charges.

It is clear that certain general defences (such as insanity and duress) are available on a charge of criminal damage and these are discussed elsewhere in this book.[135] But some particular matters call for further discussion here.

Self-defence, necessity and duress of circumstance

So far as necessity is concerned the law relating to defence of property is a particular, and well defined, instance where necessity is recognized as a defence. Are there cases in which it is permissible to destroy or damage property on the grounds of necessity in circumstances which, because there is no defence of property or belief in such a defence on the facts, would not amount to a defence under s 5 of the 1971 Act? As a starting point, it must be obvious that just as harm to the person may be justified on the grounds of self-defence of the person, so too the destruction of or damage to property may be justified in defence of the person.[136]

Where D damages property because he faces (or believes he faces) an attack involving the commission of a crime recognized by English law,[137] as will be commonly the case, the situation would be covered by s 3 of the Criminal Law Act 1967.[138] That section provides D with a defence if he uses such force as is reasonable in the circumstances in the prevention of crime. For example, if V sets his dog to attack D, and D kills the dog, D would not commit an offence of criminal damage if using reasonable force to defend himself. Section 3 in the 1967 Act is narrower than the defence under s 5 of the 1971 Act because s 3 includes an objective requirement of reasonableness.[139] D could not rely upon this section where the force used is unreasonable even though D himself honestly believed it was reasonable. Thus, there appears to be the odd situation that if D is defending his property it is enough (under s 5) that he *honestly* believed that the force used was reasonable, but if he is defending his person his honest belief will not save him unless the force used was in fact reasonable in the circumstances.[140]

Now suppose that V's dog, quite unknown to V, attacks D. If D, in self-defence, kills or injures the dog, s 3 of the Criminal Law Act can have no application since D is not seeking to prevent the commission of any crime: the dog acting of its own volition commits no crime. D must rely on the common law of self-defence. As under s 3, the question is not whether he thought his reaction was reasonable but whether it *was* reasonable. Once again this is distinct from s 5.

---

[134] *Kelleher* [2003] EWCA Crim 2486. Bizarrely, at his first trial the prosecution conceded the defence of 'lawful excuse' under s 5(2)(b) was available to D. As an indication of the difficulty if these defences are allowed to go to the jury in cases of protest, it should be noted that in that first trial the jury failed to reach a verdict.

[135] Chs 11 and 12. As to intoxication see above, p 311 et seq.

[136] So if D lawfully repelling an attack by E causes E to fall through F's window, D cannot be convicted of criminal damage to F's window: *Sears v Broome* [1986] Crim LR 461, DC.

[137] *Jones* [2006] UKHL 16.

[138] See above, p 383.

[139] See above, p 384.

[140] Perhaps, then, if D kills V's dog that has been set upon him, D should say that he feared for the safety of his trousers rather than his ankles! Section 5 would then be available.

The Law Commission knew what it was doing in creating this distinction with the 1971 Act:

We appreciate that our extended definition of lawful excuse introduces a less stringently framed defence than that of self-defence, where the force used must be reasonable when looked at objectively. There may therefore be the anomaly that different tests will apply to self-defence against bodily injury, but we do not think that this is sufficient reason to dissuade us from the present recommendation in this context.[141]

It seems unattractive for the criminal law to adopt a policy of greater generosity to those who act in protection of property than those who act in protection of personal safety.

It may also be noted that s 5(2)(b) of the Criminal Damage Act provides a wider defence in connection with offences of damage to property than is afforded by the common law defence of duress of circumstances. It appears to be the case at present that duress of circumstances is available only where D faces a threat of death or serious bodily harm or, possibly, imprisonment.[142] But s 5(2)(b), where it applies, permits a purely utilitarian calculation. Suppose there is a flood affecting the properties of X and Y and the fire service is called. Their assessment is that while X's house is not in danger there will be serious damage to Y's house by flooding unless X's fence is knocked down to allow the floodwaters to recede. A few pounds worth of damage needs to be done to the fence in order to prevent damage of several thousand pounds to the house. The firemen ask X for permission to knock down the fence, which he refuses, but the firemen nonetheless knock down the fence.[143] The firemen would have a lawful excuse to a charge of criminal damage if damaging the fence is reasonable in the circumstances. But if, additionally, the firemen have to restrain X because he resists their efforts to knock down the fence they would not be able to avail themselves of the common law defence of duress of circumstances since there is no threat of any harm to the person, let alone death or serious injury. They could rely only on the uncertain common law defence of necessity. If their action were regarded as not merely excused but justified, it may be that X would have no right to use force to defend his property.

Claim of right

It is clear that D cannot commit an offence under s 1(1) of the Act by destroying or damaging property which is, or which he believes to be, his own. The position would appear to be the same where D, though he does not believe he is the owner of the property which he destroys or damages, nevertheless acts under a claim of legal right. In *Twose*,[144] a case decided under the Malicious Damage Act, where it appeared that persons living near a common had occasionally burnt the furze in order to improve the growth of grass, it was accepted that D's belief in a right to burn the furze would be a good defence though there was no such right. Here D's belief was at least understandable, but in *Day*,[145] again under the old law, it was held that D was not guilty of an offence in maiming sheep belonging to V which he had distrained,[146] where he did so in the honest belief that he was entitled to do so upon V's refusal to pay compensation for damage done by the sheep. It would seem clear that cases such as these would be decided in the same way under the Criminal Damage Act where the clear emphasis is upon honest belief in right without any objective qualification.

---

[141] Law Com No 29, para 52.
[142] See above, p 343.
[143] The illustration is based on fact except that X readily gave his permission.
[144] (1879) 14 Cox CC 327.
[145] (1844) 8 JP 186.
[146] Taken out of V's possession pending compensation.

In similar vein, it is thought that a person who destroys or damages property found by him in circumstances where he believes the owner cannot be traced by taking reasonable steps can no more be convicted of criminal damage than he can be of theft by appropriating the property.

Protest defences

While the foregoing discussion deals with the more obvious categories of lawful excuse for damage to property there are certainly other cases. Moreover 'lawful excuse', like 'lawful authority or reasonable excuse',[147] may have an inbuilt elasticity which enables courts to stretch it to cover new situations so that it is never possible to close the categories that might constitute lawful excuse.

Criminal damage is commonly committed in the course of political protest, as in the cases of *Hill and Hall, Jones* and *Kelleher*. The courts have recently dealt with two new claims of defence to charges under the Act. First, although accepting that an act of criminal damage (such as the snipping of wire fence at a nuclear weapons base) could be regarded as an act of expression for the purposes of Art 10 of the ECHR,[148] the courts have held that the criminalization of such activity is a proportionate response to the legitimate aims in Art 10(2).[149]

Secondly, the courts have rejected attempts to argue that the commission of criminal damage is lawfully excused when in response to actions of the State which D believes to be contrary to international law.[150] In *Pritchard and others*,[151] the conduct involved possession of articles to cause damage on an RAF base. The defendants pleaded that the action was necessary and lawful to attempt to prevent what they believed was the UK's unlawful act of war against Iraq. At first instance, Grigson J held that the non-justiciability of the legality of the war did not preclude reliance on s 5 defences. On an interlocutory appeal, the Court of Appeal held that the s 5 defence would be available to D irrespective of the determination as to the legality of the war. D is entitled to defend his property against threats of a non-criminal and even of a lawful nature. The only objective element in the defence in s 5(2)(b) of the Criminal Damage Act 1971 was whether it could be said that, on the facts as the defendant believed them to be, the criminal damage alleged could amount to something done to protect another's property; subject to that the court and the jury were concerned simply with the question of a defendant's honestly held beliefs. The judge was therefore right to rule that no issue arose in relation to this defence which involved consideration of the legality of the war in Iraq. The House of Lords in the conjoined appeals of *Jones and Ayliffe*,[152] subsequently dealt with the appeals in these and related cases on the basis of pleas of necessity and self-defence (rather than under s 5) concluding that a belief in a need to protect property from action which D believes constitutes a crime in international law could not found a defence in English law.[153]

---

[147] See above, p 1022.

[148] See *Steel v UK* (1999) 28 EHRR 603.

[149] *Hutchinson v Newbury Magistrates' Court* (2000) The Independent, 20 Nov.

[150] Early cases on this included *Hutchinson v Newbury Magistrates' Court* (2000) The Independent, 20 Nov; *Pritchard and others* [2004] EWCA Crim 1981.

[151] [2004] EWCA Crim 1981.

[152] [2006] UKHL 16, [2007] AC 136.

[153] On the Court of Appeal's decision, see R Cryer, 'War and Armed Conflict: Aggression at the Court of Appeal' (2005) 10 J of Conflict and Security Law 209.

Authorized damage

At a more mundane level, clear cases arise where there is authority for the destruction or damage.[154] The typical problem is set by the sort of facts that occurred in *Workman v Cowper*.[155] D had shot a fox hound which was running wild on common land. The dog's owner was unknown at the time of the shooting. There was no evidence that the dog was attacking or likely to attack, sheep, but it was the lambing season and D thought it best, attempts to catch the dog having failed, to shoot it. On such facts as these, D's liability is unclear. There was nothing to suggest that the dog had been abandoned; D could not claim that he did not intend to destroy property *belonging* to another. Turning to the defences, since owners of healthy and expensive foxhounds do not readily consent to their destruction and there was no evidence that the dog was going to attack sheep, D would struggle to bring his conduct within s 5(2)(a). D might bring himself within the terms of s 5(2)(b) if he honestly believed that his sheep were in need of *immediate* protection. D could no doubt claim that he was acting honestly and that what he did was reasonable as a prophylactic measure – the dog, after all, might start attacking sheep. It is interesting to note that in the case itself the magistrates thought that D had acted reasonably and the Divisional Court had some sympathy for their conclusion. D was in fact convicted and it is thought that on similar facts he could still be convicted. Although there may be many who think that what he did was reasonable, even prudent, D was not acting in defence of property and it seems a necessary inference from s 5(2)(b) that unless his property is in immediate need of protection (or D honestly believes that it is) there can be no lawful excuse.

29.2 Destroying or damaging property with intent to endanger life

Section 1(2) of the Criminal Damage Act 1971 provides:

A person who without lawful excuse destroys or damages any property, whether belonging to himself or another –

(a) intending to destroy or damage any property or being reckless as to whether any property would be destroyed or damaged; and

(b) intending by the destruction or damage to endanger the life of another or being reckless as to whether the life of another would be thereby endangered,

shall be guilty of an offence.[156]

By s 4, the offence is punishable by imprisonment for life. The section creates aggravated offences of criminal damage and arson.[157]

---

[154] eg, statutory provisions for the destruction of dangerous, diseased or injured animals (Halsbury's Statutes, vol 2, tit. Animals); damage to property incidental to arrest, search and seizure (Police and Criminal Evidence Act 1984); where property is lawfully seized under statutory powers it would seem that in certain cases (firearms, offensive weapons, drugs) the police would have lawful excuse for destroying the property although the statute may not give an express power to destroy.

[155] [1961] 2 QB 143, [1961] 1 All ER 683, DC.

[156] See DW Elliott, 'Endangering Life by Destroying or Damaging Property' [1997] Crim LR 382.

[157] The trial of a person accused of arson being reckless as to whether life would be endangered must be heard by a full-time judge: *Jones (Stephen)* (1999) The Times, 20 May, CA.

This subsection incorporates what is essentially an offence against the person into the Criminal Damage Act. The Law Commission was aware of this and expected that the matter would be reviewed when offences against the person were reformed.[158] That has not occurred.

The *actus reus* is the destruction of or damage to property. The destruction or damage which occurs in fact may be quite different from that envisaged by D. Where there is such a difference, it is the destruction or damage which D intended, or as to which he was reckless, to which we must look in order to determine whether he intended to endanger, or was reckless whether he endangered, the life of another.[159] Thus, if D aimed to throw his petrol-bomb through the window of an occupied house, but the bomb hits the outer wall causing only trivial damage to the target, it is D's intended damage to the interior which is relevant. The question is as to D's state of mind when he did the act and we cannot, at that point, know for certain what, if any, destruction or damage will be caused. The offence is not committed unless D's act caused some destruction or damage – there must be an *actus reus* – but whether the terms of s 1(2)(b) are satisfied has been predetermined. The nature of the destruction or damage actually caused may be very good evidence of what D intended, or of his recklessness, but that is all.

The *actus reus* does not require that any life is in fact endangered. Thus, in *Parker*,[160] D was convicted under s 1(2) of criminal damage, being reckless as to the endangerment of his neighbours' lives when he started a fire in his semi-detached house. The fact that the neighbours were absent and therefore never at risk did not preclude conviction.

The life that D must intend or be reckless about endangering by the damage he intends or is reckless about causing must be the life of another.[161] So, D's conviction was quashed where, in order to commit suicide following the break up of his marriage, he set fire to his own car when he was in it or close to it, but parked 7–8 miles away from his wife's house. There was no evidence of an intent to endanger any life but his own by the damage that he intended to his own car in that position.[162]

The most controversial aspect of the offence is that it requires 'a dismal distinction'.[163] In *Steer*,[164] it was held that the offence requires intention or recklessness as to the endangering of life *by the damaging or destruction of property*, not merely by D's act. D fired rifle shots at the windows of a house occupied by V, against whom he had a grudge. The House of Lords held that the charge under s 1(2) was misconceived. Danger to life was caused by the bullets, not by any damage to the windows or property in the bedroom. The question, as we have seen, is not whether or how life was endangered in fact, but what D intended, or as to what result he was reckless.[165] While there was certainly cogent evidence that D was reckless as to danger to life from the bullets, he did not commit the offence unless he foresaw danger to life from, say, flying broken glass and there was no evidence of that. The contrary interpretation would also produce potential anomalies. Lord Bridge gave an example of A and B firing bullets into

[158] Law Com No 29, para 27.

[159] *Dudley* [1989] Crim LR 57 and commentary as cited with approval by the Court of Appeal in *Webster and Warwick*. The requirement is to be at least reckless as to the endangerment of the life of another. Suicide attempts with explosions and fire etc may suffice if D is reckless as to nearby residents etc.

[160] [1993] Crim LR 856.

[161] *Thakar* [2010] EWCA Crim 2136.

[162] T was drunk and it would have been open to T to argue that his consumption of a bottle and a half of vodka prevented him forming *mens rea*: reckless aggravated criminal damage being a specific intent offence according to *Heard* [2008] QB 43. See Ch 11 above.

[163] *Webster and Warwick* [1995] 2 All ER 168 at 173. Similar incidents are not uncommon – see, eg, *Ratcliffe* [2008] EWCA Crim 471.

[164] [1988] AC 111, [1987] 2 All ER 833, HL.

[165] *Dudley* [1989] Crim LR 57.

the air, being reckless whether life was endangered. It would be absurd if A alone was liable because only his bullet damaged property.

In *Webster*, D pushed a heavy stone from a bridge onto a passenger train passing below. Only a corner of the stone penetrated the roof but the passengers were showered with glass fibre and other material. The judge failed to direct the jury that D was guilty only if he foresaw danger to life from the damage to the carriage, not merely from the stone, so the conviction had to be quashed. In *Warwick*,[166] D drove a stolen car from which E threw bricks at a pursuing police car, smashing a window and showering officers with glass. It was held that there was evidence from which a jury could infer recklessness whether the police driver might lose control through being so showered, thus endangering life. Recklessness whether he might lose control through being hit by the brick would not be enough. The distinction applied in each of these cases is indeed 'dismal' but inevitable on the proper construction of the Act.

The fact that the damage may be to D's own property adds to the anomalous nature of the offence.[167] Suppose that D, the owner of a house, removing unwanted electrical equipment belonging to him, cuts a cable also belonging to him and exposes the live wire in such a way as that he foresees a risk to the life of another. The *actus reus* is the 'damage' to the cable. It is no answer that the cable belongs to D and that he is entitled to cut the cable if he wants to. It seems extraordinary that this should be an offence of damage to property, but that seems to be the implication of *Merrick*.[168] O, a householder, employed D to remove old television cable. D did so, leaving the live cable exposed for six minutes. His conviction was upheld. It would appear that the result would have been the same if O had done the act himself instead of through an agent. It would be understandable if the offence were simply the endangering of life; but the gravamen of the conduct in a case like *Merrick* has nothing to do with damage to property. Why should it be different if the danger arose not from cutting old cable but from the installation of new? The implications of the result are 'absurd and alarming'.[169]

The offence has features both of an offence against property and an offence against the person. In some circumstances (as where D severs the brake cable of V's car intending V to drive to his death) the offence will overlap with the offence of attempted murder, but it is wider than attempted murder in two respects. One is that it does not require the intent to kill which is necessary on a charge of attempted murder:[170] intention or recklessness as to the endangering of life will suffice. On facts such as those occurring in *Cunningham*,[171] for example, it could be that when D severed the gas pipe he did not intend to asphyxiate V but was reckless whether her life would be endangered; he would not be guilty of attempted murder but he would be guilty of the s 1(2) offence under the Criminal Damage Act.[172] The other is that the offence under s 1(2) may be committed where the acts done by D are too remote to constitute an attempt[173] to murder. If, for example, D were to sever the brake cable of O's car intending thereafter to induce V to drive the car to his death, D's act of damaging the car might be too

---

[166] [1995] 1 Cr App R 492.

[167] There have been a number of cases in which the charge has been laid where D has set fire to his own property intent on committing suicide, and has been reckless as to the endangerment of neighbours' lives: eg *Brewis* [2004] EWCA Crim 1919.

[168] [1996] 1 Cr App R 130, [1995] Crim LR 802.

[169] Elliott [1997] Crim LR 382 at 389.

[170] See above, p 404.

[171] [1957] 2 QB 396, [1957] 2 All ER 412, above, p 119.

[172] And also, of course, of the offence under s 23 of the Offences Against the Person Act 1861. It might be noted in passing that the toxic elements are now removed from gas used for domestic purposes and natural gas does not contain them; hence domestic gas can cause death only by asphyxiation, and even this risk is almost nil. But there remains a very high risk of explosion which is a serious danger to life.

[173] See above, p 402.

remote to support a charge of attempting to murder V but it would support a charge under the Act.

Certain general features of the offence under s 1(2) (such as destruction or damage, property, intention and recklessness) are the same as for the offence under s 1(1) which has already been discussed. The following additional matters need to be discussed in relation to the offence under s 1(2).

29.2.1 Intention and recklessness

Intention and recklessness in relation to destroying or damaging property have been discussed above.[174] That discussion applies to intention and recklessness in relation to endangering the life of another,[175] and reference may also be made to the general discussion of intention and recklessness elsewhere in this book.[176] It need not be shown that life was in fact endangered by the damage nor that the damage in fact done created any risk to life so long as D, by damaging the property, intended or was reckless as to the endangering of life.[177] Where D starts a fire in an unoccupied building with no one present, he might be reckless whether he endangers the lives of firemen, if he foresees a risk of a life being endangered by the damage.

Recklessness, following G is subjective. In *Cooper*,[178] the Court of Appeal suggested that the risk be one that was 'obvious and significant' to D. Thus, where D has realized that there is a risk but has dismissed it as negligible, it could not be said that he was taking an obvious and significant risk. This is an unusual interpretation of the subjective form of recklessness. It is submitted that the correct test is whether D has foreseen *a* risk of life being endangered by the damage that he intends or about which he is reckless and that he takes *that* risk unjustifiably. In *Castle*,[179] D had burgled an empty office, and started a fire. That spread to the unoccupied residential flats above. D pleaded guilty to burglary, but denied reckless endangerment as he claimed to have been unaware that there were residential flats above the office. The Court of Appeal confirmed that the question should have been whether D had acted recklessly with respect to: a circumstance when he was aware of a risk that had or would have existed; or a result when he was aware of a risk that it would occur, and it was in the circumstances known *to him*, unreasonable to take the risk.

Following the Court of Appeal's decision in *Heard*,[180] the element of intention or recklessness as to endangering life is an ulterior *mens rea* which means that it is not a basic intent but is a specific intent crime. Voluntary intoxication is available as a plea by D where his intoxication was such that he did not appreciate the risk of endangering life.

There must be a causal connection between the destroying or damaging of the property and the intended or reckless endangerment of life. If, to extend an example used above, D were to damage the lock in the process of entering V's garage in order to sever the brake cable of V's car, there would be no offence under s 1(2). D intends to damage the lock and he further intends to endanger V's life, but he does not intend '*by the destruction or damage to endanger the life of*' V. It is only when D damages the brake cable that he would commit the offence under s 1(2). So, in *Steer*,[181] it was held that the offence was not committed where

---

[174] At p 1019.

[175] *Hardie* [1984] 3 All ER 848, [1985] 1 WLR 64, CA.

[176] Above, Ch 5.

[177] *Sangha* [1988] 2 All ER 385, CA; *Dudley* [1989] Crim LR 57, CA. The definition of recklessness applied was that under *Caldwell*.

[178] [2004] EWCA Crim 1382.

[179] [2004] All ER (D) 289 (Oct).

[180] [2007] EWCA Crim 125, [2007] 3 All ER 306, [2007] Crim LR 654.

[181] [1988] AC 111, [1987] 2 All ER 833, HL.

D fired off some shots at V and his wife as they stood at their bedroom window. While D must have foreseen that the shooting would cause damage by smashing the bedroom window and also endanger the lives of V and his wife, D would not have foreseen that their lives would be endangered *by the damage to the window*, because it was not by that damage that they were, or were likely to be, endangered. In *Wenton*[182] W smashed a window in V's house in which V was present with children. W then threw through the window a petrol can and a burning piece of paper. The paper did not ignite the petrol canister. No fire ensued. He was convicted of an offence under s 1(2) of the 1971, namely reckless aggravated criminal damage. W appealed arguing that the damage that he caused and about which he was reckless was the broken window, there was no life endangered by that nor did he intend or was he reckless whether life would be endangered by that damage to the window. The Court of Appeal accepted this ground of appeal and quashed the conviction.[183]

On the other hand, it may be that if, having destroyed or damaged property belonging to V (for example having set fire to V's premises), D subsequently realizes that V's life is in danger, D would commit the offence under s 1(2), if, provided it lies within D's power to prevent or minimize the further harm, he then omits to do so, intending that or being reckless whether, V's life should be endangered.[184]

In *A-G's Reference (No 3 of 1992)*,[185] it was said that the property which D intends to damage need not be the same as the property which endangers life, instancing the case of a man who cuts the rope (the first property) of a crane, causing its load to crush the roof of a car (the second property) which kills the driver. But this seems to make far too heavy weather of the problem. Cutting the rope damages the crane, of which the rope is part, and the question then is whether D foresaw that the damaged crane might endanger life. It makes no difference whether the danger arises from the falling object or the car roof – it is caused by the damage to the crane.

29.2.2 Lawful excuse

Since the gist of the offence under s 1(2) lies in intending or being reckless as to the endangering of life *by* destroying or damaging property, it is understandable that D may commit the offence whether he destroys or damages the property of another or himself. The risk is just the same whether D severs the brake cable on V's car, or severs the brake cable on his own car before lending it to V to drive.

It is equally understandable that the partial definition of lawful excuse in s 5(2) should not be applicable here, and s 5 does not apply to offences under s 1(2). It ought not to be a defence to an offence of this nature that, say, D, with the assent of E, severed the brake cable on E's car before lending it to V to drive. Equally, D ought to have no lawful excuse in damaging property, although done for the purpose of protecting other property, where in so doing he knowingly creates a risk to life.

Clearly, then, the intention in framing the offence under s 1(2) was that certain matters (such as destruction by D of his own property, destruction with owner's consent, destruction

---

[182] [2010] EWCA Crim 2361.

[183] Is it impossible to argue that: (i) the canister and petrol were property, (ii) W intended to damage that property by fire (iii) he did cause some damage to that property (iv) he intended by the damage to the canister and the petrol that a life would be endangered? Equally can it be argued (i) the canister and petrol were property, (ii) W was reckless whether the petrol and canister would be damaged (iii) he damaged the property and (iv) he was reckless whether a life would be endangered by the damage about which he was reckless? Was it an attempt?

[184] *Miller* [1983] 1 All ER 978, HL, above, p 69. cf *Fuller* [1974] Crim LR 134, CA. D pleaded guilty to damaging property being reckless whether life would be endangered though warned by his brother of danger arising from a fractured gas pipe only after he had returned home. Appeal was against sentence only.

[185] (1993) 98 Cr App R 383, [1994] Crim LR 348. The case was primarily concerned with the law of attempt, above, p 407.

in defence of property) which constitute lawful excuse where D is charged with an offence under s 1(1) do not constitute lawful excuse where D is charged under s 1(2). This does not mean that there can never be a lawful excuse where D is charged under s 1(2), because s 1(2) expressly states that the offence may be committed only by one 'who *without lawful excuse* destroys or damages any property'. It follows that there may be circumstances, presumably of an exceptional character, where D would have lawful excuse for destroying or damaging property even though he does it realizing that he may endanger life. An exceptional case of this character would be where D damages property in self-defence; when it is legitimate for D to kill in order to prevent himself being killed, D would not commit an offence under s 1(2) because he happened to use, and damage, property belonging to another in killing his attacker.[186] Similarly, the police might have lawful excuse for damaging property where this was done to prevent the commission of a serious crime against the person, even though what was done might endanger the life of the criminal. And if necessity is a defence where D chooses to put one life at risk in order to save many others,[187] it would extend to damaging property to do so.

29.2.3 Endangerment offences

The problems of the s 1(2) offence stem in part from the confusion between its objective in penalizing endangerment, and the requirement for that endangerment to be founded on damage to property.[188] This has called some to question why English law does not adopt a general offence of life endangerment, and this is certainly an issue which deserves further consideration by the Law Commission.[189] To date, English law has created endangerment offences only in relation to specific activities, for example, causing explosions[190] or specific circumstances such as behaviour on an aircraft.[191] There is no general property endangerment offence.[192]

29.3 Arson

There is a separate offence of arson that is, of destroying or damaging property by fire,[193] in the Act despite the Law Commission's view that this was unnecessary.[194] Parliament preferred a specific offence.[195]

---

[186] cf *Sears v Broome* [1986] Crim LR 461, DC.

[187] See above, p 365.

[188] Despite its name it is debatable whether it is properly regarded as an endangerment offence in every case in which it can apply. See further RA Duff, 'Criminalising Endangerment', in Duff and Green, *Defining Crimes*. Duff distinguishes between crimes of attack where the intention is to harm some value of interest (and which be unconsummated as in an attempt) and endangerment offences proper which arise where D creates a significant risk that another will suffer harm. See also RA Duff, 'Criminalising Endangerment' (2005) 65 La L Rev 941.

[189] See generally KJM Smith, 'Liability for Endangerment: English Ad Hoc Pragmatism and American Innovation' [1983] Crim LR 127; D Lanham, 'Danger Down Under' [1999] Crim LR 960. The dangers are that such offences overcriminalize and render the law too vague. See generally D Husak, *Overcriminalization* (2008) 162–163.

[190] Explosive Substances Act 1883, s 2.

[191] Aviation Security Act 1982, ss 2–3. See *R(Hilali) v Governor of Whitemoor Prison* [2008] 1 AC 805.

[192] cf the Scottish Draft Criminal Code, cl 82 which provides for causing a risk of unlawful damage to property.

[193] Paper No 29, paras 28–33.

[194] The Commission proposed that such conduct would be punishable on indictment by imprisonment for life. This seemed a sensible way to meet the case and avoided complication of the substantive law.

[195] See HC, vol 817, col 1433 et seq. The reasons given for singling out damage by fire would be equally applicable to singling out damage by explosives; that 'arson' is such a splendidly evocative term cannot have been unimportant in securing its retention.

Section 1(3) of the Act provides:

An offence committed under this section by destroying or damaging property by fire shall be charged as arson.

And by s 4 it is punishable by imprisonment for life. Arguably, the retention of a separate offence was desirable to provide a more appropriate label and reflect public anxiety about the offence.[196] Arson remains disturbingly prevalent, particularly in certain types of property such as schools. In 2009/10 there were 28,954 reported arsons not endangering life and 3,625 reported arsons endangering life.[197]

The provision is a mandatory one – '*shall* be charged as arson'. Where D destroys or damages property by fire the proper course would appear to be to charge him with an offence under s 1(3).[198] Where there is also an allegation of endangerment, there should be separate counts of arson with intent to endanger life and of arson being reckless that life is endangered.[199]

The general features of arson are the same as for the offences under s 1(1) and s 1(2) except that the destruction or damage is to be by fire. For the offence to be complete some property must be destroyed or damaged by fire. The damage may of course be quite insignificant (it would be enough, for example, that wood is charred)[200] but there must be some damage *by* fire; it would not be enough that property is merely blackened by smoke though there might well be an attempt in such a case. D must intend, or be reckless as to, destruction or damage *by fire*. So if D, aided by E, throws a bottle which, unknown to E, D filled with petrol in order to set fire to V's house, D may be convicted of arson but E may not.[201] E, however, may be convicted of simple criminal damage in respect of any damage caused by the throwing of the bottle.

29.4 Racially or religiously aggravated criminal damage

Section 30 of the Crime and Disorder Act 1998 (as amended)[202] provides:

(1) A person is guilty of an offence under this section if he commits an offence under section 1(1) of the Criminal Damage Act 1971 (destroying or damaging property belonging to another) which is racially or religiously aggravated for the purposes of this section.

Definitions of 'racially aggravated' and 'religiously aggravated' and a discussion of the racial and religious aggravation offences in general are set out in Chapter 17 above. The offence is punishable on summary conviction by imprisonment for six months or a fine not exceeding the statutory maximum or both, and, on conviction on indictment, by imprisonment for 14 years or a fine or both. The offences are extremely broad and elevate what is sometimes a

---

[196] It should also be noted that arsonists may commonly be mentally unbalanced: see *Callandine* (1975) The Times, 3 Dec, CA, stating that it would be unwise to sentence for arson in the absence of a psychiatric report.

[197] See Flatley et al, *Crime in England and Wales 2009/10*, table 2.04.

[198] *Booth* [1999] Crim LR 144. *Booth* was distinguished in *Drayton* [2005] EWCA Crim 2013 D was charged under s 1(1) and (3) of the 1971 Act, but the word 'arson' did not appear in the information. The Court of Appeal held that the charge was in that context in the magistrates' court a valid charge. The use of the word 'arson' was described as desirable. The information alleged 'damage by fire' and that was synonymous with arson. It complied with the requirements of the Criminal Procedure Rules 2005, r 7.2 (now reproduced in Crim PR Rules 2010).

[199] In sentencing, the court has the more specific verdict of the jury: *Hoof* (1980) 72 Cr App R 126, CA. But cf *Flitter* [2001] Crim LR 328.

[200] cf *Parker* (1839) 9 C & P 45. No visible flame is necessary: *Stallion* (1833) 1 Mood CC 398.

[201] *Cooper (G) and Cooper (Y)* [1991] Crim LR 524, CA.

[202] By the Anti-terrorism, Crime and Security Act 2001, s 39(5)(b) and (6)(b).

trivial amount of damage (for example, a broken window caused in the course of a dispute with no racial background) into a racially or religiously aggravated offence because the offender also uses a racial or religious insult at the time of the offence.[203] The racial hostility must be roughly contemporaneous with the damage being caused.[204]

29.5 Threats to destroy or damage property

Section 2(1) of the Criminal Damage Act 1971 provides:

A person who without lawful excuse makes to another a threat, intending that that other would fear it would be carried out –

    (a) to destroy or damage any property belonging to that other or a third person; or

    (b) to destroy or damage his own property in a way which he knows is likely to endanger the life of that other or a third person; shall be guilty of an offence.

The offence is punishable by a maximum 10 years' imprisonment: s 4(2).

29.5.1 The conduct threatened

In order to constitute an offence under this section the conduct threatened must be conduct that would be an offence under s 1. D would commit the offence where, without lawful excuse, he threatened to destroy or damage the property of another (whether property of the person threatened or of a third party), or where he threatened to destroy or damage his own property in a way which he knows is likely to endanger the life of another (whether the life of a person threatened or the life of a third party).

If D is charged under s 2(1)(a) 'lawful excuse' has the meaning ascribed to it by s 5 so that D would not commit an offence where, for example, he threatens to shoot V's dog should he find it attacking his sheep.[205] But by s 5(1) the partial definition of lawful excuse in the section does not apply to an offence 'involving a threat by the person charged to destroy or damage property in a way which he knows is likely to endanger the life of another . . .' This does not mean that there cannot be a lawful excuse for an offence under s 2(1)(b), merely that the partial definition of lawful excuse in s 5 cannot apply.[206] Where D threatens to destroy property of another with intent to endanger life he would have to be charged under s 2(1)(a), and cannot be charged under s 2(1)(b). Curiously, it would seem that if in such a case D is charged under s 2(1)(a) there would be a lawful excuse if it appeared that he believed the owner would have consented to the threatened destruction or damage (s 5(2)(a)), but if he is charged under s 2(1)(b) it would not be a lawful excuse that he was threatening to destroy his own property. But the distinction can be of small practical importance: if D threatens to destroy V's property in order to endanger the life of X then it would be difficult to show that D honestly

---

[203] *DPP v M* [2005] Crim LR 392 and commentary; the offence has, of course, been used in circumstances in which it was entirely appropriate as where D spat and urinated on the Stephen Lawrence Memorial in London, *Guardian*, 20 July 1999.

[204] *Parry v DPP* [2004] EWHC 3112 (Admin) (20-minute delay between throwing nail varnish on V's door and calling him an Irish so-and-so). See also *Babbs* [2007] All ER (D) 383(Oct), where D's hostility although not contemporaneous, was evinced over a continuing period.

[205] See generally above, p 1025.

[206] As to what may therefore constitute a lawful excuse, see above, p 1022.

believed that V would have consented to the threatened destruction 'had [V] known of the destruction or damage *and its circumstances*', ie the endangerment of X's life.[207]

29.5.2 The threat

The threat may take any form. The Law Commission said:

There seems to be no good ground for limiting threats to written threats, for a telephonic threat, particularly if repeated, can cause more alarm in the recipient than any written threat. If the law is to be extended to cover telephonic threats, then logically there is no reason why it should not be extended to all threats, however made. The only limitation that needs to be imposed is that the threats should be intended to create a fear that what is threatened will be carried out.[208]

This last limitation needs to be imposed because the gist of the offence is the threat and, given that D intends that V should believe that the threat will be carried out, there ought to be no requirement that D himself should have intended to carry his threat into effect.

In *Cakmak*,[209] the accused had threatened to set fire to herself as a protest when on the London Eye. The charges were laid under s 2(1)(a), even though the threat was to set fire to herself. The Court of Appeal held that despite this the jury were entitled to find a threat of damage to property of another, because there was an implied threat to damage such property. Whether there is an implied threat is an objective question: would a reasonable person in the particular circumstances regard the words used as a threat to damage the London Eye?

If D intends that V would fear the threat would be carried out, D commits the offence only if, judged objectively, the nature of the threat would have caused V to believe that the threat would be carried out. The actual thoughts and fears of the person threatened are irrelevant (*Cakmak*). It would seem that the threat need not be a threat to do the damage immediately, but immediacy may be a relevant factor, along with other circumstances, in determining whether there is something that can be called a threat.

29.5.3 *Mens rea*

In *Cakmak*, the court held that whether an offence under s 2(1)(a) or (b) is charged, the jury must be satisfied that the defendant made a threat to another with the intention (recklessness not being a sufficient *mens rea*) that the other would fear that it would be carried out.

Section 2(1)(a) deals exclusively with the property of a person other than the defendant. It is only in relation to s 2(1)(b) that the prosecution must prove that the defendant knew that the damage or destruction threatened was likely, if carried out, to endanger the life of a person other than the defendant.

29.6 Possession offences

By s 3 of the Act:

A person who has anything in his custody or under his control intending without lawful excuse to use it or cause or permit another to use it –

  (a) to destroy or damage any property belonging to some other person; or

---

[207] Section 5(2)(a), emphasis added.
[208] Law Com No 29, para 55.
[209] [2002] 2 Cr App R 10, CA, [2002] Crim LR 581.

(b) to destroy or damage his own or the user's property in a way which he knows is likely to endanger the life of some other person;

shall be guilty of an offence.

The offence is punishable by imprisonment for a maximum 10 years: s 4(2).

In line with the offence of threatening under s 2, the possession of the thing must be for the purpose of committing an offence under s 1 of the Act. There is of course no need for the commission of an offence of destruction or damage, but there must be an intention to use the thing, or allow another to use it, for the purpose of committing what would be an offence under s 1.[210] Accordingly the same provisions apply in relation to lawful excuse as apply to charges under s 2.[211]

29.6.1 Custody or control

Although it is convenient to talk of this offence as one of possession, the section speaks only of custody or control.

Having regard to the difficulties inherent in the concept of possession, we prefer the idea of custody or control. These words are both to be found in the Statute Book, and together provide a better concept than 'possession', which is a technical term of some difficulty.[212]

It may well have been a wise decision to avoid the term 'possession', but what really helps to simplify the situation is the clear requirement for *mens rea*.

As the Law Commission observed:

Problems which may arise where a substance, such as a stick of gelignite, is slipped into a person's pocket without his knowledge will be wholly academic, because if that person has no knowledge of its presence he cannot have an intention to use it or permit or cause another to use it. If he has no intention to use it or permit or cause it to be used, he does not commit an offence...[213]

But there must be custody or control; a mere intention to use something to commit an offence of criminal damage will not suffice. D may be about to pick up stones from the road to throw through a shop window, but since at this stage he does not have custody or control of the stones he commits no offence under this provision. D need not of course be the owner of the thing in order to have custody or control of it, but he must have the charge of it. Where D is charged with permitting E to use the thing D must be in a position where, as against E, he might properly have prevented E from using it.

29.6.2 The things used

The section imports no limitation on the things which may be possessed with intent to commit criminal damage – 'anything' may do for the purpose.

The essential feature of the proposed offence is to be found not so much in the nature of the thing – for almost any everyday article, from a box of matches to a hammer or nail, can be used to destroy or damage property – as in the intention with which it is held.

---

[210] *Fancy* [1980] Crim LR 171, CC. For reform proposals, see LCCP 183, *Conspiracy and Attempts* (2007) para 16.61.

[211] Above, p 1022.

[212] Law Com No 29, para 59.

[213] ibid.

Clearly the nature of the thing may have significance in proving that D possessed the thing with intent to commit criminal damage (the possession of a box of matches may be one thing and the possession of a ton of dynamite quite another) but given that the intent can be proved the nature of the thing is immaterial.

At this point it may be noted that under s 6 of the Act a search warrant may be issued to a constable where it appears there is reasonable cause to believe that a person has anything in his control or custody or on his premises for the purpose of committing an offence under s 1. This power of search was explained by the Law Commission[214] as being parallel to the power to search for stolen goods under s 26 of the Theft Act 1968. On one view the power of search is a wide one since it extends to anything, but it is always limited by the requirement that there must be reasonable cause to believe that the thing has been used or is intended for use in committing an offence of criminal damage.[215] Powers of stop and search have also been extended to apply to this offence, in an attempt to combat graffiti.

29.6.3 *Mens rea*

The offence may be committed only where D intends to use, or cause or permit another to use, the thing to destroy or damage property. It is not enough that D realizes that the thing may be so used: he must intend or permit such use. But it is not necessary that D should intend an immediate use of the thing; the offence is aimed at proscribing what is essentially a preparatory act and it is therefore enough that D possesses the thing with the necessary intent even though he contemplates its actual use of the thing at some time in the future. And it would also seem to be clear that a conditional intent (an intention to use the thing to cause damage should it prove necessary) will suffice.[216]

29.7 Kindred offences

In keeping with the aim of codification,[217] the Criminal Damage Act 1971 contains, as near as may be, the whole of the law relating to damage to property. The Act abolished the common law offence of arson, repealed most of the provisions of the Malicious Damage Act 1861, repealed the Dockyards Protection Act 1772, and a large number of statutory provisions containing miscellaneous offences of damage to property.

But the Criminal Damage Act leaves untouched the Explosive Substances Act 1883.[218] The Law Commission had at first planned to repeal s 2 (causing an explosion likely to endanger life or to cause serious injury to property) and s 3 (possessing explosives with intent to endanger life or cause serious injury to property, and doing an act to cause an explosion likely to endanger life or cause serious injury to property) since these might easily have been brought within the scheme of the Criminal Damage Act. But in the end the Law Commission did not do this because it was felt that the Explosive Substances Act belonged to the area of public order offences, and its replacement should be considered in the context of a review of offences relating to public order. This means that on given facts there may be an offence both under the

---

[214] Paper No 29, Appendix A, notes to cl 6.

[215] But note the concerns about the breadth of s 26 expressed in *Keegan v UK* [2006] ECHR 764.

[216] *Buckingham* (1976) 63 Cr App R 159, CA; cf *Bentham* [1973] QB 357, [1972] 3 All ER 271, CA.

[217] See above, p 30.

[218] Proceedings for a crime under this Act shall not be instituted except by or with the consent of the A-G: Explosive Substances Act 1883, s 7(1).

Criminal Damage Act and the Explosive Substances Act, and it should be noted that there are differences in relation to the *mens rea* that has to be established.

The Criminal Damage Act did not repeal the following provisions of the Malicious Damage Act 1861: s 35 (placing wood etc on rail lines or obstructing signals with intent to obstruct or overturn any engine);[219] s 36 (obstructing railway engines);[220] and the retention of these offences made necessary the further retention of general provisions of the Malicious Damage Act relating to malice (s 58) and jurisdiction (s 72). It will be seen that none of these offences would necessarily (or even ordinarily) involve damage to property, though the ultimate aim may be to cause damage to property. Frequently such acts might amount to an attempt to commit criminal damage, but in so far as the acts might be merely preparatory these provisions render the preparatory acts criminal.

Nor does the Act repeal offences of damage arising under other legislation where the liability for the damage may be grounded in negligence or where there is strict liability for the damage. In particular cases, there may be thought valid policy reasons for imposing criminal liability for damage to property caused negligently, or even for imposing strict liability for offences of damage to property.[221] These offences are perhaps best considered in relation to a review of criminal liability for negligence and a review of strict liability.

29.8 Mode of trial and sentence

While the maximum punishments provided by the Act for offences of damage tried on indictment (broadly, 10 years for the simple offence, and life imprisonment for aggravated offences) may seem high, this was done merely to provide for the worst sort of case within each class and it was not intended in any way to alter previous sentencing practice. The Act provides for summary trial of offences under ss 1(1), 2 and 3, and in practice most offences will be so tried.[222]

---

[219] *See Brown* [2002] EWCA Crim 1885 for a recent application of s 35.

[220] See *Jones* [2006] EWCA Crim 2942 for a recent application of s 36.

[221] eg, s 85(1) of the Postal Services Act 2000 creates an offence to send by post a postal packet which encloses any creature, article or thing of any kind which is likely to injure other postal packets in course of their transmission by post or any person engaged in the business of a postal operator.

[222] As to summary trial of offences of damage when the value does not exceed £5,000, see above. As to offences of damage triable either way see the Magistrates' Courts Act 1980, Sch 2. The Magistrates' Courts Act 1980, s 22, affects mode of trial but has no effect on the classification of criminal damage as an 'offence triable either way': *Fennell* [2000] 2 Cr App R 318, CA approved in *Alden* [2002] 2 Cr App R (S) 74, CA; *Tuplin* [2009] EWCA Crim 1572 It can therefore be charged as an attempt in the magistrates' court where value is less than £5,000. Particular difficulties have arisen over evaluating the 'market' value of eg GM crops, *R (on the Application of the DPP) v Prestatyn Magistrates' Court* [2002] All ER (D) 421 (May). If under £5,000, criminal damage is, in practice, treated as summary only, although it remains triable either way.

30
Computer misuse offences

30.1 Introduction[1]

The impact of computer technology on society has been profound. From simple beginnings in arithmetical calculations it has spawned immense data retrieval systems; systems controlling traffic by land, sea and air; systems indispensable to the functioning of industry, healthcare, education, banking and commerce. All is to the common good or nearly all to the common good because, inevitably, some will use the technology for anti-social purposes. These may range from simple 'nosey-parkering', as where the hacker gains access to computer systems just for the fun of it (perhaps to demonstrate his computing ability), or for industrial espionage, or to perpetrate frauds, or disrupt systems with viruses, worms or Trojan horses[2] with serious commercial and possibly life-threatening consequences.

The law before the Computer Misuse Act 1990 could deal with some of these problems.[3] Appropriating property belonging to another is just as much theft[4] because it is done not by picking a pocket but by causing a computer to debit one account and to credit another. Should someone cause death or injury not with a blunt instrument but by interfering with a traffic control system, he would be equally liable to conviction for an offence against the person.

But there were gaps in the protection offered by the criminal law. The Law Commission addressed itself to these in a Working Paper published in 1988.[5] At that stage the Law Commission was primarily concerned with unauthorized access to computing systems (hacking) though it noted other problems such as the inapplicability of deception offences to computers.[6] The problem with hacking was that nosey-parkering (gaining unauthorized access to the correspondence, personal details, business records of another) is not generally an offence; invasion of privacy and industrial espionage[7] are not, as such, offences. Could a special case be made for criminalizing nosey-parkering by way of hacking into a computer

---

[1] See I Walden, *Computer Crimes and Digital Investigations* (2007) Ch 3.D; M Wasik, *Crime and the Computer* (1991) and 'The Computer Misuse Act 1990' [1990] Crim LR 767; Smith, *Property Offences* (1994) Ch 11; I Lloyd, *Information Technology Law* (4th edn, 2004) Ch 13. See also N MacEwan, 'The Computer Misuse Act 1990: Lessons from its Past and Predictions for its Future' [2008] Crim LR 955. See also www.cps.gov.uk/legal/a_to_c/computer_misuse_act_1990.

[2] For a comparative analysis of legal regulation of viruses, see M Klang, 'A Critical Look at the Regulation of Computer Viruses' (2003) 11 Int J of Law and IT 162.

[3] See C Tapper, 'Computer Crime: Scotch Mist?' [1987] Crim LR 4.

[4] cf the problem of deceiving a machine, discussed above, p 885.

[5] Working Paper No 110, *Computer Misuse*. See M Wasik, 'Law Reform Proposals on Computer Misuse' [1989] Crim LR 257.

[6] cf the similar problems in relation to forgery, above, Ch 28, and the discussion in the Fraud Act, Ch 23. On hacking see recently A Nehaluddin, 'Hackers' Criminal Behaviour and Laws Related to Hacking' (2009) 15 Computer and Telecommunications Law Review 135.

[7] See Consultation Paper No 150, *Legislating the Criminal Code: Misuse of Trade Secrets* (1997) and see J Hull, 'Stealing Secrets: A Review of the Law Commission's Consultation Paper on the Misuse of Trade Secrets' [1998] Crim LR 246.

system? The Law Commission thought that it could and it was overwhelmingly supported by commentators on the Working Paper.

The proposal in the Law Commission's Working Paper to criminalize unauthorized access was thus generally applauded. But before the publication of its final Report,[8] the Commission conducted further discussions with computer and software manufacturers and with computer users in banking and commerce. These groups convinced the Commission of the need not only for an offence of unauthorized access (hacking) but also for two further offences of: (i) unauthorized access with intent to commit or facilitate the commission of further offences and (ii) of unauthorized modification of computer material. These were enacted in the 1990 Act and have been a source of many problems.[9]

Within a decade or so of enactment commentators began to suggest that the 1990 Act had become rather dated, being drafted at a time when computers were relatively unsophisticated and the internet was in its infancy.[10] The pressure to extend the scope of the Act increased.[11] The Parliamentary All Party Internet Group reviewed and reported on the Act and made recommendations for reform.[12] The group concluded that many of the perceived problems with the Act actually stemmed from 'widespread ignorance of the current law'.[13] One particular concern was that the Act should be capable of dealing with 'denial of service attacks'[14] which lead to commercial websites being rendered unavailable to legitimate users.[15] The courts interpreted the offences in the 1990 Act as capable of applying to a denial of service attack,[16] but it was widely recognized that a more specific offence to tackle that mischief was desirable. Further pressure for reform also derived from the international treaty obligations.[17] In 2006, the Police and Justice Act made amendments to the 1990 Act offences and introduced additional offences related to computer misuse. These were further amended by those in the Serious Crime Act 2007.[18]

---

[8] Report No 186, *Computer Misuse* (1989) Cmnd 819.

[9] See MacEwan above.

[10] See, eg, S Fafinski, 'Access Denied: Computer Misuse on an Era of Technological Change' (2006) 70 J Crim L 424.

[11] Though not all were in favour of reform, cf C Holder, 'Staying One Step Ahead of the Criminals' (2002) 10(3) IT Law 17.

[12] Discussed by G Fearon, 'All Party Internet (APIG) Report on the Computer Misuse Act' (2004) 15 Comps and Law 36.

[13] Para 23.

[14] A Denial-of-Service (DoS) attack occurs 'when a deliberate attempt is made to stop a machine from performing its usual activities by having another computer create large amounts of specious traffic. The traffic may be valid requests made in an overwhelming volume or specially crafted protocol fragments that cause the serving machine to tie up significant resources to no useful purpose. In a Distributed Denial-of-Service (DDoS) attack a large number of remote computers are orchestrated into attacking a target at the same time' (APIG, para 56). These are extremely common at over 4,000 reported instances a week. See further Walden, *Computer Crimes and Digital Investigations*, para 3.284 et seq.

[15] A Private Members' Bill – the Computer Misuse (Amendment) Bill 2000 – sought to introduce a new offence of causing or intending to cause a degradation, failure or other impairment of function of a computerized system. The offence was aimed at protecting computer systems from denial of service attacks.

[16] In *DPP v Lennon* [2006] EWHC 1201 (Admin) discussed below.

[17] See especially the Convention on Cybercrime, CETS No 185 (2001) discussed by S Room, 'Criminalising Cybercrime' (2004) 154 NLJ 950. See further internet crime forum at www.internetcrimeforum.org.uk; European Convention at www.eurim.org/consult/e-crime/dec03/ECS_WP6_web_031209.htm. See also I Walden, 'Harmonising Computer Crime Laws in Europe' (2004) 12 European J of Crime Criminal Law and Criminal Justice 321; Walden, *Computer Crimes and Digital Investigations*, Ch 5 on the broader issues of international harmonization.

[18] Section 61 of the 2007 Act.

This chapter will focus on the offences created by the Computer Misuse Act 1990 as amended.[19] Analysis of the growing problem of what has become known as 'cybercrime' – offences against the person or property or of cyberobscenity – lies beyond the scope of this work.[20] Similarly, the offences under the Data Protection Act 1998 such as that of knowingly or recklessly obtaining or disclosing personal data or procuring its obtaining without the consent of the data controller,[21] are not examined here. Nor are the offences of making, possessing, distributing, etc indecent images of children.[22]

It seems safe to predict that the criminal law will continue to face difficulties in dealing with those individuals who choose to exploit the opportunities which computers, and more specifically the internet, provide for causing a wide range of harmful, or indeed illegal, activity: fraud, paedophilia, espionage, piracy, money laundering, market abuse, etc.[23]

It is difficult to assess the number of offences committed.[24] Businesses are reluctant to report offences against them as it reveals weakness in their security and might deter customers. It has been suggested that prosecutions are declining because the legislation is so complex.[25]

30.2 Unauthorized access to computer material

By s 1 of the Computer Misuse Act 1990 as amended:

(1) A person is guilty of an offence if –

    (a) he causes a computer to perform any function with intent to secure access to any program or data held in any computer;[26]

    (b) the access he intends to secure is unauthorised; and

    (c) he knows at the time when he causes the computer to perform the function that that is the case.

---

[19] See recently MacEwan [2008] Crim LR 955.

[20] See, in particular, Walden, *Computer Crimes and Digital Investigations*, Ch 2; the special edition of the Criminal Law Review [1998], edited by DS Wall; R Essen, 'Cybercrime: A Growing Problem' (2002) 66 J Crim L 269; O Ward, 'Information Technology Watch Out, There's a Hacker About' (2000) 150 NLJ 1812; D Thomas and BD Loader, *Cybercrime* (2000); Y Akdeniz, 'Cybercrime', in *E-Commerce Law & Regulation Encyclopaedia* (2003); M Wong, 'Cybertrespass and Unauthorized Access' (2007) 15 Int J of Law and IT 90. See also A Guinchard 'Crime in Virtual Worlds: The Limits of Criminal Law' (2010) 24 Int Rev of Law Computers & Technology 175 considering 'crimes' committed in virtual worlds, including: (1) the 'theft' of virtual property; (2) the 'murder', 'assault' or 'rape' of an avatar; (3) harassment by means of virtual world technology; and (4) extreme or child pornography using avatars.

[21] See s 55 of the Data Protection Act 1998 as amended by s 78 of the Criminal Justice and Immigration Act 2008.

[22] See generally P Rook and R Ward, *Sexual Offences Law and Practice* (4th edn, 2010) Ch 8.

[23] See, for discussion, S Morris, *The Future of Netcrime Now: Part 1 – Threats and Challenges* (2004) Home Office Online Report 62/04. On fraud, see A Doig, *Fraud* (2006) 62–63.

[24] See for 2007: www.publications.parliament.uk/pa/cm200809/cmhansrd/cm090916/text/90916w0015. htm#09091614000131.

[25] See www.computing.co.uk/ctg/news/1835833/computer-misuse-act-prosecution-falling.

[26] The Police and Justice Act 2006, s 35 would, if implemented, have extended the offence to include cases where D enabled another to gain access. It was designed to ensure compliance with the European Union Framework Decision on Attacks Against Information Systems, adopted by the European Union and Justice and Home Affairs Council of Ministers on 24 Feb 2005 (http://register.consilium.eu.int/pdf/en/04/st15/st15010. en04.pdf).

(2) The intent a person has to have to commit an offence under this section need not be directed at –

  (a) any particular program or data;

  (b) a program or data of any particular kind; or

  (c) a program or data held in any particular computer.

The offence carries a maximum sentence of two years' imprisonment on indictment.[27]

The idea behind this offence, in effect, is to close the door in the hacker's face. The offence is committed even if the hacker has no sinister purpose and is no more than a nosey-parker.[28] The essence of the offence under s 1 is causing a computer to perform a function with intent to secure unauthorized access. No particular computer needs to be targeted by D and it is enough that he is out fishing without a licence. Indeed, it is enough that he sets out to fish without a licence.

The scope of the offence prompts the question why it should be an offence to access files held in the office computer and not an offence to access paper files held in the filing cabinet.[29] The Law Commission thought it best to close the door on the hacker altogether in order to deter those who *might* be contemplating fraud, or who *might* go on to commit some further offence or who *might*, because of his skills, be recruited by others with more sinister motives. With respect, these are not convincing reasons; conduct is not properly penalized because it *might* lead to the commission of an offence. One reason for criminalizing such conduct is that the proprietor of the system which is accessed by an unauthorized user may be put to considerable expense to repair his defences.[30] Of course the proprietor of paper files incurs expense repairing his defences if an intruder breaks into his office to look through the files. There are, however, other important differences between the computer and the paper files: the intruder in the latter case must break into the office; he cannot access the files, as he can in the case of computer-held material, from a distant part of the country or as is frequently the case, from the other side of the world.[31] Computer systems are always vulnerable to the determined hacker. In a world that is increasingly dependent on computers, and the integrity of computer systems, it appears entirely right that the criminal law should be employed to discourage the hacker.

30.2.1 *Actus reus*

The *actus reus* consists of causing a computer to perform any function.

30.2.1.1 Computer

The Act does not define 'computer'. The Law Commission took the view that to have done so would be 'foolish'. Perhaps so, but a court, though it might be foolish to attempt a comprehensive definition, may be required to decide whether a particular contrivance is a computer. Most obviously, a computer is something that computes, but computers have long since done

---

[27] There are very few convictions under the Act. Between 1990 and 2006 there were 161: see MacEwan (above) p 962. The offence is underreported as organizations do not want to publicize failings in their security.

[28] The offence was to be extended by the Police and Justice Act to include those whose intention is to enable someone else to secure unauthorized access to a computer or to enable himself to secure unauthorized access to a computer at some later time. Those provisons were prospectively repealed by the Serious Crime Act 2007.

[29] Some regard the Act as overbroad and suggest that s 1 ought to be limited to conduct which breaches a 'security measure': S Room, 'Criminalising Cybercrime' (2004) 154 NLJ 950.

[30] The Law Com instanced a case where the restoration of a system following unauthorized access required 10,000 hours of the time of skilled staff. See recently, *Baker* [2011] EWCA Crim 928 (£ 300,000 cost to employer).

[31] On jurisdictional issues, see M Hirst, *Jurisdiction and the Ambit of the Criminal Law* (2003) 193–196.

more than merely mathematical calculations and may be used to store other information which can be processed for a wide variety of purposes ranging from legal research (Lexis and Westlaw), traffic control or manufacturing purposes. It is tentatively suggested that the defining characteristics of a computer are the abilities of the appliance (i) to store information; (ii) to retrieve the information so stored; and perhaps most importantly (iii) to process that information. Hence the abacus and the slide-rule are not computers;[32] they can be used to make calculations but they have no 'memory' and they cannot themselves process information.[33]

It is submitted that it is insufficient that a machine is programmed to perform a function or number of functions. A washing machine may be programmed to perform several varieties of wash but is not, on this view, a computer; it can only obey instructions and not process them. A computer can select a course of action on the basis of instructions given or information received. A machine which ensures that traffic lights will show red or green at stated intervals is not a computer; a machine which varies the intervals in response to information about traffic density is.

But it may be that a wider definition is felt desirable. A computer may be thought of as any machine which responds to signals (now usually electronic) to perform programmed functions. On this view, the unauthorized user of the washing machine or microwave oven would commit the offence under s 1. But such machines are not sold as, nor are they considered to be, computers. The appropriate charge for the unauthorized user of a dishwasher or microwave oven would appear to be the dishonest abstraction of electricity contrary to s 13 of the Theft Act 1968 rather than unauthorized access to computer material under s 1 of the Computer Misuse Act.

The offence is committed where D causes *any* computer to perform a function. Although often the offence is committed remotely via another computer, D also commits the offence by causing the target computer to perform a function directly.[34]

30.2.1.2 Performing a function

Once the machine in question is proved to be a computer, the *actus reus* is complete if it is caused to perform 'any' function. It is accordingly enough to switch on the computer though it may be difficult to prove *mens rea* if this is all that D has done. The strict requirements of proof are anecdotally reported to present difficulties in prosecution under the Act. It is not enough merely to view data that is already displayed on the monitor, but it is sufficient that D has, for example, accessed the internet by hitting the back key or return key when a computer has been left logged on to a university network by the previous user.[35] Expert evidence will not always be necessary to establish that a computer performed a function.[36]

---

[32] But not because these are mechanical; computers are now electronic but Babbage's computer was no less a computer because it was mechanical. See for detailed arguments about definition Walden, *Computer Crimes and Digital Investigations*, paras 3.217–3.227.

[33] The Convention on Cybercrime uses the term 'computer system'. It defines a computer as a device that runs a 'program' to process 'data' but does not define these other terms. APIG concluded that there had been no difficulties with the (lack of) definition of any of the words in the Act. The Home Office reported that they had 'never come across a case' where the courts had failed to use a 'broad definition' (para 15). It recommended retaining the current approach.

[34] *A-G's Reference (No 1 of 1991)* [1993] QB 94.

[35] See *Ellis v DPP* [2001] EWHC 362 (Admin), where D argued unsuccessfully that such conduct was akin to reading a discarded newspaper.

[36] ibid.

30.2.2 *Mens rea*

D must cause a computer to perform a function (i) with *intent* to secure access to any program or data held in any computer, and (ii) *knowing* that the access he intends to secure is unauthorized.

30.2.2.1 Intent to secure access

Intention should, it is submitted, be interpreted consistently with other offences as discussed above.[37] Recklessness is insufficient.

By s 17, 'access' is widely defined and includes any 'use' of a computer, copying or moving of a file, altering or erasing data. There is no need to prove an intention in relation to any particular program. In practice it will be common to establish that D has in fact secured access as so defined in order to establish *mens rea* but this is not a necessary element of the offence: it is complete on causing a computer to perform any function (such as switching it on) with intent to secure access.

30.2.2.2 Knowing it is unauthorized access

D must 'know'[38] that the access he intends to secure is unauthorized. By s 17(5), D's access is unauthorized if:

(i)   he is not himself entitled to control access of the kind in question to the program or data; *and*

(ii) he does not have consent to access of the kind in question to the program or data from any person who is so entitled.[39]

A person does not commit an offence where he is authorized to secure access of the kind in question to the program, but where he does so for some unauthorized purpose. Police computer operators who extracted details of the registration and ownership of cars for their private purposes were not guilty of this offence,[40] though they may have been guilty of an offence under the Data Protection Act 1984.[41] If D believes, however unreasonably, that he is entitled to control access or that his access is authorized by someone entitled to secure access, he cannot know that his access is unauthorized. Control in this context presumably means: has the power to 'authorise and forbid'.[42] More difficult is the case where D is unsure whether he is entitled to control access or, much more likely, he is unsure of the extent of his authorization to access a computer, but decides nonetheless to access the computer without checking on the nature and extent of his authorization.[43] If, as will usually be the case, D could readily ascertain the nature and extent of his authority but chooses not to do so and decides to take the risk that his access is authorized, and his access is in fact unauthorized, it may be that he does not *know* his access is unauthorized but this is only because he does not want to know. It is submitted that wilful blindness of this kind is enough to constitute knowledge. At the other

---

[37] Ch 5.

[38] See generally, above, p 128.

[39] Program includes part of a program: s 17(10).

[40] *DPP v Bignell* [1998] 1 Cr App R 1, [1998] Crim LR 53, DC. Criticized in P Spink, 'Misuse of Police Computers' (1997) 42 Juridical Review 219.

[41] See now the Data Protection Act 1998.

[42] *R v Bow Street Metropolitan Stipendiary Magistrate, ex p Government of the USA* [2000] 2 AC 216 at 224; cf *Stanford* [2006] EWCA Crim 258, [2006] 2 Cr App R 5 (considering the term 'control' in the offence of unlawful interception under the Regulation of Investigatory Powers Act 2000).

[43] This gave rise to difficulty in some early high-profile prosecutions: see P Davies, 'Computer Misuse' (1995) 145 NLJ 1776.

extreme, the fact that it crosses D's mind that he might possibly be exceeding his authority would not suffice for knowledge.

The offence may be committed where D has authority to use a computer, but not a particular program.[44] It may be committed though D is authorized to access one computer, computer X, if he does so to access another, computer Y, to which he does not have authorized access. The offence is complete when D has accessed computer X with intent to access computer Y.

Equally, the offence may be committed when D has limited authority to access the computer and he exceeds his authorization. An employee of American Express committed the offence when, having authority to access only specified accounts, she accessed other accounts.[45]

Access of any kind by any person to any program or data held in a computer is unauthorized according to s 17(5)[46] if:

(a) he is not himself entitled to control access of the kind in question to the program or data; and

(b) he does not have consent to access by him of the kind in question to the program or data from any person who is so entitled.

The offence requires both (i) that the access intended by D is in fact unauthorized; and (ii) that D knows that his access is unauthorized. If D believes his access is unauthorized when it is in fact authorized he does not commit the offence. Since the offence is now triable either way, he can be convicted of an attempt.

30.3 Unauthorized access with intent to commit or facilitate further offences

By s 2 of the Act:

(1) A person is guilty of an offence under this section if he commits an offence under section 1 above ['the unauthorized access offence'] with intent –

(a) to commit an offence to which this section applies; or

(b) to facilitate the commission of such an offence (whether by himself or by any other person);

and the offence he intends to commit or facilitate is referred to below in this section as the further offence.

The further offences to which the section applies are those for which the sentence is fixed by law; or for which a person over 21 *with no previous convictions* may be sentenced to imprisonment for a term of five years.[47] The offence requires proof of the s 1 offence together with an intent to commit the further offence or to facilitate the commission of such an offence by another. By s 2(3) it is immaterial whether the further offence is to be committed at the time of access or on some future occasion. For example, D gains unauthorized access to a computer in order to copy V's bank details so he can perpetrate a fraud if the opportunity arises.

---

[44] See *Ellis v DPP* [2001] EWHC 362 (Admin).

[45] *Bow Street Magistrate, ex p Government of USA* [2000] 2 AC 216, [2000] 1 Cr App R 61, HL, disapproving a *dictum* in *Bignell*, above, see commentary at [1999] Crim LR 971.

[46] Section 17(5) as inserted by the Police and Justice Act 2006, s 52, Sch 14, para 29(1), (4) (in force in relation to England and Wales from 1 October 2008: SI 2008/2503) applies to s 3.

[47] Or might be so sentenced but for the restrictions imposed by s 33 of the Magistrates' Courts Act 1980: Criminal Justice and Court Services Act 2000, s 74.

There is no requirement that the further offences will involve the use of a computer. The further offence need not be committed. In practical terms the offences most likely to be intended or facilitated by D will be offences against property involving dishonesty but s 2 is not restricted to those offences.[48] Arguably, at the time the 1990 Act was enacted, the Theft Acts (with an extra offence to deal with deception of machines[49]) would probably have been adequate to deal with this problem where the further offences were ones of dishonesty.[50] This was how the Law Commission initially viewed the matter when drafting the 1990 Act but it had second thoughts and concluded that it would be preferable to extend the criminal law to the hacker before he had committed a substantive offence under the Theft Acts or had reached the stage of an attempt. Like s 1, s 2 of the 1990 Act is accordingly aimed at preparatory conduct. Thus, to take examples given by the Law Commission, the hacker who, with intent to steal, is searching for the password to enter an account might not be guilty of an attempt to steal, and the hacker who seeks confidential information in order to blackmail would clearly not be guilty of an attempt to blackmail.[51] Both, however, would commit the substantive offence under s 2. It is not just the hacker in the usual sense who is caught by this offence; the employee who accesses bank data and discloses those to accomplices to enable them to commit frauds commits the offence.[52]

The Law Commission thought that the s 2 offence bore 'some relation to an attempt'[53] in that the ulterior offence needs only to be intended and not completed and accordingly s 2(4) provides that the offence may be committed even though commission of the ulterior offence is impossible. It is submitted that this provision is unnecessary but it may save argument. It will apply if D accesses V's computer to obtain his bank details, but unknown to D, that bank account was already closed by V.

Since the offence under s 2 is a substantive offence, there may, in turn, be a conspiracy, attempt or assisting and encouraging to commit the offence. These would represent extremely broad offences. D could agree with E that they would in the future access V's computer to gain information that they would, yet further in the future, use to perpetrate a crime. Given the preparatory nature of the offence, however, there is little scope for the operation of attempt.[54]

The offence is triable either way and on conviction on indictment the offence carries a maximum five years' imprisonment.

30.4 Unauthorized acts with intent to impair or recklessness as to impairment of a computer

Section 3 of the Act, as substituted by s 36 of the Police and Justice Act 2006 provides:

(1) A person is guilty of an offence if –

    (a) he does any unauthorised act in relation to a computer;

    (b) at the time when he does the act he knows that it is unauthorised; and

  either subsection (2) or subsection (3) below applies.

---

[48] A traffic or air traffic control system might be entered with intent to injure or even kill. Hacking with intent to commit treason is, perhaps, somewhat fanciful.

[49] As now in the Fraud Act 2006.

[50] See the recognition of the availability of the charge in the case of *Holmes* [2005] Crim LR 229. The APIG endorsed the need for a new fraud offence to deal with this problem (para 35) and recommended further reform on the misuse of trade secrets so as to develop a suitable framework to adequately criminalize the unlawful 'theft of data'.

[51] As in *Zezev* [2002] Crim LR 648.

[52] *Delamare* [2003] All ER (D) 127 (Feb).

[53] Law Com No 186, para 3.58.

[54] Would D be liable under s 2 by reaching for the computer power switch?

(2) This subsection applies if the person intends by doing the act –

    (a) to impair the operation of any computer;

    (b) to prevent or hinder access to any program or data held in any computer; [or[55]]

    (c) to impair the operation of any such program or the reliability of any such data; [...[56]]

    (d) to enable any of the things mentioned in paragraphs (a) to (c) above to be done

(3) This subsection applies if the person is reckless as to whether the act will do any of the things mentioned in paragraphs (a) to (c) of subsection (2) above.

(4) The intention referred to in subsection (2) above, or the recklessness referred to in subsection (3) above, need not relate to –

    (a) any particular computer;

    (b) any particular program or data; or

    (c) a program or data of any particular kind.

(5) In this section –

    (a) a reference to doing an act includes a reference to causing an act to be done;

    (b) 'act' includes a series of acts;

    (c) a reference to impairing, preventing or hindering something includes a reference to doing so temporarily.

On conviction on indictment the maximum sentence is 10 years' imprisonment or a fine or both; on summary conviction 12 months or a fine up to the statutory maximum or both: s 3(6). This is a significant increase in the sentencing powers from the original s 3.

30.4.1 Background to the s 3 offence[57]

It is, and remains, an offence under the Criminal Damage Act 1971 to destroy or damage a computer or its software as by, for example, taking a hammer and causing damage by breaking them. Where there is physical damage to tangible property there is no problem in using the 1971 Act. What though of the case where there is damage to tangible property, but that damage cannot be perceived by the senses? Say D interferes with programs so as to render the computer incapable, or less capable, of carrying out the functions the programs are designed to perform. This may be done without causing any physical damage that can be perceived by the senses.

In *Cox v Riley*,[58] it was held that D was guilty of criminal damage where he erased the program from a plastic circuit card which operated a saw to cut wood to programmed designs. D's counsel argued that the program was not 'property of a tangible nature' within the Criminal Damage Act. In this he was no doubt right but, in the view of the court, it failed to take account of the fact that D was charged not with damaging the program but with damaging the plastic card. And in *Whitely*,[59] it was held that D was properly convicted of criminal damage to computer discs where he gained unauthorized access to an academic computer system and by altering their magnetic particles caused them to delete and add files.

---

[55] As inserted by the Serious Crime Act 2007, s 61(3)(a)(i).

[56] The Serious Crime Act repealed s 3(2)(d) as such conduct will be covered by the offences under that Act of encouraging or assisting the commission of an offence or offences, above Ch 13.

[57] See, generally on the old offence, Y Akdeniz, 'Section 3 of the Computer Misuse Act 1990 – An Antidote for Computer Viruses' [1996] Web JCLI.

[58] (1986) 83 Cr App R 54, DC.

[59] [1991] Crim LR 436, CA.

His counsel's argument that only intangible information on the discs had been damaged was rejected; the discs had been damaged because their usefulness had been impaired.

These decisions might be viewed as bringing computer misuse, because of its obvious potential for harm, within the Criminal Damage Act by procrustean means,[60] but it is submitted that both decisions were defensible under the 1971 Act. The plastic circuit card in *Cox v Riley*, though it may not have been rendered useless and could have been reprogrammed to perform its original function, was temporarily unable to perform the function it was designed to perform. Though the disc was not damaged, it was rendered incapable of performing one of its programs and the case seems indistinguishable from *Fisher*.[61] Similarly, in *Whitely*,[62] the computer, though not itself damaged, had been rendered inoperable by tampering with its control mechanisms, namely the programs on the discs. That the discs could be restored is irrelevant since temporary impairment suffices.

The Law Commission, however, took the view that the problem of computer misuse should be tackled more directly. It might have been possible to deal with the problem by amending the Criminal Damage Act to include interference with data and programs[63], but the Commission decided on the creation of a new offence for two reasons. One was that 'the theoretical difficulties posed by applying the concept of damage to intangible property such as data or programs'[64] would render the law unacceptably uncertain. The other was that criminal damage may be committed recklessly[65] and the Commission did not think that the new offence should extend to a person who recklessly modified computer material.[66] In addition, as will appear, the Commission sought to clarify the relationship between the modification offence under s 3 of the Computer Misuse Act 1990 and the offence of criminal damage under the Criminal Damage Act.

The s 3 offence, in its narrower form before the recent amendments to the 1990 Act, was restricted to modifications of the computer. That form of the offence was nevertheless construed very broadly by the courts. In *Zevez*,[67] it was held that if a computer is caused to record information (an email) which shows that it comes from one person, when it in fact comes from someone else, that manifestly affects its reliability.[68] This was seen as a significant extension of the offence. The email tells a lie about itself, but it does not affect the reliability of other data on the computer. The court further extended the ambit of the offence by holding that denial of service attacks were also caught. In *DPP v Lennon*,[69] D used a 'mail-bombing' program to send five million emails to his former employer. The Divisional Court, disagreeing with the District Judge, held that D had 'caused an unauthorised modification' by adding data. The owner of a computer able to receive emails would ordinarily be taken to have consented to the sending of emails to his computer. However, such implied consent was not without limits, and the consent did not cover emails that had been sent not for the purpose of communication with the owner but to interrupt his computer system. The court suggested that this could be

---

[60] See Wasik, *Crime and the Computer*, 137–145.

[61] (1865) LR 1 CCR 7, above, p 1014.

[62] [1991] Crim LR 436, CA.

[63] Following the amendment by the Police and Justice Act 2006, s 10(5) of the Criminal Damage Act 1971 is amended to exclude 'modification of the contents of a computer' from the definition of damage unless the effect is to impair its physical condition.

[64] Law Com No 186, para 3.62.

[65] The new s 3 does extend to recklessness.

[66] See below, p 1056.

[67] [2002] Crim LR 648.

[68] D had placed in the files of a computer a bogus email purporting to come from a person which it had not. This was held to have caused a modification of the computer within s 17(7): 'A modification of the contents of any computer takes place if... any... data is added to its contents...'

[69] [2006] EWHC 1201 (Admin). See also the comment by S Fafinski (2006) 72 J Crim L 474.

tested by asking whether if D had rung his employer she would have consented to the receipt of five million emails. The new substituted s 3, as above, ensures that denial of service attacks are caught by the section,[70] and puts beyond doubt *some* of the concerns raised in the *Lennon* case.[71]

30.4.2 The new s 3 offence

There must be an unauthorized act in relation to a computer. The *extended* meaning of 'authorized' is set out in s 17(8). The impairment of the computer, program, data, etc need not actually occur. The offence is complete on the unauthorized act with intent or recklessness to achieve that impairment etc.

Essentially, s 3 is concerned with the sabotaging or impairing of computer systems by any act or series of acts specified in s 3(2). The most obvious instances will be by transferring viruses,[72] Trojan horses or worms to computer systems or by corrupting websites.[73] It is sufficient that the conduct would prevent or hinder the access of others – as, for example, by a denial of service attack or mail bomb attack which incapacitates a server. There is no longer a requirement of erasure of data or modification of anything and in that respect the offence is made much wider than as originally enacted. The concept of impairment might prove difficult to apply in some cases – how much slower must D intend the program to operate before it is properly said to be impaired? Unauthorized use may be sufficient if, for example, D intends or is reckless as to causing impairment to the reliability of the data. Causing a computer to debit V's bank account and credit D's[74] is sufficient because the data concerning V's account is now unreliable. The impairment intended or about which D is reckless need only be temporary. Again, this is a significant extension of the offence.[75]

The offence requires:

(1) that D intends is by the unauthorized act to bring about one of the consequences listed in s 3(2) (impairment, etc) or is recklessness as to whether such consequences would occur; and,

(2) knowledge that the act by which he intends or is reckless about bringing about the impairment etc is unauthorized. The knowledge must relate to the unauthorized nature of the act from which impairment is intended. It is not necessary to prove knowledge of the unauthorized nature of the impairment (as was the case with the old form of s 3 which required knowledge as to the unauthorized modification).

Intention should bear its ordinary meaning.[76] Recklessness should be understood in its subjective sense as defined in *G*.[77] The ability to commit the offence recklessly represents a significant extension by the 2006 Act. In its original form, recklessness was insufficient because the Law Commission[78] endorsed a strict *mens rea* requirement expressing concern that people could inadvertently modify the contents of a computer.

---

[70] The amendment ensure that English law complies with Art 3 of the EU Framework Decision on *Attacks Against Information Systems.*

[71] It does not deal with challenges based on consent.

[72] See, eg, *Vallor* [2004] 1 Cr App R (S) 54, spreading the third most virulent virus in the world.

[73] See, eg, *Lindesay* [2002] 1 Cr App R (S) 370, disgruntled sacked employee corrupting firm's website.

[74] cf *Thompson* [1984] 3 All ER 565, [1984] 1 WLR 962, CA.

[75] See MacEwan (above) and S Fafinski, 'Computer Misuse: The Implications of the Police and Justice Act 2006' (2006) 72 J Crim L 53.

[76] See p 107, above.

[77] [2004] AC 1034. See above, p 123.

[78] Law Com No 186, para 3.62.

D's intent or recklessness need not be directed at the proscribed impairment etc of a particular computer or program. There is concern that the offence will criminalize legitimate activities by IT security consultants.

30.5 Making, supplying or obtaining articles for use in offence under s 1 or s 3: s 3A

The Police and Justice Act 2006, s 37, introduced three new offences. The maximum sentence on conviction on indictment, is two years' imprisonment or a fine or both; on summary conviction 12 months' imprisonment or a fine up to the statutory maximum or both.

By s 3A(1) a person is guilty of an offence if he 'makes, adapts, supplies or offers to supply any article intending it to be used to commit, or to assist in the commission of, an offence under section 1 or 3'. This form of the offence mirrors closely that in s 7 of the Fraud Act 2006.[79] 'Intention' should be construed in the normal manner.

By s 3A(2), it is an offence to supply or offer to supply any article believing that it is likely to be used to commit, or to assist in the commission of, an offence under s 1 or s 3. 'Belief' should be construed as elsewhere in the criminal law, to mean a state of mind greater than one of mere suspicion but without constituting knowledge.[80] The question whether the article is 'likely to be' used for an offence under ss 1 to 3 may give rise to some difficulty in application. According to the Home Office Explanatory Notes, if D is charged in relation to a quantity of articles, the prosecution must prove its case 'in relation to any particular one or more of those articles; it would not be enough to prove that the person believed that a certain proportion of the articles was likely to be used in connection with an offence under section 1 or 3'.

Section 3A(3) provides an offence where a person obtains any article 'with a view to' its being supplied for use to commit, or to assist in the commission of, an offence under s 1 or s 3. It is submitted that the *mens rea* element may be read restrictively to mean purposive intent, as the Court of Appeal recently held in a different context.[81] This is a relatively unusual form of offence, criminalizing a 'middle man'. It is not sufficient that D merely obtains; nor is it sufficient if he possesses. This offence requires an obtaining with an ulterior purpose. It extends further than s 3A(1) by capturing D's conduct before he has got as far as to offer to supply or in fact supply the article.

For all three forms of the offence, 'article' includes any program or data held in electronic form: s 3A(4). The *mens rea* is crucial in each of these offences since the articles which could possibly be used in the commission of computer misuse offences are incredibly wide ranging – from a screwdriver to complex software, or a computer password.

The new offences were explained by the Government as being necessary to combat the market in 'hacker tools' for hacking into computer systems. Concerns have been raised about the possible criminalization of those engaged in legitimate research into computer security systems.[82] The provisions also ensure compliance with Council of Europe obligations.[83]

---

[79] At p 921.

[80] See above, p 130.

[81] See *Dooley* [2005] EWCA Crim 3093, above p 933.

[82] See House of Lords Science and Technology Report: *Personal Internet Security* (2007). See, however, the Government's subsequent response which has been heavily criticized: T Wright and D Hodgkinson 'Government Response to House of Lords Science and Technology Committee Report on Personal Internet Security' (2008) 14 Computer and Telecommunications LR 65.

[83] Art 6(1)(a) of the 2001 Council of Europe Cybercrime Convention.

31

Obscenity

Obscenity was originally an ecclesiastical offence but came to be recognized as a common law misdemeanour in *Curl*.[1] That common law offence of obscene libel was abolished by s 73 of the Coroners and Justice Act 2009.

This chapter focuses on the offences in the Obscene Publications Acts 1959 and 1964, and related offences. The offences raise interesting issues of freedom of speech as well as challenging questions about the appropriate boundaries of criminalization.

In 2009/10 there were 3,195 recorded crimes involving obscene publications and protected sexual material.[2]

31.1 Obscene publications[3]

31.1.2 Offences

It is an offence under s 2(1) of the Obscene Publications Act 1959[4] if D either:

(1) publishes an obscene article for gain or not;

or

(2) 'has' an obscene article for publication for gain (whether gain to himself or gain to another).[5]

Making an obscene article is not an offence, as such; but those who participate in its manufacture may be liable as secondary parties to the publication, or the 'having', which is a continuing offence.[6] If the article created[7] involves an image or pseudo image of a child, liability for making it will lie under the Protection of Children Act 1978. If it depicts extreme pornography or extreme images of children, the specific statutory offences discussed below (p 1076) may apply.

---

[1] (1727) 2 Stra 788; following *Sidley* (1663) 1 Sid 168, sub nom *Sydlyes' Case* 1 Keb 620, a case of an indecent exhibition.

[2] J Flatley et al, *Crime in England and Wales 2009/10, Findings from the British Crime Survey and Police Recorded Crime* (2010) 34.

[3] D Feldman, *Civil Liberties*, Ch 16. For historical accounts, see N St John Stevas, 'Obscenity and the Law' [1954] Crim LR 817; CH Rolph, *The Trial of Lady Chatterley* (1961); G Robertson, *Freedom, the Individual and the Law* (7th edn, 1993) Ch 5; DGT Williams, 'The Control of Obscenity' [1965] Crim LR 471 at 522; C Manchester, 'A History of the Crime of Obscene Libel' (1991) 12 J of Legal History 36.

[4] The Criminal Justice and Immigration Act 2008, s 71 increased the maximum sentence to five years' imprisonment

[5] ibid, s 2(1) as amended by the 1964 Act, s 1(1).

[6] *Barton* [1976] Crim LR 514, CA.

[7] This includes images merely downloaded from the internet: *Bowden* [2001] 1 QB 88.

31.1.3 Defining obscenity

The ordinary meaning of obscene is 'filthy, lewd, or disgusting'. In law, the meaning is in some respects, narrower and, in other respects, possibly wider.

Section 1(1) of the 1959 Act, provides the test of obscenity:

For the purposes of this Act an article[8] shall be deemed to be obscene if its effect or (where the article comprises two or more distinct items) the effect of any one of its items is, if taken as a whole, such as to tend to deprave and corrupt persons who are likely, having regard to all relevant circumstances, to read, see or hear the matter contained or embodied in it.

This substantially reproduces the common law test laid down by Cockburn CJ, in *Hicklin*:[9]

I think the test of obscenity is this, whether the tendency of the matter charged as obscenity is to deprave and corrupt those whose minds are open to such immoral influences, and into whose hands a publication of this sort may fall.

The element of a tendency to corrupt and deprave is important. It has been said that the test was largely ignored at common law and that, if material was found to be 'obscene' in the ordinary meaning of the word, the tendency to deprave and corrupt was presumed. If that was true, the effect of the statutory enactment of the definition in 1959 was to tighten the definition by requiring proof of an actual tendency to deprave and corrupt.[10] In *Anderson*[11] (a famous case involving a publication called the 'Oz School Kids' Issue'), the conviction was quashed because the judge left the jury with the impression that 'obscene' meant 'repulsive', 'filthy', 'loathsome' or 'lewd'. An article might be all of these and yet not have a tendency to deprave and corrupt. This should, it is submitted, be a high threshold. Sexually explicit material is not necessarily obscene.[12]

As an example of the types of conduct currently liable to be prosecuted under the Obscene Publications Act, the CPS notes that the most commonly charged categories are:[13] sexual acts with an animal; realistic portrayals of rape; sadomasochistic material which goes beyond trifling and transient infliction of injury; torture with instruments; bondage (especially where gags are used with no apparent means of withdrawing consent); dismemberment or graphic mutilation; activities involving perversion or degradation (such as drinking urine, urination or vomiting on to the body, or excretion or use of excreta); fisting. In contrast, the CPS will not normally prosecute material depicting: actual consensual sexual intercourse (vaginal or anal); oral sex; masturbation; mild bondage; simulated intercourse or buggery; fetishes which do not encourage physical abuse unless these involve the activities listed above.[14]

31.1.3.1 Aversion argument

It has been argued that if the article is so revolting that it would put anyone off the kind of depraved activity depicted then it would have no tendency to deprave.[15] The very 'obscenity' (in the popular sense) of a publication may, paradoxically, prevent it from being 'obscene'

---

[8] For the definition of 'article', see below, p 1063.

[9] (1868) LR 3 QB 360 at 371. This was an appeal from a decision of a recorder quashing an order of the justices for the destruction of certain pamphlets under the Obscenity Publications Act 1857; below, p 1071.

[10] *DPP v Whyte* [1972] 3 All ER 12 at 18, HL, per Lord Wilberforce.

[11] [1972] 1 QB 304, [1971] 3 All ER 1152. See T Palmer, *The Trials of Oz* (1971).

[12] *Darbo v DPP* [1992] Crim LR 56.

[13] As a recent example of the type of activity that is regarded as obscene see *Snowden* [2010] EWCA Crim 1200.

[14] See www.cps.gov.uk/legal/l_to_o/obscene_publications/index.html.

[15] *Calder and Boyars Ltd* [1969] 1 QB 151, [1968] 3 All ER 644; *Anderson*, above.

(in the legal sense). This is the so called 'aversion' argument. Whether this defence is available seems to depend on the nature of the article *and* the manner of publication.[16] In *Calder v Boyars*, the article in question was *Last Exit to Brooklyn*, 'a most powerfully written book, and, in some eyes...regarded as repulsive and nauseating', which was on general sale. In contrast, the defence could hardly be 'effectively run' in *Elliott*,[17] a video club case, where the material was being advertised as attractive to members of that private club.

Under the statute, it appears that the requirement that the article be 'obscene' in the ordinary meaning of the word may have disappeared and have been replaced with a technical meaning. An article may be obscene within the statute if it has a tendency to deprave and corrupt (even though it is not filthy, lewd or disgusting), but it may be found not to be obscene because it is so filthy, lewd and disgusting that it would put anyone off.

31.1.3.2 Subject matter capable of being obscene

Until 1965, the law of obscenity was only invoked in relation to sexually explicit material. The words 'deprave and corrupt' are clearly capable of bearing a wider meaning than this; and can be applied to material depicting conduct such as drug-taking. In *John Calder (Publications) Ltd v Powell*[18] the court held that a book's description of the favourable effects of drug-taking could be obscene because there was a real danger that readers might be tempted to experiment with drugs.[19]

The difficulty about extending the notion of obscenity beyond sexual morality is that it is not apparent where the law should stop. It seems obvious that an article with a tendency to induce violence may be obscene;[20] and, if taking drugs is depravity, why not drinking, or, since evidence of its harmful effects is beyond doubt, smoking? Whether the conduct to which the article relates amounts to depravity would seem to depend on how violently the judge (in deciding whether there was evidence of obscenity) and the jury (in deciding whether the article was obscene) disapproved of the conduct in question. This is an unsatisfactory state of affairs. The offence is arguably ill-defined and fails to respect the principles of certainty and fair warning. However, challenges to the offence on the basis of its incompatibility with the ECHR requirement that restrictions on freedom of expression be prescribed by law have been rejected in the English courts. In *Perrin*,[21] the Court of Appeal held that the offence was prescribed with sufficient clarity within the broad scope of the concept as described by the ECtHR in *Sunday Times v UK (No 1)*:[22]

Firstly, the law must be adequately accessible: the citizen must be able to have an indication that is adequate in the circumstances of the legal rules applicable to a given case. Secondly, a norm cannot be regarded as a 'law' unless it is formulated with sufficient precision to enable the citizen to regulate his conduct: he must be able – if need be with appropriate advice – to foresee, to a degree that is reasonable in the circumstances, the consequences which a given action may entail.

Indeed, one of the leading cases in Strasbourg jurisprudence on certainty is the obscenity case of *Handyside v UK*, in which the Court stated:

---

[16] These are factors the CPS takes into account: the printed word is less likely to be prosecuted, and where the material is displayed and to whom will be important. See www.cps.gov.uk/legal/l_to_o/obscene_publications/index.html.

[17] [1996] 1 Cr App R 432 at 436.

[18] [1965] 1 QB 509, [1965] 1 All ER 159.

[19] [1965] 1 QB 509 per Lord Parker CJ.

[20] cf *DPP v A and BC Chewing Gum Ltd* [1968] 1 QB 159, [1967] 2 All ER 504; *Calder and Boyars Ltd* [1969] 1 QB 151 at 172.

[21] [2002] EWCA Crim 747.

[22] (1979–80) 2 EHRR 245 at para 49.

Freedom of expression constitutes one of the essential foundations of…a [democratic] society, one of the basic conditions for its progress and for the development of every man. Subject to Article 10(2), it is applicable not only to 'information' or 'ideas' that are favourably received or regarded as inoffensive or as a matter of indifference, but also that offend, shock or disturb the State or any sector of the population. Such are the demands of that pluralism, tolerance and broadmindedness without which there is no 'democratic society'.[23]

31.1.3.3 Depravity defined

The core of the offence is the tendency to deprave and corrupt. It is clear that the tendency to 'deprave' may be satisfied if there is a tendency to affect a reader or viewer's mental state, without causing him to engage in conduct of any kind. Indeed, the protection of the minds of the people is the law's primary object. In *DPP v Whyte*,[24] it was found that articles which would enable readers to engage in private fantasies of their own, not involving overt sexual activity of any kind were obscene. That case also concluded that an article may be obscene although it is directed only to persons who are already depraved. It is enough that the article maintains in the viewer a state of corruption which he might otherwise have escaped. 'The Act is not merely concerned with the once for all corruption of the wholly innocent; it equally protects the less innocent from further corruption, the addict from feeding or increasing his addiction.'[25]

31.1.3.4 Proving obscenity

Expert evidence is admissible, and this most commonly occurs in the context of the 'public good' defence (discussed below). Expert evidence also has a part to play in some cases in proving the tendency to deprave, but this must be approached with caution. Expert opinion is admissible on, for example, the medical effects of cocaine and the various ways of taking it because this is a matter which is outside the experience of the ordinary jury member.[26] But whether those effects constitute depravity and corruption – that is, whether the article, whatever it is, is obscene – is exclusively a question for the jury. Expert evidence is not admissible on that issue.[27] One decision holds that exceptionally, in the case of material directed at very young children, experts in child psychiatry may be asked what the effect of certain material on the minds of children would be.[28] But that authority is to be regarded as 'highly exceptional and confined to its own circumstances'.[29] The theory seems to be that a jury is as well able as an expert to judge the effect on an adult but not on a child. This does not mean that the jury should be left without guidance on the question. It would seem right that they should be reminded that 'deprave and corrupt' are very strong words; that material which might lead one morally astray is not necessarily corrupting;[30] and they should bear in mind the current standards of ordinary decent people.[31] In the end, they have to make a judgement of what they believe to be the prevailing moral standard. On one view, this represents the deficiency

---

[23] (1979–80) 1 EHRR 737, para 49.

[24] [1972] 3 All ER 12.

[25] ibid, at 19 per Lord Wilberforce.

[26] *Skirving* [1985] QB 819, [1985] 2 All ER 705, CA, criticized by RTH Stone, 'Obscene Publications: The Problems Persist' [1986] Crim LR 139 at 142. See the Law Commission Report No 325, *Expert Evidence in Criminal Proceedings* (2011) and Criminal Evidence (Experts) Bill published March 2011.

[27] *Calder and Boyars Ltd* [1969] 1 QB 151, [1968] 3 All ER 644; *Anderson* [1972] 1 QB 304, [1971] 3 All ER 1152; *DPP v Jordan* [1977] AC 699, [1976] 3 All ER 775. For an argument that the limited availability of the expert evidence may contravene Art 6 and Arts 10 and 14 of the ECHR, see C Nowlin, 'Expert Evidence in English Obscenity Law: Implications of the Human Rights Act 1998' (2001) 30 Common Law World Review 94. See generally on expert evidence in obscenity trials F Bates, 'Pornography and the Expert Witness' (1978) 20 Crim LQ 135.

[28] *DPP v A and BC Chewing Gum Ltd* [1968] 1 QB 159, [1967] 2 All ER 504.

[29] *Anderson* [1972] 1 QB 304 at 313.

[30] *Knuller (Publishing, Printing and Promotions) Ltd v DPP* [1972] 2 All ER 898 at 932, 936.

[31] ibid, 904.

of the offence in terms of the lack of certainty and fair warning, on another view this at least preserves the flexibility of the offence and ensures the opportunity for it to evolve with contemporary moral standards.[32]

In *Reiter*,[33] the jury were asked to look at a large number of other books in order to decide whether the books which were the subject of the charge were obscene. The Court of Criminal Appeal held that this was the wrong approach. It appears that it is still not permissible, under the Act, to prove that *other* books, which are just as obscene as the one in issue, are freely circulating:[34] 'What is permitted elsewhere in the world is neither here nor there.'[35a]

But note the recent case of *Neal*,[35b] in which convictions for possession of indecent photographs of children were quashed where the photographs were all available in books of photographs by established photographers and readily available from reputable outlets.

31.1.3.5 Jury directions

Where so much power to define the scope of the wrongdoing lies with the jury, much will depend not only on an article's content, but also the content and tone of the judge's direction. In the case of *Martin Secker Warburg*,[36] concerning the publication of *The Philanderer*, Stable J gave a direction to a jury which was acclaimed in the press for its enlightened attitude and was thought to be reassuring to those who fear that the criminal law as applied by the judges was, even then, out of touch with public opinion.[37] The learned judge told the jury:[38]

the charge is a charge that the tendency of the book is to corrupt and deprave. The charge is not that the tendency of the book is either to shock or to disgust. That is not a criminal offence. The charge is that the tendency of the book is to corrupt and deprave. Then you say: 'Well, corrupt and deprave whom?' to which the answer is: those whose minds are open to such immoral influences and into whose hands a publication of this sort may fall. What, exactly, does that mean? Are we to take our literary standards as being the level of something that is suitable for the decently brought up young female aged fourteen? Or do we go even further back than that and are we to be reduced to the sort of books that one reads as a child in the nursery? The answer to that is: Of course not. A mass of literature, great literature, from many angles, is wholly unsuitable for reading by the adolescent, but that does not mean that a publisher is guilty of a criminal offence for making those works available to the general public.

Dealing with the particular book, he said:[39]

the book does deal with candour or, if you prefer it, crudity with the realities of human love and of human intercourse. There is no getting away from that, and the Crown say: 'Well, that is sheer filth.' Is it? Is the act of sexual passion sheer filth? It may be an error of taste to write about it. It may be a matter in which, perhaps, old-fashioned people would mourn the reticence that was observed in these matters yesterday, but is it sheer filth? That is a matter which you have to consider and ultimately to decide.

Perhaps surprisingly, other directions to juries in more recent times have been a good deal less liberal and it has been suggested that Stable J's is not the typical judicial attitude.[40]

---

[32] cf *Muller v Switzerland* (1991) 13 EHRR 212.

[33] [1954] 2 QB 16, [1954] 1 All ER 741.

[34] *Penguin Books* (1961); Rolph, *Trial of Lady Chatterley*, 127.

[35a] The judge was held to have correctly so directed the jury in *Elliott* [1996] 1 Cr App R 432 at 435, [1996] Crim LR 264, applying *Reiter*.

[35b] [2011] EWCA Crim 461.

[36] [1954] 2 All ER 683, [1954] 1 WLR 1138.

[37] See S Prevezer, Note (1954) 17 MLR 571.

[38] [1954] 2 All ER 683 at 686.

[39] ibid, 687, 688.

[40] H Street, *Freedom, the Individual and the Law* (7th edn, 1983) 223. For rather extreme arguments that the offence is too liberal, see S Edwards, 'A Plea for Censorship' (1991) 141 NLJ 1478.

It is now made perfectly clear by the Act that an 'item' alleged to be obscene must be 'taken as a whole' so that where an article consists of a single item,[41] like a novel, the article must be judged in its entirety. Where an article, like a magazine, comprises a number of distinct items, each item must be tested individually; and if one item is found to be obscene, the whole article is obscene.[42] In *Goring*,[43] this approach was extended to films. There is a danger with this approach that juries will be more likely to focus on individual 'purple passages', which will be given an unwarranted significance in the assessment of the overall work. The normal practice is for no more than six articles to form the basis of the indictment – that being sufficient to highlight the different types of activities portrayed or described.

31.1.3.6 Who must be at risk of being depraved?

What pool of likely readers is the jury to consider? In the lauded direction in *Warburg*,[44] reference was made to the decently brought up young female aged fourteen. Such a reader served as a convenient benchmark of the people the Act serves to protect and the judge was inviting the jury to apply that standard. It is unclear whether judges ought to encourage juries to assess obscenity by reference to such a narrow pool of likely readers or viewers.

An article is obscene if it has a tendency to deprave 'persons who are likely ... to read, see or hear the matter contained or embodied in it'. It is certainly obscene if it has a tendency to deprave 'a significant proportion' of those likely to read it.[45] Only if the number of readers likely to be corrupted is 'so small as to be negligible' is the article not obscene.[46] It would not be obscene simply on the ground that it might tend to deprave 'a minute lunatic fringe of readers'.[47] If, however, a significant, though comparatively small, number of the likely readers were decently brought up 14-year-old children, then whether the book was obscene would turn on whether it was likely to deprave them. A direction to the jury on the number of viewers/readers is not a prerequisite in all cases since there is a danger that it will confuse the jury where for example, the publication is a novel on general sale. This is a significant issue since in ECHR terms it may assist in the determination of whether the prosecution was proportionate within Art 10(2).

It has been suggested that this ambiguity over who is being protected renders the law ineffective since it offers an opportunity for many cases to be diverted away from the criminal courts.[48] In cases that do go to trial, the questions for the jury are of a highly speculative nature. How, for example, is the jury to say whether a significant proportion of the readers will be 14-year-olds? The answer seems to depend on all kinds of matters of which the jury can, at best, have imperfect knowledge. The same article may or may not be obscene depending on the manner of publication. If it has a tendency to deprave 14-year-olds, a bookseller who sells a copy to a youth club for 14-year-olds is obviously publishing an obscene article; but if he sells the same book to the local working mens' club, this may not be so.

---

[41] This is a question of law for the judge: *Goring* [1999] Crim LR 670, CA.

[42] *Anderson* [1972] 1 QB 304 at 312, above, p 1058.

[43] [1999] Crim LR 670 and commentary.

[44] [1954] 2 All ER 683, [1954] 1 WLR 1138.

[45] *Calder and Boyars Ltd* [1969] 1 QB 151 at 168.

[46] *DPP v Whyte* [1972] 3 All ER 12 at 21 and 25, per Lords Pearson and Cross. See also *O'Sullivan* [1995] 1 Cr App R 455. cf the obligations of the BBFC when classifying videos under s 4A of the Video Recordings Act 1984 [as now re-enacted following recognition of the failure of the 1984 Act: Video Recordings Act 2010], discussed in *R v Video Appeals Committee of the BBFC, ex p BBFC* [2000] EMLR 850. See C Munro, 'Sex, Laws and Videotape' [2006] Crim LR 957.

[47] ibid, 169.

[48] S Edwards, 'On the Contemporary Application of the Obscene Publications Act 1959' [1998] Crim LR 843, arguing that it renders official statistics valueless.

Since any file on the internet is theoretically available to any person of computer literate age anywhere in the world, the likelihood of material being read or viewed by a particular group in terms of age, religion, culture, etc is impossible to predict.[49] As an example of the potential reach of the offences, in one recent case 'blogger' Darryn Walker, was charged but acquitted in a prosecution based on descriptions he gave in his blog of kidnap and sexual torture of members of Girls Aloud (a pop group).[50] The BBC reported David Perry QC, prosecuting, as saying that a crucial aspect of the reasoning that led to the instigation of these proceedings was that the article in question, which was posted on the internet, was accessible to people who were particularly vulnerable – young people who were interested in a particular pop music group. 'It was this that distinguished this case from other material available on the internet.'

31.1.3.7 No requirement of an intention to corrupt

The actual intention of the author is irrelevant. If the article has a tendency to deprave a significant proportion of the readership, it does not matter how pure and noble the author's intent may have been,[51] the article is obscene. In *Martin Secker Warburg*, Stable J told the jury:[52]

You will have to consider whether ... the author was pursuing an honest purpose and an honest thread of thought or whether that was all just a bit of camouflage. ...

This was too favourable to the defence. The jury could take account of the author's intention, as it appeared in the book itself, as a factor which would have a bearing on whether people would be depraved.

31.1.3 8 Freedom of expression

A prosecution will engage the right to freedom of expression under Art 10 of the ECHR, but will be justified for the prevention of crime or the protection of morals within Art 10(2) provided it is necessary and proportionate. In *Perrin*,[53] the Court of Appeal accepted that the Obscene Publications Act offence was necessary and proportionate within the meaning in Art 10(2). A potential difficulty arises over how proportionality is to be fairly assessed in any prosecution given that the likely audience may well be unknown. For example, in *Hoare v UK*,[54] it was held that prosecution was proportionate when videotapes were sent to the intended purchaser by post because there were insufficient safeguards to ensure that only the intended purchasers would gain access to the material. It would be disproportionate otherwise where the publication is to a group voluntarily assembled with restricted access as in *Scherer v Switzerland*,[55] which involved showing a pornographic film in a private room in a sex shop.[56]

31.1.4. What is an article?

The 1959 Act provides by s 1(2):

In this Act 'article' means any description of article containing or embodying matter to be read or looked at or both, any sound record, and any film or other record of a picture or pictures.

---

[49] See on the impact the internet has had: J Rowbottom, 'Obscenity Laws and the Internet: Targeting Supply and Demand' [2006] Crim LR 97.

[50] See www.guardian.co.uk/uk/2009/jun/29/girls-aloud-blog. See BBC news reports 29 June 2009.

[51] *Calder and Boyars Ltd* [1969] 1 QB 151 at 168–169. cf *Lemon*, below, p 242.

[52] [1954] 2 All ER 683 at 688.

[53] [2002] EWCA Crim 747.

[54] [1997] EHRLR 678.

[55] (1994) 18 EHRR 276; see also *X and Y v Switzerland* (1991) 16564/90.

[56] cf *Muller v Switzerland* (1991) 13 EHRR 212 which involved displays of sexually explicit paintings in a public gallery without warnings.

This includes a video cassette,[57] a DVD,[58] and a computer disk.[59] In *Straker v DPP*,[60] it was held that while a film negative *might* be within this definition,[61] it was not kept for 'publication' as described in s 3(1) since it was not to be shown, played or projected,[62] but to be used for making prints. It could not, therefore, be forfeited under s 3. The gap left by that case is closed by s 2 of the 1964 Act which provides:

(1) The Obscene Publications Act 1959 (as amended by this Act) shall apply in relation to anything which is intended to be used, either alone or as one of a set, for the reproduction or manufacture therefrom of articles containing or embodying matter to be read, looked at or listened to, as if it were an article containing or embodying that matter so far as that matter is to be derived from it or from the set.

By s 2(2) of the 1964 Act, an article is had or kept for publication 'if it is had or kept for the reproduction or manufacture therefrom of articles for publication'. The negatives in *Straker* clearly fall within this provision.

In *Conegate Ltd v Customs and Excise Comrs*,[63] it was conceded that inflatable lifesize sex dolls, though obscene, were not 'articles'. It has been suggested that the concession was wrong because the dolls, having faces painted on them, were to be 'looked at'. However, the gist of the obscenity seems to lie in the use to which the dolls were intended to be put rather than in their appearance.

31.1.5 The offence of 'publication'

Section 1 of the Obscene Publications Act 1959,[64] provides:

(3) For the purposes of this Act a person publishes an article who —

　(a) distributes, circulates, sells, lets on hire, gives, or lends it, or who offers it for sale or for letting on hire; or

　(b) in the case of an article containing or embodying matter to be looked at or a record, shows, plays or projects it or, where the matter is data stored electronically, transmits that data.

(4) For the purpose of this Act a person also publishes an article to the extent that any matter recorded on it is included by him in a programme included in a programme service.

(5) Where the inclusion of any matter in a programme so included would, if that matter were recorded matter, constitute the publication of an obscene article for the purposes of this Act by virtue of subsection (4) above, this Act shall have effect in relation to the inclusion of that matter in that programme as if it were recorded matter.

(6) In this section 'programme' and 'programme service' have the same meaning as in the Broadcasting Act 1990.

---

[57] *A-G's Reference (No 5 of 1980)* [1980] 3 All ER 816, [1981] 1 WLR 88.

[58] See, eg, recently *Snowden* [2010] 1 Cr App R (S) 233(39).

[59] *Fellows and Arnold* [1997] 1 Cr App R 244, [1997] Crim LR 524 and commentary.

[60] [1963] 1 QB 926, [1963] 1 All ER 697, DC.

[61] Widgery LCJ had little doubt that this was so; *Derrick v Customs and Excise Comrs* [1972] 2 WLR 359 at 361.

[62] Section 1(3)(b), below.

[63] [1987] QB 254, [1986] 2 All ER 688, [1986] Crim LR 562, ECJ.

[64] As amended by the Broadcasting Act 1990, s 162(1)(b) and by the Criminal Justice and Public Order Act 1994, s 168(1) and Sch 9.

If the charge alleges publication to a named person, it must be proved that the article had a tendency to deprave and corrupt that person.[65] If the article does not have a tendency to deprave the person to whom it is published, it will be obscene only if either:

(1) (a) there are 'persons who are likely, having regard to all the relevant circumstances, to read, see or hear matter contained or embodied in it' (whether they have done so or not) *and*

(b) it will have a tendency to deprave and corrupt those persons;[66]

or

(2) D's initial publication was to a person for whom it would not have a tendency to corrupt, but subsequently it has in fact been published to a person whom it is likely to deprave and corrupt, and that publication could reasonably have been expected to follow from publication by D.[67]

If D is appropriately charged, he may then be convicted of publishing an obscene article to those persons.

In *Barker*,[68] where D published certain photographs to V, and the judge told the jury that the fact that V kept them under lock and key was unimportant, the conviction was quashed. If the jury had been told that they were to consider the tendency of the article to deprave and corrupt only V, the direction would have been unobjectionable. If, however, they were directed or left to suppose that they should consider its tendency to deprave and corrupt other people, then the direction was clearly wrong. The fact that V kept the articles under lock and key was not *conclusive* since V might have intended to produce them at some future time; but it was certainly *relevant* to the answer to proposition 1(a) above.

31.1.5.1 Internet publications

It is clear that 'transmitting data electronically' constitutes a publication. Uploading and downloading material to and from webpages is sufficient.[69] Thus, if D makes articles of an obscene nature available via a website there is a publication. D will also be held to have 'shown' obscene material by providing others with a password to access such material.[70]

The publication of material on the internet raises a difficult jurisdictional question which was, it is submitted, not adequately addressed in *Perrin*.[71] In that case, D had published material on a website in the USA which depicted coprophilia and coprophagia. X, a police officer had accessed the site in England and viewed a 'preview page' offering a sample of the material available on subscription. His viewing in England (that is, downloading) was held, without any detailed consideration, to constitute a publication by D in England. Reliance was placed on the decision in *Waddon*,[72] but the matter appears to have been conceded by counsel in that case.[73] The result is that D can be convicted of publishing obscene material in England by uploading it to a website in another jurisdiction in which such publication is legal.

---

[65] *DPP v Whyte* [1972] 3 All ER 12 at 29, per Lord Salmon.

[66] Obscene Publications Act 1959, s 1(1).

[67] ibid, s 2(6).

[68] [1962] 1 All ER 748, [1962] 1 WLR 349.

[69] *Perrin* [2002] EWCA Crim 747.

[70] See *Fellows and Arnold* [1997] 2 All ER 548, CA, drawing analogy with the individual who offers the key to his library containing obscene works.

[71] See generally M Hirst, *Jurisdiction and the Ambit of the Criminal Law* (2003) 188–190.

[72] [2000] All ER (D) 502. See also *Harrison* [2007] EWCA Crim 2976 on possession of indecent child images via 'pop ups' on screen.

[73] The court in *Waddon* declined to rule upon what the position might be in relation to 'jurisdiction if a person storing material on a website outside England intended that no transmission of that material should take place back to this country'.

The courts have recently reconsidered this issue in *Sheppard and Whittle*,[74] a prosecution under the Public Order Act for inciting racial hatred by 'publishing' anti-Semitic material on the internet. The material was written and edited in England, uploaded from England to a server in the USA and downloaded in England by a police officer. The Court of Appeal held that the English courts had jurisdiction to try the case because there was a 'substantial measure of the activity' performed in England even though the last act of 'hosting' the material was performed in the USA (and protected there by the Constitutional right to free speech).[75] The Court declined to choose between various theories of jurisdiction over internet publication: that prosecution is possible (i) in the jurisdiction where the web server upon which it is hosted is situated – the 'country of origin theory'; (ii) in any jurisdiction in which it can be downloaded – the 'country of destination theory'; (iii) in the jurisdiction where the web server upon which it is hosted is situated, and in a jurisdiction at which the publication is targeted – the 'directing and targeting theory'.[76] Each would seem to have practical problems in application. The courts will have to revisit this issue because there will clearly be cases where there is no 'substantial measure' of activity in England and Wales, as for example where D uploads obscene material in Russia to a website hosted in the USA and accessed in England. If the material is targeted at an audience in England, it is arguable that a prosecution is appropriate.

In broader terms, there is a danger that the internet will produce undesirably tight restrictions on obscenity. Since it will be almost impossible for a publisher to comply with the requirements of every jurisdiction, for safety's sake he may have to comply with the most restrictive.

31.1.5.2 Publication to whom?

Two issues have arisen in the context of the relevant recipient: does the publication have to be to a third party? And can there be a tendency to corrupt and deprave a police officer?

The Act does not require publication to a third party. Thus, the Court of Appeal held in *Taylor*[77] that there was a publication where X a photographic developer developed and printed obscene photographs which were then returned to the customer, D.[78] In *Sheppard and Whittle* (dealing with the Public Order Act 1986 offence of 'publishing'), the Court of Appeal rejected the argument that a publication requires a third party publishee (or rather sufficient publishees). The fact that an officer downloads material and is a self-publishee does not prevent there being a publication.

As regards publication to police officers, if the article has no tendency to deprave and corrupt the person to whom it is published and neither of the conditions specified above (p 1065) is satisfied, then D must be acquitted. So, in *Clayton and Halsey*,[79] where V was an experienced police officer who testified that he was not susceptible to depravity or corruption and there was no evidence of publication, or likelihood of publication, to a third party, the Court of Criminal Appeal held that the case should have been withdrawn from the jury.[80] Lord Parker CJ said:[81]

while it is no doubt theoretically possible that a jury could take the view that even a most experienced officer, despite his protestations, was susceptible to the influence of the article yet, bearing in mind

---

[74] [2010] EWCA Crim 65.

[75] Following the case of *Smith (Wallace Duncan) (No 4)* [2004] 2 Cr App R 17 on conspiracy to defraud.

[76] See further M Dyson, 'Public Order on the Internet' [2010] 2 Archbold Review 6.

[77] [1995] 1 Cr App R 131, CA.

[78] There is a resonance with the concept of supply in drugs see above, p 172.

[79] [1963] 1 QB 163, [1962] 3 All ER 500.

[80] D, of course, did not know that he was dealing with an incorruptible police officer. He had *mens rea* and might now be guilty of an attempt under the Criminal Attempts Act 1981, above, p 480. See for similar arguments *Jones* [2007] EWCA Crim 1118.

[81] [1963] 1 QB at 168, [1962] 3 All ER at 502.

the onus and degree of proof in a criminal case, it would, we think, be unsafe and therefore wrong to leave that question to the jury.

In *Perrin*, the Court of Appeal distinguished that case from one involving the publication of a single webpage offering a preview of material on offer from the site for those willing to subscribe. The court held that the trial judge had been correct to direct the jury that it was for them to determine who was likely to see the material, and the fact that the only evidence of anyone having actually seen it was that of the police officer investigating it, did not bring the case within the exception acknowledged in *Clayton and Halsey*.[82] Its availability on the internet meant that there were persons who, in the circumstances, were likely to read or see the matter *and* the jury concluded that it would have a tendency to deprave and corrupt those persons.

31.1.6 The offence of 'having' an obscene article 'for publication for gain'

This offence, separate from 'publication', was introduced by amendments made by the 1964 Act and was intended to deal with the difficulties arising from *Clayton and Halsey* where it was held that the officer was incorruptable. In fact, the accused in that case were convicted of *conspiracy*[83] to publish the articles, because the buyers they had in view were not incorruptible police officers. But the implications of the case were serious; for, where there was no evidence that D had conspired with another, it made it virtually impossible to get a conviction on the evidence of a police officer that the articles had been sold to him. Under the amended provision it is now possible to charge D with *having* the article for publication for gain; and the incorruptibility of the particular officer who purchases it will be irrelevant. The jury is unlikely to suppose that D kept these articles solely for sale to police officers; and they need only be satisfied that, having regard to all the relevant circumstances, (i) D contemplated publication to such a person as the article would have a tendency to deprave and corrupt, or (ii) that he contemplated publication from which a further publication to susceptible persons could reasonably be expected to follow (whether D in fact contemplated that further publication or not).

By s 1(3)(b) of the 1964 Act:

the question whether the article is obscene shall be determined by reference to such publication for gain of the article as in the circumstances it may reasonably be inferred he had in contemplation and to any further publication that could reasonably be expected to follow from it, but not to any other publication.

The prosecution must prove more than mere possession of the articles. The reference to 'such publication' is to that which is for gain, and this must be proved.[84]

31.1.6.1 Ownership, possession or control

The meaning of 'having' an article is elucidated by s 1(2) of the 1964 Act:

a person shall be deemed to have an article for publication for gain if with a view to such publication he has the article in his ownership, possession or control.

---

[82] See also *Sheppard and Whittle* [2010] EWCA Crim 65.

[83] The Law Officers have given an assurance that conspiracy will not be used as a charge so as to circumvent the public good defence below.

[84] *Levy* [2004] All ER (D) 321 (Apr).

Thus, the owner of the shop in which the article is stocked may be convicted as the owner of the article, as may his employee who has possession or control of it. The van driver who takes it from wholesaler to retailer may be in possession or control with a view to eventual publication for gain to another. Where articles were alleged to be held for distribution to sex shops and there bought by customers, it was necessary to prove that D contemplated that these steps would be taken. The jury had to be sure that the contemplated publication would tend to deprave and corrupt a significant proportion of the readers or viewers.[85]

31.1.6.2 'Offers' for sale

This extension of the offence overcomes another difficulty which arose under the 1959 Act as originally enacted. It was held that a person who displays an obscene article in a shop window is not guilty of publishing it.[86] Of the various ways of publishing referred to in s 1(3), the only one which could conceivably have been applicable was 'offering for sale'; and it was held that 'offer' must be construed in accordance with the law of contract,[87] under which the display of goods in a shop window is an 'invitation to treat' and not an offer.[88] This decision, of course, remains good law; but now a charge might successfully be brought of having the obscene article for publication for gain, irrespective of whether it had been displayed or not.

31.1.6.3 Film exhibitions

Film exhibitions taking place otherwise than in a private house were formerly excluded under the terms of s 1(3)(b) of the 1959 Act. Section 53 of the Criminal Law Act 1977 amended that provision so that the exhibition of a film anywhere is a publication for the purposes of the Obscene Publications Act; but no prosecution under s 2 may be brought without the consent of the DPP: where (i) the article is a moving picture film not less than 16 mm wide and (ii) publication of it took place or could reasonably be expected to take place only in the course of an exhibition of a film. 'An exhibition of a film' under s 2[89] means any exhibition of moving pictures.[90]

If the film is such as to outrage public decency then its public showing is a common law offence, and a local authority which, in performing its licensing duties, authorized the showing of an outrageously indecent film might have been guilty of aiding and abetting that offence.[91] A local authority has no duty to censor films, except in relation to children; but if it chooses to act, through its licensing powers, as a censor for adults, it must act in accordance with the law and not expressly permit the commission of an offence. Since the Criminal Law Act 1977, however, no proceedings may be brought for an offence at common law (including conspiracy) in respect of a film exhibition alleged to be obscene, indecent, offensive, disgusting or injurious to morality.[92] An indictment for *statutory* conspiracy, contrary to s 1 of the Criminal Law Act 1977,[93] would lie in appropriate circumstances.

---

[85] *O'Sullivan* [1995] 1 Cr App R 455, at 460.

[86] *Mella v Monahan* [1961] Crim LR 175, following *Fisher v Bell* [1961] 1 QB 394, [1960] 3 All ER 731.

[87] For a criticism of this ruling, see [1961] Crim LR at 181; cf *Partridge v Crittenden* [1968] 2 All ER 421, [1968] 1 WLR 1204.

[88] *Pharmaceutical Society of Great Britain v Boots Cash Chemists (Southern) Ltd* [1953] 1 QB 401, [1953] 1 All ER 482.

[89] As amended by the Cinemas Act 1985, Sch 2 and now by Sch 7, para 1 of the Licensing Act 2003. An 'exhibition of a film' now has the meaning in para 15 of Sch 1 of the Licensing Act 2003.

[90] Section 2(7) of the 1959 Act as substituted by Licensing Act 2003, Sch 6, para 28(3).

[91] *Greater London Council, ex p Blackburn* [1976] 3 All ER 184.

[92] Obscene Publications Act 1959, s 2(4A).

[93] Above, p 423.

31.1.7 Defences

31.1.7.1 No reasonable cause to believe an article obscene

By s 2(5) of the 1959 Act and s 1(3)(a) of the 1964 Act, it is a defence for D to prove[94] that he:

(i) had not examined the article, and

(ii) had no reasonable cause to suspect that it was such that his publication of it, or his having it, as the case may be, would make him liable to be convicted of an offence under s 2.

Both conditions must be satisfied; so if D has examined the article, his failure to appreciate its tendency to deprave and corrupt is no defence under these sections.[95]

31.1.7.2 Public good

Section 4 of the 1959 Act (as amended by the Criminal Law Act 1977) provides a defence of 'public good':

(1) Subject to subsection (1A) of this section a person shall not be convicted of an offence against section 2 of this Act...if it is proved that publication of the article in question is justified as being for the public good on the ground that it is in the interests of science, literature, art or learning, or of other objects of general concern.

(2) It is hereby declared that the opinion of experts as to the literary, artistic, scientific or other merits of an article may be admitted in any proceedings under this Act either to establish or negative the said ground.

The defence becomes relevant only when the jury has decided that the article is obscene – that it has a tendency to deprave a significant proportion of those likely to read it. By providing the defence, the Act assumes that this potential harm to a section of the community might nevertheless be outweighed by the other considerations referred to in the section. The jury should be directed to consider first whether an article is obscene within s 1. If not satisfied of that beyond reasonable doubt, they must acquit. If so satisfied, they should go on to consider whether, on a balance of probabilities, the publication of the article, though obscene, is for the public good.[96] The jury's task is then to:

consider, on the one hand, the number of readers they believe would tend to be depraved and corrupted by the book, the strength of the tendency to deprave and corrupt, and the nature of the depravity or corruption; on the other hand, they should assess the strength of the literary, sociological or ethical merit which they consider the book to possess. They should then weigh up all these factors and decide whether on balance the publication is proved to be justified as being for the public good.[97]

One limb of the public good defence is that the article is an object of general concern. The House of Lords held in *DPP v Jordan*[98] that expert evidence is not admissible to support a defence under s 4 to the effect that pornographic material is psychologically beneficial to persons who are sexually repressed, perverted or deviant, in that it relieves their sexual tensions and may divert them from anti-social activities. The defence applies to 'objects of general con-

---

[94] On the compatibility of reverse burdens of proof with Art 6(2) of the ECHR see p 29, above.

[95] In the case of a broadcast or transmission in a programme service under the Broadcasting Act 1990, s 162, Sch 15, para 5(1), D must show he had no knowledge or grounds to suspect that the programme included obscene content.

[96] *DPP v Jordan* [1976] 3 All ER 775. cf *Sumner* [1977] Crim LR 362 (Judge Davies).

[97] *Calder and Boyars Ltd* [1969] 1 QB 151 at 172.

[98] [1976] 3 All ER 775.

cern', but the court held that these 'objects of general concern' must fall within the same area as those specifically mentioned in the subsection ie science, literature etc. The effect on sexual behaviour and attitudes was a totally different area, covered in s 1. The Court of Appeal[99] had reached the same conclusion on the ground that the same qualities relied on by the Crown to show that the article was obscene were being relied on by the defence to show that it was for the public good. To admit such evidence would be to allow every jury to decide for itself as a matter of public policy whether obscene material should be prohibited. Parliament has decided that it should – unless it possesses certain merits; and whatever doubt there may be as to the range of those merits, they clearly cannot include obscenity itself. 'Merits' must mean qualities which show that the publication of the article is for the public good in that it tends to advance an object of general concern. In the famous *Penguin Books* case Byrne J said that merits from a sociological, ethical and educational point of view were included.[100] That decision must now be read in the light of *Jordan*.

To constitute the defence the 'other objects of general concern' must not only be such as to be conducive to the public good but must also be of 'concern' to members of the public in general. The Court of Appeal in *Jordan*[101] appears to have concluded that the public generally are not 'concerned' with, or about, the relief of the sexually repressed. It is not clear whether the term 'concerned' is interpreted to mean 'interest in' or 'activity in'. According to the court, '[t]he disposal of sewage is no doubt for the public good but it is not a matter with which the generality of the public is concerned'. The general public is certainly interested in the disposal of sewage, at least in the sense that if it were not efficiently done, they would have a great deal to say about it. On the other hand, it is difficult to suppose that the general public could ever be active in the disposal of sewage. It is submitted, however, that 'concern' ought to be interpreted to mean 'interest'. The general public are not active in literature, art or science, but the Act assumes, rightly, it is submitted, that these are objects of public concern.

Another of the limbs of the defence was considered in *A-G's Reference (No 3 of 1977)*,[102] where 'learning' was described as a noun, being the product of scholarship, something with inherent excellence gained by the work of a scholar. The judge had wrongly permitted the defence to adduce expert evidence to establish that magazines had value in relation to sex education.

In determining whether the article is in the public good because it is in the 'interests of literature', it is not permissible for D to prove that other books, which are just as obscene, are freely circulating.[103] However, evidence relating to other books may be admitted to establish the 'climate of literature' in order to assess the literary merit of the book.[104] In *Penguin Books*,[105] the prosecutor conceded in argument that the intention of the author in writing the book is relevant to the question of literary merit. If this is right, it must again[106] refer only to the author's intention as it appears in the book itself; identifying the author's private intentions would be entirely speculative.

The onus of establishing the defence is on the accused and the standard of proof required rests on a balance of probabilities.[107] The defence is not available on the common law charge of conspiracy to corrupt public morals which would often be applicable in cases covered by

---

[99] Sub nom *Staniforth* [1976] 2 All ER 714, [1976] 2 WLR 849.

[100] See Rolph, *The Trial of Lady Chatterley* at 234; *Calder and Boyars Ltd* [1969] 1 QB 151 at 172; *John Calder (Publications) Ltd v Powell* [1965] 1 All ER 159 at 161.

[101] [1976] 2 All ER 714 at 719, CA.

[102] [1978] 67 Cr App R 393, CA.

[103] *Penguin Books* (1961) Rolph, above, 127.

[104] ibid.

[105] Rolph, above, 87 and 123.

[106] As with the question whether the book is obscene. Above, p 1058.

[107] *Calder and Boyars Ltd*, above, 171.

the 1959 Act. Parliament has been assured that prosecutors will not use that common law offence so as to circumvent the statutory defence.[108]

Section 4(1) does not apply where the article is a moving picture film or moving picture soundtrack or television or sound programme.[109] In the case of these articles a similar defence of public good is provided except that the interests which may justify publication are those of drama, opera, ballet or any other art, or of literature or learning.[110]

31.1.8 *Mens rea*

31.1.8.1 At common law

In *Hicklin*,[111] it was held that it was not necessary to establish that D's motive was to deprave and corrupt; and that, if he knowingly published that which had a tendency to deprave and corrupt, it was no defence that he had an honest and laudable intention in publishing the work in question.[112] The case did not decide, as is sometimes supposed, that no *mens rea* is required. D's argument was that the publication was in his view justified by his predominant intention of exposing the errors of the Catholic Church. D did not claim that he did not know the nature of the thing published nor even that he did not know that its natural consequence was to tend to deprave and corrupt.[113] A person who knows that a certain result (being depraved and corrupted) will follow from his publication may properly be said to intend[114] it or, at the very least, to be reckless. *Hicklin*,[115] decided merely that, if D publishes material which he knows will have a tendency to deprave and corrupt, it is no defence that he did so with the best of motives. At common law *mens rea* was required.

No case before the Act of 1959 decided anything to the contrary.[116] In *Barraclough*,[117] it was held unnecessary (but desirable) that the indictment should contain an allegation of intent, because the intent was implicit in the allegation of publishing obscenity.[118] In *De Montalk*,[119] D handed to a printer some poems he had written, intending to circulate about 100 copies, mostly to young people of both sexes ('literary people'). The printer sent the poems to the police and D was convicted. His appeal on the ground that there was no sufficient direction on intent was dismissed. The headnote is misleading in asserting that the jury should not be directed that they must find an intention to corrupt public morals. Crown counsel (later Byrne J) had submitted merely that intention *was to be inferred* from the act of publication and that no affirmative evidence of intention need be given. The court dismissed the appeal, saying that the law was accurately stated in *Barraclough*.[120] In *Penguin Books*,[121] Byrne J held

---

[108] 'That should be known by all who are concerned with the operation of the criminal law', per Lord Morris in *Knuller v DPP* [1972] 2 All ER 898 at 912. See Lord Diplock's doubts as to the efficacy of the assurance (at 924) and Lord Reid's opinion that it does not apply to conspiracy to outrage public decency (at 906).

[109] 'Moving picture soundtrack' means 'any sound record designed for playing with a moving picture film, whether incorporated with the film or not', s 4(3).

[110] Section 4(1A). cf Theatres Act 1968, s 3; below, p 1083; Broadcasting Act 1990, Sch 15.

[111] (1868) LR 3 QB 360.

[112] (1868) LR 3 QB at 371, 372.

[113] Cockburn assumed that D *did* know what the effect of the publication would be: it is impossible to suppose that the man who published it must not have known and seen that the effect upon the minds of many of those into whose hands it would come would be of a mischievous and demoralizing character at 372. If the law requires knowledge, this is now clearly a question for the jury: Criminal Justice Act 1967, s 8; above, p 144.

[114] Above, p 106.

[115] Above, n 111.

[116] See *Thomson* (1900) 64 JP 456 at 457.

[117] [1906] 1 KB 201, at CCR.

[118] '... intent ... is still part of the charge or the publication would not have been lawful': per Darling J, ibid, 212.

[119] (1932) 23 Cr App R 182.

[120] Above.

[121] Above, n 100.

that, if D publishes an article which is obscene, the inference that he intends to deprave and corrupt is irrebuttable. Such an approach today would seem to be inconsistent with s 8 of the Criminal Justice Act 1967;[122] but, though Byrne J used the language of proof, he was probably saying, in substance, that intent to deprave was not a constituent of the offence.[123] He conceded that the judgment in *De Montalk* was not very clear, but stated he was bound by that decision: there was nothing in the argument that the presumption is rebuttable.

31.1.8.2 *Mens rea* under the Obscene Publications Act

In *Shaw v DPP*,[124] D was charged with publishing an obscene article in the form of the *Ladies Directory* (a catalogue of prostitutes and the services offered). His appeal to the Court of Criminal Appeal[125] on the ground that the judge did not direct the jury to take into account D's 'honesty of purpose' was dismissed. Ashworth J said:[126]

If these proceedings had been brought before the passing of the Obscene Publications Act 1959, in the form of a prosecution at common law for publishing an obscene libel, *it would no doubt have been necessary to establish an intention to corrupt*. But the Act of 1959 contains no such requirement and the test of obscenity laid down in s 1(1) of the Act is whether the effect of the article is such as to tend to deprave and corrupt persons who are likely to read it. In other words obscenity depends on the article and not upon the author.[127] (emphasis added)

This view that there is no *mens rea* requirement is inconsistent with the view of Byrne J, in *Penguin Books*.[128] In that case Byrne J thought, in holding there was no *mens rea* that he was applying the common law rule, but according to the Court of Criminal Appeal's view, he was wrong about the common law, but reached the right result by accident, the common law having been revised by the Act.[129]

It was not necessary in *Shaw* to consider the question of *mens rea*. To rule that 'honesty of purpose' is irrelevant is no more than was done in *Hicklin*. However, to decide that no *mens rea* is necessary as to depravity and corruption, is a radical departure from the common law position. Shaw's motive may have been to help the prostitutes to ply their trade, but if he knew (as he must have done) that the inevitable result of his conduct would be what the law regards[130] as depravity and corruption, he *intended* that result. Moreover, the test laid down in s 1(1) is not decisive, for this merely defines the *actus reus* and says nothing about *mens rea*. It is difficult, however, to dispute the conclusion of the Court of Criminal Appeal in the light of the defence provided by s 2(5).[131] If *mens rea* in the sense described above were required, this provision would be quite unnecessary. But the clear implication of s 2(5) is that D would be guilty (i) although he had examined the article and concluded that it had no tendency to deprave and corrupt if there were reasonable grounds on which he might have suspected that it would; (ii) although the jury thought it as likely as not that he did not suspect the arti-

---

[122] Above, n 100.
[123] See the discussion of s 8; above, p 144.
[124] [1962] AC 220, [1961] 2 All ER 446.
[125] He was refused leave to appeal to the House of Lords on this count.
[126] [1962] AC at 227, [1961] 1 All ER at 333, CCA.
[127] The reference to the author is puzzling. Presumably 'the publisher' is meant. They were one and the same in *Shaw*.
[128] Above.
[129] As a matter of fact, it seems that this was not the intention of Parliament: H Street, *Freedom, the Individual and the Law* (3rd edn, 1972) 141.
[130] Whether he knew the law so regarded it, is irrelevant. cf *Sancoff v Halford* [1973] Qd R 25.
[131] Above, p 1069.

cle's tendency;[132] and (iii) although he had examined the article and failed to appreciate its tendency. Thus it appears likely that the Act, perhaps inadvertently, has restricted the requirement of *mens rea*.

In *Anderson*,[133] the court thought it quite obvious that the jury had acquitted of the offence of conspiracy to corrupt public morals because they were not satisfied that there was the required intent to corrupt. But the court did not consider this absence of *mens rea* fatal to the charge under the Obscene Publications Act. In fact, the court considered whether to uphold the conviction under the proviso in s 2 of the Criminal Appeal Act 1968 (as it existed at the time) on the ground that no actual miscarriage of justice had occurred.[134] The court could hardly have been prepared to uphold the conviction if intention was a necessary element of the crime and the jury had found none.

31.1.9 Forfeiture of obscene articles

Section 3 of the Obscene Publications Act 1959 provides a summary procedure for the forfeiture of obscene materials. An information on oath must be laid before a magistrate that there is reasonable ground for suspecting that obscene articles are *kept* in any premises, stall or vehicle in the justice's area *for publication for gain*.[135] The magistrate may then issue a warrant authorizing a constable to search for and seize any articles which he has reason to believe to be obscene and to be kept for publication for gain. Such a warrant authorizes only a single entry and a second entry in reliance on the warrant will be unlawful; but, in the absence of evidence of 'oppression', the court has no discretion to exclude any evidence unlawfully obtained.[136]

Any articles seized must be brought before a magistrate for the same local justice area. If the magistrate, after looking at the articles, decides they are not obscene, then the matter drops and the articles[137] are, no doubt, returned.[138] But if he thinks they may be obscene (and he need not come to a decided opinion at this stage) he may issue a summons to the occupier of the premises to appear before the court and show cause why the articles should not be forfeited. If the court is satisfied[139] that the articles, at the time they were seized, were obscene articles kept for publication for gain, it must order the articles be forfeited. The power does not apply to any article which is returned to the person from whom it was seized.[140] The section applies to material destined for publication abroad.[141] The magistrates may thus be required to form an opinion as to the likely effect of the material on foreigners with different attitudes and customs but, in practice, they are likely to rely on their knowledge of human nature and are unlikely to hold an article to be obscene where it is destined for country X and not obscene where it is destined for country Y. As with the discussion of obscenity on the internet, there is a danger that this leads to the most restrictive threshold being applied.

---

[132] The onus of proof on a balance of probabilities is on D.

[133] Above, p 1058.

[134] [1971] 3 All ER 1152 at 1161.

[135] *Hicklin's* case might thus now fall outside the Act. He sold the pamphlets for the price he paid for them and this was evidently considered not to be selling for gain: (1868) LR 3 QB at 368 and 374. But cf n 111, above.

[136] *Adams* [1980] QB 575, [1980] 1 All ER 473, CA.

[137] It is not necessary for each justice to read all the material, provided the whole is discussed and considered by them: *Olympia Press Ltd v Hollis* [1974] 1 All ER 108. On an appeal to the Crown Court, the judge may take a number of articles at random to sample, showing them to the defence as an indication of the basis on which he has reached his decision: *Crown Court at Snaresbrook, ex p Metropolitan Police Comr* (1984) 79 Cr App R 184, DC. cf RTH Stone, 'Obscene Publications the Problems Persist' [1986] Crim LR 139.

[138] *Thomson v Chain Libraries Ltd* [1954] 2 All ER 616, [1954] 1 WLR 999.

[139] In *Thomson v Chain Libraries Ltd* [1954] 2 All ER 616 at 618, Hilbery J said that the onus of proof is on the person who appears to show cause. *Sed quaere*: the magistrate must be *satisfied* that the article is obscene.

[140] Criminal Law Act 1977, sch 12, s 65(4).

[141] *Gold Star Publications Ltd v DPP* [1981] 2 All ER 257, HL.

The owner, author or maker of the articles, or any other person through whose hands they had passed before being seized, is entitled to appear and show cause why they should not be forfeited; and any person who appeared or was entitled to appear to show cause against the making of the order has a right of appeal to the Crown Court.

The defence of 'public good' is available in proceedings for forfeiture;[142] but the decision is, of course, now in the hands of the magistrates and not in the hands of a jury. Thus, if proceedings for forfeiture are brought instead of an indictment, the author or publisher of a book can effectively be deprived of a right to jury trial.[143]

There is not necessarily any uniformity of decision-making. One bench may pass a magazine or picture, while another condemns it.[144] In practice, it seems that the advice of the DPP is usually taken by the police before applying for a warrant. His advice is not *necessary* since it is thought undesirable that he should be in the position of a literary or moral censor.

Where, however, the article is a moving picture film in respect of which a prosecution under s 2 of the 1959 Act could not be instituted without the consent of the Director,[145] no order for forfeiture may be made unless the warrant under which the article was seized was issued on an information laid by or on behalf of the Director.[146]

31.1.10 European matters

An argument that forfeiture is incompatible with the ECHR right to peaceful enjoyment of possessions (Art 1, protocol 1) will be unlikely to succeed.[147] If the forfeiture denied D the opportunity to have the material shown in circumstances in which there was no likelihood of corruption (for example, by removing it from general sale and making it available in a private outlet) the argument might have more substance.

As far as the EU and free movement of goods within the EU are concerned, the Divisional Court has held that once goods were within the definition of obscenity in s 1 of the 1959 Act, there was no difficulty in applying (what is now) Art 36 of the Treaty on the Functioning of the European Union to permit restriction on importation and forfeiture.[148]

31.1.11 Related offences

Numerous other statutes include offences for which summary proceedings may be, and are, instituted. These offences do not contain the safeguards of the Obscene Publications Acts. Examples include the Metropolitan Police Act 1839, s 54[149] and the Children and Young Persons (Harmful Publications) Act 1955. No doubt there are also many local Acts and by-laws which may be invoked.[150]

---

[142] Obscene Publications Act 1959, s 4(1).

[143] See the challenge in *Britton v DPP* [1996] CLY 1486, on the law officers' undertakings.

[144] The same thing could of course occur in relation to proceedings on indictment. If another publisher were to be prosecuted for publishing *Lady Chatterley*, the decision in *Penguin Books* (above, n 121) would not be relevant in evidence, let alone an estoppel; and another jury, hearing different expert evidence, might well arrive at a different conclusion.

[145] See above, p 1068.

[146] Obscene Publications Act 1959, s 3(3A).

[147] *X Co v UK* (1983) 32 DR 231.

[148] See *R v Bow Street Metropolitan Stipendiary Magistrates, ex p Noncyp Ltd* [1990] 1 QB 123; *Wright v Customs and Excise Comrs* [1999] 1 Cr App R 69. See for detailed discussion S Weatherill and P Beaumont, *EU Law* (3rd edn, 1999) Ch 16; P Craig and G de Búrca, *EU Law: Text, Cases and Materials* (4th edn, 2007) Ch 19.

[149] 'Every person who shall sell or distribute or offer for sale or distribution, or exhibit to public view, any profane, ... book, paper, print, drawing, painting or representation, or sing any profane, indecent, or obscene song or ballad, ... or use any profane, indecent or obscene language to the annoyance of the inhabitants or passengers.'

[150] See, generally, *Report of the Home Office Working Party on Vagrancy and Street Offences* (1974).

31.2 Extreme pornography

The law relating to obscenity was not reviewed in the Sexual Offences Review in 2000. It was widely regarded as being in a state of incoherence and ambiguity and in desperate need of reform. For some time suggestions had been made to reform the central test of corrupting and depraving, replacing it with schedules of prohibited material (for example, torture, coprophilia, child pornography, etc).[151] The Government announced[152] proposals to outlaw the possession of an extreme pornographic image. In August 2005, the Home Office launched a consultation paper, on the possession of extreme pornographic material stating that it was considered 'possible that such material may encourage or reinforce interest in violent and aberrant sexual activity to the detriment of society as a whole'.[153] The Home Office published a response in 2006.[154] The resulting legislative proposals were heavily criticized, not merely because they further restrict free expression, but because they are not consistent with the stated policy aim. If the concern is with extreme pornography leading to violent offending, it is strange that the offences are limited to possession of sexual but not violent imagery.[155]

The offences were enacted in the Criminal Justice and Immigration Act 2008 and came into force in January 2009.[156] They are triable either way. The offence comprises possession of extreme pornographic images. The offences are extremely controversial.[157] They are distinct from the obscenity offences above because these outlaw possession of categories of adult pornography *per se*. There is no issue of whether the individual image is obscene and likely to deprave and corrupt. The Government's focus was primarily on the harm to those participating in the activities being depicted.[158] Commentators have suggested that it is not clear what specific harm the provisions seek to prevent.[159] Unlike indecent images of children which necessarily involve depictions of child sex offences, there is not necessarily a similar *direct* harm in the depiction of all forms of extreme pornography.

Challenges under Art 10 and Art 8 seem likely. The question will be whether the offence is necessary and proportionate. Although the Obscene Publications Act offences have been

---

[151] See historically on reform the Williams Committee (1979) Cmnd 7772.

[152] In part triggered by the evidence in the prosecution of *Coutts* [2006] UKHL 39, for the manslaughter of a schoolteacher. The evidence at trial revealed that Coutts had been downloading very graphic violent pornography and that this may have been a cause of his actions.

[153] Para 27. See also J Rowbottom, 'Obscenity Laws and the Internet: Targeting Supply and Demand' [2006] Crim LR 97; S Edwards, 'A Safe Haven for Hardest Core' [1997] Ent LR 137.

[154] *Consultation on the Possession of Extreme Pornographic Material: Summary of Responses and Next Steps* (2006). See also the responses at www.scotland.gov.uk/Topics/Justice/crimes/pornography/ExtremePornograhicMateria.

[155] See also J Samiloff, 'Harmful Viewing' (2007) 157 NLJ 170. For reform of this area in Scotland, see www.scotland.gov.uk/Topics/Justice/crimes/pornography/ExtremePornograhicMateria. For views against the legislation, see www.backlash-uk.org.uk/what.html, and against the Home Office, http://news.bbc.co.uk/1/hi/7364475.stm.

[156] SI 2008/2993. See the MOJ Circular, www.justice.gov.uk/publications/docs/circular-criminal-justice-01-2009(1).pdf.

See generally on the offences C McGlynn and E Rackley, 'Criminalising Extreme Pornography: A Lost Opportunity' [2009] Crim LR 245; AD Murray 'The Reclassification of Extreme Pornographic Images' (2009) 72 MLR 73.

[157] See the discussion on the consultation responses in Murray, above, p 78.

[158] See C Itzin, A Taket and L Kelly, 'The Evidence of Harm to Adults relating to Exposure and Extreme Pornographic Material' published on the government website: www.justice.gov.uk. See also S Edwards, 'The Failure of British Obscenity Laws in the Regulation of Pornography' in C Itzin and P Cox (eds) *Pornography and Sexual Aggression* (2000).

[159] See S Forster, 'Possession of Extreme Pornographic Images, Public Perceptions and Human Rights' (2010) 15 Cov LJ 21, 25.

found compatible, this is a different offence focused on mere possession by an adult, and not the publication of material which might corrupt others.

31.2.1 Pornographic

Under s 63 of the Act, an image is 'pornographic' if it must reasonably be assumed to have been produced solely or principally for the purpose of sexual arousal (s 63(3)). Where the image appears as part of a series its potential pornographic nature is to be considered in the context of the whole (s 63(4)).[160] It is not relevant to consider D's intentions nor whether he was sexually aroused. The test is objective.

31.2.2 Extreme image

'Image' is defined to include a moving or still image (produced by any means); or data (stored by any means) which is capable of conversion into a moving or still image (s 63(8)). There is no requirement that D made or created the image. Crucially, the Act goes on to define an 'extreme image' as one which is 'grossly offensive, disgusting, or otherwise of an obscene character' and falls within the following description (s 63(7)):

(a) an act which threatens a person's life,[161]

(b) an act which results, or is likely to result in serious injury to a person's anus, breasts or genitals,[162]

(c) an act which involves sexual interference with a human corpse,

(d) a person performing an act of intercourse or oral sex with an animal (whether dead or alive),

and a reasonable person looking at the image would think that any such person or animal was real.

Classified films are excluded from the scope of the offence.[163]

The Ministry of Justice describe[164] having chosen the words 'grossly offensive and disgusting' as ordinary words, intending them to be understood in a non-technical way. The core terms – life threatening, serious injury etc – are all undefined. The Ministry of Justice note that it was not intended that serious injury relate to any class of injury under the OAPA 1861.[165]

31.2.3 Possession

In the first reported case under the Act, *Ping Chen Cheung*,[166] D was found with a laptop bag containing hundreds of DVDs bundled together by elastic bands in packs. Many were

---

[160] By s 63(5) further explanation is offered: 'where – (a) an image forms an integral part of a narrative constituted by a series of images, and (b) having regard to those images as a whole, they are not of such a nature that they must reasonably be assumed to have been produced solely or principally for the purpose of sexual arousal, the image may, by virtue of being part of that narrative, be found not to be pornographic, even though it might have been found to be pornographic if taken by itself'.

[161] eg depictions of hanging. The clause was originally much broader and included images that appeared to threaten life.

[162] Including surgically reconstructed ones: s 63(9). Examples might include penetration with sharp objects.

[163] Section 64 of the 2008 Act.

[164] Circular 2009/01, para 12.

[165] ibid, para 16.

[166] [2010] EWCA Crim 2963; see also *Wakeling* [2010] EWCA Crim 2210.

counterfeit films.[167] In the bottom of the bag was a bundle of DVDs depicting acts of bestiality. He denied knowing possession of the bestiality DVDs. The DVD covers displayed images of oral sex with animals, but these were not visible simply by opening the bag and the DVDs did not bear his fingerprints. The issue at trial was whether D had possession of them if, as he claimed, he lacked knowledge of the type of images they depicted and whether he had proved the defence under s 65 that he had not seen the image and did not know, nor had any cause to suspect, it to be an extreme pornographic image. D admitted he knew the bag contained DVDs and that it was his intention to sell them. The trial judge directed the jury in such a confused manner as to conflate several requirements and the Court of Appeal quashed the conviction.

From the Court of Appeal's judgment it is clear that the prosecution must prove (i) that D had physical possession of the DVDs (that is necessary but not sufficient for conviction); (ii) that D knew of the existence of the thing in his custody or control.[168] It is not necessary for the prosecution to prove that D knew that the DVDs contained extreme pornographic images.

> It is only if there is a real doubt as to whether the defendant believed that that which he knew he had, was of a wholly different nature from that which in fact it was, that possession would not be made out. A mere mistake as to quality of the thing which the defendant knows is in his possession or control is not enough to prevent him being in possession for the purposes of the offence under [the offence]. What amounts to something of a wholly different nature will be a question of fact and degree for the jury in a given case where this issue arises. A belief, for example, that something which is in fact a collection of DVDs is a collection of, say, floor tiles might well qualify.... In the case of a package or a box, ... the defendant's possession of it will lead to a strong inference that the defendant was in possession of its contents within the meaning of the statutory provision. [15]

Things will be more complex where the images are on a computer. Issues may arise as to whether D knew that he had *data* on his computer. Another likely challenge will be that D denies exclusive possession or control of the computer and therefore denies possession. Recent interpretations of similarly worded offences suggest that D is not in possession merely because he has the 'ability to control' the use of a computer.[169]

31.2.4 Defences

There is no defence of the image being for the public good. There are two statutory defences: one of a legitimate reason for possession (s 65) and one of participating in the consensual acts depicted (s 66).

Section 65 provides in effect three defences for D to prove: (a) that he had a legitimate reason for being in possession of the image concerned;[170] or (b) that he had not seen the image concerned and did not know, nor had any cause to suspect, it to be an extreme pornographic image; or (c) that he (i) was sent the image concerned without any prior request having been made by

---

[167] D pleaded guilty to Trade Marks Act 1994 offence in relation to these.

[168] Compare cases under s 160 of the CJA 1988: *Collier* [2004] Crim LR 1039, and *Atkins v DPP* [2000] 2 Cr App R 248. In *Atkins*, the Court held that the offence of possession under s 160 of the CJA 1988 is not committed unless the defendant knows that he has photographs in his possession. In *Collier*, it was noted that the defences in s 160(2)(a) and (c) of the CJA 1988 proceed on the assumption that the defendant is aware that the photograph is an *indecent* photograph *of a child*.

[169] *Kousar* [2009] EWCA Crim 139.

[170] This is similar to s 1(4)(a) of the Protection of Children Act 1978 and s 160(2)(a) of the Criminal Justice Act 1988. Whether D has a legitimate reason for being in possession of the image concerned is a question of fact: *Atkins v DPP* [2000] 2 Cr App R 248.

or on behalf of him, and (ii) did not keep it for an unreasonable time.[171] In *Ping Chen Cheung*[172] the Court held that the burden on D is to prove on the balance of probabilities (rather than for him to bear a mere evidential burden), but it is not clear that point was fully argued.

Under s 66 it is a defence for D to prove that the images were portrayals of acts in which D directly participated and that the acts did not involve any infliction of non-consensual harm. If D can lawfully participate in the activities it would be nonsensical to criminalize his possession of the images of his doing so.[173] This defence is not available if the images involve animals (s 63(7)(d)), or in cases in which the image portrays an act with a real corpse. Under s 66(3), 'non consensual harm' extends to harm to which a person cannot in law consent to under the decision in *Brown* (above, Chapter 17) as well as cases where there is no consent in fact.

31.2.5 Procedure[174]

The consent of the DPP will be required for a prosecution (s 63(10)). Conviction on indictment will result in a maximum sentence of three years' imprisonment where the image depicts acts in s 63(7)(a) or (b) (life threats or serious genital injury), and a maximum of two years in other cases: s 67.

31.3 Possession of prohibited images of children[175]

The latest extension of the law in this area is an offence of possession of prohibited images of children. The offence was introduced in the Coroners and Justice Act 2009, ss 62–67.[176] Detailed discussion of this offence and those of making etc and possession of indecent images of children lie beyond the scope of this work.[177]

It is, however, worth noting one unusual feature of the offence. It deals with images depicting children, but significantly, it is restricted to images which are not already caught by the indecent image offences. For the purpose of this offence, by s 65(3) 'image' does *not* include an indecent photograph, or indecent pseudo-photograph, of a child. What, therefore, is being criminalized is the possession of images of imaginary children, unlike the indecent image offences in which the image depicts a real child (or part of a child). Whereas the offences under the Protection of Children Act 1978 and the Criminal Justice Act 1988 involve direct harm to children as the images depict child sex offences, in this offence, there is no child who is directly harmed; there is no child involved in the creation of the images.[178] Ost examines

---

[171] The defence is similar to s 160(2)(c) of the CJA 1988. See *Bowden* [2000] Crim LR 381; *Collier* [2004] EWCA Crim 1411; [2004] Crim LR 1039 and commentary; see also A Gillespie, 'Tinkering With Child Pornography' [2004] Crim LR 361.

[172] [2010] EWCA Crim 2963.

[173] *Hansard*, HL, col 275, 30 April 2008, per Lord Hunt.

[174] See Ministry of Justice Circular 2009/01.

[175] See in particular the analysis in S Ost, 'Criminalising Fabricated Images of Child Pornography: A Matter of Harm or Morality?' (2010) 30 LS 230.

[176] For the background to the offence see the Home Office, *Consultation on the Possession of Non-Photographic Visual Depictions of Child Sexual Abuse* (2007) in which it is acknowledged that there is no evidence that these images lead to child sex abuse of real children. See on this the comments of the Joint Committee on Human Rights, Eighth Report, 20 March 2009, para 1.178.

[177] See generally, S Ost, *Child Pornography and Sexual Grooming: Legal and Societal Responses* (2009); M Taylor and E Quayle, *Child Pornography: An Internet Crime* (2003).

[178] The offence is about 'protecting children from abuse and to protect children and vulnerable adults from coming into contact with the material... [that] can desensitise people to child abuse and reinforce people's

in detail the possible moral bases for the offence, distinguishing (i) those cases in which the image was one of a real child which has been manipulated to disguise that and (ii) images of fantasy children. In relation to the latter, identifying a sufficient basis for criminalization is difficult. Possibilities are that the images will be used to groom children and that the images encourage the objectification of children as sex objects.[179] The parliamentary debates gave rise to some interesting discussions of whether it ought to be an offence for an adult to possess for private use images of imaginary children.

The offence under s 62 comprises (i) possession[180] (ii) of an image[181] (iii) which is a prohibited one[182] (iv) which is a pornographic[183] image (v) of a child.[184]

The maximum sentence on indictment is three years' imprisonment: s 66. The offence has a number of qualifications and safeguards: the definition in s 62 is designed to exclude genuine works of art; by s 63 the offence does not apply to classified films; the consent of the DPP is required for prosecution: s 62(9). Moreover, there is a defence in s 64 for the defendant to prove: (a) that he had a legitimate reason for being in possession of the image concerned; (b) that he had not seen the image concerned and did not know, nor had any cause to suspect, it to be a prohibited image of a child; (c) that he – (i) was sent the image concerned without any prior request having been made by or on behalf of him, and (ii) did not keep it for an unreasonable time.[185] Estimates are that there will be between 0–1 prosecutions per year.[186]

31.4 Posting indecent or obscene matter

The Postal Services Act 2000, s 85 provides:

(3) A person commits an offence if he sends by post a postal packet which encloses –

    (a) any indecent or obscene print, painting, photograph, lithograph, engraving, cinematograph film or other record of a picture or pictures, book, card or written communication, or

    (b) any other indecent or obscene article (whether or not of a similar kind to those mentioned in paragraph (a)).

(4) A person commits an offence if he sends by post a postal packet which has on the packet, or on the cover of the packet, any words, marks or designs which are of an indecent or obscene character.

inappropriate and potentially dangerous feelings towards children': Joint Committee on Human Rights, Eighth Report; 20 March 2009, para 1.175.

[179] Ost proposes an alternative form of offence focusing on creation and publication of such images.

[180] Possession will no doubt be construed as in the extreme pornographic cases (such as *Ping* discussed above) and follow closely the case law on drug possession.

[181] An image includes a moving or still image, produced by any means, and therefore sketches, or computer-generated images are within the reach of the offence (s 65(2)(a)).

[182] The image must be 'grossly offensive, disgusting or otherwise of an obscene character' (s 62(2)(c)). The language of s 62(2)(a) is identical to that in s 63(6)(b) of the 2008 Act above. The image must be one that, either (a) focuses solely or principally on a child's genitals or anal region (s 62(6)(a) and s 62(2)(a)), or (b) it portrays any of the specified acts in s 62(7) (penetration, oral sex, masturbation, bestiality etc: see s 62(6) and s 62(7)(a)).

[183] An image is 'pornographic' if it is of such a nature that it must reasonably be assumed to have been produced solely or principally for the purpose of sexual arousal: s 62(3).

[184] A 'child' means a person under the age of 18 years: s 65(5).

[185] This follows that in relation to adult extreme images in CJIA 2008, s 65.

[186] See DPP Memorandum to the PB Committee, 5 Feb 2009.

(5) A person who commits an offence under this section shall be liable –

    (a) on summary conviction, to a fine not exceeding the statutory maximum,

    (b) on conviction on indictment, to a fine or to imprisonment for a term not exceeding twelve months or to both.

The offence follows closely that under the Post Office Act 1953 which it replaces, and the authorities on that section retain significance.

31.4.1 Meaning of indecent or obscene

Under the 1953 Act, the Court of Appeal made clear in the infamous Oz Trial[187] that in the postal context, obscene takes its dictionary definition and not that adopted for the offences under the 1959 Act.[188] The Court of Appeal confirmed in *Kirk*[189] that the words indecent and obscene used in the 2000 Act are ordinary words. They are readily understood by members of the jury, and it is unnecessary, and might be misleading, for the jury to be given any interpretation of the words which might either narrow or enlarge their meaning. The defendant was an anti-vivisectionist who had sent articles to companies whom he considered to be connected with animal experimentation. The envelopes and contents of some of the packets showed graphic images of animal experiments in laboratories and the results of such experiments. The trial judge's direction followed the leading case under the previous legislation (s 11 of the 1953 Act) where it was held in *Stanley*[190] that: 'The words "indecent or obscene" convey one idea, namely offending against the recognised standards of propriety, indecent being at the lower end of the scale and obscene at the upper end of the scale […] an indecent article is not necessarily obscene, whereas an obscene article almost certainly must be indecent.'[191] In *Stanley* the verdict of a jury holding that certain cinematograph films were not obscene (for the purposes of the Obscene Publications Act) but were indecent (for the purposes of the Post Office Act) was upheld.

Kirk confirms that, as under the 1953 Act, 'obscene' bears its ordinary meaning[192] and so may not extend to material simply because it advocates drug-taking or violence[193] which would not ordinarily be described as 'indecent'.[194] On the other hand, such articles might well be said to offend against 'recognised standards of propriety'; and, for the purposes of other legislation, abusive language and shouts in church alleging hypocrisy against the reader of the lesson[195] have been held to be 'indecent'. 'Indecent' is not confined to sexual indecency, but extends to other improper matter.

The test of indecency is objective and the character of the addressee is immaterial.[196] Indeed, the object of the section seems to be the protection of Post Office employees against dangerous, deleterious or indecent articles.[197] It is evidently not limited to employees, however,

---

[187] *Anderson* [1972] 1 QB 304.

[188] Lord Widgery CJ stated expressly that obscene 'includes things that are shocking and lewd and indecent' (at 311).

[189] [2006] EWCA Crim 725, [2006] Crim LR 849.

[190] [1965] 2 QB 327, [1965] 1 All ER 1035.

[191] ibid, 333–334.

[192] *Anderson* [1971] 3 All ER 1152 at 1162. The judge's direction (above, p 1058) was thus correct so far as the 'Post Office count' was concerned. *Stamford* [1972] 2 QB 391, [1972] 2 All ER 427.

[193] Above, p 1058.

[194] *Lees v Parr* [1967] 3 All ER 181n (by-law).

[195] *Abrahams v Cavey* [1968] 1 QB 479, [1967] 3 All ER 179 (Ecclesiastical Courts Jurisdiction Act 1860, s 2); *Farrant* [1973] Crim LR 240.

[196] *Straker* [1965] Crim LR 239, CCA; *Kosmos Publications Ltd v DPP* [1975] Crim LR 345.

[197] *Stamford* [1972] 2 All ER 427 at 429.

since it is only in rare cases that they will have access to matter 'enclosed' as required by para (b). Evidence is not admissible by any person to say what the effect of the article was on him. The jury do not need assistance. They are themselves 'the custodians of the standards for the time being'.[198] The court in *Kirk* rejected a challenge to s 85 under Art 10 of the ECHR. The offence is not incompatible with Art 10 on the basis that it lacks certainty – even though the element of obscenity remains to be defined by the jury on a case-by-case basis.[199] The court's rejection of Art 10 challenges must be read with caution since it is submitted that the question whether the Article is engaged and whether the prosecution and/or punishment is necessary and proportionate will require a factual assessment in every case.

31.5 Other offensive communications offences

31.5.1 Malicious communications

The Malicious Communications Act 1988[200] created an offence of sending a letter, electronic communication[201] or article which is indecent or grossly offensive, threatening or containing information which is known or believed to be false. The Divisional Court has recently considered the scope of the offence, upholding a conviction for sending images of aborted foetuses to pharmacists selling the 'morning after pill'. In *Connolly v DPP*,[202] the court held that the words 'indecent' and 'grossly offensive' were ordinary English words. The offence does not depend on the recipient's actual reaction, but on the intention of the sender. The court also rejected the argument that on the facts of that case the prosecution infringed Arts 9 and 10 of the Convention, concluding that the right to freedom of expression does not include a right to cause distress or anxiety. The chemists were not individuals who were likely to be engaged in public reform of the abortion law.

31.5.2 Offensive communications

Under the Communications Act 2003, s 127 a person is guilty of an offence if he (a) sends by means of a public electronic communications network a message or other matter that is grossly offensive or of an indecent, obscene or menacing character; or (b) causes any such message or matter to be so sent. On summary conviction, an offender is liable to six months' imprisonment or a fine not exceeding level 5 on the standard scale, or to both.[203]

In *DPP v Collins*,[204] D telephoned the office of his MP and in the course of complaining about various issues he spoke of 'wogs', 'Pakis' and 'black bastards' during his conversations with the office members. Of those who heard the messages, one had found the language upsetting, one had not done so, and one had found it depressing. None of those people happened to be a member of an ethnic minority. The justices acquitted D on the basis that, while offensive,

---

[198] ibid, 432.

[199] *Perrin* [2002] EWCA Crim 747.

[200] See historically LC WP 84, *Criminal Libel* (1982) and Law Com Report No 147, *Poison Pen Letters* (1985).

[201] As inserted by the Criminal Justice and Police Act 2001, s 43.

[202] [2007] EWHC 237 (Admin).

[203] The Penalties for Disorderly Behaviour (Amount of Penalty) Order 2002, SI 1837 provides that an offence under s 127 may be the subject of a fixed penalty. By Sch 1, para 1 of the Penalties for Disorderly Behaviour (Amount of Penalty) (Amendment) Order 2009, SI 83, the fixed penalty is £40 only if the individual is under 16. If the person is 16 or over, the amount is £80.

[204] [2006] UKHL 40, [2006] 1 WLR 2223, [2007] Crim LR 98.

a reasonable person would not consider these messages 'grossly' offensive. The Divisional Court agreed. The House of Lords allowed the prosecutor's appeal, holding that the offence was complete when the message was sent, provided D is shown to have intended or been aware of the proscribed nature of his communication.

The purpose of this offence is not to protect against unsolicited offensive communication,[205] but to proscribe the use of public communications systems for sending messages offending against 'basic standards of society'. D's guilt did not depend on whether the message was received by a person who was deeply offended, or by a person who was not. Since there is no need for any receipt of the message to be proved, liability arises irrespective of whether the recipient was grossly offended/menaced/found it to be indecent or obscene. Indeed, logically the characteristics of the likely recipient cannot be taken into account in determining whether the *actus reus* is performed, although the expected reaction of the likely recipient (such as they are known to the sender at the time the message is sent) is *relevant* to the issue of the sender's state of mind. In terms of whether the words used were 'grossly offensive' the House held that this was for the justices to determine as a question of fact applying the standards of an open and just multi-racial society, and the words must be judged in context. The House of Lords found that C's messages were grossly offensive and would be found by a reasonable person to be so.[206]

The House of Lords also rejected a challenge based on Art 10 of the ECHR: s 127(1)(a) interferes with a person's right to freedom of expression, but is a restriction directed to a legitimate objective,[207] preventing the use of a public electronic communications network for attacking the reputations and rights of others. The offence is necessary in a democratic society to achieve that end.[208] The court must ascertain on the facts of each case whether the Article is engaged and whether the prosecution is necessary and proportionate on the facts.

The result is a far-reaching offence, extending to even solicited communications where D1 is happy to receive D2's indecent communication. This is a controversial interpretation, described by one commentator as 'fundamentally flawed' and 'a complete fallacy' because of the potential impact it will have on telephone and internet adult-chat/sex industries.[209]

31.5.3 Sending unsolicited material

Sending unsolicited matter describing human sexual techniques, or unsolicited advertisement of such matter, is an offence[210] under s 4 of the Unsolicited Goods and Services Act 1971.

---

[205] cf Sedley LJ in the Divisional Court at [9].

[206] The likelihood that the words would cause offence to those to whom they relate (not necessarily the recipients) may be relevant in evaluating their offensiveness: see Lord Bingham at [10]; Lord Carswell at [22]; Lord Brown at [26]–[27].

[207] The House placed emphasis on Art 17, which prevents a person relying on Convention rights to undermine the rights of others. For arguments that Art 17 is overused and therefore reduces the protection of Art 10, see S Turenne, 'The Compatibility of Criminal Liability with Freedom of Expression' [2007] Crim LR 866.

[208] The prosecution of informed consenting-adult sex line or internet chat-room users engaged in an indecent conversation seems unlikely in practice, but is now theoretically possible. Whether such a prosecution would withstand challenge under Art 8 of the ECHR is another matter. Could it be a proportionate response to prosecute where the individuals are adults communicating only with each other?

[209] A Gillespie [2006] Ent LR 236. Lord Brown acknowledged the problem for 'chat lines', but left this matter unresolved.

[210] *DPP v Beate Uhse (UK) Ltd* [1974] QB 158, [1974] 1 All ER 753.

31.6 Obscenity in the theatre

The Theatres Act 1968 abolished censorship of the theatre. Section 2 of the Act makes it an offence to present[211] or direct an obscene performance of a play. The maximum penalty is six months' imprisonment in the magistrates' court, and three years on indictment. The definition of obscenity is the same as in s 1(1) of the Obscene Publications Act 1959,[212] except that attention is directed to the effect of the performance on the persons who are likely to *attend* it instead of 'read, see or hear it'. A defence of 'public good' is provided by s 3 which is the same as that under s 4 of the 1959 Act,[213] except that the interests which may justify the performance are, as in the case of films, those of 'drama, opera, ballet or any other art or of literature or learning'. A performance given 'on a domestic occasion in a private dwelling' is exempted by s 7 from the provisions of s 2. If proceedings are to be brought in respect of the alleged obscenity of the performance of a play, they must be brought under the Act and not under common law offences: s 2(4). A prosecution on indictment under s 2 must be commenced within two years of the commission of the offence: s 2(3).

31.7 Indecent displays

The Indecent Displays (Control) Act 1981 makes it an offence to make, cause or permit the public display of any indecent matter. Matter displayed in, or so as to be visible from, any public place is publicly displayed. A public place is one to which the public have or are permitted to have access, whether on payment or otherwise, except (a) where the payment is or includes payment for the display, or (b) the place is a shop or part of a shop to which the public can gain access only by passing an adequate warning notice, as specified in the Act (s 1(6)). The Act is aimed at displays that people cannot avoid seeing as they go about their business – bookshop and sex shop window displays, cinema club posters, and so on. It does not apply to television broadcasts as defined in the Broadcasting Act 1990, displays visible only from within an art gallery or museum, the performance of a play within the Theatres Act 1968 or a film exhibition as defined in the Licensing Act 2003. 'Matter' is anything capable of being displayed except an actual human body or part of it. Thus 'lap dancing' or 'stripping' is not caught.[214] 'Indecent' is not defined. Whether matter is indecent will no doubt be considered a matter of fact to be determined by applying the ordinary meaning of the word.[215]

31.8 Outraging public decency[216]

The common law offence of outraging public decency is still relied upon to prosecute some displays despite the number of statutory offences available.[217]

[211] cf *Grade v DPP* [1942] 2 All ER 118.
[212] Above, p 1058.
[213] Above, p 1069.
[214] See the regulation of venues providing such services under the Policing and Crime Act 2009.
[215] Above, p 1080.
[216] See P Rook and R Ward, *Sexual Offences Law and Practice* (4th edn, 2010) Ch 14. There is a relatively brief examination of the offence in the Law Commission Consultation Paper No 193, *Simplification of Criminal Law: Public Nuisance and Outraging Public Decency* (2009) Part 3.
[217] There are reported to be 300–400 prosecutions per year, see LCCP No 193, para 4.36. The offence also overlaps with a number of sexual offences in the Sexual Offences Act 2003, see Ch 18 above. It covers diverse conduct: eg *Anderson* [2008] EWCA Crim 12 – urinating on a dying woman in the street.

The offence involves doing an act of a lewd obscene or disgusting nature which outrages public decency. The offence is triable either way.[218] An article which is sufficient for the offence of outraging public decency is not necessarily obscene. It may well outrage and disgust without having any tendency to deprave and corrupt. In such a case, a prosecution for the common law offence is not barred by s 2(4) of the Obscene Publications Act.[219] This was the conclusion of the Court in *Gibson*[220] where in a commercial art gallery D exhibited 'Human Earrings', earrings made out of freeze-dried human foetuses. It was not suggested that anyone was likely to be corrupted by the exhibition but, as the jury had found, the public would be outraged by it.

The defence of 'public good' under s 4(1) of the 1959 Act does not apply to the common law offence. An article may have a tendency both to corrupt and to cause outrage. It seems to follow that, in such a case the protection of the 1959 Act can be avoided by charging the common law offence. It can hardly be said that the 'essence of the offence' charged is that the article is obscene because the prosecution do not have to prove obscenity in order to establish it; and, if obscenity is not of the essence of the offence charged, the prosecution is not barred by s 2(4). The less grave conduct of outraging public decency therefore attracts no defence when the more serious one of corrupting and depraving does.

31.8.1 *Actus reus*

In the leading case of *Hamilton*,[221] D used a hidden camera in his bag to film up young girls' skirts while they stood in supermarket checkout queues. The Court of Appeal conducted an extensive review of the authorities. The elements of the offence were identified as being twofold.

i) The act was of such a lewd character as to outrage public decency; this element constituted the nature of the act which had to be proved before the offence could be established.

ii) It took place in a public place and must have been capable of being seen by two or more persons who were actually present, even if they had not actually seen it. This constituted the public element of the offence which had to be proved. [21]

The first element is the act of such a lewd, obscene or disgusting character that it outrages public decency.[222] An obscene act is one which offends against recognized standards of propriety and which is at a higher level of impropriety than indecency; and a disgusting act is one which fills the onlooker with loathing or extreme distaste or causes annoyance.[223] 'It is not enough that the act is lewd, obscene or disgusting and that it might shock people; it must,... be of such a character that it outrages minimum standards of public decency as judged by the jury in contemporary society.'[224] The court observed that 'outrages' is a strong word. If no such act is done, the offence is not committed, however outrageous D's intentions or fantasies, as revealed, for example, in his private diaries.[225] It might be different where the observers of ambiguous conduct are aware of the actor's purpose. They might then be outraged by acts which, if not known to be done with that purpose, would not be outrageously indecent.

---

[218] Criminal Justice Act 2003 (Commencement No 2 and Saving Provisions) Order 2004, SI 81.
[219] Above.
[220] [1991] 1 All ER 439, [1990] Crim LR 738. See also M Childs, 'Outraging Public Decency: The Offence of Offensiveness' [1991] PL 20.
[221] [2007] EWCA Crim 2062. The court conducted an extensive historical survey of the offence and its elements.
[222] *Hamilton* [2007] EWCA Crim 2062 at [31].
[223] ibid, [30].
[224] ibid, [30].
[225] *Rowley* [1991] 4 All ER 649, [1991] Crim LR 785.

Proof of the element of outrage is often by inference. In *Lunderbech*,[226] where D, masturbating in a children's playground, was seen only by two police officers who did not testify that they were outraged. The court said that where the act is plainly indecent and likely to disgust and annoy, 'the jury are entitled to infer such disgust and annoyance without affirmative evidence that anyone was disgusted and annoyed'. The so-called 'inference' is plainly fictitious. In *May*[227] (a schoolmaster 'behaving in an indecent manner with a desk' in the presence of two boys), it was held to be irrelevant that the two boys may have enjoyed the performance.[228] The effect seems to be that the offence is committed if the jury think the conduct outrageously indecent because it would disgust and annoy them, and therefore the ordinary members of the public whom they represent, if they witnessed it.[229] 'Disgusting' is that which is capable of filling the onlooker with loathing or extreme distaste or of causing the onlooker extreme annoyance.[230]

Secondly, the court in *Hamilton* concluded that the act must be done in a place to which the public has access or in a place where what is done is capable of public view and where at least two members of the public who are actually present *might* see it,[231] or hear it.[232] In *Hamilton*, the girls in the queue did not see the conduct (D secretly filming) nor did others in the vicinity, but there were more than two people present who *could* have seen it. Controversially, the court declined to restrict the offence so as to require *actual* sight or sound of the nature of the act.

The public element in the offence is satisfied if the act is done where persons are present and the nature of what is being done is *capable of being seen*; the principle is that the public are to be protected from acts of a lewd, obscene or disgusting acts which are of a nature that outrages public decency and which are capable of being seen in public.[233]

The Court of Appeal accepted that all the reported cases had involved one person *actually being present* seeing the act, but observed that the requirement was a matter of evidence rather than one of substantive law. This is technically *obiter*. As Rook and Ward observe, there remains uncertainty over whether a person must be present capable of seeing the acts or whether it is sufficient that people might come upon the act and witness it.[234]

The court's interpretation in Hamilton is surprising in that it demonstrates a willingness to extend the common law to tackle new mischief which is a practice the House of Lords had deprecated in *Rimington*[235] in the context of public nuisance.[236]

---

[226] [1991] Crim LR 784.

[227] (1989) 91 Cr App R 157, [1990] Crim LR 415.

[228] See also *Choi* [1999] EWCA Crim 1279 (filming in ladies' lavatory in supermarket).

[229] See also *Hamilton* at [31].

[230] *Choi* [1999] EWCA Crim 1279, see also *Cuthbertson* [2003] EWCA Crim 3915 (filming under cubicles in changing rooms with a mobile phone camera).

[231] *Curran* (1998) unreported, CA, 29 Oct (copulation and oral sex on bonnet of car in short stay car park at Heathrow sufficient); having sex with a stranger's dog in public: Daily Telegraph, 21 July 2010.

[232] *Hamilton* expressly accepts that this is sufficient, drawing on the statements in parliamentary debates on the Sexual Offences Bill 2003, cited by Rook and Ward, *Sexual Offences Law and Practice*, above, 14.47.

[233] *Hamilton* at [39].

[234] The Law Commission suggests the latter: LCCP 193, 3.27. See also *F* [2010] EWCA Crim sat in his car masturbating while watching children play on nearby sportsground. Whenever passers-by approached the car he covered himself. He was watched by W from an upstairs window in her house overlooking the road. The judge ruled that the two person rule was not satisfied. The CA upheld the ruling.

[235] [2006] 1 AC 459.

[236] For criticism see A Gillespie, 'Upskirts and Down Blouses' [2008] Crim LR 370, who examines whether voyeurism under s 67 of the Sexual Offences Act 2003, above Ch 18, might apply and whether England ought to adopt a new offence based on the New Zealand model to tackle upskirting.

The Divisional Court in *Rose*[237] held that the two individuals present who might see the conduct must be two other than those knowingly participating in the outrageous conduct. In that case, D and his girlfriend engaged in oral sex at 1am in a bank foyer accessible for those wishing to use ATM machines therein. Their activity was recorded on CCTV. The foyer was deserted, though well lit and passers-by could have peered in.[238] The court held that it is probably not sufficient that the only individuals who might see the conduct are able to view it via CCTV. A private recording of an act which had not previously been seen is probably insufficient to constitute the offence.[239]

It is insufficient that the act in a private dwelling is witnessed by two people,[240] or in public where only one person could see the conduct.[241]

31.8.2 *Mens rea*

To the extent that the House of Lords in *Lemon* declared blasphemy to be an offence of strict liability,[242] *Gibson* does the same for outraging public decency. D must presumably be aware of the nature of the act he is doing. If Gibson had not known that the earrings were made from human foetuses he would presumably not have been guilty. But the case decides that it was not necessary to prove that he intended or foresaw that the effect of the exhibition would be to outrage public decency.[243] As the court said, the practical effect of this ruling is not great. It is difficult to imagine a jury not being satisfied that D knew very well what the effect of his act would be. But this does not justify dispensing with *mens rea*. Rather, it demonstrates that there is not that necessity which is sometimes urged as a justification for strict liability – that is, that no one would be convicted if *mens rea* were required.

The court remarked that one reason why the early authorities are of little assistance is the existence before the enactment of s 8 of the Criminal Justice Act 1967 of the presumption that a person intends the natural and probable consequences of his actions. The court failed to draw the inevitable conclusion from this premise. Before 1967, intention need not be proved only because it was conclusively presumed, but since 1967 it is no longer presumed and must be proved.

31.8.3 ECHR

The European Commission dismissed as inadmissible an application challenging the offence in *S and G v UK*.[244] Despite the recent efforts of the courts to clarify the *actus reus* elements in *Hamilton* and *Rose* it remains doubtful whether the offence is sufficiently certain to be prescribed by law within Art 10, or necessary and proportionate within Art 10(2).[245]

---

[237] [2006] EWHC 852 (Admin).

[238] On that basis it is reconcilable with *Hamilton*.

[239] *Rose*, cf *Birch* [2007] EWCA Crim 1008, masturbating in public and witnessed on CCTV by operator who alerted police as D pursued a woman who did not see the acts. See also the possible use of s 67 of the Sexual Offences Act 2003 which criminalizes voyeurism, and see *Henderson* [2006] EWCA Crim 3264 (upskirting and filming with mobile in ladies' toilets).

[240] *W* (1995) 159 JP 509 (D masturbating in front of his daughter and her 10-year-old friend).

[241] See, eg, *Davies* (1999) No 98/5489/Y4 (D masturbating in car in remote country lane in presence of only his driving pupil). cf *Ammouchi* [2007] EWCA Crim 842, where D pleaded guilty to the offence when he masturbated outside a woman's window witnessed by her alone in the early hours of the morning.

[242] Described by the Law Commission as being as though the defendant is treated as if he had intended or been reckless. There is no explanation as to why the Commission thinks the intent is deemed. The offence is simply one of strict liability (LCCP 193, para 5.45).

[243] See, eg, *Tinley* [2004] EWCA Crim 3032, D looking up women's skirts surreptitiously using video camera.

[244] App No 17634/91 (the *Gibson* case).

[245] The Law Commission rejects the argument that the offence is potentially incompatible with the ECHR.

31.8.4 Reform

The Law Commission provisionally proposes in CP 193[246] that 'there is no *obvious* case for abolishing the offence or radically altering its conduct element, within the limits of a simplification project. It may be that a more wide-ranging and fundamental review would lead to a different view of where the offence should fit in among the wider spectrum of indecency-related offences: for example, a different rationale could be provided for penalising voyeuristic acts like those in *Hamilton*.' Rather the conclusion is that the law should be retained as it is stated in *Hamilton* with the modification that the offence be defined to require that D intentionally generates or realizes that he might generate outrage, shock or disgust in ordinary people.

31.9 Common law offences of blasphemy, libel and sedition

The common law recognized four forms of criminal libel – blasphemy, defamation, obscenity and sedition. Lord Scarman regarded them as part of a group of criminal offences designed to safeguard the internal tranquillity of the kingdom.[247]

31.9.1 Blasphemy[248]

At common law it was a misdemeanour to publish blasphemous matter. The Criminal Justice and Immigration Act 2008, s 79 abolished the offence of blasphemy and blasphemous libel.[249] For discussion of the offence see the previous edition of this work.

31.9.2 Defamatory libel[250]

By s 73 of the Coroners and Justice Act 2009, the common law crimes of libel were abolished:

The following offences under the common law of England and Wales and the common law of Northern Ireland are abolished –

(a) the offences of sedition and seditious libel;

(b) the offence of defamatory libel;

(c) the offence of obscene libel.

For discussion of these offences see the earlier edition of this work.

---

[246] See www.lawcom.gov.uk/docs/cp193.pdf.

[247] *Whitehouse v Gay News Ltd* (1979) 68 Cr App R 381 at 404 and 409, HL.

[248] For a comprehensive general discussion, see Appendix 3 and for a comparative analysis, see Appendix 5 of the House of Lords Select Committee on *Religious Offences in England and Wales First Report* (2003) vol I (HL Paper 95-I). For historical accounts, see generally: GD Nokes, *History of the Crime of Blasphemy* (1928); CS Kenny, 'The Evolution of the Law of Blasphemy' [1922] 1 CLJ 127; Stephen, II HCL, 469–476; L Blom-Cooper and G Drewry, *Law and Morality* (1976) 254–260; N Walter, *Blasphemy Ancient and Modern* (1990); R Webster, *A Brief History of Blasphemy* (1990); R Buxton, 'The Case of Blasphemous Libel' [1978] Crim LR 673.

[249] On which see R Sandberg and N Doe, 'The Strange Death of Blasphemy' (2008) 71 MLR 971.

[250] See P Milmo and W V H Rogers (eds), *Gatley on Libel and Slander* (11th edn, 2010) Ch 24.

32

Offences against public order

32.1 The Public Order Act 1986

32.1.1 Background

The Public Order Act 1986 replaced the ancient common law offences of riot, rout, unlawful assembly and affray and some statutory offences relating to public order[1] with new offences. These are, in descending order of gravity: riot, violent disorder and affray. In addition to these more serious offences the Act created offences of inducing fear of violence, and behaviour likely to cause harassment, alarm or distress which have become very heavily used. There were over 37,598 recorded public order offences in 2009/10 of those, none were for riot, and 861 for violent disorder.[2] The high volume of prosecutions reflects recent Government policing priorities focusing on low-level disorder and anti-social behaviour.[3]

It should also be noted that the offences created by the 1986 Act are not all 'public' order offences: some may be committed in private. However, as the courts have repeatedly emphasized, it is important to keep sight of the public order foundations of these offences and not treat them as merely additional offences against the person. With the lower level offences under ss 4, 4A and 5, one might question whether the real harm being protected against by these offences is one against an attack on the person or one of a more general endangering of public safety and security.[4]

32.1.2 General matters of interpretation

Though the contrary has been argued in some cases, it is clear that the general principles of secondary liability and general defences, such as private defence or the prevention of crime,

---

[1] For the law before the 1986 Act, see the 5th edition of this book, Ch 20; for the background to the 1986 Act, see the Home Office, *Review of the Public Order Act and Related Legislation* (1980) Cmnd 7891 and LCWP 82 (1982) and Report, *Offences Relating to Public Disorder* (Law Com No 123, 1983). For detailed studies of the new law at the time it was enacted, see R Card, *Public Order: The New Law* (1987) and ATH Smith, *Offences against Public Order* (1987). For a recent detailed study of the offences see P Thornton et al, *The Law of Public Order and Protest* (2010).

[2] J Flatley et al, *Crime in England and Wales 2009/10, Findings from the British Crime Survey and Police Recorded Crime* (2010) table 2.04.

[3] Anti-Social Behaviour Orders (ASBOs) are not dealt with in this book, principally because they are not crimes, rather they are civil orders backed with a criminal sanction for failure to comply. For detailed treatment of the relevant law, see M Sikand, *ASBOs: A Practitioner's Guide to Defending Anti-social Behaviour Orders* (2006).

[4] Duff suggests that the offences involve an attack on a person if they are intended to cause fear, but are endangerment offences otherwise. See R A Duff, 'Criminalising Endangerment' in Duff and Green (eds), *Defining Crimes*, 52.

are applicable to offences under the Act as they are under other statutes and at common law. In addition, the serious offences – riot, violent disorder and affray – are continuing offences, following the common law position.[5] Once the 12 people (in the case of riot) or the three (in violent disorder), as the case may be, have used or threatened violence, the offence is constituted and will continue so long as they remain together (in the case of riot, for a common purpose) and at least one of them is continuing to use or threaten violence. One is enough, since it is provided that the persons present need not use or threaten violence simultaneously.

The Act does not provide a complete code of public order offences, and some reference is made here to relevant common law offences. However, care must be taken in relying on common law interpretations. As the Court of Appeal emphasized in *Carey*[6] in the context of affray: the language of the subsections is plain and should be given its ordinary unglossed meaning. In the recent case of *NW*[7] the court referred, as guides to construction, to the Law Commission Reports which led to the enactment of the 1986 Act.

32.1.3 Riot

Riot is an indictable offence, punishable with 10 years' imprisonment, or an unlimited fine, or both. It is explained by s 1 of the Act as follows:

(1) Where 12 or more persons who are present together use or threaten unlawful violence for a common purpose and the conduct of them (taken together) is such as would cause a person of reasonable firmness present at the scene to fear for his personal safety, each of the persons using unlawful violence for the common purpose is guilty of riot.

(2) It is immaterial whether or not the 12 or more use or threaten unlawful violence simultaneously.

(3) The common purpose may be inferred from conduct.

(4) No person of reasonable firmness need actually be, or be likely to be, present at the scene.

(5) Riot may be committed in private as well as in public places.

Riot is intended for exceptionally serious cases and the consent of the DPP is necessary before a prosecution can be brought. It is, nevertheless, a very widely drafted offence. In making the decision to prosecute for riot, the CPS charging standards suggest that riot might appropriately be charged where: 'the normal forces of law and order have broken down; due to the intensity of the attacks on police and other civilian authorities, normal access by emergency services is impeded by mob activity; due to the scale and ferocity of the disorder, severe disruption and fear is caused to members of the public; the violence carries with it the potential for a significant impact upon a significant number of non-participants for a significant length of time; organized or spontaneous large scale acts of violence on people and/or property'.[8]

32.1.3.1 Twelve or more

The gravity of riot depends on the presence of large numbers. The number, 12, is arbitrary and it will not usually be necessary to offer evidence of a head-count because the offence is unlikely to be used except in the case of a large crowd, when well in excess of 12 are using or threatening violence.

---

[5] *Woodrow* (1959) 43 Cr App R 105; *Jones* (1974) 59 Cr App R 120.
[6] [2006] EWCA Crim 17.
[7] [2010] EWCA Crim 404.
[8] See www.cps.gov.uk/legal/p_to_r/public_order_offences/#Riot.

32.1.3.2 Common purpose

There is no requirement that the 12 or more should have come together in pursuance of any agreement. They may have assembled by chance, one by one, and at some point when violence is used, they are present together with a common purpose and using or threatening violence. The common purpose relates to the violence, not the coming together. If 12 or more people with a common purpose threaten unlawful violence but only one actually uses it, there is a riot but only one principal rioter. Since the 12 have a common purpose, the rest (the other 11 or more) may be guilty as secondary parties,[9] but this is not necessarily so. Suppose that they have all agreed – 'Threats, yes, but actual violence, no.' If D, for the common purpose, then uses violence, D commits riot but the rest are not necessarily guilty by their mere use of threats. And, if D has clearly gone beyond the scope of the concerted action,[10] as by producing a knife or gun that the rest did not know he had with him, they will certainly not be guilty of riot.

The common purpose need not be an unlawful one. It might be, for example, to persuade an employer to reinstate an employee whom he has wrongfully dismissed. But violence, whether used or threatened, must be unlawful. Force reasonably used or threatened by D in self-defence or for the prevention of crime cannot found a charge of riot.[11]

32.1.3.3 Violence

By s 8, in Part I of the Act 'violence' means any violent conduct, so that:

(1) it includes violent conduct towards persons and (except in the case of affray (below)) violent conduct towards property,

(2) it is not restricted to conduct causing or intended to cause injury or damage but includes any other violent conduct (for example, throwing at or towards a person a missile of a kind capable of causing injury which does not hit or falls short).

Conduct that might well have caused injury or damage will clearly be capable of amounting to violence even though it was neither intended to, nor did, cause injury or damage. 'Violent' movements of the body, where there is no possibility of any impact – as where D waves his fist at V who is across the street – is probably not 'violence' but a threat of violence.

It is immaterial whether the 12 or more use or threaten the unlawful violence simultaneously: s 1(2).

32.1.3.4 Fear for personal safety

The conduct (of the 12) must be such as would (but not necessarily did) cause a person of reasonable firmness present at the scene to fear for his personal safety; no person need actually be, or even be likely to be, at the scene.[12] Where no person is present, the court or jury has to answer a hypothetical question. It is not incumbent on the judge to direct juries on the attributes of the hypothetical reasonable person, nor to give examples of reasonable firmness.[13]

---

[9] The ordinary law of secondary participation applies to riot: *Jefferson* [1994] 1 All ER 270, [1993] Crim LR 880.

[10] Above, p 194.

[11] *Rothwell and Barton* [1993] Crim LR 626. This may prove especially problematical when DDs claim that they were taking pre-emptive action in self-defence.

[12] Sections 1(3) and (4), 2(3) and (4) and 3(3) and (4).

[13] See *Rafferty* [2004] EWCA Crim 968 on affray. The bystander who must be imagined, 'though hypothetical, is not necessarily hypothetically a white bystander': *Gray v DPP*, CO/5069/98, QB.

32.1.3.5 *Mens rea*

The mental element of riot includes the common purpose. A common purpose (which need not involve violence) must be proved in respect of all 12 persons, though not all of them are charged. It must be proved that a person charged with riot shared that common purpose and that he (but not necessarily the other 11 or more)[14] intended to use violence or was aware that his conduct might be violent,[15] and it is important that this is made clear to the jury.[16]

The Act wisely avoids the ambiguous word 'reckless' by its use of the word 'awareness'. In effect this is adopting a subjective approach akin to the *Cunningham*[17] meaning of reckless-ness, thus keeping the law of riot, violent disorder and affray in line with offences against the person generally. There is a subtle difference since the recklessness formula requires not only that D has a subjective awareness of the risk (that his conduct may be violent) but that he has taken that risk unjustifiably. With a test of awareness alone, there is no objective assessment of the justification for his taking the risk. It is doubtful whether this has significant practical implications.

Because the meaning of violence itself is uncertain it is not entirely clear what the require-ment of awareness will exclude. It is arguable that a person who was not aware that his con-duct would cause any risk of injury or damage would be held to be unaware that his conduct might be violent when it did in fact cause a risk of, or actual, damage or injury.[18]

32.1.3.6 Intoxicated rioters

Exceptionally, s 6(5) and (6) make special provision to deal with a plea of intoxication,

(5) For the purposes of this section a person whose awareness is impaired by intoxication shall be taken to be aware of that of which he would be aware if not intoxicated, unless he shows either that his intoxication was not self-induced or that it was caused solely by the taking or adminis-tration of a substance in the course of medical treatment.

(6) In subsection (5) 'intoxication' means any intoxication, whether caused by drink, drugs or other means, or by a combination of means.

The common law governs the position where D denies that he had the alleged 'purpose' because he was too drunk. Thus, if the indictment alleges only intent to use violence, that is presumably an allegation of a specific intent, so self-induced drunkenness would be an answer at common law.[19] But because of s 6(5), D is still to be taken to be aware of that of which he would be aware if not intoxicated. So, if the jury think he would have been aware that vio-lence was a virtual certainty,[20] that is evidence on which they might find that he intended it. Intoxication might not be an excuse even to an allegation of intentional violence in riot. As regard indictments alleging riot without intention – that is alleging that D was aware that his conduct may be violent – s 6 applies in full. In effect, this spells out the common law rule for offences 'of basic intent'[21] but shifts onto the defendant the onus of proving (or more probably imposes a burden on him to raise evidence) that the intoxication was involuntary.[22]

---

[14] Section 6(7); ATH Smith, *Offences Against Public Order*, para 3.03.

[15] Section 6(1).

[16] *Blackwood* [2002] EWCA Crim 3102.

[17] Above, p 118.

[18] This is, it is submitted, unlikely to succeed.

[19] Although cf *Heard* [2007] EWCA Crim 125 as discussed above, p 318.

[20] Above, p 107.

[21] Above, p 314.

[22] See above, p 29 on the post-Human Rights Act 1998 approach to reverse burdens and the greater likelihood that this is merely an evidential burden.

32.1.4 Violent disorder

Violent disorder is an offence punishable on indictment with five years' imprisonment or an unlimited fine or both or, on summary conviction, with six months' imprisonment or the statutory maximum fine, or both. It is defined as follows by s 2:

> (1) Where 3 or more persons who are present together use or threaten unlawful violence and the conduct of them (taken together) is such as would cause a person of reasonable firmness present at the scene to fear for his personal safety, each of the persons using or threatening unlawful violence is guilty of violent disorder.

> (2) It is immaterial whether or not the 3 or more use or threaten unlawful violence simultaneously.

32.1.4.1 Three or more

It is essential for the conviction of any that the jury or magistrates are sure that at least three people had been unlawfully violent during the incident.

In *Mahroof*,[23] it seems to have been assumed that if three defendants are the only persons alleged to have been involved in the disorder and one of them is acquitted, the others must also be acquitted. This will usually be the case but it is submitted that it is not necessarily so. If, for example, the acquitted person was using or threatening unlawful violence but was not guilty on some other ground, there seems to be no reason why the other two accused should not be convicted. The third person may have been acquitted because he did not so intend to, and was not aware that he might use or threaten violence (perhaps being involuntarily intoxicated) or had some defence such as duress or insanity. He will nevertheless have been involved in unlawful violence. Such cases are likely to be rare. In contrast, in *Mechen*,[24] it was acknowledged that if the jury acquits, on the grounds of self-defence, any person potentially relied on by the prosecution to constitute one of the three persons involved, that person cannot be included to make up the necessary minimum number of people using or threatening *unlawful* violence. It is for this reason that is often important to lay alternative charges of affray.[25]

In *Lemon*,[26] it was emphasized that s 2 does not require that at least two others be *convicted* of the offence before any one defendant could be convicted.[27] The judge properly directed the jury that provided they found three or more used or threatened violence, they could convict any one or more of the defendants even though they were unable to identify the three. This interpretation of the offence was reiterated in *Mbagwu*[28] with Hughes LJ explaining that 'a jury may be perfectly satisfied that there were at least 3 people participating without being able to say to the criminal standard who most of them were'.[29]

In cases of aiding and abetting violent disorder, it is crucial that the directions make clear the respective *mens rea* requirements of the principals and secondary parties.[30]

---

[23] (1988) 88 Cr App R 317, [1989] Crim LR 721; cf *Fleming and Robinson* [1989] Crim LR 658; *McGuigan* [1991] Crim LR 719.

[24] [2004] EWCA Crim 388.

[25] *Hadjisavva* [2004] EWCA Crim 1316.

[26] [2002] EWCA Crim 1661.

[27] L was one of six defendants charged under s 2. All accepted their presence at the scene, but L claimed mistaken identity, two others claimed that they had acted in self-defence and the remaining three made no comment.

[28] [2007] EWCA Crim 1068.

[29] [66].

[30] *Blackwood* [2002] EWCA Crim 3102. See also *Powell* [2006] EWCA Crim 685 on the importance of directing on *mens rea* in relation to general participation in a violent disorder.

32.1.4.2 Present together

In NW[31] the Court of Appeal held that the expression 'present together' meant no more than being in the same place at the same time. Three or more people using or threatening violence in the same place at the same time, whether for the same purpose or different purposes, were capable of creating a 'daunting prospect for those who may encounter them', simply by reason of the fact that they represented a breakdown of law and order. The phrase did not require any degree of cooperation between those using or threatening violence. The court, referring with approval to the previous edition of this work, took as guides to construction, the Law Commission Reports which led to the enactment of the 1986 Act and to the absence of any requirement in s 2 that there be a 'common purpose' among those using or threatening the use of violence. The absence of such a condition was in contrast to the requirement of a 'common purpose' in the s 1 riot offence. It is clear that the offence is not intended to be confined to situations in which the individual members of the crowd were acting together to achieve a common aim or even with a common motive. The term 'present together' involves a question of fact and if necessary, a jury should be told to give those words their ordinary meaning.

32.1.4.3 Use or threat of unlawful violence

There need be no common purpose. Each of the three or more persons may have a different purpose or no purpose. At least three must be using or threatening *unlawful* violence,[32] so if one of only three persons present is acting in self-defence or the prevention of crime, no offence is committed.[33]

It must be proved that each defendant intended to use or threaten violence or that he was aware that his conduct might be violent or threaten violence.[34] A *prima facie* case of violent disorder could be established where D was running along with a group in a populated area when D knew members of the group were armed and intent on violence.[35] There was held to be evidence of a threat of unlawful violence where three men followed another along a path for three-quarters of a mile and for three-quarters of an hour in the middle of the night, creating 'an aura of violence'.[36] The breadth of the offence has resulted in its diverse use to deal with conduct ranging from pub brawls to violent animal rights protests.[37]

Where the evidence which led to a conviction under s 2 relates to violence to property, the court must decline to substitute verdicts under s 3 since that offence is limited to violence to people.[38] The judge must then direct the jury adequately on the relevant parts of s 4 (see below).[39]

32.1.4.4 Effect of conduct

The conduct of the three must be such as would (but not necessarily did) cause a person of reasonable firmness present at the scene to fear for his personal safety, no person need actually

---

[31] [2010] EWCA Crim 404.

[32] For the meaning of 'violence', see above, p 1090.

[33] *Mechen*, above n 24.

[34] Section 6(2).

[35] *Church* (2000) 4 Archbold News 3, CA.

[36] *Brodie* [2000] Crim LR 775. See also *Casey* [2004] EWCA Crim 1853.

[37] eg *R v Oxford Crown Court, ex p Monaghan* (1998) 18 June, DC (throwing stones over the fence in an aimless manner at police and using fences as battering rams).

[38] *R v McGuigan and Cameron* [1991] Crim LR 719.

[39] *R v Perrins* [1995] Crim LR 432. The jury may return a verdict under s 4 on a count alleging s 2 if the s 4 offence has been left to them. Section 7(3) expressly provides that s 4 may be left. That section does not require that s 4 is left as an alternative in all cases: *Walton* [2006] EWCA Crim 822. See also *Mbagwu* [2007] EWCA Crim 1068.

be, or even be likely to be, at the scene.[40] Where no person is present, the court or jury has to answer a hypothetical question.

32.1.4.5 Other matters

Private defence, the prevention of crime[41] and other general defences are available to a defendant charged with this offence. The intoxicated defendant is governed by s 6(5) and (6), considered above. The offence may be committed in private as well as public.

Violent disorder is intended to be the normal charge[42] for serious outbreaks of public disorder, riot being reserved for exceptionally serious cases, but it clearly covers many relatively minor disturbances. Consequently, it is triable either way. The CPS cites as examples of the type of conduct which may be appropriate for a s 2 charge: 'fighting between three or more people involving the use of weapons, between rival groups in a place to which members of the public have access (for example a town centre or a crowded bar) causing severe disruption and/or fear to members of the public; an outbreak of violence which carries with it the potential for significant impact on a moderate scale on non-participants; serious disorder at a public event where missiles are thrown and other violence is used against and directed towards the police and other civil authorities'. The gravamen of the offence is that people are put in fear by the group action in which D participates.[43]

32.1.5 Affray[44]

Bingham LCJ (as he then was) described the nature of affray as follows:[45]

It typically involves a group of people who may well be shouting, struggling, threatening, waving weapons, throwing objects, exchanging and threatening blows and so on. Again, typically, it involves a continuous course of conduct, the criminal character of which depends on the general nature and effect of the conduct as a whole and not on particular incidents and events which may take place in the course of it. Where reliance is placed on such a continuous course of conduct, it is not necessary for the Crown to identify and prove particular incidents.

Affray is punishable on indictment with three years' imprisonment or an unlimited fine or both, or, on summary conviction, with six months' imprisonment or the statutory maximum fine or both. It is defined as follows by s 3:

(1) A person is guilty of affray if he uses or threatens unlawful violence towards another and his conduct is such as would cause a person of reasonable firmness present at the scene to fear for his personal safety.

(2) Where 2 or more persons use or threaten the unlawful violence, it is the conduct of them taken together that must be considered for the purposes of subsection (1).

(3) For the purposes of this section a threat cannot be made by the use of words alone.

---

[40] Section 2(3) and (4).

[41] *Rothwell v Barton* [1993] Crim LR 626.

[42] See CPS website for details of charging standards: www.cps.gov.uk/legal/p_to_r/public_order_offences/ #Violent.

[43] See *Grealish* [2006] EWCA Crim 1095 at [46].

[44] *Smith* [1997] 1 Cr App R 14, [1996] Crim LR 893. Where an alleged affray falls into two or more sequences – eg inside, and outside, a house – the judge must give a separate direction in relation to each sequence, for the jury may be satisfied that only one is an affray. See also *Flounders* [2002] EWCA Crim 1325.

[45] *Smith* [1997] 1 Cr App R 14 at 16. Contrast the position where parties are charged with committing an offence by a specific act in the course of a joint enterprise: *Uddin* [1998] 2 All ER 744, above, p 226.

In resolving a doubt about the meaning of the section it is permissible to refer to the definition of the common law offence – but this practice is to be approached with care.[46] The Court of Appeal in *Carey*[47] refused to interpret the offence by reference to the common law or the Law Commission paper preceding the 1986 Act.

32.1.5.1 Violence

In this offence, 'violence' is limited to violence towards another person and does not include violence towards property.[48] The overt act of carrying petrol bombs in the presence of those against whom the bombs are intended to be used may be a threat of violence.[49] The section makes it clear that the offence cannot be committed by the use of words alone, however aggressive and frightening the tone of voice.[50] If a mere threat to use violence were enough, affray would swallow the lesser offence under s 4(1) (considered below).[51] But the use of words to set a dog on another may amount to affray.[52] It seems that to say 'I am going to set the dog on you' would not be the offence, but 'Seize him Fido' would – Fido being a Pitt Bull terrier whose performance would alarm a bystander.

The violence must be unlawful, so that if the jury accept that D honestly believed or may have honestly believed that it was necessary to defend himself or others there will be no unlawful violence.[53]

32.1.5.2 Participants

The offence envisages at least three people: (i) the person using or threatening unlawful violence;[54] (ii) a person towards whom the violence or threat is directed who must be present at the scene; and (iii) a person of reasonable firmness who need not actually be, or be likely to be,[55] present. So where D swiped with a knife towards a constable, J, the question was not whether a person of reasonable firmness in J's shoes would have feared for his personal safety but whether this hypothetical third person, present in the room and seeing D's conduct towards J, would have feared for *his own* safety.[56] But where gang A marched to attack gang B, but dispersed on the arrival of the police before they came in sight of the Bs, there was no affray.[57] The question involves an objective assessment. Affray is a public order offence for the protection of the bystander. There are other offences for the protection of persons at whom

---

[46] *I, M and H v DPP* [2001] Crim LR 491, HL.

[47] [2006] EWCA Crim 17.

[48] Section 8, above, p 1090.

[49] *I, M and H v DPP*, above, n 46.

[50] *Robinson* [1993] Crim LR 581.

[51] While affray is designed to deal with imminent violence, charges under the Offences Against the Person Act 1861 are available for threats to cause harm in the future: *Lewis* [2004] EWCA Crim 1407.

[52] *Dixon* [1993] Crim LR 579, and commentary. See also *Dackers* [2000] All ER (D) 1958.

[53] See *Talland* [2003] EWCA Crim 2884. The defences of self-defence, etc will be available see *Rothwell* [1993] Crim LR 626; *Pulham* [1995] Crim LR 296; *Duffy v CC of Cleveland* [2007] EWHC 3169 (Admin).

[54] Where the only evidence is that D, having been beaten by X, returns shortly afterwards to the scene to look for X, there is no evidence of unlawful conduct for the purposes of affray: *Portela* [2007] EWCA Crim 529.

[55] *Thind* [1999] Crim LR 842. Hence the possibility of a conviction in a prison cell as in *Beaument and Correlli* (1999) 12 Feb, unreported, CACD.

[56] *Davison* [1992] Crim LR 31, CA; *Sanchez* [1996] Crim LR 572, approving the commentary on *Davison*. These commentaries were approved in *Blinkhorn* [2006] EWCA Crim 1416 in which a conviction was quashed where a bystander feared for V who was being assaulted in broad daylight, but had no fear for himself. See also *Donaldson* [2008] EWCA Crim 2457.

[57] *I, M and H v DPP*, above.

the violence is aimed. This distinction should be observed, and charges of common assault should not be elevated to affray.[58]

A striking example of this is the recent case of *Leeson v DPP*.[59] L lived with her partner V. The alleged affray comprised L saying to V, in a calm voice, that she was going to kill him with the 6 inch kitchen knife she was holding. She made no attempt to move the knife or attack him with it. The incident occurred in the bathroom of their joint home, which was securely locked with no one present nor expected in the house. V disarmed her easily, returned the knife to the kitchen, phoned a neutral friend and then called the police. V testified that he had not felt directly threatened by L nor believed that she intended to use violence towards him. L's conviction was quashed. The possibility of a bystander arriving was truly remote but that does not preclude a conviction because by s 3(4) it is unnecessary for any third person actually to be present or to be likely to be present. However, the offence does require that L's use or threat of unlawful violence against V was such as to cause a hypothetical person of reasonable firmness present at the scene to fear for his personal safety. By s 3(3) words alone cannot constitute threats, but her brandishing the knife could. The conduct may have caused V to fear for his safety but that is not enough: it is whether the hypothetical bystander would have feared for his own safety (not that of V). Account can be taken of the nature of the premises, the scene of the incident, the fact that the violence was limited to those involved and that the others present were not in fear: *Cotcher*.[60] The short, calm exchanges between L and V in private were not capable of engaging fear in another.

Subsection (2) makes it clear that, where two or more use or threaten the unlawful violence, it is the conduct of all of them which must be considered in deciding whether it would cause a person of reasonable firmness to fear for his personal safety. There is no requirement that the reasonable bystander experience 'terror' as at common law.[61]

32.1.5.3 *Mens rea*

The mental element is D's intention to use or threaten violence or his awareness that his conduct may be violent or threaten violence. Where reliance is placed by the prosecution on subs (2), it will probably be necessary to show that D's awareness extended to the conduct of the other persons or persons using or threatening violence.

The intoxicated defendant is governed by s 6(5) and (6), considered above.[62]

32.1.6 Fear or provocation of violence

It is an offence under s 4, punishable on summary conviction[63] with six months' imprisonment or a fine not exceeding level 5 on the standard scale, if a person:

(1) uses towards another person threatening, abusive or insulting words or behaviour, or

(2) distributes or displays to another person any writing, sign or other visible representation which is threatening, abusive or insulting

with intent to cause that person to believe that immediate unlawful violence will be used against him or another by any person, or to provoke the immediate use of unlawful violence

---

[58] *Plavecz* [2002] Crim LR 837. For details of CPS Charging standard, see: www.cps.gov.uk/legal/p_to_r/public_order_offences.

[59] [2010] EWHC 994. Notably, the CPS advises that 'incidents within a dwelling should not be charged as affray merely because a lesser public order charge is not available. Offences of assault are likely to be more appropriate'.

[60] (1992) The Times, 29 Dec.

[61] *Carey* [2006] EWCA Crim 17.

[62] At p 1091.

[63] Note that the racially aggravated forms of the offence discussed below are triable either way.

by that person or another, or whereby that person is likely to believe that such violence will be used or it is likely that such violence will be provoked. The fact that violence is actually used does not prevent the use of this charge.[64]

The section creates only one offence. It may be committed in a variety of ways. But the facts proved must correspond with the form alleged. If there is a substantial discrepancy between the particulars alleged and the facts found, a conviction will be quashed.[65]

32.1.6.1 Towards another

The words in s 4(1)(a), 'uses towards another person', mean 'uses in the presence of and in the direction of another person directly...' following *Atkin v DPP*[66] where D told customs officers in his house that, if the bailiff in the car outside came in, he was 'a dead un'. The bailiff, being informed, felt threatened, but the threat was not direct. Similarly, under s 4(1)(b) the distribution or display must be made directly to a person present. Writing contained in an envelope is not a 'display'.[67] For the purposes of s 4 (though not for any other offence under the Act), the words 'towards another' arguably also require that the words or behaviour be directed against that other.[68]

32.1.6.2 Threatening, abusive or insulting

This is the first of many offences under the 1986 Act of which 'threatening, abusive or insulting' conduct is a principal constituent.[69] Whether conduct has this quality seems to be governed by an objective test. This is an element of the *actus reus*. It has been explained[70] that a word describing the *actus reus* element of an offence may also imply a mental element. The Act, however, assumes that conduct or material may be threatening, abusive or insulting even though there is no evidence that the actor or author intended it to have, or was aware that it might have, that quality. The effect is to create extremely harsh offences. When proof by the prosecution of such intention or awareness is required, the Act specifically so provides;[71] and, in other cases, it puts the burden of proof (or at least an evidential one) on the defendant to show that he did not suspect or have reason to suspect that it was threatening, abusive or insulting.[72]

The words, 'threatening, abusive or insulting', which are taken from the repealed s 5 of the Public Order Act 1936, are to be given their ordinary meaning. It has been said that it is not helpful to seek to explain them by the use of synonyms or dictionary definitions because 'an ordinary sensible man knows an insult when he sees or hears it'.[73] Whether particular conduct is 'threatening' etc is a question of fact. In *Brutus v Cozens*,[74] D interrupted a tennis match to protest against apartheid and thereby angered the spectators. The House of Lords, reversing the Divisional Court, held that the finding of the magistrate that this was not 'insulting' behaviour was not an unreasonable finding of fact. If the magistrates had decided that

---

[64] See *CPS v Shabbir* [2009] EWCA Crim 2754.

[65] *Winn v DPP* (1992) 156 JP 881.

[66] (1989) 89 Cr App R 199, [1989] Crim LR 581, DC.

[67] *Chappell v DPP* (1988) 89 Cr App R 82.

[68] Thornton et al, *Public Order Law*, 1.137.

[69] Sections 4(1), 4A(1), 5(1), 18(1), 19(1), 20(1), 21(1), 22(1), 23(1).

[70] At p 48.

[71] Section 6(3) and (4).

[72] Sections 19, 20, 21, 22, 23.

[73] *Brutus v Cozens* [1973] AC 854, [1972] 2 All ER 1297 at 1300, per Lord Reid.

[74] [1973] AC 854, [1972] 2 All ER 1297.

the behaviour was insulting, it may be that their decision would have been equally beyond challenge.[75]

The section is not limited to rowdy or abusive behaviour. In *Taft*,[76] D was prosecuted having driven erratically alongside lone women drivers on country roads while masturbating. Masturbation in the sight of a stranger while in a public lavatory is capable of being insulting behaviour.[77] It is immaterial that the stranger is a policeman[78] who is on the lookout for this sort of thing, or a man, whether homosexual or not, who is not at all insulted. Words cannot be insulting (or, presumably, threatening or abusive) unless there is 'a human target which they strike' and it seems that D must be aware of that 'human target', though he need not intend the conduct to be 'insulting': *Masterson v Holden*,[79] where cuddling by two homosexual men in Oxford Street at 1.55 am, in the presence of two young men and two young women, was held capable of being insulting. It is doubtful whether this would withstand scrutiny under the Human Rights Act 1998. The gay couple could surely claim that they were being discriminated against in the exercise of their private life since it is unrealistic to assume that similar displays of heterosexual behaviour would be prosecuted.

The offence was intended to deal with 'minor acts of hooliganism' but it appears to have been applied more widely in practice.[80] In *Vigon v DPP*,[81] it was held that the offence was not limited to rowdy behaviour and was apt to cover the conduct of a market trader who peeped between the curtains of a changing room and watched his customers undressing. Such an affront to a person's dignity or modesty was 'insulting'. The fact that D did not peep, but used a video camera, made no difference. As he attempted to conceal the camera, he cannot have intended to insult; but it would be sufficient that he knew that the camera might be seen by a customer who might be insulted thereby.[82] This looks more like voyeurism under s 67 of the Sexual Offences Act 2003.[83]

The concept of 'insulting' has also given rise to difficulty in the context of protestors. In *Lewis v DPP*,[84] protestors outside an abortion clinic displayed placards including one of an aborted 21-week foetus in pools of blood. The Divisional Court held that this could constitute abusive and insulting behaviour, rejecting the argument that 'the photograph on the placard was an accurate representation of the result of an abortion, and that what is truthful cannot be abusive or insulting'. Again, challenge under the ECHR in such cases would seem likely. If the protest is peaceful and involves the depiction of factual images, it is questionable whether prosecution is a necessary and proportionate response to protect the rights of others.[85]

The breadth of the offence and the vagueness of these elements leave an enormous discretion to the police in arrest and subsequently to the magistrates and can lead to great

---

[75] Per Lord Kilbrandon at 1303. Lord Reid, *obiter*, agreed with the magistrates' finding; but it does not follow that he would have held a contrary finding to be unreasonable.

[76] (1997) 13 Jan, CA, Crim Div, unreported.

[77] *Parkin v Norman* [1982] 2 All ER 583 at 588–589, DC.

[78] And therefore presumably one who will not be readily insulted or provoked to violence.

[79] [1986] 1 WLR 1017.

[80] D Feldman, *Civil Liberties and Human Rights in England and Wales* (2nd edn, 2002) Ch 18. Emmerson, Ashworth and Macdonald, HR&CJ.

[81] [1998] Crim LR 289.

[82] For details of the CPS Charging Standard see: www.cps.gov.uk/legal/p_to_r/public_order_offences.

[83] See *Basset* [2008] EWCA Crim 1174 as discussed in Ch 18 above and *MacRitchie* [2008] NICA 26 (filming V in bikini under cubicle door at leisure centre not voyeurism as V not naked or in underwear).

[84] (1995) unreported, DC. cf *DPP v Clarke* (1991) 94 Cr App R 359, DC, where acquittals were upheld following the defendants' claims that they had not intended nor were they aware that displaying abortion images to police officers on duty outside a clinic would be threatening abusive or insulting.

[85] See on the Art 11 guarantee in the context of peaceful protest: *Brega v Modova* [2010] ECHR 52100/08; *Karabulut v Turkey* [2009] ECHR 16999/04; *Hyde Park v Moldova* [2009] ECHR 18491/07.

inconsistency in application. The circumstances and context in which the statements are made are all important. It has been held to be abusive for D to say 'fuck' twice to a police officer who was trying to arrest D's brother.[86] Describing someone of Asian appearance as 'fucking Islam' is undeniably abusive.[87]

32.1.6.3 *Mens rea*/effect on V

It must be proved that D:[88]

(1) intended his words or behaviour towards V to be, or was aware that they might be, threatening, abusive or insulting;[89] and

(2) either –

    (a) that he intended V to believe that immediate unlawful violence would be used against him or another; or

    (b) that he intended to provoke the immediate use of unlawful violence by V or another; or

    (c) that V was likely[90] to believe that such violence (that is, *immediate* unlawful violence)[91] would be used; or

    (d) that it was likely that such violence would be provoked.

Although the section creates only one offence,[92] alternatives (a) and (b) require proof of intention whereas in alternatives (c) and (d) the test focuses on the effect and is objective. The belief specified must be the belief of the person threatened.[93]

Where D's awareness that his conduct might be threatening, abusive or insulting is impaired by intoxication, s 6(5) and (6)[94] apply.

32.1.6.4 Public/private

The offence may be committed in a public or private place, except where D acts inside a dwelling[95] and V is also inside that, or another, dwelling.[96] So, in *Atkin v DPP*,[97] the threat to the

---

[86] *DPP v Southward* [2006] EWHC 3449 (Admin).

[87] *R (DPP) v Humphrey* [2005] EWHC 822 (Admin).

[88] See *Winn* (1992) 156 JP 881.

[89] Section 6(3).

[90] In construing the word 'likely', it is the state of the mind of the victim which is crucial rather than precise probability of violence actually occurring within a short space of time: *DPP v Ramos* [2000] Crim LR 768 (D sending letter bomb). See also Auld LJ in *Chief Constable of Lancashire v Potter* [2003] EWHC 2272 (Admin), para 34, considering the expression in the context of ASBOs.

[91] *Horseferry Road Metropolitan Stipendiary Magistrate, ex p Siadatan* [1991] 1 QB 260, [1990] Crim LR 598, DC (the publication of Salman Rushdie's *The Satanic Verses* was not an offence because it was not likely to provoke *immediate* violence without any intervening occurrence). Immediate does not mean instantaneous, and is generously interpreted, as in *Valentine* [1991] 1 QB 260 where V had said to a neighbour who was a prison officer 'next time you go [to work] we're going to burn your house. You are all going to fucking die.' The DC held that the magistrates were entitled to infer that these words gave rise to a fear of immediate violence. See also *Ramos*, above and *Liverpool v DPP* [2008] EWHC 2540 (Admin) – D making gun gestures with hand.

[92] Section 7(2).

[93] *Loade v DPP* [1990] 1 QB 1052 DC.

[94] Above, p 1091.

[95] Defined in s 8.

[96] Section 4(2). See *Barber* [2001] EWCA Crim 838. Delivery of a threatening letter to V's home was held to be incapable of being an offence under s 4 or s 5 in *Chappell v DPP* (1988) 89 Cr App R 82, although that decision was correct on the basis that there was no display by D. cf *DPP v Ramos* [2000] Crim LR 768 where the letter went to a business address.

[97] Above, n 66.

customs officers in D's house could not be the offence. Threatening gestures through the bedroom window to the neighbour in his bedroom window across the street do not amount to the offence. Where D is in a dwelling, it seems that, if the issue is raised, the prosecution must prove that D was aware that his conduct might be heard or seen by a person outside that dwelling or another dwelling.[98] The common parts, including a landing in a block of flats, are not part of a dwelling (this emphasizes the public order nature of the offence).[99] A police cell does not constitute a home or living accommodation and so the offence can be committed therein.[100] A laundry room used communally by tenants (each living in own flat) in sheltered housing was not a 'dwelling'. It could not properly be described as part of the structure of any individual home in the building.[101]

32.1.7 Harassment, alarm or distress[102]

It is an offence under s 5(1), punishable on summary conviction with a fine not exceeding level 3 on the standard scale,[103] if a person:

(1) uses threatening abusive or insulting words or behaviour, or disorderly behaviour, or

(2) displays any writing, sign or other visible representation which is threatening, abusive or insulting,

within the hearing or sight of a person likely to be caused harassment, alarm or distress thereby.

This offence is wider than that under s 4 in that it includes the further alternative of 'disorderly' behaviour; and it extends beyond apprehension of violence to the causing of 'harassment, alarm or distress'. When enacted it was regarded as a controversial extension of the law. It is now heavily used in policing anti-social behaviour on housing estates and in town centres.[104]

Many of the elements are discussed above in relation to s 4. 'Disorderly' is, no doubt, another ordinary word of the English language to be given its natural meaning and it will apply to acts of hooligans likely to produce the specified effect. In *Chambers and Edwards v DPP*,[105] 'disorderly' was held to be a question of fact for the trial court to determine. The CPS Charging Standards suggest that the following types of conduct may at least be capable of amounting to disorderly behaviour: 'causing a disturbance in a residential area or common part of a block of flats; persistently shouting abuse or obscenities at passers-by; pestering people waiting to catch public transport or otherwise waiting in a queue; rowdy behaviour in a street late at night which might alarm residents or passers-by, especially those who may be vulnerable, such as the elderly or members of an ethnic minority group; causing a disturbance in a shopping precinct or other area to which the public have access or might otherwise

---

[98] cf s 5(3)(b), putting the onus of proof (or at least an evidential burden) on D.

[99] *Rukwira v DPP* [1993] Crim LR 882.

[100] *CF* [2007] 1 WLR 1021, [2007] Crim LR 574.

[101] *Le Vine v DPP* [2010] EWHC 1128 (Admin).

[102] For research on the impact and operation of the offence, see D Brown and T Ellis, *Policing Low-Level Disorder: Police Use of s 5 of the Public Order Act 1986* (1994) HORS 135.

[103] The offence attracts a fixed penalty of £80 for persons aged 16 or over and £40 for persons aged under 16: The Penalties for Disorderly Behaviour (Amount of Penalty) (Amendment) Order 2009, SI 2009 No 83.

[104] Some of the more bizarre examples of purported s 5 offences include: a window display of 4 foot high Indonesian carved penis (this was reported in the Northern Echo, www.thenorthernecho.co.uk/news/7988195. Phallus_imprisonment) window displays of gollies (see A Turner, 'Golly Distressing' (2006) 170 JP 161 and logos on T shirts (FCUK)): *Woodman v French Connection Ltd* [2007] ETMR 8.

[105] [1995] Crim LR 896 (defendants standing peacefully to block surveyor's theodolite beam convicted despite absence of threat or fear of violence).

gather; and bullying'.[106] The offence can be committed in public or private, except where D and V are inside a dwelling at the time of the relevant conduct.

32.1.7.1 Harassment, alarm or distress

The terms harassment, alarm and distress were considered in the Divisional Court in *R (R) v DPP*.[107] R, aged 12 and only four feet nine inches tall, was found by the youth court to have caused distress to a police officer, V, who was 6 feet tall and weighed 17 stone, when R made 'masturbatory gestures' towards the police officer. The officer claimed that he was distressed by R being out so late and by his behaviour. The Divisional Court quashed R's conviction, accepting that his behaviour was anti-social and intended to annoy V, but that it did not cause V 'emotional disturbance or upset'.[108] The court commented that the emotional disturbance need not be serious. In contrast, where the allegation is one of harassment, there is no need to demonstrate that any person suffered real emotional disturbance or upset.[109] The element of harassment in this context requires something more than merely trivial harassment.

32.1.7.2 Victim

It is clear, that the Crown do not have to establish that the words or conduct were in fact heard or seen by a person. The prosecution must prove that D's conduct took place within the hearing or sight of a person (who might be a policeman)[110] and was likely to cause harassment, alarm (for his own or a third party's[111] safety) or distress. There must be a real, not merely a hypothetical, victim. There is no requirement that the conduct be directed 'towards another person'. It is sufficient that the conduct merely might have been seen or could possibly have been seen by a person present.[112] It has been held that the s 5 (and s 4A below) offence can be committed where there is a general confrontation between the police and protesters and the fact that the victim perceives the behaviour through CCTV at the scene does not prevent a conviction.[113]

It is for D to prove, if he can, that he had no reason to believe that there was any such person within hearing or sight, who was likely to be caused harassment, alarm or distress.[114] The requirement of a 'true' potential victim operates as a significant limitation on the breadth of the offence as compared to the public order offences discussed above where a hypothetical bystander will suffice.

In *S v DPP*,[115] the Divisional Court held that the offence was made out even if the material that caused the harassment, alarm or distress was no longer in the public domain at the time it caused someone to be harassed or distressed. In that case, material on a website was removed before the police showed it to the victim.

---

[106] See public order offences Charging Standard: www.cps.gov.uk/legal/s_to_u/stalking_and_harassment.

[107] (2006) 170 JP 661.

[108] Per Touslon J.

[109] *Southard v DPP* [2006] All ER (D) 101. The court endorsed the interpretation of distress in *R (R) v DPP*. See also *Burrell v CPS* [2005] EWHC 786 (Admin).

[110] *DPP v Orum* [1989] 1 WLR 88, DC. The court in *Southard* rejected an argument that the offence is not available when police officers are the sole audience.

[111] *Lodge v DPP* (1988) The Times, 26 Oct. See also *Chambers v DPP* [1995] Crim LR 896.

[112] *Taylor v DPP* (2006) 170 JP 485, DC. cf *Holloway v DPP* [2004] EWHC 2621 (Admin) (D videoing himself naked with group of school children on playing field in background unaware of D's presence), and see *Reda v DPP* [2011] EWHC 5 April.

[113] *Rogers and others v DPP* (1999) 22 July, DC.

[114] If D is within a dwelling, he may also rely on s 5(3)(b) below, p 1102.

[115] [2008] EWHC 438 (Admin).

32.1.7.3 *Mens rea*

It must be proved that D intended his conduct to be threatening, abusive, or insulting or disorderly or was aware that it might be so.[116] Section 6(5) and (6) apply to the intoxicated defendant.[117] The requirement at its lowest involves proof that D had an awareness of a possibility.

32.1.7.4 Defence of reasonableness

An important aspect of the crime is the defence provided in s 5(3). In addition to the opportunity to prove (a) that he had no reason to believe that there was any person within sight or hearing who was likely to be caused harassment, alarm or distress or (b) that he was inside a dwelling and had no reason to believe that his conduct would be heard or seen by a person outside that or any other dwelling, it is a defence for D to prove under s 5(3)(c) that his conduct was reasonable. This test is clearly one of an objective nature.[118] Note that the defence was not sufficient to prevent conviction in a number of cases of protest discussed in the next paragraph.

32.1.7.5 ECHR

In a number of cases the offence has been challenged as being incompatible with Art 10 of the ECHR (which guarantees the right to freedom of expression).[119] There is no doubt that the protection of freedom of expression applies widely and is engaged by 'conduct' that might not normally be considered as expression. 'Expression' includes purely physical acts of protest: *Hashman and Harrup v UK*,[120] and extends to 'the irritating, the contentious, the heretical, the unwelcome and the provocative provided it does not tend to provoke violence'.[121] The domestic courts have adopted an inconsistent application of Art 10 in this context.

In *Percy v DPP*,[122] P had desecrated the US flag as part of her protest against US defence systems in the UK. Evidence was adduced that the US military personnel witnessing P's behaviour found it distressing. The Divisional Court held that s 5 was not necessarily incompatible with Art 10 (nor could it be since the offence encompasses behaviour other than that involving freedom of expression.) The court expressly acknowledged that s 5 is drafted in such a way as to accommodate freedom of expression defences. On the facts, the District Judge had attached too much weight to the fact that P could have made the protest without the flag desecration. The court had to presume that the appellant's conduct was protected by Art 10 unless and until it was established that a restriction on her freedom of expression was strictly necessary, having regard to: P's awareness of the likely impact of her conduct, the fact that P's behaviour went beyond legitimate protest, that the behaviour had not formed part of an open expression of opinion on a matter of public interest, but had become disproportionate and unreasonable, that P knew the likely effect of her conduct upon witnesses, whom she had targeted, and the fact that she used a method of demonstration – destroying the flag – which was not necessary to convey her message or the expression of opinion.

Percy was followed in *Norwood v DPP*,[123] where N's conviction for the racially aggravated version of the offence was upheld when he displayed a British National Party poster: 'Islam out

---

[116] Section 6(3). *Ball* (1989) 90 Cr App R 378 at 381.

[117] Above p 1091.

[118] See, generally, A Geddis, 'Free Speech Martyrs or Unreasonable Threats to Social Peace? "Insulting" Expression and s 5 of the Public Order Act 1986' [2004] PL 853.

[119] See above, Ch 2. See also S Turenne, 'The Compatibility of Criminal Liability with Freedom of Expression' [2007] Crim LR 866.

[120] (1999) 30 EHRR 241, para 28 (hunt saboteurs).

[121] Per Sedley LJ in *DPP v Redmond-Bate* [1999] Crim LR 998 at 1000; and see *Handyside v UK* (1976) 1 EHRR 737, para 49.

[122] [2001] EWHC 1125 (Admin), [2002] Crim LR 835.

[123] [2003] EWHC 1564 (Admin), [2003] Crim LR 888. For criticism, see I Hare, 'Crosses, Crescents And Sacred Cows: Criminalising Incitement to Religious Hatred' [2006] PL 521 at 529–530; K Goodall, 'Incitement to

of Britain' showing an image of the terrorist attack on 11 September 2001. The Divisional Court concluded that although Art 10 was engaged, having regard to Art 10(2), prosecution was a necessary and proportionate restriction on D's freedom of expression for the prevention of disorder or crime and/or for the protection of the rights of others.[124] Norwood's application to the European Court on the grounds of an Art 10 infringement was declared inadmissible.[125]

In *Hammond v DPP*,[126] H, an evangelical Christian, carried a double-sided sign bearing the words 'Stop Immorality', 'Stop Homosexuality and Stop Lesbianism' on each side of a pole. H's preaching with the sign on display led to a gathering of 30 to 40 people shouting and becoming angry. H refused when police requested him to remove the sign, although H admitted he was aware that his sign was insulting because he had experienced a similar reaction before. H was convicted under s 5 and the conviction was upheld by the Divisional Court who concluded that H had not established that his conduct was reasonable having regard to Art 10 of the Convention and Art 9 – the right to freedom of thought, conscience and religion. This focus on the elements of the offence and the reasonableness of the conduct to be proved by D stands in contrast to the approach in *Dehal v CPS*.[127] In *Dehal,* a more robust approach was taken. D placed a notice on a notice board at a Sikh temple which he attended. The notice described the President of the Temple as a hypocrite, liar, etc. D was convicted of the s 4A offence (discussed below, but identical to s 5 for these purposes). D appealed claiming that he was expressing his views in a peaceful way as he was entitled to do under Art 10. The High Court, accepting that D intended to cause harassment, alarm or distress, found that there was no evidence that the prosecution on these facts was *necessary* in order to prevent public disorder. As such it was a disproportionate response to D's expression of opinion. Moses J, emphasized that care must be taken to avoid the use of the criminal law to unnecessarily restrict legitimate protest. His lordship concluded that it was not desirable nor possible to provide a universally applicable test as to whether conduct was legitimate protest.[128]

In the most recent decision *Abdul and others v DPP*[129] the Divisional Court provided a useful distillation of the case law. A and others were prosecuted under s 5 after demonstrating at a homecoming parade of an army regiment returning from Afghanistan and Iraq. At the parade, the defendants were close to the parading soldiers chanting slogans such as 'rapists' 'murderers', 'go to hell' etc. The police did not warn them at the time nor seek to stop them nor seize their placards. There was no evidence that the defendants were anything other than compliant with the police throughout. There was unrest as members of the public supporting the soldiers took offence; the members of the regiment did not. The judge, having regard to Art 10 of the ECHR convicted five of the seven defendants of the s 5 offence, concluding that they had gone significantly beyond the legitimate expressions of protest when viewed within

---

Religious Hatred: All Talk and No Substance' (2007) 70 MLR 89. See similarly *Kendall v DPP* [2008] EWHC 1848 (Admin) (poster saying 'illegal immigrant murder scum').

[124] If the prosecution proves that D's conduct was insulting and that he intended it to be, or was aware that it might be so, it would in most cases follow that his conduct was objectively unreasonable, especially where that conduct was motivated wholly or partly by hostility towards members of a religious group based on their membership of that group.

[125] *Norwood v UK* (2005) 40 EHRR SE11. The Court referred to the protection in Art 17 of the Convention against misuse of the protections afforded by other guarantees in the Convention. On which see Turenne, above, n 119. It referred also to the long line of cases rejecting Art 10 challenges to prosecutions for racist conduct: *Glimmerveen v Netherlands* (1982) 4 EHRR 260; *WP v Poland* (2005) 40 EHRR SE1; *Jersild v Denmark* (1994) EHRR 1.

[126] [2004] EWHC 69 (Admin), [2004] Crim LR 851.

[127] [2005] EWHC 2154 (Admin), (2005) 169) JP 581. See the comment by C Newman and B Middleton, 'Any Excuse for Certainty' (2010) 74 J Crim L 472.

[128] For a comparative analysis of the sections and a proposal for a new defence for political speech, see C Newman, 'Abusing Free Speech and Prohibiting Persecution' (2006) 70 J Crim L 329.

[129] [2011] EWHC 247 (Admin).

the context and circumstances of the day. The Divisional Court dismissed the appeal. The court identified the relevant principles governing the relationship between s 5 of the Act and Art 10 of the Convention:

i)   The starting point is the importance of the right to freedom of expression.

ii)   ... Legitimate protest can be offensive at least to some – and on occasions must be, if it is to have impact. Moreover, the right to freedom of expression would be unacceptably devalued if it did no more than protect those holding popular, mainstream views; it must plainly extend beyond that so that minority views can be freely expressed, even if distasteful.

iii)   ... interference with the right to freedom of expression must be convincingly established. Art. 10 does not confer an unqualified right to freedom of expression, but the restrictions contained in Art. 10.2 are to be narrowly construed.

iv)   There is not and cannot be any universal test for resolving when speech goes beyond legitimate protest, so attracting the sanction of the criminal law. The justification for invoking the criminal law is the threat to public order. Inevitably, the context of the particular occasion will be of the first importance.

v)   The relevance of the threat to public order should not be taken as meaning that the risk of violence by those reacting to the protest is, without more, determinative; some times it may be that protesters are to be protected. That said in striking the right balance when determining whether speech is 'threatening, abusive or insulting', the focus on minority rights should not result in overlooking the rights of the majority.

vi)   Plainly, if there is no *prima facie* case that speech was 'threatening, abusive or insulting' or that the other elements of the s.5 offence can be made good, then no question of prosecution will arise. However, even if there is otherwise a *prima facie* case for contending that an offence has been committed under s.5, it is still for the Crown to establish that prosecution is a proportionate response, necessary for the preservation of public order.

vii)   If the line between legitimate freedom of expression and a threat to public order has indeed been crossed, freedom of speech will not have been impaired by 'ruling... out' threatening, abusive or insulting speech.[130]

viii) [The High Court] should not interfere [with decisions of the magistrates'] unless, on well known grounds, the Appellants can establish that the decision to which the District Judge has come is one she could not properly have reached.[131]

The words were personal insults to the soldiers and not general statements against the war. The prosecution was proportionate to prevent public order and protect the soldiers' reputations.

It is questionable whether the current broad interpretation of s 5 strikes the right balance between free speech and protecting against threats of disorder. Several groups have called for reform, suggesting in particular that s 5 should be amended to remove reference to 'insulting' behaviour.[132] There has been no sign of legislative amendment following the Home Office consultation in 2009.[133]

---

[130] Per Lord Reid, in *Brutus v Cozens* [1973] AC 854, at 862.

[131] [2011] EWHC 247 (Admin) [49] per Gross LJ.

[132] *Liberty's response to the Home Office's 'Your Freedom' consultation*, October 2010, pp 17–18; Justice, *Response to Home Office consultation Amendment to Section 5 of the Public Order Act 1986*, September 2009; JCHR, *Demonstrating respect for rights? A human rights approach to policing protest*, HL 47/HC 320(2008–09), 23 March 2009.

[133] See HC Research Note *'Insulting words or behaviour': Section 5 of the Public Order Act 1986* (2010). See also A Bailin QC 'Criminalising Free Speech' [2011] Crim LR (forthcoming).

32.1.8 Intentional harassment, alarm or distress

The Criminal Justice and Public Order Act 1994 inserted s 4A into the 1986 Act, creating an offence of intentional harassment, alarm or distress punishable on summary conviction with imprisonment for six months or a fine not exceeding level 5 on the standard scale, or both. It requires threatening, abusive or insulting words or behaviour, as in s 5, but it also requires an *intention* to cause a person harassment, alarm or distress and actual causing of harassment, alarm or distress to that or another person. As in s 5, the offence may be committed in public or in private, with the same exception relating to a dwelling. The offence, being more severely punishable than s 5, was explained in parliamentary debates to be aimed at serious or persistent racial harassment.

The provisions relating to intoxication in s 6(5) and (6) do not apply to the offence under s 4A. The *mens rea* requires an intention, and the offence would seem therefore to be one of specific intent.

32.1.9 Racially aggravated public order offences[134]

The Crime and Disorder Act 1998, s 31, created racially aggravated versions of the offences under ss 4, 4A and 5 of the 1986 Act, and the Anti-terrorism, Crime and Security Act 2001 extended these offences to include circumstances of religious aggravation.[135] Definitions of 'racially aggravated' and 'religiously aggravated' are set out and discussed above in Chapter 17.[136] Aggravated s 4 and s 4A offences are punishable on summary conviction by six months' imprisonment, or a fine not exceeding the statutory maximum, or both; and on indictment by two years' imprisonment, or a fine, or both. An aggravated s 5 offence is triable only summarily and punishable by a fine not exceeding level 4 on the standard scale. It is CPS policy 'not to accept pleas to lesser offences, or omit or minimize admissible evidence of racial or religious aggravation for the sake of expediency'.[137]

The courts have been faced with numerous issues under the new offences, particularly as to the intentions of the defendant.[138] In *CPS v Weeks*,[139] a charge under s 4A failed on the facts where the defendant had said 'watch out the nights are getting dark' to his victim, and called him a 'black bastard'. Holland J noted that the question whether the use of words such as 'black bastard' indicates an *intention* to cause harassment, alarm or distress is a question of fact dependent on the context and circumstances in which they were used. In *DPP v McFarlane*,[140] Rose LJ found that once the 'basic' offence (that is, the public order element) was proved and that racist language was used that was hostile or threatening to the complainant, it made no difference that the defendant may have had an additional reason for using the language, the

---

[134] See, *inter alia*, M Malik, 'Racist Crime: Racially Aggravated Offences in the Crime and Disorder Act 1998 Part II' (1999) 62 MLR 409; F Brennan, 'The Crime and Disorder Act 1998: (2) Racially Motivated Crime: The Response of the Criminal Justice System' [1999] Crim LR 17 Specific guidance is provided to prosecutors by the CPS on prosecuting racially or religiously motivated crime – www.cps.gov.uk/legal/p_to_r/racist_and_religious_crime.

[135] See MM Idriss, 'Religion and the Anti-Terrorism, Crime and Security Act 2001' [2002] Crim LR 890. See also N Addison, *Religious Discrimination and Hatred Law* (2007) 131 et seq and www.religionlaw.co.uk.

[136] At p 658.

[137] See CPS guidance on prosecuting cases of racial and religious crime: www.cps.gov.uk/legal/p_to_r/racist_and_religious_crime.

[138] On which see E Burney, 'Using the Law on Racially Aggravated Offences' [2003] Crim LR 28.

[139] (2000) 14 June, DC.

[140] [2002] EWHC 485 (Admin).

test of racial hostility under s 28(1)(a) was satisfied.[141] In *DPP v Woods*,[142] it was confirmed that the fact that the motivation for the offence was something other than a racist motivation (D being refused entry by a bouncer) did not preclude conviction for the aggravated offence under s 28(1)(a).[143] That offence requires only that there is a demonstration of hostility. That is an objective test and nothing to do with D's motives, unlike s 28(1)(b) which does require proof of a racial motivation.[144] Ordinarily, the use of racially or religiously insulting remarks in the normal course of events be enough to establish a demonstration of hostility.

Arguments that such offences are an illegitimate restriction on the right to freedom of expression will be most unlikely to get off the ground. The European Court has taken the view that the direct expression of racist views is not protected under Art 10.[145]

The recent CPS Hate Crime Report[146] reveals that in the three years ending March 2008, over 33,000 defendants were prosecuted for crimes involving racial or religious aggravation; convictions in that period rose from 74 per cent in 2005–6 to 80 per cent in 2007–8; and guilty pleas increased from 64 per cent to just under 67 per cent. It revealed also that in 2007–8, the majority of defendants (85 per cent) were men; offences against the person and public order offences were the most common (84 per cent); and in that year 76 per cent of racially and religiously aggravated crime defendants were identified as belonging to the White British category.

32.1.10 Prohibited processions and assemblies

Part II of the 1986 Act makes detailed provision for the regulation of processions and assemblies. These police powers have been extended repeatedly by Parliament in recent years. Close examination of the provisions with their significant implications for public protest and civil liberties in general lies beyond the scope of this book.[147] The central focus in many of the cases under these powers is now on their ECHR compatibility.[148] Article 11 guarantees the right to organize and participate in public demonstrations and processions and to public and private meetings.[149] There is pressure for review and reform of the manner of policing protests.[150]

---

[141] See also *Greene* [2004] All ER (D) 70 (May).

[142] [2002] EWHC 85 (Admin).

[143] See also *DPP v M* [2005] Crim LR 392 and commentary.

[144] *R (Jones) v DPP* [2011] 1 WLR 833; [2010] EWHC 523 (Admin).

[145] *X v Italy* (1976) 5 DR 83; *Jersild v Denmark* [1994] EHRR 1, on which see also J Andrews and A Sherlock, 'Freedom of Expression – How Far should it Go' (1995) 20(3) EL 329. See also the important limitation in Art 17 preventing any group from performing acts designed to destroy the rights and freedoms in the Convention to a greater extent than is provided for in the Convention. This has been influential in the ECtHR's reasoning. There are similar guarantees in Art 20 of the ICCPR. For concern that it is too readily used, see Turenne, above, n 119.

[146] See www.cps.gov.uk/publications/docs/CPS_hate_crime_report_2008.pdf.

[147] D Feldman, *Civil Liberties and Human Rights in England and Wales* (2nd edn, 2002) Ch 18; DG Williams, 'Processions, Assemblies and the Freedom of the Individual' [1987] Crim LR 167; Thornton et al, *The Law of Public Order and Protest*, Ch 3.

[148] See generally: Emmerson, Ashworth and Macdonald, HR&CJ, para 8.73 et seq; D Mead, 'Right to Peaceful Protest under the ECHR' (2007) 4 EHRLR 345 examining four categories of conduct – demonstrations, marches, persuasive communications and direct – and their treatment in the ECtHR, noting how few Art 11 claims succeed.

[149] See *Rassemblement Jurassien and Unite Juriassien v Switzerland* (1979) 17 DR 93 at 119. For recent case law in Strasbourg on the protection under Art 11 of unauthorized demonstrations of a peaceful nature, see *Rosca v Moldova* (2008) ECHR 25230/02.

[150] See the Human Rights Joint Committee, Seventh Report, *Demonstrating Respect for Rights? A Human Rights Approach to Policing Protest* (2009).

32.1.10.1 Advance notice, conditions and prohibitions on processions

Section 11 requires advance notice in writing by the organizers of a procession.[151] A summary offence is committed if the requirements of the section are not complied with. Under s 12 'a senior police officer' may, in specified circumstances, impose conditions; and s 13 similarly empowers a chief officer of police to prohibit a procession altogether. An organizer,[152] or person taking part, who knowingly fails to comply with such a condition[153] or to obey such a prohibition is guilty of a summary offence.[154] It is also an offence to incite a person to commit such an offence.[155]

32.1.10.2 Conditions on assemblies

Section 14 empowers a senior police officer to impose conditions on public assemblies. Where a chief officer imposes conditions under s 14 he must identify on which limb of the section he is relying. Moreover, if the conditions are imposed under s 14(1)(a) the officer must identify which of the three grounds contained in that limb was being relied on.[156] There must be sufficient reasons given to enable a party to whom the decision is directed to understand it. Summary offences are provided for organizers, and those taking part who knowingly fail to comply with a condition.[157] It is also an offence to incite a person to commit such an offence. The courts have construed the powers widely. Thus, although the powers were originally triggered only by a group of 20 or more persons, it was held that the police were entitled to control the movements of individuals alone.[158] The courts have also acknowledged that police powers under s 14 include the power to detain and order dispersal by specified routes and detain for as long as is necessary to enable safe dispersal.[159] These controversial decisions involve an unduly narrow interpretation of Art 5 of the ECHR.[160]

The Anti-social Behaviour Act 2003, s 57,[161] altered the definition of 'public assembly' to mean an assembly of two or more. This is an astonishingly wide power to control assemblies and in many cases its proportionality may well be challenged.

---

[151] In *Kay v Metropolitan Police Commissioner* [2008] UKHL 69 the House of Lords held that the mass cycle rides that take place each month from a predetermined starting point in London, but with no fixed route were within the exception in s 11(2) and so exempt from a requirement for notice to be given. The members of the Committee took different views on the wider question whether s 11 had any application at all to the cycle rides.

[152] Sections 12(4), 13(7); *DPP v Baillie* [1995] Crim LR 426.

[153] A defence is available where D can prove that the failure to comply was a result of circumstances beyond his control.

[154] Sections 12(5), 13(8).

[155] Sections 12(6), 13(9).

[156] *R (Brehony) v CC Greater Manchester Police* [2005] EWHC 640 (Admin).

[157] Section 14(4), (5), (6). A defence is available where D can prove that the failure to comply was a result of circumstances beyond his control.

[158] *Broadwith v CC Thames Valley* [2000] Crim LR 924.

[159] *Austin v MPC* [2009] UKHL 5. See the discussion in Ch 17 above, p 668. The House of Lords construed Art 5 as being limited to protection against arbitrary detention.

[160] See on this D Mead, 'Of Kettles, Cordons and Crowd Control – Austin v Commissioner of Police for the Metropolis and the Meaning of "Deprivation of Liberty"' [2009] EHRLR 376–394; H Fenwick, 'Marginalising Human Rights: Breach of the Peace, "Kettling", the Human Rights Act and Public Protest' [2009] PL 737; D Feldman, 'Containment, Deprivation of Liberty and Breach of the Peace' [2009] CLJ 243. Art 5 of the ECHR (as well as Arts 10 and 11) may be engaged in such circumstances. The ECtHR has accepted that Art 5(1)(b) may be violated in cases where the State detains those who refuse to comply with restrictions on demonstrations: *Epple v Germany* [2005] EHRLR 431. Excessive force used in policing protest might infringe Art 3: *Muradova v Azerbaijan* [2009] ECHR 22684/05.

[161] See N Padfield, 'The Anti-Social Behaviour Act 2003: The Ultimate Nanny-state Act?' [2004] Crim LR 712.

Where s 14 conditions have been imposed, police actions in controlling the demonstration must remain within the law. In *R (Laporte) v CC of Gloucs*,[162] for example, police escorting coaches full of demonstrators away from the site of a demonstration at a US Air Force base was held by the House of Lords not to have been justified, absent any reasonable apprehension of an imminent breach of the peace. As Lord Rodger emphasized, a peaceful protestor does not 'cease to enjoy the right to peaceful assembly as a result of sporadic violence or other punishable acts committed by others in the course of a demonstration'.[163]

Kettling once again came under scrutiny in *R (Moos) v MPC*.[164] The police contained a group of peaceful protestors, fearing that another more hostile group would hijack the peaceful demonstration. The court held that the kettling was unjustified. A police officer could take steps to prevent an apprehended breach of the peace, only if the apprehended breach is imminent. The concept of imminence is not an inflexible one and depends on the circumstances. The steps the police take must be necessary, reasonable and proportionate if they are to be justified under Art 5. Keeping two or more different groups apart may be necessary, reasonable and proportionate if a combination of groups is reasonably apprehended to be likely to lead to an imminent breach of the peace, and, depending on the circumstances, where it is necessary in order to prevent an imminent breach of the peace, action may lawfully be taken which affects people who are not themselves going to be actively involved in the breach.[165]

32.1.10.3 Trespassory assemblies

Section 14A (inserted by the Criminal Justice and Public Order Act 1994) enables a chief officer of police in particular circumstances to apply to the council of the district for an order prohibiting trespassory assemblies in the district or part of it for a specified period. Again, a person who organizes or takes part in an assembly which he knows is prohibited commits a summary offence. The person who incites such an offence also commits an offence.[166] This applies only to *trespassory* assemblies, that is, assemblies which would be a trespass if no order had been made. So a peaceful assembly of 21 people on the verge of a highway adjacent to Stonehenge did not constitute a trespassory assembly since it did not amount to an unreasonable obstruction of the highway or a public nuisance.[167]

32.1.10.4 Unauthorized demonstrations

The Serious Organised Crime and Police Act 2005, s 132 disapplies s 14 of the Public Order Act in certain circumstances, replacing it with a more specific scheme to control demonstrations near Parliament. It is an offence to organize a demonstration in a public place in the designated area, or take part in a such a demonstration or carry on a demonstration by oneself in a public place in the designated area, if, when the demonstration starts, authorization for the demonstration has not been given.[168] The section was intended to have retrospective effect, particularly in respect of Mr Haw, a long-standing peace protestor camped outside Parliament. It is a very strange provision with an almost personal agenda. In *R (Haw) v Home Secretary*,[169] it was held that the purpose of s 132(6) was to replace s 14 with the provisions of ss 132 to 138 in the

---

[162] [2006] UKHL 55. See ATH Smith, 'Protecting Protest' [2007] CLJ 253.

[163] [82]. See further LH Leigh, 'Peaceful Protest and the Limits of Police Intervention' (2007) 171 JPN 260.

[164] [2011] EWCA Crim 957 (Admin).

[165] Per May P.

[166] Section 14B(1), (2), (3).

[167] *DPP v Jones* [1999] 2 AC 240, [1999] 2 All ER 257, reversing [1998] QB 563, [1997] 2 All ER 119. On which, see comments at [1999] EHRLR 223; I Hare, 'Public Assembly: The New Highway Code' [1999] CLJ 265; H Fenwick and G Philipson, 'Public Protest, the Human Rights Act, and Judicial Responses to Political Expression' [2000] PL 627; G Clayton, 'Reclaiming Public Ground: the Right to Peaceful Assembly' (2000) 63 MLR 252.

[168] Section 134(2).

[169] [2007] QB 780. See I Loveland, 'Public Protest in Parliament Square' [2007] EHRLR 252.

case of demonstrations in the designated area, *whenever they started*. The restrictions under s 132 on the right to demonstrate do not infringe the right to freedom of peaceful assembly provided in Art 11 of the ECHR, being for a legitimate purpose and justified under Art 11(2).[170]

Where a demonstration has been authorized, it is an offence to take part in, or organize a demonstration in the designated area if (a) D knowingly fails to comply with a condition imposed on him or (b) D knows or ought to have known that the demonstration is not accordance with the authorization. It is a defence to show that the breach arose from circumstances beyond D's control, or was something done by direction of a police officer.[171]

32.1.10.5 Dispersal orders

Section 30 of the Anti-social Behaviour Act 2003 enables a senior police officer to delineate an area in which there has been significant and persistent anti-social behaviour. Such an authorization may not be given without the consent of the local authority for the relevant area.[172] Publicity must be given about the authorization before the beginning of its operative period.[173] The officer may then authorize uniformed constables[174] for a period not exceeding six months to give dispersal directions to groups of persons whose public presence or behaviour in the delineated area in the reasonable belief of the officer[175] has resulted, or is likely to result, in members of the public being intimidated, harassed, alarmed or distressed. A person who knowingly contravenes a direction given to him commits a summary offence.[176]

The officer directing the dispersal must, unless exceptional circumstances apply, have a real belief that some behaviour of the group indicated that harassment, alarm, intimidation or distress would be caused.[177]

The powers of dispersal under s 30 may be used for protests within the delineated area even if the authorization had originally been made to empower police to act against a different type of disorder occurring in that area. Thus, it was available to disperse a group of Sikhs protesting at what they considered an offensive theatre production in a particular area, for which a valid dispersal order happened already to exist to combat local anti-social behaviour and alcohol related violence around Christmas.[178]

Section 30(6) empowers an officer to remove a person under the age of 16. In *R (W) v Metropolitan Police Commissioner and another*,[179] this was interpreted to mean 'take away using reasonable force if necessary'. It was emphasized that a constable exercising the power given by s 30(6) of the 2003 Act is not free to act arbitrarily and that it did not create a curfew power. The removal must be for one of the statutory purposes (that is, to protect the child from anti-social behaviour or prevent him engaging in such).

32.1.10.6 ECHR

Challenge to restrictions on public meetings and protest may include those involving freedom of religion (Art 9), freedom of expression (Art 10) and freedom of assembly (Art 11). The

---

[170] *Blum v DPP* [2006] EWHC 3209 (Admin). The case achieved notoriety as one co-appellant was convicted for failing to obtain authorization for a demonstration – reading out in Whitehall the names of British soldiers killed in Iraq. See *R(Moase) v City of Westminster Magistrates Court* [2009] EWCA Civ 1545.

[171] Section 134(8).

[172] Section 31(2). See also *Carter v CPS* [2009] EWHC 2197 (Admin).

[173] Section 31(3), (4) and (5).

[174] Designated community support officers have power to exercise the powers conferred on a uniformed constable by s 30(3) to (6) (s 33, amending the Police Reform Act 2002).

[175] See *MB v DPP* (2007) 171 JP 10.

[176] Section 32(2).

[177] *Bucknell v DPP* [2006] EWHC 1888 (Admin): quashing D's conviction for refusing to disperse when ordered by police officer to do so when group of 20 schoolmates met on street at 5 pm.

[178] See *Singh v Chief Constable of West Midlands* [2006] EWCA Crim 1118.

[179] [2006] EWCA Civ 458.

European Court has recognized that public authorities have a duty to protect the right to peaceful protest and assembly.[180] The Court has accepted that authorities might have an obligation to provide adequate policing to enable counter demonstrations to occur, rather than impose an outright ban,[181] but has held the statutory power to restrict processions to be compatible with Art 11 in particular where there is an anticipation of violence.[182] In *Pendragon v UK*,[183] Arthur U Pendragon, a druid, challenged a banning order under s 14A relating to Stonehenge. P was arrested at a service he was conducting for druids, and he claimed that his right to religion under Art 9 was infringed, along with his rights under Arts 10, 11 and 14. The European Commission found that the order under s 14A complied with a sufficiently clear procedure, was limited and could be challenged before the courts. In *Singh*, above, the court rejected a claim that Parliament could not have intended to restrict rights of protest by such vague powers. The Court of Appeal held that they had a legitimate aim – preventing crime and disorder and protecting public safety, and they were proportionate to that aim. The key issue in many cases under the statutory powers above will be on the proportionality of the restriction in the individual case.

32.1.11 Other public assembly related offences

Other public order offences such as those dealing with raves[184] (ss 63–66 of the Criminal Justice and Public Order Act 1994 as amended by the Anti-social Behaviour Act 2003, s 58) and aggravated trespass (ss 68 and 69 of the 1994 Act) are beyond the scope of this book. It should be noted that these are becoming increasingly important in dealing with protestors.[185]

32.1.12 Acts intended or likely to stir up racial or religious hatred[186]

32.1.12.1 Racial hatred[187]

Offences of inciting racial hatred were first introduced into the law by the Race Relations Act 1965 which required proof of an intention to stir up such hatred. Because of the difficulty of proving such intent, the law was amended by the Race Relations Act 1976 which replaced the requirement of intent with an objective test. It was enough that the defendant's conduct was likely to stir up racial hatred, whether he intended to do so or not. Part III of the Public Order Act 1986 replaced the old law with six new offences. These have been extended by the

---

[180] *Platform Arzte fur das Leben v Austria* (1988) 13 EHRR 204. See recently *Karabulut v Turkey* (2009) ECHR 16999/04.

[181] *Chorrer v Austria* [2006] EHRLR 583.

[182] See *Rai Allmond and 'Negotiate Now' v UK* (1995) 81 DR 146. The ECtHR relies most heavily on the risk of public disorder: see M Hamilton, 'Freedom of Assembly, Consequential Harms and the Rule of Law' (2007) 27 OJLS 75.

[183] [1999] EHRLR 223.

[184] Open air gatherings to listen to loud 'music' ('sounds wholly or predominantly characterized by the emission of a succession of repetitive beats').

[185] See *DPP v Bayer* [2003] EWHC Crim 2567 (Admin); *DPP v Tilly* [2001] EWHC 821 (Admin); *DPP v Barnard* [2000] Crim LR 371; *Nelder v DPP* (1998) The Times, 11 June. See further, S Bailey and N Taylor, *Civil Liberties Cases Material and Commentary* (2009) Ch 4; Feldman, *Civil Liberties and Human Rights*, Ch 18; Thornton et al, *The Law of Public Order and Protest*, Ch 5.

[186] See I Hare, 'Crosses, Crescents And Sacred Cows: Criminalising Incitement To Religious Hatred' [2006] PL 521, tracing the history of the common law; PS Rumney, 'The British Experience of Racist Hate Speech Regulation – A Lesson for First Amendment Absolutists?' (2003) 32 Common Law World Rev 117.

[187] Related offences include making racist chants at football games: Football (Offences) Act 1991, s 3.

Anti-terrorism, Crime and Security Act 2001.[188] They are all concerned with acts intended or likely to stir up racial hatred – the objective test is retained throughout – and, by s 17:

In this Part, 'racial hatred' means hatred against a group of persons [...[189]] defined by reference to colour, race, nationality (including citizenship) or ethnic or national origins.

It will be noted that the offences extend to stirring up hatred against members of some religious groups such as the Jewish and Sikh religions because these religions also constitute a race.[190] Under the 1976 Act it was held that the term, 'ethnic', was to be construed relatively widely and that the Sikhs, though originally a religious community, now constituted an ethnic group because they were a separate community with a long shared history and distinctive customs.[191]

In *Mandla*, Lord Fraser of Tullybelton observed that:

For a group to constitute an ethnic group in the sense of the Act of 1976, it must, in my opinion, regard itself, and be regarded by others, as a distinct community by virtue of certain characteristics. Some of these characteristics are essential; others are not essential but one or more of them will commonly be found and will help to distinguish the group from the surrounding community. The conditions which appear to me to be essential are these: (1) a long shared history, of which the group is conscious as distinguishing it from other groups, and the memory of which it keeps alive; (2) a cultural tradition of its own, including family and social customs and manners, often but not necessarily associated with religious observance. In addition to those two essential characteristics the following characteristics are, in my opinion, relevant; (3) either a common geographical origin, or descent from a small number of common ancestors; (4) a common language, not necessarily peculiar to the group; (5) a common literature peculiar to the group; (6) a common religion different from that of neighbouring groups or from the general community surrounding it; (7) being a minority or being an oppressed or a dominant group within a larger community, for example a conquered people (say the inhabitants shortly after the Norman conquest) and their conquerors might both be ethnic groups.

It has been held in an employment context that Muslims are not a racial group under this definition.[192] In *R v DPP, ex p LBC of Merton*,[193] it was held in judicial review proceedings that a declaration that Muslims were a group covered by ss 17 to 19 would not be binding on the criminal courts. The law was argued to be arbitrarily discriminatory in the protection it offers to certain religious groups within England and Wales.

The recent case of *Sheppard* and *Whittle*[194] confirms that prosecutions can occur in England and Wales if a substantial measure of the activities has taken place in England and Wales.[195] In that case the defendants had written, edited and uploaded racially offensive material in England, but it was stored on a sever in California (where First Amendment

---

[188] See also the discussion in the House of Lords Select Committee on *Religious Offences in England First Report* (2004) Ch 6.

[189] The words 'in Great Britain', in the original formulation were repealed by the Anti-terrorism, Crime and Security Act 2001, s 37.

[190] On earlier proposals to extend the offences to include inciting religious hatred, see Idriss [2002] Crim LR 890. On the difficulty of definition and application of the racial hatred offences to members of home nations, see C Munro, 'When Racism is Not Black and White' (2001) 151 NLJ 313.

[191] *Mandla v Dowell Lee* [1983] 2 AC 548, [1983] 1 All ER 1062.

[192] *JH Walker v Hussain* [1996] IRLR 11. See for an argument that British Muslims are protected KS Dobe and SS Chokar, 'Muslims, Ethnicity and the Law' (2000) 4 Int J of Discrimination and Law 369. See generally Bailey and Taylor, above, n 185, Harris and Ormerod, *Civil Liberties*, Ch 11.

[193] [1999] COD 358.

[194] [2010] EWCA Crim 65.

[195] Applying *R v Smith (Wallace Duncan) (No 4)* [2004] QB 1418. The court rejected an argument that s 42 of the Act (providing that the provisions of the Act extended to England and Wales save for some limited exceptions

free speech guarantees mean that no offence is committed in the USA). The material was downloaded in England. It was targeted at English audiences. The court was referred to, but declined to consider the merits of, three 'jurisprudential theories' as to jurisdiction over such publications on the internet.

The first is that a publication is only cognisable in the jurisdiction where the web server upon which it is hosted is situated – the country of origin theory. The second is that publication on the internet is cognisable in any jurisdiction in which it can be downloaded – the country of destination theory. The third is that while a publication is always cognisable in the jurisdiction where the web server upon which it is hosted is situated, it is also cognisable in a jurisdiction at which the publication is targeted – the directing and targeting theory.[196]

The principled basis for such offences is that, irrespective of whether they do in fact cause alarm or distress, they 'intentionally denigrate or demean those against whom' the words are directed. What makes them public wrongs is their 'blatant and derogatory denial of their victims' status as members of the polity'.[197]

32.1.12.2 The offences

Proceedings for an offence under Part III of the 1986 Act may not be instituted except by or with the consent of the Attorney General. Each offence is punishable on indictment with seven years' imprisonment[198] or an unlimited fine or both, or, on summary conviction with six months' imprisonment or a fine not exceeding the statutory maximum, or both. The offences are very rarely prosecuted.[199]

The essence of each offence is that D does an act involving the use of threatening, abusive or insulting words, behaviour or material and either:

(1) he intends thereby to stir up racial hatred, or

(2) having regard to all the circumstances racial hatred is likely to be stirred up thereby.[200]

The offences are:

s 18 – using threatening, abusive or insulting words or behaviour or displaying any written material which is threatening, abusive or insulting;

---

which mainly related to Scotland and Northern Ireland) constituted a restriction of jurisdiction to England and Wales.

[196] Some further judicial analysis of the broader questions of criminal jurisdiction for cross-border crimes on the internet would however be welcome. See generally U Kohl, *Jurisdiction and the Internet: Regulatory Competence over Online Activity* (2007). See also on the implications of the prevalent use of the internet to distribute racist material, M Horn, 'Racism and Cyber Law' (2003) 153 NLJ 777, and more generally I Walden, *Computer Crimes and Digital Investigations* (2007) 148–151.

[197] Duff, *Answering for Crime*, 134.

[198] Raised from 2 years by the Anti-terrorism, Crime and Security Act 2001, s 40.

[199] There were only 84 prosecutions between 1988 and 2007: Home Office Explanatory Notes on the Criminal Justice and Immigration Bill 2007, para 1173. For recent prosecutions see, eg, *Abu Hamza* [2007] QB 659 and the cases involving the protests outside the Danish Embassy following the publication in Denmark of the cartoons of the prophet Muhammed: *Saleem* [2007] EWCA Crim 2692.

[200] For a discussion of speech crimes as either conduct or result crimes, see J Jacconelli, 'Context Dependent Crime' [1995] Crim LR 771. Note this is a crucial difference from the religious hatred offence below.

s 19 – publishing[201] or distributing written material[202] which is threatening, abusive or insulting;

s 20 – presenting or directing the public performance of a play which involves the use of threatening, abusive or insulting words or behaviour;

s 21 – distributing or showing or playing a recording of visual images or sounds which are threatening, abusive or insulting;

s 22 – providing a programme service for, or producing, or directing, a programme involving threatening, abusive or insulting visual images or sounds, or using the offending words or behaviour therein;

s 23 – possessing written material, or a recording of visual images or sounds, which is threatening, abusive or insulting, with a view to its being displayed, published, etc.

These are specific statutory offences creating inchoate liability, and as ever with inchoates, the elements of *mens rea* take on paramount importance. This Part of the Act provides a variety of requirements of *mens rea* in relation to the 'threatening, abusive or insulting' quality of the material in question. We have seen that for offences under ss 4 and 5 the prosecution must prove that D intended his conduct to have, or was aware that it might have, that quality.[203] In Part III, this requirement is not as simple.

Under s 18 where D is shown to have intended to stir up racial hatred the test for 'threatening, abusive or insulting' is wholly objective. Where D is not shown to have intended to stir up racial hatred the prosecution must prove that D intended his conduct to have, or was aware that it might be, 'threatening, abusive or insulting'.[204]

Under s 22, where D is shown to have an intention to stir up racial hatred the test of whether it is threatening, abusive or insulting is purely objective. Where D is not shown to have intended to stir up racial hatred, the prosecution must prove that he knew or *had reason to suspect* that the material was threatening, abusive or insulting.

For offences under ss 19, 20, 21 and 23, the prosecution need prove no intention or awareness with respect to 'threatening, abusive or insulting', but it is a defence for D, who is not shown to have intended to stir up racial hatred, to prove:[205]

- for s 19, that he was not aware of the content of material and did not suspect or have reason to suspect that it was threatening, abusive or insulting;

- for s 20, that he did not know and had no reason to suspect that the offending words or behaviour were threatening, abusive or insulting;

- for s 21, that he was not aware of the content of the recording and did not suspect and had no reason to suspect that it was threatening, abusive or insulting; and

- for s 23 that he was not aware of the content of the written material or recording and did not suspect, and had no reason to suspect, that it was threatening, abusive or insulting.

---

[201] In relation to the definition of 'publication' under s 29, in *Sheppard and Whittle*, above, the court concluded that it was misconceived to argue that without a publishee there could be no publication. The Crown had to show was that there was publication to the public or a section of the public in that the material was generally accessible to all, or available to, placed before, or offered to the public, and that could be proved by the evidence of one or more witnesses: in this case one police officer.

[202] This includes material on the internet: *Sheppard and Whittle* above. This is not surprising since 'written material *includes* any sign or other visible representation'.

[203] Section 6(3) and (4).

[204] Section 6(3) and (4).

[205] Subject to the discussion in Ch 2, p 29, relating to burdens of proof resting on the accused in the light of the jurisprudence on Art 6(2) of the ECHR.

Section 26 provides a defence for fair and accurate reports of proceedings in Parliament and a contemporaneous report of proceedings in open court.

32.1.12.3 Religious hatred

The racial hatred provisions in the 1986 Act applied in a discriminatory fashion. There was no protection against inciting hatred against a religion which did not also constitute a particular racial group. Growing anxiety over increasingly common examples of Islamophobia, particularly since 9/11, led to increased pressure for a new offence of inciting religious hatred. Defining an offence with sufficient precision, and one which would infringe only to a proportionate extent on the right to freedom of expression proved difficult and controversial.[206] Draft offences were included in Bills in the Anti-terrorism, Crime and Security Act 2001, a Private Member's Bill (Religious Offences Bill) 2002, the Serious Organised Crime and Police Bill 2005, and finally in the Racial and Religious Hatred Act 2006.[207]

The 2006 Act as originally introduced was subject to very heavy criticism. The House of Lords introduced amendments which have rendered the offences much narrower and more difficult to prove.[208] The crucial amendments were (i) that unlike the racial hatred offences above, it is not enough that the conduct was 'likely' to stir up religious hatred; it must be intended to do so;[209] (ii) the offences are not satisfied by proof of abusive or insulting words or conduct, it must be 'threatening'; (iii) s 29J was introduced to ensure that comment (for example, comedy), criticism and debate on religious beliefs were protected. Section 29J provides:

Nothing in this Part shall be read or given effect in a way which prohibits or restricts discussion, criticism or expressions of antipathy, dislike, ridicule, insult or abuse of particular religions or the beliefs or practices of their adherents, or of any other belief system or the beliefs or practices of its adherents, or proselytising or urging adherents of a different religion or belief system to cease practising their religion or belief system.[210]

This provision qualifies very heavily the offence below, and it is not restricted by any element of reasonableness as to the discussion, criticism, etc.[211]

Religious hatred is defined in s 29A as hatred against a group of persons defined by reference to religious belief or lack of religious belief. The latter expression is important as it will allow for prosecutions where D incites his audience to kill 'unbelievers' meaning those who do not subscribe to his religious beliefs rather than simply atheists. The courts will have to determine whether one set of faith beliefs constitute a religion. The Home Office Explanatory Notes list religions 'widely recognised in this country' as: 'Christianity, Islam, Hinduism, Judaism, Buddhism, Sikhism, Rastafarianism, Baha'ism, Zoroastrianism and Jainism'.

---

[206] See Idriss [2002] Crim LR 890 for a full discussion; P Jepson, 'Tackling Religious Discrimination that Stirs up Racial Hatred' (1999) 149 NLJ 554; *Religious Offences in England and Wales*, House of Lords First Report (2002).

[207] The Racial and Religious Hatred Bill was granted Royal Assent on 16 February 2006. The various sections came into force by virtue of the Racial and Religious Hatred Act 2006 (Commencement No 1) Order 2007, SI 2490.

[208] See, on the Act, Goodall (2007) 70 MLR 89; Hare [2006] PL 521; Addison, *Religious Discrimination and Hatred Law*, Ch 8; D Nash and C Bakalas, 'Incitement to Religious Hatred and the Symbolic' (2007) 31 Liverpool LR 349; E Barendt, 'Religious Hatred Laws; protecting groups or beliefs?' (2011) Res Publica 41.

[209] The old offences of racial hatred which rested on an intent requirement were acknowledged to be notoriously difficult to prosecute: see B Hadfield, 'Incitement to Religious Hatred' [1984] PL 231 at 242.

[210] For discussion of defences of political and academic comment etc, see J Jaconnelli, 'Defences to Speech Crimes' [2007] EHRLR 27.

[211] See N Addison, *Religious Discrimination and Hatred Law*, at 145.

The offences, which were brought into force on 1 October 2007, are:

- s 29B: using threatening words or behaviour, or displaying any written material which is threatening, intending thereby to stir up religious hatred. The offence may be committed in a public or a private place, but no offence is committed where the words or behaviour are used or the written material is displayed by a person inside a dwelling[212] and are not heard or seen except by other persons in that or another dwelling.[213] It is a defence for D to prove that he was inside the dwelling and had no reason to believe that the words or behaviour used or the written material displayed etc would be heard or seen by a person outside that or any other dwelling;[214]

- s 29C: publishing or distributing written material which is threatening intending thereby to stir up religious hatred;

- s 29D: presenting or directing a public performance of a play which involves the use of threatening, words or behaviour, intending thereby to stir up religious hatred;[215]

- s 29E: distributing, or showing or playing, a recording of visual images or sounds which are threatening, intending thereby to stir up religious hatred;[216]

- s 29F: producing or directing a programme including threatening visual images or sounds or using in such a programme such sounds or images, intending thereby to stir up religious hatred;

- s 29G: possessing either written material which is threatening with a view to its being displayed, published, distributed, or included in a programme service whether by himself or another, or possessing a recording of visual images or sounds which are threatening with a view to its being distributed, shown, played, or included in a programme service, whether by himself or another, intending in either case religious hatred to be stirred up thereby.

The maximum sentence for the offences is seven years' imprisonment, a fine, or both; on summary conviction, the maximum is a term of imprisonment not exceeding six months, or a fine not exceeding the statutory maximum.[217] Sections 29H and 29I deal with powers of entry, search and forfeiture. There is a special saving for reports of parliamentary and judicial proceedings in s 29K. The anxiety about misuse is demonstrated by the fact that the Act amends s 24A of the Police and Criminal Evidence Act 1984 so that the powers of citizen's arrest do not apply to the offences of stirring up religious and racial hatred. In addition, the consent of the Attorney General will be necessary before any prosecution can be instituted.

None of the offences require any religious hatred to be stirred up in fact. Nor for anyone to be present being stirred up. Nevertheless, because of the limitations introduced in the House of Lords, it has been widely predicted that in practical terms the impact of the Act will be negligible. It was described by the Director of Justice as 'always irrelevant'.[218] A Government Minister described the Bill as amended by the Lords into the form in which it was to be

---

[212] 'Dwelling' means any structure or part of a structure occupied as a person's home or other living accommodation (whether the occupation is separate or shared with others) but does not include any part not so occupied, and 'structure' includes a tent, caravan, vehicle, vessel or other temporary or movable structure: s 29N.

[213] Section 29B(2).

[214] Section 29B(4).

[215] 'Play' and 'public performance' have the same meaning as in the Theatres Act 1968: s 29D(4).

[216] The offence does not apply to the showing or playing of a recording solely for the purpose of enabling it to be included in a programme services, s 29E(3).

[217] Section 29L. Section 29D limits the type of performance to which the offence applies.

[218] See P Botsford (2007) Law Soc Gazette, 7 June, 24.

enacted as 'virtually impossible to prosecute'.[219] Academic commentators agree that is it 'almost unenforceable'. The provisions mean that the law is extended so that D inciting E to hate a religion becomes criminal even if D does not incite E to act in a criminal manner on the basis of such hatred. The offences will only be of value in those cases in which the incitement is to cause hatred in another rather than to incite the other to engage in an existing criminal offence.[220]

The problem is exacerbated as lay expectations will be that the offence will apply widely, indeed there is some suggestion that there is much lay confusion about the law in this area with the racially and religiously aggravated forms of public order offence being construed as race and religion hate laws.

32.1.13 Inciting hatred on the grounds of sexual orientation

The Criminal Justice and Immigration Act 2008, s 74 extended the scope of the incitement provisions by creating a new series of offences of inciting hatred based on grounds of sexual orientation. That includes hatred against a group of people defined by reference to sexual orientation, whether towards persons of the same sex, the opposite sex or both: s 29AB. Sections 29B to 29G of the 1986 Act are amended so as to extend the offences of use of words or behaviour or display of written material (s 29B), publishing or distributing written material (s 29C), the public performance of a play (s 29D), distributing, showing or playing a recording (s 29E), broadcasting or including a programme in a programme service (s 29F) and possession of inflammatory material (s 29G).[221]

The CPS has announced the first prosecution in 2011.[222]

In relation to each extended offence the relevant act (namely words, behaviour, written material or recordings or programme) must be *threatening*, which is narrower than the offences in relation to race which include 'threatening, abusive or insulting' words or behaviour. Note also that the offences apply *only* to words or behaviour if D 'intends' to stir up hatred on grounds of sexual orientation, rather than if hatred is either intentional or 'likely' to be stirred up as in the racial offences. A provision equivalent to s 29J of the 1986 Act is included. By s 29JA the discussion or criticism of sexual conduct or practices or the urging of persons to refrain from or modify such conduct or practices shall not be taken of itself to be threatening or intended to stir up hatred.

The offences are triable either way with a maximum seven years' imprisonment on indictment. The consent of the Attorney General will be required for any prosecution to commence.

The Government has stated that it considers there to be a 'compelling case' that there is a 'pressing social need' for these offences because of the evidence of hatred against 'homosexual people being stirred up by, amongst others, some extreme political groups and song lyrics, and of widespread violence, bullying and discrimination against homosexual people'. It will therefore be compatible with Arts 9 and 10 of the ECHR.[223]

---

[219] Paul Goggins MP, *Hansard*, HC, 31 Jan 2006, col 190.

[220] K Goodall (2007) 70 MLR 84 at 93, 113.

[221] The Criminal Justice and Immigration Act 2008 (Commencement No 14) Order 2010 (SI 2010 No 712) brought into force, on 23 March 2010, s 74 and Sch 16 of the Act (offences of hatred on the grounds of sexual orientation). On the offences see I Leigh, 'Hatred, Sexual Orientation, Free Speech and Religious Liberty' (2008) 10 Ecclesiastical Law Journal 337; E Heinze, 'Cumulative Jurisprudence and Human Rights: The Example of Sexual Minorities and Hate Speech' (2009) 12 Int Jnl of Human Rights and K Goodall, 'Challenging Hate Speech' (2009) 13 Int Jnl of Human Rights 211.

[222] See CPS press release 28 January 2011, www.cps.gov.uk/news/press_releases/104-11.

[223] See Home Office Explanatory Notes, para 1167.

The Government considers that legislation which prohibits the stirring up of hatred will deter such behaviour and send a message that it is unacceptable, leading to homophobic hatred becoming less widespread and in turn reducing the number of incidents of violence, bullying and discrimination.

32.1.13.1 ECHR[224]

Challenges under Art 10 (freedom of expression) and Art 9 (freedom of religion) would seem inevitable, particularly since it has been held that there is no defence in English law that the words spoken or published are true.[225] As noted above, although the ECtHR has acknowledged that Art 10 protects the right to express views that offend, shock or disturb,[226] the Court has declined to extend the protection to direct expression of racist views. However, in the leading case of *Jersild v Denmark*,[227] the Court distinguished between those who had expressed racist views directly, and acts of those exposing these individuals and the beliefs they espoused (the prosecution of an undercover journalist was a disproportionate response). It is arguable that the present law under the Public Order Act fails adequately to reflect that distinction, and that a prosecution of a journalist under s 22 or 23 would not be a proportionate response within Art 10(2). Less concern may arise under the religious hatred provisions because of the breadth of the exclusion in s 29J.

Article 17, which prevents convention rights being relied upon to allow a person to destroy or limit the Convention rights of others, has also been important in the ECHR case law.[228] This prevents extreme racists seeking to rely on Art 10 to protect their conduct.

32.1.14 Disability hate crimes

The DPP has recently called for a change in attitudes to disability hate crimes.[229] Any criminal offence which is perceived, by the victim or any other person, to be motivated by a hostility or prejudice based on a person's disability or perceived disability will be treated as a disability hate crime and this factor will be relevant in sentencing.[230]

32.2 Public nuisance[231]

Public nuisance is a misdemeanour at common law triable either way.[232] It consists of:

an act not warranted by law or an omission to discharge a legal duty, which act or omission obstructs or causes inconvenience or damage to the public in the exercise of rights common to all Her Majesty's subjects.[233]

---

[224] See Emmerson, Ashworth and Macdonald, HR&CJ, para 8.30 et seq.

[225] *Birdwood* (1995) 6 Archbold News 2.

[226] *Muller v Switzerland* [1991] 13 EHRR 212.

[227] See *Jersild v Denmark* [1994] EHRR 1.

[228] See *Norwood v UK* (2005) 40 EHRR SE411.

[229] See www.lawgazette.co.uk/news/victims-disabilities-let-down-system-says-dpp.

[230] For guidance, see www.cps.gov.uk/publications/prosecution/disability.html and www.cps.gov.uk/news/articles/prosecuting_disability_hate_crime.

[231] I Brownlie, *Law of Public Order and National Security* (2nd edn, 1981) 75, 77. For provisional reform proposals see Law Commission Consultation Paper No 193, *Simplification of Criminal Law: Public Nuisance and Outraging Public Decency* (2010).

[232] Magistrates' Courts Act 1980, s 17 and Sch 1.

[233] Stephen, *Digest*, 184.

The House of Lords recently confirmed the continued existence of the offence. It had been described in that case by the Court of Appeal in the following terms:

A person is guilty of a public nuisance (also known as a common nuisance) who (a) does an act not warranted by law, or (b) omits to discharge a legal duty, if the effect of the act or omission is to endanger the life, health, property,[234] or comfort of the public, or to obstruct the public in the exercise or enjoyment of rights common to all Her Majesty's subjects.[235]

A person who has suffered particular damage as the result of a public nuisance can maintain an action for damages in tort, and the major importance of public nuisance today is in the civil remedy which it affords.[236]

32.2.1 Nature of nuisance

32.2.1.1 Diverse forms of offence

The most common and important instance of a public nuisance is obstruction of the highway and this is more closely considered below. But it also includes a wide variety of other interferences with the public; for example, carrying on an offensive trade which impregnates the air 'with noisome offensive and stinking smoke' to the common nuisance of the public passing along the highway;[237] polluting a river with gas so as to destroy the fish and render the water unfit for drinking;[238] unnecessarily, and with full knowledge of the facts, exposing in a public highway a person infected with a contagious disease;[239] taking a horse into a public place knowing that it has glanders and that that is an infectious disease;[240] sending food to market, knowing that it is to be sold for human consumption and that it is unfit for that purpose;[241] burning a dead body in such a place and such a manner as to be offensive to members of the public passing along a highway or other public place;[242] keeping a fierce and unruly bull in a field crossed by a public footpath;[243] keeping two pumas and a leopard in a garden;[244] discharging oil into the sea in such circumstances that it is likely to be carried on to English (*sic*) shores and beaches;[245] by causing excessive noise and dust in the course of quarrying operations;[246] by an 'acid house-party' which creates a great deal of noise so as greatly to disturb the local populace;[247] by giving false information as to the presence of explosives so as to cause actual danger or discomfort to the public;[248] by trespassing and sniffing glue in a school

---

[234] The House of Lords deleted the word 'morals' from the definition proffered by the Court of Appeal.

[235] *Goldstein* [2004] 2 All ER 589, CA, para 3. See commentary by Ashworth [2004] Crim LR 303 on the Court of Appeal.

[236] See further on the tort WVH Rogers, *Winfield and Jolowicz on Tort* (18th edn, 2010) Ch 14.

[237] *White and Ward* (1757) 1 Burr 333. See also *Tysoe v Davies* [1983] Crim LR 684 (QBD).

[238] *Medley* (1834) 6 C & P 292.

[239] *Vantandillo* (1815) 4 M & S 73.

[240] *Henson* (1852) Dears CC 24.

[241] *Stevenson* (1862) 3 F & F 106; otherwise if D did not intend it for human consumption: *Crawley* (1862) 3 F & F 109.

[242] *Price* (1884) 12 QBD 247. cf *R(Ghai) v Newcastle City Council* [2010] EWCA Civ 59.

[243] Archbold (2005) ss 31–53.

[244] *Wheeler* (1971) The Times, 17 Dec.

[245] *Southport Corpn v Esso Petroleum Co Ltd* [1954] 2 QB 182 at 197, , CA, per Denning LJ; revsd [1956] AC 218, [1955] 3 All ER 864.

[246] *A-G v PYA Quarries Ltd* [1957] 2 QB 169, [1957] 1 All ER 894.

[247] *Shorrock* [1994] QB 279, [1993] 3 All ER 917.

[248] *Madden* [1975] 3 All ER 155, CA. The court said 'potential danger' to the public was not enough but that 'actual risk' to the comfort of the public was. This is difficult to follow. Is not 'potential' danger the same as risk? And should not risk be enough?

playground even in the absence of staff and pupils;[249] by arranging to cause the abandonment of a Premiership football match by switching off the floodlights.[250]

32.2.1.2 Relationship to statute

In *Rimmington*, the House of Lords confirmed that the courts do not have the power to abolish the offence.[251] However, the House also emphasized that the offence should not ordinarily be prosecuted where there is a statutory offence covering the relevant mischief.[252] Lord Bingham referred to the numerous statutory offences, which might be available in preference to public nuisance. These include statutory offences such as: obstructing the highway under the Highways Act 1980; harassment under the Protection from Harassment Act 1997; environmental wrongdoing under the Environmental Protection Act 1990, offences dealing with pollution under the Water Resources Act 1991 (as amended); sending substances inducing someone to believe they are noxious under the Anti-terrorism, Crime and Security Act 2001; sending obscene or indecent communications under the Postal Services Act 2000; sending malicious communications under the Malicious Communications Act 1988; and improperly using a public electronic communications network under the Communications Act 2003. The common law may still be useful where no statute has intervened or where the penalty provided by statute is inadequate.[253] Its flexibility renders the offence attractive to prosecutors, particularly as it may allow them to avoid procedural restrictions which limit the use of the statutory offences.

It is this flexibility which also renders the offence subject to cogent criticism for its potential conflict with the principle of certainty.[254] The House of Lords nevertheless confirmed in *Rimmington and Goldstein*,[255] that the offence is sufficiently certain to enable a person with appropriate legal advice to regulate his conduct. As such the offence was found to be sufficiently clearly prescribed to satisfy the (rather undemanding) requirements of Art 7 of the ECHR. The House took a narrower approach than the Court of Appeal. Lord Bingham[256] observed that:

absolute certainty is unattainable, and might entail excessive rigidity since the law must be able to keep pace with changing circumstances, some degree of vagueness is inevitable and development of the law is a recognised feature of common law courts... But... existing offences may not be extended to cover facts which did not previously constitute a criminal offence. The law may be clarified and adapted to new circumstances which can reasonably be brought under the original concept of the offence.... But any development must be consistent with the essence of the offence and be reasonably foreseeable... and the criminal law must not be extensively construed to the detriment of an accused, for instance by analogy.

Previously, the offence had been used on more than one occasion as a stop-gap pending specific legislation, to prosecute activity that poses a new threat to the health and welfare of the

---

[249] *Sykes v Holmes* [1985] Crim LR 791, DC (conduct capable of being a nuisance within s 40 of the Local Government (Miscellaneous Provisions) Act 1982). Section 40 of the Local Government (Miscellaneous Provisions) Act 1982 has since been repealed by the Sch 22(3), para 1 of the Education Act 2002.

[250] *Ong* [2001] 1 Cr App R (S) 404.

[251] *Rimmington* [2006] 1 AC 459 at [31].

[252] Per Lord Bingham at [30].

[253] eg, in *Bourgass* [2007] 2 Cr App R (S) 253, where 17 years for plotting a ricin attack on the underground exceeded the maximum available under the Anti-terrorism, Crime and Security Act 2001, s 113. See also its use to regulate prostitutes: T Sagar, 'Public Nuisance Injunctions Against On-Street Workers' [2008] Crim LR 353.

[254] See JR Spencer, 'Public Nuisance – A Critical Examination' [1989] CLJ 55.

[255] [2004] 2 All ER 589, [2004] Crim LR 303.

[256] [35]. cf *W* [2010] EWCA Crim 372 refusing to dilute the *mens rea* of the common law offence of misconduct in public office.

community, for example for harassing behaviour and in some jurisdictions for such conduct as knowing HIV transmission.[257] Following *Rimmington,* this seems very doubtful.

32.2.1.3 Act or omission

A public nuisance may be committed by omission, as by permitting a house near the highway to fall into a ruinous state[258] or by allowing one's land to accumulate filth, even though it is deposited there by others for whom D is not responsible.[259]

A public nuisance can be committed by a single act or omission. What is crucial is that the acts or omissions contemplated by D are:

likely to inflict significant injury on a *substantial section of* the public exercising their ordinary rights as such.

In *DPP v Fearon,*[260] F was charged with public nuisance following his conduct in approaching an undercover police woman on a single occasion and asking her for sex. A district judge ruled that the offence of public nuisance could not be made out since this was a single incident affecting only one woman. Applying *Rimmington*[261] the central concept of public nuisance was common injury to members of the public. It was not permissible to apply the offence to multiple, separate incidents on different members of the public, let alone a single incident affecting only one woman. The court rejected the argument that the single action of the defendant should be aggregated with all other conduct of those soliciting for sex in that vice area of Nottingham. That would amount to holding F liable on the basis, in part, of the conduct of others with whom he is not acting in concert and of whose actions he has no knowledge or ability to control.

32.2.1.4 Nature of interference

The interference with the public's rights must be substantial and unreasonable. For example, not every obstruction of the highway is a public nuisance:

If an unreasonable time is occupied in the operation of delivering beer from a brewer's dray into the cellar of a publican, this is certainly a nuisance. A cart or wagon may be unloaded at a gateway; but this must be done with promptness. So to the repairing of a house; – the public must submit to the inconvenience occasioned necessarily in repairing the house; but if this inconvenience is prolonged for an unreasonable time, the public have a right to complain and the party can be indicted for a nuisance.[262]

The public right to use the highway is not limited to passing and repassing; the highway is 'a public place, on which all manner of reasonable activities may go on'. It appears to include 'such ordinary and usual activities as making a sketch, taking a photograph, handing out leaflets, collecting money for charity, singing carols, playing in a Salvation Army band, children playing a game on the pavement, having a picnic, or reading a book ...'[263]

The key word is 'reasonable'. Any interference with the public's rights must be caused by some unnecessary and unreasonable act or omission by D is an unlawful obstruction. In

---

[257] See *Kreider* (1993) 140 AR 81; *Thornton* (1991) 3 CR 4th 381.

[258] *Watts* (1703) 1 Salk 357.

[259] *A-G v Tod Heatley* [1897] 1 Ch 560.

[260] [2010] EWHC 340 (Admin).

[261] [2005] UKHL 63.

[262] *Jones* (1812) 3 Camp 230, per Lord Ellenborough. And see *Cross* (1812) 3 Camp 224: 'A stage-coach may set down or take up passengers in the street, this being necessary for the public convenience; but it must be done in a reasonable time': per Lord Ellenborough. See *Ellis v Smith* [1962] 3 All ER 954, [1962] 1 WLR 1486.

[263] *DPP v Jones* [1999] 2 All ER 257, HL, per Lord Irvine LC.

Dwyer v Mansfield,[264] it was held that, when queues formed outside D's shop because he was selling only 1lb (454g) of potatoes per ration book in view of the wartime scarcity, he was not liable because he was carrying on his business in a normal and proper way without doing anything unreasonable or unnecessary. The nuisance, if there was one, had been created not by D's conduct, but by the short supply of potatoes.[265] The result might be different if D sold ice-cream though the window of a shop, causing a crowd to gather on the pavement, because this is not a normal and proper way of carrying on business in England.[266]

32.2.2 The public

Blackstone stated that a public nuisance must be an annoyance to all the King's subjects.[267] This is obviously too wide for, if it were so, no public nuisance could ever be established. Denning LJ declared that the test is:

that a public nuisance is a nuisance which is so widespread in its range or so indiscriminate in its effect that it would not be reasonable to expect one person to take proceedings on his own responsibility to put a stop to it, but that it should be taken on the responsibility of the community at large.[268]

Whether an annoyance or injury is sufficiently widespread to amount to a public nuisance is a question of fact. In *Lloyd*,[269] where D's carrying on his trade caused annoyance to only three houses in Clifford's Inn, Lord Ellenborough said that this, if anything,[270] was a private nuisance, not being sufficiently general to support an indictment. But in the *PYA Quarries* case, the nuisance was held to be sufficiently general where the inhabitants of about 30 houses and portions of two public highways were affected by dust and vibration.

In *Rimmington*,[271] as noted, the House of Lords held that what is required is that the act of omission 'was likely to inflict significant injury on a substantial section of the public exercising their ordinary rights as such'. The House quashed Rimmington's conviction for sending 538 packages to people, some of them prominent public figures, with racist content, and in some cases threatening and obscene content. That was not a public nuisance: a series of acts involving individual members of the public cannot constitute the necessary effect on the public or a significant section of the public to constitute a public nuisance. A multiplicity of individual victims will not do.[272] Their lordships overruled *Johnson*[273] where D had made hundreds of telephone calls to at least 13 women in South Cumbria. In *Madden*, a telephone call stating that there was a bomb in a factory affected only eight security officers who could not be regarded as a class of the public.[274] If the call had stated that the bomb was in a public place, such as a highway, from which the public were consequently excluded, there would have been a public nuisance, even if few or no members of the public were in fact affected.[275]

---

[264] [1946] KB 437.

[265] *Sed quaere*. Would it be a defence to obstructing a pavement that D's lap-dancing club was the only one in town?

[266] *Fabbri v Morris* [1947] 1 All ER 315 (Highway Act 1835, s 72).

[267] *Commentaries*, iii, 216.

[268] *A-G v PYA Quarries Ltd* [1957] 2 QB 169 at 191.

[269] (1802) 4 Esp 200.

[270] The annoyance could be avoided by shutting the windows.

[271] [2006] 1 AC 459.

[272] See Lord Rodger at [48] and Baroness Hale at [58].

[273] [1996] 2 Cr App R 434.

[274] [1975] 3 All ER 155, CA. What if all the workers in the factory had been evacuated? See now, Criminal Law Act 1977, s 51(2); above, Ch 16.

[275] Lord Nicholls gave the example of a single hoax call constituting a public nuisance if it was a bomb hoax but not if it was simply to inconvenience the recipient, at [42].

The same result should apply if the place were one to which the public have access on payment, such as a sports ground. Lord Bingham stated:

> To permit a conviction of causing a public nuisance to rest on *an injury* caused to separate individuals rather than on *an injury* suffered by the community or a significant section of it as a whole was to contradict the rationale of the offence and pervert its nature.

It is not clear why if D makes 1,000 calls, each to one of the 1,000 women, inflicting the same injury on each woman, he is any *less blameworthy* than someone who sends one email to 1,000 women at once inflicting the same injury. There is an injury in each. The same injury is experienced by 1,000 women in each case.[276]

32.2.3 *Mens rea*

It was decided in *Shorrock*[277] that it is enough that D knew or *ought to have known* that a nuisance would be caused: the offence is one of negligence. The previous authorities were ambiguous and most of them were civil proceedings. D relied on *Stephens*,[278] where Mellor J said:

> in as much as the object of the indictment is not to punish the defendant, but really to prevent the nuisance from being continued, I think that the evidence which would support a civil action would be sufficient to support an indictment

arguing that as the proceedings in *Shorrock* were indeed intended to punish, *mens rea* in the sense of actual knowledge of the nuisance was required. It was accepted, however, that whether *mens rea* was required or not could not depend on the motive of the prosecutor. Despite the recent endorsement of requirements of subjective *mens rea* for serious offences,[279] including in particular the common law offence of misconduct in public offence,[280] the House of Lords in *Rimmington* approved the definition of *mens rea* in *Shorrock*. In the conjoined appeal, *Goldstein,* an ultra-orthodox Jew, bought supplies from the company of an old friend in London, Mr E, with whom he had a bantering relationship. G owed Mr E money, which the latter had pressed him to pay. G accordingly put the cheque in an envelope (addressed to Mr E) and included in the envelope a small quantity of salt. This was done in recognition of the age of the debt, salt being commonly used to preserve kosher food, and by way of reference to the very serious anthrax scare in New York following the events of 11 September 2001, which both men had discussed on the telephone shortly before. The envelope caused a security scare at the postal sorting office where it was believed to contain anthrax. The intention was to be humorous, and Mr E gave unchallenged evidence at trial that had he received the envelope he would have recognized it as a joke. G's conviction was quashed for lack of *mens rea*.

32.2.3.1 Proof

While *Shorrock* may be taken to have settled the issue of *mens rea*, it does not follow that criminal and civil proceedings for nuisance are the same in all respects. The criminal rather than the civil rules of evidence apply, particularly as to burden of proof.

---

[276] Admittedly it is harder to say at what point the nuisance becomes criminal with the individual calls, but the outcome is the same.

[277] [1994] QB 279.

[278] (1866) LR 1 QB 702 at 710.

[279] See *G* [2004] 1 AC 1034, above, p 119.

[280] *A-G's Reference (No 3 of 2003)* [2004] EWCA Crim 868, above.

Denning LJ tells us:

In an action for a public nuisance, once the nuisance is proved, and the defendant is shown to have caused it, the legal burden is shifted to the defendant to justify or excuse himself.[281]

But in a criminal prosecution the principle of *Woolmington v DPP*[282] and the guarantees in Art 6(2) of the ECHR requires that, as a general rule, there is only an evidential burden on D who sets up justification or excuse.[283]

32.2.4 Vicarious liability

In at least some types of public nuisance a master is liable for the acts of his servant, performed within the scope of employment, even though the mode of performance which creates the nuisance is contrary to the master's express orders. Thus, in *Stephens*,[284] D was held liable for the obstruction by his servants of the navigation of a public river by depositing rubbish therein. The reason given was that the proceeding was, in substance, civil, the object being not to punish D but to prevent the continuation of the nuisance.[285] But Mellor and Shee JJ thought that there may be nuisances of such a character that this rule would not be applicable. Baty[286] criticizes the ground of this decision and pertinently asks:

who is to decide whether [the] prosecution is 'substantially civil' or tinged with criminology [*sic*]?[287]

Certainly, prosecutions for obstructing the highway are by no means always civil in substance: frequently the object is the punishment of the offenders. In *Chisholm v Doulton*,[288] Field J said that *Stephens* 'must be taken to stand upon its own facts';[289] and the court held that, on a charge under the Smoke Nuisance (Metropolis) Act 1853, D was not criminally liable for the negligence of his servant in creating a nuisance. In cases of statutory nuisance D is vicariously liable only if the words of the statute require it.[290]

The rule imposing vicarious liability for public nuisance may thus be neither so firmly established nor so all-embracing as is sometimes supposed; but *Shorrock* suggests that the courts will not distinguish between different types of nuisance and that all will be held to impose vicarious liability.[291]

32.2.5 ECHR

If D's conduct involves expressing opinions or engaging in activity that might be regarded as an aspect of his private life the offence engages the rights such as the freedom of expression (Art 10) and respect for privacy (Art 8), it has been held that it is a necessary and proportionate response for the protection of the rights of others (under Arts 8(2) and 10(2)).[292] The House

[281] *Southport Corpn v Esso Petroleum Co Ltd* [1954] 2 QB 182 at 197.

[282] [1935] AC 462; above, p 28.

[283] Another obvious difference is that the civil case may be made out on a balance of probabilities, but the criminal case must be proved beyond reasonable doubt.

[284] (1866) LR 1 QB 702.

[285] Does this involve an enquiry into the motives of the prosecutor? Or does it reflect the courts' own view of what is the proper remedy for the wrong in question?

[286] *Vicarious Liability* (1916) 204.

[287] In *Russell* (1854) 3 E & B 942, Lord Campbell thought that the obstruction of navigation by building a wall was 'a grave offence'.

[288] (1889) 22 QBD 736.

[289] ibid, 740.

[290] cf *Armitage Ltd v Nicholson* (1913) 23 Cox CC 416.

[291] See also *Craik v CC of Northumbria Police* [2010] EWHC 935 (Admin).

[292] *Goldstein* [2003] EWCA Crim 3450.

of Lords, in *Rimmington*,[293] took the view that the offence of public nuisance did not breach ECHR, Art 7 on grounds of lack of certainty.

32.2.6 Reform

The Law Commission recommends retention of the offence. This conclusion is arrived at because, in the Commission's view, the offence has developed a reasonable degree of certainty. It is based on the 'core' of public nuisance in civil law. That conclusion involves the assumption that one can define a public nuisance in civil law with reasonable certainty. Even if the core can be defined with certainty by reference to the civil law, the question remains whether in terms of the appropriate boundaries of criminalization it is necessary to use criminal sanctions for such conduct. One argument is that it is necessary to use the criminal law to ensure consistency of protection. The view taken is that it may be needed by prosecution agencies and it is to be spared on pragmatic grounds. Although the Commission identifies serious cases in which public nuisance has been prosecuted,[294] these are not all strong examples. Numerous statutory offences were available in those cases.[295]

The Commission recommends a change of *mens rea* so that D must have intended to create, or realized that he or she might generate, what ordinary people would regard as a public nuisance (para 5.54). The proposal for reforming the *mens rea* echo the fault element required for dishonesty offences,[296] and as such import all the objections that are levelled at *Ghosh*: specifically that D cannot know his act constitutes a public nuisance until a jury decides as much. The Commission rejects the claim that public nuisance is contrary to the principle of legal certainty. The final report is awaited.

---

[293] [2005] UKHL 63.

[294] eg, citing *Bourgass* above.

[295] For example, *Bourgass* could have been charged under s 58 of the Terrorism Act 2000 if it really was clear that he intended to use the information he had collected in terrorist activities.

[296] Para 5.28.

33
Road traffic offences[1]

33.1 Background to the legislation

The arrival of motor vehicles on the road created problems for the laws then in force. There were some provisions of statutes which applied to motorists, but only, as it were, by chance. For example, under the Highway Act 1835, s 72, it was an offence to drive any carriage on the pavement and this could be applied to motor carriages. Under the Town Police Clauses Act 1847, s 28, the furious driving of any horse or carriage was an offence and this was applied to motorists. A further example is that it was, and remains, an offence, triable only on indictment and punishable with two years' imprisonment, under s 35 of the Offences Against the Person Act 1861 for a person, having charge of a carriage or vehicle, to cause bodily harm by wanton or furious driving.[2] In relation to more serious cases, the threat of proceedings for manslaughter might have deterred the motorist from driving with wilful disregard for human life, but where some harm less than death was caused other offences against the person were hardly pertinent at all. For the main part, the law barely concerned the motorist at all. There were no tests of driving proficiency, no registration requirements, no compulsory insurance, and virtually no driving offences. The common law could not (and rightly did not) fill gaps like these and the result is that for practical purposes the regulation of road traffic is almost entirely statutory.

The pre-existing offences which were capable of being applied to the motorist required, in the main, that the harm should be caused intentionally or recklessly. It is rare for a motorist to intend harm to the person though perhaps not so rare for him to be reckless as to whether or not he causes such harm. Though the motorist who causes harm may often be at fault,

---

[1] A detailed review of road traffic offences lies beyond the scope of this book. Readers are referred to the leading works, in particular, K McCormac (ed), *Wilkinson's Road Traffic Offences* (24th edn, 2010). A major source of reference on the major offences covered in the chapter is the Department of Transport, Home Office, *Road Traffic Law Review Report*, HMSO, 1988, hereinafter referred to as the *North Report*. See further JR Spencer, 'Road Traffic Law: A Review of the *North Report*' [1988] Crim LR 707. The more recent offences under the Road Safety Act 2006 are developed from proposals in the Consultation Paper *Review of Road Traffic Offences Involving Bad Driving* (2005). Details of reviews and reform proposals on the law are available at www.dft.gov.uk/pgr/road-safety. On the recent review of drink driving, see S Cunningham [2011] Crim LR 296.

[2] In *Okosi* [1996] Crim LR 666 and commentary, it was assumed, without deciding the point, that subjective, *Cunningham* recklessness must be proved. In *Knight* [2004] All ER (D) 149 (Oct), the court held that a jury direction referring to 'driving without sufficient thought as to the possibility of risk' represented an 'unacceptable dilution' of the *mens rea* required. This endorsement of subjective *mens rea* is to be welcomed. This provision, though rarely used, is not a complete dead letter because it applies to drivers of horse-drawn vehicles and motorists or cyclists who cannot be prosecuted for dangerous driving or cycling because their act was not done on a road or (in the case of drivers) a public place, or because they were not warned of intended prosecution. cf *Cooke* [1971] Crim LR 44, QS where D could not be charged under the road traffic legislation because the offence was not committed on a road and *Mohan* [1976] QB 1, [1975] 2 All ER 193, CA. The *North Report* recommended the repeal of s 35 but this recommendation seems to have been rejected.

the harm he causes is ordinarily both undesired and unforeseen by him. But it must not be thought that there is little or no room for offences of intention and recklessness in road traffic. There are many offences (such as speeding, driving whilst unlicensed, driving whilst uninsured) where the offence is ordinarily committed intentionally or recklessly though it does not follow that such offences will require, as a matter of law, proof of intention or recklessness. Generally it is only in relation to the causing of harm to the person or property that the motorist is neither intentional nor reckless.

Road traffic legislation is considerable, technical, and complex and it is neither possible nor appropriate in a work of this kind to deal in a comprehensive way with the plethora of offences created. Attention is accordingly concentrated on careless driving, dangerous driving, causing death by dangerous driving and some of the related offences, since a discussion of these contributes to an understanding of the general principles of the criminal law. Careless and dangerous driving are rare examples of English law providing endangerment offences.[3] The most recent additions to the legislative scheme in the Road Safety Act 2006 include some controversial new offences in which liability is imposed for a death arising while unlawfully on the roads irrespective of whether the death is due to some defect in the manner of the driving.[4]

33.2 Dangerous driving[5]

The most serious offences in this context are dangerous driving and causing death by dangerous driving. We can begin by considering dangerous driving which is governed by s 2 of the Road Traffic Act 1988, as substituted by s 1 of the Road Traffic Act 1991:

2A – (1) For the purposes of sections 1 and 2 above a person is to be regarded as driving dangerously if (and, subject to subsection (2) below, only if) –

   (a) the way he drives falls far below what would be expected of a competent and careful driver, and

   (b) it would be obvious to a competent and careful driver that driving in that way would be dangerous.

(2) A person is also to be regarded as driving dangerously for the purposes of sections 1 and 2 above if it would be obvious to a competent and careful driver that driving the vehicle in its current state would be dangerous.

(3) In subsections (1) and (2) above 'dangerous' refers to danger either of injury to any person or of serious damage to property; and in determining for the purposes of those subsections what would be expected of, or obvious to, a competent and careful driver in a particular case, regard shall be had not only to the circumstances of which he could be expected to be aware but also to any circumstances shown to have been within the knowledge of the accused.

---

[3] See, generally, on the merits of endangerment offences RA Duff, 'Criminalising Endangerment', in Duff and Green, *Defining Crimes* (2005) esp at 60–62 and the response by M Ferrante 'Criminalising Endangerment – A Comment' (2005) 65 La L R 967; Duff, *Answering for Crime*, 160–170. See also Ashworth, POCL, 297.

[4] See below p 1142 and , for criticism, PW Ferguson, 'Road Traffic Law Reform' 2007 SLT 27; S Cunningham, 'Punishing Drivers Who Kill: Putting Road Safety First' (2007) 27 LS 288; S Cunningham, 'Vehicular Homicide: A Need for a Special Offence', in S Cunningham and C Clarkson (eds), *Criminal Liability for Non-Aggressive Death* (2008); cf M Hirst, 'Causing Death by Driving and Other Offences: A Question of Balance' [2008] Crim LR 339 suggesting that the new offences are not in themselves objectionable.

[5] See generally, S Cunningham, 'Dangerous Driving a Decade On' [2002] Crim LR 945, considering reviews of the legislation.

(4) In determining for the purposes of subsection (2) above the state of a vehicle, regard may be had to anything attached to or carried on or in it and to the manner in which it is attached or carried.

The offence is based on a failure of driving which is, objectively viewed, far below the standard acceptable. In short, a person is to be regarded as driving dangerously if the way he drives falls far below what would be expected of a competent and careful driver and it would be obvious to a competent and careful driver that driving in that way would be dangerous. A person is also to be regarded as driving dangerously if it would be obvious to a competent and careful driver that driving the vehicle in its current state would be dangerous.

33.2.1 Background

Historically, there were offences of reckless, dangerous and careless driving. They were supposed to represent a hierarchy. Unfortunately, the courts failed to find a satisfactory definition for any of the offences. The James Committee[6] noted the confused state of the law and how the supposed hierarchy failed to work well.[7] In 1977, Parliament abolished dangerous driving. However, the offence of reckless driving that remained was still lacking a clear definition. The law was still unsatisfactory and the authors of the *North Report* felt that it left too many cases of bad driving to be dealt with simply as careless driving:[8]

In terms of behaviour on the road the sort of driving which we believe ought to be treated more seriously would include… such activities as driving in an aggressive or intimidatory fashion which might involve, for example, sudden lane changes, cutting into a line of vehicles or persistently driving much too close to a vehicle in front. The present reckless driving offence is too narrowly framed reliably to catch those guilty of this kind of bad driving, *particularly in that it requires investigation of the driver's state of mind at the relevant time, evidence of which may be hard to obtain.*

The italics have been supplied because, to some at least, it is not immediately apparent why in an offence carrying two years' imprisonment on conviction on indictment (and 14 years' imprisonment should death be caused) the driver's state of mind should be irrelevant. It would surely be relevant to the sentencer who would be inclined to award a sentence towards the lower end of the scale if he concluded that the driver was merely thoughtless and towards the higher end of the scale if he concluded that the driver had deliberately put at risk the persons or properties of others. And why should it be more difficult to obtain evidence as to the driver's state of mind when he is driving a car than when he is wielding other dangerous implements such as a garden fork, hedge-trimmer or chainsaw?

The *North Report* also recommended that liability ought to attach to the driver who gave thought to the risk but foolishly concluded there was none, the so-called lacuna or loophole in the *Caldwell* test of recklessness.[9] The *North Report* concluded that there should be a new 'very bad' driving offence which would be objective and would articulate the relevant

---

[6] *The Distribution of Criminal Business between the Crown Court and Magistrates' Courts*, Cmnd 6323, paras 123, 124 and Appendix K.

[7] The most unsatisfactory motoring offence at present is dangerous driving. At one end of the scale it may verge on reckless driving, at the other it may be barely distinguishable from driving without due care and attention. Appendix K, para 6.

[8] *North Report*, 5.15. This same anxiety has led, bizarrely, to suggestions for an intermediary offence of negligent driving. For cogent criticism, see Cunningham, above at n 5.

[9] As to which, see above, p 122. Some would argue that the driver in an inadvertent state is really failing to apply latent knowledge from experiences of driving and is blameworthy in that regard. For discussion see RA Duff, *Intention, Agency and Criminal Liability* (1990) 160.

standard. Section 2 of the Road Traffic Act 1988, as substituted by s 1 of the Road Traffic Act 1991, provides that.

33.2.2 The offence

The test of dangerousness is a purely objective one.[10] The CPS[11] provides the following examples of driving which may support an allegation of dangerous driving: racing or competitive driving; speed, which is highly inappropriate for the prevailing road or traffic conditions; aggressive driving, such as sudden lane changes, cutting into a line of vehicles, or driving much too close to the vehicle in front; disregard of traffic lights and other road signs, which, on an objective analysis, would appear to be deliberate; disregard of warnings from fellow passengers; overtaking which could not have been carried out safely; driving a vehicle with a load which presents a danger to other road users; where the driver is suffering from impaired ability, such as having an arm or leg in plaster, or impaired eyesight; driving when too tired to stay awake; driving a vehicle knowing it has a dangerous defect; using a hand-held mobile phone or other hand-held electronic equipment when the driver was avoidably and dangerously distracted by that use; reading a newspaper/map; talking to and looking at a passenger where the driver was avoidably and dangerously distracted by that; selecting and lighting a cigarette, or similar, in circumstances where the driver was avoidably and dangerously distracted by that.[12]

Dangerous driving is triable either way and carries a level 5 fine and/or 12 months' custody on summary conviction; in the Crown Court, the maximum penalty is two years' custody and/or an unlimited fine. Disqualification from driving for at least a year and an extended driving retest are mandatory in the absence of 'special reasons'.

The offence requires a consideration of the following matters.

33.2.2.1 The relevant standard for dangerous driving

In relation to the *driving* of the vehicle the relevant standard is entirely objective,[13] D doing his incompetent best might still render him liable for dangerous driving. The test is focused on the manner of driving and not on D's state of mind.[14]

It must be proved (i) that the way D drives falls 'far below' what would be expected of a competent and careful driver; *and*[15] (ii) that it would be obvious to a competent and careful driver that driving in that way would be dangerous. The requirements at (i) and (ii) are obviously intended to be additional and are not meant to be two ways of expressing the same thing. Dangerous driving is a more serious offence than careless driving. Careless driving may well create a risk of injury to the person or of serious damage to property but careless driving which does not fall 'far below' what would be expected of a competent driver does not suffice. Conversely, driving might fall far below the standard of the competent driver and yet not create a risk of injury to the person nor of serious damage to property. Moreover, the danger of the relevant harm must be 'obvious' to the competent and careful driver and this requires more than that the danger would have been foreseeable to the competent and careful driver; the situation must be one where the competent and careful driver would say that the danger

---

[10] *Loukes* [1996] 1 Cr App R 444.

[11] See www.cps.gov.uk/Publications/prosecution/pbd_policy.html#_09.

[12] See *Browning* [2001] EWCA Crim 1831, [2002] 1 Cr App R (S) 88.

[13] *Collins* [1997] Crim LR 578.

[14] But note the public attitude reported in the surveys discussed by Cunningham [2002] Crim LR 945 at 950 and in her 'Vehicular Homicide'. See also, B Mitchell, 'Further Evidence of the Relationship Between Legal and Public Opinion on the Law of Homicide' [2000] Crim LR 814.

[15] See *Brooks* [2001] EWCA Crim 1944.

was plain for all to see. A single inadvertent act or omission may fall so far below the standard of driving of a competent and careful driver that it constitutes dangerous driving. It is nevertheless, intended to be a high threshold, and not one applying to every slip;[16] not every breach of the Highway Code will be sufficient to establish the offence of dangerous driving, although it will be a guide as to the standard to be expected of the careful and competent driver.[17]

Clearly, the magistrates or the jury have to make a value judgement as to whether D's driving falls 'far below' the standard of the competent and careful driver. Opinions of magistrates and juries may, and no doubt will, differ on how far below is 'far below' but appellate courts are unlikely to interfere with what are said to be decisions 'of fact and degree' unless the decision is patently unreasonable. There will thus be an element of chance in whether D is convicted of dangerous driving or the lesser offence of careless.[18] This element of the offence has been heavily criticized since members of the public do not have a 'consistent perception of what is required of a competent and careful driver'.[19]

Viewed as a matter of principle the driving should be considered independently of the harm in fact caused; it is the nature of the driving and its potential to cause the stated harms that is the criterion in a conduct or endangerment crime such as dangerous driving.[20] This is supported in particular by the fact that there is a specific offence of causing death by dangerous driving.

33.2.2.2 Driving a vehicle in a dangerous state

Regardless of the manner in which a vehicle is driven, danger may be caused to the public (a) by the condition of the driver or (b) by the condition of the vehicle.[21] Under the repealed law of reckless driving the courts held, quite inconsistently, (i) that danger arising from the driver's drunken condition could not in itself amount to the offence because the recklessness must be in the manner of the driving; but (ii) that the offence was committed merely by driving a vehicle in a dangerous condition and it was immaterial that the manner of the driving was not reckless. The *North Report* recommended that, as indeed common sense seems to require, these two cases should be treated alike and either should constitute the offence. The offence:

should cover the fact that the vehicle is driven at all, as well as how it is driven. This is necessary so as to include within the offence those who decide to drive when either they themselves or their vehicles are wholly unfit to be on the road as well as those who, despite being fit to drive and having properly maintained vehicles, drive very badly.[22]

Section 2A(2) implemented this recommendation for dangerous driving but only in respect of the state of the vehicle and not in the state of the driver. The absence of any reference to the driver's condition appeared to confirm the illogical pre-Act position in this respect.

---

[16] *Conteh* [2004] RTR 1; *Few* [2005] EWCA Crim 728.

[17] *Taylor* [2004] EWCA Crim 213.

[18] It is incumbent on the trial judge to direct carefully on the difference between dangerous and careless driving: *Jeshani* [2005] EWCA Crim 146 and see *Lane* [2009] EWCA Crim 1630.

[19] Cunningham [2002] Crim LR 945 at 957, reviewing the findings of research surveys into the working of the 1991 Act.

[20] cf *Krawec* (1984) 6 Cr App R (S) 367, CA, holding that in cases of careless driving leading to death, the unforeseen and unexpected consequences are not normally relevant to penalty, the primary consideration being the extent to which the driving falls below the standard of the reasonable driver. The *North Report* (para 5.22) recommended that the dangerous driving offence 'should look directly and objectively at the quality of the driving... – was the driving really bad? – without needing to consider how or what the driver had thought about the possible consequences...'

[21] There is no need for a jury to be unanimously of the view that it was the manner or the condition of the vehicle provided the jury is sure it was dangerous driving: *Budniak* [2009] EWCA Crim 1611.

[22] At para 5.22 (iv).

It was therefore a great surprise when, in *Woodward*,[23] the court found persuasive in respect of dangerous driving the arguments which it had persistently rejected or ignored in respect of reckless driving and held that the fact that D was adversely affected by alcohol was 'a relevant circumstance' in determining whether he was driving dangerously.[24] In a final twist in this ironic tale of statutory construction, the Court of Appeal has now rightly, it is submitted, accepted in *Webster*[25] that the condition of the driver, although relevant is not conclusive proof of dangerousness. Moses LJ in the Court of Appeal stated that:

the closely drafted definition of 'dangerous driving' does not permit proof of that offence to be limited to the danger occasioned by the condition of the driver. Firstly, the wording of the statute excludes such a possibility. Section 2A(1) refers only to the manner of driving. The definition is broadened by Section 2A(2) which eschews reference to the state of the driver and is confined to the defective condition of the vehicle. Section 2A(3) permits regard to circumstances which may well include the condition of the driver. But that condition is not dispositive of the question whether the person was driving dangerously. His condition will, by virtue of subsection (3) be relevant to whether there was danger of injury or serious damage but no more.[26]

As regards the state of the vehicle, it has been acknowledged that latent defects in the vehicle will be insufficient to found the charge since they would not be obvious to a competent and careful driver.[27] The 'current state' of the vehicle implies a state altered from the manufactured or designed state.

In determining the state of the vehicle, s 2A(4) provides that regard may be had to anything attached to or carried on or in the vehicle and to the manner in which it is attached or carried. This provision may have been unnecessary but it prevents any possible argument that the 'state' of the vehicle refers only to its mechanical state and does not extend, for example, to an improperly secured trailer or an insecure load.[28]

33.2.2.3 The relevant danger

The danger created must be of 'injury to any person or of serious damage to property'. In relation to serious damage to property, given that the essence of the offence is very bad driving, it seems odd that the offence is committed only where the very bad driving creates a danger of 'serious' harm to property (assuming that no danger of personal injury is created). Very bad driving remains very bad driving if it creates a danger of any damage to property. And when does damage become *serious*? £50's worth? £100's worth? £500's worth? Of course

---

[23] [1995] 3 All ER 79, [1995] Crim LR 487. The Crim LR report wrongly treats this as a case of *reckless* driving. *Woodward* was followed in *Marison* [1997] RTR 457 (diabetic driver who was aware that there was a real risk he might have a sudden hypoglycaemic attack guilty of causing death by dangerous driving); see also *Akinyeme* [2007] EWCA Crim 3290 (epileptic failed to take medication). It was persuasively suggested that *Woodward* was a case where the court has improved the law by misreading the statute, EJ Griew (1995) 2 Archbold News 4.

[24] In *Marison* [1997] RTR 457, [1996] Crim LR 909, it was held that, for the purposes of conviction of this offence there is no relevant distinction between an incapacity induced by alcohol and one which is induced by diabetes or any other cause. The question in every case is whether the incapacity is such that it would be obvious to a competent and careful driver that it would be dangerous to drive while labouring under it. The source of the disability may be relevant to sentence. See also *Webster* [2006] EWCA Crim 415, emphasizes that *Marison* should properly be regarded as a case on the unavailability of a plea of automatism. Note also *Pleydell* [2006] 1 Cr App R 212 – admissibility of unquantified consumption of cocaine. cf the discussion below relating to the ability of the driver.

[25] [2006] EWCA Crim 415. Evidence of any consumption of alcohol may be admissible even if D is not 'over the limit': *Mari* [2009] EWCA Crim 2677.

[26] [17].

[27] *Marchant* [2004] 1 All ER 1187, [2003] Crim LR 806.

[28] cf *Crossman* [1986] RTR 49, CA (insecure load).

the courts can take refuge in the formula that 'it is all a matter of fact and degree', but in terms of statutory definition this is unsatisfactory.

33.2.2.4 The knowledge of the reasonable person assessing D's driving

The test of dangerous driving is whether D's driving falls far below the standard of the competent and careful driver and would it have been obvious to a careful and competent driver that driving in that way would be dangerous? That test is designed to be objective.

The fact that D pressed the accelerator accidentally in mistake for the brake is no defence. If no competent and careful driver would have done such a thing, that is evidence of dangerous driving.[29] Even in the case where the alleged offence is driving a vehicle in a dangerous state D cannot defend himself by showing that he was unaware of the defect in the vehicle, or that he thought the load was secure, if it would have been obvious to a careful and competent driver that the vehicle was defective or that the load was insecure.[30] Where D secured his bales of straw to the trailer in a manner that had been in use for over 25 years without mishap, it was not reasonably open to the jury to convict on the basis that it was an 'inherently dangerous' system under s 2.[31]

The danger it has been held, is 'obvious' only if it could be 'seen or realized at first glance, evident to' the competent and careful driver: *Strong*[32] where the fatal corrosion of the car, which D had bought only a few days earlier, could have been discovered only by going underneath it. The danger was not 'obvious'. The court has subsequently suggested that *Strong* was not attempting to lay down a precise formula, and that 'obvious' was an ordinary English word that did not require elaboration.[33]

If a driver is aware of facts which would not be obvious in this sense he may nevertheless be guilty since the Act provides that regard must be had to any circumstances shown to be within his knowledge. If D is reasonably unaware, for example, of the tendency of a car to swerve to the right when braked hard, D cannot be held to have driven dangerously or even carelessly, but once D becomes aware of this tendency he may properly be held to have driven dangerously if it would then be obvious to a competent and careful driver that to drive the car with this tendency would be dangerous.[34] Similarly, D's actual knowledge of an uneven road surface may count against him though other drivers would be unaware of the hazard. More may be expected of a professional driver than of the private motorist.[35] An employed driver, however, cannot generally be expected to do more than to comply with the apparently reasonable instructions of his employer.

Several cases have recently highlighted the difficulty in applying the objective test in situations where a driver has superior driving ability. Ought that to be taken into account? With an objective test, we would not take account of a driver's inexperience, so why should we take account of superior experience?

In *Milton v DPP*,[36] a police officer who was a very experienced and highly advanced driver was recorded speeding at 140 mph. He claimed to be doing so in order to improve his driving

---

[29] *A-G's Reference (No 4 of 2000)* [2001] RTR 415, [2001] Crim LR 578; cf *Cambray* [2006] EWCA Crim 1708.

[30] See *Marchant* [2004] 1 All ER 1187 on the position where the vehicle has an 'authorization for use' on the roads from the Secretary of State.

[31] *Few* [2005] EWCA Crim 728.

[32] [1995] Crim LR 428. See also *Roberts and George* [1997] RTR 462, [1997] Crim LR 209.

[33] *Marsh* [2002] EWCA Crim 137.

[34] cf *Haynes v Swain* [1975] RTR 40, DC, below, n 69.

[35] *Roberts and George* [1997] Crim LR 209.

[36] [2006] EWHC 242 (Admin).

skills for occasions when driving at such speed might be needed in an emergency situation. The District Judge acquitted him. The Crown appealed and in the Divisional Court, Hallett LJ observed that:

It matters not whether the respondent intended to drive dangerously, or believed that he could drive at grossly excessive speeds without causing danger to others because of his advanced driving skills. I repeat that the test is, what is the standard judged objectively and what would have been obvious to the independent bystander? As to whether the district judge would have been entitled to impute knowledge of the respondent's driving skills to the independent bystander on the basis of the arguments advanced before us, I can form no concluded view.[37]

The case was remitted to the magistrate who duly convicted the driver. On appeal that conviction was quashed by the Divisional Court.[38] D argued that the fact that he was a highly experienced police driver was a 'circumstance...shown to have been within the knowledge of the accused' for the purpose of s 2A(3). The Divisional Court in *Milton (No 2)* held that, just as the prosecution can rely on circumstances known to D to help establish that his driving was dangerous, so D can rely on special circumstances known to him (here, his special skill as a police driver) to help establish that it was not.[39] In the most recent case, *Bannister*[40] (also involving a speeding police officer), the Court of Appeal rejected the reasoning in *Milton (No 2)* and endorsed that in *Milton (No 1)*.

The current state of the law is, therefore, that the superior driving *ability* of the driver is irrelevant when a driver is charged with dangerous driving. To have regard to those *abilities* is inconsistent with the objective test of the competent and careful driver set out in the Act. However, the intoxicated state of the driver is relevant to determining whether the driving was dangerous because the *condition* of the driver (heavily intoxicated by alcohol) is in itself a 'circumstance' known to the accused and therefore regard had to be had to it.[41] These *are* relevant to the dangerousness test because they do not go to the *standard* of the competent and careful driver but are facts relating to the condition of the driver which were as relevant as the driver's knowledge of the unroadworthiness of a car or the conditions of the weather or the road. That distinction is a fine one. Moreover, it might be argued that the test would remain an objective one if the reasonable person were to be asked whether judged objectively, the standard of driving is dangerous taking into account the level of expertise of the driver? It takes a strained reading to include *any* such factors within the evaluation of the *dangerousness* of the driving since it is odd to describe the drunkenness of the driver as a 'circumstance within the knowledge of the accused' which is what s 2A(3) requires in order for it to be considered.[42]

---

[37] Emphasis added.

[38] [27].

[39] A jury has held that a motorist driving at 145 mph, more than twice the speed limit, was not driving dangerously, apparently having regard to the high quality of the vehicle, the ability of the driver and, presumably, the prevailing road conditions: (1999) The Times, 25 Mar.

[40] [2009] EWCA Crim 1571. See J Goudkamp [2010] CLJ 8.

[41] *Woodward* [1995] 2 Cr App R 388.

[42] *Bannister* poses other difficulties: the Court's statement that 'no emergency or police duty permits a police officer to drive dangerously' overstates the position. If a defence of necessity can legitimate killing, surely it can provide a defence to an act of objectively dangerous driving if the circumstances warrant it (eg driving the wrong way down a road to reach and defuse a terrorist bomb).

33.3 Careless and inconsiderate driving

Section 3 of the Road Traffic Act 1988, as substituted by s 2 of the Road Traffic Act 1991, provides:

If a person drives a mechanically propelled vehicle on a road or other public place without due care and attention, or without reasonable consideration for other persons using the road or place, he is guilty of an offence.

The offences are summary only and punishable by a fine at level 5.[43]

The substituted section extended the offences in two respects, first by substituting 'mechanically propelled vehicle' for 'motor vehicle', and secondly, by the addition of 'or other public place' to 'road'.[44]

For the purposes of s 3, and no doubt for the purposes of ss 1 and 2, 'other persons using the road' includes the passengers in a vehicle driven by D.[45]

Section 3 creates two distinct offences, careless driving and inconsiderate driving. In many cases the facts would constitute either offence but they are not identical since inconsiderate driving may be committed only where other persons are using the road.

33.3.1 Background to careless driving

As discussed in Chapter 6, at common law negligence is only rarely a sufficient basis for criminal liability. It is now established that manslaughter may be committed by gross negligence[46] but this is exceptional. Negligence, however gross, is not usually sufficient to ground liability for a non-fatal offence against the person or even of damage to property. A number of road traffic offences are founded on negligence. In particular, the offence discussed in detail below of driving a mechanically propelled vehicle carelessly. That offence does not require harm to person or property.[47] Why, if it is not an offence negligently to cause injury with 'a garden fork, hedge-trimmer or even a chainsaw'[48] should it be an offence to cause harm (or even not to cause harm) by the negligent use of a motor vehicle? The *North Report* conceded that there is not a great logical difference between the careless use of a chainsaw or a vehicle but defended the offence of careless driving on the grounds that:

the careless use of chainsaws does not contribute to over 5,000 deaths every year. It is because the danger associated with the widespread use of motor vehicles is so great that society has decided to attempt to restrain the use of vehicles so as to reduce this danger. And there are parallels between road traffic law and other bodies of regulatory law covering areas of activity such as health and safety at work, and building standards. Some of these areas of law contain offences which could be the result of mere carelessness such as, for example, polluting a river or leaving a machine unguarded.

---

[43] Road Safety Act 2006, s 23. The court must also either endorse the driver's licence with between 3 and 9 penalty points (unless there are 'special reasons' not to do so), or impose disqualification for a fixed period and/or until a driving test has been passed.

[44] The *North Report* recommended these extensions for the offence of dangerous driving (8.10, 8.12) but not for careless driving. On defining public place, see *May v DPP* [2005] EWHC 1280 (Admin). See also *Barrett v DPP* [2009] EWHC 423 (Admin) for a useful review of the case law.

[45] *Pawley v Wharldall* [1966] 1 QB 373, [1965] 2 All ER 757.

[46] *Adomako* [1995] AC 171. See Ch 15.

[47] It used to be that a prosecution was unlikely without such harm: 'One widespread complaint was of the mechanical nature of the prosecution decision – a bad case of careless driving may not go to court because no personal injury was caused, and conversely a very trivial case of carelessness may lead to prosecution simply because injury was caused': *North Report*, 5.27.

[48] *North Report*, 5.29.

The common element between such offences is the degree of danger that may be caused to innocent parties.[49]

Some may find this reassurance convincing, others less so. The assumption appears to be that without such an offence, road deaths attributable to careless driving would have been significantly more than 5,000, but the assumption remains unproven.[50]

One argument against such an offence is that it is unnecessary because drivers are already constrained to drive as best they can to protect their own safety, and to avoid a collision and its consequences (not least the loss of an insurance no claims bonus the cost of which may exceed any fine the court imposes). The *North Report* rejected this argument, suggesting that if the offence of careless driving were to be abolished then:

at least part of it would have to be replaced or there would be some serious instances of bad driving which would go unpunished. In our view it is likely that the issues here are confused by the amount of attention which is focused on the common shorthand term for this offence – careless driving. But what is required to establish the section 3 offence is more than this. The course of driving must be found to be lacking in *due* care or *reasonable* consideration. Cases where no accident is caused, involving momentary inattention for example, by a driver with an unblemished driving career should not, in our opinion, lead to an appearance in court. But a series of bad overtaking decisions might, if such driving came to police attention, warrant prosecution, even if no accident resulted.[51]

This passage is puzzling. It suggests that the offence of careless driving should be retained because it will deal with cases of 'bad' driving which are not bad enough to qualify as 'very bad' driving within the offence of dangerous driving. It also suggests that carelessness *per se* does not suffice for the offence; the emphasis on '*due* care' and '*reasonable* consideration' suggesting that more than mere carelessness is required to constitute the offence. This is a novel suggestion and does not appear to be one articulated in the existing case law.

33.3.2 Careless driving defined

The Road Safety Act 2006 introduced a new provision into the 1988 Act, seeking to clarify the definition of the offence. Section 30 of the 2006 Act inserts s 3ZA which provides that:[52]

(2) A person is to be regarded as driving without due care and attention if (and only if) the way he drives falls below what would be expected of a competent and careful driver.

(3) In determining for the purposes of subsection (2) above what would be expected of a careful and competent driver in a particular case, regard shall be had not only to the circumstances of which he could be expected to be aware but also to any circumstances shown to have been within the knowledge of the accused.

This codifies earlier case law and echoes the test in dangerous driving above. In that respect it is welcome since it makes clear that there is a hierarchy, with careless driving requiring conduct falling below the standard of the competent driver while the dangerous driving offence requires a falling *far* below that standard.

---

[49] *North Report*, 5.30. cf Health and Safety Act 1974 offences.

[50] The Consultation Paper preceding the 2006 Act reforms – *Review of Road Traffic Offences Involving Bad Driving* (2005) – referred to the 35,000 deaths or injuries per year on British roads. According to the Department of Transport 2,538 people were killed on the road in 2008. See www.dft.gov.uk/pgr/statistics.

[51] *North Report*, 5.31.

[52] From 24 Sept 2007.

The earlier cases had defined the test of liability for careless driving was whether D was exercising that degree of care and attention that a reasonable and prudent driver would exercise in the circumstances?[53] The relevant standard, according to Lord Hewart CJ:

is an objective standard, impersonal and universal, fixed in relation to the safety of other users of the highway. It is in no way related to the degree of proficiency or degree of experience attained by the individual driver.[54]

The courts' aim was to impose a purely objective standard, paying no heed to the inadequacies of the learner or inexperienced driver.[55] Nor was any special standard applicable to experienced drivers, such as police drivers who may be trained to meet exacting standards of proficiency,[56] even though they may have to cope with emergencies which are not the lot of ordinary drivers.[57] Faced by an emergency the issue is not whether by taking some other course of action harm may have been avoided but whether D's reaction to the emergency was a reasonable one.[58] Even if D suffers an unexplained initial loss of control (for example, resulting in the vehicle skidding), it is not improper for justices to convict him of careless driving on the basis of his reaction in braking too heavily.[59]

Lord Diplock in *Lawrence*[60] described the offence as an 'absolute offence',

in the sense in which that term is commonly used to denote an offence for which the only *mens rea* needed is simply that the prohibited physical act (*actus reus*) done by the accused was directed by a mind that was conscious of what his body was doing, it being unnecessary to show that his mind was also conscious of the possible consequences of his doing it.

This passage involves a misleading use of the term absolute offence. Offences of 'absolute', by which it is usually meant 'strict', liability are ordinarily contrasted with offences requiring a fault element, including offences which require proof of negligence.[61] In the case of an absolute offence it can be no defence to show that all reasonable care was taken but where an offence, such as careless driving, requires proof of negligence the prosecution must necessarily fail unless a want of due care is established.[62] There is a sense in which liability for careless driving might be said to be absolute. If D's driving falls short of the standard expected from the competent and careful driver, not only is it no defence for D to show that he was doing his

---

[53] Per Lord Goddard CJ in *Simpson v Peat* [1952] 2 QB 24, [1952] 1 All ER 447 at 449, DC.

[54] *McCrone v Riding* [1938] 1 All ER 157 at 158, DC. The standard is the same as that applied in a civil action for negligence – 'the obligation in the criminal law on the ... driver cannot be the subject of a more stringent test than his liability in civil law': *Scott v Warren* [1974] RTR 104, DC, per Lord Widgery CJ at 107. References in a criminal case to rules of civil law affecting the onus of proof (such as *res ipsa loquitur*) are probably best avoided though it is open to justices to infer negligence from facts affording no other reasonable explanation.

[55] *McCrone v Riding* [1938] 1 All ER 157; *Preston Justices, ex p Lyons* [1982] RTR 173, [1982] Crim LR 451, DC. See M Wasik, 'A Learner's Careless Driving' [1982] Crim LR 411. Inexperience may be relevant to sentence: *Mabley* [1965] Crim LR 377.

[56] *Woods v Richards* (1977) 65 Cr App R 300, DC.

[57] In coping with such emergencies the police driver owes the ordinary duty of care to other persons lawfully (*Gaynor v Allen* [1959] 2 QB 403, [1959] 2 All ER 644, DC) or unlawfully (*Marshall v Osmond* [1983] QB 1034, [1983] 2 All ER 225, DC) on the highway. The test is whether D is driving with due care *in all the circumstances*, including the emergency with which he is faced (*Woods v Richards* (1977) 65 Cr App R 300, DC) and the nature of the unlawful conduct with which he has to deal (*Marshall v Osmond*).

[58] *R v Bristol Crown Court, ex p Jones* (1986) 83 Cr App R 109, DC.

[59] *R (on the application of Bingham) v DPP* (2003) 167 JP 422.

[60] [1982] AC 510, HL.

[61] cf his lordship's view as expressed in *Tesco Supermarkets Ltd v Nattrass* [1971] AC 153, HL: 'negligence connotes a reprehensible state of mind – a lack of care for the consequences of his physical acts on the part of the person doing them'. See pp 181–2 above.

[62] See the discussion of the mislabelling of offences in Ch 7.

level best but also it is no defence for him to show that it was in fact impossible for him to do any better. In truth, the 'competent and careful driver' is not the average driver but a mean standard. In this limited sense careless driving might be said to be an absolute offence but it is not clear that it is in any sense helpful to so classify it. The general basis on which persons are punished for offences of negligence is that they could have done better, whereas people may be punished for offences of absolute liability even though they have taken all reasonable care.

Lord Diplock does, however, recognize that no liability can be incurred unless what was done by D was directed by a mind conscious of what he was doing. This is merely a particular instance of a general principle governing criminal liability. If D is unforeseeably afflicted by an epileptic seizure when driving he cannot be convicted of careless driving. D may thereby create considerable dangers for other road users, which perhaps explains why some cases seem to show a marked lack of sympathy to drivers raising automatism,[63] but without a real ability to control his actions D cannot be convicted of careless driving.[64] He may, however, find himself not guilty by reason of insanity if his disability arose from an 'internal factor' such as multiple sclerosis or epilepsy.[65]

Nor must it be thought that, as Lord Diplock's *dictum* might be taken to imply, the offence of careless driving requires proof of inconvenience or annoyance to other road users. Careless driving is a conduct crime and not a result crime;[66] consequently it may be committed though no one is affected by the careless driving in question.

It has always been accepted that all the circumstances (which cannot be exhaustively stated but include such factors as the state of the road, the volume of traffic, weather conditions and so on) need to be considered by the justices in determining whether D's driving falls short of the relevant standard and the question is essentially one of fact for them. Since the test is objective, and what is relevant is the driver's conduct, it cannot matter that the failure to exercise due care arose from a deliberate act of bad driving on D's part.[67] This is not to say that subjective factors must always be ruled out of account. Though no account is to be taken of such subjective factors as experience and skill,[68] knowledge of circumstances is a relevant factor.

The new s 3ZA, above, makes explicit the opportunity for the justices to consider the circumstances of the knowledge of the individual driver. A typical example would be where the driver knew that a particular road was liable to black ice, or where he knew that the brakes on the car were defective. It is clear that D could be convicted of careless driving where, for example because of his familiarity with the vehicle, he realizes that it has a tendency to pull to the right when the brakes are applied at high speed,[69] while someone who was unfamiliar with the vehicle, and who was reasonably unaware of this tendency, could not. Professor Ferguson argues that the new provision inserted by the 2006 Act creates a logical difficulty because the court must take account of the circumstances proved to have been known to D only where that operates against him (for example, knowledge of defective brakes) and not

---

[63] *Watmore v Jenkins* [1962] 2 QB 572, [1962] 2 All ER 868, DC; *Broome v Perkins* [1987] Crim LR 271, DC.

[64] But note *Moses* [2004] All ER 128 (Sept) where D was convicted of causing death by *dangerous* driving when the bus he was driving swerved onto the pavement when he was swatting a wasp that had flown into the cab.

[65] See case discussed by JC Smith in 'Individual Incapacities and Criminal Liability' (1998) 6 Med L Rev 138 at 144–145.

[66] Above, Ch 4.

[67] *Taylor v Rogers* (1960) 124 JP 217, [1960] Crim LR 271, DC.

[68] Presumably, no account is to be taken of age although D may lawfully drive a motor car at 17 years and a motorcycle at 16. No doubt the same 'impersonal and universal' standard would be applied. But what of careless cycling under s 29 where D may be only 10 years old? In civil cases generally a child must exercise the care to be expected of a child of his age but where a child is engaged in an activity such as cycling on a road there is much to be said for holding him to the standard of the reasonably experienced cyclist. cf *Bannister* above.

[69] *Haynes v Swain* [1975] RTR 40, [1974] Crim LR 483, DC.

when it amounts merely to a claim of his awareness of his own presumed superior ability (being a police driver, etc).[70]

Evidence of the amount of alcohol consumed by the driver is admissible. Where, as in *Millington*,[71] the manner of driving is in dispute, it is relevant as circumstantial evidence of that matter. An intoxicated person is more likely to have driven in the manner alleged by the prosecution than a sober person. It may also be an element in the alleged carelessness – it might not be 'careless' for a mildly intoxicated person to drive in the particular conditions at 30 mph, nor for a sober person to drive at 45 mph, but careless for that intoxicated person to drive at 45 mph.

Only where the justices reach a decision which no reasonable bench could reach on those facts will the High Court interfere.[72] Consequently, the High Court may uphold a decision to convict (or acquit) if it is one which may reasonably be reached on the facts and even though, had the decision been the reverse, that decision would equally have been upheld.[73] In criminal cases, as in civil actions for negligence, the courts resist any attempt to elevate 'to the status of propositions of law what really are particular applications to special facts of propositions of ordinary good sense'.[74] The point may be illustrated by reference to cases involving the Highway Code.[75] While the Code contains many precepts of good driving, and while the Act itself provides[76] that a failure to observe its provisions may be relied on in both criminal and civil proceedings as tending to establish or negative liability, it does not lay down for drivers a regime of inflexible imperatives. Since each case turns on its own particular facts it does not *always* (though it may usually) follow that a driver is necessarily careless in driving at such a speed that he cannot stop in the distance he sees to be clear;[77] nor in leaving insufficient braking distance between his vehicle and another's;[78] nor in failing to look behind before reversing;[79] nor in crossing a road's dividing line.[80] Though these are all precepts of driving practice set out in the Code.

D's driving is not necessarily careless merely because it constitutes some other driving offence. While the speed at which a vehicle is driven is often a relevant factor, it does not necessarily follow that D is guilty of careless driving merely because he is exceeding a speed limit.[81] Nor does it follow that a driver who is guilty of the offence of failing to accord precedence to a pedestrian on a crossing is guilty of careless driving.[82]

The following are provided by the CPS as examples of driving which *may* amount to careless driving: overtaking on the inside; driving inappropriately close to another vehicle; inadvertently driving through a red light; emerging from a side road into the path of another vehicle; tuning a car radio; using a hand-held mobile phone or other hand-held electronic

---

[70] 2007 SLT 28.

[71] [1995] Crim LR 824.

[72] *Bracegirdle v Oxley* [1947] KB 349, [1947] 1 All ER 126, DC.

[73] *Jarvis v Fuller* [1974] RTR 160, DC. The same principles apply to a charge of inconsiderate driving: *Dilks v Bowman-Shaw* [1981] RTR 4.

[74] *Easson v London and North Eastern Rly Co* [1944] 2 All ER 425 at 426, CA, per du Parcq LJ.

[75] See www.direct.gov.uk/en/TravelAndTransport/Highwaycode/DG_070202.

[76] Section 38(7).

[77] *Jarvis v Fuller* [1974] RTR 160.

[78] *Scott v Warren* [1974] RTR 104, DC. cf *Preston Justices, ex p Lyons* [1982] RTR 173, DC.

[79] *Hume v Ingleby* [1975] RTR 502, DC.

[80] *Mundi v Warwickshire Police* [2001] All ER (D) 68 (Jun), [2001] EWHC 447 (Admin).

[81] *Quinn v Scott* [1965] 2 All ER 588, [1965] 1 WLR 1004, DC. Support for this proposition is also derived from the decision of the Administrative Court in *Milton v DPP* [2007] EWHC 532 (Admin).

[82] *Gibbons v Kahl* [1956] 1 QB 59, [1955] 3 All ER 345, DC.

equipment when the driver was avoidably distracted by that use; and selecting and lighting a cigarette or similar when the driver was avoidably distracted by that use.[83]

33.3.3 Inconsiderate driving

Whereas in cases of careless driving the prosecution need not show that any other person was inconvenienced, in cases of inconsiderate driving, there must be evidence that some other user of the road or public place was actually inconvenienced. The Road Safety Act 2006 (s 3ZA(4)), provides explicitly that the offence will be made out only if those persons are inconvenienced by the driving in question.

Inconsiderate driving is the more appropriate offence where, for instance, D drives his car through a puddle which he might have avoided and drenches pedestrians. It must be the driving which is inconsiderate; other inconsiderate conduct, such as kicking a cyclist,[84] will not do. The CPS provides examples of conduct appropriate for a charge of driving without reasonable consideration: flashing of lights to *force* other drivers in front to give way; misuse of any lane to avoid queuing or gain some other advantage over other drivers; unnecessarily remaining in an overtaking lane; unnecessarily slow driving or braking without good cause; driving with undipped headlights which dazzle oncoming drivers; driving through a puddle causing pedestrians to be splashed; driving a bus in such a way as to scare the passengers.[85]

33.4 Causing death by driving[86]

There are at least six ways that a person might be held liable for causing a death by driving. At the most extreme it is possible for D to be liable for murder, as where he drives at V with intent to kill or do gbh.[87] Secondly, there is the possibility of manslaughter. There are then four statutory offences involving death by driving: causing death by dangerous driving, causing death by careless driving, causing death by careless driving while intoxicated, causing death while driving unlawfully – being disqualified, or having no licence or insurance.[88]

At common law, a motorist who by his driving causes death could always be charged with manslaughter.[89] However, in practice juries are reluctant to convict motorists of manslaughter save in the most exceptional circumstances:[90] the label is so striking that jurors balk at the

---

[83] See the CPS Policy on Bad Driving: www.cps.gov.uk/publications/prosecution/pbd_policy.html.

[84] *Downes v Fell* [1969] Crim LR 376, DC.

[85] See www.cps.gov.uk/legal/p_to_r/road_traffic_offences_guidance_on_prosecuting_cases_of_bad_driving/index.html#a15. See eg, *Curtis* [2007] EWCA Crim 2034: HGV driver attempted to overtake another HGV on a single carriageway road, causing oncoming traffic to brake, swerve off the road and collide with each other.

[86] On the application of the offences, see S Cunningham, 'The Reality of Vehicular Homicides: Convictions for Murder, Manslaughter and Causing Death by Dangerous Driving' [2001] Crim LR 679.

[87] See J Spencer, 'Motor Vehicles as Weapons of Offence' [1985] Crim LR 29. Manslaughter is more common, see *Brown* [2005] EWCA Crim 2868 (D deliberately drove his car into a head-on collision with another vehicle whilst intent on committing suicide). See also *Whitnall* [2006] EWCA Crim 2292 (car ramming) and *Bissell* [2007] EWCA Crim 2123 (manslaughter by HGV driver leaving scene); *Yaqoob* [2005] EWCA Crim 1269 (inadequate maintenance). cf the Scottish case of *HMA v Purcell* 2008 SLT 44.

[88] For a review of the greater significance of the selection of charge by the CPS, see S Cunningham, 'The Unique Nature of Prosecutions in Cases of Fatal Road Traffic Collisions' [2005] Crim LR 834 at 837. Technically an offence under the Aggravated Vehicle-Taking Act 1992 which causes death is a separate offence as it attracts a higher penalty: Theft Act 1968, s 12A(4).

[89] *United States of America Government v Jennings* [1983] 1 AC 624, [1982] 3 All ER 104, HL.

[90] See Lord Goddard, *Hansard*, 1955, vol 191, col 86; *Seymour* [1983] 2 AC 493, [1983] 2 All ER 1058, HL. See also I Brownlee and M Seneveratine, 'Killing with Cars After *Adomako*: Time for Some Alternatives' [1995] Crim

idea of convicting. Sensibly, in 1956 Parliament created a specific offence to cause death by driving a motor vehicle on a road – at that time recklessly, or at a speed or in a manner dangerous to the public – now found in the offence of causing death by dangerous driving.[91]

Clearly, following *Adomako*, a charge of manslaughter will only be appropriate where there is a risk of death from the manner of the driving; a risk of serious injury will not do. Furthermore, manslaughter will very rarely be appropriate and should be reserved for 'very grave' cases.[92] In particular, it might be appropriate where a vehicle has been used as an instrument of attack (but where D lacks the necessary intent for murder), 'or to cause fright and death results'. In addition, it may be appropriate in hit-and-run cases where the death did not arise from the manner of the defendant's driving but the subsequent failure to comply with the duty to stop under s 170 of the Road Traffic Act 1988 following an accident. Manslaughter should also be considered where the driving is otherwise than on a road or other public place, or when the vehicle driven was not mechanically propelled since in these cases the statutory offences do not apply.

Interestingly, it may be that public attitude to the use of manslaughter for driving fatalities is changing.[93] Responses to a CPS public consultation revealed support for more frequent use of gross negligence manslaughter.[94] Nevertheless, the CPS advice is still that gross negligence manslaughter should only be charged in exceptional cases, normally where there is evidence to show a very high risk of death. Further, s 33 of the Road Safety Act 2006 now allows a jury to return an alternative verdict to a charge of manslaughter for one of four offences, including causing death by dangerous driving, if they do not find that there is sufficient evidence to convict of manslaughter but think the evidence was sufficient to prove any of those four offences.

We can now turn to consider the statutory offences of causing death by driving. The necessary elements of causation and what constitutes a human being, which are important for these offences, have been considered above in relation to murder (see Chapter 14). The courts have struggled recently to apply a consistent approach to causation in relation to driving offences and attention is drawn in particular to the discussion of *L*,[95] *Barnes*,[96] *Girdler*[97] and *Williams*[98] in Chapter 4. Difficult problems of causation arise where D causes a minor crash with X and V then fails to avoid X's vehicle.

33.4.1 Causing death by dangerous driving

By s 1 of the Road Traffic Act 1988, as substituted by s 1 of the Road Traffic Act 1991:

A person who causes the death of another person by driving a mechanically propelled vehicle dangerously on a road or other public place is guilty of an offence.

LR 389. On the illogicality of the offence, see B McKenna, 'Causing Death by Reckless or Dangerous Driving' [1970] Crim LR 67.

[91] For consideration of whether manslaughter would suffice without additional statutory offences, see S Cunningham, 'Vehicular Homicide: The Need for a Special Offence', in S Cunningham and C Clarkson (eds), *Criminal Liability for Non-Aggressive Death* (2008). See also *Brown v R* [2006] UKPC 18.

[92] See also www.cps.gov.uk/publications/prosecution/pbd_policy.html#_04.

[93] See J Roberts, M Hough, J Jacobson, N Moon and A Brede, 'Public Attitudes to Sentencing Involving Death by Driving' [2008] Crim LR 339.

[94] See www.cps.gov.uk/consultations/pbd_response_index.html.

[95] [2010] EWCA Crim 1249.

[96] [2008] EWCA Crim 2726.

[97] [2009] EWCA Crim 2666.

[98] [2010] EWCA Crim 2552; [2011] Crim LR 468 and commentary.

The offence is triable only on indictment and is punishable by imprisonment for 14 years[99] and/or a fine.

The attitude of the law towards offences depending on the chance of whether a particularly evil consequence occurs, as opposed to whether D had some mental fault in relation to that particular consequence, has been considered above. This is a particularly conspicuous example of the importance attached to harm done and the *North Report*[100] canvassed the arguments for and against but concluded that the offence should be retained:

Two main factors have influenced our thinking. To abolish the offence in the absence of compelling reasons for doing so would mean that some cases of very bad driving were not dealt with appropriate seriousness. Repeal of section 1 would be seen as a down-grading of bad driving as a criminal activity. This is not a message which we wish to convey. Secondly, though logic might pull us towards arguments in favour of abolition neither English nor Scots law in fact relies entirely on intent as the basis for offences. There seems to be a strong public acceptance that, if the consequence of a culpable act is death, then this consequence should lead to a more serious charge being brought than if death had not been the result. We concur with this view.[101]

Developments since the Report have emphasized this attitude. The penalty for causing death by dangerous driving has been increased from five to 10 years, and now to 14 years' imprisonment.

33.4.2 Causing death by careless driving

In February 2005, the Government announced proposals for reform in the Consultation Paper *Review of Road Traffic Offences Involving Bad Driving*.[102] The proposals included introducing a new offence and s 20 of the Road Safety Act does so.[103] A new s 2B is inserted which provides:

A person who causes the death of another person by driving a mechanically propelled vehicle on a road or other public place without due care and attention,[104] or without reasonable consideration for other persons using the road or place, is guilty of an offence.

The aim is to fill the perceived gap created when an offender was found not guilty of causing death by dangerous driving because his driving had not fallen far enough below the standard of the competent driver.[105] The maximum penalty on conviction on indictment is five years' imprisonment or a fine, or both. This offence brings sharply into focus the question of whether punishment ought to be based on the fault of the actor or the consequences resulting. Note that the distinction between this offence and that in s 2A is that there is no need to prove that

---

[99] Criminal Justice Act 2003, s 285. Higher sentences will be imposed: *Afzal* [2005] EWCA Crim 384; *Richardson* [2007] 2 All ER 601. See, generally, on the sentencing difficulties in road traffic fatalities, the Sentencing Advisory Panel paper: www.sentencing-guidelines.gov.uk/docs/Cons-2007-01-09.pdf and the Council's guidelines published in 2008: www.sentencing-guidelines.gov.uk/docs/death-by-driving-cons-guideline.pdf.

[100] At 6.1–6.9.

[101] At 6.9.

[102] (2005). This is part of the wider Government initiative: Road Safety Strategy, *Tomorrow's Roads – Safer for Everyone* (2000). On the consultation in 2009 on making Britain's roads the safest in the world see www.dft.gov. uk/consultations/archive/2009/roadsafetyconsultation.

[103] For critical analysis of the provisions, see S Cunningham, above (2007) 27 LS 288; P Ferguson, 'Road Traffic Law Reform' 2007 SLT 27. Section 20(1) creates an offence (s 2B of the 1988 Act) of causing death by careless or inconsiderate driving.

[104] The revised definitions of careless and inconsiderate driving, as introduced by the Road Safety Act 2006 and set out above apply to these offences.

[105] See *McCallum v Hamilton* (1986) SLT 156.

it was obvious to a competent and careful driver that driving would create a risk of harm to person or property.

33.4.3 Causing death by careless or inconsiderate driving when under the influence of drink or drugs

The Road Traffic Act 1991, inserting a new s 3A into the Road Traffic Act 1988, created new offences, triable only on indictment and punishable with 10 years' imprisonment:

If a person causes the death of another person by driving a mechanically propelled vehicle on a road or other public place without due care and attention,[106] or without reasonable consideration for other persons using the road or place, and –

(a) he is, at the time when he is driving, unfit to drive through drink or drugs, or

(b) he has consumed so much alcohol that the proportion of it in his breath, blood or urine at that time exceeds the prescribed limit, or

(c) he is, within 18 hours after that time, required to provide a specimen in pursuance of section 7 of this Act, but without reasonable excuse fails to provide it; [it is not necessary that D is 'over the limit': Coe[107]]

(d) he is required by a constable to give his permission for a laboratory test of a specimen of blood taken from him under section 7A of this Act, but without reasonable excuse fails to do so; [it is not necessary that D is 'over the limit': Coe.]

he is guilty of an offence.[108]

This section appears to create eight forms of the offence. It is well established that simple careless and inconsiderate driving are separate offences and each is a further separate offence according to whether it is combined with (a), (b), (c) or (d). Where these offences are charged in the alternative to causing death by dangerous driving, the jury will need careful direction. In some instances, it will not be appropriate to leave the alternative charge of causing death by careless driving, as where the only issue is whether D was asleep.[109]

It is noteworthy that, even where the most grievous injury short of death is caused by dangerous or careless driving, the offender is punishable by only two years' imprisonment or a fine respectively.[110] When no fatality is involved, the sentence for these offences are relatively low, but a death will have a dramatic effect on the gravity of the offence. It seems, as Lord Lowry said in a different context, that it is 'the stark fact of death' which weighs so heavily.

The relevant principles of causation appear to be the same as in homicide generally and these are discussed elsewhere.[111] It is, however, worthy of note here that, where the dangerous condition of the vehicle results in its being stationary on the road, creating an obstruction which is a contributory cause of a fatal accident, the driver who ought to have known of the

---

[106] The revised definitions of careless and inconsiderate driving, as introduced by the Road Safety Act 2006 and set out above apply to these offences.

[107] [2009] EWCA Crim 1452.

[108] Added by s 31 of the Road Safety Act 2006.

[109] Hart [2003] EWCA Crim 1268.

[110] There have been calls for an offence of causing serious injury by dangerous driving. See the discussion by Cunningham above, n 86, [2001] Crim LR 679. There is, it seems, nothing to prevent charges of dangerous driving and offences against the person such as grievous bodily harm being charged together: Bain [2005] EWCA Crim 07; Stranney [2007] EWCA Crim 2847.

[111] Above, Ch 4. In this context, however, it needs to be noted that it is not enough that D brings about a death while driving dangerously; the dangerous driving must be the cause of the death. cf O'Neale [1988] Crim LR 122, CA; Hand v DPP [1991] Crim LR 473, DC.

vehicle's condition is guilty of causing death.[112] D may be convicted of causing death by dangerous driving even though it would not have been obvious to a careful and competent driver that there was any danger of personal injury so long as there was an obvious risk of serious damage to property; this seems a particularly unwarrantable extension of liability for an unforeseen death.[113]

33.4.4 Causing death while driving unlawfully

The Road Safety Act 2006 introduced in s 21 these controversial new offences of causing death while driving when unlicensed, disqualified or uninsured. The offences are triable either way with a maximum penalty on conviction on indictment of two years' imprisonment, or a fine, or both.[114] These are stark examples of constructive liability offences where the punishment is for consequence (death) unrelated to the manner of the driving or any fault involved in driving. All that needs to be proved is that the defendant was driving when he did not have a valid licence or insurance or had been disqualified from driving, and was involved in a fatal collision. Even if D's driving was flawless and the collision was solely the fault of another, or even if V was solely at fault in running out in front of D, D will be convicted of the statutory homicide offence. For example, in *Williams*,[115] W was convicted when he drove his car without a driving licence or insurance. V crossed a dual-carriageway and stepped out 3 feet in front of W's car. W argued that he could not avoid the accident. Two other drivers testified that W was not speeding and that V stepped out when W was 3 feet away. At trial the Recorder rejected a submission of no case to answer ruling that the offence could be committed without fault on the part of W. He directed the jury on the basis that the Crown did not have to prove there was any fault in the manner of W's driving. On appeal the issues for determination were whether (i) fault or another blameworthy act was required (ii) it was sufficient that W's driving was a cause of the death. The Court of Appeal held that for an offence under s 3ZB fault was not required. Moreover, 'cause' in s 3ZB was the same as in 'cause' in death by dangerous driving.[116] W's driving was 'a cause' if it was 'more than negligible or de minimis'. The Court also emphasized that the judge must explain to the jury what is meant by 'cause'. A simple reference to 'significant' or 'substantial' would in the present case have been insufficient, as the terms could easily have been misunderstood. It is evident from the jury's question that they considered 'the principal, main or major' cause of the death was V stepping into the road. Had the judge used the terms 'significant' or 'substantial', he would not have conveyed the meaning adequately. A jury must clearly understand the statutory legal requirements.

Need the offence be read quite that widely? Even if there need be no *mens rea* as to the death, there must still be proof that W caused the death by his 'driving a motor vehicle on a road'. Surely therefore there has to be a causal link between the *driving* and not just the fact that the car was on the road at that time and the death? The offence is not one of death being caused by the presence of a motor vehicle on the road; it is an offence of causing death by driving. On the facts it might not have made a difference, but it is easy to conceive of cases in which it might – as where V drives across onto D's side of the road and hits D's car moments before he would have hit the brick wall at the side of the road.

---

[112] *Skelton* [1995] Crim LR 635, rejecting an argument that, by the time of the crash, the act of dangerous driving was spent.

[113] See also *Jeshani* [2005] EWCA Crim 146.

[114] Both offences are triable either way, and disqualification upon conviction of either offence is obligatory, as is endorsement by three to 11 penalty points.

[115] [2010] EWCA Crim 2552.

[116] *Hennigan* (1971) 55 Cr App R 262.

The Court of Appeal's interpretation focuses only on the link between the fact of the vehicle being on the road and the death. The statutory wording is not limited to that fact, but requires that the act of driving is the cause of the death. In this case, what caused V's death was his voluntary act of stepping under D's wheels; it was not the fact of D driving. Consider a truly extreme case of a suicidal person jumping from a high motorway bridge and landing on D's uninsured car. Why has D's *driving* caused V's death? V's death would have arisen if he had hit V's stationary car or the road. The case of *Dalloway*,[117] which the Court dismissed, is relevant in reminding us that in an enquiry into causation, the focus must be on the relevant act – which act is it that the Crown alleges is a cause of the death? Here it is the driving not the existence of the car. In *Dalloway* it was the negligent driving not the fact of the cart on the road.

Commentators have been scathing of the breadth of the offences, with Ferguson for example, describing them as, a 'fundamental alteration of criminal law policy'.[118] Some commentators argue, however, that such offences are not objectionable in themselves because they reflect the enormity of the consequence of death, but that the sentence is inappropriately harsh.[119] The argument that the culpability of the unlawful driver for being on the road when he was uninsured poses a danger which justifies a homicide offence if a fatality arises is a weak one, and only marginally stronger in cases of unlicensed or disqualified drivers. The truth is that these offences are simply concessions to the expectations of the general public that because a death has occurred, someone ought to be blamed for it. The mismatch between fault and consequences is striking.[120]

---

[117] (1847) 2 Cox CC above p 84.

[118] ibid, 30.

[119] See Hirst [2008] Crim LR 339; cf J Roberts, M Hough, J Jacobson, N Moon and A Brede, 'Public Attitudes to the Sentencing of Offences Involving Death by Driving' [2008] Crim LR 525.

[120] See the Sentencing Advisory Panel, Consultation Document, above, para 60.

Bibliography

A comprehensive bibliography, including all references used throughout the book, is now available free online. Readers can quickly and easily locate specific references by using the online, alphabetized bibliography, or alternatively can download and print the entire listing free.

In addition to this, all references are available in full in the footnotes throughout the text.

Also available online is the list of abbreviations for quick reference when using the bibliography, as well as a list of useful websites to help guide further research.

Go to **www.oxfordtextbooks.co.uk/orc/smithhogan_textbook13e/**

Bibliography

Text size: A A A

SHARE

The following list contains all the references from the book. You can also view the list in printable PDF format (1.2mB, PDF).

A - B - C - D - E - F - G - H - I - J - K - L - M - N - O - P - Q - R - S - T - U - V - W - X - Y - Z

Abbott, C, 'The Appropriateness of Strict Liability in Environmental Law' (2004) Envl L and Management 67.

Abortion Law Reform Association, *A Guide to the Abortion Act 1967* (1971).

Adams, JN, 'Trespass under the Theft and Firearms Act' (1969) 119 NLJ 655.

Addison, N, *Religious Discrimination and Hatred Law* (2007).

Addison, N and T Lawson-Cruttenden, *Harassment Law and Practice* (1998).

Akdeniz, Y, 'Section 3 of the Computer Misuse Act 1990 – An Antidote for Computer Viruses' [1996] 3 Web Jnl CLI.

Akdeniz, Y, 'Cybercrime', in *E-Commerce Law & Regulation Encyclopaedia* (2003).

Alexander, L, 'Criminal Liability for Omissions: An Inventory of Issues' in S Shute and A Simester (eds), *Criminal Law Theory: Doctrines of the General Part* (2000).

Alldridge, P, 'Developing the Defence of Duress' [1986] Crim LR 433.

Alldridge, P, 'The Doctrine of Innocent Agency' (1990) 2 Criminal Law Forum 45.

Alldridge, P, 'Incontinent Dogs and the Law' (1990) 140 NLJ 1067.

Index

David Ormerod has raised *Smith and Hogan's Criminal Law* to a new level. He has expanded (and made more accessible) the authoritative, detailed explanations of statutes and doctrines that characterized previous editions, but he has also added theoretical depth and sophistication to the book by engaging more closely with some of the flourishing contemporary academic writing in criminal law theory.

Professor R A Duff, University of Stirling & University of Minnesota

This is *the* text to turn to on almost all points of criminal law. It offers depth, clarity, and extensive coverage.

Dr Stephen Skinner, University of Exeter

Smith and Hogan has always been the leading students' textbook but there are times when all practising lawyers need to return to basic principles and to understand the underlying thinking. David Ormerod has completely updated the work with reference to all related material and provides a ready source for the information to which all lawyers, from time to time, need to refer.

Mr Anthony Edwards, Senior Partner, TV Edwards Solicitor and Advocates

Anyone with an interest in the criminal law will profit from reading this superb book. Professor Ormerod's synthesis and analysis of the case law and legislation is characteristically outstanding. Like all classic works it is a pleasure to read.

Mr David Perry QC, 6 King's Bench Walk

Judges and practitioners have to find the right answer quickly. The key qualities they need in a reference book are practicality and accessibility combined with intellectual rigour and academic scholarship. *Smith and Hogan* has all of them.

HHJ John Phillips

From a student perspective, *Smith and Hogan's Criminal Law* provides the most comprehensive coverage of criminal law. It was refreshing to find a text where the subject matter was accessible and engaging without oversimplification. It provides a clear, current, and in-depth account of the subject, whilst offering avenues for further investigation. The critical analysis, academic views, and ideas for reform proved to be invaluable for getting the best grades in exams and assignments. It was a great starting point before accessing any of the primary sources. In my view, it is an essential companion for any undergraduate law student!

Sophie Greta Lynch, LLB Law Student, Southampton University

As a student, a barrister, and a judge I have found *Smith and Hogan's Criminal Law* an invaluable companion for more than forty years. In Professor David Ormerod it has an outstanding editor, and it is no surprise that it combines impressive learning with complete clarity of exposition. I would regard it as an essential work of reference for anyone learning about or professionally practising the criminal law.

The Hon Mr Justice Maddison

 online resource centre
www.oxfordtextbooks.co.uk/orc/
smithhogan_textbook13e/

For more information on the open access website which accompanies this book, please turn to page vi.

DAVID ORMEROD is currently a Law Commissioner. He is seconded from Queen Mary, University of London, where he is Professor of Criminal Justice.

Cover image: © John Shaw/Getty Images

ISBN 978-0-19-958649-3

OXFORD
UNIVERSITY PRESS

www.oup.com

9 780199 586493